SENIOR HIGH SCHOOL LIBRARY CATALOG

TENTH EDITION

1972

STANDARD CATALOG SERIES

ESTELLE A. FIDELL, GENERAL EDITOR

CHILDREN'S CATALOG
FICTION CATALOG
JUNIOR HIGH SCHOOL LIBRARY CATALOG
PUBLIC LIBRARY CATALOG
SENIOR HIGH SCHOOL LIBRARY CATALOG

SENIOR HIGH SCHOOL LIBRARY CATALOG

TENTH EDITION 1972

EDITED BY

ESTELLE A. FIDELL
AND
TOBY M. BERGER

NEW YORK
THE H. W. WILSON COMPANY
1972

Library of Congress Cataloging in Publication Data

Wilson, H. W., firm, publishers.
  Senior high school library catalog.

  (Its Standard catalog series)
  First-8th ed. published under title: Standard
catalog for high school libraries.

  1. Bibliography—Best books. 2. School libraries
(High school) I. Fidell, Estelle A., ed.
II. Title.
Z1035.W77 1972   028.52   72-3819
ISBN 0-8242-0475-1

PREFACE

The first edition of SENIOR HIGH SCHOOL LIBRARY CATALOG was published in 1926* and, with the exception of a six-year interval before the second edition appeared in 1932, the Catalog has been published regularly every five years. Until the eighth edition in 1962 the Catalog was called STANDARD CATALOG FOR HIGH SCHOOL LIBRARIES, but following publication of the new JUNIOR HIGH SCHOOL LIBRARY CATALOG in 1965, it became possible to change the scope of the older catalog, and, with the ninth edition in 1967, it became the SENIOR HIGH SCHOOL LIBRARY CATALOG.

Like the latest editions of JUNIOR HIGH SCHOOL LIBRARY CATALOG (1970) and CHILDREN'S CATALOG (1971), the voting list for this tenth edition was drawn up by an advisory committee of distinguished librarians. The actual voting, however, as with the other two catalogs, was done by a group of consultants. These consultants, chosen with the help of the American Association of School Libraries, comprise a group of experienced high school librarians from widely dispersed geographical areas. In addition to the tenth edition itself, the service unit includes five Supplements to be published in 1973, 1974, 1975, 1976, and 1977.

Purpose and Scope. Like the other two school catalogs that are published by The H. W. Wilson Company, this edition can be considered a core collection, with the understanding that libraries serving large systems may want to supplement this list. Users of this Catalog should consult the note at the beginning of the Fiction section (p. 476) for a suggestion on extending the list of fiction writers.

This edition includes 4,760 titles and 14,661 analytical entries. Out-of-print books have not been included, but titles that are brought back into print at a later date will be considered for inclusion in one of the annual Supplements.

Organization and Data. Part 1, the Classified Catalog, is arranged according to the Abridged Dewey Decimal Classification, and complete bibliographical information is given for each book. The form of name is, with minor exceptions, that found on the title page. References are made (in Part 2) from all known variations of the name. If a person writes under more than one form of name, *see also* references guide the user to these other forms. Prices have been obtained from the publishers and are as up to date as possible. These are always subject to change, however, and should be verified. Subject headings, based on *Sears List of Subject Headings,* are provided and are followed by an annotation which frequently includes an evaluation from a quoted source.

Part 2 is an author, title, subject, and analytical index and, in its many-faceted approach, serves as a comprehensive key to Part 1. Analytical entries are an important feature of the Catalog. Subject analytics give access to those parts of books not covered by the general subject, and author-title analytics provide a direct approach to collections, especially of plays and short stories.

Part 3 is a directory of the publishers and distributors found in Part 1 and will facilitate ordering.

FOR A FULL EXPLANATION ON THE USES OF THE CATALOG SEE P.VIII.

---

* The first edition had only an author and title index. In 1928 a fuller index appeared including, besides author and title, a subject index, as well as analytical entries for 559 books.

Acknowledgments. The H. W. Wilson Company is indebted to those publishers who generously supplied copies of their books and provided information on prices and editions. The publisher is also grateful to the editor and her cataloging staff, along with Managing Editor, Lillian Clarke, for their work in the preparation of this edition. Lastly, to the two groups that gave of their time and energy in generous measure to complete their assigned tasks: the advisory committee and the consultants, the publisher is grateful.

The advisory committee comprised:

Frances Hatfield, Supervisor of Instructional Materials
Board of Public Instruction of Broward County
Fort Lauderdale, Fla.

Marilyn Miller, Assistant Professor
Department of Librarianship
Western Michigan University
Kalamazoo, Mich.

Anne Pellowski, Director-Librarian
Information Center on Children's Cultures—UNICEF
New York, N.Y.

Elnora M. Portteus, Directing Supervisor
School Libraries
Quincy-Woodhill Building
Cleveland, Ohio

Della Thomas, Director of European Study Tours in Children's Literature
Oklahoma State University
Stillwater, Okla.

In their discussions the Committee had the benefit of advice from two experienced high school librarians who are keenly aware of the interests of present-day students: Joseph B. Benkovitz, Librarian, Springfield Gardens High School, Springfield Gardens, New York, and Michael L. Printz, Librarian, West High School Library, Topeka, Kansas.

The following consultants participated in the voting:

Marjory Bolick, Librarian
Rideau High School
Ottawa, Ont. Canada

Emma Ruth Christine, Librarian
Henry M. Gunn Senior High School
Palo Alto, Calif.

Ruth Ersted, State Supervisor of School Libraries
Minnesota Department of Education
St. Paul, Minn.

Letitia Johnson, Librarian
Missoula County High School
Missoula, Mont.

Leigh W. Ledbetter, Librarian
Junius H. Rose High School
Greenville, N.C.

Wilma Mater, Librarian
Walt Whitman High School
Bethesda, Md.

Louise Meredith, Director,
School Library Services
State Department of Education
Nashville, Tenn.

Esther Millett, Librarian
Westover School
Middlebury, Conn.

Brother Frank O'Donnell, S.M., Principal
Cardinal Gibbons High School
Baltimore, Md.

Marian Scott, Associate Professor
Graduate School of Library Service
Rutgers University
New Brunswick, N.J.

Dr. Arthur E. Soderlind
Consultant in Social Studies
State Department of Education
Hartford, Conn.

Seymour B. Stiss, Supervisor
Secondary Social Studies
Arlington County Public Schools
Arlington, Va.

Martha Stucky, Coordinator of Library Service, K-12
Manhattan Unified School District 383
Manhattan, Kan.

Travis E. Tyer
Department of Librarianship
Kansas State Teachers College
Emporia, Kan.

CONTENTS

HOW TO USE THE
SENIOR HIGH SCHOOL LIBRARY CATALOG

The SENIOR HIGH SCHOOL LIBRARY CATALOG is arranged in three parts: Part 1. Classified Catalog; Part 2. Author, Title, Subject, and Analytical Index; Part 3. Directory of Publishers and Distributors.

USES OF THE CATALOG

The SENIOR HIGH SCHOOL LIBRARY CATALOG is designed to serve as an aid in:

Purchasing. The CATALOG is designed to assist in the selection and ordering of titles. Annotations are provided for each title, and information is given concerning publisher and price as well as varying editions. Since Part 1 is arranged by the Dewey Decimal Classification, the CATALOG may be used as a checklist to determine those parts of the library collection which are weak and require additional material. The fact that the books listed have been found useful in various types of libraries throughout the country would indicate that they may also be useful in many other libraries. No library should depend, however, on one aid in book selection but should take into account particular local needs, special curriculum requirements, and the nature of the school or community.

Cataloging. Full bibliographical information is provided in Part 1. This includes recommended subject headings based upon *Sears List of Subject Headings* and a suggested classification based upon the Abridged Edition of the Dewey Decimal Classification.

Reference. This is made possible both through the annotations in Part 1 and by the subject and analytical approach in Part 2.

Rebinding, Discarding, and Replacing. It is possible to see what other titles on a subject are available, and thus help in deciding whether to discard, rebind, or replace a book.

Library Schools. The CATALOG may be useful in book selection courses.

Part 1. Classified Catalog

The Classified Catalog is arranged with non-fiction books first, classified by the Dewey Decimal Classification in sequential order from 000 to 999. The fiction books follow and are designated by the symbol "Fic." These are in turn followed by the short story collection denoted by the symbol "SC."

Each book is listed under one main entry where full information is given. Usually this is the author, although it may occasionally be the editor or even a title entry. The following main entry is typical:

Li, Dun J.
   The ageless Chinese; a history. Scribner 1971 591p illus maps $10 **951**
   1 China—History
   First published 1965
   Organized by dynasties. "After the cycle of culture, famine revolt and dynastic change has unfolded, a summarizing chapter defines the traditional Chinese society. . . . [The book] then discusses the Western impact on China and the formation of the Republic, and concludes with a view of Communist China's position vis-a-vis the Western world." Publisher's note
   "The use of Chinese metaphors in the context of Chinese thought adds much to the flavor; at the same time, the use of Western terminology makes it easy to understand. The maps are most helpful. One could not do much better in selecting this as a basic textbook on Chinese history Very highly recommended for libraries." Library J
   Suggested readings: p551-58

In this entry the name of the author is given in the form in which it appears on the title page of the book. It is inverted and is printed in dark or bold face type.

The first line in the body of the entry gives the title of the book, The ageless Chinese. The title is followed by the information that the book is published by Scribner (reference to Part 3 will show that this is Charles Scribner's Sons, 597 5th Av, New York, N.Y. 10017). This information, with the price, is useful in ordering books. The date 1971 is the date when this book was published. Further information given here is the fact that it contains 591 pages, illustrations, and maps. It sells for $10. However, prices should always be rechecked with the publishers for possible changes.

At the end of the last line in the body of the entry is the figure 951 in dark type. This is the classification number according to the Abridged Edition of the Dewey Decimal Classification. 951 is the classification for the history of China.

The one line "1 China—History" is the recommended subject heading for this book. All subject headings are based upon *Sears List of Subject Headings*. The classification and subject headings provided are useful in cataloging.

Sometimes the subject or subjects assigned to the entire book will not show that there are portions of the book which deal with more specific subjects. In this case analytics are made. In the entry above there are eleven sections of the book for which such analytics have been prepared. In Part 2 there will be entries for these portions of the book under the proper subjects, e.g. China (People's Republic of China).

Next there is a note giving a brief description of the book and its contents. The notes in this case are taken from the publisher's note and *Library Journal*. This annotation, as it is called, is useful in evaluating books for book selection. It is also useful in determining which of several books on the same subject are best suited for the individual reader.

If more than one edition of this book were currently available and were elected by the consultants, the various editions would be listed in alphabetical order by publisher.

Part 2. Author, Title, Subject, and Analytical Index

This is an alphabetical index of all the books entered in the CATALOG. Entries are made under author, subject, title, and other added entries when necessary. Also included are the subject and title analytics for the books analyzed. The classification number is the key to the location of the main entry of the book in Part 1.

The following are index entries for the book cited above:

Author

> Li, Dun J.
> The ageless Chinese   951

Title

> The **ageless** Chinese. Li, Dun J.   951

Subject

> China
> **History**
> Li, Dun J. The ageless Chinese   951

Subject analytic

> China (People's Republic of China)
> *See pages in the following book:*
> Li, Dun J. The ageless Chinese p510-49
> 951

Examples of other types of entries:

Joint author

> Lamb, Brian
> (jt. auth.) Lamb, E. The pocket encyclo-
> pedia of cacti and succulents in color
> 635.9

Author Analytic

Connell, Evan S.
    I came from yonder mountain
      In Abraham, W. ed. Fifty years of the
        American short story v 1 p220-26
                                  S C

Title Analytic

The treasure in the forest. Wells, H. G.
      In Armstrong, R. ed. Treasure and trea-
        sure hunters p32-41   910.4

Part 3. Directory of Publishers and Distributors

The name of the publisher or distributor is given in abbreviated form in each entry. This Directory lists the abbreviation and then provides the full name and address of the publisher or distributor.

PART 1

CLASSIFIED CATALOG

Outline of Classification

The following is the Second Summary of the Dewey Decimal Classification, which is reprinted here by special permission of the copyright owner, Forest Press, Inc. The non-fiction titles in Part 1 of this Catalog are arranged according to this outline, which will therefore serve as a table of contents to this portion of the Catalog. Please note, however, that the inclusion of this outline is *not* to be considered as a substitute for consulting the Dewey Decimal Classification itself.

SENIOR HIGH SCHOOL LIBRARY CATALOG

TENTH EDITION, 1972

CLASSIFIED CATALOG

000 GENERALITIES

001.5 Communication theories

Halacy, Daniel S.
Bionics; the science of "living" machines, by Daniel S. Halacy, Jr.; with illus. by David Michael Steinberg. Holiday 1965 190p illus $4.95   001.5

1 Bionics

Bionics is "the art of solving problems by discovering, recognizing and applying techniques developed by living things for the solution of similar problems." Foreword

"An excellent collection of studies in the new science of bionics, which applies animal instincts and nature's principles to men's scientific needs. This book will appeal primarily to serious science students and is one of the most advanced volumes for young people on this subject." Wis Lib Bul

Glossary: p181-84

McLuhan, Marshall
Counterblast; designed by Harley Parker. Harcourt 1969 141p $6.50   001.5

1 Communication 2 Technology and civilization

"The term 'counterblast' . . . indicates the need for a counter-environment as a means of perceiving the dominant one. Today we live invested with an electric information environment that is quite as imperceptible to us as water is to a fish. At the beginning of his work, Pavlov found that the conditioning of his dogs depended on a previous conditioning. He placed one environment within another one. Such is 'counterblast.' " p5

"In 'Counterblast' we are given a horrifying vision of a world in which media techniques are the only reality, and individual humans are only significant as their awarenesses are determined in common by communicative processes over which they can have no real control." N Y Times Bk R

Miller, Jonathan
Marshall McLuhan; ed. by Frank Kermode. Viking 1971 133p $4.95   001.5

1 McLuhan, Herbert Marshall 2 Communication
SBN 670-45876-7

"Modern masters"

This is an "assessment of the religious cultural, and intellectual values in McLuhan's life that have . . . influenced his celebrated attitudes." Publisher's note

This is a "meticulously researched essay. . . . Writing with as much bite as insight Miller . . . contends that, contrary to McLuhan's claim that he has freed himself from the 'tyranny of values,' his theories are in fact informed by the very values of his Catholic, Canadian, agrarian and literary background. . . . Yet he feels McLuhan may be 'on to something' in his media probes—if for no other reason than that 'he has successfully convened a debate on a subject that has been neglected too long.' " Newsweek

Short bibliography: p125-26

Wells, Robert
Bionics; nature's ways for man's machines; illus. with photographs and diagrams; preface by Harold S. Spielman. Dodd 1966 160p illus $4.25   001.5

1 Bionics

"Data processing computers, sensory mechanisms, and locomotion are covered, with emphasis on the nervous system and learning. There are numerous photographs and several drawings, all are black and white. The drawings of the eye, the ear, etc., are schematic rather than anatomic, but the simplifications retain accuracy. As in all semi-popular books, future possibilities seem like imminent developments. This sense of future discovery, of being at the frontiers of new adventures, of using biological knowledge to greatly improve the condition of man, adds greatly to the interest of this book for the young reader." Science Bks

011 General bibliographies

Bertalan, Frank J.
(ed.) The junior college library collection. General editor: Frank J. Bertalan; associate editor: Jessie Kitching. 1970 ed. Bro-Dart Foundation 1970 503p $34.75   011

1 Catalogs, Classified 2 Books and reading— Best books 3 Libraries, College and university
SBN 87272-012-8

First published 1968

The 1970 edition of this catalog "contains about 21,000 titles, selected as 'basic, dependable, and useful' by Frank Bertalan, with the assistance of ten assistant editors. . . . Arranged by Library of Congress classification number, with an alphabetical author index, it supplies author, title, place of publication, publisher, edition, date, pages, series title, and subject headings, but not prices for individual items. . . . [Emphasis is given] to technical and vocational subjects, such as auto mechanics, occupational therapy, nursing, data processing, police and fire service, and oceanography. Black history and culture are . . . represented, and a useful list of periodicals [is included]." Cur Ref Bks

The Booklist. A.L.A. $12   011

1 Books and reading—Best books 2 Book reviews

A semi-monthly guide to current books. The Booklist was first published 1905 with title: A.L.A. Booklist. It combined September 1956 with Subscription Books Bulletin. In September 1969 it resumed the title: The Booklist

"The Booklist section is a selected, annotated list of recent publications, recommended especially for small and medium-sized libraries. Arranged by broad classes, fiction books for young adults, children's books, new editions and series, U.S. government publications, pamphlets and paperbacks. Complete bibliographical information is given for each entry, including price. Annotations describe, evaluate, and indicate the kind of library for which the book is recommended. The reviews of the [Reference and Subscription Books Review Committee] precede the Booklist section but are not paged separately." Winchell. Guide to Reference Books. 8th edition

I

The Booklist and Subscription Books Bulletin

Subscription Books Bulletin reviews. A.L.A. 1956-1970 6v   011

1 Reference books—Bibliography 2 Book reviews

Volumes cover: 1956-1960, o.p. 1971; 1960-1962, o.p. 1971; 1962-1964, pa $2; 1964-1966, pa $2.25; 1966-1968, pa $2.25; 1968-1970 pa $2.75; with title: Reference and subscription books reviews

Reprinted from issues of The Booklist and Subscription Books Bulletin

These reviews prepared by the Subscription Book Review Committee of the A.L.A. describe and evaluate encyclopedias, dictionaries, and other major reference works "enumerating strengths and weaknesses, pointing out usefulness and limitations. This specialized buying guidance clearly states whether or not a book or set is recommended for purchase and why." Publisher's note

Junior high school library catalog. 2d ed. 1970. Ed. by Estelle A. Fidell and Gary L. Bogart. Wilson, H.W. 1970 808p $30   011

1 Catalogs, Classified 2 School libraries 3 School libraries (High school)

ISBN 0-8242-0416-6

"Standard catalog series"

Kept up to date by annual supplements which are included in the cost of the main catalog

First published 1965

Contents: Classified catalog; Author, title, subject, and analytical index; Directory of publishers and distributors

This volume "catalogs 3,412 books selected for their proven usefulness in junior high school libraries by a board of consultants nominated by the American Association of School Librarians which is both a division of the American Library Association and a department of the National Education Association." Publisher's note

Public Library Association. Starter List for New Branch & New Libraries Collection Committee

Books for public libraries; selected titles for small libraries and new branches; comp. by the Starter List for New Branch & New Libraries Collection Committee of the Public Library Association. Bowker 1970 194p $8.95   011

1 Catalogs, Classified 2 Books and reading—Best books

ISBN 0-8352-0229-1

This book is intended to be a buying guide for a core collection of non-fiction titles for use in a small public library or a new branch

Some 4500 "titles are arranged according to the Dewey classification and each major classification is subdivided into many subject headings. . . . Entries are listed alphabetically by author under these topics. Each entry provides information on author, title, publisher, edition, publication date and price. A directory of publishers with a key to their abbreviations is included." Publisher's note

Public library catalog. 5th ed. 1968. Ed. by Estelle A. Fidell. Wilson, H.W. 1969 1646p $50   011

1 Catalogs, Classified 2 Libraries

ISBN 0-8242-0392-5

"Standard catalog series"

Kept up to date by annual supplements which are included in the cost of the main catalog

First published 1918 as a catalog of social sciences; in 1928 with title: Standard catalog for public libraries

Contents: Part 1: Classified catalog; Part 2: Author, title, subject, and analytical index; Part 3: Directory of publishers and distributors

This reference work is a classified list of 11,001 nonfiction titles whose usefulness is

vouched for by a representative group of practicing librarians. Emphasis is given to the needs of small and medium-sized public and college libraries

The Reader's adviser. Bowker 2v v 1 $18.50, v2 $15.75   011

1 Books and reading—Best books 2 Literature—Bio-bibliography 3 Reference books—Bibliography

Editors: 1921-1941 Bessie Graham; 1948-1964 Hester R. Hoffman; 1968- Winifred F. Courtney

First published 1921 with title: The Bookman's manual. Title varies. Frequently revised

11th edition is in 2 volumes. Contents: v 1 A guide to the best in literature; v2 A layman's guide

A compilation of annotated bio-bibliographic information. Volume one has been arranged by such fields of literature as drama, poetry, criticism, and world literature. Volume two covers reference books, history, philosophy, science, folklore, and travel

The School Library Journal Book review. Bowker $9.95   011

1 Book reviews 2 Children's literature—Bibliography 3 Catalogs, Classified

Annual. First published for 1968-69 in 1969

A cumulation of reviews of children's books and titles for young adults written by professional librarians or subject specialists, this volume "contains complete bibliographical information on each title reviewed, as well as suggested age levels. Arrangement is by subject according to Dewey classifications, with an author-title-illustrator index." Publisher's note

015 National bibliographies and catalogs

Book review digest. Wilson, H.W. service basis   015

1 Book reviews

Reprints of 1905-1959 volumes available separately at varied prices

"An index to reviews of current books appearing in approximately 70 periodicals and journals chosen by its subscribers. Book Review Digest lists approximately 5,000 books a year. Each book is entered by author, with price, publisher, a descriptive note, citations for all reviews, and excerpts from as many reviews as are necessary to reflect the balance of critical opinion. These listings are followed by a cumulated title and subject index, in a separate alphabet. . . . Published monthly, except in February and July, with a permanent bound annual cumulation. Every fifth year, the annual volume contains a cumulated subject and title index of the books included during the previous five-year period." Publisher's note

Books in print; an author-title-series index to the Publishers' trade list annual. Bowker 2v $42.50   015

1 Catalogs, Publishers'

Annual. First published 1948

In two volumes beginning with 19th (1966) edition. Lists titles available during the current year from American publishers, supplying such information as author, co-author, title, price, publisher, year of publication. Volume 1 is arranged alphabetically by author and editor. Volume 2 is arranged alphabetically by title and series. At end of volume 2 there is an alphabetical index of the publishers, not only of those that appear in the trade catalogs of the parent Publishers' Trade List Annual, but also other active American publishers. (Publisher)

Cumulative book index; world list of books in the English language. Wilson, H.W. service basis 015

1 Bibliography

Successor to: The United States Catalog, 1928 "An author, title, and subject index to current books in the English language published in all countries. Government publications, pamphlets, miniature editions, and ephemera are excluded. Books are entered in Cumulative Book Index by author and editor, and under as many subjects as the contents demand. There are also numerous title, translator, and illustrator entries. All entries are in a single alphabetical list. Price, publisher, binding (other than cloth), paging, edition, date of publication, and Library of Congress card order number are given for each book, and a directory of publishers and distributors is appended. Cumulative Book Index is published monthly, except in August, with bound annual cumulations." Publisher's note

Landau, Robert A.

(ed.) Large type books in print; ed. by Robert A. Landau & Judith S. Nyren. Bowker 1970 193p $11.95 015

1 Large type books—Bibliography

SBN 8352-0290-9

"Today the visually or physically handicapped reader can select from a wide variety of books in type sizes ranging from 16-point to 24-point. . . . [This] bibliography, which is itself printed in 16-point type, lists approximately 1,200 books available in large type, including fiction, nonfiction, text-books, Bibles, and reference works. Entries include publisher, price, type size if it exceeds 18-point, year of publication, and, in the case of textbooks, grade level. The General Reading section is arranged by title and the Textbooks section by subject headings such as Business Skills, Foreign Languages and Social Studies. In addition, an author index to all listings—both general and text—is provided, along with a special subjects index to reference works and Bibles and commentaries." Publisher's note

The "Directory of Publishers" includes the names and addresses of seven "on demand" publishers who will produce a large type edition of almost any book submitted to them

Paperbound books in print. Bowker illus pa 015

1 Paperback books

Beginning 1972, monthly with a two-times-a-year cumulative index at $32.50 on annual subscription basis. Two cumulative issues, each $18.95

First published 1955

"A guide to . . . paperbacks, indexed by title, author, and selectively by subject. Also includes prices, names and addresses of publishers, etc." Publisher's note

Subject guide to Books in print; an index to the Publisher's trade list annual. Bowker 2v $37.50 015

1 Catalogs, Publishers' 2 Catalogs, Subject 3 Bibliography

Annual. First published 1957

"A companion volume to 'Books in Print,' classifying by Library of Congress headings . . . titles from the current trade order lists of . . . publishers. . . . Fiction and juvenile fiction are mostly not indexed though fiction collections and criticism are indexed. Bibles as such are omitted. Books priced at less than 25 cents are not listed." Pub W

Vertical file index; a subject and title index to selected pamphlet material. Wilson, H.W. pa $9 per year 015

1 Pamphlets—Bibliography 2 Pamphlets—Indexes

First published 1932 with title: Vertical file service catalog

Issued monthly except August

This "index is a list of selected pamphlets considered to be of interest to general libraries. It is not intended to be a complete list of all pamphlet material, nor does inclusion of a pamphlet constitute recommendation. Each issue contains a list of current available pamphlets, booklets, leaflets, and mimeographed material arranged alphabetically by subject, with descriptive notes and price or conditions under which they may be obtained. A title index, giving the subject heading under which each title may be found, follows the subject list." Publisher's note

015.73 National bibliographies and catalogs—U.S.

Leidy, W. Philip

A popular guide to government publications. 3d ed. Columbia Univ. Press 1968 365p $12 015.73

1 U.S.—Government publications—Bibliography

First published 1953. This edition lists over 3,000 titles issued mainly between January, 1961 and mid-1966, mostly in-print, and frequently annotated. These titles are arranged by over 100 subject headings

The publications listed are those most useful to the individual citizen and, therefore, most important to libraries and other community centers. High school students and librarians should find the book especially helpful. Among the subjects covered are education, infant and child care, carpentry, communism, astronautics, occupations, and citizenship. (Publisher)

016 Subject bibliographies

Cheney, Frances Neel

Fundamental reference sources. A.L.A. 1971 318p $8.50 016

1 Reference books—Bibliography

ISBN 0-8389-0081-X

The author "has written this textbook as 'an introduction to selected sources of bibliographical, biographical, linguistic, statistical, and geographical information.'" Preface

The titles included have been chosen on the basis of their importance in general American reference collections, and emphasize English-language sources; the cut-off date for publication is September 1970. The main body of the work is arranged by type, in accordance with traditional methodology of introductory reference courses. Additional features are a brief introduction to 'reference/information service,' an appendix of guidelines for reviewing as used by the ALA Reference and Subscription Books Review Committee, a list of readings, and an index. In view of the author's distinguished career in reference work and bibliography, this work has been awaited with interest by instructors of reference courses: they will find much to applaud, as in the excellent review of statistical sources (including 1970 census data). However, some may be disappointed . . . by certain omissions. . . . Perhaps in her next edition Cheney will be less discursive on the ways and hows of making dictionaries and encyclopedias, and more inclusive in the area of government publications and in regard to handbooks and manuals." College & Research Libs

Readings: p293-99

Enoch Pratt Free Library, Baltimore, Md.

Reference books; a brief guide for students and other users of the library. The Library illus pa $1.25 016

1 Reference books—Bibliography

First published 1938 with title: A guide to reference books. Periodically revised to keep it up to date

Compiler: 1947- Mary Neill Barton

"The aim of this guide is to present some of the salient points in regard to the more generally useful and popular reference materials, for those who want to use libraries expeditiously. No attempt is made to be exhaustive. The list is intended at all times to be suggestive rather than complete, and the 'use' and

Enoch Pratt Free Library, Baltimore, Md.
—Continued

scope of each work is emphasized rather than its technical make-up and arrangement. As in the past, inclusion, whether as a main entry or in a note describing another title, is a commendation. The grouping of similar titles is for convenience, emphasis, and to save space, and does not imply preference. . . . Since much of its usefulness has been due to the fact that it is small, compact, and highly selective, a substantially increased coverage of reference books would undoubtedly defeat its purpose. Every effort has been made therefore, with each new edition, to keep its size approximately the same and to resist the temptation to add a large number of important new reference books of unquestionable value to the large library." Preface to the sixth edition

"Intended for use in connection with courses in the use of the library and as a selection aid in small and medium-sized libraries. Well selected, with very good annotations." Winchell. Guide to Reference Books. 8th edition

Galin, Saul
Reference books: how to select and use them [by] Saul Galin and Peter Spielberg. Random House 1969 xxi, 312p $7.95   **016**

1 Reference books—Bibliography

A descriptive list of about 200 basic reference books in the humanities and social and physical sciences. The descriptions of the books listed discuss the contents and method of organization of each book; comment on its usefulness; and list related reference books. Chapters on using the library and on documentation of research papers are included

National Council of Teachers of English. Committee on College and Adult Reading List
The college and adult reading list of books in literature and the fine arts; Edward Lueders, Editorial Chairman. Washington Sq. Press 1962 446p pa 90c   **016**

1 Books and reading—Best books 2 Literature—Bibliography 3 Music—Bibliography 4 Art—Bibliography

"An annotated guide, carefully prepared by expert scholars, to help the intelligent adult increase his familiarity with the world's literature, art and music." Publisher's note

"By including works about art and music, together with works of and about literature, this reading list recognizes the interrelationship of all arts of expression and their mutual contributions to a mature view of human life and accomplishment." Introduction

Winchell, Constance M.
Guide to reference books. 8th ed. A.L.A. 1967 xx, 741p $15   **016**

1 Reference books—Bibliography

First published 1902 as: Guide to the study and use of reference books, by Alice B. Kroeger. Isadore G. Mudge kept it up to date from 1910 to 1941

"The purpose of this volume is to list reference books basic to research—general and special—and thus to serve as: (1) a reference manual for the library assistant, research worker, or other user of library resources; (2) a selection aid for the librarian; and (3) a textbook for the student . . . pursuing a systematic study of reference books. . . . [This edition] is completely revised, reorganized, and enlarged. Because of the large numbers of reference books now being published, the number of titles has been increased from some 5500 to about 7500. As in the seventh edition, the books listed are those which might be included in a large general reference collection or with which general reference librarians should be familiar. These include many scholarly works in English and in foreign languages. . . . The year 1964 was the closing date for listing new works and new editions except in a few instances." Preface

Guide to reference books. 8th ed. First supplement, 1965-1966 [by] Eugene P. Sheehy. A.L.A. 1968 122p pa $3.50   **016**

1 Reference books—Bibliography

A supplement to Winchell's Guide to reference books, entered above

"More than one thousand new titles, new editions, and supplements to titles in the parent volume have been annotated or geared in with the 'Guide' by citation. Valuable new features include the citation of LC card numbers and reference to reviews in 'The Booklist and Subscriptions Books Bulletin,' 'Choice,' and 'College and Research Libraries.' . . . The early appearance of this supplement; the intensification involved in covering a two, instead of three-year period; and the inclusion of prices all serve to increase its usefulness as a selection aid." Cur Ref Bks

Guide to reference books. 8th ed. Second supplement, 1967-1968; comp. by Eugene P. Sheehy. A.L.A. 1970 165p pa $4   **016**

1 Reference books—Bibliography

This second supplement to Winchell's Guide to reference books, entered above, includes "about 1,200 well annotated titles published here and abroad. Notable among them are a number of foreign-language dictionaries, bibliographies of literature (including those of individual authors), dictionaries and statistical sources in the social sciences, and bibliographies and encyclopedias in science and technology. . . . A notable and very convenient feature is the cumulated index to both supplements." Cur Ref Bks

016.05 Bibliographies of periodicals

Dobler, Lavinia
(ed.) The Dobler World directory of youth periodicals; comp. and ed. by Lavinia Dobler [and] Muriel Fuller. 3d enl. ed. Citation Press 1970 108p pa $4.25   **016.05**

1 Periodicals—Directories

"The successor to the Dobler International List of Periodicals for boys and girls published in 1960." Foreword

"The aim of the editors is to provide a practical, non-evaluative, and comprehensive survey of periodical literature for youth. . . . [The] 1970 edition contains nearly a thousand periodicals with a combined circulation of over 100 million, and includes a substantial increase in the number of foreign entries, especially for journals published in Eastern bloc countries, Asia, and the new African states. The section on U.S. periodicals has also been updated and expanded. Questionnaires submitted to publishers were used to ensure the accuracy of the information provided. For most entries this includes frequency of publication, price, age level, name of editor and publisher, address, and a description of content. The listings are arranged alphabetically by country, and a further breakdown of U.S. periodicals gives classroom journals by subject area." Publishers' note

Sources and references: p12-13

Katz, Bill
(comp.) Magazines for libraries; for the general reader and public, school, junior college, and college libraries [by] Bill Katz and Berry Gargal, science editor. Bowker 1969 409p $16.95   **016.05**

1 Periodicals—Bibliography
SBN 8352-0221-6

Arranged by subject, this selection guide gives publication information for about 1,000 titles, with "descriptive and critical annotation of the editorial content, point of view, and other important features of each magazine. Each entry keys the periodical to the types of libraries for which it is appropriate, thus providing public, school or college librarians with guidance toward building their own basic

Katz, Bill—*Continued*
collections. . . . Tells which authors and
features regularly appear in the columns of a
journal . . . what its strengths and weaknesses
are . . . and where it is indexed. Other details
include price, address, etc." Publisher's note
Bibliography: p378-91

Periodicals for school libraries; a guide to
magazines, newspapers, and periodical indexes; comp. and ed. by Marian H. Scott.
A.L.A. 1969 217p pa $3.50   016.05
1 Periodicals—Bibliography 2 School libraries
SBN 8389-0072-0
A selection of 429 titles culled from 1500
periodicals checked
The book "is intended as a buying guide to
periodicals and newspapers for school library
purchase. Designed to serve the needs of school
librarians and teachers, this compilation covers
all grade levels, kindergarten through twelfth
grade; it comprises a large number of titles to
keep pace with the realities of curricular demand and with the recommendations of the
'Standards for School Media Programs'; and it
includes a number of off-the-beaten-track titles
to act as a challenge to the imagination of
students and a spur to their intellectual curiosity." Preface
"It should be on every librarian's shelf,
school and public." Library Resources and
Technical Services

016.301 Bibliographies of
sociology. Contemporary problems

Dunlap, Joseph R.
(comp.) Debate index. 2d supplement.
Comp. by Joseph R. Dunlap and Martin A.
Kuhn. Wilson, H.W. 1964 176p (The Reference shelf v36, no.3) $4.50   016.301
1 Social problems—Indexes 2 Debates and
debating—Indexes
ISBN 0-8242-0081-0
Supplement to the: Debate index, first published 1929 as part of: The debaters' manual,
compiled by Edith M. Phelps
A subject index to debates, briefs, bibliographies, collections of articles, and summaries
of arguments, published between 1941 and 1960,
on contemporary problems
"The material indexed was either specifically
designed for debaters or considered to be of
use to them by Reference Shelf subscribers.
. . . The Readers' Guide to Periodical Literature' is the source of the subject headings used
in this index. . . . Under the subjects, the
entries are arranged alphabetically by series,
and chronologically within the series. To enhance the research use of this index, care has
been taken to note the presence of bibliographies wherever possible." Preface

016.3014 Bibliographies of
social groups

Johnson, Harry Alleyn
(ed.) Multimedia materials for Afro-American studies; a curriculum orientation and
annotated bibliography of resources; ed. and
comp. by Harry Alleyn Johnson. Bowker
1971 353p boards $19.95   016.3014
1 Negroes—Education—Audio-visual   aids
2 Negroes—Bibliography
ISBN 0-8352-0404-9
Some 1400 multimedia instructional materials
for a black studies curriculum from elementary
through university levels are contained in this
compilation
Divided into three parts, Part I contains
four "position papers by distinguished black
educators. These papers provide insight into
the American Negro from a sociological, educational, economical, and historical perspective.
. . . Part II, the core of this resource book,
is a selective, annotated bibliography of nonprint materials—plus a list of 100 relevant
paperbound books—which furnish an appreciation of the Afro-American and his culture,
heritage, and contributions to the growth and
development of the U.S., as well as analyzing
the many obstacles he faces today. Part III
follows the same format as Part II and centers
on the people and states of Africa, in the
present and in the past." Publisher's note

Katz, William Loren
Teachers' guide to American Negro history. Rev. ed. Quadrangle Bks. 1971 192p
illus $6.95   016.3014
1 Negroes—History—Bibliography   2 Negroes
—History—Study and teaching
First published 1968
Placing the Negro in appropriate places in
the American history curriculum, unit by unit
of study, the author lists "Dates to remember"
at the beginning of each unit and then provides
"an annotated list of related materials, both
print and audio-visual, to help pupils and
teachers understand the part Negroes played in
each event. Special features of the list include a core reference library, a list of historic landmarks associated with Negroes, locations of Negro history museums and libraries,
and lists of paperbacks and free or inexpensive
materials. Along with these rich sources of
materials, the author suggests approaches to
teaching Negro history which make it a natural
part of American history in general. Basically
a secondary school list, the 'Teachers' Guide'
provides also much help." Hodges

The **Negro** American in paperback; a selected list of paperbound books comp. and
annotated for secondary school students
[by] Joseph E. Penn, Elaine Brooks Wells
[and] Mollie L. Berch. Rev. ed. Nat. Educ.
1968 45p pa 50c   016.3014
1 Negroes—Bibliography   2 Paperback books
First published 1967
This annotated bibliography "is intended as
an aid and reference guide to teachers and
students who may have a limited background
of information on the role and contributions of
Negro Americans to the American way of life.
. . . We have tried to select books which
teachers can use for their own enrichment as
well as can their students on the secondary
school level. Books listed range from fiction
that the reluctant reader on the seventh-grade
level will enjoy to books dealing with basic
problems in American society of interest to
college-bound senior high school students. . . .
Some of the books listed will be helpful only
in a limited area of study. Other books which
have literary merit were omitted from this
list because we felt that they were not suitable
for a teaching-learning situation in a secondary
school classroom." Introduction

Porter, Dorothy B.
(comp.) The Negro in the United States;
a selected bibliography. U.S. Lib. of Congress
[for sale by the Supt. of Docs.] 1970 313p
$3.25   016.3014
1 Negroes—Bibliography
"The emphasis of this bibliography is on recent monographs in the collections of the Library of Congress, although a number of important older works, a few periodicals, and several
titles from the holdings of other American libraries are included. Entries are arranged alphabetically by author under broad subject
headings that reveal the Negro's part in numerous aspects of American life, culture, and history. An index of names and subjects is provided. Entries have been given brief annotations
where clarification seemed necessary. Because
of the increasing importance for the building
of library collections of scholarly reprints of
long unavailable classics in Negro literature
and history, indication of reprint editions has
been made where possible." Note to the User

Porter, Dorothy B.—*Continued*
"A subject and author index, LC call numbers, and location symbols add to the volume's usefulness. Updating and supplementing other bibliographies in the field, this publication is recommended for all libraries." Library J

016.3317 Bibliographies of occupations

Forrester, Gertrude
Occupational literature; an annotated bibliography. 1971 ed. Wilson, H.W. 1971 619p $15   016.3317
1 Occupations—Bibliography 2 Professions—Bibliography
First published 1946 with title: Occupations: a selected list of pamphlets, which was periodically revised and expanded
The main section is alphabetically arranged by occupations, with brief annotations. Other sections include relevant information on such topics as: schools and colleges, foreign study, apprenticeship, legislation and social security, occupations for the handicapped and professional counseling services
Lists approximately 4,500 pamphlets and 1,500 books
Directory of publishers and distributors: p589-613

016.371 Bibliographies of teaching aids. Textbooks

El-hi Textbooks in print. Bowker $13.50
016.371
1 Textbooks—Bibliography
Annual. First issued in 1872 as part of Publisher's Weekly. Formerly published with titles: The American educational catalog, and, Textbooks in print. First published 1970 with present title
Arranged alphabetically by subject with author and title indexes, this book "aims to be inclusive within its scope rather than selective. While the main emphasis in this listing is on textbooks for the classroom, appropriate reference books for use in elementary and high schools are included, as are maps, pedagogical books, teaching aids, and programmed learning materials in book form." Foreword

016.3713 Bibliographies of teaching methods

Educational Film Library Association
Film evaluation guide, 1946-1964. The Association 1965 528p $30   016.3713
1 Moving pictures—Catalogs
"Compilation of 4500 evaluations of 16mm films in all subject areas." Publisher's note
Annotations provide "information on subject, running time, price, distributor, age level, possible audience, and rating. Intended for universities, school systems, public libraries, youth-serving agencies, with film libraries or film programs. Supplements will be issued at about three-year intervals. Monthly sets of evaluation cards are available to members of the association." Pub W

Film evaluation guide; supplement [September 1, 1964-August 31, 1967] The Association 1968 157p $12   016.3713
1 Moving pictures—Catalogs
A supplement to: Film evaluation guide, 1946-1964, entered above, this contains the same type of bibliographic information
"A collection of carefully prepared evaluations of about 1200 films in current release." Introduction

George Peabody College for Teachers, Nashville, Tenn.
Free and inexpensive learning materials. The College pa $2   016.3713
1 Teaching—Aids and devices—Bibliography
2 Pamphlets—Bibliography
First published 1941. Frequently revised
"A carefully screened list of more that 3000 items useful to schools, classified by subject and accompanied by full order information. An excellent source of information for starting a vertical file collection." Hodges

Rufsvold, Margaret I.
Guides to educational media; films, filmstrips, kinescopes, phonodiscs, phonotapes, programed instruction materials, slides, transparencies, videotapes [by] Margaret I. Rufsvold and Carolyn Guss. 3d ed. A.L.A. 1971 62p pa $2.50   016.3713
1 Audio-visual education—Bibliography
First published 1961 with title: Guides to newer educational media
The annotated "compilation consists of data on catalogs other that trade catalogs, selective lists, services of professional organizations, and specialized periodicals." Booklist
"The descriptive annotations have been verified by compilers or publishers of the catalogs and lists. A helpful analytical index is appended." Cur Ref Bks

016.3719 Bibliographies of reading for the disadvantaged

Spache, George D.
Good reading for the disadvantaged reader; multi-ethnic resources. Garrard 1970 201p pa $4.25   016.3719
1 Reading—Bibliography 2 Socially handicapped children—Education
SBN 8116-6009-5
"Our concern is with ways of improving reading instruction among the disadvantaged minority groups in our population. . . . It is our hope that this book will alert teachers to the need to help pupils to find books with which they can identify—books in which they can find positive images of their race or ethnic type. . . . Our selection will seem to include the gamut of attitudes on race and human relations, from the extreme left to the far right. . . . Defamatory as well as flattering portraits of various groups are present. Appeals to the humane feelings of readers, as well as incitements to riot and revolution, are all deliberately included." Introduction

016.5 Bibliographies of science

Deason, Hilary J.
(comp.) The AAAS Science book list; 3d ed. A selected and annotated list of science and mathematics books for secondary school students, college undergraduates and non-specialists. Am. Assn. for the Advancement of Science 1970 439p $9   016.5
1 Science—Bibliography 2 Mathematics—Bibliography
ISBN 0-87168-201-X
First published 1959
Arrangement is by Dewey Decimal Classification
This guide to collateral reading and book acquisition "includes citations and annotations of 2441 titles of trade books, textbooks and references in the pure and applied science and mathematics." Publisher's note

McGraw-Hill Basic bibliography of science and technology; recent titles on more than 7000 subjects; comp. and annotated by the editors of the McGraw-Hill Encyclopedia of science and technology. McGraw 1966 738p $19.50   016.5

1 Science—Bibliography   2 Technology—Bibliography

Coordinating editor, Theodore C. Hines
Supplement to the McGraw-Hill Encyclopedia of science and technology, listed in class 503
"Lists books (non-book materials are not included) under the headings used in the 'McGraw-Hill encyclopedia of science and technology,' giving one or more annotated citations for each topic. . . . The topical guide organizes the . . . subject headings into about 100 broad areas under which the reader can find particular subject headings in his field of interest. Throughout the volume there are many cross references to related titles." N Y New Tech Bks

016.51 Bibliographies of mathematics

Schaaf, William L.
(comp.) The high school mathematics library. [4th ed] Nat. Council of Teachers of Mathematics 1970 86p pa $1.75   016.51

1 Mathematics—Bibliography

First published 1960
Contains over 800 titles, mostly published since 1965
"Intended as a guide for librarians, students, mathematics teachers, educational administrators, and parents. . . . The following points are also to be noted: (1) the increased emphasis on 'modern' topics such as computers, programming, probability, abstract algebra, contemporary geometry, and topology; (2) the increased coverage in the area of mathematical recreations; (3) the inclusion of very few highly specialized books; (4) the minimal number of out-of-print titles." Foreword [to the 4th ed]

016.8 Bibliographies of fiction

Fiction catalog. 8th ed. Edited by Estelle A. Fidell. Wilson, H.W. 1971 653p $25 (incl. 4 annual supplements)   016.8

1 Fiction—Bibliography   2 Fiction—Indexes
ISBN 0-8242-0439-5

"Standard catalog series"
First begun in 1908 as a paperback called: "English prose fiction, a selected list of about 2,000 titles, cataloged by author and title annotations"
This edition of 4,315 titles is "designed as an aid in book selection (purchasing, rebinding, discarding, replacing, etc.) and as a reference tool listing outstanding novels with critical annotations, usually giving plot outline, and supplying a subject and geographical approach as well as title indexing. . . . Books suitable for young adults are indicated." Winchell. Guide to Reference Books. 8th edition
Part 1 is the Author alphabet with full bibliographical information. Part 2 is a Title and subject index to the author listings. Part 3 is a Directory of publishers and distributors

Irwin, Leonard B.
(comp.) A guide to historical fiction; for the use of schools, libraries and the general reader. 10th ed. new & rev. McKinley 1971 255p (McKinley Bibliographies, v 1) $10
016.8

1 Historical fiction—Bibliography
SBN 910942-26-9
First edition compiled by Hannah Logasa, published 1927 with title: Historical fiction

This is a bibliography of some 2000 titles of historical novels published in the past 35 years. Arranged by broad time periods and geographical area each title is accompanied by a description of its topic and general setting. A section of juvenile novels is included with each chronological division. (Publisher)
Includes author and title indexes and a list of publishers

016.81 Bibliographies of American literature. Negro literature

Dodds, Barbara
Negro literature for high school students. Nat. Council of Teachers of English 1968 157p pa $2   016.81

1 Negro literature—Bibliography   2 Negro literature—History and criticism

"Reviews 150 books and suggests unit and lesson plans which make use of these books. Includes a discussion of junior novels and a Detroit curriculum supplement on Negro literature for grade 9." Publisher's note
Bibliography: p145-52

016.813 Bibliographies of American fiction

Dickinson, A. T.
American historical fiction. 3d ed. by A. T. Dickinson, Jr. Scarecrow 1971 380p $10   016.813

1 U.S.—History—Fiction—Bibliography 2 Historical fiction—Bibliography
ISBN 0-8108-0370-4
First published 1958
This book "contains 2,440 novels published from 1917 to 1969, arranged by period, with author-title and subject indexes. Since the brief annotations place the books in historical perspective but do not give critical judgment on the quality or the historical accuracy of the writing, the guide must be used with caution." Cur Ref Bks

016.82 Bibliographies of English literature

Watson, George
(ed.) The concise Cambridge bibliography of English literature, 600-1950. 2d ed. Cambridge 1965 269p $4.95   016.82

1 English literature—Bibliography

First published 1958
"Some 400 writers from the seventh century to 1950 are considered alphabetically within six period groups." Booklist [1965]
"More useful in high school libraries for the lists of works of the authors included than for biographical and critical material." Booklist [1966]

016.9 Bibliographies of history

Irwin, Leonard B.
(comp.) A guide to historical reading: nonfiction; for the use of schools, libraries and the general reader. 9th rev. ed. McKinley 1970 276p (McKinley Bibliographies, v2) $10   016.9

1 History—Bibliography   2 Literature—Bibliography
SBN 910942-00-5
First published 1927 as part of Hannah Logasa's "Historical fiction"

Irwin, Leonard B.—*Continued*
The purpose of this revision of the work previously titled: Historical non-fiction, and compiled by Hannah Logasa, remains that of "bibliographical assistance. . . . While the number of titles has been reduced, they have been made more selective; and more descriptive commentary has been provided for each book." Preface
Arranged by subject. Includes author and title indexes

016.95 Bibliographies of Asia

Asia Society
Asia: a guide to paperbacks. Rev. ed. [by] Ainslie T. Embree, editor [and others] The Society 1968 178p pa $1   016.95
1 Asia—Bibliography 2 Paperback books
Published 1964 with title: A guide to paperbacks on Asia
"Includes in-print titles which were listed in the original guide and the supplement, new titles which appeared between December 1965 and December 1967, those books with a 1968 publication date which were provided by some publishers, and a few titles which had been inadvertently omitted from the earlier editions. Where more than one country receives major treatment, the paperback is listed under the 'General' section. Asia here is defined as including all the countries from Afghanistan eastward to Japan. A few of the paperbacks are bibliographies and are listed by country." Preface

016.9701 Bibliographies of American Indians

Hirschfelder, Arlene B.
(comp.) American Indian authors; a representative bibliography. Assn. on Am. Indian Affairs 1970 45p pa $1   016.9701
1 Indians of North America—Bibliography
"This bibliography of oral and written literature authored by American Indians lists works under the names of the Indians who narrated or wrote them. Two supplementary sections [covering anthologies and periodic publications] follow the bibliography." Foreword

016.973 Bibliographies of American history

American history booklist for high schools; a selection for supplementary reading; ed. by Ralph and Marian Brown, with the assistance of Martin L. Fausold, Ellis A. Johnson [and] William G. Tyrrell. Nat. Council for the Social Studies 1969 207p (Nat. Council for the Social Studies bul) pa $2.50   016.973
1 U.S.—History—Bibliography
Reading list prepared "to assist the classroom teacher in her efforts to evaluate and to select those books most appropriate to supplement the program in American history." Foreword
Grouped into 17 chapters, each chapter arranged alphabetically by author, this list includes essential bibliographical data, excluding date of publication and price

Wiltz, John E.
Books in American history; a basic list for high schools. Ind. Univ. Press 1964 150p pa $1   016.973
1 U.S.—History—Bibliography

The author has compiled a "bibliography of texts and source material relating to American history. More than just a list, this bibliography gives concise but serviceable descriptions of the titles included and does not hesitate to inject a note of criticism where it is warranted. After a selection of works of an encyclopedic nature on the whole range of American history, there follows a breakdown into the significant epochs through which the country has passed. Among the many titles are outstanding biographies of Washington, Jefferson and Franklin, Bernard DeVoto's studies of the Westward movement, Allan Nevins and Bruce Catton on the Civil War, Sandburg and Thomas on Lincoln, Galbraith on the Depression, John Gunther's 'General MacArthur' and a work on the recent Cuban invasion." Library J
"A welcome and useful guide for teachers and librarians trying to make intelligent selections from the great maze of books published each year." Top of the News

016.98 Bibliographies of Latin America

Farrell, Robert V.
(comp.) Latin America; books for high schools; an annotated bibliography; comp. by Robert V. Farrell and John F. Hohenstein; ed. by Karna S. Wilgus. Center for Inter-American Relations 1969 28p pa gratis   016.98
1 Latin America—Bibliography
This selection "covers the area from Mexico and the Caribbean southward to Chile and Argentina—its history, cultural and geographic diversity, people, problems and its relations with the United States. To emphasize the region's unity and diversity, this bibliography is divided into two sections: one dealing with aspects of Latin America as a whole, and a second section covering individual countries or geographical areas. More than 1200 books—all in English—were examined. . . . Selections have also been based upon organization, usefulness, readability and such helpful aids as maps, suggestions for further reading and photographs with captions which add further dimension to the text. Price has been considered, especially for books for students, and many paperback books are included throughout." Introduction

020 Library science

The World book encyclopedia
Library. Field Enterprises illus pa gratis   020
1 Libraries 2 Library service
A reprint from: The World book encyclopedia. An explanation, with photographs, of the types, services, and use of libraries. The pamphlet includes a short history of libraries, information on careers in library work, and photographs of famous libraries

021.7 Promotion of libraries

Garvey, Mona
Library displays; their purpose, construction and use. Wilson, H.W. 1969 88p illus $7.50   021.7
1 Public relations—Libraries
ISBN 0-8242-0395-X
"Emphasis is placed on why displays should be done and how they should convey ideas; there are discussions on function and types of displays, on sources of display ideas, on design elements and principles and how they work in practice. There are also short-cut ideas for adaptable design backgrounds, multi-purpose cartoons and captions, and some fast, easy types of lettering." Introduction

8

025.2 Acquisition

Merritt, LeRoy Charles
Book selection and intellectual freedom.
Wilson, H.W. 1970 100p $6   **025.2**
1 Book selection 2 Libraries—Censorship
ISBN 0-8242-0420-4
Addressing himself to librarians the author
discusses writing and evaluating a book selection policy; the role of professional associations
and state library agencies; and professional
activity in behalf of intellectual freedom. The
book includes sample book selection policies
for adults, young adults, and children, as well
as basic documents relating to freedom to read
Bibliography: p94-96

025.3 Cataloging

Akers, Susan Grey
Simple library cataloging. 5th ed. Scarecrow 1969 345p illus $7.50   **025.3**
1 Cataloging
SBN 8108-0255-4
First published 1927 by American Library
Association
"This manual of cataloging instruction is designed especially for the inexperienced or un-
trained librarian working in the smaller
library. It contains all of the information
necessary to classify and catalog a collection
of library materials. It also serves well as an
introduction to cataloging and classification
for students in accredited library schools or in
colleges offering a few courses in library science. Fundamental classification and cataloging
rules are presented 'as clearly, simply, and
briefly as possible,' with numerous illustrations and an appendix of sample catalog cards
provided. The volume also serves as an introduction to the use of the Dewey Decimal
Classification tables, Sears List of Subject
Headings, the Anglo-American Cataloging
Rules, and the A.L.A. Rules for Filing Catalog
Cards. Recent changes in cataloging and filing
rules have been incorporated in this edition,
as well as a section dealing with centralized
and cooperative cataloging." Publisher's note
Bibliography: p332-34

Anglo-American cataloging rules, prepared
by the American Library Association, the
Library of Congress, the Library Association, and the Canadian Library Association. North American text with supplement of additions and changes. A.L.A.
1970 xxii, 409p $9.50   **025.3**
1 Cataloging
First published 1908 with title: Catalog rules:
author and title
Supersedes the A.L.A. cataloging rules for
author and title entries, and includes a revision of the Rules for descriptive cataloging
in the Library of Congress
General editor: C. Sumner Spalding
"These rules have been drawn up primarily
to respond to the needs of general research
libraries. . . . Each rule dealing with a specific
problem is to be understood in the context of
the more general rules. . . . The rules are
divided into three main parts, the first two
dealing with books and book-like materials.
Part I is concerned with entry and heading;
Part II with description. The chapters of Part
III are devoted to specific types of non-book
materials and the rules in each chapter are
normally grouped into rules of entry and rules
of description. The rules in each group are
primarily those that are either additional to or
different from those book-like materials. In no
case is a chapter of Part III completely self-
contained." Introduction
"The definitive codification of cataloging
rules for author and title entries. Appendices
include a glossary, abbreviations used in headings, rules of style for headings, and trans-
literation tables." Publisher's note

Non-book materials; the organization of integrated collections. Preliminary ed. [by]
Jean Riddle, Shirley Lewis [and] Janet
Macdonald, in consultation with the Technical Services Committee of the Canadian
School Library Association. Canadian Lib.
Assn. 1970 58p pa $3.50   **025.3**
1 Cataloging
"This manual deals with the cataloguing of
filmstrips, slides, transparencies, microforms,
pictures, charts and maps, motion pictures,
phonodiscs, phonotapes, dioramas, models and
globes, realia, games, and kits. . . . The rules
are structured so that all materials, both book
and non-book, can be integrated into a single,
unified list of holdings. Therefore, the cataloguing principles are designed to be compatible with Parts I and II of the Anglo-American Cataloging Rules." Publisher's note
Bibliography: p52-54

Piercy, Esther J.
Commonsense cataloging; a manual for
the organization of books and other materials in school and small public libraries. Wilson, H.W. 1965 223p illus $6   **025.3**
1 Cataloging
ISBN 0-8242-0009-8
Designed to serve as a manual for the beginning cataloger. The arrangement proceeds from
the general to the specific, from principles to
practice. Routines and rules are incorporated
into the several appendices
"The handbook justifies its title by consistent stress on the simple and the practical. It
recognizes that individual situations call for
individual solutions, but emphasizes the value
of standardization as a general rule because
of the current trends toward centralized
processing and use of commercial services."
Booklist
"Most libraries, especially small ones, will
want to own a copy of 'Commonsense Cataloging.' . . . The volume should also serve as an
excellent training manual for new librarians,
especially at the subprofessional level."
Library J
Bibliography: p180-86

025.33 Subject headings

Sears List of subject headings. 10th ed.
Edited by Barbara M. Westby. Wilson,
H.W. 1972 xlvi, 590p illus $10   **025.33**
1 Subject headings
ISBN 0-8242-0445-X
First published 1923 with title: List of subject headings for small libraries, by Minnie
Earl Sears. Periodically revised to keep material up to date to reflect current interests
and material
A list of headings "Which follows the library of Congress form of headings, abridged
and simplified to meet the needs of smaller
libraries." Cheney. Fundamental Reference
Sources
Contents: Subject headings: principles and
applications of the Sears list; Sample page
of checking; Directions for use [summary];
List of subject headings; Appendix: Black subject headings

025.37 Filing

ALA Rules for filing catalog cards; prepared
by the ALA Editorial Committee's Subcommittee on the ALA Rules for filing
catalog cards. Pauline A. Seely, chairman
and editor. 2d ed. A.L.A. 1968 260p $6.75
                025.37
1 Files and filing

ALA Rules for filing catalog cards—*Cont.*

First published 1942

Arranged in two parts: I Alphabetical arrangement: II Order of entries

Based on the principle of a single-alphabet arrangement, the Rules are designed to meet current library needs. This covers much specialized and foreign material. Coordination with the "Anglo-American Cataloging Rules" is emphasized with suggestions for incorporating new-form with old-form headings. Designed basically for manual filing in dictionary catalogs of any size, the rules are also suitable for divided catalogs, book catalogs, and indexes. (Publisher)

Glossary: p237-39. Bibliography: p240-47

ALA Rules for filing catalog cards. Prepared by the ALA Editorial Committee's Subcommittee on the ALA Rules for filing catalog cards. Pauline A. Seely, chairman and editor. 2d ed. abridged. A.L.A. 1968 94p pa $2   025.37

1 Files and filing

This is an abridgment of the 2d edition, also published 1968, listed above

The "edition presented herein consists of the same basic rules as the full version, but with most of the specialized and explanatory material omitted. It should be adequate for the needs of small and medium-sized general libraries, and also be useful as the basic tool for teaching filers in any size library. . . . The basic order recommended in this edition is the straight alphabetical, disregarding punctuation, with just a few exceptions." Preface

025.4   Classification

Dewey, Melvil

Dewey Decimal classification and relative index; devised by Melvil Dewey. Edition 18. Forest Press [1972 c1971] 3v (2692p) $45
                                                        025.4

1 Classification, Decimal

Also available from The H. W. Wilson Company

Title page date: 1971

First published anonymously in 1876 with title: A classification and subject index. 2d-14th editions published with title: Decimal classification and relative index. Changes in this edition include five additional auxiliary tables and new schedules particularly for law and mathematics

Contents: v 1 Introduction, Tables; v2 Schedules; v3 Relative index

Dewey Decimal classification and relative index; devised by Melvil Dewey. 10th abridged ed. Forest Press 1971 529p $12
                                                        025.4

1 Classification, Decimal

Also available from The H. W. Wilson Company

First abridged edition published 1894

"Designed primarily for small general libraries, especially elementary and secondary school and small public libraries, in English-speaking countries, libraries with up to 20,000 titles that do not expect to grow much larger. . . . As well as having shorter numbers, the present abridged edition in some places presents different classification policies and slightly different numbers from those in Edition 18." Publisher's foreword

This is the classification system used for this catalog, with modifications where necessary to conform to past Wilson Company practice

027.62   Libraries for young adults

Edwards, Margaret A.

The fair garden and the swarm of beasts; the library and the young adult. Hawthorn Bks. 1969 162p $4.95   027.62

1 Libraries, Young adults' 2 Books and reading

The author "writes of how she became acquainted with books and how she organized one of the first young-adult library departments in the country [at the Enoch Pratt Free Library in Baltimore. . . . She discusses the training of YA librarians, work in the public schools, and the city youngster and the library. In addition, she offers a practical appendix for public and school librarians on book selection, book talks, and displays, and a bibliography for the librarian working with teen-agers." Publisher's note

"This incorporates a number of previously published articles in a lively mixture of professional autobiography and a philosophy of librarianship." Booklist

027.8   School libraries

Davies, Ruth Ann

The school library; a force for educational excellence. Bowker 1969 386p illus $10.95
                                                        027.8

1 School libraries

SBN 8352-0269-0

"Defining the school librarian as team teacher, media programming engineer, and curriculum energizer, the author suggests requisite approaches and program methods for realizing this composite role and provides basic sample curriculum guides and other aids. Evaluation of library program effectiveness and supervisor's role are also covered. . . . Derived from the author's University of Pittsburgh course for both education and library students." Booklist

Bibliography: p372-78

028   Reading and reading aids

The Committee on College Reading

Good reading; a helpful guide for serious readers prepared by The Committee on College Reading. J. Sherwood Weber, editor; Anna Rothe [and others] assistant editors. New Am. Lib. pa 95c   028

1 Books and reading—Best books

"A Mentor book"

First edition 1933 by Intercollegiate Committee on Students' Reading. Other editions by National Council of Teachers of English. Variant titles: Students' guide to good reading; Guide to good reading. Frequently revised

"An annotated list of . . . titles arranged by subject areas. Gives author, title, editions, and price. A very useful, up-to-date compilation moderately priced." Winchell. Guide to Reference Books. 8th edition

028.1   Book reviews

Choice: books for college libraries. Assn. of Colleges & Research Libs. $20 a year
                                                        028.1

1 Books and reading—Best books 2 Libraries, College and university 3 Book reviews

Annual. Issued monthly, with a combined July-August issue. First published 1964

"Scope: About 5,000 appraisals of scholarly books selected from more than 28,000 books issued annually by American publishers. Covers subjects in the liberal arts curriculum. . . . Arrangement: Alphabetical by 28 broad subjects, under which entries are alphabetical by author. Bibliographic Data: Author, title, publisher, date, paging, illustrations, LC card number, price and brief reviews by teachers and librarians currently engaged in teaching courses at the undergraduate level." Cheney. Fundamental Reference Sources

028.5 Reading of young adults

Books which discuss young adults' literature are entered here. Bibliographies which also provide reading guidance are classified 028.52

Fader, Daniel N.

Hooked on books: program & proof [by] Daniel N. Fader [and] Elton B. McNeil. Putnam 1968 244p $5.95   **028.5**

1 Books and reading 2 Paperback books 3 Socially handicapped children—Education

First published 1966
Originally published as a paperback and now "rewritten and reorganized, the book is . . . a restatement of the rationale behind the English in Every Classroom program, including a progress report on the continuing program and a summary of a two-year research project directed by the book's coauthor, Dr. McNeil. . . . [The method] calls for devoted teachers committed to the proposition that English is so crucial that it should be taught every hour of the day in every classroom. It calls for a profusion of [books] . . . for a relaxation of lending rules; for an emphasis on writing and deemphasis on the blue pencil. . . . [McNeil tells of] the two-year research project, which matched the W.J. Maxey Boys' Training school with a control group in a similar boys' training school. . . . [He] demonstrates that the attitude of the teacher is of enormous importance." Library J
Includes bibliographies

Pilgrim, Geneva Hanna

Books, young people, and reading guidance [by] Geneva Hanna Pilgrim [and] Mariana K. McAllister. 2d ed. Harper 1968 241p (Exploration ser. in education) $7.50   **028.5**

1 Books and reading 2 Children's literature—History and criticism

First published 1960
This book "is designed for use by teachers, librarians, parents, and all those concerned with guiding the reading of young people of junior and senior high school age, and as a text for college courses in literature for young people. . . . This book represents the authors' firm convictions that young people can be helped to gain great satisfaction from books and that guidance into maturity through reading is important. . . . Books of interest to young people are used throughout the text to illustrate points under discussion. Emphasis is given to contemporary books, although titles chosen also include books of the past that still appeal to young people. An honest effort was made to include good titles and authors to suit the needs, although the authors have not attempted to include only the best writing." Preface
Includes bibliographies

Walker, Elinor

(comp.) Book bait; detailed notes on adult books popular with young people. 2d ed. A.L.A. 1969 129p pa $2   **028.5**

1 Books and reading—Best books 2 Book reviews

First published 1957
This book "contains synopses of 100 books ranging from the classics to modern and with each synopsis comments on the qualities that have made the book popular with teen-agers and suggests books of related interest." Booklist
The selection committee chose "the easier adult titles, which would be used as steppingstones to more mature books. . . . Although this list was made for librarians, any adult interested in promoting reading among young people can use it." Preface

028.52 Bibliographies of young adults' reading

Books for secondary school libraries; comp. by the Library Committee of the National Association of Independent Schools. 4th ed. Bowker 1971 308p $8.95   **028.52**

1 Books and reading—Best books
ISBN 0-8352-0424-3

Succeeds: 1,000 books for secondary school libraries, published 1955; 3,000 books for secondary school libraries, published 1961, and 4,000 books for secondary school libraries, published 1968
"4,000 fully cataloged books indexed by title, subject, author." On cover
A "book selection guide, on the college-bound level, for librarians, teachers, administrators, and mature students working and studying both on formal assignments and independent projects." Preface
"Valuable to those starting a new library and useful for those wishing to evaluate an established collection." Library J

Carlsen, G. Robert

Books and the teen-age reader; a guide for teachers, librarians, and parents. Rev. and updated ed. Harper 1971 247p $6.95 **028.52**

1 Books and reading—Best books

First published 1967
"Sponsored by the National Book Committee with the professional endorsement of the American Library Association, the International Reading Association and the National Council of Teachers of English." Publisher's note
This book is comprised of separate chapters which discuss different kinds of books: the adolescent novel, the classic, poetry, biography, non-fiction, ethnic literature and reference books. In addition, the author suggests ways to handle different adolescent reading problems from the teen-ager whose interest in reading is just beginning to the one who is preparing to enter college
Includes bibliographies

Emery, Raymond C.

High interest—easy reading for junior and senior high school reluctant readers, by Raymond C. Emery and Margaret B. Houshower. Nat. Council of Teachers of English 1965 40p pa $1   **028.52**

1 Books and reading—Best books 2 Literature—Bibliography

A bibliography arranged in such categories as Adventure: science; Adventure: sports; Animals: dogs; Informational; Biography; Vocational, career fiction. Reading level, interest level and a very brief descriptive comment are provided. The booklet includes lists of reading improvements series and book clubs, an interest questionnaire, and a bibliography
"The list of facts on page vii with the implications they present for the teachers has been compiled to aid teachers in locating the student's reading difficulties and to help them choose books that will meet some of the peculiar needs of reluctant readers." Foreword

National Council of Teachers of English

Books for you; a reading list for senior high school students [by] Jean A. Wilson, editorial chairman and the Committee on the Senior High School Book List of the National Council of Teachers of English. Washington Sq. Press 1971 335p illus pa 95c   **028.52**

1 Books and reading—Best books

First published 1945
"This book is intended for any high school students seeking the pleasure, knowledge and growth to be had from a wider familiarity with

National Council of Teachers of English—
—Continued

the world's greatbooks. Its purpose is to direct the young reader to those superior books—classic and modern, fiction and nonfiction—which will broaden his horizons and enrich his reading experience. . . . [It] represents the considered recommendations of a vast number of scholars, teachers, librarians, and informed students as to what is of prime value to teenage readers. Over 2,000 titles in 45 different categories and subcategories are covered, together with brief commentary and annotation. Also included are two indexes, by title and by author, and a list of publishers' addresses." [Preface to 1971 edition]

New York. Public Library

Books for the teen age. The Library illus (pa 50c   028.52

1 Books and reading—Best books 2 Literature—Bibliography

"This is a list of books, revised annually, on subjects of special interest and appeal to teenagers. Emphasis in selection of titles is on presentation which is clear, vivid, appealing, imaginative. All the books have been read and selected by the Committee on Books for Young Adults which is made up of librarians who work with teenagers in The New York Public Library. A large majority of the . . . titles have been chosen from adult publications. The juvenile titles listed either have value for all ages or are included for the younger and slower readers. Out-of-print books are included only when they are still generally available in public libraries. . . . The books are constantly tested and tried with teen-age readers in New York City." Lillian Morrison

Strang, Ruth

Gateways to readable books; an annotated graded list of books in many fields for adolescents who find reading difficult, by Ruth Strang, Ethlyne Phelps [and] Dorothy Withrow. 4th ed. Wilson, H.W. 1966 245p $7   028.52

1 Books and reading—Best books 2 Literature—Bibliography
ISBN 0-8242-0017-9

First edition, 1944, by Ruth Strang, Alice Checkovitz, Christine Gilbert and Margaret Scoggin

"Geared to adolescents who find reading difficult, the more than 1,000 titles are arranged under such categories as adventure, careers, humor, sports, music and art, science, history, and geography. Annotations are intended to arouse the interest of pupils whose reading ability falls below the level expected of them in their high school grade. The estimated grade level of difficulty is given for each title. Separate lists of texts, series, simplified editions, magazines and newspapers, and simplified dictionaries are useful selection guides in this indispensable bibliography for school and public libraries." Cur Ref Bks
Indexed by author, title, and reading difficulty

University Press Books for secondary school libraries. Am. Univ. Press Serv. pa gratis 028.52

1 Books and reading—Best books

Annual. First published 1967
This bibliography is designed to bring to the attention of secondary school librarians and teachers those current publications of university presses and such specialized institutions as museums which a selection committee of five school librarians feels would be beneficial to high school students. The titles are arranged alphabetically by subject. Entries include complete bibliographical details, price, binding, and a descriptive annotation. Critical comments are also included for many of the titles. A few select journals are cited at the end of the bibliography

028.7   Use of books and libraries as sources of information

Cook, Margaret G.

The new library key. 2d ed. Wilson, H.W. 1963 184p illus pa $2.50   028.7

1 Library service 2 Reference books
ISBN 0-8242-0037-3

First published 1956 as a replacement of: The library key, by Zaidee Brown, originally published 1928
A manual of "widely used reference books, annotated briefly under subject. Prefatory chapters . . . introduce the user to the library, the card catalog, footnotes and bibliography, dictionaries, encyclopedias and indexes." Wis Lib Bul

Downs, Robert B.

How to do library research, by Robert B. Downs, assisted by Elizabeth C. Downs. Univ. of Ill. Press 1966 179p illus $5   028.7

1 Reference books—Bibliography 2 Libraries—Handbooks, manuals, etc.
This handbook "starts by introducing the reader to the modern American library—the services provided by librarians, types of libraries, the nature of research collections, the geographic distribution of American library resources, a listing, with notes, of one hundred notable American libraries, and special services of libraries. There also are discussions of the library card catalog, classification systems, and suggestions on the practical use of reference books. The main part of the book is an extensive presentation of reference works [in such areas as biography, history, literature, periodicals, specialized subjects]." Publisher's note

Gates, Jean Key

Guide to the use of books and libraries. 2d ed. McGraw 1969 273p $5.95   028.7

1 Reference books—Bibliography 2 Library service

First published 1962
A discussion of "books and libraries, with emphasis upon the many kinds of library materials, their organization and arrangement, and their usefulness for specific purposes. Particular attention is paid to academic libraries and to ways of using them most effectively." Preface
"Beginning students will find the clear outlines of characteristics of various types of reference sources, the facsimiles of sample pages of indexes, and the emphasis on titles published since 1964 particularly useful." Cur Ref Bks
Selected guides to the literature of the subject fields: p254-56

Rossoff, Martin

Using your high school library. 2d ed. Wilson, H.W. 1964 110p illus pa $1.50   028.7

1 Reference books 2 School libraries (High school) 3 Library service
ISBN 0-8242-0052-7

First published 1952
A guide which shows "pupils how to gather and organize information for a report. The introductory chapter reviews the essential facts about a library. . . . The final chapter suggests the importance of the library as a source of inspiration and pleasure. But the major emphasis of the book is on the mechanics of individual library research." To the teacher
"The examples used from various reference sources, and the illustrations used to clarify library procedures are all excellent." PNLA Quarterly

Toser, Marie A.

Library manual; a study-work manual of lessons on the use of books and libraries. 6th ed. Wilson, H.W. 1964 118p illus map pa $2   028.7

1 Reference books 2 Library service 3 Libraries and readers—Handbooks, manuals, etc
ISBN 0-8242-0031-4

Toser, Marie A.—*Continued*
First published 1934
"Lessons for high school and junior high school students are organized in ten units, with a general review lesson, and examination questions are included in a separate envelope." Publisher's note

029.7 Library information storage and retrieval

Meetham, Roger
Information retrieval; the essential technology. Doubleday 1970 [c1969] 192p illus (Doubleday Science ser) $5.95   029.7
1 Information storage and retrieval systems
2 Libraries—Automation
First copyright 1969 in England
The author "explains present systems for storing information and how each is organized to allow easy access and recovery. He also explores the technology of the computerized library . . . describes those libraries now in use and explains why man has already reached the stage where it is the fact and not the document that is necessary for profitable communications." Publisher's note
Suggested reading: p188

031 American encyclopedias

Collier's encyclopedia; with bibliography and index. Crowell-Collier Educ. Corp. 24v illus maps $329.50   031
1 Encyclopedias and dictionaries
First published 1949-1951
"An adult encyclopedia, suitable for junior and senior high school students as well as for college and university students. Articles are well developed, well presented, and well illustrated. Arrangement is alphabetical, letter by letter. The scholarly, signed articles vary in length according to importance of subject treated. The set is especially useful for its coverage of politics, biography, fine arts, religion, philosophy, the classics, science, and technology. Small topical maps and large (many multi-colored) maps with adjacent gazetteer information accompany articles on states, provinces, and countries. The list of contributors appears in Volume 1 and notes the qualifications and writings of each specialist. Volume 24 contains the bibliography; a comprehensive, analytical index; and a study guide designed to aid the reader seeking to enlarge his knowledge on a particular subject. Bibliographies are listed under broad subject fields, explicitly sub-divided, with title entries arranged under broad or narrow subjects according to the scope of the books listed; generally the books begin at high school level and progress through college and postcollege levels, with easier or general works treated first. Continuous revision program, with several printings a year, assures up-to-dateness." ALA Reference Books for Small and Medium-sized Public Libraries
Supplemented by: Collier's Encyclopedia year book $6.95 to set owners
For a fuller review see: The Booklist and Subscription Books Bulletin, November 15, 1968

The **Columbia** encyclopedia. 3d ed. Edited by William Bridgwater and Seymour Kurtz. Columbia Univ. Press 1963 2388p illus maps $49.50, including supplement   031
1 Encyclopedias and dictionaries
First published 1935
Contains 75,000 articles with subject matter alphabetically arranged and 80,000 cross-references. (Publisher)
"A well-known one-volume encyclopedia; condensed and accurate as to scientific content. . . . Biographical sketches of scientists are good. It should not substitute for one of the major standard encyclopedias, but is a useful compact reference work for students and others. Illustrations are limited to maps and a few full-page spreads containing numerous figures." The AAAS Science Book List for Young Adults
For a more complete review see: The Booklist and Subscription Books Bulletin for May 15, 1964

The **Columbia-Viking** Desk encyclopedia; comp. and ed. at Columbia University by the staff of The Columbia Encyclopedia. William Bridgwater, editor-in-chief. 3d ed.   031
1 Encyclopedias and dictionaries
Some editions are:
Viking $9.95, thumb-indexed $10.95
Watts, F. 10v $50 Large type complete and unabridged. A Keith Jennison book. Has title: The Large type Columbia-Viking Desk encyclopedia
First published 1953
Basically an abridgment of: The Columbia encyclopedia. Alphabetically arranged articles are brief and accurate. Emphasis on people and places of importance in American history. Includes illustrations, maps, tables
For a fuller review see: The Booklist and Subscription Books Bulletin, February 15, 1961

Compton's Encyclopedia and fact-index. Compton 24v illus   031
1 Encyclopedias and dictionaries
Prices vary according to binding and terms of payment. Special prices to libraries and schools
First published 1922 with title: Compton's Pictured encyclopedia. Frequently revised
"A survey of knowledge designed for students from the middle grades onward. It is very useful for junior high and some senior high students who need an 'easy reference set.' Each volume has a text with a fact-index in the back that also provides references to material in other volumes; alphabetically arranged. The recent complete revision and expansion from 15 to 24 volumes has greatly improved the coverage." The AAAS Science Book List
Supplemented by: Compton's Yearbook $7.95
For a fuller review see: The Booklist, June 15, 1970

Encyclopaedia Britannica. Encyclopaedia Britannica Educ. Corp. 24v illus maps   031
1 Encyclopedias and dictionaries
Prices vary according to binding and terms of payment. Special prices to libraries and schools
First published in England 1768; and America 1902. Published with the editorial advice of the faculties of the University of Chicago
Annual printings are released, each one containing varying amounts of revised material
"International in scope and especially valuable in the areas of literature, science, art, geography, and history; it is the largest and most comprehensive of English language encyclopedias. Using broad topic entries, it is arranged alphabetically letter by letter. The broad subject articles, filled with minute details, are supplemented by many specific entries and are written in a dignified, scholarly style. As to its authority, it lists considerably more contributors than any other encyclopedia. Most of the articles are signed with the initials of surname of the contributing authority. 'Britannica' is accurate, dependable, and up to date. . . . Excellent bibliographies, selected and reviewed annually, follow all major articles. The outstanding index is augmented by 'see also' and direct cross references within the text. tables of contents for major articles, and the special feature 'Signpost Articles' which show related material on specific subjects. Glarefree paper, good print, fine illustrations, and dignified bindings combine to produce a superior format." Peterson. Reference Books for Elementary and Junior High School Libraries
The Atlas in volume 24 is compiled by Goode
Supplemented by: Britannica Book of the year, $9.95 to set owners
For a more complete review see: The Booklist and Subscription Books Bulletin, May 15, 1968

The Encyclopedia Americana; the international reference book. Americana 30v illus maps $375   031

1 Encyclopedias and dictionaries

Prices vary according to binding and terms of payment. Special prices to libraries and schools

First published 1829. new editions are issued annually, at which time old articles are rewritten or revised and new articles on topics of current interest are added

"Contains comprehensive subject coverage and in addition to the sciences is especially strong in topics of American interest as well as in literature, industry, and biography. Some of its special features include book-length articles on major countries, digests of literary classics and operas, comprehensive articles on the states, long entries on the centuries, literary and mythological allusions, texts of historical documents, and glossaries of technical terms. Designed for junior high and up, it is also suitable for upper elementary grade children. Arranged word by word under specific entry, it is written in excellent scholarly style, yet is easy to understand. . . . Articles are well developed on specific topics but are much longer for the more important ones. Accurate and reliable. 'Americana' maintains an impressive list of well qualified contributors whose signatures and qualifications accompany all major articles. . . . The comprehensive and accurate index is supplemented by numerous internal 'see also' references, lists of related articles, and tables of contents for major articles. Excellent glarefree, white paper and clear, easy to read print add to the appeal of the set." Peterson. Reference Books for Elementary and Junior High School Libraries

Supplemented by: Americana annual $12.95 to set owners

For a more complete review see: The Booklist, July 1, 1970

Encyclopedia international. Grolier Soc. 20v illus $275   031

1 Encyclopedias and dictionaries

First published 1963-1964

"Created for use by young people from fifth grade up, especially in high school and early college. It's balanced subject coverage is based on nationwide surveys of secondary school reference needs. Social studies receives outstanding treatment as does vocational material, sports and recreation. It includes numerous biographical entries, a high proportion of which are of contemporary persons. Alphabetically arranged, letter by letter, it contains 36,000 specific entries. The length of entry is determined by the importance of the subject, and its extensive index is supplemented by 'see' and 'see also' references and by lists of related articles. Written in clear, short-sentence style, and thoroughly tested for readability, its explanations of complicated topics are lucid and easy to understand. Up to date, reliable, and accurate, it is subject to continuous revision by its large editorial staff. . . . The set contains 19,000 illustrations. . . . Fine political, topographic, resource and other special purpose maps produced by Hammond, Inc., Jeppesen Co., Diversified Map Corp. . . . Excellent bibliographies accompany the more important articles. The format is superior, featuring clear, legible type and bold headings and subheadings." Peterson. Reference Books for Elementary and Junior High School Libraries

Kept up to date by: Encyclopedia yearbook $12; $6.95 to set owners

For a fuller review see: The Booklist and Subscription Books Bulletin, July 1, 1969

Kane, Joseph Nathan

Famous first facts; a record of first happenings, discoveries and inventions in the United States. 3d ed. Wilson, H.W. 1964 1165p $22   031

1 Encyclopedias and dictionaries 2 Curiosities
ISBN 0-8242-00152-2

First published 1933

"It includes 6,652 first happenings, discoveries, and inventions in the United States, listed and described under general subject-headings, with appropriate subheads; an index by years from 1007 to July 10, 1962, the date of the first transoceanic television program; an index by days of the month, so useful in planning displays and exhibits; an index to personal names; and a geographical index. . . . Reference librarians may wish that there were more citations to the sources of information, but the compiler's long years of effort, involving, in many cases, unpublished sources, inspire a good deal of confidence in the volume as a source of ready reference." Cur Ref Bks

The Lincoln library of essential information. Frontier Press illus maps   031

1 Encyclopedias and dictionaries

Prices vary according to binding and terms of payment

Also available in a two-volume edition

First published 1924. Continuously revised

"Designed for ready reference and as a self-instruction device for general cultural information, it is suitable for students in elementary, junior and senior high schools and in colleges. Closely correlated to school curricula, its subject coverage is comprehensive. It is especially strong on literature, fine arts, music, education, and biography. Arrangement is classified with twelve broad subject areas: English, literature, history, geography, science, mathematics, economics, government, fine arts, education, biography, and miscellany. Ease of use is facilitated by the fine analytical index and by many cross references. Tables and charts succinctly provide large quantities of information, and special dictionaries of subjects and terms provide further factual material. Many subject specialists contributed to the work. While articles are unsigned, each authority's area of responsibility is clearly stated. Written in a concise and detailed style, articles are consistently accurate and reliable. . . . No supplement, however, is available. Illustrations are minimal, but are of high quality and are well well located. An atlas section contains 24 pages of multi-color Cosmos Series maps by Rand McNally. . . . A special feature is the inclusion of thousands of test questions and answers for self-education. Sturdily bound, 'Lincoln Library' has clear, legible type on thin but strong paper. Easy to use and bountiful in current information, it is a valuable one-volume encyclopedia." Peterson. Reference Books for Elementary and Junior High School Libraries

For a more complete review see: The Booklist and Subscription Books Bulletin, January 1, 1962

The Lincoln library of social studies. Frontier Press 3v illus maps $54.50   031

1 Encyclopedias and dictionaries 2 Social sciences—Dictionaries

First published 1968. Frequently revised

"Drawn upon the 'parent' The Lincoln Library of essential information." Preface

A reference work, arranged alphabetically under subjects, designed to serve as a combination encyclopedia and handbook of facts. Test questions and bibliography at end of each section

Contents: v 1 History, government and politics; v2 Geography and travel, Economics and useful arts; v3 Biography, Miscellany, Index

The New Century Cyclopedia of names; ed. by Clarence L. Barnhart with the assistance of William D. Halsey and a staff of more than 350 consulting scholars, special editors, and other contributors. Appleton 1954 3v (xxviii, 4342p) $45   031

1 Encyclopedias and dictionaries 2 Biography—Dictionaries 3 Geography—Dictionaries 4 Names—Dictionaries

First published 1894 with title: Century Cyclopedia of names

Contents: v 1 A-Emin Pasha; v2 Em'ly-Nakuru; v3 Nalazyryanians & appendices

"Essential facts for more than 100,000 proper names of every description—persons, places, historical events, plays, operas, works of fiction, literary characters, mythological and legendary persons, etc. Volume 3 contains chronological table of world history, rulers and popes, genealogical charts, and prenames with pronunciation." ALA Reference Books for Small and Medium-sized Libraries

For a more complete review see: Subscription Books Bulletin, October 1954

Webster's Dictionary of proper names; ed.
by Geoffrey Payton. Merriam [1971 c1970]
752p $9.95   031
1 Names—Dictionaries
SBN 87779-083-3
"A Merriam-Webster"
An American adaptation of: Payton's Proper names, published 1969 in England
A guide to a wide variety of interesting or
useful names including initials, nicknames,
pen names, place names, prizes, societies, institutions, animals, and names drawn from literature, legend, the Bible, the fine and performing arts, history, politics, religion, philosophy, education, science, the armed forces, the
space program, business, economics, sports and
games, etc.

The World book encyclopedia. Field Enterprises 22v illus maps   031
1 Encyclopedias and dictionaries
Prices vary according to editions and bindings
First published 1917-1918. Beginning with
1972 edition, the set contains 22 volumes
This encyclopedia "was created to serve the
needs of the entire family, but with emphasis
on usefulness to students in the upper elementary grades through high school, and even
through beginning college. It serves libraries,
homes, and offices as an everyday reference
tool, and is as popular with adults as with
young people. . . . It deals in depth with all
areas of knowledge in an unbiased and impartial manner, while emphasizing those subjects
most often required by students in the broad
areas of the sciences (this coverage is especially fine), the arts, literature, technology,
and biography. The latter category alone comprises more than 5,000 detailed entries."
Walsh. General Encyclopedias in Print, 1971-72

032 English encyclopedias

Chambers's encyclopaedia. New rev. ed.
Pergamon Press 1966 15v illus maps 032
1 Encyclopedias and dictionaries
Prices vary according to binding
First published 1860-1868 in ten volumes.
Volume fifteen contains atlas and index. In
addition, a loose-leaf folder for the annual
world survey supplements is part of the set
Arranged alphabetically, with topical subdivisions, the articles are signed. Longer
articles include bibliographies, indexed primarily by subject with cross references inserted. (Publisher)
"The articles, written at the adult level, appear to be clear and reliable; but coverage is a
few years less up to date than that of American encyclopedias, even in the British subject
areas with which it is largely concerned. . . .
Though the atlas maps in Chambers's are less
spectacular in the rendering of relief, they are
superior in the more significant matter of detail, and there are more of them; also, the map
index includes data on all important places. The
general index is thorough, and a valuable
feature is the thirty-eight-page Classified List
of Articles, in which each broad subject is reduced to topics and subtopics." Sat R
"It is suitable for use at the senior high
school, college, and university levels." Walsh.
General Encyclopedias in Print, 1971-72
For a more complete review see: Booklist
and Subscription Books Bulletin, January 1,
1968

Guinness Book of world records [ed. by] Norris and Ross McWhirter. Sterling illus
$5.95, lib. bdg. $6.39   032
1 Encyclopedias and dictionaries 2 Curiosities
First published 1955 in England with title:
The Guinness Book of records; in the United
States, 1962. Frequently revised
Lists records of all kinds, including which
is the smallest fish ever caught, the most expensive wine, the greatest weight lifted by a
man, the world's longest horse race or the
longest river in the world
A "compilation of facts, including both the
significant and trivial, which young people
may find intriguing." Booklist

051 American periodicals and their indexes

National Geographic Magazine
Handy key to your "National Geographics";
subject and picture locater. Underhill, C.S.
pa $2.50   051
1 National Geographic Magazine—Indexes
Biennial: issued every second January and
cumulated. First published 1915. Compiler:
1954- C. S. Underhill
The purpose of this index is "to locate in a
single alphabetical listing all the incomparable
educational and pictorial wealth to be found
in the National Geographic Magazine in any
year for which requests are likely to be made,
providing at the same time a quick means of
selecting the most useful articles in order of
preference up to the last December." Foreword

Readers' guide to periodical literature. Wilson, H.W. $35 a year   051
1 American periodicals—Indexes
Also available in an abridged version with
title: Abridged Readers' guide to periodical
literature for $14
First published 1900. "Published semi-monthly from September to June and monthly in
July and August. These issues are cumulated
quarterly, and there are permanent bound annual cumulations." Publisher's note
"General and nontechnical U.S. periodicals.
These periodicals have been selected for indexing by the subscribers to the index on the
basis of their general usefulness in reference
work and represent all the important subject
fields. Author and subject entries are given,
in one alphabet, for each article, each entry
giving all the necessary information for finding
the article. Title entries are included for stories." Publisher's note

Tebbel, John
The American magazine: a compact history. Hawthorn Bks. 1969 279p $6.95   051
1 American periodicals—History
The author gives an account "of the development and growth of America's periodicals
from colonial times to the present. He traces
the vicissitudes of magazine publishing and
editing in all eras and areas: 'consumer' magazines, religious, business, professional, literary." Pub W
"An always interesting history with some
astringent commentary on the clash between
board room and editor which brought the dem-
ise of many popular magazines." Booklist
Suggested reading list: p267-68

069.025 Museums—Directories

The Official museum directory: United States
[and] Canada. Am. Assn. of Mus. & Crowell-Collier Educ. Corp. 1971 [c1970] 1022p
$35   069.025
1 Museums—Directories
Supersedes the Museums directory of the
United States and Canada, first published 1961
by the American Association of Museums and
the Smithsonian Institution
"A complete reference for all types of museums and related institutions that list name,
address, officers and department heads, founding date, major collections, special holdings,
activities, hours, admission charge, etc." AAAS
Science Book List
For a fuller review see: The Booklist, December 15, 1971

070 Journalism

Overseas Press Club of America
How I got that story, by members of the
Overseas Press Club of America; ed. by
David Brown and W. Richard Bruner. Dutton 1967 380p $6.95   070
1 Reporters and reporting 2 History, Modern
—20th century

Overseas Press Club of America—*Continued*

In the "reportorial style of 34 top newsmen and women, each story puts the reader into the global hot spots just when things are happening—Munich to Cuba, Thule to Canaveral, the Vatican or a tunnel under the Berlin Wall. The editors' aim: 'to reveal how great reporters obtained some of the world's major news stories —the preparation, the danger, the luck, the sagacity that go into making an assignment pay off.'" Pub W

070.4 Editorial management and journalistic technics

Sherwood, Hugh C.

The journalistic interview. Harper 1969 115p boards $4.95   070.4

1 Journalism

"In emphasizing the qualities necessary for the interviewer, [the author] admits interviewing is no easy job. . . . Techniques on how to obtain interviews and how to prepare record, and conduct them are discussed, with examples. Special types, such as telephone, group, and off-the-record interviews, are included." Library J

Woodward, Stanley

Sportswriter, by Stanley Woodward with Frank Graham, Jr. Foreword by Red Smith. Doubleday 1967 177p $3.50   070.4

1 Journalism as a profession

This "guide to careers in sportswriting offers a behind-the-scenes view of the field and objectively points out the disadvantages and the advantages. . . . [It] discusses the techniques of covering such sports as baseball, football, horse racing, and boxing. The appendix lists schools of journalism in the U.S. Entertaining as well as informative vocational guidance material." Booklist

071 American newspapers

Hohenberg, John

The news media: a journalist looks at his profession. Holt 1968 320p $6.95   071

1 Journalism 2 American newspapers

"This book examines the principal problems of the newspapers, wire services, news magazines, radio, and television news coverage in the United States. It considers the ethical responsibility of the journalist and the influence of his outlook on society, his duties to the nation in time of crisis, his very reasons for existence as a independent force in an open society." Publisher's note

"Provides excellent reading for all those already engaged in the profession and is necessary reading for all students of journalism." Library J

Notes and comments: p307-20

McGaffin, William

Anything but the truth; the credibility gap; how the news is managed in Washington, by William McGaffin and Erwin Knoll. Putnam 1968 250p $5.95   071

1 Journalism 2 U.S.—Politics and government

The authors "are trying to warn the public about government news management. . . . [They] document a case against government misinformation on domestic and foreign affairs and decry its increase. Cases are cited, and the appendixes illustrate the trend with excerpts from Eisenhower, Kennedy, and Johnson news conferences. It's a tidy muck rake through current [1968] concerns." Library J

Mott, Frank Luther

American journalism; a history, 1690-1960. 3d ed. Macmillan (N Y) 1962 901p illus $10.95   071

1 Journalism 2 American newspapers

First published 1941

A winner of the Pulitzer Prize provides a study of the American press during a 270-year period, 1690-1960

"An admirable and substantial history of American newspapers. . . . Necessarily rather synoptic, though there's lots of entertaining detail." New Yorker

Includes bibliographical notes

The New York Times

The New York Times Index. . . . N.Y. Times Co. semi-monthly $87.50 a year; annual cumulation $87.50; combined service $150   071

"The master-key to the news since 1851. The only service summarizing and classifying news alphabetically by subjects, persons, organizations." Title-page

It indexes by author and small subjects the last edition of the daily and Sunday issues, including the book review and magazine sections. Gives exact references to date, page and column with cross references to names and related topics. Valuable in libraries having files of one or more newspapers but also useful for answering questions of dates of events

"A carefully made subject index. . . . The brief synopses of articles answer some questions without reference to the paper itself. Indexes . . . the edition that is microfilmed and used for bound files, but also serves as an independent index to dates and even as a guide to the reporting of current happenings in other newspapers." Winchell. Guide to Reference Books. 8th edition

Solomon, Louis

America goes to press. Crowell-Collier Press 1970 166p illus $4.95   071

1 American newspapers—History

This is a "study of the history and role of American newspapers from 1690 and the 'Publick Occurances both Foreign and Domestick' to today's newspaper monopolies. The author emphasizes the philosophical and ethical problems of news reporting. The influence of special interests, the unique problems of wartime news coverage, and the news as related to the political process are discussed. Styles of journalism practiced by such greats as Greeley, Hearst and Pulitzer are analyzed." Library J

Bibliography: p159-60

Tebbel, John

The compact history of the American newspaper. New & rev. ed. Hawthorn Bks 1969 286p $6.95   071

1 American newspapers—History 2 Journalism—History

First published 1963

A study of the history and role of the American newspaper, from Boston's first broadside in 1689 to today's huge monopolies and giant newspaper chains. The author traces the problems of control and freedom of the press, the development of the newspaper as an instrument of propaganda, the growth of journalism as a business. (Publisher)

The author has put together a "workmanlike compendium, revealing how great a force the press has been and continues to be in American life." N Y Times Bk R

Suggested reading: p269-74

080 General collected essays

Essay and general literature index. Wilson, H.W. $22 per year   080

1 Essays—Indexes 2 Literature—Indexes

Continues the "A.L.A. index to general literature." The basic volume published 1934 covered the period 1900-1933. Kept up to date by semi-annual supplements, cumulating annually, with five year permanent cumulations

Essay and general literature index—*Continued*

"An author subject index to collections of essays and works of a composite nature that have reference value in many areas of knowledge, particularly in the humanities and social sciences. While all areas of the humanities are covered, literary criticism is especially emphasized. Authors of every age and nationality are included although only twentieth-century publications are indexed. Selections for inclusion in the Index are sent each month to subscribers." Publisher's note

"A monumental work, useful in several departments of library service. In cataloging it provides a usable substitute for a large amount of analysis, the cost of which would be prohibitive in the average card catalogue." Mudge

098   Prohibited works

Haight, Anne Lyon
Banned books; informal notes on some books banned for various reasons at various times and in various places. 3d ed. Bowker 1970 166p $7.95   098
1 Prohibited books—Bibliography   2 Censorship
ISBN 0-8352-0204-6
First published 1934
Here the author presents a chronological listing of banned books in order "to show the trend of censorship throughout the years and the change in thought and taste. Thus it must be judged, and so we are not surprised that 'most of the books fall under the ban of religion, politics or morality, making the offense one of heresy, treason or obscenity.' . . . Reprinted in the appendices are statements on the freedom of the press, excerpts from important court decisions, and a selected bibliography." Cur Ref Bks

100   PHILOSOPHY

103   Philosophy—Dictionaries

The Encyclopedia of philosophy. Paul Edwards, editor in chief. Macmillan (N Y) 1967 8v $219.50   103
1 Philosophy—Dictionaries
This reference tool was edited "with the assistance of an international editorial board composed of 153 distinguished scholars. . . . The 1450 signed articles are comprehensive in scope and treatment. They are arranged alphabetically and they vary in length from half a column to over 50 pages. Each major article has its own bibliography, which includes recommendations for the general reader and more scholarly citations for professional philosophers. Numerous cross references, placed immediately before the major articles, lead the curious reader on to pertinent material in other volumes." Library J
"Six and one-half years of skill have created a major English language encyclopedia of philosophy. It is authoritative and consistently clear. . . . Contents discuss past and present, East and West, agreement and controversy, men and movements. Notable features are . . . surveys of national philosophical labors (e.g. Bulgarian), rightful resurrection of forgotten men and ideas, extended comments on research tools (e.g. encyclopedias and journals) positions on contemporary issues, inclusion of thinkers in diverse fields (e.g. Toynbee, Tillich), and a simply devised, effective index." Choice

108   Philosophy—Collections

Magill, Frank N.
(ed.) Masterpieces of world philosophy in summary form. Associate editor: Ian P. McGreal. Harper 1961 xxx, 1166p boards $11.95, lib. bdg. $9.89   108
1 Philosophy

"Two hundred classic works of philosophy, chiefly Western, are digested, each prefaced by a statement of the 'principal ideas advanced' and a brief identification of the author and the type of writing. The digests are arranged in chronological order, with author and title indexes for quick references. . . . Critical comments are included within each digest, especially to point out the influences of earlier philosophers on the later. Recommended chiefly as a reference aid." Library J
Acknowledgments: p iii-vi. Glossary of common philosophical terms: p xvii-xxx

109   Philosophy—History

Boas, George
The history of ideas; an introduction. Scribner 1969 238p $5.95   109
1 Philosophy—History 2 Learning and scholarship 3 Thought and thinking
"What produces an idea, how does it exist, flourish, and affect its environment—material and spiritual—how does it survive or even die? These are some of the questions Professor Boas deals with as he explains the task of the historian of ideas. He also presents historical sketches of three ideas: The People, Monotheism and The Microcosm, each one illustrating some of the problems of intellectual historiography." News of Bks
"Flawlessly written and surprisingly absorbing book for the serious but non-specialist reader." Pub W

Durant, Will
The story of philosophy; the lives and opinions of the greater philosophers. [2d ed] Simon & Schuster 1933 412p $7.95   109
1 Philosophy—History 2 Philosophers
First published 1926
Contains chapters on Plato, Aristotle, Bacon, Spinoza, Voltaire, Kant, Schopenhauer, Spencer, Nietzsche, Bergson, Croce, Russell, Santayana, James, Dewey, Hegel
"The great philosophers are here recreated in their environment and times; their ideas are so attractively and lucidly set forth that the average person will find the volume fascinating reading." N Y Libraries
"A sense of humor, a lucid style and a surety born of familiarity combine to make the Story of Philosophy never ambiguous and always interesting." New Repub
Glossary: p399-401. Bibliography: p403-04

Russell, Bertrand
A history of Western philosophy; and its connection with political and social circumstances from the earliest times to the present day. Simon & Schuster 1945 xxiii, 895p $6 109
1 Philosophy—History 2 Philosophers
Analyzed in Essay and general literature index
Originally designed and partly delivered as lectures at the Barnes Foundation in Pennsylvania
Contents: Ancient philosophy; Catholic philosophy; Modern philosophy. A summary is given of the main contributions of each period
"My purpose is to exhibit philosophy as an integral part of social and political life; not as the isolated speculations of remarkable [philosophers and] individuals, but as both an effect and a cause of the character of the various communities in which different systems flourished." Preface

Thomas, Henry
Understanding the great philosophers. Doubleday 1962 384p boards $5.95   109
1 Philosophy—History 2 Philosophers
Analyzed in Essay and general literature index
"Because Western philosophy owes much to the East the [author] begins with chapter summaries of the wisdom of Egypt, Persia, India, China, and Israel, proceeds with the Greeks and Romans, and passes by way of Saints

Thomas, Henry—*Continued*
Paul, Augustine, and Thomas Aquinas to the
European and American philosophers. Santayana and Gandhi complete the roster." Booklist
"This is philosophy made easy and is addressed to readers to whom the subject is
fairly new. . . . The author's purpose is to
make clear the points of agreement uniting
most of the great philosophical systems. . . .
The story is told through the lives and achievements of well-known philosophers with statements of their theories in brief. Anecdotes
lighten the theory, terms are explained, and
some pronunciation is provided." Library J

128 Man

Mumford, Lewis
The conduct of life. Harcourt [1960 c1951]
342p pa $1.95   **128**
1 Life 2 Behavior
"A Harvest book"
First published 1951
"This is a consideration of the individual's
role in the new civilization; it explores the
need for a philosophy and a religion that will
teach man individual human worth and also
equip him to act as a member of a group. . . .
[The book is an] addition to the protests
against the automatism of mechanized society
and to the pleas for a renewal of human values." Booklist
Bibliography: p293-317

133 Parapsychology and occultism

Christopher, Milbourne
ESP, seers & psychics. Crowell 1970 268p
illus $6.95   **133**
1 Occult sciences 2 Psychical research
ISBN 0-690-26815-7
A survey of "the techniques and tactics used
by fortune-tellers and spiritualists of all sorts.
The book is illustrated with handbills or photographs of famous seers and psychics of the
past, and all those who achieved fame for
ESP, clairvoyance, mediumistic manifestations,
table tilting, fire walking, and living burial
are described in detail while they are exposed as being less than magic. . . . This is a
useful revelation of the methods used by those
who have seduced many otherwise rational
people away from realism. Informally, Mr.
Christopher provides a means of bringing those
who seek magic back to evidential science."
Science Bks
Bibliography: p251-57

133.1 Apparitions (Ghosts)

Holzer, Hans
Gothic ghosts; illus. by Catherine Bux-
hoeveden. Bobbs 1970 243p illus $6   **133.1**
1 Ghosts
"These 19 case histories of haunted houses
are all 'true' stories from the author's files.
Most of the ghosts have made their appearances quite recently in many parts of the
U.S.A., in 'Gothic' places like the deep South
and rural Pennsylvania, as well as such non-
Gothic areas as Port Washington, Long Island,
and New York City." Pub W

133.4 Magic, witchcraft, demonology

Boyd, Mildred
Man, myth and magic. Criterion Bks. 1969
173p $4.75   **133.4**
1 Demonology 2 Witchcraft 3 Religion, Primitive

"All through history, myth and superstition
have been used for both good and evil and
this book attempts to cover these practices. . . .
From magic in the ancient world, dark art in
the Dark Ages, the author investigates those
who dealt in satanism, including the hanging
of witches in Salem." Publisher's note
"Crammed with fascinating facts, thoroughly
researched and well written, this book's chief
strength is its logical, coherent presentation of
white and black magic and Satanism as a well-
defined aspect of humanity which has influenced men and events throughout time."
Library J
Bibliography: p166-67

Hansen, Chadwick
Witchcraft at Salem. Braziller 1969 252p
illus $6.95   **133.4**
1 Witchcraft 2 Salem, Mass.
"Focusing on witchcraft turmoil and tragedy
in Salem, Massachusetts in 1692, and re-ex-
amining germane documents of the period and
place, . . . [the author] achieves an engrossing and surprising reversal of judgment on
the witchcraft story and the role of the clergy
in contradistinction to that of the townspeople.
Anyone interested in the seventeenth-century
New England scene will appreciate this innova-
tive, readable slice of Americana." Booklist
"Hansen has done two things admirably well:
he has suggested how nearly impossible it is
to see another era clearly through the accre-
tion of prejudice and the changes of time. And
he has demonstrated that in the Salem witch
hunt, as in many others since, it was really
the people who led the leaders." Time
Selected bibliography: p242-44

Robbins, Rossell Hope
The encyclopedia of witchcraft and demonology. Crown 1959 571p illus boards $10
      133.4
1 Witchcraft—Dictionaries 2 Demonology—
Dictionaries
This book gives a "rational balanced history
of three centuries of witchcraft as a Christian
heresy, from its beginning in fifteenth century,
through its peak about 1600, to its ending in
eighteenth century." Reference Materials for
School Libraries
"The bibliography of 1,118 items is amazing,
and with the lists for further reading and
subject analysis is a work of critical scholarship itself. A grand book, the kind of encyclopedia meant to be read from beginning to
end." Library J

133.8 Extrasensory perception

Hansel, C. E. M.
ESP: a scientific evaluation; introduction
by Edwin G. Boring. Scribner 1966 xxi, 263p
illus $7.95   **133.8**
1 Extrasensory perception
"The author describes ESP, how it is examined, and the obvious experimental error in
research designs concerning it. He evaluates
what are usually presented as the crucial experiments in extrasensory perception, showing
the many possibilities for conscious or unconscious bias and, in some instances, actual
cheating." AAAS Science Book List
The author's "conclusion is not a falsification of the claims of parapsychologists, but
rather a rejection of their claims of verification. The whole argument is perhaps most
interesting as an example of how methodology
is involved in scientific controversy. . . . The
lesson to be drawn here is that there is no
such thing as a crucial, watertight experiment
for either verification or falsification. More
implicit and more important is Hansel's admitted presumption in favor of skepticism
about ESP." Commonweal

Rhine, Louisa E.
ESP in life and lab; tracing hidden channels. Macmillan (N Y) 1967 275p $6.95 **133.8**

1 Extrasensory perception

The author gives an account of all aspects of extrasensory perception and related abilities. She describes the development of research in the field, and illustrates the various forms of ESP with case histories. She also deals with psychokinesis (PK). (Publisher)
Bibliographic footnotes

142 Critical philosophy. Existentialism

Scott, Nathan A.
The unquiet vision; mirrors of man in existentialism [by] Nathan A. Scott, Jr. World Pub. 1969 208p $5.95, lib. bdg. $5.71 **142**

1 Existentialism

"Excalibur books"
The author gives "a clear, concise but not unduly simplified introduction to existentialism. After giving some historical background and defining main existentialist themes Scott traces the development of existentialist thought through profiles of five men prominent in the movement, considering Kierkegaard and Nietzsche as the great seminal figures, Camus and Sartre as representatives of existentialism in its secular mode, and Jewish philosopher Martin Buber as an example of the movement in its religious phase. In conclusion he reflects on the challenge given to the scientific interpretation of man by the existentialist outlook. An extensive list of books prepared for the nonspecialist who wishes to broaden his view of modern existentialism is appended."
Booklist

150 Psychology

Hyde, Margaret O.
Psychology in action, by Margaret O. Hyde and Edward S. Marks; illus. by Carolyn Cather. McGraw 1967 160p illus lib. bdg. $4.33 **150**

1 Psychology 2 Psychology as a profession

The authors describe the work of various kinds of psychologists (clinical, experimental, counseling, educational and others) with people of all ages and with all kinds of problems. (Publisher)
"It describes the dimensions and functions of psychology and psychologists in layman's terms. It not only defines the popular but poorly understood terminology, but shows clearly the triumphs and limitations of this inexact science." N Y Times Bk R
Suggested further readings: p154-57

Sargent, S. Stanfeld
Basic teachings of the great psychologists. Rev. ed. in collaboration with Kenneth R. Stafford. Doubleday 1965 382p pa $1.95 **150**

1 Psychology 2 Psychologists

"Dolphin books"
First published 1944
"Each of the seventeen chapters takes up an important aspect of the study of human behavior, such as the testing of intelligence or of personality, individual development, learning, perceiving, thinking and imagery motivation, mental illness, mental hygiene, social behavior, and applications of psychology to daily living. Included also are more specific topics." Preface
"The book might be called, 'Who's Who in Psychology, Past and Present.' . . . Unfortunately, it does not contain a list of carefully selected references." Science Bks

Wilson, John Rowan
The mind, by John Rowan Wilson and the editors of Time-Life Books. Time-Life Bks. 1969 200p illus (Life Science lib) lib. bdg. $7.60 **150**

1 Mind and body 2 Psychology 3 Brain

First published 1964
Partial contents: The elusive mind of man; The mind under stress and in disarray; Psychoanalysis: delving into the unconscious; How and what do we learn; Yardsticks for human intelligence; Mind and the future of man; Bibliography

150.9 Psychology—History

Watson, Robert I.
The great psychologists from Aristotle to Freud. 2d ed. Lippincott 1968 613p (Lippincott College psychology ser) $10 **150.9**

1 Psychology—History 2 Psychologists

"A history of psychology based on the lives and personalities of its major contributors. The first half covers the Greeks, medieval theologians, and later philosophers; the second deals with the development of modern psychology as a science, including contributions of James, Freud, and Jung, as well as more functional approaches, Behaviorism, and Gestalt psychology." AAAS Science Book List
"The style is clear, informative, and comprehensive. All of the major theories and systems of psychology are covered. In some areas a more systematized approach to various disciplines and more definite experimental examples could have been offered. . . . This is excellent as an original source and reference. Extensive bibliographies supplement each chapter." Science Bks

152.4 Emotions and feelings

Fromm, Erich
The art of loving. Harper 1956 133p (World perspectives) $3.95 **152.4**

1 Love

Also available in a large type edition for $6.95
"A study of all kinds of love, from narcissism to sex love and on to love of God. Dr Fromm discusses the necessity of love, and the way to achieve maturity in love." Retail Bookseller
"Many popular illustrations as to the nature of love are dispelled in this short and rewarding book." Cincinnati
Includes bibliographical footnotes

Montagu, M. F. Ashley
(ed.) Man and aggression. Oxford 1968 178p $5 **152.4**

1 Aggressiveness (Psychology) 2 Ardrey, Robert. The territorial imperative 3 Lorenz, Konrad. On aggression

Analyzed in Essay and general literature index
The authors attack the thesis of an aggressive instinct in man "in several ways—by analysis of the concept of instinct, by discussions of animal behavior, particularly territoriality, and by pointing up the problems of comparing human behavior with that of other animals. . . . The selection is excellent, but since the pieces were written for different publications, there is a great deal of repetition." N Y Times Bk R

153 Intelligence, intellectual and conscious mental processes

Elliott, H. Chandler
The shape of intelligence; the evolution of the human brain; drawings by Anthony Ravielli. Scribner 1969 303p illus $12.50 **153**

1 Intellect 2 Brain

Elliott, H. C.—*Continued*

The author discusses the relationship between psychological functions and the brain. In developing his thesis, he draws parallels between the evolutionary development of the human nervous system and those of lower organisms

"The author did not intend his book to be a technical text but rather a popular account of factual material; an account rendered in a charming, literary style, at times allegorical." Science Bks

Glossary: p265-86

Fast, Julius

Body language. Evans, M.&Co. 1970 192p $4.95 **153**

1 Nonverbal communication

"According to certain recent studies, only about 35% of what we wish to say is expressed in words. The rest is communicated through 'body language.' The author of this . . . book tells what researchers have discovered about non-verbal communication: how the body is used to send out psychological danger signals, to express emotions, to signal a member of the opposite sex, to contradict verbal communications." Book of the Month Club News

Bibliography: p191-92

153.4 Cognition (Knowledge)

Flesch, Rudolf

The art of clear thinking. Harper 1951 212p illus maps $5.95 **153.4**

1 Thought and thinking 2 Logic

"A discussion, from the psychologist's point of view but couched in ordinary layman's language, of what thinking is and how it is done. Partial contents: Robots, apes, and you; Do you see what I see; First aid for word trouble; The rise and fall of formal logic; Why argue; The harnessing of chance; Freedom from error." Book Rev Digest

"A popular approach to the problems of analyzing popaganda, with introductory material for the study of logic." A Basic Book Collection for High Schools

Includes New Yorker cartoons and a bibliography

154.6 Sleep phenomena

Luce, Gay Gaer

Sleep, by Gay Gaer Luce and Julius Segal. Coward-McCann 1966 335p illus $6.95 **154.6**

1 Sleep

"This is a semi-popular account of modern sleep research and its practical implications for physical and mental health. Each chapter is accompanied by an extensive bibliography in which certain items are designated as especially appropriate for the general reader. In addition to the discussion of the general nature of sleep, there are chapters on the effects of sleep deprivation, abnormalities of sleep, the effects of drugs, the nature of dreams, and learning during sleep. . . . It contains much imaginative speculation as the authors extrapolate from laboratory research to possible practical applications. The style of writing is interesting and lucid throughout, although at times it is needlessly repetitious." Science Bks

155.2 Individual psychology. Personality

Jung, Carl Gustav

Undiscovered self; tr. from the German by R. F. C. Hull. Little 1958 113p $4.50 **155.2**

1 Self

"An Atlantic Monthly Press book"

"This deals with the plight of the individual in today's highly organized world. Points out

man's surrender of more & more of his freedom—political freedom, religious freedom, moral & intellectual freedom—to the subjugating forces of modern mass society." Library J

A book "for the perceptive student in English, psychology, and social science." A Basic Book Collection for High Schools

Overstreet, Harry Allen

The mature mind **155.2**

1 Psychology, Applied 2 Mind and body

Some editions are:

Norton $4.95

Watts, F. $8.95 Large type edition. A Keith Jennison book

First published 1949

The author "describes most of our difficulties and conflicts as due to immaturities of attitude and conduct, and shows how the process of becoming truly mature—mentally, emotionally socially—takes place. The book is a combination of theory and application. Misbehavior is attributed neither to 'badness' nor to 'ignorance' but rather 'immature ways' of dealing with our problems. Although there is considerable technical material in the book, it is developed on the level of general understanding, and the primary appeal is for a continuous process of adult learning." Rel Bk Club Bul

155.45 Exceptional children

Buck, Pearl S.

The child who never grew. Day 1950 62p $2.95 **155.45**

1 Slow learning children 2 Mentally handicapped

A short account of the author's daughter who never grew up mentally, written especially for parents of abnormal children

D'Ambrosio, Richard

No language but a cry. Doubleday 1970 252p $6.95 **155.45**

1 Problem children

This "factual, compassionate story of the development of a warm, genuine, empathic relationship between Laura, a severly disturbed 12-year old abused child who had never spoken a word, and D'Ambrosio, a psychoanalyst, is revealed. The book uncovers the events in the troubled lives of Laura's parents which led them to the cruel act of frying her 'alive on an open flame' at the tender age of one-and-one-half years. The author tells how he rescued Laura from a life of utter misery and uselessness through seven long years of skillful clinical help which transformed her into a productive human being. This is an exceptionally well written and interesting account." Choice

West, Paul

Words for a deaf daughter. Harper 1970 188p illus boards $5.95 **155.45**

1 Deaf 2 Exceptional children 3 West, Mandy

This is the author's account of life with his "inexplicably handicapped daughter—a child of eight who is deaf and possibly brain-damaged. His account of her diagnosis and treatment is so much more than simply that. It is, without mawkishness, a masterpiece of communication, to the reader as well as to and with [his] child. . . . [Mandy] comes alive for the reader as a unique personality, and her father's book in its hard-won exaltation is a rare celebration of the human spirit that will move thousands of readers." Pub W

155.5 Adolescents

Gesell, Arnold

Youth: the years from ten to sixteen, by Arnold Gesell, Frances L. Ilg [and] Louise Bates Ames. Harper 1956 542p $7.95 **155.5**

1 Adolescence 2 Child study

"Based upon firsthand studies of a selected group of normal adolescents, it traces the development of behavior in the setting of home, school and community. Adolescence and the

Gesell, Arnold—*Continued*
years just preceding are here revealed not as a unique time of stress and strife, nor as a trackless period of conflict, but as a consistently patterned segment of the total cycle of development." Publisher's note

Smith, Sally Liberman
Nobody said it's easy; a practical guide to feelings and relationships for young people and their parents; illus. by Roy Doty. Macmillan (N Y) 1965 223p illus $4.95   **155.5**
1 Adolescence 2 Behavior 3 Family
Contents: Relations; Feeling; Fear; Anger; Guilt and guilty feeling; Rivalry and competition; Popularity and conformity; Love; Learning to live with ourselves; Some questions for further probing; Bibliography
"Since the author using an objective, psychological approach, describes problems without offering specific solutions and suggests their inevitability and the individual's responsibility for resolving his own difficulties, her book will probably be more useful to the average adolescent whose troubles are not acute, than to the seriously disturbed." Booklist

Sugarman, Daniel A.   (301-)
The Seventeen Guide to knowing yourself, by Daniel A. Sugarman and Rolaine Hochstein. Macmillan (N Y) 1967 209p $4.95 **155.5**
1 Girls 2 Psychology, Applied 3 Behavior
A "guide to self-discovery and maturity for high school girls. This is advice on emotional and social life . . . [dealing with] the topics of handling fears and anger; minimizing friction with parents; going slow in love, sex and early marriage; balancing dreaming and doing." Pub W
"Suggestions on where, when, and how to get outside help are included in a final chapter about handling crises." Booklist

155.8 Ethnopsycology and national psychology

Riesman, David
The lonely crowd; a study of the changing American character, by David Riesman in collaboration with Reuel Denney and Nathan Glazer. Yale Univ. Press 1950 386p (Yale Univ. Studies in national policy, 3) $10 **155.8**
1 National characteristics, American 2 Social psychology
"Study resulting from interdepartmental program of research in national policy organized in 1946 at Yale. Author . . . discusses the processes of social-character formation, categorizes three character types, correlating them with major changes in population and technology, and describes the social behavior at once both cause and effect of each type. Attention is given to the character-pattern of middle class urban Americans in interaction with aspects of their work, leisure, politics, and child-raising activities." Library J
"Uneven but always provocative, alternately brilliant and sluggish, exciting and exasperating." Nation
Bibliographical footnotes

158 Applied psychology

Liebman, Joshua
Peace of mind; a large type ed. Simon & Schuster [1969 c1946] 186p $6.95   **158**
1 Psychology, Applied 2 Psychology, Religious 3 Large type books
First published 1946
1946 edition analyzed in Essay and general literature index

"Drawing on his rich intellectual background [the author] . . . uses illustrative material from his consultative experiences to help the perplexed gain insight into crucial problems concerned with such subjects as love, hate, fear, death and immortality." Bookmark
"This book attempts to distill the helpful insights about human nature that psychology has discovered and the encouraging news from the scientific clinic about man's infinite capacity to change and improve himself, as well as to correlate these latest scientific discoveries with the truest religious insights and goals of the ages." Word to the reader

160 Logic

Chase, Stuart
Guides to straight thinking; with 13 common fallacies. Harper 1956 212p illus $5.95   **160**
1 Logic
An "attempt to show how to apply the logic of modern science, scientific reasoning, to the pitfalls in modern advertising, political campaigns, and pure propaganda. A plea for a saner society of straight thinkers. Outlining thirteen common fallacies and drawing on familiar examples, Stuart Chase explains how people are mentally mantrapped and offers a sensible way out." Pub W
"The general approach is so simple, lucid, and compelling that one keeps watching to see if there will be any over-simplifying. There is not. Alike for content and style, this is a work that every library, large or small, can recommend to all its adult and young adult readers." Library J
Suggested list for further reading: p207

164 Symbolic and mathematical logic

Lieber, Lillian R.
Mits, wits and logic; drawings by Hugh Gray Lieber. 3d ed. Norton 1960 240p illus $5.95   **164**
1 Logic, Symbolic and mathematical 2 Science—Philosophy
First published 1947
In this book, "the processes of modern mathematical logic reveal how men today can discover the truth found in the great world religions and philosophies when the Man in the Street, Mits, and the Woman in the Street, Wits, meet S.A.M., the best of Science, Art, and Mathematics." Bk Buyer's Guide
"A thoroughly original approach to logical thinking which emphasizes the mathematical aspects. Elementary algebra and geometry needed as prerequisites." The AAAS Science Book List for Young Adults

170 Ethics (Moral philosophy)

Camus, Albert
The rebel; with a foreword by Sir Herbert Read. Knopf 1954 273p $5.95, lib. bdg. $2.39   **170**
1 Good and evil 2 Nihilism
"Translated from the French (L'homme révolté) by Anthony Bower"
The author describes how the theories of philosophers have been used with disastrous effect by political leaders from the French Revolution through the nihilist revolutions of Russia and the governments of Lenin, Hitler and Stalin. The conclusion calls for a return to a political philosophy having as its aim the happiness and development of living human beings
The author "has written a puzzling but engrossing book about the political implications of absolutist ideas. His championship of human values against all the insidious totalitarianisms is deeply moving." New Yorker

171 Ethical systems and doctrines

Tolstoy, Leo
The law of love and the law of violence; tr. by Mary Koutouzow Tolstoy; with a foreword by Baroness Budberg. Holt 1970 101p $3.95   171

1 Christian ethics 2 Pacifism 3 Violence

"In this book, Tolstoy sees the world as violent, unjust, filled with unhappiness. Searching for its means of salvation, he rejects collective politics and revolution as merely the substitution of one violence for another, and turns instead to individual love and the deliberate elimination of self-interest." Book News

"Tolstoy's short treatise, written in 1908, two years before his death, is a summary of the beliefs he formulated in numerous works, particularly those written after 1880 when he had found his own brand of Christianity. . . . [His] essay sounds surprisingly timely; giving the lie to violence, it is an appeal to sanity and reason, as fitting now as in 1908." Choice

176 Sexual ethics

Cain, Arthur H.
Young people and sex; preface by Elisabeth K. Hoyt. Day 1967 126p $4.50   176

1 Sexual ethics 2 Sex

The author discusses "the many aspects of sex—biological, psychological and sociological. He presents . . . facts about venereal disease, pornography and prostitution. There are chapters on birth control and sexual morality and behavior. Dr. Cain traces . . . the universal significance of sex as expressed in the cultures and religions of the world." Publisher's note

"This is extremely frank and candid; occasionally it approaches the explicit description of a marriage manual." Library J
Suggested reading: p[127]

Southhard, Helen F.
Sex before twenty; new answers for young people; foreword by Mary S. Calderone. Rev. ed. Dutton 1971 121p $4.50   176

1 Sexual ethics 2 Sex instruction

First published 1967
"The author discusses dating behavior, going steady, contraceptives, abortion, premarital sex, and other subjects that young people find troublesome in relating to the opposite sex." News of Bks
Includes bibliographical references

178 Ethics of temperance and intemperance

Cain, Arthur H.
Young people and drinking; the use and abuse of beverage alcohol. Day 1970 94p boards $3.75   178

1 Temperance 2 Alcohol

First published 1963
"After telling what beverage alcohol is . . . the author describes the various forms of beverage alcohol, warns against the 'letdown of inhibitions' caused by alcohol, and gives the danger symptoms of the possible alcoholic." Bk Buyer's Guide

"Although opposed throughout the book to any immoderate abuse of alcohol, nevertheless [the author] discusses here only its normal use, pointing out some of the psychological, physiological, social and religious implications of drinking." Best Sellers
Suggested reading: p93-94

Severn, Bill
The end of the roaring twenties; prohibition and repeal; illus. with photographs. Messner 1969 191p illus $3.95, lib. bdg. $3.64   178

1 Prohibition   2 U.S.—History   3 U.S.—History—1919-1933
SBN 671-32171-4; 671-32172-2

Beginning with the early colonists' approval of liquor in moderation, "this well-organized work describes early temperance movements, their successes and failures, and the swift passage of the 18th amendment in the aftermath of World War I. The author shows how national enthusiasm for the amendment gave way to disillusionment, as enforcement became increasingly difficult when enormous profits led to 'organized' crime. Repeal was advocated as a means of ending the Great Depression, but when put into effect, it only slightly alleviated the financial crisis. Mr. Severn indicates that when Prohibition died, it left a heritage of both national cynicism toward legal restraints of all kinds and a strong, criminal underworld. An interesting, unbiased overview." Library J
Suggested further readings: p183

179 Other applications of ethics

Schweitzer, Albert
The teaching of reverence for life; tr. from the German by Richard and Clara Winston. Holt 1965 63p $2.95   179

1 Ethics 2 Life

Analyzed in Essay and general literature index
"Six essays by the German theologian and physician in Africa which set forth the central theme of his philosophy—the sacredness of life. Ethics as it demands right conduct toward all living things, a new renaissance embodying humanitarianism, the necessity for idealism in human relations, man's relationship to animals, and arguments for the outlawing of nuclear weapons are the topics of the brief pleas for implementation of Christian ideas." Booklist

181 Oriental philosophy

Creel, Herrlee Glessner
Chinese thought from Confucius to Mao Tsê-tung. Univ. of Chicago Press 1953 292p $6   181

1 Philosophy, Chinese

"A nontechnical account of the main outlines of the history of Chinese thought, especially in the period before the beginning of the Christian era." Chicago

Partial contents: Confucius and the struggle for human happiness; Mo Tzŭ and the quest for peace and order; Mencius and the emphasis on human nature; Mystical skepticism of the Taoists; Authoritarianism of Hsün Tzŭ; Eclectics of Han; Buddhism and Neo-Confucianism; Suggestions for further reading; Bibliography

"This is a book which can be understood by those who have never read anything else about China." N Y Times Bk R

Radhakrishnan, Sarvepalli
(ed.) A source book in Indian philosophy; ed. by Sarvepalli Radhakrishnan and Charles A. Moore. Princeton Univ. Press 1957 684p $12.50   181

1 Philosophy, Indic

A collection of Indian philosophical writings containing a general introduction, notes on the various texts, and a lengthy bibliography

"This by far is the best collection of Indian philosophical writing this reviewer has seen. One of its main advantages is that it quotes many more sources than previous books of that kind." Library J

191 American philosophy

Brennan, Bernard P.
William James. Twayne 1968 176p
(Twayne's United States authors ser) $5.50
191
1 James, William
The author "provides a brilliant short biography and straightforward expositions of James on truth, knowledge, pragmatism and radical empiricism, religion, metaphysics, and ethics." Choice
Bibliography: p170-72

Schneider, Herbert W.
A history of American philosophy. 2d ed.
Columbia Univ. Press 1963 590p $10 **191**
1 Philosophy, American 2 U.S.—Civilization
First published 1946
Beginning with Platonism in colonial times, this book traces the ideas and influences which have taken root in this country down to the present, with all the significant philosophers and schools of thought represented. It is a study of one branch of the general history of philosophy, a contribution to the history of American culture—especially American literature, social theory, political theory, and religion
Guide to the recent literature: p525-81

191.08 American philosophy— Collections

Kurtz, Paul
(ed.) American philosophy in the twentieth century; a sourcebook from pragmatism to philosophical analysis; ed. with an introductory survey, notes, and bibliographies. Macmillan (N Y) 1966 573p (Classics in the history of thought) $6.95 **191.08**
1 Philosophy, American
With summaries and introductions by the editor, this is an anthology of writings by such philosophers as "Charles Peirce, William James, John Dewey, George Santayana, Alfred North Whitehead, George H. Mead, Ralph Barton Perry . . . Paul Tillich, Sidney Hook, and Ernest Nagel. Movements represented include Pragmatism, the New Realism, Critical Realism, Humanisms, Materialism; Logical Positivism, Existentialism, and Philosophical Analysis." Publisher's note
Includes individual bibliographies and a general one

192 British philosophy

Price, John Valdimir
David Hume. Twayne 1969 174p (Twayne's English authors ser) $4.95 **192**
1 Hume, David
A "study of Hume not only as a philosopher but as an historian, essayist, and man of letters." Books News
Bibliography: p167-70

193 German philosophy

Kant, Immanuel
Critique of pure reason **193**
1 Knowledge, Theory of 2 Reason
Some editions are:
Dutton (Everyman's lib) $3.25 Translated by J. M. D. Meiklejohn
St Martins $11.50 Translated by Norman Kemp Smith
Original German edition, 1781
A philosophical treatise in which Kant "maintained that all sense experience must be inherently rational, and therefore, that rational knowledge about experience is possible. But although reason can understand a thing considered as an object of experience, reason cannot understand the thing-in-itself." Benet. The Reader's Encyclopedia

Nietzsche, Friedrich Wilhelm
The portable Nietzsche; selected and tr. with an introduction, prefaces, and notes, by Walter Kaufmann. Viking 1954 687p $5.50, lib. bdg. $2.25 **193**
"The Viking Portable library"
Contains new translations of the complete: Thus spoke Zarathustra; Twilight of the idols; The antichrist; Nietzsche contra Wagner. Also includes selections from 12 other works, many notes and letters, a chronology and a bibliographical note
"Mr. Kaufmann provides an informative introduction and the volume is altogether a most welcome way to enter a challenging relationship with one of the world's great minds." Spring'd Republican

Schopenhauer, Arthur
The philosophy of Schopenhauer; ed. with an introduction by Irwin Edman. Modern Lib. 1956 376p $2.95 **193**
First published 1928
Contains excerpts from: The world as will and idea, and the complete text of the essay: The metaphysics of the love of the sexes
This "German philosopher, whose extreme pessimism is expressed in The world as will and idea . . . [maintains] that the desires and drives of men, as well as the forces of nature, are manifestations of a single will, specifically the will to live, which is the essence of the world. Since operation of the will means constant striving without satisfaction, life consists of suffering. Only by controlling the will through the intellect, by suppressing the desire to reproduce can suffering be diminished." Benet. The Reader's Encyclopedia

Schweitzer, Albert
Reverence for life; an anthology of selected writings; ed. by Thomas Kiernan. Philosophical Lib. 1965 74p boards $2.75
193
Philosophical essays and quotations of the German philosopher and medical missionary about various aspects of life
Partial contents: Respect for life; Riddles of existence; The meaning of philosophy; Goethe; Religion is not a force; A new ethical system needed; Human awareness; Among the Africans; The will to live

194 French philosophy

Descartes, René
A discourse on method, and selected writings; tr. by John Veitch; introduction by A. D. Lindsay. Dutton 1951 xxx, 287p $2.95
194
1 Science—Methodology
"Everyman's library"
Contents: Discourse on the method of rightly conducting the reason and seeking truth in the sciences (1637); Meditations on the first philosophy; The principles of philosophy
Discourse on method is "divided into six parts and touches upon various matters concerning the sciences: the principal rules of Descartes' method, the rules of morality deduced from this method, proof of the existence of God and the soul, investigations in the field of physics, conclusions concerning the motion of the heart and other anatomical problems, and finally, a program for the further investigation of nature." Haydn. Thesaurus of Book Digests

200　RELIGION

203　Religion—Dictionaries

The **Oxford** Dictionary of the Christian
Church; ed. by F. L. Cross. Oxford [1966
c1957] 1492p $25　　　　　　　　**203**
　1　Christianity—Dictionaries　2　Theology—
Dictionaries
A reprint with minor corrections of the title
first published 1957
　This useful work's "aim is to provide factual
information on every aspect of Christianity,
especially in its historical development. It
contains well over 6,000 entries or articles
ranging from a few lines to about 2,500 words
in length." Publisher's note
　"Commended for its unbiased scholarship,
its broad scope, its very useful bibliographies.
Emphasis is on the historical aspects of Christianity." Enoch Pratt Free Library. Reference Books, 1966

209　Religion—Historical and geographical treatment

Parrinder, Geoffrey
　Religion in Africa. Praeger 1969 253p map
$6.50　　　　　　　　　　　　　**209**
　1　Africa—Religion
　"An informative overview of Africa's three
living religions first examines tribal or traditional religions, highlighting beliefs, rituals,
and myths that are recognizable again and
again despite local and geographic variations.
Shorter sections review Christianity's history
in Africa and its present status and Islam's
belated but highly successful transplanting on
the continent. . . . [This book] serves as a
preliminary survey rather than an in-depth
study." Booklist
　Bibliography: p239-42

220.2　Bible—Concordances and indexes

Harper's Topical concordance; comp. by
Charles R. Joy. Rev. and enl. ed. Harper
1962 628p $8.95　　　　　　　**220.2**
　1　Bible—Concordances
　First published 1940
　"Some 25,000 texts arranged under more
than 2100 topics, with cross references. Designed for the person looking for texts or quotations on a given subject." Winchell. Guide
to Reference Books. 8th edition
　"Designed to be simple, practical and convenient. . . . Only verses considered significant
and vivid are cited, and the index is of the
topic or idea sought and not necessarily of
the actual word." Bookmark

Nelson's Complete concordance of the Revised standard version Bible. Comp. under
the supervision of John W. Ellison. Nelson 1957 2157p $20　　　　　　**220.2**
　1　Bible—Concordances
　"Every means possible, both human and
mechanical, was used to guarantee accuracy
in the work. The use of a computer imposed
certain limitations upon the Concordance. Although it could be 'exhaustive' it could not
be 'analytical'; the context and location of
each and every word could be listed, but not
the Hebrew and Greek words from which they
were translated." Preface to the Concordance
of the Revised standard version Bible
　For a fuller review see: The Booklist and
Subscription Books Bulletin, February 15, 1958

Stevenson, Burton
　(comp.) Home book of Bible quotations;
selected and arranged by Burton Stevenson.
Harper 1949 xxiv, 645p $12.50　　**220.2**
　1　Bible—Concordances　2　Quotations
　This "subject treatment, giving exact location of quotation, is fully indexed, and has
the added feature of resumés of famous Bible
stories, the outstanding facts in the lives of
the principal Bible characters (all in the words
of the Bible itself), and brief explanations of
obscure references. Citations have been included from the Apocryphas of both the Old
and New Testament. The text follows the King
James Version, with a few references to the
Revised Version." Cur Ref Bks

220.3　Bible—Dictionaries

Harper's Bible dictionary, by Madeleine S.
Miller and J. Lane Miller in consultation
with eminent authorities; drawings by
Claire Valentine. Harper illus maps $9.95,
thumb indexed $10.95　　　　　**220.3**
　1　Bible—Dictionaries
　First published 1952. Frequent editions published
　A Bible dictionary covering archeology, geography, chronology, personalities, and other
fields of Biblical investigation. Includes numerous photographs, diagrams, tables, and Biblical
quotations. 18 colored maps conclude the book
　"It is not possible for a one-volume dictionary of the Bible to include every obscure individual, place-name, or site, or to discuss
every facet of biblical truth or Christian
doctrine. . . . It is our confident belief, however, that few persons, places, or topics of
moderate or major significance have been
omitted." Foreword to the seventh edition
　"Popularly written, alphabetically arranged
series of entries on a wide variety of subjects
connected with Bible study." Murphey. How
and Where to Look it Up

Hastings, James
　(ed.) Dictionary of the Bible. Rev. ed. by
Frederick C. Grant and H. H. Rowley.
Scribner 1963 1059p maps $15　　**220.3**
　1　Bible—Dictionaries
　First published 1909. Frequently reprinted
　A dictionary covering geography, history,
theology, customs, personalities, and books of
the Bible. Includes signed articles
　"This edition has been thoroughly revised in
the light of modern discoveries and scholarship. References are to the Revised Standard
version of the Bible with cross references from
the Authorized version and the Revised version." Winchell. Guide to Reference Books.
8th edition

The **New** Westminster Dictionary of the
Bible; ed. by Henry Snyder Gehman.
Westminster Press 1970 1027p illus maps
(Westminster Aids to the study of the
Scriptures) $10.95　　　　　　**220.3**
　1　Bible—Dictionaries
　SBN 664-21277-8
　Based on: A dictionary of the Bible, by J.
D. Davis first published 1898. Published in 1944
with title: The Westminster Dictionary of the
Bible
　"The standard reference work has been
greatly revised and expanded. . . . Discoveries
in recent years in archaeology and history have
greatly affected Biblical philology, interpretation, and even theology. The fruits of these
discoveries are valuably reflected in the new
edition. . . . There are hundreds of new entries,
and of the 450 illustrations, many have been
especially prepared and are wholly new. Spellings used include the King James Version,
the Revised Standard Version and the Revised
Version (English and American) The appendix includes 16 excellent full-color maps derived from the 'Westminster Historical Atlas
to the Bible.' " Pub W

220.5 Bible. Modern versions

Bible
   The Holy Bible; containing the Old and New Testaments; tr. out of the original tongues; and with the former translations diligently compared and rev. by King James's special command, 1611. Oxford prices vary   220.5
   The authorized or King James version originally published 1611

   The Jerusalem Bible. Doubleday 1966 2v in 1 maps $16.95; thumb indexed $19.95
                                              220.5
   Also available in Reader's edition for $9.95
   "General editor: Alexander Jones. . . . The principal collaborators in translation and literary revision were: Joseph Leo Alston and others."
   "The introductions to the various books and the notes are those prepared by the Dominican Biblical School in Jerusalem and published in 'La Bible de Jerusalem.' The translation of these, from the French, given here contains minor revisions, taking into account decisions and implications of the Second Vatican Council. The translation of the Biblical text, made from the Hebrew and Greek and compared with the French of 'La Bible de Jerusalem,' is concerned with meaning rather than expression." Booklist

   The new American Bible; tr. from the original languages, with critical use of all the ancient sources by members of the Catholic Biblical Association of America; sponsored by the Bishops' Committee of the Confraternity of Christian Doctrine. Kenedy 1970 1347, 401, 47p maps $9.95   220.5
   This "is a completely fresh translation from Hebrew, Greek and Aramaic texts, and makes use of both the Dead Sea Scrolls and the recently rediscovered Masada manuscript. Work on the new Bible dates from an encyclical issued by Pope Pius XII in 1943 calling for more attention to the sacred writings of the church." News of Bks
   "The textual notes, introductions to the books, and concluding essays add to the usefulness of the edition for the layman. The points of view, while basically consistent with Catholic tradition, also reveal the extent to which Catholic biblical scholars have been influenced by modern critical studies and methods." Library J

   The new English Bible. Oxford [and] Cambridge 1970 [Lib. ed] 3v Old Testament $8.95, New Testament (2d ed) $5.95, Apocrypha $4.95   220.5
   Also available in one-volume standard edition, $8.95. With Apocrypha, $9.95
   Earlier edition of New Testament, published 1961
   The work in this new translation of the Bible "has been carried out under the authority of a Joint Committee on which are representatives of the major Protestant churches of the British Isles. In the later stages the Committee was joined by observers representing the Roman Catholic Church. . . . The aim has been to present a translation which, avoiding both archaisms and transient modernisms, would provide the reader with a faithful version of the ancient texts in the language of today. In addition, the reader will find useful introductions to each volume and footnotes throughout in which the translators have noted such textual problems as alternative meanings. The major divisions within each book carry helpful descriptive headings." Publisher's note
   This "is one of the great translations. It uses fresh, living language to express the religious insights that have meant much and still mean much in the English-speaking world. . . . It is boldly accurate. At the same time, the accuracy comes through not in baldly literal or vulgar terminology but in elegant English." N Y Times Bk R

220.8 Special subjects treated in Bible

Farb, Peter
   The land, wildlife, and peoples of the Bible; illus. by Harry McNaught. Harper 1967 171p illus $3.95, lib. bdg. $3.79   220.8
   1 Bible—Natural history
   A natural history of the Holy Land in which the author uses the Bible as a chief source and relates ancient events and observations on animals, plants, climate, geography and population in the light of modern scientific and archeological knowledge. (Publisher)
   "In a final chapter [the author] cites specific examples of the Israelis' use of the Old Testament in revitalizing desert areas caused by 2,000 years of man's neglect. . . . Artistic pen-and-ink drawings." Booklist
   Suggested readings: p160-62. Index of Biblical references: p163-64

220.88 Bible as literature

Chase, Mary Ellen
   The Bible and the common reader. Rev. ed. Macmillan (N Y) 1952 325p $6.50
                                              220.88
   1 Bible as literature 2 Bible—Study
   First published 1944
   "This illuminating study of the great literature of the Bible starts with the stories of the beginning of things and continues by relating the subjects as nearly as possible to the progress of Hebrew life and thought, regardless of when the material considered was actually written. Abounding in choice quotations, the narrative considers the various types of literary forms to be found in the Old Testament and the New, though more space is given to the former. . . . List of books for reading and study." Bookmark
   "Miss Chase's account of the King James version, its origins and completion, is a good story in itself. Even more striking is her recapitulation of its wide and deep impact upon English literature and thought. Its enriching mark is upon most of the best writers in our language." Springf'd Republican

Henn, T. R.
   The Bible as literature. Oxford 1970 270p $7   220.88
   1 Bible as literature
   Based on the King James (Authorized) version of the Bible, the author analyzes the Bible's epic, narrative, lyric and dramatic qualities. "It is a valid, thoughtful study of the various kinds of literature incorporated in the Bible, but even more important are Henn's drawings on materials strongly influenced by the Bible and his discussions of the worth of the Bible in many ways other than for religious instruction." Choice

220.9 Bible—Geography, history, biography

Keller, Werner
   The Bible as history; a confirmation of the Book of Books; tr. by William Neil. Morrow 1956 xxv, 452p illus maps $8.95   220.9
   1 Bible—History of Biblical events 2 Bible—Antiquities
   Original German edition published 1955
   Only in recent years have scientific discoveries documented the Bible as history. From the Near East and the Mediterranean, Dr. Keller has gathered a mass of archaeological evidence that, step by step, reveals the historical foundations of the Old and New Testaments. (Publisher)
   "Includes beautiful photographs, drawings, maps, diagrams, and an extensive bibliography." Sec Ed Brd

Kraeling, Emil G.
Rand McNally Bible atlas. [3d ed] Rand
McNally 1966 487p illus maps $9.95   **220.9**

1 Bible—Geography 2 Bible—History of Biblical events

First published 1956
"For the general reader. The extensive text is primarily a historical discussion of geographical references in the Bible, told in the sequence of the Books of the Bible with archaeological and historical background. Many illustrations in black and white and a section of 22 maps in the center of the volume, with a geographical index to the place-names appearing on the maps and in the text." Winchell. Guide to Reference Books. 8th edition

National Geographic Society
Everyday life in Bible times. The Society 1967 448p illus maps (The Story of man lib) $9.95   **220.9**

1 Bible—History of Biblical events 2 Bible—Antiquities 3 Civilization, Ancient

Foreword by Melville Bell Grosvenor; editorial consultant: James B. Pritchard; special essays by Samuel Noah Kramer, and others. 528 illustrations, 412 in full color, 13 maps
Covers the worlds of Abraham, Moses, David, Solomon, Jesus and Paul
"Popular, widely endorsed, written largely by staff members of the Society, the book contains many essays by some of the world's leading authorities. The editors aim to 'bring Bible times to life.' There are hundreds of illustrations from photographs, old masters, and paintings commissioned for this book; some are superb, many are very unusual and would be hard to find elsewhere." Library J
Acknowledgements and reference guide: p447

The **Westminster** Historical atlas to the Bible. Rev. ed. Edited by George Ernest Wright and Floyd Vivian Filson; with an introductory article by William Foxwell Albright. Westminster Press 1956 130p illus maps $7.50   **220.9**

1 Bible—Geography

First published 1945
"A scholarly atlas, with much archaeological information, historical discussion, and illustrations. The maps are clear and well drawn. Three indexes: (1) to the text; (2) to the maps, including a topographical concordance to the Bible; and (3) to Arabic names identified with Biblical places in Syria and Palestine." Winchell. Guide to Reference Books. 8th edition
An "index of site names enables the reader to locate quickly any place mentioned in the Bible. There are 33 maps in full color. A valuable feature of the text is the historical arrangement of the materials according to the successive eras." Rel Bk Club Bul

Wright, George Ernest
Biblical archaeology. [New and rev. ed] Westminster Press 1962 291p illus maps $12.50   **220.9**

1 Bible—Antiquities

First published 1957
The author presents the Bible stories set in chronological order as the foundation and continuity for his book. To this narrative is related the archaeological discoveries that illuminate biblical history. (Publisher)
"The results of more than twenty years of intensive study of archaeological discoveries related to the Bible are embodied in this magnificent work. . . . It is delightful reading as well as an authoritative source of knowledge. It interprets all the major findings, including . . . studies of the Dead Sea Scrolls. There are 220 photographs, drawings and maps." Rel Bk Club Bul
Includes bibliographies

221.4 Dead Sea Scrolls

Burrows, Millar
Dead Sea scrolls; with translations by the author. Viking 1955 435p illus maps $8.50   **221.4**

1 Dead Sea scrolls

"The director of the American School of Oriental Research in Jerusalem at the time of the discovery [the the scrolls] outlines the story for the layman and summarizes the numerous, vehemently disputed theories about the background, contents, and writers of the scrolls." Booklist
"Clearly and simply written despite its fairly complex subject, this book has the additional advantage of being from the pen of one of the world's greatest Biblical scholars. . . This volume has extensive translations from four of the 1947 documents plus one earlier find." Christian Science Monitor

More light on the Dead Sea scrolls; new scrolls and new interpretations; with translations of important recent discoveries. Viking 1958 434p map $6.95   **221.4**

1 Dead Sea scrolls

The "author continues the story of the scrolls in the light of further discoveries and further elucidation of Biblical and non-Biblical manuscripts from the 11 caves in the Dead Sea region. . . . [He] discusses in detail the many theories which have been held or have been modified about the scrolls and their origin, and shows clearly what is tenable and what is untenable in the light of the solid evidence now provided by archaeology, palaeography and numismatics. For the most part of interpretations found in 'The Dead Sea Scrolls' [entered above] have been maintained." Library J
This book "can be read without reference to its predecessor, yet the author has continued his account with such effectiveness that the combined result may justifiably be described as two volumes of the same work. This point is made particularly clear by the fact that the index to More Light gives references to the earlier volume as well." Cath World
Bibliography: p411-24

Noble, Iris
Treasure of the caves; the story of the Dead Sea scrolls. Macmillan (N Y) 1971 214p illus maps $5.95   **221.4**

1 Dead Sea scrolls

The author relates how the Dead Sea scrolls were found by a young Bedouin shepherd in the rugged Qumran terrain. She also tells how scholars acquired the scrolls from the Bedouins and what happened when these "priceless historical clues" were pieced together. (Publisher)
"The text is greatly enriched by maps, photographs, and the author's use of names, dates, aend other specifics. Details of the contents of the scrolls are also included." Library J

Wilson, Edmund
The Dead Sea scrolls, 1946-1969. Oxford 1969 320p $6.50   **221.4**

1 Dead Sea scrolls

First published 1955 with title: The scrolls from the Dead Sea
This is an account of the origin and discovery of the Dead Sea scrolls as well as a discussion of the possible influence which the discovery will have on Biblical, political and social history. The author then discusses new findings such as an Aramaic version of Genesis which differs considerably from the Biblical version, a set of instructions for finding the locations of a variety of treasures that may have been those of the Temple. The book concludes with a description of the recent excavation of the fortress of Masada and of the Middle East as it is today. (Publisher)
"While modestly disclaiming expertise in the subject, Mr. Wilson demonstrates a fine familiarity with the scrolls and their contents, as well as the opinions and views of many students of them. As usual he writes with clarity and elegance." Best Sellers

221.9 Bible. Old Testament— Geography, history, biography

Heaton, Eric William

Everyday life in Old Testament times; illus. from drawings by Marjorie Quennell. Scribner 1956 240p illus map $8.95   **221.9**

1 Bible. Old Testament—Antiquities 2 Palestine—Social life and customs

Companion volume to A. C. Bouquet's: Everyday life in New Testament times listed in class 225.9

This survey of Israelite daily life during the period 1250-586 B.C. "describes rural and urban society and details all aspects of domestic, agricultural, industrial, military, civil, professional, and religious life in Palestine. Filled with Biblical examples and allusions but written in an energetic, informal style, the book will be an authoritative reference." Booklist

Oursler, Fulton

The greatest book ever written; the Old Testament story. Doubleday 1951 489p maps $6.95   **221.9**

1 Bible. Old Testament—History of Biblical events 2 Bible. Old Testament—Stories

Companion volume to: The greatest story ever told, entered in class 232.9

Written in everyday, modern language, this is "a narrative story of the Old Testament. . . . Protestant, Catholic and Jewish experts were consulted by Mr. Oursler." Huntting

"The author is primarily interested in the story, which he tells with a fine imaginative sweep. He discusses no historical problems; he enters into no critical examination of the Biblical text. . . . Even moral judgments are avoided. . . . There still remains the question as to whether the Bible needs an intermediary of this sort. Meanwhile, we may be glad that one more door is opened into this field of sacred literature, and the Bible made easy and not difficult to read." N Y Her Trib Books

225.9 Bible. New Testament— Geography, history, biography

Bouquet, A. C.

Everyday life in New Testament times; illus. from drawings by Marjorie Quennell. Scribner 1954 [c1953] 235p illus maps $8.95   **225.9**

1 Bible. New Testament—Antiquities 2 Palestine—Social life and customs

Companion volume to E. W. Heaton's: Everyday life in Old Testament times, listed in class 221.9

"An authoritative, factual but informal description of life in the Mediterranean world during the first century of the Christian era. . . . The text is profusely illustrated by historically accurate sketches and diagrams drawn from contemporary sources. Recommended as a reference for Biblical history, ancient literature and social studies rather than general reading." Booklist

232.9 Doctrines on family and life of Jesus Christ

Bishop, Jim

The day Christ died. Harper 1957 336p $7.50   **232.9**

1 Jesus Christ—Biography

An "hour-by-hour account of the last Supper, and Jesus' betrayal, trial and crucifixion. . . . It quotes, when direct Biblical reference is made, from the New Testament as translated by James A. Kleist and Joseph L. Lilly (Bruce).

The whole background of Jesus' life and the Jewish and Roman worlds is . . . woven in." Pub W

Bibliography: p336. Maps on lining-papers

Goodspeed, Edgar J.

A life of Jesus. Large type ed. complete and unabridged. Watts, F. [1967 c1950] 248p lib. bdg. $8.95   **232.9**

1 Jesus Christ—Biography 2 Large type books

"A Keith Jennison book"

First published 1950 by Harper

"The quality which lends importance to Dr. Goodspeed's story of Jesus is its carefulness to keep within the limits of historical facts, so far as they can be sifted by the student. . . . [An] account which is on the level of interest of any thoughtful reader. What is offered us is a trustworthy history of what the Man of Nazareth said and did [including information] about Jesus' family, birth and youth, and continuing through his public ministry down to His crucifixion and resurrection." Rel Bk Club Bul

Quotations and references: p239-48

Maus, Cynthia Pearl

(comp.) Christ and the fine arts. Rev. and enl. ed. An anthology of pictures, poetry, music, and stories centering in the life of Christ. Harper 1959 813p illus $6.95   **232.9**

1 Jesus Christ—Biography 2 Jesus Christ—Art 3 Jesus Christ—Poetry

First published 1938

Brief introductory chapters dealing with the use of the arts in religious education are followed by six parts covering every aspect of Christ's life, from the Nativity to the Ascension, and Jesus in everyday life today

Numerous indices

Oursler, Fulton

The greatest story ever told; a tale of the greatest life ever lived. Doubleday 1949 299p $6.95   **232.9**

1 Jesus Christ—Biography 2 Bible. New Testament—History of Biblical events

Companion volume to: The greatest book ever written, entered in class 221.9

"This is the story of Jesus. It is a chronology of events from the betrothal of Mary and Joseph to the days after the Resurrection, and the episodes are taken from the four Gospels. What is imaginative in the narrative is largely detail to fill in chinks left open in the Bible accounts; nothing has been included that did not seem a reasonable assumption from the records." Preface

"This reverent and vivid retelling of the story of Christ is the orthodox traditional version, yet it is as fresh as the morning newspaper." Cincinnati

242 Prayers, meditations, contemplations

Boyd, Malcolm

Are you running with me, Jesus? Prayers. Holt 1965 119p $3.95   **242**

1 Prayers

This is a "collection of prayers by an Episcopal clergyman who shows that prayer can be expressed in the language of everyday life." Cincinnati

"These are not in the least formal or prescribed prayers, but very spontaneous, expressing struggle, reluctance, weariness, or, on the obverse side, joy, hope, and determination, and always humility and faith." Pub W

Seventeen

The Seventeen Book of prayer; an anthology of inspirational prose and poetry by the editors of Seventeen Magazine. . . . Macmillan (N Y) 1965 224p illus $4.95   **242**

1 Prayers 2 Devotional literature

"With introductions on the meaning of prayer by Francis X. Connolly, Tom F. Driver, Abraham Joshua Heschel." Title page

A collection of "inspirational verse and prose, ranging from the prayers of Biblical times to thoughtful poetry of today. Selections are from the Old and New Testament, the Torah, the Koran, the Bhagavad-Gita, and the Ordination. Of special interest are the expressions of faith from leaders such as Albert Schweitzer, Winston Churchill, and John F. Kennedy. In addition, there are eight original poems by teenagers." Huntting

Includes indexes of authors, titles, and first lines

248 Personal Christian religion

Lewis, C. S.

The Screwtape letters [and] Screwtape proposes a toast. Macmillan (N Y) [1964 c1961] 185p $4.95   **248**

1 Christian life 2 Satire

Also available in a large type edition for $6.95

The Screwtape letters, first published separately, 1943. This combined edition first published 1961 in a paperback

Includes a new Screwtape piece, Screwtape proposes a toast, which continues in the same vein as the first pieces in which a witty, experienced devil in hell coaches, through his letters, an apprentice devil on earth

Merton, Thomas

Contemplation in a world of action; introduction by Jean Leclercq. Doubleday 1971 xxii, 384p $7.95   **248**

1 Spiritual life 2 Monasticism and religious orders

Merton who died in 1968 was a Trappist monk. Here, in this postumously published work, he discusses the problems involved in monastic renewal

These essays "are a call for revolution within the monastic life. . . . [They] offer many suggestions for reform, including the possibility of married men affiliating with a monastic order." N Y Times Bk R

252 Sermons

King, Martin Luther

Strength to love [by] Martin Luther King, Jr. Harper 1963 146p $5.95   **252**

1 Sermons

A collection of sermons "that preach tough-mindedness but tender-heartedness, non-violent resistance to injustice, forgiveness for one's enemies, and intellectual and moral alertness. They end with the author's personal credo and his account of its applications in his life." Pub W

"In a remarkable way these sermons combine Christian theology, Christian ethics, and strategy of Christian action in relation to a social situation. The keynote is faith in the conquering power of love. They thus represent a position of lofty Christian idealism, but it is matched by a realistic grasp of the recalcitrant social forces that have to be dealt with. . . . The two final chapters are in a somewhat different vein, summarizing in a rather dramatic way Dr. King's understanding of the Christian faith and life and his own spiritual pilgrimage." Rel Bk Club Bul

"Careful craftsmanship has made each of these 17 sermons a gem. The author has an artist's feel for colorful words and rhythmic sentences. . . . He brilliantly applies the Bible to intellectual uncertainties, emotional upsets, spiritual weaknesses." Christian Century

Sources: p143-46

Schweitzer, Albert

Reverence for life; tr. by Reginald H. Fuller. Harper 1969 153p $4.95   **252**

1 Sermons

Original German edition, 1966

"Seventeen meditations originally given at the Church of St. Nicolai in Strasbourg, 1900-19, and the first volume in English to contain only Schweitzer's sermons. . . . The messages included here are all based on New Testament scriptures and concern primarily the themes of gratitude, hope, suffering, death, missions, and ethics." Choice

"This is the essence of Schweitzer. . . . [The sermons included] communicate Schweitzer's deeply compassionate Christianity and reveal a man who [had] found his peace on earth. They never cloy, nor do they seem to preach 'at' but 'for.' [They] . . . are clear, expressively tender, not concerned with institutional doctrine." Pub W

261.8 Christianity and socio-economic problems

Berrigan, Daniel

No bars to manhood. Doubleday 1970 215p $5.95   **261.8**

1 Church and social problems 2 U.S.—Moral conditions

The American Jesuit's "recital of his personal odyssey from pleasant childhood in Minnesota to prison today and of his transformation from well-meaning unconcern to dedicated activism makes up the . . . first part of this book. The . . . second section is composed of essays on a series of 'prophets and prisoners,' Jeremiah, Gandhi, and Cleaver, among others. [Berrigan's] life at Cornell from his arrival in 1967 until after the 1969 riots is the subject of the last section before the epilogue, which makes a plea for a new humanity and a new world." Library J

270 Christian church history

Horizon Magazine

The Horizon History of Christianity, by the editors of Horizon Magazine. Editor in charge: Marshall B. Davidson; author: Roland H. Bainton. Am. Heritage 1964 432p illus boards $18.95   **270**

1 Church history

The twelve chapters of narrative are "told from the standpoint of no one denomination or doctrine. The purpose is to show . . . the evolution of the Christian faith over two millenniums and its profound influence on the course of Western civilization." Publisher's note

The author has "given the general public a book marked by judicious selectivity and a style having charity, clarity and pungency. . . . The pictures . . . make an absorbing study in themselves." Christian Century

Latourette, Kenneth Scott

A history of Christianity. Harper 1953 xxvii, 1516p maps $10   **270**

1 Church history

This book endeavors "to be a well-rounded summary of the entire history of Christianity in all its phases and in its setting in the human scene." Preface

"Comprehensive, readable and with good coverage of the 19th and 20th century." Cincinnati

Selected bibliography at end of each chapter

280 Denominations and sects

Look
Religions in America; a completely rev. and up-to-date guide to churches and religious groups in the United States; ed. by Leo Rosten. . . . Simon & Schuster 1963 415p illus maps $6.95 **280**
1 Sects 2 U.S.—Religion
First published in book form 1955 with title: A guide to the religions of America
"The famous 'Look' magazine series on Religion, greatly amplified and rewritten, plus the most complete and authoritative compilation of facts, figures, tables, charts, articles and reference material on religion in any published volume." Title page
"What is most impressive here is perhaps the sense of variety, plasticity, and freedom that comes from reading through this cross-section of contemporary religious thought." Christian Science Monitor
Selected reading list of books on religion: p330-37. Glossary of religious terms: p392-99

Mead, Frank S.
Handbook of denominations in the United States. New 5th ed. Abingdon 1970 265p $3.95 **280**
1 Sects 2 U.S.—Religion
ISBN 0-687-16568-7
First published 1951
"For those who require brief accounts of the history and doctrines, and relatively recent information on . . . [denominational] membership, this modestly priced handbook includes information on more than 250 religious bodies, the whole well indexed, and with appended list of addresses of headquarters, a glossary of terms, and a bibliography arranged by denomination." Cur Ref Bks

291 Comparative religion and mythology

Bach, Marcus
Had you been born in another faith; the story of religion as it is lived and loved by those who follow the path of their parental faith. Illus. by Polly Bolian. Prentice-Hall 1961 186p illus boards $4.95 **291**
1 Religions
The author "presents the basic elements of the world's principal contemporary religious movements by means of explaining to the reader how he would live and worship if he had happened to be born as a Hindu, a Parsi, a Buddhist, a Confucianist, a Shintoist, a Jew, a Moslem, a Roman Catholic or a Protestant." Spring'fd Republican

Bulfinch, Thomas
Bulfinch's Mythology: The age of fable, The age of chivalry, Legends of Charlemagne **291**
1 Mythology 2 Folklore—Europe 3 Chivalry 4 Charlemagne (Romances, etc.)
Some editions are:
Crowell $6.95 Illustrated by Elinore Blaisdell
Modern Lib. (Modern Lib. Giants) $4.95, lib. bdg. $3.89
Contains myths of Greece and Rome, Egypt, the Far East, Germany and the Norse myths, also legends of King Arthur, Charlemagne and Mabinogion

Cain, Arthur H.
Young people and religion. Day 1970 159p $4.95 **291**
1 Religions
The purpose of this book "is to examine the basic tenets of the great religions of the world —Christianity, Judaism, Hinduism, Buddhism, and Islam—in order to provide young readers with both the information and the inspiration to make their own religious decisions." Publisher's note
Recommended reading: p156-59

Frazer, Sir James George
The new Golden bough; a new abridgment of the classic work; ed. and with notes and foreword by Theodor H. Gaster. Phillips 1959 xxx, 738p $12.95 **291**
1 Mythology 2 Religion, Primitive 3 Superstition
First published with imprint Criterion Books
"A new edition based on the twelve volumes and . . . supplement. The revisions include deletions of obsolete material, new commentary and comprehensive annotations." Pub W
"A comparative study of world religions, magic, vegetation and fertility beliefs and rites, kingship, taboos, totemism and the like." The New Century Handbook of English Literature
"Theodor Caster has done a wonderful job of abridgment to begin with. More, however, he has reevaluated much of Frazer's basic data and interpreted them in the light of modern social anthropology." Chicago Sunday Tribune
Includes bibliographical note

Gaer, Joseph
How the great religions began. New and rev. ed. Dodd 1956 424p $5 **291**
1 Religions
First published 1929 by McBride Co.
Contents: Buddhism; Jainism; Hindustan; Confucianism; Taoism; Shinto; Zoroastrianism; Judaism; Christianity; Mohammedanism; The Reformation
"This popular guide to the study of the great religions fills a distinct need. Obviously for the average reader, these pieces cover the major religious beliefs of the earth, from earliest times to the present. Very readable." Wis Lib Bul

The wisdom of the living religions. Dodd 1956 338p $6 **291**
1 Religious literature 2 Religions
The teachings of the living religions presented through selections from their sayings, maxims and parables. The religions represented are: Buddhism, Christianity, Confucianism, Hinduism, Jainism, Judaism, Islam, Shintoism, Taoism and Zoroastrianism. (Publisher)
"The sayings are prefaced by a brief coverage of the basic principles of each faith. Each saying is given a reference number so that it can be located in the original source. Suitable for reference or for personal reading. Topical index and bibliography included." Booklist

Jurji, Edward J.
(ed.) The great religions of the modern world. . . . Princeton Univ. Press 1947 [c1946] 387p $8.50 **291**
1 Religions
Analyzed in Essay and general literature index
"Confucianism, Taoism, Hinduism, Buddhism, Shintoism, Islam, Judaism, Eastern Orthodoxy, Roman Catholicism, Protestantism." Title page
"This symposium by authorities in their fields is concerned with 'the genius, development, and spiritual core of the major contemporary religions.'" Bookmark
Selected bibliographies at end of each chapter

Larousse World mythology; ed. by Pierre Grimal. Putnam 1965 560p illus $25 **291**
1 Mythology
Originally published 1963 in France
A "presentation of the myths, cults and rites of every land from Sumer and Babylon to the islands of Oceania. Drawing upon new material uncovered by scholars in recent years . . . [this] offers a fresh interpretation of the mythologies of every religion of the world— from the dark, cave-bound rites with which prehistoric man sought to propitiate his animal quarry, through the . . . sacrificial cults of Central and South America, the magic and

Larousse World mythology—*Continued*
symbolism of Africa, and finally, the ancestor and fetish worship of Oceania." Publisher's note
"A volume of updated if not uncontroversial interpretation useful for reference and reading enrichment on mythological subjects." Booklist
Suggestions for further reading: p546-47

Savage, Katharine
The story of world religions; illus. with photographs and maps. Walck, H.Z. 1967 [c1966] 283p illus maps lib. bdg. $6   **291**
1 Religions
First published 1966 in England with title: The history of world religions
A survey of the "historical, social and geographical backgrounds of the major religions of both East and West, and the origin, rituals and tenets of each faith." Huntting
This is "a straightforward, accurate, and sympathetic account. . . . [It is] an unbiased narrative that presents belief and worship as an integral part of man's nature." Horn Bk
Bibliography: p275-78

Smith, Huston
The religions of man. Harper 1958 328p $5.95   **291**
1 Religions
The religions the author "discusses are Hinduism, Buddhism, Confucianism, Taoism, Islam, Judaism and Christianity. He has not tried to write a comparative history which will extol one at the expense of another, but to describe as succinctly as possible without sacrificing depth the meaning of each in the lives of its convinced believers. A short concluding chapter sums up the general meaning of religion in the life of man and comments illuminatingly on the likenesses of the various forms it has taken." Book of the Month Club News
Bibliographies at the end of most chapters

Smith, Ruth
(ed.) The tree of life; selections from the literature of the world's religions; with an introduction by Robert O. Ballou, and fourteen drawings by Boris Artzybasheff. Viking 1942 496p illus lib. bdg. $5.63   **291**
1 Religious literature 2 Religions
"Selected writings from religious faith of all times, from the simple legends and chants of the American Indian to complexities of the Hindu and Buddhist sacred books. Designed to show how man has striven to answer riddle of existence and to establish satisfactory relationship with his Creator and his fellow men. Thirteen sections, with introductory notes on background material. Contains songs, narratives, and precepts. Distinguished design and format. . . . Sources of text; glossary; index." Library J

Vail, Albert
Transforming light; the living heritage of world religions [by] Albert Vail and Emily McClellan Vail. Harper 1970 451p $12.50   **291**
1 Religions
With emphasis on Buddhism, Christianity, and Islam, the authors explore and accent "positive likenesses of major religions in recorded history, while making clear that the violent schisms, religious wars, inquisitions and persecutions stemmed from the loss of the true vision of religious ideals. The book is simply written and an invaluable introduction to world religions for the lay reader and young adult." Pub W

Voss, Carl Hermann
In search of meaning: living religions of the world; illus. by Eric Carle. World Pub. 1968 191p $5.95, lib. bdg. $5.70   **291**
1 Religions
"Excalibur books"
"The author discusses the origins of religion; explains Hinduism, Jainism, Buddhism, Confucianism, Taoism, Shinto, Judaism, Zoroas-

trianism, Christianity, Islam (Mohammedanism); and ventures some views of a faith for tomorrow." Am News of Bks
"In this well-written study of comparative religion, Dr. Voss first traces man's spiritual expressions from primitive times through the Roman period, including practices of the Aztecs, Incas, and Mayas. . . . Numerous quotes from sacred writings are included, and the last chapter comprises a comparison of the faiths' basic beliefs and a discussion of today's substitute religions and philosophies." Library J
Suggested reading: p173-82

291.03   Comparative religion and mythology—Dictionaries

Brandon, S. G. F.
(ed.) A dictionary of comparative religion. Scribner 1970 704p $17.50   **291.03**
1 Religions—Dictionaries
"With its short, signed articles prepared by the faculty of British universities, [this dictionary] packs in a tremendous amount of information on the beliefs, ritual, important figures, schools, councils, sacred books, and many other aspects of the world's religions, both living and dead. Extensive use of abbreviations, both in the text and in the bibliographies, and the use of many 'sees'-references helps to produce a compact volume." Cur Ref Bks
"A superb production, intelligently compiled, extremely wide ranging (for example, from ancient Greek mythology to the birth control controversy of today) and free from the usual failing of an unbalanced concentration on western religions." Economist
Includes bibliographies

New Larousse Encyclopedia of mythology; introduction by Robert Graves. Putnam [1969 c1959] 500p illus $17.95   **291.03**
1 Mythology—Dictionaries
First published 1959 by Prometheus Press with title: Larousse Encyclopedia of mythology
This comprehensive, illustrated compendium of world mythology includes prehistoric, Egyptian, Assyro-Babylonian, Roman, Celtic, Teutonic, Persian, Indian, Chinese, Japanese, African and American mythology
"Not an encyclopedia in the usual sense of the term as the material is presented in essay form with no easy approach to specific points. Includes various aspects of folklore, legend, and religious customs." Winchell. Guide to Reference Books. 8th edition
Further reading list: p486-87

292   Classical religion and mythology

Asimov, Isaac
Words from the myths; decorations by William Barss. Houghton 1961 225p illus $3.50   **292**
1 Mythology, Classical 2 English language—Etymology
The author's "informal retelling and discussion of the myths to point out the scores of words rooted in mythology and to explain their usage in the English language provide a fresh look at the myths and a better understanding of the words and expression derived from them. . . . For browsing and for reference." Booklist
Mythological index: p222-25

Bulfinch, Thomas
A book of myths; selections from Bulfinch's Age of fable; with illus. by Helen Sewell. Macmillan (N Y) 1942 126p illus $4.95   **292**
1 Mythology, Classical
"Thirty Greek myths, the text adapted with few changes from Bulfinch's Age of Fable, including such well known myths as 'The golden

Bullfinch, Thomas—*Continued*
fleece' and 'Perseus' as well as many less easily
available ... such as 'Castor and Pollux' and
'Niobe.' " Ontario Lib Rev
"Without illustrations, this would be a most
usable collection of Greek myths.... With the
illustrations, this is a truly distinguished
book." Library J

Gayley, Charles Mills
(ed.) The classic myths in English literature and in art. . . . New ed. rev. and enl.
Ginn [c1939] xli, 597p illus maps $7.95 **292**
1 Mythology, Classical
First published 1893
"Based originally on Bulfinch's 'Age of fable'
(1855) accompanied by an interpretative and
illustrative commentary." Title page
"Contains the Greek and Roman and Norse
myths and hero stories, with maps and pictures
of famous paintings and statues, and many
illustrative English and American poems. Useful for school work." Pittsburgh
For reference use rather than for general
reading, this is a valuable study of "mythology as connected with literature." Bibliography in Preface

Grant, Michael
Myths of the Greeks and Romans. Meridian Bks. [1965 c1962] xxiii, 487p illus maps
pa $3.95   **292**
1 Mythology, Classical 2 Classical literature
Original hardbound edition first published
1962 by World Publishing Company
"The myths retold, with comments on their
sources, often historical facts, with ancient versions, excerpts from modern translations, and
a chronological treatment of Greek and Latin
authors, plus ⟨a bibliography⟩ notes, appendices,
and a genealogy table." Bk Buyer's Guide
This scholarly "study of origins takes Mr.
Grant into many different fields, including archaeology and psychology as well as classical
philology [and modern literature]." Times
(London) Lit Sup

Graves, Robert
Greek myths. Braziller 1957 [c1955] 2v
in 1 map $7.50   **292**
1 Mythology, Classical
First published 1955 in two volumes by
Penguin Books
"Robert Graves retells for moderns the ancient Greek myths of the Creation, the birth
and lives of the great Olympians, the Theseus,
Oedipus, the Heracles cycles, the Argonaut voyage, the tale of Troy and others. With reference to classical sources, maps and copious
indices." Huntting
"A brilliant and stimulating compilation
which combines research in classical texts with
the findings of modern anthropology and
archaeology." Library J

Guerber, Helene Adeline
Myths of Greece & Rome. Rev. by Dorothy Margaret Stuart; with forty-nine re-
productions from famous pictures and statues. London House & Maxwell 1963 316p
illus $5.50   **292**
1 Mythology, Classical
First published 1907 in England
Contents: The beginning; Zeus; Hera; Athene;
Apollo; Artemis; Aphrodite; Hermes; Ares;
Hephæstus; Poseidon; Pluto; Bacchus (Diony-
sus); Demeter and Persephone; Hestia; Ceyx
and Halcyone; Æolus; Herakles; Perseus;
Theseus; Jason and the Golden Fleece; The
Calydonian Hunt; Œdipus, King of Thebes;
Bellerophon; The Trojan War; The Adventures
of Odysseus; Agamemnon and his family;
Virgil's "Æneid"; The lesser Gods of the
Romans; Interpretation; Glossary and Index;
Map of Greece of the myths; Map of Mediter-
ranean countries in mythical times; Genealogi-
cal table

Hamilton, Edith
Mythology   **292**
1 Mythology, Classical 2 Mythology, Norse
Some editions are:
Little $5.95
Watts, F. $12.50 Large type edition. A Keith
Jennison book
Contents: The Gods, the creation and the
earliest heroes; Stories of love and adventure;
Great heroes before the Trojan War; Heroes of
the Trojan War; Great families of mythology;
Less important myths; Mythology of the Norse-
men; Genealogical tables
"In her distinguished re-telling of the stor-
ies, the author has kept very close in style
to the originals. . . . Each story is prefaced
by a brief descriptive and informative introduction in italics." Bookmark

292.03 Classical mythology—Dictionaries

Oswalt, Sabine G.
Concise encyclopedia of Greek and Roman
mythology; introduction by Leonard Cottrell.
Follett 1969 313p illus maps (World reference lib) $3.95   **292.03**
1 Mythology, Classical—Dictionaries
Original French edition, 1965
Presented in dictionary form, this book contains "nearly 1,000 articles on the gods and
heroes' dominant themes and revered sites of
classical myths. A table of the literary sources
from Homer to Pausanias, a double-spread
map of the ancient world, 21 carefully-indexed
genealogical trees, and more than 200 captioned
photographs drawn from Greek and Roman
art supplement the text." News of Bks
"While the book should be on every student's
desk, it is an important quick reference for
libraries of all sizes." Choice

Tripp, Edward
Crowell's Handbook of classical mythology. Crowell 1970 631p maps (A Crowell
Reference bk) $10   **292.03**
1 Mythology, Classical—Dictionaries
ISBN 0-690-22608
This is "a convenient, comprehensive, and
reliable guide to classical mythology for the
layman. Its interestingly written text, with
frequent citation to source, provides an alphabetical approach to characters and events, as
well as to the places mentioned in the myths,
and to the constellations named for mythological personages, all adequately cross-referenced.
Articles range in length from a brief identification of a minor character to twenty pages for a
subject such as 'Argonauts.' Useful added features are the pronouncing index giving those
pronunciations most commonly used in the
United States ... and the five maps of the
classical world. Genealogical charts of the great
royal lines accompany appropriate articles."
Cur Ref Bks

Zimmerman, J. E.
Dictionary of classical mythology. Harper
1964 xx, 300p $5.95   **292.03**
1 Mythology, Classical—Dictionaries
This dictionary "contains nearly 2,100 personal and place names, giving pronunciation,
brief identification, and in some cases, citation to classical sources." Cur Ref Bks
It is "a handy little volume ... especially
useful for differentiating between characters
bearing the same name. . . . Well worth the
price, although not comprehensive enough to
take the place of the well-known older works
like Brewer. [Brewer's Dictionary of phrase
and fable entered in class 803]." Library J
Suggestions for further reading: p295-300

294.5　Hinduism

Coomaraswamy, Ananda K.
Myths of the Hindus & Buddhists, by Ananda K. Coomaraswamy and the Sister Nivedita (Margaret E. Noble) With 32 illus. by Indian artists under the supervision of Abanindro Nāth Tagore. Dover 1967 399p illus pa $3　　**294.5**

1 Mythology, Hindu 2 Buddha and Buddhism
Also available for $5 from Peter Smith
An unabridged republication of the work originally published 1913 by Holt
This "is a collection of the best known Indian myths, those most commonly illustrated in Indian sculpture and painting, which not only reveal national ideals and religious faith but also many universal truths that reach out to the ends of the earth." Book Rev Digest

296　Judaism

Gittelsohn, Roland B.
The meaning of Judaism. World Pub. 1970. 221p $5.95　　**296**

1 Judaism
"Excalibur books"
"A powerful essay defining the values and beliefs which are the essence of Judaism. These values and beliefs are explained in terms of the practices, morality, holidays, writings, and history of the Jewish people. Attitudes toward Israel and Zionism are explored. Gittelsohn compares Judaism to Christianity and points to differences as well as similarities." Library J

Glazer, Nathan
American Judaism. Univ. of Chicago Press 1957 175p (The Chicago History of American civilization) $3.95　　**296**

1 Jews in the U.S. 2 Judaism
"A historical survey of American Judaism from 1654, when the first Jewish families settled in New Amsterdam, to contemporary events such as the revival of Haisidism in Brooklyn." Book Rev Digest
The story is told "by an objective historical mind, yet with a fine combination of sociological insight and religious sensitivity." N Y Times Bk R

Wouk, Herman
This is my God. Doubleday 1959 356p $6.95　　**296**

1 Judaism
Also available in a 1970 deluxe edition with an afterword on the Six-Day War, for $10
An "exposition of orthodox Judaism and of the strength and inspiration it holds for the modern Jew. The . . . author sees no reason why Jewish people cannot abide by the Talmudic and Mosaic laws and still live normal and sensible western lives." Pub W
"Presents basic information in vigorous and readable fashion. Supplementary notes, a glossary, and a bibliography are appended." Booklist

297　Islam

'Azzām, 'Abd-al-Rahmān
The eternal message of Muhammad; tr. from the Arabic by Caesar E. Farah. With an introduction by Vincent Sheean. Devin-Adair 1964 297p $6.50　　**297**

1 Islam 2 Mohammed, the prophet
The author "begins his book with a brief life of the founder of Islam, clearly and simply told. . . . The rest of 'Azzam's book consists of lectures or essays clarifying for Moslems 'some of the principle and origins of their society, faith and revealed law.' . . . What emerges . . . are some valuable discussions of the Islamic attitude to social reform; to pledges, pacts and treaties; to the rules and etiquette of war; to such international instruments as the United Nations and, finally, to the whole problem of what 'Azzam calls 'the maintenance and perpetuation of civilization.' " N Y Times Bk R
Includes bibliographical footnotes

300　THE SOCIAL SCIENCES

Chase, Stuart
The proper study of mankind, by Stuart Chase in consultation with Edmund deS. Brunner. [2d rev. ed] Harper [1962 c1956] 327p $6.95　　**300**

1 Social sciences 2 Anthropology 3 Social problems
Analyzed in Essay and general literature index
First published 1948
The author "explains how we should go about putting to practical use our existing knowledge of the social sciences in the cause of better government, wiser management and more productive education and research and he leaves the reader with the optimistic sense that, aided by social science, man can yet be master of himself and the machines he has created." Huntting
"An authoritative and extremely readable discussion of the principal social sciences." Good Reading
Selected bibliography: p309-20

301　Sociology

Montagu, Ashley
On being human. Hawthorn Bks. [1967 c1966] 128p $4.95　　**301**

1 Human relations 2 Evolution 3 Sociology
First published 1950 by Abelard-Schuman
"What is the nature of life? What is meant by the expression 'survival of the fittest?' What are the basic needs of man? . . . Dr. Montagu points out that so-called civilized man of the Western world stands today on the brink of destruction—self-destruction through such deadly devices as chemical and bacteriological warfare and fission bombs. Yet all of man's problems can be solved through knowledge available to him today. . . . He discusses the normal trend among all organisms—even the simplest in the scale of evolution—toward some form of social grouping, pointing out that cooperation rather than fierce competition is the law of life and that interaction of organisms for mutual support increases their ability to survive." Publisher's note
Further reading: p122-24

301.03　Sociology—Dictionaries

Theodorson, George A.
A modern dictionary of sociology [by] George A. Theodorson and Achilles G. Theodorson. Crowell 1969 469p (A Crowell Reference bk) $10　　**301.03**

1 Sociology—Dictionaries
The entries are "from the closely related fields of psychology, social psychology, anthropology, and statistics. Economics and political science are also represented with terms that are frequently used by sociologists. The definitions [seek to] . . . explain, as well as define, the more complex terms. . . . [There are also] discussions of the present standing in the profession of many controversial or outmoded terms. Whenever appropriate the entries specify the origins of the terms and cite their sources." Publisher's note
"However brief, every entry is long enough to assure that even a layman or neophyte can understand the explanation, and specific enough to distinguish among various meanings of the same or similar terms as between legend and myth, or two senses of historicism, or the many concepts of family (atomistic, conjugal, domestic, heteronomous, etc.). The [authors] define but do not defend jargon." Sat R

32

301.15 Group behavior. Opinion formation

Chase, Stuart
American credos. Harper 1962 216p boards $5.95 **301.15**
1 Public opinion 2 Public opinion polls 3 National characteristics, American
Analyzed in Essay and general literature index
The author "analyzes the various opinion polls in order to let Americans speak for themselves. In the final chapter, he summarizes his findings in relation to foreign policy, the business system, work, politics, education, science, civil liberties, and personal problems." Wis Lib Bul
"A composite picture of what the representative American believes . . . done with Mr. Chase's usual intelligence and lively sense of social commitment." Sat R
Appendix of sources: p203-12

Choukas, Michael
Propaganda comes of age; foreword by Hadley Cantril. Public Affairs Press 1965 299p $6 **301.15**
1 Propaganda
In his evaluation of propaganda in the western world, the author endeavors "to show its true nature, its techniques, and its relation to democracy for good and for ill. . . . To sharpen the reader's understanding of the phenomenon, an account is given of its historical development, especially its evolutionary character." Preface
Professor Choukas "analyzes the vast network of domestic propaganda. . . . Many appropriate illustrations, including pamphlets, cartoons, leaflets and ads." America
References: p293-99

Huxley, Aldous
Brave new world revisited. Harper 1958 147p $5.95 **301.15**
1 Propaganda 2 Totalitarianism 3 Brainwashing
When the novel: Brave new world, first appeared in 1932, its shocking analysis of scientific dictatorship seemed a projection into the remote future. Today, however, the science of thought control and the methods for destroying individual freedom have developed to an alarming extent. In this factual survey Huxley illustrates methods of brainwashing and propaganda and shows what is being done to turn men into robots. He urges mankind to educate itself in freedom before it is too late. (Publisher)
"Huxley was always a moralist. . . . He has become a more and more thoughtful moralist, and if we have lost something in the way of entertainment, what we have gained is more important." Sat R

Liston, Robert A.
Dissent in America. McGraw 1971 158p $4.95, lib. bdg. $4.72 **301.15**
1 U.S.—Social conditions 2 U.S.—Politics and government
The author analyzes the nature of dissent in America focusing "on the past and present-day methods employed by dissenters—revolution, lawlessness, disorder, demonstrations, separatism, boycotts, influencing the media, the ballot box, and the courts." News of Bks
"Excellent discussion is included to show the great strides being made in solving the problems of control, of removing the middle element of violent repression and replacing it with forward-looking, knowledgeably organized protective legality." Library J
Selected reading: p153-54

Whyte, William H.
The organization man, by William H. Whyte, Jr. Simon & Schuster 1956 429p illus maps $6.95 **301.15**
1 Individuality 2 Loyalty 3 Social psychology

"An analysis of what is wrong with our society as seen through the life of the organization man. The author makes a plea for men to resist conformity and consult their own consciences about what is right and wrong. The last section of the book makes a complete study of suburbia." Huntting
The author "has the patience carefully to analyze malarkey. . . . His belief in the value of the individual mind lends an edge to his work, and makes his description of the ethos of the technician in America today among the best available." N Y Times Bk R
Includes bibliographies

Zeman, Z. A. B.
Nazi propaganda. Published in association with the Wiener Library [by] Oxford 1964 226p illus $6.75 **301.15**
1 Propaganda, German 2 National socialism
This study examines "the part played by the manipulation and control of public opinion in the National Socialists' capture and exercise of power in Germany, as well as of the manner in which Hitler's government employed propaganda in its bid for power abroad." Introduction
This book "recaptures the atmosphere of the period, and offers some credible explanations of how the incredible could happen." Sat R
Bibliography: p187-210

301.16 Mass communication processes

Agee, Warren K.
(ed.) Mass media in a free society. Univ. Press of Kan. 1969 96p $5 **301.16**
1 Communication 2 Telecommunication
"The William Allen White Foundation and the William Allen White School of Journalism at the University jointly sponsored the seminar, one of a series of year-long events commemorating the hundredth birthday of White"
Six "mass media specialists explore the major issues and problems of communication confronting the press, television, and motion pictures in our society. . . . In his indictment of television programming, Stan Freberg . . . suggests that America limit its TV viewing to three nights a week. . . . Bosley Crowther challenges motive-perpetuated myths concerning war and racial injustice. Bill Moyers propounds the theory that the government and the press are adversaries rather than allies. Carl Rowan, former USIA director, [examines] . . . American naïveté in general and press irresponsibility in particular. . . . Agee has presented us with a little text that makes thoughtful reading for layman and specialist alike. Highly recommended." Library J

Lineberry, William P.
(ed.) Mass communications. Wilson, H.W. 1969 206p (The Reference shelf v41, no.3) $4.50 **301.16**
1 Communication 2 Telecommunication
"This compilation is designed to explore the status of mass communications in America today—their impact on society, their achievements and shortcomings, and their potential for the future. The first section examines the impact of the mass media, for good or ill, on our daily lives. . . . The next section turns to a survey of current trends in the mass media. . . . The fourth and final section peers briefly into the future." Preface
Bibliography: p196-206

301.18 Behavior groups. Violence

Brown, Richard Maxwell
(ed.) American violence. Prentice-Hall 1970 176p $5.95 **301.18**
1 Violence 2 U.S.—Social conditions
SBN 13-031625-3

Brown, Richard M.—*Continued*

"A Spectrum book"
This survey of urban, racial, labor and agrarian violence in the United States contains eyewitness accounts and official reports of major outbreaks from the seventeenth century to the present day. (Publisher)
"This collection of documents provides a thoughtful and provocative summary of the role of violence in the American tradition. . . . The editor includes selections dealing with theories of violence to give the book a strong theoretical framework." Library J
Further readings: p173-76

Graham, Hugh Davis

(ed.) The history of violence in America: historical and comparative perspectives; ed. by Hugh Davis Graham and Ted Robert Gurr. . . . Praeger 1969 xxxvi, 822p illus $13.50   301.18
1 Violence 2 U.S.—Social conditions
"A report submitted to the National Commission on the Causes and Prevention of Violence. Special introduction by John Herbers of The New York Times." Title page
"A New York Times book"
This volume, consisting of [22] articles by various authors, examines (among other areas) "the Western tradition of violence (both Europe and America), the sources of violent behavior in America and the use of quantitative analysis to identify comparative patterns of strife that illustrate how such behavior in the U.S. compares with similar activities throughout the world." Choice
"Some essays will be frankly more rewarding for the general reader while others are intended primarily for the scholar. The report's organization makes it readily accessible to any patron seeking particular information on a specialized aspect of violence but does not encourage reading straight through." Library J
Bibliographies at end of chapters

Heaps, Willard A.

Riots, U.S.A. 1765-1970. Rev. ed. Seabury 1970 214p $4.95   301.18
1 Riots 2 U.S.—History
First published 1966
Contents: Stamp act riots; Doctors' riot; Anti-Catholic riots; Astor Place riot; Draft riots; Anti-Chinese riot; Steel lockout; Pullman strike; Miners' riot; Race riot; Police strike; The bonus army; Prison riot; The Detroit riot; Columbia University riots; The outlook for the future
"Objective, detailed, and well-organized, the text gives an interesting picture of the spectrum of causes that have moved men to violence in our history, and now in our time." Chicago. Children's Book Center
Sources and readings: p185-203

Hofstadter, Richard

(ed.) American violence; a documentary history; ed. by Richard Hofstadter and Michael Wallace. Knopf 1970 478p $10
301.18
1 Violence 2 U.S.—History
ISBN 0-394-41486-1
"This major study is outstanding for its comprehensiveness and scholarly objectivity. . . . [The editors] describe and document, frequently through eye-witness accounts, some hundred-odd separate instances of major violence in our past, placing them within the contexts of such categories as political, economic, racial, religious, anti-radical and so on. Nor are terrorism, police violence and violence in the name of 'law, order and morality' scanted." Pub W
"Though the documents are intelligently selected and many of them are hard to come by, the particular interest of this work lies in Mr. Hofstadter's long introductory essay." N Y Times Bk R

Sloan, Irving J.

Our violent past; an American chronicle; preface by Ramsey Clark. Random House 1970 234p illus $6.95   301.18
1 Violence 2 U.S.—Social conditions 3 U.S.—History

"Quoting extensively from newspapers and magazines of the past three centuries, Mr. Sloan explores the violent strain in American history characterized by the Indian massacres, the political violence of the Colonies, 19th-Century racial and abolitionist violence, frontier vigilante justice, the religious battles and anti-Chinese riots of the 19th Century, and the labor and racial struggles of this century." Publisher's note
Bibliography: p221-34

United States. National Advisory Commission on Civil Disorders

Report of the National Advisory Commission on Civil Disorders; introduction by Tom Wicker; illus. with photographs. The New York Times edition. Dutton 1968 xxv, 609p illus $7.95   301.18
1 Riots 2 U.S.—Race relations 3 U.S.—Social conditions
First published 1968 by Bantam
This report of the Commission established July, 1967 by President Johnson to investigate the causes of civil unrest in that year discusses what happened, why it happened, and what can be done to ameliorate social conditions so as to prevent a recurrence
"An important document for every American." Wis Lib Bul

United States. National Commission on the Causes and Prevention of Violence

To establish justice, to insure domestic tranquility. . . . Special introduction by James Reston; plus 32 pages of photographs. Praeger 1970 277p illus $8   301.18
1 Violence 2 U.S.—Social conditions
"The final report of the National Commission on the Causes and Prevention of Violence." Title page
"A New York Times book"
This report reviews the history of violence in America, analyzes its various manifestations, discusses modern developments, and makes specific proposals

301.2 Cultural processes

McLuhan, Marshall

Culture is our business. McGraw 1970 336p illus $10   301.2
1 Culture 2 Communication 3 Social psychology 4 U.S.—Civilization
This book "examines our civilization as it manifests itself through the century's . . . art form, advertising." Publisher's note
The author "has clipped dozens of full-page magazine ads— 'the cave art of the twentieth century.' On each right-hand page of coated paper a different product or service ad is reproduced. They are a handsome, mouth-watering collection. The facing page, in alternate paragraphs of bold and light type, carries McLuhan's comments. These may be his own, or G.K. Chesterton's or T.S. Eliot's or a sentence from Finnegans Wake. . . . Sometimes print and picture interrelate; sometimes the juxtaposing seems entirely arbitrary. The form of the book is as interesting as the content." Sat R

301.24 Social change. Technology and civilization

Diebold, John

Man and the computer; technology as an agent of social change. Praeger 1969 157p $5.95   301.24
1 Technology and civilization 2 Social change 3 Automation 4 Electronic computers
"What has always made machines truly important to man is not their individual versatility and productivity—it is the fact that

Diebold, John—*Continued*

they serve as agents of social change. They change our world. They change us. This is the theme of the present book." Preface

"This book is based on five of the author's speeches and articles: (1) 'The profound impact of science and technology;' (2) 'Educational technology and business responsibility;' (3) 'International disparities;' (4) 'The training of managers;' (5) 'The longterm questions.' Each chapter can be read independently. At the end is a list of selected readings on the impact of science and technology on individuals, institutions and societies. The author has undertaken the difficult task of giving the reader a view, in perspective, of the effect of the computer on society. . . . This short, easily read book should be especially useful as background reading for anyone interested in trends in contemporary society." Science Bks

Ferkiss, Victor C.

Technological man: the myth and the reality. Braziller 1969 336p $7.95   **301.24**

1 Technology and civilization 2 Civilization, Modern

The author examines "the interrelationship between technology and politics in the last decades of the twentieth century . . . [and] suggests the direction in which mankind must move if it is going to be able to deal with the new challenges put to the social order by technological change." Preface

"The social, political, economic, and cultural expectations for the future of man's development are examined in a learned yet literate evaluation. . . . The text reviews the societal and personal evolution of man to date, emphasizing the duality of man's scientific and cultural environment." Booklist

Bibliography: p295-327

Roszak, Theodore

The making of a counter culture; reflections on the technocratic society and its youthful opposition. Doubleday 1969 303p $7.95   **301.24**

1 Technology and civilization 2 Social change 3 U.S.—Civilization 4 Youth movement

The author "elaborates the vices of our technocratic society and its ability to reduce everything to order, and humans to objects. Second, he discusses the emergence of the counter-culture as a reaction to the technocratic society. Third, he reviews the thoughts of [Herbert] Marcuse, [Norman] Brown, [Allen] Ginsberg, [Alan] Watts and [Paul] Goodman especially, in the context of the source of man's thoughts and humanity, and as a criticism of the rational-scientific explanations. Last, he pleads for the abandonment of the 'objective consciousness' of science and the adoption of human consciousness of the visionary, the shaman. Roszak offers a concise interpretation and summary of the youth movements today." Choice

Bibliographical notes: p291-303

Silberman, Charles E.

The myths of automation [by] Charles E. Silberman and the editors of Fortune. Harper 1966 148p illus $5.95   **301.24**

1 Automation 2 U.S.—Economic conditions—20th century

This collection of essays "contains four articles related to increased mechanization in industry: its employment and unemployment effects, its relationship to changes in occupational mix, its sociological impact, and its relationship to productivity increases and labor shortages. Three essays deal with some current labor market phenomena, i.e., teenage employment, early retirement, and some aspects of the 'war' on poverty. The emphasis is on debunking some widely circulated notions in these areas. The analyses range from glossy generalizations to novel and penetrating perceptions." Library J

Toffler, Alvin

Future shock. Random House 1970 505p $8.95   **301.24**

1 Social change 2 Technology and civilization 3 Civilization, Modern

According to the author, "future shock is 'the dizzying disorientation brought on by the premature arrival of the future.' Whether we are all victims of a technological jag and doomed to a massive adaptational breakdown is something sociologists are debating. Toffler's aim is to spell out the nature of the problem we face, and to suggest how we might learn to cope. Technology within the past several decades has fed on itself and brought about an accelerating thrust of 'progress' that has already, in many ways, projected us into the future. We can anticipate cataclysmic changes in every facet of human experience. . . . Toffler outlines some interesting strategies for survival, writing in a clear popular style." Pub W

The author "has given us a revealing, exciting, encouraging, brilliant work which may satisfy many who consider man simply a biological machine, his life a brief glimmer in a dark eternity. Readers who reject that melancholy and unprovable hypothesis may nevertheless find great profit and instruction in this quite remarkable book." Christian Science Monitor

Bibliography: p461-83

301.3 Human ecology

Chasteen, Edgar R.

The case for compulsory birth control. Prentice-Hall 1971 230p $5.95   **301.3**

1 Population 2 Birth control
ISBN 0-13-115980-1

The primary focus of this book rests on the facts that people cause pollution, "that a greater number of people means a reduction in the standard of living for all people . . . and that the world can no longer afford people the 'right' to have unlimited numbers of children. . . . From these facts comes the conclusion that compulsory birth control, with absolute limitations placed on reproduction, is needed for the sake of the future. . . . The book has a bias, but it is also interesting, informative, and logically presented, with the opposing positions recognized and their arguments included." Library J

Includes bibliographical references

Disch, Robert

(ed.) The ecological conscience; values for survival. Prentice-Hall 1970 206p $5.95   **301.3**

1 Ecology
SBN 13-222828-9
"A Spectrum book"

Analyzed in Essay and general literature index

"A collection of ecologically oriented writings with one basic purpose: to awaken the public to the fact that man must reestablish his sense of values if this society is not to undergo an 'ecological suicide.' It emphasizes the conscious human values involved more than the actual ecological results of man's past failures." Choice

Suggested readings: p205-06

Dubos, René

So human an animal. Scribner 1968 267p $6.95   **301.3**

1 Ecology 2 Man—Influence of environment 3 Technology and civilization

Awarded Pulitzer Prize. 1969

The author, a microbiologist, discusses "how man responds to his physical and social surroundings (overpopulation, overcrowding, air and water pollution, transportation breakdowns). . . . He writes of the failure of science through its game of 'overpromise' stresses the need for harmony with nature." Pub W

The author "recommends conservation, planning, and restraints on mechanization as essential checks on the ultimate decay of civilization. A nontechnical treatment, suitable

Dubos, René—*Continued*

for informed laymen and for students.'' Booklist
    Bibliography in Reference notes: p243-57

Ehrlich, Paul R.

Population, resources, environment; issues
in human ecology [by] Paul R. Ehrlich
[and] Anne H. Ehrlich. Freeman 1970 383p
illus (A Series of books in biology) $8.95
                               301.3
    1 Population   2 Natural resources
    ISBN 0-7167-0680-6
    This is an analysis of the "crisis of over-
population and the resulting demands on food,
resources, and the environment." Publisher's
note
    "This is the best single descriptive and ana-
lytic treatment of the subject that I have yet
seen." N Y Rev of Books
    General bibliography: p360-63. Bibliographies
at ends of chapters

**Friends, Society of. American Friends Ser-
vice Committee**

Who shall live? Man's control over birth
and death; a report. Hill & Wang 1970
144p illus $3.95   **301.3**
    1 Birth control   2 Abortion   3 Social ethics
    4 Medical ethics
    SBN 8096-9706-0
    "A report approved in October 1969 by the
board of directors of the American Friends
Service Committee which grew out of a concern about the implications of abortion but expanded to a consideration of the quality of life
in the family and society, contraception, sexual morality, genetic counselling, and the religious and moral issues arising from scientific
advances in the control of death and birth."
Booklist
    "The Report favors open dissemination of
information and materials regarding contraception; it also concludes that no woman should
be forced to bear an unwanted child. On death
control it poses more questions than it answers, but there is agreement that no life
should be artificially prolonged when there is
conclusive evidence that a patient has suffered
irreversible brain damage." Pub W
    Bibliography: p115-36

Goldston, Robert

Suburbia: civic denial; a portrait in urban
civilization; illus. by Donald Carrick. Macmillan (N Y) 1970 184p illus map lib.
bdg. $5.95   **301.3**
    1 Suburban life   2 Metropolitan areas
    "By examining the development of suburbia
within the megalopolitan area that stretches
from Boston to Philadelphia—its impact on
cities, towns and countryside, its life patterns,
its possible future . . . [the author presents a]
case for regional planning, a redefinition of
land use and a recommitment to public rather
than private well-being." Publisher's note
    This book "comes across as a good work-
manlike examination. It combines demograph-
ic, historic, economic, and sociologic detail into
a mélange that is readable, informative, and
entertaining." Library J

Green, Constance McLaughlin

The rise of urban America. Harper 1965
208p $6.95   **301.3**
    1 Cities and towns—U.S.   2 U.S.—Social con-
ditions
    An analysis of "the rise of cities in the
United States from the early seventeenth century to the 1960s. . . . [The author] traces the
forces—economic, political, social—that led to
today's urban civilization, beginning with the
growth of colonial seaports and local government, the rise of new cities that competed for
wealth and power with the older cities, the
spread of industrialization, transportation and
communications that made complex city life
possible." Publisher's note
    Bare-bones bibliography: p197

Hyde, Margaret O.

This crowded planet; illus. by Mildred
Waltrip. McGraw 1961 159p illus maps $3.95
lib. bdg. $3.83   **301.3**
    1 Population   2 Natural resources
    "Whittlesey House publications"
    An explanation of "the ways in which sci-
ence is preparing to meet demands for food, resources, shelter, and space for the world's rapidly growing population." Bk Buyer's Guide
    "The author ably presents both the dimen-
sions of the problem and the prospects for
meeting it through expansion of resources and
food supply. The challenge this offers research
scientists is well described." Christian Science
Monitor

Isenberg, Irwin

(ed.) The city in crisis. Wilson, H.W.
1968 246p map (The Reference shelf v40,
no.1) $4.50   **301.3**
    1 Sociology, Urban   2 Urban renewal   3 Ne-
groes—Moral and social conditions   4 Riots
    The 32 articles in this book "highlight a
multiplicity of urban problems, from slum housing and racial disturbances to air and water
pollution and financing a city's operations, and
give representative suggestions for meeting the
challenge with large-scale plans and some
specifics. A 12-page bibliography is appended."
Booklist

Mumford, Lewis

The city in history; its origin, its transformation, and its prospects. Harcourt 1961
657p illus $15   **301.3**
    1 Cities and towns—History   2 Civilization
—History
    "After looking at the nomadic and agricul-
tural civilizations of the ancients Mumford
discusses the forms, functions, and purpose
of the earliest cities; then does the same for
Greek, Egyptian, Minoan, Roman, Christian,
medieval, Victorian, and modern cities; the
medieval city would seem to be highest in his
estimation, with Rome and the twentieth-century city of today and perhaps, tomorrow,
far down the list." Booklist
    "Plumbs both the life-giving and death-
dealing aspects of urban civilization through
depths of time and expanses of space which no
other writer has explored in quite this particular way, analyzing both the spiritual and
physical remains of cities. As such, the book is
more than urban history: it is moral philosophy of a high order and tragic poetry." N Y
Times Bk R
    Bibliography: p579-634

The highway and the city. Harcourt 1963
246p pa $1.95   **301.3**
    1 Metropolitan areas   2 Cities and towns—
History
    "A Harvest book"
    This account of the urban community cen-
ters "on the problems of architecture, city
planning, highway control, and other related
subjects." Publisher's note
    "Gathered in one volume, Mumford's saga-
cious challenges of certain clichés and misconceptions . . . are even more powerfully persuasive than they were when these essays appeared piecemeal in 'The New Yorker' and
elsewhere over the past decade." Library J

Osborn, Fairfield

(ed.) Our crowded planet; essays on the
pressures of population. Sponsored by the
Conservation Foundation. Doubleday 1962
240p $4.50   **301.3**
    1 Population
    Analyzed in Essay and general literature
index
    A collection of essays "pointing out the dan-
gers that world overpopulation poses to specific
areas of human concern and pounding away at
the points that the whole human species is at
stake and that it is up to mankind to do something about it. Among the contributors are

Osborn, Fairfield—*Continued*
Marston Bates, Eugene R. Black, Arnold J. Toynbee, Enrique Beltran, Rev. Robert I. Gannon . . . Joseph Wood Krutch, and others." Pub W

"The essays are short, averaging twelve pages each, but their calculated conciseness adds to their punch. . . . The impressive effect of this book is a new awareness of the political, economic, social and ethical consequences of a crowded world." N Y Her Trib Books
Includes bibliography

Ridgeway, James
The politics of ecology. Dutton 1970 222p $5.95
301.3
1 Environmental policy—U.S. 2 Natural resources—U.S. U.S.—Social conditions
ISBN 0-525-08108-3

This is a "collection of short reports . . . on the oil industry, industrial water pollution, sewer-construction abuses, and the . . . games corporations play with government at the expense of the environment. . . . [The author seeks to reveal the] collaboration between government and business in [the ecology movement]. . . . Ridgeway's suggestions for reforms . . . [include] changes in fuels policies, new rules for mineral-rights leases, a new low-pollutant auto engine, and so forth." Book World

"This book highlights the hypocrisies of business and government on the ecology issue." Christian Century

Toynbee, Arnold
Cities on the move. Oxford 1970 257p $6.75
301.3
1 Cities and towns—History
ISBN 0-19-215251-3

"Dr. Toynbee provides an informative and highly readable discourse upon the characteristics, distinctive features, and development of cities, from their beginnings in prehistory up to the present. He considers the cultures they expressed, their natural surroundings, the ways in which they were built, the lives of their inhabitants, and their commercial, military, political and religious organization." News of Bks

United States. Department of Agriculture
A place to live; the yearbook of agriculture, 1963. U.S. Govt. Ptg. Off. 1963 xxiii, 584p illus maps boards $3
301.3
1 Sociology, Rural 2 Sociology, Urban 3 Agriculture—Economic aspects

"Written 'to inform all Americans about the effects of urbanization and industrialization on rural America and the need for plans and action so that people will have a proper place to live.' Describes many natural and social changes that have occurred as a result of growing cities, and gives suggestions for action to guide these changes. Though general in scope, some of the articles are fairly technical and require knowledge of the fundamentals of agriculture and economics." The AAAS Science Book List for Young Adults
Includes bibliographies

United States. Farm Security Administration
The bitter years: 1935-1941; rural America as seen by the photographers of the Farm Security Administration; ed. by Edward Steichen. Mus. of Modern Art; [distributed by N.Y. Graphic] 1962 unp illus pa $1.25
301.3
1 Sociology, Rural 2 U.S.—Social conditions —Pictures, illustrations, etc.

"A selection of 27 outstanding photographs in the Museum . . . exhibition which shows many phases of life in rural and urban America during the depression. With an introduction by Rexford Guy Tugwell." Publisher's note

301.4 Institutions and groups

Howard, Jane
Please touch; a guided tour of the human potential movement. McGraw 1970 271p $6.95
301.4
1 Human relations 2 Social group work

This book examines the "human potential movement—the philosophies behind it; the almost endless varietiesof groups; the leaders who run them; the people who join them; the enthusiasts who believe in them and the critics who think they are a fraud." Book News

This "is the best comprehensive guide to the human potential movement available. Miss Howard has a capacity for gathering huge masses of facts and making sense of them with wit and style." Sat R

301.41 The sexes

Mead, Margaret
Male and female; a study of the sexes in a changing world. Morrow 1949 477p $7.50
301.41
1 Sex 2 Man 3 Woman

"The substance of this book was given as the Jacob Gimbel lectures in sex psychology under the auspices of Stanford University and the University of California, San Francisco, California, November, 1946." p vi

An explanation of the role of the sexes as it relates to preliterate Pacific peoples, and essentially as it operates today in our American pattern of culture. Includes background material on seven Pacific island cultures: Samoa, Manus, Arapesh, Mundugumor, Iatmu, Tchambull, Bali

Bibliographical references in Notes to chapters: p387-463

United States. President's Commission on the Status of Women
American women; the report of the President's Commission on the Status of Women and other publications of the Commission. Ed. by Margaret Mead and Frances Balgley Kaplan, with an introduction and an epilogue by Margaret Mead. Scribner 1965 274p illus map $8.95
301.41
1 Women in the U.S.

The Report "is accompanied by an account of the work of the commission's seven committees, amplifying and documenting the commission's decisions and treating subjects in the same order as in the 'Report.' The epilog summarizes and interprets the 'Report,' and appendixes provide pertinent papers, documents, statistical tables, rosters of the commission and committees, and sources." Booklist

Some of the topics covered are education, employment, law, community activities. "These are major social documents of the 20th century and should be widely available." Library J

301.42 Marriage and family

Avery, Curtis E.
Love and marriage; a guide for young people, by Curtis E. Avery and Theodore B. Johannis, Jr. Harcourt 1971 170p illus $4.95
301.42
1 Marriage
ISBN 0-15-249531-2

"Curriculum-related books"

In this book, the authors discuss the various problem areas in marriage—"finance, parenthood, relationships with friends and family, and the use of leisure time. They also examine the evolution of marriage as a social institution, describe the changes it has undergone in America, and attempt to fit it into the broader context of our society as a whole." Publisher's note

Avery, Curtis E.—*Continued*

"It is not a 'how-to' marriage manual; its purpose is to help the young to discover their own ideas about marriage and, if necessary, adjust them in accordance with the basic principles of marriage. There are ten categories of ideas based on what social scientists consider to be the ten most important areas of married life. No set formulae are offered, but factors that may influence the attitudes of young people are examined and some reports of typical situations are provided to stimulate thought and discussion." Best Sellers

Sources: p169-70

Cain, Arthur H.

Young people and parents. Day 1971 148p $4.95   301.42

1 Conflict of generations

In this book addressed to young people, the author suggests ways to overcome the "Battle of the Generations." (Publisher)

Partial contents: Parents around the world; Too permissive or too repressive; Nonparents and parent substitutes, good and bad; How to rehabilitate a delinquent parent; Recommended reading

Duvall, Evelyn Millis

Faith in families. Rand McNally 1970 206p $4.95   301.42

1 Family

In this guide to family living, the author describes what a family is and discusses such topics as happiness in marriage, child rearing, "the adolescent, learning to live with differences in the family, establishing communication between family members, and approaches to solving family problems." Publisher's note

Notes and references: p193-206

Duvall, Sylvanus M.

Before you marry. New rev ed. Assn. Press 1959 252p boards $3.50   301.42

1 Marriage

First published 1949

"This book is addressed mainly to 'young people' for whom marriage in the not too distant future is a definite possibility. It is designed to help them at two points—(1) in their selection of a mate and (2) in what to expect of marriage and how to plan for it in advance." Preface

Partial contents: How do you know it's love; Fact and fiction about sex; Financing your marriage; Personality and mental health; What about mixed marriages; Emergencies and crises

"Of potential help . . . also to ministers in premarital counseling, this book is a wise and witty discussion of the subject in question and answer form." Religious Book Club Bul

Suggestions for further reading: p251-52

Mead, Margaret

Family, by Margaret Mead and Ken Heyman. Macmillan (N Y) 1965 208p illus $10   301.42

1 Family   2 Family—Pictures, illustrations, etc.

An "anthropologist draws on her lifetime of observation and thought to write about humanity's basic unit—the family—as it exists in every part of our world. . . . Miss Mead stresses the similarities in familial relationships while noting the differences." Huntting

Arranged in such sections as: Fathers, Grandparents, The child alone. "One reads a section of text for the background and the mood, and then patiently enjoys the photographs in which he can read much more than words can tell about warm personal relationships that occur among members of families everywhere. Ken Heyman visited 45 countries over a period of 7 years to obtain the photographs which, as reproduced here, constitute an unparalleled exhibition." Science Bks

Pike, James A.

If you marry outside your faith; counsel on mixed marriages. Rev. ed. Harper 1962 159p boards $3.50   301.42

1 Marriage, Mixed

First published 1954

In this guide for young adults, Bishop Pike includes material on: "positions of non-Roman Catholic churches on mixed marriages; moral views on birth control [and abortion]; legal status of prenuptial marriage agreements about religious observance, religious training for children, etc." Publisher's note

Brief case studies and a bibliography are included

Shedd, Charlie W.

Letters to Karen: on keeping love in marriage. Abingdon 1965 159p $3   301.42

1 Marriage

"Karen Shedd asked her father for his honest counsel about marriage—what holds it together, what can tear it apart, what a wife and husband must contribute (or sacrifice) to make it meaningful. These letters [on sex, tact, housekeeping, etc.] are the author's frank response, based on his [ministerial experience]." Huntting

301.43 Minors. Youth

Bernstein, Saul

Alternatives to violence; alienated youth and riots, race, and poverty. Assn. Press 1967 192p $4.95   301.43

1 Youth   2 Riots   3 U.S.—Social conditions   4 Poverty   5 U.S.—Race relations

A report made between December 1965 and June 1966 during which time the author visited nine major cities, including New York, Los Angeles and Detroit, in order to study the meaning and effects of previous riots on its underprivileged and alienated young people. The author also examines possible strategies for change and practical ways out of poverty, the roots of discontent and violence. (Publisher)

Bibliography: p187-92

Fortune (Periodical)

Youth in turmoil; adapted from a special issue of Fortune. Time-Life Bks. 1969 159p illus lib. bdg. $3.95   301.43

1 Youth   2 U.S.—Social conditions

In this collection of essays, sociologists and scholars examine various aspects of the current youth "rebellion" in the United States. The authors consider the ideology of the present younger generation, the role of youth in the universities and pop culture, and the relation of the young to their elders, including their parents and teachers

Keniston, Kenneth

Young radicals; notes on committed youth. Harcourt 1968 368p $6.95   301.43

1 Youth   2 Students—U.S.

The author observed "a number of young people who worked from June to September 1967, for Vietnam Summer, an organization opposing American involvement in Southeast Asia. The focus of the book is on the psychological development of these young men and women and on the impact upon them of their experiences in the New Left." Publisher's note

This book "is unusually clear and free of psychological jargon. In trying to understand the development of a radical personality, the author begins by examining the 'red-diaper baby' and the 'radical-rebel' theories, and finds both inadequate. From these hypotheses he moves to a broader interpretation of the forces which combine to produce the particular set of radical-personality traits. . . . [The book's] greatest usefulness in the long run may be as an historical analysis of a particular faction of a larger movement." Yale R

Bibliography: p361-68

Lukas, J. Anthony

Don't shoot—we are your children! Random House 1971 461p $8.95   301.43

1 Youth   2 U.S.—Biography
ISBN 0-394-46287-5

Lukas, J. A.—*Continued*

The author examines the lives of 10 young Americans and their families and finds that the cliché "generation gap" masks far more complex relationships. Included are a wealthy businessman's daughter and an ex-gang leader found murdered in New York's Greenwich Village, a Harvard SDS leader, a white Southern civil rights activist, a leader of the Brandeis Afro-American organization, and a founder of the Yippies

"His eloquence as a writer, his tenacity in research, his respect for other human beings, have combined to give us a beautiful and important book which I think may become a classic." N Y Times Bk R

Mead, Margaret

Culture and commitment; a study of the generation gap. . . . Natural Hist. Press/ Doubleday 1970 xxvii, 113p $5   **301.43**

1 Youth 2 Conflict of generations 3 Culture
4 Social change

"Published for the American Museum of Natural History"

The author maintains that the present conflict between generations is unique, without a past parallel, and world-wide. She "establishes models of three kinds of societies and their methods of transition from one generation to the other. The oldest she calls 'postfigurative,' in which grandchildren, parents, and children exist together. Wisdom resides in the old. . . . The 'configurative,' like the United States before 1940, . . . was a society in which adults and children alike learned from their peers, a society of mobility and improvisation. This society we are still trying to perpetuate after its day is past. What we now require and what Mead . . . believes is coming is the 'prefigurative' society, worldwide, in which the role of parents . . . is only to nurture the child, to be custodians of the world and the child until he is old enough to teach us." Harper

"Many readers will find this an inspiring, fearlessly realistic book." Book of the Month Club News

Bibliographical note: p100-02

Montessori, Maria

The child in the family; tr. by Nancy Rockmore Cirillo. Regnery 1970 120p $4.95
          301.43

1 Child study 2 Parent and child

Original Italian edition, 1956

"A noted educator summarizes her concepts relating to a child's mental development, the adult-child relationship, Montessori teaching methods, a child's environment, the character of a child, and the child in a family context." Booklist

Time, inc.

The hippies, by the correspondents of Time; ed. by Joe David Brown. The author 1967 220p illus pa $1.95   **301.43**

1 Hippies 2 Youth 3 U.S.—Social conditions

Analyzed in Essay and general literature index

"This report on the hippies, their historical and philosophic roots, their heroes, their foods, their sexual and drug habits, and the other phenomena associated with the 300,000 or so members of this subculture in America, Europe, and Asia makes a modest and extremely useful encyclopedia. . . . [The writers] are not scholars, but reports in the aggregate make a remarkably concise compendium of hard fact and clear observation. . . . There is fortunately little philosophizing about what the movement will lead to, and the final report in the book wisely quotes Arnold Toynbee's remark that the hippies are 'a red light warning to American society.' This will undoubtedly remain one of the best books on the hippies." Library J

Glossary of hippie terms: p217-20

Wein, Bibi

The runaway generation. McKay 1970 309p $6.95   **301.43**

1 Youth 2 Narcotic habit

The author "contrasts the life style of youngsters in her Pennsylvania high school days (1956-1959) with that of today's youngsters in the same school, including one group of seven completely immersed in the drug culture. While the author's interest in the subject was aroused by children she saw in New York's East Village, she followed the trail to Los Angeles and San Francisco as well." Library J

301.44 Systems and criteria of social distinction and stratification

Coles, Robert

The middle Americans; proud and uncertain; photographs by Jon Erikson. Little 1971 181p illus $12.50   **301.44**

1 Middle classes 2 U.S.—Social conditions

"An Atlantic Monthly Press book"

Based on tape-recorded interviews, this book attempts to describe the views and life style of some members of working class families of the United States. "Coles condenses talk and comment, going back as much as five years, with a handful of workingmen and their wives —a steam fitter, a policeman, a filling-station operator, a machinist, a fireman, a welder, a druggist and a bank-loan arranger, the only white-collar man in the group." Time

"Coles is content simply to observe, which he does in just 75 pages of text . . . some dozen people among the many he spoke with over the years. The text is an extended caption for the 155 splendid photographs by Erikson, which depict Middle America at work and play." Newsweek

Harrington, Michael

The other America; poverty in the United States. Macmillan (N Y) 1962 191p $4.95
          301.44

1 Poverty 2 Social problems 3 U.S.—Economic conditions

"A wrathful book about the condition of the poor in the United States, the 'subculture of misery' under the affluent surface of this country. Takes the main segments of the worst-off poor—the unskilled, the migrants and some other farm workers, the aged, and minority peoples—describing the predicament of each group and summarizing the vicious circle of poverty, why the poor stay poor, and what can be done to help them." Pub W

"The author has thoroughly studied his source material: his statistics are grimly impressive and his scholarship is sound." Nation

Packard, Vance

The status seekers; an exploration of class behavior in America and the hidden barriers that affect you, your community, your future. McKay 1959 376p $7.95   **301.44**

1 Social classes 2 U.S.—Social life and customs

Dividing American society into five classes grouped under the broad headings of the "diplomatic elite" and the "supporting classes," the author "tells about the new class system whose tone is set by the big corporation, the union, the real estate developer, the advertiser, and most important, the diploma mill, often called a college. . . . Mr Packard considers such American status symbols as the church (where the social layering is most apparent), the motorcar, shopping, clubs, lodges, schools, political parties." Book of the Month Club News

"His book is journalism of the highest rank, an ordered compendium of his own researches and the findings of dozens of sociologists and investigators, with his interpretations and opinions clearly identified as such." N Y Times Bk R

Reference notes: p361-68

301.45 Nondominant groups. Prejudice

Baruch, Dorothy W.

Glass house of prejudice. Morrow 1946
205p $5.95   301.45

1 Prejudices and antipathies 2 U.S.—Race relations 3 Minorities

The author describes "the causes and effects of prejudice. She uses numerous examples to show its unhappy influence, especially among children. Her suggestions for its cures are both workable and sensible." Booklist
References and supplementary materials: p185-205

Bosworth, Allan R.

America's concentration camps; introduction by Roger Baldwin. Norton 1967 283p illus $6.95   301.45

1 Japanese in the U.S. 2 World War, 1939-1945—Evacuation of civilians 3 Concentration camps 4 World War, 1939-1945—U.S.

"In 1942, caught in the grip of war hysteria, the American government moved the entire West Coast Japanese population, both aliens and native-born citizens, to detention camps. In an angry and well-documented study, Allan Bosworth exposes this shameful and usually ignored chapter of American history. He details how the government succumbed to pressure from economic and racist groups . . . overlooked the heroic record of the 442nd Nisei (American-born boys of Japanese parentage) Regiment fighting for the U.S. Army in Europe. . . . Parts of the story are told through excerpts from moving, tragic diaries of innocent Japanese-Americans caught in this persecution." Pub W
Bibliography: p258-61

Glazer, Nathan

Beyond the melting pot; the Negroes, Puerto Ricans, Jews, Italians, and Irish of New York City. 2d ed. By Nathan Glazer and Daniel Patrick Moynihan. MIT Press 1970 xcviii, 363p $10   301.45

1 New York (City)—Foreign population 2 Minorities
ISBN 0-262-07039-1

First published 1963
Based on a study of ethnic groups in New York City, this book examines the thesis that the United States is a "melting pot" of minorities. The authors argue that such assimilation does not occur
"Each group is 'not a survival from the age of mass imigration but a new social form.' The analysis of these new social forms is continuously interesting, the conclusions are often startling." Book of the Month Club News
Bibliographical references included in Notes: p325-47. Map on lining-papers

Glock, Charles Y.

(ed.) Prejudice U.S.A. Ed. by Charles Y. Glock and Ellen Siegelman. Praeger 1969 xxii, 196p $5.95   301.45

1 Prejudices and antipathies

Analyzed in Essay and general literature index
"The book consists of perceptive essays by Dore Schary, Saunders Redding, Seymour Lipset, Rodney Stark, M. Brewster Smith, Charles Silberman and Richard Hatcher, exploring prejudice in American political life, in the blacks' struggle for equality, in churches, the mass media, schools and the marketplace. Professed ideals are in contrast to painful reality in every area discussed; but the book's context is dynamic and optimistic." Pub W

Greeley, Andrew M.

Why can't they be like us? America's white ethnic groups. Dutton 1971 223p $6.95   301.45

1 Minorities 2 U.S.—Foreign population
ISBN 0-525-23370-9

In this study the author "concurs with many who have noted that America's melting pot has not melted 'a nation of immigrants,' but has instead, in our century at least, tended to sustain diversity of ethnic groups—Irish, Italians, Poles, Germans, Jews and blacks—which are in various phases of adaptation or assimilation and which enrich our nation with their sub-structures and life styles. Greeley stresses the reasons why white ethnic groups are 'deeply committed' to the American system and calls the failure of liberal elites to understand the relevance of the law and order issue a disastrous political and social mistakes which has played into the hands of demagogues." Pub W
Bibliography: p216-18

Handlin, Oscar

The American people in the twentieth century. 2d ed. rev. Harvard Univ. Press 1966 [c1963] 248p (Library of Congress Ser. in American civilization) $5.50   301.45

1 U.S.—Foreign population 2 U.S.—Race relations 3 U.S.—Civilization

First published 1954
This is a "study of immigration waves in America from the seventeenth to the nineteenth centuries and their aftermath. The pattern of these movements, their ethnic content, places of settlement, and the problems of the various national groups are all analyzed, as well as the way they were affected by and reacted to events such as the Depression, the New Deal, and the two world wars." A Guide to Reading in Am History
The author "develops a picture of a population which is more nearly homogenous and integrated as a result of the crises of the last half-century." Booklist
Bibliographical references included in Notes: p237-39

The newcomers: Negroes and Puerto Ricans in a changing metropolis. Harvard Univ. Press 1959 171p illus (New York metropolitan region study) $4.50   301.45

1 Negroes—New York (City) 2 Puerto Ricans in New York (City)

"The patterns and problems of adjustment of Negroes and Puerto Ricans in New York are discussed against the background of earlier immigrations by Irish, German, Jewish and Italian groups. The similarities are pointed out and the difficulties caused by racial difference and metropolitan changes are discussed. Various population tables are included in an appendix." Pub W
"The study as a whole contrasts in mood with most discussions of the subject; it is written, after all, by a historian who relates the present to the experiences of the past. But there is more that perspective; there is also faith. Mr. Handlin looks for will and energy on the part of the newer immigrants, and tolerance on the part of their settled neighbors." N Y Times Bk R
Includes bibliography

Howard, John R.

(ed.) Awakening minorities: American Indians, Mexican Americans, Puerto Ricans. Aldine Pub. 1970 189p $5.95   301.45

1 Indians of North America 2 Mexicans in the U.S. 3 Puerto Ricans in the U.S.

"Trans-action books"
Contents: Introduction: Ethnic stratification systems, by J. R. Howard; American Indians: goodby to Tonto, by J. R. Howard; The warrior dropouts, by R. H. Wax; Renaissance and repression: the Oklahoma Cherokee, by A. L. Wahrhaftig; White rites and Indian rights, by A. D. Fisher; Seminole girl, by M. S. Gabarino; Mexican Americans: the road to Huelga, by J. R. Howard; La raza: Mexican Americans in rebellion, by J. L. Love; Puerto Ricans: the making of a minority group, by J. R. Howard; Even the saints cry, by O. Lewis; The Puerto Rican independence movement, by A. Liebman; The death of Dolores, by O. Lewis
Includes bibliographical references

Huthmacher, J. Joseph

A nation of newcomers; ethnic minorities in American history. Delacorte Press [1969 c1967] 132p illus boards $3.95   **301.45**

1 U.S.—Foreign population 2 Minorities
First published 1967 by Dell in paperback
"An informative survey of the treatment that has been accorded representative minority groups in the U.S. Looking at the Catholic Irish, Italians, Chinese and Japanese, Puerto Ricans, and Negroes, Huthmacher examines the means by which each group earned or tried to earn recognition and respect from society and shows how each contributed out of its particular culture to the enrichment of American culture. A chronology and suggestions for further reading are included in the appendixes." Booklist

Stalvey, Lois Mark

The education of a WASP. Morrow 1970 327p boards $6.95   **301.45**

1 Prejudices and antipathies 2 U.S.—Race relations 3 Discrimination
"The author with her husband and three children were a White Anglo-Saxon Protestant family living in Omaha in 1961. When they tried to help some black friends find a home in their community, they paid the price in a series of personal disasters." Pub W
"Mrs. Stalvey has written a remarkable story. She exposes the naive beliefs that she held about the treatment of Negroes at the beginning of this story and the views she gained through personal experience throughout the years. Hers is no hearsay evidence. She lived it. . . . [Her] book is a giant step in the education of Americans so that racial justice can be achieved in the United States." Best Sellers

301.451 Ethnic groups. Blacks

Aptheker, Herbert

(ed.) A documentary history of the Negro people in the United States; preface by W. E. B. Du Bois. Citadel 1969 942p $10   **301.451**

1 Negroes—History—Sources 2 Slavery in the United States 3 Negroes—Civil rights
First published 1951
"A compilation of documents, petitions, speeches, letters, and editorials prepared by Negroes and addressed sometimes to the world at large, sometimes to other Negroes, but most often to those who had the power to bring them relief. The earliest was addressed to the 'Noble Right Honourable Director-General and Lord Councillors of New Netherlands' in 1661, and the latest inclusion is DuBois's first editorial from the first number of 'The Crisis' (November, 1910), the official organ of the N.A.A.C.P." A Guide to Reading in Am History
"Subject to the well-known limitations of a source-book, the [work] seems, in view of its purpose and fulfillment, to admit of little, if any, special criticism. The student and many of the general public should find it exceptionally useful. It is a highly valuable contribution to the literature of its field." Am Hist R

Baldwin, James

The fire next time   **301.451**

1 Negroes 2 U.S.—Race relations 3 Black Muslims
Some editions are:
Dial Press $3.95
Watts, F. $7.95 Large type edition. A Keith Jennison book
First published 1963
" 'My Dungeon Shook,' the short essay which opens this small book, first appeared in The Progressive and is written in the form of a 'Letter to My Nephew on the 100th Anniversary of the Emancipation.' . . . The longer second essay, now entitled 'Down at the Cross,' formerly appeared in The New Yorker. . . . [It is] part autobiographical, part philosophical . . . [with a] section on the Black Muslim movement and Baldwin's meeting with its leader, Elijah Muhammad." Library J

"Forcefully and emotionally Baldwin describes Negro anger and disillusionment, pleads for a solution to race problems, and warns of the danger inherent in the current situation." Wis Lib Bul

Nobody knows my name; more notes of a native son. Dial Press 1961 241p boards $4.95   **301.451**

1 Negroes 2 U.S.—Race relations
First-person essays by the Negro author "in which he deals astutely and candidly with the relationship between black and white and between the writer and society. Drawing on his own experiences and observations in the U.S. and Europe he writes of American majorities and minorities . . . [and] novelists Richard Wright and Norman Mailer." Booklist
"The essays are uneven; some are slight and dated already because of their subject, some simply deserve more thought than Baldwin has devoted to them. But in this book . . . he has frequently written with a combination of passion, insight and intelligence to which his prose is equal." Commonweal

Notes of a native son. Dial Press 1963 158p $4.95   **301.451**

1 Negroes 2 U.S.—Race relations 3 Europe —Race relations
A reissue of the paperback edition first published 1955 by Beacon Press
The author's essays depicting the Negro experience in America and Europe
"This sheaf of personal essays, written with bitter clarity and uncommon grace, is an effort to retrieve the Negro from the abstractions of the do-gooders and the nogoods." Time
Contents: Autobiographical notes; Everybody's protest novel; Many thousands gone; Carmen Jones: the dark is light enough; The Harlem ghetto; Journey to Atlanta; Notes of a native son; Encounter on the Seine: black meets brown; A question of identity; Equal in Paris; Stranger in the village

Bennett, Lerone

Before the Mayflower: a history of the Negro in America, 1619- [by] Lerone Bennett, Jr. Johnson Pub. (Chicago) illus maps $6.95   **301.451**

1 Negroes—History
First published 1962 and periodically revised to bring it up-to-date
The author traces "the story from the ancient history of Africa to the present-day breakthroughs in desegregation. Emphasis is on slavery; miscegenation; plantation life . . . the fugitive slaves; the Negro troops who fought in the Revolution and the Civil War; Reconstruction; and Jim Crow laws and customs." Pub W
"Out of his journalistic background [the author] brings to history the pace and tang of newspaper language. . . . Bennett exercises restrained judgment. In the main he lets the facts speak for themselves, but he selects those facts which have an emotional as well as an intellectual impact." Christian Century
Includes bibliography

Bergman, Peter M.

The chronological history of the Negro in America, by Peter M. Bergman, assisted by a staff of compilers under the direction of Mort N. Bergman. Harper 1969 698p $12   **301.451**

1 Negroes—History
"A Bergman book"
This handbook "comprises a history of the Negro American. It is a record of 500 years, and brings together events, ideas, laws, and legislation, as well as literature. . . . The arrangement is chronological by year: from 1441, when the Portuguese began the slave trade by importing Africans into Europe, to 1968, when 1702 Negroes held elective or appointive positions in government below the federal level." Publisher's note

41

Bergman, Peter M.—*Continued*

"Each event generates rings of additional information, some swelling into lengthy stories, and most of it unfamiliar. [This is] a readable, invaluable account of events, at every level, and of Negroes in all fields." Sat R

Bibliography of bibliographies: p617-24

Bontemps, Arna

Anyplace but here [by] Arna Bontemps and Jack Conroy. Hill & Wang 1966 372p $5.95   301.451

1 Negroes—History   2 Negroes—Biography 3 Migration, Internal

First published 1945 with title: They seek a city

The authors discuss the migration of Negroes from the South to other regions in the United States, beginning with the 1700's and continuing to the present. Included are examinations of recent [1966] urban racial disturbances

"In effect the book is a compendium of pieces about Negro city dwellers whose exploits have in one fashion or another . . . affected the course of American history. Although mainly biographical, the essays do project . . . impressions of American social, racial and political developments." Library J

A selected list of references and sources: p349-60

100 years of Negro freedom. Dodd 1961 276p illus $5   301.451

1 Negroes—Moral and social conditions 2 Negroes—Biography

"The Negro's ideas and advances since the Civil War with Frederick Douglass, Booker T. Washington, W.E.B. Du Bois, the NAACP, the Urban League representing various goals and experiments. For the student ready for solid reading." N Y Pub Lib

"An interesting, well-documented account supplemented by a bibliography." Booklist

Bracey, John H.

(ed.) Black nationalism in America; ed. by John H. Bracey, Jr., August Meier [and] Elliott Rudwick. Bobbs 1970 512p (American Heritage ser) $8.50   301.451

1 Negroes 2 U.S.—Race relations

The editors "have gathered considerable long-neglected material in their anthology, the first collection of original writings devoted entirely to black nationalism. . . . The book is divided into five main sections, covering the origins, maturation, flowering, eclipse, and revival of black nationalism from . . . the late 1700s to the Revolutionary Action Movement and the Black Panthers. Its seventy-seven documents are drawn from speeches, manifestos, letters, leaflets, poems, books, Negro newspapers, and the proceedings of colored people's conventions." Sat R

Brink, William

Black and white; a study of U.S. racial attitudes today [by] William Brink [and] Louis Harris. Simon & Schuster 1967 285p $5.95   301.451

1 U.S.—Race relations 2 Negroes—Civil rights 3 Negroes—Politics and suffrage

A report on race relations in America, based on a 1966 Newsweek Magazine survey. It covers dissensions within the civil rights movement, the rising white backlash, the Negro extremist factions and "how the next stages of this revolution are likely to affect politics, the American family system, housing in our big cities, the U.S. Army, and many other vital aspects of our lives." Publisher's note

The book "is dispassionate reportage. It is well larded with statistics and tables gleaned from Harris's survey of both white and Negro attitudes, but pungent quotes, personality sketches and a terse writing style make the statistics highly palatable." N Y Times Bk R

Chambers, Bradford

(ed.) Chronicles of Negro protest; a background book for young people documenting the history of Black power; comp. and ed. with a commentary by Bradford Chambers. Parents Mag. Press 1968 319p illus $4.50, lib. bdg. $4.12   301.451

1 Negroes—History   2 Negroes—Civil rights 3 Negroes—Moral and social condtions

The author uses historical documents to survey the background of Negro protest. "The book includes such documents as: the first Negro Senator speaks to the Senate; Marcus Garvey outlines his program for a Negro nation; Dr. Martin Luther King describes his pilgrimage to nonviolence; Malcolm X, Stokely Carmichael, H. Rap Brown and others explain what 'Black Power' really means to them." Publisher's note

"Some of these documents are well known, some less so . . . but many of the earlier documents by Negroes are unknown. They touch upon every aspect of the race problem." N Y Times Bk R

Available sources of the documents: p309-12

Clark, Kenneth B.

Dark ghetto; dilemmas of social power; foreword by Gunnar Myrdal. Harper 1965 xxix, 251p $5.95   301.451

1 Negroes—New York (City) 2 Harlem, New York (City)—Social conditions 3 Negroes—Segregation

The author uses Harlem as a focal point to analyze "the Negro power structure—political, religious, economic, intellectual—and dissects the effectiveness and ineffectiveness of civil rights strategies. There are . . . profiles of Adam Clayton Powell, J. Raymond Jones, Martin Luther King, and others, and a probing interpretation of the psychology of the ghetto and of the ambivalent relationship between the Negro and the white liberal." Publisher's note

A book "which indicates that permanent solutions to the ghetto's multiple problems will invoke a radical transformation of U.S. society." Booklist

Clarke, John Henrik

(ed.) Malcolm X; the man and his times; ed. with an introduction and commentary, by John Henrik Clarke; assisted by A. Peter Bailey and Earl Grant. Macmillan (N Y) 1969 xxiv, 360p $6.95   301.451

1 Malcolm X 2 Black Muslims

"An anthology of personal reflections, dialogs, articles, speeches, and manifestos by Malcolm X and by his Black supporters throughout the world." Bk Buyer's Guide

"Appended materials include a definition of the aims and objectives of the Organization of Afro-American Unity, and the outline of a petition to the U.N. Several of the articles were previously published in periodicals, the rest written expressly for the book." Booklist

A selected bibliography of books and articles relating to the life of Malcolm X: p352-56

Cleaver, Eldridge

Soul on ice; with an introduction by Maxwell Geismar. McGraw 1968 210p $5.95   301.451

1 Negroes

"A Ramparts book"

"In a collection of essays and open letters written from California's Folsom State Prison, the author, an Afro-American . . ., writes about the forces which shaped his life." Book Rev Digest

There are sections "on the Watts riots, on Cleaver's religious conversion, on the black man's stake in the Vietnam War, on fellow-writers and white women." Sat R

Cole, Ernest
House of bondage, by Ernest Cole with Thomas Flaherty; introduction by Joseph Lelyveld. Random House 1967 187p illus $12.50 **301.451**

1 Africa, South—Race relations 2 Africa, South—Social conditions

"A Ridge Press book"

In this photographic essay, "a South African, who has left his native land, describes the mistreatment of the black people; the pass system, the lack of education, and his people's futile efforts to win justice." Bk Buyer's Guide

"An extraordinary achievement in photojournalism. . . . Mr. Cole's photo album describes the South Africa which few whites, whether citizens or visitors have ever seen or know anything about." Christian Science Monitor

Coles, Robert
Children of crisis; a study of courage and fear. Little 1967 401p illus $8.50 **301.451**

1 Negroes—Integration 2 Negroes—Segregation

"An Atlantic Monthly Press book"

"The author investigates and analyzes some twenty persons who represent the spectrum of the South—the Negro children who faced the howling mobs when they attended white schools, their classmates, some hostile, some protective. Teachers, by-standers, staunch segregationists and integrationists are examined and the roots of their prejudice explored. The results of his study make worthwhile and interesting reading." English-Speaking Union

References: p383-92

Davis, John P.
(ed.) The American Negro reference book. Prentice-Hall 1966 xxii, 969p illus map $24.95 **301.451**

1 Negroes

Analyzed in Essay and general literature index

Following a chapter on American Negro history, different contributors "survey the American Negro's role in various fields of activity (e.g., agriculture, politics, fine arts), the status of various groups of American Negroes (e.g., urban Negro families, Negro women), the presence and effect of prejudice, and the religion, economic position and legal status of the American Negro." Pub W

Includes "a list of honors won by Negroes and of the All-American team references." Cur Ref Bks

Includes bibliographical footnotes

Draper, Theodore
The rediscovery of Black nationalism. Viking 1970 211p $5.95 **301.451**

1 Negroes 2 U.S.—Race relations

"Drawing largely on secondary historical sources and some of the arguments of W.E.B. DuBois and Harold Cruse, [the author] brings together and analyzes a number of recurring themes in the history of American black nationalism. . . . [He also reviews its] dilemmas, contradictions, failures, and occasional excesses." Sat R

Bibliography included in Reference notes: p183-203

Du Bois, W. E. B.
The souls of Black folk; essays and sketches; with illus. of the author, his environment, and the setting of the book, together with an introduction by Saunders Redding. Dodd [1970 c1961] 199p illus $4.95 **301.451**

1 Negroes

"Great illustrated classics"

First published 1903 by McClurg

"A collection of essays. . . . This influential volume gives, affectingly and impressively, the point of view of a Negro who believes it is beneath the dignity of a human being to beg

for those rights that belong to all mankind. Du Bois presents with courage and insight the cause of the Negro in America." Herzberg. The Reader's Encyclopedia of Am Lit

W. E. B. Du Bois: a reader; ed. and with an introduction by Meyer Weinberg. Harper 1970 471p $8.95 **301.451**

1 Negroes

"An Urban Affairs book under the general editorship of Kenneth B. Clark. The Urban Affairs Series is cosponsored by the Metropolitan Applied Research Center, Inc, and Harper & Row." Verso of title page

This "selection of DuBois' work is in excellent taste. . . . Most of these works will be new to the followers of DuBois, and this newness will provide greater understanding of the profound depth and scope of that great black leader's philosophy. The readings cover the field, incorporating works dealing with black manners, politics, race relations, and African heritage, and a surprising criticism of the 'talented tenth' which DuBois advocated at the turn of the century. While one might wonder why more attention was not given to pan-Africanism as a unit, the overall impression left by Weinberg's editing is favourable." Choice

A selected bibliography of W. E. B. Du Bois: p445-59

Ducas, George
(ed.) Great documents in Black American history; ed. by George Ducas with Charles Van Doren; introduction by C. Eric Lincoln, editorial consultant. Praeger 1970 321p illus $12.50 **301.451**

1 Negroes—History—Sources

Analyzed in Essay and general literature index

"From an essay by Quaker John Woolman of Colonial days to a contemporary piece by LeRoi Jones, this anthology of familiar and unfamiliar significant writings, some first fully published here, reflects black-white attitudes and interactions over the years and mirrors from different points of view the experiences and hopes of Americans who happen to be black and whose history is a valid if suppressed part of American history. The black viewpoint and black destiny are underscored in the general introduction and in editorial observations prefacing each piece in a volume intent on placing black history trends and movements in their rightful American history context." Booklist

Sources: p317-18

Ebony
The Negro handbook; comp. by the editors of Ebony. Johnson Pub. (Chicago) 1966 535p $12.50 **301.451**

1 Negroes—Handbooks, manuals, etc.

A compilation offering a "variety of information on American Negroes. Figures on population, crime, education, employment and other economic matters, and housing are mingled with reports on aspects of the civil rights struggle, lists of Negro office holders, publications, colleges, monuments, graduates of service academies, and artists. [There is a] career guide and lists of scholarships, loan funds, and preparatory schools available to Negroes. . . . Negro obituaries, biographies of 130 Negroes of current significance, and an annotated bibliography of books by and about Negroes." Choice

For a more complete review see: The Booklist and Subscription Books Bulletin for September 1, 1967

Fishel, Leslie H.
(ed.) The Black American; a documentary history [ed. by] Leslie H. Fishel, Jr. [and] Benjamin Quarles. Rev. ed. of The Negro American. Morrow 1970 608p illus $10 **301.451**

1 Negroes—History—Sources

Fishel, Leslie H.—*Continued*
First published 1968 with title: The Negro
American
This collection of documents traces "the history of the black American from his African
background through Colonial America and the
Revolution, slavery and abolition, Reconstruction, urbanization and renaissance, the New
Deal to the March on Washington and the
assertion of black power." Publisher's note
"The special values of this book are its convenient collection of material not hitherto
easily available and its numerous and well
chosen illustrations." Pub W

Franklin, John Hope
From slavery to freedom; a history of Negro Americans. 3d ed. Knopf 1967 xxii,
686, xliii p illus $12   301.451
1 Negroes—History 2 Slavery in the U.S.
First published 1947
The author "traces the record from Negro
origins in Africa, through slavery, to freedom
in the Western Hemisphere, including the West
Indies, Latin America, Canada, and the United
States." Publisher's note
"The book is forthright and honest, and
contains material about the Negro, which will
surprise those having only a casual acquaintance with his history." N Y Times Bk R
Bibliographical notes: p653-86

An illustrated history of Black Americans,
by John Hope Franklin and the editors of
Time-Life Books. Time-Life Bks. [distrib-
uted by Little] 1970 192p illus map
boards $7.95   301.451
1 Negroes—History 2 Slavery in the U.S.
"This is a much shorter version of [the
author's] widely praised work 'From Slavery
to Freedom' [entered above] . . . which he has
now popularized and profusely illustrated." Library J
A "portrait of our American social order and
how it evolved. In a text amplified by illustrations, picture essays, and selections from
diaries and memoirs of the times, John Hope
Franklin sketches the growth of slavery in the
United States, the rise of the plantation economy, the Civil War as seen from the blacks'
perspective, and the years since: Reconstruction, the eras of the KKK and the Great Depression, the contrasting period of the Harlem
renaissance, as well as the latest developments
in black power, black studies and the resurgence of interest in African roots." Publisher's
note
Bibliography: p188

Frazier, E. Franklin
The Negro family in the United States.
Rev. and abridged ed. Foreword by Nathan
Glazer. Univ. of Chicago Press 1966 xxii,
372p $6   301.451
1 Negroes—Moral and social conditions
2 Family
Originally published 1939. This abridged edition first published 1948
"This classic study of the Negro family in
America from slavery days to the mid-twentieth century demonstrates the Negroes' historic ability to evolve stable family forms out
of total dependence and disruption." Publisher's note
It is "of current value not only for the historical survey it affords but only for the insight into recent developments." Booklist
Bibliographical footnotes

Goldman, Peter
Report from Black America. Simon &
Schuster 1970 282p $6.95   301.451
1 Negroes 2 U.S.—Race relations
SBN 671-20609-5
"Based on the results of a summer 1969
Gallup poll taken for 'Newsweek' magazine
this is a concise, objective survey of Negro
opinion on a variety of important issues including discrimination, black leadership, techniques in the civil rights movement, rioting,
attitude toward whites, and probable develop-

ments in the racial situation during the 1970s.
Interspersed throughout are seven personal in-
terviews with such blacks influential in today's
movement as Harry Edwards, Charles Evers,
Jesse Jackson, and Bayard Rustin." Booklist
Includes bibliographical references

Griffin, John Howard
Black like me. Houghton 1961 176p $4.95
                                          301.451
1 Negroes—Southern States
The author, "who is white, a Catholic, and
a Texan, conceived and carried out the unusual notion of blackening his skin with, a
newly developed pigment drug and traveling
through the Deep South as a Negro. This book,
part of which appeared in the Negro magazine
Sepia, is a journal account of that experience."
New Yorker
"The story of this incredible adventure is
told here in bare, unemotional pedestrian prose
which gains in its drama from its very sparse-
ness." San Francisco Chronicle

Hughes, Langston
A pictorial history of the Negro in America, by Langston Hughes & Milton Meltzer.
3d rev. ed. Crown 1968 380p illus maps
boards $5.95   301.451
1 Negroes—History 2 Slavery in the U.S.
First published 1956: this revision by C. Eric
Lincoln and Milton Meltzer
A "picture panorama, with text, of all aspects of American Negro life from African
origins through slavery days to the present
[integration efforts]. The pictures were collected . . . from prints, engravings, woodcuts,
photographs, paintings." Pub W
"Since relatively few people read and learn
from history as written by scholars, the fast-
paced narrative style of Hughes' text may be
all to the good. The pictures . . . compound
the value." N Y Her Trib Books
Bibliography: p375

Lomax, Louis E.
The Negro revolt. Harper 1962 271p
boards $6.50   301.451
1 Negroes—Moral and social conditions
2 Negroes—Civil rights 3 U.S.—Race relations
The author's premise in this work is that
the American Negro revolt is directed not only
against the white world but against the old-
guard Negro organizations. Writing in the
early 1960's, Lomax examined the Negro leadership organizations as it was then, who ran
them, where they got their support, what their
goals and problems were. Presented also are
prominent Negro leaders from the late Martin
Luther King to Elijah Muhammad. (Publisher)
"Mr Lomax's book is a first-rate guide to
the differences between the Urban League, the
NAACP, CORE, SNICK, SCLC and the Black
Muslims. His own sympathies lie with the
advocates of direct action, but he does justice
to the older leaders, educators and organisa-
tions now being brushed aside by a race that
is on the move at last. His book is full of
interesting points. . . . One of the virtues of
Mr Lomax's book is that he does not deny that
subjection has made many Negroes apathetic,
immoral and prone to crime and that he recognizes that they must become much more
responsible." Economist
Bibliography: p261-62

Malcolm X
The autobiography of Malcolm X; with
the assistance of Alex Haley. Introduction
by M. S. Handler; epilogue by Alex Haley.
Grove [1965 c1964] 455p illus $7.50 301.451
1 Black Muslims 2 U.S.—Race relations
An account of his life and of the Black
Muslims completed shortly before the violent
death of Malcolm Little, commonly known as
Malcolm X. Malcolm X recalls his early childhood, introduction to sordid Harlem, years in
prison when he became a disciple of Elijah
Muhammad, the Black Muslims, and his eventual break with Muhammad
"An important document in American Negro
history as well as an intensely personal, honest, and revealing account of the Black Nationalist's amazing life." N Y Pub Lib

Meier, August

From plantation to ghetto, by August Meier and Elliott Rudwick. Rev. ed. Hill & Wang 1970 340p maps $8.95   **301.451**

1 Negroes—History 2 Negroes—Civil rights 3 U.S.—Race relations
ISBN 0-8090-4791-8
"American century series"
First published 1966
This discussion of Negro ideologies and movements in America emphasizes the work of such twentieth century Negro leaders as A. Philip Randolph and Martin Luther King, and such organizations as the NAACP, CORE and SNCC. (Publisher)
Selected bibliography: p299-326

Negro thought in America, 1880-1915; racial ideologies in the age of Booker T. Washington. Univ. of Mich. Press 1963 336p $7.95
301.451

1 Negroes—History 2 Washington, Booker Taliaferro
"This is an interestingly presented historical review of the Negro's attitudes toward the social, economic, educational, and political development of his race in the U.S. from the Reconstruction to the period just preceding the country's entry into World War I." Booklist
"The style is at times heavy and reminiscent of the jargon of the sociologists, but the book makes fascinating reading in spite of this. . . . This is not a biography of Booker T. Washington, but it is the best book on that enigmatic figure which has yet appeared." J Am Hist
Bibliographical note: p280-82. Bibliographical references in Notes: p283-316

Meltzer, Milton

(ed.) In their own words; a history of the American Negro. Crowell 1964-1967 3v illus ea $4.95   **301.451**

1 Negroes—History
Contents: v 1: 1619-1865; v2: 1865-1916; v3: 1916-1966
A "history of the American Negro from 1619 to [1966] is told in his own words through selections from letters, diaries, journals, speeches, and other documents. Helpful background information and commentary introduce each of the pieces, some of which have been edited for easier reading, and the source is given at the end of each document. A calendar of Negro history . . . and an annotated reading list are appended [in each of the three volumes]." Booklist
"The collection is occasionally distinguished by a simple eloquence and despite the underlying sadness, is notably lacking in bitterness. . . . [Many will find] inspiration to work for solutions to current problems." Horn Bk

Myrdal, Gunnar

An American dilemma; the Negro problem and modern democracy. With the assistance of Richard Sterner and Arnold Rose. 20th anniversary ed. Harper 1962 lxxxiii, 1483p illus $16.50   **301.451**

1 Negroes 2 U.S.—Race relations
First published 1944
This lengthy analysis of "American attitudes and actions with respect to the Negro presents social, economic, and political factors of the Negro question and their interrelation with the whole of American life. The dilemma is the conflict between American ideals and actual behavior and, in the author's interpretation, indicates a moral lag that is the core of the problem." Booklist
Extensive footnotes. List of books, pamphlets, periodicals and other material referred to in this book: p1144-80

Olsen, Jack

The Black athlete; a shameful story; the myth of integration in American sport. Time-Life Bks. 1968 223p boards $4.95
301.451

1 Negroes—Integration 2 Negro athletes

An expanded version of the series of articles published in Sports Illustrated about discrimination against black athletes. The author presents the case of the black athlete as a microcosm of the total racial problem in the U.S. (Publisher)
"This book is filled with first-hand material obtained from interviews and observations by the author and is written in a convincing and interest-sustaining journalistic style. The author offers no remedies, no solutions, no panaceas—this is up to the public which his book will indubitably help to enlighten." Science Bks

Quarles, Benjamin

The Negro in the making of America. Rev. ed. Collier Bks. 1969 318p pa $1.25   **301.451**

1 Negroes—History
First published 1964
"A readable account of the black man's role in plantation life, his participation in the Revolutionary and Civil War, and his struggle for equality." Negro in the U.S.
Bibliography: p291-96

Silberman, Charles E.

Crisis in black and white. Random House 1964 370p $5.95   **301.451**

1 Negroes—Moral and social conditions 2 U.S. —Race relations
A book which grapples "with the hard and pressing problems of the Negro hatred of the white and of himself and with white prejudice against the Negro, in the U.S. How slavery and its aftermath distorted Negro personality and suppressed Negro mentality is one of the author's main points. He shows how oppression has crippled the Negro with feelings of inferiority and apathy. The Black Muslim movement is carefully evaluated. When proposing means of giving the Negro his due, the author is emphatic about job opportunities and proper education. This survey of the past, present, and possible future of the Negro in the U.S. is one of the most plain-spoken accounts yet to appear on the subject. Much of the material originated in an assignment for 'Fortune.'" Pub W
It "is a perceptively accurate diagnosis of the situation, in which there is no sustained preaching or special pleading. Yet both are implicit in Mr. Silberman's painstaking study." Christian Science Monitor
Bibliographical footnotes

Silver, James W.

Mississippi: the closed society. New enl. ed. Harcourt 1966 xxix, 375p illus map $5.75
301.451

1 Mississippi—Race relations 2 Mississippi—Politics and government
First published 1964
On September 30, 1962 the author witnessed the "riot that exploded on the campus of the University of Mississippi at Oxford, when students, and, later, adults with no connection with the university, attacked United States marshalls sent to the campus to protect James H. Meredith, the first Negro to attend Ole Miss. . . . [Professor Silver describes the] state's commitment to the doctrine of white supremacy." Publisher's note
Commendable are "the force of Mr. Silver's indictment and the depth of his examination of the mentality of a closed society." New Yorker
"Mr Silver's originality and power consist in his putting each circumstance into relation with all the other circumstances—an operation that results in many new insights. He is especially good on the subject of the Citizens Council. . . . Indeed, the entire book is made lively and persuasive by detail. Personalities are sketched, speeches and press stories quoted, and stories of blackmail and lynching included where relevant and verifiable." Book Week
Bibliographical footnotes

White, William

Lost boundaries. Harcourt 1948 91p boards $3.95   **301.451**

1 Negroes 2 Johnston family

White, William—*Continued*
"The straightforward, unadorned story of a real New England family which 'passed' as white until the father's application for a Navy commission was rejected and his Negro blood was revealed. The effect of this revelation on the children, who had been brought up as whites, and their decisions to 'pass' or declare their race, are the sober issues of this slight but important book." Retail Bookseller

Woodward, C. Vann
The strange career of Jim Crow. 2d rev ed. Oxford 1966 205p $5.75   **301.451**
1 Negroes—Segregation
First published 1955
An "account of segregation in the South from 1877 to the present. The problem is analyzed as to origins and developments of Jim Crowism. Refutes the belief that Southern segregation laws were imposed when the Reconstruction period ended in the 1870's. Involved are class war, Whigs, Populism, Tom Watson, and the New South." A Guide to Reading in Am History
"No informed person will question Dr. Woodward's facts. It may, nevertheless, be that he has put too much emphasis on segregation by law. . . . Dr. Woodward's objective but often eloquent book deserves a wide reading today. If it throws no flashing illumination on the past, it does provide a basis for the clearer seeing of the problem now." Yale R
Notes on reading: p193-96

Year
Pictorial history of the Black American. Year, inc. 1968 154p illus maps $4.95
          301.451
1 Negroes—History 2 Negroes—Civil rights 3 Negroes—Moral and social conditions
First published 1965 by C. S. Hammond with title: Year's Pictorial history of the American Negro
Edited by Balwin H. Ward
Using pictures, text, and documents, this book summarizes the history and social and economic conditions of the American Negro, beginning with his African background and concluding with the civil rights movement of the 1960's
"A brief bibliography, and an index to persons, places, and events append the lively text accompanying the clear but small photographs which fill the pages with evidence of the mounting tension." Cur Ref Bks
Bibliography: p152

301.453 Nondominant groups of specific national origin

Lewis, Oscar, 1914-1970
La vida; a Puerto Rican family in the culture of poverty—San Juan and New York. Random House 1966 lix, 669p $12.50
          301.453
1 Puerto Ricans in New York (City) 2 New York (City)—Social conditions 3 San Juan, P.R.—Social conditions
First person biographies of a mother and her grown children all of whom have lived in poverty in Puerto Rico and New York City. (Publisher)
"The San Juan slum . . . is made unforgettable while 'the culture of poverty' in New York City and the Bronx remains, to put it politely, vague. Yet the overall impact is genuine and frightening." New Repub
Bibliography included in Notes: p liii-lv

Moore, Joan W.
Mexican Americans [by] Joan W. Moore with Alfredo Cuéllar. Prentice-Hall 1970 172p (Ethnic groups in American life ser) $5.95   **301.453**
1 Mexicans in the New Southwest

This book considers "the history and current status of the Mexican-American population of the U.S. Southwest. . . . The first third is devoted to a brief survey ofthe history of Mexican Americans in the Southwest, following a profile of employment, education, and income, the roles of the educational, religious, and law enforcement institutions are considered. Separate chapters are then concerned with the family, and community, language and culture, and finally politics." Choice
Selected bibliography: p163-64

O'Connor, Richard
The German-Americans; an informal history. Little 1968 484p illus boards $8.95
          301.453
1 Germans in the U.S.
"An informal social history of one of the largest ethnic minorities in America, from their arrival early in this country's history to the present. Today [mid-60's] one out of six Americans is either partly or wholly of German ancestry, including such diverse personalities as Eric Hoffer, Walter Lippmann, Dwight D. Eisenhower, Rod Steiger and the Rockefellers. German influence has touched America's labor movement, political doctrines, religions, its music and education." Am News of Bks
The author "tells his story in minute detail and with engaging fluency. He is never tedious and he leavens his narrative with many a refreshing anecdote." Christian Science Monitor
Bibliography: p475-78

Senior, Clarence
The Puerto Ricans: strangers—then neighbors; foreword by Hubert H. Humphrey. Quadrangle Bks. 1965 128p illus maps $4.50
          301.453
1 Puerto Ricans in the U.S. 2 U.S.—Foreign population 3 U.S.—Social conditions 4 U.S.—Race relations
"Published in cooperation with the Anti-Defamation League of B'nai B'rith"
First published by Freedom Books in 1961 with title: Strangers—then neighbors
The author "reviews every aspect of life among this group including education, economics, housing, welfare, criminality, and the multiplicity of labels applied to this latest group of immigrants." Library J
"Certainly Dr. Senior's book belongs in every public or school library. . . . In addition to giving the reader an authoritative, if somewhat simplified, over-view of the Puerto Ricans in our stress-ridden urban society, it also contains conclusive answers to the timeworn but still circulating canards." Book Week
Bibliography: p112-23

Shannon, William V.
The American Irish. [Rev. ed] Macmillan (N Y) 1966 484p illus $9.95   **301.453**
1 Irish in the U.S. 2 National characteristics, Irish
Analyzed in Essay and general literature index
First published 1963
"After a brief history of the Irish and an explanation of their racial character, the author covers the exodus to America, their varying fortunes here, and picks out such individuals as John L. Sullivan, Father Coughlin, James Curley, John O'Hara, and of course, John F. Kennedy for special mention." Bk Buyer's Guide
"He has worked mainly from original, not secondary, sources, he is not uncritical (as a highly interesting chapter on McCarthyism demonstrates), and his witty . . . style goes well with his subject." Pub W
Bibliographical references included in Notes: p439-67

Steiner, Stan
La Raza; the Mexican Americans. Harper 1970 418p illus $8.95   **301.453**
1 Mexicans in the U.S.
Making use of numerous interviews in this account of an exploited minority group in the U.S., the author describes "the continuing struggle of Cesar Chavez and his striking California grape-pickers, Tijerina's fiery leadership of his people in New Mexico, the Denver 'chicano' movement led by boxer-poet-playwright

Steiner, Stan—*Continued*

Rodolfo 'Corky' Gonzales, and many others. Here [too] are descriptions of the traumatic experience of the 150,000 'braceros' who cross the border annually to work as field laborers." Pub W

"All in all, it is one of the most important books about Mexican-Americans." Choice
Sources: p393-406

303 Social sciences—Dictionaries

Encyclopaedia of the social sciences; editor-in-chief, Edwin R. A. Seligman; associate editor, Alvin Johnson. Macmillan (N Y) 1937 15v in 8 $195 **303**
1 Social sciences—Dictionaries
Originally published 1930-1935 in 15 volumes
"The first comprehensive encyclopedia of the whole field of the social sciences, projected and prepared under the auspices of 10 learned societies. Aims to cover all important topics in the fields of political science, economics, law, anthropology, sociology, penology, and social work, and the social aspects of ethics, education, philosophy, psychology, biology, geography, medicine, art, etc. International in scope and treatment, but fuller for the English-speaking world and western Europe than for other regions or interests. Articles are by specialists and signed; bibliographies in the main are adequate and in unusually good form. About 50 percent of the articles are biographical; includes many biographies of deceased persons." Winchell. Guide to Reference Books. 8th edition

International Encyclopedia of the social sciences; David L. Sills, ed. Macmillan (N Y) 1968 17v illus $495 **303**
1 Social sciences—Dictionaries 2 Encyclopedias and dictionaries
This encyclopedia, which complements the Encyclopedia of the social sciences, published 1930-1935, reflects "thirty years' growth in fields of the social sciences: anthropology, economics, geography, history, law, political science, psychiatry, psychology, sociology, and statistics. Emphasis is placed upon the analytical and comparative rather than historical and descriptive aspects of topics treated. . . . The alphabetical arrangement of entries is augmented by copious cross-references both within the text and appended to articles; by a detailed index volume; and by grouping under a single heading of several specific articles having in common a general subject matter. . . . All articles are signed and accompanied by lengthy bibliographies intended both to document the text and to suggest material for further reading." Coll & Res Lib

309.1485 Social conditions of Sweden

Jenkins, David

Sweden and the price of progress. Coward-McCann 1968 286p $6.50 **309.1485**
1 Sweden—Social conditions
"A description of how labor works together with management through its labor peace apparatus, how the capitalists cooperate with the socialists who run the welfare state, and how Sweden's complex of organizations affects and partially runs the government." McClurg. Book News

309.151 Social conditions of China

Myrdal, Jan

Chinese journey; photographs by Gun Kessle. Pantheon Bks. 1965 160p illus map $9.95 **309.151**
1 China (People's Republic of China)—Social conditions 2 China (People's Republic of China)—Description and travel

"The aim of this book is an extension of 'Report from A Chinese Village' . . . to show through the lives of the common people what Chinese Communism is all about." Publisher's note

"This is not meant as a profound interpretation of China today but as a reflection of people at work, at school, at home. Many of Gun Kessle's beautiful photographs are in color; all of them together show the present [early 1960's] face of China." Horn Bk

309.152 Social conditions of Japan

Kahn, Herman

The emerging Japanese superstate: challenge and response. Prentice-Hall 1970 274p illus $7.95 **309.152**
1 Japan—Economic conditions 2 Japan—Social conditions 3 Japan—Foreign relations
ISBN 0-13-274738-3
This account of modern Japan explores the following: "Japanese 'national character' and social attitudes; the post-war 'economic miracle'; the future of Japan Inc.'; the emerging 'Japanese superstate'; and the potential challenge represented by Japan in about [the year] 2000." Choice
The author "succeeds admirably in his stated goal of opening up rather than settling discussion. . . . [This book] will be acknowledged as invaluable to anyone interested in Japan, and as a book which should be read straight-away by anyone concerned with geopolitics." Nat R
Selected bibliography: p247-50

309.172 Social conditions of Mexico

Lewis, Oscar, 1914-1970

The children of Sánchez; autobiography of a Mexican family **309.172**
1 Mexico (City)—Social conditions 2 Mexico (City)—Poor 3 Family
Some editions are:
Modern Lib. $4.95 (Modern Lib. Giant)
Random House $12.50
First published 1961
"First-person autobiographical narratives by the members of a poor family in Mexico City. One by one, the father and his four grown children told the anthropologist-author their stories of fights, sex, struggles for jobs, bitterness, hate, sickness, death, and only a little happiness. The book has tremendous force as a picture of living, suffering people and of the effect of urbanization, slum-living, on the poor." Pub W

A death in the Sánchez family. Random House 1969 119p $4.95 **309.172**
1 Mexico (City)—Social conditions 2 Mexico (City)—Poor 3 Death 4 Funeral rites and ceremonies
The author "goes back to the Sanchez family which he portrayed so vividly in his 'Children of Sanchez,' focusing this time on Guadalupe, the aunt whose death brings two nephews and a niece together to view her body and lament over their lack of consideration for her while she lived. Once more using a tape recorder and his own notes, Lewis draws a heartrending portrait of the young Guadalupe, starving, beaten, caring for the children of others and bearing her own as one man after another deserts her and she is left, old and ailing, in one of the slums of Mexico City—caring even then for a much younger man who is her last common-law husband." Pub W

309.173 Social conditions of the U.S.

Addams, Jane

The social thought of Jane Addams; ed. by Christopher Lasch. Bobbs 1965 xxxvii, 266p (The American heritage ser) $7.50 **309.173**

Addams, Jane—*Continued*

A collection of some of the author's "writings on politics, the city, the revolt of youth, immigrants, social work, civil rights, pacifism, and family life. From her letters, lectures, articles, and books, Professor Lasch has given us the materials that warrant a fresh assessment of Jane Addams as more than the universal maiden aunt who founded Hull-House, won a Nobel Peace Prize, and aroused the social conscience of America." Foreword
Bibliography: p xxxiii-xxxv

Deloria, Vine

We talk, you listen; new tribes, new turf, by Vine Deloria, Jr. Macmillan (N Y) 1970 227p $5.95   **309.173**

1 U.S.—Social conditions 2 Indians of North America 3 Minorities

An Indian spokesman "sees racial conflict, inflation, the ecological crisis, and power groups as symptoms rather than causes of the American malaise. . . . His proposed solution to the legacy of genocide, imperialism, capitalism, feudalism, and . . . liberalism centers around . . . [an] Indian idea—that group identity and . . . community development are a kind of neo-tribalism, and that the elements of American society are . . . a collection of tribes: Indians, Chicanos, blacks, hippies, and others." Publisher's note

Gardner, John W.

No easy victories; ed. by Helen Rowan. Harper 1968 177p boards $4.95   **309.173**

1 U.S.—Social conditions

The author, former U.S. Secretary of Health, Education, and Welfare, "probes those areas of national concern which are his special province. He is strongly outspoken on social and racial injustice; rejecting violence of thought and deed. . . . He espouses community involvement, challenging lay leaders and universities to guide our society toward enlightenment and fulfillment." Pub W
"This book is a well-selected mosaic of connected passages from [the author's] numerous addresses and papers prepared during the last four crowded years. . . . They should be taken in small doses. They are to be read leisurely after the day's work is over and not hastily gulped at one reading." Book World

Goldston, Robert

The Great Depression; the United States in the thirties; illus. with photographs and drawings by Donald Carrick. Bobbs 1968 218p illus $5   **309.173**

1 U.S.—Social conditions 2 U.S.—Economic conditions—1919-1933 3 U.S.—Economic conditions—1933-1945

"A long, hard look at the grim years that followed the crash of 1929, prefaced by a description of the United States in the optimistic decade that preceded the disaster. The author examines in authoritative detail the political and financial intricacies of the depression: the role of the farmers and of organized labor, and futile efforts of the Hoover administration and the turbulent activity of the New Deal, the actions of the Congress and of big business. Carefully written, objective and analytical, this is an absorbing and important book from both financial and historical viewpoints. An extensive bibliography and index are appended." Chicago. Children's Book Center

Hoffer, Eric

First things, last things. Harper 1971 132p boards $4.95   **309.173**

1 U.S.—Social conditions 2 Social change
SBN 06-011916-0

"A Cass Canfield book"
These nine short "essays are vaguely related to a central theme: change is the cause, rather than the result, of revolution. This thesis is defended by appeals to incidental illustrations arbitrarily selected from man's history—past, present, and envisioned future. The American 'madhouse of change' is described as involving the 'Latin-Americanization of the universities, the Africanization of the big cities, the decline of efficiency in manufacturing and service, the incapacity to maintain the social plant in good repair, the tax-cheating rich and the swaggering intelligentsia." Choice

King, Martin Luther

The trumpet of conscience [by] Martin Luther King, Jr. [1968 c1967] 78p $4.95   **309.173**

1 U.S.—Social conditions 2 U.S.—Race relations 3 U.S.—Moral conditions

Analyzed in Essay and general literature index

Five talks "broadcast during November and December, 1967, over the Canadian Broadcasting Corporation as the seventh annual series of Massey Lectures." p ix
"In his last statement of creed, the late Dr. King examines his feelings on the Vietnam War, race relations, youth and social action, nonviolence and concludes with a Christmas sermon on peace." Cincinnati

Michener, James A.

The quality of life. Lippincott 1970 127p boards $4.95   **309.173**

1 U.S.—Social conditions

This exploration of the problems racking our society examines our cities, education, race conflict, youth, the population crises and conservation as well as television and the role of the free press. (Publisher)
"Michener is writing for the general public, or that segment of it which reads books, not for specialists. . . . We must applaud what [he] sets out to do and the deep love of country that drives him to do it. His sense of style and occasional insights also deserve appreciation." Best Sellers

Polenberg, Richard

(ed.) America at war: the home front, 1941-1945. Prentice-Hall 1968 175p pa $1.95   **309.173**

1 U.S.—Social conditions 2 World War, 1939-1945—U.S. 3 U.S.—History—1933-1945—Sources

"A Spectrum book"
"A source book on the effect of World War II on American society, consisting of contemporary material from the 'Congressional Record,' President Roosevelt's official papers, Federal and state documents, magazine articles, and books. Varied and often conflicting opinions are expressed in areas such as morale building, war economy, labor, agriculture, bipartisan politics, civil liberties, increased family mobility and employment of women, and war aims, with many familiar names among the authors, including, in addition to the President, Stuart Chase, Robert Taft, Earl Warren, Thurgood Marshall, Henry Wallace, and Walter Lippmann. Useful as reference material though limited in general reader appeal." Booklist

Terkel, Studs

Hard times; an oral history of the Great Depression. Pantheon Bks. 1970 462p $8.95   **309.173**

1 U.S.—Social conditions 2 U.S.—History—1919-1933 3 U.S.—History—1933-1945

This book consists of "several hundred reminiscences, reflecting every stripe of vocation, background and reaction, captured by Studs Terkel's tape recorder. . . . The brief vignettes, with their authentic speech patterns, their frequent dry understanding, spell out a terrible chapter in American history. Here is the Depression with all its despair and bitterness: the apple salesmen on the street corners, the Bonus March on Washington, the Hoovervilles, the stirrings of organized labor (and the violent squelchings), the drumbeat of the humiliation of American citizens. But here also—such is the human spirit—are humor, fellow feelings. even nostalgia." Book of the Month Club News

Tocqueville, Alexis de
Democracy in America   309.173
1 U.S.—Social conditions 2 U.S.—Politics and government 3 Democracy 4 National characteristics, American

Some editions are:
Harper $15 Edited by J. P. Mayer and Max Lerner. A new translation by George Lawrence
Knopf 2v $12.50 set The Henry Reeve text as revised by Francis Bowen, now further corrected and edited with introduction, editorial notes, and bibliographies by Phillips Bradley; foreword by Harold J. Laski
Oxford $3.50 (World's classics) Translated by Henry Reeve; edited with introduction by Henry Steele Commager
Random House (Vintage) 2v lib. bdg. ea $2.39 Edited by Phillips Bradley; translated by Henry Reeve

First part originally published 1835 in Paris, the second, 1840
"The pertinent views of a shrewd, observant Frenchman on American government and American political behavior in the Age of Jackson." Good Reading
"No better study of a nation's institutions and culture . . . has ever been written by a foreign observer." A Guide to Reading in Am History

Weinberg, Arthur
(ed.) The Muckrakers. . . . Ed. and with notes by Arthur and Lila Weinberg. Capricorn Bks. [1964 c1961] 449p pa $2.85
                                  309.173
1 U.S.—Social conditions 2 Corruption (in politics) 3 Social problems

Analyzed in Essay and general literature index
First published 1961 by Simon and Schuster
The collection of articles "by America's most famous writers for reform who flourished only from about 1902 to 1912. . . . Among them were Lincoln Steffens, Ida Tarbell, Upton Sinclair, Samuel Hopkins Adams, Edwin Markham, Mark Sullivan, Will Irwin, Charles Edward Russell, Thomas W. Lawson and Ray Stannard Baker ('David Grayson') of Amherst. These were the writers in such magazines as McClure's, Collier's, the Cosmopolitan, the American, and Everybody's, who shocked Americans from a state of lethargy about big business, racial inequalities, health rackets, food production and utilities into what became the Progressive Movement." Springf'd Republican

Bibliography: p441-49

309.175 Social conditions of Appalachia

Caudill, Rebecca
My Appalachia; a reminiscence; photographs by Edward Wallowitch. Holt 1966 90p illus $4.95
                                  309.175
1 Appalachian Mountains—Social conditions 2 Mountain life—Southern States 3 Harlan County, Ky.

The author, who grew up there, contrasts life in Appalachia, before the mines came, with life in Appalachia now, showing how and why it has become a poverty-stricken area. (Publisher)
"A book like this is valuable in pointing up, readably and at times dramatically, the mindless way in which the devastation of land and the contamination of rivers . . . have left great parts of the country a shambles; and simultaneously in suggesting dispassionately what can be done to ameliorate the human degradation in these wastelands." Book Week

309.2 Social planning. Peace Corps

The American Assembly
The states and the urban crisis. Prentice-Hall 1970 215p $5.95   309.2
1 U.S.—Social policy 2 State governments 3 Local government 4 City planning
SBN 13-844480-3
"A Spectrum book"
Edited by Alan K. Campbell
"In focusing upon two units of government that are of major interest to both political scientists and the public, this anthology on the linkages between cities and states provides a useful introduction to a problem of theoretical and current significance. Following an introductory essay on emerging social trends that have worked to the benefits of suburbs and to the disadvantage of central cities, several writers explore the constitutional, fiscal, and governmental barriers that have prevented states from responding actively to pressing urban problems." Choice
Bibliography: p210-12

Ashabranner, Brent
A moment in history: the first ten years of the Peace Corps. Doubleday 1971 392p $7.95
                                  309.2
1 U.S. Peace Corps
A former Deputy Director of the Peace Corps presents an "account of the Corps' initial philosophy, its organizational stages, its growing-pains, its problems, successes, failures and lessening interest among youth in recent years." Pub W
"The writing is lively and 'inside' but not particularly analytical or critical [Ashabranner] is particularly good on the P.C.'s inception and the bureaucratic infighting that accompanied it." N Y Times Bk R

Carey, Robert G.
The Peace Corps; foreword by Joseph H. Blatchford. Praeger 1970 274p illus maps (Praeger Lib. of U.S. Government departments and agencies) $8.95   309.2
1 U.S. Peace Corps
In this book, the author reviews the records of both the Peace Corps volunteer and the Peace Corps as a government agency. He traces the agency's development from its first period under Sargent Shriver to the present. He explains how volunteers are recruited and trained and describes the different programs in which they work. (Publisher)
The author "has given both facts and color to his exposition. Appendixes include President Kennedy's original executive order, the Peace Corps Act, and a summary of volunteers (2553) by countries (60) and programs (250) as of May 1, 1969." Library J
Bibliography: p267-70

Gardner, John W.
The recovery of confidence. Norton 1970 189p $5   309.2
1 U.S.—Social policy 2 U.S.—Social conditions
SBN 393-05407-1
"This book, a revised version of the Godkin lectures which [the author] delivered at Harvard in March 1969, is a discussion of the ability of Americans to deal effectively with problems in the areas of peace, discrimination, poverty, and pollution control. An appendix contains a useful list of liberal program suggestions to deal with various urban problems." Library J

Higbee, Edward
A question of priorities; new strategies for our urbanized world; with an introduction by R. Buckminster Fuller. Morrow 1970 214p boards $6   309.2
1 U.S.—Social policy 2 Sociology, Urban 3 Technology and civilization 4 U.S.—Economic policy

Higbee, Edward—*Continued*
The author argues that our nation's social policies are suitable only to our rural, nineteenth-century past, and are now outmoded. He urges that we remodel our social, economic and political institutions to meet the human requirements of an irreversibly urban age. (Publisher)
"A fresh approach to a newer world, this volume is an appeal to develop our institutions of intelligence and resource development. Adding to this excellent account is an introduction . . . on 'information pollution.' Good index and appendix of quoted source materials." Science Bks

Millikan, Max F.
(ed.) The emerging nations: their growth and United States policy; ed. by Max F. Millikan and Donald L. M. Blackmer. Little 1961 171p pa $2.95   **309.2**
1 Underdeveloped areas 2 Social change 3 Social policy
A study from the Center for International Studies, Massachusetts Institute of Technology
"This is an analysis of economic, political and social changes in the world's developing nations, and the forces that are causing these changes." N Y Her Trib Books
Selected bibliography: p161-67

Scientific American
Cities. Knopf 1965 211p illus maps $5.95
                                                          309.2
1 City planning 2 Cities and towns
"A Scientific American book"
Analyzed in Essay and general literature index
"The twelve chapters in this book originally appeared as articles in the September 1965 issue of Scientific American." Verso of title page
The authors "discuss Stockholm, a planned city; Guayana, a 'created' city; Calcutta; our own Megalopolis, stretching from Boston to Washington; London; San Francisco; the [planning] history, functions, and problems of cities." Bk Buyer's Guide
Bibliography: p203-06

310.25 Statistics—Yearbooks

The **Statesman's** year-book; statistical and historical annual of the states of the world. St Martins $13.50   **310.25**
1 Statistics—Yearbooks 2 Political science—Yearbooks 3 Encyclopedias and dictionaries
Annual. First published 1864 in Great Britain
"Not an almanac of miscellaneous statistics but a concise and reliable manual of descriptive and statistical information about the governments of the world. Contents vary somewhat but usually give: (1) British Commonwealth and Empire; (2) United States; (3) Other countries, arranged alphabetically. For each country [this] gives information about its ruler, constitution and government, area, population, religion, social welfare, instruction, justice and crime, state finance, defence, production and industry, agriculture, commerce, navigation, communications, banking and credit, money, weights and measures, diplomatic representatives, etc. A valuable feature is the selected bibliography of statistical and other books of reference given for each country. Recent volumes include information on the United Nations. The most useful of all the general yearbooks; indispensable in any type of library." Winchell. Guide to Reference Books. 8th edition

United Nations. Statistical Office
Statistical yearbook. The Office $22
                                                          310.25
1 Statistics—Yearbooks
First published 1948. Text in English and French
An annual giving statistics under the following headings: Population; Manpower; Production summary; Agriculture; Forestry; Fishing; Mining, quarrying; Manufacturing; Construction; Electricity, gas, consumption; Transport;

Communications; Internal trade; External trade; Balance of payments; International economic aid; Wages and prices; National income; Public finance; Housing statistics; Education, culture

311   Statistical method

Huff, Darrell
How to lie with statistics; pictures by Irving Geis. Norton 1954 142p illus maps $3.95   **311**
1 Statistics
A "humorous dissertation on statistical prevarication. The sample with the built-in bias, the well-chosen average, the insignificant difference, the one-dimensional picture, and the unwarranted assumption are among the subjects treated." Huntting
Mr. Huff's treatment "is a reminder for prudent executives that statistics, surveys, and tests are tools to work with, not mechanical substitutes for human judgment. . . . This book needed to be written, and makes its points in an entertaining, highly readable manner." Management R

312   Statistics of population. Census

Scott, Ann Herbert
Census, U.S.A.; fact finding for the American people, 1790-1970; charts and graphs by Randolph Chitwood. Seabury 1968 228p illus maps $5.95   **312**
1 U.S.—Census 2 U.S. Bureau of the Census
An overview of American census taking from the first census in 1790 to plans for the census of 1970. The author describes technological development and pioneering techniques employed by the Census staff in converting millions of individual census questionnaires into statistical tabulations. (Publisher)
"All stages in the taking of a major census are described: planning, fact-gathering, processing, and evaluation. Discussion of population projections and the application of statistics by government and private industry round out the text." Library J
Sources and suggested reading: p207-14. Census statistics and where to find them: p215-17. Glossary: p218-21

317.3   General statistics of the United States

Information please almanac. Planned and supervised by Dan Golenpaul Associates. Simon & Schuster $3.95   **317.3**
1 U.S.—Statistics 2 Statistics—Yearbooks 3 Almanacs
Annual. First published 1947 by Doubleday
Editor: 1947-1951, John Kieran
"There are special timely articles in each volume; reviews of the year in Washington, sports, theater, fiction, screen, music, etc., written by specialists; statistical and historical descriptions of the various countries of the world; sports records; and many kinds of general information. Sources for many of the tables and special articles are noted." Winchell. Guide to Reference Books. 8th edition
A popular basic reference book and a history emphasizing the highlights of the year
Maps on lining-papers

The New York Times
The New York Times Encyclopedic almanac. Produced by The New York Times Bk. & Educ. Division [distributed by World Pub.] $4.95   **317.3**
1 U.S.—Statistics 2 Statistics—Yearbooks 3 Almanacs

The New York Times—*Continued*

"A New York Times book"
Annual. First edition 1970 published 1969
Editor in chief, 1970-   Seymour Kurtz
This "up-to-date, well organized and extremely well rounded almanac-encyclopedia drawing on the editorial and research facilities of the 'New York Times' contains the usual reference features plus more unusual material such as signed articles by authorities writing on various aspects of history and contemporary life." Booklist
This "almanac has been organized on the principle that a reference work can be read for pleasure as well as for accurate information." Library J

United States. Bureau of the Census

Statistical abstract of the United States. Supt. of Docs. $5.75   317.3
   1 U.S.—Statistics
Annual. First issued for the year 1878. The volumes covering the years 1913-1937 were issued by the Bureau of Foreign and Domestic Commerce
"A valuable compendium covering population, agriculture, manufacturing, mining, exports, imports, finance, climate, banking, and many other topics. The figures in most instances cover a period of at least two decades, and in some instances go back to the beginning of the government. Well indexed." Special Libraries

The World almanac and book of facts.

Newspaper Enterprise Assn. [distributed by Doubleday] $3.95   317.3
   1 U.S.—Statistics   2   Statistics—Yearbooks
   3 Almanacs
Annual. First issued 1868
A useful compilation of statistics and general information whose "especially useful sections are: the sports records, summarizing the year's events in every major field and many minor ones and including past records; a chronicle of advances in medicine and science; and information on finance, labor, the United Nations, population, education, and religion." Pub W
It is advisable to retain older volumes since all subjects are not repeated each year
Maps on lining-papers

320   Political science

Machiavelli, Niccolò

The prince   320
   1 Political science 2 Political ethics
Some editions are:
Dutton $2.95 (Everyman's lib) Translated by W. K. Marriott
Modern Lib. $2.95, lib. bdg. $2.69 With an introduction by Max Lerner. Has title: The prince and The discourses
Oxford $2.95 (The world's classics) Translated by Luigi Ricci; revised by E. R. P. Vincent
First written 1513
"A handbook of advice on the acquisition, use, and maintenance of political power, dedicated to Lorenzo de Medici by the Florentine Machiavelli, once active in government, but at the time of writing out of favor. Rules are set down for governing the various kinds of monarchies as well as conquered territory. Methods for insuring military strength are proposed. The young Prince is advised, further, in such matters as the type of personal behavior which will gain him respect without incurring hatred; whom to trust; how to make his ministers competent and faithful; how to be prepared for changes of fortune." Haydn. Thesaurus of Book Digests

Paine, Thomas

Common sense, and other political writings; ed. with an introduction by Nelson F. Adkins. Liberal Arts [1953] liii, 184p $5
                     320
   1 U.S.—Politics and government 2 Political science

"The American Heritage series"
Analyzed in Essay and general literaure index
Contains the title essay first published 1776; excerpts from The American crisis; selections from the Rights of man; and Dissertation on first principles of government
Common sense, a political tract published in 1776, urged American independence from Britain. The American crisis is concerned with issues of the Revolution, while the Rights of man is a defense of the French Revolution against the attacks of British statesman Edmund Burke
Includes a chronology of Paine's life and works, selected bibliography and notes

Ward, Barbara

Five ideas that change the world. Published for the University College of Ghana by Norton 1959 188p boards $4.50   320
   1 Political science 2 World politics
Analyzed in Essay and general literature index
Based on lectures given at the University College of Ghana in 1957, this is an "account of the impact of colonialism, Communism, industrialization, internationalism and nationalism on the world today, with speculation about future developments." Minnesota
Barbara Ward's "analysis of the changing world is not exceptionally original . . . but if is consistently reasonable and just, as well as lucid and humane." N Y Times Bk R

320.03   Political science— Dictionaries

Plano, Jack C.

The American political dictionary [by] Jack C. Plano [and] Milton Greenberg. Rev. and expanded. Holt 1967 401p $6.95   320.03
   1 U.S.—Politics and   government—Dictionaries
First published 1962
Defining over 1100 terms from the vocabulary of American government, the volume is organized into broad subject areas. Each definition includes a paragraph of comment on the significance of the entry in light of contemporary American political life and history, and each chapter concludes with an explanation of relevant Supreme Court cases, federal statutes, and the important agencies concerned. (Publisher)
"Provides a well-selected working vocabulary for American political institutions, conveniently arranged and adequately treated. It is recommended for high school, college, and public libraries." Booklist

Safire, William

The new language of politics: an anecdotal dictionary of catchwords, slogans, and political usage. Random House 1968 528p $15
                    320.03
   1 U.S.—Politics and   government—Dictionaries
The text abounds "in anecdote, quotations, and original research that makes it far more than a reference book: each of the 1,000 definitions is accompanied by an informative and . . . self-contained essay. The emphasis of the essays is on current American political usage. Historical and etymological information is given in abundance, and controversial matters [are included]." Publisher's note
"In herding together, classifying and clarifying the epidemic of catchwords and phrases that infects the news media, [the author] sketches a pointillist portrait of the American political landscape. . . . Despite its rather austere double-column format and small type, the book is not essentially scholarly. . . . Read selectively, [it] is both an interesting commentary on the mood of America now and a scrapbook of American history." Newsweek
Bibliography: p505-10

Smith, Edward C.

(ed.) Dictionary of American politics; [ed. by] Edward C. Smith and Arnold J. Zurcher. 2d ed. Barnes & Noble 1968 434p illus maps $4.95 **320.03**

1 U.S.—Politics and government—Dictionaries

"Everyday handbook series"

First published 1888 under the editorship of Everit Brown and Albert Strauss

"Gives brief concise definitions and also includes slogans, political slang, nicknames, etc." Winchell. Guide to Reference Books. 8th edition

This useful reference guide includes a list of the presidents and texts of the Constitution of the United States and the Declaration of Independence

320.1 The state. Nationalism

Ward, Barbara

Nationalism and ideology. Norton 1966 125p $3.75 **320.1**

1 The State 2 Political science 3 Nationalism

"A world view of the nature of capitalism and Communism and the history of human forms of government, from tribal to imperial, up to modern times. In most of the book, Miss Ward is leading up to consideration of the little attention given to the hard realities of international order in the prevalent nationalism. She tries to find the seeds of a new world among the 'renewers and reconcilers,' such as the Peace Corps and the ecumenicists." Pub W

"It is easy to see why Miss Ward's vision will win support and admiration. When she deals with past and present she is admirably able to see communism and capitalism alike with an elegant dispassion. When she paints a picture of the modern world she is vivid and convincing, if sometimes a trifle school-marmish. . . . It is when she turns to the future that I find the sharp sense of realism giving way to a kind of wishful, not to say pietistic, thinking." Book Week

320.5 Political theories and ideologies

Mao, Tsê-tung

The political thought of Mao Tse-tung. Rev. and enl. ed. [edited by] Stuart R. Schram. Praeger 1969 479p $9.50 **320.5**

1 Communism—China (People's Republic of China) 2 China (People's Republic of China)—Politics and government

First published 1963

In addition to the documents by Mao expounding his thoughts on Communism, China, its relationships with other countries, and the West, the book includes an introduction which examines the evolution of Mao's thought and the development of China under his leadership. (Publisher)

Bibliography: p448-60

Quotations from Chairman Mao Tse-tung; ed. and with an introductory essay and notes by Stuart R. Schram; foreword by A. Doak Barnett. Praeger 1967 xxxiv, 182p $5 **320.5**

1 Communism—China (People's Republic of China) 2 China (People's Republic of China)—Politics and government

First American edition published 1967 in paper by Bantam Books

A collection of extracts from the author's four volumes of Selected Works. This edition "contains the complete original text of the translation published and distributed by Foreign Languages Press in Peking [in 1966]. Stuart Schram [has written an] introduction and annotated this edition; he has also translated the Foreword to the 1966 Chinese edition of quotations (omitted from Peking's English-language

edition). . . . By tracing the individual quotations to their original sources and determining the periods in which these works were written, Mr. Schram . . . [attempts to show] what the text reveals about Mao Tse-tung himself and about the aims of the Cultural Revolution." Publisher's note

Includes bibliographical references

Rossiter, Clinton

Conservatism in America; the thankless persuasion. 2d ed. rev. Knopf 1962 306p $6.95 **320.5**

1 Conservatism 2 U.S.—Politics and government

First published 1955

The viewpoint "presented here is that the political needs of our country . . . can best be served by a return to a mature, constructive conservatism. After reviewing past conservative traditions, the author sets forth principles and a future program which would provide just and orderly government." Cincinnati

"It deals with abstractions and is closely reasoned, yet it eschews the technical language of political theory. It reveals a fine talent for well-turned phrases, and striking summaries, yet it avoids the effusive language and endless historical and philosophical allusions of similar works." N Y Her Trib Books

Bibliography: p271-92

Sigler, Jay A.

(ed.) The conservative tradition in American thought; an anthology, selected and ed. by Jay A. Sigler. Putnam 1969 375p $6.95 **320.5**

1 Conservatism 2 U.S.—Politics and government

Companion volume to: The liberal tradition in American thought, by W. E. Volkomer, listed below

"This anthology summarizes conservative thought in America from Colonial days to the present. It defines the character of American conservatism, exploring its origins and its particular qualities, showing how it differs from and relates to European conservatism." Publisher's note

Suggestions for further reading: p371-75

Volkomer, Walter E.

(ed.) The liberal tradition in American thought; an anthology, selected and ed. by Walter E. Volkomer. Putnam 1969 352p $6.95 **320.5**

1 Liberalism 2 U.S.—Politics and government

Companion volume to: The conservative tradition in American thought, by J. A. Sigler, listed above

Through the essays, speeches and letters of American political figures, the editor traces the development of liberal thought in the United States. He includes Jefferson's draft of the Declaration of Independence, William Lloyd Garrison's abolitionist articles, Thoreau's "Civil disobedience," Lincoln's statements on slavery, and articles by Franklin Delano Roosevelt, John Kenneth Galbraith and Earl Warren

"At a time when political liberals seem at bay, this survey provides a service to readers whose knowledge of the liberal tradition needs filling in." Pub W

Suggestions for further reading: p351-52

321 Types and forms of states

More, Thomas

Utopia **321**

1 Utopias

Some editions are:

Oxford $2 Edited with introduction and notes by J. Rawson Lumby. Has title: Sir Thomas More's Utopia

More, Thomas—*Continued*

St Martins $2.25 Translated by Ralph Robinson with introduction and notes by H. B. Cotterill. Has title: Utopia of Sir Thomas More
Yale Univ. Press (The Yale Edition of the works of St Thomas More: selected works) $15 Edited with introduction and notes by Edward Surtz

Originally published 1516 in Latin; 1551 in English

In his study of the ideal state, "More assigns the narrative to a Raphael Hythloday ('Hythloday' is Greek for 'talker of nonsense'). . . . Book I treats of the evils of the world and asserts the need for an ideal commonwealth, which Book II describes. Utopia has the advantages of isolation, being a completely self-contained island almost immune to external forces. As the author regards property as the root of all evil, he banishes private property and all luxuries in his ideal state." Haydn. Thesaurus of Book Digests

321.8 Representative democracy

Ketchum, Richard M.

(ed.) What is democracy? Introduction by Grayson Kirk. (New ed.) Art director: Will Anderson; picture editor: Ruth Traurig. Dutton 1968 191p illus $5.95   **321.8**

1 Democracy 2 Liberty

First published 1955

Companion volume to the author's: What is communism, entered in class 335.4

Text and illustrations present the record of democracy: its solid achievements, its opportunities, its obligations and its occasional failures. (Publisher)

A selected list of works on democracy: p190-91

Padover, Saul K.

The meaning of democracy; an appraisal of the American experience. Praeger 1963 139p $4.50   **321.8**

1 Democracy 2 U.S.—Politics and government

In this volume which begins with a brief history of the term 'democracy,' "Professor Padover stresses that understanding of Jeffersonian democracy is essential to knowing 'the quintessence of the democratic philosophy.' . . . He devotes more than one-third of the book to 'Selected Quotations on the Concepts of Democracy, Equality, and Liberty.' from Aristotle to J.F.K." Library J

A book "which is positive, but not uncritical." Minnesota

Selected bibliography: p123-31

Scholastic Magazines

What you should know about democracy—and why, by the editors of Scholastic Magazines. Four Winds [1965 c1964] 189p illus $3.95   **321.8**

1 Democracy

"The authors explore the roots of our heritage, describes the origins, growth, and flowering of democracy, and follow its evolution from Greece to the present. They . . . contrast democracy with communism and other forms of totalitarianism and clarify the challenge that democracy faces today." Publisher's note

"The authors have written a persuasive essay in praise of democracy. Most effective are a history of democracy and an account of the relations between the individual and a democratic government. Less effective . . . is an analysis of democracy." Library J

323 Relation of state to individuals and groups

Beals, Carleton

The nature of revolution. Crowell 1970 296p $8.95   **323**

1 Revolutions 2 World history

The author examines the causes and methods, aims and results of the major revolutions of the past two centuries, "beginning with the American Revolution, the French Revolution, the Latin American struggle for independence, and the Paris Commune through the Chinese and Russian revolutions, Mussolini's March on Rome, the Spanish Civil War, Africa, Cuba, and the present stirrings in the United States." Publisher's note

Books for parallel reading: p275-83

Douglas, William O.

Points of rebellion. Random House 1970 97p $4.95   **323**

1 Civil rights 2 U.S.—Social conditions 3 Passive resistance to government 4 Youth

The author speaks out "in behalf of the waves of rebellion that are sweeping the nation and . . . the entire world. Justice Douglas argues that young people are right to rise up against widespread poverty, segregation, inequitable laws, and inadequate education. They are right to protest the pollution of America. . . . He points out that although violence has no constitutional sanction, it is often the only effective response when grievances keep mounting and most elected spokesmen represent the Establishment." Publisher's note

"The book is a classic statement of the civil libertarian viewpoint and indeed of traditional American liberalism grounded in the Bill of Rights, our revolutionary heritage, and revolutionary spirit which overthrew George III." Pub W

Gandhi, Mohandas K.

Gandhi on non-violence; selected texts from Mohandas K. Gandhi's Non-violence in peace and war; ed. with an introduction by Thomas Merton. New Directions 1965 82p pa $1.50   **323**

1 Passive resistance to government 2 India—Politics and government

"A New Directions paperbook"

"Thomas Merton has selected the basic statements of principle and interpretation which made up Gandhi's philosophy of non-violence (Ahimsa) and non-violent action (Satyagraha). . . . In his long introduction to this book Father Merton shows how Gandhi linked the thought of East and West in his search for universal truth, and how, for him, non-violence sprang from realization of spiritual unity in the individual." Publisher's note

Lynd, Staughton

(ed.) Nonviolence in America: a documentary history. Bobbs 1966 xlix, 535p (The American Heritage ser) $7.50   **323**

1 Passive resistance to government

Analyzed in Essay and general literature index

This book presents "original documentary material from the 17th to the 20th century." Pub W

Partial contents: Quakers; Abolitionists; Anarchists; Progressives; Conscientious objectors; World War I; Trade unionists; Direct action for civil rights, post-World War II; Nonviolent revolution

"A volume in the American Heritage series, and an excellent one. . . . Here are not only the classic texts of nonviolence, from Penn and Thoreau to Muste and Rustin, but many new and unfamiliar documents. A moving and disquieting collection." New Yorker

Selected bibliography: p xlvii-xlviii

323.2 Revolutionary and subversive groups and individuals

Epstein, Benjamin R.

The radical Right; report on the John Birch Society and its allies [by] Benjamin R. Epstein and Arnold Forster. Random House 1967 239p $6.95   **323.2**

1 Right and left (Political science) 2 John Birch Society

Epstein, Benjamin R.—*Continued*

This "report on the menace of right-wing movements in the U.S. brings up to date the authors' 1966 'Report on the John Birch Society' and sketches other activities of the far-right wing—the Liberty Lobby, the Conservative Society of America, the Minutemen, the Patriotic Party, and other groups. The Birchites, the authors report, are now making hay on the Vietnam issue, with the country's divided state of opinion about the Vietnam war. Also Birchers are trying increasingly for political power; some hold office, some are political candidates. The authors' material or right-wing groups has been documented and analyzed with the help of the Anti-Defamation League of B'nai B'rith." Pub W

Lowe, David

Ku Klux Klan: the invisible empire; with an introduction and epilogue by Haynes Johnson. Norton 1967 128p illus $4.95 **323.2**

1 Ku Klux Klan (1915-   )

This book, an examination of the principles and often violent methods of the Ku Klux Klan through photographs, interviews and text, stems from the author's "documentary which he wrote and produced for CBS in September, 1965. Haynes Johnson . . . [deals] with events since the HUAC [House Unamerican Activities Committee] investigation of the Klan." Pub W

"Both browsers and report-writers will find this brief, pictorial exposé of the Ku Klux Klan very significant. . . . The book contains numerous excellent photographs and a lucid, though brief, text." Library J

A Klan glossary: p125-26

323.4   Civil rights

Belfrage, Sally

Freedom summer. Viking 1965 246p $5 **323.4**

1 Civil rights 2 Mississippi—Race relations 3 Negroes 4 Student Non-violent Coordinating Committee

An account of a young writer's "summer in Greenwood, Mississippi, working on the Student Nonviolent Coordinating Committee's Mississippi Summer Project. She tended the library in the crude community center, lived with a Negro family and became their close friend, taught Negroes to read, picketed for voter-registration, and was jailed for five horrible, hungry days. Most of her book is simply about human relations and feelings . . . the awakening of the local Negroes to political action and a hunger for knowledge, the fierce hate shown by most white southerners, and the volunteers' exhaustion, apprehension, and fear." Pub W

"What she says about callousness and cruelty in arrests and jailings is sharp and biting but it says nothing different from all the other reports—only the personal experiences give it force." Horn Bk

Douglas, William O.

An almanac of liberty. Doubleday 1954 xx, 409p illus $6.50 **323.4**

1 Civil rights 2 U.S.—Constitutional law

"Justice Douglas' chronicle of civil liberties has an entry for each day in the year, beginning with the Fourth of July. The year dates run from 1215—the Magna Carta—down to mid-1954, which marks the unanimous decision of the Supreme Court outlawing school segregation." Library J

"Selections include sermons, documents, speeches, decisions, and ideas illustrating various methods of preserving the freedom and democratic principles to which Americans have committed themselves. An impressive record useful to libraries, discussion groups, students, teachers, and families." Booklist

Ebony

The white problem in America, by the editors of Ebony. Johnson Pub. (Chicago) 1966 181p $3.50 **323.4**

1 Negroes—Civil rights 2 U.S.—Race relations

"First published in a special issue of Ebony Magazine for August, 1965. Among the authors are James Baldwin, J. O. Killens, C. T. Rowan, and Martin Luther King, Jr." Book Rev Digest

"The so-called 'white backlash' is seen as part of a long continuum, rather than as a transitory political phenomenon; the book stresses throughout that the white American 'must change before the Negro can change.' " Choice

Fromm, Erich

Escape from freedom. Rinehart 1941 305p $6.50 **323.4**

1 Liberty 2 Social psychology 3 Totalitarianism

"A searching inquiry into the meaning of freedom for modern man, part of a broad study to be completed later [see The sane society, entered below] of the character structure of man in our culture. The author stresses the role of psychological factors in the social process, interpreting the historical development of freedom in terms of man's awareness of himself as a significant separate being." Library J

This "is the best diagnosis of the psychological aberrations of Nazism I have seen. . . . It is also a distinguished contribution to our understanding of history. . . . [The author's] brief analysis of the psychological basis of the Protestant Reformation contains some of the most brilliant and illuminating pages that have ever been written on the subject." Sat R

Bibliographical footnotes

The sane society. Rinehart 1955 370p $7.95 **323.4**

1 Liberty 2 Civilization, Occidental 3 Social psychology

The book is a continuation of: Escape from freedom, in which "I tried to show that the totalitarian movements appealed to a deepseated craving to escape from the freedom man had achieved in the modern world; that modern man, free from medieval ties, was not free to build a meaningful life based on reason and love, hence sought new security in submission to a leader, race or state. In The Sane Society I try to show that life in twentieth-century Democracy constitutes in many ways another escape from freedom, and the analysis of this particular escape, centered around the concept of alienation, constitutes a good part of this book." Foreword

"Erich Fromm attempts in this book to evaluate the condition of man in the Western World and more particularly in the United States of today. . . . For myself I will say that this utterly sincere, unselfish and loving book comes as something of a shock to me. I hadn't realized that the situation was so bad or that the remedy need be so radical." N Y Her Trib Books

Handlin, Oscar

Fire-bell in the night; the crisis in civil rights. Little 1964 110p boards $3.75 **323.4**

1 Negroes—Civil rights 2 U.S.—Race relations

"An Atlantic Monthly Press book"

In this analysis of the development of our present racial attitudes, the author discusses the threat to national unity posed by the racism of both white supremists and Black Muslims. He indicates "the necessity of providing equality of opportunity for the Negro in education, employment and urban life in the same terms that we have granted it to . . . many other racial minorities." Publisher's note

I have a dream; the story of Martin Luther King in text and pictures. Time-Life Bks. 1968 96p illus map lib. bdg. $3.39 **323.4**

1 King, Martin Luther 2 Negroes—Civil rights

In this book, text and photographs memorialize "the highlights of Dr. King's life. Although more comprehensive biographies exist . . . this . . . captures the essence of Dr. King's contributions to social and racial justice. Pictures of police brutality against demonstrators, the funeral of Medgar Evers, Dr. King leading the Montgomery march in the rain and many others exemplify photographic journalism at its best." Library J

Kellogg, Charles Flint

NAACP; a history of the National Association for the Advancement of Colored People: volume I, 1909-1920. Johns Hopkins Press 1967 332p illus $10   323.4

  1 National Association for the Advancement of Colored People

The author "traces the development of the NAACP from its founding in 1909 by Oswald Garrison Villard, W.E.B. Du Bois, and the Committee of Forty to its acceptance by Negroes [at the end of its first decade of existence] as the most effective organization in the United States working for political and social equality." Publisher's note

Although the author "does not bring alive the spirit and commitment powering the nascent Negro-rights movement, he presents a balanced, creditable picture of [its] leaders . . . and he clearly depicts substantive issues confronting the 'organization.'" J Am Hist

Bibliographical notes: p309-15

King, Martin Luther

Stride toward freedom; the Montgomery story, by Martin Luther King, Jr. Harper 1958 230p illus boards $4.95   323.4

  1 Negroes—Segregation 2 Montgomery, Ala.—Race relations

A "description of the Montgomery, Alabama, bus boycott organized by Montgomery Negroes in December, 1955, as a protest against discourtesy from the bus drivers and inequalities in the seating. . . . This is eloquent testimony to the Negro community's self respect, unity, and self control. Particularly memorable is a chapter on the author's personal intellectual pilgrimage to belief in nonviolent resistance to evil." Pub W

"Naturally this book does not purport to give the white position and attitudes with impartiality. It is primarily a documentation of the Negro side of the dispute and an important, detailed study of a significant . . .; development in race relations in our times." Christian Science Monitor

Where do we go from here: chaos or community? [By] Martin Luther King, Jr. Harper 1967 209p boards $4.95   323.4

  1 Negroes—Civil rights 2 U.S.—Race relations 3 Negroes—History

The author reaffirms his belief in the power of nonviolence to achieve full citizenship for the Negro in America and defines his attitude toward the Black Power movement and the white backlash. (Publisher)

"It is quite clear from [this] book that the present de-escalation of the freedom movement could easily lead to chaos. But it is far less clear precisely how community rather than chaos can be achieved by America's 21 million citizens of African ancestry. Dr. King is definite—and persuasive—in his repudiation of two forces that are impeding and even destroying the Negro's march toward equality: the illusion of 'black power' and the pervasiveness of white 'backlash.' Dr. King's analysis of the implications of the black power movement is possibly the most reasoned rejection of that concept by any major civil rights leader in the country." America

Bibliography included in Note: p203-04

Why we can't wait [by] Martin Luther King, Jr. Harper 1964 178p illus boards $4.95   323.4

  1 Negroes—Civil rights 2 Birmingham, Ala.—Race relations 3 Negroes—Moral and social conditions

The author first reviews the background of the 1963 civil rights demands. He then describes the strategy of the Birmingham campaign and outlines what can be expected in future action. (Publisher)

Dr King "includes his cogent 'Letter from a Birmingham Jail,' which tells precisely why the Negro demands his rights now, why he himself urges a national war upon poverty and ignorance, and why he sees non-violence as a weapon not only for winning civil and human rights but also for winning world peace." Horn Bk

"A moving, beautifully written book which will certainly be a classic account of that vital year in the history of Negro rights." Pub W

McClellan, Grant S.

(ed.) Civil rights. Wilson, H.W. 1964 192p (The Reference shelf v36, no.6) $4.50   323.4

  1 Civil rights 2 Negroes—Civil rights

This compilation of articles, speeches, and excerpts from books "surveys the Negroes' demands for advances in recognition of their civil rights in American society. It also considers advances made in the protection of traditional civil rights, the claims for the extension of rights into new areas, and the efforts toward achievement of human rights on a global basis." Preface

"The book is designed largely as a handbook for debaters and could be useful for such purpose." Choice

Includes the text of the Universal Declaration of Human Rights

Bibliography: p188-92

Paine, Thomas

The rights of man. Dutton [1935 c1915] 290p $2.95   323.4

  1 Liberty 2 France—History—Revolution, 1789-1799 3 Great Britain—Politics and government—1714-1837

"Everyman's library"

First published 1791-1792 in England; in this edition 1915

This political tract consists of two parts. The first is a defense of the French Revolution against the attack of the British statesman Edmund Burke in his: Reflections on the revolution in France. In the second section Paine presents his views on the rights of man. He believes that "sovereignty inheres in the will of the present majority, as a continuous compact reaffirmed by each generation. . . . Civil authority should interfere with the natural freedom of individuals only in so far as is required to insure and protect the security and happiness of the majority of the people." The Oxford Companion to American Literature

The works of Thomas Paine: p xiv-xv

323.44 Personal liberty and freedom of the press

American Library Association. Intellectual Freedom Committee

Freedom of inquiry; supporting the Library bill of rights. Proceedings of the Conference on Intellectual Freedom, January 23-24, 1965, Washington, D.C. Sponsored by the American Library Association, Intellectual Freedom Committee. A.L.A. 1965 70p pa $1.50   323.44

  1 Censorship

"Originally printed in the ALA Bulletin, June, 1965." Verso of title page

"The papers of the various participants discuss the freedom to read and censorship as these are related to the problem of obscenity, religious, racial, and political problems, to instruction in the public schools, to the law courts, and to juvenile delinquency. . . . At times [this] is an exceedingly startling and provocative summary of the most recent thinking in the area of intellectual freedom." Bookmark

Includes bibliographical references and text of the Library bill of rights

Commager, Henry Steele

Freedom, loyalty, dissent. Oxford 1954 155p boards $5   323.44

  1 Liberty 2 Loyalty

"The essays now collected in this volume were written at different times and for different occasions over a period of six years, but all are bound together by a common theme and unified point of view. The theme . . . is the necessity of freedom in a society such as the American." Preface

Commager, Henry—*Continued*
Contents: Necessity of freedom; Necessity of experimentation; Free enterprise in ideas; Guilt by association; Who is loyal to America
"Mr. Commager's provocative book constitutes an admirable primer on just what is the essence of Americanism." N Y Times Bk R

Downs, Robert B.
(ed.) The first freedom; liberty and justice in the world of books and reading. A.L.A. 1960 469p $8.50   323.44
1 Censorship 2 Books
Analyzed in Essay and general literature index
A collection of 88 "twentieth-century American and British writings on literary censorship and intellectual freedom. The twelve chapters treat such aspects of censorship as the historical setting, issues at stake, famous legal decisions, pressure groups, obscenity, political subversion, attitudes of librarians and writers, censorship in schools, censorship in Ireland, and a look at the future." Publisher's note
"In preparing and publishing this volume the American Library Association renders a . . . service to the book world by making available so handy a store of ammunition in the battle to defend our basic freedom." Sat R
Bibliographical footnotes

Hohenberg, John
Free press/free people; the best cause. Columbia Univ. Press 1971 514p $9.95
                                                  323.44
1 Freedom of the press
ISBN 0-231-03315-X
The author "begins with the dissemination of news in the days before print and carries the story . . . to the present day, showing in each episode the interaction between press and event. . . . His purpose is to show the press through wars, revolutions, domestic crises, dictatorial suppressions, and modern technological upheaval. . . . The book proceeds on two tracks—one tracing the theme of a free press, the other historical happenings." Sat R

Levy, Leonard W.
(ed.) Freedom of the press from Zenger to Jefferson; early American libertarian theories. Bobbs 1966 lxxxiii, 409p (The American Heritage ser) $7.50   323.44
1 Freedom of the press
Companion volume to H. L. Nelson's: Freedom of the press from Hamilton to the Warren Court, entered below
"This anthology is valuable on two levels. On the one it is the first compendium of the classic American statements on freedom of the press from Andrew Hamilton's defense in the Zenger case (1735) to Alexander Hamilton's defense in the Croswell case (1804), including the full texts of oft-quoted opinions of Benjamin Franklin, James Madison, and Thomas Jefferson. On the second level, Professor Levy offers a documentary defense of his provocative thesis. Thus here are assembled a representative selection of . . . substantial writings that enable us to weigh the intent of the drafters of the first amendment—James Wilson, Richard Henry Lee, William Cushing, and John Adams." Foreword
Bibliographical footnotes

McClellan, Grant S.
(ed.) Censorship in the United States. Wilson, H.W. 1967 222p (The Reference shelf v39, no.3) $4.50   323.44
1 Censorship
This "compilation shows how our freedom to read and freedom of speech are currently affected by censorship activities, public or private." Preface
Arranged topically under the following headings: Censorship: the current debate; The Supreme Court: more freedom or less; Censorship and politics; Censorship and intellectual freedom; Censorship and education
Bibliography: p214-22

Nelson, Harold L.
(ed.) Freedom of the press from Hamilton to the Warren Court. Bobbs 1967 lxvii, 420p (The American Heritage ser) $7.50
                                                  323.44
1 Freedom of the press
Companion volume to L. W. Levy's: Freedom of the press from Zenger to Jefferson, entered above
"Avoiding the 'war horse' arguments (e.g. Milton's 'Areopagitica') for freedom of the press, Nelson has compiled and annotated an amazing variety of documents—legal rulings, pamphlets, essays, editorials, executive orders —woven together to tell the story of rises and declines in U.S. press freedom from 1800 to now. Aside from his introductory summary of that history, Nelson uses only primary sources and his notes on them. [The book presents] many original and complete texts, making it an indispensable reference tool for any undergraduate work in this area." Choice
Bibliography: p lv-lxv

Packard, Vance
The naked society. McKay 1964 369p $6.95   323.44
1 Privacy, Right of 2 Liberty
The author exposes the current invasion of individual privacy. Many persons "are victimized, Packard says, by over-curious questionnaires, 'bugged' telephones, concealed TV cameras . . . lie detectors, and exchanges, either officially or by bribery, of private information on file about individuals. The government is doing this; so are credit bureaus, ex-FBI men freelance or organized in companies, large industrial or business concerns, and others." Pub W
This book "clearly shows our Bill of Rights is being flaunted daily and suggests what we should do to change the situation that is rapidly developing." Library J
At the core of this book "is a topic worthy of thoughtful attention, and there are ample references to other, more philosophical works for the reader who, wants to get deeper into the underlying issues." Christian Science Monitor
Reference notes: p343-48

Reston, James
The artillery of the press; its influence on American foreign policy. Published for the Council on Foreign Relations by Harper 1967 116p boards $3.95   323.44
1 Freedom of the press 2 U.S.—Foreign relations 3 Journalism
"Based on three lectures given in the Elihu Root series before the members of the Council on Foreign Relations in New York City in 1966." Introduction
The author "discusses the inevitable conflict between those who make news—and often try to suppress or disguise it—and those who report it." Bk Buyer's Guide
A "penetrating analysis of the influence of American newspapers on our foreign policy." Atlantic

324.73 Suffrage—U.S.

Chute, Marchette
The first liberty; a history of the right to vote in America, 1619-1850. Dutton 1969 371p $8.95   324.73
1 Suffrage—History 2 U.S.—Politics and government
This book "chronicles in detail the early history of suffrage for the white male in America showing that the first colonial governments, beginning in Jamestown in 1619, followed English parliamentary law and stipulated property ownership for franchise. Chute traces the modification of this political principle by later American bodies noting that by 1850 the general assemblies of the states had mainly abandoned the property qualification for voting in America. The appended identification of quotations is a partial bibliography." Booklist

Chute, Marchette—*Continued*

The author's "history is a tapestry which explains the past as the weaver sees it, with bright threads of curious knowledge to enliven the picture. Her taste and her freedom from academic jargon make the book a pleasure." Book World

Sayre, Wallace S.

Voting for President; the electoral college and the American political system [by] Wallace S. Sayre and Judith H. Parris. Brookings 1970 169p (Studies in Presidential selection) $5.95   **324.73**

1 Presidents—U.S.—Election 2 Politics, Practical
ISBN 0-8157-7720-5

The authors "examine the present structure of the Electoral College and its effects on the electoral system. There follows a discussion of numerous proposals, to alter (or abolish) the Electoral College—the direct-vote plan, the automatic plan, the district plan, and the proportional plan. . . . [Sayre and Parris] recommend retention of the present system with minor alterations." Choice
Selected bibliography: p161-63

325.73 Immigration to the U.S.

Fermi, Laura

Illustrious immigrants; the intellectual migration from Europe, 1930-41. Univ. of Chicago Press 1968 440p illus $7.95   **325.73**

1 U.S.—Foreign population 2 U.S.—Intellectual life 3 U.S.—Civilization

The author describes the variety of intellectuals who came to this country, their cultural and national background, their escape routes and the organizations and individuals who assisted them. She then discusses the achievements of these immigrants in the fields of psychoanalysis, atomic science, art, literature, natural science, social science and other areas. The newcomers included Einstein, Bruno Walter, Marcel Duchamp, Paul Tillich, Hans Morgenthau, Bruno Bettelheim, John Von Neumann, Enrico Fermi and others." Book Rev Digest

"A splendid and useful book, tackling with imagination, industry and a rare combination of personal concern and emotional detachment a subject that would frighten—indeed thus far has frightened—professional social historians by its magnitude and complexity." Science
Includes bibliography and index of persons

Handlin, Oscar

(ed.) Children of the uprooted; selected and ed. with an introduction and notes by Oscar Handlin. Braziller 1966 xxii, 551p $15
                                        325.73

1 U.S.—Foreign population 2 Acculturation 3 Literature—Collections

An anthology of writing produced by 34 offspring of immigrants to the United States, and published between 1887 and 1964. The literature reflects the immigrant's tendency to live suspended between two cultures. Authors include David Belasco, Joel Chandler Harris, Thorstein Veblen, Walter Reuther, William Saroyan

"Apart from the sociological and historical impact of the book as a 'casebook,' the excerpts in themselves read . . . as an anthology of fiction and nonfiction, prose, and a little poetry." Library J

The uprooted; the epic story of the great migrations that made the American people. Little 1951 310p $5.95   **325.73**

1 U.S.—Foreign population 2 Acculturation

"An Atlantic Monthy Press book"
Awarded the Pulitzer Prize for history, 1952
"A composite account of immigration to the U.S., written in a flowing style. Describes life in the agricultural villages of middle Europe, and shows the peasant forced by economic pressures to emigrate to America, where he found his old values and customs so unsuitable that he became a confused, rootless person, a foreigner even to his own Americanized children." Booklist
Bibliography included in Acknowledgements: p308-10

Kennedy, John F.

A nation of immigrants; introduction by Robert F. Kennedy. Rev. and enl. ed. Harper 1964 111p illus map lib. bdg. $3.79
                                        325.73

1 U.S.—Immigration and emigration 2 U.S.—Foreign population

A reissue of a booklet written 1958 for the "One Nation Library" series of the Anti-Defamation League of B'nai B'rith

"An account of the struggles of successive waves of immigrants, their contributions to America, and their repeated triumphs over prejudice and discrimination. Expounds the need for an enlargement of our immigration laws." A Guide to Reading in Am History

"Written for popular understanding, using historic data supplemented by concise commentary. . . . As the final literary work of a beloved public figure, this book has even greater appeal than the specialized subject it covers so well. It is a poem of praise to a growing America that would have pleased Walt Whitman." Sat R
Suggested readings: p95-101

Orth, Samuel P.

Our foreigners; a chronicle of Americans in the making. U.S. Pubs. Assn. 1920 225p front (The Chronicles of America ser. v35) $3.95   **325.73**

1 U.S.—Immigration and emigration 2 U.S.—Foreign population

First published by Yale University Press
Contents: Opening the door; American stock; The Negro; Utopias in America; Irish invasion; Teutonic tide; Call of the lands; City builders; The oriental; Racial infiltration; Guarded door; Bibliographical note

326 Slavery

Douglass, Frederick

The mind and heart of Frederick Douglass; excerpts from speeches of the great Negro orator; adapted by Barbara Ritchie. Crowell 1968 201p $4.50   **326**

1 Slavery in the U.S.

"The penetrating mind and prophetic vision of the great nineteenth-century Afro-American orator and reformer are revealed in these well-chosen excerpts from his speeches against slavery and against the country's continued denial of equal civil rights to Negroes following the Civil War. Since Douglass interpreted the injustices and hypocrisy of his time in terms of the basic issues underlying prejudice and the vital significance of human freedom, his words have a timeless, universal quality that make them equally pertinent for today." Booklist

Speeches, addresses, lectures and orations from which selections were taken: p196-97

Furnas, J. C.

Goodbye to Uncle Tom. Morrow [1964 c1956] 435p illus pa $2.95   **326**

1 Slavery in the U.S. 2 Negroes 3 Stowe, Harriet Elizabeth (Beecher). Uncle Tom's cabin 4 U.S.—Race relations

"Apollo editions"
First published 1956

An analysis of slavery in America and "of the myths pertaining to the American Negro, from their origins to the misconceptions of today. The role of 'Uncle Tom's Cabin' provides the author a point of departure. Highly provocative." A Guide to Reading in Am History

References: p389-96. Works consulted: p397-418

Liston, Robert
Slavery in America; the history of slavery.
McGraw 1970 128p illus (Of Black America
ser) $4.95, lib. bdg. $4.72   326
1 Slavery in the U.S.
This book "traces the history of American
slavery from its beginnings in Africa to Latin
America and then on to the American colonies. . . . The author traces the horrors of
the slave trade and the treatment of slaves
in the North as well as in the South." Huntting
Books for further reading: p125

Quarles, Benjamin
Black abolitionists.   Oxford 1969   310p
$7.95   326
1 Abolitionists
The author "deals with the Negro preachers
and writers who promoted abolition and the
Negro societies that supported it, with the
Negro agitator's role abroad, with Negroes
who operated the fugitive slave law and John
the effect of the fugitive slave law and John
Brown's raid on Negro opinion, and with the
effects of Negro activity and opinion on all
levels of political life." Publisher's note
The author is "one of the leading historians
of Afro-American history. . . . Contrary to
general belief, black abolitionists played a significant role alongside William Lloyd Garrison
and others. . . . Professor Quarles has drawn
his facts mainly from primary sources. Written clearly and persuasively, the book is recommended for most libraries." Library J
Notes on bibliographical literature: p251-92

327 International relations.
Espionage

Armbrister, Trevor
A matter of accountability; the true story
of the Pueblo affair. Coward-McCann 1970
408p illus $7.95   327
1 Pueblo (Ship)
"The author affords the reader a clear, objective, and detailed look at the Pueblo incident, from the time the ill-fated vessel was
converted to an electronics spy ship to the
aftermath of the court of inquiry. Throughout
the book Armbrister carefully adheres to his
main purpose of determining accountability for
the seizure of the ship by the North Koreans
in January 1968 by tracing the actions and
reactions of those involved, including officers
and officials from the bridge of the USS
'Pueblo' to the basement of the White House."
Library J
Map on lining-papers

Bucher, Lloyd M.
Bucher: my story, by Lloyd M. Bucher
with Mark Rascovich. Doubleday 1970 447p
illus $7.95   327
1 Pueblo (Ship)
The story of events leading up to and following the capture of the U.S. intelligence ship
"Pueblo," by the North Koreans, as told by
the ship's captain. It includes a brief account
of Bucher's personal life previous to the
"Pueblo" assignment
This account "necessarily contains less detail about events in Washington and considerably more information about the crew's experiences in the hands of the North Koreans.
Bucher's chronicle is often emotional; it could
hardly be otherwise." Sat R
Glossary: p443-47. Map on lining-papers

Dulles, Allen
The craft of intelligence. Harper 1963
277p illus $6.95   327
1 Spies 2 U.S. Central Intelligence Agency
"The nature of an intelligence service in
general is described in [this] analysis of the

function and methods of the U.S. Central Intelligence Agency. After a brief history of international espionage, Dulles explains the need
for secret information, how it is collected . . .
how reported data are processed and used, and
how agents and other personnel are selected
and trained. He concludes with a . . . defense
of the Central Intelligence Agency against
criticisms such as the charges that it exceeds
its authority by making policy and supporting
dictators . . . and that the Soviet spy system
is superior to that of the U.S." Booklist
"Every technical term which might be unfamiliar to the non-professional is explained
briefly, while a wealth of personal anecdotes
. . . sheds light on many hitherto obscure
events in the . . . past." Best Sellers
Bibliography: p265-67

(ed.) Great true spy stories. Harper 1968
393p $6.95   327
1 Spies
"A Giniger book"
A collection of thirty-nine true spy stories
ranging in time from Greek antiquity into the
Cold War, many of them excerpts from larger
works. "The book is divided into sections
representing the different elements of intelligence work, such as networks, counter-espionage, double agents, penetration, evaluation, codes and ciphers, and the technology
of espionage." Publisher's note
"Introductory remarks to each section are
short, lucid and commonsensical. . . . Inevitably, some of the selections are too fragmentary. . . . [But] both average reader and
serious student will find rich rewards." N Y
Times Bk R

Powers, Francis Gary
Operation Overflight; the U-2 spy pilot
tells his story for the first time [by] Francis
Gary Powers with Curt Gentry. Holt 1970
375p illus map $6.95   327
1 U-2 Incident 1960
SBN 03-083945-1
This is Gary Powers' story "from the day in
1956 when he accepted a high-paying CIA job—
flying the U-2 without actually knowing what
the job was, to his return from [imprisonment
in] Russia and his [recent] job, testing U-2s
for Lockheed." Pub W
"The story he writes is immensely personal,
filled at various times with pride, fears, and
misgivings." Library J

Snyder, Louis Leo
(ed.) Fifty major documents of the twentieth century. Van Nostrand 1955 185p
pa $1.95   327
1 International relations 2 History, Modern—
20th century—Sources
"An Anvil original"
A "compilation, including the Austro-Hun-
garian ultimatum to Serbia in 1914, the Munich
agreement of 1939, the enfranchisement of women in Britain and the United States in 1918-19,
the Nuremberg Laws on race, Churchill's
'Blood, Toil, Tears, and Sweat' address, the
secret Yalta agreement, and the Truman Doctrine." Good Reading

Stevenson, Adlai
An ethic for survival; Adlai Stevenson
speaks on international affairs, 1936-1965; ed.
with introduction and commentary by
Michael H. Proser; assisted by Lawrence H.
Sherlick. Morrow 1969 571p front $15 327
1 International relations 2 United Nations
3 U.S.—Foreign relations
The book contains fifty of Stevenson's speeches—many previously unpublished. The majority
of the speeches concern the U.N. and foreign
relations, although there are anniversary addresses as well as explanations of U.S. foreign
policy
It is good "to have the speeches on foreign
affairs culled from all the rest. Many of these
were . . . delivered in the years before the
Stevenson manner became a public institution.
. . . (The Ambassadorial addresses to the

Stevenson, Adlai—*Continued*

United Nations are in this context less interesting; they are clearly committee-crafted and may not be precisely what Stevenson wanted to say). . . . They bespeak a simple and direct, though supple, and highly serious mind. They are not particularly witty, nor even very much touched by that self-conscious will to elegance with which memory associates his campaign oratory. . . . Stevenson's message on foreign affairs, though not without a certain resolute good humor, was no fun. It seems terribly important now to see this in the light of all that has happened." Harper

Bibliography: p553-66

327.47   Russian foreign policy

Isenberg, Irwin
  (ed.) The Russian-Chinese rift; its impact on world affairs. Wilson, H.W. 1966 221p maps (The Reference shelf v38, no.2) $4.50
                                         327.47
  1 Russia—Foreign relations—China (People's Republic of China) 2 China (People's Republic of China)—Foreign relations—Russia
  "The [29] articles in this book trace the development of the rift, consider what its impact on world affairs has been, and discuss possible Western policy responses." Preface
  Contents: The rise and fall of the monolith; Moscow vs. Peking: the worldwide competition; Documenting the rift; Dealing with the Communist world; Bibliography
  These "articles from Soviet, Chinese, and American sources show that the Sino-Soviet rift has compounded the difficulties of American foreign policy. . . . High school and adult groups will find this book useful for debate and discussion background." Scholastic Teacher

Kennan, George F.
  Russia and the West under Lenin and Stalin. Little 1961 411p $8.50   327.47
  1 Russia—Foreign relations 2 World politics
  "An Atlantic Monthly Press book"
  The material in this book was drawn from lectures delivered at Oxford University in 1957-58 and at Harvard University in 1960
  A history of Soviet-Western relations from the Russian Revolution of 1917 to the end of World War II. The author examines in detail such things as: the Allied intervention in Russia in World War I; the Versailles treaty; Lenin's versus Stalin's methods of advancing Communism; the rise of Hitler; the German-Russian pact of 1939; and, the Yalta Conference. (Publisher)
  "There is so much that is useful in this volume . . . that even those who have reservations about one or another of the judgments in it will welcome it warmly as a significant contribution." N Y Times Bk R
  Bibliographical references in Notes: p399-403

Salisbury, Harrison E.
  War between Russia and China. Norton 1969 224p illus maps $4.95   327.47
  1 Russia—Foreign relations—China (People's Republic of China) 2 China (People's Republic of China)—Foreign relations—Russia
  SBN 393-05394-6
  "This book has been written out of concern over the tension between Russia and China and the proliferation of signs that the two sister-states are headed toward a collision course and war. . . . The United States can profoundly influence this struggle and will be influenced by it. . . . By employing our superior weight and influence we can transform impending disaster into the foundation of a new stable world structure. It is to that objective that this work is dedicated." Foreword
  This volume consists of "the musings of an experienced observer of Russia and a student of the massive scope of world history. It is a broad and interpretative topic. Taken in that context, [the book] can be a valuable and interesting addition to the bibliography of current events and future prospects. While many

of the author's concepts, ideas and theories are provocative and perhaps even utopian in outlook, the book generates thought and discussion." Best Sellers

327.52   Japanese foreign policy

Tamarin, Alfred
  Japan and the United States; early encounters, 1791-1860. Macmillan (N Y) 1970 260p illus maps $6.95   327.52
  1 U.S.—Foreign relations—Japan 2 Japan—Foreign relations—U.S.
  This is "an account of the opening of Japan to international trade and diplomacy. . . . [The author gives] details from both the Japanese and the American points of view, the unofficial contacts that paved the way for Commodore Perry's arrival in 1835 and the experiences of Townsend Harris." Book News
  For further reading: p255

327.73   U.S. foreign policy

Beale, Howard K.
  Theodore Rosevelt and the rise of America to world power. John Hopkins Press 1956 600p $10   327.73
  1 Roosevelt, Theodore, President U.S. 2 U.S.—Foreign relations
  At head of title: The Albert Shaw Lectures on diplomatic history, 1953
  "Analyzes the extent of Theodore Roosevelt's impact upon the formation of American foreign policy; his knowledge of the field, his attitudes towards various nations and his manner in dealing with foreign problems and foreign representatives." Pub W
  "Criticisms are . . . made, but this is a book favorable to Roosevelt." A Guide to Reading in Am History
  Notes: p463-579

Beard, Charles A.
  American foreign policy in the making, 1932-1940; a study in responsibilities. Archon Bks. 1968 [c1946] 336p $10   327.73
  1 U.S.—Foreign relations 2 U.S.—Politics and government—1933-1945 3 Roosevelt, Franklin Delano, President U.S.
  "What Mr Beard examines is the process leading to the participation of the United States in the second World War. . . . It is an account of programs, pronouncements and measures of foreign policy, and particularly of the words and deeds of President Roosevelt." N Y Times Bk R
  "Whether one does or does not agree with Dr. Beard's conclusions regarding the authorship of American foreign policy, one cannot but admire the degree of documentation and mass of data which, marshalled in support of his thesis, he places before the reader." U S Quarterly Bk R
  Bibliographical footnotes

Bowles, Chester
  The conscience of a liberal; selected writings and speeches; introduced and ed. by Henry Steele Commager. Harper 1962 xxiv, 351p $5.95   327.73
  1 U.S.—Foreign relations 2 U.S.—Social conditions 3 World politics—1945-
  These selections, pertaining to both domestic and international issues, include such "topics as economics, Negro rights, politics as a career, food and population problems, communism, isolationism, and the many revolutionary forces and ideas of the present times. Mr. Bowles is never at a loss for a striking statement of position or an uncompromising assignment of responsibility. He . . . deserves our thoughtful attention." Library J
  "Perhaps the most significant contribution in the book is the author's analysis of the arms race, delivered at the Los Angeles Modern Forum in 1960. Bowles gives priority to the control of nuclear arms over every other problem facing mankind." Sat R

Chomsky, Noam

American power and the new mandarins. Pantheon Bks. 1969 404p $7.95   **327.73**

1 U.S.—Foreign relations 2 Vietnamese Conflict, 1961- 3 U.S.—Intellectual life 4 World politics—1945-

"The failure of liberal scholarship and our academic mandarins to provide an intellectual leadership directing this country away from its imperialistic war policies is a unifying theme in this collection. . . . Vietnam occupies much of the book and two of the author's 1967 articles from 'Ramparts' are reprinted." Library J

The "new mandarins" whom the author "sears are Arthur Schlesinger, Jr., Kenneth Young of the Asia Society, Morton Halprin of the Harvard Center for International Affairs—and scores more. . . . His concern is with the growth of violence and militarism in our society, and the probable consequences." Pub W

Bibliographical footnotes

Divine, Robert A.

(ed.) American foreign policy since 1945; ed. with an introduction by Robert A. Divine. Quadrangle Bks. 1969 248p $6.95

                              327.73

1 U.S.—Foreign relations

"A New York Times book"

"This is a compilation of articles from the 'New York Times Magazine.' First published in the years 1945 to 1967, the material here includes pieces on the atom bomb, U.S. policy in the Far East, the Cold War, Castro, and the U.N. by Robert Oppenheimer, John Foster Dulles, Adlai Stevenson, George McGovern, Averell Harriman and others." Booklist

Suggested reading: p241-42

Dozer, Donald Marquand

(ed.) The Monroe Doctrine; its modern significance. Knopf 1965 208p (Borzoi Bks. on Latin America) $4.50   **327.73**

1 Monroe Doctrine 2 U.S.—Foreign relations 3 Pan-Americanism

Contains source readings and several essays translated into English for the first time

Bibliographical footnotes

Dulles, Foster R.

America's rise to world power, 1898-1954. Harper 1955 314p illus maps (New American nation ser) $7.95   **327.73**

1 U.S.—Foreign relations

Traces those developments in United States foreign policy that have marked this nation's rise to world power. The underlying theme is the conflict between isolationism and internationalism. Concluding chapters stress America's current search for the basis of a durable peace

This book "is unusually good in its analysis of intellectual currents, or sectional and partisan attitudes, and of public opinion in general. . . . Nineteen pages of critical bibliography enhance its usefulness." Pol Sci Q

"This is a useful and attractive overview, more noteworthy for breadth than depth. . . . Mr. Dulles' most important contributions are in synthesis, emphasis, and readability." Am Hist R

Fish, Carl Russell

The path of empire; a chronicle of the United States as a world power. U.S. Pubs. Assn. 1919 305p (The Chronicles of America ser. v46) $3.95   **327.73**

1 U.S.—Foreign relations 2 U.S.—Territorial expansion

First published by Yale University Press

Contents: Monroe Doctrine; Controversies with Great Britain; Alaska and its problems; Blaine and Pan-Americanism; United States and the Pacific; Venezuela; Outbreak of the war with Spain; Dewey and Manila Bay; Blockade of Cuba; Preparation of the army; Campaign of Santiago de Cuba; Close of the war; Peace which meant war; Open door; Panama Canal; Problems of the Caribbean; World relationships; Bibliographical note

Foreign Policy Association

A cartoon history of United States foreign policy since World War I, by the editors of the Foreign Policy Association; introduction by Richard H. Rovere. Random House [1968 c1967] 252p illus $10   **327.73**

1 U.S.—Foreign relations 2 Cartoons and caricatures

"Linked by brief explanatory passages the cartoons collected here trace the changes in American attitudes toward foreign affairs as viewed by political cartoonists during the past 50 years. The book includes the work of such well-known cartoonists as Herblock, Mauldin, Fischetti, Fitzpatrick, Gropper, Orr, McCutcheon, and David Low, the only non-American represented. An entertaining as well as informative adjunct to histories of the period for student or browser." Booklist

Fulbright, J. William

The arrogance of power. Random House [1967 c1966] 264p boards $5.95   **327.73**

1 U.S.—Foreign relations 2 World politics—1945-

"After examining some of our major foreign policies, and particularly our relations with revolutionary movements in Latin America and Asia, the author . . . puts forth various suggestions about the direction our foreign policy should take." Preface

The author "maintains that the U.S. too often approaches less-advanced countries with power but without understanding [and] persuasively shows that this increasing arrogance also infects other U.S. international relations as well as domestic affairs." Booklist

Bibliography included in Notes: p259-64

Galbraith, John Kenneth

Ambassador's journal; a personal account of the Kennedy years; illus. with photographs and maps drawn by Samuel H. Bryant. Houghton 1969 xx, 656p illus maps $10   **327.73**

1 U.S.—Foreign relations—India 2 India—Foreign relations—U.S.

The author records his experiences as Ambassador to India during the years 1961-1963, describing his work, the problems of India, and his relations with his own government at home

"It is arrogance of a sort, tinged with the saving grace of self-satire, that makes [this] book one of the most refreshing and witty personal accounts to be published so far by a member of the Kennedy Administration. . . . Perhaps the greatest value of the 'Journal' is the picture it gives of [the author's] routine in New Delhi: almost daily conversations with Nehru, ceremonial appearances with officials, foreign and domestic, tricky matters of precedence and protocol within the Embassy itself (including the problems raised by staff members who doubled as CIA agents). Major events of the Galbraith Ambassadorship included Jacqueline Kennedy's state visit, India's invasion of Goa, fighting along the Indian-Chinese border and, of course, continual tension between India and Pakistan." Book of the Month Club News

Harriman, W. Averell

America and Russia in a changing world; a half century of personal observation; introduction by Arthur M. Schlesinger, Jr. Doubleday 1971 218p $5.95   **327.73**

1 U.S.—Foreign relations—Russia 2 Russia—Foreign relations—U.S. 3 World politics—1945-

An account of the author's "Russian experiences and an indication of what policies and attitudes he believes the United States should adopt in future dealings with the Soviet Union. He also expresses forthright opinions about Stalin, Molotov, Khrushchev, and other Soviet leaders, about FDR, Truman, Dulles, Eisenhower, LBJ, and Nixon, and about the shortcomings of American policy. . . . The book itself is based upon three talks Mr. Harriman gave . . . to students at Lehigh University, with some of the questions and answers they brought forth, plus more detailed background material and afterthoughts." Pub W

Kennan, George F.

American diplomacy, 1900-1950. Univ. of Chicago Press 1951 146p $4.95 **327.73**

1 U.S.—Foreign relations 2 Russia—Foreign relations

Analyzed in Essay and general literature index

Charles R. Walgreen Foundation lectures

"A cogent analysis and appraisal of foreign relations during the first half of the twentiet century. Included are chapters on the Open Door Policy, the war with Spain, and how to deal with the Russians. Here is a knowledgeable evaluation of U.S. principles and policies, and most importantly, recommendations for future American policy." A Guide to Reading in Am History

Realities of American foreign policy. Norton 1966 119p pa $1.25 **327.73**

1 U.S.—Foreign relations 2 World politics—1945-

"The Norton library"

First published 1954 by Princeton University press

The Stafford Little lectures given at Princeton University, March 1954

Contents: The two planes of international reality; The non-Soviet world; The problem of Soviet power; The unifying factor

A personal philosophy of foreign policy in which the author "relates current problems of foreign policy both to realities outside the U.S., and to the nature and goals of American society." Booklist

Kissinger, Henry A.

American foreign policy; three essays. Norton 1969 143p $3.95 **327.73**

1 U.S.—Foreign relations 2 Vietnamese Conflict, 1961-

"This book contains three previously published essays. The first . . . examines the impact of domestic structures and leadership styles on foreign policy and on the prospects of world order. The second . . . discusses the 'central issues of American foreign policy' today, in a world in which military bipolarity coexists with political multipolarity. The third . . . deals with Vietnam and suggests three levels of negotiations: between the United States and North Vietnam, between Saigon and N.L.F., and an international conference on guarantees and safeguards." Book World

"Essays from a conservative point of view. . . . Recommended for students of government and politics." Booklist

Lederer, William J.

A nation of sheep. Norton 1961 194p illus boards $4.95 **327.73**

1 U.S.—Foreign relations 2 World politics—1945- 3 Journalism

"First viewing events in Laos, Korea, Thailand, and Formosa that have, in his opinion, been misrepresented or mismanaged by the U.S. press or government, the author next regards weaknesses in the government and press and ends with specific recommendations for improving news coverage of and public and personal links with foreign countries." Booklist

"A bit shrill and subjective but effective in arousing a more intelligent interest in our place in the world and a more critical awareness of the press at home." Top of the News

Neumann, William L.

America encounters Japan: from Perry to MacArthur. Johns Hopkins Press 1963 353p $8 **327.73**

1 U.S.—Foreign relations—Japan 2 Japan—Foreign relations—U.S.

"The Goucher College series"

"The ideas and attitudes which shaped and influenced American foreign policy in respect to Japan and the Far East over the past century and a half are the primary concern of this book. . . . Japanese policy is treated only secondarily and when necessary for the understanding of American reactions. Particular emphasis is given to those ideas, attitudes, and events which are related to the coming of war in 1941." Preface

"A scholarly and readable book . . . written with a detachment unlikely to ingratiate partisans of official American policy in its various historic changes of attitude toward Japan. Professor Neumann points out stereotyped opinions held by Americans concerning the Japanese and other Oriental nations and thereby uncovers some submerged facts of U.S. history." Booklist

Bibliographic essay: p315-43

Nevins, Allan

The New Deal and world affairs; a chronicle of international affairs, 1933-1945. U.S. Pubs. Assn. 1950 332p (The Chronicles of America ser. v56) $3.95 **327.73**

1 U.S.—Foreign relations 2 World politics 3 World War, 1939-1945—Diplomatic history

First published by Yale University Press

Contents: The New Deal and the London Conference; Roosevelt's good neighbor policy; Years of false realism, 1933-37; Experiments in neutrality; Nation comes to its senses; World on the brink, 1938-39; European cataclysm begins; War and global diplomacy; Diplomacy of wartime cooperation; Rough road to victory; New world order; Bibliographical note

The United States in a chaotic world; a chronicle of international affairs, 1918-1933. U.S. Pubs. Assn. 1951 [c1950] 252p (The Chronicles of America ser. v55) $3.95 **327.73**

1 U.S.—Foreign relations 2 World politics

First published by Yale University Press

Contents: Guiding traditions of foreign policy; Lost peace; Dollars and cents in foreign policy; Plans for exorcising war; Turn for the worse; Japan defies the world; American neighbors; Breakdown of disarmament; Bibliographical note

Reischauer, Edwin O.

Beyond Vietnam: the United States and Asia. Knopf 1967 242p maps $4.95 **327.73**

1 U.S.—Foreign relations—Asia 2 Asia—Foreign relations—U.S.

"A reasoned re-thinking of the Far Eastern policy of the United States, by a historian and diplomat who . . . was American Ambassador to Japan, 1961-1966. His is a middle-of-the-road approach, though it has more of a chance of approval from the doves than from the hawks. The author begins with Vietnam, analyzing how our involvement there developed from World War II on. . . . From Vietnam, the author ranges over the whole of Asia, proposing intelligent, flexible ways of improving U.S. relationships with nations in the Far East, ways of fending off trouble and helping less developed countries to solve their worst problems." Pub W

"No reviewer can do justice to all Mr. Reischauer's ideas; there are too many. And, obviously, nobody is going to agree with all his conclusions. The singular excellence of his book is its treatment of our policy in East Asia and the Western Pacific as an integrated whole. Thus, to appreciate his position, fully, [this book] must be read in its entirety." Sat R

The United States and Japan. 3d ed. Harvard Univ. Press 1965 xxv, 396p maps (The American foreign policy lib) $6.50 **327.73**

1 U.S.—Foreign relations—Japan 2 Japan—Foreign relations—U.S.

First published 1950

"A careful description of Japanese economic, political, and social institutions and traditions; and a full account of U.S.-Japanese relations." Good Reading

The book is "amplified by a section on the postwar Japanese, primarily an analysis of the spectacular Japanese economic boom." Pub W

"This is certainly one of the most readable and authoritative books on this subject available and is particularly for use by the general reader." Library J

Bibliography: p382-84

Schlesinger, Arthur M. 1917-

The bitter heritage; Vietnam and American democracy, 1941-1966 [by] A. M. Schlesinger, Jr. Houghton 1967 [c1966] 126p $3.95   **327.73**

1 U.S.—Foreign relations—Vietnam 2 Vietnam—History 3 U.S.—Politics and government—1961-

An "analysis of our present dilemma and a series of suggestions for a political rather than a military solution. . . . [The author] assesses the wider implications of the Russo-Chinese split for American policy [and] the potential impact of the war in Vietnam on civil freedom in the United States and the uses of history as a means of prediction." Publisher's note

The author "frames the issues with precision and analyzes our current policies with a relentless logic. If it offers no solutions, it is nonetheless an important contribution to the creation of an informed electorate." Book Week

Bibliographical footnotes

Tuchman, Barbara W.

Stilwell and the American experience in China, 1911-45. Macmillan (N Y) 1971 621p illus maps $10   **327.73**

1 Stilwell, Joseph Warren 2 U.S.—Foreign relations—China 3 China—Foreign relations—U.S. 4 World War, 1939-1945—China

The author "interweaves brilliant narrative history with superb biography in this major new book which takes as its theme America's relation to China. The dominant figure in her story is General Joseph 'Vinegar Joe' Stilwell, whose connection with China spanned the period from the dramatic opening moment of 1911, the year of the Revolution, to 1944, the decisive year in the decline of the Nationalist government. The battles, the victories and defeats, the flaming drama of the war in the China-India-Burma theater are vividly recounted." News of Bks

Tuchman "has used masses of previously unavailable material for . . . [her] early chapters, particularly the full range of Stilwell's diaries, and his letters to his wife. The descriptions of American Army life on Chinese soil in the 20's and 30's coupled with Stilwell's notes of his lengthy treks and his careful observations of the encroaching Japanese Army, constitute a new and valuable historical source." N Y Times Bk R

Bibliography and other sources: p541-52

Warren, Sidney

The President as world leader. Lippincott 1964 480p $8.95   **327.73**

1 U.S.—Foreign relations 2 Presidents—U.S. 3 World politics

This study of our chief executives in their vital roles "is also a history of United States foreign policy over the last six decades. The author analyzes the policies, the achievements and failures of the President from the first inauguration of Theodore Roosevelt to the death of John F. Kennedy, Theodore Roosevelt and the Panama Canal, Wilson and the League of Nations, Franklin D. Roosevelt and Lend-Lease, Truman and the Korean War, Kennedy and the Cuba missile crisis [are covered]." Publisher's note

"Helpful information for history and political science students." Booklist

A selected bibliography: p458-70

328.1 Parliamentary rules and procedure

Cushing, Luther Stearns

Manual of parliamentary practice; rules of proceeding and debate in deliberative assemblies. Rev. and amplified by Paul E. Lowe. . . . McKay [1957 c1925] 318p $2.95   **328.1**

1 Parliamentary practice

First published 1845

"Containing comprehensive instructions and explanations for organizing and conducting the proceedings of conventions and other deliberative bodies. Also exemplar of the proceedings of a meeting in actual operation, and model forms for the drafting of constitutions and by-laws." Title page

Robert, Henry M.

Robert's Rules of order; newly rev. A new and enl. ed. by Sarah Corbin Robert, with the assistance of Henry M. Robert III, James W. Cleary [and] William J. Evans. Scott 1970 xlii, 594p $5.95   **328.1**

1 Parliamentary practice

First published 1876 as: Pocket manual of rules of order for deliberative assemblies

"This book embodies a codification of the present-day general parliamentary law (omitting provisions having no application outside legislative bodies). The book is also designed as a manual to be adopted by organizations or assemblies as their parliamentary authority." Introduction

"The standard handbook, although not necessarily the easiest to use." Winchell. Guide to Reference Books. 8th edition

328.73 Legislative branch of U.S. government

Goodman, Walter

The Committee; the extraordinary career of the House Committee on Un-American Activities; foreword by Richard H. Rovere. Farrar, Straus 1968 564p illus $10   **328.73**

1 U.S. Congress. House. Committee on Un-American Activities 2 Governmental investigations 3 Subversive activities

A narrative of the thirty years' history of the House Committee on Un-American Activities and its often controversial investigations and activities concerning the political Left and Right in America. (Publisher)

The author "does not do full justice to the perfectly genuine wreckage which the Committee at various times made of the lives of people who had done no harm to anyone. . . . In its own terms, however, 'The Committee' is a first-rate historical study—exhaustive in research, cool in judgment, brilliantly perceptive and eminently readable." Book World

Selected bibliography: p549-50

Morrow, William L.

Congressional committees. Scribner 1969 261p $6.95   **328.73**

1 U.S. Congress—Committees

"The role of Congressional committees is described and analyzed in a businesslike study that gives a general, wide-angle view of the entire committee system and its relation to the political order rather than a close look at the workings of a specific committee. . . . The chapter citations of . . . sources augment the book's usefulness." Booklist

United States. Congress

Official Congressional directory. U.S. Govt. Ptg. Off. illus maps $4   **328.73**

1 U.S. Congress—Directories 2 U.S. Congress—Biography

"Appears once during each Congressional session. Contents vary but you will usually find biographical sketches of current members of Congress and of principal officers of the executive department. Members of Congressional committees are named, and other principal officers of the executive and judicial branches of the government are listed." Murphey. How and Where to Look it Up

Partial contents (approximately the same in recent volumes though sometimes in different order): Biographical sketches; State delegations; Terms of service; Committees, commissions, and boards; Statistical information; The

United States. Congress—*Continued*
Capitol; Executive departments; Independent offices, agencies, and establishments; Judiciary; District of Columbia; Foreign diplomatic representatives and foreign consular offices in the United States; U.S. foreign service and consular offices; Maps of congressional districts

Wright, Jim
You and your Congressman. Coward-McCann 1965 282p $4.95 **328.73**
1 U.S. Congress
While discussing both the Senate and the House of Representatives the author "tells how Congress functions, how bills are introduced, and what Representatives do both in Congress and in offices and committee rooms to help their constituents." Bk Buyer's Guide
Includes index of names

329   Practical politics

Abels, Jules
The degeneration of our Presidential election; a history and analysis of an American institution, in trouble. Macmillan (N Y) 1968 322p $6.95 **329**
1 Presidents—U.S.—Election
"The three main sections to the book are: a look at our archaic voting machinery; a historical review of presidential campaigns with their lies, and compromised reputations; a look at various proposals for vitally needed reforms." McClurg. Book News
"The value of the . . . book lies in the diagnosis and analysis rather than the speculation about the future. . . . Do the highly tentative and general schemes that Abels advances give any assurance of improvement? . . . Whatever the answer . . . [he has] contributed to a valuable dialogue that must be expanded and continued in the future." Sat R

Chambers, William Nisbet
(ed.) The American party systems; stages of political development; ed. by William Nisbet Chambers and Walter Dean Burnham. Contributors: Frank J. Sorauf [and others] Oxford 1967 321p illus $7.50 **329**
1 Political parties
Outgrowth of a conference on American political party development, held at Washington University, St Louis, in April, 1966
"The value of this collection does not lie so much in the presentation of new material or new ideas; in general, each essay represents an extension of ideas already formulated and of work already undertaken and published by the respective authors. The great merit of the book is that the results of these labors have been brought together in a meaningful interdisciplinary synthesis. . . . Students of American politics, historical or contemporary, would do well to read the book." J Am Hist

Political parties in a new nation: the American experience, 1776-1809. Oxford 1963 231p $5 **329**
1 Political parties 2 U.S.—Politics and government—Revolution 3 U.S.—Politics and government—1783-1809

"The growth of the political party system in our country is seen as an American phenomenon which began with the Federalists, reflecting Alexander Hamilton's philosophy and politics, and the Republicans, who opposed them." Bk Buyer's Guide
"Chambers believes that the new nations which are committed to the development of democratic institutions have much to learn from the American experience. . . . There is much in this analysis which is thought-provoking." Va Q R

Chester, Lewis
An American melodrama; the Presidential campaign of 1968 [by] Lewis Chester, Godfrey Hodgson [and] Bruce Page. Viking 1969 814p $10 **329**
1 Presidents—U.S.—Election 2 Politics, Practical
The authors have written this account of the 1968 American Presidential election based on impressions which they gathered while covering the campaign for the London Times. They begin with President Johnson's decision not to run, and go on to analyze each of the candidates and the events which occurred
"Though packed with detail, [the book] is clear, well written, and easy to read. It has depth, analysis, and insight, and is entertaining. Its generalizations are often of high quality. . . . The authors have tried to convey (1) 'the gap between rhetoric and reality' and (2) the 'humor' uproarious diversity and plain enjoyment' characterizing American political life." Choice

Cunningham, Noble E.
(ed.) The making of the American party system, 1789-1809; ed. by Noble E. Cunningham, Jr. Prentice-Hall 1965 177p pa $1.95 **329**
1 Political parties 2 U.S.—Politics and government—1783-1809
"A Spectrum book"
"A collection of primary source documents which show how national political parties were formulated and operated during the United States' first 20 years under the Constitution." Pub W
The materials treat such topics as "concept of party, issues and ideas in early party conflicts, party managers, the press, machinery for politics, nominations, campaigns, securing funds, and Jefferson's patronage. The coverage is uneven, but this is satisfactory for use as a source book to be sold at reasonable cost." Library J

Hesseltine, William Best
Third-party movements in the United States. Van Nostrand 1962 192p pa $1.45 **329**
1 Political parties 2 U.S.—Politics and government
"An Anvil original"
"Historical survey and documents of protest, 1827-1948." A Guide to Reading in Am History
Includes bibliography

Hicks, John Donald
The Populist revolt; a history of the Farmers' Alliance and the People's Party. Univ. of Neb. Press 1961 [c1959] 473p pa $1.75 **329**
1 Populist Party 2 Farmers' Alliance 3 Agriculture—Economic aspects 4 U.S.—Politics and government—1865-1898
"A Bison book"
First published 1931 by the University of Minnesota Press
"This is required reading for an understanding of American politics and economics. The Populists failed but they were fore-runners of reforms adopted by later parties in context of the role of the third-party in the United States. This is . . . [a] study of the movement that stirred the farming regions of the West and South." A Guide to Reading in Am History
Includes bibliography

Lubell, Samuel
The hidden crisis in American politics. Norton 1970 306p $5.95 **329**
1 Presidents—U.S.—Elections 2 U.S.—Politics and government—1961- 3 U.S.—Social conditions
SBN 393-05370-9
Structured around the meaning of the 1968 Presidential election and the "four 'conflicts on the run' which divide the nation: deepening

Lubell, Samuel—*Continued*

white-black antagonisms, our youth and university crisis, competition over how to divide the economic resources, and new isolationism, this is an analysis of the 'strange new politics of impatience' that is transforming political life today." Book News

Lubell "combines the skills of an expert analyst of voting behavior . . . a sensitive interviewer and a shrewd observer of American politicians." Newsweek

McCarthy, Eugene J.

The year of the people. Doubleday 1969
323p $6.95   **329**

1 Presidents—U.S.—Election 2 Politics, Practical

This is Senator McCarthy's election chronicle of the 1968 Democratic Presidential nomination. He discusses the issues which he fought for and against during the campaign and "quoting critics and supporters . . . he weighs each nuance and shift of events in relation to the developing campaign—its confusions, misunderstandings, restrained rancor, the tragedy of RFK, [and] the bitterness of Chicago." Pub W

"Reflective, impassioned, ironic, candid, a bit quirky, and unfailingly literate, it is a political memoir that can be read with pleasure and intellectual profit whether one believed in The Movement or abhorred it." N Y Times Bk R

Orth, Samuel P.

The boss and the machine; a chronicle of the politicians and party organization. U.S. Pubs. Assn. 1919 203p (The Chronicles of America ser. v43) $3.95   **329**

1 Political parties 2 U.S.—Politics and government

First published by Yale University Press
Contents: Rise of the party: Rise of the machine; Tide of materialism; Politician and the city; Tammany Hall; Lesser oligarchies; Legislative omnipotence; National hierarchy; The awakening; Party reform; Expert at last

Political handbook and atlas of the world; parliaments, parties and press. Published for the Council on Foreign Relations by Simon & Schuster $19.95   **329**

1 Political science—Handbooks, manuals, etc. 2 Political parties 3 Newspapers—Directories

Annual. First published 1927 with title: A political handbook of Europe. Title, editor and publisher varies

This handbook, which covered more than 125 countries in its 1966 edition, is "designed to furnish the necessary factual information for understanding political events in all countries which have independent governments—colonies and trust territories are not included." Foreword to the 1966 edition

The following information is provided: "the composition of governments; the programs of political parties; their leaders; political affiliations of editors and leading newspapers and periodicals; and a summary of recent political events, both domestic and foreign. In addition, the book describes in detail the form, membership and personnel of the United Nations affiliated international agencies." Publisher's note

Roseboom, Eugene H.

A history of Presidential elections; from George Washington to Richard M. Nixon. [3d ed] Macmillan (N Y) 1970 639p $10
    329

1 Presidents—U.S.—Election 2 U.S.—Politics and government

First published 1957
The author describes the political developments between elections, the conventions, campaigns and elections themselves, the leadership capabilities of each President, and the rise and decline of political parties. (Publisher)

"Though written in a sprightly and sometimes colloquial style, Mr. Roseboom's book is stamped with . . . painstaking scholarship." N Y Times Bk R [Review of second edition]
Selective bibliography: p614-23

Scammon, Richard M.

The real majority [by] Richard M. Scammon and Ben J. Wattenberg. Coward-McCann 1970 347p illus map $7.95   **329**

1 Politics, Practical 2 Elections—U.S. 3 Public opinion

The authors examine the attitudes of American voters, as revealed in recent polls and elections, particularly in the 1968 Presidential election. They conclude that the American voter is still basically moderate in his social and political views and that, in order to be successful, candidates must appeal to the political center

Includes sections on "Lyndon Johnson, the Wisconsin primary or the zenith of Eugene McCarthy, other presidential primaries and the national conventions of 1968 in Miami and Chicago. The icing on this part is provided by the authors in their discussions of the campaigns of Humphrey, Wallace and Nixon. . . . [This] is a competent work written in journalistic style. . . . One would be all the poorer if he neglected this engrossing guide to current American politics." Best Sellers

U.S. politics—inside and out. U.S. News & World Report [distributed by Macmillan (N Y)] 1970 221p illus maps pa $2.95
    329

1 Elections—U.S. 2 U.S.—Politics and government—1961-

"Asserting that the levers of public power are in the hands of a relatively small group rather than the electorate this well-organized survey of the U.S. political scene examines shady and corrupt political practices and the workings of the electoral system on local, state, and national levels. The book looks into a variety of problems areas; among them campaign costs, power groups and lobbyists, the 'selling' of a candidate, vote buying, party machines, and the voting behavior of members of Congress. The concluding section makes an urgent plea for an informed electorate that registers, votes, and mobilizes on issues and suggests steps that can be taken by individuals to work for an improved political picture." Booklist
Includes bibliographical references

White, Theodore H.

The making of the President, 1960. Atheneum Pubs. 1961 400p $10   **329**

1 Presidents—U.S.—Election 2 U.S.—Politics and government—1953-1961

Companion volume to the author's: The making of the President, 1964, and The making of the President, 1968, listed below

The author reports on who the "Presidential candidates were, how they campaigned, and the factors that hurt or helped them—like great wealth or the lack of it, political connections, experience, previous publicity, etc. A dramatic revelation of our great political machines working at top speed." Bk Buyer's Guide

"A sensitive, often intimate, account of what the candidates went through in seeking nomination and election as President. The machinery of politics, the ambitions of politicians, and the powerful subsurface influences among the electorate are all interpreted by Mr. White with a sympathetic attitude toward American politics." A Guide to Reading in Am History

The making of the President, 1964. Atheneum Pubs. 1965 431p $10   **329**

1 Presidents—U.S.—Election 2 U.S.—Politics and government—1961-

"A masterly report, with an occasional lapse into flamboyance, of the personalities, conventions, planning, issues, and outcome of the 1964 Presidential election. . . . This is an invaluable record that illuminates deftly the national psyche. Of particular interest is the author's hope that the issues he feels Goldwater wished to raise but failed to express be kept before the public. Appended is a tabulation of the popular vote and the Graham memorandum on Johnson's selection in 1960 as Vice-president." Booklist

White, Theodore H.—*Continued*

The making of the President, 1968. Atheneum Pubs. 1969 459p $10   **329**

1 Presidents—U.S.—Election 2 U.S.—Politics and government—1961-

This is a chronological account and analysis of the 1968 Presidential campaign—the preliminaries, the conventions, the issues, the men involved, and the outcome

"What makes White's book so good is his solid grasp of the American political scene, his personal acquaintance with hosts of political figures from the Kennedys to Nixon, Finch and some who will be heard from as their time arrives. Here he makes his immense canvas come to life because he takes the time to give both the human and political contexts in which Richard Nixon, Eugene McCarthy and Bobby Kennedy made their decisions and conducted their so-different campaigns." Pub W

Maps on lining-papers

The **World** this year. 1971 supplement to the Political handbook and atlas of the world; governments and intergovernmental agencies as of January 1, 1971. Ed. by Richard P. Stebbins and Alba Amoia with the assistance of Sheila Low-Beer. Published for the Council on Foreign Relations by Simon & Schuster 1971 168p $9.95   **329**

1 Political science—Handbooks, manuals, etc.
SBN 671-20953-1

"This volume presents the essential facts about the world's governments and leading intergovernmental organizations as they existed on January 1, 1971. . . . While designed . . . to supplement . . . The Political handbook and atlas of the world . . . [it] is entirely suited for independent use as a guide to the global politics of the current period." Preface

330 Economics

Galbraith, John Kenneth

The affluent society. 2d ed. rev. Houghton 1969 xxxii, 333p $6.95   **330**

1 Economics 2 U.S.—Economic conditions
First published 1958

An "attack on existing ideas & attitudes in economics. [The] author believes these ideas were developed for a world of bleak poverty & shows how imperfectly & reluctantly the ideas appropriate to that world have been modified for today." Library J

"The original arguments and merits of the first edition have been maintained and strengthened. . . . [The author] challenges our traditional thinking not only about economic and social organization, but about ends, as well. . . . It is not imperative that the second edition . . . be purchased if the original is available." Choice

Bibliographical footnotes

330.1 Economics—General systems, principles, theories

Boardman, Fon W.

Economics: ideas and men [by] Fon W. Boardman, Jr. Walck, H.Z. 1966 133p $5   **330.1**

1 Economics—History

"A survey of the history of economics from ancient times to the near present. Schools of thought like the Mercantilists and Physiocrats are defined, and there are the men who developed theories and explanations of their economic times. A chapter is given to Adam Smith, another to Karl Marx and also to John Maynard Keynes." Bk Buyer's Guide

"The extreme urgency for teaching economics in high school is pointed out. . . . It is imperative that students understand at least the fundamentals of economics and this book is an excellent starting point." Best Sellers

Reading list: p125-26

Galbraith, John Kenneth

American capitalism; the concept of countervailing power. Rev. ed. Houghton 1956 208p $4   **330.1**

1 Capitalism 2 U.S.—Economic conditions
First published 1952

"A modern economist presents an interesting theory about American economic development primarily since World War II. He believes American capitalism has survived its test and though changed in places has come up with 'countervailing power.' (Labor unions against great corporations, strong buyers against weak sellers)." Cincinnati

Heilbroner, Robert L.

The worldly philosophers; the lives, times, and ideas of the great economic thinkers   **330.1**

1 Economists 2 Economics—History
Some editions are:
Simon & Schuster $6.95
Watts, F. $12.50 Large type edition. A Keith Jennison book
First published 1953
Analyzed in Essay and general literature index

"This introduction to economic thought . . . dramatizes the biographies of the great economists and their ideas which, translated into political action, helped shape the modern world. The author, who indulges in no special pleading, gives an equal hearing to both the orthodox and the unorthodox; he invites the reader to judge for himself from the evidence, as he presents one economic viewpoint after the other. A lucid and forceful handbook, which stimulates while it entertains." Booklist

Guide to further reading: p307-12

Smith, Adam

An inquiry into the nature and causes of the wealth of nations   **330.1**

1 Economics
Some editions are:
Dutton (Everyman's lib) 2v ea $2.95 Introduction by Edwin R. Seligman
Modern Lib. (Modern Lib. giant) $4.95 Edited with an introduction, notes, marginal summary and an enlarged index by Edwin Cannan; with an introduction by Max Lerner
First published 1776

This treatise "is the first comprehensive treatment of the whole subject of political economy, and is remarkable for its breadth of view. . . . [In it, the author presents an] attack on the mercantile system, and an advocacy of freedom of commerce and industry. His political economy is essentially individualistic; self-interest is the proper criterion of economic action. But the universal pursuit of one's own advantage contributes, in his view, to the public interest." Oxford Companion to English Literature

Veblen, Thorstein

The portable Veblen; ed. and with an introduction by Max Lerner. Viking 1948 632p $5.95   **330.1**

1 Economics

"The Viking Portable library"

"Contains the first seven chapters of the Theory of the Leisure Class, large selections from The Place of Science and Absentee Ownership, and articles from six other books." Book Rev Digest

The editor's purpose has been "to give the greater emphasis to [Veblen's] commentaries on social institutions and current practices—in short, to keep in mind the lay reader rather than the technical one . . . to show both Veblen the elusive ironist and Veblen the explicit radical; and finally—and perhaps most to

Veblen, Thorstein—*Continued*
the point—to give the selections I happen to
like and remember best, which means those
that shook up my own thinking and left scars
on it." Editor's note
List of Veblen's books: p629-30. Further
reading on Veblen: p630-32

330.3   Economics—Dictionaries

The McGraw-Hill Dictionary of modern
economics; a handbook of terms and organizations [by] Douglas Greenwald, in
collaboration with Jack McCroskey [and
others] McGraw 1965 697p illus $14.75
330.3

1 Economics—Dictionaries
Contains "1,300 well-selected and fully-de-
fined terms which reflect the considered judgment of the book's eight well-qualified compilers. These terms range from 'ability-to-pay
principle of taxation' to economic schools of
thought, e.g. 'classical school,' 'neoclassical
school.' Added features include: references to
books and articles which provide a more detailed explanation of the terms: charts, tables,
and diagrams; and well-written descriptions of
about 200 private, public, and nonprofit agencies, associations, and research organizations
concerned with economics and marketing, including a few outside the United States. Intended for students, housewives, and businessmen, as well as instructors, it is a valuable,
up-to-date addition to school, college, and public libraries." Cur Ref Bks

Paradis, Adrian A.
The economics reference book. Chilton
Bks. 1970 191p $5.95, lib. bdg. $5.73   **330.3**

1 Economics—Dictionaries
ISBN 0-8019-5528-9; 0-8019-5529-7
"This book was written for the high school
student and the layman who may be puzzled
by the meaning of various economic terms
encountered in their daily study or reading."
To the Reader
Paradis supplies definitions on "technical
programs, monopoly, markets, laws, policies,
systems, controls, currency, stock exchanges,
profit and loss, tariff, war on poverty, careers
in economics, and so on . . . [and] thumbnail
sketches of leading economists and the part
they played in monetary and sociological systems." Publisher's note
Suggested readings: p174-84

330.94   Europe—Economic conditions

Isenberg, Irwin
(ed.) The outlook for western Europe.
Wilson, H.W. 1970 213p map (The Reference shelf v42, no.2) $4.50   **330.94**

1 Europe—Economic conditions 2 Europe—
Politics—1945-
ISBN 0-8242-0410-7
This compilation deals mainly with western
Europe's economic conditions (including the
problems of the European Economic Community) and the political questions it faces, such
as the possibility of federation. Several articles on western Europe's foreign relations,
with both East and West are also discussed
Bibliography: p203-13

330.973   U.S.—Economic conditions

Chamberlain, John
The enterprising Americans: a business
history of the United States. Harper 1963
282p illus $7.95   **330.973**

1 U.S.—Economic conditions 2 Business—
History

"A Colophon book"
An "account of the growth of American business, from its mercantile beginnings in New
England and along the Delaware and James
River valleys to the great trade and industrial complexes which span the free world today. . . . [In this record] virtual unknowns
such as Sir William Pepperrell take their
place with the more famous Eli Whitney,
Carnegie, Ford, and J. P. Morgan." Publisher's note
"An exciting as well as scholarly account.
. . . The author does not allow prejudice to
sway his story; he treats scoundrels and heroes
with equal fairness and has done a good job
of research behind the scenes. The telling is
lively and will certainly interest students of
American history or modern problems." Library J
Bibliography: p265-72

Coles, Robert
Still hungry in America; photographs by
Al Clayton; introduction by Edward M.
Kennedy. World Pub. 1969 115p illus $7.95
330.973

1 U.S.—Economic conditions 2 Poverty
3 Nutrition
"An NAL book"
"This collection of eloquent photographs and
accompanying commentary documents the
hunger and malnutrition still prevalent among
many of the poor in the United States." Cincinnati
"An important social document and merits
wide purchase by libraries." Library J

Davis, Kenneth S.
(ed.) The paradox of poverty in America.
Wilson, H.W. 1969 224p (The Reference
shelf v41, no.2) $4.50   **330.973**

1 U.S.—Economic conditions 2 Poverty
3 Economic assistance, Domestic
The articles included discuss the nature and
extent of poverty in the United States; the
experience of being poor, measures undertaken
by government and private enterprise to
eliminate poverty, and proposed new approaches to the question
Bibliography: p212-24

Gladwin, Thomas
Poverty U.S.A.   Little   1967   182p
boards $4.75   **330.973**

1 U.S.—Economic conditions 2 U.S.—Social
conditions 3 Economic assistance, Domestic
4 Poverty
This is "an appraisal of the accomplishments
of the War on Poverty to date, with background on the New Deal programs and explanation of the interrelationships between anti-
poverty and civil rights goals. Some of the
proposals which the author discusses favorably
and convincingly are the guaranteed income,
major welfare reforms, educational reforms,
and a better image for the neglected 'service'
occupations as a source for wide employment.
The whole book is a careful and sensible explanation—the information cries out for mass
communication and acceptance. Yet . . . the
author rarely achieves the popular, palatable
touch." Pub W

Leuchtenburg, William E.
The perils of prosperity, 1914-32. Univ.
of Chicago Press 1958 313p (The Chicago
history of American civilization) $4.50
330.973

1 U.S.—Economic conditions 2 European War,
1914-1918—U.S. 3 U.S.—Civilization
"This book traces the political economic, social and cultural phenomena that transformed
America from an agrarian, primarily decen-
tralized, moralistic isolationist nation into an
industrial, urban, morally liberalized nation
involved in foreign affairs in spite of itself."
Publisher's note
"An extensively-documented though informal
history depicting the jazz age of prosperity."
Chicago
Includes bibliography

Rublowsky, John

After the Crash; America in the Great Depression. Crowell-Collier Press 1970 186p illus $4.95   **330.973**

1 U.S.—Economic conditions—1919-1933 2 U.S.—Social conditions 3 Depressions

In this account of the Crash of 1929 and the Depression that followed, the author describes the collapse of the American economy, the richest the world had known, and the early efforts of President Roosevelt to start the country on the road to recovery with his New Deal program. (Publisher)

"A useful, lucid explanation of the stockmarket crash. . . . Psychological factors, and the recovery and growth of organized labor, are treated in some detail." Library J

Bibliography: p179-80

Shannon, David A.

(ed.) The Great Depression. Prentice-Hall 1960 171p pa $1.95   **330.973**

1 U.S.—Economic conditions—1919-1933—2 Depressions

"A Spectrum book"

"The subject of this book is the impact of the Great Depression of 1929 and thereafter upon the American people. It does not concentrate upon economics, nor politics, nor social and intellectual matters, although there is something here of all these. Its emphasis is the effects of the depression upon its victims, and much of the material allows the reader to see the events of the 1930's through the eyes of these victims." Introduction

Contents: Crash; The farmer in the depression; America's shame: the crisis of relief; Nomads of the depression; The middle classes: bank failure and unemployment; The depression and education; Will there be a revolution; Some case histories

331.6 Special classes of workers: Migrant labor

Heaps, Willard A.

Wandering workers; the story of American migrant farm workers and their problems. Crown 1968 192p map $4.95   **331.6**

1 Migrant labor

"Young Adult Books from Crown"

This book consists of "taped interviews of workers, obtained by the author in migrant camps in New Jersey, Maryland, Virginia, Indiana, Illinois, Texas and California. . . . The migrants describe who they are, where they are from, where they travel, their work, their lives, and the problems of housing, health, community acceptance, and their children's welfare and education." Publisher note

"A piercing look at a grim picture. The author's extensive research is obvious. . . . The spelling in these interviews (attempting to replicate dialect) is the only weak point of the book: 'specials' is spelled 'speshuls,' and 'auto,' 'otto.' " Chicago. Children's Book Center

Sources and reading: p178-87

Moore, Truman

The slaves we rent; photographs by the author. Random House 1965 171p illus $7.75   **331.6**

1 Migrant labor 2 Agriculture—U.S.

"The world of the migrant, its economic and physical characteristics and consequences, is detailed with clarity and compassion. Moore discusses the activities and attitudes of crew leaders and produce growers; he covers the rise of large farms and their impact on the economy; he explores the possibilities and problems of migrant unions and outlines . . . efforts on behalf of the migrant." Library J

Bibliography: p161-66

331.7 Labor by occupation

Arnold, Arnold

Career choices for the '70s. Crowell-Collier Press 1971 151p $4.95   **331.7**

1 Vocational guidance

"This book does not suggest any single career area. It . . . is intended to make you aware of the need to choose early and to acquaint you with the choices available." Introduction

Partial contents: Minorities and careers; Girls and careers; Summer and part-time jobs; How to match who you are to who you would like to become; Educational routes to careers; What will be expected of you on the job

Asbell, Bernard

Careers in urban affairs: six young people talk about their professions in the inner city. Wyden, P.H. 1970 111p $3.95   **331.7**

1 U.S.—Occupations 2 Social work as a profession

In this book, six urban specialists explain their jobs and discuss what they like and dislike about their work. Represented here are a school social worker, a community organizer, a public-housing expert, two city planners, and an assistant to a mayor. (Publisher)

The National Observer

Careers . . . for the seventies; close-ups of 20 ways Americans earn a living; from the pages of The National Observer; ed. by Jerrold K. Footlick. Dow Jones Bks. 1969 211p pa $1.85   **331.7**

1 U.S.—Occupations

"These articles discuss careers by describing the people in them—their backgrounds, their education, their family life, and money they make, their dreams and aspirations." Introduction

Contents: Advertising creator; Archeologist; Architect; Artist; Banker; Baseball player; Dancer; Foreign Service officer; Government official; Inventor; Librarian; Musical theater performer; Musician; Politician; Popular singer; Stewardess; Stockbroker; Traveling salesman; Veterinarian; Woman scientist

Summer

employment directory of the United States. Nat. Directory Service illus pa $5.95   **331.7**

1 U.S.—Occupations

Annual. First published 1954. Title varies

This directory "is arranged alphabetically according to states, types of organizations within the states, and the names of the organizations. Listed under the name of organization is the location, whom they employ, the positions open, the total number of openings (shown in parenthesis), salary or salary range, and the name and address of the person to whom one should make application." General Information and Suggestions

United States. Bureau of Labor Statistics

Occupational outlook handbook; employment information on major occupations for use in guidance. U.S. Govt. Ptg. Off. illus maps pa $6.25   **331.7**

1 Occupations 2 Vocational guidance

Prepared in cooperation with the Veterans Administration

First published 1949. Biennial revisions kept up to date by: Occupational outlook, published four times a year

Information about employment opportunities and jobs in professions, trades, business, industry, agriculture and government

Contains "much statistical information. Comprehensive index and bibliography are included for each field." Murphey. How and Where to Look it Up

331.703 Labor by occupation— Dictionaries

United States. Employment Service
Dictionary of occupational titles. 3d ed.
U.S. Dept. of Labor, Manpower Administration, Bureau of Employment Security.
U.S. Govt. Ptg. Off. 1965 2v   **331.703**
  1 Occupations—Dictionaries
  First published 1939-1944
  Contents: v 1: Definitions of titles; v2: Occupational classification and industry index
  "This publication consists of an alphabetical listing of standard titles of occupations, trades, and professions, with a concise description of what type of work is involved in each listing. Numerous cross references from alternate titles." Murphey. How and Where to Look it Up

331.88 Labor organizations

Hutchinson, John
The imperfect union; a history of corruption in American trade unions. Dutton 1970
477p $12.50   **331.88**
  1 Labor unions—History 2 Racketeering
  The author surveys the history of unions and labor-management relations from 1890 to the early 1960's. He "focuses a magnifying glass on corruption in the building, longshoremen's, garment, service, and road transportation unions and offers . . . commentary on the reasons for it." Library J
  Hutchinson "deserves high praise for assembling the facts of this sorry tale, and especially for doing so in a spirit of balance and probity. Moreover, he writes extraordinary well." Sat R
  Bibliography included in Notes and comments: p393-428

Kennedy, Robert F.
The enemy within. Harper 1960 338p illus
$7.95   **331.88**
  1 Labor unions 2 U.S. Congress. Senate. Select Committee on Improper Activities in the Labor or Management Field
  "A hard-hitting report on the work of a Congressional investigation committee, the Select Committee on Improper Activities in the Labor or Management Field. Robert Kennedy . . . devotes half of this stark and revealing book to the Teamsters' Union, the corruption of Dave Beck and James Hoffa, and the Teamsters' ties with racketeers. The other half of the book describes the way the Senate committee works and many of its other cases." Pub W
  "The tone of the book is sober and not sensational." Bk Buyer's Guide

Marx, Herbert L.
(ed.) American labor today; ed. by Herbert L. Marx, Jr. Wilson, H.W. 1965 208p
(The Reference shelf v37, no.5) $4.50 **331.88**
  1 Labor unions
  A compilation of articles concerning American labor's position in the 1960's prosperous economic situation, the rise of membership, independence within unions, collective bargaining, developments in labor law
  If the tone of this book "is mainly critical of unionism, if the weaknesses of the institution appear to outweigh its strengths, this is less the result of editorial bias as it is a reflection of the current trend in 'labor research.' . . . One section is devoted to new approaches to collective bargaining, another to the non-bargaining activities of trade unions, and a third to current issues in labor law. These sections are brief and to the point. . . . The heart of the volume lies, however, in the remaining sections which deal primarily with the forces affecting union growth and the prospects for unionism in the economy of the future. . . . It is to be hoped that the careful reader of this volume will discover—as many of labor's more ardent detractors apparently have not—that democracy in unions is a far from simple issue." Dartmouth Alumni Magazine
  Bibliography: p197-208

Orth, Samuel P.
The armies of labor; a chronicle of the organized wage-earners. U.S. Pubs. Assn. 1949 279p (The Chronicles of America ser. v40) $3.95   **331.88**
  1 Labor unions—History
  First published by Yale University Press
  Contents: The background; Formative years; Transition years; Amalgamation; Federation; Trade union; Railway brotherhoods; Issues and warfare; New terrorism; The I.W.W.; Labor and politics

Taft, Philip
Organized labor in American history. Harper 1964 xxi, 818p $12.50   **331.88**
  1 Labor unions—History
  "A history of American labor from its infancy . . . covering the Knights of Labor, Dual Unionism, the I.W.W., the A F of L and C.I.O., [minority groups] and the chief labor leaders." Bk Buyer's Guide
  A "work of reference . . . based on solid knowledge and a command of historical method." Sat R

Werstein, Irving
The great struggle; labor in America. Scribner 1965 190p illus lib. bdg. $3.63   **331.88**
  1 Labor unions—History 2 Labor and laboring classes—U.S.
  The author "traces the growth of the American labor movement from colonial times to 1965 and the merger of the AF of L and the CIO, stressing the general unrest among workers and the blood shed for better working conditions. He covers such . . . events as the Haymarket Square protest and the Pullman strike and shows the role played by Samuel Gompers, Eugene Debs, 'Big Bill' Haywood, and other labor leaders. Reproductions of historical pictures complement the text. A list of adult books for further reading is appended." Booklist

332.5 Paper money

Shafer, Neil
A guide book of modern United States currency. . . . Western Pub. Co. illus boards $2.50   **332.5**
  1 Paper money

  First published 1965 by Whitman. Frequently revised to bring material up to date
  "A comprehensive illustrated valuation catalog of all modern-size United States paper money from 1929 to the present, with historical data and official totals. Also includes complete catalog listing of U.S. military payment certificates." Title page [of 1971 edition]
  Includes glossary and bibliography

332.6 Investment finance

Friedlander, Joanne K.
Stockmarket ABC [by] Joanne K. Friedlander and Jean Neal; illus. by Tom Dunnington. Follett 1969 96p illus $2.95, lib. bdg. $2.97   **332.6**
  1 Stock exchange 2 Stocks

  The authors discuss "the operations on the floor of the New York Stock Exchange, common and preferred stocks, mutual funds, over-the-counter sales, the role of the stockholder, investments other than stock, market terminology, and translation of the financial pages of newspapers." Sat R

Moody, John
The masters of capital; a chronicle of Wall Street. U.S. Pubs. Assn. 1919 234p (The Chronicles of America ser. v41) $3.95 **332.6**
1 Finance 2 Capitalists and financiers 3 Wall Street
First published by Yale University Press
Contents: Rise of the house of Morgan; Morgan and the railroads; The ironmasters; Standard Oil and Wall Street; Steel trust merger; Harriman and Hill; Apex of "High Finance"; Panic of 1907 and after; Wall Street and the World War; Bibliographical note

Tyler, Poyntz
(ed.) Securities, exchanges, and the SEC. Wilson, H.W. 1965 201p (The Reference shelf v37, no.3) $4.50 **332.6**
1 Securities 2 Stock exchange 3 U.S. Securities and Exchange Commission
"The purpose of this book is to introduce the reader to the methods used in trading securities and commodities, the exchanges where such trading is conducted, and the Federal Government's machinery for regulating both trading and the exchanges." Preface
Articles cover stock market operations, stocks, bonds, investment clubs, mutual funds, and related subjects
Bibliography: p186-93. A short lexicon of investing: p194-201

332.7 Credit

Black, Hillel
Buy now, pay later. Morrow 1961 240p boards $5.95 **332.7**
1 Credit 2 Instalment plan
An "exposé of credit-buying in the United States: what debt-living is doing to Americans, the rise of the all-purpose credit card, the tragedies that can result from mountainous bills, and the warping of values among the easy-credit consumers, and among the 'debt merchants' or credit agents of various kinds." Pub W
"A first class reporting job. . . . The book is so clear, so interesting, and so valuable, that the reader will wonder why he has been wasting his money when a little information could have saved him hundreds of dollars." Best Sellers

333 Land

McClellan, Grant S.
(ed.) Land use in the United States; exploitation or conservation. Wilson, H.W. 1971 253p (The Reference shelf v43, no.2) $4.50 **333**
1 Land 2 U.S.—Public lands
ISBN 0-8242-0447-6
"The first section touches on our emerging land use policies. Section II, A Land To Live In, briefly raises the issue of a new urban-rural balance and the building or rebuilding of our cities. Questions of conservation and proper use of our water, forest, and mining resources are dealt with in Section III. Brief reference in Section IV is made to our national parks, wilderness areas, and other scenic lands." Preface
Bibliography: p245-53

333.7 Surface resources and general conservation policies

Allen, Durward L.
Our wildlife legacy. Rev. ed. Funk 1962 422p illus $8.95 **333.7**
1 Wild life—Conservation

First published 1954
"Considers conservation of living natural resources in relation to the often conflicting interests of sportsmen and fishermen, the administrators, and public officials. Dr Allen communicates his keen insights into how renewable resources can be managed successfully and used for satisfying other interests. He also deals with questions of predicator control and artificial propagation and rearing." The AAAS Book List for Young Adults
Reference notes: p341-78. Bibliography: p379-408

Douglas, William O.
A wilderness bill of rights; with photos. Little 1965 192p illus boards $6.75 **333.7**
1 Natural resources—U.S. 2 Natural resources—Laws and regulations 3 Wilderness areas 4 Wild life—Conservation
The author surveys conservation in the United States, its history and present problems. He examines county, state and municipal parks, Indian reservations, and bird and animal sanctuaries. He then urges the establishment of an Office of Conservation and outlines a Wilderness Bill of Rights incorporating proposed laws to check the encroachment of vested interests and careless citizens. (Publisher)
"There is an abundance of useful information, statistics of our land resources, sketches of public policy . . . [and] regulations affecting wilderness land use." Book Week
Justice Douglas is "at times poetic and lyrical. . . . The book is ideally suited for those with serious interest in conservation of natural resources and will undoubtedly serve its purpose of alerting certain elements of the public to the need for a balance between commercial, Federal and private interests." Science Bks
Major acts of Congress in the conservation field: p177-79

Ecotactics: the Sierra Club handbook for environment activists; ed. by John G. Mitchell with Constance L. Stallings; and with an introduction by Ralph Nader. Simon & Schuster 1970 288p pa $1.95 **333.7**
1 Natural resources—U.S. 2 Ecology
SBN 671-20779-2
"Ecotactics—the science of arranging and maneuvering all available forces in action against enemies of the earth. . . . The collected essays, some written for this work, tell how the individual can fight, via the law, the media, rapping, teach-ins, and education, to save the earth. Many of the essays were written by college student activists in this field as well as veterans, such as Nader. The text is appended by an excellent conservation bibliography; a roster of conservation organizations, key governmental agencies, the various Sierra Club chapters. This may be the most valuable book young adults inheriting the earth can read." Library J

Fisher, James
Wildlife in danger, by James Fisher [and others]. Foreword by Harold J. Coolidge and Peter Scott; preface by Joseph Wood Krutch. Viking 1969 368p illus $12.95 **333.7**
1 Wild life—Conservation 2 Zoology
"A Studio book"
Based on reports by members and correspondents of the Survival Service Commission of the International Union for Conservation of Nature and Natural Resources, this book offers an account on the current status of mammals, birds, reptiles, amphibians, fishes and plants around the world that are threatened with extinction
"The book should serve as a standard reference work in its field." Science Bks

McClung, Robert M.
Lost wild America; the story of our extinct and vanishing wildlife; illus. by Bob Hines. Morrow 1969 240p illus $5.95 **333.7**
1 Wild life—Conservation 2 Animals—U.S. 3 Rare animals
The book presents "the past, the present and the future of America's wildlife. The author relates the destruction of the abundant animal

McClung, Robert M.—*Continued*

life that took place as civilization spread across the continent. He also traces the development of the conservation movement, which began toward the end of the nineteenth century and describes both private and government efforts in the field." Publisher's note

"Vignettes of about 70 extinct or endangered animal species are narrated here with excellent chapters on current problems in environmental quality control. Good illustrations maintain an awareness of the animal under discussion. The book and its bibliography could serve many students as a stimulating start in a research project on wildlife management or concerning the influence of man on other species." Science Bks

Murphy, Robert

Wild sanctuaries; our national wildlife refuges—a heritage restored; foreword by Stewart L. Udall. Dutton 1968 288p illus maps $22.50   333.7

1 Wild life—Conservation 2 Natural resources —U.S. 3 Game preserves

"A remarkably thorough and attractive story of the initial exploitation of America's wildlife and the extermination of certain species, which was followed by the biological surveys and inventories of the late 1800's and early 1900's. The result was initiation of large scale conservation programs. The illustrations are numerous and of excellent quality." AAAS Science Book List

Philip, Duke of Edinburgh

Wildlife crisis [by] Philip, Duke of Edinburgh and James Fisher; forewords by the Prince of the Netherlands and Peter Scott; epilogue by Stewart L. Udall. Published with the cooperation of the World Wildlife Fund. Cowles 1970 256p illus maps $14.95   333.7

1 Wild life—Conservation 2 Rare animals 3 Extinct animals
ISBN 0-402-12511-8

The narrative by Fisher "traces human history from the beginning of man as a species some 200,000 years ago to the present, describes man's relations with wild animals and the problems of maintaining the world's wildlife today and what we can do about them. . . . [There is a preface and] personal testimonial—'Life and Wildlife'—by Prince Philip, with reproductions in black and white of 30 or more of his . . . wildlife photographs." N Y Times Bk R
Includes bibliography

Roosevelt, Nicholas

Conservation: now or never. Dodd 1970 238p $5.95   333.7

1 Natural resources—U.S. 2 Landscape protection

The main emphasis of the book is on the conservation of scenic resources in various areas of the United States. In this connection, the author surveys the conservation movement from the 19th century to the present, describes the work of leading conservations, and discusses specific conservation problems, past and present

Udall, Stewart L.

The quiet crisis; introduction by John F. Kennedy. Holt 1963 209p illus $5   333.7

1 Natural resources—U.S.

The author reviews "the land-and-people story of our continent. He begins with the history: the men who explored the land, either with an acquisitive or an appreciative eye; the great names of conservation history, from George Perkins Marsh to Gifford Pinchot; on the other hand, the raiders and despoilers; the problems of preserving green spaces in cities as well as countrysides; and problems of water and air pollution." Pub W

"Anyone who loves the natural beauty of the earth and understands even in the least degree mankind's responsibility as stewards of this beauty, will find this volume both absorbing and demanding. . . . With the addition of

magnificent photographs, some in color. Secretary Udall has, when the case is summed up, made his plea eloquent. This book is one to value oneself, and to share with those who care." Christian Science Monitor

United States. Department of Agriculture

Outdoors USA. U.S. Govt. Ptg. Off. [1967] xxxix, 408p illus map lib. bdg. $2.75   333.7

1 Natural resources—U.S. 2 Outdoor recreation

"This Yearbook of agriculture is a handbook of resource conservation, a guide to the American outdoors with its great recreation potential, and a primer of natural beauty. It tells its story largely in terms of people. It covers all the U.S. Department of Agriculture's activities serving farmers and the general public in developing our natural resources so that they can be enhanced while being used productively. . . . As a conservation document, . . . [this book] naturally falls into four divisions: The Big Woods (forests and mountains), Water, Beautification, and The Countryside." Preface
Includes bibliographies

Walsh, John

Time is short and the water rises, by John Walsh with Robert Gannon; foreword by Carlton E. Buttrick. Dutton 1967 224p illus maps $7.95   333.7

1 Wild life—Conservation 2 Surinam—Description and travel 3 Animals—Surinam

At head of title: Operation Gwamba: the story of the rescue of 10,000 animals from certain death in a South American rain forest

"A dramatic and instructive account of what happened after the Afobaka Dam was closed in Surinam. Walsh's mission, a dangerous and demanding 18-month task, was to rescue as many armadillos, opossums, ocelots, sloths, jaguars, brocket deer, tamanduas, porcupines and other animals as possible before they were trapped and drowned by the rising waters. . . . [The book is also] an excellent account of the natural history of Surinam and of its Bushnegro population." Science Bks

"Popularly written and illustrated with striking photographs, many in color, this vivid account will appeal not only to readers with an interest in conservation of wildlife but also to those who enjoy personal narratives of true adventure in exotic places. The appendix lists the animals saved." Booklist

333.7069   Careers in conservation

Dodd, Ed

Careers for the '70s: conservation; foreword by Theodore Roosevelt III. Crowell-Collier Press 1971 181p illus boards $4.95   333.7069

1 Natural resources 2 Vocational guidance

The author "issues a clear call-to-action for youth interested in conservation careers. Written in the first person, the text incorporates quotes, gives statistics, and cites specific levels of education, income and experience of actual conservationists in the U.S. Forest Service, wildlife agents, and conservation artists, writers and photographers. Short chapters provide a quick survey of the varied job areas . . . summer jobs, opportunities in Canada, careers for nonprofessionals, and sources of job information. A directory of colleges offering degrees in conservation studies is appended." Library J
Suggestions for further reading: p159-60

333.9   Other natural resources. Water

Bardach, John

Harvest of the sea. Harper 1968 301p illus $6.95   333.9

1 Marine resources 2 Oceanography

Bardach, John—*Continued*

"A popular study of developments in ocean science, of sea life and its potential for food and industry. . . . [The author] explains the movements of the seas—waves, tides and currents; describes the instruments and machines used in exploration, then moves to the products of the sea. . . . He traces the development of the fishing industry (worldwide) from the family boat operation to the modern factory afloat; discusses fisheries research, conservation, and utilization of marine resources." Pub W

Bardach's account "is greatly enhanced by well-chosen illustrations. It is a sober, well-written and very informative book, but it holds out no hope that exploitation of the seas will solve all of our problems, though certainly we could get much more from them than we now do. The danger is that we may mistreat the seas as we have the land." N Y Times Bk R
Bibliography: p281-89

Davies, Delwyn

Fresh water; the precious resource. Natural Hist. Press 1969 [c1967] 155p illus maps (Nature and science lib) boards $5.95, lib. bdg. $6.70   333.9

1 Water 2 Water supply
"Published for The American Museum of Natural History"
First published 1967 in England
"In a somewhat diffuse but sound, thorough report, Davies explains the properties, distribution, and uses of water including purification, irrigation, desalination, reuse, and pollution. He also examines some of the problems arising from increased demands on the world's water supply in the light of man's essential physiological needs and modern industrialized society's requirements. The book contains numerous well-correlated, informative prints, photographs, maps, and diagrams." Booklist

Goldman, Marshall I.

(ed.) Controlling pollution; the economics of a cleaner America. Prentice-Hall 1967 175p pa $1.95   333.9

1 Air—Pollution 2 Water—Pollution
"A Spectrum book"
This collection of writings, many published first as magazine articles or conference papers, "deals with economic aspects of water, air, and scenic pollution caused by the activities of producers and consumers, and the role of government in disputes over environmental quality." Choice

Halacy, D. S.

The water crisis [by] D. S. Halacy, Jr. Illus. with drawings by George H. Buehler and photographs. Dutton 1966 192p illus maps $4.95, lib. bdg. $4.90   333.9

1 Water supply 2 Water resources development
A "simplified overview of the world's water problems which should give interested young people and students a background knowledge and lead to further reading. Halacy discusses . . . such topics as the present water supply, pollution, conservation, and future sources of water. A list of agencies offering positions in hydrology and a bibliography are appended." Booklist

Moss, Frank E.

The water crisis; foreword by Paul H. Douglas. Praeger 1967 305p illus maps $8.50   333.9

1 Water resources development 2 Water supply
The author "defines problems of water pollution, shortage, variability . . . and waste. He describes how rivers have been used as waste dumps; states have lagged in cooperation in water problems; federal water-management agencies are Balkanized. He expands on the possibilities of research into desalination and weather modification and the use of some Canadian water." Pub W
Bibliography: p291-96

Nikolaieff, George A.

(ed.) The water crisis. Wilson, H.W. 1967 192p (The Reference shelf v38, no.6) $4.50   333.9

1 Water supply 2 Water resources development 3 Water—Pollution
A compilation of articles dealing with the nature of water; the water supply, pollution and other factors limiting it; methods of increasing the supply, and sources of financing them
Bibliography: p183-92

Overman, Michael

Water; solutions to a problem of supply and demand. Doubleday [1969 c1968] 192p illus maps (Doubleday Science ser) $6.95   333.9

1 Water supply 2 Water conservation
First copyright 1968 in England
"A thorough, lucid survey of worldwide water problems by a British technical journalist . . . Calling attention to the growing need for water caused by both increased population and greater percapita demand, Overman discusses methods employed or available to maintain a balanced distribution adequate for agricultural and industrial requirements as well as for man's personal needs. Information on dams, irrigation, the hydrologic cycle, hydroelectric power, desalination, and pollution is included." Booklist
Suggested readings: p187

Wright, Jim

The coming water famine. Coward-McCann 1966 255p $6.95   333.9

1 Water supply 2 Water resources development 3 Water—Pollution 4 Water—Conservation
Mr Wright reviews current water problems in the United States. He "discusses the immediate crisis, water usage, pollution, flood control, and future planning. . . He recommends an intensification of our desalination program, a much-expanded pollution control program, more small upstream dams, and planning for long-distance transport of water." Pub W
The book "is masterfully written by one who knows the facts and should be required reading for all public officials, teachers, members of service clubs, chambers of commerce, conservationists, industrialists and students. It is indexed, but has no bibliography." Science Bks

335 Collectivist systems and schools

Ebenstein, William

Today's isms; communism, fascism, capitalism, socialism. Prentice-Hall illus $6.95   335

1 Communism 2 Fascism 3 Capitalism 4 Socialism
SBN 13-924431-X
First published 1954. Frequently revised
"This book is a discussion of the main representatives of each side—communism and fascism on the totalitarian side, capitalism and socialism on the democratic. . . . The psychological roots of totalitarianism and democracy are given particularly close attention, since it is difficult to understand either system without understanding both the personality traits and psychological motivations to which each system appeals." Preface
"In spite of Dr. Ebenstein's strong admiration for American capitalism and British socialism, he is not unwilling to criticize their weaknesses, in particular the . . . trend towards conformity and the dangers of concentration of ownership in America, and the tendency towards isolationism on the part of British socialism. On the whole, however, this tract for the times presents a warm and sensible defense of democracy." U.S. Quarterly Bk R

335.4 Marxian systems

Cohen, Arthur A.
The communism of Mao Tse-tung. Univ.
of Chicago Press 1964 210p $6   335.4
1 Mao, Tse-tung   2 Communism—China
(People's Republic of China)
The author provides an "account of Mao's
thinking on revolution, transition to Communism, dictatorship of the proletariat, contradictions in socialist society. He describes Mao's
pragmatic talents as well as his brilliance as
a tactician in carrying on a revolutionary war
from self-sustaining rural bases." N Y Rev of
Books
The author "has been able to show, through
extensive documentation, how much of Mao's
reputation as an original thinker is built on
sheer sycophancy and in which areas of Communist revolutionary thought and action he
has made genuine contribution." Sat R
Includes bibliographical footnotes

Djilas, Milovan
The new class; an analysis of the communist system. Praeger 1957 214p $4.95
335.4
1 Communism
"A description of contemporary Communism
in Russia and Yugoslavia by a prominent
Yugoslav who was once a high-ranking Communist in his country. . . . He states that he
is becoming increasingly estranged from the
reality of contemporary Communism and closer to the idea of democratic socialism." Pub
W
"The author never wrote so informatively
as a Communist propagandist; among other
things, this volume is a fine example of how
lucid a man's thoughts can be when they
reflect his true convictions." N Y Times Bk R

Draper, Theodore
The roots of American communism. Viking [1963 c1957] 498p illus (Communism
in American life) pa $1.95   335.4
1 Communism—U.S.   2 Communist Party of
the United States of America
First published 1957
"A revealing and documented survey of the
formative years [to 1923] of the Communist
party in America. The author discusses the
people who actually made up its membership,
its structure and operation, factional differences within, and its activities." Huntting
"Regarded as a chronicle and a source
book, . . . [it] is admirable. Mr. Draper
writes simply and clearly." Nation
Bibliographical references in Notes: p399-
458

Hoover, J. Edgar
Masters of deceit; the story of communism
in America and how to fight it. Holt 1958
374p $6.95   335.4
1 Communism—U.S.   2 Communist Party of
the United States of America
In this account of communism in the United
States, Mr Hoover shows the organization
and operation of the Communist Party and
tells who the Communists are and what they
claim. He describes Communist strategy and
tactics, methods of mass agitation and underground infiltration, espionage and sabotage.
He also tells how to combat communism.
(Publisher)
"The book is not the last word on communism and how to fight it. But it is sound,
practical and detailed." N Y Her Trib Books
Glossary: p339-51. Bibliography of major
Communist "classics": p353-57. International
Communist organizations and publications:
p361-62

Ketchum, Richard M.
(ed.) What is communism? A picture
survey of world communism. . . . New rev.
ed. Dutton 1963 192p illus maps boards $4.95
335.4
1 Communism

First published 1955
"Newly revised and brought up to date by
Abraham Brumberg; art director: Will Anderson, first edition; picture editors: Ruth
Traurig, first edition; [and] Pierce G. Fredericks, revised edition." Title page
Companion volume to the author's: What is
Democracy, entered in class 321.8
"A simple pictorial survey of communism
designed to convey through pictures, captions,
and text the evils of collectivism and the
threat of communist imperialism. The editor
states the basic tenets of communism and
points out its appeals, reviews its history,
describes the present structure of the Soviet
Union, and demonstrates the methods used
to further communist expansion. His broadly
popular treatment, plainly stressing the vicious effects of the doctrine, is a convincing
indictment of communism as opposed to
democracy." Booklist
Includes a glossary and bibliography

336.2 Taxation

Nikolaieff, George A.
(ed.) Taxation and the economy. Wilson,
H.W. 1968 212p (The Reference shelf v39,
no.6) $4.50   336.2
1 Taxation—U.S.   2 U.S.—Economic policy
The purpose of this book "is to view the
role of taxation as an economic tool. At the
same time, because the two are so closely interwoven, the book also concerns itself with
the fundamental economic assumptions that
underlie our Government's actions in the economic sphere." Preface
Bibliography: p203-12

338 Production

Hendrick, Burton J.
The age of big business; a chronicle of the
captains of industry. U.S. Pubs. Assn. 1919
196p (The Chronicles of America ser. v39)
$3.95   338
1 U.S.—Industries—History
First published by Yale University Press
Contents: Industrial America at the end of
the Civil War; First great American trust;
Epic of steel; The telephone: America's most
poetical achievement; Development of public
utilities; Making the world's agricultural machinery; Democratization of the automobile
In this useful authoritative book "the heroes
(often not quite immaculate heroes) of our
tremendous industrial expansion appear in
their habit as they lived. There is no extenuation of their faults, but neither is Mr Hendrick a muckraker for the pleasure of it. He
sees the work of these men in their entirety."
N Y Times Bk R

338.1 Agricultural production. Food supply

Cochrane, Willard W.
The world food problem; a guardedly optimistic view. Crowell 1969 331p map (The
Crowell Economics ser) $7.95   338.1
1 Food supply 2 Population
"This book analyzes the relationship of food
production to consumption in both developed
and undeveloped countries. . . . Data presented
concludes that the future ratio of food produced per capita can be kept near the present
level if technical skill and personal determination remain strong. It is assumed that birth
control will aid in the struggle. This is a book
with a rich supply of data concerning food
production and consumption in various countries of the world. It is well edited, clearly
printed, and useful for those interested in
world food problems." Science Bks

Dumont, René
The hungry future [by] René Dumont and Bernard Rosier; tr. from the French by Rosamund Linell and R. B. Sutcliffe; foreword by Thomas Balogh. Praeger 1969 271p $6.95
338.1
1 Food supply 2 Population
Original French edition, 1966
"The authors predict that 1980 will be a point of no return in food production, and advocate world-coordinated trade, the extensive application of technically advanced agricultural methods, intensified use of fertilizers, land reform, the development of new sources of nutrition, and birth or population control." AAAS Science Book List
"The book's chapters on technical matters . . . are fascinating, as is the survey of the world's agricultural economy today. But the best thing about it is the positive tone the authors take: there are ways to surmount our predicament, they say; the scientific tools are at hand, and it is merely a matter of putting them to work." New Yorker
Bibliography: p262-63

Freeman, Orville L.
World without hunger. Praeger 1968 190p illus $6.50
338.1
1 Food supply 2 Agriculture 3 Technical assistance
The author "outlines the history of U.S. food relief to foreign countries back to World War I, traces the history of the Food for Peace Act (a food assistance program linked to other U.S. aid in developing countries), of U.S. technical assistance in agriculture, and of American private and voluntary projects to help agriculture abroad. He sees the world food crisis as bad, and worsening, but finds great hope in measures taken by the U.S. and other advanced countries to help the underdeveloped countries to help them help themselves." Pub W
Bibliography: p181-85

Paddock, William
Famine—1975! America's decision: who will survive? By William and Paul Paddock. Little 1967 276p illus boards $6.95 **338.1**
1 Food supply 2 Underdeveloped areas 3 Agriculture and state
The authors predict that "catastrophic famines are inevitable by 1975; they will last for years . . . and incite economic upheaval, social turmoil and revolution over large areas of Asia, Africa and Latin America. . . . Only the United States will be in a position to help. Even so, it will not have enough food to keep alive all the starving and must therefore decide which countries to save. In the 'Time of Famines,' the book concludes, supremacy in world affairs will lie with the nation that has the most food and the resolve to use it as a source of power." N Y Times Bk R
References: p249-62

Stone, Archie A.
Careers in agribusiness and industry. Interstate 1970 [2d ed] xxiii, 352p illus $7.95
338.1
1 Agriculture industries and trade 2 Agriculture as a profession
First published 1965
The author offers practical information and advice about various career and business aspects of agriculture. Included are chapters on the food, dairy, grain, feed, livestock, cotton, and farm equipment industries, ornamental horticulture, government services, farm cooperatives and rural electrification

United States. Department of Agriculture
Farmer's world; the yearbook of agriculture. U.S. Govt. Ptg. Off. 1964 592p maps boards $3
338.1
1 Agriculture—Economic aspects 2 Agriculture—U.S. 3 Agricultural administration

"This book reveals the vital stake everybody in the United States has in a healthy export trade for American agriculture, not only because farmers have so much to sell and because the livelihood of so many Americans besides farmers depends on it, but also because the world so greatly needs what we can offer." Foreword
Partial contents: Production; Marketing; World trade; Our trade; Assistance

338.54 Business cycles

Galbraith, John Kenneth
The great Crash, 1929. Houghton 1955 212p $4.95
338.54
1 Business cycles 2 Depressions 3 U.S.—Economic conditions—1919-1933
"1929 was a year marked for a fame that is beyond the ordinary. . . . The author guides the reader from the ascent of the Coolidge and Hoover bull market through the frantic days of the stock market crash, analyzing and reappraising the causes and weighing the chances of its happening again." McClurg. Book News
"Good reading for those who know little or nothing of the period, and for those who have grown complacent about the present." Nation
Includes bibliographical footnotes

338.8 Combinations. Monopolies

Kefauver, Estes
In a few hands: monopoly power in America [by] Estes Kefauver with the assistance of Irene Till; with cartoons by Herblock. Pantheon Bks. 1965 239p boards $6.95
338.8
1 Monopolies 2 Trusts, Industrial 3 U.S. Congress. Senate. Subcommittee on Antitrust and Monopoly
This is an exposé of the evils of a monopoly grip on essential commodities and products: drugs, steel, automobiles and bread. . . . Shocking in its revelations [it] is based upon the proceedings of the Senate Subcommittee on Antitrust and Monopoly, which [the late] Senator Kefauver chaired, 1957-1963. . . . The drug-price hearings were front-page news and produced much corrective legislation. It is good that these hearings and their counterparts about other products can be available in such an incisive book." Pub W
Includes bibliographical footnotes

338.9 Production programs and policies

Galbraith, John Kenneth
Economic development. Harvard Univ. Press 1964 109p $2.95
338.9
1 Economic policy
First published 1962 with title: Economic development in perspective
Contents: The purpose of economic development; The causes of poverty; The choice; Development as a process; Developing and development planning and practice; Education and economic development; Development and the industrial corporation; A postscript on population
"For someone who wishes to make a first acquaintance with the complexities of the most important economic problem of our time, these speeches, wise, moderate and humane, are just the thing. Moreover, below the calm surface there are nicely placed rocks to stub the toes of more experienced swimmers who make a living out of studying, teaching and preaching economic development." New Statesman

338.91 International economic policies

Isenberg, Irwin
(ed.) The developing nations; poverty and progress. Wilson, H.W. 1969 205p (The Reference shelf v41, no.1) $4.50 **338.91**
1 Underdeveloped areas
Divided into four sections (The development decade; What underdevelopment means; Too many people, too little food; and Development and the future) this volume gathers together articles on the problems of nation-building and the prospects for the economic development of emerging nations
Bibliography: p194-205

Myrdal, Gunnar
The challenge of world poverty; a world anti-poverty program in outline; with a foreword by Francis O. Wilcox. Pantheon Bks. 1970 518p $8.95 **338.91**
1 Underdeveloped areas 2 Economic assistance 3 Asia—Economic conditions
"The Christian A. Herter Lecture series"
This book is "based on a series of lectures which Dr. Myrdal delivered at the Johns Hopkins School of Advanced International Studies in 1969." Publisher's note
The author "returns to an earlier work, his monumental 'Asian Drama,' summarizing his analyses of world poverty in that study—with heavy emphasis on anti-Communist India and Pakistan—and going on to develop his suggested solutions on a world-wide scale. Repeatedly Myrdal stresses the self-help theme. . . . He runs the gamut of problems, from the abstract notion of national status to the very concrete issue each country must resolve in population control, education, agriculture and administration. Myrdal also examines trade and capital investment, and has some criticism for the opportunistic juggling of aid statistics by Western powers." Pub W
Bibliography included in Notes: p491-518

Ward, Barbara
The rich nations and the poor nations. Norton 1962 159p $3.75 **338.91**
1 Underdeveloped areas 2 Economic policy 3 World politics—1945-
The author believes that the progressive political and economic advances of the richer nations of the world during the past two centuries are occuring simultaneously in the underdeveloped world at breakneck speed today. Without outside help they may succumb to Communism. Why and how the West must meet this challenge is the theme of the book. (Publisher)
"Miss Ward's cool detachment and preciseness are most refreshing. In a short book . . . she manages to hack a trail through a thicket of isms and problems of truly global scope, without either over-powering or over-simplifying. We emerge on the other side at least on speaking terms with the issues. And en route one may pick up some fascinating baubles of history." Christian Science Monitor

338.973 U.S.—Economic policy

Forman, Brenda
America's place in the world economy. Harcourt 1969 127p illus $3.50 **338.973**
1 U.S.—Economic policy 2 International economic relations 3 U.S.—Economic conditions
"Curriculum-related books"
"Well-organized, comprehensive, clear, and detailed, this is a fine introduction to a complex topic. The first section deals with the sources and extent of American economic power; the second discusses our commitments to the world economy in treaties, foreign aid, military aid, and the United Nations; the third describes the limitations and pressures that

result; the final section discusses the complicated (and apparently insoluble) problems of our payments deficit. The writing is objective and authoritative; the book is all the more useful because it considers the political causes and implications of economic relationships." Chicago. Children's Book Center

Galbraith, John Kenneth
The new industrial state. 2d ed. rev. Houghton 1971 xxii, 423p $8.95 **338.973**
1 Industry and state—U.S. 2 U.S.—Economic policy 3 Corporations
ISBN 0-395-12475-1
First published 1967
The author "insists that the imperatives of technology and growth of giant corporations are bringing about a planned economy. He sees government increasingly allied to industry and sees marketplace dictates and the entrepreneur displaced. Management is viewed as the new directing force, its decision making assisted by the 'technostructure' of educated, experienced specialists. Galbraith poses questions regarding the impact of these changes on education and social and political behavior and regarding reforms or remedies to keep human needs paramount." Booklist
"The crucial question in evaluating [the author's theory] is whether corporate enterprise and government have in fact achieved the degree of control he attributes to them. . . . [Nevertheless his book] deserves the widest possible attention and discussion." N Y Times Bk R

339 Distribution of capital goods and consumption of consumer goods

Miller, Herman Phillip
Rich man, poor man. Crowell 1971 305p $8.95 **339**
1 Income 2 U.S.—Economic conditions—1945-
ISBN 0-690-70039-3
First published 1964
The author has analyzed U.S. income statistics "and has produced some interesting comparative studies of poverty, wealth, occupational trends, and earning power based on age, sex, race, education, and other factors. Though he mainly evaluates past and present conditions he does venture some predictions for the two decades ahead and pinpoints some sociological and economic problems arising, out of present income drifts." Booklist
"Miller's commentary is informed by American liberalism. He assumes that the American system's economic growth remains impressive, that the government is generally responsible to the people, and that the system's faults can be remedied if we do not hide them from ourselves. Miller takes a calm, statistical view of our income distribution, outlining the problem of poverty without raising his voice." Choice

Veblen, Thorstein
The theory of the leisure class; introduction by Robert Lekachman. Viking 1967 400p pa $1.95 **339**
1 Leisure class
"A Viking Compass book"
First published 1899 by Macmillan
In this economic treatise. "Veblen held that the feudal subdivision of classes had continued into modern times, the lords employing themselves uselessly . . . while the lower classes labored at industrial pursuits to support the whole of society. The leisure class, Veblen said, justifies itself solely by practicing 'conspicuous leisure and conspicuous consumption'; he defined waste as any activity not contributing to material productivity." Benét. The Reader's Encyclopedia
"Whatever may be the deficiencies of Veblen in the scientific role which he assumed, the effect of his work has been to stimulate some of the best scientific work of the present century in the field of the social sciences." Odum's Am Masters of Social Science

74

339.4 Consumption and conservation of income and wealth

McClellan, Grant S.
(ed.) The consuming public. Wilson, H.W. 1968 219p (The Reference shelf v40, no.3) $4.50 **339.4**
1 Consumer protection 2 Consumption (Economics)
This compilation deals with consumer problems and protection in America, from the standpoint of government, business and consumers' organizations
Arranged topically under the following headings: The citizen as consumer; The role of government as protector; Business and consumer protection; Consumer concerns; The consumer interest movement; Bibliography

Packard, Vance
The waste makers. McKay 1960 340p $6.50 **339.4**
1 Consumption (Economics) 2 U.S.—Economic conditions—20th century
In this survey of waste in our economic life due, he says, to overproduction, the author questions the morality and economic validity of a system that in order to exist depends upon artificially shortening the useful life of its products. In his analysis of this philosophy of waste he tells who the waste makers are, how they operate, and what they do to us. (Publisher)
"Mr. Packard offers some suggestions on how the trend to wastefulness can be curbed. . . . Take or leave the author's remedies, however, he must be credited with an outsanding journalistic effort in stating the problem, in speaking out boldly against our scandalous prodigality. There are few wasted words in this book." Best Sellers
Reference notes: p329-30

Smith, Carlton
The Time-Life Book of family finance, by Carlton Smith, Richard Putnam Pratt and the editors of Time-Life Books; illus. by Lionel Kalish. Time-Life Bks. [1970 c1969] 415p illus $11.95 **339.4**
1 Finance, Personal
Contents: Money; Credit; Daily expenses; Automobiles; Life insurance; Second incomes; Your house; Vacations; The younger generation; Income tax; Savings; Investor's guide; Your estate; Retirement; Bibliography
"Many tables, sketches, forms, and other visual inserts add greatly to the understanding of the chapters and help to set the book in a class by itself." Library J

Trump, Fred
Buyer beware! Abingdon 1965 207p $3.50 **339.4**
1 Consumer education 2 Fraud 3 Consumer protection
"An exposé of common confidence games and other ways the public has been defrauded; by fake guarantees; magazine salesmen using sob stories; 'homework' schemes; home improvement rackets; franchise and repair rackets; health quackery; food fads; investment, real estate and insurance trickery; and the false lure of the vanity press in publishing. The author tells succinctly how to avoid being defrauded and where to turn for help. Much of the information came from Better Business Bureaus. A very useful book." Pub W
Publications: p198-202

340 Law

Holmes, Oliver Wendell, 1841-1935
The mind and faith of Justice Holmes; his speeches, essays, letters, and judicial opinions; selected and ed. with introduction and commentary by Max Lerner. Modern Lib. [1954 c1943] 474p $4.95, lib. bdg. $3.89 **340**
1 Law—U.S. 2 U.S.—Constitutional law

"The Modern Library of the world's best books"
Selections "chosen to reveal the great jurist not only as a leader in legal thinking but also as a fine human being." Booklist
"Mr. Lerner has provided for us a comprehensive and reasonably complete record. His interpretations, analyses, and the excerpts he has selected, usually fairly in relation to their context, are, of course, his own. The reader is afforded a valuable opportunity to reach his own conclusions and to weigh them in the balance, for or against those quite eloquently and convincingly set down by an expert." Christian Science Monitor
Bibliography: p452-60

Sloan, Irving J.
Youth and the law; rights, privileges and obligations. [New rev. ed] Oceana 1970 122p (Legal almanac ser) $3 **340**
1 Law—U.S.
ISBN 0-379-11073-3
Replaces: Legal status of young adults, by Parnell J. T. Callahan
"This Almanac is written to give young people an opportunity to gain some measure of knowledge concerning their legal rights and corresponding obligations. Among the subjects explored are: citizenship, selective service, voting, marriage, divorce and annulment, support, drugs, and criminal law." Publisher's note
Includes a glossary of legal terms

340.69 Law as a profession

Asbell, Bernard
What lawyers really do: six lawyers talk about their life and work. Wyden, P.H. 1970 114p $3.95 **340.69**
1 Law as a profession
"Six young attorneys tell in the first person exactly what they do, how they do it, how they got where they are, and what they like and dislike about their work. Each one is engaged in a different phase of his profession—a small-town family lawyer; a partner in a Wall Street law firm; a house counsel employed by a large corporation; a defense attorney in criminal law; a prosecutor; and an attorney experienced in providing legal services to the poor." Publisher's note

341 International law

Morgenthau, Hans J.
Politics among nations; the struggle for power and peace. 4th ed. Knopf 1967 xxiv, 615, xxiii p illus maps $12.95 **341**
1 International relations 2 Power (Social sciences)
First published 1948
"This book developed from lectures in international politics which I have given at the University of Chicago since 1943. Though it covers the traditional subject matter of courses in international relations, special emphasis is placed on basic problems of international law, international organization, and diplomatic history." Foreword to the first edition
"The classic defense of the power-centered view of international relations. Not hammock reading, the book argues powerfully for pursuing the national self-interest and suffering any consequences." Good Reading
Bibliography: p597-610. Historical glossary: p611-30

341.13 United Nations

Comay, Joan
The UN in action; foreword by Adlai E. Stevenson. Macmillan (N Y) 1965 150p illus maps $4.50 **341.13**
1 United Nations

Comay, Joan—*Continued*

The author discusses the functions of the United Nations by first describing its various peace keeping operations in the Israel-Arab conflict, Korea, the Suez-Sinai crisis, Kashmir, the Congo, Yemen, Cyprus, Jordan and Lebanon. She then explains the activities of the United Nations' agencies dealing with food; health; work; child care; education, science and culture; money; atomic energy; and other areas

"A simplified yet graphic description of the U.N. in the field rather than in session. . . . A chart of the U.N. and its related agencies . . . are appended. Illustrated with maps and many photographs." Booklist

Coyle, David Cushman

The United Nations and how it works. Columbia Univ. Press $7.50   341.13

1 United Nations

First published 1955 by the New American Library. Periodically revised to bring it up to date

The author surveys the principles and activities of the United Nations, its agencies, and its related organizations and analyzes the debate and recommendations of the UN on various world problems. Includes complete charter and other important documents

Eichelberger, Clark M.

UN. Harper boards $5.95   341.13

1 United Nations

First published 1955 as: UN: the first ten years, and revised at five year intervals, with variable subtitles

The author sketches the history of the United Nations and evaluates its current strengths and weaknesses and his hope for its future." Publisher's note

Stevenson, Adlai E. 1900-1965

Looking outward; years of crisis at the United Nations; ed. with commentary by Robert L. and Selma Schiffer; preface by John F. Kennedy. Harper 1963 xx, 295p $5.95   341.13

1 United Nations   2 U.S.—Foreign relations

Analyzed in Essay and general literature index

"A selection of Mr. Stevenson's speeches and statements as United States representative to the UN. They are a record of American sentiments and stands on some of the great issues of our time—The Common Market, Cuba, Latin America, recognition of Red China—as they came up and were dealt with in the U.N. The speeches are really spoken essays in Mr. Stevenson's own straight-forward and eloquent style. Most of the writing comes from Stevenson the diplomat, but the memorial tributes to Eleanor Roosevelt and Dag Hammarskjold are Stevenson the man." Library J

United Nations. Office of Public Information

Everyman's United Nations. The Author $6   341.13

1 United Nations

First published 1948. Frequently revised

A complete handbook of the activities and evolution of the United Nations and its related agencies, [the book] is divided into three main parts: Part I provides an introduction to the Organization as a whole—its founding, its purposes and principles, its main organs and their functions. Part II covers the work of the United Nations and Part III describes the structure and activities of the Inter-Governmental Agencies related to the United Nations. (Publisher)

Yearbook. The Author illus $25   341.13

1 United Nations—Yearbooks

Annual. First published 1947

"Describes the proceedings and activities of the United Nations and its related inter-governmental agencies during [the year]. . . . Political, security, economic, social, legal, administrative, and budgetry questions are covered." Pub W

Vincent, Jack E.

A handbook of the United Nations. Barrons Educ. Ser. 1969 211p $5.25   341.13

1 United Nations

This book is intended as a survey of the major organs and functions of the United Nations. The entries are alphabetically arranged under headings such as General Assembly, Substantive question, Veto

"In addition to articles on the structure, function, concepts, and principal agencies of the U.N. system, summaries of all decisions and advisory opinions of the International Court of Justice, and the text of the charter are included." Booklist

341.18   Regional associations. Atlantic community

Cleveland, Harlan

NATO: the transatlantic bargain. Harper 1970 204p map $6.95   341.18

1 North Atlantic Treaty Organization

"The former U.S. Ambassador to NATO from 1965 to 1969 describes the challenges the alliance faced during his four years: the ABM debate, arms limitation talks, and the nonproliferation treaty, as well as the three crises occasioned by French withdrawal, U.S. intentions of reducing its forces in Europe, and the Warsaw Pact invasion of Czechoslovakia." Library J

"This is an interesting . . . inquiry into the 'bargain' by which 14 NATO Allies share the burdens of 'nuclear uncertainty.' Cleveland puts his sharpest focus on the day-to-day consultations among these allies, which he credits with sustaining a 'generation of peace' in Europe." Pub W

Bibliography included in Notes: p191-98

MacCloskey, Monro

North Atlantic Treaty Organization; guardian of peace and security. Rosen, R. 1960 127p illus (Military research ser) lib. bdg. $3.78   341.18

1 North Atlantic Treaty Organization

"It is the purpose of this book to tell the story of NATO: why it was created; what the provisions of the Treaty are; how it is organized; what some of its problems are; and what it is accomplishing." Introduction

341.4   International criminal law

Columbia Broadcasting System, inc. CBS News

Trial at Nuremberg, by the staff of CBS News. Based on the CBS News television series "The Twentieth Century"; project editor, William E. Shapiro; illus. with photographs. Watts, F. 1967 66p illus maps $2.95   341.4

1 Nuremberg Trial of Major German War Criminals, 1945-1946   2 World War, 1939-1945 —Atrocities

At head of title: The Twentieth Century

In 1945 twenty-four men and six Nazi organizations were indicted for conspiracy, war crimes and crimes against humanity. This is the story of the trial and of the infamous men and women who were sentenced. (Publisher)

"A brief, bare, objective, well-illustrated book. . . . The trial of Nuremberg was an embarrassment to civilized mankind. It is outlined here formally and circumspectly." N Y Times Bk R

341.6 Pacific settlement of disputes

Douglas, William O.
International dissent: six steps toward world peace. Random House 1971 155p $4.95 **341.6**

1 Peace 2 International relations

The author is concerned with the global crisis in international relations and the need to find non-military solutions for it. He provides a step-by-step analysis of the problems standing in the way of international accord, together with a program for their solution. (Publisher)

He tells us, "lucidly and cogently and unpretentiously, what should be done to make the world a viable community. Perhaps some of the young may listen—or, if not the young, then at least the concerned citizen. . . . The author does not quail at the implications of the abandonment of the war system. . . . The task is indeed 'onerous,' but Douglas would say it can be done because it must. His is a telling tract for the times." Sat R

342.73 U.S.—Constitution and Constitutional law

Barker, Lucius J.
(ed.) Civil liberties and the Constitution; cases and commentaries [ed. by] Lucius J. Barker [and] Twiley W. Barker, Jr. Prentice-Hall 1970 471p $8.95 **342.73**

1 Civil rights 2 U.S. Supreme Court 3 U.S.—Constitutional law
SBN 13-168211-3

"This book focuses on some basic issues in civil liberties: free exercise of religion and church-state relations; freedom of expression and association; rights of persons accused of crime; and problems related to racial justice. Each major problem area is treated first in an introductory commentary. These commentaries summarize the development of case law and provide historical perspective [1833-1968] for examining and evaluating the issues presented. In short, this volume points up civil-liberties issues as they have been expounded by and in leading judicial decisions, primarily those of the Supreme Court." Preface
Includes bibliographies

Beard, Charles A.
An economic interpretation of the Constitution of the United States; with new introduction. Macmillan (N Y) 1935 xxi, 330p $6.95 **342.73**

1 U.S. Constitution 2 U.S.—Constitutional history 3 U.S.—Economic conditions
First published 1913

"A book for the special student in which the author places the whole emphasis upon four groups of personality interests, money, public securities, manufactures and trade and shipping, as instrumental in the framing and acceptance of the Constitution." Booklist

"The book is convincing, and will occupy a distinguished position among the mass of works in which the 'materialist conception' is elaborated." Athenæum

The Supreme Court and the Constitution; with an introduction and bibliographies by Alan F. Westin. Prentice-Hall 1962 149p (Classics in history ser) pa $1.95 **342.73**

1 U.S. Supreme Court 2 U.S. Constitution 3 U.S.—Constitutional history

"A Spectrum book"
First published 1912

"Timely discussion of the question as to whether the framers of the Constitution intended that the Supreme Court should have the power to declare laws unconstitutional. In proving that such was their intent the author cites seventeen out of the twenty-five leaders of the Constitutional Convention of 1787 as being in favor of judicial control." Booklist

"For a brief and quite impersonal piece of historical research the book is eminently readable." Independent

Bowen, Catherine Drinker
Miracle at Philadelphia; the story of the Constitutional Convention, May to September 1787. Little 1966 346p illus map $7.50 **342.73**

1 U.S. Constitutional Convention, 1787 2 U.S.—Constitutional history

"An Atlantic Monthly Press book"

"Writing from sources—delegates' letters and diaries; contemporary reports; James Madison's faithful minutes—Catherine Drinker Bowen draws [a] . . . picture of the men, issues and background of the Constitutional Convention held at Philadelphia in the hot summer of 1787." Pub W

"The author is brilliantly successful in placing the reader right there in the Pennsylvania State House during those four sweltering months. She not only brings the principal actors to life; she helps us to sense the feeling and attitudes of the times." Christian Science Monitor

Bibliography included in Author's note: p327-30

Chidsey, Donald Barr
The birth of the Constitution; an informal history. Crown 1964 207p illus $3.95 **342.73**

1 U.S. Constitutional Convention, 1787 2 U.S. Constitution

This narrative of the making of the Constitution develops the conflict of factions and personal interests as if the reader were in Philadelphia in 1787 hearing the arguments over a permanent replacement for the Articles of Confederation

"The personalities of the delegates are skillfully presented in a lively, colloquial style and the conflicts of interest between large and small states and rural and urban communities are clearly indicated, as are also the slow, laborious steps by which the important compromises were finally reached. Interesting and informative history for the general reader. . . . Appendixes include résumés of the Virginia and New Jersey plans, the text of the Constitution, and a bibliography." Booklist

Creamer, J. Shane
A citizen's guide to legal rights. Holt 1971 336p $7.95 **342.73**

1 U.S.—Constitutional law 2 Civil rights 3 Criminal investigation
SBN 03-085057-6

The author "offers an extremely informative discussion of man's constitutional rights. In a succinct and easily understandable presentation replete with citations and quotations, he explains probable cause, investigative methods, arrest, search, seizure, and the Suppression of Evidence Rule. He further treats a selected number of Supreme Court cases involving the Fourth, Fifth, and Sixth Amendments." Library J

Douglas, William O.
A living Bill of Rights; drawings by Douglas Gorsline. Doubleday 1961 72p illus $2.95 **342.73**

1 U.S. Constitution—Amendments 2 Civil rights

"An evaluation of the first ten Amendments to the Constitution. It relates the principles of today's major issues: education, our racial problems, and the Anti-Communist and loyalty questions." Huntting

"This is a book admirably suited for high school students or college freshmen, although it could be profitably read by all adults. The style is somewhat wooden and the philosophic concepts behind the Bill of Rights are rather over-simplified, but Justice Douglas's ardor and sincerity more than make up for these deficiencies." Sat R

Bibliography included in Appendix: p70-72

Farrand, Max
The framing of the Constitution of the United States. Yale Univ. Press 1913 281p $6.50   **342.73**

1 U.S. Constitutional Convention, 1787 2 U.S. Constitution

"Drawing from the daily records of the Convention, the private correspondence of important delegates, Pierce's character sketches of his fellow delegates, contemporary pamphlets, and other sources, this is an account of great merit. Reporting chronologically rather than topically, Farrand compares the Constitution with the Articles of Confederation and does not see a great difference. Emphasis is also placed on the Great Compromise." A Guide to Reading in Am History

"While the narrative is made simple and references are omitted, the book is the result of a scholarly investigation." Dial

Full index and appendix containing text of the Constitution and other documents

The Federalist
The Federalist; or, The new Constitution, by Alexander Hamilton, James Madison and John Jay   **342.73**

1 U.S. Constitution

Some editions are:
Dutton (Everyman's lib) $2.95 Introduction by W. R. Brock
Harvard Univ. Press (The John Harvard lib) $7.50 Edited by Benjamin Fletcher Wright
Modern Lib. $2.95, lib. bdg. $2.69 With an introduction by Edward Mead Earle
Wesleyan Univ. Press $15 Edited with an introduction and notes by Jacob E. Cooke

"From 27 Oct. 1787 to 2 April 1788, 77 essays were published in the semi-weekly 'Independent Journal' of New York, entitled 'The Federalist,' and signed first 'A Citizen of New York' then 'Publius.' Eight more were added when they were collected in book form. . . . They were so acute and massively learned in their exposition of the true intent of the Constitution, that even the courts have accepted them as authoritative comments in doubtful cases; and they are held by all the civilized world as among the noblest storehouses of political philosophy in existence, a classic textbook of political science." Encyclopedia Americana

Garraty, John A.
(ed.) Quarrels that have shaped the Constitution. Harper 1964 276p $4.95   **342.73**

1 U.S.—Constitutional law 2 U.S.—Constitutional history 3 U.S. Supreme Court

Analyzed in Essay and general literature index

Sixteen historians analyze Supreme Court decisions. "The cases covered here, ranging from the time of Chief Justice John Marshall to Chief Justice Earl Warren, dramatize how the Supreme Court, in casual and unplanned fashion, has increased its power until today its influence affects every aspect of American life. Civil rights cases from Dred Scott through the school desegregation case, are highlighted." Publisher's note

Hand, Learned
The Bill of Rights. Harvard Univ. Press 1958 82p $2.50   **342.73**

1 U.S. Constitution—Amendments 2 Civil rights 3 U.S. Supreme Court

"Oliver Wendell Holmes lectures, 1958"

"Judge Hand, in three lectures delivered before the Harvard Law School examines the function of the Supreme Court in declaring invalid statutes of Congress and of States, because of conflict with the Bill of Rights. He finds no ground in the Constitution for the invalidating power, but considers it an historical necessity, maintaining that without some arbiter whose decisions would be final, the whole system of government would collapse." Library J

"Learned Hand is beyond challenge in his devotion to the values of freedom but nearly a half-century as a Federal judge makes him skeptical of judicial omnicompetence to correct democratic error." N Y Times Bk R

Konvitz, Milton R.
(ed.) Bill of Rights reader; leading Constitutional cases. 4th ed. rev. and enl. Cornell Univ. Press 1968 xxiv, 1198p (Cornell Studies in civil liberty) $15   **342.73**

1 U.S. Constitution—Amendments 2 Civil rights 3 U.S.—Constitutional law

First published 1957

This source book of cases dealing with the constitutional amendments "should be of great value to any teacher who deals with the subject of civil rights and civil liberties with his students. It is not only a good resource book to consult for the thinking and opinions of the Court, but it is a book which can be read with profit by the more able high school student." Social Educ

Rossiter, Clinton
Alexander Hamilton and the Constitution. Harcourt 1964 372p $6.75   **342.73**

1 U.S.—Constitutional law 2 Hamilton, Alexander

"A reappraisal of the ideas and achievements of Alexander Hamilton by a scholarly writer who has carefully documented an impressive amount of evidence to prove that Hamilton sincerely labored for a powerful federal government that could thrive in a prosperous industrial America. . . . [An] advanced [book]." Library J

Bibliographical references included in Notes: p259-348

Seedtime of the Republic; the origin of the American tradition of political liberty. Harcourt 1953 558p $8.50   **342.73**

1 U.S.—Constitutional history 2 U.S.—Politics and government 3 Liberty

Written from the viewpoint of Constitutional history, this study concerns "the origin and rise of the American tradition of political liberty. The book is divided into three parts: a background study of liberty in the Colonies; chapters on the 'most notable thinkers' of the Colonial period: and political theories expressed and acted upon, 1765-1776." Book Rev Digest

"Though long, the book is so arranged . . . that students and their teachers should find this a useful introduction." Am Hist R

1787: the grand Convention. Macmillan (N Y) 1966 443p illus (The New American history ser) $7.95   **342.73**

1 U.S. Constitutional Convention, 1787 2 U.S. Constitution 3 U.S.—Politics and government

The author gives a "complete account of the meeting in Philadelphia of fifty-five delegates from twelve states to produce the Constitution of the United States." Bk Buyer's Guide

"A devotee of personality sketches, the author sprinkles his pages with anecdotes about the [Founding] Fathers as they move on and off his stage. He has skillfully molded his main characters. . . . Rossiter sets forth his theme unperturbed, by historiographic controversies." Sat R

A select bibliography: p337-48. Documents: p349-410. Notes: p411-24

Van Doren, Carl
The great rehearsal; the story of the making and ratifying of the Constitution of the United States. Viking 1948 336p illus $5   **342.73**

1 U.S. Constitutional Convention, 1787 2 U.S. Constitution

The author "has taken the great episode of the making of the United States Constitution and followed it—step by step—in terms of the personalities who took part and the conflicts of interest which had to be reconciled." Hunting

"This lively account of the problems facing the Colonial Confederation in 1787 makes that period both understandable and surprisingly close to the present. For mature high school students." Minnesota

Sources and acknowledgments: p321-22

343 Criminal law. Punishment. Trials

Aymar, Brandt
A pictorial history of the world's great trials; from Socrates to Eichmann [by] Brandt Aymar and Edward Sagarin. Crown 1967 373p illus $10   **343**

1 Trials
"Here, in the thirty-one trials we have chosen, we have sought to find both the significant and the cross-sectional, that would capture both the spirit of courts and the spirits of many types of courts; those of many nations, civilian and military, and even of an unofficial or 'rump' nature." Introduction
Bibliography: p559-64

Bedau, Hugo Adam
(ed.) The death penalty in America; an anthology. Rev. ed. Aldine Pub. [1968 c1967] 584p illus $9.50   **343**

1 Capital punishment
First published 1964
1964 edition analyzed in Essay and general literature index
A volume of "selections covering the pros and cons, public opinion, deterrence, the success of abolition in states which have tried it, and the viewpoints of penology, law enforcement, sociology, psychology, and religion, plus essays by Dr. Bedau written especially to cover aspects on which no published material was available." Library J
"Admittedly weighted toward the abolitionist position, this volume nevertheless contains a wealth of objective information on the death penalty, well-indexed." Ann Am Acad
"An essential purchase for all schools still using the subject as a debate topic." Minnesota
Bibliography: p565-74

Berrigan, Daniel
The trial of the Catonsville Nine. Beacon Press 1970 122p illus $5.95   **343**

1 Trials
SBN 8070-0548-7
Father Berrigan presents "the unfolding record of his trial—along with eight companions, including his brother, Father Philip Berrigan—following their raid on a Selective Service office in Catonsville, Md., in which they dramatized their resistance to the draft and the Vietnam war by burning draft files with napalm. The 'raid' occurred in May, 1968; the trial ended in verdicts of guilty. . . . Berrigan conceives and treats this compelling trial-drama along the formal lines of a secular passion play." Pub W

De Camp, L. Sprague
The great monkey trial. Doubleday 1968 538p illus map $7.95   **343**

1 Trials 2 Evolution 3 Scopes, John Thomas
"An exhaustive account of the trial in 1925 of a Tennessee schoolteacher for teaching evolution in the public schools. . . . [The account is] based on archives of the American Civil Liberties Union, which cooperated with the defense, on newspaper articles, on correspondence and interviews with participants, and on a variety of secondary sources." Booklist
"This broadly inclusive, thoroughly documented narrative . . . is without doubt to be rated as the definitive account. . . . There are numerous interesting details not found in any of the half-dozen books previously written on the subject." Science
Bibliography: p517-23

Ernst, Morris L.
Censorship: the search for the obscene, by Morris L. Ernst and Alan U. Schwartz. With an introduction by Philip Scharper. Macmillan (N Y) 1964 288p (Milestones of law ser) $6.95   **343**

1 Obscenity (Law) 2 Censorship

"For reader and writer, film-maker and theatergoer—for everyone concerned in the field of communications—here is [an] account of the centuries-long battle between freedom of expression and the watchdogs of public morality. [The authors convey] the history of what, in law, has been considered obscene, pornographic, prurient, indecent, and 'dirty.' From 'notorious' novels to naturalistic movies, from sex education for juveniles to sex magazines for adults—all phases of the controversial field are covered. The role of censorship—official and private—is documented in terms of actual cases, briefs, and judicial decisions." Publisher's note
"It consists in good part of excerpts from famous judicial opinions. . . . Technicalities are pruned and the result is a solid work, informative and easy to follow." N Y Times Bk R

Nizer, Louis
My life in court. Doubleday 1961 542p $6.95   **343**

1 Trials
An "account by a successful trial lawyer of the legal drama, in preparation and in the courtroom, of seven of his important cases. Nizer . . . evokes sympathy for the cause of his clients and respect for the high standards of an ethical legal practitioner, at the same time revealing delight in the contest and the ego gratification of final victory. . . . The largest single section is the narration of the libel suit of news correspondent Quentin Reynolds against columnist Westbrook Pegler. [Includes selections of court transcript]." Booklist
"Nizer is interested in the drama, including the human reactions of the people involved as well as the quirks in the law. No murder cases are here. There are divorce, libel, plagiarism, and the negligence of a physician." N Y Her Trib Books

Scopes, John T.
Center of the storm; memoirs of John T. Scopes [by] John T. Scopes and James Presley. Holt 1967 277p $5.95   **343**

1 Trials 2 Evolution
"The defendant in the famous 'Monkey Trial' of 1925 . . . [gives his] personal account of the trial, and of the social milieu in which it took place." Publisher's note
"42 years later, the man who sat in 'the center of the storm' writes . . . a casual account of the entire controversy that goes down as easily as a drink of branch water. A shot of Mencken's sour-mash prose would be needed to make a decent highball of this amiable recollection, but [the] . . . memoir-unsensational and unpretentious—is quietly perceptive." Newsweek
"Scopes' clear strengths as a man—self-effacement, gentle irony to all sides—are, equally clearly, his shortcomings as a memoirist. He lacks the conviction of the unique importance of 'his' life-in-history. . . . [He] seems also to lack—charmingly but baffling and a little disturbingly—an imaginative sense of the enduring importance, permanence, and virulence of the conflict of which he was a brief center." Book Week

347.9 Judicial system. Supreme Court

Acheson, Patricia C.
The Supreme Court; America's judicial heritage. Dodd 1961 270p illus $4   **347.9**

1 U.S. Supreme Court
"This is not a book on constitutional law. It is primarily an attempt to [explain] . . . the role of the Supreme Court in the nation's history, the political and economic origins of some of the cases decided by that court and the impact of those decisions on the life of the nation." Preface
"The author writes with interest and competence; the material is well-organized. . . . Not a book for the browsing reader, this will be one that is most valuable to the serious student of

Acheson, Patricia C.—*Continued*

American history. Appended are the Constitution, a list of judges of the Supreme Court arranged by presidential appointment, a list of sources for cases cited in the book, and an appendix in which case citations are italicized." Chicago. Children's Book Center

Frankfurter, Felix

Mr Justice Holmes and the Supreme Court. 2d ed. Harvard Univ. Press 1961 112p front $3   347.9

1 Holmes, Oliver Wendell, 1841-1935   2 U.S. Supreme Court   3 U.S.—Constitutional law

One section "consists of a series of three lectures delivered at Harvard in 1938 by Professor Frankfurter, which have since gone out of print. The [other section] is a biographical essay [of Holmes] written for the Dictionary of American Biography in 1944, and reprinted in this volume. Both contributions have a timelessness. . . . Under the headings 'Property and Society,' 'Civil Liberties and the Individual,' and the 'Federal System,' the lectures offer much information about Mr. Justice Frankfurter's own philosophy." Library J

Fribourg, Marjorie G.

The Supreme Court in American history; ten great decisions: the people, the times and the issues. Macrae Smith Co. 1965 193p $4.25   347.9

1 U.S. Supreme Court   2 U.S.—Constitutional history

Analyzed in Essay and general literature index

"In a lively, understandable examination of 10 cases brought before the U.S. Supreme Court, the author demonstrates the flexibility of the Constitution in filling the needs of a changing society. Spanning the years from the decision in 'Marbury' v. 'Madison' which established the authority of the Court, to 'Baker' v. 'Carr,' which provided for reapportionment, the account includes well-known decisions about interstate commerce, monopolies, and integration. Each case is preceded by a brief description of the times and the issues and followed by a bibliography of sources. . . . Suggestions for further reading are appended." Booklist

Habenstreit, Barbara

Changing America and the Supreme Court. Messner 1970 191p $3.95, lib. bdg. $3.64
                                                    347.9

1 U.S. Supreme Court
SBN 671-32209-5; 671-32210-9

The aim of this book, "to show the development of the United States Supreme Court in a country undergoing change, is accomplished in a competent manner. Through becoming acquainted with the failures and successes of the Court, the reader becomes familiar with the political, social and economic conditions in the U.S. from 1790 to the present." Best Sellers
Suggested further reading: p188

James, Howard

Crisis in the courts. . . . Rev. ed. McKay 1971 267p $6.95   347.9

1 Courts—U.S.   2 Justice, Administration of

"This book is based on a series of articles that appeared weekly in "The Christian Science Monitor," April to July, 1967." Title page
First published 1968

In this "specific, pointed criticism of state courts across the U.S. . . . [the author] finds: backlogs and delays frustrate justice; the adversary system of trial often does not get at the truth; the police and the courtroom staff are often below-standard; the ethical conduct of lawyers is not always above question. [James] cites names and places all over the country, in this review of defective American justice." Pub W

"This is a revealing and important book. The frightening aspect of it is that James . . . did not have to delve into behind-the-scenes machinations and courthouse corruptions

. . . to document the depressing failure of one-third of this nation's constitutional government. . . . The book has its faults. . . . But the important thing is that [it reminds us that the criminal court] is—and must remain—open to examination, and that responsibility for its operations and end products lies not only with lawyers and judges but with all of us." Book World

Lewis, Anthony

Gideon's trumpet. Random House 1964 262p $6.95   347.9

1 U.S. Supreme Court   2 Law—U.S.   3 Gideon, Clarence Earl

The author "tells the story of Earl Gideon, prisoner, who charged that his sentence was unconstitutional because he had had no legal representation, [and who] carried his case to the Supreme Court, and won." Bk Buyer's Guide

"In these days of momentous decisions, 'Gideon's Trumpet' besides telling of one of those decisions and how it was reached, is a layman's primer on how the Supreme Court is constituted, its restrictions, its powers and how it uses them." Best Sellers
Notes: p239-52. Suggested readings: p253-56

McCart, Samuel W.

Trial by jury; a complete guide to the jury system. [2d ed. rev] Chilton Bks. 1965 204p $4.95   347.9

1 Jury
First published 1964

"The author explains the qualifications and requirements of jury service, with a description of the jury trial system, and a brief history of all phases of a trial by jury." Bk Buyer's Guide

"Mr. McCart has set himself the nearly impossible task of making his book a 'complete' guide and therefore wanders down side roads in an effort to cover every question, every rule, every exception. All in all, however, his book is 'relevant, material and competent.'" Christian Century

United States. Supreme Court

Historic decisions of the Supreme Court [by] Carl Brent Swisher. Van Nostrand 1958 192p pa $1.95   347.9

1 U.S.—Constitutional law
"An Anvil original"

"Contains the essence of historic decisions of the Supreme Court in chronological order. The author gives introductions for each question upon which a decision was made. Illuminates the vital role of the court in American history." A Guide to Reading in Am History

350   Public administration

Marx, Herbert L.

(ed.) Collective bargaining for public employees, by Herbert L. Marx, Jr. Wilson, H.W. 1969 215p (The Reference shelf v41, no.5) $4.50   350

1 Civil service   2 Collective bargaining
SBN 8242-0110-8

The articles included discuss the background of public sector unionism, unions in public employment, teachers and collective bargaining, strikes, the law, and public unionism abroad
Bibliography: p202-15

351.7   Central government. Public order and security

Tully, Andrew

CIA: the inside story. Morrow 1962 276p boards $6.95   351.7

1 U.S. Central Intelligence Agency

Tully, Andrew—*Continued*

"A crisp . . . description of some of the Central Intelligence Agency's espionage activities. Tully . . . admits some of the C.I.A.'s fiascos, notably in the Cuban invasion, but he comes to its defense as giving adequate warning in tense situations abroad. Of the startling operations which he describes, the recruitment of C.I.A. agents within Russia itself is outstanding. Tully notes that he has fictionalized some names and disguised some techniques." Pub W

This "is an extremely readable book. Its contents, however obviously were garnered outside and not inside our country's most publicized secret organization." N Y Times Bk R

352   Local units of government. Police

Arm, Walter

The policeman; an inside look at his role in a modern society. Dutton 1969 160p illus $4.95, lib. bdg. $4.90   352

1 Police 2 New York (City)—Police

This book, using as an example the New York City Police Department, "gives a complete behind-the-scenes look at the police department in operation—from sample questions on the police examination to a description of how a detective solves a seemingly anonymous murder." Publisher's note

Steffens, Lincoln

The shame of the cities; introduction by Louis Joughin. Hill & Wang 1957 214p pa $1.50   352

1 Municipal government 2 Corruption (in politics)

Also available for $4 from Peter Smith "American century series"

First published 1904 by McClure

The author tells "how American cities were being corrupted one by one in our industrial and impersonal society. A casebook for the practice of political reform." A Guide to Reading in Am History

Wood, James Playsted

Scotland Yard. Hawthorn Bks. 1970 211p $5.95   352

1 Great Britain. Metropolitan Police Office. Criminal Investigation Department 2 Crime and criminals—Great Britain

This account of England's crime detection force traces the history and development of the criminal investigation department and describes present-day methods and equipment. Also included are stories of the Yard's cases and chapters on English thieves' jargon and on murder-mystery heroes who deal with a fictional Scotland Yard. (Publisher)

"Included is a worthwhile discussion of Doyle's Sherlock Holmes stories and other detective fiction in which Scotland Yard men have appeared." Booklist

Bibliography: p206-08

353   United States federal and state governments

Acheson, Patricia C.

Our federal government: how it works; an introduction to the United States government; illus. with drawings by Everett Raymond Kinstler. Rev. and enl. ed. Dodd 1969 210p illus $4.50   353

1 U.S.—Politics and government

First published 1958

The author describes the major divisions of our Washington government and explains how they function. He discusses the Constitutional construction of the federal government and development of the executive departments through the years. (Publisher)

"Not detailed enough to be an extensive reference tool, this nonetheless has use as a timely overview of government." Library J

Bailey, Stephen K.

(ed.) American politics and government; essays in essentials. Basic Bks. 1965 284p $5.95   353

1 U.S.—Politics and government 2 Political science

"Various aspects of political science are discussed in the 20 essays included in this volume. Among the contributors are Hans J. Morgenthau, James M. Burns, Avery Leiserson and other authorities in their fields. . . . Among the subjects covered are the Presidency, Congress, the party system, interest groups, state government, international relations, and foreign policy." Library J

Harvey, Donald R.

The Civil Service Commission; foreword by John W. Macy, Jr. Praeger [1969 c1970] 233p illus map (Praeger Lib. of U.S. Government departments and agencies) $6.95   353

1 U.S. Civil Service Commission

The author "explains the structure of the governmental agency established by the Pendleton Act in 1883 to provide a policy of personnel administration. . . . [He] discusses such topics as the wide range of federal occupations, the role of the . . . commission in relation to the President and Congress, [and] the problems of enforcement." Booklist

Additional information in appendixes includes: Career opportunities in personnel management; U.S. Civil Service regions; Civil Service laws; Civil Service commissioners

Bibliography: p227-29

353.03   Executive branch of the federal government

Cunliffe, Marcus

The American Heritage History of the Presidency, by Marcus Cunliffe and the editors of American Heritage, the Magazine of History. Editor in charge: Kenneth W. Leish. Am. Heritage 1968 384p illus $16.50   353.03

1 Executive power—U.S. 2 Presidents—U.S.

This is an "account of the evolution of the Presidency, the influence of the Presidents upon the office, and the changes in the office necessitated by the nation's growth from recent colonial status to the world's greatest power." Bk Buyer's Guide

"A sensible literate, uncontroversial text and a lively variety of illustrations, making altogether a nice comfortable creation, if one can stand the color printing, which lurches unpredictably from decent to frightful." Atlantic

Bibliography: p377

Pusey, Merlo J.

The way we go to war. Houghton 1969 202p $5.95   353.03

1 Executive power—U.S. 2 U.S. Congress 3 U.S.—History, Military

In considering the use of war powers by our Presidents, the author discusses "the original intent of the framers of the Constitution in granting war-making powers to Congress; [and] . . . the disregard of Constitutional law by various Presidents—from Polk, who in 1846 goaded Mexico into war by sending an army into disputed territory, to LBJ, . . . [and his] executive actions in Vietnam, the Congo and the Dominican Republic." Pub W

The author "presents a bristling critique of the 'inherent powers' doctrine which Presidents have seized upon to justify 'executive war-making.' . . . [This is] a thought-provoking book for the citizen concerned about American foreign policy, past and future." Choice

Bibliographical footnotes included

Rossiter, Clinton
The American Presidency. 2d ed. Harcourt 1960 281p $4.50   353.03
  1 Presidents—U.S. 2 Executive power—U.S.
First published 1956
"A revised version of six lectures given on the Charles R. Walgreen Foundation at the University of Chicago, April 23-May 3, 1956." The author
"With clarity and wit [the author] . . . examines the American Presidency and its incumbents. Emphasizing throughout the democratic nature of the office and its tested workability, he discusses the President's multiple duties in domestic and international life and the safeguarding limitations placed upon his powers, traces the historical development of the Presidency, shows the new dimensions added in modern times, and evaluates the policies and achievements of Roosevelt, Truman, and Eisenhower. An informative and stimulating analysis directed toward the general reader." Booklist
Includes bibliography

Schlesinger, Arthur M. 1917-
Congress and the Presidency: their role in modern times [by] Arthur M. Schlesinger, Jr. [and] Alfred De Grazia. Am. Enterprise Inst. 1967 192p (Rational debate seminars) $4.50   353.03
  1 Executive power—U.S. 2 U.S. Congress
"Few political issues are more fundamental or controversial than the question of what roles Congress and the presidency should play in governing our country in modern times. This [debate between Alfred de Grazia and Arthur Schlesinger, Jr] was not designed to resolve disagreements on this issue but to bare their roots in the form of conflicting matters of fact, value, or judgment. . . . This book now brings the debate, just as it took place, into the homes on the general public. Only the sequence has been rearranged, the lectures and rebuttals of Professors Schlesinger and De Grazia being grouped together to make it easier for the reader to follow the basic argument without interruption." Preface
Bibliographical references included in Footnotes: p191-92

353.061   Permanent U.S. government organizations

Brundage, Percival Flack
The Bureau of the Budget; foreword by Robert P. Mayo. Praeger 1970 327p (Praeger Lib. of U.S. Government departments and agencies) $10   353.061
  1 U.S. Bureau of the Budget 2 Budget—U.S.
This "book explains the operations of one of the least known and least understood agencies in the federal government. The author outlines the budget processes, using actual figures to demonstrate the changes a national budget undergoes from its formulation in separate government agencies to its journey through Congress." News of Bks
"While many of the complicated government operations described here may not concern high school students, the explanation of how federal programs are inaugurated and evaluated will be useful." Booklist
Bibliography: p315-20

Henderson, John W.
The United States Information Agency. Praeger 1969 324p (Praeger Lib. of U.S. Government departments and agencies) $8.50   353.061
  1 U.S. Information Agency
The author "describes all aspects of the U.S.I.A. the agency responsible for the expression and support of U.S. policy abroad. He traces its history; incisively analyzes its techniques, its current operations, and its organization in Washington and overseas; and outlines the activities of the Voice of America." Am News of Bks

"For students of history and government, for those who appreciate detail, for the person seeking a career in the USIA, this is a very important book. The appendixes, listing career opportunities in the agency, summarizing laws and regulations specifically relating to the USIA, and giving the agency's fiscal budgets for the years 1954 to 1967, are invaluable sources of information. A bibliography is also included." Library J

353.1   U.S. Department of State

Blancké, W. Wendell
The Foreign Service of the United States; foreword by Loy W. Henderson. Praeger 1969 286p illus (Praeger Lib. of U.S. Government departments and agencies) $7.95   353.1
  1 U.S. Department of State. Foreign Service 2 U.S.—Diplomatic and consular service
An account "of the service's history, duties and responsibilities, organizational structure, daily operations, problems, and relations with other United States agencies such as the CIA and USIS." Library J
"Detailed, authoritative career information is combined with a survey for the general reader. . . . Appendixes include a list of foreign service posts and a short bibliography." Booklist

Simpson, Smith
Anatomy of the State Department. Houghton 1967 285p $5.95   353.1
  1 U.S. Department of State
The author raises "questions about State Department recruiting, training, administration, and planning. He points to the chaos caused by automatic thoughtless rotation of personnel . . . and the terrible impact of the government's dictum of 'move up or out,' achieve promotion or resign, which has made the State man think only of his own personal career. Simpson cites specific blunders and shortcomings." Pub W
Bibliographies included in Notes: p249-68

353.2   U.S. Department of the Treasury. Internal Revenue Service

Chommie, John C.
The Internal Revenue Service. Praeger 1970 267p illus map (Praeger Lib. of U.S. Government departments and agencies) $9.50   353.2
  1 U.S. Internal Revenue Service 2 Taxation—U.S.
After giving a brief history of taxes and tax-collecting in the United States from the Whisky Rebellion of 1794 to recent computer applications, the author describes the organization and functions of the Internal Revenue Service, the work of the Intelligence Enforcement Division and the Alcohol, Tobacco and Firearms Division, the Service's international activities, its future and its career opportunities
Bibliography: p257-61

353.3   U.S. Department of Interior. Bureau of Land Management

Clawson, Marion
The Bureau of Land Management. Praeger 1971 209p illus map (Praeger Lib. of U.S. Government departments and agencies) $8.50   353.3
  1 U.S. Bureau of Land Management

Clawson, Marion—*Continued*
"Gives the only comprehensive but compact presentation of the origins and responsibilities of a lesser known, newer, but a most important bureau of the government. . . . A very informative account is given of its activities which include grazing, forestry, mining and mineral leasing, geological and land survey, and outdoor recreation." Choice
Bibliography: p203-04

353.4   U.S. Post Office Department

Cullinan, Gerald
The Post Office Department; foreword by James A. Farley. Praeger 1968 272p illus (Praeger Lib. of U.S. Government departments and agencies) $7.50   353.4
1 U.S. Post Office Department 2 Postal service
An "historical analysis of the post office from its inception in 1639 to [1968]. . . . The author describes its functions, organization, relationship with Congress and other government agencies, and with the public." McClurg.
Book News
Appendixes include a summary of important postal laws and a bibliography

353.5   U.S. Department of Justice. F.B.I.

Harris, Richard
Justice; the crisis of law, order, and freedom in America. Dutton 1970 268p $6.95
353.5
1 U.S. Department of Justice 2 Clark, Ramsey 3 Mitchell, John Newton
This "serenely written, wonderfully composed and morally outraged report gives an account of what Justice (both as a government department and as a human activity) became under the direction of Ramsey Clark and what it would become under that of John N. Mitchell." Newsweek
"Contemporary in setting, [this] book is perennial in substance, part of the ageless drama of man's struggle to find the meaning of the just life and of the debts he owes as a citizen and a man. It is superfluous to say that such a book is worth reading. It may well be essential." N Y Times Bk R

Huston, Luther A.
The Department of Justice. Praeger 1967 270p illus (Praeger Lib. of U.S. Government departments and agencies) $8.50   353.5
1 U.S. Department of Justice
"The author provides a brief history of the Department and examines the operation of its various divisions, including the FBI, Bureau of Prisons, Immigration and Naturalization Service, Antitrust and Civil Rights divisions." Huntting
Appendixes include a list of Attorney Generals of the United States, a discussion of career opportunities within the Department and a bibliography

Overstreet, Harry
The FBI in our open society [by] Harry and Bonaro Overstreet. Norton 1969 400p $6.95
353.5
1 U.S. Federal Bureau of Investigation
The authors discuss the structure and performance of the agency chiefly responsible for the enforcement of federal laws—the Federal Bureau of Investigation. They consider its war against organized crime and the extreme right and left, as well as its role in the civil rights struggle

"Throughout a strong sense of fairness asserts itself and the FBI emerges looking like a fine organization, most of its critics looking rather foolish. . . . Occasional statistics are given, but, in the main, the reliance is upon the anecdotal approach and analysis of illustrative cases and problems. The Overstreets write with cool logic." Best Sellers

Terrell, John Upton
The United States Department of Justice; a story of crime, courts and counterspies. Duell 1965 120p $3.95   353.5
1 U.S. Department of Justice
The author presents a "picture of the Department of Justice, explaining its historical evolution to its present important position, the duties of its employees, its environment in American life, the Federal Bureau of Investigation, and the evolution of the role of Attorney General and the history of those who have held this office." Publisher's note

Tully, Andrew
The FBI's most famous cases; with an introduction and comments by J. Edgar Hoover. Morrow 1965 242p illus boards $4.95
353.5
1 U.S. Federal Bureau of Investigation
2 Crime and criminals—U.S.
"Descriptions of the FBI at work in selected cases. The cases include several kidnappings (one is that of Frank Sinatra, Jr.), bank robberies, hijacking, spy and sabotage cases, an airplane bombing, and three cases in the civil rights battle in the South. Most of the cases are recent, since 1960." Pub W
"Much of the material presented is very familiar; the reader of the newspaper finds himself already well acquainted with a great deal of the stock included. . . . Perhaps 'The FBI's Least Famous Cases' would have offered more potential for documented exploration. However, Mr. Tully's book is what it is supposed to be which is a goal frequently missed. It is a worthwhile addition to any library." Best Sellers

353.6   U.S. Department of Defense

Borklund, C. W.
The Department of Defense. Praeger 1968 342p illus (Praeger Lib. of U.S. Government departments and agencies) $8.50   353.6
1 U.S. Department of Defense
"This is a first-rate, thorough, objective and readable study of the . . . Department of Defense. . . . [The author] covers very well the reasons why the department was established in 1947, the effects of wars, crises and technology on it, its relations with Congress, commentators and the public (poor) and with the President and State Department (excellent), the need for constant reorganization and other pertinent subjects." Library J
Appendices include: Secretaries of Defense; Deputy Secretaries of Defense; The Joint Chiefs of Staff; National Security Act of 1947; Bibliography

Proxmire, William
Report from wasteland; America's military-industrial complex; foreword by Paul H. Douglas. Praeger 1970 248p front $6.95
353.6
1 U.S. Department of Defense   2 Munitions 3 Industry and state—U.S.   4 Waste (Economics)
The author "discusses at length the military budget, outlines the feeble constraints Congress places on military budget review, and offers specific suggestions for bringing that budget under control. He also discusses the men in the military-industrial complex; the

Proxmire, William—*Continued*
civilians in the Pentagon, the officers in industry, and those few brave cost analysts who attempt 'to bell the cat,' often at the cost of their own jobs. Other chapters are concerned with the arms race, and an initial chapter provides an excellent introduction to the power of the Pentagon." Library J
"A well-written, logically presented and copiously documented indictment of the economic waste incurred in the procurement of military materials." Best Sellers

353.81   U.S. Department of Agriculture

Simms, D. Harper
The Soil Conservation Service. Praeger 1970 238p illus (Praeger Lib. of U.S. Government departments and agencies) $8.50
         353.81
1 U.S. Soil Conservation Service 2 Soil Conservation
"The agency's first task was to correct the conditions responsible for the terrible dust storms of the 1930's. [The author] briefly sketches the events leading up to those years and relates how the Soil Conservation Service [of the Dept. of Agriculture] which grew out of the more than fifty-year-old Bureau of Soils program 'to construct terraces to reduce soil erosion,' has developed into a complete land-use program." Publisher's note
Bibliography: p230-32

Terrell, John Upton
The United States Department of Agriculture; a story of food, farms and forests. Duell 1966 130p $3.95   353.81
1 U.S. Department of Agriculture
"The entire spectrum of American agriculture as well as the activities of the U.S. Department of Agriculture are described clearly and briefly. The author ranges from the vast scientific achievements to the technical training of foreign farmers. The abrupt changes brought by World War I, the Great Depression, and World War II are all explored briefly but frankly. He covers especially well the activities of the Department in protecting urban consumers from fraud and disease. The book concludes with discussions of nutrition, school lunches, the Extension Service, 4-H Clubs, the Forest Service, and the agricultural colleges." Science Bks

United States. Department of Agriculture
After a hundred years; the yearbook of agriculture, 1962. U.S. Govt. Ptg. Off. 1962 688p illus maps $3   353.81
1 U.S. Department of Agriculture—History 2 Agriculture—U.S.
"A history of the Agriculture Department and the story of agriculture in the United States over the past 100 years, with numerous photographs illustrating progress in farming. Main topics include plants, conservation, forests, animals, insects, technologies, markets, and economics." The AAAS Science Book List for Young Adults

353.82   U.S. Department of Commerce. Patent Office

Jones, Stacy V.
The Patent Office. Praeger 1971 234p illus (Praeger Lib. of U.S. Government departments and agencies) $8.50   353.82
1 U.S. Patent Office 2 Patents
Discussed in this account of the Patent Office from its early days to the present are: the "basic categories of patents; the rights conferred by a patent (or a trade-mark); how

patents are applied for, issued, and sometimes fought over in the courts. . . . Famous patents are covered (the telephone, the flying machine, the rocket) as are patents for devices that lie just this side of insanity." Publisher's note
Bibliography: p226-29

353.84   U.S. Department of Health, Education, and Welfare

Terrell, John Upton
The United States Department of Health, Education, and Welfare; a story of protecting and preserving human resources. Duell 1965 138p boards $3.95   353.84
1 U.S. Department of Health, Education, and Welfare
The author "describes the growing and diverse problems of our society that led to the formation of HEW; he discusses the resistance to its establishment and the reasons for that resistance. The major part of the text is devoted to the agencies of HEW: their structure, their services, their research, their problems and goals." Chicago. Children's Book Center

353.85   U.S. Department of Housing and Urban Development

Willmann, John B.
The Department of Housing and Urban Development. Praeger 1967 207p illus map (Praeger Lib. of U.S. Government departments and agencies) $7.50   353.85
1 U.S. Department of Housing and Urban Development 2 Urban renewal
The author "describes the structure and workings of the department, including its relationships with Congress and with the powerful housing lobbies. Individual chapters deal with HUD's divisions for mortgage credit, housing assistance, metropolitan development, as well as the 'model cities' program." Publisher's note
Bibliography: p197-201

353.9   State governments

The **Book** of the States. Council of State Govs. $12.50, with supplements $16   353.9
1 State governments—Yearbooks
Biennial. Began publication 1935
"Gives both statistical and directory information on constitutions and elections; legislatures and legislation; the judiciary; administrative organization; finance; intergovernmental relations; state services. Issued biennially in even-numbered years, with supplements in odd-numbered years updating directory information on elected officials and legislators." Cheney. Fundamental Reference Sources

355.02   War and warfare

Armour, Richard
It all started with stones and clubs. . . . McGraw 1967 147p boards $4.50   355.02
1 War—Anecdotes, facetiae, satire, etc.
"Being a short history of war and weaponry from earliest times to the present, noting the gratifying progress made by man since his first crude, small-scale efforts to do away with those who disagreed with him." Title page
Covering every great war or battle except Armageddon, the author concludes that war is for everybody. (Publisher)
"Never has soldiering seemed so silly. The satire grows very sharp indeed on modern warfare." Pub W
Bibliography: p145-47

355.03 U.S.—Military policy

Davis, Kenneth S.
(ed.) Arms, industry and America. Wilson, H.W. 1971 232p (The Reference shelf v43, no. 1) $4.50   355.03
1 U.S.—Military policy   2 U.S.—Defenses
ISBN 0-8242-0446-8
This compilation surveys the origin and development of our military-industrial complex grouped around the following headings: The rise of American militarism; The military-industrial complex: critical descriptions; In defense of the military-industrial complex; The struggle for control
Bibliography: p224-32

Galbraith, John Kenneth
How to control the military. Doubleday 1969 69p $3.95   355.03
1 U.S.—Military policy   2 U.S.—Politics and government
The author claims that the military-industrial complex must be restrained and brought under close public scrutiny if the United States is to fulfill its national priorities. He makes a number of specific suggestions on what can be done to control the military, including making the problem a political issue and mobilizing independent scientific judgment to provide the final word on guidelines for military spending. (Publisher)
"Galbraith has written a small interesting book on a controversial and timely topic. . . . This book should stimulate discussion." Library J
Includes bibliographical footnotes

Knoll, Erwin
(ed.) American militarism, 1970. . . . Ed. by Erwin Knoll and Judith Nies McFadden; epilogue by J. William Fulbright. Viking 1969 150p $4.95   355.03
1 U.S.—Military policy   2 Militarism
"A dialogue on the distortion of our national priorities and the need to reassert control over the defense establishment." Title page
"Sets forth the ideas of such noted persons as Senators George McGovern, Gaylord Nelson, and William Fulbright; Representatives Phillip Burton and Robert Kastenmeier; Professors Hans Morgenthau and John Kenneth Galbraith; and others. Some of the points discussed include the need to restore general meaningful dialogue on American foreign and military policies, and the importance of re-evaluating the meaning of and need for classified information. Brief biographical information on each contributor is appended." Library J

355.09 Military history

Dupuy, R. Ernest
The encyclopedia of military history; from 3500 B.C. to the present [by] R. Ernest Dupuy and Trevor N. Dupuy. Harper 1970 1406p illus maps $20   355.09
1 Military history—Dictionaries
Divided chronologically and by region this "history summarizes the highlights of each period, outstanding leaders, unusual developments, tactical and strategical trends—followed by a continent-by-continent assessment of wars and battles, putting each major operation in political and social perspective." Book News
"A massive, authoritative, and usable encyclopedia. . . . The maps, line drawings, and pictures are quite helpful and the book is a genuine military historian's, not an antiquarian's, encyclopedia." Choice
Includes a bibliography, a general index, an index of battles and sieges, and an index of wars

Norman, A. V. B.
A history of war and weapons, 449 to 1660; English warfare from the Anglo-Saxons to Cromwell [by] A. V. B. Norman and Don Pottinger. Crowell 1966 224p illus $6.95   355.09
1 Arms and armor—History   2 Military art and science—History   3 Great Britain—History, Military
Published in England with title: Warrior to soldier 449-1660
"The English fighting man's equipment, tactics and fortifications, reviewed in text and pictures from the Anglo-Saxon invasion to the emergence of the standing army in Cromwell's time." McClurg. Book News
"A purely introductory study. The topic is exceedingly broad for so brief a work, and the normal scholarly accouterments of a bibliography and footnotes are missing. . . . However, the authors admit these limitations at the outset, and within the limited scope of the book there is much to recommend to the student lacking a background in military history." Choice

355.1 Military life. Insignia, medals, badges and decorations

Kerrigan, Evans E.
American badges and insignia; with illus. by the author. Viking 1967 286p illus $7.95   355.1
1 U.S.—Armed Forces—Insignia   2 U.S.—Armed Forces—Medals, badges, decorations, etc.
A guide to Army, Navy, Marine, and Coast Guard insignia of the United States from Revolutionary War days to the Vietnam Conflict
The author "has illustrated his encyclopedic guide on American military badges and insignia with more than 1000 drawings." Library J
Bibliography: p263

355.2 Military resources

Janeway, Eliot
The struggle for survival   355.2
1 Industrial mobilization   2 World War, 1939-1945—Economic aspects   3 U.S.—Economic policy
Some editions are:
U.S. Pubs. Assn. (The Chronicles of America ser. v53) $4.95 Has title: The struggle for survival: a chronicle of economic mobilization in World War II
Weybright & Talley (The Chronicles of America ser. v53) Includes a new foreword and epilogue by the author
Originally published by Yale University Press
"The story of America's economic mobilization in World War II—how it was accomplished and how American production became a decisive factor in the victory." Huntting
"It is a book about which students of politics will long debate. Some of them may disagree with Mr. Janeway's analysis, but none of them will find it dull." Sat R
Bibliographical note: p362-72

Liston, Robert
Greeting: you are hereby ordered for induction; the draft in America. McGraw 1970 159p $5.50, lib. bdg. $5.33   355.2
1 Military service, Compulsory
"Clearly and objectively explaining the Selective Service System in the U.S. Liston traces the historical background of conscription, describes the current operation of the draft, and puts forth the criticisms as well as suggestions for improvement that have been made. . . . Although he proposes no solutions he offers concrete information, both pro and con, on the draft laying the groundwork for an intelligent evaluation of the matter." Booklist

Reeves, Thomas
The end of the draft . . . [by] Thomas
Reeves and Karl Hess; prefaces by Mark O.
Hatfield & George McGovern. Random
House 1970 200p $6.95   355.2
  1 Military service, Compulsory
  "A proposal for abolishing conscription and
for a volunteer army, for popular resistance
to militarism and the restoration of individual
freedom." Title page
  Discusses the abuses, arbitrariness, and inequities, of the current system. It also points
out how it induces a war economy and increases influence of the military on our lives.
(Publisher)
  The authors have "done an important service
to legislators and citizens in producing this
factual, lucid and concise book—an indispensable aid in considering a critical public question." America
  Bibliographical references in Notes, at end
of the chapters

355.4 Attack and defense plans and operations. Guerrilla warfare

Sully, François
  Age of the guerrilla; the new warfare.
Parents Mag. Press 1968 255p $4.50, lib.
bdg. $4.19   355.4
  1 Guerrilla warfare
  "A Background book"
  "A profound and fascinating study of guerrilla warfare in contemporary society, with detailed examinations of insurrection in the
Arab world, Vietnam, Cuba, Israel, Southeast
Asia, South America, and in European areas
that have been torn by civil war and insur-
gency. The author, whose many years as a
correspondent have given personal experience
in many of the troubled areas of the world,
analyzes with intelligent objectivity and several
motivations of guerrilla fighters and he describes events with dispassionate vigor. A number of documents (interviews, speeches, and
writing) are appended, as are some appendices
(explanatory and summary) and an index."
Chicago. Children's Book Center

359.9 U.S. Marine Corps

Donovan, James A.
  The United States Marine Corps, by
James A. Donovan, Jr. Praeger 1967 246p
illus (Praeger Lib. of U.S. Government departments and agencies) $8.50   359.9
  1 U.S. Marine Corps—History
  The author, a former Marine, "explains the
doctrines and concepts that have shaped the
history of the USMC from Tripoli and Montezuma to Vietnam; shows how the Corps is organized and trained; and details how it acquired its well-known traditions, esprit de
corps, slogans and uniform." Huntting
  Marine terms and expressions: p228-32. Bibliography: p233-38

361 Social welfare work

Addams, Jane
  Twenty years at Hull-House; with autobiographical notes; with illus. by Norah
Hamilton. Macmillan (N Y) [1966 c1910]
462p illus $6.95   361
  1 Hull House, Chicago   2 Chicago—Social
conditions
  A reissue of a book first published 1910
  "This classic of the reform era is actually
an autobiography of the woman who practically founded social service work in this country.

. . . It tells her life story, but the greater
part of it is devoted to the setting up of
Chicago's Hull House, the first settlement
house in the United States." A Guide to Reading in Am History
  "The book is a lively account of a remarkably fruitful social project and reveals a woman
who was profoundly concerned with the welfare
of humanity." Herzberg. The Reader's Encyclopedia of Am Lit

361.069 Social welfare work as a profession

Perlman, Helen Harris
  So you want to be a social worker. (Rev.
ed) Harper 1970 177p boards $4.95, lib.
bdg. $4.43   361.069
  1 Social work as a profession
  First published 1962
  The author describes the different types of
social workers and social work as a profession.
She then discusses the necessary details about
the training required, the salary and working
conditions in the field, and the opportunities
for advancement. Her final chapter lists other
sources, including books, where additional information may be obtained

362.1 Welfare services to the physically ill

Crichton, Michael
  Five patients; the hospital explained.
Knopf 1970 231p $5.95   362.1
  1 Massachusetts General Hospital, Boston
  2 Medical care
  The author "takes us here on what amounts
to a guided tour of the Massachusetts General
Hospital, where he trained. His book illuminates a host of matters from diagnostic
procedures to blood banks to teaching techniques, and includes explanations for the sky-
rocketing costs of medical care ('The fastest-
rising item in the consumer price index in
recent years') and even helpful pointers on
health insurance. . . . The five patients of the
title reflect some of the ways in which medicine is now changing. . . . Throughout Dr.
Crichton manages to interweave fascinating bits
of medical history, even touches of humor."
Book of the Month Club News
  Glossary: p219-24. Bibliography: p225-31

Elliott, Lawrence
  The legacy of Tom Dooley. World Pub.
1969 238p illus $5.95   362.1
  1 Hospitals—Asia, Southeastern   2 The
Thomas A. Dooley Foundation, Inc.
  After the death of Dr Tom Dooley, the
Thomas A. Dooley Foundation was established,
in his memory, to carry on his work. This
is the story of the volunteers who went to the
areas of Southeastern Asia where Dr Dooley
had set up hospitals and medical stations for
the poor and ill. They cleaned and repaired
the hospitals, which had fallen into a state of
decay, and are now attempting to carry on
his work
  The author "lifts his account well above the
stickiness of 'inspirational' stories; he gets the
pictures across in simple language, so that the
reader is moved with images of thatch-roofed
jungle dispensaries, inexperienced young people
going 'into the field,' volunteer doctors who
gave up lucrative practices to go where the real
treasure is." Pub W

Hartog, Jan de
  The hospital. Atheneum Pubs. 1964 337p
$5.95   362.1
  1 Ben Taub General Hospital, Houston, Tex.
  "From his experiences as a volunteer in
Houston's city-county charity hospital, a popular novelist-playwright paints . . . the heartbreak and horror that infiltrate an under-
staffed, neglected public hospital. He recounts

Hartog, Jan de—*Continued*
the battle he and his wife helped launch to promote an effective volunteer corps and to break through public apathy, political irresponsibility, and professional suspiciousness." Booklist

"Whatever its stylistic faults. The Hospital is a powerful and disturbing book. . . . It gradually convinces the reader that such conditions, however unbelievable at first mention, might exist in the public hospital of any city in the United States." Book Week

Walsh, William B.
A ship called Hope. Dutton 1964 224p illus map $5.95   **362.1**

1 Hope (Hospital ship) 2 Indonesia—Social conditions 3 Vietnam—Social conditions

Edited by Suzanne Gleaves and Lael Wertenbaker

An account of the first voyage of the borrowed U.S. Navy hospital ship to Indonesia and Vietnam. "The staff treated thousands of desperately ill patients, made friends, melted resistance even in strongholds of Communism, taught flexible medical practice to local nurses and doctors, and learned from them, too. An especially appealing case, among many told here, is a cure of a hunch-backed boy made straight as an arrow. The book is a touching report on American generosity and medical know-how that did endless good abroad." Pub W

"Inevitably, since such a report is a kind of 'thank you' to helpers and a report to contributors, the author names many names and cites many problems. But there is so much drama in the many stories of patients, doctors, nurses, and others . . . a reader is proud of these practical idealists. Dr. Walsh reminds me of Dr. Tom Dooley in his concern for people who suffer and his conviction that we are indeed 'our brother's keeper.'" Horn Bk

362.7 Welfare services to the young (Child welfare) Adoption

Braithwaite, E. R.
Paid servant. McGraw [1968 c1962] 219p $5.95   **362.7**

1 Child welfare 2 Adoption 3 Great Britain —Race relations

First published 1962 in England

The author describes his experiences as a welfare officer in London's Department of Child Welfare and relates some cases, particularly that of the adoption of Rodwell Williams, a 4½ year old mulatto

"To Braithwaite the social worker is the 'paid servant' of the poor, and his book is a plea for friendlier treatment and greater understanding of the disadvantaged of all races. Despite the poignant subject, it is written with an underlying cheerfulness and optimism and a wealth of lively anecdotes." America

Chinnock, Frank W.
Kim: a gift from Vietnam. World Pub. 1969 211p illus $4.95   **362.7**

1 Adoption

The author "tells about his family's adoption of an orphaned Vietnamese child. Chinnock went to Vietnam and found little Ninh— who became 'Kim' to the family (Chinnock's wife Jan and their three young sons) when she was brought to her new home in Westchester. [Included is a] recital of the problems of Kim's adaptation." Pub W

"The story of Kim's adjustment to an American home with three older brothers is an infinitely touching record of patience and love. . . . The section of photographs showing a gay, charming child, laughing and confident, are pictorial corroboration of Kim's transformation from a bewildered Vietnamese waif to the sturdy youngest child of an affectionate American family." Sat R

362.8 Unmarried mothers

Pierce, Ruth I.
Single and pregnant. Beacon Press 1970 222p boards $5.95   **362.8**

1 Unmarried mothers 2 Pregnancy
ISBN 0-8070-2778-2

"An experienced counselor and trained social worker steps outside traditional moralizing to outline each of the roads the single pregnant girl can take—abortion—adoption—marriage— single parenthood—and what to expect from each. A comprehensive listing of where to go for counseling, medical, legal and financial help is included." Book News

Suggested readings: p216

364 Criminology

United States. President's Commission on Law Enforcement and Administration of Justice
The challenge of crime in a free society; a report by the President's Commission on Law Enforcement and Administration of Justice; introduction and afterword by Isidore Silver. Dutton [1969] c1968 814p $10   **364**

1 Crime and criminals—U.S. 2 Law enforcement 3 Justice, Administration of

The text of the report on crime, and relevant sections from the Task Force Reports. Recommendations for future actions are given

Partial contents: Juvenile delinquency and youth crime; The police; The courts; Corrections; Organized crime; Narcotics and drug abuse

"The commission established by President Johnson in July, 1965, and chaired by Nicholas Katzenbach makes a summary but formal and extensive report of their findings with the promise of additional volumes containing the details of research and analysis upon which the present volume is based." Booklist

364.1 Criminal offenses

Capote, Truman
In cold blood; a true account of a multiple murder and its consequences   **364.1**

1 Murder 2 Clutter family 3 Hickock, Richard Eugene 4 Smith, Perry Edward

Some editions are:
Modern Lib. $2.95
Random House $6.95

First published 1966

A documented "nonfiction novel" of mass murder. "In deceptively simple style, Truman Capote builds his report about the [1959] murder of the Herbert Clutter family of Holcomb, Kansas, by introducing the victims—four members of a greatly liked and respected family— and then cross-cutting to the two psychotic young men who killed the family, to the investigators who solve the crime, and back to the killers." Pub W

"Suspense is maintained throughout a skillful, intricately plotted, and objective reconstruction of a much-publicized crime. Although this book has popular appeal, sociological overtones make it provocative fare for the mature reader." Top of the News

Clark, Ramsey
Crime in America; observations on its nature, causes, prevention and control; with an introduction by Tom Wicker. Simon & Schuster 1970 346p $6.95   **364.1**

1 Crime and criminals—U.S. 2 Police—U.S.
SBN 671-20407-6

In this book, "the former Attorney General of the United States . . . spells out the facts

Clark, Ramsey—*Continued*
of the problem, diagnoses the roots of anti-social behavior in American society, and proposes the specific measures the nation must take if we are to banish the causes of crime American style." Publisher's note
"Clark's discussion of the police and their relationship to the genesis of crime is well done and shows an appreciation of the nuances of social interrelationships. His call to a much needed reordering of national priorities is forcefully and convincingly presented. Should be widely read, and, more importantly it should be critically discussed." Choice

Ehrmann, Herbert B.
The case that will not die; Commonwealth vs. Sacco and Vanzetti; with maps and illus. Little 1969 xxix, 576p illus maps $12.50 **364.1**
1 Sacco-Vanzetti case
The author, a lawyer in the Sacco-Vanzetti case examines the case from its origins until after the death of the two accused. Court records, withheld evidence, unfair practices—all are brought to light to form a picture of what has been considered a classic miscarriage of justice. (Publisher)
The author's "book is probably the most definitive study of the subject available. . . . Sacco and Vanzetti themselves emerge in Ehrmann's highly readable book as passionately convinced men of principle, amazingly eloquent in an unfamiliar language." Pub W
Bibliography: p547-50

Lewin, Stephen
(ed.) Crime and its prevention. Wilson, H.W. 1968 244p (The Reference shelf v40, no.4) $4.50 **364.1**
1 Crime and criminals—U.S. 2 Law enforcement 3 Punishment
"This book is an attempt . . . to explain problems in law enforcement, punishment, and crime prevention. The first two sections are devoted to a discussion of crime itself . . . the third section discusses the lot of the policeman; the fourth, the role of the courts. The last section examines various suggestions for halting the steadily increasing crime rate." Preface
Bibliography: p230-44

Maas, Peter
The Valachi papers. Putnam 1968 285p illus $6.95 **364.1**
1 Valachi, Joseph 2 Mafia 3 Crime and criminals—U.S.
"Composed of direct interviews with Joseph Valachi, these 'papers' relate the life of crime led by the . . . informer who revealed for the first time the existence of the 'Cosa Nostra,' more popularly known as the 'Mafia.' . . . Valachi recounts the organizational structure of the 'Cosa Nostra,' naming individuals at the head of various units." Library J
"This highly readable narrative . . . confirms the stereotype of the Cosa Nostra that has been diffused by the news stories, films and television series of the past fews years. . . . What makes this book such grimly fascinating reading is the picture of Valachi as hero and narrator relating in his own Runyonesque diction his incredible survival in the continuing cross fire of gang wars. . . . It is a story littered with bodies and unsolved crimes, betrayals and beatings, oaths, ritual and revenge." Newsweek

Toland, John
The Dillinger days. Random House 1963 371p illus maps $10 **364.1**
1 Crime and criminals—U.S. 2 Dillinger, John
"Back in the 1930's John Dillinger and his gang terrorized the middle West; this is the story behind the headlines. In search of information, the author has followed Dillinger's trail through thirty states. His account brings to life the notorious figures of the depression—Machine Gun Kelly, Ma Barker and her boys, Pretty Boy Floyd and many others." Huntting

"As a stylist, Mr. Toland is undistinguished, but the uproar of his material will probably console any reader with the faintest interest in the mechanics of sticking up a bank." Atlantic

Tyler, Gus
(ed.) Organized crime in America; a book of readings; introduction by Estes Kefauver. Univ. of Mich. Press 1962 421p pa $3.25 **364.1**
1 Crime and criminals—U.S. 2 Juvenile delinquency 3 Mafia
"This reader is the by-product of a study commissioned by the Fund for the Republic (now the Center for the Study of Democratic Institutions) on the impact of organized crime on our democratic institutions. . . . [The editor's] views and conclusions are expressed in the introductory essays to the seven parts." Preface
This "is a sobering historical, sociological and political study of the sources and trends of organized crime in the U.S., illustrated with testimony from congressional investigations, analytical essays, newspaper reports, criminal confessions and other material. Several sections concern the Mafia, and others are about youth gangs." Pub W

United States. National Commission on the Causes and Prevention of Violence
Violent crime; homicide, assault, rape, robbery; the report of the National Commission on the Causes and Prevention of Violence. . . . Braziller [1970 c1969] 85p boards $3 **364.1**
1 Crime and criminals—U.S. 2 Violence
"With an introduction: 'Toward a national urban policy' by Daniel P. Moynihan." Title page
The report "succinctly discusses the characteristics, causes, continued increase, and possible remedies for violent crime in today's U.S., making it explicit that nothing less than a restructuring of urban life will bring about genuine improvement. Moynihan's introduction . . . almost as long as the report itself, sets forth a ten-point national urban policy designed to coordinate and increase federal-local action on urban problems." Booklist
"Many Americans, accustomed to having their society's faults screamed at them have simply tuned out. Therefore, they may find the statements of this calm and deliberative report all the more alarming. . . . Moynihan's essay . . . is a useful and thought-provoking adjunct to the report." Library J
Includes bibliographical references

West, Rebecca
The new meaning of treason. Viking 1964 374p $6.95 **364.1**
1 Treason 2 Trials
First published 1947 with title: The meaning of treason
Analyzing espionage cases in Britain and the United States during and after World War II, the author discusses the activities and trials of John Amery, William Joyce, Guy Burgess, Ethel and Julius Rosenberg, Stephen Ward, and others
"It is a meticulously accurate account of some of the most astounding and disturbing events in this disturbed age." Sat R

364.12 Detection. Investigation of crime

Horan, James D.
The Pinkertons; the detective dynasty that made history. Crown [1968 c1967] 564p illus maps $7.95 **364.12**
1 Pinkerton's National Detective Agency, Incorporated 2 Crime and criminals—U.S. 3 Pinkerton, Allan
The author relates the story of the Pinkerton National Detective Agency (now Pinkerton's Inc.) from its beginnings until the present. He describes the protection against the

Horan, James D.—*Continued*
assassination of Lincoln on his trip to Washington, the conflict with the Molly Maguires and later with the Mafia, and the never-ending battle against robbery. The author bases much of his information on the correspondence of Allan Pinkerton and his sons
He "has made this biography also a study of Pinkerton's methods, and they are fascinating. [P]inkerton himself was an amazing man: a stickler for detail, he lived a life of epic proportions. . . . Included are 100 photographs and documents." Pub W
Bibliography: p551-60

Sterling, Claire
The Masaryk case. Harper 1969 366p illus $7.95   **364.12**
1 Masaryk, Jan Garrigue 2 Czechoslovak Republic—Politics and government
The author "has thoroughly re-researched the mass of complex and contradictory evidence concerning the grotesque death by defenestration of Jan Masaryk, Foreign Minister of Czechoslovakia, in 1948, shortly following the Communist takeover of the country. She has studied the written records available to her, interviewed all of the still-living witnesses on both sides of the Iron Curtain, and discovered new and crucial documentary evidence hitherto kept secret. Her shrewd investigations and the opinions of expert criminologists have led her to reject the official governmental verdict of suicide and to charge Communist-directed murder. Her recreation of the crime is stunningly convincing. . . . Background history is adequately presented, and the sinister climate of Czechoslovakia in 1948 and the exhilarating one in 1968 (the year of liberalization during which the case was reopened) are skillfully captured." Choice
Characters: p xi-xvii. Bibliography: p351-53

United States. Warren Commission on the Assassination of President Kennedy
The official Warren Commission report on the assassination of President John F. Kennedy. With an analysis and commentary by Louis Nizer and a historical afterword by Bruce Catton. Doubleday 1964 xxiv, 888, xxxii p illus $5.95   **364.12**
1 Kennedy, John Fitzgerald, President U.S.—Assassination 2 Oswald, Lee Harvey
"On November 22, 1963, the 35th President of the United States was shot to death in Dallas. . . . For eight painstaking months the [new] President's commission, with the complete cooperation and vast resources of all federal bureaus and agencies at their disposal, weighed every theory, tracked down every lead, however remote, and took the testimony of more than 400 witnesses, plus thousands of investigation reports and at least 800 items of physical evidence. This book contains the full summary report of that investigation." Publisher's note

364.36   Juvenile delinquency

James, Howard
Children in trouble. . . . McKay 1970 340p $6.95   **364.36**
1 Juvenile delinquency
"This book is based on a series of articles that appeared weekly in 'The Christian Science Monitor,' March 31 to July 7, 1969." Title page
This book "concerns children in trouble—not only those involved in crime, but the homeless, neglected and abused. It is a detailed report on what happens when they become the pawns of 'justice.' Visiting some 44 states, the author looked at institutions and agencies: courts, jails, reform schools, public schools, welfare offices, and police stations. He talked to administrators, workers in the field, and the children themselves. Case history after case history reveals that 'no community in America is doing enough for children in trouble.' . . .

This is a shocking indictment of the inadequacies and failures of our method of handling juvenile problems. It is an alert to the American public of the urgent need for improving the system." Library J

Loble, Lester H.
Delinquency can be stopped [by] Lester H. Loble and Max Wylie. McGraw 1967 148p front $5.95   **364.36**
1 Juvenile delinquency 2 Punishment
Judge Loble from Montana speaks up against the pampering of the criminal youth by social workers, psychologists and do-gooders, who see in the juvenile delinquent always the misguided and disadvantaged youth, never a criminal. He recommends stronger methods such as the abolishment of the secrecy in youth trials, a weekend in solitary confinement, as a taste of prison life, supplemented by trade schools and more discipline by parents and educators. (Publisher)
"A controversial book but an interesting theory with proven results." English Speaking Union

Steel, Ronald
(ed.) New light on juvenile delinquency. Wilson, H.W. 1967 221p (The Reference shelf v39, no.4) $4.50   **364.36**
1 Juvenile delinquency 2 Youth
This compilation begins with articles on the causes and manifestations of juvenile delinquency, describes the delinquent's world of gangs, truants and drug addicts, then examines the phenomenon of a separate youth culture and the conflict between youth and society. The concluding chapters describe various means of preventing and dealing with juvenile delinquency.
Bibliography: p212-21

364.8   Discharged offenders

Sands, Bill
My shadow ran fast. Prentice-Hall 1964 212p boards $6.95   **364.8**
1 Crime and criminals—Rehabilitation 2 California State Prison, San Quentin
"A plea for rehabilitating as opposed to punitive penology is voiced in this true story of a life brought from criminality to useful and idealistic citizenship. Rejected by his parents Sands found himself in his early twenties an inmate of San Quentin convicted of armed robbery. His rehabilitation through the efforts of Warden Clinton Duffy and his subsequent adventures and efforts in behalf of other convicts are movingly described in a popularly written narrative." Booklist

365   Penology

Bennett, James V.
I chose prison; ed. by Rodney Campbell. Knopf 1970 229p illus $5.95   **365**
1 Prisons—U.S.
"For nearly three decades—he was director of the federal Bureau of Prisons from 1937 to 1964—James V. Bennett was deeply involved with the treatment of criminals in America. Believing that the business of penology is the rehabilitation of the convict rather than the enforcement of society's retribution, he introduced numerous controversial—but successful—prison reforms. . . . [Here] he writes forthrightly about his career, about the men he knew and dealt with on both sides of the law, from J. Edgar Hoover to Al Capone and Joe Valachi to Julius and Ethel Rosenberg." News of Books
"This book is a lucid and highly readable treatment of the problems and conditions of American prisons. The work is designed for popular reading and focuses on many prison topics ranging from capital punishment to prisons without bars." Choice

369.43   Boy Scouts

Boy Scouts of America
Fieldbook for Boy Scouts, explorers, scouters, educators, outdoorsmen. [2d ed] The author [distributed by McGraw] 1967 565p illus maps $4.95   **369.43**
1 Boy Scouts
Title on cover: Fieldbook for boys and men
First edition 1944 by James E. West and William Hillcourt published with title: Scout field book
This handbook contains information on such subjects as scouting, camping, hiking, cooking, survival methods, map reading, conservation, weather, plants, and astronomy. (Publisher)

370   Education

Postman, Neil
Teaching as a subversive activity [by] Neil Postman [and] Charles Weingartner. Delacorte Press 1969 219p boards $5.95   **370**
1 Education—U.S.   2 Teaching
"An attack upon teaching methods the authors consider outdated, drawing upon their own experience and the opinions of such writers as Marshall McLuhan, Norbert Wiener, and others with specific suggestions for improvement." Bk Buyer's Guide
"The book contains a good many prescriptions for schools and teachers: Eliminate textbooks, tests, grades, 'courses' and requirements. . . . What is notable about these suggestions is not that most of them are new or that teachers will rush to adopt them (neither is the case) but that Postman and Weingartner believe them still worth making at all —that the existing school system can be reformed. They propose just what the title suggests: a form of subversion—teaching kids to ask real (and therefore often unwelcome and threatening) questions." N Y Times Bk R

Silberman, Charles E.
Crisis in the classroom; the remaking of American education. Random House 1970 552p $10   **370**
1 Education—U.S.   2 Education—Aims and objectives   3 Teaching
"The author indicts all levels of education in the United States. In part one he argues that American schools are failing. Part two is concerned with education and equality, education and docility. He presents suggestions for change in primary and secondary schools in part three. The education of educators, part four, analyzes the need for reform in teacher education and in higher education." Book Rev Digest
"Silberman's charges have been made before and with much of the insight he provides; but the value and importance of his book lies in the richness of his analysis on every educational level. He is concrete, specific, keenly observant, and he brings a broad grasp of our educational needs to the reader while suggesting future directions." Pub W
Includes bibliographical references

Slosson, Edwin E.
The American spirit in education; a chronicle of great teachers. U.S. Pubs. Assn. 1921 309p (The Chronicles of America ser. v33) $3.95   **370**
1 Education—U.S.
First published by Yale University Press
Partial contents: School days in early New England; Schools of the middle and southern colonies; Jefferson and state education; Horace Mann and the American school; De Witt Clinton and the free school; Catholic education in America; Rise of technical education; University of today; Bibliographical note

370.1   Education—Philosophy, theories, principles

Dewey, John
John Dewey on education; selected writings; ed. and with an introduction by Reginald D. Archambault. Modern Lib. 1964 xxx, 439p $2.95, lib. bdg. $2.69   **370.1**
1 Education—Philosophy
The book "contains chapters from several of Dewey's most important books, some of which have never before been included in any collection, and many selections from books and periodicals which have long been out of print. . . . The editor has made selections of Dewey's work in the several branches of philosophy that nourish educational theory, including ethics, epistemology, aesthetics, political theory and a major section on pedagogy." Publisher's note

Holt, John
What do I do Monday? Dutton 1970 318p $6.95   **370.1**
1 Education—Philosophy   2 Education—U.S.
ISBN 0-525-23140-4
"Destroying the false dichotomy between work and play [the author] demonstrates how children may learn by doing, by touching and trying, and shows how conditions may be created—by use of art, films, tape-recorders, bringing in outside people who help make studies relevant to the adult world—which foster the child's sense of the wholeness and openness of life." Pub W
Bibliography: p313-18

Parker, Don H.
Schooling for what? McGraw 1970 270p $7.95   **370.1**
1 Education—Aims and objectives   2 Education—U.S.
SBN 07-048483-X
"Based on 1000 interviews with people in many fields, Dr. Parker has explored the thoughts of people regarding schooling and its relationship to society. The findings from these interviews have convinced him that the educational establishment must face up to a clear-cut choice: stop defending the educational status quo and inaugurate change quickly or prepare for revolution. To prevent this revolution, the author suggests three major improvements: more student involvement in curriculum-making, more attention paid to individual student needs, and more relevance of the curriculum to the world in which students live." News of Bks

370.19   Sociological aspects of education. Segregation

Meredith, James
Three years in Mississippi. Ind. Univ. Press 1966 328p $7.50   **370.19**
1 Mississippi. University   2 Segregation in education   3 Mississippi—Race relations
"James Meredith recapitulates the steps in his progress towards a degree (awarded him in 1963) at the hitherto all-white University of Mississippi. He begins with his home background, the farming town of Kosciusko, Mississippi. . . . He leads the reader through the court briefs, the testimony and the embattled tactics that won his entrance into the university." Pub W
"Meredith writes carefully, deliberately—perhaps a bit stuffily—making sure each point is crystal-clear before he continues. His setting of the scene . . . and his recounting of the events are precise and evocative, but the emotion has been screened out. This dispassionate quality, however, gives the book even more force." Newsweek

370.25 Education—Directories

Handbook of private schools; an annual descriptive survey of independent education. Sargent illus maps $14   370.25

1 Private schools—Directories

First published 1915 with title: Handbook of the best private schools of the United States and Canada

Presents, by articles, maps, cross-references and indexes, a survey of more than 2,500 private elementary and secondary schools in the U.S. and Canada, their tuition, programs, scholarships, facilities, and administrative personnel. The arrangement is by state. (Publisher)

Private independent schools; the American private schools for boys and girls. Bunting & Lyon illus $15   370.25

1 Education—U.S.—Directories   2 Private schools—Directories

Annual. First published 1943 with title: Independent schools, a directory. Title varies

"A directory and guide for parents and teachers. Boarding schools, day schools, and military schools, with or without church affiliations and operating for the most part as educational corporations under state charters." Title page [to 1968 edition]

The editors include such information as location, the history and development of the academic program, the campus and physical plant, the nature of the faculty and staff, the composition of the student body, the admission procedures and charges, and the extra-curricular activities

"The descriptions of the schools in this book are supplied by the schools themselves; subscribers get expanded space, up to four pages as opposed to the brief paragraph alloted to nonsubscribers." Library J

370.7 Teachers—Training

Conant, James Bryant

The education of American teachers. [New enl. ed] McGraw 1964 319p (The Carnegie ser. in American education) $5   370.7

1 Teachers—Training

First published 1963, this book is the result of a two year study of state certification policies and teacher training programs

Partial contents: A quarrel among educators; The academic preparation of teachers; The theory and practice of teaching; The education of elementary school teachers; Continuing and in-service education of teachers

"Dr. Conant does not just offer vague formulas for improving teacher education. His book abounds in specific recommendations ... and his long experience as a professor and university president are evident in the sureness and common sense of his suggestions." America

370.8 Education—Collections

Gross, Beatrice

(ed.) Radical school reform; ed. by Beatrice Gross and Ronald Gross. Simon & Schuster [1970 c1969] 350p $7.95   370.8

1 Education—U.S.

SBN 671-20412-2

Analyzed in Essay and general literature index

"This three-part anthology consists of 23 articles. Part 1 describes the urban and suburban 'nightmare,' with selections from James Herndon, Jonathan Kozol, John Holt, and Jules Henry. Part 2 gives theories of such authors as Paul Goodman, George Leonard, and Sylvia Ashton-Warner. Part 3, by Joseph Featherstone, George Dennison, and others tells about current practices. If a person must rely on an anthology for his information of the school crisis, he will find this to be one of the better of the many now flooding the market, as it gives a succinct survey of both sides of the picture: ghetto problems and the weaknesses of the more prosperous schools." Library J

Bibliography: p347-48

Lineberry, William P.

(ed.) New trends in the schools. Wilson, H.W. 1967 211p illus (The Reference shelf v.39, no.2) $4.50   370.8

1 Education—U.S. 2 Education, Elementary 3 Education, Secondary

"In the first section—a broad overview of the current educational scene—the backdrop against which reforms and innovations are taking place is reviewed. . . . The second section throws the spotlight on some of the forces working for reform. . . . A major force for change—the Federal Government and its growing involvement in education—is given separate treatment in Section III. Sections IV and V focus on the new trends themselves." Preface

Bibliography: p198-211

371 The school

Popenoe, Joshua

Inside Summerhill; with candid photographs by the author. Hart 1970 111p illus $7.50   371

1 Summerhill School, Leiston, England

SBN 8055-0112-6

This book was written by a sixteen-year-old American boy "who spent four years at this controversial school. He tells forthrightly, in his own naive and charming and revealing manner, what Summerhill is all about. Here is day-by-day description of how the school operates, how the students feel, how they react to visitors, how they react to classes, what their interests are, and what their hopes are." Publisher's note

371.1 Teaching and teaching personnel

Barzun, Jacques

Teacher in America. Little 1945 321p $6.95   371.1

1 Teaching   2 Education, Higher   3 U.S.—Intellectual life

Analyzed in Essay and general literature index

The author "analyzes for the intelligent layman the 'basic facts of teaching' and its wider implications in the United States today. . . . [He writes] of the questionable prestige of the teaching profession, of classroom methods, of such essential subjects as the classics, philosophy, science and history, of the Ph.D. fetish, examinations and tests, educational goals for women, recognition and financial reward. Bibliographical note." Bookmark

The chapters "are provocative, witty and entertainingly readable. Wholly free from the jargon and mechanics of pedagogy, they should interest laymen as well as teachers." Library J

Biegeleisen, J. I.

Careers and opportunities in teaching; illus. with photographs. Dutton 1969 255p illus $4.95   371.1

1 Teaching as a profession

"Information and advice on teaching positions of all types are presented. General conditions of teaching are discussed and specifics of preschool teaching, kindergarten, elementary, secondary, junior college, college, and university teaching are considered. Pros and cons of public and private schools are weighed and various overseas teaching assignments are listed. Very little consideration of problems and difficulties is given, as the approach is to present the most favorable aspect in a clear and simple fashion." Choice

Bibliography: p231-37

Highet, Gilbert
The art of teaching   371.1
Some editions are:
Knopf $5.95
Vintage lib. bdg. $2.39
First published 1950
"Teaching is an art, not a science; Highet
proceeds to spell out the artist and his work.
Basically a book on the methods of teaching.
An attempt to work out the principles by which
a subject can be well taught.   It is not a
book of educational theory, but a book of suggestions drawn from practice. Considers the
character and abilities that make a good professional teacher. Famous teachers and their
influence are examined—Plato, Aristotle, Jesus
of Nazareth; then the teachers of the Renaissance to the best nineteenth-and twentieth-
century teachers; and finally the fathers of
great men who taught their sons to be great.
Last of all, a look at teaching in everyday
life—parents, doctors, priests, and politicians."
A Guide to Reading in Am History
"A delightful and stimulating discussion.
. . . [The author] believes that teaching itself
is an education that the good teacher not
only must know his subject, he must also continue to learn more about it." Cincinnati
Bibliographical references included in Notes:
p283-91

Ryan, Kevin
(ed.) Don't smile until Christmas; accounts of the first year of teaching; with
contributions by John Canfield [and oth-
ers]. Univ. of Chcago Press 1970 190p $5.95
                                      371.1
1 Teachers 2 Teaching
ISBN 0-226-73230-4
"Irresistible forces meet movable objects in
six candid records kept by beginning high-
school teachers, who found themselves unpre-
pared for the realities of the classroom and,
in some cases, the obduracy of the faculty
against innovation. How does a white teacher
cope in a black school? How does a new teacher
achieve authority without becoming a martinet?
How does a male teacher handle a coquette?
How does one stir the apathetic? Quell the
disorderly? Face one's own inadequacy." Sat R

Taylor, Harold
The world as teacher. Doubleday 1969
322p $6.95   371.1
1 Teacher—Training   2 Intercultural education
This book, the result of a two year study of
the education of American teachers in world affairs, "calls for a large scale revision in
the way teachers are educated . . . beginning with the formation of a nation-wide
volunteer Student Corps . . . with service and
study in foreign and American communities
considered as a regular part of the student's
program. . . . [The author] provides an analysis
of the problems . . . in the system of teacher
certification, in the professional education
courses, practice teaching, urban education, the
arts and sciences curriculum, teacher recruit-
ments, graduate schools of education and
methods of instruction." Publisher's note
This is "imaginative, insistently radical and
brilliantly persuasive . . . [going] beyond theory and philosophy to a welcome and practical
concreteness. . . . Taylor is less interested in
the formal preparation of teachers in such subjects as international relations and world history than in developing teachers who think
globally and who are alert to the ways in
which their own country is deeply implicated
in world society." N Y Times Bk R
Bibliography included in footnotes

371.2 Dropouts

Cervantes, Lucius F.
The dropout: causes and cures, by Lucius
F. Cervantes; with the assistance of Grace
Platts Hustad. Univ. of Mich. Press 1965
244p $5.95   371.2
1 Dropouts 2 Youth

"An unusual book in which the dropout
speaks for himself, and his views are compared
with those of a high school graduate having the
same I.Q. and similiar background. The emotional problems and attitudes towards families,
friends and teachers and his position as a
citizen are some of the issues discussed about
the dropout that have far reaching effects in
many communities." Huntting
Bibliographical references included in Notes:
p229-39

371.26 Educational tests and measurements

Brownstein, Samuel C.
Barron's How to prepare for college entrance examinations. Barrons Educ. Ser.
$7.50   371.26
1 Colleges and universities—Entrance requirements 2 Examinations
First published 1954 with title: How to prepare for college entrance examinations. Frequently revised to bring information up to date
"This book clears the mystery surrounding
entrance examinations. It contains extensive
drill material with answers and also gives practice with typical examinations. It explains the
mechanics of the interview and furnishes hints
which are invaluable to the student who is
anticipating the interview." Preface [to the
1954 edition]

Turner, David R.
Scoring high on college entrance tests;
the complete study guide.   Arco lib.
bdg. $6.50   371.26
1 Colleges and universities—Entrance requirements 2 Examinations
First edition 1950 by Alison S. Peters, a
pseudonym of Nathan H. Mager. Frequently revised to bring information up to date. Title
varies
"Here is a most complete and authoritative
study manual to prepare a student for every
possible type of college entrance examination
he may have to take. . . . Thousands of sample
questions patterned after actual exams—with
answer keys—cover math, vocabulary, English
usage, reading comprehension, mechanical insight, spatial relations, graph interpretation,
and non-verbal reasoning. Proven study methods for scoring high are clearly set forth so
that this wealth of material may be used to
best advantage." Publisher's note

371.27 Evaluation of pupils' progress

Farley, Eugene J.
Barron's How to prepare for the high
school equivalency examination reading interpretation tests. Barrons Educ. Ser. 1970
477p illus $8   371.27
1 Reading—Examinations, questions, etc.
"Planned for adults who have not completed
high school but also useful for high school
students who wish to extend basic skills in
reading and interpretation. Initial chapters
provide information on the equivalency cer-
tificate and requirements of the General Educational Development Tests. Social studies,
science, and literature are the subject areas
covered. Their general and special skills and
techniques are clarified; pertinent sample passages of material at three levels of difficulty
are given; questions (with answers listed
separately) check reader comprehension; explanations describe reasoning process to figure
out answers; and cautions warn against false
reasoning. Application information by state
and territories; sources of reading passages."
Booklist

371.3 Methods of instruction

Beggs, David W.
  (ed.) Team teaching; bold new venture; introduction by Harold Spears. Ind. Univ. Press 1964 192p illus $6.50   **371.3**
    1 Teaching teams
  "Exploring significant new developments and ideas in education, this study brings together a thought-provoking presentation by practitioners of what happens in a school when team teaching is employed." Publisher's note
    Bibliography: p179-87

Kohl, Herbert R.
  The open classroom; a practical guide to a new way of teaching. A New York Review Book, distributed by Vintage [1970 c1969] 116p pa $1.65   **371.3**
    1 Teaching
  "This book is a handbook for teachers who want to work in an open environment. . . . In an open situation the teacher tries to express what he feels and to deal with each situation as a communal problem. [The] book is based upon the experience of teachers: their problems, failures, and frustrations, as well as their successes. It is about the battles with self and system that teachers encounter in the schools. But it is not a handbook that gives teachers a step-by-step account of how to change their classrooms and themselves. . . . [It] does, however, try to anticipate problems, to present possibilities and make suggestions." Introduction

371.33 Audio-visual materials for teaching. Bulletin boards

American Association of School Librarians
  Standards for school media programs; prepared by the American Association of School Librarians and the Department of Audiovisual Instruction of the National Education Association in cooperation with representatives of the American Association of School Administrators [and others]. A.L.A. 1969 66p pa $2   **371.33**
    1 Audio-visual education   2 School libraries
  First published 1960 with title: Standards for school library programs
  "Two objectives that have motivated this project are: (1) to bring standards in line with the needs and requirements of today's educational goals and (2) to coordinate standards for school library and audiovisual programs. . . . The standards presented . . . describe the services of the media program in the school and note the requirements for the staff, resources, and facilities needed to implement the program effectively. Standards for personnel, resources, expenditures, and facilities are presented for a unified media program, but are applicable in schools having separate school libraries and audiovisual centers. The standards apply to schools having 250 or more students, but can also serve as valid guidelines for superior schools with fewer than 250 students that have or are planning a functional media program." Preface
  Bibliographical footnotes included. Definitions: p xv-xvi

Audio visual market place; a multimedia guide. Bowker pa $15   **371.33**
    1 Audio-visual education—Directories 2 Teaching—Aids and devices
  Annual. First published 1969
  Editor: 1969- Olga S. Weber
  Designed primarily for educators, this directory of the audio visual industry "brings together information on the U.S. companies, associations, and services dealing with films and other nonprint materials. . . . Listings cover professional and commercial associations, [producers and distributors] educational radio and television, film libraries, 'hardware' manufacturers, pertinent books and other reference sources, review services, and miscellaneous services. Listings in some sections are also classified by type of media." Booklist

Coplan, Kate
  Guide to better bulletin boards; time and labor-saving ideas for teachers and librarians, by Kate Coplan and Constance Rosenthal. Oceana 1970 xxii, 232p illus $17.50   **371.33**
    1 Bulletin boards
  ISBN 0-379-00369-4
  The primary purpose of this volume is "to put at the disposal of teachers and librarians everywhere those techniques and design elements which would assist them in producing constructive visual aids easily and swiftly. . . . Though intended mainly for teachers and librarians in the elementary schools . . . many of the ideas presented . . . may be adapted with minor changes to the needs of the higher grades, as well. . . . In addition, workers in public libraries, museums, art schools, book stores, religious schools, and other book-oriented establishments, should find the concepts depicted here useful in developing their own exhibits skills for their own particular purposes." Introduction
  Related readings: p219-20

National Information Center for Educational Media
  Index to 8mm motion cartridges. Bowker 1969 402p $19.50   **371.33**
    1 Moving pictures in education—Catalogs
  SBN 8352-0276-3
  "Lists and describes . . . educational 8mm motion cartridges, with the following information: Annotations, Running time, Year of release, Audience level, Producer/distributor codes, Series listings, Whether film is silent, has optical or magnetic sound track." Publisher's note

  Index to overhead transparencies. Bowker 1969 552p $22.50   **371.33**
    1 Audio-visual education—Catalogs   2 Slides (Photography)—Catalogs
  SBN 8352-0277-1
  This guide to commercially produced transparencies gives "Descriptive annotations; Series listings; Physical size; Type (prepared, operable, polarized); Number of overlays; Color; Audience level; Producer/distributor codes; Year of release." Publisher's note

  Index to 16mm educational films. 2d ed. Bowker 1969 1111p $39.50   **371.33**
    1 Moving pictures in education—Catalogs
    2 Filmstrips—Catalogs
  SBN 8352-0275-5
  First published 1967 by McGraw
  "Lists alphabetically by title 27,400 films. Each entry includes a brief description; codes indicating producer and distributor; whether in color or black and white; running time; series title reference; edition if other than first; year of U.S. release in 16mm; and, in many cases, audience level. Library of Congress card catalog numbers are included, where available. In addition to individual title entries, series title entries are given, with a listing of films in the series." Publisher's note
  Includes subject guide and directory of producers and distributors

  Index to 35mm filmstrips. 2d ed. Bowker 1970 872p $34   **371.33**
    1 Moving pictures in education—Catalogs
    2 Filmstrips—Catalogs
  SBN 8352-0278-X
  First published 1968 by McGraw
  This index lists and describes educational filmstrips. "The Alphabetical Title section

National Information Center for Educational Media—*Continued*
indicates: The number of frames for each title; The Series; Whether it is captioned or accompanied by record, script, or audio tape. Other . . . information is provided, such as annotation, date of release in the U.S. and producer/distributor codes." Publisher's note

Oates, Stanton C.
Audiovisual equipment; self-instruction manual. Illus. by George Cohen. 2d ed. Brown, W.C. 1971 226p illus pa $3.95   371.33
1 Teaching—Aids and devices 2 Projectors 3 Sound—Recording and reproducing
ISBN 0-697-06042-X
Spiral binding
First published 1966
Using this manual the reader can, first, learn by himself "the operation of audiovisual equipment. Second, through the use of the indexes, one may quickly locate the information needed to adjust equipment that is not performing properly in the classroom. . . . The pages that follow cover the basic principles of the operation of filmstrip-slide projectors, tape recorders, motion-picture projectors, opaque projectors, overhead projectors, record players and portable projection screens. . . . At the end of each of these sections there is a quiz to test understanding and comprehension. Then following the basic information sections are specific directions on selected makes and models." Preface

371.42 Educational and vocational guidance

Lovejoy, Clarence E.
Lovejoy's Career and vocational school guide; a source book, clue book and directory of job training opportunities. Simon & Schuster $6.50   371.42
1 Vocational education—Directories
First published 1955 with title: Lovejoy's Vocational school guide
A guide to public and private vocational schools which "list training facilities for different occupations by state. Includes those offering free, or nominal tuition courses, home study courses, and training for the handicapped." Pub W

Russell, Max M.
(ed.) The blue book of occupational educations; Max M. Russell, editorial director. CCM Information Corp. 1971 897p $29.95   371.42
1 Vocational education—Directories
This book "presents descriptive information on almost twelve thousand occupational schools of the United States. . . . The composite of information included in this volume is the result of requests, recommendations, and directions of State vocational education personnel, by those engaged in occupational counseling, by school counselors, and finally by thirty years of personal experience in public education." Preface

371.8 The student

Libarle, Marc
(ed.) The high school revolutionaries [ed. by] Marc Libarle and Tom Seligson. Random House 1970 xxxi, 276p $6.95   371.8
1 Students—U.S. 2 High schools 3 Youth movement
"A Scanlan's book"

This is a "collection of taped interviews and previously unpublished essays by 21 radical high school and junior high students of different backgrounds from around the U.S. Some talk about what it is that leads to rebellion in privileged suburban and private high schools, some about the problems in ghetto schools and racism. Others speak out on the 'cultural revolution,' junior high radicalism, religion, the politics of the high school movement, and women's liberation." Booklist
"The quality of the collection is uneven, but at least five pieces are exceptionally well-argued and provocative." N Y Times Bk R

371.89 School activities. School journalism

Loken, Newt
Cheerleading. 2d ed. Ronald 1961 92p illus (Ronald Sports lib) boards $5   371.89
1 Cheers and cheerleading
First published 1945 by A. S. Barnes as: Cheerleading & marching bands, by Newt Loken and Otis Dypwick
This introduction to cheerleading offers a "collection of traditional and novelty cheers and a thorough discussion of how to lead them. Stunts and tumbling routines . . . skits and stunts for pep rallies are presented." Preface

Magmer, James
Photograph & printed word; a new language for the student journalist, editors, writers, photographers working on the school newspaper, yearbook, magazine. David Falconer, photographer. Midwest Pub. Co. 1969 150p illus $7.95   371.89
1 College and school journalism 2 Photography, Journalistic
"A practical, elementary guide for schools with journalism courses and extensive publication programs shows student journalists how to combine photographs and text effectively. It stresses the importance of team work among editors, writers, and photographers, suggests ways to achieve the desired collaboration, and, in line with its thesis that photographs are a necessary tool in school journalism, uses them copiously to illustrate principles set forth in the text. Technical problems, including choice of type, layout, methods of photographic reproduction and the use of color are also covered, with a glossary supplied." Booklist

Medlin, C. J.
Yearbook editing, layout, and management. Iowa State Univ. Press 1966 244p illus $8.50   371.89
1 College and school journalism 2 Yearbooks
A "handbook on the production of high school and college annuals, for faculty advisers and student staff. . . . The illustrations reproduce pages from school yearbooks which demonstrate practices recommended in the text; other features include . . . surveys of high school yearbook production costs and income, and an abbreviated style book." Booklist

Shaff, A. L.
The student journalist and the critical review. Rosen, R. 1970 117p (The Student journalist guide ser) lib. bdg. $3.99 371.89
1 College and school journalism 2 Criticism
This book discusses "three basic ideas for the young critic: Why he should be a critic; how he should prepare himself to become a critic; and how he actually goes about writing literary, musical, or film criticism. . . . It is written with the student journalist specifically in mind." Preface
Included are sample reviews of specific works

371.9 Special education

Ashton-Warner, Sylvia
Teacher. Simon & Schuster 1963 224p
illus $5.95   **371.9**
1 Maoris—Education   2 Education—Experimental methods 3 Teaching

"As a teacher of the Maori children in New Zealand, the author found it necessary to experiment with new and different teaching methods to prepare her pupils for the difficult transition at a relatively early age from a simple, rather primitive culture to that of the complex modern world. The first half of the book is an explanation, a justification, of her Creative Teaching Scheme, an organic process based on the intensity of the child's interest and of her Maori reader series. . . . Her methods are illustrated by brief case studies. The second half consists of stories of the Maori children, their families, their daily activities, their recreation, but most of all, their school life." Library J

"A vivid journal of incidents, personalities, sudden moments of insight, and a philosophy of education in old cultures and new nations, upon experiences. It should have great value not only for those interested in the problems of education in old cultures and new nations, but also for those concerned with the future of civilization." N Y Times Bk R

Decker, Sunny
An empty spoon; photographs by Tana Hoban. Harper 1969 115p illus $4.95 **371.9**
1 Negroes—Education   2 Teaching   3 Philadelphia—Public schools

This is a document of the experiences and growing pains of a white teacher in an all Negro high school in Philadelphia. The author discusses her own inadequacies and those of her fellow teachers, as well as the moral and social pressures under which the children she taught lived

Kohl, Herbert
36 children; illus. by Robert George Jackson, III. New Am. Lib. [distributed by World Pub] 1967 227p illus boards $5.95
                                              371.9
1 Negroes—Education   2 New York (City)—Public schools 3 Teaching

The author "tells of his years spent teaching children in a Harlem school, from his own fear and confusion on the first day (baffled by his pupils apathy or resentment) to the progress of his thirty-six children during the next four years. He makes . . . comments on teaching methods and materials and explains his changes from academic traditions." Bk Buyer's Guide

This sometimes heartbreaking book is as much by the children as by the author. Starting with simple descriptions of their surroundings, some progressed to the perceptive stories, fables and poems that comprise about half the text." N Y Times Bk R

Kozol, Jonathan
Death at an early age; the destruction of the hearts and minds of Negro children in the Boston public schools. Houghton 1967 240p $5.95   **371.9**
1 Negroes—Education 2 Boston—Public schools 3 Discrimination in education

National Book Award winner, 1968

The author "writes of a year spent in a predominantly Negro school in Boston, where the children were subjected to fear, humiliation and discrimination, thus killing both mind and spirit. The author attempted to impart learning and pride of being, but was defeated by the unwritten yet clearly defined anti-Negro policies of the local school board. A moving indictment of segregation, Northern style." Books for Brotherhood

"The finest moments in this book are those in which the author quite openly examines his own, ordinary ('normal,' if you will) willingness to go along with the rest, to submit to the very mean and stupid practices he so clearly recognized." N Y Times Bk R

Bibliography included in Notes: p235-40

373.1 The secondary school

Birmingham, John
(ed.) Our time is now. Notes from the high school underground. Introduction [by] Kurt Vonnegut, Jr. Praeger 1970 262p illus $5.95   **373.1**
1 College and school journalism 2 Students—U.S.

As editor of his high school's two newspapers (an "overground" and an underground) the author "became aware of the extent and intensity of high school students' growing concern with their own roles, the quality of their education, and the controls they feel are imposed upon them. Quite deftly tied together by his comments and explanations, the text consists of excerpts from underground papers all over the United States. They range from satirical applause for the System and reasoned editorials to biting criticism and inflamed (possibly inflammatory) diatribes. In various ways they ask (or demand) student power, freedom from the dicta of authority, a voice in the shaping of curricula, less rigid attendance requirements, etc. The editorial comments are informative and astute, the book an eye-opener." Chicago. Children's Book Center

373.2 Junior high schools

Herndon, James
How to survive in your native land. Simon & Schuster 1971 192p $5.95   **373.2**
1 Junior high schools 2 Education—U.S.
SBN 671-20864-0

This book describes the experiences of a teacher in a white middle-class California suburb. "He makes some of the 'problem children' come alive, and you wonder whether it is the child or the system that is really the problem. His conclusions . . . [are that] children need direction; when they are given freedom to do what they wish, they do nothing. But when the teachers are busy doing things that they, as adults, are interested in, the children want to get in on the act. 'Teachers ought to know something about what they are doing. They can't "depend" on the kids to show them how to teach.' " Library J

373.73 Secondary education—U.S.

Conant, James B.
The comprehensive high school; a second report to interested citizens. McGraw 1967 95p $3.95   **373.73**
1 High schools 2 Education, Secondary

In a second report to the public (the first was The American high school today, published 1959), the author "finds that the situation regarding academic studies in a great many schools is better than it was a decade ago but that only a few schools can be regarded as highly satisfactory. This work, based on a questionnaire sent to public high school principals in 50 states, centers on staff-student ratios, the elective system, and general education in the high school. General trends in public education and statistical data conclude a concise but probing inquiry." Booklist

374   Adult education

Wellman, Henry Q.
The teenager and home study; a practical guide to correspondence education for young people and guidance counselors. Rosen, R. 1970 155p illus lib. bdg. $3.99   **374**
1 Correspondence schools and courses 2 Vocational guidance
SBN 8239-0204-8
The author discusses the correspondence method of education and how to choose the right school. Some of the courses covered are in airlines, data processing, drafting, medical office assisting, banking. There are also chapters on learning a hobby, finishing high school, and taking college-level courses at home. An appendix lists accredited correspondence schools
Bibliography: p155

378.1   Colleges and universities

Bander, Edward J.
(ed.) Turmoil on the campus. Wilson, H.W. 1970 276p (The Reference shelf v42, no.3) $4.50   **378.1**
1 Students—U.S. 2 Colleges and universities —U.S.
ISBN 0-8242-0411-5
Educators, representatives of the government, social scientists and political observers discuss various aspects of student unrest in the United States and the implications of this unrest for the country and for the universities. Among the topics covered are causes of the unrest, Black studies, law and order, and the events at Kent State University and Jackson State College
Bibliography: p261-76

Fine, Benjamin
How to be accepted by the college of your choice. Appleton boards $4.95   **378.1**
1 Colleges and universities—Entrance requirements
First published 1957 by Channel Press. Periodically revised to bring information up to date
Detailed advice and information on all aspects of college entrance requirements. Includes a state by state analysis of the entrance standards of accredited colleges
Includes sample applications and test questions

Foster, Julian
(ed.) Protest! Student activism in America; ed. by Julian Foster and Durward Long. Morrow 1970 596p $10   **378.1**
1 Students—U.S. 2 Youth movement
This is a "study of student protest movements during the past decade. . . . Essays cover historical background, the faculty role in student activities, and the actions of the SDS, BSU, TWAF, and other student organizations. Also included are psycho-sociological studies of causes and motivations, and case histories of confrontations at several campuses, including Indiana University, the University of Wisconsin, and San Francisco State College. One chapter is a discussion of research sources on student protest." Library J
"Both serious students as well as the general reader will want to refer to this important and convenient source whenever American activism is discussed." Choice

Kampen, Irene
Due to lack of interest tomorrow has been canceled. Doubleday 1969 168p $3.95 **378.1**
1 Students—Anecdotes, facetiae, satire, etc.
Returning to the University of Wisconsin at the age of 45 to pick up six or seven credits

to her long-delayed degree [the author] finds herself living amidst a group of student agitators, taking alarmingly Freudian literature courses, and being a wallflower at her compulsory folk-dance class. Student protestors, 'with-it' religion, 'artsy' faculty, and 'out-of-it' alumnae are all exposed in this . . . [satire of] life on campus." Library J
"The view from the older generation is not critical, but amused and sympathetic. [The author] does not make judgments, she merely presents a scene and lets the reader draw his own conclusion. The writing is spritely with comic situations handled by understatement." Best Sellers

Kunen, James Simon
The strawberry statement—notes of a college revolutionary. Random House 1969 150p $4.95   **378.1**
1 Students—U.S. 2 Columbia University
This journal, written by a Columbian sophomore "before, during and after [the 1968] student rebellion at Columbia University, is a . . . collection of diary entries, aphorisms and occasional musings on youth, student radicalism, baseball, long hair and the problems of American society. The title is inspired by a Columbia dean's . . . remark, in the midst of the student uprising that 'whether student's vote 'yes' or 'no' on an issue is like telling me they like strawberries." Newsweek
The author "writes in a natural, articulate way that conveys confidence in his own voice and attitudes, and little else. . . . His writing [is] directly personal rather than pretentious . . . and [this] makes him worth listening to. His the language is terse, his thoughts fragmentary and tentative, both keyed to the immediacy of the here and now." New Repub

United States. President's Commission on Campus Unrest
The report of the President's Commission on Campus Unrest; including special reports: The killings at Jackson State [and] The Kent State tragedy. Arno Press 1970 537p illus maps $5.95   **378.1**
1 Students—U.S. 2 Colleges and universities —U.S.
ISBN 0-405-01712-X
The report and recommendations of the Commission established by President Nixon on June 13, 1970 under the chairmanship of William W. Scranton
This "is a thorough, unbiased, well documented, and generally accurate document. . . . The bulk of the report deals with the student movement—its history, development in the 1960's, and specific aspects such as the black student movement. The report's recommendations deal largely with how academic institutions and government should respond to student unrest and broader crises. The suggestions are generally moderate, and place the burden of responsibility on the universities themselves, rather than on government intervention. . . . A must for any library, and indeed, for anyone concerned with understanding the campus crisis." Choice
Bibliography: p466-518

379.102 Colleges and universities— Handbooks, manuals, etc.

Lass, Abraham H.
The college student's handbook. Rev. ed. [by] Abraham H. Lass and Eugene S. Wilson. White 1970 201p $6.95   **378.102**
1 Colleges and universities—U.S.—Handbooks, manuals, etc. 2 Students
SBN 87250-007-1
First published 1965
A "guide which identifies and treats the academic, financial and social problems facing all college students. With . . . material on campus activism, sexual freedom and drugs." Publisher's note
Where to get career information: p190-201

378.3 Student costs and finances

Angel, Juvenal L.
How and where to get scholarships &
loans. 2d ed. Regents Pub. 1968 221p $6.50
378.3

1 Scholarships, fellowships, etc. 2 Education
—Finance

First published 1964
"A compilation of 'all' the available data
on current scholarships and loans. For easy
reference, it is organized into five major sections: (1) A broad, general survey of the whole
field of scholarships and loans: how and where
to find them, information on the steps to
take and the material to submit, when applying. (2) A complete alphabetic guide to scholarships and loans for undergraduate college
training, including colleges, foundations and
other organizations. (3) An index to Section
2, arranged alphabetically by states so that
the student can readily locate the area in
which he is interested. (4) A list of specialized
sources of financial aid, classified, according
to race, religion, nationality, region, etc. (5)
A reference list of publications concerned with
undergraduate student financial aid, offered
here as a convenience for those who wish to
make further inquiries." Introduction

Garraty, John A.
The new guide to study abroad [by] John
A. Garraty, Walter Adams [and] Cyril J. H.
Taylor. Harper $7.95
378.3

1 Scholarships, fellowships, etc. 2 Colleges
and universities—Europe

First published 1962 by Channel Press with
title: A guide to study abroad. Periodically revised
This handbook for high school and college
students and teachers evaluates programs and
provides "information on sponsorship, language
requirements, academic credits, dates, costs,
and where to obtain further information or send
one's application. . . . Work-study programs
are also treated, and there are helpful suggestions for combining education with tourism."
Publisher's note

Lovejoy, Clarence E.
Lovejoy's Scholarship guide. Simon &
Schuster 1964 91p $4.95
378.3

1 Scholarships, fellowships, etc. 2 Colleges
and universities—U.S.

First published 1957 with title: Lovejoy-Jones
College scholarship guide
Contains lists of scholarships, fellowships,
loan funds and other financial aids, arranged
alphabetically and numbered serially, with
names and addresses of donors and sponsors.
Full index and cross references
"A convenient compilation for school and
public libraries." Booklist

Proia, Nicholas C.
Barron's Handbook of American college
financial aid, by Nicholas C. Proia [and]
Vincent M. Di Gaspari. Barrons Educ. Ser.
1971 701p pa $6.95
378.3

1 Scholarships, fellowships, etc. 2 Student
loan funds

This "is a comprehensive review of approximately 1200 four-year private and public colleges who offer financial assistance to high
school graduates and those who transfer from
a two- or four-year college to a four-year college. . . . Also, you will find herein answers
to questions that confront the college-bound
student. 'Where do I start?' 'How do I go
about applying?' 'What are the qualifications?'
'Who offers the assistance best suited to my
needs?' 'When do I apply?' " Introduction

Barron's Handbook of junior and community college financial aid, by Nicholas C.
Proia [and] Vincent M. Di Gaspari. Barrons Educ. Ser. 1970 697p pa $6.95
378.3

1 Scholarships, fellowships, etc. 2 Student
loan funds

The topics covered in this guide are: "what
to consider in determining college cost, the
financial aid 'package,' the independent student, the married student, how to obtain application forms, when to apply for aid, a glossary of financial terms, types and conditions of
grants and loans, complete information on
financial aid at over 800 two-year junior and
community colleges." Publisher's note

Study abroad; international guide; fellowships, scholarships, educational exchange.
UNESCO pa $6
378.3

1 Scholarships, fellowships, etc. 2 International education

Biennial. First published 1948. Issued annually until 1966
"Gives details of available fellowships and
scholarships for international study, including:
name, field of study, value, duration, number
available, where to send application, and date
limit. Arranged according to donors of awards,
by administering agency or by country in which
donor is located. Includes a list of organizations, arranged alphabetically. In English,
French, and Spanish." Winchell. Guide to Reference Books. 8th edition

378.73 Higher education—U.S.

American Council on Education
Accredited institutions of higher education. Published for Federation of Regional
Accrediting Commissions of Higher Education. The Council pa $4.50
378.73

1 Colleges and universities—U.S.—Directories

Semiannual. First published 1964
Supersedes a publication of the same title
issued annually by the National Committee of
Regional Accrediting Commissions of Higher
Education
Lists "institutions of higher education in
the United States that are accredited by the
nation's six regional associations of schools
and colleges, and two institutions in Mexico
that are so accredited." Preface
"The specialized accreditation noted in this
directory is limited to the twenty-eight professional fields whose accrediting agencies are
recognized by the National Commission on Accrediting." p xiv

American junior colleges. Am. Council on
Educ. $14
378.73

1 Junior colleges—Directories 2 Education—
U.S.—Directories

First published 1940. Frequently revised and
brought up to date
"Arranged alphabetically by state, [this di-
rectory] provides for each college a brief history, requirements, fees, student aid, staff, . . .
enrollment statistics, number of foreign students, library facilities, publications finances,
buildings and grounds, and names of chief
administrative offices. An introductory summary for each state. [Canal Zone, Guam,
Puerto Rico and District of Columbia is included.]" Cur Ref Bks

American universities and colleges. Am.
Council on Educ. $22
378.73

1 Colleges and universities—U.S.—Directories
2 Education—U.S.—Directories

First published 1928. Frequently revised to
bring the information on requirements, tuition, courses, and new institutions up to date
"The most generally useful educational directory for higher education, presenting a
summary of the present resources of American
colleges and universities in three main sections: (1) Survey articles on higher education
in the United States, including chapters on
selecting a college; undergraduate, graduate,
and professional education; the federal government and higher education; the foreign student, etc.; (2) Professional education; (3) Descriptions of . . . institutions arranged alphabetically by state, giving for each: definite
information about its history, organization,

American universities and colleges—*Cont.*
calendar, admission and degree requirements, fees, graduate work, departments and teaching staff, distinctive educational programs and activities, degrees conferred, enrollment, foreign students, library resources, publications, student financial aid, finances, buildings and grounds, administrative offices, etc." Winchell. Guide to Reference Books. 8th edition

Barron's Guide to the two-year colleges. Barrons Educ. Ser. illus maps $8   **378.73**
1 Junior colleges—Directories
First published 1960, and completely revised 1966, under the authorship of Seymour Eskow. Periodically revised to keep up to date
Part one covers such topics as planning to go to a two-year college, counting the cost, and exploring individual motives, preferences and chances of success in such a college. Part two discusses such subjects as the history and patterns of the two-year college, and choosing a two-year college. The third and largest part of the book contains both regional and alphabetical lists of American two-year colleges

Barzun, Jacques
The American university; how it runs, where it is going. Harper 1968 319p $7.95
  378.73
1 Colleges and universities—U.S. 2 Education, Higher
The author "describes the American university, its changing shape and its complexity, and tries to foresee something of its future." Book of the Month Club News
The author "bewails the fantastically rapid rate of growth of the university since World War II, and sees 'bigger' as not necessarily 'better.' . . . Nevertheless, a most urbane and enlightening volume by an establishment leader." Choice
Bibliography: p295-302

Cass, James
Comparative guide to American colleges; for students, parents, and counselors by James Cass and Max Birnbaum. Harper $10
  378.73
1 Colleges and universities—U.S.—Directories
2 Education—U.S.—Directories
First published 1964. Periodically revised to keep information up to date
This handbook covers "Admission requirements; Academic opportunities offered by the Institution; Faculty qualifications; Enrollment figures; Degrees offered; Special programs [and intellectual, social, religious, and cultural environment." Publisher's note
The authors have provided a "business-like introduction and put their stress on standards of quality in assessment. No other general or popular directory of our vast array of colleges tells as much about the students, faculty or campus life of U.S. colleges." Library J
Includes bibliographies

Comparative guide to two-year colleges & four-year specialized schools and programs, by James Cass and Max Birnbaum. Harper 1969 xxii, 275p $7.95   **378.73**
1 Colleges and universities—U.S.—Directories
2 Junior colleges—Directories 3 Education—U.S.—Directories
Companion volume to: Comparative guide to American colleges, entered above
This handbook provides information about specialized schools and programs in the visual, performing and communication arts, as well as two-year colleges
"In addition to supplying the usual information about schools, the authors rather successfully attempt to provide the flavor of each individual school by furnishing information on such matters as anticipated growth, average ACT and SAT test scores of entering students, percentage of students going on to four-year schools, and so forth." Library J

The **College** blue book. CCM Information Corp. [distributed by Crowell-Collier Press] 10v $99   **378.73**
1 Colleges and universities—U.S.—Directories
2 Education—U.S.—Directories
Available separately as follows: volumes 2, 5, 6, 10, each $9.95; volume 3, $14.50; volumes 4, 9, each $12.50
First published 1923, edited by Christian E. Burckel; roughly biennial since 1947. The 12th edition is the first complete computerized revision; 1969/1970, editorial director: Max Russell
Contents: v 1: Guide and index; v2: U.S. colleges: tabular data; v3: U.S. colleges: narrative description; v4: Degrees offered, by subject; v5: Degrees offered, by college; v6: College atlas; v7: Specialized educational programs; v8: Professors, careers, and accreditation; v9 Scholarships, fellowships, and grants; v10: Secondary schools in the U.S.

College Entrance Examination Board
A chance to go to college; a directory of 800 colleges that have special help for students from minorities and low-income families. The Board 1971 248p pa $3   **378.73**
1 Colleges and universities—U.S.—Directories
2 Education—U.S.—Directories
Alphabetical listing by state of 829 colleges which offer various kinds of aid (financial, special tutoring services, etc.) to members of minority groups and low-income families. (Publisher)

Fine, Benjamin
Barron's Profiles of American colleges. Barrons Educ. Ser. $9.95   **378.73**
1 Colleges and universities—U.S.—Directories
2 Education—U.S.—Directories
First published 1964. Periodically revised
"It gives enrollment, educational philosophy, physical plant, costs, programs of study, admission requirements, and extracurricular activities for [approximately 1300] colleges and universities accredited by one of the six regional accrediting associations. . . . The book provides a great deal of information." Cur Ref Bks
Includes bibliography

Hawes, Gene R.
The New American Guide to colleges. Columbia Univ. Press $10   **378.73**
1 Colleges and universities—U.S.—Directories
2 Education—U.S.—Directories
First published 1959 by the New American Library of World Literature. Frequently revised
This book includes more than 2,000 "institutions recognized by the United States Office of Education in 1964. In addition, it describes a number of colleges not recognized by the U.S. Office. Separate entries are included for several hundred constituent colleges of universities as well; also included are entries for a few foreign universities of special interest to American students [and entries for graduate schools in the United States]." p13 (1966 edition)
For each college, the following information is given: general character of the college; student life; degrees, programs of study, and academic life; tuition and boarding charges; scholarships and other financial aid; admission policies and levels of academic demands; enrollment; graduate schools
Includes bibliography

Lovejoy, Clarence E.
Lovejoy's College guide. . . . Simon & Schuster $6.50   **378.73**
1 Colleges and universities—U.S.—Directories 2 Education—U.S.—Directories
First published 1940 with title: So you're going to college. Frequently revised
"A complete reference book to . . . American colleges and universities for use by students, parents, teachers, reference libraries, churches, parish houses, youth agencies, guidance coun-

Lovejoy, Clarence E.—*Continued*
selors, industrial corporations, foundations,
Army, Navy, Air Force, other federal services
and by foreign governments and agencies."
Title page of 1970 edition
"This book will tell you how to: Choose a
college—location, size, facilities; Be admitted
—when to apply, entrance tests, credits, mid-
year transfers; Get scholarships, loans, grants-
in-aid; Obtain guidance, career-planning information; Estimate expenses—tuition, board,
room, extras; Work your way through college."
Publisher's note

Pope, Loren
The right college; how to get in, stay in,
or get back in. Macmillan (N Y) 1970 209p
$6.95   378.73
1 Colleges and universities—U.S.   2 Students
—U.S.
This assessment of the nation's college scene
discusses "the college lottery—a cultural time
bomb; why the problem has grown; the student—the underachiever; the high school,
where the problem often starts; colleges and
the sellers' market; how to select a college;
junior colleges; resurrecting a disastrous se-
mester; the blessings of dropping or flunking
out; shifting gears for college; and dealing
with the draft board." Publisher's note
Bibliography: p201-02

379 Governmental supervision and financial support of education

Isenberg, Irwin
(ed.) The drive against illiteracy. Wilson,
H.W. 1964 164p (The Reference shelf v36,
no.5) $4.50   379
1 Illiteracy   2 Poverty
Analyzed in Essay and general literature index
A collection of 29 articles concerning illiteracy, poverty, and their interrelationship. The
material is arranged under the following headings: The world-wide struggle against illiteracy; The undereducated millions; The underprivileged; Literacy campaign for the United
States
Bibliography: p157-64

380.5 Transportation services

Owen, Wilfred
Wheels, by Wilfred Owen, Ezra Bowen
and the editors of Time-Life Books. Time-
Life Bks. [1968 c1967] 200p illus (Life Science lib) lib. bdg. $7.60   380.5
1 Transportation—History   2 Wheels
"A Stonehenge book"
First published 1967
"This volume surveys that [technological]
progress from the solid wheeled oxcarts of ancient times to the 130-mph Tokaido express and
turbine-powered trucks. It traces the many
turns of the wheel's development, and points to
innovations that are likely to shape human society in the future." About this book
"The appendices show construction profiles
of great bridges, the power systems of the automobile, and suggestions for reading (which
could have been improved). The book is a
blend of engineering, economics, and sociology
that provides a coherent and interesting treatment of a subject that is of concern to almost
everybody." Science Bks

Reische, Diana
(ed.) Problems of mass transportation.
Wilson, H.W. 1970 208p (The Reference
shelf v42, no.5) $4.50   380.5
1 Transportation   2 Local transit
ISBN 0-8242-0413-1
"Both urban and interurban transportation
in the U.S. are examined for the causes of the
present situation and various trends in automobile, bus, train, and air transportation that
may ameliorate or worsen conditions. Most of
the 30 articles are selected from general news
magazines and newspapers." Booklist
Bibliography: p199-208

Ridley, Anthony
An illustrated history of transportation.
Day 1969 186p illus $5.95   380.5
1 Transportation—History
"How transportation has developed from the
days when prehistoric man paddled a fallen
log, to the jumbo jet and space ship is surveyed in this comprehensive and attractive
volume." News of Bks
"This is a copiously illustrated book of transportation. . . . The illustrations are well chosen
and make the book quite worthwhile. Those
who pick it up will find it hard to put down
since it contains so many interesting details."
Best Sellers

381.061 U.S. Federal Trade Commission

Cox, Edward F.
'The Nader report' on the Federal Trade
Commission, by Edward F. Cox, Robert C.
Fellmeth [and] John E. Schulz. Preface by
Ralph Nader. Richard W. Baron 1969 241p
$5.95   381.061
1 U.S. Federal Trade Commission   2 Consumer protection
Ralph Nader "sent a team of seven young
law students in the summer of 1968 to find out
why deceptive business practices and advertising can continue all but unchallenged to take
millions annually out of the pockets of American consumers, especially the ghetto poor.
They released a report of their investigation of
the Federal Trade Commission in January
1969. This is an updated and expanded version
of that report prepared by three members of
the team." Book Rev Digest
This is a "controversial but thoroughly documented survey. . . . The statement given by
[FTC] Chairman Paul Rand Dixon when the
data were released and the authors' reply are
reprinted in full with an overview of the FTC
and statistical analyses appended." Booklist

Wagner, Susan
The Federal Trade Commission. Praeger
1971 261p illus (Praeger Lib. of U.S. Government departments and agencies) $9
                                        381.061
1 U.S. Federal Trade Commission   2 U.S.—
Commerce
"A brief history of the Federal Trade Commission, its reorganization as of July 1, 1970,
and the evolution of its purpose precedes the
author's exploration of the work of the FTC
discussing its investigation of the meat-pack-
ing, oil, drug, and cigarette industries in addition to cases brought against specific companies. She considers such topics as unfair
trade practices, mergers, price discrimination,
false advertising, truth-in-packaging, and
truth-in-lending and explains various regulatory trade laws and their application." Booklist
Appendixes include information on careers in
trade regulation and the Federal Trade Commission Act
Bibliography: p251-55

382 International commerce

Savage, Katharine
The story of the Common Market; illus.
with photographs and maps. Walck, H.Z.
[1970 c1969] 192p illus maps $6   382
1 European Economic Community
ISBN 0-8098-3091-4
First published 1969 in England with title:
The history of the Common Market

Savage, Katharine—*Continued*
This is the story of the creation by Belgium, West Germany, France, Italy, Luxembourg and the Netherlands "of the European Economic Community—better known as the Common Market. . . . [The author] describes the first attempts at cooperation between countries, and the actual founding of the Market . . . [and gives a] picture of how the Market works—its roles in industry, agriculture, trade and atomic energy." Publisher's note
"A clear and readable presentation. . . . The influences of numerous European personages in developing and spreading the original idea is ably shown. It is full of information logically presented, and yet uncluttered by exhaustive detail. There is appropriate emphasis given both the accomplishments and problems of the Common Market." Best Sellers
Bibliography: p185-86

383.2 Postage stamps

Bloomgarden, Henry S.
American history through commemorative stamps. Arco 1969 141p lib. bdg. $5.95
383.2
1 Postage stamps 2 U.S.—History
The author "arranges 68 full-page reproductions of U.S. commemorative postage stamps to chronicle significant personalities, events, places, and causes of American history from Columbus' voyage to the first U.S. orbital space flight. Noting the historical importance of each topic memorialized in this representative selection of U.S. commemorative postage stamps, the author provides further information about each stamp: when and where and in what denomination it was first issued, the name of the artist, and the picture or drawing reproduced. Interesting as Americana and as an aid for stamp collectors." Booklist

Reinfeld, Fred
Stamp collectors' handbook; adapted by Burton Hobson. Doubleday 1970 152p illus $3.95
383.2
1 Postage stamps
Profusely illustrated, this guide to collecting American stamps serves also as a detailed catalog of current values through January 1970 for all United States regular issues, commemoratives, air mails and special delivery stamps

Scott Publications, inc.
Scott's Standard postage stamp catalogue. The Company 2v in 1 illus $15
383.2
1 Postage stamps
An annual publication giving date of issue, color, shape, and value of all stamps ever issued by any government. A basic catalogue for collectors
Contents: v 1 The Americas and the British Commonwealth of Nations; v2 Nations of Europe, Africa, Asia and colonies

Scott's New handbook for philatelists. Simon & Schuster 1967 192p illus boards $5
383.2
1 Postage stamps
"A general book for the stamp collector on keeping up with philatelic news, founding or joining study groups, preparing collections, etc. With a stamp identifier, a glossary, a list of philatelic publications around the world." Bk Buyer's Guide

384.55 Television broadcasting

Friendly, Fred W.
Due to circumstances beyond our control. . . . Random House 1967 xxvi, 325p $8.95
384.55
1 Television broadcasting 2 Columbia Broadcasting System

In this "occupational memoir" of 16 years in television, the author evaluates the networks' current programming, analyzes the profits gained by broadcasters, and condemns the FCC for failure to police the industry. (Publisher)
This is "a loosely constructed volume, compounded of history, memoir, polemic, and pleading. . . . It is a forceful book, enormously informed, tartly analytical, astute, passionate, and disturbing. No one can read it without a sharply heightened sense of the tragedy of American TV." Book Week

Johnson, Nicholas
How to talk back to your television set. Little 1970 228p $5.75
384.55
1 Television broadcasting 2 U.S. Federal Communications Commission
"An Atlantic Monthly Press book"
The essays included range "from an analysis of TV's influence on private citizens and society in general to [discussions of] the current and future problems posed by technology (cable TV) and the dangers arising from increasing ownership in the hands of a few 'media barons.' . . . [The author] discusses nearly all the medium's inadequacies as licensed servant of J. Q. Public, and . . . [criticizes] both the broadcasting industry 'and' the FCC's bureaucratic sluggishness." Pub W

385.09 Railroad transportation—History

Moody, John
The railroad builders; a chronicle of the welding of the states. U.S. Pubs. Assn. 1919 257p (The Chronicles of America ser. v38) $4.45
385.09
1 Railroads—History
Originally published by Yale University Press
Contents: Century of railroad building; Commodore and the New York Central; Great Pennsylvania system; Erie railroad; Crossing the Appalachian range; Linking the oceans; Penetrating the Pacific Northwest; Building along the Santa Fé Trail; Growth of the Hill lines; Railroad system of the South; Life work of Edward H. Harriman; American railroad problem
"A piece of high-class journalistic history that avoids obvious pitfalls. . . . Mr Moody's volume is entitled to rank among the best of our summaries. His bibliography is sensible." Mississippi Valley Hist R

387.2 Ships

National Geographic Society
Men, ships and the sea, by Alan Villiers, and other adventurers on the sea. . . . The Society 1962 436p illus maps (The Story of man lib) $9.85
387.2
1 Ships 2 Voyages and travels 3 Seafaring life
"Prepared by National Geographic Book Service. Merle Severy, chief; foreword by Melville Bell Grosvenor." Title page
Articles are divided into the following topics: Man learns to sail; He discovers new worlds; He turns oceans into highways; He perfects his ships; He employs the power of steam; Man sails again for pleasure
"Magnificent illustrations. . . . There are lists of maritime museums and of historic ships still to be seen. The selection, of necessity, is episodic." Library J

387.5 Merchant marine. Salvage operations

Mowat, Farley
The grey seas under. Little 1958 341p illus boards $5.95   387.5
1 Salvage 2 Foundation Franklin (Tugboat)
"An Atlantic Monthly Press book"
"The author chronicles the history of the oceangoing [salvage] tug 'Foundation Franklin' and those who manned her. . . . The small but resolute vessel was employed from 1930 to 1947 in the hazardous business of aiding ships disabled in the storm-swept, treacherous North Atlantic. . . . Often dramatic, her story constitutes a true epic of the eternal battle between the rescue ships and the 'grey seas under.'" Booklist
Map on lining-papers

Paine, Ralph D.
The old merchant marine; a chronicle of American ships and sailors. U.S. Pubs. Assn. 1919 214p (The Chronicles of America ser. v36) $4.45   387.5
1 Merchant marine—U.S.
Originally published by Yale University Press
Contents: Colonial adventurers in little ships; Privateers of '76; Out cutlases and board! Famous days of Salem port; Yankee vikings and new trade routes; "Free trade and sailors' rights"; Brilliant era of 1812; Packet ships of the "Roaring Forties"; The stately clipper and her glory; Bound coastwise; Bibliographical note
"This is a splendid book with its animated and picturesque narrative. . . . The chapter on 'The clipper and her glory' is a joy to read and typical of the book as a whole." N Y Times Bk R

391 Costume

Wilcox, R. Turner
Folk and festival costume of the world. Scribner 1965 unp illus $10   391
1 Costume
This "survey of traditional dress from all over the world ranges—alphabetically—from Afghanistan to Yugoslavia. . . . In addition to all countries where native dress is still worn it also covers those countries and ethnic groups whose folk costumes have been replaced by conventional Western attire but who preserve their traditional garb for festive occasions." Publisher's note
A page of text accompanies each of the one hundred eleven plates which in turn have six or more black-and-white drawings. Useful for art and costume design classes
Includes bibliography

391.03 Costume—Dictionaries

Cunnington, C. Willett
A dictionary of English costume, by C. Willett Cunnington, Phillis Cunnington and Charles Beard. Dufour 1960 281p $8.95
                391.03
1 Costume—Dictionaries 2 Costume—History
"Brief entries, often illustrated by line drawings, are alphabetically arranged under the names of articles of clothing, styles, or terms used in tailoring or dressmaking. Hats, hairstyles, shoes, and other costume accessories are included. Information supplied includes dates when garment or style was popular, a description—frequently supplemented by a quotation from contemporary literature—and whether worn as sport attire or for formal or informal dress. A glossary lists, defines, and dates the costume materials used. A handy reference

source for students of English history and literature, costume designers, and those concerned with staging period plays." Booklist

Wilcox, R. Turner
The dictionary of costume. Scribner 1969 406p illus $15   391.03
1 Costume—Dictionaries
Incorporating many foreign words in the fashion world this book "not only describes briefly more than 3,000 articles of clothing, many of them with black-and-white drawings by the author, but also includes brief biographies of top couturiers of the twentieth century—Chanel, Dior, Cassini. Perhaps illustrations were included for less familiar clothing, for American-Indian costume is illustrated only with the head of an Indian in war paint, while Eighteenth Century costume is represented by dozens of corsets, chemises, and bustles. Adequate cross-references and convenient alphabetical arrangement of entries recommend it for quick identification of the 'New Look' or an angel sleeve." Cur Ref Bks
Bibliography: p405-06

391.09 Costume—History

Cunnington, C. Willett
Handbook of English mediaeval costume, by C. Willett Cunnington and Phillis Cunnington; with illus. by Barbara Phillipson and Catherine Lucas. [Rev. ed] Plays, inc. 1969 210p illus $8.95   391.09
1 Costume—History
First published 1952 in England
The period covered dates from 800-1500 A.D. and includes descriptions of men, women's, children's and working people's clothing
"As a reference book the arrangement of the material has been designed to facilitate accurate and ready dating of mediaeval illustrations, effigies, brasses, etc. It may also serve as a companion to the larger works on the subject and as a convenient guide to the stage costumier." Preface to first edition
Glossary: p182-89. Bibliography: p190-94

Cunnington, Phillis
Costumes of the seventeenth and eighteenth century. Plays, inc. [1971 c1968] 120p illus boards $3.95   391.09
1 Costume—History
ISBN 0-8238-0086-5
Copyright 1968 by the author. Published in England with title: Your book of seventeenth and eighteenth century costume
The book "describes the costumes of English men, women and children in the seventeenth and eighteenth centuries and covers details like hats and shoes as well as the main garments. It is very fully illustrated with authentic and attractive line drawings and it is also entertaining to read, for Dr. Cunnington draws on her wide knowledge of the literature of the period for amusing quotations and anecdotes about the fashions she describes." Publisher's note

Costumes of the nineteenth century. Plays, inc. 1971 [c1970] 80p illus boards $3.95
                391.09
1 Costume—History
ISBN 0-8238-0093-8
First published 1970 in England with title: Your book of nineteenth century costume
Companion volume to: Costumes of the seventeenth and eighteenth century, entered above
Here the author "has devoted a complete book to a single century, since fashions in the nineteenth century were particularly elaborate and fast-changing. [It] describes the clothes of men, women and children, including hats, shoes, accessories and hairstyles, and it is illustrated with many authentic and charming line drawings." Publisher's note

Cunnington, Phillis—*Continued*
Medieval and Tudor costume. Plays, inc.
1969 77p illus $3.95   391.09
1 Costume—History
"The Your book series"
First published 1968 with title: Your book
of medieval and Tudor costume
Covering the periods between the Norman
Conquest to the end of the reign of Elizabeth
I, this book describes "the clothes of the work-
ing people as well as fashionable costumes, and
the text includes shoes, gloves, hats, and hair
styles as well as the main garments." Choice
'Descriptions and accompanying illustrations
are useful and clear, but the binding is weak."
Library J

Evans, Mary
Costume throughout the ages. [Rev. ed]
Lippincott 1950 360p illus $8.95   391.09
1 Costume—History
First published 1930
"A textbook of costume, showing its develop-
ment from the ancient Egyptians and Assyrians
to the early twentieth century. Part one deals
with the historic dress of the ancients, the
French, the English, and the Americans; part
two with national costume in Europe, northern
Africa, Asia and the Americas." Book Rev
Digest
"A survey useful for those interested in de-
sign, in drama and/or the life at court and in
the alleys." Library J
Bibliography of the history of costume: p320-
31

Gorsline, Douglas
What people wore; a visual history of
dress from ancient times to twentieth-century America; written and illus. by Douglas
Gorsline. Viking 1952 266p illus $12.95
                                        391.09
1 Costume—History
"Beginning with a brief review of the ancient
world, this book traces in greater detail European costume trends from the medieval period to World War I—including such specialized items as armor, headgear, etc." McClurg.
Book News
"These hundreds of drawings, and the references to each of them in the back of the
book, add up to a very useful service which
Mr. Gorsline has performed pleasantly." N Y
Her Trib Books
Bibliography: p254-56

Harris, Christie
Figleafing through history: the dynamics
of dress [by] Christie Harris and Moira
Johnston; illus. by Moira Johnston. Atheneum Pubs. 1971 246p illus map $6.95
                                        391.09
1 Costume—History 2 Clothing and dress
Since earliest times dress "has been an expression of what men felt they were. It has
been an indicator of class and status, sometimes a sign of rebellion, and always an indication of the life style of the wearer. In their
book [the authors have taken a broad look
at the whole history of mankind . . . describing the clothes that went with the events."
Publisher's note
Selected bibliography: p229-35

Laver, James
The concise history of costume and fashion. Abrams [1969] 288p illus $7.50   391.09
1 Costume—History
"Discusses major changes in the form and
material of clothing throughout the development of Western civilization, pointing out
modifications in the original basic draped garment worn by men and women and the emer-

gence late in the fourteenth century of fashion
in the form of fitted clothing. Effectively combining text and illustrations. Laver shows the
reflection in costume and fashion of economic
and political conditions, noting the characteristics of contemporary styles and predicting further innovations in clothing fashion due to
social and cultural changes. A select bibliography is appended." Booklist

Costume through the ages; 1000 illus. in-
troduced by James Laver. Simon & Schuster [1964 c1963] 144p illus $5.95   391.09
1 Costume—History
Originally published 1961 in Germany; first
English translation published 1963 in England.
The plates were drawn and arranged by Erhard
Klepper
"A pictorial encyclopedia of representative
costumes from the first century up to 1 8
. . . Sources of the drawings are furnished in
the back of the book." Huntting
"Planned with student, illustrator, and
stage or film designer in mind, this should also
be a boon to producers of amateur theatricals."
Booklist

Lester, Katherine Morris
Historic costumes; a resumé of style and
fashion from remote times to the nineteen-
sixties [by] Katherine Morris Lester and
Rose Netzorg Kerr. Bennett illus $6.44
                                        391.09
1 Costume—History
First published 1925. Periodically revised
and brought up to date. Subtitles vary
"The aim has been to cover the periods of
costume as represented by those nations most
influential in matters of dress from remote times
to the present, emphasizing the most marked
of these influences and touching upon minor
details. The work deals primarily with the variation and development in the costume of women. Men's dress is also considered, and the
most important changes noted and closely
followed." Preface of the first edition
The book "is filled with interesting and curious information. The text is clear and readable. The use of historic incidents and literary
quotations is especially apt and commendable.
The book will prove serviceable to directors of
school plays in which historical characters appear. It will also be of value as supplementary
material to teachers of art, literature, history,
and costume design." School R

Lister, Margot
Costume: an illustrated survey from ancient times to the twentieth century. Plays,
inc. 1968 346p illus boards $12.95   391.09
1 Costume—History
"A comprehensive reference work on costume
from the old Egyptian kingdom to 1914, effectively illustrated with line drawings. Attention
to details such as hair style, footwear, jewelry,
colors and materials, suggestions for construct-
ing the garments, and inclusion of the dress of
all classes of society give it practical value. . . .
A glossary and list of authorities are included."
Booklist

Wilcox, R. Turner
Five centuries of American costume.
Scribner 1963 207p illus $10   391.09
1 Costume—History
A study of North and South "American
everyday costume from American Indian wear
to modern children's clothes. There are four
chapters on military costumes and there is a
lot about men's wear as well as women's
clothes. Each chapter is followed by 10 or 12
pages of handsome black and white drawings."
Pub W
"It is an excellent source for children's
clothes from the sixteenth century [on] for
cowboy dress, for [the dress of] Indians and
midshipmen. Illustrations are so clearly drawn
that they can be used by theatrical designers
as well as students and teachers." Cur Ref Bks
Bibliography: p203-07

392 Customs of life cycle

Emrich, Duncan
(comp.) The folklore of weddings and
marriage . . . illus. by Tomie de Paola. Am.
Heritage Press [distributed by McGraw]
1970 51p illus boards $1.95   **392**
1 Marriage customs and rites
SBN 8281-0057-8
"The traditional beliefs, customs, superstitions, charms, and omens of marriage and
marriage ceremonies." Subtitle
Bibliography: p[52]

393 Death customs

Mitford, Jessica
The American way of death. Simon &
Schuster 1963 333p $4.95   **393**
1 Funeral rites and ceremonies 2 Undertakers
and undertaking
The "inner workings of our Funeral Industry
are laid bare—its extraordinary public-relations
techniques, its embalming fashions, its attempts
to keep the 'nosy clergy' from standing between the mourner and the undertaker's sales
talk, the propaganda and the cemetery, coffin
and vault promotions." Huntting
Miss Mitford "constructs a brilliant journalistic case against the whole funeral industry. Her book is long and repetitious but
provides a helpful index of the few remaining
means of returning to dust with dignity."
New Yorker
Bibliography: p321-25

394.2 Festivals and anniversaries

Douglas, George W.
The American book of days. . . . [2d ed]
Rev. by Helen Douglas Compton. Wilson,
H.W. 1948 xxii, 697p illus $10   **394.2**
1 Holidays 2 Fasts and feasts 3 Festivals—
U.S.
ISBN 0-8242-0002-0
First published 1937
"A compendium of information about holidays, festivals, notable anniversaries and Christian and Jewish holy days with notes on other
American anniversaries worthy of remembrance." Subtitle
"Birthdays of outstanding people are included; Jewish holidays, church festivals, and
local celebrations are fully described. Origin of
names for months and days is given; holidays
in the United States are listed. Excellent index
and table of contents make this a valuable book
for all reference collections." Library J

Hazeltine, Mary E.
Anniversaries and holidays; a calendar of
days and how to observe them. 2d ed. completely rev. with the editorial assistance of
Judith K. Sollenberger. A.L.A. 1944 316p $7
                                                394.2
1 Holidays—Bibliography   2 Birthdays—Bibliography 3 Calendars
First published 1928
A "calendar arrangement of important holidays, holy days, historical events, birthdays
of important personages, and special days and
weeks with information about them and lists of
materials for their observance. In five parts:
The Calendar; Books about Holidays, Special
Days, and Seasons; and Books about Persons
Referred to in the Calendar. Part IV and V are
a classified index and a general index. Code
numbers correlate Parts I, II, and III." Publisher's note
The indexes "make the wealth of material
readily accessible. Major holidays are treated
at length." Wis Lib Bul

Krythe, Maymie R.
All about the months. Harper 1966 222p
boards $5.95   **394.2**
1 Months 2 Manners and customs
"In a readable ready reference book the
author . . . gives a history of each month telling
how it was named, lists noted individuals born
in the month, important events which occurred,
and holidays which fall during each month, and
provides facts about the birthstones and flowers.
A bibliography of books, encyclopedias, magazine articles, and pamphlets is appended."
Booklist

Meyer, Robert
Festivals U.S.A. & Canada [by] Robert
Meyer, Jr. Rev. ed. Washburn 1970 280p
$5.95   **394.2**
1 Festivals—U.S. 2 Festivals—Canada
First published 1950 with title: Festivals
U.S.A.
This guide to annual festivities and events
celebrated in various states and in Canada is
arranged by categories or type of festival, such
as agriculaural festivals, community festivals,
drama festivals, etc. There is also a listing of
festivals by state and province

394.26 Holidays

Becker, May Lamberton
(ed.) The home book of Christmas. Dodd
1941 xx, 746p $6   **394.26**
1 Christmas
A compendium of Christmas stories, poems,
essays, songs, carols, etc. listed under such
headings as: Christmas Eve; The Magi; The
tree; Santa Claus; Food and fun; Songs and
verses; How they spent Christmas
Contains many of the same stories found in
her series of "Golden tales"
"The range is from reverent devotion to
hilarious fun." N Y Her Trib Books
Includes author, title and first line indexes

Schauffler, Robert Haven
(ed.) Christmas; its origin, celebration and
significance as related in prose and verse.
Dodd 1907 332p (Our American holidays)
$3.50   **394.26**
1 Christmas
"Selections grouped under: Origin; Celebration; Significance and spirit; Stories; Old carols
and exercises. . . . Principally valuable from
the literary point of view as the author has
selected from English literature of all periods.
There are, however, many selections suitable
for reading and speaking, some fine old hymns
and carols (words only). . . . A valuable and
interesting collection." Booklist

Wernecke, Herbert H.
(ed.) Celebrating Christmas around the
world. Westminster Press 1962 246p illus
$3.95   **394.26**
1 Christmas 2 Christmas stories
This collection of articles and stories about
Christmas customs is arranged alphabetically
by continent and country. The editor goes
from Africa; "to Asia, which is treated in considerable detail for Armenia, China, Iraq, and
Thailand; to Europe; North America, touching
on Labrador, Guatemala and Nicaragua; and
ends with four South American countries. Descriptions vary greatly in scope—some stories
by well-known authors are included as examples, in addition to an occasional hymn
[and missionary reports]." Library J

Christmas customs around the world.
Westminster Press 1959 188p illus $3.50
                                               394.26
1 Christmas
The first chapter traces the history of Christmas from the early centuries to the time of

Wernecke, Herbert H.—*Continued*

Colonial America, and explains the development of symbols and legends. Succeeding chapters describe both the religious and purely festive customs of sixty-six different countries grouped according to large geographic areas; Chapters on "Recipes from around the world," and Christmas programs are included. (Publisher)

"Other than providing another general source for information on Christmas customs, this book . . . provides material that is difficult to find." Wis Lib Bul

Indexed by countries, subjects, and names. Bibliography: p175-76

395   Etiquette

Haupt, Enid A.

The new Seventeen Book of etiquette and young living. McKay 1970 325p illus $7.95

            395

  1 Etiquette

"More than a guide to good manners; [this] is a combination of teen-age psychology, personality development, and etiquette for young people on various occasions. . . . The first few chapters tell the reader ways of making and keeping friends and getting along with the family and relatives. There is a highly recommended chapter on prejudice . . . relationships with boys, the proper way to act on a date, including dining in a restaurant. Introductions, letter writing, telephoning, dressing, traveling, and giving parties are other topics covered." Best Sellers

"An informal style of writing and a detailed index enhance this handbook." Cur Ref Bks

The Seventeen Book of etiquette & entertaining. McKay 1963 307p illus $7.95   395

  1 Etiquette 2 Adolescence 3 Behavior

Partial contents: Nice people: the habits they have: Nice to be with: in your home and neighborhood; When you go to proms and dances; On the move: planes, trains, busses; motels, hotels and ships: When you speak: When you telephone: Good guestmanship; Table manners that take you anywhere; Getting along successfully in a job; A treasury of entertaining ideas

"Certainly school and public libraries will find it a ready source of information, since its analytical index brings out points included in the 26 chapters which cover the habits of well-mannered people." Cur Ref Bks

Post, Elizabeth L.

The Emily Post Book of etiquette for young people. Funk 1967 238p illus $5.95

            395

  1 Etiquette

The author offers advice to teenagers on how to behave at home, at restaurants, theaters, movies and sports events, on trips, and in other situations. Included are chapters on good grooming, the art of conversation, and correspondence

"Every High School library (Junior or Senior) will be well advised to invest in a copy of this excellent book. . . . A chapter on Dating is . . . sensible without being didactic." Choice

The wonderful world of weddings; the complete guide to wedding etiquette. Funk 1970 218p illus $10   395

  1 Etiquette 2 Marriage customs and rites

The author "explains the right thing to do from the moment the engagement is decided upon until the reception is over—including what to do if the engagement is broken or the wedding canceled. Step-by-step planning of all kinds of weddings, from the simplest to the most formal, is made easy by the book's many check lists, charts, and examples." Publisher's note

Post, Emily

Emily Post's Etiquette. Funk illus $6.95

            395

  1 Etiquette

11th-12th editions edited by Elizabeth L. Post

First published 1922 with title: Etiquette in society, in business, in politics and at home. Periodically revised to keep material up to date

An authoritative guide covering principles of good taste, manners, and etiquette

"Long the most famous of guides to etiquette, this book is still preferred by many who favor the continued adherence to more traditional and formal behavior, though Mrs. Post has considerably modified many of her views [and has added up-to-date topics] since the first edition of her book was published." Murphey. How and Where to Look it Up

Vanderbilt, Amy

Amy Vanderbilt's etiquette. Doubleday illus $7.95   395

  1 Etiquette

First published 1952 with title: Amy Vanderbilt's Complete book of etiquette, and frequently revised. Titles vary

Contents: The ceremonies of life; Dress and manners; Home entertaining; Household management; Correspondence; The family and social education of the children; Your public life; Official etiquette for civilians; Travel etiquette at home and abroad

"It is my hope that this book answers as fully and simply as possible all the major questions of etiquette and most of the minor ones too. It is the largest and most complete book of etiquette ever written." Introduction to the original edition

Vogue's Book of etiquette and good manners. Published by Condé Nast in association with Simon & Schuster 1969 749p illus $9.95   395

  1 Etiquette

First published 1924 with title: Vogue's Book of etiquette

"Etiquette, as interpreted in these pages, is a combination of consideration, good taste, respect for established traditions, and a thorough knowledge of good manners." Publisher's note

Partial contents: A woman alone; Great happy occasions; Running a house; Entertaining; Correspondence and cards; Manners in business; Moving and traveling; Formality and protocol

"Each chapter concludes with an amusing 'Customs and Curiosites' section." Sat R

Wilson, Barbara

The complete book of engagement and wedding etiquette. [New and rev. ed] Hawthorn Bks. 1970 480p illus $6.95   395

  1 Etiquette 2 Marriage customs and rites

First published 1959 with title: The Brides' School Complete book of engagement and wedding etiquette

In question and answer form, the author offers practical advice to the bride and groom, their parents, friends and guests in every wedding situation

Bibliography: p459-61

397   Gipsies

Esty, Katharine

The Gypsies, wanderers in time. Meredith 1969 152p illus $4.95   397

  1 Gypsies

A "picture of the Gypsies, from their first characteristically abrupt appearance in the Western world to the present. Drawn from many sources—ancient town records; the accounts of Romany Ryes; the few Gajos who have earned Gypsy trust; studies of scholars; and reports of modern experts . . . the book tells of early attitudes toward the wanderers; describes how their language provided the key to their homeland; gives the story of George Borrow and the romantic literature tradition, the revelations of Milos, the 'black arts,' their

Esty, Katharine—*Continued*
music and dance, the World War II persecutions, their religion, twentieth-century problems, the Romany Ryes, and the Gypsies in America." Publisher's note
A "well written, sympathetic, and interest-rousing introduction to Gypsy history and lore. . . . Enhanced by a wide-ranging further reading list." Library J

McDowell, Bart
Gypsies: wanderers of the world; with illus. by Bruce Dale; foreword by an English Gypsy, Clifford Lee. Prepared by the Special Publications Division, Robert L. Breeden, chief. Nat. Geographic Soc. 1970 215p illus maps $4.65   397

1 Gypsies
SBN 87044-088-8
"This is an informal, anecdotal account of [the author's] 13,000-mile motor trip following gypsy routes from Great Britain to India, homeland of the gypsies. Accompanied on the journey by an English gypsy couple, McDowell visited and talked with gypsies and scholars in 13 countries and incorporates some history and gypsy lore into the descriptive narrative. Enhanced by many handsome, captioned, color photographs the book can be enjoyed by the armchair traveler, browser, or reader interested in the gypsies' way of life." Booklist

Yoors, Jan
The Gypsies. Simon & Schuster 1967 256p $6.95   397

1 Gypsies
"The author, who ran away with a band of gypsies when he was twelve . . . describes their customs, their language, their social and religious life, and stubborn determination to preserve their way of life." Bk Buyer's Guide
It is "an exciting firsthand impression of life in a Gypsy camp forever on the move. . . . This book is an elaboration of the material gathered in [Yoors'] 10 years of Gypsying. Limiting his study to the group with whom he was directly in contact, he has made a most valuable and original contribution to Gypsy scholarship by his descriptions of rituals, taboos and birth, marriage and death ceremonies." N Y Times Bk R

398   Folklore

Botkin, B. A.
(ed.) A treasury of American folklore; stories, ballads, and traditions of the people; with a foreword by Carl Sandburg. Crown 1944 xxvii, 932p music $5.95   398

1 Folklore—U.S.
"Tall tales, and true, of frontier characters and sea captains, recurring American jokes and expressions, ballads of railroad men and miners, Negro songs and stories, and a wealth of other material are assembled in this [volume]." Literary Guild
"The running comment throughout the book is terse, good-humored and for the most part lacking the irritating academic tone with which only too much American folklore has been burdened." N Y Her Trib Books
Index of authors, titles, and first lines of songs: p919-26. Index of subjects and names: p926-32. Bibliographical footnotes

(ed.) A treasury of New England folklore; stories, ballads, and traditions of Yankee folk. Rev. ed. Crown 1965 xxii, 618p music $7.50   398

1 Folklore—New England
First published 1947
Here are the tales the New Englanders tell "and the songs they sing, their myths and mythology in folk tale and folk speech. These are their heroes and sages, showmen and tricksters, eccentrics and strong men—Israel Putnam, Ethan Allen, Timothy Dexter, P. T. Barnum,

Cal Coolidge, and a host of local characters about whom a body of lively anecdote and colorful legend has grown up." Publisher's note
Index of authors, collectors, informants, titles, and first lines of songs: p605-13. Index of subjects and names: p613-17. Geographical index: p617-18. Includes bibliographical footnotes

(ed.) A treasury of Southern folklore; stories, ballads, traditions, and folkways of the people of the South; ed. and with an introduction by B. A. Botkin; with a foreword by Douglas Southall Freeman. Crown 1949 xxiv, 776p music $5.95   398

1 Folklore—Southern States 2 Southern States—Social life and customs
More than 500 tales and over 75 folk songs present the full cast of characters of the varied South, including heroes like Patrick Henry, Davy Crockett, Sam Houston, Stonewall Jackson
"Basic to the book is the view of folklore as a part of folk culture. . . . Traditionally, folklore in the South has been associated with three relatively uneducated groups: the mountaineer, the poor white, and the Negro. . . . The present book adds a fourth group; the 'quality.'" Introduction
Includes an Index of authors, titles, and first lines of songs, and an Index of subjects, names, and places

(ed.) A treasury of Western folklore; foreword by Bernard DeVoto. Crown 1951 xxvi, 806p music $5.95   398

1 Folklore—The West
"Mr. Botkin scans his West both geographically and chronologically. His thousands of stories, selections from books, tales collected by heresay—all of it relates to one West or another, in place of time. The range West? There's a whole section on it here. . . . The bad-man West, complete with bandits, killers and, of course, Marshalls and Sheriffs? That's here, too, as is the 'vigilante' West." San Francisco Chronicle
"The book contains amusing and salty reading in copious measure. Moreover, its value as a reference tool is enormously enhanced by two excellent indexes, one of Authors, Titles and First Lines of Songs, the other listing Subjects, Names and Places." N Y Her Trib Books
Bibliographical footnotes

Brewer, J. Mason
American Negro folklore; illus. by Richard Lowe. Quadrangle Bks. 1968 386p illus $12.50   398

1 Folklore, Negro 2 Folklore—U.S.
In this anthology, which is divided into ten parts: Tales; The Negro's religion; Songs; Personal experiences; Superstitions; Proverbs; Rhymes; Riddles; Names; Children's rhymes and pastimes, "Dr. Brewer explains the historical background and peculiar characteristics of the type of folklore, then lets the reader savor a . . . variety of selected source material." McClurg. Book News
"A wonderfully readable collection and a significant source for understanding the black man's experience in America." Chicago

Coffin, Tristram P.
(ed.) Folklore in America. . . . Selected and ed. by Tristram P. Coffin and Hennig Cohen from the "Journal of American Folklore." Doubleday 1966 xxiii, 256p music $4.95   398

1 Folklore—U.S.
"Tales, songs [17 with melodies] superstitions, proverbs, riddles, games, folk drama and folk festivals." Title page
"It is regrettable that many of the items presented are identified and dated only in the notes at the back of the book; brief and consistent headnotes would have made the collection more pleasant reading. Nevertheless, this is a book of considerable merit." Library J
Notes on sources. p227-46

Colum, Padraic
(ed.) A treasury of Irish folklore; the
stories, traditions, legends, humor, wisdom,
ballads and songs of the Irish people; ed.
with an introduction by Padraic Colum. 2d
rev. ed. Crown 1967 xx, 620p $5.95   **398**

1 Folklore—Ireland
First published 1954
A selection of stories and ballads about the
saints and heroes, the ways and traditions of
the Irish people, grouped under such headings
as: The Irish edge; Great chiefs and uncrowned
kings; Ireland without leaders; Fireside tales;
Ballads and songs
"Everything that's here represents careful
weighing and judging at the hands of the man
best qualified to do the job. An on top of that,
when you have such a collection edited by a
distinguished poet and prose writer who has
himself a beautiful sense of humor—well, then,
you've got something extra." San Francisco
Chronicle
Bibliographical footnotes

Hughes, Langston
(ed.) The book of Negro folklore; ed. by
Langston Hughes and Arna Bontemps.
Dodd 1958 624p $7.50   **398**

1 Folklore, Negro 2 Folklore—U.S.
Selections from the folklore of the Negro in
the United States, from ante-bellum days to
the present. The selections come from the plantation and the levee, old New Orleans, Chicago,
and Harlem, and includes animal tales and
rhymes, games, spirituals, blues, modern gospel songs., jazz, jive, early slave memories,
contemporary folk tales, songs, poetry and
prose." Pub W
"It is a rich, varied contribution indeed, full
of surprises, lore so integrated into the American scene that of much of it one forgets it was
first the Negroes'. Perhaps this is the really
important point of this collection, one answer to
what the editors label 'The Problem.' " San
Francisco Chronicle
Arranged by subject or type of selection.
There is no index

Toor, Frances
A treasury of Mexican folkways. . . . Illus.
with 10 color plates, 100 drawings by Carlos
Merida, and 170 photographs. Crown 1947
xxxii, 566p illus map $8.50   **398**

1 Folklore—Mexico 2 Mexico—Social life and
customs
"The customs, myths, folklore, traditions,
beliefs, fiestas, dances, and songs of the Mexican people." Subtitle
"After an introductory account of the history, Miss Toor describes the economic life of
the people; then their social and religious organization; then their music and dance; and
finally, their literature in all its forms. . . .
Fascinating." Cur Ref Bks
Bibliography: p547-51. Glossary: p552-60

398.03 Folklore—Dictionaries

Funk & Wagnalls Standard dictionary of
folklore, mythology and legend. Maria
Leach, editor; Jerome Fried, associate
editor. Funk 1949-1950 2v (1196p) $20
398.03

1 Folklore—Dictionaries 2 Legends—Dictionaries 3 Mythology—Dictionaries
"A representative selection of gods, heroes,
tales, motifs, customs, beliefs, songs, dances,
games, proverbs, etc., of the cultures of the
world. Volume 1 includes 23 'survey articles'
with bibliographies on regions and on special
subjects (ballad, dance, fairy tale) written by
specialists." Winchell. Guide to Reference
Books. 8th edition
For a more complete review see: The Booklist and Subscription Books Bulletin for April
1951

398.2 Folklore—Tales and legends

Arabian nights
The Arabian nights' entertainment; or,
The book of a thousand nights and a night;
a selection of the most famous and representative of these tales from the plain and
literal translations by Richard F. Burton;
the stories have been chosen and arranged
by Bennett A. Cerf and are printed complete
and unabridged with many of Burton's notes;
introductory essay by Ben Ray Redman.
Modern Lib. 1932 823p $2.95, lib. bdg. $2.69
398.2

1 Folklore—Arabia
"The frame tale of this collection of Eastern
Stories in the Arabic language was evidently
of Indian origin, transmitted first to the Persians, then to the Arabs. . . . The stories are
supposed to be told to a cruel Sultan, Schariar,
by his wife, Scheherazade, who feared death
at his hands and sought by 1001 nightly tales
left unfinished to delay the order of her execution. The collection numbering in the most
complete form 263, includes fairy tales, tales
of strange voyages and adventures and of
courtly love, animal fables, moral and historical anecdotes and long romances. They vary
considerably ranging from extreme coarseness
or obscenity to delicate sentimentality. The
best known are those of Ali Baba, Sinbad the
Sailor and Aladdin." Bookman's Manual

Dobie, James Frank
(ed.) Tales of old-time Texas; illus. by
Barbara Latham. Little 1955 336p illus $6.95
398.2

1 Folklore—Texas
"Stories of ranching and pioneering days of
the Southwest. Tall tales interspersed with history and folklore." A Guide to Reading in Am
History
The author exhibits, "a mind sensitive to
the speech of the earth as it talks to those
who can hear, and with a Hemingway-like
respect for a simple, even a sandpapered style."
N Y Times Bk R
Includes bibliography

Malory, Sir Thomas
Le morte d'Arthur. Dutton 2v ea $2.95
398.2

1 Arthur, King
"Everyman's library"
Originally published 1485. This edition first
published 1906
"The work is a skilful selection and blending of materials taken from the mass of Arthurian legends. The central story consists of
two main elements: the reign of King Arthur
ending in catastrophe and the dissolution of
the Round Table; and the quest of the Holy
Grail." Harvey. The Oxford Companion to
English Literature

Marriott, Alice
American Indian mythology [by] Alice
Marriott and Carol K. Rachlin. Crowell
1968 211p illus $7.95   **398.2**

1 Indians of North America—Legends
"A fascinating collection of myths, legends
and contemporary folklore which the authors
have obtained in most cases directly from Indians. . . . With each tale there is a brief introduction to the tribe. Subjects include myths
of creation; the world and the hereafter; 'how-
and-why' stories told to children; historic legends and witchcraft. Among the tribes represented are Cheyenne, Modoc, Ponca, Hopi,
Kiowa, Comanche and Zuni." Pub W
The authors "seek to present the best of two
worlds, accurate background on the main Indian groups in America, and a sort of literary
telling of their myths and legends. The viewpoint is that of the anthropologist rather than
of the folklorist. The stories do not have an
Indian flavor but, this makes for somewhat
smoother reading." Library J
Bibliography: p207-11

Megas, Georgios A.
(ed.) Folktales of Greece; tr. by Helen
Colaclides; foreword by Richard M. Dorson. Univ. of Chicago Press 1970 lvii, 287p
(Folktales of the world) $9.95   **398.2**
1 Folklore—Greece, Modern
ISBN 0-226-51785-3
"A charming collection of folktales that
should not be confused with the classical
myths of the Greek gods. . . . [Included here
are] animal tales, wonder stories, the adventures of princes and kings, morality tales,
jokes, tales of fate, religion and legend."
Pub W
Glossary: p253-56. Bibliography: p257-63

Nahmad, H. M.
(ed.) A portion in paradise, and other Jewish folktales; [ed. and] tr. by H. M. Nahmad. Norton 1970 170p (The B'nai B'rith
Jewish heritage classics) $6   **398.2**
1 Folklore, Jewish
SBN 393-04329-0
A collection of stories, legends, and folktales
from ancient Biblical and secular sources of
the East and West grouped in the following
categories: Tales of the Prophet Elijah; Tales
of David and Solomon; The wisdom and folly
of women; The righteous and the pious; Tales
of wit and wisdom; The golem
"Nahmad accompanies his simple, popular
versions with discussions of historical background and the distinctive qualities of folk
literature." Booklist

Noy, Dov
(ed.) Folktales of Israel; ed. by Dov Noy,
with the assistance of Dan Ben-Amos. Tr.
by Gene Baharav. Univ. of Chicago Press
1963 221p (Folktales of the world) $5.95
398.2
1 Folklore, Jewish
"A selection of 71 tales . . . about the
righteous, the covetous, talking animals, kings
and commoners, clever Jews, husbands and
wives, heroes and heroines, wise men, and
numbskulls represent the two main sources
from which the modern Israeli folklore tradition derives: oral legends, parables, and metaphors which express many facets of the Jewish popular faith and the variegated body of
tales and songs, customs, and beliefs brought
into Israel by her immigrants." Booklist

Paredes, Américo
(ed.) Folktales of Mexico; ed. and tr. by
Américo Paredes; foreword by Richard M.
Dorson. Univ. of Chicago Press 1970 lxxxiii,
282p (Folktales of the world) $9.75   **398.2**
1 Folklore—Mexico
ISBN 0-226-64571-1
"Here is a scholarly but generally interesting collection of some 80 Mexican folktales
ranging from the sacred to the scatological,
with the 'belief' tale, the joke and the legendary anecdote predominating and with religion
a continuing source of humor. Several stories
revolve around Pedro de Urdemalas, the Mexican counterpart of the Spanish 'picaro' or
trickster—Pedro usually seen besting a 'gringo.'
In his translations, Paredes seeks to capture
the narrator's style and flavor intact, which
may in part account for a certain unevenness
in narrative quality. But this is authentic material of unquestionable value, often absorbing."
Pub W
"The scholarly aids are excellent including
notes to individual tales, a glossary, helpful
bibliography, indices of motifs and tale types,
and a general index." Choice

Rees, Ennis
Fables from Aesop; with illus. by J. J.
Grandville. Oxford 1966 210p illus $7.50
398.2
1 Aesop—Adaptations

"This collection of 187 of Aesop's fables,
mostly in rhymed couplets, is an attempt to update, simplify and provide their . . . re-creation. Modern idiom, slang, and puns are used
with good effect." Library J
Illustrated with wood engravings done for
an 1838 edition of La Fontaine's Fables

Rugoff, Milton
(ed.) Harvest of world folk tales; with
illus. and decorations by Joseph Low. Viking 1949 734p illus $5.25   **398.2**
1 Folklore
Selections are under these headings: African,
American, American Indian, Arabian and Turkish, Chinese, Egyptian, English, Finnish,
French, German, Greek, Indian, Irish, Italian,
Jewish, Latin American, Russian, Scandinavian, Spanish
"There is a complete representation of the
various categories of legend as well, including
parables, fairy tales, drolls, fables, fantasies,
ghost stories, and all the rest." N Y Times
Bk R
Bibliographical note: p729

Sutcliff, Rosemary
Beowulf; retold by Rosemary Sutcliff;
with drawings by Charles Keeping. Dutton
[1962 c1961] 93p illus $3.50, lib. bdg. $3.46
398.2
1 Beowulf
First published 1961 in England
A prose retelling of "the Anglo-Saxon epic
of Beowulf, of the Sea-Hag and of Grendel the
monster." Cincinnati
"Hewing closely to the original plot, but adding a few interpretations of her own [the
author] has given new literary life to [the]
story. . . . Excellent supplementary reading for
students of English literature." Library J

398.9   Proverbs

The Macmillan Book of proverbs, maxims,
and famous phrases; ed. by Burton Stevenson. Macmillan (N Y) [1965 c1948] 2957p
$25   **398.9**
1 Proverbs
First published 1948, with title: The home
book of proverbs, maxims and familiar phrases
The author "has taken all the proverbs,
maxims, and familiar phrases that are commonly used in America and England, and arranged them alphabetically by subject. He
traces each back to its source in early Greek,
Latin, and Hebrew writings, or in medieval
or Renaissance England. From this first, frequently crude expression of the idea, he follows it through the variations and perversions
until he arrives at the modern streamlined
form." Huntting
A facile source "for tracing chronologically
the development of an idea from its first expression or finding quickly and together a
variety of proverbs, maxims and quotations on
a subject." Library J

The Oxford Dictionary of English proverbs.
3d ed. rev. by F. P. Wilson; with an introduction by Joanna Wilson. Oxford 1970
930p $16   **398.9**
1 Proverbs
First published 1935. The first two editions
were compiled by William George Smith
Proverbs are "alphabetized under significant
words (usually the first), with the preceding
words, if any, transferred to the end or, occasionally, to an intermediate point. Liberal
cross references are included from all other
significant words, usually with enough of the
phrase so that it is readily identifiable. Dated
references are given for each proverb to the
earliest uses and sources found, with variant
usage at succeeding times, shown by examples
from the literature." Winchell. Guide to Reference Books. 8th edition

399   Customs of war

Tunis, Edwin
Weapons; a pictorial history; written and illus. by Edwin Tunis. World Pub. 1954 152p illus $6.95, lib. bdg. $7.70   399
1 Arms and armor—History 2 Munitions—History
The story, in text and picture, of arms through the ages—from the first tied stone thrown by prehistoric man to the super bombs of our own day
The author-illustrator "emphasizes the offensive rather than the defensive weapon in his narrative which omits strategy due to space limitations, but does include fortifications. He clearly explains with diagrams and text how the mechanism of the weapons operates. Whether it is used for reference or browsing, this handsomely illustrated book will engage the interest of the nonmilitary-minded as well as the hobbyist or weapons collector." Booklist

400   LANGUAGE

Laird, Helene
The tree of language, by Helene and Charlton Laird; illus. by Ervine Metzl. World Pub. 1957 233p illus $4.95   400
1 Language and languages 2 English language
"Beginning with a discussion of what life would be like without language, the authors then proceed to the beginnings of language; the beginnings of the English language; Anglo-Saxon; Chaucer, Shakespeare and Modern English; the history of the alphabet; the how and why of English spelling; the history of printing; the development of names; and some odd things about words. The final section consists of one hundred 'Word Stories' in which the derivations of words are traced and changes in meaning discussed. There is much here to stimulate the reader to further study of the origins and development of words and word usages." Chicago. Children's Book Center

Pei, Mario
All about language; decorations by Donat Ivanovsky. Lippincott 1954 186p illus maps $3.50   400
1 Language and languages
The book summarizes "the important facts about language—its history, diversity, distribution, and importance. It discusses entertainingly slang, dialects, and the advantages of a universal language. The usefulness of foreign language study is emphasized, with criteria for choice." Library J
"Solidly informative and fascinating. Its value is enormous for the boy or girl just beginning the study of unfamiliar languages, whether classical or modern. Also it is an aid to richer understanding of our own English." N Y Times Bk R

Language for everybody; what it is and how to master it. Devin-Adair 1956 340p illus maps pa $2.75   400
1 Language and languages
"An introduction to all the languages of the world, past and present, with emphasis on the world's 100 most important ones. [The author] tells just what language is, the part it play in our everyday lives, how to improve our own written and spoken tongue, and how to save time and energy in learning the most useful foreign languages." Huntting
"Dr. Pei is incapable of being dull; the vivacity of his approach to a weighty subject is as refreshing as it is unusual." Sec Ed Brd
Selective bibliography: p327-30

The story of language. Rev. ed. Lippincott 1965 491p $7.50   400
1 Language and languages
First published 1949
"This book deals with the origins and family relationships of languages, with dialects, place names, personal names, slang and the structure of language." McClurg. Book News
"It is difficult to imagine anyone who will not find something of interest in this book. It sharpens one's sense of one's own control over language; and it is full of fresh and often surprising information about the words we use. Enjoyable merely to browse through, it is also valuable as a work of reference." Book of the Month Club News

407   Language—Study and teaching

Pei, Mario
How to learn languages and what languages to learn. Harper 1966 245p $5.95   407
1 Language and languages—Study and teaching
"Here is a book that deals with 'language-learning' methods rather than with 'language-teaching' methods. Dr. Pei discusses the advantages and disadvantages of each method of learning a language and stresses the usefulness of learning aids. He describes the many languages that are being taught today—from French to Arabic and Urdu—and explains what languages may be learned simultaneously, and the special difficulties of each. He also illustrates how to apply the rules and vocabulary of one language in studying others." Publisher's note
This book "is definitely intended for the layman and deliberately avoids technical expressions. The style is easy, clear and interesting. . . . As usual Mario Pei has written a book that is informative, interesting and eminently practical." Mod Lang J

410   Linguistics

Gallant, Roy A.
Man must speak; the story of language and how we use it. Random House 1969 177p illus $3.95, lib. bdg. $3.89   410
1 Language and languages 2 Animal communication
"Starting with a chapter on How Animals Communicate, Professor Gallant examines the various theories about the origin of language, then discusses the invention of writing and the various forms it has taken over the millenia and in various parts of the world. After that he talks about words that are the vehicle of description and narration, long many-syllabled words and 'genteelisms' with a short consideration of the mass media as languages." Best Sellers

Pei, Mario
Invitation to linguistics; a basic introduction to the science of language. Doubleday 1965 266p $5.95   410
1 Language and languages 2 Grammar 3 Language and languages—Research
The basic terminology and methodology of three branches of linguistics are presented. The first two are "descriptive linguistics, the study of how a language is formed, written, and spoken; and historical linguistics, the study of how a given language has developed. Dr. Pei . . . programs the future of the . . . third—geolinguistics. This last branch is the study of the present status of the world's languages: how many people speak them and where they are spoken; and the significance of this knowledge in governmental, business, legal, cultural, and military fields." Publisher's note

Pei, Mario—*Continued*

"Appendixes include a chart of the international phonetic alphabet . . . forms of writing, a table of alphabetic development, and a geolinguistic survey of the nations of the world. . . . [Long annotated] bibliography; Index." Book Rev Digest

"It would be hard to find a more concise yet comprehensive introduction to this new science." Christian Science Monitor

(ed.) Language today; a survey of current linguistic thought. Mario Pei, editor and chief contributor. Other contributors: William F. Marquardt, Katharine Le Mée [and] Don L. F. Nilsen. Funk 1967 150p illus $5.95   **410**

1 Language and languages 2 English language
Analyzed in Essay and general literature index

The author "states, in a short foreword, the purpose of this book: 'to present in simplified form and in layman's language a few of the more important language problems facing today's speakers of English.' He then discusses briefly what he believes are the more important problems—usage, spelling, semantics, communications, and grammar. Each of the five problems is treated by an expert with Pei covering spelling and semantics and also engaging in an interesting exchange on usage and abusage with William F. Marquardt. . . . The layman will find these essays informative and provocative." Choice
Bibliography: p147-49

411 Notations (Alphabets and ideographs)

Fairbank, Alfred

The story of handwriting; origins and development. Watson-Guptill 1970 108p illus $7.95   **411**

1 Writing—History

The author "traces the history of writing from its beginning in Sumer, Egypt, and China, to the present day. He discusses the deciphering of ancient scripts, the Phoenician invention of the alphabet, the Latin, Carolingian, Mediaeval, and Renaissance scripts, as well as print-script, the italic hand of today, and the revival of formal calligraphy. . . . Fairbank then considers the basic principles involved in good handwriting . . . and the writer's tools." Publisher's note

This book "is a remarkable performance, and as, avowedly, an introduction it should be widely welcomed." Times (London) Lit Sup
Some books to consult: p102-03

Ogg, Oscar

The 26 letters. Rev. ed. Crowell 1971 294p illus $6.95   **411**

1 Alphabet 2 Writing—History 3 Printing—History
ISBN 0-690-84115-9

First published 1948
Starting with the earliest cave drawings, the author traces the development of writing up to today's new methods of printing and the new designs and techniques involved in modern typography

412 Etymology. Semantics

Chase, Stuart

Danger—men talking! A background book on semantics and communication. Parents Mag. Press 1969 215p $4.50, lib. bdg. $4.12   **412**

1 Semantics 2 Communication

"His goal better communications among men, the author analyzes the pitfalls and posts the warning signs that will help the reader clarify his thinking and structure his arguments. He discusses linguistic theories, the deviousness of human speech, the channels of communication, and semantics." Sat R
Recommended reading list: p201-06

Power of words, by Stuart Chase, in collaboration with Marian Tyler Chase. Harcourt 1954 308p $7.95   **412**

1 Semantics 2 Communication

Analyzed in Essay and general literature index

"This book grew out of my earlier work, 'The Tyranny of Words,' published in 1938 [and entered below]." Foreword

"The author discusses semantics and other branches of communication, such as cybernetics, linguistics, brain physiology, etc. After describing the new findings, he applies them to various fields, ranging from mass media to Russian propaganda." McClurg. Book News

This book is "not technical, but it is limited to serious and literate readers." Wis Lib Bul
Includes bibliographies

The tyranny of words. Harcourt 1938 396p illus $6.50   **412**

1 Semantics 2 Thought and thinking

The author delves into the science of semantics. "In the first half of the book, he has made a popularization of the science itself, based on the authoritative works of four experts in this field. From this study he builds a semantic discipline which the reader may apply to philosophy, economics, law, logic and politcs. The second half of the book is a practical application of the discipline to the confused use of abstractions such as idealism, liberty, New Deal, Fascism, etc. used by orators, editorial writers, diplomats and judges." Book Rev Digest
Bibliography: p385-86

Hayakawa, S. I.

Language in thought and action. 3d ed. [by] S. I. Hayakawa, in consultation with Arthur Asa Berger and Arthur Chandler. Harcourt 1972 289p illus pa $3.95   **412**

1 Semantics 2 Thought and thinking

Based on the author's: Language in action, first published 1939

"Hayakawa analyzes both the pitfalls and the possibilities of language, and gives . . . advice on how to think clearly and how to say and write what one means and what is true. His revision . . . gives special attention to developments in social psychology." Publisher's note

In this standard work on semantics "technical terms, though abundant, are carefully explained." Springf'd Republican
Selected bibliography: p331-36

418 Polygot languages—Usage

Pei, Mario

Talking your way around the world. Enl. 3d ed. Harper 1971 249p $5.95   **418**

1 Languages, Modern—Conversation and phrase books 2 Language and languages
SBN 06-013327-9

First published 1961
The author provides profiles of the world's great languages which form a world guide to the principal languages of Europe, Africa, Asia and the Middle East: English, German, Russian, Latin, Swahili, Chinese, Japanese, Arabic and Hebrew. Each chapter includes phrases of the type the tourist finds useful, and there is a concluding chapter on Pidgin languages throughout the world. (Publisher)

420.9 English language—History

Pei, Mario

The story of the English language. [Rev. ed] Lippincott 1967 430p $7.95   **420.9**

1 English language—History

First published 1952 with title: The story of English

Pei, Mario—*Continued*

The author describes the growth of the English language from Anglo-Saxon to modern English. He also discusses uses and reforms, English as a class tool, proper names, American English, and related topics

"The story as [Mr. Pei] tells it deals as much with the present as with the past and ends by speculating at some length on the future. It does this with wide knowledge, careful judgment and in a fashion that should capture and hold the interest of any literate reader." N Y Times Bk R

List of works most frequently consulted: p385-92

421 English language—Written and spoken codes

NBC Handbook of pronunciation. 3d ed. Originally comp. by James F. Bender for the National Broadcasting Company. Rev. by Thomas Lee Crowell, Jr. Crowell 1964 418p $7.95   **421**

1 English language—Pronunciation

First published 1943

"Entries include words or proper names frequently used by broadcasters, common words often mispronounced, and 'difficult' names from history and the arts. Names of persons who have come to the attention of American audiences in recent years are listed in a supplement of 'Names in the News.' " Library J

"This is handy, ready reference record of how words 'are' pronounced by educated speakers across the greater part of the United States. It does not prescribe how words 'should' be pronounced." Cur Ref Bks

421.03 English language—Written and spoken codes—Dictionaries

Gale Research Company

Acronyms and initialisms dictionary. . . . 3d ed. Edited by Ellen T. Crowley and Robert C. Thomas. Contributing editors: Harry Schecter [and] Harvey Wolf. The Company 1970 484p $22.50   **421.03**

1 Abbreviations—Dictionaries

First published 1960 with title: Acronyms dictionary. Kept up to date by annual supplements

"A guide to alphabetic designations, contractions, acronyms, initialisms, and similar condensed appellations covering: aerospace, associations, biochemistry, business and trade, domestic and international affairs, education, electronics, genetics, government, labor, medicine, military, pharmacy, physiology, politics, religion, science, societies, sports, technical drawings and specifications, transportation, and other fields." Subtitle

Schwartz, Robert J.

(comp.) The complete dictionary of abbreviations. [Enlarged-type ed] Crowell [1959 c1955] 211p $7.95   **421.03**

1 Abbreviations—Dictionaries 2 Large-type books

First published 1955

"Contains more than 25,000 entries arranged in one alphabet. . . . Covers not only the common abbreviated expressions, but all other abbreviations in every conceivable field. . . . These fields include: business, law, science, education, music, geography, Army, Navy, foreign, U.S. government, religion, fraternal orders, stock market, book trade, shipping, medicine, pharmacy." Publisher's note

422 English language—Etymology

Funk, Charles Earle, 1881-1957

Thereby hangs a tale; stories of curious word origins. Harper 1950 303p $6.95   **422**

1 English language—Etymology

This book contains "hundreds of words arranged alphabetically, with their derivations, and the circumstances that brought them into our language." Wis Lib Bul

"An admirable collection of little essays—no more than a paragraph apiece—on 600 words." N Y Times Bk R

Funk, Wilfred

Word origins and their romantic stories. Funk, W. 1950 432p $5.95   **422**

1 English language—Etymology

"The life stories of over three thousand words in use in English today." Book Rev Digest

Partial contents: Romance behind business terms; Word histories of your garden; Word stories about your dining table; Political terms and the origins; War words and their histories; Romantic stories of words about women; Terms of religion and their beginnings; Origin of the terms of art, music and the drama

Bibliographical references included in "A note of thanks": p405-08

422.03 English language—Etymology—Dictionaries

Bliss, A. J.

Dictionary of foreign words and phrases in current English. Dutton 1966 389p boards $6.95   **422.03**

1 English language—Foreign words and phrases—Dictionaries

In this dictionary of over 5000 terms "I have tried to supply the needs of the general reader in search of a single work of reference which will explain at least the majority of the foreign words and phrases likely to be encountered in current English, both written and spoken . . . excluding expressions which are either obsolete or have only a limited technical currency. For this reason I have found it necessary to compile the list of words and phrases to be included without reference to earlier dictionaries. . . . With very few exceptions all the words and phrases in this dictionary have been culled from recent books and journals." Introduction

"There is a lengthy scholarly introduction . . . which, perhaps for the first time, succinctly and authoritatively discusses the character and status of 'foreign words and phrases.' There is a useful appendix in which the entries are arranged by centuries and by countries. This book deserves purchase by all libraries, large and small, and by any individual seriously interested in the English language." Library J

Morris, William

Dictionary of word and phrase origins, by William and Mary Morris. Harper 1962-1971 3v v 1 $7.50, lib. bdg. $6.48; v2 $7.50, lib. bdg. $6.48; v3 $7.95   **422.03**

1 English language—Etymology—Dictionaries 2 English language—Terms and phrases—Dictionaries

Each volume is arranged alphabetical from A to Z containing more than 5,500 "little known stories behind everyday words and expressions, ranging from the earliest years of the English language to the Space Age. Answered are many questions about latest usage, differences between similar words, derivations and inconsistencies." Publisher's note

"The familiar style, the effort to select colorful words and phrases, and the popular approach will attract the general reader more than the student of language." Cur Ref Bks

The **Oxford** Dictionary of English etymology; ed. by C. T. Onions; with the assistance of G. W. S. Friedrichsen and R. W. Burchfield. Oxford 1966 1024p $16.50   **422.03**

1 English language—Etymology—Dictionaries

In this "etymological dictionary the pronunciation of each word is given, the present-day meaning, the date of its first record, the chronology of the development of its sense, and its earliest form in written English." Bk Buyer's Guide

"In subsequent editions there will doubtless be many alterations; but the dictionary will not be superseded in our lifetime. . . . It is reasonably but not absolutely up-to-date. . . . [Special advisers] should be recruited for all off-beat languages." Economist

For a more complete review, see The Booklist and Subscription Books Bulletin, November 1, 1966

423   English language— Dictionaries

The **American** college dictionary; C. L. Barnhart, editor-in-chief; Jess Stein, managing editor. Random House illus maps $5.95, thumb indexed $6.95   **423**

1 English language—Dictionaries

First published 1947, and frequently revised

The entries in this dictionary including foreign phrases, place names, famous people and abbreviations are in one alphabet. Prepared "to meet the essential needs of the reader, speaker, and writer who want to know the meaning of a word, how to pronounce it, how to spell it, its history, or some important fact of usage." General introduction

Appendices contain: Common signs and symbols; Given names; List of United States colleges and universities

"A favorite with pupils because of all inclusive alphabet and clear type. . . . Particularly strong on scientific and technical terms, new words and etymologies." English Language Dictionaries in Print

"It represents an imposing combination of publishing acumen and scholarly devotion, the culminating triumph of a semantic approach to language based upon our American-born pragmatic philosophy." Chicago Sunday Tribune

For a fuller review see: Subscription Books Bulletin Reviews, June 1, 1963

The **American** Heritage Dictionary of the English language. William Morris, ed. Published by Am. Heritage and Houghton 1969 1, 1550p illus maps $7.95, thumb indexed $8.95   **423**

1 English language—Dictionaries

The preliminary section includes articles on the origin, dialects, usage, grammar, spelling and pronunciation of the English language. The alphabetical listing of over one hundred thousand entries includes geographical and biographical entries and definitions of new words from the world of science and technology. (Publisher)

"Definitions are clearly expressed, and in the case of multiple numbered ones, the first definition is the central meaning about which the other senses may be most logically ordered. . . . Field, regional, and usage labels are freely used, and 800 usage notes are appended to certain controversial words, based on the opinions of the panel of writers [made up of one hundred novelists, journalists and others with a recognized ability to speak and write good English]. Synonyms are carefully treated, with discriminations in use." Cur Ref Bks

This "is perhaps the handsomest dictionary in English. Beautifully printed, with unusually large and clear print, with illustrations (including large numbers of photographs) running down each outer margin, with easily turnable paper . . . it includes a wider range of four-letter Anglo-Saxon words than does Webster's offering the justification that the

politics of 'confrontation' makes this obligatory. But it neither sanctions them nor the tongue's most egregious illiteracies." Christian Science Monitor

The **Concise** Oxford Dictionary of current English; ed. by H. W. Fowler and F. G. Fowler. Based on the Oxford Dictionary. 5th ed. rev. by E. McIntosh; etymologies rev. by G. W. S. Friedrichsen. Oxford 1964 1558p   **423**

1 English language—Dictionaries

Prices vary according to binding

First published 1911

"Definitions are given in historical order, with the most common meaning last, and are followed by etymologies, copious quotations illustrating usage, and synonyms. Main alphabet includes foreign words and phrases and slang expressions, but, like most British dictionaries, omits biographical and geographical entries. Abbreviations are contained in an appendix. A good system of pronunciation is employed." English Language Dictionaries in Print

In the 1964 edition "American terms and usages are taken into account more than ever before. . . . Conversely, it is an ideal source for British terms likely to be neglected in American dictionaries of comparable scope. It is for this purpose and for its insight into current British usage that it is highly recommended to North American libraries and individuals as a supplement to one or more of the good dictionaries they already have." Library J

It "is still the same attractively tubby little volume, the nicest looking among the smaller dictionaries." Times (London) Lit Sup

Funk & Wagnalls New Standard dictionary of the English language. Funk illus $47.50   **423**

1 English language—Dictionaries

First published 1893 with title: A standard dictionary of the English language. Frequently reprinted with corrections and additions

"A serviceable one volume work. Its special feature is emphasis upon current information, i.e. present day meaning, pronunciation, spelling, and the subordination of the historical to the current information. Full vocabulary, about [450,000] words including [over] 65,000 proper names. . . . Contains considerable encyclopedic information and many illustrations and good colored plates." Winchell. Guide to Reference Books. 8th edition

For a fuller review see: The Booklist and Subscription Books Bulletin, July 1, 1957

Funk & Wagnalls Standard college dictionary. Funk illus maps   **423**

1 English language—Dictionaries

Prices vary according to binding

First published 1963, based on Funk & Wagnall's Standard dictionary, International edition, entered below. Frequently revised

A dictionary whose entries "include geographical, biographical, and mythological terms in the same alphabet with the vocabulary. . . . Word division is shown by a center period; pronunciation is clearly indicated by use of letters of the alphabet and certain standard diacritical marks; order of definitions of words having several senses is determined by frequency of use; [and] etymologies are given after the definition." Cur Ref Bks

"Excellent for scientific and mathematical terms that can be explained succinctly in a short definition." The AAAS Science Book List for Young Adults

For a fuller review see: The Booklist and Subscription Books Bulletin Reviews, June 15, 1964

Funk & Wagnalls Standard dictionary of the English language. International ed. Funk illus $24.50, 2v ed $35   **423**

1 English language—Dictionaries

First published 1958 and frequently revised for corrections and additions

"A new 'between-size' Standard dictionary attempting to include 'the established word

Funk & Wagnalls Standard dictionary of the English language—*Continued*
stock of English and of the rapidly expanding vocabularies of the arts, sciences, trades, and professions,' as well as slang, colloquialisms, regional and local dialects, etc. Gives, in one alphabet, words; personal, proper, and geographical names; foreign phrases, etc. Alphabetization is letter by letter. A list of some 5000 commonly used abbreviations follows the main text." Winchell
"Especially notable is its strong coverage of recent scientific and technical terms and also new works in other fields." English Language Dictionaries in Print

Johnson, Samuel
Johnson's dictionary; a modern selection, by E. L. McAdam, Jr. & George Milne. Pantheon Bks. 1963 464p illus $6.50   423
1 English language—Dictionaries
This "first modern edition of Samuel Johnson's 'English Dictionary' . . . retains most of the definitions unavailable in modern dictionaries; the items which reflected Johnson's own taste and prejudices; the entire preface; and all entries under the letter Z." Bk Buyer's Guide
"The most sensible way of making the dictionary available is the book we have here—a selection by two Johnsonians devoted enough to have read the 2,300 doubled-columned pages and judicious enough to have carved out a handy volume. . . . The purist or the scholar may grumble about any 'modern selection,' and prefer all or nothing; but this selection does succeed in giving the reader a sampling of a uniquely great man and great work, as well as a more extensive view of the landscape of lexicography." Sat R

Oxford Illustrated dictionary; text ed. by J. Coulson [and others] illus. ed. by Helen Mary Petter. Oxford 1962 974p illus $12.50   423
1 English language—Dictionaries
Based upon vocabulary of the Concise Oxford dictionary. "This is the first Oxford dictionary to be illustrated. Dispersed through the text are some 1,700 text-figures of plant and animal forms, the parts of the human body, geometrical figures, machines, architectural details, costumes, and other works of man and nature.
. . . . [The book] lays emphasis upon the 'things' which words denote, rather than the words themselves and their usage. . . . There are [also] entries on proper names—persons of the Bible and of legend, statesmen, writers, famous places, [and] historical incidents. Further information, varying in kind from the dates of the Popes to the atomic weights of the chemical elements, is tabulated at the end of the volume." Publisher's note
This volume "is decidedly British in its spellings and meanings." Christian Science Monitor
"As always in a work of this kind, it is not clear why certain words are illustrated and others not. . . . Still, this is a sturdy, attractive and useful book." Sci Am

The **Random** House Dictionary of the English language. Jess Stein, editor in chief; Laurence Urdang, managing editor. Random House 1966 xxxii, 2059p illus maps $30   423
1 English language—Dictionary
"More than 260,000 entries emphasizing words in current use, including 'foreign words and phrases, biographical terms, geographical terms, abbreviations, titles of major literary works and many other types of information." Preface
Appended are four concise bilingual foreign dictionaries; an atlas; a gazetteer; lists of national parks, colleges, and universities; presidents and vice presidents of the United States; reference books; signs and symbols; a basic style manual; and miscellaneous tables. . . . This is the first general dictionary to use electronic data processing equipment in its production." Cheney. Fundamental Reference Sources

Includes section: Atlas of the world
For additional critical material see Booklist and Subscription Books Bulletin, April 1, 1967

The Random House Dictionary of the English language. College ed. Laurence Urdang, editor in chief; Stuart Berg Flexner, managing editor. Random House 1968 xxxii, 1568p illus maps $6.95, thumb indexed $7.95   423
1 English language—Dictionaries
"Based on The Random House Dictionary of the English language. The unabridged ed. Jess Stein, editor in chief; Laurence Urdang, managing editor." Facing title page
"The type is small but clear: getting more than 155,000 entries into a single volume, and doing it thoroughly, is miracle enough. Designed for college use, the book keeps abreast of the orbiting Young Generation with 6000 idiomatic expressions and phrases and the latest technical, general and slang words, Synonyms and antonyms; a fine style manual; a pronunciation guide and a guide to common English spellings; 6500 geographical entries, 10,000 scientific terms and 700 biographical entries of famous people: it's complete, authoritative and well organized." Pub W

Thorndike-Barnhart Comprehensive desk dictionary; ed. by Clarence L. Barnhart. Doubleday illus $3.95, thumb indexed $4.95   423
1 English language—Dictionaries
First published 1951. Frequently revised
A dictionary of over 80,000 words. For each entry this dictionary includes usage notes, phrases, and sentences as examples of usage, word origins, pronunciation keys, synonyms, antonyms, biographical and geographical information and idioms
"Particularly good on examples of usage. . . . Selection of words excellent, based on Thorndike-Lorge word counts." English Language Dictionaries in Print

Webster's New twentieth century dictionary of the English language, unabridged. Based on the broad foundations laid down by Noah Webster. Extensively rev. by the publisher's editorial staff under the general supervision of Jean L. McKechnie. 2d ed. World Pub. 1960 2129, 160p illus maps thumb indexed $39.50, 2v ed $39.50   423
1 English language—Dictionaries
First published with this title, 1941, by the Publisers Guild, inc. "400,000 entries emphasizing current vocabulary, including biographical and geographical names. Appended are a dictionary of biography, of geography, of noted names in fiction, mythology, and legend of foreign words and phrases, of scriptural proper names and foreign words, forms of address, weights and measures, signs and symbols, lists of U.S. presidents, vice presidents, and cabinet officers, etc." Cheney. Fundamental Reference Sources
For a fuller review see: The Booklist and Subscription Books Bulletin, December 1, 1957

Webster's New World dictionary of the American language. 2d college ed. David B. Guralnik, editor-in-chief. World Pub. 1970 xxxvi, 1692p illus $7.95, thumb indexed $8.95   423
1 English language—Dictionaries
First published 1953, based upon Webster's New World dictionary of the English language, Encyclopedic edition
This edition consists of a "single alphabetical listing ⸢which includes⸣ biographical and geographical entries, proper names and abbreviations. . . . ⸢The vocabulary⸣ was chosen to meet the needs of students and

Webster's New World dictionary of the American language—*Continued*
others . . . [and so] there is a heavier proportion of terms from the sciences than was true for the previous edition." Foreword
"Claiming 'over 157,000 entries,' which would put it a couple of notches above the competition, it is standard size, set in clearer type than others, and, rather than being a revision of the first edition, is a completely new and greater reference work. We recommend it with only the pettiest reservations." Sat R

Webster's Seventh new collegiate dictionary. Based on Webster's Third new international dictionary. Merriam illus **423**
1 English language—Dictionaries
"A Merriam-Webster"
Prices vary according to binding
First published 1898 with variant titles: Webster's Collegiate dictionary, and Webster's New collegiate dictionary. Frequently revised
This dictionary "reflects the new concepts and policies of that dictionary [Webster's Third new international dictionary]. Emphasis is on 'standard language,' with only a small selection of slang and colloquial terms and meanings; colloquial terms usually are not so designated. Pronunciation is indicated by a diacritical system, the key to which is given in full on the front and back endpapers and in abbreviated form at the bottom of every other page. Etymologies are full and given at the beginning of the entry; definitions follow in chronological order, the modern meaning coming last. Synonyms are given but not antonyms. Appendixes include: Abbreviations; Arbitrary signs and symbols; Biographical names (more than 5000 names with pronunciation, dates, and identifying phrase); Pronouncing gazetteer containing more than 10,000 names of places; forms of address; Pronouncing vocabulary of common English given names; Vocabulary rhymes; Spelling, punctuation, etc.; Colleges and universities in the United States and Canada." Winchell. Guide to Reference Books.
For a fuller review see: The Booklist and Subscription Books Bulletin, July 15, 1963

Webster's Third new international dictionary of the English language; unabridged. Merriam illus **423**
1 English language—Dictionaries
"A Merriam-Webster"
Prices vary according to binding
First published 1828 by S. Converse as: An American dictionary of the English language, by Noah Webster. Also appeared with titles: Webster's Unabridged dictionary, Webster's International dictionary of the English language, and Webster's New international dictionary of the English language. This edition first published 1961. Frequently reprinted with additions and changes to keep it up to date
Editor in chief: 1961- Philip Babcock Gove and the Merriam Webster editorial staff
This work "is evidently intended as a dictionary for our times, for its more than 450,000 entries include 100,000 newly added terms and exclude words obsolete before 1755. Its more than 200,000 quotations illustrate contemporary usage, drawing on many modern writers. Instead of encyclopedic treatment at one place of a group of related terms, each term is defined at its own place in the alphabet with an analytical one-phrase definition. . . . Gone are the biographical and geographical sections, the key to pronunciation at the bottom of each page, while only 3,000 new illustrations replace the 12,000 found in the earlier edition. . . . Thus the dictionary must stand on its true dictionary features—as a source of etymology, pronunciation, syllabication and definition.' Cur Ref Bks
"Much is included, often without qualification, which may be regarded by many as colloquial, vulgar, or incorrect. . . . Regardless of varying opinions of editorial judgment, this edition will be wanted in most American libraries, though the 2d edition will be wisely retained as well." Winchell. Guide to Reference Books. 8th edition
For a fuller review see: The Booklist and Subscription Books Bulletin, July 1, 1963

The **World** book dictionary; Clarence L. Barnhart, editor in chief. Prepared in cooperation with Field Enterprises Educational Corporation. Field Enterprises 2v illus $51.20 **423**
1 English language—Dictionaries
"A Thorndike-Barnhart dictionary"
First published 1963 with title: The World Book Encyclopedia dictionary. Revised annually
"This dictionary gives information about the meaning, spelling and pronunciation of the most important and most frequently used words and phrases in the English language. It records facts about the use of these words in both the spoken and written language. . . . The editors have prepared this dictionary especially for use with The World Book Encyclopedia. Because information about persons and places in fully presented in the encyclopedia, this dictionary does not include biographical and geographical entries. . . . The dictionary includes the names and definitions of plants and animals." What's special About This Dictionary
Definitions are given in terms of the age of those most likely to look them up and "include illustrative quotations, usage notes, and restrictive labels (slang, obsolete, informal, etc.) Preceding vocabulary are extensive sections on how to write, vocabulary building at all grade levels, and handbook of usage." Library J
For a fuller review see: Subscription Books Bulletin, September 1, 1963

424 Synonyms, antonyms, homonyms

Fernald, James C.
Funk & Wagnalls Standard handbook of synonyms, antonyms, and prepositions. Completely rev. ed. Funk 1947 515p $6.95 **424**
1 English language—Synonyms and antonyms
First published 1896 with title: English synonyms, antonyms, and prepositions
Arranged alphabetically under key words. Compares or contrasts synonymous words, explains their difference of meaning or usage and shows in what connection one or the other may be most specifically applied. Alphabetic index

Funk & Wagnalls Modern guide to synonyms and related words; lists of antonyms, copious cross-references, a complete and legible index [ed. by] S. I. Hayakawa and the Funk & Wagnalls Dictionary staff. Funk 1968 726p $8.95 **424**
1 English language—Synonyms and antonyms
"Over 1,000 key words are presented, and under these are grouped 6,000 synonyms and related words. The meaning and nuances of the synonyms are described in short essays that provide concise definitions and illustrative sentences. An index at the end of the book lists both the key and related words, with the key word printed in small capitals. A list of antonyms are also listed at the end of most essays, but these are not indexed unless they occur elsewhere as key or related words." Cur Ref Bks
"There have been more thorough compilations—and a good standard dictionary will contain much of this material—but few are as conveniently arranged or as pleasant to consult. To the careful writer and speaker, the book can be invaluable." Sat R
For a more complete review see: The Booklist and Subscription Books Bulletin, June 15, 1968

The **New** American Roget's College thesaurus in dictionary form. [Prepared and ed. by the National Lexicographic Board; Albert H. Morehead, chairman and general editor] Grosset 1958 433p $3.98 **424**
1 English language—Synonyms and antonyms
"This thesaurus is based on American rather than British usage. Synonyms are arranged in alphabetic order but Roget's original categories

The **New** American Roget's College thesaurus in dictionary form—*Continued*

are retained in the back of the book and are keyed to the alphabetic text." Pub W

"This edition of 'Roget's Thesaurus' is both a dictionary of synonyms and antonyms and a thesaurus or 'treasury' of related words. To use it, simply look up the word for which you wish to have a synonym, an antonym, or a word related in some other way." How to use this thesaurus

The **New** Roget's Thesaurus of the English language in dictionary form. Rev. greatly enl. ed. Edited by Norman Lewis. . . . Putnam [1965 c1964] 552p $3.75, thumb indexed $4.50; lib. bdg. $4.75, thumb indexed $5.50   **424**

1 English language—Synonyms and antonyms

"Based on C. O. Sylvester Mawson's alphabetical arrangement of the famous Roget system of word classification." Title page

This alphabetically arranged revision of P. M. Roget's Thesaurus of English language in dictionary form, was first published 1931 under the editorship of C. O. S. Mawson. The 1961 edition of about 17,000 individual entries includes many new or recently coined words

A standard dictionary of synonyms and antonyms

The **Original** Roget's Thesaurus of English words and phrases. New ed. completely rev. and modernized by Robert A. Dutch. For the first time American spelling and usage are incorporated in the original Roget. St Martins [1965 c1962] lxxx, 1405p $6.95, thumb indexed $7.95   **424**

1 English language—Synonyms and antonyms

First published 1852. This is a reissue of the 1962 edition published in England with title: Roget's Thesaurus of English words and phrases

In this edition of a standard dictionary of antonyms and synonyms, Roget's preface and introduction to the original edition and a tabular synopsis of the 990 categories are included. "The vocabulary has been enlarged by some 50,000 entries. These are not all new in the sense that none of them has previously appeared anywhere in the text. The majority are old words in new places. . . . Deletions were, by comparison, very much fewer. . . . The axe fell mainly on the numerous French and Latin expressions which have not become anglicized, and on the 'phrases.' . . . Within the subheads, great care has been given to the ordering of vocabulary in context, and to the provisions of a multiplicity of cross-references." Preface to the revised edition 1962

Roget, Peter

Everyman's Thesaurus of English words and phrases; rev. from Peter Roget by D. C. Browning. Dutton 1952 572p (Everyman's reference lib) $4.95   **424**

1 English language—Synonyms and antonyms

A revision of the standard reference work first published 1852

In this edition the opportunity has been taken to give the work "as complete a revision as was possible, short of doing the whole compilation afresh. Every paragraph has been carefully reviewed, over 10,000 words and phrases have been added, and the articles have 'tidied up' so that all additions follow the logical order which agrees with the original plan." Introduction

Roget's International thesaurus. 3d ed. Crowell 1962 xx, 1258p front (A Crowell Reference bk) $5.95, thumb indexed $6.95 **424**

1 English language—Synonyms and antonyms

First copyright edition published 1911 with title: The standard thesaurus of English words and phrases classified and arranged so as to facilitate the expression of ideas and assist in literary composition

"This handy reference work has a trick rapid reference system of numbers to enable the user to track down quickly the elusive word that fits his need. It contains [over] 200,000 words and phrases, modern quotations and the new words that have come into the language. The Index Guide alone requires 500 pages." Cur Hist

Webster's New dictionary of synonyms; a dictionary of discriminated synonyms with antonyms and contrasted words. Merriam 1968 31a, 909p $7.95   **424**

1 English language—Synonyms and antonyms

"A Merriam Webster"

First published 1942 with title: Webster's Dictionary of Synonyms

"The core of this book is the discriminating articles. It is not its purpose to assemble mere word-finding lists for consultants with but a vague notion of the sort of word they seek, but rather to provide them with the means of making clear comparisons between words of a common denotation and to enable them to distinguish the differences in implications, connotations, and applications among such words and to choose for their purposes the precisely suitable words. . . . Every word discussed in an article of synonymy is entered in its own alphabetical place and is followed by a list of its synonyms, with a reference (by means of an asterisk or a direction introduced by 'see') to the entry where the discussion of these listed words is to be found. The words listed as analogous and those listed as contrasted are always displayed in groups, each group having a clear reference (asterisk or 'see') to the term under which an article of synonymy is to be found." Preface

426 Prosody

Walker, J.

Rhyming dictionary of the English language. . . . Rev. and enl. ed. by Lawrence H. Dawson. Dutton 1924 549p $6.95   **426**

1 English language—Rhyme—Dictionaries

First published 1775

"In which the whole language is arranged according to its terminations, with an index to allowable rhymes." Subtitle

"Excellent book for music teachers in improvising songs appropriate for certain occasions." California

427 Nonstandard English. Slang

Mathews, Mitford M.

American words; illus. by Lorence Bjorklund. World Pub. 1959 246p illus $4.50 **427**

1 Americanisms 2 English language—Etymology

The author "shows how American English has developed during the past 350 years. After discussing ways in which the language has been modified and enlarged to meet the needs of the people and the growth of the country, he takes up 200 American words and phrases—ranging from Conestoga wagon, hoecake, and Yankee to G man, juke box, and skyscraper—telling the derivation or story behind each. A good introduction to etymology, with some colorful side lights on American history and culture." Booklist

Mencken, H. L.

The American language; an inquiry into the development of English in the United States. . . . Knopf 1963 xxv, 777, cxxiv p $12.95   **427**

1 Americanisms 2 English language 3 Names

At head of title: One-volume abridged edition

"The fourth edition and the two supplements, abridged, with annotations and new material, by Raven I. McDavid, Jr. with the assistance of David W. Maurer." Title page

Mencken, H. L.—*Continued*

"Professor McDavid has done an extremely able job of combining and abridging the massive elements. . . . [He has also included] annotations and new material which bring Mencken's monumental study . . . completely up to date [1963]." Chicago Sch J

An historical treatment of the development of American English covering such subjects as pronunciation and spelling, slang, proper names, and common speech

Bibliographic footnotes

Partridge, Eric

A dictionary of slang and unconventional English; colloquialisms and catch-phrases, solecisms and catachreses, nicknames, vulgarisms and such Americanisms as have been naturalized. Macmillan (N Y) $18.50   427

1 English language—Slang—Dictionaries 2 Americanisms

First published 1937. Periodically revised
Contents: The dictionary; The supplement

"The Supplement incorporates into one alphabet the addenda of the 2d, 3d, and 4th editions (with some revisions) and new material running to some 100,000 words. These additions consist mainly of new words and phrases with the emphasis on slang, particularly of World War II." Winchell. Guide to Reference Books. 8th edition

It "deals not only with slang but with [some] foul language as well, such as is found in the works of Joyce and James T. Farrell." The Reader's Adviser

Slang to-day and yesterday; with a short historical sketch and vocabularies of English, American, and Australian slang. 4th ed. rev. and brought up to date. Barnes & Noble 1970 476p $14.50   427

1 English language—Slang
SBN 389-03977-2

First published 1934 by Routledge
This book may be used "as a source of wise and witty commentary on the history and characteristics of various kinds of slang—Cockney, publicity, the church, circus, soldiers, and so forth." Cur Ref Bks

Wentworth, Harold

(ed.) Dictionary of American slang; comp. and ed. by Harold Wentworth and Stuart Berg Flexner. With a supplement by Stuart Berg Flexner. Crowell 1967 718p $7.95   427

1 English language—Slang—Dictionaries 2 Americanisms

First published 1960
Together this "compilation and the supplement contain more than 21,000 definitions, illustrated by quotations from published sources. Terms long in use are cited with both early and recent quotations, often with examples selected at ten-year intervals. . . . Expressions from all strata of society are here, including the special terms of all vocations and avocations, and many regionalisms and colloquialisms. America's most recent concerns, from the sit-ins through the war in Vietnam to LSD and 'ski bunnies,' are reflected in the supplement, which also encompasses a surprising number of Spanish, Yiddish, and Negro expressions coming into use. . . . [Mr Flexner's] preface contains a discussion of what slang is, why and how it is created, how the choice of words reveals one's character, and the relationship of American slang to the national character." Publisher's note

"A short appendix to the supplement provides a useful insight into the formation of new slang terms. A selected bibliography accompanies this supplement. This is an indispensable dictionary for any reference collection which includes American English." Library J

428 Standard English usage (Applied linguistics)

Bernstein, Theodore M.

Watch your language; a lively, informal guide to better writing, emanating from the news room of the New York Times. Atheneum Pubs. 1965 [c1958] 276p $4.50   428

1 English language—Errors   2 English language—Idioms 3 Journalism

"A Leonard Harris book"
First published 1958 by Channel Press
"The kindness and good humor with which the pointing out is done make the dose palatable. But [the author] is sometimes pedantic and sometimes far from current American usage. . . . The student of journalism will find the book indispensable and—if he watches Mr. Bernstein's language as well as his own—instructive. The common reader will find it delightful. The linguist will find it at least stimulating." N Y Times Bk R

Bryant, Margaret M.

(ed.) Current American usage. Funk [1962] xxiv, 290p $5   428

1 Americanisms 2 English language—Idioms

"A comprehensive study of the various uses employed in speech and writing in different parts of the United States. Entries are arranged alphabetically, and each entry begins with a summary and then proceeds with a general discussion followed by fully annotated citations. The book does not presume to prescribe 'good' usage; the reader is presented with the evidence and can draw his own conclusions." Huntting

"Useful for moot matters upon which current textbooks give inadequate or misleading information." Good Reading
Bibliography: p281-90

Evans, Bergen

A dictionary of contemporary American usage, by Bergen Evans and Cornelia Evans. Random House 1957 567p $7.95   428

1 Americanisms   2 English language—Idioms 3 English language—Dictionaries

"This dictionary is intended as a reference book on current English in the United States. It is designed for people who speak standard English but are uncertain about some details. . . . It also contains a full discussion of English grammar, a discussion which does not assume that the student can already read and write Latin." Preface

A "lively and sophisticated word and phrase list characterized by sprightly definitions, scholarly derivations, and unhackneyed examples of usage drawn from everyday speech, the classics, and contemporary literature. . . . This book also gives both British and American usage, but always from the American viewpoint. For reference or browsing." Booklist

Follett, Wilson

Modern American usage; a guide. Ed. and completed by Jacques Barzun, in collaboration with Carlos Baker [and others]. Hill & Wang 1966 436p $7.50   428

1 English language—Terms and phrases 2 English language—Idioms 3 English language—Grammar

This compilation "seeks to serve two related purposes. By analyzing structural errors and ambiguities it reminds writers and speakers of grammatical norms that are frequently flouted; and by discussing words and idioms it provides a list of distinctions and suggestions in the realm of tact. . . . It concentrates on the prevailing faults of current speech and prose." The author

"There has never been such an assault on the integrity of the English language as there is today. Each of the professions has its own jargon, intended both to impress and to bewilder the laity. . . . [This volume] is concerned rather with the possibilities of making mistakes than with the opportunities for saying something fresh and impressive. . . . [However]

Follett, Wilson—*Continued*

it is] a sturdy weapon against the incoherence . . . of the mass media." Sat R
Short titles of books cited in the text: p xi

Fowler, H. W.
A dictionary of modern English usage. 2d ed. rev. by Sir Ernest Gowers. Oxford 1965 xx, 725p $6   **428**
1 English language—Etymology   2 English language—Idioms

First published 1926

Covers current practice in pronunciation, idiom, and spelling. Includes information on the historical origin, and usage of words and comparisons between American and British pronunciation and usage

This indispensable work "has been a byword since the 1920's. An examination of the contents will reveal the restraint with which Sir Ernest Gowers approached its up-dating, destroying none of the flavor of the original author. Reference librarians who have never mastered Fowler's enigmatic headings will welcome the classified guide which allows a more conventional approach to the contents. Also useful among the 373 added articles are the many new comparisons between British and American usage and pronunciation." Cur Ref Bks

Lewis, Norman
Thirty days to better English. Doubleday 1965 200p $4.95   **428**
1 English language   2 Vocabulary

Thirty lessons on spelling, vocabulary building, "pronunciation and the use of words, with suggested tricks for memorizing, self-tests, and tips on grammar." Bk Buyer's Guide

"It is readable. . . . As do most self-help books, this has blanks to be filled in by the reader, but, despite this drawback, it will be useful in . . . libraries." Library J

Nicholson, Margaret
A dictionary of American-English usage; based on Fowler's Modern English usage. Oxford 1957 671p $6.50   **428**
1 Americanisms   2 English language—Idioms 3 English language—Dictionaries

Title on spine: American-English usage

The present volume is an adaptation, but not a replacement, of H. W. Fowler's "A dictionary of modern English usage" entered above. . . . It includes American variations of spelling, pronunciation, and usage not recorded by Fowler, and adds new entries on words and idiomatic usage, both English and American. (Publisher)

A ready reference guide, with entries arranged in one alphabet, to the correct use of both written and spoken English

"Miss Nicholson has added many short entries which show definite divergencies in usage between British and American practices: spelling variants, pronunciation shifts which affect syllabication." Library J

428.2   Vocabulary

Funk, Peter V. K.
It pays to increase your word power. Funk 1968 205p $4.95   **428.2**
1 Vocabulary

"A self-help manual for readers who want to increase their vocabularies, consisting of a series of word tests and exercises accompanied by definitions and correct answers. The material, based on the author's regular 'Reader's Digest' feature, is similar to that of other vocabulary books and will be useful where more are needed." Booklist

428.4   Reading

Lewis, Norman
How to read better and faster. 3d ed. completely rev. Crowell 1958 398p illus $5.95   **428.4**
1 Reading

First published 1944

"How an average reader many improve his reading ability, speed, [vocabulary] and comprehension is presented in a series of lessons." Chicago

"Intended for the home scholar as well as for the one in the school or group, but if it is tackled by the individual he must be prepared to devote himself to its study with the regularity and concentration that he would bestow upon work in the classroom. For the normal reader the book is difficult to take, for it means slowing down his reading, but for the one who needs to gain speed, its general principles and specific examples, if conscientiously applied, ought to prove exceedingly helpful." Book of the Month Club News

Includes bibliographies

433   German language— Dictionaries

Cassell's New compact German-English, English-German dictionary. Comp. by H. C. Sasse, J. Horne [and] Charlotte Dixon. Funk 1966 541p $3.95   **433**
1 German language—Dictionaries

A "dictionary with an extensive and up-to-date vocabulary. [Includes] phonetic transcriptions using the symbols of the international Phonetics Association." Bk Buyer's Guide

"The main emphasis, says the foreword, is on 'straightforward contemporary German,' though as it is designed primarily for school and university students at a not very advanced level, provision is also made for the words they are likely to find in their set texts." Times (London) Lit Sup

The **New** Cassell's German dictionary: German-English, English-German. Based on the editions by Karl Breul. Completely rev. and re-edited by Harold T. Betteridge. With a foreword by Gerhard Cordes. Funk $7.95, thumb indexed $9.50   **433**
1 German language—Dictionaries

First compiled 1888 by Elizabeth Weir and published by Heath. Periodically revised

A "reference designed for maximum coverage of modern German language developments, while maintaining the high standard of scholarship set by its precursor, the 'Breul.' . . . [Includes] terms which have become accepted parts of contemporary literary, practical, and colloquial German [in science, politics, technology, etc.]." Publisher's note

"This popularly priced volume will be indispensable for the scientist and the student of German affairs and German literature; it should be purchased by reference departments of public, college, and high school libraries regardless of size." Library J

443   French language— Dictionaries

Mansion's Shorter French and English dictionary. Holt [1947] 2v in 1 $8.50   **443**
1 French language—Dictionaries

Abridged edition of Mansion's Standard French and English dictionary. Published in England with title: Harrap's Shorter French and English dictionary

Contents: v 1 French-English. v2 English-French

Includes material necessary and useful to the student and general reader. It deals fully with points of grammar, idiom, and pronunciation. There are thousands of terms in the fields of modern science and invention, industry and commerce, motoring, aviation, sports, movies, radio and other facets of modern life

The **New** Cassell's French dictionary: French-English, English-French. Completely rev. by Denis Girard with the assistance of Gaston Dulong, Oliver Van Oss, and Charles Guinness. Funk $7.95, thumb indexed $9.50   **443**
1 French language—Dictionaries
First published 1920 with title: Cassell's French-English, English-French dictionary. Periodically revised and brought up to date
Contains the basic vocabulary needed for the study of classical French literature. Also includes "words and phrases stemming from recent scientific developments, as well as many . . . colloquial expressions [and] French-Canadian terms. . . . Pronunciation of both French and English words is indicated." Publisher's note
Includes bibliography

453 Italian language—Dictionaries

Cassell's Italian dictionary: Italian-English, English-Italian. Comp. by Piero Rebora with the assistance of Francis M. Guercio and Arthur L. Hayward. Funk $7.50, thumb indexed $8.50   **453**
1 Spanish language—Dictionaries
First published 1958 in England with title: Cassell's Italian-English, English-Italian dictionary. Frequently revised
The dictionary includes "colloquialisms and words brought into use by the war, by recent political and social changes, and by industrial and technical advancements, as well as obsolete words used by classic Italian authors." McClurg. Book News

463 Spanish language—Dictionaries

Cassell's New compact Spanish-English, English-Spanish dictionary. Comp. by Brian Dutton, L. P. Harvey and Roger M. Walker. Funk 1969 444p $3.95   **463**
1 Spanish language—Dictionaries
Published in England with title: Cassell's Compact Spanish-English, English-Spanish dictionary
This is a "new dictionary, not an abridgement of the larger Cassell's Spanish dictionary. . . . Emphasis [is] on Latin-American usage and current colloquialisms, as well as the standard vocabulary." News of Bks
"Students and travelers should find the 55,000 entries and the verb tables adequate for general needs." Sat R

Cassell's Spanish dictionary: Spanish-English, English-Spanish. Ed. by Edgar Allison Peers [and others]. Funk $7.95, thumb indexed $9.50   **463**
1 Spanish language—Dictionaries
First published 1959 in England. Frequently revised. Title varies
"Intended to be used for the reading of both the classics and of standard modern English, for the comprehension of current colloquialisms in both English and Spanish, and for a wide range of modern technical usage." Pub W
This dictionary "gives special prominence to the Spanish of Latin America, includes the vocabulary of both classical and literary Spanish as well as the language of the modern Spanish-speaking world. The Spanish section, somewhat longer than the English, shows part of speech, field and stratum of language to which a word belongs. . . . The scope and up-to-dateness recommend it for serious consideration." Cur Ref Bks

Crowell's Spanish-English & English-Spanish dictionary, by Gerd A. Gillhoff. Crowell 1963 1261p illus $6.95, thumb indexed $7.95   **463**
1 Spanish language—Dictionaries
A "dictionary of Spanish and English as they are spoken in the Americas. There are more than 80,000 entries. It has wide coverage of business, legal and scientific terms, it identifies by locality Latin-American words and phrases, and it has a good representation of slang words." Pub W

Cuyás, Arturo
Appleton's New Cuyás English-Spanish and Spanish-English dictionary. Rev. and enl. by Lewis E. Brett (Part 1) and Helen S. Eaton (Part 2) with the assistance of Walter Beveraggi-Allende. Revision editor, Catherine B. Avery. Appleton 2v in 1 $7.95, thumb indexed $8.95   **463**
1 Spanish language—Dictionaries
First published 1903 with title: Appleton's New English-Spanish and Spanish-English dictionary. Periodically revised and brought up to date. Title varies
"Includes 7,500 new entries, a . . . table of model Spanish regular and irregular verbs, a list of geographical names in English and Spanish, colloquial pet names and proper names, and abbreviations." Bk Buyer's Guide

The **New** World Spanish-English and English-Spanish dictionary; prepared under the supervision of Mario A. Pei; Salvatore Ramondino, editor. World Pub. [1969 c1968] 2v in 1 $6.95, thumb indexed $7.95   **463**
1 Spanish language—Dictionaries
In this dictionary "American English and Americanisms in Spanish are stressed; when an English word has several meanings, each is shown in use; pronunciations are given for all words in both languages. . . . [Contains] more than 70,000 entries." Bk Buyer's Guide

Velázquez de la Cadena, Mariano
(comp.) New revised Velázquez Spanish and English dictionary, by Mariano Velázquez de la Cadena, Edward Gray, and Juan L. Iribas. Follett 2v in 1 $7.95, thumb indexed $8.95   **463**
1 Spanish language—Dictionaries
First published in this edition 1959. Periodically revised
"Newly revised by Ida Navarro Hinojosa, Manuel Blanco-Gonzalez, and Richard John Wiezell." Title page for 1967 edition
A bilingual dictionary in which the thousands of English and Castilian Spanish entries cover up-to-date words in all fields including science. Particular attention has been paid to terms and idioms commonly used in the United States and Spanish America. Appendix includes geographic terms, proper nouns, weights and measures, etc.

473 Latin language—Dictionaries

Cassell's New compact Latin-English, English-Latin dictionary; comp. by D. P. Simpson. Funk [1964 c1963] 379p $3.50   **473**
1 Latin language—Dictionaries
An abridgment of: Cassell's New Latin dictionary, entered below
"Mr. Simpson has retained amazing amounts from his more extensive version. There is no discrimination against authors; only very rare words are missing, and not all of those; names represent the largest category of the outs, but

Cassell's New compact Latin-English, En-
lish-Latin dictionary—*Continued*
many of them are still in, too. The cutting lies
more in meanings, and in all references to
writers, though many idioms are still there in
both languages. Indications of origin are gone;
those of length, plus identifying forms and
principal parts are present. The print is smaller.
High school students and other beginners may
find this 'compact' edition valuable, though
they normally get vocabularies in their texts."
Library J

Cassell's New Latin dictionary: Latin-English, English-Latin [comp] by D. P.
Simpson. Funk [1960 c1959] 883p $7.50,
thumb indexed $8.50   **473**

1 Latin language—Dictionaries
Cassell's Latin dictionary was first published
1854; Cassell's Latin-English dictionary revised,
1886. This 1960 edition, which was first published
in England in 1959, is a complete revision of
the two sections of the dictionary as it appeared
in 1892
"My aim has been to conform to the fashions
of the present day, both in English idiom and in
Latin spelling; to introduce fresh material from
various sources; and in matters of explanation
and arrangement to go part of the way back to
the simplicity of the first edition. Yet while rewriting much, I have tried to adhere throughout to the traditional principle that 'classical'
Latin, the language of what we still consider
the best period, should be the prime concern of
both parts of 'Cassell's New Latin Dictionary.'
The first part is intended primarily to help
the student in the reading of such Latin, the
second part to help him in the writing of it."
Preface

483 Greek language—Dictionaries

The **Oxford** Dictionary of modern Greek
(Greek-English). Oxford 1965 219p $5.75
                                                483

1 Greek language, Modern—Dictionaries
This "is primarily a dictionary of the popular language but it contains, also, many terms
from the learned tradition which have entered
the language of the people." Class World
This "manages to pack an extraordinary
amount into a handy pocket format. . . . On
'untranslatable' terms this unpretentious little
lexicon is quite as good as we have any right
to expect." Times (London) Lit Sup

491.7 Russian language— Dictionaries

Müller, V. K.
(comp.) English-Russian dictionary. Dut-
ton $10.95   **491.7**
1 Russian language—Dictionaries
First published in the United States 1944.
Periodically revised
This dictionary is arranged alphabetically by
the English word. Russian translations are
derived from the actual literary, conversational, and specialized vocabularies of English,
American and Australian works. Separate lists
of names, geographical terms, initials
Includes bibliography

500 PURE SCIENCES

Asimov, Isaac
The new intelligent man's guide to science;
foreword by George W. Beadle. Basic Bks.
1965 864p illus maps $12.50   **500**
1 Science

First published in two volumes 1960 with
title: The intelligent man's guide to science
A panoramic picture of the modern physical
and biological sciences, explaining basic ideas,
highlighting important developments and scientists, and pointing out the meaning of scientific
discoveries for life today
"The breadth and perspective of the treatment of the field of science will give the student an orientation to further study." Wis Lib
Bul
Bibliography: p815-23

Twentieth century discovery. Doubleday
1969 178p $4.95   **500**
1 Science
The author surveys recent scientific development in entomology, biology, physics, astronomy and space travel. He includes material on
insecticides and pesticides, the structure of the
atom, and the use of microwaves to measure
distances between planets
"One of Asimov's purposes in writing the
book was to demonstrate the rapid rate at
which scientific discoveries are being made, and
this he has clearly done. The essays are of
even high quality and much of the material
will be new to the general reader." Library J

Gamow, George
One two three . . . infinity; facts & speculations of science; rev. ed. Illus. by the
author. Viking 1961 340p illus $4.75   **500**
1 Science
First published 1947
"Numbers, space and time, the fourth dimension, atomic theory, ideas in astronomy, and
other topics are discussed in an interesting . . .
fashion." A Basic Book Collection for High
Schools
"This book is for the lay-reader, but no one
who desires only light reading about the wonders of science should pick it up." Library J

Time-Life Books
A guide to science, and Index to the Life
Science library, by the editors of Time-Life
Books. Time-Life Bks. [1969 c1967] 208p
illus (Life Science lib) lib. bdg. $7.60   **500**
1 Science 2 Science—Indexes
"A Stonehenge book"
First published 1967
This twenty-fifth and final volume of the
Life Science library contains a survey of the
history of science and picture essays on phys-
ics, chemistry, microbiology, anatomy, mind
and body, technology, geology and astronomy.
The second part of the book indexes the entire
series. (Publisher)
"Excellent colored photographs, pictures, tables. For the general reader, school and public
libraries." N Y New Tech Bks

Warshofsky, Fred
The new age of exploration. Viking 1969
173p illus (The 21st century) $6.95   **500**
1 Science and civilization 2 Technology and
civilization
Based upon a CBS television series
The author "presents the thesis that the expanding uses of the computer, the atom, and
the laser will delimit life in the 21st Century,
and explores the feasibility and methods of
colonizing and utilizing various celestial bodies
and exploiting the resources of earth's ocean.
. . . [He] also presents theories of the origin
of the cosmos and the nature of matter." Library J
"Lacking the visual impact of the telecast
series [the author's] text is at a disadvantage;
but the book, while it is diminished in 'popular'
appeal, gains from continuity of the printed
medium. . . . The book amounts to a major
primer for space-age." Pub W

501 Science—Philosophy and theory

Ruchlis, Hy
  Discovering scientific method; with science puzzle pictures; illus. with drawings by Jean Krulis and with photographs. Harper 1963 190p illus $3.95, lib. bdg. $3.79   501
    1 Science—Methodology

Using puzzle pictures, the author "introduces young people to the development and principles of scientific method. . . . These pictures pose problems that can be solved by a combination of careful observation, knowledge of pertinent facts, formulation of hypotheses, designing of experiments, and measurement." Publisher's note
"Although the reader is asked to devise his own questions, the author poses excellent ones and demonstrates how to bring the problems to logical conlusions." Library J

503 Science—Dictionaries

Asimov, Isaac
  Words of science, and the history behind them; illus. by William Barss. Houghton 1959 266p illus lib. bdg. $2.97   503
    1 Science—Dictionaries 2 English language—Etymology

A book "both for the reader interested in science and the reader interested in language and words. Two hundred and fifty words [arranged alphabetically] are given one-page explanations, but each word is used as a starting point for giving the histories and derivations of other words related by concept or etymology. The choice of words is, of necessity, rather arbitrary, but the selection is well-balanced and comprehensive; the author has defined his field broadly. . . . Format is attractive, and [there is an] excellent index." Chicago. Children's Book Center

The Harper Encyclopedia of science; ed. by James R. Newman; Managing editor: Jerome Wyckoff. Associate editors: Roger G. Menges [and] Edmund H. Harvey, Jr. Board of editorial consultants: John Tyler Bonner [and others]. Rev. ed. Harper 1967 1379p illus maps 2v $32.95; 2v in 1 $40   503
    1 Science—Dictionaries 2 Technology—Dictionaries

First published 1962 in 4 volumes
"This reference work covers, in alphabetical order by subject, the physical sciences, mathematics, logic, the history and philosophy of science and the lives of leading scientists." Book Rev Digest
"Concisely titled articles employ scientific terms that are likely to be encountered by general readers, and were prepared according to correlated entry lists covering the various branches of science. Cross-references and an accurate general index add to ease of use. Spot checking revealed up-to-date information as well as historical background. . . . Short biographies of scientists and a separate bibliography for each of the ten major scientific disciplines covered in the encyclopedia are included, the latter being arranged under form division, e.g. bibliographies, reference works, survey texts, etc, principally recent titles. Among the . . . illustrations, many in full color, are reproductions from old sources (such as the dedication page of Galileo's 'Dialogo') as well as remarkable clear photographs." Cur Ref Bks

McGraw-Hill Encyclopedia of science and technology. McGraw 15v illus maps $360   503
    1 Science—Dictionaries 2 Technology—Dictionaries

First published 1960 and periodically revised. Accompanied by Study guide and Reader's guide
"The subject matter of the various disciplines or branches of science and technology is organized systematically: a general article provides a broad survey of the field, and a number of separate articles, alphabetically arranged, cover its main subdivisions and more specific aspects." Suggestions to the readers
Supplemented by: McGraw-Hill Yearbook of science and technology, $27.50

Van Nostrand's Scientific encyclopedia. . . . 4th ed. Van Nostrand 1968 2008p illus $42.75   503
    1 Science—Dictionaries 2 Technology—Dictionaries

First published 1938
Entries cover "aeronautics, astronomy, biochemistry, botany, chemical engineering, chemistry, civil engineering, computer technology, electrical engineering, electronics, geology, guided missiles, mathematics, mechanical engineering, medicine, metallurgy, meteorology, mineralogy, navigation, nuclear science and engineering, photoelectronics, photography, physics, planetary explorations, radio and television, rocketry, space travel, statistics, zoology." Subtitle

505 Science—Serial publications

Britannica Yearbook of science and the future. Encyclopaedia Britannica illus $12.50   505
    1 Science—Yearbooks 2 Technology—Yearbooks

Annual. First published 1969
This yearbook "has been designed to provide those who have little or no background in science with authoritative, up-to-date, comprehensive information about current scientific and technological efforts and achievements. It includes in-depth articles prepared by noted authorities but written and illustrated in a manner that makes each subject clearly understandable to those who are unfamiliar with scientific principles and terminology." Publisher's note
"With its abundance of photographs and diagrams, broad nontechnical treatment, and variety of subject matter, this yearbook will appeal to browsers more than to serious students." Booklist

Science year; the World book science annual. Field Enterprises illus $7.95, lib. bdg. $6.95   505
    1 Science—Yearbooks

First published 1965
Consists of signed articles describing the latest achievements in science and technology with pertinent bibliographies. A second section: Science file consists of alphabetically arranged briefer articles

507.2 Science—Experiments

United Nations Educational, Scientific and Cultural Organization
  700 science experiments for everyone. Rev. and enl. ed. Comp. by UNESCO; foreword by Gerald Wendt. Doubleday [1964 c1962] 250p illus $4.50, lib. bdg. $5.25   507.2
    1 Science—Experiments

"Originally published as UNESCO Source book for science teaching." Title page
First published 1956 by UNESCO; in 1958 by Doubleday
Partial contents: How to make some general pieces of equipment; Plant study; Animal study; Rocks, soils, minerals and fossils; Astronomy; Air and air pressure; Weather; Water; Machines; Forces and inertia; Sound; Heat; Magnetism; Electricity; Light; The human body

United Nations Educational, Scientific and
Cultural Organization—*Continued*
The metric system is followed for all measurements
"A rare find for scientifically inclined youth.
It is complete, fascinating and comprehensive."
San Francisco Chronicle
Books from a science master's library: p225-27. Periodicals for science teaching and science
club libraries: p228-33

507.4 Science museums and exhibits

Oehser, Paul H.
The Smithsonian Institution. Praeger 1970
275p illus map (Praeger Lib. of U.S. Government departments and agencies) $8.95
507.4
1 Smithsonian Institution
"Persons important in Smithsonian history,
the organizational structure, research activities, the institution's complex of museums and
galleries, fiscal operations, and related topics
are brought into an instructive and well-organized book that includes among its appended material career opportunities at the Smithsonian and a selected list of its publications."
Booklist
"A book of this length could not be expected
to cover so large a topic in depth. But the coverage it does offer is informative and entertaining." Library J
Bibliography: p264-68

508 Science—Collections

Asimov, Isaac
The solar system and back. Doubleday
1970 246p illus $5.95
508
1 Science
The author offers a collection of essays
which were first published in The Magazine of
Fantasy and Science Fiction. "The portion
which corresponds to the first half of the title,
'To The Solar System,' is first-rate Asimov
popularization of solar system astronomy. For
serious, inquiring minds, unschooled in the
ways of traditional science, Asimov is a master
explainer; accurate, profound, and at the same
time exciting. . . . The topics follow the author's curiosity; nonetheless, they provide a
feeling for the fun, and difficulty, and the rewards of solar system research. The final third
of the book, the 'and Black' part, touches on
such topics as dinosaurs, metals in the ancient
world, the validity of giant creatures in science
fiction stories, and even the future role of
women in society. The quality again is good."
Choice

The stars in their courses. Doubleday
1971 199p $5.95
508
1 Science
A "collection of 17 essays on astronomy,
physics, chemistry and sociology, all reprinted
from 'The Magazine of Fantasy and Science
Fiction,' where they appeared in 1969-1970."
Pub W
In this book, the author "does what he
does best: debunking irrational scientific theories and practices, starting out with a multimegaton debunk of astrology. He draws on
his encyclopedic knowledge of the sciences and
their history to cut down anything that smacks
slightly of irrationality or scientific impossibility. He is the master of the devasting refutation. . . . He is a middle-man for the sciences. And as such, there is none better."
Christian Science Monitor

Ley, Willy
Another look at Atlantis, and fifteen other
essays. Doubleday 1969 229p illus maps
$5.95
508
1 Science 2 Natural history

"Atlantis, a new look at a lost continent,
the building of the Great Pyramid, the dodos,
the moas, and the pangolins, the sound of meteors, the legal question of who will own the
planets, these are just a few of the subjects
discussed in this new collection of sixteen
science and natural history essays." Publisher's note
The author's essays "are as delightful as
they are learned, and his range is from the
trivial—the extinct Dodo and other birds—to
such cosmic contemplations as the death of
the sun." Pub W

Newman, James R.
(ed.) What is science? Twelve eminent
scientists and philosophers explain their
various fields to the layman. Simon & Schuster 1955 493p illus pa $1.95
508
1 Science—Addresses and essays
Analyzed in Essay and general literature index
"This is a collection of essays on one of the
most pervasive influences shaping the world
today—natural science and the knowledge
gained from its researches. It is also an indirect introduction to the natural scientists themselves." Christian Science Monitor
Some of the contributors are: Bertrand Russell, Hermann Bondi, John Read, Julian S.
Huxley, Edwin G. Boring and Erich Fromm
"The book is by no means easy reading, but
it provides . . . [an] introduction to an understanding of scientific thinking." New Yorker
Includes bibliography

Science looks at itself. Comp. and ed. by
National Science Teachers Association.
Scribner 1970 122p $5.95
508
1 Science and civilization 2 Technology and
civilization
This book is the "result of a series of programs called Silver Symposia sponsored by
the National Science Teachers Association
. . . April 1969 in more than 100 meetings in
honor of the Association's 25th anniversary."
Preface
The papers were selected and reviewed by
Milton O. Pella, Mary C. Hawkins and Sally
L. Banks. The text "indicts the anarchy of
technology, the power and self-interest of private enterprise, and the apathy of individuals
for many of the present environmental crises
and explores new courses of action to safeguard the natural world." Publisher's note
Reference notes: p113-14

509 Science—History

Dampier, Sir William Cecil
A history of science and its relations with
philosophy & religion. 4th ed. reprinted with
a postscript by I. Bernard Cohen. Cambridge 1966 xxvii, 544p illus $9.50
509
1 Science—History 2 Philosophy
First published 1929 in England
A scholarly history of the evolution of scientific thought "tracing the subject from ancient times through the developments of modern physics, biology, and anthropology." N Y
New Tech Bks
The author's "valuable philosophic excursuses seem sometimes to fit rather loosely in
their context. In fact, he is not a 'layman's
writer' and his method makes his material
somewhat inaccessible to those without a scientific training." Spectator

Sarton, George
A history of science. Harvard Univ. Press
1952-1959 2v illus maps ea $15
509
1 Science—History   2 Civilization, Ancient
3 Hellenism
Analyzed in Essay and general literature index
Contents: v 1 Ancient science through the
Golden Age of Greece; v2 Hellenistic science in
the last three centuries B.C.

Sarton, George—*Continued*

These are the first two volumes in a projected eight-or-nine volume series in which the author, who died in 1956, planned to present the growth of scientific thought and activity from the earliest beginnings to the present. The author considers the history of the scientist in the context of ancient and Hellenistic culture

"A rather loosely connected mass of encyclopaedic information, conveyed eruditely, enthusiastically, and clearly, excellent in the scientific parts. . . . A good introduction to the science of the period." Manchester Guardian

510   Mathematics

Bergamini, David

Mathematics, by David Bergamini and the editors of Time-Life Books. Time-Life Bks. 1970 200p illus maps (Life science lib) lib. bdg. $7.60   510

1 Mathematics

First published 1963

An historical survey of mathematics including its role in art and nature and treating computing, calculus, probability and chance, topology, and outstanding mathematicians. (Publisher)

It is a popular account and, "hopefully, the rich detail woven into the visually delightful presentation may lead many to read other books." Science

Bibliography: p196

Hartkopf, Roy

Math without tears. Emerson 1971 247p illus $4.95   510

1 Mathematics

First published 1965 in Australia with title: Maths for those who hate it

"In lively non-technical language the author . . . [presents] many of the everyday applications of mathematics. Emphasizing the practical aspects of math, the author avoids mathematical terms and jargon and takes the reader from simple counting to trigonometry and calculus." News of Bks

Hogben, Lancelot

Mathematics for the million [4th ed] extensively rev. with additional material and completely re-illustrated. Norton [1968 c1967] 648p illus $8.95   510

1 Mathematics   2 Mathematics—History   3 Civilization

First published 1937

"Stressing the historical and social aspects of mathematics, this book was written primarily to popularize mathematics. Examples are given to show how many of life's problems may be solved mathematically." Cincinnati

"Professor Hogben has succeeded in writing a novel book. . . . His book should be read by all who wish to lose their fear of mathematics. Thousands of ordinary readers, ten of thousands of school children. and quite a number of teachers should discover from it what mathematics is really all about." Manchester Guardian

Lieber, Lillian R.

The education of T. C. Mits; drawings by Hugh Gray Lieber, words by Lillian R. Lieber. [Rev. and enl. ed] Norton 1944 230p illus $4.95   510

1 Mathematics

First published 1942 by Galois Institute Press

An elementary presentation of the postulational method. In verse, stressing the implications of method for daily life

The hero of this book "is The Celebrated Man in the Street, and its purpose is far more than to provide a painless introduction to the strange new algebras and geometries of modern mathematics. . . . Half of the book is an exposition of classical mathematics with its demonstration of the practical effectiveness of abstract thinking. Half is concerned with the new mathematics in which 'twice two is not four,' and by virtue of which we may 'speak of living in a four-dimensional world without being either confused or mystical.' Words and drawings combine to give an enticing demonstration of the fact 'that modern art has infinitely more variety than old-fashioned art, just as mathematics today has infinitely more variety that it used to have.' " Scientific Bk Club R

National Council of Teachers of Mathematics

Enrichment mathematics for high school. The Council 1963 388p illus $4   510

1 Mathematics

"Twenty-eighth yearbook"

Twenty-seven articles, by different authors, on various aspects of mathematics. Divided into two sections: The high school years, and, The transition to college, this book includes selections on number theory, primes, abstract mathematics, lunar eclipse, the geometry of color, linear programming, generating functions, etc. Diagrams, problems, answers, and references are provided. In addition, there are bibliographies of books for school libraries, magazine articles, and books for the teacher of gifted students

"A valuable book for secondary school libraries, for the teacher working with talented students, or for the student who wishes to explore on his own." The AAAS Science Book List for Young Adults

Includes bibliographies

Polya, G.

How to solve it; a new aspect of mathematics. 2d ed. Doubleday 1957 253p pa $1.45   510

1 Mathematics

"Doubleday Anchor book"

First published 1945 by Princeton Univ. Press

The author "shows how to use heuristic reasoning—an incisive, constant, and logical approach to any given problem. . . . Includes a short dictionary that supplies the history, techniques, and terminology of heuristic, and a . . . section of nineteen Problems, Hints, and Solutions." Publisher's note

510.21   Mathematics—Tables and related material

Barlow, Peter

Barlow's Tables of squares, cubes, square roots, cube roots and reciprocals of all integers, up to 12,500; ed. by L. J. Comrie. 4th ed. E. & F. N. Spon [distributed by Barnes & Noble] 258p pa $3.25   510.21

1 Mathematics—Tables, etc.

SBN 412-201100

A standard work first published 1814 in England and frequently reprinted with minor emendations

Handbook of mathematical tables. Chemical Rubber Co. $24.50   510.21

1 Mathematics—Tables, etc.

First published 1962. A supplement to: CRC Handbook of chemistry and physics, entered in class 540.21

Includes tables of logarithms, trigonometric functions, numerical constants, mathematical formulae and equations "plus such specialized topics as spherical harmonics, the binomial and Poisson distributions, and information on elliptic planetary orbits." The AAAS Science Book List for Young Adults

510.3 Mathematics—Dictionaries and encyclopedias

James, Glenn
(ed.) James & James Mathematics dictionary. . . . 3d ed. Van Nostrand 1968 446p illus $13.50   510.3
1 Mathematics—Dictionaries
First published 1942 by Digest Press
"Contributors: Armen A. Alchian, Edwin F. Beckenbach [and others]. Translators: J. George Adashko [and others]." Title page
"A complete, one volume, popularly priced mathematical dictionary, defining and illustrating fully all mathematical terms, and including advance material in physics, chemistry and engineering." Huntting
"A table of contents appears for the first time, a welcome guide to the appendix. As before, the appendix has several numerical tables, a list of symbols and abbreviations, and formulas for differentiation and integration." Choice

The Universal encyclopedia of mathematics; with a foreword by James R. Newman. Simon & Schuster 1964 715p illus $9.95
                                        510.3
1 Mathematics—Dictionaries   2 Mathematics
—Tables, etc.
Adapted from the original German edition published 1960
This alphabetically arranged volume "encompasses many branches of mathematics from arithmetic through the calculus and includes a collection of essential formulae and tables." Foreword
"For use of high school and college students, and as a refresher course for graduates. . . . Arranged for easy reference and cross-indexed." Am News of Bks

510.78 Computation instruments and machines

Adler, Irving
Thinking machines; a layman's introduction to logic, Boolean algebra, and computers; with diagrams by Ruth Adler. Day 1961 189p illus $5.50   510.78
1 Electronic computers
In this introduction to the theory of computers, the author "first explains algebra, the binary scale of numerals, Boolean algebra, and its use in design circuits that 'think.'" Bk Buyer's Guide
Adler's "remarkable ability to explain mathematical ideas to people who don't know any mathematics is once again evident in this introduction into the science of those calculating machines which are presently generating a second industrial revolution." San Francisco Chronicle
Bibliography: p185-86

Asimov, Isaac
An easy introduction to the slide rule; with diagrams by William Barss. Houghton 1965 187p illus $3.50   510.78
1 Slide rule
"The author familiarizes the reader with the basic scales on standard slide rules for addition, subtraction, multiplication, and division and then moves to the more complicated squares, cubes, etc." Bk Buyer's Guide
"Isaac Asimov has brought his lively and detailed writing style to the dull topic. . . . [He treats] the historical theoretical considerations which permit the calculator to operate effectively. . . . For the serious student." Library J

Crowley, Thomas H.
Understanding computers. McGraw 1967 142p illus $4.95   510.78
1 Electronic computers

The book explains "how modern, digital computers operate, what they can and can't do, and how they are affecting our society. . . . The basic functions of memory, control, processing, input, and output are explained, and the devices which are used in a computer to perform these functions are discussed." Publisher's note
"It is possible to describe the organization and operation of a computer in some detail without making use of any background of mathematical or other technical knowledge. And that is just what this book attempts to do. . . . In addition . . . this book is intended to emphasize some fundamental principles, or characteristics, of computers which are not commonly known or at least not properly appreciated." Introduction
Selected general bibliography on computers: p137-39

Cundy, H. Martyn
Mathematical models, by H. Martyn Cundy and A. P. Rollett. 2d ed. Oxford 1961 286p illus $6.50   510.78
1 Mathematical models
First published 1962
"The book gives detailed instructions for making a wide variety of models illustrating elementary mathematics. . . . Dissections, paperfolding, curve-stitching, the drawing of loci and envelopes, the construction of plane tessellations, polyhedra, and ruled surfaces are all included. Complete plans and nets are given for all regular, Archimedean, and stellated polyhedra, together with compound solids of various kinds." Publisher's note
Bibliography: p279-80

Halacy, D. S.
Computers—the machines we think with. Rev. ed. [by] D. S. Halacy, Jr. Harper 1969 279p illus $6.95   510.78
1 Electronic computers 2 Electronic data processing
First published 1962
The author "covers the history of computers—from the discovery of the abacus, through Jacquard and his use of punched cards in weaving, to the latest developments and the enormous potential for the future. He discusses . . . the basic theories and operation of digital and analog computers and shows them at work in business, industry, and education." Publisher's note

Nikolaieff, George A.
(ed.) Computers and society. Wilson, H.W. 1970 226p (The Reference shelf v41, no.6) $4.50   510.78
1 Electronic computers 2 Technology and civilization
SBN 13-165498-5
"The first section of the book notes that we have crossed an invisible line in our technology development, entering a phase characterized by the rapidly expanding use of computers. . . . The second section describes how the computer works. The third deals with the history of events that made computers . . . possible. The fourth section considers the immediate impact that widespread use of the computer has had on our society." Preface
This book "should be in every library and should be so marked that it would attract the attention of all who are interested in the place of computers in the society of today. It will give a very good introduction to many areas and does not require any technical background in any way." Choice
Bibliography: p214-26

510.8 Mathematics—Collections

Newman, James R.
(ed.) The world of mathematics. . . . Simon & Schuster 1956 4v (2535p) illus $30
                                        510.8
1 Mathematics
"A small library of the literature of mathematics from A'h-musé the Scribe to Albert Einstein, presented with commentaries and notes by James R. Newman." Subtitle

Newman, James R.—*Continued*

"I have tried in this book to show the range of mathematics, the richness of its ideas and multiplicity of its aspects. It presents mathematics as a tool, a language and a map; as a work of art and an end in itself; as a fulfillment of the passion for perfection." Introduction

Bibliographical footnotes. Index in v4

510.9 Mathematics—History

Bell, Eric Temple

Mathematics; queen and servant of science. McGraw 1951 xx, 437p illus $7.95
510.9

1 Mathematics—History 2 Mathematics

"This book is a thorough revision and a very considerable amplification of two popular accounts of mathematics, 'The Queen of the Sciences,' 1931 . . . [and] 'The Handmaiden of the Sciences,' 1937." To the reader

Here is the story of the developments in pure and applied mathematics from the geometry of Euclid 2200 years ago to . . . [mid-twentieth century] developments in mathematical physics. Over two hundred mathematicians are represented. The material is so organized that the reader can omit difficult or uninteresting sections

"The author has succeeded very well in relating mathematics to the other sciences. Moreover, he has explained such abstruse mathematical concepts as matrices so that they can be grasped by non-mathematical minds." Library J

512 Algebra. Theory of numbers

Adler, Irving

A new look at arithmetic; with diagrams by Ruth Adler. Day 1964 309p $8.50   512

1 Arithmetic 2 Numbers, Theory of

This book "is built around developing an understanding of the structure of the number system. It introduces the layman to significant concepts at the same time that it strengthens his skill in computation. It presupposes no knowledge of mathematics at all beyond the ability to read numbers, because it reconstructs all of elementary school arithmetic." Publisher's note

"The book is divided into two parts: natural numbers and integers, and rational numbers and real numbers. Includes historical material and advanced topics. Chapter exercises; answers provided." N Y New Tech Bks

Asimov, Isaac

Realm of algebra; diagrams by Robert Belmore. Houghton 1961 230p illus $3.50
512

1 Algebra

The author proceeds "from the most basic concepts of algebra to the more refined considerations of quadratic and cubic equations, simultaneous equations, and those involving imaginary and transcendental numbers." Publisher's note

With its "easily understood explanations, this book will be useful as a supplement to the textbook for beginning algebra students or as a review for those more advanced." Library J

Dantzig, Tobias

Number, the language of science; a critical survey written for the cultured non-mathematician. 4th ed. rev. and augmented. Macmillan (N Y) 1954 340p illus $7.50   512

1 Numbers, Theory of

First published 1930

"In a series of brilliant and arresting chapters the author unfolds the evolution of the concept of numbers. . . . Some of the chapters

deal with history, others with philosophical questions; still others deal with symbol and form and the ideas which are back of them." Cincinnati

"Technicalities are avoided as far as possible, and any reader with a foundation of high school mathematics should be able to follow much, perhaps not all, of it." Wis Lib Bul

Includes indexes of names and subjects

513 Geometry

Abbott, Edwin A.

Flatland; a romance of many dimensions; with illus. by the author, a square; with introduction by William Garnett. 5th ed. rev. Barnes & Noble 1963 108p illus $2.25   513

1 Fourth dimension

First published 1884

"A unique book based on the assumption that but two dimensions exist, length and breadth, consequently the people are all geometric figures." Publisher's note

"Much of it will be read with amusement, as satire, by those who do not appreciate its scientific bearing. . . . The assumption of the author is worked out with wonderful consistency and his mathematics are thoroughly sound." Spectator

519 Probabilities. Game theory

Adler, Irving

Probability and statistics for everyman; how to understand and use the laws of chance; with diagrams by Ruth Adler. Day 1963 256p illus $7.95   519

1 Probabilities 2 Statistics

"The approach to probability theory is through the modern use of point set theory, which is explained . . . in the first part of the book. Probability models with dice, coins, and cards are then explained and several more difficult problems are solved. In the counting and computing chapter, the usual discussion of permutations and combinations is supplemented by the more difficult problems concerning the number of ways in which (r) objects can be put in (m) cells. Such modern concepts in physics as Maxwell-Boltzmann, Bose-Einstein and Fermi-Dirac statistics follow. . . . Sampling theory and the normal and Poisson continuous distributions form his final chapters." Library J

Bibliography: p241

Davis, Morton D.

Game theory; a nontechnical introduction; with a foreword by Oskar Morgenstern. Basic Bks. 1970 208p illus (Science and discovery) $6.95   519

1 Game theory

SBN 465-02626-5

"Introduces inquiring readers of limited mathematical background to various theories that actually comprise the theory of games, their basic concepts, strategies, rules, and applications to assorted practical situations and fields. Games are discussed and illustrated according to size (number of people participating) as a major game characteristic. Emphasis is placed on the fact that unless game theory is rooted in human behavior it is meaningless except as pure mathematics." Booklist

Bibliography: p199-204

Huff, Darrell

How to take a chance; illus. by Irving Geis. Norton 1959 173p illus $4.95   519

1 Probabilities

"Norton Primers for our time"

"Chapters on how to control chance, the strategy of winning, how to look at a statistic, and the mystery of extra-sensory perception are included." Management R

Huff, Darrell—*Continued*

"Although written in a most amusing fashion, the book is soundly based on mathematics, and can give some surprising information to people who think that 'taking a chance' is just a matter of luck. . . . The clever drawings by Mr. Geis, including sketches, diagrams and charts, perfectly complement the entertaining text." Springf'd Republican

520   Astronomy

Scientific American

Frontiers in astronomy; readings from Scientific American; with introductions by Owen Gingerich. Freeman 1970 370p illus maps $11   **520**

1 Astronomy
ISBN 0-7167-0948-1

"This collection of articles from the Scientific American documents . . . recent developments in astronomy. Half the articles appeared since 1964; some describe developments so new that they are scarcely mentioned in textbooks." Preface

Contents: The earth and moon; The planetary system; The sun; Stellar evolution; The Milky Way; Galaxies; The new astronomy; Cosmology; Biographical notes and bibliographies

520.3   Astronomy—Encyclopedias

Rudaux, Lucien

Larousse Encyclopedia of astronomy, by Lucien Rudaux and G. De Vaucouleurs. 2d ed. With an introduction by F. L. Whipple. Prometheus Press [distributed by Putnam] 1962 506p illus $17.50   **520.3**

1 Astronomy

First English language edition published 1959
Title on spine: Astronomy

"Basics of astronomy, very thoroughly explained for the intelligent layman. After an introductory chapter, the authors describe the solar systems, the stars, the galaxy and theories about the universe, and astronomical instruments and techniques. Translated by Michael Guest and John B. Sidgwick and revised by Z. Kopal from the [1948] 'Larousse Astromie.'" Pub W

522   Practical and spherical astronomy. Telescopes

Howard, Neale E.

The telescope handbook and star atlas. Crowell 1967 226p illus $12   **522**

1 Telescope 2 Stars—Atlases 3 Astronomy

"Coverage includes topics on the sky and co-ordinates, the solar system, double stars, variables, galaxies, comets, aurorae, and photography. Accurate and up to date, this is a complete summary for the beginning student and amateur astronomer. An atlas of the whole sky, tables, bibliography, index and glossary are included." The AAAS Science Book List

Woodbury, David O.

The glass giant of Palomar; illus. with drawings by the author, sketches by Russell W. Porter, and photographs. [Rev. ed.] Dodd 1970 390p illus $7.50   **522**

1 Telescope 2 Palomar Observatory, Calif. 3 Hale, George Ellery
ISBN 0-396-01919-6

First published 1939

The story of the planning and building of the giant 200-inch telescope of Palomar Mountain, California. 'Not only is this book a record of [Dr George Ellery Hale's] devotion to

a great ideal but . . . it recounts the erection of the Yerkes and Mt Wilson Observatories and gives appreciative glimpses of the men who fought so valiantly for their completion. Continuing, it starts its major theme—the events which led to the final triumph on the top of an isolated mountain in California." Springf'd Republican

523   Descriptive astronomy

Alter, Dinsmore

Pictorial astronomy [by] Dinsmore Alter, Clarence H. Cleminshaw, and John G. Phillips. 3d rev. ed. Crowell 1969 328p illus maps $10   **523**

1 Astronomy

First published 1948 as a collection of articles culled from the magazine, Griffith Observatory

The "sixty chapters are divided into sections on the sun, the earth, the moon, eclipses, the planets, comets and meteors, and stars and the nebulae. Of particular interest . . . will be the convenient reference charts scattered throughout the text that give, in compact form, basic data on the sun, the stars, the planets, and other areas of knowledge in astronomy." Publisher's note

"The articles are not only well written, but they bring a wealth of interest in astronomy to the lay reader. Particularly good are the sections dealing with phenomena in the sky. There is much interesting historical material as well. Although not truly modern, the book is authoritative, interesting and informative." Science Bks

Glossary: p313-20

Calder, Nigel

Violent universe; an eyewitness account of the new astronomy. Viking [1970 c1969] 160p illus $8.95   **523**

1 Astronomy
SBN 670-74720-3

First published 1969 in England

The author traces in "detail the newest discoveries and speculations about the stellar universe . . . pulsars, quasars, the mysteries of microwave background radiation, the sometimes 'rude' debates among astronomers themselves as they argue the Big Bang theory of an 'exploding universe' versus the 'steady state' theory." Pub W

"There is a little historical background, plus a lot of excellent photographs and illustrations. The author has reduced a very complex subject to an understandable, readable and highly interesting survey." Library J

Hodge, Paul W.

The revolution in astronomy. Holiday 1970 189p illus $4.95   **523**

1 Astronomy

"This is an account of recent discoveries, techniques, and fields of research in astronomy. Seventeen brief chapters describe the development of radio astronomy, quasars, exploding galaxies, the cosmic background radiation, pulsars, radio radiation from Jupiter, radar astronomy, the discovery of infrared stars, rocket and satellite observations of ultraviolet radiation, X-rays and gamma rays, observations of neutrinos and cosmic rays, orbiting solar and astronomical observatories, and space exploration of the moon and planets. The book is easy to read and up-to-date." Science Bks

Suggested reading: p176-80. Glossary: p181-85

Menzel, Donald H.

A field guide to the stars and planets; including the moon, satellites, comets, and other features of the universe. With photographs and with sky maps and other illus. by Ching Sung Yü. Houghton 1964 397p illus $5.95   **523**

1 Astronomy

"The Peterson Field guide series"

"Here is every amateur astronomer's guide. . . . The stress is on the stars: there are

Menzel, Donald H.—*Continued*

monthly sky maps for both Northern and Southern hemispheres. Each of the sky maps appears twice, once as seen in the telescope and again with the name of the stars superimposed on the map. This same method is used for photographic atlas charts (54 in number) to identify the fainter stars, and 12 moon maps (for some reason not including the Russian chart of the other side of the moon) which show every surface marking of the moon. . . . Radio astronomy is not included." Library J

"A glossary of terms, a selective bibliography, and an index which gives page references to constellations under both their Latin and English-equivalent names are helpful features. Added chapters on time, how to use a telescope, and photography in astronomy accompany this handy aid." Cur Ref Bks

Moore, Patrick

Amateur astronomy. Norton 1968 328p illus (The Amateur astronomer's lib) $6.95
523

1 Astronomy

A rewriting of the version first published 1957 with title: The amateur astronomer

"Organized for ease of reading and reference, it discusses the equipment of the amateur, provides a course in the nature of the skies, the solar system, the stars, and the universe. It contains maps, charts, and tables needed by the observer, together with a large number of diagrams and photographic illustrations." Publisher's note

Bibliography: p314-18

The atlas of the universe; foreword by Bernard Lovell; epilogue by Thomas O. Paine. Rand McNally 1970 272p illus $35
523

1 Astronomy

This publication contains "sections on all the physical bodies of the universe, ranging from interstellar matter to giant stellar systems. Historical background material is also . . . supplied." Library J

"The sectional arrangement and choice of topics are sensible and helpful. The order is from the known to the unknown, outward from the earth, and before tackling any of the scientific results we have a look at the tools (many types of telescopes and accessories) and the behavior of light. . . . The Atlas is as up-to-date as it could be, just missing the new International Astronomical Union list of named far-side lunar features but including descriptions of quasars, pulsars, and a number of strange galaxies. . . . The language is simple and well chosen, and the Atlas is a joy to look at." Science

Suns, myths and men. Norton [1969 c1968] 236p illus (The Amateur astronomer's lib) $7.95
523

1 Astronomy

Originally published 1954 in England. First American edition published 1955 with title: The story of man and the stars

The author "explores the mysticism and superstition of primitive men everywhere concerning phenomena such as the sun, moon, stars, eclipses, etc. . . . [Includes a] section on modern observatories, astronauts, the newest discoveries about the galaxies, current theories of the universe, and a . . . look at the future." Pub W

523.09 Astronomy—History

Ley, Willy

Watchers of the skies; an informal history of astronomy from Babylon to the space age. Viking 1963 528p illus maps $8.50
523.09

1 Astronomy—History 2 Astronomers

Also available in paperback (A Viking Compass book) with a new foreword, published 1969

Includes an "historical section on discoveries in astronomy up to the late 18th century, a section, the largest, on the solar system, planet by planet, and a section of special problems about our own and other galaxies. Especially interesting: the intriguing speculations about Mars, the record of meteoritic traces on earth, the question of whether other civilizations exist in the stars. Clear and well written, so that the interested layman can follow it with absorption." Pub W

Appendixes include scientific tables, a chronological list of great astronomers from Pythagoras to recent times, a brief note on radio astronomy, and an annotated bibliography

523.1 Physical universe

Bergamini, David

The universe, by David Bergamini and the editors of Time-Life Books. Time-Life Bks. [1971 c1962] 192p illus (Life Nature lib) lib. bdg. $7.60
523.1

1 Universe 2 Astronomy

First published 1962

Contents: Myths and misconceptions; Probing the universe; Planets, meteorites and comets; Biography of the sun; What our galaxy is made of; The birth and death of stars; Beyond the Milky Way: Space time and the universe; Glossary and tables; Bibliography

This "is a beautiful book. Its illustrations are lavish, well chosen, and largely well reproduced." Natur Hist

"The writing style is solid and scholarly, so that the book will be most useful to the reader with a special interest or with previous knowledge in the subject." Chicago. Children's Book Center

Bondi, Hermann

The universe at large. Anchor Bks. 1960 154p illus (Science study ser) pa $1.45 **523.1**

1 Universe

Partial contents: The expansion of the universe; Why is it dark at night; Theories of cosmology; Between the stars; The earth's radiation belts; The motion of celestial bodies; The earth: motion and magnetism

A "speculation on the findings of modern astronomy which examines the theories of Einstein, Eddington, Hoyle, Hubble, Lemaitre and others." Publisher's note

Gamow, George

The creation of the universe. Rev. ed. Viking 1961 147p illus $5.75
523.1

1 Universe

First published 1952

The author "examines the origins of galaxies, stars and planets in the light of known nuclear reactions—is concerned with the fundamental question of whether the universe had a beginning in time and whether it has an end in space." Am News of Bks

"Dr. Gamow's book is stimulating. It is clearly written and undertakes faithfully to say what is factual and what is speculative. It commends itself especially to the scientist and the general reader who has some preparation in physics. . . . Critical readers will perhaps not agree with all the conclusions." Sat R

Jastrow, Robert

Red giants and white dwarfs; man's descent from the stars. Rev. ed. Harper 1971 190p illus boards $6.95
523.1

1 Universe 2 Life—Origin 3 Evolution

First published 1967 with subtitle: The evolution of stars, planets and life

This book describes "the birth and death of stars and planets and the emergence of intelligent life [on earth]. The prospects for life on other planets and the chances for contact with intelligent beings in other solar systems are discussed. The author's observations of Rutherford, Darwin, Urey, and other pioneer scientists add a compelling human element to the story." Publisher's note

Jastrow, Robert—*Continued*
"Probably the most successful account yet
published for the layman of the continuous
thread of events that led from the beginnings
of the universe to the appearance of man on
this planet." Natur Hist

Sullivan, Walter
We are not alone; the search for intelligent life on other worlds. Rev. ed. McGraw
1966 325p illus boards $8.95   **523.1**
1 Life on other planets
First published 1964
Scientific speculation "about new astronomical
and biochemical tools and new thinking about
the origins of life. Among the questions it discusses: will other civilizations be more ·ad-
vanced than ours? (yes); is there life on Mars
(impediments are formidable but it's possible);
is interstellar travel feasible (is this trip
necessary if radio communication can be
achieved?)." Pub W
References: p292-311

523.2 Solar system

Edson, Lee
Worlds around the sun; consultant: Carl
Sagan; published by Am. Heritage in association with the Smithsonian Inst. [dis-
tributed by Van Nostrand-Reinhold] 1969
159p illus boards $4.95   **523.2**
1 Solar system
SBN 8281-0001-2
"The Smithsonian library"
This book "describes the results of the recent
upsurge in planetary astronomy as a result of
modern space exploration and research. Emphasis is on the work of the Smithsonian As-
trophysical Observatory. Discusses some of the
major problems and how they have been
solved or the current theories concerning
them. There is a brief introductory history of
the solar system and an appendix on telescopes." Choice

523.4 Planets

Moore, Patrick
The planets. Norton 1962 189p illus maps
$5.95   **523.4**
1 Planets
Supersedes the author's: A guide to the
planets, first published 1954
"How the planets came into being, with a
description of each planet, its satellites, the
possibility of space travel, and the problems of
the amateur astronomer." Bk Buyer's Guide
Planetary literature: p178-79

Nourse, Alan E.
Nine planets; paintings by Mel Hunter.
Rev. ed. Harper 1970 322p illus $8.95   **523.4**
1 Planets 2 Solar system
First published 1960
"We will attempt to develop step by step a
complete, realistic and stimulating picture of
the physical nature of our solar system: the
nine known planets, their satellites and their
Sun. With established facts and convincing
probabilities as a background, we will specu-
late about the things we may reasonably expect to find in the course of the forthcoming
exploration of that solar system." Introduction
"It is by no means comprehensive but is
quite complete for the readers it will attract.
Although it is not intended for light reading it
could serve more as an introduction to the
subject rather than a foundation for the serious student. It includes an appendix of comparative statistics of the planets, a glossary
and 12 full-page paintings of an artist's idea of
the surface of various planets." Science Bks

523.8 Stars. Quasars

Bova, Ben
In quest of quasars; an introduction to
stars and starlike objects. Crowell-Collier
Press [1970 c1969] 198p illus $5.95   **523.8**
1 Quasars 2 Stars 3 Universe
"Modern astronomy for the general reader is
presented in this excellent book. Only the first
and last two chapters deal with quasars. The
main body of the book is devoted to the physical constitution, energy production and evolution of the sun and other stars, galaxies of all
types, and various views in cosmology and
their basis. It is against this background that
the newly discovered quasars are discussed.
The book is well illustrated and includes an excellent collection of astronomical photographs."
Science Bks
For further reading: p190-92

525 Earth (Astronomical geography) Tides

Clancy, Edward P.
The tides; pulse of the earth; illus. by
Warren H. Maxfield. Doubleday 1968 228p
illus (The Science study ser) $5.95   **525**
1 Tides
The author describes "what makes the tides,
how we see them here and there in the world,
how they complicate the life of the sailor, how
men are harnessing them to generate power,
and how they affect the future of the earth
and of the moon." Prologue
"The book does a fine interdisciplinary service of placing tidal information within a
broad background of physics and astronomy."
Science Bks
Suggestions for additional reading: p222-23

526.8 Map projections

Brown, Lloyd A.
Map making; the art that became a science. Little 1960 217p illus maps $4.95 **526.8**
1 Map drawing 2 Maps
A "survey of the development of cartography from earliest times to the beginning of the
twentieth century. The discussion takes into
account discovery and geography, measuring
instruments (including the compass), clocks,
navigation by the stars and related topics. Authenticated with reproductions of old prints."
The AAAS Science Book List for Young Adults

529 Chronology

Asimov, Isaac
The clock we live on. Rev. ed. Illus. with
diagrams by John Bradford. Abelard-Schuman 1965 172p illus map $4   **529**
1 Time 2 Calendars 3 Clocks and watches
First published 1959
The author presents the "story of time, describing the complications that can arise from
such simple things as the earth's rotation on its
axis. He explains why the moon was the basis
for the first year, why the lunar year doesn't
match the seasons. . . . The numbering of
years, naming of days of the week, vagaries of
Easter, and calendar reform are [covered]."
Publisher's note
"Historical development of timepieces
is more briefly discussed than is the evolution
of the present-day calendar [and the motions
of the earth]." Chicago. Children's Book Center

530.1 Physics—Theories

Barnett, Lincoln
The universe and Dr Einstein; with a foreword by Albert Einstein. [2d rev. ed] Sloane 1957 127p illus $6   530.1
1 Relativity (Physics) 2 Einstein, Albert
First published 1948
"Mr. Barnett discusses the earlier theories, discoveries and experiments of such men as Max Planck, A. A. Michelson and E. W. Morley, that formed a starting point for Dr. Einstein's work. In terms comprehensible to the layman, he elucidates the General Theory of Relativity. . . . From Einstein's famous equation, E=mc², (which led to the atomic bomb) to the fourth dimension and beyond, all is explained." Publisher's note
"Brilliant, relatively easy-to-grasp exposition of the quantum theory and relativity." Good Reading
Reading list: p117-19

Bondi, Hermann
Relativity and common sense; a new approach to Einstein. Anchor Bks. 1964 177p illus (Science study ser) pa $1.25   530.1
1 Relativity (Physics)
"Einstein's theory of relativity, since it accounts for matter and energy at high velocities, is more relevant than ever in these days of nuclear reactions, space flight, and cosmological speculation. Professor Bondi, the British mathematician, presents a lucid and fascinating study showing how the relativity theory can be largely derived from classical Newtonian physics." Publisher's note

Einstein, Albert
The meaning of relativity. 5th ed. including the Relativistic theory of the non-symmetric field. Princeton Univ. Press 1956 166p $6   530.1
1 Relativity (Physics)
The Stafford Little lectures of Princeton University, May 1921
First published 1922. Translated by Edwin Plimpton Adams, Ernst G. Straus and Bruria Kaufman
"Though few can understand it, most readers in physics and librarians in charge of science collections know this book as one of the land marks of modern knowledge. . . . The book is not intended for general reading. Instead it is addressed to . . . [those whose training enables] them to understand the mathematical expressions of relativity." N Y New Tech Bks

Gamow, George
Thirty years that shook physics; the story of quantum theory; illus. by the author. Doubleday 1966 224p illus $5.95   530.1
1 Quantum theory
"Reviewing the evolution of the still-incomplete quantum theory of energy and matter from its inception in 1900 to the peak of its theoretical development in the 1930's, Gamow relates the quantum theory to relativity and indicates differences between classical and modern physics. . . . [Covers] evaluations of eight physicists whose work he considers preeminent in quantum research and most of whom he has known personally, including Max Planck, Niels Bohr, and Enrico Fermi. Diagrammatic sketches and drawings furnish appropriate illustrations." Booklist
Contains "the script of a play that was written and performed by several pupils of Bohr. . . . The theme of this dramatic masterpiece has Pauli '(Mephistopheles)' trying to sell to the unbelieving Ehrenfest '(Faust)' the idea of the weightless neutrino '(Gretchen).'" Prefatory remarks
Notes on the text: p215-18

Gardner, Martin
Relativity for the million; illus. by Anthony Ravielli. Macmillan (N Y) 1962 182p illus $6.95   530.1
1 Relativity (Physics)
The author examines "contemporary developments in the field of relativity . . . as well as illuminating the history, concepts and practical conclusions of Einstein's theory." Publisher's note
"Without mathematics or complicated technical arguments [the author] manages to convey the significance and basic meaning of Einstein's relativity." Christian Science Monitor
Glossary: p169-73. Suggestions for further reading: p175-79

Lieber, Lillian R.
The Einstein theory of relativity; drawings by Hugh Gray Lieber. Rinehart 1945 324p illus $3.95   530.1
1 Relativity (Physics) 2 Einstein, Albert 3 Mathematics
Part I of this book was first published in 1936
"The authors combine a remarkably lucid text with skilful diagrams and 'funny' drawings that help greatly to illuminate the subject. . . . The book is in two parts. The first deals with the special theory by means of which Einstein extended the principle of relativity, long applied to mechanical motion, [to] the electromagnetic phenomena, and thus laid the foundation for the concept of a four-dimensional space-time continuum. . . . The second and larger part of the book deals with Einstein's general theory." Sci Bk Club R
Some interesting reading: p324

530.4 States of matter

Lapp, Ralph E.
Matter, by Ralph E. Lapp and the editors of Time-Life Books. Time-Life Bks. 1969 200p illus (Life Science lib) lib. bdg. $7.60   530.4
1 Matter
"A Stonehenge book"
First published 1963
Contents: An endless searching for substance; The basic ingredients of a complex world; The wayward, willful ways of gas; The restless surge of the liquid state; A deceptive facade of solidity; Mapping the terrain of the atom; The nucleus: enigmatic heart of matter; The start of an unfinished chain reaction; Bibliography
"Up-to-date material colorfully illustrated for high school students studying physics. . . . Excellent periodic tables." Library J

530.9 Physics—History

Gamow, George
Biography of physics. Harper 1961 338p illus (Harper Modern science ser) $6.50   530.9
1 Physics—History 2 Physicists
"A survey of physics from the days of the 'ancient Greeks' (Pythagoras, Democritus and Archimedes) to the relativistic revolution, the law of quantum, and the modern concepts of the atomic nucleus and elementary particles (more than half of the book is devoted to the latter.) Each of the eight chapters centers its discussion around one or two scientists of the period, with other physicists and their contributions forming the background of the development and progress of the science. The author combines successfully the historical, biographical . . . factual and theoretical aspects of physics in a continuous and highly readable narrative." School Science & Math
Sources: p330

Nourse, Alan E.

Universe, earth, and atom; the story of physics. Harper 1969 688p illus $10   530.9

1 Physics—History

In this history of physics from the earliest times to the present, the author describes the nature of physics, its tools and the development of the 'scientific method,' classical physics and the Einstein revolution. In addition to discussing concepts such as motion, friction and inertia, gravity, energy, time, and relativity, he analyzes the practical applications of physics, in lasers, transistors, and solar batteries. (Publisher)

"A comprehensive survey in which physics is made intelligible . . . by concentration on principles and the general direction in which physical knowledge has progressed and by the omission of mathematical formulas and technical details." Booklist

531 Mechanics

Gamow, George

Gravity; illus. by the author. Anchor Bks. 1962 157p illus (Science study ser) pa $1.25
531

1 Gravitation

The author studies the nature of gravity, explaining how the work of Galileo, Newton and Einstein helped in understanding it, introduces the principles of calculus, and discusses some theories about the relation of gravity to physical phenomena like electromagnetic fields. (Publisher)

An account written with Gamow's "characteristic popular and whimsical style. . . . He concludes with a discussion of 'unsolved' problems of gravity." The AAAS Science Book List for Young Adults

Wilson, Mitchell

Energy, by Mitchell Wilson and the editors of Time-Life Books. Time-Life Bks. [1968 c1967] 200p illus (Life Science lib) lib. bdg. $7.60   531

1 Force and energy

First published 1963

The authors explain that energy can appear as energy of motion, in the form of heat, or "on an atomic or molecular scale as chemical energy. It can appear in the flow of electrical current. On a nuclear scale it can appear in one of the most fearsome forms." Introduction

"The last part of the book describes some of our newer energy sources and predicts what may be in store for the future. Many exquisite color photographs and drawings." The AAAS Science Book List for Young Adults

Bibliography: p196

534 Sound and related vibrations

Kock, Winston E.

Sound waves and light waves. Anchor Bks. 1965 165p illus (Science study ser) pa $1.25   534

1 Sound waves 2 Light 3 Wave mechanics

"The similarities between sound and light or radio waves are used to explain the behavior of each type. It begins with definitions and descriptions, then proceeds to such topics as diffraction, wave and group velocities, microwave lenses, wave guides, delay lines, etc. The presentation is non-mathematical. A full appreciation will be obtained only if the reader had considerable knowledge of the subject. This book will be valuable to one who wishes only a glimpse of the physical phenomena involved or a general impression of the technology that has been developed." Science Bks

The book also covers "applications of knowledge of wave properties. Well illustrated with drawings and photographs." Booklist

Further reading: p153

Stevens, S. S.

Sound and hearing, by S. S. Stevens, Fred Warshofsky and the editors of Time-Life Books. Time-Life Bks. [1971 c1965] 200p illus (Life Science lib) lib. bdg. $7.60   534

1 Sound 2 Hearing

"A Stonehenge book"

First published 1965

"The world of sounds and the sense of hearing are the subjects of this book. It analyzes the physical nature of sound, describes the way ear and brain translate vibrations into music, information or noise, and shows how man's understanding of sound and hearing have enabled him to put them to use for both practical and esthetic purposes." About this book

The interrelated subjects "are presented in this well-planned, admirably executed book. Complex material is discussed with restrained use of mathematical or technical processing. . . . Each chapter and picture essay discusses historical, physical, and experimental data which often are not readily accessible." Science Bks

Further reading: p196

Van Bergeijk, Willem A.

Waves and the ear [by] Willem A. Van Bergeijk, John R. Pierce and Edward E. David, Jr. Anchor Bks. 1960 235p illus (Science study ser) pa $1.45   534

1 Sound waves 2 Hearing

A discussion of "the physical nature of sound waves and the physiology of the ear itself. . . . [Here are blended] together the latest findings of acoustics, anatomy, electronics, psychology, hydro-mechanics, zoology, phonetics, and hi-fi engineering." Publisher's note

A "concise . . . book, sponsored by the Physical Science Study Committee." The AAAS Science Book List for Young Adults

Suggested reading: p222-25

535 Visible light and paraphotic phenomena

Froman, Robert

Science, art, and visual illusions; drawings by Laszlo Kubinyi. Simon & Schuster 1970 127p illus $4.50, lib. bdg. $4.29   535

1 Optical illusions 2 Art—Psychology

SBN 671-65085-8

"Painters have been creating the illusion of depth in their paintings for centuries; recently they have been experimenting with other visual illusions, as in the field of Op Art. Scientists studying how people perceive the world around them have made useful and fascinating insights from experiments with visual illusions." Hunting

"While there are many books that deal with visual illusions, this is the first attempt at a complete multidisciplinary analysis." Science Bks

Bibliography: p121-23

Mueller, Conrad G.

Light and vision, by Conrad G. Mueller, Mae Rudolph and the editors of Life. Time, inc. 1966 200p illus (Life Science lib) lib. bdg. $7.60   535

1 Light 2 Vision

"A Stonehenge book"

"Lucidly written and delightfully illustrated the book reviews historical and fundamental background material in light, visual physiology and the psychology of perception. Though not medically oriented, it embraces necessary facets of ophthalmic anatomy with precision and understandable simplification. . . . Light and vision are explored as the link between the

Mueller, Conrad G.—*Continued*
animal world and its environment. The extraordinary diagrams and photographs portray the subject vividly. The development of visual organs and their relations to photographic or camera functions is clearly depicted. The contradictory concepts in color perception are well recounted both in text and illustration. Major emphasis is directed to the brain and psychological aspects of vision. . . . The volume is recommended for its broad and attractive introductory usefulness." Science Bks
Bibliography: p196

535.5 Beams and their modification. Holography

Klein, H. Arthur
Holography; with an introduction to the optics of diffraction, interference, and phase differences. Lippincott 1970 192p illus (Introducing modern science) lib. bdg. $4.95
535.5
1 Optics
"This is a sound explanation of holography and the hologram (a 'curious kind of "frozen" photograph' which reveals 'the inmost secrets of vibrations, fluctuations, combustions, explosions,' etc. that are 'too rapid, energetic, or violent to be analyzed otherwise'). Historical development is given along with a presentation of basic technical material; also included are the many varied applications of holography in research and industry." Library J

Kock, Winston E.
Lasers and holography; an introduction to coherent optics. Doubleday 1969 103p illus (Science study ser) pa $1.45
535.5
1 Lasers 2 Optics
An "explanation of light amplification by the stimulated emission of radiation (laser) and use of this light in making a three-dimensional image." Booklist
This "is an excellent summary of the history, development, and anatomy of the revolutionary techniques of image recording and retrieval called holography. The author has skillfully described the various methods, techniques and components of the holograph, using language which can readily be understood by high school and junior high school students. The clear diagrams and well-described plates contribute to the ease of understanding an otherwise esoteric subject." Science Bks

535.6 Color

Hellman, Hal
The art and science of color; illus. by Mark Binn. McGraw 1967 175p illus $5.95, lib. bdg. $5.72
535.6
1 Color
"Clearly a most excellent book . . . full of facts about the phenomenon of color not readily available. The author obviously took great care in his work and for the most part achieved a rare level of craftsmanship in his explanations. Besides establishing the basics of physical principles of light and the relationship of wavelength to color, he has accurately described that less understood area of the physiological and subjective appearance of color to the eye and mind where many paradoxes abound. The four pages of color plates whet the appetite. It's regrettable that for this subject, particularly, more color figures were not used. The line drawings are abundant, relevant, and support the text well, however." Appraisal
Suggestions for further reading: p167-69

538 Magnetism

Bitter, Francis
Magnets: the education of a physicist. Anchor Bks. 1959 155p illus (Science study ser) pa $1.45
538
1 Magnetism
The autobiography of a physicist "whose productive career has included extensive explorations of theoretical and applied problems of magnetism, and . . . magnetic aspects of the nuclei of atoms." The AAAS Science Book List for Young Adults
The book includes "a comprehensive résumé of our knowledge of magnetism. Highly recommended for subject reading as well as for vocational reading for young people interested in the sciences." Library J

539 Modern physics

Adler, Irving
The elementary mathematics of the atom; with diagrams by Ruth Adler. Day 1965 147p illus $4.95
539
1 Atoms 2 Mathematics
For the student with one year of high school algebra, the author "develops the molecular theory of matter and the periodic table of the elements, their utilizing principles of motion, electricity, and light, develops the Bohr model of the atom, and then goes on to describe the quantum mechanical model of the atom together with . . . [other] discoveries of atomic physics." Library J
"The book should be most appealing to mathematics students and others interested in the applications of math to science." Best Sellers

539.7 Nuclear physics

Asimov, Isaac
The neutrino; ghost particle of the atom. Doubleday 1966 223p illus $5.50
539.7
1 Nuclear physics
"The neutrino was invented by scientists in 1931 to explain the composition of an atom, but further research proved that this 'little neutral one' really exists, that it has no mass, no electric charge, moves as fast as light, and can penetrate lead walls with ease." Bk Buyer's Guide
"The subject is introduced with excellent background. . . . It is a lucid and intriguing presentation for anyone with a rudimentary physics background." Science Bks
Included is an explanation of exponential numbers

Glasstone, Samuel
Sourcebook on atomic energy. 3d ed. Van Nostrand 1967 883p illus $13.95
539.7
1 Atomic energy 2 Nuclear physics
First published 1950
Beginning with the earliest theories of the atom and its structure, the text "describes the growth of thought and knowledge in the field, the development of the theories of the phenomenon of radioactivity, and so through the study of isotopes to the construction and operation of cyclotrons, synchrotrons, and nuclear reactors for research and for power. New discoveries in research and development—the identification of hitherto unknown fundamental particles, the production of new elements, advances in the use of isotopes, and vastly improved experimental techniques and equipment—are . . . presented." Publisher's note
"A standard reference book on atomic and nuclear science which was originally prepared under the sponsorship of the U. S. Atomic Energy Commission." The AAAS Science Book List for Young Adults

Romer, Alfred
The restless atom. Anchor Bks. 1960 198p
illus (Science study ser) pa $1.25　　539.7
1 Nuclear physics 2 Atoms 3 Radiation
This book about nuclear physics "traces
briefly the development of knowledge about
X-rays, radium and the atom." Booklist
"A stimulating nonmathematical account of
the development of man's knowledge of atomic
particles from 1890 to 1916." The AAAS Science
Book List for Young Adults
Suggested readings: p192

540.21　Chemistry—Tables, etc.

CRC Handbook of chemistry and physics;
a ready-reference book of chemical and
physical data. Chemical Rubber Co. $24.95
540.21
1 Chemistry—Tables, etc. 2 Physics—Tables,
etc.
First published 1913. Periodically revised
Supplemented by: Handbook of mathematical
tables, entered in class 510.21
"A useful handbook usually revised annually
giving the constants and formulae used in
chemistry and physics, including mathematical
and conversion tables." Winchell. Guide to
Reference Books
"This work is as basic to secondary school,
public, technical, and academic library collections as an unabridged dictionary." Science
Bks
Includes bibliographical references

540.3　Chemistry—Dictionaries

The Condensed chemical dictionary. Reinhold $27.50　　540.3
1 Chemistry—Dictionaries
First published 1919 and frequently revised
to bring it up to date
"A reference volume for all requiring quick
access to essential data regarding chemical and
other substances used in manufacturing and
research, and to terms in general use in chemistry and the process industries." Subtitle of
5th edition
"An excellent source of information about
official pharmaceuticals and drugs, and trademarks and generic names which are not yet official." N Y New Tech Bks

Hackh's Chemical dictionary, American and
British usage. . . . 4th ed. completely rev.
and ed. by Julius Grant. McGraw 1969
738p illus $29.50　　540.3
1 Chemistry—Dictionaries
First published 1929 by Blakiston under the
authorship of Ingo Waldemar Dagobert Hackh
"Containing the words generally used in
chemistry, and many of the terms used in the
related sciences of physics, astrophysics, mineralogy, pharmacy, agriculture, biology, medicine, engineering, etc., based on recent chemical literature." Title page
"The book is attractive, possesses a good
format, is strongly bound, and has small but
clear print. There are defined the familiar, unfamiliar, new, old, short, long, easy, and hard
words. Many of the words have encyclopedic-
type definitions. Treatment is balanced with
due respect to the British and American usage.
. . . The meanings of listed words, are summarized and extended by numerous tables such
as: a historical table of elements, energy conversion factors, insecticides, common indicators and their properties, properties of liquid
fuels, fungicides, primary constants, colloidal
systems, amino acids, and more." Science Bks

International encyclopedia of chemical science. Van Nostrand 1964 1331p illus
$32.95　　540.3
1 Chemistry—Dictionaries

Title on dust jacket: Van Nostrand's International encyclopedia of chemical science
This book "is intended to integrate recent
developments in theory with the practical reference information needed in plant and laboratory, in research and design, in schools and
universities. . . . In content it ranges from sim-
ply-described tests, e.g. bromine test, to highly complicated (at least for the non-chemist)
articles on nucleic acids. The long section on
organic chemistry nomenclature is reprinted
from the 1960 volume of 'Journal of the American Society.' Studded with formulas, adequately cross-referenced, and supplied with multilingual indexes in German, Spanish, French
and Russian, the book is a ready . . . source
of both theory and practice in chemistry."
Cur Ref Bks

540.72　Chemistry—Experiments

Coulson, E. H.
Test tubes and beakers; chemistry for
young experimenters [by] E. H. Coulson,
A. E. J. Trinder, and Aaron E. Klein.
Doubleday 1971 134p illus $4.95, lib.
bdg. $5.70　　540.72
1 Chemistry—Experiments
First published 1963 in England with title:
Experiments for young chemists
Partial contents: Setting up your chemistry
set; The Bunsen burner and glass working; A
study of gases and related substances; Acids,
alkalis, and salts; Electricity and chemistry;
Experiments with carbon compounds; Chemicals required for the experiments listed in this
book; Sources of equipment and chemicals

540.8　Chemistry—Addresses, essays, lectures

Faraday, Michael
Chemical history of a candle; illus. by
Jeanyee Wong; foreword by E. N. daC.
Andrade; biographical introduction by Sir
J. Arthur Thomson. Crowell 1957 158p illus
$3.50　　540.8
1 Chemistry—Addresses and essays 2 Candles
First published 1861 with title: A course of
six lectures on the chemical behavior of a candle
The author "talks about a candle, how it is
made and what happens as a result of its combustions. The result is that, as he says, 'there
is not a law under which any part of this universe is governed which does not come into
play.' A fine book for the curious, for the science shelf as supplementary reading, for those
who have had a little introductory chemistry."
N Y Her Trib Books

541　Physical and theoretical chemistry

Pauling, Linus
The architecture of molecules [by] Linus
Pauling and Roger Hayward. Freeman 1964
unp illus $10　　541
1 Molecules
"Shows how atoms are arranged and inter-
connected in molecules and crystals; emphasizes the significance of molecular structure to
life." Reference Materials for School Libraries
"An eminent chemist and gifted architect
have collaborated in a fascinating volume, designed to provide insight in the inherent beauty
of molecular architecture." Science Bks

546 Inorganic chemistry

Asimov, Isaac
Building blocks of the universe. Rev. ed.
Abelard-Schuman 1961 280p illus $4.50   **546**
  1 Chemical elements
  First published 1957
  The author discusses all of the known chemical elements, some separately and some in groups. He tells of their discovery, naming, uses, and why some are dangerous. (Publisher)
  "Included are many familiar, as well as a host of unfamiliar elements including gladolinium, yttrium, einsteinium. . . . Readable and informative, with many interesting asides— and not too senior." Ontario Lib Rev

547 Organic chemistry

Asimov, Isaac
Photosynthesis. Basic Bks. [1969 c1968] 193p illus (Science & discovery) $5.95   **547**
  1 Photosynthesis 2 Chemistry, Organic
  The author "provides a look through the chemist's eyes at the process upon which life in all its forms is utterly dependent. . . . [He] explains the vital process of photosynthesis and traces the efforts of scientists to understand its role in the fundamental chemistry of life." Publisher's note
  "Once again, Asimov has written a technical but readily understandable book on a complex subject. . . . This book is recommended to all persons with an interest in the natural sciences, even though certain technical portions of the book will be difficult for the young reader." Science Bks

548 Crystallography

Wohlrabe, Raymond A.
Crystals. Helen Hale, editorial consultant. Lippincott 1962 128p illus $3.50   **548**
  1 Crystallography
  An "introduction to the science which deals with crystals, explaining how crystals are formed, how they function, and what man has done and hopes to do with them once he has learned more about these complex structures. With methods for growing crystals and suggestions on acquiring a collection." Bk Buyer's Guide
  "The book does not require background knowledge . . . but it will make the text more easily comprehensible." Chicago. Children's Book Center

549 Mineralogy

Dana's Manual of mineralogy. Wiley illus $14.95   **549**
  1 Mineralogy
  First published 1848 and frequently revised. Revised by Cornelius S. Hurlbut, Jr. beginning with the 15th edition
  This is a standard introductory reference book for the use of students and collectors. It covers physical, chemical, determinative, and descriptive mineralogy, discusses mineral occurrence, association, and use, and includes both a subject and mineral index

Loomis, Frederic Brewster
Field book of common rocks and minerals. . . . [Rev] With 47 colored specimens and over 100 other illus. from photographs by W. E. Corbin and drawings by the author. Putnam 1948 352p illus 73 plates (Putnam's Nature field bks) $5.95   **549**
  1 Mineralogy 2 Rocks

First published 1923
  "For identifying the rocks and minerals of the United States and interpreting their origins and meanings." Subtitle
  "A useful guide to observation, collection, and study which requires little background or equipment. The minerals are grouped according to their chemical composition, appearance, specific gravity, and many other distinguishing characteristics. Uses, natural combinations, and important national deposits are discussed. The rocks are then taken up and grouped by origin, giving their composition, visible features, and natural occurrence." The AAAS Science Book List for Young Adults
  Bibliography: p270-71

Pough, Frederick H.
A field guide to rocks and minerals. 3d ed. Houghton 1960 349p illus 46 plates maps $5.95   **549**
  1 Mineralogy 2 Rocks
  "The Peterson Field guide series"
  First published 1953
  Emphasis is "on immediate identification in the field. Chapters on crystallography and mineral environments provide an introduction to the basic material on which a proper visual identification can usually be made." Publisher's note
  "More advanced than Loomis [Field book of common rocks and minerals, entered above] with much greater emphasis on minerals, this book can also be used by beginners while easily accommodating the needs of the serious collector. Explains many specific procedures. . . . Illustrated with many line drawings and photographs, often in color." The AAAS Science Book List for Young Adults
  Glossary: p333-38. Bibliography: p339-40

550 Earth sciences

Bertin, Leon
Larousse Encyclopedia of the earth. . . . Prometheus Press [distributed by Putnam] 1961 419p illus maps $17.50   **550**
  1 Earth 2 Geology
  Title on spine: The earth
  Originally published 1956 in France
  "Foreword by Sir Vivian Fuchs; introduction by Carroll Lane Fenton; editorial consultants (English edition) Norman Harris [and others]." Title page
  "The structure of the earth from atmosphere to interior, the characteristics of various formations and their origins in ages past, the mineral and other economic resources of the earth, and paleontology are covered in topically arranged sections." Booklist
  "There is some unevenness of coverage, particularly and unfortunately in paleontology, the topic least well covered. All things considered, the 'Encyclopedia' should answer the need in large science collections for a general up-to-date survey of earth science." Library J

551 Physical and dynamic geology

Beiser, Arthur
The earth, by Arthur Beiser and the editors of Time-Life Books. Time-Life Bks. [1969 c1963] 192p illus maps (Life Nature lib) lib. bdg. $7.60   **551**
  1 Earth 2 Geology
  First published 1962
  Contents: A small but extraordinary planet; Cloudy beginnings; Anatomy of the skies; The emergence of the crust; Shaping of the landscape; The record of the rocks; An uncertain destiny; Bibliography; A geologic tour of the U.S.
  "A readable study. . . . Laymen and young students interested in geography, geology, geophysics, astronomy, fossils, and rock and gem hunting will find the volume full of carefully digested material well illustrated with photographs, 106 in full color." Booklist

Chapman, Sydney
IGY: year of discovery; the story of the International Geophysical Year. Univ. of Mich. Press 1959 111p illus $4.95   **551**

1 International Geophysical Year, 1957-1958
2 Geophysics

"This book offers a popular account of some scientific aspects of the earth and sun—in special connection with the 1957-58 enterprise called the International Geophysical Year (IGY). The text, based on four lectures given in October 1958 at The University of Michigan, is addressed in the first place to an American audience." Preface

Written by the president of the international committee that directed the IGY, the book covers such topics as: The earth and oceans; The solid and liquid earth; The atmosphere; The ionosphere; Cosmic rays, the sun, and nuclear radiation; The growth of natural science

Gamow, George
A planet called earth. Viking 1963 247p illus maps $5.75   **551**

1 Earth 2 Geology 3 Universe

Replaces the author's: Biography of the earth, first published 1941

The author ranges "through the scientific disciplines, discussing theories of planetary formation, composition of the bodies of our solar system, geologic changes, weather, evolution, the living cell, and future of the earth. Maps, photographs, and diagrams are excellent." Chicago. Children's Book Center

"As is true with all [Gamow's] books this one does an excellent job of making a mass of scientific information not only informative but interesting to the average reader." Sec Ed Brd

Hammond, Incorporated
Earth and space. The author 1970 192p illus maps $12.95   **551**

1 Geophysics 2 Space sciences

A one-volume graphic encyclopedia of earth and space science designed to explain the physical workings of both the Planet Earth and the greater universe of which it is a part. This work is organized into four main sections—astronomy, earth science, oceanography and meteorology. (Publisher)

Glossary of terms: p184-87

Scientific American
The biosphere. Freeman 1970 134p illus $6.50   **551**

1 Geophysics 2 Geochemistry 3 Ecology
ISBN 0-7167-0946-5

"A Scientific American book"

These articles, first published in the September 1970 issue, concerning man's environment—the thin film of air and water and soil and life surrounding the earth which is called the biosphere—discuss the energy cycles of the earth and the biosphere, the water, carbon, oxygen, nitrogen and mineral cycles, and human food, energy and materials production

"The text is current and will undoubtedly serve as the basis for statements to be found in the spate of semi-popular books dealing with ecology that are becoming so common." Science Bks

Bibliographies: p129-30

The planet earth, by the editors of Scientific American. Simon & Schuster 1957 168p illus pa $1.45   **551**

1 Earth 2 Geophysics 3 International Geophysical Year, 1957-1958

"Articles [first published in the 'Scientific American'] on the earth's formation, the lithosphere, the hydrosphere, the atmosphere and the edge of space. By noted American, English and Australian scientists." Pub W

551.09 Physical and dynamic geology—History

Moore, Ruth
The earth we live on; the story of geological discovery; drawings by Sue Allen. 2d ed. substantially rev. Knopf 1971 437p illus $8.95   **551.09**

1 Geology—History 2 Geologists
ISBN 0-394-46968-2

First published 1956

The text is presented here "largely through the story of the scholars and field workers, from earliest times to the present, who made geological discoveries and formulated great theories about the origin and evolution of the earth." Pub W

Note on books and materials: p430-37

551.2 Plutonic phenomena

Wilcoxson, Kent H.
Chains of fire; the story of volcanoes. Chilton Co. 1966 235p illus map $6.95   **551.2**

1 Volcanoes

"Primarily a nontechnical description of volcanic eruptions in which most of the chapters are each devoted to a specific volcano or volcanic area. Interspersed are four chapters devoted to theory and discussions of volcanism in general. Intentionally omits the majority of the world's volcanoes and concentrates only on the few dozen that have had spectacular or well-documented eruptive histories. A very good job of presenting numerous and detailed eye-witness accounts of eruptions." The AAAS Science Book List

Glossary: p223-25. Bibliography: p227-32

551.4 Geomorphology

Behrman, Daniel
The new world of the oceans; men and oceanography; with photographs. Little 1969 436p illus $8.95   **551.4**

1 Oceanography 2 Oceanography—Research

The author "introduces his readers to the men and the ways of life at numerous major 'stations' in America: Scripps in La Jolla, California; Woods Hole, Massachusetts; the University of Miami. He makes the people real personalities, describes their enthusiasms, their endless efforts to get to know everything there is to know about the sea. He shares their knowledge . . . [and] in the oceanographers' own jargon, he communicates some of their musings on sea, earth, tides, catastrophes possible in the epochs ahead as the sea in its 'awful opacity' is moved from changelessness by unpredictable nature or heedless men." Pub W

Some further reading: p421-25

Carson, Rachel L.
The sea around us   **551.4**

1 Ocean

Some editions are:
Oxford $6.50
Watts, F. $8.95 Large type edition. A Keith Jennison book

First published 1951

Beginning with a description of how the earth acquired its oceans, the book covers such topics as how life began in the primeval sea; the hidden lands; the life recently discovered in the abyss by highly delicate sounding apparatus; currents and tides; mineral resources; etc.

"The accuracy of a scientist and the imagination of a storyteller combine to make this description of the 'sweet mystery' of the sea fascinating, informative reading." N Y Pub Lib

Includes bibliography

Cousteau, Jacques-Yves
Jacques-Yves Cousteau's World without
sun; ed. by James Dugan. Harper 1965 202p
illus map $15   551.4

1 Oceanography—Research 2 Diving vehicles
3 Marine animals

Original French edition, 1964
A "documentary of Continental Shelf Station Number Two, where oceanauts lived and
worked for a month on the floor of the Red
Sea in man's first underwater colony." Top of
the News

"Richly illustrated with 102 color photographs and 140 monochrome plates. . . . After
a ten-page Foreword by M. Cousteau, the book
uses its pictures and a running commentary on
them to tell the story of the building of the undersea structures and of the life of the men underwater. It is an absorbing account, sparked
by humor as well as spiced with quiet courage." Best Sellers

Life and death in a coral sea [by] Jacques-
Yves Cousteau with Philippe Diolé; tr. from
the French by J. F. Bernard. Doubleday
1971 302p illus maps (The Undersea discoveries of Jacques-Yves Cousteau) $8.95
                                                    551.4

1 Oceanography   2 Coral reefs and islands
3 Marine biology

A companion volume to the author's The
shark: splendid savage of the sea entered in
class 597

"With his 30-man team of divers, technicians
and scientists, Cousteau made numerous expeditions to explore the coral reefs deep in the
Red Sea and in the Indian Ocean around the
Seychelles and elsewhere—partly to learn what
inroads man-made pollution had made on coral
formations he had first seen nearly two decades earlier. The Red Sea in particular he
found a trap for the debris of civilization, with
coral formations deteriorating or already dead.
Its scientific importance aside, Cousteau's
book makes consistently absorbing reading
for the adventure buff, especially in its descriptions of the deep-water exploration and filming of coral grottoes by tiny saucer-shaped
subs called Fleas." Pub W

Illustrated glossary: p277-98

Dugan, James
World beneath the sea, by James Dugan
[and others]; foreword by Gilbert M. Grosvenor; prepared by Special Publications Division, Robert L. Breeden, chief. Nat. Geographic Soc. 1967 204p illus maps $4.25
                                                    551.4

1 Oceanography—Research

The authors "highlight experiences with the
United States Navy Sealab project and give
a chapter to . . . submersibles (submarinos).
. . . In other chapters they cover underwater
photography, archaeological discoveries, and
undersea wildlife." Library J
Additional references: p202

Engel, Leonard
The sea, by Leonard Engel and the editors of Time-Life Books. Time-Life Bks.
1968 190p illus maps (Life Nature lib) lib.
bdg. $7.60   551.4

1 Ocean 2 Marine biology
First published 1961

"The text discusses the earth's oceans in detail, their origins, currents, waves and tides,
the animals and plants in them, and their possibilities for man's future." N Y Her Trib
Books

A profusely illustrated "attractive addition
to any library. . . . Part of the book, and perhaps a disproportionate part of it, is devoted
to sharks and other oceanic killers." N Y Times
Bk R

Includes bibliography, chronology, lists of
principal oceans, rivers, lakes

Fairbridge, Rhodes W.
(ed.) The encyclopedia of oceanography.
Reinhold 1966 1021p illus maps (Encyclopedia of earth sciences ser. v 1) $25   551.4

1 Oceanography—Dictionaries

"Contains 245 original articles 'intended for
the use of all scientists, young and old.' The
contributors were selected by the editor . . .
from scientists throughout the world who are
leaders in their various fields. The general articles are intended to span the field for the
novice. . . . The entries are under broad subjects, e.g., ocean waves, Gulf of Carpentaria,
English Channel, tides, etc., and are well illustrated with black-and-white charts and diagrams." Cur Ref Bks

French, Herbert E.
Of rivers and the sea. Putnam 1970 318p
boards $6.95   551.4

1 Water

Among the topics discussed in this history
of the world of water "are the variety and dimensions of oceans; the ecological battle between sea, land and air; the origins and mechanics of lakes, rivers, waterfalls, hot and
cold springs. There are chapters on man's use
of water through the centuries—for sport,
convenience and health, with . . . references to
water closets, mudpie-making and skin-div-
ing." Pub W

"Both anecdotal and informative, the work
is an indepth presentation of water in all its
forms: from oceans to snow, waterfalls to
fountains, and yet the topic is tastefully done
and geared to the layman rather than the serious scientist." Choice
Bibliography: p299-304

Gaskell, T. F.
World beneath the oceans; with paintings
by Barry Evans. Natural Hist. Press [1965
c1964] 154p illus maps (Nature and science
lib: The earth) boards $5.95, lib. bdg. $6.70
                                                    551.4

1 Oceanography 2 Ocean

"Published for the American Museum of Natural History"

"Waves and currents of the sea, movement
of tides, minerals of the sea, pioneers of oceanography, and the future of research beneath
the waves are a few of the subjects which
make this book a fascinating one. Many fine
illustrations are an aid to understanding." Wis
Lib Bul

"The writing is marred by unevenness—simplicity in some explanations, complexity in
others. . . . [But] it is obviously a learned work
based on many hours of reference library research." Natur Hist

Gordon, Bernard L.
(ed.) Man and the sea; classic accounts of
marine explorations; foreword by Paul M.
Fye. Natural Hist. Press 1970 xxiv, 498p
illus maps $9.95   551.4

1 Ocean 2 Oceanography

"Published for The American Museum of Natural History"

"A selection of writings of marine explorers
throughout history. The accounts of men of
the past, such as Franklin, Halley, and Agassiz,
provide insights into the growth and development of oceanography; contemporary explorers, such as Cousteau and Piccard, provide a
vision of our future with this last frontier on
earth." News of Bks

"Chapters are specific and short, each by an
authority. Most have appeared elsewhere and
are presented together for the first time in an
integrated history of oceanography and oceanology." Science Bks

Larson, Peggy
Deserts of America; illus. by Stanley
Wyatt. Prentice-Hall 1970 340p illus $9.95
                                                    551.4

1 Deserts 2 Ecology
SBN 13-199851-X

"In the two introductory chapters, deserts of
the world are defined and described in general

Larson, Peggy—*Continued*

terms, and then, more particularly, the deserts of North America. The next 18 chapters present an immense number of statements and statistics concerning meteorological and geographical features, plants and animals, their methods of surviving both as individuals and as species, the communities they form, historical notes, and finally, wishful prospects for the future of desert lands. . . . The illustrations are numerous and, for the most part, excellent." Choice

Leopold, A. Starker

The desert, by A. Starker Leopold and the editors of Time-Life Books. Time-Life Bks. [1969 c1962] 192p illus maps (Life Nature lib) lib. bdg. $7.60   551.4

1 Deserts 2 Desert animals 3 Desert plants

First published 1961

Contents: Scorched belts on the earth; The creation of deserts; Plants under the sun; The world of desert animals; Water: the eternal problem; Life patterns in arid lands; Man against desert; The desert tamed

Many excellent photographs, some in color, picture "stretches of desolate sand dunes, dry lakes, distant buttes shimmering in the heat . . . native plants, animals and even humans, as well as some of the world's most awe-inspiring scenery." Introduction

Bibliography: p186

Leopold, Luna B.

Water, by Luna B. Leopold, Kenneth S. Davis and the editors of Time-Life Books. Time-Life Bks. [1968 c1966] 200p illus maps (Life Science lib) lib. bdg. $7.60   551.4

1 Water

"A Stonehenge book"

The authors "show graphically why water is the most important substance essential to life. Starting with the chemical nature of water, they continue with discussions of the water cycle, underground water, the geological effects of erosion, water as the original source of life, the influence of water supply, man's use and abuse of his water supply, and possible ways to overcome scarcity. . . . A short bibliography and glossary are appended." Booklist

Copiously illustrated, "it is not a book which must be read from cover to cover. A dipperful at any point along its course will be refreshing." Library J

Milne, Lorus

Water and life [by] Lorus & Margery Milne; drawings by Kenneth Gosner. Atheneum Pubs. 1964 275p illus $5.75   551.4

1 Water

This "writing team explores the importance of water to the human body and its many other uses. They tell of the large amount of water used by each individual, of water shortages and their dangers. Ways of meeting the danger are presented." Cincinnati

The authors have provided "general background, and some fresh and provocative points of view." N Y Times Bk R

Bibliographical sources included in Grace notes: p259-63

Piccard, Jacques

The sun beneath the sea; tr. from the French by Denver Lindley. Scribner 1971 xxxix, 405p illus map $12.50   551.4

1 Oceanography—Research 2 Ben Franklin (Research submarine) 3 Gulf Stream

SBN 684-31101-1

"Here is an informative account of the design and voyages of the mid-water diving vehicle 'Ben Franklin' which in 1968 . . . made a 30-day scientific cruise of 1,500 miles submerged in the Gulf Stream. . . . Unique in scope the book belongs among classics of the sea. Well-illustrated with an adequate index and table

of contents but no bibliography . . . often amusing in its dealing with unavoidable frustrations, the Gulf Stream Drift Mission is described as an ideal blend of industrial and scientific effort." Choice

Platt, Rutherford

Water: the wonder of life; line drawings by Stanley Wyatt. Prentice-Hall 1971 274p illus $8.95   551.4

1 Water

ISBN 0-13-945808-5

The author "explores the mysteries of water: how it covered the earth in oceans, lakes, rivers, and glaciers, and why it is essential to the physical and cultural development of man." News of Bks

Platt "has immense erudition, keen insight and a spontaneous gift for making the most scientifically difficult explanations both lucid and entertaining. His new volume on that most deceptively commonplace subject, water, is brilliant." Pub W

Includes bibliographical references

Scientific American

The ocean. Freeman 1969 140p illus maps $6.50   551.4

1 Ocean 2 Marine resources

SBN 7167-0998-8

"A Scientific American book"

"The 10 chapters in this volume originally appeared as articles in the September 1969 issue of Scientific American. Each chapter is written by an outstanding authority and presents the current thinking on various aspects of the ocean. Some of these are the origin of the ocean, the atmosphere and ocean interaction, the physical and biological resources and the problems of international relations associated with the resource utilization. The quality of illustrations is the usual high standard of 'Scientific American.' Highly recommended to anyone who wishes to become familiar with various aspects of the current thinking on the oceanic environment of our planet." Choice

Bibliographies: p135-36

Soule, Gardner

The greatest depths; probing the seas to 20,000 feet and below. Macrae Smith Co. 1970 194p illus map $5.95   551.4

1 Oceanography—Research 2 Diving vehicles

SBN 8255-8350-0

This study of underwater exploration describes the research submarines now being used and the efforts deep-sea probers are making to discover "new clues to the earth's formation, some exotic animals, and a more complete knowledge of the earth's elements . . . [plus] possibilities of future ocean farming and mining." Publisher's note

"Although it is not a lengthy book . . . it is easy nontechnical reading and is suitably illustrated and indexed. The six pages of bibliographic and reference sources should be entirely sufficient for any who wish to pursue the subject further. Soule has produced a very readable volume on a seldom written of aspect of marine science; nowhere has he sacrificed scientific and technical assuracy in details; the book maintains high reader interest and is thoroughly enjoyable." Science Bks

551.5 Descriptive and dynamic meteorology

Chandler, T. J.

The air around us; man looks at his atmosphere. Natural Hist. Press 1969 156p illus map (Nature and science lib) $5.95, lib. bdg. $6.70   551.5

1 Atmosphere 2 Weather 3 Climate

"Published for The American Museum of Natural History"

First published 1967 in England

Chandler, T. J.—*Continued*
This book "is primarily a story-text on meteorology and climatology, written simply, clearly, and interestingly, but not patronizingly, by one who obviously knows his subject matter. The book is well illustrated with diagrams, maps, and photographs that enhance its usefulness. . . . Starting with a description of the structure and composition of the atmosphere, the presentation follows a logical course through expositions on wind patterns, energy balances between earth and sky, hydrological cycles and accompanying effects, and theories of the development of climate and of weather to the measurement and forecasting of weather phenomena (clouds, rain, snow, hail, tornadoes, storms). The effects of climate on man—physical, social, economic—and man's effect on climate as caused, for example, by the creation of large city land masses or attempts at rainmaking, are appropriate closing chapters for this delightful book." Science Bks

Thompson, Philip D.
Weather, by Philip D. Thompson, Robert O'Brien and the editors of Time-Life Books. Time-Life Bks. 1968 200p illus maps (Life Science lib) lib. bdg. $7.60 **551.5**
1 Meteorology
"A Stenehenge book"
First published 1965
"This book traces the basic circulation of heat and winds from equator to poles, and explains the many phenomena of weather, from hailstones to hurricanes. It describes how modern meteorologists armed with such tools as radar, laser beams and computers, may change civilization itself as they make more accurate predictions and possibly modify the weather." p4
"Of special interest to the general reader and amateur meteorologist is the photo essay, 'The Home Weatherman' which describes a 13-year old's prize-winning (national science contest) weather station." N Y New Tech Bks
Further reading: p196

551.59 Climatology and weather

Barrett, E. C.
Viewing weather from space. Praeger 1967 140p illus maps (Praeger Monographs in geography) $6 **551.59**
1 Meteorology in aeronautics 2 Meteorology 3 Weather forecasting
"A useful introduction to satellite meteorology. The emphasis is on weather systems and the surface of the earth as these are sensed by the satellites and portrayed by receiving stations. . . . The book is organized into three unequal sections: Part 1 (three chapters) on satellite equipment and new data; Part 2 (six chapters) focusing on atmospheric phenomena, the forecast problem, and the earth's surface; and Part 3 (one chapter) suggesting future needs and developments. Each chapter has a short, partially annotated bibliography, and there is appended tabular material on instrumentation, storm systems, surface characteristics, and remote sensor experiments. Index: carefully done line drawings; good sample of photos from several different types of sensors." Choice

Battan, Louis J.
Cloud physics and cloud seeding. Anchor Bks. 1962 144p illus (Science study ser) pa $1.25 **551.59**
1 Weather control 2 Clouds
"Explains the things we know or need to know about the natural processes of atmospheric condensation and precipitation in order to artificially squeeze more water from the clouds to meet our ever-increasing needs. The physics of condensation nuclei, cloud formation, and the production of different forms of precipitation are explained, as well as the actual attempts made so far to stimulate these processes chemically." The AAAS Science Book List for Young Adults
Includes a bibliography

Harvesting the clouds; advances in weather modification. Doubleday 1969 148p illus (Science study ser) $4.95 **551.59**
1 Weather control
The author discusses some of the proposals advanced by scientists who are seeking ways to control the weather and change the climate. He reviews the fundamental processes of rain formation and techniques of cloud seeding; discusses early attempts at weather control; and gives an account of some of the tested or still speculative ways that may change the course of rain, snow, hail, lightning, and hurricanes. (Publisher)
"Although nontechnical, its review of past and present research problems and procedures also makes it valuable for science oriented students and professionals as well." Choice
For additional information: p143

Claiborne, Robert
Climate, man, and history. Norton 1970 444p illus $8.95 **551.59**
1 Climate
SBN 393-06370-4
"After an account of what climate is and what determines it, the author examines the interrelationship of man's evolution and climatic change. . . . The impact of climate on history—the end of the Roman Empire, the rise and fall of the Vikings, and the Hanseatic League, among other events—is discussed [as well as possible future control of climate]." Publisher's note
Selected bibliography: p427-32. Map on lining-papers

552 Petrology

Fenton, Carroll Lane
The rock book, by Carroll Lane Fenton and Mildred Adams Fenton; illus. with color plates, photographs and line drawings. Doubleday 1940 357p illus maps $9.95 **552**
1 Rocks 2 Mineralogy
Partial contents: Rocks in our world: Atoms to minerals; Important minerals; Coarse-grained igneous rocks; Fine-grained, glassy and fragmental rocks; Rocks from the sky; Clastic rocks; Rocks from solutions; Limestones and related rocks; Records in strata; Ores and their origins; Collect, travel and read
"A practical nature guide combined with the romantic story of the earth's surface, with a useful chapter on rock collecting." Ontario Lib Rev

553 Economic geology

Brown, Mary L. T.
Gems for the taking; mine your own treasure. Macmillan (N Y) 1971 193p $5.95 **553**
1 Prospecting 2 Precious stones
A book on where to mine your own gems in the United States. Emphasizing surface mining, the author covers site examination, how to plan a gem-mining vacation, types of stones, tools needed, etc.
"The author's enthusiasm for the hobby is real, and her chatty, low-key style makes it ideal for the casual reader. . . . Some of the incidental information on the history of gem minerals and man's use of them is of potential reference value." Library J

Sinkankas, John
Prospecting for gemstones and minerals. Van Nostrand-Reinhold 1970 397p illus $10.95 **553**
1 Precious stones 2 Mineralogy 3 Prospecting
First published 1961 with title: Gemstones and minerals: how and where to find them

Sinkankas, John—*Continued*
A guide for the amateur prospector, with information on planning a trip, choosing equipment, the formation, appearance, and classification of rocks and minerals, and extracting, preparing, storing and marketing specimens
Includes lists of useful addresses and libraries and a bibliography

560 Paleontology

Fenton, Carroll Lane
The fossil book; a record of prehisotric life [by] Carroll Lane Fenton and Mildred Adams Fenton. Doubleday 1958 482p illus $17.50 **560**
1 Fossils
This "survey of the fossil remains of plants, beasts, birds, insects, and various forms of marine and animal life progresses from the simplest to the most complex specimens. . . . The fossils and their restorations are compared not only with those of other prehistoric creatures but also with related species which still survive. Generously supplied with photographs and drawings which are well coordinated with the text. Not a popular treatment, will be most useful as a reference work or student guide." Booklist
Read, see and collect: p448-58. Glossary: p459-65

568 Fossil reptiles

Colbert, Edwin H.
Men and dinosaurs; the search in field and laboratory. Dutton 1968 283p illus maps $8.95 **568**
1 Dinosaurs 2 Naturalists
The author "focuses on the men who have engaged in the search for and study of dinosaurs during the 150 years that have passed since a dinosaur was first scientifically described. Through anecdotes which reveal the personalities as well as the achievements of the scientists he traces the growth of man's knowledge about dinosaurs. Many excellent photographs, drawings, maps, charts round out the presentation." Booklist
An "interesting story which laymen as well as scientists can enjoy. The bibliography, principally of primary sources, is invaluable to students." Science Bks

569 Fossil mammals

Silverberg, Robert
Mammoths, mastodons, and man; illus. by Dale Grabel. McGraw 1970 223p illus $5.50, lib. bdg. $5.33 **569**
1 Mammoth 2 Mastodon 3 Man, Prehistoric
The author "discusses the discovery and study of mammoth and mastodon remains from the first known finds during the Middle Ages to the present-day scientific study of prehistoric animals. He describes important and interesting discoveries and quests for information around the world and traces the ongoing controversy surrounding the huge bones, including the early giant theory and the turmoil created in religious circles." Booklist
Bibliography: p217-19

570.3 Biological sciences— Dictionaries

Compton's Dictionary of the natural sciences; fully illus. & fully indexed. Editor in chief: Charles A. Ford; editorial director: Paul E. Klinge; executive editor: Leo Charles Fay. Compton 1966 2v illus maps $24.95 **570.3**
1 Natural history—Dictionaries

Contents: v 1 A-N; v2 O-Z
"The fields of science represented in the dictionary include astronomy, biology, botany, earth science, geology, meteorology, microbiology, mineralogy, oceanography, paleontology and zoology. . . . The first section is the main text, consisting of 2,360 articles identifying, defining, describing, and illustrating terms from the life and earth sciences. . . . The second section consists of 17 charts and tables. . . . The third section is the illustrated index and glossary of terms." Booklist

The Encycopedia of the biological sciences; 2d ed. edited by Peter Gray. Van Nostrand-Reinhold 1970 xxv, 1027p illus $24.95 **570.3**
1 Biology—Dictionaries
First published 1961
Arranged alphabetically, these articles of 500 or more words each "cover the broad field of the biological sciences as viewed by experts in their developmental, ecological, functional, genetic, structural, and taxonomic aspects." Introduction
"As a compendium, it is well done: over 500 specialists have written succinctly and inclusively on some 800 topics. Well edited, each article nonetheless has a distinctive style and quality, bespeaking its original author." Choice
"There are many brief biographical sketches —limited to their subjects' scientific work and contribution. Hence, details of their personal lives should be sought in other sources." Science Bks

572 Human races (Ethnology)

Benedict, Ruth, 1887-1948
Patterns of culture. Houghton 1934 290p $5.95 **572**
1 Anthropology 2 Society, Primitive 3 Zuñi Indians 4 Kwakiutl Indians 5 Dobu Island
"The first part of this anthropological classic introduces the concept 'culture' and tells some ways in which it is studied. The middle chapters describe the three cultural groups the book is based on—Zuni Indians of New Mexico, the Dobuans of Melanesia, and the Kwakiutl of Vancouver Island—and points out contrasts among them, while the last two chapters deal with the nature of society and the place of the individual in culture, drawing on findings from the groups studied." The AAAS Science Book List for Young Adults
"This is an important and revealing book, . . . Dr. Benedict's work is based upon a scholarly knowledge of the sources, combined with first-hand experience of American Indian tribes." Nation
References: p279-86

Race: science and politics. Rev. ed.—with The races of mankind, by Ruth Benedict and Gene Weltfish. Viking 1947 [c1945] 206p $5 **572**
1 Anthropology 2 Race problems
First published 1940 by Modern Age Books
"This book for the general reader reviews both the science of race and the history of racism. Typical examples of the ideas of both scientists and racists range in time from the writings of Cicero to those of Franz Boas and the maunderings of the Third Reich propagandists." Cincinnati
For further reading: p192-93

Coon, Carleton S.
The living races of man, by Carleton S. Coon with Edward E. Hunt, Jr. Knopf 1965 xxxii, 344, xx p illus maps $12.50 **572**
1 Race 2 Ethnology
A companion volume to the author's: The story of man, entered below
The author "traces the races of man from their five cradles at the end of the last glacial period to their present distribution. He summarizes the 'racial composition of people of the world' and discusses factors important in differentiation of races, adding a warning

Coon, Carleton S.—*Continued*
against any use of this book to promote any specific cause or dogma." Cincinnati
"Coon is an internationally known authority in his field and, although his views are controversial, he effectively presents data from various fields (archaeology, linguistics physical anthropology, geography, and genetics) to substantiate his thesis. . . . One-third of the book consists of photographic plates of human physical types distributed over selected geographic regions; these vary from excellent to very poor. . . . The maps and tables are very good, and the glossary and bibliography are worth the price of the book. This is a valuable contribution—for the lay reader, the student, and the specialist." Choice

The origin of races. Knopf 1962 xli, 724, xxi p illus maps $12.50   572
1 Ethnology 2 Race 3 Man—Origin and antiquity
Dr Coon presents his theory "that early man, 'Homo erectus,' divided into five geographic races, or subspecies, which then separately evolved into 'Homo sapiens.' The author . . . reviews some of the principles of evolution, describes the primates, and traces the origins and evolutionary progress of the five lines or races of human descent which he sees." Pub W
Making use of material from many fields, this "is an important book . . . because it provides a detailed and critical review of what is known about fossil man, and in such a way as to create order and a system in a field of study that has traditionally suffered from an accumulation of disconnected and undigested observations. It is the subject of controversy because Professor Coon states some of his conclusions in a way that makes his work susceptible to misuse by racists, white supremecists and other special pleaders." Sci Am
Bibliography: p686-710. Glossary: p711-24

The story of man; from the first human to primitive culture and beyond. 2d ed. rev. Line drawings by Richard Albany; photographs by Reuben Goldberg. Knopf 1962 xxii, 438p illus maps $8.95   572
1 Anthropology 2 Civilization—History
First published 1954
The story of the races of man and of his customs and beliefs during 50,000 years of growth and change, from ape men to the atomic era. (Publisher)
"Here we have history presented in something like its proper proportion—with great attention to that long period of man's cultural infancy which is none the less history because it is prehistoric. Professor Coon sees clearly the inevitability and importance of cultural change, and he makes an earnest plea for the development in men of that alertness of mind which will be able to grasp the meaning and value of change." Book of the Month Club News

Goldsby, Richard A.
Race and races. Macmillan (N Y) 1971 132p illus maps $5.95   572
1 Race
According to the author "the book is 'intended to be an introductory survey of the contributions, both factual and conceptual, various areas of biology have made to the study of race in man.' The style is easy, and the text flows and reads well. . . . The seven chapters deal . . . with the origin, concepts, and definition of race and races, human variability, and genetic traits." Natur Hist
Includes a bibliography

Montagu, Ashley
Man: his first two million years; a brief introduction to anthropology. Columbia Univ. Press 1969 262p illus maps $7.50   572
1 Anthropology
First published 1957 by World with title: Man: his first million years

"The book is an introduction to what anthropology has discovered about man: his primate ancestors, his differentiation into the varied ethnic groups which we know today, and his diverse cultural response to his environment." Publisher's note
"Here, in a book that stands midway between textbook and a straight popularized primer on anthropology [the author] writes with his usual clarity and wit. . . . Even when he is presenting the facts and nothing but the facts, Montagu is an engaging writer." Pub W
For further reading: p239-51

National Geographic Society
Vanishing peoples of the earth; foreword by Leonard Carmichael; produced by the National Geographic Special Publications Division, Robert L. Breeden, chief. The Society 1968 207p illus maps $4.25   572
1 Ethnology 2 Society, Primitive
Text and illustrations portray the lives, tribal customs and traditions of the Lapps, Bushmen, Eskimos, Nilgiri peoples of India, Japan's Ainu, Australia's Aborigines and others
"The book contains 187 color photographs and will serve to record the disappearing traditions of these peoples. It will be an asset for any library because of its revelations on how modern life has altered ancient and cherished beliefs and customs." Library J
Additional references: p206

572.97 Races in North America

Mead, Margaret
(ed.) The golden age of American anthropology; selected and ed. with introduction and notes by Margaret Mead and Ruth L. Bunzel. Braziller 1960 630p illus $12.50
572.97
1 Anthropology 2 Indians of North America
Analyzed in Essay and general literature index
This compendium by about 50 authors spans over 400 years and includes the most important writings about the American Indian from Diaz del Castillo to Franz Boas. It covers different Indian tribes and cultures as well as the methods of anthropology
"Fascinating reading for all who are interested in the Indians of our continent and for all who are interested in anthropology." Wis Lib Bul
Suggestions for further reading: p629-30

572.996 Races in Polynesia

Heyerdahl, Thor
Aku-aku; the secret of Easter Island. Rand McNally 1958 384p illus maps $8.95
572.996
1 Easter Island—Antiquities 2 Anthropogeography 3 Polynesians
"Fast and fascinating as Heyerdahl explores Easter Island with its strange colossal stone figures and, by applying to people, legends, and artifacts the imaginative speculation of his Kon-Tiki, comes up with some specific conclusions about the history and cultures of this place. He makes friends with the natives who finally reveal to him the secrets of the island; he makes breath-taking descents into caves so narrow that he has to slide down feet first with his arms over his head; he demonstrates how the huge figures were quarried and moved. This is a long book and I can't vouch for its archaeology but it is a vigorous adventure story with all the lure of mysteries to be solved." Horn Bk
"An absorbing . . . tale beautifully illustrated with colored photographs." Top of the News

573 Physical anthropology

Bates, Marston
Man in nature. 2d ed. Prentice-Hall 1964
116p illus maps (Foundations of modern
biology ser) $3.95   **573**
1 Man—Origin and antiquity 2 Botany, Economic 3 Ecology
First published 1961
"Deals primarily with the broad problem of
human activities within the framework of nature in its entirety. In terms of their special
relation to the rest of nature, the book discusses human evolution and variations, populations, agriculture, domestication, conservation, medicine, and the utilization of natural
resources." Publisher's note
"A small and succinct volume in which Professor Bates gives an admirable introduction
to biology for the layman. Not biology in the
schoolbook sense, but biology of man." Library J
Selected readings: p112

573.2 Organic evolution of man

Howell, F. Clark
Early man, by F. Clark Howell and the
editors of Time-Life Books. Time-Life Bks.
[1970] 200p illus (Life nature lib) lib.
bdg. $7.60   **573.2**
1 Man—Origin and antiquity 2 Evolution
3 Stone age
First published 1965
The book traces "the development of man
from the earliest known forerunners to the
dawn of modern man and the present-day primitive African Bushmen. Also included is discussion of the early beliefs about the beginnings of man and the development of the tools
of stone age man." Booklist
"The illustrations, consisting of paintings
of primitive human societies and men, and
photographs of their art and artifacts and of
present-day primitive societies, are revealing.
. . . This is a book primarily for the student
and non-professional layman who need an elementary introduction to paleoanthropology.
The bibliography suggests additional reading,
and the detailed index enhances the use of the
book as a reference." Science Bks

Moore, Ruth
Man, time, and fossils; the story of evolution; drawings by Sue Richert. 2d ed. significantly rev. and enl. Knopf 1961 436p illus
maps $8.95   **573.2**
1 Man—Origin and antiquity 2 Evolution
3 Naturalists
Analyzed in Essay and general literature index
First published 1953
"A history of evolutionary theory and significant experiments, discoveries and formulations which have contributed to current understanding of man's origins." Booklist
"The author, one of the better-known popularizers of the science of life [has] revised
. . . her excellent and widely read book (1953).
The story of scientific evolution is told
through the work and contributions of Charles
Darwin and the brilliant evolutionists who
came after him. . . . [This account] tells of
man's goal—to learn about himself, his origin
and evolution." School Sci & Math
Selected bibliography: p429-36

Simak, Clifford D.
Prehistoric man; illus. by Murray Tinkelman. St Martins 1971 192p illus $5.95 **573.2**
1 Man—Origin and antiquity
In this survey of man's prehistoric rise to
civilization the author deals with such subjects

as the evolution of the human body, the origin
and purposes of cave art, how men first
learned to trust each other, how dogs may
have "domesticated" man, the unique characteristics of flint, and pre-historic religions.
(Publisher)

Vlahos, Olivia
Human beginnings; illus. by Kyuzo Tsugami. Viking 1966 255p illus $5.95   **573.2**
1 Man—Origin and antiquity 2 Evolution
3 Man, Prehistoric
"What does it mean to be human? What
type of evolutionary processes have come between the first land vertebrate and man? The
author answers these and other questions in
his discussion of man's biological and cultural
evolution." Bk Buyer's Guide
Suggestions for further reading: p245-47

574 Biology. Natural history

Carson, Rachel
The sense of wonder; photographs by
Charles Pratt and others. Harper [1965
c1956] 89p illus $5.95, lib. bdg. $5.11   **574**
1 Nature study 2 Nature photography
This "is a warm, personal account of [the
author's] walks along the seashore, through
the fields, into the coastal woods of Maine,
with her young nephew." Science Bks
In this book, the author "affirms her belief
that those who live with the mysteries of
earth, sea and sky are never alone or weary
of life. . . . Her narrative and the photographs
that accompany it chart the paths which adult
and child can take together on this journey
of discovery." Publisher's note
The book is "truly inspiring . . . with nearly
one hundred photographs." Huntting

Darwin, Charles Robert
Darwin for today; the essence of his
works; ed. and with an introduction by
Stanley Edgar Hyman. Viking 1963 435p
$7.50   **574**
1 Biology
"This collection contains excerpts from Darwin's most significant writings, ranging from
his '1844 Essay' and its famous successor 'Origin of Species,' to 'Formation of Vegetable
Mold Through Worms.' Beginning with the
Tierra del Fuego and Galapagos chapters from
'Voyage of the "Beagle,"' it also includes generous samplings from the 'Autobiography.' The
editor's introduction seems to justify and interpret the selections, and it ties them together into a neat biographical and critical sketch.
Includes a chronology of Darwin's life and
works. For those who want to read the basic
Darwin story without the . . . textbook approach." Library J
Bibliographical footnotes

The Darwin reader; ed. by Marston Bates
and Philip S. Humphrey. Scribner 1956 470p
illus $8.95   **574**
1 Biology 2 Evolution
"A carefully edited, one-volume Reader containing selections from Darwin's best known
books—the Autobiography, The Voyage of the
Beagle, The Origin of the Species, The Descent
of Man, and The Expression of the Emotions.
The excerpts were chosen for readability and
to illustrate the biologist's most important
ideas. A bibliography of critical appraisals of
Darwin and his work is included." N Y Her
Trib Books
"This condensation of Darwin's principal
works retains all of the moving drama, charm,
and essential facts of the originals, and has eliminated the less interesting detail. Recommended as a first assignment which will whet the
appetite for reading the originals later on."
The AAAS Science Book List for Young Adults

Halacy, D. S.

Man alive [by] D. S. Halacy, Jr. Macrae Smith Co. 1970 183p illus (The Nature of man ser) $4.95   574
1 Life (Biology) 2 Man
SBN 8255-4040-2
This "is a nontechnical discussion of man—his origin, his structure, his responses to the outside world, his physical needs, and the mental processes that set him far above the other living things on earth. . . . Development of a human being from fertilization to birth is described. Man's marvelous—and awkward—anatomy is described; as is his physiology, including his plumbing in the form of blood vessels, lungs, alimentary system, and the nervous system crowned by man's fantastic brain. The brain's functions of memory, learning, and intelligence are briefly covered. Anthropology is touched on, with reference to evolution, mutations, the variations among men, and the concept of race, and so on." Foreword
Bibliography: p175

Handler, Philip

(ed.) Biology and the future of man. Oxford 1970 xxiv, 936p illus $12.50   574
1 Biology
"A comprehensive survey of the life sciences prepared by 175 leading biologists under the auspices of the National Academy of Sciences. Summarizes the whole of modern basic biology; surveys the main areas of applied biology: 'On Feeding Mankind,' 'Environmental Health' and so on; sums up the ways in which the life sciences are 'likely to serve and to shape the future of man.'" Book of the Month Club News

Life (Periodical)

The wonders of life on earth, by the editors of Life and Lincoln Barnett. [Rev. ed] Time-Life Bks. [distributed by Little] 1968 238p illus maps $12.95   574
1 Natural history—Pictures, illustrations, etc. 2 Evolution 3 Darwin, Charles Robert
First published 1960. "The 1968 edition is an abridged reprint of the 1960 book." Science Bks
Following the route of Darwin's expedition and studies, this book, in text and many illustrations, tells the "story of the evolution of life: how it has shaped living things through ceaseless change and proliferation, and given rise to the infinitely diverse flora and fauna that blanket the globe today." Foreword

Time-Life Books

A guide to the natural world, and Index to the Life Nature library, by the editors of Time-Life Books. Time-Life Bks. [1968 c1965] 210p illus (Life Nature lib) lib. bdg. $7.60   574
1 Natural history—Handbooks, manuals, etc.
Title on spine: Index and guide
First published 1965
This twenty-fifth and final volume of the Life Nature library consists of two sections. The first summarizes the major groups within the five natural kingdoms: the kingdoms of the monerans and protistans: of the plants: of the animals; and of the rocks and minerals. The second part indexes the entire series

574.01 Biology—Philosophy

Eiseley, Loren

The unexpected universe. Harcourt 1969 239p $5.75   574.01
1 Natural history—Philosophy 2 Science—Philosophy
The author "narrates a naturalist's encounter with unexpected and symbolic aspects of the universe, ranging from seeds, and the hieroglyphs on shells, to such disparate things as

the microscopic components of our bodies, the ice age, lost tombs, the goddess Circe, city dumps, and Neanderthal man. Through it all, like a hidden thread, binding the book together, runs the theme of desolation and renewal in the planet's history." Publisher's note
"Written with rich imagery and poetic prose, it reflects Eiseley's profound insight into the meanings of his life work in anthropology as well as his keen sense of history. . . . Philosophical and intuitive but profound. . . Of value for any library that includes science interpretation as well as scientific facts." Choice
Bibliography: p235-39

574.028 Biology—Techniques, apparatus, equipment

Berger, Melvin

Tools of modern biology; illus. by Robert Smith. Crowell 1970 215p illus $4.50
574.028
1 Scientific apparatus and instruments 2 Biology—Research
This is an account of the development of such tools "as invisible utrasonic waves, biometrics, electron microscopes, classification systems and computers, centrifuge, chromatography, radiation tracers, and the like, used by the modern biologist." Best Sellers
Includes bibliography

574.03 Biology—Dictionaries

Encyclopedia of the life sciences. Doubleday 1964-1966 8v illus ea $9.95, lib. bdg. $10.70   574.03
1 Biology—Dictionaries
Original French edition. 1961-1963. This translation first published 1964-1966 in England
"Oversize volumes, profusely illustrated with diagrams, drawings, and photographs, contain selections from the writings of American and European scientists which present specific aspects of biology rather than a comprehensive treatment. Current research is emphasized and while some articles are more technical than others, all are intended for the layman who has a basic knowledge of science." Booklist
The volumes are: The living organism; The animal world; The world of plants; The world of microbes; The human machine: Disorders; The human machine: Mechanisms; The human machine: Adjustments; Man of tomorrow
Includes glossaries

Henderson, I. F.

A dictionary of biological terms . . . by I. F. Henderson and W. D. Henderson. Van Nostrand $12.50   574.03
1 Biology—Dictionaries
First published 1920 with title: A dictionary of scientific terms
"Pronunciation, derivation, and definitions of terms in biology, botany, zoology, anatomy, cytology, genetics, embryology; physiology." Title page
Volumes since 1939 revised periodically and edited by J. H. Kenneth

574.09 Biology—History

Moore, Ruth

The coil of life; the story of the great discoveries in the life sciences; drawings by Patricia M. Jackson. Knopf 1961 418p illus $6.95   574.09
1 Biology—History 2 Biochemistry 3 Life (Biology) 4 Scientists
This book tells "the story of the great discoveries in the life sciences of the last 200 years which have brought us to the threshold

Moore, Ruth—*Continued*

of solving the secret of life. It includes the work and contributions by Lavoisier, Wohler and Liebig, Schleiden and Schwann, Fischer and Buchner, Beadle, Tatum, Crick and Watson, Ochoa, Pauling, Sanger, Kornberg, and others, some of whom researched into the most elemental problems of life." School Sci & Math

This "is an interesting, topical, and highly readable book. Intricate concepts are presented with facility and clarity. The flavor of the excitement of scientific discovery bursts from almost every page." Chicago Sunday Tribune

Note on books and materials: p411-18

574.1 Biophysics

Klein, H. Arthur

Bioluminescence; Helen Hale, editorial consultant; illus. by the author and Lewis Zacks. Lippincott 1965 184p illus $4.25 **574.1**

1 Bioluminescence

The "author explains the nature of bioluminescence, which is the emission of light from plants and animals, and, proceeding from the lower to the higher forms, describes organisms which are luminescent. He also traces discoveries made through the study of the phenomenon showing how an understanding of bioluminescence contributes to scientific research in other areas." Booklist

"Scientific terminology is not shunned, rather it is presented in a manner easily understood by the layman. . . . This book, supplemented by additional reading, will dispel misconceptions related to luminescence." Science Bks

Ward, Ritchie R.

The living clocks. Knopf 1971 385p illus maps $8.95 **574.1**

1 Biology 2 Animals—Habits and behavior
ISBN 0-394-41695-3

The author discusses the "biological clocks" that govern the behavior of all life from the barnacle to man. He explains how these living clocks account for the sleep of leaves, the difference between a rose at noon and at midnight, and altered human reactions after a prolonged sojourn underground. (Publisher)

The author "has provided a fascinating panorama of research in one often overlooked area of biology." Book World

Includes bibliographical footnotes

574.5 Ecology

Bates, Marston

The forest and the sea; a look at the economy of nature and the ecology of man. Random House 1960 277p boards $4.95, lib. bdg. $2.39 **574.5**

1 Ecology 2 Natural history

"Drawing on his field researches in tropical forests, coral reefs, and environments between the two extremes, the biologist reveals the astonishing parallel between forest and ocean ecology, then, in widening circles extends the parallel to show the interdependence of all natural things—earth plant life, insects, parasites, wild and domestic animals, and man." Booklist

"Since the author's two favorite kinds of places in the world are coral reefs and rain forests . . . he writes brilliantly about these two environments. Skin divers should be fascinated with what he says about tropical sea life. Throughout, there are touches of humor and flashes of colorful description." Pub W

Notes and sources: p263-68

Farb, Peter

Ecology, by Peter Farb and the editors of Time-Life Books. Time-Life Bks. [1970] 192p illus maps (Life Nature lib) lib. bdg. $7.60 **574.5**

1 Ecology

First published 1963

Dr Farb describes "the vital connections each living creature makes with the other living creatures in and with the physical environment. Here are classic illustrations of the workings of the law of natural selection, of competition and cooperation, conflict and coexistence in the different natural communities—sea and shore, desert, grassland, and mountaintop. Also here are some fundamental considerations as to the future of the human population on this planet, given its biocidal tendencies. The presentation . . . [is] for browsing or serious, provocative reading." Library J

The book is "illustrated by photographs in color and in black and white, and by precise drawings and diagrams. . . . The writing is solid—saved from stolidity by the subject-matter-itself—and the material very well organized." Chicago. Children's Book Center

Bibliography: p183

Halacy, D. S.

Habitat [by] D. S. Halacy, Jr. Macrae Smith Co. 1970 186p illus (The Nature of man ser) $4.95 **574.5**

1 Ecology
SBN 8255-4029-1

The author "discusses at some length the inanimate physical environment of earth from theories on the origin of the universe to natural resources and briefly considers forms of plant, animal, and bacterial life which share this environment with man. He then explains concepts of ecology which are fundamental to man's existence and examines current problems of pollution and their possible solution." Booklist

Bibliography: p178-79

Ketchum, Richard M.

The secret life of the forest; conceived and produced in cooperation with the St Regis Paper Company. Am. Heritage Press 1970 108p illus maps $7.95 **574.5**

1 Ecology 2 Forests and forestry 3 Trees
ISBN 0-07-34418-3

This book explores the complex life within the woodland community. It contains nearly one hundred "color illustrations of forest trees, ferns, shrubs, wildflowers, animals, birds, and insects, all of which depend for survival upon the miraculous cycle of photosynthesis, which provides oxygen for the air we breathe." News of Bks

"The book is well and concisely written, and the illustrations are incomparable. It has to rank as the most informative popular book on forest life and forestry available." Choice

574.8 Histology and cytology

Lessing, Lawrence

DNA: at the core of life itself, by Lawrence Lessing and the editors of Fortune; illus. by Max Gschwind. Macmillan (N Y) 1967 85p illus $3.95 **574.8**

1 DNA 2 RNA

This is a collection of articles, originally published in Fortune Magazine, about "DNA and RNA molecules and their possible significance in curing disease and in changing human heredity. In reasonably nontechnical terms, for the informed layman, Lessing outlines the steps involved in deciphering the genetic code of DNA, the extent of what is known today, the mysteries still unsolved, and the ethical moral, legal, and social issues that will arise if control of heredity becomes a reality. Effective diagrams with detailed captions illustrate the text." Booklist

Pfeiffer, John
The cell, by John Pfeiffer and the editors of Time-Life Books. Time-Life Bks. [1970 c1964] 200p illus (Life Science lib) lib. bdg. $7.60   **574.8**
1 Cells
"A Stonehenge book"
First published 1964
"A good text is enchanced by a superb selection of photographs, photomicrographs, diagrams, and magnifications. The material is presented in reverse of the usual order in biology books: such subjects as photosynthesis, ATP, DNA, and genetics are discussed in the first part of the book. The text then examines the evolution of animal life, ontogenic changes, the complexities of human physiology and the functioning of the various systems of the human body. The book concludes with a chapter on the cell in sickness, this section being the only one that treats its topic rather superficially. A 'Vocabulary of Cellular Biology,' a full-page diagram of a cell, a brief bibliography, and a good relative index are appended." Chicago. Children's Book Center

Scientific American
The living cell; readings from Scientific American. With introductions by Donald Kennedy. Freeman 1965 296p illus (Freeman Bks. in biology) $10   **574.8**
1 Cells
24 articles by different authors report basic facts and discoveries concerning cell biology. The readings are grouped under the following headings: Levels of complexity; Organelles; Energetics; Synthesis; Division and differentiation; Special activities
"Authoritative articles originally published between 1958 and 1964 and suitable for the reader with some knowledge of biology. . . . With an introduction to each topic supplied by the editor. Diagrams and illustrations which accompanied the articles in 'Scientific American' are included." Booklist
Biographical notes and bibliographies: p290-96

574.9 Regional and geographical treatment of natural history

Carlquist, Sherwin
Hawaii: a natural history; geology, climate, native flora and fauna above the shoreline; illus. by Sherwin Carlquist and Jeanne R. Janish. Natural Hist. Press 1970 463p illus maps $19.95   **574.9**
1 Natural history—Hawaii
"Published for the American Museum of Natural History"
"The author first sets the stage of his natural history study by reviewing the geology and climate, and explaining the volcanic origin of the islands and other salient features of the geographic history. Then follows a discussion of biological phenomena. . . . [And] discussions of the various ecological regions of the main islands. There are brief descriptions of a few field trips a tourist might take, and a bibliography and index. This is a very useful book for students who wish to learn something about the flora and fauna of Hawaii which are unique in many respects." Science Bks

Carr, Archie
The land and wildlife of Africa, by Archie Carr and the editors of Life. Time, inc. 1964 200p illus maps (Life Nature lib) lib. bdg. $7.60   **574.9**
1 Natural history—Africa 2 Africa—Description and travel 3 Ecology
The African land, flora, and fauna, "are surveyed in an informed, businesslike text . . . and in numerous photographs, some in color. . . . African ecology, the diversity of animal

and insect life, and recent developments and needs in the continent's conservation program are major motifs. Two chapters deal with the island of Madagascar." Booklist
Bibliography: p195

Durrell, Gerald
Birds, beasts, and relatives. Viking 1969 248p boards $5.95   **574.9**
1 Natural history—Corfu 2 Corfu—Description and travel
The author relates his experiences at the age of ten, before World War II, when he and his family lived on the island of Corfu. He describes the animals he befriended: a donkey, a white barn owl, three mongrels, five baby hedgehogs, a snarl of scorpions, and a spade footed toad. (Publisher)
"Especially vivid are the accounts of spider crabs planting seaweed on their backs for camouflage and of a remarkable silver and brown spider which builds an air-filled nest under water. All these creatures are described in a luminously accurate prose. Less interesting, though still amusing, are the episodes about the family (among whom of course the eldest brother is the novelist-to-be, Lawrence Durrell)." Book of the Month Club News

Farb, Peter
The land and wildlife of North America, by Peter Farb and the editors of Time-Life Books. Time-Life Bks. [1968 c1966] 200p illus maps (Life Nature lib) lib. bdg. $7.60
                                         574.9
1 Natural history—North America 2 Natural resources—North America 3 Wild life—Conservation
First published 1964
Title on spine: North America
An account of the mammals and birds that were the original endowment of the continent, of the history of how some have vanished and . . . of the efforts being made to preserve the vestiges of American wilderness that remain." p16
Text "and numerous captioned photographs, some in color, effectively portray the scope and variety of North America's landscape and wildlife. Appended is a bibliography and an annotated list of the principal national parks and national monuments in Canada and the U.S." Booklist

Krutch, Joseph Wood
The best nature writing of Joseph Wood Krutch; illus. by Lydia Rosier. Morrow 1970 384p illus $8.50   **574.9**
1 Natural history—U.S. 2 Nature
Title page date: 1969
"In this volume, the author has selected thirty-four essays he likes best from his nature writings of the past two decades. In them and his introduction, he discusses what our relationship is and what it ought to be to the natural world, particularly to those living creatures that inhabit the world with us." Book News
"A pleasant sampling that may serve to introduce new readers to his earlier works." Booklist

Maxwell, Gavin
Ring of bright water. Dutton [1961 c1960] 211p illus $6.95   **574.9**
1 Natural history—Scotland 2 Otters
First published 1960 in England
The author describes his life in a lonely cottage on the northwest coast of Scotland. "He tells of the sea and the seashore, of the coming of spring, and the bird, animal and fish migrations that the changing seasons bring, and of the creatures of the sea that he observes from his doorstep. . . . But the hero and heroine of the book are by all odds Maxwell's incomparable otters, Mijbil and Edal." Publisher's note

Maxwell, Gavin—*Continued*

"What emerges from the book is not only an intimate study of the semidomesticated otter and of the wild life of the remoter Highlands but also a self portrait of an animal lover of some integrity. . . . Mr Maxwell stands out for his ability to treat an otter as a creature in its own right and not as though it were some eccentric or inadequate human being. He writes with enthusiasm, and it makes, with some excellent photographs, an enchanting and original story." Guardian

Peterson, Roger Tory

Wild America. . . . By Roger Tory Peterson and James Fisher; illus. by Roger Tory Peterson. Houghton 1955 434p illus maps $7.95   **574.9**

1 Natural history—North America 2 North America—Description and travel

"The record of a 30,000-mile journey around the continent by a distinguished naturalist and his British colleague." Subtitle

The authors, an American naturalist and an English ornithologist, have recorded their observations of the birds and other wild life, as well as the natural wonders of the North American continent, taken on a journey from Newfoundland southward to Florida, then west to Mexico, and north to California and Alaska. (Publisher)

"A bountiful book both in text and illustrations, the latter superb examples of Mr. Peterson's scratchboard art. It is a long book but not too long. The reader ends with the feeling of having been one of the party, of having joined two fortunate naturalists during great days of their lives." N Y Times Bk R

Sanderson, Ivan T.

The continent we live on; photographs by Eliot Porter [and others]. Random House 1961 299p illus maps boards $20   **574.9**

1 Natural history—North America

"A Chanticleer Press edition"

"The land, waters, flora, fauna, and bird life of Canada, the U.S., and Mexico are graphically described. . . . Devoting a chapter to each of the 21 'natural provinces' [the author] concentrates on the most remarkable aspects of each area." Booklist

"Both the black and whites and the colored [photographs] are beautifully rendered and the selections fresh and unconventional. . . . This is the kind of conservation argument that is most effective." Library J

Glossary: p293

Teale, Edwin Way

Autumn across America. . . . Dodd 1956 386p illus (The American seasons) $6.95   **574.9**

1 Natural history—U.S. 2 Autumn

Companion volume to: North with the spring, entered below

"A naturalist's record of a 20,000-mile journey through the North American autumn. With photographs by the author." Subtitle

"The harbingers of fall and the autumnal birds and animals, trees and flowers are vividly described as are the larger vistas of mountain, ocean, plain, and forest. The quiet, frequently poetic, prose reflects not only the author's scientific curiosity but his love of the delightfully varied world of nature." Booklist

Map on lining-papers

Journey into summer. . . . With photographs by the author. Dodd 1960 366p illus (The American seasons) $6.95   **574.9**

1 Natural history—U.S. 2 Summer

"A naturalist's record of a 19,000-mile journey through the North American summer." Subtitle

The third book in the author's series on the American seasons "takes the reader through twenty-six states from New England to the Rocky Mountains. Mayflowers and prairie dogs, ladyslippers and woodpeckers, falling stars and fossil dragonflies—all are described." Cincinnati

"A most pleasurable and joyful journey through a vast variety of scenery and wild life. . . . Teale's prose is smooth and flowing as always." Pub W

Map on lining-papers

North with the spring. . . . Illus. with photographs by the author. Dodd 1951 366p illus (The American seasons) $6.95   **574.9**

1 Natural history—U.S. 2 Spring

Analyzed in Essay and general literature index

First, chronologically, in the authors' series: The American seasons

"A naturalist's record of a 17,000-mile journey with the North-American spring." Subtitle

Starting in the vast Everglades, where the seasons overlap and spring begins for the United States, the author and his wife traveled through 23 states for 130 days. The story of their adventures forms a natural history of the spring, a biography of the world's favorite season

"Written beautifully, and written out of a wide knowledge of nature. . . . More, it is superbly illustrated with photographs." Sat R

Map on lining-papers

Wandering through winter. . . . With photographs by the author. Dodd 1965 xx, 370p illus (The American seasons) $6.95   **574.9**

1 Natural history—U.S. 2 Winter

The Pulitzer Prize for nonfiction, 1965

The fourth book in the author's series: The American seasons

"A naturalist's record of a 20,000-mile journey through the North American winter." Subtitle

"Whooping cranes, migrating whales, the eagles of a Mississippi ice jam and the other myriad faces of winter in North America are arrestingly presented. . . . [Mr Teale begins his] tour in Southern California and travels through plains, mountains and deserts to snowbound Caribou, Maine." Huntting

"Edwin Teale has a way of making you want to watch, of making you glad you are alive, making you itch to fill the tank and retrace the routes he followed." Best Sellers

Maps on lining-papers

Thoreau, Henry David

America the beautiful; in the words of Henry David Thoreau, by the editors of Country Beautiful. Editorial direction: Michael P. Dineen; ed. by Robert L. Polley; art direction: Robert W. Pradt. Published by Country Beautiful Foundation: in association with Morrow 1966 97p illus boards $7.95   **574.9**

1 Natural history—U.S. 2 United States

"Thoreau's prose and poetry about the beauty of the American land, its wildlife and his reflections on the relationship of man and nature. Included are excerpts from his classic, 'Walden,' as well as lesser known works, 'Cape Cod,' 'A Week on the Concord and Merrimack Rivers' and 'The Maine Woods.' Many selections are from his famous journal, which he kept for most of his adult life. . . . Brilliantly illustrated with over 50 color photographs and many others in monochrome." Publisher's note

574.92   Marine biology

Amos, William H.

The life of the pond. Published in cooperation with The World Book Encyclopedia. McGraw 1967 232p illus (Our living world of nature) boards $4.95   **574.92**

1 Fresh-water biology 2 Ecology

"Produced with the cooperation of The United States Department of the Interior." Preceding title page

Amos, William H.—*Continued*

This book describes how "living things flourish in the constantly changing pond environment, and how these plants and animals have developed remarkable characteristics that ideally suit them to fresh-water life. . . . [Full-color, black-and-white, and duotone photographs, plus line drawings, show the] variety . . . from predatory birds and fish to delicate insects and strange creatures that burrow in the bottom mud." Publisher's note

Glossary: p222-26. Bibliography: p227

Carson, Rachel

The edge of the sea; with illus. by Bob Hines. Houghton 1955 276p illus $5.95
574.92

1 Marine biology

"The seashores of the world may be divided into three basic types: the rugged shores of rock, the sand beaches, and the coral reefs and all their associated features. Each has its typical community of plants and animals. The Atlantic coast of the United States [provides] clear examples of each of these types. I have chosen it as the setting for my pictures of shore life." Preface

"It is a truly extraordinary world which Miss Carson vividly unfolds to us and which is admirably illustrated in Bob Hines' drawings; a world full of marvels such as the tiny periwinkle, which has 3500 teeth, and the sea pansy which has responded to the struggle for survival by turning itself from an individual into a colony." Atlantic

"Again author Carson has shown her remarkable talent for catching the life breath of science on the still glass of poetry." Time

Classification: p251-70

575 Organic evolution

Huxley, Thomas Henry

On a piece of chalk; ed. & with an introduction & notes by Loren Eiseley; drawings by Rudolf Freund. Scribner 1967 90p illus $6.95
575

1 Evolution

"First delivered in 1868 as a lecture to the working men of Norwich during the meeting of the British Association for the Advancement of Science." Introduction

The author uses the role of minute animals in forming the chalk beds of Europe and North Africa as a basis for a lesson in evolution

This work "itself is a scientific and literary gem. Loren Eiseley's introduction which provides a warm personal insight into the man Huxley and his contemporaries is equally beautiful. Eiseley also has provided helpful explanatory notes for the text and a bibliography." Science Bks

Moore, Ruth

Evolution, by Ruth Moore and the editors of Time-Life Books. Time-Life Bks. [1968 c1964] 192p illus (Life Nature lib) lib. bdg. $7.60
575

1 Evolution

First published 1962

"An oversize book, profusely illustrated with drawings, reproductions, diagrams, and photographs; some of the photographic illustrations in full color are superb. The text discusses all aspects of evolution, giving some of the development of theories on evolution and genetics, with a good section on DNA. The arrangement of chapters is somewhat arbitrary, but this is easily compensated for by an excellent and extensive index. A divided bibliography is also appended." Chicago. Children's Book Center

575.1 Genetics

Asimov, Isaac

The genetic code. Orion 1962 187p illus boards $4.50
575.1

1 Genetics 2 Biochemistry 3 Cells

The author explains the story of the breakthrough in molecular biology which began with the discovery in 1944 of deoxyribonucleic acid or DNA. He explores the complex function of cell, chromosome, molecule, and protein, shows how the blueprint contained within the chromosome dictates the characteristics of an individual, and discusses the meaning of these developments and their implications for the future. (Publisher)

This is "popular science of a high caliber for intelligent nonscientists. . . . [And is] extremely well constructed and organized. . . . The book is not everything, however. It is short; sometimes it teases rather than satisfies. There is little mention in it of the people who have done the molecular unraveling; Asimov chooses brevity and the plain facts instead." Science

Beadle, George

The language of life; an introduction to the science of genetics, by George and Muriel Beadle. Doubleday 1966 242p illus $5.95
575.1

1 Genetics

A book "about genes, chromosomes, viruses, nucleic acids, DNA, RNA, and about the transmission of genetic information from generation to generation." Bk Buyer's Guide

An "authoritative book on genetics; written with only the necessary minimum of scientific terminology and illustrated with diagrams that are carefully labelled and placed. . . . The authors give enough background information and scientific history to place research and discovery in genetics in perspective in relation to the state of scientific knowledge." Chicago. Children's Book Center

Bibliographical footnotes

Fried, John J.

The mystery of heredity; foreword by Norton Zinder. Day 1971 180p illus (The Frontiers of science ser) $6.95
575.1

1 Genetics

"An authoritative, lucidly written history and explanation of one of the most difficult of disciplines, the science of genetics. Persistent readers with any bent at all toward this fascinating subject will find John Fried's book rewarding. He ranges from the trail-blazing work of Mendel to the astonishing exploratory work in today's laboratories." Pub W

Scheinfeld, Amram

Your heredity and environment; assisted in research and editing by Herbert L. Cooper and by others herein mentioned; illus. by the author. Lippincott 1965 xxiv, 830p illus $16.95
575.1

1 Heredity

First published 1939 with title: You and heredity, revised 1950 with title: The New You and heredity

The author communicates to "students and non-specialist adults the essential facts of human embryology, genetics, heredity, and eugenics. . . . [The bibliography is] keyed to the various chapters of the book—a great asset to the reader. Well-indexed." Science Bks

"The title indicates the attention in the text to reexamining some social problems such as delinquency and drug addiction from the standpoint of contributory genetic predispositions." Booklist

Glossary: p731

Scientific American

Facets of genetics; readings from Scientific American; selected and introduced by Adrian M. Srb, Ray D. Owen [and] Robert S. Edgar. Freeman 1970 354p illus $10

575.1

1 Genetics
SBN 7167-0950-3

This compilation of reprinted articles "covering the last 20 years emphasizes molecular, biochemical, bacterial, and viral genetics." Choice

"The well-selected papers are conveniently organized into five chapters, each with an introduction. . . . Although limited in scope by restriction to material previously published in Scientific American, this volume represents a readable survey of the recent advances in genetics and it should prove useful to those wishing an introduction to the field." Library J

Biographical notes and bibliographies: p353-65

576   Microbiology

Anderson, M. D.

Through the microscope; science probes an unseen world. Natural Hist. Press [distributed by Doubleday] 1965 155p illus (Nature and science lib) $5.95

576

1 Microbiology 2 Microscope and microscopy

"Published for the American Museum of Natural History"

Partial contents: The microscope and how it works; Every living cell comes from a cell; Microbes at work; Microbes harmful to man; Microbes useful to man; The viruses; Inside the cell

"The writing is clear and crisp. The illustrations, many in color, are interesting and descriptive of the text." The AAAS Science Book List

577   General properties of living matter

Taylor, Gordon Rattray

The biological time bomb. World Pub. 1968 240p $6.95

577

1 Life (Biology) 2 Biology—Research 3 Medicine—Research

"An NAL book"

The author discusses some of the new biological discoveries that may revolutionize human life in the near future. (Publisher)

Contents: Where are biologists taking us; Is sex necessary; The modified man; Is death necessary; New minds for old; The genetic engineers; Can we create life; The future, if any

"A well written, popular science book on new discoveries and the about-to-be discovered phenomena in the field of modern biology. Although easy reading, the text is very interesting and contains a great amount of established biological fact." Choice

578   Microscopes and microscopy

Gray, Peter

Handbook of basic microtechnique. 3d ed. McGraw 1964 302p illus (McGraw-Hill Publications in the biological sciences) $9.95

578

1 Microscope and microscopy

First published 1952 in England

"Gives information on the use of the microscope and the preparation of slides, and shows examples of slide making." A Basic Book Collection for High Schools

579   Taxidermy

Grantz, Gerald J.

Home book of taxidermy and tanning. Stackpole Bks. 1969 160p illus $7.95   579

1 Taxidermy 2 Tanning
SBN 8177-0805-5

"The art of preparing animal mounts is covered in this book. . . . It is a well-rounded treatment of taxidermy methods, with tips and tricks which will help the beginner gain the confidence and skill necessary for a good job. Separate chapters deal with tools of the trade, the preparation of fish, birds, small and large mammals, and study skins. The last two chapters present an introduction to tanning. A listing of taxidermy supply sources and tanning services is provided." Science Bks

Glossary of terms: p154-58

581   Botany

Farb, Peter

The forest, by Peter Farb and the editors of Time-Life Books. Time-Life Bks. [1967 c1963] 192p illus (Life Nature lib) lib. bdg. $7.60   581

1 Botany—Ecology 2 Forests and forestry 3 Natural history

First published 1961

This book presents "the concept of the forest as a community of living things whose lives are inextricably intertwined with one another and bound to their physical environment." Introduction

Some of the topics covered are the cycle of the seasons, fossil records, tree structure, plant and animal life, types of forests, lumbering

"The writing is eloquent, often poetic, yet free from sentimentality. . . . The writers politely dismiss old folklore about forest plants and animals and replace it with the latest scientific data." N Y Times Bk R

Bibliography: p183. A key to tree recognition: p184-88

Harlow, William M.

Patterns of life; prologue by Paul B. Sears. Harper 1966 128p illus $6.95   581

1 Botany—Pictures, illustrations, etc.

At head of title: The unseen world of plants

"A collection of over 80 black-and-white photographs of buds, twigs, leaves, and flowers as seen through a magnifying lens." Pub W

"The pictures on the following pages not only reveal beauty of structure but in many cases show how plants respond or adapt to their environment, not only during the lifetime of the individual plant but also over millions of years. These plant patterns . . . may provide students, designers, and others with new and exciting departures for creative expression." Preface

Hylander, Clarence J.

The world of plant life. 2d ed. Macmillan (N Y) 1956 653p illus $12.95   581

1 Botany

First published 1939

"Written to familiarize the layman with some of the interesting native and introduced plants in the United States. The material is presented with a minimum of scientific terminology; it gives the distribution, habits, uses, and structures of many types of plants from bacteria to orchids." Booklist

"This is not only a general reading book; it also contains aids in the identification of and important information on plant evolution, morphology, and physiology." The AAAS Science Book List for Young Adults

The **Oxford** Book of food plants; illus. by B. E. Nicholson; text by S. G. Harrison, G. B. Masefield [and] Michael Wallis. Oxford [1970 c1969] 206p illus $11   581
1 Plants, Edible
Title page date: 1969
"The authors have organized the text into origin, domestication, geographical distribution, botany and nutritional contribution of more than 400 plant varieties nourishing humans. A botanical glossary and an index serve as bonus. The nineteen classifications include grain, sugar, oil, beverage, salad and tropical root crops, nuts, legumes, fruits, fruit vegetables, spices and flavorings, herbs, leaf, stem, inflorescence, bulb, and root vegetables, sago and sugar palms, seaweeds, mushrooms, truffles, exotic water plants and wild British food plants. The illustrations by B .E. Nicholson elevate the quality of the text to superior rating. From seedlings through the flowering stage to maturity, the drawings note details valuable to both learner and teacher." Science Bks

Scientific American
Plant agriculture; readings from Scientific American; selected and introduced by Jules Janick [and others]. Freeman 1970 246p illus maps $10   581
1 Botany 2 Botany, Economic 3 Plant physiology
SBN 7167-0996-1
"Articles from 'Scientific American' dealing with the origins of agriculture, the physiology of plants, environmental requirements, the technology of crop production, and the world food problem. Noteworthy for their timely significance are pieces on pesticides, mechanical harvesting, human population, and new methods of increasing food production." Booklist
"Students of crop plants and general botany will find this anthology of carefully selected . . . articles a means of exploring and amplifying a wide variety of pertinent subject areas." Choice
Biographical notes and bibliographies: p233-41

Sears, Paul B.
Lands beyond the forest; illus. by Stanley Wyatt. Prentice-Hall 1969 206p illus $7.95   581
1 Natural history 2 Grasses 3 Botany—Ecology
"Ostensibly an ecological study of non-forest areas this book is so much more than just a study of plant and animal communities. Sears has produced a study of ecology, anthropology, evolution, history, and economics. No aspect of the land has been omitted. . . . The pictures are beautiful, though much is lost in black and white that would be overwhelming in color. Stanley Wyatt's illustrations are pleasant. The index is excellent." Science Bks

Went, Frits W.
The plants, by Frits W. Went and the editors of Life. Time, inc. 1963 194p illus (Life Nature lib) lib. bdg. $7.60   581
1 Botany
In this book "the author discusses the diversity of the plant kingdom, evolution and classification, photosynthesis, growth factors, symbiosis, plant oddities, man's use of plants, and many aspects of botanical experimentation. An illustrated 5-page guide to the plant kingdom is appended, as are a bibliography (with paperback editions noted) and a good relative index." Chicago. Children's Book Center

Zim, Herbert S.
Plants; a guide to plant hobbies; illus. by John W. Brainerd. Harcourt 1947 398p illus $5.25   581
1 Botany 2 Plants—Collection and preservation

"After giving a clear picture of the plant world—its classification and identification—Dr Zim makes a survey of practical hobbies in the plant kingdom, and shows how, with simple equipment, there are many things an amateur can do, whether he lives in the country or in the city. An important feature of the book is a geographical list of places in the United States which are of particular interest to the plant enthusiast." Huntting
Bibliography at end of each chapter

582 Toxonomic botany
Seed-bearing plants

Gray, Asa
Gray's Manual of botany . . . . 8th (centennial) ed. Largely rewritten and expanded by Merritt Lyndon Fernald; with assistance of specialists in some groups. Am. Bk. 1950 lxiv, 1632p illus $24.95   582
1 Botany
First published 1848
"A handbook of the flowering plants and ferns of the central and northeastern United States and adjacent Canada." Subtitle
This standard reference work "includes all the changes in our knowledge of plants and in the requirements of the International Rules of Botanical Nomenclature since the last edition 42 years ago." Pub W

Kieran, John
An introduction to wild flowers; illus. by Tabea Hofmann. Doubleday 1965 77p illus $4.50   582
1 Wild flowers
First published 1952 by Hanover House
"One hundred of the most common wild flowers of this country and Canada are described. . . . They are presented in the order of their blooming and there is information on where each plant is likely to be found, its growth characteristics, and the length of its blooming season." Huntting

The **Macmillan** Wild flower book; descriptive text by Clarence J. Hylander; illus. by Edith Farrington Johnston. Macmillan (N Y) 1954 480p illus $12.95   582
1 Wild flowers
In this comprehensive guide "the plants described cover the region from the East Coast to the Rockies and often beyond, and from Florida to Southern Canada, with a number in Alaska and Labrador. Information on each plant includes the botanical name, the common name, a description of size and general appearance, location or type of environment, where it can be grown, and the exact geographical area where it grows." Publisher's note
"Outstandingly beautiful colored illustrations. . . . While too cumbersome for use in the field, it is . . . . useful in the library or at home." The AAAS Science Book List for Children

Peterson, Roger Tory
A field guide to wildflowers of northeastern and north-central North America, by Roger Tory Peterson and Margaret McKenny; a visual approach arranged by color, form, and detail; illus. by Roger Tory Peterson. Houghton 1968 xxviii, 420p illus map $5.95   582
1 Wild flowers
"The Peterson Field guide series"
"Almost 1300 species of herbaceous plants and a few showy flowering shrubs and woody vines are included. The family to which each

Peterson, Roger T.—*Continued*

species belongs is recognized at a glance by means of a symbol placed alongside the family name in the text. At the front of the book each symbol is linked to a brief and nontechnical description of each of the 84 families represented. Through this method association of symbol and family the user of the book soon learns to categorize the families of most flowers." Publisher's note

"The authors of this compact book have succeeded in preparing an excellent guide. . . . The book is for those interested in the out-of-doors, but who are not professional biologists. The material is accurate and the authors have used only a small number of technical terms." Science Bks

Glossary: p xiii-xiv

Petrides, George A.

A field guide to trees and shrubs. . . . Illus. by George A. Petrides (leaf and twig plates) [and] Roger Tory Peterson (flowers, fruits, silhouettes) Houghton 1958 xxix, 431p illus $5.95   582

1 Trees—North America 2 Shrubs 3 Climbing plants

"The Peterson Field guide series"

"Field marks of all trees, shrubs, and woody vines that grow wild in the northeastern and north-central United States and in southeastern and south-central Canada." Title page

Follows the Peterson system of identification which emphasizes visual differences between species. Information on individual species includes growth habits, environment and uses by man and animals

"Terminology is made fairly simple, for the layman. An especially valuable feature is keys to winter identification." Pub W

Platt, Rutherford

Discover American trees. . . . With drawings by Margaret L. Cosgrove; photographs by the author. Dodd 1968 256p illus $4.50
582

1 Trees—U.S.

"A revised edition of the book originally published [1952] as American trees." Title page

This book aims at giving the name of every tree to be seen in every part of the United States, including the Southwestern deserts, and the heritage of ancient trees along the California coast. The trees are grouped according to the areas in which they grow

A guide to the quick identification of trees: p231-42. Index lists popular as well as Latin names

Preston, Richard J.

North American trees (exclusive of Mexico and tropical United States) [by] Richard J. Preston, Jr. . . . [2d ed] Iowa State Univ. Press 1961 xxxii, 395p illus maps $4.50 582

1 Trees—North America

First published 1948

"A handbook designed for field use, with plates and distribution maps." Title page

"135 genera containing 568 species are treated. Drawings showing descriptive characters, distribution maps, and concise descriptions of botanical and silvical characters have been included for 232 species of trees. . . . An additional 336 less important species are either briefly described or included in the complete keys." Preface

Glossary: p373-81

586 Seedless plants

The **Oxford** Book of flowerless plants; ferns, fungi, mosses and liverworts, lichens, and seaweeds; illus. by B. E. Nicholson; text by Frank H. Brightman. Oxford [1967] 1966 208p illus $10.50   586

1 Plants

First published 1966 in England

The book contains descriptions, with color pictures on facing pages, of plants found in England. "Arrangement is by the natural localities in which the plants grow. . . . Plant names are in Latin, with some common names in parenthesis. The index is by Latin and common names." Pub W

Suggestions for further reading: p201

587 Ferns

Cobb, Boughton

A field guide to the ferns and their related families of northeastern and central North America; with a section on species also found in the British Isles and western Europe; illus. by Laura Louise Foster. Houghton 1956 281p illus $5.95   587

1 Ferns

"The Peterson Field guide series"

All the species are illustrated with drawings of the full plant as well as detailed sketches of spore cases, leaf patterns and other points of identification. Included also are descriptions of the morphology and life cycle of a fern, a cross reference key to closely related species in Europe and a bibliography. (Publisher)

"Clear enough for the beginning naturalists, full enough for the professional biologist. . . . The Peterson system of visual identification is used." Pub W

589 Molds. Mushrooms

Christensen, Clyde M.

The molds and man; an introduction to the fungi. [3d ed. rev] Univ. of Minn. Press 1965 284p illus $6   589

1 Fungi

First published 1951

"A layman's introduction to the biology of the fungi, to their role as parasites of various plants and animals, and to their destructive role in stored foods, in building materials, and in textiles. . . . For students and biology teachers there is [a] . . . chapter on experiments with fungi, sources of culture materials and laboratory equipment, and references. The final chapter is devoted to a summary classification of fungi." Science Bks

Bibliography at the end of each chapter

Kavaler, Lucy

Mushrooms, molds, and miracles; the strange realm of fungi. Day 1965 318p illus $7.50   589

1 Fungi 2 Mushrooms 3 Molds (Botany)

The author describes the vast number and diversity of fungi: the mushrooms, mildews, yeasts and molds, and tells "how fungi make survival possible for all life on earth and their strangely complex role in destruction and healing and nutrition." Bk Buyer's Guide

"Often entertaining as well as informative, this is excellent science writing for the layman: informal without being popularized. The material is well-organized and the subject is handled authoritatively. . . . One of these, a chapter on LSD and other psychedelic drugs, is particularly good, and objective and quite full report. An extensive bibliography and a good index are appended." Chicago. Children's Book Center

590 Zoological sciences

Ley, Willy

Dawn of zoology. Prentice-Hall 1968 280p illus $7.95   590

1 Zoology—History 2 Naturalists

The author discusses "the landmarks in the literature of zoology, beginning with early folklore and ending with the publication of the

Ley, Willy—_Continued_

theories of Darwin and Spencer. He presents [an] . . . analysis of the works, giving background data on the authors and the conditions under which their books were written." Library J

"Well illustrated and informative, this is an ideal source for young people of up-to-date information about the whole animal world." Huntting

Bibliography included in Notes: p255-76

590.74 Zoological gardens

Kirchshofer, Rosl

(ed.) The world of zoos; a survey and gazetteer; introduction by Bernhard Grzimek. Viking [1968 c1966] 327p illus $12.95
590.74

1 Zoological gardens

Original German edition, 1966. Translated by Hilda Morris

"A collection of ten essays by various authors, each a recognized authority dealing with the theory and philosophy of modern zookeeping, aquarium management, animal trade, veterinary medicine, etc. The second section is a survey of zoological gardens and public aquariums throughout the world with descriptive details and other information for prospective visitors. Outstanding illustrations, some in color." AAAS Science Book List

591 Zoology

Ardrey, Robert

The territorial imperative; a personal inquiry into the animal origins of property and nations; drawings by Berdine Ardrey. Atheneum Pubs. 1966 390p illus $9.95 **591**

1 Animals—Habits and behavior 2 Behaviorism (Psychology) 3 Instinct

"A territory is an area of space which an animal guards as its exclusive possession and which it will defend against all members of its kind. . . . [The author presents] scientific observations of this form of behavior, and demonstrates that man obeys the same laws as . . . many another animal species." Publisher's note

The author "discusses with much insight what he considers to be the dominant, and to him, unsound teaching of American cultural anthropology. He is especially critical of the idea that human behavior is not dependent on instinct or other genetic determination, but only on learned ways of life that are derived from 'culture.' There are some gaps in the scientific argument of the book, but its thesis is worthy of serious consideration." Science Bks

Bibliography: p361-73

Burton, Robert

Animal senses. Taplinger 1970 183p illus $7.95 **591**

1 Animals—Habits and behavior 2 Senses and sensation
SBN 8008-0260-8

"How animals use their senses to regulate their lives and relate to their environment is explained and the sense organs of a variety of species are described. . . . In the discussion of animal senses, including both the familiar five and the temperature sense, detection of electrical fields, animal solar systems, and orientation and migration mechanisms, the problems and limitations of experimenting with animals are emphasized and the gaps in current knowledge concerning their sense organs are pointed out. Illustrations include photographs and diagrams, and a bibliography of scientific material is appended." Booklist

Durrell, Gerald

Two in the bush; illus. by B. L. Driscoll. Viking 1966 255p illus $5.95 **591**

1 Rare animals 2 Zoology 3 Wild life—Conservation

The author describes his adventures with strange birds, animals, and reptiles on a 45,000 mile trip through New Zealand, Australia, and Malaya. He also discusses what is being done in these countries to protect such exotic creatures as the three-eyed lizard, the lyrebird, and leadbeater's possum. (Publisher)

"The book is made amusing and fascinating by Durrell's enthralled enjoyment of the birds and animals, his gift for the vivid phrase or analogy that perfectly sums up a wild creature, and his descriptions of the weird, hilarious mishaps of cameramen and scientists stalking elusive wild creatures." Pub W

Durrell, Jacquie

Beasts in my bed; with footnotes by Gerald Durrell. Atheneum Pubs. 1967 178p illus boards $4.95 **591**

1 Animals—Habits and behavior 2 Durrell, Gerald Malcolm

The author tells of life with her animal-collecting husband, Gerald Durrell, and of adventures with animals from anteater to gorilla

The book "has the same entertaining liveness as [her husband's] books . . . Mrs. Durrell is naturally very much involved with the animals, and fond of them, but her book is much more an account of daily problems of life, travel, visas, and money than it is an animal book." Pub W

The **Larousse** Encyclopedia of animal life; foreword by Robert Cushman Murphy. McGraw 1967 640p illus $25 **591**

1 Zoology

Based in part on the title by Léon Bertin published 1949 in France

"A handsomely-printed, well-illustrated volume, with entries arranged in taxonomic sequence. Classes, order, and families are briefly and clearly described, with pertinent data on reproduction, nutrition, physiology, and behavior. An immense amount of useful information is offered in highly organized and readable form. . . . There are high quality color plates and good black-and-white photographs, and occasional diagrams are inserted appropriately throughout the text." Science Bks

Glossary: p618-20. Further reading list: p621-22

Lorenz, Konrad Z.

King Solomon's ring; new light on animal ways; illus. by the author and with a foreword by Julian Huxley. Crowell 1952 202p illus $6.95 **591**

1 Animals—Habits and behavior

Translated from the German by Marjorie Kerr Wilson

The author "feels that animals inhibited by confining chains and pens will not reveal their true, full and free nature. Here are the findings through the application of his 'inverse cage principle' which allows his pets the freedom of his household." McClurg. Book News

"Blending scientific observation with skillful presentation, a distinguished naturalist describes the 'private lives' of birds, animals and fishes. Merry drawings by the author. Index." Bookmark

Murie, Olaus J.

A field guide to animal tracks; illus. by the author. Houghton 1954 xxii, 374p illus $5.95 **591**

1 Animals—Habits and behavior 2 Tracking and trailing

"The Peterson Field guide series"

This handbook includes "drawings of the tracks and droppings of North and Central American mammals and some 30 birds, some reptiles, and a few insects. Each animal is sketched, in addition, and some of its charisteristic habits are described." Pub W

Bibliography: p359-67. Key to tracks: p xiii-xvii

Orr, Robert T.
Animals in migration. Macmillan (N Y)
1970 303p illus maps $12.50   **591**
1 Animals—Migration
"A comprehensive, up-to-date account of
the movements—great and small and often
tragic—that stir the populations of the animal
world. Whereas most previous books on this
subject have been confined to the population
movements of a single class of organism, i.e.
insects, birds, fish—this text treats the basic
principles underlying all population movements." News of Bks
Bibliography: p271-88

Ricard, Matthieu
The mystery of animal migration. English
version by Peter J. Whitehead. Hill &
Wang 1969 209p illus maps $5.95   **591**
1 Animals—Migration 2 Birds—Migration
SBN 8090-7190-8
Original French edition, 1968
"Describes migratory patterns as observed
in mammals, birds, fishes, insects, amphibians,
and a few lesser known animal groups. The
emphasis is on bird migration, and such topics as orientation, physiology of flight and
influence of external conditions are considered.
The migration problem is approached from a
nontechnical point of view. . . . The book is
of value as an elementary introduction to the
fascinating topic of migration, and will lead
the reader to the more definitive works in the
field." Choice
Bibliography: p195-96

Silverberg, Robert
Forgotten by time: a book of living fossils; illus. by Leonard Everett Fisher.
Crowell 1966 215p illus $3.95   **591**
1 Rare animals 2 Plants
"Mr. Silverberg describes many of the unusual insects, fish, animals, and plants which
defy evolution. He provides a clear description and the history of each 'living fossil,' as
well as the story behind its discovery in modern times. Oddities such as the duck-billed
platypus, the cockroach, the two-toed and
three-toed sloth, the ginkgo tree, and many
others are included." Publisher's note
"The book is readable. . . . Some of the historical notes are of interest. However, in making the book readable, the author has simplified . . . at the cost of accuracy." Science Bks
For further reading: p204-07

Tinbergen, Niko
Animal behavior, by Niko Tinbergen and
the editors of Time-Life Books. Time-Life
Bks. [1969 c1965] 200p illus (Life Nature
lib) lib. bdg. $7.60   **591**
1 Animals—Habits and behavior
First published 1965
"This survey of animal behavior studies begins with an historical study of the four pioneers Darwin, Fabre, C. Lloyd Morgan, and
Pavlov, then proceeds to review the work of
many contemporaries: Von Frisch on color
vision of bees; Schneirla on learning in ants;
Harlow on rhesus monkeys; and many others.
The major topics are sense organs, stimuli, the
machinery of behavior, instinct versus learning and evolution. A bibliography and an index complete this very useful survey of experimental psychology which will serve as an introduction to a diversified and increasingly
important field." Science Bks

591.92   Marine zoology

Bridges, William
The New York Aquarium Book of the
water world; a guide to representative fishes,
aquatic invertebrates, reptiles, birds, and
mammals. Published for the New York
Zoological Society [by] Am. Heritage Press
1970 287p illus $6.95   **591.92**
1 Marine animals 2 Fresh-water animals

"Although there are five sections . . . the
allotment of 200 pages to fish life makes the
book basically a guide to fishes. Filled with
hundreds of color plates, it is an extremely accurate reference work for the identification
of fish." Library J
This "guide to animals of the sea, rivers,
lakes, marshes, and swamps describes selected
species in concise, informative, lively paragraph. . . . For the zoology student or aquarium hobbyist." Booklist

Carson, Rachel
Under the sea-wind; a naturalist's picture
of ocean life. [New ed. with corrections]
Oxford 1952 [c1941] 314p illus $6.50   **591.92**
1 Marine animals
First published 1941 by Simon and Schuster
"In a series of narratives [the author] describes the life of the shore, the open sea, and
the sea bottom. Her portrait of the birds and
fishes that inhabit the eastern rim of our continent begins with the hush of a spring twilight along the North Carolina coast." Huntting
"A storyteller's gift with words and a scientist's observant eye distinguish these stories
of the sea and the creatures who live in it."
N Y Pub Lib
Glossary: p273-314

592   Invertebrates

Buchsbaum, Ralph
The lower animals; living invertebrates
of the world, by Ralph Buchsbaum and
Lorus J. Milne; in collaboration with Mar-
gery Milne. . . . Doubleday [1960] 303p
illus (The World of nature ser) $14.95   **592**
1 Invertebrates
"A Chanticleer Press edition"
"With photographs by Ralph Buchsbaum,
Douglas P. W. Wilson, Fritz Goro, and others.
Line drawings by Kenneth Gosner." Title page
A natural history of the invertebrates excepting the insects "arranged systematically
group by group, proceeding from the primitive
forms to the most specialized ones." Preface
"The first half was written by Ralph and
Mildred Buchsbaum; the second half by Lorus
and Margery Milne. . . . [It gives] informa-
tion about all manner of creatures from fa-
miliar protozoans, jelly fishes, sea anemones,
crabs, and spiders. Striking illustrations." San
Francisco Chronicle
Bibliography: p291-92

593   Protozoa

Hall, Richard P.
Protozoa; the simplest of all animals.
Holt 1964 123p illus (Holt Lib. of science)
$2.50   **593**
1 Protozoa
The author "describes the ecology, variations, and many of the vital life processes of
these interesting animals." McClurg. Book
News
"Practical organization makes this book suitable for high school students: includes a classification of protozoans, glossary, [bibliography]
and numerous labeled drawings. The method
of presentation appears, however, to be typical
of textbook science series." Library J

594   Mollusca and molluscoidea

Morris, Percy A.
A field guide to shells of the Pacific Coast
and Hawaii; including shells of the Gulf of
California; illus. with photographs. 2d ed. rev.
and enl. Sponsored by the National Audubon
Society and National Wildlife Federation.
Houghton 1966 xxxiii, 297p illus $5.95   **594**
1 Shells 2 Mollusks
"The Peterson Field guide series"

Morris, Percy A.—*Continued*

Companion volume to: A field guide to the Atlantic and Gulf coasts, entered below
First published 1952
"The basic plan of the book is in three parts. The first part covers the marine shells occurring from Alaska to southern California, the range of some extending to Baja California and even to Panama; the second includes the Gulf of California, with some species that may be found as well on the Pacific coast of Baja California; and the third part deals with the shells of Hawaii. A total of 945 species are described and illustrated by one or more photographs." About this book
Both common and scientific names are given
Includes a glossary and a bibliography

A field guide to the shells of our Atlantic and Gulf Coasts. Rev. and enl. ed. Illus. with photographs. Houghton 1951 236p illus $5.95
594

1 Shells 2 Mollusks
"The Peterson Field guide series"
Companion volume to: A field guide to shells of the Pacific Coast and Hawaii, listed above
First published 1947 with title: Field guide to the shells of our Atlantic Coast
"A guide to all of the larger and more common species of the marine clams and snails found along the east coast from Labrador to Texas. Includes some of the minute, rare, and deep-water varieties. Gives shape, size, distribution, color, distinctive markings. The clear photographs in black and white or natural color refer to the descriptions of the individual species. Glossary of terms." Booklist
"A book to delight both the gatherer of sea shells and the conchologist. The illustrations, most of them in color, are outstandingly good and the descriptions of the shells are complete and lucid." Christian Science Monitor

595.7 Insects

Barker, Will

Familiar insects of America; illus. by Carl Burger; schematic drawings by Nancy Lloyd. Foreword by Hilary J. Deason. Harper 1960 236p illus boards $5.95, lib. bdg. $5.11
595.7

1 Insects
The author "describes the evolutionary development, reproduction, and influence on other living things of such insects as grasshoppers, crickets, katydids, butterflies, skippers, moths, ants, wasps, bees, and fleas. More interesting reading than field books, and should supplement them." A Basic Book Collection for High Schools
Glossary: p225-28 Suggested reading and references: p228-31

Borror, Donald J.

A field guide to the insects of America north of Mexico, by Donald J. Borror and Richard E. White; color and shaded drawings by Richard E. White; line drawings by the authors. Houghton 1970 404p illus $5.95
595.7

1 Insects
"The Peterson Field guide series"
The authors "have brought field identification of insects and museum study together in a book that will still fit in a pocket. . . . The item of most importance is simplified identification of the more common of the 88,000 species that have been identified in North America. Of great use is the chapter on the collecting and preserving of insects. Also useful is the chapter on observing insects in the field. Sufficient information on the structure of the insect is given. . . . The last part of the book consists of insect orders with descriptions of the order and the families in them. Of special use is the section of 16 color plates of the insects in the

middle of the book. Elsewhere are line drawings emphasizing the key characters by which the order is identified. . . . The guide is very well done for its intended use." Science Bks
Bibliography: p373-70

Callahan, Philip S.

Insect behavior; illus. and photographs by the author. Four Winds 1970 155p illus $4.95
595.7

1 Insects
"This book serves as a brief introduction to the complex field of insect behavior. There are chapters on environment, morphology, reproduction, feeding, migration, camouflage, habitats, flight, communication, and economic importance. The last chapter presents various projects for the beginner in studying insects and their behavior. A list of selected readings, a glossary, and an index are included. . . . The author's unproven theories on insect detection of various infrared and microwave frequencies as part of their behavior patterns and his experiments offer the reader interesting insight into the workings of science. Errors and misleading statements are generally of a minor nature." Science Bks

Insects and how they function; with illus. and photographs by the author. Holiday 1971 191p illus $4.95
595.7

1 Insects
ISBN 0-8234-0181-2
"Nature lovers of all ages will be rewarded by this small attractive volume if they have some interest in learning anything (or everything) about this largest group of animals in creation. With precision . . . the author tells about the anatomy and physiology, the strange life-cycles and unique adaptations of this amazing phylum. The book is enriched with many of the author's own illustrations, including some electron photomicrographs that would delight any photographer. The final chapter shows how we can all become amateur entomologists, explaining easy experiments that can be devised with simple equipment, using only the woods and fields for a laboratory." Best Sellers
Includes a bibliography

Chauvin, Rémy

The world of ants; a science-fiction universe; tr. by George Ordish. Hill & Wang [1971 c1970] 216p illus $5.95
595.7

1 Ants
ISBN 0-8090-9810-5
Original French edition, 1969
"An informative yet easily read account of the highly diversified, prolific ant covers all aspects of the insect's life and touches on its beneficial relationship to man. Accompanied by numerous diagrams and a few photographs the British study opens with information on major classifications of ant species followed by a chapter on habits of the familiar red ant. Other more or less likable ants, such as the African driver ant, are described fully with information on fungus cultivating ants, slave-making species, and others that store grain also included." Booklist

Evans, Howard E.

The wasps, by Howard E. Evans and Mary Jane West Eberhard; drawings by Sarah Landry. Univ. of Mich. Press 1970 265p illus $7.95
595.7

1 Wasps
ISBN 0-472-00118-3
"Both social and solitary wasps are included in the presentation. These are compared with ants, bees, and other insects. The place of the wasp as a predator is included and in turn the role as prey for other creatures is explored. The parasitic wasps are discussed as an ally of man. Of great interest is the finely attuned adaptation of the chalcid wasps to live inside of the small alfalfa seed. There are numerous photographs, line drawings, charts, and tables throughout to assist the reader in grasping the ideas presented. . . . It is a great book for the naturalist and the ecologist." Science Bks

Fabre, Henri

The insect world of J. Henri Fabre; with introduction and interpretive comments by Edwin Way Teale. Dodd 1949 333p $4

595.7

1 Insects

This "volume brings into the compass of a single book the most famous of Fabre's studies, many of them now out of print. In some instances, material has been shortened but nothing has been added." Foreword

"Fascinating insect stories of the celebrated naturalist selected by a foremost nature writer of today. For browsing or reference." Library J

Klots, Alexander B.

A field guide to the butterflies of North America, east of the Great Plains. . . . Houghton 1951 349p illus $5.95   595.7

1 Butterflies

"The Peterson Field guide series"

"Illustrated with color paintings of 247 species by Marjorie Statham and 232 photographs by Florence Longworth." Title page

Describes and tells the reader how to identify butterflies found east of the Great Plains from Greenland to Mexico; it tells about the habits, the range, the food plant of the caterpillar, the type of country in which the butterfly is likely to be found

This "natural history and field guide . . . deals also with life zones, ecology, principles of taxonomy, and geographic variation." The AAAS Science Book List for Young Adults

Bibliography: p301-08. Checklist of butterflies: p308-28

Lutz, Frank E.

Field book of insects of the United States and Canada, aiming to answer common questions. 3d ed. rewritten to include much additional material, with about 800 illus. many in color. Putnam 1935 510p illus (Putnam's Nature field bks) $5.75   595.7

1 Insects

First published 1918

"Describes all of the principal families, many genera, and most of the common species. . . . Condensed information on natural history of aerial, aquatic, and terrestrial insects." The AAAS Science Book List for Young Adults

"A most valuable handbook for younger as well as older amateur entomologists. It is comprehensive in scope . . . with innumerable illustrations including many coloured plates." Toronto

Maeterlinck, Maurice

The life of the bee; tr. by Alfred Sutro. Dodd 1913 427p $3   595.7

1 Bees

First published 1901

"An artist's study of bees in which philosophy, fancy, and natural history join to make a book of rare fascination." Pratt Alcove

Bibliography: p423-27

597 Fishes. Sharks

Burgess, Robert F.

The sharks. Doubleday 1970 159p illus $3.95   597

1 Sharks

"Despite the fact that the shark has existed for a far longer time than man, it has remained a very mysterious as well as terrifying animal. The author does a commendable job in trying to dispel some of the mystery. A list of some three dozen current references to shark literature further aids the treatment of the subject." Best Sellers

Cochran, Doris M.

Living amphibians of the world; with photographs by Robert S. Simmons, and others. Doubleday 1961 199p illus (The World of nature ser) $14.95   597

1 Amphibia 2 Frogs 3 Salamanders

"A Chanticleer Press edition"

Arranged by orders of amphibians, this book "presents understandable and informative material on caecilians, salamanders, frogs, and toads. The author . . . offers general remarks on some biological aspects of amphibians in a final section. . . . The text is supplemented by handsome photographs in black and white and in color." Booklist

Selected bibliography: p195

Cousteau, Jacques-Yves

The shark: splendid savage of the sea [by] Jacques-Yves Cousteau and Philippe Cousteau. Doubleday 1970 277p illus map (The Undersea discoveries of Jacques-Yves Cousteau) $7.95   597

1 Sharks

"Translated from the French by Francis Price." Verso of title page

The first of a projected six book series

A blend of narrative text and 124 color photographs describes the observations of underwater explorer Jacques-Yves Cousteau, his son Philippe and the crew of the "Calypso" during an expedition in which they conducted research on the life of the shark

"Outstanding for its photographs and very well translated from the French. . . . There is a table of contents, an introduction by Cousteau, Sr., appendices on photography, a variety of things from uses of shark skin to geological timetables, and an adequate index." Choice

Herald, Earl S.

Living fishes of the world; with photographs by Fritz Goro [and others]. Doubleday 1961 303p illus (The World of nature ser) $14.95   597

1 Fishes

"A Chanticleer Press edition"

In this survey, the world's fishes are classified by species and arranged in groups according to structure, i.e. jawless, cartilage, and bony fishes. The author covers such basic matters for each species as habits, range, feeding and life cycles. (Publisher)

"An effort was made to avoid going over material ably covered in many books on tropical fish, and more emphasis is placed on groups less often covered in popular works." Preface

"A handsome volume with many illustrations and interesting text." Ontario Lib Rev

Glossary: p293. Bibliography: p295-96

National Geographic Society

Wondrous world of fishes. New enl. ed. The Society 1969 373p illus (Natural science lib) $9.95   597

1 Fishes 2 Fishing

First published 1965

Editor and art director: Leonard J. Grant

Partial contents: Fishes and how they live, by L. P. Schultz; Angling in the United States, by L. Marden; Ice fishing's frigid charms, by T. J. Abercrombie; America's first park in the sea, by C. M. Brookfield; Florida meets a walking catfish, by C. P. Idyll; Aquarium fishes; enchanting entertainers, by T. Y. Canby; Gallery of sharks and Hawaiian fishes; Guide to fish cookery, by J. A. Beard

"Colorfully illustrated articles and underwater exploration in and around North America from Newfoundland to Hawaii." Reference Materials for School Libraries

Ommanney, F. D.

The fishes, by F. D. Ommanney and the editors of Time-Life Books. Time-Life Bks. 1970 192p illus map (Life Nature lib) lib. bdg. $7.60   **597**

1 Fishes

First published 1963

In this introduction to fish—their biology and commercial importance, "the drawings are good, the photographs—especially those in color—are superb, all of the illustrative material being fully captioned. The text is solid and serious. . . . Among the topics discussed are physiology and morphology, habits and habitat, reproduction and adaptation, patterns of hunting and spawning, migratory patterns, and the fishing industry around the world. Appended are an extensive relative index, a divided bibliography, and a list of fish names, alphabetized by common name, with the scientific name following." Chicago. Children's Book Center

"A skillful synthesis of separate articles. . . . More suited for reading adventures than reference work." The AAAS Science Book List for Young Adults

598 Birds

Audubon, John James

The birds of America; with a foreword and descriptive captions by William Vogt. Macmillan (N Y) 1953 [c1937] xxvi p 435 plates $12.50   **598**

1 Birds—North America 2 Birds—Pictures, illustrations, etc.

The 435 plates in this volume were originally published by Audubon, in London, during the years 1827-1838

"William Vogt has written an excellent introduction and a brief descriptive note for each plate. The names, both common and scientific, accompanying each plate, are those found in the 'Check-List' of the American ornithologists' union. Index is to common names only." Booklist

"The book is a remarkable combination of beauty and usefulness, in which every student of birds will rejoice." Scientific Bk Club R

Headstrom, Richard

A complete field guide to nests in the United States. . . . Washburn 1970 xlii, 451p illus $10   **598**

1 Birds—Eggs and nests 2 Animals—Habitations

"Including those of birds, mammals, insects, fishes, reptiles and amphibians." Subtitle

Based on the author's 'Birds' nests, and his Birds' nests of the West, first published 1949 and 1951 respectively

McNulty, Faith

The whooping crane; the bird that defies extinction; introduction by Stewart L. Udall. Dutton 1966 190p illus maps boards $5.95
598

1 Whooping cranes 2 Aransas National Wildlife Refuge 3 Birds—Protection

Winner of the Dutton Annual Book Award, 1966

A "history of the whooping crane, its habits and habitats, which traces the efforts made by many persons and agencies, both private and governmental, to save the crane from extinction by locating and protecting the northern nesting grounds and providing a safe sanctuary on the wintering grounds in [Aransas] Texas. The account covers the plight of both the remaining wild birds and the few living in captivity and makes a strong plea for the conservation of the species." Booklist

Mannix, Dan

The last eagle; illus. by Russell Peterson. McGraw 1966 149p illus $4.95   **598**

1 Bald eagle 2 Birds—Protection

The author follows the life of a "bald eagle from his birth through his growth, his training by his parents and by disappointing or jarring experience, and his maturity. The eagle spends most of his adult years around his nest on a midwestern farm." Pub W

"The author has a real social purpose in writing this novel of sorts, for the species is threatened with extinction in our country. . . . The diversified diet of the bald eagle permits a wide latitude of incidents and the author seems to have done a fine job of culling and integrating scientific particulars." Best Sellers

Includes bibliography

Milne, Lorus

North American birds, by Lorus and Margery Milne; paintings by Marie Nonnast Bohlen. Prentice-Hall 1969 340p illus $25
598

1 Birds—North America

SBN 13-623769-X

The volume depicts the birds in full-color painting "size-marked for readier identification. . . . After a chapter on the familiar birds come those of, respectively, the forest, grasslands, deserts, mountains, the Far North, inland waters, and the seashore." Sat R

"A truly beautiful book of birds that should prove irresistible to anyone with more than a casual interest in the subject. . . . The book is divided into habitats . . . and discusses migration habits, song, food and plumage. For some species this book may someday serve as a memorial rather than a guide, for the Milne's have included a notable number of endangered birds. Though the price of the volume is high, in this case, it is well worth it." Natur Hist

National Geographic Society

Song and garden birds of North America, by Alexander Wetmore and other eminent ornithologists; foreword by Melville Bell Grosvenor. The Society 1964 400p illus (Natural science lib) $11.95   **598**

1 Birds—North America 2 Birds—Pictures, illustrations, etc.

At head of title: 327 species portrayed in color and fully described

The major portion of the book consists of sections on the different "species—nearly all that breed north of Mexico. . . . [There are] 555 illustrations that show each bird to best advantage for identification. Where the female's plumage differs significantly from the male's, both sexes are portrayed." Preface

"There are also some general articles on families, and on subjects such as 'Courtship and Nesting Behavior.' A pocket inside the back cover contains a small album of 6 vinyl records presenting songs for 70 species." Library J

Map on lining-paper

Water, prey, and game birds of North America, by Alexander Wetmore and other eminent ornithologists; foreword by Melville Bell Grosvenor. The Society 1965 464p illus maps (Natural science lib) $11.95 **598**

1 Water birds 2 Birds of prey 3 Game and game birds

At head of title: 329 species portrayed in color and fully described

Life histories, breeding and feeding habits, range and characteristics of ducks, seabirds, hawks, geese, vultures and others. (Publisher)

Copiously illustrated. "Seven maps locate wildlife refuges and trace migration routes. The illustrated biographies of the many species . . . are organized in family groupings. The accounts combine humor and anecdotes with history." Publisher's note

Album of 6 vinyl records in pocket contains 97 bird sounds

Acknowledgments: p463

Peterson, Roger Tory
The birds, by Roger Tory Peterson and the editors of Time-Life Books. Time-Life Bks. 1968 192p illus (Life Nature lib) lib. bdg. $7.60   598
1 Birds 2 Birds—Pictures, illustrations, etc.

First published 1963
The author "discusses the evolution and existing orders of birds, their methods of flight, feeding habits, migration, songs and other means of communication, the bird census, bird development from egg to adult, and their relation to man. Profusely illustrated with excellent diagrams, sketches, and photographs in both black and white and in color. A bibliography classified by subject, is included." Booklist
"The writing of a well-known naturalist is enhanced by attractive artwork and superb color photography. Facts of natural history, anatomy and physiology are woven into the descriptive and informative text." The AAAS Science Book List for Children

A field guide to the birds; giving field marks of all species found east of the Rockies; text and illus. by Roger Tory Peterson. 2d rev. and enl. ed. Sponsored by the National Audubon Society. Houghton 1947 xxiv, 290p illus maps $5.95   598
1 Birds—North America

Companion volume to: A field guide to Western birds, listed below
First published 1934
A "guide to the field marks of Eastern birds, designed to help in identifying live birds at a distance. . . . The text gives field marks, such as range, habits, manner of flight, etc., that can not be pictured. In addition it mentions birds that might in any instance be confused with a given species." N Y Libraries
The book is "outstanding for its superior system of bird identification and style of writing." A Basic Book Collection for High Schools
Home reference suggestions: p273-74

A field guide to Western birds. . . . Text and illus. by Roger Tory Peterson. 2d ed. rev. and enl. Sponsored by the National Audubon Society and National Wildlife Federation. Houghton 1961 xxvi, 366p illus map $5.95   598
1 Birds—The West
"The Peterson Field guide series"
First published 1941
"Field marks of all species found in North America west of the 100th meridian, with a section on the birds of the Hawaiian Islands." Title page
"This compact but complete little work employs . . . [a] system of field identification based upon the characteristic features of the birds and facilitating quick recognition at a distance." Springf'd Republican

How to know the birds; an introduction to bird recognition. 2d ed. newly enl. and with 72 new full-color illus. by the author and more than 400 line drawings. Endorsed by the National Audubon Society. Houghton 1962 [c1957] 168p illus $3.95   598
1 Birds
First published 1949
Contents: Introducing the birds; What to look for: The families of birds; Habitats (Where to look for birds); Silhouettes of common birds
"A valuable orientation course which points out the short cuts—and which will in a few months enable the beginner to gain a background that would otherwise take him several years of trial and error to acquire." Huntting

Rue, Leonard Lee
Pictorial guide to the birds of North America; text and photographs by Leonard Lee Rue III. Crowell 1970 368p illus $12.50   598
1 Birds—North America

This guide to North American birds includes data on their appearance, habitat, the range of various orders and families of birds, migration and nesting habits as well as anecdotes based on bird myths and legends. (Publisher)
This "book is rich with factual data and the kind of observations that add dimension to any kind of scientific writing." Pub W
Bibliography and suggested reading: p361-63

Sparks, John
Owls: their natural and unnatural history [by] John Sparks and Tony Soper; illus. by Robert Gillmor. Taplinger 1970 206p illus $5.95   598
1 Owls
ISBN 0-8008-6170-1
The owl's anatomy, nocturnal adaptation, appearance, "habits of hunting, feeding, courting, nesting, and breeding are [described followed by a discussion] of owls in the wild, in captivity, and in folklore and mythology." Publisher's note
"A wide-ranging and scholarly account which will be enjoyed by the general reader as well as the naturalist." Times (London) Lit Sup
Reference sources: p198-201

598.1 Reptiles

Cochran, Doris M.
The new field book of reptiles and amphibians [by] Doris M. Cochran [and] Coleman J. Goin; more than 200 photographs and diagrams. Putnam 1970 359p illus $5.95
598.1
1 Reptiles 2 Amphibia
This is a guide to the identification of every known species of snake, lizard, alligator, crocodile, salamander, newt, turtle, frog and toad in the United States. It provides descriptions of their distinguishing characteristics, habits, geographical ranges, voices, mating habits, and habitat preferences as well as glossaries for each animal. (Publisher)
This volume is "beautifully and accurately illustrated with the use of 96 full-color photographs, 100 black-and-white photographs and six drawings. The text introduces each group of amphibians reptiles in a language which is easily read and understood by both laymen and scientists. . . . Accurately indexed. Handy size for field use." Choice
Selected references: p339

Conant, Roger
A field guide to reptiles and amphibians of the United States and Canada east of the 100th meridian; illus. by Isabelle Hunt Conant. Houghton 1958 366p illus maps $5.95
598.1
1 Reptiles 2 Amphibia
"The Peterson Field guide series"
An "authoritative guide to the species of turtles, crocodiles, alligators, lizards, snakes, salamanders, newts, frogs and toads in the area indicated in the title. Introductory notes on habitat, collection, transportation and care, as well as the appended glossary and bibliography, make it valuable to the amateur collector and natural history student." The AAAS Science Book List for Young Adults
Contains "over 1,100 illustrations, more than 400 of them in full color." Pub W

Ditmars, Raymond L.
The reptiles of North America. . . . 8 plates in color and more than 400 photographs from life. Doubleday 1936 476p illus $12.95
598.1
1 Reptiles
First published 1907
"A review of the crocodilians, lizards, snakes, turtles and tortoises inhabiting the United States and northern Mexico." Title page

Ditmars, Raymond L.—*Continued*

"While this work follows a scientific trend, the thought has been to simplify the identification of the North American reptiles, thus assisting the beginner in such studies and the reader seeking scattered points of information about reptile life." Introduction

"Although professionals consider the taxonomy out-of-date, the basic natural history information is reliable and very readable." The AAAS Science Book List for Young Adults

Bibliography: p451-53

Reptiles of the world; the crocodilians, lizards, snakes, turtles and tortoises of the eastern and western hemispheres. New rev. ed. . . . Macmillan (N Y) 1933 xx, 321p illus $8.50   598.1

1 Reptiles

First published 1910

"With a frontispiece and nearly 200 illustrations, from photographs taken by the author and from the files of the New York Zoological Society." Subtitle

"The scope of the book prevents it from being . . . primarily a volume intended to be used for identification purposes; it is here designed to consider the class of reptiles as a whole and in a general way. But for purposes of identification the profuse illustrations cannot fail to be serviceable in a high degree." Preface

The work is "comprehensive, well arranged, accurate and giving the information most in demand among ordinary readers." Booklist

Snakes of the world; with illus. from life. Macmillan (N Y) 1931 207p illus $7.50   598.1

1 Snakes

Although not intended as a guide to identification, this book provides a "general description of snakes with discussion of habits, and recital of personal experiences with [the reptiles]." Pittsburgh

The "book is as untechnical as is compatible with definite and exact information; yet, in the interest of the latter, it comprises and arranges a great deal of value and technical information expressed in necessarily technical terminology, principally as regards nomenclature. . . . The photogravures, beginning with the frontpiece of a pair of king cobras, are superlatively clear." N Y Times Bk R

Harrison, Hal H.

The world of the snake; with text and photographs by Hal H. Harrison; line drawings by Mada M. Harrison. Lippincott 1971 160p illus (Living world bks) boards $5.95, lib. bdg. $5.82   598.1

1 Snakes

The author deals with the species of snakes found in the United States and Canada. He "clears up a number of misconceptions about snakes and reveals a host of interesting facts as he discusses anatomy, reproduction, diet, defense mechanisms, and behavioral idiosyncracies." Publisher's note

Partial contents: Meet the snake; Nonpoisonous snakes; Poisonous snakes; Snake facts and fallacies; Snakes and men; A check list of the snakes of the United States and Canada; Bibliography

Stebbens, Robert C.

A field guide to Western reptiles and amphibians; field marks of all species in western North America; text and illus. by Robert C. Stebbins. Sponsored by the National Audubon Society and National Wildlife Federation. Houghton 1966 279p illus maps $4.95   598.1

1 Reptiles 2 Amphibia

"The Peterson Field guide series"

This book describes more than 200 species of salamanders, frogs, toads, turtles, lizards, and snakes. "Beginning with short chapters on collecting and keeping records, most of the text is devoted to brief descriptions of species,

with some ecological information. For each family there are several paragraphs of general information. Illustrations are in three major sections, the largest being an excellent center section of both colored and black-and-white plates. These are cross-referenced to the text. Other illustrations include range maps and characteristics of juvenile stages, including eggs and mouthparts. The book is best used by a person in the field for quick identification, or by a beginner for brief life history notes. Intended as a field guide, not as a text, it seems to serve its purpose admirably." Science Bks

Glossary: p217-21. References: p222-23

599 Mammals

Adamson, Joy

Born free; a lioness of two worlds. Pantheon Bks. 1960 220p illus map $6.95   599

1 Lions 2 Kenya Colony and Protectorate—Description and travel

This "is the story of how the author and her husband, warden of a Kenya game preserve, found a baby lioness, brought it up as a household pet and at last set it free [to roam the jungle]." Bk Buyer's Guide

"The stellar role in this real-life drama is played by [the] young lioness, Elsa. . . . This rambling, delightfully simple story has no real plot except the unique relationship between man and beast. As a study in animal psychology or an episodic tale of Africa, it appeals to most young adults as soon as they glance at the [many] photographs." Doors to More Mature Reading

The spotted sphinx. Harcourt 1969 313p illus $7.95   599

1 Cheetahs 2 Kenya—Description and travel

"A Helen and Kurt Wolff book"

In this work the author "recounts the trials and tribulations of taking an 8-month-old cheetah, Pippa, who has been house-trained and thoroughly petted and spoiled, and teaching her finally to fend for herself in the wilderness." Pub W

"The book is enhanced by excellent black-and-white and color photographs." Science Bks

Map on lining-papers

Andersen, Harald T.

(ed.) The biology of marine mammals. Academic Press 1969 511p illus $21.50   599

1 Mammals 2 Marine animals

"A distinguished group of active investigators in the biology of marine mammals have produced this book in which seven sections deal with physiological activities of marine mammals to bring out their marked differences from land mammals. Four additional sections deal with unique activities of marine mammals." AAAS Science Book List

Topics included are: Age determination of marine mammals; Deep diving; Temperature regulation in marine mammals; Marine mammal communication; Reproduction and reproductive organs

Includes bibliographies

Barbour, John A.

In the wake of the whale. Macmillan (N Y) 1969 102p illus lib. bdg. $3.95   599

1 Whales 2 Whaling

"Surveyor books"

"This well written account of the whales as a biological resource of great commercial value, and the over-exploitation of the most economically valuable species to the point of near extinction, is a needed addition to . . . literature. . . . The gradual development of the whaling industry, its technical improvement and mechanization, and the eventual commercial exhaustion of the most valuable species, despite international agreements and stringent conservation regulations, are discussed." The AAAS Science Book List

For further reading: p99

Bourlière, François
The natural history of mammals. 3d ed. rev. Tr. from the French by H. M. Parshley with revisions in English by the author. Knopf 1964 xxi, 387p illus maps $7.95   599
  1 Mammals 2 Animals—Habits and behavior
  Original French publication 1951. First English translation published 1954
  "An account of the life and habits of mammals the world over: their feeding habits; sex life and care of the young; social organization, migratory habits, and population dynamics and structure." McClurg. Book News
  Taxonomic list of species: p337-48. Bibliography: p349-83.

Burt, William Henry
A field guide to the mammals. . . . Text and maps by William Henry Burt; illus. by Richard Philip Grossenheider. 2d ed. rev. and enl. Sponsored by the National Audubon Society and National Wildlife Federation. Houghton 1964 xxiii, 284p illus $5.95   599
  1 Mammals
  "The Petersen Field guide series"
  First published 1952
  "Field marks of all species found north of the Mexican boundary." Title page
  This "handbook provides information on 378 species to be found in North America and surrounding waters. Contains . . . maps showing present distribution, beautiful and detailed color plates of each animal, and many other aids to quick and accurate identification through tracks, skulls, teeth, nests, and distinguishing physical characteristics. Each description also gives the animal's habits, habitat, economic importance, and similar easily-confused species." The AAAS Science Book List for Young Adults
  Includes alternate common names
  References: p267-72

Carrington, Richard
The mammals, by Richard Carrington and the editors of Time-Life Books. Time-Life Bks. [1968 c1963] 192p illus maps (Life Nature lib) lib. bdg. $7.60   599
  1 Mammals
  First published 1963
  Ranging over "the whole gamut of the natural group of mammals . . . the text describes the evolution of mammals, their relationship to man, protective devices, [mating] and living habits." Library J
  "The author does not propose to be comprehensive, but to examine variations, differences, and similarities among types and species. . . . Since the first two chapters describe mammalian variety and evolution, and since the index is good, the book should have some quick reference use as well as being good browsing material. Illustrations are profuse and informative; a substantial divided bibliography is included." Chicago. Children's Book Center

Eimerl, Sarel
The primates, by Sarel Eimerl and Irven DeVore and the editors of Time-Life Books. Time-Life Bks. [1969 c1965] 220p illus (Life Nature lib) lib. bdg. $7.60   599
  1 Primates
  First published 1965
  The primates "are described in words and pictures including facts obtained from research on new fossils, recent anatomical and physiological studies, and current investigations of primate behavior. The drawings that illustrate biological principles, anatomical features, and research findings as well as the magnificent photographs (many in color) of the animals under natural and experimental conditions are well chosen and greatly amplify the necessarily condensed text. The bibliography and the very detailed analytical index are great assets." Science Bks

Haynes, Bessie Doak
(ed.) The grizzly bear; portraits from life; ed. and with an introduction by Bessie Doak Haynes and Edgar Haynes; with drawings by Mary Baker. Univ. of Okla. Press 1966 xxi, 386p illus $7.95   599
  1 Bears 2 Literature—Collections
  This anthology about the grizzly bear contains "excerpts from such noted writers as T. Roosevelt, Enos Mills, John Muir, Frank Dobie and a host of others; much of it . . . hunter's tales and folklore." Library J
  Bibliography: p372-76

Jordan, E. L.
Animal atlas of the world. Hammond 1969 224p illus maps $16.95   599
  1 Mammals 2 Animals—Habits and behavior
  This book describes the habits and behavior of mammals in the mountains and tundras, deserts and oceans, rain forests and ice caps of the world. It also includes distribution maps, showing the range of the species; a geologic time chart of all orders; an article by the author on the world's major wildlife areas; and a zoological breakdown of the orders of mammals. (Publisher)

Leslie, Robert Franklin
The bears and I; raising three cubs in the north woods; illus. by Theodore A. Xaras. Dutton 1968 224p illus $5.95   599
  1 Bears 2 British Columbia—Description and travel
  While panning for gold in the mountain wilderness of British Columbia, the author was adopted by three orphaned bear cubs. "Trying to assume the responsibilities of a mother bear, he taught the cubs to find berries, to fish, and to climb the nearest tree when danger was near. Even as they shared his cabin, his larder (and occasionally even his bunk), he prepared them for the freedom that would someday be theirs." Publisher's note
  "From a scientific point of view, one could say this is a fine study in the behavior of young bears—which it is—but from a layman's view it is a wonderfully human story of animals and men in a grand and rugged wilderness." Pub W

Littlewood, Cyril
The world's vanishing animals: the mammals; illus. by D. W. Ovenden; foreword by Thomas L. Kimball. Arco 1970 62p illus lib. bdg. $4.50   599
  1 Mammals
  ISBN 0-668-0220-9
  "An attractive brief factual source of information focusing our attention on 69 mammals of the world that are fast becoming extinct. The animals are arranged by continent, also included are vanishing ocean mammals. The physical characteristics, geographic environment, and habits of each animal are described. An accompanying map on every second page locates the animals' places of origin and keys the area where they presently survive. Color illustrations of each animal contribute immensely to the value of this volume. . . It is useful as a reference book for public and school libraries as a source of brief facts concerning a current problem of social concern." Science Bks

Morris, Desmond
The mammals; a guide to the living species. Harper 1965 448p illus maps $12.95   599
  1 Mammals
  "There would appear to be 4,237 species of mammals living today and from these a representative cross-section of 300 types has been selected for more detailed treatment. Each of these is allocated a full page, with a photograph and brief descriptive text." Preface
  Includes distributional charts and a bibliography for zoologists

Mowat, Farley

Never cry wolf. Little 1963 247p
boards $4.95   599

1 Wolves 2 Keewatin

"An Atlantic Monthly Press book"
"The story centers on [the author's] long
stay in Wolf House Bay as a government biologist. His official duties included the obligation to study the habits of wolves who were
thought to be preying on the once copious
bands of caribou. Mowat records his observations on one family of wolves and the many
incidents and adventures that occurred during
his study. In his study he was helped by an
Eskimo, Ootek, who had a deep knowledge of
wolves and their ways." Best Sellers
"In spite of occasional lapses into whimsy-
whimsy, this is an absorbing and reliable book
about a much misunderstood animal." Library J

National Geographic Society

Wild animals of North America. The Society 1960 400p illus (Natural science lib)
$7.75   599

1 Mammals

"Edited and prepared by the National Geographic Book Service. . . . 409 illustrations,
258 in full color, by Walter A. Weber, Louis
Agassiz Fuertes, and other artists and photographers." Verso of title page
Chapters by various writers grouped under
the following headings: Animals in fur; The
hoofed mammals; The meat eaters; Gnawing
mammals; Survivors of ancient orders; Ocean
dwellers
"This is an attractive informative compilation for readers of all ages and is especially
good for browsing." Booklist
Map on lining-papers

North, Sterling

Raccoons are the brightest people; illus.
with photographs. Dutton 1966 192p illus
$5.95   599

1 Raccoons

"This entertaining narrative of the author's
experiences with raccoons reveals their unusual intelligence. Diet, behavior and habitat
are also described." Chicago
The book "includes many delightful photographs. . . . In addition, nearly one-quarter of
the book is devoted to Carl Marty and his syl-
van resort, Northernaire, in Wisconsin. Mr.
Marty has fawns, bears, otters, dogs, etc., in
an unusual 'peaceable kingdom' set-up." Library J
Map on lining-papers

Olsen, Jack

Night of the grizzlies. Putnam 1969 254p
illus $6.95   599

1 Bears 2 Glacier National Park

"In the early hours of August 13, 1967, two
young women camping in Glacier National
Park were killed by grizzly bears, the first such
incidents in the park's history. . . . [The author recreates] the events of this night of terror and the factors that made it inevitable:
the grizzly is a wilderness animal; the park has
ceased to be a true wilderness, bringing man
and bear into conflict." Library J
Maps on lining-papers

Park, Ed

The world of the otter; with text and
photographs by Ed Park. Lippincott 1971
159p illus (Living world bks) $5.95, lib.
bdg. $5.82   599

1 Otters

In text and pictures, the author records the
seasonal daily life of otters. "He discusses
their physical characteristics, their environment, and their life cycle, as well as those aspects of their existence at which we can still
only guess, including their gestation period
and their eating habits." Publisher's note
Bibliography:p149-54

Sanderson, Ivan T.

How to know the American mammals; with
full line drawings by the author and full-color
plates by Louis Agassiz Fuertes. Little 1951
164p illus $4.95   599

1 Mammals

"An illustrated manual, written primarily for
the amateur naturalist who wants concise information about the mammals as well as identification in the field. . . . Ten full pages of
animal tracks, all North American mammals,
are included." Huntting
"One would not always know from reading
these pages that the author possessed a wealth
of field experience. Rather does he sound like
a well-trained museum lecturer taking a crowd
of us from one handsomely mounted specimen
to another, pausing before each to deliver a
lucid, reliable, brief account." Sat R

Living mammals of the world; photographs
by John Markham [and others]. Doubleday
1955 303p illus $14.95   599

1 Mammals

First published by Garden City Books
"All (or as much as can be said with any
certainty) about wombats, tenrecs, flying foxes, bushbabies, pikas, jerboas, servals, ror-
quals, tapirs, klipspringers, and the several hundred other extant members (including man) of
the animal kingdom that are distinguished
from the rest of animate life by a four-cham-
bered heart, true hair, and the capacity to
suckle their young. The book is laid out something like an encyclopedia, the difference being
that the order is evolutionary rather than alphabetical." New Yorker
This book "is chiefly distinguished for its
330 magnificent photographs, 190 of them in
full color. A lively text, world-wide scope, the
author's popular reputation, and the excellent
format will recommend it to public libraries."
Cur Ref Bks

Schaller, George B.

The year of the gorilla; with line drawings
by the author. Univ. of Chicago Press 1964
260p illus maps $7.50   599

1 Gorillas 2 Natural history—Africa, Central
3 Natural history—Africa, East

The author's account of his two years of
travel and observation in East and Central
Africa. Particularly this is a "description of the
way of life of that gentle beast, the upland gorilla, and of the African terrain and people."
Publisher's note
"The book is full of fascinating observations, well illustrated with photographs and
drawings." Book Week
Selected reading: p259-60

Scheffer, Victor B.

The year of the whale; decorations by Leonard Everett Fisher. Scribner 1969 213p illus
$7.95   599

1 Whales

In fictional form, based on fact, the author
"tells the story of a year in the life of a sperm
whale calf—from its birth in equatorial waters
through the first months of its suckling life, its
growth, its awareness of the whale herd swimming through thousands of miles of seas (tropical and arctic) and its first recognition of that
mysterious creature, man who comes in ships."
Pub W
The author "infers from the known facts
without seeming to fictionalize, and at intervals introduces scientific detail based on his
own deep-sea and laboratory researches. He
writes with great clarity and style, and sometimes with painful vividness as he tells how
Leviathan in general is bombed, harpooned,
disemboweled, sliced up and boiled down by the
modern commercial whaler." Book of the
Month Club News
"Reference notes: p199-204. Seven whaling
classics: a selected and annotated bibliography: p205-08

Van Gelder, Richard G.
Biology of mammals. Scribner 1969 197p
$5.95   599
1 Mammals
"Utilizing the theme of adaptations to
stresses of various environments, Van Gelder
presents information on birth, growth, development, dispersal, home range, territory, and
shelter; the problems of obtaining air, water,
and food; mechanisms of defense and protection, the maintenance of social structure and
populations, and mating, reproduction and
gestation." Choice

Zappler, Lisbeth
The world after the dinosaurs; the evolution of mammals [by] Lisbeth and Georg
Zappler. Natural Hist. Press 1970 183p illus
$4.95, lib. bdg. $5.70   599
1 Mammals 2 Evolution
"Published for the American Museum of
Natural History"
"The authors have succeeded in selecting
and presenting an abundance of interesting material. . . . The introductory chapter briefly
covers animal classification to show where
mammals fit into the scheme of things. Also
included in the chapter is a short history of
land vertebrates up to the last days of the
dinosaurs. The second chapter describes what
a mammal is, and several species are used as
examples. In the subsequent chapters the authors have grouped mammals into flesh eaters,
plant eaters, rodents, peg-toothed forms . . .
elephants, marine mammals, reptile-like mammals, monkeys, and man. Ancestral and modern species from each group are described and
their behavior, food sources, and habitats are
discussed. Characteristics are given to distinguish each group from the preceding one."
Science Bks

600 TECHNOLOGY
(APPLIED SCIENCES)

603 Technology—Dictionaries

Crispin, Frederic Swing
Dictionary of technical terms. Bruce Pub.
$6.95   603
1 Technology—Dictionaries
First published 1929 and periodically revised
to keep it up to date
Prepared for the use of students, draftsmen,
mechanics, builders, electricians and for workmen generally, the dictionary includes terms
used in modern trades, technical procedures,
industry, shopwork, and occupations of mass
production. (Publisher)

Pugh, Eric
A dictionary of acronyms & abbreviations;
some abbreviations in management, technology, and information science. 2d rev. and
expanded ed. Archon Bks. 1970 389p $15 603
1 Technology—Dictionaries 2 Management—
Dictionaries 3 Acronyms
First published 1968
A dictionary of more than 5,000 alphabetically arranged "abbreviations now current in the
fields of management, technology, and information science excluding, in the main, commercial companies. Principal attention is given
to organizations and institutions in the U.K.
and U.S., although those in the Commonwealth and other industrialized countries are
included. A selective subject index makes it
possible to search acronym lists relating to
chemistry, statistics, water, etc." Choice

608 Patents. Inventions

Cooper, Margaret
The inventions of Leonardo da Vinci. Macmillan (N Y) 1965 182p illus maps lib.
bdg. $6.95   608
1 Inventions 2 Leonardo da Vinci
"This book demonstrates clearly that Leonardo da Vinci went far beyond his contemporaries in versatility and originality, even
though many of his inventions never got beyond the planning stage. It describes his work
in such diverse fields as musical instruments,
construction tools, industrial machinery, optics, measuring devices and many others, using
Leonardo's drawings and photographs of his
models as illustrations." Booklist
A "physical defect of the book is the use of
very long captions that are in the same format
(a column of print two-thirds of the page wide)
as the text. Most of the material is utterly fascinating, but much of it is accompanied by prefatory conversational irrelevancies." Chicago.
Children's Book Center
"This book is visual proof that there are no
boundaries to the world of imagination." Pub
W

National Geographic Society
Those inventive Americans; foreword by
Leonard Carmichael. Produced by the National Geographic Special Publications Division, Robert L. Breeden, chief. The Society
1971 231p illus $4.25   608
1 Inventors 2 Inventions 3 Technology
SBN 87044-089-6
"A collection of biographical sketches of inventors which differs from others on the same
subject in three ways, namely, a few almost unknown but important men have been included
with the usual selection, the colored illustrations and portraits are excellent, and the illustrations often show not only the original invention but its modern counterpart." Booklist
Partial contents: Inventors of a new nation;
the beginners; Frontier of power: steam and
its heroes; Agriculture: new machines for new
lands; "The Lightnin' Wire"—telegraphy conquers time; Magic to order: electricity for
America; The yielding sky: exploration leaves
the earth

Thompson, Holland
The age of invention; a chronicle of mechanical conquest. U.S. Pub. Assn. 1921 267p
(The Chronicles of America ser. v37) $4.45
                                                         608
1 Inventions 2 Inventors
Originally published by Yale University Press
"The purpose of this book is to outline the
personalities of some of the outstanding American inventors and indicate the significance of
their achievements." Prefatory note
Contents: Benjamin Franklin and his times;
Eli Whitney and the cotton gin; Steam in captivity; Spindle, loom, and needle in New England; Agricultural revolution; Agents of communication; Story of rubber; Pioneers of the
machine shop; Fathers of electricity; Conquest
of the air; Bibliographical note

609 Technology—History

Daumas, Maurice
(ed.) A history of technology & invention;
progress through the ages; tr. by Eileen B.
Hennessy. Crown [1970 c1969] 2v illus maps
ea $12.50   609
1 Technology—History 2 Civilization—History
Volume one and two of a projected four volume set
Original French edition of volume one and
two published 1962 and 1964 respectively
Contents: v 1 The origins of technological
civilization; v2 The first stages of mechanization

Daumas, Maurice—*Continued*
"For solid popular-level reading, browsing, and reference. . . . The basic aim is description of techniques and their development, with political, social, and economic environment mentioned only as essential to the account." Booklist
Includes bibliography

Hodges, Henry
Technology in the ancient world; with drawings by Judith Newcomer. Knopf 1970 287p illus $10   609
1 Technology—History
In this survey of the development of ancient technology the author traces "the evolutions of man's tools and machines. He describes firemaking and stone-working, and the development of the tools of agriculture, navigation, transportation and military conquest in Egypt and Mesopotamia. His narrative carries through the period . . . in Assyria and Babylon, around 1000 B.C. . . . [to a] study of the contributions of Archimedes." Pub W
Developments "are invariably handled in relation to environment and social organization. . . .Particularly recommended are the fine illustrations and maps with their accompanying texts. They help to make Hodge's book a real joy to read." Science Bks
Bibliographical note: p285-87

Morison, Elting E.
Men, machines, and modern times. MIT Press 1966 235p $5.95   609
1 Technology and civilization 2 Inventions
Based upon a series of lectures held at California Institute of Technology between 1950 and 1966
"Several historical events which involved technical innovations are recounted, analyzed, and disserted upon. . . . The effects of the introduction of gun sights on naval bombardment in 1900, of the introduction of milk pasteurization, and the relationship of the development of the Bessemer converter to the production of steel, are three of the themes. In developing them the author emphasizes the reactions of organizations and individuals to innovations. . . . Those who are willing to plow through the text may receive some insights helpful to discussion of an important contemporary problem." Science Bks

610 Medical sciences

Lasagna, Louis
Life, death, and the doctor. Knopf 1968 322p $6.95   610
1 Medicine 2 Public health 3 Medical ethics
A "view of important medical issues that pleads for the medical professions to assume a greater role in the public issues created by new medical advances. [The author] criticizes medical education and medical practice as unsatisfactory for the community-wide medicine as practiced and demanded by modern society. The ethical and social issues of artificial organs, organ transplants, abortion, birth control, artificial insemination and genetic control are discussed." The AAAS Science Book List
"The volume is suitable for high school and college students seeking encouraging views of modern medicine and society in rapid transition, and for the intelligent layman asking for humanistic guidelines to emotional issues of the day affecting everyone. Despite some personal positions taken, especially the anti-establishment ones, the book is recommended." Science Bks

Longmore, Donald
Machines in medicine; the medical practice of the future; ed. and illus. by M. Ross-Macdonald. Doubleday 1970 [c1969] 192p illus (Doubleday Science ser) $6.95   610
1 Medical technology 2 Medicine—Automation

First copyrighted 1969 in England
"In the future the core of the hospital function will be a central computer monitoring each patient's vital processes and allowing one computer expert to free large numbers of nursing personnel. . . . [The author] tells how these modern medical instruments work, their varying ranges of reliability, and the many possible applications of the future." Publisher's note
"Entertaining reading but poses a real challenge to the bioengineer of the present and future." Choice
Suggested reading: p186-87

610.3 Medical sciences— Dictionaries

Dorland's Illustrated medical dictionary. Saunders illus thumb indexed, flexible bdg. $13.50   610.3
1 Medicine—Dictionaries
First published 1900 with title: American illustrated dictionary, by W. A. N. Dorland. Frequently revised to incorporate recent discoveries
This standard reference includes terms used in medicine, surgery, dentistry, pharmacy, chemistry, nursing, veterinary science, biology and medical biology. Pronunciation, derivation and definitions are given

610.69 Medical professions

Lee, Russel V.
The physician, by Russel V. Lee, Sarel Eimerl and the editors of Time-Life Books. Time-Life Bks. [1968 c1967] 200p illus (Life Science lib) lib. bdg. $7.60   610.69
1 Medicine as a profession
First published 1967
This book traces the emergence of the modern physician from the primitive medicine man. "It pays particular attention to the latest trends in medicine—the growth of specialization, and the increasing tendency of physicians to practice in groups rather than individually. Finally it examines [new medical techniques]. . . . The text chapters of the book are supplemented by picture essays." About this book
"There are balanced presentations of issues avoided in most surveys of medicine. . . . [This] readable book can advantageously be used by counsellors seeking to interest students in a future medical career." Choice
Further reading: p196

610.73 Nursing profession

Dodge, Bertha S.
The story of nursing; illus. by Barbara Corrigan. New ed. Little 1965 244p illus $4.95   610.73
1 Nurses and nursing—History 2 Nursing as as profession
First published 1954
Part one tells about the heritage of the nursing profession—of such women as Florence Nightingale, Clara Barton, Linda Richards, Lillian Wald, and Mary Breckinridge. Part two tells about present conditions and plans for the future in private, hospital, and public health nursing
"The account does full justice to the glamor that this profession has for many girls, but it also gives a clear, accurate picture of the difficulties of both the training and the work itself." Chicago. Children's Book Center
Bibliography: p233-38

611   Human anatomy

Gray, Henry
Gray's Anatomy of the human body. Lea illus $22.50   611

1 Anatomy

First published 1858 in England with title: Anatomy, descriptive and surgical. Frequently revised to keep material up to date

A comprehensive standard reference work with illustrations, descriptions and definitions

"Holds its place as a major authoritative text on systematic anatomy." Annals of Internal Medicine

Includes bibliographies

612   Human physiology

Asimov, Isaac
The chemicals of life; enzymes, vitamins, hormones. Abelard-Schuman 1954 159p illus $4   612

1 Physiological chemistry 2 Biochemistry

The author "explains how enzymes control the functioning of living tissue and are themselves aided by vitamins and hormones, how deficiency diseases arise, and how the modern wonder drugs work. A readable introduction to biochemistry which should be especially useful in school libraries." Booklist

The human body; its structure and operation; illus. by Anthony Ravielli. Houghton 1963 340p illus $6.95   612

1 Physiology 2 Anatomy

In this "introduction to human biology . . . the author defines man's genealogy, shows his place in nature and fully describes the parts, composition and dynamics of the body, except for the nervous system which he [covers in 'The human brain' entered below]." Pub W

The author "gives a thorough and carefully detailed study of human anatomy and of the corresponding physiology of our heads, limbs, points, muscles, lungs, heart, circulatory vessels, blood, intestines, kidneys, skin, and genital organs. The book should be appealing on two counts. First, it is excellently written and beautifully illustrated (although some drawings could be more completely labeled). Asimov gives an academically and scientifically accurate account. He defines and gives the Greek or Latin derivations of the scientific terminology. Secondly, his book encompasses a topic of extreme interest to the . . . reader, but seldom covered in his classroom biology text." Best Sellers

The human brain; its capacities and functions; illus. by Anthony Ravielli. Houghton 1964 [c1963] 357p illus $5.95   612

1 Brain 2 Physiology

Companion volume to the author's: The human body, entered above

This book on the human brain, nervous system, and sense organs is devoted "to the organization that makes multicellular life possible and, in particular, to the organization that makes the human body a dynamic living thing and not merely a collection of cells. The brain is not the only organ involved in such organization, but it is by far the most important." Introduction

This is not "a simple factual account, for Asimov is able to communicate his own awe and enthusiasm for that which is not yet known. The intelligent layman, to whom the book is directed, will be grateful for the derivation and pronunciation of technical terms and for the attractive and useful illustrations. For all libraries with readers interested in non-technical science." Library J

"Obviously, the picture is incomplete and Dr. Asimov is the first to emphasize this point. . . . [The book will serve] one hopes, to stimulate further study." Best Sellers

Life and energy. Doubleday 1962 380p illus boards $5.95   612

1 Biochemistry 2 Biophysics

An introduction to the biochemistry and biophysics of the human body "devoted to the understanding of the life processes and in particular the working of the human body as a specific example of life. The first half of this book is concerned with the mechanics and thermodynamics of the inanimate world. In the second half, Asimov uses these concepts as a means of explaining the inner workings of living tissue." Publisher's note

"This is written so as to be understandable to the layman, despite the highly technical nature of the subject." Springf'd Republican

Brooks, Stewart M.
The sea inside us: water in the life processes. Meredith 1968 116p illus $3.95   612

1 Body fluids 2 Diseases

The "story of the composition and functions of . . . body fluids and . . . the diseases that an imbalance of fluid may cause—diabetes insipidus, Addison's disease, hemophilia, coronary thrombosis, and many others. The human body is mostly water, but too much water, too little water, or water in the wrong place will reveal itself in disease." Publisher's note

"In some places, such as in the discussion of osmosis, the writing is too technical for beginners and should have included simpler definitions of terms and concepts. However, with its informative diagrams and sketches, this is a good supplement to books on human biology." Library J

Calder, Nigel
The mind of man. . . . Viking [1971 c1970] 288p illus $8.95   612

1 Brain 2 Psychology, Physiological
SBN 670-47640-4

First published 1970 in England, this book is an expansion of a BBC television script by the author

"An investigation into current research on the brain and human nature." Subtitle

Magnificently illustrated with photos and two-tone drawings and diagrams, the volume is a prime example of excellent scientific writing for the general reader. In its three parts Calder explains the brain as an enormously subtle 'electric machine' in its relation to human functions and passions, studies what experts have learned and are now learning of the intricate 'maze' of the mind through brain-damaged victims . . . and finally examines in depth the many subtle aspects of the human brain in its development from infancy to 'creative intellect.' " Pub W

Suggestions for further reading included in Author's note: p7

Halacy, D. S.
Man and memory [by] D. S. Halacy, Jr. Harper 1970 259p illus $6.95   612

1 Brain 2 Memory

In this book the author "surveys the history of brain studies and shows the relationship of remembering, learning, forgetting, intelligence, dreaming, drugs, and memory. He covers physiological and molecular theories of memory and the . . . research now being carried on." Publisher's note

"Halacy has written a charming, intelligent, informative balanced book on the psychology and biology of learning and memory. . . . His book is illustrated with a reasonable number of interesting and informative photographs and drawings, both contemporary and historical, including photos of several researchers at work. . . . This is not a 'how-to-remember' book, but rather a clear and entertaining presentation of important scientific research." Science Bks

Nourse, Alan E.
The body, by Alan E. Nourse and the editors of Time-Life Books. Time-Life Bks. [1971] 200p illus (Life Science lib) lib. bdg. $7.60   612

1 Physiology 2 Anatomy
First published 1964

Nourse, Alan E.—*Continued*

"The two fundamental approaches to a study of the human body are comprehended in this attractive introduction: how the body is constructed and how it functions. Eight picture essays tell the story, and the final one: 'The Making of a Doctor,' is valuable career background for students and guidance personnel. The bodily measurements and bibliography in the appendices are interesting and useful." The AAAS Science Book List for Young Adults

Bibliography: p196

Seeman, Bernard

Your sight; folklore, fact and common sense. Little 1968 242p illus boards $5.95 612

1 Vision 2 Eye

"Beginning with the actual mechanics of sight the author then takes up the various defects or mishaps that impede or threaten vision. Glaucoma, cataract, detached retina, far- and near-sightedness, the effects of aging—in down-to-earth, direct language [he] sets forth the symptoms, care and effects of each, telling readers what to watch for and what steps to take when trouble is suspected. He also discusses the various superstitions and occult powers attached to the eye, some of which are still believed. The care and protection of children's eyes is discussed and the whys and hows of corrective lenses are dealt with." Publisher's note

The appendix includes lists of groups working to prevent blindness and to help the blind, a glossary and a bibliography

Snively, William D.

The sea of life, by William D. Snively, Jr. with Jan Thuerbach. McKay 1969 240p $5.50
612

1 Body fluids 2 Metabolism

The author discusses man's development from a one-celled sea creature to the complex beings we have become; the discovery of the importance of body fluids; and how these extraordinary substances work within us and help determine how well we look, work, and feel. His book answers such questions as what inexpensive protein foods we can substitute for a more costly meat, and what vital substances we lose when we stay in bed too long. (Publisher)

"The presentation is enlivened with many examples, some from Dr. Snively's practice, and will be intelligible to non-scientists. Under illustrated, but nevertheless pleasantly entertaining as well as informative." Library J

Vroman, Leo

Blood. Natural Hist. Press 1967 178p illus $5.50
612

1 Blood

"Published for The American Museum of Natural History"

The author "takes the reader into his laboratory and together they unravel all sorts of phenomena relating to blood on a basis of equality in interest and appreciation, if not in knowledge and experience. Dr. Vroman ranges widely in his discourse on blood, covering its components, their structure and some abnormalities. His explanations are augmented by delightful sketches; his illustrations of some complex protein molecules are especially good. While this is a scientific book, it has a light-hearted approach to its subject." Pub W

Some literature: p172-73

612.6 Reproductive system and developmental periods

Bohannan, Paul

Love, sex and being human; a book about the human condition for young people. Doubleday 1969 144p illus $4.95   612.6

1 Sex instruction 2 Sexual ethics

"The first half describes . . . the anatomy and physiology of human sex organs, conception, and growth of a human organism from embryo to sexually mature individual. The second half provides a basis for teenage discussion and development of a modern morality grounded on an understanding of human biology and social organization." Am News of Bks

The second section of the book "is written without taking a moral position, yet pushing for moral responsibility and moral decision. The book is perhaps the best popular text on sexuality available. It is highly recommended as a springboard for discussion." Science Bks

Further reading: p143-44

Dalton, Katharina

The menstrual cycle. Pantheon Bks. [1971 c1969] 149p illus $4.95
612.6

1 Woman—Health and hygiene
ISBN 0-394-46867-8

First published 1969 in England

"There are a number of variations in the patterns of menstruation which come within the bounds of normality, but have attendant discomfort and suffering, both physical and mental. These variations are rarely to be found in any textbook but have a considerable sociological impact on society: they and their consequences are the subject of this book. It is my hope that by opening up this subject to a wider audience I may induce women to appreciate that there is an answer to much of today's unnecessary suffering; that men may gain a sympathetic understanding of the problems of the opposite sex." Preface

References: p139. Glossary: p140-42

Guttmacher, Alan F.

Understanding sex: a young person's guide; with a foreword by Millicent McIntosh. Harper 1970 140p boards $4.95   612.6

1 Sex instruction

This book describes the female and male reproductive organs and their functions, and discusses such topics as petting, intercourse, homosexuality, masturbation, fertilization, pregnancy and birth, contraception, and venereal disease, and concludes with some remarks on premarital sex. (Publisher)

Johnson, Eric W.

Love and sex in plain language; illus. by Edward C. Smith; foreword by Joseph Stokes, Jr. Rev. ed. Lippincott 1967 68p illus $3.95
612.6

1 Sex instruction

First published 1965

This book gives young people basic facts about sex relations, conception, contraception and reproduction

This book should appeal to youngsters approaching adulthood "and to their parents, for whom it may provide the springboard for good, free discussion within the family." Foreword

Companies offering educational literature about menstruation: p66

Pomeroy, Wardell B.

Boys and sex. Delacorte Press 1968 157p $4.95
612.6

1 Sex instruction

The book takes up such "matters as masturbation, petting as a means of fulfillment instead of actual intercourse, protection for the girl partner, the necessity of reporting venereal disease immediately, and other related topics." Bk Buyer's Guide

"Dr. Pomeroy, the father of three children and coauthor of the two Kinsey Reports, seems well qualified to give advice to boys and their parents about sexual problems. . . . He is frank to the point of using the slang words boys all recognize in naming the sexual act and the parts of the body related to it, and, although it is obvious that Dr. Pomeroy favors love in marriage, he refrains from moralizing. This is indeed a 'modern' guide, probably too advanced for some parents but it makes sense and should be widely purchased by school and public libraries." Library J

Pomeroy, Wardell B.—*Continued*

Girls and sex. Delacorte Press [1970 c1969] 159p $4.95   **612.6**

1 Sex instruction

Companion volume to: Boys and sex, entered above

The author describes the developmental patterns and sexual behavior of girls. Topics covered include dating, petting, intercourse, masturbation and homosexuality

The book succeeds "because of the author's mild, non-preaching tone, his urging of readers to exercise similar rationality, and his full and sympathetic treatment of the psychological factors in girls' sexual development." Library J

Tanner, James M.

Growth, by James M. Tanner, Gordon Rattray Taylor and the editors of Time-Life Books. Time-Life Bks. [1968] 200p illus (Life Science lib) lib. bdg. $7.60   **612.6**

1 Growth 2 Physiology

First published 1965

"The complex, intricate process of human growth is the subject of this book. . . . [Text and illustrations] trace the timetable of human development from conception to maturity, describe the many patterns that growth displays and explore the frontiers of new research which may enable man to influence growth." Publisher's note

"The most outstanding feature of this work are the colored photographs of Lennart Nilsson, showing various states in the development of the human fetus." Science Bks

Further reading: p194

613.2 Food and health

Bolian, Polly

Growing up slim. Am. Heritage Press 1971 150p illus $3.95   **613.2**

1 Weight control

SBN 07-006380-X

This book, discussing weight control through a program of balanced eating and exercise, examines the "Basic Six" elements in food and where to find them. A calorie chart, menus, recipes and specific exercises are included as well as grooming hints

West, Ruth

The teen-age diet book; illus. by Don Trawin. Messner 1969 182p illus $3   **613.2**

1 Weight control

SBN 671-32204-4

First published 1958

"Half of the book is devoted to 'do and don't' suggestions and a few 'why' statements for activity and well-balanced diets. The other half implements this device with recipes and calorie contents of foods. . . . The unnumbered section ('Personal Dope Sheet') at the end of the book could have been the most tantalizing, but it is documented only for girls." Science Bks

613.7 Rest, exercise, physical fitness

American Association for Health, Physical Education, and Recreation

Physical education for high school students; a book of sports, athletics, and recreational activities for teen-age boys and girls. 2d ed. The Association [distributed by Nat. Educ.] 1970 400p illus $5   **613.7**

1 Physical education and training 2 Recreation

First published 1955

Designed to serve either as textbook or supplementary reading, this book "covers history, rules, skills and strategy, equipment, safety, and sportsmanship for 20 sports, major and minor, group and individual. Also considers folk, square, social, and modern dance, intramural and interscholastic athletics, recreational games . . . and physical education as a career." Booklist

Includes bibliographies

Cooper, Kenneth H.

Aerobics; with a foreword by Richard L. Bohannon; and a preface by William Proxmire. Published by Evans, M.& Co. and distributed in association with Lippincott 1968 253p boards $4.95   **613.7**

1 Exercise 2 Physical fitness

"A graded system of exercises particularly for men, tested by Cooper in a program for the U.S. Air Force, explained in a straight-forward but enthusiastic manner. Cooper defines aerobics as exercises for increasing one's supply of oxygen through measured techniques in order to improve general health. He recommends cycling, walking, stationary running, handball, basketball, and squash and gives detailed charts for checking progress for each exercise. A chapter titled 'The clinical conditions' discusses the role of exercise in heart, ulcer, diabetic, and other disease therapy. Expanded point value charts appended. No index." Booklist

Bibliographic notes: p243-53

The new Aerobics. Published by Evans, M.& C. and distributed in association with Lippincott 1970 191p $5.95   **613.7**

1 Exercise 2 Physical fitness

Companion volume to: Aerobics, entered above

"This present book is perhaps best described as being a supplement to the original 'Aerobics' volume. . . . A greater variety of exercises has been tabulated and calibrated for possible use. Different exercise series have now been made up for different age groups. Also some of the rates of progression through an exercise series have been altered on the basis of experience. . . . [However] much of the enthusiasm and motivational 'zing' of the original have been dropped by the wayside." Choice

Bibliography: p188-91

Wilkinson, Bud

Bud Wilkinson's Guide to modern physical fitness; illus. by George Ford. Viking 1967 176p illus boards $4.95   **613.7**

1 Physical fitness

Title on spine: Modern physical fitness

This guide for laymen on how to keep fit with an exercise program includes chapters on individual sports and diet, plus physical fitness tests and calorie tables. Includes a special section for women

613.8 Addictions and health

Brenner, Joseph H.

Drugs & youth; medical, psychiatric and legal facts [by] Joseph H. Brenner, Robert Coles [and] Dermot Meagher. Liveright 1970 258p illus $4.95   **613.8**

1 Drugs 2 Narcotics 3 Narcotics—Laws and regulations

SBN 87140-501-6

The book begins with explanations of terms like "tolerance" and "dependence." Then various drugs and their effects are described. The last third of the book is a discussion of drugs and the law, ending with a summary of the laws in each of the fifty states. (Publisher)

"A good portion of the book is devoted to statements by youngsters—drug users, nonusers, ex-users. And their candid thoughts, feelings, and reactions form the basis for sincere and honest discussion and speculation by the author." Library J

Selected bibliography: p249-51

Cain, Arthur H.

Young people and drugs. Day 1969 160p $4.75   613.8

1 Narcotic habit 2 Drugs

"This book deals with the effects, both psychological and physiological, of such drugs or practices as amphetamines, barbiturates, marijuana, LSD, and glue sniffing. Dr. Cain cites cases, gives advice, compares marijuana with tobacco and alcohol, and argues for life without drugs. The information is relatively accurate, but his style is often very condescending." Library J

Suggested readings: p156. Glossary: p157-60

Young people and smoking; the use and abuse of cigarette tobacco. Day 1964 96p $3.95   613.8

1 Smoking 2 Cigarettes

"There is sufficient evidence—if presented in an unbiased, unemotional manner—to enable most people to make a sensible decision concerning smoking. This volume presents [material to help a young person reach] . . . his own personal decision in reference to cigarettes and health." Preface

"The author objectively sets forth pertinent facts. . . . In a matter-of-fact presentation Dr. Cain discusses the psychological, social, and the physical factors involved in smoking, comments on the different types of smokers, and gives pointers on breaking the habit. Will be helpful to counselors and parents as well as young adults." Booklist

Includes a summary of the Surgeon General's Report. Suggested reading: p95-96

Consumer Reports

The Consumers Union report on smoking and the public interest, by Ruth and Edward Brecher [and others] . . . and the editors of Consumer Reports. Simon & Schuster 1963 222p illus pa $1.50   613.8

1 Smoking 2 Cigarettes 3 Cancer

"A review of the facts for and against the current charge that smoking induces lung cancer and the tobacco industry's stand in the matter. With suggestions for individual and government action." Bk Buyer's Guide

This is "a thorough, carefully worded study containing documented evidence." Booklist

Diehl, Harold S.

Tobacco & your health: the smoking controversy. McGraw 1969 271p illus (McGraw-Hill Ser. in health education) $4.95   613.8

1 Smoking 2 Cigarettes

This "book is not a diatribe, but neither is it a presentation of pro and con designed to allow the reader to draw his own conclusion. The author believes, as do most medical doctors, that cigarette smoking is a serious health hazard. After an initial chapter which gives the opinions of medical authorities on tobacco and health, the author describes the origins and uses of tobacco, the early medical evidence connecting tobacco with disease, and more recent studies relating the use of tobacco to increased death rates. Next, the substances present in tobacco smoke and their immediate effects are described, followed by chapters on the relationship of tobacco to cancer, cardiovascular disease, chronic bronchitis, emphysema, other diseases, and general illness and disability. A single chapter of dissenting opinions is presented. The remaining portion of the text tells of reasons for smoking and aids for giving up smoking." Science Bks

Suggested reference: p209-13. Glossary: p255-61

Fort, Joel

The pleasure seekers: the drug crisis, youth and society. Bobbs 1969 255p $6.50   613.8

1 Narcotic habit 2 Drugs

A "study of the mind-altering drugs—marihuana, LSD, barbiturates, tranquilizers, amphetamine, alcohol and others—their use and abuse, and the ineffective and harmful social policies which have been used to 'control' drugs in the United States and elsewhere." News of Bks

The author "is vigorous in his attack upon the irrational and hypocritical in our approach to the drug scene. The indictment of the Federal Bureau of Narcotics, C.I.A., and the State Department is restrained but blistering. . . . Fort writes well, has much data, is biased (especially in favor of marijuana), and is a crusader. The book is a good antidote to the spate of drug scare books and articles but must be taken with its own grain of salt." Science Bks

Bibliography: p245-50

Grinspoon, Lester

Marihuana reconsidered. Harvard Univ. Press 1971 443p $9.95   613.8

1 Marihuana
ISBN 0-674-54835-3

"In well-ordered chapters, . . . [the author] explores with lucidity and thoroughness the history of 'Cannabis' through its transmutations in America, leading up to its first widespread use as a 'psychoactive' drug in the 1930s by black jazz musicians and its nationwide use by the young in recent years. Dr. Grinspoon is extraordinarily knowledgeable about the chemistry of the 'weed' and is able to reveal the ignorance and prejudice involved in most 'scientific' reports on the subject." Pub W

"The volume is exhaustively and exhaustingly thorough. No one is going to read it for thrills. That very solidity and stuffiness is what makes [this book] so potent a weapon in the hands of those who want marihuana legalized." Book World

Includes bibliography

Houser, Norman W.

Drugs; facts on their use and abuse [by] Norman W. Houser in consultation with Julius B. Richmond. . . . Lothrop 1969 48p illus $3.95, lib. bdg. $3.78   613.8

1 Drugs 2 Narcotics

"Hal Kearney, art director; Ed Bedno, designer [and] Jane Bedno, illustrator." Title page

"The purpose of this book is to provide concise, accurate answers to questions about the various stimulants, depressants, hallucinogens, narcotics, and other chemicals on the drug scene, and to describe their effects on the body and mind." Publisher's note

"A very short, but highly readable and accurate outline of drugs currently being abused in the United States. The book, simply written and imaginatively illustrated, will appeal to reluctant readers and be useful in the classroom." Library J

Glossary: p45-47. Reading list: p48

Hyde, Margaret O.

(ed.) Mind drugs. McGraw 1968 150p $4.95, lib. bdg. $4.46   613.8

1 Narcotic habit 2 Drugs

Experts from the fields of psychiatry, social psychology, medicine, and public health discuss the nature of marijuana, LSD, heroin and alcohol, and their psychological and physical effects

"Addressed to young people and adults working with young people this contains a series of objective, factual articles about mind-altering drugs. . . . The final piece describes attempts to expand human awareness without drugs." Booklist

"The tone is consistently objective, neither adjuring the reader nor indulging in man-to-man-let's-lick-this-thing-together heartiness. A glossary, reading list, and index are appended, as is a list of places to get help in New York City." Chicago. Children's Book Center

Jones, Kenneth L.

Drugs and alcohol, by Kenneth L. Jones, Louis W. Shainberg and Curtis O. Byer. Harper 1969 132p illus pa $2.75   613.8

1 Narcotic habit 2 Alcoholism

"The authors discuss alcohol in a more comprehensive manner than any other drug

Jones, Kenneth L.—*Continued*

(two out of five chapters) and the two chapters devoted to alcohol are well done. The first three chapters on 'Use of Drugs,' 'Physical Aspects of Drug Abuse,' and 'Special Aspects of Drug Abuse' are somewhat of a conglomerate evidently designed to meet the market demand. . . . The glossary definition of terms and the bibliography citing other references to drugs that are subjected to abuse may prove of value to those interested in drug abuse." Science Bks

Lingeman, Richard R.

Drugs from A to Z: a dictionary. McGraw 1969 277p $6.95   613.8

1 Drugs—Dictionaries

"The Preface clearly defines . . . [the scope of this book which is] an alphabetical listing of the drugs of abuse (hallucinogens, opiates, barbiturates and other central nervous system depressants) and central stimulants employed illegally for their pleasurable and euphoric properties. Roughly 1,100 slang or otherwise esoteric names, initials, or expressions dealing with the drug addict, hippie, chemist, pharmacologist, and pharmacist are defined in clear, succinct language for the layman. More than a dictionary, the book often explains in depth certain terms that have become household words, e.g., glue sniffing, heroin, marijuana, Synanon, with their origins, if known. No syllabifications nor pronunciations are provided. Trademarks of the most commonly abused prescription drugs, a description of dose forms, physical appearance, and the strengths available from legitimate sources are also listed." Science Bks

Bibliography included in Acknowledgements

Louria, Donald B.

The drug scene. McGraw 1968 215p boards $5.95   613.8

1 Narcotic habit 2 Hallucinogenic drugs

"An informative account of the use and abuse of drugs—primarily marijuana, LSD, and opiates—in the United States, England, and Sweden. [The author] has found that fellow students or contemporaries play a large role in starting a person on drugs, and that television, newspapers, and radio exert a considerable suggestive force. He stresses the need for firm and fair laws, and especially for a strong, reasonable stand by college administrators. . . . [Louria] concludes his study by saying that a change in the drug scene in the United States can be accomplished effectively only by a complete reorientation of society's attitude. This factual, unemotional, and well-thought-out book should be in public, senior high school, and college libraries." Library J

Glossary of terms: p207-10. Bibliography: p211-14

Overcoming drugs; a program for action. McGraw 1971 233p $6.95   613.8

1 Narcotic habit 2 Drugs
ISBN 0-07-038779-6

The author presents a program for dealing with the proliferating traffic in narcotics. He gives "advice to parents who wish to discuss the use of drugs with their children . . . [and answers] questions concerning the chemical and addictive properties of the various amphetamines, barbiturates, and hallucinogens, and about the effects they have on the human brain and central nervous system." Publisher's note

"Louria considers the various causes of drug addiction and illustrates the adverse effects drugs can have on the individual. . . . Although he has not presented significantly new ideas on the problems of drug use and abuse, this volume is written in an open manner, and Louria refrains from making any personal evaluation of the user per se. If for this reason alone, the volume is worthwhile." Library J

Bibliography: p229-33

Marin, Peter

Understanding drug use; an adult's guide to drugs and the young [by] Peter Marin and Allan Y. Cohen. Harper 1971 163p boards $5.95   613.8

1 Drugs 2 Narcotic habit 3 Adolescence

Written to help parents and other concerned adults to deal with drugs, this book assumes that at one time or another most children will try drugs. Arguing that attempts to suppress drug use entirely are doomed to failure, it concentrates on the minimization of drug misuse. It discusses drugs, their effects and the American adolescent. (Publisher)

"This present text gains power because it is scientific rather than moralizing. To these authors, the taking of drugs is not only dangerous and harmful; it is silly and even stupid. If they belabor parents who unconsciously push their young ones toward this chemical excitement and anti-social culture, then they neatly balance their ideas by giving proper advice on how to prevent drug use before it starts, as well as how to handle it once the addiction has been discovered. This is an exceptionally well written book, even though it exposes a seamy segment of American life that is very disturbing." Best Sellers

Glossary: p149-51. Bibliography: p153-57

Ochsner, Alton

Smoking: your choice between life and death. Simon & Schuster [1971 c1970] 224p illus $3   613.8

1 Smoking 2 Cancer
SBN 671-20698-2

First published 1954 by Messner. Title varies

"An evaluation and interpretation of the most recent findings by the U.S. and Great Britain. All of the damaging evidence of the U.S. Surgeon General's report is appraised." Publisher's note

"Dr. Ochsner is definitely (almost vehemently) against smoking which he avers is responsible for heart trouble, respiratory troubles, and a multitude of other physical ailments. Well documented." Library J

References: p136-39

Oursler, Will

Marijuana: the facts, the truth. Eriksson 1968 240p $5.95   613.8

1 Marihuana

"Through interviews with leading authorities, through case histories and special reports, Mr. Oursler presents . . . [a] portrait of marijuana, and shows how it is being used in our educational institutions, in our upper-class suburbs, in our ghettoes and slums. . . . Here are the facts about 'pot'—here are the answers to the question 'is marijuana dangerous?'" Publisher's note

"Carefully researched and documented study of the latest data on marijuana. In view of the increasing use and the many extremely vocal people who defend the drug's use, this should be read by both young people and their elders." Huntting

United States. Surgeon General's Advisory Committee on Smoking and Health

Smoking and health; report of the Advisory Committee to the Surgeon General of the Public Health Service. Van Nostrand 1964 387p illus $6.95   613.8

1 Smoking 2 Cigarettes

Originally issued as the official report of the Committee, in a paper edition for sale by the Superintendent of Documents

A book "concerned with the relationship between cigarette smoking and health, certain respiratory, circulatory and other diseases. Scientifically sound, objective, well documented." Cincinnati

Includes bibliographies

Vermes, Hal
Helping youth avoid four great dangers: smoking, drinking, VD, narcotics addiction, by Hal and Jean Vermes. Assn. Press 1965 157p $3.95   613.8
1 Hygiene 2 Youth
Partial contents: The campaign against cigarettes; The facts about drinking; The importance of education in the attack on alcohol; The stand on social disease; VD—effective methods of prevention; The assault on narcotics; References and sources
A study addressed to adolescents, as well as parents, educators, clergy, and counselors, in the belief that "if a young person is acquainted with the full facts and, as a result, decides not to indulge in drinking, smoking, narcotics, and illicit sex, there is a chance that he may never do so." p.14

What everyone needs to know about drugs. Joseph Newman, directing editor. U.S. News & World Report 1970 239p illus map $2.95   613.8
1 Narcotic habit 2 Drugs 3 Youth
Partial contents: What the experts say: a judge's view of marihuana, by G. T. Tauro; Speed: the risk you run, by S. Cohen; A psychiatrist looks at LSD, by D. X. Freedman; Youth and family, by A. Mandelbaum; Youth and drugs, by C. Chamberlin; If your child takes drugs, by R. H. Blum; Drug use and student values, by K. Keniston; Drugs: do they produce open or closed minds, by D. L. Farnsworth
Includes bibliographical references

614 Public health.
Noise pollution

Aylesworth, Thomas G.
This vital air, this vital water; man's environmental crisis; illus. with photographs. Rand McNally 1968 192p illus $4.95   614
1 Air—Pollution 2 Water—Pollution
The author explores "the causes and effects of air and water pollution, describes the visible effects of pollution and explains why the other, invisible pollutants, may be even more dangerous." Publisher's note
"A realistic report on the fatal consequences to human beings of pollution in various parts of the world, including the U.S. . . . He urges young people to consider careers in pollution control and indicates the types of positions open to them as scientists, engineers, technicians, or clerical workers." Booklist
Bibliography: p182

Berland, Theodore
The fight for quiet. Prentice-Hall 1970 370p $8.95   614
1 Noise pollution
The author "says, in effect, that as a nation we are literally going deaf because of the prevalence of man-made noise. There is evidence to indicate that the booming music of today's youth is causing a surprising amount of deafness, but deafness is only a part of the story. What sonic booms can do to windows and even masonry, the common noises of our mechanized society can do (and do) to our mental stability." Pub W
Bibliography: p309-44

Herber, Lewis
Crisis in our cities. Prentice-Hall 1965 239p illus maps $5.95   614
1 Air—Pollution   2 Public health—U.S.
3 Water—Pollution 4 Cities and towns—U.S.

"The author describes the effects on human health when pesticides, chemicals, tons of sewage, and detergents are dumped into waterways and describes the results of air pollution [and social stress] in many large cities." Bk Buyer's Guide
The book "is not pleasant reading: but its message is urgent and compelling." Best Sellers
Notes: p201-23

Linton, Ron M.
Terracide; America's destruction of her living environment. Little 1970 376p $7.95   614
1 Water—Pollution 2 Air—Pollution 3 Technology and civilization
Section one of this book deals with human reactions to the overcrowded and polluted environment. "Section two deals with commercial and industrial sins of pollution and a discussion of the specific abuses to our wildlife and natural resources that the 'new technology' has produced. The third and concluding section . . . tells what must be done to solve our environmental problems." Publisher's note
"A more widely ranging and partisan account of the problem [of pollution] than most of the flood of publications on this popular and pressing subject. Useful bibliography, listing significant government publications separately from other books and articles, so that it may also be used as a guide to some of the authoritative sources; good index." Choice

McClellan, Grant S.
(ed.) Protecting our environment. Wilson, H.W. 1970 218p (The Reference shelf v42, no. 1) $4.50   614
1 Environmental policy—U.S. 2 Air—Pollution 3 Water—Pollution 4 Natural resources
ISBN 0-8242-04009-3
The contributors to this volume examine the global aspects of pollution problems as well as American environmental issues such as air and water pollution. They also consider the national measures being undertaken to deal with the conservation of our natural resources, as well as foreign and international attempts to protect man's environment
Bibliography: p211-18

Our poisoned planet: can we save it? U.S. News & World Report 1970 256p illus pa $2.95   614
1 Environmental policy—U.S. 2 Natural resources—U.S.
Part I deals with various forms of pollution facing the environment today: too many people, chemicals that kill, our dying lakes and rivers, the garbage explosion, and the plague of noise. Part II discusses roles which industry, government and individuals can take in working to overcome the problem of pollution
Environmental reading list: p245-46

Still, Henry
In quest of quiet; meeting the menace of noise pollution; call to citizen action. Fred Kerner/Publishing Projects in association with Stackpole Bks. 1970 221p illus $6.95 614
1 Noise pollution
ISBN 0-8117-0891-8
Here are "facts about noise and its adverse effects on the nervous system, the heart and the blood vessels, plus the results of studies indicating the development of gradual and partial deafness in more than half the country's population and surgical evidence of physical damage caused by rock music. Other kinds of noise pollution discussed result from freeway traffic, industry, and the wide world of jets. It is a sad commentary that our society, already highly restrictive, may need more laws to prevent people from losing their hearing acuity." Library J
References and Bibliography: p215-[23]

Winter, Ruth

Poisons in your food; with an introduction by Walter Frederick Mondale. Crown 1969 248p illus $5.95   **614**

1 Food adulteration and inspection 2 Food poisoning

The author discusses the dangers of the poisons found in our foods today. She examines "raw foods and their processing, meats, packaged foods, water supply, vending machines, restaurants, fertilizers, pesticides, additives, sanitary practices, and new foods and ingredients introduced without inspection." Publisher's note

"Quiet and positive are probably the best two words to describe this book. . . . Mrs. Winter gives chapter and verse for the incidents she discusses and cites pertinent literature. In each section or chapter she makes positive suggestions for consumers to adopt in their daily lives. This book should be in every public, college, high school, and home library." Library J

Bibliographies at end of chapters

614.069 Careers in public health

Fanning, Odom

Opportunities in environmental careers. Vocational Guidance 1971 271p $5.75 **614.069**

1 Environmental policy—U.S. 2 Occupations

Partial contents: Careers in ecology; Careers in earth sciences; Careers in resources and recreation; Careers in environmental design; Careers in environmental protection; Environmental policy and programs

"Stressing the necessity for each group of environmental careers the author surveys briefly . . . fields of environmental involvement giving educational requirements, present and future opportunities, and earnings and working conditions. He cites opportunities in all fields for blacks and mentions specifically the chances women have in finding such employment. . . . The appendix includes a bibliography of inexpensive items, a list of periodicals on environment, voluntary organizations open to public membership, key government agencies, and institutions offering training for environmental careers." Booklist

614.4 Control of disease

Deschin, Celia S.

The teenager and VD; a social symptom of our times. Rosen, R. 1969 130p illus lib. bdg. $3.99   **614.4**

1 Venereal diseases 2 Sexual ethics

"The purpose of this book is to provide a basic understanding that will help teenagers realize the seriousness of venereal disease; but also to stimulate them to think about their sexual behavior and its effect on their total development as people—their career, marriage, and happiness, quite aside from the possibility of contracting VD." Introduction

References: p129-30

614.8 Accidents and their prevention. First aid

Bolton, William

What to do until the doctor comes. Rev. ed. Reilly & Lee 1960 158p $3.95   **614.8**

1 First aid in illness and injury

First published 1953

A compendium of advisory medical articles, alphabetically arranged, extending from accidents and emergencies to X-rays. Articles of general interest include material on such topics as: atomic bombing, swallowing foreign bodies, bathing and baths, blood types, cancer, diets, (13 special), first aid, and infant care

Henderson, John

Emergency medical guide. Neil Hardy, medical illustrator. 2d ed. McGraw [1968 c1969] 556p $7.95   **614.8**

1 First aid in illness and injury

First published 1963

"The book 'offers detailed instructions for meeting most medical emergencies.' What to do in case of: Acute-heart failure, auto accident, unattended childbirth, bleeding, drowning, fractures, poisoning, shock." Science and Tech

Bibliography: p540-45

Red Cross. United States. American National Red Cross

Basic first aid. Doubleday 1971 4v illus pa set $2.95   **614.8**

1 First aid in illness and injury

This is "a series of four books of programmed material which covers the whole basic course of first aid. The material consists of questions and answers, with illustrations, that demonstrate techniques—from applying a tourniquet to treating shock victims." Publisher's note

615 Therapeutics and pharmacology

Cohen, Sidney

The drug dilemma. McGraw [1968 c1969] 139p (McGraw-Hill Paperback ser. in health education) $5.50   **615**

1 Drugs 2 Narcotics 3 Narcotic habit

This book "attempts to present the current drug scene within the context of our past experience with mind-altering chemicals. The trends and foreseeable future developments are described. The effects, side effects, treatment and prevention of all abused drugs are presented. These include the sedatives, narcotics, psychedelics, stimulants, solvents, etc." Publisher's note

"Characterized by clear definitions, logical classifications, and understandable explanations, this book is an excellent contribution to the problem of drug use and abuse. . . . Interesting exhaustive glossary . . . and a comprehensive table, 'Summary of Drug Effects.' Good bibliography; no index. Emphatically recommended to all parents, teachers, and students on all levels." Choice

Hechtlinger, Adelaide

(comp.) The great patent medicine era; or, Without benefit of doctor. Grosset 1970 248p illus $14.95   **615**

1 Patent medicines 2 Medicine, Popular

Selections of Americana from various books, magazines, almanacs, newspapers, etc.

Contents: Books to aid afflicted; Parts of the body; Home remedy books; Indian doctor's dispensatory; The Indian doctor; Passions and sex; The guide board; Health and disease; Book advertisements; Almanacs of patent medicines; Labels of old patent medicines; Sears & Roebuck; Aphrodisiacs; Electricity; Dr Pierce; The Indian vegetable family instructor; Dr Chase's recipes; Medicology; Advertisements; Trading cards; Medicinal plants; Medical folklore

Modell, Walter

Drugs, by Walter Modell, Alfred Lansing and the editors of Time-Life Books. [Rev] Time-Life Bks. [1969 c1967] 200p illus (Life Science lib) lib. bdg. $7.60   **615**

1 Drugs

First published 1967

"How drugs have been used—and misused—is the subject matter of this volume, which traces the origins of modern drugs and exam-

Modell, Walter—*Continued*
ines some of the most important and common ones: alcohol, antibiotics, tranquilizers and contraceptives. Each text chapter of the book is accompanied by a picture essay." About this book

"While the content is necessarily journalistic and highly selective, it does provide historical orientation and emphasizes both popular and professional current interests in drugs and their use. Suggestions for further reading are included." Science Bks

616.5 Dermatology

Sternberg, Thomas H.
More than skin deep. Doubleday 1970 330p $7.95   616.5

1 Skin 2 Skin—Diseases

"An exceedingly comprehensive layman's guide to the skin and its care by an outstanding authority and teacher of dermatology. In three parts, it covers first, aspects of the skin in beauty and appearance, then everyday health subjects affecting the skin, and finally diseases of the skin and their detection and management." Book News

Woodburn, John H.
Know your skin; illus. by Lee Ames. Putnam 1967 159p illus (A Science survey bk) lib. bdg. $3.79   616.5

1 Skin

This book "deals with the basic functions of the human integument: anatomy, texture, and color; cytology, texture, and color of hair; blushing and blanching; common skin infections; skin poisons and bites; and relation of tactile stimulation to emotional and affective states." The AAAS Science Bk list

616.8 Diseases of nervous system

Killilea, Marie
Karen. Prentice-Hall 1952 314p $4.95   616.8

1 Cerebral palsy 2 Killilea, Karen 3 United Cerebral Palsy Association, inc.

The "story of a victorious battle against cerebral palsy, as Marie and Jim proved that twenty-odd famous doctors were wrong about baby Karen, whom they taught to talk, walk and write. There is also a good deal about the work of the United Cerebral Palsy Association." Retail Bookseller

"Karen's story is symbolic of the many less articulate victims of cerebral palsy who will live in life's shadows unless our entire people give them aid; the rewards of such aid are positively presented by Mrs. Killilea, who not only writes well, but presents a message of considerable merit." Library J

Followed by: With love from Karen, listed below

With love from Karen. Prentice-Hall 1963 371p $4.95   616.8

1 Cerebral palsy 2 Killilea, Karen

This account brings Karen, a victim of cerebral palsy, "through medical and spiritual trials to her twentieth birthday. Though Karen and her problems remain central, this is truly a family portrait . . . of firm Catholic faith, courage, resourcefulness, joyousness, and self-discipline, typified by [adopted] daughter Gloria's behavior in the face of what appeared to be a doomed love, as much as by any other member of the household." Booklist

"Mrs. Killilea has an uncanny knack for making her family come alive for her readers. . . . The book is very readable, entertaining and absorbing." Best Sellers

Lang, Gladys Engel
(ed.) Mental health. Wilson, H.W. 1958 192p (The Reference shelf v30, no. 1) $4.50
616.8

1 Mental illness 2 Mentally ill—Care and treatment

In this symposium "most of the articles concern mental illness. What are the roots of mental disorder? How widespread is it? What are the major kinds of treatment and, in particular, what facilities do we have for the mentally ill, in the form of hospitals, clinics, and the like. . . . In these few pages we can define the problems and trends only in the broadest outline." Preface

"A comprehensive examination of many facets of the mental health problem." Pub W
Bibliography: p184-92

616.86 Psychoneurotic addictions to narcotics

Hentoff, Nat
A doctor among the addicts. Rand McNally 1968 135p illus $4.95   616.86

1 Nyswander, Marie E. 2 Narcotic habit

"Hentoff discusses the problems of narcotics and addicts, telling of the Methadone Maintenance Treatment Program started and maintained in Harlem by Dr. Marie Nyswander, who feels that this drug can be an important means of rehabilitating the addicted. . . . The book includes a brief history of drugs, drug laws and addiction in the United States." Library J

"As the success story of an extraordinary physician, Nat Hentoff's account is mostly good news; as an expose of our national head-in-the-sand attitude over much of the past 50 years it is shockingly bad news." N Y Times Bk R

616.89 Psychotherapy

Rogers, Carl R.
Carl Rogers on encounter groups. Harper 1970 172p boards $5.95   616.89

1 Psychotherapy

The author "first traces the history of encounter groups, then turns to the experiences of groups in which he has participated. His account is filled with illustrative 'scenes' from actual groups, so that the reader can sample the flavor of group life and understand why so many different individuals find encounter groups meaningful." Publisher's note

"Carl Rogers is an excellent guide to the group movement—sensible, knowledgeable, committed yet not fanatic, an acknowledged expert who writes clearly and without jargon." Christian Century

616.9 Other diseases

Blanzaco, André
VD: facts you should know [by] André Blanzaco in consultation with William F. Schwartz and Julius B. Richmond. Robert Lipman, designer. Lothrop 1970 63p illus $3.95, lib. bdg. $3.78   616.9

1 Venereal diseases

This book provides young people with information about venereal diseases. It discusses their effects on the body and how they are caused, cured and prevented. A brief historical note is included as well as the steps which should be taken by a person who contracts a venereal disease. (Publisher)
Glossary: p61-63

Marks, Geoffrey
The medieval plague; the black death of the Middle Ages. Doubleday 1971 155p $3.95
616.9

1 Plague

"The story of the plague that ravaged fourteenth century Europe is one of disaster and horror, and in this book [the author] examines the medical aspects of the plague, describing the role of rats and rodents in the plague's cycle, and then delves into the moral and social implications of the situation which the 'black death' left behind. He demonstrates the human desolation and depravity which evolved as family ties were broken down, religious values were lost, and priests, lawyers, and doctors failed the people." News of Bks
Bibliography: p147-48. Map on lining-papers

Zinsser, Hans
Rats, lice and history. . . . Little 1935 301p $6.95
616.9

1 Typhus fever 2 Contagion and contagious diseases

"Being a study in biography, which after twelve preliminary chapters indispensable for the preparation of the lay reader, deals with the life history of typhus fever." Subtitle
"Following his 'inquisitive nose' into many a diverting side issue, the author, a bacteriologist, has written with frequent ironic and timely comment, an illuminating, nontechnical 'life history' of typhus fever. Typhus and other epidemic diseases are shown to have exerted great influence on political and military history. The fact that the hiding places of typhus in rats and lice have been discovered and that modern science is learning to cope with the disease does not mean typhus is dead. 'It will continue to break into the open whenever human stupidity and brutality give it a chance.' " N Y Libraries
"This book will appeal to three classes of readers. First, those miserable sinners who like popular science. Secondly, amateurs of history who enjoy novel viewpoints and curious anecdotes rather than ponderous and systematic works. Thirdly, people who like to study the reactions of a vigorous human mind to its environment." Sat R

617 Surgery

Longmore, Donald
Spare-part surgery; the surgical practice of the future. Ed. and illus. by M. Ross-Macdonald. Doubleday 1968 192p illus (Doubleday Science ser) $6.95
617

1 Transplantation of organs, tissues, etc.

"Longmore discusses the 'surgical practice of the future' in chapters on the immune reactions, heart-lung and kidney machines, new prosthetic limbs, mechanical implants including energy sources, simple and complex homografts, and finally ethical, legal, and economic considerations. In general discussions, with much solid data, the author manages to convey the essence of modern forefront surgery. Excellent colored diagrams and pictures." Choice

Nolen, William A.
The making of a surgeon. Random House 1970 269p $6.95
617

1 Surgery

"After graduation from a medical school, a would-be surgeon (as with other doctors) spends four additional years in a hospital mastering his craft. These four years, beginning with his internship and culminating in a head residency, are the subject of Nolen's book. As he shows us, these are likely to be hard, grueling years, both physically and mentally exhausting, and only gradually getting easier as

one learns the routines and his competence increases and status improves with seniority. Nolen's is a fascinating story, told in a straightforward and sometimes earthy fashion; shocking at times perhaps, but always engrossing." Choice

619 Comparative and experimental medicine

Heller, John H.
Of mice, men and molecules. Scribner 1960 176p illus $4.50
619

1 Medicine—Research 2 Research

"In a strong, almost impassioned, plea for support of basic research, the founder of the New England Institute for Medical Research addresses himself to the layman with no background in science. . . . Using the layman's vocabulary, he describes medical research at the molecular and cellular levels where a transdisciplinary approach is imperative, tells how his own institution started with practically no funds and certainly no facilities, enumerates the problems involved in setting up and maintaining such a laboratory, and gives progress to date of some of the researches undertaken. . . . Young people blessed with curiosity, would-be scientists, future physicians who read the book will get a clear-cut idea of what is involved in current medical research and of the problems and intangible rewards that await the researcher. They will pick up some interesting general medical information along the way, as well." Best Sellers

620 Engineering

Furnas, C. C.
The engineer, by C. C. Furnas, Joe McCarthy and the editors of Time-Life Books. Time-Life Bks. [1971] 200p illus maps (Life Science lib) lib. bdg. $7.60
620

1 Engineering 2 Engineering as a profession
First published 1966
A brief survey of some outstanding accomplishments, old and new, in various engineering fields, interspersed with descriptions of the work of leading engineers
An "instructive series of essays. . . . An especially lucid discussion of Thomas Edison's contributions. Will serve as career inspiration for high school students." N Y New Tech Bks
Further reading: p196

621 Applied physics

Sterland, E. G.
Energy into power; the story of man and machines. Natural Hist. Press 1967 252p illus (Nature and science lib) boards $6.95
621

1 Force and energy 2 Power (Mechanics) 3 Machinery

"Published for the American Museum of Natural History"
"The first section of this book deals with the sources of energy that can be turned into power. The second section presents the scientific principles that lie behind the conversion of energy into power. This section also shows how and why different kinds of machines have been developed. . . . The third section looks into the future." p15
"An appendix, somewhat more technical than the remainder of the book, explains the laws of thermodynamics. A text of such broad scope must necessarily be somewhat superficial, and for the most part, it is scientifically precise. . . . The illustrations and diagrams, some in color, are attractive and informative. The mathematical background necessary for comprehension is minimal." Science Bks

621.3 Electrical, electronic engineering

Buban, Peter
Understanding electricity and electronics [by] Peter Buban and Marshall L. Schmitt. 2d ed. McGraw 1969 438p illus (McGraw-Hill Publications in industrial education) $7.96   621.3

1 Electric engineering 2 Electronics
First published 1962
"Begins with information on basic procedures such as soldering and the use of tools, and explains the operation of many common electrical appliances. Good diagrams and experiments assure comprehension." The AAAS Science Book List

621.302 Electrical, electronic engineering—Handbooks, manuals, etc.

Graham, Frank D.
Audels Handy book of practical electricity with wiring diagrams; ready reference for professional electricians, students, and all electrical workers. Audel illus $5.95   621.302

1 Electric engineering—Handbooks, manuals, etc.
First published 1924. Frequently revised to conform with up-to-date practices
Principles and applications of electricity and descriptions of electric machinery components are contained in this ready-reference manual

621.32 Light and illumination engineering. Lasers

Brown, Ronald
Lasers: tools of modern technology. Doubleday [1969 c1968] 192p illus (Doubleday Science ser) $5.95   621.32

1 Lasers
The author "explains the theory of the laser and its development in the 1960s into specific tools having applications in the fields of medicine, communications, engineering, and manufacturing." Publisher's note
The author's "explanation of the basic laser science, while qualitative, would be an excellent introduction to more detailed classroom discussions. His discussion of laser applications with the suggested reading list would be a first-rate start for an assigned paper on supplementary reading." Choice
Suggested reading: p188

Carroll, John M.
The story of the laser. New ed. rev. and enl. Dutton 1970 213p illus $5.95   621.32

1 Lasers
First published 1964
A history which covers "the first attempts to link the phenomena of light and electricity, one hundred years ago, to the scientific and engineering efforts of today. It explores the more important uses of the laser, both actual and potential, in national defense, space exploration, communications, data processing, medicine, and manufacturing." Preface
Bibliography: p199-205

Larsen, Egon
Lasers work like this; illus. by Charles Green. Roy Pubs. 1969 54p illus (The 'Science works like this' ser) $3.95   621.32

1 Lasers

"Presents a very interesting, easily read narrative on the history of laser development, from the first concepts of Dr. Charles Townes in 1951 to the myriad of applications in recent years. . . . Larsen's description of laser operation is presented clearly and correctly, drawing on concepts from quantum mechanics only enough to prevent misleading the reader with generalizations. . . . Applications for lasers are continuously increasing. Typical fields of interest include astronomy, geodesy, communications and television, stone cutting, welding, mining and tunnelling, high-voltage power measurement, medical surgery, dentistry, and earthquake prediction. Larsen concludes with a macabre postscript concerning military application." Science Bks

621.3803 Electronic and communication engineering— Dictionaries

Funk & Wagnalls Dictionary of electronics. Funk 1969 230p illus $6.95   621.3803

1 Electronics—Dictionaries
Companion volume to Funk & Wagnalls Dictionary of data processing, by Harold A. Rodgers, entered in class 651.803
"Electronics and electrical terms are defined to show their relation to the root concepts of physics and mathematics. Definitions are written in a style that allows the interested layman to ignore technical information and yet comprehend the basics. Careful attention has been paid to digital circuitry and to computers." Publisher's note
"This dictionary contains a modest, but well-chosen, number of electronics terms. Definitions are generally clear, accurate, and concise." Library J

621.381 Electronic engineering

Pearce, W. E.
Transistors and circuits; electronics for young experimenters [by] W. E. Pearce and Aaron E. Klein. Doubleday 1971 156p illus $4.95, lib. bdg. $5.70   621.381

1 Electronics 2 Electronic apparatus and appliances
First published 1966 in England with title: Electronics for young experimenters
"This is a logically organized, clearly diagramed collection of 71 experiments progressing from simple procedures for charging by friction such things as nylons and plastic bags to the building of elementary transistor circuits; the later experiments hinge on knowledge gained in earlier ones. The book contains experiments involving the construction of apparatus, the use of the apparatus, and the measuring of results. Tips for soldering, circuit color codes, and supply sources are appended. For science student or beginning electronics hobbyist." Booklist

Steckler, Larry
Simple transistor projects for hobbyists & students. G/L Tab Bks. 1970 192p illus $7.95
621.381

1 Transistors 2 Electronic circuits 3 Electronic apparatus and appliances
The "hobbyist will find all sorts of devices to build with diodes, SCRs, LASCRs, transistors, Triacs, Diacs, Trigacs, and integrated circuits. The first Section offers suggestions for building or breadboarding circuits. Section 2, 3, and 4 describes a wide range of devices for the car, home, office, or anywhere electronics devices are used. . . . Section 5 describes Trigacs and how to use them in a variety of circuits for switching and control functions, and Section 6 is devoted to integrated-circuit projects." Publisher's note

621.3841   Radio

Collins, A. Frederick
The radio amateur's handbook. Crowell
illus $5.95   621.3841
1 Radio—Handbooks, manuals, etc.
First published 1922. Frequently revised to
bring material up to date
"A valuable aid to the beginning or experienced radio amateur. Covers fundamentals of
construction techniques, elementary electronic
theory, and FCC regulations, plus information
on more complicated apparatus. The concluding
chapters deal with mobile transmitters, transistors, tunnel diodes and solid-state devices.
Glossary and index included." The AAAS Science Book List

The **Radio** amateur's handbook. Am. Radio
illus $4.50   621.3841
1 Radio—Handbooks, manuals, etc.
Annual. Edited by E. E. Handy, 1926-1930;
1931-date by the headquarters staff of the
American Radio Relay League
This is the standard manual of amateur radio
communication. Reprinted each year with revisions to keep the material up to date. The
"Handbook" is intended both as reference
work for member-operators of the American
Radio Relay League and other skilled amateurs and as a source of information to those
wishing to participate in amateur radio activ-
ies

Simon, Bert
Ham radio incentive licensing guide. G/L
Tab Bks. 1969 160p illus $6.95   621.3841
1 Radio—Examinations, questions, etc.
"A handbook for ham radio operators that
gives instruction on how to get an initial start
in amateur radio and how to advance to higher
licenses. Suggestions on learning the Morse
code and a chapter each on the various license
requirements, sample examinations with answers, and directions for applying for licenses
with lists of locations where examinations are
held are included." Booklist

621.389   Sound recording and reproducing systems

Zuckerman, Art
Tape recording for the hobbyist. [2d ed]
Sams 1967 160p illus pa $3.95   621.389
1 Tape and wire recorders
"A Howard W. Sams Photofact publication"
First published 1963 with title: Magnetic recording for the hobbyist
The author includes directions and advice
for the amateur on all aspects of tape recording, suggesting what to record and how to edit
in addition to describing the mechanics of tap-
ing and the correct care of tapes

621.48   Nuclear engineering

Curtis, Richard
Perils of the peaceful atom; the myth of
safe nuclear power plants, by Richard Curtis
and Elizabeth Hogan. Doubleday 1969 274p
$5.95   621.48
1 Atomic power plants 2 Nuclear reactors
3 Radioactivity
Documenting "their statements and contentions with quotes from AEC reports, congressional testimony and scientific journals [the
authors] cite instances of inadequate planning
in the utilization of nuclear energy for electrical power; they stress the dangers of imperfect workmanship, human error and natural
disasters to nuclear plants located near urban
centers." Pub W

"Includes a complete set of footnotes documenting the case and lists the principal sources
used by the authors. Well and clearly written.
The argument [presented] will surely serve to
stimulate public awareness of and concern
over the consequences possible from large scale
nuclear power installations." Choice
Principal sources: p258-68. Maps on lining-
papers

Fermi, Laura
Atoms for the world; United States participation in the Conference on the Peaceful
Uses of Atomic Energy. Univ. of Chicago
Press 1957 227p $4.50   621.48
1 International Conference on the Peaceful
Uses of Atomic Energy, Geneva, 1955 2 Nuclear engineering 3 Atomic energy
The widow of the atomic scientist presents
"the story of the first conference on the peaceful uses of atomic energy. Atomic energy is
discussed in non-technical terms in connection
with events of this conference which was
a milestone in man's quest for peace." The
AAAS Science Book List
"It is not in any sense a definitive 'history'
of the conference itself or even of the United
States delegation. Instead it is the warm appreciative account of a sensitive observer who
shared the enthusiasm and hopes of the other
delegates." Christian Science Monitor

Stokley, James
The new world of the atom. Rev. and enl.
ed. Washburn 1970 333p illus map $8.95
621.48
1 Nuclear engineering 2 Atomic energy
First published 1957
This book tells the story of man's harnessing
of atomic energy, describes its uses in war and
peace, discusses contemporary developments
throughout the world, and projects what lies
ahead. (Publisher)
"The descriptions and explanations of peaceful uses of atomic energy in power plants, for
transportation, and in industry and medicine,
and other areas are stated in clear, simple
terms for the layman or beginning student."
Booklist

621.5   Low temperature technology. Cryogenics

Boyd, Waldo T.
The world of cryogenics; the story of heat-
lessness. Putnam [1969 c1968] 191p illus
(Science survey ser) lib. bdg. $3.96   621.5
1 Low temperatures
"The author explores what has been found
out about the world of heatlessness since
Michael Faraday began investigating it more
than a century ago. He also forecasts the uses
of cryogenics in years to come." Huntting
"Clearly written, well-organized survey. . . .
Helpful diagrams and photographs are included
throughout." Library J
Glossary of cryogenic terms: p182-88

621.9   Machine tools

Black, Perry O.
Audels Machinists library. Audel 1965-1966
3v illus ea $5.95   621.9
1 Machine tools 2 Machine shop practice
3 Machinery—Handbooks, manuals, etc.
Contents: v 1 Basic machine shop practice;
v2 Machine shop; v3 Toolmakers handybook
The first volume of this series covers basic
principles and practices of machine operation.
Comprehensive discussions on the major machines and their setups and the operations
are given in the second volume. The third volume encompasses toolmaking procedures, in-

Black, Perry O.—*Continued*
cluding layouts, drawing of specifications, jigs
and fixtures, gear forming, cams and dies, and
heat treating. Of use to students, beginners and
active workers in the field as a reference and
study source. (Publisher)

O'Brien, Robert
Machines, by Robert O'Brien and the editors of Time-Life Books. Time-Life Bks.
1968 200p illus (Life Science lib) lib.
bdg. $7.60   621.9

1 Machinery 2 Technology—History
First published 1964
Partial contents: A seasoned instrument for
war or peace; Assembly-line avenues to abundance; The quickened world of internal combustion; Master keys to an age of communication; The promise and problems of automation; Bibliography
"This contains photographs and drawings of
many of the notable machines which have aided
and at times controlled our lives and live-
lihoods." Library J

622.09 Mining engineering and operations—History

Sloane, Howard N.
A pictorial history of American mining; the
adventure and drama of finding and extracting nature's wealth from the earth, from pre-
Columbian times to the present, by Howard
N. and Lucille L. Sloane. Crown 1970 342p
illus $12.50   622.09

1 Mines and mineral resources—U.S.—History
"In addition to details of discoveries and descriptions of mining operations and techniques
through history, are the camps and trails
themselves: The folklore, the swindles, strikes,
disasters, adventurers, child labor, women, outlaws bankers, entrepreneurs, magnates—all
part of this living panoramic history." Book
News
Bibliography: p325-29

623.4 Military ordnance

Baar, James
Polaris! By James Baar and William E.
Howard. Harcourt 1960 245p illus $4.95
                                                 623.4

1 Polaris (Missile) 2 Atomic submarines
"The birth, development, and accomplishments of the Polaris missile program are chronicled in this informative, nontechnical account.
. . . Preliminary work in the Navy's Special
Projects Office, the leaders in the Polaris program, the successful testing of the missile,
life aboard the missile-carrying submarine
are described." Booklist

623.7 Military aircraft

Green, William
The warplanes of the Third Reich; with
line drawings by Dennis Punnett. Doubleday
1970 672p illus $25   623.7

1 Airplanes, Military 2 Germany. Air Force
"This monumental study of German warplanes from 1933 to 1945 is the result of 20 years
of research by the author, and it will undoubtedly stand as the definitive work on this subject. . . . [The author] has devoted a section to
each of the warplanes developed in Germany,
including experimental prototypes, and has

traced the development and career of the aircraft. These sections are profusely illustrated
with superb photographs, cutaway drawings,
and Punnett's excellent profile and plan view
drawings. . . . A provocative introduction
traces succinctly the rise and decline of the
Luftwaffe." Library J

623.82 Ships and boats

Anderson, William R.
Nautilus 90 north, by William R. Anderson
with Clay Blair, Jr. Photographs by John
Krawczyk. World Pub. 1959 251p illus $5.95
                                                 623.82

1 Nautilus (Atomic submarine) 2 Arctic regions
"The skipper of the nuclear submarine that
found a new Northwest Passage from Seattle
to England under the Arctic ice . . . tells briskly about his ship [crew] . . . the preparatory
mission and the final achievement." Pub W
"It is packed with details about the structure and operation of the 'Nautilus' . . . and
the problems of secrecy and rumor. Commander
Anderson recreates the day-to-day events,
hours of suspense, tension, even practical jokes
and finally, recognizes the accomplishment and
implications of this voyage." Doors to More
Mature Reading
Map on lining-papers

Landström, Björn
The ship; an illustrated history, written
and illus. by Björn Landström. Doubleday
1961 309p illus $17.95   623.82

1 Shipbuilding 2 Ships—History
Translated from the Swedish by Michael Phillips
The author "traces the development of water transportation over a period of six thousand years—from the ancient Egyptian up to
the age of nuclear propulsion. Björn Landström, a Scandinavian author and artist, supplies both text and pictures . . . the latter consisting largely of diagrammatic drawings." N Y
Times Bk R
"This is a notable contribution to the history of sail. . . . [The author's] illustrations,
over 800 in full color and in black-and-white,
are beautifully drawn and exquisite in detail.
Time after time Landström pauses to identify
carefully the various parts of a ship and of its
rigging." Best Sellers
Sources: p311-12

Sweeney, James B.
A pictorial history of oceanographic submersibles. Crown 1970 310p illus $9.95
                                                 623.82

1 Submarines 2 Diving vehicles 3 Oceanography—Research
"From the bizarre devices the Greeks, Romans and Persians used to survive underwater
(and to attack enemy ships) to the newest
submersible, 'Deep Quest,' which planted an
American flag at the deepest level of Pacific
ocean-bottom in 1968 [the author] tells the
story of the first use of every sort of submarine invention in recorded history." Pub W
Glossary of terms: p301-05. Bibliography:
p306-08

623.88 Seamanship. Knotcraft

Snyder, Paul
Knots & lines [by] Paul and Arthur Snyder.
[Rev. enl. ed] De Graff [1970 c1967] 104p
illus $6.95   623.88

1 Knots and splices
ISBN 0-8286-0046-5
First published 1967 by Van Nostrand
"The purpose of this manual is to teach a
beginner 'how' to tie basic knots on board the

Snyder, Paul—*Continued*
cruising and racing sailboat. . . . Where practical each knot and each line handling operation has: 1. A brief general description; 2. An outline of a typical use with an illustration. . . . 3. A specific description, numbered step by step, of how to tie the knot or how to perform the operation, with corresponding numbered illustrations." Introduction
Glossary: p95-102. Bibliographical references included in Acknowledgment: p104

624 Civil engineering

Jacobs, David
Bridges, canals & tunnels, by David Jacobs and Anthony E. Neville; consultant: Robert M. Vogel. Published by American Heritage in association with The Smithsonian Inst. Am. Heritage 1968 159p illus maps (The Smithsonian Lib) boards $4.95, lib. bdg. $4.98
                                      624

1 Civil engineering   2 Bridges   3 Tunnels 4 Canals
"Describes the network of inland paths, passages and crossings on the North American continent, within an historical framework, but with the chief focus on the actual technological processes of civil engineering." McClurg. Book News
"The superb illustrations, many of them historic, show construction details as well as historic scenes and events. An appended section of special features includes a chronology of American engineering accomplishments, a history of song of canal construction, a discussion of the essentials of bridge engineering design, and reports of celebrations that accompanied the completion of historic projects." Science Bks
Further reading: p152

Overman, Michael
Roads, bridges, and tunnels; modern approaches to road engineering. Doubleday 1968 191p illus (Doubleday Science ser) $5.95   624
1 Civil engineering   2 Roads   3 Bridges 4 Tunnels
"History and techniques of civil engineering are presented in a manner that demonstrates how basic mathematical procedures, as well as scientific principles, and business methods are involved in the design and construction of highways, tunnels and bridges. There is also a history of the profession and excellent explanatory diagrams and colored illustrations." The AAAS Science Book List
Bibliography: p187

Smith, H. Shirley
The world's great bridges. Rev. ed. with 24 line drawings by Rowland J. Mainstone and 43 photo plates. Harper [1965 c1964] 250p illus $5.95   624
1 Bridges
First published 1953 in England
Partial contents: The beginnings; Roman bridges; Persia, China, and Japan; The Middle Ages; Birth of the modern bridge; Reinforced concrete bridges; The cantilever era; Big steel arches; The great suspension bridges of America; Bibliography
"It is a book for the layman who likes a bit of solid information with his reading." San Francisco Chronicle

625.7 Highway engineering

Von Hagen, Victor W.
Roman roads; photographs by Adolfo Tomeucci; maps and drawings by Dino Rigolo. World Pub. 1966 189p illus maps $4.95, lib. bdg. $5.20   625.7
1 Roads 2 Rome—History

"The Roman roads were among the great engineering feats of the ancient world. Here is the fascinating story of how they were built, as well as an informal survey of the great historic events—from the 4th century B.C. . . in which these roads fulfilled a vital function." Hunting
A selected bibliography: p183-84

627 Hydraulic engineering and construction works

Munzer, Martha E.
Valley of vision; the TVA years; illus. with contemporary prints, photographs & maps. Knopf 1969 199p illus maps (The Living history lib) $3.95, lib. bdg. $3.74 627
1 Tennessee Valley Authority
This account of the Tennessee Valley Authority, established in 1933 to harness the Tennessee River and to revitalize the land through which it flows, discusses the process by which the plan became a reality and the related problems of relocation of the families in the area, flood control, and demonstration farming. Much of the story is told in the words of people involved or affected by the plan. (Publisher)
"That [the author] has a good grasp on T.V.A. affairs is apparent in this very readable and informative book. . . . Very useful as a reference." Bk Buyer's Guide
Bibliography: p189-92

627.7 Underwater operations

Cousteau, Jacques-Yves
(ed.) Captain Cousteau's Underwater treasury; ed. by Jacques-Yves Cousteau and James Dugan. Harper 1959 xx, 415p $10
                                      627.7
1 Bathyscaphe 2 Skin and scuba diving
"A generous sampling from the literature of underwater adventure and exploration brings together over 50 articles and book excerpts, consisting predominantly of true first-person accounts, interspersed with poems, quotations, and curiosa. Writers ranging from Aristotle, Darwin, and Jules Verne to Beebe, Quilici, Hass, Rachel Carson, and the compilers themselves describe the wonders of the marine world and the many activities—scientific investigation, warfare, rescue and salvage work, treasure diving, spearfishing and submarine archaeology, photography, agriculture, and industry—which man has carried on beneath the sea." Booklist

The living sea, by Jacques-Yves Cousteau with James Dugan. Harper 1963 325p illus map $7.95   627.7
1 Diving vehicles 2 Marine biology 3 Archeology 4 Photography, Submarine 5 Calypso (Ship)
"Adventures on and near the sea research ship 'Calypso,' which Cousteau designed to carry out undersea photography, scientific work, and, incidentally, marine archaeology. These are bright . . . memories of exploration, danger, and discoveries in the Mediterranean, the Red Sea, the Indian Ocean, the Persian Gulf, and other seas. The 'Calypso's crew had some fascinating experiences with dolphins [and] sharks. . . . [There are] 24 pages of color photographs which originally appeared in 'National Geographic,' and . . . 64 pages of black and white photographs." Pub W
"It offers both adventure and science in abundance with the added bonuses of fine writing and magnificent photographs. A 'must' for any young adult collection." Library J

Cousteau, Jacques Y.—*Continued*

The silent world, by J. Y. Cousteau with Frédéric Dumas; illus. with photographs. Harper 1953 266p illus $7.95, lib. bdg. $5.79

627.7

1 Skin and scuba diving 2 Marine biology 3 Photography, Submarine

"The author describes the development of the aqualung during the war in occupied France, exploration of sunken ships as well as natural wonders, diving for ancient art treasures, and experiments in the depths of the Atlantic Ocean and the Red Sea." Booklist

This "is a fascinating book, the distillation of Cousteau's experiences undersea. . . . Captain Cousteau succeeds admirably in giving his readers a sense of personal participation in these explorations of a strange world. We feel that we know what a diver sees, feels, and thinks as he descends into the blue twilight of the sea." N Y Her Trib Books

The book "supplements the newness [of experiences] with photographs of things never seen before—65 pages of them, 17 in color. Its style has the French clarity and wit." Christian Science Monitor

629.13   Aeronautics

American Heritage

The American Heritage History of flight, by the editors of American Heritage, The Magazine of History. Editor in charge: Alvin M. Josephy, Jr. Narrative by Arthur Gordon. . . . Am. Heritage 1962 416p illus maps boards $16.50

629.13

1 Aeronautics—History

"With two chapters by Marvin W. McFarland; introduction by Carl Spatz and Ira C. Eaker." Title page

This "covers the history of aviation from the earliest times to the beginning of the space age. It is especially strong in the early endeavors, when ballooning lifted man above his earthly domain and the earliest pioneers experimented with their strange machines. The book also includes excerpts from the reminiscences of these pioneers as well as interviews with those still living. Many of the drawings were especially commissioned for this work." Library J

Includes bibliography

Bonney, Walter T.

The heritage of Kitty Hawk. Norton 1962 211p illus $8.50

629.13

1 Aeronautics—History   2 Airplanes—History

This is a history of aviation from its beginnings to the first airplane exploits of World War I. "Here are Glenn Curtiss, [the] Lilienthals, Langley, Glenn Martin, the Wrights, and others who began with gliders, flapping wings, and other crude devices but finally put man into the air." Bk Buyer's Guide

"The second half of the book . . . tells about the early research laboratories, about the development of the early engines, and about the first uses of the airplane as a military weapon." Library J

Harris, Sherwood

The first to fly; aviation's pioneer days. Simon & Schuster 1970 316p illus $6.95

629.13

1 Aeronautics—History

SBN 671-20474-2

Through diaries, letters, newspaper stories and interviews, the author presents a history of aviation. He begins with the "experiments that culminated in Wilbur and Orville Wright's first successful flight; he continues through the years when the . . . Frenchmen Voisin and Blériot and the Brazilian Santos-Dumont dominated the skies; and in the final [longest] sec-

tion he follows the course of flying between 1908 and this country's entrance into World War I." Publisher's note

Bibliography included in Acknowledgments: p297-99

Lindbergh, Anne Morrow

Listen! The wind; with foreword and map drawings by Charles A. Lindbergh. Harcourt [1940 c1938] 275p illus maps $3.95

629.13

1 Aeronautics—Flights 2 Bathhurst, Gambia 3 Natal, Brazil 4 Santiago (Island)

"Harbrace edition"

"The story of a survey flight around the North Atlantic Ocean in 1933. It is a true and accurate account of various incidents which occurred in flying from Africa to South America. The purpose of the flight was to study the air-routes between America and Europe." Foreword

"There is a strong appeal to every reader whether interested in the practicalness of aviation or the thrill of a truly exciting air flight. . . . The touches of humor that show the companionship and the reliance upon each other's abilities—and last but not least the unconscious beauty of poetry and poetic thinking that runs throughout the book make it a story that all should read." Churchman

North to the Orient; with maps by Charles A. Lindbergh. Harcourt 1949 [c1935] 255p maps $2.95

629.13

1 Aeronautics—Flights 2 East (Far East) 3 Arctic regions

"Harbrace Modern classics"

First published 1935

"There is so much of the personality of the author in this book that it is much more than a volume of travel or of aviation. It tells the story of the flight to the Orient by the Great Circle route in the summer of 1931, with information about equipment and incidents from the trip, mingled with personal reflections and impressions." Wis Lib Bul

This "has intrinsic value for girls as a revelation of character, imagination, and humor combined with rare powers of observation." N Y Pub Lib

Lindbergh, Charles A.

The Spirit of St Louis. Scribner 1953 562p illus $7.95

629.13

1 Aeronautics—Flights 2 Spirit of St Louis (Airplane)

Awarded the Pulitzer Prize for biography, 1954

"An important American autobiography providing a complete account of the most superb adventure of our time'—the first solo transatlantic flight from New York to Paris, as well as a detailed description of the preparation for the flight which in turn mirrors aviation in the 1920's. A very long book, but an exciting one." Minnesota

"Mature boys who appreciate Saint Exupery's books [two of which are entered below] will like the fine writing as well as the aeronautical details in Lindbergh's story of his aviation experiences." Booklist

Appendix includes log of the flight, engineering data, copies of headlines from the world press, and an extensive bibliography

Saint Exupéry, Antoine de

Airman's odyssey. Harcourt [1959 c1942] 437p illus $7.50

629.13

1 Aeronautics—Flights

First published 1942 by Reynal and Hitchcock

A reprint in one volume of the following books: Wind, sand, and stars, listed separately below; Night flight; Flight to Arras

Night flight was translated from the French by Stuart Gilbert; the other two books were translated by Lewis Galantière

"The first tells of flying in Africa and South America, the third of war-flying in France. 'Night Flight' is cast in novel form, but . . .

Saint Exupéry, Antoine de—*Continued*
it, too, grew directly out of the author's own life." Huntting
What these books "really are is poetic expression of what flying means to a man of meditative, sensitive nature." Twentieth Century Authors

Wind, sand, and stars; tr. from the French by Lewis Galantière; illus. by John O'H. Cosgrave II. Illus. ed. Harcourt 1949 [c1940] 306p illus $2.95   629.13

1 Aeronautics—Flights
First published 1940 by Reynal & Hitchcock
"Harbrace Modern classics"
"The author's enthusiasm for flying is dramatized in his descriptions of his own flights, crashes, and narrow escapes. He flew the mail over the Sahara and across the Andes in all weather conditions. He knew danger and loneliness, but he reveled in the beauty he saw and the rapture he felt. One of his most memorable experiences was on the Paris-Saigon flight. . . . Saint Exupéry discusses the early planes, the elements and the comradeship of the pilots, as well as his adventures in Spain during the Civil War. Through all of this he has woven philosophical musings, often speaking poetically about those thoughts which touched him deeply. Because 'Wind, Sand and Stars' is concerned fundamentally with human relationships and motives, it is not dated. . . . The book's adventures appeal to those who who want action, but the beautiful image and meditative passages make it more appropriate for the poetic, sensitive individual." Doors to More Mature Reading

629.132 Principles of flight

Stever, H. Guyford
Flight, by H. Guyford Stever, James J. Haggerty and the editors of Time-Life Books. Time-Life Bks. 1971 200p illus (Life Science lib) lib. bdg. $7.60   629.132

1 Flight 2 Airplanes
First published 1965
"The world of manned flight—from its primitive beginnings through the sophisticated present to the science-fiction future—makes up the scope of this book. It covers the history of flight, the theory of aerodynamics, propulsion, navigation and air-traffic control, testing [and] design. . . . The volume consists of alternating text chapters and picture essays. . . . The appendix comprises a glossary of airmen's slang and a chronological list of the highlights of manned flight." About this book
Further reading: p196

629.133 Aircraft. Flying saucers

Colorado. University
Final report of the scientific study of unidentified flying objects; conducted by the University of Colorado under contract to the United States Air Force; Edward U. Condon, scientific director. . . . Dutton [1969 c1968] xiv, 967p illus $12.95   629.133

1 Flying saucers
"This research was supported by the Air Force Office of Scientific Research. Office of Aerospace Research, USAF, under contract F44620-67 C-0035. Daniel S. Gillmor, editor: with an introduction by Walter Sullivan of the New York Times." Title page
"In addition to the many details of the studies of UFO's completed during 1966-68 at the University of Colorado, the report contains an excellent brief summary of the Colorado Project, a detailed history of UFO studies during the past two decades, a brief discussion of UFO reports throughout recorded history, and extensive treatment of the scientific knowledge which can be useful in the interpretation of UFO reports. . . . A brief bibliography, 24 appendices containing supplementary documents, and an extensive index are included." Choice
"This compendium is so complete and detailed that it supersedes all previous compendia and analyses as a reference work." Science Bks

Klass, Philip J.
UFOs—identified. Random House 1968 290p illus map $7.95   629.133

1 Flying saucers
The author presents his theory that many UFO's, or so-called flying saucers, may be natural plasmas of ionized air caused by electrical discharge along power lines, and are related to St Elmo's fire and ball lightning
Klass "deserves the fullest credit for recording a thoughtful and thoroughly documented scientific investigation covering all principal ufological areas, incidents, and personalities, and then coming up with an equally well-documented scientific explanation. And all successfully combining technicality with readability." Christian Science Monitor

Soule, Gardner
UFOs and IFOs; a factual report on flying saucers. Putnam 1967 189p illus lib. bdg. $3.49   629.133

1 Flying saucers
The author "probes the complex question of UFOs [unidentified flying objects]. Are they really hurled into space by a planet more technically advanced than ours? Conflicting opinions are contained in this book along with instructions for laymen about how to be more scientific in recording details if and when UFOs are spotted." Huntting
Many readers "will be fascinated with this book which is just what the title suggests. Of particular scientific interest will be the chapter 'What to do if you see a UFO.'" Ontario Lib Rev
Bibliography: p[190]

629.2 Motor land vehicles. Automobiles

Hot Rod
The complete book of engines, by the editors of Hot Rod magazine. Petersen Pub. illus $2 plus 25¢ postage and handling 629.2

1 Automobiles—Engines
"Hot Rod Magazine Technical library"
Annual. First published 1965
The editors describe over twenty car models in detail, giving specifications on their component engine parts, including optional pieces, and performance. Includes an essay: How to blueprint an engine. (Publisher)
The tables have been compiled "from data contained in the Automobile Manufacturer's Association official specifications. . . . The specifications for 125 basic engines have been tabulated." Introduction to the 1966 edition

Nader, Ralph
Unsafe at any speed; the designed-in dangers of the American automobile. Grossman Pubs. 1965 365p illus $5.95   629.2

1 Automobiles—Design and construction 2 Automobile industry and trade
The author tells the "story of how and why cars kill and why the automobile manufacturers have failed to make cars safe. . . . It is the thesis of this book that it is easier to redesign automobiles to make them safe than to revise the nature of the people who drive them." Publisher's note
"This book is a starter in informing the general public of the built-in dangers in the cars that it drives, and it should serve as a stimulus to the various government officials responsible for the protection of life and property of the American people to exercise their duties and responsibilities with greater care." Best Sellers

629.209 Automobiles—History

Bird, Anthony
Antique automobiles. Dutton 1967 168p
illus $7.95   **629.209**

1 Automobiles—History

This "attractive introduction to early cars
in Europe and America notes major developments in car engineering and design, characteristics of individual models, and pioneer
names in the car industry. Captioned colorplates of cars reinforce this text." Booklist

Burness, Tad
Cars of the early twenties. Chilton Co.
1968 270p illus $17.50   **629.209**

1 Automobiles—History

"The good old days are evoked by these
wonderful old automobile advertisements
which recall a world of lovely people and comfortable neighborhoods filled with classical gardens and imposing homes, a world that never
wholly existed, perhaps, except in those advertisements. . . . [The author] has fitted much of
his text around some 100 advertisements from
the early 1920's and what they tell us about the
cars of the times, not to mention our society!
He also covers those early innovations which
we now take for granted. Included is a list of
266 marques produced in 1920!" Library J

629.22 Types of motor vehicles

Edmonds, I. G.
Hot rodding for beginners; illus. by Francis A. Chauncy. Macrae Smith Co. 1970 181p
illus $4.95, lib. bdg. $4.79   **629.22**

1 Automobiles 2 Automobile racing
SBN 8255-3000-8; 8255-3001-6

"Defining a hot rod as a car that has been
modified and altered with loving care and emphasizing the need for a prospective hot
rodder to become a good mechanic first, an
experienced enthusiast offers beginners an informal, though detailed guide to hot rodding.
Edmonds gives step-by-step instructions for
improving an engine's performance and for
building and customizing a hot rod. He also
provides description of drag and stock competition, a glossary, and a list of books for
additional specialized information. Profusely
illustrated with clear diagrams, drawings, and
photographs this is a basic introduction for
the interested teenager." Booklist

Georgano, G. N.
(ed.) Encyclopedia of American automobiles. Contributors: Glenn Baechler [and
others]. Dutton 1971 222p illus $12.50 **629.22**

1 Automobiles—Dictionaries 2 Automobiles—
History
SBN 0-525-097929

"The material in this book, emended and
fully revised, has been extracted from 'The
Complete Encyclopedia of Motorcars,' first
published [1968]." Verso of title page
American and Canadian makes, past and
present, are concisely described. Varieties of
design are represented." Publisher's note

Hertz, Louis H.
The complete book of building and collecting model automobiles. Crown 1970 310p
illus $9.95   **629.22**

1 Automobiles—Models

The construction of model automobile
whether from commercial kits or from raw materials is explained as well as the history and
terminology, basic specifications, scale and
proportion of this hobby

"Illustrated with photographs of vintage
models, reproductions of pages from toy catalogs, and facsimiles of advertisements for
model vehicles. The appendixes include a list of
model automobile builders' and collectors' organizations. Comments on other books on
model cars, and a short glossary." Booklist

Musciano, Walter A.
Building and operating model cars. 2d ed.
Funk 1970 192p illus $4.95   **629.22**

1 Automobiles—Models
First published 1956

"The author presents a comprehensive description of all phases of model-car construction and operation from the simplest models to
increasingly complex projects. Each of the
models described is an operating type, pro-
pelled by standard methods ranging from electric motors through internal combustion engines to jet propulsion." Publisher's note

Nader, Ralph
What to do with your bad car; an action
manual for lemon owners, by Ralph Nader,
Lowell Dodge [and] Ralf Hotchkiss. Grossman Pubs. [1971 c1970] 175p illus $8.95
       629.22

1 Automobiles 2 Automobile industry and
trade 3 Consumer education

"With the aid of more than 4000 letters from
lemon owners, Lowell Dodge, Ralf Hotchkiss
and I have prepared a set of materials that describes, first, how you may avoid the lemon experience and, failing that, how best to get your
defective vehicle fixed or replaced. There are
no easy ways to achieve these objectives, and
this book does not pretend otherwise. What it
does strive to do is to offer some hope to the
embattled car buyer, to challenge the legal profession to take a greater interest in these cases,
and to push for more basic reforms of the laws
and remedies to protect the new car buyer.
Consumers are the key to all these objectives."
Preface
A lemon "can be got rid of, with luck and a
lawyer in the right corner, and if this brisk
little illustrated manual incites enough outraged owners to action, the production of lem-
ons may even begin to decline." Atlantic
Bibliography: p148-51

Oliver, Smith Hempstone
The Smithsonian collection of automobiles
and motorcycles, by Smith Hempstone
Oliver and Donald H. Berkebile. Smith-
sonian Inst. Press, distributed by Random
House 1968 164p illus $4.95   **629.22**

1 Automobiles—History 2 Motorcycles—History

"Smithsonian publication"
"An expansion and revision in enlarged format of the Smithsonian's U.S. National Museum Bulletin 213, 'Automobiles and motorcycles
in the U.S. National Museum.' . . . The design
and mechanism of the over 40 pieces—passenger cars, motorcycles, trucks, and other mechanized vehicles—are described concisely and
illustrated with one or more photographs for
the benefit of antique-car enthusiasts." Booklist
Includes bibliography

Yerkow, Charles
Motorcycles: how they work. Putnam
1971 95p illus (How it works) lib. bdg. $3.86
       629.22

1 Motorcycles

Illustrated with photographs and diagrams,
this book covers such topics as how a motorcycle works, how to care for and repair it,
and how to ride it even on the roughest terrain. Also included are tips on how to select a
motorcycle

629.28 Operation, maintenance, and repair of motor vehicles

Allen, Willard A.
Know your car. 2d ed. Am. Tech. Soc. 1967 184p illus $4.95   629.28
1 Automobiles—Handbooks, manuals, etc.
2 Automobiles—Repairing

First published 1960
Text, photographs, and drawings provide information on the fundamentals of engines, fuel systems, ignition systems, electrical systems, chassis, and preventive maintenance for owners, drivers, and beginning mechanics

Anderson, Edwin P.
Audels Foreign auto repair manual. [2d ed] Audel 1966 584p illus $5.95   629.28
1 Automobiles—Repairing 2 Automobiles—Handbooks, manuals, etc.

First published 1964
Contains "service and repair data for the most popular imported makes, including Fiat, Hillman Minx, M.G., Opel, Peugot, Renault, SAAB, Simca, Volkswagen, and Volvo. Introductory chapters provide complete data on operation and maintenance of fuel and ignition systems." Publisher's note
"For mechanics, students, hobbyists, and owners. . . . Well illustrated and clearly written; simple step-by-step instructions and procedures." N Y New Tech Bks

Chilton's Auto repair manual. Chilton Bks. illus $10.95   629.28
1 Automobiles—Repairing 2 Automobiles—Handbooks, manuals, etc.

Annual. First published 1953 under the Chilton imprint
"A highly compact guide to the repair of American passenger cars and the Volkswagen. . . . Covers all systems of each model describes each, with detailed instructions for removal and installation. A large part of the book deals with the various types of transmissions and major units, including troubleshooting charts, and instructions for assembly and reassembly. Profusely illustrated with exploded drawings, diagrams, and photographs. Many charts and tables with data and specifications." N Y New Tech Bks

Fales, E. D.
The book of expert driving, by E. D. Fales, Jr. Foreword by John R. Whiting; introduction by William J. Toth. Hawthorn Bks. 1970 178p illus $6.95   629.28
1 Automobile drivers

"The fine points of driving under normal and dangerous conditions, at high speeds, in the rain or fog, and on turnpikes are presented, along with some controversial recommendations based on the author's wide experience with highway patrolmen and professional drivers. . . . [The author] explodes some old ideas and presents challenging new ones." News of Bks

Felsen, Henry Gregor
To my son, the teen-age driver. Dodd 1964 124p $3.50   629.28
1 Automobile drivers

"Assuming that the reader has learned to drive and understands the mechanism of a car, the author offers straightforward, sensible advice on driving behavior and ethics. Stressing responsibility and a mature attitude, he discusses the value of experience and caution, and explains the dangers of overconfidence, of using a car to express hostile emotions, and of developing an excessive interest in the automobile as a way of life and status symbol." Booklist
"The wisdom and help offered . . . will be appreciated and will help many young people see the 'light' in prudent and safe driving." Best Sellers

Glenn, Harold T.
Glenn's Foreign car repair manual. With thousands of illus. Chilton Co. 1966 1280p illus $17.50   629.28
1 Automobiles—Repairing 2 Automobiles—Handbooks, manuals, etc.

On cover: Revised and enlarged second edition
First published 1963
"Contains specifications and service notes for more than 30 foreign automobiles, including . . . coverage of rear drive mechanisms and flat rate time schedules for commonly performed service jobs. Illustrated with exploded views of mechanical and electrical units, wiring diagrams, and comprehensive tables of specifications." Bk Buyer's Guide
"A must for every up-to-date auto service and repair collection." Huntting

Honda: repair & tune-up guide. Cowles 1968 85p illus (A Cowles Repair bk) $4.95   629.28
1 Motorcycles—Repairing 2 Motorcycles—Handbooks, manuals, etc.

"A self-help manual for Honda owners. Its excellent close-up photographs and drawings of parts and procedures and its precise textual directions, wiring diagrams, and specification tables clarify diagnostic and tune-up and repair methods, measures, and precautions for the various unit components of a one-cylinder engine cycle. Push-rod and overhead-cam variety of engines and manual as well as automatic clutches are dealt with." Booklist

Glenn's Auto repair manual. Chilton Co. illus $9.95   629.28
1 Automobiles—Repairing 2 Automobiles—Handbooks, manuals, etc.

Annual. First published 1960 with title: Chilton's New auto repair manual. Title varies
This is "a standard manual covering every essential repair process in the service field arranged by topic." Chicago
Includes wiring diagrams, as well as information on trucks

Kearney, Paul W.
How to drive better and avoid accidents. 3d rev. ed. Crowell 1969 259p illus $6.95   629.28
1 Automobile drivers 2 Traffic accidents

First published 1953
"This book is designed to help the average motorist understand better what happens when he drives and help him improve his driving skill by anticipating close calls." Publisher's note
This practical guide "includes tests to try on quiet roads to measure car control; rules for car care, safe parking, stopping a skid, controlling automobile fires; and expert tips on tires, gas conservation, touring, driving in winter and night." McClurg. Book News

Mechanix Illustrated
Car care; by the editors of Mechanix Illustrated. Arco 1969 111p illus lib. bdg. $3.50   629.28
1 Automobiles—Repairing

"First suggesting 10 special tools for the week-end backyard automobile mechanic, the editors furnish 28 well-illustrated articles comprising a step-by-step guide to professional car maintenance with the overall aim of reducing repair costs, and insuring for the car an easy start, good performance, and better mileage. Information included explains the specific care of parts including spark plugs, carburetors, tires, brakes, water pumps, filters, air conditioners, alternators, and mufflers. The final chapter outlines a six-step spring tune-up for all cars." Booklist

Purdy, Ken W.
Young people and driving; the use and abuse of the automobile; foreword by Stirling Moss. Day 1967 92p $3.95   629.28

1 Automobile drivers

The author tells learners and young drivers what they ought to know about the machine, about the techniques of driving, and about themselves in order to be good drivers. He describes how to anticipate what will go wrong on the road; how to handle an automobile in an accident; when and how to skid; and gives many other tips. (Publisher)

"Most young people think of the automobile as everything but what it really is: a lethal machine in need of constant control. Mr. Purdy views this killer with loving respect and writes to instill this same feeling in younger drivers. His advice is easy to follow, if taken, and will certainly save lives." Library J

Ritch, Ocee
Chilton's Harley-Davidson repair and tune-up guide. Chilton Bks. 1968 126p illus $4.95
                                              629.28

1 Motorcycles—Repairing

Contains repair and service data for the various models of Harley-Davidson motorcycles. Labeled diagrams illustrate such motor parts as the electrical system, the clutch and the transmission

Chilton's Motorcycle troubleshooting guide. Chilton Co. 1966 94p illus $4.95   629.28

1 Motorcycles—Repairing

"To help the mechanic find the defective unit as quickly as possible, this manual is divided into two sections, one covering two-stroke motorcycle engines, the other covering four-stroke engines." Bk Buyer's Guide

Illustrated with step by step photographs

Smith, LeRoi
How to fix up old cars. Dodd 1968 210p illus $4.50   629.28

1 Automobiles—Repairing

"The book tells how to buy a used car and used parts, plan the work in advance, and figure costs and with the aid of . . . diagrams and photographs, gives instruction in the actual mechanics involved." Booklist

The author "combines solid knowledge of subject matter with writing ability. The highly readable results, while offering vast amounts of useable technical knowledge in 210 pages, at no time becomes patronizing. A center spread of illustrative photographs is supported by clear, informative diagrams throughout. An index and two appendices (sources of car parts and a list of special car clubs) are included." Science Bks

Stapley, Ray
The car owner's handbook; illus. by Blair Drawson. Doubleday 1971 312p illus $6.95
                                              629.28

1 Automobiles—Handbooks, manuals, etc.
2 Automobiles—Repairing

Answering questions ranging from how to buy a new or used car to when to change the oil, this book provides descriptions of the workings of all the systems in the car as well as explanations of what can go wrong and how the car can be fixed. (Publisher)

Wallach, Theresa
Easy motorcycle riding; illus. by Maggie MacGowan. Sterling 1970 144p illus $3.95, lib. bdg. $3.99   629.28

1 Motorcycles
ISBN 0-8069-4038-7

This book "traces the pathway to correct and easy riding. Never before has the right kind of information reached the beginner in time to prevent an accident for which the mo-

torcycle was not to blame. This book is written for motorcycle riders everywhere. The aim is to prepare the beginner for a safe learning period and also to bring present owners of motorcycles a little closer to fully understanding their mounts." p8

"While the image of young women and motorcycles in this country is sometimes less than charming and ladylike, the English Miss Wallach makes clear her determination to ride motorcycles expertly and remain a 'lady' at the same time." Library J

629.3 Air-cushion vehicles

Gunston, Bill
Hydrofoils and hovercraft; new vehicles for sea and land. Doubleday 1970 [c1969] 192p illus (Doubleday Science ser) $6.95   629.3

1 Hydrofoil boats 2 Ground effect machines

First published 1969 in England

"A thorough introduction to the characteristics of hydrofoil and hovercraft or air cushion vehicles. The historical development, advantages, disadvantages, and present and potential future applications of these vehicles are described in an easily readable format. The important technical aspects of the vehicles are covered in a clear and simple manner by a noted journalist. . . . An outstanding series of high quality color and black-and-white illustrations, a short glossary of technical terms, a table listing the important characteristics of the principal hydrofoil and air cushion vehicles in the world and a brief index are included." Choice

629.4 Astronautics

Clarke, Arthur C.
Man and space, by Arthur C. Clarke and the editors of Time-Life Books. Time-Life Bks. [1969] 200p illus maps (Life Science lib) lib. bdg. $7.60   629.4

1 Space flight 2 Outer space—Exploration
3 Manned space flight

First published 1964

This book "reviews the history of man's interest in space and analyzes the technological developments that have enabled him to explore this new frontier. The book also discusses the future—not only describing travel to the moon and beyond but also reporting changes that may occur on earth as a consequence of experiments in space." About this book

The vocabulary of space: p193. Bibliography: p196

Lewis, Richard S.
Appointment on the moon; the full story of Americans in space, from Explorer I to the lunar landing and beyond. [Rev. ed] Viking 1969 560p illus map $10   629.4

1 Astronautics—U.S. 2 U.S. National Aeronautics and Space Administration—History
3 Space flight to the moon

First published 1968

This book traces the American space program "from its beginnings shortly after World War II, through the Mercury and Gemini projects, and on to the Apollo 11 flight." Publisher's note

"Quotes of conversations between astronauts, supporting scientists, technicians, government officials and businessmen make the book lively and interesting. The excellent photographs and diagrams, and extensive reference and index sections add greatly to the value of this accurate book for collateral reading and reference." Science Bks

Reference notes: p541-46

Ley, Willy
Rockets, missiles, and men in space. Viking illus maps $10.95   629.4
1 Rocketry 2 Space flight
First published 1944 with title: Rockets. Frequently revised with variant titles
"A classic and definitive history of space flight. . . . Its only near equal is History of Rocketry and Space Travel by [W.] Von Braun and [F.] Ordway [entered in class, 629.409]. Much new material has been added on space exploration since 1961, and future developments are discussed. . . . The bibliography is extensive and up to date, indexing is excellent, and illustrations are profuse. Ley's writing style is readable and lucid." Choice

Shelton, William R.
Man's conquest of space; foreword by James E. Webb; prepared by National Geographic Special Publications Division, Robert L. Breeden, chief. Nat. Geographic Soc. 1968 199p illus $4.25   629.4
1 Astronautics 2 Manned space flight 3 Outer space—Exploration
The author describes the whole pageant of space flight, from the mythical flight of Icarus, the gunpowder rockets of the 19th century, Yuri Gagarin's trip around the earth and the first simple satellites to today's astronauts and their complex spacecraft. (Publisher)
"In this volume [the author] has compiled a balanced, up-to-tomorrow's-headlines summary of his subject. . . . An outstanding popular presentation capitalizing in spectacular fashion . . . on the pictorial nature of its subject." Library J
Additional references: p199

Von Braun, Wernher
Space frontier. New ed. completely rev. and updated. Holt 1971 307p illus $5.95   629.4
1 Space sciences 2 Outer space—Exploration 3 Rocketry
SBN 03-063705-8
First published 1967
Contents: Launch and ascent; Flight through space; Safety in space; Stations in space; Flight to the moon; Bonanzas on the way to the moon; To the Planets—and beyond
"No attempt was made at a systematic, orderly development of the subject. However, the resulting melange of facts constitutes a sweeping, and highly commendable, portrayal of the vast variety of considerations and disciplines involved in the exploration of space. This work is essentially nontechnical and its content will be understood even by younger students." Science Bks

629.403 Astronautics— Dictionaries and encyclopedias

The **McGraw**-Hill Encyclopedia of space; foreword by M. Scott Carpenter. McGraw 1968 831p illus $27.50   629.403
1 Outer space—Exploration—Dictionaries 2 Space sciences—Dictionaries 3 Astronautics —Dictionaries
Originally published 1967 in France
This encyclopedia covers the fundamentals of space science as well as current space exploration. "The main section headings include The Rocket, Artificial Satellites, Space Navigation and Electronics, Man in Space, Life in the Universe, Astronomy—Astrophysics, Conquest of the Moon, Towards Other Worlds, and Astronautics in the World of Today." Publisher's note
"The text is rather technical and heavy-going in most places, of high school level difficulty at least, but this should not dissuade the serious reader." Science Bks

The **New** Space encyclopaedia; a guide to astronomy and space exploration. Dutton 1969 316p illus $13.95   629.403
1 Astronautics—Dictionaries 2 Space flight —Dictionaries 3 Astronomy—Dictionaries
First published 1957 with title: The Space encyclopaedia
The entries in this book "vary in length from a two-line identification (Faculae) to a nine-page study (Space Medicine), and in topic from Tektites to life or the Apollo Project, without neglecting pulsars, quasars, quarks, or anti-matter." Sat R
This edition is "well illustrated with astronomical photos, spectra, diagrams, photos of spacecraft and components, this book has articles on over 800 terms, mostly astronomical. . . . All are up to date (1969), and in language appropriate from junior high school to graduate students. The book contains valuable tabular material on planets, asteroids, satellites and cosmic abundances. . . . Coverage of astronomy and astrophysics is excellent, including telescopes and instruments. . . . Cross-referencing between articles is good, but terms not listed alphabetically are hard to find. There is no single book that matches this coverage of space terms." Science Bks

Turnill, Reginald
The language of space; a dictionary of astronautics. Day [1971 c1970] xxxiv, 165p $6.95   629.403
1 Astronautics—Dictionaries
First published 1970 in England
Containing about 100 terms "the book concentrates on the jargon of the American space program, and it covers even more of the astronauts' slang. Also, under such general headings as 'fire' and 'Mars,' it offers capsule histories of past events. . . . [A] prefatory chapter sketches the next 20 years in space." Library J

629.409 Astronautics—History

Von Braun, Wernher
History of rocketry & space travel [by] Wernher von Braun [and] Frederick I. Ordway III. Rev. ed. Original illus. by Harry H-K. Lange; intoduction by Frederick C. Durant III. Crowell 1969 276p illus $17.50
629.409
1 Rocketry—History 2 Space flight—History
First published 1966
A panoramic review of man's conquest of space. This "volume ranges from ancient Babylonian and Greek concepts of the universe through the development of rockets by Chinese, Arabic, and medieval European experimenters to today's plans for manned missions to the Moon, Mars, and Venus." Publisher's note
A reference work written in an "interesting style and supported by extensive documentation and superb illustrations. Numerous tables." N Y New Tech Bks
Bibliography: p255-70

629.43 Flight of unmanned vehicles

Bester, Alfred
The life and death of a satellite; with photographs. Little [1967 c1966] 239p illus boards $5.95   629.43
1 Artificial satellites, American
"In this biography of a satellite Bester concentrates on tracing the construction-through-launching progress of one family of satellites, but also fills in background information on space-program personnel, conflicts, and issues." Booklist
Selected bibliography: p223-27

629.45 Flight of manned vehicles

Associated Press

Footprints on the moon; by the writers and editors of the Associated Press; manuscript by John Barbour. [The Press 1969] 214p illus $5   629.45

1 Apollo project 2 Space flight to the moon

A "documentary account of all of the major events of manned space flight, including programs of the U.S.A. and the U.S.S.R. The many remarkable photographs in color are from the Associated Press, NASA, Tass and Novosti. The dramatic narrative moves smoothly from event to event, including unadorned facts, favorable or unfavorable. The mistakes, disappointments, frustrations, failures and tragedies are recounted in proper perspective and sequence along with all of the triumphs and achievement. . . . The book is well-indexed and a good quick reference to events, dates, persons and places." Science Bks

First on the moon; a voyage with Neil Armstrong, Michael Collins [and] Edwin E. Aldrin, Jr; written with Gene Farmer and Dora Jane Hamblin; epilogue by Arthur C. Clarke; with photographs. Little 1970 434 illus $7.95   629.45

1 Apollo project

"Life editor Gene Farmer and Life staff writer Dora Jane Hamblin spent months living with the astronauts and their families. They interweave here an account of the moon flight itself with the recorded transcript of the astronauts conversations and descriptions of the atmosphere in the astronauts' homes during the flight." Book Rev Digest

"The epilogue, written by the well-known space writer, Arthur C. Clarke, is excellent reading material not only for elementary astronomy courses, but also for courses on sociology, since it gives a rationale for the space program, exposes its influence on life in this country, and analyzes future events in space." Choice

Glossary: p xi-xiii. Notes: p425-34

Gagarin, Yuri

Survival in space, by Yuri Gagarin and Vladimir Lebedev; tr. from the Russian by Gabriella Azrael. Praeger 1969 166p illus $5.95   629.45

1 Manned space flight 2 Astronauts 3 Life support systems (Space environment) 4 Man—Influence of environment

The book "describes the problems man faces living in space. . . . Although there is some discussion of life support—oxygen, food, temperature control, and so on—the book deals primarily with the psychological problems such as the effects of prolonged isolation or weightlessness which space travelers must overcome. The emphasis, naturally, is upon Russian space flights and experiments." Library J

"A considerable part of the book is devoted to describing man's reaction to stress and the unusual, and how these reactions are tested to determine if an applicant would be suitable as an astronaut. . . . The limitations of machines are discussed as well as the frustrations and psychological effects they can produce when they do not perform as expected. There are many references to work done in the NASA manned space flight program and the authors show considerable knowledge of U.S. literature." Science Bks

Haggerty, James J.

Apollo: lunar landing. Rand McNally 1969 159p illus maps $4.95, lib. bdg. $4.79   629.45

1 Apollo project

Illustrated with photographs and drawings, this "book tells us, in non-technical terms, the why, what, and how of America's Apollo flight program. Why was it undertaken? What does the nation get in return for its [multibillion] dollar investment? The author takes us from launch pad through actual lunar landing, with . . . explanations about each stage of the program." Publisher's note

"The style is easy and breezy. No mathematics is used, nor is there any mathematical point of view. Considerable jargon appears, but all terms are explained." Science Bks

Apollo glossary: p153-55

Mailer, Norman

Of a fire on the moon. Little [1971 c1970] 472p $7.95   629.45

1 Apollo project 2 Space flight to the moon 3 Astronauts 4 U.S.—Civilization

This book includes "personal reportage of the background, techniques, planning, and achievement of the first moonshot, together with commentary on the political and psychological effects, and philosophical significance of man's greatest adventure in space." Book News

"Concerned as always with the fundamental conflicts represented by 20th-century America, Mailer proceeds to view our country and our century from a number of vantage points; political, sexual, mystical. Through a prose which is both precise and metaphorically lush, he succeeds in evoking in the reader a sense of awe at the massive achievement represented by the moon shot, and in leading him through some of the fascinating, labyrinthine passages of the author's own mind." Choice

Mallan, Lloyd

Suiting up for space; the evolution of the space suit. Day 1971 262p illus $9.95   629.45

1 Astronauts—Clothing 2 Life support systems (Space environment)

Tracing the space suit's development from the 1930's to the present the author "gives full credit to all the scientists and engineers who worked hopefully, tirelessly, and frequently under great discomfort and even pain. A chapter is devoted to the monkeys, dogs, rats and other animals which participated in the space program. Mallan shows that the rapid, continuing development of the space suit has been necessary, for the suits used in Project Mercury would have been totally inadequate for the moon landing. Much of the information presented is fairly technical, but good writing makes this a book to be enjoyed." Library J

Moore, Patrick

Moon flight atlas. Rand McNally 1969 48p illus $6.95   629.45

1 Apollo project 2 Moon

"A Mitchell Beazley book"

This book "maps not only Man's first trips around the Moon, but even his first exploratory steps on Earth's natural satellite, and reveals the amazing technology which has made possible these great moments of human exploration." Publisher's note

Moore's book "expresses its ideas and information mainly by photographs, diagrams of spacecraft and orbits, and maps. The text is decidedly subordinate, though very far from negligible." Horn Bk

Ruzic, Neil P.

Where the winds sleep; man's future on the moon: a projected history; with a foreword by Wernher von Braun and illus. by Donald G. Lewis. Doubleday 1970 236p illus $4.95   629.45

1 Lunar bases

The author "traces the history of man's colonization of the moon from 1975 to 2045: why we went to Luna, how we lived there, and what we gained. His story is not science fiction but extrapolated science; based on the most current programs of NASA, it is a . . . projection of what we can expect from our life on this other world." Publisher's note

"Underground cities, moon mines and farms, levitation roads, huge pressurized astrodomes, a University of the Moon, and a flourishing

Ruzic, Neil P.—*Continued*

tourist industry are some of the developments
he forecasts for a multiworld, peaceful civilization in which the mechanics of slow motion,
extremes of light and dark, heat and cold, and
other lunar idiosyncrasies have been overcome
or used to advantage." Booklist

Sharpe, Mitchell R.

Living in space; the astronaut and his environment.   Doubleday   1969   192p   illus
(Doubleday Science ser) $5.95   **629.45**

1 Manned space flight 2 Life support systems
(Space environment) 3 Space medicine

"A comprehensive survey of the psycho-
physiological problems involved in sending men
into space and of the solutions that have been
successfully used. Discussion of psychological
stresses, such physical hazards as extreme temperatures, radiation, and weightlessness, and
the testing and training of astronauts to meet
these conditions is followed by detailed information on the life support systems, including
provision for food, water, and waste disposal,
the space suit, and the telemetric systems for
maintaining contact between space vehicle and
mission control. As evidence of the value of
the manned space program, new medical knowledge and techniques derived from aerospace
research and technology are reviewed. The general reader will find the material timely and
understandable in spite of a somewhat technical vocabulary." Booklist

We seven, by the astronauts themselves:
M. Scott Carpenter [and others]. Simon &
Schuster 1962 352p illus $7.50   **629.45**

1 Astronauts 2 Mercury project 3 Manned
space flight

Astronauts Carpenter, Cooper, Glenn, Gris-
som, Schirra, Shepard, and Slayton "talk, individually, about their background, recruiting,
testing and training, shedding light on their
personalities and reactions, and on the intricacies of Project Mercury. They describe how
they have worked together in planning and testing equipment and have continued this cooperation so that each man in orbit has been
backed by six prime helpers on the ground.
Even the layman with little scientific knowledge
can follow most of their remarkably clear explanations of the mechanics of space trips."
Pub W

"The result is an interesting insight into the
similarities and differences in the men who
make up the space team as well as a glance
at the space program itself. Something for the
boys." Horn Bk

630   Agriculture and agricultural
industries

United States. Department of Agriculture

Contours of change. [Supt. of Docs. 1970]
xl, 366p illus (The Yearbook of Agriculture)
$3.50   **630**

1 Agriculture—U.S.

"The book looks not only at the technological
revolution in agriculture, the changing face of
Rural America, and the growing importance of
America's role in world agriculture; it peers
also into the 1970's and, to some extent, into
the long-term future." Foreword

630.72   Agriculture—Research

United States. Department of Agriculture

Science for better living. U.S. Govt. Ptg.
Off. 1968 xlvi, 386p illus (Yearbook of agriculture, 1968)   **630.72**

1 Agriculture—Research 2 Natural resources
3 Natural resources—U.S.

"The yearbook describes the many kinds of
research activities of the U.S. Department of

Agriculture that are improving the quality and
quantity of food production, clothing, and
shelter. The introduction by . . . Orville L.
Freeman, tells of scientific research conducted by the department and the implementation
of the research findings into agricultural and
processing practices, new and improved food
and pharmaceutical products, revitalization of
communities, development of new textiles. . . .
The book is divided into five major sections:
'Abundance for All,' 'City and Country,' 'Natural Resources, 'Growing Nations and World
Trade,' 'For Better Living,' " Science Bks

631.3   Farm tools, machinery,
appliances

United States. Department of Agriculture

Power to produce; the yearbook of agriculture, 1960. U.S. Govt. Ptg. Off. 1960 480p
illus $2.25   **631.3**

1 Agricultural engineering 2 Agricultural machinery

"Summarizes and explains the use of power
in agriculture, particularly that derived from
the internal combustion engine and electric
motors. Describes the workings, the historical
development, and the uses of tractors, irrigation devices, agricultural aircraft, barn inventions, and an assortment of harvesters, cutters.
diggers, vibrators, and cultivators. Profuse
photographs and an even, clearly written text
make it valuable for reference or straight reading, even by city-dwellers." The AAAS Science
Book List for Young Adults

631.4   Soil and soil conservation

United States. Department of Agriculture

Soil; the yearbook of agriculture, 1957. U.S.
Govt. Ptg. Off. 1957 784p illus maps   **631.4**

1 Soils

"A new and adapted variety of 'Soils and
men,' the 1938 Yearbook of Agriculture." Preface

Eighty-eight articles reflecting research in
soil management under the following categories: Principles; Fertility; Practices; Soil care;
Moisture; System; Regions; Special uses

Glossary: p751-70

631.5   Crop production

United States. Department of Agriculture

Seeds; the yearbook of agriculture, 1961.
U.S. Govt. Ptg. Off. 1961 591p illus   **631.5**

1 Seeds

This volume on seeds, with chapters by different authors, covers the importance of, life
processes, production, processing, certification,
testing, and marketing of seeds

"There is a 48-page section of good photographs and many diagrams in the text, making
the book a valuable one for reference and for
reading by anyone interested in agriculture.
Many valuable appendices and a long, explicit
glossary." The AAAS Science Book List for
Young Adults

631.7   Irrigation and water
conservation

United States. Department of Agriculture

Water. U.S. Govt. Ptg. Off. 1955? 751p
illus map   **631.7**

1 Water 2 Irrigation

At head of title: Yearbook of agriculture,
1955

The chief "purpose of this Yearbook is to
supply as much information as we can about
water in a practical, useful way for farmers
and others who use water." Preface

United States. Department of Agriculture— —*Continued*

Contains 96 articles on such subjects as the sources, needs, uses and conservation of water, irrigation, and drainage

Includes bibliographies

631.8 Fertilizers and soil conditioners

Slack, A. V.
Defense against famine; the role of the fertilizer industry. Doubleday 1970 232p illus (Chemistry in action ser) $5.95   631.8

1 Fertilizers and manures

"Prepared under the sponsorship of the Manufacturing Chemists' Association"

"Brief history of the fertilizer industry, showing that nourishing food products and better grazing land are but two of the results of the chemical industry's efforts to provide food for the world's burgeoning population." Publisher's note

632 Plant injuries, diseases, pests, and their control

Carson, Rachel
Silent spring; drawings by Lois and Louis Darling. Houghton 1962 368p illus $5.95 632

1 Insecticides 2 Ecology 3 Poisons

"An important, controversial account, written for the layman, of the way in which man's use of poisons to control insect pests and unwanted vegetation is changing the balance of nature. Stressing ecology—the interrelationships and interdependencies of man, plants, birds, animals, fishes, and insects—the author discusses how our eradication programs have destroyed friendly as well as unfriendly living things and cites ironic instances in which the insects we have tried to destroy have developed immunity and increased in numbers." Booklist

One might discount the criticism of distortion "somewhat if it came only from those with a vested interest in the chemicals. But reputable scientists . . . make similar criticisms too. . . . Miss Carson has undeniably sketched a [dramatic but] one-sided picture." Christian Science Monitor

Written in a "readable style and with a minimum of technical terminology, this is a book which presents an important problem. . . . There is no hesitation in recommending it to all readers." Best Sellers

List of principal sources: p299-355

Graham, Frank
Since Silent spring. Houghton 1970 333p $6.95   632

1 Pesticides 2 Ecology 3 Carson, Rachel Louise. Silent spring

Paying tribute to Rachel Carson's Silent spring, the author "provides absorbing information about the steps that led to her book, and many insights into her personality. The reception her best-seller received is included as well as a factual, low-key account of each aspect of chemical pollution of the environment as it has unfolded in the years since 1962. Ten and one-half pages of references allow the interested reader to go back to primary sources. An excellent index provides easy access to information." Science Bks

The author indicates "that scientists are not without their biases, that the source of one's keep does affect one's view, and that there is 'politics' in science and technology. Graham's book may be almost as hotly argued as Carson's." Library J

Harmer, Ruth Mulvey
Unfit for human consumption. Prentice-Hall 1971 374p $6.95   632

1 Pesticides 2 Public health—U.S. 3 Food supply
ISBN 0-13-936906-6

The author "describes the 'tide of poisons unbelievable in magnitude and uncontrollable in consequence' that she, along with many others, says is engulfing us. Her focus is on the chemicals—pesticides particularly—that are making much of our foods not merely unfit for human consumption but downright dangerous on the long haul. Some of her accounts of little-publicized 'accidents' that have occurred during the spraying, storing and shipping of foodstuffs read like sci-fi horror tales. Pointing a finger at the pesticide industry, the legislators whom it lobbies, regulatory agencies such as FDA and USDA, scientists and others, she challenges the contentions that the risks incurred by modern techniques of chemical control of agriculture are worth taking in view of what has demonstrably happened and the safer measures available to the industry." Pub W

Bibliography: p353-60

Swan, Lester A.
Beneficial insects; nature's alternatives to chemical insecticides: animal predation, parasitism, disease organisms. Harper 1964 429p illus $7.95   632

1 Insects, Injurious and beneficial

This book is intended to supply the general reader with "the information required to understand biological control and to appreciate both its present role in pest control and its great future potential. It is, besides, . . . [an] account of the lives and behavior of insects that live at the expense of others and to our benefit, as well as of the phenomena of parasitism and predation in general." Foreword

"Rachel Carson's Silent Spring [listed above] brought the attention of the public to the effects of DDT and other insecticides. . . . The present work by Swan offers some positive approach to a few of the problems posed by Miss Carson. . . . Young people will not find this book as easy to read as the works of Carson; but individual sections are packed with information and the interested student will profit from a study of the author's presentation." Best Sellers

United States. Department of Agriculture
Insects; the yearbook of agriculture, 1952. U.S. Govt. Ptg. Off. 1952? 780p illus   632

1 Insects, Injurious and beneficial 2 Insecticides

Contents: Introducing the insects: How to know an insect; Insects as helpers; Insects as destroyers; Nature of insecticides; Applying insecticides; Warnings as to insecticides; Resistance to insecticides; Fumigants; Quarantines; Other controls; Economic entomology; Insects, man, and homes; Insects on cotton; Insects and vegetables; Insects on fruit; Insects on field crops; Pests on ornamentals; Livestock and insects; Forests, trees, and pests; Insects and wildlife; Bibliography and appendix; Some important insects

Plant diseases; the yearbook of agriculture, 1953. U.S. Govt. Ptg. Off. 1953? 940p illus   632

1 Plant diseases

"Some 30,000 different diseases attack our economic plants—the plants grown for sale or use as foods, feeds, clothing, and lumber. Others spoil or destroy our flowers, shade trees and shrubs. In this book we present information on the causes and control of many diseases of our important crop plants." Preface

Contents: Costs and causes; Bases of controls; Growing healthier plants; Grasses and legumes; Cotton; Food and feed grains; Vegetable crops; Sugar crops; Tobacco plant; Some ornamentals; Fruits and nuts; After harvest; Some others

Glossary: p897-907

633   Field crops

United States. Department of Agriculture
Grass; the yearbook of agriculture, 1948.
U.S. Govt. Ptg. Off. 1948 892p illus   **633**

1 Grasses 2 Forage plants

The book "has many articles on how farmers, ranchers, poultrymen, livestock raisers, dairymen, and the conservationists can grow and use grasses and legumes. And because those plants are so basic to farming and living, discussions of them must include a great deal about soils, geography, agricultural history, economics and marketing, genetics, public programs, and natural resources. . . . It contains information on grass for lawns, parks, roadsides, playgrounds, and so on." Editor's preface

List of plant names: p823-54. For further reference: p855-78

634.9   Forestry

United States. Department of Agriculture
Trees; the yearbook of agriculture, 1949.
U.S. Govt. Ptg. Off. 1949 944p illus maps
   634.9

1 Trees—U.S.   2 Forests and forestry—U.S.

The book considers "first the tree as a unit, a living thing; next, the tree as a member of a small group—in cities and around homes; finally, trees growing together in wood lots, groves, and forests, large and small. The main section of the book ends with chapters on specific problems and values—insects, fire, recreation, wildlife, forestry, and economic importance." The editor to the reader

For further reference: p901-10. Some words woodsmen use: p911-16

635.03   Garden crops (Horticulture)—Dictionaries

Wyman, Donald
Wyman's Gardening encyclopedia. Macmillan (N Y) 1971 1222p illus $17.50   **635.03**

1 Gardening—Dictionaries 2 Plants, Cultivated—Dictionaries

A "reference book for gardeners, it lists thousands of plants with descriptions and scientific names, and provides the latest information on selecting the proper plants, on growing specialized groups of plants satisfactorily, and on new techniques, fertilizers and pesticides." Book News

Map on lining-papers

635.9   Flowers and ornamental plants (Floriculture)

Coats, Alice M.
Flowers and their histories. McGraw [1971 c1968] 346p illus $10   **635.9**

1 Flowers—History 2 Herbs—History 3 Plant lore

ISBN 0-07-011476-5

First published 1956 in England

A compilation of fact and folklore. "Included is a section of short biographies of distinguished writers, from antiquity through the twentieth century, whose works on gardening and botany have made an important contribution to garden literature. There is also . . . an index of English names." Publisher's note

This book is "suitable as a reference work for a multidisciplinary course in landscape gardening, garden design, history of gardening and horticulture, etc. The author is familiar with classical and modern sources of information. Occasionally, American gardens are mem-

tioned, yet most remarks are derived from the author's experience in Great Britain. . . . The writing is highly subjective and personal, which adds to its readability." Science Bks

Bibliography: p331-35

Lamb, Edgar
The pocket encyclopedia of cacti and succulents in color [by] Edgar and Brian Lamb; with 326 photographs reproduced in full color. Macmillan (N Y) [1970 c1969] 217p illus $4.95
   635.9

1 Cactus 2 Succulent plants

First published 1969 in England

Designed for the beginner, this handbook gives instructions for cacti and succulent cultivation—soil mixture, watering, pests and diseases, greenhouse plants, vegetative propagation, grafting techniques and raising from seed. A planting calendar and descriptions of individual species are included. (Publisher)

"It would best be considered a useful and not too technical background book for student projects, or for students who are looking for an interesting hobby." Science Bks

636   Livestock and domestic animals

Henley, Diana
ASPCA guide to pet care. Taplinger 1970 70p illus pa $1.25   **636**

1 Pets

SBN 8008-0453-8

"This book is an up-to-date guide for pet owners and for those who would like to be and are wondering what type of pet to choose. The book covers a wide range of animals including reptiles, small mammals and fish, as well as dogs and cats. Because of the many pets described, with some of them we can hope to do little more than stimulate your interest. By all means seek more lengthy and detailed information once you have selected the pet that is 'just right' for you." Foreword

636.089   Veterinary sciences

Yates, Elizabeth
Is there a doctor in the barn? A day in the life of Forrest F. Tenney, D.V.M. Illus. by Guy Fleming. Dutton 1966 207p $4.95
   636.089

1 Tenney, Forrest F. 2 Veterinary medicine

"The author follows [New Hampshire vet] Dr. Tenney on his rounds from farm to farm and back to his office for the treatment of pets and small animals while flashbacks fill in the doctor's boyhood and years of training. The doctor's love and respect for animals is apparent as is his emphasis on animals as an economic investment. Primarily for those interested in veterinary medicine or farm animals but pet lovers may also enjoy it." Booklist

636.1   Horses

Brady, Irene
America's horses and ponies; written and illus. by Irene Brady. Houghton 1969 202p illus $7.95   **636.1**

1 Horses 2 Ponies

"This is not a pretentious book and is one that will be frequently consulted in homes and libraries. Adults will enjoy it, young children will be fascinated by the drawings, and young horse lovers will look, read, and dream. The author covers each breed with a pencil drawing (to scale), a table of outstanding conformations, and a short commentary on the breed's 'character' and 'flavor' as well as its

Brady, Irene—*Continued*

history. The commentaries are generally informative, but not heavy reading. The author has a nice easy style. The drawings are excellent, and the 'poses' are fairly constant, so that one might compare the various horses, ponies, etc. There is a short section on the evolution of the horse, a diagram of the parts of the horse, and a table describing points of conformation to be used in comparative judging." Science Bks

Bibliography: p202

636.109 Horses—History

Haines, Francis

Horses in America. Crowell 1971 213p illus map $7.95   636.109

1 Horses—History
ISBN 0-690-40253-8

"An engrossing panoramic history of the horse in America from Colonial times to the age of the automobile. Francis Haines writes with authority and color of the horse in war, on the frontier, on farms, in towns and cities. The author . . . traces vividly the use of horses by Indians, the Pony Express, ranchers and rustlers. He describes the role of trail riders in opening the West, the use of cavalry in the Civil War. . . . Included too is a fascinating account of the long history of the use of the horse for pleasure in our country: trotters, racing thoroughbreds, circus and other horses right up to currently popular light riding horses." Pub W

Selected bibliography: p202-03

Nagler, Barney

The American horse. Macmillan (N Y) 1966 182p illus $5.95   636.109

1 Horses—History

This book "tells the origin and development of all the major American breeds. The history begins with the introduction of the horse into America by the early Spanish expeditions and ranges through the years until the mid 1960s when a horse named Kelso piled up a record $1,977,396 in winnings." Publisher's note

"Mr. Nagler has done an excellent job of selecting, condensing, and interpreting a great mass of material in order to produce this survey of the role of the horse in America." Library J

Glossary: p171-72. Bibliography: p173-74

636.7 Dogs

American Kennel Club

The complete dog book. . . . Doubleday illus $6   636.7

1 Dogs

First published 1935 by Garden City Books as a combination of: Pure bred dogs, first published 1929 by G. Watt, and The care, handling, and feeding of dogs, compiled by E. R. Blamey. Frequently revised and brought up to date

"The histories and standards of breeds admitted to AKC registration, and the feeding, training, care, breeding, and health of pure-bred dogs." Title page

Borland, Hal

The dog who came to stay; with drawings by Taylor Oughton. Lippincott 1962 220p illus $5.95   636.7

1 Dogs 2 Country life—Connecticut

First published 1961

The dog, Pat, "came to the Borland's farm one sleety night and stayed in spite of their qualms. Among many exploits are hunting and fishing expeditions, brushes with skunks and poachers, an encounter with a man who claimed he was Pat's former owner." Cincinnati

"A leisurely narrative interspersed with descriptions of life and nature in [the author's] Connecticut land. . . . It has enough understanding and quality to appeal to the real dog lovers, especially to those who like dogs more than exciting stories in which dogs figure." Horn Bk

Fiennes, Richard

The natural history of dogs [by] Richard and Alice Fiennes. Natural Hist. Press 1970 [c1968] 237p illus boards $7.95   636.7

1 Dogs

"Published for The American Museum of Natural History"

First published 1968 in England

"Beginning with that first nebulous relationship between Stone Age man and wolves, the authors describe the different races of dogs; their origins and dispersal from the Paleolithic to the present; and the roles dogs have played in ancient, classical, and modern times; [as well as] the zoology of the dog." Publisher's note

Bibliography: p225-28

Frank, Morris

First lady of the Seeing Eye, by Morris Frank and Blake Clark; illus. with photographs. Holt 1957 156p illus $3.95   636.7

1 Seeing eye dogs 2 Seeing Eye, Incorporated, Morristown, N.J. 3 Blind

"Morris Frank had the first Seeing Eye dog in America and tells of their twelve years together. Frank was twenty when he read an article explaining how Germans had trained shepherd dogs to lead the blind. Immediately he wrote to the author, Mrs. Eustis, to ask how he could get such a dog. With her help he went to Switzerland and met Buddy. That was the beginning not only of a successful life for him but also of the Seeing Eye Foundation in America. His determination and Buddy's intelligence moved thousands of people who saw and listened to support this new aid for the blind. . . . With details of Buddy's training and examples of her almost human reasoning." Horn Bk

Hartwell, Dickson

Dogs against darkness; the story of the Seeing Eye. Enl. ed. Dodd 1968 278p illus $5   636.7

1 Seeing eye dogs 2 Seeing Eye, Incorporated, Morristown, N.J. 3 Blind

First published 1942

Story of the training of the "Seeing Eye" dogs who guide blind people in the home and through traffic. It is also an account of the persons who founded the organization in Morristown, New Jersey, as well as the "Fortunate Fields" in Switzerland

"Mr. Hartwell tells his story simply. . . . If certain passages lump your throat the effect comes from the situation, not from literary trimming." N Y Times Bk R

National Geographic Society

Man's best friend; National Geographic Book of dogs. Rev. ed. . . . The Society [1971] 432p illus (Natural science lib) $9.85   636.7

1 Dogs 2 Dogs—Pictures, illustrations, etc.

First published 1958 with title: The National Geographic Book of dogs

"Foreword by Melville Bell Grosvenor. Chapters by John W. Cross, Jr. [and others]. Paintings by Walter A. Weber and other artists. Photographs by Walter Chandoha and others." Title page

Over one hundred breeds "are pictured in paintings and photographs, in color and in black and white. The text covers briefly the history of dogs and selection and care as well as descriptions of the individual breeds. The book brings together in a convenient and attractive compilation much material familiar to readers of the 'National Geographic Magazine.'" Booklist (Review of 1958 edition)

Orbaan, Albert

Dogs against crime. . . . Illus. with photographs and with drawings by the author. Day 1968 234p illus $6.95   **636.7**

1 Dogs—Training 2 Criminal investigation

"True accounts of canine training and exploits in worldwide police work, past and present." Subtitle

The accounts describe the use of dogs in police work in New York City, "Australia, Rome, London, Chicago, Copenhagen, [and] Baltimore, . . . and from such breeding and training centers as operate in Bloomfield, Connecticut, Bonn, West Germany, and Freeport, Long Island." Sat R

"In addition to the exploits of the dogs, the author also gives some interesting background and the various methods used in training dogs." Best Sellers

Bibliography: p229-30

Saunders, Blanche

Training you to train your dog. New rev. ed. Illus. by Louise Branch and J. Kilburn King; preface by Walter Lippmann. Doubleday 1965 299p illus $5.95   **636.7**

1 Dogs—Training

First published 1946

"The purpose of this book is to give the owner the technique and fundamentals of training. It is intended to teach the humane and just method to use in enforcing obedience and to help the unskilled owner become a successful disciplinarian." p 1

Sports Illustrated

Sports Illustrated Book of dog training, by the editors of Sports Illustrated. Lippincott 1960 |c1959] 88p illus $2.95   **636.7**

1 Dogs—Training

Title on spine: Dog training

"The first section of the book deals with training the family dog from puppyhood to maturity. . . . The second part of the book deals with field training and gives detailed guidance on the proper training of flushing spaniels, trailing hounds, retrievers and pointing dogs." Publisher's note

Whitney, Leon F.

How to select, train, and breed your dog. McKay 1969 242p illus $6.95   **636.7**

1 Dogs 2 Dogs—Training

First published 1955 with title: Your puppy: how to select, raise and train him

"A layman's guide to dog ownership, giving descriptions of all types of dogs and complete information on training and care." Am News of Bks

The author "emphasizes the medical aspects of dog care. He disagrees with the American Kennel Club's division of dogs into six groups and has devised his own grouping scheme. . . . This is an excellent book to put in the hands of a new dog owner; it is not too technical nor yet too elementary." Library J

636.8 Cats

Amberson, Rosanne

Raising your cat; a complete illustrated guide. Crown 1969 288p illus $5.95   **636.8**

1 Cats

"Regarding the nutrition and health of cats, new research during the past few years at veterinary colleges has turned up some surprising facts. These findings have led to a revolution in the production of cat foods and medicines. The author, owner of some three hundred cats at different times, has obtained this information directly from these sources and now makes it available to all cat owners, along with valuable nutrient charts and tables." News of Bks

Bryant, Doris

Doris Bryant's New cat book. Washburn 1969 181p illus $4.50   **636.8**

1 Cats

"A well-known authority on the subject of cats and their care, Doris Bryant has updated an earlier book on cats [Pet cats: their care and handling, published 1963] and has included much additional information on breeding." Book News

Denham, Sidney

The complete book of the Siamese cat [by] Sidney and Helen Denham. Barnes, A.S. 1970 [c1968] 173p illus $5.95   **636.8**

1 Siamese cat

SBN 498-07505-2

First published 1968 in England

"Distinctive qualities and history of Siamese cats and abundant pointers on selecting and on attending them in health, sickness, and disaster comprise a portion of . . . [this] guide for potential and novice Siamese cat owners. Consideration is also given to Siamese breeders and breeding, genetics and colors evolved (a table of 45 litter expectations included), British cat clubs, and show standards and opportunities. . . . Though costs, clubs, and standards are chiefly British, the book's general instructional value makes it a useful acquisition for extensive pet shelves in U.S. libraries." Booklist

Whitney, Leon F.

The complete book of cat care. Doubleday 1953 284p illus $5.95   **636.8**

1 Cats

"In non-technical language, one of the country's leading veterinarians presents a complete guide for the cat owner. Instructions are given on feeding, first aid, diagnosis and treatment of disease." Huntting

"In addition he discusses some matters not always included in the cat owner's handbook, such as hospitalization, boarding, shows, what you can and cannot catch from the cat, and heredity in cats." Booklist

639 Nondomesticated animals. Fisheries. Tropical fish. Whaling

Axelrod, Herbert R.

Axelrod's Tropical fish book. Photos and descriptions of over 180 aquarium fishes. Arco [1965 c1964] 112p illus (Arco Hobby lib) lib. bdg. $3.50   **639**

1 Tropical fish 2 Aquariums

"This book is not an easy way out for the serious person interested in learning about fishes. It can help the novice keep his fishes alive easier and more successfully, it can help him identify them and breed them, but it can't help him recognize the first symptom of a disease or assist him in selecting a ripe female and an active male to set up for spawning." Introduction

"Emphasis on starting an aquarium and on its accouterments [rather] than on individual fish species . . . is proper and desirable for the potential reader." Library J

Indexes to fishes by popular and scientific names

Idyll, C. P.

The sea against hunger. Crowell 1970 221p illus maps $7.95   **639**

1 Fisheries 2 Food supply 3 Marine resources 4 Fish culture

ISBN 0-690-72264-8

"An International Oceanographic Foundation selection"

The author "discusses numerous potentials for nutrition contained in the oceans: plankton and seaweed, techniques of fish transplantations, the use of fish meal and fish protein concentrates, and sea-farming." Pub W

Idyll, C. P.—*Continued*
In "this authoritative examination of food resources in the oceans [the author's general verdict is]: . . . if we ever intend to exploit the sea, we'd first better stop polluting it." Christian Century
Additional reading: p207-10

Wainwright, Neil
Tropical aquariums; with 12 plates in colour by Ernest C. Mansell and 12 pages of black and white photographs; line drawings in the text by Baz East. Warne 1970 110p illus boards $3.95   **639**
1 Aquariums 2 Tropical fish
ISBN 0-7232-1263-5
Supersedes A. L. Wells' Tropical aquariums, plants and fishes, first published 1937 in England
The author describes how to set up, heat and maintain an aquarium, listing suitable plants with which to stock it and giving useful advice on the feeding, tending and breeding of tropical fishes
Bibliography: p101-02

The Whale [by Leonard Harrison Matthews, and others]. Simon & Schuster 1968 287p illus maps $20   **639**
1 Whales 2 Whaling
"The result of an international cooperative effort in that 16 experts, representing 10 countries, have combined to produce a book that should appeal to the general reader as well as the scientist. Largely pictorial but contains a wealth of textual material written concisely but with depth. Three of the 10 chapters treat the biology of cetaceans, five are devoted to aspects of whaling, and two discuss the folklore and literature of whales and whaling. The book is important in the attention it calls to the need for conservation of whales. Many of the 340 illustrations and photographs are in color. All are well chosen to give a balanced treatment of the subject. The glossary is brief but helpful in dealing with whaling terminology. The bibliography contains 200 selected entries. No index." Choice

640 Domestic arts and sciences

Bradford, Barbara Taylor
The complete encyclopedia of homemaking ideas. Meredith 1968 624p illus $9.95   **640**
1 Home economics 2 Interior decoration
"An Edward Ernest book"
"Prepared with the cooperation of the National Design Center"
"Such topics as home safety, the importance of insurance, decoration problems, gardening, making use of storage space, and keeping on a budget are all covered in this guide to all phases of running a house." Bk Buyer's Guide
"Whether designing a new home, remodeling a present residence, rearranging and adding furnishings, or just managing a home, the reader will find here practical, interesting, and individually styled suggestions. The book is virtually a picture gallery with more than 400 photographs, many in sharp, clear color, which accurately support the text." Library J

Gillies, Mary Davis
The new How to keep house; illus. by Cobean. Harper 1968 335p illus $6.95   **640**
1 Home economics
First published 1948 with title: How to keep house
The book contains "material on what makes a house run smoothly—cleaning, laundering, cooking, household management, entertaining . . . [and it] incorporates . . . information on advances in mechanical and electrical equipment, furniture, floor coverings, and other aids available to the housewife." Library J

640.3 Domestic art and sciences —Dictionaries

Good Housekeeping
Good Housekeeping's Guide for young homemakers; an up-to-the minute handbook of successful home management; ed. by William Laas with the editors of Good Housekeeping. Harper 1966 431p illus $5.95   **640.3**
1 Home economics—Dictionaries
"Advice on basic questions and problems that arise in home management and related areas is the foundation of a ready-reference book addressed to the inexperienced homemaker. Its 175 articles are arranged in dictionary fashion, with a table of contents by categories, cross-references, and an index augmenting reference use. Twenty-three categories range from appliances, food preparation, and housekeeping to money management, shopping guides, and stain removal." Booklist

640.73 Consumer education

Klamkin, Charles
If it doesn't work, read the instructions. Stein & Day 1970 191p boards $4.95   **640.73**
1 Consumer education 2 Household appliances, Electric
SBN 8128-1285-9
This brief work is intended to put the buyer on guard in purchasing major electrical appliances (only), namely, refrigerators, TV sets . . . dishwashers, electric stoves, and hi-fi's. Klamkin has two targets, both of which he takes to task in a frank and humorous way: the manufacturer and the retailer. Of shoddy manufacture, poor design, frequent and unnecessary design changes, costly frills, conflicting warranty claims, and uncertain service. To the latter he attributes advertising gimmicks, price doubletalk, costly financial arrangements, and fraudulent sales pitches and dodges." Choice

United States. Department of Agriculture
Consumers all. U.S. Govt. Ptg. Off. 1965 496p illus (Yearbook of agriculture) boards $2.75   **640.73**
1 Consumer education
This volume tells "about buying, using, or making food, clothing, household furnishings, and equipment; managing money; caring for yards, gardens, and houses; bettering communities; using leisure time; and staying healthy." Preface
"Secretary of Agriculture Orville Freeman notes in his foreword to this work that 'the impressive variety of . . . consumer services available from the "People's Department" must be extended to many more Americans everywhere . . . yet the consumer must know what these services are, where they are and how to obtain them.' An excellent start towards this goal has been made in this compendium of ideas for everyday living. Material is concise, easy-to-read and practical, and gives the best methods for obtaining and using the goods and services we often take for granted. . . . Many bibliographies are included." Library J

641 Food

United States. Department of Agriculture
Food for us all. U.S. Govt. Ptg. Off. 1969 xxxix, 360p illus (Yearbook of agriculture)   **641**
1 Food supply 2 Farm produce—Marketing 3 Cookery
"This Yearbook tells agriculture's story in terms of food—how it's produced by the farmer, how it's marketed, and how the consumer can use it to best advantage in the home. . . .

United States. Department of Agriculture—
—*Continued*

'Food From Farm to You,' first section of the Yearbook, describes the economics of food, from the farmer's field to the supermarket. The second section, 'Buying and Cooking Food,' is divided into the major food classes, from meat and poultry on to dairy products, fruits, vegetables, and ultimately—pickles, spices, and herbs. Housewives may find the tips on buying and the recipes especially helpful. Nutrition and planning meals are major components of the third section." Preface

"The book is introduced by over 20 pages of colored photographs, and there are black-and-white photographs, drawings, and other illustrations liberally distributed throughout the text where they are needed or useful. The level of sophistication of the individual articles varies." Science Bks

641.1   Applied nutrition

Arnold, Pauline

Food facts for young people [by] Pauline Arnold and Percival White; drawings by Gilbert Etheredge. Holiday 1968 256p illus map $4.95   **641.1**

1 Food 2 Nutrition

"The authors promote a positive, wholesome attitude toward food and nutrition in this book. . . . [It] is divided into four sections: components of and needs for food; problem areas, including weight control, food misinformation, and food related illnesses; world population and food supply; and eating well in the United States. A glossary, bibliography, and index are included." Science Bks

Kraus, Barbara

Calories and carbohydrates; foreword by Edward B. Greenspan. Grosset 1971 322p illus $7.95   **641.1**

1 Nutrition 2 Food—Analysis
ISBN 0-448-01982-5

"This dictionary of foods lists several thousand brand-name products and basic foods with their caloric and carbohydrate content. . . . Foods are listed alphabetically by brand name or by the name of the food. The singular form is used for the entries, that is, blackberry instead of blackberries. Most items are listed individually though a few are grouped. . . . All brand-name products have been italicized and company names appear in parentheses." Introduction

"An interesting feature is the inclusion of drawings of meat portions so that dieters may learn to recognize calorie content by the size of the portion rather than by its weight. The book should be of considerable interest to dietitians, physicians, and dieters." Library J
Bibliography: p318

Sebrell, William H.

Food and nutrition, by William H. Sebrell, Jr., James J. Haggerty and the editors of Time-Life Books. Time-Life Bks. [1970 c1967] 200p illus maps (Life Science lib) lib. bdg. $7.60   **641.1**

1 Food 2 Nutrition

Reissue of a title published 1967
"The first part of the book deals with the universality of man's nutritional requirements, the diversity of diet around the world, and developments in food production and preservation. There are excellent chapters on digestion and conversion of food in the body and on milestones in vitamin history. Dietary nostrums and food fads are evaluated and discussed lucidly. Also covered are important current nutrition problems of the world." Science Bks

Further reading: p196

641.3   Foods and foodstuffs

United States. Department of Agriculture

Protecting our food. U.S. Govt. Ptg. Off. 1966 386p illus (Yearbook of agriculture) $2.50   **641.3**

1 Food 2 Food supply 3 Food industry and trade

"The yearbook begins with the world and national food situations. The story continues through the battles for abundance against insects, decay, drought, and frost. It ranges from on-farm production to shipping and handling; from processing to packaging to refrigeration; from warehouse to supermarket to protecting food in the home and restaurant. The marketing marvel, military and space food problems, and safeguarding the sportsman's paradise are part of the story." Preface

641.5   General cookery

Adams, Charlotte

The teen-ager's menu cookbook; drawings by Ragna Tischler Goddard. Dodd 1969 214p illus $3.95   **641.5**

1 Cookery 2 Menus

This book "presents teen-agers, both girl and boy . . . with the menu for family dinners, special holiday dinners, dinners featuring various national specialties, casserole dinners, suggested menus for a beach picnic, after the football game snacks, Christmas tree trimming supper, birthday party, Sunday brunch and others. After the menu is set forth, the marketing list is given, check-list of staples to be needed and the utensils required. Then a schedule of timing for the preparation of the recipes which follow." Best Sellers
A glossary of cooking terms: p7-14

American Heritage

The American Heritage cookbook, by the editors of American Heritage, The Magazine of History. Recipes editor: Helen McCully; associate recipes editor: Eleanor Noderer; historical foods consultant: Helen Duprey Bullock. Am. Heritage 1969 245p illus boards $6.95   **641.5**

1 Cookery
SBN 8281-0006-3

Based on: The American Heritage cookbook, and illustrated history of American eating & drinking, entered below

"A collection of American recipes selected from old cookbooks and adapted to present methods and equipment." Book Rev Digest

"The anecdotes are well-chosen, there is no 'cute' commentary, and the non-working verbiage is set off by a different color printing from the actual recipes, a real time and muddlesaver. . . . For anyone disenchanted with the glib non-cookery of modern 'basic' volumes." Canadian Forum

The American Heritage cookbook, and illustrated history of American eating & drinking, by the editors of American Heritage, The Magazine of History. . . . Am. Heritage 1964 629p illus $12.50   **641.5**

1 Cookery 2 Menus

"With chapters by Cleveland Amory [and others]. Historical foods consultant: Helen Duprey Bullock; recipes editor: Helen McCully; associate: Eleanor Noderer." Title page

"500 traditional recipes are served against a background of American history and art." Huntting

Bailey, Adrian

The cooking of the British Isles, by Adrian Bailey and the editors of Time-Life Books; photographed by Anthony Blake. Time-Life Bks. [distributed by Little] 1969 208p illus map (Foods of the world) boards $7.95 **641.5**

1 Cookery, British

Bailey, Adrian—*Continued*

This work presents "traditional English Scottish, Welsh, and some Irish recipes for meats and meat-pies, dumplings, puddings, trifles, with porridge and scones and seed-cakes, marmalades and so forth. . . . [The accompanying] spiral-bound handbook . . . contains 110 [indexed] recipes, of which only 86 appear in the parent volume." Best Sellers

Better Homes and Gardens

Better Homes & Gardens New cook book. [Rev. ed] Meredith 1965 400p illus $6.95

641.5

1 Cookery

First published 1930 with title: My Better Homes and Gardens Cook book
Loose leaf, spiral binding
This cook book "includes 20 sections, each with its own index tab. Here is a new collection of 1,403 thoroughly tested recipes." McClurg. Book News
"Easy to use guides for preparation of nutritious meals, many of which contain bargain foods. There are excellent sections of tested recipes for appetizers and beverages, breads, cakes, casseroles and one dish meals, jiffy cooking, outdoor cooking, pastry and pies, salads. Beautifully illustrated." Cincinnati

Brown, Dale

American cooking, by Dale Brown and the editors of Time-Life Books. Photographed by Mark Kauffman. Time-Life Bks. [distributed by Little] 1968 208p illus maps (Foods of the world) boards $7.95

641.5

1 Cookery

"From apple pie to old-fashioned lemonade, from sourdough biscuits to pecan pie, from clam bakes to home-made vanilla ice cream, from barbecued beef to baked bourbon-glazed ham . . . many of America's dishes are included and are beautifully illustrated. . . . Gives the young adult a good background to American foods." Catholic Library World
"The historical chapters make fascinating reading. . . . As with the other books in the series the recipes come in a separate spiral-bound booklet for easier use in the kitchen." Library J

The cooking of Scandinavia, by Dale Brown and the editors of Time-Life Books; photographed by Richard Meek. Time-Life Bks. [distributed by Little] 1968 206p illus (Foods of the world) boards $7.95

641.5

1 Cookery, Scandinavian

"For prospective or returned travelers as well as adventurous cooks, an impressive presentation in beautiful color photography and informative text of culinary and related customs, eating habits, and distinctive dishes of Denmark, Norway, Sweden, and Finland and the diversities of terrain, traditions, and way of life from which they stem. At each chapter end, explicit recipes well adapted for the American kitchen are supplied for dishes mentioned." Booklist

Child, Julia

The French Chef cookbook; drawings and photos by Paul Child. Knopf 1968 xxxiii, 424p illus $6.95

641.5

1 Cookery, French

"This book grew out of the educational television series 'The French Chef.' . . . It ranges from sauces, stews, and meats to appetizers, vegetables, desserts, cakes and pastries, and from the very simple to the fairly complicated. The book represents 119 programs . . . and the recipes are printed in the order that the shows were produced. Although about a third were taken from Mastering the Art of French Cooking [by Simone Beck, Louisette Bertholle and Julia Child] some of the television recipes differ slightly from the book recipes." Introduction

In "Julia Child's new and delightful book, . . . the simplest soups and the most complicated patisseries are treated with the same loving, meticulous care. One immediately has the impression that nobody wants the amateur cook to succeed with each recipe more than the author herself." Book World

Crocker, Betty

Betty Crocker's Good and easy cookbook; photography directors: Len Weiss [and] Stephen Manville. Golden Press 1971 151p illus lib. bdg. $5.95

641.5

1 Cookery

First published 1954 by Simon & Schuster
"Here are more than 400 no-fuss, no-muss recipes to streamline your way through the business of three-meals-a-day-every-day. Learn how to use the very latest frozen, canned and packaged foods in creative, unusual and delicious ways—with a minimum of time and effort and a maximum of satisfaction." News of Bks

De Knight, Freda

The Ebony cookbook: a date with a dish. . . . With a foreword by Gertrude Blair. Johnson Pub. (Chicago) 1962 390p illus $4.95   641.5

1 Cookery 2 Cookery, Negro

"A cookbook of American Negro recipes." Title page

Farmer, Fannie

The Fannie Farmer cookbook. Little illus $7.95

641.5

1 Cookery

First published 1896 with title: Boston Cooking School Cook book. Titles vary slightly with editions. Latest edition revised by Wilma Lord Perkins
A standard, comprehensive cookbook comprising a ready reference to the selection, preparation, and serving of a wide variety of foods
"Any book which has had 10 editions since its first in 1896, and which has sold only a little under 3 million copies, needs no other praise, really." Christian Science Monitor

Feibleman, Peter S.

The cooking of Spain and Portugal, by Peter S. Feibleman and the editors of Time-Life Books. Photographed by Dmitri Kessel and Brian Seed. Time-Life Bks. [distributed by Little 1970 c1969] 208p illus (Foods of the world) boards $7.95

641.5

1 Cookery, Spanish 2 Cookery, Portuguese

First published 1969
"A hardcover book discussing the cuisine, customs and countryside of these two nations is accompanied by a spiral-bound volume of about one hundred recipes. English recipe index Spanish and Portuguese recipe index, and general index." Book Rev Digest
"The two regions of Portugal and 13 regions of Spain that contribute Iberian cooking to world cuisine are described here with a skillful traveler's careful attention to details." Christian Science Monitor

Field, Michael

A quintet of cuisines, by Michael and Frances Field and the editors of Time-Life Books; photographed by Sheldon Cotler and Richard Jeffery; photography in Poland by Eliot Elisofon. Time-Life Bks. [distributed by Little] 1970 208p illus (Foods of the world) boards $7.95

641.5

1 Cookery

The cooking of five regions, including 10 countries are included in this book: "Switzerland, the Low Countries (Belgium-Luxembourg-Netherlands), Poland, Bulgaria, Romania, North Africa (Tunisia-Algeria-Morocco)." Publisher's note

Field, Michael—*Continued*
"The Recipe Booklet that accompanies this volume has been designed for use in the kitchen. It contains all of the 60 recipes printed in this book plus 91 more. It has a wipe-clean cover and a spiral binding so that it can either stand up or lie flat when open." p5

Fisher, M. F. K.
The cooking of provincial France, by M. F. K. Fisher and the editors of Time-Life Books. Photographed by Mark Kauffman. Time-Life Bks. [distributed by Little] 1968 208p illus (Foods of the world) boards $7.95
         641.5

1 Cookery, French
"Traditional cooking of provincial France, and its relationship to closely knit French patterns of family life are described with verve and authority by an American gastronome . . . who lived for years in France. There is a 100-page recipe booklet . . . and a 64-page kitchen guide. This cookbook has advice on basic everyday dishes and also on elegant specialties. Recipes and shopping instructions are calculated for the American market. Wines recommended are French." Pub W

Good Housekeeping Institute, New York
The new Good Housekeeping cookbook; ed. by Dorothy B. Marsh; illus. by Bill Goldsmith. Harcourt 1963 805p illus $8.50
         641.5

1 Cookery
First published 1942 with title: Good Housekeeping cookbook
A guide to meal preparation from planning and purchasing to serving. The book also includes information on low-calorie dishes, quantity cookery, freezing methods, barbecue techniques, plus recipes for teen-age cooks. (Publisher)
"An unusually fine index adds to the usefulness of this . . . cookbook." Library J
Cook's vocabulary: p4-12

Hahn, Emily
The cooking of China, by Emily Hahn and the editors of Time-Life Books. Photographed by Michael Rougier. Time-Life Bks. [distributed by Little] 1968 206p illus (Foods of the world) boards $7.95
         641.5

1 Cookery, Chinese
On spine: Chinese cooking
"Anecdotes about her own life in prerevolutionary China are mingled with down-to-earth cooking instruction in Miss Hahn's book. From Peking Duck to Chicken Velvet, the book contains tested recipes representative of the four major schools of Chinese cooking." McClurg. Book News
"The photographer, Michael Rougier, deserves a special round of applause: the book is a work of art. In it, are excellent sections on hors d'oeuvres and Dim Sum, the use of ingredients, mail-order sources, and the philosophy of Chinese cooking. An extremely useful 120-page spiral-bound recipe booklet accompanies the book." Library J

Hale, William Harlan
The Horizon Cookbook and illustrated history of eating and drinking throughout the ages, by William Harlan Hale and the editors of Horizon Magazine; editor in charge: Wendy Buehr; recipes editor: Tatiana McKenna; historical foods consultant: Mimi Sheraton. Am. Heritage [distributed by Doubleday] 1968 768p illus map $16.50 **641.5**

1 Cookery 2 Cookery—History 3 Menus
Part 1 by William Harlan Hale and the editors of Horizon Magazine. Part 2 by the editors of Horizon Magazine. This book traces the evolution of wining and dining and displays a collection of more than 675 recipes and menus from the world's cuisines, past and present. (Publisher)

Hazelton, Nika Standen
The cooking of Germany, by Nika Standen Hazelton and the editors of Time-Life Books. Photographed by Ralph Crane and Henry Groskinsky. Time-Life Bks. [distributed by Little] 1969 208p illus maps (Foods of the world) boards $7.95
         641.5

1 Cookery, German
"A panoramic survey of German cuisine, from delicate 'vorspeisen' of mushrooms and puff pastry, through the magnificence of roasts and the delicacy of 'schnitzel', to the superb custards and cakes that end a meal. Other chapters describe the five meals of the German day; dining out in some of the world's finest restaurants and in country inns and 'rathskellers;' and German entertaining from the casual elegance of a wine party to the pagan splendor of a hunt. A historical discussion traces some of the great German creations such as 'hasenpfeffer' back to late medieval times. In a tour of the nation's three major culinary regions, the reader visits a North German market for pork and smoked eels, attends a robust breakfast of Westphalian ham and schnapps, and hunts mushrooms in the Black Forest." Publisher's note

Leonard, Jonathan Norton
American cooking: New England; with supplementary chapters on the cooking of Eastern Canada, by Jonathan Norton Leonard and the editors of Time-Life Books; photographed by Constantine Manos and Richard Jeffery. Time-Life Bks. [distributed by Little 1971 c1970] 208p illus maps (Foods of the world) boards $7.95 **641.5**

1 Cookery—New England
First published 1970
Text and color photographs describe New England cooking, including Indian crops (corn, squash, and beans), sea food, cranberries, pies, preserves, and maple syrup. Recipes accompany the text and also appear in a spiral-bound booklet which accompanies the basic volume. The booklet contains 106 additional recipes

Latin American cooking, by Jonathan Norton Leonard and the editors of Time-Life Books; photographed by Milton Greene. Time-Life Bks. [distributed by Little] 1968 206p illus maps (Foods of the world) boards $7.95
         641.5

1 Cookery, Latin American
This "illustrated volume gives interesting information on the chief foods and drinks of the people in nine South American countries and Mexico. Most chapters are by region, but three are devoted to distinctive foods—fruits, sweets and drinks." Publisher's note
Includes a glossary

McCall's
McCall's Cook book, by the food editors of McCall's. Random House 1963 786p illus $6.95
         641.5

1 Cookery
A beginner's step-by-step cook book in double-columned text containing "nearly 2,000 recipes, an herb chart, sections on dieting, nutrition, menu-planning, shopping, outdoor cooking, wines, using frozen foods, etc. With 1,000 drawings [and] 24 full-color photographs." Bk Buyer's Guide

Mazda, Maideh
In a Persian kitchen; favorite recipes from the Near East. Illus. by M. Kuwata. Tuttle 1960 175p $3.75
         641.5

1 Cookery, Iranian
SBN 8048-0260-2
This is a "collection of Near Eastern specialties adapted for American kitchens by the Persian-born author who includes . . . com-

Mazda, Maideh—*Continued*

mentary on Persian food and customs. There are directions for preparing yogurt, appetizers, soups, many stuffed vegetables and fruits, many pilafs and sauces for them, egg casserole dishes, meat and fowl, desserts and salads. Eight representative menus are included. An appendix describes the unusual ingredients, spices and herbs." Library J

Mendes, Helen

The African heritage cookbook. Macmillan (NY) 1971 247p illus $7.95   **641.5**

1 Cookery, Negro 2 Cookery, African

"A fascinating and delightful history/cookbook that traces the evolution of 16th and 17th century West African culinary style into what is now known as soul cooking, and provides the best collection of soul recipes available. More than 200 recipes, contributed by soul people, include such favorites as barbecued spareribs, Chitterlings, shrimp gumbo, hopping john, blackberry pudding, sweet potatoe pie, and breads, cakes, and pies of all kinds." News of Bks

Bibliography: p233-37

Miller, Jill Nhu Huong

Vietnamese cookery. Tuttle 1968 118p illus pa $3.95   **641.5**

1 Cookery, Vietnamese
SBN 8048-0617-9

Spiral binding

"Hors d'oeuvres, soup, salad and main-dish recipes make up this authentic collection. Added features are a brief description of Vietnamese cookery; equipment needed; and a glossary providing substitutes for hard-to-find foods. The only illustration shows how to fold dough for crab or other rolls." Minnesota

Nickles, Harry G.

Middle Eastern cooking, by Harry G. Nickles and the editors of Time-Life Books. Photographed by David Lees and Richard Jeffery. Time-Life Bks. [distributed by Little] 1969 206p illus (Foods of the world) boards $7.95   **641.5**

1 Cookery, Near East

The author describes "Middle Eastern cooking, basing his account largely upon an extensive culinary journey through Greece, Turkey, Lebanon, Jordan, Israel, Syria, Iraq, Iran, and Egypt. Noting that each of the nine nations has its own character and cuisine, Nickles concludes that Middle Eastern cooking is simultaneously homogeneous and diverse, lavish and thrifty, plain and well seasoned. He notes that sweets, coffee, and spices are popular throughout the region and that favorite foods include lamb, wheat, eggplant, and yogurt. A glossary and mail-order sources of ingredients are appended, and a spiral-bound booklet containing 121 recipes accompanies the volume." Booklist

Papashvily, Helen

Russian cooking, by Helen and George Papashvily, and the editors of Time-Life Books; photographed by Eliot Elisofon and Richard Jeffery. Time-Life Bks. [distributed by Little] 1969 206p illus map (Foods of the world) boards $7.95   **641.5**

1 Cookery, Russian

"Informal, informative text and handsome color photographs depict the culinary habits of Great Russia; the Baltic Republics of Estonia, Latvia, and Lithuania; the Ukraine; Armenia and Georgia in the Caucasus; and the four states of Central Asia together with neighboring Kazakhstan. The accompanying spiral-bound book is an indexed collection of the recipes scattered throughout the volume." Booklist

Rama Rau, Santha

The cooking of India, by Santha Rama Rau and the editors of Time-Life Books; photographed by Eliot Elisofon. Time-Life Bks. [distributed by Little] 1969 208p illus (Foods of the world) boards $7.95   **641.5**

1 Cookery, Indic

"Photographs, a narrative and recipes comprise this description of Indian cooking culture." Book Rev Digest

The recipes "were adapted to the 'western' kitchen. A special chapter on Pakistan cooking [is included]. . . . [The book is] beautifully printed with exceptional color photographs, sturdily bound . . . and accompanied by a spiral bound Recipe Book, which includes, actually, more recipes than those given in the hardbound larger book. . . . The book [is] valuable not only as cookbook but as observant and informative description of the land and the people." Best Sellers

The "book has recipes which often require unusual ingredients or implements, but [it] lists mail order sources for these items." Library J

Rombauer, Irma S.

Joy of cooking [by] Irma S. Rombauer [and] Marion Rombauer Becker; illus. by Ginnie Hofman and Beverly Warner. Bobbs illus $6.95   **641.5**

1 Cookery

First published 1931 and periodically revised to include new recipes and modern methods of cooking

A compilation of recipes in double column pages covering also such related topics as: Cocktails; Herbs; Pressure cookery; Electric blender; High altitude cookery; Nutrition and calorie chart; Definitions and tables

"An all-purpose cookbook, containing more than 4000 recipes with sections on menus, table-setting, canning, salting and smoking, freezing foods, etc." Winchell. Guide to Reference Books. 8th ed.

Root, Waverly

The cooking of Italy, by Waverly Root and the editors of Time-Life Books. Photographed by Fred Lyon. Time-Life Bks. [distributed by Little] 1968 208p illus (Foods of the world) boards $7.95   **641.5**

1 Cookery, Italian

"An introduction by Barzini, author of 'The Italians' . . . on the character of Italian cooking and a history of Italian cookery as the source of all other Western cuisine precedes a presentation of Italian recipes by region. Visually beautiful with many colorplates and gastronomically tempting." Booklist

Spiral bound booklet of recipes accompanies volume

Steinberg, Rafael

The cooking of Japan, by Rafael Steinberg and the editors of Time-Life Books; photographed by Eliot Elisofon. Time-Life Bks. [distributed by Little] 1971 c1970] 208p illus map (Foods of the world) boards $7.95 **641.5**

1 Cookery, Japanese

First published 1969

"Japanese cooking—the author asserts—can be ranked with the French and the Chinese as one of the three great cuisines of the world. True Japanese-style food remains comparatively unknown, because Japanese hosts assume that visiting foreigners will not like their subtle and delicate cookery. . . . The author offers a sympathetic account of the niceties of Japanese food preparation, cooking and serving, and lists the authentic Japanese foodstuffs (all of which can be obtained in the U.S.). [He] cites the 'dipping sauce' as the heart of Japan's cuisine, and extols the healthful qualities of the vegetarian-oriented diet." Publisher's note

Steinberg, Rafael—*Continued*

This is "beautifully printed with exceptional color photographs [and is] sturdily bound. . . . [The book is] valuable not only as [a] cookbook, but as [an] observant and informative description of the land and the people [of Japan]." Best Sellers

Accompanied by spiral-bound booklet of the recipes, some of which are in the main text

Pacific and Southeast Asian cooking, by Rafael Steinberg and the editors of Time-Life Books; photographed by Anthony Blake [and others]. Time-Life Bks. [distributed by Little] 1970 208p illus map (Foods of the world) boards $7.95   **641.5**

1 Cookery, Oriental

"In an area-by-area geographical tour, the reader is introduced to an intriguing collection of exotic foods; suckling pig roasted in an underground oven in Tahiti; taro leaves combined with coconut, baked fish and bananas in Samoa; 'rijstaafel' in Indonesia; turtle 'sate' in Bali; hot curries in Sumatra; 'adobo' (marinated chicken and pork) in the Philippines; and 'mie krob,' a national dish of Thailand, which blends noodles, shrimp, pork and bean sprouts. The book also shows how copra, spice and rice influenced history—how the demand for spices, for example, helped launch the early voyages of exploration." Publisher's note

Van der Post, Laurens

African cooking, by Laurens van der Post and the editors of Time-Life Books. Photographed by Brian Seed and Richard Jeffery. Time-Life Bks. [distributed by Little] 1970 208p illus maps (Foods of the world) boards $7.95   **641.5**

1 Cookery, African

"Africa is almost the only remaining spot on the globe where eating styles range from the Stone Age to sophisticated modern. The author singles out for special mention the varied cooking of Ethiopia, which has the longest recorded history south of the Mediterranean. The book conducts a gastronomic tour from Senegal through French Guinea, Sierra Leone, the Ivory Coast, Ghana and Nigeria, and across into Uganda, Kenya and Tanganyika. Along the way, the reader will discover the foods of Portuguese Africa and the rich South African cuisine; the Cape-Malay-Javanese tradition of the Cape of Good Hope peninsula, which reflects the impact of the Far East; the blend of Huguenot French and Dutch styles in the Western Province; and the cooking of the interior—Natal, Orange Free State, Transvaal, and Southern Rhodesia, with a selection of dishes from Zambia and Malawi." Publisher's note

Spiral bound booklet of recipes accompanies volume

Walter, Eugene, 1926-

American cooking: Southern style; by Eugene Walter and the editors of Time-Life Books; studio photographs by Mark Kauffman. Time-Life Bks. [distributed by Little] 1971 208p illus map (Foods of the world) boards $7.95   **641.5**

1 Cookery—Southern States

This book "takes the reader to a Southern style breakfast at the Kentucky Derby, a classic soul food dinner in South Carolina, to a national fried chicken festival in the 'Delmarva' belt, to a Thomas Jefferson vintage repast at Monticello, on a shorghum syrup hunt in Tar Heel territory, to a bourbon distillery in Kentucky, and on a palm tree hunt deep in Florida." Publisher's note

A spiral-bound booklet accompanies this volume which includes 60 recipes from the book plus 90 more

Wilson, José

American cooking: the Eastern heartland; New York, New Jersey, Pennsylvania, Ohio, Michigan, Indiana, Illinois, by José Wilson and the editors of Time-Life Books. Photographed by Richard Jeffery [and others]. Time-Life Bks. [distributed by Little] 1971 208p illus map (Foods of the world) boards $7.95   **641.5**

1 Cookery

The cooking indigenous to these seven states "is stick-to-the-ribs stuff, more plain than fancy, given to substantial meat dishes, dumplings, breads, pies. It does not have the austere background of the New England style, or the glamorous background of some of the Southern style; but it is hearty, appetizing, often exciting and always good." Introduction

Wilson, Marie M.

Siamese cookery. Tuttle 1965 109p illus $3.95   **641.5**

1 Cookery, Thai
SBN 8048-0530-X

"The introduction to this recipe book tells about Thai foods and eating customs. There is a pronunciation guide for the names of the dishes given in transliterated Thai and English. The selection of recipes is geared to Western kitchens and supermarkets. Illustrations typify Thai sights and customs." Minnesota

Wolfe, Linda

The cooking of the Caribbean Islands, by Linda Wolfe and the editors of Time-Life Books. Photographed by Richard Meek. Time-Life Bks. [distributed by Little] 1970 208p illus map (Foods of the world) boards $7.95   **641.5**

1 Cookery, Caribbean

Text and color photographs describe cooking and its traditions in the Caribbean area. Included are chapters about tropical fruits, sea food, and rum. Eighty-five recipes accompany the text and also appear in a spiral-bound booklet which accompanies the basic volume; the booklet contains fifty-eight additional recipes

Glossary: p197-99

641.503 Cookery—Dictionaries

De Sola, Ralph

(comp.) A dictionary of cooking. . . . Comp. by Ralph and Dorothy De Sola; with an introduction by Peg Bracken. Meredith 1969 246p $7.95   **641.503**

1 Cookery—Dictionaries
SBN 696-58012-8

"Approximately eight thousand definitions of culinary ingredients, methods, terms, and utensils." Title page

"Culinary terms are concisely defined in this continental dictionary which attempts to identify food terms rather than to give encyclopedic information on them. If the term is other than American, the country of origin is cited. Colloquial, slang, and, in some cases, misspelled words are given referring the reader to the proper word. . . . The foods span the centuries, from yogurt to engineered food, but few historical notes are included. Both the novice cook and the seasoned chef will appreciate this uncluttered reference book." Library J

641.6 Special cookery and materials

Rosengarten, Frederic

The book of spices [by] Frederic Rosengarten, Jr. Livingston Pub. distributed by Macrae Smith Co. 1969 489p illus maps $20   **641.6**

1 Spices 2 Cookery
SBN 87098-031-9

Rosengarten, Frederic—*Continued*

This title will be "of value to scientists and historians as well as gourmet cooks and home-makers (it includes more than 200 recipes). . . . The major portion of the book consists of chapters on the 35 most important spices and herbs. For each spice there is a complete description accompanied by a colored botanical print, along with the Latin binomial, followed where possible by the name in 11 other modern languages." Library J

"The special bonus in this lavishly illustrated book . . . is Rosengarten's informative and extremely interesting discussion of the nature and history of spices from Egypt, where they were used in embalming, to the modern spice trade. The book rates A-1 on the subject." Pub W

Glossary: p469-72. Bibliography: p473-79

641.8 Composite dishes

Better Homes and Gardens

Better Homes and Gardens Pies and cakes. Meredith 1966 92p illus $1.95   **641.8**

1 Pastry 2 Cake

200 "recipes for pies, cakes and frostings! Includes tips on making . . . pie crusts, decorating cakes, hints on freezing and a special guide to high-altitude baking." Publisher's note

"Tempting pies and cakes in great variety may be made from the excellent recipes in this book. It contains new ideas for both experienced and novice bakers." Cincinnati

642 Food and meal service. Table service and decor

Hirsch, Sylvia

The art of table setting and flower arrangement. New expanded ed. Crowell 1967 168p illus $7.95   **642**

1 Table 2 Flower arrangement

First published 1962

This book "emphasizes modern trends in flower arrangement and table decor and . . . chapters discuss the use of color and space in design today. With sections on table settings for flower show exhibitions and on the relation of menus to table settings." Bk Buyer's Guide

643 The home and its equipment

Gladstone, Bernard

The New York Times Complete manual of home repair. Macmillan (N Y) 1966 438p illus $7.95   **643**

1 Houses—Repairing

Contents: Tools and materials; Interior repairs: Exterior repairs; Painting and papering; Plumbing and heating; Electrical repairs: Furniture repairs and refinishing

"Although it is based on the 'Home Improvement' columns of the Sunday 'Times,' this is essentially an original book. . . . From a practical background in maintenance and repair it has been written in language as simple and non-technical as possible. The many photographs and drawings which illustrate the various subjects have been chosen carefully." Introduction

646 Clothing

Carson, Byrta

How you look and dress. 4th ed. McGraw 1969 310p illus (American home and family ser) $6.60   **646**

1 Clothing and dress 2 Dressmaking

First published 1949

A practical book on grooming, poise and charm, clothing care, color, design, textiles, hand sewing, machine sewing, construction and other aspects of dressmaking

Textile glossary: p96-99

646.4 Clothing construction

Better Homes and Gardens

Better Homes and Gardens Sewing book; professional methods to simplify creative sewing and to help you to make clothes with a "custom-made" look for the entire family. [2d ed] Meredith 1970 360p illus boards, spiral binding $7.95   **646.4**

1 Dressmaking 2 Sewing

SBN 696-00100-4

First published 1961

Partial contents: Basic sewing equipment; The commercial pattern; The alteration pattern; Cutting the dress; Professional sewing tips; Finishing details; Sewing with special fabrics; Making sportswear; Tailoring the suit; Sewing for children; Wardrobe planning; Ready-to-wear clothes; Sewing for the home

"Practical, well illustrated sewing guide for the novice. Each step in garment construction is clearly explained and fully illustrated. Equipment, tools, supplies, working space and methods are also discussed and illustrated. Of use to any beginning seamstress, regardless of age." Ontario Lib Rev

Cunningham, Gladys

Singer Sewing book. Prepared under the supervision of Jessie Hutton. Book design, art direction, and production supervision: Claire F. Valentine. Editor: Mary Skemp Perkins. Singer distributed by Golden Press 1969 428p illus $7.95   **646.4**

1 Sewing

"Directed to the novice as well as the experienced seamstress. Among topics covered are pattern choice and assembly, buttonholes, decorative touches, use of special fabrics such as suede, silk, and the wash and wear materials; sewing of drapes, curtains, slipcovers, and bedspreads is also explained. Tables defining the generic classification, trademark name, manufacturer or source of man-made materials or yarns and a list of appropriate fabrics for interfacing are given; an extensive glossary is appended." Booklist

"An up-to-date, comprehensive manual with detailed instructions and exceptionally clear illustrations. . . . Many of the sewing tricks found in each of the sections must usually be learned either by trial and error or by picking the brains of other sewers. The sections on pressing and tailoring are particularly clear and informative." Library J

Johnson, Mary

Sewing the easy way. New, completely rev. and enl. ed. New illus. by Mary Johnson; rendered by Jeanette Foletar. Dutton 1966 256p illus $5.95   **646.4**

1 Dressmaking 2 Sewing

First published 1958

Step-by-step detailed sewing instructions with stress on time-saving techniques. Information on making dresses and suits, collars, sleeves, trimming, etc. There are also chapters on fabrics and sizes. Pictures are limited to parts of patterns and garments so the book will not become dated. (Publisher)

McCall's Sewing book. Random House 1968 308p illus $6.95   **646.4**

1 Dressmaking 2 Sewing

"A Random House book"

First published 1963

"A completely revised guide to: Dressmaking; Tailoring; Mending; Embroidery; Home decorating." Publisher's note

McCall's Sewing book—*Continued*

Included is information on such "factors as the latest sewing tools and the new fabrics, particularly knits, fake fur, and stretch fabrics. The vogue for women's pants is recognized in several pages of fitting instructions; repairing and remodeling are also stressed, and there is a brief but excellent section on decorator skills." Booklist

Includes glossary

Margolis, Adele P.

How to make clothes that fit and flatter. Doubleday 1969 296p illus $6.95   **646.4**

1 Sewing 2 Dressmaking

Of "all the problems faced by the home sewer, the most difficult is securing proper fit. The author . . . focuses on the methods of making well-fitting clothes. She discusses selection of good styles and appropriate fabrics and patterns, details the many possible pattern alterations and how to select the best, and describes the making and use of dress forms and trial muslins. There are clear sketches and diagrams to illustrate methods." Library J

Rosenberg, Sharon

The illustrated hassle-free make your own clothes book, by Sharon Rosenberg and Joan Wiener. Straight Arrow Bks. distributed by World Pub. 1971 154p illus $7.95   **646.4**

1 Sewing 2 Dressmaking

This book "assumes a reader has some knowledge of sewing (not too much) and wants to do his or her thing by making his or her own clothes. There are simple patterns for pants, kaftans, hooded capes, ponchos, children's clothes, pillows." Library J

"Intended for dartless, ungusseted commune types, this book is anybody's sound introduction to sewing." Atlantic

Simplicity Sewing book. Simplicity Pattern [distributed by Doubleday 1971] c1970 224p illus boards $4.95   **646.4**

1 Sewing 2 Dressmaking

For the beginning or advanced dressmaker, this book contains many sewing tips with photographs to illustrate

Partial contents: Equipment; Picking a proper pattern; To line or underline; Fitting facts; Customizing your patterns; Details make the difference

646.7 Care of body (Toilet)

Angeloglou, Maggie

A history of make-up. Macmillan (N Y) 1970 143p illus $8.95   **646.7**

1 Cosmetics—History

"A highly entertaining illustrated history of body decoration the world over—from the ancient Egyptians (the first cosmetic chemists) to our modern-day mass industry and changing attitudes in cosmetic styles, marketing, and preparations. . . . It is also about religions, magic, and beautiful people." News of Bks

"The judiciously selected black-and-white plates and colorplates show works of art illustrating changing modes of cosmetic usage, types of equipment, and historic and contemporary advertisements for various products." Booklist

Includes a bibliography

Archer, Elsie

Let's face it; the guide to good grooming for girls of color. Rev. ed. Lippincott 1968 208p $4.95   **646.7**

1 Grooming, Personal

First published 1959

Designed specifically for the Black adolescent girl, here is concrete information on hair care and styling, makeup and complexion care

and on choosing clothes for one's personal skin color and budget. Includes chapters on speech, manners and personal relationships. (Publisher)

Esquire

Esquire Good grooming for men, by the editors of Esquire magazine; illus. by Harlan Krakovitz. Grosset 1969 248p illus $5.95 **646.7**

1 Grooming, Personal 2 Clothing and dress

The book presents "many pointers on dress and grooming to enable the modern man to choose wisely from the many styles, products, and colors now being offered to the male buyer." Bk Buyer's Guide

"This is a good book that goes into considerable detail, interestingly and in pace with the times, on every essential of man's good grooming." Pub W

Seventeen

The Seventeen Book of fashion and beauty, by the editors of Seventeen; introduction by Enid A. Haupt. Rev. ed. Macmillan (N Y) 1970 265p illus $7.95   **646.7**

1 Grooming, Personal 2 Clothing and dress

First published 1967

This book on good grooming, good looks, and good taste covers such topics as skin care, hair styles, makeup, glasses, figures, diets, fashion, colors, accessories, a girl's smile and voice

649 Child rearing and home nursing

Better Homes and Gardens

Better Homes & Gardens Baby book. Meredith illus $4.95, lib. bdg. $4.31   **649**

1 Infants—Care and hygiene 2 Children—Care and hygiene

First edition by Gladys Denny Shultz published 1943. Periodically revised to keep material up to date

Information on the care of the baby and child from the prenatal period to the sixth year. Illustrations show equipment and methods

Includes bibliography

Kraft, Ivor

When teenagers take care of children; the official guide for baby sitters; with illus. by Bob Parker. Macrae Smith Co. 1965 64p illus $3.75   **649**

1 Baby sitters

"Starting with the startling statistic that there are over one million teenagers babysitting in our country today, the value of such pointers about getting along with parents and their children, on feeding, playing and bedtime habits are [discussed]. . . . A valuable chapter emphasizes first aid treatment for minor accidents." Best Sellers

Lowndes, Marion

A manual for baby sitters. Rev. ed. Little 1961 185p $4.50   **649**

1 Baby sitters

First published 1949

"Describes how to care for babies and young children, up to the age of eight and nine, both indoors and out. Includes a reference section which suggests books to read aloud; games for all ages; and simple meals and how to cook them." Book Rev Digest

The New Encyclopedia of child care and guidance. Sidone Matsner Gruenberg, editor; Pauline Rush Evans, associate editor; Frances Ullmann DeArmand, managing editor. Doubleday 1968 1016p illus $10   **649**

1 Children—Management 2 Children—Care and hygiene 3 Child study

The **New** Encyclopedia of child care and guidance—*Continued*

First published 1954 with title: The Encyclopedia of child care and guidance

Contents: pt. 1: Ready references to child care and guidance; pt. 2: Basic aspects of child development [chapters by Margaret Mead, Benjamin Spock and others]

Short articles combined with longer basic ones, arranged alphabetically by topic. The alphabetical section emphasizes the practical considerations of day-to-day living, while the thirty-one basic chapters are designed to give the fundamental background of how children develop at different stages and an understanding of the interlocking influence of the home, school, church, community, and the child's inner drives. All the articles and chapters are cross-referenced so that the reader can get further information and grasp the close relationship of one subject to another. (Publisher)

Spock, Benjamin

Baby and child care. Meredith 1968 620p illus boards $6.95   **649**

1 Infants—Care and hygiene 2 Children—Care and hygiene

First published 1946 by Duell with title: The common sense book of baby and child care

This handbook for parents gives advice on everyday problems that arise in the physical and psychological care of babies and children. Material is topically arranged according to age and subjects covered range from breast feeding to questions of discipline and spoiling, from natural toilet training to the problem of adjustment to school, from infant care to helping a child be sociable and happy, from sleep problems to prevention of accidents. Special problems, including the premature baby, twins, separated parents, the working mother, the handicapped children are also dealt with

"Libraries will want reference and circulating copies of the new edition with its thoughtful appraisal of the purpose of human existence along with the explicit answers to thousands of everyday and emergency situations which have made this book invaluable to a generation of parents." Library J

649.8   Home nursing

Red Cross. United States. American National Red Cross

American Red Cross Home nursing textbook. Doubleday $1.75   **649.8**

1 Home nursing 2 Hygiene

First published 1913 by Blakiston. Periodically revised to keep material up to date

Covers home care of the sick and aged, maintenance of good health (especially in later years), how to meet emergencies, survival and care of disaster victims

Includes glossary and bibliography

651.02   Office services— Handbooks, manuals, etc.

Becker, Esther R.

The successful secretary's handbook, by Esther R. Becker and Evelyn Anders. Harper 1971 418p illus $7.95   **651.02**

1 Office management—Handbooks, manuals, etc. 2 Secretaries

This handbook "is based on the actual requirements of a diversified group of secretaries who generously cooperated with us. . . . To find practical answers, [to their questions] we consulted scores of authorities and sources on the most modern techniques of secretarial science. We also studied dozens of handbooks or manuals compiled by all types of organizations as guides for their secretaries." Author's note

This guide provides a "grounding in [correspondence techniques] basic procedures, technical skills, handling insurance and tax records and serving as the boss's personal assistant." Book News

Doris, Lillian

Complete secretary's handbook, by Lillian Doris and Besse May Miller. 3d ed. Prentice-Hall 1970 xxii, 528p illus $6.95   **651.02**

1 Office management—Handbooks, manuals, etc. 2 Secretaries

First published 1951

"A complete manual for business or personal use. It gives tips on handling mail and telephone, training assistants, preparing or correcting copy, how to address dignitaries and officials, rules of grammar, an alphabetical list of bothersome words, etc." Retail Bookseller

Hutchinson, Lois

Standard handbook for secretaries. McGraw illus $7.95   **651.02**

1 Office management—Handbooks, manuals, etc. 2 Secretaries

First published 1936. Periodically revised to bring it up to date

A desk reference book which provides secretaries and office personnel with up-to-date information on a wide variety of business subjects from correct grammar and letter writing to postal services and filing procedures. (Publisher)

Includes bibliographies

Ingoldsby, Patricia

The executive secretary: handbook to success [by] Patricia Ingoldsby and Joseph Focarino. Doubleday 1969 348p $6.95 **651.02**

1 Secretaries   2 Office management—Handbooks, manuals, etc.

"Based on actual, on-the-job experience . . . [this book] presents the arts and skills, the diplomatic and psychological subtleties, and the varied business techniques necessary for mastering the challenging but rewarding job of secretary to a top executive." Publisher's note

Bibliography included in Appendix: p317-35

651.7   Business communication

Cloke, Marjane

The modern business letter writer's manual [by] Marjane Cloke and Robert Wallace. Doubleday 1969 215p illus $4.95   **651.7**

1 Business letters

The authors discuss the general problems involved in writing business letters and techniques useful in writing specific types of letters, such as collection and discount letters, follow-up letters, complaints, and others. A chapter on speechmaking is included. (Publisher)

"This book, written by two authorities in the field of business communications, reveals the 'new' approach to business letter writing. A basic book, with emphasis on writing modern letters that get action." Am News of Bks

Taintor, Sarah Augusta

The secretary's handbook; a manual of correct usage [by] Sarah Augusta Taintor and Kate M. Monro. Macmillan (N Y) illus $5.95   **651.7**

1 Business letters 2 Secretaries 3 Rhetoric

First published 1929. Periodically revised to keep material up to date

This manual stresses the importance of correct English in the writing of letters and other business forms

"Material designed to conform to modern practice. One of the most useful of the secretary's manuals." Winchell. Guide to Reference Books. 8th ed.

651.8 Data processing

Benice, Daniel D.
Introduction to computers and data processing. Prentice-Hall 1970 370p illus (Prentice-Hall Series in applied mathematics) $8.50
651.8

1 Electronic computers 2 Electronic data processing

The text requires "no previous experience with computers [and] contains history of computer science and discussion of its basic concepts as well as a survey of the machines and systems currently in use. Punched cards and the machines to process them are described through step-by-step instructions, and number systems, codes, and programming languages are explained and illustrated with examples and exercises. An annotated bibliography is appended." Booklist

Computer science; a primer [by] Alexandra I. Forsythe [and others]. Wiley 1969 403p illus $7.95
651.8

1 Programming (Electronic computers) 2 Mathematics—Electronic data processing

Based on: Algorithms, computation, and mathematics, by the School Mathematics Study Group

A shortened version of: Computer science: A first course

This book "centers around the study of computing rather than computers. [It] deals with such basic concepts as the algorithm, flow-chart and flow-chart language plus additional concepts for computation and data organization. [It] also covers numerical applications." Publisher's note

Cross, Wilbur
A job with a future in computers; introduction by John Diebold. Grosset 1969 127p illus (Jobs with a future) lib. bdg. $3.59
651.8

1 Electronic data processing 2 Electronic computers

"Emphasizing the importance of planning long-range objectives rather than seeking immediate rewards the author outlines career opportunities in the rapidly expanding and changing computer industry. He considers the amount of education required, examining the reliability of computer schools, describes the aptitudes needed, and gives brief job descriptions for basic positions in programming, computer operation, and other computer-oriented occupations. A discussion of how computers work, their many uses, and their role in the future rounds out this realistic introductory view. Sources of additional information and a glossary of computer terms are appended." Booklist

Gildersleeve, Thomas R.
Computer data processing and programming. Prentice-Hall 1970 170p illus $8.95
651.8

1 Electronic data processing 2 RPG (Computer program language)

"This book is an introduction to computer data processing. Crucial to this subject is an understanding of the concept of computer programming, necessitating the use of a programming language. The one chosen is Report Program Generator (RPG) language. Thus this book also serves as an introduction to RPG programming." Publisher's note

651.803 Data processing—Dictionaries

Rodgers, Harold A.
Funk & Wagnalls Dictionary of data processing terms. Funk 1970 151p illus $7.95
651.803

1 Electronic data processing—Dictionaries

Companion volume to Funk & Wagnalls Dictionary of electronics, entered in class 621.3803

"The terms defined in this work are those referring to hardware, programming, software, logic, and Boolean algebra; also related terms in such subjects as data communications and mathematics. Illustrations for clarification appear where the compiler feels the necessity. Appended are a list of mathematical symbols, codes, flowcharts and flowchart symbols, and conversion tables." Booklist

655 Printing and related activities

Stevenson, George A.
Graphic arts encyclopedia. McGraw 1968 492p illus $16.50
655

1 Printing—Dictionaries 2 Graphic arts—Dictionaries

"The alphabetical arrangement of the material in the main section and the tabular form of appended information make this guide best suited for ready reference. Materials, equipment, and processes are defined and described concisely and shown where needed in drawings or photographs. All types of printing are covered although the main purpose is to give a working knowledge of the preparation and reproduction of graphic illustration for student or practicing artist, designer, or printer. Trade journals, a product index, and a manufacturer's index are among the appended sections." Booklist

Biography: p421-22

655.061 U.S. Government Printing Office

Kling, Robert E.
The Government Printing Office [by] Robert E. Kling, Jr. Foreword by James L. Harrison. Praeger 1970 242p (Praeger Lib. of U.S. Government departments and agencies) $9
655.061

1 U.S. Government Printing Office

"While it includes chapters on the GPO's history and even on early printing in America, this work chiefly details the GPO's internal workings and its relations with other governmental units and the public." Library J

Photographs and organizational charts are included in this work as well as information on careers at the GPO and laws and regulations governing public printing

655.2 Typography and composition

Chicago. University. Press
A manual of style. Univ. of Chicago Press $10
655.2

1 Printing—Style manuals 2 Authorship—Handbooks, manuals, etc.

First published 1906. Frequently reprinted with minor revisions

"Containing typographical and other rules for authors, printers, and publishers, recommended by the University of Chicago Press, together with specimens of type." Title page

United States. Government Printing Office
Style manual. U.S. Govt. Ptg. Off.
655.2

1 Printing—Style manuals 2 Authorship—Handbooks, manuals, etc.

Abridged edition also available

Frequently revised with minor changes

Covers the style and form used in the printing of United States government publications, including capitalization, spelling, compound words, abbreviation of numerals, symbols, punctuation, tabulation work, date marks, italics, etc.

658.4 Management at executive levels

Townsend, Robert
Up the organization. Knopf 1970 202p
boards $5.95   **658.4**

1 Executive ability 2 Management
"How to stop the corporation from stifling
people and strangling profits." Title page
The author offers his tongue-in-cheek "suggestions for running a business organization
sensibly, humanely and profitably. . . . The
book runs alphabetically from A to W and . . .
in a succession of brief memos, discusses every kind of problem a top corporate executive
encounters." Pub W
This "is an entertaining book which scores
heavily off the absurdities of large organizational structures and the pretensions and vanities of those associated with them, from the
busboys to the directors." Book World

658.87 Retail (Consumer) marketing

Cross, Jennifer
The supermarket trap; the consumer and
the food industry; drawings by Helen Fulker-
son. Ind. Univ. Press 1970 258p illus $6.95
                                              658.87

1 Supermarkets 2 Food industry and trade
SBN 253-14495-7
"An extraordinarily sharp-eyed survey of
our nation's food industry and the top 10
chains that own and run our supermarkets
from coast to coast. . . . [The author] entertains as she informs, describing the 1966 nationwide revolt of women against zooming
prices for food, how the big chain stores got
that way, the common deceptions in packaging, the way supermarket 'money games' work,
and just about everything the lady pushing
the supermarket cart wants to know for her
own protection. She's remarkably well informed, names names, and in a series of appendices backs up everything she has to say
with charts, cost break-downs and inside facts
that are eye-openers." Pub W
Bibliography: p219-26

Mahoney, Tom
The great merchants; America's foremost
retail institutions and the people who made
them great, by Tom Mahoney and Leonard
Sloane. New and enl. ed. Harper 1966 374p
$8.95   **658.87**

1 Retail trade 2 Department stores
Analyzed in Essay and general literature in-
dex
First published 1955
"The 23 chapters, arranged chronologically
by date of company origin, include accounts
of the oldest retailer in America, the Hudson's
Bay Company, through Brooks Brothers, Tiffany's, the Singer Company, Filene's, Marshall
Field, Brentano's, Macy's, the supermarkets,
F. W. Woolworth, J. L. Hudson, Sears, Lane
Bryant, Bullock's, I. Magnin, and Neiman-
Marcus, to the present-day mass-merchandis-
ing discount houses." Library J
"There is little that is new in the individual
histories of these firms, as Mr. Mahoney tells
them, but they are interestingly written,
packed with facts (which are generally accu-
rate) and which are not elsewhere accessible
to the general reader in a single volume."
Sat R
Bibliography included in Notes: p351-61

659.1 Advertising

Packard, Vance
The hidden persuaders. McKay 1957 275p
$7.50   **659.1**

1 Advertising 2 Propaganda

"An account of the motivation research
people, the advertising agency psychologists
who analyze consumer desires and find out how
to make people buy—or vote, or think—the
things the agencies are paid to promote.
Personalities, techniques, symbols, and approaches are discussed and some of the leading
ad psychologists are interviewed." Pub W
"The various ways in which M. R. operates,
the findings it has produced, and their applications to selling goods (and political candidates) are described by Mr. Packard with a
wealth of documentation which is often appalling, often very funny, and continuously
fascinating. His book deserves to be widely
read." Atlantic

659.15 Fashion modeling

Jones, Candy
Modeling and other glamour careers. Har-
per 1969 227p illus $5.95   **659.15**

1 Models, Fashion
Discusses the world of professional modeling throughout the United States. Gives helping information and answers questions most
frequently asked by aspiring models. One
chapter is devoted to other glamour careers:
Company good-will ambassadors, receptionists,
traveling hostess and others
"Basic, down-to-earth, and up-to-date advice for the girl or young woman considering
a career as a model." Booklist

Lenz, Bernie
The complete book of fashion modeling.
Crown 1969 278p illus $7.50   **659.15**

1 Models, Fashion
"Written in an easy conversational style. . . .
All types of modeling are satisfactorily detailed with more than 200 photographs and
diagrams coinciding with the commentary.
Some of the subject areas covered are model
types and figures: stage, runway, group, photography and television modeling; learning
techniques for developing personality and
style; procedures for modeling various costumes from coats to accessories; preparing
for assignments; beauty care and personal
wardrobe; necessary forms and promotion."
Library J

660.21 Chemical technology— Tabulated and related material

Lange, Norbert Adolph
(ed.) Handbook of chemistry. . . . Comp.
and ed. by Norbert Adolph Lange, assisted
by Gordon M Forker. McGraw $12   **660.21**

1 Chemistry, Technical—Tables, etc. 2 Mathematics—Tables, etc.
First published 1934 by Handbook Pubs. Periodically revised to bring material up to date
"A reference volume for all requiring ready
access to chemical and physical data used in
laboratory work and manufacturing." Subtitle
This handbook "covers a large amount of
miscellaneous data. . . . The usual tables of
chemical and physical properties of a wide
variety of materials are supplemented by such
items as first aid and safety advice, an outline
for qualitative analysis, photographic and
laboratory formulas and recipes, definitions
and conversion factors, seven mathematics
tables, and a 300-year calendar." Science Bks
"Written for those who lack the facilities of
a large technical library. For the professional
chemist or student of chemistry." Science and
Tech

664 Food technology

Hunter, Beatrice Trum
Consumer beware! Your food and what's been done to it. Simon & Schuster 1971 442p $8.95 **664**

1 Food adulteration and inspection 2 Food industry and trade
SBN 671-20797-0

A survey of the deterioration of our basic foods as a result of aspects of twentieth century production, processing, packaging, labeling and distribution methods. The author explores the scientific, industrial and economic forces that have shaped the "Food Revolution" and suggests how to improve the quality and safety of food

"The style and content are good and it is very well documented, effectively organized, and interesting. The book is not sensationalistic, nor is it the 'health nut, food faddist' type of book." Choice

Bibliographic references included in Notes: p377-428. Suggested reading: p429-30

666 Ceramic and allied industries

Chandler, Maurice
Ceramics in the modern world; man's first technology comes of age. Doubleday 1968 192p illus (Doubleday Science ser) $6.95 **666**

1 Clay industries

"A lucid explanation of ceramics technology. The author discusses the physical properties of ceramics, the techniques of producing them, and the prospects for ceramic material in the future." McClurg. Book News

Suggested reading: p7

Maloney, F. J. Terence
Glass in the modern world; a study in materials development. Doubleday 1968 [c1967] 192p illus (Doubleday Science ser) $6.95 **666**

1 Glass 2 Glass manufacture

This is a "brief, balanced, and lively account of the history of glassmaking, the properties of glasses, and the varied applications made possible by its properties. . . . The interplay of the science of the glassy state, the art of glass fabrication, and technological refinement of production techniques is described in a way that explains why the glasses have contributed extensively to the commonplace aspects of life as well as to a great variety of specialized applications. The illustrations are numerous and well chosen." Science Bks

Suggested reading: p5

668.4 Plastics

Kaufman, Morris
Giant molecules; the technology of plastics, fibers, and rubber. Doubleday 1968 187p illus (Doubleday Science ser) $6.95 **668.4**

1 Plastics 2 Polymers and polymerization

"This well-written study of polymer chemistry begins with a brief but interesting history of the subject then examines what a polymer is, the chemistry involved, and the technology of producing useful articles from raw materials. The stereo chemistry of polymers is also examined. An eight page summary table itemizes many of the topics central to the discussion of polymers." The AAAS Science Book List

Bibliography: p[188]

Mark, Herman F.
Giant molecules, by Herman F. Mark and the editors of Time-Life Books. Time-Life Bks. [1968 c1966] 200p illus (Life Science lib) lib. bdg. $7.60 **668.4**

1 Chemistry, Technical 2 Polymers and polymerization 3 Synthetic products

First published 1966

"The history of synthetics traced through the discoveries which led chemists to an understanding of the structure of molecules, and from there to the creation of pre-designed polymers, or giant molecules. . . . The properties of such products as bakelite, nylon, plastics, synthetic rubber, spandex, and the petro-chemicals used in their production are described, and the methods by which these products were developed are explained. As in other volumes in this series, each chapter is followed by a 'picture essay.'" Booklist

A polymer primer: p194-95. Further reading: p196

669.1 Metallurgy. Steel

Fisher, Douglas Alan
Steel: from the iron age to the space age; illus. with photographs, diagrams, and engravings. Harper 1967 200p illus lib. bdg. $4.79 **669.1**

1 Steel

"The author traces the history of steel, from its first use by man to the modern blast furnace and the Bessemer process, and its effect on American industry." Bk Buyer's Guide

"This book virtually exhausts the subject. . . . The biggest hurdle the author has to surmount is the subject itself, not only is it highly specialized, but it is hard to get [a reader] worked up about the Bessemer process, alloys, and blast furnaces. But given the handicap, Mr. Fisher does well." Christian Science Monitor

674 Lumber

Edlin, Herbert L.
What wood is that? A manual of wood identification, with 40 actual wood samples and 79 illus. in the text. Viking 1969 160p illus $7.95 **674**

1 Wood

"A Studio book"

"A brief résumé of man's use and treatment of wood throughout history precedes full discussion of its general properties and modern processing methods for timbers commonly used in the U.S. Keys to the identification of various woods by color, grain, hardness, and other qualities make up part two and are illustrated with a foldout of samples attached to the front cover, while part three catalogs 40 trees, describing their physical characteristics, growth rate, and uses. A practical handbook for woodworking hobbyist, cabinetmakers, and carpenters." Booklist

677.03 Textiles—Dictionaries

Fairchild's Dictionary of textiles; ed. by Isabel B. Wingate. Fairchild 1967 662p $35 **677.03**

1 Textile industry and fabrics—Dictionaries

First published 1959 under the editorship of Stephen S. Marks

"This dictionary defines . . . words and phrases used currently in the textile industry. Derived from the pioneer work of Louis Harmuth, its coverage includes description and, frequently, historical treatment of natural and man-made fibers, fabrics including lace, and finishes. Linguistic differences in meaning have been reconciled; botanical names in Latin are

Fairchild's Dictionary of textiles—*Continued*
given wherever possible for the vegetable fibers. Obsolete fabrics are described, but 'garments, sewing, needle work and embroidery,' pattern, color and all but basic information on textile machinery and equipment are omitted. Cross indexing is plentiful. . . . Its comprehensive treatment makes the work a basic tool for persons engaged in the textile industry or merchandising as well as for large public, college and university libraries." Library J

681 Precision mechanisms. Time pieces

Bruton, Eric
Clocks and watches, 1400-1900. Praeger 1967 208p illus $10   **681**
    1 Clocks and watches
    "For the collector, a history of the timepiece from ancient times to the present, with instructions on how to determine the age of a clock or watch, its authenticity, and its worth. Also included is a chronological chart and explanation of the care of timepieces and their decorative uses. Illustrated with photographs and drawings." Bk Buyer's Guide

684 Home workshops. Woodworking

Adams, Jeannette T.
Complete woodworking handbook, by Jeannette T. Adams and Emanuele Stieri; drawings by John G. Marinac. Arco 1960 568p illus $5.95   **684**
    1 Woodwork
    "This woodworking reference and guide book places emphasis upon 'providing complete directions for using and maintaining every hand-and power-driven wood-working tool used in the workshop.' Chapters are heavily illustrated, providing step-by-step instructions for completing projects." Pub W

Bridge, Paul
Designs in wood [by] Paul Bridge and Austin Crossland. Praeger [1970 c1969] 88p illus $4.95   **684**
    1 Woodwork
    First published 1969 in England
    A "treatise on the aesthetic principles governing the execution of wooden objects emphasizes creativity over the learning of tool manipulation which is described as a means to a specific end. Diagrams and photographs are skillfully used in chapters devoted to defining concepts such as visual form, recognition of negative and positive shapes, the methods used to suit construction to a desired material, techniques such as turning and cutting, and methods for making various surface designs by use of the chisel and plane." Booklist

Groneman, Chris H.
General woodworking. 4th ed. McGraw 1971 434p illus (McGraw-Hill Publications in industrial education) $7.96   **684**
    1 Woodwork 2 Cabinet work
    First published 1952
    This guide covers hand tool processes as well as machine tool processes used in woodworking. Projects from the elementary to the complicated are also presented

Hammond, James J.
Woodworking technology [by] James J. Hammond [and others]. 2d ed. McKnight [distributed by Taplinger] 1966 427p illus $7.96   **684**
    1 Woodwork

First published 1961
Arranged by 198 topics, this book covers design, woods, patternmaking and finishing. (Publisher)
Includes bibliographies

698 Detail finishing

Goodheart-Willcox's Painting and decorating encyclopedia. . . . Ed. by William Brushwell. Goodheart-Willcox 1964 288p illus map $5.54   **698**
    1 House painting 2 Interior decoration
    First published 1959
    "A complete library of professional know-how on painting, decorating, and wood finishing in one easy-to-use-volume." Subtitle

698.3 Finishing woodwork

Newell, Adnah Clifton
Coloring, finishing and painting wood; rev. by William F. Holtrop. Bennett 1961 478p illus $8.16   **698.3**
    1 Wood finishing 2 Varnish and varnishing 3 Stains and staining 4 Painting, Industrial
    First published 1930
    This handbook, which can be used by the amateur as well as the teacher in the field, gives information on mixing stains, colors, varnishes, enamels, lacquers, and paints
    Bibliographical references included

700 THE ARTS

Faulkner, Ray
Art today; an introduction to the visual arts [by] Ray Faulkner [and] Edwin Ziegfeld. Holt illus $14.95   **700**
    1 Art 2 Art industries and trade 3 Esthetics
    First published 1941 and frequently revised. Original edition analyzed in Essay and general literature index
    This is "an interesting, practical book, intended for both laymen and students. How to appreciate the influence of modern and historic art products, materials, processes, and problems in such fields as city planning, architecture, painting, printing, sculpture industry, and commerce is told, with the application of art to the needs of each." Booklist
    Includes glossary and bibliography

Janson, H. W.
A history of art & music, by H. W. Janson with Dora Jane Janson [and] Joseph Kerman. Abrams 1968 xxii, 318p illus $12.95   **700**
    1 Art—History 2 Music—History and criticism
    The authors cover the development of art and music in the Western World from primitive times to modern
    The "text is both scholarly and readable with well chosen and reproduced illustrations. Kerman's shorter section on music history gives a concise summary of the major composers and discusses examples of their representative works. . . . [This] book can be recommended for an undergraduate collection to expand its holdings in interdisciplinary studies." Choice
    Synopsis of art and music terms: p xi-xxii. Books for further reading on art: p302-03. Books for further reading on music: p304-05

701 Art—Philosophy and theory

Gombrich, E. H.
Art and illusion; a study in the psychology of pictorial representation. [2d ed] Princeton Univ. Press [1969] xxxi, 466p illus $12.50
701

1 Art 2 Art—Psychology
"Bollingen series"
Analyzed in Essay and general literature index
First published 1960 by Pantheon Books
"The A. W. Mellon lectures in the Fine Arts, 1956." Title page
"This book, a study in the psychology of pictorial representation, is directed to all those who seek for a meeting ground between science and the humanities. Searching for a rational explanation of the changing styles of art, the author is led to re-examine many current ideas on the imitation of nature, the function of tradition, and other problems." Chicago
"His thoughts, integrating the latest advances of psychology, are developed in a meandering, difficult text with rather involved language. . . . The illustrations are very good and well placed, and the book is handsome. Recommended for all larger libraries for serious readers in aesthetics, in psychology, or in the history of art." Library J
Bibliographical references included in Notes: p397-439

Kuh, Katherine
Art has many faces; the nature of art presented visually. Harper 1951 185p illus $10.95
701

1 Art 2 Art—History—20th century
This "pictorial guide to understanding and appreciating art uses many photographs of paintings, sculpture, drawings, prints, and other photographs, and a minimum of text. It does not interpret famous works of art but demonstrates the possibility of variations resulting from the artist's individuality, his environment, and his materials." Booklist
"A persuasive introduction for those who resist art because of the seeming confusion of styles and the baffling of complexity in the chronological sequences of most big museums." New Repub

703 Art—Dictionaries

Encyclopedia of world art. McGraw 1959-1968 15v illus maps
703
1 Art—Dictionaries
For sale in sets only, each volume costing $39.80
Volume 15 is the index
Added title page in Italian. All articles have been translated into English from the original language and correlated with the final editorial work of the Italian edition. Contributors are specialists from many parts of the world. Articles are signed and include extensive bibliographies. Approximately the last half of each volume consists of plates arranged to illustrate the articles in the first half
"The subject matter of the Encyclopedia consists of the representational arts in the broadest sense, that is, architecture, sculpture, and painting, and every other man made object that, regardless of its purpose or technique, enters the field of esthetic judgment because of its form or decoration. No limits of any kind have been set with regard to the time, place or cultural environment of the manifestations of artistic interest." Preface
"The scholarly, monographic articles (with fragmentation reduced whenever possible) and detailed bibliographies are of great value and the encyclopedia's usefulness is increased by a feature of prime importance in art reference—the plates." Enoch Pratt Free Library. Reference Books, 1966
For a fuller review of volume 1 see. Subscription Books Bulletin Reviews, 1956-1960

Mayer, Ralph
A dictionary of art terms and techniques. Crowell 1969 447p illus (A Crowell Reference bk) $8.95
703
1 Art—Dictionaries
This book "emphasizes materials and methods in its 3,200 definitions and in this respect supplements various art dictionaries and encyclopedias. Processes are described in some detail, while schools, styles and periods, readily available in other sources, are treated more briefly. The volume is well edited, with adequate cross-references, and appended bibliography, and diagrams, drawings, and small reproductions accompanying some of the entries." Cur Ref Bks

Murray, Peter
Dictionary of art and artists [by] Peter and Linda Murray; 1250 illustrations in color and black-and-white. Praeger [1966 c1965] 464p 48 plates illus $14.95
703

1 Art—Dictionaries 2 Artists—Dictionaries
"An extended version of the 'Penguin Reference Book' of the same title (published in 1959. . . .) It is a biographical and general dictionary of the arts of painting, sculpture, drawing and the other graphic processes, chiefly in Western Europe. It is intended to cover the period from the year 1300 to the present. There are 1250 illustrations . . . including a superb color section with reproductions showing the major techniques in color. Among the biographies of over 1000 artists, there is emphasis on English artists." Pub W
"This is a handsome work as well as one that will prove most valuable for reference and is hereby recommended for every library particularly the college and university and public libraries." Best Sellers
Classified bibliography: p435-39. Alphabetical bibliography: p440-64

The **Oxford** Companion to art; ed. by Harold Osborne. Oxford 1970 1277p illus map $25
703

1 Art—Dictionaries 2 Artists—Dictionaries
A compilation "with many contributors who, while acknowledged experts in their fields, presume no sophisticated knowledge on their readers' parts, the nearly 1300-page volume contains over 3000 entries on art history, artists, sculptors, architects, schools of art, styles, techniques, design and iconography. We find it excellently organized, handily cross-referenced, and soundly based in its emphasis on major aspects of art as opposed to aberrations and transient 'fads' and gimmicks. With 393 illustrations, 81 figures and numerous maps, plus extensive bibliographies, the book is a very good reference work." Pub W

The **Praeger** Picture encyclopedia of art; a comprehensive survey of painting, sculpture, architecture and crafts, their methods, styles and technical terms, from the earliest times to the present day; with 192 plates in full color and 416 illus. in monochrome. Praeger 1958 584p illus $13.95
703
1 Art—Dictionaries 2 Art—History
The work "is divided into eight parts. The first is a general introduction dealing with the nature of art, its forms and styles. This is followed by six sections on the great periods: Antiquity, the Middle Ages, the Renaissance, Baroque and Rococo, the 19th and the 20th century, and a final section on Art outside Europe. Each section opens with a survey of the period covered, the sources of its forms and the historical background and is followed by a comprehensive glossary of technical terms artists and their works, movements in art, etc An extensive easy-reference index covers every subject dealt with in both the narrative texts and the sectional glossaries, besides providing additional short self-contained entries." How to use the Encyclopedia
"While recommended certainly for all large collections, this would also serve well as a one-volume reference book for . . . small libraries." Library J

Quick, John
Artists' and illustrators' encyclopedia. Mc-Graw 1969 273p illus $11.50   703
1 Art—Dictionaries
Alphabetically arranged, this volume contains a series of definitions and descriptions of the methods and materials commonly used today in commercial and fine art, photography, the graphic arts, and printing. The book discusses recent developments in these fields, such as the new acrylic paints and the latest plastics. (Publisher)
Bibliography: p235-39

704.94 Symbolism and allegory in art

War and peace; published in the United States with the sponsorship of the World Confederation of Organizations of the Teaching Profession (WCOTP) and with the financial help of UNESCO. N.Y. Graphic 1964 64p illus (Man through his art, v 1) $8.95
704.94
1 Art 2 War 3 Peace
In this series "the editors are endeavoring to present, by means of various art media, man through the ages. . . . Vol. I includes a Tassili rock painting, an Egyptian relief, a Greek vase painting, a Chinese wall painting, a Japanese scroll, and works by Da Vinci, Velazquez Rubens, Goya, Monet, Hicks and Picasso. Each item is described by an expert. Peace is represented in fewer than one-fourth of the works." Library J
Includes bibliographies

708 Galleries, museums, private collections

Christensen, Erwin O.
A guide to art museums in the United States. . . . Dodd 1968 303p illus $7.95   708
1 U.S.—Galleries and museums
"Basic information about eighty-eight major and regional art museums in fifty-nine cities of the United States, including over 500 illustrations of representative works of art for identification." Title page
"The first part of the text gives . . . consideration to major museums of the East, Middle West, and Pacific Coast, presenting the history and background of the collections with the location and description of representative works. . . . The second part gives more general information about regional and more specialized museums. In both parts administrative information about hours of operation and admission is included, as well as lists of art museums connected with colleges and universities, [and] a list of museum directories and regional guides." Publisher's note
"The extent of treatment varies according to the importance of the museum, and reflects the author's many years of experience as museum curator and art historian. The convenient size of the guide must recommend it to gallery goers as well as to reference collections in all types of libraries." Cur Ref Bks
Museum directories and regional guides to art museums: p289

Huyghe, René
Art treasures of the Louvre. Text adapted from the French of René Huyghe. Commentary by Mme René Huyghe. With a brief history of the Louvre by Milton S. Fox. Abrams 1960 211p illus $25   708
1 Paris. Musée national du Louvre 2 Art, French
First published 1951

"Includes brief histories of the Louvre, of Italian, Flemish, Dutch, English, Spanish, German, and French painting, and excellent notes on the 100 works which are shown in color. The color reproduction maintains the standard Abrams has set for his house." Booklist

National Gallery, London. Newsweek. distribution by Simon & Schuster [1970 1969] 171p illus (Great museums of the world) $10   708
1 London. National Gallery 2 Paintings
Texts by Gigetta Dalli Regoli and others
"The paintings represented are selected to emphasize the balance of the collection of some 2000 paintings in the National Gallery. . . . [They] are gathered into sections representing, chronologically, the origin of the painters—Italy, Flanders-Holland, Germany, France, Spain, and England. The color plates are superb and the running texts are by seven Italian writers under the direction of Carlo Ludovico Ragghianti. There are also brief descriptions of the paintings, their provenance and size and the medium used; together with a History of the Collections, and essay on the Building . . . a select Bibliography, and Indices of the Illustrations and of Names." Best Sellers

New York (City) Metropolitan Museum of Art
Great paintings from the Metropolitan Museum of Art; a selection from the European collections, presented by the curatorial staff. Abrams 1959 38p illus $25   703
1 Paintings
A revised excerpt from: Art treasures of the Metropolitan published 1952 under the same authorship
"Basically composed of 60 large and excellent color plates chosen to survey the history of European painting; a brief introduction by Edith Standen describes the formation of the Museum's collection and mentions those individuals most responsible for its present importance. Notable are the short commentaries for each painting, admirably telescoping popular and scholarly information." Library J

Spaeth, Eloise
American art museums; an introduction to looking. Rev. ed. McGraw 1969 321p illus $8.95   708
1 U.S.—Galleries and museums
First published 1960 by Harper & Row with title: American art museums and galleries
Covers aspects "of the art world in America, from the history of collecting to the actual directions on how to get to a given museum, whether or not it charges admission, and the hours that it is open to the public. Ideal for planning an itinerary, it is also a fund of information about [local] treasures." Publisher's note
Bibliography: p293-95

Walker, John
National Gallery of Art, Washington, D.C. Abrams 1963 347p illus $7.50   708
1 U.S. National Gallery of Art 2 Paintings
"A history of its genesis with pictures and diagrams, a description of the Mellon, Widener, Kress, Rosenwald, and Chester Dale collections, brief notations on the smaller collections, and a review of the museum's other cultural activities comprise the first part of the work with over 100 color plates accompanied by a full-page explication following. Approximately 30 pages of small black-and-white reproductions and a list of the illustrations arranged alphabetically by artist are appended. [Includes floor plans]." Booklist

709 Art—History

Cheney, Sheldon
A new world history of art. [Completely rev. ed. with additional text] Viking 1956 xxvi, 676p illus $15.95 **709**

1 Art—History

First published 1937 with title: A world history of art

Covers painting, sculpture, architecture, and the minor arts from the dawn of history to the present. (Publisher)

"A lavishly illustrated history that is easy reading for the layman but not unduly popularized in style. It is well integrated, and, while chiefly concerned with painting and sculpture, includes also architecture and such minor arts as illumination, prints, and pottery." Booklist

"This is the most ambitious of Mr. Cheney's books on the visual arts, and . . . excepting only those on the theater, his seems the most interesting and the most successful. It is also art history with a difference. Geography and time are treated with an elasticity which permits greater concentration on the experiences afforded by the various arts as they have historically occurred." Sat R

Maps on lining-papers

Clark, Kenneth
Civilisation; a personal view. Harper 1970 [c1969] 359p illus $15 **709**

1 Art—History 2 Civilization—History

"Developed from a series of 13 lectures on art given by Clark in 1969 for the British Broadcasting Corporation, the text traces the emergence of human values during crucial periods of man's history from the seventh century until nearly the present, emphasizing Western European culture with a few selections of U.S. works. Genial, knowledgeable, and anxious to convey his carefully trained viewpoint, Clark's interpretations of representative paintings, sculpture, architectural masterpieces, and such small pieces as reliquaries and manuscript afford an urbane review of archetypes of the past." Booklist

"Nothing could be pleasanter, though we must not expect any searching analysis or what he perhaps too grandly calls 'civilisation.' . . . In speaking of the more remote historical periods he gives us his most satisfactory passages." Book World

Gardner, Helen
Gardner's Art through the ages. 5th ed. Rev. by Horst de la Croix & Richard G. Tansey. Harcourt 1970 801p illus maps $11.50 **709**

1 Art—History

First published 1926

This standard introductory survey traces the history of western art from the Stone age to the present. Architecture, sculpture and painting are emphasized. Some attention is given to the decorative arts

Includes glossary and bibliography

Gombrich, E. H.
The story of art. Phaidon illus $8.50 **709**

1 Art—History

First published 1950. Frequently reprinted with slight revisions

"This beautifully made, beautifully illustrated book tells in simple language the story of art from prehistoric and primitive times to the present. Intended for those discovering a new field, it stresses the well-known masterpieces." Ontario Lib Rev

Includes bibliographies and glossary

Janson, H. W.
History of art . . . [by] H. W. Janson with Dora Jane Janson. [Rev. and enl] Abrams 1969 616p illus $18.50 **709**

1 Art—History

First published 1962

"A survey of the major visual arts from the dawn of history to the present day." Title page

Painting, architecture, and sculpture are surveyed "from paleolithic art to abstract expressionism, from the cave to the glass and prestressed concrete skyscraper, from primitive clay figurines to mobiles and 'assembled' sculptures." Publisher's note

"Illustrations, particularly the color plates, are excellent both from an aesthetic and technical point of view. They closely integrate with a text which is at once authoritative and readable. . . . Closes with a list of recent and comprehensive books for further reading." Booklist

Maps on lining-papers

New York (City) Museum of Primitive Art
Art of Oceania, Africa, and the Americas, from the Museum of Primitive Art; an exhibition at the Metropolitan Museum of Art, May 10-August 17, 1969. Metropolitan Museum of Art [distributed by N.Y. Graphic 1970] unp illus map $9.95 **709**

1 Art, Primitive—Exhibitions

The book contains "650 of the finest objects in the collection. . . . Ranging from gold figurines to colossal wood sculptures, from ceremonial pottery to dark masks, the material is presented in fifteen geographical groups, each provided with an introduction and a map." Publisher's note

Time-Life Books
Seven centuries of art; survey and index, by the editors of Time-Life Books. Time-Life Bks. [distributed by Little] 1970 191p illus (Time-Life Lib. of art) boards $7.95 **709**

1 Art—History 2 Paintings 3 Art—Indexes

The last part of this volume is an index to the entire Time-Life Library of art series. The rest is devoted to . . . picture essays that cover the entire span of art history surveyed in the series, i.e., 1300-1970. . . . This volume also includes, the work of artists not discussed elsewhere in the series." Publisher's note

Also provided is a list of museums and galleries in Europe and the United States giving brief descriptions of their collections

709.01 Art of primitive peoples and ancient times

Larousse Encyclopedia of prehistoric and ancient art; ed. by René Huyghe. Prometheus Press [distributed by Putnam] 1962 414p illus maps $17.95 **709.01**

1 Art, Ancient 2 Art—History

At head of title: Art and mankind

Translated by Michael Heron. Corinne Lambert, and Wendela Schurmann from the original French edition, 1957

A "survey of the development of artistic form and of aesthetic concepts, relating art to the history of civilization and carrying the narrative up to the late Roman Empire. There is a chapter on primitive art (African, Oceanic and pre-Columbian) and one on the development of art in Asia. The book is arranged in long essays, interwoven with historical and geographical summaries. There are 750 illustrations, 32 in full color." Pub W

"It is a most scrupulous synthesis of the scholarship of many diverse fields and subjects." Library J

709.02   Art—History, 500-1500

Batterberry, Michael
Art of the early Renaissance; adapted by
Michael Batterberry; foreword by Howard
Conant. McGraw [1970 c1968] 191p illus
(Discovering Art ser) $9.95   709.02
1 Art, Renaissance
Portions of the text adapted from the magazine series: Discovering Art, and from the original Italian text
A survey of the early Renaissance artists and
their works. Beginning with a definition of
the term Renaissance, the author explores new
techniques of perspective, color scheme and
more truthful anatomy which spread from Italy to Northern Europe. (Publisher)
"Profusely illustrated with full color reproductions of the paintings, sculpture, and architecture, the elaborate beauty of small, jew-
eled art objects and the ornate interiors of the
early Renaissance. The text discusses artists
and techniques as well as individual works,
most of the material organized by region or
city. A list of illustrations, with locations, and
an index are appended." Chicago. Children's
Book Center

Larousse Encyclopedia of Byzantine and
medieval art; ed. by René Huyghe. Prometheus Press [distributed by Putnam] 1963
416p illus maps $17.95   709.02
1 Art, Medieval 2 Art, Byzantine 3 Art—History
At head of title: Art and mankind
"Translated by Dennis Gilbert, Ilse Schreier
and Wendela Schurmann from the French original [1958]." Verso of title page
"From early Christian art to the age of the
Gothic cathedrals here are articles by experts
on periods and places, as well as on paintings,
sculpture, architecture, etc." Bk Buyer's Guide
There are over 1000 "illustrations in black
and white and color. The insistence upon the
part of the editor and various contributors
that medieval art should be seen within the
total context of not only Western Europe but
also the Near, Middle, and Far East provides
a refreshing reorientation of the cross-currents
of influence which were flowering between Europe and the East. . . . It would have been
helpful to have had at least a minimal bibliographic section following each of the major
divisions." Library J

Souchal, François
Art of the early Middle Ages; with an introduction by Hans H. Hofstätter. Abrams
1968 263p illus (Panorama of world art)
$7.95   709.02
1 Art, Medieval 2 Art, Romanesque
Original French edition published in Germany
"Text translated from the French by Ronald
Millen; introduction translated from the German by Robert Erich Wolf." Verso of title page
"A mistified picture book actually dealing
with individual monuments from Romanesque
and early Gothic times. . . . The 242 plates
(over half in color) are excellent and the
strongest part of the book: a good balance of
architecture, painting, sculpture, and the minor
arts. Separate countries are treated individually. This is a good introduction to Romanesque
art but cannot be used for detailed study."
Choice
Bibliography: p258-59

709.03   Art—History, 1500-1900

Canaday, John
Mainstreams of modern art: David to
Picasso. Simon & Schuster 1959 xxiv, 576p
illus $15   709.03
1 Modernism (Art) 2 Art—History—20th century 3 Art, French

The author "analyzes specific works and interprets trends in art from the French Revolution to the present day. Includes 700 photographs and 15 color reproductions." Pub W
The author "surveys the nineteenth century
expansively yet in penetrating detail, but he
merely summarizes art of the last sixty years.
. . . Repeatedly one is distressed by this writer's peremptory evaluations of such pioneer
modern leaders as Brancusi, Delaunay, Duchamp, Ernst, Arp, and the Futurists. However, his handling of nineteenth-century masters, in contrast, is often wise, generous, and
knowledgeable. . . . Though Canaday's text is
filled with voluminous information, he does not
pretend to be breaking new ground. His approach is 'teacherly,' his audience the layman."
Sat R

Cheney, Sheldon
A primer of modern art. Liveright illus
$9.50   709.03
1 Modernism (Art) 2 Art—History—20th century 3 Painting
First published 1924 and periodically revised
While emphasizing painting, this volume also analyzes the underlying principles of modern architecture, sculpture, and the theater.
Starting with its theoretical and historical
backgrounds, the book traces "modernism as
a matter of techniques and objectives, rather
than contemporaneousness, from the discoveries of Cézanne through the subsequent icono-
clastic movements of Cubism, Surrealism and
Abstraction." Publisher's note
Cheney's "sound judgment, and his infectious enthusiasm will continue to recommend
the volume to any beginning student of the
subject." Cur Ref Bks

The story of modern art. Rev. and enl.
mid-century ed. Viking 1958 723p illus $8.50
    709.03
1 Art—History—20th century   2 Modernism
(Art)
First published 1941
A "history of the development of the modern movement from the French Revolution to
[1950]. . . . Before introducing his numerous
lead characters, the author etches in with concise, graphic strokes, each artist's setting in
terms of concurrent political and artistic history. Then follows a brief biography. . . . The
artist, having been thus introduced before a
backdrop of his own environment, is summed
up by Cheney with insight into his individual
contribution to the over-all picture of modern
art." N Y Her Trib Books

Larousse Encyclopedia of modern art; from
1800 to the present day; ed. by René
Huyghe. Prometheus Press [distributed
by Putnam] 1965 444p illus $20   709.03
1 Art—History—20th century   2 Modernism
(Art)
Original French edition published 1961
At head of title: Art and mankind
"English text prepared by Emily Evershed,
Dennis Gilbert, Hugh Newbury, Ralph de Sa-
ram, Richard Waterhouse and Katherine Watson." Verso of title page
This volume covers the varied facets of
world art, including paintings, architecture,
sculpture, design, and the minor arts. The articles range from classicism and the romantic
movement to impressionism, fauvism, cubism,
surrealism, and abstract expressionism
"The book as a whole treats schools, movements, and artists, which someday will, or
should have a better term than merely 'modern art' and the presentation is quite authoritative, lucid, and well organized. While there
is reference to the new school of 'pop art,'
no mention is made of the latest trend, 'op
art.' . . . Unfortunately the book has no bibliography, although there are many book and
periodical references cited in the text itself.
. . . The 16-page Index, with five columns to
the page, is an essential feature in a book of
this type which is in fact a collection of essays
rather than an encyclopedia." Booklist

Larousse Encyclopedia of Renaissance and
Baroque art; ed. by René Huyghe. Prometheus Press [distributed by Putnam] 1964
444p illus maps $20   709.03

1 Art, Renaissance 2 Art, Baroque

At head of title: Art and mankind

"English text prepared by Emily Evershed
[and others] from [v3 of] the French original
[1961]." Verso of title page

A "panorama of Western Art from the late
middle ages to the end of the 17th century.
The encyclopedia is organized into four main
[historical] sections. . . . After an introductory
chapter by René Huyghe who discusses the
major forms and the intellectual and economic
forces that shaped them, each section contains
papers by contributing scholars who discuss
the epoch from its various aspects and geographic centers. Each section also contains
historical summaries with attention given to
architecture, miniatures, tapestry, the graphic
arts, and the minor arts, in addition to the
emphasis on painting and sculpture. . . . A
valuable book for reference and quick reviews
of the periods concerned, interesting for browsing." Library J

Ruskin, Ariane

Nineteenth century art; adapted by Ariane
Ruskin; foreword by Howard Conant. Mc-
Graw [1969 c1968] 192p illus (Discovering
Art ser) lib. bdg. $8.95   709.03

1 Art—History 2 Nineteenth century

Text adapted from the British magazine series: Discovering Art, and from the original
Italian work

"Beginning with painters of the Neo-Classi-
cal school, . . . [the author] traces the development of Romanticism, Realism and the Pre-
Raphaelites, Impressionism, and the Post-Impressionist schools. Painters of each persuasion are discussed in detail, and significant so-
cio-political influences are correlated, writing,
based on thorough research, is highly entertaining, and there is an excellent index. Almost every work which is mentioned is
beautifully reproduced in full color, and references to plate numbers are scattered liberally
throughout the text." Library J

17th & 18th century art; adapted by Ariane
Ruskin; foreword by Howard Conant. Mc-
Graw 1969 191p illus (Discovering Art ser)
$8.95   709.03

1 Art—History 2 Seventeenth century 3 Eighteenth century

Text adapted from the British magazine series: Discovering Art, and from the original
Italian work

This book "surveys the course of the fine
arts in Western Europe between the Renaissance and the French revolution. . . . The account is divided into considerations of the development of painting . . . sculpture and architecture . . . [in] Italy, Spain, the Netherlands
and Germany, England, and France." Horn Bk

"Lavishly illustrated with full-color reproductions of paintings and photographs of buildings and sculpture. . . . Ariane Ruskin writes
with literary skill, smoothly combining biographical material, technical analysis, and historical background to give two centuries of
art history continuity and colorful details."
Sat R

Bibliographical footnotes

709.04 Art—History, 1900-

Batterberry, Michael

Twentieth century art; foreword by Howard Conant. McGraw [1970 c1969] 191p illus
(Discovering Art ser) $8.95   709.04

1 Art—History—20th century

Text adapted from the British magazine:
Discovering Art, and from the original Italian
work

"The book contains discussion of major
styles, schools, movements, and individual art-

ists' works from the turn of the century to
the present with the emphasis on European
painters and sculptors; Americans are given
a summary treatment." Booklist

This is "adapted for a general audience, especially a youthful one. . . . The color reproductions . . . vary in quality from the atrocious to the superb. . . . [A] lively review, free
of both preciousness and condescension." Sat
R

Hamilton, George Heard

19th and 20th century art: painting, sculpture, architecture. Abrams 1970 483p illus
(Lib. of art history) $18.50   709.04

1 Art—History 2 Art—History—20th century

"This survey begins with Romantic Classicism in the early nineteenth century and continues to the varied art of today. The author
shows how the tremendous revolutionary upheavals in every area of life—social, political,
technological—are reflected in painting, sculpture, and architecture. All the major figures
and movements are discussed and illustrated.
Bibliography." Book Rev Digest

"A handsome and admirably organized volume in which the major emphasis falls on the
present century and within that, on the past
twenty-five years. Hamilton takes the opportunity to expatiate appreciatively and seriously on the soup-can, comic-strip, color-
swatch and eye-dazzle schools, all handsomely reproduced among the book's 487 illustrations (sixty-four in color) just as if they were
fine art." Sat R

Lippard, Lucy R.

(ed.) Pop art; with contributions by Law-
rence Alloway, Nancy Marmer [and] Nicolas
Calas. Praeger 1966 216p illus (Praeger
World of art ser) $7.50   709.04

1 Art—History—20th century

Analyzed in Essay and general literature index

This "informal group of essays by four 'au-
courant' art experts clarifies for the uninitiated the basic character and substance of pop
art, its precursor and allied movements and
artists, phases, similarities, and differences in
development in various pop art centers in
North America and over seas, with England,
New York, and California mainly discussed as
the most active centers. Specific practitioners
are identified and their methods and certain of
their works are described in some detail."
Booklist

"Until now there has been no really good
book to present to the teen age the phenomenon of pop art, which, says the author, may
mean nothing or a great deal. . . . Some of the
text may be too analytical to hold the interest
of young people, but for the most part it is extremely informative and follows the pictures
nicely. At least the reader can see enough pop
art in this book to begin to make up his own
mind about its worth." Horn Bk

Bibliography: p206-08

709.38 History of ancient Greek art

Richter, Gisela M. A.

A handbook of Greek art. Phaidon illus
maps $10   709.38

1 Art, Greek

First published 1959 and frequently revised

"A concise but comprehensive survey for the
student or prospective traveler. The major art
forms are shown in their development from the
archaic through the classical and Hellenistic
periods. There are also chapters on some of
the minor arts such as furniture, textiles,
[coins] and glass. The history is liberally supplied with excellent photographs." Booklist

Includes bibliographies

Ruskin, Ariane
Greek & Roman art; adapted by Ariane Ruskin and Michael Batterberry; foreword by Howard Conant. McGraw 1968 192p illus maps (Discovering Art ser) $8.95   709.38
1 Art, Greek 2 Art, Roman 3 Classical antiquities
Text adapted from the magazine series: Discovering Art, and from the original Italian work
"Description of the social and political climate of the times and of important archaeological finds is incorporated into a brisk chronological overview of Greek and Roman painting, sculpture, and architecture from the earlier Cretan, Mycenean, and Etruscan civilizations to the collapse of the Roman Empire." Booklist
"This book serves as a beautifully constructed introductory guide to classical art." Horn Bk

Schoder, Raymond V.
Masterpieces of Greek art. Text and color photography, by Raymond V. Schoder. 2d. ed. rev. N.Y. Graphic 1965 15p 96 plates $14.50   709.38
1 Art, Greek
The author presents "his photographs of Greek architecture, sculpture, pottery, paintings, mosaics, jewelry, coins, glassware and other objects covering the entire range of ancient Greek art. Each plate is accompanied by a facing page of text in which the subject, technique, history and importance of the illustrated work are informally described or discussed. And there is an introduction on the history and modern relevance of Greek art." Library J
"The book could hardly be bettered as an introduction to Greek art in its many phases and forms." Times (London) Lit Sup
Bibliography: p14-15. Maps on lining-papers

709.39 History of Minoan and Mycenaean art

Higgins, Reynold
Minoan and Mycenaean art. Praeger 1967 216p illus map (Praeger World of art ser) $7.50   709.39
1 Art, Minoan 2 Art, Mycenaean 3 Classical antiquities
A "survey of the art and architecture of the principal Bronze Age civilizations of the Aegean, not only . . . the important Cretan and Mycenaean cultures but also the culture of the Cycladic Islands. The period covered begins shortly after 3000 B.C. and ends with the Dorian invasions of mainland Greece." Publisher's note
The author "gives an impartial account of the excavations and their controversies as well as a lucid analysis of the stylistic problems of the objects." Choice
Selected bibliography: p195

709.42 History of British art

Halliday, F. E.
An illustrated cultural history of England; with 378 plates. Viking 1967 320p illus $8.95   709.42
1 Art, British 2 Great Britain—Intellectual life
"A Studio book"
The artistic and cultural stages "through which Britain has passed from prehistoric times to the present are surveyed in this book which is illustrated throughout with sketches, photographs, and reproductions which increase the value of the excellent text. The fine index will help a student locate the material he needs for a report, or the general reader who would travel historic paths either actually or in his armchair." Library J

709.44 History of French art

Art treasures in France; monuments, masterpieces, commissions, and collections; introduced by Germain Bazin. [General editors: Bernard S. Myers and Trewin Copplestone]. McGraw 1969 176p illus $6.95   709.44
1 Art, French
The volume "traces the history of art and architecture, of taste and patronage in France from the cave paintings of prehistoric man to the architecture of Le Corbusier. The works which are familiar to us as examples of styles and periods in art are here examined in their historical setting. Who owned them and what was the cultural climate of the periods in which they were produced? . . . [There is] a list of the chateaux, palaces, town houses, churches and museums grouped geographically at the end of the book . . . giving brief histories of each building and mentioning the important work they house." Publisher's note
A "useful, workmanlike book that records where treasure is to be found. . . . [The] illustrations are still a delight. Even when they do not promise to reproduce the glory of the original they serve to remind us of it." Christian Science Monitor
Maps on lining-papers

709.47 History of Russian art

Horizon Magazine
The Horizon Book of the arts of Russia, by the editors of Horizon Magazine. Editor: Thomas Froncek; introductory essay by James H. Billington. Consultant: S. Frederick Starr. Am. Heritage 1970 383p illus map $16.95   709.47
1 Art, Russian
ISBN 0-8281-0100-0
"The arts [here] have been interpreted very broadly to include virtually all expressions of the creative urge—the graphic and plastic arts, architecture, theater, dance, music, film and literature—on all levels of society, from the tastemakers at court to the peasant craftsmen, and in all historical periodss down to the present day. This is a tall order, but it has been filled with great thought, care, and considerable originality. Nearly 300 illustrations (many in full color and some published for the first time) are combined with a generous sampling of literary excerpts; the total effect is genuinely evocative of the Russian cultural milieu." Choice
Includes bibliography

709.5 History of Oriental art

Batterberry, Michael
Chinese & Oriental art; adapted by Michael Batterberry; foreword by Howard Conant. McGraw [1969 c1968] 192p illus maps (Discovering Art ser) $8.95   709.5
1 Art, Oriental 2 Art, Chinese
Illustrations adapted from the British magazine "Discovering Art" and from the original Italian work published 1968
In this "history of the art of China, Korea, Japan and India . . . [the author] has included both religious and decorative art in a great variety of media—delicate jade carvings, rich porcelain vases, ornate temples, bronze urns and statuettes, miniature pictures, silk tapestries, lacquered boxes, and prints." Publisher's note

709.6 History of African art

Trowell, Margaret
African and Oceanic art; text by Margaret Trowell and Hans Nevermann. Abrams [1968] 264p illus maps (Panorama of world art) $7.95 **709.6**

1 Art, African 2 Art—Islands of the Pacific

Part one examines the art of Africa. "Dance masks, fetish figures, reliquaries, and purely decorative objects . . . are related to the geographical, religious, and social conditions that inspired them. . . . [Part two examines] the art of Oceania . . . the whole vast area that includes New Guinea, Melanesia, Micronesia, and Polynesia. Stressing its fundamentally religious and magical purposes . . . [the author] traces the complex interrelationships of the great diversity of styles." Publisher's note

"Beautifully illustrated with many annotated color and black-and-white plates." Booklist

Bibliography: p259-60

709.72 History of Mexican art

Fernandez, Justino
A guide to Mexican art: from its beginnings to the present; tr. by Joshua C. Taylor. Univ. of Chicago Press 1969 398p illus $8.75 **709.72**

1 Art, Mexican 2 Indians of Mexico—Art 3 Mexico—Antiquities

Original Spanish edition, 1958

"An authority in the field describes four major periods of art, pre-Columbian, colonial, modern, and contemporary. Each section contains a brief up-to-date bibliography divided into English and Spanish sources. The 183 black-and-white illustrations of adequate quality follow the text. Each is numbered for convenient referral. Art history is well integrated with the descriptions of individual works which include many of Mexico's masterpieces of all kinds—sculpture, paintings, buildings, murals, and monuments. The reader who knows the art may often be surprised by the deftness and 'rightness' of the stylistic analyses and critical appraisals. Specialists and students alike will find this synthesis and overview rewarding." Library J

709.73 History of art in the U.S.

The Arts in America: the colonial period [by] Louis B. Wright [and others]. Scribner 1966 368p illus $20 **709.73**

1 Art, American

"Abundantly illustrated essays perceptively relate the arts of the Colonial period to the times." Booklist

"Architecture, painting and the decorative arts are treated in some detail and with ample photographs [including] . . . major colonial buildings and [the work] of such painters as Copley, Trumbull, Stuart and West. . . . The chapter on colonial furniture and metal work is especially revealing. These arts, while less known, are judged by many critics to be the 'major American artistic accomplishment of the period.' " America

Bibliography: p353-57

Dover, Cedric
American Negro art. N.Y. Graphic 1960 186p illus $12 **709.73**

1 Negro art 2 Art, American 3 Negro artists

"An anthology of Negro American art which the author calls a 'picture book of responses to needs, situations, surroundings and ideas,' offering a glimpse of the 'shape of Negro things to come.' The first section, entitled 'Perspectives,' is a literary analysis and interpretation of various facets of the artistic world and the problems it poses. The second section includes the illustrations, which range from a late 18th century portrait to very recent work." Pub W

"An exceptional survey, both in text and illustrations, of the American Negro artist from colonial times to the present." Chicago

Bibliography: p57-60

Larkin, Oliver W.
Art and life in America. Rev. and enl. ed. Holt 1960 559p illus $17.75 **709.73**

1 Art, American 2 U.S.—Civilization

First published 1949. Awarded Pulitzer Prize in history, 1950

The history of this country from the beginning to the present, told in terms of its paintings, sculpture and architecture, and of its minor arts and crafts

"A competent, well illustrated reference book that will be read as much for enjoyment as information." Chicago Sunday Tribune

Bibliographical notes: p491-525

Mendelowitz, Daniel M.
A history of American art. 2d ed. Holt 1970 522p illus maps $17.95 **709.73**

1 Art, American

SBN 03-081835-4

First published 1960

"My particular aim has been to produce a broadly conceived, well-illustrated survey of the development of architecture, painting, sculpture, prints, the decorative arts and crafts, and photography from Pre-Columbian times to today." Preface

Bibliography: p510-12

Morris, Jerrold
On the enjoyment of modern art; an illustrated introduction to contemporary American styles. N.Y. Graphic 1968 55, 31p illus $3.50 **709.73**

1 Art—History—20th century 2 Art, American

The author "offers a concise two-part guide to the appreciation of modern art for gallery and museum visitor, student, or teacher. The first part is a lucid, introductory essay on the historical background of contemporary art and its sources. The second section deals informally but specifically with some of modern art's more important manifestations and contains a representative selection of adequate but not outstanding reproductions of American works covering a period of about 20 years." Booklist

Myron, Robert
Art in America; from colonial days through the nineteenth century [by] Robert Myron [and] Abner Sundell. Crowell-Collier Press 1969 186p illus lib. bdg. $4.95 **709.73**

1 Art, American

This "survey traces the distinctively American forms of art and architecture that developed from the craft-based, European-influenced colonial styles. . . . [The authors present an] account of the changing pattern of American taste over a 250-year period which shows how the development of visual arts reflected the political and socioeconomic attitudes of the American people, from the Puritans to the Victorians." Publisher's note

"The authors devote most of the text to painting, and there is attention given to architecture, but there is no reference to sculpture (little though there was) or to the distinctive work done in glass." Chicago. Children's Book Center

Bibliography: p183

Rose, Barbara
American art since 1900; a critical history. Praeger 1967 320p illus (Praeger World of art ser) $7.50 **709.73**

1 Art, American

"The history of American art in the twentieth century is one of revolt, of conflict. It is the story of the American artist's attempt to

Rose, Barbara—*Continued*
free himself from European models yet at the
same time join the mainstream of Western art.
. . . Miss Rose traces the evolution of American
art within the context of social, historical, and
intellectual events." Publisher's note

"Being a working critic and part of the contemporary scene, the author loses little time in
making clear her tastes and preferences. She
is decidedly of the nonfigurative persuasion,
has little use for optical art, and barely mentions the vast number of current American fig-
urative painters." Book World
Includes bibliography and index of names

709.8 History of Latin American art

Castedo, Leopoldo
A history of Latin American art and architecture; from pre-Columbian times to the
present; tr. and ed. by Phyllis Freeman.
Praeger 1969 320p illus maps (Praeger
World of art ser) $8.95   709.8
1 Art, Latin American—History 2 Architec-
ture, Latin American—History

This volume "surveys 3,000 years, from the
monoliths of the Olmecs through the fabled
cities of the Aztecs and Incas to today's soaring, modern Latin American capitals. Throughout, the author traces the constants and variants in Latin American art, with its fusion of
Indian, European, and African elements." Publisher's note
Selected bibliography: p297-99

711 Area planning

Hellman, Hal
The city in the world of the future. Evans,
M.&Co. 1970 186p illus $4.95   711
1 City planning 2 Cities and towns
The book tells how scientists and engineers
must plan to accommodate—in housing,
schools, transportation, public health and recreation—a world population that is expected
to double in the next thirty years. It describes
where new cities will have to be built and
how, as well as the kinds of cities required
"The many photographs, drawings, and dis-
grams enhance the text, and an extensive bibliography adds to the usefulness of the book."
Booklist

McHarg, Ian L.
Design with nature. Natural Hist. Press
1969 197p illus $19.95   711
1 Regional planning 2 City planning 3 Landscape protection 4 Environmental policy—
U.S.
"Published for the American Museum of Natural History"
McHarg is a "city and regional planner with
the ecological outlook—we must design our
cities and suburban areas with nature, taking
advantage of the values of the natural landscape, its geology, watersheds, shores, forests,
wildlife. We must leave open spaces for re-
plenishment of the water table and nourishment of the soul. Only in this way can we hope
to avoid additional urban blight and ugliness
and eventual destruction of our landscape. Mc-
Harg shows how intelligent ecological planning can provide us with living areas that are
a joy rather than a disaster." Choice

Mumford, Lewis
The urban prospect. Harcourt 1968 xx, 255p
$5.95   711
1 City planning 2 Sociology, Urban 3 Cities
and towns
"A selection of lectures and essays dating
from 1925 to the present, [1968], reprinted because the discussions of urban problems, the

solutions offered, and the warnings uttered are
still pertinent. The final chapter reproduces
Mumford's statement on the history of urban
frustration made to the Ribicoff committee on
governmental expenditures in 1967, and a postscript amplifies this theme." Booklist
"Mumford does not have all the answers and
retreats to generalizations when talking of solutions. But, if he is not optimistic about the
future, he seems to be pointing in the right
direction. Few would disagree with the need
to make our cities desirable places for living,
working, and recreation; controversy exists
only over the ways and means." Best Sellers

Rudofsky, Bernard
Streets for people; a primer for Americans;
photographs by the author. Doubleday 1969
351p illus $14.95   711
1 Streets 2 Cities and towns 3 City planning
"Lamenting the lack of civilized streets in
the U.S., [the author] sets out to write a primer for Americans about streets by tracing their
origins and contrasting American streets of
today with examples from other countries. In
the process, he exposes the reader to a multitude of subjects, including the art of walking,
promenades, covered streets, diversified forms
of street life, street names, stairs, bridges,
street furniture, street flooring, and sidewalk
cafés—the main theme being that the street
does not exist in a vacuum but is inseparable
from the environment as well as a reflection
of a way of life. The book offers no solutions
and is somewhat limited in scope (to pedestrian
streets)." Choice
"In showing us the human value of streets
Rudofsky leans heavily on Italian examples.
. . . [His book] is such an elegant essay and
so handsomely illustrated that it should appeal even to those who tire of indictments and
controversies about America's urban mess."
Library J
Text references: p343-48

720.1 Architecture—Philosophy

Sullivan, Louis
The testament of stone; themes of idealism
and indignation from the writings of Louis
Sullivan; ed. with an introduction by Maurice
English. Northwestern Univ. Press 1963
xxvii, 227p $6.50   720.1
1 Architecture 2 Art and society 3 Democ-
racy
"A revealing picture of one of the founders
of modern architecture as shown through a
group of his writings, giving an insight into
his thoughts on democracy and education."
Cincinnati

720.9 Architecture—History

Fletcher, Sir Banister
A history of architecture on the comparative method. Scribner illus maps $18.95
                                                   720.9
1 Architecture—History
First published 1896. Periodically revised and
reprinted to keep material up to date
A comprehensive analytical and comparative
method of studying international architecture.
The book "aims at displaying clearly the characteristic features of the architecture of each
country by comparing the buildings of each
period and by giving due prominence to the
influences—geographical, geological, climatic,
religious, social, and historical—which have
contributed to the formation of particular
styles." Preface [to the 1961 edition]
"A profusely illustrated standard reference
work." Winchell. Guide to Reference Books.
8th edition
Includes bibliographies

Hamlin, Talbot Faulkner

Architecture through the ages. [Rev. ed]
Putnam 1953 li, 648p illus $9.50   720.9

1 Architecture—History

First published 1940
The author surveys the history of architecture from the dawn of civilization to Frank Lloyd Wright. He is concerned with the development of architecture in its relation to social and cultural history and helps the layman to understand why and how a certain style expresses the spirit of an age. Written in nontechnical language
Bibliography: p vii-viii

Jordan, R. Furneaux

A concise history of Western architecture.
Harcourt [1970 c1969] 359p illus $7.50   720.9

1 Architecture—History

First published 1969 in England
"A survey of historical developments in the form, structure, and cultural significance of buildings throughout Western civilization. After discussing the design of the pyramids and temples in ancient Egypt, Greece, and Rome, Jordan depicts the architectural influence of ecclesiastical, secular, and industrial societies in Europe and the New World . . . describing outstanding features of Byzantine, Gothic, baroque, neoclassic, Victorian, and modern architecture. He concludes that contemporary architecture in combining art, crafts, and technology is reflecting the emergence of a world culture. A lucid text, profusely illustrated." Booklist
A short bibliography: p338-39

Mansbridge, John

Graphic history of architecture.   Viking
1967 192p illus maps $9.95   720.9

1 Architecture—History

"A Studio book"
This survey of Western architecture "consists almost exclusively of drawings, diagrams, details, plans and illustrations of buildings from ancient Egypt to contemporary U.S.A. Index at the beginning of the book is divided into (1) Places and buildings (2) Architects (3) Architectural terms, styles and materials."
Books for School Libraries, 1968
Short bibliography: p192

720.973 Architecture of the U.S.

Mumford, Lewis

Sticks and stones; a study of American architecture and civilization. [2d rev. ed]
Dover 1955 238p illus pa $2   720.973

1 Architecture, American

First published 1924 by Boni and Liveright
"A discussion of the import of the changes that have come in American architecture and the way it reflects the social and industrial characteristics of each period, from the early New England village to the city skyscraper. Provocative in subject matter, and facile in style." N Y State Lib

The Rise of an American architecture [by]
Henry-Russell Hitchcock [and others].
Ed. with an introduction and exhibition notes by Edgar Kaufmann, Jr. Praeger
1970 241p illus maps $10   720.973

1 Architecture, American 2 Architecture, Modern—20th century

Contents: American influence abroad, by H. R. Hitchcock; The American city: the ideal and the real, by A. Fein; A new view of skyscraper history, by W. Weisman; American houses: Thomas Jefferson to Frank Lloyd Wright, by V. Scully
This book "was conceived as counterpart to an exhibition of the same name that opened at The Metropolitan Museum of Art in May, 1970." Publisher's note
The four essays, written by prominent architectural historians, focus upon "the under-

standing of nineteenth-century American architecture in those special areas that represent advances valid today: buildings for commerce, small homes, and city parks." Introduction
Bibliography: p210

Scully, Vincent

Frank Lloyd Wright, by Vincent Scully, Jr. Braziller 1960 125p illus (The Masters of world architecture ser) $5.95   720.973

1 Wright, Frank Lloyd 2 Architecture, American 3 Architecture, Modern—20th century

"The great number of unique and advanced designs produced by Frank Lloyd Wright are considered here as they contributed to modern architecture." Bk Buyer's Guide
"Vincent Scully has risen to the very considerable challenge of writing something new about Wright with an essay that is itself Wrightian, brimming with allusions to the whole range of architecture past and present, as well as to literature, music and the graphic arts, brilliantly (sometimes, perhaps, striving too hard after brilliance as Wright himself did) tracing the architect's affinities with Whitman and Nietzsche, Crete and Yucatan." N Y Times Bk R
Bibliographical note: p117-18

Smith, Norris Kelly

Frank Lloyd Wright; a study in architectural content. Prentice-Hall 1966 178p illus $5.95   720.973

1 Wright, Frank Lloyd 2 Architecture, Modern—20th century 3 Architecture, American

"A Spectrum book"
"Examining Wright's frustrations, failures, and uncertainties in trying to embody his philosophical principles in architectural metaphors, Smith portrays Wright as a figure deeply concerned with the continuing quest for perfection and harmony amidst man's seeming inadequacy and discord." Publisher's note
"Wright a modern architect? In Smith's view he was a romantic conservative. The treatment is a mite superficial and the documentation more or less random, but Smith does make his point." Christian Century
Bibliographical footnotes

Whiffen, Marcus

American architecture since 1780; a guide to the styles. MIT Press 1969 313p illus $7.95   720.973

1 Architecture, American

"This, the author points out, is a buildingwatchers' guide and not a history or work of criticism. Whiffen . . . puts American architecture into 38 style categories, from 'The Adam Style' and 'Jeffersonian Classicism' which 'reached their zenith in 1780-1820' to 'Brutalism' which is one of five styles 'that have flourished since 1945.' " Library J
"The most concise, yet comprehensive attempt at classifying American architecture according to styles. . . . The directness of the approach and the systematic presentation make the volume a valuable addition to the general reference material on American architecture." Choice
Bibliography: p281-89

Wright, Frank Lloyd

Frank Lloyd Wright: writings and buildings; selected by Edgar Kaufmann and Ben Raeburn. Horizon Press 1960 346p illus map $5.95   720.973

1 Architecture—Addresses and essays 2 Architecture, American

Partially analyzed in Essay and general literature index

"A representative selection of the American architect's writings on such topics as prairie architecture, the nature of materials, the young man in architecture, style, and the grammar of architecture. Generously illustrated with photographs, plans, perspective drawings, and sketches of a number of buildings span-

Wright, Frank L.—*Continued*
ning the architect's long career. A feature of the book is the appended inventory which lists, geographically, structures built by Frank Lloyd Wright and still standing in 1960." Booklist
"To this reviewer it seems the best survey course yet offered in the basic philosophy, style, diversity, and technical virtuosity of this voluble genius of modern American architecture." Christian Science Monitor

724.9　Modern 20th century architecture

Le Corbusier
Towards a new architecture; tr. from the French by Frederick Etchells. Praeger 1970 269p illus $7.50　　724.9
1 Architecture, Modern—20th century
Original French edition published 1923. This translation first published 1927 in England
In this book on the modernist movement in architecture, the author discusses "the significance and the potentiality of the new engineering architecture, which includes not only houses, but ocean liners, airplanes and automobiles." Providence
"The book is illustrated with a great many interesting photographs of buildings and of machinery and factories and the like." Times (London) Lit Sup

724.903　Modern 20th century architecture—Dictionaries

Encyclopedia of modern architecture; ed. by Wolfgang Pehnt. Contributors: Kyösti Alander [and others]. Abrams 1964 336p illus $15　　724.903
1 Architecture, Modern—20th century—Dictionaries
Original German edition, 1963. English version, 1963, edited by Gerd Hatje and Wolfgang Pehnt
This work includes biographical entries and entries dealing with "places, with episodes in the history or development of modern architecture . . . or with technical developments." Times (London) Lit Sup
The text "has been written by competent contributors from almost as many different countries as the numerous illustrations." Economist
"Several judicious articles have been added [to those in the original edition] by such authorities as Henry Russell Hitchcock, William H. Jordy and John M. Jacobus, but the volume would have profited by an all-out revision. . . . And although individual bibliographies are rewarding the bibliography at the end of Abrams volume is trifling." Sat R

726　Buildings for religious purposes

Adams, Henry
Mont-Saint-Michel and Chartres; with an introduction by Ralph Adams Cram. Houghton 1936 397p illus $6　　726
1 Mont St Michel, France 2 Chartres, France. Notre Dame (Cathedral) 3 Middle Ages
First published 1913
A study, made with considerable insight, of the philosophy and religion of the Middle Ages as expressed in literature and art and especially in the architecture of such cathedrals as Chartres and Mont-Saint-Michel

Horizon Magazine
The Horizon Book of great cathedrals, by the editors of Horizon Magazine. Editor in charge: Jay Jacobs. Introduction by Zoe Oldenbourg. Am. Heritage 1968 384p illus maps $20　　726
1 Cathedrals—Europe
Each of the five chapters "is devoted to the greatest churches of one European nation—France, England, Germany, Spain, and Italy. The history of 43 magnificent cathedrals is related. . . . In addition s,even portfolios throughout the book describe various aspects of the construction of cathedrals and the beliefs that inspired their builders. . . . The 446 pictures, 50 in color, include architectural photographs, paintings of cathedral interiors and exteriors, manuscript illuminations, designs for cathedral construction, and stained glass, mosaics, and murals from cathedral interiors." Publisher's note

728　Residential buildings

Wright, Frank Lloyd
The natural house. Horizon Press 1954 223p illus $7.50　　728
1 Architecture, Domestic 2 Architecture, Domestic—Designs and plans 3 Architecture, Modern—20th century
"This book is convincing evidence that Wright did not build only for the rich. Herein he tells about and illustrates his "Usonian" houses which are moderate-cost dwellings of infinite variety. Included are actual photographs, floor plans, and sketches." The AAAS Science Book List for Young Adults

728.6　Dwellings of suburban and rural types

House & Garden
House & Garden Book of modern houses and conversions. Editor: Robert Harling; art editor: Alex Kroll; editorial assistants: Léonie Higton, Martin Simmons [and] Caroline Wilcox. [St Martins 1967] c1966 256p illus $22.50　　728.6
1 Architecture, Domestic—Designs and plans 2 Architecture, Modern—20th century 3 Building—Repair and reconstruction
First published 1966 in England
"Articles, pictures and plans of over [seventy-five] new homes built in Britain, the United States, Scandinavia, Italy and France. Includes a section on older houses which have been converted so as to conform with modern standards of comfort and taste." Pub W
Includes a section on home heating

730.9　History of sculpture

Cheney, Sheldon
Sculpture of the world; a history. Viking 1968 538p illus $12.95　　730.9
1 Sculpture—History
A "history of sculpture in pictures and words, from the caveman to today, including the Oriental, African, and Amerindian along with the Near Eastern and the more familiar Western development." Publisher's note
This "history is illustrated with good black-and-white photographs. Save for Lippold's Sun, which is reversed, it is a well-designed and compact book, with an excellent bibliography. Mr. Cheney is a fluent writer, and this, his latest book on art, can be useful as a textbook introduction." Sat R
Maps on lining-papers

730.942 History of British sculpture

Read, Herbert
Henry Moore; a study of his life and work. Praeger [1966 c1965] 284p illus (A Praeger World of art profile) $7.50   730.942
1 Moore, Henry
First published 1965 in England
The author "introduces the reader to Moore's life and the formative influences on him of education and art and gives a detailed review of his work. Dividing his works into six periods of his work. Dividing his work into six periods from 1921 to 1964 the author meticulously examines the sculptures, show the origins of approach. . . . Appended are notes, a bibliography, and a descriptive list of plates." Booklist
This "adds little to what has already been related. It fights shy of the debate about whether or not Henry Moore's art is still evolving. Nevertheless it is authoritative. . . . Practically all the 200 or so illustrations of his works in the volume are reproduced from the sculptor's own photographs." Economist

730.973 History of American sculpture

Craven, Wayne
Sculpture in America. Crowell 1968 722p illus $18.50   730.973
1 Sculpture, American
This "first complete survey of American sculpture in more than sixty years, provides a well-written text and more than 280 well-chosen photographs; both efficiently indexed for the quick location of biocriticism of individual artists, and works, which are given in their cultural significance. The complete survey, in accordance with its enthusiastic author's hopes, should stimulate interest in and enjoyment of American sculpture." Cur Ref Bks
"Scholars and students of American studies and art will welcome Mr. Craven's book for its documentation, bibliography and index; all readers should find the work a delight for the author's lively narrative is laced with provocative and entertaining news items, letters and conversations." Sat R
Bibliography: p675-90

New York (City). Metropolitan Museum of Art
American sculpture; a catalogue of the collection of the Metropolitan Museum of Art [by] Albert TenEyck Gardner. N.Y. Graphic 1965 192p illus $10   730.973
1 Sculpture, American 2 Sculptors, American
This catalog "contains biographies of major American sculptors and a discussion of more than 350 works. . . . Arranged chronologically by date of birth of the artist, it has an excellent index." Cur Ref Bks
"Previous exhibitions of the works, bibliographical references, and replicas are indicated and excellent illustrations help to identify most works." Library J

731 Sculpture—Processes and representations. Mobiles

Moorey, Anne
Making mobiles [by] Anne & Christopher Moorey. Watson-Guptill 1966 95p illus $2.50   731
1 Mobiles (Sculpture)
The authors "explain the basic structure of a mobile, and then demonstrate some of the many variations possible with different shapes or materials. There are full instructions for making some 40 mobiles, with photographs or drawings of the finished result and step-by-step diagrams." Publisher's note

731.4 Sculpture—Techniques

Lynch, John
Metal sculpture; new forms, new techniques. Studio 1957 145p illus $4.95   731.4
1 Metalwork 2 Sculpture—Technique
Contents: Development of contemporary metal sculpture; Sculpture with shears and pliers (wire and light metals); Introduction to soft-soldering; Silver-soldering; Constructions, mobiles, stabiles and kinetic sculpture; Sculpture with oxyacetylene welding
"Designed to start the beginner on the way to making mobiles and working in the medium of metal, the book contains much information on appreciation and the development of this art form. The photographs are numerous, well organized, and add much to the text." Sec Ed Brd

Rich, Jack C.
Sculpture in wood. Oxford 1970 155p illus $15   731.4
1 Wood carving 2 Sculpture—Technique
"The book, designed to meet the need for a basic modern manual on wood carving, contains a wealth of simply presented factual material that will be invaluable both to the student sculptor and to the practicing artist. It describes the many varieties of wood that are generally available for sculpture, and, in detail, the tools employed (chisels, gouges, files, rasps, riffers, scrapers, etc.), as well as the methods of using and caring for tools. It also discusses wood seasoning, the finishing of wood carvings, and the preservation of wood." News of Bks
"The text is crisp and to the point. The 51 illustrations are modest in size but excellently chosen." Choice
Bibliography: p141-42. Map on lining-paper

735 Sculpture—Modern period, 1400-

Goldwater, Robert
What is modern sculpture? Mus. of Modern Art distributed by N.Y. Graphic 1970 [c1969] 146p illus $7.95   735
1 Sculpture
"This book serves as an introduction to the sculpture of the 20th Century and does not propose to be a history of the subject. In 20 sections, each with a brief text and clear black-and-white illustrations, the book surveys the major trends and developments of the past 75 years. Various sections consider visual themes of sculpture (the torso, the reclining figure, the head) or major movements (symbolism, constructivism, Futurism, Cubism, Dada) and there is a closing section on sculpture in relief, monuments, and architecture as sculpture. The book concludes with a list of 78 sculptors, giving brief biographical entries and listing works illustrated in the text along with their dimensions, material, and location." Library J
Bibliography: p[147]

Read, Herbert
A concise history of modern sculpture. Praeger 1964 310p illus (Praeger World of art ser) $7.50   735
1 Sculpture—History
Companion volume to the author's: A concise history of modern painting, entered in class 759.06
"A chronological survey, beginning with Rodin, of modern sculptors and their work. Applying the term 'modern' to artists who

Read, Herbert—_Continued_

have broken with tradition. [the author] concentrates his attention on those who introduced or influenced stylistic movements such as cubism, constructivism, futurism, and surrealism; describing assemblages, metalwork, and other postwar innovations he questions their validity as sculpture." Booklist

Text reference: p279-82. Bibliography: p283-85

736 Carving and carvings. Wood

Graveney, Charles

Woodcarving for beginners. Watson-Guptill 1967 103p illus $2.50   **736**

1 Wood carving

"Studio Vista"

"This manual's specific directions may not be easy for the absolute novice to follow, but it will serve him and others well in terms of the foundation of understanding it lays down concerning the possibilities and problems presented by different woods, tools, equipment, carving techniques whether carving in relief, chip and surface carving, or other methods, and by textures and finish. A chapter on lettering, a short reading list, a brief list of British and U.S. suppliers, and numerous illustrations of past and present professional work and student work complete the book." Booklist

737.4 Coins

Davis, Norman M.

The complete book of the United States coin collecting. Macmillan (N Y) 1971 336p illus $7.95   **737.4**

1 Coins

This "handbook for the beginner of the veteran collector covers every phase of American coin collecting, including basic information and tips; identification; best investments for profit; gold and silver coins; mints and mint marks; counterfeits; medals; tokens; and other 'collectables.' With a table of mints, a complete star-line and marginals list, a Collector's Vocabulary, and a bibliography." News of Bks

Hobson, Burton

Illustrated encyclopedia of world coins [by] Burton Hobson and Robert Obojski. Doubleday 1970 512p illus $12.95   **737.4**

1 Coins—Dictionaries

A "one-volume reference work to treat in depth all the diverse topics that comprise the fascinating world of numismatics. With hundreds of entries, over 175,000 words of text, and nearly 2500 photographs, it will be an invaluable tool for both the experienced coin collector and the beginner." Book News

Alphabetically arranged by country or region of the world

Reed, Mort

Cowles Complete encyclopedia of U.S. coins; foreword by Gilroy Roberts. Cowles 1969 xx, 300p illus $7.95   **737.4**

1 Coins

SBN 402-01111-2

"A complete survey of all U.S. coins, minting dates, mineral content, with photos and information about the minting and value plus information about counterfeiting, collecting, etc." News of Bks

Glossary: p xv-xx. Bibliography: p293-94

Reinfeld, Fred

A catalogue of the world's most popular coins. Doubleday illus $8.95   **737.4**

1 Coins

First published 1956 by Sterling. Periodically revised to bring the material up to date. Recent editions revised by Burton Hobson

This book lists and pictures ancient, modern, American, and foreign coins, with current values. (Publisher)

"In addition to the country-by-country listings Mr. Reinfeld speaks of inscriptions and identification, and in the concluding pages describes coins that are particularly difficult to identify." Booklist

Coin collectors' handbook. Doubleday illus $3.95   **737.4**

1 Coins

First published 1954 by Sterling. Frequently revised to bring it up to date on prices and issues. Latest editions revised by Burton Hobson

This book tells how to acquire coins for fun and investment, how to store collections, preserve rarities, and sell coins profitably. In the catalog section of the book are up-to-date values for every condition of every United States and Canadian coin, along with the quantities issued. (Publisher)

Includes glossary

How to build a coin collection. [Rev. ed] Sterling 1966 159p illus $3.50, lib. bdg. $3.69   **737.4**

1 Coins

"Revised by Burton Hobson"

First published 1958

Contains "information necessary to start, build, and maintain a good coin collection. With a sample collection, the author shows how to select coins, and how to build through careful investment and by replacement with coins in superior condition. How to recognize and identify mint marks, how to grade, classify, and determine the condition of coins, and how to care for and store a coin collection are other facets covered." Huntting

Foreign coins, price lists and glossary are included

A treasury of American coins. Hanover House 1961 124p illus $5.95   **737.4**

1 Coins

"The complete illustrated story of American coins and private money. The origin and development of coin types and a selection of outstanding coins for investment." p9

An "historical survey of those American coins most in demand by collectors. Both the expert and the casual user will find the book an easy one in which to locate information, including market value, about specific issues." Booklist

Glossary: p7-8

Treasury of the world's coins. Sterling illus $4.95, lib. bdg. $4.80   **737.4**

1 Coins

First published 1953. Periodically revised to keep material up to date

Arranged by country, here is "a comprehensive photographic guide to the world's most interesting coins. This book tells you the colorful story behind each coin and the country issuing it." Huntting

739.27 Jewelry

Baxter, William T.

Jewelry, gem cutting, and metalcraft. 3d ed. rev. and enl. McGraw 1950 334p illus $7.95   **739.27**

1 Jewelry 2 Metalwork 3 Gems 4 Handicraft

"Whittlesey House publications"

First published 1938

"It is written for beginners, but is not oversimplified. It does not contain as much information on gem-cutting as some of the available specialized books; on the other hand, it covers all of the crafts which enter into jewelry-making by hand." Library J

Magazines devoted to mineralogy and gem cutting: p325. Books of interest: p327

741.2 Pencil drawing

Guptill, Arthur L.
Pencil drawing step-by-step. 2d ed. Reinhold 1959 147p illus $10.95   **741.2**

1 Pencil drawing

First published 1949
This book "covers lead pencil, charcoal and scratchboard drawing, and contains many examples by well-known artists." Cleveland Open Shelf
"Mr. Guptill's teaching background gives him insight for anticipating the needs of the beginner and skilled artist alike." School Arts

Loomis, Andrew
Fun with a pencil. Viking 1939 119p illus $4.95   **741.2**

1 Pencil drawing

"The fundamentals of drawing caricatures and popular figures are explained and demonstrated with many step-by-step illustrations for the beginner. Though intended only to provide a pastime, it may be useful in learning commercial art work." Booklist

741.5 Cartoons, caricatures, comics

Mendelson, Lee
Charlie Brown & Charlie Schulz; in celebration of the 20th anniversary of Peanuts, by Lee Mendelson in association with Charles M. Schulz. World Pub. 1970 160p illus $6.95   **741.5**

A biography of the creator of the comic strip "Peanuts" plus an examination of the popularity of the Peanuts phenomenon. Illustrated with 95 photographs and 75 of the cartoonist's drawings

The New Yorker
The New Yorker album, 1955-1965, fortieth anniversary. Harper 1965 $7.50   **741.5**

1 American wit and humor, Pictorial

Containing work by both well-know cartoonists and newcomers, this "collection of [some 700] 'New Yorker' cartoons is suggested as entertainment for sophisticated young adults." Booklist

Rogers, W. G.
Mightier than the sword; cartoon, caricature, social comment. Harcourt 1969 287p illus $5.25   **741.5**

1 Cartoons and caricatures—History

This is a "history of the artists who have used this medium [ranging] from sixteenth-century Arcimboldo to Goya. Hogarth to Herblock, Daumier to Mauldin, Tenniel to Thurber. The author . . . describes their work in relation to their times and the influence each had on the contemporary scene." Publisher's note
"There are too few examples of the cartoons, caricatures, and drawings that influenced generations of readers. But the text supplies for the lack of picturization. A bibliography, a listing of museums where the originals may be viewed and an Index are helpful for teen-age study of the question." Best Sellers

Schulz, Charles M.
Peanuts classics. Holt 1970 unp illus $6.95   **741.5**

1 Comic books, strips, etc.

Companion volume to the author's: Peanuts treasury, entered below
This is a collection of the author's "most popular daily strips plus ninety-two pages of his best Sunday features reproduced for the first time in any book in full color. Here are the further adventures (and misadventures) of the internationally famous 'Peanuts' gang, featuring good ol' Charlie Brown, Snoopy—Head Beagle, World Famous Author, World War I flying ace and just plain (almost) dog—Lucy, Linus, Peppermint Patty, Schroeder, and all the rest." Publisher's note

Peanuts treasury; foreword by Johnny Hart. Holt 1968 unp illus $4.95   **741.5**

1 Comic books, strips, etc.

This is a "selection of Schulz's own favorite cartoons taken from strips which originally appeared from 1959 through 1967. Included among the more than 600 cartoons are strips that feature Charlie Brown as baseball team manager and kite flier not so par excellence, Lucy in her role as neighborhood psychiatrist and inspiration to all the crabby people of the world, Snoopy as a World War I flying ace, and the rest of the Peanuts gang as they cope with life." Booklist

Thurber, James
Thurber & company; introduction by Helen Thurber. Harper 1966 208p illus $6.95   **741.5**

1 American wit and humor, Pictorial

"Cartoons and drawings 'of male and female animals, including the human,' many never before published in book form and some never published at all." Bk Buyer's Guide
"The magic that was Thurber comes through beautifully in this appealing book. . . . I strongly suspect that a new generation of Thurber fans may spring up as a result of this book. Young adult readers will especially appreciate the more satiric touches, as in 'American Folk Dance,' 'Destinations,' and the section entitled 'Famous Poems Illustrated.' " Library J

741.67 Posters

Mills, Vernon
Making posters. Watson-Guptill 1967 104p illus (Watson-Guptill Art and craft handbks) lib. bdg. $2.50   **741.67**

1 Posters

This book "explains how to organize and present material so that it attracts, interests, and informs. The author describes basic materials and equipment; shows infallible shortcuts to lettering; offers advice on layout; describes how to manufacture posters in limited runs. Detailed illustrations show elements of basic design, the difference between weak and strong designs, use of proportion and contrast." Publisher's note
"An excellent introduction to the practical aspects of poster making, with fine examples." Chicago
For further reading: p102-03

743 Freehand drawing and drawings by subject

Hogarth, Burne
Drawing the human head. Watson-Guptill 1965 156p illus $9.95   **743**

1 Drawing 2 Head

The author analyzes the basic structure, proportions, anatomy, and changes of the human head; defines head types according to structure and explains what features go with these types; and demonstrates how to draw the head from every angle. (Publisher)

Loomis, Andrew
Drawing the head and hands. Viking 1956 154p illus $6.95   **743**

1 Drawing 2 Head 3 Hand

In this manual for self-instruction or classroom study the author leads into the subject

Loomis, Andrew—*Continued*
of drawing the head through the fundamentals of anatomical construction. He then proceeds to the specifics of expression, gesture, light effects etc. In a brief final section he provides a similar study of hands. (Publisher)
The author "knows all the little tricks that make for success in this field, and . . . passes them on to the reader. The book is basically sound, and easily comprehended." Chicago Sunday Tribune

745.1 Antiques

American Heritage
The American Heritage History of American antiques from the Revolution to the Civil War, by the editors of American Heritage, The Magazine of History. Author and editor in charge: Marshall B. Davidson. Am. Heritage 1968 416p illus $17.50   745.1
1 Antiques 2 Art objects
Covers architectural and furnishing styles of the period, Britannia ware, clocks, cased glass, funerary embroidery and quilts
"Illustrated with paintings, aquatints, daguerreotypes, drawings, lithographs, and photographs, more than 100 in color." Pub W
Glossary of terms: p385-95. Bibliography included in Acknowledgments: p402
The American Heritage History of colonial antiques, by the editors of American Heritage, The Magazine of History. Author and editor in charge: Marshall B. Davidson. Am. Heritage 1967 384p illus boards $16.50
745.1
1 Antiques 2 Art objects
This work "is a rich, rhythmic counterpoint of color illustration and anecdote, tracing the steady convergence of comfort and culture through the various colonial periods. . . . A fine emphasis is put on the rewards resulting from the intermingling of stylistic influences that came to America through its bustling trade and busy immigration." Book World
"More than 800 excellently chosen examples show the skilled craftsmanship and understanding of design in this early period. The illustrations are superior. This book is as much American history as it is a book on antiques." Library J
Glossary of terms: p353-63

745.54 Papercraft. Origami

Randlett, Samuel
The art of origami; paper folding, traditional and modern; illus. by Jean Randlett; preface by Lillian Oppenheimer; introduction by Edward Kallop. Dutton 1961 192p illus $6.95   745.54
1 Paper crafts
The introduction to this book outlines "the history of paper-folding as an art. . . . The body of the book contains illustrations and instructions for beginners as well as practiced craftsmen. There are plenty of clear diagrams with the instructions and also photographs of particularly artistic origami figures. One chapter gives suggestions on how to teach origami. For all craft collections." Library J
Bibliography: p188-90. Sources of paper: p191

745.59 Making specific objects. Collages

Lynch, John
How to make collages. Viking 1961 136p illus $5.95   745.59
1 Collage

"A Studio book"
"Collage designs can be worked out with bits of colored paper, fabrics, cut-outs from magazines, photographs, scraps of odd materials, arranged and rearranged in a pleasing combination and then pasted down to form a permanent picture. John Lynch shows many kinds of collages, from the simplest to the most complicated. He suggests materials to use, gives sources of design, and takes the reader step-by-step through many projects." Huntting

745.6 Lettering

Biegeleisen, J. I.
The ABC of lettering. 4th ed. Harper 1971 266p illus boards $12.50   745.6
1 Lettering
Spiral binding
First published 1940
Contents: Equipment; Lettering terminology; Lettering exercises; Anatomy of lettering; Spacing; Reproduction lettering; Series of alphabets; Shop hints and safety precautions; Selling your lettering; Supplement of type faces; Supplement of photo-lettering; Supplement of antique and decorative alphabets
"These lessons for the beginner in lettering seem unusually complete and detailed; they give careful instructions on strokes, with exercises, and information about materials." Booklist

745.92 Floral arts. Flower arrangement

Rockwell, F. F.
The Rockwells' New complete book of flower arrangement [by] F. F. Rockwell and Esther C. Grayson; with 92 full color reproductions and more than 150 photographs and diagrams. Doubleday 1960 336p illus $6.95
745.92
1 Flower arrangement
"An American Garden Guild book"
First published 1947 with title: The complete book of flower arrangement
This book for both the beginning and the practiced arranger provides information on "types of arrangements, the principles of color combinations and design, hints on what judges are looking for, etc." Bk Buyer's Guide

746 Textiles handicrafts

Better Homes and Gardens
Better Homes & Gardens Stitchery and crafts; a complete guide to the most rewarding stitchery and craft projects for the whole family. Meredith 1966 168p illus $5.95   746
1 Handicraft 2 Needlework 3 Weaving
In addition to projects in knitting, weaving, and other forms of needlecraft, this book includes directions for "making pinatas, picture frames, photograms, articles in rope or plastic, seed and mosaic work, cement painting, wire sculpture, and articles in other media." Pub W

746.1 Weaving

Wilson, Jean
Weaving is fun; a guide for teachers, children & beginning weavers; about yarns, baskets, cloth & tapestry. Van Nostrand-Reinhold 1971 140p illus $8.95   746.1
1 Weaving 2 Textile industry and fabrics
SBN 289-70196-1
The author includes chapters on the sources of yarn and the various processes used to

Wilson, Jean—*Continued*
transform yarns into fabric; basket weaving from original material to finished product; descriptions of many kinds of handwoven cloth; and one entitled, "Learning by doing"
Glossary: p137. List of useful reference publications: p138

746.3 Tapestry making

Denny, Norman
The Bayeux Tapestry; the story of the Norman conquest: 1066 [by] Norman Denny & Josephine Filmer-Sankey. Atheneum Pubs. 1966 unp illus $7.95   **746.3**
1 Bayeux tapestry 2 Hastings, Battle of, 1066
The "tapestry shows, from the Norman point of view, the tragic epic of Harold the noble warrior, whose betrayal of William the Conqueror profoundly changed the course of English history. . . . The complete tapestry—actually not a tapestry at all but a magnificent work of embroidery, two hundred and thirty feet long—is reproduced in sequential order as a unified historical narrative instead of a collection of individual pictures. The text is twofold: on every page, a paragraph in large type narrates the events revealed in the illustrations; and on most of the pages a second paragraph in smaller type adds a commentary on the historical background and elucidates obscure details. The reproduction is impressive for its color and clarity; there are pictorial end-paper maps." Horn Bk
Bibliography contained in Acknowledgments

746.4 Textile handicrafts. Needlework. Macramé

Andes, Eugene
Practical macramé; all macramé articles pictured are the work of Gene and Ellen Andes. Van Nostrand-Reinhold 1971 118p illus $7.95   **746.4**
1 Macramé
ISBN 0-289-701945
This book is designed to help the beginner through a series of projects of increasing difficulty and sophistication. Discussed are materials, basic knots, suppliers, and projects, including hats, belts, purses, vests and bikinis

Bucher, Jo
The complete guide to embroidery stitches and crewel. Meredith 1971 353p illus $8.95   **746.4**
1 Embroidery
SBN 696-16500-7
"Creative Home Library in association with Better Homes and Gardens"
The author gives diagrams and directions for over 300 surface stitches, plus more than 1000 suggestions for how to create with them. Also included are instructions for left-handed people, advice on equipment, directions for applying designs to fabrics and guidelines for blocking completed work. (Publisher)
Terms used in embroidery: p333-39. Bibliography: p347

747 Interior decoration

Better Homes and Gardens
Better Homes & Gardens Decorating book. [Rev. ed]. Meredith 1968 400p illus $7.95 **747**
1 Interior decoration
Loose-leaf binding with tab index
First published 1956
This book presents practical down-to-earth ideas for making a home beautiful. There are photographs which show the work of leading interior designers to illustrate how these professionals create inviting rooms and solve decorating problems. (Publisher)
Partial contents: The color families; Furniture arrangement; Apartment planning; Walls; Window fashions; Dollarwise decorating

751.4 Painting with specific mediums. Water color painting

Richmond, Leonard
Fundamentals of watercolor painting, by Leonard Richmond and J. Littlejohns. Watson-Guptill 1970 143p illus $15   **751.4**
1 Water color painting
First published 1925 in England with title: The technique of water-colour painting
Topics discussed by the author include: materials, laying a flat wash, combining colors, outline and wash, wash and outline, transparent wash, dry method and scratching out, paste methods, charcoal and watercolor, granulated wash, opaque watercolor, painting with dry pigment, lucky accidents
Bibliography: p140

759 Painting—Historical and geographical treatment

Catalogue of colour reproductions of paintings prior to 1860. UNESCO illus pa $8.50   **759**
1 Color prints—Catalogs 2 Paintings—Catalogs
First published 1950 and frequently revised to bring it up to date
This list of color reproductions in UNESCO's archives is arranged alphabetically by artist. The title page and text are in French, English and Spanish
UNESCO's object in undertaking the publication of this catalogue and its complement, the Catalogue of color reproductions of paintings from 1860 to date [entered below] was to make the masterpieces of painting more widely known by promoting the production and distribution of high-quality colour reproductions on a world scale. (Publisher)

Catalogue of colour reproductions of paintings—1860 to [date] UNESCO illus pa $8.50   **759**
1 Color prints—Catalogs 2 Paintings—Catalogs
First published 1949. Frequently revised
A listing of color reproductions in the UNESCO's archives, arranged alphabetically by artist. Title page and text in French, English and Spanish
"The purpose of these catalogues, however, apart from encouraging the distribution of the best available reproductions, is also to secure a steady improvement in their quality and to coordinate their production. The welcome these catalogues have received from teachers, students and art lovers of all kinds is sufficient proof of their usefulness. But they are perhaps most valuable to art publishers themselves, because they indicate both the trend of taste and the gaps that have to be filled." Preface [to third edition]
Includes indexes of artists, publishers and printers

Craven, Thomas
(ed.) A treasury of art masterpieces; from the Renaissance to the present day. [New and rev. ed] Simon & Schuster 1958 327p illus $9.95   **759**
1 Paintings 2 Painters
First published 1939
There is a general historical introduction, description and appreciation of each painting by the editor

Craven, Thomas—*Continued*
"No pains have been spared to make the selections truly representative; to illustrate not only general tendencies but diversities in styles and subject matter . . . from the thirteenth to the twentieth century." Introduction
"The phrase 'are masterpieces' can be applied with perfect justice to the great majority of Mr. Craven's selections but not to all of them." New Yorker

759.04 Painting—1600-1800

Schwarz, Michael
The age of the Rococo; tr. by Gerald Onn. Praeger 1971 194p illus $9.95   **759.04**
1 Art, Rococo 2 Painting—History
Original German edition 1969
"The Age of Rococo is usually identified with the eighteenth century, although there are [overlappings] into the previous and the following centuries. . . . This work traces the various elements of the painting of the period which has sometimes been dubbed, rather superciliously, as the 'decay of the baroque.' After an introductory chapter on the Spirit of the Times, Michael Schwarz studies Genre Painting, Satirical Art, Portraiture, Townscapes, Landscapes, Still-Life Painting, Religious and Mythological Painting. Watteau, Boucher, Fragonard, Chardin, Hogarth, Goya. Greuze, Canaletto, Gainsborough, Reynolds, Guardi Tiepolo, Piazzetta, and many other less familiar names are representative of this period. The book is illustrated with forty full-page color plates, forty more in black-and-white, with another forty 'text illustrations.' An index of artists and a list of illustrations are appended." Best Sellers

759.05 Painting—1800-1900

Rewald, John
The history of impressionism. Rev. and enl. ed. Mus. of Modern Art 1961 662p illus $25
        759.05
1 Impressionism (Art)
First published 1946
This history "describes the meetings, aims, methods and exhibitions of the painters who came to be known as impressionists, and traces their decades of struggle for recognition and their disbandment after their eighth group show in 1886." Book of the Month Club News
"Reads like fiction in spite of its scholarly conception." School Arts
Bibliography: p608-44. Map on lining-papers

759.06 Painting—1900-

Read, Herbert
A concise history of modern painting. [Rev. and enl. ed] Praeger [1969 c1968] 380p illus (Praeger World of art ser) $8.50   **759.06**
1 Painting—History 2 Modernism (Art)
Companion volume to: A concise history of modern sculpture, entered in class 735
First published 1959
"The art historian traces the development of styles such as cubism, surrealism, dadaism, constructivism, and nonobjectivism. The artists whose work is analyzed range from Cézanne to Pollock and in their diversity have in common an awareness of the problems of our time and the ability 'to present a clear and distinct visual image' of their insights and experiences. The author has excluded certain contemporary movements such as academic realism and the primitive or naive styles because he feels they are more traditional than modern." Booklist
Bibliography: p350-52

759.13 Painting—United States

Atkinson, J. Edward
(ed.) Black dimensions in contemporary American art; comp. and ed. by J. Edward Atkinson. New Am. Lib. 1971 126p illus pa $3.95   **759.13**
1 Painting, American 2 Negro art 3 Negro artists
"A Plume book"
"The artists whose works appear in this volume are from every region of the United States. Their paintings represent a wide variety of styles and themes which, in turn, reflect every major trend in modern American art. Yet the diversity of style, theme, and locale presented in this . . . collection is unified by one immutable link—each artist is black and living in 20th-century America. Each, too, is acutely aware of the various qualities which define the American experience—among them, violence, conflict, and racism." Publisher's note
For each of the 50 artists represented there is a brief career description and one or two color illustrations

Baigell, Matthew
A history of American painting. Praeger 1971 288p illus (Praeger World of art ser) $9.95   **759.13**
1 Painting, American—History
This history "is traced from its origins as a provincial offshoot of the European Baroque to its international triumph in the twentieth century. The author shows how each succeeding generation of artists defined the range of possibilities open to it and how certain characteristics of style and vision persisted from one generation to another." News of Bks
"For the general reader [the author's] book is excellent: his characterizations of the periods are well made, and he presents just enough of each painter's work so that one senses that artist's richness. The illustrations, which are clearly correlated with the text, are of good quality. The notes and bibliography represent very recent books and articles and make it possible for the reader to explore each of the periods further." Library J

Geldzahler, Henry
American painting in the twentieth century. Metropolitan Mus. [distributed by N.Y. Graphic] 1965 236p illus $7.50   **759.13**
1 Painting, American 2 Painters, American
"A concise chronological survey from 1900 to 1960 of significant groups of U.S. painters and the European or other ties each member of the group manifested and the innovations he introduced. The author . . . supplies 155 utilitarian reproductions in black and white from originals held in most cases in the Museum's permanent collection. . . . [Contains] biographical capsules and bibliography." Booklist

Time-Life Books
American painting, 1900-1970, by the editors of Time-Life Books. Time-Life Bks. [distributed by Little] 1970 192p illus (Time-Life Lib. of art) $7.95   **759.13**
1 Painting, American 2 Painters, American
A "survey in text and illustrations of the past seven decades of painting in the U.S.—a time when American art came of age. The book begins with the Ashcan School, swiftly moves to the new abstraction, the social realism, of the 1930's, Abstract Expressionism, and pop art . . . and concludes with a few pages on op paintings." Library J
"A good introductory survey, if necessarily sketchy, in its attempt to cover so much ground. . . . Illustrations are first-rate, many in full color, well balanced in showing the many strands and phases of the exciting American art scene." Pub W
Chronology: Artists of the 20th century: p186-87. Bibliography: p187

759.4 French painting

Guichard-Meili, Jean
Matisse. Praeger 1967 256p illus (Praeger World of art profile) $7.50   759.4
1 Matisse, Henri
Translated from the French by Caroline Moorehead
In this "voluminously illustrated and instructive introductory survey of [Matisse's] work and development as an artist [the author] briefly establishes the milieu in which Matisse began his career. Then citing representative examples, he concisely describes and analyzes the subjects, media, and treatment that were preoccupying Matisse at given sequential periods. Reference numbers link text and illustrations. A closing chapter indicates numerous museum collections of Matisse in the U.S. and abroad and some private collections." Booklist
Includes bibliographical references

Kelder, Diane
The French impressionists and their century. . . . Praeger [1970 c1967] 191p illus $8.50
                759.4
1 Impressionism (Art) 2 Painters, French
"A new text based on Die Maler des grossen Lichtes, by Hans Platte [published 1967 in Germany]" Title page
This is an "informative survey of developments in painting during the nineteenth and early twentieth centuries. Moving from Delacroix and Ingres to Picasso the account describes the contributions to modernism made by Manet, Monet, Degas, Pissarro, Van Gogh, Gauguin, Cézanne, and Matisse, among others, and traces the evolution of the various schools of painting from Impressionism to Cubism. The reproductions, some in color, are adequate and useful for identification, and the text is keyed to the illustrations. . . . Appended are a bibliography, a glossary, and a biographical index of artists." Booklist

760.9 Prints and print making

Goodrich, Lloyd
Winslow Homer's America. Tudor 1969 192p illus $15   760.9
1 Homer, Winslow 2 U.S.—Social life and customs—Pictures, illustrations, etc.
The book contains many of the wood engravings and lithographs which the artist made to illustrate stories in magazines, newspapers, and books. The illustrations span the years 1857-1880 and cover such topics as the Civil War, resort areas, and everyday life on the farms. The text includes descriptions of American social life and customs during this period. (Publisher)

769 Print collections

Museum of Graphic Art
American printmaking, the first 150 years. Preface by A. Hyatt Mayor. Foreword by Donald H. Karshan. Introduction by J. William Middendorf II. Text by Wendy J. Shadwell. [Smithsonian Inst. distributed by Random House 1969] 180p illus $12.50   769
1 Engravings
"The prints include portraits, pictures of historical events, views of cities, and broadsides. Notes on the prints indicate provenance of imprints. Appended are a résumé of holdings of major collections and a selected bibliography." Booklist

770.2 Photography—Handbooks, manuals, etc.

The **Amateur** photographer's handbook. Crowell illus $6.95   770.2
1 Photography—Handbooks, manuals, etc.
First published 1925. Written by A. F. Collins through 1941; by A. Sussman from 1948 on. Frequently revised to bring material up to date
The book covers many aspects of photography: equipment, exposure, developing negatives, and making prints, enlargements and slides. (Publisher)
"A good book for the amateur. . . . Should be very useful in a library." Wis Lib Bul
Includes a supplementary glossary

Eastman Kodak Company, Rochester, N.Y.
How to make good pictures. The Company illus pa $1.50   770.2
1 Photography—Handbooks, manuals, etc.
Frequently revised. Subtitles vary
"The book's approach is simple: to help you see the picture possibilities that exist all around you, and then to help you make the most of these possibilities, through wise choice of viewpoint, lighting, good subject arrangement, and correct operation of your camera. In Part Two there's a good deal of information about specific picture-making projects—under widely various conditions. . . . Part Three goes into the darkroom to brief you on the processes of developing, printing, enlarging, and a number of other operations. Part Four provides some indication of the many ways you can use the pictures your camera and your darkroom work have produced." What this book is all about
"An elementary book of instruction for the beginner: sound advice in a humorous vein combined with hundreds of well-chosen illustrations." Sec Ed Brd

Feininger, Andreas
The complete photographer. Prentice-Hall 1965 344p illus $8.95   770.2
1 Photography—Handbooks, manuals, etc.
"Information on the essentials of modern photography, from advice on the selection of equipment to the interrelationship of many technical factors involved in making a photograph. Material from several of Feininger's earlier phototechnical texts . . . has been reorganized and brought up to date to cover recent developments and trends." Booklist
"Feininger has 32 charming pages of plates, half in color, but some text figures would be a welcome relief to the pages of solid text in sans serif type. A praise worthy feature is the numerous callouts in the margin referring the reader to related material on other pages—a sort of concordance. The author discusses color photography as well as monochrome but fails to furnish a bibliography." Science Bks

770.28 Photography techniques

Time-Life Books
Light and film, by the editors of Time-Life Books. Time-Life Bks. [distributed by Morgan & Morgan] [1971 c1970] 227p illus (Life Lib. of photography) boards $9.95   770.28
1 Photography—Lighting 2 Photography—Apparatus and supplies
First published 1970, revised 1971
This volume "deals with the nature of light: the evolution of modern film since the early discoveries of light's effect on sensitive substances; the types of film now available and their uses; light meters and their operation in the determination of accurate exposure; sources of artificial light; and the creation of pleasing light patterns. These topics cover the basic problems faced in taking a photograph. By

Time-Life Books—*Continued*
exploring them in orderly fashion this book shows how the technical objectives of a 'good' negative can be combined with the esthetic aims of an outstanding picture." Introduction
Bibliography: p223

770.9 Photography—History

Pollack, Peter
The picture history of photography, from the earliest beginnings to the present day. Rev. and enl. ed. Abrams 1969 108p illus $25
770.9
1 Photography—History
First published 1958
The book discusses all aspects of photography: "portraiture, journalism, documentary, 'pictorial,' scientific, abstract, interpretive. A special section is devoted to the new dimension of color. Chief emphasis, however, is on the great photographs made by the most inspired cameramen, each using the process available to him at his own time. Each of these major figures is the subject of a 'profile' and a display of some of his best work." Publisher's note
"Magnificent is the word for this important and scholarly volume. . . . Pollack does a superb and fascinating job of making his history well knit and logical, with generous samplings of the work of scores of the world's greatest cameramen, living and dead." Chicago Sunday Tribune (Review of first edition)
Bibliography: p698-701

771.3 Cameras

Time-Life Books
The camera, by the editors of Time-Life Books. Time-Life Bks. [distributed by Morgan & Morgan] 1970 236p illus (Life Lib. of photography) boards $9.95
771.3
1 Cameras 2 Photography
This book "begins with a discussion of 'The many levels of Photography,' with illustrations that chronicle the history and the uses of photography. It then goes on to explain the major types of cameras, tells how to choose a camera, explains the camera's 'controls' and how to use them creatively, and explains lenses with illustrations. Interesting historical notes, 'talks with photographers,' and other details complete the book." Science Bks
Bibliography: p231

778 Specific fields of photography

Time-Life Books
Photojournalism, by the editors of Time-Life Books. Time-Life Bks. [distributed by Morgan & Morgan] 1971 227p illus (Life Lib. of photography) boards $9.95
778
1 Photography, Journalistic
This "is a lavishly illustrated exploration of the uses of the camera in covering news, telling stories, making 'pictures that persuade,' and carrying out such amateur or professional assignments as photographing for poster art, greeting cards and advertisements. . . . Brief section on equipment; bibliography, index." Pub W

The studio, by the editors of Time-Life Books. Time-Life Bks. [distributed by Morgan & Morgan] 1971 236p illus (Life Lib. of photography) boards $9.95
778
1 Photography
Examining "one of the most specialized and demanding areas of photographic activity, this volume defines studio photography, illustrates how it evolved, looks at its subjects, examines the techniques of recognized masters and includes instruction on organizing a studio and on using special studio equipment." Publisher's note
Bibliography: p233

778.3 Scientific and technological photographic applications

Eastman Kodak Company, Rochester, N.Y.
Close-up photography. The Company 1969 88p illus (Close-up photography and photomacrography v 1) pa $2.75
778.3
1 Photography
Volume 1 of a two-volume set
"This book deals generally with the equipment and techniques common to photographic applications in all fields, and includes specifically the methods for the particular fields. Still photography only is described, nevertheless, many sections will prove helpful to cinematographers. Volume I covers close-up photography and incorporates basic treatments of cameras, films, and lighting." About this book
References: p86-87

778.5 Motion pictures. Photography

Eastman Kodak Company, Rochester, N.Y.
Home movies made easy. The Company 1970 128p illus pa $1.95
778.5
1 Moving picture photography
"Covers the basics of home movie-making, plus tips on taking movies of children, vacations, sports. Includes simple techniques for slow motion, animation, existing-light movies. Tips on editing." Publisher's note

Ferguson, Robert
How to make movies; a practical guide to group film-making. Viking 1969 88p illus $5.95
778.5
1 Moving picture photography 2 Moving pictures
SBN 289-79574-5
"A Studio book"
"Deals with the practical aspects of film-making: editing, script-writing, shooting, directing, acting, lighting, sound synchronization, and how to choose a subject and project it convincingly." Book News

Kinsey, Anthony
How to make animated movies. Viking 1970 95p illus $6.95
778.5
1 Moving picture cartoons 2 Moving picture photography
SBN 670-38391-0
"A Studio book"
"A basic, introductory guide with easy to understand explanations of types of and techniques in animation. The author offers a brief history and discussion of perception and illusion, and describes pixilation, animating without a camera, lettering and how to use gels. Finally, he presents the development of a film step by step, from storyboard to sound. There is an overabundance of diagrams and illustrated examples, but these do not cause confusion." Library J
Bibliography: p93

Lowndes, Douglas
Film making in schools. Watson-Guptill 1968 128p illus $8.95
778.5
1 Moving picture photography
Intended as a guide for both teachers and students, the book describes film equipment and gives instructions in its use. (Publisher)

Smallman, Kirk
Creative film-making. Macmillan (N Y) 1969 245p illus $6.95   **778.5**
1 Moving picture photography
"A guide to the basic principles and techniques of professional film making which includes a sample script, step-by-step directions and estimated costs for making a low-budget film." Booklist

778.6 Color photography

Time-Life Books
Color, by the editors of Time-Life Books. Time-Life Bks. [distributed by Morgan & Morgan] 1970 240p illus (Life Lib. of photography) boards $9.95   **778.6**
1 Color photography
Included in this book is information on "how color film works, the history of color film, techniques of color photography, innovation in color photography, a guide to home processing of color film and printmaking, synthetic color, and an appendix on projectors." Science Bks
Bibliography: p235

779 Collections of photographs

Cartier-Bresson, Henri
The world of Henri Cartier Bresson. Viking 1968 210p $14   **779**
1 Photography, Artistic
"A Studio book"
"Cartier-Bresson has had two major exhibitions of photographs at the Museum of Modern Art, one in 1946 and one in 1968. This book is a retrospective collection of his work from 1929 to the present day and consists of two-hundred ten photographs taken in Europe, America, Asia and Africa. The major part of the text is a reworking of the ideas on photography set forth in Cartier-Bresson's The Decisive Moment." Book Rev Digest
This volume "is a strong, endlessly fascinating statement comprised of his greatest pictures." Am News of Bks

New York (City) Museum of Modern Art
The family of man. . . . Mus. of Modern Art 1955 192p illus $4.95   **779**
1 Photography—Exhibitions
"The greatest photographic exhibition of all time—503 pictures from 68 Countries-created by Edward Steichen for the Museum of Modern Art." Subtitle
Reproductions of the photographs in the exhibition held at the Museum from January 26 to May 8, 1955. Depicts men, women and children playing, working, dreaming, fighting. (Publisher)
"By excellent reproduction and superb layout, the book achieves its purpose of showing 'men in relation to his environment, to the beauty and richness of the earth and what he has done with this inheritance, the good and the great things, the stupid and the destructive things.' " Christian Science Monitor

Parks, Gordon
Gordon Parks: a poet and his camera. Preface: Stephen Spender; introduction: Philip B. Kunhardt, Jr. Viking 1968 unp illus $8.95   **779**
1 Photography, Artistic
"A Studio book"
This book "is the author's first one using creative photography as its theme. It combines many of Parks' world-famous color photographs with his poetry, which evokes or extends the mood of the pictures." Publisher's note

Each poem, whether it searches the face of a 'hunger-eyed and sallow-cheeked' child or slices the night sky above the Nubian desert, has a surface thought and sub-surface mysteries. Likewise, in Parks' photography a picture does not merely duplicate a sight somewhere sometime, but demands repeated viewings to behold color, oblivious and almost-hidden elements, and the message of the man behind the camera." Horn Bk

Steichen, Edward
A life in photography. Published in collaboration with the Museum of Modern Art. Doubleday 1963 unp illus $9.95   **779**
1 Photography, Artistic
"Included are gravure productions of 250 of Steichen's photographs [of war, nature, personalities, etc.] culled from 30,000. The text, sprinkled with anecdotes, provides insights into the role of photography and presents an autobiographical record of Steichen's career." Hunting
"A breathtaking gallery of personalities, abstractions, still life, war pictures, nature, which comprise the testament of the man who, more than any other, has influenced the standards for creative photography in the twentieth century." Chicago

780.1 Music—
Philosophy and esthetics

Bernstein, Leonard
The infinite variety of music. Simon & Schuster 1966 286p illus music $6.50   **780.1**
1 Music—Analysis, appreciation
"A companion volume to 'The Joy of Music' [listed below]. It includes the scripts of his TV programs on Mozart, Romanticism, Jazz in Serious Music, etc., plus an explanation of four great symphonies by Beethoven, Tschaikovsky, Brahms, and Dvorak." Bk Buyer's Guide
"The many pages of music are meaningless in printed form unless one reads music easily. Although the writing reflects Bernstein's boundless vitality, this is recommended only for specialized music collections within YA departments." Library J

The joy of music. Simon & Schuster 1959 303p illus music $6.50   **780.1**
1 Music—Analysis, appreciation
"Seven scripts for Bernstein's 'Omnibus' TV show—dealing with conducting, Bach, modern music, etc.—plus an introduction and four essays written for this book." Bk Buyer's Guide
"The style varies from the profound to the pert, and the text is copiously illustrated with bars of music. . . . Even for those who do not have a musical background or ability there is much appeal." Doors to More Mature Reading

Boyden, David D.
An introduction to music; foreword by Percy A. Scholes. 2d ed. Knopf 1970 xxviii, 554, xxxvii p illus music $8.95   **780.1**
1 Music—Analysis, appreciation 2 Music—History and criticism
First published 1956 in England
A survey of music in 33 chapters extending to the present day, with emphasis on Western music

Copland, Aaron
What to listen for in music. [Rev. ed] McGraw 1957 307p illus music $5.95   **780.1**
1 Music—Analysis, appreciation
First published 1939
This book based on a series of lectures delivered at the New School for Social Research in New York City "is designed to give the average adult, intelligent, ignorant music lover a sufficient initiation into the mysteries of musical composition to enable him to listen

Copland, Aaron—*Continued*

with pleasure and profit. . . . [Copland] discusses the three planes of listening—the sensuous, the expressive, and the sheerly musical. He discusses the question of where composers get their ideas and what they do about them. He describes the four elements of music. He discusses tone color in a chapter on the orchestra that is a miniature masterpiece of communicative writing." Yale R

"Mr. Copland succeeds wonderfully well in giving the layman glimpses into the mind of the composer, which, he emphasizes, is not so mysterious as it is sometimes said to be." San Francisco Chronicle

Includes a chapter on film music, bibliography, and list of recordings

Ewen, David

(ed.) The complete book of classical music. Prentice-Hall 1965 xx, 946p $14.95 **780.1**
1 Music—Analysis, appreciation 2 Music—History and criticism 3 Composers

This "chronologically arranged reading reference guide, contains over 1,000 works by 118 composers ranging from the fourteen century to Richard Strauss. Critical evaluations and biographical sketches of each composer preface commentaries on major works, arranged in order of composition. Less familiar periods such as pre-Bach and Baroque are well represented as are minor composers worthy of attention." Booklist

The "book's chief value lies in the detailed studies of the musical pieces, whether of a violin sonata in a paragraph or a complete opera in a few pages. . . . For the advanced student." Sat R

Bibliography: p907-16

The world of twentieth century music. Prentice-Hall 1968 xxxi, 989p $14.95 **780.1**
1 Music—Analysis, appreciation 2 Music—History and criticism 3 Composers

This work is a replacement for the author's previous "The complete book of twentieth century music" originally published in 1952. Less than ten percent of the material from the earlier volume has been retained

A representation of works of major composers; brief biographies are followed by composers' works, chronologically arranged, with programmatic and analytical information

"Ewen keeps his discussions of each composition non-technical, which should reassure the layman or the beginning student; on the other hand he remains sufficiently informative to interest the trained musician. The book's purpose—to offer a broad, knowledgeable chronology of the important music composed in our century, and to summarize composers and their works in relation to the contemporary development of music—is a useful one, competently achieved." Pub W

Sources: p923-28

The New York Times

Guide to listening pleasure; ed. and with an introduction by Howard Taubman. Macmillan (N Y) 1968 xxiv, 328p $6.95 **780.1**
1 Music—Analysis, appreciation 2 Music—Discography

"A New York Times Book"

Nine commentators have contributed to this guide. Each writes about his own speciality, recommending performing groups as well as specific titles. The topics covered include opera, orchestral music, chamber music, choral music, the musical theater and light music

"But while the contributors to this book pay deserved tribute to so many of the fine programs of WQXR, we find that the revised material we enjoyed as an accompaniment to the programs we loved contains value judgments too rarely supported by sufficient evidence. Even the general reading public for whom this guide is designed will realize the bias found in the lists of recordings." Library J

Discography: p225-319

780.3 Music—Dictionaries

Apel, Willi

The Harvard Brief dictionary of music, by Willi Apel and Ralph T. Daniel. Harvard Univ. Press 1960 341p illus music $5.95
780.3
1 Music—Dictionaries

"Intended for people actively interested in music but having no specialized training. Defines terms, describes instruments, identifies composers, their works and styles, and provides historical and national information." Pub W

"A sound dictionary, certainly; simply and clearly written; and probably more with the student's own desk than his college or public library in mind. This does not mean, however, that libraries should skip it." Library J
Includes bibliographical references

Grove's Dictionary of music and musicians. 5th ed. Edited by Eric Blom. St Martins 1955 [c1954] 9v illus music ea $15, set $149.50 (incl suppl) **780.3**
1 Music—Dictionaries 2 Musicians—Dictionaries

First published 1878-1889 under the editorship of Sir George Grove

"Includes in one alphabet signed articles by specialists on the history, theory and practice of music, terminology, instruments, biographies of musicians, individual compositions, songs, and operas. Lists composers' works. An appendix, arranged by year, gives the names of composers from 1400 to the present with birth and death dates. Many cross-references." Minnesota. The Use of Books and Libraries

It is "assumed by this reviewer that any sizable general collection will purchase [this set], for it is not only the basic current tool in music, but also one that will assist the cultivated general reader and the scholar in borderline fields." Library J

Volume 10 (Supplement) entered below is available separately for $15

Grove's Dictionary of music and musicians; supplementary volume to the 5th ed. Edited by Eric Blom; associate editor: Denis Stevens. St Martins 1961 xxxii, 493p illus music $15 **780.3**
1 Music—Dictionaries 2 Musicians—Dictionaries

"To bring the fifth edition of 1954 completely up to date has not been the principal aim in the planning of the present volume. No consistent attempt has been made, for instance, to complete all the catalogues of composers, and authors works down to the year 1960, or indeed any year between 1954 and now. . . . Nevertheless, catalogues have in a great many cases been improved, and important new works, as well as many not so important, have been entered so far as information has been available. . . . What 'has' been added, though admittedly in an inevitably haphazard, hand-to-mouth kind of way, will often, I am sure, be found very useful, so much so that the absence of other accessions will, I hope, to be thought excusable as well as understandable." Preface

Scholes, Percy A.

The concise Oxford Dictionary of music. 2d ed. Edited by John Owen Ward. Oxford 1964 xxx, 636p illus music $7 **780.3**
1 Music—Dictionaries 2 Musicians—Dictionaries

First published 1952 as a condensation of the author's: The Oxford Companion to music, listed below

"It may be recommended particularly to students and small libraries with limited budgets. The definitions of foreign terms are particularly helpful." Music Lib Assn Notes

Scholes, Percy A.—*Continued*

The Oxford Companion to music; ed. by John Owen Ward. 10th ed. rev. and reset. Oxford 1970 1189p illus music $25   780.3

1 Music—Dictionaries 2 Musicians—Dictionaries

First published 1938

Alphabetically arranged by subject, this volume contains biographies of composers and articles on every aspect of music, with thousands of cross-references to related entries and subjects, and detailed accounts of opera plots

Thompson, Oscar

(ed.) The international cyclopedia of music and musicians. Dodd illus $35   780.3

1 Music—Dictionaries 2 Musicians—Dictionaries

First published 1939. Periodically revised to keep material up to date

"Alphabetically arranged. Most of the articles are short, but there are also included, in the same alphabet, signed monographs of considerable length—written by authorities—on the more important composers and also on special subjects such as the history of music, music criticism, folk music, opera, etc. Each of the biographical articles is followed by a calendar of the composer's life and a classified list of his works. The work is strong in biography, and many contemporary names are included." Winchell. Guide to Reference Books. 8th edition

9th edition edited by Robert Sabin shows American emphasis

780.7   Music—Study and teaching

Moses, Harry E.

Developing and administering a comprehensive high school music program. Parker Pub. [1971 c1970] 221p illus music $8.95   780.7

1 Music—Study and teaching
ISBN 0-13-204156-1

Outlined here is a curriculum "in which a variety of courses are offered, all interrelated and growing out of the General Music Course which serves as its base. The music program which it advocates puts the specialties such as the Choir and Band in proper perspective, each as a part of the larger educational plan." Publisher's note

Partial contents: Basing the program on the general music course; Developing the vocal music program; Developing the instrumental music program; Teaching music appreciation and music literature; Organizing effective assembly programs; Performing in concerts, festivals, and contests; Scheduling and giving credit for music subjects; Developing the music teacher; Evaluating and organizing facilities, equipment, and materials

780.9   Music—History

Bauer, Marion

Music through the ages; an introduction to music history [by] Marion Bauer and Ethel R. Peyser; ed. and rev. by Elizabeth E. Rogers. 3d ed. completely rev. Putnam 1967 748p illus map music $8.95   780.9

1 Music—History and criticism 2 Musicians

First published 1932

This book "is an understandable study of the fascinating aspects of music history linking past to present. . . . It guides the reader to the salient points in the long and vivid story of music stimulating him to continue reading about its varying phases since its genesis to the era of the twentieth century." Publisher's note

"There is remarkable fullness of detail in the treatment of all the more important phases of music, ancient and modern. The discussions and explanations are in clear, attractive and not too technical language and throw the kind of light on the subject that the not too technical reader would most desire." N Y Times Bk R

General bibliography: p725-27

Copland, Aaron

The new music, 1900-1960. Rev. and enl. ed. Norton 1968 194p music $5.50   780.9

1 Music—History and criticism 2 Music, American—History and criticism

First published 1941 with title: Our new music

In this work the author provides an introduction to the formative ideas of our century, and a survey of recent and current trends. He shows how contemporary music grew out of the work of such masters as Debussy, Stravinsky, and Bartok, and discusses individually certain leading composers of Europe and America. (Publisher)

"The fact that Mr. Copland's assessment the state of music [in 1941] still makes very good sense today is a proof of his discrimination and insight. . . . Several chapters deal with American music only." Times (London) Lit Sup

Ewen, David

David Ewen introduces modern music; a history and appreciation—from Wagner to the avant-garde. Rev. and enl. ed. Chilton Co. 1969 323p illus $5.50   780.9

1 Music—History and criticism 2 Composers

First published 1962.

"Beginning with the upheaval created by Richard Wagner and his mighty musical dramas, the author describes and analyzes the forces and counterforces that have governed the making of music in all parts of the Western world during the twentieth century." Publisher's note

Shippen, Katherine B.

The heritage of music, by Katherine B. Shippen & Anca Seidlova; illus. by Otto van Eersel. Viking 1963 311p illus $6, lib. bdg. $5.63   780.9

1 Music—History and criticism 2 Composers

A history of music from primitive times to the modern musician's electronic compositions. The authors trace the changing fashions in serious music, the development of various musical instruments as well as orchestral and vocal forms, the progress of music in America. They provide sketches of Bach, Berlioz, Haydn, Monteverdi, Mozart, Stravinsky, Verdi, and other composers. (Publisher)

"An engagingly written history. . . . Miss Shippen's method is that of the biographical sketch and anecdote and, in this respect, her choice of detail is felicitous and her narrative continuously interesting." Library J

The meaning of some musical terms: p289-300

781.5   Musical forms.   Jazz

Cohn, Nik

Rock from the beginning. Stein & Day 1969 256p illus $5.95   781.5

1 Jazz music 2 Music, Popular (Songs, etc.)

Offering "critique and characterization of both personalities and styles [the author] considers such performers as Bill Haley, Elvis Presley, P. J. Proby, the Beatles, Bob Dylan, and the Who and such sounds as Classic rock, highschool, California pop, soul, rhythm-and-blues, and folk rock." Booklist

Feather, Leonard
The book of jazz: from then till now; a guide to the entire field. Horizon Press 1965 280p music boards $5.95   **781.5**
1 Jazz music 2 Musicians, American
First published 1957
This book covers the history, nature, sources, instruments, sounds, performers, composers, and the future of jazz. (Publisher)
Includes a section "giving musical illustrations of the jazz improvisations of 17 of the great soloists such as Louis Armstrong, Charlie Parker, Jack Teagarden, etc. Intended for both beginner and expert." Cur Ref Bks
Notes: p265-66

Hopkins, Jerry
Festival! The book of American music celebrations. . . . Macmillan (N Y) 1970 191p illus $7.95   **781.5**
1 Music festivals 2 Jazz music 3 Music, Popular (Songs, etc.)
"San Jose Rock Festival/Newport Folk Festival/Woodstock Music & Art Fair/Monterey Jazz Festival/Ann Arbor Blues Festival/Memphis Blues Festival/Big Sur Folk Festival/Salinas Country and Western Music Festival/Galax, Va. Fiddlers Convention/North Carolina Bluegrass and Square Dance Festival/Mt. Clemens Pop Festival/Berkeley Folk Festival, Amen!" Title page
Photographs by Jim Marshall and Baron Wolman
This book "was written and photographed by three people connected with 'Rolling Stone' magazine, where much of the material in the book originally appeared. Their prime concern is the rock festival—where it came from, how it happens, where it is going. Most of the text is occupied with reportage of the dozens of festivals that have taken place—or tried to—since the birth of the phenomenon in 1967." Library J

Shaw, Arnold
The rock revolution. Crowell-Collier Press 1969 215p illus lib. bdg. $4.95   **781.5**
1 Jazz music 2 Music, Popular (Songs, etc.)
The author writes about the development of rock music from its beginnings in the 50's until the present time. He discusses Elvis Presley, Bob Dylan, the Beatles, electronic rock, psychedelic rock, and soul. He also mentions the relation of rock music to the social environment of the day
"Arnold Shaw is a veteran music publisher and song writer who knows the entertainment business and is well equipped to write one of the first histories of our current popular music. . . . What is lacking is a critical stand on the part of Mr. Shaw (enthusiasm, disgust, etc.); but for facts quick frozen, the book is valuable." Library J
A glossary of rock: p196-205. Discography: p206-11

Ulanov, Barry
A handbook of jazz. Viking 1957 248p $3.50   **781.5**
1 Jazz music 2 Musicians, American
"A survey of jazz, its musicians, instruments, purposes and schools. With . . . sections on recordings and biographical sketches of its famous personalities." Pub W
"This is an engagingly written book which except in its sometimes pedantic passages, achieves the rare feat of interpreting jazz sounds in language that should (regardless of agreement or disagreement with the author's thesis) enable the nonprofessional enthusiast to listen to jazz with a fuller appreciation of its musical values." N Y Times Bk R
Jazz glossary: p106-11. Further reading: p227-30

Williams, Martin
(ed.) The art of jazz; essays on the nature and development of jazz. Oxford 1959 248p $6   **781.5**
1 Jazz music 2 Musicians

Analyzed in Essay and general literature index
A collection of articles dealing "with every phase of jazz—from Ragtime to Bop, through Dixieland, the Blues, and Modern Jazz Quartet." Pub W
"Hardly half a dozen are in any real sense critical evaluations. The rest are historical, biographical, or merely appreciative essays. These are interesting enough . . . of a certain documentary value, but the critical pieces . . . are much the most rewarding." New Yorker

Jazz masters in transition, 1957-69. Macmillan (N Y) 1970 288p illus (The Macmillan Jazz masters ser) $6.95   **781.5**
1 Jazz music 2 Negro musicians
This volume "covers one of the most important decades in the development of jazz. It includes reviews; interviews; narratives of rehearsals, recording dates, television tapings, nightclub performances; and profiles of such personalities as Thelonious Monk, Miles Davis, Ella Fitzgerald, Dave Brubeck, Ray Charles, and Duke Ellington, as well as young artists newly arrived on the scene. Together, these present a fascinating portrait of a time when new careers were born, established ones flourished, and jazz moved from one great era into another." News of Bks

The jazz tradition. Oxford 1970 232p $6.50   **781.5**
1 Jazz music 2 Musicians, American
Analyzed in Essay and general literature index
These essays on sixteen major jazz figures—players and composers—describe their music and evaluate their individual contributions and show how they influenced one another. (Publisher)
"The discography is important and can be used as the basis for building a library or individual collection. Unfortunately there is no bibliography, and bibliographic notes within the text are skimpy. However, the book does have much to commend it for use in a high school or college jazz course." Library J
Discographical notes: p221-32

781.503 Jazz music—Dictionaries

Feather, Leonard
The encyclopedia of jazz in the sixties; foreword by John Lewis. Horizon Press 1966 312p illus $15   **781.503**
1 Jazz music—Dictionaries 2 Musicians—Dictionaries
This survey contains 1100 biographies of active jazz musicians; a short review of the jazz scene from 1960 to the present, and an article on folk blues. In addition, it includes a list of recordings of the sixties and one of jazz record companies. (Publisher)
"Unfortunately, the book is presented as a retrospective view of the 1960's at a time when there was still a good four years of jazz development left in the decade. Future users will have to remember that the book does not go beyond 1966. Feather's work is probably the only encyclopedia of its kind compiled by one man. Therefore it reflects his own opinions. In a field where factual information is difficult to obtain, Feather has done a remarkable job. There is no other place to get this material." Library J
Bibliography: p311-12

The new edition of The encyclopedia of jazz. Completely rev. enl. and brought up to date. Appreciations by Duke Ellington, Benny Goodman and John Hammond. Horizon Press 1960 527p illus music $15   **781.503**
1 Jazz music—Dictionaries 2 Musicians—Dictionaries 3 Phonograph records
First published 1955 with title: The encyclopedia of jazz
The major part of this reference book is a biographical dictionary of over 2000 jazz musicians. Also included are a brief history of

Feather, Leonard—*Continued*
jazz, an annotated discography and a bibliography and other short articles
"Here is the one book a jazz fan can put his hand upon as if it were a bible." Chicago Sunday Tribune

781.7 Music of ethnic and national orientation

Jones, LeRoi
Black music. Morrow [1967] 221p illus $7.95   **781.7**
1 Negro musicians 2 Jazz music
"Essays, reviews, and notes on modern Negro jazz musicians written by the author between 1959 and 1967. Covered here is the work of such great musicians as John Coltrane, Ornette Coleman, Cecil Taylor, and Thelonious Monk. Illustrated with photographs. Discography." Bk Buyer's Guide
"Sometimes Jones has the musicians speak for themselves, about their art and about their lives. There are voices that White America does not often hear—voices that America needs to hear more. Sometimes Mr. Jones speaks in his own voice (about be-bop, the jazz avant-garde, about musicians he loves). 'Black Music' is lyrical and polemical, visceral and intellectual." Pub W

Blues people; Negro music in white America. Morrow 1963 244p $7.95   **781.7**
1 Negro musicians 2 Blues (Songs, etc.) 3 Jazz music
"I am trying in this book, by means of analogy and some attention to historical example, to establish certain general conclusions about [the Negro] segment of American society. . . . The Negro as slave is one thing. The Negro as American is quite another. But the path the slave took to 'citizenship' is what I want to look at. And I make my analogy through the slave citizen's music—through the music that is most closely associated with him; blues and a later, but parallel development, jazz. . . . If the Negro represents, or is symbolic of something in and about the nature of American culture, this certainly should be revealed by his characteristic music." Introduction

Shankar, Ravi
My music, my life: with an introduction by Yehudi Menuhin. Simon & Schuster 1968 160p illus map music $6.95   **781.7**
1 Music, Indic—History and criticism
The author "writes with remarkable candor of himself, of his spiritual journey, of the music of his people, of his struggle for mastery of the sitar—and of the young people of many lands who have turned to him and his music to bring meaning into their lives." McClurg. Book News
"Many illustrations of musical instruments and of Indian art having to do with music enrich the presentation." Choice

Shaw, Arnold
The world of soul; Black America's contribution to the pop music scene. Cowles 1970 306p illus $6.95   **781.7**
1 Negro musicians 2 Blues (Songs, etc.) 3 Singers
This book "offers an encyclopedic, much needed roster of names, anecdotes, records, quotes and definitions illuminating the story of 'black musical originators' and their 'white polishers and popularizers.' The corrective Shaw gives the subject restores blacks to their rightful important position on the pop music scene, and it even brings to light the neglected role of black disc jockeys and black radio. Generous dollops of history enliven the book—minstrelsy, ragtime, Dixieland jazz, rock 'n' roll—as Shaw . . . conducts his readers through Blues country, the black pop realm of Billy Eckstine and Nat King Cole, Rhythm and Blues, Soul, Gospel and on down to James

Brown, Otis Redding, Aretha Franklin." Pub W
Discography: p295-300

Southern, Eileen
The music of Black Americans: a history. Norton 1971 552p illus music $10   **781.7**
1 Music, American—History and criticism 2 Negro musicians
SBN 393-02156-4
This survey "is so gracefully written and its information so enormously exciting that it could have a wide general readership. Dr. Southern covers everything from the first black music after 1619, with its West African heritage, music in the colonies, during the Revolution, slave festivals and gatherings, plantation entertainments, the anonymous slave composers, the ballad writers of the Gay Nineties, jazzmen of the 20th century, down to today's symphonic composers. There is a combination bibliography and discography that is alone worth the price of the book for its careful choice of pieces of music to be listened to and understood. Many texts of songs, music illustrations and 16 pages of pictorial illustrations." Pub W

781.9 Musical instruments. Words to be sung with music

Dietz, Betty Warner
Musical instruments of Africa; their nature, use, and place in the life of a deeply musical people [by] Betty Warner Dietz and Michael Babatunde Olatunji; illus. by Richard M. Powers. Day 1965 115p illus map music $6.50   **781.9**
1 Musical instruments 2 Music, African
"An introduction by Colin Turnbull sets the pace for this book with its enormous amount of interesting and unusual information on indigenous African musical instruments. Photographs of drums, rattles, and xylophones are generously interspersed with textual material. The reader gets an exciting introductory survey of African musical systems." Library J
List of recordings: p109-10. Books for further reading: p111-12. Additional books for adults: p113-14

Guthrie, Arlo
Alice's restaurant; drawings by Marvin Glass. Grove 1968 unp illus music pa $1.50   **781.9**
"The biggest hit on [Arlo Guthrie's] first recording was a monolog about an arrest and conviction for littering that later kept him out of the draft, a classic tale of sly innocence defeating mindless bureaucracy. Here is the song. 'Alice's Restaurant,' transcribed in all its marvelous ramblings and set to witty, slap-dash two-color drawings. This is an almost new genre, the young adult cartoon book. It will also be an instant hit and a minor classic." Library J
Includes melody with words

782.1 Opera

Cross, Milton
Milton Cross' More stories of the great operas [by] Milton Cross and Karl Kohrs. Doubleday 1971 752p $6.95   **782.1**
1 Operas—Stories, plots, etc.
A companion volume to: The new Milton Cross' Complete stories of the great operas
This book contains interpretations of 45 operas being presented today. Included are 15 classic operas being given on the concert stage, a section of brief histories of the careers of nearly 700 leading singers (past and present), a glossary and a bibliography. (Publisher)

Cross, Milton—*Continued*

The new Milton Cross' Complete stories of the great operas. Rev. and enl. ed. Edited by Karl Kohrs. Doubleday 1955 688p $5.95
782.1

1 Operas—Stories, plots, etc.

Successor to: Milton Cross' Complete stories of the great operas, first published 1947
"Detailed descriptions of [76] famous operas, covering plot, dialogue and every important area. There is a short history of the development of the opera and the ballet as a traditional part of opera. In a chapter on how to enjoy an opera. Mr. Cross has given some advice on what to listen to and look for." Wis Lib Bul
Bibliographies: p670-72

Kobbé, Gustav

Kobbé's Complete opera book; ed. and rev. by the Earl of Harewood. Putnam [1964 c1954] 1262p illus music $10.95
782.1

1 Operas—Stories, plots, etc.

First published 1919
"Discusses the development of opera, giving the stories of more than 200 operas, brief notes on the composers, musical motives, etc. Includes older operas which are still being produced, and modern works which will probably 'be seen by English-speaking audiences during, say, the next ten or fifteen years.' The most complete general guide available." Winchell. Guide to Reference Books. 8th edition
Arranged by centuries, subdivided into countries with all the works of each composer grouped together

782.103 Opera—Dictionaries

Ewen, David

The new Encyclopedia of the opera. Hill & Wang 1971 759p $15
782.103

1 Opera—Dictionaries
ISBN 0-8090-7262-9
First published 1955 by Wyn with title: Encyclopedia of the opera
A "handy source of more than one hundred opera stories, characters, passages brief biographies of composers, librettists, singers, conductors, stage directors, impresarios, teachers, critics, and musicologists, definitions of terms, literary sources, history of opera, and special articles, such as children's operas. . . . It is certain to be enthusiastically acclaimed as a popular guide." Cur Ref Bks

782.8 Theater music

Ewen, David

New Complete book of the American musical theater. Holt 1970 xxv, 800p illus $15
782.8

1 Musical revues, comedies, etc. 2 Composers, American
SBN 03-085060-6
First published 1958 with title: Complete book of the American musical theater
Part one covers over 500 musical shows with details of composer, lyricist, choreographer, performances, stars, hit songs and theater. Part two contains biographies of librettists, lyricists and composers. Appendices include a chronology of the musical theater and a list of outstanding songs and the stars who introduced them. (Publisher)

The story of America's musical theater. [Rev. ed] Chilton Co. 1968 278p $5.50   782.8

1 Musical revues, comedies, etc. 2 Composers, American
First published 1961
A "panorama of musical entertainment in this country. We are introduced to the earliest forms of indigenous musical theater—the burlesque and the minstrel show—and how they helped create the traditions and ritual which have governed our musical theater. We see the birth of American comic opera and American operetta with Reginald De Koven and John Philip Sousa, and are witness to its full flowering with Victor Herbert, Sigmund Romberg, and Rudolf Friml. We are shown how the revue, the musical comedy, and the musical play came into being. . . . This is also the story of many of our theater's foremost composers, from Victor Herbert to Leonard Bernstein, as well as foremost librettists and lyricists." Publisher's note

Gilbert, Sir William Schwenck

The complete plays of Gilbert and Sullivan. Modern Lib. 711p illus $4.95
782.8

1 Operas—Librettos
"Modern Library giant"
"This volume contains the complete, authorized text of the fourteen operas for which Gilbert wrote the librettos and Sullivan the music, with the original illustrations by W. S. Gilbert." Publisher's note

Martyn Green's Treasury of Gilbert & Sullivan. . . . Ed. and annotated by Martyn Green; illus. by Lucille Corcos; arrangements by Albert Sirmay. Simon & Schuster 1961 717p illus music boards $19.95
782.8

1 Operas—Librettos 2 Songs
"The complete librettos of eleven operettas. The words and the music of one hundred and two favorite songs." Subtitle
"Complete libretto of Trial by Jury; The Sorcerer; H.M.S. Pinafore; The Pirates of Penzance; Patience; Iolanthe; Princess Ida; The Mikado; Ruddigore; The Yeomen of the Guard; and the Gondoliers. Selected songs are arranged for piano and voice, and the book also contains 'many of Gilbert's "Bab" sketches, and a text by Martyn Green commenting on the history and background of each operetta, its staging and performance.'" N Y Her Trib Books
"Songs arranged quite simply for voice and piano, lively illustrations (many colored) that are much in the vein, and comments (historical, descriptive, explanatory, and reminiscent) by the knowing editor. . . . No indexes." Library J

Rodgers, Richard

The Rodgers and Hammerstein Song book. . . . Simon & Schuster 1968 320p illus music boards $12.50
782.8

1 Musical revues, comedies, etc. 2 Songs, American
First published 1958
"The stories of the principal musical plays and commentary by Newman Levy. Arrangements by Albert Sirmay, with an introduction by Richard Rodgers and Oscar Hammerstein II. Illustrated by Frederick E. Banbery." Title page
"Here are the words and music of 55 great songs in easily playable arrangements for the piano (with guitar chords for strummers), along with the stories and settings of such earlier triumphs as 'Oklahoma!,' 'Carousel,' 'The King and I,' 'Allegro,' 'South Pacific' and 'State Fair.'" Publisher's note

784 Vocal music

Bacharach, Burt

The Bacharach and David Song book, by Burt Bacharach and Hal David; music edited by Norman Monath; with an introduction by Dionne Warwick. Simon & Schuster 1970 127p music boards $7.50
784

1 Songs 2 Music, Popular (Songs, etc.)
"This large-sized songbook contains 37 songs by composer Burt Bacharach and lyricist Hal David. All of the favorites are included: 'What the World Needs Now,' 'Alfie,'

Bacharach, Burt—*Continued*
... 'Raindrops Keep Fallin' on my Head,' 'Do You Know the Way to San Jose?,' etc. Included are melody lines, piano accompaniments, guitar chord lettering, and lyrics. Pages are nicely laid out: the book opens flat, the notes are large, clear and easily read from a distance." Library J

Ewen, David
The life and death of Tin Pan Alley; the golden age of American popular music. Funk 1964 380p boards $5.95　　**784**
1 Music, Popular (Songs, etc.) 2 Composers, American
From approximately 1885 until 1930 the center of American music publishing was Twenty-eighth Street between Fifth Avenue and Broadway in New York. Tracing "Tin Pan Alley's" rise and fall, this book covers Civil War songs, barbershop harmonies, topical songs, operettas, jazz, the blues, as well as composers, publishers, and performers. (Publisher)
"A detailed index and lists of songs, composers and lyricists, as well as a fairly comprehensive bibliography on popular music give this work ... reference value." Library J

784.03　Vocal music—Dictionaries

Ewen, David
(ed.) American popular songs; from the Revolutionary War to the present. Random House 1966 507p $10　　**784.03**
1 Music, Popular (Songs, etc.)—Dictionaries
2 Songs, American—Dictionaries
Provides basic information on all the great songs "together with anecdotal and historical material of pertinent interest. The over four thousand entries include such information as the names of the authors of lyrics and music; the name of the one who introduced it or made it famous; and when possible, human-interest material about the way the song came to be written and how it first became popular." Publisher's note
There is an "emphasis on Tin Pan Alley, Broadway, and vaudeville, rather than indigenous jazz and folk music." Pub W
"Good browsing, first-rate American social history." Best Sellers

784.09　Vocal music— History and criticism

Krythe, Maymie R.
Sampler of American songs. Harper 1969 245p music $5.95　　**784.09**
1 Songs, American—History and criticism
2 National songs, American—History and criticism
This "exploration of the American past presents the background and folklore of eighteen songs from 'Yankee Doodle Dandy' to 'White Christmas.' The author tells how the songs came to be written, how they have been sung and enjoyed through the years, and little known facts about the lives of the composers." Book News
Bibliography: p233-38

Spaeth, Sigmund
A history of popular music in America. Random House 1948 729p $8.95　　**784.09**
1 Music, Popular (Songs, etc.) 2 Music, American—History and criticism 3 Jazz music
A "serious record, chronologically arranged, of popular song titles which are important artistically or historically, or which the average reader might consider important. Biographical material is inserted at convenient points with emphasis on men who have helped to develop our popular music. Includes foreign importations and outstanding examples of folk music." Booklist

"The author emphasizes patriotic songs, political and martial airs, and then goes into the obscure background of some familiar melodies. There is a complete listing of popular music and an index of songs and instrumental numbers arranged by title and also by composer." Wis Lib Bul
Additional popular music from Colonial times to the present: p587-657. Bibliography: p658-62

784.4　Folk songs

American Heritage
The American Heritage Songbook, by the editors of American Heritage, The Magazine of History. ... Am. Heritage 1969 223p illus music boards $7.95　　**784.4**
1 Folk songs—U.S. 2 Songs, American
SBN 8281-0024-1
"Songs compiled and arranged by Ruth and Norman Lloyd; editor in charge: Kenneth W. Leish; managing editor: Charles W. Folds." Title page
Partial contents: Songs of early America; Frontier songs of work and play; Folk hymns and love songs; Songs of the minstrel stage; Songs of the American Negro; Songs; Songs for the parlor piano; Songs of the Civil War; Songs across the continent; Songs of the turning century; Index of titles and first lines
"In this useful, interesting collection of American songs, each song is accompanied by a short historical note and illustrative diagram or etching. Of special interest is the section dealing with songs of the American Negro. The editors have attempted to portray the songs in their original form without altering lyrics or music. Arrangements for piano and guitar are included, but browsing without benefit of musical background is also entertaining and enlightening." Library J

Boni, Margaret Bradford
(ed.) Fireside book of folk songs; selected and ed. by Margaret Bradford Boni; arranged for the piano by Norman Lloyd; illus. by Alice and Martin Provensen. Simon & Schuster [1966 c1947] 323p illus music $7.95　　**784.4**
1 Folk songs
Reprint of the 1947 edition with guitar chords added
"Words, music and bright pictures: 147 favorite [international folk] songs: Ballads, work songs, marching songs, spirituals, hymns and carols." Los Angeles. School Libraries
"This is a good cross-section lot, no two ways about it. ... One of the best things about the volume is the spirited, colorful way in which it is illustrated." San Francisco Chronicle
There are indexes of first lines and titles

Lomax, Alan
(ed.) The folk songs of North America in the English language. ... Doubleday 1960 xxx, 623p illus music $10　　**784.4**
1 Folk songs—U.S.
"Melodies and guitar chords transcribed by Peggy Seeger; with one hundred piano arrangements by Matyas Seiber and Don Banks. Illustrated by Michael Leonard; editorial assistant: Shirley Collins." Title page
Includes words, music, and origins of over 300 American folk songs including ballads, work songs and spirituals, as well as a book list, guitar guide, and a discography
"Divides his material into four sections— 'The North,' 'The Southern Mountains and Backwoods,' 'The West,' and 'The Negro South.' ... There is not a single important folk-song type practiced by the English-speaking people of the United States which is not represented here." San Francisco Chronicle
Maps on lining-papers

Lomax, John A.

(comp.) American ballads and folk songs; collected and comp. by John A. Lomax and Alan Lomax; with a foreword by George Lyman Kittredge. Macmillan (N Y) 1934 xxxix, 625p music $8.95   784.4

1 Folk songs—U.S.   2 Ballads, American 3 Negro spirituals

A "collection of nearly 300 American ballads and folk songs, many of them with music. It includes Creole French and Texan-Spanish songs as indigenous, but excludes the English and Scottish ballads of the southern Appalachians as importations. Songs of the American Indian are omitted. In the case of variants the compilers have attempted to present 'the best examples of the most noteworthy types, words and tunes.'" Book Rev Digest

"Professor Lomax shares the experiences of the collector with great freshness and charm. People, scenes and ways of existence come to life in his running sketches. He uncompromisingly states that these songs belong to literature, and so they do." New Republic

Bibliography compiled by Harold W. Thompson: p613-21

(comp.) Cowboy songs and other frontier ballads. Rev. and enl. Collected by John A. Lomax and Alan Lomax. Macmillan (N Y) 1938 xxxvii, 431p illus music $8.95   784.4

1 Cowboys—Songs and music   2 Ballads, American 3 Folk songs—U.S.

Slightly enlarged edition of a collection first published 1910

"Professor Lomax has collected more than 150 songs which were orally preserved on remote cattle ranches of the Southwest. They deal with a variety of themes, including logging, the saw-mill, the Mexican war, outlaws, gold-mining, stage-driving and cow-punching." Pittsburgh

This "collection of songs and ballads by the Lomaxes, noted for their pioneer work in this area, will be welcomed by librarians, folklorists, and Americana enthusiasts." Library J

(ed.) Folk song: U.S.A.; the 111 best American ballads; collected, adapted and arranged by John A. Lomax and Alan Lomax; Alan Lomax, editor; Charles Seeger and Ruth Crawford Seeger, music editors. Duell 1947 407p music $10   784.4

1 Folk songs—U.S. 2 Ballads, American

"American folk songs collected by the famous father-son team, each section prefaced by a long and lively introduction. There are chapters on Spirituals, Railroad Songs, Farmers' Tunes, Lumberjack Ballads, Sailors' Chanteys, Love Songs, Work Songs, and Cowboy Ditties." Retail Bookseller

Includes music for piano and guitar

Makeba, Miriam

(ed.) The world of African song; music edited by Jonas Gwangwa and E. John Miller, Jr. Introduction and notes by Solomon Mbabi-Katana; illus. by Dean Alexander. Quadrangle Bks. 1971 119p illus music $10   784.4

1 Folk songs, African
SBN 8129-0138-X

These 25 African folk songs, selected by singer Miriam Makeba, are "arranged for piano, guitar and percussion, with brief notes that explain the meaning of each song and describe its rhythm pattern. Lyrics are provided in the authentic African language (with a pronunciation guide) and also in English." News of Bks

"African songs, mainly of the Zulu and Xhosa peoples, chosen from the repertoire of Miriam Makeba. Sonomon Mbabi-Katana's introduction contains illuminating comments on black folk music. . . . [The] illustrations are superb. The musical notation and transliterated lyrics are large and clear." N Y Times Bk R

Index of first lines: p117. Discography: p119

Sandburg, Carl

(ed.) The American songbag. Harcourt 1927 xxiii, 495p illus music $7.95   784.4

1 Folk songs—U.S. 2 Ballads, American

The song history of America is traced through this "collection of 280 songs. . . . The music includes not merely airs and melodies, but complete harmonizations or piano accompaniments." Introduction

"Songs and ballads from every section of the country which reflect the spirit of the time and place as well as the mood of the singer—songs of the Negro, the pioneer, the Irish immigrant, the Southern mountaineer, the Great Lakes bargeman, the jailbird, the hobo, the section hand, the lumberjack, the soldier. the college student. The collection is a commentary on American life with sidelights on American history." Book Rev Digest

"Each song is introduced by Mr Sandburg, who in a few words gives the story of his discovery or of its origin. Those notes make fascinating reading, and they can be enjoyed by those who cannot read notes." Springf'd Republican

784.7 Other kinds of songs

Johnson, James Weldon

(ed.) The books of American Negro spirituals. . . . [By] James Weldon Johnson and J. Rosamond Johnson. Viking 1940 2v in 1 music $6.95   784.7

1 Negro spirituals

A re-issue of the volumes first published separately in 1925 and 1926. Each volume has special title page

Includes "The book of American Negro spirituals" (1925) and "The second book of Negro spirituals" (1926). Contains words and music of 120 spirituals. Spiral binding

Music arrangements by J. Rosamond Johnson, additional numbers by Lawrence Brown

Shaw, Martin

(ed.) National anthems of the world; ed. by Martin Shaw, Henry Coleman and T. M. Cartledge. [3d and rev. ed] Pitman 1969 456p music $12.50   784.7

1 National songs

First published 1960

"Each anthem is presented with the words in the original language (or languages) set to the music and where necessary with a transliterated phonetic version, so that it may be sung by people of other tongues. The English translations are placed within the music or, in a few instances, set at the foot in a free translation. . . . The present edition contains 150 anthems, including 20 new anthems in all." Publisher's note

"Brief but vital footnotes throughout make this a useful guide to adoption dates, composers, general usage of anthems et al." Music J

790 Recreation (Recreational arts)

Mulac, Margaret E.

Games and stunts for schools, camps, and playgrounds; illus. by Julianne. Harper 1964 362p illus music $5.95   790

1 Games

"The major sections of the book cover: classroom games and activities; circle and line; hide and seek; tag and chase games; picnic games and contests; dance mixers; sidewalk games; group stunts; word and spelling games. . . . Piano score is included for many games." Publisher's note

"The book will prove invaluable to parents, teachers, counselors and recreation workers." Books of the Year 1965

791.3   Circuses

Fenner, Mildred Sandison
(ed.) The circus, lure and legend; comp. and ed. by Mildred Sandison Fenner and Wolcott Fenner. Prentice-Hall 1970 208p illus $9.95   **791.3**

1 Circus
ISBN 0-13-134551-6

This book offers "a lively and varied assortment of stories about circuses, circus life, circus people, legends, oddities, animal acts and the apparently endless history of man's most ancient form of mass entertainment. The Fenners draw from many sources, including bits and excerpts from Carl Sandburg, E. B. White, Tarkington, Saroyan and even Hemingway, and go as far back as Pompey. . . . P. T. Barnum, of course, along with his Tom Thumb and his Siamese Twins and unabashedly flamboyant hokum, gets a big play in the book—which carries right through the 1950s, when the modern circus began to suffer the inroads of TV. This promises to be a . . . book of some appeal, with some 50 photos and illustrations supporting a nostalgia that will probably outlive our age of computerized sophistication." Pub W

791.43   Motion-picture entertainment

Colman, Hila
Making movies: student films to features; illus. by George Guzzi. World Pub. 1969 191p illus (Careers in the making ser) $4.95, lib. bdg. $5.20   **791.43**

1 Moving pictures as a profession

In this book, actors, directors, producers, cameramen, costume designers, and script girls tell of their careers. Chapters cover different types of films, as well as details on the education, training, and union requirements for jobs in the film industry. (Publisher)

"Films referred to and film-makers interviewed are well-chosen and current (e.g. 'Alice's Restaurant,' Tim Hunter); however, still photographs would have supplemented these interviews far more aptly than do the gray and white line drawings." Library J

Gessner, Robert
The moving image; a guide to cinematic literacy. Dutton 1968 444p illus $8.95   **791.43**

1 Moving picture plays—History and criticism

"Maintaining that 'the key that can unlock most of the secrets of cinema is the shooting script,' Mr. Gessner systematically studies cinema as a story-telling art form. Focusing on 'conflict,' he elaborates his thesis in the first six chapters by using the salient features of the shooting script. The remaining seven chapters also contribute immeasurably to give the reader guidelines to evolve seeing into perceiving. This 'shot-awareness' of a film is necessary for any appreciative understanding of 'the ninth art.' . . . A knowledgeable, practical, enlightening, readable book, [this] is a major contribution to the film as art." Best Sellers
Bibliography: p409-20. Glossary: p421-25

Griffith, Richard
The movies, by Richard Griffith and Arthur Mayer, with the assistance of Eileen Bowser. Rev. ed. Simon & Schuster 1970 494p illus $19.95   **791.43**

1 Moving pictures—History
First published 1957

"The best popular work on American cinema available. . . . The book can certainly stand on its own as a comprehensive guide to movies and the moviemaking industry in this country from the days of Edwin S. Porter and the Edison Company to today's low-budget films and

highly independent directors. But it is not basically a critical reference work: too little is said about the foreign film and its effect upon the American industry (although the updated section has remedied this somewhat); virtually no attention is given experimental cinema (names like Belson and Mekas are not to found): and there are the occasional, inevitable inaccuracies. . . . Rather, this is a book to lean back with, to browse through, to 'enjoy.' " Library J

International motion picture almanac. Quigley illus $13   **791.43**

1 Moving pictures—Directories 2 Moving pictures—Biography

Annual. First published 1929 with title: Motion picture almanac
Title: 1952-1954. Motion picture and television almanac

Contains a Who's who of motion-picture world personalities: "also lists directories of corporations, theater circuits, members of the press dealing with motion pictures, syndicates, and agencies of various kinds. It also lists motion pictures of all types produced during the year covered and surveys the industry in various countries of the world, giving some statistical data. Also sections on codes and censorship and a buyers' guide to motion-picture and theater supplies and equipment." Murphey. How and Where to Look it Up

Jacobs, Lewis
(ed.) The movies as medium; selected, arranged and introduced by Lewis Jacobs. Farrar, Straus 1970 335p illus $8.95   **791.43**

1 Moving pictures
Analyzed in Essay and general literature index

This is a compilation of essays on various aspects of filmmaking by such people as Sergei Eisenstein, Arthur Goldsmith, Stanley Kubrick and Michelangelo Antonioni. The "five main sections are Image, Movement (mostly of the camera) Time and Space, Color, and Sound, each section with an introductory article by Jacobs. . . . The book begins with a [series] of short statements by directors, and it closes, in summation, with a section called The Plastic Structure." New Repub

"The presentation is unified not only by Jacobs' incisive introduction to each section but also by each essayist's consistent interest in the effect of these processes on an audience. [The book] can be recommended with assurance to anyone wishing to learn about the aesthetics of film." Library J
Selected bibliography: p323-28

Larson, Rodger
Young filmmakers, by Rodger Larson with Ellen Meade; original photographs by Marcelo Montealegre. Dutton 1969 190p illus $5.95, lib. bdg. $5.89   **791.43**

1 Moving pictures 2 Moving picture photography

This book begins with "descriptions of some of the films that teen-agers are making today and goes on to discuss various techniques, the nature of visual language, types and selection of equipment, the sequence of steps involved in shooting a film, problems of casting and directing, the responsibilities of director and cameraman, editing the film, and ways of creating a sound track." Horn Bk
Glossary: p174-83

792   Theater (Stage presentations)

Cole, Toby
(ed.) Actors on acting. . . . Ed. with introductions & biographical notes by Toby Cole and Helen Krich Chinoy. New rev. ed. Crown 1970 715p $8.95   **792**

1 Acting 2 Actors and actresses
1949 edition analyzed in Essay and general literature index

Cole, Toby—*Continued*

First published 1949
"The theories, techniques, and practices of the great actors of all times as told in their own words." Title page
This collection contains over 100 selections ranging "from ancient Greece and Rome to present-day U.S. but only Western countries are represented; arrangement is by country. In some cases quotations from authors or critics amplify an actors' statements and the editors preface each selection with further explanatory data. The bibliography is extensive and is arranged by country." Booklist

Cornberg, Sol

A stage crew handbook, by Sol Cornberg and Emanuel L. Gebauer; drawings by Jack Forman. Rev. ed. Harper 1957 291p illus $5.95
         792

1 Theaters—Stage setting and scenery 2 Theaters—Lighting 3 Theater—Production and direction

First published 1941
The "book covers the technical processes and problems of the stage, especially for the apprentice learning to build scenery and to operate lights. Sections on the technical director and the designer are for those skilled in play production." Booklist

Corson, Richard

Stage makeup. 4th ed. Appleton 1967 xxii, 456p illus $12.50
         792

1 Make-up, Theatrical

First published 1942
The author discusses the various aspects of theatrical makeup, including character analysis, facial anatomy, color, light and shade, rubber prosthesis, beards and mustaches, hair and wigs, and fashions in makeup. Appendices include a list of makeup materials, sources of such materials, period hair styles, and a make-up color chart
"He has given excellent examples, both textual and pictorial. The careful color chart, though complicated, is thorough. . . . Problems are realistically treated and sample kits are outlined." Library J

Guthrie, Tyrone

Tyrone Guthrie on acting. Viking 1971 96p illus $8.95
         792

1 Acting 2 Theater
SBN 670-73832-8
"A Studio book"
This book "written mainly for young actors and for amateurs, teachers, and students of acting, argues the case for a serious professional approach to theatre. . . . After establishing that good acting is as much a matter of technique as of imagination or intuition and can therefore, at least to some extent, be taught, the author analyzes the relation between student and teacher as well as methods of teaching. . . . [He discusses] stage craft, . . . technique, make-up, movement, vocal training; . . . the real value of improvisation; [and] the legitimate theatre as opposed to mass media." Publisher's note
"Guthrie's relevant stories of some of the great performers of his youth (Duse, Bernhardt) are enlivened by a large folio of photos ranging from early in the century to a 1970 Café La Mama production." Pub W

Kelly, F. M.

Shakespearian costume. Completely rev. by Alan Mansfield. [2d ed. rev. and reset] Theatre Arts 1970 123p illus $8.75
         792

1 Costume—History 2 Shakespeare, William —Stage setting and scenery

First published 1938 in England with title: Shakespearian costume for stage and screen
"There are here chapters on men's and women's clothes of the period 1570-1620 in England, and, remembering that various of Shakespeare's plays have foreign settings, a chapter on the characteristics of foreign dress. The long section on arms and armour is celebrated, and shoes, headwear and the dressing

of the hair are also dealt with. Specific suggestions for the costuming and staging of the more frequently produced plays of Shakespeare are put forward. . . . Mr. Kelly gives helpful suggestions to aid actors in breaking through that irrational, but deeprooted, apprehension that in wearing unfamiliar raiment they are only playing the fool. There is also a helpful 'Don't' checklist of frequently committed gaffes." Publisher's note

Tompkins, Julia

Stage costumes and how to make them. Plays, inc. [1969 c1968] 160p illus $4.95   792

1 Costume

First copyright 1968 in England
The author explains "how costumes needed to dress any production from Saxon times to the nineteen-thirties can be made up simply and cheaply from quite simple basic patterns. Her diagrams follow the conventions of modern pattern layouts, with average measurements clearly laid out for the needlewoman with no experience of pattern-making. There is a chapter on the construction of farthingales, hoops, crinolines and bustles, and advice is also given on stripping and dyeing materials." Publisher's note
"Unpretentious and practical this is a handbook to be welcomed by the amateur or student faced with costume making." Booklist

792.025   Theater—Annuals

Theatre world. Crown illus $8.95   792.025

1 Theater—U.S.

Annual. First published 1944/45. Editor: 1944/45-1963/64, Daniel Blum; 1964/65-date [1971] John Willis
Each issue includes: Broadway calendar, Plays from other seasons that ran through this season, Plays from other seasons that closed during this season, Plays that opened out of town but did not arrive on Broadway, Theatre World Award winners, Portraits of promising personalities, Biographies of players, Obituaries, and other features

792.03   Theater—Dictionaries

The Oxford Companion to the theatre; ed. by Phyllis Hartnoll. 3d ed. Oxford 1967 1088p illus $15
         792.03

1 Theater—Dictionaries

First published 1951
"Articles include names of actors, playwrights, scene designers, and sometimes producers; titles of plays and dates of first performances, descriptions of playhouses and touring companies; and comments on the effect on the theater of changing times and ideologies. There are separate articles on actors and dramatists, on music, ballet, and puppetry, on technical and structural aspects of production, and on every subject pertaining to the theater. All these articles are delightful to read and, since the 57 contributors are experts on the theater, factually correct. . . . Actors, students, playgoers, and playhouse personnel will find this handbook a source of pleasure as well as information." Cur Ref Bks
Select list of theater books: p1029-74

792.09   Theater—History

Adams, John Cranford

The Globe Playhouse; its design and equipment. [2d ed] Barnes & Noble 1961 435p illus $8.50
         792.09

1 Southwark, England. Globe Theatre 2 Theater—Great Britain—History 3 Shakespeare, William—Stage history

First published 1942
"The aim of this book is to reconstruct as fully as possible the design and equipment of the Globe Playhouse. . . . This study was based

Adams, John C.—*Continued*

primarily on two assumptions: the first that the requirements of Elizabethan plays—requirements both explicit and implicit—necessarily reflect the design, equipment, and conventions of the stages for which they were written; and the second that as far as possible 'all' the evidence should be taken into account." Preface

"From Mr. Adams' patient marshaling and evaluation of minutiae there emerges a vivid picture of the many-leveled, complex and flexible Elizabethan stage." Theatre Arts

Includes bibliographical footnotes

Blum, Daniel

A pictorial history of the American theatre, 1860-1970. New 3d ed. enl. and rev. by John Willis. Crown 1969 416p illus $12.50   792.09

1 Theater—U.S.—History 2 Actors and actresses—Pictures, illustrations, etc.

First published 1950 by Greenberg

Photographs present the stars of the 100 years covered. There is also a brief commentary concerning the hit plays and the stars of each year

Includes index to plays and players

Ernst, Earle

The Kabuki theatre. Oxford 1956 xxiii, 296p illus $7.50   792.09

1 Theater—Japan—History 2 Japanese drama —History and criticism

"The influences of the Japanese puppet theater, aristocratic Nō plays, and modern Western drama on the kabuki theater are discussed in a detailed review. Acting conventions, favorite themes, mechanical devices, and staging are explained as well as the basic function of kabuki as one expression of Japanese life and culture. Particularly helpful to the student are a glossary of theater terms and a bibliography of titles in Western languages." Booklist

"Mr. Ernst's is an excellent account and the illustrations are a pleasure to behold. This is definitely a book to be included in any library of the theater." N Y Her Trib Books

Freedley, George

A history of the theatre [by] George Freedley and John A. Reeves; 3d newly rev. ed. with a supplementary section by George Freedley and a group of eminent scholars and critics; with hundreds of illustrations from photographs, playbills, contemporary prints, etc. Crown 1968 1008p illus $10   792.09

1 Theater—History

First published 1941

"An up-to-date history of world theatre from pre-Greek days to the most modern American, and a highly readable account of each form, type, and artistic movement in the drama." McClurg. Book News

The "whole story is here in rich condensation, sympathetically analyzed and soundly appraised, with good working supplements in the form of an extended bibliography and a voluminous index." Christian Science Monitor

Hartnoll, Phyllis

The concise history of theatre. Abrams 1968 288p illus $7.50   792.09

1 Theater—History

"An authoritative, readable survey of the theater of Europe and America from ancient Greece to the present by an English theatrical historian. Concentrating on play production rather than on drama as literature, Hartnoll follows the evolution of theater architecture, scenery, costume, stagecraft, direction and acting, noting innovations as they appear and devoting as much attention to outstanding actors, managers, and directors as to playwrights. Numerous and varied illustrations in color and black and white with explanatory captions are helpfully tied in with the text by marginal notations." Booklist

Bibliography: p283-84

Hewitt, Barnard

History of the theatre from 1800 to the present. Random House 1970 210p illus (An Original Random House Study on the history of the theatre) pa $3.95   792.09

1 Theater—History

First volume in a planned series of concise studies on theater history. "Concerned with the development of Western theater from 1800 to the present, it is surprisingly detailed on the growth of theatrical styles in playwriting, directing, acting, and production. Framed in correlative matter on economic, political, and social change throughout the last century, Hewitt's work describes the indebtedness of today's theater and cites contemporary innovations. Special attention is given to influential plays and playwrights, managers, directors, actors, designers, critics, and theorists. . . . Almost 40 carefully selected illustrations and an informative bibliography complete this." Choice

Hodges, C. Walter

Shakespeare's theatre; written and illus. by C. Walter Hodges. Coward-McCann 1964 103p illus map $5.95   792.09

1 Theater—Great Britain—History 2 Shakespeare, William—Stage history 3 Southwark, England. Globe Theatre

The author "describes in word and picture how the idea of the theatre in Shakespeare's time developed gradually from pagan festivals and religious drama to the playhouses of the sixteenth century. One playhouse in particular [is described]. . . . This was Shakespeare's theatre; the place where his plays were staged and he himself acted in them. The author [also] describes a typical performance of 'Julius Caesar' at The Globe." Publisher's note

"Typography, format, text and illustrations are handsome; the beautiful pictures are filled with informative detail and are well-placed in relation to the textual reference. The text is written with simplicity and authority, describing the emergence of Elizabethan theatre from the travelling companies that developed after the early Mysteries and Moralities. The last part of the book is particularly interesting, since it gives unusual information about theatres of Shakespeare's period, information about mechanical devices used in production or about unusual architectural details." Chicago. Children's Book Center

Laver, James

Costume in the theatre. Hill & Wang [1965c 1964] 212p illus $6.50   792.09

1 Costume—History

"The author traces the history of theatre costume from primitive times through the Greek and Roman theatres, medieval mysteries, Shakespeare, opera, ballet, etc., up to the present." Bk Buyer's Guide

This "is almost a history of theatre itself. . . . The select bibliography (four pages) is from Mr. Laver's sources and should be of great value in retreading the ground he has covered. . . . [The book] will be of great importance to schools and universities offering courses in theatrical costume." Library J

No glossary or index

Samachson, Dorothy

The dramatic story of the theatre [by] Dorothy & Joseph Samachson. Abelard-Schuman 1955 168p illus $4.95   792.09

1 Theater—History 2 Drama—History and criticism

A "well-documented history of the theatre, from ancient Greece and Rome to the present day. The authors describe the theater of Shakespeare and the major developments of dramatic production in Norway, Moscow, Dublin, Germany and the United States. There is a brief discussion of the drama of the Far East, particularly China. The book closes with strong pleas for the re-vitalization of the theater in America." Chicago. Children's Book Center

"This short history of world theater relates its actors, audiences, playwrights, and dramas to changing social trends. . . . A somewhat cursory review useful for the reader without

Samachson, Dorothy—*Continued*

the time or patience for longer, more substantial histories of world theater." Booklist
Selected bibliography: p162

Smith, Irwin

Shakespeare's Globe Playhouse; a modern reconstruction in text and scale drawings. Based upon the reconstruction of the Globe by John Cranford Adams; with an introduction by James G. McManaway. Scribner [1962 c1956] xxiii, 240p illus maps $12.50
                                                        792.09

1 Shakespeare, William—Stage history 2 Southwark, England. Globe Theatre

First published 1956
The author presents "a full discussion of the acting area, the seating capacity, the robing rooms and production methods; indications of how well suited this particular stage was to the sequence of scenes in many of the plays; discussion of the style and techniques of the carpenters and builders, the use of hoists and trapdoors—in brief as thorough a book on the Elizabethan stage as has come to hand in decades and one of absorbing interest to anyone who knows or would like to know Shakespeare as a dramatist and playwright." Best Sellers
"The special feature of this study is the set of scale drawings developed from the model which will be of help to Shakespearean students of any age interested in making similar scale models. Notes on producing Shakespeare's plays on the Globe's stage will interest theater groups." Booklist
Bibliography: p225-28

Taubman, Howard

The making of the American theatre; with a foreword by Richard Rodgers. Rev. ed. Coward-McCann 1967 402p illus $10   792.09

1 Theater—U.S.—History

First published 1965
The book traces "the rise of the American theatre from Colonial times to the forces that revolutionized the U.S. theatre in the twentieth century—Eugene O'Neill and the artistic awakening of the 1920's, the development of the Broadway musical the flowering of Off Broadway in the 1950's, and the burgeoning national repertory movement of the 1960's." Publisher's note
"Immensely informative, frank, responsible, provocative and full of warm nostalgia. . . . The achievement of the book is the grand, panoramic view it provides of two centuries of theatre in this country." N Y Times Bk R

Thorndike, Ashley H.

Shakespeare's theater. Macmillan (N Y) 1916 472p illus map $6.95   792.09

1 Theater—Great Britain—History 2 Shakespeare, William—Stage history

"The author's aim has been to bring together in one volume all that is known about the theater in Shakespeare's time. The work contains about thirty illustrations and sixteen pages of bibliographical notes." Cleveland
"It seems to us that Professor Thorndike has given us [one of] the truest pictures we have of the conditions under which Shakespeare and his fellows composed their plays, of the characteristics of the histrionic art of the age and of the distinctive qualities and outlook of the audiences they addressed." Nation

792.8 Ballet

Balanchine, George

Balanchine's New complete stories of the great ballets; ed. by Francis Mason; drawings by Marta Becket. Doubleday 1968 xxi, 626p illus $10   792.8

1 Ballets—Stories, plots, etc. 2 Ballet

First published 1954 with title: Balanchine's Complete stories of the great ballets
Besides stories of over two hundred ballets, there are sections on how to enjoy the ballet, a history of the ballet with a chronology of outstanding events since 1469, guides to selected readings and recordings and an illustrated glossary. (Publisher)
The stories "range through the whole repertory of other people's ballets as well as his own. The style is charming, and the author often makes comments on an intimate feature that reflect his long association with choreographers and dancers." New Yorker
Glossary: p559-79. Annotated selection of ballet recordings: p581-98. Selected reading guide: p599-605

De Mille, Agnes

To a young dancer; a handbook; illus. by Milton Johnson. Little 1962 175p illus $4.95
                                                        792.8

1 Ballet—Handbooks, manuals, etc. 2 Dancing

"An Atlantic Monthly Press book"
"A direct, succinct, wise, witty handbook for the would-be dancer. . . . It covers every aspect of a career—from early training and evaluation of schools [and colleges] to good manners, human relationships, and acceptance of criticism. There is much sage advice on how to dance and how to choreograph; there is no jargon at all. Because the approach to dancing turns out to be the approach to any discipline (approach, really, to living), this book has appeal and meaning for readers beyond the specialized group of aspiring dancers." Horn Bk
Suggested reading: p147-48. Commerical films: p165-75

793 Indoor games and amusements

Gibson, Walter

Family games America plays; illus. by Murray Keshner and Robert Michaels. Doubleday 1970 275p illus $5.95   793

1 Games

"For parents, young people, and group recreational leaders of young people, a compendium of [seventy-four] popular and less commonly known games with their basic rules, sample plays, and permissible variations clearly stated, outlined, and diagrammed. Contents cover group games, games for two people, board games, card games, assorted domino games, mah-jongg, and such games as darts, tiddlywinks, and others that require varied equipment." Booklist

793.3 Dancing

Haskell, Arnold L.

The wonderful world of dance. Doubleday 1969 96p illus boards $3.95, lib. bdg. $4.70
                                                        793.3

1 Dancing—History

First published 1960
The author explains how dance began and why different dances grew up throughout the world, over the centuries. He then explores ritual dancing, dancing as a way of building minds and bodies, and dancing as entertainment. (Publisher)
"Of special interest to the devotee of the dance, the book is also admirably suited to the reader who has only general interest and background; it never becomes too technical." Chicago. Children's Book Center
Glossary: p75-93

McDonagh, Don

The rise and fall and rise of modern dance. Outerbridge & Dienstfrey; distributed by Dutton 1970 344p illus $6.95   793.3

1 Modern dance
ISBN 0-87690-013-9

McDonagh, Don—*Continued*

This book "summarizes the history and current state of modern dance, tracing its development from . . . Isadora Duncan, Loie Fuller and Ruth St. Denis, to . . . Martha Graham, Doris Humphrey and Charles Weidman, . . . Merce Cunningham and on to the current avant-garde." Newsweek

793.3025 Dancing—Annuals

Dance world. Crown illus $10   **793.3025**

1 Dancing—U.S. 2 Dancers

Annual. First published 1966. Editor: 1966— John Willis

"A comprehensive, pictorial, and statistical record of the dance in America. In addition to the photographs of dance scenes and stars, there are repertoires, lists of dancers in ballet, modern, and ethnic company performances, regional companies, festivals, and biographies of choreographers and featured dancers." Book News

793.7 Mathematical games and recreations

Bakst, Aaron

Mathematical puzzles and pastimes. 2d ed. Van Nostrand 1965 242p illus $6.95   **793.7**

1 Mathematical recreations

First published 1954

"The present volume represents a systematic discussion of various mathematical recreations with the view toward developing and systematizing the methods for the solution and treatment of recreational material." Preface

"All mathematical principles have been meticulously preserved and simplified for easy comprehension. Special applications discussed by the author include such things as electronic computing machines with an analysis of the various abaci and relations between the Roman, Mayan, Chinese and Japanese systems of numeration, all of great importance in modern computation devices." Publisher's note

Ball, W. W. Rouse

Mathematical recreations & essays; rev. ed. H. S. M. Coxeter. 11th ed. Macmillan (N Y) 1939 418p illus $6   **793.7**

1 Mathematical recreations

"This has been a standard work since 1892 for those seeking recreation by solving mathematical problems having, according to the author little or no practical use. . . . [It preserves] the entertainment provided by previous editions . . . and maintains the character of the original." N Y New Tech Bks

Contents: Arithmetical recreations; Geometrical recreations; Polyhedra; Chessboard recreations; Magic squares; Map-coloring problems; Unicursal problems; Kirkman's schoolgirls problem; Miscellaneous problems; Three classical geometrical problems; Calculating prodigies; Cryptography and cryptanalysis

Friend, J. Newton

More Numbers: fun & facts. Scribner 1961 201p illus $3.50   **793.7**

1 Mathematical recreations 2 Arithmetic

"The first half of the book includes chapters on digits and primes, problems with digits and letters, squares magic and otherwise. . . . The second half presents 100 problems [posed in anecdote form] of varying degrees of difficulty." Publisher's note

Incidents frequently refer to English customs

Numbers: fun & facts. Scribner 1954 208p illus $3.50   **793.7**

1 Mathematical recreations 2 Arithmetic

"Tells how numbers originated, and of the traditions, legends and superstitions that have collected around numbers." The AAAS Science Book List for Young Adults

"A book of entertaining mathematical puzzles and oddities with their scientific explanations. Appealing to those interested in cryptography and mathematics." A Basic Book Collection for High Schools

Still More Numbers: fun & facts. Scribner 1964 206p illus $3.50   **793.7**

1 Mathematical recreations 2 Arithmetic

"Material on mathematical prodigies, prime numbers, and digit conversions is included in a book containing 90 problems. Answers are appended." Booklist

Gardner, Martin

Martin Gardner's New mathematical diversions from Scientific American. Simon & Schuster 1966 253p illus boards $5.95   **793.7**

1 Mathematical recreations

This collection of 20 expanded and revised magazine columns ranges "in scope from fun with the binary system and pi to group theory, paper cutting, packing spheres, Graeco-Latin squares, color cubes, and the calculus of finite differences. Most of the problems are from classical mathematics out of which has arisen some of the newer, modern mathematics. Solutions are given to the problems and many of these solutions are truly ingenious." Library J

Gardner's "talent for ferreting out new problems, genius for expounding them, and above all, his wonderful good humor, challenge and exhilarate. From a teacher's viewpoint, there is something here for everyone." Science Bks

References for further reading: p247-53

The unexpected hanging, and other mathematical diversions. Simon & Schuster 1969 255p illus $5.95   **793.7**

1 Mathematical recreations

The author's "collection of mathematical puzzles takes the reader into mysterious worlds: The Chicago Magic Convention and the Church of the Fourth Dimension, gambling methods and geometric dissections, a Matchbox-Game. Learning machine; Borromean Rings and replicating figures to the transcendental number e." Am News of Bks

Kadesch, Robert R.

Math menagerie; drawings by Mark A. Binn; illus. with photographs. Harper 1970 112p illus $4.50   **793.7**

1 Mathematical recreations

"By using inexpensive materials in twenty-five experiments, the reader learns how mathematics works. The topics treated in the seven independent sections are probability, binary numerals, unusual numbers, menagerie of shapes, soap-film mathematics, mappings and transformations, and mathematical machines. Even without doing the experiments, an interested . . . student can get the taste and feel of modern mathematics and learn a few tricks in the process." Best Sellers

Latcha, Alfred G.

How do you figure it? Modern mental exercises in logic and reasoning. Barnes, A.S. 1970 69p illus $3.95   **793.7**

1 Puzzles 2 Mathematical recreations

SBN 498-06964-8

This collection contains one hundred and twenty posers which "are neither puzzles, riddles, tricks, nor problems in mathematics, but are statements of facts from which people with no special knowledge can reason to a logical conclusion." Publisher's note

"Solutions are found at the back of a book suitable for either individual or group use." Booklist

Longley-Cook, L. H.

New math puzzle book. Van Nostrand 1970 176p illus map $4.95   **793.7**

1 Mathematical recreations

"A collection of 100 puzzles ranging from very simple to fairly complex comprises this

Longley-Cook, L. H.—*Continued*
book. The mathematical concepts involved include simple logic, elementary number theory, symmetry, and such topological notions as that of the Mobius strip.'' Science Bks
''Since familiarity with new mathematics is not required, puzzle fans of all ages will find the problems a stimulating challenge to their powers of concentration and logical thought.'' Booklist

794.1 Chess

Horowitz, I. A.
First book of chess, with pocket chessboard, by I. A. Horowitz and Fred Reinfeld. Barnes & Noble [1958 c1952] 128p illus pa $1.25   794.1
1 Chess
''Everyday handbook series''
First published 1950 by the editors of ''Chess Review'' with title: Let's play chess! This edition published 1952 by Sterling
Two chess champions cover first steps and different moves, giving concise instructions that make it possible to learn to play in a few sittings. They show how to mount an attack, discuss tactical moves and their values, give 29 different kinds of openings and defenses, each with diagrams

Reinfeld, Fred
Chess for young people. Holt 1961 111p illus $3.95   794.1
1 Chess
After giving a brief history of chess, telling of famous players, championship matches, and chess-playing organizations throughout the world, the author then identifies each chess piece and explains its role in the game. Opening, middle game, and endgame plays are covered. Chess problems and endgame compositions are also included. (Publisher)
Illustrated with diagrams, this is a ''concise instructional guide for amateurs of any age.'' Booklist

The complete chessplayer. Prentice-Hall 1953 292p illus $6.95   794.1
1 Chess
''Useful information for chess players of all abilities, from the beginner to the seasoned player. . . . A special feature of the book is the inclusion of almost a score of illustrated games, showing various kinds of offense and defense.'' Huntting

795 Games of chance

Foster, R. F.
Foster's Complete Hoyle; an encyclopedia of games. Lippincott illus $5.95   795
1 Cards 2 Games
First published 1897; periodically revised and brought up to date for newer games
''Including all indoor games played today, with suggestions for good play, illustrative hands and all official laws to date.'' Subtitle
An encyclopedia of indoor games played with cards, dice, tiles or men, chips, etc. It includes the rules of not only such games as bridge, 500, hearts, whist, chess, checkers, dominoes, mah jong, billiards, cribbage, faro, craps and poker, but also European games such as baccara, bézique, vingt-et-un, écarté, roulette, piquet and skat. There are directions for playing some familiar games for which it is difficult to find rules elsewhere, such as author, old maid, I doubt it, and fan tan. Only a very few varieties of solitaire or patience are included

795.4 Card games

Gibson, Walter B.
Hoyle's Simplified guide to the popular card games; with complete explanation of terms, rules, and procedures. Newly rev. and enl. with recent games and a glossary. Doubleday 1971 312p $6.95   795.4
1 Cards
First published 1963
Partial contents: Cassino, gin rummy, canasta, cribbage, Russian bank, numerous kinds of poker, whist, pinochle, contract bridge, glossary-index of card games and terms

Goren, Charles H.
Goren's Bridge complete; a major revision of the standard work for all bridge players. Doubleday 1963 561p illus thumb indexed $6.95   795.4
1 Bridge (Game)
''A Chancellor Hall Book''
First published 1951 with title: Contract bridge complete
''Designed for the new player and the experienced devotee of bridge, this is an encyclopedic coverage of the game by one of its masters.'' Cincinnati

796 Athletic and outdoor sports and games

Best sports stories. Dutton illus   796
1 Sports
For availability and prices of volumes, consult publisher's catalog
Annual. First published for the year 1944. Editors: 1945 to date [1971]: Irving T. Marsh and Edward Ehre
''News stories and magazine articles . . . of baseball, football, boxing, basketball, golf, horse racing, track and field, tennis, yachting, and auto racing. Profiles, action stories and feature articles are included, many by well-known sports writers.'' Booklist

Friendlich, Dick
Panorama of sports in America; Gabriele Wunderlich, picture editor. Funk 1970 205p illus boards $10   796
1 Sports
Illustrated by numerous photographs, this book describes the origins, growth, and some professional and amateur participants of fifteen sports. Included are baseball, football, golf, tennis, boxing, bowling, swimming, hockey, skiing and skating, handball, horse racing and auto racing. Records and statistics are also provided

Sports Illustrated
The wonderful world of sports. . . . Time-Life Bks. 1967 324p illus $19.95   796
1 Sports
''A phenomenon of the second half of the twentieth century as discovered, explored and interpreted by the editors, writers, reporters, photographers and artists of Sports Illustrated. Additional commentary by Alden Clarke, Sidney L. James and Paul O'Neil; art direction and design by Richard Cummings.'' Title page
''An absorbing book which gives a comprehensive review of 'Sports Illustrated's' 13 years of interpreting the sports scene. A profusely illustrated volume depicting some of the most exciting moments in the world of sports. Many full-page color photographs comprise the first section, with stories and articles in the second by such distinguished writers as John Dos Passos, Ogden Nash, William Faulkner, George Plimpton, and others.'' Library J

796.03 Sports—Encyclopedias

Menke, Frank G.
The encyclopedia of sports. Barnes, A.S. illus $20   **796.03**

1 Sports—Dictionaries

First published 1939. Periodically revised to bring material up to date

The author presents historical facts about indoor and outdoor sports and games, rules, records, and lists of champions, attendance totals, salaries

This work is "comprehensive, well compiled, and easy to consult in spite of its wealth of content.... Indispensable to any library interested in sports and sporting records." Library J

Pratt, John Lowell
(ed.) The official encyclopedia of sports, [ed] by John Lowell Pratt and Jim Benagh; illus. with line drawings and photographs. Watts, F. 1964 344, 90p illus (The Watts Sports lib) lib. bdg. $6.95   **796.03**

1 Sports—Dictionaries

"A sparkling collection of background material, biographical sketches, and records of 33 participation sports, including badminton, water skiing, and weightlifting.... The informal style, good organization and clear photographs, ensure maximum usage by young sports enthusiasts. In fact, the book may kindle new interests. Appendant to each section is the name of the governing association for the sport. A list of books and magazines for further study and a 'Record Section' are included.... An excellent purchase for both circulation and reference collections, for there are just enough facts for the intended audience." Library J

Includes bibliography

796.09 Sports—History

Brasch, R.
How did sports begin? A look at the origins of man at play. McKay 1970 434p $8.95   **796.09**

1 Sports—History

"You may know where and how golf began, but why is the cup exactly 4 1/4 inches in diameter? And how did 'love' find its way into tennis scoring or the bull's eye into archery? Forty-five different sports are given their genesis here, ranging from badminton and baseball to water-skiing and wrestling. Here is ... lore on the origin and history of sports, from earliest times till now." News of Bks

"All those interested in the origins of sports will find this compilation of facts and opinions intensely absorbing." Choice

Durant, John
Pictorial history of American sports; from colonial times to the present [by] John Durant and Otto Bettmann. Rev. ed. Barnes, A.S. 1965 312p illus $10   **196.09**

1 Sports—History

First published 1952

From the moment in 1621 when Governor William Bradford of the Plymouth Colony spoke out against sports to the present day, the authors have collaborated to make this historical, pictorial and narrative record complete. They have uncovered little known facts about sports in the early days and have produced a book that is not only the story of sports but also the story of one phase of America

"Full of fascinating and excellently reproduced photographs, cartoons and sketches, with a sprightly running commentary by the compilers. Librarians familiar with the Bettmann Archive will be aware of the wide range of pictorial sources available to the compilers." Cur Ref Bks

796.32 Basketball

Hollander, Zander
(ed.) Basketball's greatest games. Prentice-Hall 1971 242p illus (The Official NBA lib) $6.95   **796.32**

1 Basketball—History

ISBN 0-13-072306-1

"An Associated Features book"

"Not everyone will agree that the 21 games chosen by Hollander are the greatest but he thinks at least 10 of these games will appear on everyone's list. In these college and professional contests many of the players who have risen to stardom since 1940 appear—Alcindor, Chamberlain, Baylor, Reed, West, and Bradley, to name a few. The account of each game was written by a journalist who attended the game or had close contact with some of the contenders." Booklist

Sports Illustrated
Sports Illustrated Basketball, by the editors of Sports Illustrated. [Rev. ed] Lippincott 1971 93p illus (The Sports Illustrated lib) $3.95   **796.32**

1 Basketball

First published 1962 with title: Sports Illustrated Book of basketball

This book offers an up-to-date analysis of offensive and defensive play in basketball, based on the methods of coaches and players. Included are discussions of floor positions, blocking, switching, UCLA's zone defense, free throws and basic shots. Action drawings follow every step of the instructions. (Publisher)

796.33 Football

Kramer, Jerry
Instant replay; the Green Bay diary of Jerry Kramer; ed. by Dick Schaap; photographs by John and Vernon J. Biever. World Pub. 1968 286p illus $6.95   **796.33**

1 Green Bay Packers (Football team)

"An NAL book"

Cover title: The Green Bay diary of Jerry Kramer

"A personal diary kept by Jerry Kramer, offense lineman for the Green Bay Packers, spanning the 1967 football season. He tells of his actions and reactions, after returning to professional football following 22 operations, and gives an insight into what professional football means to the players." Bk Buyer's Guide

This book "deserves more than a first glance, because the Green Bay Packers of 1967 were no ordinary team and, more important, because Jerry Kramer is an extraordinary right guard—thoughtful, literate and highly observant. Kramer gives you the guts of interior line play, but he sees it through an unusually detached eye.... Not many pro football players are as interested—or as interesting—as Kramer.... In the end, the book is most fascinating in its revelation of the unique love-hate relationship between the Packers and their coach, Vince Lombardi." Newsweek

Plimpton, George
Paper Lion. Harper 1966 362p illus $5.95   **796.33**

1 Football

Also available in a Large type edition for $9.95

"In order to explore the world of the professional football player, 'Paris Review' editor, George Plimpton, joined the Detroit Lions at summer training in 1963. His four weeks of experience as last-string quarter-back are recounted." Cincinnati

"The book is much more than the real treatment of every football fan's dream of direct participation; it is a vivid insight into the triumphs and tragedies, joys, sorrows, and daily monotonies that make up the life of the professional athlete. Plimpton is a perceptive observer and a compelling writer, and the book goes not only behind the scenes but into the nature of the actors. Illustrated, with a glossary and a team roster." Pub W

Sports Illustrated

Sports Illustrated Book of football, by the editors of Sports Illustrated. Lippincott 1960 86p illus $3.50
796.33

1 Football

Title on spine: Football

Contents: The big picture: how to watch football; The T-formation quarterback, by Y. A. Tittle; End play on offense, by R. Berry; Place kicking, by L. Groza; Line play, by T. Maule

796.34 Racket games

King, Billie Jean

Tennis to win [by] Billie Jean King with Kim Chapin; drawings by Gerald McConnell. Harper 1970 157p illus boards $5.95
796.34

1 Tennis

A champion tennis player takes the reader "from the fundamentals of the game to some of the most sophisticated aspects of modern strategy. She devotes special attention to the intricacies of percentage tennis and offers . . . advice on practice and conditioning, tennis psychology, and playing [one's] best on different court surfaces." Publisher's note

"The helpful hints from a champion are interesting, and the section on practice drills is very good. . . . Although the readers may be looking for more about King and Chapin's actual tennis experiences, the information is generally sound." Choice

Sports Illustrated

Sports Illustrated Book of badminton, by the editors of Sports Illustrated. Lippincott 1967 96p illus $2.95
796.34

1 Badminton

Text by J. Frank Devlin with Rex Lardner. Illustrations by J. George Janes

"A basic guide to badminton for beginners and more experienced players. The authors give tips on equipment and clothing, explain the rules and scoring, cover the fundamentals of play, and suggest tactics for both doubles and singles games. Diagrams and action drawings complement the clear instructions. The American Badminton Association's Laws of Badminton and a glossary are appended." Booklist

Talbert, William F.

Sports Illustrated Tennis, by William F. Talbert and the editors of Sports Illustrated; illus. by Ed Vebell. [Rev. ed] Lippincott 1972 96p illus (The Sports Illustrated lib) $3.95
796.34

1 Tennis

First published 1961 with title: Sports Illustrated Book of tennis

This book of tennis instruction "covers tactics of offensive and defensive play, and includes drawings and diagrams of singles, doubles and mixed-doubles." Publisher's note

796.352 Golf

Golf Magazine

Golf Magazine's Tips from the teaching pros, by the editors of Golf Magazine; illus. by Dom Lupo and Lealand Gustavson. Harper 1969 228p illus $6.50
796.352

1 Golf

"More than 50 professional golfers who are trained to analyze golf swings, spot faults, and suggest helpful remedies are the authors of these popularly written, short articles. Lew Worsham, Jim Turnesa, Alice Kirby, Peggy Kirk Bell, and Tony Kowski are among the professional golf teachers giving pointers to the average golfer on improving his game. Several chapters give information on the care of golf equipment, how to put more fun in the game, and golf rules." Booklist

Golf Magazine's Encyclopedia of golf; ed. by Robert Scharff and the editors of Golf Magazine; assisted by Peter D. Eaton. Harper 1970 424p illus $13.95
796.352

1 Golf

"Most of the material in this volume appeared in Golf magazine during the 10 years of its publication but some of the material was previously published in other periodicals, books, and company and association publications." Booklist

This is "an oversize book, truly encyclopedic, alphabetically arranged for quick reference: the history of golf, latest official rules, equipment, playing techniques, [short] biographies of famous golfers, descriptions of championship courses, results of major tournaments, a glossary of golf terms and much more." News of Bks

Plimpton, George

The bogey man. Harper 1968 306p illus $5.95
796.352

1 Golf—Anecdotes, facetiae, satire, etc.

This account of the author's "month on the professional golf circuit . . . [tells of] the amateurs, pros, caddies, officials, fans, and hangers-on he met; the golf legends, adventures, stroke-saving theories, superstitions, and other golfing lore which he absorbed; and his actual experiences as a player from tee to green." Publisher's note

"This is a well-written literate book that rises above the stylistic level of most sports journalism. . . . Plimpton has a remarkably keen sense of humor and it pervades the entire book." Best Sellers

Sports Illustrated

Sports Illustrated Book of golf, by the editors of Sports Illustrated and Charles Price. Lippincott 1970 73p illus $3.50
796.352

1 Golf

"Here is everything the beginner needs to know about the game, from learning the rules of play, selecting the right clubs, and teeing off to holing out on the eighteenth green." News of Bks

796.357 Baseball

Allen, Lee

The American League story. Rev. ed. Hill & Wang 1965 248p illus $4.95
796.357

1 American League of Professional Baseball Clubs 2 Baseball—History

First published 1962

An account of the American League from its founding "in 1901 to the assault of Roger Maris on Babe Ruth's record and the expansion of the league in the sixties." Publisher's note

The National League story; the official history; foreword by Warren Giles. Rev. ed. Hill & Wang 1965 293p illus $4.95
796.357

1 National League of Professional Baseball Clubs 2 Baseball—History

First published 1961

A "history of baseball's National League, full of anecdotes and the old-time, all-time greats like Cap Anson, Honus Wagner, John J. McGraw, Cy Young, Mel Ott, and others, and covering the organization of the League, and much more." Bk Buyer's Guide

"The book provides a concise and colorful account of the great and not-so-great days of the elder of the two Big Leagues." N Y Her Trib Books

The **Baseball** encyclopedia; the complete and official record of major league baseball. Macmillan (N Y) 1969 2337p $25
796.357

1 Baseball—Statistics

Going back to baseball's beginning in 1869, this volume covers such material as batting averages, game regulations, team rosters. It

The Baseball encyclopedia—*Continued*
"is the first to use the computer [to] process literally millions of statistics. . . . The statistics and records contained in The Baseball Encyclopedia are now accepted by both the National and American Leagues as official." News of Bks
Also included is a history of special decisions and changes in baseball rules

Durso, Joseph
Amazing: the miracle of the Mets; illus. with photographs. Houghton 1970 242p illus $5.95   796.357
1 New York Mets
The author chronicles the rise of the New York Mets to baseball's world championship in 1969 after seven years of being regarded as comical losers. He focuses on the lives of the players, managers and owners, their reactions to joining the Mets, to the lean years, and to the final triumph as well as on the public's frenetic reaction to the team
"Unlike many of the books about the Mets and their realization of the impossible dream, this one was not turned out quickly to cash in on the market. That is one of its strongest points. . . . What the Mets did is too well known to bear repetition, but how they did it and how they felt while doing it are not so well known; Durso takes care of these aspects." Library J

Mays, Willie
My secrets of playing baseball, by Willie Mays with Howard Liss; photographs by David Sutton. Viking 1967 89p illus $4.95
796.357
1 Baseball
"Written primarily for sand-lot, leagues and teenage players, this demonstrates the fundamentals of baseball in a brief but clear text. It covers defensive playing, position by position, and is illustrated by action photographs and filmed sequences." Bruno. Books for School Libraries, 1968

Sports Illustrated
Sports Illustrated Baseball, by the editors of Sports Illustrated; illus. by Ed Vebell. [Rev. ed] Lippincott 1972 93p illus (The Sports Illustrated lib) $3.95   796.357
1 Baseball
ISBN 0-397-00857-0
First published 1960 with title: Sports Illustrated Book of baseball. Text revisions by Roy Blount
"Personal coaching by major league stars is the keynote of this baseball book, written especially for the developing player. Harmon Killebrew gives batting advice. . . . Pitcher Dave McNally provides guidelines for an effective motion and discusses the strategy of pitching to different hitters and handling base runners. Brooks Robinson offers advice on how to play the infield positions. . . . Tim McCarver discusses the relationship between the catcher and the pitcher . . . [and] Tommie Agee explains how to play the three outfield positions and how to back up the infielders." Publisher's note

796.4 Track athletics

Cretzmeyer, Francis X.
Bresnahan and Tuttle's Track and field athletics [by] Francis X. Cretzmeyer, Louis E. Alley [and] Charles M. Tipton. 7th ed. Mosby 1969 317p illus $8.95   796.4
1 Track athletics 2 Athletics
First published 1937. Previous editions written by George T. Bresnahan and W. W. Tuttle
The book "covers the modern procedures and techniques in the events on the track and field program which are most frequently encountered in not only the United States, but also throughout the world. Furthermore, the

book contains up-to-the-minute material on aids in physical conditioning, diet, training schedules (both American and European), and construction plans for a track and field layout. . . . It is designed as a basic text for institutions offering undergraduate teacher training courses in physical education." Publisher's note
Includes bibliographies

Dunaway, James O.
Sports Illustrated Track and field: running events, by James O. Dunaway and the editors of Sports Illustrated. [Rev. ed] Lippincott 1972 96p illus (The Sports Illustrated lib) $3.95   796.4
1 Track athletics
ISBN 0-397-00889-9
Drawings by J. George Janes
First published 1968 with title: Sports Illustrated Book of track and field: running events
Chapters of this instructional book "are devoted to sprinting, hurdling, middle- and long-distance running. The authors cover the theory, technique, and strategy of competitive running. Action drawings illustrate and supplement the text." Library J
"The running events are described in detail, with techniques and training procedures given for the various distances. . . . The volume will be of interest to track buffs as well as those actively competing." Best Sellers

Fogel, Samuel J.
Gymnastics handbook. Parker Pub. 1971 220p illus $8.95   796.4
1 Gymnastics
ISBN 0-13-371815-8
"There are many gymnastics books that present individual stunts for all events, but the uniqueness of this handbook is the emphasis on basic routines. It is written for the secondary school gymnast, and lists skills of varying degrees of difficulty in varying combinations. The evaluation of routines and individual skills will, hopefully, aid gymnastics officiating." Choice

Kieran, John
The story of the Olympic games: 776 B.C. to [date] by John Kieran and Arthur Daley. Lippincott illus $7.95   796.4
1 Olympic games
First published 1936 by Stokes. Periodically revised to keep material up to date
Covers the birth of the Olympic games in ancient Greece and each of the modern Olympics since 1896, with statistical records. (Publisher)

Ryan, Frank
Weight training. Viking 1969 84p illus (The Viking Lib. of sports skills) boards $4.95
796.4
1 Weight lifting
The author "explains the process of physical development by using weights, stressing the need for safety and protection from injury. He shows how the needs of an athlete in a sport may be analyzed and a program worked out to achieve the desired muscular development." Publisher's note
"The book has many fine illustrations, showing the actual steps in the various weight training skills. These illustrations are a highlight of the book and are a primary, differentiating feature from other standard works on weight training." Choice

796.5 Outdoor life

Noyce, Wilfrid
(ed.) World atlas of mountaineering; ed. by Wilfrid Noyce and Ian McMorrin. Macmillan (N Y) [1970 c1969] 224p illus maps $14.95   796.5
1 Mountains 2 Mountaineering

Noyce, Wilfrid—*Continued.*

"The six continents and the polar regions are subdivided into smaller areas for treatment by the ten contributors, who write . . . of some of the most difficult climbing in the world. Their accounts of past expeditions are interwoven with advice to novices." Sat R

"Each contributor has concentrated on the mountaineering and related exploratory activities in the regions about which he has written and has also included information on ethnology, anthropology, history, physical geology, and the flora and fauna in accordance with his professional competence and personal interest. . . . The beautiful book seems to be of major interest to those who like to read about mountain climbing and exploratory travels and who enjoy beautiful photographs." Science Bks

Ormond, Clyde

Outdoorsman's handbook; ed. by Henry Gross; illus. by Nicholas Amorosi. Outdoor Life; distributed by Dutton [1971 c1970] 336p illus $5.95 **796.5**

1 Outdoor life

The author provides "practical ideas, tips, and techniques for living in the outdoors and putting nature's raw materials to practical or decorative use. Outdoor activities covered . . . include hunting, fishing, camping, cooking, hiking, back-packing, photography, and handling horses and horse gear." News of Bks

"This compact source of information should be welcomed by those who like to meet the challenge of wilderness recreation with creativity and ingenuity." Library J

Ullman, James Ramsey

The age of mountaineering. [New ed] Lippincott 1964 364p illus maps $8.95 **796.5**

1 Mountaineering

Revised edition of a 1954 book based on the author's: High conquest, published 1941

Covering the major mountaineering expeditions of the last hundred years, the author describes "the pioneer ascents in the Alps and the disastrous conquest of the Matterhorn; the famous climbs and explorations in the Rockies and Andes, Africa and Alaska . . . the great Himalayan ascents. . . . There is also a discussion of the craft of mountaineering and a description of some of America's most attractive and challenging mountain regions." Publisher's note

Appendices include: One hundred famous mountains; Glossary of mountaineering terms; Reading list

796.7 Driving motor vehicles for racing

Engel, Lyle Kenyon

The Indianapolis "500"; the world's most exciting auto race; produced by Lyle Kenyon Engel and the editors of Auto Racing magazine. Four Winds 1970 223p illus $6.95 **796.7**

1 Indianapolis Speedway Race

"With many photographs and minimal text, this focuses primarily on the 1963-69 races. Complete charts of all races (1911-1969) are appended, showing entrants, positions, speed, etc." Library J

796.8 Combat sports

Maertz, Richard C.

Wrestling techniques: takedowns. Barnes, A.S. 1970 113p illus $6.95 **796.8**

1 Wrestling
SBN 498-07501-X

"The author has analyzed more than 50 different takedown moves and arranged them in easy-to-follow sequential order. Each move discussed is accompanied by an illustration and a concise explanation that seldom runs longer than one paragraph. . . . The chapters of this book are arranged according to the areas of attack—arms, head, legs, for example —and the stances are also . . . explored." Publisher's note

"Wrestlers and coaches will be interested in this well-illustrated book." Library J

Pfluger, A.

Karate: basic principles. Sterling 1967 144p illus $3.95, lib. bdg. $3.99 **796.8**

1 Karate

"Translated by Dale S. Cunningham and Paul Kuttner from the German edition." Verso of title page

"Concise, well-organized instruction book. The description of each technique is supplemented with clear photographs and diagrams. The author emphasizes the positive developments in intellectual discipline as well as physical strength that can result from learning Karate." Library J

796.9 Ice and snow sports. Skiing

Iselin, Fred

Invitation to modern skiing, by Fred Iselin and A. C. Spectorsky; with action photographs by John O'Rear and drawings by S. Fleishman. Simon & Schuster 1965 207p illus $5.95 **796.9**

1 Skis and skiing

First published 1947 with title: Invitation to skiing

The authors cover each "aspect of skiing today, from wedeln and the snake turn to metal skis and new bindings." Publisher's note

Jerome, John

Sports Illustrated Skiing, by John Jerome and the editors of Sports Illustrated. [New ed] Lippincott 1971 96p illus (The Sports Illustrated lib) $3.95 **796.9**

1 Skis and skiing

First published by the editors of Sports Illustrated 1957 with title: Sports Illustrated Book of skiing

The author "offers some sound advice for beginners on such basics as balance and stance, edge control, sideslipping, traversing and the snowplow. He also describes all the turns a skier uses to control his speed and to negotiate different terrains and conditions. Finally, the author gives valuable tips to the skier who has mastered the fundamentals and is ready to perfect his own style." Publisher's note

Ski Magazine

America's ski book, by the editors of Ski Magazine and John Henry Auran; with an introduction by Willy Schaeffler. Scribner 1966 473p illus $10 **796.9**

1 Skis and skiing

"Exposition and analysis of the sport, with information and instruction for beginner, intermediate, and expert. Includes sections on the history of the sport, equipment, major ski areas, and competitions." Pub W

"Handsomely produced . . . the book suffers only from attempting to cover too much ground in too little space." N Y Times Bk R

Glossary: p435-42. Books, journals and films: p451-52

Ski Magazine's Encyclopedia of skiing; ed. by Robert Scharff and the editors of Ski Magazine. Harper 1970 427p illus $13.95 **796.9**

1 Skis and skiing

Ski Magazine—*Continued*

Contents: The history of skiing; Ski equipment; Principles of skiing; Ski competition Where to ski; Glossary, lexicon, and ski associations

"This is a valuable book for the skier, whether beginner or expert. It is, however, encyclopedic in content rather than in arrangement. Instead of having the traditional alphabetical listing, the book is broken down into sections. . . . Nearly everything a skier would want to know is included in this volume." Library J

The skier's handbook, by the editors of Ski Magazine. Harper 1965 262p illus boards $6.95   **796.9**

1 Skis and skiing

Using the "American Technique" as a framework, the editors present a step-by-step guide that takes the pupil from walking on level ground and rising after a fall to wedeln and racing. Photographs and line drawings illustrate the way to make maneuvers. (Publisher)

Glossary of abbreviations of names of ski organizations: p262

797.1   Surfing

Dixon, Peter L.

Where the surfers are; a guide to the world's great surfing spots. Coward-McCann 1968 234p illus maps $6.95   **797.1**

1 Surfing

The author "provides current [1968] information on the world's surfing areas, covering the U.S. coastlines and the Caribbean, Mexico, the Hawaiian Islands, Australia and New Zealand, Africa, Europe, and South America. For each surfing spot he notes location, surf size, type of ride, seasonal considerations, potential hazards, living accommodations available, transportation required, and, often, persons to contact or sources of up-to-date knowledge. An informal guide suitable for the weekend surfer or the serious surfer." Booklist

797.2   Swimming

Sports Illustrated

Sports Illustrated Book of swimming, by the editors of Sports Illustrated. Lippincott [1961 c1960] 90p illus $2.95   **797.2**

1 Swimming

Title on spine: Swimming

"Text by Matt Mann with Coles Phinizy. Illustrations by Ed Vebell"

Contents: You, the teacher: The crawl kick; The crawl arm action; The crawl breathing action; The backstroke; The breaststroke

"A nine-year-old girl is the model in the illustrations but the methods are applicable in working with girls or boys." Booklist

797.5 Parachuting (skydiving)

Dwiggins, Don

Bailout; the story of parachuting and skydiving. Crowell-Collier Press 1969 196p illus (America in the making) $4.50   **797.5**

1 Parachuting—History

This history of parachuting contains accounts of "those who pioneered the use of parachutes as tactical and life-saving equipment during wartime, as a device for recovering space vehicles, and as standard gear for the most daring sport of all—skydiving." Publisher's note

Bibliography: p191-92

798   Horsemanship

Chenevix Trench, Charles

A history of horsemanship. Doubleday 1970 320p illus $14.95   **798**

1 Horsemanship—History

"How, why, where, and when men (and women) have ridden horses, from the Sumerians to today's Pony Clubbers, chronicled in a unique authoritative work written with a style and wit that make it highly entertaining as well as informative. Illustrated with a copious, original selection of photographs and works of art." News of Bks

Bibliography: p317

Self, Margaret Cabell

The complete book of horses & ponies; illus. by R. W. Mutch. McGraw 1963 316p illus $5.95   **798**

1 Horsemanship 2 Horses 3 Ponies

A "round-up of facts about horses—evolution, structure, types and breeds, behavior, care and handling, training, riding techniques, etc.—presented in question and answer format." Bk Buyer's Guide

Glossary: p305-07

Sports Illustrated

Sports Illustrated Horseback riding, by the editors of Sports Illustrated. [Rev. ed] Lippincott 1971 94p illus (The Sports Illustrated lib) $3.95   **798**

1 Horsemanship

Text by Gordon Wright with Alice Higgins. Illustrated by Sam Savitt

First published 1960 with title: Sports Illustrated Book of horseback riding

"A beginner's book on horseback riding with many valuable tips on the correct method of instruction for young people. . . . Includes information on equipment for both horse and rider, the care and handling of horses, mounting and dismounting, how to post the trot and sit the canter." Publisher's note

798.03 Horsemanship—Encyclopedias

Self, Margaret Cabell

The horseman's encyclopedia. New and rev. ed. Barnes, A.S. 1963 428p illus (The Sportsman's lib) $9.75   **798.03**

1 Horsemanship—Dictionaries 2 Horses—Dictionaries

First published 1946

Comprehensive information about horses and riding, arranged alphabetically. "Statistics pertaining to the Quarter Horse, to racing (harness, flat, and hurdle), recognized hunts and shows, and steeplechase and hunt associations will be found in the appendix." Preface

799 Fishing, hunting, shooting

Bateman, James

Animal traps and trapping. Stackpole Bks. 1971 286p illus $8.50   **799**

1 Trapping

ISBN 0-8117-0103-4

The author examines both simple and complex devices for trapping insects, birds, fish, and mammals. Also discussed are the traps of nature, baits, the ethics of trapping and related legislation

Bibliography: p270-73

Bryant, Nelson
Fresh air, bright water; adventures in Wood, field, and stream. Am. Heritage Press 1971 283p illus $6.95   **799**
1 Hunting 2 Fishing 3 Outdoor life
ISBN 0-07-008605-2
A "selection of 125 'Wood, Field and Stream' columns that Bryant has written for the New York 'Times' during the past four years. The man has a job Jupiter would envy; he does it justice, too, packing his gear and getting off on fishing or hunting jaunts to the New England woods, Canada's lakes and streams, Florida, the Caribbean, even to Scotland. Bryant can be evocative in a few lines, and he writes with an accomplished sportsman's know-how whether with rifle or rod. More important for his readers, he is able to communicate his affinity with the outdoors." Pub W

799.3 Shooting other than game

Sports Illustrated
Sports Illustrated Book of the shotgun, by the editors of Sports Illustrated. Lippincott 1967 89p illus $2.95   **799.3**
1 Shotguns 2 Shooting
Text by Virginia Kraft. Illustrations by Ed Vebell and Burt Silverman
This book covers "the basic types of shotguns, their uses and price ranges, how the gauge of a gun is measured, how the choke works, how barrel length influences accuracy. There is a guide to selecting ammunition. . . . [The book also explains how to] master shooting form, and shoot targets." Publisher's note

800 LITERATURE

801 Literature—Philosophy and theory

Daiches, David
English literature. Prentice-Hall 1964 174p (The Princeton studies: humanistic scholarship in America) $6.50   **801**
1 Criticism 2 English literature—Research 3 English literature—History and criticism
Analyzed in Essay and general literature index
A "survey of American criticism and scholarship in English literature during the last thirty years or so. Evaluating the major trends in almost every area of literary inquiry in America, Mr. Daiches finds a complex of deficiencies in our academic, professional, and cultural attitudes that account, in part, for both a minimal accomplishment in some types of study and an unfortunate proliferation in others." Publisher's note
Partial contents: Milton; Shakespeare; Literary criticism and literary history; Critics as teachers; Biography and letters; The industrious scholar; The paperback revolution

803 Literature—Dictionaries and encyclopedias

Brewer, E. Cobham
The reader's handbook of famous names in fiction, allusions, references, proverbs, plots, stories, and poems; a new ed. rev. throughout and greatly enlarged. Lippincott 1899; republished by Gale Res. 1966 2v (1243p) set $29.50   **803**
1 Literature—Dictionaries 2 Allusions 3 Fiction—Dictionaries

This reprint was first published 1899 by Lippincott
"The object of this Handbook is to supply readers and speakers with a lucid but very brief account of such names as are used in allusions and references . . . the plot of popular dramas, the story of epic poems, and the outline of well-known tales. . . . Another striking and interesting feature of the book is the revelation of the source from which dramatists and romances have derived their stories, and the strange repetitions of historic incidents." Preface

Brewer's Dictionary of phrase and fable. Centenary ed. Rev. by Ivor H. Evans. Harper 1970 1175p front $10   **803**
1 Literature—Dictionaries 2 Allusions
First published 1870
"It contains: a history of the chief figures of mythology: a record of superstitions and customs, ancient and modern; explanations of commonly-used English phrases of native origin or borrowed from other tongues; etymological information: more common words of old and modern slang in everyday use; a glossary of scientific, historical, political, and archaeological terms and events." Huntting
"Includes colloquial and proverbial phrases, biographical and mythological references, fictitious characters, titles, etc . . . including many terms used in World War II." Winchell. Guide to Reference Books. 8th edition

Cassell's Encyclopaedia of world literature; editor: S. H. Steinberg. Funk 1954 2v (xxiv, 2086p) $25   **803**
1 Literature—Dictionaries 2 Literature—Biobibliography 3 Authors
First published 1953 in England with title: Cassell's Encyclopaedia of literature
An historical survey of world literature from the earliest oral tradition to the present. Arrangement is alphabetical under these three headings: Histories of the literatures of the world and general literary subjects; Biographies of writers who died before 1 August 1914; Biographies of authors who were living on 1 August 1914 or who were born after that date
"The articles were written by more than 200 'scholars and critics.' . . . The biographical sections devote more than the usual attention to Asian and Central European writers. Cassell's' brings together much factual and critical material on world literature and often furnishes a 'first' source. Selected bibliographies are included." Minnesota. The Use of Books and Libraries

The Concise encyclopedia of modern world literature; ed. by Geoffrey Grigson. [2d ed] Hawthorn Bks. [1971 c1963] 430p $12.95   **803**
1 Literature—Dictionaries 2 Literature—Biobibliography 3 Literature, Modern—History and criticism
First published 1963
A volume of over 300 brief introductions to various novelists and poets of the twentieth century, who in the opinion of the editor and contributors, are worth reading. Greater space is given to writers in English. "To enable the reader to see these authors in a wider context of development an introductory section is provided. It describes the growth of the major national literatures and the characteristic literary forms of our time. The book is fully indexed by both authors and titles." Publisher's note
"An uneven but fascinating book at a good price." Library J

Magill, Frank N.
(ed.) Cyclopedia of literary characters. Harper 1963 1280, 50p $11.95, lib. bdg. $9.89   **803**
1 Characters and characteristics in literature 2 Literature—Indexes 3 Literature—Stories, plots, etc.
Also available from Salem, with title: Masterplots Cyclopedia of literary characters, in 2 volumes, at $15

Magill, Frank N.—*Continued*

A volume of identification and description, alphabetically arranged by title of the work, "of more than sixteen thousand [major and minor] characters from some thirteen hundred novels, dramas, and epics drawn from world literature. . . . Pronunciation is given for names likely to be mispronounced and for unfamiliar foreign names." Preface

For a fuller review see: The Booklist and Subscription Books Bulletin, October 1, 1964

The Reader's encyclopedia. 2d ed. Crowell 1965 1118p illus $8.95   803

1 Literature—Dictionaries 2 Art—Dictionaries 3 Music—Dictionaries

First published 1948, edited by William Rose Benét

Replaces: Crowell's Handbook for readers and writers, edited by Henrietta Gerwig

"One-volume encyclopedia of world literature and the arts. Contains . . . articles covering mythology, drama, history, literature, music, art, odd facts. . . . It gives plots, themes, characters, dates, names, biographical information, etc. . . . All articles are alphabetically arranged with convenient cross references." Huntting

It "will serve as a well organized supplementary memory and an explanation of many literary allusions." Cleveland

For a fuller review see: The Booklist and Subscription Books Bulletin for April 15, 1965

Shipley, Joseph T.

(ed.) Dictionary of world literary terms; forms, technique, criticism; completely rev. and enl. ed. With contributions by 260 authorities. Writer 1970 466p $12.95   803

1 Literature—Dictionaries
ISBN 0-87116-012-9

First published 1943 by Philosophical Library with title: Dictionary of world literature

Arranged in alphabetical order. "The first part of the book . . . is devoted to terms, forms, and types, definitions, techniques, and genres. Part II offers . . . critical surveys of American, English, French, German, Greek, Italian, Latin, Medieval, Russian, and Spanish criticism. And Part III includes selected lists of critics and works, bibliographies . . . for the literature of 25 different countries." Publisher's note

807.9 Literary competitions

Literary and library prizes. Bowker $10.95
807.9

1 Literary prizes

First published 1935 and frequently revised to account for yearly winners and newly established awards

Title varies: 1935-1939, Famous literary prizes and their winners; 1946, Literary prizes and their winners

Prizes are listed under four main divisions: International, American, British, and Canadian prizes. American prizes are subdivided into various categories. Other sections list only the major literary awards given. Includes an index to prizes and winners

808 Rhetoric

Flesch, Rudolf

How to be brief; an index to simple writing. Harper 1962 114p $5.95   808

1 Rhetoric 2 English language

"Alphabetically arranged tips on trimming one's writing, especially of business letters, to the bone. Cites words that can be omitted, simple words to use in place of pompous ones, and space-saving abbreviations. In spite of its dictionary arrangement, this is best read straight through." Pub W

How to write, speak, and think more effectively. Harper 1960 362p illus boards $5.95
808

1 English language—Composition and exercises 2 Rhetoric 3 Thought and thinking

Includes material from: The art of plain talk; The art of readable writing; The art of clear thinking; How to test readability; and, A new way to better English

Divided into two parts: Lessons; and hints and devices. Part One contains 30 chapters based on the author's older books. Part Two discusses how to write; how to say it; how to test readability; and, how to raise readability. (Publisher)

"A lucid, stimulating book that gives concrete help to its readers. Using a scientifically tested system designed to improve the three mental activites mentioned in the title he incorporates in his discussion analyses, specific examples, tests, exercises, and similar aids to learning. The final chapters are devoted to formulas and tests for readability." Booklist

Strunk, William

The elements of style, by William Strunk, Jr. With revisions, an introduction, and a new chapter on writing, by E. B. White. Macmillan (N Y) 1959 71p $2.95   808

1 Rhetoric

First appeared 1918, privately printed; trade edition first published 1920 by Harcourt

"The book consists of a short introduction, eight rules of usage, ten principles of composition, a few matters of form, a list of words and expressions commonly misused, a list of words commonly misspelled." Introduction

"In the introduction Mr. White says that this was Professor Strunk's 'attempt to cut the vast tangle of English rhetoric down to size and write its rules and principles on the head of a pin.' He himself always referred to it as 'the little book.' As the editor says, it is clear, brief, and bold, pithy and pungent, very useful and very readable." Library J

808.02 Authorship and editorial techniques

Barzun, Jacques

The modern researcher [by] Jacques Barzun & Henry F. Graff. Rev. ed. Harcourt 1970 430p $8.50   808.02

1 Research 2 Report writing
ISBN 0-15-161482-2

First published 1957

"Using examples from fields as diverse as medicine and music, science and politics, literature and painting, [the authors] illustrate and illuminate the principles by which facts are assembled, sifted, and organized into a readable finished product. The book tells how to use a library, how to judge the accuracy of sources, how to confront the computer and microbook, how to translate foreign sources, and how to prepare footnotes and bibliography." Publisher's note

For further reading: p387-407

Engle, Paul

(ed.) On creative writing. Dutton 1964 244p $5.95   808.02

1 Authorship

Analyzed in Essay and general literature index

The "editor has assembled a group of essays on creative writing accompanied by literary examples. . . . Such writers as R. V. Cassill, Donald Justice, and Lionel Abel contribute short but rewarding discussions of the various literary forms. Examples of short stories, poems, and articles are by such authors as Chekhov, Tolstoi, Richard Wilbur, William Carlos Williams. This work may be useful for writing classes, and it will also be helpful for students and the general public requiring information and sensible discussion of literary forms." Library J

Hook, Lucyle
The research paper; gathering library material, organizing and preparing the manuscript [by] Lucyle Hook [and] Mary Virginia Gaver. 4th ed. Prentice-Hall 1969 120p pa $2.95   **808.02**
1 Report writing 2 Libraries and readers
3 Reference books
SBN 13-774448-X
First published 1944 by Edwards Brothers with title: The source theme
This text "offers a visual presentation of the correct way to prepare and present a documented paper. The book is designed to guide the student graphically through the successive steps of learning the use of various library reference tools, selecting the working bibliography, preparing an outline, footnotes and bibliography, and culminating in a completed theme." Publisher's note

Markman, Roberta H.
10 steps in writing the research paper, by Roberta H. Markman and Marie L. Waddell. Rev. Barrons Educ. Ser. 1971 142p $4 **808.02**
1 Report writing
First published 1965
"We have attempted to present clear and complete step-by-step instructions for the writing of a research paper and to give models for all necessary research forms. Our arrangement outlines each step in the research process and puts all information concerning each step in the process together in the same section; everything about bibliographies is in one section; all information about footnotes is in another, and so on." Preface
Appendices include a glossary and a bibliography

Turabian, Kate L.
A manual for writers of term papers, theses and dissertations. 3d ed. rev. Univ. of Chicago Press 1967 164p $3.50   **808.02**
1 Report writing 2 Dissertations, Academic
First published 1937 with title: A manual for writers of dissertations
"Designed to serve as a guide to suitable style in the presentation of formal papers—term papers, reports, articles, theses, dissertations—both in scientific and in non-scientific fields. . . . In the main, the manual is addressed to the writers of the papers, who have the major responsibility for their organization and form in general. The section on typing is addressed especially to the typists who have the responsibility for preparing the final copies." Foreword

The **Writer's** handbook. Writer $10   **808.02**
1 Authorship—Handbooks, manuals, etc.
2 Publishers and publishing
Some earlier editions analyzed in Essay and general literature index
Editors: 1936 S. G. Houghton and U. G. Olsen. 1941- A. S. Burack
First published 1936. Frequently revised to include new articles
"In two parts. Pt. 1 is made up of articles by various writers, which appeared originally in 'The writer,' on various phases of professional writing including fiction, nonfiction, and specialties [juveniles, verse, etc.]. Some articles are carried over from earlier editions, some are new, none are dated. Pt. 2 is a market guide, mainly to the periodical field, giving for each periodical: address, editor, and type of material accepted with indication of rate of payment. Also has section for radio and television, and for book publishers." Winchell. Guide to Reference Books. 8th edition

The **Writer's** market. Writers Digest $8.95
808.02
1 Authorship—Handbooks, manuals, etc.
2 Publishers and publishing
Annual. First published 1930
Contains names, addresses, rates of payment, editorial requirements, style rules, and preferences of firms that buy the works of free lance writers in the fields of art, music, aviation, photography, newspapers, magazines, and television

808.06 Composition for specific purposes and types of readers

Bowen, Catherine Drinker
Biography: the craft and the calling. Little 1969 174p $5.95   **808.06**
1 Biography (as a literary form)
"An Atlantic Press book"
The author "demonstrates that biography is an authentic art form that demands the utmost of its practitioners. . . . [She writes] of the problems every biographer encounters, from choice of subject through research, interpretation and significant form right down to the pitfalls that must be avoided along the way—and how to make your subject come alive." Pub W
"A fluent and candid little book. . . . [Mrs. Bowen's] brief and helpful chapters are musings in a workshop. . . . [Her] book, rich in experience, offers signposts to critics and students of biography and aspirants in that art." Book World

Mathieu, Aron M.
(ed.) The creative writer. Rev. ed. Writers Digest 1968 416p illus $6.95   **808.06**
1 Authorship 2 Fiction—Technique
SBN 911654-07-0
First published 1961
This compilation "offers a variety of functional, stimulating ideas for those concerned with writing, editing and issuing magazines. Contains markets, ideas, and inspiration in the fields of syndicates, fiction, novels, newspapers, plays, trade journals." McClurg. Book News

808.1 Poetry

Aristotle
Poetics   **808.1**
1 Poetics
Some editions are:
Clarendon Press $2.40 With an introduction and explanations by W. Hamilton Fyfe. Has title: Aristotle's Art of poetry, a Greek view of poetry and drama
Dutton (Everyman's library) $2.75 Edited and Translated by John Warrington
Hill & Wang $3.50 Translated by S. H. Butcher; introduction by Francis Fergusson
Oxford $7 With an introduction, commentary and appendixes by D. W. Lucas
Univ. of Mich. Press $4.50 Translated, with an introduction and notes by Gerald F. Else
In this basic work of literary criticism, Aristotle discusses the fundamental principles of poetry and its various forms, emphasizing tragedy and the epic

Deutsch, Babette
Poetry handbook; a dictionary of terms. 3d ed. rev. and enl. Funk 1969 201p $5.95
808.1
1 Poetics 2 Poetry—Dictionaries
First published 1957
"Alphabetically arranged, the special vocabulary of poetry is easily accessible to the student, reader, or practicing poet. The definitions of poetic forms and techniques, with illustrative models taken from the ancients to the avant-garde, [beat poetry, and contemporary poets] are particularly helpful. Concise and clearly written, the handbook satisfies a need for a versifiers' tool and reference book." Booklist
"For anyone dealing with poetry, or interested in reading it carefully, the book's usefulness is obvious." Christian Science Monitor

Drew, Elizabeth
Discovering poetry. Norton 1933 224p illus $3.95   **808.1**
1 Poetry 2 English poetry—History and criticism

Drew, Elizabeth—*Continued*

"The book is an effort to discover the secret of the delight that poetry gives us, in what the magic of the poetic imagination consists, and in what ways we may best train ourselves to recognize and enjoy it." Book Rev Digest

"Such a book as this will suggest, even to those who have long made companions of the poets, fresh points of view and richer meanings. To those who for whatever reason, because poetry seems difficult, or what not, have avoided poetry, it opens new and lovely paths to reluctant feet. By means of the abundance of poetry quoted—on a rough guess perhaps even as much as one-fourth of the book is quoted —the author lures one along the enchanted way." N Y Times Bk R
Bibliography: p211-16

Poetry: a modern guide to its understanding and enjoyment. Norton 1959 287p $5.95
808.1

1 Poetry 2 English poetry—History and criticism 3 American poetry—History and criticism

The "first chapters speak of the poetic process: language, symbolism, and rhythms. The rest of the book is devoted to a collection and discussion of poems on the great human themes —love, religion, humanity. . . . Included are poems, English and American, ranging from the sixteenth century to the twentieth, with a generous proportion from contemporary poets." Publisher's note

"One of its most pleasant features is the way in which the traditional and the modern appear together amicably and helpfully in each chapter." N Y Her Trib Books
The alphabetical list of poets serves as an index. Bibliography: p283-85

Eastman, Max

Enjoyment of poetry, with Anthology for Enjoyment of poetry. One-volume ed. Scribner 1951 2v in 1 $7.50
808.1

1 Poetry 2 Esthetics 3 American poetry— Collections 4 English poetry—Collections

A reprint in an omnibus volume with a new preface of two books: Enjoyment of poetry, first published 1913, and Anthology for the Enjoyment of poetry, published 1939

"A popular expository study of the history, artistic techniques, aesthetic values and appreciation of poetry; [with] an anthology of 218 poems especially selected to accompany the foregoing work." Publisher's note
General notes and references: v 1 p275-308

Eliot, T. S.

On poetry and poets. Farrar, Straus 1957 308p $4.50
808.1

1 Poetry 2 Poetry—Addresses and essays 3 Poetry—History and criticism

Analyzed in Essay and general literature index

"The present book is a collection of seven essays on poetry and nine on poets. Two of the latter, on Goethe and Dr. Johnson have not been easily available; the rest, such as the Minnesota lecture on 'The Frontiers of Criticism' and the preface to Kipling's poems are well known." N Y Times Bk R

"They are distinguished, literary, and urbane. . . . Will appeal most to the reader with some background in the subject." Booklist

Hillyer, Robert

In pursuit of poetry. McGraw 1960 229p $5.50
808.1

1 Poetry—History and criticism 2 Poetics

"Starting with a description of the essential spirit of poetry, Robert Hillyer explains just what poets attempt to do, the means they use, and ways to judge the success of their efforts. He analyzes the techniques of the poet's craft and explains . . . many of the mechanical devices of which the average reader may be unaware. In discussing the forms of poetry he offers a wealth of illustrations from some of the greatest works in the English language." Publisher's note

A "guide to the enjoyment and appreciation of poetry. . . . Particularly helpful are the suggestions on how to read a poem aloud." Booklist
Some recommended reading: p219-21

Untermeyer, Louis

The forms of poetry; a pocket dictionary of verse. 2d (rev.) ed. Harcourt 1926 166p $3.50
808.1

1 Poetics 2 Poetry 3 English poetry—History and criticism 4 American poetry—History and criticism

Here are, in alphabetical order, definitions of all terms which one may need for a profitable study or discussion of poetry. A section of the book is given over to a presentation of verse forms, diagrammed and exampled. The closing third covers briefly the history of English and American verse. A bibliography and an index complete the volume

"The handbook is terse and accurate. It is lively and readable." N Y Times Bk R

The pursuit of poetry. . . . Simon & Schuster 1969 318p $6.95
808.1

1 Poetry 2 Poetics 3 Poetry—History and criticism
SBN 671-20409-2

"A guide to its understanding and appreciation with an explanation of its forms and a dictionary of poetic terms." Title page

This volume is "divided into two sections. The first is an examination of poetry: how it is conceived, shaped by the conscious mind; how it can be apprehended, appreciated and enjoyed. The second is a poetry handbook: an explanation of techniques, plus an encyclopedia of poetic terms, with examples of every form from ballads to free verse." News of Bks

"In a foreword Mr. Untermeyer notes that his book is not for the advanced scholar, and he is absolutely right, but it is a good and useful book for almost anyone else interested in the subject, authoritative without being dogmatic, tolerant of novelty yet respectful of tradition, full of pleasantly apt quotations for reading and mulling." Book of the Month Club News
A selected bibliography: p307-09

808.2 Drama technique

Kline, Peter

The theatre student: playwriting. Rosen, R. 1970 186p (The Theatre student ser) lib. bdg. $5.97
808.2

1 Drama—Technique
SBN 8239-0196-3

This book is "designed as an adjunct to classwork and as a collection of resource materials rather than as a textbook. Kline's unorthodox, informal teaching methods, reflecting his expertise in acting, directing, and producing as well as in teaching, emphasize student development rather than rules for writing good plays and employ group consultation and improvisation as devices for working out dramatic ideas. Where discussions of plot, characters, and dialog occur, they are frequently illustrated with selections from students' plays. A useful guide for teachers and students." Booklist
Bibliography: p180-86

808.3 Fiction technique

Dickson, Frank A.

(ed.) Handbook of short story writing; ed. by Frank A. Dickson and Sandra Smythe. Writers Digest 1970 238p boards $5.95 **808.3**

1 Short story
SBN 911654-15-1

"The organization of the book presupposes nothing on the part of the beginning writer but pencil, paper, enthusiasm, and talent. Everything else—getting the idea and finding

Dickson, Frank A.—*Continued*
the time to write, developing and using characters, writing scenes, building plots, writing description, managing story pacing, story openings, story endings, transitions, flashbacks, emotion, theme, and meaning—has been covered." Publisher's note
The book "has an aura of the authentic and the reliable, though some of the authors are not among the most familiar. . . . While this well-organized group of articles of suggestions and advice may bear some resemblance to a factual text, it is good, stimulating, mentally appetizing writing, and fun to read. . . . This book communicates." Library J

Forster, E. M.
Aspects of the novel. Harcourt 1927 250p $5.75
808.3
1 Fiction 2 English fiction—History and criticism
Clark lectures delivered under the auspices of Trinity College, Cambridge, in the spring of 1927
Informal discussions of the novel including the story, characters, plot, fantasy, prophecy, pattern, and rhythm
These essays are "provocative, and often the provocation, for the widely-read reader, will be to dissent." Wis Lib Bul

808.51 Public speaking (Oratory)

Buehler, E. C.
Building the contest oration, by E. C. Buehler and Richard L. Johannesen. Wilson, H.W. 1965 202p $5.50
808.51
1 Public speaking 2 Orations
ISBN 0-8242-0008-X
"This book is designed to meet the needs of the growing number of high school students who participate every year in some form of competitive educational oratory." Preface
Part I explains the nature of oratory. Part II presents the procedures for preparing and delivering the oration. Part III includes five high school and two college winning contest orations
Selected sources on the American Constitution: p196-97

808.53 Debate and public discussion

Musgrave, George McCoy
Competitive debate; rules and techniques. 3d ed. Wilson, H.W. 1957 170p $4.50 808.53
1 Debates and debating
ISBN 0-8242-0010-1
First published 1945
"Consideration has been given both the elementary techniques that every neophyte should learn at once, and the advanced techniques." Preface
In this book "the rules of debate are listed and customs and procedures, case presentations, cross examination, strategy, judging, and administration are examined." Publisher's note
Bibliography: p150-66

808.8 Literature—Collections

Fadiman, Clifton
(ed.) Fantasia mathematica. . . . Assembled and ed. with an introduction. Simon & Schuster 1958 298p illus $6
808.8
1 Literature—Collections 2 Mathematics
"Being a set of stories, together with a group of oddments and diversions, all drawn from the universe of mathematics." Title page

"These are, for the most part, entertainment rather than science for the nontechnical reader; some pieces are science fiction, some pay tribute to mathematics as an art, others comment on methods of teaching and the layman's awe of mathematics. They can, however, give the reader new appreciation and lead to further investigation." Booklist
(ed.) The mathematical magpie. . . . Assembled and ed. with an introduction and commentaries, by Clifton Fadiman. Simon & Schuster [1964 c1962] 300p illus pa $1.95
808.8
1 Literature—Collections 2 Mathematics
First published 1962
"Being more stories, mainly transcendental, plus subsets of essays, rhymes, music, anecdotes, epigrams, and other prime oddments and diversions, rational or irrational, all derived from the infinite domain of mathematics." Title page
"An unconventional and wide-ranging assortment, it includes selections from Bertrand Russell, Richard Hughes, Samuel Clemens, and George Santayana as well as from the more-to-be expected Isaac Asimov, Lewis Carroll, and Arthur Clarke." Horn Bk

Magill, Frank N.
(ed.) Masterpieces of world literature in digest form. [1st-4th ser] ed. by Frank N. Magill with the assistance of Dayton Kohler and staff. Harper 1952-1969 4v ea $11.95, lib. bdg. ea $9.89
808.8
1 Literature—Stories, plots, etc.
2d-4th series also available from Salem Press, with title: Masterplots. 2 volumes in each series at $15 per series
Essay reviews and plot synopses of novels, epic poems, stories, plays, poetry, philosophy and other classics. Arranged alphabetically by title with author indexes only

808.81 Poetry—Collections

Brewton, Sara
(comp.) Christmas bells are ringing; a treasury of Christmas poetry, selected by Sara and John E. Brewton; illus. by Decie Merwin. Macmillan (N Y) 1951 114p illus $4.50
808.81
1 Christmas poetry
"About 100 poems are included in this inviting and varied anthology of Christmas poetry. Under such headings as In the week when Christmas comes and Who will kneel them gently down, there are selections for all ages, gay verses as well as reverent poems. Author, title, and first-line indexes." Booklist

Creekmore, Hubert
(ed.) A little treasury of world poetry; tr. from the great poets of other languages, 2600 B.C. to 1950 A.D. Ed. with an introduction by Hubert Creekmore. Scribner 1952 xl, 904p illus $7
808.81
1 Poetry—Collections
"The Little treasury series"
"A selection of the best translations into English of the outstanding poetry written in foreign languages. They range from the earliest Babylonian hymns to the poets of our own day." Huntting
Original poetry in the English language is excluded. Poems are arranged in language sections and chronologically by poets within the sections. Includes indexes of authors and titles, languages and translators

Granger's Index to poetry. 5th ed. completely rev. and enl. indexing anthologies published through June 30, 1960; ed. by William F. Bernhardt. Columbia Univ. Press 1962 xxxix, 2123p $65
808.81
1 Poetry—Indexes

Granger's Index to poetry—*Continued*

First published 1904 by McClurg with title: Index to poetry and recitations

Indexes 574 volumes of poetry anthologies. Includes separate subject index, combined title and first-line index, and author index

"A very useful index important in public, college, and school libraries as it indexes a large number of standard and popular collections of poetry (the 1st-3d editions also indexed prose selections). . . . Because of the number of titles indexed in earlier editions, but omitted in later ones, most libraries will find it advantageous to keep all." Winchell. Guide to Reference Books. 8th edition

Granger's Index to poetry: supplement to the fifth edition; indexing anthologies published from July 1, 1960 to December 31, 1965. Ed. by William F. Bernhardt and Kathryn W. Sewny. Columbia Univ. Press 1967 416p $35   **808.81**

1 Poetry—Indexes

Indexes 97 anthologies and "follows the arrangement and style of the Fifth Edition [listed above] with the exception of one change in the 'Subject Index.' . . . Listings of poems with the same title as the subject have been omitted from the 'Subject Index.' " Preface

Lomax, Alan

(ed.) 3000 years of Black poetry; an anthology; ed. by Alan Lomax and Raoul Abdul. Dodd 1970 xxvi, 261p $6.95   **808.81**

1 Negro poetry

The selections in this anthology have been gathered from the black kings of ancient Egypt and the poets of the Moslem conquest through the salons of eighteenth century Europe to the black cultures of modern Africa and America. Each section is preceded by an historical, cultural introduction, and a brief biography is given for each poet. (Publisher)

"Here's an anthology which opens doors to a virtual Biblical treasury of human intensities, love, tenderness and human pride. . . . The beauty is in the harmonious whole, the revelation through the writings of poets of an ages-old aristocracy of warm eloquence and pride that will be an eye-opener to many readers, white and black alike." Pub W

Morrison, Lillian

(comp.) Sprints and distances; sports in poetry and the poetry in sport; illus. by Clare and John Ross. Crowell 1965 211p illus $4.95   **808.81**

1 Sports—Poetry 2 Poetry—Collections

"The poems included here range from memorable newspaper verse to pieces by Pindar, Virgil, Wordsworth, and Yeats. They vary in form from simple quatrains to intricate modern verse. No attempt was made to include every sport though many are represented, from baseball to falconry." Prefatory note

Includes author, title, first line, and sport indexes

Plotz, Helen

(comp.) The earth is the Lord's; poems of the spirit; illus. with wood engravings by Clare Leighton. Crowell 1965 223p illus $5   **808.81**

1 Religious poetry

A collection of religious "poems of grief and splendor and questioning . . . cries of rebellion and despair, prayers and hymns of praise, tales of the saints. . . . The poems are drawn from the literature of many lands and ages, with particular emphasis on contemporary poets—John Updike, Theodore Roethke, and many others." Publisher's note

"A book essential to any poetry collection. . . . Each section is preceded by a handsome wood engraving. Dip in anywhere and the force of the poets overwhelms." Book Week

Indexes of authors, titles, first lines

(comp.) Imagination's other place; poems of science and mathematics; illus. with wood engravings by Clare Leighton. Crowell 1955 200p illus $4.50   **808.81**

1 Poetry—Collections 2 Science—Poetry

A collection of "poems about astronomy, geography, and physics; about chemistry, biology, and medicine. And there are poems about the scientists themselves—from Euclid to Einstein." Publisher's note

"Unusual in theme and provocative in approach, this anthology offers a wide variety of humorous as well as serious selections ranging from ancient through contemporary poetry, with emphasis upon the latter. In a stimulating preface and introductions to each of the four sections, the compiler breaks down the artificial dichotomy between scientist and poet, showing how both seek to find order and meaning in the creation of the world, the forms of nature, and the animal kingdom, and how the vision of each has illuminated human knowledge of the universe." Booklist

Van Doren, Mark

(ed.) An anthology of world poetry; in English translations by Chaucer, Swinburne, Dowson, Symons, Rossetti, Waley, Herrick, Pope, Francis Thompson, E. A. Robinson and others. Rev. and enl. ed. Harcourt 1936 lxii, 1467p $12.50   **808.81**

1 Poetry—Collections

First published 1928 by Boni

This is a selection from the best English translations of poetry of sixteen ancient and modern languages. Arranged in chronological sequence from the thirty-fifth century B.C. to the twentieth century A.D.

The author "has handled a difficult task with an admirable blend of comprehensiveness and selective taste." Spring'd Republican

(ed.) The world's best poems; ed. by Mark Van Doren and Garibaldi M. Lapolla. World Pub. 1946 [c1929] xlv, 672p $7.95   **808.81**

1 Poetry—Collections

1929 copyright held by Boni

First published 1932

The scope of this anthology ranges "in time from the thirty-fifth century A.D. and in space from China and Japan around through India, Persia, Arabia, Palestine, Egypt, Greece, and Rome to Europe and America. . . . This is an anthology of the world's best poetry in the best English I could unearth, and when I found no good English at all I left the poet out. . . . The arrangement [of the poems] is by countries, or rather by languages, and within each section the order of poets is chronological, the name of the translator being given at the end of each poem in parentheses. Occasionally I have prefixed a note to a poet's work in its proper place, not so much to give information about that poet as to suggest his quality and to make him stand out." Preface

The **Viking** Book of folk ballads of the English-speaking world; ed. by Albert B. Friedman. Viking 1956 xxxv, 473p $4.95   **808.81**

1 Ballads

"A rich collection of folk ballads, British, American, Canadian, Australian, and West Indian, for reading, for singing (with musical annotations for typical ballads), and for reference (with a discography, notes and glossaries). They are grouped by subject, from ballads of the supernatural to cowboy and frontier ballads." Pub W

"Explanatory notes and musical notations add to the pleasure and usefulness for student, specialist, or amateur." Booklist

808.82 Drama—Collections

Bentley, Eric
(comp.) The great playwrights; twenty-five plays with commentaries by critics and scholars chosen and introduced by Eric Bentley. Doubleday 1970 2v (2265p) $22.50
808.82

1 Drama—Collections
This is an anthology of plays "by the most significant dramatists of Western literature. From Aeschylus to Bertolt Brecht, Eric Bentley's main concern in assembling this collection was to choose those works most meaningful to the modern reader. The commentaries which accompany them are intended to point up their particular relevance to contemporary society." News of Bks
Includes bibliographical references

The **Best** plays of 1919/1920-1970/1971. . . . Dodd 1919-1971 52v illus 1919/1920-1969/1970 ea $10; 1970/1971 $12.50   **808.82**

1 Drama—Collections 2 Drama 3 Theater—Yearbooks
Volumes for 1919/1920-1955/1956 were analyzed in the Index to the Best plays series, 1899-1956, both currently out-of-print. Index to the Best plays series, 1949-1960 can be consulted for earlier volumes
Editors: 1919/1920-1947/1948 Burns Mantle and John Chapman; 1949/1950-1951/1952 John Chapman; 1952/1953-1960/1961 Louis Kronenberger; 1961/1962-1963/1964 Henry Hewes; 1964/1965 to date Otis L. Guernsey, Jr.
"Each volume includes by excerpt and summary, the ten most representative plays of the Broadway season. In addition it lists the full casts for each production of the year, the number of performances of each play, date on which it opened and the theater in which it played. There are also the usual statistical summary of the season, the plays that have run over five hundred performances on Broadway, the birthplace and birth date of prominent actors, and the 'necrology.'" Publisher's note

The **Best** short plays, 1968-1971; ed. by Stanley Richards. Chilton Bk. Co. 1968-1971 4v 1968-1970 ea $6.95, 1971 $7.50
808.82

1 Drama—Collections 2 One-act plays
"The Margaret Mayorga series"
This series of annual collections was begun in 1937 under the editorship of Margaret Mayorga with title: Best one-act plays, and published by Dodd through 1955. Beacon Press published the volumes from 1956 through 1961, when publication was suspended. Resumed 1968 under the present editorship
The editor's intent is "to include plays that are both entertaining and dramatically stimulating. Plays that restore a sense of reality, immediacy, dramatic excitement and personal involvement to the theatre. Plays that convey the author's sense of life to us, for a work of art is a direct extension of the personality of the artist. Plays that offer pertinent commentary and dramatically striking ideas, spoken in original and articulate voices." Introduction to 1968 volume
Contains brief biographical and bibliographical data about each dramatist represented

Block, Haskell M.
(ed.) Masters of modern drama; ed. with introductions and notes, by Haskell M. Block and Robert G. Shedd. Random House 1962 1198p illus $15.75   **808.82**

1 Drama—Collections
"An anthology of 45 plays, a few one-act, of contemporary and artistic significance. The arrangement is chronological with an introduction to each play. . . . The anthology begins with Ibsen's 'Peer Gynt,' 1867, and extends to 1958 but makes no attempt to include every country or well-publicized playwright. . . . The selective bibliography consists of important works in English on modern drama and the theater." Booklist

Cerf, Bennett A.
(comp.) Sixteen famous European plays; comp. by Bennett A. Cerf and Van H. Cartmell; with an introduction by John Anderson. Modern Lib. 1947 [c1943] xxv, 1052p (Modern Lib. giant) $4.95, lib. bdg. $3.89
808.82

1 Drama—Collections
A reprint of a book first published 1943 by Garden City Publishing Company
"This collection of plays [by Ibsen, Hauptmann, Rostand, Capek, Synge, and others] would be cheap at twice the price since it contains at least a dozen plays which should be found in the most modest theatrical library." Book Week

(ed.) Thirty famous one-act plays; ed. by Bennett Cerf and Van H. Cartmell; with an introduction by Richard Watts, Jr. Modern Lib. 1949 [c1943] xxii, 617p (Modern Lib. giant) $4.95, lib. bdg. $3.89   **808.82**

1 Drama—Collections 2 One-act plays
A reprint of a book first published 1943 by Garden City Publishing Company
This anthology, with biographical sketches ranges from plays by Anatole France and Strindberg through Schnitzler, O'Neill, Kaufman, Coward to Saroyan and Irwin Shaw

(ed.) 24 favorite one-act plays; ed. by Bennett Cerf and Van H. Cartmell. Doubleday 1958 455p $5.95   **808.82**

1 Drama—Collections 2 One-act plays
"This wide assortment of one-act plays includes comedies, tragedies, new and old, Irish, American, Russian, English, and Austrian. Includes the work of such playwrights as Eugene O'Neill, Noel Coward, George S. Kaufman, William Inge, Dorothy Parker, etc." McClurg. Book News
"A good collection showing the variety of form and subject used by modern masters of the short play." Good Reading

Chicorel Theater index to plays in anthologies, periodicals, discs and tapes. Chicorel Lib. Pub. Corp. 1970-1971 2v v 1 $38.25, v2 $42.50   **808.82**

1 Drama—Indexes
SBN 87729-001-6
Volume 1 edited by Marietta Chicorel and Veronica Hall; volume 2, by Marietta Chicorel and Richard Samuelson
"Indexes over 5,000 different plays by more than 2,000 authors in approximately 1,000 anthologies and 21 periodicals. All are in English or in English translation." Publisher's note
"Augmenting, but not replacing Ottemiller's 'Index to Plays in Collections' or Firkins' 'Play Index,' it is distinguished for its excellent format and ease of use. 'Based on primary sources, impeccably researched and verified with publishers, librarians, and by personal examination of the books and records provided by the publishers' it supplies complete bibliographic data, including price, for each entry, and indicates those available in paperback. The index is conveniently arranged in one alphabet under both author's and editor's names, and by titles of both plays and anthologies, with appended lists of authors, editors, and titles of plays, a list of publishers, and a subject indicators index." Cur Ref Bks

Dickinson, Thomas H.
(ed.) Chief contemporary dramatists [first series]. . . . Selected and ed. by Thomas H. Dickinson. Houghton 1915 676p $9.50
808.82

1 Drama—Collections
"Twenty plays from the recent drama of England, Ireland, America, Germany, France, Belgium, Norway, Sweden, and Russia." Title page

Dickinson, Thomas H.—*Continued*

"An excellent selection. . . . The appendix material is valuable for any library having much demand for material on the drama, including notes on the production of the plays, a reading list, a working book list and an index of characters." Wis lib Bul
Second series, published 1921, o.p. 1971

(ed.) Chief contemporary dramatists, third series. . . . Selected and ed. by Thomas H. Dickinson. Houghton 1930 698p $9.50
808.82

1 Drama—Collections

"Twenty plays from the recent drama of the United States, Great Britain, Germany, Austria, France, Italy, Spain, Russia, Hungary, Czechoslovakia, the Yiddish theatre, and Scandinavia." Title page
"This volume is the third in the series of collections of contemporary plays published under the general title of 'Chief Contemporary Dramatists,' of which the first was issued in 1915 [listed above] and the second in 1921." Introduction

Drury's Guide to best plays. 2d ed. by James M. Salem. Scarecrow 1969 512p $15
808.82

1 Drama—Indexes 2 Drama—Bibliography 3 Plots (Drama, fiction, etc.)
SBN 8108-0254-6

First published 1953, under editorship of F. K. W. Drury
This book "offers an easy-to-use guide for locating the plays most often performed by amateur and educational theater groups. The information provided is clear and practical: under an [alphabetical] author listing, one can find the plays, publisher, cast breakdown and some indication of setting required, plot synopsis, current holder of play, and royalty fee. The indexes provide listings under coauthors, lists of plays most popular among the producing groups and lists of play publishers." Library J

Gassner, John

(ed.) Twenty best European plays on the American stage; ed. with an introduction by John Gassner. Crown 1957 733p $6.95
808.82

1 Drama—Collections

"The present anthology is intended primarily for the study of the American stage. . . . I say 'study,' because a comparison between the plays printed here and their original form will instruct the careful reader about Broadway's way of dealing with its imports. It may also dismay him at times, and that can be instructive, too." Preface
Among the playwrights represented in this collection of twentieth-century European drama are Giraudoux, Anouilh, Chekhov, Sartre, S. Zweig, Molnar, and Benevente

Ireland, Norma Olin

Index to full length plays, 1944 to 1964. Faxon 1965 xxxii, 296p (Useful reference ser) $10
808.82

1 Drama—Indexes

A continuation of: Index to full length plays, by Ruth Gibbons Thomson
In this selected list, approximately 952 books have been indexed, including 798 individual plays and 154 collections. Approximately 979 different authors, 1187 titles, and 1062 subjects are arranged in a single alphabet. Includes a bibliography of individual plays analyzed
"Readily available plays in English by established playwrights and a representative sampling of 'pamphlet plays' for groups are indexed. . . . Main entries give title, author, adaptation, and number of acts and characters and indicate if illustrated or digested. A basic reference tool." Booklist

Ottemiller's Index to plays in collections; an author and title index to plays appearing in collections published between 1900 and mid-1970, by John M. Connor and Billie M. Connor. 5th ed. rev. and enl. Scarecrow 1971 452p $11
808.82

1 Drama—Indexes
ISBN 0-8108-0447-6

First edition compiled by John H. Ottemiller published 1943 by The H.W. Wilson Company
An index to full length plays published in the United States and England.
"The index covers play from earliest times to the present . . . which have been published in play anthologies and collections of literature." Publisher's note

Play index, 1949-1952; an index to 2616 plays in 1138 volumes; comp. by Dorothy Herbert West [and] Dorothy Margaret Peake. Wilson, H.W. 1953 239p $8
808.82

1 Drama—Indexes

"Includes plays for both children and adults, plays in collections and single plays, one-act plays and full-length plays, radio plays and those written for television, trade editions of Broadway plays and paper-bound plays for amateur production." Preface
Part I, arranged in one alphabet, has author, title and subject entries for all plays indexed; Part II lists the collections; Part III is the cast analysis; Part IV, Directory of publishers
"All types of plays are indexed, including translations into English. The dictionary catalog arrangement and the large amount of subject indexing are particularly helpful." Winchell. Guide to Reference Books. 8th edition

Play index, 1953-1960; an index to 4592 plays in 1735 volumes; ed. by Estelle A. Fidell [and] Dorothy Margaret Peake. Wilson, H.W. 1963 404p illus $11
808.82

1 Drama—Indexes
A supplement to the basic volume, 1949-1952, entered above. Arranged by the same categories

Play index, 1961-1967; an index to 4,793 plays; ed. by Estelle A. Fidell. Wilson, H.W. 1968 464p $16
808.82

1 Drama—Indexes
A supplement to the basic volume, 1949-1952. Arrangement the same as preceding volumes

Richards, Stanley

(ed.) Best plays of the sixties; ed. with an introductory note and prefaces to the plays. Doubleday 1970 1036p illus $10
808.82

1 Drama—Collections

Here are ten plays ranging from comedy to modern epic, representing both long established authors and gifted newcomers. "Contains the complete text of all ten plays, each one accompanied by a preface that provides a wealth of background information on the play itself, its production, and its playwright. In addition, Stanley Richards has . . . compiled a bibliography of other noteworthy plays of the decade." Publisher's note

(ed.) Best short plays of the world theatre, 1958-1967; ed. with an introduction and prefaces to the plays by Stanley Richards. Crown 1968 331p $6.50
808.82

1 Drama—Collections 2 One-act plays

"Twenty short plays selected from the thousands produced during the last ten years, each an outstanding presentation for one reason or another. All are complete. They include work by Jean Anouilh, Sean O'Casey, Brendan Behan, Brigid Brophy, William Inge, LeRoi Jones, Robert Lowell, and others." Bk Buyer's Guide
The editor "has supplied a splendid introduction to each [play]. These make the collection more valuable as a study of an important area of current drama." Library J

Tucker, S. Marion
(ed.) Twenty-five modern plays. 3d ed. by Alan S. Downer. Harper 1953 xx, 1008p illus $11.95 **808.82**

1 Drama—Collections

First published 1931
Among the playwrights represented in this collection are Henrik Ibsen, Eugene O'Neill, August Strindberg, Oscar Wilde, Anton Chekhov, Ferenc Molnár, Tennessee Williams, Sean O'Casey and Jean Cocteau
Includes: List of suggested readings

808.83 Short stories—Indexes

Short story index; an index to 60,000 stories in 4,320 collections; comp. by Dorothy E. Cook and Isabel S. Monro. Wilson, H.W. 1953 1553p $20 **808.83**

1 Short stories—Indexes
Supersedes the Index to short stories compiled by Ina Ten Eyck Firkins (1923) and its Supplements (1929 and 1936)
In two parts. The first part is an index by author, title and subject to the stories included in more than 4,000 collections published 1949 or earlier. The second part is a list of the collections indexed

Short story index; supplement, 1950-1954; an index to 9,575 stories in 549 collections; comp. by Dorothy E. Cook [and] Estelle A. Fidell. Wilson, H.W. 1956 394p $10 **808.83**

1 Short stories—Indexes
This supplement follows the pattern of the basic volume, entered above, with some changes in typography
Part I is an alphabetical index by author, title and subject to the stories included in the collections indexed. Part II is a list of the collections indexed. Part III is a directory of publishers

Short story index: supplement, 1955-1958; an index to 6,392 stories in 376 collections; comp. by Estelle A. Fidell [and] Esther V. Flory. Wilson, H.W. 1960 341p $10 **808.83**

1 Short stories—Indexes
A supplment to the basic volume and the 1950-1954 supplement. Follows the same arrangement

Short story index: supplement, 1959-1963; an index to 9,068 stories in 582 collections; comp. by Estelle A. Fidell. Wilson, H.W. 1965 487p $13 **808.83**

1 Short stories—Indexes
A continuation of the basic volume and the 1950-1954 and 1955-1958 supplements, which follows the same pattern

Short story index: supplement, 1964-1968; an index to 11,301 stories in 793 collections; comp. by Estelle A. Fidell. Wilson, H.W. 1969 599p $16 **808.83**

1 Short stories—Indexes
A continuation of the basic edition and its three supplements

808.851 Public speaking— Collections

Peterson, Houston
(ed.) A treasury of the world's great speeches. . . . Rev. and enl. ed. Simon & Schuster 1965 xxix, 866p $7.50 **808.851**

1 Orations

First published 1954
"Each speech prefaced with its dramatic and biographical setting and placed in its full historical perspective." Title page
"A comprehensive anthology of famous orations from Moses and Demosthenes to Churchill and Kennedy . . . [including] speeches by Khrushchev, Martin Luther King and President Johnson." Publisher's note

808.86 Collections of letters

Schuster, M. Lincoln
(ed.) A treasury of the world's great letters, from ancient days to our own time. . . . Simon & Schuster 1960 [c1940] xlviii, 562p illus pa $3.45 **808.86**

1 Letters
"Containing the characteristic and crucial communications, and intimate exchanges and cycles of correspondence, of many of the outstanding figures of world history, and some notable contemporaries, selected, edited, and integrated with biographical backgrounds and historical settings and consequences." Title page
"An interesting, voluminous collection, from the letters of Alexander the Great and King Darius III to an indictment of Hitler by Thomas Mann. Some are more intimate than 'great.'" Booklist

808.88 Collections of literature. Quotations

Barlett, John
(comp.) Familiar quotations. Little $15 **808.88**

1 Quotations
First published 1855. Periodically revised and brought up to date. Editors vary
"A collection of passages, phrases and proverbs traced to their sources in ancient and modern literature." Subtitle [of 14th edition]
Authors are arranged in chronological order from ancient times to the present so that the quotations may be considered in the context of the author's work and period. Includes author and key word indexes
"A standard collection, comprehensive and well selected. . . . One of the best books of quotations with a long history." Winchell. Guide to Reference Books. 8th edition

Bohle, Bruce
(comp.) The home book of American quotations; selected and arranged by Bruce Bohle. Dodd 1967 512p $10 **808.88**

1 Quotations
A collection of documented American quotations arranged first alphabetically by subject, and within subject alphabetically by author. It reflects "a lively American interest in politics and humor . . . [and] there is generous representation of the thoughts of Emerson, Thoreau, Franklin, Jefferson, Lincoln, Santayana, the Roosevelts, Woodrow Wilson, John F. Kennedy, Adlai Stevenson, and many others, together with selections from authors ranging from Longfellow to Robert Frost." Prefatory note

Brussell, Eugene E.
(ed.) Dictionary of quotable definitions. Prentice-Hall 1970 xl, 627p $19.95 **808.88**

1 Quotations
ISBN 0-13210633-7
Arranged alphabetically by topic, this is a collection of quotations which define the many aspects of man's condition, ranging from ability and absurdity to Zionism and zoo. The definitions are by individuals from all countries and many walks of life, including Casy Stengel and Walter Slezak as well as Shakespeare and Emerson. (Publisher)

Brusssell, Eugene E.—*Continued*

This "might well be titled a dictionary of aphorisms and metaphors, since these make up the body of the quotations arrayed under about 1,500 subjects. Since only authors' names, including many an 'Anon' are cited, it is more useful for those looking for pertinent phrases to enliven a speech or article, than for identification." Cur Ref Bks

Dictionary of foreign phrases and abbreviations; comp. and tr. by Kevin Guinagh. 2d ed. Wilson, H.W. 1972 352p   **808.88**

1 Quotations 2 English language—Foreign words and phrases—Dictionaries 3 Abbreviations

First published 1965

About 4500 "frequently used phrases, proverbs, quotations, mottoes and abbreviations; [approximately] 2000 of these are from Latin. Entry consists of phrase, language, translation . . . and source (if any). Greek phrases are in romanized form. Appended list of phrases arranged by languages." Walford. Guide to Reference Material, 2d edition

"The predominance of Latin quotations . . . is evidence that in spite of its being viewed as a dead language, Latin is still used by some writers. Next frequently quoted in this collection are French and Italian phrases, with a sprinkling of German, Irish, Greek, Spanish, and a few other languages. The selection reflects the tastes and interests of the compiler, who was influenced to some extent by the frequency of usage." Cur Ref Bks

"This book is one that I must have here in the office as well as at home." N Y Times Bk R

Evans, Bergen

(ed.) Dictionary of quotations; collected and arranged and with comments by Bergen Evans. Delacorte Press 1968 lxxxix, 2029p $15   **808.88**

1 Quotations

"This volume is arranged alphabetically. There is a typical index which is followed by the main section of quotations under topical headings which are arranged in chronological order to show the development in an idea. Index of authors." Book Rev Digest

The volume includes an "immense subject index—the structure is very satisfactory. Of the content, one can only say that it's a hard heart that will grumble at omissions. . . . This is a very good book indeed—exact, encyclopaedic, human, humorous, wise, urbane, American, [and] universal." Book World

Flesch, Rudolf

(ed.) The new book of unusual quotations. Selected and ed. by Rudolf Flesch. Harper 1966 448pp $7.50   **808.88**

1 Quotations

First published 1957 with title: The book of unusual quotations

"This is intended to be 'the exact opposite of a standard collection of quotations': i.e., instead of verifying or identifying a 'familiar' quotation, it assembles unfamiliar quotations to promote thinking. The quotations (all prose) are grouped under a multitude of alphabetically listed subjects and are often followed by references to similar or antithetical entries. The arrangement under subject appears to be random, and no citations of works quoted are given in the text." Library J

Hoyt, Jehiel Keeler

Hoyt's New cyclopedia of practical quotations. . . . Comp. by Kate Louise Roberts. Funk 1940 xxxi, 1343p $8.50, thumb indexed $9.25   **808.88**

1 Quotations

First published 1882

"Drawn from the speech and literature of all nations, ancient and modern, classic and popular, in English and foreign text. With the names, dates, and nationality of quoted authors, and copious indexes." Title page

In three main divisions: (1) Quotations arranged alphabetically by general subjects; (2) Index of quoted authors with brief biographical data; (3) Concordance of quotations

"A very comprehensive collection of some 21,000 quotations given with exact references. Omits quotations from the Bible. The indexes are excellent. Though now more than 40 years old, still useful except for contemporary writers." Winchell. Guide to Reference Books. 8th edition

Magill, Frank N.

(ed.) Magill's Quotations in context. [1st-2d ser]; associate editor: Tench Francis Tilghman. Harper 1965-1969 2v ea $11.95   **808.88**

1 Quotations

Also available from Salem Press in two, two-volume sets at $15 per set

Over 3500 quotations drawn from world literature explaining who said what, when, where, why and under what circumstances. (Publisher)

Entries are arranged alphabetically by quotation without regard to author or chronology. Includes indexes of quotations, key words, and authors

Mencken, H. L.

(ed.) A new dictionary of quotations on historical principles from ancient and modern sources. Knopf 1942 1347p $15   **808.88**

1 Quotations

Quotations in prose and poetry arranged under subjects. The quotations are dated and names of authors and titles of books quoted are given in full

"Since Mr. Mencken gives no index of authors quoted, it is impossible to look for a given author's opinions unless you already know what they are in something like his own words. But for the nibblers and lingerers, it will perhaps not matter." N Y Her Trib Books

The Oxford Dictionary of quotations. 2d ed. [rev] Oxford 1953 1003p $11   **808.88**

1 Quotations

First published 1941

"Alphabetical arrangement by author, with special sections of quotations from the Book of Common prayer, the Bible, and from foreign languages. Indexed by key words." Booklist

"A remarkable compilation. . . . It will not necessarily supersede Bartlett but is certainly as valuable. Familiarity rather than merit has been the test of inclusion." New Yorker

Prochnow, Herbert V. 1897-

(comp.) A treasury of humorous quotations; for speakers, writers, and home reference, by Herbert V. Prochnow and Herbert V. Prochnow, Jr. Harper 1969 398p $6.95   **808.88**

1 Quotations 2 Wit and humor

More than 6000 [numbered] humorous bits and pieces arranged alphabetically by subject, i.e. 'husbands,' 'money,' 'women,' and others, quoted from the Bible, Plato, Mark Twain, Oscar Wilde, Adlai Stevenson, John F. Kennedy, and others." Bk Buyer's Guide

Index refers to numbers of the quotes

Stevenson, Burton

(ed.) The home book of quotations; classical and modern. Dodd $35   **808.88**

1 Quotations

First published 1934 and periodically revised

"A comprehensive and well-chosen collection of more than 50,000 quotations, arranged alphabetically by subject with subarrangement by smaller topics. Usually gives exact citation. Includes an index of authors—giving full name, identifying phrase, and dates of birth and death, with reference to all quotations cited—and a word index, which indexes the quotation by leading words, usually nouns, though in some cases verbs and adjectives are also

Stevenson, Burton—*Continued*

used. Boldface entries are given for some of the smaller subjects. The quotations under these are not indexed separately, and one must, therefore, turn to the subject and run through the entries. This practice must be remembered when using this index." Winchell. Guide to Reference Books. 8th edition

Tripp, Rhoda Thomas
(comp.) The international thesaurus of quotations. Crowell 1970 1088p (A Crowell Reference bk) $8.95, thumb indexed $10
808.88

1 Quotations
ISBN 0-690-44584-9; 0-690-44585-7
Companion volume to: Roget's International thesaurus, class 424
Arranged alphabetically by categories of meaning with cross-references to related subject categories, this thesaurus contains 16,000 sayings, with more than 6,000 from this century, the rest chosen for their relevance to today's concerns. (Publisher)
"Since more than a third of the quotations are from twentieth-century sources, and since older writers in other languages are often represented in recent translations and by material chosen for its usefulness to writers and speakers today, the big new treasury is as fresh as it is unique. It is typical that, in addition to those in the general Racial Prejudice category, relevant quotations can be found under Minorities, Whites, and Blacks, and that the seventeen quotations under Blacks are from James Baldwin, Le Roi Jones, Michael Harrington, and others of their stature." Sat R
Includes indexes of authors and sources, key words and categories

The **Viking** Book of aphorisms; a personal selection by W. H. Auden and Louis Kronenberger. Viking 1962 405p $6.50
808.88

1 Aphorisms and apothegms
Aphorisms "have been collected by the editors from the works of Santayana, Shaw, Bertrand Russell, Ogden Nash, and others and divided into categories." Bk Buyer's Guide
"A very interesting collection. . . . It is too bad that the editors did not indicate where in an author's works a specific quotation appears. Also many authors are identified only by their last names." Library J
Index of authors: p397-405

Wallis, Charles L.
(ed.) Our American heritage. Harper 1970 222p illus boards $4.95
808.88

1 Quotations
In this book "songs and poems, and the words of leaders from Washington to Lincoln to Kennedy and Nixon tell of a remarkable past and prescribe confidence for a troubled present." News of Bks
Includes indexes of photographs, familiar quotations, authors, poetry and topics

809 Literature—History, description, critical appraisal, biographical treatment

Downs, Robert B.
Books that changed the world. A.L.A. 1956 200p $2.25
809

1 Literature—History and criticism 2 Books and reading
Analyzed in Essay and general literature index
"To demonstrate the dynamic power of books a librarian has selected for study 16 books which can be credited with concrete results and actions in national and international affairs. The books are selected from science and the social sciences, and range from the

Renaissance to the present. The author presents the books without measuring them for moral values or literary quality but clearly designates their power in shaping events. The books are: The prince, by Machiavelli; Common sense, by Paine; Wealth of nations, by Smith; Essay on the principle of population, by Malthus; Civil disobedience, by Thoreau; Uncle Tom's cabin, by Stowe; Das Kapital, by Marx; The influence of sea power upon history, by Mahan; The geographical pivot of history, by Mackinder; Mein Kampf, by Hitler; De revolutions orbium coelestium, by Copernicus; De motu cordis, by Harvey; Principia mathematica, by Newton; Origin of species, by Darwin; The interpretation of dreams, by Freud; and Relativity, by Einstein." Booklist
Bibliographical notes: p194-95

Durant, Will
Interpretations of life; a survey of contemporary literature. . . . By Will and Ariel Durant. Simon & Schuster 1970 384p $8.95 **809**

1 Literature—History and criticism
"The lives and opinions of some major authors of our time: Faulkner, Hemingway, Steinbeck, Sinclair, O'Neill, Jeffers, Pound, Joyce, Eliot, Maugham, Proust, Gide, Wittgenstein, Kierkegaard, Husserl, Heidegger, Sartre, de Beauvoir, Camus, Mann, Kafka, Kazantzakis, Sholokhov, Pasternak, Solzhenitsyn, and Yevtushenko." Title page
The authors' "judgments are, if conventional, generally sensible. There is little pretense to profound scholarship. If there is one idea unifying this pleasant series of personal commentaries, it is that modern literature has been produced in the climate of a world whence God has fled, presumably permanently. The Durants' work will be of value to the general reader." Book of the Month Club News
Bibliographical guide to the Notes: p345-51

Highet, Gilbert
The classical tradition; Greek and Roman influences on western literature. Oxford 1949 xxxviii, 763p $12.50 **809**

1 Literature—History and criticism 2 Literature, Comparative
Analyzed in Essay and general literature index
The author "traces the history of the Greco-Roman classic tradition and its influence on the various ages of literature, with special emphasis upon such moderns as Joyce, Pound, Eliot, Gide, O'Neill, Sartre, etc." Retail Bookseller
This book "collects, sifts, compresses, and applies an immense accumulation of technical study that most readers have neither the time nor the training to examine for themselves and that too frequently is inaccessible to those who could make use of it." Nation
Brief bibliography: p550-55 Bibliographical references included in Notes: p556-705

People, places and books. Oxford 1953 277p $6.75 **809**

1 Books and reading 2 Literature—Addresses and essays
Analyzed in Essay and general literature index
"Adapted from the author's radio broadcasts, these thirty-odd pieces touch on nearly everything in the world of books, from the art of translation to science fiction." Retail Bookseller

Macy, John
The story of the world's literature; illus. by Onorio Ruotolo. [Rev. ed] Liveright 1961 615p illus $6.95 **809**

1 Literature—History and criticism
First published 1925
"A clearly written and decidedly entertaining outline of most of the world's principal national literatures, with relatively more space devoted to English and American literature." Cleveland
Bibliography: p565-92

Trilling, Lionel
The opposing self; nine essays in criticism.
Viking 1955 232p $5.75   809
1 Literature—History and criticism 2 Literature—Addresses and essays
Analyzed in Essay and general literature index
"Most of these essays were written as introductions to books." Preface
Contents: The poet as hero: Keats in his letters; Little Dorrit; Anna Karenina; William Dean Howells and the roots of modern taste; The Bostonians; Wordsworth and the Rabbis; George Orwell and the politics of truth; Flaubert's last testament; Mansfield Park

Wilson, Edmund
Axel's castle; a study in the imaginative literature of 1870-1930. Scribner 1931 319p $4.50   809
1 Literature—History and criticism 2 Symbolism in literature
Analyzed in Essay and general literature index
"A discussion of symbolism in literature is followed by masterly analyses of the work of the writers who in the author's opinion are the outstanding figures of the movement today." Pittsburgh
Contents: Symbolism; W. B. Yeats; Paul Valéry; T. S. Eliot; Marcel Proust; James Joyce; Gertrude Stein; Axel and Rimbaud

809.1 History and criticism of poetry

Auslander, Joseph
The winged horse; the story of the poets and their poetry, by Joseph Auslander and Frank Ernest Hill; with decorations by Paul Honoré and a bibliography by Theresa West Elemendorf. Doubleday 1928 [c1927] 451p illus $4.95   809.1
1 Poetry—History and criticism 2 Poets
Companion volume to the authors': The winged horse anthology, class 821.08
"Representative selections illustrating the qualities which made each poet great are introduced into the narrative." Pittsburgh
Includes material on the following poets: Blake, Browning, Burns, Byron, Chaucer, Dante, Homer, Horace, Keats, Milton, Petrarch, Poe, Shakespeare, Shelley, Spenser, Tennyson, Virgil, Whitman, Wordsworth

Highet, Gilbert
The powers of poetry. Oxford 1960 356p $7.95   809.1
1 Poetry—History and criticism 2 Poets
Analyzed in Essay and general literature index
Contains 39 essays on poets and poetry, beginning with three chapters on poetic technique. "Next is a group of essays on individual poets, from Shakespeare to Dylan Thomas, discussing their characters . . . and some of the experiences that profoundly affected their work. . . . In the third part there are twenty-one studies of poems [from several languages]." Preface
"The student and teacher of literature will find in it many reiterations of what they have heard and said, but exchanging past experiences with old friends is still a rewarding pleasure." Best Sellers

MacLeish, Archibald
Poetry and experience. Houghton 1961 [c1960] 204p $5.95   809.1
1 Poetry—History and criticism 2 Poetry
Analyzed in Essay and general literature index
"A poet's statement of what poetry is, what it can be, and what it can do. The first four chapters of the book constitute an introduction to the appreciation of poetry; the four

final chapters center around the work of Emily Dickinson, W. B. Yeats, Arthur Rimbaud, and John Keats." Huntting
"Although the book retains the lucidity and fervor of the best public address, it is a serious and provocative contribution to the theory of poetry." N Y Times Bk R

809.2 History and criticism of drama

Gassner, John
Masters of the drama. 3d rev. and enl. ed. Dover 1954 xxi, 890p illus $7.50   809.2
1 Drama—History and criticism 2 Dramatists
First published 1940 by Random House
"A history of the theater from ancient times to the present [1954] in which emphasis is laid on drama and dramatists, rather than on its associated arts." Book Rev Digest
"It is a readable useful book, including in one text critical commentaries, biographical sketches of dramatists, brief plots of outstanding plays, and highlights of historical tendencies and cultural trends." Booklist

Nicoll, Allardyce
World drama; from Aeschylus to Anouilh; with sixty-four plates in half-tone. Harcourt [1950] 1000p illus $9.75   809.2
1 Drama—History and criticism
This one-volume history of the theater "includes the Greek theatre, religious drama, the French classic theatre, the triumph of Realism, the theatre of China and Japan, and ends with the postwar theatre in America, England and France." Huntting
"This is an extraordinarily interesting and authoritative history of world drama. . . . Highly recommended to theatre and drama collections regardless of size." Library J

809.203 History and criticism of drama—Dictionaries and encyclopedias

The Reader's encyclopedia of world drama; ed. by John Gassner & Edward Quinn. Crowell 1969 1030p illus (A Crowell Reference bk) $15   809.203
1 Drama—Dictionaries 2 Drama—History and criticism
This compilation "emphasizes drama as literature, with biocriticisms of playwrights, plots of plays, articles on genres, and historical surveys of national drama, usually under the name of the country. . . . Most of the articles are signed giving initials for the list of about one hundred contributors, many of whom are from American universities, with a few from abroad." Cur Ref Bks
"If few of the articles are exhaustive, those on important individual plays may be consulted for provocative comments and well-told plots. A 100-page appendix is the repository of a couple of dozen 'basic documents in dramatic theory.'" Sat R

809.7 History and criticism of satire

Highet, Gilbert
The anatomy of satire. Princeton Univ. Press 1962 301p illus $6   809.7
1 Satire—History and criticism
"The outgrowth of a series of lectures given at Princeton University under the sponsorship of the Spencer Trask Lecture Fund, an information-packed study by a well-known classicist and literary critic analyzes by definitions, descriptions, and examples the three

Highet, Gilbert—*Continued*
main forms of satire: monolog, parody, and narrative. Highet takes as the scope of his work the entire range of satirical literature from ancient Greece to contemporary America, from Aristophanes to Henry Miller." Booklist

810.3 American literature— Dictionaries and encyclopedias

Hart, James D.
The Oxford Companion to American literature. 4th ed. [rev. and enl] Oxford 1965 991p $12.50   810.3
1 American literature—Dictionaries 2 American literature—Bio-bibliography
Companion volume to: The Oxford Companion to American history by Thomas H. Johnson, class 973.03
First published 1941
"Included are: short biographies and bibliographies of American authors, with information on their style and subject matter: summaries and descriptions of hundreds of American novels, stories, essays, poems and plays; definitions and historical outlines of literary schools and movements; and information on literary societies, magazines, anthologies, cooperative publications, literary awards, book collectors, printers, and other matters relating to writing in America. Entries are alphabetically arranged." Huntting
"An invaluable reference book. . . . There must be omissions—there could not help but be—yet if there are, they in no way make the book less good, for there is so much here." Commonweal

The **Reader's** encyclopedia of American literature, by Max J. Herzberg and the staff of the Thomas Y. Crowell Company. Crowell 1962 1280p illus (A Crowell Reference bk) $15   810.3
1 American literature—Dictionaries 2 American literature—Bio-bibliography
"An encyclopedia of American authors, past and present, and their important works, American literary groups and movements, and other literary topics. With [over 6000] subjects and people included, some authors are given four or five paragraphs, most get one or two. Biographical entries give the facts of the subject's life, deal individually with his chief works, provide critical comment, and supply bibliographic references." Pub W
"There are also a fair sprinkling of photographs of authors, a few reproductions of pages from famous books or magazines, and a good, though highly selective, glossary. And there are some good, long signed articles by some 44 special contributors. . . . This is a valuable addition to the reference shelves of any type of library." Library J

810.8 American literature— Collections

Fadiman, Clifton
(ed.) The American treasury, 1455-1955; selected, arranged, and ed. by Clifton Fadiman; assisted by Charles Van Doren. Harper 1955 xxxii, 1108p $9.95   810.8
1 American literature—Collections 2 U.S.—Civilization
"Contains some 6000 selections from about 1300 authors. Divided into three parts: (1) About ourselves and our country (2) An anthology of poetry and song; (3) What we have said about the world and human life in general." (Publisher)
"An excellent anthology for browsing or reference works consisting of short quotations. . . . As, always, Mr. Fadiman's taste is impeccable." Cincinnati
Includes indexes of subjects, familiar words and phrases, authors and titles

Jones, LeRoi
(ed.) Black fire; an anthology of Afro-American writing; ed. by LeRoi Jones and Larry Neal. Morrow 1968 670p boards $10
810.8
1 Negro literature 2 American literature—Collections
"Unlike other anthologies of black writers, the editors of this volume make no pretense that their selections constitute a fair sampling. Very frankly the contents by youthful writers —essays, poems, plays, short fiction—are political, celebrating black nationalism, black militancy and negritude." Choice
"The volume places in sharp focus the old controversy between the particular and the universal relevance of esthetic standards, and makes one consider afresh the relationship between political and cultural programs and the human imagination." Sat R

Joseph, Stephen M.
(ed.) The me nobody knows; children's voices from the ghetto. World Pub. 1969 143p boards $4.95   810.8
1 Children as authors
"The children whose writing appears in this book live in the slums. Their ages range from seven to eighteen and most of them are Black or Puerto Rican. . . . This anthology resulted from my growing awareness that the children I had been teaching were something special. All children are. It became important to me to make other people aware of this. . . . This book is primarily for them and for the children and teachers whom I hope it will encourage to be freer in their writing and teaching." Introduction
"The book is divided into four sections: one containing pieces on self, family, friends, and school; another on the ghetto neighborhood; the third on the world outside the ghetto; and the last on ideas about death, sleep, love, science, sex, and God." Booklist

Kearns, Francis E.
(ed.) The Black experience; an anthology of American literature for the 1970's; ed. with an introduction and notes by Francis E. Kearns; foreword by Arna Bontemps. Viking 1970 xx, 650p $10   810.8
1 Negro literature 2 American literature—Collections
SBN 670-17148-4
"A first-rate collection of imaginative writing by both black and white writers focuses on the influence of the black identity and experience on American literary tradition and shows the shifts in literary attitudes toward race in the U.S. from pre-Civil War times to the present. Containing short stories, poems, plays, extracts from novels, a few essays, and a selection of Negro songs, the anthology includes works by 42 writers. . . . Kearns provides a general explanatory introduction and brief notes on each writer and his works." Booklist
Bibliography: p639-50

Margolies, Edward
(ed.) A native sons reader. Lippincott 1970 361p $6.95   810.8
1 Negro literature 2 American literature—Collections
"This is not a collection of militant or even aesthetically avant-garde writing by American Negroes, but simply Margolies' personal selection of the typical writings—essays, poems, stories, excerpts from larger works—by black authors who, from DuBois, Dunbar and Langston Hughes to James Baldwin, Gwen Brooks and Eldridge Cleaver, have expressed the 'black experience in America' in personal terms. Margolies places his selections under such headings as 'Roots,' 'South: Slavery and After,' 'Migration,' 'City,' 'Church,' 'Music' and so on. Rather than being a mirror of the Negro's mood today, the book fulfills Margolies' aim to transcend skin and 'suggest the possibilities' of black literary expression as a rich part of the American heritage." Pub W

Miller, Perry
   (ed.) The American Puritans: their prose
and poetry. Doubleday 1956 346p pa $1.75
                                              810.8

   1 American literature—Collections 2 Puritans
   "Doubleday Anchor books"
   "In this collection of journals, sermons, poe-
   try, and personal narrative, prominent Puri-
   tans discuss their first hundred years in the
   New World and their convictions about reli-
   gion, the state and society, literature, and ed-
   ucation. Among the authors included are: Wil-
   liam Bradford, John Winthrop, Cotton Mather,
   John Cotton, Thomas Hooker, Samuel Sewall,
   Anne Bradstreet, Michael Wigglesworth, and
   Edward Taylor." Publisher's note

810.9 American literature—
History and criticism

Brooks, Van Wyck
   The confident years: 1885-1915. Dutton
1955 620p $3.50   810.9

   1 American literature—History and criticism
   "Everyman's library New American edition"
   First published 1952
   "With 'The Confident Years' I bring to a
   close the series of [five] historical volumes
   that bears the general title 'Makers and Find-
   ers: a History of the Writer in America, 1800-
   1915.' . . . I have tried to define the American
   tradition in letters." Note
   An inclusive picture of the American literary
   scene from New York to San Francisco, from
   Chicago to New Orleans discussing such authors as: Stephen Crane, Ambrose Bierce,
   Frank Norris, Jack London, Lafcadio Hearn,
   O. Henry, Edith Wharton, Theodore Dreiser,
   H. L. Mencken, Eugene O'Neill and many others
   "In Mr. Brooks one finds united, to an unusual degree, the talents of an indefatigable
   scholar, historian, psychologist, biographer,
   genre-painter, sociologist, critic, and literary
   artist. . . . He brings the cultural past to life
   in all its interrelated aspects; illuminates it by
   an act of vivid re-creation." Atlantic

   The flowering of New England. Dutton
1952 563p $3.50   810.9

   1 American literature—New England 2 American literature—History and criticism 3 New
   England—Civilization
   "Everyman's library New American edition"
   Sequel to: The world of Washington Irving
   First published 1936. Awarded Pulitzer Prize,
   1937
   The second volume of the author's five volume series: Makers and finders; a history of
   the writer in America, 1800-1915
   "Van Wyck Brooks has fused into a glowing
   narrative, not only the atmosphere of the period [from 1815-1865] but also charming, mellow and authentic portraits of the leading figures from Ticknor, Prescott, Hawthorne,
   Emerson, on through [Thoreau, Longfellow]
   Lowell, Motley and Holmes. There are brilliant summaries of each one's work; and there
   are delightful recreations of groups gathered
   in clubs or at Brooks Farm, and of friendly
   talk on a walking trip. As the chronicle length-
   ens, changing phases are noted in the times,
   as well as in individuals and their writings."
   N Y Libraries
   Followed by: The times of Melville and Whitman

   New England: Indian summer. Dutton
1950 569p $3.50   810.9

   1 American literature—New England 2 American literature—History and criticism 3 New
   England—Civilization
   "Everyman's library New American edition"
   First published 1940
   Although this is the fourth volume in the
   author's series: Makers and finders; a history
   of the writer in America, 1800-1915, it constitutes a sequel to: The flowering of New England; taking up to the thread of the previous
   volume

   Partial contents: Howells in Cambridge;
Henry Adams; Henry James; Aldrich and his
circle; Emily Dickinson; Boston in the nineties; Pre-war years
   The author "has lovingly resurrected his
hosts of authors and brought the warmth of
his intense antiquarian zeal to all their acts
and works. His scenes show his superb felicity
in genre and milieu. . . . His quotations and
footnotes alone make his book unrivaled."
Nation
   Followed by: The confident years, 1885-1915

   Our literary heritage; a pictorial history
of the writer in America, by Van Wyck
Brooks and Otto L. Bettmann. Dutton 1956
241p illus $9.95   810.9

   1 American literature—History and criticism
   "One sixth of the material in the five volume of 'Makers and finders: a history of the
   writer in America, 1800-1915' is compressed
   into a book studded with photographs and
   drawings from the Bettmann Archive. Lack of
   room forces out the lesser figures but the major authors and eras in American literary history are not slighted; both text and pictures
   capture the spirit of American literature."
   Booklist
   Condensations of: The world of Washington
   Irving; The flowering of New England; New
   England: Indian summer [and] The confident
   years: 1885-1915, all entered separately
   Source of illustrations: p240

   The times of Melville and Whitman. Dutton 1953 499p $3.50   810.9

   1 American literature—History and criticism
   2 U.S.—Civilization
   "Everyman's library New American edition"
   Sequel to: The flowering of New England
   First published 1947
   Analyzed in Essay and general literature index
   Intended as the third volume of his series on
   American literary history, this covers the period 1840-1890 in the literary history of the
   whole country—New York, the Middle West,
   the South and Far West
   "As in previous volumes there is especial
   attention to rural America and emphasis on
   our early naturalists—the poets and artists
   who pictured the countryside." Wis Lib Bul
   Followed by: New England: Indian summer

   The world of Washington Irving. Dutton
1950 514p $3.50   810.9

   1 American literature—History and criticism
   2 U.S.—Civilization
   "Everyman's library New American edition"
   First published 1944
   The first volume of the author's series:
   Makers and finders: a history of the writer in
   America, 1800-1915. "The period covered is
   from 1800 to the 1840's. It deals with the litera-
   ture of New York, the Middle States, the
   South and the West." Book Rev Digest
   Discusses the literary output and personali-
   ties of John James Audubon, William Cullen
   Bryant, James Fenimore Cooper, Thomas Jef-
   ferson, Edgar Allan Poe. William Dunlap,
   Washington Irving, William Gilmore Simms
   and Nathaniel Parker Willis
   Followed by: The flowering of New England

   The **Cambridge** History of American literature; ed. by William Peterfield Trent
[and others]. . . . Imperial ed. Macmillan
(N Y) 3v in 1 $9.95   810.9

   1 American literature—History and criticism
   Contents: v 1 Colonial and Revolutionary
   literature—Early national literature: pt. 1; v2
   Early national literature: pt 2, Later national
   literature: pt. 1; v3 Later national literature:
   pt. 2-3
   "Still an important history of American literature, necessary in all types of general libraries. Covers the early period with unusual
   thoroughness; treats the ordinary literary forms and subjects, standard writers, etc.
   with great detail; and includes adequate treatment of many subjects not covered in the customary literary histories, e.g., accounts of the
   early travelers, explorers, and observers; colonial newspapers; literary annuals and gift

The **Cambridge** History of American literature—*Continued*
books; later magazines and newspapers; children's literature; oral literature; the English
language in America; non-English writings,
i.e., German, French, Yiddish, aboriginal.
Each chapter is by a specialist, and the bibliographies . . . . are very full, although not now
up to date." Winchell. Guide to Reference
Books. 8th edition

Curley, Dorothy Nyren
(ed.) A library of literary criticism: Modern American literature; comp. and ed. by
Dorothy Nyren Curley, Maurice Kramer
[and] Elaine Fialka Kramer. 4th enl. ed.
Ungar 1969 3v $45   810.9
1 American literature—History and criticism
2 Criticism
First published 1960 under Nyren
Contents: v 1 A-F; v2 G-O; v3 P-Z
"This very valuable source book and index
excerpts hundreds of critical books, essays,
articles, and reviews dealing with the works
of nearly 300 important 20th-Century American
novelists, poets, dramatists, and essayists, with
citations to original sources. . . . A judiciously
chosen, representative survey of and key to
modern criticism of American authors of our
century, this is recommended for all libraries."
Library J

Downs, Robert B.
Books that changed America. Macmillan
(N Y) 1970 280p $6.95   810.9
1 American literature—History and criticism
2 U.S.—Civilization 3 Books and reading
Analyzed in Essay and general literature index
The author "discusses 25 titles which in his
judgment have effected changes in American
life, usually for the good, but not without
pain and suffering and bitter controversy. The
titles range from Tom Paine's 'Common Sense'
to Rachel Carson's 'Silent Spring.' Others are
Mrs Stowe's 'Uncle Tom's Cabin,' Upton Sinclair's 'The Jungle,' and John K. Galbraith's
'The Affluent Society.' Political and economic
treatises mingle with fiction, scientific reports,
and legal essays." Library J
Bibliography: p269-71

Kazin, Alfred
On native grounds; an interpretation of
modern American prose literature. Harcourt
1942 541p $7.50   810.9
1 American prose literature—History and
criticism 2 American literature—History and
criticism 3 Authors, American
Analyzed in Essay and general literature index
Contents: Opening struggle for realism;
American fin de siècle; Two educations: Edith
Wharton and Theodore Dreiser; Progressivism:
the superman and the muckrake; Progressivism:
some insurgent scholars; Joyous season; Post-
war scene; New realism: Sherwood Anderson
and Sinclair Lewis; Exquisites; Elegy and
satire: Willa Cather and Ellen Glasgow; Liberals and new humanists: Into the thirties;
Revival of naturalism: Criticism at the poles;
Rhetoric and the agony; America! America!
"A full-length, brilliantly sustained history
of the relation between American prosewriters
and our developing society in the years between
1890 and the present." New Yorker

Literary history of the United States. Editors: Robert E. Spiller [and others]. 3d
ed. rev. Macmillan (N Y) [1965-1966
c1963] 3v in 2 v 1 $17.50, v2 $16.50   810.9
1 American literature—History and criticism
2 American literature—Bibliography
Volumes one and two first published 1948 in
three volumes. Volume three, the Bibliography
supplement, published 1959 was revised by Robert Ludwig
Contents: v 1: History; v2: Bibliography;
v3: Bibliography supplement

The history "presents a survey from colonial
times to the present day in a series of chapters
written by authorities and integrated into a
whole by a board of editors. The chapters are
not signed, but a list of them with the author
of each is given. . . . Also includes a highly
selected bibliography for the general reader,
p.1446-81. v.2, 'Bibliography', consists of bibliographical essays organized to develop the
treatment of the text." Winchell. Guide to
Reference Books. 8th edition
"Not limited to belles lettres, it examines
also the more important literature of travel
and exploration, historical and political writing, folklore, and the work of speculative
thinkers." Library J

Margolies, Edward
Native sons; a critical study of twentieth-
century Negro American authors: W. E. B.
Du Bois [and others] Lippincott 1968 210p
$5.95   810.9
1 Negro literature—History and criticism
2 Negro authors
Analyzed in Essay and general literature index
The author discusses the work of a number
of Negro American authors—including Richard
Wright, Chester Himes, Ralph Ellison, and
LeRoi Jones, among others—both in terms of
its literary significance and in terms of what
it tells us about American life. (Publisher)
"The main concern is with those [writers]
who have appeared since 1940. . . . [Margolies']
concern with quality instead of quantity is
clearly what raises his work above those of
many of his predecessors. . . . He has rediscovered some long-forgotten works of high
artistic value, such as Attaway's Blood on the
Forge. . . . Margolies reminds us once again
of the vitally important part the Negro has
played in the growth of American literature.
Over and over he tells us that these writers are
worth reading." Sat R
Bibliography: p201-02

Parrington, Vernon L.
Main currents in American thought; an
interpretation of American literature from
the beginnings to 1920. Harcourt [1939] 3v
in 1 $11.50   810.9
1 American literature—History and criticism
2 Philosophy, American 3 U.S.—Civilization
4 U.S.—Politics and government 5 U.S.—
Religion
Reprint in one volume of a set first published
1927-30 in three volumes
Contents: v 1 Colonial mind, 1620-1800;
v2 Romantic revolution in America, 1800-1860;
v3 Beginnings of critical realism in America,
1860-1920, completed to 1900 only
"A history of American ideas as revealed by
literary production. Parrington, a liberal, evaluated American writing by a economic and
social interpretation. His critical sweep of the
scene has originality and accuracy. The first
two volumes received the Pulitzer Prize for
1928." Haydn. Thesaurus of Book Digests
Bibliography at end of each volume

Spiller, Robert E.
(ed.) The American literary revolution,
1783-1837; ed. with a preface and explanatory notes. N.Y. Univ. Press 1967 500p
(Documents in American civilization ser)
$10   810.9
1 American literature—History and criticism
Analyzed in Essay and general literature index
First published by Anchor Books
"Contemporary documents selected to show
the development of American literary independence and literary criticism in the immediate
post-Revolutionary era. . . . The papers consist of prefaces, prologs, essays, and addresses
by such writers as William Cullen Bryant,
Washington Irving, Noah Webster, Henry Wadsworth Longfellow, Edgar Allan Poe, and Ralph
Waldo Emerson. Contemporary lists of book
orders and library holdings are also included.
A bibliographic note is appended." Booklist

811 American poetry

Agee, James
The collected poems of James Agee; ed. and with an introduction by Robert Fitzgerald. Houghton 1968 179p $4.95   **811**

"Employing a variety of forms, including short lyrics, sonnets, and Byronic 'ottava rima.' Agee's poetry reflects his cinematic perception of natural beauty as well as his religious spirit. Reprinted in full is 'Permit me voyage.' published in 1934, followed by poems chosen by the editor as suitable for a never-realized second book, as explained in the introduction. The third section, John Carter: 1932-1936, was Agee's project for an unsuccessful Guggenheim Fellowship application. The final selections, dating from 1929 to 1955 are fugitive poems and draft lyrics for the musical 'Candide.' " Booklist

Aiken, Conrad
Collected poems. 2d ed. Oxford 1970 1049p front $15   **811**

First published 1953
This volume contains all of the poet's published verse written since 1953 and the verse he has chosen to preserve from more than five decades of previously published work. The arrangement is chronological
"The currently complete work of one of the masters of our time, a poet who can charm, surprise, enlighten, or terrify, varying but never losing a harpsichordist's elegance of touch." Atlantic
Includes index of first lines

Selected poems. Oxford 1961 274p $6.75   **811**

Contains more than 150 poems which Aiken considers representative of his most important work since 1917. Arranged for the most part in chronological order this collection includes selections from earlier volumes of his work
"At times the language turns soft and rhetorical in the manner of early Yeats. But the bulk of his work is a steady enrichment of our literary culture." N Y Her Trib Books
Includes an index of first lines

Benét, Rosemary
A book of Americans, by Rosemary and Stephen Vincent Benét; illus. by Charles Child. Rinehart 1933 114p illus $3.95, lib. bdg. $3.59   **811**

1 U.S.—Biography—Poetry   2 U.S.—History—Poetry
"Clever light verse on prominent figures in America's story and equally clever illustrations. . . . A glint of seriousness beneath the sophisticated froth reveals an understanding of deeper things in our historic personages than the idiosyncracies so amusingly sketched." Cincinnati

Benét, Stephen Vincent
John Brown's body. Holt 1928 376p $4.50   **811**

1 Brown, John, 1800-1859—Poetry   2 U.S.—History—Civil War—Poetry
First published by Doubleday and awarded the Pulitzer Prize in 1929
"A long narrative poem of great energy and sweep, which swings into view the whole course of the Civil War, throwing into relief against the war background individual figures of both North and South, soldiers and civilians." Book Rev Digest
"The poem has lyric beauty, strong imagery and good drama. It is fiery, convincing and completely readable." Open Shelf

Brooks, Gwendolyn
In the Mecca; poems. Harper 1968 54p $4.95   **811**

1 Negroes—Poetry
The main work in this volume of poems tells the story "of a [Negro] mother's efforts to find a lost child. Although the woman fails to discover her daughter, her search reveals the lost and tragic lives of her neighbors. . . . [Among other poems included are ones] of appreciation to Medgar Evers and Malcolm X." Library J
Clarity, dignity, humor, and drama characterize both the portrait of the inhabitants of the now demolished Mecca apartment building and Brooks's shorter poems, Malcolm X and Martin Luther King together with local Chicago residents and monuments are memorably introduced with imagery reflecting an honest examination of life on contemporary terms." Booklist

Selected poems. Harper 1963 127p $4.95   **811**

1 Negroes—Poetry
Selections from three of the poet's earlier books, A street in Bronzeville, Annie Allen, and The bean eaters . . . plus several new poems. Love, domestic scenes, and the Negro's place in American society are the central themes. The selections vary in depth and impact but the best fuse sensibility with style." Booklist

Ciardi, John
Person to person. Rutgers Univ. Press 1964 83p boards $3.50   **811**

"The best [of these 57] poems include some that are painfully autobiographical, three meditative poems on death and its meaning for the survivors, a lovely small poem about birdsong, and another about a small boy running in a field of daisies." Pub W
Partial contents: The size of song; Gulls land and cease to be; When a man dies; Person to person; A blaze for everything and everything in its blaze; Possibilities; and The colossus in quicksand

This strangest everything. Rutgers Univ. Press 1966 104p $3.75   **811**

Lyric poems about daily life, people, nature, science, and poetry itself
"This volume not only confirms Mr. Ciardi's wide range of subject matter but also reveals his continuing search to produce graceful amusing and sometimes powerful poems." McClurg. Book News

Crane, Stephen
The poems of Stephen Crane; selected by Gerald D. McDonald; woodcuts by Nonny Hogrogian. Crowell 1964 61p illus $3.50, lib. bdg. $4.25   **811**

The editor has chosen, from Crane's unpublished poems and his two volumes of poetry, "these poems which best illustrate Crane's ideas, his varied techniques, and his closeness to our own time." p xiii
"Approximately half of the number [of poems] Crane wrote are included in a beautiful small book. His poetry seems to belong to young people, for most of them share his rebellions against pretense, his searchings for God and truth. An appreciation of Crane and a brief biographical sketch introduce an excellent, representative selection. The severe simplicity of the woodcuts is appropriate." Horn Bk
Index of first lines: p60-61

Cullen, Countee
On these I stand. . . . Harper 1947 197p $4.95   **811**

1 Negroes—Poetry
"An anthology of the best poems of Countee Cullen. Selected by himself and including six new poems never before published." Title page
"Ranging in mood from bitterness and a sense of injustice to puckish humor and love, the poems are marked by deep feeling, singing rhythm and sensitive awareness of both beauty and evil." Bookmark

Cummings, E. E.
95 poems. Harcourt 1958 95p $4.75   **811**

The poet "continues to celebrate the birds and the flowers, the rain, the snow, the moon, spring and love. He continues to damn the

Cummings, E. E.—*Continued*

tribes of Grundy and of Pangloss and their uglier descendants, those who would regiment or atomize mankind." N Y Her Trib Books

73 poems. Harcourt 1963 unp $5.75 **811**

A posthumously published collection of the poet's last work, some of which appeared in periodicals. "The nature of life, of love, of death; the glory of the human spirit; the joys and wonders of experience—all these Cummings explores." Publisher's note

Deutsch, Babette

The collected poems of Babette Deutsch. Doubleday 1969 xxii, 230p $5.95 **811**

The poems in this collection include selections from the poet's "earlier books, ten new poems composed since 1963, some previously unpublished work, a short section of light verse, and translations from twenty foreign poets, from Heraclitus to Eeva-Liisa Manner." Publisher's note

"Admirers of Babette Deutsch's poetry will be pleased with the poet's selection for this volume. . . . Readers not familiar with Miss Deutsch's work will be delighted with the breadth of her poetic concern, the sensitivity of her perceptions, and the artistry of her accomplishments. Miss Deutsch is equally effective with the short or long poem, the lyric, or the philosophic mood. The poems written in honor of poets and artists are among the best of their kind, and those written in response to nature are usually fresh." Library J

Dickinson, Emily

Final harvest; Emily Dickinson's poems; selection and introduction by Thomas H. Johnson. Little 1961 331p $5.95 **811**

A selection of 575 poems from: The complete poems of Emily Dickinson. The editor's aim has been to allow the reader to realize the full scope and diversity of the poet's work. (Publisher)

"Emily Dickinson assesses the problems of anxiety and loneliness, the editor submits; also 'the extremity of pain and its duration and redemptive quality, and she thereby steadily participated in the issues of existing.' . . . One can accept or ignore the profounder interpretation of her poetry and read her for the sheer old-fashioned delight of it. This large and pleasant collection is a good place to start." San Francisco Chronicle

Index of first lines: p325-31

Poems; including variant readings critically compared with all known manuscripts; ed. by Thomas H. Johnson. Harvard Univ. Press 1955 3v (lxviii, 1266p) illus $30 **811**

"Belknap Press book"

"This edition of the poetry of Emily Dickinson includes all the seventeen hundred seventy-five poems, together with the variants, that she is known to have written. Since the greater part of her manuscripts survive, it has been possible to assign to most of the poems a relative chronology. The dating of them is conjectural and for the most part will always remain so." Foreword

Indexed by subject and first line

Poems of Emily Dickinson; selected by Helen Plotz; drawings by Robert Kipniss. Crowell 1964 157p illus (The Crowell Poets) $3.50, lib. bdg. $4.25 **811**

Selected poems which "reflect the myriad interests that were part of Emily Dickinson's quiet life. The book is divided into five sections: the temporal world, the world of nature, the world of love, the world within, and the eternal world." Publisher's note

The book is "prefaced by a brief but perceptive discussion of the poet's life and some paradoxical aspects of her work. . . . The gemlike poems reveal Dickinson's linguistic originality, emotional intensity, and freshness of view. Delicate drawings enhance the book's attractiveness, and an index of first lines is appended." Booklist

Dunbar, Paul Laurence

The complete poems of Paul Laurence Dunbar; with the introduction to "Lyrics of lowly life," by W. B. Howells. Dodd 1955 [c1913] xxxiv, 479p $4.50 **811**

1 Negroes—Poetry

First published 1913

Includes: Lyrics of lowly life, Lyrics of the hearthside, Lyrics of love and laughter, and Lyrics of sunshine and shadow, with a few other poems

"Dunbar [was] the first American Negro of pure African blood to reveal innate distinction in literature; as W. D. Howells has said, 'to feel the Negro life esthetically and express it lyrically.' His dialect pieces are delightful." Review of Reviews

Eliot, T. S.

Collected poems, 1909-1962. Harcourt 1963 221p $6.95 **811**

The author was awarded the Nobel Prize for literature, 1948

"A new edition of T. S. Eliot's 'Collected Poems, 1909-1935.' with the complete text of 'Four Quartets' [1943] and some previously uncollected poems added to make a full compilation of all the poetry through 1962 which the poet wishes to preserve." Bk Buyer's Guide

"Now surely, is the time to remember that, for all our current bland acceptance of him and for all his steady talk about tradition, [T. S. Eliot] is likely to go down in history as a revolutionist. . . . The proof of the success of Mr. Eliot's revolution is that we do take it so for granted. His sort of poetry—subtly supported by his enormously influential criticism—became the status quo so long ago that it is difficult to remember what things must have been like [before]. . . . There is a hard leanness to Eliot's poetry and to his whole endeavor." Christian Science Monitor

Poems written in early youth. Farrar, Straus 1967 38p $3.95 **811**

"These early poems were collected by John Hayward and privately printed in an edition limited to twelve copies by Albert Bonniers of Stockholm in 1950." Note

"This collection contains all the surviving poems written by T. S. Eliot between the winter of 1904 and the spring of 1910; that is to say, between his sixteenth and twenty-second birthdays. . . . [It also includes] 'The Death of Saint Narcissus.' which was suppressed in proof and never published, [and] is of a slightly later date. . . . The sources of the text of the present authorized collection are given in the Notes at the end." Introduction

The wasteland, and other poems. Harcourt 1934 88p pa $1.25 **811**

"Harvest books"

This long poem, which first appeared in an issue of Dial, won the Dial's award for poetry in 1922. "The power of suggesting intolerable tragedy at the heart of the trivial or the sordid is used with a skill little less than miraculous in The Waste Land, and the power is the more moving because of the attendant conviction that this terrible resembling contrast between nobility and baseness is an agony in the mind of Mr Eliot of which only a portion is transferred to that of the reader." Literary Rev

Emerson, Ralph Waldo

Poems of Ralph Waldo Emerson; selected by J. Donald Adams; drawings by Virgil Burnett. Crowell 1965 112p illus (The Crowell Poets) $3.50 **811**

Contents: Nature; The search for truth; Patriotism and public affairs; The conduct of life

"The editor briefly but lucidly discusses the nature of Emerson's work and the relevancy of his thought in today's world. He intersperses prose excerpts, correlated with the poetic expression of similar ideas and concepts, from Emerson's essays and journal and adds a judicious selection of aphorisms and maxims." Booklist

"This slender volume will provide a happy introduction to the lyrical side of Ralph Waldo Emerson. . . . In format the book is a delight." Library J

Frost, Robert

Come in & other poems; selection, biographical introduction and commentary by Louis Untermeyer; illus. by John O'Hara Cosgrave II. Large type ed. complete and unabridged. Watts, F. 1967 192p illus lib. bdg. $8.95   **811**

1 Large type books

"A Keith Jennison book"

First published 1943 by Holt

The eighty-three poems in this volume are from: A boy's will, North of Boston, Mountain interval, New Hampshire, West-running brook, A further range, and A witness tree

Complete poems of Robert Frost, 1949. Holt 1949 xxi, 642p front $8   **811**

The author was awarded the Pulitzer Prize for three collections included in this volume: New Hampshire (awarded 1924); A further range, 1937; A witness tree; 1943

To Collected poems, published 1939, have been added the two volumes of lyrics: A witness tree and Steeple bush, several new poems; and the two verse plays: A masque of reason and A masque of mercy

"Woods at evening, a crumbling wall, a lonely boy in the country, snow, birch trees, wandering tramps, a prize chicken, fear of storms, trees, a sugar orchard—all these and many, many more ideas, pictures, people, and stories come and go in the simplest way through Robert Frost's poetry. . . . In at least one of the twenty-five subdivisions of this delightful book almost anyone can find lines which mean something special to him." Doors to More Mature Reading

In the clearing. Holt 1962 101p $4.95   **811**

In this collection of poems "the New England poet restates his belief in nature, love, and the American heritage. . . . Included here [are 'Kitty Hawk,' and] the poem 'The gift outright,' the conclusion of 'For John F. Kennedy his inauguration.'" Booklist

"Feel for rhythm and command of language [in these poems] are as sensitive as ever. The subjects are widely varied. . . . Cool gaiety pervades the entire book. Connoisseurs of gentle satire are directed to the elegant paragraph on free verse, in which Frost hints what he thinks about Whitman and Sandburg." Book of the Month Club News

The poetry of Robert Frost; ed. by Edward Connery Lathem. Holt 1969 607p $10.95 **811**

"This edition follows basically the organization of 'Complete Poems of Robert Frost' (1949) [entered above] with the addition of 'In the Clearing' (1962), which has been placed in sequence immediately before 'A Masque of Reason' and 'A Masque of Mercy,' thus allowing the two 'Masques' to stand together at the end of the overall collection, as in 'Complete Poems.' The bibliographical and textual notes are arranged according to the order within this volume of the elements to which they relate. Entries for individual poems are prefixed by a citation giving, first, the page on which the poem appears or begins, then, its title." Editor's statement

"The poems are line-numbered as they were not previously—an advantage to critics and teachers, especially when dealing with longer poems. . . . Mr. Lathem is also responsible for 'changes introduced . . . that constitute departures from copy-texts.' . . . [He] has seen fit to correct or improve Frost's punctuation of his own poems." Atlantic

"The qualities of plain speech and a human simplicity that always understates whatever doubt and torment Frost undoubtedly knew in his lifetime create a spell that marks him as one of our enduring poets." Pub W

Index of first lines & titles: p583-607

The road not taken. . . . Illus. by John O'Hara Cosgrave II. Holt 1951 xxxvii, 282p illus $4   **811**

"An introduction to Robert Frost; a selection of Robert Frost's poems; with a biographical preface and running commentary by Louis Untermeyer." Title page

This book "is an enlargement of ['Come in, & other poems,' entered above]. More than fifty poems have been added, the commentary has been greatly amplified, the introductory biography has been entirely recast, enlarged, and brought up to date." Publisher's note

You come too; favorite poems for young readers; with wood engravings by Thomas W. Nason. Holt 1959 94p illus $3.50, lib. bdg. $3.27   **811**

Frost's "simplicity, wisdom, and humanity, as well as his craftsmanship, come clear in some half-hundred poems, among them 'Mending Wall,' 'The Death of the Hired Man,' and 'Tree at My Window.'" Library J

"Despite the subtitle this is an admirable introduction to Frost for young adults as well as children." Booklist

Index of titles: p93-94

Holmes, Oliver Wendell, 1809-1894

The complete poetical works of Oliver Wendell Holmes. Houghton 1895 xxi, 352p front $6.50   **811**

"Cambridge edition"

Title on spine: The poems of Holmes

"From his poetry many delightfully humorous, sentimental, and pathetic pieces may be selected. . . . Holmes yields to no one as the laureate of a college, of a cultured city, and of graceful old age, and to few as an urbane writer of familiar verse." W. P. Trent's Short History of American Literature

Horgan, Paul

Songs after Lincoln. Farrar, Straus 1965 74p $4.95   **811**

1 U.S.—History—Civil War—Poetry   2 Lincoln, Abraham, President U.S.—Poetry

The author's work is a collection of "poems reflecting his impressions of Abraham Lincoln and the Civil War as suggested by photographs, drawings, and books of the period, and the poetry of Walt Whitman. The pieces . . . are grouped in three parts, 'The War,' 'The Casualty,' concerning a dead soldier, and 'The President.' Some of these poems have already been adapted by folk singers." Library J

Bibliographical references included in Notes and comments: p67-74

Hughes, Langston

The panther & the lash; poems of our times. Knopf 1967 101p $4.50   **811**

The seventy poems included here deal mainly with race relations in the United States in the . . . [fifties and sixties]. The poet writes of freedom marches, sit-ins, speeches, prayers, violence, and nonviolence, from Alabama to New York. (Publisher)

Selected poems of Langston Hughes; drawings by E. McKnight Kauffer. Knopf 1959 297p illus $6.95   **811**

1 Negroes—Poetry

This collection represents Langston Hughes' own decisions as to which of his poems he wants to preserve and reprint. It contains not only selections from his published books (including private publication) but also poems that either have never been published before or have appeared only in periodicals. (Publisher)

"Unlike many anthologies or collections, one is not here conscious so much of omissions as of the consistent fineness of what has been chosen for the book. Between his opening Afro-American Fragment ('So long./ So far away/ Is Africa') and his closing, Freedom's Plough, we have some of the saddest, most humorous and beautiful insights ever given into the heart of a race." San Francisco Chronicle

Jarrell, Randall

The complete poems. Farrar, Straus 1969 507p $10   **811**

A posthumous collection which includes "'Selected Poems' (1955); 'The Woman at the Washington Zoo' (1960), which won him the National Book Award; 'The Lost World' (1965) plus poems from his earlier books, poems published from 1934 to 1964 but never collected, and some poems never before published." Bk Buyer's Guide

Jarrell, Randall—*Continued*

"There are so many good things about Jarrell's poems and they are all here in this important volume. The fine and rare qualities of Jarrell's sensibility: the heartbreaking but poignantly meaningful loneliness, the irrecoverable wanderings and wise knowings of childhood, his own Rilkeen pursuit of inner things, his tempestuous and open Thomas-like vulnerability. . . . 'The Complete Poems' is one of those rarely meaningful publishing events, and anyone who knows or wants to know anything about modern poetry ought to own it." Choice

Johnson, James Weldon

God's trombones; seven Negro sermons in verse; drawings by Aaron Douglas, lettering by C. B. Falls. Viking 1927 56p illus $3.95
811

1 Negroes—Poetry

"Seven Negro sermons in verse inspired by memories of sermons by Negro preachers heard by Mr Johnson in childhood. His themes are similar and the poems are written after the manner of the primitive sermons, but not in dialect. The illustrations are by a Negro artist." Book Rev Digest
"The poet here has admirably risen to his intentions and his needs; entombed in this bright mausoleum the Negro preacher of an older day can never pass entirely deathward. This verse is simple and awful as once, the grand diapason of a musician playing on an organ with far more than two keys." Bookmark

Kilmer, Joyce

Trees, and other poems. Doubleday 1914 75p $2.95
811

"Homeliness of theme and simplicity of form characterize the poems in this slight volume. The twelve-forty-five, Pennies, Trees, Old poets. Delicatessen, The apartment house, The house with nobody in it; Alarm clocks—these are some of the titles." Book Rev Digest

Lindbergh, Anne Morrow

The unicorn, and other poems, 1935-1955. Pantheon Bks. 1956 86p $5.95
811

A representative selection of the author's poetry written between 1935 and 1955. Here is her response to life, love and death, to the joy of flight, to art and nature, to the impact of a world at war, and other moods. (Publisher)
"Her prose is often markedly poetic; at times her poems are prosaic. But if artistry and eloquence occasionally flag, sensibility never does. At their best, her lines flash with beauty and brightness." Time

Lindsay, Vachel

Collected poems. Rev. and illus. ed. Macmillan (N Y) lxii, 464p illus $7.95
811

First published 1923
"Most of the poems are presented as chants, and in effect they are not unlike the chants of the old time minstrel, who, wandering from house to house, recited the happenings of his day. This collection brings together the contents of all previously published volumes, including occasional poems scattered through the author's prose works, preceded by an autobiographical foreword entitled 'Adventures while singing these songs.'" Booklist

The selected poems of Vachel Lindsay; ed. by Mark Harris. Macmillan (N Y) 1963 xxvii, 210p boards $5.95
811

Poems grouped under the following headings: United States rhythms; Home town; Runes of the road; Politics; Songs, prayers, & supplications to the muse
The editor gives "an attractive selection of the poems on which Lindsay's reputation should be based . . . [and a] witty introductory biographical and appreciative essay." Library J

Longfellow, Henry Wadsworth

The complete poetical works of Henry Wadsworth Longfellow. Houghton 1922 xxi, 689p front $8
811

Has spine title: The poems of Longfellow
First published in this edition 1893
"The present edition of Mr Longfellow's poetical writings is based upon the Riverside [edition]. It contains the entire text as published in the six volumes of verse, and such condensed bibliographical and other notes as seem desirable for the general reader and compatible with the limitations of a one-ovlume edition. A biographical sketch introduces the volume." Publisher's note

Evangeline; ed. by Mina Lewiton; illus. by Howard Simon. Duell [1966] 113p illus $3.95
811

1 Acadians—Poetry

First published 1847
In this epic poem, Longfellow describes the mid-eighteenth century expulsion from their homes of the inhabitants of Nova Scotia, and the doomed search of Evangeline, a gentle Acadian girl, for her lost lover, Gabriel
Longfellow "is at once the most patriotic and the least patriotic of our poets—least patriotic because he drew upon European legend and story for so much of his material, and most patriotic because he first introduced American history into American poetry. [One of] his three most popular narrative poems thoroughly native to our soil [is] 'Evangeline,' 'the flower of American idylls.'" The Reader's Adviser

Lowell, Amy

The complete poetical works of Amy Lowell; with an introduction by Louis Untermeyer. Houghton 1955 xxix, 607p $10   811

In addition to six poems not previously published in book form, this volume contains the following volumes of the author's previously published verse: A dome of many-coloured glass; Sword blades and poppy seed; Men, women and ghosts; Can Grande's castle; Pictures of the floating world; Legends; Fir-flower tablets; Critical fable; What's o'clock; East wind; and, Ballads for sale
"Her lucid word pictures infuse an imaginative quality into the most commonplace subjects and her use of everyday speech proclaims that poetry, after all, is woven from life itself." Booklist
"The small print and double-column page make casual reading difficult, but students will find a one-volume source convenient." Wis Lib Bul
Contains title and first line indexes

Lowell, Robert

Notebook. [3d ed. rev. and expanded] Farrar, Straus 1970 265p $7.50   811
SBN 374-2-2323-1

First published with title: Notebook 1967-68
This volume includes poems the author "has written out of his experiences, remembrances, reflections and impressions during the past [three] years. . . . Breadth and depth redeem his poetry even when, as occasionally happens here, the reader wishes a variation—a change of pace, style, tone—from his unflagging fourteen line quasisonnet scheme. But this is major poetry that wears the skin of the times and often touches the pulse, as in his poems on the Columbia University violence, Robert Kennedy's murder, King's, the street-fighting in Chicago." Pub W

McGinley, Phyllis

Love letters of Phyllis McGinley. Viking 1954 116p $5.95
811

A "collection of light verse, largely reprinted from magazines, which reaffirms its author's ability both to pinpoint the innately humorous and to stir a light ripple on the surface of more serious matters. Commonplace subjects, approached in moods varying from the gently whimsical to the satiric and adroitly exhibited in a variety of forms and meters, are presented with malice toward none and a good deal of charitable wit for all." Booklist

McGinley, Phyllis—Continued

Times three; selected verse from three decades, with seventy new poems. Foreword by W. H. Auden. Viking 1960 304p $5.50   **811**

Awarded the Pulitzer Prize, 1961
"Three hundred poems arranged chronologically according to decades: the 50's, the 40's and the 30's including 70 poems . . . previously unpublished. In the foreword, W. H. Auden defines, with the aid of her poetry, Phyllis McGinley's distinctive style, and distinguishes between the male and female creative imaginations." Pub W
"Ranging widely over diverse themes, [these] poems of varying length deal lightly and perspicaciously with everyday concrete themes." Bookmark
Indexed by title and first line

A wreath of Christmas legends; illus. by Leonard Weisgard. Macmillan (N Y) 1967 62p illus $4.95   **811**

1 Christmas poetry 2 Jesus Christ—Nativity —Poetry
A "lilting book of old stories of the Christ Child and the young in heart, retold in poetry. . . . Miss McGinley has searched for and found medieval tales—out of Russia and Ireland and all places in between where man and beast lived close together—and in her inimitable style re-created them into direct and charming poetry. It is verse of today with the ring of yesterday, as if these stories might always have been sung this way." Book of the Month Club News

McKuen, Rod

Lonesome cities. Random House 1967 111p boards $4.50   **811**

This volume of poetry "details a man's journey around the world in an attempt to find himself. . . . In addition to Mr. McKuen's exploration of cities, large and small, there are thirteen lyrics from his most recent songs." Publisher's note
The author's "books have reached nearly 1 million in sales, a figure that places him in sheer volume among the immortals of the English language. He isn't. In fact, McKuen is an antipoet by his own admission. . . . [He] answers the outdated modes of poetry with a verse that drawls in country cadences from one shapeless line to the next, carrying the rusticated innocence of a Carl Sandburg thickened by the treacle of a man who prefers to prettify the world before he describes it." Newsweek

MacLeish, Archibald

Collected poems, 1917-1952. Houghton 1952 407p $6   **811**

Pulitzer Prize award for poetry, 1953
Gathered in this volume for the first time are the poet's long poems: The pot of earth (1925); The Hamlet of A. MacLeish (1928); Einstein (1929); Conquistador (1932); Pulitzer Prize, 1933); Elpenor (1933); America was promises, (1939); Colloquy for the states (1943) and Act-five (1948). A number of new poems which have not appeared in book form are also included
"This volume, covering the work of thirty-five years, shows the direct, wiry and forceful nature of MacLeish's talent and will be indispensable to the full understanding of his life. He has an Elizabethan sort of exuberance which has been exercised on nonliterary fields as well as on poetry and prose." N Y Times Bk R
Contains the verse drama: The Trojan horse, first published 1952

Masters, Edgar Lee

The new Spoon River; introduction by Willis Barnstone. Macmillan (N Y) 1968 xxvi, 325p $5.95   **811**

First published 1924 by Boni and Liveright
This "continuation of his famous 'Spoon River Anthology,' describes in 322 microbiographies the spiritual and physical disintegration of a small American town." Publisher's note

"The best poems in 'The New Spoon River' are superior to any in the first book; they are more desperate and violent, more tragic. . . . These confessional monologues of tragic existence are closer to the world of Theodore Roethke, Robert Lowell, and Sylvia Plath than to poems by any of Masters' contemporaries." Introduction

Spoon River anthology   **811**

Some editions are:
Macmillan (N Y) $4.95
Macmillan (N Y) $7.95. Woodcuts by John Ross and Clare Romano Ross
First published 1915
"A series of character sketches which reveal the life of a village community in the Middle West. They are in the form of epitaphs in a kind of 'free verse.' " Pratt Quarterly
"An extraordinary book, which will delight some readers as its cynicism—or realism—will offend others." N Y Pub Lib

Merriam, Eve

Finding a poem; illus. by Seymour Chwast. Atheneum Pubs. 1970 68p illus $5.25   **811**

"There are poems of despair, cries of a poet, 'in a plastic age of time for everything and time for nothing, of masses of people and lonely individuals, of new discovery and numbing sameness.' There are poems as bright as quicksilver that in a few words reveal a mood of awe, of surprise, of wonder. And there is a record, noted down step by step, word by word, of how she created a poem, that is as fascinating to follow as the birth of a baby." Pub W

Millay, Edna St Vincent

Collected poems; ed. by Norma Millay. Harper 1956 xxi, 738p $10   **811**

"The definitive edition of the American woman poet's sonnets and lyrics, edited with taste and discrimination by her sister. jincludes all the poems which have appeared in earlier selections and 16 not published in previous collections of her poetry, but excludes the plays, translations, and childhood verse. The poems are divided into two separate sections of lyrics and sonnets, arranged chronologically and printed in groups under the titles of the original volumes, ranging from 'Renascence' of 1917 to 'Mine the harvest,' published in 1954, four years after the poet's death. Large, clear print and attractive format." Booklist

Collected sonnets. Harper 1941 161p $7.50   **811**

This collection includes three poems not published before in book form and sonnets from the following volumes: Renascence; Few figs from thistles; Second April; Harp-weaver; Buck in the snow; Fatal interview; Wine from these grapes; Huntsman, what quarry; Make bright the arrows
This "is the work of a minor poet who impresses a personality on everything she writes, who is often a most accomplished technician in the sonnet form, and whose best examples will always find a place in any anthology of romantic verse." Atlantic Bookshelf

Moore, Marianne

The complete poems of Marianne Moore. Macmillan (N Y) [distributed by Viking] 1967 305p $8.50   **811**

The 120 poems contained in this volume are taken from earlier volumes. They include: Collected poems, 1951; Like a bulwark, 1956; O to be a dragon, 1959; Tell me, tell me, 1966, class 818; four poems hitherto uncollected, and selections from Miss Moore's translation of: The fables of La Fontaine, 1954, class 841. (Publisher)
The poet's "work will, I think continue to be read as poetry when much of the major poetry of our time has become part of the history of literature. . . . When we examine any of the poems that comprise the Moore canon —poems like 'The Steeple-Jack,' 'The Fish,' 'Novices,' 'Marriage,' 'The Monkeys,' 'Bow's,' 'In the Days of Prismatic Color'—we are brought up against a mastery which defies attempts to analyze it, an intelligence which

Moore, Marianne—*Continued*

plays just beyond our reach. . . . Perhaps it is in her translations of La Fontaine, which I confess I prefer to the originals, that one sees most clearly her gift for language-making. . . . [Marianne Moore] has set about poetry with all the tools at her disposal . . . and a mastery of form that outpaces the most devoted reader." N Y Times Bk R
Index of titles and opening lines: p299-305

Nash, Ogden

Everyone but thee and me; illus. by John Alcorn. Little 1962 171p illus $4.25   811
"A fresh collection, culled from various magazines, of slightly mad verses displaying a typically astronomical range of subjects treated in Nash verse forms. The line drawings are appropriately absurd or fey." Booklist
"Ogden Nash fans and the public in general will not be disappointed. . . . Nash continues to work wonders with the English language." Library J

Family reunion. Little 1950 146p $4.50 811
Poems about families, parents and children, husbands and wives
"The poems in this book are drawn with revisions, from ten previous books by Ogden Nash. They are prefaced by a foreword so disarming, so genuinely modest, and at the same time so penetrating and intelligent that the foreword itself is virtually a sufficient review of the book and in better prose than book reviews generally exhibit." N Y Her Trib Books

Parents keep out; elderly poems for youngerly readers; drawings by Barbara Corrigan. Little 1951 137p illus $3.95   811
"Light verse, chiefly celebrating the confusion of the elderly vis-a-vis the younger generation." Book Rev Digest
"Elderly readers of the poems, who naturally will have no intention of staying out of them, will recognize many old favorites. Youngerly readers, in case they haven't already done so, will find in Mr Nash a good companion and a cheerful influence." Springf'd Republican

You can't get there from here; drawings by Maurice Sendak. Little 1957 190p illus $4.95
                                                    811
The poems include: Oafishness sells goods, Like an advertisement should; Come on in, the senility is fine; Chacun à son Berlitz, etc.
"More poems by the Laureate. His wit never fails: The hilarity is as fresh and as incisive as it has always been." Sec Ed Brd
Index of first lines

Parker, Dorothy

The collected poetry of Dorothy Parker. Modern Lib. 1944 210p $2.95, lib. bdg. $2.69
                                                    811
First published 1936 by Viking
Contains the poems which appeared in the author's former volumes: Enough rope (1926), Sunset gun (1928), and Death and taxes (1931), together with several new verses not hitherto published in book form
With "its clean bite, its perfectly conscious —and hence delightful—archness, [this poetry] stands re-reading amply." N Y Times Bk R
Indexed by first line only

Parks, Gordon, 1912-

Gordon Parks: whispers of intimate things; introduction: Philip B. Kunhardt, Jr. Viking 1971 unp illus $8.95   811
SBN 670-34667-5
"A Studio book"
A collection of interwoven poems and color photographs. The photographer-poet's "subjects range from peace symbolized by a dove in nocturnal flight to stacked wheat . . . to houses by the sea, with widowhood, lonely men, 'last season's leaves' [and] his father's funeral [also included]." Pub W

The "color photographs, mostly haunting representations of romantic symbols, are exquisite revelations of [the author's] artistic vision. And in reading his poetry, one begins to sense the fully visual character of his art: even his words seem to be translated through a creative camera lens, and the rich pictorial imagery works well to conjure up each photograph even as it is being looked at." Best Sellers

Poe, Edgar Allan

Poems of Edgar Allan Poe; selected by Dwight Macdonald; drawings by Ellen Raskin. Crowell 1965 169p illus $3.50, lib. bdg. $4.25   811
The editor "has collected Poe's most interesting or important poetry for this volume, adding a number of pieces that are poems in every way except typographically. There is also a rich selection of Poe's critical writing on poets and poetry." Publisher's note
Includes a "critical introduction adding much to the reader's appreciation of the personality of the man, his poetry and theory of poetics, and his influence upon the French symbolists." Library J
Includes title and first line indexes

Pound, Ezra

Selected poems. A new ed. New Directions 1957 184p pa $1.50   811
First published 1949
This "provides a good sampling of the Pound who wrote 'A Virginal,' the latter-day Renaissance poet, as well as the reincarnate Li Po and the other 'personae' that Ezra wore during the years he spent absorbing the styles (and not the political thinking) of other centuries. But . . . I suggest that in subsequent issues of this volume the New Directions editors get down off their high Pegasuses and exclude the lament of 'Ben [ito] and La Clara' and the more scatological sections of Cantos XIV and XV." Sat R

Ransom, John Crowe

Selected poems. 3d ed. rev. and enl. Knopf 1969 159p $5.95   811
First published 1945
"This third edition of Selected Poems represents the poet's . . . refining of the second edition [published 1963]. It also contains about twenty poems from Mr Ransom's earlier volumes, Poems About God, Chills and Fever, and Two Gentlemen in Bonds, which he has revised and added to this collection. The final section is made up of eight 'pairings'—original texts of poems side by side with later revisions. In each instance Mr Ransom provides an informal commentary." Publisher's note
This poets "world is mostly the South . . . a might-have-been South, a vision of gentleness in all senses of that Chaucerian word. . . . I hope any aspiring poet who wished some first-rate shop talk will read the sixteen pairs of poems and Ransom's commentaries at the end of the book. Here he plunges into the nitty-gritty of the process of writing and revising verse." Book World

Rexroth, Kenneth

The collected shorter poems. New Directions [1967 c1966] 348p $7.50   811
"This volume brings together all Kenneth Rexroth's shorter poems from 1920 to the present, including a group of new poems not previously published. It is drawn from seven earlier books." Publisher's note
"Rexroth is probably one of the most learned autodidacts we have. His love poems are unquestionably great. They celebrate woman's body, mutual happiness, the sacramental character of love, and give a naturalist's lyricism which surpasses Keats. Other poems treat the supernatural, the macabre, the evil, and the great events of man's life with a sure, sharp, cerebral skill that is personal and unique. Rexroth is not a stylist and is seldom delicate, but his delicacy will become an ornament in the history of American letters." Choice

Robinson, Edwin Arlington

The collected poems of Edwin Arlington Robinson. Macmillan (N Y) 1937 1498p front $12.50   811

First published 1929
Contains the following volumes of the poet's verse: The man against the sky (1916); The children of the night (1897); Capitain Craig (1902); Merlin (1917); The town down the river (1910); Lancelot (1920); The three taverns (1920); Avon's harvest (1921); Tristram (1927; Pulitzer Prize (1928); Roman Bartholow (1923); Dionysus in doubt (1925); The man who died twice (1924; Pulitzer Prize, 1925); Cavender's house (1929); The glory of the nightingales (1930); Matthias at the door (1931); Nicodemus (1932); Talifer (1933); Amaranth (1934); King Jasper (1935)
Readers "will be a little surprised to notice that about a third of it was written after 'Tristram' brought [Robinson] his first great popular recognition. . . . Austere as he was, his total volume swarms with the multitude of life." N Y Times Bk R

Roethke, Theodore

The collected poems of Theodore Roethke. Doubleday 1966 274p $7.95   811

Contains "all the poems from the late [poet's] previous books, each poem given under the title of the book in which it first appeared, and 16 new poems . . . selected from Roethke's unpublished and uncollected poems." Pub W
In this book "we have what is certain to be the definitive text of Roethke's work. . . . It is a poetry of terrible struggle and of redeeming exaltation and vision, of death and rebirth, though interspersed with wit and humor." N Y Times Bk R

Sandburg, Carl

The complete poems of Carl Sandburg; rev. and expanded ed. Harcourt 1970 xxxi, 797p $12.50   811

ISBN 0-15-120773-9
Awarded the Pulitzer Prize, 1951
First published 1950
A collection of seven of the author's books: Chicago poems, 1916; Cornhuskers, 1918; Smoke and steel, 1920; Slabs of the sunburnt West, 1922; Good morning, America, 1925; The people, yes, 1936; Honey and salt, 1963
"Known for his free verse, written under the influence of Walt Whitman and celebrating industrial and agricultural America, American geography and landscape, figures in American history, and the American common people, [Sandburg] frequently makes use of contemporary American slang and colloquialisms." The Reader's Encyclopedia
Includes indexes of titles and first lines

Honey and salt. Harcourt 1963 111p $5.50   811

A collection of seventy-seven "poems of the prairies, poems on the nature of love, poems about many other topics, and a . . . long, chanting poem, 'Timesweep,' about many incarnations of life over the ages." Pub W
The poems "combine mellow lyricism and the tang of wisdom, the seeming ease and unrelenting mystery of the craftsman who knows and loves his material and whose fire is still burning. The forms are free but disciplined—'self-structured' might describe them—each built to its own inner specifications." Best Sellers
"We open the book and know immediately whose hands we are in. . . . [We hear] the voice that is really two voices, as though Sandburg were both a recorder of American lingo and an impressionist painter." N Y Her Trib Books

The people, yes. Harcourt 1936 286p $5.75   811

"Being several stories and psalms nobody would want to laugh at, interspersed with memoranda variations worth a second look, along with sayings and yarns traveling on grief and laughter, running sometimes as a fugitive air in the classic manner, breaking into jig time and tap dancing nohow classical, and further broken by plain and irregular sounds and echoes from the roar and whirl of street crowds, work gangs, sidewalk clamor, with interludes of midnight cool blue and inviolable stars over the phantom frames of skyscrapers." The author
"The longest and most sustained piece of work [the author] has yet done in verse. It is a book that will irritate some; and some will find it meaningless. . . . It is as honest as it is questioning and it speaks its deep convictions in a tongue we know." N Y Her Trib Books

Service, Robert

Collected poems of Robert Service. Dodd 1958 735p $6   811

Earlier edition first published with title: Complete poems of Robert Service
A reprint of six books: The spell of the Yukon, and other verses (1916); Ballads of a Cheechako (1917); Rhymes of a rolling stone (1912); Rhymes of a Red Cross man (1916); Ballads of a Bohemian (1912); Bar-room ballads (1940)
Service's verses "are characterized by a simple ballad meter, vigorous love of adventure, and heroic emotions and primal instincts." The Oxford Companion to American Literature

Later collected verses. Dodd 1965 477p $6   811

This "collection contains all the poems in 'Carols of the old codger' [1954] and 'Rhymes for my rags' [1956] with a number of verses from his prose writings and an entire section of previously unpublished verse. . . . [It presents some] of the verse which has made Robert Service one of the most widely read poets throughout the world." Am News of Bks
This volume together with the two earlier volumes listed in this class form a complete collection of the poet's verse

More collected verse. Dodd 1955 5v in 1 $5   811

"A companion volume to Service's Collected poems. . . . This includes Songs of a sunlover, Rhymes of a roughneck, Lyrics of a low brow, Rhymes of a rebel, and Songs for my supper." Booklist

Shapiro, Karl

Selected poems. Random House 1968 333p $7.95   811

"This volume contains over two hundred poems selected from the author's seven previously published books as well as twenty-five new and uncollected poems." Book Rev Digest
This "is a splendidly edited model. . . . Shapiro has chosen generously from his past work, and equally from each phase of it; he has declined to revise old poems. Consequently this book, unlike most such books, is a genuinely useful compendium." N Y Times Bk R

Teasdale, Sara

The collected poems of Sara Teasdale. Macmillan (N Y) 1966 xxxii, 224p $5.95   811

First published 1937
In this collection may be found most of the poems from eight of the author's books; Helen of Troy; Rivers to the sea; Love songs; Flame and shadow; Dark of the moon; Strange victory; and Sonnets to Duse. Ten of the twenty-five poems found in Stars tonight are included. The few poems not included were omitted in accordance with Miss Teasdale's wishes
"All these are moving, as is the sound of an old tune, tender, nostalgic, and, if you will, sentimental. . . . The unwise reader who plods doggedly through this volume may well close the book with a sick heart, heavy with so much pain, so much loss. But he who reads with discretion will find an echo for many moods; pride, joy in nature, laughter and zest for life . . . they are all here." Springf'd Republican

Van Doren, Mark

Collected and new poems, 1924-1963. Hill & Wang 1963 615p $10   811

More than 800 poems, many from earlier collections, chosen by the author from forty

Van Doren, Mark—*Continued*
years of creative work. " 'New Poems,' the last
section of the volume, includes poems never
before published." Publisher's note
    What Van Doren "lacks in pioneering verve
he makes up for in the old-fashioned virtues
of clarity and polish." Christian Science Monitor

    Mark Van Doren: 100 poems; selected by
the author. Hill & Wang 1967 128p $3.50 **811**
    "American century series"
    This "representative selection of Van Do-
ren's work shows his sensitivity to nature, his
crisp use of conventional form, and his humanistic bent." Booklist
    Includes Index of titles and Index of first
lines

Whitman, Walt
    Leaves of grass   **811**
    Some editions are:
Doubleday $5.50 Edited by Emory Holloway
Dutton (Everyman's lib) $3.25 New and com-
prehensive edition. Edited with introduction
and notes by Emory Holloway
Modern Lib. (Modern Lib. Giant) $4.95
Viking $5 First (1885) ["Brooklyn"] ed. Edited,
with an introduction by Malcolm Cowley
    "The reader who would get at the spirit and
meaning of 'Leaves of Grass' must remember
that its animating principle, from first to last,
is Democracy—that it is a work conceived and
carried forward in the spirit of the genius of
humanity that is now in full career in the New
World. Whitman is the 'poet of the ever-beck-
oning future, the ever expanding, ever insati-
able spirit of man.' " Pratt Alcove

Whittier, John Greenleaf
    The complete poetical works of John Green-
leaf Whittier. Cambridge ed. Houghton 1895
xxii, 542p front $7   **811**
    "Whether his work is poetry or rhymed
propaganda, it is literature, for it expresses a
man and events in words that are today alive
with emotion." Macy's Spirit of American Literature

Wylie, Elinor
    Collected poems. Knopf 1932 311p illus
$7.95   **811**
    A combined edition of the author's four
books of poems: Nets to catch the wind (1921),
Black armour (1923), Trivial breath (1928), and
Angels and earthly creatures (1929). An additional section contains poems not previously
published in book form, and one bit of poetic
prose: The heart's desire

811.08 American poetry— Collections

Adoff, Arnold
    (ed.) Black out loud; an anthology of mod-
ern poems by Black Americans; drawings by
Alvin Hollingsworth. Macmillan (N Y) 1970
86p illus lib. bdg. $4.95   **811.08**
    1 Negro poetry 2 American poetry—Collec-
tions
    This compilation "contains 67 short, sharp
poems by 36 poets, among them Langston
Hughes, Gwendolyn Brooks, LeRoi Jones,
Margaret Walker, Victor Hernandez Cruz, and
other lesser known poets. Arranged in six sections, each embellished by a striking drawing,
the poems are concerned with black pride, the
poet, famous blacks, life in white America, the
black experience, and love and anger." Booklist
    Biographical notes: p77-81. Includes an In-
dex to authors, titles, and first lines

    (ed.) I am the darker brother; an anthology
of modern poems by Negro Americans; drawings by Benny Andrews; foreword by Charlemae Rollins. Macmillan (N Y) 1968 128p
illus $4.95   **811.08**
    1 Negro poetry 2 American poetry—Collec-
tions
    "This strong, singing work contains sixty-
four poems by twenty-nine poets of the twentieth century. A few of their names are familiar, but most of them are little known. The
poems explore how Negro Americans feel
about themselves and about the Negro's role
in America's past, present, and future. There
are poems of fear and anger, of joy and uncertainty; poems that mourn the sufferings of the
slaves; poems that celebrate the heroes—Frederick Douglass, Harriet Tubman, Malcolm X
and others. Some of the poems confront the
reality of violence and death by beating, lynching, burning. Some recount the ironies and
frustrations that Negroes face as they try to
grasp the freedom of America's promise. Others laugh at white America's presumptions and
sound an affirmation of the Negro American's
spirit, of his roots in the land. And finally, some of the poems tell of Negro dreams."
Horn Bk
    Includes Notes, Biographies, Indexes to au-
thors and first lines

Aiken, Conrad
    (ed.) A comprehensive anthology of Amer-
ican poetry. Modern Lib. 1944 xxii, 490p
$2.95, lib. bdg. $2.69   **811.08**
    1 American poetry—Collections
    First published 1929
    Ralph Waldo Emerson, Trumbull Stickney,
Robert Frost, Wallace Stevens, Ezra Pound,
T. S. Eliot and Jose Garcia Villa are among
the eighty-nine poets represented in this collection of over 280 poems
    The editor "has been rather hard on certain
national favorites: it will be thought by some
that he has been too drastic with Longfellow
and Holmes and Whittier and Lowell and Lanier; that he has been too generous with Poe
and Whitman and Dickinson; and that he has
erred in proportion by giving to the poetry of
the last twenty years so much more space
than he has given to that of any preceding
era." Introduction
    Includes indexes of poets and first lines

    (ed.) Twentieth-century American poetry,
ed. and with a preface by Conrad Aiken.
[Newly rev. ed.] Modern Lib. 1963 xxii, 552p
$2.95, lib. bdg. $2.69   **811.08**
    1 American poetry—Collections
    An enlarged edition of the editor's: Modern
American poets, first published 1922 in England, 1927 in the United States
    In this anthology eighty-one poets are re-
presented "and of these twenty-three now appear in an anthology for the first time. As in
the earlier editions, the editor has when possible preferred to include such poets as could
best be represented by a group of poems, and
with few exceptions, to avoid the one-poem
poet. . . . If Auden is not present, it is simply
because he is no more an American poet than
Eliot [who is included] is an English one."
Preface
    Index of poets: p543. Index of first lines:
p545-52

Bontemps, Arna
    (ed.) American Negro poetry; ed. and with
an introduction by Arna Bontemps. Hill &
Wang 1963 197p $4.95   **811.08**
    1 Negro poetry 2 American poetry—Collec-
tions
    A collection of over 170 poems by more than
50 prominent and less well-known "American
Negro poets, from the end of the 19th century
to the . . . [mid-twentieth century]. Especially
strong in what the editor calls the Harlem Renaissance of the 1920's—Countee Cullen, Jean
Toomer, Helene Johnson, Frank Horne and
others." Pub W

Bontemps, Arna—*Continued*

The book is "An interesting, valuable [one]. . . . The poems vary in form and quality. They vary also in subject matter although the Negro experience in this country naturally looms large." Horn Bk

Poems "reflecting both sombre and bright Americana. Biographical sketches and an informative introduction by the editor." Top of the News

Ciardi, John

(ed.) Mid-century American poets. Twayne 1950 336p (Twayne Lib. of modern poetry) $6
811.08

1 American poetry—Collections

"This is a book of verse and prose by fifteen . . . American writers: two women and thirteen men. The prose in each case serves as explanatory statement to the verse which follows, an attempt on the part of each writer to make clear what he is at. The result is a treatise on the poem that should be of the greatest interest to the student as well as the curious reader who has begun to wonder what all this pother about modern verse signifies." N Y Times Bk R

Dunning, Stephen

(comp.) Reflections on a gift of watermelon pickle . . . and other modern verse [comp. by] Stephen Dunning, Edward Lueders [and] Hugh Smith. Lothrop 1967 [c1966] 139p illus boards $4.50
811.08

1 American poetry—Collections

Text edition of this title first published 1966 by Scott, Foresman

The compilers have included 114 poems on a variety of topics. Chosen by students . . . many of the poems are by unfamiliar poets

"The articulated thoughts are clear and lovely—the world's truth expressed as it can only be—in poetry. Illustrated with unusually beautiful photographs. The design is by Donald Marvine. A most outstanding anthology." Bk Buyer's Guide

Author-title index

(comp.) Some haystacks don't even have any needle, and other complete modern poems; comp. by Stephen Dunning, Edward Lueders [and] Hugh Smith. . . . Lothrop 1969 192p illus boards $5.95
811.08

1 American poetry—Collections

"Editorial direction: Leo Kneer; development: Nora Rotzoll, Philip Brantingham, Ronald Mochel; design: Don Marvine." Title page

"The book contains more than 125 modern poems from magazines including the 'New Yorker, Harpers', and the 'little' magazines. . . . Tasteful, ingenious, the varied, relevant poems . . . will turn on even confirmed poety haters. The coy title and the lack of first-line index are small faults in a book as praiseworthy as this one—the poems about trivia and tragedy, garbage and glory, intriguingly patterned on the pages and complemented by scattered color reproductions of modern art, constitute a happening for today and a lasting delight." Library J

Index of titles: p188-89. Index of authors: p190-92

Fife, Austin

(ed.) Ballads of the great West; ed. with commentary by Austin & Alta Fife; with line drawings by Glen Rounds. Am. West 1970 271p illus $10
811.08

1 Ballads, American 2 The West—Poetry
ISBN 0-910118-17-5

Divided into four parts (The physical and human environment; The cowboy and other western types; Dramatic situations and events; and Code of the cowboy), this anthology of ballads, songs and verse provides a picture of the Old West. (Publisher)

"Although some of the folk poetry is known to us through song, much of the verse included is relatively unfamiliar; it has been gleaned from wide and varied sources of authentic Western Americana. . . . Also included are an excellent glossary of Western vocabulary, a title/first-line index, and a brief, incisive commentary for each selection which justifies its place in the anthology and enlightens the reader as to nuances, origins, and source." Library J

Hughes, Langston

(ed.) New Negro poets U.S.A. Foreword by Gwendolyn Brooks. Ind. Univ. Press 1964 127p $5.95
811.08

1 Negro poetry 2 American poetry—Collections

"Thirty-seven relatively young poets appear in an anthology whose five divisions are described in the foreword as 'lyrical, protest, personal and general descriptions, and personal, reflective statements.'. . . Some pieces are purely universal in theme, but in the main the book reflects the hurts, hopes, roots, and passions of its composite Negro authorship. Biographical notes appear at the back." Booklist

(ed.) The poetry of the Negro, 1746-1970; an anthology; ed. by Langston Hughes and Arna Bontemps. [Rev. ed] Doubleday 1970 xxiv, 645p $8.95
811.08

1 Negro poetry 2 American poetry—Collections

First published 1949

This collection is divided into two sections: Negro poets of the U.S.A. arranged chronologically from pre-Revolutionary times to the present; and Tributary poems by non-Negroes. Biographical notes on the poets appear at the end of the volume

Includes Author index and First line index

Johnson, James Weldon

(ed.) The book of American Negro poetry; chosen and ed. with an essay on the Negro's creative genius. [Rev. ed] Harcourt 1931 300p illus $5.95
811.08

1 Negro poetry 2 American poetry—Collections

First published 1922

"Contains selections from the work of forty writers. . . . The sketches of the poets included have been made critical as well as biographical, and a list of references for supplementary reading has been added." Preface to revised edition

Striking poems "with a finely suggestive historical and critical introductory essay." N Y State Lib

Books suggested for collateral reading: p295-96

Lee, Al

(ed.) The major young poets; selected and introduced by Al Lee. World Pub. 1971 200p $7.95
811.08

1 American poetry—Collections

A representative selection from the works of the following eight American poets: Marvin Bell, Michael Benedikt, William Brown, Charles Simic, Mark Strand, James Tate, C. K. Williams and David P. Young. A brief biography and bibliography precede the actual poetry

"Some like William Brown, C. K. Williams, and David P. Young, are poets of social protest. Others, like Michael Benedikt and James Tate, are followers of Franco-American modernism, painting a surreal world. . . . These poets are bizarre, serio-comic, Rabelaisian, Kafkaesque." Christian Science Monitor

Index of first lines and index of titles are provided

Lowenfels, Walter

(ed.) The writing on the wall; 108 American poems of protest. Doubleday 1969 189p $4.95
811.08

1 American poetry—Collections 2 Social problems—Poetry

"An excellent anthology, diverse in style and form, echoing the tempo of our times; some of the poets are of past generations but of

Lowenfels, Walter—*Continued*
contemporary vision, but most are the poets of today. The selections reflect the restlessness of youth and its rejection of ephemeral values, the protest against war and racial injustice, the isolation of man from fellow man." Chicago. Children's Book Center
"Among poets represented are Whitman, Dickinson, Pound, Cummings, Millay, Sandburg, Ginsberg, and Ferlinghetti." Publisher's note

The **Oxford** Book of American verse; chosen and with an introduction by F. O. Matthiessen. Oxford 1950 lvi, 1132p $7.50   811.08
1 American poetry—Collections
Completely new anthology, replacing Oxford Book of American verse, edited by Bliss Carman (1927)
This anthology covers, in 571 selections, the whole range of American poetry from colonial times to the present, with selections by fifty-one poets
The editor "devotes more than half of [the pages] to the 20th century. Nothing gets in on historical or sentimental grounds alone. He includes many long poems when they speak best for the poet. His basic plan is to present fewer poets with more space to each. . . . Emily Dickinson, Whitman, Emerson, Frost, Robinson, Cummings and Stevens have the most pages. . . . Throughout, the anthology is representative of mid-century critical taste." Library J
Bibliography: p1107-15. Index of first lines: p1119-32

Schreiber, Ron
(ed.) 31 new American poets; ed. and with an introduction by Ron Schreiber; foreword by Denise Levertov. Hill & Wang 1969 xxvi, 260p $5.95   811.08
1 American poetry—Collections
"American century series"
"New York School, San Francisco School, Black Mountain School, protest, hip, pop, concrete, lyrical poetry—all are represented in this collection of the best of America's unrecognized poets. The poets range in age from twenty-two to fifty; most are under thirty-five. . . . Each poet in the collection is represented by a number of poems—from five to nine pages —enough to give readers an impression of the variety of verse he is capable of writing." Publisher's note
"A wide variety of form and subject make this a vital collection. Most of the poems have previously appeared in literary periodicals and collections." Booklist

Shapiro, Karl
(ed.) American poetry. Crowell 1960 265p (Reader's bookshelf of American literature) $6.95   811.08
1 American poetry—Collections
Contains selections from more than 50 American poets, arranged chronologically from the 17th century to the present. Among the poets represented are Anne Bradstreet; Philip Freneau, Henry Wadsworth Longfellow, Walt Whitman, Emily Dickinson, Edgar Lee Masters, Robert Frost, Ezra Pound, E. E. Cummings, Hart Crane, and Allen Ginsberg
Includes notes on the poets, suggested critical readings, and indexes of poets and titles

Untermeyer, Louis
(ed.) An anthology of the New England poets; from colonial times to the present day; ed. with biographical and critical commentaries. Random House 1948 xx, 636p $10   811.08
1 American poetry—Collections
Selections from the writings of more than 30 distinguished New England poets, from the seventeenth century of Anne Bradstreet to the time of Emerson and Thoreau and today's Robert Frost, Edna St Vincent Millay and Robert Lowell. Includes index to authors, titles and first lines

"Because of its discriminating selection, (e.g. much Frost, little Coffin), and its well written critical sketches of the three dozen poets included, it should take its place on the reference shelves along with the compiler's other well known anthologies." Cur Ref Bks

(ed.) Modern American poetry. New and enl. ed. (Harcourt 1962 xxvi, 701p $7.95   811.08
1 American poetry—Collections 2 Poets, American
First published 1919
Companion volume to: Modern British poets, listed in class 821.08
"The chief aim of this collection is to express not only the national range but the rich diversity of recent American poetry. The object, in short, is to present a panormous in which outstanding figures assume logical prominence, but in which the valuable lesser personalities are not lost." Preface [to the 1950 edition]
Arranged chronologically. Preface discusses tendencies and schools of the period covered in the volume. The lengthy biographical and critical sketches preceding each poet are a valuable feature of this anthology. Author and title indexes

Williams, Oscar
(ed.) A little treasury of American poetry; the chief poets from Colonial times to the present day. Rev. ed. Edited with an introduction by Oscar Williams. Scribner [1952 c1948] xxxvi, 860p illus $7   811.08
1 American poetry—Collections
First published 1948
"An anthology of the works of the chief American poets. . . . More than 400 poems, by such writers as Whitman, Ezra Pound, T. S. Eliot, Poe, Millay, Frost . . . have been arranged in chronological order to give a history of American poetry." Retail Bookseller
Appendix contains portraits of 67 poets followed by an index of authors and titles

811.09 American poetry—History and criticism

Allen, Gay Wilson
A reader's guide to Walt Whitman. Farrar, Straus 1970 234p $5.95   811.09
1 Whitman, Walt
"Of special value to students of U.S. poetry, the study of the corpus of Whitman's work is a sensitively balanced, analytical introduction to the basic tenets of the poet's thought. After appraisal of the evolutionary influences on Whitman's writing, Allen reviews each of the nine editions of 'Leaves of grass,' published during Whitman's lifetime, then examines the root-center of his work from literary, cultural, religious, and psychological standpoints, quoting not only from the poems but from past and present criticism; the form and structure of Whitman's poetry is the subject of the final chapter." Booklist
Includes bibliography

Brittin, Norman A.
Edna St Vincent Millay. Twayne 1967 192p (Twayne's United States authors ser) $5.50   811.09
1 Millay, Edna St Vincent
The author "emphasizes Millay's solid achievements as the creator of a wide variety of poetry. He elucidates her high skill as a craftsman and, importantly, her real gift in the use of language. By tracing various themes in Millay's work, including the verse dramas, which here receive serious consideration as an important part of her poetry, Brittin gives the intellectual content the thoughtful consideration called for by Edmund Wilson and Max Eastman. The book is well annotated." Choice
Selected bibliography: p180-87

Burney, William
Wallace Stevens. Twayne 1968 190p
(Twayne's United States authors ser)
boards $5.50   811.09
1 Stevens, Wallace
In this volume, the author attempts "a complete paraphrase of 'The Collected Poems of Wallace Stevens.' Except for 'Harmonium,' selections from which are used to illustrate the major themes of death, life, and the vulgar in a systematic way, the poems are taken up in the order in which they are printed in 'The Collected Poems.' Because of the chronological approach, William Burney's study can be said to trace the spiritual biography of Stevens as well as to give interpretations of the poetry as a coherent whole. Burney is particularly interested in following the evolution of symbolic characters in the poems." Publisher's note
Selected bibliography: p184-86

Cox, James M.
(ed.) Robert Frost; a collection of critical essays. Prentice-Hall 1962 205p $5.95 811.09
1 Frost, Robert
"Twentieth century views. A Spectrum book."
Analyzed in Essay and general literature index
"These eleven critical views appraising the poet's work range from high praise to severe judgment." Chicago

Fein, Richard J.
Robert Lowell. Twayne 1970 173p
(Twayne's United States authors ser)
boards $5.50   811.09
1 Lowell, Robert
"This study tracing the development of Lowell's poetry strives for an overall view of his work and for a sense of his position in American literature and in modern poetry. The book combines application of the tools of 'new criticism' with discussions of the broader significance of Lowell's poetic themes." Publisher's note

Gerber, Philip L.
Robert Frost. Twayne [1967 c1966] 192p
(Twayne's United States authors ser)
boards $5.50   811.09
1 Frost, Robert
"Probing beneath the surface of the poet who encouraged his 'simple' image, this study reveals his complexities and great sophistication. There is close scrutiny of individual poems and an investigation of Frost's relationship with his colleagues." McClurg. Book News
"The general reader, the teacher, and particularly the student, it is hoped, will find the volume to be of some worth in placing Frost within his times and his profession. If it serves as that much of a definition of the man behind the poems and of the poetry itself, it will have fulfilled its chief end." Preface
Selected bibliography: p177-85

Kenner, Hugh
(ed.) T. S. Eliot; a collection of critical essays. Prentice-Hall 1962 210p $5.95   811.09
1 Eliot, Thomas Stearns
"Twentieth century views. A Spectrum book"
Analyzed in Essay and general literature index
"A selection covering the chief works and touching upon aspects of Eliot's activity as poet, playwright, critic, and personality." Chicago

Larrick, Nancy
(ed.) Somebody turned on a tap in these kids; poetry and young people today. Delacorte Press 1971 178p $5.95   811.09
1 American poetry—History and criticism
2 Children as authors
"Here are essays about . . . [teachers'] experiences, largely in inner-city classrooms, 'doing poetry' with an eager, excited bunch of

kids of assorted ethnic make-up and background. . . . The kids' poems quoted in the essays are lively, honest, sometimes pungent and strikingly original. A rap session on poetry by students at an all-black Philadelphia high school is an especially vivid evocation of the surprisingly vital youth scene today." Pub W
Includes bibliographical references

Miller, James E.
Walt Whitman, by James E. Miller, Jr. Twayne 1962 188p (Twayne's United States authors ser) boards $5.50   811.09
1 Whitman, Walt
"A critical essay on Whitman which studies first his views of himself and the major events of his life as related to his poetry. Subsequently the structure, language, recurring images, and democratic tone of his poetry are reviewed. Finally considered are the sexuality and mysticism that infused his work. A chronology precedes the text while notes and bibliography follow." Booklist

Sewall, Richard B.
(ed.) Emily Dickinson, a collection of critical essays. Prentice-Hall 1963 182p $5.95
                                           811.09
1 Dickinson, Emily
"Twentieth century views. A Spectrum book"
Sixteen analytical essays previously published in journals and books. "Among the contributors are such prominent literary names as Conrad Aiken, John Crowe Ransom, Louise Bogan, and Archibald MacLeish. . . . A chronology of important dates, notes on the authors, and a selected bibliography conclude a study that, aside from its intrinsic value as a kaleidoscope of critical insight, should be useful . . . for a range of material not likely otherwise to be available in a limited collection." Booklist

Tate, Allen
(ed.) T. S. Eliot: the man and his work; a critical evaluation by twenty-six distinguished writers. Delacorte Press 1966 400p illus $6.50
                                           811.09
1 Eliot, Thomas Stearns
"A Seymour Lawrence book"
Analyzed in Essay and general literature index
A "tribute to T. S. Eliot and his great contribution to twentieth-century literature, this book is in the form of appreciative essays, personal reminiscences, poems of tribute and literary criticism." McClurg. Book News
"The memoires represent a generation of thought in the literary arts; the essays and poems are from respected and loved poets of Eliot's generation; the art of the essay is displayed in an impressive variety of ways. This, then, is a consistently significant contribution to Eliot's biography, to the literary history of his period, and to the history of the spiritual impact of the events early in the 20th century." Library J
The works of T. S. Eliot: p395-97

Tomlinson, Charles
(ed.) Marianne Moore; a collection of critical essays. Prentice-Hall [1970 c1969] 185p $5.95   811.09
1 Moore, Marianne
"A Spectrum book"
The essays in this book "analyze the style, methods, motives, and motifs of Miss Moore's poetry, emphasizing her unique sensitivity and keen wit." Publisher's note
"Probably the single most useful book of criticism on Moore, and therefore essential for all libraries. Although, in keeping with the policy of this series, it is not intended as an introduction, the editor's introductory essay and the nature of several of the included pieces (such as Donald Hall's interview) make this volume useful even to those who are approaching Moore for the first time." Choice
Selected bibliography: p184-85

Unger, Leonard
(ed.) Seven modern American poets; an
introduction. Univ. of Minn. Press 1967 303p
$6.50   811.09
1 American poetry—History and criticism
Analyzed in Essay and general literature index
This collection "brings together in convenient book form the material from 7 pamphlets: 'Robert Frost' by Lawrance Thompson
'Wallace Stevens' by Wiliam Van O'Connor,
'John Crowe Ransom' by John L. Stewart,
'T. S. Eliot' by Leonard Unger, 'Allen Tate'
by George Hemphill, [William Carlos Williams
by John Malcolm Brinnin, and Ezra Pound by
William Van O'Connor]." Huntting
Selected bibliographies: p267-81

Wegner, Robert E.
The poetry and prose of E. E. Cummings.
Harcourt 1965 177p $4.95   811.09
1 Cummings, Edward Estlin
"Despite the title Wegner concentrates on
Cummings' poetry. . . . He explains for the student Cummings' theories of typographical
meaning and their concomitant appearance in
the poet's experiments with type placement
and punctuation marks and explores his themes
and use of satire. Appended are a chronology
of Cummings' work, an index to first lines to
poems referred to in the text, and a subject index." Booklist

812 American drama

Albee, Edward
The American dream, a play. Coward-Mc-
Cann 1961 93p (Coward-McCann Contempo-
rary drama) pa $1.95   812
Characters: 3 women, 2 men. 2 acts. First
produced at the York Playhouse, New York,
January 24, 1961
A satirical comedy of contemporary Amer-
Ican life which attacks a family's substitution
of artificial for real values

The zoo story, The death of Bessie Smith
[and] The sandbox; three plays, introduced
by the author. Coward-McCann 1960 158p
pa $2.25   812
In the first play, a mentally disturbed man
forms a terrible plan when he sees a placid
man reading a newspaper on a park bench.
Set in the South. "The death of Bessie Smith"
concerns the emotional conflict between an
intern and a nurse in a hospital for white people. In "The sandbox" a couple go to the beach
with the wife's aged mother

Anderson, Maxwell
Eleven verse plays, 1929-1939. Harcourt
[1940] 11v in 1 illus $12.50   812
Contents: Elizabeth the Queen (1930); Night
over Taos (1932); Mary of Scotland (1933);
Valley Forge (1934); Winterset (1935); Wing-
less victory (1936); High Tor (1937); The Masque of kings (1936); Feast of Ortolans (1938);
Key Largo (1939); Second overture (1940)

Baldwin,, James
Blues for Mister Charlie; a play. Dial Press
1964 121p $4.50   812
1 Negroes—Drama
Characters: 10 men, 3 women, and others.
3 acts. First produced at the ANTA Theatre,
New York, on April 23, 1964
"When a Negro drug addict from the North
returns to his southern home and is killed, a
service in the church places the blame on whites
and Negroes alike for his murder." Bk Buyer's
Guide
"Is the play propaganda? I suppose that it
is, to the extent that Baldwin hopes to have
a specific effect on an audience of Mister
Charlies—to make them change, to make them
see that the present crisis makes change imperative." Sat R

Connelly, Marc
The green pastures; a fable suggested by
Roark Bradford's Southern sketches, "Ol'
man Adam an' his chillun." Holt 1929 173p
$3.95   812
1 Negroes—Drama
Awarded the Pulitzer Prize for 1930
First produced February 26th, 1930 at the
Mansfield Theatre, New York. 59 characters
"A play in two parts and seventeen scenes,
more or less based on Roark Bradford's two
books of sketches of the deep South. It is a
Negro interpretation of the Bible as it shows
progressively God's dealings with his sinning
suffering earth-people, from the Creation to
the Redemption." Cleveland

Eliot, T. S.
The complete plays of T. S. Eliot. Harcourt 1969 355p $7.50   812
Contents: Murder in the cathedral; The family
reunion; The cocktail party; The confidential
clerk; The elder statesman
Published in England with title: Collected
plays

Murder in the cathedral. Harcourt 1935 87p
$3.50   812
1 Great Britain—History—Plantagenets, 1154-
1399—Drama 2 Thomas à Becket, Saint, Abp.
of Canterbury—Drama
Characters: 2 men, women's chorus and extras; 2 parts, 14 scenes, 2 interiors. First produced at the Canterbury Festival, England
June 1935
This verse drama of the conflict between
church and state in 12th century England, [un-
der Henry II] culminates in the murder of
Thomas à Becket in Canterbury Cathedral
"Mr. Eliot has admirably brought to maturity his long experimenting for a dramatic style,
the chief merit of which lies in his writing for
a chorus." Times (London) Lit Sup

Gesner, Clark
You're a good man, Charlie Brown; music
and lyrics by Clark Gesner. . . . Random
House 1967 88p illus boards $5.50   812
"Based on the comic strip 'Peanuts' by
Charles M. Schulz." Title page
Characters: 3 men, 2 women, extra. Two acts.
First produced March 7, 1967 at Theatre 80
St Marks, New York
Musical comedy depicting incidents in the
lives of five-year-old Charlie Brown, his friends
and dog Snoopy
The play "successfully renders the flavor
and mood typical of the comic strip it is based
on by effective characterizations interacting
convincingly in a series of vignettelike scene
that fade one into another." Booklist

Gibson, William
The miracle worker; a play for television.
Knopf 1957 131p boards $4.95   812
1 Keller, Helen Adams—Drama 2 Macy, Anne
(Sullivan)—Drama
Characters: 6 men, 5 women
"A dramatization of the miracle wrought by
Annie Sullivan, the young teacher of Helen
Keller, encompasses the first year of their
long association and reaches its climax when
after months of patient effort Helen speaks her
first word." Booklist
"The present text is meant for reading, and
differs from the telecast version in that I have
restored some passages that read better than
they play and others omitted in performance
for simple lack of time." Author's note
"What comes through is the great intelligence
of two extraordinary [young] people. . . . Recommended for general collections, as well as
theatre, cinema and television sections." Library J

Goodrich, Frances

The diary of Anne Frank; dramatized by Frances Goodrich and Albert Hackett; based upon the book, Anne Frank: Diary of a young girl; with a foreword by Brooks Atkinson. Random House 1956 174p illus $5.50   812

1 Netherlands—History—German occupation, 1940-1945—Drama 2 World War, 1939-1945—Jews—Drama 3 Jews in the Netherlands—Drama

Awarded the Pulitzer Prize and the New York Drama Critics Circle Award for 1956
Characters: 5 women, 5 men. 2 acts. One set of scenery. First produced at the Cort Theatre, New York, October 5, 1955
The play dramatizes the autobiography of Anne "the youngest of a group of eight Jews who for two years and one month hid in a cramped attic over a warehouse to escape the Gestapo." Foreword
"Using the device of spoken passages from the actual diary, together with more conventionally staged scenes . . . [the authors] have translated the fire and evanescence of a fifteen year-old's secret thoughts into a forceful and workmanlike drama. As in the original book, the horrors of war and genocide, and the poverty of narrow souls are the more poignant for being seen through such naive and hopeful eyes." Booklist

Hammerstein, Oscar, 1895-1960

6 plays, by Rodgers and Hammerstein. Modern Lib. 1959 527p $2.95   812

A reissue of the title first published 1955 by Random House
The scripts and lyrics of six of their most popular musicals: Oklahoma; Carousel; Allegro; South Pacific; The king and I; Me and Juliet

Hansberry, Lorraine

A raisin in the sun; a drama in three acts. Random House 1959 142p illus boards $5.50   812

1 Negroes—Drama

Awarded the New York Drama Critics Circle Award for the 1958-1959 season
Characters: 3 women, 8 men, 6 scenes in 3 acts. One set of scenery. First produced at the Ethel Barrymore Theatre, New York. March 11, 1959
"A play about the tensions and explosive drama in a middle-class Negro family in Chicago, when they come into possession of a legacy." Pub W
"More than just a plea for integration, this play reveals how a family can be revitalized, not by a sudden financial windfall, but by mutual love and understanding." Doors to More Mature Reading

To be young, gifted and Black; Lorraine Hansberry in her own words; adapted by Robert Nemiroff; with original drawings and art by Miss Hansberry; and an introduction by James Baldwin. Prentice-Hall 1969 xxii, 266p illus $8.95   812

SBN 13-923003-3

"This moving compilation of Miss Hansberry's letters, excerpts from plays, autobiographical essays, speeches, and interviews is the text for the off-Broadway play of the same name. A good introduction to Miss Hansberry's unique, impassioned, talented personality." Library J

Hughes, Langston

Five plays; ed. with an introduction by Webster Smalley. Ind. Univ. Press 1963 258p $6.95   812

"These folk plays, most of them full length, for all Negro casts, include fantasy, melodrama, comedy, and musical comedy. . . . The same qualities that make them interesting as drama make them enjoyable reading; an earthiness, a basic respect for human beings, and an indigenous American idiom both precise and revealing." Booklist

Inge, William

Four plays. Random House 1958 304p $7.50   812

The author was awarded the Pulitzer Prize, 1953, for: Picnic
Contents: Come back, Little Sheba; Picnic; Bus stop; The dark at the top of the stairs

Laurents, Arthur

West Side story; a musical (based on a conception of Jerome Robbins). . . . Random House 1958 143p illus boards $5.50   812

1 New York (City)—Drama

"Book by Arthur Laurents: music by Leonard Bernstein lyrics by Stephen Sondheim entire production directed and choreographed by Jerome Robbins." Title page
Characters: 14 women, 25 men. One set of scenery. First produced at the Winter Garden Theatre, New York, September 26, 1957
The feud between two New York teenage gangs "abruptly ends the brief happiness shared by Maria, a Puerto Rican girl, and Tony, a member of the Jets. In his attempt to defend a fellow Jet Tony kills Maria's brother and shortly thereafter is killed by Maria's rejected fiancé. The romantic dreams of the two young lovers and the idiom and the activities of the rival teenage gangs are effectively contrasted in a piognant and witty play that deals unobtrusively but tellingly with a contemporary social problem." Booklist

Lawrence, Jerome

Mame; book by Jerome Lawrence and Robert E. Lee; music and lyrics by Jerry Herman. Based on the novel by Patrick Dennis and the play "Auntie Mame" by Lawrence and Lee. Random House 1967 137p illus $4.95   812

Characters: Large mixed cast. 16 scenes in 2 acts. First produced at the Winter Garden Theatre, New York City, May 24, 1966
A musical comedy about a young boy, orphaned at ten, who is being brought up by his gay, warmhearted but eccentric aunt

Lerner, Alan Jay

Camelot; a new musical; book and lyrics by Alan Jay Lerner. Music by Frederick Loewe. . . . Random House 1961 115p illus boards $5.50   812

1 Arthur, King—Drama

Characters: 14 men, 5 women, extras. Nineteen scenes in two acts. First produced at the Majestic Theatre, New York, on December 3, 1960
"Based on The once and future king, by T. H. White." Title page
A recreation of the Arthurian legend "from the marriage of Arthur and Guenevere to the wars following Lancelot and Guenevere's defections." Booklist

My fair lady; a musical play in two acts. . . . Coward-McCann 1956 186p front $4.50   812

Recipient of the New York Drama Critics Circle Award for 1956
"Based on 'Pygmalion' by Bernard Shaw; adaptation and lyrics by Alan Jay Lerner: music by Frederick Loewe." Title page
Characters: 28 men, 14 women. First produced on March 15: 1956 at the Mark Hellinger Theatre, New York
"A British professor of phonetics transforms a Covent Garden flower girl into the semblance of a duchess." Ontario
"Nourishing and palatable fare for a reading group or an individual reader. This musical play . . . is written in witty dialogue and revealing scenes, which point up some of the foibles in our society, especially in the area of communication." Wis Lib Bul

Levin, Ira

No time for sergeants <adapted from the novel by Mac Hyman> Random House 1956 176p illus $5.95   812

Characters: 36 men, 2 women. One set of scenery. First produced October 20, 1955 at the Alvin Theatre, New York City

Levin, Ira—*Continued*
This farce depicts the trials and tribulations of Will Stockdale, a good-natured hillbilly from Georgia, as an inductee in the U.S. Army
"The humor of Will's blunders, the commentary on prejudice, and the satire on military life combine to produce a readable and unique drama." Doors to More Mature Reading

Lindsay, Howard
Clarence Day's Life with father and Life with mother; made into plays by Howard Lindsay and Russel Crouse. With an introduction by Brooks Atkinson. [1st combined ed] Knopf 1953 2v in 1 illus $7.95   812
An omnibus volume reprinting the following volumes: Clarence Day's Life with father (1940) and Clarence Day's Life with mother (1949)
These two comedies are based on Clarence Day's amusing books about his despotic father and about the Day family life, particularly his mother's scheming to acquire an engagement ring

The sound of music; a new musical play. . . . Music by Richard Rodgers; lyrics by Oscar Hammerstein II; book by Howard Lindsay and Russel Crouse. Random House 1960 141p illus boards $5.50   812

1 Trapp family—Drama

"(Suggested by the Trapp family singers by Maria Augusta Trapp)." Title page
Characters: 10 women, 7 men, 7 children. Two acts, twenty scenes. First produced at the Lunt-Fontanne Theatre, New York City, on November 16, 1959
This musical "tells the story of Maria Rainer, a young postulant in Austria who leaves the convent to make a final decision regarding her future. As governess to Captain von Trapp's motherless children she begins a new life that leads to her marriage with the captain. The family's escape from Nazi soldiers ends a play filled with exuberant lyrics and warm sentiment." Booklist

Lowell, Robert
Prometheus bound. Derived from Aeschylus. Farrar, Straus 1969 67p $5.95   812
Characters: 6 men, 1 woman, extras. First presented by the Yale School of Drama, New Haven, Connecticut, May 9, 1967
An adaptation of a Greek tragedy based on the legend in which the demi-god Prometheus is punished for stealing fire from Heaven for man
Robert Lowell "here succeeds movingly in 'marrying' the great play by Aeschylus to his own ideas on the Promethean drama. . . . [This] is a modern man's rendering, in tempered prose that avoids the 'poetic eloquence' of Aeschylus, that goes as far as any contemporary can in doing nearly-colloquial justice to the original without succumbing to the obvious temptations of tasteless 'modernization.' " Pub W

MacInnes, Helen
Home is the hunter; a comedy in two acts. Harcourt 1964 199p $4.75   812

1 Ulysses—Drama 2 Homer—Adaptations 3 Homer—Parodies, travesties, etc.

Characters: 7 men, 4 women and extras. 2 acts, 6 scenes
The author "sets forth her version of the homecoming of Ulysses after his extended 'delay en route' from the siege of Troy. . . . The years have taken a toll of Ulysses' strength and the legendary Great Bow that . . . no one but Ulysses could draw is now too much for him; so the suitors have to be dispatched via the sword rather than the arrow." Best Sellers
"Told in the modern idiom with shrewd psychological touches and good-natured deflation of the Homeric version. . . . Homer himself appears intermittently." Booklist

Miller, Arthur
The crucible; a play in four acts. Viking [1964 c1953] 145p $3.50   812

1 Witchcraft—Drama 2 Salem, Mass.—Drama

A reissue of a book published 1953
Characters: 11 men, 10 women. First presented at the Martin Beck Theatre in New York, January 22, 1953
"A play based on the Salem witchcraft trials of 1692. It deals particularly with the hounding to death of the nonconformist John Proctor." Book Rev Digest
"The terrifying consequences of fear and insecurity are explored here in a drama of . . . the Puritan world." Ontario Lib Rev
"This play is recommended for mature senior high school students who are interested in early American history." Doors to More Mature Reading

Death of a salesman; certain private conversations in two acts and a requiem. Viking 1949 139p $3.50   812

1 Salesmen and salesmanship—Drama

Winner of the Pulitzer Prize and the New York Drama Critics Circle award 1949
Characters: 8 men, 5 women. First produced at the Morosco Theatre in New York on February 10, 1949
"The tragedy of a typical American—salesman who at the age of sixty-three is faced with what he cannot face: defeat and disillusionment. It is a bitter and moving experience of groping for values and for material success." Cleveland

The price; a play. Viking 1968 116p $4.50   812

Characters: 3 men, 1 woman. First produced at the Morosco Theater, New York, February 7, 1968
"Engrossing play about two estranged brothers who meet after . . . [many] years to dispose of their deceased parents' furniture. One sacrificed a science career and became a policeman to support their father during the depression while the other studied to become a surgeon. Questions of self-sacrifice, self-interest, responsibility, and illusions are explored but left for the reader to resolve." Wis Lib Bul

Odets, Clifford
Six plays; with a preface by the author. Modern Lib. 443p $2.95, lib. bdg. $2.69   812
A reprint of the title first published by Random House
Contents: Waiting for Lefty; Awake and sing; Till the day I die; Paradise lost; Golden Boy; Rocket to the moon
"Mr. Odets seems to me best in handling characters whom he is willing to treat as definitely individual." N Y Her Trib Books

O'Neill, Eugene, 1888-1953
The author was awarded the Nobel Prize in literature, 1936

Ah, wilderness! And two other plays: All God's chillun got wings, and Beyond the horizon. Modern Lib. [1964] 306p $2.95, lib. bdg. $2.69   812
A collection of three plays first copyrighted 1933, 1924, and 1920 respectively. Beyond the horizon was awarded the Pulitzer Prize, 1920
"Ah wilderness" concerns family life in a small town and a couple's reactions to their son's ideas. "All God's chillun got wings" is about a tragic marriage between a white woman and a Negro. "Beyond the horizon" is a tragedy contrasting the characters of two brothers on the family farm

The Emperor Jones, Anna Christie [and] The hairy ape; introduction by Lionel Trilling. Modern Lib. 1937 260p $2.95, lib. bdg. $2.69   812
The first play portrays a Negro tyrant in the West Indies, overthrown by the natives; Anna Christie, 1922 Pulitzer Prize winner, dramatizes life of ex-prostitute who joins barge captain father. The hairy ape is expressionistic play about Yank, stoker on transatlantic liner, in search of identity

O'Neill, Eugene—*Continued*

The iceman cometh; a play. Vintage 1946
260p lib. bdg. $2.29   812

A reprint of the title first published by Random House

Characters: 16 men, 3 women. First produced October 9th, 1946

The author dramatizes the thoughts and actions of a group of derelicts who inhabit the barroom of a New York city saloon in 1912

"The compelling quality of the play is that, for all this shockingness, instinctively we recognize and identify them as only too human." Book Week

Long day's journey into night. Yale Univ.
Press 1956 [c1955] 176p $6.75   812

Awarded the Pulitzer Prize, 1957

Characters: 3 men, 2 women. Five scenes in four acts. First produced in Stockholm, Sweden, February 1956

"First publication of a four-act play written by the . . . playwright in 1940. Dramatizes the tragedy of O'Neill's own earlier life in which he and those closest to him were mutually involved but with varying degrees of guilt." Retail Bookseller

The long voyage home; seven plays of the sea. Modern Lib. 1946 217p $2.95, lib. bdg. $2.69   812

1 Seafaring life—Drama

Contents: The moon of the Caribbees; Bound east for Cardiff; The long voyage home; In the zone; Ile; Where the cross is made; The rope

Nine plays; selected by the author; introduction by Joseph Wood Krutch. Modern Lib. 1941 xxii, 867p $4.95, lib. bdg. $3.89 812

Reprint of a book first published 1932 by Random House

Contents: The Emperor Jones; "The hairy ape"; All God's chillun got wings; Desire under the elms; "Marco Millions"; The great god Brown; Lazarus laughed; Strange interlude (1928 Pulitzer Prize winner); Mourning becomes Electra

Plays. Random House 1951 3v $25 boxed, ea $9   812

"The Random House Lifetime library"

First published 1941

A collection of 29 representative O'Neill plays

Contents: v 1: Strange interlude; Desire under the elms; Lazarus laughed; The fountain; Moon of the Caribbees; Bound east for Cardiff; Long voyage home; In the zone; Ile; Where the cross is made; The rope; Dreamy kid; Before breakfast. v2: Mourning becomes Electra; Ah wilderness; All God's chillun got wings; Marco millions; Welded; Different; First man; Gold. v3: "Anna Christie"; Beyond the horizon; Emperor Jones; Hairy ape; Great god Brown; The straw; Dynamo; Days without end

Selected plays of Eugene O'Neill. Random House 1969 758p $12.50   812

A "new collection of eight plays by the major American playwright who won three Pulitzer Prizes and a Nobel Prize." Booklist

Contents: The Emperor Jones; Anna Christie; The hairy ape; Desire under the elms; The great god Brown; Strange interlude; Mourning becomes Electra; The iceman cometh

Patrick, John

The Teahouse of the August Moon; a play adapted from the novel by Vern Sneider. Putnam [1954 c1952] 180p front $3.95   812

Pulitzer Prize for drama, 1954 and the 1953-54 New York Critics Circle award

Characters: 13 men, 5 women and several minor characters. First produced at the Martin Beck Theatre, October 15, 1953

"Captain Fisby, ordered to build a school and to teach democracy in a village on Okinawa, succumbs to the influence of Lotus Blossom, a geisha girl, and builds a teahouse to the consternation of his commanding officer." Cleveland

"This is the complete text of a thoroughly original and amusing play. But it is also wise, witty, and thought-provoking." Sec Ed Brd

Sackler, Howard

The great white hope; a play. Dial Press
[1968] 264p $4.95   812

1 Johnson, Jack—Drama 2 Boxing—Drama 3 Race problems—Drama

Awarded the Pulitzer Prize, 1969

Characters: Large mixed cast. 19 scenes in 3 acts. First produced at the Arena Stage in Washington, D.C. December 12,1967

A play "based on the rise and fall of Jack Johnson, first Negro heavyweight champion of the world, who eventually took his white wife to Europe to escape race-hatred and lost his title to 'the great white hope.'" Bk Buyer's Guide

Schary, Dore

Sunrise at Campobello; a play in three acts. Random House 1958 109p illus boards $5.50
                                        812

1 Roosevelt, Franklin Delano, President U.S. —Drama 2 Roosevelt family—Drama

Characters: 19 men, 5 women. First produced at the Cort Theatre, New York City, January 30, 1958

Deals with Franklin Delano Roosevelt's personal and family life during the years 1921-1924 when he was stricken, with infantile paralysis and fought his way back to active life

Includes photographs of the original Broadway production

Sherwood, Robert Emmet

Abe Lincoln in Illinois; a play in twelve scenes; with a foreword by Carl Sandburg. Scribner 1939 250p $4.95   812

1 Lincoln, Abraham, President U.S.—Drama

Awarded the Pulitzer Prize, 1939

Characters: 25 men, 7 women. First produced October 3, 1938

Deals with Lincoln's life from his first meeting with Ann Rutledge until he left Springfield to take office as President

In the last act "Mr. Sherwood's drama suddenly moves into epic proportions, taking on body and imaginative power. In the opening scene of the Lincoln-Douglas debate, in the scenes of his candidacy for the presidency, and above all his final adieu to his fellow citizens of Springfield as he leaves for Washington, this final act is informed with a rare dignity, even a majesty." Commonweal

Simon, Neil

Barefoot in the park; a new comedy. Random House 1964 143p illus $5.50   812

Characters: 4 men, 2 women, 3 acts. First produced at the Biltmore Theatre, New York City, October 23, 1963

A 'comedy about a young married couple in which a slight plot is disguised in quick, amusing lines. A fifth-floor, walk-up with, idiosyncracies, a lovers' quarrel, and a love affair between the girl's mother and a zany neighbor all contribute to an enjoyable entertainment." Booklist

Stein, Joseph

Fiddler on the roof; book by Joseph Stein; music by Jerry Bock; lyrics by Sheldon Harnick. . . . Crown 1964 116p illus $3.95   812

1 Jews in Russia—Drama

"Based on Sholom Aleichem's stories." Title page

Large cast. 2 acts, 18 scenes. First produced at the Imperial Theatre, New York, September 22, 1964

A drama of Jewish life in a Russian village, 1905

Stone, Peter

1776; a musical play (based on a conception of Sherman Edwards). Book by Peter Stone; music and lyrics by Sherman Edwards. Viking 1970 171p illus $5   812

SBN 670-63657-6

Stone, Peter—*Continued*

Characters: 25 men, 2 women. One set of scenery. Seven scenes. First produced at the Forty-Sixth Street Theater on March 16, 1969

"1776 takes place in one continuous flow of action, during the months from May 8 to July 4 in Philadelphia, when the Second Continental Congress argued, voted and signed the Declaration of Independence." News of Bks

"Lines of pithy humor, witty lyrics, a smidgen of fantasy, and entertainingly vivid characterization allow Edwards and Stone to zero in most refreshingly on the very human traits of the now mythically exalted members of the Continental Congress and their hassles through three crucial months of 1776." Booklist

Vidal, Gore

Visit to a small planet, and other television plays. Little 1956 278p $4.95   **812**

1 Television plays

"Reading versions of eight television plays by Vidal, including five original dramas and three adaptations." Theatre Arts

"The impressive thing in this collection—which includes the author's own enlightening commentary—is the breadth of his experience and the variety of his subject matter." Chicago Sunday Tribune

Wasserman, Dale

Man of La Mancha; a musical play; lyrics by Joe Darion; music by Mitch Leigh. Random House 1966 82p illus $5.50   **812**

Winner of the New York Drama Critics award "Best Musical 1966"

Chararcters: 14 men, 5 women and extras. First produced at the ANTA Washington Square Theatre, New York City, November 22, 1965

This musical play-adaptation of Don Quixote is built around Cervantes' defense, when imprisoned and held for inquisition. He arranges a mock trial performance to present his case

The author "fails to do much with Cervantes but he has found an ingenious means of bringing to the stage some of the poetic elements and famous events in the great novel. The play evokes man's idealism, his striving to be better than he is. This theme is epitomized by author Wasserman's conceit that 'Facts are the enemy of truth.' While this may not be all that 'Man of La Mancha' is about, on its own terms it's a successful musical play, sure to be popular among regional and community theaters throughout the country." Library J

White, Theodore H.

Caesar at the Rubicon; a play about politics. Atheneum Pubs. 1968 174p $5   **812**

1 Caesar, Caius Julius—Drama 2 Rome—History—Republic, 510-30 B.C.—Drama

This drama depicts "six weeks of Roman politics as Caesar decided whether or not he should cross the Rubicon, defying Rome." Bk Buyer's Guide

A bibliography of Julius Caesar: p171-74

Wilder, Thornton

Our town; a play in three acts   **812**

Some editions are:
Harper $4.95
Watts, F. $9.95 Large type edition. A Keith Jennison book

Awarded the Pulitzer Prize, 1938

First published 1938 by Coward-McCann

Characters: Large mixed cast. First produced at McCarter's Theatre, Princeton, New Jersey, on January 22, 1938

"Drama of life in a small New Hampshire village, called Groper's Corners. The people of the village go about their daily affairs, thru a few years in the early 1900s and then some of them experience death. Altho when produced little or no scenery is used, the play has a stage manager who links together the separate parts of the action with running comment, somewhat in the manner of the Greek Chorus." Booklist

Three plays; Our town, The skin of our teeth [and] The matchmaker; with a preface. Harper 1957 401p boards $7.95   **812**

Wilder was awarded the Pulitzer Prize, 1938 for: Our town, and 1943 for: The skin of our teeth

A collection of three titles first copyrighted 1938, 1942, and 1955 respectively. An earlier version of: the matchmaker, was first copyrighted 1939 with title: The merchant of Yonkers

In: Our town, the dead of a New Hampshire village of the early 1900s, appreciate life more than the living. The skin of our teeth is an allegorical fantasy about man's struggle to survive. The matchmaker is a romantic farce set in the 1880's

Williams, Tennessee

The glass menagerie; a play. New Directions [1949 c1945] 124p illus (The New classics) pa $1.50   **812**

Awarded the New York Drama Critics Circle Award for 1945

A reprint of the edition first published 1945 by Random House, with the addition of a brief essay entitled; The catastrophe of success

Characters: 2 men, 2 women, 2 parts. First produced at the Civic Theatre, Chicago on December 26, 1944. One set of scenery

A play about a Southern woman who is anxious for her crippled daughter to be married and the daughter's experiences with the man whom her brother brings home at the mother's request. Each character lives with a different set of illusions

"Mr. Williams has succeeded in projecting his people above and beyond their airless world: all of them are universals in the best sense of the term, yet all are compellingly real as persons, too." N Y Times Bk R

A streetcar named Desire. New Directions 1947 171p $5.25   **812**

Awarded the Pulitzer Prize, 1948

Characters: 6 women, 7 men, scenes. First produced December 3, 1947 at the Barrymore Theatre in New York

"The drama of a widowed young woman, whose unfortunate marriage and home life have unbalanced her mind, and of her conflict with the sister and brother-in-law whom she goes to live with." Huntting

Wouk, Herman

The Caine mutiny court-martial; a play based on his novel "The Caine mutiny." Doubleday 1954 128p $4.95   **812**

1 World War, 1939-1945—Drama

Characters: 13 men, 2 acts. First produced October 12, 1953 at the Granada Theatre in Santa Barbara, Calif.

Lieutenant Maryk of the United States Navy stands trial for having taken over from incompetent Captain Queeg, command of the minesweeper "Caine," caught in a typhoon during World War II

"The text of Wouk's smash-hit Broadway play based on his Pulitzer Prize novel, and certainly one of the tensest reading experiences of the year. To the student, it should also be most revealing to compare the play with the novel and notice the enormous gains made by dramatic compression." Sec Ed Brd

812.08   American drama—Collections

Cerf, Bennett A.

(ed.) Plays of our time. Random House 1967 782p $10   **812.08**

1 American drama—Collections

Contents: The iceman cometh, by E. O'Neill; A streetcar named Desire, by T. Williams; Death of a salesman, by A. Miller; Mister Roberts, by T. Heggen; Come back, Little Sheba, by W. Inge; Look back in anger, by J. Osborne; A raisin in the sun, by L. Hansberry; A man for all seasons, by R. Bolt; Luv, by M. Schisgal

Cerf, Bennett A.—*Continued*

(ed.) Six American plays for today; selected and with biographical notes by Bennett Cerf. Modern Lib. 1961 599p $2.95   812.08

1 American drama—Collections

Contents: Camino Real, by T. Williams: The dark at the top of the stairs, by W. Inge; Sunrise at Campobello, by D. Schary; A raisin in the sun, by L. Hansberry; The tenth man, by P. Chayefsky; Toys in the attic, by L. Hellman

(ed.) Sixteen famous American plays; ed. by Bennett A. Cerf and Van H. Cartmell; with an introduction by Brooks Atkinson. Modern Lib. 1942 [c1941] 1049p $4.95   812.08

1 American drama—Collections

"Modern Library giants"

Reprint of a title first published 1941 by Garden City Publishing Company

This collection was chosen from a period of "twenty years beginning with 'They Knew What They Wanted' (1924), and ending with 'Life with Father.' . . . There is no major playwright of the . . . two decades who is not represented, and well represented: and to go through this volume is to realize that, whatever the faults of this period, it is one of great vitality in the theatre." Book of the Month Club News

Gassner, John

(ed.) Best American plays; 3d series—1945-1951; ed. with an introduction by John Gassner. Crown 1952 xxviii, 707p $6.95   812.08

1 American drama—Collections

This collection "includes Arthur Miller's 'Death of a Salesman,' Tennessee Williams' 'A Streetcar Named Desire,' William Inge's 'Come Back. Little Sheba' and 14 others." Pub W

Supplementary list of American non-musical plays. Bibliography

(ed.) Best American plays; 4th series—1951-1957; ed. with an introduction by John Gassner. Crown 1958 xxii, 648p $6.95 812.08

1 American drama—Collections

"Contains the complete reading texts of 17 plays which were . . . successful stage productions. An introductory essay by the editor assesses trends and achievements in the American theater during the period covered. Each play is prefaced by a brief introduction." Booklist

Selective bibliography. Supplementary list of plays

(ed.) Best American plays; 5th series—1957-1963; ed. with an introduction and prefaces to the plays by John Gassner. Crown 1963 xxiv, 678p $6.95   812.08

1 American drama—Collections

The editor's brief evaluation "of American drama introduces complete texts of 17 plays. . . . Selected lists of Broadway and off-Broadway plays during the period are included." Booklist

Represented in this series for the first time are Paddy Chayefsky, Edward Albee, and Arthur Kopit

(ed.) Best American plays; 6th series—1963-1967; ed. by John Gassner and Clive Barnes; with an introduction and prefaces to the plays by Clive Barnes. Crown 1971 594p (Best American plays ser) $7.95   812.08

1 American drama—Collections

An anthology of seventeen plays, produced on and off Broadway

(ed.) Best American plays; supplementary volume, 1918-1958; ed. with an introduction. Crown 1961 687p $6.95   812.08

1 American drama—Collections

"Seventeen plays not included in the author's previous 'Best plays' collections with a general introduction and a brief [critical] introduction for each play." Book Rev Digest

(ed.) Best plays of the early American theatre; from the beginning to 1916; ed. with introductions, by John Gassner in association with Mollie Gassner. Crown 1967 xlviii, 716p front $6.95   812.08

1 American drama—Collections

Sixteen "plays from the beginning of the American theater to the coming of Eugene 'Neill—including, among others, 'Salvation Nell,' 'The Octoroon,' 'The Count of Monte Cristo.' 'Uncle Tom's Cabin,' 'The Scarecrow,' 'The Great Divide,' and 'The Witching Hour.' " Bk Buyer's Guide

This book, "in all reality, constitutes the cornerstone of our national theater. The plays are not often performed, but that is no excuse for not including this book in every library claiming a section on the American theater." Library J

A selective bibliography: p xlvii-xlviii

(ed.) Best plays of the modern American theatre; 2d series; ed. with an introduction. Crown 1947 xxx, 776p $6.95   812.08

1 American drama—Collections

The editor "surveys the plays that represent the theater of the turbulent period of 1939-1945. . . . He analyzes the effects of the war, and presents . . . [complete texts of 17] plays as his choices for the best." Cleveland

Includes bibliography

(ed.) Twenty best plays of the modern American theatre; ed. with an introduction. Crown 1939 xxii, 874p $6.95   812.08

1 American drama—Collections

Complete text of 20 successful plays

"Mr. Gassner's vivid and pungent preface adds greatly to the value of a book which succeeds in presenting the diversity and intrinsic vigor of Broadway [of the times]." Theatre Arts

Plays by authors represented: p869-71. Plays by other authors, 1930-1940: p871-72. Bibliography: p873-74

(ed.) Twenty-five best plays of the modern American theatre; early series; ed. with an introduction. Crown 1949 xxviii, 756p $6.95   812.08

1 American drama—Collections

"Selected from work produced from 1916 through 1929. The editor has represented most of the important dramatists who had established reputations before 1930 and has tried to give a cross-section of theatrical writing during those years. Includes The hairy ape, Desire under the elms, What price glory? Porgy, and, The front page. The introduction gives a good, brief history of the period and there are biographical notes on the playwrights." Booklist

Supplementary list of plays: p754-55. Bibliography: p756

Quinn, Arthur Hobson

(ed.) Representative American plays; from 1767 to the present day; ed. with introductions and notes. 7th ed. rev. and enl. Appleton 1953 1248p $9.75   812.08

1 American drama—Collections

First published 1917

A reference collection of 31 plays which illustrate the development of our native drama from its beginning to the present

General bibliography of the American drama: p1243-48

Six modern American plays; introduction by Allan G. Halline. Modern Lib. 1951 xxviii, 419p $2.95, lib. bdg. $2.69   812.08

1 American drama—Collections

Contents: The Emperor Jones, by E. O'Neill; Winterset, by M. Anderson; The man who came to dinner, by G. S. Kaufman; The little foxes, by L. Hellman; The glass menagerie, by T. Williams; Mister Roberts, by T. Heggen

Bibliography: p xxvii-xxviii

812.09 American drama— History and criticism

Amacher, Richard E.
Edward Albee. Twayne 1969 190p (Twayne's United States authors ser) boards $5.50   **812.09**
1 Albee, Edward
"A scholarly analysis of the dramatic writings of the leading American representative of 'theater of the absurd.' Also included are a chapter on Albee's life and on his literary views." Publisher's note
Includes bibliography

Carpenter, Frederic I.
Eugene O'Neill. Twayne 1964 191p (Twayne's United States author ser) boards $5.50   **812.09**
1 O'Neill, Eugene Gladstone, 1888-1953
After a long discussion of the relationship between O'Neill's life and plays, the author "suggests that there is a kind of 'pattern' which runs through the succession of individual tragedies which O'Neill wrote. This pattern was biographical in origin. . . . The central chapters of this book (Chapter Three through Seven) describe and criticize O'Neill's best plays individually. The descriptions and critiques, are as concrete and detailed as possible. . . . The concluding chapter of this book discusses the chief criticism of his work." Preface
Notes and references: p180-83. Selected bibliography: p184-87.

Corrigan, Robert W.
(ed.) Arthur Miller; a collection of critical essays. Prentice-Hall 1969 176p $5.95 **812.09**
1 Miller, Arthur
"Twentieth century views. A Spectrum book"
"The dominant themes of Miller's dramas, and his personal and theatrical development are explored in 10 articles. Corrigan's analytical introduction traces the thematic progression of Miller's writing from his earliest plays through the pivotal work 'The misfits' . . . to his most recent productions. Other contributors survey Miller's strengths and weaknesses and examine the implications for the liberal conscience evident in 'The crucible, a play in four acts.' . . . Harold Clurman's director's notes for Miller's 'Incident at Vichy' are included." Booklist
Includes bibliographical references

Falk, Signi Lenea
Tennessee Williams. Twayne [1962 c1961] 224p (Twayne's United States authors ser) boards $5.50   **812.09**
1 Williams, Tennessee
This literary study "contains critical comment on Tennessee Williams' work. It also assesses his position among contemporary Southern writers. The critical comment on Williams' major plays is arranged by four types of characters which reappear in them: The Southern gentlewoman, the Southern wench, the lonely, fugitive hero, and degenerate artist. A Williams chronology and a bibliography of primary and secondary sources round out the objective appraisal." Booklist

Gould, Jean
Modern American playwrights; illus. with photographs. Dodd 1966 302p illus $6.50   **812.09**
1 American drama—History and criticism
2 Dramatists, American
Analyzed in Essay and general literature index
"This book provides a summary of the 'realistic' theater from [Elmer] Rice to the currently [in] theater of the Absurd or abstract, with its exotic symbolism. The Province-towners, Barry, Anderson, Hellman, Sherwood, Odets, Saroyan and Williams, and Albee and his group, are covered with interpretations of their work in terms of their backgrounds." Library J
A selected bibliography: p291-92

Krutch, Joseph Wood
The American drama since 1918; an informal history. Braziller 1957 344p $6 **812.09**
1 American drama—History and criticism
Analyzed in Essay and general literature index
First published 1939 by Random House
"Since 1918 we have had a succession of playwrights who deserve to be called 'serious' in a sense that few of their predecessors do, and we are still part of the tradition which was established then. This book is an attempt to describe them as a group, to define differences and to trace trends. . . . A section has been added to continue the story up to the end of 1956." Foreword to the revised edition
This noted critic "emphasizes the drama as a literary form rather than as a vehicle of ideas and measures the success of the playwright in terms of his ability to make his characters credible." Cincinnati

Moss, Leonard
Arthur Miller. Twayne 1967 160p (Twayne's United States authors ser) boards $5.50   **812.09**
1 Miller, Arthur
"As an analysis of a playwright's distinctive 'way of looking,' this discussion centers its attention upon Miller's technical resources—dialogue styles, narrative conventions, symbolic devices, and structural principles—and undertakes to judge the success with which the progressions of personality, theme, and tension have been executed and interrelated." Preface
Selected bibliography: p135-53

Nolan, Paul T.
Marc Connelly. Twayne 1969 175p (Twayne's United States authors ser) boards $5.50   **812.09**
1 Connelly, Marcus Cook
"Noting that up until now there has not been a full length study of Marc Connelly's plays Nolan attempts to fill the gap in this general discussion of early works, plays written in collaboration with George S. Kaufman, the Pulitzer Prize winning play 'The green pastures.' and the less successful dramas of later years. . . . The book is helpful in bringing together material for drama students and others needing factual information. Bibliography." Booklist

813.09 American fiction— History and criticism

Auchincloss, Louis
Pioneers & caretakers; a study of 9 American women novelists. Univ. of Minn. Press 1965 202p $4.95   **813.09**
1 American fiction—History and criticism 2 Authors, American 3 Women as authors
Analyzed in Essay and general literature index
"These are critical studies with liberal biographical interspersings of nine American women novelists from Sarah Orne Jewett to Mary McCarthy. Mr. Auchincloss, himself a novelist, has a writer's insights into the technical and thematic problems involved in their works. He has, moreover, wisely judged their 'influences,' literary and otherwise—and has assigned them a conservative role in the mainstream of American life and letters." Library J
Contents: Sarah Orne Jewett; Edith Wharton; Ellen Glasgow; Willa Cather; Elizabeth Madox Roberts; Katherine Anne Porter; Jean Stafford; Carson McCullers; Mary McCarthy

Baker, Carlos
Hemingway: the writer as artist. [3d ed]
Princeton Univ. Press 1963 xx, 379p $8.50
813.09
1 Hemingway, Ernest
First published 1952
"Begins with the young Hemingway, the veteran of the Italian fighting who returned to Chicago in 1919 and entered upon his literary apprenticeship. As the title indicates, the subject of the book is Hemingway, the writer as artist, rather than the man as writer, and one looks in vain for any biographical discussion that is not immediately related to the study of a literary work. . . . Between the chapters devoted to the novels, short stories, and nonfiction appear essays in interpretation of Hemingway's philosophy." Chicago Sunday Tribune

Baker, Sheridan
Ernest Hemingway; an introduction and interpretation. Barnes & Noble 1967 150p illus (American authors and critics ser) $4
813.09
1 Hemingway, Ernest
The author sees in Hemingway "two different modes, the soft and the hard, the inner and the outer and . . . two distinct heroes—the early, beaten one, and the emerging unbeaten one, the man who is, in Hemingway's own term, 'undefeated' in spite of loss." Introduction
In this book Baker documents his view through an examination of Hemingway's life as a writer and the characters he created
Selected bibliography: p137-42

Brooks, Cleanth
William Faulkner: the Yoknapatawpha country. Yale Univ. Press 1963 499p map $12.50
813.09
1 Faulkner, William
"A well-known American critic focuses on Faulkner's stories and novels of Yoknapatawpha County in this fruitful and searching study. Introductory chapters contrast Faulkner with various other regional writers, comment on the social structure in his novels, and discuss his poetic treatment of nature. 'Sanctuary,' 'Light in August,' 'The sound and the fury,' 'Absalom, Absalom!' and other works are analyzed in remaining chapters. Genealogies and a character index are included." Booklist
Notes: p369-446. Includes bibliographical references

Burbank, Rex
Thornton Wilder. Twayne 1961 156p (Twayne's United States authors ser) boards $5.50
813.09
1 Wilder, Thornton Niven
A critical study of Thornton Wilder that attempts "to clear away some of the critical platitudes that have obscured him, to measure his achievement against his total artistic intent, and to place him where he belongs in the American tradition." Preface
"Wilder's five novels and four full-length plays are analyzed in detail and the shorter plays are briefly described and discussed; a final chapter reviews the writer's limitations and achievements. Notes, bibliography, chronology." Booklist

Cady, Edwin Harrison
Stephen Crane. Twayne 1962 186p (Twayne's United States authors ser) boards $5.50
813.09
1 Crane, Stephen
"Chapters one and two survey Crane's life, aiming to bring out considerations the biographical tradition has hitherto neglected or misemphasized. Chapter three studies Crane's ideas as I think no one has previously done. And the final three chapters undertake to summarize the principal modes of Crane criticism and to match their trends of judgment against my own considered responses to Crane's literary art." Preface
Selected bibliography: p169-80

Chase, Richard
Melville; a collection of critical essays.
Prentice-Hall 1962 168p $5.95
813.09
1 Melville, Herman
"Twentieth century views. A Spectrum book"
Analyzed in Essay and general literature index
Essays about Herman Melville and such works of his as Benito Cereno, Billy Budd, The confidence-man, Mardi, Moby Dick, Omoo, Redburn, Typee, and White-Jacket. Marius Bewley, Richard Palmer Blackmur, Robert Penn Warren, Francis Otto Matthiessen, D. H. Lawrence, Daniel G. Hoffman and Alfred Kazin are among the contributors
Includes chronology of important dates and a bibliography

Current-Garcia, Eugene
O. Henry. Twayne 1965 192p (Twayne's United States authors ser) boards $5.50
813.09
1 Porter, William Sydney
An "examination that relates O. Henry's stories to four decisive phases or periods in his life: Southern upbringing, apprentice years in the West, fulfilling final stage in New York City, and prison experience. A biographical summary and O. Henry's technical achievements and posthumous reputation open and close [the book]." Booklist
Selected bibliography: p182-87

Day, A. Grove
James A. Michener. Twayne 1964 175p (Twayne's United States authors ser) boards $5.50
813.09
1 Michener, James Albert
A "study of the life and writings of [novelist] Michener, which includes analyses of all his books, and many of his shorter pieces." Publisher's note
Selected bibliography: p157-67

Dooley, D. J.
The art of Sinclair Lewis. Univ. of Neb.
Press 1967 286p $5.50
813.09
1 Lewis, Sinclair
This "stimulating, objective work of criticism intended as an introduction rather than a last word concentrates primarily on Lewis' individual books but sets the discussion within a biographical framework and enlarges it by an assessment of the varied critical opinion regarding Lewis. . . . [It] concludes with the reflection that Lewis 'went far beyond most of his more illustrious contemporaries in raising questions of enduring importance to the national life.'" Booklist
Selected bibliography: p269-77

Doyle, Paul A.
Pearl S. Buck. Twayne 1965 175p (Twayne's United States authors ser) boards $5.50
813.09
1 Buck, Pearl (Sydenstricker)
"Since she has written so much and has been so moved by thematic interests, this study of her work will give special attention to her plots, themes, and arguments, as well as to the more standard matters of characterization and style. Her short stories and 'talk books' have not been considered. . . . A final aim of 'Pearl S. Buck' has been to give as much biographical and general background as is consonant with her literary work." Preface
This study "examines the reasons for her critical neglect . . . points out her strengths and weaknesses as a writer, and analyzes the 'House of Earth' trilogy. . . . Her importance as chronicler of turbulent twentieth-century China is also assessed." Publisher's note
Notes and references: p157-68. Selected bibliography: p169-70

Eble, Kenneth
F. Scott Fitzgerald. Twayne 1963 174p
(Twayne's United States authors ser)
boards $5.50   **813.09**
1 Fitzgerald, Francis Scott Key
Contents: The boy from St. Paul; Princeton;
Early success; A touch of disaster; The Great
Gatsby; "The Carnival by the Sea"; Stories
and articles: 1926-34; Tender is the Night; The
Crack-up and after; Final assessment
Primarily a survey of F. Scott Fitzgerald's
work and reputation . . . this book "provides
a fresh and useful approach by giving more
attention to the short stories than they usually receive." Am Lit
Includes bibliography

Foster, Richard
(ed.) Six American novelists of the nineteenth century; an introduction. Univ. of
Minn. Press 1968 270p $6.50   **813.09**
1 American fiction—History and criticism
2 Authors, American
Analyzed in Essay and general literature index
"Based on material in the university's 'Pamphlets on American Writers,' for students this
is an extremely valuable volume about six of
the most important American novelists of the
19th century . . . Cooper, Hawthorne, Melville,
Twain, Howell, Gibson and James. Biographical information is included for each, as well as
critical discussions of the author's work." Hunting
Selected bibliographies: p229-47

French, Warren
J. D. Salinger. Twayne 1963 191p
(Twayne's United States authors ser)
boards $5.50   **813.09**
1 Salinger, Jerome David
"In his preface the author states that he
writes not for Salinger devotees but for parents, teachers, and other representatives of the
older generation who are puzzled by Salinger's
impact on the young. The critic, who obviously
does not regard Salinger as a demigod, fares
much better when he turns from rather queru-
lous psychoanalysis to a detailed criticism of
the stories and novels. Although he feels it is
premature—indeed impossible—to assess Salinger's permanent worth as a novelist he finds
much to admire in several of the short stories
and in 'The catcher in the rye.' " Booklist
Includes bibliography

Gaston, Edwin W.
Conrad Richter, by Edwin W. Gaston, Jr.
Twayne 1965 176p (Twayne's United States
authors ser) boards $5.50   **813.09**
1 Richter, Conrad
"A chronology, brief biographical summary,
bibliography, and extensive critical analysis of
Richter's work emphasizing the lack of sound-
ness in the philosophical theories of his essays
and the excellence of the art with which his
best fiction, notably his historical works, out-
soared his attempted application of these theories to his creative writing. Scarcity of material on Richter makes this book worth considering." Booklist

Geismar, Maxwell
American moderns: from rebellion to conformity. Hill & Wang 1958 265p $4.50 **813.09**
1 American fiction—History and criticism
2 Novelists, American
Analyzed in Essay and general literature index
This volume of literary criticism "consists
largely of reprinted reviews, articles, and critical introductions, sometimes with additional
notes; but there is also some new material. . . .
The most interesting part of the volume is the
last third, in which the author discusses such
young writers as Styron, Salinger, Jones, Griffin, Bellow, and others." Library J

Writers in crisis; the American novel between two wars. Houghton 1942 299p $6.95
                                    813.09
1 American fiction—History and criticism
2 Novelists, American
Analyzed in Essay and general literature index
These critical essays show "the rapidly changing phases of American life, from Lardner's
boom period in the 1920's to Steinbeck's powerful social studies of the 1940's. Mr. Geismar
treats each writer [including Hemingway, Dos
Passos, Faulkner, and Wolfe] with humor . . .
and sound critical ability." Library J

Gellens, Jay
(ed.) Twentieth century interpretations of
A farewell to arms; a collection of critical
essays. Prentice-Hall 1970 121p $4.95 **813.09**
1 Hemingway, Ernest. A farewell to arms
SBN 13-303091-2
"A Spectrum book"
"Hemingway's style, symbolism, and treatment of war are recurring subjects in the articles that date from 1940 to 1966; the authors
represented include Carlos Baker, Wyndham
Lewis, Malcolm Cowley, and a number of
lesser-known university professors or instructors." Booklist
Selected bibliography: p121

Grebstein, Sheldon Norman
Sinclair Lewis. Twayne 1962 192p
(Twayne's United States authors ser)
boards $5.50   **813.09**
1 Lewis, Sinclair
A "study of Lewis' life, career, and ambivalent attitudes toward American conditions. . . .
Starts with a 'psychograph' of the writer and
then presents in chronological order each of
the novels, stressing particularly those written
from 1920-1929—the works upon which Grebstein feels Lewis' reputation will rest—as the
conscience of his generation, novels which
again have meaning in the 1960's." Booklist
Includes bibliography

Gurko, Leo
Ernest Hemingway and the pursuit of heroism. Crowell 1968 247p (Twentieth century
American writers) $4.75   **813.09**
1 Hemingway, Ernest
The organization of this book "is both
functional and scholarly, it can make absorbing reading as a whole, but it is well suited
to consultation for specific information and
critiques. The first chapter outlines Hemingway's life, focusing on his background, his
friends, his marriages, and the important influences on his personal and literary life. It
concludes with his tragic final years and death.
The remaining chapters discuss in turn his
novels, short stories, and nonfiction. There is
an entire chapter on each of his major novels.
. . . The final chapter evaluates Hemingway as
artist, his techniques, motivation, and philosophy." Library J
A selected bibliography: p240-42

Hendrick, George
Katherine Anne Porter. Twayne 1965 176p
(Twayne's United States authors ser)
boards $5.50   **813.09**
1 Porter, Katherine Anne
"A brief, appreciative working analysis of
Katherine Anne Porter's stories, one novel, and
essays by a professor of English . . . who considers her 'a conscious artist, in the tradition
of James and Joyce.' The mixed reception by
American, English, and German critics of 'Ship
of fools' is reviewed at some length." Booklist
"In retelling the stories and discussing their
themes, Professor Hendrick may not seem to
search deeply, but he gets to the heart of the
matter. His observations bring out deeper
meanings which many readers may have overlooked." Library J
Bibliography: p161-71

Hillway, Tyrus

Herman Melville. Twayne 1963 176p
(Twayne's United States authors ser)
boards $5.50   813.09

1 Melville, Herman

This book attempts "to introduce to its readers authenticated information about Melville's
life and works, a brief review of recent research, and a summary of the author's personal
critical judgments. . . . [The author examines]
Melville's works one by one, beginning with
Typee (1846)." Preface

"A good account of important events and influences in Melville's life. The criticism provides an introduction to plots, characters, and
dominant themes that should be helpful to
many readers, but special students of Melville
will undoubtedly take issue with some of Mr.
Hillway's personal judgments on controversial
points." Am Lit

Selected bibliography: p154-61

Howarth, William L.

(ed.) Twentieth century interpretations of
Poe's tales; a collection of critical essays.
Prentice-Hall 1971 116p $4.95   813.09

1 Poe, Edgar Allan
SBN 13-684654-8

"A Spectrum book"

In the introduction the editor discusses Poe's
life and the method and meaning of the tales.
The essays which follow represent a variety of
critical approaches: historical, theoretical and
technical. Viewpoints by such critics as Harry
Levin, Yvor Winters, and William Carlos Williams are followed by essays on "The narrative
of A. Gordon Pym," by Charles O'Donnell;
"The fall of the House of Usher," by I. M.
Walker and John S. Hill; "Ligeia," by Clark
Griffith, John Lauber and Donald Barlow Stauffer; "The black cat," by James W. Gargano;
"The tell-tale heart," by E. Arthur Robinson;
and Poe's detective, Dupin, by Robert Daniel

Chronology of important dates: p111-12. Selected bibliography: p115-16

Howe, Irving

(ed.) Edith Wharton; a collection of critical essays. Prentice-Hall 1962 181p $5.95
           813.09

1 Wharton, Edith Newbold (Jones)

"Twentieth century views. A Spectrum book"
Analyzed in Essay and general literature index

Contributors of these essays about Edith
Wharton and her works include such critics
as: Edmund Wilson, Louis S. Auchincloss, Al-
fred Kazin, Queenie Dorothy Leavis, Vernon
Louis Parrington, Louis Osborne Coxe, Diana
Trilling, and Henry James

Includes a chronology of important dates
and a bibliography

Martin, Terrence

Nathaniel Hawthorne. Twayne 1965 205p
(Twayne's United States authors ser)
boards $5.50   813.09

1 Hawthorne, Nathaniel

The author "reviews Hawthorne's personal
history and his progress as a writer who remains, after a century, one of the major American authors. Concerned mainly with establishing the nature and extent of his subject's
achievement in fiction, Martin stresses such
characteristics as emphasis on the past, guilt
and isolation, the protean nature of pride, the
redeeming possibilities of love, the ambiguity
of experience and the ambivalence of motive."
Booklist

Selected bibliography: p185-201

Miller, James E.

A reader's guide to Herman Melville, by
James E. Miller, Jr. Farrar, Straus 1962 266p
$6.95   813.09

1 Melville, Herman

"A detailed explication of Melville's novels
and poetry. The author traces the difficult
symbolism through all Melville's work and

shows that the novelist is concerned always
with the problem of evil and man's necessary
compromise with his ideals when confronted
with evil. Parts of the book have appeared in
a different form in various literary journals."
Booklist

Includes bibliography

Minter, David L.

(ed.) Twentieth century interpretations of
Light in August; a collection of critical essays. Prentice-Hall 1969 120p $4.95   813.09

1 Faulkner, William. Light in August
SBN 13-536615-1

"A Spectrum book"

"Five enlightening essays representing a
variety of approaches to Faulkner's 1932 novel
'Light in August' consider characterization,
style, psychological and social themes, plot,
and other aspects of the work. The short excerpts in part two present varying critical
views on the significance of the novel's major
characters and the role it gives to sex, religion,
and women. An outline of the narrative structure of 'Light in August' is appended along
with important dates in Faulkner's career and
era." Booklist

Selected bibliography: p119-20

Mizener, Arthur

(ed.) F. Scott Fitzgerald; a collection of
critical essays. Prentice-Hall 1963 174p $5.95
           813.09

1 Fitzgerald, Francis Scott Key

"Twentieth century views. A Spectrum book"
Authors of these essays about the American
author include such writers as Lionel Trilling,
William Troy, Edwin Fussell, Malcolm Cowley,
Leslie Fiedler, Edmund Wilson, James E. Miller, Jr., John Henry Raleigh, Tom Burnam,
and D. S. Savage

Includes chronology of important dates and
a selected bibliography

O'Connor, William Van

(ed.) Seven modern American novelists; an
introduction. Univ. of Minn. Press 1964 302p
$6.50   813.09

1 American fiction—History and criticism
2 Novelists, American

Analyzed in Essay and general literature index

Contents: Edith Wharton, by L. Auchincloss;
Sinclair Lewis, by M. Schorer; F. Scott Fitz-
gerald, by C. E. Shain; William Faulkner, by
W. V. O'Connor, Ernest Hemingway, by P.
Young; Thomas Wolfe, by C. H. Holman; Na-
thanael West, by S. E. Hyman

"Each article treats the author's principal
works seriatim, provides a critical sketch of
the material, relates it to the author's background, and attempts to give a key to the
work as a whole and an estimate of the writer's significance." Library J

Selected bibliographies: p265-79

Quinn, Arthur Hobson

American fiction; an historical and critical
survey. Appleton 1936 xxiii, 805p $7   813.09

1 American fiction—History and criticism

"A chronological study with careful and conservative estimates of the work of both major and minor writers. Does not take account
of authors who began writing after 1920, but
to this point is quite comprehensive, covering both novel and short story. With its bibliographies and an adequate index will add
valuable reference and study club material."
Cur Ref Bks

Richman, Sidney

Bernard Malamud. Twayne [1967 c1966]
160p (Twayne's United States authors ser)
boards $5.50   813.09

1 Malamud, Bernard

"This book is quite frankly intended as an
introductory study—a novel-by-novel, story-
by-story analysis—which will supply the reader with as thorough an exposure to Malamud's

Richman, Sidney—*Continued*

fiction as space allows. . . . With one exception, I have avoided all but occasional biographical or historical references. The exception is the short first chapter." Preface

Malamud's work is examined "with emphasis upon the intricacies of his style and his affirmation of the dignity that man may achieve through suffering." McClurg. Book News
Selected bibliography: p150-53

Rovit, Earl H.

Ernest Hemingway. Twayne 1963 192p (Twayne's United States authors ser) boards $5.50 **813.09**

1 Hemingway, Ernest

"Hemingway's work is presented through an analysis of the Hemingway style, his characteristic employment of narrational structures, recurrent theme, and the Hemingway 'code' as elements in his total achievement." Huntting

"Amid a spate of critical material appearing since Hemingway's death in 1961 Rovit's insights on his subject's work, if not arresting, are at least discussable and provide a good overview of the Hemingway corpus." Booklist
Notes and references: p174-83. Bibliography: p184-88

Sanders, David

John Hersey. Twayne 1967 159p (Twayne's United States authors ser) boards $5.50
813.09

1 Hersey, John Richard

"This book is an introduction to the work of a writer who has described himself as a 'novelist of contemporary history.' Hersey is one of many such novelists, but his approach is distinctive. He has not written the kind of novel in which the protagonist defines the conditions of the time in the process of discovering himself. He has not written fiction as the record of his own effort at such a definition. Nor has he been driven merely to work up material on a succession of topical issues. . . . This study moves from his reporter's background into separate analyses of the novels." Preface
Selected bibliography: p150-56

Smith, Henry Nash

(ed.) Mark Twain; a collection of critical essays. Prentice-Hall 1963 179p $5.95 **813.09**

1 Clemens, Samuel Langhorne

"Twentieth century views. A Spectrum book" This collection of essays includes Van Wyck Brooks on Twain's humor, James M. Cox on A Connecticut Yankee, Kenneth Lynn on Roughing it, and Walter Blair on Tom Sawyer. Other contributors are the editor, Maurice Le Breton, Leo Marx, Daniel G. Hoffman, W. H. Auden, Leslie Fiedler, Bernard DeVoto and Tony Tanner
Includes chronology of important dates and a bibliographical note

Stegner, Wallace

(ed.) The American novel; from James Fenimore Cooper to William Faulkner. Basic Bks. 1965 236p $5.95 **813.09**

1 American fiction—History and criticism
Analyzed in Essay and general literature index

"Sixteen scholars, authorities on the authors they analyze, sum up 19 outstanding American novels (up to 1929). These essays, designed originally for oral presentation over the Voice of America, keep within the general reader's comprehension and interest. Stegner, the editor, discusses Willa Cather's 'My Antonia.' David Levin writes about Nathaniel Hawthorne's 'The Scarlet Letter.' Carlos Baker, about Ernest Hemingway's 'A Farewell to Arms.' Arthur Mizener about F. Scott Fitzgerald's 'The Great Gatsby.' These and the others try very succesfully to cast light on the American mind and personality as seen in important American novels." Pub W
Bibliographical footnotes

Steinbeck, John

Journal of a novel; the "East of Eden" letters. Viking 1969 182p $7.50 **813.09**

1 Steinbeck, John. East of Eden
SBN 670-40939-1

While working on this novel: East of Eden, John Steinbeck began each day by writing a letter to his editor and friend, Pascal Covici. These letters contain "random thoughts, trial flights of wordsmanship, nuggets of information and comment for his friend about the surrounding events of the moment, both personal and public. But the letters were also full of serious thinking about this novel . . . [and] about novel-writing in general." Publisher's note

The letters "reveal much about Steinbeck the man, about his relationship with those closest to him, about his art in general and East of Eden in particular. I believe they will be indispensable to future studies of his work. The autobiographical details are of course invaluable in the absence of any biography. . . . [For the general reader] the Journal provides . . . a telephoto close-up of a fabulist seriously engaged in the 'silly business' of writing. The most eloquent passages in the letters come when Steinbeck discusses this business at length." Sat R

Stuckey, W. J.

The Pulitzer Prize novels; a critical backward look. Univ. of Okla. Press 1966 224p $5.95 **813.09**

1 American fiction—History and criticism
2 Literary prizes

"The author analyzes the themes, ideas and sentiments of the prizewinning novels from 1917 to 1962, and enquires into the motives behind the awards." Book Rev Digest

It is an adult, "honest and conscientious study, but it provides little guidance for the critic." Sat R
Bibliographical footnotes

Van Doren, Carl

The American novel, 1789-1939. Rev. and enl. ed. Macmillan (N Y) 1940 406p $6.25
813.09

1 American fiction—History and criticism
Analyzed in Essay and general literature index

First published 1921. Contains some parts of the author's Contemporary American novelists: 1900-1920, published 1922

A history of the progress of native fiction with chapters on the following novelists: Cooper, Hawthorne, Melville, Howells, Clemens, James, Dreiser, Wharton, Cather, Lewis, Cabell, Wolfe

"The chapters on such writers as Cooper and Mark Twain are admirably vigorous and meaty." New Republic
Bibliography: p367-82

Vincent, Howard P.

(ed.) Twentieth century interpretations of Billy Budd; a collection of critical essays. Prentice-Hall 1971 112p $4.95 **813.09**

1 Melville, Herman. Billy Budd
SBN 13-084715-1

"A Spectrum book"
Interpretations and view points on Billy Budd by such literary critics as W. H. Auden, Werner Berthoff, Edward H. Rosenberry, John Seelye, William York Tindall, Ray B. West, Jr., and others
Selected bibliography: p111-12

Wagenknecht, Edward

Cavalcade of the American novel; from the birth of the nation to the middle of the twentieth century. Holt 1952 575p front $11.95
813.09

1 American fiction—history and criticism
Analyzed in Essay and general literature index

Wagenknecht, Edward—*Continued*

"It begins with the birth of our nation and takes [it] down to the middle of the present century. It offers interpretive comment on nearly all of our foremost novelists." Hunting

Novelists discussed are: Cabell, Cather, Clemens, Cooper, Dreiser, Glasgow, Hawthorne, Hemingway, Howells, James, Lewis, Melville, Stowe, Wharton

There are two indexes, one by names and one by titles

Selected bibliography with annotations: p497-555

814   American essays

Emerson, Ralph Waldo

Essays, first and second series   814

Some editions are:
Crowell $4.95 With introduction by Irwin Edman
Houghton $6.95 (Riverside lib)

First published 1929

Contents: First series: History; Self-reliance; Compensation; Spiritual laws; Love; Friendship; Prudence; Heroism; Over-soul; Circles; Intellect; Art. Second series: The poet; Experience; Character; Manners; Gifts; Nature; Politics; Nominalist and realist; New England reformers

Twain, Mark

The complete essays of Mark Twain; now collected for the first time; ed. and with an introduction by Charles Neider; drawings by Mark Twain. Doubleday 1963 xxv, 705p illus boards $6.95   814

Analyzed in Essay and general literature index

Some of the 68 essays are: The Sandwich Islands; English as she is taught; Mental telegraphy; The German Chicago; Queen Victoria's jubilee; What is man; Taxes and morals; The bee; Concerning tobacco; Adam's soliloquy; Down the Rhône; Dueling; Letters to Satan; Some national stupidities; The war prayer; Letter from the recording angel

"I have also included nine speeches which possess the characteristic style of Clemens's essays. . . . The contents of the present volume . . . are arranged chronologically according to the years of first publication, and alphabetically within a given year whenever more than one item was published in that year." Editor's note

"Punch said it first and ever since Mark Twain has been generally regarded as this country's finest humorist. Yet as this gathering of his miscellaneous essays confirms, he is also one of our finest essayists. Not in the pure sense of the genre, of course, for here he was rather a fumbler. His notorious generalization, his impatience and illogic make much of what he says absurd. But in the way he says things, his witty, vital, colorful style, he is unchallenged." Critic

815.08   Speeches—Collections

Hurd, Charles

(comp.) A treasury of great American speeches; new and rev. ed. Selected by Charles Hurd; rev. and ed. by Andrew Bauer. Hawthorn Bks. 1970 411p $10   815.08

1 American orations 2 U.S.—History—Addresses and essays

First published 1959

This chronologically arranged selection of famous American speeches from 1645 to 1969 includes the most vital parts of each speech and a news report introduction setting each speech in its historical time and place. (Publisher)

Includes list of speakers and list of speeches by categories

Lott, Davis Newton

(ed.) The Presidents speak; the inaugural addresses of the American Presidents. . . . Annotated by Davis Newton Lott. Holt illus $10   815.08

1 American orations 2 Presidents—U.S. 3 U.S.—History

First published 1961 with title: The inaugural addresses of the American Presidents. Periodically revised to bring it up to date

In addition to the annotated text of the addresses there are notes describing each President and the state of the nation and the world. Also included are the Declaration of Independence, Articles of Confederation and the Constitution

Representative American speeches. Wilson, H.W. (The Reference shelf) $4.50   815.08

1 American orations 2 Speeches, addresses, etc.

Annual. First published for the year 1937-1938. Editors: 1938-1959 A. Craig Baird; 1960-1970 Lester Thonssen; 1971- Waldo W. Braden

A compilation containing a selection of speeches of the year made by eminent men and women on major trends and events. Each speech is prefaced by a note about the speaker and the occasion. The appendix in each volume contains biographical notes

817   American satire and humor

Armour, Richard

The classics reclassified. . . . McGraw 1960 146p illus $4.95   817

1 Parodies

"In which certain famous books are not so much digested as indigested, together with mercifully brief biographies of their authors, a few unnecessary footnotes, and questions which it might be helpful not to answer; nostalgically illustrated by Campbell Grant." Title page

"Burlesque accounts of seven classics of the 'required reading' type: 'The Iliad,' 'Julius Caesar,' 'Ivanhoe,' 'The Scarlet Letter,' 'David Copperfield,' 'Silas Marner,' and 'Moby Dick.' After irreverent . . . short biographies of the authors, [Armour] retells the plots of their masterpieces." N Y Her Trib Books

English lit relit. . . . Irreverently illus. by Campbell Grant. McGraw 1969 151p illus boards $4.50   817

1 English literature—Anecdotes, facetiae, satire, etc. 2 Authors, English—Anecdotes, facetiae. satire, etc.

"A short history of English literature from the Precursors (before swearing) to the Pre-Raphaelites and a little after, intended to help students see the thing through, or see through the thing, and omitting nothing unimportant." Title page

"Students will appreciate the light, punning hand Armour turns toward subjects which are treated with grave reverence in the classroom. The illustrations . . . are a witty accompaniment to the text." Library J

Going around in academic circles; a low view of higher education; with illus. by Leo Hershfield. McGraw 1965 140p illus $4.95   817

1 Education, Higher—Anecdotes, facetiae, satire, etc.

"In order that prospective students may have some light on college education, the author first gives its history from the Stone Age (when the only clubs were carried by the students) on to modern times. Next he takes up the matter of choosing the college, the tricks of field representatives, the college catalogue, its campus, etc. . . . 'Cheerful light humor.' " Bk Buyer's Guide

Benchley, Robert

The Benchley roundup; a selection by Nathaniel Benchley of his favorites; drawings by Gluyas Williams. Harper 1954 333p illus $5.95   817

These ninety-odd pieces were chosen from thirty years of Robert Benchley's humorous pieces by his son. He selected the pieces he felt had the most enduring appeal and those which he, himself, liked best

"The passage of time has not staled the special appeal of Benchley's humor, with its talent for amused self-depreciation and impatience with modern gadgetry. He was, perhaps, at his best when he parodied the literary affectations of his contemporaries." Booklist

Chips off the old Benchley; with an introduction by Frank Sullivan and drawings by Gluyas Williams. Harper 1949 273p illus $5.95   817

"Benchley was truly one of the great wits of our time and it is a real joy to be offered this collection of his hitherto unpublished pieces. Here, true to form, he is being gently but ironically indignant over taxes, banks, hay fever, daylight saving—in short most of the trying situations with which we all cope daily. But how Mr. Benchley does cope—to the delight and entertainment of all!" Ontario Lib Rev

Buchwald, Art

Getting high in government circles. Putnam 1971 254p $5.95   817

1 U.S.—Politics and government—Anecdotes, facetiae, satire, etc. 2 U.S.—Social conditions—Anecdotes, facetiae, satire, etc.

"Selections from the author's columns, which have appeared in various American newspapers from 1968 to 1971, commenting on politics, students, television, fashions, movies, foreign affairs, family life, sports and politicians." Book Rev Digest

"The folks who are familiar with [these] syndicated columns in the daily newspapers will find this book a welcome addition to their libraries. For readers who are not acquainted with the author's fare, there is a treat in store. . . . [This is a] witty book." Best Sellers

Have I ever lied to you? Putnam 1968 256p $5.95   817

1 U.S.—Civilization—Anecdotes, facetiae, satire, etc.

Humorous comments on various aspects of life in the United States today, ranging from the relations of parents and children to the Vietnam War

This "book of short articles is funny and thought provoking, appropriate to our age of crisis after crisis. With tongue in cheek, the author pokes fun at everyone, himself included. The material is useful for history, government and literature students as well as general readers." Bruno. Books for School Libraries, 1968

Holmes, Oliver Wendell, 1809-1894

The autocrat of the breakfast table. Dutton 1906 300p $2.95   817

"Everyman's library"

This is the first and most famous of the Breakfast-table series. It consists of "delightful essays of wholesome and genial philosophy first contributed to the Atlantic Monthly." Pratt Alcove

"One of America's great essayists and critics addresses his fellow boarders on wide-ranging topics of religion, education, philosophy, and psychology—and the reader has an opportunity to share in the conversations, which took place in 1857." A Guide to Reading in Am History

Hudson, Virginia Cary

O ye jigs & juleps! Illus. by Karla Kuskin. Macmillan (N Y) 1962 50p illus boards $2.95   817

The author "was a sprite of ten back in 1904 when she wrote these essays . . . [expressing her] concepts of school, the sacraments, church etiquette, everlasting life, spring, the library, personal appearance, strolling, and the religions of China (Mr. Confucius', Mr. Tao's, Mr. Buddha's.)" Publisher's note

"A frank and funny diary of a church-going, Episcopalian, but not overly pious . . . [small town] girl. . . . A cheerful little book, about her friends, of all ages, her mischief-making, and her insight into the grown-ups' lives." Pub W

Kerr, Jean

Please don't eat the daisies; with drawings by Carl Rose. Doubleday 1957 192p illus $3.50   817

"Mrs Kerr, playwright, mother, wife of dramatic critic and bon vivant, has written . . . these [sketches]. They concern the care and feeding of children, the wear and tear of parenthood, fads of dieting and decor, the art of theatre reviewing, and a couple of biting burlesque of modern writing, etc." Library J

"The best of her humor is directed toward the Kerr family itself. Both men and women will enjoy the variety of stories, Mrs. Kerr has to tell." Massachusetts

The snake has all the lines; with drawings by Whitney Darrow, Jr. Doubleday 1960 168p illus $4.50   817

"Jean Kerr presents a delightful commentary on the family life of a career girl and housewife. Her zany humor sparks interest in her misadventures as she tries to combine a writing career with a family." Wis Lib Bul

"It's the surprise that's funny. Mrs. Kerr living in the midst of a familiar and usual world, writing on conventional, even banal themes, is still surprising." N Y Times Bk R

Leacock, Stephen

Laugh with Leacock; an anthology of the best work of Stephen Leacock. Dodd [1961 c1930] 339p pa $2.25   817

"Apollo editions"

A reprint of an edition first published 1930

A representative selection of Leacock's humorous essays, sketches and parodies

"Those of us who have at times despaired because the professor talked too fluently to talk wittily will welcome this book, in which he talks at his best." N Y World

The Leacock roundabout; a treasury of the best works of Stephen Leacock. Dodd 1946 [c1945] 422p $5   817

Analyzed in Essay and general literature index

Divided into the following parts: Personal experiences and recollections; Nonsense novels and model memoirs; Detective stories; Fishing and other madness; Friends and relatives; Drama; Homer and humbug; Lectures; Foibles and follies

"This book is Leacock in his humor as he lived, alternately given to horse play and to horse sense, and equally admirable in either. You'll find your favorites here, from the historical drama on Napoleon to the noble series of parodies on the mystery novel. The ideal book for the bedside table in the guest-room—where you'll bed yourself down till you've finished it." San Francisco Chronicle

McKenney, Ruth

My sister Eileen   817

Some editions are:

Harcourt $4.95

Watts, F. lib. bdg. $8.95 Large type edition. A Keith Jennison book

Sketches from the New Yorker "purporting to describe the adventures of the author and her sister from childhood experiences at the movies to their grown up trials with suitors [in Greenwich Village]." Book Rev Digest

"Miss McKenney writes with refreshing good humor and an authentic sense of fun." Springf'd Republican

Marquis, Don

Archy and Mehitabel. Doubleday 1930 264p illus $3.50   **817**

First published 1927

"This is the free verse of archy, the cockroach. archy has the soul of a poet, and he cannot resist the temptation to express himself in verse. . . archy has a lot to say about insects and beasts and human beings in general—but especially about mehitabel the cat. mehitabel is a feline to the tips of her claws, and her adventures are romantic, capricious, and corybantic, but though toujours gai, she is always a lady." Publisher's note

"It takes something approaching genius to make a cockroach and an alley cat understandable and sympathetic characters, and that is what Mr. Marquis has done." North American Rev

The lives and times of Archy & Mehitabel; with pictures by George Herriman and an introduction by E. B. White. Doubleday 1950 xxiv, 477p illus $4.95   **817**

A reprint of three books formerly published separately: Archy and Mehitabel (1927) entered above; Archy's life of Mehitabel (1933); Archy does his part (1935) They are all concerned with the antics of the famous cat, Mehitabel, and with Archy, the literary cockroach

Peter, Laurence J.

The Peter Principle, by Laurence J. Peter & Raymond Hull. Morrow 1969 179p illus boards $4.95   **817**

1 Management—Anecdotes, facetiae, satire, etc.

"In a delightful spoof of administrative inefficiency in both public and private enterprise, the authors expound their theory known as the Peter Principle—'in a hierarchy every employee tends to rise to his level of incompetence.' From this they develop their science of hierarchiology. For those who enjoy Parkinson and Stephen Potter." Cincinnati

"Horrible examples of [the Peter Principle] at work fill most of the book. But an extraordinary number of other flaws in our systems get a nasty nod from Dr. Peter. The tongue is obviously, sometimes too obviously, in the cheek, but readers and skimmers will relish spotting a familiar situation or two." Christian Science Monitor

Glossary: p169-74

Ross, Leonard Q.

The education of H*Y*M*A*N K*A*P*L*A*N. Harcourt 1937 176p (Harbrace Modern classics) $2.95   **817**

1 Adult education—Anecdotes, facetiae, satire, etc.

"These sketches from the 'New Yorker' record the progress of Mr Kaplan, a student in the American Night Preparatory School for Adults. It is Mr Kaplan who declines the verb 'to fail' as 'fail, failed, bankrupt,' and gave the plural of dog as dogies, Library as Public library, and cat as Katz. Enough to indicate the characteristic and amusing Jewish humor." Wis Lib Bul

Runyon, Damon

A treasury of Damon Runyon; selected, with an introduction by Clark Kinnaird. Modern Lib. 1958 428p $2.95, lib. bdg. $2.69 **817**

A series of humorous sketches taken from various magazines in which they first appeared

Thurber, James

Lanterns & lances. Harper 1961 215p illus boards $5.95   **817**

"These 24 'pieces' originally published in a variety of magazines, (with two exceptions, which are here appearing for the first time in print), are all a delight to the mind and heart. The involvements one gets into at cocktail parties, particularly with determined ladies who want to argue a point or to talk above their tipsy heads, the dangers of waking at three-in-the-morning, the depreciation of the English language, the decline of comedy into the snake pits, the horrors of the film ads, the logic of tots and the illogic of females, are only some of the topics our favorite author has taken a lantern or a lance to. Those who know and enjoy Mr. Thurber need only be told about this new collection; those who have not heretofore made his acquaintance will find this as good an introduction as any to many other wonderful books." Best Sellers

My life and hard times. Harper 1933 153p illus $5.95   **817**

"A collection of incidents from James Thurber's life—illustrated by his own whimsical drawings." Books for You

Contents: The night the bed fell; The car we had to push; The day the dam broke; The night the ghost got in; More alarms at night; Sequence of servants; The dog that bit people; University days: Draft board nights; Note at the end

The author "has a sense of the wildly incredible things that happen to human beings who think all the time that they are acting with the greatest prudence and common sense." Sat R

The Thurber carnival   **817**

Some editions are:

Harper $5.95, lib. bdg. $5.49 Written and illustrated by James Thurber

Modern Lib. $2.95, lib. bdg. $2.69

First published 1945

A Thurber omnibus containing some stories not collected before in book form; and others from: My world and welcome to it; Let your mind alone; The middle-aged man on the flying trapeze; My life and hard times [entered above] Fables for our time and famous poems illustrated; The owl in the attic; The seal in the bedroom; Men, women and dogs; The war between men and women

"Most of the laughter in Thurber is friendly laughter. But he is not only a humorist, he is also a satirist who can toss a bomb while he appears to be tipping his hat." N Y Times Bk R

Thurber country; a new collection of pieces about males and females, mainly of our own species. Simon & Schuster 1953 276p illus $6.50   **817**

Also available in a large type edition for $7.95

"Twenty-six pieces from 'The New Yorker' plus 8 pieces never before published here. All in the famous humorist's engaging style and with his own incomparable illustrations." Retail Bookseller

Thurber's dogs. . . . Simon & Schuster 1955 294p illus $3.95   **817**

1 Dogs

"A collection of the master's dogs, written and drawn, real and imaginery, living and long ago." Title page

Contains 24 humorous articles and stories and drawings about dogs, most of which appeared originally in The New Yorker

"Anyone who owns a dog or anyone who would like to own one will find this book entertaining." Huntting

Twain, Mark

The complete humorous sketches and tales of Mark Twain; now collected for the first time; ed. and with an introduction by Charles Neider; drawings by Mark Twain. Hanover House 1961 722p illus $6.50   **817**

Contains 136 sketches and stories written by Mark Twain between the years 1862 and 1904. Thirty of these selections have been taken from the following books: Roughing it; Innocents abroad; A tramp abroad; Life on the Mississippi; and, Following the equator

The innocents abroad; or, The new Pilgrims' progress, being some account of the steamship Quaker City's pleasure excursion to Europe and the Holy Land. Harper 2v in 1 illus $6.95   **817**

1 Voyages and travels 2 Europe—Description and travel 3 Near East

Twain, Mark—*Continued*

One of the author's earliest successes, first published 1869
"Humorous account of a voyage through the Mediterranean and travel in the bordering countries." Pittsburgh

Life on the Mississippi   **817**

1 Mississippi River 2 Mississippi Valley— Social life and customs

Some editions are:
Dodd (Great illustrated classics) $4.50 With biographical illustrations and drawings from the first edition of the book together with an introduction by Guy A. Cardwell. Samuel L. Clemens on title page
Harper $5.50
Harper [Holiday ed] $4.95, lib. bdg. $4.43 Illustrated by Walter Stewart
Oxford (The World's classics) $1.75 With an introduction by Harold Beaver
First published 1874
Mark Twain's famous account of life of the Mississippi in the old steamboat days and his own experiences as a pilot
"Its historical sketches, its frequent passages of vivid description, and its humorous episodes combine to make [this] a masterpiece of the literature of the Middle West." English and Pope's What to read

Roughing it. Harper [1913] 2v in 1 illus $5.95   **817**

1 Hawaii—Description and travel 2 The West —Description and travel
Written in 1872
A humorous account of a trip across the plains to California and then to Hawaii in the early 1860's, full of grotesque exaggeration, drollery and rollicking spirits

817.08 American satire and humor—Collections

Cerf, Bennett

(comp.) Bennett Cerf's The sound of laughter; with illus. by Michael K. Frith. Doubleday 1970 463p illus $6.95   **817.08**

1 American wit and humor 2 Anecdotes
The subjects for this collection of jokes, anecdotes, puns and stories "include the credibility gap (everybody's), animals, history, politics, religion, the military, showbiz, authors, celebrities, farmers, sportsmen." Pub W
"As one would expect, some of the jokes are a bit motheaten, but there are also some which are 'with it' in the humor of today." Best Sellers

(ed.) Good for a laugh; a collection of humorous tidbits and anecdotes from Aardvark to Zythum; with illus. by Doug Anderson. Hanover House 1952 220p illus $4.50   **817.08**

1 American wit and humor 2 Anecdotes
"Many of the stories in this book are reprinted, with permission, from my 'Cerf Board,' column in 'This Week Magazine,' 'Trade Winds' in the 'Saturday Review,' and my daily stint, 'Try and Stop Me' for the King Features Syndicate." Foreword
"Another collection of jokes, shaggy dog stories, puns and other humorous confections by by the cheerful benefactor of mankind." Springf'd Republican
"Arranged for the convenience of after-dinner speakers, alphabetically by subject." Pub W

(ed.) Laugh day; a new treasury of over 1000 humorous stories and anecdotes; with illus. by Michael R. Frith   **817.08**

1 American wit and humor 2 Anecdotes
Some editions are:
Doubleday $5.95
Watts, F. $7.95 Large type edition complete and unabridged. A Keith Jennison book
A collection arranged under such headings as: All the world's a stage; Animals galore;

Battle of the sexes; The great society; The professions; The printed word; Punsters on parade; Right up the riddle; Still out on a limerick; Military orders; Wide, wide world; Index by categories
"This is a book that can be read and enjoyed by anyone of any age at anytime. It is also a wonderful reference book for anyone who needs a good story for some occasion." Hunting

Hughes, Langston

(ed.) The book of Negro humor; selected and ed. by Langston Hughes. Dodd 1966 265p illus $5   **817.08**

1 American wit and humor 2 Negro literature 3 Negroes in literature and art
"For his panorama of humor, Mr Hughes reaches from Old New Orleans to Harlem and into the lives of such men as Booker T. Washington, Jackie Robinson, and Martin Luther King. The fourteen sections of this book contain as well, nonsense verses, ballads and songs, stanzas of the Blues, poetry, Harlem party cards, and tales from the world of jazz, all of which enrich the legacy of Negro humor." Am News of Bks
"This generous assortment of traditional and modern Negro humor is an odd mixture—of tradition and the latest word, of dialect and bop. Both old and new humor tend towards the sardonic. There are, unfortunately, a few long dull stretches." Pub W

Lewin, Leonard C.

(ed.) A treasury of American political humor. Delacorte Press 1964 480p $6.50 **817.08**

1 U.S.—Politics and government—Anecdotes, facetiae, satire, etc.
The material for this collection is "drawn from the writings of columnists, humorists, and politicians and [covers] the political scene from the Revolution to [the sixties]." Library J
"American political humor is as old as American politics, and the best of it has been collected in this volume. What strikes a reader as funny, writes Editor Leonard Lewin, depends on whose 'sacred cow is gored.' So he has selected his material from the right, the left and the middle, showing that political wit knows no ideology." Time
Bibliographical references included in Acknowledgments: p4-8

White, E. B.

(ed.) A subtreasury of American humor; ed. and abridged by E. B. White and Katharine S. White. Capricorn Bks. [1962 c1941] 369p illus pa $2.15   **817.08**

1 American wit and humor 2 Short stories
"This shorter version of the original book [published 1941 by Coward-McCann] was selected by the original editors." Verso of Title Page
A collection of humor in prose and verse arranged under: Stories and people: Fables and other moral tales; All sorts of dilemmas: Parodies and burlesque; For (or against) children; Satire—broad and otherwise; Nonsense; Verse; Reminiscence

817.09 American wit and humor— History and criticism

Morsberger, Robert E.

James Thurber. Twayne 1964 224p (Twayne's United States authors ser) boards $5.50   **817.09**

1 Thurber, James
This critical study of the work of the American humorist "attempts to show how Thurber's timorous husbands, aggressive wives, amiable dogs, irascible conversationalists, the fabulous and the familiar, the craftsman's prose and casual cartoons, political liberalism

Morsberger, Robert E.—*Continued*
and nostalgic conservatism, contemporary commentary and escapist fantasy can add up to a coherent statement about the human condition." Publisher's note
Notes and references: p200-06. Selected bibliography: p207-18

Rourke, Constance
American humor; a study of national character. Doubleday 1953 [c1931] 253p pa $1.25
817.09

1 American wit and humor—History and criticism 2 National characteristics, American 3 American literature—History and criticism
"A Doubleday Anchor book"
First published 1931 by Harcourt
This study "was the first to uncover the folk origins of American drama and literature, describing the styles and psychology of the humor of the Yankee, the backwoodsman, the minstrel, and the 'stroller' in colonial and frontier America, and tracing the dominant themes through major novels and poetry of the late nineteenth and early twentieth centuries." A Guide to Reading in Am History

Yates, Norris W.
Robert Benchley. Twayne 1968 175p (Twayne's United States authors ser) boards $5.50   817.09

1 Benchley, Robert Charles
"Starting with Benchley's acting, editing, drawing, and writing at Harvard the author . . . brings his own liveliness and a knowledge of humor to an analysis of Benchley's career. Yates reviews the development of Benchley's style, his achievements as author and columnist, his themes and ideas, and his motion-picture shorts. A chronology precedes the text, and notes . . . are appended." Booklist
Bibliography: p161-70

818   American miscellany

Adams, John R.
Harriet Beecher Stowe. Twayne 1963 172p (Twayne's United States authors ser) boards $5.50   818

1 Stowe, Harriet Elizabeth (Beecher)
In this evaluation of Mrs Stowe's cultural and literary significance, the author surveys her writings, analyzing her books and referring to uncollected contributions to magazines and newspapers. The book also includes biographical information. (Publisher)
"Thorough documentation and detailed treatment of her whole literary output, . . . will recommend it to students of American literature." Booklist
Selected bibliography: p159-67

Anderson, David D.
Abraham Lincoln. Twayne 1970 205p (Twayne's United States authors ser) boards $5.50   818

1 Lincoln, Abraham, President U.S.
This is "a well-researched study of the writings of Abraham Lincoln correlating the events of Lincoln's personal and political life with the development of his thought and prose. . . . A chronology precedes and a selected bibliography of primary and secondary sources is appended." Booklist

Bassan, Maurice
(ed.) Stephen Crane; a collection of critical essays. Prentice-Hall 1967 184p $5.95   818

1 Crane, Stephen
"Twentieth century views. A Spectrum book"
Analyzed in Essay and general literature index
"Eighteen critics examine the structure and themes of Crane's most important prose and poetry and provide psychological studies of the man and his works." Bk Buyer's Guide

"A good collection of scholarly criticism for students and others familiar with the work of an American writer." Booklist
Selected bibliography: p181-84

Benét, Stephen Vincent
Selected works of Stephen Vincent Benét. Rinehart [1959] 2v in 1 $8.50   818

First published 1942 by Farrar & Rinehart in two volumes
Contents: v 1 Poetry; v2 Prose
The first volume "contains all of John Brown's Body, and selections from his other published ballads and verse. Volume two has all of his stories of American history, and selections from his other prose works." Book Rev Digest

Bohner, Charles H.
Robert Penn Warren. Twayne [1965 c1964] 175p (Twayne's United States authors ser) boards $5.50   818

1 Warren, Robert Penn
This study emphasizes the shaping influence of the Southern heritage on Warren and is "the first book-length study to discuss systematically both the range of Warren's talents and the growth of his artistic development. The author argues that despite the variety of forms Warren has employed, his work is concerned with several underlying themes: the problem of evil, the meaning of history, the human penchant for violence, the search for self-knowledge, and the need for self-fulfillment." Publisher's note
Selected bibliography: p166-68

Boyd, Malcolm
Malcolm Boyd's Book of days. Random House 1968 215p $5.95   818

Arranged chronologically with a thought or two for each day, the author is "concerned not with traditional religious problems, but with secular realities—Vietnam, Black Revolution, sexual freedom, worldly hypocrisy, anti-Semitism, and the Underground Church. 'Minutes and hours, people and places, family problems and human revolutions, work and leisure, straws of life and confrontation of moral issues, joy and pain, are the stuff making up a book of days." Publisher's note
"Many of the ideas used are quite short, but require much thought to be fully appreciated [and have] immediate relevance to young people's concerns." Library J

Brooks, Van Wyck
The ordeal of Mark Twain; introduction by James R. Vitelli. Dutton [1970 c1947] 324p pa $2.25   818

1 Clemens, Samuel Langhorne
First published 1920
"This book is primarily a psychological study and yet it is full of biographical detail related to the career of Mark Twain." N Y Times Bk R
"Although it is easy to dissent from Mr. Brooks's interpretation of Clemens's biography, the book aims to provide something of the serious criticism which is so essential not only to American letters but to American culture." Springf'd Republican

Crowder, Richard
Carl Sandburg. Twayne 1964 176p (Twayne's United States authors ser) boards $5.50   818

1 Sandburg, Carl
"The object of this present book is five-fold: (1) to give the details of Sandburg's life that are relevant to his writing; (2) to summarize the prose and sample the verse content of his books; (3) to review the critics' reception of each major work; (4) to analyze the themes and the craftsmanship in each volume; and (5) to appraise Sandburg's achievement; that is to determine, in so far as is possible with an author who is still publishing, his permanent position in American letters." Preface
Selected bibliography: p163-68

Day, Clarence

The best of Clarence Day.... Knopf 1948 451p illus $6.95 **818**

"Including God and my father, Life with father, Life with mother, This simian world, and selections from Thoughts without words." Title page

"Close to half of Mr. Day's total output, including . . . his long essay on man's wobbly trajectory toward the good society, called 'This Simian World.' There are also a few pages of jingles, embellished with drawings by the author, from the collection 'Thoughts Without Words.'" New Yorker

Life with father **818**

1 Fathers

Some editions are:
Knopf $4.95
Watts, F. $7.95 Large type edition A Keith Jennison book
First published 1935
Reminiscences of New York City in the late 1800's. "Life in the Day family was frequently a stormy but spirited affair because father had strong feelings and 'they always came out with a bang.' Father's eldest son, with just the right tang of humorous understanding, recalls a variety of major and minor earthquakes when guests disturb father's peace and comfort, when he has a bad night, when his pet rug is removed, or when he tries to make mother like figures." N Y Libraries

"Done with affection and gusto, with here and there a touch of lovely, unsweetened tenderness, always with kind, unflinching eyes and the friendliest laughter. And while we read we also laugh, often uncontrollably, in outbursts. . . . It is written for the ear, it sounds like the best talk, it has a casual air, its nonchalance invites you to ignore the subtlety of its cadences. A delightful book alive with energy." New Repub

Eliot, T. S.

The complete poems and plays, 1909-1950. Harcourt 1952 392p $8.50 **818**

This book is made up of six individual titles formerly published separately: Collected poems (1909-1935); Four quartets: Old Possum's book of practical cats; Murder in the cathedral; Family reunion; Cocktail party

"To have all this in one volume is convenient. And the most casual glance through these poems, both lyric and dramatic, serves to remind us of Eliot's stature and significance." N Y Her Trib Books

Index to titles: p389-90. Index to first lines: p390-92

Floan, Howard R.

William Saroyan. Twayne 1966 176p (Twayne's United States authors ser) boards $5.50 **818**

1 Saroyan, William

"An appraisal of this author's contributions to literature and the American theater." Chicago

This book "surveys the entire body of his work but gives especially close attention to the young Saroyan's search for a subject and for a suitable technique. The inimitable appeal of William Saroyan and the obvious staying power of this appeal are clearly defined. While the distinguishing qualities of Saroyan's art are emphasized, its limitations are not ignored. The reader will find here . . . [an] exploration to the center of a unique literary accomplishment." Publisher's note

Selected bibliography: p164-67

Foster, Ruel E.

Jesse Stuart. Twayne 1968 168p (Twayne's United States authors ser) boards $5.50 **818**

1 Stuart, Jesse

"This volume describes and evaluates the work of Jesse Stuart, a prolific writer hitherto ignored by most serious literary critics. Stuart holds a position as chief exemplar and elegist of a lost way of life in the Appalachian world." Publisher's note

Bibliography: p160-61

Frank, Charles P.

Edmund Wilson. Twayne 1970 213p (Twayne's United States authors ser) boards $5.50 **818**

1 Wilson, Edmund

"Because there is so little book-length material on Wilson—certainly one of the most significant and provocative literary critics of the 20th century—this volume should be welcomed by libraries. The facts, notes, and bibliography are here. Frank has obviously availed himself of the most recent periodical sources where much commentary on Wilson must be found. Wilson's reputation as 'the public critic' and his penchant for controversy are looked at, as well. Yet Frank does Wilson an unintentional disservice. By placing undue emphasis on minor achievements in poetry, drama, and fiction, the biographer dilutes the very strength of his subject. Frank claims too much for Wilson's fiction, which is deservedly neglected by commentators." Choice

Franklin, Benjamin

The autobiography, and other writings of Benjamin Franklin.... Dodd 1963 312p illus (Great illustrated classics) $4.50 **818**

1 Statesmen, American 2 Authors, American

"With selections from 'Poor Richard's almanac' and papers relating to the 'Junto,' together with sixteen pages of illustrations and commentary by Frank Donovan." Title page

In the third section, "Franklin describes how he organized his 'ingenious acquaintances into a club of mutual improvement,' which he called the Junto. Actually, the Junto was much more than this. It was a combination debating society, forum, social group, business service club and junior Chamber of Commerce." p221

Poor Richard's almanac. . . . McKay 132p (The Pocket classics) $2.25 **818**

A collection of items—maxims, proverbs, etc. —which appeared in Poor Richard's almanack, written by Benjamin Franklin, under the pseudonym Richard Saunders, from 1733-1757

Frost, Robert

Selected prose of Robert Frost; ed. by Hyde Cox and Edward Connery Lathem. Holt 1966 119p $4.50 **818**

Among the fifteen selections included are "The figure a poem makes," introductions to volumes of poetry, "Perfect day—a day of prowess" with which Frost introduced a magazine article on baseball, and two essays reflecting his philosophical position—"Letter to The Amherst Student'" and "On Emerson." (Publisher)

"Essays in this volume have not been collected before and add substantially to the picture we have of Frost as a major literary figure as well as a poet." Huntting

Gale, Robert L.

Richard Henry Dana, Jr. Twayne 1969 191p (Twayne's United States authors ser) boards $5.50 **818**

1 Dana, Richard Henry, 1815-1882

The author "combines a well-researched biography of Richard Henry Dana, nineteenth-century American lawyer-politician with a critical analysis of the major literary writings of Dana, including 'Two years before the mast.' Chronicling Dana's childhood in Boston, education at Harvard, two years in California and at sea, study of law, marriage, political activities, and further travels, Gale evaluates the structure and content of 'Two years before the mast,' concluding that the narrative is graphic, universally popular, and the most enduring literary accomplishment of a public spirited, articulate Brahmin. A chronology precedes, and an annotated selected bibliography is appended." Booklist

Hemingway, Ernest

The Fifth Column, and four stories of the Spanish Civil War. Scribner 1969 151p $4.95
                                                            818

1 Short stories 2 Spain—History—Civil War, 1936-1939—Drama   3 Spain—History—Civil War, 1936-1939—Fiction

"Re-reading Hemingway's one major effort at playwriting, one is moved more by a renewal of contact with the Hemingway essence than by any unique power in the play. 'The Fifth Column' [first published 1938] is absorbing, make no mistake. It possesses every prime Hemingway ingredient. Its setting, Madrid under siege during the Spanish Civil War, is the 'presence of death' that was Hemingway's real milieu. Rawlings, the tough American who works in counter-espionage against Fascists inside the city by day and is a womb-crawler by night, reflects Hemingway's own agonized dichotomy. . . . Of the four stories, each set in the same Madrid under siege, 'The Denunciation' and 'The Butterfly and the Tank' are tragic-comic sketches: but 'Night Before Battle' is a beautifully sustained and wildly boozy picture of men-of-war trying to drown the knowledge that in the morning they will probably die, and 'Under the Ridge' dramatizes the absolute hatred of a Spanish fighter for all foreigners with a terrible poignancy that has meaning today." Pub W

Hughes, Langston

The Langston Hughes reader. Braziller 1958 501p $5.95
                                                            818

1 Negroes 2 U.S.—Race relations

The selections in this anthology, some never before published in book form, include short stories, poems, song lyrics, articles and speeches, portions of the autobiographical works The big sea, and I wonder as I wander; and selections from the Simple trilogy: Simple takes a wife, Simple speaks his mind, and Simple stakes a claim. Also included are the complete texts of Simply heavenly, a musical comedy, Soul gone home, a one-act play, The glory of Negro history, a pageant, and Montage of a dream deferred, a long poem about the Harlem community

"Since Mr. Hughes is a Negro who writes mostly about Negroes, seeing some thirty years of his work spread out before you is like attending an unusually subtle tolerance lecture—perhaps the last thing Mr. Hughes had in mind—for what is most striking about his book is that his American Negroes are remarkably unexotic and unalien." New Yorker

Jackson, Shirley

The magic of Shirley Jackson; ed. by Stanley Edgar Hyman. Farrar, Straus 1966 753p $10
                                                            818

1 Short stories

Contains eleven short stories and three earlier titles: The bird's nest, a novel, published 1954, and two family chronicles: Life among the savages, 1953, and Raising demons, 1957

"The posthumous selection by the author's husband shows Shirley Jackson's range of mood from macabre to comic." Booklist

Konvitz, Milton R.

(ed.) Emerson; a collection of critical essays; ed. by Milton R. Konvitz and Stephen E. Whicher. Prentice-Hall 1962 184p $5.95
                                                            818

1 Emerson, Ralph Waldo

"Twentieth century views. A Spectrum book" Analyzed in Essay and general literature essay

Includes selections by the editors, Newton Arvin, John Dewey, Charles Feidelson, Norman Foerster, Robert Frost, William James, Francis Otto Matthiessen, Perry Miller, Henry Bamford Parkes, Sherman Paul, George Santayana and Henry Nash Smith

Includes a chronology of important dates and a bibliography

Lincoln, Abraham

A treasury of Lincoln quotations; comp. and ed. by Fred Kerner. Doubleday 1965 320p $4.95
                                                            818

1 Quotations

A selection of the famous and "the little-known quotations from Lincoln. These statements, arranged alphabetically by subject matter and indexed for easy reference, are taken from speeches, letters, and other writings. They range from reflections on his own background and family to opinions on the paramount issues of the day—slavery, states' rights, and war." Publisher's note

"Quotations are given at whatever length is necessary to prevent their being misconstrued out of proper context. Attribution and date are cited for each entry. An index of familiar phrases closes a volume that is both a valuable reference tool and a source of rewarding browsing." Booklist

Lindbergh, Anne Morrow

Earth shine. Harcourt 1969 73p illus $5.75
                                                            818

1 Apollo project 2 Zoology—Africa, East

"A Helen and Kurt Wolff book"

"Two brief essays—'The heron and the astronaut' and 'Immersion in life'—describe a trip to Cape Kennedy for the launching of Apollo 8 and a month long safari in an East African game preserve. At first glance, there is no apparent connection between the two events but as Lindbergh develops her theme of interrelatedness the gap between the natural world and technological achievement lessens. 'Life' magazine originally published earlier versions of both essays." Booklist

Gift from the sea
                                                            818

1 Life

Some editions are:
Pantheon Bks. $4.50
Watts, F. lib. bdg. $7.95 Large type edition. A Keith Jennison book

The setting is the sea shore; the time, a brief vacation which had lifted the author from the distractions of everyday existence into the sphere of meditation. As the sea tosses up its gifts—shells rare and perfect—so the mind, left to its ponderings, brings up its own treasures of the deep. And the shells become symbols here for the various aspects of life she is contemplating

"Reflections on the writer's search for outward simplicity, inner integrity, yet fuller relationships with family and friends. The observations are expressed with poetic sensitiveness and will find sympathetic response among readers striving for a balance in fulfilling their obligations to a family and to themselves as individuals." Booklist

McGinley, Phyllis

Sixpence in her shoe. Macmillan (N Y) 1964 281p (A Macmillan Career bk) $4.95 818

1 Home economics

Sharing with readers her experiences, problems and joys of the domestic life, the author divides her material into three parts: The wife, The house, and The family. Phyllis McGinley discusses such subjects as higher education for women, thrift, and domestic help

"Reassuring amusing reading for American women, though everyone won't agree with Miss McGinley's basic premise about housewifery as a noble career." Pub W

MacLeish, Archibald

A continuing journey. Houghton 1968 [c1967] 374p $5.95
                                                            818

1 Twentieth century

Analyzed in Essay and general literature index

This collection of essays written during the past quarter century covers "a wide range of subjects: individual and national behavior, education, Communism and Democracy, poetry and people. One section of the book contains brief portraits of people, including tributes to Mrs. Roosevelt, Adlai Stevenson and Felix Frankfurter." Pub W

Bibliography included in Acknowledgments: p371-74

Mencken, H. L.

The American scene; a reader; selected and ed. and with an introduction and commentary, by Huntington Cairns. Knopf 1965 xxvii, 542p $10 **818**

1 U.S.—Civilization

Analyzed in Essay and general literature index

"Selections from the Baltimore bad boy who invented such insults as 'the booboisie' to express his disgust with democracy and its stodgier conventions. Here are articles on Theodore Dreiser, William Jennings Bryan, the American language, the nature and origin of religion, Mark Twain, Ambrose Bierce, Upton Sinclair, with some of his letters. It's a wonderful collection that may irritate some but will certainly amuse and delight many thousands." Bk Buyer's Guide

Bibliography: p541-42

Mowat, Farley

The dog who wouldn't be; illus. by Paul Galdone. Little 1957 238p illus $4.95 **818**

1 Dogs

"Mutt, a dog who shared 10 years of the writer's happy boyhood in Saskatchewan, Canada, persistently refused to be a mere canine. . . . While centered on the exploits of Mutt, these fresh, sometimes riotously funny reminiscences also relate the author's experiences with two owls named Weeps and Wol and other highly individualistic pets." Booklist

"A book full of wholesome, outdoor fun, the lessons of nature, and the nonmeddlesome wisdom of parents. For the basic collection." Wis Lib Bul

Poe, Edgar Allan

Selected poetry and prose; ed. with an introduction by T. O. Mabbott. Modern Lib. 1951 428p $2.95 **818**

1 Short stories

Contains poems, tales, essays and criticism

Porter, Katherine Anne

The collected essays and occasional writings of Katherine Anne Porter. Delacorte Press 1970 496p $12.50 **818**

Analyzed in Essay and general literature index

"A Seymour Lawrence book"

"An immensely engaging collection of critical essays, book reviews, letters, biographical and autobiographical sketches, and poems written over the past four decades or so gives access into the mind and life of a discerning writer and compelling human being. Whether seeing the praiseworthy in Willa Cather's work or the pretentious in Gertrude Stein's, or commenting on the insanity of war or her partiality for certain landscapes, Porter reveals herself as a woman wise about literature and life and as perceptive about herself as about others." Booklist

"Of these, her critical essays—'On a Criticism of Thomas Hardy' and 'A Wreath for the Gamekeeper' are my favorites—bid for an enduring place. They lead off this collection, as it happens, bringing to view her tough-minded humanism and the autobiographical springs of her criticism." Harper

Regan, Robert

(ed.) Poe; a collection of critical essays. Prentice-Hall 1967 183p $5.95 **818**

1 Poe, Edgar Allan

"Twentieth century views. A Spectrum book" This collection consists of more than ten articles on Poe as a poet and "as a major writer. Among the contributors are Joseph Wood Krutch, Aldous Huxley, Allen Tate, Jean-Paul Weber, and Floyd Stovall." Booklist

Includes bibliographical references

Rosten, Leo

The many worlds of L*E*O R*O*S*T*E*N. . . . Harper 1964 329p $6.95 **818**

"Stories, humor, social commentary, travelogues, satire, memoirs, profiles, and sundry entertainments never before published; with a special introduction, background notes, revelations and confessions, all hand-written and themselves worth the price of admission." Title page

"Leo Rosten's creative imagination and his writing is vivid and entertaining and provides the body and substance of this anthology." Library J

Ruland, Richard

(ed.) Twentieth century interpretations of Walden; a collection of critical essays. Prentice-Hall 1968 119p $4.95 **818**

1 Thoreau, Henry David. Walden

"A Spectrum book"

This book contains "an introductory section of brief comments and opinions. Beyond its balanced selection of essays, it would remain justified by a single statement in its short introduction: 'Certainly a good four-fifths of the writing on Thoreau is either undiscriminating appreciation or sentimental testimonial.'" Choice

"Among the contributors are Reginald L. Cook, Norman Foerster, Robert Frost, F. O. Matthiessen, Perry Miller, and E. B. White." Pub W

Includes bibliographical references

Saroyan, William

Days of life and death and escape to the moon. Dial Press 1970 139p boards $5.95 **818**

In this personal journal, kept during August 1967 in Paris and November-December, 1968 in Fresno, California, the author records his thoughts on many subjects—life, death, space travel and time, work, honor and the phenomenon of growing older. (Publisher)

"Throughout his new book Saroyan writes with his usual beautiful simplicity of old friends on whom time has run out. . . . A graceful and affecting book." Pub W

Steinbeck, John

The portable Steinbeck. Rev. selected and introduced by Pascal Covici, Jr. Viking 1971 xlii, 692p $6.25 **818**

SBN 670-66960-1

"The Viking Portable library"

First published 1943 with title: Steinbeck

The author was awarded the Nobel prize in literature, 1962; The grapes of wrath received the Pulitzer Prize, 1940

A collection of the author's works, mainly fiction, some complete, some excerpted

A sampling of the titles included are: The long valley; The Pastures of Heaven; Tortilla Flat; In dubious battle; Of mice and men; The red pony; The grapes of wrath; Sea of Cortez; East of Eden; Travels with Charley in search of America; The language of awareness

Stroud, Parry

Stephen Vincent Benét. Twayne [1963 c1962] 173p (Twayne's United States authors ser) boards $5.50 **818**

1 Benét, Stephen Vincent

"Critical appraisal of the writer's important works, including representative poems and short stories and most of his work in other genres." Pub W

Notes and references: p158-64. Selected bibliography: p165-68

Stuart, Jesse

A Jesse Stuart reader; stories and poems selected and introduced by Jesse Stuart. Foreword: Max Bogart. McGraw 1961 310p $5.25 **818**

1 Kentucky 2 Mountain life—Southern States

Stuart, Jesse—*Continued*

The hills of Kentucky and the people who
live there form the background for this collection of poems, stories and biographical excerpts. The author tells of their compassions,
hardships, conflict and cruelties. For each of
his stories he has written an introduction commenting on the reasons for his choice and recalling its particular place in his life. (Publisher)

Read these pieces "for humor, for a glimpse
of a way of life that has all but disappeared
from America, for any reason you like; but
read them." Sec Ed Brd

Thoreau, Henry David

Henry David Thoreau; a man for our time;
selections and drawings by James Daugherty.
Viking 1967 111p illus $4.50, lib. bdg. $4.13
                                              818

A brief biography and excerpts from
Thoreau's writings "show how Thoreau influenced such men as Gandhi, Martin Luther King
and other American civil rights leaders. This
handsome book, illustrated by the author,
serves as an excellent introduction to Thoreau's
philosophy." Cincinnati

Thoreau: people, principles, and politics;
ed. by Milton Meltzer. Hill & Wang 1963
235p $3.95
                                              818

"American century series"
"Selections from Thoreau's speeches, journals, and letters showing his beliefs on the
controversial subjects of his day. There are
many often needed writings (e.g. 'Civil Disobedience') that teachers and librarians may
find pertinent to our times. Civil War and
slavery items can also be used in high schools.
. . . List of short biographical sketches."
Library J

Walden   **818**

Some editions are:
Dodd (Great illustrated classics) $4.50 With
an introduction, interpretive comments, photo-
graphs and descriptive captions by Edwin Way
Teale
Twayne $5 Annotated and with an introduc-
tion by Walter Harding. Has title: The vario-
rum Walden
Watts, F. $8.95 Large type edition. A Keith
Jennison book
First published 1854
"Philosophy of life and observations of na-
ture drawn from the author's solitary sojourn
of two years in a cabin on Walden Pond near
Concord, Massachusetts." Pratt Alcove

Walden, and other writings; introduced by
Nat Hentoff. Doubleday 1970 368p $6.95 **818**

"Here is a collection of writings that show
Thoreau as social philosopher, rather than
poet-naturalist—writings with a special significance to the modern reader." Book News

Thurber, James

Alarms and diversions. Harper 1957 367p
illus $5.95
                                              818

"The prose of James Thurber presented here
includes short stories, essays in which hilarity is blended with serious comedy (and occasionally pointed up with satire), and exciting
factual articles. Contains 180 Thurber drawings." McClurg. Book News

"An especially good selection of cartoons is
included, along with the essay 'The Lady on
the Bookcase,' which explains how and why
Thurber cartoons come into being. And not
the least of this book's attractiveness stems
from the inclusion in its entirety of 'The
Last Flower,' Mr. Thurber's picture-parable
of war and peace." N Y Her Trib Books

Credos and curios. Harper 1962 180p illus
$5.95
                                              818

This collection contains "twenty one short
articles by James Thurber, with a foreword by
his widow. All have been published before,
three in books, the others in periodicals. . . .
The book is short and easy to read." Best Sellers

The Thurber album; a new collection of
pieces about people. Simon & Schuster 1952
346p illus $5.50
                                              818

In this book Thurber offers "sketches of
relatives, friends, teachers, and colleagues—
'the lovely and colorful people of whom I am
especially fond.' The album is nostalgic, recalling the 'good old days' in the Middle West.
Most of the pieces appeared originally in 'The
New Yorker.'" Wis Lib Bul

"The chronological arrangement, beginning
in the early nineteenth century, gives us not
only a glimpse of the development of historical events, but the American character. Though
the sketches are of one family in one area in
Ohio they have a quaint, timeless folklore
quality." Library J

Tobias, Richard C.

The art of James Thurber. Ohio Univ.
Press 1970 196p $7.50
                                              818

1 Thurber, James 2 Comedy
SBN 8214-0058-4

"Using an authoritative knowledge of the
art of comedy and studding his discussion
with literary allusions Tobias has crafted an
enjoyable and informative study of Thurber's
writing. With a chronological approach he
demonstrates the differences in the humorist's
life interpretations from the 1920s to the 1950s.
A bibliography is appended." Booklist

Tomkins, Calvin

Eric Hoffer: an American odyssey; intro-
duction by Eric Sevareid; photographs by
George Knight; aphorisms by Eric Hoffer.
Dutton 1968 68p illus $4.95
                                              818

1 Hoffer, Eric

In the author's "sympathetic portrait Hoffer
emerges as a true original. Born of German
parents in New York City, he has been a migrant worker, miner, and longshoreman on the
West Coast. Self-educated and dedicated to an
austere life, he has formed his outlook and
writings from his unique experience. Photographs of Hoffer and a selection of his aphorisms follow Tomkins' sketch [p69-115]."
Booklist

Vitelli, James R.

Van Wyck Brooks. Twayne 1969 191p
(Twayne's United States authors ser)
boards $5.50
                                              818

1 Brooks, Van Wyck

"An introduction to the works and career
of Van Wyck Brooks, critic and historian of
the literary life in America. Each of his books
is described and analyzed." Publisher's note
Includes bibliography

Wagenknecht, Edward

Washington Irving: moderation displayed.
Oxford 1962 223p $6.50
                                              818

1 Irving, Washington

This book draws "on manuscript materials
and benefits from unpublished dissertations as
well as recent literature on Irving. . . . Wagenknecht captures something of Irving's own ur-
banity in delineating his mastery of 'a middle
region which he surveyed and described with
a winning, companionable charm.'" Library J
Includes bibliography

Whitaker, Thomas R.

William Carlos Williams. Twayne 1968
183p (Twayne's United States authors ser)
boards $5.50
                                              818

1 Williams, William Carlos

"The first full-length critical assessment of
the poetry and prose. . . . The author shows
how Williams sought to abandon shielding
habits and conventions and thus renew contact with 'that eternal moment in which we
alone live.'" Publisher's note

"One of the better books in this series,
Whitaker's appraisals of Williams can be appreciated without necessarily agreeing with
them." Choice

White, E. B.

An E. B. White reader; ed. with commentary and questions by William W. Watt and Robert W. Bradford. Harper 1966 342p pa $4.95 **818**

A representative selection of the author's essays, verse, editorials, letters, and comments on usage, published from 1936 to 1963. The book includes the editor's notes, questions for discussion, and suggestions for writing

"The fusion of a far-ranging subject matter and a free and fluid style is the hallmark of this collection of White's essays." Choice

"While intended as a college textbook, it provides a delightful and stimulating collection of short pieces for the general reader." Booklist

One man's meat. A new and enl. ed. Harper 1944 350p $6.95 **818**

Analyzed in Essay and general literature index

"A new edition of the author's book of essays which first appeared in 1942. The ten new essays are: Song-birds; Questionnaire; Aunt Poo; Book learning; Morningtime and eveningtime; Getting ready for a cow; Bond rally; A week in November; Control; Cold weather." Book Rev Digest

"It is clear that beneath the deceptively gentle tenor of his writing lies a deep awareness of the dreadful things that are happening in the world and a stinging irritation with man's reaction to them, his own, perhaps, included." N Y Times Bk R

The points of my compass; letters from the East, the West, the North, the South. Harper 1962 240p boards $4.95 **818**

Contains 18 of the author's pieces which have appeared in the New Yorker, purportedly as the letters of a self-appointed foreign correspondent who elected to stay home. These reports deal with such things as a hurricane in New England, a visit to the circus in its winter quarters, disarmament, and the decline of railroading. (Publisher)

"Good readers who appreciate style as well as content in writing will enjoy these polished, perceptive, and often entertaining essays on a variety of topics." Booklist

The second tree from the corner. Harper 1954 253p $6.50, lib. bdg. $4.43 **818**

Partially analyzed in Essay and general literature index

"Whoever sets pen to paper writes of himself, whether knowingly or not, and this is a book of revelations: essays, poems, stories, opinions, reports, drawn from the past, the present, the future, the city, and the country." Foreword

"Mr. White is an essayist in the Sheridan and Steele tradition: witty, tolerant, easygoing, urbane, and intelligent without being intellectual. Together, they form a commentary on our country." Wis Lib Bul

White, Ray Lewis

Gore Vidal. Twayne 1968 157p (Twayne's United States authors ser) boards $5.50 **818**

1 Vidal, Gore

"First study of a writer in mid-career, and therefore, despite short-comings, a valuable reference tool. Biographical matter is adequate, but there is heavy emphasis on plot summary, and the commentary-analysis is rather thin, ingenuous, and often awkwardly written. White does, however, present a convincing pattern to Vidal's varied career, a pattern that fits others of the 'after-the-lost-generation' writers: (1) early and 'brilliant' success with postwar novels in the Hemingway manner; (2) rejection, experiment, search for a style, and career crisis during the decade of McCarthy and the Silent Generation, and (3) an almost spectacular comeback in the sixties as successful public man of letters." Choice

Bibliography: p147-52

Whitman, Walt

Walt Whitman's America; being selections from Leaves of grass, Democratic vistas, Specimen days and Portraits of Lincoln [ed.] by James Daugherty. World Pub. 1964 110p illus $4.95 **818**

"Selected prose and poetry of Walt Whitman. Partial contents: I hear America singing; Song of myself (excerpt); Crossing Brooklyn ferry (excerpt); Pioneers! O pioneers! (excerpt); The people; The battle of Bull Run, July 1861; The first time I ever saw Abraham Lincoln; The assassination." Book Rev Digest

The works of Walt Whitman; in two volumes as prepared by him for the deathbed edition; with a foreword and an introduction by Malcolm Cowley. Funk 1968 2v ea $7.95 **818**

These volumes "were first issued in 1948 by the [then] newly founded publishing house of Pellegrini and Cudahy . . . which had a short life—later its list was taken over by Farrar, Straus and Giroux." Foreword: 1968

Contents: v 1 The collected poetry; v2 The collected prose

"During the last year of his life (1891-1892) Walt Whitman prepared the final text of his writings, in two volumes, which became known as the Deathbed Edition. The two volumes contained everything of Whitman's that he wanted to save, in the final form in which he wanted it to appear." Publisher's note

"The volumes are rather jampacked, with resultant slender margins; but that fact, and even the lack of an index, is compensated for by the reasonable price." Pub W

820.3 English literature—Dictionaries

The **Concise** Oxford Dictionary of English literature. 2d ed. Oxford 1970 628p $8 **820.3**

1 English literature—Dictionaries 2 American literature—Dictionaries

First published 1939 as an abridged dictionary of Sir Paul Harvey's Oxford Companion to English literature. This edition is based on the fourth edition of the larger work, and revised by Dorothy Eagle

Entries include authors and their works, mythological and historical subjects related to English literature, references to sources for over one thousand characters in books and plays and short articles on general literary terms and topics. (Publisher)

The **New** Century Handbook of English literature; ed. by Clarence L. Barnhart with the assistance of William D. Halsey. Rev. ed. Appleton [distributed by Hawthorn Bks.] 1967 1167p $14.95 **820.3**

1 English literature—Dictionaries 2 Authors

First published 1958

A one-volume encyclopedia that "seeks to answer those questions about English writers, works of literature, characters from works of literature, and various related (but not necessarily English) items which are most likely to be raised by modern American readers of English literature." Preface

"A useful, carefully compiled reference book containing more than 14,000 entries that are briefly but adequately identified. In addition to English writers whose works are likely to be included in standard anthologies this includes the great Irish writers. 'Anglo-Americans' such as Henry James, authors representing British dominions, and contemporary Britons acclaimed by reviewers." Booklist

The **Oxford** Companion to English literature;
comp. and ed. by Sir Paul Harvey. 4th ed.
rev. by Dorothy Eagle. Oxford 1967 961p
$12.50   **820.3**
1 English literature—Dictionaries 2 English
literature—Bio-bibliography   3 American literature—Dictionaries   4 American literature
—Bio-bibliography
First published 1932
This reference work includes in alphabetical
arrangement a list of English authors, literary
works and literary societies which have historical or present importance. A number of
American authors are included. Under each
author are given facts bearing on his life and
literary activity. Under the title of a work is
given an indication of its nature and for the
important works of literature of the past,
poetry, prose, drama, there is a brief sketch of
the plot. These brief summaries may, at times,
make the use of the book questionable. Contains
also an explanation of allusions mostly limited
to those containing proper names and occurring
in English literature
For a fuller review see: The Booklist and
Subscription Books Bulletin Review, June 15,
1968

820.9   English literature—
History and criticism

Daiches, David
A critical history of English literature. 2d
ed. Ronald 1970 2v (1169p) $13.50   **820.9**
1 English literature—History and criticism
First published 1960
From Anglo-Saxon times to the present, the
poetry, prose, and drama of each period of
English literature come to new life under the
author's critical scrutiny. Stress is placed on
the important works of major authors with numerous, aptly chosen quotations. The literature
of each period is related to the historical background in order to provide a sense of continuity of English literature. (Publisher)
No bibliography, few footnotes

More literary essays. Univ. of Chicago
Press 1968 274p $7.50   **820.9**
1 English literature—History and criticism
Analyzed in Essay and general literature index
This volume "contains pieces on Shakespeare's Antony and Cleopatra, Marlowe's Tamburlaine, Milton, Robert Burns, Thomas Carlyle, Whitman, Mark Twain, and the modern
Scottish poet Hugh MacDiarmid. Daiches also
includes a portrait of his own teacher, the
editor of Donne, H. J. C. Grierson." Publisher's note
"I think that some of [Daiches'] most valuable writing has been on questions of general
critical theory. His essay on 'Myth, Metaphor, and Poetry' . . . is a model of lucidity and
discernment. . . . [The excellence] of his essay
on Marlowe's Tamburlaine is the result of his
ability to connect patterns of language and
gesture within the play and then to relate these
to what he knows of the nature of human experience. . . . Though there is much one can
be impatient with in Daiches, for such moments
of fine critical illumination, when they come
any reader must be grateful." Commentary

Sampson, George
The concise Cambridge History of English
literature. 3d ed. . . . Cambridge 1970 976p
$9.95   **820.9**
1 English literature—History and criticism
SBN 521-07385-5
First published 1941
"Revised throughout and with additional
chapters on the literature of the United States
of America and the mid-twentieth-century literature of the English-speaking world by R. C.
Churchill." Title page [of the 3d ed]

"The literature of the U.S.A. is now surveyed 'in extenso' and in its own right. The
literatures in English of Ireland, India,
Pakistan, Ceylon, Malaysia, Canada, Australia, New Zealand, the West Indies, South Africa and the new African states are also treated." Publisher's note
"As a work of reference, as a handbook for
beginners this volume, in so far as it is an epitome, cannot be too highly praised. But the
book is more than an epitome, and its fresh
pages, lively as they often are, provocative,
sensitive, a little too severe at moments, cannot be so thoroughly commended." Sat R

Ward, Alfred Charles
Illustrated history of English literature;
illus. collected by Elizabeth Williams. McKay
1953-1955 3v illus ea $10   **820.9**
1 English literature—History and criticism
First published by Longmans
Content: v 1 Chaucer to Shakespeare; v2 Ben
Jonson to Samuel Johnson; v3 Blake to Bernard
Shaw
The present volumes are "designed to provide the general reader with a small-scale survey of the extensive territory of mind and imagination with which English literature has
been concerned through the centuries up to
1950." Author to the reader v 1
Includes bibliographies

821   English poetry

Auden, W. H.
The collected poetry of W. H. Auden. Random House 1945 466p $8.95   **821**
"These 225 poems, selected by the [poet] . . .
as the ones he wishes to preserve from his
writings thus far, range widely in thought and
technique. . . . Two of his most recent and
lengthy works, the Christmas oratorio 'For the
time being,' a searching analysis of the spiritual ills of our time, and 'The sea and the
mirror,' subtitled 'a commentary on Shakespeare's The tempest,' are included in their entirety. The arrangement although not completely consistent seems to be by form, not
chronology. No index." Booklist
"This is a convenient edition of Auden, and
those previously unacquainted with him would
do well to begin with it." N Y Times Bk R

Collected shorter poems: 1927-1957. Random House [1967 c1966] 351p $8.95   **821**
The poet "has arranged in a single volume
the shorter poems he wishes to preserve. The
poems, printed chronologically, are taken from
all his previous volumes, and include sections
of book-length poems." Publisher's note
The material written since 1944 "spans a
period which no one would advance as Mr
Auden's most gripping or purposeful. The nervous energy of his Marxist-Freudian days has
drained into Anglo-Catholicism. . . . A saviour
of dereliction hangs about this later, so-firmly-
unpolitical Auden." New Statesman
Index of first lines: p343-51

Blake, William
Poems of William Blake; selected by
Amelia H. Munson; illus. by William Blake.
Crowell 1964 151p illus (The Crowell Poets)
$3.50, lib. bdg. $4.25   **821**
"Some of the poems that Blake wrote as a
very young man are here, many of the great
ones of his later years, the 'Songs of Inno-
cence' and 'Songs of Experience,' and illumi-
nating selections from the 'Prophetic Books.' "
Publisher's note
Includes indexes of titles and first lines

William Blake; an introduction; ed. by
Anne Malcolmson; with illus. from Blake's
paintings and engravings. Harcourt 1967 127p
illus $4.50   **821**
"For this perceptive introduction to Blake the
editor has selected important poems and passages, grouped in seven sections, from 'Songs
of innocence,' 'Songs of experience,' 'Poetical

Blake, William—*Continued*

sketches,' the manuscripts. 'The marriage of heaven and hell,' 'America: a prophecy,' and the later prophetic books. In addition to an excellent biographical and critical sketch of the eighteenth-century visionary artist-poet, she has provided prefatory notes for each section and for many individual poems, explaining Blake's philosophy, themes, symbolism, and historical allusions.'' Booklist
Acknowledgments and bibliography: p123-24.
Index of first lines: p125-27

Brooke, Rupert

The collected poems of Rupert Brooke; with an introduction by George Edward Woodberry and biographical note by Margaret Lavington. Dodd 1930 192p front $3.95
821

First published 1915
"Rupert Brooke, soldier, died April 23, 1915; Rupert Brooke, poet, lives in poems of youthful hopes and aspirations.'' Cincinnati

Browning, Elizabeth Barrett

The Brownings: letters and poetry; selected and with an introduction by Christopher Ricks; illus. by Barnett I. Plotkin. Doubleday 1970 726p illus $7.95
821

"Of the almost 600 letters that passed between Robert Browning and Elizabeth Barrett before their marriage, the 50 here reprinted . . . reveal very well the characters of the poets, their love for each other, and the dangers of their courtship. The effects of these on their poetry are brilliantly analyzed in Christopher Ricks' short, unfootnoted introduction, which is written apparently without a lapse into either sentimentality or scholar's jargon. Ricks also gives 27 complete poems by Mrs. Browning and more than 80 by Browning, plus selections from their longer works, all chosen in the light of recent criticism, Ricks' analysis, and his sensitivity to the best in their writing.'' Choice

The complete poetical works of Elizabeth Barrett Browning. Cambridge ed. Houghton 1900 530p illus $6
821

Title on spine: The poems of Browning
Contains a biographical sketch, notes, indexes, and portraits. Edited by Harriet Waters Preston
This poet's "themes were dictated by her broad humanitarian interests; a deep if unorthodox religious feeling; her affection for her adopted country, Italy; and . . . her love for [her husband].'' The Reader's Encyclopedia

Sonnets from the Portuguese. Harper 1932 44p $2.95
821

First published 1850
A series of sonnets which "were written during a period of seven years and are considered by some scholars to have been inspired by her love for her husband [poet Robert Browning].'' New Century Handbook of English Literature

Browning, Robert

The complete poetic and dramatic works of Robert Browning. Cambridge ed. Houghton 1895 1033p front $9
821

Title on spine: The poems of Browning
This edition contains a biographical sketch, notes, and indexes; and, in an appendix, Browning's suppressed essay on Shelley

Poems of Robert Browning; selected by Rosemary Sprague; drawings by Robert Galster. Crowell 1964 152p illus (The Crowell Poets) $3.50, lib. bdg. $4.25
821

A selection of Browning's poems grouped under the following headings: Men and women speak: "Two hearts beating each to each''; "Boot, saddle, to horse and away''; "Oh, the wild joys of living.'' Includes indexes of first lines and titles

Poetical works, 1833-1864; ed. by Ian Jack. Oxford 1970 952p $8.50
821

"The aim of this edition is to present all the volumes and pamphlets of poetry which Browning published up to the year 1864, in the order in which they first made their appearance. The text, however, is that of the collected edition which he published at the end of his life. . . . In the present edition a table . . . lists the poems in the three categories of 'Dramatic Lyrics', 'Dramatic Romances', and 'Men and Women' in the collected editions, so that the reader can easily follow Browning's own attempt at classification. . . . No textual apparatus is included, but changes in the titles of the poems are carefully recorded.'' Introduction

Burns, Robert

Poems of Robert Burns; selected by Lloyd Frankenberg; drawings by Joseph Low. Crowell 1967 136p illus (The Crowell Poets) $3.50, lib. bdg. $4.25
821

This collection of over 50 poems in dialect is divided into the following sections: Scotch, Scottish, and Scots; an introduction to Robert Burns: "Aye rowth o' rhymes''; 'Tam o' Shanter; The jolly beggars; "Gin a body kiss a body''; Glossary; Index of titles; Index of first lines
This book "reveals the exuberant spirit of Robert Burns whose poetry depicts the everyday life of the Scottish countryside.'' McClurg. Book News

The poetical works of Robert Burns
821

Some editions are:
Houghton (Cambridge ed) $6 Edited by W. E. Henley. Has title: The complete poetical works of Robert Burns
Oxford (Oxford Standard authors) $4.50 Edited by J. L. Robertson
"The greatest of Scottish lyrical poets and song writers. He wrote mainly in dialect. His poems show warm passions and sympathies, and an intense love for man and nature.'' Pratt Alcove

Byron, George Gordon Noël Byron, 6th Baron

Poems of George Gordon, Lord Byron; selected by Horace Gregory; drawings by Virgil Burnett. Crowell 1969 117p illus (The Crowell Poets) $3.50, lib. bdg. $4.25
821

Contents: Introduction; Occasional pieces; From "Childe Harold's Pilgrimage''; From "Don Juan''; "Beppo''; Letters; Index of titles; Index of first lines
"Horace Gregory's urbane commentary, in both the book's general introduction (in which he points up Byron's modernity) and the brief explanations preceding major sections, is the chief virtue of the selection; the letters . . . further illumine the man presented to readers in the poetry and introductions. Well executed, moody line drawings punctuate the text.'' Library J

Chaucer, Geoffrey

The Canterbury tales
821

Some editions are.
Doubleday $5.95 Rendered into modern English by J. U. Richardson. With illustrations by Rockwell Kent and an introduction by Gordon Hall Gerould
Modern Lib. $2.95 Edited by Walter W. Skeat; introduction by Louis Untermeyer
Random House $10 A prose version in modern English by David Wright
"A collection of twenty-four stories, all but two of which are in verse, written by Geoffrey Chaucer mainly between 1386 and his death in 1400. The stories are supposed to be related by members of a company of thirty-one pilgrims (including the poet himself) who are on their way to the shrine of St. Thomas at Canterbury. The prologue which tells of their assembly at the Tabard Inn in Southwark and their arrangement that each shall tell two stories on the way to Canterbury and two on the return journey, is a remarkable picture of English social life in the fourteenth century, inasmuch as every class is represented from the gentlefolks to the peasantry.'' Keller's Reader's Digest of Books

Chaucer, Geoffrey—*Continued*

The modern reader's Chaucer; the complete poetical works of Geoffrey Chaucer, now first put into modern English by John S. P. Tatlock and Percy MacKaye; illus. by Warwick Goble. Macmillan (N Y) 1950 [c1940] 607p illus $7.95   821

First published 1912
"A prose rendering in modern language for the general reader. Besides the 'Canterbury Tales,' this volume includes transcriptions of all of Chaucer's poetry and prose except a few doubtful and repetitious elements." Pratt Alcove
"It is a pleasure to acknowledge that Messrs Tatlock and MacKaye have done their work well. To those for whom the book was planned it may be heartily commended." Nation
Glossary and notes: p597-607

The poetical works of Chaucer; ed. by F. N. Robinson. Cambridge ed. Houghton 1933 1133p (The Cambridge ed. of the poets) $12
821

This collection is a carefully edited version with full notes, glossary and a brief bibliography

The portable Chaucer; selected, tr. and ed. by Theodore Morrison. Viking 1949 600p $4.95   821

"The Viking Portable library"
A new verse translation bringing to the modern reader the pleasure that Chaucer's contemporaries enjoyed, including: The Canterbury tales the prologue and 12 of the best tales; with summaries of the others, and all of the connecting links about the pilgrims along the way; Troilus and Cressida (a brilliant modern version, complete in itself) and selections from other long poems and short poems
Bibliography: p56-57

A taste of Chaucer; selections from The Canterbury tales; chosen and ed. by Anne Malcolmson; illus. by Enrico Arno. Harcourt 1964 184p illus $3.95   821

This book "offers portions of the Prologue and [nine] of the Tales. Although the language has been modernized, the actual words of Chaucer have been retained whenever possible despite the risk of unfamiliarity. But the glossary and notes supply simple explanations of the vocabulary and the allusions. Preceded by a quotation from Chaucer's text so that the opening lines of each selection may be compared with the original, the character studies and the tales are introduced by commentaries. Supplementary to the text [is] a biographical sketch of Chaucer. . . . The choice of stories is discreet. . . . A few Pilgrims have been omitted from the Prologue, but they will scarcely be missed from the lively company." Horn Bk

Coleridge, Samuel Taylor

Poems of Samuel Taylor Coleridge; selected by Babette Deutsch; woodcuts by Jacques Hnizdovsky. Crowell 1967 139p (The Crowell Poets) $3.50, lib. bdg. $4.25   821

"In addition to critical and biographical material, . . . short introductions are presented here for three major poems. 'The Rime of the Ancient Mariner,' 'Christabel' and 'Kubla Khan.' The other selections include both familiar and unfamiliar poems such as 'Reflections on Having Left a Place of Retirement,' 'To William Wordsworth' and 'Youth and Age.' Several of Coleridge's critical essays are also included." Library J

De La Mare, Walter

The complete poems of Walter De La Mare. Knopf 1970 [c1969] 948p $17.50   821

First published 1969 in England
This "volume contains all of Walter de la Mare's poetry, brought together in one book for the first time. It includes over two hundred poems that were omitted from his two collected volumes published in the early forties. (Collected poems and Collected rhymes and verses) and . . . all the poetry that he published between that time and his death in 1956." Publisher's note
Bibliographical appendix: p889-99. Includes indexes of first lines and titles

Gilbert, W. S.

Poems of W. S. Gilbert; selected by William Cole; illus. by W. S. Gilbert "Bab." Crowell 1967 163p illus (The Crowell Poets) $3.50, lib. bdg. $4.25   821

A collection of humorous poems, from the Bab Ballads and the Gilbert and Sullivan operettas arranged under such headings as: "He led his regiment from behind"; "Never, never sick at sea"; and "The meaning doesn't matter"
Includes notes and indexes of titles and first lines

Graves, Robert

Poems, 1938-1945. Farrar, Straus [1967 c1946] 58p $3.95   821

A reprint of a title first published 1946 in England by Creative Age Press
A collection of 40 poems by a poet who claims he writes "poems for poets, and satires or grotesques for wits." Foreword
These poems "show the author unsentimental and determined to attain some personal reality, and there is an occasional tone of bitterness—but not despair." Times (London) Lit Sup

Poems, 1965-1968. Doubleday 1969 [c1968] 97p $4.95   821

First published 1968 in England
"These four groups of poems are additions to my 'Collected Poems' 1965 (Cassell)." Foreword
"In this collection. Graves includes songs, Latin and French verse, and poems in tribute to nature. But above all, he continues to sing in praise of the power and mysticism of love." Publisher's note

Herrick, Robert

Poems of Robert Herrick; selected by Winfield Townley Scott; drawings by Ellen Raskin. Crowell 1967 126p illus (The Crowell Poets) $3.50, lib. bdg. $4.25   821

A collection of over one hundred poems which "represents Herrick in all his moods as a poet and his skills as a craftsman and . . . contains much of his most beautiful verse. . . . The text here has been modernized as faithfully to Herrick's text as I could make it." Prefatory note
"This is a volume in which the poems have been chosen with discrimination. The lively and informative essay gives biographical information and astute literary comment. . . . Separate title and first line indexes are appended." Chicago. Children's Book Center

Hopkins, Gerard Manley

The poems of Gerard Manley Hopkins. 4th ed. . . . Oxford 1967 lxvi, 362p $7.95 821

"Based on the first edition of 1918 and enlarged to incorporate all known poems and fragments; edited with additional notes, a foreword on the revised text, and a new biographical and critical introduction by W. H. Gardner and N. H. MacKenzie." Title page
First published 1918 in England: first American edition, 1948
This book "brings together all the known poems and verse fragments, including the early verses first published in the poet's Journals and Papers' (1959), the remainder of his Latin verse—now printed for the first time—together with translations into English of all the Latin poems which are entirely original compositions." Publisher's note

Housman, A. E.
The collected poems of A. E. Housman.
Holt 1965 254p front $6   821

This anthology "constitutes the authorized
canon of A. E. Housman's verse as established
in 1939." Note on the text
"It contains A Shropshire lad (1896), Last
poems (1922), More poems (1936), the Additional poems (eighteen first published in Laurence Housman's 'Memoir of his brother' in
1937; five in the collected edition of 1939), and
the three translations from A. W. Pollard's
anthology 'Odes from the Greek dramatists'
(1890)." Publisher's note
"This is the first and definitive edition of
A. E. Housman's poetry, authorized by the
Housman Estate and newly introduced by
John Carter." Am News of Bks
"One outgrows Housman, but does not stop
reading him. His range is narrow, but his
music clear, almost always bravely and gravely
so." Sat R
Index of first lines and titles

Keats, John
Poems of John Keats; selected by Stanley
Kunitz; woodcuts by Jacques Hnizdovsky.
Crowell 1964 148p illus $3.50   821

"The arrangement of the poems, in eight
sections, is intended to show the general development of Keats as a poet, while at the
same time grouping, as far as possible, those
poems that are related to one another in form
or in theme. Excerpts from the letters of
Keats are distributed throughout the text
where they are pertinent." Prefatory note
Indexes of first lines and titles
The poetical works   821

Some editions are:
Houghton (Cambridge ed) $7 Illustrated. Edited
by H. E. Scudder. Has title: The complete
poetical works and letters of John Keats
Modern Lib. $2.95 With an introduction by
Harold Edgar Briggs. Has title: Complete
poetry and selected prose
"An inspired genius who wrote a lifetime of
great poetry in a few years." Good Reading

Kipling, Rudyard
Rudyard Kipling's verse. Definitive ed.
Doubleday 1940 852p front $7.95   821

This edition includes all Kipling's published
poetry and, in addition, more than 20 poems
which have not previously appeared in the inclusive edition of his verse. Index to first lines
"Poems that sing themselves, that breathe of
the open and free, poems of adventure and
romance that are of the very soul of youth."
Pratt Alcove

Langland, William
Vision of Piers Plowman   821

Some editions are:
Dutton (Everyman's lib) $2.95 Translated into
modern English by Donald and Rachel Att-
water, edited by Rachel Attwater. Has title:
The book concerning Piers the Plowman
Oxford $2.70 Translated into modern English
by Nevill Coghill. Has title: Visions from
Piers Plowman
Random House $10 Translated and with an in-
troduction by Margaret Williams. Has title:
Piers the Plowman
"This long allegorical alliterative poem by
an author (or authors) contemporary with
Chaucer describes all sorts of human types
and throws much light upon social and re-
ligious institutions in 14th Century England."
Dickinson

Lawrence, D. H.
D. H. Lawrence: poems selected for young
people, by William Cole; drawings by Ellen
Raskin. Viking 1967 120p illus $3.95, lib.
bdg. $3.77   821

"William Cole has found forty-odd poems to
provide an introduction to one of the most
remarkable poets of our time and, with his
usual gift for sensing the occasion, has done his
work effectively. Grouping the poems under
four headings—'Animals,' 'Man, Woman,
Child,' 'Celebrations and Condemnations,' and

'Love'—he manages to show Lawrence's intensity and compassion, wit and humor, and
'reverence for life' with surprising fullness.
His introduction, although useful and informative, is a little uncomfortable; and the drawings by Ellen Raskin seem a little pretty
for the poems. Yet the text itself is handsomely presented." Horn Bk
Index of first lines: p119-20

Masefield, John
Poems. Complete ed. with recent poems.
Macmillan (N Y) 1953 2v in 1 $10.50   821

First published 1929
"As for the poems here presented again,
there can be no question that certain of them,
lyrics, sonnets, and narratives alike, will live
for some time. The stamp of a powerful and
impressive personality is upon them. Masefield
is no great philosopher, but he is a noble one;
and he knows the true springs of song and is
a natural narrator." Sat R

Salt-water poems and ballads; illus. by
Charles Pears. Macmillan (N Y) 1916 163p
illus $4.95   821

1 Seafaring life—Poetry
First published 1902 in England
This book of racy lyrics and stirring narrative poems is a popular selection containing
Salt-water ballads; Sea pictures; Salt-water
poems
"Most of these [poems] derive from Kipling,
with sailors' chanteys substituted for barrack-
room ditties. . . . In the proem to this collection . . . [the author] 'consecrated' himself
to themes of the lowly, the burdened, and
the forlorn." A Literary History of England
Glossary: p161-63

Milton, John
The complete poetical works of John Milton
821

Some editions are:
Houghton (Cambridge ed) $10.25 Edited by
Douglas Bush
N.Y. Univ. Press (Stuart editions) $10 Ar-
ranged in chronological order with an introduction, notes, variants, and literal translations of the foreign language poems by
John T. Shawcross. Has title: The complete
English poetry of John Milton
Oxford (Oxford Standard editions) $5 Edited
by Helen Darbishire. With translations of
the Italian, Latin and Greek poems from
the Columbia University edition. Has title:
Poetical works
"Every form that Milton attempted—the
masque, the elegy, the sonnet, the long epic,
the short epic, the verse drama—seemingly
achieved its potentiality at his hands. And
distinguishable as Milton's various periods
might be from each other, each is unmistakably
'Miltonic,' an epithet suggesting a standard of
poetic power and intellect never since challenged." The College and Adult Reading List

Rossetti, Christina
Selected poems of Christina Rossetti; ed.
and with an introduction by Marya Zaturen-
ska. Macmillan (N Y) 1970 152p illus $5.95
821

This collection of poems is divided "into the
following categories: Love Poems; Devotional
Poems; Poems of Nature, Experience, Time
and Eternity; and Children's verse from 'Sing-
Song.'" Publisher's note
"Christina, sister of Pre-Raphaelite Dante
Gabriel Rossetti, is an interesting if minor
figure on the Victorian landscape. . . . Zaturen-
ska has chosen her selections well and does
offer a glowing introduction." Library J
Indexed by titles and first lines

Scott, Sir Walter
The poetical works of Sir Walter Scott;
with the author's introduction and notes; ed.
by L. Logie Robertson. Oxford 981p
front (Oxford Standard authors) $6   821

First published 1904 in this edition
Believed to contain every known poem and
verse, including mottoes and lyrical fragments
of the novels

Shakespeare, William

The sonnets, songs & poems of Shakespeare; ed. with introduction, running commentary, glosses and notes by Oscar James Campbell; illus. with 25 woodcuts. Schocken [1965 c1964] 378p illus $5 **821**

First published 1964 by Bantam Books
Contents: The sonnets: Songs from the plays; Venus and Adonis; The rape of Lucrece; The phoenix and the turtle; The passionate pilgrim; A lover's complaint; Chronology of Shakespeare's life; Bibliography
The editor "places for the reader each one [of the poems in] its original dramatic setting. His comments on them are full of taste." N Y Times Bk R

Shelley, Percy Bysshe

The complete poetical works of Percy Bysshe Shelley **821**

Some editions are:
Dutton (Everyman's lib) 2v ea $3.25 Introduction by A. H. Koszul. Has title: The poetical works
Houghton (Cambridge ed) $8 Edited with notes and an introduction by George Edward Woodberry
Oxford (Oxford Standard authors) $7 Edited by Thomas Hutchinson
"Poetry of sheer beauty with urgent messages to all mankind." Good Reading

Poems of Percy Bysshe Shelley; selected by Leo Gurko; drawings by Lars Bo. Crowell 1968 150p illus (The Crowell Poets) $3.50, lib. bdg. $4.25 **821**

"Mr. Gurko has gathered the best of Shelley's poems into five sections: The Corrupt Present and the Visionary Future; The Dazzling Face of Nature; Love and Friendship; Loss and Lamentation; The Imaginative Ideal." Publisher's note
"The editor has included excerpts from the longer poems as well as the better-known odes and short lyrics. The biographical and critical introduction emphasizes the similarity of Shelley's idealism to that of many of today's youth." Booklist
Includes indexes of titles and first lines

Spender, Stephen

Collected poems, 1928-1953. Random House 1955 204p $6.50 **821**

The poet has collected and arranged all the poems he wishes to preserve. They are gathered from "Poems," "Ruins and visions," "Trial of a judge," "Poems of dedication," "The edge of being" and from occasional magazine contributions
"Some of the poems are excursions into autobiography, others are exercises in introspection. Almost all of them deal with the sufferings of persons caught in the agonies of modern history." Booklist

Tennyson, Alfred Tennyson, 1st Baron

The complete poetical works of Alfred, Lord Tennyson. Cambridge ed. Houghton [1947 c1898] 887p $8 **821**

Title on spine: The poems of Tennyson. This edition originally published with title: The poetic and dramatic works of Alfred, Lord Tennyson. Edited with a biographical sketch and notes by W. J. Rolfe
"Tennyson has made the widest appeal of any English poet of the nineteenth century. His verse is graceful, romantic, elegant, of great pictorial beauty, and imbued with deep religious feeling. Tennyson's poetry perfectly mirrored the spirit of his era in England." Pratt Alcove

Idylls of the King; in twelve books; with a preface, introduction and notes, by J. H. Fowler. St Martins 1966 [c1930] xxvi, 343p (Macmillan's English classics) $2.75 **821**

1 Arthur, King—Poetry
First copyrighted in this edition 1930
The story in verse of King Arthur and the members of his court. "The Arthurian material was reworked in . . . [an] elaborately

allegorical structure . . . . released in parts between 1859 and 1870." The College and Adult Reading List

Thomas, Dylan

A child's Christmas in Wales. Illus. by Fritz Eichenberg. New Directions [1969 c1954] 31p illus $4 **821**

1 Christmas poetry 2 Wales—Poetry
"A New Directions book"
First published 1954
A portrait of Christmas Day in a small Welsh town and of the author's childhood there
For any season of the year "the language is enchanting and the poetry shines with an unearthly radiance." N Y Times Bk R

Collected poems of Dylan Thomas. New Directions 1957 203p front $4.25 **821**

First published 1953
"Among the poems which the poet has written and published, those chosen for this collection are the ones he would most like to preserve." Booklist
"Mr. Thomas is a warlock, as a poet should be, and no matter how he chooses to construct his poems when he takes hold of an old theme —love or joy or the fear of death or the reach for God—it turns magically new and flashes like the phoenix." Atlantic

Wordsworth, William

The complete poetical works of William Wordsworth **821**

Some editions are:
Dutton (Everyman's lib) 3v ea $3.25 Edited with an introduction by Philip Wayne. Has title: Poems
Houghton (Cambridge ed) $8.50 Edited by A. J. George
Oxford (Oxford Standard authors) $5 With introduction and notes, edited by Thomas Hutchinson. New ed. rev. by Ernest De Selincourt. Has title: Poetical works
First published 1904
"One of England's greatest poets, who revealed the extraordinary beauty and significance of simple people and things." Good Reading

Poems of William Wordsworth; selected by Elinor Parker; wood engravings by Diana Bloomfield. Crowell 1964 147p illus $3.50 **821**

"Most of Wordsworth's best lyric and narrative poems and a number of his lesser known pieces celebrating nature and simple rural people are included. . . . The editor's introduction incorporates Wordsworth's own statement of his poetic theories, and comments on individual poems, taken from his journal or that of his sister Dorothy, are interspersed throughout. Pleasing format. . . . Indexes by title and first line." Booklist

Yeats, William Butler

Collected poems. Definitive ed. with the author's final revisions. 2d ed. rev. Macmillan (N Y) 1956 480p front $6.95 **821**

First published 1933
"In this volume . . . one has the opportunity of seeing in its entirety the poetic contribution of a rich and subtle mind. Here are Yeats' lyrics . . . his broodings over the thoughts and beliefs of ancient times; his poems inspired by the changes which have fallen on the world; his dramatic retellings of the beliefs and legends of country folks in Ireland; his musings on age and youth and the passions and moods of men." Publisher's note
The author "has rewritten much of his early poetry. In every case the changes are good. And they are made always to bring his early work into agreement with his mature philosophy. A vague, dreamlike phrase gives place to an exact and sometimes harsh image. Melody is broken by rhythms more nervous and more dramatic. One can learn more about poetry by tracing through these revisions than by reading a dozen essays on the art." Nation

821.03 English poetry— Encyclopedias and dictionaries

Spender, Stephen
(ed.) The concise encyclopedia of English and American poets and poetry; ed. by Stephen Spender and Donald Hall. Hawthorn Bks. 1963 415p illus $16.95 **821.03**

1 English poetry—Dictionaries 2 American poetry—Dictionaries 3 Poets, English—Dictionaries 4 Poets, American—Dictionaries

"Intended to represent the best contemporary critical opinion of about 300 poets, old and new, with 32 general articles on aspects of poetic form and techniques, literary history and the relationship of poetry to other subjects. Treatment ranges from short, unsigned paragraphs for some poets, e.g. Belloc, Benét, Henley, Hillyer, to long signed articles which emphasize the poet's work and quote from it, e.g. Andrew Marvell, Shelley, Hardy, Yeats. The editors have exercised discriminating judgment in the selection of the 78 contributors in an effort to represent both English and American opinion by informed critics and scholars. Photographs or reproductions of portraits for 96 of the poets handsomely illustrate the volume and must be located through the adequate general index, which also includes references to the appended topical bibliography arranged by the name of poet and subjects of articles, e.g. Anglo Saxon poetry." Cur Ref Bks

"Though the stress is on the 'concise,' the editors achieve a wonder of poetic criticism and biography." Library J

Bibliography: p367-92

821.08 English poetry— Collections

Auslander, Joseph
(comp.) The winged horse anthology, by Joseph Auslander and Frank Ernest Hill; with decorations by Paul Honoré. Doubleday 1929 xxxi, 669p $5.95 **821.08**

1 English poetry—Collections 2 American poetry—Collections

Following closely the order of: The winged horse, class 809.1, this book gathers together examples of the best verse of the authors covered in that volume

"Designed for the use of younger readers who have still to climb the slopes of Parnassus and older readers who neglected to climb them during their youth." N Y Her Trib Books

Benét, William Rose
(ed.) An anthology of famous English and American poetry; ed. with introductions, by William Rose Benét and Conrad Aiken. Modern Lib. 1945 xxvi, 951p $4.95, lib. bdg. $3.89 **821.08**

1 English poetry—Collections 2 American poetry—Collections

"Modern Library Giants"
First published 1944

A collection of Anglo-American poetry from Chaucer to Auden in England and from our own Revolutionary time through the Second World War

"Includes 670 poems by 103 poets, the English ones selected by W. R. Benét, and the American by Conrad Aiken." Booklist

Index of poets and Index of first lines

Brinnin, John Malcolm
(ed.) Twentieth century poetry: American and British (1900-1970); an American-British anthology; ed. by John Malcolm Brinnin and Bill Read, and with photographs by Rollie McKenna. McGraw [1971 c1970] xx, 515p illus $8.95 **821.08**

1 English poetry—Collections 2 American poetry—Collections
SBN 07-007909-9

First published 1963 with title: The modern poets: an American-British anthology

"This collection is weighted on the side of pleasure—the pleasure of first encounter, the pleasure of old acquaintance, the pleasure of poems that speak with . . . particularly human resonance." Preface

Nearly one hundred poets are represented, including Conrad Aiken, T. S. Eliot, Robert Frost, David Ignatow, Stephen Spender, and Wallace Stevens

Index of titles and first lines: p505-15

Brooks, Cleanth
(ed.) Understanding poetry; ed. by Cleanth Brooks [and] Robert Penn Warren. 3d ed. Holt 1960 xxiv, 584p $10.95 **821.08**

1 English poetry—Collections 2 American poetry—Collections 3 Poetry—Collections

First published 1938

"The teaching of poetry was revolutionized twenty years ago by the publication of 'Understanding Poetry' by Brooks and Warren. Their thoughtful selection of 200 poems and their provocative analyses provided then, as now, a complete orientation to the nature and methods of poetry." Publisher's note

Glossary: p551-61. Index of authors and titles: p571-84

Ciardi, John
(ed.) How does a poem mean? Houghton 1960 [c1959] p663-1028 boards $4 **821.08**

1 English poetry—Collections 2 American poetry—Collections 3 Poetry—History and criticism

" 'How does a poem mean?' was originally published by Houghton Mifflin Company as one section of a collaborative volume entitled 'Introduction to literature.' . . . The reader will observe that the pagination of the original printing has been retained. In this book, Mr Ciardi discusses the value and nature of poetry, its kinds, structure, and techniques, in a way which will be illuminating for anyone who enjoys poetry or wants to. Basing all his arguments on the specific discussion or particular poems, he also builds the entire book around a generous selection of English and American poems from six centuries." Publisher's note

Coffin, Charles M.
(ed.) The major poets: English and American. Harcourt 1954 xxi, 553p $4.95 **821.08**

1 English poetry—Collections 2 American poetry—Collections

"This book is an 'anthology' of poets rather than of poems. . . . It represents poetry in English from Chaucer to the present with a generous selection from a limited number of our best poets. . . . In assembling the particular titles, I have simply tried to include typical and important poems, representative so far as possible of different phases of a poet's career and of the different conditions of his art." To the reader

Principal text sources: p540-43. Index of authors, titles and first lines

Cole, William
(ed.) A book of love poems; illus. by Lars Bo. Viking 1965 188p illus $3.95, lib. bdg. $3.77 **821.08**

1 Love poetry 2 English poetry—Collections 3 American poetry—Collections

"Ranging in type from conventional lyrics and ballads to popular songs, and in mood from the romantic to the disillusioned and

Cole, William—*Continued*

cynical, the pieces represent both traditional and contemporary poets, mostly British and American. Arranged under section headings indicating different aspects of love and contrasting attitudes toward it the selections emphasize love's endless variety." Booklist

"An imaginative collection with the right quality and tone for teen-agers. Author index. Title index." Wis Lib Bull

(ed.) The fireside book of humorous poetry. . . . Simon & Schuster 1959 522p illus $8.50
821.08

1 English poetry—Collections 2 American poetry—Collections 3 Wit and humor

"With the original illustrations by Tenniel, Bab, Lear, A. B. Frost, Oliver Herford, George Herriman, Nicolas Bentley and others." Title page

Contains more than 450 English and American humorous poems including nonsense verse, fantasy, parody, and zany improvisations. Among the writers represented are Ogden Nash, Don Marquis, Lewis Carroll, Hilaire Belloc, John Updike, Samuel Hoffenstein, Edward Lear, and Oliver Herford

Two indexes of authors, and titles and first lines

Engle, Paul

(ed.) Poet's choice; ed. by Paul Engle and Joseph Langland. Dial Press 1962 303p $7.50
821.08

1 English poetry—Collections 2 American poetry—Collections

An anthology of "103 poems chosen as their own favorites from their own work by 103 poets of today." Christian Century

"Each poet tells the reason for his choice. Brief biographies of the contributors are appended." Book Rev Digest

"The selections do not do justice to the talents of their authors, and they are hardly representative. However, the reasons each poet adduces in making his selection give the reader a notion of what the poet values in his own work and provide useful insight into some problems of genesis and craft." N Y Her Trib Books

Felleman, Hazel

(ed.) Poems that live forever. Doubleday 1965 xxiv, 454p $4.95
821.08

1 English poetry—Collections 2 American poetry—Collections

An anthology of favorite poetry largely by English and American authors

"Arrangement is by subject under such headings as stories and ballads, love, friendship, home and family, patriotism and war, humor, death, faith and inspiration, others." Pub W

Author, title and first line indexes

Nash, Ogden

(ed.) Everybody ought to know. Verses selected and introduced by Ogden Nash; illus. by Rose Shirvanian. Lippincott 1961 186p illus $4.25
821.08

1 English poetry—Collections 2 American poetry—Collections

"The range of authors includes Shakespeare, T. S. Eliot, Don Marquis, e.e. cummings, William McGonagall, John Ciardi and a fellow named Ogden Nash, to name but a few. Mother Goose is also here." Publisher's note

Some of these poets "make strange companions, but their very contrasts add spice to the collection. This is an anthology for the family to enjoy together; individually it is most likely to appeal to the more sophisticated poetry fans of junior high and high school age. Shirvanian's drawings add a subtle touch of humor in keeping with the tone of the poems." Booklist

Indexes of authors, titles, first lines

The **Oxford** Book of ballads; newly selected and ed. by James Kinsley. Oxford 1969 711p music $8.50
821.08

1 Ballads, English 2 Ballads, Scottish

Supersedes The Oxford Book of ballads, comp. by Sir Arthur Quiller-Couch, published 1910

The editor "includes some street ballads and some composed by such literary figures as Blake, Swinburne, and Rosetti. He gives us 150 ballads, more than half of them with their tunes." Library J

Bibliography included in Notes: p695-706. Index of titles: p707-11

The **Oxford** Book of English verse, 1250-1918; chosen and ed. by Sir Arthur Quiller-Couch. New ed. Oxford 1939 xxviii, 1171p $9.50
821.08

1 English poetry—Collections

First published 1900

"A discriminating anthology of poetry in the English language, British and American, ranging from before Chaucer to the end of the nineteenth century." Pratt Alcove

"The table of contents is arranged chronologically, and there are author and first line indexes." Book Rev Digest

The poems "supply the best panorama (from the British point of view) of the development of poetry in the English language." N Y Times Bk R

The **Oxford** Book of light verse, chosen by W. H. Auden. Oxford 1938 xxiv, 553p $6
821.08

1 English poetry—Collections 2 American poetry—Collections

"Three kinds of poetry have been included: (1) Poetry written for performance, to be spoken or sung before an audience; (2) Poetry intended to be read, but having for its subject-matter the everyday social life of its period or the experiences of the poet as an ordinary human being; (3) Such nonsense poetry as, through its properties and technique, has a general appeal." Introduction

Every sort of poetry which Mr. Auden could consider as light has been included. An original and provocative collection." Ontario Lib Rev

Indexes of authors, titles and first lines

The **Oxford** Book of medieval English verse; chosen and ed. by Celia and Kenneth Sisam. Clarendon Press 1970 xxiii, 617p $8.50
821.08

1 English poetry—Collections

"Selections from the works of well-known authors—Chaucer, Gower, Langland, and the 'Gawain' poet—make up the heart of this member of the 'Oxford Books of Verse.' But the volume contains also a multiplicity of other pieces, mostly anonymous. . . . The selection extends from the end of the twelfth century, when post-Conquest English verse begins, to the late fifteenth century, which ushered in the Renaissance." Publisher's note

This volume "is intended for the general reader, and to that purpose the editors have generously glossed difficult words and passages on the same pages as the texts, resorting occasionally to full prose translations of such difficult excerpts as those from Layamon's 'Brut,' the Pearl Poet's poems, and 'The owl and the nightingale.' The selections are mostly lyrics and excerpts from longer narrative poems; a final section of 'snatches' gives a miscellany of curious and often humorous short rhymes infrequently anthologized." Choice

Includes index of first lines

The **Oxford** Book of modern verse, 1892-1935; chosen by W. B. Yeats. Oxford 1936 xlv, 454p $6
821.08

1 English poetry—Collections 2 American poetry—Collections

The **Oxford** Book of modern verse, 1892-
1935—*Continued*

"Includes 378 poems by some 98 poets of
whom 77 are not represented in the 'Oxford
book of English verse.' Has index of authors,
and index of first lines, but no index of
titles." Mudge
"One reads and rereads this collection, quar-
reling here and there with Yeats's judgment,
grateful now and then for included fine selections from little-known minor poets." Nation

The **Oxford** Book of nineteenth-century English verse; chosen by John Hayward. Oxford 1964 xxxv, 969p $10   821.08
1 English poetry—Collections
The material "hitherto divided between 'The
Oxford Book of English verse of the romantic period' (1928) and 'The Oxford Book of
Victorian verse' (1912) is now represented in
a single volume." Publisher's note
In this anthology, "Victorian verse is more
fully represented by the use of longer poems
and by substantial extracts from poems. Some
600 poems and extracts by 85 poets have been
selected in the light of current taste and critical opinion. . . . Arranged chronologically by
birth date of the poet, and with first line and
author indexes." Cur Ref Bks
"Like other Oxford books of verse this will
be useful to students and poetry lovers."
Booklist

The **Oxford** Book of Scottish verse; chosen
by John MacQueen and Tom Scott. Oxford
[1967 c1966] xxix, 633p $9.50   821.08
1 Scottish poetry—Collections
First published 1966 in England
One of the editors purposes "is to lay the
greater empasis on verse written in Scots as
opposed to English. The other is . . . to give
as fair a representation to verse written before 1603 as to that which came afterwards."
Publisher's note
Some features of pronunciation: p x-xii. Indexes of authors and first lines

The **Oxford** Book of seventeenth century
verse, chosen by H. J. C. Grierson and G.
Bullough. Oxford 1934 974p $6   821.08
1 English poetry—Collections
"Professor Grierson and Mr. Bullough give
us . . . more than 600 poems from more than
100 poets; the texts carefully prepared, the
spelling modified from the originals in a manner which, though a little hard to justify in
theory, in practice gives no offence. The selection from the major poets is a full one, and
all the minor poets who deserve a place are
here." Times (London) Lit Sup
Indexed by author and first line

Palgrave, Francis Turner
(comp.) The golden treasury of the best
songs & lyrical poems in the English language;
selected and arranged by Francis Turner Palgrave, with a Fifth book selected by John
Press. 5th ed. Oxford 1964 xxi, 615p $5.75
821.08
1 English poetry—Collections
First published 1961 in England
"The fifth edition of Oxford's publication of
Palgrave contains a 250-page selection of
works by British and Irish poets alive in 1861
and thus excluded from the original publication and by those born after that date." Booklist
"An anthology of English lyrical poetry selected with almost faultless discrimination."
Pratt Alcove
Bibliographical references included in Notes:
p569-83

Reeves, James
(ed.) The Cassell Book of English poetry;
selected and introduced by James Reeves.
Harper 1965 unp $8.95   821.08
1 English poetry—Collections 2 American
poetry—Collections

"In this book you will find a thousand of
the best poems in English [from Chaucer on].
. . . No poet has been included unless he was
born not later than 1900 or, if born in the present century, has already died. . . .This book is
confined, for obvious reasons, to comparatively
short poems. Most of them are what are called
lyrics, apart from certain narrative poems, es-
pecialy ballads." Foreword
Indexes of authors, titles, and first lines

Sitwell, Edith
(ed.) The Atlantic Book of British and
American poetry. Little 1958 xliii, 1092p $15
821.08
1 English poetry—Collections 2 American
poetry—Collections
"An Atlantic Monthly Press book"
Dame Edith's "highly individual selection of
American and British poetry, including some
translations from the classics, which is in general arranged chronologically. Features of the
compilation are a generous representation of
early lyrics and ballads and excerpts from
Shakespearean and other longer poetic works.
Brief prefaces introduce the work of the poets
the compiler most admires." Booklist
"It is especially rich and wondrous in its exploration of the Elizabethans and their predecessors." Library J
Indexes of authors and titles, and first lines

Stevenson, Burton Egbert
(comp.) The home book of modern verse.
. . . Comp. and arranged by Burton Egbert
Stevenson. 2d ed. Holt [1966 c1953] xlix,
1124p $10.95   821.08
1 English poetry—Collections 2 American
poetry—Collections
First published 1925
"An extension of 'The home book of verse';
[entered below] being a selection from American and English poetry of the twentieth century." Title page
The poems in this collection are arranged by
such subjects as: Poems of youth and age,
Poems of love, Poems of nature, Familiar verse
and poems humorous and satiric, Poems of patriotism, history and legend, Poems of sentiment and reflection, Poems of sorrow, death,
and immortality
"One of the most extensive collections, with
coverage from the last part of the 16th century
to the first part of the 20th century. Arranged
by large subjects, with full indexes of authors,
titles. and first lines." Winchell. Guide to Reference Books. 8th edition

(comp.) The home book of verse, American and English; with an appendix containing
a few well-known poems in other languages;
selected and arranged by Burton Egbert
Stevenson. 9th ed. . . . Holt 1953 2v (lxxxiv,
4013p) $30   821.08
1 English poetry—Collections 2 American
poetry—Collections
First published 1912
"Extended in The home book of modern
verse." Title page
Contents: Poems of youth and age; Poems of
love; Poems of nature; Familiar verse, and
poems humorous and satiric; Poems of patriotism. history, and legend; Poems of sentiment and reflection; Poems of sorrow. death,
and immortality
Expensive, but very useful as a reference
book. Contains many modern poems not often
included in anthologies. Very inclusive, with
full indices of authors, first lines and titles

Untermeyer, Louis
(ed.) Men and women: the poetry of love;
illus. by Robert J. Lee. Am. Heritage 1970
224p illus $6.95   821.08
1 Love poetry
SBN 8281-0037-3
"The prevailing theme of this excellent anthology, which ranges from the 'Greek Anthology' and Song of Songs to the works of Anne
Sexton and Judith Viorst, is romance. Lee's

287

Untermeyer, Louis—*Continued*

romantic line drawings accompany these beautiful though occasionally bitter or sarcastic poems. Untermeyer has salted the familiar with the new, and readers will find this a good subject anthology—surely a candidate for Granger. Indexes by titles of poems, poets, and first lines." Library J

(ed.) Modern American poetry [and] Modern British poetry. Combined new and enl. ed. Harcourt 1962 2v in 1 text ed. $10.95

821.08

1 American poetry—Collections 2 English poetry—Collections 3 Poets

A combined edition of: Modern American poetry, class 811.08, and Modern British poetry, entered below, first published in combined edition 1922 with title: Modern American and British poetry. In the 1962 edition biographical and critical material has been brought up to date; some poets and poems have been omitted and others added, in both volumes

Contains about 772 poems by 76 poets in the American volume and about 775 poems by 80 poets in the British volume, all arranged chronologically. In each volume the preface provides a critical introduction and there is an index of authors and titles

(ed.) Modern British poetry. New and enl. ed. Harcourt 1962 xxiii, 541p $7.95   821.08

1 English poetry—Collections 2 Poets, English

First published 1920

Companion volume to: Modern American poetry, listed in class 811.08

Contains more than 775 poems by 80 poets, arranged chronologically from Thomas Hardy to Charles Tomlinson. The preface provides a critical introduction and there is an index of authors and titles. Includes bibliographical index

(ed.) A treasury of great poems: English and American. . . . Rev. and enl. Simon & Schuster 1955 lviii, 1286p $12.50   821.08

1 English poetry—Collections 2 American poetry—Collections

First published 1942

"From the foundations of the English spirit to the outstanding poetry of our own time, with lives of the poets and historical settings selected and integrated." Title page

"The poems in this large anthology are in general the ones usually selected with some personal variations in choice, but the book is distinctive for the interpretive text which accompanies the poems. In this the compiler characterizes the poet, appraises his work, and gives some biographical data." Booklist

Sources of reference: p1240-41. Index: p1242-67. Index of first lines: p1268-86

Van Doren, Mark

Introduction to poetry; commentaries on thirty poems. Hill & Wang [1968 c1966] 136p $3.95   821.08

1 English poetry—Collections 2 English poetry—History and criticism 3 American poetry—Collections 4 American poetry—History and criticism

An abridgment of the title first published 1951 by Sloane

The author "believes that the best way to evaluate poetry in general is to study specific poems. Among the thirty poems evaluated are works by Robert Burns, Emily Dickinson, John Donne, Robert Frost, and William Blake." Bk Buyer's Guide

Williams, Oscar

(ed.) A little treasury of British poetry; the chief poets from 1500 to 1950; ed. with an introduction. Scribner 1951 xxii, 874p illus $7

821.08

1 English poetry—Collections

"The Little treasury series"

A comprehensive collection of more than 700 great English poems, covering four and a half centuries. Arranged chronologically

"It is my hope that this anthology will offer the reader a new perspective by showing the natural culmination of the tradition, that is, 'modern' British poetry, in its organic relationship with the past." Introduction

Contains a section of portraits of poets represented and an index of authors and titles

(ed.) A little treasury of great poetry, English and American, from Chaucer to the present day. Scribner 1947 816p illus $7.50

821.08

1 English poetry—Collections 2 American poetry—Collections

"A companion volume to the . . . [author's] 'A Little Treasury of Modern Poetry' [entered below]. It contains over 500 great English and American poems of seven centuries, selections to suit all tastes. . . . With 64 portraits of the poets." Retail Bookseller

"Includes both long and short narrative and lyric, ballads, songs, and passages from great plays." Huntting

Indexed by author, title and first line

(ed.) A little treasury of modern poetry, English & American. 3d ed. Edited with an introduction. Scribner 1970 liv, 937p illus $4.75   821.08

1 English poetry—Collections 2 American poetry—Collections

"The Little Treasury series"

First published 1946

This collection of poems is organized in four main sections: A little treasury of the chief modern poets of England and America; A little treasury of modern lyrics; A little treasury of poetry in progress; Appendix. Part I lists works by poets from Emily Dickinson to Richard Wilbur in roughly chronological order. Part II is arranged alphabetically by name and includes works by poets who do not have a large body of work but have written individual poems of importance. Part III contains works by the new and younger poets of the forties, fifties and sixties, who are listed in alphabetical order. The appendix contains statements by poets on poetry, a bibliography of modern poetic criticism, and photographs of the poets. There is an index of authors and titles

821.09   English poetry— History and criticism

Cox, C. B.

(ed.) Dylan Thomas; a collection of critical essays. Prentice-Hall 1966 186p $5.95 821.09

1 Thomas, Dylan

"Twentieth century views. A Spectrum book" Analyzed in Essay and general literature index

"Dylan Thomas's early admirers were mesmerized by the music of his rhetoric, while his detractors found in the flash and plunge of his work only incoherence. . . . These essays represent high points in the controversy. Favoring serious evaluations of the poems over biographical anecdotes about the poet, the writers give detailed attention to Thomas's language and technique, analyze the merits of individual works, and provide parallels and perspectives on the body of his poetry." Publisher's note

Selected bibliography: p185-86

Daiches, David

Robert Burns. [Rev. ed] Macmillan (N Y) [1967 c1966] 334p boards $8.95   821.09

1 Burns, Robert

First published 1950 by Rinehart

This is primarily a critical examination of the poetical achievement of Robert Burns, although some biographical material is included to explain his development as a poet. The author discusses Burn's poetry as well as his place in the Scottish literary tradition

Bibliographical references included in Notes: p321-23

Haber, Tom Burns

A. E. Housman. Twayne 1967 223p
('Twayne's English authors ser) boards $4.95
821.09

1 Housman, Alfred Edward

The author examines the interrelationships
between Housman's poetical work and his life,
first as a schoolboy and then as a professor
of Latin. Dr. Haber also discusses the mechanics of Housman's poetic composition. (Publisher)
Selected bibliography: p212-14

Hussey, Maurice

(comp.) Chaucer's world; a pictorial companion; photographs and maps comp. and introduced by Maurice Hussey. Cambridge 1967
172p illus maps $6.50
821.09

1 Chaucer, Geoffrey—Contemporary England
2 Civilization, Medieval—Pictures, illustrations, etc.

"Pictures and interpretive text intended as
background for readers of the 'Canterbury
tales' portray the pilgrims, explain the institutions which they represent and illustrate the
life of the period. . . . Illustrations of architecture, paintings, sculpture, and manuscripts
represent aspects of medieval culture, religion,
and science relevant to Chaucer's writing."
Booklist
Taking it further: p164-67

Kissane, James D.

Alfred Tennyson. Twayne 1970 183p
('Twayne's English authors ser) boards $4.95
821.09

1 Tennyson, Alfred Tennyson, 1st Baron

The author's introduction to Tennyson's work
"is an excellent one. He writes pleasantly, he
blends criticism and biography in an informative way, and his judgments, while cautious,
are invariably sound." Choice

Reiman, Donald H.

Percy Bysshe Shelley. Twayne 1969 188p
('Twayne's English authors ser) boards $4.95
821.09

1 Shelley, Percy Bysshe

"A well-documented study, correlating a biographical account of the life of nineteenth-century English essayist-poet, Percy Bysshe Shelley, with a critical analysis of the structure
and content of his writings. Stating that the
chronological plan clearly reflects Shelley's
growth as an artist, Reiman bases his final
evaluation of Shelley's life and work on the
great extent to which Shelley's mythic formulations such as his concepts of natural phenomena including the west wind, a cloud, and
a skylark, have been diffused into the general
cultural imagination. A chronology precedes
and a partially annotated, selected bibliography is appended." Booklist

Rosenthal, M. L.

The new poets; American and British
poetry since World War II. Oxford 1967
350p $7.95
821.09

1 English poetry—History and criticism
2 American poetry—History and criticism

Analyzed in Essay and general literature index
The author "distinguishes between modern
poetry in general and the poetry since World
War II. He discusses 'confessional' poetry, in
particular Robert Lowell, and poetry of the
'projectivist' movement by studying the work
of selected poets. Contemporary British and
Irish poetry are also considered." Book Rev
Digest
Selective bibliography: individual volumes by
poets discussed: p334-40

Serraillier, Ian

Chaucer and his world. Walck, H.Z. 1968
[c1967] 45p illus lib. bdg. $4.50
821.09

1 Chaucer, Geoffrey—Contemporary England
2 Civilization, Medieval—Pictures, illustrations, etc.

First published 1967 in England

"Using the facts of Chaucer's life as a point
of departure, he states briefly, specifically,
and clearly the social, historical, and cultural
developments of the period. Hints in 'The Canterbury Tales' (frequently quoted) are amplified to suggest the importance of such events
as the Black Death or the Peasants' Revolt,
or to signify the rank or importance of the
characters. There is at least one photograph
on almost every page: Portraits, manuscripts,
architecture, utensils, clothing, weapons illuminate the text and point up the medieval
heritage and milieu of the poet." Horn Bk
Bibliography included in Acknowledgments

Trueblood, Paul G.

Lord Byron. Twayne 1969 177p (Twayne's
English authors ser) boards $4.95   821.09

1 Byron, George Gordon Noël Byron, 6th Baron

"The first biographical-critical study of Lord
Byron intended for the general audience as
well as for teachers and students. Its purpose
is to encourage appreciation of the work of one
of the most attractive and 'modern' of the
Romantic poets." Publisher's note
Includes bibliographical references

Wagenknecht, Edward

The personality of Chaucer. Univ. of Okla.
Press 1968 155p $5   821.09

1 Chaucer, Geoffrey

"Enthusiasm, perception, and scholarship
mark this excursion into the character of
Chaucer by a prolific critic of English and
American literature. . . . The medieval temperament in its earthiness, wisdom, and sweetness as personified and interpreted by Chaucer is vivified by reference to Chaucer's work
and Chaucerian scholarship and is pinpointed
in such topics as Chaucer's appearance, habits,
background, interests, his attitudes on love,
virtue, and religion, and his uses of satire
and sympathy. For both the general reader
and the student a convincing profile." Booklist

Wright, George T.

W. H. Auden. Twayne 1969 180p (Twayne's
United States authors ser) boards $5.50
821.09

1 Auden, Wystan Hugh

"A convincing portrait of Auden as a consistent, serious, and developing poet. The author discusses Auden's quest for a poetry that
avoids vague Romantic symbolism and self-concern, but which nevertheless achieves impressiveness and scope." Publisher's note

822   English drama

Barrie, J. M.

The plays of J. M. Barrie. Scribner 1928
871p front $8.95   822

"Twenty plays which comprise all of Barrie's
dramas that have been published, with the exception of 'Der Tag.'" Cleveland
"No English dramatic writer during the past
generation, except perhaps Pinero, has approached the level of Barrie's instinctive
stagecraft. For there is something about all
his work that seems to be instinctive. He gets
his effect without any sign of effort." New
Statesman & Nation

Besier, Rudolf

The Barretts of Wimpole Street; a comedy
in five acts. Little 1930 165p $4.50   822

1 Browning, Elizabeth (Barrett)—Drama
2 Browning, Robert—Drama

Characters: 13 men, 4 women. One set of
scenery. First produced in England at the
Malvern Festival on August 20, 1930
"The long-famous courtship and elopement
of Elizabeth Barrett and Robert Browning
furnish the theme for this drama. . . . The
author has reproduced the known facts faithfully
and yet has succeeded in creating a play which
is of commanding interest in itself." Pittsburgh

Bolt, Robert
A man for all seasons; a play in two acts.
Random House 1962 xxv, 163p illus
boards $5.50   **822**

1 More, Sir Thomas, Saint—Drama 2 Great Britain—History—Tudors, 1485-1603—Drama
Characters: 11 men, 2 women. One set. First produced in the United States at the ANTA Theatre, New York, on November 22, 1961
Set in sixteenth century England, this is a play about Sir Thomas More, a devout Catholic, and his conflict with Henry VIII
Portrays "a man of sharp wit and deep sensitivity, who wound up going to his death rather than betray his conscience. . . . [The drama] radiates a faith everyone who witnesses (or reads) the play will envy and respect." Best Sellers

Fry, Christopher
The lady's not for burning; a comedy. 2d ed. rev. Oxford 1950 95p $3.95   **822**

1 Witchcraft—Drama
First published 1949
Play in verse. Characters: 8 men, 3 women. Three acts, one set of scenery. First produced in London
"The time of the play is 1400. . . . The hero is a returned soldier who tries to get himself hanged because he has no use for the human race. He confesses to a murder he hasn't committed. The heroine is a pretty creature condemned to be burned as a witch. But she bewitches everybody in the modern sense of the term, including the hero." N Y Her Trib Books

Galsworthy, John
Plays. Scribner 1928 698p $10   **822**
"Nineteen long and six short plays. Galsworthy's complete dramatic works in one volume. Printed closely on double column pages and so not entirely satisfactory as a reading volume, nevertheless useful to have in libraries." Wis Lib Bul
"Obviously some compression in the physical process of book-making has been necessary. The indispensable economy has been affected by using a small though legible type." Springf'd Republican

Goldsmith, Oliver
She stoops to conquer; ed. by Arthur Friedman. Oxford 1968 104p pa $1.25   **822**
First produced on March 15, 1773 at Covent Garden, London
Characters: 6 men, 4 women, extras. Five acts, 3 interiors and 1 exterior
Written in a day when sentimental comedy reigned, this play is a pure farce presenting contemporary characters of the time in a purportedly realistic framework. It is the story of the Hardcastle family's mishaps and adventures in their undertaking to wed a single daughter
"The author's masterpiece. A delightful example of the best type of English society comedy." Pratt Alcove

Marlowe, Christopher
The plays of Christopher Marlowe. Oxford 1939 467p (The World's classics) $2.75 **822**
Contents: Tamburlaine the Great (First and Second parts); The tragical history of Doctor Faustus; The Jew of Malta; Edward the Second; The massacre at Paris; The tragedy of Dido, Queen of Carthage
Each play has a facsimile title page

O'Casey, Sean
Three plays: Juno and the paycock, The shadow of a gunman, The plough and the stars. St Martins 1957 218p pa $1.25   **822**
"St Martins library"
Juno and the paycock is a study of a Dublin tenement family in the struggle between Free Staters and Republicans in 1922. The shadow of a gunman is a tragedy in which a young Irish woman is killed by the Black and Tans during a raid in the Anglo-Irish War of 1920.

The plough and the stars concerns an incident in the Sinn Fein Rebellion, 1916. Irish dialect in all three plays

Rama Rau, Santha
A passage to India; from the novel by E. M. Forster. Harcourt [1961 c1960] 112p $3.95   **822**

1 British in India—Drama 2 India—Drama
First published 1960 in England
Characters: 13 men, 8 women, and others. Three acts, 5 scenes. First produced at the Playhouse, Oxford, on January 19, 1960
A drama about two women who visit India hoping to learn about the country, only to come face-to-face with the misunderstandings dividing Briton and Indian, Moslem and Hindu, and human beings from one another

Shaw, Bernard
Androcles and the lion, Overruled, Pygmalion. Dodd 1916 cxxvii, 224p $5   **822**
First published by Brentano
" 'Androcles and the lion' is at once a hilarious farce and a deeply challenging play on the ideals of Christianity. 'Overruled' is a farce comedy with a dissertation on sex for [the] preface. 'Pygmalion' is the comedy of a cockney flower girl made into a lady by a professor of philology." A L A Catalog 1929
"The prefaces are as long as the plays and deal vigorously and with the usual Shavian exaggeration with the large phases of the subjects of the pays." Wis Lib Bul

Bernard Shaw's plays; Major Barbara, Heartbreak House, Saint Joan, Too true to be good; with backgrounds and criticism; ed. by Warren Sylvester Smith. Norton 1970 494p $8   **822**
SBN 393-04323-1
"A Norton Critical edition"
Four of Shaw's plays are accompanied by commentary and background by "John Gassner, Martin Meisel, Julian B. Kaye, Stanley Weintraub, G. K. Chesterton, Barbara Watson, Sidney P. Albert, Michael J. Mendelsohn, Louis Crompton, Alice Griffin, Katherine Haynes Gatch, and Frederick P. W. McDowell. A special feature is Luigi Pirandello's review of the New York premiere of 'Saint Joan.' " Publisher's note

Complete plays, with prefaces. Dodd 1962 6v illus ea $7.50   **822**
"A definitive edition of all the plays, playlets, and prefaces of George Bernard Shaw, many of which have never been included in selected editions or have never appeared in book form in this country. With a cross-index, dates of first performances in England and America, and photographs of Shaw at various stages in his career." Bk Buyer's Guide

Four plays. Introduction by Louis Kronenberger. Modern Lib. 1953 473p $2.95, lib. bdg. $2.69   **822**
Contents: Candida; Caesar and Cleopatra; Pygmalion; Heartbreak House
Candida is a domestic comedy about a clergyman who is appalled to find his wife idealized by an 18-year-old poet. An old sea captain in Heartbreak House takes a dim view of early 20th century English society, as shown by the lives of his daughters and their guests. Pygmalion is a comedy of manners involving the transformation of a Cockney flower girl into the semblance of a duchess, and Caesar and Cleopatra is about the meeting of the aged Roman conqueror and the youthful Egyptian queen

Pygmalion, and other plays. With sixteen pages of illustrations from the plays and an introduction by Alan S. Downer. Dodd 1967 359p illus (Great illustrated classics) $4.50 822
Contents: Pygmalion; The Devil's disciple; Caesar and Cleopatra

Shaw, Bernard—*Continued*

This "edition contains the complete text of three of Bernard Shaw's most popular plays, including his prefaces and notes. For 'Pygmalion' . . . the additional dialogue Shaw wrote for the film has been added to the text of the stage play. A short background for each play is provided." Publisher's note

Saint Joan, Major Barbara, Androcles and the lion. Modern Lib. 1956 479p $2.95, lib. bdg. $2.69   **822**

Saint Joan depicts the trial, burning at the stake and canonization of Joan of Arc. In Major Barbara a Salvation Army daughter changes her mind about capitalism's role in breeding poverty and converts to the views of her munitions maker father. Androcles and the lion is described above

Seven plays; with prefaces and notes. Dodd 1951 xxvi, 911p $10   **822**

"The text in this volume is that of the Ayot St Lawrence Edition, which is the latest revised edition." Publisher's note
Contents: Mrs Warren's profession; Arms and the man; Candida; The Devil's disciple; Caesar and Cleopatra; Man and superman; Saint Joan

Sheridan, Richard Brinsley

The rivals; ed. by Vincent F. Hopper and Gerald B. Lahey, with a note on the staging [by] George L. Hersey; illus. by Fritz Kredel. Barrons Educ. Ser. [1958] 176p illus (Theatre classics for the modern reader) $3.50   **822**

In this comedy, first presented in 1775, two gentlemen woo Lydia Languish, a young woman with highly romantic ideas concerning love whose fortune will be forfeited if she marries without the consent of her aunt. The aunt, Mrs. Malaprop, has become famous for her eccentric use of the English language
"The play is Sheridan's satire on the pretentiousness and sentimentality of his age." Magill. Masterpieces of World Literature in Digest Form

Stoppard, Tom

Rosencrantz & Guildenstern are dead. Grove 1967 126p $3.95   **822**

1 Shakespeare, William. Hamlet—Parodies, travesties, etc.
Characters: 13 men, 2 women, extras. First produced in this form April 11, 1967 in London
The author "takes a new look at Hamlet through the eyes of Rosencrantz and Guildenstern as the unfortunate pair stumble toward a seemingly arranged destiny. Gradually, Guildenstern comes to the knowledge that they are instruments whose smallest action sets off another. Awakened before dawn by a messenger from Claudius, the pair hurry to the palace where the king asks them to spy on Hamlet. There they meet the strolling players who rehearse before them Hamlet's removal to England by two spies who then are killed. These spies, the player muses, may be 'traitors hoist by their own petard? Or victims of the gods? We shall never know!'" Library J

Thomas, Dylan

Under milk wood; a play for voices. New Directions 1954 107p front music pa $1.35   **822**

1 Wales—Drama
The complete text of the late Welsh poet's prose radio play
"While studded with his special capering marks and turns of style, enjoyable inventions all, it relates in a saucy love of life the carryings on around the clock of some typical characters in a Welsh seacoast village." N Y Times Bk R
It "is delightful and not difficult to understand." Nation
Music for the songs: p100-07

Van Druten, John

I remember mama; a play in two acts; adapted from Kathryn Forbes' book Mama's bank account. Harcourt 1945 177p $3.95 **822**

1 Norwegians in the U.S.—Drama

Characters: 9 men, 13 women. First produced October 19th, 1944 at the Music Box Theatre, New York
The story of a Norwegian-American family living in San Francisco
"Mama's vehicle is still a 'natural'—a Broadway winner that can probably go on playing in little theatres forever, with a fat part for nearly everyone." N Y Times Bk R

Wilde, Oscar

The importance of being Earnest; ed. by Vincent P. Hopper and Gerald B. Lahey; with a note on the staging [by] George L. Hersey; illus. by Fritz Kredel. Barrons Educ. Ser. 1959 148p illus (Theatre classics for the modern reader) $3.50   **822**

Satirical social comedy set in England in the 1890's. The theme is an attack on earnestness, in the Victorian sense. After much confusion a young man discovers who he really is

The plays of Oscar Wilde; introduction by Edgar Saltus. Modern Lib. [1932] 2v in 1 $2.95, lib. bdg. $2.69   **822**

Contents: Salomé; The importance of being Earnest; Lady Windermere's fan; An ideal husband; A woman of no importance

Yeats, W. B.

Collected plays of W. B. Yeats. New ed. with five additional plays. Macmillan (N Y) 1953 446p front $6.95   **822**

First published 1934
Twenty-six plays designated for hearers and readers. "Some of the plays are developed in greater detail while others are . . . written in lilting verse as opposed to earlier prose forms." Cincinnati
"The reader finds in these plays . . . such magnificence of poetry, such suggestiveness of symbolism that they are an enduring delight." N Y Her Trib Books

822.08 English drama—Collections

Cerf, Bennett A.

(comp.) Sixteen famous British plays; comp. by Bennett A. Cerf and Van H. Cartmell; with an introduction by John Mason Brown. Modern Lib. 1943 [c1942] xx, 1000p $4.95, lib. bdg. $3.89   **822.08**

1 English drama—Collections
"Modern Library Giants"
First published 1942 by Garden City Books
"These plays were all, save 'Cavalcade,' 'popular' successes on both sides of the Atlantic: representative of the theater as people remember it, from Pinero to Emlyn Williams." Library J

822.09 English drama—History and criticism

Boyle, Ted E.

Brendan Behan. Twayne 1969 150p (Twayne's English authors ser) boards $4.95   **822.09**

1 Behan, Brendan
"A critical assessment of Behan's personal and literary career delineates the influences that shaped Behan's character and talent and places his idiosyncrasies in perspective to show that despite the acknowledged vagaries of his personality, his plays, autobiography, and other writings are the efforts of a recognized master. Each of his major works is studied in a separate chapter; a chronology from 1923 to 1965 precedes the text, and an annotated bibliography is appended." Booklist

Hinchliffe, Arnold P.
Harold Pinter. Twayne 1967 190p
(Twayne's English authors ser) $4.95 822.09
1 Pinter, Harold
"This book traces the assimilation of the
Absurb Drama into the British way of life
in the hands of Harold Pinter, and it shows
Pinter's development toward a kind of tragi-
comedy that is purely his own." Publisher's
note
Selected bibliography: p181-86

Kaufmann, R. J.
(ed.) G. B. Shaw; a collection of critical
essays. Prentice-Hall 1965 182p $5.95 822.09
1 Shaw, George Bernard
"Twentieth century views. A Spectrum book"
Analyzed in Essay and general literature index
"These essays, all of which have appeared
since World War II, utilize contemporary critical techniques to arrive at the heart of Shaw's
immense range of interests and his relationship to modern political and religious thought.
. . . The essays [also] point up his singular
achievements in serio-comic theater." Publisher's note
Selected bibliography: p182

Knoll, Robert E.
Christopher Marlowe. Twayne 1969 160p
(Twayne's English authors ser) $4.95 822.09
1 Marlowe, Christopher
This introduction to the playwright's work
outlines his life and briefly discusses his minor
works but gives primary attention to his plays:
Tamburlaine the Great, Doctor Faustus, The
Jew of Malta, Edward II, The massacre at
Paris
Includes bibliography

Levin, Milton
Noel Coward. Twayne 1968 158p (Twayne's
English authors ser) $4.95   822.09
1 Coward, Noël Pierce
"The first critical study to attempt a comprehensive overview of Coward's writing, along
with detailed analyses of individual titles. A
biographical sketch and a brief description of
the theater during the first decades of this
century provide an introduction." Book News
Bibliography: p149-53

Nicoll, Allardyce
British drama. 5th ed. rev. and reset.
Barnes & Noble [1963 c1962] 365p illus $5
822.09
1 English drama—History and criticism 2 Theater—Great Britain
First published 1925
"A general—and thoroughly enjoyable—survey of drama in Great Britain. For the layman
and student." Cincinnati

A history of English drama, 1660-1900.
Cambridge 1952-1959 6v ea $14.50 822.09
1 English drama—History and criticism
2 Theater—Great Britain
Contents: v 1 Restoration drama, 1660-1700.
4th ed. v2 Early eighteenth century drama. 3d
ed. v3 Late eighteenth century drama, 1750-
1800. 2d ed. v4 Early nineteenth century drama,
1800-1840. 2d ed. v5 Late nineteenth century
drama, 1850-1900. 2d ed. v6 A short-title alphabetical catalogue of plays produced or printed
in England from 1660 to 1900
Includes bibliographies and bibliographical
footnotes

822.3   William Shakespeare

Listed here are works by and about Shakespeare, with the exception of his sonnets. The
latter are entered in Class 821

Bentley, Gerald E.
Shakespeare and his theatre. Univ. of Neb.
Press 1964 128p pa $1.95   822.3
1 Shakespeare, William—Stage history
2 Theater—London—History

"A noted scholar's compact and crystalline
essays on Shakespeare's acting company, the
Globe and Blackfriars theaters, changes in
theater audiences in the generation following
Shakespeare's death, and corollary matters. As
Bentley himself notes he deliberately uses
familiar examples, minimal documentation, and
an unpedantic style in selections originally
given as lectures in England and the U.S."
Booklist

Brown, Ivor
Shakespeare and his world. Walck, H.Z.
1964 46p illus map $4.50   822.3
1 Shakespeare, William—Contemporary England 2 Great Britain—Social life and customs
3 Great Britain—History—Tudors, 1485-1603
A view of Shakespeare set against the background of the Elizabethan Age showing "him
in his proper setting—the town in which he
was born, the school he attended, the types
of houses in which he stayed, the books he
used, the London to which he came, his
friends and the figures of the day, the entertainments of the people and the climate
and events affecting their lives." Publisher's
note
Many excellent photographs . . . amplify the
text. For the reader of any age lacking background in the life of the Elizabethan period."
Horn Bk

Shakespeare in his time. Nelson 1960 238p
illus maps $6   822.3
1 Shakespeare, William—Contemporary England 2 Great Britain—Social life and customs
3 Great Britain—History—Tudors, 1485-1603
The author "presents a readable introduction
to the playwright, his work, and his times.
Homely details about dress, food, city life,
and other aspects of the Elizabethan scene are
given along with material on actors and play
production and comments on references in
some of the Shakespearean plays." Booklist
"A valuable addition, especially to the high
school library, of books on Shakespeare [and
the period]. . . . Index and illustrations all
aid in the use of this informative and interesting book." Library J

The women in Shakespeare's life. Coward-
McCann [1969 c1968] 224p $5.95   822.3
1 Shakespeare, William—Biography
First published 1968 in England
The author portrays Shakespeare's "mother,
his wife, his daughters, and the flittering ladies
of London's theatrical set, women of great
learning and high fashion. . . . It was in London's theatrical world that Shakespeare came
into his own . . . and it was there he met
Mary Fitton, Elizabeth's bold and captivating
young maid of honor, who was destined for
twelve years to be the most important of the
women in his life." Publisher's note
Ivor Brown "knows that any study of the
actual life of Shakespeare must lean on guess-
work. Perhaps that's why he is so engagingly
good-humored about his speculations." Pub W
Principal books consulted: p216-17

Chapman, Gerald W.
(ed.) Essays on Shakespeare [by] Robert
B. Heilman [and others]. Princeton Univ.
Press 1965 176p $5   822.3
1 Shakespeare, William—Criticism, interpretation, etc.
Analyzed in Essay and general literature in-
dex
"The essays in this volume were first pre-
sented as lectures at the University of Denver
during the spring of 1964." Preface
Contents: The role we give Shakespeare, by
R. B. Heilman; Nature and nothing, by N. Frye;
Shakespeare's nomenclature, by H. Levin;
"With that facility": false starts and revisions
in "Love's labour's lost", by J. V. Cunning-
ham; Judgment in "Hamlet" by G. Boklund;
"We came crying hither": an essay on some
characteristics of "King Lear" by M. Mack
Bibliographical footnotes

Chute, Marchette

An introduction to Shakespeare. Dutton 1951 123p front $3.50 **822.3**

1 Shakespeare, William –Criticism, interpretation, etc. 2 Shakespeare, William—Stage history

"This slender volume emphasizes Shakespeare's plays and the theater rather than the man and the social life of the period. Miss Chute analyzes the plays individually, source, plot development, and themes; how they were produced [acted, and costumed]: what the theater meant to London of that time, and Shakespeare's influence." Horn Bk

"For young people first meeting Shakespeare, the book is a sound and revealing guide." N Y Times Bk R

Shakespeare of London. Dutton 1949 397p front $7.95 **822.3**

1 Shakespeare, William—Biography 2 Dramatists, English

"Retelling of Shakespeare's life, reconstructed from documentary evidence and a sound knowledge of Shakespeare's England . . . . The author's Shakespeare is a young man of talent, who made good at a congenial occupation at a time when the political and cultural atmosphere was conducive to the development of literary, and dramatic talent." Booklist

"The author, who is noted for her careful scholarship, is also noted for her ability to write entertainingly. Her Shakespeare is not a dead immortal but a very human personality. A valuable addition to the high school collection." Minnesota

Selected bibliography: p363-72. Map on lining-papers

Stories from Shakespeare. World Pub. 1956 351p illus $5.95, lib. bdg. $5.90 **822.3**

1 Shakespeare, William—Adaptations

A retelling of the plays, comedies, tragedies, and histories included in Shakespeare's "First folio." "Its purpose is to give the reader a preliminary idea of each of the thirty-six plays by telling the stories and explaining in a general way the intentions and points of view of the characters." Introduction

"These resumés . . . with a few explanatory paragraphs about the intent or background of each play, keep more to the dramatic form than do Lamb's 'Tales' and are for older young people. Less space is given to each play; plot outlines are very clear and the characters genuinely Shakespeare's. Full index of names." Library J

The worlds of Shakespeare, by Marchette Chute and Ernestine Perrie; drawings by Frederick Franck. Dutton 1963 128p illus boards $3.95 **822.3**

1 Shakespeare, William—Adaptations

"A distillation of all Shakespeare drama in the form of a two-act play constructed out of selections from 12 of the plays. The first act presents six love scenes and the second, the world of music. The play is adapted for two actors. The authors have . . . made slight alterations in spelling and punctuation." Library J

"The introductions are brief, and graceful. The excerpts are largely from the more familiar plays, and the book will be of interest chiefly as an introduction for high school students and general readers not well acquainted with Shakespeare." Pub W

Deutsch, Babette

The reader's Shakespeare; with decorations by Warren Chappell. Messner 1946 510p illus $5 **822.3**

1 Shakespeare, William—Adaptations

"A reworking of fifteen of Shakespeare's plays, relating them in straight narrative form." Book Rev Digest

"Miss Deutsch has deftly introduced a minimum of interpretation and explanation. Occasionally she supplies background information that helps to clarify the motives of the characters or the social forces implicit in the action." N Y Her Trib Books

Reading list: p509-10

Frye, Roland Mushat

Shakespeare's life and times; a pictorial record. Princeton Univ. Press 1967 unp illus map $10 **822.3**

1 Shakespeare, William—Biography 2 Shakespeare, William—Contemporary England

A biography which provides a "view of Shakespeare as he lived his life, faced his problems, reared his family, made friends and enemies, invested his money, acted, and wrote. Narratives and pictures follow Shakespeare from his birth and boyhood through the last years of his life." McClurg. Book News

"A book for illustrating Shakespeare's life, not for studying it. There is only an approximate chronology to the illustrations, and the majority of them deal more or less with Shakespeare's environment and his contemporaries, not with his life. Nevertheless, the book is unique in the quality and variety of the predominately Elizabethan illustrations which it brings together under one cover." Choice

Bibliographical note

Halliday, F. E.

Shakespeare; a pictorial biography. Viking 1964 147p illus maps $6.95 **822.3**

1 Shakespeare, William—Biography 2 Dramatists, English

"A Studio book"

First published 1956 in England

This book "remains one of the more successful pictorial biographies extant, and the illustrations of Elizabethan personalities, maps of London, and pages from the early folios tend to round out the playwright's life in lieu of the many unknown facts. . . . Halliday knows all there is to know and he presents his knowledge engagingly." Library J

Shakespeare in his age. Yoseloff [1964 c1956] 362p illus map $6 **822.3**

1 Shakespeare, William—Contemporary England 2 English drama—History and criticism 3 Great Britain—History—Tudors, 1485-1603

First published 1956 in England

"An exploration of the English setting in which Shakespeare lived and worked. . . . Major events as well as the political, religious, and cultural heritage and climate of the day are noted for their influence through the years on art, music, literature, and particularly drama, dramatists, and theater companies of the realm, with significant personalities introduced throughout." Booklist

"This book is an inexhaustible mine of fascinating detail, though it is the age rather than the poet which is in the foreground." N Y Times Bk R

Harbage, Alfred

(ed.) Shakespeare: the tragedies; a collection of critical essays. Prentice-Hall 1964 181p $5.95 **822.3**

1 Shakespeare, William—Tragedies

"Twentieth century views. A Spectrum book"

Analyzed in Essay and general literature index

A companion volume to Shakespeare: the comedies; ed. by Kenneth Muir, entered below

Contents: Humanism and mystery, by H. B. Charlton; The tragic qualm, by W. Franham; Construction in Titus Andronicus, by H. T. Price; The school of love: Romeo and Juliet, by D. A. Stauffer; "Or else were this a savage spectacle" (ritual in Julius Caesar) by B. Stirling; The world of Hamlet, by M. Mack; The historical approach: Hamlet, by H. Gardner; Death in Hamlet, by C. S. Lewis; Othello: an introduction, by A. Kernan; Iago revisited, by B. Spivak; Macbeth, by L. C. Knights; Macbeth as the imitation of an actor, by F. Ferguson; King Lear: an introduction, by A. Harbage; King Lear and the comedy of the grotesque, by G. W. Knight; Character and society in King Lear, by A. Sewell; Timon of Athens, by M. Van Doren; Antony and Cleopatra, by S. L. Bethell; Coriolanus: an introduction, by H. Levin

Harbage, Alfred—*Continued*
"Provocative for student or reader seeking analytical understanding of Shakespearean tragedy. Suggestions for further reading occur in text and footnote references and bibliography." Booklist

Hodges, C. Walter
Shakespeare & the players; written and illus. by C. Walter Hodges. 2d ed. Coward-McCann 1970 110p illus map $2.80   822.3

1 Shakespeare, William—Stage history
2 Southwark, England. Globe Theatre
3 Theater—Great Britain—History

First published 1948 in England
"From the shows of the strolling players, Mr Hodges traces the growth of the theater in Elizabethan times, illustrating how the famous London playhouses may have looked when a play was put on. He . . . outlines Shakespeare's connection with the plays themselves, imagining a day at the Globe when Richard III was given. Brief sketches of Ben Jonson and other well-known playwrights are included and there is a short chapter on Stage Music." Horn Bk
"Provocatve text and illustrations recreate the playhouse of Shakespeare's time and serve as an invitation to reading his plays." N Y Pub Lib

Horizon Magazine
Shakespeare's England, by the editors of Horizon Magazine, in consultation with Louis B. Wright; illus. with paintings, drawings, and engravings of the period. Am. Heritage 1964 153p illus maps boards $5.95, lib. bdg. $5.49   822.3

1 Shakespeare, William—Contemporary England   2 Theater—Great Britain—History
3 Great Britain—History—Tudors, 1485-1603

"A Horizon Caravel book"
"The purpose of this book is not to challenge the debatable points of Shakespeare's biography or to probe his literary reputation. It is, rather, to present the playwright as a man of his day against the colorful tapestry of his England; the kingdom under Elizabeth I and James I." Foreword
"A book that should enthrall the student of English history as much as it does the reader interested in theatre. The illustrations [many from European sources] are handsome, varied, and carefully placed and captioned. The text . . . gives, especially, interesting material about touring companies, patronage, literary criticism, and the intrigue and competition in the world of Elizabethan actors and playwrights. . . . Photographs of the several memorial theatres are included. A bibliography, an index and a list of plays—arranged by original performance date—are appended." Chicago. Children's Book Center

Muir, Kenneth
(ed.) A new companion to Shakespeare studies; ed. by Kenneth Muir and S. Schoenbaum. Cambridge 1971 297p illus $12.50 822.3

1 Shakespeare, William—Criticism, interpretation, etc.
ISBN 0-521-07941-1

Analyzed in Essay and general literature index
Supersedes the title first published 1934 under the editorship of Harley Granville-Barker with title: A companion to Shakespeare studies
These "well written essays, covering all important aspects of Shakespeare's life and works, are so well indexed and so well appended with notes and reading lists, and a chronology, that . . . [the collection] will have considerable value . . . as an authoritative introduction to the whole field of Shakespeare studies." Cur Ref Bks

(ed.) Shakespeare: the comedies; a collection of critical essays. Prentice-Hall 1965 183p $5.95   822.3

1 Shakespeare, William—Comedies
"Twentieth century views. A Spectrum book"
Analyzed in Essay and general literature index
"This book is a companion to 'Shakespeare: The Tragedies' [ed. by Alfred Harbage, entered above] . . . recommended earlier for both adult and young adult reading. . . . [It] 'attempts to give a cross-section of twentieth century criticism of the comedies.' Twelve essays of different kinds on all the major plays by such authorities as Helen Gardner, G. Wilson Knight and J. Middleton Murry have been included. . . . The bibliography lists the books and articles from which the final choice was made. For varying reasons there is nothing on the imagery, the relationship between Shakespeare's comedies and those of his contemporaries, nor Shakespearian Comedy in general, but those libraries which have the first volume should have the second, and any student of the Bard will find this of considerable interest." Library J

Onions, C. T.
A Shakespeare glossary. 2d ed. rev. Oxford 1919 259p $5   822.3

1 Shakespeare, William—Dictionaries
First published 1911 in England
"An excellent small dictionary. . . . The aim of the glossary is to supply (1) definitions or illustrations of words or senses now obsolete or surviving only in archaic or provincial use. (2) explanations of other words involving allusions not generally familiar. (3) explanations of proper names carrying with them some connotative significance, etc. . . . Includes also obsolete and technical terms which occur only in the stage directions." Winchell. Guide to Reference Books. 8th edition

The **Reader's** encyclopedia of Shakespeare; ed. by Oscar James Campbell. Associate editor: Edward G. Quinn. Crowell 1966 1014p illus (A Crowell Reference bk) $15   822.3

1 Shakespeare, William—Dictionaries
This work "has bee compiled in the hope of offering in a single volume all the essential information available about every feature of Shakespeare's life and works. . . . [It] contains an entry for nearly every individual with whom Shakespeare is known or suspected to have established a relationship, for the playwrights thought to have influenced him or been influenced by him, for every significant character in the plays, for important actors remembered for performances in principal roles of the plays, for celebrated critics or editors of his works. Many essays [were] written for the volume by . . . scholars on the subjects of their particular competence." Preface
For "fact-and-quotation hunters, this volume is a godsend. . . . Familiar entries may trouble one." N Y Times Bk R
Bibliography: p983-1014

Rowse, A. L.
William Shakespeare; a biography. Harper 1963 484p illus map $8.95   822.3

1 Shakespeare, William—Biography 2 Shakespeare, William—Criticism, interpretation, etc.

"An authority on Elizabethan England undertakes to apply a historian's method of research to illuminate Shakespeare's life and work. Documentary evidence and Shakespeare's writings are cited extensively, and Rowse comments freely from his wide knowledge of the period on social and political matters. Rowse contends that his research gives positive evidence that Shakespeare's sonnets were written for Southampton." Booklist
"Its readable style, meticulous documentation, and good indexing commend it to high school collections." Library J
"Despite its excellence, this is not a book for the beginners." Best Sellers
Bibliographical references included in Notes: p467-78

Shakespeare, William

The complete works of William Shakespeare **822.3**

Some editions are:
Crowell (Player ed) $15 Edited by George Lyman Kittredge
Doubleday $8.95 Illustrated by Rockwell Kent. Preface by Christopher Morley
Harcourt $12.95 General editor: Sylvan Barnet; contributing editors: John Arthos [and others]. Has title: The complete Signet classic Shakespeare
Harper $10 Including a biographical and general introduction, glossary and index of characters. Edited by Charles Jasper Sisson
Houghton (Cambridge ed) $15 Edited with an introduction and notes by William Allan Neilson and Charles Jarvis Hill. Has title: The complete plays and poems of William Shakespeare
Oxford (Shakespeare Head Press ed) $6.50
Oxford (Oxford Standard authors) Prices vary according to paper and binding. Edited with a glossary by W. J. Craig. Known as the Oxford Shakespeare
Oxford (Oxford Standard authors) 3v ea $7 Prepared by W. J. Craig, with a general introduction by Charles Algernon Swinburne. Introductory studies to each play by Edward Dowden
Oxford $11.50 With 32 full page plates from modern stage productions
Random House $7.95 Edited by Peter Alexander
Tudor $6.95 Edited by A. H. Bullen
World Pub. $8.95 With the Temple notes; containing all the plays and poems of William Shakespeare, the history of his life, his will, an introduction to each play, and an index to characters. Original designs by T. M. Matterson; engravings by Alexander Anderson
For an exhaustive comparison of the editions of Shakespeare see: The Reader's adviser

Everyman's Dictionary of Shakespeare quotations; comp. by D. C. Browning. Dutton 1953 560p $6 **822.3**

1 Shakespeare, William—Quotations
"Everyman's Reference library"
"An indispensable reference guide to the greatest passages in Shakespear.' Arranged by act and scene from each play; and in order of composition from the sonnets and poems. Fully and conveniently indexed." Sec Ed Brd

Shakespeare's songs; ed. by Alfred [Harbage: illus. with the original musical settings. Macrae Smith Co. 1970 96p $5.95 **822.3**

1 Shakespeare, William—Songs and music
SBN 8255-4110-7
"Lyric, comic, and drinking songs from Shakespeare's plays are accompanied by the original scores where they are extant. A foreword, a listing by first lines, notes, appended modern scores, and an index by first line and source enhance the usefulness of the attractively produced collection." Booklist

Shakespeare's England; an account of the life and manners of his age; ed. by Sir Walter Raleigh, Sir Sidney Lee, and C. T. Onions. Oxford 1916 2v illus $16.80 **822.3**

1 Shakespeare, William—Contemporary England 2 Great Britain—Social life and customs 3 Great Britain—History—Tudors, 1485-1603
"A veritable cyclopedia of the life and manners of Shakespeare's age, comprising thirty scholarly essays on as many topics, each written by one or more noted authorities, and nearly two hundred illustrations taken largely from contemporary prints and paintings." Booklist
"A book not to read, but to consult." Times (London) Lit Sup
Includes a bibliography at end of each chapter; indexes of passages cited from Shakespeare's works, proper names, subjects and technical terms

Webster, Margaret

Shakespeare without tears; introduction by John Mason Brown. [Rev. ed] World Pub. 1955 318p $6.95 **822.3**

1 Shakespeare, William—Criticism, interpretation, etc. 2 Shakespeare, William—Technique

First published 1942 by Whittlesey House
Discusses Shakespeare, the Elizabethan theater, general problems of Shakespearean acting and production from the Elizabethan age to the present, and then analyzes in detail each of the plays
"Miss Webster's book has just the combination of traditional wisdom and scholarship and practical theatre sense that her direction has consistently exhibited." Theatre Arts

823.09 English fiction—History and criticism

Craik, W. A.

Jane Austen in her time. Nelson 1969 192p illus map boards $7.50 **823.09**

1 Austen, Jane 2 Austen, Jane—Contemporary England 3 England—Social life and customs
"Background information on life in the England of Jane Austen's novels which, the author suggests, is not essential to an understanding of the Austen works but is likely to increase the reader's appreciation and enjoyment of them. Using as her sources contemporary writing, letters, and the novels themselves, Craik describes the English middle class of the late eighteenth and early nineteenth century, particularly the landed gentry, in terms of its basic patterns, codes of manners and morals, economy, and attitudes toward religion, marriage, money, education, and the arts. Short synopses of the six novels and a brief biography of Miss Austen are appended." Booklist

Creeger, George R.

(ed.) George Eliot; a collection of critical essays. Prentice-Hall 1970 182p $5.95 **823.09**

1 Eliot, George
"Twentieth century views. A Spectrum book"
Contents: George Eliot's religion of humanity, by B. J. Paris; The authority of the past in George Eliot's novels, by T. Pinney; The moment of disenchantment in George Eliot's novels, by B. Hardy; George Eliot's conception of "form," by D. Mansell; George Eliot, Feuerbach, and the question of criticism, by U. C. Knoepflmacher; An interpretation of Adam Bede, by G. R. Creeger; Intelligence as deception: The mill on the floss, by G. Levine; Felix Holt: society as protagonist, by D. R. Carroll; George Eliot in Middlemarch, by Q. Anderson; Daniel Deronda: A conversation, by H. James; Selected bibliography

Daiches, David

The novel and the modern world. Rev. ed. Univ. of Chicago Press 1960 220p illus $5.95 **823.09**

1 English fiction—History and criticism
Analyzed in Essay and general literature index
First published 1939
"Combining intellectual history and critical analysis, the author illuminates the attitudes and techniques of these great experimenters who changed the course of the novel during the first thirty years of this century. . . . He shows us that four writers above all—Conrad, Joyce, Lawrence, and Woolf—fully responded, though in very different ways, to the intellectual and psychological climate of their age, and demonstrates how, in so doing, they radically extended the possibilities of fiction." Publisher's note

Daly, Saralyn R.

Katherine Mansfield. Twayne 1965 143p (Twayne's English authors ser) $4.95 **823.09**

1 Mansfield, Katherine
"A critical study of the fiction of Katherine Mansfield in terms of her short stories, considering her other writings only as they cast light on her fiction. After brief view of Mansfield's literary career and the personal experiences and other influences that shaped her work, Daly analyzes in detail many of her stories, treating them chronologically to follow her developing techniques, examines characteristic themes, and evaluates her influence on modern fiction." Booklist
Bibliography: p133-38

Drew, Elizabeth

The novel; a modern guide to fifteen English masterpieces. Norton [1964 c1963] 287p $4.50   823.09

1 English fiction—History and criticism

Analyzed in Essay and general literature index

Discussions of Defoe's Moll Flanders; Richardson's Clarissa; Fielding's Tom Jones; Sterne's Tristram Shandy; Jane Austen's Emma; Thackeray's Vanity fair; Eliot's The mill on the Floss; Hardy's Far from the madding crowd; Conrad's Lord Jim; Emily Brontë's Wuthering Heights; Dickens' Great expectations; D. H. Lawrence's Women in love; Henry James's The portrait of a lady; James Joyce's A portrait of the artist as a young man and Virginia Woolf's To the lighthouse

"Coming to her texts with an open intelligence [Miss Drew] allows the individual work to make its impressions upon her. She is sensible rather than clever, helpful rather than dazzling. Yet steadily, quietly she informs and illuminates." Christian Science Monitor

Suggestions for further reading: p285-87

Gregor, Ian

(ed.) The Brontës; a collection of critical essays. Prentice-Hall 1970 179p $5.95   823.09

1 Brontë, Charlotte 2 Brontë, Emily Jane
SBN 13-083899-3

"A Spectrum book"

Ten essays examine the influences, structure, imagery and writing styles of Charlotte and Emily Brontë. Wuthering Heights and Jane Eyre are among the works discussed

Selected bibliography: p177-79

Hewish, John

Emily Brontë: a critical and biographical study. St Martins 1969 204p boards $8.50
                                      823.09

1 Brontë, Emily Jane

The author "is concerned in the biographical portion of his study with patterns of contradiction in the evidence, resulting from 'afterthoughts by various witnesses' and particularly from [her sister] Charlotte's distortions. In the critical portion he attempts to show that Emily Brontë, far from being a primitive, did have models and sources for 'Wuthering Heights,' though not such as would place it in a genre. His analysis is thoughtful, modest, essayistic, inconclusive, and rather engaging." Library J

Bibliography: p177-89

Karl, Frederick R.

An age of fiction: the nineteenth century British novel. Farrar, Straus 1964 374p $7.50
                                      823.09

1 English fiction—History and criticism

Analyzed in Essay and general literature index

Contents: An age of fiction; Jane Austen: the necessity of wit; Sir Walter Scott: the moral dilemma; The Brontës: the outsider as protagonist; Charles Dickens: the Victorian Quixote; Thackeray's Vanity fair: all the world's a stage; George Meredith: an English ordeal; George Eliot: the sacred nature of duty; Thomas Hardy's "Mayor" and the changing novel; Five Victorian novelists; Bibliography: works and selected criticism and scholarship; Character Index

Sprague, Claire

(ed.) Virginia Woolf; a collection of critical essays. Prentice-Hall 1971 185p $5.95
                                      823.09

1 Woolf, Virginia (Stephen)
SBN 13-962837-1

"A Spectrum book"

"Did feminism really detract from her work? Was Virginia Woolf actually a poet writing in novel form? Did her mental illness affect her writing? How much of her technique was her own and how much did she borrow from Joyce and Proust? . . . These and other questions [are discussed] in an effort to interpret the work of this controversial and original author." Publisher's note

"An intelligent and representative gathering of extracts (and some complete articles and chapters) from the better and best critical studies of Virginia Woolf, from Auerbach and Brower through Edel and Guiguet to Schaefer and Wilkinson. Prefaced with a competent introduction useful to serious beginning students." Choice

Bibliography: p183-85

Vogler, Thomas A.

(ed.) Twentieth century interpretations of Wuthering Heights; a collection of critical essays. Prentice-Hall 1968 $4.95   823.09

1 Brontë, Emily Jane. Wuthering Heights

"Twentieth century interpretations. A Spectrum book"

"Evaluations of Emily Brontë's novel by distinguished critics, most of whom are associated with universities in the U.S. or Great Britain. The essays, of varying length, express diverse but not conflicting opinions and all recognize the brilliance and psychological depth of the novel. Among the contributors are Mark Schorer, Albert J. Guérard, Virginia Woolf, V. S. Pritchett, and David Daiches." Booklist

Selected bibliography: p121-22

Wagenknecht, Edward

Cavalcade of the English novel; 1954 ed. with supplementary bibliography. Holt 1954 686p illus $11.95   823.09

1 English fiction—History and criticism

First published 1943

Includes the following novelists: Defoe, Richardson, Fielding, Smollett, Sterne, Austen, Scott, Dickens, Thackeray, Trollope, the Brontë family, Eliot, Meredith, Hardy, Stevenson, Conrad, Bennett, Wells, Galsworthy, Lawrence, De La Mare

"For students the book will provide an excellent summary and critical appraisal of the development of English fiction from the 16th century well into the 20th. In a library it will have many reference uses, one of them to supply information about the lesser novelists, nearly 100 of whom are treated briefly in an appendix, followed by an extensive bibliography for the major writers." Wis Lib Bul

Selected bibliography with annotations: p577-619. Supplementary bibliography: p620-60

Wilson, Angus

The world of Charles Dickens. Viking 1970 301p illus boards $14.95   823.09

1 Dickens, Charles

"A Studio book"

The author "traces Dickens's career from his birth in a small, lower-middle-class terrace house in Portsmouth to his death, an internationally recognized and revered figure. He quotes extensively from Dickens's letters and writings, he shows Dickens's life, experience, and obsessions were transmuted into the great art of his novels." Publisher's note

"A wonderfully stimulating guide to the exploration of Dickens's imaginative system. However familiar he may be with recent Dickens criticism, the reader will find something fresh, revealing and provocative in every chapter. . . . The numerous pictures . . . have been most skillfully chosen not merely to supplement the text but to illuminate it. . . . They combine to recreate vividly the atmosphere of Victorian England." Book World

824   English essays

Carlyle, Thomas

On heroes, hero-worship and the heroic in history. Oxford 1928 245p $1.75   824

1 Heroes

"The World's classics"

First published 1841; in this edition 1904

By means of sketches on Mahomet, Dante, Shakespeare, Luther, Samuel Johnson, Cromwell, Napoleon and others, Carlyle aims to prove the importance of the great man in history and to show that the essential heroic qualities have been the same in all great men

Lamb, Charles

The essays of Elia and The last essays of Elia; ed. by Ernest Rhys with an introduction by Augustine Birrell. Dutton 1932 327p $2.95   **824**

Another edition analyzed in Essay and general literature index
"Everyman's library"
First published in this edition 1906
"Written for the most part on trivial subjects, with no purpose but to please, they bring us close to the lovable nature of the man, full, indeed, of sadness, but full, too, of a refined and kindly humour, ready to flash out in a pun, or to light up with a warm and gentle glow the cloud that overhangs him." H. S. Pancoast's Introduction to English Literature

Orwell, George

A collection of essays. Doubleday 1954 320p pa $1.95   **824**

"An Anchor book"
"Fourteen of the best essays by one of the great writers of our time, the man whom V. S. Pritchett called 'the conscience of his generation.' Included are essays on Dickens,' Kipling, and Gandhi, shooting an elephant, politics and the English language, and others." Publisher's note

The Spectator, by Joseph Addison, Richard Steele, & others. Dutton 1907 4v ea $2.95   **824**

"Everyman's library"
"A daily journal published from March, 1711, to December, 1712, embodying the brilliant contributions of Joseph Addison and Richard Steele. Addison's essays predominate in The Spectator. They are considered models of English style." Pratt Alcove
"One of the most famous of essayists, Addison is at his best here." Trinity College List
The essays concern manners, political science, religion, literary criticism, etc. of English society during the period of Queen Anne

824.08   English essays— Collections

Parker, Elinor

(ed.) I was just thinking—a book of essays; wood engravings by Clare Leighton. Crowell 1959 180p illus $4.50   **824.08**

1 English essays 2 American essays
Part I, Reading, writing and talking, consists of essays by such writers as Charles Lamb, Francis Bacon and Christopher Morley. In Part II, out of doors, the reader can take a literary excursion with such essayists as Hilaire Belloc, Henry Thoreau and Joseph Wood Krutch. Part III, Traveling, presents short trips by James Thurber, Logan Pearsall Smith, and others. Part IV This and that, is a potpourri
"Thoughtful selection and attractive format recommend the book for personal reading as well as school use." Booklist

826   English letters

Chesterfield, Philip Dormer Stanhope, 4th Earl of

Letters of Lord Chesterfield to his son. Dutton 1929 312p $2.75   **826**

1 Behavior
"Everyman's library"
"Selections from the famous letters of this man of fashion admonishing his son in the art of graces of the finished gentleman according to the standards to the times of George III." Pratt Alcove

Lewis, C. S.

Letters of C. S. Lewis; ed. with a memoir, by W. H. Lewis. Harcourt 1966 308p illus $6.95   **826**

"The brother of C.S. Lewis has selected a group of the writer's letters, keeping in mind the general reader rather than the scholar. Included are letters reflecting his views on literature, religion, philosophy, and education. Often the correspondence reads like essays on various topics." Library J
"The letters cover a period of over forty years from 1915 when he first discovered George Macdonald's Phantasies, through October, 1963, shortly before his death." Book Rev Digest
The several hundred letters "seem to capture the complete man, and the editor-brother has captured at least part of the man . . . in a 25-page biographical foreword." Book of the Month Club News

827   English satire and humor

Churchill, Winston S.

The Churchill wit; ed. by Bill Adler. Coward-McCann 1965 85p illus $3   **827**

"An amusing compilation of Churchill's quips and barbs; many of the comments or brief speeches are prefaced by notes explaining the circumstances, others need no explanation. The editor has divided the material into four areas: politics, the war, personal remarks, and comments made about the United States or made while in this country." Chicago. Children's Book Center
Mr Churchill's comments "prove to be more enjoyable than the work of many a professional humorist. Even though some of these may be well known to Churchill enthusiasts, they still are not stale, and it is good to have them collected conveniently in one place." Library J

Parkinson, C. Northcote

Parkinson's law, and other studies in administration; illus. by Robert C. Osborn. Houghton 1957 112p illus $3.50   **827**

"A book which solemnly searches out the absurdities of cocktail parties, big organizations, questionnaires, and other impressive landmarks in contemporary life. Advice on such vital problems as securing committee votes, spotting important people at a party, and discriminating between important and unimportant organizations is freely given by an English author . . . [of] dust-dry humor." Booklist
"The entire book consists of a series of shockingly improbable assertions, which are promptly backed up by incontrovertible evidence. The tone varies from savage glee to coldly amused brutality. The style is faultless, arrogant, didactic." N Y Times Bk R

828   English miscellany

Arnold, Matthew

The portable Matthew Arnold; ed. and with an introduction by Lionel Trilling. Viking 1949 659p $5.50   **828**

"The Viking Portable library"
"Selections from the poems, critical essays, political works, and letters of Matthew Arnold." Book Rev Digest
"Mr. Trilling begins his capital introduction to the present volume with the assertion that 'of the literary men of the great English nineteenth century there are few who have stayed quite so fresh, so immediate, and so relevant as Matthew Arnold,' and this statement is fully justified by the six hundred and more pages of poetry and prose that follow. Arnold is fresh and immediate and relevant because his predicament is ours—he merely knew it a little earlier." Sat R
A note on bibliography: p34-36

Blake, William

The portable Blake; selected and arranged with an introduction by Alfred Kazin. Viking [1968 c1946] 713p illus $5.50　　　828

"The Viking Portable library"
"The editor has combined selections from Blake's poetry, prose, and drawings into a comprehensive single volume. Included are the 'Songs of Innocence and of Experience' complete; most of the verses and fragments from the Rossetti and Pickering mss.; and nine of the longer works from the Prophetic Books, with selections from the others, including 'Jerusalem.' The rest of the short poems are also well represented." Huntting
Bibliography: p700-02

Clifford, James L.

(ed.) Twentieth century interpretations of Boswell's Life of Johnson; a collection of critical essays. Prentice-Hall 1970 123p $4.95
828

1 Boswell, James. The life of Samuel Johnson

"A Spectrum book"
These essays discuss the strengths and weaknesses of the biography, explore Boswell's materials and techniques and examine "how faithful the Life is to the historic Dr. Johnson and what was contributed by Boswell's creative imagination." Publisher's note
Selected bibliography: p122-23

Coleridge, Samuel Taylor

The portable Coleridge; ed. and with an introduction by I. A. Richards. Viking 1950 630p $4.95　　　828

"The Viking Portable library"
Includes: The rime of the ancient mariner (1875); Christabel; Kubla Khan; and most of the shorter poems; ample representation of the "Biographia literaria," generous selections from the other literary criticism, political essays, notebooks, and letters; also a lengthy biographical introduction
Partial bibliography; p56-57

Conrad, Joseph

The portable Conrad; ed. and with an introduction and notes, by Morton Dauwen Zabel. Viking 1947 760p $6.50　　　828

"The Viking Portable library"
Contains two novels: The Nigger of the "Narcissus," and Typhoon; three long stories; six shorter stories; and a selection from Conrad's prefaces, letters and autobiographical writings
Bibliographical note: p758-60

Goldsmith, Oliver

The Vicar of Wakefield, and other writings; ed. with an introduction and notes by Frederick W. Hilles. Modern Lib. 1955 xxv, 580p $2.75　　　828

"Contains a selection of essays, criticisms, and poems; She stoops to conquer; selections from The citizen of the world; an abridgment of The life of Nash; and The Vicar of Wakefield." Booklist
The first title in this combined edition was first published 1776. "Written in a style of perfect quiet and simplicity, its hold is due to its domesticity and idyllic charm. 'Its motive is to enforce the truth that heroism of soul may rise triumphant over the vanities and trials of daily life.' " Pratt Alcove
The play: She stoops to conquer, [also entered separately; class 822] was first produced in Covent Garden, London on March 15, 1773. It relates the Hardcastle family's mishaps and adventures in their undertaking to wed a single daughter

Greene, Donald

Samuel Johnson. Twayne 1970 245p (Twayne's English authors ser) $4.95　　　828
1 Johnson, Samuel, 1709-1784

"In a pleasingly nonsimplistic, stimulating topical overview the . . . author introduces students and other novice inquirers to the significant concepts, views, style, and accomplishments of Johnson's major and minor work as poet, journalist, biographer, moralist, political writer, lexicographer, critic, and essayist. Scholars' corrections of longstanding misconceptions about Johnson's work are cited. Recapitulation of references to Johnson's modernity appears at the close and includes such matters as his forward-looking political views and their social extensions. An initial chapter discusses Johnson's life and person." Booklist
Bibliography: p235-39

Hunting, Robert

Jonathan Swift. Twayne 1967 149p (Twayne's English authors ser) $4.95　　　828
1 Swift, Jonathan

"Confining his analysis and assessment of Swift to those writings which in his opinion transcend the occasion that produced them and are of greatest interest to contemporary readers. Hunting discusses 'A tale of a tub,' 'The journal to Stella.' 'Gulliver's travels,' and selected poems and comments briefly on a few other works." Booklist
Chronology: p13-15. Notes and references: p129-38. Selected bibliography: p139-44

Johnson, Samuel

The portable Johnson & Boswell; ed. and with an introduction by Louis Kronenberger. Viking 1947 762p $5.50　　　828

"The Viking Portable library"
"A collection, made up of a chunk of Boswell's 'Life of Samuel Johnson,' some selections from Boswell's journal of the tour of the Hebrides that he made with the usually comfort-loving Doctor, and a sprinkling of Johnson's own writings—lives of Pope and Savage, prefaces, letters, and poems. The book provides an opportunity to compare the Johnson of Boswell's biography (which has been called one of the great novels of all time) with the Doctor as he revealed himself when he ponderously took his pen in hand." New Yorker

Korg, Jacob

Dylan Thomas. Twayne 1965 205p (Twayne's English authors ser) $4.95　　　828
1 Thomas, Dylan

"A brief introductory guide to and defense of Dylan Thomas' much challenged work by an [author] . . . who appreciates Thomas most for the 'balanced collaboration' between his mysticism and passion for words. Korg provides a biographical sketch, analysis of style and survey and occasional explication of poetry, stories, and plays, with maximal attention to the poetry. Throughout his text he comments on more complete or contradictory material by other scholars, thus providing a useful résumé of pertinent literature." Booklist
Bibliography: p192-97

Lamb, Charles

The portable Charles Lamb; ed. and with an introduction by John Mason Brown. Viking 1949 594p $4.95　　　828

"The Viking Portable library"
A selection of Lamb's letters and essays arranged to present the character of the man, his work and his interests
Contents: Letters; Himself, his youth and his family; London; Fantasies and tales; Men, "characters," and places; Books and paintings; In general; Poems; Playgoing and the drama
A short bibliography: p593-94

Milton, John

The portable Milton; ed. and with an introduction by Douglas Bush. Viking 1949 693p $5.50　　　828

"The Viking Portable library"
Here in one volume is the cream of the early poems and sonnets; "Areopagitica" complete, and lengthy selections from the other chief

Milton, John—*Continued*
prose works; the three major poems—"Paradise lost," "Paradise regained," and "Samson Agonistes" complete
    Glossary of words and proper names: p667-93. Bibliography: p28-33. Chronology: p33-36

O'Casey, Sean
    The Sean O'Casey reader; plays, autobiographies, opinions; ed. with an introduction by Brooks Atkinson. St Martins 1968 xxiv, 1008p $12.50   **828**
    This volume contains the text of nine plays: "Juno and the Paycock, The Plough and the Stars, The Silver Tassie, Within the Gates, Purple Dust, Red Roses for Me, Cock-a-Doodle Dandy, Bedtime Story, and The Drums of Father Ned. Then there are . . . excerpts from the autobiographies, from I Knock at the Door, Pictures in the Hallway, Drums Under the Windows, Inishfallen Fare Thee Well, Rose and Crown, Sunset and Evening Star; to which are added eight essays of Opinions and a short story. Mr Atkinson contributes the Introduction with a brief biography and a discerning and warm estimate of O'Casey as a man and as an author, particularly as a playwright." Best Sellers
    "We can see the pattern of irony, satire and imagination, and above all, the magic that can be wrought with popular speech. O'Casey the man is central too. . . . The plays show his empathy, his profound knowledge of the human experience as comic and tragic, real and visionary: the prose writings give us embattled words, in his own commentary on the plays, and empathy again in his own human story." N Y Times Bk R
    A Sean O'Casey bibliography: p993-99

829   Anglo-Saxon (Old English literature)

Beowulf
    Beowulf; tr. by Kevin Crossley-Holland and introduced by Bruce Mitchell. Farrar, Straus 1968 146p illus map $5.95   **829**
    "The Anglo-Saxon epic of a dragonslaying hero is of Scandinavian origin and might be called the first milestone along the highway of English literature. It is the very oldest poem of any size and scope in any modern language." A. D. Dickinson
    "The introductory notes are a concise compendium of valuable scholarly material, and the appendices are more than adequate for any educational purpose. Crossley—Holland specifically states in his introduction that he does not want what he has written to stand in the way of the reader who comes to the poem for the first time. He need have no fear; he aids our own understanding of Beowulf—indeed of Anglo-Saxon literature in general—and of all poetry in his masterful translation." Choice
    Bibliography: p143-46

831   German poetry

Hesse, Hermann
    Poems; selected and tr. by James Wright. Farrar, Straus 1970 79p $4.95   **831**
    "A collection of translations of some of his poems, all written on the theme of homesickness. . . . Like his novels, the poems unite the romantic and the tragic with precision. . . . For more scholarly YA's the original German is provided on facing pages." Library J

833.09   German fiction—History and criticism

Field, George Wallis
    Hermann Hesse. Twayne 1970 198p (Twayne's World authors ser) $5.50   **833.09**
    1 Hesse, Hermann

"I have attempted to deal with the major works as fully as possible, while at the same time trying to give a total picture of Hesse's personality and his output in many genres. Thus Chapter Nine deals briefly with the lyric poet, the literary critic, and the political thinker and essayist, Chapter Five concentrates on three major 'novellas,' and in the early part of Chapter Six some attention is paid to a 'Märchen' which bears on the discussion of 'Siddhartha.' The first three chapters deal with the biographical background and the major and minor works of the first decade and a half in Hesse's literary career." Preface
Bibliography: p188-93

839.3   Dutch literature

Frank, Anne
    The works of Anne Frank; introduction by Ann Birstein and Alfred Kazin; drawings by Peter Spier. Doubleday 1959 332p illus $5.95   **839.3**
    1 World War, 1939-1945—Jews 2 Netherlands
    Collected here for the first time are the contents of two notebooks. One notebook contained Anne Frank's now famous "Diary," originally published in 1952, and entered in class 940.54. In the other notebook were Anne's personal reminiscences, stories, fairy tales, formal essays, and attempts at "adult" fiction. (Publisher)
    "The diary remains strong and impressive. Of the shorter pieces, some seem a fictional reworking of episodes [of school days or life in Amsterdam] recorded in the diary, others are more or less conventional schoolgirl exercises. [The] introduction . . . is sympathetic and informative." Booklist

839.7   Swedish literature

Hammarskjöld, Dag
    The light and the rock; the vision of Dag Hammarskjöld; ed. by T. S. Settel. Dutton 1966 157p boards $4.50   **839.7**
    This is "a collection of very brief statements which reflect Dag Hammarskjöld's innermost thoughts and briefs. . . . [The late Secretary-General of the United Nations discusses] maturity, responsibility, the life of the man of public service, the conditions and obligations of freedom, religion, art, literature, history, the precise observation of the natural world . . . and the role of the United Nations." Introduction
    Sources: p147-57

    Markings; tr. from the Swedish by Leif Sjöberg & W. H. Auden; with a foreword by W. H. Auden. Knopf 1964 221p $5.95   **839.7**
    1 Spiritual life
    First published 1963 in Sweden
    The author described this account as a sort of white book concerning his negotiations with himself and with God. "A record of his inner life, it opens with a poem he wrote around 1925; most of the entries were made during . . . the nineteen forties and fifties—and the book ends with a poem written only a few weeks before his plane crashed." Publisher's note
    "I have no hesitancy in calling this work the noblest, self-disclosure of spiritual struggle and triumph, perhaps the greatest testament of personal devotion, published in this century. History may judge its author no less preeminent as a man of faith than as a man of action. . . . Beyond its astonishing intrinsic worth, just here lies the marvel of this work—that reflections on life and destiny, fate and faith which would merit enduring recognition had they issued from monastic retreat and prolonged meditation were, in fact, hammered out during the contemporary world's most urgent business." N Y Times Bk R

839.8   Norwegian literature

Ibsen, Henrik

Eleven plays of Henrik Ibsen; introduction by H. L. Mencken. Modern Lib. 1935 1185p $4.95   839.8

"Modern Library Giants"

Contents: A doll's house; Ghosts; An enemy of the people; The master builder; Pillars of society; Hedda Gabler; John Gabriel Borkman; The wild duck; League of youth; Rosmersholm; Peer Gynt

Four plays of Ibsen; tr. from the Norwegian by R. V. Forslund. Chilton Bks. 1968 306p $6.95   839.8

When we dead awaken, The master builder, Little Eyolf, and The wild duck "are translated into acceptable contemporary American idiom without doing violence to Ibsen's manner or meaning. In fact, the translation is a corrective to more florid versions available." Booklist

Six plays. Newly tr. and with an introduction by Eva Le Gallienne. Modern Lib. 1957 xxxiii, 510p $2.95   839.8

Contents: A doll's house; Ghosts; An enemy of the people; Rosmersholm; Hedda Gabler; The master builder

840.3   French literature—Dictionaries

The **Oxford** Companion to French literature; comp. and ed. by Sir Paul Harvey and J. E. Heseltine. Oxford 1959 771p maps $12.50   840.3

1 French literature—Dictionaries 2 French literature—Bio-bibliography

"Covers French literature from medieval times to approximately 1939, in the manner of other Oxford 'Companions,' including: (1) articles on authors, critics, historians, religious writers, savants, scientists, etc.; (2) articles on individual works, allusions, places, and institutions; and (3) general survey articles on phrases or aspects of French literary life, movements, etc." Winchell. Guide to Reference Books. 8th edition

Pointers to the study of French literature and its background: p765-71

840.9   French literature—History and criticism

Cazamian, Louis

A history of French literature. Oxford 1955 464p $9   840.9

1 French literature—History and criticism

"This history starts with the ninth century and traces the development and character of French literature down to the middle of the twentieth century." Publisher's note

Maurois, André

From Proust to Camus; profiles of modern French writers; tr. by Carl Morse and Renaud Bruce. Doubleday [1968 c1966] 342p illus pa $1.45   840.9

1 French literature—History and criticism 2 Authors, French

"A Doubleday Anchor book"

Original English hardbound edition, published 1966, analyzed in Essay and general literature index

"The original [1963] French edition . . . did not include the articles on Gide, Sartre, and Simone de Beauvoir, which appear in this volume." Publisher's note

"These early sketches (originally lectures to American students) tend more to eulogy than to criticism, with the emphasis on the man rather than on the work. As such, they are good introductions to the greatest of twentieth-century French authors." Cincinnati

842   French drama

Anouilh, Jean

The lark; tr. by Christopher Fry. Oxford 1956 [c1955] 103p $3.75   842

1 Joan of Arc, Saint—Drama

Characters: 16 men, 5 women. One set of scenery. First produced in France

"Moving dramatization of the trial of Joan of Arc which . . . evokes the spirit of the ingenious peasant girl without attempting to explain her vision and dedication." Bookmark

"The translation is a work of art in its own right." Sec Ed Brd

Camus, Albert

Caligula & 3 other plays; tr. from the French by Stuart Gilbert; with a preface written specially for this edition and tr. by Justin O'Brien. Knopf 1958 302p $5.95   842

"Four of the author's best-known plays, written between 1938 and 1950. 'Caligula,' about the infamous emperor's self-destroying rebellion against fate; 'The Misunderstanding,' about the murder of a man by his ghoulish mother and sister, 'The Just Assassins,' on the self-questionings of terrorists; and 'State of Siege,' an allegory about the refusal of one individual in a plague-stricken city to compromise with evil." Pub W

"The total impression these plays make, despite their defects as organic drama, is one of spiritual vigor and integrity." N Y Times Bk R

The possessed; a play in three parts; tr. from the French by Justin O'Brien. Knopf 1960 182p $4.95, lib. bdg. $2.39   842

Characters: 18 men, 6 women

A re-creation, "for the theatre, of Dostoevsky's novel. Camus has foreshortened the Dostoevsky novel so that it emerges as a vehicle for his own ideas, his own philosophy. It is a forceful and lucid work (however long as a play) that bears a deep and complex message for modern man." Pub W

Ionesco, Eugene

Four plays; tr. by Donald M. Allen. Grove 1958 160p pa $1.95   842

"Evergreen books"

Originally published 1954 in France

Contents: The bald soprano; The lesson; Jack; or, The submission; The chairs

The bald soprano is a comedy satirizing English middle class life, while Jack, concerns a sulky young man who disappoints his family by refusing to marry the girl of their choice. An avante garde drama, The chairs focuses on an old couple who receive many imaginary guests. The murder of a young student by his elderly teacher ends a bizarre lesson in The lesson

Rostand, Edmond

Cyrano de Bergerac   842

1 Cyrano de Bergerac, Savinien—Drama

Some editions are:

Heritage $6.95 In a new English version by Louis Untermeyer; with illustrations drawn by Pierre Brissaud

Holt $4.50 A new version in English verse by Brian Hooker. Prepared by Walter Hampden with a prefatory gesture by Clayton Hamilton

Modern Lib. $2.95 lib. bdg. $2.69 Translated by Brian Hooker

First presented in 1897

"The nose of the famous French guardsman, Cyrano de Bergerac, was of such amazingly heroic proportions that the man's very behavior was shaped and directed by it. His courage, which seemed almost foolhardy, and his ability

Rostand, Edmond—*Continued*
to compose poetry even during a duel more than compensated for his ugliness. Cyrano was not a man to be taunted or disparaged without dire consequences. Beneath the braggadocio and swaggering courage, however, lay a sensitive soul yearning for but one prize—the love of the beautiful Roxanne. . . . This drama is set in seventeenth-century Paris is full of the court intrigue of the time." Doors to More Mature Reading

844 French essays

Camus, Albert
Lyrical and critical essays; ed. and with notes by Philip Thody; tr. from the French by Ellen Conroy Kennedy. Knopf 1968 365p $6.95 **844**
Analyzed in Essay and general literature index
A "consolidation of much of Camus's major reflective prose—L'Envers et L'Endroit, Noces, L'Eté—with selections from his critical writings on Sartre, Silone, Gide, Melville, Faulkner, Jean Grenier, all of which are joined by Camus's comments about himself, including three interviews." Library J
"Well-chosen selection of personal and critical pieces suitable for high school libraries." Booklist

The myth of Sisyphus, and other essays; tr. from the French by Justin O'Brien. Knopf 1955 212p $5.95, lib. bdg. $2.29 **844**
Analyzed in Essay and general literature index
"The fundamental subject of 'The Myth of Sisyphus' is this: it is legitimate and necessary to wonder whether life has a meaning: therefore it is legitimate to meet the problem of suicide face to face. The answer, underlying and appearing through the paradoxes which cover it, is this: even if one does not believe in God, suicide is not legitimate. Written fifteen years ago, in 1940, amid the French and European disaster, this book declares that even within the limits of nihilism it is possible to find the means to proceed beyond nihilism. . . . It has been thought possible to append to this philosophical argument a series of essays, of a kind I have never ceased writing, which are somewhat marginal to my other books. In a more lyrical form, they all illustrate that essential fluctuation from assent to refusal which, in my view, defines the artist and his difficult calling." Preface

Resistance, rebellion and death; tr. from the French and with an introduction by Justin O'Brien **844**
1 Europe—Politics 2 Good and evil
Some editions are:
Knopf $5.95
Modern Lib. $2.95
Knopf edition analyzed in Essay and general literature index
"A selection of forthright essays on contemporary world politics, on capital punishment and the relations of the state and the individual, and on art, chosen from the three volumes of 'Actuelles,' published in France between 1950 and 1958. Includes editorials from 'Combat,' discussions of the French-Algerian problem, observations on the abortive Hungarian revolution, and essays and interviews." Pub W

848 French miscellany

Camus, Albert
Notebooks. . . . Knopf 1963-1965 2v ea $5.95 **848**
Also available in Modern Library editions for $2.95 each
Published in England with title: Carnets
Contents: [v 1] 1935-1942, translated from the French and with a preface and notes by Philip Thody (1963); [v2] 1942-1951, translated from the French and annotated by Justin O'Brien (1965)

Camus "was no Boswell interested in a narrative of his personal affairs. Instead, he has left the diary of a writer, full of his aesthetic ideas, plans for his work, snatches of conversation showing an acute sense of what makes good dialogue, quotations from reading that interested him, and impressions of persons, places, and things. . . . This is the record of a probing, searching mind." N Y Her Trib Books

Esslin, Martin
(ed.) Samuel Beckett; a collection of critical essays. Prentice-Hall 1965 182p $5.95 **848**
1 Beckett, Samuel
"Twentieth century views. A Spectrum book"
The essays here analyze such subjects as "the theatrical effect of 'Waiting for Godot,' the conflict between the rational and the irrational in 'Watt,' or the modifications in the Beckett persona from its appearance in 'Molloy' to its virtual disappearance in 'The Unnamable.' . . . These essays illuminate Beckett's subterranean world while providing a . . . view of contemporary criticism." Publisher's note
Selected bibliography: p181-82

Keating, L. Clark
Andre Maurois. Twayne 1969 172p (Twayne's World authors ser) $5.50 **848**
1 Maurois, Andre
After a "survey of the writer's life, Professor Keating presents us his works by genre. Each chapter offers a summary and a critical analysis of the various works within the genre. It also contains references to the critics' as well as to the public's reaction to the major books." Mod Lang J
Bibliography: p159-66

Rhein, Phillip H.
Albert Camus. Twayne 1969 148p (Twayne's World authors ser) $5.50 **848**
1 Camus, Albert
"The purpose of this study is to analyze the gradual evolution of Camus' thought into an art and a philosophy that bears his particular seal." Publisher's note
Partial contents: The Algerian summer; Man and the absurd; The theater of the absurd; The theater of revolt; Man and the rebellion; Selected bibliography

Voltaire, François Marie Arouet de
The portable Voltaire; ed. with an introduction by Ben Ray Redman. Viking [1968 c1949] 570p $4.95 **848**
"The Viking Portable library"
"The selections from Voltaire's works include: Candide, part one; Three stories: Zadig; Micromegas; and Story of a good Brahmin; Letters, and selections from the Philosophical Dictionary and other works. The editor's introduction gives a biographical sketch of Voltaire." Book Rev Digest

851 Italian poetry

Dante Alighieri
The portable Dante. . . . Ed. and with an introduction by Paolo Milano. Viking 1947 xlii, 662p $5.50 **851**
"The Viking Portable library"
"The Divine comedy, complete, translated by Laurence Binyon, with notes from C. H. Grandgent; La vita nuova, [The new life] complete, translated by D. G. Rossetti; Excerpts from the Latin prose works." Subtitle
Bibliographical note: p661-62

851.09 Italian poetry—History and criticism

Bergin, Thomas G.
Petrarch. Twayne 1970 213p (Twayne's World authors ser) $5.50   851.09
1 Petrarch, Francesco
"A biographical-critical study of the great 14th-century poet and humanist, with an assessment of his enduring significance in world literature and the culture of the West." Book News
"Three chapters critically review each of his works; the book closes with an assessment of Petrarch's enduring influence on cultural and literary traditions. A chronology from 1304 to 1377 is included and a Latin, Italian, and English bibliography is appended." Booklist

860.8 Spanish and Latin-American literature—Collections

Cohen, J. M.
(ed.) Latin American writing today. Penguin [hardbound distributed by Peter Smith] 1967 267p $3.25   860.8
1 Latin American literature—Collections
An anthology of poetry and short stories
Short stories included are: The handwriting of God, by J. L. Borges; Dreaded hell, by J. C. Onetti; Journey to the seed, by A. Carpentier; Bestiary, by J. Cortázar; The third bank of the river, by J. G. Rosa; Aura, by C. Fuentes; The Iriartes, by M. Benedetti; Ana María, by J. Donoso; They gave us the land, by J. Rulfo; The day after Saturday, by G. García Márquez; At the great 'Ecbo,' by G. Cabrera Infante; Sun, by C. V. Maia; João Urso, by B. Accioly; It's a long time ago, by O. J. Cardoso

860.9 Spanish and Latin American literature—History and criticism

Franco, Jean
An introduction to Spanish American literature. Cambridge 1969 390p $9.50   860.9
1 Latin American literature—History and criticism
ISBN 0-521-07374-X
"All Spanish-American literature from the Conquest to the present is surveyed, but the 20th Century dominates the greater part of the volume. The author traces the influence of cultural dependence on Europe, frequent links between politics and literature, traditional bondage to the conventions of the Spanish language (that is, literary Spanish often far removed from the spoken languages of Latin America), and the subsequent decisiveness of the Modernist movement as a turning point in the development of Spanish-American literatures. The form is that of broad categories which lend themselves to chronological arrangement within which brief entries on major writers constitute the nuclei of the book." Library J
Includes bibliography

Stamm, James R.
A short history of Spanish literature. Doubleday 1967 267p $5.95   860.9
1 Spanish literature—History and criticism
"A chronological survey covering the most important writers, movements, ideas, and works in Spanish literature, from its beginnings to the present." Booklist
Selected bibliography of works in English: p247-51

861.08 Spanish poetry—Collections

Lewis, Richard
(ed.) Still waters of the air; poems by three modern Spanish poets; drawings by Arvis Stewart. Dial Press 1970 95p $4.50, lib. bdg. $4.17   861.08
1 Spanish poetry—Collections
"An inviting bilingual collection of poems by the noted Spanish poets Juan Ramon Jimenez, Federico Garcia Lorca, and Antonio Machado. [The editor] states that it is the marriage between human experience and nature that has suggested the format of the book, and, consequently, the poems are not grouped by poet but are arranged loosely to follow the course of changing seasons and the ages of man from childhood to death. Brief profiles of the three poets and a list of adult books about them are appended." Booklist
"The poems represent the tendency of the early 20th Century toward a sincerely felt lyricism and honesty of perceptions and feelings. Young readers with a fair knowledge of Spanish will enjoy the original poems . . . for their rhythm and brilliant images." Library J

Resnick, Seymour
(ed.) Spanish-American poetry; a bilingual selection; illus. by Anne Marie Jauss. Harvey House 1964 96p illus $3.50, lib. bdg. $3.36   861.08
1 Latin American poetry—Collections
"The forty poems are selected from the best of five centuries of Spanish-American poetry, by poets from Chile to Mexico, from the sixteenth-century Ercilla to the famous moderns, Neruda and Mistral. The bilingual format is designed for both enjoyment and the development of reading techniques." Publisher's note

863.09 Spanish fiction—History and criticism

Nelson, Lowry
(ed.) Cervantes; a collection of critical essays; ed. by Lowry Nelson, Jr. Prentice-Hall 1969 176p $5.95   863.09
1 Cervantes Saavedra, Miguel de. Don Quixote de la Mancha
SBN 13-123299-1
"Twentieth century views. A Spectrum book"
"This collection of essays by such well-known critics and commentators as Leo Spitzer, Thomas Mann, W. H. Auden, and Erich Auerbach testifies to Cervantes' remarkable genius and reveals the immense influence of his masterpiece on the development of modern fiction. In articles ranging from a short biographical sketch of Cervantes to an examination of the picaresque mode in 'Don Quixote' these experts pay critical tribute to Cervantes' story of the mad, idealistic knight and his shrewd squire." Publisher's note
"In this collection of essays, a range of perspectives is offered—from biographical to analytical—by eminent contemporary men of letters. . . . These re-presentations, of great quality and authority, are supplemented by a brief chronology of Cervantes' life and a selected bibliography. Of interest to both the scholar and the general reader." Choice

870.8 Latin literature—Collections

Davenport, Basil
(ed.) The portable Roman reader; ed. and with an introduction. Viking 1951 656p $5.50   870.8
1 Latin literature—Collections

Davenport, Basil—*Continued*
"The Viking Portable library"
"Readers who once found Latin unendurable may be surprised and delighted to discover how much the Romans contributed to the world's stock of significant and entertaining writing." N Y Her Trib Books
"Complete plays by Plautus and Terence; excerpts from Apuleius, Boethius, and St. Augustine; portions of Caesar and Cicero, Virgil, Livy, Ovid, Petronius, Martial, Juvenal; Seneca, Lucan, Tacitus; the lyric poets, Horace and Catullus; Lucretius; [and] the complete 'Pervigilius Veneris.' " Retail Bookseller

870.9 Latin literature— History and criticism

Hamilton, Edith
The Roman way. Norton 1932 281p $5.50
870.9
Latin literature—History and criticism
2 Rome—Civilization
Companion volume to: The Greek way, class 880.9
An interpretation of Roman life from the descriptions in the works of great writers from Plautus and Terence to Virgil and Juvenal
"Few books in this field can be read with more ease and pleasure. It was written apparently with enthusiasm and a sufficiently competent mastery of the material." N Y Her Trib Books

871 Latin poetry

Ovid
Metamorphoses **871**
Some editions are:
Ind. Univ. Press $7.50 Translated by Rolfe Humphries
Macmillan (N Y) (Classics of Greece and Rome) $7.95 The Arthur Golding translation, 1567. Edited, with an introduction and notes by John Frederick Nims
"A series of tales in Latin verse. . . . Dealing with mythological legendary, and historical figures, they are written in hexameters, in 15 books, beginning with the creation of the world and ending with the deification of Caesar and the reign of Augustus." Benét. The Reader's Encyclopedia
"Professional men of letters have always liked Ovid for his sincerity, his vivacity, his imagination. His imagination, is at its best in the 'Metamorphoses' in which he put together many of the Greek and Graeco-Roman myths. . . . Perhaps Ovid never wrote a stunningly great line . . . but he was a born story-teller and a poet of really extraordinary facility. His work as a whole had an incalculable influence on the literature of modern countries, unsurpassed even by the influence of Virgil." J. Macy's Story of the World's Literature

873 Latin epic poetry

Virgil
The Aeneid of Virgil **873**
1 Aeneas
Some editions are:
Dutton (Everyman's lib. Classical) $2.95 Translated and annotated by Michael Oakley. With an introduction by E. M. Forster
Ind. Univ. Press (Indiana Univ. Greek and Latin classics) $8.50 Translated by L. R. Lind. Has subtitle: An epic poem of Rome
"This is the story of a band of Trojan refugees and their leaders, Aeneas; their last-ditch fight in the collapsing city; their exodus and odyssey; and their founding of the new empire of Rome. The whole poem is built around the legendary figure of Aeneas—exemplar of Roman manhood. . . . The 'Aeneid' is a marvelous book, full of the exuberance of life, of the burden of hard labor, of tears at the passing of things." The College and Adult Reading List

880.3 Classical literature— Dictionaries

Feder, Lillian
Crowell's Handbook of classical literature. Crowell 1964 448p maps (A Crowell Reference bk) $7.95 **880.3**
1 Classical literature—Dictionaries
An alphabetically arranged "guide to the drama, poetry, and prose of Greece and Rome, with biographies of their authors. Mythical figures are briefly described or identified, as are places; but the emphasis is on . . . the literature itself." Huntting
This guide "is increasingly important as a reference source in these days when readers know little Latin and less Greek. Biographies of the authors are included. . . . The 950 entries in Crowell are devoted almost entirely to the writers and their writings, with separate entries identifying the characters. . . . The book is most useful as a digest of classical writing and for identification of characters." Cur Ref Bks

The **Oxford** Companion to classical literature; comp. and ed. by Sir Paul Harvey. Oxford [1966 c1937] 468p illus maps $5.75 **880.3**
1 Classical literature—Dictionaries
A reprint with corrections of the title first published 1937
"The aim of this book is to present, in convenient form, information which the ordinary reader not only of the literatures of Greece and Rome, but also of that large proportion of modern European literature which teems with classical allusions, may find useful. It endeavors to do two things: in the first place to bring together what he may wish to know about the evolution of classical literature, the principal authors, and their chief works; in the second place, to depict so much of the historical, political, social, and religious background as may help to make the classics understood." Preface [to 1937 edition]
"Arrangement is alphabetical, with cross references. English pronunciation is given." Booklist

880.8 Greek literature— Collections

Auden, W. H.
(ed.) The portable Greek reader. Viking 1948 726p $5.50 **880.8**
1 Greek literature—Collections
"The Viking Portable library"
"Selections from representative Greek writers from Homer to Galen, aimed at providing the reader with an introduction to all facets of Greek culture, rather than to its literature alone. Mr Auden's preface deals chiefly with the various Greek concepts of the hero, in comparison with our own, and points up the imense differences between the two civilizations." New Yorker

880.9 Greek literature— History and criticism

Hamilton, Edith
The echo of Greece. Norton 1957 224p $4.95
880.9
1 Greek literature—History and criticism
2 Civilization, Greek
An "interpretation of Greek life and thought into the period just following the Periclean Age. The author writes of Athens and the Greeks of the fourth century [specifically] . . . of Plato and Aristotle, of Demosthenes and Alexander the Great, of the much-loved playwright Menander, of the Stoics, and finally of Plutarch." Publisher's note

Hamilton, Edith—*Continued*

"The only fault I can find in the book is a fault unavoidable in so swift a study: oversimplification. Greek freedom and lack of cruelty are stressed. Greek tyranny and mass executions are skipped. . . . But what a gift for simplification Miss Hamilton has, and what a flair for plain powerful truths." N Y Times Bk R

The Greek way   **880.9**

1 Greek literature—History and criticism 2 Civilization, Greek

Some editions are:
Modern Lib. $2.95
Norton $5.95
Watts, F. lib. bdg. $9.95 Large type edition complete and unabridged. A Keith Jennison book

First published 1930. Variant title: The great age of Greek literature
Companion volume to: The Roman way, class 870.9
An account of writers and literary forms of the Periclean Age including discussions of Pindar, Aristophanes, Aeschylus, tragedy, Greek religion and philosophy, etc.
"This book is no mere literary compendium but a penetrating study of the Greek mind and spirit in relation to both the ancient and the modern worlds. It is beautifully written." Springf'd Republican

882.08   Greek dramatic poetry and drama—Collections

Fitts, Dudley

(ed.) Greek plays in modern translation; ed. with an introduction by Dudley Fitts. Dial Press 1947 596p $7.50   **882.08**

1 Greek drama—Collections

"Permanent library series"
The translation of eleven famous Greek plays of Aeschylus, Sophocles, and Euripides "outstanding for their clarity and poetic interpretation." Ontario Lib Rev
"The book is designed primarily for the reader with little or no Greek who is nevertheless interested in one of the most significant treasures of our European heritage." Introduction
Includes commentaries by the translators and an index of proper names

Oates, Whitney J.

(ed.) The complete Greek drama. . . . ed. by Whitney J. Oates and Eugene O'Neill, Jr. Random House 1938 2v front ea $11
     882.08

1 Greek drama—Collections

"All the extant tragedies of Aeschylus, Sophocles and Euripides, and the comedies of Aristophanes and Menander, in a variety of translations." Title page
"A general introduction surveys the subject; a brief special introduction accompanies each play. The translations of E. D. A. Morshead, R. C. Jebb, E. P. Coleridge, Robert Potter, L. A. Post, and Gilbert Murray are most frequently used." Booklist
Contents: v 1 Aeschylus; Sophocles; Euripides. v2 Euripides; Aristophanes; Menander

883   Epic poetry and fiction

Graves, Robert

The siege and fall of Troy; illus. by C. Walter Hodges. Doubleday 1962 128p illus map $3.50, lib. bdg. $4.25   **883**

1 Troy 2 Trojan War

This is the story of Troy from its foundation to the return of the victorious Greeks, including the details of the genealogies of the characters, the incidents leading to the epic clash and the aftermath. (Publisher)

"Homer's poems are by no means the sole source of the legend; in fact, about two-thirds of this book is taken from various other Greek and Latin authors." Introduction
"While it in no way replaces the classic retellings of 'The Iliad' and 'The Odyssey' this [is a] brisk modernization." Booklist

Homer

The complete works of Homer; The Iliad, tr. by Andrew Lang, Walter Leaf, Ernest Myers; The Odyssey, tr. by S. H. Butcher and Andrew Lang. Modern Lib. 1950 2v in 1 $4.95   **883**

1 Trojan War 2 Ulysses
"Modern Library giants"
Also entered separately below

The Iliad   **883**

1 Trojan War

Some editions are:
Doubleday $6.95 Translation by Robert Graves. Illustrated by Ronald Searle. Has title: The anger of Achilles
Dutton (Everyman's lib) $3.25 Translated by S. O. Andrew and M. J. Oakley. With an introduction by John Warrington. Preface by M. J. Oakley
Macmillan (N Y) $4.50 With introduction by Louise Pound. Translations by Lang, Leaf and Myers
Modern Lib. $2.95
"The materials for the epic were drawn from the Trojan legend which told how the barbarian city of Troy, or Ilium, was besieged for ten years by an army of Greeks and finally captured and sacked to regain Helen [of Troy] and avenge her abduction from King Menelaus by the Trojan prince, Paris." Haydn. Thesaurus of Book Digests

The Odyssey   **883**

1 Ulysses

Some editions are:
Dodd (Great illustrated classics) $4.50 Translated by S. H. Butcher and Andrew Lang. With a portrait of a bust of Homer and reproductions of early drawings of the narrative together with an introduction by James I. Armstrong
Dutton (Everyman's lib) $3.25 Translated by S. O. Andrew With an introduction by John Warrington
Doubleday $5.50 Translated by Robert Fitzgerald. With drawings by Hans Erni
Harper $8.95 Translated with an introduction by Richard Lattimore. Has title: The Odyssey of Homer
Macmillan (N Y) $3.95 Done into English prose by S. Butcher and A. Lang
Modern Lib. $2.95 Translated by Ennis Rees
Norton $6 A new verse translation by Albert Cook
Watts, F. lib. bdg. $7.95 Large type edition. A Keith Jennison book. Done into English prose by S. H. Butcher and A. Lang
"An epic poem in Greek hexameters. . . . The 'Odyssey' is a sequel to the 'Iliad' and narrates the ten years' adventures of Ulysses during his return journey from Troy to his own kingdom, the island of Ithaca." Keller's Reader's Digest of Books

888   Greek miscellany

Aristotle

The basic works of Aristotle; ed. and with an introduction by Richard McKeon. Random House 1941 xxxix, 1487p front $12.50
     888

1 Philosophy, Ancient
Follows the Oxford translation of 1931
Contains entire text of the following: Physica; De generatione et corruptione; De anima; Parva naturalia; Metaphysica; Ethica Nicomachea; Politica; De poetica
Some chapters have been omitted from the following included works: Organon; De caelo; Historia animalium; De partibus animalium; De generatione animalium; Rhetorica

Aristotle—*Continued*

"The translators present the philosopher for what he means to us today and show him in full figure. Together, with the help of the editor, they accomplish what no one of them could begin to do alone. Their book is a long job for a reader to tackle, but every moment of perusal brings reward." Christian Science Monitor

Bibliography: p xxxv-xxxix

Plato

The Republic   888

1 Utopias 2 Political science

Some editions are:
Cambridge $4.75 Edited and translated by I. A. Richards. Has title: Plato's Republic
Modern Lib. $2.95 Translated into English by B. Jowett. Has title: Plato's The Republic
St Martins $3.25 Translated into English, with an analysis and notes by David James Vaughan and John Llewelyn Davies. Has title: The Republic of Plato

In this section of the celebrated Dialogues in which Socrates is represented as interlocutor. Plato develops in his views of the ideal state. "Political thought in Europe has been more or less consciously influenced by the Republic for twenty-three centuries." A. D. Dickinson

891   Indic poetry

Aldan, Daisy

(comp.) Poems from India; illus. by Joseph Low. Crowell 1969 158p illus (Poems of the world) $3.50, lib. bdg. $4.25   891

1 Indic poetry—Collections

Here is a glimpse into the world of Indian poetry ranging from verses from the Hindu scriptures, passages from the epic "Mahabharata" and the "Ramayana," medieval poems in classical style, to contemporary poems from the many different states of modern India. (Publisher)

"This sampling of the storehouse of Indian poetry is made more valuable by the introduction, in which [the author] briefly surveys the ancient classics which, like ancient Indian art, are permeated with religion, before moving on through the centuries to contemporary verse. . . . [Modern poems constitute] by far the longest section and the most varied. The contemporary poetry has comparatively little humor but is rich in imagery and romantic idealism, often bittersweet, often passionate in self-examination." Sat R

Indexed by titles, authors, translators

891.4   Literature of modern Indic languages

Tagore, Rabindranath

Collected poems and plays of Rabindranath Tagore. Macmillan (N Y) 1937 577p $7 891.4

"Eight moralistic plays and the collected poems of the Hindu philosopher, poet, and educator. [No explanatory notes]." Book Rev Digest

A Tagore reader; ed. by Amiya Chakravarty. Beacon Press [1966 c1961] 401p pa $2.45
                                                             891.4

"UNESCO Collection of representative works: Indian series"
First published 1961 by Macmillan (N Y)
"Selections from the travel writings, letters, short stories, fables, drama, poetry and philosophical, literary, authobiographical writings of an Indian Nobel Prize winner." Pub W

891.5   Persian literature

Omar Khayyam

Rubaiyat   891.5

Some editions are:
Crowell $5 The 1st and 4th editions in English verse by Edward Fitzgerald. With illustrations by Eugene Karlin. Introduction by T. Cuyler Young
Doubleday $5 A new translation with critical commentaries by Robert Graves and Omar Ali-Shah. Has title: The original Rubaiyyat of Omar Khayaam
Garden City Bks. $3.95 Rendered into English verse by Edward Fitzgerald, with illustrations by Edmund Dulac
Grosset $2.95 Rendered into English verse by Edward Fitzgerald, with paintings and decorations by Sarkis Katchadourian

" 'The Rubáiyát' (Quatrains) of Omar the Tentmaker, of Persia, is composed of a series of stanzas forming 'a medley of love and tavern songs, tinged with Sufi mysticism, and with the melancholy of Eastern fatalism.' " A. D. Dickinson

891.7   Russian literature

Chekhov, Anton

Best plays; tr. and with an introduction by Stark Young. Modern Lib. 1956 296p $2.95
                                                             891.7

Contents: The sea gull; Uncle Vanya; The three sisters; The cherry orchard
These plays are set in 19th century Russia

Pasternak, Boris

In the interlude, poems, 1945-1960; tr. into English verse by Henry Kamen; with a foreword by Maurice Bowra, and notes by George Katkov. Oxford 1962 250p $8   891.7

"Sixty-nine English verse translations of Pasternak's later poetry by a young Oxford scholar. Includes the poems of Dr. Zhivago, published previously as part of the novel, and the full text of the 'When the skies clear' collection, with Russian and English text on facing pages and explanatory notes. . . . These final poems [are] mainly autobiographical." Booklist

Yevtushenko, Yevgeny

Yevtushenko poems; introduction by Yevgeny Yevtushenko. Authorized translation by Herbert Marshall. Bilingual ed. Dutton 1966 191p $4.95   891.7

In this bilingual collection, the poet "writes of love, war, Russia, and a myriad of other themes. . . . There are 30 poems here plus a part of his epic, 'Bratsky Ges', presented for the first time in English translation." Library J

"Most of the poems have not been previously translated into English. . . . In this book you will come across poems from different periods of my literary life. . . . The poems are quite varied, both in the means of substantiation and their themes." Author's introduction

892.49   Yiddish literature

Howe, Irving

(ed.) A treasury of Yiddish poetry; ed. by Irving Howe and Eliezer Greenberg. Holt 1969 xx, 378p $10   892.49

1 Yiddish poetry—Collections
SBN 03-066425-X

The poems, translated by such writers as John Hollander, Stanley Kunitz, Karl Shapiro, are arranged chronologically from the earliest Yiddish poets to those still writing. Included are "the poems of Reisen, Yehoash, Einhorn, Mani & Leib, Leivick, Halpern, the European and Russian Yiddish 'moderns' and the Yiddish Israeli poets." Pub W

Howe, Irving—*Continued*
"The poems are sensitively chosen with an eye for variety in form, mood and theme. The translations of the poems are generally competent and often strikingly good." Choice
Glossary: p370-71. Indexes of poets and titles

892.7   North Arabic literature

Gibran, Khalil
The Prophet. Knopf 1923 107p front $4.50
892.7

Consisting of twenty-eight prose poems or preachments by 'The Prophet'. . . this work is composed in the highly embroidered style common to Near-Eastern literature. Its tone is lofty, its ideas vague, resplendent in glittering metaphor and lush imagery." Hadyn. Thesaurus of Book Digests

895.1   Chinese literature

Douglas, Alfred
How to consult the I Ching; the Oracle of Change; illus. by David Sheridan. Putnam 1971 251p illus $6.95
895.1
1 Divination
Published in England with title: The Oracle of Change
This book examines the history, wisdom, and influence of the Chinese Oracle of Change, gives instructions on how to use and understand it and includes a new translation of the basic text. (Publisher)
The author "addresses the reader primarily interested in divination. His text is clear and avoids the mystifying symbolism of a more literal translation. His introduction is informative, and the instructions for using the 'I Ching' are easy to follow." Library J

Rexroth, Kenneth
(ed.) One hundred poems from the Chinese. New Directions 1956 159p $5
895.1
1 Chinese poetry—Collections
"Nine poets, who lived centuries ago, speak with the poignancy of understatement of unchanging things: the brevity of life, the richness of friendship, the beauties of nature, the inevitability of old age and death." Booklist

895.6   Japanese literature

Henderson, Harold G.
(ed.) An introduction to haiku; an anthology of poems and poets from Bashō to Shiki. Doubleday 1958 179p illus $4.95
895.6
1 Haiku
Original Japanese words are given in footnotes
"One of the most satisfactory books on this important part of the Japanese literary tradition. Well written, based on careful scholarship with excellent selection and translation." Asia: A Guide to Paperbacks

896   Literature of African languages

Angoff, Charles
(ed.) African writing today; Ethiopia, Ghana, Kenya, Nigeria, Sierra Leone, Uganda, Zambia; selected and ed. by Charles Angoff [and] John Povey. Manyland Bks. 1969 304p illus $6.95
896
1 African literature
SBN 87141

"A Literary Review book"
This anthology contains poems, short stories and a novella written by various authors from sub-Saharan Africa and an introductory essay on: The quality of African writing today, by John Povey. The bulk of the contents comprised the Africa number of The Literary Review
"Compared with other collections, this book has several characteristics. . . . It taps the post colonial writing of English speaking Africans, as opposed to those writing in French, Arabic, or other African languages. . . . It is contemporary in orientation rather than ethnographic or archaic. . . . It is not generally political, ideological, polemical, or racist anti-white—unlike much African French writing. . . . Many of the stories and some of the poems are quite moving or entertaining and should be enjoyed by students or the general public." Choice

Hughes, Langston
(ed.) Poems from Black Africa. . . . Ind. Univ. Press 1963 158p illus $5.95
896
1 African poetry—Collections
"UNESCO Collection of contemporary works"
"Ethiopia, South Rhodesia, Sierra Leone, Madagascar, Ivory Coast, Nigeria, Kenya, Gabon, Senegal, Nyasaland, Mozambique, South Africa, Congo, Ghana, Liberia." Subtitle
"Here is a collection of poems from the fabled dark continent, dazzling in their primary colors, strong in contrasts, and pulsing with emotion. They give powerful expression to the new nationalism of the African people." N Y Her Trib Books

897   Literature of the North American Indian

Day, A. Grove
(ed.) The sky clears: poetry of the American Indians. Univ. of Neb. Press [1964 c1951] 204p pa $1.75
897
1 Indians of North America—Poetry
First published 1951 in hard cover by Macmillan (N Y)
"Some 200 examples of American Indian songs and chants have been assembled by the editor. The translations have been studied as contributions to American literature. The introductory material to the poems provides a review of the form and content of this poetry. Bibliography." Book Rev Digest

900   GEOGRAPHY AND HISTORY

901   Philosophy and theory

Durant, Will
The lessons of history, by Will and Ariel Durant. Simon & Schuster 1968 117p $5 901
1 History—Philosophy
The authors "ask what history has to say about the nature, the conduct and the prospects of man, seeking in the great lives, the great ideas, the great events of the past for the meaning of man's long journey through war, conquest and creation." Publisher's note
"A modest balanced and helpful statement of the beliefs and values that have resulted from the Durants' immersion in historical investigation these many years. Here are their fairmindedness, their respect for human dignity, their exaltation of reason, their horror of bigotry and their faith in education as the clue to the betterment of the human condition." N Y Times Bk R
Guide to books: p103-04

901.9   Civilization

Brinton, Crane
Ideas and men; the story of Western thought. 2d ed. Prentice-Hall 1963 484p $10.95   **901.9**

1 Civilization, Occidental 2 Civilization—History

First edition, published 1950, analyzed in Essay and general literature index

"A discussion of the evolution of Western thought from its origins in Hebrew and Greek civilization to the present day. It considers the fundamental ideas of our culture and examines the answers Western man has given to persisting questions of ethics, religion, politics and science." Publisher's note

Includes: Suggestions for further study; How to use this book; Annotated list of proper names

Foreign Policy Association
Toward the year 2018. Ed. by the Foreign Policy Association. Cowles 1968 177p $5.95   **901.9**

1 Twenty-first century 2 Technology and civilization 3 Progress

"Although no precise predictions are made, attention is focused upon a number of trends which point in the direction of the changes that are being affected [in the fields of weather, space, food, communications and energy]. This book will make the reader become more aware of how the changes and developments in technology of today are most likely to affect the living modes of people not only in the United States but more so in other countries over the world." Best Sellers

Includes bibliographical references

Horizon Magazine
The light of the past. A treasury of Horizon: a Magazine of the Arts. Am. Heritage 1965 288p illus maps boards $13.95   **901.9**

1 Civilization—History 2 Culture

Analyzed in Essay and general literature index

Twenty-eight articles by different authors selected from Horizon Magazine and ranging through many centuries and cultures. Homer's age, the Sumerians, the cave dwellers, the 20th century ideologies of Toynbee and Spengler are among the topics covered. (Publisher)

"The volume permits pleasant visual and intellectual dipping and browsing. . . . Among contributors are such familiar names as C. M. Bowra, Geoffrey Bibby, Alfred Duggan, Basil Davidson, and Gilbert Highet." Booklist

McNeill, William H.
A world history. 2d ed. Oxford 1971 550p illus maps $15   **901.9**

1 World history 2 Civilization—History

First published 1967

A large-type "Keith Jennison" edition of the earliest edition is available from Watts for $12.50

In this survey of world history from the age of early man to the present, the author shows how powerful or attractive cultures have influenced world events. He also demonstrates the importance of geography, communication, and technological and artistic development in the course of civilization. (Publisher)

Includes bibliographical essays

Mumford, Lewis
The myth of the machine. Harcourt 1967-1970 2v illus v 1 $12, v2 $12.95   **901.9**

1 Civilization—History 2 Technology and civilization

Contents: v 1 Technics and human development; v2 The pentagon of power

In this historical survey of the development of man from prehistoric times through the Space Age, the author explores the forces that have shaped technology, taking "life itself to be the primary phenomenon, and creativity,

rather than the 'conquest of nature,' as the ultimate criterion of man's biological and cultural success." Author's note

"This work is not an attack on modern technology per se, but rather on its misuses. Mumford is concerned with saving what is valuable from the irrational obsessions and compulsions that characterize the prevailing applications of science and technology. . . . As in the past, Mumford's work is most illuminating." Choice

Includes bibliographies

Ortega y Gasset, José
The revolt of the masses; authorised tr. from the Spanish. [25th anniversary ed] Norton [1957 c1932] 190p $5.95   **901.9**

1 Civilization 2 Europe—Civilization 2 Proletariat

First published 1930 in Spanish; in English translation, 1932

This famous Spanish intellectual sees the control of government by the masses as a menace to civilization, drowning out the voice of the cultured few who are a country's "saving grace"

"This particular analysis of the modern world's predicament is complex, brilliant, original, and anything but easy to follow. It will probably be attacked from all sides and especially from the Marxist camp. . . . The Revolt of the Masses is an extraordinarily stimulating book, even if one completely disagrees with its thesis." Forum

Bibliography in footnotes

Parkinson, C. Northcote
East and West. Houghton 1963 xxii, 330p maps $5   **901.9**

1 Civilization—History 2 East and West

The author "reviews history from Sumerian days to the present time to show that throughout its course, East and West have alternately been dominant, the periodic decline of one civilization creating a cultural vacuum that was filled by the adjacent rising culture. The new civilization thus evolved in turn decayed, causing the reascendancy of the first, by now revived." Publisher's note

"In covering a period stretching from 3000 B.C. to the present, the author has necessarily practiced selection and condensation, which is not the most persuasive way to document a large, amorphous thesis, since almost any given episode used to support a statement turns out to be only a partial version of the known facts." Atlantic

Bibliography: p303-08

901.92   Civilization—500-1500

Hindley, Geoffrey
The medieval establishment, 1200-1500. Putnam 1970 128p illus (The Putnam Pictorial sources ser) $4.95   **901.92**

1 Civilization, Medieval 2 Middle Ages

"Manuscripts, woodcuts, tapestries, and other authentic visual material of the medieval period are incorporated here in a volume which examines the role of authority at the time: the relationships between king and courtier, priest and layman, church and state. . . . [The author] demonstrates how these different forms of authority interacted upon each other and how the resulting changes in social, economic and religious structure were to provide the groundwork for the Renaissance." New of Bks

Further reading: p125

901.93   Civilization—1500-1900

Brinton, Crane
The shaping of modern thought. Prentice-Hall 1963 249p pa $1.95   **901.93**

1 Civilization, Modern

Brinton, Crane—*Continued*

"A Spectrum book"
Originally published 1959 as: The shaping of
the modern mind, a reprint of the concluding
half of the author's: Ideas and men, listed in
class 901.9
"This is a book about the world-views of
men in our Western tradition, the ideas they
have held and still hold on the Big Questions—
cosmological questions, which ask whether
the universe makes sense in terms of human
capacity to comprehend and, if so, what kind
of sense; theological and metaphysical questions . . . and ethical and aesthetic questions."
Introduction
Includes discussions of such subjects as humanism, Protestantism, rationalism, the Enlightenment, Victorian thought, The Right
and Left during the 19th century and anti-intellectualism

Gay, Peter
Age of Enlightenment, by Peter Gay and
the editors of Time-Life Books. Time, inc.
[1967 c1966] 192p illus map (Great ages of
man: a history of the world's cultures) lib.
bdg. $7.60   **901.93**
1 Eighteenth century 2 Civilization, Modern
3 Europe—Intellectual life
The author portrays 18th century Western
civilization, especially that of Europe, in terms
of its revolutionary philosophies, arts, sciences,
and intellectual and political leaders
The book also includes "the representative
men and women of the century, among them
Frederick and Catherine, Jefferson and Franklin, Newton, Voltaire, Diderot, Rousseau,
Goethe, Lessing, and many others. The illustrations, including the Hogarths, turn the reader into a participant in all the activities at-
tainments, conditions, and problems of 18th
century Europe." Library J
Bibliography: p186

901.94 Civilization—1900-

Colton, Joel G.
Twentieth century, by Joel G. Colton and
the editors of Time-Life Books. Time-Life
Bks. 1968 208p illus maps (Great ages of man:
a history of the world's cultures) lib. bdg. $7.60
901.94
1 Twentieth century 2 Civilization, Modern
"The book is divided into six major sections
each subdivided into text and Picture Essay.
The West in Command centers on the colonial
expansion of the European powers before
World War I. The Lights Go Out carries the
account through the war and its aftermath up
to the Thirties. Scourge of the Depression
centers its picture essay on Lindbergh's successful flight over the Atlantic. A World at
War covers World War II. An Awakening of
Nations starts with the formation of the
United Nations and the collapse of colonial
administration in the face of rising national
spirit across Africa, Asia, Malaysia, Indonesia. A New Balance of Power takes a look at
China and the rest of the world and centers
its picture essay mostly on modern art." Best
Sellers
"Both high school and public libraries will
certainly use [this] attractive, well-laid-out-
book." Library J
Bibliography: p174. Index to the series: p178-
208

902 History—Miscellany. Chronologies

Canning, John
(ed.) 100 great events that changed the
world; from Babylonia to the space age. Hawthorn Bks. [1966 c1965] 672p illus $8.95 **902**
1 Chronology, Historical 2 History—Dictionaries 3 Biography

First published 1965 in England
"Depicts 100 of the world's most important
events, from the formation of Hammurabi's
Code 4,000 years ago to the space walk of the
present era and shows how each event was a
product of its time." Bk Buyer's Guide
"The pieces vary in depth and style . . . the
authors are not identified, and [there is] no
source bibliography. In addition there is a
slight English bias as to who the 'Makers' were
and are. Many fields are represented." Choice

Langer, William L.
(ed.) An encyclopedia of world history; ancient, medieval, and modern; chronologically
arranged; comp. and ed. by William L.
Langer. 4th ed. rev. and enl. with maps and
genealogical tables. Houghton 1968 xxxix,
1504p $15   **902**
1 Chronology, Historical 2 History—Outlines,
syllabi, etc.
First published 1940
Replaces "Manual of universal history" by
K. J. Ploetz which was also published under
the title of "Ploetz's Epitome"
"This encyclopedia covers the history and
civilization of the world from the Paleolithic
period to the middle of 1964." Publisher's note

903 History—Dictionaries

Everyman's dictionary of dates. Dutton $6.50
903
1 History—Dictionaries 2 Chronology, Historical
First published 1911 as: A dictionary of
dates; comp. by Eric Smith. Frequently revised
Alphabetically arranged by subject. "The
basic purpose of this work is to make useful
dates accessible to the general reader. Broadly speaking there are three types of headings: short entries relating to particular mat-
ters, e.g. 'coach'; narratives, e.g. 'United
States of America'; and classified entries, e.g.
'Sieges.'" Preface [to 6th edition, revised by
Audrey Butler]

904 Collected accounts of specific events

Creasy, Sir Edward S.
Fifteen decisive battles of the world. Stack-
pole Bks. 1955 471p maps $4   **904**
1 Battles
Analyzed in Essay and general literature in-
dex
First published 1851
Contents: Marathon, 490 B.C.; Syracuse, 413
B.C.; Arbela, 331 B.C.; Metaurus, 207 B.C.;
Arminius, A.D. 9; Châlons, 451; Tours, 732;
Hastings, 1066; Orléans, 1429; Spanish Armada,
1588; Blenheim, 1704; Pultowa, 1709; Saratoga,
1777; Valmy, 1792; Waterloo, 1815

Eggenberger, David
A dictionary of battles. Crowell 1967 526p
maps $14.95   **904**
1 Battles—Dictionaries 2 Military history—
Dictionaries
This book "provides essential information
on some 1,500 military engagements from the
first battle of Megiddo in 1479 B.C. to the Is-
raeli-Arab War, June 1967. Illustrated by about
one hundred battle maps, the book includes
chronologies of major battles in major wars.
Adequate cross-references for variant spellings
of place-names under which battles are listed
alphabetically, a detailed index of military leaders, a few slogans and battle cries, and an appended list of recent books add to the usefulness of this factual account." Cur Ref Bks

Mitchell, Joseph B.
Twenty decisive battles of the world [by] Joseph B. Mitchell [and] Sir Edward S. Creasy; illus. with maps. Macmillan (N Y) 1964 365p illus maps $7.95   904

1 Battles

Based on Creasy's Fifteen decisive battles of the world, entered above
"Mitchell has abridged and edited to a limited extent the fifteen accounts by Creasy, revised the synopses between these accounts, and added, in 94 pages, accounts of five battles of modern times." Booklist
Includes the battles of: Marathon, 490 B.C.; Syracuse, 415-413 B.C.; Arbela, 331 B.C.; Metaurus, 207 B.C.; Arminius, 9 A.D.; Châlons, 451; Tours, 732; Hastings, 1066; Orléans, 1429; Spanish Armada, 1588; Blenheim, 1704; Poltava, 1709; Saratoga, 1777; Valmy, 1792; Waterloo, 1815; Vicksburg, 1863; Sadowa, 1866; First Battle of the Marne, 1914; Midway, 1942; Stalingrad, 1942-1943
Bibliography: p339-46

Roscoe, Theodore
True tales of bold escapes. Prentice-Hall 1965 235p $5.95   904

1 Escapes

"Five true suspense tales of daring escapes, ranging from that of the 17th-century Dutch scholar Grotius to that of an American submarine [the U.S.S. Puffer] in World War II." Pub W
Bibliographical references included in Notes: p228-35

907 History—Study and teaching. Historiography

Nevins, Allan
The gateway to history. Quadrangle Bks. 1963 [c1962] 440p $5.95   907

1 Historiography

First published 1938
The author "defines the scope and variety of his field and outlines his views on history's objectives both as a science and as an art. . . . He sets apart the different approaches to history—biographical, cultural, intellectual, geographical, and political—illuminating the peculiar goals, problems, and development of each discipline. . . . He spans the history of the collection and use of records—including the mischief of 'garbled' and 'cheating' documents." Publisher's note
Includes bibliographies

908 History—Collections and anthologies

Prescott, Orville
(ed.) History as literature; ed. and with an introduction by Orville Prescott. Harper [1971 c1970] 412p $12.50   908

1 History—Collections

The editor "has assembled an anthology that is both entertaining and of high literary quality. His selections from the works of the great historians are intended to provide a sound representation of major historical periods, and they do: but Prescott has chosen first those who write well and on a high level. . . . Included are choice excerpts from Herodotus, Thucydides, Livy, Plutarch, Tacitus, Suetonius, and among later writers, Gibbon, Macaulay, Voltaire, Parkman, Mattingly, Catton and Flexner." Pub W

909 World history

Asimov, Isaac
Words from history; decorations by William Barss. Houghton 1968 265p illus $5.95   909

1 World history—Dictionaries 2 English language—Etymology

"Attractive and informative volume consisting of one-page articles which define etymologically each of 250 words, alphabetically arranged, selected for inclusion because of their relevance to world history both ancient and modern. The author . . . traces the development of every listed word from its earliest known use in any language to the present, indicating its transmission to other languages and its current connotation." Booklist

Larousse Encyclopedia of ancient and medieval history. General editor: Marcel Dunan; English advisory editor: John Bowle; foreword by Arnold Toynbee. Harper 1963 413p illus maps $25   909

1 History, Ancient 2 Middle Ages—History

Contributors: Jean Piveteau, Jean Delorme, Robert Fossier, Georges Ruhlmann. Translated by Delano Ames and Geoffrey Sainsbury
"Man's progress from prehistory to the late Middle Ages is encompassed in this . . . account of men and empires. A universal rather than sectional history, the book chronicles the interaction of races and civilizations and the consequences in cultural, [religious] historical, and political terms. . . . [Price is one of the] factors in purchase considerations." Library J
Its "contributors give attention to the East as well as the West. . . . [The book is distinguished] for the number, clarity, and interest of the illustrations." Cur Ref Bks

Larousse Encyclopedia of modern history, from 1500 to the present day. General editor: Marcel Dunan. English advisory editor: John Roberts; foreword by Hugh Trevor-Roper. Harper 1964 405p illus maps $25   909

1 History, Modern 2 World history

Translated from the French by Delano Ames
"Beginning with the breakdown of the feudal aristocracies in 15th-century Europe, this volume follows the rise of nations through warfare and conquest as well as through peaceful colonization, up to the present [early 1960's]. More than a history, it provides a record of man's achievements in the arts. With more than 500 illustrations, including 32 in color plates." Huntting
"This volume, as are nearly all Larousse publications, is richly illustrated and printed on paper of fine quality. . . . [The editor] has provided the general reader with an exceptionally well-written book which vividly unfolds the complex drama of modern history. Librarians will find this a handy reference work suitable for the college university and large public library." Library J

The **New** Cambridge Modern history. Cambridge 1957-1970 13v v 1-12 ea $14.50, v14 $27.50   909

1 History, Modern

This projected fourteen volume set supersedes: The Cambridge Modern history, first published 1902-1912 by Macmillan in thirteen volumes
Contents: v 1 The Renaissance, 1493-1520, ed. by G. R. Potter; v2 The Reformation, 1520-1559, ed. by G. R. Elton; v3 The Counter-Reformation and price revolution, 1559-1610, ed. by R. B. Wernham; v4 The decline of Spain and the Thirty Years War, 1609-48/59, ed. by J. P. Cooper; v5 The ascendancy of France, 1648-88, ed. by F. L. Carsten; v6 The rise of Great Britain and Russia, 1688-1715/25, ed. by J. S. Bromley; v7 The old regime, 1713-63, ed. by J. O. Lindsay; v8 The American and French

The **New** Cambridge Modern history—*Cont.*
revolutions, 1763-93, ed. by A. Goodwin; v9
War and peace in an age of upheaval, 1793-
1830, ed. by C. W. Crawley; v10 The zenith of
European power, 1830-70, ed. by J. P. T. Bury;
v11 Material progress and world-wide problems,
1870-1898, ed. by F. H. Hinsley: v12 The shifting
balance of world forces, 1898-1945, ed. by C. L.
Mowat; v14 Atlas, ed. by H. C. Darby

Van Loon, Hendrik Willem
The story of mankind. [New & enl. ed]
Liveright 1967 xxiv, 550p illus maps $7.95
                                         909

1 World history
Awarded the Newbery Medal, 1922
First published 1921
An account of universal history from prehistoric times to the present. Over 150 illustrations and maps by the author are a notable addition to the book. A chronology (500,000
B.C.-2000 A.D.) and an index are included
"The author deals primarily with movements
and ideas not with heroes and picturesque incidents. Nevertheless it reads like a fascinating story told by a master story teller. Knowledge, humor, imagination are brought into
play to explain how a medieval commune got
its charter, why people died for their religion,
what the French revolution did for Europe,
why a scientist is a greater hero than a general." Nation

Wells, H. G.
The outline of history; being a plain history of life and mankind. Rev. and brought
up to date by Raymond Postgate and G. P.
Wells; with maps and plans by J. F. Hor-
rabin. Doubleday 1971 xxii, 1103p illus maps
$5.95
                                         909

1 World history
First published 1920 by Macmillan (N Y)
"Beginning with the position of the earth in
space it covers geologic time and human history down to the present." Wis Lib Bul
What Wells has done "is to state the evolutionary concept of history as a continuing,
growing entity, in terms readily understandable
of the common man." Bookmark

909.08   World history—Modern, 1450/1500-

Harper Encyclopedia of the modern world;
a concise reference history from 1760 to
the present; ed. by Richard B. Morris and
Graham W. Irwin. Harper 1970 xxxii,
1271p maps $17.50
                                     909.08

1 History, Modern 2 World history
The book offers a summary of world history
in two parts—"a Basic Chronology which presents political, military, and diplomatic history
by state, region, and area, and a Topical
Chronology covering, on a worldwide basis,
economic, social, and constitutional history, and
the history of science, thought, and culture."
Publisher's note
"Valuable for ready reference, the volume
also lends itself for browsing." Booklist

909.82   World history, 1900-

Cronkite, Walter
Eye on the world. Cowles 1971 310p illus
$8.95
                                     909.82

1 History, Modern—20th century 2 U.S.—
Social conditions
Covering such topics and personalities as the
environmental crisis, the Middle East and
Southeast Asia conflicts, Kent State, the Chicago 7 and Manson trials, the women's liberation movement, Spiro Agnew, Angela Davis,
the deaths of De Gaulle and Nasser, this book
illustrates the most newsworthy events of 1970
Illustrated "with transcripts of actual tele-
casts introduced, explained and 'bridged' by
Cronkite. . . . Cronkite's book is an engrossing
playback that suggests TV, for all its weaknesses, plays the news game professionally
and seldom slices its drives." Pub W

Halle, Louis J.
The cold war as history. Harper 1967
434p $6.95
                                     909.82

1 History, Modern—20th century 2 World
politics—1945-
Covering the period from 1945 until shortly
after the Cuban Missile Crisis of 1962, this
book describes the origins, the underlying
forces and trends, the principal events, and
the vital participants of the cold war from the
standpoint of history. (Publisher)
"Although Mr. Halle's able and judicious
book cannot be accepted as a history of the
cold war, it is nevertheless a serious contribution to scholarship. Above all it is humane
and compassionate to both sides." Times (London) Lit Sup
Publications cited: p419-21

**National Broadcasting Company, inc. NBC
News**
NBC News Picture book of the year.
Crown illus $10
                                     909.82

1 History—Yearbooks
Editor: 1967- Ben Grauer
Annual. First published 1967
A yearbook which contains pictures and
articles, covering news events in major areas
for the preceding year

News dictionary. Facts on File $9.50 **909.82**

1 History, Modern—20th century—Yearbooks
"A Facts on File publication"
Annual. Supersedes: News year, published
1960-1963
Editor: 1964- L. A. Sobel
This yearbook "provides easy access to the
world events of [the current year] in its alphabetically arranged topical entries under
persons, places, and other subjects, giving information drawn from the daily press, news
magazines, Facts on File, and other professional reference services. According to its compilers, 'it has been assembled, written and edited
with care to avoid distortion or bias.' . . .
Cross-references are given from large subjects, e.g. 'arts,' to specific entries, e.g. 'See
also Academy Awards, Nobel Prizes. . . .' Obituaries are listed under the subject, with 'see'
references under the names of those listed
there. This is a most useful ready-reference
source for answering such questions as: 'What
happened in Cambodia in 1964?' 'How was
the Republic nominee for President selected?'
'What was the school prayer controversy?' "
Cur Ref Bks

Tuchman, Barbara W.
The proud tower; a portrait of the world
before the war, 1890-1914. Macmillan (N Y)
1966 528p illus $7.95
                                     909.82

1 World history 2 Europe—Social conditions
3 U.S.—Social conditions
The author has written "a social history of
the major powers before the first World War
. . . France, England, Germany, The Netherlands, and the United States are minutely scru-
tinized. Concentration is on the social mores of
the late Victorian and Edwardian eras. Each
chapter is concerned with a major power. The
leading political, military and purely bon-vi-
vant hop and skip through the pages of this
[book]." Best Sellers
"Miss Tuchman shows the seeds of hate and
the proliferation of mindless force in an era
often dubbed halcyon. In a world view of rulers, anarchists, labor leaders, pacifists, peace
promoters, and socialists the author writes a
history of tragedy flecked with wry comic relief that is unfailingly interesting." Booklist

Tuchman, Barbara W.—*Continued*

"This is amateur history at its zenith. . . . Certainly a professional historian might have done it differently, but I doubt if there is one living who could have done it half as well." Sat R
References: p465-510

Year: the encyclopedia news annual. Year, inc. illus maps $7.95   **909.82**

1 History, Modern—20th century—Yearbooks 2 History—Yearbooks

Annual. First published 1948. Subtitle varies
A survey of world affairs and major domestic issues, giving background information on developments in the news and an analysis of trends and events with long-term significance

910   General geography

Life (Periodical)

Handbook of the nations and international organizations, by the editors of Life. Time, inc. 1966 176p illus maps (Life World lib) boards $4.95   **910**

1 Geography 2 International organization

This volume describes the geography, history, economy and social structure of 18 countries, and "provides a survey of the world's principal international organizations and a gazetteer of all the nations." Publisher's note
Includes bibliographies

United States. Department of State

The U.S. Department of State Fact book of the countries of the world; introduction by Gene Gurney. Crown 1970 792p illus maps $7.95   **910**

1 World politics—1945- 2 Almanacs

"The background notes on most countries of the world, prepared by officials of the State Department: the land, people, history, government, political parties, economy, etc. A map and reading list for each country." Publisher's note

910.2   Geography—Miscellany. Travel

Additional travel information for the American motorist is obtainable from many oil and gas companies as well as automobile clubs

Baedeker, Karl

Autoguides. Macmillan (N Y)   **910.2**

"Being promoted as the guides for people who have been there more than once . . . [these] books have a unique arrangement of principal routes, alternate routes and digressions, enabling readers to plan their tours selectively." Neal. Reference Guide for Travellers
Countries and areas covered by these autoguides are: Austria; Benelux; Italy; Scandinavia; Spain and Portugal; Switzerland; Turkey; and Yugoslavia

Handbooks. Macmillan (N Y)   **910.2**

This series includes guide books for: Great Britain, France, Berlin and Southern Bavaria
These books "published in English, French, and German editions, and originating in Germany . . . [have] long been regarded as the most authentic and complete guide for the serious traveler. . . . The handbooks [are] written in a concise, informative style . . . and are especially useful for their maps, city plans and diagrams." Winchell. Guide to Reference Books. 8th edition

The **Blue** guides. Rand McNally   **910.2**

Popularly known as: Muirhead's Blue guides
Included in this series are guide books for: Athens and environs; Belgium & Luxembourg; Bernese Oberland & Lucerne; Denmark; England; France, Northwestern; France, The South of; Greece; Holland; Ireland; Italy, Northern; Italy, Southern; London; Malta; Paris; Rome; Scotland; Spain, Northern; Spain, Southern; Wales; Yugoslavia
The books "are mainly guides to European countries, cities, and environs. Similar to Baedeker in style and coverage, they include excellent maps and plans." Winchell. Guide to Reference Books. 8th edition

Clark, Sydney

All the best in. . . . Dodd   **910.2**

Frequently revised guide books to: Bermuda, the Bahamas, Puerto Rico and the Virgin Islands; Britain; the Caribbean; Central America; Europe; France; Germany; Hawaii; Italy; Japan and the Orient; the Mediterranean; Mexico; Scandinavia; South America—East Coast; South America—West Coast; the South Pacific; Spain and Portugal

Fodor's Modern guides. McKay   **910.2**

This series includes guide books for: Austria; Belgium and Luxembourg; Caribbean, Bahamas and Bermuda; Czechoslovakia; Europe; France; Germany; Great Britain; Greece; Hawaii; Holland; Hungary; India; Ireland; Israel; Italy; Japan and East Asia; Morocco; Portugal; Scandinavia; South America; Spain; Switzerland; Turkey; Yugoslavia
These travel guides, edited by Eugene Fodor, are "illustrated and revised annually, [as well as] modern in format and style." Winchell. Guide to Reference Books. 8th edition

Michelin Guides [distributed by French & European Publications]   **910.2**

Michelin publishes two kinds of travel guides. The first, known as Michelin Red guides in four languages, are revised annually and provide "the latest, most up-to-date information on European accommodations . . . [including] town plans, maps, main sights, distances, garages, etc. For accommodations, there is a selection of hotels and restaurants to suit all pockets, with details of agreed prices, comfort, [and] standard of cuisine." Publisher's note
The second series, Michelin Green guides, are not revised annually and are mainly concerned with sightseeing. They "point out places of interest and attractive routes, plans of towns and buildings, and suggest itineraries based on the amount of time the tourist has to spend in a given area." Publisher's note
The Red guides are: Benelux; France; Paris; Spain; Germany; Italy
The Green guides available in English include: Austria; Brittany; Chateaux of the Loire; French Riviera; Germany; Italy; Normandy; Paris; Portugal; Switzerland

910.3   Geography—Dictionaries

The **Columbia** Lippincott Gazetteer of the world; ed. by Leon E. Seltzer; with the Geophysical Research Staff of Columbia University Press and with the cooperation of the American Geographical Society. With 1961 supplement. Columbia Univ. Press 1962 2148p $75   **910.3**

1 Geography—Dictionaries

Based on the 1905 edition of Lippincott's New gazetteer, which superseded the 1855 Lippincott's Pronouncing gazetteer
"Includes 130,000 articles with over 30,000 cross-references in a 3-column, thumb-indexed, buckram bound cyclopedia of places. The new 'Gazetteer' has half again as much material as its godfather, 'Lippincott's Gazetteer' of 1905. All places of any importance, alphabetically arranged, past and present, are identified. Long, comprehensive articles are devoted to large and significant geographic

The **Columbia** Lippincott Gazetteer of the world—*Continued*

areas with shorter articles on smaller areas. Geographic features of the world are described thoroughly and a wide coverage with essential facts about each place, is apparent. Ancient. Biblical, and archeological sites, as well as modern communities, all over the world, are included. The main entry is under an English name when it has one. Transliterated names furnish parallel listings hard to find elsewhere. Pronunciations are given with simple symbols to make [it] as usable as possible. Three preliminary pages give abbreviations and keys to population figures and pronunciation." Cur Ref Bks

Kane, Joseph Nathan
Nicknames and sobriquets of U.S. cities and states, by Joseph Nathan Kane and Gerard L. Alexander. 2d ed. Scarecrow 1970 456p $10   **910.3**

1 Names, Geographical 2 Nicknames
ISBN 0-8108-0325-9

First published 1965 with title: Nicknames of cities and states of the U.S.

An enlargement of a section of Kane's "1000 facts worth knowing" plus Alexander's "Nicknames of American cities, towns and villages (past and present)"

"An unusual reference tool composed of a selective list of official and unofficial sobriquets of U.S. cities and states by two men who previously and independently published now out-of-print material in this area. A geographical index, arranged alphabetically by state and then city, with city nicknames listed, is followed by an alphabetical index of city nicknames. Similar indexes for states follow after a list of 'All-American cities.' When known and not obvious, explanations of source, origin, and reason for selection are given in the geographical indexes." Booklist

Monkhouse, F. J.
A dictionary of geography. 2d ed. Aldine Pub. 1970 378p illus maps $7.95   **910.3**

1 Geography—Dictionaries
First published 1965

A "dictionary of 3,400 entries based on actual usage, including tables of statistical material, cross-references and specific terms which differ from general practice, illustrated with 225 specially compiled and drawn maps and diagrams. The main categories of entry include landforms, oceanography, climate and weather, cartography and surveying, the earth as a spheroid, units and dimensions, soil, vegetation and biogeography, political, economic and cultural geography, archeology, and geographical theory. . . . Cross-references are given to assist the user in tracing cognate and supplementary entries." Publisher's note

Stewart, George R.
American place-names; a concise and selective dictionary for the continental United States of America. Oxford 1970 xl, 550p $12.50   **910.3**

1 Names, Geographical—Dictionaries

"Designed for the 'general public,' the work includes three categories of place-name information: well-known places, such as Philadelphia; repeated names which appear in many localities . . . and unusual names, such as Kokomo, Piaski, Goodnight. Emphasis is on names rather than places. Following each of the 12,000 entries is the name derivation, the state where pertinent, and explication with historical, geographical and/or folk interpretations." Library J

"For lovers and students of Americana and for many who undoubtedly will be interested in learning something of the early history and lore of their own regions, it is a comprehensive if necessarily selective, reference work." Pub W

Webster's Geographical dictionary; a dictionary of names of places, with geographical and historical information and pronunciations. Merriam maps $8.50   **910.3**

1 Geography—Dictionaries

First published 1949. Periodically revised to bring it up to date

"A pronouncing dictionary of more than 40,000 geographical names, including not only current but also historical names from Biblical times, ancient Greece and Rome, medieval Europe, and World Wars I and II. Cross references are given for equivalent and alternative spellings of names that have been changed. Gives the usual gazetteer information, e.g., location, area, population, altitudes of mountains, etc.; for the largest cities, important countries, and each of the United States, also gives geographical features, historical monuments, and a concise history. Includes full-page, and smaller, inset maps and an appendix of historical maps in color. Introductory material includes a list of geographical terms with their equivalents in various foreign languages." Winchell. Guide to Reference Books. 8th edition

"For use as a quick and convenient reference book. . . . It takes the place of the old familiar gazetteer in about half the space, with the addition of many maps and considerable statistical material on the principal countries of the world." N Y Times Bk R

Worldmark Encyclopedia of the nations. Editor and publisher: Moshe Y. Sachs. World Press [distributed by Harper] 5v illus maps $59.95   **910.3**

1 Geography—Dictionaries 2 World history—Dictionaries 3 United Nations 4 World politics—1945-

First published 1960 in one volume, arranged in one alphabet. The five volumes are divided by continent, with the countries appearing in alphabetical order. Periodically revised to bring material up to date

"Vol. 1 of this compilation is devoted to the United Nations System and its agencies and vols. 2-5 to the nations of the world. It covers somewhat the same ground as the 'Statesman's Year-Book,' [entered in class 310.25] but the two works supplement each other usefully. A vast amount of information for each country is treated under 50 numbered arbitrary headings. Thus it is easy to compare the judicial systems, labor, social welfare, tourism, for example, of any given countries. These headings include geographical, historical, political, social and economic information. The bibliographies are helpful, and there are certain unexpected features such as brief information on famous persons in each country's history. Particularly helpful for the newer countries." Enoch Pratt Free Library. Reference Books, 1966

910.4 Accounts of travel

Armstrong, Richard
(ed.) Treasure and treasure hunters. White 1969 203p $4.75, lib. bdg. $4.56 **910.4**

1 Buried treasure

"A David White collection"

The editor "has gathered together a fascinating collection of treasure-hunting stories that display man's courage and endurance, but also the extreme lengths to which greed can lead him." News of Bks

Contents: The law of treasure trove: The cryptograph, by E. A. Poe; The treasure in the forest, by H. G. Wells: The treasure of Axayacatl, by W. H. Prescott; Mogul silver, by A. C Clarke; Where the trail forks, by J. London; Famous treasures; The magic calabash, by R. Armstrong; Nothing is hidden, nothing lost, by V. Hugo; The treasure hunt, by R. L. Stevenson; Adventure on Cocos Island, by R. Charroux; Oak Island, by E. Burke; Pacific plunder, by C. Lloyd; An epic of treasure recovery, by R. H. Davis

Burgess, Robert F.
Sinkings, salvages, and shipwrecks. Am. Heritage Press 1970 188p illus map $6.95   **910.4**

1 Shipwrecks 2 Salvage 3 Buried treasure
ISBN 0-07-008956-6

Burgess, Robert F.—*Continued*

"Burgess is thoroughly engrossing in his yarn-spinning about 'the archaeology of shipwrecks.' He tells of ancient ships discovered, with their artifacts and treasures, where they had lain buried in sea-muck for centuries or millenia; he relates more recent instances, for example, Commander Keeble's extraordinarily dangerous feat in diving to find a secret device believed inside a German U-boat sunk in World War II. His detailed accounts of the 1715 hurricane-sinking of a Spanish treasure armada off Florida, its discovery and the salvage of some of its gold in recent years, the search for the famous 'Monitor' of Civil War days, the excavation of the city-beneath-the-sea, Port Royal in Jamaica, destroyed in an earthquake in 1692, are only some of his intriguing tales." Pub W
Bibliography: p[191-92]

Chichester, Sir Francis
Gipsy Moth circles the world. Coward-McCann [1968 c1967] 269p illus maps $6.95
910.4

1 Voyages around the world 2 Gipsy Moth IV (Ketch) 3 Sailing
First published 1967 in England
The author's account of his nine-month voyage alone around the world in the ketch Gipsy Moth IV. Starting from Plymouth, England in August 1966, he sailed round the Cape of Good Hope to Sydney, from there around stormy Cape Horn and north through the Atlantic back to Plymouth
"An intensely detailed personal document. There is an almost minute-by-minute recapitulation of events, carrying, in addition to a brave man's personal reactions and emotions, a vast amount of technical nautical material. This can be fascinating to the experienced offshore yachtsman, but a reader without this background, more interested in romance and adventure, may find some of it heavy going." N Y Times Bk R

Dana, Richard Henry
Two years before the mast
910.4

1 Seafaring life 2 Voyages and travels
Some editions are:
Dodd (Great illustrated classics) $4.50 With authentic illustrations of the period and a biographical sketch of the author by his grandson. H. W. L. Dana
World Pub. (Rainbow classics) $3.95. lib. bdg. $3.90 Illustrated by Alexander Dobkin, with an introduction by May Lamberton Becker
Published anonymously in 1840, this book "is written in the form of an extended diary, based on a journal that the author kept during his voyage [as a seaman] for the purpose of presenting 'the life of a common sailor as it really is.' . . . A concluding chapter furnishes a general statement of conditions prevailing on merchant ships at the time, and suggests measures to diminish the hardships of the sailors' daily lives." Oxford Companion to American Literature
"The book dwells on the brutality of the ship's captain and the sailors' lack of redress. It did much to arouse public opinion, and led to legal action." The Reader's Encyclopedia
Includes an account of California in Spanish days

Freuchen, Peter
Peter Freuchen's Book of the Seven Seas, by Peter Freuchen with David Loth. Messner 1957 512p illus maps $9.95
910.4

1 Ocean 2 Voyages and travels 3 Discoveries (in geography)
"Here I have tried to set forth something of both the science and the dreams—the facts and the fancies which make the Seven Seas endlessly fascinating." Foreword
"The seas' geography, curious facts about its plant and animal life, its weather, winds, waves, seagoing ships, the sea's effect on man, famous sea battles, exploration, whaling days, tales of sunken treasure and of the slave trade, yarns of the late author's own days in sail and steam, and much older fact and anecdote about the oceans are related in simple narrative style and there are more than 100 illustrations from many sources." Pub W

Halliburton, Richard
Richard Halliburton's Complete book of marvels. Bobbs 1960 2v in 1 (640p) illus maps boards $6.95
910.4

1 Voyages and travels
First issued in two separate volumes: Richard Halliburton's Book of marvels: the Occident, published 1937, and Second book of marvels: the Orient, published 1938
The author describes such scenic wonders of the world, natural or man-made, as the Pyramids, Mecca, the Taj Mahal, Lhasa, Yosemite Falls, the Grand Canyon, New York, Popocatepetl and Gibraltar

Heyerdahl, Thor
Kon-Tiki; across the Pacific by raft; tr. by F. H. Lyon
910.4

1 Kon-Tiki Expedition, 1947 2 Pacific Ocean 3 Ocean currents—Pacific Ocean 4 Ethnology —Polynesia
Some editions are:
Rand McNally $6.95
Watts, F. lib. bdg. $9.95 Large type edition. A Keith Jennison book
First published 1948 in Norway
"The Norwegian author had a theory that civilization had come to the South Sea Islands from South America with the prevailing winds and currents. And there was a Polynesian legend of a great Chief Tiki who had come from the east. So he built a balsa log raft lashed together with ropes, just as the old chief's men would have built it, and with five companions and a parrot set out to drift across the Pacific Ocean. The 4300-mile trip took almost 100 days, but the raft did land in Polynesia. The writing here is taut and vivid; there is no padding." Horn Bk

Lord, Walter
A night to remember
910.4

1 Titanic (Steamship)
Some editions are:
Holt $5.95 Illustrated with photographs
Watts, F. lib. bdg. $8.95 Large type edition complete and unabridged. A Keith Jennison book
A detailed account of "the tragic drama of that terrible night—April 14, 1912—when the 'Titanic,' the unsinkable ship, struck an iceberg and went down in the icy waters of the Atlantic." Library J
"Using every available scrap of evidence that archive and memory can bring to the surface, [the author] has set out to tell, simply and chronologically, the events of the night of the sinking. The result is a stunning book, incomparably the best on its subject and one of the most exciting books of this or any year." N Y Times Bk R

Marcus, Geoffrey
The maiden voyage. Viking 1969 320p illus map $8.95
910.4

1 Titanic (Steamship)
The author discusses the tragedy of the Titanic from the period of embarkation until after the inquiries into its sinking were completed on both sides of the ocean. He describes the provisions made for the wealthy passengers, the ignored messages, and the faulty seamanship which precipitated the disaster. (Publisher)
"The book is explained, and sometimes illuminated, by notes. . . . Contemporary photographs show monochrome glimpses of that day; and a pocket inside the back cover holds a lift-out facsimile plan of the Titanic's first-class accommodation. Even after all these years the story remains enthralling. Wisely, Mr. Marcus lets it tell itself in verbal pictures." Christian Science Monitor
References and notes: p299-316

Mowat, Farley

The boat who wouldn't float. Little 1970
241p boards $5.95   **910.4**

1 Sailing 2 Newfoundland—Description and
travel

"An Atlantic Monthly Press book"

This book tells of the author's "sea-going
experiences with 'Happy Adventure,' a small
two-masted schooner, painted an appalling
shade of green, of a class known in the foggy
little fishing village of Muddy Hole in Newfoundland as a 'Southern Shore bummer.' . . .
The schooner didn't float too well, but perseverance, pumps and repairs—a saga in itself
—overcame all [as he explored the coast of
Newfoundland]." Pub W

"Farley Mowat's effort here is to show that
a vessel may have a mind of its own such as
to constitute a continuing frustration to its
owner. . . . Mowat's style is impeccable, his
ear and eye for people and places are sharp
and faithful instruments of recordation, and
his humor is evident." Best Sellers

Map on lining-papers

Rawicz, Slavomir

The long walk; a gamble for life, by
Slavomir Rawicz as told to Ronald Downing. Harper 1956 239p illus map boards $5.95
                                      910.4

1 Escapes 2 Asia, Central—Description and
travel 3 Prisons

"With death a constant companion the Pole,
Slavomir Rawicz, and his fellow escapees from
a Siberian labor camp follow a tortuous path
to freedom through Mongolia and the Himalayas. Grim narrative is lightened by the
camaraderie among them. Special attention is
given to their encounter with the Abominable
Snowman." Cincinnati

Rickenbacker, Edward V.

Seven came through; Rickenbacker's full
story; with an introduction by W. L. White.
Doubleday 1943 118p illus $3   **910.4**

1 Survival (after airplane accidents, shipwrecks, etc.) 2 Pacific Ocean 3 World War,
1939-1945—Personal narratives

"Captain Rickenbacker tells from memory of
his 21 days on a raft on the Pacific in Octo-
ber-November, 1942. He relates briefly the reason for his being a passenger on a flight
south-westward from Hawaii and incidents of
the trip to the time the plane was forced
down. He describes in a matter-of-fact way
the days on the raft in shark-filled waters, the
condition and reactions of the men, and the
rescue, and carries his story through completion of his mission in the combat areas."
Booklist

"This is really the story of the personality
of a strong man . . . whoever may disagree
. . . although he talks much more of his companions than of himself, of their suffering and
stoicism and bravery in the face of black despair." N Y Times Bk R

910.9 Voyages and travel— History. Discovery and exploration

Armstrong, Richard

A history of seafaring. Praeger [1967-
1969] 3v illus maps ea $4.95   **910.9**

1 Voyages and travels 2 Ships —History

Published respectively, 1967, 1968, 1969 in England; 1968 (v 1) and 1969 in the U.S.

Contents: v 1 The early mariners; v2 The discoverers; v3 The merchantmen

Volume one "chronicles the beginning of seafaring from prehistoric times to the fourteenth century, tracing the development of ship
building and navigation instruments and describing the maritime exploits of such early
peoples as the Egyptians, Phoenicians, Greeks,

Carthagenians, and the Vikings. Volume two,
. . . shows how an increasing awareness of the
sea led men, from the fifteenth to the seventeenth centuries, to become maritime explorers
and recounts the achievements and discoveries
of the great mariners. [Volume three] chronicles the activities of merchant seamen from
the seventeenth to the twentieth centuries.
In detailing the development of ships as cargo
and passenger carriers he discusses their use
in the transportation of emigrants from Europe
to the New World and Australia and in the
slave trade, and points out technological advances in navigation and ship construction, particularly the change from sail to steam." Booklist

A bibliography is included in each volume

Hale, John R.

Age of exploration, by John R. Hale and
the editors of Time-Life Books. Time-Life
Bks. [1971] 192p illus maps (Great ages of
man: a history of the world's cultures) lib.
bdg. $7.60   **910.9**

1 Discoveries (in geography) 2 Voyages and
travels 3 Renaissance 4 Explorers

First published 1966

"Identifying the years 1420 to 1620 as the
great period of discovery in Western history
and pointing out that Europe in this era possessed the unique conditions necessary for
great explorations, an English scholar reviews
succinctly the achievements of the Portuguese
under Henry the Navigator, the voyages of
Columbus, and other persistent efforts to find
a sea route to the Orient, rounding out his account with the eighteenth-century discoveries
of Captain Cook. Picture essays, handsomely
illustrated in the manner of other Time-Life
volumes, depict the sea and its hazards, maps
and ships of the period, the home of a prosperous Dutch trader, and the American Indian."
Booklist

Bibliography: p186

Hermann, Paul

Conquest by man; tr. from the German
by Michael Bullock. Harper 1954 xxiii, 455p
illus maps lib. bdg. $6.48   **910.9**

1 Discoveries (in geography)

First published 1952 in Germany

"The story of exploration from the times of
ancient man to the beginning of the age of discovery. It describes Marco Polo's travels, the
voyages of the Chinese, the Viking trips to
North America, and smaller movements of peoples, such as the Javanese emigration to Madagascar." Book Rev Digest

"In this packed, fascinating brightly written
and audaciously speculative book . . . [the
author] deals with the travels and discoveries
of man, from the earliest time to the Portuguese voyages of the fifteen century. The
author admits that it is meant to be a popular
work, that he has tried 'to make the book
rather more entertaining than is usual in works
dealing with such a forbidding subject as ancient history.' " Christian Science Monitor

Bibliography: p433-40

Masselman, George

The Atlantic: sea of darkness. McGraw
1969 127p illus maps $4.95, lib. bdg. $4.72
                                      910.9

1 Atlantic Ocean 2 Discoveries (in geography)

"A brief but illuminating history of man's exploration of the Atlantic Ocean, from the 8th
Century B.C. until the end of the 15th Century.
The author discusses two controversial topics—
the Vinland Map and Parahyba stone of Brazil
—and gives detailed accounts of the explorations
of the early Vikings, the activities of Henry
the Navigator, and the voyages of Diaz, Columbus, Vespucci and Cabot. Material on the beginnings of slave trade in Africa during the middle
of the 15th Century will interest students in
African Studies programs." Library J

Further reading: p123-24

National Geographic Society

Great adventures with National Geographic; exploring land, sea, and sky. The Society 1963 504p illus maps (Story of man lib) $7.95   910.9

1 Discoveries (in geography) 2 Adventure and adventurers 3 Voyages and travels

"Melville Bell Grosvenor, editor-in-chief; Merle Severy, editor and art director." Verso of title page

"To mark its seventy-fifth anniversary, the Society presents in one volume, the principal adventures and explorations chronicled over the years in the National Geographic. . . . There is a list of National Geographic expeditions and scientific researches, and of medals awarded by the Society." Book Rev Digest

"Here are Peary's race to the North Pole. Carl Akeley's elephant hunting expeditions, as well as newer epics in bathyscaphe and space capsule . . . with the dear, familiar makeup known to millions. . . . May there always be a National Geographic." N Y Times Bk R

Sanderson, Ivan T.

Ivan Sanderson's Book of great jungles, by Ivan T. Sanderson with David Loth. Messner 1965 480p illus maps $9.95   910.9

1 Tropics 2 Natural history—Tropics

In this book about the world's great tropical rain forests, the author describes their inhabitants, flora, animals, resources, explorers, and ancient civilizations

"Many personal observations, some adventures, and hints of a few mysteries still unsolved make good browsing as well as [a] . . . guide to adventure and to possible careers in the natural sciences." Horn Bk

Stefánsson, Vilhjalmur

(ed.) Great adventures and explorations. . . . New rev. ed. Edited with an introduction and comments by Vilhjalmur Stefánsson; with the collaboration of Olive Rathbun Wilcox; maps designed by Richard Edes Harrison. Dial Press 1952 788p maps $7.50   910.9

1 Discoveries (in geography) 2 Explorers

First published 1947, and analyzed in Essay and general literature index

"From the earliest times to the present as told by the explorers themselves." Subtitle

Partial contents: The Polynesians cross the Pacific; Europe proves that the world is round; The discovery of the Amazon and the first crossing of South America; Discovery of the Northwest Passage; The attainment of the North Pole

This book "has endeavored to secure historical continuity by leading from one major narrative to the next through summaries of less important ones that belong in between, and by occasional passages of interpretation which seek to give the reader a needed perspective." Introduction

Thomas, Lowell, 1892-

Lowell Thomas' Book of the high mountains. Messner 1964 512p illus maps $10
910.9

1 Mountains 2 Discoveries (in geography)

This is "not only a history of mountains in the making, but the story of the men who have climbed them, their avalanches and volcanoes, their plant and animal life, and the . . . legends about them." Bk Buyer's Guide

"This is nontechnical, with the emphasis on adventure and the unusual." Horn Bk

911 Historical geography

Adams, James Truslow

(ed.) Atlas of American history; R. V. Coleman, managing ed. Scribner 1943 360p maps $17.50   911

1 U.S.—Historical geography—Maps

Available only from the publisher by direct subscription

This atlas enables the user to locate "with relation of other places of importance in the same area and period every event of geographical importance in American history. . . . An index of some 10,000 locations guides the user instantly to the proper map on which to find the place for which he is looking." Huntting

"Intended to meet the need for a concise, easy to use authoritative atlas, its chronologically arranged, clearly drawn maps give evidence of the careful editorial work of 64 historians. There is no commentary except brief paragraphs on the maps themselves. The place index is a valuable guide to names no longer in use in this country." Cur Ref Bks

American Heritage

The American Heritage Pictorial atlas of United States history, by the editors of American Heritage, The Magazine of History. Editor in charge: Hilde Heun Kagan; chapter texts by Roger Butterfield [and others]; consultant: Richard B. Morris. Am. Heritage 1966 424p illus maps $16.50   911

1 U.S.—Historical geography—Maps 2 U.S.—Maps

Maps, historical illustrations, and commentary relate geographic and historical causes and effects in American history from the Ice Age to the Space Age. (Publisher)

"Indian cultures, explorers' routes, military campaigns, national expansion, industrial and agricultural patterns, population and voting trends and much other historical and sociological data are given in clear, informative maps and charts. . . . Special sections or portfolios, (battle grounds, mid-19th-century cities, national parks) are a bonus." Library J

"The 60,000 word text is supplemented by . . . historical pictures and documents." McClurg. Book News

Gilbert, Martin

American history atlas; cartography by Arthur Banks. Macmillan (N Y) [1969 c1968] 112p maps $4.95   911

1 U.S.—Historical geography—Maps

First published 1968 in England

This "atlas contains maps that depict the history of America from the origin of settlements in 50,000 B.C. to the present day. The maps [show] . . . changes in the political, social, religious, and economic development of America as well as major wars, battles, explorations, alliances, and the growth and expansion of various aspects of American life, such as transportation, trade, agriculture, and industry." Publisher's note

Jewish history atlas; cartography by Arthur Banks. Macmillan (N Y) 1969 112p maps $4.95   911

1 Jews—History—Maps 2 Israel—Historical geography—Maps

"Jewish and Christian students of Jewish history, interested general readers, and reference questioners are uniquely and graphically served by 112 sharply drawn maps that chronologically chart major and significant minor vicissitudes in 4,000 years of Jewish migrations and destiny. The themes, multiple legends, and statistics of each map convey fortunate conditions and creative contributions as well as oppression and tragedy. Typical of the wide variety of topics mapped are the Jews of Italy, 1000-1600; nine prominent Jewish thinkers, 882-1939; other Zions, 1652-1946; and Jewish city dwellers, 1966. Index of themes and places." Booklist

"A helpful popular work, which may be certainly recommended though with reservations." Choice

Bibliography: p126-31

Recent history atlas: 1870 to the present day; cartography by John R. Flower. Macmillan (N Y) [1969 c1966] 121p maps $4.95
911

1 Atlases, Historical 2 History, Modern

Gilbert, Martin—*Continued*

First published 1966 in England
"A chronologically arranged presentation of
. . . maps, which are specially designed to
help explain some of the main historical developments and important episodes in world
history of the last 100 years. The author, gives
information concerning wars, battles, treaties,
alliances, population problems and political
confrontations for each continent. He includes
a time chart which tabulates by decades from
1860 to 1960-1970 historical events and dates
for Great Britain, Germany, France, Italy, the
U.S., Russia, and other nations." Booklist

Hammond, Incorporated
    History atlas of America. Hammond illus
maps $2.50   911
    1 U.S.—Historical geography—Maps
    First published 1948. Title varies
    "On the written story of history which tells
'What' happened, this atlas superimposes maps
showing 'Where' it happened." Title page [of
1959 edition]
    "Beginning between 10,000 and 20,000 years
ago when America was reached by visitors from
across the Pacific, the [atlas] illustrates geographically by means of a collection of maps
the most significant periods and events in the
development of Western Civilization. . . . The
American child, as well as many adults—especially those of foreign extraction—will now
learn visually and with the insight only maps
can supply, the history of our [country]."
Publisher's note

Heyden, A. A. M. van der
    (ed.) Atlas of the classical world. Ed. by
A. A. M. van der Heyden and H. H. Scullard. Nelson 1959 221p illus maps $18   911
    1 Geography, Ancient—Maps 2 Civilization,
Greek 3 Rome—Civilization
    "The purpose of the Atlas is to present for
student, teacher, and general reader a vivid
picture of the history and culture of Greece
and Rome and to demonstrate their lasting influence on Western civilization. The 'generous
interpretation of the word "Atlas"' has al-
lowed the work to cover geographical, ethnological, political, economic, military, religious, literary, and artistic aspects of the classical world and to present them through
maps, illustrations, and the explanatory text.
. . . A 60,000-word text is interwoven with
the maps and plates. . . . The use of current
photographs contrasted with reconstructions
or drawings of the ancient buildings or scenes
contribute greatly to the understanding of the
ancient world. . . . The writing is concise and
crisp, scholarly yet readable. . . . The maps
are on still heavier paper and are remarkably
clear and legible even though unusually full of
information. . . . It succeeds admirably in its
purpose of offering a graphic introduction to
the classical world . . . its achievments, its remains, and its lasting importance." Booklist
    This book is "in the last resort, somewhat
baffling work of reference: at once much more
and much less than what is usually meant by
the term 'atlas.' . . . It tells you everything
except what you consult it for: it has all the
luxuries and none of the necessities." Times
(London) Lit Sup

Historical atlas of the world. Barnes &
Noble 1970 unp maps $4.50   911
    1 Atlases, Historical
    SBN 389-01087-1
    Original Norwegian edition, 1962
    "108 small-scale maps cover the period from
the spread of civilization in ancient times to
1968, half of them devoted to the last five centuries. . . . An index of over 7,000 entries contains all the place names on the maps, names
of peoples, historical events, military expeditions, and voyages of discovery, giving location by letter and number. Countries, provinces, and regions are given several references
in chronological order so that their development may be traced." Cur Ref Bks
    In this "handy, compact, and comprehensive
historical atlas . . . colors are clear and effective, even in the small detail maps." Booklist

Rand McNally and Company
    Rand McNally Atlas of world history;
ed. by R. R. Palmer; contributing editors:
Knight Biggerstaff [and others]. The Company 1965 216p maps $7.95   911
    1 Atlases, Historical
    First published 1947
    A presentation of world history from an-
cient times to the end of World War II prepared by outstanding authorities in the field
of history, the scores of new maps and the
concise text cover the political, economic, social, military and religious phases of world
history. (Publisher)
    "Europe and the U.S. are treated in more
detail than other parts of the world. The concise explanatory text and appended population
data add to an understanding of the maps although they are not covered by the index. A
convenient one-volume atlas for circulation."
Booklist
    Bibliography: p192

Shepherd, William R.
    Historical atlas. Barnes & Noble maps
$17.50   911
    1 Atlases, Historical
    **First published 1911 by Holt and periodically
revised.** Editions published from 1956 include
maps for period since 1929, prepared by C. S.
Hammond and Company
    "Because of its scholarly accuracy, compre-
hensiveness both as to field and detail, its
clearness and the fact that it has been arranged especially for use in American schools
and colleges, this atlas is [recommended]. . . .
The time range is from Greece of the Mycenean period and the Orient in 1450 B.C. to
present-day Europe and the United States."
Booklist
    "The best of the smaller general historical
atlases. . . . Full general index of names."
Winchell. Guide to Reference Books. 8th edition
    Includes bibliography

Vries, S. de
    An atlas of world history [by] S. de Vries,
T. Luykx [and] W. O. Henderson. Nelson
1965 183p illus maps $10   911
    1 Atlases, Historical 2 World history—Pic-
tures, illustrations, etc.
    Based on a work published 1964 in the Neth-
erlands
    This atlas "opens with 8 pages of maps
showing Britain from the first to the twentieth century. These are followed by maps of
world history from the earliest civilisations
right up to subjects of contemporary significance, such as the dissolution of the British
and French Empires. . . . The maps are supplemented by 6 pages of black-and-white sketch
maps showing selected battlefields and the
historical growth of towns. A special feature
of this atlas is the . . . introductory section—
over 300 black-and-white illustrations of objects, scenes and personalities. A running commentary explains the pictures and links them
with the maps." Publisher's note

912 Atlases

    The major publishers of atlases have vari-
ant editions, suitable for various libraries.
For detailed information, see Publishers' catalogs

Britannica atlas. Encyclopaedia Britannica
1969 various paging illus maps $35   912
    1 Atlases
    Supersedes the Encyclopaedia Britannica
World atlas, first published 1942, and the 1965
changed title: Encyclopaedia Britannica World
atlas international. Periodically revised
    This "atlas presents in sequence: the world;
the oceans; the continents; three series of regional maps at progressively larger scales; and,
finally, a section of maps of the world's great

Britannica atlas—*Continued*

cities. . . . Maps in the most extensive section of the atlas—the regional map section—employ special design characteristics for each of three basic series, thus making maps in each series easily distinguishable from the others. . . . A 40-page section . . . deals graphically with economic, political, and cultural data that transcend national boundaries. This is the section students consult for information on distribution of population, religions, natural resources, and so on." Publisher's note

Goode, John Paul

Goode's World atlas. Rand McNally illus maps $10.95   912

1 Atlases 2 Geography, Commercial—Maps

All editions, from the first in 1922 to 1949, published with title: Goode's School atlas. Through the eighth edition compiled by John Paul Goode, thereafter edited by Edward B. Espenshade, Jr. Periodically revised

"A long time favorite and standard work in schools and educational material centers. One of the best atlas values available and certainly the best inexpensive small atlas for home use. More a true atlas than most works. . . . Very well balanced, includes a wealth of statistical information on climate, soils, resources, industries, population, etc. Especially useful are the maps of cities and their environs. Maps are clear, easily read, usually attractive, beautifully reproduced, with excellent relief features. This atlas is on practically all approved lists." General World Atlases in Print

Includes a glossary

Hammond, Incorporated

Hammond Contemporary world atlas. New census ed. Doubleday illus maps $12.50 912

1 Atlases

First published 1967. Subtitle varies with revisoins of statistics, maps and/or ploitical data

The full-color maps, tables, charts, glossaries and other important data for each area of the world are located on consecutive pages. Also included are the postal zip code numbers for the cities and towns of the United States. (Publisher)

Hammond World atlas. The Company 1971 2v illus maps $39.95   912

1 Atlases

"Hallmark edition"

"Hammond World Atlas is organized to make the retrieval of information as simple and quick as possible. The guiding principle in organizing the atlas material has been to present separate subjects on 'separate' maps. In this way, each individual map topic is shown with the greatest degree of clarity, unencumbered with extraneous information that is best revealed on separate maps. Of equal importance from the standpoint of good atlas design is the treatment of all current information on a given country or state as a single atlas unit. Thus, the basic reference map of an area is accompanied on adjacent pages by all supplementary information pertaining to that area. . . . An outstanding new feature of the atlas is the addition of ZIP codes to the index entries for each of the legion of communities shown on the state maps. . . . [Moreover] the results of the latest census [are here for the United States and 85 other countries]." Introduction

Hammond's Ambassador world atlas. The Company illus maps $14.95   912

1 Atlases

First published 1954 and frequently revised

"Contains political and physical maps, including those showing rainfall, vegetation, population, etc. Arranged by continents with separate maps for individual countries and states. The index gazetteer lists the cities of the world with inset city street maps of some of the larger cities, topographic features, such as rivers, mountains, lakes, etc., and includes some very brief gazetteer information about some places." Winchell. Guide to Reference Books. 8th edition

National Geographic Society

National Geographic Atlas of the world. The Society illus maps $18.75   912

1 Atlases

First published 1963, periodically revised to keep it up to date. Editor-in-chief: Melville Bell Grosvenor

Maps and text of this atlas "treat the world by geographic regions. Each region is discussed first as a unit, followed by individual vignettes of the political divisions that make it up. . . . Statistical digests follow the country summaries. . . . The digest for each country gives its population, in latest figures from the most authoritative source. . . . [Also facts as to] the religion and racial background of a nation's people [is given along with] what the climate is, what industries and natural resources exist. The population—within city limits—of the country's largest city, with other major cities listed after it according to size and an address to write to for travel or other information from an agency of the country itself [is included]." Introduction to third edition

Rand McNally and Company

The international atlas. The Company 1969 liv, 280, 223p illus maps $35   912

1 Atlases

Title page and text in English, German, Spanish and French. Edited by Russell L. Voisin and others

This atlas has been designed "with international use in mind . . . for those whose native tongue is German, Spanish or French, as well as English. . . . This international approach has been carried into the maps themselves through the utilization of the metric system of measurement, and particularly by a strong emphasis on the use of local forms for geographic names. . . . The space allotted to each region reflects its relative economic and cultural significance on the world scene, as well as its total population and area. . . . The sequence of maps in the Atlas begins with the series of world, continent, and ocean maps. Next are the three series of regional maps, grouped together in regional sequence, and . . . [a] metropolitan map series." Foreword

Includes glossary

Rand McNally Cosmopolitan world atlas. The Company illus maps $19.95   912

1 Atlases

First published 1949. Periodically revised. 1965-1967 appeared with title: Rand McNally New Cosmopolitan world atlas. Frequently referred to as: Cosmopolitan world atlas

"Map types include physical, political, metropolitan area, and oceanographic. . . . A superior general atlas, with exceptionally comprehensive coverage." Library J

Rand McNally Pictorial world atlas. The Company 1967 160p illus maps boards $4.95
912

1 Atlases

"Text, pictures and maps are combined in an atlas that has been specifically designed to give maximum information about today's world. Facts about world transportation, languages, races, religions, vegetation, climates and land forms are made more meaningful through the inclusion of 75 colorful photographs and special maps." Huntting

Time-Life Books

Atlas of the world, by the editors of Time-Life Books and Rand McNally. Time-Life Bks. [1968 c1966] 160p maps (Life World lib) lib. bdg. $7.60   912

1 Atlases

First published 1966

This atlas contains maps of the countries and political areas of the world

"Here also will be found a group of special maps dealing on a worldwide basis with such topics as population, climate and economics. . . . [Another section] contains up-to-date statistics on the countries and major cities of

Time-Life Books—*Continued*
the world. The special 63-page Index, containing more than 25,000 place names, is an unusually large one for an atlas of this scope. Together with the maps that make up the bulk of the book, this all adds up to a volume which can stand on its own but which is also . . . [an] able adjunct to the other World Library volumes." Introduction

The Times, London
The Times Atlas of the world. Comprehensive ed. produced by the Times of London in collaboration with John Bartholomew & Son, Ltd. Edinburgh. 2d ed. rev. Houghton 1971 [c1968] xliii, 272p maps $6   912

1 Atlases

First published 1967
This is a one-volume edition based on the five-volume third edition published from 1955-1960
This is a sturdy 12-pounder and stands a foot-and-a-half high. . . . The book is generous to Americans in the way that matters: in giving fullest treatment to places less familiar to us than America. The intensity of coverage is impressive. . . . [The] index is implemented by a list of convenient abbreviations. . . . What is more impressive, there is a glossary explaining some 2,300 terms from 47 languages. This is useful in view of the policy of favoring native designations on the maps. The packing of information into the maps has been aided also by another device: a detached plastic panel summarizing the map conventions of color, abbreviation, and other symbols. . . . The maps are an inexhaustible store of lore and an unflagging delight to the eye." Book World
For a fuller review see: The Booklist and Subscription Books Bulletin Review, July 15, 1968

913 Geography of the ancient world. Prehistoric archeology

Bowman, John S.
The quest for Atlantis. Doubleday 1971 182p ilus maps $4.50, lib. bdg. $5.25   913

1 Atlantis

Following the trail of all the other searchers for Atlantis, this book gives an account of the legendary island from mythology to present-day research. The names of some of the searchers encountered include the familiar—Plato, Homer, Columbus—and the less familiar—St Brendan, Madame Blavatsky, Diodorus Siculus. (Publisher)
"This work is at least as much a history of Western thought as it is a chronicle of the Atlantis problem. In several instances Atlantis becomes an example, demonstrating some philosophical position, rather than forming the primary subject matter. This book is not a set of crackpot hypotheses. It is an objective and well-reasoned effort." Science Bks

Deetz, James
Invitation to archaeology; with illus. by Eric G. Engstrom. Natural Hist. Press 1967 150p illus $4.50   913

1 Archeology

"Published for the American Museum of Natural History"
The author "links archaeology to anthropology in an absorbing account of what an archaeologist does, and where and why he does it. Uses many interesting examples to explain the complexities of the profession today, and includes a number of drawings. For laymen, and for career-seeking students." N Y New Tech Bk.
Selected readings: p141-42

Müller, Artur
The Seven Wonders of the World; five thousand years of culture and history in the ancient world; photographs by Rolf Ammon; introduction by Michael Grant; tr. by David Ash. McGraw [1969 c1966] 336p illus $14.95   913

1 Civilization, Ancient 2 Art, Ancient
Original German edition, 1966
"Descriptions and histories of the seven wonders of the world: the Hanging Gardens of Babylon, the Statue of Zeus from Olympia, the Temple of Artemis in Ephesus, the Mausoleum of Halicarnassus, the Colossus of Rhodes, the Pharos of Alexandria, and the Pyramids of Gizeh (the only one still extant)." Bk Buyer's Guide
Index and glossary: p331-36

Poole, Lynn
Carbon-14, and other science methods that date the past, by Lynn and Gray Poole; illus. by P. A. Hutchison. McGraw 1961 160p illus maps $4.50   913

1 Archeology 2 Radiochemistry
"Whittlesey House publications"
An "easy-to-read explanation of the method of dating ancient objects through the use of carbon 14. Its use in modern times to trace the development of man and evaluate in writing the timetable of history are illustrated by means of interesting descriptions of dating remnants of antiquity. Although dealing primarily with carbon 14, other dating devices are introduced: archeomagnetism, dating of obsidian by hydration rate, and of clay, pottery, and earth materials by thermoluminescence." Chicago Sch J

913.03   Archeology

Bibby, Geoffrey
Four thousand years ago; a world panorama of life in the second millenium B.C. Knopf 1961 398p illus maps $7.95   913.03

1 Civilization, Ancient
A picture of everyday life "as the ordinary man experienced it, not only in the civilizations of Egypt, Crete, Asia Minor and Mesopotamia, but also among the hunters of northern Europe, horsemen of the Russian steppes and the merchants and seafaring men. Also chronicles the important events." Ontario Lib Rev

Looking for Dilmun. Knopf [1970 c1969] 383p illus maps $10   913.03

1 Dilmun 2 Excavations (Archeology) 3 Persian Gulf region—Antiquities
The state of Dilmun, which was referred to in Gilgamesh, left some material artifacts of its 20 centuries of existence. "Archaeologists have been digging up these remains, and using them to reconstruct the history of Dilmun, which was in its day an important trading center for much of the Middle East. . . . One of its modern excavators here tells the story of his fifteen years' struggle." Book of the Month Club News
"An archaeological project in the Persian Gulf region is described in a lively, detailed, personal report that digresses occasionally to review the history revealed by earlier digging in the area and to explain how archaeologists determine the meaning of their findings." Booklist

Bordaz, Jacques
Tools of the old and new stone age; photographs by Lee Boltin. Natural Hist. Press 1970 145p illus $5.95   913.03

1 Stone implements 2 Stone age
"Published for the American Museum of Natural History"
This book gives a "résumé of our knowledge concerning the manufacture and use of prehistoric stone implements in the Old World

Bordaz, Jacques—_Continued_

which started about two million years ago. . . . The majority of the drawings have been prepared by Mr. Marcel Smit." Preface
Bibliography: p117-41

Bray, Warwick

The American Heritage Guide to archaeology [by] Warwick Bray [and] David Trump; drawings by Judith Newcomer. Am. Heritage Press 1970 269p illus maps $6.95
913.03

1 Archeology—Dictionaries
ISBN 0-07-007348-1
Published in England under title: A dictionary of archaeology

This encyclopedic dictionary written by two British archaeologists "is designed to aid readers who may find standard works too technical and to serve serious students who wish to go beyond their immediate specializations. The authors' greatest problem was to avoid omitting anything essential and still produce a book that would be compact and not too expensive. Classical, medieval, and industrial archaeology have in general been excluded; coverage is world-wide and the emphasis is on the prehistoric. However, the authors obviously write for an English audience and include therefore many entries for Roman and Anglo-Saxon times. The text contains about 1600 entries and 211 figures, and there are almost 100 additional pages of photographs and maps. There is no bibliography." Library J

Ceram, C. W.

Gods, graves, and scholars; the story of archaeology; tr. from the German by E. B. Garside and Sophie Wilkins. 2d rev. and substantially enl. ed. Knopf 1967 441p illus maps $8.95
913.03

1 Archeology—History
Original German edition published 1949. First edition in English 1951

"The story of Champollion and the reading of the Rosetta Stone, the decipherment of the inscriptions on the monument of Darius the Great, Leonard Woolley's famous excavations at Ur, and John Lloyd Stephens' discovery of the ruins of a great Mayan city are . . . told in this book, which has been arranged by cultural area rather than by chronological order. . . . This volume shows the human side of many personalities who have made significant contributions to scholarship." Doors to More Mature Reading

A "popular survey of archaeological work. His stories are interesting and instructive, sometimes downright exciting, revealing a genuine respect for scholarship." Sat R
Bibliography: p433-41

(ed.) Hands on the past; pioneer archaeologists tell their own story. Knopf 1966 434p illus $10
913.03

1 Excavations (Archeology) 2 Archeology 3 Archeologists
Published in England with title: The world of archaeology

"This book is confined almost entirely to the authentic writings of the archaeologists themselves. . . . Our book covers the period of the first systematic excavations up to the present day, when the excavator with a spade has suddenly had his work made easier and more effective by complicated technical advances. We have restricted ourselves regionally to Europe, North Africa, the Near East and both the Americas. Prehistoric discoveries have not been included." Foreword

"None of the selections is unduly technical although the writing skill of the authors varies." Library J
Sources: p421-25

The march of archaeology; tr. from the German by Richard and Clara Winston. Knopf 1958 326p illus maps $17.95
913.03

1 Archeology—History

Originally published 1957 in Germany
The author "records the accomplishments of archaeology by tracing 'the historical and cultural continuity that extends from Sumeria through Babylonia, Assyria, Crete, Greece, and Rome down to our own times. . . . Will be popular by reason of its approach and the unusual format in which text and photographs are displayed to mutual advantage." Booklist
Chronological table: p307-15. Bibliographical note: p316-17

The **Concise** encyclopedia of archaeology; ed. by Leonard Cottrell. 2d ed. Hawthorn Bks. 1971 xxv, 430p illus maps $16.95
913.03

1 Archeology—Dictionaries
First published 1960
"Although this book is aimed principally at amateurs, professional archaeologists will find that it contains many useful, readily available data. A brief essay, 'What is archaeology?', defines the subject and describes archaeological work. Some American students will be surprised at his differentiating between archaeology and prehistory; others would disagree with his statements about Neanderthal man. Entries include archaeologists, sites, peoples and cultures, dating techniques, and hundreds of others. Using amendments and additions the editor attempts to cover archaeological research and developments during the 11 years since the first edition." Choice
Bibliography: p413-25

Cottrell, Leonard

Lost cities. Grosset [1963 c1957] 251p illus pa $2.25
913.03

1 Archeology 2 Cities and towns, Ruined, extinct etc.
"Grosset's Universal library"
First published 1957 by Holt
"The Assyrian cities of Nimrud and Nineveh, ancient Hittite sites in Turkey, Babylon, Ur, and other cities of Babylon—these are explored in all the suspense of their discovery. Also included are findings at Macchu Picchu, the last great capital of the Inca Empire, and Chichen Itza, sacrificial site of the Mayas." The AAAS Science Book List for Young Adults
Bibliography: p237-41

Falls, C. B.

The first 3000 years: ancient civilizations of the Tigris, Euphrates, and Nile River valleys, and the Mediterranean Sea; written & illus. by C. B. Falls. Viking 1960 220p illus maps $5.95
913.03

1 Civilization, Ancient
This is a "history of civilization from 4,000 B.C. to 14 A.D. It is far more than the dreary facts of wars and conquests, dynasties and kings. Its scope is wide, including ordinary citizens and how they lived as well as the great leaders. Mores, social customs, trade and commerce, art, architecture, and military enterprises are among aspects included. Ten beautifully colored maps relate events of text closely. Many striking drawings with humor and informative captions. . . . Excellent table of contents with dates, detailed index including pronunciation key, and annotated, classified bibliography (adult books)." Massachusetts

Horizon Magazine

The search for early man, by the editors of Horizon Magazine. Author: John E. Pfeiffer; consultant: Carleton S. Coon. . . . Am. Heritage 1963 153p illus maps boards $5.95, lib. bdg. $5.49
913.03

1 Archeology 2 Man, Prehistoric
"A Horizon Caravel book"
"Illustrated with many paintings, engravings, and sculptures from prehistoric times." Title page
An account of the evolution of prehistoric man which "describes discoveries of artifacts and remains in the Dordogne area of France and Olduvai Gorge in Africa." Publisher's note

Horizon Magazine—*Continued*

"Mr. Pfeiffer's summary of [the] infinitely patient and laborious [archeological] achievement spares no technical detail. Also, as intended, it leaves the impression that life in Paleolithic times was much more complex and represented a much higher accomplishment, than had once been imagined." N Y Times Bk R

Further reference: p151

Quennell, Marjorie

Everyday life in prehistoric times, by Marjorie & C. H. B. Quennell. Putnam 1959 225p illus maps $4   913.03

1 Man, Prehistoric 2 Stone age
First published 1921-1922 in England
"The present volume is a new edition, incorporating 'Everyday Life in the Old Stone Age' and 'Everyday Life in the New Stone, Bronze, and Early Iron Ages,' revised and edited by G. de G. Sieveking. . . . The subject matter has been brought up to date, and more illustrations have been added." Publisher's note
Describes the everyday life of prehistoric man with special emphasis on the cave dwellers and their art
Bibliography: p21

Schreiber, Hermann

Vanished cities [by] Hermann and Georg Schreiber; tr. from the German by Richard and Clara Winston. Knopf 1957 344p illus maps $7.95   913.03

1 Cities and towns, Ruined, extinct, etc.
Original German edition published 1955 in Vienna
The authors reconstruct the life of such vanished cities as Palmyra, Sybaris, Tarshish, Zimbabwe, Cumae, Sodom and Gomorrah, Troy, Vineta and Tiahuanaco. (Publisher)
"Translation, type, illustrations, and bookmaking are all of the highest quality. . . . Contains over a hundred line-cuts and photographs." N Y Her Trib Books
Chronological table: p340-44

Silverberg, Robert

Frontiers in archaeology; maps by Dorothy de Fontaine. Chilton Co. 1966 182p illus maps $4.95   913.03

1 Archeology
"Six archeological sites or cultures are chosen to illustrate the process of discovery, investigation and interpretation of the remains: Jericho and Ugarit in the Middle East, Anyang in China, Zimbabwe in east Africa, the Aztec civilization of Mexico, and the prehistoric remains of Easter Island. . . . A reliable, well-organized and readable book. Conveys some of the fascination of archeology without distorting the facts." Science Bks
Selected bibliography p171-75

Throckmorton, Peter

Shipwrecks and archaeology; the unharvested sea. Little 1970 270p illus maps $6.95   913.03

1 Archeology 2 Shipwrecks 3 Skin and scuba diving
"An Atlantic Monthly Press book"
The author begins with a "section on 'The Sea Change,' in which he describes what happens to a ship and its contents which have been lying under the sea for centuries or even millennia. . . . [Following a description] of marine archaeology, explaining many of the techniques, dangers, disappointments and difficulties, Throckmorton proceeds to [analyze] . . . a number of investigations in which he himself has taken part." Book World
Selected bibliography: p257-58

White, Anne T.

Lost worlds; adventures in archaeology. Random House 1941 316p illus maps $3.95, lib. bdg. $4.49   913.03

1 Archeology 2 Civilization, Ancient

A "book which not only brings to life famous archeologists and their contributions to history but reveals as well the driving power behind and the mystery and excitement attendant upon their discoveries. With enthusiasm and authenticity the author describes the reconstruction of four vast, buried civilizations—the Minos, Egypt of the Pharaohs, Babylonia-Assyria, and the Maya." Booklist
"This absorbing book . . . contains all the thrills of a great mystery. Illustrated with photographs and drawings. Well printed and designed." N Y Pub Lib
Some books to read: p307-09

913.31   Civilization of Ancient China

Loewe, Michael

Everyday life in early Imperial China; during the Han period 202 BC-AD 220; drawings by Eva Wilson. Putnam 1968 208p illus maps $4.50   913.31

1 China—Civilization
The book covers "a period of great historical importance, for the institutions that stabilized in these 400 years set sacrosanct precedents for China's succeeding dynasties. Loewe's book does not fail to touch upon any of the features of governmental or personal life which remain to us from records. These facts are presented clearly, arranged under appropriate headings—such as 'Life in the cities,' 'The officials,' 'Industry and technology'—and supplemented by many clear drawings of Han artifacts and buildings. The book thus provides a convenient catalogue of the period." Library J

This book is "to be read by people who are not specialists. . . . From it there emerges an outline of what we know most about and what we know least about in Han China." Times (London) Lit Sup
Suggestions for further reading: p200-01

Schafer, Edward H.

Ancient China, by Edward H. Schafer and the editors of Time-Life Books. Time-Life Bks. 1967 191p illus maps (Great ages of man: a history of the world's cultures) $6.95, lib. bdg. $7.20   913.31

1 China—Civilization 2 China—Antiquities
"A superb introduction to early Chinese civilization. The scope of the book, which ranges from the Shang through the T'ang dynasties, exceeds the period usually designated as ancient China, but still provides a cohesive and very rewarding subject matter. Schafer has not attempted a thorough coverage of all aspects in the limited space allotted to his well written text, but has focused on daily life, religion, philosophy, major technical innovations, literature, and contacts with the world outside of China. The material on religion and daily life is much fuller than that found in most books on China's early culture. The text is ably supplemented by a large number of illustrations, many grouped as picture essays on such topics as the role of women in society, painting, and Buddhist sculpture." Choice
Bibliography: p186

913.32   Civilization of Ancient Egypt—To 640 A.D.

Casson, Lionel

Ancient Egypt, by Lionel Casson and the editors of Time-Life Books. Time, inc. 1965 192p illus maps (Great ages of man: a history of the world's cultures) boards $6.95   913.32

1 Egypt—Antiquities 2 Egypt—Civilization

Casson, Lionel—*Continued*

This book pictures the civilization, history, daily life, religious beliefs, art, and architecture of the ancient Egyptians as revealed through archeological discoveries. (Publisher)

"The description of pyramid building, a simplified explanation of hieroglyphs, and other information about a still entrancing civilization will fascinate even the jaded. Librarians familiar with other works in the series will recognize the format—many charts, diagrams, and pictures, together with a simplified but clear and interesting text." Library J
Bibliography: p186

Chubb, Mary

Nefertiti lived here; with illus. by Ralph Lavers. Crowell 1955 [c1954] 195p illus map $5.95   **913.32**

1 Egypt—Antiquities 2 Tell el-Amarna 3 Nefertiti, Queen of Egypt

First published 1954 in England

"A young woman serves as secretary and jack-of-all-trades for a group of archeologists on an expedition to Egypt to explore the site where Queen Nefertiti lived." Cleveland

"As she tells of the expedition's six weeks at Tell el Amarna, the reader too feels present at the diggings, discoveries, and impromptu lectures that brought Nefertiti and her contemporaries alive for the expedition's newest members. A fresh flowing style makes this read like fiction." Booklist

Cottrell, Leonard

Five queens of ancient Egypt. Bobbs 1969 181p illus $5   **913.32**

1 Queens 2 Egypt—Civilization 3 Egypt—Antiquities

A version for younger readers of the original book first published 1967 with title: Lady of the two lands

The author has reconstructed from a few scattered clues, a picture of the lives and times of Hashepsowe, Tiye, Nefertiti, Ankhesnamun, and Nefertari, five Egyptian queens who achieved much power

"Although this book is devoid of the personal lives of these five queens, the author gives a broad and fairly detailed account of the esteem in which they were held and of the power with which they were endowed, either by their own ingenuity or through their royal husbands. Although the Egyptian history is sparse, Mr. Cottrell has successfully compiled events and details which portray and relate interesting and informative reading for young people." Best Sellers
Bibliography: p173-75

Life under the Pharaohs. Holt 1960 255p illus $5   **913.32**

1 Egypt—Antiquities 2 Egypt—Civilization

An account of life in ancient Egypt as seen in the household of a nobleman, the Vizier Rekmire, who lived during the reign of Thutmose III in 1500 B.C. From the wall paintings and inscriptions on Rekhmire's tomb, translations of ancient records, and antiquities unearthed by archeologists, the author has created this picture of the civilization of ancient Egypt. (Publisher)

"Chapters alternate, one giving a straightforward account of a subject such as 'The Land, The People, and Their Gods,' 'Houses and Furniture,' . . . and the next a fictional account of various characters, as they lived and worked, gave a party, bought and sold on the market, and so forth. This device is surprisingly effective, and result is an interesting, readable, and informative book. It will appeal to the library patron everywhere who is looking for something 'not too ponderous' about ancient Egypt. The book was first published in Great Britain in 1955." Library J
Bibliography: p245-47

The lost Pharaohs. Holt 1961 250p illus $5   **913.32**

1 Egypt—Antiquities

First published 1950 in England

"An archaeological survey of Egypt, including the land itself, its history, some important 'digs,' and the work of the Egyptologists in

piecing together evidence to uncover the story of this civilization that began over 3,000 years before Christ." The AAAS Science Book List for Young Adults

Illustrated with photographs, this account is "a lively travel book, and an introduction to the fascinations of archeology that should lure many a reader to consider making a career of it." Sec Ed Brd

The secrets of Tutankhamen's tomb; drawings by Raymond Cruz. N.Y. Graphic 1964 139p illus map $4.50   **913.32**

1 Egypt—Antiquities 2 Tutenkhamûn, King of Egypt

The story "of the discovery of the Tutankhamen Tomb [in Egypt] by Howard Carter and Lord Carnarvon and the archaeological detective work involved in the discovery." Bk Buyer's Guide

A "selection to exemplify the contribution of archeology to ancient history or as a specialized reference work at junior or senior high school level. Note, however, that it is a book on a single specific topic, and not a general survey." Science Bks

Murray, Margaret A.

The splendor that was Egypt; a general survey of Egyptian culture and civilization. New and rev. ed. Praeger [1969 c1964] xxii, 256p illus $9.50   **913.32**

1 Egypt—Antiquities 2 Egypt—Civilization

First published 1949 by Philosophical Library. This is a reissue of the 1963 edition published by Hawthorn Books

"A study of Egyptian culture and the dynastic complications of Egypt in its three main periods. Building, agriculture, horticulture, clothing, cooking, science, law, government and religion are all covered." Huntting

"'A scholarly, yet thoroughly readable work, which will appeal both to historian and general reader.' Superbly illustrated." Cincinnati
Includes bibliography. Maps on lining-papers

White, Jon Manchip

Everyday life in ancient Egypt; drawings by Helen Nixon Fairfield. Putnam [1964 c1963] 200p illus maps $4.50   **913.32**

1 Egypt—Social life and customs

"With the remarkable abundance of discoveries and writings on hand, the author is able to give a complete picture of life in ancient Egypt throughout the Dynastic times. With little change throughout the period, the picture is uniform and aspects of daily life are closely examined. The author gives four main divisions: the geography and character of the people, the areas of dwellings, the homes and familial customs, and finally the various strata of society. The concluding section takes in the private life of an ordinary family." Best Sellers

The author "is very sharp with those who regard the Egyptians as cynical religious pessimists: constantly he emphasizes the gaiety of their lives and the sustaining quality of their faith. At times, perhaps, this counter-movement takes him a little too far the other way." Times (London) Lit Sup
Books for further reading: p192

913.33   Civilization of Palestine to 70 A.D.

Horizon Magazine

The Holy Land in the time of Jesus, by the editors of Horizon Magazine. Author: Norman Kotker; consultant: Frederick C. Grant. Am. Heritage 1967 151p illus map boards $5.95, lib. bdg. $5.49   **913.33**

1 Palestine—Antiquities 2 Church history—Primitive and early church

"A Horizon Caravel book"

This is "the turbulent history of the Holy Lands at the beginning of the Christian era,

Horizon Magazine—*Continued*
when the power of the Romans became dominant and the persecution of Jews and Christians strengthened their faith." Horn Bk
"Beautifully and profusely illustrated . . .
[events are] told with discernment and vigor,
giving a broad yet detailed picture of the
political, religious, and historical intricacies."
Chicago. Children's Book Center
Further reading: p151

Pearlman, Moshe
The Zealots of Masada; story of a dig.
Scribner 1967 216p illus map $5.95, lib.
bdg. $5.09   913.33
1 Excavations (Archeology)—Israel 2 Masada, Israel
An account of Masada, which towers over the
Dead Sea in Israel. This "story of the 1963-1965
dig, led by . . . Professor Yigael Yadin, re-
creates one of the great [archeological]
searches into the distant past and vividly depicts the events that made Masada both a
fortress and a symbol of heroism." Huntting

913.34 Civilization of India to 647 A.D.

Edwardes, Michael
Everyday life in early India; drawings by
Oliver Williams. Putnam 1969 176p illus
map $4   913.34
1 India—Antiquities 2 India—Social life and
customs 3 India—Civilization
"A detailed look at life in early India and its
background from roughly the third century
B.C. to the eighth century A.D. Drawing on
Indian literature as well as the discoveries of
archaeologists, epigraphers, and social anthropologists Edwardes pieces together the history
of the period and the daily life in a civilization
he characterizes as refined, brilliant, lusty, and
incomparable rather than gloomy, oppressed by
a rigid caste system, and conditioned into accepting unhappiness." Booklist

913.35 Civilization of Mesopota- mia and Iranian Plateau to 642 A.D.

Cottrell, Leonard
The quest for Sumer. Putnam 1965 222p
illus $4.95   913.35
1 Sumerians 2 Archeology
The author describes the rediscovery of Sumer in southern Mesopotamia through archeological excavations and through the decoding
of the Sumerian language. He gives an account
of the knowledge that was gained about Sumerian life, religion, government, and art.
(Publisher)
In this popular account "there are occasional
lapses of accuracy and misemphasis. . . .
[Despite these] it is an excellent survey for the
layman and should whet the student's appetite
for more. The latter's wants can be supplied
from the good bibliography appended." Choice

Culican, William
The Medes and Persians. Praeger 1965
260p illus maps (Ancient peoples and places)
$8.50   913.35
1 Iran—Antiquities 2 Iran—Civilization
"By following the evolution of the Luristan
bronzes and other metalwork found in southwestern Iran, Mr. Culican traces the transformation of the Medes and Persians from a
relatively primitive people into a great nation.
He provides . . . [a] panorama of the mature
Achaemenid civilization—and of its empire
builders (Darius, Xerxes, Artaxerxes, and Cyrus

the Great), its satrapy system, its . . . arts and
architecture, and its decline and fall." Publisher's note
Bibliography: p178-90

Kramer, Samuel Noah
Cradle of civilization, by Samuel Noah
Kramer and the editors of Time-Life Books.
Time-Life Bks. [distributed by Little 1971
c1967] 183p illus maps (Great ages of man:
a history of the world's cultures)
boards $6.95   913.35
1 Mesopotamia—Civilization
Reprint of a title first published 1967
"Sumerian, Babylonian, and Assyrian cultures are traced to show how the growth of
agriculture in the fertile Tigris-Euphrates valley led to the founding of great cities like Nineveh and Babylon where writing and wheeled
vehicles were invented and music, architecture,
and literature flourished. The archaeological
techniques used in excavating these sites are
described, and . . . an abundance of excellent
illustrations amplifies the text." Booklist
Bibliography: p179

Saggs, H. W. F.
Everyday life in Babylonia & Assyria;
drawings by Helen Nixon Fairfield. Putnam 1965 207p illus maps $4   913.35
1 Civilization, Assyro-Babylonian
"After giving an outline account of Mesopotamian history from 3000 to 300 B.C., the
author describes in detail life at an Amorite
court . . . agriculture, crafts and industries;
law, trade and commerce; life in the city of
Babylon at the time of Nebuchadnezzar; and
finally religion." Publisher's note
"Only a very serious and interested student
will read the book cover-to-cover, but the
detail, illustrations and index make the work
ideal for reference." Best Sellers
Books for further reading: p199-200

913.36 Civilization of Europe north and west of the Italian peninsula

Arribas, Antonio
The Iberians. Praeger [1964 c1963] 274p
illus maps (Ancient peoples and places)
$8.50   913.36
1 Spain—Antiquities
Translated from the Spanish by Celia Topp
This volume sums up "knowledge about the
Iron Age coastal peoples living between the
Rhone in Southern France and the Pillars of
Hercules on the Iberian Peninsula. It describes
daily habits; homes; political, social, and
economic life; religion; crafts; and art. A
survey of studies, tables of events, drawings,
photographs, an appendix of sources, and an
international bibliography." Booklist

Hagen, Anders
Norway. Praeger 1967 205p illus maps
(Ancient peoples and places) $8.50 913.36
1 Norway—Antiquities 2 Iron age
Translated from the Norwegian by Elizabeth
Seeger
This book traces the archeological history of
Norway, beginning with the Early Stone Age
Fosna and Komsa people. "Professor Hagen
pursues his story . . . by way of the Neolithic
Age and the first farmers, past the sub-
Neolithic cultures and the Bronze Age with
their marked overlappings, on to the defined
periods of the Iron Age—always with the pro-
viso that the less accessible regions of the
country lagged well behind the south." Times
(London) Lit Sup
Bibliography: p158-60

Hawkins, Gerald S.

Stonehenge decoded; [by] Gerald S. Hawkins in collaboration with John B. White. Doubleday 1965 202p illus maps $5.95
913.36

1 Stonehenge 2 Great Britain—Antiquities 3 Astronomy

"It is the contention of the astronomer-author, after computer analysis, that the circle of great stones on the Salisbury Plain—long believed to be an ancient religious monument—is really an astronomical observatory." Bk Buyer's Guide

"Dr. Hawkins' complex theory of Stonehenge's purpose stands at the heart of his fascinating and often exciting book, but he also includes an outline of what has been written about the monument: legends from early myths to the romanticisms of recent poets; theories of how it was built, including his own on how the huge stones were brought from Milford Haven in Wales; guesses about its use." Book of the Month Club News

Bibliography: p191-94

Hodges, Henry

Ancient Britons; how they lived. Pictures by Marjorie Maitland Howard; text by Henry Hodges and Edward Pyddoke. Praeger [1970 c1969] 92p illus $3.95   **913.36**

1 Great Britain—Antiquities 2 Man, Prehistoric

First published 1969 in England

The authors' purpose is "to re-create everyday life in the British Isles as it was before writing was known. The authors reconstruct the story of early man from the beginning of the Old Stone Age, about 250,000 years ago, to the invasions by the Romans, about 55 B.C. to A.D. 43 (when history, as distinct from prehistory, began), by piecing together the evidence provided by his artifacts and other remains." Publisher's note

"The drawings are equally important, as each chapter has an illustration depicting typical activities and is followed by drawings of artifacts of that particular period." Pub W

Jazdzewski, Konrad

Poland. Praeger 1965 240p illus maps (Ancient peoples and places) $8.50   **913.36**

1 Poland—Antiquities

Translated from the Polish by Maria Abramowicz and Robin Place

"A concise, chronological survey of ancient Polish history from paleolithic times through late Iron Age stages as revealed by interpretations of archaeological materials concerning the environment, way of life, and tools of each period and the social, cultural, and other changes from one period to another." Booklist

Bibliography: p178-90

Savory, H. N.

Spain and Portugal; the prehistory of the Iberian peninsula. Praeger 1968 324p illus (Ancient peoples and places) $10   **913.36**

1 Spain—Antiquities 2 Portugal—Antiquities 3 Man, Prehistoric

The book reviews "the present state of research into the prehistory of the Iberian peninsula, from its beginnings until the arrival of the Celts and the shaping of the historical Iberian culture." Publisher's note

"It is without question a book more useful to the specialized student or professional than to the layman. . . . It must also be remarked that this is one of the few English language sources devoted to Iberian prehistory." Choice

Bibliography: p262-71

913.37 Civilization of Ancient Italian peninsula and adjacent territories to 476 A.D.

Arnott, Peter D.

The Romans and their world. St Martins 1970 318p illus $6.95   **913.37**

1 Rome—Civilization

Published in England with title: An introduction to the Roman world

This "profile of Rome and the Romans ranging from the legendary Romulus and Remus through almost twelve hundred years of triumph and decay until the fall . . . [focuses] on the people, the daily events, the culture and society—not on the warmaking." Publisher's note

"The leading personalities of Roman times are presented realistically rather than as stereotypes to give a feel for the atmosphere of ancient Rome beyond a recitation of names and dates of interest only to specialists. Photographs of architectural and landscape sites in Rome and elsewhere convey the impact of Roman presence that still remains." Booklist

Bailey, Cyril

(ed.) The legacy of Rome; essays by C. Foligno [and others]. With an introduction by H. H. Asquith. Oxford [1928] 512p illus maps $6   **913.37**

1 Rome—Civilization

First published 1923

"This book is an endeavour to trace in many fields [commerce, law, social life, religion, science, the arts, engineering, etc.] the extent of the inheritance which the modern world owes to ancient Rome." Editor's note

Bibliographies at the end of most of the essays

Bloch, Raymond

The Etruscans. Praeger 1958 260p illus (Ancient peoples and places) $8.50   **913.37**

1 Etrurians

Translated by Stuart Hood

"A general historical survey of Etruscology, a probing of the key questions still unanswered about the origins and language of the Etruscan people, and a description of the different aspects of Etruscan civilization." Pub W

"Written primarily as a reference work for the student, its quick and facile style makes it equally attractive to the general reader with cultivated interests." N Y Times Bk R

Critical bibliography: p189-93

The origins of Rome. Praeger 1960 212p illus maps (Ancient peoples and places) $8.50   **913.37**

1 Rome—Antiquities

Translated by Margaret Shenfield

Original French edition published 1946

"Professor Bloch describes the migrations and the economic and strategical factors that caused Rome, among a whole outcrop of different early cultures, to rise to a position of supreme importance in the ancient world. Having emphasized the influence of Greece on the one hand, and that of Etruria on the other, he . . . reconstructs life in Rome up to the beginning of the Republic—its culture, language, law and religion, the Etruscan invasions, the Tarquinian kings." Publisher's note

Bibliography: p152-60

Cowell, F. R.

Everyday life in ancient Rome; illus. from drawings by D. Stredder Bist. Putnam 1961 207p illus $4   **913.37**

1 Rome—Social life and customs 2 Rome—Civilization

"Designed to stimulate further interest in Roman history, this introduction attempts to picture the main aspects of everyday life in ancient Rome, as it developed at all levels of society, from the days of the early Republic

Cowell, F. R.—*Continued*

down through the decline of the Empire. The British author covers architecture and domestic furnishings, home and family life, education, slavery, occupations, cultural interests, recreational activities, and religion. His scholarly and detailed yet readable discussion incorporates illuminating quotations from contemporary writers and is illustrated with numerous photographs and drawings. A vivid recreation for supplementary use in junior high and high school." Booklist

Davis, William Stearns

A day in old Rome; a picture of Roman life. Biblo & Tannen 1959 xxiv, 482p illus maps $4.50   **913.37**

1 Rome—Social life and customs 2 Rome—Civilization

A reprint of the title first published 1925 by Allyn

Describes "what an intelligent person would have witnessed in Ancient Rome if . . . he had been translated to the Second Christian Century, and conducted about the imperial city under competent guidance." Preface

Depicts the daily life and customs of all classes—government, religion, games, courts and orators, country life, phases of Roman occupations

Payne, Robert

Ancient Rome. Am. Heritage Press [1971 c1970] 343p illus maps $6.95   **913.37**

1 Rome—Civilization 2 Rome—History
SBN 07-048936-X

First published 1966 under auspices of Horizon Magazine with title: The Horizon Book of ancient Rome

"The reader follows the course of Rome's rise, reign, and collapse from the mysterious Etruscan precursors through the clashes and conquests of the early republic, the advent of the Caesars, the 200-year-long grandeur of the 'pax Romana,' the excesses of the declining empire, the influence of Christianity and the 'barbarian' invasions, and the role of Constantinople as the custodian of classical culture after the fall of the western empire. The people of Rome . . . are introduced in vivid word portraits and anecdote. . . . [Included are] details of Roman statecraft, commerce, provinces, domestic life, warfare, amusements, and social customs." Publisher's note

Treble, H. A.

Everyday life in Rome in the time of Caesar and Cicero, by H. A. Treble and K. M. King. Oxford 1930 160p illus maps $1.95   **913.37**

1 Rome—Social life and customs 2 Rome—Civilization

Companion volume to: Robinson's: Everyday life in ancient Greece, class 913.38

Intended primarily for pupils beginning the study of Latin, this book will also be of interest to the reader interested in the period. Subjects discussed include amusements, social customs, military organization, religion, festivals, and law

Trump, David

Central and southern Italy before Rome. Praeger 1966 244p illus maps (Ancient peoples and places) $8.50   **913.37**

1 Italy—Antiquities

Describes "the peoples [of prehistoric Italy] who produced late Palaeolithic cave drawings, gaudily painted neolithic ceramics, Copper Age flint daggers, and numerous bronze artifacts throughout the Bronze and Iron Ages. It is Dr. Trump's thesis that this prehistoric period was mainly an era of assimilation, not of foreign domination. Drawing on evidence obtained from . . . recent excavations he spans the time when the first human settlement appeared on the Italian peninsula down to the time when archeological records become involved with those of classical Greece." Library J

Bibliography: p185-89

913.38 Civilization of Greece to 323 A.D.

Baumann, Hans

Lion gate and labyrinth; tr. by Stella Humphries. Pantheon Bks. 1967 182p illus maps $4.95, lib. bdg. $5.59   **913.38**

1 Civilization, Mycenaean 2 Crete—Antiquities 3 Evans, Sir Arthur John 4 Schliemann, Heinrich

Original German edition published 1966

In this account of the excavation of Mycenae and Knossos, "the author not only describes the work of Schliemann and Evans (and some other archeologists) but incorporates into his accounts some of the myths and legends pertaining to those cultures. The photographs, maps and diagrams are excellent; the writing style is lively and informed." Chicago. Children's Book Center

Glossary of proper names and terms used: p177-81

Davis, William Stearns

A day in old Athens; a picture of Athenian life. Biblo & Tannen 1960 242p illus maps $4.50   **913.38**

1 Athens—Social life and customs 2 Civilization, Greek

A reprint of a title first published 1914 by Allyn

"Tries to describe what an intelligent person would see and hear in ancient Athens, if by some legerdemain he were translated to the fourth century B.C. and conducted about the city under competent guidance." Preface

Though of "value for school reference, it is so vivacious in style . . . as to make it readable for any one." Wis Lib Bul

Horizon Magazine

The Horizon Book of ancient Greece, by the editors of Horizon Magazine; William Harlan Hale: author and editor in charge. Am. Heritage 1965 415p illus maps boards $18.95   **913.38**

1 Civilization, Greek 2 Greece—Antiquities

This volume on Greek civilization "combines history, art, and great writings of the period. Includes a glossary of basic concepts, innovations in mathematics and science, evolution of the Greek alphabet, chronology of Greek history, and genealogy of the gods." Pub W

"Magnificent photographs and color prints. Hale's perceptive and abundant articles . . . combine in this wonderful sampler to evoke the spell of ancient Greece for modern man." Booklist

Bibliographical references in Acknowledgments: p402-03

National Geographic Society

Greece and Rome: builders of our world. The Society 1968 448p illus maps (The story of man lib) $11.95   **913.38**

1 Civilization, Greek 2 Rome—Civilization

Foreword by Melville Bell Grosvenor; editorial consultant; Paul MacKendrick; special essays by Emily Vermeule and others

Covers the worlds of Odysseus, Pericles, Alexander, the Etruscans, Hannibal, and Caesar

Acknowledgments and reference guide: p447

Payne, Robert

Ancient Greece; the triumph of culture. Norton 1964 449p illus $10   **913.38**

1 Civilization, Greece 2 Greece—History

A "readable history of the ancient Greek peoples, told from the evidence of their artifacts and using many quotations from and synopses of their literature. The narrative is brought up to the death of Alexander the Great. It incorporates the findings of much present-day scholarship, about the Greeks." Pub W

Bibliographical note: p435-39. Map on lining-papers

Quennell, Marjorie

Everyday things in ancient Greece, by Majorie & C. H. B. Quennell. [2d ed] Rev. by Kathleen Freeman. Putnam 1954 256p illus maps $4   913.38

1 Greece—Social life and customs 2 Civilization, Greek 3 Greece—Antiquities

"Condensation into one volume of the three books on Greece: Homeric, Archaic, and classical [1930-1933]. The editor states that the addition of material on archaeological discoveries of the past 20 years is very limited. The bibliography is revised to include books on these recent materials." Booklist

The subjects covered are: religion, sports, houses, clothes, schools, music, travel, the theatre, warfare, life after death. Notable people discussed are Herodotus, Homer, Thucydides and Odysseus

The "book is a kind of Science Museum of the Hellenic world, which employs ingenious diagrams, town plans and reconstructions to serve as working models." Times (London) Lit Sup

Robinson, C. E.

Everyday life in ancient Greece. Oxford 1933 159p illus maps $1.95   913.38

1 Greece—Social life and customs 2 Civilization, Greek

Companion volume to Treble's: Everyday life in Rome in the time of Caesar and Cicero, class 913.37

"This concise account of Greek civilization will serve both the classical beginner and the non-classical student. . . . The development of society is traced from the earliest times to the end of the classical age. Naturally most of the book concerns classical Athens, but there is a chapter on Sparta. There are chapters on politics, society, trades, art and recreations, religion and education." Times (London) Lit Sup

Stobart, J. C.

The glory that was Greece; a survey of Hellenic culture and civilization. 4th ed. rev. By R. J. Hopper. Hawthorn Bks. 1964 xxxix, 265p illus maps $12   913.38

1 Civilization, Greek 2 Art, Greek

First published 1911

This well illustrated book "tells the story of Greece and its people from Neolithic times to the Roman conquest of 146 B.C. . . . Stobart's emphasis is not on military or political events but rather on Greek achievements in the art, literature and philosophy and on Greek attitudes toward religion, government and society." Publisher's note

Bibliography: p241-45

Webster, T. B. L.

Everyday life in classical Athens; drawings by Eva Wilson. Putnam 1969 192p illus maps $4   913.38

1 Athens—Social life and customs 2 Civilization, Greek

"Ranging over the whole Classical period (480-330 B.C.) the book tells how the Athenians worked and lived, how they brought up their families and how they looked after their homes, how they worshipped their gods and their heroes. This is Athens, from the Persian wars to the conquests of Alexander the Great, a society remembered above all for art and poetry." Publisher's note

Books for further reading: p186-88

913.3803 Ancient Greece— Dictionaries

The New Century Classical handbook; ed. by Catherine B. Avery; editorial consultant, Jotham Johnson. Appleton 1962 1162p illus $17.95   913.3803

1 Classical dictionaries

Contains "6,000 entries in alphabetical order describing the great personalities, ideas and accomplishments of Classical Greece and Rome. . . . The entries range over the fields of archaeology, architecture, art, geography, history, literature, mythology, philosophy, religion and science." Publisher's note

"Pronunciation and variant spellings with cross-references are given when required. . . . Illustrations include 114 line drawings . . . [and] over 100 scattered photographs of art and architecture." Cur Ref Bks

Maps on lining-papers

The **Oxford** Classical dictionary; ed. by N. G. L. Hammond and H. H. Scullard. 2d ed. Oxford 1970 xxii, 1176p $26 913.3803

1 Classical dictionaries

First published 1949

This classical dictionary is an "eminent scholarly compendium. . . . Although it emphasizes the biographical and literary, and devotes longer articles to broad subjects, the dictionary can be consulted on ancient cults and religious practices, on myths and legendary characters, on towns and geographical features, on politics and historical events, on musical instruments and art forms, on pets and papyrology." Sat R

Includes bibliographies and Index of names: p1154-73

The **Praeger** Encyclopedia of ancient Greek civilization [by] Pierre Devambez with the collaboration of Robert Flacelière, Pierre-Maxime Schuhl [and] Roland Martin. Praeger 1967 491p illus $15   913.3803

1 Civilization, Greek—Dictionaries 2 Classical dictionaries

Original French edition published 1966

This dictionary covers, "in more than 750 entries, such far ranging topics as warfare, athletics, mythology, daily life, place names, divination, and mysteries. Drama and epic poetry are explained in terms of playwrights and poets as well as in terms of the characters they created; the sections on art, ceramics, and sculpture are major entries amply illustrated with significant photographs. The articles, all signed, are fresh approaches to fascinating subjects. Thoroughly cross-referenced." Library J

Maps on lining-papers

913.39 Civilization of other parts of ancient world to ca. 640 A.D.

Berciu, D.

Romania. Praeger 1967 215p illus maps (Ancient peoples and places) $8.50   913.39

1 Rumania—Antiquities

"A history of the Rumanian peoples from the Old Stone Age, through the Bronze and Iron Age to the arrival of the Celts." Bk Buyer's Guide

"The chapters on agricultural times are the best ones. A common failing for all chapters is that, due to the multitude of cultural subgroupings in the area and the limited space . . . reading becomes almost impossible for the uninitiated and is at best hard going for the fairly advanced reader. Nevertheless, the work is definitely most usable for the latter as a start for really serious involvement. For the expert, the concise descriptions of each group make this work a very handy reference volume." Choice

Bibliography: p163-70

Charles-Picard, Gilbert

Daily life in Carthage at the time of Hannibal [by] Gilbert and Colette Charles-Picard; tr. from the French by A. E. Foster. Macmillan (N Y) 1961 263p illus map (Daily life ser) $5   913.39

1 Carthage—Civilization 2 Carthage—Social life and customs

Charles-Picard, Gilbert—*Continued*
Original French edition 1958
Contents: An outline history of Carthage;
The city of Carthage; Carthaginian society;
the ruling classes; The people, industry, and
the social problem; Everyday life; Traders and
commerce; Diplomacy, army and navy; Great
expeditions; Conclusion; Bibliography

Cottrell, Leonard
The mystery of Minoan civilization. World
Pub. 1971 128p illus $4.95, lib. bdg. $5.22
913.39
1 Civilization, Minoan 2 Crete—Civilization
3 Crete—Antiquities
This introduction to Minoan Crete "describes
the many puzzles that together make up the
mystery of Minoan Civilization—where did the
Minoans come from? What was their social organization? Why, and when, did their empire
collapse?" News of Bks
Includes bibliographical footnotes

Moscati, Sabatino
The world of the Phoenicians; tr. from the
Italian by Alastair Hamilton. Praeger 1968
281p illus maps (Praeger History of civilization) $10   913.39
1 Phenicians
The author 'surveys Phoenician civilization
from 1200 B.C. when the Phoenicians were located along the east coast of the Mediterranean through their colonizing adventures and
the move from the homeland to Carthage. His
scholarly panorama of their culture stresses as
distinctive their maritime prestige, commercial
skill, development and spread of the alphabet,
and considerable artistic achievements." Booklist
The author's "accomplishment is in showing
the special contributions and unique qualities
of the Phoenician civilization. . . . His well
done . . . investigation necessarily relies heavily upon archaeological evidence as well as art
and materials found outside the Phoenician
homeland." Choice
Bibliography: p264-71

Phillips, E. D.
The Mongols. Praeger 1969 208p illus maps
(Ancient peoples and places) $8.50   913.39
1 Mongols
This is a general "history of the early Mongols, from the twelfth to the sixteenth centuries." Public Affairs
"Concentrating on [the Mongol's] period of
expansion and brilliance in the 13th century,
[the book is] extended somewhat in each direction to put that period in a general context.
Its brevity and telescoped form are both an asset and a liability as they give a valuable overview on one hand, yet also occasionally give
the impression of a catalogue of rising and
falling figures never fully explained." Choice
Bibliography: p157-60

Taylour, Lord William
The Mycenaeans. Praeger 1964 243p illus
maps (Ancient peoples and places) $8.50
913.39
1 Mycenae 2 Civilization, Mycenaean
The author "has worked with Blegen at
Pylos, and is currently engaged in clearing one
of the few unexplored regions on the Acropolis
of Mycenae. . . . He touches on [aspects] of
Mycenaean life, and includes the evidence of
the Linear B tablets; he has found room to
mention the most recent archaeological discoveries, such as the Dendra corslet, the temple on Keos with its cult statues, and the surprisingly early 'tholos' tomb at Karditsa in
Thessaly." Times (London) Lit Sup
Bibliography: p179-87

Willetts, R. F.
Everyday life in ancient Crete; drawings by
Eva Wilson. Putnam 1969 191p illus maps
$4.50   913.39
1 Crete—Social life and customs 2 Crete—
Civilization 3 Crete—Antiquities

In this book, based upon archeological discoveries, the author discusses Cretan life from
the Stone Age until the Roman conquest 7,000
years later. He describes Minoan civilization
during the Bronze Age and the growth of city-
states during the Iron Age and discusses the
main social groups, including the position of
women and slaves; the growth of trade; the
organization of law and government; and the
role of religious belief and ritual. (Publisher)
Books for further reading: p181

913.42 Civilization of Ancient Britain

Ashe, Geoffrey
The quest for Arthur's Britain [by] Geoffrey Ashe [and others]. Praeger 1968 282p
illus maps $13.50   913.42
1 Great Britain—Antiquities 2 Arthur, King
3 Great Britain—History—To 1066
"The Arthurian legend has enjoyed a long
lived popularity among professional archeologists as well as with the general public. Hence,
this well-written and finely illustrated book
should find an exceptionally well disposed
readership. The contributors are experts in
archeology and British history and all have
worked extensively on the legend and fact of
King Arthur's existence. In 11 chapters, they
discuss questions in which they are most expert: the Arthurian fact; Wales in the Arthurian Age; excavations at Glastonbury Abbey
and Glastonbury Tor; the postulate that Cad-
bury was the fabled Camelot; life in the Arthurian Age; Arthur and English history; and
the new 'Matter of Britain.' The discussions
are engrossing and very well narrated; the text
is never pedantic or abstruse. Many excellent
drawings, photographs, and maps are correlated with the text material." Science Bks
Bibliography: p262-69

Horizon Magazine
The search for King Arthur, by the editors
of Horizon Magazine. Author: Christopher
Hibbert; consultant: Charles Thomas. Am.
Heritage 1969 153p illus maps $5.95, lib.
bdg. $5.49   913.42
1 Arthur, King 2 Great Britain—Antiquities
3 English literature—History and criticism
"A Horizon Caravel book"
"One of the most pervasive legends in the
world—King Arthur—has inspired writers and
artists for more than a thousand years. From
medieval chronicles to the 'Camelot' of Lerner
and Loewe, the Arthurian legend has received
numerous and varied treatments. . . . [This
book] fully explores the background of the
myth, and in addition, attempts to separate
Arthurian fancy from historical fact. . . . [Fur-
thermore] the book looks at efforts to substantiate the existence of a 'real' King Arthur.
Mr. Hibbert examines the discovery in 1962 of
the apparent site of Arthur's grave . . . and
recounts the archaeological efforts to pinpoint
the legendary Camelot." Publisher's note
"The writing is competent, the material so
organized that there is some overlapping; in
toto, however, the text has not only historical
and literary interest, but an element of detec-
tive-story appeal." Chicago. Children's Book
Center
Further reading: p148

Quennell, Marjorie
Everyday life in Roman and Anglo-Saxon
times; including Viking and Norman times,
by Marjorie & C. H. B. Quennell. [Rev. ed]
Putnam 1959 235p illus maps (Everyday life
ser) $4   913.42
1 Great Britain—Social life and customs
2 Great Britain—Antiquities 3 Great Britain
—Civilization
The present volume incorporates two books:
Everyday life in Roman Britain, and, Everyday life in Anglo-Saxon, Viking and Norman
times

Quennell, Marjorie—*Continued*

Describes the contributions of Romans, Anglo-Saxons, Danes, Norwegians, and Normans to British civilization covering architecture, literature, religion, dress, games, commerce, the army, etc.

"For those who conceive of Anglo-Saxon days as a period of unrelieved cultural gloom, the . . . Quennell books will come as a happy surprise. They will learn that not only did the Anglo-Saxons develop an artistic sense which equaled that to be found elsewhere in the Europe of that day, but that the time even came when England was recognized as one of the great intellectual centers of the Middle Ages." Christian Science Monitor

Includes a bibliography

Wilson, David

The Anglo-Saxons. Praeger 1960 231p illus map (Ancient peoples and places) $8.50 **913.42**

1 Great Britain—Antiquities 2 Anglo-Saxons

"In this book, the archaeology of the Anglo-Saxon period, from the departure of the Romans to the coming of the Normans, is . . . treated as a whole. Here the finest archaeological treasure ever recovered from English soil, that found at Sutton Hoo, is discussed and fitted into its historical and cultural background. Here the work of . . . the illuminator of the Lindisfarne Gospels is examined. Here also are examined the humbler products of the peasants of the Anglo-Saxon period." Publisher's note

Bibliography: p165-69

913.47 Civilization of Ancient Eastern Europe

Gimbutas, Marija Alseikaite

The Balts. Praeger 1963 286p illus maps (Ancient peoples and places) $8.50 **913.47**

1 Baltic region—Antiquities

"Covers the period from prehistory until the 13th century A.D. Examines language, folklore, cultural traits, religion, their jewelry, and their weapons." Pub W

Bibliography: p214-23

913.471 Civilization of Ancient Finland

Kivikoski, Ella

Finland; 66 photographs, 16 line drawings, 13 maps, 1 table. Praeger 1967 204p illus maps (Ancient peoples and places) $8.50 **913.471**

1 Finland—Antiquities

Translated from the original 1961 Swedish edition by Alan Binns

"An account of Finland's prehistory and early history from the land's emergence from glaciation around 8,000 B.C. to the Swedish conquest of ca. A.D. 1150." Book Rev Digest

Bibliography: p157-60

913.48 Civilization of Ancient Scandinavia

Davidson, H. R. Ellis

Pagan Scandinavia. Praeger 1967 214p illus (Ancient peoples and places) $8.50 **913.48**

1 Scandinavia—Antiquities 2 Scandinavia—Religion

"The aim of this book is to trace the history of religious cults and symbols in Scandinavia from the earliest archaeological records until the close of the heathen period." Publisher's note

"She has made an impressive historical reconstruction. . . . The line drawings and the photographic plates allied to her simple and elegant style greatly enhance the quality of this study. Even a nonspecialist is likely to find the book entrancing." Library J

Bibliography: p149-59

913.485 Civilization of Ancient Sweden

Stenberger, Marten

Sweden; tr. from the Swedish by Alan Binns. Praeger [1963 c1962] 229p illus (Ancient peoples and places) $8.50 **913.485**

1 Sweden—Antiquities 2 Sweden—History

First published 1962 in England

"A concise account of developments in Sweden from the close of the ice age 12,000 years ago to the beginning of the Viking period in about A.D. 800. . . . The body of the work is based on archaeological finds and is introduced by a summary of the geology of prehistory. A chart of periods and related climates, a topical bibliography, and notes on the plates accompany the text." Booklist

913.489 Civilization of Ancient Norway

Klindt-Jensen, Ole

Denmark before the Vikings. Praeger 1957 212p illus maps (Ancient peoples and places) $8.50 **913.489**

1 Denmark—Antiquities

Translated by Eva and David Wilson

"The first record of man in Jutland dates from about 5,000 B.C. He hunted with flint tools and lived in tents. At the close of the Ice Age Denmark was left bounded on three sides by the sea and forests spread over the land, but agriculture didn't arrive until the Neolithic period. By 1500 B.C. bronze-casting had spread to southern Denmark. Excavations have turned up imported objects side-by-side with locally-manufactured tools indicating that there was a channel for trading during this period of pre-history. As the Bronze Age came to a close, trade with the Celts stagnated, and Denmark's isolation wasn't ended until the country became linked by trade with the Roman Empire. The survey ends with the Germanic Iron Age." Library J

"In a hundred rewarding ways, Dr. Klindt-Jensen reports his findings and leaves the reader to draw his own conclusions. . . . We leave his book wanting more. . . . The illustrations are superb." Ann Am Acad

Bibliography: p144-46

913.52 Civilization of Ancient Japan

Kidder, J. E.

Japan before Buddhism, by J. E. Kidder, Jr. [Rev. ed] Praeger 1966 284p illus maps (Ancient peoples and places) $8.50 **913.52**

Japan—Antiquities 2 Japan—Civilization

First published 1959

This book is a "review of Japanese archeology in English. Beginning with the first traces of people in Japan, the author traces the archeological record into the historic period, after which time archeology is supplemented with the written sources to correlate Japanese and Chinese events. . . . It is well illustrated with line drawings and photographs and is written in a readable but not flamboyant style." Science Bks

Bibliography: p208-18

913.6 Civilization of Ancient Africa

Clark, J. Desmond
   The prehistory of Africa. . . . Praeger 1970
302p illus maps (Ancient peoples and places)
$10   913.6
   1 Africa—Antiquities 2 Man, Prehistoric
   "48 photographs. 62 line drawings. 10 maps."
Title page
   The author "explains the techniques and
theories currently being used to investigate the
African fossil record, which is bringing about
a . . . revision of established conceptions regarding human origins and behavior. He provides . . . [an account of the] finds that are
coming to light in many parts of the African
continent and an analysis of their significance
for an understanding of the physical and cultural evolution of man in what is believed to
be his earliest habitat." Publisher's note
   This "is an authoritative and stimulating
outline of the present state of African prehistory, and moreover, with its extensive notes
to the text and selected bibliography, it
should also prove to be a valuable introduction." Times (London) Lit Sup

Davidson, Basil
   The lost cities of Africa; with maps and illus. Rev. ed. Little 1970 xxiii, 366p illus maps
$7.95   913.6
   1 Africa—Civilization 2 Africa—Antiquities
   "An Atlantic Monthly Press book"
First published 1959
   "This book is about Africa and Africans
south of the Sahara Desert, during the fifteen
hundred years or so before the colonial period
began. Its aim is to present in outline what is
now known and what it now seems reasonable
to believe about some leading aspects and
achievements of African life and civilization
during that time." p xx
   The author "presents a sober view of old
Africa based on careful reading of the archaeological and historical evidence and intelligent
speculation from it. . . . [The book] contains
first-hand accounts and impressions and
throughout shows a vigorous and intelligent
understanding of the problems, potentialities,
and limitations of the evidence available." New
Statesman
   General bibliography: p339-57

913.7 Civilization of Ancient America

Ceram, C. W.
   The first American; a story of North American archaeology. Harcourt 1971 xxi, 357p
illus maps $9.95   913.7
   1 America—Antiquities 2 Indians of North
America—Antiquities 3 Excavations (Archeology)—North America
   ISBN 0-15-131250-8
   Translated from the German by Richard and
Clara Winston
   An "introduction to North American archaeology for readers unfamiliar with the subject.
. . . The author describes the work of Bande-
lier, Kidder, Fewkes and others whose field
work focused in the Southwest (Folsom, San-
dia, Clovis) that place homo sapiens and Ice
Age animals together; and discusses more recent finds that have pushed the archaeological
clock back some 30,000 years. There is plenty
to engross the average reader in Ceram's highly informative book, which closes on a note
more dramatically anthropological than archaeological with the story of Ishi, the last 'wild
Indian.'" Pub W
   "Although it is a popular account, it is well
referenced with citations and suggestions for
further reading. There are extensive notes, index, and numerous illustrations. This book
fills a void in an underpublished field." Choice

Leonard, Jonathan Norton
   Ancient America, by Jonathan Norton Leonard and the editors of Time-Life Books.
Time, inc. 1967 192p illus maps (Great ages
of man: a history of the world's cultures) $6.95
                                           913.7
   1 America—Antiquities 2 Indians of Mexico—
Antiquities 3 Indians of South America—Antiquities
   This is "an account of the rise and fall of
the ancient Indian cultures of Latin America,
including the Aztecs, Mayas, and Incas, based
on the testimony of early Spanish chroniclers,
travelers, sociologists, and modern archeologists and anthropologists. Included is a pic-
ture-book depicting the legendary adventures
of a Mixtec chieftain." Bk Buyer's Guide
   "A well written text that is accurate and up
to date. The most useful feature of the book
is the large number of excellent photographs
of sites, works of art, artifacts, codices, etc."
Choice
   Bibliography: p186

Stuart, George E.
   Discovering man's past in the Americas, by
George E. Stuart and Gene S. Stuart; foreword by Matthew W. Stirling; produced by
the Special Publications Division, Robert L.
Breeden chief. Nat. Geographic Soc. 1969 211p
illus maps $4.25   913.7
   1 America—Antiquities 2 Indians—Antiquities
   Text and numerous photographs follow the
"mysterious nomad hunters through the mists
of prehistory as they cross from Siberia to
Alaska to become the first Americans. . . . [The
authors] trace the footsteps of early man from
the frigid Arctic to the scorching deserts of
South America. They recreate the flowering of
New World civilizations such as the Maya,
the Aztec, and the Inca." Publisher's note
   Additional references: p209

Vlahos, Olivia
   New world beginnings; Indian cultures in
the Americas; illus. by George Ford. Viking
1970 320p illus maps $6.50, lib. bdg. $5.96
                                           913.7
   1 Indians—Antiquities
   SBN 670-50839-X; 670-50840-3
   On the basis of archeological discoveries and
ancient customs that are still preserved today,
the author describes the cultures of the Indians
of both North and South America as they were
before the arrival of Europeans, grouping them
by their way of life: hunters, fishermen, gath-
erers, farmers, empire builders. (Publisher)
   "A solid but readable anthropological survey. . . . Reference maps and distinctive accurate drawings enhance the book's value."
Booklist
   Bibliography: p305-14

913.7074 Civilization of Ancient America—Museums and exhibits

Folsom, Franklin
   America's ancient treasures; guide to archeological sites and museums. Rand Mc-
Nally 1971 202p illus boards $4.95   913.7074
   1 Indians of North America—Antiquities
2 Excavations (Archeology)—North America
3 North America—Galleries and museums
   "Rand McNally Guide to archeological sites
and museums." On cover
   "The author delineates the major prehistoric
culture areas, and then addresses himself to
specific cultures, archeological sites, and museums within each culture area. The discussion
of early peoples and extinct cultures, largely in
the United States and the adjacent parts of
Canada, is enriched by ethnological data and
historical evidence, where available, and by

Folsom, Franklin—*Continued*

pertinent notes on prehistoric technology and selected archeological methods of dating. This is not an introduction to archeology or its techniques but a useful guide to the available sites and other protected treasures." Science Bks

Bibliography: p191-94

913.85 Civilization of Ancient Peru

Bingham, Hiram

Lost city of the Incas; the story of Machu Picchu and its builders. Atheneum Pubs. 1963 240p pa $2.65   913.85

1 Machu Picchu, Peru 2 Peru—Antiquities 3 Incas

First published 1948 by Duell
"In 1911 Bingham, an American explorer, found the Inca city of Machu Picchu, which had been lost for 300 years. In this volume he tells of its origin, how it came to be lost and how it was finally discovered. He has endeavored to tell the story in 'popular form', and the general public may be interested; but the book, rather full of details, is more likely to interest the archeologist and the student of Latin American history." Library J

914 Geography of Europe

The **Age** of chivalry. Nat. Geographic Soc. 1969 378p illus maps (Story of man lib) $11.95   914

1 Civilization, Medieval

Special essays by Kenneth M. Scott and others

"Combining travelog and popular history, a panel of scholars and members of the National Geographic staff survey the Middle Ages, featuring Charlemagne, William the Conqueror, Bernard of Clairvaux, Richard the Lionheart, Joan of Arc, cathedrals, universities, and monasteries, and the countries where they lived or flourished. A simple text is lavishly illustrated with photographs of present-day scenes, paintings by staff artists, maps, and reproductions of medieval art, including a 16-page spread of the Bayeux tapestry." Booklist
Bibliography: p377

Fielding's Travel guide to Europe. Fielding Publications illus $7.95   914

1 Europe—Description and travel

Annual. First published 1948 by Sloane; title varies
"A really practical guide for the American visitor to Europe, the concentration on how to travel, although there is information also on where to go and what to see. Its hints on tipping, eating, customs, dress, language, drinks, rackets, etc., will save the traveler money and grief." Retail Bookseller
Map on lining-papers

Rowling, Marjorie

Everyday life in medieval times; drawings by John Mansbridge. Putnam 1968 227p illus map $4   914

1 Civilization, Medieval 2 Europe—Social life and customs

A volume "that deserves a place in the high school library. It gives a vivid account of the people of the period and their lives, covering the broad spectrum from the traders to the scientists. While covering the types of people the author also recounts their work and their home, their hopes and expectations. Illustrations, index and bibliography all serve the book and help make it more of a reference tool." Best Sellers

Skinner, Cornelia Otis

Our hearts were young and gay, by Cornelia Otis Skinner and Emily Kimbrough; drawings by Alajálov. Dodd 1942 247p illus $4   914

1 Europe—Description and travel

The apt title tells the story—a book of youth, when everything is either very funny or very serious. The two authors went on their first trip to Europe in the '20's, when they themselves were not quite in their twenties. Here they tell of sightseeing and the people they met and the things they did

"The book is compact of little nothings, made electric by the irresistible delight of youth in life and adventure. We defy anyone to read it without laughter or recall it without a smile." Sat R

914.15 Geography of Ireland

Connery, Donald S.

The Irish. Simon & Schuster 1968 304p illus $5.95   914.15

1 Ireland—Civilization 2 National characteristics, Irish

"Blending anecdote and history, [the author] draws upon numerous interviews with people in nearly every phase of Irish life, from government leaders and schoolmasters to farmers, housewives and parish priests. The result is a . . . portrait of the reality of Irish life in the sixties." Pub W

The author "has presented a reasoned, objective study of the 'new Ireland' which has emerged within the past decade. . . . Mr. Connery writes with charm and humor of Irish character, of Irish conversation, of the arts, of the beauties of the Irish countryside, and of the complex business of courtship and marriage: and he includes a most revealing chapter on 'The Neurotic North.' Anyone interested in what has been happening in Ireland during the past few years will find 'The Irish' a most rewarding reading experience." Best Sellers

McCarthy, Joe

Ireland, by Joe McCarthy and the editors of Life. Time, inc. 1964 160p illus maps (Life World lib) boards $4.95, lib. bdg. $7.60   914.15

1 Ireland—Description and travel

Pictures and text combine to describe Ireland's history, culture, politics and government, economy, and social life and customs

"Interesting are the chapters on Irish writers and on Irish Catholicism: the book also gives a thoroughly detailed analysis of the Irish-English relationship." Chicago. Children's Book Center

For further reading: p153-54

914.2 Geography of the British Isles

Ashley, Maurice

Life in Stuart England. Putnam 1964 178p illus maps (English life ser) $4   914.2

1 Great Britain—Social life and customs 2 Great Britain—History—Stuarts, 1603-1714

The author "presents a detailed description of occupations, beliefs, recreations, politics, education, and literary interests during the Stuart period [in England] with emphasis on the striking contrasts among the various social classes. He uses quotations and actual examples to enliven the portrayal of typical laborers, farmers, merchants, professional men, and members of the nobility and gentry." Booklist

Bibliography at the end of each chapter

Avery, Gillian

Victorian people; in life and in literature. Holt 1970 255p illus $6.50, lib. bdg. $5.97
914.2

1 Great Britain—Social conditions 2 Great Britain—Civilization
SBN 03-066655-4; 03-066660-0

The Victorians are "portrayed here through their own literature and through the eyes of such foreigners as de Tocqueville and Hawthorne. All segments of society are discussed: the aristocracy; clergy; squirearchy; cottages; middle class (upper, middle, and lower); industrialists; workingmen; poor; and criminals. Disraeli, Trollope, Mrs. Gaskell, Thackeray, Dickens, Gosse, and Edgeworth are among the writers whose works are used to describe the social scene." Library J

"The chapters on the various social gradations . . . are excellent. . . . There is an acute and knowledgeable section on the Church and its divisions, and a particularly vivid one on the railways. . . . [The quotations that Miss Avery] uses through the book are always compelling." Times (London) Lit Sup

Bagley, J. J.

Life in medieval England. Putnam 1960 175p illus $4
914.2

1 England—Social life and customs 2 Middle Ages

In this book "there are quotations from contemporary sources and humorous medieval art reproductions in addition to excellent photographs. In all its detail of everyday life in castle, court, and peasant quarters, the development of university and monastery, gilds and crafts, it offers background rich in human interest for the teen-age reader of English historical fiction and medieval legends." Chicago. Children's Book Center
Bibliography at end of each chapter

Brown, Ivor

Dickens and his world. Walck, H.Z. 1970 47p illus lib. bdg. $5
914.2

1 Dickens, Charles—Contemporary England 2 Great Britain—Social life and customs
ISBN 0-8098-3043-0

"A brief biography of Dickens is followed by a rambling, often interesting discussion of aspects of the Victorian world in which he lived —some of this information more pertinent to Charles Dickens than other, peripheral facts. The literary, political, and social facets of Victorian life are pertinent; the description of clothing and vehicles less so—although all of the cultural and period details are reflected in Dickens' writings. The text is capably written, continuous, profusely illustrated with reproductions of old prints, photographs, portraits, and drawings. There is no index, or table of contents." Chicago. Children's Book Center

Dr Johnson and his world. Walck, H.Z. 1966 [c1965] 47p illus $4.50
914.2

1 Johnson, Samuel—Contemporary England 2 England—Social life and customs
First published 1965 in England

"Although Samuel Johnson was unique as a literary figure, he was very much a man of his age, and Ivor Brown has placed him in his setting in a . . . re-creation of eighteenth century England. The concise text describes noisy bustling London and the slower-paced countryside; discusses food, clothes, politics, literature and the arts." Publisher's note

Burton, Elizabeth

The pageant of Elizabethan England; illus. by Felix Kelly. Scribner 1958 276p illus $6.95
914.2

1 England—Social life and customs 2 Great Britain—History—Tudors, 1485-1603
English edition has title: The Elizabethans at home

The author describes such aspects of life in Elizabethan England as houses, and furnishings, food and drink, pastimes, gardens, cosmetics and perfumes

A study "with some amused asides calling attention to parallels with the current Elizabethan reign." Booklist
Selected bibliography: p262-63. Sources: p264-67

The pageant of Georgian England; illus. by Felix Kelly. Scribner [1968 c1967] 422p illus $6.95
914.2

1 England—Social life and customs
First published 1967 in England with title: The Georgians at home

The author presents a "social history of 18th-Century and early 19th-Century England. Her discussions of the houses, furniture and gardens, foods, medicines, and diversions are interlaced with excerpts from contemporary letters, diaries, journals, and memoirs." Library J
Bibliography: p391-96

Cecil, Robert

Life in Edwardian England. Putnam [1970 c1969] 211p illus (English life ser) $4
914.2

1 Great Britain—Social life and customs 2 Great Britain—History—20th century

"Edward VII came to the throne of what was then the world's most thriving empire, but an empire that was becoming increasingly unpopular throughout the world. It was 1901, and although Britain was to continue to win its wars, the sun was beginning to set on the British Empire. Here is what it was to live in England during that period [up to the start of World War I]." Publisher's note

"In a scholarly but often amusing history which incorporates excerpts from contemporary accounts Cecil characterizes Edwardian England as a period of upheaval with the voice of social conscience becoming louder and politically effective after the relative stability of the Victorian era. . . . Many contemporary photographs enhance the text." Booklist
Short bibliography: p202

Davis, William Stearns

Life in Elizabethan days; a picture of a typical English community at the end of the sixteenth century. Harper 1930 376p illus lib. bdg. $5.11
914.2

1 England—Social life and customs 2 Great Britain—History—Tudors, 1485-1603

"The author takes an imaginary person. Sir Walter Hollydean of Boroughport, and around this central figure and his intimates weaves a picture of the typical modes, manners and customs of an English community in the time of Queen Elizabeth." Book Rev Digest

"Food, clothing, weddings, religious practices, schools, plagues, doctors, printings, housing, vagabonds, law, ships, the stage, and all that went to make up the daily life of classes are presented. . . . Every library needs this." Booklist

Hart, Roger

English life in the seventeenth century. Putnam 1970 128p illus maps (The English heritage ser) boards $4.95
914.2

1 England—Social life and customs 2 Great Britain—History—Stuarts, 1603-1714 3 Great Britain—History—Civil War and Commonwealth, 1642-1660

The author captures "in words and pictures the character of the people, the quality of life, and the meaning of the pivotal historical events of seventeenth-century England. He conveys the essence of an era, from the prosperity of the early years of the century through the autocratic rules of James I and Charles I, the terrible years of civil war and the emergence of the Puritan reign of Oliver Cromwell, to the . . . period of the Restoration, and lastly the Age of Marlborough. The beauties and delights of the age are discussed as well as the political upheaval and the Great Fire and the Plague that swept London and decimated the population." Publisher's note

Hart, Roger—*Continued*

"The illustrations are excellent, of a quality, abundance, and size . . . altogether surprising for a book at this price. They give a good composite picture of the age. The text is, of course a summary, but it contains a great deal of information, and is very well balanced." Best Sellers
Further reading: p126

English life in the eighteenth century. Putnam 1970 128p illus (The English heritage ser) boards $4.95   914.2
1 England—Social life and customs 2 Great Britain—History—1714-1837
ISBN 0-85340-002-4
The author describes how the various 'classes lived and worked—tradesmen, craftsmen and shopkeepers, Whig and Tory parliamentarians, East India Company merchants and adventurers, coffee house politicians and speculators, farmers, the criminal classes, and the down-and-out. . . . 'Eyewitness' accounts from diaries, newspapers, books, letters, posters, broadsheets and pamphlets, [are included]." Publisher's note
This account "is enhanced by hundreds of well-chosen, well-reproduced contemporary pictures, with 16 pages in color." Library J
Bibliography: p125

A History of everyday things in England. Putnam [1956-1959] 5v illus ea $4.50 914.2
1 Great Britain—Social life and customs
First published 1918
Contents: v 1 1066-1499; v2 1500-1799; v3 1733-1851; v4 1851-1914; v5 1914-1968
Volumes 1-4 written by Marjorie and C. H. B. Quennell; volume 5 written by S. E. Ellacott
Includes bibliographies

Loomis, Roger Sherman

A mirror of Chaucer's world. Princeton Univ. Press 1965 unp illus $12.50   914.2
1 Chaucer, Geoffrey—Contemporary England
2 Civilization, Medieval—Pictures, illustrations, etc.
A pictorial companion to Chaucer. "Portrayals of Chaucer, his friends and associates, the poets he admired, and the places he knew, are followed by photographs and a large number of medieval miniatures showing scenes, persons, and things to which Chaucer refers. . . . Each of the 179 illustrations is accompanied by indications of source and date, and often by explanatory and reference material. [They are] drawn mainly from the period 1340 to 1415." Publisher's note
"This mirror or window on mediaevalism . . . is an appropriate presentation for this poet of rich visual imagery, and the result is so . . . delightful that the reader does not at once fully appreciate the scholarship and art in the arrangement." Choice

Osborne, John, 1907-

Britain, by John Osborne and the editors of Time-Life Books. Time-Life Bks. [distributed by Little] 1970 176p illus maps (Life World lib.) boards $4.95   914.2
1 Great Britain
First published 1961
Text and numerous photographs, many in color, combine to describe Great Britain's history, culture, politics and government, economy, and social life and customs
For further reading: p169

Page, R. I.

Life in Anglo-Saxon England. Putnam 1970 179p illus (English life ser) $4 914.2
1 England—Social life and customs 2 Civilization, Anglo-Saxon
The author describes the Anglo-Saxons who were "often violent, brutish, and superstitious, but sometimes pious, intellectual and refined. Included is an account of the daily struggle

for food and existence, of the coming of Christianity, and the complicated set of rules that governed the conduct of life for all." Publisher's note
Bibliographies follow each chapter

Priestley, J. B.

The Edwardians. Harper 1970 302p illus $15   914.2
1 Great Britain—Social life and customs
2 Edward VII, King of Great Britain
SBN 06-013414-3
This book surveys English life from the accession of King Edward VII in 1901 to the outbreak of the first World War. The first part of the book examines the personality of the monarch who gave his name to the era and analyzes the contrasts between High Society and what were then regarded as the Lower Orders. The second part, covering the years 1906 to 1910, ranges over such aspects of Edwardian life as politics, the press, the achievements of such writers as Shaw and Wells, the acting of Sarah Bernhardt, the singing of Caruso and the delights of the music hall, and concludes with the portrayal of a society drifting into dissolution. (Publisher)
"Forty-eight pages of color pictures and innumerable half-tones. . . . Mr. Priestley's text is knowledgeable, acute, effortlessly urbane." Atlantic
Select bibliography: p291

Reader, W. J.

Life in Victorian England. Putnam 1964 176p illus (English life ser) $4.50   914.2
1 Great Britain—Social life and customs
2 Great Britain—History—19th century
"A British author emphasizes the energetic, confident, and youthful character of England during the [approximately] 60 years of Queen Victoria's reign and in a graphic view contrasts the existing extremes of poverty and affluence. He shows the effect of increasing urbanization and industrialization upon the entire complexion of the country in his description of the typical occupations and concerns of the various classes." Booklist
A "quite advanced list of 'further reading' is at the end of each chapter; interesting period reproductions." Library J

Tomkeieff, O. G.

Life in Norman England. Putnam 1966 178p illus maps (English life ser) $4 914.2
1 England—Social life and customs 2 Great Britain—History—Norman period, 1066-1154
3 Great Britain—History—Plantagenets, 1154-1399
A view of the Norman impact upon English society, running approximately from Edward the Confessor's accession in 1042 to the early years of the thirteenth century
Partial contents: The village; The Church; Learning and literature; The building crafts; Arts and entertainments
The material is presented in such a way "that the reader will be able to distinguish . . . between established fact and what must needs be conjecture." Preface
"A vivid, panoramic picture of English life. . . . Over one hundred illustrations and photos, including many of the Bayeux tapestry, add to the value of the textual presentation." Huntting
Bibliographies at end of each chapter

Wedgwood, C. V.

Milton and his world. Walck, H.Z. 1969 48p illus $4.50   914.2
1 Milton, John 2 Milton, John—Contemporary England 3 England—Social life and customs
The author examines Milton's life against the background of 17th century England and discusses the events of this time and their effect on Milton's writings. The illustrations picture everyday life—clothes, buildings, people and places. (Publisher)
This "is a slender volume which aims at presenting England's second-greatest poet in an era loaded with lessons for the 20th century. Considering that this is attempted in under 50 pages, it succeeds extraordinarily well—partly because of the lucidity of the text." Christian Science Monitor

914.2-914.4 SENIOR HIGH SCHOOL LIBRARY CATALOG
TENTH EDITION, 1972

White, R. J.
Life in Regency England. Putnam [1964 c1963] 176p illus (English life ser) $4   914.2
1 Great Britain—Social life and customs 2 Great Britain—History—1714-1837
First published 1963 in England
"The period covered is that of the beginning of the 19th Century, taking in the transition period before the famous Victorian era. Various strata of society are considered, a picture of London is given, and then the author covers the topics of manners and morals, politics, provincial life and the Puritan revival." Best Sellers
Includes bibliographies, "quotations from well-known writers and more than 150 reproductions of contemporary woodcuts, silhouettes, drawings and paintings." Bk Buyer's Guide

Williams, Penry
Life in Tudor England. Putnam [1965 c1964] 178p illus map (English life ser) $4   914.2
1 England—Social life and customs 2 Great Britain—History—Tudors, 1485-1603
First published 1964 in England
Contents: The land; Trade, industry and agriculture; The order of society; Castles, palaces and houses; Doctors, disease and diet; School and college; Church and people; Change and rebellion
Concentrating on the years from 1520 to 1570, this "is an authoritative picture of life at all levels of society." Booklist
Bibliography at the end of each chapter

914.21   Geography of London

Hibbert, Christopher
London: the biography of a city. Morrow [1970 c1969] 290p illus maps $12.50   914.21
1 London
This book on London starts with "its prehistoric beginning, follows through the Roman occupation of nearly 400 years . . . the Saxon invasions, the middle ages and the Norman conquest, emerges into the Tudor period, and the successive centuries after it to the present rebuilding after the devastation of the World War II bombings." Best Sellers
"It is social history that interests Mr. Hibbert, but as the reader progresses through his stories of kings and whores, crooks and eccentrics, ordinary and extraordinary people, the topography of the city falls into place, piece by piece, until it is all there." New Yorker
Bibliography: p270-76

Robertson, D. W.
Chaucer's London [by] D. W. Robertson, Jr. Wiley 1968 241p illus (New dimensions in history: historical cities) $7.95   914.21
1 London—Social life and customs 2 Chaucer, Geoffrey—Contemporary England
SBN 471-72730-X
"This history presents an account of London during the second half of the fourteenth century—the London of Chaucer. In its descriptions and commentaries, it stresses the principle that people were basically different in the Middle Ages than they are today; that human nature is not universal. The world and society of that time were considerably different than they are now, and human values and ideas differed from those we now hold." Publisher's note
"In touching on many customs and events, the narrative seems in part rather loose and undisciplined, and Robertson devotes surprisingly little space to topics which seem central to his theme—the total population of the city, and customs affecting family life, such as courtship, marriage, child raising, and the like. But those weaknesses are more than compensated by the author's rich learning, and the book will be instructive for any reader interested in medieval England and in Chaucer." Choice
Bibliographical note: p223-24

914.3   Geography of Germany

Childs, David
East Germany. Praeger 1969 286p illus map (Nations of the modern world) $8.50   914.3
1 Germany (Democratic Republic)
In this analysis of the evolution of the German Democratic Republic since 1945, the author "presents a judicious appraisal of the political and constitutional developments of the last quarter century. Also his chapters on the new economic system and the living standards are based on sound evidence. . . . Childs offers also valuable observations on East German education and cultural trends. The book concludes with a fair discussion of the international position of the German Democratic Republic." Library J
"An informed and reliable, albeit sometimes colorless, account of the state of affairs of what can no longer be called the Soviet zone in the present." Choice

Prittie, Terence
Germany, by Terence Prittie and the editors of Time-Life Books. Time-Life Bks. [distributed by Little 1968] 176p illus maps (Life World lib) boards $4.95   914.3
1 Germany
First published 1961
Contents: A people of discipline and energy; The unresolved quest for unity; The construction of a stable state; A prosperity reborn; In the shadow of the Soviet; A capital without a country; The peaceable small man; An undercurrent of uncertainty; A resurgence of intellect; The unsettled and perilous future
For further reading: p169

Rees, Goronwy
The Rhine. Putnam 1967 186p illus map (Great rivers of the world) $4.95   914.3
1 Rhine River and Valley—Description and travel
A "portrait of Europe's greatest historic river from its source high in the Alps to its mouth in the North Sea and an . . . account of the 2000 years of history played out along its banks. Included are biographical sketches of such famous Rhinelanders as Beethoven, Goethe, Marx, Schiller, Heine and Adenauer." Huntting

Walton, Henry
Germany; with 33 illus. and 2 maps. Walker & Co. 1969 222p illus maps (Nations and peoples) $7.50   914.3
1 Germany (Federal Republic)
"A nicely written and well illustrated introduction to contemporary West Germany. It seldom errs—Walton holds high credentials in both scholarship and journalism. . . . Chapters on political institutions, economy, society, literature, etc." Choice
Select bibliography: p206

914.4   Geography of France

Bishop, Claire Huchet
Here is France. Farrar, Straus 1969 215p illus $3.75   914.4
1 France
"An Ariel book"
The author writes about "various aspects of France. Some, she knows, are often little understood; others are of special interest to American young people—such as life in France, today, its international role, and such contemporary issues as environmental planning and university and industrial unrest." Publisher's note
"Thirty-six photographs, a list of French scientific accomplishments from 1517 on, and a detailed index add to the usefulness of this book." Library J

Brogan, D. W.
France, by D. W. Brogan [and] the editors of Time-Life Books. Time-Life Bks [distributed by Little 1971] 176p illus maps (Life World lib) boards $4.95   914.4

1 France
First published 1960 by the editors of Life
"Color and black-and-white photographs supplemented by an informative text view high lights of French history, the past and present literary scene, modern intellectual trends, new developments in agriculture, and other aspects of the French scene. An interesting survey reinforced by a historical chronology, a bibliography, and a list of famous French cultural figures and their principal works." Booklist

Carroll, Joseph T.
The French; how they live and work. [Rev. ed] Praeger [1971 c1970] 179p illus map (How they live and work) $5.50   914.4

1 France
First published 1968 in England. First American edition 1969
Beginning with a brief discussion of French history and geography, the book goes on to describe the people, their origins, language, national characteristics, government and politics and social conditions. Included is a brief appendix: Hints for visitors

Gies, Joseph
Life in a medieval city [by] Joseph and Frances Gies. Crowell 1969 274p illus maps $6.95   914.4

1 France—Civilization 2 Civilization, Medieval 3 Cities and towns—France
The authors depict "what it was like to live in a prosperous city of Northwest Europe in the midst of the Commercial Revolution of the twelfth and thirteenth centuries. The time is A.D. 1250. The city is Troyes, capital of the county of Champagne, site of two of the cycle of Champagne Fairs—the 'Hot Fair' in August and the 'Cold Fair' in December." Publisher's note
"The work is a pleasing narrative about life and death, midwives and funerals, business, books and authors, and town government. But the authors limit their evidence to neither Troyes nor the 13th century. They draw on Paris, Sicily, England, and Provence." Choice
Bibliography: p246-61

Robiquet, Jean
Daily life in the French Revolution; tr. from the French by James Kirkup. Macmillan (N Y) 1965 [c1964] 246p illus (Dairy life ser) $6.95   914.4

1 France—Social life and customs 2 France—History—Revolution, 1789-1799
Original French edition 1938. This translation first published 1964 in England
In addition to picturing middle and upper class characters, the author mirrors "the life of common people—soldiers, criminals, artisans, prostitutes, shopkeepers—in a . . . cross-section of the swarming, passionate, optimistic revolutionary crowds both in Paris and the provinces." Publisher's note
"The index permits the volume to be used for reference, since very few students would find the time or inclination to read the volume cover-to-cover. Some of the observations on the moral climate of the times would seem to restrict the volume to more mature students." Best Sellers
Notes: p234-41

914.43 Geography of Paris metropolitan area

Glyn, Anthony
The Seine. Putnam [1967 c1966] 204p illus map (Great rivers of the world) $4.95   914.43
1 Seine River

First published 1966 in England
An account of the history, geography, peoples, and legends of the Seine from Roman times to the present. The author describes life along the Seine—its bridges, cities and towns, fishermen, bookstalls, courting couples, the artists it has nurtured, and Paris. (Publisher)
"A journey from the source of the Seine to its mouth, with a witty Englishman who writes crisply, humorously and with imagination." Pub W

Levron, Jacques
Daily life at Versailles in the seventeenth and eighteenth centuries; tr. by Claire Eliane Engel. Macmillan (N Y) 1968 239p illus $5.95   914.43

1 Versailles 2 France—Social life and customs 3 France—History—Bourbons, 1589-1789
Original French edition, 1965
"The author first describes the Court of Henry IV, then discusses the beginning of Versailles under Louis XIV: its construction and the finishing of its interiors, and concludes with the reign of Louis XVI." McClurg. Book News
"A colorful picture of a fabulous era, focusing not only on the royal family and courtiers but also on guards, police, pages, kitchen help and townspeople." Booklist
Sources and bibliography: p231

914.5 Geography of Italy

Bryant, Andrew
The Italians; how they live and work. Rev. ed. Praeger 1971 164p illus maps (How they live and work) $5.95   914.5

1 Italy
First published 1968 in England. First American edition 1969
Beginning with a brief discussion of Italy's history and geography, the book goes on to describe the people, their origins, language, national characteristics, government and politics, and social conditions. (Publisher)

Kubly, Herbert
Italy, by Herbert Kubly and the editors of Time Life Books. Time-Life Bks. [distributed by Little 1968] 160p illus maps (Life World lib) boards $4.95   914.5

1 Italy
First published 1961
"The background text for this book was written by Herbert Kubly, the picture essays by Henry Moscow"
Pictures and text combine to describe the history, culture, social life and customs, and economy of Italy
For further reading: p153

914.6 Geography of Spain and Iberian Peninsula

Michener, James A.
Iberia; Spanish travels and reflections; photographs by Robert Vavra. Random House 1968 818p illus maps $12.50   914.6

1 Spain—Description and travel 2 Spain—Civilization
"Within a general framework of visiting different rural areas and the big cities of Toledo, Seville, Madrid, Barcelona and the sites of special events—Pamplona, Teruel, Compostela—Michener includes everything. Wherever he goes, he reaches back into antiquity and gives the full history in detail; he visits the well-known museums and the isolated Madonna in a remote convent chapel; he comments on literature, architecture, politics, the balance-by tension power of church, military, police, politicians, and the rich, on corridas and bullfighters, on fiestas and on the great religious processions, on agriculture and conservation and land spoilage, on black poverty and insensitive wealth." Pub W

Michener, James A.—*Continued*

"As a work of history it has little value. However, taken as a vivid picture of the cities, towns, countryside, and people framed by a sensitive writer with an enduring interest in the country, 'Iberia' is entertaining and occasionly profound reading." Choice

Perceval, Michael

The Spaniards; how they live and work. Praeger 1969 192p illus maps (How they live and work) $4.95   914.6

1 Spain—Civilization 2 National characteristics, Spanish

The author "offers well-organized information about life in contemporary Spain. After pointing out the political stability during the past decade that has helped in the developing industrialization of the country, [he] notes the varied geographical regions and climates of Spain. He perceptively describes the life of people in urban and rural Spain particularly in relation to their national and local government, living conditions, work, education, transportation, and recreation. Hints for visitors to Spain and a bibliography are appended." Booklist

Thomas, Hugh

Spain, by Hugh Thomas and the editors of Life. Time, inc. [distributed by Little] 1966 160p illus maps (Life World lib) boards $4.95   914.6

1 Spain

A discussion of the history of Spain the character of the people, the political traditions, the modern economic and social conditions. King Ferdinand, Queen Isabella, Charles I, Philip II, General Franco, the poets, the painters, the nobles and the poor also appear here. (Publisher)

A "well-organized text; several excellent maps are included in the illustrative material, which is chiefly photographic, and a chapter on the arts has reproductions of paintings. . . . The author writes for the mature and sophisticated reader." Chicago. Children's Book Center

For further reading: p153

914.7 Geography of Russia

Jacob, Alaric

A Russian journey; from Suzdal to Samarkand; drawings by Paul Hogarth. Hill & Wang 1969 160p illus map $10   914.7

1 Russia—Description and travel
SBN 8090-8350-7

This account of a trip to Russia in 1967 describes the experiences of both the author and illustrator as they travelled to Central Asia, the Ukraine, Georgia, Leningrad and Moscow. The book also records their conversations with individuals in all walks of life. (Publisher)

Koningsberger, Hans

Along the roads of the new Russia. Farrar, Straus 1968 195p boards $5.50   914.7

1 Russia—Description and travel

For several months the author traveled through European Russia in an old Army truck. In this book, he writes about the people and scenes he observed and "about churches and religion, restaurants and hotels, vacationing and shopping, how the young people think about America, about the literary freeze, and about the changing landscape." Publisher's note

"Included is Koningsberger's conversation with Ilya Ehrenberg about America and about John Steinbeck. The author was impressed by the deep reaction of the ordinary Russian to President Kennedy's assassination, and gives his theories for this. A casual, tolerant, perceptive book by an amiable traveller." Pub W

Koutaissoff, Elisabeth

The Soviet Union. Praeger 1971 288p illus maps (Nations of the modern world) $8.50   914.7

1 Russia

The author examines "Soviet contemporary political, economic, and social-cultural institutions and their functioning since 1965. . . . The presentation is accurate and well balanced. . . . It successfully provides a useful setting against which the still outstanding difficulties in the path of modernization of the various aspects of Soviet society can be placed and evaluated. Foreign relations are not considered here; however, perceptive and enlightening comparisons are drawn with advanced Western countries. A chronology of events and a brief description of personalities mentioned in the text are provided." Choice
Bibliography: p276-79

Rama Rau, Santha

My Russian journey. Harper 1959 300p boards $5.95   914.7

1 Russia—Description and travel 2 Russia—Social life and customs

A report on a trip to Russia taken by the famous Indian author, in 1957, with her American husband, their son, and his Negro nurse

The author offers "intimate glimpses of the friendly Russians and interesting comment on the theater, art and literature of the Soviet Union." Bookmark

Rieber, Alfred J.

A study of the USSR and communism: an historical approach, by Alfred J. Rieber and Robert C. Nelson. Putnam [1964 c1962] 256p illus maps $4.50   914.7

1 Russia—Civilization 2 Communism—Russia
First published 1962 by Scott, Foresman

A survey of "Russia: its people, history, ideology, political structure, economy, cultural life, and international relations. Photographs, maps, and charts add vividness. . . . A few factual errors are noticeable . . . but, in general, the authors have managed to convey a great deal of significant information with a high degree of accuracy." Library J

Salisbury, Harrison E.

(ed.) The Soviet Union: the fifty years. Harcourt 1967 xxii, 484p illus $10   914.7

1 Russia
"A New York Times book"
Analyzed in Essay and general literature index

On the fiftieth anniversary of the Russian Revolution, reporters of "The New York Times" describe the progress and the current situation in the Soviet Union in education, the arts, science, housing, sports and religion. Their observations are based on trips to Russia in 1967

The emphasis "is on cultural and social aspects; the political and economic sides, more familiar to the average newspaper reader, receive much less attention. . . . The most serious gap in this book is the absence of any treatment of the non-Russian nationalities." N Y Times Bk R
Maps on lining-papers

Thayer, Charles W.

Russia, by Charles W. Thayer and the editors of Life. Time, inc. [Distributed by Little] 1965 176p illus (Life World lib) boards $4.95   914.7

1 Russia
First published 1960
"A former U.S. foreign service official writes . . . about farm and city life, education, the structure of the Communist party, arts and letters, living conditions, and other phases of the subject. . . . A historical chronology, a topically arranged bibliography, and other material are appended. End-paper maps." Booklist

"A skeletal account, largely pictorial, with emphasis on the human rather than the political side." Pub W

Van der Post, Laurens

A portrait of all the Russias; photographs by Burt Glinn. Morrow 1967 175p illus $13.95
914.7

1 Russia—Description and travel

"The text is drawn from the author's 'A view of all the Russias' . . . . [It] is used here to accompany a pictorial essay consisting of photographs taken by Glinn on a separate journey. The 56 full-page and eight double-spread color photographs added to the brief text give a vivid impression of the USSR's variety and vastness." Booklist

Vladimirov, Leonid

The Russians. Praeger 1968 249p $6.95
914.7

1 Russia 2 Communism—Russia

"In this colorful portrait of his countrymen, Leonid Vladimirov captures the mood and spirit of the Russian people today; workers and farmers, intelligentsia and scientists, writers and artists, the government bureaucracy and Party officials. He explains what the people really think about their government and its officials; the story behind the guerrilla war between writers and the state; attitudes toward marriage and divorce, sex and prostitution; Russian youth and their special conflicts with the older generation." Am News of Bks

914.71 Geography of Finland

Mead, W. R.

Finland. Praeger 1968 256p illus maps (Nations of the modern world) $6.50 **914.71**

1 Finland

The author surveys the nation's "geography, history, literature, politics, economics, and social conditions." Library J

"Mead presents a wide range of factual detail which is perceptively interpreted and enables the reader to understand the emergence and present day existence of this modern, progressive industrialized democracy in the northern latitudes of Europe. . . . About three-fifths of the book is devoted to Finland before 1917-1918, although the early chapters contains a great many references to the years since World War I. The writing is enviably clear throughout." Ann Am Acad

Bibliography: p237-47

914.8 Geography of Scandinavia. Vikings

Arbman, Holger

The Vikings; tr and ed. with an introduction by Alan Binns. Praeger 1961 212p illus maps (Ancient peoples and places) $8.50
914.8

1 Northmen

The author "examines sites in the Scandinavian countries, the British Isles and Atlantic islands, the European continent, Russia and other lands bordering the Caspian Sea, and Iceland, Greenland, and North America, concluding with an evaluation of Viking art and its relation to contemporary art in England and Ireland." Booklist

"The book is well illustrated and the plates and line drawings provide a perfect foil for the authority and liveliness of the text. The introduction . . . gives a summary of Viking culture as seen through the eyes of an Englishman: it is a useful summary." Times (London) Lit Sup

Includes bibliography

Innes, Hammond

Scandinavia, by Hammond Innes and the editors of Life. Time. inc. [distributed by Little] 1963 160p illus maps (Life World lib) boards $4.95
914.8

1 Scandinavia

Contents: Kingdoms of the North; The Viking Age; A struggle toward unity; The urbane Danes; Children of the midnight sun; The industrious Swedes; Personalities of peace; Timber, snow and sea; Culture in a cold climate; Today and tomorrow

"Written at a fairly mature level and in clear style, although the organization of material is not as careful as it is in other books in the series. Printed in double columns of rather small print, and with an occasional boxed insert of information in very small print." Chicago. Children's Book Center

Copiously illustrated. For further reading: p53

Simpson, Jacqueline

Everyday life in the Viking age; drawings by Eva Wilson. Putnam [1968 c1967] 208p illus maps boards $4.50
914.8

1 Northmen 2 Scandinavia—Antiquities

First published 1967 in England

The author relates early archeological discoveries "to literature dealing with the early Scandinavian and Icelandic civilizations. The format and size of the book suggest juvenile literature, but it is not. It is an excellent summary of information on Viking life for mature students and adults. . . . Two introductory chapters are devoted to Viking history, and these are followed by chapters on agriculture, seafaring, mercantilism, weapons and warriors, family and society, games, arts and poetry, religious practices and funerary rites. Its only visible shortcoming is the author's failure to cite all of the resources she has used, and the bibliography which is a brief list of major works only." Science Bks

Wilson, David M.

The Vikings and their origins; Scandinavia in the first millennium. McGraw 1970 144p illus maps (Lib. of early medieval civilizations) $5.95
914.8

1 Northmen 2 Scandinavia—Civilization

An expansion of a chapter in: The dawn of European civilization: the Dark Ages, ed. by David Talbot Rice, published 1965

"While dating the Viking era from the eighth to the eleventh centuries, Wilson describes the preceding Scandinavian life and culture through the Roman Iron Age and the migratory period before embarking on the history of the Vikings. Their trading expeditions, navigation skills, discoveries of Iceland, Greenland, and North America, and raids and conquests in Western Europe are noted but the emphasis is on conditions in their homeland where flourishing towns, agriculture, and creative arts were developed. Maps, diagrams, and captioned color and black-and-white photographs of artifacts and other archaeological remains supplement the text." Booklist

Select bibliography: p133-38

914.85 Geography of Sweden

Austin, Paul Britten

The Swedes; how they live and work. Praeger 1970 167p illus map (How they live and work) $5.50
914.85

1 Sweden

"A comprehensive, factual description of Sweden. . . . In discussing government, economics, education, the arts, recreation, and the intellectual climate, Austin stresses recent developments that have changed Sweden from a poor agricultural country to a prosperous industrialized and urbanized state with a high standard of living and ultramodern ideas, and while he points out some apparent paradoxes between theory and practice, he is consistently objective in his treatment of Swedish neutrality in foreign affairs, the welfare state, the permissive attitude toward sex, and Swedish life in general." Booklist

914.92 Geography of the Netherlands

Rachlis, Eugene
  The Low Countries, by Eugene Rachlis and the editors of Time-Life Books. Time-Life Bks. [distributed by Little 1968] 160p illus maps (Life World lib) boards $4.95
    914.92
    1 Netherlands 2 Belgium 3 Luxemburg
  First published 1963
  Picture essays supplement this survey of the history, geography, ethnology, economic conditions, politics, religion, art and architecture of the Netherlands, Belgium and Luxemburg
  Rachlis' "sense of humor, used sparingly, is most effective in brightening a straightforward and competent assessment. . . . Maps are plentiful: language maps, maps of religious divisions, full-page relief maps, and political maps." Chicago. Children's Book Center
  For further reading: p153

914.94 Geography of Switzerland

Kubly, Herbert
  Switzerland, by Herbert Kubly and the editors of Time-Life Books. Time-Life Bks. [distributed by Little 1969] 160p illus maps (Life World lib) boards $4.95   914.94
    1 Switzerland
  First published 1964 by the editors of Life
  "The book covers geography and history, political and economic analysis of Switzerland today, industry and agriculture, and the people: their diversity, their recreation, their education, their cultural interests. Some of the illustrations are, of course, breathtakingly lovely; some of the text is most unusual, also, in the topics discussed: the hotel schools, the tourist trade, the international organizations, and the country's remarkable recent history of peace and stability. . . . A list of important dates, a bibliography divided by chapters, a list of famous Swiss cultural figures, and an index are appended." Chicago. Children's Book Center

914.95 Geography of Greece

Eliot, Alexander
  Greece, by Alexander Eliot and the editors of Time-Life Books. Time-Life Bks. [distributed by Little 1968] 160p illus maps (Life World lib) boards $4.95   914.95
    1 Greece, Modern 2 Civilization, Greek
  First published 1963
  A "survey of Greece past and present, with long, detailed chapters on Grecian history and an exceptionally good chapter on Greece today. The second part of the text comprises chapters on the Byzantine influence, Greek literature, the distinguished great people from other lands who have loved Greece, and the changes in Greek religion from pagan times to today. . . . A list of dates, a list of famous cultural figures, and a divided bibliography are included." Chicago. Children's Book Center
  "This too is a pictorial book. . . . The author emphasizes the classical heritage of Greece." Introduction

914.96 Geography of the Balkan Peninsula

Stillman, Edmund
  The Balkans, by Edmund Stillman and the editors of Life. Time, inc. [distributed by Little] 1964 160p illus maps (Life World lib) boards $4.95   914.96
    1 Balkan Peninsula

"A Stonehenge book"
  Introduction to the geography, races, history, languages, religions, economics and politics of the region—Yugoslavia, Albania, Rumania and Bulgaria
  A "detailed discussion. . . . The photographs are profuse and informative, especially interesting because some of the scenes are rather rare—such as those of the Albanian capital." Chicago. Children's Book Center
  For further reading: p153-54

915 Geography of Asia

Polo, Marco
  The travels of Marco Polo   915
    1 Asia—Description and travel 2 Voyages and travels
  Some editions are:
  AMS Press $17.50. The translation of Marsden, revised, with a selection of his notes. Edited by Thomas Wright
  Dutton (Everyman's lib) $3.25. Introduction by John Masefield
  Liveright $5.95 Revised from Marsden's translation and edited with an introduction by Manuel Komroff
  Modern Lib. $2.95, lib. bdg. $2.69 Revised from Marsden's translation and edited with an introduction by Manuel Komroff
  First Italian edition 1496
  Marco Polo's tale of his travels in Asia in the thirteenth century, received with great incredulity by his contemporaries in Venice, has become one of the unique records in travel literature. "Time has fully credited the veracity of all he wrote. The book was written while he was a prison inmate at Genoa during the war between Venice and Genoa. It was dictated to a fellow prisoner entirely in French. It was immediately translated into many languages, the Marsden translation being the first English translation." The Reader's Adviser and Bookman's Manual

Reischauer, Edwin O.
  A history of East Asian civilization. Houghton 1960-1965 2v illus maps ea $15.25
    915
    1 Civilization, Oriental
  Contents: v 1 East Asia: the great tradition, by Edwin O. Reischauer and John K. Fairbank; v2 East Asia: the modern transformation, by John K. Fairbank, Edwin O. Reischauer and Albert H. Craig
  In the first volume "the authors have dealt with the civilization that arose in China and have covered its developments in China, Korea, and Japan down to the irruption of the Occident in the nineteenth century. They regard that civilization as a unit and confine themselves almost entirely to peoples embraced in it." Am Hist R
  Covering Chinese, Japanese and Korean history of "the last century and a half, [the second volume] concludes with sections on the Sino-Soviet dispute and Taiwan." Bookweek
  Includes bibliographies

915.1 Geography of China

Buck, Pearl S.
  China as I see it; comp. and ed. by Theodore F. Harris. Day 1970 305p $7.95 915.1
    1 China
  A selection of the author's writings and speeches on Chinese civilization and politics beginning in the 1930's and ending with a "final chapter newly written to summarize the Communist take-over, its background and its consequences." Publisher's note
  The author's "viewpoints are intuitive, and the book is infused with a mellow sense of humanity." Pub W

Fessler, Loren
  China, by Loren Fessler and the editors of Life. Time, inc. [distributed by Little] 1963 176p illus maps (Life World lib) $5.70 915.1
    1 China

Fessler, Loren—*Continued*

The authors discuss "ancient and modern China's social, political, cultural, and religious highlights. . . . Approximately one half of the text deals with twentieth-century events. The interesting collection of photographs includes some handsome reproductions of ancient Chinese paintings." Booklist

For further reading: p169-70

Fitzgerald, C. P.

China: a short cultural history. [4th rev. ed] Praeger 1954 621p illus maps $12.50
915.1

1 China—Civilization 2 China—History 3 Art, Chinese 4 China—Religion

First published 1935 in England. First American edition published 1938 by Appleton-Century

"A readable cultural history of China from antiquity to about the 19th century. Chapters on thought, art, social and economic conditions from 'Feudal China' through 'China under the Manchus.'" Asia. A Guide to Paperbacks

Horizon Magazine

The Horizon History of China, by the editors of Horizon Magazine. Editor in charge: Norman Kotker; author: C. P. Fitzgerald. Am. Heritage 1969 415p illus maps boards $22
915.1

1 China—Civilization 2 China—History
SBN 8291-0005-5

In this book, the text "is a broad survey, finely balanced, of those areas of Chinese history and culture of greatest interest to the layman. The chronology of Chinese history is divided into five chapters in which political developments are outlined. Interspersed among the chapters are topical essays, pictorial portfolios, and anthologies of translations on subjects essential to an appreciation and understanding of China's past and present. There are studies of philosophy, religion, the family, technology and invention, the city, poetry, painting, the scholar, the impact of the West, and the Communization of China. . . . There are acknowledgments, which might serve as a guide to further reading, and a useful index." Choice

Liu, James T. C.

(ed.) Traditional China; ed. by James T. C. Liu and Wei-ming Tu. Prentice-Hall 1970 179p (Asian civilization) $5.95
915.1

1 China—Civilization
SBN 13-926014-5

"A Spectrum book"

"This work which focuses on the theme of the integration of traditional culture and civilization consists of 16 intellectually stimulating essays written by specialists in Chinese studies. . . . [It covers] topics, such as isolated geographic conditions, the urban-rural continuum, state monopolies and capitalism, the 'closed society,' civil service systems, peasant rebellions, law and propriety, and the so-called 'three teachings,' Confucianism, Taoism and Buddhism before the dawn of China's modern period. This work offers one a good background for understanding the cultural legacy of modern-day China." Library J

Includes bibliographical footnotes

Salisbury, Harrison E.

Orbit of China. Harper 1967 204p illus map $5.95
915.1

1 China (People's Republic of China) 2 East (Far East)

The journalist-author "traveled more than 25,000 miles along China's frontiers from the jungles of Southeast Asia to the bristling Siberian-Chinese border. Wherever he went—remote Himalayan villages or glittering Hong Kong—Mr. Salisbury sought from peasants and princes the story of China—her explosive impact on Asia and the world." Publisher's note

"An astute and superbly trained observer, he has written a chilling but rewarding report. . . . For those who have read little on the Far East, to date, this book presents a superb opportunity to make a start; for those who have made such a start, the report gives an overview and summary. . . . This book is essential reading for all concerned adults." Library J

Snow, Edgar

Red China today. Rev. and updated ed. of The other side of the river. Random House [1971 c1970] 749p illus maps $20
915.1

1 China (People's Republic of China)
ISBN 0-394-46261-0

First published 1962

Edgar Snow writes in his Preface: China in the 1970's: "It is hoped that the page which follow will help to show why and how China's historical problems conditioned the political means available for their solution." The author was present at the birth of Communist China and in 1960 he was the only American writer accredited by the U.S. State Department and the Peking government to travel throughout that country. Having revisited China in 1964-1965 and again in 1970, he has revised and updated the book which he wrote after his 1960 trip. On farms, in factories, in rural and urban communes, hospitals and schools, at dam projects, tree farms and steel mills, he studies all aspects of New China. Among his many interviews were lengthy discussions with Mao Tse-tung and Premier Chou En-Lai. (Publisher)

"His first-person narrative is a mixture of conversations, epitomes of history, reminiscent personal flashbacks, analyses of institutions, and comments on policy. . . . No other volume on Communist China has covered so broad a range with so much perception." Atlantic

Bibliography: p725-34

915.15 Geography of Tibet

Harrer, Heinrich

Seven years in Tibet; tr. by Richard Graves. Dutton 1954 [c1953] 314p illus map $7.95
915.15

1 Tibet—Description and travel

First published 1952 in Austria

An "Austrian mountaineer, interned in India in 1939, gives a colourful and exciting account of his escape to Tibet, and of his experience there until his second escape from the invading Chinese Communists. [In Tibet] he became tutor to the Dalai Lama." Ontario Lib Rev

"One finds in this book what a travel book cannot give, what can only be had from years of eating and sleeping and living with people in their homes. In addition, there are beautiful photographs of Tibetan life." Sat R

915.2 Geography of Japan

Benedict, Ruth

The chrysanthemum and the sword; patterns of Japanese culture. Houghton 1946 324p $4.95
915.2

1 Japan—Civilization 2 Japan—Social life and customs 3 National characteristics, Japanese

In this book an anthropologist writes of the Japanese view of life and of themselves. She sketches in the main outlines of their society and then describes their system of practical ethics, their ideas of good and evil, and the disciplines which make them able to live according to their code

"Because it pictures a Japan that exists more in tradition than in reality, Miss Benedict's book must be considered to be primarily of historical interest." N Y Times Bk R

Bibliographical foot-notes. Glossary: p317-20

Buck, Pearl S.

The people of Japan; photographs by Stuart Fox. Simon & Schuster 1966 255p illus boards $7.95
915.2

1 Japan—Civilization 2 Japan—Social life and customs

Buck, Pearl S.—*Continued*
The author "writes of the customs, traditions, change in culture, and western influence in Japan." Pub W
"In spite of her obvious affection for Asiatic people, Mrs. Buck writes with candor and objectivity on topics from Shinto to sex." Library J

Dunn, C. J.
Everyday life in traditional Japan; drawings by Laurence Broderick. Putnam 1969 197p illus map $4   915.2
1 Japan—Social life and customs 2 Japan—Civilization
"A description of Japanese life during the stable, . . . reign of the Tokugawa shoguns [1600-1850] which provides a basis for our understanding of the 'typical' or traditional Japanese flavor of today." Cincinnati
The author's "study of the country's deliberate isolation from outside influences, of the four basic classes—samurai, farmers, craftsmen, merchants, and of the people of the court, the temples and the theaters—is richly informative. The text is illustrated by several photographs of surviving locations . . . [and] by drawings." Best Sellers
Notes on further reading: p191

Halloran, Richard
Japan: images and realities. Knopf 1969 xxiv, 281p map $6.95   915.2
1 Japan 2 National characteristics, Japanese
This account of present day Japan explores "Japanese history, economics, sociology, education, politics, personalities and business practices." Pub W
"Halloran dramatically treats images of Japan's dynamic cities, booming economy, advanced technology; of jazz, TV, traffic jams, and Coca-Cola—all creating an illusion of a Westernized nation. He also effectively analyzes the realities of Japan's establishment, with its complex decision-making and economic mentality; of a regulated press consensus, and policies—all verifying that the way of life flows from ideas, ethics, customs, and institutions deep in traditional culture. The result is perhaps the best study of Japanese 'national character' written to date." Choice

Leonard, Jonathan Norton
Early Japan, by Jonathan Norton Leonard and the editors of Time-Life Books. Time-Life Bks. [distributed by Little] 1968 191p illus maps (Great ages of man: a history of the world's cultures) $6.95   915.2
1 Japan—Civilization 2 Japan—History—To 1867
Text and picture essays cover "the period from Japan's shadowy beginnings as a backward land on the edges of the civilized world, to the time when the pattern of its own cultural greatness had become well set by the early 17th Century." Introduction
Bibliography: p186

Lifton, Betty Jean
Return to Hiroshima; photographs by Eikoh Hosoe. Atheneum Pubs. 1970 90p illus $5.95, lib. bdg. $5.69   915.2
1 Hiroshima
Today Hiroshima "has the appearance of a modern Western city. But among its population of five hundred thousand are ninety thousand survivors of the [first atomic bomb]. Some of these survivors are still suffering from ailments caused by the bomb, and others are never absolutely certain they will avoid being affected. The documentary volume devoted to Hiroshima and its people is elegant in format, and at least half of the clear and sharply detailed photographs are associated with informal case-history reports of individual survivors: their ways of coping with life and their genuine desire for universal peace." Horn Bk
"The writing is sober and matter-of-fact, yet the effect of the whole poetic—an elegy in black and white." Sat R

Seidensticker, Edward
Japan, by Edward Seidensticker and the editors of Time-Life Books. Time-Life Bks. [distributed by Little 1968] 160p illus maps (Life World lib) boards $4.95   915.2
1 Japan
First published 1961
Contents: The crowded country; The heritage of a long isolation; Storm and calm in politics; A resilient and growing economy; Upheavals in family and society; Traces of spirit; Diversions borrowed and preserved; The tolerant believers; Powerful molders of young minds; A nation in the balance
"This is a brief, eye-catching, and authoritative survey of a country and its people. A chronology and a diversified list of books for further reading cap a report which owes as much to the photographs, some in color . . . as to a smoothly flowing text." Booklist

Van der Post, Laurens
A portrait of Japan. Photographs by Burt Glinn. Morrow 1968 176p illus map $13.95   915.2
1 Japan—Description and travel—Views
The author describes his earlier encounters with Japan: the first in 1926, and the second as a prisoner of the Japanese during World War II. He seeks "to reconcile his two earlier conflicting encounters—the bright enchantment of the youthful sojourn; the darkness of the war years. To do so, he deals first with . . . Tokyo—the head of Japan, as he terms it; then with Kyoto, its heart and 'the capital of the world within;' and finally with the 'body', . . . Nara . . . Nikku . . . and Kyushu." Publisher's note
"The beautifully written book reflects his sharp perception and warm understanding about the people, architecture, industry, gardens, religion, and arts. The photographs of the land and the people are extraordinary." Library J

915.3 Geography of Arabian Peninsula

Stewart, Desmond
The Arab world, by Desmond Stewart and the editors of Time-Life Books. Time-Life Bks. [distributed by Little 1968] 160p illus maps (Life World lib) boards $4.95   915.3
1 Arabs 2 Civilization, Arab
First published 1964
The Arab world with its rich religious, cultural and scientific tradition "is an extraordinarily complicated one. Inspired by new leaders, enriched by modern technology . . . . it is solving its problems in ways often baffling to western onlookers. . . . [This book attempts to provide an] insight into Arab problems and aspirations." Introduction
For further reading: p153

915.4 Geography of India

Bartholomew, Carol
My heart has seventeen rooms. Macmillan (N Y) 1959 177p boards $4.95   915.4
1 India—Social life and customs 2 India—Social conditions
"The wife of an American engineer writes of their two and a half years in Punjab, Northern India. Drawn by curiosity to visit the hospital next door, Carol Bartholomew lost her heart to the people, both staff and patients, who crowded into its seventeen rooms. As she worked there, she came to understand and appreciate the Indians. Her account is full of incidents which illustrate their ways of life and thought, and of character sketches. She comes to many conclusions about Americans and Indians, seeing the faults but also the many good points of both." Horn Bk

Bartholomew, Carol—*Continued*

"This is a warmly human and richly informative account. . . . The hospital episodes and descriptions of family life in a foreign land appeal to nursing enthusiasts as well as to girls who enjoyed the Santha Rama Rau books [entered below]." Doors to More Mature Reading

Bowles, Chester

Ambassador's report. Harper 1954 415p illus maps $6.95   **915.4**

1 India—Description and travel 2 India—Social conditions 3 India—Politics and government 4 U.S.—Foreign relations—India

An "analysis of India's problems based on the author's experiences as American ambassador [from 1951 to 1953]. . . . Mr. Bowles traveled extensively throughout the country and talked with people from all walks of life. From them he gained considerable understanding of Asian goals and aspirations. In his book he argues for a constructive nonpartisan American policy which recognizes the national interests of Asiatic countries and encourages the democratic forces at work." Cincinnati

"The experiences of his own family, their contacts and school attendance add human interest and readability." Massachusetts

Suggested reading: p403-06

Bowles, Cynthia

At home in India; illus. with photographs. Harcourt 1956 180p illus maps $4.50 **915.4**

1 India—Description and travel 2 India—Social life and customs

"When her father was appointed Ambassador to India in 1951, fifteen-year-old Cynthia went with her family to New Delhi. From that time until she returned to America in 1953, Cynthia attended school with Indians her own age, visited friends in their homes, lived in villages and saw the work of public health nurses and the India Village Service, studied Hindustani, and did volunteer service in one of Delhi's hospitals. Her book is an excellent report on the young people of India. She herself says: 'These friendships have taught me not simply that East and West 'can' meet, but that the very difference between the girl from India and the girl from America is not so great as I thought. Deep down, I realized, my Indian friends and I are very much the same.' At home in India' might well be a handbook for any young Americans who hope to serve as unofficial ambassadors anywhere." Horn Bk

Glossary of Hindustani terms: p179-80

Brown, Joe David

India, by Joe David Brown and the editors of Time-Life Books. Time-Life Bks. [distributed by Little 1967 c1964] 160p illus maps (Life World lib) boards $4.95   **915.4**

1 India

First published 1961

"With independence the new India opened its windows to the world. . . . How the new India government and people have embarked on this great adventure—something of their problems, the immense difficulties encountered, their frustrations and failures, but also their achievements and victories—will be found here." Introduction

A profusely illustrated account useful for social studies classes and as background for current events

For further reading: p153

Hazari

Untouchable; the autobiography of an Indian outcaste; introduction by Beatrice Pitney Lamb. Praeger [1969 c1951] 198p map $5.95   **915.4**

1 India—Social life and customs 2 Caste

First published 1951 in England with title: I was an outcaste

"Born into the untouchable caste in a Hindu community in north India early in the twentieth century, the writer recalls his childhood and youth, portraying his family life, school

days, work, and marriage. He tells of his life in Delhi and Simla as a servant to the British, of assuming the Muslim faith and Muslim name of Harzari in order to conceal his identity, and at the conclusion of the narrative, of sailing from Bombay to Paris where he was to study for three years. Beatrice Pitney Lamb . . . [the editor] contributes an introduction giving information about the caste system in India and noting the legal abolition of untouchability in 1955." Booklist

"Lively, absorbing, informative, this book with appeal to those who demand that what they read be relevant to their own lives. Comparisons between Indian untouchability and American racial discrimination are unavoidable." N Y Times Bk R

Glossary: p195-98

Herzog, Maurice

Annapurna; first conquest of an 8000-meter peak <26,493 feet>. . . . Dutton 1953 [c1952] 316p illus maps $7.50   **915.4**

1 Annapurna 2 Expédition française á l'Himalaya, 1950 3 Mountaineering

"Translated from the French by Nea Morin and Janet Adam Smith; cartographic and photographic documentation by Marcel Ichac; with an introduction by Eric Shipton; illustrations in color and monochrome-gravure." Title page

"The account of the French Himalayan Expedition which in 1950 conquered the 26,493 foot peak of Annapurna. . . . Nothing about the feat was easy. A lot of precious time was spent in finding Annapurna, since the country through which the men traveled was largely unmapped. The route to the top led through snow fields, across glaciers, up sheer ice and rock walls. At one time, Herzog was swept to the edge of a precipice and saved only by a loop of rope around his neck and leg. The two men who reached the peak suffered frostbite of hands and feet and knew the agony of a perilous descent in a race against death. A book of triumph and courage." Horn Bk

Glossary: p313-14

Hunt, John

The conquest of Everest; with a chapter on the final assault by Sir Edmund Hillary; foreword by H.R.H. the Duke of Edinburgh. Dutton 1954 [c1953] xx, 300p illus maps $8.95 **915.4**

1 Everest, Mount 2 Mount Everest Expedition, 1953 3 Mountaineering

First published 1953 in England with title: The ascent of Everest

"The leader of the British group that attacked Mount Everest in May 1953 recounts with care the meticulous planning and preparations, and the progress of the expedition in its successful ascent. He pays special tribute to the men both British and Sherpa, who worked together so well, and to the contribution of all previous expeditions. . . . Appendixes give technical information on equipment." Booklist

"This book stands in sharp contrast to 'Annapurna.' [entered above]. It is objective, where 'Annapurna' is almost tearfully emotional; it is like a military narrative in which the human beings involved almost disappear, whereas 'Annapurna' stresses the human relationships almost to the point of strain." Book of the Month Club News

Glossary: p289-90

Mehta, Ved

Portrait of India. Farrar, Straus 1970 544p $12.95   **915.4**

1 India

Based on a visit to India in 1965-66 by the blind expatriate Indian author and "consisting of nearly 50 'New Yorker' essays . . . Mehta's book is a highly personal collage of scenes and impressions that embrace almost every aspect of contemporary India." Pub W

This is "a book that has fascinated, entertained, moved, and very much edified me. . . . Without unduly retarding the narrative flow, Mehta weaves in a great deal of diverse information. Besides history he includes geography, mythology, anthropology, esthetics, and much material on caste, religion, agriculture, industry, and education." Sat R

Glossary: p521-25. Map on lining-paper

Moore, Clark D.

(ed.) India yesterday and today; ed. by Clark D. Moore and David Eldredge. Praeger 1970 368p map (The George School Readings on developing lands) $7.95   **915.4**

1 India—Civilization 2 India—History

"A wide-ranging survey of India containing numerous short selections, primarily historical in focus. The readings deal with the caste system, the rise of nationalism, the steps toward independence and Buddhism. Continuity is provided by connecting passages written by the author." Book News

Bibliography of sources; p346-48. Glossary of foreign words: p349-56

Rama Rau, Santha

Home to India. Harper 1945 236p $4.50, lib. bdg. $4.11   **915.4**

1 India—Description and travel 2 India—Social life and customs

A report on India "as seen by a young girl educated in England and unable to speak the language of the relatives to whose house she returns [in 1939 at the age of 16].... Her family connections assure an inside view of Congress, interviews with Nehru and Lord Linlithgow, and a picturesque glimpse of Indian household." Literary Guild

"A more delightful more honest little book it is hard to imagine.... It is enjoyable narrative, not instructive exposition, and has the flavor of private letters, written, perhaps to some school friend far away, avid for answers to questions about customs and personal affairs." N Y Her Trib Books

This is India. Harper 1954 155p illus maps lib. bdg. $3.79   **915.4**

1 India—Description and travel

"A personal report on Malabar, North India, Kashmir, New and Old Delhi, and other parts of the country, the people, their customs, and their condition." Retail Bookseller

"Within the pages of her slim book, Miss Rama Rau has savored, to a remarkable degree the full flavor of this land of contrasts." Christian Science Monitor

Taylor, Edmond

Richer by Asia. 2d ed. Houghton 1964 420p $6.50   **915.4**

1 India—Civilization 2 Asia—Civilization 3 World War, 1939-1945—Asia

First published 1947

Impressions of the peoples and cultures of Asia, especially India, and of World War II in this area. The author concludes "that the only way to peace between East and West is understanding, and especially understanding the Asiatics as people." Bk Buyer's Guide

"In this volume, Taylor has woven together what are essentially two different books. One is a rambling compound of philosophy, introspection and fantasy. The other, and vastly superior book, is the narrative that reports his movement, his work and his visual observation. The narrative portion of the book is written with graceful, fluent ease." New Repub

Ullman, James Ramsey

Americans on Everest; the official account of the ascent led by Norman G. Dyhrenfurth, by James Ramsey Ullman and other members of the expedition. Lippincott 1964 xxi, 429p illus maps $10   **915.4**

1 Everest, Mount 2 Mount Everest Expedition, 1963 3 Mountaineering

"An exciting, detailed report on the major, successful campaign of 18 Americans and one Englishman to climb Everest from Nepal in 1963 by two routes. Six men, one of them a Sherpa, reached the summit." Pub W

"Although Ullman, the official scribe, stayed on lower levels, he saw the diaries of the climbers, got constant reports by radio, and utilized verbal accounts. He describes vividly and skillfully the complexities of such an undertaking." Library J

915.5   Geography of Iran

Mehdevi, Anne Sinclair

Persia revisited; illus. by Milton Glaser. Knopf 1964 271p illus $5.95   **915.5**

1 Iran—Social life and customs

Sequel to: Persian adventure, listed below

After eleven years, Mrs Mehdevi, the American wife of a Persian diplomat, returns "to Teheran to her father-in-law, Hajji Malek, whose household shelters ninety relatives. She shows him as a towering symbolic figure—a man who by sheer force of personality preserved, in his lifetime, the traditional Persian way of life against the erosion of time." Publisher's note

"One wonders why Mrs. Mehdevi in all these years has not learned her husband's language; it would add so greatly to understanding and pleasure. But, although this is not the real Persia, which is made up of elements far more permanent and profound than are visible under the fleeting modern fashions of Teheran, the book is so . . . agreeable that one can even forgive the misspelling of nearly every Persian word." Sat R

Persian adventure. Knopf 1953 271p $5.95   **915.5**

1 Iran—Social life and customs 2 Iran—Description and travel

"A girl from Wichita married a member of the Iranian mission to the U.N.; ultimately the young couple were summoned 'home,' and the girl from Wichita discovered a rich, feudal society, tenaciously clinging to ancient custom or as persistently striving toward modern ideas." Retail Bookseller

This book "is a very personal book. But within its self-imposed limits, it peers deeply into the differences between East and West. It seems to say that with enough delicacy of insight they can be fathomed and a 'modus vivendi' found." N Y Her Trib Books

915.6   Geography of the Middle East

Stewart, Desmond

Early Islam, by Desmond Stewart and the editors of Time-Life Books. Time, inc. [distributed by Little] 1967 192p illus maps (Great ages of man: a history of the world's cultures) $6.95   **915.6**

1 Islam 2 Civilization, Islamic

This profusely illustrated book presents "the background and early theological and political development of Islam coupled with a series of chapters devoted to the culture, science, and art of the early Islamic world. The only criticism which may be leveled at the book is that for one reason or another Mr. Stewart has stretched his concept of early Islam to include what amounts to a complete history of Islam up to the late 19th century." Library J

Bibliography: p186

915.61   Geography of Turkey

Stewart, Desmond

Turkey, by Desmond Stewart and the editors of Time-Life Books. Time-Life Bks. [distributed by Little] 1969 c1965] 160p illus maps (Life World lib) boards $4.95   **915.61**

1 Turkey

First published 1965

This "pictorial guide to Turkey contains description of the physical features of the land, ancient history, a biographical sketch of Atatürk, known as the creator of modern Turkey, modern history and the struggle toward democracy, and an appraisal of the possibilities for the future. Appendixes include historical dates, suggestions for further reading, and a list of famous Turkish cultural figures and their principal works." Booklist

Copiously and attractively illustrated with colored and black-and-white photographs that reveal the Turkish way of life

915.66 Geography of Armenia

Der Nersessian, Sirarpie
The Armenians. Praeger [1970 c1969] 216p illus maps (Ancient peoples and places) $8.50
915.66

1 Armenia—Civilization 2 Armenia—History
This is a "history of Armenia beginning with the Urartians, the first inhabitants of the area, to the creation of the Kingdom of Cilicia in the eleventh century. . . . In separate chapters, the author describes the political organization, religion, literature, and the Armenian contributions in the fields of architecture, sculpture, and painting." Best Sellers
"It is in the chapters on architecture, sculpture and manuscripts of the Christian period that Professor der Nersessian is most at home and these . . . are the best in the book: those on the earlier phases are less personal and have more the character of a summary." Times (London) Lit Sup
Bibliography: p155-63

915.694 Geography of Israel

Feigenbaum, Lawrence H.
Israel: crossroads of conflict, by Lawrence H. Feigenbaum and Kalman Seigel; illus. with photographs and maps. Rand McNally 1968 176p illus maps $4.50
915.694

1 Israel
"After a brief history of the land of Palestine from Biblical times through the establishment of the modern state of Israel, the reader is introduced to life there today. Political structure, religion, economics, defense, science, music, theater, and, perhaps most fascinating, archaeology, with its recent discoveries, are covered. Many aspects of Israel's often troubled scene are explained clearly, to interest both Jews and non-Jews. . . . There are many uncommon photographs and a number of useful maps." Pub W
"Israelis aid to emergent nations is touched on, and the 1967 war is briefly mentioned. Some 70 clear photographs are included. The tone is enthusiastically pro-Israel." Library J

Payne, Robert
The splendor of Israel. Harper 1963 222p illus $9.95
915.694

1 Israel—Description and travel
"The journey begins with the ancient fortress of Jerusalem and wends its way to ancient places such as Caesarea, Beth Shearim, Nazareth, Tiberias, and Lake Galilee. Although he makes minor references to the modern-day state of Israel, Mr. Payne's primary concern is with the ancient sites and their religious and archaeological significance." Library J
"Not a study in depth yet one that re-creates atmosphere and effectively contrasts the country's ancient and modern elements." Booklist
Maps on lining-papers

St John, Robert
Israel, by Robert St John and the editors of Time-Life Books. Time-Life Bks. [distributed by Little 1968 c1962] 160p illus maps (Life World lib) boards $4.95
915.694

1 Israel
First published 1962
A "survey of Israel's history and of the present political problems, cultural development: and industrial growth. The writing style is objective and analytical, the many photographs are—almost all of them—of excellent quality, handsome and informative. A useful and interesting book with an extensive index and with lists of important holidays, historical dates, and famous Israeli cultural figures. A bibliography is included; endpapers are double-spread maps." Chicago. Children's Book Center

915.7 Geography of Siberia

Mowat, Farley
The Siberians. Little [1971 c1970] 360p maps $7.95
915.7

1 Siberia—Description and travel
"An Atlantic Monthly Press book"
The author challenges the myth of Siberia as being merely a desolate wilderness of trackless forests and snow-covered tundra inhabited by wolves and political prisoners, showing that since World War II it has become a teeming and productive country. He describes his talks with riverboat captains, reindeer herdswomen, Arctic specialists, students and teachers, dissidents and pioneers, and others who have helped make Siberia what it is

915.9 Geography of Southeast Asia

Karnow, Stanley
Southeast Asia, by Stanley Karnow and the editors of Time-Life Books. Time-Life Bks. [distributed by Little 1969 c1967] 169p illus map (Life World lib) boards $4.95
915.9

1 Asia, Southeastern
First published 1962
"A serious and rather heavy text that surveys the separated and diverse countries of southeast Asia: their past kingdoms, their colonial periods, their political and religious variations, their arts and their industries. Each of the chapters includes a text . . . followed by a section of photographs." Chicago. Children's Book Center
For further reading: p153-54

915.93 Geography of Thailand

Landon, Margaret
Anna and the King of Siam; illus. by Margaret Ayer. Day 1944 391p illus map $7.94, lib. bdg. $6.29
915.93

1 Thailand—Social life and customs 2 Leonowens, Anna Harriette (Crawford) 3 Mongkut, King of Siam
Anna Leonowen's experiences at the Siamese court in the 1860's. From her experiences she wrote two books: The English governess at the Siamese court, and The romance of the harem. The author has put these two books into one story with additions to make a complete tale
"An inviting escape into an unfamiliar, exotic past. . . . The suppressed inner life of the harem, the unspeakable cruelties . . . the brazen color come to us as perpetual astonishment." N Y Times Bk R

Thompson, Virginia
Thailand: the new Siam. 2d ed. Paragon Bk. 1967 xxxii, 865p map $17.50
915.93

1 Thailand
A reprint of the first edition published 1941 by Macmillan (N Y)
This study of the land, people and culture of Thailand "discusses Thai history, ethnography, agricultural, commercial, industrial and political development, the organization of the government, and examines such major social problems as opium, education, and public health." Asia. A Guide to Paperbacks
A "careful, comprehensive view of that little known country, a book that will be a storehouse of information and interest for present and future generations." Churchman
Bibliography: p807-25

915.97 Geography of Vietnam

Hammer, Ellen
Vietnam: yesterday and today. Holt 1966
282p illus maps (Contemporary civilizations
ser) $3.95   **915.97**
1 Vietnam
The author "goes back to Vietnam's break
from China in the fifteenth century, covers
the French occupation and Vietnam's 1954 victory, and brings her history up to the present
conflict." Bk Buyer's Guide
Includes chapters on the land, the people,
social and economic institutions
This blends "history with expert though
sometimes controversial opinion." Booklist
Glossary: p270-71. Bibliography: p272-74

Salisbury, Harrison E.
Behind the lines—Hanoi, December 23,
1966-January 7, 1967. Harper 1967 243p illus
maps boards $5.95   **915.97**
1 Vietnam (Democratic Republic) 2 Vietnamese Conflict, 1961-
An enlargement of the dispatches which the
author sent to The New York Times from
Hanoi in 1966. He "saw much of the bombing
damage, and interviewed Premier Pham Van
Dong. His main conclusion . . . was that the
American bombing was not justified by its
military, political or psychological results, and
may even have had negative effects." Pub W
A "thoughtful, balanced and dispassionate
account of North Vietnamese thoughts about
the . . . war." Choice

Schell, Jonathan
The village of Ben Suc. Knopf 1967 132p
map $4.95   **915.97**
1 Ben Suc, Vietnam 2 Vietnamese Conflict,
1961-
This book tells "how the Americans transferred the 3500 inhabitants of Ben Suc, on the
edge of the Iron Triangle, from their homes
and farms to a refugee camp and destroyed
the village so that it could not serve as a hide-
out for the Vietcong." Bk Buyer's Guide
Schell's account, much of which appeared
first in the "New Yorker" magazine, "is written with a skill that many a veteran war reporter will envy, eloquently sensitive, subtly
clothed in an aura of detachment, understated,
extraordinarily persuasive." N Y Times Bk R

Sheehan, Susan
Ten Vietnamese. Knopf 1967 204p map
$6.95   **915.97**
1 Vietnamese Conflict, 1961- —Personal narratives 2 Vietnam—Social conditions 3 Vietnam—Biography
From October 1965 through May 1966 the author, a journalist, interviewed ten Vietnamese: a peasant, a landlord, a refugee, a politician, a Montagnard, an orphan, a Buddhist
monk, a South Vietnamese soldier, a Viet
Cong, and a North Vietnamese prisoner. Their
lives provide a multisided view of conditions
in Vietnam
This book "is the unglamorous story of the
war shattered common man only dimly cog-
nizant of the anguish that engulfs him. The
reader looking for a commentary on the Viet
Nam situation will be disappointed in this
book. Miss Sheehan makes no attempt at political analysis. Writing in a direct and factual
style, she faithfully reports external details."
Best Sellers

916 Geography of Africa

Clark, Leon E.
(ed.) Through African eyes: cultures in
change. Praeger 1971 744p illus maps $12.50
   916
1 Africa—Civilization

"Tribal customs, urbanization, ancient African kingdoms, colonization, the rise of nationalism and struggle for independence, and post-
independence nation-building are the six general subject units around which approximately
85 firsthand accounts of sub-Saharan Africa
are arranged. (The six units [originally published between 1969-70] are also available as individual paperbacks.)" Library J
"Almost all the selections in this book were
written by Africans. Non-African writing has
been used only when African material did not
exist or when it seemed appropriate to illustrate a European point of view, as in the section dealing with colonial attitudes. The selections are drawn from a variety of sources,
including historical documents, autobiographies, journalistic accounts, novels, poems,
and studies by social scientists." Preface and
Acknowledgments

Davidson, Basil
The African genius; an introduction to African cultural and social history. Little [1970
c1969] 367p illus map $7.95   **916**
1 Africa—Civilization
"An Atlantic Monthly Press book"
Published in England with title: The Africans
The author "describes the influence of ecology on the development of African character
and institutions, the manner in which resilient
social and ideological structures were built
how Africans came to their concepts of Good
and Evil and their multiplicity of religions, and
the origins of misconceptions about Africa that
have endured to this day." Pub W
"This is very far from being just another
academic study, of interest only to an exclusive circle of anthropologists. Both learned
and readable, it forms a valuable contribution
to a better composite understanding of modern African problems. . . . Davidson establishes
very convincingly that African achievements
are as notable as those of anyone else, and the
point is worth making." Economist
Notes and references: p321-44. Select bibliography: p345-53

Moore, Clark D.
(ed.) Africa yesterday and today, ed. by
Clark D. Moore and Ann Dunbar. Praeger
1969 [c1968] 394p (The George School
Readings on developing lands) $7.95   **916**
1 Africa
This compilation "on Africa south of the
Sahara covers geography, culture, history, economics, African reaction to European culture
and the colonial system, and modern political
development. Varied points of view are represented in the selections, some of which are
general in scope while others discuss British,
French, Belgian, and Portuguese colonial policies, with special attention given to the Congo,
South Africa, Tanzania, Nigeria, and French
Equatorial Africa. The editors provide explanatory material where needed." Booklist
Bibliography: p377-82

Moorehead, Alan
No room in the ark. Harper 1959 227p illus
maps $6.95   **916**
1 Africa—Description and travel 2 Animals—
Africa
"The author reports on four extensive trips
into Southern and Central Africa concentrating
on the vanishing wild animals, and also on the
more primitive tribes encountered in remote
areas." Ontario Lib Rev
"Along the way, he gives some devasting
glimpses of the white man's social and political attitudes as well as sympathetic glimpses
of native peoples. Not everyone's book but
well worth introducing to (boys and girls as
well) who will appreciate its special blend of
literary quality, travel, animal life, and relationships of people." Horn Bk

916.1 Geography of Libya

Keith, Agnes Newton
Children of Allah; sketches by the author.
Little 1966 467p illus $7.95   **916.1**
1 Libya—Social life and customs 2 Libya—
Description and travel

"An Atlantic Monthly Press book"
The author lived for almost nine years in
Libya where her husband worked for the
United Nations. In this book, she describes
present day life in Libya, and field trips into
the Sahara. (Publisher)
"An account of [the author's] discovery of
the strangely beautiful desert landscape and
her awakening friendship for the people of Libya. Girls, especially, will enjoy meeting Libyan
girls and women who are still [1966] wearing
long, enveloping veils." Horn Bk
Map on lining-papers

916.2 Geography of Egypt and Sudan

Brander, Bruce
The River Nile; foreword by Melville Bell
Grosvenor; prepared by National Geographic
Special Publications Division, Robert L.
Breeden, chief. Nat. Geographic Soc. 1966
208p illus maps $4.25   **916.2**
1 Nile River 2 Egypt 3 Sudan
The author explored the Nile and its basin
by felucca, river-launch, truck, and camel. His
chronicle tells of ancient kingdoms and of
countries newly independent. It covers more
than a million square miles—the area drained
by the Nile. The account contains hundreds of
illustrations, most of them in color. (Publisher)

Cottrell, Leonard
Egypt; with 100 heliogravure illus. and
6 coloured plates. Oxford 1966 280p illus
map $15   **916.2**
1 Egypt—Description and travel
First published 1965 in France
"The terrain and people of Egypt, ancient
and modern, in word and picture." Christian
Century
"This book contains superb descriptions
of scenery, monuments and archaeological discoveries . . . complemented by beautiful illustrations. . . . Includes a section on the monuments threatened by the Aswan Dam." Library J

916.6 Geography of West Africa

Hoepli, Nancy L.
(ed.) West Africa today. Wilson, H.W.
1971 197p map (The Reference shelf v42, no.6)
$4.50   **916.6**
1 Africa, West
ISBN 0-8242-0414-X
African, American, British and French correspondents, scholars, students and leaders
discuss the first ten years of the independence
of West Africa. Their articles deal with the political and economic problems of the region;
with its foreign relations; and with the civil
war in Nigeria
Bibliography: p185-97

Krüger, Christoph
(ed.) Sahara; ed. by Christoph Krüger, in
collaboration with Alfons Gabriel [and
others]. Putnam 1969 183p illus $15   **916.6**
1 Sahara
"A description and history of the fabulous
Sahara Desert, its people, its animals, its
plants, the caravans and wild tribes and its

romantic past, and the new era, with irrigation
and atomic bomb tests in the future. With more
than 100 illustrations in one color and 63
plates in four colors." Bk Buyer's Guide
"The book is a first-rate education in Sa-
hariana from rock-drawings, nomads and
camels to the latest oil strike." Pub W

916.69 Geography of Nigeria

Niven, Sir Rex
Nigeria. Praeger 1967 268p map (Nations
of the modern world) $7   **916.69**
1 Nigeria
"Concise introduction to resources, current
problems and future prospects." Publisher's
note
Bibliography: p253-55

916.7 Geography of Central Africa

Coughlan, Robert
Tropical Africa, by Robert Coughlan and
the editors of Time-Life Books. Time-Life
Bks. [1970 c1962] 176p illus maps (Life
World lib) boards $4.95   **916.7**
1 Africa
First published 1962
This colorfully illustrated, "simplified account
of Africa . . . [emphasizes] history: the inter-
weavings through migrations and warfare, exploitation by slavers and colonists, and the
surge to independence and nationalism." Booklist
For further reading: p169-70

Martelli, George
Livingstone's river; a history of the Zambezi Expedition, 1858-1864. Simon & Schuster
[1970 c1969] 186p front maps $7.50   **916.7**
1 Livingstone, David 2 Zambezi River 3 Africa, Central—Description and travel
SBN 671-20466-1
This account of the ill-fated Zambezi Expedition focuses on the personality of Dr David
Livingstone, the African explorer whose exploits held an almost obsessive hold over the
imagination of Victorian England. (Publisher)
"Martelli provides us with an excellent character portrait of Dr. David Livingstone . . .
and a depressing but accurate picture of what
a quagmire the expedition turned out to be.
. . . Although well constructed, the book is
written in a pedestrian style. But the general
reader as well as the specialist may enjoy it."
Library J
Principal sources: p267-68

916.76 Geography of Kenya

Roberts, John S.
A land full of people; life in Kenya today.
Praeger [1968 c1966] 240p illus maps $7.50
          916.76
1 Kenya
Copyright 1966 in England
"Writing with the purpose of disposing of
some stereotyped ideas about Kenya, Roberts
presents various facets of Kenyan life by showing the people of the land. He illuminates
the difficulties and successes of the experiment of Asians, Europeans, and Kenyans trying to live together and touches on politics,
the arts, national character, and education.
A crisply written sympathetic, and informative essay." Booklist

916.8 Geography of South Africa

Hopkinson, Tom

South Africa, by Tom Hopkinson and the editors of Time-Life Books. Time-Life Bks. [distributed by Little] 1969 160p illus maps (Life World lib) boards $4.95   **916.8**

1 Africa, South

First published 1964

"Vivid pictures plus the impressionistic captions and commentary of a British journalist . . . convey to the uninformed reader an adequate introduction to South Africa's terrain, the ethnic stratification of its populace, its fragmented cultural life, and other distinctive and disturbing factors in the violent contrasts and ambiguities of its social-economic, and political way of life since the advent of Europeans to the land." Booklist

For further reading: p153-54

Van der Post, Laurens

The heart of the hunter. Morrow 1961 268p illus $5   **916.8**

1 Kalahari Desert—Description and travel
2 Bushmen

The author "relates how his party of explorers, on their way out of the Kalahari desert, saved a group of starving Bushmen; then the author turns to tales of magic, creation, and the Bushmen's animal pantheon, as the tales are still told among the dwindling numbers of aboriginal Bushmen." Pub W

"The author has been fighting a gallant battle against the forces of stupidity that have almost killed off the Bushmen; and if any of these notable little people survive, it will be due largely to him. His campaign, described here, does something to sweeten the ugly story of South Africa in our time. This work, however, is intended to be read on two levels. On the deeper level it is another venture into the interior; Mr Van der Post's exploration of the labyrinths of his unconscious." New Statesman

White, Jon Manchip

The land God made in anger; reflections on a journey through South West Africa. Rand McNally 1969 308p illus maps $7.95   **916.8**

1 Africa, Southwest—Description and travel

"South West Africa is a vast region of burning deserts, towns spaced hundreds of miles apart, its populated areas an odd mixture of German, British and black natives of the Hottentot, Herero and Bushmen tribes. . . . In a land rover, with two Afrikaans as guides, [the author] visited towns and regions normally shunned . . . [he] noted rare flora and fauna, asked questions, got to know people, how they lived, their struggle against a blistering environment, their politics and prejudices." Pub W

917.1 Geography of Canada

Angier, Bradford

How to live in the woods on pennies a day. Stackpole Bks. 1971 191p illus $6.95   **917.1**

1 Canada—Description and travel 2 Alaska—Description and travel 3 Outdoor life
ISBN 0-811-0845-0

The author explains how to obtain land for little or nothing in the northern wilderness areas of Canada and Alaska, how to build a home and basic furniture, how to find food and preserve it, how to find employment or live off the land, and even how to get a mail-order education

Clark, Gerald

Canada: the uneasy neighbor. McKay 1965 433p $6.50   **917.1**

1 Canada—Civilization 2 Canada—Foreign relations—U.S.

In addition to analyzing Canada's political, economic and cultural relations with the United States, this book interprets many phases of Canadian life. It ranges over the country "from Newfoundland to the Pacific to the Arctic Ocean with sharp delineations of the strikingly different problems of each region and its cultural, political, and economic aspirations." Publisher's note

Moore, Brian

Canada, by Brian Moore and the editors of Time-Life Books. Time-Life Bks. [distributed by Little 1968] 160p illus maps (Life World lib) boards $4.95   **917.1**

1 Canada

First published 1963

"An excellent survey of Canada's history and of the Canadian scene today—analytical, objective, comprehensive, and written in crisp, straightforward style. The photographs are handsome and informative; chapters of text alternate with sections of well-captioned illustrations, a format that is just slightly disruptive for the reader. Mr Moore has done an especially good job in the sections that deal with the cultural resurgence in Canadian life and with the problems that have arisen since Canada has assumed a growing international importance—such problems as nuclear warfare and relationship to the Common Market. Political and relief maps are included; an index, a bibliography, and several lists of statistical and historical facts are appended." Chicago. Children's Book Center

Mowat, Farley

Canada north. Little [1968 c1967] 127p illus maps boards $4.95   **917.1**

1 Canada

"An Atlantic Monthly Press book"

First published 1967 in Canada

The author "is indignant at the apathy and ignorance of southern Canada in regard to her northern regions and their people and attempts to correct misconceptions concerning climate, resources, and inhabitants. His description of arctic geography, archaeology, flora, and fauna is combined with a variety of excellent illustrations, including maps photographs, paintings, and a few Eskimo drawings." Booklist

National Geographic Society

Exploring Canada from sea to sea; foreword by Melville Bell Grosvenor; produced by National Geographic, Special Publications Division, Robert T. Breeden, chief. The Society 1967 208p illus map $4.25   **917.1**

1 Canada—Description and travel

"A centenary tribute to Canada. . . . The reader is taken to every corner of Canada, is told something of its history and introduced to a few of its people. . . . Although quite a few of the illustrations are of winter scenes, they dispel the idea that Canada is a snowy wilderness. Canada has vast underdeveloped areas and, of course, these receive considerable attention. However, as much, and perhaps more, attention is given to the country's great cultural and economic achievements." Library J

917.18 Geography of New Foundland

Mowat, Farley

This rock within the sea: a heritage lost. [Photographs by] John De Visser. Little [1969 c1968] unp illus $12.50   **917.18**

1 Newfoundland—Social life and customs

"An Atlantic Monthly Press book"

"Mowat has written clearly and movingly about a people and a way of life he views with affection and nostalgia—and anger about their unhappy future. John de Visser's 157 marvelous black-and-white photographs add exquisite detail at the end of each chapter. All the pictures were taken, appropriately enough, in the winter, since the portrait offered 'is of a people in the winter of their time.' This informative and beautiful book will be of interest to a great many people." Library J

917.2 Geography of Mexico

Coe, Michael D.
Mexico. Praeger 1962 244p illus maps (Ancient peoples and places) $8.50   **917.2**

1 Mexico—Civilization 2 Mexico—Antiquities 3 Indians of Mexico

The author "traces the development of the ancient cultures of Mexico from approximately 7000 B.C. to the conquest of Cortes, excluding the ancient Maya, whose boundaries lay partly in Mexico, and giving comparatively little space to the late-coming Aztecs. The emphasis is on archaeological and anthropological discoveries and implications. The book is well illustrated with line drawings, maps, and plates. A chronology of reigning Aztec monarchs and a select bibliography are appended." Booklist

Johnson, William Weber
Mexico, by William Weber Johnson and the editors of Time-Life Books. Time-Life Bks. [distributed by Little 1971 c1966] 160p illus maps (Life World lib) boards $4.95
917.2

1 Mexico

First published 1966
Illustrated with numerous photographs, many of them in color, this book presents a political, historical, economic, social, and cultural tour of Mexico

"Not enough U.S. citizens perceive what U.S. policy makers have to understand about the primal political and social energies that have made and are continually remaking modern Mexico. This book will, I hope, help U.S. citizens to comprehend the Mexico with which the U.S. of this generation must live." Introduction

For further reading: p153-54

Treviño, Elizabeth Borton de
Here is Mexico. Farrar, Straus 1970 198p illus $4.50   **917.2**

1 Mexico

"An Ariel book"
An account of Mexico, past and present, which attempts to give "an idea of the taste, smell, feeling, and rhythm of Mexico; and perhaps a few basic ideas about Mexico's history, sociology, and geography." Author's apology

Maps on lining-papers

917.28 Geography of Central America

Lavine, Harold
Central America, by Harold Lavine and the editors of Life. Time, inc. [distributed by Little] 1968 160p illus maps (Life World lib) boards $4.95   **917.28**

1 Central America

First published 1964
"Colorful introduction in photographs, maps, and interpretive text to Central America's six nations, Panama, Costa Rica, Guatemala, El Salvador, Honduras, and Nicaragua, their past civilizations and relics as well as current conditions, preoccupations, and customs. . . . Historical dates, suggested readings, and major political units listed in appendix." Booklist

917.291 Geography of Cuba

Lockwood, Lee
Castro's Cuba, Cuba's Fidel; an American journalist's inside look at today's Cuba—in text and picture. Macmillan (N Y) 1967 288p illus $9.95   **917.291**

1 Cuba 2 Castro, Fidel

A lengthy interview with Fidel Castro touching on "agriculture, industralization, agrarian reform, the small farmer, the counter-revolution, the city, education, Cuba's relations with the United States and with the Soviet Union, revolution in Latin America, The Bay of Pigs, the missile crisis, the CIA, political prisoners." Publisher's note

This book "is fascinating because it is much more personal experience and personal observation than political polemics. In general, Lockwood is very sympathetic to Castro although the book is certainly not hero-worship. . . . Whether you like Castro or what's happening in Cuba, the book is extremely valuable since it presents a first-hand picture of Cuba today, and a picture far different from what is generally presented in American news media." Pub W

917.3 Geography of the United States

American Heritage
The American Heritage Book of great historic places. Narrative by Richard M. Ketchum; introduction by Bruce Catton. Am. Heritage 1957 376p illus maps $16.50   **917.3**

1 U.S.—Civilization 2 U.S.—Description and travel 3 U.S.—Historic houses, etc.

"The story of America's past is told in terms of the fascinating places where history was made. The book is divided into nine geographic sections, each followed by a map of the area and a listing of the important places to visit in the towns and cities of each [state]. . . . More than 700 pictures—160 in full color—show where the events actually occurred." Huntting

"A monumental work, not so much in its physical aspect as in its delightful condensation and deft selection." Chicago Sunday Tribune

The American Heritage History of the 20's & 30's, by the editors of American Heritage. Editor in charge: Ralph K. Andrist. Narrative: Edmund Stillman; with two chapters by Marshall Davidson. Pictorial commentary: Nancy Kelly. Am. Heritage 1970 416p illus $19.95   **917.3**

1 U.S.—Civilization 2 U.S.—History—1919-1933 3 U.S.—History—1933-1945

"Alternating narratives and pictorial portfolios vividly evoke the ferment of the times in a colorful panorama of life in the U.S. between the two world wars. Beginning with President Wilson's 1918 European visit the book explores various aspects of small town America, the transformation of the social scene brought about by the automobile, the euphoric Jazz Age, Prohibition, the Depression, the New Deal, and the coming of the second war. It is given an immediacy by the numerous contemporary photographs, cartoons, drawings, and paintings, many in full color; the excerpts from popular writings of the period ranging from novels to periodical articles; and the short informal profiles of such personalities as F. Scott Fitzgerald, Al Capone, Texas Guinan, and Joe Lewis." Booklist

The nineties; glimpses of a lost but lively world, by the editors of American Heritage. Am. Heritage 1967 144p illus map $4.95 **917.3**

1 U.S.—Social life and customs 2 U.S.—History—1865-1898

"Staff for this book: Oliver Jensen, editor in charge"

The leading figures, spirit and meaning of the decade that marked the passing of Victorian life and the beginnings of modern America are portrayed. (Publisher)

"Colorfully illustrated articles by capable authors on a very flamboyant period in American history. Topics cover urban and rural life, finance and politics, arts and literature, war and peace." Library J

Andrews, Charles M.

Colonial folkways; a chronicle of American life in the reign of the Georges. U.S. Pubs. Assn. 1919 255p (The Chronicles of America ser. v9) $3.95   **917.3**

1 U.S.—Social life and customs—Colonial period

First published by Yale University Press
Contents: Land and the people; Town and country; Colonial houses; Habiliments and habits; Everyday needs and diversions; Intellectual life; Cure of souls; Problem of labor; Colonial travel; Bibliographical note

Boorstin, Daniel J.

The Americans: The colonial experience. Random House 1958 434p $12.50   **917.3**

1 U.S.—Civilization 2 U.S.—History—Colonial period 3 National characteristics, American 4 U.S.—Intellectual life

The first volume of a projected trilogy entitled: The Americans
"This study of colonial America attempts to show that it was not merely an offshoot of the mother country, but a new civilization. Particularly mindful of the intellectual realm, the author centers his highly informative work on colonial education, the special qualities of American speech, and the growth of a distinct culture." Booklist
Includes bibliography
Followed by: The Americans: The national experience, entered below

The Americans: The national experience. Random House 1965 517p $8.95   **917.3**

1 U.S.—Civilization 2 National characteristics, American 3 U.S.—Intellectual life

The second volume of a projected trilogy entitled: The Americans
A cultural interpretation of American history, this book traces "the roots of contemporary American life to the years between the Revolution and the Civil War. Boorstin's approach is twofold: a . . . view of regional characteristics and an examination of aspects of nationality as influenced by geography, American language, the necessity for symbols, and the tension between the theories of decentralization and centrality in government." Booklist
Bibliographical notes: p433-95

Butcher, Devereux

Our national parks in color. 2d ed. rev. and augmented. Potter, C.N. 1968 194p illus maps $5.95   **917.3**

1 National parks and reserves—U.S. 2 Natural monuments—U.S.

First published 1965
"The book describes not only the 29 great national parks, but also the National Park Service's 33 national nature monuments and 18 archeological monuments, and tells how to get there and where to stay." Publisher's note
"With the growing hordes of tourists frequenting our national parks, public libraries will find this a picture book with a purpose that of teaching Americans how to know and enjoy their parks." Cur Ref Bks
For further reading: p189-90

Cable, Mary

American manners & morals; a picture history of how we behaved and misbehaved, by Mary Cable and the editors of American Heritage. Am. Heritage 1969 399p illus $18   **917.3**

1 U.S.—Social life and customs

A history "of the manners, customs and mores of our country from the days of the Pilgrim Fathers to contemporary youth whose 'hippie' garb and rebellious ways seem, in the light of all their early American forefathers did and were, hardly outlandish at all. In more than one way a book such as this throws highlights on certain facets of our history that one never thinks about." Pub W

"Fun to look at, this is good ammunition for YA's, who find it necessary to defend some of their antics to parents who have forgotten what they themselves did 20 or 30 years ago." Library J

Colby, Vineta

(ed.) American culture in the sixties. Wilson, H.W. 1964 199p (The Reference shelf v36, no. 1) $4.50   **917.3**

1 U.S.—Civilization 2 U.S.—Intellectual life

Analyzed in Essay and general literature index
"It is the purpose of this compilation to survey the phenomenon of American culture in the sixties and to attempt to single out for closer scrutiny and evaluation some of the specific areas of its development—art, literature, theatre, music, ballet, and the mass media of motion pictures and television." Preface
Bibliography: p191-99

Commager, Henry Steele

The American mind; an interpretation of American thought and character since the 1880's. Yale Univ. Press 1950 476p front $12.50   **917.3**

1 U.S.—Intellectual life 2 U.S.—Civilization 3 National characteristics, American

Analyzed in Essay and general literature index
This work "may be described as an interpretation of American thought and character since 1880. Mr. Commager . . . examines the work of the great and the small among our philosophers, clergymen, novelists, poets, and men of letters. It is a full bodied book of staunch opinions and shrewd observations, bringing both understanding and excitement to its interpretation of the American mind and the forces that made it. Annotated bibliography." Huntting
This is an "important and readable book . . . which is itself an education. Its only limitation is that, quite properly, its consideration of literature is essentially a study of meaning rather than art." Book of the Month Club News

Country Beautiful

America's historic houses; the living past, by the editors of Country Beautiful. Editorial direction: Michael P. Dineen; ed. by Robert L. Polley; managing editor; Charles R. Fowler. Putnam 1967 194p illus $12.95 **917.3**

1 U.S.—Historic houses, etc. 2 Architecture, Domestic

About 90 American houses "are included for a variety of reasons: some because of the occupant's political or military fame, or social, literary or business prestige; others because the houses represent a meaningful way of life. New England, the Middle Atlantic and the South are well covered, the Midwestern section a little less so. The West gets scanty coverage, and there is nothing from San Francisco. Pictures of both exteriors and interiors are included." Pub W

Curti, Merle

The growth of American thought. 3d ed. Harper 1964 xx, 939p illus $12.50   **917.3**

1 U.S.—Intellectual life 2 U.S.—Civilization

First published 1943
Awarded the Pulitzer Prize for history, 1944
This "is an account of the growth of the thought of all the American people . . . as shaped by the various factors and forces—geographical, economic, social and personal—of American history. It is in fact what Professor Curti intended it to be 'a social history of American thought.' This means that the work . . . reaches out to include man's thought about the world and himself, about his origin and destiny, about the true, the good and the beautiful. It includes the growth of thought in the fields of technology, natural science, philosophy and theology." New Repub
Includes bibliography

Douglas, William O.

America challenged. Princeton Univ. Press 1960 74p $2.50   **917.3**

1 Conformity 2 U.S.—Civilization 3 U.S.—Foreign relations

Analyzed in Essay and general literature index

The Walter E. Edge lectures, 1960

"This is a concentrated, angry exhortation to Americans, covering major aspects of foreign and domestic policy, as well as people's basic attitudes. [The author] concludes, 'The complacency, the mediocrity, and the intolerance that have possessed us are our greatest enemies.' " Pub W

Bibliographical footnotes

Freeman, Orville L.

The national forests of America, by Orville L. Freeman and Michael Frome. Published by Putnam: in association with Country Beautiful Foundation 1968 194p illus maps $12.95
917.3

1 National parks and reserves—U.S. 2 Natural resources—U.S.

This book "presents a well-illustrated history of the national forest, the national forest movement and the U.S. Forest Service. Also included are glimpses of the forests and their resources, including wildlife. Various appendices are the primary reference assets of the book, the text and illustrations are good for reading for recreation and general enlightenment." The AAAS Science Book List

Frost, David

The Americans. Stein & Day 1970 250p boards $6.95   **917.3**

1 U.S.—Civilization 2 National characteristics, American
SBN 8128-1334-0

A collection of edited transcripts from the television talk show conducted by the English born interviewer with a number of well-known Americans. The book is "interspersed with general remarks by Mr. Frost. Some of the people interviewed are Truman Capote. Orson Welles, Spiro Agnew, Adam Clayton Powell, Chet Huntley, Jesse Jackson, and a couple of dozen others." N Y Times Bk R

This book "is a lively cluster of personalities and ideas. Relevant if not elegant, it is both bright and trite. Left and Right, Black and White. And rarely dull." Christian Science Monitor

Furnas, J. C.

The Americans; a social history of the United States, 1587-1914. Putnam 1969 1015p illus $12.95   **917.3**

1 U.S.—Civilization 2 National characteristics, American

"This is a popularly-written and richly impressionistic social portrait of America from early days up to the First World War. . . . [The author] writes vividly and with verve of the teeming variety of our country and our people. . . . [He] shows how the destiny of the early colonists was shaped by the great forests of the eastern seaboard. He takes up the contributions of the ethnic or national groups that came in successive waves to the New World. He is even contagiously enthusiastic about colonial cookery and devotes a whole section to it. He draws upon novels, stories, plays, uses every available source to document our eccentricities, customs and mores, our westward expansion, our railroads, the world of 'tramps,' feminist movements, the Negro as slave and freeman, arts and entertainment. Bibliography and notes." Pub W

Golden, Harry

Only in America; foreword by Carl Sandburg. World Pub. 1958 317p $6.95   **917.3**

1 U.S.—Civilization 2 U.S.—Social life and customs

"Short pieces about life in America as observed by a Jewish newspaper editor who seasons his writing with humor, common sense, and priceless anecdotes." Pub W

"These pieces are some of the results of [the author's] observations and cogitations on Jews, Negroes, politicians, and presidents, the old East Side and the new South, and the mores, folkways and foibles of our times and our people." Library J

Good things about the U.S. today. Macmillan (N Y) 1970 247p illus $5.95   **917.3**

1 U.S.—Civilization

"A U.S. News & World Report book"

This is a "survey of all those aspects of strength, validity and leadership which continue to make this country one of the greatest nation's on earth." Publisher's note

Contents: The greatest good of all; The horn of plenty; The boom in education; Winning the war on disease; Explosion in the arts; Culture for the millions; Lending a helping hand; Supremacy in technology; Conquering space; Americans at play; Land of opportunity

Handlin, Oscar

(ed.) This was America; true accounts of people and places, manners and customs, as recorded by European travelers to the western shore in the eighteenth, nineteenth, and twentieth centuries. Harvard Univ. Press [1969 c1949] 602p illus maps $12.50   **917.3**

1 U.S.—Description and travel 2 U.S.—Social life and customs

A reissue of the 1949 edition with a new preface

Analyzed in Essay and general literature index

"From the observations of an unknown 18th century Hollander, who lived among the Indians, to the 1939 impressions of the cosmopolitan André Maurois, here is a delightful account of America—its people, and places, manners and customs—as seen through the perspicacious eyes of Europeans who have loved and hated it." Hunting

Includes bibliographical notes

Hofstadter, Richard

Anti-intellectualism in American life. Knopf 1963 434p $7.95   **917.3**

1 U.S.—Intellectual life 2 U.S.—Civilization

Awarded Pulitzer Prize, 1964

The author "uses the idea of anti-intellectualism as a device for looking at several of the less attractive aspects of American life. This is not a formal history of a single idea, but rather an extended personal essay which explores various features of the American character. Mr. Hofstadter deals, in turn, with the peculiarly dismal anti-intellectual climate of the 1950's; with the evangelical religious movements from the Great Awakening to Billy Graham . . . with anti-intellectualism in education—the absurdities of life-adjustment theory and the uses and misuses of John Dewey." Publisher's note

"The book is thoroughly documented, admirably planned, gracefully written and everywhere clarifying to past and present. . . . Professor Hofstadter judges with fairness and sympathy and with his eye on the complexity of the issues. He judges the intellectuals as well as their opponents, especially in the long concluding section." Commonweal

Bibliographical footnotes

Langdon, William C.

Everyday things in American life, 1607-1776. Scribner 1937 xx, 353p illus map $7.95
917.3

1 U.S.—Social life and customs—Colonial period

"How the early colonists lived, what they ate, what they worked at, how they travelled, all helped out with a variety of illustrative material." New Yorker

Some of the chapter headings are: Shelters and first houses; Pennsylvania German farms; Handwork at Ephrata; Eighteenth-century furniture; Silversmiths and silverware; Measures of value; Colonial glass; New England ships; Trails and roads; Agriculture in the colonies; The colonial town

Langdon, Willam C.—*Continued*

"The survey possesses admirable geographical range as well as range of subjects." Springf'd Republican
Bibliography: p335-40

Everyday things in American life, 1776-1876. Scribner 1941 398p illus map $7.95
917.3

1 U.S.—Social life and customs

"This second work continues through the first hundred years of national life, ending with the Philadelphia Centennial. The emphasis naturally is on expansion, with chapters on Roads and turnpikes, Covered bridges, River transportation, the passing of canals, The development of steam. Other chapters treat of home life upstairs and down, clothes and their materials, and the improvements in farm machinery, all illustrated with well chosen pictures." Wis Lib Bul
Bibliography: p383-84

Leighton, Isabel

(ed.) The aspirin age, 1919-1941; written by Samuel Hopkins Adams [and others]. Simon & Schuster 1963 [c1949] 491p pa $2.25
917.3

1 U.S.—Civilization

"A Clarion book"

1949 edition analyzed in Essay and general literature index

A reissue of the title first published 1949 in hard covers

"Story of America between two wars told in terms of the most significant, typical, or fantastic news events of the gaudy and chaotic years that separated Versailles and Pearl Harbor. Re-creation of a period of time by twenty-two prominent authors who were closely connected with the period. For example: 'My Fights with Jack Dempsey,' Gene Tunney; 'The Lindbergh Legends,' John Lardner; and 'Huey Long; American Dictator,' Hodding Carter." A Guide to Reading in Am History

Matthews, William H.

A guide to the national parks; their landscape and geology [by] William H. Matthews III; foreword by Paul M. Tilden. Natural Hist. Press 1968 2v illus maps v 1 $9.95, v2 $7.95 ~~Supp has rev.~~
917.3

1 National parks and reserves—U.S. 2 Geology—U.S.

"Published for the American Museum of Natural History"

Contents: v 1 The Western parks; v2 The Eastern parks

"A good general introduction to the national park system for people who do not have very much time to spend in a single park but would like to understand a little about the park's natural formations and wildlife. The geology and natural history are described in a nontechnical language and the visitor is guided to museums, nature trails, campgrounds, etc." Pub W

Montagu, Ashley

The American way of life. Putnam 1967 352p $5.95
917.3

1 U.S.—Civilization   2 National characteristics, American

The author "has opinions on a great many things: conformity, television, sex, honorary degrees, Hollywood, courtesy, manners, the American magazine, the American newspaper, teen-age culture, secondhand bookstores, cocktail parties, Christmas, scientists, etc. A few of these he likes or admires, the others he dislikes and tells us why in capsule essays." Pub W

He "is at his best when coming to grips with the actual or potential disasters posed by entrenched ignorance, selfishness, bias or myth. . . . [The book] is vigorous, intelligent and humane, however open-ended." N Y Times Bk R

Moyers, Bill

Listening to America; a traveler rediscovers his country. Harpers Mag. Press 1971 342p $7.95
917.3

1 U.S.—Description and travel 2 U.S.—Social life and customs
SBN 06-126400-8

This record of the author's 13,000 mile journey across America last summer describes his impressions and reports on his meetings with "college presidents, student radicals, American Legionnaires, street people, union rebels, clergymen, drug addicts, black spokesmen, political candidates, unemployed executives, business leaders, country doctors, hardworking cops [and] ordinary citizens." Publisher's note

This is a "'now book.' Its overtones and implications, however, may be something more than that. I doubt very much if there is or will be, of the traveling-around-asking-questions-to-all-kinds-of-people type of book, a more relevant . . . one than this. A great deal of its value stems from Moyers's own personality, and his gifts as a reporter." N Y Times Bk R

National Geographic Society

America's historylands; touring our landmarks of liberty. . . . New ed. The Society 1967 576p illus maps (The World in color lib) $9.95
917.3

1 U.S.—Description and travel 2 U.S.—Historic houses, etc. 3 U.S.—History

The companion volume to: America's wonderlands, entered below

"Prepared by National Geographic Book Service; foreword by Melville Bell Grosvenor; introduction by Conrad L. Wirth." Title page

First published 1962

A report on hundreds of national historic sites, state parks, battle fields, towns, homes and restorations in the United States with an explanation of their historic significance

"The text, to which Carl Sandburg, Louis B. Wright, Earl Schenck Miers, Stewart Holbrook and Frank Freidel contribute, sparkles with wit, wisdom, and good sense. . . . The book is designed to appeal to all ages and all types of readers." Library J

America's wonderlands; the scenic national parks and monuments of the United States. . . . New enl. ed. 524 illus 465 in full color; contributors: Daniel B. Beard [and others]. The Society 1966 552p illus maps (World in color lib) $9.95
917.3

1 National parks and reserves—U.S. 2 National monuments—U.S.

"Prepared by the National Geographic Book Service, Merle Severy, chief; foreword by Melville Bell Grosvenor; introduction by George B. Hartzog, Jr. [and] Conrad L. Wirth." Title page

First published 1959

Contents: The Rocky Mountains; The great plateau; The Southwest; The golden West; The Pacific Northwest; The East; Alaska, Hawaii, and the Virgin Islands; Travel tips

"A beautiful volume of photographs of and articles about our national parks and monuments [including wildlife as well as scenic attractions]. Material has appeared in the 'National Geographic Magazine,' but it is most useful to have it collected in one volume. For travellers, nature lovers, budding scientists, and all young adult and school library collections." Library J

Vacationland U.S.A. The Society 1970 424p illus maps (World in color lib) $10.55 **917.3**

1 U.S.—Description and travel
SBN 87044-083-7

"This book was created under the guidance of Franc Shor." Verso of title page

"Lavishly illustrated with unexcelled color photographs in 'National Geographic Magazine' style, this guide book offers a year-round panorama of vacation activities in all 50 states. There are over 500 full-color illustrations, 17 diagrammatic maps locating vacation spots, and a large pocket map supplement showing U.S. national and state parks, forests, game refuges, Indian reservations, and other

National Geographic Society—*Continued*

features. Special sections list fairs, festivals, pageants, regattas, rodeos, and winter carnivals, and tell where to write for further information. Most articles are first-person accounts of family vacation experiences written and illustrated by members of the National Geographic Society staff." Library J

Nye, Russel

The cultural life of the new Nation, 1776-1830. Harper 1960 324p illus (The New American Nation ser) $7.95   **917.3**

1 U.S.—Civilization 2 U.S.—History—1783-1865 3 U.S.—Intellectual life

Companion volume to: The cultural life of the American colonies, 1607-1763, by L. B. Wright, entered below

"Mr Nye makes vividly clear the period's underlying patterns of thought, indicating . . . the profound influence of European Romanticism, although American experience itself precluded the Old World's pessimism; how new discoveries in science were gradually wrecking the grand Newtonian scheme of the universe; and how all these changes affected religion, manners, education and the arts." Publisher's note

Includes bibliographies

The unembarrassed muse: the popular arts in America. Dial Press 1970 497p illus (Two centuries of American life: a bicentennial ser) $12.50   **917.3**

1 U.S.—Civilization

This is a "history and analysis of American mass culture: theatre, fiction (including westerns, detective novels and science fiction), the pulps, comic books and comic strips, popular music, radio and television, and movies." News of Bks

"Fascinating, comprehensive, lively, colorful, entertaining—and still an excellent reference work on a subject. . . . Nye's book is both history and analysis of the best sort." Pub W

Bibliography and sources: p421-37

Reich, Charles A.

The greening of America; how the youth revolution is trying to make America livable. Random House 1970 399p $7.95   **917.3**

1 U.S.—Civilization 2 Youth movement

The author "analyzes the youth culture which is changing America and predicts a revolution of the new generation, 'a revolution of consciousness' that would 'offer a new way of life that is nothing less than a new vision of human existence—freedom, creativity, humor, love, community—made possible and necessary by technology.' This book . . . is full of insights as to the future." Open Shelf

Bibliography included in Acknowledgments: p397-99

Schlesinger, Arthur M. 1888-1965

The birth of the Nation; a portrait of the American people on the eve of independence; with an introduction by Arthur M. Schlesinger, Jr. Knopf 1968 258p $5.95   **917.3**

1 U.S.—Social life and customs—Colonial period 2 U.S.—History—Colonial period 3 National characteristics, American

"In displaying the character of American folkways and institutions just before the Revolution, Professor Schlesinger shows how social, political, and intellectual changes in the century and three quarters of America's colonial history had by 1776 created a distinctive American character and a separate American society." Publisher's note

Includes bibliography

Segal, Ronald

The Americans: a conflict of creed and reality. Viking 1969 340p $6.95   **917.3**

1 U.S.—Civilization 2 National characteristics, American

First published 1968 in England with title: American's receding future

In this survey of the United States today, the author, a white man, born in South Africa and educated at Cambridge, England, discusses "racial collisions, disunity over the war in Vietnam, [the] deep and widespread poverty in the midst of conspicuous wealth, [and] the disintegration of the cities." Publisher's note

Reference notes: p325-31

Smith, Richard Austin

The frontier states: Alaska [and] Hawaii, by Richard Austin Smith and the editors of Time-Life Books. Time-Life Bks. [distributed by Little 1968] 192p illus maps (Time-Life Lib of America) boards $6.95   **917.3**

1 Alaska 2 Hawaii

"This lucid and comprehensive volume, filled with many colored and black-and-white photographs, offers a rare, perspicacious analysis of the two [newest] States and their people. Some of the information is common knowledge to many readers, but most of it is new and interesting. The author has shown a surprising number of similarities in the two cultures, as sweeping changes overtake both and indicate trends for future development. Virtually every aspect of life in Alaska and Hawaii is analyzed, from the small industries that dot the land, to the people at work and in their leisure activities." Science Bks

Appendixes include suggested tours, pronouncing glossary, and bibliography

Steinbeck, John

Travels with Charley; in search of America   **917.3**

1 U.S.—Description and travel

Some editions are:
Viking $4.95
Watts, F. lib. bdg. $8.95. Large type edition. A Keith Jennison book

"John Steinbeck, accompanied by a French poodle named Charley, set out in a three-quarter-ton pickup [truck] equipped with a miniature ship's cabin to see what changes had occurred in the country he had been writing about for twenty years. His course took him to almost 40 states; as always, his concern was with the people." Huntting

"The book is entertaining, occasionally informative, frequently thoughtful and thought-provoking. Mr. Steinbeck writes with lively ease of the people he meets and with appreciation of the beauty he sees in the countryside. There is some disgressive writing . . . but much of the social commentary is poignant." Chicago. Children's Book Center

Time-Life Books

This fabulous century, by the editors of Time-Life Books. The author [distributed by Little 1970] 8v illus maps boards ea $9.95 **917.3**

1 U.S.—Civilization

Everyone "will delight in this popular pictorial history of America's last 100 years. The set will doubtless be in demand, for history comes vibrantly alive through the carefully chosen photographs and illustrations of American life as it was and is. It's all here: the old hometown, all that jazz, boom and bust, radio, the movies, television, suburbia, culture, the youth trip, assassins, black emergence, doves and hawks, science." Library J

Bibliographies included

The U.S. overseas; Puerto Rico; territories; cumulative index; by the editors of Time-Life Books. The author [distributed by Little 1969] 192p illus map (Time-Life Lib. of America) boards $6.95   **917.3**

1 U.S.—Territories and possessions

The book discusses areas such as Puerto Rico, the Panama Canal Zone, the Virgin Islands, and others, which are still under U.S. domain. It provides brief histories of these areas, as well as information about their social and economic development

Includes the cumulative index to all volumes of the Time-Life Library of America

Bibliography: p161-62

Time-Life Books—*Continued*

The USA; a visitor's handbook, by the editors of Time-Life Books. Time-Life Bks. [distributed by Little] 1969 348p maps boards $4.95   **917.3**

1 U.S.—Description and travel

"Part one of the guide has many thoughtful hints for persons unfamiliar with U.S. mores such as rules for the woman alone, automobile and other transportation information, a glossary, tipping customs, a list of holidays, liquor laws, and arrival and departure regulations. Part two contains essential information and personality profiles of eight major cities and 23 regional cities of special interest. A suggested 21-day tour with a description of the six sections of the U.S. brings the book to a close." Booklist

Tunis, Edwin

Colonial living; written and illus. by Edwin Tunis. World Pub. 1957 155p illus $6.95, lib. bdg. $7.70   **917.3**

1 U.S.—Social life and customs—Colonial period

"A comprehensive portrayal of the details of life in the United States in the 17th and 18th centuries. Over 200 detailed drawings supplement and amplify the text. Among the aspects of colonial life described in the book are food and dress architecture and industries, tools and utensils, communications and customs. An excellent reference book; the smooth writing and occasional bits of humor provide reading that is enjoyable as well as informative." Chicago. Children's Book Center

Udall, Stewart L.

The national parks of America [by] Stewart L. Udall and the editors of Country Beautiful. Published by Putnam: in association with Country Beautiful Foundation 1966 225p illus maps $15.95   **917.3**

1 National parks and reserves—U.S. 2 U.S.—Description and travel

At head of title: The editors of Country Beautiful. Editorial direction: Michael P. Dineen; edited by Robert L. Polley; managing editor: Charles R. Fowler; contributing editors: Joseph Dever, Frank Sullivan, William Bibber

This "briefly sketches the history of each of the national parks and the special charm and attraction of each (without, however, indicating the perils which some of the parks [face]). . . . With each essay there are photographs [some of them] full-color photographs of good quality." Pub W

The **United** States, by Patrick O'Donovan [and others] and the editors of Time-Life Books. Time-Life Bks. [distributed by Little 1968] 192p illus (Life World lib) boards $4.95   **917.3**

1 U.S.—Civilization

First published 1965 by the editors of Life

Nine foreign-born experts examine different aspects of American civilization including the religious zeal, the political system, the economy of a democracy, the search for leisure, the sense of history, the problems of education, etc.

"Each piece is followed by a section of captioned, topically oriented photographs, some in color. Lists of historical dates, cultural figures, and books for further reading are appended. A provocative interpretation of the American scene for the thoughtful reader." Booklist

Map on lining-papers

Walker, Robert H.

Everyday life in the age of enterprise, 1865-1900; ed. by Louis B. Wright. Putnam 1967 255p illus (Life in America) $4.50   **917.3**

1 U.S.—Social life and customs 2 U.S.—History—1865-1898

The author "describes social life, artifacts, and customs in the United States between the years 1865 and 1900, when this country changed from an isolated, agricultural, regionalized society to a more centralized and industrial nation. There is also information about the influence of newspapers, the impact of railroads, and the effect of electricity, steam, steel, and coal on American life and the economy. This well researched study covers a period for which such detailed material is hard to find in one place. A good bibliography, index, and contemporary photographs are included." Library J

Wish, Harvey

Society and thought in America. McKay 1950-1962 2v illus ea $9.50   **917.3**

1 U.S.—Civilization 2 U.S.—Intellectual life 3 U.S.—Social life and customs

First published 1950-1952 by Longmans

"A social and intellectual history of the American people . . . showing how Americans developed into the people they are today. Personalities, anecdotes, customs in dress, controversies of the times, economic conflicts, literary and religious trends are viewed as part of the colorful, developing scene." Retail Bookseller

Contents: v 1 Society and thought in early America: a social and intellectual history of the American people through 1865. v2 Society and thought in modern America: a social and intellectual history of the American people from 1865. 2d ed.

Selected bibliography at end of each volume

Wright, Louis B.

The cultural life of the American colonies, 1607-1763. Harper 1957 292p illus (The New American Nation ser) $7.95   **917.3**

1 U.S.—Civilization 2 U.S.—History—Colonial period 3 U.S.—Intellectual life

Analyzed in Essay and general literature index

Companion volume to: The cultural life of the new Nation, 1766-1830, by R. B. Nye, entered above

This volume "gives an account of ideas, manners and institutions from 1607 to 1763. Dr Wright is mainly concerned with how the colonists lived, earned a living and enriched their lives." Huntting

Includes a bibliography

Everyday life in colonial America. Putnam [1966 c1965] 255p illus maps (Life in America) $4   **917.3**

1 U.S.—Social life and customs—Colonial period

"The book covers the living conditions during the Colonial period, and discusses the way of life on farms, religion, sports and pastimes, careers and the military events of the era." Huntting

"The account is written in a rich and vivid style, illustrated with photographic plates." Best Sellers

Suggested readings: p247-50. Further readings: p250

917.4 Geography of New England and Middle Atlantic states

Bowen, Ezra

The Middle Atlantic States; Delaware, Maryland, Pennsylvania, by Ezra Bowen and the editors of Time-Life Books. Time-Life Bks. [distributed by Little 1970] 192p illus maps (Time-Life Lib. of America) $6.95   **917.4**

1 Pennsylvania 2 Delaware 3 Maryland

Bowen, Ezra—*Continued*

"This is a survey of Delaware, Maryland, and Pennsylvania. The text, accompanied by numerous pictorial sections, traces the history of the area with emphasis on the economic difficulties early in the century, recent efforts to stimulate the economy, and urban developments since World War II. . . . Suggested tours, lists of museums, galleries, and wildlife, and statistics are appended." Booklist
Bibliography: p188

McCarthy, Joe

New England: Connecticut, Maine, Massachusetts, New Hampshire, Rhode Island, Vermont, by Joe McCarthy and the editors of Time-Life Books. Time, inc. [distributed by Little] 1967 192p illus maps (Time-Life Lib. of America) $6.95   **917.4**

1 New England—Description and travel

A "survey [of] New England showing the geographical cohesiveness and common history of the six states and covering the area's economy, intellectual growth, politics, ethnic groups, and social progress. The appendix lists suggested tours, museums and galleries, local festivals and events, wildlife, statistics, and books for further reading." Booklist

Miller, Perry

The New England mind: From colony to province. Harvard Univ. Press 1953 513p front $8   **917.4**

1 New England—Intellectual life 2 New England—History—Colonial period 3 Puritans 4 American literature—New England

Companion volume to: The New England mind: The seventeenth century, entered below
"An intellectual history of the interregnum between Richard Mather's farewell sermon in 1657, which ended the era of the founding fathers, and Jonathan Edwards' Harvard lecture in 1731, which began a new (if less extreme) era of certainty. The book is centered on Boston, and, within Boston, on the ambiguous and fascinating figure of Cotton Mather. . . . Subordinating social and economic realities, Mr. Miller concerns himself extensively with theological controversy." New Yorker
The author "appraises the Salem witchcraft debacle, the inoculation controversy, and countless other developments in the light of contemporary standards. He has written with sympathy and understanding of men whose tastes and ways of thinking are obviously remote from his own." Ann Am Acad
Bibliographical notes: p487-98

The New England mind: The seventeenth century. Harvard Univ. Press 1954 528p $8   **917.4**

1 Puritans 2 Religious literature 3 American literature—History and criticism 4 American literature—New England

Reprint of edition first published 1939
Companion volume to: The New England mind: From colony to province, entered above
"This volume is no mere defense of the Puritans from charges they were unduly austere or lugubrious in their attitude toward life and its amenities. What the author attempts, rather, is to prove they were normal people with normal interest in becoming prosperous and enjoying the good things of this world—but people who were also endowed with an intellectual and theological outlook which distinguished them in some ways from most other groups. This outlook Prof Miller examines in great detail and from many angles, being convinced it is the key to a proper understanding of early New England." Springf'd Republican
Bibliographical references included in Appendix A-B and Notes: p493-523

917.47 Geography of New York (State)

Boyle, Robert H.

The Hudson River; a natural and unnatural history. Norton 1969 304p illus $7.95   **917.47**

1 Hudson River 2 Hudson Valley 3 Natural history—Hudson River

This is a description "of the Hudson in all its colorful aspects and phases from wilderness days to the present. . . . [The author describes] the Hudson's pollution and its disastrous effects, and strikes out against modern industrial carelessness in general and in particular against Con Ed's proposed nuclear plant on the river's shores." Pub W
A "highly entertaining and informative book in a style which is easily read and grasped by the layman. Frequent quotes from original manuscripts make the documentation of historical events very enjoyable." Choice
Bibliography: p282-96. Map on lining-papers

917.5 Geography of Southern and Southeastern states

Clark, Thomas D.

The emerging south. 2d ed. Oxford 1968 341p $7.50   **917.5**

1 Southern States—Civilization 2 Southern States—Social conditions

First published 1961
This discussion of the development of the American South discusses agriculture and capital farming, industrial gains and the effect of technology, urbanization, and race relations, civil rights and education
Selected bibliography: p311-28

Dykeman, Wilma

The border states; Kentucky, North Carolina, Tennessee, Virginia, West Virginia, by Wilma Dykeman and James Stokely and the editors of Time-Life Books. Time-Life Bks. [distributed by Little] 1968 192p illus maps (Time-Life Lib. of America) $6.95   **917.5**

1 Kentucky 2 North Carolina 3 Tennessee 4 Virginia 5 West Virginia

"A chronicle of the history of the border states (Kentucky, North Carolina, Tennessee, Virginia and West Virginia) and a candid report on those places today—where the Civil War is still a bitter heritage and poverty a way of life. Lavishly illustrated with photos." Huntting
Among the highlights "are text and picture essays on Appalachia, native handicrafts, the Tennessee Valley Authority, 'country music,' and the horse farms of Kentucky." Booklist
Pronunciation glossary: p186-87. Bibliography: p188

McGill, Ralph

The South and the Southerner. Little 1963 307p $6.95   **917.5**

1 Southern States—Civilization 2 Southern States—Race relations

"An Atlantic Monthly Press book"
An autobiography in part, as well as an account of social and economic progress and retrogression in the South from the Civil War onwards, markedly in the 1930's, 1940's, and 1950's." Pub W
The author describes "the effect on the South of the 'separate-but-equal' doctrine, explains the origin of the Ku Klux Klan and White Citizen's Councils, and discusses the attitude of the churches and of politicians, both good and bad, to the integration problem." Booklist

Osborne, John, 1907-
The old South; Alabama, Florida, Georgia, Mississippi, South Carolina, by John Osborne and the editors of Time-Life Books. Time-Life Bks. [distributed by Little] 1968 192p illus maps (Time-Life Lib. of America) $6.95   917.5

1 Southern States—Description and travel

Pictures and text depict the land, people—their life and religion—industries, social conditions, and great writers of the Southern States

As the author "describes the the Old South, it is an abstraction, having more to do with communal custom and posture than with geography, and subject to definition pretty much as the definer chooses." McClurg. Book News

Appendix includes suggested tours, museums and galleries, glossary and bibliography

917.53 Geography of Washington, D.C.

Weisberger, Bernard A.
The District of Columbia; the seat of government, by Bernard A. Weisberger and the editors of Time-Life Books. Time-Life Bks. [distributed by Little 1969 c1968] 192p illus maps (Time-Life Lib. of America) boards $6.95   917.53

1 Washington, D.C.

"The institutions, the customs, and traditions, the different kinds of people that form Washington's galaxy are presented in this book against the shifting and developing backdrop of the city's monumental and history-laden buildings." McClurg. Book News

"In this perceptive portrait of the District of Columbia, Bernard Weisberger describes Washington as 'perhaps the most electric 70 square miles of urban America.' . . . [The author] has spelled out the atmosphere of crisis an ferment and expectancy that excite everyone in this driving, pulsing town. He has also given us a feeling of the complexity of the government and the dedication of its personnel. These are things the American people should know about, and they will find what they are looking for in this volume." Introduction

Bibliography: p188

917.6 Geography of South Central states

Goodwyn, Lawrence
The South Central States; Arkansas, Louisiana, Oklahoma, Texas, by Lawrence Goodwyn and the editors of Time-Life Books. Time, inc. [distributed by Little] 1967 192p illus maps (Time-Life Lib. of America) boards $6.95   917.6

1 Arkansas 2 Louisiana 3 Oklahoma 4 Texas

Pictures and text depict the diversified population, geography, history, industries, and Western folklore of Arkansas, Louisiana, Oklahoma, and Texas. Mapped tours, museums, local events, wildlife, statistics, glossary, and bibliography are included in the appendix

917.7 Geography of Middle West

Carter, Hodding
Man and the river: the Mississippi; photography by Dan Guravich. Rand McNally 1970 174p illus map $14.95   917.7

1 Mississippi River 2 Mississippi Valley

"This story of the Mississippi River is divided into eight chapters followed by an outstanding color pictorial review of the river from its origin, called 'The Everlasting Flowing.' The author has skillfully blended many historical, geological, geographical, biological, and economic facts into a story that will appeal to the high school student and layman. The chapters subdivide this information into interesting discussions entitled 'The River,' 'The Wildlife,' 'The People,' 'Romance,' 'The Towns,' 'The River Bounty,' 'Blow for a Landing,' and 'Mastering the River.'" Science Bks

Keating, Bern
The mighty Mississippi; photographs by James L. Stanfield. Prepared by the National Geographic Society's Special Publications Division, Robert L. Breeden, chief; foreword by Melville Bell Grosvenor, editor-in-chief. Nat. Geographic Soc. 1971 199p illus map $4.25   917.7

1 Mississippi River 2 Mississippi Valley
SBN 87044-096-9

"Over 2,000 miles of the Mississippi River from its source just south of the Canadian border to the Gulf of Mexico described in touristic manner . . . and revealed in color photographs of exceptional quality. . . . The power and productivity of the major waterway and the ports, ships, and people to whom it gave life in the past and gives sustenance in the present are enlivened by a felicitous text, historical illustrations, and pleasing photographs. Additional references are found in the index section." Booklist

917.8 Geography of Western and Plains states

Hollon, W. Eugene
The Great American Desert; then and now. Oxford 1966 284p illus maps $6   917.8

1 The West—History 2 Rocky Mountain region 3 Deserts

The author "traces the history of the arid region bounded by central Kansas, the Sierra Nevada mountains, northern Montana and the Mexican border." Book Rev Digest

"Much of the book is concerned with the area as it is today, and tells how such things as innovations in farming and cattle raising, modern transportation facilities, and air conditioning are urbanizing the desert." Publisher's note

Bibliographical notes: p254-74

Jones, Evan
The Plains States; Iowa, Kansas, Minnesota, Missouri, Nebraska, North Dakota [and] South Dakota, by Evan Jones and the editors of Time-Life Books. Time-Life Bks. [distributed by Little] 1968 192p illus maps (Time-Life Lib. of America) boards $6.95   917.8

1 Great Plains

Text and picture essays describe the terrain, climate, historical and economic development, social and political changes, and the Indians of the seven Plains States. (Publisher)

Bibliography: p188

Remington, Frederic
Frederic Remington's own West; written and illus. by Frederic Remington; ed. and with an introduction by Harold McCracken. Dial Press 1960 254p illus $7.50   917.8

1 The West 2 Frontier and pioneer life—The West 3 Indians of North America

This collection of twenty-six "of Frederic Remington's articles and stories, with his own illustrations, presents Remington as a writer as well as a painter of the Far West of

Remington, Frederic—*Continued*

the 1880's and 1890's. Indians, white trappers and cowboys, rangers, army men, Mexican vaqueros, cow ponies, and cattle are the subjects of the writings and the art work." Booklist

"The material in the book is arranged to follow the sequence of Remington's life, thus approximating an autobiography of the extraordinary Western artist-writer." Pub W

Santee, Ross

Cowboy; illus. by the author. Hastings House 1964 257p illus $4.95   **917.8**

1 Arizona 2 Ranch life 3 Cowboys

Original 1928 edition published by Cosmopolitan Book Corporation

This is "the saga of a range-struck youngster who rides away from home and grows to manhood on a ranch in the Arizona hills." Dalls Pub Lib

"One gets a singularly intensive and intimate picture of the cowboy and the things that make up his existence." N Y Her Trib Books

Sprague, Marshall

The Mountain States; Arizona, Colorado, Idaho, Montana, Nevada, New Mexico, Utah, Wyoming, by Marshall Sprague and the editors of Time-Life Books. Time-Life Bks. [distributed by Little] 1967 192p illus maps (Time-Life Lib. of America) $6.95   **917.8**

1 Rocky Mountain region 2 Southwest, New

This book is "a very brief geography, geology and history of the [eight Mountain States], with a graphic survey of Indian life and splendid pictorial coverage of Indian arts, and chapters on ranching, mining, the Mormons, the desert, and the need to preserve the best of the West's wilderness." Pub W

Appendix includes suggested tours, museums and galleries, glossary and bibliography

Williams, Brad

Lost legends of the West [by] Brad Williams & Choral Pepper. Holt 1970 192p illus $5.95   **917.8**

1 The West 2 Folklore—U.S.
SBN 03-081867-2

The authors "examine many little-known stories and legends of the American West. . . . The lost secrets of Charles Hatfield—super rainmaker, who twice nearly washed San Diego off the map of California—the lost site of the Calavaras skull, and the mystery of the Port Oxford meteorite are but a few of the phenomena discussed." Publisher's note

917.98 Geography of Alaska

Keating, Bern

Alaska; illus. by George F. Mobley; produced by the National Geographic Special Publications Division, Robert L. Breeden, chief. [2d ed] Nat. Geographic Soc. 1971 207p illus maps $4.25   **917.98**

1 Alaska—Description and travel
SBN 87044-076-4

First published 1969

In text and illustrations, the book describes the people, the land and natural resources, and the cities, towns, and industries of Alaska.

"The photographs are up to the 'National Geographic's' usual standard of excellence. The book is handsomely bound and contains a good index and a short bibliography. An added bonus is the Society's map of Alaska, with the top of the world printed on the back, a most useful and welcome addition though libraries might wish a pocket had been included to house the map." Library J

918   Geography of South America

Ferguson, J. Halcro

The River Plate republics; Argentina, Paraguay, Uruguay, by J. Halcro Ferguson and the editors of Time-Life Books. Time-Life Bks. [distributed by Little 1971] 160p illus maps (Life World lib) boards $4.95 **918**

1 Argentine Republic 2 Paraguay 3 Uruguay

First published 1965

"Historical background is briefly reviewed but this attractive, plentifully illustrated introduction . . . emphasizes recent and present-day political, cultural, and social developments. Names and works of the area's important writers and artists are among the appended material." Booklist

For further reading: p153-54

Johnson, William Weber

The Andean republics; Bolivia, Chile, Ecuador, Peru, by William Weber Johnson and the editors of Life. Time, inc. [distributed by Little] 1965 160p illus maps (Life World lib) boards $4.95   **918**

1 Bolivia 2 Chile 3 Ecuador 4 Peru

In pictures and text, this book describes the history, politics, economy, social life and culture of the Andean countries

"Fully captioned effective photographs, many in color, augment the text. Appendix, list of historic dates, and suggested readings." Booklist

MacEoin, Gary

Colombia and Venezuela and the Guianas, by Gary MacEoin and the editors of Time-Life Books. Time-Life Bks. [distributed by Little 1971] 160p illus maps (Life World lib) boards $4.95   **918**

1 Colombia 2 Venezuela 3 Guiana

First published 1965

In this profusely illustrated book, the authors survey the history and contemporary economy, culture, politics, social life, and customs of Colombia, Venezuela, and the Guianas

For further reading: p153

Schneider, Ronald M.

An atlas of Latin American affairs. Text by Ronald M. Schneider; maps by Robert C. Kingsbury. Praeger 1965 136p maps (Praeger Ser. of world-affairs atlases) $4   **918**

1 Latin America 2 Law America—Maps

"General information on geography, history, politics, demography, trade patterns, foreign investment, and social conditions. . . . The authors first survey, in striking maps and . . . text, the problems of economic, political, and social unrest that plague all of Latin America. They then focus on the individual nations." Publisher's note

Schreider, Helen

Exploring the Amazon, by Helen and Frank Schreider; with photographs by the authors; foreword by Gilbert M. Grosvenor; produced by the Special Publications Division, Robert L. Breeden, chief. Nat. Geographic Soc. 1970 207p illus maps $4.25 **918**

1 Amazon River 2 Amazon Valley
SBN 87044-078-0

This pictorial travelogue "describes an eight-month journey down what may be the world's longest river, beginning in the Peruvian Andes at the Amazon's source and ending at Belém, Brazil. Excellent color photographs, taken by the authors, fill about half the book. The text is brief, descriptive, and spiced with historical anecdotes." Library J

The South American handbook. Rand McNally boards $6.95   **918**

1 Latin America—Statistics 2 Latin America —Yearbooks 3 South America

Annual. First published 1924
Some libraries may prefer to class this yearbook with statistical handbooks in class 318. Based on the Anglo-South American handbook, edited by W. H. Koebel
"An annual traveller's guide to the countries and economies of South America, Central America, Mexico, Caribbean and West Indies." Subtitle to 1968 ed.
The guide "is arranged alphabetically by country and each chapter includes material on history and geography, commerce, communications, political and economic conditions and cultural matters." Library J

918.1   Geography of Brazil

Bishop, Elizabeth
Brazil, by Elizabeth Bishop and the editors of Life. Time, inc. [distributed by Little] 1967 160p illus maps (Life World lib) boards $4.95   **918.1**

1 Brazil

First published 1962
History, description, politics, economic conditions, cultural and social aspects of Brazilian civilization are delineated in this survey, supplemented by picture essays
Includes appendixes of historical dates, noted Brazilians in literature, music, art, and architecture
For further reading: p153-54

Furneaux, Robin
The Amazon; the story of a great river; foreword by Peter Fleming. Putnam [1970 c1969] 258p illus maps $6.95   **918.1**

1 Amazon River

First published 1969 in England
This is a description of the Amazon River and its history, the animals and men that live on its banks, the explorers and adventurers it has attracted since its discovery in 1499 by Vicente Pinzón from Pizarro to twentieth century explorers like Theodore Roosevelt. (Publisher)
"Romance, adventure, exotic scenes, hardship, tragedy, comedy and the vagaries of human nature are combined in [this] fluent, colorful history." Booklist
Bibliography: p249-52

918.95   Geography of Uruguay

Alisky, Marvin
Uruguay, a contemporary survey. Praeger 1969 174p illus map $8   **918.95**

1 Uruguay

"Of value as an introduction to a major Latin American nation the account traces the social, economic, and political developments in Uruguay emphasizing primarily recent events both national and foreign that affect Uruguay. Drawn from research that included a tour of the country in 1967 the account touches on the basic character of the people and the 1966 constitutional reform, describes important Protestant and Jewish communities, and closes with informed speculation on future changes in the country's structure. Spanish-English bibliography." Booklist

919   Geography of Pacific Ocean islands

Shadbolt, Maurice
Isles of the South Pacific, by Maurice Shadbolt and Olaf Ruhen; prepared by National Geographic Special Publications Division, Robert L. Breeden, chief. Nat. Geographic Soc. 1968 211p illus maps $4.25   **919**

1 Islands of the Pacific

Text and color illustrations convey the enchantment of the islands of Polynesia: Tahiti, the Cook Islands, Samoa, Tonga and New Zealand and that of Melanesia, picturing Fiji, New Caledonia, New Hebrides, the Solomons and New Guinea

919.11   Geography of Borneo

Keith, Agnes Newton
The land below the wind; sketches by the author. Little 1939 371p illus maps $8.50   **919.11**

1 Borneo

Story "of the humorous adjustments of a Californian to life in [Borneo] and life with an English administrator. Most of the comedy comes from the personnel of her household staff . . . and from the delightful animals that live in her house and who are as much characters of the story as anyone else" Book of the Month Club News
Followed by: Three came home, class 940.54

White man returns; sketches by the author. Little 1951 310p illus $6.95   **919.11**

1 Borneo—Social life and customs

Sequel to: Three came home, class 940.5
"With humor, good sense and warm friendliness, Mrs. Keith tells of her family's return to Borneo, by way of Hong Kong. She tells of the changed position of white men, her experiences with polyglot people of Borneo and her conviction that people of all races can be friends if they wish." Los Angeles

919.31   Geography of New Zealand

Rowe, James W.
New Zealand, by James W. Rowe and Margaret A. Rowe. Praeger 1968 192p illus maps (Nations of the modern world) $6.50   **919.31**

1 New Zealand

Two native New Zealanders "tell the story of New Zealand's development around three themes—the geography, multiracial character of the people, and the emergence of the welfare state. They cover political, economic and cultural aspects of New Zealand, and provide an evaluation of this nation's direction in the 20th century." Library J

919.4   Geography of Australia

Brander, Bruce
Australia, by Bruce Brander, Mary Ann Harrell, and Hector Holthouse; foreword by Gilbert M. Grosvenor; prepared by National Geographic Special Publications Division: Robert L. Breeden, chief. Nat. Geographic Soc. 1968 219p illus maps $4.25 **919.4**

1 Australia

Brander, Bruce—*Continued*
This book is the work of three writers and three photographers, who spanned the country to produce an up-to-date book on the southern continent. Text and illustrations portray the land, flora and fauna, cities, and life and customs of the people of Australia

MacInnes, Colin
Australia and New Zealand, by Colin Mac-Innes and the editors of Life. Time, inc. 1966 160p illus maps (Life World lib) boards $4.95   **919.4**

1 Australia 2 New Zealand
"A Stonehenge book"
First published 1964
A British writer "reviews the geography, history, native races, politics, economy, sports, and culture of both countries. His concise informative text is complemented by maps and photographs, in color and black and white." Booklist
For further reading: p153

Spate, O. H. K.
Australia. Praeger 1968 328p illus maps (Nations of the modern world) $8   **919.4**

1 Australia

A series of essays "on all aspects of contemporary Australia from the problems of northern development to the social mores of the Australian pub. The entire book is informed by Mr. Spate's profound respect for the harshness of the environment . . . and by his deep understanding of Australian social and cultural history. Mr. Spate of course, does not ignore politics and students of American foreign policy will find here a generous sample of Australian opinion on the Vietnam war." Library J
Includes bibliographical references

919.6 Geography of Easter Island

Dos Passos, John
Easter Island; island of enigmas. Doubleday 1971 150p illus $6.95   **919.6**

1 Easter Island

The author "traces the history of Easter Island and the attempts by such men as Captain Cook and Thor Heyerdahl to solve the mystery of the highly advanced civilization which flourished and perished there, leaving as its sole visible trace a number of gigantic statues. He also describes his own visit to the island." Book Rev Digest
"His book is at once a personal expression of his own enthusiasm and an excellent piece of adventure reading about a fabled place and people." Pub W

919.69 Geography of Hawaii

Day, A. Grove
(ed.) The spell of Hawaii; selected and ed. by A. Grove Day and Carl Stroven. Meredith 1968 338p $6.95   **919.69**

1 Hawaii 2 Literature—Collections

The editors "bring together 24 fictional and nonfictional pieces that . . . reveal Hawaiian history and life. The selections are arranged chronologically by time described and represent such authors as Michener, Robert Louis Stevenson, Mark Twain, Jack London, and Eugene Burdick. A brief introduction to each selection notes the significance of the piece and the writer's connection with Hawaii." Booklist
Glossary of Hawaiian words: p337

Graves, William
Hawaii; with illus. by James L. Amos; foreword by Gilbert M. Grosvenor, associate editor; produced by the Special Publications Division, Robert L. Breeden, chief. Nat. Geographic Soc. 1970 203p illus maps $4.25   **919.69**

1 Hawaii
SBN 87044-086-1
"Ethnography, anthropology, history, natural history of flora and fauna, geography, geology, and economics are all interwoven disciplinary aspects in a beautiful pictorial book about the fiftieth state. It is based on . . . [the author's] visit to the islands during which he traveled extensively among them and viewed their varied wonders—beaches, volcanoes, mountains, flower gardens, forestlands, and underwater life." Science Bks

919.8 Geography of Arctic regions

Freuchen, Peter
Peter Freuchen's Adventures in the Arctic; ed. by Dagmar Freuchen. Messner 1960 383p illus $4.95   **919.8**

1 Greenland 2 Arctic regions 3 Eskimos—Social life and customs

"Here is not only all the best of 'Arctic Adventure'—Freuchen's great classic narrative long out of print—but many other autobiographical accounts of his further adventures in the north. In these fascinating pages, Peter Freuchen tells of his battles against snow and ice, bears, wolves, walrus and narwhal in a land where he faced death many times. He tells of his explorations across the uncharted Arctic wilderness, stories of incredible hardship, hunger and danger. He writes of the Eskimo girl he married, of the ways of the Eskimo people, their superstitions and customs, their astonishingly appealing moral code. He shows the effects—good and bad—of the whiteman's entry into the Arctic and the reaction of the Eskimos to it." Publisher's note

Ley, Willy
The Poles, by Willy Ley and the editors of Time-Life Books. Time-Life Bks. 1971 192p illus maps (Life Nature lib) lib. bdg. $7.60   **919.8**

1 Polar regions
First published 1962
"Except for the two long sections on the exploratory work at each of the poles, most of the material in the [profusely illustrated] book covers both regions: polar animals, man at high latitudes, rigors of polar life. The concluding chapter describe the experimental work being done at the poles today, and discuss some of the possibilities of the future for colonization, exploitation of resources, and scientific research. A double-page spread headed 'Polar Do's and Don't's' is interesting if not useful to many readers; a bibliography is appended." Chicago. Children's Book Center

919.9 Geography of Antarctic regions

Dufek, George J.
Operation Deepfreeze. Harcourt 1957 243p illus maps $5.75   **919.9**

1 U.S. Navy. Task Force 43 2 Antarctic regions 3 Scientific expeditions

"In 1956, Task Force 43 began its second year of Antarctic operations. Admiral Dufek—the first man in history to land by plane at the South Pole—gives an account of the dangers of the Antarctic, his own close encounters with death, the planes that were lost and the men who led it. Illustrated with photographs, maps and base plans." Huntting
Includes bibliography

920 BIOGRAPHY

Books of biography are arranged as follows:
1 Biographical collections (920) 2 Biographies of individuals arranged alphabetically by names of biographees (92)

920 Collective biography

Adams, Russell L.
Great Negroes, past and present. 3d ed. Illus. by Eugene Winslow; ed. by David P. Ross, Jr. Afro-Am Pub. Co. 1969 212p illus $6.95   920

1 Negroes—Biography
SBN 910030-07-3
First published 1963
Contains 175 documented "biographies of great Negroes of all times and places, and in every field of achievement. In addition, each of the . . . sections of the book has an introductory essay, chronologically arranged, which puts the names and achievements of many other Negroes into a historical frame of reference. . . . This book is unique in its gathering of so much biographical and historical information about Negroes inside one cover." Chicago Sch J
Bibliography: p207-08

Alexander, Rae Pace
(comp.) Young and Black in America; introductory notes by Julius Lester. Random House 1970 139p illus $3.95, lib. bdg. $4.41   920

1 Negroes—Biography
SBN 394-90482-6
"Eight black Americans describe childhood or young adult experiences in the U.S. in these selections drawn from larger autobiographical works." Book Rev Digest
Contents: Teaching myself to read and write, by F. Douglass; Apprentice, by R. Wright; How my mother died, by D. Bates; Turning point, by Malcolm X; I was a teen-age warlord, by J. Brown; Sitting in and hiding out, by A. Moody; The revolt of the Black athlete, by H. Edwards; G.I. in Vietnam, by D. Parks; Bibliography

Alexander, Robert J.
Prophets of the revolution; profiles of Latin American leaders. Macmillan (N Y) 1962 322p $5.95   920

1 Latin America—Biography 2 Latin America—Politics
"A gallery of 12 portraits of twentieth century leaders in Latin America, including Cárdenas, Betancourt. Perón and Castro." Foreign Affairs
"Each of the 'prophets' is set against an effectively sketched panorama of events, ideas, and forces of the times—all interacting in the fascinating unfoldment of revolution." Am Pol Sci R
Bibliographical note: p305-10

American Heritage
The American Heritage Pictorial history of the Presidents of the United States, by the editors of American Heritage, The Magazine of History. Editor in charge: Kenneth W. Leish; foreword by Bruce Catton. Am. Heritage 1968 2v (1023p) illus maps $18.50
920

1 Presidents—U.S.   2 U.S.—History—Biography
Contents: v 1 George Washington through Rutherford B. Hayes; v2 James A. Garfield through Lyndon B. Johnson
In addition to data on the thirty-five Presidents, and fact summaries of their administrations, the set includes brief biographies of many other famous Americans

"Each of the Chief Executives is treated with sympathy, but without blind adulation. . . . [The portaits are] often refreshingly unfamiliar." N Y Times Bk R

Armbruster, Maxim Ethan
The Presidents of the United States, and their administrations from Washington to Nixon. 4th ed. rev. Horizon Press 1969 372p illus $6.50   920

1 Presidents—U.S. 2 U.S.—History—Biography
First published 1960
A guide to the inner history of the United States, through its Presidents
The author "has read the standard treatments of the men and their times and summarized them adequately. The work is therefore a fairly handy reference work on the presidents. The facts are generally accurate and the interpretations defensible. It is, however, a study of the Presidents, not the Presidency." Choice
Bibliography: p357-64

Associated Press
Triumph and tragedy; the story of the Kennedys, by the writers, photographers, and editors of The Associated Press. The Press [distributed by Morrow] 1968 256p illus $5.95   920

1 Kennedy family 2 Kennedy, John Fitzgerald, President U.S. 3 Kennedy, Robert Francis
Editor: Sidney C. Moody, Jr.
"A graphic narrative, tells of the lives of the members of the Joseph P. Kennedy family, from their origins in Ireland to their present-day activities. The arrival in Boston of Patrick Kennedy from Dunganstown, Ireland in 1848, the subsequent development of a successive family cohesiveness, and individual and group achievements in political, economic, educational, and social areas are clearly portrayed. The contrasting times of tragedy, of illness, and of violent death are also described in this comprehensive chronicle of a contemporary American family." Booklist
Bibliography: p256

Bakeless, John
Signers of the Declaration [by] John and Katherine Bakeless. Houghton 1969 300p $3.95   920

1 U.S.—Biography 2 U.S. Declaration of Independence
The authors present a brief history of the events that led to the signing of the Declaration of Independence, and the life stories of the 56 men, from the thirteen original colonies, who conceived and signed it. (Publisher)
"So inclusive is the book, that it could be used, with the help of a few additional titles, as the basis for a study of the formation of the Union, replacing traditional history texts. A very useful reference tool." Library J
Bibliography: p299-300

Bassett, Margaret
Profiles & portraits of American Presidents & their wives; with an introduction on "the Presidency" by Henry F. Graff. Bond Wheelwright, distributed by Grosset 1969 449p illus $10   920

1 Presidents—U.S. 2 Presidents—U.S.—Wives
"The text on the Presidents in Bassett's 'Profiles & portraits of America Presidents,' published in 1964 . . . is expanded here to include President Nixon, and material is added on the wife of each President from Washington down. A portrait of each President accompanies the text about him and portraits of all but eight of the Presidents' wives are included. A select bibliography on the men and their wives is appended." Booklist

Beard, Annie E. S.

Our foreign-born citizens. 6th ed. Crowell 1968 276p $4.50   920

1 U.S.—Biography

First published 1922

Through the life stories of over twenty foreign-born citizens, the author demonstrates the importance of the immigrants to the development of the United States. "Their influence is felt in every phase of the nation's life: in art, music, industry, science, politics, philosophy, and literature." Publisher's note

Contents: John James Audubon; Andrew Carnegie; John Muir; Alexander Graham Bell; Joseph Pulitzer; Augustus St Gaudens; Samuel Gompers; Felix Adler; Ottmar Mergenthaler; Charles Proteus Steinmetz; Hideyo Noguchi; Albert Einstein; Hans Hofmann; Walter Gropius; Philip Murray; Igor Sikorsky; David Dubinsky; Raymond Loewy; Spyros Skouras; Alfred Hitchcock; Enrico Fermi; W. H. Auden; Erich Leinsdorf

Bell, E. T.

Men of mathematics. Simon & Schuster 1937 xxi, 592p illus $7.95   920

1 Mathematicians

Analyzed in Essay and general literature index

"Intimate, well-written biographies of some of the founders of modern mathematics with brief accounts of their notable contributions. They are Zeno, Eudoxus, Archimedes, Descartes, Fermat, Pascal, Newton, Leibniz, the Bernoullis, Euler, Lagrange, Laplace, Monge, Fourier, Poncelet, Gauss, Cauchy, Lobatchewsky, Abel Jacobi, Hamilton, Galois, Sylvester, Cayley, Weierstrass, Kowalewski, Boole, Hermite, Kronecker, Riemann, Kummer, Dedekind, Poincare, and Cantor." N Y New Tech Bks

Bentley, Phyllis

The Brontës and their world. Viking 1969 144p illus $6.95   920

1 Brontë family

"Lavishly illustrated with pictures of the Brontës and their friends and with scenes typical of the times, a fascinating biography of the sisters who produced, out of a genteel and cloistered environment, the passionate creativity of their shared art. The author writes with verve and polish . . . the discussion of the Brontës' work acute and perceptive. A chronology, notes on the pictures, and an index are appended." Chicago. Children's Book Center

Bontemps, Arna

(ed.) Great slave narratives; selected and introduced by Arna Bontemps. Beacon Press 1969 331p pa $2.95   920

1 Slavery in the U.S. 2 Negroes—Biography

A collection of autobiographies written by slaves. Contents: The slave narrative: an American genre, by A. Bontemps; The life of Olaudah Equiano; or, Gustavus Vassa, the African written by himself; The fugitive blacksmith; or, Events in the history of James W. C. Pennington, pastor of a Presbyterian church, New York, formerly a slave in the State of Maryland; Running a thousand miles for freedom; or, The escape of William and Ellen Craft from slavery

"The books here reprinted . . . are among the works which show us slavery through nonwhite eyes. . . . [Only one of the] authors was African-born. He was Olaudah Equiano . . . sold to a British naval officer and later to a West Indies trader. . . . His is an up-from-adversity tale in the manner of Defoe. The other narratives are all by nineteenth-century American slaves who escaped. The Rev. James Pennington, a pious blacksmith, tells his story in the manner of an apostle. . . . [William and Ellen Craft] were of the slave elite. She was nearly white and he was a skilled cabinetmaker. Their flight was romantic suspense fiction, suitably moralized." Book World

We have tomorrow; illus. with photographs by Marian Palfi. Houghton 1945 131p illus $3.95   920

1 Negroes—Biography

"These brief, inspiring biographies are of young Negroes who have succeeded in breaking through the color barrier to become successful army officers, lawyers, engineers." Books for You

Includes biographies of E. Simms Campbell, Mildred E. Blount, Horace R. Clayton, Beatrice Johnson Trammell, Dean Dixon, Sylvestre C. Watkins, Douglas Watson, Emmett M. May, Hazel Scott, Algernon P. Henry, James E. LuValle, Benjamin Davis, Jr.

Bowen, Catherine Drinker

Family portrait. Little 1970 301p illus $7.50   920

1 Drinker family

"An Atlantic Monthly Press book"

This account "moves from an easy salute to the 18th-Century ancestors of the Pennsylvania Drinker family down to the 20th-Century travails and accomplishments of the generation that included the developer of the iron lung, a preeminent member of the bar, and a gifted biographer, Catherine Drinker Bowen herself." Library J

This "is an intricate multiple picture of many men and women, powerful personalities, admirable if not always likable; written with wisdom, depth, truthfulness and an artless freshness like the unsullied air of the early century when Mrs. Bowen was young. This is a book to be read and savored in layers, a book within a book." N Y Times Bk R

Canaday, John

The lives of the painters. Norton 1969 4v illus $40   920

1 Painters

Contents: v 1 Late Gothic to High Renaissance; v2 Baroque; v3 Neoclassic to post-impressionist; v4 Plates and index

"One of the most practical and up-to-date reference books for art students and for the interested layman." Best Sellers

Carr, Albert

Men of power; a book of dictators; illus. by Marc Simont. Rev. ed. Viking 1956 298p illus lib. bdg. $4.13   920

1 Dictators

First published 1940

Stories of how Richelieu, Cromwell, Frederick the Great, Napoleon, Bolivar, Bismarck, Mussolini, Stalin, Hitler, Perón, Franco, and Mao Tse-tung got their power and rose to dictatorship. (Publisher)

Carr, William H. A.

The du Ponts of Delaware; illus. with photographs and a map. Dodd 1964 368p illus map $7.95   920

1 Du Pont de Nemours family   2 Du Pont de Nemours (E. I.) and Company

The author traces the family's history from its French background through the du Ponts' arrival in America in 1800 to the present. Interwoven with family feuds and biographies is an account of the giant company, its activities during World War I and World War II and antitrust actions. (Publisher)

Bibliography: p352-56

Chapin, Victor

Giants of the keyboard. Lippincott 1967 189p illus $4.95   920

1 Pianists

"Here are the biographies of 16 pianists who were selected to coincide with the important developments in the evolution of the piano as an instrument. Thus, the history of the piano and social history as it affected musicians is incorporated in the various biographies. Included are life stories of such keyboard giants as Clementi, Hummel, Field, Czerny, Liszt, Clara Schumann, Anton Rubenstein, Paderewski, Busoni, Schnabel." Hunting

Recommended recordings: p181-82

Chapin, Victor—*Continued*

The violin and its masters. Lippincott 1969 192p illus boards $4.75   920

1 Violinists, violoncellists, etc.   2 Composers

'The evolution and development of the sixteenth-century Italian invention the violin, and the music composed for it are combined with biographies of the instrument's greatest masters. Among them are Lully, Corelli, Vivaldi, Tartini, Viotti, Kreutzer, Paganini, Spohr, Joachim, and Kreisler most of whom were great composers as well as virtuoso violinists." News of Bks

Glossary: p183-88

Churchill, Allen

The Roosevelts: American aristocrats. Harper 1965 341p illus $10   920

1 Roosevelt family

"A colorfully detailed, highly readable history of the Roosevelt family from the 1640's in New Amsterdam to the 1960's in Oyster Bay, New York City, and points west. A history of New York City up to the 20th century is, of necessity, woven into this account of the family. The emphasis is on . . . the two Presidents and Eleanor Roosevelt, and on the record of public and political service first set by Isaac Roosevelt on Revolutionary times and so successfully carried on by his descendants." Pub W

Bibliography: p319-23

Clapesattle, Helen

The Doctors Mayo. [2d ed. condensed] Univ. of Minn. Press 1954 [c1941] 426p illus map $8.50   920

1 Mayo, Charles Horace   2 Mayo, William James   3 Mayo, William Worrall   4 Mayo Clinic, Rochester, Minn.

First published 1941

The authorized story of the Mayos, father and sons and of the Mayo Clinic in Rochester, Minnesota which grew from a private practice into a world-famous medical institution

"In conjunction with the story of the careers of these men, many anecdotes and incidents in their private lives are given. . . . Their family life, their hobbies and recreations: their travels and honors all take their chronological place. Dr. Charlie's supreme gift for human contacts, Dr. Will's more studied kindness, the difference in physical appearance, the peculiar genius of each, and above all their teamwork are described with vigor and sympathy." Sci Bk Club R

Clark, Ronald, W.

The Huxleys. McGraw 1968 398p illus $9.95   920

1 Huxley family   2 Huxley, Aldous Leonard   3 Huxley, Sir Julian Sorell   4 Huxley, Thomas Henry

The author "traces the development of the ideas of the Huxley family as expressed in their writings and their work In the modern period, he focuses on Julian and Aldous Huxley." Pub W

"The book is workmanlike and readable. It is best, as one would expect, on the scientific side; but, even on Aldous Huxley, the facts are there." Economist

Select bibliography: p367-73

Commager, Henry Steele

Crusaders for freedom; illus. by Mimi Korach. Doubleday 1962 240p illus $3.95, lib. bdg. $4.70   920

1 Biography   2 Liberty

Stories of the men and women who fought for the freedoms we know today such as the freedom of speech, of religion, and of asylum and fair trial, are told here. Prominent among them are: Tom Paine, William Penn, Harriet Tubman, Horace Mann, Voltaire, Susan Anthony, Fridtjof Nansen, John Quincy Adams ,and Eleanor Roosevelt. (Publisher)

Coolidge, Olivia

Lives of famous Romans; illus. by Milton Johnson. Houghton 1964 248p illus $3.50   920

1 Rome—Biography   2 Rome—History

The author presents a "panoramic view of the Roman world from about 86 B.C. to the death of Constantine in 337 A.D. She ably depicts the personalities of Cicero, Julius Caesar, Augustus, Virgil, Horace, Nero, Seneca, Trajan, Hadrian, Marcus Aurelius, Diocletian, and Constantine, pointing out their weaknesses as well as their strengths and relating them to each other and to their world." Booklist

"The writing is mature, dignified, and scholarly; the tone is candid and the material is handled with authoritative familiarity. The book gives a broad and sweeping view of the intrigues and complexities of Roman history yet creates, with vivid details, vignettes of incidents or situations and innumerable characterizations that are sharply perceptive." Chicago. Children's Book Center

David, Jay

(ed.) Growing up Jewish. Morrow 1969 341p $7.50   920

1 Jews—Biography

"Twenty-five brief and yet thoughtful vignettes, of famous Jews who grew up in various parts of the world. Though a few took place in the Middle Ages, most experiences 'in growing up' in this volume actually took place in the last 100 years. We read young Chaim Weizman's reaction to the Kishinev Pogrom, and Isaac Bashevis Singer's youth in Warsaw. Robert Briscoe's interesting experiences in Dublin are matched by David Daiches' youth in Edinburgh. Harry Golden writes of his young love affair with the lower East Side, and Alfred Kazin has a beautiful selection of his early years in Brownsville that is both eloquently and meaningfully sketched in just a few short pages. There are many gems in these autobiographical sketches that span the far away countries, starting in the Old World, continuing in the New World, and ending in the Promised Land." Choice

Davies, Hunter

The Beatles; the authorized biography. McGraw 1968 357p illus $6.95   920

1 The Beatles

"An in-depth survey of famous Liverpudlians from their school days to the present, with photographs, song manuscripts, and much little-known information." Chicago

The author "capitalizes on his position of privilege to interview seriously John, Paul, George and Ringo, their friends, family and associates, with the sole object of putting together an honest account. His hard work and the obvious trust the Beatles have in him allow us to see the young musicians for the first time as interesting, fallible, corporeal creatures, each quite different from the others, each with his own history and hang-ups and hopes." Newsweek

De Kruif, Paul

Men against death. Harcourt 1932 363p illus $6.50   920

1 Scientists   2 Medicine—History

Analyzed in Essay and general literature index

These thirteen physicians and scientists whose discoveries in the field of medicine have prevented fatalities from certain diseases are: Semmelweis; Banting; Minot; Spencer; Evans; McCoy; Schaudinn; Bordet; Wagner-Jauregg; Finsen; Rollier; Strandberg; Coburn

"It is a proud record, and magnificently told. Dr. de Kruif has a splendid gift for making these stories exciting and human. The steps by which success was eventually gained, the puzzles, the difficulties along the way, the human qualities of the discoverers and their associates, are arranged with masterly narrative skill." N Y Her Trib Books

De Kruif, Paul—*Continued*

Microbe hunters. Harcourt 1926 363p illus $6.50   920

1 Scientists 2 Bacteriology

Analyzed in Essay and general literature index

"A series of biographical sketches involving epoch-making scientific discoveries, it is as discerning in its studies of temperament as it is accurate in its information on research. As for tragedy, thrills, suspense, and the like, just try it." Sat R

Contents: Leeuwenhoek; Spallanzani; Pasteur; Koch; Roux and Behring; Metchnikolff; Theobald Smith; Bruce; Ross vs. Grassi; Walter Reed; Paul Ehrlich

Dictionary of American biography

The American Plutarch; 18 lives selected from the Dictionary of American biography; ed. by Edward T. James; with an introduction by Howard Mumford Jones. Scribner [1965 c1964] xxiii, 408p $7.95   920

1 U.S.—Biography 2 Statesmen, American

Various authors have contributed articles on: Benjamin Franklin; George Washington; Thomas Jefferson; Alexander Hamilton; John Jay; James Madison; John Marshall; Andrew Jackson; Henry Clay; John C. Calhoun; Jefferson Davis; Abraham Lincoln; Robert E. Lee; Ulysses S. Grant; Woodrow Wilson; Theodore Roosevelt; Oliver Wendell Holmes; William H. Taft

Drotning, Phillip T.

Up from the ghetto, by Phillip T. Drotning and Wesley W. South. Cowles 1970 207p illus $5.95   920

1 Negroes—Biography

This book was written "to discover whether there are consistent elements of human behavior that enable some [individuals] to succeed while others fail. Selected, at random, without any detailed knowledge of their early years [were] fourteen black men and women who [had] won contemporary recognition for achievement in a variety of fields. . . . All proved to be the product of impoverished ghetto environments, and many of uneducated if not illiterate parents." Introduction

Included are: Ernie Banks; Jesse Jackson; Anna Langford; James Tilmon; James Brown; Richard Hatcher; Frederic Davison; M. Earl Grant; Shirley Chisholm; John Shepherd; Manford Byrd; Gwendolyn Brooks; John H. Johnson; James Farmer

Durant, John

Pictorial history of American Presidents, by John and Alice Durant. Barnes, A.S. illus maps $12.50   920

1 Presidents—U.S.

First published 1955, and periodically brought up to date

Arranged chronologically, this book presents the careers of the American Presidents from George Washington to date, including the events of their administrations and characteristics of their personalities

"By obliging with all their homey detail, the Durants have put together an entertaining, visually attractive story." N Y Times Bk R

Ewen, David

Composers for the American musical theatre; illus. with photographs. Dodd 1968 270p illus $5   920

1 Composers, American

"A brief history of the development of the American musical theater from 1735 serves as an introduction to this collection of biographical studies of 14 composers of operettas and musical comedies in America in the twentieth century. The author . . . writes of the lives and the musical careers of each of the following: Victor Herbert, Rudolf Friml, Sigmund

Romberg, George M. Cohan, Jerome Kern, Irving Berlin, George Gershwin, Cole Porter, Richard Rodgers, Kurt Weill, Frederick Loewe, Frank Loesser, Jerry Bock, and Leonard Bernstein." Booklist

Composers of tomorrow's music; a non-technical introduction to the musical avant-garde movement; illus. with photographs. Dodd 1971 176p illus $5   920

1 Composers 2 Music—History and criticism

ISBN 0-396-06286-5

This volume describes "the new forms of avant-garde music, sketching the lives and theories of ten of its leading exponents." Publisher's note

The composers considered are Charles Ives, Arnold Schoenberg, Anton Webern, Pierre Boulez, Edgard Varèse, Karlheinz Stockhausen, Yannis Xenakis, Milton Babbitt, John Cage and Harry Partch

The author "explains very simply the 12-tone system, serialism, the use of noise as a creative process, electronic music, music for computer and synthesizer, chance music, and the new dadaism, all techniques used by one or more of these composers." Booklist

Famous modern conductors; illus. with photographs. Dodd 1967 159p illus (Famous biographies for young people) $3.50   920

1 Conductors (Music)

The author describes the careers of twelve leading conductors of both the American and European musical scene. Included are: Leopold Stokowski; Eugene Ormandy; Charles Munch; Erich Leinsdorf; George Szell; Leonard Bernstein; William Steinberg; Joseph Krips; Herbert von Karajan; Otto Klemperer; Lorin Maazel; Zubin Mehta

Great men of American popular song; the history of the American popular song told through the lives, careers, achievements, and personalities of its foremost composers and lyricists—from William Billings of the Revolutionary War to the "folk-rock" of Bob Dylan. Prentice-Hall 1970 387p $12.95   920

1 Music, Popular (Songs, etc.) 2 Composers, American 3 Songs, American

SBN 13-364174-0

"A comprehensive, nostalgia-loaded history. . . . War songs, ballads, minstrel go-rounds, dance tunes, ragtime, songs for musical comedy, movies, radio and television are among the types of music that Ewen explores. There are readable biographies not only of the big names —Stephen Foster, Irving Berlin, George M. Cohan, George Gershwin, Jerome Kern, Cole Porter, Vincent Youmans, Rodgers and Hart (and later Hammerstein)—but also of hosts of others celebrated in their day but now largely forgotten: George F. Root ('Rally 'Round the Flag'), James Bland ('Carry Me Back to Ol' Virginny'), Gus Edwards ('School Days') and von Tilzer ('I want a Girl Just Like the Girl')." Pub W

(ed.) The new book of modern composers. 3d ed. rev. and enl. Knopf 1961 491p $10   920

1 Composers

First published 1942 with title: The book of modern composers

For most of these 32 composers of the late nineteenth or twentieth century there is a note by the composer himself and perhaps a comment by a contemporary and for each a brief biography and a critique. A long introductory essay by Nicolas Slonimsky discusses the styles and techniques of modern music. Includes lists of the composers' principal works and a bibliography

"In most cases there was an abundance of material and Mr. Ewen's task was to winnow it. He has done his job skillfully. He has obtained critical essays from recognized authorities, men who knew well the composer and his music. The personality sketches are from the hands of capable reporters." N Y Times Bk R

Ewen, David—Continued

(ed.) The world of great composers. Prentice-Hall 1962 576p $5   920

1 Composers

"Thirty-seven of the world's greatest composers [from the Renaissance to the 20th century] are described from four points of view: a brief biography, an informal and intimate portrait of the man by a contemporary, a critical essay by a top musicologist, and a statement from the composer himself." Huntting

Includes a list of the principal works of each composer and a bibliography

Forsee, Aylesa

Men of modern architecture; giants in glass, steel, and stone. Macrae Smith Co. 1966 223p illus $4.75   920

1 Architects   2 Architecture, Modern—20th century 3 Architecture, American

Illustrated with photographs

The author presents modern American architecture by recounting the lives of the following eight architects who were American by birth or adoption: Louis Sullivan; Frank Lloyd Wright; Walter Gropius; Mies van der Rohe; Eric Mendelsohn; Richard Neutra; Edward Durell Stone [and] Eero Saarinen

Pronunciation guide: p9. Glossary: p219-20.

Selected bibliography: p221-22

Gitler, Ira

Jazz masters of the forties. Macmillan (N Y) 1966 290p illus (The Macmillan Jazz masters ser) $5.95   920

1 Musicians, American 2 Jazz music

The author describes "the emergence in the 1940's of bebop . . . [and of its exponents] Charlie 'Yardbird' Parker and Dizzy Gillespie. . . . [To their story the author adds those of the jazz musicians of the period]: pianists Bud Powell and Lennie Tristano, tenor saxophonist Dexter Gordon and alto saxophonist Lee Konitz, J. J. Johnson and his trombone, bass player Oscar Pettiford, drummers Kenny Clarke and Max Roach, and composer-arranger Tadd Dameron." Publisher's note

Bibliography: p83-85. Includes discographies at end of chapters

Goldberg, Joe

Jazz masters of the fifties. Macmillan (N Y) 1965 246p (The Macmillan Jazz masters ser) $5.95   920

1 Musicians, American 2 Jazz music 3 Negro musicians

This book describes "the 'cool' jazz of Gerry Mulligan and sketches of such leaders as Thelonious Monk, Miles Davis, Sonny Rollins, Charles Mingus, and Ray Charles. With anecdotes and non-technical discussions of music." Bk Buyer's Guide

"Some of the anecdotes show the abuse which Negroes had to endure in the South as well as their subtle rejection in the North." Library J

Selected discography at end of each chapter

Grant, Michael

The ancient historians. Scribner 1970 486p illus maps $12.50   920

1 Historians, Greek   2 Historians, Roman
3 History, Ancient

The author discusses the work of Greek and Latin historians from about 500 B.C. to 500 A.D. Beginning with Herodotus and Thucydides he "discusses over a dozen major historians as well as several minor ones. The discussion of each writer is accompanied by a sketch of the major events that provided the background for his work." Publisher's note

Grant "has done a magnificent critical job. Though he is concise, he tells us all sorts of things we need or want to know, including how ancient historians earned their living, how their contemporaries assessed their veracity, and what excellences each man contributed to the historian's art." New Yorker

Bibliography: p467-71

Hadlock, Richard

Jazz masters of the twenties. Macmillan (N Y) 1965 255p illus (The Macmillan Jazz masters ser) $5.95   920

1 Musicians, American 2 Jazz music

For jazz buffs this "covers the era that saw the emergence of jazz both as a social and a musical force in America. Among the jazz men included are: Louis Armstrong, Earl Hines, Bix Beiderbecke, Jack Teagarden, James P. Johnson, Bessie Smith, Fats Waller, Eddie Lang and many other all-time greats." Huntting

Bibliography and discography at end of chapters

Holbrook, Stewart H.

The age of the moguls. Doubleday 1953 373p illus $5.95   920

1 Capitalists and financiers 2 U.S.—Industries—History

"Mainstream of America series"

"Deals with the great tycoons of the nineteenth and early twentieth centuries, and the way in which they built their great fortunes and changed the history of America." Huntting

Acknowledgements and bibliography: p364-66

Lost men of American history. Macmillan (N Y) 1946 370p illus $6.95   920

1 U.S.—Biography   2 U.S.—History—Biography

Analyzed in Essay and general literature index.

"An anecdotal and debunking study of some history events and personages in our history, ranging from the introduction of log cabins by the Swedes in 1638 . . . to a few well-chosen facts about H. L. Mencken." Book Rev Digest

"Unabashed journalism is Mr. Holbrook's style—perhaps usefully and happily so, since a prodigious array of personalities . . . crowd the pages of this lively harangue." N Y Times Bk R

Acknowledgements and bibliography: p349-59

Jones, Bessie Zaban

(ed.) The golden age of science; thirty portraits of the giants of 19th-century science, by their scientific contemporaries; with an introduction by Everett Mendelsohn. Simon & Schuster [1967 c1966] xxxiii, 659p $12   920

1 Scientists 2 Science—History

"Nonscientist and student interested in history of science will find that this volume of personality and achievement profiles of 30 notable nineteenth-century scientists, give or take a few years, imparts a sense of the scientific ferment and diversity of the period in addition to introducing certain participants. The essays stem from a series that appeared in the Smithsonian Institution annual reports from 1858 to 1931. . . . Arranged chronologically by birth date of the subject." Booklist

Bibliographical footnotes included

Josephson, Matthew

The robber barons; the great American capitalists, 1861-1901. Harcourt 1962 474p pa $2.85   920

1 Capitalists and financiers 2 U.S.—Industries—History 3 Railroads—History

"A Harvest book"

First published 1934

"The men whose fortunes form the subject of this history were the capitalists who seized power in the United States after the Civil War, men who thru their command of capital became commanders of industry and banking and of the government itself. The dominating figures of this era and this book are Jay Gould, the Vanderbilts, J. P. Morgan, Andrew Carnegie, John D. Rockefeller, James J. Hill, Collis P. Huntington, E. H. Harriman, Henry C. Frick, and others." Book Rev Digest

What the author "has written is not a mere series of biographies but a genuine history, with the stories of the great American capitalists skillfully interwoven, and with an eye always on the broader social background. He

Josephson, Matthew—*Continued*

has digested an immense mass of material, and he is particularly to be congratulated upon the lucidity with which he sets forth the complex financial transactions and the uncanny legerdemain by which most of the barons built up their fortunes." N Y Times Bk R

Bibliography: p455-60

Kane, Joseph Nathan

Facts about the Presidents; a compilation of biographical and historical data. 2d ed. Wilson, H.W. 1968 384p illus $10   920

1 Presidents—U.S.
ISBN 0-8242-0014-4
First published 1959

In Part I a chapter is devoted to each President from Washington to Lyndon Baines Johnson. Information on the President's family history is followed by data on elections, congressional sessions, cabinet appointments, the Vice President, and highlights of the President's life and administration. Part II gives comparative data and statistics on the Presidents as individuals and on the office of the Presidency. (Publisher)

"A fascinating compendium." Sat R

Kennedy, John F.

Profiles in courage. Memorial ed.   920

1 Statesmen, American   2 U.S.—Politics and government   3 Courage

Some editions are:
Harper $5, lib. bdg. $4.43
Watts, F. lib. bdg. $8.95 Large type edition.
A Keith Jennison book

First published 1956. Awarded Pulitzer prize for biography, 1957. Includes a special foreword by Robert F. Kennedy

This series of profiles of Americans who took courageous stands at crucial moments in public life includes John Quincy Adams, Daniel Webster, Thomas Hart Benton, Sam Houston, Edmund G. Ross, Lucius Q. C. Lamar, George Norris, Robert A. Taft and others

"Moral courage, the courage of one's convictions, is the subject of far fewer books than physical courage but here, at last, is a tribute to Americans in politics who took the stand they thought right regardless of consequences." Horn Bk

Kenworthy, Leonard S.

Leaders of new nations [by] Leonard S. Kenworthy and Erma Ferrari; illus. by Michael Lowenbein. Doubleday 1968 373p illus $4.95   920

1 Statesmen   2 States, New
First published 1959

"Sketches of sixteen of [the] new nations, seen through the lives of the leaders who guided them to independence." Huntting

"In telling of the forces that shaped the lives of these leaders and of the problems they met and are still meeting, Mr. Kenworthy gives a clear, unbiased picture of each country as it is today. As these countries are mentioned almost daily in our newspapers, . . . [students] will welcome such a compact, yet, interesting, source of background material." Horn Bk

Map on lining-papers

Lamb, Beatrice Pitney

The Nehrus of India; three generations of leadership. Macmillan (N Y) 1967 276p illus map lib. bdg. $5.95   920

1 Nehru, Motilal   2 Nehru, Jawaharlal
3 Gandhi, Indira (Nehru)   4 India—Politics and government

"A portrait of the Nehru family of India telling of the contributions of Motilal Nehru, one of the architects of free India; of his son, Jawaharlal, who became Prime Minister after the Nation's independence from Britain; and of [Jawaharlal's] daughter Indira . . . the present Prime Minister of India." Bk Buyer's Guide

For further reading: p262-64

Mantle, Mickey

The quality of courage. Doubleday 1964 185p $4.50   920

1 Baseball—Biography   2 Courage

"Casey Stengel, Jimmy Piersall, and Roy Campanella are among those included in this collection of stories of baseball players [and others] who did not give way to defeat when adversity struck." Top of the News

"In the course of the book Mantle gives glimpses of his own boyhood and early struggles and pays tribute to his father." Horn Bk

Maynard, Olga

American modern dancers: the pioneers. . . . Little 1965 218p illus $4.50   920

1 Dancers   2 Dancing—History

"An Atlantic Monthly Press book"

"An introduction to Modern Dance through the biographical studies of the first creative dancers of that art. Related in narrative form, it is also arranged for teacher-student use in dance classes, complete with Notes. Illustrated with eight photographs of the dancers." Title page

The "famous names [essentially American] dance through a variety of choreographic schemes and ideas. This book is for serious students of the dance who have ability and aspirations of adult maturity." Chicago Sch J

Metcalf, George R.

Black profiles. Expanded ed. McGraw 1970 405p illus $7.95   920

1 Negroes—Civil rights   2 Negroes—Biography
First published 1968

Included among these portraits of Black Americans who have fought against racial injustice are: Martin Luther King, Jr., William E. B. Du Bois, Roy Wilkins, Thurgood Marshall, Jackie Robinson, Harriet Tubman, Medgar Evers, James Meredith, Rosa Parks, Edward W. Brooke, Whitney Young, Jr., Eldridge Cleaver and Malcolm X

"Intended to be inspirational these somewhat superficial, laudatory sketches of 11 civil rights leaders will be most useful as an introduction to those profiled or as a source of biographical material." Booklist

A note on sources: p401-05

Morgan, James

Our Presidents. 3d ed. Chapters on Kennedy and Johnson by Herbert S. Parmet. Macmillan (N Y) 1969 xx, 548p illus $8.95 920

1 Presidents—U.S.
First published 1924

In addition to biographies of the thirty-five chief executives, the book contains a tabulated history of the American Presidency

National Geographic Society

Our country's Presidents, by Frank Freidel; introduction by Richard M. Nixon; foreword by Melville Bell Grosvenor; prepared by National Geographic Special Publications Division. [2d ed] The Society 1969 258p illus $4.25   920

1 Presidents—U.S.   2 U.S.—History—Biography
First published 1966

"Several interesting sidelights and particular mode of each administration are graphically illustrated by 285 paintings and photographs. The social reforms, diplomatic and domestic achievements, and the characteristics of each presidential family are detailed in a six to ten page profile." Library J

Orr, Jack

The Black athlete: his story in American history; introduction by Jackie Robinson. Lion 1969 157p illus boards $3.95, lib. bdg. $4.17   920

1 Negro athletes   2 Sports—History

Orr, Jack—*Continued*

This book describes the achievements of the black man as an athlete in United States sports history from the days of the plantation slave to the completion of the 1968 Olympic Games. It discusses the accomplishments of such athletes as Joe Louis, Althea Gibson and Arthur Ashe, Wilt Chamberlain, Jackie Robinson and others in such sports as boxing, tennis, basketball, and baseball. (Publisher)

Bibliography: p149

Padwe, Sandy

Basketball's Hall of Fame. Prentice-Hall 1970 193p illus boards $6.95   920

1 Basketball—Biography

"An Associated Features book"

Most of the book "consists of chapters dealing with the best-known individual members of the Basketball Hall of Fame; each chapter is limited to a description of the man's contributions as player, coach, or promoter. The first chapter concerns James Naismith, inventor of the game, and the major improvements made in the rules since its invention. The last section consists of brief biographies of all individual and team members of the Hall of Fame. This unique method of presentation provides interesting and entertaining information on the development of basketball as a major sport as related to the people who helped it grow." Library J

Contents: Dr James Naismith; George Mikan; Nat Holman; Hank Luisetti; Ned Irish; Bob Kurland; Forrest "Phog" Allen; Ed Macauley; Joe Lapchick; Andy Phillip; Henry Iba; John Wooden; Adolph Rupp; Red Auerbach; Clair Bee; Directory of Hall of Fame members

Pepe, Phil

Greatest stars of the NBA. Prentice-Hall 1970 218p illus boards $6.95   920

1 Basketball—Biography   2 National Basketball Association
SBN 13-364935-0

"The Official NBA Library. An Associated Features book"

"The fifteen players in this volume span the entire history of the NBA, from the great ones who helped establish the league—Joe Fulks and George Mikan—through the heroes of the NBA's greatest years—Bob Cousy, Bob Pettit, Bill Russell, Wilt Chamberlain, Oscar Robertson, Elgin Baylor, Jerry West, Dolph Schayes, Paul Arizin, John Havlicek—to the stars of today who will go on to even greater heights tomorrow—Earl Monroe, Elvin Hayes, Willis Reed. As the game evolved, so did the characteristics of the players—their styles, techniques, and approaches to the game. . . . [This book] details these changes by taking a close look at the men and their exciting accomplishments." Publisher's note

Polatnick, Florence T.

Shapers of Africa . . . [by] Florence T. Polatnick and Alberta L. Saletan; maps and illus. Messner 1969 184p illus maps $3.50, lib. bdg $3.34   920

1 Africa—Biography   2 Africa—History
SBN 671-32193-5; 671-32194-3

"Mansa Musa: Mali Empire; Queen Nzinga: Angola; Samuel Ajayi Crowther: Nigeria; Moshoeshoe: Lesotho; Tom Mboya: Kenya." Title page

Spanning seven centuries of African history, these biographies recount the lives and achievements of five leaders of their people. (Publisher)

"Although the authors cover only five individuals, they manage to give in the process an overall look at Africa. . . . [There are] separate indexes for the five individuals covered in the volume." Best Sellers

Suggested further reading: p[185]

Plutarch

Lives from Plutarch; the modern American edition of twelve lives; ed. and abridged, with an introduction by John W. McFarland, Pleasant & Audrey Graves. Random House [1967 c1966] xx, 284p $7.95   920

1 Greece—Biography   2 Rome—Biography

These shortened biographies are based on the Dryden translation and Clough revision of Plutarch's Lives

Contents: Lycurgus; Aristides: Cimon; Pericles; Alcibiades; Alexander; Coriolanus; Marcus Cato; The Gracchi; Cicero; Caesar; Antony

The editors have kept "the 'interesting' parts, omitting mere historical or biographical detail, and have rewritten [the Lives] in language not especially simplified except in syntax. They prefer short, straightforward sentences. The result is highly readable, and every page immediately holds one's attention." Choice

Posell, Elsa Z.

Russian authors; illus. with photographs. Houghton 1970 253p illus $4.25   920

1 Authors, Russian

"Spanning a period of history from the late 1700's to the present [the author] discusses the lives and work of eleven of Russia's greatest authors. Included are Pushkin, Dostoyevsky, Tolstoy, Chekhov, Gogol, Turgenev, Gorky, as well as more recent writers like Pasternak, Sholokhov, Solzhenitsyn, and Yevtushenko." Publisher's note

Suggested reading: p[255-58]

Roland, Albert

Profiles from the new Asia. Macmillan (N Y) 1970 184p illus map $4.95   920

1 Asia—Biography   2 Asia—Social conditions

"By focusing on a film director, a magazine publisher, an urban developer, a journalist and a team of credit union managers [the author] presents the major problems of the new Asia. . . . [These biographies provide a] portrait of Asia today—the hopeful signs of economic development, social improvement and regional cooperation." Publisher's note

Ross, Ishbel

An American family: the Tafts, 1678 to 1964. World Pub. 1964 468p illus $8.95   920

1 Taft family   2 Taft, William Howard, President U.S.   3 U.S.—Politics and government

This book reveals the public careers and the private lives of such widely different Tafts as the twenty-seventh President of the United States, William Howard Taft, and his wife Nellie, Horace Dutton Taft, founder of the world-famous Taft School, the ultra-conservative Senator Robert Taft, 'Mr. Republican' and young Robert Taft, Jr., who won the 1963 election for Ohio's Congressman-at-Large. (Publisher)

"Political controversies involving the Tafts are not stressed; the accent is upon the individuals themselves." Best Sellers

Sources: p415-41. Bibliography: p443-50

Rowse, A. L.

The Churchills: the story of a family. Harper 1966 577p illus $8.95   920

1 Churchill family   2 Churchill, Sir Winston Leonard Spencer   3 Churchill, Sir Winston, 1620?-1688   4 Marlborough, John Churchill, 1st Duke of   5 Marlborough, Sarah (Jennings) Duchess

First published 1966 in England

An abridgement of: The early Churchills, and The Churchills, published 1956 and 1958, respectively

A history of the Churchill family, from the 17th century to the death of Sir Winston, which in its "prose and colorful tapestry does justice to the remarkable line which produced those two superbly extraordinary individuals, The Duke of Marlborough, and Sir Winston Churchill." Christian Science Monitor

Seroff, Victor

Men who made musical history. Funk [1970 c1969] 176p illus boards $5.95   920

1 Composers

Nine "composers—Haydn, Mozart, Beethoven, Schumann, Mendelsohn, Chopin, Weber, Schubert, and Brahms—are brought to life in this collection of biographies. . . . Each of the composers is pictured not only as a master musician but as a man in his historical setting." Publisher's note

Stirling, Nora

Who wrote the modern classics? Day 1970 288p illus $6.95   920

1 Authors, American

The book includes brief biographies of six American authors—Sinclair Lewis, Willa Cather, Eugene O'Neill, Thomas Wolfe, F. Scott Fitzgerald and Ernest Hemingway, as well as a biography of British author W. Somerset Maugham

The author "has shown great skill in selection and arranging and she writes in an easy, graceful style. . . . These writers are all going to be around for a while, and these essays form an ideal introduction to them." Best Sellers

Bibliography: p285-88

Stoddard, Hope

Famous American women; illus. with photographs and prints. Crowell 1970 461p illus $7.50   920

1 Women in the U.S.—Biography

"From Jane Addams to Babe Didrikson Zaharias, forty-two women who have contributed to widely varied fields in American history (sociology, music, art, religion, literature, sports, medicine, public life, etc.) are described in brief and lively biographical sketches, each preceded by a synopsis of facts and a statement about the subject's contribution and followed by a bibliography. The index indicates reference use but the book makes its mark even more as stimulating reading." Sat R

Stone, Irving

They also ran; the story of the men who were defeated for the Presidency. [Rev. ed] Doubleday 1966 434p illus $5.95   920

1 U.S.—Biography 2 U.S.—Politics and government

First published 1943

An account of the "lives, careers, and campaigns of 20 men from Henry Clay through . . . [Barry Goldwater] who ran for the Presidency and lost. [The author tells] why they failed and how failure might have been avoided." A Guide to Reading in Am History

"The processes by which these men were selected and the conduct of their candidacies make for lively and profitable reading both for the sociological student and the voter." Book Week

Source notes: p415-27. Selected bibliography: p428-29

Sullivan, George

Pro football's all-time greats; the immortals in Pro Football's Hall of Fame. Putnam 1968 251p $5.95   920

1 Football—Biography 2 Canton, Ohio. National Pro Football Hall of Fame

"A description of professional football's Hall of Fame, located in Canton, Ohio, effectively introduces the biographical sketches of 54 professional football players who have been honored with membership in the Hall of Fame since the dedication of the building in 1963. Red Grange, George Halas, and Jim Thorpe were among the first group of players named to the Hall of Fame. Players added in 1968 include Cliff Battles, Art Donovan, Elroy Hirsch, Wayne Millner, Marion Motley, Charley Trippi, and Art Wojciechowicz." Booklist

Sutcliff, Rosemary

Heroes and history; illus. by Charles Keeping. Putnam [1966 c1965] 152p illus boards $3.75   920

1 Heroes 2 Great Britain—Biography

First published 1965 in England

The heroes of whom the author "writes in this book are Caratacus, Arthur, Alfred, Hereward, Llewellin, Robin Hood, William Wallace, Robert the Bruce, Owen Glyndwr and Montrose. These are the figures, in England, Scotland and Wales, whose lives still have a national and legendary vitality." Publisher's note

Tharp, Louise Hall

The Peabody sisters of Salem. Little 1950 372p illus $7.50   920

1 Peabody family 2 Peabody, Elizabeth Palmer 3 Mann, Mary Tyler (Peabody) 4 Hawthorne, Sophia Amelia (Peabody)

"The three famous Peabody sisters—Elizabeth who founded the American kindergarten, Mary who married Horace Mann, and Sophia who became the wife of Nathaniel Hawthorne—are the key figures in this fascinating picture of their times." Books for You

The author "has written an intelligent and vivid appraisal of the Peabody sisters and has also sketched many fascinating personalities of the period. Emerson Alcott, the publisher Fields, the Unitarian leader Channing come into her pages and she has used little known letters and unpublished manuscripts with considerable effect." Chicago Sun

Three saints and a sinner: Julia Ward Howe, Louisa, Annie, and Sam Ward. Little 1956 406p illus $6.95   920

1 Ward family 2 Howe, Julia (Ward) 3 Terry, Louisa (Ward) 4 Mailliard, Anne Eliza (Ward) 5 Ward, Samuel

This story of the Ward family tells much about the renowned Julia, her marriage to the social reformer, Samuel Gridley Howe, her own subsequent career as a crusader for freedom, and her writing of the "Battle Hymn of the Republic." It recounts also the stories of Louisa who married the sculptor, Thomas Crawford, of Anna who married the grandson of Napoleon Bonaparte, and of Sam whose come and go fortunes also involved the inheritance of his sisters. (Publisher)

"Absorbing collective biography . . . providing an authentic picture of late 19th century notables in New York and Boston. Photographs." Bookmark

Sources: p373-74

Thomas, Norman

Great dissenters. Norton 1961 220p $5.95   920

1 Biography

"An American dissenter presents this account of five men whose dissents have helped shape the western world—Socrates, Galileo, Tom Paine, Wendell Phillips, and Gandhi. He tells their stories and explores their heresies with a deep awareness of the implications of our time." Huntting

Trease, Geoffrey

Seven sovereign queens. Vanguard [1971 c1968] 178p illus maps $4.95   920

1 Queens

First published 1968 in England

The personal stories of: Cleopatra, "Lass Unparalleled"; Boudicca, Queen of the Iceni; Galla Placidia, the Empress in the West; Isabella of Spain; Christina of Sweden; Maria Theresa, the Empress-Queen; Catherine the Great

"Each biography is narrated in a vivid, frank, humorous style and centered—as far as ascertainable facts will allow—on the personality of the sovereign queen. And the necessary political, military, and cultural facts are skillfully subordinated and at the same time cogently employed to make the individual queens psychologically as well as historically understandable." Horn Bk

Suggestions for further reading: p[179]

Trease, Geoffrey—*Continued*

Seven stages; illus. with photographs. Vanguard [1965 c1964] 194p illus $3.95   920

1 Theater—Biography
First published 1964 in England
"A collective biography that reflects three centuries of theater life, since it begins with Marlowe and describes the careers of Molière, Siddons, Verdi, Lind, Irving, and Pavlova. The writing has authority, vivacity, and style; in covering so many different facets of theater, Mr. Trease has also given the book unusual color and variety. . . . A brief list of suggestions for further reading are appended." Eakin. Good Books for Children
Suggestions for further reading: p[195]

Untermeyer, Louis

Lives of the poets; the story of one thousand years of English and American poetry. Simon & Schuster 1959 757p $7.95   920

1 Poets, English 2 Poets, American 3 English poetry—History and criticism 4 American poetry—History and criticism
"Brief biographies of 133 poets, from Langland to Dylan Thomas. The author covers their personal lives and appraises their places in the history of poetry." Bk Buyer's Guide
"Invaluable for reference, the book also is useful as a record of changing poetic manner and theme. Untermeyer's lifelong devotion to the art of poetry makes him a perfect biographer, for he sees what is important both in the poet and in the poem." Chicago Sunday Tribune

Makers of the modern world. . . . Simon & Schuster 1955 809p $7.95   920

1 Biography
"The lives of ninety-two writers, artists, scientists, statesmen, inventors, philosophers, composers, and other creators who formed the pattern of our century." Subtitle
"A dazzling gallery of the great and near-great, selected by a well-known poet and anthologist. . . . All the way from Darwin to Dylan Thomas, the author provides powerfully, excitingly written vignettes which should enlighten and entertain a large reading audience for many years to come." Library J
Selected bibliography: p758-78

The paths of poetry; twenty-five poets and their poems. Delacorte Press 1966 250p $3.95   920

1 Poets, English 2 Poets, American 3 English poetry—History and criticism 4 American poetry—History and criticism
"Brief, intensive biographical surveys of 25 major poets. Quoting liberally from their poems, Mr. Untermeyer has brought new insight into the tempestuous careers of the greatest poets in the English language [from Chaucer to Frost]." Huntting
"The approach is heavily biographical, suited to those young readers who have yet to find that poems can be as exciting as poets. The 20th century is represented disappointingly, only by Kipling, Yeats, and Frost. Mr. Untermeyer's unpretentious discussions are more lively, understandably, when he is dealing with good poets who led interesting lives (like Byron) than when he is confined to mediocre poets who led conventional lives (like Bryant)." N Y Times Bk R
For further reading: p231-36

Vance, Marguerite

The lamp lighters; women in the Hall of Fame; foreword by Sarah Gibson Blanding; illus. by J. Luis Pellicer. Dutton 1960 254p illus $4.50   920

1 Women in the U.S.—Biography 2 New York University. Hall of Fame
These sketches portray "the lives of the eight courageous women whose names are enrolled in the Hall of Fame. . . . [Here are] the dreams and accomplishments of Emma Willard, Mary Lyon, Maria Mitchell and Alice Freeman Palmer. And [here also are] the lives of Harriet Beecher Stowe, Charlotte Cushman, Susan B. Anthony and Frances Willard." Foreword

Vasari, Giorgio

The lives of the painters, sculptors and architects; ed. with an introduction by William Gaunt. Dutton 1963 4v ea $2.95   920

1 Artists, Italian 2 Art, Italian
"Everyman's library"
An edition of a classic work on 15th and 16th century Italian artists by a contemporary of that period
Vasari "deals with the life and work of nearly two hundred Italian artists, and any reader making a specialized study of the art of Italy will have just cause to commend him, for he deals with minor as well as major practitioners. Vasari, in giving observations of critical merit and supplying reliable facts, also presents them with an unbiased mind." Publisher's note
Select bibliography and glossary in volume one

White, Ralphe M.

The royal family; a personal portrait, by Ralphe M. White and Graham Fisher. McKay 1969 275p $6.50   920

1 Elizabeth II, Queen of Great Britain 2 Windsor, House of
The book describes the royal family " 'as a family:' a fabulously wealthy family, to be sure, with a colossal servant problem and thousands of official and ceremonial duties light-years removed from ordinary life, but a family still, with domestic crises and domestic joys, and even troublesome in-laws like the rest of us." Publisher's note
"What's intriguing is [the] description of how Buckingham Palace is run; its vast organization relies on a tangle of ancient practices and modern convenience—it's an eighth of a mile from kitchens to dining rooms." Pub W

Whitney, David C.

The graphic story of The American Presidents; ed. by Thomas C. Jones. Ferguson; distributed by Doubleday 1971 540p illus $14.95   920

1 Presidents—U.S.
First published 1967 by Doubleday with title: The American Presidents
This is a collection of personal and political biographies of the Presidents. "Each president is accorded a chapter devoted to major biographical events and his career, accompanied by a profusion of captioned illustrations of the times and isolated lists of his cabinet members. Article subheadings are provided for easy reference." Library J

Worcester, Donald E.

Makers of Latin America. Dutton 1966 222p illus maps $4.95, lib. bdg. $4.90   920

1 Latin America—Biography 2 Latin America—History
"The biographies of twenty men and one woman who have especially influenced the course of Mexican, Central American and South American history from the Conquest to the twentieth century." Publisher's note
"Donald Worcester's book is a valuable contribution—he not only charts new fields but does it well." Christian Science Monitor

920.02   Biography—Indexes

Biography index; a cumulative index to biographical material in books and magazines. Wilson, H.W. annual subscription $25   920.02

1 Biography—Indexes 2 Biography—Bibliography
First issued September 1946
Published quarterly, November, February, May, and August, with bound annual and permanent three-year cumulations. Permanent volumes $50 each
Editor: 1946-1963: Bea Joseph; 1964-date: Rita Volmer Louis

Biography index—*Continued*

"It includes current books in the English language wherever published; biographical material from the 1500 periodicals now regularly indexed in the Wilson indexes, plus a selected list of professional journals in the fields of law and medicine; obituaries of national and international interest from the 'New York Times.' All types of biographical material are covered: pure biography, critical material of biographical significance, autobiography, letters, diaries, memoirs, journals, genealogies, fiction, drama, poetry, bibliographies, obituaries, pictorial works and juvenile literature. Works of collective biography are fully analyzed. Incidental biographical material such as prefaces and chapters in otherwise nonbiographical books is included." Preface

"Index is in two sections: (1) Name alphabet, giving for each biographee, insofar as possible, full name, dates, nationality, and occupation or profession with index references; (2) Index by profession and occupation. Large categories, such as authors, are divided by nationality." Winchell. Guide to Reference Books. 8th edition

Nicholsen, Margaret E.

People in books; a selective guide to biographical literature arranged by vocations and other fields of reader interest. Wilson, H.W. 1969 498p $12   920.02

1 Biography—Indexes 2 Biography—Bibliography
ISBN 0-8242-0394-1

This reference tool designed for libraries serving children, young adults and adults "has a main section arranged by vocation or activity, a country-century appendix which indexes by country and by century the persons whose biographies are listed in the main section, a second appendix listing alphabetically by author books of an autobiographical nature and an index listing all those persons about whom a book or part of a collective biography is included in the main section." Preface

920.03 Biography—Dictionaries

American men and women of science. . . . Ed. by The Jaques Cattell Press. 12th ed. v 1-2 The physical and biological sciences. Bowker 1971-1972 2v ea $35   920.03

1 Scientists—Dictionaries

"Formerly American men of science; a biographical directory founded in 1906." Title page
First published by Science Press in one volume
Volume one and two of a projected six-volume set, to be sold for $210
Alphabetically arranged in two columns per page this compilation lists leading American and Canadian scientists. The fields covered range from biochemistry to ecology to medicine. The following information is included for each biographee: name, current address, field of specialization, research interests, past and present positions, birthplace, degrees, and professional memberships

American men of science; a biographical directory; ed. by The Jaques Cattell Press. 11th ed. [v7-8] The social and behavioral sciences. Bowker 1968 2v ea $33   920.03

1 Scientists—Dictionaries
Supplementary volume available at $18
"30,000 biographies of U.S. and Canadian men and women in the social and behavioral sciences." Publisher's note

Asimov, Isaac

Asimov's Biographical encyclopedia of science and technology. . . . New rev. ed. Doubleday 1972 xxviii, 805p illus $12.95   920.03

1 Scientists—Dictionaries
First published 1964
"The lives and achievements of 1195 great scientists from ancient times to the present chronologically arranged." Title page

"In this book the history of science is told through biographies (biographies that concentrate on the subjects' scientific labors, of course, rather than their private lives). . . . There is no attempt to divide the sciences into separate categories and devote chapters to each, as is often done in histories of science. When this is done, the sense of the panorama is easily lost. The scientists included in this book are listed in chronological order of birth. You will encounter what might seem a bewildering succession of chemists, mathematicians, inventors, explorers, physicists, astronomers, biologists, and physicians. . . . I have resisted, to a greater extent than is usual, the temptation to fade off as modern times are approached." From the Preface to the first edition

Chambers's Biographical dictionary; ed. by J. O. Thorne. St Martins $22.50   920.03

1 Biography—Dictionaries

First published 1897 and periodically brought up to date
A standard reference work containing biographies of over 15,000 men and women, contemporary and past, of all nations. "Essential basic information—surname (Bold capitals), christian names and titles (small bold), pronunciation (where given), dates, designation, birth place (where known)—now commences each entry.... Bibliographical notes giving useful suggestions for further reading appear at the end of most articles. The supplementary [subject] index . . . will be an invaluable aid for devotees of quiz games and the crosswords, for settling arguments, or for the idle pursuit of general knowledge." Preface to 1962 edition

Concise Dictionary of American biography. Advisory editorial board: Frederick Burkhardt [and others] managing editor: Joseph G. E. Hopkins; assistants: Antoinette Boysen [and] Edythe Greissman; editorial associates: George Basalla [and others]. Scribner 1964 1273p $25   920.03

1 U.S.—Biography—Dictionaries

This one-volume abridgement of the: Dictionary of American biography, entered below, includes the 14,870 entries of the parent work in reduced form. Coverage is limited to persons no longer living and includes "explorers, frontiersmen, artists and scientists, craftsmen, inventors, businessmen, surgeons and physicians, feminists, scholars, politicians and statesmen." Publisher's note
The articles "have been shortened to contain just pertinent facts. Reference work for college students, others." Pub W

Contemporary authors; a bio-bibliographical guide to current authors and their works. [First revision] Gale Res. 1967-1969 8v in 2 ea $25   920.03

1 Authors, American—Dictionaries 2 U.S.—Bio-bibliography

Contents: v 1-4, edited by James M. Ethridge and Barbara Kopala; v5-8, edited by Barbara Harte and Carolyn Riley

Volume 1-4 "represents a complete revision and consolidation into one alphabet of bio-graphical material which originally appeared in four separate quarterly issues of 'Contemporary Authors,' volumes 1, 2, 3, and 4, published in 1962 and 1963. The revised material is down to date, and in most cases, through spring, 1967." Preface to volume 1-4
Volume 5-8 "represents a complete revision and a consolidation into one alphabet of biographical material which originally appeared in two separate semi-annual issues of 'Contemporary Authors,' volumes 5-6 and 7-8, published in 1963. The revised material is up to date in most cases, through fall 1969." Preface to volume 5-8

Contemporary authors—*Continued*

Established "to provide information about as many nontechnical writers as possible whose work is being published, read, and discussed currently." Preface to volume 1-4

Will be kept up to date by the addition of about 3,500 new sketches each year, to be published in two semiannual volumes. See entry below

Contemporary authors; the bio-bibliographical guide to current authors and their works. Gale Res. $25 a year   920.03

1 Authors, American—Dictionaries 2 U.S.—Bio-bibliography

Semi-annual. First published 1962 as a quarterly

Editor: 1962-1968, James M. Ethridge

An alphabetically arranged "directory intended to supply biographical and bibliographical information on published 'authors of fiction, juvenile books—both fiction and nonfiction, poetry, texts outside the physical and biological sciences and technology but including the social sciences, and general nonfiction.' The sketches vary in length from a dozen lines to several columns, depending on the amount of material supplied by the author though all follow a pattern of headings in the following order: personal, career, writings. In many cases, added paragraphs cover awards and honors, membership in associations, sidelights and work in progress." Cur Ref Bks

Cross, Milton

The Milton Cross New encyclopedia of the great composers and their music [by] Milton Cross and David Ewen. Rev. and expanded. Doubleday 1969 2v (1284p) $11.95   920.03

1 Composers—Dictionaries

First published 1953 with title: Milton Cross' Encyclopedia of the great composers and their music

A dictionary of biographies with musical analyses for 67 composers. Also includes sections on music before and since Bach; the anatomy of the symphony orchestra; a discography, a dictionary of musical forms, a glossary, and a bibliography

Current biography yearbook. Wilson, H.W. illus $10   920.03

1 Biography—Dictionaries

Annual, first published 1940 with title: Current biography

Presents articles on the life and work of people in the news—in national and international affairs, the sciences, the arts, labor, and industry. Sources of information for the articles are newspapers, magazines, books, and, in most cases, the biographees themselves. The heading of each article includes the pronunciation of the name if it is unusual, date of birth, occupation, and address. Source references are given at the end of each article. Brief obituary notices with a reference to New York Times obituary, are given for persons whose biographies have previously appeared in Current biography. Each yearbook contains an index by profession, a necrology, and a cumulated index which includes names in all previous yearbooks

Also issued monthly except August. Subscription price $12 per year. Earlier reprinted yearbooks are obtainable: 1940-1943, ea $24; 1944-1945 ea $20

Dictionary of American biography, under the auspices of the American Council of Learned Societies; ed. by Allen Johnson and Dumas Malone. Scribner 1958 11v $290   920.03

1 U.S.—Biography—Dictionaries

Handled through Scribner's Subscription Department

A notable reference work originally published in 20 volumes and an index, now no longer available. Two supplements, edited by Harris E. Starr and Robert Livingston Schuyler, respectively, bringing the material up to 1940, are now included in volume 11

"Planned on the lines of the English 'Dictionary of national biography' and so includes only persons no longer living. Scope includes noteworthy persons of all periods who lived in the territory that is known as the United States, excluding British officers serving in America after the colonies declared their independence. Signed articles. Bibliographies." Mudge

The Dictionary of national biography, founded in 1882 by George Smith. The concise dictionary. . . being an epitome of the main work and its Supplement. Oxford 1953 pt. 1 $12.50   920.03

1 Great Britain—Biography—Dictionaries 2 Great Britain—Bio-bibliography

Half title: The concise dictionary of national biography

First published as an index to the basic set

"Since 1913 'The Concise Dictionary of National Biography' has been printed in two parts: one covering lives up to 1900 and the other, in succession, those of the first three decades of the twentieth century. Up to 1950 these two parts were bound together and sold in one volume." Preface

Now available separately. Part two is entered below

The Dictionary of national biography: The concise dictionary; pt. 2, 1901-1950; being an epitome of the Twentieth century D.N.B. down to the end of 1950. Oxford 1961 528p $8.80   920.03

1 Great Britain—Biography—Dictionaries 2 Great Britain—Bio-bibliography

Part one is entered above

"The opportunity has been taken to make some corrections in those portions of the text which have appeared in print before. At the end of the volume there is a select subject index. The entries are not intended to be comprehensive but may serve as signposts to set the inquirer upon his way." Note

Dictionary of scientific biography. Charles Coulston Gillespie, editor-in-chief. Scribner 4v illus ea $35   920.03

1 Scientists—Dictionaries

"Published under the auspices of the American Council of Learned Societies." Facing title page

Here are the first four "volumes of a projected 12-volume compendium (plus index) which will describe and evaluate the lives and contributions of over 4500 scientists and mathematicians. Provides coverage of selected scientific figures from every region and period. The presentations are similar to those of the DNB and DAB, and entries give precise, essential biographical data plus information on the subject's contributions in relation to his predecessors, contemporaries, and successors. Entries vary in length, but all have selective bibliographies which identify primary and secondary literature relative to the subject." Library J

Contents: v 1 Pierre Abaillard—L. S. Berg (1970); v2 Hans Berger—Christoph Ballot (1970); v3 Pierre Cabanis—Heinrich von Dechen (1971); v4 Dedekind to Firmicus Maternus (1971)

Ewen, David

(ed.) Composers since 1900; a biographical and critical guide; comp. and ed. by David Ewen. Wilson, H.W. 1969 639p illus $17   920.03

1 Composers—Dictionaries 2 Music—Bio-bibliography
ISBN 0-8242-0400-X

Companion volume to the author's: Great composers, 1300-1900, entered below

This volume replaces: Composers of today, American composers today, and European composers today, originally published 1934, 1949 and 1954, respectively

Ewen, David—*Continued*

"This work contains biographical sketches of 220 principal composers of the twentieth century. Included among traditionalists, innovators, eclectics, and romanticists are the avant-garde—those doing significant work with aleatory music, electronic music, directional music, organized sound, and other modern methods of composition. More than half the composers have been personally interviewed. Two appendixes are included: Major Schools of Composers and Specific Techniques, Idioms, and Styles; and A Select Bibliography." Publisher's note

(ed.) Great composers, 1300-1900; a biographical and critical guide comp. and ed. by David Ewen. Wilson, H.W. 1966 429p illus $12   **920.03**

1 Composers—Dictionaries 2 Music—Bio-bibliography
ISBN 0-8242-0018-7

This volume is intended as a "replacement for 'Composers of Yesterday,' published in 1937." Introduction
A reference book which furnishes biographical, critical, analytical, and historical information on about 200 composers of the past, both the musical giants and lesser masters. Entries, alphabetically arranged by composer, incorporate principal works and bibliographies. Appendixes offer a chronological listing of composers, and a listing by nationality
"Indispensable for all libraries but don't discard the 1937 [edition, now out-of-print]." Library J

(ed.) Popular American composers, from Revolutionary times to the present; a biographical and critical guide; comp. and ed. by David Ewen. With an index of songs and other compositions. Wilson, H.W. 1962 217p illus $8   **920.03**

1 Composers, American—Dictionaries 2 Music, Popular (Songs, etc.)—Bio-bibliography
ISBN 0-8242-0040-3

A biographical guide to 130 American popular composers arranged alphabetically "from Richard Adler to Victor Young. Approximately two thirds of the composers represented in this volume belong to the past; only one third are still alive." Introduction
The editor "has personally interviewed 41 of the 54 living composers, selected for their success, their productiveness and their contribution to popular music. Many of the sketches are accompanied by photographs and additional references." Cur Ref Bks
A chronological list of popular American composers: p193-94

Fuller, Muriel

(ed.) More junior authors. Wilson, H.W. 1963 235p illus (The Authors ser) $8 **920.03**

1 Authors—Dictionaries   2 Illustrators—Dictionaries   3 Children's literature—Bio-bibliography
ISBN 0-8242-0036-5

"This work is designed to be a companion volume to 'The Junior Book of Authors,' second edition, edited by Stanley J. Kunitz and Howard Haycraft [entered below]. Includes biographical or autobiographical sketches [arranged alphabetically] of 268 authors and illustrators of books for children and young people. The great majority are authors and illustrators who have become prominent since the publication of the second edition." Preface
"Selected from a preliminary list of almost 1,200 names, by a distinguished group of librarians working with children and young people in school and public libraries, the sketches represent only the most familiar and popular names. Photographs of many of the writers accompany the well-written accounts which should appeal to young people because of their personal flavor. Only partial lists of works by, and none about, the authors are given." Cur Ref Bks

Kunitz, Stanley J.

(ed.) American authors, 1600-1900; a biographical dictionary of American literature; ed. by Stanley J. Kunitz and Howard Haycraft. Complete in one volume with 1300 biographies and 400 portraits. Wilson, H.W. 1938 846p illus (The Authors ser) $12 **920.03**

1 Authors, American—Dictionaries
ISBN 0-8242-0001-2

"Contains, in all, biographies of almost 1300 authors, of both major and minor significance, who participated in the making of our literary history from the time of the first English settlement at Jamestown in 1607 to the close of the 19th century. No living authors are included." Preface
"Nearly every American who has written anything of value . . . is included. The major writers, of course, receive proportionately more space and attention and generally a photograph from the Frederick H. Meserve Collection. The minor writers are presented skillfully and with charm. At the end of each sketch are appended two bibliographies, labeled 'Principal Works' and 'About.'" Shores

(ed.) British authors before 1800; a biographical dictionary; ed. by Stanley J. Kunitz and Howard Haycraft. Complete in one volume with 650 biographies and 220 portraits. Wilson, H.W. 1952 584p illus (The Authors ser) $10   **920.03**

1 Authors, English—Dictionaries
ISBN 0-8242-0006-3

Precedes the editors': British authors of the nineteenth century, listed below. Their "purpose is to bring together in one place in concise and convenient form, pertinent biographical and critical information about the literary figures of the period defined." Preface
"The information is attractively presented and is generally correct and abreast of current scholarly research. As a reference work it seems to be directed to the beginning student or to the general reader and to be designed for the small library which does not possess the Dictionary of National Biography, [etc].
. . . In choosing 650 authors out of a vast number who flourished in England before 1800, the editors have generally selected wisely, not omitting the standard literary figures and also including a great many minor writers." Library Q

(ed.) British authors of the nineteenth century; ed. by Stanley J. Kunitz, associate ed. Howard Haycraft. Complete in one volume with 1000 biographies and 350 portraits. Wilson, H.W. 1936 677p illus (The Authors ser) $12   **920.03**

1 Authors, English—Dictionaries
ISBN 0-8242-0007-1

"The purpose of this work is to provide in a single volume brief, readable accounts of the lives of the major and minor British authors of the nineteenth century concerning whom students and amateurs of English literature are likely at any time to desire information." Preface
"Most of the sketches are short, but there has been a general effort both to make a really lifelike presentation of these writers and to offer a sound, though brief, critical judgment of their work. The book is thus genuinely interesting." N Y Times Bk R

(ed.) European authors, 1000-1900; a biographical dictionary of European literature; ed. by Stanley J. Kunitz and Vineta Colby. . . . Wilson, H.W. 1967 1016p illus (The Authors ser) $24   **920.03**

1 Authors, European—Dictionaries
ISBN 0-8242-0013-6

"Complete in one volume with 967 biographies and 309 portraits." Title page
Includes continental European writers born after the year 1000 and dead before 1925. Nearly a thousand major and minor contributors to thirty-one different literatures are discussed

Kunitz, Stanley J.—*Continued*

"Main criteria for inclusion rests on the individual's influence on European letters. (France and Germany have the most entries, followed by Italy, Spain, and Russia.) Importance determines entry length; and the entries, alphabetical and popular in style, include highlights, brief bibliographies of English translations, books about the biographees, and some diacritical pronunciations. . . . These biographies provide quick, satisfactory introductions to a staggering variety of authors and literatures. Senior high school libraries and up will use it for just this reason." Choice

(ed.) The junior book of authors. 2d ed. rev. Edited by Stanley J. Kunitz and Howard Haycraft; illus. with 232 photographs and drawings. Wilson, H.W. 1951 309p illus (The Authors ser) $8   920.03

1 Authors—Dictionaries 2 Illustrators—Dictionaries 3 Children's literature—Bio-bibliography
ISBN 0-8242-0028-4

"First published in 1934, this contains 289 biographical sketches of authors and illustrators of children's books. . . . Many people using the book will, of course, miss some favorite authors, even though the selection was carefully made by a large committee of librarians and other specialists in children's books; but all will agree that this is an indispensable reference tool for schools and libraries." Horn Bk

Each account gives birth date, death date—if subject is deceased, author's background, mention of his work, and a photograph or drawing. Many of the articles are autobiographical

(ed.) Twentieth century authors; a biographical dictionary of modern literature; ed. by Stanley J. Kunitz and Howard Haycraft. Complete in one volume with 1850 biographies and 1700 portraits. Wilson, H.W. 1942 1577p illus (The Authors ser) $22   920.03

1 Authors—Dictionaries
ISBN 0-8242-0049-7

This work "aims to provide a foundation-volume of authentic biographical information on the writers of this century, of all nations, whose books are familiar to readers of English. . . . [It] supersedes two out-of-print preliminary volumes, 'Living Authors' (1931) and 'Authors Today and Yesterday' (1933)." Preface

"This contains twice as many authors as the other two and each sketch has been rewritten. The combination of sprightliness and accuracy, which appears as a result of four years' preparation—and such years—is a monument to its editors." Cur Ref Bks

(ed.) Twentieth century authors: first supplement; a biographical dictionary of modern literature; ed. by Stanley J. Kunitz; assistant ed. Vineta Colby. Wilson, H.W. 1955 1123p illus (The Authors ser) $18   920.03

1 Authors—Dictionaries
ISBN 0-8242-0050-0

Original volume, edited by Stanley J. Kunitz and Howard Haycraft, listed above

"The present First Supplement brings the original biographies and bibliographies up to date and contains some 700 new biographies, 670 with portraits, mostly of authors who have come into prominence since 1942." Preface

An "invaluable library tool. . . . [Lists] the approximately 2,500 names in a single alphabet with reference to the main sketch if located in the original volume." Bookmark

McGraw-Hill Modern men of science; 426 leading contemporary scientists, presented by the editors of the McGraw-Hill Encyclopedia of science and technology. McGraw 1966-1968 2v illus ea $19.50 920.03

1 Scientists—Dictionaries

"In both volumes most of the sketches are autobiographies, and the remainder have been written by knowledgeable persons and whenever possible have been checked by the biographees. The emphasis in these accounts, each prefaced by a small portrait drawing, is on the scientific enterprises in which the individual was engaged and on his specific achievements. Pertinent references to colleagues, contemporaries and events of historical value are included. Chronological personal details normally found in biographical directories are condensed in a final paragraph or two. For those who desire more detailed background on scientific concepts, ideas, or terminology, there are references to articles in 'The McGraw-Hill Encyclopedia of Science and Technology' [class 503]." Science Bks

Magill, Frank N.

(ed.) Cyclopedia of world authors. Associate editor: Dayton Kohler. Harper 1958 1198p $11.95, lib. bdg. $9.89   920.03

1 Authors—Dictionaries 2 Literature—Dictionaries

Also available in 2 volumes at $15 per set from Salem Press, with title: Masterplots cyclopedia of world authors

"Critical biographies of 753 authors . . . whose works are covered in 'Masterpieces of World Literature,' series one [through four entered in class 808.8] also edited by Frank N. Magill. The biographies, each 200 to 1,000 words long, sketch in facts about the details of the authors' lives and times, and evaluations of their works." Pub W

Bibliography at end of each sketch

Murphy, Rosalie

(ed.) Contemporary poets of the English language; with a preface by C. Day Lewis; deputy editor: James Vinson. St James Press 1970 1243p $25   920.03

1 Poets—Dictionaries 2 English poetry—Bio-bibliography

This dictionary provides "biographical and bibliographical information about [1100] poets now writing in the English language. . . . [Brief] articles by a variety of critics have been included on about three hundred of the poets, those who, in the view of the advisers, are the outstanding poets currently writing in English, as well as those about whom critical comment is often difficult to obtain." Editor's note

Thomas, Henry

Biographical encyclopedia of philosophy. Doubleday 1965 273p $5.95   920.03

1 Philosophers—Dictionaries

Arranged in alphabetical order, this dictionary contains studies of more than four hundred philosophers. Included are such well-known thinkers as Confucius, Santayana, Socrates and Kant along with "some surprising names" —Browning, Burroughs, and Hamilton. (Publisher)

"While there is uneveness in treatment—Sartre gets less space than Will Durant,—some notable omissions, such as Karl Jaspers and Gabriel Marcel, and some questionable inclusions, the book . . . will be useful in high school libraries." Library J

Webster's Biographical dictionary; a dictionary of names of noteworthy persons with pronunciations and concise biographies. Merriam $9.50   920.03

1 Biography—Dictionaries

William Allan Neilson, editor in chief

First published 1943 and frequently revised

"Contains some 40,000 concise biographies of notable men and women from every country and period of history—all within the compass of a single volume. Alphabetically arranged, it is a handy guide to essential facts—birth and death dates, important accomplishments, family relationships, influence on history. A valuable quick reference source book for every course in the curriculum." Publisher's note

Webster's Biographical dictionary—*Continued*

The entries "vary from a few lines to a full page. Concise and clearly written, the sketches are unsigned but considered trustworthy and adequate. Liberal cross references aid the user in locating information. Also included are tables of popes, American government officials, and rulers of various countries." Peterson. Reference Books for Elementary and Junior High School Libraries

Who was who in America; a companion biographical reference work to Who's who in America. . . . Marquis 1942-68 4v ea $34.50   **920.03**

1 U.S.—Biography—Dictionaries

Contents: v 1 1897-1942; v2 1943-1950; v3 1951-1960; v4 1961-1968

"Includes sketches removed because of death from 'Who's who in America' with dates of death and often interment location appended." Winchell. Guide to Reference Books. 8th edition

Who was who in America: historical volume, 1607-1896. Rev. ed. 1967; a component volume of Who's Who in American history. . . . Marquis 1967 689p $30   **920.03**

1 U.S.—Biography—Dictionaries

First published 1963. Precedes Who was who in America, entered above

"A compilation of sketches of individuals, both of the United States of America and other countries, who have made contribution to, or whose activity was in some manner related to, the history of the United States, from the founding of Jamestown Colony to the year of continuation by 'Volume I of Who was who'" Subtitle

"This is an extremely useful addition to the working libraries of scholars, colleges [and] newspapers. . . . It is not so scholarly a work as the recent one-volume epitome of the Dictionary of American Biography, and does not cover so much ground. But it has a utility that the Dictionary has not got, for it is less choosy in its choice of subjects and it is often the rightfully obscure that the reader wants to identify." Times (London) Lit Sup

Map on lining-papers

Who's who; an annual biographical dictionary. St Martins $35   **920.03**

1 Great Britain—Biography—Dictionaries

Annual. First published 1849

"The pioneer work of the who's who type and still one of the most important. Until 1897, it was a handbook of titled and official classes and included list of names rather than biographical sketches. With 1897, called 'First year of new issue.' it changed its character and became a biographical dictionary of prominent persons in many fields. It has been developed and enlarged along these lines ever since. It is principally British, but a few prominent names of other nationalities are included. Biographies are reliable and fairly detailed; they give main facts, addresses, and in case of authors, lists of works." Winchell Guide to Reference Books. 8th edition

Who's who in America; a biographical dictionary of notable living men and women. A component volume of Who's who in American history. Rev. and reissued biennially. Marquis $49.50   **920.03**

1 U.S.—Biography—Dictionaries

First published 1899

"The standard dictionary of contemporary biography, containing concise biographical data, prepared according to established practices, with addresses and, in case of authors, lists of works. Issued biennially and constantly expanded since 1899. The standards of admission are high, aiming to include the 'best-known men and women in all lines of useful and reputable achievement' including (1) those selected on account of special prominence in creditable lines of effort . . . and (2) those

included arbitrarily on account of official position. . . . Volumes up to v.22 (1942/1943) included geographical indexes." Winchell. Guide to Reference Books. 8th edition

Although this "is the basic reference work in contemporary American biography, outstanding foreigners in many walks of life, including all chiefs of state, are [now] listed. . . . Appropriately to the times, greater emphasis is given some of the more technical types of professions and businesses, and some research sciences." Preface

Who's who in the world. Marquis $44.95   **920.03**

1 Biography—Dictionaries

First published 1970 for coverage of the years 1971-1972

A listing of about 25,000 noteworthy men and women whose achievements are shaping today's world. Data is furnished by the listees, more than 150 countries being represented. Includes a table of abbreviations, and a geographical index of biographees

92   Individual biography

Lives of individuals are arranged alphabetically under the names of the persons written about

A number of subjects have been added to the titles in this section to help in curriculum work. It is not necessarily recommended that these subjects be used in the card catalog

Acheson, Dean

Morning and noon; illus. with photographs. Houghton 1965 288p illus $6   **92**

1 Statesmen, American

An autobiography "which stretches from Acheson's happy turn-of-the-century childhood in Middletown, Connecticut, to his acceptance of a position as Assistant Secretary of State for Economic Affairs in 1941. . . . [Mr. Acheson recalls] his years a law clerk, a lawyer, and an economic expert. From his middle years, the personalities he best recalls are Justice Louis Brandeis, Felix Frankfurter, and President Franklin D. Roosevelt." Pub W

"There are many sketches, done with sharp perception, remarkable economy and a clarity that the tender-minded will not be altogether wrong in calling ruthless. The gallery of the Nine Old Men . . . is remarkable." Book Week

Bibliography in Notes: p231-78

Adams, Henry

The education of Henry Adams   **92**

Some editions are:

Houghton $6.95 Editor's preface by Henry Cabot Lodge

Modern Lib. $2.95 Introduction by James Truslow Adams

Awarded the Pulitzer Prize, 1919

First published in a popular edition 1918

"Henry Adams was the son of Charles Francis Adams, U. S. Minister to Britain during the Civil War, and a grandson of John Quincy Adams. His 'education' consists of everything that happened to him or about him from his birth to his death and his frank, somewhat cynical descriptions and comments are fascinating." St Louis Mo Bul

"The book is not a complete autobiography; it omits any mention of the 13 years of Adams' marriage, and the seven years following his wife's suicide. It does, however, present a vivid picture of places and people the author knew." Benét. The Reader's Encyclopedia

Adams, John, President U.S.

The John Adams papers; selected, ed. and interpreted by Frank Donovan. Dodd 1965 335p illus (The Papers of the Founding Fathers) $5   **92**

1 Presidents—U.S. 2 U.S.—History—Biography

"Excerpts from speeches, reports, and letters to and from John Adams, which, with the editor's commentary and relevant background information, constitute a comprehensive though fragmentary biography. The short

Adams, John, President U.S.—_Continued_

chronologically arranged selections, only a sampling from the voluminous John Adams papers, were chosen . . . for their significance in revealing the writer's character." Booklist

Bowen, Catherine Drinker. John Adams and the American Revolution. Little 1950 699p illus $8.95   92

1 Presidents—U.S. 2 U.S.—History—Revolution—Biography

"Concerned with the first 40 years of Adams' life. The author re-creates the life of the period, the events through which Adams lived and closes with the signing of the Declaration of Independence." Los Angeles. School Libraries

"The author states that her reading and research for this book were directed toward the understanding of Adams' character, and of how it felt to be a citizen of the eighteenth century. She succeeds in conveying that understanding to her readers in this portrait of a passionate and brilliant man, an ardent patriot and astute statesman, who was also Abigail Adams' devoted but frequently exasperating husband. Abigail herself, many others of Adams' intimates, and the prominent figures of the times, are drawn with equal clarity." Booklist

Notes: p609-40. Word about sources and methods: p642-76. Map on lining-papers

Addams, Jane

Meigs, Cornelia. Jane Addams: pioneer for social justice; a biography. Little 1970 274p illus $5.95   92

1 Hull House, Chicago

"This book deals with Jane Addams' recognition of the social inequities at the turn of the century. It follows her establishment of the Hull House in Chicago, to the founding of the Women's International League for Peace and Freedom." Book News

"The story is inspiring. . . . [It is a] good source of information for students researching the period of rising industrialism—its evils and its reformers." Library J

Wise, Winifred E. Jane Addams of Hull-House; a biography. Harcourt 1935 255p illus $4.75   92

1 Hull House, Chicago

"The material for this biography has been drawn from Miss Addams's published books, her papers, and letters. The author has built up a simple, direct account of Jane Addams's early life and school days, her work at Hull House and her championship of various social and humanitarian causes." Booklist

"There is in Miss Wise's book only just enough of the long struggle, the constantly recurring misunderstandings that met Jane Addams, the successive adjustments of the public mind regarding her, to prepare a young reader for books that will tell him how many other things Jane Addams was called besides 'America's Joan of Arc' in her long working life." N Y Her Trib Books

Agee, James

Letters of James Agee to Father Flye; with a new preface and previously unpublished letters by Father Flye. 2d ed. Houghton 1971 267p illus $5.95   92

First published 1962 by Braziller

"This book contains some ninety letters written over the shaping years of the author's life to the Episcopalian priest who was his oldest friend. Beginning in 1925, when Agee was a student at boarding school, they annotate his growth as a writer and a human being up to the day of his death thirty years later. They move through Harvard, Greenwich Village, Hollywood, and back to Manhattan in step with his career as a reporter for 'Fortune,' film critic, scriptwriter, novelist, and poet." Publisher's note

Agnew, Spiro T.

Lucas, Jim G. Agnew: profile in conflict. Award Bks. distributed by Scribner 1970 160p $5.95   92

1 Vice-Presidents—U.S.

The author "traces the life of Spiro T. Agnew from his formative years in Baltimore as the son of a Greek immigrant through his governorship of Maryland and headline-making role as the 37th Vice President." Publisher's note

The author "focuses naturally on Agnew the political man." Pub W

Marsh, Robert. Agnew, the unexamined man; a political profile. Evans, M.&Co. 1971 182p $5.95   92

1 Vice-Presidents—U.S.

The author, who was on Agnew's staff during the 1966 Maryland gubernatorial campaign, traces Agnew's political progress from Republican convert in 1956 to Republican Vice President in 1969. (Publisher)

"Marsh makes clear Agnew is his own man. He portrays him as a philosophically shallow, hypersensitive and unbending paragon of rectitude who has been extremely lucky politically." Pub W

Akihito, Crown Prince of Japan

Simon, Charlie May. The sun and the birch; the story of Crown Prince Akihito and Crown Princess Michiko. Chapter headings by Grisha; illus. with photographs. Dutton 1960 192p illus $3.95   92

1 Michiko, consort of Akihito, Crown Prince of Japan 2 Japan—Social life and customs

This biography "traces the early years and backgrounds of the prince and princess and shows the two young people devoted to the traditions of their parents and yet realizing they must face the changes that have come about in Japan's civilization and culture. Author has a delightful style, and the illustrations throughout the book tend to keep the Japanese flavor." Library J

Vining, Elizabeth Gray. Windows for the Crown Prince. Lippincott 1952 320p illus $7.95   92

1 Japan—Social life and customs

A record of the author's four years at the Japanese Imperial Court, where she helped to teach and guide the young Prince from a chubby child to a poised, attractive youth with a high sense of responsibility

"The author brings to the reader a real understanding of the liking for Japan and the Japanese people that should help develop a similar liking and appreciation in American young people." Chicago. Children's Book Center

Alexander the Great

Horizon Magazine. Alexander the Great, by the editors of Horizon Magazine; author: Charles Mercer; consultant: Cornelius C. Vermeule III. . . . Am. Heritage 1962 153p illus maps boards $5.95, lib. bdg. $5.49   92

1 Kings and rulers

"A Horizon Caravel book"

"Illustrated with many paintings, mosaics, sculptures, and maps of the period." Title page

The life and adventures of the military genius and empire builder, Alexander of Macedon

The abundant "illustrative material [is] drawn largely from works of art. As a lure into the excitement of history and art, this should be highly successful. As a biography, it simply records an assortment of different images and interpretations of Alexander." Pub W

Further reference: p151

Lamb, Harold. Alexander of Macedon; the journey to world's end. Doubleday 1946 402p illus maps $5.95   92

1 Kings and rulers

Alexander the Great—*Continued*

"Scholarly assembling of the facts and legends about a brilliant military genius who crossed the Hellespont into Persia to conquer the known world. One sees him first as a studious, absent-minded boy, tutored by Aristotle, and at the end as the conqueror who brought Greek culture to Asia Minor and whose split personality led him to acts of violence, followed by periods of self-loathing." Cincinnati

Alliluyeva, Anna

The Alliluyev memoirs; recollections of Svetlana Stalina's maternal aunt Anna Alliluyeva and her grandfather Sergei Alliluyev; tr. and ed. by David Tutaev. Putnam 1968 222p illus $4.95   92

1 Russia—History
Originally published 1946 in Russia in separate volumes
These memoirs "cover the period prior to and through the Russian Revolution and the Kerensky period, with intimate views of Stalin and Lenin." Publisher's note
They "are interesting not only in what they contain but also because of what knowledgeable readers will realize they omit." Library J
Bibliographical references included in Notes: p214-22

Alliluyeva, Svetlana

Only one year; tr. from the Russian by Paul Chavchavadze. Harper 1969 444p $7.95
92

On December 19, 1966, Svetlana Alliluyeva left Moscow for a month's trip to India, to deposit her husband's ashes. One year later she celebrated her first year of freedom in the U.S. In this book she describes her Moscow friends and the ordeal she went through when she decided to renounce her past and start a new life in the U.S.
This new book "is outspoken to an astonishing degree, and [is] a unique historical document, which will take its place, I believe, among the great Russian autobiographical works. . . . The book is close-packed with incident, with ideas, and with information. I do not know how far consciously its scheme was planned, but the result is immensely effective: the Russian instinct for storytelling and dramatic presentation makes it a [moving] narrative . . . [Svetlana] makes an attempt to explain her father which, since she knew his Georgian mother and had family information about his early life, makes some genuine contribution to the subject. . . . [This is] a book which I believe will reverberate through the whole contemporary world." New Yorker

Twenty letters to a friend; tr. by Priscilla Johnson McMillan. Harper 1967 246p illus $5.95   92

1 Stalin, Iosif 2 Russia—Politics and government, 1925-1953
This is not a real biography or a connected story, but memories cast in letter form, dated from Mme Svetlana Alliluyeva's summer place near Moscow in 1963, and addressed supposedly to an unnamed friend. The author tells of her relationship with her father and describes her life with him. His entourage and political activities are also dealt with. (Publisher)
"Undoubtedly honest and as accurate as possible, she has given us an illuminating picture of the mysterious and controversial Stalin, his family, and a more general idea of Russia's upper echelon." Library J

Andersen, Hans Christian

Godden, Rumer. Hans Christian Andersen; a great life in brief. Knopf 1955 [c1954] 206p (Great lives in brief) $3.95   92

1 Authors, Danish
This biography recreates Andersen's life in terms of his own faith in himself and his dream of becoming a great writer. The author shows how his early struggles in Copenhagen and his later travels in Germany, France and Italy provided him with material for his stories and fairy tales

Miss Godden "has triumphed over all of the difficulties much as Andersen himself triumphed over the difficulties that surrounded him—by penetrating sympathetically and tenderly to Andersen's character." N Y Times Bk R

Anderson, Marian

My Lord, what a morning; an autobiography   92

1 Singers 2 Negroes—Biography
Some editions are:
Viking $5.75
Watts, F. $8.95 Large type edition. A Keith Jennison book
"With sincerity and simplicity Marian Anderson tells the story of her long struggle to become a concert singer. Sharing both her personal and professional life she recalls her childhood in South Philadelphia, describes her studies in America and abroad, recounts experiences of her concert tours, offers observations on vocal technique, gives her feeling about race prejudice, and expresses her hopes for the future of the Negro. An autobiography which reflects the warmth of its writer's personality and the depth of her artistic integrity." Booklist

Andretti, Mario

What's it like out there? [By] Mario Andretti with Bob Collins. Regnery 1970 282p $5.95   92

1 Automobile racing—Biography 2 Indianapolis Speedway Race
Although born in Italy, Andretti "started racing in Nazareth, Pennsylvania and came up from stock car and midget racing to win the Indianapolis 500 in 1969. . . . Racing is Andretti's whole life and his book is a chronological conversation about his rides, his cars, his relationships with other drivers, and his struggle to the top. Happily for his readers, Andretti is truthful about himself and his profession." Library J

Engel, Lyle Kenyon. Mario Andretti; the man who can win any kind of race; produced by Lyle Kenyon Engel and the editorial staff of Auto Racing magazine. [Rev. ed] Arco 1972 159p illus lib. bdg. $4.95 92

1 Automobile racing—Biography
ISBN 0-668-02193-4
First published 1970
"This biography of Mario Andretti characterizes the driver as the foremost example of the new breed in American championship auto racing. The account traces Andretti's driving career from his early years in Italy through the victorious 1969 season paying attention to his cohorts, backers, cars, and races. Pertinent photographs, including many action shots, share the space about equally with the narrative and statistical racing records." Booklist

Angelou, Maya

I know why the caged bird sings. Random House [1970 c1969] 281p $5.95   92

1 Negroes—Biography
A "memoir by a black author who is now a well-known actress and dancer. Maya Angelou's book is an elegantly written flesh-and-blood memoir of her earliest childhood in Arkansas—cigarbox guitars, hog mash and 'po' white trash kids'—and her later growing-up years in St. Louis and San Francisco, and a still-later wild, mysterious fiesta with her father in Mexico. She moved to St. Louis to live for the first time with her mother, at the age of eight and was raped by her mother's lover; in San Francisco she became, at 16, the first of her race to work on that city's cable cars. Courage and sophistication without bitterness are woven into Miss Angelou's intimate story." Pub W

Anne, Queen of Great Britain

Green, David. Queen Anne. Scribner [1971 c1970] 399p illus $8.95   92

1 Queens 2 Great Britain—History—Stuarts, 1603-1714

Anne, Queen of Great Britain—*Continued*

"This account of the personal and public life and career of Queen Anne portrays the political and military achievements of her reign." Book Rev Digest

The author "possesses admirable insight into character and he writes with clarity and skill. His control of the political background is less sure, but adequate to his purpose, and certainly this is a wonderful book about one of the most powerful Court dramas of English history." N Y Times Bk R

Antin, Mary

The promised land; with a foreword by Oscar Handlin. 2d ed. Houghton 1969 [c1912] xxii, 373p illus $5.95   92

1 Jews in the U.S. 2 Russia—Social life and customs

First published 1912

This is a "frankly introspective autobiography of a young Jewess of genius who was brought from Russia to America . . . lived for years in the Boston slums, gained an education which included a college course, and grew into [an adult with] a wonderfully beautiful feeling for America, her spiritual mother-country. The gift of poetic expression which the author's verses have shown adds to the appeal which the clear picture of life in Russia and of the attitude of the immigrant toward America make." Booklist

Glossary: p367-73

Aristotle

Farrington, Benjamin. Aristotle; founder of scientific philosophy. Praeger [1969 c1965] 118p illus maps (Praeger Pathfinder biographies) $4.50   92

1 Philosophers, Ancient

First published 1965 in England

The author discusses the philosopher's boyhood and youth against the background of Hellenic Greece; his work as a teacher and as head of the Lyceum at Athens; and his contributions to logic, physics, metaphysics, ethics and politics

"Written in light and readable style. There are pictures of Aristotle, Socrates, Plato, Philip II, Alexander, et al, the various men who figure prominently in the philosopher's life. In addition, the reader will be grateful for graphs and illustrations of Aristotle's four elements." Choice

Suggestions for further reading: p113-14

Audubon, John James

Audubon, by himself; a profile of John James Audubon; from writings selected, arranged, and ed. by Alice Ford. Natural Hist. Press 1969 276p illus $8.95   92

"Published for the American Museum of Natural History"

"The letters, journals and published works by the great American naturalist, John James Audubon . . . [have been compiled in] this 'autobiography'—a chronicle of almost sixty incredible and adventurous years. Audubon tells of his first attempt to draw, comments constantly on the America of the early 1800's and recreates scenes of the frontier." News of Bks

"Handsomely illustrated with 36 black and white photographs." N Y Times Bk R

Bibliography: p263-64

Austen, Jane

Becker, May Lamberton. Presenting Miss Jane Austen; illus. by Edward Price. Dodd 1952 204p illus $3.75   92

1 Authors, English

Jane Austen's life at Steventon Parsonage, her brief adventure at school and her real education at home, family theatricals in the barn with her cousin, the Countess from the Court of France, as leading lady—all these are in this book

"An ingratiating introduction to Jane Austen's family, era and works by an author whose familiarity with source materials and magic enthusiasm bring Jane Austen completely before us." Horn Bk

A selective list of books consulted: p199-204

Laski, Marghanita. Jane Austen and her world. Viking 1969 143p illus map $6.95   92

1 Authors, English 2 Austen, Jane—Contemporary England

"A Studio book"

The author portrays the life of Jane Austen against her background—that of "the upper-middle-class society of late eighteenth-century southern England. This society—self-contained, orthodox in morals and religion, generally Tory in politics, depending for its strength on the professions and on the ownership of land . . . [is the milieu] which she describes . . . in her novels." Publisher's note

"Profusely illustrated with pictures of Jane Austen, her friends and family, the homes and spas they lived in and visited, and with scenes of late eighteenth-century England, an excellent biography. . . . The writing is skilful, based on scholarship but not pedantic, the tone objective. A chronology, a list of notes on the illustrations, a bibliography of works by and about Austen, and an index are appended." Chicago. Children's Book Center

Aylward, Gladys

Burgess, Alan. The small woman; with illus. and maps. Dutton 1957 256p illus boards $4.95   92

1 Missionaries

The "true story of Gladys Aylward, a woman of energy, determination, spiritual strength, warm heart, and a consuming ambition to be a missionary in China. Pursuing this dream, she left her domestic-servant job in England, made her way to China's wild northern mountains, won converts and wide love and admiration, and then helped her people, as many as she could, escape the Japanese invaders." Pub W

Maps on lining-papers

Bacon, Francis, Viscount St Albans

Bowen, Catherine Drinker. Francis Bacon; the temper of a man. Little 1963 245p illus $7.50   92

1 Great Britain—History—Tudors, 1485-1603

"An Atlantic Monthly Press book"

In presenting this portrait of the Elizabethan thinker, writer, legal colleague of Coke, and aspirant of royal favor, "I have culled and taken from the existing material such facts and scenes, be they large or trivial, as may reveal the man. My chapters are cast in biographical form, yet they are in essence essays of opinion, the expression of one person's thinking about Francis Bacon." Author's note

"Shakespearean controversy is omitted purposely, but Bacon is briefly defended against claims of homosexuality. The predominant impression is that of Bacon's genius." Library J

Bader, Douglas

Brickhill, Paul. Reach for the sky; the story of Douglas Bader, legless ace of the Battle of Britain. Norton 1954 312p illus $5.95   92

1 Air pilots 2 Physically handicapped 3 World War, 1939-1945—Aerial operations

The story of an aviator who lost both legs in an air crash in 1931 and who fought his way back to become one of the great British heroes of the second World War

"Brickhill, himself a pilot, writes vividly of Bader's courageous fight against his handicap and of his brilliant flying." Horn Bk

Baez, Joan

Daybreak. Dial Press 1968 159p $3.95 92

1 Singers

In these autobiographical essays the folk singer and supporter of nonviolent resistance gives her impressions of her own life and of our times. Among the sketches included are those of fellow prisoners; group therapy sessions: an AWOL Army private; and children at the Perkins Institute for the Blind

Baez, Joan—*Continued*

"Though disjointed and sketchy, her memoirs manage to coalesce into a clear picture of an agitated, courageous, unconventional life and of her commitment to draft resistance, to antinationalism, and to defiance of the 'liberal middle class mold.' " Pub W

Baker, Louise

Out on a limb. McGraw 1946 213p $4.95
92

1 Physically handicapped

"Whittlesey House publications"

"Loss of a leg at the age of eight years proved no handicap to Mrs. Baker, who counted tennis, swimming, horseback riding, newspaper reporting amongst her many accomplishments. A delightfully human and humorous biography." Ontario Lib Rev

Balchen, Bernt

Come north with me; an autobiography. Dutton 1958 318p illus maps $6.95　92

1 Air pilots 2 Arctic regions

The "Norwegian-born flyer engagingly recounts his adventures with Amundsen and Byrd, bush flights in the Canadian wilderness and later operations as a U.S. Air Force officer in charge of Greenland bases and supplydrops into Norway to aid the Resistance in World War II." Bookmark

Bannister, Roger

The four minute mile; illus. with photographs. Dodd 1955 252p illus $4　92

1 Track athletics—Biography

"The great English runner tells how he ran the mile in less than four minutes, the first man ever to do so. However, since he is sensitive, intelligent, and articulate, he does far more than describe his training and the races all over the world in which he has taken part. He explains why men run and why they must ever seek to break new barriers." Horn Bk

Barnum, Phineas Taylor

Wallace, Irving. The fabulous showman; the life and times of P. T. Barnum. Knopf 1959 317p illus $6.95　92

This biography presents Barnum as a public figure, a great showman, a circus man, an impresario, and a swindler. It also tells of Barnum the private man who led a life as fascinating as one of his exhibits. (Publisher)

Acknowledgments and bibliography: p307-17

Barton, Clara Harlowe

Ross, Ishbel. Angel of the battlefield; the life of Clara Barton. Harper 1956 305p illus $5.95　92

1 Nurses and nursing—Biography 2 Red Cross. U.S. American National Red Cross

The life story of Clara Barton, called the "Angel of the battlefield" because of her work in bringing help to wounded soldiers at the front in three wars, the American Civil War, the Franco-Prussian War, and the Spanish American War. Out of her experiences in these wars and in disaster relief work at home and abroad grew her greatest achievement, the establishment of the American Red Cross. (Publisher)

She is "a compelling figure, immortalized here as a tiny, painfully shy spinster with a powerful conscience, defenseless on her own behalf, but indomitable in a humanitarian cause." Booklist

Bibliography: p291-94

Baruch, Bernard Mannes

Baruch: my own story. Holt 1957 337p illus $6.95　92

"The first volume [the only one still in print] of a two-volume autobiography of the well-known American financier and philanthropist, Bernard M. Baruch. Beginning with the story of his physician-father's part in the Civil War,

the author covers his own early years and education, his business career, marriage, and the building of his South Carolina estate, Hobcaw Barony. He closes with some statement of his philosophy." Book Rev Digest

"One thing stands out of the pages of the first volume. The author never forgot a kindness to himself or any member of his family and he never nursed hatred. He concludes with a moving expression of belief in reason, not because of the wisdom men have demonstrated in the past, but because reason remains as man's best tool for governing himself." Chicago Sunday Tribune

Beaconsfield, Benjamin Disraeli, 1st Earl of

Grant, Neil. Benjamin Disraeli; Prime Minister extraordinary. Watts, F. 1969 245p illus (Immortals of history) lib. bdg. $4.50
92

1 Great Britain—Politics and government—19th century 2 Statesmen, British

This biography traces Disraeli's life with particular emphasis on politics. "For forty years the House of Commons was the center of his existence, and he acquired a mastery of its workings that has seldom been equaled. Overcoming disadvantages of birth, reputation, and political circumstance, he became the leader of his party and, eventually, prime minister of England." Introduction

"The biographer sees Disraeli through no rose-colored glasses, and he is drawn as a man of tremendous wit, ability, charm, caprice, ambition, pride, and—in his earlier days—arrogance and flamboyance. The writing is plum-pudding style: a rather heavy consistency but studded with juicy raisins of anecdotes and Disraeli's quips. A brief bibliography and a relative index are appended." Chicago. Children's Book Center

Beethoven, Ludwig van

Marek, George R. Beethoven, biography of a genius. Funk 1969 696p illus $12.50　92

1 Composers, German

"Marek has a rare gift of communicating in literate, urbane and sensitive prose the nobler strains within Beethoven that warred with the more dubious frailities of his character. . . . One of the distinguished features of Marek's book is his excerpting of Beethoven's letters and his generous use of extracts from the 'Conversation Books': The composer, deaf by the age of 28, conversed with his friends by writing in these notebooks. As Marek observes in a moving final chapter, Beethoven has been curiously free from passing trends and tastes." Pub W

Bell, Alexander Graham

Costain, Thomas B. The chord of steel; the story of the invention of the telephone. Doubleday 1960 238p illus $5.50　92

1 Bell family 2 Telephone 3 Brantford, Ontario

"A native of Brantford, Ontario focuses on the brief period in which Alexander Graham Bell and his family lived in that town and declares, as do his quotations from Bell, that the telephone was invented in Brantford. A simply written account highlighting the Bell Family's 1870 arrival in Brantford, their interests in social and scientific problems, and Bell's first successful experiments with his new invention. Not designed as a biography but gives a clear picture of an important period in the inventor's life." Booklist

"Almost as fascinating as the story of Alexander Graham Bell's work as an inventor (not by any means restricted to telephones) is the account of what his father, Alexander [Melville] Bell, did to help the deaf." Pub W

Ben-Gurion, David

Memoirs: David Ben-Gurion; comp. by Thomas R. Bransten. World Pub. 1970 216p illus $6.95　92

1 Statesmen, Israeli 2 Israel—Politics and government

Ben-Gurion, David—*Continued*

"Derived from interviews conducted during the filming of a motion picture on his life, Ben-Gurion's succinct essays state his philosophy, define his aspirations for Israel, and explain his interpretation of the correct role of a modern Jew." Booklist

"It serves as a prelude to the memoirs he is in the process of writing. . . . Set within the context of the story of his life are discussions of Zionism's appeal in the early 20th Century, the genesis and role of Israel Defense Force as a civilian force, the Palestinian cause (which he sees as an individualistic claim to land rather than a true nationalist movement), and the central role of the Negev in the future of Israel. A fascinating book which whets one's appetite for the fuller story." Library J

Bibliography: p215-16

St John, Robert. Ben-Gurion; a biography. Doubleday 1971 360p $6.95   **92**

1 Statesmen, Israeli 2 Israel—Politics and government

First published 1959 with title: Ben-Gurion; the biography of an extraordinary man

A report "on the volatile, energetic, courageous Jewish leader, David Ben-Gurion, who helped create the new state of Israel . . . this biography gives a great deal of information about Ben-Gurion, Zionism and Israel." Pub W

Benítez Pérez, Manuel

Collins, Larry. Or I'll dress you in mourning [by] Larry Collins and Dominique Lapierre. Simon & Schuster 1968 349p $6.95   **92**

1 Bullfights 2 Spain—Civilization

The authors describe the life of the matador, Manual Benítez Pérez, known as El Cordobés; the world of the bullfight; and the changing conditions in Spain following the Spanish Civil War. (Publisher)

This "is far more than just a splendid book about a bullfighter. Woven into its fabric is the story of Spain during the last 32 years. . . . Insofar as a single volume could encapsulate so much history, it succeeds admirably and in the most readable fashion imaginable." N Y Times Bk R

Glossary of bullfighting terms: p341-45. Map on lining-papers

Bernhardt, Sarah

Skinner, Cornelia Otis. Madame Sarah   **92**

1 Actors and actresses

Some editions are:

Houghton $6.95

Watts, F. $8.95 Large type edition complete and unabridged. A Keith Jennison book

The "author tells the story of the incomparable Sarah Bernhardt, illegitimate daughter of a Dutch-Jewish demi-mondaine, who began life as a filthy waif in Paris and reigned as undisputed queen of the theater for some sixty years, feted by royalty as well as by mobs of common folk." Bk Buyer's Guide

The author "catches Bernhardt's compelling charm and her contradictory kindness and cruelty, egocentricity and self-sacrifice, and materialism and devout patriotism. The author's detailed characterization necessarily covers a wide range of social settings and nineteenth-and early twentieth-century public figures." Booklist

Bibliography: p343-46

Bernini, Giovanni Lorenzo

Wallace, Robert, 1919-   The world of Bernini, 1598-1680, by Robert Wallace and the editors of Time-Life Books. Time-Life Bks. [distributed by Little] 1970 192p illus (Time-Life Lib. of art) boards $7.95   **92**

1 Sculptors, Italian 2 Art, Italian

"Bernini lived from 1598 to 1680 and is probably the greatest sculptor of that extraordinary period which contained Rembrandt, Hals, Vermeer, Poussin, Rubens, Van Dyck, Velazquez. [Wallace] has written an exceptionally fine text, which adheres to the title, 'The

World of Bernini,' so that he can discuss Caravaggio and the Fountains of Rome, as well as the works of Bernini which are still the wonder of Rome. . . . [This volume is] handsomely illustrated in color and in monochrome. There are appended also a Chronology of Artists of the period, a selected Bibliography, as well as an Index." Best Sellers

Bernstein, Leonard

Ewen, David. Leonard Bernstein; a biography for young people. [Rev. ed] Chilton Co. 1967 180p illus $4.25   **92**

1 Conductors (Music) 2 Composers, American

First published 1960

A biography of the "wonder-child," the first American conductor of the New York Philharmonic: his childhood and early struggles, his rise to fame on Broadway and in the ballet, his role in the world of music

"One wonders why it is 'a biography for young people,' since it is not remarkably different from the author's other adult books which aim to popularize music. Could be useful to meet teen-age interests in music or current biography, but would be superseded by a deeper or more perceptive portrait." Library J

Includes lists of Bernstein's works and recordings and a bibliography

Berry, Martha McChesney

Kane, Harnett T. Miracle in the mountains, by Harnett T. Kane with Inez Henry. Doubleday 1956 320p $4.95   **92**

1 Berry Schools, Mount Berry, Ga. 2 Educators

"Harnett Kane, a devoted Southerner, writes an intimate story of the amazing Martha Berry who was born to plantation wealth but could not ignore those forgotten Americans living in the Georgian hills. Starting with a log cabin school, she built a unique educational institution." Cincinnati

"Skillfully written, the tale of this schoolroom Joan of Arc moves smoothly from one climatic moment to another. It is spiced with laughter and studded with tears and ever inspiring admiration for a great woman." Chicago Sunday Tribune

Bethune, Mary (McLeod)

Holt, Rackham. Mary McLeod Bethune; a biography. Doubleday 1964 306p illus $5.95   **92**

1 Educators 2 Negroes—Biography

"The life story of a woman who devoted her long life to the cause of racial equality. Her three great achievements were: the founding of the small girls' school that grew into coeducational Bethune-Cookman College; dedicated service to the National Youth Administration as Director of the Division of Negro Affairs; and two decades of labor on behalf of the National Council of Negro Women which she founded in 1935." Huntting

Bismarck, Otto, Fürst von

Hollyday, Frederic B. M. ed. Bismarck. Prentice-Hall 1970 180p (Great lives observed) $5.95   **92**

1 Germany—History—1866-
SBN 13-077362-X

"A Spectrum book"

Divided into three parts, this book "includes selections showing what Bismarck thought about issues, what contemporaries thought about him, and how historians have judged him. The editor has selected items that focus on specific aspects of Bismarck's life and work." Choice

"Hollyday introduces each selection with a brief explanatory paragraph and concludes the volume with a brief afterword covering Bismarck's final years and a thorough annotated bibliography." Library J

Blake, William

Daugherty, James. William Blake; with reproductions of drawings by William Blake. Viking 1960 128p illus $4.95   **92**

1 Artists, British 2 Poets, English

Blake, William—*Continued*

"An interesting biography of a colorful subject, with emphasis on Blake's work rather than on his personal life, although the latter is quite adequately covered. The author's attitude toward Blake as a man is objective, his enthusiastic appreciation being reserved for the artist's verses and engravings. An unpaged section at the back of the book gives 21 reproductions of Blake's illustrations for the Book of Job; these are shown on a full page, with a descriptive paragraph on the facing page. Appended is a list of the Blake collections in the United States." Chicago. Children's Book Center

Bolívar, Simón

Bushnell, Davis, ed. The liberator, Simón Bolívar; man and image; ed. with an introduction. Knopf 1970 xxxiv, 218p front map (Borzoi Books on Latin America) $3.95   92

1 Statesmen, South American 2 South America —History

"A balanced anthology of Bolívar's life, legends, and accomplishments that is a very instructive contribution to our knowledge of the independence of South America. It includes selections from the Liberator's writing and works as well as contemporary and current assessments of his historic achievements. . . . Generally, it provides the most modern and meaningful analysis of the man and his mark on South America." Choice

Selected bibliography and historiography: p212-18

Bond, Julian

Neary, John. Julian Bond: Black rebel. Morrow 1971 256p boards $5.95   92

1 Negroes—Biography

A biography of the politician, civil rights activist and poet who was ousted from the Georgia State legislature in 1966 because of his opposition to the Vietnam War, and returned to that body by a Supreme Court order. He fought for and led the first fully integrated delegation to the 1968 Democratic convention, and was the first Black man to be nominated for the Vice-Presidency

"A straightforward biography of the young black politician with emphasis on the political rather than the personal." Booklist

Borland, Hal

Country editor's boy. Lippincott 1970 313p boards $5.95   92

1 Colorado

"This sequel to High, Wide and Lonesome [entered below] tells the story of the author's high school years. He recalls the years from 1915 to 1918, the years following his family's move to Flagler, a small town in the High Plains of Colorado, where his father became the owner and editor of a weekly newspaper." Book Rev Digest

"This is homespun Americana of the best sort—intelligent, aware, never sentimentally sloppy, a portrait of a time and a place and a modest backward look at a boy changing into a man that should give hours of reading pleasure to many." Pub W

High, wide and lonesome. Lippincott 1956 251p $6.95   92

1 Frontier and pioneer life—Colorado 2 Colorado

The story of the author's boyhood on the plains of eastern Colorado where his family homesteaded in 1909 when he was nine years old. There were few neighbors and many chores but Hal found much to interest him in the birds, the animals, and the changing seasons. It was a hard life for the family in that dry, short-grass region but they persisted until they gained their own land. (Publisher)

"Hal Borland tells, without a word of self-pity, the story of hardship, courage, honesty and determination which have made America." N Y Her Trib Books

Bourke-White, Margaret

Portrait of myself. Simon & Schuster 1963 383p illus boards $6.95   92

1 Photographers 2 Paralysis agitans

This is the autobiography of Margaret Bourke-White who was "an innovator in the fields of architectural and industrial photography and a magnificent portrayer of people and places. Her devotion to photography led her into dangerous areas, dangerous situations, dangerous wars. From all, she brought back breath-taking pictures and vivid reports. [In this book] she is specific and engrossing about her art, somewhat aloof and completely unsentimental about her personal life, though always honest. . . . She developed Parkinson's disease and underwent surgery and therapy—all of which she describes in report and photograph with the same dispassionate interest in detail she would have for an intricate architectural construction. From her story emerges a woman of iron will, daring, courage, discipline, and dedication." Horn Bk

Bouton, Jim

Ball four; my life and hard times throwing the knuckleball in the Big Leagues; ed. by Leonard Shecter. World Pub. 1970 400p illus $6.95   92

1 Baseball—Biography

"A lively, often funny account of the antics of baseball players, managers and coaches. . . . Sports fans will enjoy his candid inside looks at the world of baseball, and most will be glad that baseball's equation with Mom and Apple Pie has finally been laid to rest." Library J

"His book sparkles with anecdotes, candid profiles of some of baseball's big stars, and some dialog that Ring Lardner or Hemingway might like to have written." Pub W

Bowles, Chester

Promises to keep; my years in public life: 1941-1969. Harper 1971 657p illus $12.95 92

1 U.S.—Politics and government

The author, who served six Presidents and held state and federal offices in wartime and in peace, at home and abroad, describes his experiences. His autobiography is also the story of the currents of change and of the opposition to change that have characterized America since Pearl Harbor. (Publisher)

The author's "experience as Governor of Connecticut makes instructive reading. . . . His career in foreign affairs is somewhat sadder, for, though he did well and greatly enjoyed his terms as Ambassador to India from 1951 to 1953 and again from 1963 to 1969, his instinct and opinions about American foreign policy were at variance with those of the Kennedy and Johnson Administrations. . . . Mr. Bowles' tone, nevertheless, is enthusiastic or hopeful; disillusion and despair are not his stlye. The book, by the way, includes a number of entertaining lifelike portraits of historic figures, ranging from Harold Ickes at his stormiest to Nehru at his most knowledgeable." New Yorker

Boyd, Malcolm

As I live and breathe; stages of an autobiography. Random House [1970 c1969] 276p $6.95   92

1 Clergy

The author, an Episcopalian priest, writes of his life from the time he was giving up his career as a producer-publicist in Hollywood, through his years in seminary training, his first parish, his discovery of the civil rights movement, his interlude at a nightclub in San Francisco, the writing of his book, "Are you running with me, Jesus," his mission to an all-Black parish in Washington, D.C. and his days with students at Yale University. (Publisher)

This "is a story of our times. The vibrations of church and society and race and war are so tightly interwoven that you can never separate them into manageable categories. . . . [Boyd's autobiography] gives you a good sampling of this priest who writes for Variety as well as Ave Maria, The Wall Street Journal and Christian Herald." N Y Times Bk R

Braithwaite, E. R.

To Sir, with love. Prentice-Hall 1959 216p $4.95   92

1 Teaching 2 Negroes in Great Britain 3 London—Social conditions

The "recollections of a cultured young Negro from British Guiana who got a job teaching in a school for difficult teen-agers in London's East End. He was a great success at being both teacher and friend to these young people from a slum neighborhood, but it was not easy, and his experience with anti-Negro prejudice in London made things even harder for him." Pub W

"Mr. Braithwaite is no literary stylist but his narrative shines with simplicity and frankness and, understandably, with occasional flashes of self-righteousness. His personal romance is an adult and moving one, properly subordinated to the story of his first class." N Y Her Trib Books

Brontë, Charlotte

Gaskell, Elizabeth Cleghorn. The life of Charlotte Brontë   92

1 Authors, English

Some editions are:
Dutton (Everyman's lib) $2.75 Introduction by May Sinclair
Oxford Univ. Press (The World's classics) $2.25 With an introduction by Clement Shorter

First published 1857

"In the whole of English biographical literature there is no book that can compare in widespread interest with the 'Life of Charlotte Brontë' by Mrs Gaskell. . . . As far as mere readers are concerned, it may indeed claim its hundreds as against the tens of intrinsically more important rivals. Mrs Gaskell was herself a popular novelist, who commanded a very wide audience. She brought to bear upon the biography of Charlotte Brontë all those literary gifts which had made the charm of her seven volumes of romance. And these gifts were employed upon a romance of real life, not less fascinating than anything which imagination could have furnished. . . . It is quite certain that Charlotte Brontë would not stand on so splendid a pedestal today but for the single-minded devotion of her accomplished biographer." Clement K. Shorter

Brown, Claude

Manchild in the promised land. Macmillan (N Y) 1965 415p $6.95   92

1 Harlem, New York (City)—Social conditions 2 Negroes—Biography

This is "the autobiography of a young Negro raised in Harlem. A realistic description of life in the ghetto. Claude Brown began stealing at the age of five, was taught to rob cash registers by his friends at eight, and progressed steadily through the curriculum of the streets. . . . The core of the book concerns the 'plague' of heroin addiction that swept through Harlem in the 1950's taking the lives of many of Brown's contemporaries. The subject matter of the book is sordid, tragic and compelling." Pub W

Brown, John, 1800-1859

Oates, Stephen B. To purge this land with blood; a biography of John Brown. Harper 1970 434p illus $10   92

1 Abolitionists 2 Negroes—Biography

Based on contemporary letters, diaries, journals, newspapers, published reports, and recollections of eyewitnesses, this book provides a description of Brown's early life and career, as well as an account of his life and its culmination at Harpers Ferry. (Publisher)

"Brown emerges as an orthodox, nineteenth-century New England Calvinist who believed that slavery was a 'great sin against God' and who could feel a divinely appointed mission to end that 'sum of villainies.'" Newsweek

Bibliography included in Notes: p363-415

Browning, Elizabeth (Barrett)

Winwar, Frances. The immortal lovers: Elizabeth Barrett and Robert Browning; a biography. Harper 1950 344p front $7.95   92

1 Browning, Robert 2 Poets, English

The author tells the intertwining story in its entirety, tracing the lives of the Brownings from their separate, but similar, childhoods through their romance and the years of their marriage

"To one of the great love stories of literary history, Frances Winwar has brought not only her thorough knowledge of the setting, the period, the atmosphere of the times, but also flavorful, zestful appreciation of the glamorous romance. One reads the familiar love story of Elizabeth and Robert Browning as though for the first time." Cincinnati

Bibliography: p327-35

Woolf, Virginia. Flush, a biography. Harcourt 1933 185p illus $4.75   92

1 Dogs

A biography of E. B. Browning's dog

"When Flush first penetrates the quiet of Miss Barrett's bedroom, he is 'a very spirited, very inquisitive, very well-bred' young spaniel, but in an instant he surrenders all to his new mistress. And thus it is that the experiences that come to Flush for the rest of his days, are often adroitly revelatory of the life of Elizabeth Barrett Browning. It is, however, as a dissection of a dog's awareness and sensations that this tour de force is so constantly witty, constantly original, and daringly interpretative." N Y Libraries

Browning, Robert

How do I love thee? The love-letters of Robert Browning and Elizabeth Barrett; selected and with an introduction by V. E. Stack. Putnam 1969 xxvi, 230p $5.95   92

First published in England with title: The love-letters of Robert Browning and Elizabeth Barrett

The letters were "written between January, 1845 and September, 1846, when they were secretly married. They are charming letters which really breathe life into that fabled love story. Also included are EBB's 'Sonnets from the Portuguese,' written during the same period." Library J

Sprague, Rosemary. Forever in joy; the life of Robert Browning. Chilton Co. 1965 171p illus $4.95   92

1 Browning, Elizabeth (Barrett) 2 Poets, English

"Robert Browning, who destroyed the majority of his personal papers to prevent his biography from being written, is the subject of this readable study which relies on his poetry and the background of the age to explain his personality and character." Baltimore. Best Bks

"Written in a serious style, with almost no fictionalization and no dialogue." Chicago. Children's Book Center

Bibliography: p161-62

Brueghel, Peeter, the elder

Foote, Timothy. The world of Bruegel, c.1525-1569, by Timothy Foote and the editors of Time-Life Books. Time-Life Bks. [distributed by Little 1968] 192p illus maps (Time-Life Lib. of art) boards $7.95   92

1 Painters, Flemish 2 Painting, Flemish

Text and illustrations portray the work of the 16th century Flemish master who is best known as a "peasant" painter and a landscape artist. The author whose text blends biography and art criticism with history, probes the forces at work in Bruegel's world. (Publisher)

"By comparing Northern and Southern renaissance styles and relating the problems of 16th-Century Northern Europe to those faced by 20th-Century man, [the author] provides the layman with an excellent résumé of Bruegel's art and times." Library J

Bibliography: p187

Bryan, William Jennings

Koenig, Louis W. Bryan; a political biography of William Jennings Bryan. Putnam 1971 736p $14.95   92

1 U.S.—Politics and government

"A thorough, fair-minded biography of William Jennings Bryan [who was] a pioneer of major social and political reforms—women's suffrage, the graduated income tax, the direct election of United States Senators—a humanitarian and a moralist whose ideas influenced much of the legislation that shapes life today in the United States. . . . [The author presents] a full-length portrait, from his birth in an Illinois prairie town to his pathetic death in the wake of the Scopes trial, stressing his education . . . his virtues of compassion, courage and high-mindedness, his limitations in intellectual capacity and curiosity. The stage on which he moved is portrayed in fascinating detail, with a cast of the politicians, journalists and tycoons . . . who made up the world around him." Book of the Month Club News
Bibliographical references in Notes and Sources: p663-719

Buber, Martin

Simon, Charlie May. Martin Buber; wisdom in our time; the story of an outstanding Jewish thinker and humanist. Dutton 1969 191p illus $4.50, lib. bdg. $4.45   92

1 Philosophers, Jewish

This biography of the philosopher describes his boyhood in Lemberg, his university years in Vienna and Berlin, the beginning of his literary and teaching career in Germany, his family life and, finally, his life in Israel from 1939 until his death in 1965. (Publisher)
"A serious and lucid analysis of Buber's philosophy as well as a biography. . . . Dwelling at more length on his writings and on the influence his work had on many prominent people of our time. The tone is reverent, the writing style capable." Chicago. Children's Book Center
Bibliography: p181-83

Buck, Pearl (Sydenstricker)

My several worlds; a personal record. Day 1954 407p $8.95   92

1 Authors, American 2 China

Born of missionary parents and brought up in China the author devotes the major part of this autobiography to a social and political description of China, from the Boxer Rebellion to 1953. The last part of the book tells of her return to the United States, her interest in helping the unwanted children of the world, her work for international understanding. Through it all there are her books and her own family life
"No doubt the immediate popular appeal of her books lay in the color and strangeness of their background, and in her gift for narrative. But Mrs. Buck's real concern has always been to reach across the gap between East and West, to bring the knowledge of each home to the other." N Y Times Bk R

Harris, Theodore F. Pearl S. Buck; a biography by Theodore F. Harris in consultation with Pearl S. Buck. Day 1969-1971 2v front v 1 $8.95, v2 $9.95   92

1 Authors, American

The first volume traces Pearl Buck's life beginning with her early years in China through the time after the Nobel Prize award when she devoted herself largely to her various humanitarian activities. Volume two: her philosophy as expressed in her letters is a select group of letters "along with a few speeches and articles, mostly written in the 1940's and 1950's, to convey her opinions and thinking on such issues as racial prejudice, world peace, religion, the family and marriage, and retarded and displaced children." Library J
Bibliography of books by Pearl S. Buck: [v 1] p367-72

Burns, Robert

Fitzhugh, Robert T. Robert Burns: the man and the poet; a round, unvarnished account. Houghton 1970 508p illus $10   92

1 Poets, Scottish

This biography of the Scottish poet makes "extensive use of quotations—not only from Burns's own writings, but from the letters, journals, and memoirs of his contemporaries. . . . Also included are the texts of a number of . . . poems that influenced Burns, a new analysis of Burns's health by a physician, Burns's autobiographical letter, and evidence concerning the child in Highland Mary's grave." Library J
"Fitzhugh aims to 'deliver a round, unvarnished account' and that he does; his biography is scrupulous, steady, and earthy. There's no whitewashing and such literary criticism as there is 'is' diffidently offered." Book World
Bibliography: p443-82

Burr, Aaron

Parmet, Herbert S. Aaron Burr; portrait of an ambitious man, by Herbert S. Parmet & Marie B. Hecht. Macmillan (N Y) 1967 399p illus $8.95   92

1 Vice-Presidents—U.S. 2 U.S.—Politics and government—1783-1865

The authors draw upon Burr's own journals and letters to describe Burr's role in the Revolutionary War; his success as a politician; his term as Vice-President under Jefferson; his feud and duel with Alexander Hamilton; his effort to start a secession movement; his trial for treason, escape to Europe, and return to America; and his second marriage. (Publisher)
"Fascinating as all revisions of myths must be [this one] makes no attempt to whitewash Burr. . . . Was Burr a child of the Puritan tradition—a grandson of Jonathan Edwards—who mischievously rebounded on his sources? Was he the spirit of the frontier turned a little too recklessly adventurous? Whatever flawed variation he represented, he was, Parmet and Hecht persuasively suggest, less a villain than a near-miss hero." Christian Science Monitor
Bibliography: p377-88

Byrd, Richard E.

Alone; decorations by Richard E. Harrison. Putnam 1938 296p illus maps $6.50 92

1 Antarctic regions 2 Byrd Antarctic Expedition, 2d, 1933-1935 3 Explorers

"An account of Byrd's five month's isolation at Advance Base, the place, far south of Little America and where in 1934 he nearly died. Advance Base was to be an observation post manned by scientists whose task would be to study weather on the polar cap,—but the original plan never developed as the critical ice conditions so exhausted the men that Byrd had to face the choice of giving up the base or else manning it alone. This he did fully conscious of the danger, but determined to find out what lay in the world's darkest dark and coldest cold." Ontario Lib Rev
"This story in its events is a breathless and almost shattering drama, one of the most intense and moving dramas of our own or any time." N Y Her Trib Books

Byron, George Gordon Noël Byron, 6th Baron

Marchand, Leslie A. Byron: a portrait. Knopf 1970 518, xxxiv p illus $13.95   92

1 Poets, English

A condensed rewritten version of the author's three volume study of the poet published in 1957 with title: Byron: a biography
The author traces Byron's life, examines his dramatic career and engaging personality and describes his love affairs, his wanderings and his romantic and adventurous commitment to the cause of Greek independence. (Publisher)
Bibliography: p514-18

Byron, George G. N. B. 6th Baron—*Cont.*

Parker, Derek. Byron and his world. Viking [1969 c1968] 143p illus $6.95   92

1 Poets, English
"A Studio book"
First published 1968 in England
The author "traces Byron's life and literary career, from his childhood years of poverty in Scotland to his death in the fever-ridden swamps of Missolonghi. . . . He shows how Byron, while leading the life of the hero of a romantic novel, was at once a Lothario and a prey to an almost Calvinist conscience—the dichotomy which was at the root of his genius." Publisher's note
Bibliographical note: p141

Caracciola, Rudolf

A racing car driver's world. Farrar, Straus 1961 232p illus $5.95   92

1 Automobile racing—Biography
First published 1958 in Germany
"The autobiography of one of Europe's great racing car champions, finished before his death in 1959 and published with an epilog which summarizes the years following his retirement from competition. The German driver's account of his career, from his first race in 1922 through his final one as a member of the Mercedes-Benz team in 1939, is filled with vivid descriptions of individual courses and events, sidelights on the development of automobile racing, and glimpses of other famous members of the international racing fraternity. Caracciola's complete racing record is appended." Booklist

Carnegie, Andrew

Simon, Charlie May. The Andrew Carnegie story; illus. with photographs. Dutton 1965 224p illus lib. bdg. $4.70   92

1 Philanthropists
"A biography of Andrew Carnegie, great American steel tycoon and philanthropist who began as a bobbin boy in a cotton mill and retired years later to spend some of his great fortune in the pursuit of cultural enrichment for the world." Bk Buyer's Guide

Carver, George Washington

Elliott, Lawrence. George Washington Carver; the man who overcame. Prentice-Hall 1966 256p front $5.95   92

1 Scientists 2 Negroes—Biography
An "attractive biography of the great scientist who spent so many years of dedicated service at Tuskegee Institute. His struggle for education is vividly recounted. And the years when he joined the efforts of Booker T. Washington at Tuskegee from 1896 are described in detail. While his dedication to science is well known, in this volume the readers will also come to understand his grasp of the theory of science as well as its practical aspects. The multi-talented Carver comes to life within the pages of the book." Best Sellers

Holt, Rackham. George Washington Carver; an American biography. Rev. ed. Doubleday 1963 360p illus $4.95   92

1 Scientists 2 Negroes—Biography
First published 1943
Biography of one of the outstanding Negroes of modern times, who was born in slavery, and, at death, had attained distinction as an educator and scientist, director of the department of agricultural science, Tuskegee Institute. His laboratory experiments won him world-wide fame; and his profound knowledge of botany, agriculture, and soil economy enabled him to help his people in the south to better ways of living

Casals, Pablo

Forsee, Aylesa. Pablo Casals: cellist for freedom. Crowell 1965 229p illus $4.50   92

1 Violinists, violoncellists, etc.

Biographical account of Pablo Casals, the Spanish cellist, from his early childhood interest in music to his voluntary exile first to France and then Puerto Rico
"The biography is detailed, serious, and admiring; much of the text, although related to Casals, is interesting general information about the world of music or about the Spanish political scene. A section of photographs is bound into the book; a reading list and an index are appended." Chicago. Children's Book Center

Castro, Fidel

Matthews, Herbert L. Fidel Castro. Simon & Schuster 1969 382p $6.95   92

1 Cuba—History—1959-
A political biography by the former "New York Times reporter who first interviewed [Castro] in the Sierra Maestra mountains in 1957. . . . [It presents the] story of the man, his political philosophy, his plans and hopes for the first communist country in this hemisphere. For ten years . . . Matthews continued to see . . . . [Castro] in Havana. They had long talks about where Castro and Cuba are now headed, about United States policies, and about the world. These talks are reported here. . . . [There are new] details here of Che Guevara, and of other Cuban revolutionary leaders, of the differences among them in the past and at present, and of the strengths and weaknesses of the regime." Publisher's note
Bibliography: p365-67

Catharine of Aragon, consort of Henry VIII, King of England

Roll, Winifred. The pomegranate and the rose; the story of Katharine of Aragon. Prentice-Hall 1970 288p illus maps $4.95   92

1 Great Britain—History—Tudors, 1485-1603
2 Henry VIII, King of England
ISBN 0-13-686238-1
The youngest child of King Ferdinand and Queen Isabella of Spain, Katharine of Aragon was destined to be a political tool. This is the story of her betrothal to Crown Prince Arthur of England, her marriage and widowhood, her second marriage to Henry VIII of England and the subsequent divorce with its far-reaching personal and political implications. (Publisher)
The author "presents a scholarly, documented study, based on 'contemporary or near-contemporary sources' from which she quotes fascinating and often touching passages, which reveal a tragic but not a pathetic woman determined to save her good name and her soul." Horn Bk
Selected reading list: p270-73

Cather, Willa Sibert

Brown, Marion Marsh. Willa Cather; the woman and her works [by] Marion Marsh Brown and Ruth Crone. Scribner 1970 160p $4.50   92

1 Authors, American
Willa Cather grew up with an intense desire to write. This biography describes how she fulfilled this desire as a teacher, a newspaper reporter, a magazine writer and as one of America's foremost novelists
Suggestions for further reading: p157-58

Catherine II, Empress of Russia

Oldenbourg, Zoé. Catherine the Great; tr. from the French by Anne Carter. Pantheon Bks. 1965 378p illus $8.95   92

1 Queens 2 Russia—History
"This picture of the Russian ruler seeks to depict Catherine the woman by concentrating on her early years in which intrigue after intrigue followed this minor German princess. The conflicts surrounding Catherine in this period were such that she had to rule or perish and by demonstrating this fact Zoé Oldenbourg demonstrates that the eventual murder of her husband and her dizzying succession of lovers were only the outward scandalous events at a court and in an era still shockingly brutal and primitive." Pub W

Catherine II, Empress of Russia—*Continued*

"Though she is called Catherine the Great . . . the best thing she ever did was to write her autobiography, in which she described herself with painful honesty and lucidity. By basing herself very largely on the autobiography, Miss Oldenbourg has succeeded in giving a portrait in depth of one of the few tyrants intelligent enough to know what she was doing." N Y Times Bk R

Bibliography: p370-71

Cellini, Benvenuto

The autobiography of Benvenuto Cellini; ed. by Alfred Tamarin; abridged and adapted from the translation by John Addington Symonds. Macmillan (N Y) 1969 164p illus maps $5.95   92

1 Artists, Italian   2 Art, Renaissance

The sixteenth-century sculptor and goldsmith describes life in Renaissance Italy and his adventures and exploits, trials and triumphs, and the behind-the-scenes intrigues of the patrons of the arts whose purse strings controlled the artistic creations of his era. (Publisher)

Cervantes Saavedra, Miguel de

Busoni, Rafaello. The man who was Don Quixote; the story of Miguel Cervantes; written and illus. by Rafaello Busoni, editorially assisted by Johanna Johnston. Prentice-Hall 1958 209p illus $4.95   92

1 Authors, Spanish

"A biography of Miguel Cervantes showing him as the son of an impoverished nobleman, soldier, captive, and in later life as the tax collector and author of 'Don Quixote.' " Huntting

"A rather romanticized but very interesting biography of Cervantes. . . . The author's very lively sketches appear on almost every page." Pub W

Diaz-Plaja, Fernando. Cervantes: the life of a genius; tr. from the Spanish by Sue Matz Soterakos. Scribner 1970 144p $3.95   92

1 Authors, Spanish

"This well-written biography by the author of 'Don Quixote' not only gives in detail the man's eventful life, which was battered by persecution, injustice, and plain bad luck almost until its end, but also serves as an excellent social and political outline of the period. . . . [Included are selections from Cervantes'] writings to show how greatly the author drew upon his own experiences to enrich his narratives and elucidate his ideas." Booklist

Cézanne, Paul

Murphy, Richard W. The world of Cézanne, 1839-1906, by Richard W. Murphy and the editors of Time-Life Books. Time-Life Bks. [distributed by Little 1968] 192p illus maps (Time-Life Lib. of art) boards $7.95   92

1 Painters, French 2 Painting, French

This is a study of the life and work of the artist who influenced Fauvism, Cubism, Expressionism and other 20th century art. (Publisher)

"Chapters of biography and historical and critical commentary alternate with sections of generously captioned illustrations including color reproductions of paintings by Cézanne's contemporaries as well as his own work." Booklist

Bibliography: p187

Charlemagne

Horizon Magazine. Charlemagne, by the editors of Horizon Magazine. Author: Richard Winston; consultant: Harry Bober. Am. Heritage 1968 153p illus map $5.95, lib. bdg. $5.49   92

1 Kings and rulers 2 Holy Roman Empire 3 Civilization, Medieval

"A Horizon Caravel book"

A biography of the Middle Ages ruler who conquered and unified much of Europe, protected Christianity against medieval heresy, established schools and encouraged scholars and artists

"The text in this biography of the great king, emperor, conqueror of Europe in the eighth century is as colorful as the volume's 64 pictures in color. Charlemagne's character as patron of arts and protector of religious faith is also enhanced by the pictures, not only those from contemporary sources, but also modern ones of jewels, art objects, and other treasures. There are 73 additional pictures in black and white." Pub W

For further reading: p148

Chaucer, Geoffrey

Chute, Marchette. Geoffrey Chaucer of England; written and decorated by Marchette Chute. Dutton 1946 347p $6.50   92

1 Poets, English 2 Chaucer, Geoffrey—Contemporary England

A "biography of Chaucer, incorporating all the known facts of his life. It also probes into the reasons why he wrote in English, although he was attached to the court, and French was the language of the court. Includes critical analysis of his writings." Book Rev Digest

Against all the magnificence and pageantry of 14th century England, the author places Chaucer, not simply as poet, but as businessman and diplomat, and chronicles his rise from obscurity to a position of considerable prestige in the court of the king

Selected bibliography: p323-32. Map on lining-papers

Halliday, F. E. Chaucer and his world. Viking [1969 c1968] 144p illus maps $7.50   92

1 Poets, English 2 Chaucer, Geoffrey—Contemporary England 3 England—Social life and customs

"A Studio book"

First published 1968 in England

"Chaucer spent all his life in royal service—under Edward III, Richard II and Henry IV successively. Courtier, soldier, diplomat and civil servant by turns, he was at the centre of events . . . in that troubled age of luxury and corruption, foreign war and domestic revolt. It is in this context that Mr Halliday traces Chaucer's life and his poetic career." Publisher's note

"The pictures are good in general, although they suffer the bane of all such low-priced volumes which depend on plates, in that the illustrations are much too small. . . . None are in color, again a great loss. The text weaves the poet's biography with his works, always with intelligence and skilled prose." Library J

A short bibliography: p129. Glossary: p132

Chennault, Anna

A thousand springs; the biography of a marriage; introduction by Lin Yutang. Eriksson 1962 318p illus $5.95   92

1 Chennault, Claire Lee 2 China

"A tribute to her late husband, by General Claire Chennault's widow, an account of their brief marriage, cut short by the General's death from cancer in 1958, and Mrs. Chennault's story of her own schoolgirl experiences in wartime China, fleeing the Japanese. . . . It is also a . . . report of her husband's war service, his intramural conflict with General Stilwell, and his personal efforts, exerted mostly through his Chinese airline, in opposition to communism in China after the war." Pub W

"As a chapter of Chinese history, or even as biography, it may sometimes fall short of impartiality. As a love story, it has its own perfection." N Y Her Trib Books

Chiang, Kai-shek

Curtis, Richard. Chiang Kai-shek. Hawthorn Bks. 1969 272p illus $5.95   92

1 China—History

Chiang, Kai-shek—*Continued*

Against the background of the history of modern China this biography "traces Chiang's life from his humble birth to his island exile on Formosa. It examines Chiang's early influences and motivations, his conversion to the philosophy of Dr. Sun, his relationship with the Communists and his rule of Nationalist China." Huntting

"The biography is well documented, is illustrated by selected photographs and has a bibliography and index, as well as a convenient listing of the proper names (Chinese) which appear in the book with a brief note on each." Best Sellers

Chisholm, Shirley

Unbought and unbossed. Houghton 1970 177p $4.95 　　　　　　　　　　　　**92**

1 U.S.—Politics and government—1961- 2 Politics, Practical 3 Negroes—Biography

The author describes "her life, her career, her opinions of the political scene in the United States, and her thoughts on some of the major issues of our . . . time. She discusses . . . the militant young, black politicians, the subjugation of women, and the lack of response and sensitivity on the part of those in power." Sat R

"Topical, lucidly written autobiography and assessment of her role by the first black Congresswoman in U.S. History. Provides a vivid account of how both roles of inferior status—female and black—affect what it is she has done, is doing, and will do to change the way the leaders of this country deal with the citizenry." Choice

Churchill, Clementine Ogilvy (Hozier) Spencer, Lady

Fishman, Jack. My darling Clementine; the story of Lady Churchill; with an introduction by Eleanor Roosevelt. McKay 1963 384p illus $5.95 　　　　　　　　　　　　**92**

1 Churchill, Sir Winston Leonard Spencer

"From her first meeting with the young Churchill and his proposal for her in the gardens of Blenheim Palace, the story of Clementine Churchill covers their lives together. It is filled with intimate details of their days of struggle, disaster, and glory." Publisher's note

"It has many appealing pictures, including one memorable sequence of six showing Lady Churchill's expressive face when her husband refers to her during a speech." Pub W

Bibliography: p375-76

Churchill, Jennie (Jerome) Lady Randolph Churchill

Martin, Ralph G. Jennie: the life of Lady Randolph Churchill; v 1 The romantic years, 1854-1895. Prentice-Hall 1969 404p illus $8.95 　　　　　　　　　　　　**92**

1 Great Britain—Social life and customs
SBN 13-509737-1

"This is the first volume of a proposed two-volume biography of the wife of Lord Randolph Churchill and mother of Sir Winston Churchill." Book Rev Digest

The author "has produced a volume in which not only Jennie, but the world in which she lived, dance before the reader in magnificent display. [He] makes one realize the extraordinary impact this girl from Brooklyn made upon the English scene. Every famous political figure of the time appears in these pages." Book World

Includes bibliographical references

Churchill, Sir Winston Leonard Spencer

Churchill, Randolph S. Winston S. Churchill; illus. with photographs and maps. Houghton 1966-1967 2v illus maps ea $10　**92**

1 Statesmen, British

Volume one and two of a projected five volume biography; volume three, by Martin Gilbert is entered below

Contents: v 1 Youth, 1874-1900; v2 The young statesman, 1901-1914

Written by Sir Winston's son, the data is based largely on his father's letters and papers. They trace the statesman's life from boyhood, youth and his early political career through his post as First Lord of the Admiralty and his efforts in preparing the fleet on the eve of the First World War

Gilbert, Martin. Winston S. Churchill, v3: The challenge of war, 1914-1916; illus. with photographs and maps. Houghton 1971 xxxvi, 988p illus maps $15　　　　　**92**

1 Statesmen, British

This third volume of a projected five volume biography; volume one and two by Randolph S. Churchill entered above

This volume "takes the story of Winston Churchill's life from the eve of war in 1914 to his return from the trenches in 1916 and his repeated attempts to regain his lost influence." Publisher's note

Life (Periodical) The unforgettable Winston Churchill; giant of the century; by the editors of Life. Time, inc. [distributed by Silver] 1965 128p illus (A Life News bk) pa $1.95　　　　　　　　　　　　**92**

1 Statesmen, British

"This commemorative volume begins with a twelve-page, full-color account of the first state funeral ever granted to any commoner other than the great Gladstone. The balance of the book represents a review of Sir Winston's life and is lavishly illustrated with over 200 pictures." Huntting

The Times, London. The Churchill years, 1874-1965, by the editors of the Viking Press; text by the Times of London; with a foreword by Lord Butler of Saffron Walden. Viking 1965 264p illus $16.50　　　　　**92**

1 Statesmen, British 2 Great Britain—Politics and government—20th century

A collection of "photographs of a heroic and photogenic man, from childhood to old age. Some of the text and many of the captions incorporate quotations from Churchill's speeches and writings. This partly explains the cumulatively moving effect of the text." Pub W

Clemens, Samuel Langhorne

The autobiography of Mark Twain; including chapters now published for the first time, as arranged and ed. with an introduction and notes, by Charles Neider. Harper 1959 xxvi, 388p illus $10　　　　**92**

1 Authors, American

"In this third working of the materials left by Clemens as his autobiography, the editor has selected the items he considers most truly autobiographical, has used some material not used by either Paine in 1924 or DeVoto in 1940, and has arranged the selections in coordinated chronological order, ending with the death of Clemens' daughter Jean in December, 1909. Much of the material is anecdotal and reveals Clemens' distinctive personality." Booklist

"The whole adds up to a book filled with richness of humor and tragedy, of disappointment and triumph, of sweetness and bitterness, and all in that unsurpassed American prose." N Y Her Trib Books

Kaplan, Justin. Mr Clemens and Mark Twain; a biography. Simon & Schuster 1966 424p illus $7.95　　　　　　　　　**92**

1 Authors, American

Awarded the Pulitzer Prize for biography, 1967

"Although this biography of Mark Twain begins when Twain is 31 . . . the book is a full account of Twain, his life and his work, related both to his early years and to the 'Gilded Age' of his mature life." Pub W

"A finely rendered portrait of a man and a personality, not an anatomy chart." N Y Rev of Books

Bibliography included in Notes: p389-410

Clemens, Samuel L.—*Continued*

Wecter, Dixon. Sam Clemens of Hannibal. Houghton 1952 335p front $5.50   **92**

1 Authors, American

"The first volume of what promised to be the definitive biography of Mark Twain until the author, who was working on the second volume at the time, died. . . . This one takes Sam Clemens only to his eighteenth year, when he left his home town in Missouri, but it covers the period that was the fountainhead of Mark Twain's best writing." New Yorker

"As literary editor of the Mark Twain estate, Wecter had access to the priceless wealth of unpublished Mark Twain papers. He drew upon them with fine discrimination." Chicago Sunday Tribune

Bibliography: p317-22

Cleveland, Grover, President U.S.

Tugwell, Rexford G. Grover Cleveland. Macmillan (N Y) 1968 298p illus $6.95   **92**

1 U.S.—Politics and government—1865-1898
2 Presidents—U.S.

The author's "well-written, keen interpretation of Cleveland's character and his record as President amply justify a fresh analysis of an enigmatic personality. Cleveland is portrayed as industrious, dependable, and above all honest but also stubborn, ill-informed, and ill-prepared to cope with the complex problems confronting him during his two terms in the White House. Though even his virtues were sometimes tragically turned by circumstances into faults, he is credited with restoring integrity to politics." Booklist

Cocteau, Jean

Steegmuller, Francis. Cocteau; a biography. Little 1970 583p illus $12.50   **92**

National book award, 1970
"An Atlantic Monthly Press book"

A life of the man who spent fifty-eight years of his life in the arts, as a poet, novelist, playwright, and filmmaker. It discusses his work in these various fields and the contradictions and paradoxes of his private life. (Publisher)

The author "probes for the facts and tries to see beyond the legend of Cocteau. His book is vastly entertaining and informative, written stylishly and wittily. . . . The demythified Jean Cocteau who emerges from this book is a complex, fascinating, exasperating, and all in all very human figure who must resemble the 'real' Cocteau closely. It is a major biographical achievement." Sat R

Bibliography: p531-39

Cody, William Frederick

Buffalo Bill's life story (Colonel W. F. Cody); illus. by N. C. Wyeth. Rinehart 328p illus lib. bdg. $3.59   **92**

1 The West—History 2 Frontier and pioneer life

Reprint of a book published 1920 by Cosmopolitan Book with title: Autobiography of Buffalo Bill

"Story of adventurous days in the old West, with the author as pony express rider, Indian fighter, buffalo hunter, army scout, and showman. An interesting epitome of the transition of the West from wilderness conditions to civilized life within a single lifetime." N Y State Lib

Columbus, Christopher

Morison, Samuel Eliot. Admiral of the ocean sea; a life of Christopher Columbus; maps by Erwin Raisz; drawings by Bertram Greene. Little 1942 xx, 680p illus maps $15   **92**

1 Explorers 2 America—Discovery and exploration

Awarded Pulitzer Prize, 1943
"An Atlantic Monthly Press book"

A condensation of the author's two-volume work with same title also published in 1942 but now out of print

"An authoritative . . . biography of Columbus which is also decidedly original in its emphasis on the ability of Columbus as seaman and navigator and in the amount of space given to tracing the routes of the voyages and landings." Library J

"Scholarly but highly readable biography." Good Reading

Morison, Samuel Eliot. Christopher Columbus, mariner; maps by Erwin Raisz. Little 1955 224p maps $4.95   **92**

1 Explorers 2 America—Discovery and exploration

A rewritten text of the author's "Admiral of the ocean sea" his definitive biography of Columbus published 1942, entered above

"Dispensing with footnotes and other scholarly paraphernalia but maintaining a primarily nautical approach, [Mr Morison] re-creates Columbus' life and voyages in a . . . narrative that evidences his knowledge of fifteenth-century navigational methods and his personal familiarity with the routes which Columbus followed." Booklist

"An old familiar story is made fresh and exciting under the skilled hand of a scholarly historian." Current Hist

Conrad, Joseph

Gurko, Leo. The two lives of Joseph Conrad. Crowell 1965 209p $3.75   **92**

1 Authors, English 2 Seamen

"Throughout this story of Conrad's life, Mr. Gurko points to many true situations that later appeared in the author's books. Conrad is presented to us as a man who excelled in both the physical sphere (as an expert seaman) and the world of the mind (as a gifted writer). . . . [The author also analyzes] many of [Conrad's] well-known and lesser-known works." Publisher's note

A selected bibliography: p198-202

Cook, James, 1728-1779

Villiers, Alan. Captain James Cook. Scribner 1967 307p illus maps $7.50   **92**

1 Explorers 2 Voyages around the world

James Cook, in the author's opinion, "is 'the greatest ship seaman there ever was.' This account of the voyages is a very human story of captain and crew and of the scientists who accompanied Cook." Pub W

"In his explanation of naval affairs, seamanship, and navigation, Villiers, well qualified by his own career as a deep-water sailing ship man, makes his most valuable contribution. A chapter summarizing the historiography of the Pacific Ocean to 1768 is helpful. . . . The style, always pleasing, ranges from the poetic to the conversational, with liberal dashes of sea-faring phrases." Choice

Copland, Aaron

Dobrin, Arnold. Aaron Copland: his life and times. Crowell 1967 211p illus $4.50   **92**

1 Composers, American

"A biography that is particularly interesting because it reflects, in Copland's career, the awakening interest in innovatory composition, both in the United States and abroad. There is little melodrama in Copland's life: he recognized his own goals when a boy and never deviated from the path; he didn't achieve instant or complete success, but there were always those who recognized his abilities, and by the 1930's Copland was well on his way to financial stability and an eminent position as a composer and critic. Not an effusive book but a warm and enthusiastic one; the subject emerges as a vivid personality despite the book's emphasis on musical achievement." Chicago. Children's Book Center

Musical works by Aaron Copland: p197-201. Books by Aaron Copland: p205

Crane, Stephen

Franchere, Ruth. Stephen Crane; the story of an American writer. Crowell 1961 216p $4.50   **92**

1 Authors, American

Crane, Stephen—*Continued*

"Covering the principal events of the American writer's life, from the time he was a restless college student already frequenting police courts and slums in an effort to observe and depict life realistically to his early death from tuberculosis, this perceptive biography shows the genesis of [his most famous works]. . . . Throughout it reveals Crane as a talented, improvident, and sometimes irresponsible nonconformist, tormented by inner conflicts but passionately dedicated to writing. A difficult subject portrayed with understanding, honesty, and good taste." Booklist
Sources: p215

Cromwell, Oliver

Ashley, Maurice, ed. Cromwell. Prentice-Hall 1969 177p (Great lives observed) $5.95
92

1 Great Britain—Politics and government—Civil War and Commonwealth, 1642-1660

"A Spectrum book"
A compilation of "representative opinions on the character and accomplishments of the seventeenth-century British military and political leader beginning with a selection of passages from Cromwell's letters and speeches. [The editor] includes views of Cromwell by . . . his contemporaries and appraisals of Cromwell's leadership by eighteenth-, nineteenth-, and twentieth-century historians. . . . [He] furnishes an analytical introduction and chronology of the life of Oliver Cromwell, an afterword, and a bibliographical note." Booklist

Curie, Marie (Sklodowska)

Curie, Eve. Madame Curie, a biography; tr. by Vincent Sheean. Doubleday 1949 [c1937] 412p illus $5.95
92

1 Scientists

First published 1937
"Into the writing of this definitive biography of the great woman scientist, Eve Curie has brought the skill of a trained writer, the research of a scientist, and the love of a daughter. She describes her mother's early years in which she surmounted all hardships to pursue the course she had chosen, then the tragic death of her husband, and finally her pressing on to new and greater heights of achievement, totally oblivious to fame, honour and health. The world knows the record of her career, but for the first time reads of her background and private life." Ontario Lib Rev
"One does not even feel it necessary to discount statements because of a daughter's prejudice or affection. Rather it seems as if some of the keen judgment which the mother displayed in science has influenced her daughter in her selection of material and in the depth of insight she displays in interpreting her mother's character." Scientific Bk Club R

Custer, Elizabeth (Bacon)

Boots and saddles; or, Life in Dakota with General Custer
92

1 Custer, George Armstrong 2 Frontier and pioneer life 3 U.S. Army—Military life

Some editions are:
Harper $4.95
Univ. of Okla. Press (The Western frontier lib) $2.95 With an introduction by Jane R. Stewart

First published 1885
"The honeymoon of Elizabeth Bacon and George Armstrong Custer was interrupted in 1864 by his call to duty. She begged to go along, and from that time on she accompanied Custer on his major assignments, aside from the Indian campaigns. This is her journal." McClurg. Book News

Randall, Ruth Painter. I Elizabeth. . . . Little 1966 260p illus $4.50
92

1 Custer, George Armstrong

"A biography of the girl who married General George Armstrong Custer of 'Custer's Last Stand.'" Title page
"Based on the writings and diaries of Elizabeth Custer, this is a vivid account of her life,

a . . . portrait of the tragic years of the Civil War and the difficult times of the reconstruction in which she lived." Huntting
Bibliographical references in Acknowledgements

Dahl, Borghild

I wanted to see; with a foreword by William L. Benedict. Macmillan (N Y) 1944 210p $4.95
92

1 Blind

"The author was nearly blind from childhood. . . . Despite her handicap she finished her college course, became a teacher in high school and then college; lectured, and reviewed books. Finally two operations at the Mayo clinic gave her more sight than she has ever had before. Her book describes her life from childhood, to the operation which saved her sight." Book Rev Digest
"Told modestly and with no plea for sympathy, but the total effect of it should communicate something of her heroic determination to any person who labors under a handicap." Christian Century

Dai, Hsiao-ai

Bennett, Gordon A. Red Guard; the political biography of Dai Hsiao-ai, by Gordon A. Bennett and Ronald N. Montaperto. Doubleday 1971 xx, 267p $5.95
92

1 China (People's Republic of China)—Politics and government 2 Communism—China (People's Republic of China)

This is an account of the Chinese Cultural Revolution by a Red Guard Student Activist leader. Told largely in Dai's own words this book "traces his initial enthusiasm for Chairman Mao's Revolution, his trips across China to mass demonstrations in Peking, his growing role as a faction leader when infighting developed between competing groups of Red Guards, and the ultimate disillusionment that led him to leave family and comrades behind and defect to Hong Kong." Publisher's note
"Millions of students were sent mysteriously on the rampage, tormenting innocent people, destroying works of art, defying Communist authorities. Dai Hsiao-ai was one of those students. His story is neither pleasant nor easy reading. Yet it succeeds far better than anything yet published in transforming that frightening mass of unhinged automatons into boys and girls with human faces." Time
Selected bibliography: p255-56

Dalai Lama XIV

My land and my people, by His Holiness, the Dalai Lama of Tibet. McGraw 1962 271p illus map boards $7.95
92

1 Tibet—Politics and government
The Dalai Lama of Tibet relates the story of his brief tumultuous reign climaxed by the appalling humiliation and systematic murder of his people by the Communists. He writes of the simple Tibetan life into which he was born, his unique boyhood when he ruled with the help of a regent, and how he struggled during the 1950's to preserve his country from the Chinese Communists only to face defeat in the end and exile in India. (Publisher)
This memoir "is the chronicle of a national tragedy. Yet it is also a most inspiring book for it relates this story in a spirit of tolerance and gentleness." Sat R

Darrow, Clarence Seward

The story of my life. Scribner [1965 c1960] 495p pa $3.95
92

1 Lawyers 2 Trials
SBN 684-71745-X
"The Scribner library"
First published 1932
"The story of his great cases—Eugene Debs, Haywood, Moyer and Pettibone, the McNamaras, Loeb-Leopold, Dayton—his opinions on crime and punishment and other problems, and the personality of the man, cynical yet compassionate, make this an unusual autobiography." Wis Lib Bul
This book will give students of history, law, and crime a first-hand account of some prominent events in American life

Darrow, Clarence S.—*Continued*

Gurko, Miriam. Clarence Darrow. Crowell 1965 280p $4.50   92

1 Lawyers 2 Trials

"Biography of a famous trial lawyer which, after describing his small town origins and slow-starting legal career, concentrates on his most famous cases, including his defense of Debs, Haywood, Leopold and Loeb, and Scopes. In discussing these cases, the author makes clear the principles behind each and explains the background of the issues, which usually involved causes unpopular in Darrow's time." Booklist

"The book is worth reading for the description of the Scopes trial alone." Chicago. Children's Book Center

Selected bibliography: p269-72

Darwin, Charles Robert

Horizon Magazine. Charles Darwin and The origin of species, by the editors of Horizon Magazine. Author: Walker Karp; consultant: J. W. Burrow. Am. Heritage 1968 153p illus maps boards $5.95, lib. bdg. $5.49   92

1 Naturalists 2 Evolution

"A Horizon Caravel book"

This biography of the naturalist Charles Darwin "is the story of one man's devotion to science and his courage in presenting a new and almost incredible theory about man's origins." Publisher's note

A "beautifully illustrated book. . . . Students of biology should find [it] informative and intriguing." Best Sellers

Further reading: p150

Huxley, Julian. Charles Darwin and his world, by Julian Huxley and H. B. D. Kettlewell. Viking 1965 144p illus map $6.50   92

1 Naturalists

"A Studio book"

"This brief biographical sketch of Darwin, based on his original notebooks and published works as well as the recollections of his granddaughter, Lady Barlow, possesses the authenticity and unadorned factual literary style characteristic of two eminent biologists who have the necessary depth of background to produce a scholarly work of this nature. The reader should have a general background in the natural sciences and in history of science to appreciate fully this appraisal of Darwin the man, his education, his contemporaries and professional associates, his life, and his work. The appendices contain a chronology of the important events in Darwin's life, explanations of the illustrations, and an index." Science Bks

Davis, Sammy

Yes I can; the story of Sammy Davis, Jr. by Sammy Davis, Jr. and Jane & Burt Boyar. Farrar, Straus 1965 612p illus $7.95   92

1 Entertainers 2 Negro actors

"Early in his life Sammy Davis, Jr. decided not to live his life as a 'Negro,' but as a 'man,' and it has made 'Sammy run' through a gamut of experiences; tragic accident, conversion to Judaism, glittering Broadway success, marriage to a lovely white woman. The raw nerves show in this fast paced life story, at once successful and tragic." Baltimore. Best Bks

Dayan, Moshe

Moshe Dayan; a portrait; ed. by Pinchas Jurman. Dodd [1969 c1968] unp illus $10 92

First published 1968 in Israel

"This pictorial biography tells in photographs, quotations from its subject, and [additional text providing] . . . historical continuity the story of Moshe Dayan . . . who, as one of Israel's . . . leaders, has participated in the critical periods of the history of his nation." Publisher's note

"An unusually good pictorial biography of the Israeli military leader, victor in the Arab war, currently a major figure in Israeli political life. . . . The large-format book vividly captures the sweep of Dayan's life. . . . The excellent photographs are informal, candid and revealing of the man's dynamic character; they are necessarily of varying sizes and quality, but are on the whole well reproduced and arranged." Pub W

Debs, Eugene Victor

Radosh, Ronald, ed. Debs. Prentice-Hall 1971 (Great lives observed) 181p $5.95   92

1 Socialism—U.S.

SBN 13-197681-8

"A Spectrum book"

This book "combines the intimacy of autobiography, the immediacy of eyewitness observation, and the objectivity of modern scholarship. . . . [It] presents Eugene Debs's own words, the views of his contemporaries, and analyses in retrospect by leading historians and political scientists." Publisher's note

Includes bibliographical references

De Mille, Agnes

And promenade home; with photographs. Little 1958 301p illus $6.50   92

1 Ballet 2 Dancers

"An Atlantic Monthly Press book"

A continuation of the autobiography of the American dancer and choreographer which was begun in "dance of the piper," listed below

This book is the account of Agnes de Mille's war-time romance and marriage to Walter F. Prude, and of the work she has done in the maturity of her career. It is also the story, as she writes, "of the conflict between the life of a woman as wife and as artist." (Publisher)

Dance to the piper. Little 1952 342p illus $6.50   92

1 Ballet 2 Dancers

"An Atlantic Monthly Press book"

Autobiography of a "choreographer who introduced a new concept of dance to the American stage. Tells of her many ups and downs, and includes descriptions of Hollywood in its infancy. Brimming with famous names, and fascinating backgrounds. The author is the niece of Cecil B. de Mille, and the granddaughter of Henry George." Huntting

"Miss De Mille's history of a triumphant career is rich, racy, and often hilarious, yet it is frank in its recital of the arduous training, the effort, and the discouragements that attend the dancer's climb to success." U S Quarterly Bk R

De Valera, Eamonn, President Ireland

Steffan, Jack. The Long Fellow; the story of the great Irish patriot, Eamon De Valera. Macmillan (N Y) 1966 xxv, 197p illus $3.95, lib. bdg. $3.94   92

1 Ireland—Presidents 2 Ireland—History

Eamonn de Valera "who is the 'long fellow' of this book, was brought up on the Irish legend that Ireland's salvation would come from Spain. Born of Irish and Spanish parents in America, de Valera has proved the legend to be true. The whole story of the country's half century of struggle for freedom is told through the life of her great patriot and leader." Huntting

Glossary: p185-89. Selected bibliography: p190-93

Devlin, Bernadette

The price of my soul. Knopf 1969 224p $5.95   92

1 Northern Ireland—Politics and government

The author "tells about her family, her girlhood, her schooling with the nuns and at college, her Catholicism, her political awakening in the student movement culminating in the bloody Londonderry march . . . [her] entry into the House of Commons . . . [and] her days and nights on the barricades in August 1969 as the frustration of Northern Ireland's Catholics finally burst forth into active protest." Publisher's note

Devlin, Bernadette—*Continued*
This "is a narrative in which bitterness, understandable bitterness is offset by charm and a genuine sense of the comic. The author is to be commended for this, her first work to appear in print." Best Sellers

Dickens, Charles
Becker, May Lamberton. Introducing Charles Dickens; illus. by Oscar Ogg. Dodd 1940 250p illus $4   **92**
1 Authors, English
"A delightful biography which brings to life the personality of the man and shows how the fusion of his genius, his circumstances, and the England of his day created . . . [his] novels." Booklist

Priestley, J. B. Charles Dickens; a pictorial biography. Viking [1962 c1961] 144p illus $6.95   **92**
1 Authors, English
"A Studio book"
First published 1961 in England
"A brief account of the tribulations that turned Charles Dickens into a humorous but compassionate social commentator by the contemporary novelist often likened to him. With 132 gravure illustrations." Bk Buyer's Guide
"Appended are a chronological list of events in Dickens' life, a series of notes on the pictures within the book, and an index of names. The book would be valuable for the illustrations alone; it would be a wonderfully stimulating biography were it without illustration." Chicago. Children's Book Center

Wagenknecht, Edward. The man Charles Dickens; a Victorian portrait. New & rev. ed. Univ. of Okla. Press 1966 269p illus $5.95   **92**
1 Authors, English
First published 1929 by Houghton
"An interpretation, or psychography—as the author terms it—of Dicken's character. Bits of personal incident in the man's daily life, his social relationships, his unhappy love affairs, his individual habits and peculiarities, are the material with which the biographer works." Book Rev Digest
"Despite all the flourishes, it is a sane and essentially lucid series of questions and answers about Dickens's character and personality." Spring'd Republican
Bibliography: p249-58

Dickinson, Emily
Longsworth, Polly. Emily Dickinson; her letter to the world. Crowell 1965 170p $3.50   **92**
1 Poets, American
"The important forces in Emily Dickinson's life—her Puritan background, her family, her friends, and her beloved books—are woven into a [biography that includes brief selections of her poetry]." Publisher's note
"A distinguished biography, deceptively simple to read but offering something new on each rereading." Book Week
Reading list: p162-64

Di Maggio, Joseph Paul
Silverman, Al. Joe Di Maggio: the golden year, 1941. Prentice-Hall 1969 234p illus $5.95   **92**
1 Baseball—Biography
SBN 13-510032-1
The author tells "the story of Joe's golden year, 1941, when he hit safely in 56 straight games. . . . He begins with the streak's beginning. The interwoven chapters flash back to his boyhood, his first professional game, his rookie year with the Yankees." Pub W
"The suspense, the excitement, and the mounting tension of the year . . . are vividly conveyed. . . . The book is, however, not improved by sections that move back in time to another segment of Di Maggio's career, or by the staccato interpolations, here and there, of a page of headlines and quotations reflecting

events then current. Game descriptions are good, and the author establishes Di Maggio's character deftly, although there is a minimum of personal material in the text. Statistical tables are appended." Chicago. Children's Book Center

Disney, Walt
Schickel, Richard. The Disney version; the life, times, art and commerce of Walt Disney. Simon & Schuster 1968 384p $6.50   **92**
1 Moving picture industry
This "revealing biographical narrative is interlaced with pointed social and aesthetic insight into the America that made the man who, in turn, projected upon it so much of his own personality." McClurg. Book News
The author "has not written the last word on Disney but he conceives a view of Disney that shows his many dimensions and many contradictions. Disney comes out at the end larger than the book, and Mr. Schickel deserves vast credit for this fact. He has demeaned the man, but he has also seen positive values along with the contradictions." America
Bibliographical note: p367-74

Dobie, J. Frank
Some part of myself. Little 1967 282p illus $7.50   **92**
1 Ranch life 2 Texas
"The 'some part' of Texas' great collector of western stories and legends is his youth—a ranch boyhood in the brush country of southwest Texas at the turn of the century. This major section of the [autobiography] is a grand nostalgic memoir of peaceful times, rough but beautiful country, hard work, good eating, and fine parents. . . . The Dobies' life was not the wild shoot-'em-up ranch life of TV, yet it had flavor and gusto, and Dobie tells many robust, salty, true stories of Texas neighbors." Pub W

Dooley, Thomas A.
Dr Tom Dooley's three great books; Deliver us from evil, The edge of tomorrow, The night they burned the mountain. Farrar, Straus [1960] 383p illus map boards $7.95   **92**
1 Physicians 2 Hospitals—Laos 3 Laos—Social conditions 4 Vietnam 5 Refugees, Vietnamese
First published separately in 1956, 1958 and 1960 respectively
In the three books Dr Dooley describes his experiences helping his fellow men in southeastern Asia. In Vietnam in 1954 and 1955 he worked as a U.S. Navy doctor to help the refugees fleeing the Communists when Indochina was divided. In 1956 he set up a medical mission in Laos and later established hospitals in other parts of the country

Doss, Helen
The family nobody wanted. Little 1954 267p $5.95   **92**
1 Adoption
Several years ago Carl Doss, a Methodist minister, and his wife Helen adopted a baby boy. Now they have a dozen children—all adopted, although considered "unadoptable" because of mixed racial parentage. The author tells how these children all fit into one happy family

Douglas, Wiliam O.
Of men and mountains. Harper 1950 338p front $7.95   **92**
1 Mountaineering 2 Cascade Range
"An informal autobiography of Supreme Court Justice Douglas. The book stresses his experiences as mountaineer and fisherman, and the years of his boyhood in Yakima, Washington. There is very little space given to his legal work, the S.E.C., or his work in the Supreme Court." Book Rev Digest

Douglas, William O.—*Continued*

"There are many good stories of mountain rambles, and one hair-raising passage on rock climbing I found, to my taste . . . too much botanical cataloguing. But to compensate, there are good backwoods anecdotes and football character sketches." N Y Times Bk R
　Glossary: p330-38. Maps on lining-papers

Douglass, Frederick

Life and times of Frederick Douglass; ed. and abridged by Genevieve S. Gray; illus. by Scott Duncan. Grosset 1970 181p illus $4.50, lib. bdg. $4.59　　　　92
　1 Slavery in the U.S. 2 Abolitionists 3 Negroes —Biography
　Abridged edition of the author's autobiography as adapted from his: My bondage and my freedom
　"This classic autobiography of a runaway slave carries all of the impact of Frederick Douglass' turbulent life, including his relationship with John Brown's Raiders, his activity as an abolitionist, his recruitment of Negro troops and his significance as an adviser to President Lincoln." News of Bks

Bontemps, Arna. Free at last; the life of Frederick Douglass; illus. with photographs. Dodd 1971 310p illus map $7.95　　　92
　1 Abolitionists 2 Negroes—Biography
　ISBN 0-396-06308-X
　This is a biography of Frederick Douglass, a fugitive slave who became a leader of the abolitionist movement. At various times in his life he was an orator, journalist, revolutionary and statesman; he was also constantly involved in agitation for racial and sexual equality, Irish freedom, and temperance

Hoexter, Corinne K. Black crusader: Frederick Douglass; illus. with photographs and prints. Rand McNally 1970 224p illus $4.95　　　92
　1 Slavery in the U.S. 2 Abolitionists 3 Negroes—Biography
　This biography of Frederick Douglass examines his life from his early harrowing adventures as a slave to his years as United States Minister to Haiti. The author presents the many-faceted career of the Black abolitionist as lecturer, activist, editor, public servant, and spokesman for many causes, including universal education and women's rights. (Publisher)
　"Interesting not only as a portrait of a courageous, dedicated man, but also as a history of the abolitionist movement in nineteenth-century America." Booklist
　Bibliography: p215-18

Quarles, Benjamin, ed. Frederick Douglass. Prentice-Hall 1968 184p (Great lives observed) $5.95　　　92
　1 Slavery in the U.S. 2 Abolitionists 3 Negroes—Biography
　"A Spectrum book"
　The story of the famous Negro abolitionist, who had himself been a slave, presented in his own words, in the views of his contemporaries, and analyzed in retrospect by leading historians and political scientists. (Publisher)
　"The editor summarizes Douglass' life in the introduction and, in an afterword, effectively shows Douglass' influence on the current civil rights movement. Chronology of the life of Frederick Douglass. Bibliographical note." Booklist

Doyle, Sir Arthur Conan

Hardwick, Michael. The man who was Sherlock Holmes [by] Michael and Mollie Hardwick. Doubleday 1964 92p illus $3.50　　　92
　1 Authors, English
　This dual profile of Sir Arthur Conan Doyle and Sherlock Holmes, his literary creation, shows how the author "developed the names and attributes of Sherlock Holmes and Doctor Watson, and . . . how Doyle pursued justice

personally in behalf of hundreds of people who came to him for help in criminal matters." Publisher's note

Dreyfus, Alfred

Werstein, Irving. I accuse; the story of the Dreyfus case; illus. with photographs. Messner 1967 191p illus $3.95, lib. bdg. $3.64　　　92
　1 Treason 2 France—History—Third Republic, 1870-1940
　"On December 22, 1894, a French military court declared Captain Alfred Dreyfus guilty of selling military secrets to Germany . . . and sentenced [him] to life imprisonment in the . . . penal colony of Devil's Island. The Dreyfus Case seemed ended. But in reality it had only just begun. For in the decade to follow, the question of Alfred Dreyfus' guilt was to divide the . . . French nation into two bitterly opposing camps. . . . [This is] the story of the eventual vindication of Dreyfus and of those who risked all to aid him." Publisher's note

Du Bois, William Edward Burghardt

Lacy, Leslie Alexander. Cheer the lonesome traveler; the life of W. E. B. Du Bois. Illus. by James Barkley and with photographs. Dial Press 1970 183p illus $4.95　　92
　1 Negroes—Biography
　This biography of the famous Black scholar, writer, civil rights leader, and spokesman for Africa and persons of African descent, attempts to show the relevance of his beliefs and teachings to the present-day Black movement. It runs from Du Bois' birth in New England in 1868 to his death in Ghana in 1963
　"Late in life . . . William Du Bois became a communist. This action, like others in his career, the biographer neither defends nor apologizes for, but attempts to interpret. A good study of one of the greatest black leaders." Sat R
　Includes bibliography of books and articles by and about Du Bois

Dumas, Alexandre, 1802-1870

Maurois, Andre. Alexandre Dumas; a great life in brief. Knopf 1955 [c1954] 198p (Great lives in brief) $3.95　　　92
　1 Authors, French
　Translated from the French by Jack Palmer White
　Dumas, as the author says "was a hero out of his own novels: naïve, phenomenal, charming and outsize. At 28 he was already the most celebrated playwright of his time. Within a few more years he had established himself as a world-renowned tycoon of the historical novel, as a drawing-room wit, as a champion of the bedchamber, as a gourmet of note. . . . M. Maurois, using a Gallic style as rapid as swordplay, had done as much with Dumas' life as the brief compass of his book allows him. . . . [It is] unfailingly readable." Book of the Month Club News

Dürer, Albrecht

Russell, Francis. The world of Dürer, 1471-1528, by Francis Russell and the editors of Time-Life Books. Time, inc. [distributed by Little] 1967 183p illus maps (Time-Life Lib. of art) boards $7.95　　92
　1 Artists, German 2 Art, German
　"A general introduction to Dürer and his immediate predecessors and followers in painting and printmaking, rather than to Dürer and the economic, social, political, and other conditions of his time, as the title suggests." Choice

Earhart, Amelia

Burke, John. Winged legend; the story of Amelia Earhart. Putnam 1970 255p illus $6.95　　　92
　1 Air pilots

Earhart, Amelia—*Continued*

"Drawing on her flight logs, on records, published books and the reminiscences of her flying colleagues, her sister and her surviving husband George Putnam, [the author] provides a . . . portrait which covers [Amelia Earhart's] family background—an alcoholic father, an aristocratic mother—and her youthful experiences as a World War I nurse and, after the war, as a settlement-house worker. [He also] describes her flying career, [particularly] her setting of numerous aerial records early in the 1920s." Pub W
A note on sources and bibliography: p245-46

Goerner, Fred. The search for Amelia Earhart. Doubleday 1966 326p illus map $7.95   **92**

1 Air pilots
"When Amelia Earhart disappeared over the Pacific on her round-the-world flight in 1937, there ensued what was probably the greatest air and water search ever made. There have been all sorts of rumors and wild conjectures about her fate, and here the man who spent six years investigating the case for CBS tells what he found out, from trips to the islands, examination of military files, and official interviews." Bk Buyer's Guide
"The world still awaits the full story. Her memory deserves the recognition that is due for 'service beyond the call of duty.' That is the real purpose of this book. But the story will more than repay reading, for its own sake." Best Sellers

Eisenhower, Dwight David, President U.S.

The White House years. Doubleday 1963-1965 2v illus maps v 1 $8.95, v2 $7.95   **92**

1 Presidents—U.S. 2 U.S. Politics and government—1953-1961 3 U.S.—Foreign relations
Contents: v 1 Mandate for change, 1953-1956; v2 Waging peace, 1956-1961
The autobiography covers President Eisenhower's two terms in the White House from the first suggestion of candidacy in 1943 to the inauguration of President Kennedy and describes the political events and decisions of this period as Eisenhower saw them. Included are Suez, the Korean War, McCarthyism, the Rosenberg case, Little Rock, Hungary and the U-2 affair
"The former President's long and detailed report on the foreign and domestic events of his . . . [two terms] in office has interest for the general reader as well as the student of politics. Excerpts from his diary, letters, and official records are made use of in a work that gives some attention to personal life but is, on the whole, a public profile. Despite the occasional awkwardness of style Eisenhower's personality and philosophy are effectively conveyed." Booklist

American Heritage. Eisenhower, American hero; the historical record of his life, by the editors of American Heritage Magazine and United Press International; introduction by Bruce Catton; biographical narrative by Kenneth S. Davis. Am. Heritage [distributed by McGraw] 1969 144p illus $4.95   **92**

1 Presidents—U.S. 2 Generals
The biography of Dwight D. Eisenhower from his childhood until his death—with special emphasis on his service as the Supreme Commander of the Allied Forces during part of World War II
Davis "manages to make a few sound critical statements despite his restricted space. The major feature of the book is its black-and-white and color photographs. Occupying more space than the actual text is a second feature, 10 distinguished contemporaries' 'Recollections' of particular phases of Ike's life." Choice

Eleanor of Aquitaine, consort of Henry II

Kelly, Amy. Eleanor of Aquitaine and the four kings. Harvard Univ. Press 1950 431p illus $10   **92**

1 Queens 2 Great Britain—History—Plantagenets, 1154-1399

A "biography of the exceptional woman who, as Queen of France, accompanied Louis VII on the disastrous Second Crusade, who later married Henry Plantagenet and became involved in the conflict over Thomas Becket, and whose sons were Richard Coeur-de-Lion and John 'Lackland' of Magna Carta fame." Rel Bk Club Bul
"A well-balanced, documented, and highly literate saga of a remarkable woman and of her times." U.S. Quarterly Bk R
Bibliography: p407-17. Map on lining-papers

Pernoud, Regine. Eleanor of Aquitaine; tr. by Peter Wiles. Coward-McCann [1968 c1967] 286p illus maps $6.50   **92**

1 Queens 2 Middle Ages 3 Henry II, King of England
Original French edition, 1965. This translation first published 1967 in England
"More than just the story of Eleanor, the book vividly shows the medieval world (1122-1204) of troubadours, rebellious barons, rising bourgeoisie, and crusaders. The struggle between Henry II, Eleanor's second husband, and Becket is presented from her viewpoint. Based on original sources this is a beautifully written, highly informed account." Library J
Bibliographical note: p271-73

Eliot, John, 1604-1690

Winslow, Ola Elizabeth. John Eliot: "apostle to the Indians"; illus. with photographs. Houghton 1968 225p illus $5.95   **92**

1 Algonquian Indians 2 U.S.—History—Colonial period—Biography
This is the biography of John Eliot, a preacher from Colonial Roxbury, Massachusetts who "wanted to tell the Algonquian Indians about God, but the Algonquians had no written language. He put their language into writing and translated the Bible into it. He preached to them in Algonquian and before long there were fourteen 'Praying Indian' towns." Bk Buyer's Guide
Selected bibliography: p213-18

Elizabeth I, Queen of England

Jenkins, Elizabeth. Elizabeth the Great. Coward-McCann 1959 [c1958] 336p illus $6.95   **92**

1 Queens 2 Great Britain—History—Tudors, 1485-1603
First published 1958 in England
"A lively portrait of Elizabeth I of England and of the age which took its name from hers. The materials for the biography, all collected from previously published sources, have been selected and interpreted by the author with understanding and insight. Elizabeth's appearance, personality, her genius for ruling, her loves, her intrigues, and the myths which have grown up about her are here examined with a fresh and discerning eye." Booklist
Bibliography: p325-28

Strachey, Lytton. Elizabeth and Essex: a tragic history. Harcourt 1928 296p illus $3.95   **92**

1 Essex, Robert Devereux, Earl of 2 Queens 3 Great Britain—History—Tudors, 1485-1603
The story "begins where the conventional biography recedes, when the queen at fifty-three falls in love with a lad of twenty—a favorite whom she forgives again and again and sends at last to the scaffold." Chicago
The author's "Elizabeth is a real woman, and Essex is a real man. Neither is a mere lay figure, an automation moved about at the will of the biographer. Both are strong, both are powerful, both are mighty, Elizabeth holding herself continuously beyond the permanent grasp of the man who sought to wield authority through a woman." Boston Transcript
Bibliography: p287-88

Emerson, Ralph Waldo

Journals; abridged and ed. with an introduction by Robert N. Linscott. Modern Lib. 1960 463p $2.95, lib. bdg. $2.69   **92**

1 Authors, American

Emerson, Ralph W.—Continued

Originally edited by the author's son and W. E. Forbes in 10 volumes, from 1909-1914 "Records begun in early youth and continued, though at the close in the form of brief memoranda, to the end of his life. . . . There is of course much variety of matter in the Journals—shrewd observations on men and books, chronicles of the day's events, etc.—but through it all runs this thread of self-communion, the poetry, it might be called, of the New England conscience deprived of its concrete deity and buoying itself on gleams and suggestions of eternal beauty and holiness." Cambridge Hist of Am Lit

Derleth, August. Emerson, our contemporary. Crowell-Collier Press 1970 168p $4.95   92

1 Authors, American

"Do not expect a biography in the strict sense of the word, for August Derleth has collected Emerson's thoughts and words and laced them with commentary. . . . Above all the book is an excellent introduction to further reading." Pub W
Bibliographical notes: p163-65

Everest, Frank K.

The fastest man alive, by Frank K. Everest, Jr.; as told to John Guenther; foreword by Albert Boyd. Dutton 1958 252p illus $5.95   92

1 Air pilots 2 Aeronautics, Military

An American test pilot describes "his boyhood in West Virginia, his combat service in World War II, and his recent achievements with the supersonic planes at Edwards Air Force Base." Cleveland
"Those interested in jet and rocket flight will enjoy this account by Lt. Colonel Everest who has earned the title with his record flight of 1900 miles an hour [in 1956]." Massachusetts

Evers, Medgar Wiley

Evers, Mrs Medgar. For us, the living, by Mrs Medgar Evers with William Peters. Doubleday 1967 378p $6.95   92

1 Mississippi—Race relations 2 Negroes—Biography

"Evers, Mississippi field secretary of the NAACP, was shot and killed from ambush as he entered his home on night in June, 1963. Racial strife and tension in Mississippi and Evers' own premonition of death had foreshadowed the assassination. Mrs Evers recalls this nightmare period in her book after she has probed her memories for her husband's background—what in his childhood made him an intelligent fighter against injustice—and for their college-years courtship and years of marriage. She also tells tragic stories of Mississippi Negroes who have suffered for their courageous stands in recent years against desegregation." Pub W

Ferber, Edna

A peculiar treasure. Doubleday 1960 383p illus $5.95   92

1 Authors, American

First published 1939
This autobiography of the author is, in her own words, "the story of an American Jewish family in the past half-century, and as such is really a story about America which I know and love"
"Just the sort of informal biography one would expect from Edna Ferber—honest, hearty, full of conscious lapses in 'good taste,' and pleasantly extroverted. . . . Much interesting light is thrown on the origin of her best-selling novels. If there is one single motif that dominates Miss Ferber's brisk walk through her past, it is an unforced and contagious love for her country." New Yorker

Fermi, Enrico

Fermi, Laura. Atoms in the family; my life with Enrico Fermi. Univ. of Chicago Press 1954 267p illus $5   92

1 Physicists 2 Nuclear physics

"These reminiscences begin in Italy where Laura Fermi met and married Enrico Fermi, who became one of the world's great physicists. His work in nuclear physics which won him a Nobel prize, his escape to the United States from Mussolini's Italy, and his aid to America in the development of the atom bomb are combined with affectionate description of the man himself." Horn Bk
To most of us, great scientists seem more machines than men, minds remote from the laughter or the grief of everyday life. In this simply written, tender, but amusingly unimpressed human picture of her husband, Laura Fermi has made all scientists human." Chicago Sunday Tribune

Segrè, Emilio. Enrico Fermi: physicist. Univ. of Chicago Press 1970 276p illus $6.95   92

1 Physicists 2 Nuclear physics

A "survey of Fermi's work in Italy and in the U.S. Fermi's experimentation and resulting discoveries in statistics, beta rays, and chain reaction are fully described, including his work at the University of Chicago and at Los Alamos, and his subsequent involvement in decisions concerning the use of the atom bomb and the postwar control of atomic energy are discussed. Segre . . . a pupil, associate, and friend of Fermi's, bases his analytical narrative on personal recollection, documents, and Fermi's published papers. Appendixes contain some early Fermi letters, two of his speeches, and a bibliography of his articles and lectures. Though much technical information is included, enough attention is paid to Fermi's personal life and character to interest the informed layman as well as the student and physicist." Booklist

Fitzgerald, Francis Scott Key

Mizener, Arthur. The far side of paradise; a biography of F. Scott Fitzgerald. 2d ed. Houghton 1965 xxviii, 416p illus $5.95   92

1 Authors, American

First published 1951
"A full length biography of F. Scott Fitzgerald which incorporates some critical study of his writings. The author has had access to Fitzgerald's papers, and to the reminiscences of his daughter and of his friends." Book Rev Digest
"Sympathy for Fitzgerald's physical, emotional, financial and professional crack-up is evident while understated on almost every page, along with a thoughtful evaluation of his artistic accomplishments and aspirations." N Y Times Bk R
Notes and references: p353-99. Fitzgerald's published work: p400-07

Fitzgerald, Zelda (Sayre)

Milford, Nancy. Zelda: a biography. Harper 1970 424p illus $10   92

1 Fitzgerald, Francis Scott Key

This biography of Zelda Sayre Fitzgerald, the wife of F. Scott Fitzgerald, draws upon many unpublished letters and interviews with friends of the Fitzgeralds, such as Edmund Wilson and Carl Van Vechten. It traces the life of Zelda Sayre through her marriage to Fitzgerald and their relationship, to her breakdown and, finally, her death in a sanatorium fire
"Milford has written the most authoritative study yet done of Zelda Fitzgerald, the wife of one of the century's major novelists. . . . Cultural historians and students of modern literature will find the book central. The general reader will find it lively, but its main character pathetic." Choice
Includes bibliographical references

Ford, Henry, 1863-1947

Nevins, Allan. Ford, by Allan Nevins and Frank Ernest Hill. Scribner 1954-1963 3v illus ea $12.50　　　　92

1 Automobile industry and trade 2 Ford Motor Company

Contents: v 1 The times, the man, the company; v2 Expansion and challenge, 1915-1933; v3 Decline and rebirth, 1933-1962; research associates: Mira Wilkins, George G. Heliker and William Greenleaf

This biography of Henry Ford is also a history of the Ford Motor Company and the automotive industry

Bibliographical footnotes. Bibliography: v 1, p653-64

Foyt, A. J.

Engel, Lyle Kenyon. The incredible A. J. Foyt; produced by Lyle Kenyon Engel and the editors of Auto Racing magazine. Arco 1970 160p illus lib. bdg. $4.95　　　　92

1 Automobile racing—Biography
ISBN 0-668-02195-0

This is a biography "of a sensational American automobile race driver who besides breaking many other records is the only man to win the Indianapolis '500' three times since World War II. Foyt's career is traced from his first prize-winning victory in 1956, when he won $68 in a midget race, through bad years and good to 1969. . . . Photographs of famous drivers and cars share the space about equally with the narrative and statistical racing records." Booklist

Francis of Assisi, Saint

Almedingen, E. M. St Francis of Assisi; a great life in brief. Knopf 1967 229p (Great lives in brief) $4.95　　　　92

Published in England with title: Francis of Assisi; a portrait

A "portrait of Francis as he was, full of joy and simplicity, sometimes disillusioned and blundering, but always touched by a divine charisma. . . . His pilgrimages to the Holy Land, his visions, and the stigmata that made him a virtual cripple are all recorded in this work." Publisher's note

The author "tells the familiar story with an engaging lyricism, that is not without its occasional rhetoric. . . . The historical and geographical background is adequately indicated." Times (London) Lit Sup

A note on bibliography: p227-29

Frank, Anne

Schnabel, Ernst. Anne Frank: a portrait in courage; tr. from the German by Richard and Clara Winston. Harcourt 1958 192p illus boards $5.95　　　　92

1 Concentration camps 2 World War, 1939-1945—Jews 3 World War, 1939-1945—Netherlands

To fill out the story of Anne Frank after the events recorded in her "Diary of a young girl" [entered in class 940.54] the author interviewed 42 people who had known her. Based on these interviews, this book "tells about Anne's experiences at Auschwitz and Belsen and of her death at the latter [German concentration] camp. It gives first-hand accounts of what Anne Frank was like." Pub W

The author "quotes Anne's stories and sketches, which give further proof of her talent. This book is a shattering document." Book of the Month Club News

Steenmeijer, Anna G. ed. A tribute to Anne Frank; ed. by Anna G. Steenmeijer in collaboration with Otto Frank [and] Henri van Praag. Doubleday 1971 [c1970] 120p illus $8.95　　　　92

1 World War, 1939-1945—Jews

Originally published 1970 in the Netherlands

"A most interesting compilation of articles, poetry, essays, comments, and drawings dealing with Anne Frank and her diary. Any young person who has read the diary and is interested in more information will find this illuminating and, in its own way, quite moving." Library J

Frankfurter, Felix

Baker, Liva. Felix Frankfurter. Coward-McCann 1969 376p illus $8.95　　　　92

1 Judges 2 U.S. Supreme Court

The author relates the life story "of a Jewish immigrant who grew up at the turn of the century in New York's Lower East Side, worked his way through City College, went on to Harvard Law School, and eventually distinguished himself as teacher, lawyer, presidential adviser, and Supreme Court jurist. He fought throughout his life for causes in which he believed and steadily evolved a philosophy of law whose roots lay not in abstractions and logic but in experience." Publisher's note

This is "not a lightweight book devoted to the gossipy aspects of Frankfurter's career. The anecdotes are balanced by serious reflection on the values Frankfurter pursued in his long life. Mrs. Baker also selects sensibly among the 723 opinions Frankfurter wrote during his years on the Court, and manages a good and useful essay on the paradoxes of power that beset the Supreme Court justice." Book World

A note on sources: p335-39

Franklin, Benjamin

The autobiography of Benjamin Franklin　　　　92

1 Statesmen, American 2 Authors, American

Some editions are:
Dutton (Everyman's lib) $2.95
Watts, F. lib. bdg. $7.95 Large type edition. A. Keith Jennison book
Yale Univ. Press $15 Edited by Leonard W. Labaree and others

Written between 1771 and 1788

"The style of this work is inimitable: it is as simple, direct, idiomatic as Bunyan's. It is the straightforward life-story of a typically American character endowed with the great powers developed by self-education, who exerted vast influence as a citizen and statesman for his own day and for the future of his country." Pratt Alcove

Frederick II, the Great, King of Prussia

Mitford, Nancy. Frederick the Great; picture research by Joy Law. Harper 1970 304p illus maps $15　　　　92

1 Prussia—Kings and rulers
ISBN 06-012986-7

The author portrays Frederick as "not merely a brilliant military strategist and statesman, but also a scholar, musician and patron of the arts. . . . [She] presents the known facts of his life objectively, including his homosexuality, drawing almost all her material from contemporary sources." Publisher's note

Sources: p292

Frémont, Jessie (Benton)

Randall, Ruth Painter. I Jessie; a biography of the girl who married John Charles Frémont, famous explorer of the West. Little 1963 223p illus $4.95　　　　92

1 Frémont, John Charles

"A good biography of Jessie Benton Fremont, albeit mildly adulatory. As the daughter of a wealthy senator, Jessie Benton was well educated and socially prominent as well as being pretty and lively; her love match with a dashing soldier and explorer provides more drama than would be credible in a work of fiction. The Fremonts lived sometimes in luxurious urban surroundings, sometimes in rude frontier homes. They lived at times honored by the social and political leaders of their day, at times in disgrace or in seclusion. Good writing style, and good . . . characterization. The sources for historical details are quoted in a preface by the author." Chicago. Children's Book Center

Freud, Sigmund

Stoutenburg, Adrien. Explorer of the unconscious: Sigmund Freud, by Adrien Stoutenburg and Laura Nelson Baker. Scribner 1965 202p front lib. bdg. $3.63   92

1 Psychoanalysis

"This biography, based on research into Freud's own works, journals, and letters, focuses upon both the man and his theories and teachings in the field of psychoanalysis." McClurg. Book News

The authors "have not only been able to give a clear picture of Freud, but also an uncomplicated idea of the progression of his philosophy and analysis from an art to a possible science. Much of Freud's life is seen through his own ideas of psychoanalysis; his personality, eccentricities and courage are shown in family episodes that are humorous, touching and revealing. A few of the authors' statements are open to criticism, but in a work so succinct they may be overlooked." Best Sellers

Glossary: p183-90. Selected bibliography: p191-92

Frost, Robert

The letters of Robert Frost to Louis Untermeyer. Holt 1963 388p $7   92

1 Poets, American

Starting in 1915 and continuing until Frost's death in 1962, these letters reveal what Frost "thought about poetry, critics, fellow poets (he could be caustic as well as admiring), politics, his family, lecturing, farming, all the concerns of his long life. They are in effect an autobiography." Pub W

"It is also a testimony to Louis Untermeyer for being the sort of man with whom Frost, in a correspondence that lasted nearly 50 years, would try to 'localize' some of his private pain and many of the more public threats to his ultimate triumph." Book Week

Fuller, Richard Buckminster

Rosen, Sidney. Wizard of the dome: R. Buckminster Fuller, designer for the future. Little 1969 189p illus $4.95   92

1 Inventors

"This is an account of the life and career of R. Buckminster Fuller, the American architect who designed the Dymaxion house and the geodesic dome." Sat R

"The book has a good balance of personal life, career and professional information, and discussion of Fuller's theories; written in an informal but dignified style, it makes clear the importance and the innovatory quality of Fuller's work without being adulatory, and it is as candid about Fuller's days of despair as it is about the basic ebullience of his nature." Chicago. Children's Book Center

Bibliography: p185-86

Galilei, Galileo

Fermi, Laura. Galileo and the scientific revolution [by] Laura Fermi and Gilberto Bernardini. Basic Bks. 1961 150p illus (Science and discovery) $4.50   92

1 Astronomers 2 Science—History

"A clear exposition of Galileo's discoveries, experiments, and methods is accompanied by diagrams and quotations from his writings. His contribution toward promoting freedom in the field of scientific research is stressed, and his conflict with the Church is treated sympathetically and with considerable detail. A final chapter summarizes Galileo's contributions to the science of physics." Library J

Bibliography: p144-45

Geymonat, Ludovico. Galileo Galilei; a biography and inquiry into his philosophy of science; foreword by Giorgio de Santillana; text tr. from the Italian with additional notes and appendix by Stillman Drake. McGraw 1965 260p $6.50   92

1 Astronomers

"The biographical details of this scholarly and readable work serve as a framework for a consideration of Galileo's complex philosophy of science which must be understood and appreciated to evaluate Galileo's achievements. The translator is an eminent U.S. authority on Galileo who has appended historical notes for the introduction and each chapter that greatly enhance the value of the book." Science Bks

Bibliography included in Notes: p227-51

Gandhi, Indira (Nehru)

Mohan, Anand. Indira Gandhi; a personal and political biography. Meredith 1967 303p boards $6.95   92

1 Statesmen, East Indian 2 Nehru, Jawaharlal 3 India—Politics and government

The life "of the woman who is [currently] the leader of the world's second largest nation. The author tells of Indira Gandhi's childhood, of her rise to fame in the political world, and of the influence that her father, Nehru, and Shastri had upon her." Bk Buyer's Guide

A glossary of Indic terms: p291-95. Maps on lining-papers

Gandhi, Mohandas Karamchand

All men are brothers; life and thoughts of Mahatma Gandhi as told in his own words. Columbus Univ. Press 1958 196p illus $7   92

1 Statesmen, East Indian 2 India—Politics and government

"Excerpts from Gandhi's own writings and speeches form a partial autobiography of the Mahatma. The stress is on his moral, spiritual, and political experiments rather than on personal matters, although these are sometimes briefly mentioned. The selections are grouped under the themes which were some of Gandhi's main concerns in life, such as religion and truth, nonviolence, self-discipline, international peace, poverty, democracy, education, and the role of women." Booklist

Gandhi's autobiography; the story of my experiments with truth; tr. from the original in Gujarati by Mahadev Desai. Public Affairs Press 1954 640p $6   92

1 Statesmen, East Indian 2 India—Politics and government

First published in two volumes 1927-1929 in England with title: The story of my experiments with truth

This book reveals the basic forces and factors which moulded Gandhi's life. It describes his colorful childhood, his varied education, his singular career as a lawyer, his complex religious and intellectual development, his championship of the Untouchables of his native land, and his epic fight for Indian independence

Written during a prison term in the early '20s, "Gandhi bares his soul with deep humility and merciless honesty. He tells the innermost secrets of his personal life—holding back nothing, embellishing nothing." Publisher's note

Payne, Robert. The life and death of Mahatma Gandhi. Dutton 1969 703p illus maps $12.95   92

1 Statesmen, East Indian 2 India—Politics and government

"A massively researched narrative of Gandhi's inner and public life, it tends to stagger the imagination—it is both trivial and titanic, exhaustive and monumental. . . . Payne draws the dedicated political and spiritual man profoundly in context—which means India, Gandhi's beginnings, his compassionate identification with the Untouchables, his voluntary poverty no less than his negotiations with viceroys, his friendships with the great. In sweep, in completeness, Payne's book may be the one that tells it all in a way most readers would like it told. Glossary, genealogy, bibliography, chronology." Pub W

Garland, Hamlin

A son of the middle border; ed. and with an introduction by Henry M. Christman. Macmillan (N Y) 1962 401p $5.95   92

1 Frontier and pioneer life 2 Middle West

Garland, Hamlin—*Continued*

First published 1917

"A narrative of a youth spent in toil among the hard, homely pioneer conditions in Wisconsin and Iowa after the Civil war and of later struggles in Boston to become a professional man of letters." Cleveland

"As you read it you realize it is the memorial of a generation, of a whole order of American experience; as you review it you perceive it an epic of such mood and make as has not been imagined before." N Y Times Bk R

Gaulle, Charles de, President France

Schoenbrun, David. The three lives of Charles de Gaulle. Atheneum Pubs. 1966 [c1965] 373p pa $3.95   92

1 France—Presidents 2 France—Politics and government 3 World War, 1939-1945—France

"The biographer focuses upon de Gaulle as a soldier of the Third Republic, liberator of the Fourth and creator of the Fifth." Chicago

The author's "opinions are backed by his 25 years' acquaintance with de Gaulle, by a detailed study of de Gaulle's essays and memoirs, and by a profound knowledge of contemporary French history. There is exclusive inside information in this book, especially dealing with de Gaulle's relations with the U.S. during the Eisenhower administration. A . . . thoughtful journalistic analysis." Pub W

Geronimo, Apache chief

Geronimo: his own story; ed. by S. M. Barrett; newly ed. with an introduction and notes by Frederick W. Turner, III. Dutton 1970 190p illus $6.95   92

1 Apache Indians
ISBN 0-525-11308-8

First published 1906 with title: Geronimo's story of his life

"In his Christianized old age (1905-1906, to be definite), the . . . Apache warrior dictated his autobiography. . . . [The book] tells of Apache motives for the various flights and uprisings led, or fomented, by Geronimo." Atlantic

"At the time he dictated [this story] to S. M. Barrett in 1906 [Geronimo] still longed for repatriation to Arizona and was careful not to incur the wrath of his American captors by boasting of his depredations against them. Mexicans, not Americans, were the source of his troubles, as he spun his yarn. . . . The fresh introduction prepared by Frederick W. Turner, a folklorist, tells us much more about Geronimo and Apache life than anything the old warrior has to say." Book World

A selected bibliography: p[191]

Gershwin, George

Ewen, David. George Gershwin: his journey to greatness. Prentice-Hall 1970 xxx, 354p illus $7.95   92

1 Composers, American
ISBN 0-13-353854-0

"This biography first appeared in 1956 under the title of 'A Journey to greatness: the life and music of George Gershwin'." Preface

In this portrait the author "traces the development of George Gershwin from his childhood in New York's East Side through the introduction of his vital new music, to his present status as one of America's most beloved composers. . . . [The book contains] information obtained from the Gershwin family, personal letters, scrapbooks, diaries, and interviews with famous contemporaries." News of Bks

"An excellent and readable, important and authoritative biography, which also gives due credit to the composer's modest brother, lyricist Ira Gershwin." Best Sellers

Gibson, Althea

I always wanted to be somebody; ed. by Ed Fitzgerald. Harper 1958 176p illus boards $4.95, lib. bdg. $4.43   92

1 Tennis—Biography 2 Negroes—Biography

"Althea Gibson tells of traveling the rough, tough road from the back streets of Harlem to the royal courts of Wimbledon and Forest Hills." Books for You

"She is frank in her descriptions of her Harlem childhood and her family life, or lack of it. She is outspoken in her attitude toward race. Some of her comments on her first introductions to the polite formalities of tennis are very funny." Horn Bk

Gibson, Bob

From ghetto to glory: the story of Bob Gibson [by] Bob Gibson with Phil Pepe. Prentice-Hall 1968 200p illus boards $6.95 92

1 Baseball—Biography 2 Negroes—Biography

The Negro pitching star traces his career from a Nebraska ghetto to the ballparks of the major leagues. He talks about the players, the fans, his opponents, his differences with the working press, and reveals his pitching strategy. (Publisher)

"The sensational pitcher for the . . . St. Louis Cardinals baseball team here gives his personal story into the capable hands of sportswriter Phil Pepe . . . with results a shade better than most books of its kind can show. That may be because there's so much more to tell than usual. . . . The book is equally divided between the drama of baseball and the human drama of being a Negro in America." Pub W

Gilbreth, Frank Bunker, 1868-1924

Gilbreth, Frank B. 1911- Cheaper by the dozen [by] Frank B. Gilbreth, Jr. and Ernestine Gilbreth Carey; drawings by Vasiliu. [Updated ed] Crowell 1963 245p illus $4.95   92

1 Gilbreth family

First published 1948

"Reminiscences of the twelve Gilbreth children, of Montclair, N.J., and their adventures with their boisterous big-boy genius of a father, who trained typists, surgeons, machinegunners, and others in efficiency and tried to use the same principles in his domestic life." Retail Bookseller

"A gay and lighthearted book, with some serious overtones. Cast in the mold of 'Life with Father,' it stands up very well on its own." Chicago Sun

Gilbreth, Frank B. 1911- Cheaper by the dozen |by] Frank B. Gilbreth, Jr. and Ernestine Gilbreth Carey; illus. by Donald McKay. Large type ed. complete and unabridged. Watts, F. [1968 c1948] 237p illus lib. bdg. $8.95   92

1 Gilbreth family 2 Large type books

"A Keith Jennison book"

A reissue in large type of the title first published 1948 by Crowell. The 1963 updated edition is entered above

Gilbreth, Lillian Evelyn (Moller)

Gilbreth, Frank B. 1911- Belles on their toes [by] Frank B. Gilbreth, Jr. and Ernestine Gilbreth Carey; illus. by Donald McKay. Crowell 1950 237p illus $5.95   92

1 Gilbreth family

"The authors of 'Cheaper by the dozen' [listed above] . . . resume the family story at the point where the first book left off, with the father's death. The mother took her husband's place as family authority (but with more democracy) and as breadwinner, saw all the children through college and into marriage." Booklist

"As a whole, this delightful book is as clean, clever and cheerful as a story about Mom and her kids should be. From start to finish, it is a reading joy." Chicago Sunday Tribune

Gilbreth, Frank B. 1911- Time out for happiness [by] Frank B. Gilbreth, Jr. Crowell 1970 254p $5.95   92

1 Gilbreth, Frank Bunker, 1868-1924
ISBN 0-690-82517-X

Gilbreth, Lillian E. M.—*Continued*

A companion volume to: Cheaper by the dozen, and Belles on their toes, entered above

In this book the author concentrates on the lives and accomplishments of his parents, Lillian and Frank Gilbreth. "Both mother and father Gilbreth were famous in the engineering management fields. . . . [They] worked right along with each other in their business and professions, in managing their home in Montclair, N.J., and raising their brood of [12] children." Pub W

Godden, Jon

Two under the Indian sun, by Jon and Rumer Godden. Knopf [distributed by Viking] 1966 240p boards $5.50   92

1 Authors, English 2 India—Social life and customs

"In November 1914 the two small sisters, Jon and Rumer Godden, returned to India. This book, a unique collaboration, is a remembrance of the five years that followed in the village of Narayangunj." Hunting

"There is the delight of reading not only of the life and sights and sounds and smells of India as they existed then, but of the leisurely domestic side of the forever vanished world of Englishmen in India. The two little girls, now distinguished authors, are able today to remember in tranquility, and to evoke the moment with passion." Harper

Gogh, Vincent van

Van Gogh's "diary"; the artist's life in his own words and art; ed. by Jan Hulsker. Morrow 1971 [c1970] 168p illus boards $12.50   92

1 Painters, Dutch 2 Painting, Dutch

"A juxtaposition of illustration with artist's comments relating to the work highlights a discerning portrait of Van Gogh taken from the artist's own pen and brush. Several of the hundreds of letters by Van Gogh, 19 colorplates, and 260 black-and-white illustrations reveal feelings toward his life, art, and family." Booklist

Wallace, Robert, 1919-   The world of Van Gogh, 1853-1890, by Robert Wallace and the editors of Time-Life Books. Time-Life Bks. [distributed by Little] 1969 192p illus (Time-Life Lib. of art) boards $7.95   92

1 Painters, Dutch 2 Painting, Dutch

Accompanying a selection of Van Gogh's works is a text which describes the life and art of the man who became a pioneer of expressionistic art. Also included are pictorial essays on the lives and works of his two friends, Gauguin and Toulouse-Lautrec

Bibliography: p184

Goya y Lucientes, Francisco José de

Schickel, Richard. The world of Goya, 1746-1828, by Richard Schickel and the editors of Time-Life Books. Time-Life Bks. [distributed by Little] 1968 192p illus (Time-Life Lib. of art) boards $7.95   92

1 Painters, Spanish 2 Painting, Spanish

The author provides a biography of the artist; a discussion of his work, including his later masterpieces; and a sketch of Spain at the time of the Inquisition

"Of the little that is known of Goya's life, [the author] manages to write an absorbing semi-biography that is, at the same time, an excellent impressionistic sketch of Spanish history at the time of the Inquisition." Pub W

Bibliography: p187

Granatelli, Anthony

They call me Mister 500, by Anthony (Andy) Granatelli. Regnery 1969 341p illus $6.95   92

1 Automobile racing—Biography

"Describing his flamboyant life in appropriate prose Granatelli reveals his effervescent egotism and effectively conveys the excitement and flavor of automobile racing. He recounts his rise from a Chicago slum to the top of the racing business giving, along the way, a vivid, inside picture of the race pit and tracks and showing why he is called Mister 500, 'the most controversial figure at the Indianapolis Motor Speedway.' " Booklist

Grant, Ulysses Simpson, President U.S.

Catton, Bruce. Grant moves south; with maps by Samuel H. Bryant. Little 1960 564p front maps $10   92

1 Generals 2 Presidents—U.S. 3 U.S.—History—Civil War—Campaigns and battles

This "is not only the chronological account of a series of battles which freed the Mississippi for the Union: it is also a story of a man's personal development. It describes Grant's progress from a reluctant but dedicated soldier to a forceful General, conscious of his own worth and confident of his future." Publisher's note

"Although Catton focuses attention on military strategy and tactics more sharply than other biographers of Grant have done, he never loses sight of the many complex problems which plagued his subject. . . . The author's discussions of these problems are full and revealing, as is his entire writing about Grant during the period dealt with in his book." Ann Am Acad

Bibliography: p539-47

Followed by: Grant takes command

Catton, Bruce. Grant takes command; with maps by Samuel H. Bryant. Little 1969 556p front maps $10   92

1 Generals 2 Presidents—U.S. 3 U.S.—History—Civil War—Campaigns and battles

Sequel to: Captain Sam Grant, by Lloyd Lewis and the author's Grant moves south

The author "takes up Ulysses S. Grant's career just after his capture of Vicksburg in 1863, a hard-won victory which split the Confederacy and perked up Lincoln's interest in his then relatively little-known general. . . . It carries the action right up to Richmond and Lee's surrender at Appomatox." Pub W

"The narrative is fascinating and by no means all concerned with the movement of troops. . . . [It is] a highly artistic and highly analytical examination of the qualities of a great man, achieved by perceptively watching him in action." Sat R

Bibliography: p527-34

Catton, Bruce. U. S. Grant and the American military tradition. Little 1954 201p (Lib. of American biography) $5   92

1 Generals 2 Presidents—U.S. 3 U.S.—History—Civil War—Biography

The author "analyzes factors which made Grant an excellent general but a less satisfactory President. Some of these factors, claims the author, were inherent in Grant's direct unsubtle personality, while others were peculiar to the spirit of uncontrolled expansionism and to the bitter hostilities which followed the war between the states." Booklist

Lewis, Lloyd. Captain Sam Grant. Little 1950 512p front $10   92

1 Generals 2 Presidents—U.S. 3 U.S.—History—War with Mexico, 1845-1848—Biography

"This biography of Ulysses S. Grant covers in detail his background and his life up to June, 1861, when he was named colonel of an Illinois regiment." Book Rev Digest

"The portrait that emerges is of Grant as a human being: it weighs the evidence of his inadequacies, his weaknesses, his frailties. Perhaps the most important part of the record is the story of the Mexican War, told in great detail through records of contemporaries and through Grant's letters." Cincinnati

Bibliography: p473-84

Followed by Bruce Catton's: Grant moves south

Gregory, Dick

Nigger; an autobiography, by Dick Gregory with Robert Lipsyte. Dutton 1964 224p illus $5.95   92

1 Negroes—Biography

"A strong, forceful book that explains why Richard Claxton Gregory has faced ugly southern crowds and gone to prison for the cause of Negro freedom. It tells how he grew up (on relief in St. Louis, brought up by his mother, his father a runaway). . . . It tells of his trouble getting started as a comedian, and the first poverty-ridden years of his marriage. The pages are full of pent-up fury, humiliation, the tragic sadness and finally anger for his whole people, not just himself." Pub W

Grey, Anthony

Hostage in Peking.   Doubleday   1971 [c1970] 365p illus $7.95   92

1 Political prisoners 2 British in China (People's Republic of China) 3 Journalists

First published 1970 in England

On August 18, 1967 "200 Red Guards smashed into the Peking home of Reuters correspondent, Anthony Grey, subjecting him to intensive physical abuse and imprisoning him for what ultimately became 26 long and torturous months in solitary confinement. . . . [The author] tells the story of that terrible time when he was both pawn and victim in an international dispute between Britain and Red China." Publisher's note

The author "conveys poignantly the torment of 'living in a void.' His knowledge of China was perforce largely confined to the tiny dot he lived in, but his experience made up in intensity for what it lacked in geographical breadth. By describing his guards and the few officials he saw, he brings out the physical and psychological impact of Mao and Mao's 'cultural revolution' on the Chinese people. . . . His book seems to provide much insight into the current Red Chinese psyche." Book of the Month Club News

Guevara, Ernesto

Harris, Richard. Death of a revolutionary; Che Guevara's last mission. Norton 1970 219p illus map $5.95   92

1 Bolivia—History 2 Guerrilla warfare

This "study of Che's life and his doomed campaign in Bolivia . . . deals with the essential question: When Che Guevara was killed by the Bolivian Army in October 1967, did he die a hero, a martyr, or the victim of his own errors? In reaching his controversial conclusions, Professor Harris explores Che's youth and early political indoctrination, his association with Fidel Castro, his activities as Cuba's Minister of State, and his relationships with the Cuban and the Soviet Communist parties." News of Bks

Sinclair, Andrew. Che Guevara. Viking 1970 115p $4.95   92

1 Cuba—History—1959-
SBN 670-21391-8

"Modern masters"

"A study of the life, ideas and influence of the Argentinian-born revolutionary who died in Bolivia in 1968." Book Rev Digest

"The present volume is a rather sketchy essay on his life and thought, but it nonetheless has one distinct advantage over similar efforts—Guevara emerges whole." N Y Times Bk R

Short bibliography: p109

Gunther, John, 1929-1947

Gunther, John, 1901-1970. Death be not proud   92

Some editions are:

Harper $4.95, lib. bdg. $4.11 Has subtitle: a memoir

Harper $7.50 Large type edition. Has subtitle: a memoir

Harper $6.95 Memorial edition. Preface by Cass Canfield

Modern Lib. $2.95 Has subtitle: a memoir

First published 1949

A memoir dedicated to John Gunther's seventeen-year-old son, who died after a series of operations for brain tumor. Not only a tribute to remarkable boy but an account of a brave fight against disease

"It is as painful a story as one could well read, for Mr. Gunther spares neither himself nor his reader. It is also a story of great unselfishness and great heroism. If we can stand literal descriptions of battles, we ought to be able to stand this. Still, it is not easy. . . . If courage is an antidote to pain and grief, the disease and the cure are both in this book. Those who can endure this strong medicine will be the stronger if they read this book." N Y Times Bk R

Hannibal

Cottrell, Leonard.   Hannibal, enemy of Rome. Holt 1961 257p illus maps $5.50   92

1 Punic War, 2d, 218-201 B.C.

First published 1960 in England with title: Enemy of Rome

This biography follows the exploits of Hannibal, the great military genius, particularly in the Second Punic War. Beginning with Hannibal's departure from Spain in command of the Carthaginian armies in 218 B.C. and continuing through Hannibal's seventeen years of combat in Italy, the narrative emphasizes Hannibal's feat of leading his army with elephants across the Alps. Despite many victories, however, Hannibal failed to achieve his goal, the annihilation of Rome. (Publisher)

Further readings: p249

Lamb, Harold.   Hannibal: one   man against Rome. Doubleday 1958 310p illus maps $4.95   92

1 Punic War, 2d, 218-201 B.C.

"A biographical narrative set in the ancient world of Rome and Carthage and centered on an incomparable military strategist most famous for his feat of leading an army with elephants over the Alps [during the second Punic War]. Since very little is known of Hannibal's personal history or character but much about his . . . exploits in war, the book is largely one of military history and, as such, is very interesting." Pub W

Harding, Warren Gamaliel, President U.S.

Russell, Francis.   The shadow of Blooming Grove; Warren G. Harding in his times. McGraw 1968 691p $12.50   92

1 Presidents—U.S. 2 U.S.—Politics and government—1919-1933

"Our twenty-ninth President, handsome, weak, and ultimately destroyed by scandal, is explained as the product of his place and time, of smalltown hoopla and big city politics in an America frantically pursuing the almighty dollar, unhindered by scruples." Bk Buyer's Guide

"Russell's biography has many fine qualities. It neither condones nor apologizes for Harding. It is packed with interesting anecdotes and vivid character sketches of dozens of politicos. Russell succeeds particularly well in evaluating the villains who crossed Harding's path. . . . Yet [the book] also has exasperating weaknesses. . . . It contains neither footnotes nor organized bibliography. . . . [The author's] judgements about the reliability of sources and his allocation of space to various topics are also erratic." N Y Times Bk R

Bibliography included in Notes: p667-72

Hart, Moss

Act one; an autobiography   92

1 Dramatists, American 2 Theater—U.S.

Some editions are:
Modern Lib. $2.95
Random House $7.95

First published 1959

"A hilarious account of the playwright's youth and first experiences in the theater. In the portrayals of his abortive attempt at acting and the failure of his first play and in the character sketches of the more eccentric members of his family, his impressions of celebrities and

Hart, Moss—*Continued*

theater folk, and his funny but informative record of his collaboration with the redoubtable George S. Kaufman on the successful play 'Once in a lifetime,' the writer displays the same comic and satiric gifts that mark his later Broadway triumphs. A candid personal history and an affectionate backward glance at the theater of the 1930's." Booklist

Harte, Bret

O'Connor, Richard. Bret Harte; a biography. Little 1966 331p illus boards $6.95 **92**

1 Authors, American

A life of Bret Harte, which gives "him credit for originating, 'westerns' in 'The Luck of Roaring Camp' and his other tales of the Sierra foothills mining camps. O'Connor sheds . . . light on Harte's unhappy henpecked marital life, his extramarital liaisons, his quarrel with Mark Twain, and the downhill slide of his writing career after his first success in San Francisco." Pub W

"Biographer O'Connor . . . sensibly confines himself to the life and the figure of the man." Time

Selected bibliography: p323-24

Hatano, Isoko

Mother and son; the wartime correspondence of Isoko and Ichiro Hatano. Houghton 1962 195p map $4.50 **92**

1 Japan—Social life and customs

First published 1950 in Japan. Translated from the French by Margaret Shenfield

"Letters between a Hiroshima high school boy and his mother, exchanged in the . . . period from 1944 to 1948." Pub W

A "sensitive and revealing collection of notes and letters. . . . The deep and universal struggles of all young people come through Ichiro's specific problems." Horn Bk

Hawthorne, Nathaniel

Wagenknecht, Edward. Nathaniel Hawthorne: man and writer. Oxford 1961 233p front $6.50 **92**

1 Authors, American

"This book is neither a chronological biography nor a critical study. . . . [It is] a study of Hawthorne's character and personality, based on his writings, his letters and journals and on all that has been written about him." Preface

"This penetrative and generally sympathetic book surely contributes to a better understanding of this intensely reserved New Englander whose character has often been misrepresented and his works misinterpreted." Springf'd Republican

Includes bibliography

Hayes, Helen

On reflection; an autobiography [by] Helen Hayes with Sandford Dody **92**

1 Actors and actresses

Some editions are:
Evans, M.&Co. $5.95
Lanewood Press. Lanewood Largetype $7.50

First published 1968

The actress presents these memoirs "as a legacy for her grandchildren, to be read one day when they are grown. . . . [She describes] the family stories, the backstage anecdotes and her recollections of spiritual struggle." Publisher's note

It "is a thoroughly readable small volume, chiefly because it is liberally sprinkled with Miss Hayes's own salty wit and graphic images. Lines on stage may be written for her; offstage she comes through with her own, and they are just as pungent. And if her readers want glimpses of the people she has known well, Miss Hayes offers warmly evocative memories." Christian Science Monitor

Hearst, William Randolph

Swanberg, W. A. Citizen Hearst, a biography of William Randolph Hearst. Scribner 1961 555p illus $12.95 **92**

1 Journalists

When William Randolph Hearst died at eighty-eight in the summer of 1951, one of the most flamboyant characters in American history vanished from the scene. In this book the author examines every side of his subject: Hearst the millionaire, the newspaper tycoon, the politician, the kingmaker; his influence on the Spanish-American War, his sumptuous life at San Simeon, and his art collecting. (Publisher)

Includes bibliographies

Heiser, Victor

An American doctor's odyssey; adventures in forty-five countries. Norton 1936 544p illus $12 **92**

1 Physicians

Published in England with title: Doctor's Odyssey

Dr Heiser "studied disease, fought epidemics and carried the gospel of health all over the globe. The narrative is not confined to experiences connected with this work, fascinating and informing as it is, but there are many incidents, some dramatic, some amusing, arising out of the author's travels, as well as descriptions of people and places in both civilized and primitive countries. Photographs." N Y Libraries

Hemingway, Ernest

A moveable feast. Scribner 1964 211p illus boards $4.95 **92**

1 Authors, American 2 Paris—Description

A posthumously published collection of sketches, which Hemingway said might be regarded as fiction, about the author's early life in Paris during the 1920's. In addition to picturing the Parisian scene, Hemingway portrays Gertrude Stein, Ezra Pound, Ford Madox Ford, and others. (Publisher)

"This is a book of love, loathing and bitterness. . . . More than a quarter of the book [is] devoted to Scott Fitzgerald." N Y Times Bk R

Baker, Carlos. Ernest Hemingway; a life story. Scribner 1969 697p illus $10 **92**

1 Authors, American

"Most of the story is drawn directly or indirectly from manuscript sources, including many pages of his unpublished work, approximately 2500 of his letters, and at least an equal number of letters to him from friends, members of his family, and chance associates. These materials have been supplemented with numerous interviews." Foreword

The author "has done what was expected, a superb job of research. He has, moreover, organized his book in such a way that it can be enjoyed by the general reader and at the same time used by scholars: the notes, a hundred pages of them, are in the back of the book, out of the way, and yet are so arranged that one can readily discover the source of any statement. The writing is sound and unpretentious." Sat R

Sources and notes: p567-668

Hotchner, A. E. Papa Hemingway; a personal memoir. Random House 1966 304p illus $7.95 **92**

1 Authors, American

The book reveals "personal information about Ernest Hemingway, his working habits, his friends, his ways of relaxing, his sex life, and the way he died. All this is [in] A. E. Hotchner's reports of conversations with Hemingway, vacations with him, and business conferences about his books." Pub W

"Primarily a moving, tragic book of keen insights, this biography, though seasoned with hilarity (some of it 'not' for the squeamish), presents a complex personality. . . . [It] promotes a reader's serious reflections on human motives, weaknesses and nobility; reflections on the high price paid for fame, for solid achievement, or for independence of thought and action; and even more: the losing battle to defend privacy." Best Sellers

Sanford, Marcelline Hemingway. At the Hemingways; a family portrait; with photographs. Little 1962 244p illus $5.95 **92**

1 Authors, American 2 Hemingway family

Hemingway, Ernest—*Continued*

"An Atlantic Monthly Press book"
"Ernest Hemingway's sister paints a portrait of her brother—his high spirit and the deep bond between the boy and his father. The story reaches its high point on Ernest's return from Italy and his convalescence at home [after World War I] and comes to an end in 1928, the year of his father's death." Huntting
This biography can also be read "as an account of family life in a bygone age." Library J

Henry VIII, King of England

Bowle, John. Henry VIII; a biography. Little [1965 c1964] 316p illus $7.50   92

1 Great Britain—Kings and rulers 2 Great Britain—History—Tudors, 1485-1603
First published 1964 in England
A portrait of Henry VIII against the background of Tudor England which shows him a tyrannical but able ruler who destroyed the power of the Papacy in England, founded the British Navy, and secured the throne for the Tudor dynasty. (Publisher)
"An extraordinary feature of Mr. Bowle's book is its copious use of the language of the Tudor period." N Y Times Bk R
Notes on sources: p301-03

Hess, Rudolf

Hutton, J. Bernard. Hess; the man and his mission; introduction by Airey Neave. Macmillan (N Y) [1971 c1970] 262p illus $6.95   92

1 World War, 1939-1945—Germany
First published 1970 in England
The author attempts "to determine what motivated Rudolf Hess, Deputy Führer of the Third Reich, to undertake his mysterious flight to Scotland on the evening of the tenth of May, 1941. Dr. Albrecht Haushofer . . . had encouraged Hess to make peace with Great Britain so that Germany could attack Russia. . . . When it became evident to Berlin that Churchill would not seriously consider Hess's proposal the German Government officially declared Hess to be insane and a traitor." Best Sellers
The author "has a most dramatic story to tell. Some people will approve, and others disapprove, his apparent determination to tell it as if it were fiction." Christian Science Monitor

Heyerdahl, Thor

Jacoby, Arnold. Señor Kon-Tiki; the biography of Thor Heyerdahl. Rand McNally 1967 424p illus $7.95   92

1 Kon-Tiki Expedition, 1947
"This definitive biography of Thor Heyerdahl tells of his boyhood and youth; his war-time service; his growing conviction that the prevalent scientific opinion about the South Sea islander's origin was wrong; and how he set out to prove his theory. It includes behind-the-scenes stories of the 'Kon-Tiki' voyage and the scientific controversy it stimulated." Books for School Libraries, 1968

Himmler, Heinrich

Smith, Bradley F. Heinrich Himmler: a Nazi in the making, 1900-1926. Hoover Inst. Press 1971 211p $6.95   92

1 Germany—Politics and government
SBN 8179-1931-7
"This early life of Himmler portrays him as 'the obedient son of a typical Bavarian bourgeois family with . . . social ambitions, a . . . loyalty to the Wittelsbach dynasty, and rigid standards of morality. He frees himself gradually of inherited religious beliefs and traditional political concepts. Under the impact of the counter-revolutionary propaganda in Bavaria and on the basis of his wide readings of nationalistic and anti-Semitic literature, in the early 1920's he embraces the cause of National Socialism and turns to uninhibited Jew-hating and 'Nordic' racialism.'" Library J
Bibliography: p201-03

Hirohito, Emperor of Japan

Mosley, Leonard. Hirohito, Emperor of Japan. Prentice-Hall 1966 371p illus $7.95   92

1 Japan—Kings and rulers

"The author traces the Emperor's role in the secret policy-making meetings held among the military and civilian officials of the Japanese government prior to World War II and describes Hirohito's early upbringing as Crown Prince and the post-war period with General Douglas MacArthur." Huntting
Bibliography: p357-61

Hitler, Adolf

Mein Kampf; tr. by Ralph Manheim. Houghton 1943 xxi, 694p $10   92

1 National socialism 2 Germany—Politics and government—1918-1933 3 Germany—Politics and government—1933-1945

"Written not as propaganda but for the instruction of those committed to the Nazi movement. It is a significant historical document in which the leader of a successful revolution tells the story of his life [and] traces the growth of his social, economic and political philosophy." Publisher's note
Most of Hitler's individual style has been retained. However, there are "certain traits of Hitler's style that are peculiarly German and do present a problem in translation. . . . The translation follows the first edition. The more interesting changes made in later German editions have been indicated in the notes. Where Hitler's formulations challenge the reader's credulity, I have quoted the German original in the notes." Translator's note
"The book may well be called a kind of satanic Bible. . . . To give back to these noble [Aryan] races their former consciousness of superiority by inculcating the principle that men are 'not' equal is the theoretical purpose of 'Mein Kampf.' . . . Compared to the spirit of the book, the pragmatical parts are of less importance. . . . What gives 'Mein Kampf' its terrific import is not the aims but the methods." Introduction

Bullock, Alan. Hitler; a study in tyranny. Completely rev. ed. Harper [1964 c1962] 848p illus maps $10   92

1 National socialism 2 Germany—Politics and government—1933-1945

First published 1952
This biography covers Hitler's career and the role of Germany in World War II. Sources for the book include the "German archives, evidence given at the Nuremberg trials, and countless documents, speeches, memoirs and diaries of men in close contact with the Führer." Publisher's note
"This volume must be carefully read and thoughtfully pondered by all who would hope, somehow and ultimately, to understand Hitler and Hitlerism—which Bullock sees as not merely a German disease but a disease of Europe and of all our world." New Republic
Bibliography: p809-15

Ho-chi Minh, President Democratic Republic of Vietnam

Halberstam, David. Ho. Random House 1971 118p $4.95   92

1 Vietnam (Democratic Republic)
ISBN 0-394-46275-0

"The present highly readable and accurate book offers a fine portrait of a humble yet determined revolutionary from birth to his entry in a triumphant but simple style into Hanoi after the 1954 Indochina Conference. . . . It gives a wealth of information and a fine analysis of Vietnamese nationalism and the rise of Viet Minh as a people's army. It concludes that both the French and the Americans never really understood this war but only thought of it in terms of terrain controlled, bodies counted." Choice
Bibliography: p[119]

Ho-chi Minh, President Democratic Republic of Vietnam—*Continued*

Lacouture, Jean. Ho Chi Minh; a political biography; tr. from the French by Peter Wiles; translation ed. by Jane Clark Seitz. Random House 1968 313p $7.95　　92

1 Vietnam (Democratic Republic)

Original French edition, 1967

This biography of the President of North Vietnam traces his development from peasant to revolutionary to leader of his people against the French and finally against the United States. (Publisher)

"This is a sympathetic biography, but Lacouture has made a clear effort to be objective, incorporating even Trotskyite criticism and emphasizing Ho's willingness to apply ruthless measures when he considered them politically necessary. [The] translation appears to be a good one, reflecting Lacouture's clarity and liveliness of style." N Y Times Bk R

Bibliographical references included in footnotes

Holmes, Oliver Wendell, 1841-1935

Bowen, Catherine Drinker. Yankee from Olympus; Justice Holmes and his family. Little 1944 475p illus $8.50　　92

1 Judges 2 U.S. Supreme Court

"An Atlantic Monthly Press book"

"The rare quality of Justice Holmes, the background from which he came, the grim days of Civil War service, all the wealth of his human relationships and his clear and vivid interpretation of the law are reflected in this engrossing biography written with sympathy and imagination. The two portrayals, a cultivated New England home of an earlier generation with its literary aspects and exasperations, and the development of a great legal tradition make the book of wide interest." Library J

Includes bibliography

Homer, Winslow

Flexner, James Thomas. The world of Winslow Homer, 1836-1910, by James Thomas Flexner and the editors of Time-Life Books. Time, inc. [distributed by Little 1966] 190p illus (Time-Life Lib. of art) boards $7.95　　92

1 Painters, American 2 Painting, American

The author combines a description of the life of the American painter and watercolorist with a critical analysis of his work

"An agreeably popular, authoritative introduction to the background, world, work, and fellow artists of Winslow Homer. . . . Text, reproductions, and accompanying remarks by Dale Brown enrich this informal art vista." Booklist

Bibliography: p185

Hoover, Herbert

Memoirs. Macmillan (N Y) 1951-52 3v illus ea $8.95　　92

1 Presidents—U.S. 2 U.S.—Politics and government 3 Depressions

Contents: v 1 Years of adventure, 1874-1920; v2 Cabinet and the Presidency, 1920-1933; v3 Great depression, 1929-1941

Volume 1 tells of his boyhood in Iowa and Oregon, his college life at Stanford, his marriage, his engineering career, through the first World War. Volume 2 covers his official activities from 1919 and those aspects of his Presidency concerned with reconstruction, national development and foreign policy. Volume 3 analyzes the causes of depression and criticizes economic measures taken by the New Deal

Horne, Lena

Lena, by Lena Horne and Richard Schickel. Doubleday 1965 300p illus $5.95　　92

1 Singers 2 Negroes—Biography

Although Lena Horne "writes of both her professional and her personal life, her recurrent theme is her struggle for recognition as a singer and actress and against the second-class treatment and real cruelty she has experienced because she is Negro." Pub W

"The book has an earnest and modest tone and is much less gossipy than these things are wont to be." Harper

Houdini, Harry

Christopher, Milbourne. Houdini; the untold story. Crowell 1969 281p illus $6.95　　92

1 Magic

"The 'untold story' in this biography is not how Houdini did his tricks (except for those with which he showed up the fakery of seance manifestations). Mr. Christopher, who is himself a past national president of the Society of American Magicians, is scrupulously loyal to the code of his profession. But his thirty years of research have unearthed many little-known incidents of Houdini's life and aspects of his character . . . his extremely sensitive 'amour-propre,' his bitter resentment of people who stole tricks from others . . . and his egotism. Mr. Christopher's book moves as swiftly . . . as Houdini slipping out of a set of Scotland Yard's best manacles." Book World

Bibliography: p268-72

Hughes, Langston

Meltzer, Milton. Langston Hughes; a biography. Crowell 1968 281p $4.50　　92

1 Poets, American 2 Negroes—Biography

"In this book we see the growth of a poet and a man. . . . Here is the young man exploring the world of life and letters; here is the burning vigor of the Black Renaissance; here is Simple, speaking his mind on the problems of 'white folks, colored folks, and just plain folks.' " Publisher's note

"An excellent biography, written with vigor and clarity, about the gifted and prolific writer whose life and writing were a testament to his belief that it was a proud thing to be black. Any book about Hughes would be fascinating because of his travels, his friends in the literary world, his involvement in causes; Milton Meltzer has added to that by making vivid the poet's passion for justice and truth." Chicago. Children's Book Center

"The author, who had collaborated with Langston Hughes on two books dealing with American Negro history, was working on a biography of his friend when Hughes suddenly died. Partly because the poet's literary executors immediately denied access to his unpublished papers and partly because Hughes' two autobiographical volumes cover only his first thirty-five years, the emphasis of this present book is largely on the early half of his life." Horn Bk

Bibliography: p269-74

Rollins, Charlemae H. Black troubadour: Langston Hughes; illus. with photographs. Rand McNally [1971 c1970] 143p illus $4.95, lib. bdg. $4.79　　92

1 Authors, American 2 Negroes—Biography

"This is a readable account which presents an affectionate portrait of [Langston Hughes] and a competent assessment of his works. Rollins traces the poet's life from boyhood, drawing mainly on information found in Hughes' two autobiographies, and discusses his stories, novels, plays, and poems underlining his distinctive qualities as an interpreter of both the black and universal human experience. The book contains a chronological listing of the honors and awards accorded Hughes, a list of his published works including an annotated section of plays and musicals for amateur dramatic groups, and photographs of Hughes, his family, and friends." Booklist

Hugo, Victor Mario, comte

Maurois, André. Victor Hugo and his world. Viking 1966 143p illus $6.95　　92

1 Authors, French

"A Studio book"

Text based on the author's: Olympio: the life of Victor Hugo, published 1956 by Harper. This book was translated from the French by Oliver Bernard. (Publisher)

Hugo, Victor M. comte—*Continued*

"More than a mere chronicle of [biographical] events and more than an essay in literary criticism, this book provides a balanced view of Victor Hugo and his achievements. The result is a sensitive and most readable work that gives a convincing and complete picture of Hugo. 113 black-and-white illustrations." Huntting

Huxley, Julian

Memories. Harper [1971 c1970] 296p illus $8.95   92

SBN 06-012132-7

First published 1970 in England

In this first volume (up to 1945) of a projected two-volume autobiography, "Huxley offers insights into the enterprise of science and the process by which he came to make it his life's work. . . . He evokes family life at the turn of the century and youth and education in [the] . . . years before World War I. Huxley describes his careers as scientist, teacher, writer, and traveler and his association with some of the great men of 20th Century biological science. . . . [Also included are] Huxley's remembrances of D. H. Lawrence, H. G. Wells, Lady Ottoline Morrell and the Bloomsbury group, and his brother Aldous." Library J

This autobiography "promises to be one of the most interesting records of the emergence of science as a dominating influence in the culture of our time." Times (London) Lit Sup

Jackson, George

Soledad brother; the prison letters of George Jackson; introduction by Jean Genet. Coward-McCann 1970 330p illus $5.95   92

1 Prisons—U.S. 2 Negroes—Biography

"A prison guard was killed at Soledad Prison. Jackson was one of three black convicts accused of murdering the white guard. The three have become known as the Soledad Brothers. . . . On Aug. 7 [1970] George Jackson's younger brother, Jonathan, led the . . . raid on the Marin County Courthouse. That event . . . brought the case of . . . George Jackson into the national news. This book is composed of letters written by Jackson to his mother, his father, Jonathan, Angela Davis, Fay Stender, his attorney and others from 1964 to two days after Jonathan's death. . . . His letters tell the story of one man's solitary act of willing himself to exist on the basis of his rage at what had been done to him as a black." N Y Times Bk R

James, Will

Lone cowboy; my life story; illus. by the author. Scribner 1932 [c1930] 431p illus $6 92

1 Cowboys

"Scribner Illustrated classics"

First published 1930

"Left an orphan at the age of five, Will James was taken in hand by the kindly 'Bopy,' a French Canadian trapper who taught him . . . outdoor lore and habits of life which stood him in good stead during his years as a wandering cowboy. . . . The book tells of his cowboy activities, of breaking into the movies as an extra, of his service in the army." Cleveland

Jefferson, Thomas, President U.S.

The Thomas Jefferson papers; selected, with commentary by Frank Donovan. Dodd [1964 c1963] 304p illus pa $1.95   92

1 Presidents—U.S. 2 U.S.—History—1783-1865 —Biography

"Apollo editions"

First published 1963 by Dodd

"Selections from Jefferson's writings in many fields, including some material addressed to the Virginian, arranged, in general, in chronological order with a running commentary by Donovan. The historic exchanges between John Adams and Jefferson . . . are duly represented." Booklist

Fleming, Thomas. The man from Monticello; an intimate life of Thomas Jefferson. Morrow 1969 409p illus boards $12.50   92

1 Presidents—U.S. 2 U.S.—History—1783-1865 —Biography

The book focuses on both the public and private life of Jefferson, analyzing their interrelationship. [The author] sees America's third President as a man who started with an ambivalent attitude towards the political life, then rose to an understanding of politics as a means to his goal of a free society." Publisher's note

This "biography is designed to entertain, and it does. Leaving to sober historians the heavier emphasis usually given to Jefferson's public life, Fleming nicely balances the statesman with the 'intimate' man. Even historic details of importance are given with a relatively light touch." Pub W

Bibliography: p391-93

Koch, Adrienne, ed. Jefferson. Prentice-Hall 1971 180p (Great lives observed) $5.95
92

1 Presidents—U.S. 2 U.S.—History—1783-1865 —Biography

ISBN 0-13509810-6

"A Spectrum book"

In this account of the President and universal man, the editor "presents Thomas Jefferson's own words, the view of his contemporaries, and analyses in retrospect by leading historians and political scientists to create a threefold perspective." Publisher's note

Bibliographical note: p176-77

Lisitzky, Gene. Thomas Jefferson. Viking 1933 358p illus lib. bdg. $4.13   92

1 Presidents—U.S. 2 U.S.—History—1783-1865 —Biography

"The life story of an amazing American, ingenious and versatile, with broad interests in national and world affairs and equally intense love for home and all its associations. The visionary writer of the Declaration of Independence becomes a human individual as pictured in these pages." Wis Lib Bul

Jenghis Khan

Lamb, Harold. Genghis Khan, the emperor of all men. Doubleday 1952 [c1927] 270p illus $4.95   92

1 Kings and rulers 2 Mongols—History

A reprint of the title first published 1927 by R. M. McBride & Company

"An account of the rise and conquest of this master strategist who marched his army across Tibet, over the Pamirs, through Afghanistan, Turkestan, Persia, Armenia, across Russia and into Poland and Hungary. This march has been acknowledged the greatest military feat in all history." N Y Times Bk R

Mr Lamb "has brought to life in the pages of a thoroughly readable book the career of a warrior whose place in history has been thus far fixed for us by the hostile accounts of three great groups of enemies whom he overthrew—Chinese, Arabic-Persian, and European." Sat R

Bibliography: p247-57

John XXIII, Pope

Trevor, Meriol. Pope John. Doubleday 1967 312p $5.95   92

1 Popes

First published 1965 in England

"A biography of the late pope which shuns sentimentality while interpreting his character in the light of his experiences and placing him in historical relation to both political and ecclesiastical events of his lifetime. . . . The brief appended bibliography includes books by and about Pope John and general references." Booklist

Johnson, Lady Bird

A White House diary. Holt 1970 806p illus $10.95   92

1 Johnson, Lyndon Baines, President U.S.
2 U.S.—Politics and government—1961-
3 Washington, D.C.—Social life and customs
4 Presidents—U.S.—Wives

SBN 03-085254-4

Johnson, Lady B.—*Continued*

This chronicle of the First Lady's days in the White House, from November 22, 1963, when the tragedy in Dallas unexpectedly altered the Johnson's lives, to January 20, 1969 when her husband left office, records both historical and family events. (Publisher)

"What a simply splendid account Lady Bird has given us of Lyndon Johnson's, and her own, five years in the White House. There has never been, and perhaps never will be, such an intimate glimpse of power in its private moments. . . . [This book] is a story for America. Part history, part family album, part the self-portrait of an exceptional woman." Book World

Johnson, Osa

I married adventure; the lives and adventures of Martin and Osa Johnson. 83 aquatone illus. Lippincott 1940 376p illus $6.95

92

1 Johnson, Martin Elmer 2 Africa—Description and travel 3 Photography of animals

The lives of Martin and Osa Johnson who for 20 years faced life and adventure in dangerous jungles in all corners of the world

"It is a good travel book, a good adventure book, a good book about animals, a good book on photography and, best of all, it is a good human story about two extremely likable people, told by one of them with simplicity, humor, warmth." N Y Her Trib Books

Johnson, Samuel, 1709-1784

Boswell, James. The life of Samuel Johnson

92

1 Authors, English

Some editions are:

Dutton (Everyman's lib) 2v ea $2.45 Introduction by Sir Sydney Roberts; index by Alan Dent

Modern Lib. (Modern Lib. Giants) $4.95 With an introduction by Herbert Askwith

Oxford (Oxford Standard authors) 2v in 1 $8 With an introduction by Chauncey Brewster Tinker

First published 1791

"The most famous biography in the English language. It is an intimate and minute delineation of the great lexicographer's life, character and person, enlivened with small-talk, gossip and bits of familiar correspondence. It is also an admirable portrayal of the society of which Johnson was the outstanding figure." Pratt Alcove

Halliday, F. E. Doctor Johnson and his world. Viking 1968 144p illus $6.95　　92

1 Authors, English

"A Studio book"

This illustrated chronicle of events in the life of Samuel Johnson includes material written about him by his friends and excerpts from his own writings

Bibliographical notes: p129

Jones, John Paul

Morison, Samuel Eliot. John Paul Jones; a sailor's biography; with charts and diagrams by Erwin Raisz and with photographs. Little 1959 xxii, 453p illus maps $8.95　　92

1 U.S. Navy—Biography 2 U.S.—History, Naval

"An Atlantic Monthly Press book"

Awarded Pulitzer Prize, 1960

"Morison gives the reader an authenticated and detailed picture of America's famous sea captain: his fiery temper, his loneliness, his charm and love of women." Huntting

He "has destroyed the myth of John Paul Jones but has left us a more human, more understandable character, who through his sailing and his fighting, showed that he truly deserved to be called the 'Father of the U.S. Navy.' " Best Sellers

Bibliography: p431-43

Jonson, Ben

Chute, Marchette. Ben Jonson of Westminster. Dutton 1953 380p front $6.95　　92

1 Authors, English

A "re-creation of the life and times of one of England's great literary figures, this gives abundant evidence of prodigious research and makes both the man and the world in which he lived intensely real." Booklist

"To read this book is to visit England in the time of Queen Elizabeth and King James, to learn how people lived, talked and thought, to know as intimately as one's own friends the leading writers, nobility, and royalty of the period, and especially the fascinating and vigorous central character." Sec Ed Brd

Selected bibliography: p351-60. Map on lining-papers

Joyce, James

Anderson, Chester G. James Joyce and his world. Viking [1968 c1967] 144p illus map $6.95　　92

1 Authors, Irish 2 Dublin—Social life and customs

"A Studio book"

First published 1967 in England

This illustrated biography explores the details of Joyce's life from his Dublin childhood to his self-imposed exile in Switzerland and France, and relates his life to his work. (Publisher)

"A good text, careful, accurate and perceptive. . . . The 124 illustrations have in many cases an almost magical power of evocation of Dublin in 1904. Quite a number of them are unfamiliar, and in the midst of such riches a few old, bad ones can be tolerated. . . . An outstanding picture book." Economist

Bibliographical notes: p133

Kaiulani, Princess of Hawaii

Webb, Nancy. Kaiulani: Crown Princess of Hawaii [by] Nancy and Jean Francis Webb. Viking 1962 218p $4.50　　92

1 Hawaii—History

"Kaiulani, niece of the last reigning monarch of Hawaii, Queen Liliuokalani, and heir apparent to the throne, is shown here as a beautiful, sweet, dignified person, always popular with her people but never called upon to do anything or be anything but a symbol of futile hopes. . . . As a young girl she left Hawaii to attend school in England and thus entered what proved to be a ten-year period of troubled but uneventful exile. After the annexation of Hawaii to the U.S., she returned home but died shortly afterward at the age of twenty-four. In telling the story of Hawaiian annexation, the authors make no pretense of presenting both sides—they are definitely in sympathy with the opposition; however, their attitude will not detract from the value of the book as a romantic story with interesting historical background." Booklist

Keats, John, 1795-1821

Hilton, Timothy. Keats and his world. Viking 1971 144p illus maps $7.95　　92

1 Poets, English

SBN 670-41196-5

"A Studio book"

The author "combines biography with literary criticism and relates both to the places that Keats knew, and to the people and books that molded his personality. Engravings, photographs, portraits, and reproductions of the poet's own manuscripts illustrate almost every stage of his career—from his childhood to . . . the last tragic journey to Rome." Publisher's note

Bibliography: p131

Ward, Aileen. John Keats; the making of a poet. Viking 1963 450p illus $8.95　　92

1 Poets, English

The author presents an "image of the artist engaged in a significant process of 'self-making.' She traces Keats's developing awareness of identity from his years as a medical apprentice on: through his decision to become a poet, and his struggle for personal as well as poetic mastery; through family trials, the death of his loved younger brother, the beginnings of his passionate attachment to Fanny Brawne; to its final triumphant expression in his last poems, written on the eve of his decline into illness and death." Publisher's note

Notes: p416-40. Selective bibliography: p441-42

Keller, Helen Adams

The story of my life. . . . Introduction by Ralph Barton Perry. Doubleday 1954 382p illus $5.95   92

1 Blind 2 Deaf

First published 1903

"With letters (1887-1901) and a supplementary account of her education, including passages from the reports and letters of her teacher, Anne Mansfield Sullivan, by John Albert Macy." Title page

"The book is indeed unique. The story itself and the years of effort which have made its telling possible, the personality which it reveals, and the creation of that personality—these are things which seem little short of miraculous. The narrative of a young woman who has been deaf and blind from infancy is written in a style which is not only idiomatic, but individual and rhythmical." Pittsburgh

Waite, Helen E. Valiant companions: Helen Keller and Anne Sullivan Macy. Macrae Smith Co. 1959 223p $4.25   92

1 Macy, Anne (Sullivan) 2 Deaf—Education 3 Blind—Education

"The story of Helen Keller and her teacher, Anne Sullivan, who was engaged when the blind and deaf child was only seven. Through a combination of patience and hard work, the teacher helped Helen to overcome her afflictions and go on to become one of the outstanding women of our age. Based on new information found during the author's research." Bk Buyer's Guide

Bibliography: p223

Kemble, Francis Anne

Rushmore, Robert. Fanny Kemble. Crowell-Collier Press 1970 213p front lib. bdg. $4.95   92

A biography of the famed 19th century British actress, Fanny Kemble. Married at the height of her career to a Philadelphian who owned Southern plantations, Fanny's outrage over existing conditions was recorded in a journal. When her marriage ended because of the couple's conflicting views on slavery, Fanny resumed her acting career, returned to England, and published her journal which was credited with swinging British sympathies from the Confederate to the Union side

"This is a sensitive, beautifully-written book, exceptional for its picture of slavery and for a truthful, moving account of its subject's marriage." N Y Times Bk R

Recommended reading: p209

Kennedy, John Fitzgerald, President U.S.

Bishop, Jim. A day in the life of President Kennedy. Random House 1964 108p boards $5.95   92

1 Presidents—U.S. 2 Kennedy family

The author "tells how each hour of a particular day was spent by the President, Mrs. Kennedy, the children, and the office and domestic White House staff." Pubisher's note

"Jim Bishop has presented his subject in so many and diverse aspects of his personality that both friends and foes of the Kennedys will discover some new insights into the man himself." Best Sellers

Bishop, Jim. The day Kennedy was shot. Funk 1968 713p $7.95   92

1 Kennedy, John Fitzgerald, President U.S. —Assassination 2 Presidents—U.S.

"An extremely detailed hour-by-hour, kaleidoscopic recapitulation of the day President Kennedy was assassinated and the actions and reactions of the principals involved. Journalistic in style, compelling in minutiae of content, and based on extensive research and numerous interviews, including one with President Johnson, the book agrees, on the whole, with the Warren Commission Report and offers little in the way of new revelations." Booklist

The author "re-creates the scene, events, and characters from the words of the common man and brings the scene to the common man. He is more real than television. In other ways, Jim Bishop leads with his chin. Some of his scenes are overemotional; the Kennedy autopsy is described in too vivid detail . . . he is repetitive. The almost 700-page book could have done with some judicious cutting." Pub W

Source material: p689-93. Maps on lining-papers

The Kennedy years; text by The New York Times; photographs by Jacques Lowe and others. . . . Viking 1964 327p illus $16.50   92

1 Presidents—U.S.

Aso available in a reduced format for $6.95

"Text prepared under the direction of Harold Faber with contributions by John Corry, Paul Greenfeder, Lee Kanner, Alvin Shuster, Warren Weaver, Jr. Introduction by Tom Wicker; contributing photographer George Tames." Title page

Text and photographs record the individuals and events of Kennedy's life and administration

This large-sized "book on Kennedy and his time in government is neither history nor on-the-spot reporting. It is a combination—a . . . souvenir and a recapitulation of intelligent reporting." Book Week

Manchester, William. The death of a President, November 20-November 25, 1963. Harper 1967 710p illus maps $10   92

1 Kennedy, John Fitzgerald, President U.S.— Assassination 2 Presidents—U.S.

William Manchester "has at the suggestion of the Kennedy family undertaken to report the most tragic event of recent years. After an introductory sketch of President Kennedy's life in the White House, the first part of the book covers events from the President's departure for Texas until the stricken widow, her entourage, and President Johnson embark on the return flight from Dallas. Part two includes the flight, arrival in Washington, and the funeral ceremonies. Both parts provide a vivid and very detailed account of what happened in those fateful days. It involves a great number of places and personalities, and some readers may be confused by the many minor figures that appear from time to time; but Manchester's ability to reflect the reactions of such varied people throughout the nation enhances the interest and grips the attention. Readers also gain a glimpse behind the scenes of leading circles in Washington. In such moments of crisis an individual's true nature and certain personal and political differences become apparent. Time will tell where errors and misunderstandings have arisen." Library J

Glossary: p x-xvi. Sources: p659-77

Manchester, William. Portrait of a President; John F. Kennedy in profile. Rev. ed. with a new introduction and epilogue   92

1 Presidents—U.S. 2 U.S.—Politics and government—1961-

Some editions are:

Little $5.95

Watts, F. $10 Large type edition. A Keith Jennsion book

First published 1962

The period covered is April 1961 to April 1962, but the author points out that this is not a chronological account. In this detailed close-up of the late President, the reader gains new insight into his early life, his family, the war years, the years in Congress, and his rise to the most powerful office in the world. (Publisher)

"It is a study of the development of character under terrific stress." New Repub

Includes bibliography

Salinger, Pierre. With Kennedy. Doubleday 1966 391p illus $5.95   92

1 Presidents—U.S. 2 U.S.—History—20th century—Biography

"Beginning with the news of John F. Kennedy's assassination, the author backtracks to his days as an investigating reporter from 1946 on, his work with Robert Kennedy inquiring into the activities of corrupt officials of the Teamsters Union, and his association with JFK as Press Secretary, covering the Presidential campaign, the Cuban crisis, etc. With photographic illustrations, transcripts, and index." Bk Buyer's Guide

Kennedy, John F. President U.S.—*Continued*

"There is a certain amount of triviality, too, but even this will prove of eventual value to the full-dress historian. The style is that of a busy reporter with rolled-up sleeves, but in recollections like this, one cannot demand deathless prose." Book of the Month Club News

Sorensen, Theodore C. Kennedy. Harper 1965 783p front $10   **92**

1 Presidents—U.S. 2 U.S.—Politics and government

Recollections of the late President by his Special Counsel. Covering the 1953-63 period this is a "portrait of Kennedy's emergence into political maturity and of his increased knowledge of the country, of world affairs, of his own abilities and of administrative tactics as he fought the tough political battles of 1956-1960. Most of all, the book shows the man at work in the Presidency." Pub W

"Written in a scholarly style it is probably the most important overall evaluation of the Kennedy incumbency to date. Readers can see a John F. Kennedy complete with pride, sensitivity, and even a trace of vindictiveness arise from its pages. Openly partisan in treating civil rights and domestic economic policy, Sorensen skillfully shows that since Kennedy's philosophy of government was keyed to power, he viewed the Presidency as the fulfilment of that goal not as a matter of personal ambition but of national obligation." Best Sellers

"Appended are actions of the 86th and 87th Congresses and a chronology of Kennedy's Presidency." Booklist

United Press International. Four days; the historical record of the death of President Kennedy; comp. by United Press International and American Heritage Magazine. Am. Heritage 1964 143p illus boards $2.95   **92**

1 Kennedy, John Fitzgerald, President U.S.—Assassination 2 Presidents—U.S.

Introduction by Bruce Catton

"This record of the four days from November 22 to November 25, 1963 includes the report of the assassination of President Kennedy by United Press reporter Merriman Smith, eulogies, and comments from the world press. Photographs record the death of the President, the funeral, and the shooting of Lee Harvey Oswald in the police station at Dallas." Book Rev Digest

"A restrained, well-designed, very moving record." Atlantic

Kennedy, Robert Francis

Halberstam, David. The unfinished odyssey of Robert Kennedy. Random House [1969 c1968] 211p boards $4.95   **92**

1 U.S.—Politics and government—1961-

A "study of the growth of Robert Kennedy as a politician and human being, of the huge distance between the young man who admired Joe McCarthy and the presidential candidate who had to contend with the conflicting forces and ambitions of a spectrum ranging from Cesar Chavez and Charles Evers to Mayor Daley—and yet who exemplified the aspirations of the unlikely coalition." Publisher's note

"Halberstam's extremely readable book shows him to be an admirer of the late Bobby Kennedy who does not demean his memory by any attempt to nourish a 'legend' or to paint out the warts in the portrait." Pub W

Newfield, Jack. Robert Kennedy; a memoir. Dutton 1969 318p $6.95   **92**

1 U.S.—Politics and government—1961-
ISBN 0-525-19315-4

This book "is a chronicle and analysis of Robert Kennedy's politics and character between the gunshots of Dallas and Los Angeles. It is therefore necessarily a book about the changes and convulsions in America between 1963 and 1968—a half-decade of war, violence, racism, and social chaos." Publisher's note

"Newfield was quite close to RFK, and the depth of his affection is measured by the honesty of his portrait: Kennedy's flaws are there, but seen as human traits that in some ways

incapacitated him for politics. . . . [The author's] intimate glimpses and insights add up affectingly to a picture of Robert Kennedy as a man 'becoming'—a man who, agonizing and indecisive after the Dallas tragedy, grew with each experience." Pub W

Stein, Jean. American journey; the times of Robert Kennedy; interviews by Jean Stein; ed. by George Plimpton. Harcourt 1970 372p $8.95   **92**

"Senator Robert Kennedy was buried in Arlington Cemetery on June 8, 1969. His body had been transported by train from New York City to Washington. The subject of this book is the train, the people on it, the mourners and the curious along the tracks, and the friends, enemies, and associates of Robert Kennedy. Over two hundred people were contacted for their opinions on this last ride; the question was, how did they think of Kennedy himself." Best Sellers

Kennedy, Rose (Fitzgerald)

Cameron, Gail. Rose; a biography of Rose Fitzgerald Kennedy. Putnam 1971 247p illus $6.95   **92**

Kennedy family

This biography of the matriarch of one of America's greatest political families portrays her as "a figure of striking paradoxes: a devout daily communicant in somber black, a woman of spectacular beauty, a leader in the world of fashion. For years she has drawn searching questions: How did she raise such a remarkable family? Is she the real 'power' behind the Kennedys? How can she bear over and over such unspeakable tragedies?" Publisher's note

Khrushchev, Nikita Sergeevich

Crankshaw, Edward. Khrushchev; a career. Viking 1966 311p illus $7.50   **92**

1 Dictators 2 Russia—Politics and government—1917-

The author "tells of Khrushchev's long road to power, his rise as yes-man to Stalin until he destroyed his benefactor's name, and the mixture of expediency, idealism, and corruption that made him a powerful leader but chained him to political intrigue." Bk Buyer's Guide

"Crankshaw does not absolve Khrushchev . . . of most of the well-known faults of an autocrat. It is possible that this will stand as the best biography of Khrushchev. At any rate, it is an impressive portrait in depth, set against the background of Soviet Russian history, 1919-1964." Pub W

Bibliography included in Notes: p293-302

King, Coretta Scott

My life with Martin Luther King, Jr. Holt 1969 372p illus $6.95   **92**

1 King, Martin Luther 2 Negroes—Biography
SBN 03-081022-1

An autobiography by the widow of Martin Luther King, Jr. which discusses her girlhood, their meeting and marriage and the life they shared. It also describes the ordeal which began for them so soon after marriage and which became a constant part of their lives because of their dedication to an ideal

"On the whole, a calm, gentle and graceful sequence of reminiscences and reflections, [this book] is less important as a chronicle of the movement and an assessment of King's impact on the country, than as a widow's epitaph, characterized by a decorous restraint, for a husband who happened to be a hero." Book World

King, Martin Luther

Bennett, Lerone. What manner of man; a biography of Martin Luther King, Jr. by Lerone Bennett, Jr. with an introduction by Benjamin E. Mays. [3d rev. ed] Johnson Pub. (Chicago) 1968 251p illus $5.95   **92**

1 Negroes—Biography   2 Negroes—Civil rights

King, Martin L.—*Continued*

First published 1964

The author recalls Martin Luther King's childhood, education, accomplishments as a Baptist minister, his leadership in the Negro Civil Rights movement, his winning the 1964 Nobel Peace Prize and his tragic end in 1968

"Lerone Bennett's biography is a competent, thoughtful presentation of the facts of King's life as well as various influences, characteristics and decisions that help the reader to understand who King [was]." Critic

Lincoln, C. Eric, ed. Martin Luther King, Jr. A profile. Hill & Wang 1970 232p (American profiles) $5.95   92

1 Negroes—Biography 2 Negroes—Civil rights
SBN 8090-6351-4

"American century series"

"Selection from three biographies and such diverse periodicals as 'Reader's Digest' and 'New Politics' follow C. Eric Lincoln's introduction and brief biography.... These [thirteen] essays ... examine, from several viewpoints, his philosophy of non-violence, his changing role in the Negro revolution, and his opposition to the war in Vietnam." Library J

Bibliography: p229-30

Lahr, Bert

Lahr, John. Notes on a cowardly lion; the biography of Bert Lahr. Knopf 1969 394p illus $8.95   92

1 Actors and actresses

A biography of Bert Lahr, the famed lion in: The Wizard of Oz. This book covers Lahr's career from his early vaudeville days through his Hollywood trials and tribulations to his later stage roles including his part in: Waiting for Godot

"The writing throughout ... is excellent. Most biographies of stage luminaries are adulatory, congratulatory and trivial. What strikes me forcibly in John Lahr's book is the fact that some of the descriptions of his father's performances he could not have seen (because too young) are often more telling than those by reviewers who did see them. The past becomes present in this biography, so that we come to know and understand the actor as clearly as the man." N Y Times Bk R

Laubach, Frank Charles

Medary, Marjorie. Each one teach one; Frank Laubach, friend to millions. McKay 1954 227p illus $4.95   92

1 Illiteracy 2 Missionaries

First published by Longmans

The missionary "whose campaigns have helped to teach sixty million people of Asia, Africa and South America to read is the subject of this enthusiastic biographical sketch. He began his work among the illiterate and half-savage Moro tribes of the Philippines, for whom he devised a simple system of charts and key words for teaching them to read quickly. Since then he has prepared similar lessons in 245 tongues and dialects." Rel Bk Club Bul

"This informative volume on a revolutionary technique to adult education—whereby when one person is taught, he teaches another, and so on—presents a personal challenge and appeal to help perform a gigantic and rewarding task." Library J

Bibliography: p225-27

Leakey, Louis Seymour Bazett

Mulvey, Mina White. Digging up Adam; the story of L. S. B. Leakey; illus. with photographs; map and decoration by Russ Anderson. McKay 1969 216p illus map $4.95, lib. bdg. $4.19   92

1 Anthropologists 2 Man, Prehistoric 3 Archeology 4 Kenya

"A biography of the anthropologist L. S. B. Leakey, born in Kenya of missionary parents and now through choice a citizen of Kenya, can hardly fail to be a fascinating account. While the insights and historical perspective

provided of the people of this new African state are important, they are secondary to the account of Leakey's determined and eventually successful search for early man and the ancestors of early man in East Africa. The author has admirably traced the broader development of our knowledge of man's ancestry and cultural evolution as a background to the unfolding of Leakey's career." Science Bks

Books for further reading: p208-09

Lee, Robert Edward

Commager, Henry Steele. America's Robert E. Lee [by] Henry Steele Commager & Lynd Ward. Houghton 1951 111p illus $4.25, lib. bdg. $3.73   92

1 Generals 2 U.S.—History—Civil War—Biography

"The story of the great Confederate general, his childhood, his career at West Point, and his choice between the united country he served so well, and the Southern traditions he loved." McClurg. Book News

Freeman, Douglas Southall. Lee of Virginia. Scribner 1958 243p illus lib. bdg. $4.05   92

1 Generals 2 U.S.—History—Civil War—Biography

"The major portion of the book is devoted to the Civil War years, but the stress, even during that period, is on the character of the man rather than on his career. In serious, but highly effective style. Mr. Freeman presents Lee as West Point student, family man, Mexican campaigner, Confederate general, and college president." Chicago. Children's Book Center

"Mr. Freeman includes many anecdotes, quotations and colorful incidents relating to Lee, his family and associates that enliven the narrative. At the same time he slights none of the important elements in Lee's own life and character or the stirring events of the period as these related to his subject." N Y Times Bk R

Miers, Earl Schenck. Robert E. Lee; a great life in brief. Knopf 1956 203p map (Great lives in brief) $3.95   92

1 Generals 2 U.S.—History—Civil War—Biography

"In tracing the influences that molded Lee—the aristocratic, idealistic Virginian, the supremely gifted military leader, the gentle and intensely human husband, father, and friend—the author has given us not only a portrait of the man, but also an insight into the dark and dramatic events that called forth the full expression of his genius." Publisher's note

The aim is to present "a concise and authoritative record intended for the reader for whom an encyclopedia account is too brief and a standard biography is too detailed. Mr. Miers's book more than fills the bill." Sat R

Includes bibliography

Lenin, Vladimir Il'ich

Payne, Robert. The life and death of Lenin. Simon & Schuster 1964 672p illus $8.50   92

1 Dictators 2 Communism—Russia 3 Russia—History—Revolution, 1917-1921

This biography of Lenin covers his "years of power: the July Days, the October Revolution, the Civil War, the Kronstadt mutiny, the intricate web of decrees, laws, executions and assassinations that followed the birth of the Soviet Republic." Publisher's note

"Payne concentrates on Lenin the man. Lenin the politician, planner, and pamphleteer is given less attention, and Payne tends to evaluate Lenin's writing almost as much for its style as for its content. This popularized biography is fluent and highly readable." Pub W

Bibliography: p641-44. Map on lining-papers

Trotsky, Leon. Lenin; notes for a biographer; with an introduction by Bertram D. Wolfe; tr. from the Russian and annotated by Tamara Deutscher. Putnam 1971 224p $5.95   92

1 Dictators   2 Russia—History   3 Russia—History—Revolution, 1917-1921

Lenin, Vladimir I.—*Continued*

Originally published in Russian. First English translation published 1925 by Minton, Balch & Company

This book "consists of sketches and fragments relating chiefly to two periods in Lenin's life during which he and Trotsky were closely associated: first, their work together in London, during 1902, on Iskra, a journal published under Lenin's direction; second, recollections of the decisive year of the October revolution in Russia. Trotsky reveals frankly the course of their relations during these two periods, and adds several articles and speeches characterizing Lenin, the man." Book Rev Digest

"This is a series of reflections by one who was very close to the . . . Soviet leader. It is as revealing of the author as it is of its subject, perhaps more. Deutscher's . . . notes should prove useful to the reader encountering either Trotsky, Lenin, or Russian Marxism for the first time. Bertram Wolfe's introduction is perceptive and helps put these notes into the larger perspective of Trotsky's life and work." Choice

Leonardo da Vinci

Horizon Magazine. Leonardo da Vinci, by the editors of Horizon Magazine. Author: Jay Williams; consultant: Bates Lowry. . . . Am. Heritage 1965 153p ,illus map boards $5.95, lib. bdg. $5.49   92

1 Painters, Italian 2 Renaissance

"A Horizon Caraval book"

"Illustrated with the paintings, drawings, and diagrams of Leonardo da Vinci." Title page

This "text follows Leonardo's progress back and forth between Florence and Milan and later to Rome and France, describing and evaluating his scientific and engineering projects as well as his paintings and other artistic achievements. . . . Excellent illustrations." Booklist

Further reference: p149

Wallace, Robert, 1919-   The world of Leonardo, 1452-1519, by Robert Wallace and the editors of Time-Life Books. Time, inc. [distributed by Little] 1966 192p illus (Time-Life Lib. of art) boards $7.95   92

1 Art, Italian

"Selection of the works of Leonardo the artist, the scientist and anticipator of the modern age of technology and invention is accompanied by a text which presents and analyzes the stages of Leonardo's life and growth, including numerous quotations from his own notes and writings. We follow this representative life against the social and artistic background of his century from Leonardo's Florentine period to the zenith of his career in the service of the Duke of Milan and his later years in Venice. . . . Equally impressive is the long series of his drawings included in this volume, which reflect the vast range of his technological imagination; further his late self-portrait, archetype of the thinking man; and the drawings showing the aging genius's uncanny visions of a cosmic deluge." Library J

Bibliography: p187-88

Lewis, Meriwether

Dillon, Richard. Meriwether Lewis; a biography. Capricorn Bks. [1968 c1965] 364p illus pa $2.25   92

1 Clark, William, 1770-1838 2 Lewis and Clark Expedition

First published 1965 by Coward-McCann

The author chronicles Lewis' expedition with William Clark up the Missouri River, a feat which opened up the American West. Mr. Dillon also recalls Lewis' "youth in Virginia, his close relationship with Thomas Jefferson, his preparation for the expedition, his turbulent career as Governor of the Louisiana Territory, and his tragic and mysterious death." Publisher's note

"Lewis's gracefulness as a writer and skill as a diplomat among the Indians are also pointed out by a biographer whose . . . . reconstruction often makes use of Lewis' own journals." Booklist

Bibliographical note: p353-55

Lewis, Sinclair

O'Connor, Richard. Sinclair Lewis. McGraw 1971 144p front (American writers) lib. bdg. $4.75   92

1 Authors, American
SBN 07-047535-0

An account of the life and work of the 20th century American novelist who "repeatedly returned to the small town atmosphere of Main Street and peopled it with a host of memorable characters such as Carol and Will Kennicott, George Babbitt, Elmer Gantry, Sam and Fran Dodsworth, Cass and Ginny Timberlane." Publisher's note

Bibliography: p140

Schorer, Mark. Sinclair Lewis; an American life. McGraw 1961 xxiii, 867p illus $2.98   92

1 Authors, American 2 U.S.—Social life and customs

"A biography of Harry Sinclair Lewis, from Sauk City, Minnesota; mixed up, a failure as a husband, a hard drinker, lonely, yet a brilant success as a novelist—the man who refused the Pulitzer Prize, won the Nobel Prize, and wrote 'Main Street,' 'Elmer Gantry,' 'Arrowsmith,' and other novels both good and bad." Bk Buyer's Guide

This "masterly study is not merely a life of Lewis, it is a panorama of twentieth-century America, before World War II, a social history as well as a 'life,' a biography that fuses into a single whole, acute psychological penetration and a profound grasp of American culture in the period under survey." Christian Science Monitor

Lincoln, Abraham, President U.S.

Bishop, Jim. The day Lincoln was shot; with illus. selected and arranged by Stefan Lorant. Harper 1955 304p illus maps $6.95, lib. bdg. $5.79   92

1 Lincoln, Abraham, President U.S.—Assassination 2 Presidents—U.S.

The complete record of the dramatic events which occurred on the day Lincoln was shot in Ford's Theatre. The chapters start with one for 7 A.M. April 14, 1865 and close with one for 7 A.M. April 15, 1865

"A dramatically detailed account of the conspiracy which led to Lincoln's assassination and the tragic events of the day on which it took place. The author's vast research on the subject combined with his ability to make the reader feel 'he is there' add up to a fascinating account of an important event." Library J

Horgan, Paul. Citizen of New Salem; illus. by Douglas Gorsline. Farrar, Straus 1961 89p illus boards $3.75   92

1 Presidents—U.S.

Written in honor of the centennial of Lincoln's first inauguration on March 4, 1861, this biography chronicles his years in New Salem, Illinois. Lincoln was twenty-one when he came there as a flatboatman and he was twenty-eight when he left for Springfield as a new counsellor at law. His development during these crucial years is seen against a background of frontier society. (Publisher)

Acknowledgement: p[93]

Lorant, Stefan. Lincoln; a picture story of his life. Rev. enl. ed. Norton 1969 336p illus map $10   92

1 Presidents—U.S.   2 U.S.—History—Civil War—Pictures, illustrations, etc.
SBN 393-07446-3

First published 1952

The Lincoln story is told through more than 700 pictures with a running text arranged chronologically

"One of the indispensable and fascinating works of Lincoln hagiography." Nation

Contents and bibliography: p329-34

Lincoln, Abraham, President U.S.—Cont.

Plowden, David, comp. Lincoln and his America, 1809-1865; with the words of Abraham Lincoln. Arranged by David Plowden and the editors of the Viking Press; foreword by John Gunther. Viking 1970 352p illus maps $22.50   92

1 Presidents—U.S. 2 U.S.—History—Civil War —Pictures, illustrations, etc.
SBN 670-42933-3

"A Studio book"
"Hundreds of contemporary and modern-day photographs, drawings, and paintings portray Lincoln and the persons, events, and scenes associated with him, with excerpts from his own writings and speeches quoted liberally throughout the accompanying text. . . . Pictures and text are well selected and arranged and the illustrations beautifully reproduced to make an attractive though heavy book for browsing. A chronology of national events during Lincoln's lifetime and key events in his life and a one-page bibliography of sources are appended." Booklist

Sandburg, Carl. Abe Lincoln grows up. . . . With illus. by James Daugherty. Harcourt 1928 222p illus $4.25   92

1 Presidents—U.S. 2 Frontier and pioneer life
"Reprinted from Abraham Lincoln: The prairie years." Title page
Includes "the first twenty-seven chapters of the original work, apparently with some necessary adaptation, thus telling the story of Lincoln's birth and childhood in Kentucky, the family migration to Indiana and their life there, the removal to Illinois and young Abe's activities of many sorts up to the time in 1831 of his flatboat trip to New Orleans and return, and ending with his departure for New Salem to start life on his own account." N Y Times Bk R
"The illustrations by James Daugherty catch the spirit of the book and of the times." Wis Lib Bul

Sandburg, Carl. Abraham Lincoln: The prairie years; with illus. from photographs, and many cartoons, sketches, maps and letters. Abridged ed. in one volume. Harcourt 1929 [c1926] 604p illus maps $10   92

1 Presidents—U.S. 2 Frontier and pioneer life
This abridgment of the original edition in two volumes published 1926, has been reduced about one tenth and many illustrations have been omitted, although about forty still remain
"The extreme simplicity of Mr Sandburg's style and his poetic interpretation of the great but simple life of his subject makes this biography admirably suited to youthful readers. Not a juvenile book but a child-like one." Cleveland

Sandburg, Carl. Abraham Lincoln: The prairie years and The war years. Illustrated ed. Harcourt 1970 640p illus maps $12.95   92

1 Presidents—U.S. 2 Frontier and pioneer life 3 U.S.—History—Civil War—Biography
First published 1954
A condensation of the two volumes of "The prairie years" and the four volumes of "The war years. The author has taken advantage of material recently made available to include in this edition of his lifetime study of Lincoln
"A biography that as a whole is superior to the longer life. This one volume has a form which the six lacked. It is a tighter and tidier book. It retains the superb qualities of the original work without the faults of the latter." Sat R
Sources of acknowledgments: p743-47

Lincoln, Mary (Todd)

Randall, Ruth Painter. I Mary; a biography of the girl who married Abraham Lincoln. Little 1959 242p illus $3.95   92

1 Presidents—U.S.—Wives 2 Lincoln, Abraham, President U.S.
A portrait of the rich little fun-loving girl who grew up to be one of the country's first

ladies, at a time of national crisis. This biography presents both the gaiety and tragedy in the lives of Mary and "Mr Lincoln." (Publisher)
"Photographs of the Lincolns and other contemporary photographs and prints are woven into the text, giving the book a kind of Victorian atmosphere. Mrs. Randall is very sympathetic toward her subject though she does not omit stories of her extravagance and vanity. She deals very sensibly with Mrs. Lincoln's insanity, and she quietly demolishes the Ann Rutledge legend." Pub W
Bibliography: p219-29

Randall, Ruth Painter. Mary Lincoln; biography of a marriage. Little 1953 555p illus $8.95   92

1 Presidents—U.S.—Wives 2 Lincoln, Abraham, President U.S.
"A biography of the wife of Abraham Lincoln, based on all available documents, which presents her case in a different light than that of her detractors. It is also the story of a marriage and of the homelife of the Lincolns." Book Rev Digest
"The real value of her book is not the execution it does among the slanderers. It is her marvelous ability to make the reader understand the torment to which an emotionally unstable woman was subjected in Mary Todd Lincoln's situation." New Repub
Bibliography: p517-29

Lind, Jenny

Benét, Laura. Enchanting Jenny Lind. Illus. with decorations by George Gillett Whitney and photographs. Dodd 1939 452p illus $5   92

1 Singers

"My desire has been, not to write a fictional account but an authentic biography of Jenny Lind's first thirty years." Acknowledgment
"While the author shows clearly, as a background, the very different period in which the singer lived, she makes her a real person with whom the girl of today will feel at home." N Y Times Bk R

Lindbergh, Charles Augustus, 1902-

The wartime journals of Charles A. Lindbergh. Harcourt 1970 xx, 1038p illus $12.95   92

1 World War, 1939-1945—Personal narratives
ISBN 0-15-194625-6

The journals "cover the pre-World War II period, when the celebrated flier was in Europe surveying military aviation . . . [and] the war years when . . . he served as a civilian aeronautical expert in private industry and the Pacific, also managing to work in 50 combat missions; and the weeks just after the Nazi surrender, which found him again in Europe, attached to a Naval Mission studying wartime developments in plane design and missiles. . . . Not a sentence excoriates Nazism as a general credo or poses it as a menace to civilization in any tenable definition of the word, including Lindbergh's own. . . . Lindbergh emerges from the journals something of an American original, a first rate mind who was widely informed yet retained certain key areas of naivete." N Y Times Bk R
Glossary: p1003-12. Map on lining-papers

"We." . . . With a foreword by Myron T. Herrick; fully illustrated. Putnam 1927 318p illus $5.95   92

1 Aeronautics—Flights

"The famous flier's own story of his life, and his transatlantic flight, together with his views on the future of aviation." Subtitle
"Simple, straightforward story of his life, especially the training and experiments in aviation. . . . Lindbergh's own chapters are supplemented by Fitzhugh Green's account of the unparalleled ovation accorded him abroad and at home. . . . Interesting illustrations from photographs." Cleveland

Lindbergh, Charles A.—*Continued*

Ross, Walter S. The last hero: Charles A. Lindbergh. Harper 1968 402p illus $7.95   **92**

1 Aeronautics

"The revealing story of the man who is an unwilling legend in his own time—his spectacular solo flight across the Atlantic; the tragic kidnapping and death of his infant son; his controversial stand against U.S. involvement in World War II; his combat service in the Pacific war—his contributions to such widely-differing fields as medicine and rocketry." Literary Guide

Ross "has constructed a fair and thoughtful biography of a grossly misunderstood, pursued, idolized, and abused man. . . . [He] has immersed himself in Lindbergh's life, going to old records and recent books and articles, to memoirs by friends and acquaintances, and to people willing to be interviewed. . . . What he has learned is presented to us in that direct, old-fashioned way which allows the reader to comprehend a child's struggles, a man's achievements and failures, without being made to feel that any life is only an excuse for the elaboration of this or that 'larger' historical or psychological or economic theory." New Republic

Sources and acknowledgments: p371-72

Lindsay, John Vliet

Hentoff, Nat. A political life; the education of John V. Lindsay. Knopf 1969 354p $6.95   **92**

1 Mayors 2 New York (City)—Politics and government

The author describes the career of John Lindsay as a congressman and as Mayor of the City of New York. He considers that the fundamental drama of Lindsay has been the conflict between his own moral views and the complex, often contradictory demands of his job as Mayor, and reports on this conflict as he himself has observed it in conversations with the Mayor, his colleagues, friends, admirers, and enemies. (Publisher)

"Most of the text is a highly personal evaluation, often critical of Lindsay's policies and practices at particular times, but more pleasing to the mayor's friends than his foes. Hentoff uses his conversations with insiders skillfully (though without documentation) to make a readable narrative for anyone concerned with New York City politics or with urban problems in general." Library J

Lloyd George, David Lloyd George, 1st Earl

Gilbert, Martin, ed. Lloyd George. Prentice-Hall 1968 182p (Great lives observed) $5.95   **92**

1 Statesmen, British

"A Spectrum book"

This is "a detailed study presenting contemporary and modern views of Lloyd George, British political leader and statesman during World War I. Included are excerpts from the speeches and writings of Lloyd George expressing his thoughts on war, social justice, peacemaking, and diplomacy. Extracted opinions of Winston Churchill, Stanley Baldwin, and others indicate the impact of Lloyd George upon his contemporaries. Seven essays by modern British and American historians critically appraise the political accomplishments of Lloyd George. The editor provides a biographical introduction, an afterword, a chronology of the life of Lloyd George, and a bibliographical note." Booklist

Lombardi, Vince

Kramer, Jerry, ed. Lombardi: winning is the only thing. [Maddick Manuscripts, inc.; distributed by] World Pub. 1970 173p illus $6.95   **92**

1 Football—Biography

"This book, edited by one of Lombardi's most notable players, is composed of reminiscences by some two dozen colleagues and players who knew Lombardi best. Earl H. (Red) Blaik recalls Lombardi's years as an assistant coach at West Point. Paul Hornung, Bart Starr, Willie Davis, Henry Jordan, and others tell how it was to be a member of the 'Pack' in those fabulous years during the 1960's." Library J

"With regard to sport, it is a fact-full and action-full account of the most successful and intelligent coach his sport has ever seen. It is the penetrating story of the last great super-coach of this space age." Best Sellers

London, Jack

O'Connor, Richard. Jack London; a biography. Little 1964 430p illus boards $6.75   **92**

1 Authors, American

"A most compelling [biography] with excellent source material on the youth, seafaring adventures, two marriages, and the extensive literary career of an amazing author. O'Connor gives a fine, documented, journalistic account of a complex personality, pathetic in his groping for fulfillment of human needs and overpowering in his energetic drives toward accomplishing his goals." Library J

Selected bibliography: p411-14

Long, Huey Pierce

Graham, Hugh Davis, ed. Huey Long. Prentice-Hall 1970 184p (Great lives observed) $5.95   **92**

1 Louisiana—Politics and government

"A Spectrum book"

"Huey Long was labeled at various times a demagogue, a fascist, a communist, a dictator, and a populist democrat. . . . Through writings by Long himself, by his friends and enemies, and by more objective historians and biographers, this volume reveals the . . . personality of the 'Louisiana Kingfish' that prompted such diverse reactions." Publisher's note

Bibliographical note: p179-81

Longfellow, Henry Wadsworth

Wagenknecht, Edward. Henry Wadsworth Longfellow: portrait of an American humanist. Oxford 1966 252p front $6.50   **92**

1 Poets, American

First published 1955 by Longmans with title: Longfellow: a full-length portrait. This shorter edition "contains the essence of the earlier book, reorganized and with some added material." Pub W

"A study of Longfellow based on research in primary sources and covering all of the poet's life." McClurg. Book News

"It will be welcomed as a brief, fair, and sensible account of the life of an American poet too little appreciated in this century." Va Q R

Selected bibliography: p237-41

Louix XIV, King of France

Cronin, Vincent. Louis XIV. Houghton 1965 [c1964] 384p illus maps $6.95   **92**

1 France—Kings and rulers 2 France—Civilization

First published 1964 in England

The author presents Louis as the personification of a glorious era in which architecture, painting, sculpture, and literature flourished. "The King's activities in war and politics are relegated to the periphery. While the complex figure of Louis himself occupies the center of the stage, Mr. Cronin studies in enlightening portraits such figures as Racine, Molière, Lully; Mignard, Mansart, Le Nôtre, Vauban, Cassini." Publisher's note

Sources and notes: p355-71

Lowell, James Russell

Wagenknecht, Edward. James Russell Lowell; portrait of a many-sided man. Oxford 1971 276p front $7.50   **92**

The author presents a portrait of one of 19th century America's leading men of letters, showing him as "poet and critic; philologist, teacher and editor; diplomat and political satirist; abolitionist, brilliant conversationalist, husband and father." Publisher's note

Wagenknecht, "sensibly does not try to pass off Lowell for what he was not, but manages to weave together the seeming inconsistencies of the man and to delineate his inner coherence." Pub W

Selected bibliography: p259-65

Lumumba, Patrice Emergy

McKown, Robin. Lumumba; a biography. Introduction by Herbert F. Weiss. Doubleday 1969 202p illus maps $3.95   92

1 Congo (Democratic Republic)

"A political biography of a dynamic and dedicated African leader who was chosen to be the Congo's first Prime Minister, was murdered during the chaotic months following the country's independence, and has since become a symbol of liberty throughout Africa." Hunting

"Although the sympathetic tone verges on the adulatory in some passages, this is an excellent biography. . . . The history of Congolese independence is complicated; this is as clear as it is possible to be about the factions, successes, reversals, compromises, and betrayals. . . . A bibliography and an index are appended." Chicago. Children's Book Center

Luther, Martin

Bainton, Roland Herbert. Here I stand; a life of Martin Luther. Abingdon 1950 422p illus $6.95   92

1 Reformation 2 Europe—Church history

Here is the "life of the monk who cried out against the corruption of the medieval church and changed the history of the world, with a full background of the period and church affairs, quotations from Luther's writings, etc." Retail Bookseller

"A sound but somewhat pedestrian biography. . . . However, the fascinating contemporary woodcuts and engravings and the generous extracts from Luther's writings are well worth the price of the book." Nation

Cowie, Leonard W. Martin Luther: leader of the reformation. Praeger 1969 122p illus (Praeger Pathfinder biographies) $4.75   92

1 Reformation

The author tells the story of Martin Luther's public and private life. He describes "Luther's school days, his early life as a monk, his controversial insights and their effects on his people and on religious history, his marriage, and his declining years." Publisher's note

Suggestions for further reading: p120

Luthuli, Albert

Let my people go. McGraw 1962 255p illus boards $5.95   92

1 Africa, South—Race relations 2 Africa, South—Politics and government

A former Zulu chief "tells of his education at an American missionary college, of his becoming a chief of his people, and of his long battle against racial discrimination for which he received the Nobel Peace Prize in 1961." Bk Buyer's Guide

"His moral and spiritual insights combined with his devotion to the African people and his political statesmanship make this one of the most striking testimonies to the tragedy in . . . South Africa." Rel Bk Club Bul

MacArthur, Douglas

Reminiscences. McGraw 1964 438p illus maps $7.95   92

1 Generals 2 U.S.—History, Military

"The late General MacArthur recalls high points of his life from his boyhood on Army posts to his return to the US after President Harry Truman's dismissal of him from Far Eastern command . . . MacArthur criticizes the Navy for lack of support of the Philippines in World War II; he criticizes Yalta; he recalls his battles with Harold Ickes; but he saves his biggest guns for Truman and the Korean War strategy." Pub W

Gunther, John, 1901-1970. The riddle of MacArthur; Japan, Korea and the Far East. Harper 1951 240p $6.95   92

1 Generals 2 East (Far East)—Politics 3 Japan—History—Allied occupation, 1945-1952

MacArthur is revealed not only in his 1951 situation but through the pattern of his life and those persons who influenced it. With an understanding of the figure who has been directing our Far Eastern military strategy the author has been able to analyze the background of the Korean War and the broader aspects of the situation in the seething, vitally important area that is Asia today

"Expert reporting makes this interpretation of MacArthur and his place in Far Eastern affairs a natural choice for popular reading." Booklist

McCarthy, Joseph Raymond

Matusow, Allen J. ed. Joseph R. McCarthy. Prentice-Hall 1970 181p (Great lives observed) $5.95   92

1 U.S.—Politics and government—1945-1953
SBN 13-566729-1

"A Spectrum book"

"Documenting McCarthy's rise and fall by direct quotations from speeches and hearings, [the author] has chosen very well from the plethora of available material. He divides his second section, an appraisal, between proponents and opponents. The third section traces the effects of McCarthyism, particularly its impact on the development of the New Conservatism." Library J

Bibliography: p175-77

Macdonald, Flora (Macdonald)

Vining, Elizabeth Gray. Flora: a biography. Lippincott 1966 208p illus maps boards $7.95   92

"The life of Flora MacDonald, who in her twenties earned undying fame in Scotland by helping Prince Charles escape to Skye from the island of South Uist in the Hebrides. . . . She and her husband, Allan MacDonald, emigrated to North Carolina and were leaders there at the time of the Revolution. Paradoxically, the MacDonalds were on the Loyalist side in America. This quietly written, pithy biography, based solidly on source materials, shows Flora against a background of the people, the crowded events, and the distressed wartorn conditions of her time." Pub W

A key to the MacDonalds and MacLeods: p15-17. Notes: p199-208

Macy, Anne (Sullivan)

Keller, Helen. Teacher: Anne Sullivan Macy; a tribute by the foster-child of her mind; introduction by Nella Braddy Henney. Doubleday 1955 247p illus $4.50   92

When Helen Keller, a blind deaf-mute, was six years old, Anne Sullivan, an Irish immigrant girl, came to be her teacher-companion. This book tells of their early years, together as teacher and pupil, Helen's years at Radcliffe, Anne's marriage to John Macy, and their work together for the blind. (Publisher)

"Here, in the fullest acknowledgment yet made to her beloved teacher and closest friend for fifty memorable years, Helen Keller rights the balance between what she considers has been too great adulation of herself and too little intelligent evaluation of Anne Sullivan Macy's brilliant inventiveness." N Y Her Trib Books

Manet, Édouard

Schneider, Pierre. The world of Manet, 1832-1883, by Pierre Schneider and the editors of Time-Life Books. Time-Life Bks. [distributed by Little 1968 c1968] 192p illus (Time-Life Lib. of art) boards $7.95   92

1 Painters, French 2 Painting, French 3 Impressionism (Art)

This book "explains how Manet put paint on canvas in such dazzling new ways, without totally rejecting subject matter, that he invented what amounts to a new way of looking at the world." McClurg. Book News

"This study of the life and painting of Edouard Manet and his contemporaries (insofar as they exerted a mutual influence on each other) is illustrated with 64 pages in excellent

Manet, Édouard—*Continued*

color, many more black-and-white reproductions of sketches, engravings, drawings, paintings and several daguerrotypes. The text is uniformly well written and emphasizes, perhaps too much, the effect of Manet's revolutionary ideas of painting as the beginnings of the Impressionist school of painting." Best Sellers

Chronology: Artists of Manet's era: p185.

Bibliography: p186

Mantle, Mickey

The education of a baseball player. Simon & Schuster 1967 219p illus boards $4.95   92

1 Baseball 2 Baseball—Biography

Mickey Mantle tells his story—from his boyhood in Oklahoma to the spring of 1967. His easy, personal style will keep his present fans interested and will probably win him new ones. Interspersed in the text are Mantle's tips on how to play baseball." Cincinnati

Mao, Tsê-tung

Ch'en, Jerome, ed. Mao. Prentice-Hall 1969 176p (Great lives observed) $5.95   92

1 China (People's Republic of China)

"A Spectrum book"

"The selections in this book present a threefold view of Mao. Through his own writings and speeches, many never before published outside China, Mao reveals his often elusive ideology, his revolutionary fervor, and his anti-imperialist and anti-'revisionist' vehemence. Articles by Oriental and Western contemporaries, including Lin Piao, Leonid Brezhnev, André Malraux, and scholars of international reputation, further explain Mao's philosophy, evaluate his contribution to Marxism-Leninism, and analyze his program for uninterrupted world-wide revolution." Publisher's note

Bibliographical note: p168-74

Schram, Stuart. Mao Tse-tung. Simon & Schuster [1967 c1966] 351p illus maps $7.95   92

1 Mao, Tsê-tung   2 China (People's Republic of China)   3 Communism—China (People's Republic of China)

First published 1966 in England

This political biography of Mao Tse-tung is at once a description of his life, an account of modern Chinese history, and an "analysis of the ways in which essentially Western ideas—specifically Marxism-Leninism—were adapted and applied to the vastly different social and political conditions of the Chinese." Publisher's note

"Primarily academic in orientation and interest, the book is a rich source of research for any reader interested in Mao as a political philosopher and evolutionary social thinker." Pub W

Bibliography included in Notes: p327-36

Marshall, John, 1755-1835

Severn, Bill. John Marshall; the man who made the Court supreme. McKay 1969 248p $4.95   92

1 U.S. Supreme Court 2 Judges

This biography of the Chief Justice whose historic decisions established the power and durability of the Supreme Court also portrays his private life. It describes Marshall's interest in poetry and the theater, his non-conformism in manner and dress, and his lifelong courtship of the girl he married. (Publisher)

Some other books about John Marshall: p241

Marshall, Peter

Marshall, Catherine. A man called Peter; the story of Peter Marshall. McGraw 1951 354p front $6.95   92

1 Clergy

"Chaplain of the Senate, minister in Atlanta and Washington, D.C., a preacher noted for his pungent metaphors and vigorous faith . . . Peter Marshall made an indelible impression on the religious life of the country. In

this biography his wife reveals much of his personal side and a great deal of herself. . . . Many of Dr Marshall's prayers and sermons are included." Booklist

"It can scarcely be claimed that any man's wife is well equipped to be his most objective biographer. In the present case this does not matter, since objectivity is not essential in portraying a beloved person for a multitude of others who also loved him. Catherine Marshall writes extremely well. Those who do not accept her religious viewpoint will nevertheless admit that she presents it with grace and charm." N Y Times Bk R

Mary Stuart, Queen of the Scots

Fraser, Antonia. Mary, Queen of Scots. Delacorte Press 1969 613p illus $10   92

1 Queens 2 Great Britain—History—Tudors, 1485-1603

A biography which presents Mary as a tragic figure "betrayed by those closest to her. Her golden years as a French princess . . . and her brief marriage to the French King Francis II present a . . . contrast to the bitterness and . . . hatred she faced when she left the adoptive land to reenter Protestant Scotland, as its Catholic ruler. [The book describes how] her ill-fated marriages to Darnley and Bothwell, her incessant struggle with political and religious saboteurs, her flight to England and subsequent imprisonment . . . led to her execution at Fotheringhay." Publisher's note

Bibliography: p585-94. Includes genealogical tables

Matisse, Henri

Russell, John. The world of Matisse, 1869-1954, by John Russell and the editors of Time-Life Books. Time-Life Bks. [distributed by Little] 1969 190p illus (Time-Life Lib. of art) boards $7.95   92

1 Painters, French 2 Painting, French

"Eight pictorial essays portray the works of Matisse and his colleagues. [The author] notes the late beginning of Matisse in art after a study of law, his innovations in the use of color, and his development of the art of paper cutouts." Booklist

"An extremely lucid tracing of the life and progressive development of one of the most unique modern artists. . . . The profusion of full-color plates fully represents Matisse's changing styles; particularly brilliant in reproduction are his 'Odalisque In Red Trousers' and 'Red Still Life with Magnolia.' Some colorplates of works by Derain, Seurat and others are included." Pub W

Bibliography: p185

Maurois, André

Memoirs, 1885-1967; tr. from the French by Denver Lindley. Harper 1970 439p $10   92

"A Cass Canfield book"

The first half of this work was published 1942 with title: I remember, I remember. The author has made extensive revisions for this edition

"This account of Maurois' literary life and career begins with his family background and his education. Included are his military service in both World wars, his life in the United States, and his return to France where he continued to travel, to teach and to write." Book Rev Digest

"The memoirs show Maurois's humane faith in the written word and in the enduring qualities of the literary imagination, as well as his passionate love for the glory of great lives. These are, moreover, honest memoirs. There is no posturing, no self-deception, no dramatization." Sat R

Maximilian, Emperor of Mexico

O'Connor, Richard. The cactus throne; the tragedy of Maximilian and Carlotta. Putnam 1971 375p illus $7.95   92

1 Charlotte, consort of Maximilian, Emperor of Mexico 2 Mexico—History

Maximilian, Emperor of Mexico—*Continued*

This is the story of Maximilian and Carlotta, two nineteenth-century royal innocents hurled into a revolution they were ill-equipped to understand. It tells of Emperor Napoleon III and Eugenie; the Hapsburgs; the clerics and aristocrats of Mexico determined to turn back the clock; the generals who tried and failed to learn the lessons of fighting a guerrilla war; and the men of the Paris Bourse who profited from the intervention into Mexican politics. (Publisher)

O'Connor "has a real taste for the characters, both sympathetic and seamy, around whom the ill-fated venture unfolded, and he recounts the tale with warmth, humor and adequate depth, although his book is obviously geared to a popular . . . market." Nat R

Selected bibliography: p361-62

Mays, Willie

Willie Mays: my life in and out of baseball [by] Willie Mays as told to Charles Einstein. Dutton 1966 320p illus $5.95   92

1 Baseball—Biography 2 Negroes—Biography

Willie Mays "won the Most Valuable Player Award in 1954 and again in 1965. He writes of this, of his life as a boy, a baseball star, and a father, he gives his ideas on Civil Rights; and he describes many of his fellow players. With . . . photographs, a chart of every home run he has hit, and his complete baseball statistics." Bk Buyer's Guide

"The emphasis is on baseball, not race problems. . . . Mays has advice for boys who want to play baseball for fun or as a career." Pub W

Medici, Lorenzo de', il Magnifico, 1449-1492

Horizon Magazine. Lorenzo de' Medici and the Renaissance; by the editors of Horizon Magazine. Author: Charles L. Mee; consultant: John Walker. Am. Heritage 1969 153p illus map $5.95, lib. bdg. $5.49   92

1 Renaissance 2 Florence—History 3 Italy—History—To 1559

"A Horizon Caravel book"

The book tells the story of Lorenzo de Medici's brief life and of the time in which he lived—the very apex of the Renaissance. His personality "and his thought touched nearly all who lived in his age: Michelangelo, Botticelli, Leonardo, the Strozzi and Pitti families in Florence, the Sforza in Milan, the kings of Naples, the popes in Rome." Foreword

"Attractive for its quality reproductions, . . . this noteworthy book relates the political and cultural history of Florence during its golden period of creativity under the leadership of the benevolent despot." Library J

Further reading: p149

Meir, Golda

Mann, Peggy. Golda; the life of Israel's Prime Minister. Coward-McCann & Geoghegan 1971 287p front $5.95   92

1 Israel—Politics and government

This biography relates the life of Israel's Prime Minister from her early childhood in Russia to her present position

"The author has done a marvelous piece of work in tracing the twentieth-century history of Israel along with the life of one of its greatest political figures. The book gives a fascinating presentation of the present Arab-Israeli conflict." Best Sellers

Bibliography: p282

Syrkin, Marie. Golda Meir: Israel's leader. [New rev. ed] Putnam 1969 366p illus $6.95 92

1 Israel—Politics and government

First published 1963 with title: Golda Meir: woman with a cause

This biography of the woman who has dedicated her life to the founding and survival of Israel describes her life from her childhood and youth in the United States to her present role as Prime Minister of her adopted country. (Publisher)

Merton, Thomas

The seven storey mountain. Harcourt 1948 429p $6.95   92

1 Converts, Catholic 2 Monasticism and religious orders

"The story of a man who became a Trappist monk at the age of 26. Thomas Merton lived a varied and disturbed life as his artist father moved the family from Paris to London and New York. He became a typical Columbia University student chiefly interested in jazz and night clubs but gradually came to appreciate literature and Catholic writers." Ontario Lib Rev

Michelangelo Buonarroti

Coughlan, Robert. The world of Michelangelo, 1475-1564, by Robert Coughlan and the editors of Time-Life Books. Time, inc. [distributed by Little] 1966 202p illus maps (Time-Life Lib. of art) boards $7.95   92

1 Artists, Italian 2 Italy—History—To 1559

This volume follows in text and pictures the various stages of the life and major works of Michelangelo against the background of the Italian Renaissance and shows "him in his relations to his Florentine and Roman contemporaries from Lorenzo de' Medici to the Popes Julius II, Leo X, and Paul III, as well as the great masters of Italian art from Giotto, Masaccio, and Donatello to Botticelli, Verrocchio, and Raphael. The works reveal not only his unsurpassed artistic mastery . . . but even more the depth of his religious emotions." Library J

Millay, Edna St Vincent

Gurko, Miriam. Restless spirit; the life of Edna St Vincent Millay. Crowell 1962 271p $4.50   92

1 Poets, American

"Covering the successive stages of Edna St Vincent Millay's life this . . . biography sheds light on her personal life and on her personality as it developed over the years, analyzes her poetry, and shows how her work and her views affected and were affected by the period in which she lived. It also provides an illuminating picture of other literary figures of the day, particularly those of her Greenwich Village years." Booklist

"Includes many quotations from Millay's writings. . . . With a good index and an extensive bibliography." Chicago. Children's Book Center

Moody, Ralph

Little Britches; Father and I were ranchers; illus. by Edward Shenton. Norton 1950 260p illus lib. bdg. $5.95   92

1 Ranch life 2 Colorado

As a youngster, the oldest boy of a big family, Ralph Moody lived valiantly through the ordeal of helping to establish the family on a barren Colorado ranch, starting from scratch in a broken-down three-room house. He tells their story of struggles and hardship

Man of the family; illus. by Edward Shenton. Norton 1951 272p illus $5.95   92

1 Ranch life

Sequel to: Little Britches

"It describes the boy's brave struggle to help his mother in her efforts to support herself and her children after the death of the head of the family. It begins when 'Little Britches' was eleven and ends when he was thirteen." Book Rev Digest

Moses, Anna Mary Robertson

Grandma Moses; my life's history; ed. by Otto Kallir. Harper 1952 140p illus $8.95 92

1 Painters, American

The autobiography of the woman who began to paint when she was 80 and could no longer do fancy work, and who first exhibited her paintings, now known to everybody, at the

Moses, Anna M. R.—*Continued*
village drugstore. The book is rather like her pictures in its nostalgic charm and ingeniousness and also shows the resourcefulness and energy that carried her through life

Mozart, Johann Chrysostom Wolfgang Amadeus
Valentin, Erich. Mozart and his world. Viking [1970 c1959] 143p illus $6.95　　92

1 Composers, Austrian
SBN 670-49215-9
"A Studio book"
Reprint of an edition orginally published 1959 in Germany and first published 1960 in the United States with title: Mozart
"Photographs and reproductions of paintings, prints, sculpture and such—all adequately documented—are the feature of this short biography. . . . Family, friends, patrons, performers, manuscripts, homes, opera houses, concert halls and cities are some of the subjects drawn upon and tied in with the text." Library J

Musial, Stan
Stan Musial: "The Man's" own story, as told to Bob Broeg. Doubleday 1964 328p illus $5.95　　92

1 Baseball—Biography 2 St Louis Cardinals (Baseball Club)
The author's life "in the minors and twenty-two years in the majors, with the story of his early trials, his sudden popularity. . . . He also comments on players, changes, and the way to success on the diamond." Bk Buyer's Guide
Full of "advice for our younger generation regarding such things as marriage, college education, discipline, respect for others, and frugal living as the beginning of a successful life." Best Sellers

Mussolini, Benito
Fermi, Laura. Mussolini. Univ. of Chicago Press 1961 477p illus maps $6.95　　92

1 Dictators 2 Italy—Politics and government—1914-1946 3 World War, 1939-1945—Italy
The author "portrays the fascist dictator's life from childhood in a poor Romagnese village, through his seizure of power in 1922, to death by execution in 1945. Final chapters examine the Mussolini-Hitler alliance during World War II." Booklist
"A serious and sensitive biography. . . . Better in dealing with Mussolini as an individual than with his role in the setting of Italian and world politics." Foreign Affairs
Selected bibliography: p461-67

Napoléon I, Emperor of the French
Maurois, André. Napoleon; a pictorial biography. Viking [1964 c1963] 160p illus map $6.95　　92

1 Kings and rulers 2 France—History—Consulate and Empire, 1799-1815
"A Studio book"
This edition translated from the French by D. J. S. Thomson and copyrighted 1963 in England
"The story of Napoleon's lightning career, from his childhood in Corsica, his education at the Military School in France, and his swift rise to power following the triumphant campaigns in Italy. . . . [The pictures also show] the Russian campaign, Elba, the return to France in 1815, Waterloo, and the final exile on St Helena." Publisher's note
"André Maurois has been inclined to make a Napoleon after his own image: suave, ironic, a knowing artist who shaped his career like a complex play. The interesting thing is how well he makes the interpretation stick." Christian Science Monitor

Napoléon III, Emperor of the French
Guérard, Albert L. Napoleon III; a great life in brief. Knopf 1955 207p illus (Great lives in brief) $3.95　　92

1 Kings and rulers 2 France—History—Second Empire, 1852-1870

"A brief but authoritative biography of the nephew of the first Napoleon and husband of the beautiful Eugénie, who became Napoleon III." Book Rev Digest
"Its chronicle of the triumph and tragedy of the Second Empire is gripping; its portrait of the Emperor, whose 'career, glittering and tragic, was a picaresque romance on an epic scale,' is vivid though surprisingly sympathetic." Nation
Notes on sources: p203-07

Nefertiti, Queen of Egypt
Wells, Evelyn. Nefertiti. Doubleday 1964 300p illus $5.95　　92

1 Queens 2 Egypt—Antiquities
This is a "biography of the hauntingly beautiful queen who, with her husband Akhenaton, ruled Egypt in the 14th century B.C. Nefertiti took part in Akhenaton's revolt against the pagan gods of Egypt and in his acceptance of monotheism. With Akhenaton, she moved from Thebes to the new city of Amarna dedicated to culture and the one god, Aton." Publisher's note
"When liberties are taken in ascribing emotions and reactions, these are generally identified as assumptions made plausible by the evidence." Booklist
Glossary: p285-87. Bibliography: p288-90

Nehru, Jawaharlal
Shorter, Bani. Nehru; a voice for mankind. Day 1970 312p illus $7.95　　92

1 India—Politics and government 2 Statesmen, East Indian
This story of Nehru is also the story of India's struggle for independence. The author provides historical background and then discusses some of the important events in Nehru's political life—his prewar civil disobedience and subsequent imprisonment; his break with Gandhi; and his fight against imperialism wherever it appeared in the world. (Publisher)
"Valuable chiefly because it is beautifully written and was planned in discussions with Nehru himself before the latter's death. Shorter's book is a good if somewhat too adulatory biography of the great Indian leader." Pub W

Nelson, Horatio Nelson, Viscount
Horizon Magazine. Nelson and the age of fighting sail, by the editors of Horizon Magazine. Author: Oliver Warner; consultant: Chester W. Nimitz. . . . Am. Heritage 1963 153p illus maps $5.95, lib. bdg. $5.49　　92

1 Admirals 2 Great Britain—History, Naval
"A Horizon Caravel book"
"Illustrated with paintings, drawings, letters, and maps of the period." Title page
The story of Lord Horatio Nelson, hero of the British Navy, up to the time of the triumph and tragedy of Trafalgar. (Publisher)
"Mr. Warner has an easy and sophisticated writing style that sets off to best advantage the exceedingly romantic and adventurous truth. Nelson's love affair with Emma Hamilton is handled with restraint, the naval battle scenes are superbly described, and the broader pictures of the Napoleonic war and the role played by sailing ships are vividly drawn." Chicago. Children's Book Center
Further reference: p149

Nicholas II, Emperor of Russia
Massie, Robert K. Nicholas and Alexandra. Atheneum Pubs. 1967 584p illus $12.50　　92

1 Alexandra, consort of Nicholas II, Emperor of Russia 2 Russia—Kings and rulers
"The tragedy of the last of the Romanovs is here postulated on the hemophilia of Alexis, the heir to the throne. Massie contends that the disease which gave Rasputin such power over the Czarina through his supposed success in treating Alexis was the crucial factor in alienating the Romanovs and their subjects." Booklist

Nicholas II, Emperor of Russia—*Continued*

"Readers skeptical of this hypothesis may still enjoy this [book]. . . . Massie gives an absorbing account of a vital period in Russian history and of a rather well-meaning, pious, old-fashioned family caught in the tragedy of their times." Book of the Month Club News

Bibliography: p563-68. Maps on lining-papers

Nicklaus, Jack

The greatest game of all my life in golf, by Jack Nicklaus with Herbert Warren Wind; foreword by Robert Tyre Jones, Jr. Simon & Schuster 1969 416p illus $7.50   92

1 Golf—Biography

Recalling his career, the author writes of "particular players, including a boyhood hero named Bobby Jones, pro tours and tournaments, fairway tactics and greens techniques, and even the business side of being a big time golfer." Book of the Month Club News

"Different from other books on golf because, in addition to following the career of a great golfer, one may receive better than average instruction in how to execute the swing and improve his game. The illustrations in the instructional portion of the book are excellent." Choice

Nightingale, Florence

Woodham Smith, Cecil. Lonely crusader; the life of Florence Nightingale, 1820-1910. . . . McGraw 1951 255p illus $3.95   92

1 Nurses and nursing—Biography

"Whittlesey House publications"

"An abridged edition of the definitive biography 'Florence Nightingale' by the same author." Title page

The "author has shortened the original book by cutting some of the details of Miss Nightingale's later years and putting the emphasis on her girlhood and her experiences during the Crimean War. The result is an excellent biography that will be read with pleasure and interest." Chicago. Children's Book Center

Sources: p243-48

O'Casey, Sean

Fallon, Gabriel. Sean O'Casey: the man I knew. Little 1965 213p illus $5   92

1 Dramatists, Irish

The author portrays O'Casey's personal struggles and his progress as a playwright, particularly in his early years. O'Casey's association with the Abbey Theatre in the 1920's, and with such famous figures as William Butler Yeats and George Bernard Shaw are related. (Publisher)

Mr Fallon believes "O'Casey's later plays represent a decline in his talent. Whether or not one agrees with his estimate of O'Casey as a dramatist, he certainly does no injustice to O'Casey as a great, if sometimes intemperate, personality." Library J

O'Neill, Eugene Gladstone, 1888-1953

Coolidge, Olivia. Eugene O'Neill. Scribner 1966 223p front $3.95, lib. bdg. $3.63   92

1 Dramatists, American

"In a biography of great merit the author presents Eugene O'Neill as an individual genius and as a representative of 'the turmoil of a whole generation.' She sees him, an Irish-American, as 'a man who has lost his rudder,' just as his characters are 'lost in a world which is too big for them.' Her aim is to explain O'Neill's 'world, inheritance, and life,' since his dramas 'reflect both how he lived and what he saw.' . . . Because his career as playwright was also the career of the Provincetown group and the Theatre Guild, which his plays did much to support, this is also a history of the American theater in his time and an analysis of his contributions to it. . . . [Included is a key to] O'Neill's plays." Horn Bk

Orwell, George

Williams, Raymond. George Orwell; ed. by Frank Kermode. Viking 1971 102p $4.95   92

1 Authors, English
SBN 670-33702-1

"Modern masters"

"George Orwell has become a hero to diverse and often opposing elements in Anglo-American life. What is the nature of his paradoxical legacy? In this . . . essay, Raymond Williams offers an . . . account of the 'conscious double vision' that makes Orwell's life and work inseparable." Publisher's note

Short bibliography: p99-100

Paine, Thomas

Coolidge, Olivia. Tom Paine, revolutionary. Scribner 1969 213p front $3.95, lib. bdg. $3.63   92

1 U.S.—History—Revolution—Biography

Tom Paine devoted his life to three great causes: the American Revolution, the rights of man, and the reform of religion. In this biography, the author describes the life and work of this dynamic—and difficult—genius, bringing into focus the many facets of a man considered a failure by his contemporaries, but whose passionate defense of man's liberties helped create the modern world. (Publisher)

"A well-balanced, laudably unbiased, portrait. . . . This is also an excellent history of the period, and the information, complete and accurate, is presented in an informal, highly readable style." Library J

Suggestions for wider reading: p207-08

Papashvily, George

Anything can happen, by George and Helen Papashvily. Harper 1945 202p $4.95, lib. bdg. $4.43   92

1 Russians in the U.S.

Also available in a large type edition for $7.50

"A new and delightful variation of the familiar immigrant-in-America theme. The American wife seems to have done the writing but she uses her husband's words and seems to have caught remarkably both his inflections and his light-hearted philosophy. Arriving in New York with no money in his pocket, he had looked to America as a country where anything can happen and isn't disappointed. Anything does, even to happy marriage with an American girl and success as an inventor." Wis Lib Bul

Pasteur, Louis

Vallery-Radot, Pasteur. Louis Pasteur; a great life in brief. Knopf 1958 199p (Great lives in brief) $3.95   92

1 Scientists

Original French edition published 1956

In this biography, Pasteur's grandson tells how as a young man Pasteur gave up the notion of becoming an artist to study chemistry. After making some startling discoveries about crystals he turned his attention to the cause of fermentations and to the nature of microbes. Later he found means of fighting deadly anthrax but his greatest achievement was the preparation of an effective rabies vaccine. (Publisher)

This brief biography is "human and personal without being sentimental or over-dramatic." Ontario Lib Rev

Sources: p199

Paton, Doris Francis

Paton, Alan. For you departed. Scribner 1969 156p $5.95   92

Paton's book is an epistle of sixty-nine "episodes composed for his wife, who died in 1967. In substance it is a memoir [of] . . . their love, their friction, and their anguish." Atlantic

This work "has as its underlying theme the inner struggle to overcome conventional white South African prejudices. But this deep and fearless book . . . is also a singular, elegiac work of art, lyric in mode and paradoxically triumphant in mood." Sat R

Patterson, Floyd

Victory over myself, by Floyd Patterson with Milton Gross. Geis 1962 244p illus $4.95

92

1 Boxing—Biography

"Born on the fringes of destitution, with a childhood record of truancy and petty theft, Patterson could neither read nor write when he was committed to Wiltwyck School in 1945. He considers that the turning point in his life . . . [because of] the people who helped him there. He rose to be heavyweight champion of the world." Pub W

"More an individual triumph than a sports story." Bookmark

Penn, William

Gray, Elizabeth Janet. Penn; illus. by George Gillett Whitney. Viking 1938 298p illus maps $4.50

92

1 Friends, Society of 2 Pennsylvania—History

A biography of the man who renounced wealth and position to become a Quaker, and who became governor and proprietor of the new colony of Pennsylvania

"Readable and authentic." Horn Bk

Selected list of authorities: p283-87

Pepys, Samuel

Everybody's Pepys; the diary of Samuel Pepys, 1660-1669; abridged from the complete copyright text and ed. by O. F. Morshead; with 60 illus. by Ernest H. Shepard. Bell, G. [distributed by British Bk. Centre] xxiv, 570p illus $5.25

92

1 Great Britain—History—Stuarts, 1603-1714
2 Great Britain—Social life and customs

First published in this version 1926 in England

"This abridgement of the famous diary is made from the standard Wheatley text and illustrated by E. H. Shepard." Book Rev Digest

A picture of life in England under Charles II
Map on lining-papers

Peter I, the Great, Emperor of Russia

Grey, Ian. Peter the Great: Emperor of all Russia. Lippincott 1960 505p $7.50   **92**

1 Russia—Kings and rulers

The author "discusses Peter I's complex and autocratic personality and relates his military campaigns, his political, social, and economic reforms, and particularly notes that under this czar Russia for the first time began to take a place in European affairs." Booklist

Picasso, Pablo

Wertenbaker, Lael. The world of Picasso, 1881- by Lael Wertenbaker and the editors of Time-Life Books. Time-Life Bks. [distributed by Little] 1967 190p illus (Time-Life Lib. of art) boards $7.95

92

1 Artists, Spanish 2 Art, Spanish

"An introduction to Picasso combining personal and artistic biography with art history. The many illustrations, accompanied by descriptive and explanatory captions, include Picasso's paintings, drawings, sculpture, and ceramics and also some examples of work by contemporary artists." Booklist

Bibliography: p185-86

Piersall, Jim

Fear strikes out; the Jim Piersall story, by Jim Piersall and Al Hirshberg. Little 1955 217p $4.95

92

1 Baseball—Biography 2 Mental illness

"The story of a man who became mentally 'sick,' and how, through competent medical care, the help of a sympathetic and most understanding wife, the patience and encouragement of manager, teammates and fans, above all his own splendid courage, he made a complete recovery and resumed his baseball career." Library J

"An inspiring biography which will do much to dispel the stigma of mental illness." Massachusetts

Pocahontas

Woodward, Grace Steele. Pocahontas. Univ. of Okla. Press 1969 227p illus (The Civilization of the American Indian ser) $6.95

92

1 Powhatan Indians 2 U.S.—History—Colonial period—Biography

"A researched and documented study of the life of the Powhatan Indian princess, Pocahontas, reveals the romantic and dramatic truth about this Indian maid who saved the life of Captain John Smith, prevented the destruction of Jamestown by the Powhatan Indians, married John Rolfe, and journeyed to London to help the settlers in their efforts to increase interest in the colony." Bk Buyer's Guide

Bibliography: p196-214. Map on lining-papers

Poe, Edgar Allan

Wagenknecht, Edward. Edgar Allan Poe; the man behind the legend. Oxford 1963 276p front $7.50

92

1 Authors, American

"A critical biography of the controversial 19th-century literary figure, studying in particular Poe's nature and personality as reflected in his writings, accounts of persons who knew him, and available records concerning him." Bk Buyer's Guide

Notes: p223-60. A note on bibliography: p261-66

Porter, Cole

Ewen, David. The Cole Porter story. Holt 1965 192p front $3.95

92

1 Music, Popular (Songs, etc.)

A biography of the American composer and lyricist whose musical career stretched from his undergraduate years at Yale through the 1950's

"The book captures the tone of the era as well as the uniqueness of Cole Porter's talent." Wis Lib Bul

Appendixes include stage, motion picture, television productions; Cole Porter's greatest songs; selected recordings, and a select bibliography

Porter, William Sydney

O'Connor, Richard. O. Henry; the legendary life of William S. Porter. Doubleday 1970 252p illus $6.95

92

1 Authors, American

In this portrayal of the man who turned "out the short stories that made his 'nom de plume' a byword and earned him the cognomen, Caliph of Bagdad-on-the-Subway' . . . [O'Connor traces] O. Henry's career from his birth in Asheville, N.C., in 1862, through his sad marriage to a tubercular young woman, his arrest for embezzlement, his exile to Honduras after jumping bail, his return to serve time in an Ohio prison, and his frenzied, lonely last years in the New York jungle." Pub W

"In a highly entertaining, anecdotal biography. . . . O'Connor's chief focus is the last eight years (1902-10) of the writer's life. . . . Brief synopses of several short stories provide much of the material of the book; somewhat detailed quoting from literary assessments of O. Henry comprises much of the material in the . . . concluding chapter." Choice

Bibliography: p245-46

Rama Rau, Santha

Gifts of passage. Harper 1961 223p boards $5.95

92

1 Voyages and travels

"This 'informal autobiography' is actually a collection of [the author's] best personal essays (mostly from the New Yorker) pieced together with explanatory bridge passages. . . . Miss Rama Rau starts by telling a bit about her grandmother's . . . household and her father's travels as a senior Indian civil servant. . . . The family moved with her father's assignments. She and her . . . American husband, Faubion Bowers, subsequently continued to

Rama Rau, Santha—*Continued*

travel widely, and she has included pieces . . . on episodes in northwest China, Spain, Russia, Kenya, Ceylon, Indonesia and Afghanistan." Christian Science Monitor

"A rare view of people east and west by one who understands both." Bookmark

Rembrandt Hermanszoon van Rijn

Wallace, Robert, 1919- The world of Rembrandt, 1606-1669, by Robert Wallace and the editors of Time-Life Books. Time-Life Bks. [distributed by Little] 1968 188p illus maps (Time-Life Lib. of art) boards $7.95 **92**

1 Painters, Dutch

"Some very good writing, an apt critical survey, and glowing reproductions characterize this summary of Rembrandt's life, work, and times. The text not only gives the basic facts of Rembrandt's life and work but delves beyond these to deflate a few legends and to sketch the background of his country, his era, and his contemporaries in art. Works of Rembrandt and of other artists of his period are reproduced both in full and in detail. There is a sequence of Rembrandt's self-portraits of himself from youth to age." Pub W

Bibliography: p183

White, Christopher. Rembrandt and his world. Viking 1964 144p illus maps $6.95 **92**

1 Painters, Dutch

"A Studio book"

"The artist's milieu, the places where he lived, his family, his friends, his career as an artist and his splendor and poverty are described, based on the few preserved original documents and supplemented by the information taken from contemporary sources of deduced from his artistic work. . . . Rembrandt's art itself is not the subject of this book." Library J

Renoir, Auguste

Hanson, Lawrence. Renoir: the man, the painter, and his world. Dodd 1968 332p illus $8.50 **92**

1 Painters, French

"Though a popularized rather than scholarly biography, this account is somewhat more pedestrian than colorful or eloquent. It manages, however, to convey the significant events in Renoir's life, his enterprising, practical, sensual, and spirited character, his friends and fellow artists, and his development as a painter distinguished for his studies of women and his medley of colors in reproducing their flesh." Booklist

Bibliography: p297-301

Reuther, Walter Philip

Cormier, Frank. Reuther [by] Frank Cormier and William J. Eaton. Prentice-Hall 1970 475p $10 **92**

1 International Union, United Automobile, Aircraft and Agricultural Workers of America

"Drawn from extensive interviews, the account traces the career of Reuther from a childhood influenced by his trade unionist father to early years in the automobile industry and on to the major role he played in shaping the United Automobile Workers. The narrative includes quotations from past and present union figures and examples of some union songs that add color to the portrayal of Reuther's life; Reuther's untimely death is described in the final pages. Bibliography and extensive chapter notes are appended." Booklist

Revere, Paul

Forbes, Esther. Paul Revere & the world he lived in. Houghton 1942 510p illus $9.50 **92**

1 Boston—History 2 U.S.—History—Revolution —Biography 3 Silversmithing

Awarded the Pulitzer Prize for history, 1943

Not only a biography of Paul Revere, diligent patriot, silversmith, soldier, but also a picture of his time, a panorama of 18th century Boston and its life

"Brings Paul Revere to life as a full-bodied personality, offers a rich storehouse of information about his times, retells many of the stirring incidents of the pre-revolutionary period, in addition to the famous ride, and provides an informal history of the American revolution. A generous book in every way. The Paul Revere portrait by Copley, reproduced in color, sets the scene for the book." Wis Lib Bul

Bibliography: p491-96. Maps on lining-papers

Richthofen, Manfred, Freiherr von

The Red Baron; tr. by Peter Kilduff. Doubleday 1969 240p illus (Air combat classics) $5.95 **92**

1 Air pilots 2 European War, 1914-1918—Aerial operations

Original German edition, 1918

This is the autobiography of Manfred von Richthofen, the famed Red Knight of Germany. During three years of combat in World War I, he shot down more aircraft than any other aviator on either side of the war, and became a legend in his own time. (Publisher)

"There is a chapter by Manfred's brother, Lothar, and a description of the 'Red Baron's' final combat by Capt. A. Roy Brown, the Canadian pilot who is credited with shooting him down. . . . [An] appendix lists Richthofen's victories, names the leading German [Austro-Hungarian and Allied] aces, . . . contains a chronology of World War I [and gives] three-view drawings and vital statistics of German and Allied fighter planes." Library J

Rickenbacker, Edward V.

Rickenbacker. Prentice-Hall 1967 458p illus $7.95 **92**

The life story "of one of the great American military heroes and industrial leaders, a man famous also for surviving an impressive number of brushes with death. Eddie Rickenbacker reviews his career from its Horatio Alger-style beginning through his work on early autos, his World War I flying service, his leadership in Eastern Air Lines and the secret missions he undertook for the U. S. Government in World War II. High points are the adventure and tenseness of autoracing, World War I combat flights, a very bad air crash in Atlanta, Georgia, in 1941, and the famous episode of Rickenbacker's survival on a raft after his plane was forced down over the Pacific in October, 1942." Pub W

"Moving with certainty and enhanced by the nonprofessional slickness of Rickenbacker's writing, the book grows in interest as we watch a boy grow up in America from the turn of the century, believing in God, in mother, in country—and in himself. It is the tale of an old-fashioned boy with dreams that come true. Enjoyable reading and, most of all, a personalized history of the U.S. from around 1900 to the present which—as Captain Eddie presents it—is pretty hard to beat." Choice

Riis, Jacob August

The making of an American. A new ed. with an epilogue by J. Riis Owre. Macmillan (N Y) 1970 347p illus $6.95 **92**

1 New York (City)—Social conditions

A reissue of the title first published 1901

"The famed autobiography of a self-made man, with all of the honesty, warmth, sentiment and spirit that has made the book endure for nearly 70 years. For the first time, the story of Jacob Riis's life is told in full, completed by his grandson. It is a story that covers the death of Riis's first wife, Elizabeth, his second marriage, later years of fame marred by illness and, finally, his death." News of Bks

"A classic in the literature of U.S. immigrants." Good Reading

Robinson, Frank

My life is baseball, by Frank Robinson with Al Silverman. Doubleday 1968 225p illus $5.95   92

1 Baseball—Biography

Frank Robinson tells the story of his "growth as a professional athlete and as a person. He tells what it is like to hear the cheers —and the boos—of the crowd, what it is like in the dugout and the clubhouse after a key victory or loss, and the reaction a man feels when he is traded." Publisher's note

"From the playgrounds of his ghetto neighborhood, to high school, to the minor leagues, and on to the big leagues, his eventful career in baseball has been candidly described. A chart of Frank Robinson's minor league and major league record, covering the years 1953-1967, is included." Booklist

Robinson, Sugar Ray

Sugar Ray [by] Sugar Ray Robinson with Dave Anderson. Viking 1970 376p $6.95   92

1 Boxing—Biography 2 Negroes—Biography
SBN 670-68141-5

"This book relates the life and career of Sugar Ray Robinson from the days of his youth in the ghettos in Detroit and New York to his winning of two world boxing championships. Included also is an account of how he spent four million dollars while at the height of his fame." Book Rev Digest

"The Sugar Ray Robinson story—like most true-life fables, is often incredible. But it is, withal, a very human story—a story of poverty and riches, success and failure, pride and humility, good and bad. It is, in its early years, a study of Afro-American . . . life as it was, as it is, lived in the ghetto." N Y Times Bk R

Rodgers, Richard

Ewen, David. With a song in his heart; the story of Richard Rodgers. Holt 1963 216p illus lib. bdg. $3.59   92

1 Composers, American   2 Musical reviews, comedies, etc.

The book "is filled with fascinating information about a remarkable man. [The author] has added a splendid section at the end, listing the dates of all [Rodgers'] stage productions, his motion pictures, his greatest songs, instrumental music, recommended recordings, song collections and a bibliography." Book Week

"A fascinating account of Richard Rodgers' collaboration and eventual break-up with [Lorenz] Hart, his association with [Oscar] Hammerstein, and his personal life." Wis Lib Bul

Rodin, Auguste

Hale, William Harlan. The world of Rodin, 1840-1917, by William Harlan Hale and the editors of Time-Life Books; with photographs by Lee Boltin and Dmitri Kessel. Time-Life Bks. [distributed by Little 1970 c1969] 192p illus (Time-Life Lib. of art) boards $7.95   92

1 Sculptors, French 2 Sculpture, French

"Hale presents Rodin, the man and the artist, in all his vitality in this account of the artist's life and times coupled with numerous striking reproductions of Rodin's work and that of other artists. The author skillfully interweaves the chronicle of Rodin's professional and personal life and loves with discussion of his artistic development, ability to convey emotion and movement, and his artistic successes and failures. A chronology of the artists of Rodin's era and a bibliography are appended." Booklist

Rogers, Will

The autobiography of Will Rogers; selected and ed. by Donald Day; with a foreword by Bill and Jim Rogers. Houghton 1949 410p front $6.95   92

1 Humorists

"Will Rogers was writing his autobiography in his daily columns, his stage shows, his humorous books, and his movies. He had begun to write a formal one, too, that was left unfinished. To this, Donald Day has added the best of a rich store of published and unpublished material." Cincinnati

"The selections have been made skillfully and arranged logically. There are notes enough to provide continuity, but not so many as to interrupt or obscure the humorist himself. It is an excellent job of editing." N Y Her Trib Books

Rommel, Edwin

Young Desmond. Rommel, the desert fox; foreword by Sir Claude Auchinleck. Harper 1951 [c1950] 264p illus maps $5.95, lib. bdg. $5.11   92

1 Generals 2 World War, 1930-1945—Campaigns and battles

Also available in a large type edition for $7.95

First published 1950 in England

This biography, written by a wartime enemy of the late Field-Marshal who led the German and Italian troops in the African campaign, reveals the life and adventures—and strange death—of a man who has become a legend in his time

"Young's book is distinguished by a graceful style and by the author's admirable ability to make very confused military situations understandable. His battle pieces are without exception informative and exciting." N Y Her Trib Books

Romulo, Carlos P.

I walked with heroes; illus. with photographs. Holt 1961 342p illus $5   92

1 Statesmen, Philippine 2 Philippine Islands

"This book is the personal chronicle of Carlos Romulo's rise from the obscurity of a Luzon hill town to the international position and fame he so well deserved. In the interval he lived 'many lifetimes.' His story is an immensely moving human document that is remarkable for its candor and for the deep humanity of its sentiments. . . . This autobiography is much more than a recital of the 'success story' of the little Filipino. It recounts the trials and triumphs of a wise and kind man with an unquenchable zest for living and a hatred of all evil and injustice." Sat R

Roosevelt, Eleanor (Roosevelt)

The autobiography of Eleanor Roosevelt. Harper 1961 454p illus $8.95   92

1 Presidents—U.S.—Wives 2 Roosevelt, Franklin Delano, President U.S.

This book consists of material from Mrs Roosevelt's three previous autobiographical volumes: This is my story (1937), out of print, 1967: This I remember (1949) and On my own (1958). The present volume represents an elimination of material of only passing interest and an addition of new material bringing the book up to date

"In 'This Is My Story' I covered my early years, the vanishing world in which I grew up, the influences and the values that dominated that era. In 'This I Remember' I dealt with a broader and more vital period concerned for the most part with my husband's political life during one of the most dramatic and eventful times in history, and with the gradual broadening of my own activities. In 'On My Own,' I tried to give some picture of the changing world as I have seen it during recent years and of the various jobs into which I plunged." Preface

MacLeish, Archibald. The Eleanor Roosevelt story. Houghton 1965 101p illus $5   92

1 Presidents—U.S.—Wives

"The text and illustrations in this book are from the motion picture: The Eleanor Roosevelt Story, produced by Mr. Sidney Glazier." Verso of title page

This pictorial biography of Eleanor Roosevelt covers her shy childhood and youth, marriage to Franklin Delano Roosevelt and the period following his death. (Publisher)

Roosevelt, Franklin Delano, President U.S.

Burns, James MacGregor. Roosevelt: the lion and the fox. Harcourt 1956 553p illus $9.50   **92**

1 Presidents—U.S. 2 U.S.—Politics and government—1933-1945

"That Franklin D. Roosevelt was a master of the fine art of politics and displayed on occasion qualities of the lion and the fox is the underlying theme of Mr. Burns' . . analysis of the complex character and political career of our only four-term President. The author focuses his attention on FDR's career from 1933 through the election of 1940 and points out both Mr. Roosevelt's strengths and weaknesses as a President and political leader." Library J

"This is a major contribution to the study of political leadership and one of the ablest works yet to appear on Roosevelt." N Y Times Bk R

Includes bibliographies

Burns, James MacGregor. Roosevelt: the soldier of freedom. Harcourt 1970 722p illus $10   **92**

1 Presidents—U.S. 2 U.S.—Politics and government—1933-1945
ISBN 0-15-178871-5

Sequel to the author's: Roosevelt: the lion and the fox, entered above

This study of FDR as a war-time President portrays him as a deeply divided man—divided by principle, ideals, faith, Realpolitik, prudence, and manageable goals—a man intent on protecting his power and authority in a world at war, a world of shifting moods and capricious fortune. (Publisher)

"There is not, and may never be a better one-volume presentation of the diplomatic and political aspects of the great war that raged in those years. As historiography, also, the book commands admiration. Its documentation is ample, and invariably apposite. . . . He has written a very fine book." Book World

General bibliography and chapter bibliographies with basic book list: p617-85

Roosevelt, Theodore, President U.S.

The autobiography of Theodore Roosevelt; condensed from the original edition; supplemented by letters, speeches, and other writings; and ed. with an introduction by Wayne Andrews. Centennial ed. Scribner 1958 372p illus $7.95   **92**

1 Presidents—U.S.

An "autobiography replete with quotations from [Roosevelt's] voluminous [writings]. No story of a man so colorful, who did so much, can easily be reduced to a single volume. Some might prefer more about the man, less about his politics and his policies. It is well worth reading." Best Sellers

Bibliography: p359-62

Chessman, G. Wallace. Theodore Roosevelt and the politics of power; ed. by Oscar Handlin. Little 1969 214p (The Library of American biography) $5   **92**

1 Presidents—U.S. 2 U.S.—Politics and government—1898-1919

The author scrutinizes the early career of Theodore Roosevelt, examining his political development and his understanding of executive power. He "stood at a strategic point in the emergence of modern America. His career thus throws light on the problems of transition of the nation from the nineteen to the twentieth century." Editor's preface

"Not so much a biography as a serious study of how fiercely independent 'Teddy' Roosevelt rose from New York State Assemblyman to become our 26th President, and how he used the great power of that office." Pub W

A note on the sources: p200-05

Grantham, Dewey W. ed. Theodore Roosevelt. Prentice-Hall 1971 181p (Great lives observed) $5.95   **92**

1 Presidents—U.S.
SBN 13-783241-9

"A Spectrum book"

"This volume reveals this unique president as he really was, distinguishing between the man and the symbol. Roosevelt's speeches and letters show how sincere he was in admonishing national duty and physical and moral strength. La Follette and Clemenceau, among others, stress the courage with which Roosevelt saw through his reforms, while present-day historians show how deeply his policies affected the future course of American history." News of Bks

Bibliographical note: p172-76

Hagedorn, Hermann. The Roosevelt family of Sagamore Hill. Macmillan (N Y) 1954 435p illus $7.50   **92**

1 Presidents—U.S. 2 Oyster Bay, N.Y. 3 Roosevelt (Theodore) family

"An account of the home life of the Theodore Roosevelt family from the time of Roosevelt's second marriage to his death. The home at Oyster Bay is the focal point but the scene shifts to the White House for the years of Roosevelt's Presidency. The account is alive with anecdotes about the six children." Booklist

"An informal biography showing the former president as a forceful character both at home and in public life." Massachusetts

Ruark, Robert

The Old Man and the boy; illus. with line drawings by Walter Dower. Holt 1957 393p illus $5.95   **92**

1 Authors, American 2 Country life—North Carolina

The author "describes his happy boyhood years in the coastal region of North Carolina some thirty years ago, where he was taught a philosophy of life, plus the rudiments of hunting and fishing, by an understanding grandfather." Book Rev Digest

"There is delight in the book's record of sounds, smells and sights in the countryside and coast the boy loved so much before he discovered the delight of books as well. 'The Old Man and the Boy' offers sheer poetry within the terms of the comprehension of a boy. It also has homespun humor and salty common sense." N Y Her Trib Books

Rubens, Sir Peter Paul

Wedgwood, C. V. The world of Rubens, 1577-1640, by C. V. Wedgwood and the editors of Time-Life Books. Time-Life Bks. [distributed by Little 1971 c1967] 192p illus map (Time-Life Lib. of art) boards $7.95   **92**

1 Painters, Flemish

First published 1967

The author discusses the work of the Baroque painter, whose style influenced Watteau, Delacroix and Renoir. She also portrays his personal life, as a Catholic, businessman, devotee of classical antiquity, and intimate of Europe's leading intellectuals. (Publisher)

Bibliography: p187

Profusely illustrated with photographs, sketches, and reproductions, many in color, of Ruben's works

Sandburg, Carl

Always the young strangers. Harcourt 1953 445p $7.50   **92**

1 Authors, American 2 Swedes in the U.S.

"In this book Carl Sandburg tells the story of his life in the small town of Galesburg [Illinois] in which he was born, of his family, and of his neighbors there. It is Sandburg's personal story; it is the story of life in a typical American town of the period; and it is an account of the part played by the Swedes in the settling of the Midwest." Huntting

"The fond recollections of his boyhood and youth end with his return from service in the Spanish-American War and enrollment at a small local college." Pub W

Golden, Harry. Carl Sandburg. World Pub. 1961 287p illus $7.95   **92**

1 Authors, American

Sandburg, Carl—*Continued*

Written in column-size vignettes by his long-time friend and neighbor, this tribute to Carl Sandburg describes his many roles—poet, journalist, biographer, novelist, and singer of folk songs. Based on letters, journals, documents and some hitherto unpublished material this study emphasizes Sandburg's championship of the workingman in his struggle for social justice. (Publisher)

Rogers, W. G. Carl Sandburg, yes; poet, historian, novelist, songster; illus. with photographs. Harcourt 1970 212p illus map $4.95   **92**

1 Authors, American
ISBN 0-15-214470-6
This book "which traces the poet's life from his birth at Galesburg, Illinois, to his death at his farm-home in North Carolina, is obviously well-researched and lovingly presented yet, unfortunately, slightly condescending. . . . [The author] seeks out the people and places which influenced Sandburg and concentrates more on the shape and doings of his days than on the complexion of his work. At times Sandburg seems lost in a plethora of detail; despite all the difficulties, however, Sandburg's genuinely fascinating life carries the book along on mounting interest." Best Sellers
Bibliography: p201-04

Sanger, Margaret (Higgins)

Kennedy, David M. Birth control in America; the career of Margaret Sanger. Yale Univ. Press 1970 320p (Yale Pubs. in Am. studies) $8.75   **92**

1 Birth control
The author "reviews the earlier phases of birth control in America and relates in detail the determination and perseverance of Margaret Sanger, pioneer and leader in the field. Despite ridicule, defamation, and imprisonment she lived to receive long-overdue accolades and to be accepted as one who had led man far along the path toward the geneticists' goal. Many original sources of information on Margaret Sanger are given. All are combined to create a readable, informative book of value to the student and lay reader alike." Science Bks
Bibliography: p294-95

Lader, Lawrence. Margaret Sanger: pioneer of birth control [by] Lawrence Lader [and] Milton Meltzer; illus. with photographs. Crowell 1969 174p illus (Women of America) $4.50   **92**

1 Birth control
"Margaret Sanger realized the need for birth control in the early 1900's. She fought the laws and established birth-control clinics, having travelled abroad to locate effective birth control methods. The authors tell the story of her struggle and eventual success." The AAAS Science Book List
This biography "provides straightforward, explicit information about the birth control methods available at various points in history. This makes the whole story of Margaret Sanger's crusades much more understandable. . . . [The authors] also use quotes from Mrs. Sanger . . . to convey why she worked so hard and sacrificed her personal happiness for the movement she created." Library J
Bibliography: p164-66

Sartre, Jean Paul

The words; tr. from the French by Bernard Frechtman. Braziller 1964 255p $5   **92**

1 Authors, French
In telling of his childhood, the author "presents a vivid picture of his family—his mother, his father's death, his mother's parents to whose house the widow brought her small son. Why have I spent my life writing, Sartre asks, and shows that for him everything was already decided by the time he was ten years old." Huntting
"An inconclusive book, partly ideological, partly psychological in a narrow sense, anti-literary at times but inconsistently so." N Y Rev of Books

Schumann, Clara Josephine (Wieck)

White, Hilda. Song without end; the love story of Clara and Robert Schumann. Dutton 1959 300p front $4.50   **92**

1 Schumann, Robert Alexander 2 Musicians, German

"An accomplished concert pianist, Clara Wieck had to face the conflict between her father's desire for his daughter to have a successful career and her own desire to marry the penniless but gifted composer, Robert Schumann." Cleveland

Schweitzer, Albert

Out of my life and thought; an autobiography; tr. by C. T. Campion; postscript by Everett Skillings. Holt 1949 274p $4.95   **92**

1 Missionaries 2 Physicians

First published 1933. English title: My life and thought
"Autobiography of the Alsatian medical missionary who renounced the rewards of his great gifts as philosopher, theologian, organist and writer, to minister to the sick natives of Equatorial Africa, alternating his service there with trips to Europe to earn money thru lectures and organ recitals to carry on the work of his hospital at Lambarene." Book Rev Digest
"Rarely does a man who writes an autobiography succeed in giving so much of himself as Schweitzer has here. The simplicity of the writing reflects the simplicity of the man; the range of the topics treated reflects the range of his mind; the record of events reflects his incredible vigor and his capacity to accomplish the seemingly impossible." Christian Century

Payne, Robert. The three worlds of Albert Schweitzer. Nelson 1957 252p $3.95 **92**

1 Missionaries 2 Physicians

This "biography covers Albert Schweitzer's achievements in music, theology and medicine. It also sketches the African background of his medical career." Huntting
"Mr. Payne has succeeded in writing a book of profound insight, of sensitive awareness and appreciation, which is yet marked by an objective balancing of fact and interpretation." Sat R

Scott, Sir Walter, bart.

Pearson, Hesketh. Sir Walter Scott: his life and personality. Harper 1954 295p illus $6.95   **92**

1 Authors, Scottish

First published in England with title: Walter Scott: his life and personality
"A genial biography of Sir Walter Scott, which takes as its theme the parallels between Sir Walter, a Napoleon of letters, and his contemporary, Napoleon Bonaparte. The biographer does not begrudge Sir Walter the benevolence and sweetness that earned for him the idolatry of his family, dogs, friends, and servants. But he points out that Sir Walter also enjoyed a drink and a bawdy joke with the boys as much as the next man. He has thus made Sir Walter Scott into a three-dimensional figure in whom lurked the dual spirit of Sancho Panza and Don Quixote." Booklist

Shaw, Wilbur

Gentlemen, start your engines. Coward-McCann 1955 320p illus $6.95   **92**

1 Automobile racing—Biography

"Three times winner of the famous 500-mile classic at Indianapolis and former President of the Motor Speedway, Wilbur Shaw, describes the hard work of automobile racing, the tension, the races won and lost, and the thrill that always came when he heard the command, 'Gentlemen, start your engines.'" Cleveland

Smith, John

Smith, Bradford. Captain John Smith: his life & legend. Lippincott 1953 375p front $5
92

"Much of what we know of Captain Smith comes entirely from his own writings. Because they could not verify his accounts elsewhere some scholars during the past century have refused to accept, in whole or in part, the statements of his adventures in Hungary and Turkey and have ridiculed the romantic story of Pocahontas. With the assistance of Dr. Laura Polanyi Striker, who contributes a brilliant thirty page essay on John Smith in Hungary, Bradford Smith conducts a painstaking investigation of the controversies and finds the evidence very much in the Captain's favor." Library J

Bibliography: p351-63

Socrates

Turlington, Bayly. Socrates: the father of Western philosophy. Watts, F. 1969 245p map (Immortals of philosophy and religion) lib. bdg. $4.50
92

1 Philosophers, Ancient

The author "shows how the story of Socrates that has come down to us from Plato and Xenophon came to be, and infers, from such evidence as exists, that the story is very likely true. He details Socrates' philosophic method and thought, and clearly presents background, the life, government, culture, and religion of 5th-Century B.C. Athens." Library J

Includes: The apology of Socrates, by Plato

Solzhenifsyn, Aleksandr Isaevich

Labedz, Leopold, ed. Solzhenitsyn: a documentary record; ed. and with an introduction by Leopold Labedz; foreword by Harrison E. Salisbury. Harper 1971 xxiv, 229p $7.95
92

1 Russia—Intellectual life 2 Authors, Russian
SBN 06-012487-3

"A prodigious compilation of excerpts from correspondence, conversations, speeches, articles, reviews, tributes, and other related materials conveys the intensity of controversy surrounding the Russian winner of the 1970 Nobel Prize. . . . The record begins with Solzhenitsyn's 1957 rehabilitation after political imprisonment and exile, continues with his denunciation of Soviet censorship in an open letter to delegates of the fourth Soviet Writers' Congress and his expulsion from the Soviet Writers' Union in 1969, and ends with a 1970 'Pravda' castigation of Solzhenitsyn as a spiritual alien hostile to the Soviet society." Booklist

Includes bibliographical references

Sone, Monica

Nisei daughter. Little 1953 238p $5.95   92

1 Japanese in the U.S.

The author, "American-born Kozuko Itoi, tells of a happy childhood spent with brothers and sisters in her father's hotel on the Seattle waterfront. Pearl Harbor brought the unsettling realization that her feeling of identity as an American was seriously questioned by those who evacuated her family with the other Japanese to relocation centers. . . . Through the experiences of this girl we see life on Seattle's waterfront, the mores of a Japanese community in a Western city, the isolation and bitterness of a relocation center, and finally her experiences in a large Midwestern city." Reading Ladders

Stalin, Iosif

Deutscher, Isaac. Stalin; a political biography. 2d ed. Oxford 1967 [c1966] 661p illus $13.50
92

1 Dictators 2 Russia—Politics and government—1925-1953

First published 1949

This biography is neither an apologia for, nor an indictment of, Stalin, but an attempt to describe and analyze his complex role and personality with as much detachment as is possible in the portrayal of a contemporary and highly controversial figure. The author ahows the forces that shaped Stalin's life and placed him in the dominating position on the Russian scene and in the Communist movement for more than a quarter of a century

"Deutscher has mastered his source materials, in Russian and in other languages. . . . He has historical perspective, psychological insight, and a talent for shrewd evaluation." Chicago Sun

Bibliography: p631-36

Payne, Robert. The rise and fall of Stalin. Simon & Schuster 1965 767p illus $10   92

1 Dictators 2 Russia—History

A "biography of Stalin, the seminary student, thief, revolutionary, and—with Churchill and Roosevelt—one of the three top Allied leaders. The author writes of Stalin's paranoia, his slaughter of . . . Russians, his ruthless treatment of his own family." Bk Buyer's Guide

"Accuracy in minor detail is not one of Mr. Payne's strong points. . . . Yet, if there are countless lacunae, distortions, and downright errors in the Payne book, it must be added that few writers have come closer to capturing the spiritual essence of their subject." Sat R

Bibliography: p725-29. Map on lining-papers

Warth, Robert D. Joseph Stalin. Twayne 1969 176p (Twayne's Rulers & statesmen of the world ser) $4.95
92

1 Dictators 2 Russia—History

This "popularly-written biography of Stalin emphasizes his rise to power and the foreign policy he pursued during his long reign." Book News

Includes bibliographical references

Steffens, Lincoln

The autobiography of Lincoln Steffens. Harcourt 1931 884p illus $12
92

1 Journalists

First published in 2 volumes

"The life story of an American reporter, journalist, student of ethics and politics, a 'muck-raker' in the days of the early 20th century attempts to reform government. He was a friend of presidents, city bosses, foreign dictators, youthful radicals; a disillusioned, loving optimist." Book Rev Digest

"Here is a text-book on journalism: a treasure house for the historian of that wave of social idealism that shook the United States from 1900 to 1917; a casebook for the psychologist of political types. Above all it is the vivid diary of a bold and humane pilgrim who so loved his fellowmen that he has never been able to condemn them." Survey

Steinbeck, John, 1946-

In touch [by] John Steinbeck IV. Knopf 1969 202p $4.95
92

1 Vietnamese Conflict, 1961- 2 Marihuana

The author, son of John Steinbeck, writes of the feelings of today's generation as seen through his own experience at age twenty. He writes of his experiences in Vietnam, of his article on marijuana with regards to American soldiers, his subsequent arrest, trial, and acquittal on a drug charge and his trip West

Steinbeck "also talks about meditation, why he finds it more of a mind expander than drugs, and what he feels individuals and society at large can gain from its practice. Written casually, directly, the book is an absolute must: it's the intimate, sincere, significant statement of a man distinctly of his times." Library J

Stevenson, Adlai Ewing, 1900-1965

Severn, Bill. Adlai Stevenson: citizen of the world; illus. with photographs. McKay 1966 184p illus $4.75
92

1 Statesmen, American

Stevenson, Adlai E.—*Continued*

"A good biography of Stevenson, with a balanced treatment of personal life and legal career and of public life in elective, appointive, or voluntary positions. . . . There is much that is of historical importance in the background material of this biography, particularly material about the United Nations." Chicago. Children's Book Center

"This is one of the better biographies for young people to appear in recent months. The author's account is highly readable and, while giving the facts of Stevenson's life, also manages to create an attractive picture of a man who was totally dedicated to his country." Best Sellers

Some other books by and about Adlai Stevenson: p177-78

Stowe, Harriet Elizabeth (Beecher)

Wagenknecht, Edward. Harriet Beecher Stowe: the known and the unknown. Oxford 1965 267p front $6.50　　　92

1 Authors, American

"A sympathetic portrait of a complex woman which looks behind the stereotype of the author of 'Uncle Tom's Cabin' to a talented, contradictory, and loving person and her roles of daughter, sister, wife, friend, mother, aesthete, and reformer. Wagenknecht takes a new look at the literary value of her most famous novel and interprets Mrs. Stowe's character and relationships through her inherited Calvinism, her humane softening of its harshness, and her genuine Christ-centered religiosity. The introduction lists primary sources, and notes and bibliography are appended." Booklist

"Mr. Wagenknecht will send many readers back to Mrs. Stowe's own writings and to other studies of her character, and this will be both a tribute to his own skill and a justification of his method." Times (London) Lit Sup

Stuart, Jesse

The thread that runs so true. Scribner 1958 [c1949] 293p $4.50　　　92

1 Authors, American 2 Teaching

A reprint of the 1949 edition with a new preface by the author

"The poet-novelist describes his turbulent career as a teacher, which he abandoned after almost 20 years because it didn't pay enough to permit him to marry. This is a vigorous account of his progress from his first day in charge of a one-room rural school in Kentucky when he had to establish discipline with his fists, through increasingly responsible conditions." Booklist

"His joy for living illuminates each page even those detailing the rather complicated quarrels about educational theory and practice. The writing is for the most part simple, strong and direct." Chicago Sun

To teach, to love. World Pub. 1970 317p $5.95　　　92

1 Teachers 2 Teaching

The author "writes about his boyhood [in Kentucky in the 1930's] his elementary-school and high-school experiences, his days at Lincoln Memorial College and Vanderbilt University. . . . [He describes] teaching in one-room rural schoolhouses . . . [and] recounts his experiences as a country school superintendent and as a high-school principal. [He] describes his stay at the American University in Cairo, Egypt, where he taught creative writing. He explains what classroom methods worked best, and why, and speculates on what has gone wrong in American schools today." Publisher's note

The author "has succeeded in communicating the depths of his emotional experiences with teaching. . . . To this reviewer, at least, Stuart's remedies for the major problems confronting education today . . . are more emotionally-based than Stuart would probably admit. Actually he has not offered solutions, only further descriptions of these problems." Best Sellers

Sugimoto, Etsu Inagaki

A daughter of the Samurai; how a daughter of feudal Japan, living hundreds of years in one generation, became a modern American. Frontispiece by Ichiro Hori. Tuttle 1966 314p illus front $4.95　　　92

1 Japanese in the U.S. 2 Japan—Social life and customs

First published 1925 by Doubleday

"A daughter of feudal Japan tells of her education and home life, and the first impressions of her new country when she becomes a modern American." Ontario Lib Rev

Tenzing, Norgay

Tiger of the snows; the autobiography of Tenzing of Everest; written in collaboration with James Ramsey Ullman. Putnam 1955 294p illus maps $5.95　　　92

1 Mount Everest Expedition, 1953 2 Everest, Mount 3 Mountaineering

"Tenzing, the Sherpa who reached the top of Everest with Hillary, was born only a day's march from the great peak in harsh and stony country. . . . He recounts his life to James Ramsey Ullman. The result is a fascinating, sometimes rambling, chronicle of his rise from porter to sirdar (chief of porters) to Tiger (high-climbing Sherpa) to member of the Everest assault team. Tenzing emerges as a man of thoughtfulness and integrity—and a first-rate climber." Horn Bk

Thant, U

Bingham, June. U Thant; the search for peace. Knopf 1966 xxii, 300p illus map $5.95　　　92

1 Statesmen, Burmese 2 Burma

A "concise biography of the [former] Secretary-General of the United Nations, characterizing U Thant as a humanitarian pragmatist, praising his integrity and charm, and describing the political and economic struggles which made his life in Burma a testing ground for his present position. Alternating chapters describe U Thant and his background." Pub W

Bibliography: p293-300

Thomas à Becket, Saint, Abp. of Canterbury

Duggan, Alfred. The falcon and the dove; a life of Thomas Becket of Canterbury; decorations by Anne Marie Jauss. Pantheon Bks. 1966 217p illus lib. bdg. $4.19　　　92

1 Henry II, King of England

First published 1952 in England with title: Thomas Becket of Canterbury

Set in twelfth-century England, this account tells "of the life of Thomas Becket, of his friendship with King Henry [II] and of the struggle between them which eventually led to Thomas's martyrdom." Preceding title page

"Although the [author] begins his biography like a fairy-tale . . . he carefully places the conflict of two strong-minded men in the context of times. Sometimes he digresses, sometimes tries to tell too much, out of his vast knowledge of things medieval. But he builds up a convincing hero." Book Week

Bibliography: p216-17

Thomas, Dylan

Selected letters of Dylan Thomas; ed. and with commentary by Constantine Fitzgibbon. New Directions [1967 c1966] 420p $8.50　92

1 Poets, Welsh

First published 1966 in England

"On the theory that Dylan Thomas's primary claim on our attention is the value of his poetry, Mr. FitzGibbon has aimed to present all letters that bear directly on his methods of composing poems and on his views of poetry in general. Others were chosen to illustrate Thomas's prose style, and many to broaden our picture of Thomas the man." Publisher's note

Thomas, Dylan—*Continued*

In this book "brilliantly edited by Mr. Fitz-Gibbon, the tensions and dynamics of Thomas's creative life . . are made clear. Though the roaring boy does not wholly vanish—he is painfully coy, tail-between-the-legs and blubbering in his apologies and begging letters—we are drawn much closer to the glorious, often hilarious, writer of short stories as well as to the maker of some of the best poems written in our century." N Y Times Bk R

FitzGibbon, Constantine. The life of Dylan Thomas; with photographs. Little 1965 370p illus $8.95   92

1 Poets, Welsh

"An Atlantic Monthly Press book"

This documented biography of Dylan Thomas which covers his life from childhood in Wales to his death in New York in 1953 acknowledges him as a great poet and human being. It reduces the famous lurid American tours at the end of his life to their proper perspective. (Publisher)

"A deep and real affection for his subject underlies Mr. FizGibbon's astringent honesty and his firmly objective tone." Times (London) Lit Sup

Appendixes contain broadcasts, film scripts and lectures and readings from America by Dylan Thomas

Thoreau, Henry David

Derleth, August. Concord rebel; a life of Henry D. Thoreau. Chilton Co. 1962 213p front $3.95   92

1 Authors, American

The author shows how Thoreau, by rejecting all external compulsions in a kind of spiritual anarchism, has become an inspiration to those who rebel at the pressures of our material civilization. He discusses Thoreau's youth, his years at Harvard, his experiment in simple living at Walden Pond, and his arrest and imprisonment for his refusal to pay a poll tax. (Publisher)

"The author quotes Thoreau throughout the book, and gives a broad picture of the literary atmosphere and personalities of the times." Chicago. Children's Book Center

Bibliographical notes: p205-06. Map on lining papers

Norman, Charles. To a different drum; the story of Henry David Thoreau; pictures by Margaret Bloy Graham. Harper 1954 113p illus lib. bdg. $3.27   92

1 Authors, American

A "biography of Henry David Thoreau, emphasizing his trip down the Concord-Merrimack Rivers and his life at Walden Pond. Excerpts from his writings are used throughout, especially for descriptions of the countryside. No attempt is made to give a critical look at the man, his philosophy or his writings." Chicago. Children's Book Center

Titian

Williams, Jay. The world of Titian, c.1488-1576, by Jay Williams and the editors of Time-Life Books. Time-Life Bks. [distributed by Little] 1968 192p illus (Time-Life Lib. of art) boards $7.95   92

1 Painters, Italian 2 Painting, Italian

Text and picture essays portray Venice at the height of her power and the Venetian painters, focusing on the paintings of Titian

"The excellent selection of Titian's most significant works (many full and double-paged in color) reveals the Christian and the neo-pagan traditions and rediscoveries of the age. The wide range of portraits included in this volume indicates his unsurpassed mastery in this field and his close association with the men who made the history and the culture of the later Renaissance. Other pictures and text illustrate the artist's city, Venice, in its growth and grandeur, and the great masters of Venetian painting before and after Titian, from Bellini and Carpaccio to Tintoretto, Paolo

Veronese and Guardi. Particular emphasis has been on the unique genius of Giorgione." Library J

Bibliography: p187

Tolstoĭ, Lev Nikolaevich, graf

Philipson, Morris. The count who wished he were a peasant; a life of Leo Tolstoy; illus. with photographs. Pantheon Bks. 1967 170p illus (A Pantheon Portrait) lib. bdg. $5.17   92

1 Authors, Russian

"A comprehensive account of the many phases and activities of the life of one of Russia's greatest writers. The brief résumé of Russian history up to his time provides the setting for the problems that were to absorb so much of his energy: government, social customs, established religion, the lot of the peasants, and education." Horn Bk

Suggested reading list: p167-70

Trapp, Maria Augusta

The story of the Trapp Family Singers. Lippincott 1949 309p illus $5.95   92

1 Trapp Family Singers

"Baroness Trapp describes her coming as governess to a retired Austrian captain's seven motherless children, her marriage, the development of the 'Trapp Family Singers,' their tours in Europe and America and music camp at Stowe, Vermont." Bookmark

"It is an amusing, sometimes serious, always highly personal record of one of the distinguished musical families of our time, and it is also an intimate, friendly, completely engaging story of how an indomitable woman (for the author, as the reader will see, is and has been the moving spirit of the whole enterprise) met adversity and triumphed." San Francisco Chronicle

Treviño, Elizabeth Borton de

My heart lies south; the story of my Mexican marriage. Crowell 1953 248p illus $5.95   92

1 Americans in Mexico 2 Mexico—Social life and customs

"A young American [newspaper] woman marries a Mexican engineer and adopts a completely Mexican way of life. Some humourous but sympathetic comparisons are made between American and Mexican personalities and customs. Each chapter deals with one phase of family or community life." Top of the News

Where the heart is. Doubleday 1962 286p $4.95   92

1 Americans in Mexico 2 Mexico—Social life and customs

The author, an American married to a Mexican, presents sketches "of her education as Mexican wife and mother. . . . Through anecdotes of her boys, her husband and mother-in-law and the rest of her big Mexican family, her friends, and the people who work in her household, she shows Mexican daily life as well as the thoughts, feelings, and traditions which mold it. . . . She has gained much insight into Mexican and American characters; under her humorous accounts lies a shrewd analysis of the traits which make the two peoples alternately appreciate and resent one another." Horn Bk

Truman, Harry S. President U.S.

Memoirs. Doubleday 1955-1956 2v $6.95 92

1 Presidents—U.S. 2 U.S.—Politics and government—1945-1953

Contents: v 1 Year of decisions; v2 Years of trial and hope

A "record of the former President's tumultuous years in office, his early days in Missouri . . . glimpses of his family life, appraisals of world leaders, and . . . about the background of national and international events." Publisher's note

"Perhaps the cardinal value of the book indeed, lies in its frank depiction of Mr. Truman's mind and character. As a literary performance it does not achieve a place among the best memoirs of our times. . . . Nevertheless, this is a volume of distinction. It has force, clarity and

Truman, Harry S. President U.S.—*Continued*

sincerity. It contains numerous comments of incisive shrewdness and anecdotes both apt and revealing. It is lighted up by bits of informal, folksy writing." Book of the Month Club News

Gies, Joseph. Harry S. Truman; a pictorial biography. Doubleday 1968 178p illus $6.95

92

1 Presidents—U.S. 2 U.S.—Politics and government—1945-1953

This biography of the 33rd President of the United States begins with his early days in rural Missouri and goes on to follow his political career with focus on his years in the White House. (Publisher)

"Here is a good, if not profound and not very searching, biography of former President Truman. . . . In all fairness, this is intended as a pictorial biography (there are 125 illustrations revealing Truman against the background of his times). This being so, its failure to inquire too deeply into many aspects of Truman's personality and his career (including some genuine accomplishments as well as his awesome decision to drop the first A-bomb) cannot be faulted strongly. Certainly the book will serve to introduce to the younger generation a man who was struck by presidential lightning and stood up rather magnificently." Pub W

Velázquez, Diego Rodríguez de Silva y

Brown, Dale. The world of Velázquez, 1599-1660, by Dale Brown and the editors of Time-Life Books. Time-Life Bks. [distributed by Little] 1969 192p illus maps (Time-Life Lib. of art) boards $7.95

92

1 Painters, Spanish 2 Painting, Spanish

Text and illustrations portray the work of the 17th century Spanish master who served King Philip IV through four decades. Velázquez painted the royal family, court notables, court jesters, and dwarfs in a realistic style that dignified his subjects. (Publisher)

Bibliography: p187

Vermeer, Johannes

Koningsberger, Hans. The world of Vermeer, 1632-1675, by Hans Koningsberger and the editors of Time-Life Books. Time, inc. [distributed by Little] 1967 192p illus map (Time-Life Lib. of art) boards $7.95

92

1 Painters, Dutch 2 Art, Dutch

In discussing the artist's life, the author describes 17th century Holland and the Dutch artists who preceded Vermeer or who were his contemporaries. The main part of the book is devoted to analyses of Vermeer's paintings. (Publisher)

"Particularly interesting are the sections on the history of Holland's fight for freedom from Spain and the resulting golden age, and those explaining the quality of light and realism in painting . . . and the story of the Van Meegeren forgeries during World War II." Library J

Bibliography: p187

Victoria, Queen of Great Britain

Strachey, Lytton. Queen Victoria. Harcourt 1921 434p $2.95

92

1 Queens 2 Great Britain—History—19th century

"Harbrace Modern classics"

A "presentation of Queen Victoria and her time, characterizations of Lord Melbourne, Palmerston, Gladstone and Disraeli, and a very impressive and convincing portrait of the prince consort." Booklist

"The aim is not new knowledge, but a new interpretation of facts already known. . . . His method is more that of a novelist than of a biographer. . . . Nothing is admitted that might appear dull; nothing is excluded that can add piquancy to the narrative. In temper, Mr. Strachey's art is not so much English as French. There is doubtless another Victoria. It yet remains for a finer if less brilliant mind to trace the Queen in all her subtle influences on her age." W. L. Cross's Outline of Biography

Bibliography: p425-29

Vining, Elizabeth Gray

Quiet pilgrimage. Lippincott 1970 410p illus $8.95

92

The author relates her childhood and Quaker upbringing in Pennsylvania, her warm relationship with her sister, her happy but brief marriage, her experiences in postwar Tokyo as the tutor of Japan's crown prince, and her writing

"This is a gentle and muted book that takes a quiet grip on the reader and will give genuine pleasure to the author's many followers." Pub W

Von Braun, Wernher

David, Heather M. Wernher von Braun. Putnam 1967 255p front (Lives to remember) lib. bdg. $3.64

92

1 Scientists 2 Space sciences

A "biography of von Braun, from his early days in Germany where he successfully launched the V-2 rocket, to his entry and expansion of America's space projects. The technical problems of rocketry as well as the political climate affecting our program are . . . presented." Publisher's note

"An excellent, well-written, biography. . . . It should interest anyone intrigued with space flight." Science Bks

Bibliography: p241-44

Washington, Booker Taliaferro

Up from slavery; an autobiography

92

1 Negroes—Biography 2 Educators 3 Tuskegee Institute

Some editions are:

Dodd (Great illustrated classics) $4.50 With illustrations of the author and his environment, together with an introduction by Langston Hughes

Doubleday $4.95

First published 1901

"The classic autobiography of the man who, though born in slavery, educated himself and went on to found Tuskegee Institute." N Y Pub Lib

"In no other respect is this book more impressive and effective than in that of his complete identification of himself with his people. . . . The vicissitudes and achievements of the Tuskegee school are exhibited in a series of pictures and contrasts that must sometimes make the reader's heart beat fast and sometimes dim his eyes." Nation

Thornbrough, Emma Lou, ed. Booker T. Washington. Prentice-Hall 1969 184p (Great lives observed) $5.95

92

1 Negroes—Biography

"A Spectrum book"

This "selection of writings by and about . . . [Booker T. Washington] are presented, after a brief biography, under various headings, among them Washington viewed by whites and Negroes, Washington's place in history. . . . [The author's] comments are judicious throughout; and her emphasis on the complexity of Washington's character and her rejection of the idea that he was a mere 'Uncle Tom' are refreshing." Library J

Bibliographical note: p178-82

Washington, George, President U.S.

Flexner, James Thomas. George Washington and the new nation (1783-1793): with photographs. Little 1970 466p illus map $12.50

92

1 Presidents—U.S. 2 U.S.—History—1783-1809—Biography

This is the third of four projected volumes of the author's study of the First President's life begun in George Washington: the forge of experience, and George Washington, entered below. This volume "reaffirms and clarifies two major contributions by Washington during the period covered: his pervasive influence at the Constitutional Convention and his calm good sense in guiding the nation in its first four years under the Constitution." Library J

Bibliography: p431-37

Washington, George, President U.S.—Cont.

Flexner, James Thomas. George Washington in the American Revolution (1775-1783). Little 1968 599p illus maps $12.50   92

1 Presidents—U.S. 2 U.S.—History—Revolution—Biography

"Continuing his analysis of the Revolutionary War leader begun in 'George Washington: the forge of experience' . . . [the author] interprets the personality, philosophy, and war conduct of Washington during eight crucial years and shows the effect of a military career thrust on Washington the citizen of Virginia. By probing the character of Washington's subordinates and associates he illustrates Washington's qualities as a general. Changing attitudes among Colonial leaders as the revolution ended and Washington's role are examined in concluding chapters." Booklist
Bibliography: p557-63

Flexner, James Thomas. George Washington: the forge of experience (1732-1775). Little 1965 390p illus $12.50   92

1 Presidents—U.S. 2 U.S.—History—Colonial period—Biography

This first volume of the author's study on the life of George Washington describes his childhood, youth, the influence of his mother and brother, his part in the French and Indian Wars as well as his life as the husband of a wealthy widow

A portrait "not skimping on his infatuation with his neighbor's wife, Sally Fairfax . . . but also showing him to be amiable and sociable and not the 'marble image' in which history has preserved him." Pub W
Source references: p361-77. Map on lining-papers

Watteau, Jean Antoine

Schneider, Pierre. The world of Watteau, 1684-1721, by Pierre Schneider and the editors of Time-Life Books. Time, inc. [distributed by Little] 1967 191p illus (Time-Life Lib. of art) boards $7.95   92

1 Painters, French 2 Painting, French

Combined with Schneider's account of Watteau's tragic life are 146 illustrations, 54 of them in full color. Sixty pictures display a broad range of Watteau's sketches, etchings, and his creation—the "fête galante." Watteau's notable artistic successors are also presented. (Publisher)

"Useful for undergraduates in the scope of its coverage and its readable presentation. Although not as penetrating in its analysis as some recent essays on the 19th century . . . it still presents a perfectly well balanced account of the period. The selection of illustrations is satisfactory, although their quality cannot be compared with that in other more expensive volumes." Choice
Bibliography: p185

Wharton, Edith Newbold (Jones)

Coolidge, Olivia. Edith Wharton, 1862-1937. Scribner 1964 221p front lib. bdg. $3.63   92

1 Authors, American

A biography of the daughter of a prominent New York family who "earned lasting fame as one of the most distinguished writers of her time. Even as a child . . . Edith displayed an intelligence and energy that were not expected of her. Later . . . she found the formal structure of American society stifling. She was happier in Europe, among friends such as Henry James and Walter Berry." Publisher's note

"The discussion of her works as a part of her development as a woman is sensible and restrained and serves as an inducement to their reading. Not only for confirmed Wharton fans, this is a fine introduction to a woman and her times." Library J
Recommended reading: p213-14

Whistler, James Abbott McNeill

Prideaux, Tom. The world of Whistler, 1834-1903, by Tom Prideaux and the editors of Time-Life Books. Time-Life Bks. [distributed by Little] 1970 191p illus (Time-Life Lib. of art) boards $7.95   92

1 Painters, American

The author "has been attracted to the theatricality of his subject's character and career. Prideaux's biographical text limns Whistler as a man at bay against the miscomprehensions of his time, and an artist who intuitively was moving toward modern non-representational art." Pub W
Bibliography: p187

White, Terence Hanbury

Warner, Sylvia Townsend. T. H. White; a biography. Viking [1968 c1967] 352p illus $6.50   92

1 Authors, English

"Though best known as the author of 'The Once and Future King.' White was a variety of other persons as well: poet, mythologist, sailor, and, as this fine biography notes, an unusual human being. The author notes White's compulsive seeking after new, unfamiliar areas of knowledge and his equally great hesitance at personal intimacy, whether romantic or merely friendly. Based on numerous letters and private diaries, as well as the memories of those who knew White, Warner's biography is genuinely moving and thoroughly engrossing. While little is said about White's literary craft his life is brilliantly brought alive, a feat not always found in biographies." Choice
Bibliography: p346-48

White, William Allen

The autobiography of William Allen White. Macmillan (N Y) 1946 669p illus $6.95   92

1 Journalists

Pulitzer Prize for biography, 1947
The life of William Allen White inevitably forms a chapter in American history, for he not only participated in the making of much of the history of his era, but was a keen observer of a great deal more. Included are characterizations of leaders like Mark Hanna and Theodore Roosevelt, of lesser men like McKinley, of writers and editors, of the Progressives, of Harding, of the Versailles Peace Conference which Mr White attended, and of America in the throes of its greatest period of growth and change

Williams, Ted

My turn at bat; the story of my life, by Ted Williams with John Underwood. Simon & Schuster 1969 288p illus boards $5.95   92

1 Baseball—Biography
SBN 671-20228-6

The life of one of baseball's all-time greats from his childhood days in San Diego through his career with the Boston Red Sox to his managing of the Washington Senators
This "will be enjoyed by most sports fans for its candor and insight into the game as well as for the biographical approach." Library J

Wilson, Woodrow, President U.S.

Hoover, Herbert. The ordeal of Woodrow Wilson. McGraw 1958 318p illus $6.95   92

1 Presidents—U.S. 2 U.S.—Foreign relations

Herbert Hoover was a close advisor to President Wilson during World War I and the years immediately following. He presents "a tribute to Woodrow Wilson's personal qualities and administrative genius and a highly sympathetic account of his tragic difficulties in connection with the League of Nations, and the attempt to get the United States to join the League." Pub W
Bibliography: p305-07

Wilson, Woodrow, President U.S.—*Cont.*

Link, Arthur S. Woodrow Wilson; a brief biography. World Pub. 1963 191p front $5.95
92

1 Presidents—U.S. 2 U.S.—Politics and government—1898-1919

The author "discusses all the facets of Wilson's formidable career—his early years, his reforms as president of Princeton University, his political campaigns for the governorship of New Jersey and later the Presidency, his New Freedom program, his neutrality and leadership during World War I, his Fourteen Points and championship of the League of Nations, and more." Publisher's note

Additional reading: p181-84

Wolfe, Thomas

Turnbull, Andrew. Thomas Wolfe. Scribner [1968 c1967] 374p illus $7.95
92

1 Authors, American

"Not a definitive study, but a readable portrait of a giant of a man with an enormous capacity for life and filled with the conflicts of genius—cruel, tender, generous, and crass. His relations with his family, his mistress Aline Bernstein and Maxwell Perkins, his editor, during his adult years are given attention with perspective, reflecting the passionate Wolfe of the spilling novels, yet in a smooth-flowing narrative." Library J

Sources and acknowledgments: p348-54

Wong, Jade Snow

Fifth Chinese daughter; with illus. by Kathryn Uhl. Harper 1950 246p illus $5.95, lib. bdg. $4.43
92

1 Chinese in the U.S.

Jade Snow Wong's autobiography "has a unique story to tell of growing up between the Old World and the New in San Francisco's Chinatown. As a daughter brought up in the narrow traditions of the old family ways, she only slowly found her identity . . . as a student at Mills College, later as a wartime shipyard worker and, finally, as a creative artist." Hunting

"An engrossing story, related with the same skill the author apparently manifests in her . . .; occupation of designing and making pottery." New Yorker

Wordsworth, William

Halliday, F. E. Wordsworth and his world. Viking 1970 143p illus map $6.95
92

1 Poets, English 2 Wordsworth, William—Contemporary England
SBN 670-78256-4

"A Studio book"

A biography of the poet who was a central figure in the English Romantic movement. "The text is supported by contemporary illustrations of the Lake District, France during the darkest hour of the Revolution . . . and many writers and public figures whom [Wordsworth] knew." Publisher's note

A short bibliography: p129

Wright, Richard

Black boy; a record of childhood and youth. Harper 1964 285p $6
92

1 Negroes—Moral and social conditions 2 Negroes—Biography

First published 1945 by World Publishing Company

The "moving and harrowing autobiography of a Negro who drifted from Natchez to Chicago to Brooklyn. His later life and evolution of thought and his solutions to the problem of the Negro in America are relevant today." A Guide to Reading in Am History

Webb, Constance. Richard Wright; a biography. Putnam 1968 443p illus $9.95
92

1 Authors, American 2 Negroes—Moral and social conditions 3 Negroes—Biography

Based upon Wright's diaries, letters, speeches, unpublished work, and conversations with his wife, this biography combines personal reminiscence and literary analysis. (Publisher)

"Marred by a personal and sometimes sentimental approach to its subject together with recorded thoughts by Wright which lend it a fictional aspect, this biography is nevertheless valuable in the details of the fruitful yet tragic life of an American Negro novelist." Booklist
Bibliography: p423-29

Williams, John A. The most native of sons; a biography of Richard Wright. Dorothy Sterling, editorial consultant. Doubleday 1970 141p front $3.95, lib. bdg. $4.70
92

1 Authors, American 2 Negroes—Moral and social conditions 3 Negroes—Biography

"A Perspective book"

"The first half of the book describes Richard Wright's impoverished childhood—a childhood of despair and misery that set the scene for his writings about the black man in a white society. The author has done an admirable job (without sentimentality) of telling his story and analyzing his works." Pub W

A selected bibliography of the works of Richard Wright: p136

Wyeth, Andrew

Logsdon, Gene. Wyeth people; a portrait of Andrew Wyeth as he is seen by his friends and neighbors; illus. with photographs by the author. Doubleday 1971 159p illus $5.95
92

1 Painters, American

The author traveled in Pennsylvania and Maine among people Andrew Wyeth has known. He describes that journey, recording his encounters with the scenes, the men, and the women Wyeth has painted. Through the author's informal conversations with these people, he portrays Wyeth—the man and the artist. (Publisher)

Ybarra, T. R.

Young man of Caracas; foreword by Elmer Davis. Washburn 1941 324p illus $4
92

1 Caracas, Venezuela

Story of the author's early years in Caracas and of his father, a general in the Venezuelan army, and his mother, a Bostonian beauty

"It is Tom Ybarra's autobiography, but the book is really about his mother and father, two sharply contrasted characters and their lifelong love story. It is a 'Life with Father' in Venezuela with personalities as surprising and delightful as in Clarence Day's book." Book of the Month Club News

929.4   Personal names

Lambert, Eloise

Our names; where they came from and what they mean, by Eloise Lambert and Mario Pei. Lothrop 1960 192p $3.50
929.4

1 Names 2 Names, Personal

Divided into three parts: First names, Family names, and Thing names, this book discusses sources and meanings of names, the role of mythology, religion, race, appearance, location and occupation in establishing names, and the spelling of names. It includes animal, seasonal, national group, and abbreviated names

Latham, Edward

A dictionary of names, nicknames, and surnames of persons, places and things. Dutton 1904 Republished by Gale Res. 1966 334p $9.50
929.4

1 Names—Dictionaries 2 Nicknames—Dictionaries 3 Names, Personal—Dictionaries

Compiled as a supplement to "the ordinary dictionaries of biography, geography, mythology, etc. [wherein] a person or place is often alluded to by means of a surname or nickname without any clue being given to the reader, who does not happen to be aware of the actual name of the person or place." Preface

Shankle, George Earlie

American nicknames; their origin and significance. 2d ed. Wilson, H.W. 1955 524p $10

929.4

1 Nicknames 2 Names, Geographical 3 Names, Personal—U.S.
ISBN 0-8242-0004-7

"More than 4000 nicknames, belonging to famous Americans, cities and states, political organizations, and military regiments, arranged in dictionary form with cross references, with sources given in footnotes." Booklist

"While the work is not flawless, the average reader may be surprised at the number of entertaining subjects to which he will be introduced. . . . [The reader] will find interest in scanning here the nicknames that at one time or another have had lively significance in American affairs." Springf'd Republican

Smith, Elsdon C.

American surnames. Chilton Co. 1969 xx, 370p $9.95

929.4

1 Names, Personal—U.S.

In this study of the roots and derivations of American surnames, the author examines "abbreviated names, immigrant alterations, surnames from animals, change of names by immigrants, surnames without vowels, those from Christian first names, landscape names, town names, soldier names, Jewish surnames, surnames from periods of time, comic or odd names, and hyphenated names." Publisher's note

Bibliography: p327-29

929.9   Flags

Flags of the world; ed. by E. M. C. Barraclough. With 370 flags in full colour and over 375 text drawings. [Rev. ed] Warne 1969 284p illus $12.95

929.9

1 Flags
SBN 7232-1101-9

First published 1897 in England under the authorship of F. E. Hulme

The book contains "an introductory chapter on the history of flags, followed by the flags of Great Britain and her Dependencies, and flags of North America, Latin America, the West Indies, Europe, Africa, the Middle East, Asia and Oceania; there are also chapters on International and Signal flags, and flags worn by merchant ships and yachts." Publisher's note

Bibliography: p269

Pedersen, Christian Fogd

The international flag book in color; color plates: Wilhelm Petersen; editor of the English language edition: John Bedells. Morrow 1971 237p illus $5.95

929.9

1 Flags

Translated by Frederick and Christine Crowley

Original Danish edition, 1970

Supersedes Preben Kannik's: The flag book, first published 1957 by Barrows

National, state, naval and mercantile flags in use today, currently recognized official flags, and national coats of arms are illustrated by 853 colored reproductions arranged geographically and keyed to an explanatory text at the end of the book

"The information is accurate and up-to-date, the colors are surprisingly good for so inexpensive a book, relative dimensions are given for many flags, and special terminology is explained in a glossary." Library J

Quaife, Milo M.

The history of the United States flag; from the Revolution to the present, including a guide to its use and display, by Milo M. Quaife, Melvin J. Weig, and Roy E. Appleman. . . . [2d ed] Published in co-operation with the Eastern National Park and Monument Association. Harper [1964 c1961] 190p illus $6.95, lib. bdg. $5.79

929.9

1 Flags

First published 1961

"With contributions by Charles E. Shedd, John A. Hussey, and George C. Mackenzie; foreword by Roger Butterfield. Original drawings by Elmo Jones." Title page

"This book describes the various flags adopted by the American Colonies during the Revolution; the earliest regimental colors; naval pennants, mercantile flags; and the origin of the Stars and Stripes and its many changes through the 19th and 20th centuries. Included are inspiring stories of Francis Scott Key, John Paul Jones, and others." Huntting

Bibliographical references included in Notes: p179-86

Smith, Whitney

The flag book of the United States; illus. by Louis Loynes & Lucien Philippe. Morrow 1970 306p illus $12.95

929.9

1 Flags

"The director of the Flag Research Center has written a useful flag book, beautifully illustrated and printed, showing that a study of flags can tell us much about the history of a country. Smith includes flags of the colonial powers, the history of the development of the U.S. flag, the history of the various state and Confederate flags, government, military, local, private, and—never before shown—flags of the Indian nations. Included in the appendixes are the dates that each of the various U.S. flags were flown as well as information on other flags flown over the states, flag etiquette, and a glossary." Library J

Bibliography: p279-80

930-999   HISTORY

930   The ancient world to ca. 500 A.D.

The **Cambridge** Ancient history; ed. by J. B. Bury [and others]. Cambridge 1923-1970 13v illus maps v 1 pts 1-2 ea $23.50, v3-12 ea $23.50

930

1 History, Ancient

New edition in preparation for volume 2

Contents: v 1 pt 1 Prolegomena and prehistory; v 1 pt2 The early history of the Middle East; in preparation; v2 Egyptian and Hittite empires to c. 1000 B.C. (o.p. 1971); v3 Assyrian empire; v4 Persian empire and the West; v5 Athens, 478-401 B.C.; v6 Macedon, 401-301 B.C.; v7 The Hellenistic monarchies and the rise of Rome; v8 Rome and the Mediterranean, 218-133 B.C.; v9 The Roman republic, 133-44 B.C.; v10 Augustan empire, 44 B.C.-A.D. 70; v11 The imperial peace, A.D. 70-192; v12 The imperial crises and recovery A.D. 193-324

Volume 1 pt 1 edited by I. E. S. Edwards, C. J. Gadd, and N. G. L. Hammond; v2-6 edited by J. B. Burr, S. A. Cook and F. E. Adcock; v7-11 edited by S. A. Cook, F. E. Adcock, and M. P. Charlesworth; v12 edited by S. A. Cook, F. E. Adcock, M. P. Charlesworth and N. H. Baynes

"Volumes I and II of the Cambridge Ancient History have had to be entirely re-written as a result of the very considerable additions to knowledge which have accrued in the past forty-five years. For the same reason it has also been necessary to increase the size of the volumes and to divide each of them into two parts." Publisher's note

An "excellent reference history, each chapter written by a specialist, with full bibliographies at the end of each volume." Winchell. Guide to Reference Books. 8th edition

Robinson, Charles Alexander
Ancient history from prehistoric times to the death of Justinian. 2d ed. prepared by Alan L. Boegehold. Macmillan (N Y) 1967 xxv, 740p illus maps $9.95   **930**
1 History, Ancient 2 Civilization, Ancient
First published 1951
The author relates the history, government, politics, and wars of ancient times to the civilization in terms of art, literature, law, economic development, the reasons for growth, failure and decay of the countries
Select bibliography: p703-20

932 Egypt to 640 A.D.

Cottrell, Leonard
The warrior Pharaohs. Putnam 1969 137p illus map lib. bdg. $3.49   **932**
1 Egypt—Kings and rulers 2 Egypt—History, Military
First published 1968 in England
This history "focuses on the activities and exploits of the pharaohs [during a period of 2,000 years]. How these priest-kings built an empire that stretched through northeastern Africa and much of the Near East and the manners, morals, and mores of their subjects and soldiers are examined and explained." Publisher's note
The author's "lively interpretations of archaeological findings and ancient records of the period effectively show the strength and resilience of the ancient Egyptian civilization." Booklist

Horizon Magazine
Pharaohs of Egypt, by the editors of Horizon Magazine. Author: Jacquetta Hawkes; consultant: Bernard V. Bothmer. . . . Am. Heritage 1965 153p illus maps boards $5.95, lib. bdg. $5.49   **932**
1 Egypt—History 2 Egypt—Kings and rulers
"A Horizon Caravel book"
"Illustrated with reliefs, sculptures, wall paintings, and monuments of ancient Egypt." Title page
"Describes the beginning of civilization in the Nile Valley, with emphasis on the period of the New Kingdom when the Pharaohs were at the height of their power. Notable for illustrations of wall paintings, sculptures, reliefs, and monuments of the period." Hodges
"The reigning kings are treated in historical perspective—from the unification of Upper and Lower Egypt by Narmer (the legendary Menes) in 3100 B.C. to the closing days of the New Kingdom. Special treatment is given to Zoser, who with his vizier Imhotep, raised the first pyramid, to Cheops and Chephren, to Mentuhotep II, Tuthmosis I, Amenhotep III, and the brilliant Akhenaten." Science Bks
Further reference: p149

936 Europe north and west of Italian peninsula

Powell, Thomas George Eyre
The Celts. Praeger 1958 282p illus map (Ancient peoples and places ser) $8.50   **936**
1 Celts
"We begin with a survey of European prehistory which explains the background and circumstances antecedent to the emergence of the people who were to be known as the Celts from the fifth century BC onwards, then examine the material culture of the various phases of Celtic development, their art and trade, and the manner of their living, before turning to a . . . description of what can be deduced of the pagan Celtic religion and a discussion of the survival of the Celtic world on and beyond the fringes of the Roman Empire in the west and north, until the beginning of the mediaeval world." Spec

"With a masterful touch which reveals a full command of the sources—both literary and archaeological . . . the author, while avoiding excessive details, fruitless controversy, and dogmatic conclusions, has given us a lucid and highly informative treatment of his subject." Ann Am Acad
Bibliography: p189-200

937 Rome

Asimov, Isaac
The Roman Empire. Houghton 1967 277p illus maps $4.50   **937**
1 Rome—History—Empire, 30 B.C.-476 A.D. 2 Roman emperors
A continuation of: The Roman Republic, entered below
An account of Rome's history and culture "from its beginnings as a small uncivilized tribe to the magnificent Roman Empire in existence just 500 years later." Bk Buyer's Guide
"The author skates over a large and he skates well and vigorously over so large a surface. He is perhaps better at facts than at judgments, some of which seem dogmatic and a few wrong. . . . But in straight, rapid narration Mr. Asimov is very good indeed and he writes with an infectious kind of enthusiasm." Book Week
Genealogies: p255-58. A table of dates: p259-69

The Roman Republic. Houghton 1966 257p illus maps $4.50   **937**
1 Rome—History—Republic, 510-30 B.C.
A "chronicle of Rome's rise to power from the founding of the city to 27 B.C. . . . Focusing mainly on military and political activity, the author . . . interprets historic events in the light of the abilities, motives, ideas, and actions of the men who dominated them." Booklist
"The text gives an enormous amount of information, yet it has a conversational quality. . . . A table of dates (both the Christian year and the year from the founding of Rome) and an extensive index are appended." Chicago. Children's Book Center

Coolidge, Olivia
Caesar's Gallic War. Houghton 1961 245p illus maps $3.75   **937**
1 Rome—History—Republic, 510-30 B.C. 2 Caesar, Caius Julius
This "presentation of the Gallic War from 58 B.C. through 52 B.C. combines the political history of the period with military information from Julius Caesar's 'Commentaries on the Gallic War.' Told through a fictitious narrator, a former officer in Caesar's army, the account vitalizes some of the people mentioned in Caesar's 'Commentaries,' includes invented characters to show types, and depicts Caesar, not only as a man ambitious of power, but also as deliverer, conqueror, and avenger. A praiseworthy book which may be useful in connection with the study of ancient Roman history and Latin. Illustrated with maps and with effective decorations adapted from old engravings." Booklist
Place names used in the text [and] their Roman equivalents: p[246]

Duggan, Alfred
The Romans; illus. by Richard M. Powers. World Pub. 1964 125p illus map $4.95, lib. bdg. $5.20   **937**
1 Rome—History
"A chronological history of Rome covering the legends of Romulus and Remus, the Etruscan kings, the Republic, the Punic Wars with Carthage, the civil wars, the growth and decay of the empire, and fall of the city to the Goths. Should foster understanding of the unique character of the Romans, their courage, discipline, patriotism, judicial system as well as the common culture uniting sovereign countries developed by the empire. Striking illustrations." Library J
Bibliography: p120-21

Durant, Will
Caesar and Christ. . . . Simon & Schuster
1944 751p illus maps (The Story of civilization: pt.3) $10   **937**

1 Rome—Civilization 2 Church history

"A history of Roman civilization and of
Christianity from their beginnings to A.D. 325."
Title page
The author "has reinterpreted and synthe-
sized an entire culture with conscientious ob-
jectivity." Sat R
Bibliographical guide: p673-80

Gibbon, Edward
The decline and fall of the Roman Empire
     937

1 Rome—History—Empire, 30 B.C.-476 A.D.
2 Byzantine Empire

Some editions are:
Dutton (Everyman's lib) 6v ea $3.25 Notes by
Oliphant Smeaton; introduction by Christopher Dawson
Modern Lib. (Modern Lib. Giant) 3v ea $4.95
First published 1776-1788 in England
In this substantial history of the Roman Empire, Gibbon "bridges the abyss between the
ancient and the modern world. It is the one
historical work of the eighteenth century that
is still accepted as authoritative. It covers thirteen centuries of history, during which time
paganism was breaking down and Christianity
was taking its place." The Reader's Adviser
and Bookman's Manual

The decline and fall of the Roman Empire;
an abridgment by D. M. Low. Harcourt 1960
924p $10   **937**

1 Rome—History—Empire, 30 B.C.-476 A.D.
2 Byzantine Empire

A one-volume abridged edition of title entered above
"It is certain that Mr. Low's streamlined
version will encourage many more to embark,
and he still offers a handsome voyage. Little
of the flavour of bigness (though some of the
eighteenth century) is lost by cutting Gibbon
to about one-third of his original length."
Times (London) Lit Sup
Bibliographical note: p904. Map on lining-
papers

Hadas, Moses
Imperial Rome, by Moses Hadas and the
editors of Time-Life Books. Time-Life Bks.
[distributed by Little 1969 c1965] 190p illus
maps (Great ages of man: A history of the
world's cultures) boards $6.95   **937**

1 Rome—History 2 Rome—Civilization

First published 1965
Text and numerous illustrations, many in
color, describe the history of ancient Rome,
from its legendary founding to the decline of
the Empire
The author presents with "sympathy the
many aspects of the Roman record and the
Roman character." Introduction
Bibliography: p184

Mills, Dorothy
The book of the ancient Romans; an introduction to the history and civilization of
Rome from the traditional date of the founding of the city to its fall in 476 A.D. Putnam
1927 464p illus map $4   **937**

1 Rome—History 2 Rome—Civilization

This history is similar in scope and treatment to the author's: The book of the ancient
Greeks, entered in class 938. A chronological
chart at the end of this volume includes the
events from 8th century B.C. to the fall of the
Roman Empire
Books for further reading: p455-56

938   Greece to 323 A.D.

Asimov, Isaac
The Greeks: a great adventure. Houghton
1965 326p illus maps $4.95   **938**

1 Greece—History 2 Civilization, Greek

"The history of the Greek civilization which
began more than 4,000 years ago, and whose influence—in culture, politics, philosophy, etc.
—encompassed half the world." Bk Buyer's
Guide
"The last pages of the book bring the history of Greece up to date. . . . Despite the dis-
tracting use of parenthetical guides to pronunciation, the . . . text is enjoyable because
of the conversational quality of the writing."
Chicago. Children's Book Center

Bowra, C. M.
Classical Greece, by C. M. Bowra and the
editors of Time-Life Books. Time, inc. [dis-
tributed by Little] 1965 192p illus maps (Great
ages of man: a history of the world's cultures) boards $6.95   **938**

1 Greece—History 2 Civilization, Greek

"This offers both textually and pictorially
a fine survey of all that made Greece great.
Emphasizing the 6th and 5th centuries B.C., it
covers the years through the Peloponnesian
War and the reign of Alexander the Great. . . .
Of great value for the money. The appendixes
are full of information in a variety of forms."
Library J

Bury, John Bagnell
A history of Greece to the death of Alex-
ander the Great. 3d ed. rev. by Russell
Meiggs. St Martins 1951 xxv, 925p illus $6 **938**

1 Greece—History

First published 1900
A political history of Greece
Partial contents: Beginnings of Greece and
the heroic age; Growth of Sparta; Growth of
Athens; Advance of Persia to the Aegean;
Perils of Greece; The War of Athens with the
Peloponnesians; Hegemony of Thebes; Rise of
Macedonia; Conquest of Persia; Conquest of
the Far East
Notes and references (Bibliographical): p851-
900

Durant, Will
The life of Greece. . . . Simon & Schuster
1939 754p illus (The Story of civilization:
pt.2) $10   **938**

1 Greece—History 2 Civilization, Greek

"Being a history of Greek civilization from
the beginnings, and of civilization in the Near
East from the death of Alexander, to the Roman conquest; with an introduction on the prehistoric culture of Crete." Title page
"Colorful and alive in characterization and
description, the life of Greece . . . is seen 'both
in the mutual interplay of its cultural elements, and in the immense five-act drama of
its rise and fall.' " Bookmark
Glossary: p672. Bibliography: p673-79. Maps
on lining-papers

Herodotus
The histories of Herodotus. Tr. by George
Rawlinson; ed. by E. H. Blakeney; introduction by John Warrington. Dutton [1964]
2v ea $2.95   **938**

1 History, Ancient 2 Greece—History—Persian Wars, 500-449 B.C.

"Everyman's library"
"The history falls into two chief parts. The
first five books are an introduction, tracing
the rise and growth of the Persian power. The
last four books relate the Persian invasions of
Greece under Darius and Xerxers. . . . As a
historian, he fails chiefly by inattention or insensibility to political cause and effect. . . .
And he tells us little or nothing about constitutional change. His charm of style is all the
greater for his almost child-like simplicity,
and he is one of the most delightful story-tell-
ers." R. C. Jebb's Greek literature

Mills, Dorothy

The book of the ancient Greeks; an introduction to the history and civilization of Greece from the coming of the Greeks to the conquest of Corinth by Rome in 146 B.C. With sixteen illus. and a map. Putnam 1925 420p illus map $4   **938**

1 Greece—History 2 Civilization, Greek

"An introduction to the history and civilization of Greece from the coming of the Greeks to the conquest of Corinth by Rome in 146 B.C. The emphasis of the book is not on wars but on the life of the people, their literature and art and the heritage that they left." Book Rev Digest

Thucydides

The history of the Peloponnesian War **938**

1 Greece—History—Peloponnesian War, 431-404 B.C.

Some editions are:
Dutton (Everyman's lib) $2.95 Translated by Richard Crawley
Univ. of Mich. Press 2v $6.95 The Thomas Hobbes translation. Edited by David Grene, with an introduction by Bertrand de Jouvenel. Has title: The Peloponnesian War
"A perceptive analytical yet stirring account of the fateful struggle between Athens and Sparta." Good Reading

939 Other parts of ancient world to ca. 640 A.D.

Asimov, Isaac

The Near East; 10,000 years of history. Houghton 1968 277p illus maps $4.95   **939**

1 Near East—History 2 Near East—Civilization

The author "reviews what is known of the ancient civilizations in and around the area called The Near East—the Eastern end of the Mediterranean eastward into Persia,—the civilizations of the Sumerians, Akkadians, Amorites, Assyrians, Chaldeans, Persians, Macedonians, Parthians, Sassanids, then quickly sketches the more recent history of the Arabs, Turks, Russians, Germans and Israel. . . . Illustrated with maps and drawings; chronological table and index." Best Sellers
"Asimov demonstrates, as in all his books, rare ability to bring to life the long dead past with his enthusiastic lively and lucid prose." Books for School Libraries, 1968

Ceram, C. W.

The secret of the Hittites; the discovery of an ancient empire. Tr. from the German by Richard and Clara Winston. Knopf 1956 [c1955] xxi, 281p illus maps $6.95   **939**

1 Hittites

Originally published in German
"A continuation of the panorama of the most ancient world presented in 'Gods, Graves, and Scholars [entered in class 913.031].'" Publisher's note
A reconstruction of the part the Hittites played in ancient (2000 B.C.) history based on archeological findings discovered on the 1954 expedition to the ancient Hittite empire in Central Turkey. (Publisher)
Ceram "is able to make every page interesting by intimate knowledge of the subject and skill of presentation rather than by exploitation of bizarre side issues." Sat R
Bibliography: p261-81

940-990 THE MODERN WORLD

940.1 Europe—Middle Ages, 476-1453

Asimov, Isaac

The Dark Ages. Houghton 1968 256p maps $4.75   **940.1**

1 Middle Ages

"With the close of the second century, the Roman Empire became a thing of the past. The Germanic tribes of Northern Europe made their mark on the crumbling empire and what is now called the 'Dark Ages' began. [The author] explores this obscure period of history [and the influence of personalities such as Alaric, Charlemagne, and Charlemagne's successors]." Publisher's note
"Asimov's tracings of the origins of place names . . . are especially interesting. An excellent index makes this a good reference tool as well as absorbing general reading. Charts of the Merovingian, Pepin, and Carolingian dynasties are included, as are useful maps and a comprehensive table of dates." Library J

Bishop, Morris

The Middle Ages. Am. Heritage Press 1970 386p illus $6.95   **940.1**

1 Middle Ages 2 Civilization, Medieval

A reissue in a new format of the book first published 1968 with title: The Horizon Book of the Middle Ages, entered below

The **Cambridge** Medieval history; planned by J. B. Bury; ed. by H. M. Gwatkin [and] J. P. Whitney. Cambridge 1922-1967 8v in 9 maps v 1-3 ea $19.50, v4 $42.50 (2pts pt 1 $25, pt2 $17.50) v5-8 ea $19.50   **940.1**

1 Middle Ages—History

Contents: v 1 The Christian Roman Empire and the foundation of the Teutonic kingdoms, 2d ed. (1924); v2 The rise of the Saracens and the foundation of the Western empire; v3 Germany and the Western empire; v4 The Byzantine Empire. 2d ed. Pt. 1 Byzantium and its neighbours (1966); Pt. 2 Government, church and civilisation (1967); v5 Contest of empire and papacy; v6 Victory of the papacy; v7 Decline of the empire and papacy; v8 Close of the Middle Ages
Volume 3 edited by H. M. Gwatkin, J. P. Whitney, J. R. Tanner, C. W. Previté-Orton; v4 edited by J. M. Hussey; v5-7 edited by J. R. Tanner, C. W. Previté-Orton, Z. N. Brooke; v8 edited by C. W. Previté-Orton, Z. N. Brooke
"An excellent reference history written by specialists, with full bibliographies at the end of each volume." Winchell. Guide to Reference Books. 8th edition

Duggan, Alfred

The story of the crusades, 1097-1291; with drawings by C. Walter Hodges. Pantheon Bks. [1964 c1963] 263p illus maps $5.95 **940.1**

1 Crusades

First published 1963 in England
"An account of the Holy War . . . emphasizing the strategy, tactics, and objectives of the Crusaders." Chicago
"For source material he has drawn on Runciman, Oman, Smail, and Oakeshott—thereby insuring authenticity of facts. . . . Most of all, Duggan succeeds admirably in disclosing the national and diplomatic intrigue." Library J
Note on sources: p7

Durant, Will

The age of faith. . . . Simon & Schuster 1950 1196p illus (The Story of civilization: pt.4) $12   **940.1**

1 Civilization, Medieval 2 Religion

"A history of medieval civilization—Christian, Islamic, and Judaic—from Constantine to Dante: A.D. 325-1300." Title page

Durant, Will—*Continued*
"The outstanding merit of this book is that it does present the medieval chapter in the story of civilization substantially as a whole, vividly, intelligibly, and honestly." Sat R
Bibliographical guide: p1087-1100. Maps on lining-papers

Eastern and Western Europe in the Middle Ages [by] F. Graus [and others] ; ed. with an introduction by Geoffrey Barraclough; with 132 illus. 16 in color. Harcourt 1970 216p illus maps (History of European civilization lib) $6.95   **940.1**
1 Europe—Civilization 2 Civilization, Medieval 3 Civilization, Slavic 4 Civilization, Germanic
ISBN 0-15-12762-X
Emphasizing the process of assimilation and cooperation, five historians from East and West discuss the different aspects of East-West relations: the contacts and settlements of Slavs and Germans in the early centuries; the political relationships; the impact of Christianity; the economic patterns of East-West trade; and cultural exchanges. (Publisher)
Bibliographical notes: p207-10

Fremantle, Anne
Age of faith, by Anne Fremantle and the editors of Time-Life Books. Time, inc. [distributed by Little] 1965 192p illus maps (Great ages of man: a history of the world's cultures) boards $6.95   **940.1**
1 Civilization, Medieval 2 Middle Ages—History
During the Middle Ages, a period running from the second half of the 5th century to the first half of the 15th, Europe became the cradle of Western civilization. This profusely illustrated book touches many aspects of medieval life: religion; art; literature; economics and politics; philosophy, and science. (Publisher)
"Anne Fremantle brings out the main lines of this story with remarkable . . . competence." Robert S. Lopez
Bibliography: p186

Horizon Magazine
The Horizon Book of the Middle Ages, by the editors of Horizon Magazine. Editor in charge: Norman Kotker; author: Morris Bishop. Am. Heritage 1968 416p illus $22.50   **940.1**
1 Middle Ages   2 Civilization, Medieval
"This volume covers the period from the conversion of Constantine in 312 A.D. through the conclusion of the Hundred Years War in 1461." Book Rev Digest
Contents: The long dark; The high Middle Ages; Knights in battle; The noble's life; An age of faith; Towns and trade; The life of labor; The life of thought; The artists' legacy; End of an era
The author's "presentation, accompanied by 329 pictures of contemporary art and architecture . . . turns the reader into a participant in that unique pageant of European history which took place during the Middle Ages." Library J

Lamb, Harold
The crusades. . . . Doubleday 1945 [c1930-1931] 2v in 1 illus maps $7   **940.1**
1 Crusades
First published 1930-1931
"The whole story of the crusades originally published in two volumes in Iron men and saints and The flame of Islam." Subtitle
Volume 1 covers mainly the first crusade; v2 begins in 1169 and tells the story of the next 150 years
"Without idealization, colorfully and in interesting detail, the author makes the reader realize the background and achievement of the first and greatest of the crusades. The other four are touched upon in a brief section." Providence
Selected bibliography: v 1 p351-58; v2 p469-75

Mills, Dorothy
The Middle Ages. Putnam 1935 360p illus maps $4.50   **940.1**
1 Middle Ages—History
Covers, roughly, the period between 300 and 1500, with discussions of the church, Charlemagne, the Norsemen, monasteries, chivalry, the crusader, medieval town, trade, travel, education, and government
The author employs an "informal, intimate style of history writing . . . frequent use of quotations from contemporary chronicles . . . [and] fine illustrations." Michigan School Librarian

The **Shorter** Cambridge Medieval history. Cambridge 1952 2v (xx, 1202p) illus maps $17.50   **940.1**
1 Middle Ages—History
"A condensation of the 8-volume 'Cambridge Medieval History,' by one of its original editors. . . . [Includes] histories of the ten centuries between the fall of the Roman Empire and the Renaissance, covering the invention of gunpowder and the printing press, the rise of such men as Genghis Khan, Saladin, Saint Augustine, Dante, Chaucer, etc." Retail Bookseller
Contents: v 1 Later Roman Empire to the twelfth century; v2 Twelfth century to the Renaissance
"There can be no question that as a work of concise and primary reference this book ranks high. . . . Colour and individuality have often, and inevitably, been sacrificed, but . . . the factual accuracy of this account is throughout wholly admirable, and within the limitations of its space its detail is remarkable." Times (London) Lit Sup

Simons, Gerald
Barbarian Europe, by Gerald Simons and the editors of Time-Life Bks. [distributed by Little] 1968 192p illus maps (Great ages of man: a history of the world's cultures) boards $6.95   **940.1**
1 Europe—History—476-1492
This history of Europe from 406 A.D. to the 11th century describes "the slow conversion of the barbarian tribes to Christianity; the emergence of new political forms; the . . . expansion of commerce; the rebirth of urban society and education [and] innovations in art and architecture." Introduction
Bibliography: p186

Thorndike, Lynn
The history of medieval Europe. 3d ed. Houghton 1949 750p illus maps $9.50   **940.1**
1 Europe—History 2 Middle Ages—History 3 Civilization, Medieval
First published 1917
"This book will trace the history of Europe and of the parts of Asia and Africa adjacent to the Mediterranean and thus closely connected with Europe." Introduction
Time: From the decline of the Roman Empire to about 1500
Includes bibliographies

Treece, Henry
The crusades. Random House [1963 c1962] 334p $4.95   **940.1**
1 Crusades
A condensed account of two hundred years of wars, some of them sacred journeys, but others merely quests for quick riches. "The author traces the changing moods of each campaign; the fiery aspirations of those who led and those who followed . . . [such as] Charlemagne, Haroun-al-Raschid Peter the Hermit, Richard Lion-Heart, Raymond of Toulouse, Bohemond, Saladin, Mourschild, Henry Dandolo, Frederick II, Louis the Pious and Jenghis Khan." Publisher's note
The author "endeavors to show that religious motives were only one group of factors out of many, that economic motives were also significant, and that the Crusaders were often anything but religious or noble, and he does this with charm, skill, and accuracy." Library J
Map on lining-paper

940.2 Europe. Modern period, 1453-

Blitzer, Charles
Age of kings, by Charles Blitzer and the editors of Time-Life Books. Time, inc. 1967 192p illus maps (Great ages of man: a history of the world's cultures) lib. bdg. $7.60   940.2
1 Europe—History—1492-1789 2 Seventeenth century 3 Kings and rulers
The author gives an account of the seventeenth century, which produced great artistic and scientific achievements and led to the first attempt at government by public participation. (Publisher)
Bibliography: p186

Chamberlin, E. R.
Everyday life in Renaissance times; drawings by Helen Nixon Fairfield. Putnam [1966 c1965] 200p illus map boards $4   940.2
1 Renaissance 2 Europe—Social life and customs
First published 1965 in England
A survey of the social background of the cultural and intellectual achievements of the Renaissance. (Publisher)
Partial contents: The court; The merchant; The common man; The city; The world of learning; The city of God
"Another of an excellent social-history series, which will probably be used more by teachers planning study units than by young students." Horn Bk
Select bibliography: p11-12

Cheyney, Edward Potts
European background of American history, 1300-1600. Ungar [1966] 343p front maps $7.50   940.2
1 America—Discovery and exploration 2 Commerce—History 3 Reformation 4 Great Britain—Politics and government
"American classics"
A reprint of the 1904 edition first published by Harper
The first chapters present those aspects of medieval and Renaissance trade and exploration that inspired the discovery of America. As the sixteenth and seventeenth centuries wore on, religion became the ever more dominant factor in colonization. The final section is devoted to an examination of the English governmental institutions the colonists left behind them. (Publisher)
Bibliographical references included in Critical essay on authorities: p316-31

Durant, Will
The age of Louis XIV. . . . By Will and Ariel Durant. Simon & Schuster 1963 802p illus (The Story of civilization: pt.8) $10   940.2
1 Europe—History—1492-1789
"A history of European civilization in the period of Pascal, Molière, Cromwell, Milton, Peter the Great, Newton, and Spinoza: 1648-1715." Title page
Emphasis falls "on the famous lives, particularly on the creative writers and great thinkers. The underlying concern is with the development of science and scholarship in conflict with superstition and religion. . . . The style is sprightly and cheerfully unobtrusive, thus rendering the whole eminently palatable. For the general, and informed reader and young people's collections." Library J
Bibliographical guide: p723-32. Maps on lining-papers

The age of reason begins. . . . By Will and Ariel Durant. Simon & Schuster 1961 732p illus (The Story of civilization: pt.7) $10   940.2
1 Europe—History—1492-1789
"A history of European civilization in the period of Shakespeare, Bacon,, Montaigne, Galileo, and Descartes: 1558-1648." Title page
"With great erudition and in a deft, smooth style of writing, the authors have produced an immensely readable . . . cultural and political history of this richly eventful period of world history. Special emphasis is put on the spreading contest between faith and reason." Pub W
Bibliographical guide: p649-59. Maps on lining-papers

The age of Voltaire. . . . By Will and Ariel Durant. Simon & Schuster 1965 898p illus (The Story of civilization: pt.9) $12   940.2
1 Europe—History—1492-1789 2 Europe—Civilization 3 Voltaire, François Marie Arouet de
"A history of civilization in Western Europe from 1715 to 1756, with special emphasis on the conflict between religion and philosophy." Title page
Following discussion of France, England and Middle Europe in this era "developments in many other areas of human activity are brought into a lengthy work rewarding for both the student and attentive general reader." Booklist
Bibliographical guide: p799-809. Notes: p811-36. Maps on lining-papers

The Reformation. . . . Simon & Schuster 1957 1025p illus (The Story of civilization: pt.6) $12   940.2
1 Reformation 2 Europe—History—476-1492 3 Europe—History—1492-1789
"A history of European civilization from Wyclif to Calvin: 1300-1564." Title page
Discusses also the following personalities: Calvin, Charles V, Chaucer, Columbus, Dürer, Erasmus, Henry VIII, Joan of Arc, Knox, Luther, Mary I, More, Rabelais, Wolsey
The author's "prose has a bright speed that carries its load of facts like an effortless burden. Deft allusions and the spice of humor transmute hours of research into a few sparkling phrases." N Y Times Bk R
Bibliographical guide: p941-52. Maps on lining-papers

The Renaissance. . . . Simon & Schuster 1953 776p illus (The Story of civilization: pt.5) $10   940.2
1 Renaissance 2 Italy—Civilization
"A history of civilization in Italy from 1304-1576 A.D." Title page
An "interesting but disconnected narrative, a mosaic of biographical sketches interspersed with lively passages on manners, morals, dress, food, festivals, plagues, pastimes and artistic preferences among the Italian élite, during some eight generations." N Y Her Trib Books
"The author presents a vivid engrossing picture of the Renaissance in Italy from the birth of Petrarch in 1304 to the death of Titian in 1576. The splendid pageant of a great age is made real through sharply etched portraits of popes, princes and tyrants, poets, artists and sculptors." Cincinnati
Bibliographical guide: p729-34

Rousseau and revolution. . . . By Will and Ariel Durant. Simon & Schuster 1967 xx, 1091p illus (The Story of civilization: pt.10) $15   940.2
1 Europe—History—1492-1789
"A history of civilization in France, England, and Germany from 1756, and in the remainder of Europe from 1715 to 1789." Title page
There is "no popular history that is so encyclopedic in scope, so brightly readable in style. . . . The authors find Rousseau less repulsive as a man than some do. Their analysis of his ideas, which were instrumental in producing both the Romantic movement and the French Revolution, is first-rate." Sat R
Bibliographical guide: p967-81. Maps on lining-papers

Hale, John R.
Renaissance, by John R. Hale and the editors of Time-Life Books. Time-Life Bks. [1969 c1965] 192p illus map (Great ages of man: a history of the world's cultures) lib. bdg. $7.60   940.2
1 Renaissance

Hale, John R.—*Continued*

First published 1965
A history of the Renaissance focusing mainly upon Italy and the city of Florence in the 15th century
Contents: The break with the Middle Ages; The variety of Italy; Manners and morals; Florence: intellectual dynamo; The triumph of art; A creative elite; War and politics; Renaissance in the North
Readers "will enjoy the brilliant pictures and clear text." Library J
Bibliography: p186

Hayes, Carlton J. H.

Contemporary Europe since 1870. Rev. ed. Macmillan (N Y) 1958 835p illus maps $8.95
940.2

1 Europe—History—1789-1900 2 Europe—History—20th century
Companion volume to: Modern Europe to 1870, entered below. Based on volume II of the author's: Political and cultural history of modern Europe
First published 1953
A standard work which "not only records political and military happenings but explains them by reference to their social, economic, and ideological setting" Foreword
Select bibliography: p785-812

History of Western civilization since 1500 [by] Carlton J. H. Hayes, Marshall Whithed Baldwin [and] Charles Woolsey Cole. Macmillan (N Y) 1962 574p illus maps $8.95 940.2

1 Europe—History 2 Civilization, Occidental
First published 1949 with title: History of Europe since 1500
In this history, from the time of Charles V and Luther to President Kennedy, "the course of European events is traced not only in political and economic terms, but also through . . . [the] integration of these with religious, philosophical, and artistic currents. Yet Western Civilization is not narrowly confined to Europe. . . . The authors have sought to treat these [wider] areas and their civilizations in sufficient detail to relate Europe to the rest of the world and to provide a clearer background for understanding today's international situation." Publisher's note
Includes bibliographies and a list of European sovereigns

Modern Europe to 1870. Macmillan (N Y) 1953 837p illus maps $8.95
940.2

1 Europe—History
Companion volume to the author's: Contemporary Europe since 1870
"It reinterprets the historical evolution of Europe from the standpoint of the Atlantic Community which has been developing since the sixteenth century and especially of the crisis in that Community resulting from the world wars and revolutions of our own time." Foreword
Select bibliography: p786-815

Horizon Magazine

The Battle of Waterloo, by the editors of Horizon Magazine. Author: J. Christopher Herold; consultant: Gordon Wright. Am. Heritage 1967 153p illus maps boards $5.95, lib. bdg. $5.49
940.2

1 Waterloo, Battle of, 1815
"A Horizon Caravel book"
This "story of the dramatic Hundred Days after Napoleon's return from exile on the island of Elba and of the great battle that ended his whirlwind bid for power . . . stresses the importance of the personalities of the major opponents in deciding Europe's fate." Publisher's note
"The battle that decided in one fearful tragic day, the future of Europe, is brilliantly recounted and superbly illustrated with contemporary pictures, cartoons, artifacts created from imaginations which were ignited by this historic spectacle." Pub W
Further reading: p151

The Horizon Book of The Elizabethan world, by the editors of Horizon Magazine. Editor in charge: Norman Kotker; author: Lacey Baldwin Smith. Am. Heritage 1967 416p illus maps $22.50
940.2

1 Great Britain—History—Tudors, 1485-1603 2 Europe—History—1492-1789
Also available with fewer illustrations for $6.50 with title: The Elizabethan world
"The author has collaborated with the editors of Horizon magazine to create this portrait of life not only in England during the sixteenth century but also in Spain, the Netherlands, and Scotland. With three sixteen-page anthologies of Elizabethan writings, and more than 400 illustrations of the era, over 100 in full color." Bk Buyer's Guide
"Lavishly illustrated and beautifully designed, this survey of the Elizabethan world is also lucid and readable. . . . In spite of its price, this volume certainly deserves a place in all libraries, and young adults will find it useful for both browsing and assignments." Library J
Bibliographical references included in Acknowledgments: p401-03

The Horizon Book of the Renaissance, by the editors of Horizon Magazine. Editor in charge: Richard M. Ketchum; author: J. H. Plumb; with biographical essays by Morris Bishop [and others]. Am. Heritage 1961 431p illus maps boards $17.50
940.2

1 Renaissance 2 Art, Italian
A picture history of the artistic, social, cultural, and political aspects of the Renaissance. The narrative text is arranged in 12 chapters, nine of which are supplemented by biographical essays on such outstanding leaders of the Renaissance as: Beatrice and Isabella d'Este, Foscari, Leonardo da Vinci, Machiavelli, Lorenzo Medici, Michelangelo, Montefeltro, Petrarch, and Pius II
"The hundreds of well-chosen and reproduced works of art (many among them full page and in color) are the greatest glory of the book. This visual approach is particularly important for the understanding of an age in which the visual arts play such a paramount part in reflecting the life and thought." Library J

Langer, William L.

Political and social upheaval, 1832-1852. Harper 1969 674p illus maps (The Rise of modern Europe) $10
940.2

1 Europe—Politics—1789-1900 2 Europe—Intellectual life
"A survey of the 20-year period in European history when the roots of liberalism, enlightenment, social reform and middle-class power were laid down or developed, culminating in a cycle of revolution whose main event was the Paris revolt in 1848, which was the signal for upheavals all over Europe." Pub W
Bibliographical essay: p615-55

Mills, Dorothy

Renaissance and Reformation times. Putnam 1939 xx, 345p illus maps $4.50 940.2

1 Renaissance 2 Reformation
"The period from the thirteenth through the sixteenth century is one of the hardest to present to young people with vigor if it is also to be presented—as it should be—without prejudice. It is also one of the most exhilarating to young people if its political, religious and economic changes can be shown . . . as they are here." N Y Her Trib Books

National Geographic Society

The Renaissance; maker of modern man. The Society 1970 402p illus maps (The Story of man lib) boards $11.95
940.2

1 Renaissance
SBN 87044-091-8
Foreword by Franc Shor. Editorial consultant: Kenneth M. Setton. Essays by Vincent Cronin, Merle Severy and others cover such figures as Michelangelo and Leonardo da Vinci, as well as historical periods such as Elizabethan England and the Reformation

National Geographic Society—*Continued*

"As would be expected, the visual effects in this survey of the Renaissance done by the National Geographic Society are outstanding. The full color illustrations, including a special section on Michelangelo's ceiling, with the binding make a beautiful book. . . . This work includes a text which is both very readable and historically accurate, based as it is on the work of solid and respected scholars. The style leads the reader into sharing the excitement the writers felt about the achievements of Renaissance Europe. The reader is left with the impression that he has been led on a tour of Renaissance Europe guided by some of its greatest admirers." Choice

Acknowledgments and reference guide: p401

Simon, Edith

The Reformation, by Edith Simon and the editors of Time-Life Books. Time-Life Bks. [distributed by Little 1969 c1966] 191p illus maps (Great ages of man: a history of the world's cultures) boards $6.95 **940.2**

1 Reformation

First published 1966

During the 16th century a movement started that culminated in the founding of Protestantism. "The story of ecclesiastical reform as it developed into contending factions, and as it interacted with the political, social, economic and philosophical currents of the age, is unfolded in this book." Introduction

"There is considerable emphasis on the major events, conditions, and personalities in the cultural, political, and scientific field, including a brief analysis of representative writers from Machiavelli to Montaigne and Cervantes. Among the merits of the book are numerous significant contemporary illustrations, many of them chosen from great masters such as Dürer, Brueghel, and El Greco, reflecting the lives of princes, burghers, and peasants." Library J

Bibliography: p186

940.3 World War I, 1914-1918

American Heritage

The American Heritage History of World War I, by the editors of American Heritage, The Magazine of History; narrative by S. L. A. Marshall, with a prologue by Edmund Stillman. . . . Am. Heritage 1964 384p illus maps boards $16.50 **940.3**

1 European War, 1914-1918

"Editor in charge: Alvin M. Josephy, Jr; managing editor Joseph L. Gardner." Title page

An analysis of the origins, course, and aftermath of World War I

"Historical and pictorial elements are interwoven into a year-by-year display of various aspects of World War I. While this overview covers both home-front and battle-front, the focus is on the campaigns, strategies, and personalities. Marshall's narrative is a . . . distillation and re-creation of the war's character and its economic, political, and social consequences. Other works will be more detailed about particular events, but few will be as readable or as graphic." Library J

Fay, Sidney Bradshaw

The origins of the World War. 2d ed. rev. Free Press 1966 2v maps pa v 1 $3.65, v2 $2.95 **940.3**

1 European War, 1914-1918—Causes 2 Europe —Politics—20th century

"A Free Press paperback"

First published 1928 by Macmillan (N Y)

"It is based upon knowledge . . . of the diplomatic correspondence and the personal narratives of leading diplomatists; in method and

in spirit it conforms closely to the highest standards of historical investigation and exposition." Guide to Historical Literature

Bibliographical footnotes

Parkinson, Roger

The origins of World War One. Putnam 1970 128p illus maps (The Putnam Documentary history ser) $4.95 **940.3**

1 European War, 1914-1918—Causes 2 Europe —Politics—20th century

"In tracing the origins of the First World War, the author goes back to the Germany of Bismarck and the Junkers, the Anti-Socialist Law of 1878, and focuses in succession on England's economic crisis of 1909, rumblings of impending social upheaval in Turkey and Russia, the consequences in France and in Germany of the Franco-Prussian War and the harsh peace terms of 1871, and the welter of crises and diplomatic exchanges and behind-the-scenes moves prior to and surrounding the assassination of Archduke Ferdinand in Sarajevo on June 28, 1914." Pub W

Further reading: p119

Snyder, Louis Leo

(ed.) Historic documents of World War I. Van Nostrand [1958] 192p pa $1.95 **940.3**

1 European War, 1914-1918—Sources

"Introductory notes place each document in its historical setting—documents that illustrate the origins and development of the war. Valuable in that it helps the reader form his own conclusions about the causes of the war." A Guide to Reading in Am History

Tuchman, Barbara W.

The guns of August. Macmillan (N Y) 1962 511p illus maps $8.95 **940.3**

1 European War, 1914-1918

Also available in a large type edition for $8.95

Pulitzer Prize 1963

A "history of the negotiations that preceded World War I and the course of the war's first month, up through the Battle of the Marne. Begins with an intimate and sometimes caustic view of the leaders in power as war came and of the actual making of war and continues with a critique of generals, equipment and tactics and a survey of the first confused and hideous battles." Pub W

A "valuable look at the first days of World War I from the British, French, Belgian, Russian, and German points of view." Top of the News

"The mature young adult who enjoys history appreciates this intensive, documented study. . . . The participants are drawn objectively, and the story is told with authority and a dramatic flair. Much of the book reads like a novel, and superior students find it stimulating and revealing." Doors to More Mature Reading

Sources: p441-55

The Zimmermann telegram. [New ed] Macmillan (N Y) 1966 244p illus $6.95 **940.3**

1 European War, 1914-1918—Causes 2 Zimmermann, Alfred

First published 1958

During the First World War, "the British intercepted a telegram in which German agents in Mexico were instructed to promise that country U.S. territories if she would create diversionary strife on the American continent. . . . The author tells how the telegram was decoded, and how its sensational message . . . [was] an important factor in the U.S. decision to enter the war." Booklist

"It should be required reading for any student of that period's history, and would that all required reading were as interesting as this." San Francisco Chronicle

Sources: p205-12

940.4 World War I, 1914-1918 (Military conduct of the war)

Horne, Alistair

Death of a generation; from Neuve Chapelle to Verdun and the Somme. Am. Heritage Press 1970 127p illus maps $3.95   **940.4**

1 Verdun, Battle of, 1916 2 Somme, Battle of the, 1916

"Library of the 20th century"

"In a concise account of the western front in World War I during 1914, 1915, and 1916 the author . . . stresses the futility of trench warfare and traces the fruitless attacks and counterattacks that were eventually climaxed at Verdun and the Somme. These two battles, lasting nearly a year and ending in deadlock, are characterized by Horne as 'the great and tragic watershed of the war.' His description, with full details of mistakes, casualties, destruction, and demoralizing effect experienced by Allies and Germans alike, is copiously illustrated with black-and-white photographs and with maps, posters, and representative paintings in color."
Booklist

Hough, Richard

The long pursuit. Harper 1969 173p illus $5.95   **940.4**

1 European War, 1914-1918—Naval operations

First published in England with title: The pursuit of Admiral von Spee

"The author chronicles the 1914 British naval defeat off the Coronel Islands at the hands of the German Admiral von Spee and the subsequent British destruction of von Spee's East Asiatic squadron later that year." Book Rev Digest

The author "is an expert on naval warfare . . . but he even more interestingly conveys the patriotic fervor and the touching sense of chivalry that incredibly survived (at least at the officer level) into the twentieth century." New Yorker

Select bibliography: p167-68. Maps on lining-papers

Lawrence, T. E.

Seven pillars of wisdom; a triumph. Doubleday 1966 [c1935] 622p maps $6.95   **940.4**

1 European War, 1914-1918—Campaigns and battles—Turkey and the Near East 2 Arabia—Social life and customs 3 Arabs 4 Bedouins 5 Wahhabis

Also available in an illustrated edition for $10

First published 1926 in England in a private edition

"Not only a history of the Arab revolt during the [first] World War, but a commentary on the national characteristics and political policies of Arabs, Turks and British." Cleveland

"With its packed pages of battles and raids, waterless deserts, strange peoples, the antics of rulers and ruled, prophets and robber chiefs, cruelties, sufferings and brief joys, there is no book by which to measure its worth as a whole. It is an extraordinary work." Times (London) Lit Sup

Reynolds, Quentin

They fought for the sky; the dramatic story of the first war in the air. Rinehart 1957 304p illus boards $5.95   **940.4**

1 European War, 1914-1918—Aerial operations 2 Air pilots

"This popular history of the first war in the air, 1914-1918, covers the activities of the air forces employed by both the Allies and the Germans. . . . It is in no way a definitive history of air fighting during World War I, but as the author himself admits, is, 'in the main a story of the airplanes and the men who flew them.' Its main emphasis is upon the individual exploits of aces on both sides—Nungesser, the Frenchman; Richthofen, the German; Rickenbacker, the American; and McCudden, the Englishman." Library J

"Skillfully integrating anecdotes of their personal exploits and methods with the rapid technical advances in aviation and the progress of the war in the air, [the author] achieves an informative and stirring record."
Booklist

Rickenbacker, Eddie V.

Fighting the Flying Circus; ed. and with a foreword by Arch Whitehouse. Doubleday 1965 296p illus maps $6.50   **940.4**

1 U.S. Army. 94th Aerosquadron 2 European War, 1914-1918—Aerial operations

First published 1919

The story of America's Hat-in-the-Ring Squadron during World War I. By downing 69 enemy aircraft, Captain Rickenbacker "and his 94th Pursuit Squadron became living legends; but they faced an equally renowned and deadly foe: Baron von Richthofen's notorious Flying Circus." Publisher's note

Glossary of expressions used in early aviation: p 1

940.53 World War, 1939-1945

Churchill, Winston S. 1874-1965

Closing the ring. Houghton 1951 749p maps (The Second World War v5) $6.50   **940.53**

1 World War, 1939-1945 2 World War, 1939-1945—Great Britain

"'Closing the Ring' sets forth the year of conflict from June 1943 to June 1944. Aided by the command of the oceans, the mastery of the U-boats, and our ever growing superiority in the air, the Western Allies were able to conquer Sicily and invade Italy, with the result that Mussolini was overthrown and the Italian nation came over to our side." Preface

"This is the raw stuff of history, refined, worked and molded into imperishable form by a master craftsman who [was] also one of the greatest participants in the scene he has so brilliantly reproduced." San Francisco Chronicle

The gathering storm. Published in association with the Cooperation Pub. Co. by Houghton 1948 784p maps (The Second World War v 1) $6.50   **940.53**

1 World War, 1939-1945 2 World War, 1939-1945—Great Britain

"Divided into two parts, the first covers the period 1919-1939 and includes chapters on the mistakes of the Allies after World War I, the rise and rearmament of the dictators, Spain, and the failure to preserve Austria and uphold Czechoslovakia. The second part covers the twilight war, 1939-1940 and is devoted largely to military matters." Library J

"Few books belong in the category of great events, and this is one of them. Few books makes history in the sense that the epoch they depict will always live as they saw it. This is such a book." N Y Times Bk R

The grand alliance. Houghton 1950 903p maps (The Second World War v3) $6.50   **940.53**

1 World War, 1939-1945 2 World War, 1939-1945—Great Britain

The history begun with: The gathering storm and continued with: Their finest hour, now broadens its sweep and reaches a climax wit' Pearl Harbor and the historic Christmas of 1941 at the White House

"The source material alone makes this book essential to any student of the Second Wor'· War and its literary style is magnificently in keeping with its heroic theme." Cath World

The hinge of fate. Houghton 1950 1000p illus maps (The Second World War v4) $6.50   **940.53**

1 World War, 1939-1945 2 World War, 1939-1945—Great Britain

Churchill, Winston S.—*Continued*

The author "tells of the year 1942 that led to the invasion of Sicily, through the ebb and flow of warfare in Africa, and the discouragingly slow job of reconquest. There are revealing accounts of meetings with F.D.R., and determined efforts at collaboration with Stalin." Retail Bookseller

"This book is as fine a description of the salient events of the titanic struggle as has yet been given us, written by the man best qualified to tell them." Christian Science Monitor

Memoirs of the Second World War. . . . Houghton 1959 1065p illus maps $10 **940.53**

1 World War, 1939-1945 2 World War, 1939-1945—Great Britain

"An abridgment of the six volumes of 'The Second World War' with an epilogue by the author on the postwar years written for this volume. Illustrated with maps and diagrams." Title page

This abridgment has been prepared by Denis Kelly from the original volumes: The gathering storm; Their finest hour; The grand alliance; The hinge of fate; Closing the ring; and, Triumph and tragedy, all entered in this class

"School libraries and larger young people's departments in public libraries, particularly those which do not have the six-volume history, will probably want this." Booklist

Their finest hour. Published in association with the Cooperation Pub. Co. [by] Houghton 1949 751p maps (The Second World War v2) $6.50 **940.53**

1 World War, 1939-1945 2 World War, 1939-1945—Great Britain

This volume starts with the problems confronted by Churchill as he assumed the office of Prime Minister in 1940; it continues with the Battle of France; the tragic glory of Dunkirk; the Battle of Britain; the rebuilding of England's army; the triumph over the "Graf Spee"; the desperate struggle to maintain England's supply lines against the increasing U-boat campaign; and finally the victorious African campaign ending at Tobruk

"Throughout the book there are, of course, estimates of men and events, judgments on the grand process of history, too many to consider here, around which controversy will doubtless always revolve. There are the brilliant sidelights and the vivid personal details. . . . But above all this there is the power of the majestic story itself." N Y Her Trib Books

Triumph and tragedy. Houghton 1953 800p maps (The Second World War v6) $6.50 **940.53**

1 World War, 1939-1945 2 World War, 1939-1945—Great Britain

"The final volume in Churchill's history of the war, beginning with D-Day [1944]. It includes an appraisal of F.D.R., descriptions of Yalta and the Potsdam conference, and the British elections of 1945." Retail Bookseller

"It is as magnificent a narrative as the best of its predecessors." Atlantic

Mosley, Leonard

On borrowed time; how World War II began. Random House 1969 509p illus maps $8.95 **940.53**

1 World War, 1939-1945—Causes

This examination of the diplomatic, political and military maneuvers during the year preceding the outbreak of World War II starts with the obscure "incident at Eger" in 1938 and continues to the invasion of Poland in September 1939

"Most of the information in [this book] is available elsewhere. But one would have to read dozens of books to discover what Mr. Mosley has compiled in one immensely readable package. In doing so, he has performed an eminently useful service." Christian Science Monitor

Sources: p469-75

Parkinson, Roger

The origins of World War Two. Putnam 1970 128p illus map (The Putnam Documentary history ser) $4.95 **940.53**

1 World War, 1939-1945—Causes

"Edited documents from all major sources are presented to reveal the events and personalities responsible for the beginnings of World War II. The activities of the Germans, Italians, French, English and Japanese are thoroughly covered in Mr. Parkinson's selections, demonstrating the political and social conflicts which precipitated the second major clash of the twentieth century." Publisher's note

Further reading: p125

Reeder, Red

The story of the Second World War; with maps and photographs. Hawthorn Bks. 1969-1970 2v illus maps v 1 $4.95, v2 $5.95 **940.53**

1 World War, 1939-1945

Contents: v 1 The Axis strikes (1939-1942) published by Meredith; v2 The Allies conquer (1942-1945)

Volume one tells of the war's early phases in Europe and the East. Volume two takes up the story in 1942, when Eisenhower arrives in London and continues through the end of the war. (Publisher)

Bibliographies included

Taylor, Alan John Percivale

The origins of the Second World War. Atheneum Pubs. 1962 [c1961] 296p illus $6.95 **940.53**

1 World War, 1939-1945—Causes

Professor Taylor's main thesis "is that Hitler did not wish any war from the time of his accession to power in 1933 until the outbreak of hostilities in September 1939. What he desired was a peaceful revision of the Treaty of Versailles, which the Allies had refused to bring about for thirteen years despite their promises to do so. . . . Taylor concludes that the Second World War can best be described as 'the unwanted war.' It was the product of blunders on all sides and without any notable heroes or villains." Am Hist R

"As a vigorous rebuttal to the previous devilish theory of how the Second World War was all Hitler's fault this book is of value. But it is very far from being the last word upon the subject." Canadian Forum

Toland, John

The last 100 days. Random House 1966 622p illus $10 **940.53**

1 World War, 1939-1945—Europe

Basing his report on hundreds of interviews with eyewitnesses from 21 countries and on several thousand primary sources, the author relates the military and diplomatic strategy that defeated Nazism and fascism at the close of World War II. Within the 100 days Roosevelt, Mussolini, and Hitler died. Mr Toland describes them as well as such military leaders as Patton and Montgomery

Events "have been handled with great skill; the pace is swift but seldom frantic, the style is lucid and controlled, and sharply controversial episodes are presented with unfailing good taste." Sat R

Bibliographical references included in Notes: p595-609. Map on lining-papers

Wright, Gordon

The ordeal to total war, 1939-1945. Harper 1968 315p illus maps (The Rise of modern Europe) $7.95 **940.53**

1 World War, 1939-1945 2 Europe—History—1914-1945

A study of Europe during the Second World War. The author "explores the economic, psychological, and scientific dimensions of the struggle . . . discusses Germany's plans for consolidating its conquests after the occupation of virtually all continental Europe, and . . . analyzes Europe's response to conquest, which

Wright, Gordon—*Continued*

ranged from . . . collaboration to armed resistance. In a concluding chapter, the author summarizes the War's . . . impact on European political and social institutions, on attitudes, and on forms of intellectual and cultural expression." Publisher's note

"We still do not know how much the war really cost us. . . . What Professor Wright has tried to do here is to sketch the broad canvas. . . . With one important exception he has succeeded admirably. He has demonstrated the German conquest, like that of Ghengis Khan, had no real plan or design: it was an impulse."
Va Q R
Bibliography: p269-305

940.54 World War II, 1939-1945 (Military conduct of the war)

The Army Times

D-Day; the greatest invasion, by the editors of The Army Times. Putnam 1969 192p illus maps $5.95   **940.54**

1 Normandy, Attack on, 1944

"An action-packed account of Operation Overlord [which began June 6, 1944] and its decisive effect in winning World War II in Europe for the Allies. . . . In full and dramatic detail and graphic, on-the-scene photographs, here is the inspiring story of that invasion from its inception after the disasterous Allied evacuation of Dunkerque in 1940 through its aftermath, final victory in Europe." Am News of Bks
Glossary: p183-84. Bibliography: p185-86

Beach, Edward L.

Submarine! Holt 1952 301p $5.50 **940.54**

1 Trigger (Submarine) 2 World War, 1939-1945—Naval operations—Submarine 3 World War, 1939-1945—Pacific Ocean

The true story of USS "Trigger," of those who sailed her against the enemy, and of her life and death in the Pacific. Interwoven with the story of "Trigger" are tales of other battle-hardened submarines, and of the officers and enlisted men who fought in them against the Japanese

"Each attack is told in clear, precise language, orders are repeated in Navy style until the landsman reader becomes so thoroughly introduced to the mysteries of range finding and ship handling that he is part of the crew." N Y Her Trib Books

Brickhill, Paul

The great escape; introduction by George Harsh. Norton 1950 264p illus map $5.95
940.54

1 World War, 1939-1945—Prisoners and prisons 2 Escapes 3 World War, 1939-1945—Personal narratives

"Exciting story behind the escape of nearly 100 British prisoners of war from Stalag Luft III in 1944. Over 600 prisoners worked secretly on this great venture for a year digging 'Tom,' 'Dick' and 'Harry,' three tunnels, 30 feet deep and nearly 200 feet long, forging identification papers, setting up a tailor shop to provide civilian clothes, and creating a system of alarms. One of the most astounding tales of the war." Cincinnati

"Since it turned out that all but three of these gallant men would have been better off to keep on waiting instead of forcing the issue, the reader may be impressed with the futility as well as the daring of the attempt. He may also experience a stifled feeling as the tension mounts." Springf'd Republican

Chennault, Anna

Chennault and the Flying Tigers; introduction by Thomas G. Corcoran. Eriksson 1963 xx, 298p illus $5.95   **940.54**

1 World War, 1939-1945—Aerial operations 2 Chennault, Claire Lee 3 World War, 1939-1945—China

This is the story of the "American pilots known as 'The Flying Tigers'—and of the famous American General, Claire Lee Chennault, whose genius formed these fighters into the most formidable military groups in American aviation history. . . . [Here is] the defense of China against the overwhelming active Japanese air arm by the American Volunteer Group [later known as] the Fourteenth Air Force." Publisher's note

"Although it presents a one-sided view of a controversial figure, Mrs. Chennault's [story] of her husband seems to be a reasonably accurate account . . . .based on his records and diaries. . . . [A] picture of the tragic as well as adventurous aspect of the war in China." Booklist
Map on lining-papers

Chinnock, Frank W.

Nagasaki: the forgotten bomb. World Pub. 1969 304p boards $7.95   **940.54**

1 Nagasaki—Bombardment, 1945 2 Atomic bomb 3 World War, 1939-1945—Japan

"An NAL book"

"On August 9, 1945, an entire industrial city was devastated, the bulk of its population killed or wounded, its earth and air contaminated with radiation, and its survivors branded with lingering illness or the living scar of memory. . . . Using diaries, written accounts, and the actual words of hundreds of Japanese who lived through the holocaust, Frank Chinnock has constructed a . . . narrative of Nagasaki's ordeal on that day." Publisher's note

"On questions of the morality and the political history of the atomic bombing of Nagasaki, Chinnock does not contribute much that is new. . . . What sticks in the reader's mind is the graphic, horrible detail of the Nagasaki bombing and the courage of its victims in the face of it. It inspires the hope that the story may live not because this was the second time a nuclear weapon was deliberately used against people, but because it was the last." Sat R
Bibliography: p302-04

Collier, Basil

The Second World War; a military history; from Munich to Hiroshima—in one volume. . . . Morrow 1967 640p maps $8.95
940.54

1 World War, 1939-1945—Campaigns and battles

"British title: A short history of the Second World War." Title page

Starting with the events which led up to World War II, the author proceeds with descriptions of the war in Europe and Asia. (Publisher)

A "readable, old-fashioned British military-planning, campaigns, and battles—history. It is very good on land and air operations, and fair on the war at sea." Choice
Bibliography: p569-78

Donovan, Robert J.

PT 109; John F. Kennedy in World War II. McGraw 1961 247p illus $6.95 **940.54**

1 Kennedy, John Fitzgerald, President U.S. 2 World War, 1939-1945—Naval operations

"A full account of Kennedy's command of PT boat 109 in World War II in the Pacific and his heroic efforts to get his crew rescued after their boat was shot up by the Japanese. . . . [Written] from private interviews given the author by the [late] President and from interviews with surviving members of the crew." Pub W

"A reasonably true-to-life account of how the alternate dullness and tension of combat was survived with grit and occasional good humor." A Guide to Reading in Am History
Maps on lining-papers

Eisenhower, Dwight D.

Crusade in Europe. Doubleday 1948 559p illus maps $6.95   **940.54**

1 World War, 1939-1945—Campaigns and battles 2 World War, 1939-1945—Personal narratives

Eisenhower, Dwight D.—*Continued*

The complete story of the war in Europe as Eisenhower planned it and lived it. Through his eyes is seen the whole gigantic drama of the war—the strategy, the battles, the moments of fateful decision. Covers the years 1941-1945

This "is set off from all memoirs written by military leaders—it is the least military and most democratic of them all. It is the report of a citizen who led other citizens in a difficult task of restoring order and peace. When its author describes military actions he writes not for the archives of West Point but for the understanding of Americans who sent their sons into battle." Survey

Bibliographic references included in Footnotes: p481-510. Glossary of military code names: p518-22.

Eisenhower, John S. D.

The bitter woods. . . . Putnam 1969 506p illus maps $10   940.54

1 Ardennes, Battle of the, 1944-1945

"The dramatic story, told at all echelons—from supreme command to squad leader—of the crisis that shook the western coalition: Hitler's surprise Ardennes offensive." Title page

This narrative of the European campaign during World War II focuses on the Battle of the Bulge and portrays both Allied and German commanders

The author "offers some choice portraits of both Allied and Nazi figures and brings belated recognition to some unsung heroes on varied levels of rank. Historians and reviewers may fault him for favoritism or misplaced emphasis, but he cannot be accused of writing dully. His book is thorough, well-researched and downright suspenseful at its climax." Pub W

Bibliography: p471-79

Frank, Anne

The diary of a young girl; tr. from the Dutch by B. M. Mooyaart-Doubleday; with an introduction by Eleanor Roosevelt 940.54

1 World War, 1939-1945—Netherlands 2 World War, 1939-1945—Jews 3 Jews in the Netherlands

Some editions are:
Doubleday $5.95
Modern Lib. $2.95
Watts, F. $8.95 Large type edition complete and unabridged. A Keith Jennison book

First published 1947 in Holland

Two Jewish "families went into hiding in the abandoned half of a warehouse in Amsterdam during the Nazi occupation. Anne, the thirteen-year-old, recorded what she saw and felt about the relationships of eight people living under the strain of hunger, of crowded housing, and fear of discovery and death. . . . [This story tells of Anne's] shifting relationship to her parents and sister [and young Peter Van Doan] and her growing self-awareness." Reading Ladders

"A book that derives its lasting interest less from its war background . . . than as an unaffected, often moving account of the dreams and soul searchings of an adolescent." Ontario Lib Rev

Glines, Carroll V.

Doolittle's Tokyo Raiders. Van Nostrand 1964 447p illus maps $6.95   940.54

1 Tokyo—Bombardment, 1942 2 Doolittle, James Harold

An account of "the American surprise air attack on Japan. April, 1942. Planning details and first-hand accounts by crew members of the B-25 planes are followed by an evaluation of the raid's effect and its aftermath." Pub W

Bibliography: p440

Hachiya, Michihiko

Hiroshima diary; the journal of a Japanese physician, August 6-September 30, 1945; tr. and ed. by Warner Wells. Univ. of N.C. Press 1955 238p $4   940.54

1 Hiroshima—Bombardment, 1945 2 Atomic bomb—Physiological effect 3 World War, 1939-1945—Personal narratives

An eyewitness account of the atomic bombing of Hiroshima, Japan, in World War II and the ensuing seven weeks, by the Director of the Hiroshima Communications Hospital. Wounded and with his hospital gutted by fire, Dr Hachiya faced the task of keeping his hospital running and of trying to discover the radioactive effects of the bomb

"Although Hiroshima Diary necessarily is full of horrors, it is not a depressing book. Frightening, certainly; but the courage, patience, unselfishness, and resourcefulness it records would make the grimmest misanthrope proud of the human race." Atlantic

Glossary: p235-38. Map on lining-papers

Hersey, John

Hiroshima   940.54

1 Hiroshima—Bombardment, 1945 2 Atomic bomb—Physiological effect

Some editions are:
Knopf $4
Modern Lib. $2.95

First published in the New Yorker issue of August 31, 1946, this is an account of the ruin of a city and the wreck of human lives by one atomic bomb. The report focuses on six individuals who survived in that city

The purpose of the book "is to move everyone to take time to consider the terrible implications of [the bomb's] use. . . . Its aftereffect for the reader is one of numbed shock, which in turn becomes the first step in forcing us to consider seriously the grave responsibility we as a country have assumed in using the atom bomb." Literary Guild

Into the valley; a skirmish of the Marines; illus. by Donald L. Dickson. Knopf 1943 138p illus $3.95   940.54

1 World War, 1939-1945—Solomon Islands 2 U.S. Marine Corps 3 World War, 1939-1945—Personal narratives

"Story of the deeds of one company of marines during a small, unimportant battle on Guadalcanal, as told by a reporter. . . . The story is simply and briefly told but gives many details, concerning the sights and sounds of the jungle, the conversation and reactions of men ready for battle and in the thick of the fight, of how the wounded were evacuated, and other work of unsung heroes." Book Rev Digest

Howarth, David

D Day, the sixth of June, 1944. McGraw 1959 251p illus maps boards $5.95   940.54

1 Normandy, Attack on, 1944 2 World War, 1939-1945—Amphibious operations

"The greatest day of World War II . . . when the Allies landed in France, described blow by blow as parachutists, glider troops, infantry, air forces and naval commands concentrated on the French Coast. Any number of personal accounts by officers and men and by some of the Germans are skilfully worked into this engrossing chronicle." Pub W

The sledge patrol. Macmillan (N Y) 1957 233p illus maps $5.50   940.54

1 World War, 1939-1945—Greenland

The true "story of a murderous game of hide and seek between Danes and Germans fighting for weather stations in the ice and snow of northeast Greenland in World War II." Pub W

The author "has skillfully reconstructed the unique struggle. . . . His perceptive analysis of the moral conflicts of men, including the German commander Ritter, who could not reconcile their wartime duties with the arctic traditions of human brotherhood gives depth to a stirring true adventure story." Booklist

We die alone. Macmillan (N Y) 1955 231p illus $5.95   940.54

1 World War, 1939-1945—Norway 2 Baalsrud, Jan

"A sabotage mission to Norway in 1943 was a gamble that failed but it proved the almost incredible stamina of the one man who survived. When the crew and his three Commando partners were all killed by Nazis on the Arctic Norwegian coast, Jan Baalsrud fled into the snowy wastes. Although he was aided by various

Howarth, David—*Continued*
countrymen at the risk of their own lives, he reached Sweden only after such ordeals as being buried in an avalanche, wandering senseless and frozen for days, lying in a snow cave for a month, almost dying of frost bite. It is a grim record which highlights courage and does not play up the horrible sufferings." Horn Bk

Keith, Agnes Newton
Three came home; sketches by the author and Don Johnston. Little 1947 316p illus $7.50　　940.54

　1 World War, 1939-1945—Borneo 2 World War, 1939-1945—Prisoners and prisons 3 World War, 1939-1945—Personal narratives
"An Atlantic Monthly Press book"
Sequel to: Land below the wind, class 919.11
"When the Japanese invaded North Borneo in 1941, three who couldn't get away were Agnes Keith, her husband Harry and their baby son, George. In a series of Japanese prison camps, life became primitive, the most important question being how to get enough food to stay alive. That all three were alive when the Australians arrived four years later was almost a miracle of survival. A moving and courageous story suitable for older students." Ontario Lib Rev
Followed by: White man returns, class 919.11

Liddell Hart, B. H.
History of the Second World War. Putnam [1971 c1970] 768p maps $12.50　940.54

　1 World War, 1939-1945
First published 1970 in England
This account of World War II explores its military and political aspects "ranging from the frustrating events preceding the war, through all the campaigns and battles of seven turbulent years, to the final conclusion of hostilities." Publisher's note
This book "is a work of art, deceptively simple and plain. . . . The narrative of the course of the war both in Europe and the Far East is terse and disciplined. The comments pop up almost as incidentals, but this adds to their point and effectiveness. This is not, in other words, a book of easy, strategic generalisations. Rather it is a detailed, critical analysis, describing what happened and showing why it need not have done so." Economist
Books referred to in the text: p715-16

Lord, Walter
Day of infamy; illus. with photographs. Holt 1957 243p illus boards $4.50　940.54

　1 Pearl Harbor, Attack on, 1941
The author "recreates each minute of the day just before and just after the bombing of Pearl Harbor by the Japanese on December 7, 1941. He has built up a vast panorama by stopping for a second at a time to record the actions, thoughts, and emotions of hundreds of civilians, soldiers, generals, sailors, pilots, etc. He focuses attention on specific men." Horn Bk
"Based on exhaustive research and the eyewitness reports of over 500 participants, his vivid minute-by-minute chronicle depicts with detached objectivity both the daring enemy coup and the stunned reactions of American military personnel and the civilian populace of Hawaii." Booklist
Acknowledgments: p221-24. Maps on lining-papers

　Incredible victory. Harper 1967 331p illus $5.95　　940.54

　1 Midway, Battle of, 1942
Large type edition also available for $5.95
A "description of the sea battle of Midway in June, 1942, the turning point of the Pacific in World War II. . . . The fortunes of many individual men, American or Japanese, are followed through the battle." Pub W
The author's "details are drawn from interviews with some four hundred survivors of the action and from war diaries, charts, and letters. Written in his graphic, breathless style,

the story, as true as he can make it, mounts with almost unbelievable tension as the converging fleets draw near." Atlantic
Bibliography included in Acknowledgments: p301-07. Maps on lining-papers

Montagu, Ewen
The man who never was; with a foreword by Lord Ismay. [New ed] Lippincott 1967 [c1953] 176p illus $6.50　　940.54

　1 World War, 1939-1945—Secret service 2 World War, 1939-1945—Personal narratives
A reprint of a title first published 1953, with a new postscript explaining how the book came to be written
A "now it can be told" story of secret Operation Mincemeat. This was a carefully prepared ruse involving planted documents on a floating body which successfully misled the German commanders as to the Sicily invasion. Told by the British naval officer who originated the plot
"A true episode to outdo any spy novel. Fast, simple reading for all adventure lovers." Horn Bk
Includes "an appendix of communications in reference to the operation taken from official German documents." Pub W

Morison, Samuel Eliot
The two-ocean war; a short history of the United States Navy in the Second World War. Little 1963 xxvii, 611p illus maps $15　　940.54

　1 World War, 1939-1945—Naval operations
"An Atlantic Monthly Press book"
"In the hope of reaching new readers the author of the 15-volume 'History of the United States naval operations in World War II' has reduced the story of the war to one substantial volume, selecting the most important campaigns and battles. . . . Written with authority and vitality, this summary of World War II naval operations will be read by those interested in the overall situation but not the exhaustive detail of the larger work." Booklist
Abbreviations: p xxv-xxvii

Newcomb, Richard F.
Iwo Jima; foreword by Harry Schmidt. Holt 1965 338p illus maps $5.95　　940.54

　1 Iwo Jima, Battle of, 1945 2 U.S. Marine Corps
The author uses material from both American and Japanese sources in this account of the United States' capture of the island of Iwo Jima during World War II. In the 36 days of fighting, there were 28,686 American casualties, 25,851 of whom were Marines
"It is not a pretty story, for death is on every page in every imaginable form. The writing is skillful, charged with the drama of the events, but Mr. Newcomb never loses sight of the general struggle for the island while he draws the reader intimately into the private hell of individual men." Library J
Place names on Iwo Jima: p323. Bibliography: p325-27

Ogburn, Charlton
The Marauders. Harper 1959 307p illus maps boards $6.95, lib. bdg. $5.79　　940.54

　1 World War, 1939-1945—Burma 2 World War, 1939-1945—Personal narratives
A "moving narrative . . . [and] account of jungle warfare. Ogburn was communications officer in Merrill's Marauders, an ill-supplied group of three American battalions that fought the Japanese bravely and threw them back but succumbed by the dozen to undernourishment and disease in the bamboo forests of northern Burma in World War II. This is mostly Ogburn's personal story of the tense raids and battles . . . [and] the bright heroism of many of the Marauders." Pub W

Osada, Arata

(comp.) Children of the A-bomb; the testament of the boys and girls of Hiroshima. Tr. by Jean Dan and Ruth Sieben-Morgen; illus. by Mr and Mrs Minoru Kuroki. Putnam [1963 c1959] 256p illus $5.95   940.54

1 Atomic bomb 2 Hiroshima—Bombardment, 1945 3 World War, 1939-1945—Personal narratives

First published 1959 in Japan

In these accounts school children and youth of Hiroshima write about the A-bomb, the destruction of their homes, the terror of their experiences, and their hopes for world understanding

"It does not make pleasant reading, but it does vividly describe the horrors of atomic warfare." Library J

Map on lining-papers

Perrault, Gilles

The secret of D-Day; tr. from the French by Len Ortzen. Little 1965 249p $6.50
                                                   940.54

1 World War, 1939-1945—Secret service 2 Normandy, Attack on, 1944 3 Spies

Originally published 1964 in France

This is an account of "the deadly espionage duel between the Allies and the Germans just before D-Day. . . . Sorties of German spies did badly in England. Meanwhile, thousands of French informants funneled German defense plans into London. . . . On the other hand, there were Allied breaches of security and, as D-Day approached, the Allied command suffered some nervous moments. . . . [This] book about a secret battle before a battle has more suspense than a good spy novel." Pub W

Bibliography: p242-44. Map on lining-papers

Pratt, Fletcher

War for the world; a chronicle of our fighting forces in World War II. U.S. Pubs. Assn. 1950 364p (The Chronicles of America ser. v54) $4.45   940.54

1 World War, 1939-1945—U.S.

Originally published by Yale University Press

Contents: Japanese attack; Men and materials; Campaign of the carriers; Guadalcanal; Europe and the periphery, 1942; Campaign in Tunisia; Italian battleground; Sea and air, 1943; Island hopping toward Japan; Island chain broken; Secondary theaters and the submarine war, 1944; Imperial defense-line collapses; Great invasion; France set free; End of the Japanese navy; Reconquest of the Philippines; European enemy breaks; End of Japan; Bibliographical note

Reid, P. R.

The Colditz story. Lippincott 1953 [c1952] 288p front $6   940.54

1 Colditz, Germany. Castle 2 World War, 1939-1945—Prisoners and prisons

"Colditz Castle, built on a high cliff with walls seven feet thick, was the 'escape-proof' fortress. . . . Reid was one of the men who engineered several successful escapes and finally got away himself. This is an amazing description of how prisoners could manufacture tools, papers and clothing under the very eyes of the guards and how they could plan movements to a split second." Horn Bk

Map on lining-papers

Ryan, Cornelius

The last battle. Simon & Schuster 1966 571p illus maps $7.50   940.54

1 Berlin, Battle of, 1945

This is an "account of the encirclement of Berlin and its fall in the last days before the German surrender in early May of 1945. [The author] has interviewed or otherwise obtained information from eyewitnesses and participants,

American, British, Russian, German, the survivors of Berlin. . . . All this he has put together, with selected photographs (of individuals mostly), into a running account divided into five parts: The City, The General, The Objective, The Decision, The Battle. He discloses why the American and western Allied Forces stopped at the Elbe, when they might easily have pushed on the hundred or so miles to Berlin ahead of the two huge Russian armies driving toward it from the east. His accounts of the stupidities of the Reichskanzler Hitler and his sycophantic advisors, of the devastation of the much-bombed and eventually shell-razed city, of the courage and despair, the sufferings and stubborn endurance of the Berliners are clear and absorbing reading." Best Sellers

Bibliography: p541-51

The longest day: June 6, 1944. Simon & Schuster 1959 350p illus maps boards $7.95
                                                   940.54

1 Normandy, Attack on, 1944

Also available in a large type edition for $9.95

A detailed account of Operation Overload, the Allied invasion of Normandy on June 6, 1944 in World War II. Based on interviews with hundreds of men on both sides and on official records, including German war diaries, this book is not military history but the story of people: the men of the Allied forces, the enemy they fought, and the civilians caught up in the confusion of battle. (Publisher)

"Mr. Ryan's research is commendable. He has the ability to relate for the reader the drama of high-level planning with the chaos of personal combat." A Guide to Reading in Am History

Bibliography: p336-39

Salisbury, Harrison E.

The 900 days; the siege of Leningrad. Harper 1969 635p illus maps $10   940.54

1 Leningrad—Siege, 1941-1944

"This is the story of how Hitler turned on his sometime ally, finding the Russian people unsuspecting and ill-prepared, their leaders fully warned but nevertheless unbelieving, and how subsequently a million and a half Russians perished in Leningrad, chiefly by starving, during the winter siege of 1941-42." Book of the Month Club News

"The human story is all here, with its heroism and sacrifice, its horror and depravity, its bullheaded obstinacy and its tender touches." Library J

Bibliography: p597-610

Sims, Edward H.

American aces in great fighter battles of World War II; foreword by Nathan F. Twining. Harper 1958 xxv, 256p illus maps lib. bdg. $5.11   940.54

1 World War, 1939-1945—Aerial operations

In this book the author "records the most thrilling fighter missions flown by the twelve top U.S. Army Air Force fliers who survived World War II—missions which ranged all over Germany and France, in the skies over China, New Guinea and the Philippines." McClurg. Book News

"Excellent pictorial charts, in three-dimensional perspective, illustrate each action and carry an inset map to show its location. There are photo portraits of the twelve pilots, of the types of planes involved and photos of actual combat, some taken from the planes' wing cameras." N Y Times Bk R

Steiner, Jean-François

Treblinka; prefaced by Simone de Beauvoir; tr. from the French by Helen Weaver. Simon & Schuster 1967 415p $5.95   940.54

1 Treblinka (Concentration camp) 2 World War, 1939-1945—Jews

Original French edition, 1966

The story of Treblinka, a Nazi concentration camp in Poland set up to exterminate Jews in large numbers. "The book tells how Treblinka was organized, how it operated, and, finally, how its Jewish slave laborers, 1000 strong, rose up against their German and Ukrainian guards [in 1943] and destroyed the camp." Library J

Steiner, Jean F.—*Continued*

"There is no way of 'understanding' Treblinka and Steiner's attempts at an account acceptable to reason are no more adequate (though they are more admirable) than those of the official apologists." N Y Times Bk R

Toland, John

Battle: the story of the Bulge. Random House 1959 400p illus maps $6.95   **940.54**

1 Ardennes, Battle of, 1944-1945

"Basing his narrative on interviews with more than 1,000 people in 10 countries, civilians as well as soldiers of all ranks, and quoting even the conversational inanities engraved on their minds by the tensions of battle, the author . . . begins with a description of the still, cold night of December 15, 1944, in a Luxembourg town, introduces the violent contrast of the first German assault, then proceeds day by day, and in some cases hour by hour, through the story of what he designates the greatest pitched battle ever fought by the U.S." Booklist

But not in shame; the six months after Pearl Harbor. Random House 1961 427p illus maps $8.95   **940.54**

1 World War, 1939-1945—Pacific Ocean

"Tracing. region by region, the Japanese attack in the Pacific in World War II and the American and Allied crushing first defeats, and first reprisals, Toland incorporates dozens of personal adventure stories of heroism and desperation. He deflates some legends and tries to settle some of the praise-or-blame controversies of these early days of the Pacific war." Pub W

Notes: p406-18

Van der Post, Laurens

The prisoner and the bomb. Morrow 1971 152p $5   **940.54**

1 World War, 1939-1945—Prisoners and prisons 2 World War, 1939-1945—Personal narratives

First published, 1970 in England with title: The night of the new moon

The author "a South African serving with the British forces during World War II, was—along with thousands of other members of the Allied forces—a Japanese prisoner of war in Java when the atomic bomb was dropped on Hiroshima. This book presents his view of the value of the dropping of the bomb in relation to the war in general and to the prisoners of war in particular." Best Sellers

Werstein, Irving

The uprising of the Warsaw Ghetto, November 1940-May 1943. Norton [distributed by Grosset] 1968 157p illus map $4.95   **940.54**

1 World War, 1939-1945—Jews 2 Jews in Warsaw

"The true story of the remnant of the Jews of the Warsaw Ghetto, who chose to fight and die with honor." Bruno. Books for Schools Libraries, 1968

"Drawn from trial records, contemporary sources, and interviews, this vivid and accurate report shows both the collaborators and the heroes, the inhuman and the humane. While Mr. Werstein does not lift the guilt from the perpetrators of these atrocities, his ultimate judgment is directed less against the individuals than against the philosophy they served." Library J

A note on sources: p149-50

White, W. L.

They were expendable. Harcourt 1942 209p $4.75   **940.54**

1 World War, 1939-1945—Philippine Islands 2 U.S. Navy. Motor Torpedo Boat Squadron

"The story of the part played by MTB Squadron 3 in the Philippine campaign, as told to the author by four of its young officers: Bulkeley, Kelly, Akers, and Cox. These men were responsible for transporting General MacArthur safely to Australia. This and their many other exploits from the time when the first Japanese planes came over Manila Bay until the end of their brave little flotilla, has as its background 'the whole tragic panorama of the Philippine campaign—America's little Dunkirk.' " Book Rev Digest

"An account of America's disastrous Philippine campaign that is almost unbearably painful at times, yet so engrossing that few who begin it will be able to put it down until they have finished. . . . Inextricably intermingled with it is the living, flesh-and-blood picture of what went on in those terrible months when the Japanese tide kept flowing ever southward." N Y Times Bk R

940.55 Later 20th century, 1945-

White, Theodore H.

Fire in the ashes; Europe in mid-century; with an introduction by Ernest R. May. [1968 c1953] 405p pa $3.95   **940.55**

1 Europe—Politics—1945- 2 Reconstruction (1939-1951)—Europe 3 U.S.—Foreign relations

"Apollo editions"

Analyzed in Essay and general literature index

First published 1953 by Sloane

The author gives an "exposition of the dramatic regeneration which has taken place during the past six years on the old continent. By an analysis of the situation in France, Germany and England he proves that the danger of communism exists only while there are weaknesses within the free world itself." Library J

"The value of this book lies not so much in its portrait of post-war Europe—vivid though that is—as in its appraisal of American policy since 1948, when the United States embarked upon its great venture in European construction. And as a foreign correspondent in Europe . . . Theodore White . . . reveals a sympathetic understanding of American responsibility . . . [in its] role of leader of the Western world." N Y Times Bk R

941.5 Ireland

Lyons, F. S. L.

Ireland since the famine. Scribner 1971 852p $17.50   **941.5**

1 Ireland—History 2 Ireland—Politics and government

SBN 684-10369-9

"Tracing Irelands history from 1847 to 1969, "the author discusses the state of the Union, the demands for Home Rule, the violence and the compromises ending in a divided Ireland, and the evolutions of Eire and Ulster in the fifty years since their separation." Publisher's note

The "book strikes an unusually good balance between the political and the economic and social elements in the Irish story, right through from the terrible rural scene of the famine period to the republic's industrial take-off in the 1960's, the portentous approach to membership of the European common market, and the mushroom growth of British subsidising of Northern Ireland's ailing economy." Economist

Select bibliography: p803-24

942 British Isles

Ashley, Maurice

Great Britain to 1688; a modern history. Univ. of Mich. Press 1961 444, xxii p maps (The Univ. of Mich. History of the modern world ser.) $7.50   **942**

1 Great Britain—History

A companion volume to: Great Britain since 1688, by K. B. Smellie, entered below

Ashley, Maurice—*Continued*

"Britain from Roman times through the late seventeenth century is surveyed by an English journalist who studied British history at Oxford University. Brief character sketches of England's rulers are conventionally presented yet readable work but the emphasis is on political, social, economic, and religious changes. . . . Contains a bibliography [and] list of sovereigns." Booklist

"Clearly and ably written, 'Great Britain to 1688' is one of the very best of the works to appear so far in . . . a series which is making a signal contribution to our knowledge of man and his past and present." Christian Science Monitor

Bowle, John

England; a portrait. Praeger 1966 262p (Nations of the modern world) $7.50   942

1 Great Britain—History 2 Great Britain—Civilization

The author traces the traditions of his country "from their Anglo-Saxon basis through medieval restlessness, sixteenth-century expansion, and eighteenth-century enterprise to the Victorian era of riches, respectability, and empire . . . [and concludes] with a survey of English life today." Publisher's note
Includes bibliographical footnotes

Churchill, Winston S. 1874-1965

Churchill's History of the English-speaking peoples; arranged for one volume by Henry Steele Commager. Dodd 1965 475p illus maps $7.95   942

1 Great Britain—History

An abridged version of the original four volume edition entered below
The author has arranged the text "so that, by judicious omission of such passages as those dealing with the phantom kings of Britain before Alfred the Great and with the Boer War in more recent times, a single inclusive volume has been made available. . . . There has been no editing or rewriting of the text." Am News of Bks

A history of the English-speaking peoples. Dodd 1956-1958 4v maps ea $6.95, set $25   942

1 Great Britain—History

A four volume history of the British Empire from the Roman invasions to the death of Queen Victoria and its influence upon the other English-speaking peoples of the world. (Publisher)
Contents: v 1 The birth of Britain; v2 The new world; v3 The age of revolution; v4 The great democracies
"The great English statesman presents in his inimitable style the history of England, the United States, and the British Commonwealth as a unified story." Good Reading

Halliday, F. E.

A concise history of England; from Stonehenge to the atomic age; with 225 illus. Viking [1965 c1964] 240p illus maps $7.50   942

1 Great Britain—History

"A Studio book"
First published 1964 in England
A history of England including the role of prominent persons and their creative achievements
Its purpose is to "provide a basic historical framework for the reading of detailed works. . . . The more than 200 black-and-white illustrations from contemporary sources are well chosen." Library J
Suggestions for further reading: p225-27

Smellie, K. B.

Great Britain since 1688; a modern history. Univ. of Mich. Press 1962 462p maps (The Univ. of Mich. History of the modern world ser.) $7.50   942

1 Great Britain—History

A companion volume to: Great Britain to 1688, by Maurice Ashley, entered above
"From William III to Harold Macmillan—the ideas, events, and personalities that [have] shaped Britain [are here analyzed]." Publisher's note
"Professor Smellie's approach is reflective rather than sociological. Much the best part of the book, running through it like a thread, is the account of how the British state gradually and, in retrospect at least, inevitably became a 'welfare state.'" New Statesman
Includes bibliography

Trevelyan, George Macaulay

English social history; a survey of six centuries, Chaucer to Queen Victoria. Barnes & Noble 1946 628p maps $11   942

1 Great Britain—History 2 Great Britain—Social conditions

First published 1942 by Longmans
"The daily life of the British people from Wat Tyler and John Ball down through six hundred years to Kipling and Lloyd George—this is Mr. Trevelyan's theme. . . . All the British types are here: the sheep-farmer, the sea rover, the Oxford fellow, the Scottish mosstrooper, the fox-hunting squire, the London merchant . . . and Lancashire factory-owners. . . . The book is . . . strongest in its ample use of literature, newspapers, popular art, traditions, and old diaries to illuminate the daily life of the past." Book of the Month Club News
"Mr. Trevelyan is a master of the art of writing history in which a subject of enormous extent is condensed and clarified. Only one who has read widely in the field—or rather many fields—here surveyed can realize the immense amount of material that has been brought under contribution, English life in town and country in all its phases is passed under review." N Y Her Trib Books

History of England. [3d ed. Reissue with minor corrections] Doubleday 1953 3v illus pa ea $1.45   942

1 Great Britain—History

"Doubleday Anchor books"
First published 1926 by Longmans
Contents: v 1: From the earliest times to the Reformation; v2: The Tudors and the Stuart era; v3: From Utrecht to modern times: the Industrial Revolution and the transition to democracy
"A classic synthesis written by an outstanding English historian. Presupposes some knowledge of English history." Good Reading
Includes bibliographies

Illustrated English social history; illustrations selected by Ruth C. Wright. McKay 1949-1952 4v illus maps ea $11.95   942

1 Great Britain—History 2 Great Britain—Social conditions

First published by Longmans
An illustrated edition of: English social history, a one volume work, entered above
Contents: v 1 Chaucer's England and the early Tudors; v2 Age of Shakespeare and the Stuart period; v3 Eighteenth century; v4 Nineteenth century
"In selecting these illustrations to form a pictorial commentary on the text, I have been guided by two considerations, first, that they should be drawn as far as might be from English sources as distinct from European sources generally, and secondly, that they should be as nearly contemporary as possible with the scenes they represent." Prefatory note to illustrations

Illustrated History of England; illustrations selected by St John Gore. McKay 1956 xxiv, 758p illus maps $14.50   942

1 Great Britain—History

First published by Longmans
An illustrated edition of: History of England, entered above
Covers the history of England from the days of the Iberians and the Celts through the end of World War I
Includes bibliographies

942.03 British—House of Plantagenet, 1154-1399

Costain, Thomas B.

The conquering family. Doubleday 1962 291p illus maps (A History of the Plantagenets) $6.95　　942.03

1 Great Britain—History—Plantagenets, 1154-1399 2 Great Britain—History—Norman period, 1066-1154

First published 1949 in The Pageant of England series with title: The conquerors

This history begins with the conquest of England by William the Conqueror in 1066 and closes with the end of the reign of John in 1216, when the full merging of Norman and Saxon had taken place and the conquest was complete

"Though not a well-rounded picture of the times, it is a successful presentation of strong and diverse personalities. Useful with young people." Wis Lib Bul

Selected bibliography: p403-07

The last Plantagenets. Doubleday 1962 424p maps (A History of the Plantagenets) $6.95　　942.03

1 Great Britain—History—Plantagenets, 1154-1399 2 Great Britain—History—Lancaster and York, 1399-1485 3 Richard III, King of England

First published in The Pageant of England series

"The author follows Plantagenet fortunes, 1377-1485, from the rule of Richard II to the end of the dynasty in Richard III who, Costain agrees, has been maligned by history." Pub W

"The author presents an orderly commentary on this eventful period. It is no easy task to assemble coherently all the happenings during this age. . . . He describes admirably the domestic strife which beset England, notably the Peasants Revolt in 1381 and the inordinate political activity of religious leaders. The author is best when dealing with the personalities who walked the stage then." Springf'd Republican

The magnificent century. Doubleday 1962 [c1951] 324p illus (A History of the Plantagenets) $6.95　　942.03

1 Great Britain—History—Plantagenets, 1154-1399 2 Henry III, King of England

First published 1951 in The Pageant of England series

"Covers the reign of Henry III [1216-1272] his French wars, but mostly [concerned] with the efforts of such leaders as Hubert de Burgs and Simon de Montfort to limit the powers of the King: a time when England took remarkable strides in the direction of freedom and the establishment of democratic principles." Library J

"A superb narrative history of England in the turbulent days of Henry the Third. . . . Written as dramatically as the author's novels." Los Angeles. School Libraries

Selected bibliography: p364-68

The three Edwards. Doubleday 1962 419p illus maps (A History of the Plantagenets) $7.95　　942.03

1 Great Britain—History—Plantagenets, 1154-1399 2 Edward I, King of England 3 Edward II, King of England 4 Edward III, King of England

First published 1958 in The Pageant of England series

"Between 1272 and 1377 three Edwards ruled England: Edward I took England out of the Middle Ages into new ideas in clothes, government, culture, and law; Edward II had a tragic reign but gave his country Edward III, who ruled gloriously if violently." The Bookseller

"To both good and evil Costain gives due weight, not sparing the sickening brutalities in an attempt to attach false glamor to a past easily romanticized." Chicago Sunday Tribune

942.05 British Isles— Tudor period, 1485-1603

Horizon Magazine

The Spanish Armada, by the editors of Horizon Magazine. Author: Jay Williams; consultant: Lacey Baldwin Smith. Am. Heritage 1966 153p illus maps boards $5.95, lib. bdg. $5.49　　942.05

1 Armada, 1588

"A Horizon Caravel book"

In 1588, "the massed fleets of Protestant England and Catholic Spain met in a gigantic naval duel. . . . [Here is a] view of this encounter." Publisher's note

"A superbly illustrated and colorfully written account of one of the great battles of history, the text giving more than adequate prefatory and background material to enable the reader to understand both the causes and the consequences of the defeat of the armada. As always in this series, the illustrations are varied, well-placed, and adequately captioned. The writing is lucid, and the coverage is comprehensive." Chicago. Children's Book Center

Further reference: p149

Lewis, Michael

The Spanish Armada. Crowell [1968 c1960] 216p illus maps $6.95　　942.05

1 Armada, 1588

First published 1960 by Macmillan (N Y)

The author "concentrates on the purely naval aspects of the Armada episode and draws heavily on both contemporary sources and his own extensive researches. . . . He concludes that the rival fleets were much more evenly matched in ship and cannon strength than usually thought, yet he believes that it was English seapower, rather than any 'Protestant wind,' that drove off the Spanish Armada. This account complements Mattingly's more detailed and diplomacy oriented The Armada [entered below]." Choice

Mattingly, Garrett

The Armada. Houghton 1959 443p illus maps $7.50　　942.05

1 Armada, 1588

Set against the background of 16th century Europe, this account of the defeat of the Spanish Armada by the British in 1588 describes in detail the "military measures and actions, the sentiments and passions of the public, political intrigue, and the motives and maneuvering of the royal figures involved, notably Elizabeth." Pub W

An account combining "scholarship and literary artistry. Reading and reference." Cleveland

General note on sources: p405-09

942.06 British Isles— Stuart period, 1603-1714

Notestein, Wallace

The English people on the eve of colonization, 1603-1630. Harper 1954 302p illus maps (The New American nation ser) $7.95 942.06

1 Great Britain—History—Stuarts, 1603-1714 2 Great Britain—Social conditions

"Deals almost exclusively with English institutions and life during the reigns of James I and Charles I. There is scarcely a facet of English culture and political, economic and legal patterns which the author has left untouched." Current Hist

"Designed for the historian [this book] is almost equally suitable for any serious reader whose background of English history of the era is above average. Even so, it is good reading for the completely uninitiated, if he goes slowly." Wis Lib Bul

Bibliography: p267-79

942.082 British Isles—
20th century, 1901-

Churchill, Sir Winston
Great destiny; sixty years of the memorable events in the life of the man of the century recounted in his own incomparable words; ed. by F. W. Heath. Putnam 1965 720p illus $8.95   **942.082**
1 Great Britain—History—20th century 2 Statesmen, British
First published 1962 in England with title: Churchill anthology
"This book consists of extracts from all Churchill's books other than 'The Second World War' [entered in class 940.53] and 'A History of the English-Speaking Peoples' [entered in class 942]. There are also extracts from his most famous speeches, and through these it has been possible to present his life as recorded by him. . . . It gives much data on Churchill and the memorable events of the 20th century." Library J

Cross, Colin
The fall of the British Empire, 1918-1968. Coward-McCann [1969 c1968] 359p illus $8.95   **942.082**
1 Great Britain—History—20th century 2 Great Britain—Colonies 3 Commonwealth of Nations
First published 1968 in England
The author "describes the long sunset of the British Empire from the first major signs of decline (coincident with the United States' ascendency) in 1918. The account is carried through the shift to dominion status for Canada, Australia, New Zealand and South Africa, and Gandhi's long struggle for Indian independence, to the post-World War II shift in the balance of world power. Washington and Moscow became the decisive influences and England, economically drained by the war, was forced to make concessions to her territories in a holding operation that could not last. When India was lost, four-fifths of the Empire went with it. Cross' study is comprehensive and, for a narrative of contemporary history that doesn't play to the galleries, frequently vivid in its descriptions and consistently good reading." Pub W
Maps on lining-papers

943 Germany

Dill, Marshall
Germany; a modern history, by Marshall Dill, Jr. New ed. rev. and enl. Univ. of Mich. Press 1970 490, xxiii p maps (The Univ. of Mich. History of the modern world ser) $10   **943**
1 Germany—History
ISBN 0-472-07101-7
First published 1961
A "succinct history of Germany designed for the interested general reader, the undergraduate student, and the teacher of history. . . . Begins with the fifth century A.D. but concentrates on political, military, intellectual, economic, and social developments in the twentieth century." Booklist
Suggested readings: p479-90

Maurois, André
An illustrated history of Germany; tr. from the French by Stephen Hardman. Viking 1966 295p illus $22.50   **943**
1 Germany—History—Pictures, illustrations, etc.
Original French edition published 1965
In text and pictures the author describes German history from prehistoric and Roman times to the present
The illustrations are "nearly all interestingly chosen although not always well presented and

reproduced. . . . If the text here is regarded as merely the explanation of the pictures, then it is more than adequate. But if one had nothing else this would indeed give a sketchy idea of German history." Times (London) Lit Sup

943.08 Germany since 1866

Kurtz, Harold
The Second Reich: Kaiser Wilhelm II and his Germany. Am. Heritage Press 1970 127p illus maps (Lib. of the 20th century) $3.95   **943.08**
1 William II, German Emperor 2 Germany—History—1866-
"Kurtz characterizes Wilhelm as a simple and sensible human beneath the theatrical apparition playing a role as a personalizing egocrat and lays the blame, at least in part, on Wilhelm's disturbing childhood and his constant need to overcome physical deformities and appear normal. The author delves into the background of Wilhelm's rule and surveys the issues and events of the Second Reich, but does not go into detail about World War I." Booklist
Includes bibliographical references

943.086 Germany—
Third Reich, 1933-1945

Goldston, Robert
The life and death of Nazi Germany; illus. with photographs and drawings by Donald Carrick. Bobbs 1967 224p illus maps $5   **943.086**
1 Germany—Politics and government—1933-1945 2 Hitler, Adolf
"The history of Germany is covered in enough detail to give the reader an understanding of the forces and factors that made possible the emergence of a Hitler and the subservience of a people whose cultural achievements and heritage should have made them impervious to demagoguery. . . . The rise of the Nazi party and the course of events that led to the war are described in great detail. . . . The author gives a broad picture of the roles of other nations and of the forces and important figures within the country. Intelligent, lucid, and dramatic—an absorbing and important book." Chicago. Children's Book Center
Bibliography: p213-16

Herzstein, Robert Edwin
(ed.) Adolf Hitler and the Third Reich, 1933-1945. Houghton 1971 283p maps (New perspectives in history) pa $3.95   **943.086**
1 Hitler, Adolf 2 Germany—History—1933-1945 3 World War, 1939-1945—Germany
This book containing documents and historical interpretations relevant to the study of Adolf Hitler's Third Reich is grouped as follows: The New Germany and its institutions; The diplomacy of expansion; The Third Reich at War, 1939-1945
Suggestions for further reading: p277-83

Shirer, William L.
The rise and fall of the Third Reich; a history of Nazi Germany. Simon & Schuster 1960 1245p $12.50   **943.086**
1 Germany—History—1933-1945 2 World War, 1939-1945—Germany 3 Hitler, Adolf
This is a comprehensive, documented history of Germany from the beginning of the Nazi party in 1918 to the World War II defeat of Germany in 1945. Here is a detailed account of the events, and the leading figures of the Nazi era, especially Adolf Hitler. (Publisher)
"Throughout his work Shirer reveals his flair for the drama of history as reflected in representative scenes. Much of the narrative is based

Shirer, William L.—*Continued*

on his first-hand contact with the protagonists
of this tragedy, including the 'Fuhrer.' There
is a thorough documentation by contemporary
sources such as Hitler's speeches and 'Mein
Kampf.' " Library J
Bibliography: p1181-91. Maps on lining-papers

Speer, Albert

Inside the Third Reich; memoirs. Tr. from
the German by Richard and Clara Winston;
introduction by Eugene Davidson. Macmillan (N Y) 1970 xxiii, 596p illus $12.50
943.086

1 Hitler, Adolf 2 Germany—Politics and government—1933-1945 3 World War, 1939-1945—
Germany

"Albert Speer, the only defendant at the
Nuremberg Trials to assume full responsibility
for his role in Nazi war crimes, was released
from Spandau Prison in 1965 after having served
a 20-year sentence. Now, in memoirs begun
while he was in prison, he reveals in great detail his 15-year-long association with Hitler—
first as the architect chosen to execute the
Führer's grandiose plan for the post-war rebuilding of Berlin and later as Nazi Germany's
Minister for Armaments and War Production."
News of Bks
This "is not only the most significant personal German account to come out of the war
but the most revealing document on the Hitler phenomenon yet written. It takes the reader inside Nazi Germany on four different levels: Hitler's inner circle, National Socialism
as a whole, the area of wartime production
and the inner struggle of Albert Speer. The
author does not try to make excuses, even by
implication, and is as unrelenting toward himself as to his associates." N Y Times Bk R
Bibliographical references in Notes: p527-70

943.087 Germany—
Later 20th century, 1945-

Heaps, Willard A.

The wall of shame. Duell 1964 175p illus
map $3.95   943.087

1 Berlin wall (1961-)

"True stories of escapes through, under or
over the infamous Wall which the Communists
built to divide East from West Germany in 1961.
Geared both to adults and to teen-agers, this
. . . shows the desperation of the trapped, the
fury and resentment of the West Germans, and
the inhumanity that conceived and maintains
the Wall." Pub W
"Offers little that readers of newspapers do
not know already, but [the author's] compilation has an impressive cumulative effect."
Christian Century

943.6 Austria

Stadler, Karl R.

Austria. Praeger 1971 346p illus maps
(Nations of the modern world) $9.50 943.6

1 Austria—History

The author "concentrates on the formative
influences that have made Austrians into what
they are today [and] places their story in the
regional context of East-Central Europe. . . .
The thesis [of this book] is that throughout
her history Austria was a state without a nation, and that it took the turbulent events of
the last half-century to awaken a sense of national purpose among a people bitterly divided
on all major issues." Preface
Bibliography: p327-35

943.7 Czechoslovak Republic

Szulc, Tad

Czechoslovakia since World War II. Vi-
king 1971 503p $14   943.7

1 Czechoslovak Republic—History
SBN 670-25332-4

Szulc "has written an incisive survey of the
unfolding drama of Czechoslovakia from 1945
to the present. He begins with the approach of
Patton's army to Prague, an aborted march
that ended with an order from General Eisenhower—based on reasons that Szulc explains.
. . . [He describes the] attempts of President
Benes and the foreign minister to cope with
the Communist coup of February, 1948 . . . [and
depicts] dramatically the great Communist
purges of the 1950s and the dire impact of the
aborted Hungarian revolt on Czechoslovakia's
later struggle to achieve 'Socialism with a human face.' Dubcek's courageous efforts to lib-
eralize his country, only to succumb to the
massive Soviet invasion of August, 1968, carries the mood of Greek tragedy in Szulc's detailed account." Pub W
Bibliography: p481-83

943.9 Hungary

Michener, James A.

The bridge at Andau. Random House 1957
270p map $5.95   943.9

1 Hungary—History—Revolution, 1956 2 Refugees, Hungarian

"A first-hand account of the revolt against
the Soviets in Hungary [in 1956]. The author
obtained a good deal of the material from
Hungarian refugees in Vienna [who had
crossed the bridge at Andau to freedom]." Retail Bookseller
"Obviously written in white heat, his book
at the same time is more than pamphleteering.
It is a dramatic, chilling and enraging document made so chiefly by the author's disciplined detachment. Later, perhaps, the Hungarian story will be analyzed more thoroughly, but hardly with anything approaching the
emotional wallop of this." San Francisco
Chronicle

944 France

Guérard, Albert

France; a short history. Norton 1946 274p
maps $4.95   944

1 France—History

"Here is the ideal book for the reader who
wants a brief history of France. Its . . . pages
document the author's interpretation of the
living French spirit with cultural and political
data from pre-history to 1945. Guérard's
standing as historian and critic makes the
book all the more acceptable. Summary tables
of significant dates, maps, well annotated
reading list and index enhance its value for
quick reference." Library J

Johnson, Douglas

A concise history of France. Viking 1971
191p illus maps $9.50   944

1 France—History
ISBN 0-670-23645-4

"A Studio book"

"The history of France has been marked by
periods of unity under a strong ruler—Charlemagne, Louis XIV, Bonaparte, de Gaulle—interspersed with periods of anarchy. This de-
viation is reflected in the dichotomy between
vigorous nationalism and equally fierce individualism seen in its people, which in turn
helps to explain France's unusually dramatic
history. Proceeding from this interpretation,
Douglas Johnson has provided a stimulating
narrative essay on the French character."
News of Bks

944.04 France—
Revolution, 1789-1804

Carlyle, Thomas
The French Revolution; a history   **944.04**
1 France—History—Revolution, 1789-1799
Some editions are:
Dutton (Everyman's lib) 2v ea $3.25
Modern Lib. (Modern Lib. Giants) $4.95, lib. bdg.
$3.89
Originally published 1837
"This is a magnificent prose poem rather
than a history in the strict sense of the word.
It abounds in descriptive passages which, for
vividness, have never been surpassed." W. W.
Davies's How to Read History

Horizon Magazine
The French Revolution, by the editors of
Horizon Magazine in consultation with
David L. Dowd. . . . Am. Heritage 1965 150p
illus maps boards $5.95, lib. bdg. $5.49
944.04

1 France—History—Revolution, 1789-1799
"A Horizon Caravel book"
"Illustrated with paintings, drawings, and
documents of the period." Title page
"A simple, lucid text describes the historical
events, political ideologies and personalities
that motivated the ideals and atrocities of the
revolutionary period from 1789 to 1795." Booklist
"Despite the enormous detail, events
smoothly follow one another and reflect careful research. Although the editors condemn
distortions that frequently mark fictional accounts, they themselves [resort to] . . . inter-
polating descriptions of people's thoughts, actions, and motives, without citing any contemporary source as authority. The selection
of prints and other illustrations is excellent,
and the entire format lives up to the high
standard of this series." Library J
Further reference: p[151]

The Horizon Book of The age of Napoleon, by the editors of Horizon Magazine. Editor in charge: Marshall B. Davidson. Author: J. Christopher Herold. Am.
Heritage 1963 420p illus maps boards $18.95
944.04

1 France—History—Consulate and Empire,
1799-1815 2 Napoléon I, Emperor of the
French
Also available with only sixteen pages of illustrations, for $7.50 with title: The age of
Napoleon
A panorama of Napoleon and of France, her
allies and enemies, "from 1793 to 1815—from
the bloody license of the Terror through the
glitter of the [French] Empire to Waterloo."
Bk Buyer's Guide
"Opulent in quality of text and illustrations
—maps, reproductions in color and also in
black and white of contemporary paintings and
prints, and modern photographs—this is an
aesthetically satisfying book in the gift item
category. But it is also, because of its detailed
pictures, a valuable tool for research as to how
people lived, worked, and amused themselves
in the Napoleonic period." Booklist

Loomis, Stanley
Paris in the terror, June 1793-July 1794.
Lippincott 1964 415p $7.95   **944.04**

1 France — History — Revolution, 1789-1799
2 Paris—History—Revolution, 1789-1799
"French Revolutionary history told through
the lives of some of its most influential personages, beginning with Charlotte Corday, as-
sassin of Jean-Paul Marat. Mme. Manon Roland, Georges-Jacques Danton, Maximilien
Robespierre, they all met violent deaths in a
terror which dominated Paris and which the
three, with Marat, and a few others, largely
engineered." Pub W
Bibliography: p405-08

944.05 France—
First Empire, 1804-

Delderfield, R. F.
The retreat from Moscow. Atheneum
Pubs. 1967 256p illus maps $5.95   **944.05**
1 Napoléon I, Emperor of the French—Invasion of Russia, 1812
"Napoleon's 1812 attack on Russia was his
biggest campaign—and also his greatest mistake. A well-known British historian presents
the story of both that campaign and its subsequent disaster." Huntting
The sources of this book: p237-40

944.081 France—
Third Republic, 1870-1945

Collins, Larry
Is Paris burning? [By] Larry Collins and
Dominique Lapierre. Simon & Schuster
1965 376p illus $6.95   **944.081**
1 France—History—German occupation,
1940-1945 2 Paris—History—1940-1945
The liberation of Paris on August 25, 1944
was the result "of an extraordinary and fateful interplay of circumstances that saved the
city, its population and its priceless treasures
from Hitler's vengeful sentence of destruction
and death." Publisher's note
"The authors have told this fascinating story
day by day, with frequent scene-shifts and innumerable vignettes of individual adventure.
. . . The acknowledgments reveal that the book
is the product of nearly three years of work
entailing extensive documentary research and
countless interviews with surviving participants
in those great events." N Y Times Bk R
Sources: p351-57. Map on lining-papers

Schechter, Betty
The Dreyfus affair; a national scandal;
illus. with photographs. Houghton 1965 264p
illus $3.50   **944.081**
1 Dreyfus, Alfred 2 France—History—Third
Republic, 1870-1940 3 Jewish question
The author describes the circumstances of
the court-martial of the French Army officer
Alfred Dreyfus who was unjustly accused and
convicted of treason in 1894, but later vindi-
cated after a national political uproar initiated
by Emile Zola
"Interspersed with unobtrusive biographical
and historical material on French politics and
anti-Semitism, the scandal is recalled here with
vibrant immediacy." Library J
A note on sources: p258-60

Shirer, William L.
The collapse of the Third Republic; an
inquiry into the fall of France in 1940. Simon
& Schuster 1969 1082p maps $12.50 **944.081**
1 France—History—Third Republic, 1870-1940
2 World War, 1939-1945—France
SBN 671-20337-1
The author covers the history of the Third
Republic from its birth in 1870 to its end in
1940, stressing the political, social and economic factors leading to its collapse. The larger
portion of the book, however, is given to the
last years of the Republic and particularly to
the events of 1939 and 1940
"Shirer is able to weigh the conflicting accounts and recriminations to provide the most
complete and dispassionate narrative of those
agonizing days. . . . [And he] gives us, through
the records of the French generals and journalists, the real feeling of how different the
war looked from France. . . . Shirer succeeds
magnificently in the main [task] he sets himself. . . . He is fair, scholarly, and superbly dramatic." Atlantic
Bibliography: p997-1010

945 Italy

Grindrod, Muriel

Italy. Praeger 1968 260p illus maps (Nations of the modern world) $7   **945**

1 Italy

The first part of this book discusses the history of Italy from the early beginnings to the end of World War II. The author's emphasis "is on the postwar years. . . . She describes the political parties . . . [the] efforts of modern Italian statesmen . . . Italy's economic resources, its foreign trade, and the efforts of the Cassa per il Mezzogiorno to revivify the South. In addition, she explains the Italian educational system, the position of women in Italian society, relations between Church and State, and the special problems posed by Sicily and Sardinia." Publisher's note

Bibliography: p242-44

Jucker, Ninetta

Italy; with 32 illus. & 2 maps. Walker & Co. 1970 208p illus maps (Nations & peoples) $7.50   **945**

1 Italy—History

"The history of united Italy is the story of how a nation found itself a hundred years ago, then fell into the abyss of fascism; and struggled out from war, chaos, and defeat. The cast of characters includes Garibaldi, D'Annunzio, and Danilo Dolci." Book News

"Her account of the post-war Italian political scene is excellent. The general reader, with little background in Italian history, may find the book at times confusing because the author has been forced to compress so many names and events into a tight narrative." Choice

946 Spain

Horizon Magazine

Ferdinand and Isabella, by the editors of Horizon Magazine. Author: Melveena McKendrick; consultant: J. H. Elliott. Am. Heritage 1968 151p illus maps boards $5.95, lib. bdg. $5.49   **946**

1 Spain—History 2 Ferdinand V, King of Spain 3 Isabel I, Queen of Spain

"A Horizon Caravel book"

"The year 1492 was the most important year in the reign of Ferdinand and Isabella of Spain —for it was the year of Columbus' voyage to the Americas, of the conquest of Granada, and of the expulsion of Jews from Spain. This is an examination of the events of that year, of the circumstances leading up to them, and of the actions that resulted from them." Bk Buyer's Guide

"A superb rendering of the history of Spain during the last years of the attempt, successful in the end, to drive the Moors out of Spain. The heroes are, of course, King Ferdinand (Fernando) of Aragon and his consort Isabella (of Castille) out of Spain. Christopher Columbus figures among others. But the major emphasis is on the two 'kings' of Spain who succeeded in uniting the Iberian peninsula into one kingdom." Best Sellers

Further reading: p149

Lloyd, Alan

The Spanish centuries. Doubleday 1968 395p (The Mainstream of the modern world) $7.95   **946**

1 Spain—History

"A history of Spain and its colonial empire from the time of the Carthaginians up to the present [1968]." Pub W

The author "has given us a work that is engagingly readable, historically accurate, and wellbalanced. His treatment is not superficial, for he continually looks at people and their feelings and not only at high-level policies and ideas. The book . . . [displays on] artistic interweaving of anedcotal biography, of Cervantes and of Goya, for example, with the customary political and military history." Library J

Bibliography: **p373-86**

946.081 Spain— Second Republic, 1931-1939

Werstein, Irving

The cruel years; the story of the Spanish Civil War; illus. with photographs and maps Messner 1969 189p illus map $3.95, lib. bdg. $4.29   **946.081**

1 Spain—History—Civil War, 1936-1939

The author chronicles the events leading to the Spanish Civil War and describes in detail the struggle which resulted in one million deaths and the fascist dictatorship of General Franco

"The author's advocacy of the Loyalist cause is clearly evident in this treatment of the Spanish Civil War. . . . He sympathetically portrays the military activities of American volunteers who joined the army of the Republican government, incorporating some of the personal reminiscences of veterans of the Abraham Lincoln Brigade." Booklist

Suggested further reading: p181-82

947 Russia

Horizon Magazine

The Horizon History of Russia, by the editors of Horizon Magazine. Editor in charge: Wendy Buehr; author: Ian Grey. Am. Heritage 1970 404p illus maps $22   **947**

1 Russia—History

SBN 8281-0098-5

"Nearly three-fourths of the book is devoted to the Pre-Soviet period, and most of that to the pre-19th-Century era. . . . [There is a] coverage of early history—the Kievan Rus of the 10th Century, the succeeding Mongol invasions, and the rise of Muscovy, all mirrored in reproductions of contemporary icons, miniatures, and artifacts. . . . [Included also are] excerpts from the chronicles of peripatetic monks and foreign visitors who explored Russia before Peter the Great opened a window on the West with the building of St. Petersburg (now Leningrad)." Library J

"Grey tells his long tale largely by concentrating on a few key periods and characters. . . . This is a book which ably sketches in the gorgeous, generous, selfish, brutal glorious, tragic background of a super-power." Christian Science Monitor

Oliva, L. Jay

Russia in the era of Peter the Great. Prentice-Hall 1969 184p (New insights in history ser) boards $5.95   **947**

1 Peter I, the Great, Emperor of Russia 2 Russia—History

"A Spectrum book"

"An enlightening and well-organized introductory study of Peter the Great's era examines that period within the context of Europe's changing eighteenth-century environment, taking issue with the view that Peter was an isolated phenomenon without historical antecedents. Oliva looks first at the world of Muscovite Russia from which Peter emerged; subsequent chapters discuss Tsar Peter's military involvements and analyze Peterine Russia in terms of governmental administration and finance, the composition of the social order, commerce and industry, and the church and secular culture." Booklist

Suggested reading: p177-80

Salisbury, Harrison E.

Russia. Atheneum Pubs. 1965 144p map $3.95   **947**

1 Russia—History 2 Russia—Politics and government

"A New York Times Byline book"

"A succinct, lucid recapitulation of Russia's rise from a primitive nation under Mongol domination to a major world power under Communist rule includes not only a political history with analysis of key figures but also discussion of such aspects as topographical characteristics, the various ethnic groups, and the creative art." Booklist

Wallace, Robert, 1919

Rise of Russia, by Robert Wallace and the editors of Time-Life Books. Time, inc. [distributed by Litte] 1967 184p illus maps (Great ages of man: a history of the world's cultures) lib. bdg. $6.95   **947**

1 Russia—History 2 Russia—Civilization

Through text and picture essays this book traces Russian history and civilization from the invasions of the Scythians in 700 B.C. through the conquests of the Varangians, the rise and fall of Kievan Russia, the slow growth of Moscow and the reigns of the two Ivans. It also surveys the Europeanization of Western Russia by Peter the Great. (Publisher)

Bibliography: p178

Walsh, Warren B.

Russia and the Soviet Union; a modern history. New ed. rev. and enl. Univ. of Mich. Press 1968 682, xxiv p maps (The Univ. of Mich. History of the modern world ser) $10   **947**

1 Russia—History

First published 1958

The author "describes the rapid metamorphosis of the Russian nation from an agriculturally oriented society into a mighty industrial power. He discusses the personalities of contemporary Russia and analyzes the major changes in policy and ideology that have occurred during the last two decades. Changes in economic priorities and attitudes, the relaxation, however slight, of traditional controls over Soviet intellectual life, and startling advances in science and technology have changed the relationship of the Soviet government to its own people and have greatly influenced its relation with other countries." Publisher's note

Bibliographical references included in Notes: p615-31. Suggested readings: p633-82

947.08   Russia since 1855

Westwood, J. N.

Russia, 1917-1964. Harper 1966 208p maps $5.95   **947.08**

1 Russia—History—1917-

In the opening chapters, the "author goes back as far as the 10th century to give the necessary background to the nature of Czarist Russia at the time of World War I. The next handful of pages depict the situation in Russia during World War I and prior to 1917. From then on, it is a rushing panorama of the history of the Soviet Union. . . . [Covers] not only the political aspects, but the military, social, economic, religious and cultural ones as well." Library J

Bibliography: p197-99

947.084   Russia— Communist regime, 1917-

Conquest, Robert

The great terror; Stalin's purge of the thirties. Macmillan (N Y) 1968 633p illus $9.95   **947.084**

1 Russia—Politics and government—1925-1953 2 Stalin, Iosif

"The book develops through a series of bloody . . . episodes, starting with the murder of Sergei Kirov, head of the Party in Leningrad. Then come the 'show trials' of Zinoviev and Pyatakov, the Ordzhonikidze 'suicide,' the last attempt to block Stalin in February 1937, the slaughter of the Army Command, the crushing of the Party, the fantastic Bukharin Trial, and the murderous climax of 1938." Publisher's note

"A masterpiece of historical detection. . . . Not the least merit of Mr Conquest's study is that, while preserving commendable objectivity and restraint, he draws the only moral possible in the circumstances. He pays respect to the martyred millions, especially to those who, whatever their own sins, showed courage and honesty by resisting their tormentors. Still more relevant is his eloquent warning of the continuing threat to civilised values represented by totalitarian rule." Economist

Select bibliography: p572-77

Goldston, Robert

The Russian Revolution; with drawings by Donald Carrick and photographs. Bobbs 1966 224p illus maps $5   **947.084**

1 Russia—History—Revolution, 1917-1921

"Beginning with a brief but clear picture of Czarist Russia and the prevailing conditions which fostered the rise of Marxism, the author covers events immediately preceding and following the Bolshevik Revolution of 1917 as well as the revolution itself. He includes comprehensible descriptions of Marxism, Bolshevism, and other political ideologies of the times and sketches in the personalities of prominent participants." Booklist

"This is a pleasant surprise—a literate, lucid account of the Russian Revolution which manages to sustain interest without talking down to its young adult audience. . . . He emphasizes issues rather than personalities, and attempts to place the Revolution in a realistic historical and ideological context." Library J

Bibliography: p214-18

Khrushchev, Nikita Sergeevich

Khrushchev remembers; with an introduction, commentary and notes by Edward Crankshaw; tr. and ed. by Strobe Talbott. Illus. with photographs. Little 1970 639p illus $10   **947.084**

1 Russia—Politics and government—1917-

"This book is made up of material emanating from various sources at various times and in various circumstances. The publisher is convinced beyond any doubt, and has taken pains to confirm, that this is an authentic record of Nikita Khrushchev's words." Publisher's note

The book describes the historical and political events in Russia since the Revolution, and portrays many of the leading figures of this period, including Stalin, Bulganin, Molotov, Malenkov, and Zhukov

"These memoirs are not objective history. Primarily they are Khrushchev's effort to justify himself and his career. . . . [He] emerges from this volume—as he did during his years on center stage—as one of the most complex and contradictory major figures of the mid-twentieth century." Sat R

Kohler, Foy D.

Understanding the Russians; a citizen's primer. Harper 1970 441p $10   **947.084**

1 Russia—Politics and government—1917- 2 Russia—Foreign relations

In this survey of the Soviet system, the author, who was U.S. Ambassador to the U.S.S.R., gives his views of the apparatus of international communism, Soviet expansionist ambitions and methods, and U.S.-Soviet relationships. (Publisher)

It is the author's "contention that the Soviet Union will not be able to compete with us militarily and in space and at the same time meet the domestic needs of their people. . . . It is an easily read book that summarizes briefly Russia old and new. It is basic and yet enjoyable reading, spiced with personal interpretations. A good introduction to understanding the Russians." Best Sellers

948.9   Denmark

Jones, W. Glyn

Denmark. Praeger 1970 256p illus map (Nations of the modern world) $8   **948.9**

1 Denmark

This is a "splendid work on modern Denmark, stressing political and economic events rather than literary. No history of modern

Jones, W. G.—_Continued_
Denmark compares with this small volume, either in style or content, and the reader feels drawn into an appreciation of 20th-century Danish problems. The work stresses the ease of transition from a rural, agricultural economy to modern industrialism. The story of World War II is handled with understanding, and complex problems are carefully examined with tolerance toward opposing groups. Events since 1945 are well covered. Appendices on Greenland, the West Indies, and the Faeroe Islands give some notion of the spread of Danish influence." Choice
Bibliography: p247-48

949.4   Switzerland

Martin, William
Switzerland, from Roman times to the present; with additional chapters by Pierre Béguin; tr. from the French by Jocasta Innes. Praeger 1971 355p map $10   949.4
1 Switzerland—History
First published 1929. This translation is from 6th edition published 1966 in Switzerland
This history of Switzerland "is an analytical reconstruction of the central events and forces in each main period of the country's past. . . . [The author] shows the growth of Swiss unity from its roots in medieval parochialism, through the religious hatred of the Reformation and the conflicts between dominant merchant towns and fiercely resistant peasant cantons, to the conservative neutrality of today." Publisher's note

949.5   Modern Greece. Byzantium

Papandreou, Andreas
Democracy at gunpoint: the Greek front. Doubleday 1970 365p $7.95   949.5
1 Greece, Modern—Politics and government
In this examination of Greek politics, "the former elected chief of state of the democratic Greek government under King Constantine . . . [tells the] story of the events leading up to the military coup of April 21, 1967. . . .[Papandreou also] describes his own ordeal through eight months of imprisonment." Pub W
"Papandreou's account is valuable both for the information it provides us about what was said and done by influential Greeks in the Sixties, and for what it manages to display (sometimes inadvertantly) of the sporadic turbulence and irresponsibility of Greek politics." Book World

Sherrard, Philip
Byzantium, by Philip Sherrard and the editors of Time-Life Books. Time, inc. 1966 192p illus maps (Great ages of man: a history of the world's cultures) lib. bdg. $7.60   949.5
1 Byzantine Empire
An introduction to the political and cultural history of the Byzantine Empire, which combined Greek, Roman, Christian, and Oriental elements and lasted for over 1000 years
Partial contents: The new Rome; Constantine's city; An emperor under God; The holy establishment; The round of Byzantine life; The final centuries; Chronologies; Bibliography

949.6   Turkey in Europe. Constantinople

Asimov, Isaac
Constantinople; the forgotten empire. Houghton 1970 293p illus maps $4.75   949.6
1 Istanbul—History 2 Byzantine Empire

The author "tells the story of the Byzantine Empire, successor to the Roman Empire, in an extremely clear manner. He brings into concise description the vast sweeps of Eastern European and Eastern Mediterranean history since the official founding of the 'New Rome' by Constantine in 330 A.D. and outlines briefly the previous history of Byzantium." Science Bks

950   Asia

Durant, Will
Our Oriental heritage. . . . Simon & Schuster 1935 1049p illus (The Story of civilization: pt. 1) $12   950
1 Civilization, Oriental
"Being a history of civilization in Egypt and the Near East to the death of Alexander, and in India, China and Japan from the beginning to our own day; with an introduction on the nature and foundations of civilization." Title page
"Dr. Durant's opus on the inception of civilization is as masterly and scholarly a study as the author . . . would be expected to write. It must never be forgotten that he writes with the popular demand in mind, and presents his material not for the profound, mature student, but for those who attempt culture and education through contact with secondary sources." Boston Transcript
Glossary: p939-44.   Bibliography: p945-55.
Maps on lining-papers

Fitzgerald, C. P.
A concise history of East Asia. Praeger 1966 306p illus maps $8.50   950
1 East (Far East)—History
This book "encompasses prehistory to the present time. . . . [It is] necessarily selective but nonetheless informative. . . . The subject is divided into three areas: China, Japan and Korea, and Southeast Asia." Booklist

Latourette, Kenneth Scott
A short history of the Far East. Macmillan (N Y) maps $9.95   950
1 East (Far East)—History
First published 1946. Periodically revised to bring material up to date
Comprehensive history of the Far East, with emphasis on China and Japan. Covers the political history, economics and culture of the people of the area. (Publisher)
"Any weakness which this survey has is more than balanced by the clarity of style with which it is composed and the objectivity with which the author has drawn his outlines and his conclusions. The brief bibliographical references at the chapter ends are carefully chosen." Ann Am Acad

951   China

Latourette, Kenneth Scott
China. Prentice-Hall 1964 152p map (The Modern nations in historical perspective) $5.95   951
1 China—History 2 Communism—China
"A Spectrum book"
The author surveys the history of China's great civilization. "Today, Communist China is mobilizing for a momentous confrontation with the West and with Russia while the Nationalist Chinese government on Taiwan struggles to maintain its claim. . . . This book [closely] reviews the history of the Kuomintang's fight to hold the mainland and Communism's ultimate triumph." Publisher's note
Suggested readings: p144-46

Li, Dun J
The ageless Chinese; a history. Scribner 1971 591p illus maps $10   951
1 China—History

Li Dun J.—*Continued*

First published 1965

Organized by dynasties. "After the cycle of culture, famine revolt and dynastic change has unfolded, a summarizing chapter defines the traditional Chinese society. . . . [The book] then discusses the Western impact on China and the formation of the Republic, and concludes with a view of Communist China's position vis-a-vis the Western world." Publisher's note

"The use of Chinese metaphors in the context of Chinese thought adds much to the flavor; at the same time, the use of Western terminology makes it easy to understand. The maps are most helpful. One could not do much better in selecting this as a basic textbook on Chinese history. Very highly recommended for libraries." Library J

Suggested readings: p551-58

951.04 China—Early 20th century, 1912-1949

Snow, Edgar

Red star over China. 1st rev. and enl. ed. Grove 1968 543p illus $10   **951.04**

1 China—History—Republic, 1912-1949 2 Communism—China

First published 1938

The author describes China in 1936 and 1937, when he, the first Westerner to enter "Red China," interviewed the Communist leaders and reported to the world on the events which culminated in the present People's Republic. (Publisher)

"The author's main conclusions have stood the test of time surprisingly well. . . . In many cases the [new] biographies are already outdated by the cultural revolution, and many of them seem to be based on secondhand newspaper accounts." Sat R

Bibliography: p517-21. Maps on lining-papers

951.05 China. People's Republic, 1949-

Baum, Richard

(ed.) China in ferment; perspectives on the cultural revolution; ed. by Richard Baum with Louise B. Bennett. Prentice-Hall 1971 246p $6.95   **951.05**

1 China (People's Republic of China)—Politics and government

ISBN 0-13-132688-0

"A Spectrum book"

In this volume, the editor "has collected writings by political scientists, government leaders, and scholars from both China and the United States, which probe the events leading up to the revolution and which [seek to] assess its impact on the political, economic, and social life of China. The essays—including a government tract by Chinese leader Lin Piao —argue the strengths and weaknesses of Mao's influence on the Red Guards, the need for army interference to keep the revolution under control, and the effect the revolution could have on future Chinese political and military behavior." Publisher's note

These 1967-1970 writings provide "a stimulating variety of viewpoints." Sat R

Chronology of events (1957-1970): p237-41. Selected bibliography: p242-45

Elegant, Robert S.

Mao's great revolution. World Pub. 1971 478p $12.50   **951.05**

1 China (People's Republic of China)—Politics and government 2 Mao, Tsê-tung

An "exploration of events inside Communist China, and the 'princess of the Communist hierarchy' who rose or fell with the unfolding drama of those events, beginning with the 1959 Plenary Session of the Central Communist Party and carrying right through Great Proletarian Cultural Revolution unleashed by Mao

seven years later. While Elegant's writing may be suspect by some (he leans toward the 'popular' and is, like most contemporary China-watchers, compelled to draw on Hong Kong and Taiwanese sources whose reliability falls short of 100-proof), he is consistently interesting and at times perceptive in his portraits of key figures in the Cultural Revolution—Chiang Chin, Mao's 56-year-old wife, for instance, and Wu Han, the Peking Mayor whose acts precipitated the Red Guards' sweep through China." Pub W

952 Japan

Reischauer, Edwin O.

Japan: the story of a nation. Knopf 1970 345, xx p maps $4.95   **952**

1 Japan—History

"This book is a successor volume to my 'Japan: Past and Present,' which was first published in 1946 and was expanded and brought up to date in two revised editions, in 1953 and again in 1964." Preface

This history of the Japanese people from their origins to the present examines their civilization, cultural heritage, militarism, and the effect of the American occupation, and the recovery of the postwar economy. (Publisher)

"In lucid if unexciting language, Mr. Reischauer (until recently U.S. Ambassador to Japan) skillfully and authoritatively summarizes Japanese history." Sat R

Bibliographical note: p341-45

952.03 Japan—Re-establishment of imperial power, 1868-1945

Terasaki, Gwen

Bridge to the sun. Univ. of N.C. Press 1957 260p $4.95   **952.03**

1 World War, 1939-1945—Japan 2 Terasaki, Hidenari 3 Japan—History—Allied occupation, 1945-1952

"An American woman met and married an aristocratic Japanese diplomat in Washington in 1937. Her husband worked for peace and, with his colleagues, had planned the cable to the Emperor which might have averted the Pearl Harbor attack. After Pearl Harbor, she went with her husband to Japan. As an intimate picture of the Japanese in war, this is informative: as vignettes of Japanese statesmen and diplomats who disagreed with the militarists, this is heartening; but its greatest appeal is as the human story of a mixed marriage where love overcame all the problems. Older girls—and some boys—will like and respect Mrs Terasaki and her family." Horn Bk

953 Arabian Peninsula

Glubb, Sir John

A short history of the Arab peoples. Stein & Day 1969 318p maps boards $8.95   **953**

1 Arabs—History 2 Civilization, Arab

This is "the essence of the British author's four-volume history of the Arabs, covering the time from the beginning of the seventh century to the middle of the twentieth—the swift spread of the Bedouin empire from the Atlantic Ocean to China, the advance of science and culture while Europe was going through the Dark Ages, up to the arrival of the Mongol conquerors and after." Bk Buyer's Guide

The author "writes with assurance, familiarity, and a broad and deep knowledge of his subject. The many maps lend a great deal to his narrative, indicating the change of places and flow of people and events in Islam throughout 13 centuries. This is an excellent short introduction to the older history of the Arabs." Library J

A short bibliography: p301-03

Hitti, Philip K.
The Arabs; a short history. 5th ed. St
Martins 1968 211p maps $5.95   **953**

1 Arabs—History 2 Civilization, Arab

This title, first published 1943 by Princeton
University Press, is a condensation of the author's: History of the Arabs, published 1937

These pages "tell, very briefly, the story of
the rise of Islam in the Middle Ages, its conquests, its empire, its time of greatness and of
decay." Preface

The book "is from its very start provocative
as well as informative. . . . The method employed is not one of straight chronology but of
broad subjects. . . . As such it is excellent for
the purpose in hand. Necessarily the book covers much ground at a rapid rate." N Y Times
Bk R

954   India

Schulberg, Lucille
Historic India, by Lucille Schulberg and
the editors of Time-Life Books. Time-Life
Bks. 1968 192p illus maps (Great ages of
man: a history of the world's cultures) lib.
bdg. $7.60   **954**

1 India—History 2 India—Civilization

"An enlightening survey of Indian history
from about 2500 B.C. to the turn of the eighteenth century. Complemented by handsome
pictorial sections the text traces the political,
social, and cultural development of India and
shows the successful synthesization of diverse
forces and influences through the dominance
of Hinduism as a religion and a mode of living. A chronological listing of significant
events, a Hindu pantheon, and a bibliography
are appended." Booklist

954.04   India—Independence and partition, 1947-

Griffiths, Sir Percival
Modern India. 4th ed. Praeger 1965 311p
maps (Nations of the modern world) $8
954.04

1 India—History 2 India—Politics and government 3 India—Economic conditions

First published 1957

"India's second Five Year Plan, her difficulties with Pakistan over Kashmir, and her relations with Russia, Great Britain, and the U.S.
since her independence in 1947 are reviewed by
a veteran of military and civil service in India.
Judicious light is thrown upon such controversial areas in current India affairs as neutral-
ism, economic aid, and social reforms." Booklist

954.9   Pakistan

Stephens, Ian
Pakistan. 3d ed. Praeger 1967 304p illus
maps (Nations of the modern world) $8
954.9

1 Pakistan—History 2 Pakistan—Politics and
government

First published 1963

The author "begins by showing the idea behind the creation of an independent Pakistan
and continues by describing her complex geography and social problems. The second part of
his book . . . traces events from the Indian
Mutiny to 1946 and then gives a study . . . of
the dramatic events which led to the end of
the British Raj and the bloodsoaked partition-
ing of a subcontinent in 1947. Finally, he deals
with the emergence of the new state, the Kashmir conflict, and later events including the
military revolution of 1958." Publisher's note

"He plainly holds that it is impossible to
understand Pakistan without a clear grasp of
the factors which led to her emergence and
which later shaped her evolution. Accordingly,
he has devoted by far the greater portion of
this book to the past rather than to the present. . . . The reader who has no local knowledge may find this immensely intricate narrative rather heavy going. This is a pity, because when Mr Stephens turns his attention
to what is happening in Pakistan today his
gift of concise narration makes the reader want
more detail." Times (London) Lit Sup

Bibliography: p277-83

954.93   Ceylon

Pakeman, Sidney Arnold
Ceylon. Praeger 1964 256p map (Nations
of the modern world) $6.95   **954.93**

1 Ceylon—History 2 Ceylon—Politics and
government 3 Ceylon—Social conditions

"The scene of early influence from Portugal
and the Netherlands, Ceylon came finally under British influence and in the early 20th century became a kind of advanced British experiment in colonialism. This is the core of the
history which Mr. Pakeman tells. . . . For all
libraries needing an authoritative case study of
colonism or record of modern Ceylonese
government and adminstration." Library J

"Mr Pakeman has obviously done a good
deal of research into Ceylon's history and recent progress, and his last two chapters are
particularly interesting as they focus attention
on the problems confronting the nation today. . . . He has given a fair, balanced, picture, neither exaggerating nor minimising present difficulties and past mistakes." Economist

Includes bibliographical references

956   Middle East

Churchill, Randolph S.
The six day war, by Randolph S. Churchill
and Winston S. Churchill. Houghton 1967
250p maps $4.95   **956**

1 Israel-Arab War, 1967-

"The Churchill father-son writing team present a remarkably factual and detailed book
describing how Israel won the 'instant' war.
By nightfall of the second day, for example,
Israel had destroyed 416 enemy aircraft. Using
the 'mailed fist' military strategy, Israeli arm-
or then raced into Egypt. The Egyptians frequently were disorganized and fettered by rigid preplanned strategy; the Jordanians fought
well with heavy casualties, but without air
protection they had no chance. The statistics
of war are incredible, exemplified by the winning of the war by a country of two and one-
half million while surrounded by 40 million enemies. Well documented with statistics. military maps, diagrams, index. Son Winston covered on-the-spot reporting, and father Randolph (now deceased) interpreted the diplomatic and political maneuvers." Choice

"It is all from one side, but the Israeli generals are obviously the best source, and no
doubt they are professional as well as justifiably proud. The narrative is lucid, colorful,
filled with good quotations, devastating—the
reader feels as if he were riding an avenging
hurricane." Christian Science Monitor

Hitti, Philip K.
The Near East in history; a 5000 year
story. Van Nostrand 1961 574p illus maps
$11.95   **956**

1 Near East—History

A "record of the Near East, from the dawn
of civilization to the present cold war, is recounted in this . . . book: a political, social,
and cultural history of that part of the world
which now includes Turkey, Iran, Iraq, Syria,
Lebanon, Jordan, Israel, Egypt, and Arabia."
Publisher's note

"This book is surprisingly pungent and vivid
considering the tremendous . . . reservoir of
data woven into its six sections." Library J

Includes bibliographies

Hitti, Philip K.—*Continued*

A short history of the Near East. Van Nostrand 1966 278p illus maps $7.95   **956**

1 Near East—History

Based on the author's: The Near East in history, entered above, this political and cultural history concentrates on the modern era, although it also discusses the past. (Publisher)

"High school libraries will find this a condensed but well-balanced . . . history." Booklist

Readings: p253-57

Hussein, King of Jordan

Hussein of Jordan: My "war" with Israel; as told to and with additional material by Vick Vance and Pierre Lauer; tr. by June P. Wilson and Walter B. Michaels. Morrow 1969 170p illus map $5.95   **956**

1 Israel-Arab War, 1967- 2 Jordan—History

Original French edition, 1968

"This strangely constructed book, consisting of taped interviews with King Hussein and selected members of his staff, along with other key Jordanians, as well as leaders of the Palestine Liberation Organization, contributes to an understanding of how Arab division, lack of communications, unwillingness to bury political rivalries, as well as the failure of Arab intelligence, all brought about the crushing defeat in the June War of 1967. The book also provides an understanding of the disintegration of Hussein's political authority in the postwar period as a result of the extension of Israel's boundaries to the Jordan and its seizure of Jerusalem. . . . While the book provides some insights into the Arab dilemma, it is of limited scholarly usefulness." Choice

956.94 Israel

Eban, Abba

Voice of Israel. Horizon Press 1969 398p $6.95   **956.94**

1 Israel—History 2 Israel—Foreign relations

First published 1957

In a series of addresses made during the past twenty years, Israel's prominent statesman surveys all that has befallen his nation since its establishment. "The chronicle reveals Israel's position on security in the Middle East; on the Arab refugee problem; on Jerusalem and the Holy Places; on the Suez Canal; on border clashes and their remedy; [and] on American-Israel relations." Publisher's note

959.1 Burma

Donnison, F. S. V.

Burma. Praeger 1970 263p illus map (Nations of the modern world) $8   **959.1**

1 Burma—History 2 Burma—Civilization

The author "explains how Burma has changed from the remote, self-sufficient, and almost medieval country it was before the British annexation to the one-party, quasi-Marxist dictatorship it is today. . . . [He provides] insights into Burmese cultural, social, and religious life." Publisher's note

Such is Burma's self-imposed isolation these days under the leadership of General Ne Win that evaluating the nation's condition and recent history in broad perspective is a difficult job. Within the restricted limits of available information, Donnison has produced a readable work that is particularly authoritative wherever British colonialism is involved." Choice

Bibliography: p253-54

959.4 Laos

Fall, Bernard B.

Anatomy of a crisis; the Laotian crisis of 1960-1961; ed. with an epilogue by Roger M. Smith. Doubleday 1969 283p maps $5.95   **959.4**

1 Laos

"This is the dissection of a crisis. It deals with the events in Laos leading up to the clashes between the Pathet-Lao and Royal Government forces in 1960 and 1961. . . . [The author] reconstructs the origins, major actions, and probable consequences—for Asia, the United States, and the rest of the world—of this still precarious situation." Publisher's note

Although his book is involved "with complex and serious events, Fall writes in a sprightly, journalistic style that makes for easy reading and wide appeal. On occasion his judgments are too quick and easy to satisfy the professional scholar, but both the scholar and the layman will find much . . . on which to ponder." Book World

Bibliography: p264-66

959.5 Malaysia

Gullick, J. M.

Malaysia. Praeger 1969 304p illus map (Nations of the modern world) $7.50   **959.5**

1 Malaya—History 2 Malaysia—Politics and government

First published 1963 with title: Malaya

"An excellent introduction for the general reader to the history, economy, and political organization of Malaysia. Unfortunately the 1969 election and the racial rioting and governmental changes that followed have outdated this volume and badly shattered the basis of Gullick's optimism. . . . However, the book is an extremely useful general reference for the reader who knows nothing of this tangled multiracial polity and its history." Choice

Bibliography: p289-91

959.7 Vietnam

Fall, Bernard B.

Hell in a very small place; the siege of Dien Bien Phu. Lippincott 1967 [c1966] 515p illus maps (Great battles of history) $8.95   **959.7**

1 Dien Bien Phu, Vietnam

"A searing, detailed account of the French disaster at Dien Bien Phu. The parallels the author draws between the French experience with the Vietminh—ambush, hit-and-run attack, deadly anti-aircraft artillery, masterful camouflage, miraculous supply—and the American experience in South Vietnam are painfully obvious." Huntting

The author, who was killed in Viet Nam, "has written a thorough account of a brave sanguinary battle that has since turned out to have immense historic importance." New Yorker

Bibliography: p491-92

The two Viet-Nams; a political and military analysis. 2d rev. ed. Praeger 1967 507p illus maps $10   **959.7**

1 Vietnam—History 2 Vietnam—Politics and government

First published 1963

The author has written this book "simply to attempt to bring some understanding of the plight of a valiant people that happens to find itself, no doubt much against its will, at one of the focal points of a world-wide struggle. . . . [It] is devoted to a comparison of the governmental and economic institutions of both zones not as they have been designed on paper to impress their friends and fool their foes, but as they 'really operate' in everyday practice." Preface

Bibliography: p492-97

Hersh, Seymour M.
My Lai 4; a report on the massacre and its aftermath. Random House 1970 210p $5.95   959.7
  1 Vietnamese Conflict, 1961-   —Atrocities
2 Songmy, Vietnam
  Awarded Pulitzer Prize, 1970
  The author bases this report primarily on interviews with American soldiers who participated in the March 16, 1968 attack on the civilians of My Lai, a hamlet in Songmy, Vietnam. He discusses the significance of the massacre and the war as well as the events and personalities involved
  The author's report "is solidly documented and well written, full of relevant facts and figures." Sat R
  Bibliographical references included in Notes: p189-210

Knoll, Erwin
  (ed.) War crimes and the American conscience; ed. by Erwin Knoll and Judith Nies McFadden. Holt 1970 208p $5.95   959.7
  1 Vietnamese Conflict, 1961-   —Atrocities
  "Not until the accounts of the killing of hundreds of helpless men, women and children by GIs at My Lai leaked out last year [1969] did numbers of the American people experience enough of a shock to search their individual consciences concerning their support of our government's role in Vietnam. In February of this year a notable conference of concerned legislators, churchmen, political scientists, lawyers, psychologists, biologists and others convened to discuss the profound moral, legal and social issues raised by what has become the most unpopular war in our history. This book is an edited transcript of the proceedings together with supplementary material. It is possibly the most valuable and important single-volume collection of relevant source material available on this crucial subject, and should be read soberly by Americans of every shade of conviction." Pub W

960   Africa

Davidson, Basil
  Africa in history; themes and outlines. Macmillan (N Y) [1969 c1968] 318p illus maps $6.95   960
  1 Africa—History
  Expanded and updated edition of "Africa: history of a continent," published in 1966. This edition first pubished 1968 in England
  The author presents a chronological synthesis for the history of the entire African continent. He offers an account of the old civilization, traces the history of the various cultures, and concludes with the growth of African nationalism after World War II. (Publisher)
  The author's account "ranges from the origins of that unique civilization to its critically renascent present, Davidson describes the influence of ecology on the development of African character and institutions, the manner in which resilient social and ideological structures were built, how Africans came to their concepts of Good and Evil and their multiplicity of religions, and the origins of misconceptions about Africa that have endured to this day. In discussing the African colonial period he stresses largely what Africans 'did,' rather than what was done to them." Pub W
  Brief guide to further reading: p299-307

  African kingdoms, by Basil Davidson and the editors of Time-Life Books. Time-Life Bks. [distributed by Little 1971] 192p illus maps (Great ages of man: a history of the world's cultures) boards $6.95   960
  1 Africa—History 2 Africa—Civilization
  First published 1966
  The author explores "not only the large centralized states that once existed in Africa, but

also the past of its simple village societies. The history of these societies [is] presented by taking examples from the present and weaving into them impressions and reflections gained from the wider story." Introduction
  "Half a dozen sets of photographs, largely in color, display among other things the stunning rock paintings of the Sahara and the great bronze sculpture of Benin." Sci Am
  Includes bibliography

Hallett, Robin
  Africa to 1875; a modern history. Univ. of Mich. Press 1970 483, xx p maps (The Univ. of Mich. History of the modern world) $8.95   960
  1 Africa—History
  SBN 472-07160-2
  "Broad, enlightening, readable general history embracing the continent of Africa and adjoining islands from remote times to 1875. It discusses African societies and politics, indigenous developments, foreign incursions and influences, and manifestations of change region by region and underlines the differences between and among the regions that make generalizations about Africa absurd." Booklist
  Suggested readings: p427-83

McEwan, P. J. M.
  (comp.) Twentieth century Africa; maps drawn by Regmarad. Oxford 1968 xxiv, 517p maps (Readings in African history) $9   960
  1 Africa—History
  In this volume "the general aspects of nationalism and Pan Africanism are presented." Library J
  "In all there are 50 contributions, mostly from American and British scholars but 11 are by white South Africans, three by Africans (if one includes President Nasser as an African), and three by French authors in translation. . . . It is to be noted that a preponderance of the contributors are political scientists rather than historians, 'pace' the title. All articles included were previously published in journals or symposia. . . . The readings are well selected and representative of modern scholarship. . . . Clear maps; useful chronological table; comprehensive index." Choice
  Bibliography: p484-86

Thompson, Elizabeth Bartlett
  Africa: past and present. Houghton 1966 330p illus maps $5.95   960
  1 Africa—History
  "After briefly describing the physical characteristics of Africa the author provides an . . . introductory survey of African history. She begins with prehistoric Africa and highlights important events and trends through the emergence of the new, modern Africa. . . . The list of books for further reading includes fiction and nonfiction for adults and children." Booklist

961   North Africa. Libya

Wright, John
  Libya. Praeger 1969 304p illus maps (Nations of the modern world) $7.50   961
  1 Libya—History
  A history of Libya "beginning with the years prior to 1800 [and concentrating] on the period from 1800 to 1968, with one third of the text covering the developments from 1945 to 1968. Economic and social factors are discussed throughout." Library J
  "A multilingual bibliography is appended." Booklist

962   Egypt and Sudan

Horizon Magazine
Building the Suez Canal, by the editors of Horizon Magazine. Author: S. C. Burchell; consultant: Charles Issawi. . . . Am. Heritage 1966 153p illus maps $5.95, lib. bdg. $5.49
962

1 Suez Canal 2 Lesseps, Ferdinand Marie, vicomte de
"A Horizon Caravel book"
"The history of the Suez Canal and its builder, Ferdinand de Lesseps, with many contemporary photographs, drawings, maps, and etchings." Title page
"The text is accurate and readable and makes much of the role of the Egyptian government in supplying money and labor in building the canal. . . . The bibliography lists several recent books which dig deeper into the technical, political and economic implications of the Suez Canal." Science Bks

Moorehead, Alan
The White Nile. [Rev. ed] Harper 1971 368p illus maps $15
962

1 Nile River 2 Africa—Discovery and exploration 3 Africa—History 4 Explorers
First published 1960
"The story of the exploration of the Nile from the Mountains of the Moon to the Mediterranean. [The author] . . . recreates the excitement of discovery and the realities of nineteenth-century politics as played out by a handful of remarkable and idiosyncratic individuals." Publisher's note
This "popularly written account catches the drama of the various expeditions and assesses the political, economic, and religious consequences for the native peoples as well as the invading explorers and exploiters." Booklist
Select bibliography: p360-62

962.6   Blue Nile

Moorehead, Alan
The Blue Nile. Harper 1962 308p illus maps $7.50
962.6

1 Blue Nile River 2 Africa—Discovery and exploration 3 Africa—History
The author's earlier book: The White Nile, entered in class 962, covered the period from 1856 to 1900. The present volume covers the period from 1798 through the nineteenth century. It describes the exploration and conquest by the Turks, the French, and the British, of those regions watered by the Nile from Lake Tana in Abyssinia to the Mediterranean
"The most exciting parts of 'The Blue Nile' are those dealing with Napoleon and Napier. . . . Those with a deep interest in the social history of Africa might find Mr. Moorehead a little superficial when he writes of the ordinary people of Egypt, the Sudan and Ethiopia." Christian Science Monitor
Sources: p291-95

966.9   Nigeria

Hatch, John
Nigeria; the seeds of disaster. Regnery 1970 313p map $6.95
966.9

1 Nigeria—History
Hatch "traces the growth of the present west African state: from the first African immigrants to the great empires such as Benin, the slave trade, the coming of the Europeans, the British age [and] independent statehood." Publisher's note
"This engagingly written new work is a survey of Nigeria's past which effectively places the recent civil war in historical perspective. . . . Hatch demonstrates why the unfortunate colonial experience was eventually destined to produce serious trouble. Lugard and British

supporters of his policies come under heavy attack, but the overall indictment is judiciously balanced as shortsighted, self-seeking Nigerian leaders share the blame." Choice
Select bibliography: p299-306

967   Central Africa

Davidson, Basil
Black mother; the years of the African slave trade. Little 1961 311p illus $8.50   967

1 Congo (Democratic Republic)—History 2 Africa, West—History 3 Africa, East—History 4 Slave trade
The author "analyzes 'The Black Mother' as he metaphorically refers to the continent. In [an] . . . analysis of the African genesis of slave cargoes, he describes the disgorgement of some forty million (his estimate) offspring from the continental womb. . . . He examines three regions which present contrasts and parallels and permit more precise measurement of the effects of this drainage of humanity from its native habitat. These are the old states of the Congo, the East African coastal city-states and trading empires, and parts of the Guinea Coast, now West Africa." Sat R
Includes bibliography

967.6   Kenya

MacPhee, A. Marshall
Kenya. Praeger 1968 238p illus map (Nations of the modern world) $6.50   967.6

1 Kenya—History
In showing the social, racial and economic stresses which exist today "and are embedded in Kenya's history, [the author] divides the book into four parts. In the first, he takes account of the history from the early Hamitic invasions to the Portuguese and Arab conquests, after which East Africa became a target for Chinese, European, and American traders, explorers, and missionaries. He next discusses British colonial rule and the concept of White Kenya. The third and fourth parts deal with the Mau Mau rebellion, its defeat and the ensuing struggle for independence, with special reference to the career of Jomo Kenyatta." Publisher's note
Bibliography: p221-23

968   South Africa

Marquard, Leo
A short history of South Africa. [Rev. ed.] Praeger 1968 272p illus maps (Praeger Short histories) $6.50
968

1 Africa, South—History
First published 1955 by Roy Pubs. with title: The story of South Africa. This is a reissue of the English edition
Various peoples have contributed to the making of modern South Africa: the native Bushmen and Hottentots; the Dutch settlers . . . French Huguenots; English governors and, later on, English settlers; and, in the twentieth century, immigrants from other Commonwealth countries and from many parts of Europe. And, of course, in larger numbers than all the preceding were Bantu-speaking Africans, who began to settle South Africa at an early period and who now form two-thirds of the present population. . . . [The author] traces the story of these many different peoples, describes the main events in that story, and reassesses some of those events." Publisher's note
"Objectivity is the keynote of South African writer Leo Marquard's history of his country and the people who built it. Deductions are left to the reader. But with such clarity and breadth are the facts presented by this liberal intellectual that one cannot but gain a more appreciative view of the cause of many South African problems, and thus of the problems themselves." Christian Science Monitor
Bibliographical footnotes

Paton, Alan

The long view; ed. by Edward Callan. Praeger 1968 295p boards $6.95   **968**

1 Africa, South—Politics and government
2 Africa, South—Race relations

"An informative collection of essays about the whole subject of Apartheid in South Africa —which has particular interest for the U.S. today." Wis Lib Bul

"These essays are very moving. They are written out of specific moments of crisis or dismay. Some are hastily written, some are less affecting than others, but they are all concerned with the deepest human values, and this gives them an indelible freshness." Christian Science Monitor

Bibliography: p283-84

970.1 Indians of North America

American Heritage

The American Heritage Book of Indians, by the editors of American Heritage, The Magazine of History. . . . Am. Heritage 1961 424p illus maps boards $17.50   **970.1**

1 Indians

"Editor in charge: Alvin M. Josephy, Jr; narrative by William Brandon; introduction by John F. Kennedy." Title page

A "book about the American Indian and his history. Organized mostly by regions, with two chapters on the Inca, Maya and Aztec and one on the social and economic status of the Indian since 1890. . . . The 500 illustrations include reproductions of paintings and photographs, many of them rare, 125 in color and the rest in black and white." Pub W

"The origin of the Indians, migrations over the continents, and strong cultures are highlighted; the conflict with the white man in the nineteenth century is kept largely to the U.S. area, and only a token chapter summarizes the condition of the Indian in the U.S. today." Booklist

Baity, Elizabeth Chesley

Americans before Columbus; illus. with drawings and maps by C. B. Falls and with 32 pages of photographs. Viking 1961 272p illus maps lib. bdg. $4.13   **970.1**

1 Indians

First published 1951

A study of American Indian civilization from the earliest Asiatic migrations to the coming of Columbus. It tells how they lived, what they wore, what they built, the different art objects they created, and even something of what they thought

Suggested readings: p261. Glossary: p262-63

Daniels, Walter M.

(comp.) American Indians. Wilson, H.W. 1957 219p (The Reference shelf v29, no.4) boards $4.50   **970.1**

1 Indians of North America

Contains 44 articles grouped under the following headings: Indian culture; History of Indian-White relations; Legal status and property rights; Termination of the Federal Trusts; Relocation program; Suggested programs

Bibliography: p211-19

Debo, Angie

A history of the Indians of the United States. Univ. of Okla. Press 1970 386p illus maps (Civilization of the American Indian ser) $8.95   **970.1**

1 Indians of North America—History
ISBN 0-8061-0911-4

This is an "historical survey of the Indians of the United States, including the Eskimos and Aleuts of Alaska, which isolates and analyzes the problems which have beset these people since their first contacts with Europeans. . . . In the book are described the first

meetings of Indians with explorers, the dispossession of the Indians by colonial expansion, their involvement in imperial rivalries, their beginning relations with the new American republic, and the ensuing century of war and encroachment. The most recent aspects of government Indian policy are also detailed— the good and bad administrative practices and measures to which the Indians have been subjected and their present situation." Publisher's note

The book "overemphasizes the Five Civilized Tribes [of Oklahoma] . . . provides very little on the reservation period so critical for many tribes, and ignores the current red power movement. Nevertheless, it is a valuable book containing a wealth of information on a subject that should be of concern to all Americans." Library J

Selected readings: p359-63

Deloria, Vine

Custer died for your sins; an Indian manifesto, by Vine Deloria, Jr. Macmillan (N Y) 1969 279p $5.95   **970.1**

1 Indians of North America

"The author, a young Standing Rock Sioux Indian . . . calls for a new Indian program which would acknowledge the right of Indians to live in peace, free of harassment. Highly critical of America's treatment of the Indian people and its failure to keep treaties, Mr. Deloria pinpoints constructive action which he believes this nation should take." Open Shelf

"Although Deloria's subject is serious, he approaches it non-informally. In fact, he devotes a chapter to Indian humor. . . . If more voices as strong as Deloria's are heard, there may yet be a place in America for Indians." Best Sellers

Driver, Harold E.

Indians of North America. 2d ed. rev. Univ. of Chicago Press 1969 632p illus maps $12.50   **970.1**

1 Indians
ISBN 0-226-16466-7

First published 1961

The author examines Indian life and culture, from the Arctic to Panama, drawing upon old sources as well as recent discoveries and interpretations. Languages, food, clothing, shelters, crafts and many aspects of social structure and culture are described. Included are chapters concerning government and social control, Indian-white relations in the United States, and cultural changes in Mexico, the United States, Canada, Alaska and Greenland

Bibliography: p567-93

Hagan, William T.

American Indians. Univ. of Chicago Press [1961] 190p illus (The Chicago History of American civilization) $5.75   **970.1**

1 Indians of North America—History 2 Indians of North America—Government relations

The author "describes the American Indian's relations with whites from the Colonial years to after the New Deal. His thesis is that the relationship between the Indian and the white man was doomed at the start by the conflict of cultures. He suggests that our Indian policies have been significant for their impact on the white man as well as the Indian, and shows how they reflect our entire social, political, and economic scheme of values." A Guide to Reading in Am History

Includes bibliography

Huntington, Ellsworth

The red man's continent; a chronicle of aboriginal America. U.S. Pubs. Assn. 1919 183p (The Chronicles of America ser. v 1) $4.45   **970.1**

1 Indians of North America 2 Anthropogeography 3 Physical geography—North America

Originally published by Yale University Press

"In writing this book the author has aimed first to present in readable form the main facts

Huntington, Ellsworth—*Continued*

about the geographical environment of American history. . . . The influence of geographical conditions upon the life of the primitive Indians has been emphasized." Preface
Bibliographical note: p173-75

Josephy, Alvin M.

The Indian heritage of America [by] Alvin M. Josephy, Jr. Knopf 1968 384p illus maps $10   **970.1**

1 Indians—History

The author "tries in this very readable book to define the true identity of the Indian as against the stereotype. . . . He narrates the separate stories of virtually all branches of the Indians as a people, beginning with the Eskimos and ending with the nomadic tribes of South America. He traces languages and the beginnings of agriculture as well. . . . This is a survey with a great sweep and a genuine authority, and will serve as a stimulant to a much-needed awareness of the Indians living among us today." Pub W
Bibliography: p367-84

La Farge, Oliver

A pictorial history of the American Indian. Crown 1956 272p illus map $7.50   **970.1**

1 Indians of North America—History 2 Indians of North America—Pictures, illustrations, etc.

A panoramic portrait "of the Indians of North America from the time the first white man landed to the [mid 1950's]. . . . All the great events, major developments and notable chiefs and heroes of Indian history are covered. The wars among the tribes, their leagues, their fighting and alliances with the British, the French, the Spanish and the American settlers [etc.] are recounted." Publisher's note

Terrell, John Upton

American Indian almanac. World Pub. 1971 494p illus maps $12.50   **970.1**

1 Indians of North America

"The author embarks on a comprehensive survey of prehistoric Indians in ten geographic areas, showing how each discovery has pushed the clock backwards in our knowledge of American Indian prehistory, migrations and culture. Terrell's scientific data and his reconstructions of the tribes of each region, their languages, social structures and material cultures are clearly described for laymen." Pub W

"A highly readable mix of anecdotes, vignette, and fact. . . . [The author] has thrown in enough archeology, scientific notes, maps, and charts to keep us oriented to straight facts. But this book's appeal lies in the stories he weaves into the two or three pages devoted to each tribe." Christian Science Monitor

A selected bibliography: p455-66. Glossary of names and terms: p467-80

Wax, Murray L.

Indian Americans: unity and diversity. Prentice-Hall 1971 236p (Ethnic groups in American life ser) $5.95   **970.1**

1 Indians of North America 2 Indians of North America—Social conditions
SBN 13-456988-1

This "book reveals how the identity of being an 'Indian' has emerged out of the relationship between the native peoples of the Americas and the White invaders from the time of Cortez. While emphasizing the contemporary American Indian, the author bases his analysis of the topic on an ecological, historical, and conceptual understructure." Publisher's note
Bibliographic and related source materials: p199-204. A list of suggested readings follows each chapter

Wissler, Clark

Indians of the United States. Rev. ed. Revisions prepared by Lucy Wales Kluckhohn. Doubleday 1966 336p illus map $5.95   **970.1**

1 Indians of North America—History

First published 1940

A popular history from prehistoric times to date "of the American Indian, showing him at the height of his strength and culture and at the depths of his humiliation. The author develops the histories of important tribes, depicts the Indian way of life, and gives biographical sketches of famous Indian chiefs." Library J
Bibliography: p303-19

970.3 Specific North American Indian tribes

Coe, Michael D.

America's first civilizations; consultant: Richard B. Woodbury. Am. Heritage 1968 159p illus maps boards $4.95   **970.3**

1 Olmecs 2 Mexico—Antiquities

"The Smithsonian library"

"Discoveries made during the last 50 years and as recently as the 1960's concerning the Olmec Indians of southern Mexico are reviewed by [an] . . . archaeologist who had a major role in digging up the remains of their culture. Coe describes excavations at San Lorenzo and La Venta which uncovered massive building stones and sculptured figures radio-carbon dated as early as 1100 B.C. and proved to his satisfaction and that of many though not all experts that the Olmec civilization was the sources of all pre-Spanish civilizations of Mesoamerica, including those of the Mayans, Toltecs, and Aztecs. Maps, charts, and photographs of archaeological finds illustrate the evolution of these cultures." Booklist

"The style is agreeable, the illustrations pleasing, and the factual content high. Appealing features include a number of hitherto unpublished sketches by the Mexican artist and art historian Miguel Covarrubias." Science Bks
Further reading: p153

Wauchope, Robert

(ed.) The Indian background of Latin American history; the Maya, Aztec, Inca, and their predecessors; ed. with an introduction by Robert Wauchope. Knopf 1970 211p maps (Borzoi Books on Latin America) $4.50   **970.3**

1 Aztecs 2 Mayas 3 Incas

"This book brings together authoritative readings on the archaeology, art history, and ethnohistory of the Aztec, the Maya, and the Inca civilizations of Latin America. . . . The subjects discussed include: the role of environment in culture; the development of urbanism and empire; the settlement patterns as they reflect ancient social, political, and economic organization; native art, pottery and artifacts as tools to reconstruct unwritten history; and the cooperative efforts of archaeologists, ethnologists, art historians, and ethnohistorians to understand the past." Publisher's note

Glossary: p203-07. Bibliography of selected general works: p209-11

970.4 Indians in specific places

Brown, Dee

Bury my heart at Wounded Knee; an Indian history of the American West. Holt 1970 487p illus $10.95   **970.4**

1 Indians of North America—The West 2 The West—History 3 Indians of North America—Wars
SBN 03-085322-2

"To put it quickly and plainly, this is nothing less than a thirty-year crime story, a blow-by-blow account of the destruction, between 1860 and 1890, of the culture and civilization of the Indian of the American West. It opens with the butchery of the Navahos in the Southwest and closes with the massacre

Brown, Dee—*Continued*
of the Sioux at Wounded Knee in South Dakota. . . . To me sure, much hass been written about this terrible record, but seldom from the Indian point of view. What distinguishes Mr. Brown's excellent work is that the Indian's voice, seldom heard in American history, enters these pages through excerpts from the records of treaty councils and other meetings."
Book of the Month Club News
Bibliography: p465-73

Burnford, Sheila
Without reserve; with drawings by Susan Ross. Little 1969 242p illus map $6.50   **970.4**
1 Indians of North America—Canada 2 Cree Indians 3 Chippewa Indians
"An Atlantic Monthly Press book"
"A wise sympathetic record of visits made by . . . [the author and illustrator] to the remote Reserves of the Cree and Ojibwa Indians in northwestern Ontario. The brief accounts, drawn from her journals and expanded for clarity, reflect an appreciation for the quiet dignity, humor, and richness of Indian culture, qualities perceptively captured in the drawings. In a postscript Burnford speculates on the future of Indians in Canada." Booklist

Silverberg, Robert
Mound builders of ancient America; the archaeology of a myth. N.Y. Graphic 1968 369p illus maps $10   **970.4**
1 Mounds and mound builders 2 U.S.—Antiquities
"Our forebears, finding large, incomprehensible earthworks scattered down the Mississippi Valley, refused to believe they were built by the aborigines who still cluttered up the place and impeded settlement. Mr. Silverberg describes . . . the nineteenth-century literature of speculation which attributed these monuments to Phoenicians, stray Vikings, the lost tribes of Israel, refugees from Atlantis, an extinct race of giants, and Welshmen. The book . . . ends with a history of the archeological work which gave the mounds back to the Indians." Atlantic
"The present book goes far toward meeting our need for a history of American archeology." Science

970.5 Government relations with Indians

Josephy, Alvin M.
(ed.) Red power; the American Indians' fight for freedom; ed. by Alvin M. Josephy, Jr. Am. Heritage Press 1971 259p $13.50   **970.5**
1 Indians of North America—Government relations
ISBN 0-07-033052-2
Includes Mr Josephy's paper "with several dozen other documents bearing on the issues to which Red Power is addressing itself today: the Indian's right to a voice in the policies and decisions affecting the laws under which he lives, his right to better health measures and to an education that will serve him in an economy where he is largely an outsider. Is he on the way to these? In this symposium Mr. Joseph and his fellow contributors suggest that he may be. . . . But new voices are being heard, speaking forcefully at gatherings like those of the National Indian Youth Council. Their words, and those of elders recalling the culture in which they were raised, are in these pages." Book of the Month Club News

Van Every, Dale
Disinherited: the lost birthright of the American Indian. Morrow 1966 279p maps boards $8.50   **970.5**
1 Indians of North America—Government relations 2 Five Civilized Tribes 3 Cherokee Indians—Government relations

The author tells the story of the expulsion of the Five Civilized Tribes—the Cherokee, Choctaw, Cree, Chickasaw and Seminole Indians—from the Southern States to the plains by the passage in Congress in 1830 of the Indian Removal Bill. He concentrates chiefly upon the Cherokee, the talented and progressive Indians who fought longest to retain their homeland. (Publisher)
"The federal record on Indian Affairs is bleak. The author is definitely in sympathy with the Indian and he writes with literary gusto. His sentences sing justified indignation." Best Sellers
Bibliography: p267-69

970.6 Specific subjects in relation to Indians. Arts and crafts

Dockstader, Frederick J.
Indian art in America; the arts and crafts of the North American Indian. [3d ed] N.Y. Graphic 1966 224p illus map $27.50   **970.6**
1 Indians of North America—Art 2 Indians of North America—Industries
First published 1961
"This illustrated study covers the development of Indian arts from Alaska to Florida and includes some work of the Eskimos. The introduction makes enlightening observations on the Indian as an artist and characteristics of Indian art before and after contact with the white man. The illustrative photographs are grouped to show work before the white man came and after, and a short note accompanies each of the . . . illustrations to explain origin, use, or development in style or technique of the sculpture, painting, textile, woodwork, or other type of work shown." Booklist
An "authoritative book for every art and cultural collection in American libraries—even those which must hesitate before buying expensive books such as this." Library J

971 Canada

Brebner, J. Bartlet
Canada; a modern history. New ed. rev. and enl. by Donald C. Masters. Univ. of Mich. Press 1970 570p maps (The Univ. of Mich. History of the modern world) $10   **971**
1 Canada—History
SBN 472-07091-6
First published 1960
A chronicle of Canadian history from the earliest explorations to the crises and achievements of today. (Publisher)
Suggested readings: p561-70

Peck, Anne Merriman
The pageant of Canadian history; illus. with photogravures and a map. 2d ed. McKay 1963 386p illus map $6.50   **971**
1 Canada—History
First published 1943
This informal history is related as "the story of peoples of various racial stocks who, through their activities, ambitions and cultures, have created the nation of Canada. . . . Relations between Canadians and Americans of the United States run through the history, and problems for continued friendly cooperation between two neighbor nations, that exist at the present time, [1963] are considered." Publisher's note
Includes bibliography

971.01 Canada—Early history to 1763

Costain, Thomas B.
The white and the gold; the French regime in Canada. Doubleday 1954 482p illus maps $5.95 **971.01**
1 Canada—History—To 1763 (New France)
This volume covers the history of Canada from the early discoveries through the end of the seventeenth century. The author tells the story in terms of the people who lived it—Richelieu, Louis XIV, Frontenac, the Jesuit martyrs, the Indians, the coureurs, etc.
"A popular, well written and needed history of the period." Massachusetts

Wrong, George M.
The conquest of New France; a chronicle of the colonial wars. U.S. Pubs. Assn. 1918 246p (The Chronicles of America ser. v10) $4.45 **971.01**
1 Canada—History—To 1763 (New France)
2 U.S.—History—Colonial period
Originally published by Yale University Press
Contents: Conflict opens; Frontenac and Phips; Quebec and Boston; France loses Acadia; Louisbourg and Boston; Great West; Valley of the Ohio; Expulsion of the Acadians; Victories of Montcalm; Montcalm at Quebec; Strategy of Pitt; Fall of Canada; Bibliographical note

972 Mexico

Quirk, Robert E.
Mexico. Prentice-Hall 1971 152p maps (The Modern nations in historical perspective) $5.95 **972**
1 Mexico—History
"A Spectrum book"
"A history of Mexico from the earliest times to the present. Explains contemporary Mexico in terms of its cultural, political, economic, and social development." News of Bks
"Bibliographical essay:" p126-47

972.9 West Indies (Antilles)

Williams, Eric
From Columbus to Castro: the history of the Caribbean, 1492-1969. Harper [1971 c1970] 576p illus maps boards $10.95 **972.9**
1 Caribbean area—History
SBN 0601-4668-0
First published 1970 in England
The book's "scope is the entire West Indian area, including the Guianas—whether their connections have been or are British or French, Spanish or American, Dutch or Danish or whether they have discarded or are about to discard the alien rule of previous centuries."
Introduction
Written by the Prime Minister of Trinidad and Tobago, this is "an interesting and well-written essay on slavery and sugarcane cultivation and the effects of their interaction on the peoples of the Caribbean. . . . [He also comments] on present conditions in the West Indies and his suggestions for the future." Times (London) Lit Sup
Select bibliography: p516-58

972.91 Cuba

Archer, Jules
Thorn in our flesh: Castro's Cuba. Cowles 1970 193p illus $4.95 **972.91**
1 Cuba—History
SBN 402-14181-4

The author "recounts the events that led to the victory of the rebels headed by Fidel Castro, his brother Raul, and Che Guevara, against the dictatorship of Fulgencio Battista; then continues with a survey of the history of Cuba since then, including the disastrous Bay of Pigs attempt, the missile crisis of 1962, and the disappearance from the government of Che Guevara to foment revolution in South America." Best Sellers
Bibliography: p185-87

Williams, Byron
Cuba: the continuing revolution. Parents Mag. Press 1969 271p illus maps $4.50 **972.91**
1 Cuba—History
In this historical survey the author examines the perspective within which Fidel Castro is but one of a long line of Cuban revolutionaries who have fought—since early in the sixteenth century when white men colonized the island—to restore Cuba to the Cubans. He also presents an analysis of almost ten years of Castroism in Cuba. (Publisher)
This book "is especially valuable because, unlike most historical accounts, it has focused on the conditions and roles of the oppressed black and Indian populations both during the colonization as well as during the revolution." Choice
Documents: p217-64

973 United States

Adams, James Truslow
The epic of America. 2d ed. Little 1933 446p illus $8.95 **973**
1 U.S.—History
First published 1931
"An illuminating and suggestive volume. Mr. Adams's 'Epic of America' is difficult to classify. It is not, in the conventional sense, history, nor is it precisely philosophical interpretation, but something of both. It is an attempt to segregate and interpret the significant experiences, to discover the origin and explanation of the abiding characteristics of the American people." N Y Libraries

The march of democracy; a history of the United States. Scribner 1965 7v illus maps $95 direct subscription only **973**
1 U.S.—History
A continuation of the title originally published 1932-1933
Contents: v 1 The rise of the Union; v2 A half-century of expansion; v3 Civil War and aftermath; v4 America—a world power; v5 New Deal and global war, continued by J. E. Cooke, R. W. Daly and A. F. Davis; v6 Age of responsibility, continued by J. E. Cooke, R. W. Daly and A. F. Davis; v7 The Kennedy years, continued by J. E. Cooke
Although "we are the youngest of the great peoples, our history is neither simple, short, nor unimportant. The prime historical concern of the citizen of any country is to know the past, the ideals, the great events and the great men of his own land, but the importance of American history transcends the merely local. . . . To understand the whole world in this critical period in which we live, we must have a clear idea of the part which America has played." Preface

Album of American history. Scribner 1969 6v illus $120 direct subscription only **973**
1 U.S.—History—Pictures, illustrations, etc.
2 U.S.—Social life and customs
Volumes 1-4 and volume 5 (index volume) first published between 1944-1949 and edited by James Truslow Adams
Contents: v 1 Colonial period; v2 1783-1853; v3 1853-1893; v4 End of an era [1893-1917]; v5 1917-1953; v6 1953-1968; and General Index
A pictorial survey, "illustrating American society on all levels, from the earliest Colonial settlements to present times." Publisher's note

American Heritage

The American Heritage History of the making of the Nation, by the editors of American Heritage; editor in charge: Ralph K. Andrist; narrative: Francis Russell; pictorial commentary: Rex Lardner. Am. Heritage 1968 416p illus maps boards $20   **973**

1 U.S.—History—1783-1865

This book spans the period from George Washington's inauguration to Lincoln's departure from Springfield for his inauguration. It includes picture portfolios showing "the young Navy between 1794 and 1805; . . . the perils of travel; rural life; the rise of mills and factories; the burgeoning cities; [and] the look of America on the eve of the Civil War. . . . Selections [of contemporary writings] range from Benjamin Franklin's explanation of the American character, to a note John Brown wrote while he was awaiting execution." Publisher's note

"Major events—social, political, cultural, military—are woven into a pattern that evolves and unfolds naturally from generation to generation." N Y Times Bk R

The **Annals** of America. Encyclopaedia Britannica 1968 21v illus maps $174.50   **973**

1 U.S.—History—Sources

Contents: v 1 1493-1754: Discovering a new world; v2 1755-1783: Resistance and revolution; v3 1784-1796: Organizing the new Nation; v4 1797-1820: Domestic expansion and foreign entanglements; v5 1821-1832: Steps toward equalitarianism; v6 1833-1840: The challenge of a continent; v7 1841-1849: Manifest destiny; v8 1850-1857: A house dividing; v9 1858-1865: The crisis of the Union; v10 1866-1883: Reconstruction and industrialization; v11 1884-1894: Agrarianism and urbanization; v12 1895-1904: Populism, imperialism, and reform; v13 1905-1915: The progressive era; v14 1916-1928: World War and prosperity; v15 1929-1939: The great depression; v16 1940-1949: The Second World War and after; v17 1950-1960: Cold war in the nuclear age; v18 1961-1968: The burdens of world power; v19-20: Great issues in American life; a conspectus; v21: Index

The first eighteen volumes contain official documents (15%), "reprints, poems, songs, short stories, and the writings of leaders in philosophy, art, economics, education, race relations, pacifism, journalism, and other fields—more than 2,000 pieces by 1,110 authors grouped by year of publication." Sat R

Includes bibliographical references

Archer, Jules

The extremists: gadflies of American society; illus. with political cartoons and the old prints. Hawthorn Bks. 1969 197p illus $6.95   **973**

1 U.S.—History 2 U.S.—Biography

"Viewing extremists as those who pursue their goals by unlawful, unjust, or extravagant means whether against the power structure, in defense of the power structure, or against another group in society, [the author] covers extremism from Colonial times to the present. Along the way he looks at such groups as the Puritans, Founding Fathers, abolitionists, Nat Turner and his followers, the suffragettes, Ku Klux Klan, Know Nothings, prohibitionists, monopolists, Hitlerites, Birchers, and the present-day Far Right and Far Left." Booklist

Bibliography: p185-87

Armstrong, O. K.

The fifteen decisive battles of the United States; maps by James Macdonald. McKay 1961 370p maps $5.95   **973**

1 U.S.—History, Military 2 Battles

First published by Longmans

Includes the following battles, campaigns, and sieges: Bloody Marsh, St Simon's Island; Quebec; Saratoga; Yorktown; Lake Erie; New Orleans, 1815; The Alamo; Buena Vista; Vicksburg; Gettysburg; Manila Bay; The Aisne and the Marne, 1918, in the European War; and, Midway and the Coral Sea and finally D-Day in World War II

For the boys, "Mr. Armstrong presents the background and significance as well as a lively recreation of these decisive battles. . . . Useful [also] for reference." Library J

Beard, Charles A.

The Beards' New basic history of the United States [by] Charles A. Beard and Mary R. Beard. Doubleday illus maps $7.95   **973**

1 U.S.—History 2 U.S.—Civilization

First published 1944 with title: A basic history of the United States. Periodically revised to bring material up to date. 1968 edition revised by son, William Beard

Portrays "those events and circumstances—physical, social, military, economic, political, spiritual—which produced our American civilization." Cincinnati

"This work at its remarkably low price is a book for every library. It strikes a happy balance between histories which are too heavy on the side of facts and those which go too far in the way of interpretation." Wis Lib Bul

Includes Selected documents from American history

The rise of American civilizatiion, by Charles A. Beard & Mary R. Beard. Decorations by Wilfred Jones. New ed. rev. and enl. Macmillan (N Y) 1949 2v in 1 illus maps $10.95   **973**

1 U.S.—History 2 U.S.—Civilization

First published 1927 in 2 volumes

Emphasis in this history is on tendencies, movements and major aspects of life, mainly accounted for by the action of social and economic forces

"There is in the book an excess of intellectual irony. . . . Possibly the difficulties of the work arise from the attempt to combine the academic and the popular. Yet there is much in the work which attains the authors' purpose of illuminating, from a critical point of view, the developing social currents in the course of American civilization from Indian aborigines down to technocracy." Springf'd Republican

Includes bibliography

Billington, Ray Allen

Westward expansion; a history of the American frontier [by] Ray Allen Billington with the collaboration of the late James Blaine Hedges. 3d ed. Macmillan (N Y) 1967 933p maps $11.95   **973**

1 U.S.—Territorial expansion 2 U.S.—History 3 Mississippi Valley—History 4 The West—History

First published 1949

The author "traces the advance of the frontier across America from colonial beginnings along the Atlantic Coast in the 16th Century to the closing of the frontier nearly four hundred years later." Publisher's note

This "is a distinguished performance. It reveals clearly the qualities of the Americans who brought greatness to our country, and the political and economic conditions that must prevail before the seeds of greatness, no matter how often planted, will grow. It is a book which, by treating the history of the American frontier in detail, supports a theory and explains much that is best in America to-day." San Francisco Chronicle

Bibliographical notes: p761-93

Boorstin, Daniel J.

(ed.) An American primer. Univ. of Chicago Press 1966 2v (994p) $22.50   **973**

1 U.S.—History—Sources

Selections and accompanying commentaries by approximately 80 historians illuminate the American past "from the Mayflower compact through the Ballad of John Henry and the Sears Company's advertisement to President Johnson's Voting Rights Address." McClurg. Book News

This primer "is mainly intended for home purchase as a 'book of Citizen's History.' However, its discriminating and varied selec-

Boorstin, Daniel J.—*Continued*

tion of 83 significant documents, reproduced from an authoritative text, with source cited; its broad scope . . . including laws, letters, speeches, songs, poems, etc.; and its comment on each document provided by an eminent historian, will make it a valuable reference source in school and public libraries. Particularly useful for those in search of a quotation is the index of words and phrases which supplements the index of authors, titles, and editors, and the general index of subjects." Cur Ref Bks

The genius of American politics. Univ. of Chicago Press 1953 201p (Charles R. Walgreen Foundation lectures) $5.50   **973**

1 U.S.—Politics and government—Addresses and essays   2 Political science—Addresses and essays

Originally delivered 1952 as lectures at the University of Chicago under the Charles R. Walgreen Foundation for the Study of American Institutions

The book describes "the uniqueness of American thought and explains, after a close look at the American past, why we have not produced and are not likely to produce grand political theories or successful propaganda." A Guide to Reading in Am History

Contents: How belief in the existence of an American theory has made a theory superfluous; The Puritans: from providence to pride; The American Revolution; Revolution without dogma; The Civil War and the spirit of compromise; The mingling of political and religious thought; Our cultural hypochondria and how to cure it

Commager, Henry Steele

(ed.) Documents of American history. Appleton 2v in 1 $12.95   **973**

1 U.S.—History—Sources

First published 1934 by Crofts. Frequently revised to include new material

The documents included trace the course of American history from Columbus to the present. They "are generally supplied with a brief introductory paragraph giving the setting, historical connection, bibliography and references to other pertinent documents." Book Rev Digest

"Commager's 'Documents,' we dare to prophesy, will be cited everywhere as a convenient form in which most basic sources of our political history may be consulted." Foreword by the general editor

"An excellent one volume supplement to . . . U.S. history for general reference use." Special Libraries

(ed.) The heritage of America, ed. by Henry Steele Commager and Allan Nevins. Rev. and enl. ed. Little 1949 xxiv, 1227p illus $15   **973**

1 U.S.—History—Sources 2 American literature—Collections

Analyzed in Essay and general literature index

First published 1939

History told almost entirely by men who saw the scenes they describe. This book consists of 269 readings in American history grouped into thirty-five sections, each with an introduction that gives the historical setting

"Messrs. Commager and Nevins have done a fine [job]. Here is the stream, with its eddies and its turbulence, with queer straws floating in it and a few lasting landmarks—the stream of American history from the days of Leif to today. If you want to know something about it, this must be one of your books." Sat R

Bibliography: p1203-18

(ed.) Living ideas in America; ed. and with commentary by Henry Steele Commager. New, enl. ed. Harper 1964 xx, 872p $8.95   **973**

1 U.S.—History—Sources 2 U.S.—Civilization 3 U.S.—Politics and government 4 American literature—Collections

First published 1951

The author brings together, in readable form and with extensive connecting commentary of his own, the basic writings both old and new

which describe and interpret the American idea —memoirs, stories, autobiographical fragments, speeches, documents and historical accounts. Organized around three basic concepts: the people and their country: political principles, traditions and institutions; and America as a world power

"A treasury of source material." Los Angeles. School Libraries

Bibliography: p835-55

Degler, Carl N.

Out of our past; the forces that shaped modern America. Rev. ed. Harper 1970 xx, 546p $10   **973**

1 U.S.—History

First published 1959

"This book seeks an answer to the question 'How did Americans get to be the way they are . . . [today]?' In other words, the multitudinous events of the American past are here seen through the lens of the present. . . . History viewed through the eyes of the present is understandably different from history written from the standpoint of the past. Persons and events which in other treatments might remain unnoticed or unappreciated now spring into focus. Therefore, in this book events and developments usually ignored or subordinated in standard accounts of American history now move to the center of the stage." Preface [to the first edition]

Critical bibliographical essay: p466-513

Dos Passos, John

The shackles of power; three Jeffersonian decades. Doubleday 1966 426p (Mainstream of America ser) $7.95   **973**

1 U.S.—History—1783-1865 2 Jefferson, Thomas, President U.S.

In this historical account, Mr. Dos Passos "interweaves the story of Thomas Jefferson with those of Madison, Monroe, and John Quincy Adams, who followed him, and through whom he dominated the first quarter of the nineteenth century. . . . [The author also provides a] sampling of the scoundrels and scandals of the period." Am News of Bks

"Mr. Dos Passos does a tremendous job of character analysis. . . . He documents many of his statements with quotations from letters or diaries. The book is, indeed, packed with long quotations which might, for reader interest, be curtailed somewhat. . . . To sum up, however, this book is a magnificent survey of a period of American history." Best Sellers

Reading on the Jeffersonian era: p409-12. Maps on lining-papers

Dulles, Foster Rhea

The United States since 1865. New ed. rev. and enl. Univ. of Mich. Press 1969 562, xx p maps (The Univ. of Mich. History of the modern world) $8.95   **973**

1 U.S.—History

First published 1959

Companion volume to: The United States to 1865, by Michael Kraus, listed below

A history of the United States from the Civil War to 1968. The author covers economic, intellectual and industrial as well as political history

"The style is clear and forceful and, in the relation of some episodes, sparkling and witty. Moreover, the emphasis on social and intellectual trends is unusual; and the stress on diplomacy is the mark of a modern text." Chicago Sunday Tribune

Suggested reading: p549-62

Handlin, Oscar

The Americans; a new history of the people of the United States; with illus. by Samuel H. Bryant. Little 1963 434p illus $8.95   **973**

1 U.S.—History 2 U.S.—Civilization

"An Atlantic Monthly Press book"

The author gives an account of the influence of migration upon the people of the United States. "The experience of the people— in all their variety—provides the continuity of

Handlin, Oscar—*Continued*

the narrative. The characters are men and women, exceptional and ordinary, whose lives responded to the pressure of the great social forces of their times. But the focus is fixed upon the context and on developments common to the whole people, rather than on the individual. What impelled men to move and how they earned their livelihood, their thoughts of life and death and the ways in which they expressed themselves are among the subjects that reveal some aspect of that common experience." Preface

"The book will undoubtedly satisfy the needs of many. Those who are already well read in history will find it a fascinating change of pace. And most readers will probably consider it an appetizer for following up on the host of interesting stories led by Mr. Handlin." Christian Science Monitor

Hart, Albert Bushnell

(ed.) American history told by contemporaries. Macmillan (N Y) 1897-1929 5v ea $9.50; set $45   **973**

1 U.S.—History—Sources

Contents: v 1 Era of colonization 1492-1689; v2 Building of the republic 1689-1783; v3 National expansion 1783-1845; v4 Welding of the nation 1845-1900; v5 Twentieth century United States, 1900-1929, with the collaboration of J. G. Curtis. General index in volume 4

"The object of these volumes is to furnish a collection of sources for the study of American history. . . . Few public documents are given, but rather extracts from diaries and contemporary narratives. . . . The selections will be of great service in furnishing illustrative material for teachers or for students who are reading modern authors. Each selection is preceded by a very short statement concerning the life of the author." Larned's Literature of American History

Hofstadter, Richard

The American political tradition and the men who made it. Knopf 1948 378p $7.95   **973**

1 U.S.—Politics and government 2 U.S.—Biography

Analyzed in Essay and general literature index

A study of men and ideas in American politics. The biographies deal with: Founding fathers; Thomas Jefferson; Andrew Jackson; John C. Calhoun; Abraham Lincoln; Wendell Phillips; The spoilsmen; William Jennings Bryan; Theodore Roosevelt; Woodrow Wilson; Herbert Hoover; Franklin D. Roosevelt

"A thoughtful, penetrating controversial study." Library J

Bibliographical essay: p349-78

(ed.) Great issues in American history; a documentary record. Vintage 1958 2v pa ea $2.45   **973**

1 U.S.—History—Sources

Contents: v 1 1765-1865; v2 1864-1957

"Documentary selections with general introductions that put the documents in historical context. Debating of the issues through the words of judges, statesmen, private individuals, and legislative bodies. Political controversy is the focus. Divided into units such as Progressivism and Federalism. Closes with Eisenhower's Second Inaugural Address." A Guide to Reading in Am History

Holbrook, Stewart H.

Dreamers of the American dream. Doubleday 1957 369p (Mainstream of America ser) $6.95   **973**

1 U.S.—History 2 U.S.—Biography 3 U.S.—Social conditions

The account begins "with the true tale of John Noyes' 'Perfectionists,' who became the Oneida Community and practiced communal ownership of everything, including wives and husbands. Then the author moves back and forth in history to other 'dreamers' who were 'uncommon disturbers' of the peace of mind of the nation—Miss Frances Willard

as temperance advocate, for instance, Ethan Allen, Henry George, many others." Pub W

Bibliography: p350-53

Kraus, Michael

The United States to 1865. New ed. rev. and enl. Univ. of Mich. Press 1969 548p maps (The Univ. of Mich. History of the modern world) $8.50   **973**

1 U.S.—History

First published 1959

Companion volume to: The United States since 1865, by Foster Rhea Dulles, listed above

"Smoothly narrated chronological history which brings out salient factors of social development as well as political history. A basic history for general reading [which contains material on the Negro's contribution to American history and culture]." Booklist

Suggested readings: p533-48

Life (Periodical)

The Life History of the United States. Consulting editor, Henry F. Graff. Time, inc. 1963-1964 12v illus maps lib. bdg. ea $7.60, ser. $91.20   **973**

1 U.S.—History

"A Stonehenge book"

A series of broad, personalized interpretations of American history, copiously illustrated

Contents: v 1 The new world: prehistory to 1744, by R. B. Morris; v2 The making of a nation: 1775-1789, by R. B. Morris; v3 The growing years: 1789-1829, by M. L. Coit; v4 The sweep westward: 1829-1849, by M. L. Coit; v5 The Union sundered: 1849-1865, by T. H. Williams; v6 The Union restored: 1861-1876, by T. H. Williams; v7 The age of steel and stream: 1877-1890, by B. A. Weisberger; v8 Reaching for empire: 1890-1901, by B. A. Weisberger; v9 The progressive era: 1901-1917, by E. R. May; v10 War, boom and bust: 1917-1932, by E. R. May; v11 New Deal and global war: 1933-1945, by W. Leuchtenburg; v12 The great age of change: from 1945, by W. Leuchtenburg

Includes bibliographies

Morison, Samuel Eliot

Dissent in three American wars [by] Samuel Eliot Morison, Frederick Merk [and] Frank Freidel. Harvard Univ. Press 1970 104p illus $4.95   **973**

1 U.S.—Politics and government 2 U.S.—History—War of 1812 3 U.S.—History—War with Mexico, 1845-1848 4 U.S.—History—War of 1898

"Focusing on the War of 1812, the Mexican War, and the Spanish-American War, [the authors] . . . remind us that internal disagreement with American involvement in war is not a recent phenomenon. They [argue] that dissenters have sometimes been able to effect changes in national policy, although failing to achieve their primary goal of immediate withdrawal from conflict. Certain recurring points of dissent stand out; e.g., charges of war's drain on national resources, to the neglect of urgent domestic needs, were heard in the past and Americans were urged not to contribute their services or resources to a war they felt was morally wrong." Library J

Includes bibliographical references

The growth of the American Republic [by] Samuel Eliot Morison and [others]. Oxford 2v illus maps ea $9.50   **973**

1 U.S.—History

First published 1930 in a single volume, and periodically revised

A "political, military, economic, social, literary, and spiritual history of the United States." Bk Buyer's Guide

Includes bibliographies

The Oxford History of the American people. Oxford 1965 xxvii, 1150p illus maps $15   **973**

1 U.S.—History 2 U.S.—Civilization

Morison, Samuel E.—*Continued*

A political, social, and military history of the United States from prehistoric man to President Kennedy's assassination, including such aspects of American life as sports, science, art, and music. Includes comments also on Canadian history. (Publisher)

"A panoramic history. . . . Morison achieves amazing compression without using a shorthand English. In fact, his flowing style is one of the pleasures of this book. . . . [His] wit and his views on how the course of history might have been better managed season his book." Pub W

List of songs: p xxiii-xxvii. Bibliographical footnotes

Morris, Richard B.

(ed.) Basic documents in American history. Rev. ed. Van Nostrand 1965 193p pa $1.95   973

1 U.S.—History—Sources
"An Anvil original"
First published 1956
There is an analysis for each of the documents and an evaluation of its historical significance. Covers documents from the Mayflower Compact in 1620 to President Kennedy's 1962 proclamation of a quarantine of offensive weapons to Cuba

(ed.) Great Presidential decisions; state papers that changed the course of history. [Rev. ed] Lippincott 1967 448p $7.50   973

1 U.S.—History—Sources 2 Presidents—U.S.
First published 1960
"This book is concerned with [38] presidential decisions, their formulation and the way they were announced. Professor Morris has collected these famous state papers to demonstrate the way presidential leadership can be exercised and the decisive influence it can have. . . . They are printed in full with long introductory comments by the editor. While such collections as this have inherent value as reference material, the long editorial comments give this work an independence and coherence which make it more generally useful. The papers begin with Washington's on the Whisky Insurrection and conclude with [Johnson's decision to fight a land war in Asia]." Library J

List of sources: p448

Nevins, Allan

A short history of the United States, by Allan Nevins and Henry Steele Commager. 5th ed. rev. and enl. Knopf 1966 669, xxvi p illus $10   973

1 U.S.—History
First published 1942 by Little with title: America, the story of a free people
A history that covers the period up to the 1964 election of Johnson. "It is designed to meet the need for a short narrative history of the American people. . . . [The authors] have not conceived American history to be primarily political or economic, or as a series of problems, but as the story of the evolution of a free society." Preface to original edition
This "readable summary . . . in its inclusion of details may be just what the average reader needs to brush up or integrate his knowledge of our backgrounds." Wis Lib Bul
Bibliography: p653-69

Pageant of America; a pictorial history of the United States; ed. by Ralph Henry Gabriel and others. Independence ed. U.S. Pubs. Assn. 1925-1929 15v illus ea $12.75; set $175   973

1 U.S.—History—Pictures, illustrations, etc.
2 U.S.—Civilization
Originally published by Yale University Press
Contents: v 1 Adventures in the wilderness, by C. Wissler; v2 Lure of the frontier by R. H. Gabriel; v3 Toilers of land and sea, by R. H. Gabriel; v4 March of commerce, by M. Keir; v5 Epic of industry, by M. Keir; v6 Winning of freedom, by W. Wood; v7 In defense of liberty, by W. Wood; v8 Builders of the republic,

by F. A. Ogg; v9 Makers of a new nation, by J. S. Bassett; v10 American idealism, by L. A. Weigle; v11 American spirit in letters, by S. T. Williams; v12 American spirit in art, by F. J. Mather; v13 American spirit in architecture, by T. F. Hamlin; v14 The American stage, by O. S. Coad; v15 Annals of American sport, by J. A. Krout

"The outstanding merit of the set . . . is the bringing together in one place of a large number of pictures of many types, illustrations of historic events, of the life of the people, of industrial and agricultural processes, of works of art, portraits, cartoons, maps and of facsimile reproductions of documents of various kinds. . . . No other single set of books contains a collection of pictures in American history which approaches this in size. An especially valuable feature is the inclusion of a reference to the source from which each illustration has been taken. The printed word is used only to describe the pictures, not to give a connected written history." Library J

973.03 U.S.—History— Dictionaries

Carruth, Gorton

(ed.) The encyclopedia of American facts and dates; ed. by Gorton Carruth and associates. Crowell $7.95   973.03

1 U.S.—History—Dictionaries 2 Chronology, Historical
"A Crowell Reference book"
First published 1956. Periodically revised
"The most important facts and trends of American history, arranged chronologically on a four-column page across which the eye can follow at a glance the events in politics and government, and the developments in culture, learning and religion, and manner of everyday life in any one year." Pub W

Dictionary of American history; James Truslow Adams, editor in chief. Scribner 1940-1961 6v and index $120   973.03

1 U.S.—History—Dictionaries
Supplement one, published 1961 becomes volume six, formerly index volume; the index now being the 7th volume
Consists of "articles each dealing with a separate and definite aspect of American history and each signed with full name of contributor. Also contains a number of articles on broader subjects, which include cross references to related articles on specific aspects. Covers political, economic, social, industrial, and cultural history, but omits biography. . . . However, the activities of prominent persons may frequently be traced through the references under their names in the analytical index. Includes many catchwords and popular names of bills and laws." Winchell. Guide to Reference Books. 8th edition
"One of the most authoritative and most useful sources of essential reference data in the field of U.S. history. . . . The brief bibliographies were selected generally speaking for their availability." Murphey. How and Where to Look it Up

Johnson, Thomas H.

The Oxford Companion to American history [by] Thomas H. Johnson in consultation with Harvey Wish. Oxford 1966 906p $12.50   973.03

1 U.S.—History—Dictionaries
Companion volume to: The Oxford Companion to American literature, by James D. Hart, class 810.3
This reference book includes "summaries of lives, events, and places significant in the founding and growth of the nation. It gives attention to social, political, and labor movements, the observations of travelers . . . art, science, commerce, literature, education, and law. There are also articles dealing with sports and entertainment." Preface

Johnson, Thomas H.—*Continued*

This "is a convenient reference volume. It covers . . . [its subjects] through a judicious mixture of biographical and subject entries, almost 5000 in number. The standard of accuracy is high, the information is concisely and clearly presented, and the format is handy." Atlantic

The author's "attention to the small matters of the past which can suggest the larger issues in our society makes this dictionary extremely valuable." New Repub

Morris, Richard B.

(ed.) Encyclopedia of American history. Harper illus maps $12.50, lib. bdg. $9.89

973.03

1 U.S.—History—Dictionaries 2 Chronology, Historical

First published 1953 and periodically revised "The aim of this 'Encyclopedia' is to provide in a single handy volume the essential historical facts about American life and institutions. The organization is both chronological and topical. 'Dates, events, achievements,' and 'persons' stand out, but the text is designed to be read as a narrative." How to Use This Book

"A chronological manual rather than an encyclopedia as usually understood. No bibliography and no reference to sources." Winchell. Guide to Reference Books. 8th edition

Webster's Guide to American history; a chronological, geographical and biographical survey and compendium. Editors: Charles Van Doren and Robert McHenry; assistant editor: Carolee Benefico; general editor: Mortimer J. Adler; consulting editor: John William Ward. Merriam 1971 1428p illus maps $14.95

973.03

1 U.S.—History—Dictionaries 2 Chronology, Historial 3 U.S.—Biography—Dictionaries

"A Merriam-Webster"

"This is a one-volume summary of U.S. history consisting basically of short factual statements. The chronology is adapted from the 20-volume 'The annals of America,' 1969, [entered in class 973] In this abridgment literary excerpts from each period are in columns adjacent to the chronology, all maps are grouped together, and biographical sketches conclude the volume." Booklist

973.05 U.S.—History—Periodicals

American Heritage. Am. Heritage illus maps ea $5, $20 a year

973.05

1 U.S.—History—Periodicals 2 U.S.—Civilization

Editor: 1954-date, Bruce Catton

Bi-monthly. First published 1947. Sponsored by the American Association for State & Local History and Society of American Historians. Beginning with December 1954 issue, in book form

Recreates textually and pictorially scenes from America's past

"The articles are written by authorities on popular subjects of historical interest." Massachusetts

973.08 Mexicans in the U.S.— History

Moquin, Wayne

(ed.) A documentary history of the Mexican Americans; ed. by Wayne Moquin with Charles Van Doren; introduction by Feliciano Rivera, consulting editor. Praeger 1971 399p illus $13.50

973.08

1 Mexicans in the U.S.—History

This collection "provides excellent insights into the history of the Mexican Americans. The editors have selected judiciously. . . . The selections are all pertinent to the theme of the development of the Mexican-American heritage. The last section of readings is of particular value, as it provides a wealth of information for understanding the directions that the La Raza movement has been taking in the last few years." Library J

Bibliography: p393-94

973.1 U.S.—Discovery and exploration to 1607

De Voto, Bernard

The course of empire; with maps by Erwin Raisz. Houghton 1952 647p maps $8.50

973.1

1 America—Discovery and exploration 2 U.S.—Territorial expansion 3 Indians of North America

A "definitive account of westward conquest and exploration from Balboa to Lewis and Clark. Geography and Indians are included in appraising the Spanish, French, British, and United States exploits determining the course of empire. Excellent introductory essay by Wallace Stegner." A Guide to Reading in Am History

Bibliographical notes: p561-631

Horgan, Paul

Conquistadors in North American history. Farrar, Straus 1963 303p $6.95

973.1

1 America—Discovery and exploration 2 Mexico—History

This account of the northward movement of conquest and conquistadors into what are now the territorial boundaries of the U.S. begins on the flagship of Columbus in 1492 and ends over 200 years later in New Mexico. The period between is filled with violent events and tragic encounters like that of the Indian Montezuma and the Spaniard Cortés. (Publisher)

"If there are any reservations about the book, they are only that the treatment is too short. . . . The story of man's greed and cruelty is not sufficiently detailed." Best Sellers

Bibliography: p292-95. Maps on lining-papers

Innes, Hammond

The Conquistadors. Knopf 1969 336p illus maps $17.50

973.1

1 America—Discovery and exploration 2 Cortés, Hernando 3 Pizarro, Francisco, marqués 4 Peru—History 5 Mexico—History

The author "captures the epic sweep of the brutal destruction of the Aztec and Inca civilizations in Mexico and Peru under the swords of two of Spain's most ruthless explorer-conquerors, Cortes and Pizarro. . . . His depiction of the incredible rivalries, jealousies and intrigues surrounding Cortes and Pizarro in their voyages, and their confrontations with Montezuma and Atahualpa, is both historically accurate and endlessly absorbing." Pub W

Bibliography included in Author's notes: p321-25

Lamb, Harold

New found world; how North America was discovered & explored. Doubleday 1955 336p maps (Mainstream of America ser) $6.95

973.1

1 America—Discovery and exploration 2 North America—History

"Based on contemporary accounts, this interesting survey interprets for the general reader events from Indian migrations in prehistoric times to European conquest and colonization before 1600." Bookmark

"It is primarily concerned with the portion of the new-found world comprising the modern United States and Canada." Foreword

Note on further reading: p324-28. Map on lining-papers

Richman, Irving Berdine

The Spanish conquerors; a chronicle of the dawn of empire overseas. U.S. Pubs. Assn. 1919 238p maps (The Chronicles of America ser. v2) $4.45   **973.1**

1 America—Discovery and exploration 2 Latin America—History 3 Spain—Colonies

Originally published by Yale University Press
Contents: West and East; Columbus and new lands; Balboa and the Pacific; Cortés and Mexico; Spanish conquerors in Central America; Pizarro and the Incas; Bibliographical note

Wood, William

Elizabethan sea-dogs; chronicle of Drake and his companions. U.S. Pubs. Assn. 1918 252p (The Chronicles of America ser. v3) $4.45   **973.1**

1 Drake, Sir Francis 2 America—Discovery and exploration 3 Great Britain—History—Tudors, 1485-1603

Originally published by Yale University Press
"It was during the reign of Elizabeth, the last of the Tudor sovereigns of England, that Englishmen won the command of the sea, under the consummate leadership of Sir Francis Drake, the first of modern admirals. . . . And Anglo-American history begins with that century of maritime adventure and naval war." Prefatory note
Bibliographical note: p241-45

973.2 U.S.—Colonial period, 1607-1775

Acheson, Patricia C.

America's colonial heritage; illus. by Lois K. Williams. Dodd 1957 201p illus map $4.50   **973.2**

1 U.S.—History—Colonial period

"The forces that impelled the colonization of the New World and drove the American colonists to fight for independence can be traced centuries back on the continent of Europe. . . . [The author tells the] story of the varied paths of history that form the rich heritage of this nation." Publisher's note

American Heritage

The American Heritage History of the thirteen colonies, by the editors of American Heritage, The Magazine of History. Editor in charge: Michael Blow; narrative: Louis B. Wright; pictorial commentary: Ralph K. Andrist. Am. Heritage 1967 384p illus maps boards $16.50   **973.2**

1 U.S.—History—Colonial period

This volume is "not just a history of the thirteen colonies, [but] a history of the time from Columbus to the Declaration of Independence, Canada and its settlement is covered as well; also Florida. The prime emphasis, however, is on the 13 colonies which eventually became English colonies and which revolted. An outstanding feature of the book is the four sections . . . that quote from writings of the time—letters, books, diaries, etc. The illustrations are also outstanding: more than 300 paintings, maps, drawings, woodcuts, watercolors and especially commissioned landscape renderings. A good book that covers well what it is meant to cover." Pub W
"The contemporary documents that enrich Wright's narrative reveal good taste and often wit." N Y Times Bk R

Andrews, Charles M.

The colonial background of the American Revolution; four essays in American colonial history. Rev. ed. Yale Univ. Press 1931 220p $6.50   **973.2**

1 U.S.—History—Colonial period 2 Great Britain—Colonies 3 U.S.—History—Revolution —Causes

First published 1924
"A balanced study of Colonial conditions and British policy which led to the Revolution. The author feels the British did not understand the stage of development that the colonies had reached and therefore tried to apply ill-advised solutions." A Guide to Reading in Am History

Becker, Carl

The eve of the Revolution; a chronicle of the breach with England. U.S. Pubs. Assn. 1918 267p (The Chronicles of America ser. v11) $4.45   **973.2**

1 U.S.—History—Colonial period 2 U.S.—History—Revolution 3 U.S.—Politics and government

Originally published by Yale University Press
"I have chiefly endeavored to convey to the reader, not a record of what men did, but a sense of how they thought and felt about what they did." Preface
Contents: Patriot of 1763; Burden of empire; Rights of a nation; Defining the issue; Little discreet conduct; Testing the issue; Bibliographical note

Chidsey, Donald Barr

The French and Indian War; an informal history. Crown 1969 176p illus $4.50   **973.2**

1 U.S.—History—French and Indian War, 1755-1763

"The French and Indian War was the first major conflict in the new world. It was a bloody and long-drawn-out war, marked by massacres, full-blown sieges, and innumerable guerrilla actions. It also prepared many Americans for a later war: for here George Washington and a host of other subsequent heroes of the American Revolution gained invaluable experience. . . . [This book] recreates the causes, the conflicts, the facts, and the personalities of this dramatic war." Am News of Bks
This is "a vigorous, narrative-style history that may over-simplify but nevertheless makes its points clearly." Pub W
Glossary of eighteenth century military terms: p159-63. Bibliography: p164-72

The great separation. . . . Crown 1965 194p illus $4.50   **973.2**

1 U.S.—History—Colonial period 2 U.S.—History—Revolution—Causes 3 Boston—History

"The story of the Boston Tea Party and the beginning of the American Revolution." Title page
An account of the events preceding and leading up to the Revolutionary War. "Not only does the reader participate in the . . . Boston Tea Party, but he learns what was happening in Commons and how the merchants in England and the Colonies thought. The background of the so-called Navigation Acts, the Molasses Act, the Sugar Act and the Stamp Act is discussed." Publisher's note
Notes: p167-80. Bibliography: p181-90

Craven, Wesley Frank

The colonies in transition, 1660-1713. Harper 1968 363p illus maps (The New American Nation ser) $7.95   **973.2**

1 U.S.—History—Colonial period

The book "traces the effect upon the American Colonies of the Restoration, Britain's wars with France, and British political changes, emphasizing the fact that Colonial restlessness was not yet a move toward Revolution." Bk Buyer's Guide
"Not only does Professor Craven summarize past scholarship, but he also provides fresh and original insights, as in his account of the granting of colonial charters. This book will be of value for, and of interest to, students of history and laymen." Library J
Bibliographical essay: p331-51

Fisher, Sydney G.

The Quaker colonies; a chronicle of the proprietors of the Delaware. U.S. Pubs. Assn. 1919 244p (The Chronicles of America ser. v8) $4.45   **973.2**

1 Pennsylvania—History 2 New Jersey—History 3 Delaware—History 4 Friends, Society of

Fisher, Sydney G.—*Continued*

Originally published by Yale University Press
Contents: Birth of Pennsylvania; Penn sails
for the Delaware; Life in Philadelphia; Types
of the population; Troubles of Penn and his
sons; French and Indian War; Decline of
Quaker government; Beginning of New Jersey; Planters and traders of southern Jersey;
Scotch covenanters and others in east Jersey;
United Jerseys; Little Delaware; English conquest; Bibliography

Gipson, Lawrence Henry

The coming of the Revolution, 1763-1775.
Harper 1954 287p illus map (The New
American Nation ser) $7.95   **973.2**

1 U.S.—History—Colonial period 2 U.S.—History—Revolution—Causes

The author "re-examines the causes of the
great war for independence, and traces the ir-
ritants and counter-irritants which plagued
British-American relations between the Peace
of Paris and the calling of the Continental
Congress in 1774." Huntting
"Emphasizes the growing spirit of nationalism and federalism in the American Colonies.
. . . Less emphasis on particular issues of disagreement. A good view of the Revolution
through British eyes." A Guide to Reading in
Am History
Bibliography: p235-78

Hamilton, Edward P.

The French and Indian Wars; the story of
battles and forts in the wilderness. Doubleday 1962 318p maps (Mainstream of America ser) $7.95   **973.2**

1 U.S.—History—French and Indian War,
1755-1763 2 U.S.—History—Colonial period

The author reconstructs the picture of the
ragged men, the battles and sieges during this
long series of wars which began in the 1690's.
He shows how the French colonies spanned
the continent while the English lay on the seacoast, and points out that the basic conflict
occurred as the English desperately tried to
penetrate the barrier of the Appalachians. He
also discusses the controversial role of the Indian in these wars. (Publisher)

973.3 U.S.—Revolution and confederation, 1775-1789

Alden, John Richard

The American Revolution, 1775-1783. Harper 1954 294p illus maps (The New American Nation ser) $7.95   **973.3**

1 U.S.—History—Revolution

The author presents an outline of the Revolution's background and then gives a history of the war itself. The book covers the
military, political, including events in England, economic and social aspects of the period
"The battle accounts are well documented
and illustrated with detailed maps. They are
also colorfully written." San Francisco Chronicle
Bibliography: p269-83

American Heritage

The American Heritage Book of the Revolution, by the editors of American Heritage,
The Magazine of History. Editor in charge:
Richard M. Ketchum; narrative by Bruce
Lancaster with a chapter by J. H. Plumb;
introduction by Bruce Catton. Am. Heritage
1971 384p illus maps boards $19.95   **973.3**

1 U.S.—History—Revolution

A reissue of the title first published 1958
America's fight for independence, the full
story of the Revolutionary War, from Lexington to Yorktown, is told in text and more
than 600 pictures, 183 in full color. (Publisher)
"Here is as sane and illuminating a general
account of the American Revolution as can be

found. Its illustrations do not overshadow the
text—as is so often the case with picture
books—but reinforce it and bring to it an additional actuality. As a book for the ordinary
reader it could scarely be bettered. . . . As for
the illustrations they are lavish, the usual fine
standard of American Heritage." Christian Science Monitor

Becker, Carl

The Declaration of Independence; a study
in the history of political ideas. Knopf 1942
286p $5.95   **973.3**

1 U.S. Declaration of Independence 2 U.S.—
Politics and government—Revolution 3 Jefferson, Thomas, President U.S.

Reprint, with a new preface, of a book first
published 1922
"A study of the Declaration, the philosophy
that lay behind it, the history of its several
drafts, an estimate of its literary quality." Wis
Lib Bul
"I have chiefly endeavored to convey to the
reader, not a record of what men did, but a
sense of how they thought and felt about what
they did." Preface
Bibliographical footnotes

Commager, Henry Steele

(ed.) The spirit of 'seventy-six; the story
of the American Revolution as told by participants; ed. by Henry Steele Commager
and Richard B. Morris. Harper 1967 liii,
1348p illus maps $20   **973.3**

1 U.S.—History—Revolution—Personal narratives 2 U.S.—History—Revolution—Sources

A reissue in one volume of the text first published 1958 in two volumes by Bobbs
"Here are nearly one thousand selections
from official records, diaries, letters, and the
like giving contemporary views of the Revolution. its causes and its aims." The Bookseller
Acknowledgements, bibliography and indexes: p1297-1319

Farrand, Max

The fathers of the Constitution; a chronicle
of the establishment of the Union. U.S. Pubs.
Assn. 1921 242p (The Chronicles of America ser. v13) $4.45   **973.3**

1 U.S.—History—1783-1809 2 U.S.—Constitutional history

Originally published by Yale University Press
Contents: Treaty of peace; Trade and indus-
try; The Confederation; Northwest ordinance;
Darkness before dawn; Federal convention;
Finishing the work; Union established; Bib-
liographical note

Furneaux, Rupert

The Battle of Saratoga. Stein & Day 1971
304p illus maps (Great battles of the modern world) boards $7.95   **973.3**

1 Sarotoga Campaign, 1777 2 Burgoyne's Invasion, 1777
SBN 8128-1305-7

The author recounts what is considered "the
pivotal battle of the American Revolution. In
this battle British General Burgoyne, moving
down from Canada, failed to link forces with
Howe's troops moving up from Pennsylvania,
and surrendered at Saratoga on October 17,
1777." Pub W
"This book is a useful survey of the Saratoga campaign for the nonspecialist in Revolutionary War and military history. . . . The
quotations are well selected and add a feeling
of immediacy to Furneaux's own well written
passasges." Choice
Bibliography: p294-99

McDowell, Bart

The Revolutionary War; America's fight
for freedom; prepared by Special Publications Division, Robert L. Breeden, chief. Nat.
Geographic Soc. 1967 199p illus maps $4.25
          973.3

1 U.S.—History—Revolution

McDowell, Bart—*Continued*

Drawing upon archival material, letters, and contemporary art and records, the author "narrates the dramatic events from Braddock's ill-fated expedition of 1755, through the years of growing discontent in the colonies and ministerial intransigence in London, the first blood at Lexington; the implacable spread of the conflict north, south, and west; the famous battles from Bunker Hill to Yorktown. . . . The nearly 200 illustrations are superb; maps are uncluttered and skillfully drawn, and the several panoramic paintings of key battles are extraordinarily apt and revealing." Library J

Additional references: p198

Morris, Richard B.

The American Revolution reconsidered. Harper 1967 178p $5   **973.3**

1 U.S.—History—Revolution 2 U.S.—Constitutional history

A "re-examination of the American Revolution [in which] Mr. Morris argues that the war not only heralded the end of parochial colonialism and the fulfillment of nationhood, but that it had a social and ideological dimension as well. This understanding of the dual character of the War for Independence, he says, makes the American Revolution not an event in American history alone, but a turning point in world history." Publisher's note

"A scholarly reappraisal with extensive notes and bibliography following each essay." Booklist

Peckham, Howard H.

The War for Independence; a military history. Univ. of Chicago Press 1958 226p (The Chicago History of American civilization) $5   **973.3**

1 U.S.—History—Revolution—Campaigns and battles

Written for the layman this "history of the American Revolution characterizes leading protagonists, describes major battles and campaigns, and illuminates the events and conditions that shaped America's ultimate victory. Includes inside cover maps and a chronological list of important dates." Booklist

This book "is especially good on the British side of the struggle. . . . The American side of the conflict is not handled with quite so much authority." Am Hist R

Bibliographical notes: p210-17

Trevelyan, George

The American Revolution; a condensation into one volume of the original six-volume work. Edited, arranged, and with an introduction and notes by Richard B. Morris. McKay 1964 xxiii, 580p $12.50   **973.3**

1 U.S.—History—Revolution

The original work was first written 1899

Emphasis of this abridgment is on politics, manners, and ideas, omitting most of the military aspects of the Revolution

"The device of giving both the American and British point of view and stressing the connection of events in both countries gives a much more complete and understandable picture then the usual British or American account would convey." Best Sellers

Bibliographical footnotes

Wrong, George M.

Washington and his comrades in arms; a chronicle of the War of Independence. U.S. Pubs. Assn. 1921 295p (The Chronicles of America ser. v12) $4.45   **973.3**

1 U.S.—History—Revolution 2 Washington, George, President U.S.

Originally published by Yale University Press

Contents: The Commander-in-Chief; Boston and Quebec; Independence; Loss of New York; Loss of Philadelphia; First great British disaster; Washington and his comrades at Valley Forge; Alliance with France and its results; War in the South; France to the rescue; Yorktown; Bibliographical note

973.4   U.S.—Constitutional period, 1789-1809

Bowers, Claude G.

Jefferson and Hamilton; the struggle for democracy in America. Houghton 1925 531p illus $8.50   **973.4**

1 Jefferson, Thomas, President U.S. 2 Hamilton, Alexander 3 U.S.—Politics and government—1783-1809

This second volume of the author's trilogy on Jefferson covers "the twelve years' struggle between the conflicting ideals of Hamilton and of Jefferson and the imprint they left on the character of the new republic. . . . Mr Bowers paints living portraits of the two great protagonists and their associates in the struggle, against a background of the social life of the times." Book Rev Digest

"All students of American history should read this book, and the general reader will not be wasting time or thought if he tackles it. For it is a masterly exposition of the practical working of ideas which are still alive to-day, and still have meaning for us." Nation and Atheneum

Bibliography: p513-18

Jefferson in power; the death struggle of the Federalists. Houghton 1936 538p illus $8.50   **973.4**

1 Jefferson, Thomas, President U.S. 2 U.S.—Politics and government—1783-1809

This concluding volume of the author's trilogy on Jefferson is a "chronicle of Jefferson's eight Presidential years, as vigorous and picturesque as anything Mr. Bowers has done. The accents are on the extremely lively social life of the period, on the duel between Jefferson and Hamilton, and on the dramatic degeneration of the Federalist Party. Mr. Bowers succeeds in his desire 'to picture the actors off the stage out of their full-dress uniforms.'" New Yorker

The young Jefferson, 1743-1789. Houghton 1945 xxx, 544p illus $8.50   **973.4**

1 Jefferson, Thomas, President U.S. 2 U.S.—Politics and government—1783-1809

"This book which covers Jefferson's career up to his return from France in 1789 to become Secretary of State in Washington's cabinet, fits in with the author's two previous books, 'Jefferson and Hamilton,' and 'Jefferson in power,' to form a complete trilogy covering his life. Puts special stress on his accomplishments in Virginia, in breaking down the power of aristocracy and establishing the principles of religious liberty. The years in France and his relation to the French Revolution are also treated in full." Wis Lib Bul

Chidsey, Donald Barr

The great conspiracy; Aaron Burr and his strange doings in the West. Crown 1967 166p illus $4.50   **973.4**

1 Burr, Aaron 2 Burr Conspiracy, 1805-1807 3 Trials

The author describes the circumstances surrounding the duel with Hamilton; Burr's plots with leading figures of the day; Burr's trip south with his small "army" and the great Virginia trial at which he was charged with conspiracy. (Publisher)

The author "attempts to explain this loophole in history. . . . Pedants may find Mr. Chidsey's enthusiasms for his subject slightly overwhelming, but because his approach is so readable he cannot severely be called to task on this score. However, sentences such as 'Burr even had time for a romance, reputedly with a maiden called Madeline Price; but then, he always had time for things like that,' are something else; and will cause historians' brows to wrinkle." Library J

Bibliography: p156-61

Lewis and Clark; the great adventure. Crown 1970 191p illus maps $4.50   **973.4**

1 Lewis and Clark Expedition 2 Clark, William, 1770-1838 3 Lewis, Meriwether

Chidsey, Donald B.—*Continued*

The author "presents a lively account of the [1804-1806] expedition . . . of Meriwether Lewis and William Clark, the men commissioned by President Thomas Jefferson to explore the Missouri River for the purpose of locating a possible Northwest passage to the Pacific. Chidsey describes the members of the historic Corps of Discovery, chronicles their perilous journey to the Columbia River and their return, incorporating excerpts from the diaries and journals of Lewis and Clark and including information concerning their lives following the expedition." Booklist

Bibliography: p183-86

Corwin, Edward S.

John Marshall and the Constitution; a chronicle of the Supreme Court. U.S. Pubs. Assn. 1919 242p (The Chronicles of America ser. v16) $4.45   **973.4**

1 Marshall, John, 1755-1835   2 U.S. Constitution 3 U.S. Supreme Court 4 U.S.—History—1783-1809

Originally published by Yale University Press

Contents: Establishment of the national judiciary; Marshall's early years; Jefferson's war on the judiciary; Trial of Aaron Burr; Tenets of nationalism; Sanctity of contracts; Menace of state rights; Among friends and neighbors; Epilogue; Bibliographical note

Dos Passos, John

The men who made the nation. Doubleday 1957 469p (Mainstream of America ser) $7.50   **973.4**

1 U.S.—History—1783-1809   2 U.S.—Biography

The years between Yorktown in 1781 and the Louisiana Purchase in 1803 determined the future of our country. The author interweaves the history of those critical years with the stories of the men who shaped the times—such men as Washington, Jefferson, Hamilton, Franklin, Adams, Madison, Monroe, Marshall and Morris. (Publisher)

"Mr. Dos Passos has now written a special blend of American history and American biography, done in his well-known impressionistic manner. From a storytelling standpoint, the result is most effective, for Mr. Dos Passos is an unequaled storyteller, and his impressionistic method permits the use of lavish color. But in the writing of history, the impressionistic method does have its limitations." Book of the Month Club News

Ford, Henry Jones

Washington and his colleagues; a chronicle of the rise and fall of federalism. U.S. Pubs. Assn. 1918 235p (The Chronicles of America ser. v14) $4.45   **973.4**

1 U.S.—History—1783-1809   2 Washington, George, President U.S. 3 Federal Party

Originally published by Yale University Press

Contents: Imitation court; Great decisions; Master builder; Alarums and excursions; Tribute to the Algerines; French designs on America; Settlement with England; Party violence; Personal rule of John Adams; Bibliographical note

Johnson, Allen

Jefferson and his colleagues; a chronicle of the Virginia dynasty. U.S. Pubs. Assn. 1921 343p (The Chronicles of America ser. v15) $4.45   **973.4**

1 U.S.—History—1783-1865   2   Jefferson, Thomas, President U.S.

Originally published by Yale University Press

Contents: President Jefferson's court; Putting the ship on her republican tack; Corsairs of the Mediterranean; Shadow of the First Consul; In pursuit of the Floridas; American Catiline; Abuse of hospitality; Pacifists of 1807; Last phase of peaceable coercion; War-hawks; President Madison under fire; The peacemakers; Spanish derelicts in the New World; Framing an American policy; End of an era; Bibliographical note

Miller, John C.

The Federalist era, 1789-1801. Harper 1960 304p illus map (The New American Nation ser) $7.95   **973.4**

1 U.S.—History—1783-1809 2 Federal Party

This detailed study "chronicles the administrations of George Washington and John Adams. . . . [The author] believes that historians have tended to side with either Hamilton or Jefferson, the two most influential political thinkers of the period; agreeing sometimes with one and sometimes with the other he examines the Federalist era with regard to measures that promoted the growth, prosperity, and cohesion of the U.S. and those worked out to protect the individual's constitutional rights." Booklist

Bibliography: p279-98

Smelser, Marshall

The Democratic Republic, 1801-1815. Harper 1968 369p illus maps (The New American Nation ser) $7.95   **973.4**

1 U.S.—History—1783-1865

This "history presents a revisionist point of view on American foreign and domestic policies in the crucial age of world wars between 'the Tiger and the Shark,' when France and Britain tried to make the United States a satellite nation. To save the identity of the young republic, Jefferson and Madison in turn led a struggle which engaged many characters, both honorable and rascally." Publisher's note

"For too many years we have been without a short, scholarly, readable account of the years of the Jefferson and Madison Administrations. The void has now been filled by Smelser's text which sparkles with interest as well as being authoritative, concise, and indicating exhaustive research. He has included the latest interpretations on most of the points of controversy and has ventured a number of personal observations and conclusions, all of which seem sound." Choice

Select bibliography: p325-58

Snyder, Gerald S.

In the footsteps of Lewis and Clark; photographs by Dick Durrance II; illus. by Richard Schlecht; foreword by Donald Jackson. . . . Nat. Geographic Soc. 1970 215p illus maps $4.25   **973.4**

1 Lewis and Clark Expedition

SBN 87044-087-X

"Produced by the Special Publications Division, Robert L. Breeden, Chief [of] National Geographic Society." Title page

A narrative based on research and the personal retracing of the trail up the Missouri River and on to the Pacific by the author and his family. There are historical illustrations by artists of pioneer times as well as present-day photographs and specially commissioned drawings depicting major etvents described in the journals of expedition members

Bibliography: p215

973.5 U.S.—Early 19th century, 1809-1845

Dangerfield, George

The awakening of American nationalism, 1815-1828. Harper 1965 331p illus maps (The New American Nation ser) $7.95   **973.5**

1 U.S.—History—1815-1861 2 Democracy 3 Nationalism

"How the United States, after the War of 1812, gradually developed democratic nationalism, especially under the aegis of President Andrew Jackson." Bk Buyer's Guide

Partial contents: Madison and Monroe; Secretary Adams, General Jackson, and the Transcontinental Treaty; The Panic of 1819; The Missouri Compromises; The Monroe Doctrine; The election of 1828; Bibliographical essay

"Resource material written at the college level. For able and interessted history students." Minnesota

Forester, C. S.

The age of fighting sail; the story of the naval War of 1812. Doubleday 1956 284p (Mainstream of America ser) $5.95   **973.5**

1 U.S.—History—War of 1812 2 U.S.—History, Naval

This "report makes the War of 1812 sound like a near-contemporary event. Not only are the sailing vessels, their masters and men, and the ballistics of the early nineteenth century described in detail, but the complex political drama of the young colonies is realistically presented. Several . . . parallels with recent history are suggested." Booklist

Maps on lining-papers

Lawson, Don

The War of 1812; America's second war for independence; illus. with photographs and maps by Richard Howard. Abelard-Schuman 1966 160p illus maps $4.50 **973.5**

1 U.S.—History—War of 1812

An "engrossing account. . . . The coverage is concise, with chapters on prewar controversy and naval and military encounters and thumbnail sketches of American, Indian, and British men involved in the conflict. Written in episodic fashion, with emphasis on William Henry Harrison and his conflict and battles with the Indians, notably Tecumseh, the account includes chapters on the war in the northwest, the battles of Lake Erie and New Orleans, the free trade and sailors' rights cause, the sea fight between the ironclads, and writing of the 'Star-spangled Banner.'" Library J

Books about the War of 1812: p149-52

Ogg, Frederic Austin

The reign of Andrew Jackson; a chronicle of the frontier in politics. U.S. Pubs. Assn. 1919 249p (The Chronicles of America ser. v20) $4.45 **973.5**

1 U.S. History—1815-1861 2 Jackson, Andrew, President U.S.

Originally published by Yale University Press

Contents: Jackson the frontiersman; Creek War and the victory of New Orleans; "Conquest" of Florida; Death of "King Caucus"; Democratic triumph; "Reign" begins; Webster-Hayne debate; Tariff and nullification; War on the United States Bank; Removal of the Southern Indians; Jacksonian succession; Bibliographical note

Paine, Ralph D.

The fight for a free sea; a chronicle of the War of 1812. U.S. Pubs. Assn. 1920 235p (The Chronicles of America ser. v17) $4.45 **973.5**

1 U.S.—History—War of 1812

Originally published by Yale University Press

Contents: "On to Canada": Lost ground regained; Perry and Lake Erie; Ebb and flow on the northern front; Navy on blue water; Matchless frigates and their duels; "Don't give up the ship"; Last cruise of the Essex; Victory on Lake Champlain; Peace with honor; Bibliographical note

Schlesinger, Arthur M. 1917-

The age of Jackson, by Arthur M. Schlesinger, Jr. Little 1945 577p $8.50 **973.5**

1 Jackson, Andrew, President U.S. 2 U.S.—Politics and government—1815-1861

Awarded the Pulitzer Prize for history, 1946

Begins with the end of the Jeffersonian agricultural era and paints the slow rise of industrialism and its radical effects on the national economy. The author shows the relation of Jacksonian democracy to law, industrialism, religion and literature, the beginning of the Free Soil movement and the growing intensity of sectional disputes

"The Age of Jackson will delight the advanced student of American history, but its plenitude of detail and its author's interest in

ideologies may weary the general reader." U.S. Quarterly Bk R

Bibliography: p529-59

Wellman, Paul I.

The house divides; the age of Jackson and Lincoln, from the War of 1812 to the Civil War. Doubleday 1966 488p maps (Mainstream of America ser) $6.95 **973.5**

1 U.S.—History—1815-1861 2 Jackson, Andrew, President U.S. 3 Lincoln, Abraham, President U.S.

The author pictures primarily "the world of Andrew Jackson, hero of the Battle of New Orleans, President, and proponent of many of our continuing policies in a period of expansion and surging power." Bk Buyer's Guide

The author "leans heavily on political and military history, following the traditional approach in American history. . . . If the book has a weakness, it is in the failure of the author to emphasize social and cultural history." Best Sellers

Notes on bibliography: p467-69

973.6   U.S.—Middle 19th century, 1845-1861

Catton, William

Two roads to Sumter, by William and Bruce Catton. McGraw 1963 285p $6.50

973.6

1 U.S.—History—Civil War—Causes 2 U.S.—History—1815-1861 3 Lincoln, Abraham, President U.S. 4 Davis, Jefferson

"This study of the United States in the 1850's describes the thinking of Abraham Lincoln and Jefferson Davis and their 'two roads' to the Civil War." Christian Science Monitor

"What caused their different attitudes, the authors think, was not their education, but their homes and environment." Pub W

Chidsey, Donald Barr

The War with Mexico. Crown 1968 192p illus $4.50 **973.6**

1 U.S.—History—War with Mexico, 1845-1848

"In vivid terms, Chidsey re-creates the wanton massacre of a whole company of American troops, the heroic defense and fall of the Alamo, the dramatic battles of Buena Vista and Monterey, the siege and shelling of Vera Cruz, and the invasion of Mexico." Am News of Bks

"This is a brisk and brief account of one of this country's lesser-known but more consequential wars . . . [written in] a clear and simple style. . . . In such short space [the author] can deal only briefly with most events and individuals, and they are often described or characterized in a few pithy words or sentences. . . . Not a book for scholars, but the general reader and the young adult should enjoy it." Library J

Bibliography: p181-88

Lincoln, Abraham

The Lincoln-Douglas debates of 1858, ed. by Robert W. Johannsen. Oxford 1965 330p pa $2.75 **973.6**

1 Lincoln-Douglas debates, 1858 2 U.S.—Politics and government—1815-1861

With introductions to give perspective, this "includes the seven debates of 1858 as well as Douglas's speech in Chicago that set the tone for the debates." A Guide to Reading in Am History

Suggestions for further reading: p330

Macy, Jesse

The anti-slavery crusade; a chronicle of the gathering storm. U.S. Pubs. Assn. 1919 245p (The Chronicles of America ser. v28) $4.45 **973.6**

1 U.S.—History—1815-1861 2 Slavery in the U.S. 3 Abolitionists

Macy, Jesse—*Continued*

Originally published by Yale University Press

Contents: Introduction; Geography of the crusade; Early crusaders; Turning point; Vindication of liberty; Slavery issue in politics; Passing of the Whig Party; Underground Railroad; Books as anti-slavery weapons; "Bleeding Kansas"; Charles Sumner; Kansas and Buchanan; Supreme Court in politics; John Brown; Bibliographical note

Nevins, Allan

Ordeal of the Union. Scribner 1947 2v illus maps ea $12.50   **973.6**

1 Slavery in the U.S. 2 U.S.—History—Civil War—Causes 3 U.S. History—1815-1861

"Winner of the $10,000 Scribner prize in American history this study . . . traces the course of an extremely important period in our history." Library J

"The years between the close of the Mexican War and the beginning of the 'irrepressible conflict' described and explained in terms of political, social and economic life." Chicago

Contents: v 1 Fruits of manifest destiny, 1847-1852; v2 House dividing, 1852-1857

Note on the sources: v 1 p561-62

Stephenson, Nathaniel W.

Texas and the Mexican War; a chronicle of the winning of the Southwest. U.S. Pubs. Assn. 1921 273p (The Chronicles of America ser. v24) $4.45   **973.6**

1 Texas—History 2 U.S.—History—War with Mexico, 1845-1848

Originally published by Yale University Press

Contents: The empressarios; Turning point; The incompatibles; Texas secedes; Recognition; Mexican shadow; England as peacemaker; International crisis of 1844; Domestic crisis of 1844; Adventure in imperialism; "Hero of Buena Vista"; Stroke from the East; Pivotal action; Conquered peace; Bibliographical note

973.7 U.S.—Administration of Lincoln, 1861-1865 (Civil War)

American Heritage

The American Heritage Picture history of the Civil War, by the editors of American Heritage, The Magazine of History; editor in charge: Richard M. Ketchum. Narrative by Bruce Catton. Am. Heritage 1960 630p illus maps boards $24.95   **973.7**

1 U.S.—History—Civil War—Pictures, illustrations, etc.

"Eight writers, researchers, and artists, under the direction of Editor Richard M. Ketchum have searched for more than two years through libraries, museums and private collections in both the U.S.A. and Europe for the pictures and factual background of the book. . . . A third of the pictures are in color. The narrative covers the story of the war from start to finish: the military campaigns, the political atmosphere of the 1860's, the changing objectives of the war, the leaders on both sides, the economic and social forces involved. Detailed picture captions complement Catton's text. . . . Two special chapters break the chronological sequence of the book to cover in considerable pictorial detail the look of The Armies and The Navies. In addition, six . . . photographers were sent by American Heritage to photograph the major Civil War battlefields in color at the same time of year and in the same kind of weather as when the battles were fought. Eighty-four such photographs are reproduced." Publisher's note

"One special feature of this history is a newly perfected technique for maps designed to present a succession of battle movements against a realistic background. . . . What the maps lack in old-fashioned accuracy they

more than provide in clarity and in dramatic character. The editors have given us maps for every battle of importance and it is a safe prophecy that many readers will find that now for the first time they really understand the troop movements. This is a magnificent collection of pictures, but it is far more than a picture book. . . . The text itself is everything we have come to expect . . . from the practiced hand of Bruce Catton: scholarly, judicious, clear and unfailingly interesting. It would be difficult to find a better introduction to the Civil War than this sumptuous book." N Y Times Bk R

Bakeless, John

Spies of the Confederacy. Lippincott 1970 456p $7.95   **973.7**

1 Spies 2 Confederate States of America—Biography

"An entertaining look at the group of amateurs, opportunists, daredevils, dewy-eyed maidens, cunning chaplains, simple soldiers and patriotic countryfolk who all belonged to the loosely organized spy system of the Confederacy during the Civil War. John Bakeless tells their stories, from Sumter to Appomattox." Pub W

Bibliography included in Notes; p397-436

Botkin, B. A.

(ed.) A Civil War treasury of tales, legends and folklore; ed. with an introduction by B. A. Botkin; illus. by Warren Chappell. Random House 1960 xx, 625p illus $10
973.7

1 U.S.—History—Civil War 2 Folklore—U.S.

"Based on a wide variety of contemporary sources. To supply the historical framework the selections have been arranged in six parts, corresponding to the years of the war and the aftermath. These parts are in turn divided into forty-four sections, representing main aspects of the war. Within these sections the selections are arranged by date, when known. The whole constitutes a collective saga of the human side of the Civil War." Introduction

Notes: p577-607

Catton, Bruce

America goes to war. Wesleyan Univ. Press [1958] 126p illus pa $1.45   **973.7**

1 U.S.—History—Civil War

The book "is based on a series of lectures given by the author at Wesleyan University. In these essays Mr. Catton ranges . . . through such Civil-War related topics as the impact of the new weapons introduced in the conflict on tactics, the employment of political generals in the North, the psychology of the citizen soldier, the repression of civil liberties in wartime and the career of U.S. Grant as President." N Y Times Bk R

"A simple, beautifully narrated little volume." Chicago Sunday Tribune

The coming fury. Doubleday 1961 565p illus maps (The Centennial history of the Civil War v 1) $10   **973.7**

1 U.S.—History—Civil War

The first book in a trilogy

"Chronicles the break between the South and North leading to the Civil War, from the Democratic Convention in April, 1860, to First Bull Run in July, 1861. The highlight is an . . . account of Sumter. Lincoln's formulation of policy in the early days of the administration is followed almost day by day." Pub W

"The book has, throughout its pages, the ring of authority and authenticity. The writing is based upon extensive research in primary as well as secondary sources." N Y Her Trib Books

Bibliography: p509-47

Followed by: Terrible swift sword

Glory Road; the bloody route from Fredericksburg to Gettysburg. Doubleday 1952 416p maps $6.95   **973.7**

1 U.S.—History—Civil War—Campaigns and battles

Catton, Bruce—*Continued*

Sequel to: Mr Lincoln's Army
"A record of the Army of the Potomac during the period between autumn, 1862, in which the fortunes of war turned from defeat to the beginning of victory for the Union cause. A story of privates and generals under fire and in camp, derived from letters, diaries and other official and personal recollections." Pub W
"There is close attention to the hours, the days, the weeks, not given over to fighting. . . . Once again Mr. Catton lays about him unsparingly, but there is more depth, more understanding." N Y Her Trib Books
Bibliography: p363-70
Followed by: A stillness at Appomattox

Mr Lincoln's army. Doubleday 1951 372p maps $6.95   **973.7**

1 U.S.—History—Civil War—Campaigns and battles 2 McClellan, George Brinton
First volume of a trilogy on the Civil War. The trilogy entitled: The army of the Potomac, is available as a boxed set for $14.95
This is the story of Lincoln's famous army of the Potomac during the early years of the Civil War, when it was under the command of dashing General George B. McClellan. It is an account, gathered from diaries and letters and published reports, of the ordinary foot soldiers
"Mr. Catton tells the story in journalistic order, beginning with Pope's fiasco at Second Bull Run, then going back to pick up the narrative of McClellan's rise. . . . He has the rare gift of doing enormous research and then, presenting it in what is almost a motion picture in color of march, camp and field, with brief vivid closeups of generals." N Y Times Bk R
Bibliography: p341-47
Followed by: Glory Road

Never call retreat. Doubleday 1965 555p maps (The Centennial history of the Civil War v3) $7.95   **973.7**

1 U.S.—History—Civil War
Sequel to: Terrible swift sword
An account of the South's decline in strength and unity from December, 1862, to Lee's surrender
"Frequent shifting from the dramatic description of a battle or march to conditions in Washington or Richmond, a Northern farm or Southern plantation is so artistically done that the reader has a clearer view of the whole picture and a better understanding of why this battle was fought or this political maneuver was made. . . . The footnotes are at the end of the text and there is a helpful index." Best Sellers
Bibliography: p517-34

Prefaces to history. Doubleday 1970 192p $6   **973.7**

1 U.S.—History—Civil War
Analyzed in Essay and general literature index
"A collection of Catton's introductions to his own and other writers' books together with asssorted essays and addresses reveals the wide range of his interests, from his lifelong dedication to the interpretation of the men and events influencing the Civil War, to the voyages of Columbus and Joshua Slocum, the game of baseball, and the history of his home state of Michigan. Throughout the selections Catton's narrative skill, graceful prose, and unobtrusive scholarship are pleasingly evident." Booklist

A stillness at Appomattox. Doubleday 1953 438p maps $6.95   **973.7**

1 U.S.—History—Civil War—Campaigns and battles
Sequel to: Glory Road
Awarded the Pulitzer Prize for history, 1954
"The final volume of this detailed and intensely interesting study of the Army of the Potomac covers the period from early 1864 to April, 1865." Library J
"What Mr. Catton has done is to write the life history of an army. . . . Any serious student of the Civil War must read many books, some for their factual content, some for their character portrayals, a few for their new ideas. Mr. Catton's history of the Army of the Potomac deserves reading on all these counts. But

these superb volumes are not merely accurate and provocative history; the combination of literary brilliance and deep human compassion makes them a memorable and moving saga of Americans at war." Nation
Bibliography: p383-91

Terrible swift sword. Doubleday 1963 559p maps (The Centennial history of the Civil War v2) $7.50   **973.7**

1 U.S.—History—Civil War
Sequel to: The coming fury
This volume begins just after the Battle of Bull Run in 1861 and continues until General McClellan was relieved of his command of the Army of the Potomac in 1862. The author makes two main points; how the war slowly but steadily got out of control, and how all out conflict changed the war's purpose and made it a war for human freedom. (Publisher)
"Most of the book is devoted to interpretation, to reflections on the underlying meaning of events, the impact of various personalities. . . . All these threads are skillfully woven into a dramatic and absorbing tale, a story any reader will find thrilling and thought provoking." Best Sellers
Bibliography: p529-44
Followed by: Never call retreat

This hallowed ground; the story of the Union side of the Civil War. Doubleday 1956 437p maps (Mainstream of America ser) $7.95   **973.7**

1 U.S.—History—Civil War
This history deals with the entire scope of the Civil War—from the months of unrest and hysteria that led to Fort Sumter through the Union victory. (Publisher)
"It is a fine study, military and political, of the Civil War, filled with intimate details based on thorough knowledge of the subject. Unlike so many histories it is a book to be read more for pleasure than as a textbook or a reference work. The subtitle does not imply a partisan approach, for incidents and characters though molded by the author's organization of material and literary style, are treated with great fairness. Highly recommended as a particularly readable history of the Civil War." Library J
Bibliography: p424-29

Commager, Henry Steele

(ed.) The Blue and the Gray; the story of the Civil War as told by participants. Bobbs 1954 [c1950] xxxviii, 1201p illus maps $11.95   **973.7**

1 U.S.—History—Civil War—Personal narratives
This 1954 edition is a reprint in one volume of the two volume edition published 1950
"Story of the Civil War as told by participants in 400 separate contributions—North and South—begins with the election of Lincoln and the secession of the Southern states and carries through to Appomattox. In these volumes is a living record of the economic, social and military history of the Civil War . . . in all its fury of battle, social unheaval, humorous, personal and national, movements." Huntting
Bibliography and acknowledgements: p1155-86

(ed.) Fifty basic Civil War documents. Van Nostrand 1965 192p pa $1.75   **973.7**

1 U.S.—History—Civil War—Sources
"An Anvil original"
This collection presents "a history of the Civil War in the words of those who fought it. It is not restricted to military accounts but includes social history as well. Each section is preceded by an introductory statement." A Guide to Reading in Am History
Includes bibliographical footnotes

Davis, Burke

To Appomattox; nine April days, 1865. Rinehart 1959 433p illus maps $8.95   **973.7**

1 U.S.—History—Civil War 2 Appomattox Campaign, 1865

Davis, Burke—*Continued*

"April 1 through April 9, 1865, saw the fall of Richmond, the defeat of the Army of Northern Virginia, the disintegration of all the Confederacy's troops, and Lee's surrender to Grant. By tying together the eye-witness accounts of many individuals on both sides and following these individuals from day to day through the nine days, the author gives a vivid report on the times as these people in the midst of them saw and felt what was happening. There are close-ups of Lincoln, Grant, Lee, Custer, and Sherman, as well as of more humble captains, couriers, soldiers, and private citizens. The book is detailed, as are all these minute-by-minute and person-by-person reports, but is well organized and very dramatic in its emphasis on human actions and reactions." Horn Bk

Bibliography: p413-22

Freeman, Douglas Southall

Lee's lieutenants; a study in command. Scribner 1942-1944 3v illus maps ea $17.50
973.7

1 U.S.—History—Civil War—Campaigns and battles 2 U.S.—History—Civil War—Biography 3 Confederate States of America—Biography

Contents: v 1 Manassas to Malvern Hill; v2 Cedar Mountain to Chancellorsville; v3 Gettysburg to Appomattox

A "detailed treatment of the military history of the Civil War as seen through the performance of the Confederate officers. The clarity of Freeman's description of battles lies in his use of only the information known to the Confederate officers at the time of the battle. Following the story of each major battle is a summary which . . . forms a critique of the Confederate officers engaged." Enoch Pratt

Select critical bibliography: v3 p799-825

Kane, Harnett T.

Spies for the Blue and Gray. Hanover House 1954 311p $5.50
973.7

1 U.S.—History—Civil War—Secret service 2 Confederate States of America—Biography 3 Spies

The civilian spies and secret agents described are: Rose O'Neal Greenhow, Allan Pinkerton, Mrs E. H. Baker, Timothy Webster, Lafayette C. Baker, Belle Boyd, Walter Bowie, Pauline Cushman, Philip Henson, Spencer K. Brown, Elizabeth Van Lew, Sam Davis, Ginnie and Lottie Moon

"While the episodes read like escape fiction, the book is a most solid contribution to an understanding of the relatively primitive and highly personal systems of espionage evolved in an internecine war." Sat R

Bibliography: p291-301

Sandburg, Carl

Storm over the land; a profile of the Civil War; taken mainly from "Abraham Lincoln: the war years"; with 60 halftones from photographs, and 98 drawings, maps, and sketches. Harcourt 1942 440p illus maps $7.50
973.7

1 U.S.—History—Civil War

"For the sake of brevity and sequence the author has rewritten some sections of the larger work. . . . [Comparison] shows that whole paragraphs have been lifted from the chapters having to do with the campaigns and battles of the war, omitting all extraneous matter and adding connecting paragraphs where needed. May be read by some to whom the four volumes looked formidable or by others interested primarily in military history." Wis Lib Bul

Stephenson, Nathaniel W.

Abraham Lincoln and the Union; a chronicle of the embattled North. U.S. Pubs. Assn. 1918 272p (The Chronicles of America ser. v29) $4.45
973.7

1 U.S.—History—Civil War 2 U.S.—Politics and government—Civil War 3 Lincoln, Abraham, President U.S.

Originally published by Yale University Press

"The task imposed upon the volume resolves itself, at bottom, into just two questions: Why was there a war? Why was the Lincoln Government successful? With these two questions always in mind I have endeavored, on one hand, to select and consolidate the pertinent facts; on the other, to make clear . . . their relations in the historical sequence of cause and effect." Preface

Bibliographical note: p261-64

The day of the Confederacy; a chronicle of the embattled South. U.S. Pubs. Assn. 1920 214p (The Chronicles of America ser. v30) $4.45
973.7

1 Confederate States of America—History

Originally published by Yale University Press

Contents: Secession movement; Davis government; Fall of King Cotton; Reaction against Richmond; Critical year; Life in the Confederacy; Turning of the tide; Game of chance; Desperate remedies; Disintegration; Attempted revolution; Last word; Bibliographical note

Wood, William

Captains of the Civil War; a chronicle of the Blue and the Gray. U.S. Pubs. Assn. 1921 424p front maps (The Chronicles of America ser. v31) $4.45
973.7

1 U.S.—History—Civil War—Biography 2 U.S.—History—Civil War—Campaigns and battles

Originally published by Yale University Press

Contents: The clash: 1861; The combatants; Naval war: 1862; River war: 1862; Lincoln: war statesman; Lee and Jackson: 1862-3; Grant wins the River war: 1863; Gettysburg: 1863; Farragut and the navy: 1863-4; Grant attacks the front: 1864; Sherman destroys the base: 1864; The end: 1865; Bibliographical note

973.703 U.S.—Administration of Lincoln, 1861-1865 (Civil War)—Dictionaries

Boatner, Mark Mayo

The Civil War dictionary; maps and diagrams by Allen C. Northrop and Lowell I. Miller. McKay 1959 974p illus maps $15
973.703

1 U.S.—History—Civil War—Dictionaries

"A monumental reference work on the Civil War, its personalities, campaigns, battles, military organizations, weapons, and political events. For the researcher and the serious student of the Civil War period of American history. Included among the other material are about 2,000 brief biographical sketches of major Civil War personalities, military and civil. . . . Extensively cross-referenced." Pub W

Bibliography: p970-74

973.8 U.S.—Later 19th century, 1865-1901

American Heritage

The American Heritage History of the confident years, by the editors of American Heritage, The Magazine of History. Editor in charge: Ralph K. Andrist; narrative: Francis Russell; pictorial commentary: Michael Harwood. Am. Heritage 1969 400p illus boards $17.50
973.8

1 U.S.—History—1865-1898 2 U.S.—History—1898-1919

This "large-format volume is attractive popular history. The 'confident years' were those years from the end of the Civil War up to

American Heritage—*Continued*
America's emergence into the 20th century—
the frontier years when America was largely
rural (even in its thinking), the 'Robber Barons' grabbed financial empires and both Indians and newly-freed Negroes were firmly
put into their 'places' as second-class citizens.
These were also the years when America became a melting pot for ethnic groups, and the
Horatio Alger image was fixed in every young
American's mind. It was, as Francis Russell
notes in his last chapter heading, the time of
'twilight on Elm Street'—out of a jingoistic
war with Spain, America stood up in full confidence, unaware of future wars, nuclear
bombs and sex revolutions." Pub W

Beth, Loren P.
The development of the American Constitution, 1877-1917. Harper 1971 xxvi, 280p
illus (The New American Nation ser) $7.95
                                                        973.8

1 U.S.—Politics and government—1865-1898
2 U.S.—Politics and government—1898-1919
3 U.S.—Constitution
SBN 06-910314-0
"The author traces the evolution of American constitutional institutions and practices
in this period and surveys the events and ideas
which produced the need for constitutional
change. . . . [He suggests that] perhaps the
most important force for change was the
growth of an urban-industrial society." Publisher's note
"Beth presents a very good synopsis of the
interrelationships between the branches of the
Federal government and between Federal,
state, and local governments." Choice
Bibliographical essay: p255-64

Bowers, Claude G.
The tragic era; the revolution after Lincoln. Houghton 1929 xxii, 567p illus $6.95
                                                        973.8

1 U.S.—Politics and government—1865-1898
2 Reconstruction 3 Johnsson, Andrew, President U.S.
"This history recreates the Reconstruction
period after the Civil War, the twelve tragic
years that stretched from the death of Lincoln
to the close of the Grant administration. The
period lives again in this dramatic and fully
documented account of the political corruption of the times." Book Rev Digest
"It bears the unmistakable authenticity of
careful scholarship, hardwork, heartbreaking
research among musty records and forgotten
documents. Yet it moves swiftly. There are few
dull spots among its five hundred pages." Outlook
Manuscripts, books, and newspapers consulted and cited: p541-47

Buck, Paul H.
The road to reunion, 1865-1900. Little
[1964 c1937] 320p pa $1.95   **973.8**
1 U.S.—History—1865-1898   2 U.S.—Politics
and government—1865-1898 3 Reconstruction
First published 1937
Pulitzer Prize, 1938
"This is a treatment of the reconciliation of
North and South in the generation following
the Civil War. Describes economic, social, and
cultural factors. Shows how they wove a new
pattern of national unity. For the first time in
our history we were called upon to deal with
a disaffected people who had aspired to independence and failed." A Guide to Reading in
Am History
Bibliographical footnotes

Faulkner, Harold Underwood
Politics, reform and expansion, 1890-1900.
Harper 1959 312p illus maps (The New American Nation ser) $7.95   **973.8**
1 U.S.—Politics and government—1865-1898
2 U.S.—History—1865-1898
This volume "deals almost exclusively with
the years 1890 to 1900. It is essentially concerned with the politics of the decade, with

the economic history of the period, with efforts to reform and improve many areas of the
existing society, and finally with the new
burst of territorial expansion resulting in part
from the Spanish-American War." Preface
"The author does justice to the intellectual
and political high points of the period. . . . Impressive evidence of primary sources in the
bibliographical essay." Library J

Fleming, Walter Lynwood
The sequel of Appomattox; a chronicle of
the reunion of the states. U.S. Pubs. Assn.
1919 332p (The Chronicles of America ser.
v32) $4.45   **973.8**

1 U.S.—History—1865-1898 2 Reconstruction

Originally published by Yale University Press
Contents: Aftermath of war; When freedom
cried out; Work of the presidents; Wards of
the nation; Victory of the radicals; Rule of the
major generals; Trial of President Johnson;
Union League of America; Church and school;
Carpetbag and Negro rule; Ku Klux movement; Changing South; Restoration of home
rule; Bibliographical note

Ford, Henry Jones
The Cleveland era; a chronicle of the new
order in politics. U.S. Pubs. Assn. 1919 232p
(The Chronicles of America ser. v44) $4.45
                                                        973.8

1 U.S.—History—1865-1898   2 U.S.—Politics
and government—1865-1898

Originally published by Yale University Press
Contents: Transition period; Political groping and party fluctuation; Advent of Cleveland;
Constitutional crisis; Party policy in Congress; Presidential knight-errantry; Public
discontents; Republican opportunity; Free silver revolt; Law and order upheld; Bibliographical note

Franklin, John Hope
Reconstruction: after the Civil War. Univ.
of Chicago Press 1961 258p illus (The Chicago History of American civilization) $5
                                                        973.8

1 Reconstruction   2 U.S.—History—1865-1898

The author treats Reconstruction as a tributary of the main stream of American civilization with its source in the ante bellum period.
He examines the subtleties of the period and
reduces the exaggeration of former views,
points out many fallacies which still impede
the solution of problems left by the Civil War.
He concludes the ending of Reconstruction is
traced to a combination of Southern corruption
and lack of interest of the North. (Publisher)
"Although individual phases of Reconstruction history have been revised, no dispassionate general account incorporating these findings has ever been published. It is only now
that this need has been filled by the appearance of Professor Franklin's excellent book."
Am Hist R
Suggested reading: p232-42

Reeder, Red
The story of the Spanish-American War.
Duell 1966 179p maps $4.95   **973.8**

1 U.S.—History—War of 1898

The author "goes into the background of
the war, including the tremendous influence of
the yellow press in urging the conflict on the
United States. Since the volume is short, only
the highlights of the campaign can be covered,
with the scene shifting about the world from
Manila Bay to San Juan Hill. Desspite its brevity the volume covers the war and perhaps
will lead . . . readers to more detailed accounts
as found in the books listed in the bibliography." Best Sellers

Sandoz, Mari

The Battle of the Little Bighorn. Lippincott 1966 191p maps (Great battles of history ser) boards $5.95   **973.8**

1 Little Big Horn, Battle of the, 1876 2 Custer, George Armstrong

In this account of the defeat of Custer's troops by the Sioux Indianss, the author analyzes Custer's motives and "the underlying reason for the Army expedition and for the convocation of Indians on the Little Bighorn that particular year." Publisher's note

"A stern criticism of Lt. Col. George Armstrong Custer for his military blunders. . . . This book is not tactics nor logistics but stark tragedy." Pub W

Selected bibliography for the general reader: p185-88

973.9 U.S.—20th century, 1901-

Filler, Louis

(ed.) The President speaks: from William McKinley to Lyndon B. Johnson; ed. with an introduction by Louis Filler. Putnam 1964 416p illus pa $2.25   **973.9**

1 U.S.—History—20th century—Sources 2 Presidents—U.S.—Messages

"A Capricorn Giant"

A reprint of the title first published 1964

Beginning with the editor's essay on the President's role as national spokesman, this book is a collection of statements of twelve American presidents of the twentieth century. Subjetcts of their speeches include progressivism, the first and second World War, the cold war, and the search for peace. (Publisher)

"The point of the anthology is to sum up the United States' situation and problems through the century, as seen by the country's top spokesmen. There are candid short biographies of the Presidents, also." Pub W

973.91 U.S.—Early 20th century, 1901-1953

Allen, Frederick Lewis

The big change; America transforms itself, 1900-1950. Harper 1952 308p boards $6.95, lib. bdg. $5.79   **973.91**

1 U.S.—History—20th century 2 U.S.—Social conditions 3 U.S.—Economic conditions

Sketches of "some of the major changes that took place in the United States during the years 1900-1950. Art, literature, manners morals, sports, business, politics, and the everyday living that took place during this period come under the scrutiny of the author."

A Guide to Reading in Am History

"With great skill in selecting specific facts, conditions and trends, Mr. Allen has painted a series of panoramic pictures, significant individuals in the foreground, representative activities in the middle distance and general ideas in the background. . . . It is so well organized and so briskly presented that it makes for continuosly interesting, and often illuminating, reading." N Y Times Bk R

Sources and obligations: p295-98

Only yesterday; an informal history of the nineteen-twenties. Harper 1957 370p $6.95, lib. bdg. $5.11   **973.91**

1 U.S.—History—1919-1933 2 U.S.—Social conditions 3 U.S.—Economic conditions—1919-1933

First published 1931

"A swiftly moving, well-integrated American chronicle, recording with wit and sagacity 'the fads and fashions and follies of the time, the things which millions of people thought about, and talked about and became excited about and which at once touched their daily lives,' while indicating fundamental trends in national life and thought. . . . Bibliography." N Y Libraries

Daniels, Jonathan

The time between the wars; Armistice to Pearl Harbor. Doubleday 1966 372p illus (Mainstream of America ser) $6.95   **973.91**

1 U.S.—History—1919-1933 2 U.S.—History—1933-1945

This book "begins with the return of Woodrow Wilson bearing the covenant of the League of Nations and the determined opposition of Senator Lodge, with the coming of prohibition and Secretary of the Navy Joseph Daniels' 'cleaning up' of New Orleans. It tells of Lucy Mercer, the 'other woman' of FDR's married life, of labor, bootleggers, Charles Lindbergh, and the coming of WW II." Bk Buyer's Guide

This period "is replete with drama; but, to the uninitiated, a welter of confusion. Under the . . . guidance of Mr. Daniels, however, the confusion is resolved." Best Sellers

Sources and acknowledgments: p347-53

Dos Passos, John

Mr Wilson's war. Doubleday 1962 517p illus (Mainstream of America ser) $7.50   **973.91**

1 Wilson, Woodrow, President U.S. 2 European War, 1914-1918 3 U.S.—Politics and government—1898-1919

An account of "American and world history from McKinley's assassination, 1901, through the first world war and the failure of the League of Nations to Wilson's death in 1924. Dos Passos has sketched briefly but unforgettably Theodore Roosevelt, William Jennings Bryan, Colonel Edward House, Edith Wilson, the President, Clemenceau, David Lloyd George, and many others." Booklist

"Here is taut, selective, but readable history. . . . It is necessarily a condensation. . . . [The author's] method has succeeded in making a concentrated—sometimes too concentrated whole of the momentous events in our early twentieth-century history." Harper

Notes on sources: p499-502. Maps on lining-papers

Faulkner, Harold Underwood

From Versailles to the New Deal; a chronicle of the Harding-Coolidge-Hoover era. U.S. Pubs. Assn. 1950 388p (The Chronicles of America ser. v51) $4.45   **973.91**

1 U.S.—History—1919-1933 2 Harding, Warren Gamaliel, President U.S. 3 Coolidge, Calvin, President U.S. 4 Hoover, Herbert Clark, President U.S.

Originally published by Yale University Press

Contents: End of the great crusade; Isolation and laissez-faire; Normalcy and nationalism; Advance of prosperity; Social confusion; Political corruption; From Harding to Coolidge; Government and business; Plight of farmer and laborer; End of an era; Interlude; Bibliographical note

The author "stresses the political and economic aspects (giving, it must be said, full attention to the brighter phases of this period of national expansion), but he does not neglect the social and cultural flow." N Y Times Bk R

Hofstadter, Richard

The age of reform; from Bryan to F.D.R. Knopf 1955 328, xx p $6.95   **973.91**

1 U.S.—Politics and government—1898-1919 2 U.S.—Politics and government—1919-1933

Awarded Pulitzer Prize, 1956

This analysis of the reform movements in American politics from 1890-1940 reviews: (1) The agrarian uprising that found its expression in the Populist movement of the 1890's; (2) The Progressive movement from about 1900-1914; (3) The New Deal of the 1930's. Emphasis is placed upon the ideas of the leading political reformers, their aims and techniques, and the combined effect of all of these things upon American thinking

"By concentrating upon what reformers thought rather than upon their political antics Hofstadter has made a unique and valuable contribution." Sat R

Bibliographical footnotes

Howland, Harold

Theodore Roosevelt and his times; a chronicle of the progressive movement. U.S. Pubs. Assn. 1921 289p (The Chronicles of America ser. v47) $4.45 973.91

1 U.S.—History—1898-1919 2 Roosevelt, Theodore, President U.S. 3 U.S.—Politics and government—1898-1919

Originally published by Yale University Press

Contents: Young fighter; In the New York Assembly; Champion of civil service reform; Haroun Al Roosevelt; Fighting and breakfasting with Platt; Roosevelt becomes president; Square deal for business; Square deal for labor; Reclamation and conservation; Being wise in time; Rights, duties, and revolutions; Taft administration; Progressive Party; Glorious failure; Fighting edge; Last four years; Bibliographical note

Link, Arthur S.

Woodrow Wilson and the progressive era, 1910-1917. Harper 1954 331p illus maps (New American Nation ser) $7.95 973.91

1 U.S.—History—1898-1919 2 Wilson, Woodrow, President U.S.

"This book represents an attempt to comprehend and recreate the political and diplomatic history of the United States from the beginning of the disruption of the Republican party in 1910 to the entrance of the United States into the First World War in 1917." Preface

Essay on sources: p283-313

Lord, Walter

The good years; from 1900 to the First World War. Harper 1960 369p illus maps lib. bdg. $5.79 973.91

1 U.S.—History—1898-1919 2 U.S.—Civilization

In this account of the United States from 1900-1914, the author concentrates on such major episodes as "the Americans beseiged along with other nationals in the Boxer rebellion; McKinley's assassination; railroad speculation; the Wrights' new flying machine; the San Francisco earthquake-fire; union troubles; the bank panic of 1907; Peary's expedition to the North Pole; the woman suffrage movement." Pub W

"It is a series of brilliantly written chapters which add up to a fascinating picture of American life. While not profound or outwardly scholarly, it is nevertheless an accurate and at the same time lively story. . . . The book is history and reading entertainment at its best." Christian Century

Published material: p348-54

Mowry, George E.

The era of Theodore Roosevelt, 1900-1912. Harper 1958 330p illus (The New American Nation ser) $7.95 973.91

1 Roosevelt, Theodore, President U.S. 2 U.S.—Politics and government—1898-1919

"The first group of chapters deals with the economic, intellectual and political currents of the period and culminates in [an] analysis of 'the progressive profile.' The central section covers the years of Roosevelt's Presidency, with emphasis upon politics, legislation and foreign policy. The final chapters take up the administration of 'the troubled Taft' and the confused political cross-currents that so rapidly led to Republican decline and ultimately opened the door to the Democrats' triumphant return to political power in 1913." N Y Times Bk R

"Of the great scholarship so admirably put to work it is hardly necessary to speak. There are one or two odd errors. . . . It is possible that Taft is too severely treated. . . . But these are trivial blemishes in a masterly and very readable book." Times (London) Lit Sup

Bibliography: p297-316

Schlesinger, Arthur M. 1917-

The crisis of the old order, 1919-1933, by Arthur M. Schlesinger, Jr. Houghton 1957 557p (The Age of Roosevelt, v 1) $10 973.91

1 U.S.—History—1919-1933 2 Roosevelt, Franklin Delano, President U.S.

The first of a series "interpreting the . . . history of our times in terms of Franklin Delano Roosevelt the controversial figure who became its spokesman and its symbol." Publisher's note

"This brilliantly written work covers the period from 1920 to FDR's inauguration. Rich in anecdote and conversation, it is also admirable in describing the conditions which led to the New Deal. Both friendly to Roosevelt and critical of him. Long, but not too long." Sec Ed Brd

Notes: p489-542

Followed by: The coming of the New Deal, and The politics of upheaval, class 973.917

Seymour, Charles

Woodrow Wilson and the World War; a chronicle of our own times. U.S. Pubs. Assn. 1921 382p (The Chronicles of America ser. v48) $4.45 973.91

1 Wilson, Woodrow, President U.S. 2 European War, 1914-1918—U.S.

Originally published by Yale University Press

Contents: Wilson the executive; Neutrality; The submarine; Plots and preparedness; America decides; Nation in arms; Home front; Fighting front; Path to peace; Ways of the Peace Conference; Balance of power or League of Nations; The settlement; Senate and the treaty; Conclusion; Bibliographical note

Shannon, David A.

Between the wars: America, 1919-1941. Houghton 1965 259p illus (Houghton Mifflin Books in American history) pa $3.50 973.91

1 U.S.—History—1919-1933 2 U.S.—History—1933-1945

"This present volume might well be subtitled 'a study in recent historical myth and counter-myth.' For at the start of each chapter Professor Shannon has listed the misconceptions about the period between the two great World Wars which prevailed among contemporaries. The most important of these, according to the author, were the assumptions that the Republicans were responsible for inaugurating post-World War I conservatism, that these same Republicans sought to turn social problems back to the nineteenth century, that Franklin Roosevelt was victorious over the great depression, and that he was either a far-sighted statesman or [a demagogue]. . . . The author proceeds to examine each of these beliefs and many more in the light of the most recent scholarship." Editorial foreword

Selected bibliography: p243-51

973.917 U.S.—Administration of Franklin D. Roosevelt, 1933-1945

Baker, Leonard

Roosevelt and Pearl Harbor. Macmillan (N Y) 1970 356p illus $8.95 973.917

1 U.S.—History—1933-1945 2 Roosevelt, Franklin Delano, President U.S. 3 World War, 1939-1945—Causes 4 Pearl Harbor, Attack on, 1941

"The book is a thorough and detailed study of relevant developments from FDR's third inauguration in January, 1941, to the approach of Japanese squadrons to Pearl Harbor on December 7. . . . [The author] offers a firm picture and a reasoned justification for FDR's balancing act on the home front between interventionists and isolationists." Pub W

Acknowledgments, sources, and notes: p314-44

Brogan, Denis William

The era of Franklin D. Roosevelt; a chronicle of the New Deal and global war. U.S. Pubs. Assn. 1950 382p (The Chronicles of America ser. v52) $4.45   973.917

1 U.S.—History—1933-1945 2 Roosevelt, Franklin Delano, President U.S. 3 U.S.—Politics and government—1933-1945

Originally published by Yale University Press
Contents: Panic and depression, 1930-1933; Election of Roosevelt; Meeting the crisis; Light that failed; NRS; Needy and the insecure; Some emergency problems; Bankrupt farmers and the AAA; Revolt of labor; Second Roosevelt landslide; Battle over the Supreme Court; Dazzling TVA; Storm and stress, 1936-1939; Recession in a darkening world; Third-term battle; Question of national unity; War tasks of the Roosevelt administration, 1940-1944; Fourth campaign; Roosevelt's death; Bibliographical note

Freidel, Frank

(ed.) The New Deal and the American people. Prentice-Hall 1964 151p (Eyewitness accounts of American history) pa $1.95   973.917

1 U.S.—Politics and government—1933-1945 2 U.S.—Economic conditions—1933-1945

"A Spectrum book"
A "cross section of popular opinion on the New Deal. Freidel includes the writings of small men and of critical analysts such as Sherwood Anderson and William Kiplinger. Of particular worth are the words of the migrant workers, the midwestern pig farmers, and the CCC campers. This is a human record of the thirties." A Guide to Reading in Am History

Leuchtenburg, William E.

Franklin D. Roosevelt and the New Deal, 1932-1940. Harper 1963 393p illus (The New American Nation ser) $7.95   973.917

1 U.S.—History—1933-1945 2 Roosevelt, Franklin Delano, President U.S. 3 U.S.—Economic conditions—1933-1945

This study concerns "what happened to American society during the Great Depression. . . . [It] gives a penetrating picture of the Depression and the immense changes the thirties brought about: the growth of big government, of labor and farm group empires, of a new concern for social welfare, and of the increased political and social importance of ethnic groups." Huntting
"The author's bias, in spite of reasonably successful attempts to present both sides of major controversies, is plainly pro-Roosevelt. . . . The New Deal's failures, however, are as honestly described as its successes." Library J
Bibliography: p349-63

Schlesinger, Arthur M. 1917-

The coming of the New Deal, by Arthur M. Schlesinger, Jr. Houghton 1959 [c1958] 669p (The Age of Roosevelt, v2) $10   973.917

1 U.S.—History—1933-1945 2 Roosevelt, Franklin Delano, President U.S.

"The second volume in 'The Age of Roosevelt' [following: The crisis of the old order, in class 973.91] tells of the years following F.D.R.'s inauguration with the author's incisive observations on New Deal policies and their success as well as the detractors and antagonists with whom the President had to struggle." The Bookseller
"The impact of the depression on private lives and the government's response to great need in the shadow of great peril—the whole story of a society in trouble—are the subjects. . . . It is a brilliant union of political, social economic and intellectual history." Library J
Notes: p589-639
Followed by: The politics of upheaval, listed below

The politics of upheaval, by Arthur M. Schlesinger, Jr. Houghton 1960 749p (The Age of Roosevelt, v3) $10   973.917

1 U.S.—History—1933-1945 2 Roosevelt, Franklin Delano, President U.S.

The third volume of: The age of Roosevelt, following: The crisis of the old order, class 973.91, and The coming of the New Deal, entered above
"The continuing ferment, experimentation, excitement—and some setbacks and internal feuds—of Roosevelt's New Deal in 1935 and 1936 form the body of this chronicle. . . . Schlesinger's brilliant account brings together all the threads of the country's economic and political life, when it was still depressed but recovering. There are views of the most important political figures of the day, from Frankfurter to Landon; excellent evaluations of the Supreme Court's anti-New Deal decisions, of the TVA's evolution, of the reorganization of the Democratic Party. . . . [It is] absorbing historical writing." Pub W
Notes: p659-717

Sherwood, Robert E.

Roosevelt and Hopkins; an intimate history. Rev. ed. Harper 1950 1002p illus map $15   973.917

1 U.S.—Politics and government—1933-1945 2 Roosevelt, Franklin Delano, President U.S. 3 Hopkins, Harry Lloyd 4 World War, 1939-1945—U.S.

First published 1948. Awarded Pulitzer Prize, 1949
The inside story about the Second World War and the critical years 1941-1945. "This is the story Harry Hopkins would have told had he lived . . . the full story . . . from the point of view of one who stood at the center with Roosevelt and saw it whole. With 32 pages of illustrations and reproductions of documents and letters." Huntting
"A distinguished biography that is too long for the casual reader but should be brought to the attention of older young people with broad interests." Booklist
Bibliographical references included in Notes: p937-84

Tugwell, Rexford G.

FDR: architect of an era. Macmillan (N Y) 1967 270p illus $4.95   973.917

1 Roosevelt, Franklin Delano, President U.S. 2 U.S.—Politics and government—1933-1945 3 U.S.—Social policy

This book "is meant to describe the transformations that took place during the Roosevelt years, to speak of his education in politics, and to show how he used its arts to achieve the well-being of the nation, then peace. His intention was to start something that would never end. This record is meant to show what that was, and how it was brought about." Introduction
"There is very little new material here, and Tugwell does not dwell on any of the controversies which have developed around the Roosevelt Administration. Tugwell's warm admiration and friendship for Roosevelt and his flowing style make for pleasurable reading." Library J
Some additional readings: p265-66

Wecter, Dixon

The age of the great depression, 1929-1941. Macmillan (N Y) 1948 362p illus (History of American life ser) $8.95   973.917

1 Depressions 2 U.S.—Economic conditions 3 U.S.—Social life and customs 4 U.S.—Politics and government—1933-1945

A social, "economic and political panorama of the United States from 1929 to 1941 with the New Deal as the focal point." Cincinnati
"As a source book on the depression under Hoover and Roosevelt, what it did to America physically and spiritually, [this] will long be used by students. A tendency toward academic stuffiness is more than balanced by its solid factual contribution." N Y Times Bk R
Critical essay on authorities: p317-42

973.918 U.S.—Administration of Truman, 1945-1953

Acheson, Dean
Present at the creation; my years in the State Department. Norton 1969 798p illus maps $12.50   973.918
1 U.S.—Politics and government—1945-1953
2 U.S. Department of State 3 U.S.—Foreign relations
SBN 393-07448-X
Awarded Pulitzer Prize, 1970
During a period that included World War II, European reconstruction, Israel's independence, the Korean War, the formation of the U.N., and McCarthyism, Acheson served in the State Department—leaving as the Secretary of State in 1953. In his book he recounts these events and their political significance
"Mr. Acheson's insights into the administrations under which he served and the perspective that he has retained through the years provide an invaluable contribution to the annals of history." Cincinnati
Bibliography included in References: p770-78

973.92 U.S.—Later 20th century, 1953-

Lester, Julius
Search for a new land; history as subjective experience. Dial Press 1969 195p $4.95
                    973.92
1 U.S.—History—20th century
"Combining autobiography, contemporary history, and 'found' poetry, a sensitive black militant reveals the frustrations of his life, the sickness in American society, and a revolutionary hope for the future." Top of the News
"Readers will get an idea of what it's like to be black, but they will also get a compassionate explanation of white middle-aged cops, beatniks, and hippies. Mr. Lester has articulated difficult emotions and experiences in a deceptively simple style. Some librarians may need to read the book before purchasing, as there are a number of expressions often considered obscene." Library J

973.922 U.S.—Administration of Kennedy, 1961-1963

Kennedy, John F.
The burden and the glory. . . . Ed. by Allan Nevins; foreword by Lyndon B. Johnson. Harper 1964 293p $6   973.922
1 U.S.—Politics and government—1961- 2 U.S.—Foreign relations
"The hopes and purposes of President Kennedy's second and third years in office as revealed in his public statements and addresses." Title page
"The speeches range from a 'State of the Union' message to the speech that was to be made in Dallas on Nov. 22, 1963, and Nevins' brief and informal explanatory notes set each speech in perspective." Library J
Kennedy's "visions and extraordinary personality are both reflected in these speeches." Best Sellers

Kennedy, Robert F.
Thirteen days; a memoir of the Cuban missile crisis; with introductions by Robert S. McNamara and Harold Macmillan   973.922
1 U.S.—Politics and government—1961- 2 U.S.—Foreign relations—Russia 3 Russia—Foreign relations—U.S. 4 Cuba—History—1959-
Some editions are:
Norton $5.50
Watts, F. $8.95 Large type edition

The late Senator Kennedy wrote this "account of the October, 1962, Cuban missile crisis in the fall of 1967, from his diaries and recollections. It brings to the world a fuller understanding of the events and their sequence than might otherwise have been possible, and of the decisive and statesmanlike action of President Kennedy. The drama is in the events themselves." Pub W

Schlesinger, Arthur M. 1917-
A thousand days; John F. Kennedy in the White House [by] Arthur M. Schlesinger, Jr. Houghton 1965 1087p $9   973.922
1 Kennedy, John Fitzgerald, President U.S.
2 U.S.—Politics and government—1961-
Awarded the Pulitzer Prize for biography, 1965
This account of John F. Kennedy's Presidency reveals the personality and politics of the late President and describes the men of his administration. It covers the campaign and trips abroad, the issues of Cuba, civil rights, and other crises. (Publisher)
"Schlesinger is not an altogether dispassionate chronicler. . . . But if he frequently hymns the Kennedy Administration, he also limns it with objectivity and perception. . . . [He] has managed—by using state papers, letters and personal interviews—to reconstruct the period so skillfully that the result is not so much a personal memoir as a penetrating, balanced ledger of the Kennedy Administration. . . . Schlesinger excels at providing the illuminating stray quote or the odd fact that firmly fixes a character in the reader's mind. . . . Kennedy indeed saw himself and his office in princely Shakespearean verse. The prose of attendant-lord Schlesinger does him no disservice." Time
Bibliographical footnotes

Sorensen, Theodore C.
The Kennedy legacy. Macmillan (N Y) 1969 414p $6.95   973.922
1 Kennedy, John Fitzgerald, President U.S.
2 U.S.—Politics and government—1961-
3 Kennedy, Robert Francis
"Basing his observations on his long association with the Kennedy brothers, Sorensen analyzes the gifts of ideas, beliefs, dreams, and hopes left by John and Robert Kennedy. . . . [He] traces the Kennedy ideas as they evolved from the brothers' education, their wealth, their family, and all the associations which these brought. He gives interesting insights into the methods of approach on the Vietnam conflict developed by the two brothers. The book is a plea for the Kennedy legacy of human rights, of peace all over the world, of reform in our governmental institutions, of better quality in our culture and environment and of faith in our youth. The emphasis on youth and what must be done to 'connect' with the young people today is a dominant theme." Library J

973.923 U.S.—Administration of Lyndon B. Johnson, 1963-1969

Goldman, Eric F.
The tragedy of Lyndon Johnson. Knopf 1969 531, xxi p $8.95   973.923
1 Johnson, Lyndon Baines, President U.S.
2 U.S.—Politics and government—1961-
The author, who served as Special Consultant to President Johnson in the latter's effort to establish a link between the federal government and the American intellectual community describes his experiences. He discusses the national and international political events that he was witness to, and the effect of President Johnson's complex nature on those events and on those around him
"The big events are here, described much as we might view intimate newsreels of yesterday's headlines today: the railway strike, the Vietnam escalation, Santo Domingo, the White House Festival of the Arts . . . even Lady Bird's beautification program. Goldman is more moved than mocking; he writes with understanding of LBJ's dilemmas." Pub W

974   Northeastern states. New England

Andrews, Charles M.
The fathers of New England; a chronicle of the Puritan commonwealths. U.S. Pubs. Assn. 1919 210p (The Chronicles of America ser. v6) $4.45   **974**

1 New England—History—Colonial period

Originally published by Yale University Press
Contents: Coming of the Pilgrims; Bay Colony; Completing the work of settlement; Early New England life; Attempt at colonial union; Winning the charters; Massachusetts defiant; Wars with the Indians; Bay Colony disciplined; Andros régime in New England; End of an era; Bibliographical note

974.7   New York (State)

Carmer, Carl
The Hudson; illus. by Stow Wengenroth. Farrar 1939 434p illus map (Rivers of America) $6   **974.7**

1 Hudson River 2 Hudson Valley—History 3 New York (State)—Social life and customs

"Famous boats, eminent men, beautiful scenery, and hot political strife have combined to make the Hudson one of the most storied rivers in this country, and Mr. Carmer has captured most engagingly its charm and its spirit." Cincinnati
Bibliography: p408-21

Goodwin, Maud Wilder
The Dutch and English on the Hudson; a chronicle of colonial New York. U.S. Pubs. Assn. 1919 243p (The Chronicles of America ser. v7) $4.45   **974.7**

1 New York (State)—History 2 Dutch in the U.S.

Originally published by Yale University Press
Contents: Up the great river; Traders and settlers; Patroons and lords of the manor; The directors; Domines and school-teachers; The burghers; Neighbors of New Netherland; Early English governors; Leisler; Privateers and pirates; Colonial government in the eighteenth century; Zenger trial; Negro plots; Sir William Johnson; Bibliographical note

Irving, Washington
Knickerbocker's History of New York; ed. by Anne Carroll Moore; with pictorial pleasantries by James Daugherty. Ungar [1959 c1956] 427p illus $6.50   **974.7**

1 New York (State)—History

First published 1928 by Doubleday
"In this charming and especially readable edition available again after many years, noted writer and editor Anne Carroll Moore has created a shorter, simpler version that makes Knickerbocker more accessible to today's readers. . . . Irving concentrated on a considerable amount of the history of old New Amsterdam and the Hudson Valley region in his humorous history, which starts with the momentous voyage of Henry Hudson and ends with the defeat of gallant Peter Stuyvesant, the Dutch governor, by the British." Publisher's note

974.71   New York (City)

Lindsay, John V.
The city. Norton 1970 240p $5.95   **974.71**

1 New York (City)—Politics and government 2 New York (City)—Social conditions 3 Municipal government—U.S.
SBN 393-05387-3

The author uses his specific New York City experiences in municipal politics to survey the broader problem. He explains "what the conditions are that have led New York City to its present state, and why he believes that the reforms he has tried to make can come to grips with the problems confronting the city. . . . [Topics included are] urban renewal, housing and rent control, municipal reorganization, finance, education and decentralization, crime, police reallocation, cultural development, and welfare." Publisher's note
Lindsay "displays a rare literacy, humor and wit throughout [the book]." Pub W

975   Southeastern states

Dodd, William E.
The cotton kingdom; a chronicle of the Old South. U.S. Pubs. Assn. 1919 161p (The Chronicles of America ser. v27) $4.45   **975**

1 Southern States—History 2 Cotton

Originally published by Yale University Press
Contents: The lower South in 1850; Rise of the cotton magnates; Social philosophy of the cotton-planter; Life and literature in the lower South; Religion and education; Planter in politics; Bibliographical note

Johnston, Mary
Pioneers of the Old South; a chronicle of English colonial beginnings. U.S. Pubs. Assn. 1918 260p (The Chronicles of America ser. v5) $4.45   **975**

1 Southern States—History

Originally published by Yale University Press
Contents: Three ships sail; The adventurers; Jamestown; John Smith; "Sea adventure"; Sir Thomas Dale; Young Virginia; Royal government: Maryland; Church and kingdom; Commonwealth and Restoration; Nathaniel Bacon; Rebellion and change; The Carolinas; Alexander Spotswood; Georgia; Navigation laws; Bibliographical notes

Thompson, Holland
The new South; a chronicle of social and industrial evolution. U.S. Pubs. Assn. 1919 250p (The Chronicles of America ser. v42) $4.45   **975**

1 Southern States—History 2 Southern States—Social conditions

Originally published by Yale University Press
Contents: The background; The Confederate soldier takes charge; Revolt of the common man; The farmer and the land; Industrial development; Labor conditions; Problem of black and white; Educational progress; South of today; Repudiation of state debts; Bibliographical note

975.3   Washington, D.C. White House

Jensen, Amy La Follette
The White House and its . . . families; Howard C. Jensen, art editor. McGraw illus $14.95   **975.3**

1 Washington, D.C. White House 2 Presidents —U.S.

First published 1958 and periodically revised to keep up to date
Hundreds of photographs and text describe the changes that have taken place in the building, decor, and use of the White House as well as the lives of its occupants since 1800
Bibliography: p[323-25]

We, the people: the story of the United States Capitol, its past and its promise. United States Capitol Historical Society. [distributed by Grosset] illus maps $3.95   **975.3**

1 Washington, D.C.—Capitol

We, the people: the story of the United States Capitol, its past and its promise —*Continued*

Text by Lonnelle Aikman. Produced by the National Geographic Society

Annual. First published 1963

A portrait of the Capitol and its significance in American history. "A map indicating the use of each room in the building and detailed photographs of architectural curiosities are examples of the many features in this handsome book." Library J

Efforts "have been taken to make it an accurate and graphic portrait of a structure within whose walls . . . a Government truly 'of the people' has evolved." Foreword to the first edition

White House Historical Association, Washington, D.C.

The White House; an historic guide. The Association [distributed by Grosset] illus lib. bdg. $4.59   975.3

1 Washington, D.C. White House

Published with the cooperation of the National Geographic Society

First published 1962. Frequently revised

This book traces the changing appearance of the White House through many administrations. It describes life in the White House under different presidents as well as its great furniture, paintings, collections of china, vermeil, and the furnishings of the official rooms

"Pictorial guide filled with excellent color plates." Library J

Maps on lining-papers

Wolff, Perry

A tour of the White House with Mrs John F. Kennedy. Doubleday 1962 258p illus $10   975.3

1 Washington, D.C. White House 2 Onassis, Jacqueline Lee (Bouvier) Kennedy

A description of Mrs Kennedy's television tour of the White House in February 1962. It consists, in part, of her answers to Charles Collingwood's questions about the house, its furnishings, and its history, with some comments made by the late President. (Publisher)

This is "an extremely handsome book with a great amount of fascinating information, much of which, the chapter on the first ladies, for example, was not in the TV broadcast. . . . Illustrations, 158 in black and white and eight in color, are selected from the electronic pictures plus some 300 unposed photographs taken during the TV tour. Floor plans." Pub W

Bibliography: p251-53

975.5   Virginia

American Heritage

Jamestown; first English colony, by the editors of American Heritage, The Magazine of History. Author: Marshall W. Fishwick; consultant: Parke Rouse, Jr. Am. Heritage 1965 151p illus maps boards $5.95, lib. bdg. $5.49   975.5

1 Jamestown, Va.—History

"American Heritage Junior library"

Illustrated with numerous maps, prints, and photographs, this is "the story of Jamestown, from the early days under Captain John Smith to 1699, when England's first overseas colony became the capital of the prosperous colony of Virginia." Bk Buyer's Guide

"The writing is crisply straightforward, and it is objective in treating of such often-dramatized subjects as Pocahontas, the Lost Colony, and the Starving Time." Chicago. Children's Book Center

Further reading: p151

Barbour, Philip L.

Pocahontas and her world; a chronicle of America's first settlement in which is related the story of the Indians and the Englishmen, particularly Captain John Smith, Captain Samuel Argall, and Master John Rolfe. Houghton 1970 [c1969] xx, 320p illus maps $7.95   975.5

1 Jamestown, Va.—History 2 Pocahontas

This is "a history intended to pinpoint Pocahontas as a personality and to emphasize her contribution to American history. Because of the dearth of documentation concerning his heroine, Barbour is forced to rely largely on speculation and though he demonstrates her part in furthering friendly relations between the Indians and colonists, she remains a dim figure and after her voyage to England a rather pathetic one. For the most part the book is a detailed report on the fortunes of the troubled colony and the men who controlled them." Booklist

"The legend of Pocahontas has continued to exert fascination on generations of American students. . . . Mr. Barbour has here written an account that changes some aspects of the legend and clarifies others. . . . [The book] has considerable value for anyone interested in knowing more of the early days of the Virginia Colony." America

Bibliography: p283-99

976   South central states. Old Southwest

Skinner, Constance Lindsay

Pioneers of the Old Southwest; a chronicle of the dark and bloody ground. U.S. Pubs. Assn. 1919 304p (The Chronicles of America ser. v18) $4.45   976

1 [Southwest, Old   2 Kentucky—History 3 Tennessee—History   4 Boone, Daniel

Originally published by Yale University Press

"This narrative is founded largely on original sources—on the writings and journals of pioneers and contemporary observers." Acknowledgment

Contents: Tread of pioneers; Folkways; The trader; Passing of the French peril; Boone, the wanderer; Fight for Kentucky; Dark and bloody ground; Tennessee; King's Mountain; Sevier, the statemaker; Boone's last days; Bibliographical note

976.4   Texas

Fehrenbach, T. R.

Lone Star; a history of Texas and the Texans. Macmillan (N Y) 1968 751p $10   976.4

1 Texas—History

This title "traces the history of Texas from the arrival of the earliest Old American race 40,000 years ago through the agonies of the Spanish and French invasions and the heyday of the cotton, cattle, and oil empires of the 19th and 20th centuries to the tragic Kennedy assassination in 1963 and its aftermath." Publisher's note

"Footnotes and bibliography are regrettably lacking but Mr. Fehrenbach's scholarship is broad and substantial; above all, he brings to what is so often told as a largely conventional record of wars and politics numerous stimulating sociological, sharply contemporary, analyses of the past." Va Q R

Map on lining-papers

Lord, Walter

A time to stand. Harper 1961 255p illus maps lib. bdg. $5.49   976.4

1 Alamo—Siege, 1836

Lord, Walter—*Continued*

On the morning of March 6, 1836, in an abandoned mission called the Alamo, a small Texas garrison fought to the death rather than yield to an overwhelming army of Mexicans. This detailed account of the siege of the Alamo tells much about the men on both sides who played their part in the struggle. (Publisher)

"Well-written, based on perusal of much material previously unused . . . [this] presents both sides with care and understanding. . . . Beyond apt characterizations, 'A Time to Stand' is marked by good balance between narrative and analysis. One of the best contributions is Mr. Lord's account of why the Texans stayed in the Alamo." N Y Times Bk R

Sources: p227-46

977 North central states

Havighurst, Walter

(ed.) The Great Lakes reader. Macmillan (N Y) 1966 421p illus $7.95   977

1 Great Lakes 2 American prose literature

This collection of Americana "includes the tales of Indian traders, field notes of geologists and surveyors, stories of landlookers and prospectors, records of Indian agents, the logs of schoonermen and steamboat captains, the diaries of travelers and emigrants, accounts of the building of canals and harbors and of the surging freshwater commerce . . . [as well as] accounts by historians and biographers who see their story in context and perspective. But original sources are the best, and the first aim of this 'Reader' is to recall men and moments from the past." Introduction

"The source material in this anthology has more than regional value for high school history students." Booklist

Map on lining-papers

The heartland: Ohio, Indiana, Illinois; illus. by Grattan Condon. Harper 1962 400p illus map (A Regions of America bk) $8.95   977

1 Illinois—History 2 Indiana—History 3 Ohio—History

A history in which "giant industry is contrasted with somnolent, fertile fields of giant agriculture. Ohio, Indiana and Illinois emerge as entities and yet are integrally identified with the character of the Midwest. Adventurers and dreamers, agitators and responsible statesmen, Southern Hoosiers and Yankee pioneers, men of many nations and many tongues [who] shaped the destiny of America's heartland [are portrayed]." Publisher's note

"A complete social history results, with economic and political factors all included. . . . A pleasure to read." Library J

Bibliography: p379-88

Ogg, Frederic Austin

The Old Northwest; a chronicle of the Ohio Valley and beyond. U.S. Pubs. Assn. 1919 220p (The Chronicles of America ser. v19) $4.45   977

1 Northwest, Old 2 Ohio Valley—History

Originally published by Yale University Press
Contents: Pontiac's conspiracy; "A lair of wild beasts": The Revolution begins; Conquest completed; Wayne, the scourge of the Indians; Great migration; Pioneer days and ways; Tecumseh; War of 1812 and the New West; Sectional cross currents; Upper Mississippi Valley; Bibliographical note

978 Western states

American Heritage

The American Heritage Book of great adventures of the Old West; comp. by the editors of American Heritage; introduction by Archibald Hanna, Jr. Am. Heritage 1969 384p illus maps $8.95   978

1 The West—History 2 Adventure and adventurers

SBN 8281-0010-1

These 20 stories of adventure "include the gold fever begun near San Francisco in 1847, the saga of the Butterfield stage that first carried mail to California, the storming of the Alamo, tales of mountain men, Lewis and Clark, Indian massacres and battles, Brigham Young's settling of Great Salt Lake valley with his Mormon followers, Chief Geronimo's final surrender to the white man's will." Pub W

"Some of the events described are familiar; others, such as the explorations of David Thompson, are less well known. The readability of these historical studies and the perennial appeal of the subject should attract many." Library J

Billington, Ray Allen

America's frontier heritage. Holt 1966 302p (The Histories of the American frontier) $8.95   978

1 Frontier and pioneer life—The West 2 National characteristics, American

"In this scholarly analysis of America's westward movement . . . [the author] explores the reasons why men moved west, covers the sociological aspects of the frontier life, and discusses the men who flourished in its atmosphere. Extensive notes on each chapter and bibliographical notes [are included]." Library J

The far Western frontier, 1830-1860. Harper 1956 324p illus maps (The New American Nations ser) $7.95   978

1 The West—History 2 Frontier and pioneer life—The West 3 U.S.—Territorial expansion

This history presents a pageant of westward exploration, military conquest, commercial penetration, exploitation and settlement. It also considers the various types of frontiersmen, fur trappers, missionaries, Mormons, forty-niners, etc. and their types of adjustment to the new environment. (Publisher)

It considers "the Frederick Jackson Turner thesis of the frontier as a major influence upon American civilization." A Guide to Reading in Am History

Bibliography: p293-311

De Voto, Bernard

Across the wide Missouri; illus. with paintings by Alfred Jacob Miller, Charles Bodmer and George Catlin; with an account of the discovery of the Miller collection by Mae Reed Porter. Houghton 1947 xxvii, 483p illus $12.50   978

1 The West—History 2 Fur trade 3 Indians of North America

Awarded Pulitzer Prize, 1948

"Narrative of the Rocky Mountain fur trade, 1832-1838, in its relation to western expansion of the United States. These years saw the climax and decline of the trade, but the mountain men, wandering from the Missouri to the Pacific, had by 1838 blazed the trails and opened the country for emigration." Library J

The author's "book is documented carefully; his notes and bibliography are in themselves enough to start any interested reader off on half a lifetime of reading in the field." San Francisco Chronicle

Maps on lining-papers

The year of decision: 1846. Houghton [1950 c1943] 538p maps $7.50   978

1 The West—History 2 U.S.—History—War with Mexico, 1845-1848

A reprint of a title first published 1943 by Little

"A big colorful picture of America west of the Mississippi in the year the Mexican War broke out. A great migration to California and Oregon was afoot, and episodes such as the Donner party tragedy occurred—all related parts, in Mr. De Voto's view, of the culmination of the national movement from the Atlantic to the Pacific. Mr. De Voto researched hard-to-come-by diaries and journals for eye-witness accounts and used them to make the course of history seem dramatic and personal. He shows how from 1845 to 1847 we gained

De Voto, Bernard—*Continued*

the entire Pacific coast when in 1845 we had no land beyond the Rockies." A Guide to Reading in Am History
Statement on bibliography: p523-27

Durham, Philip

The Negro cowboys, by Philip Durham and Everett L. Jones. Dodd 1965 278p illus maps $5   978

1 Negroes—The West 2 Cowboys 3 The West —History

An "account of the Negroes who became trail-hands, heroes, villains, hunted wild horses, and helped to build the new western lands." Bk Buyer's Guide

"The role of the Negro in taming the range country in and north of Texas, is vividly described here. Some of the best mid-19th century riders, ropers, wranglers and cooks—and a few of the most villainous cowboys—were Negroes, the authors say. They estimate that more than 5,000 Negroes rode the range in Texas in the years following the Civil War. . . . Fine true stories of heroism or humor are scattered through this graphic account of the old West." Pub W

Notes: p231-53. Bibliography: p254-70

Haines, Francis

The buffalo. Crowell 1970 242p illus map $7.95   978

1 Bison 2 Frontier and pioneer life—The West 3 Indians of North America

"This is a grand panoramic account of the bison in America from prehistoric times through the heyday of the Plains Indians to the vanishing herds and the recovery of the species. It is also the dramatic story of the horse in Indian culture, and its influence on different tribes. Professor Haines vividly describes buffalo hunts by primitive man, by Indians, and by white pioneers." Pub W

Hough, Emerson

The passing of the frontier; a chronicle of the Old West. U.S. Pubs. Assn. 1918 181p (The Chronicles of America ser. v26) $4.45
978

1 The West—History 2 Frontier and pioneer life—The West

Originally published by Yale University Press

Contents: Frontier in history; The range; Cattle trails; The cowboys; The mines; Pathways o fthe West; Indian Wars; Cattle kings; The homesteader; Bibliographical note

Parkman, Francis

The Oregon Trail   978

1 Oregon Trail 2 The West—Description and travel 3 Frontier and pioneer life—The West 4 Indians of North America

Some editions are:
Dodd (Great illustrated classics) $4.50 With biographical illustrations and pictures of the setting of the book, together with an introduction by Harry Sinclair Drago. Has subtitle: Sketches of prairie and Rocky-Mountain life
Holt $5.50 With an introduction by Mark Van Doren; illustrated by James Daugherty
Watts, F. $7.95 Large type edition, complete and unabridged. A Keith Jennison book

First published in book form, 1849, with title: The California and Oregon Trail

A "true record of the adventures of Parkman and his four companions as they join the great western movement that took place in 1846. He tells of life on the prairie encounters with hostile Indians, buffalo hunts, and the like." Right Book for the Right Child

"The picture of the American prairies in the old savage days before the advent of the railroad and the barbed-wire fence; is historically priceless; and the author's adventurous enthusiasm and indomitable resolution give the autobiography intense interest." Keller's Reader's Digest of Books

Turner, Frederick Jackson

The frontier in American history; with foreword by Ray Allen Billington. Holt 1962 xx, 375p $5.95   978

1 The West—History 2 Frontier and pioneer life—The West

First published 1920 and analyzed in Essay and general literature index

This collection of studies presents the author's thesis "that the significant fact in American history has been the steadily advancing westward frontier. Our national character and ideals and the nature of our democracy have been shaped by it. The volume consists of reprinted papers bearing closely on this theme. There is inevitably some repetition." Wis Lib Bul

"No one volume has done more to reshape the writing of American history or to recast the popularly held image of the American past than this collection." Foreword

979.1   Southwest, New

Hall-Quest, Olga

Conquistadors and Pueblos; the story of the American Southwest, 1540-1848; illus. by Marian Ebert. Dutton 1969 256p map $4.95
979.1

1 Southwest, New—History

A history of the colonization and exploration of our Southwest, primarily of the area in and around New Mexico. The story of this area lies within four civilizations—Indian, Spanish, Mexican and Anglo-American. (Publisher)

"A well-written, authentic and exciting study of the important periods in Southwestern American history. . . . Particularly good is the author's even-handed treatment of both Indian revolts and personalities, and Spanish figures." Library J

Bibliography: p245-47

Stone, Irving

Men to match my mountains; the opening of the Far West, 1840-1900. Doubleday 1956 459p illus (Mainstream of America ser) $8.95
979.1

1 Southwest, New—History 2 Southwest, New —Biography

A history of the settlement of the present states of California, Nevada, Utah and Colorado, told in terms of the people who shaped that history. Included are the stories of such men and events as Sutter and the California gold rush, Brigham Young and the settlement of Utah, and the tragic Donner Party. (Publisher)

"It is a staggering project, boldly handled. Faced with [varying] cultures . . . Mr. Stone has sought unity by following a rigorous chronological progression. At times the device has him jumping from theme to theme and back again with almost bewildering virtuosity. Though results at first seem rather chaotic, the reader is soon won by the author's deft narrative touch." N Y Her Trib Books

Bibliography and sources: p436-42. Maps on lining-papers

Wellman, Paul I.

Glory, God and gold; a narrative history. Doubleday 1954 402p maps (Mainstream of America ser) $7.95   979.1

1 Southwest, New—History

The beginning was in 1540, when Coronado marched north from Mexico into the unexplored territory of the Southwest. The Spanish, French, Indians, Mexicans, and Americans fought for supremacy of this rich land. Massacres, raids, forays and six-shooter battles marked its course from cutlasses and arrows at Chichilticalli to nuclear fission at Los Alamos

"No new discoveries are here, and few deductions that have not been made before, but it is an admirable summary, well organized." N Y Her Trib Books

Some books to read: p389-90

979.4   California

Chidsey, Donald Barr

The California gold rush; an informal history. Crown 1968 208p illus $4.50   **979.4**

1 California—Gold discoveries

"The California Gold Rush of 1848 and 1849 was one of the most electrifying events in American history. When word spread from Sutter's Mill that gold had been discovered, thousands upon thousands of people left home and job and often family to flock to California. The author tells the whole dramatic story." Am News of Bks

Bibliography: p200-04

Thomas, Gordon

The San Fancisco earthquake [by] Gordon Thomas and Max Morgan Witts. Stein & Day 1971 316p illus boards $7.95   **979.4**

1 San Francisco—Earthquake and fire, 1906
SBN 8128-1360-X

In this account of the earthquake, the authors "draw on eye-witness accounts and hitherto untapped historical sources. . . . [They include] not only vignettes of the ordinary man-on-the-crumbling-street, but descriptions of the frenzied activities of San Francisco's Mayor [and] the not always salubrious results of the calling of troops into the stricken city." Pub W

They "have pieced together a mosaic of courage, compassion, ingenuity, and the miraculous." Atlantic

Bibliography: p299-309. Map on lining-papers

White, Stewart Edward

The Forty-niners; a chronicle of the California Trail and El Dorado. U.S. Pubs. Assn. 1918 273p (The Chronicles of America ser. v25) $4.45   **979.4**

1 California—History 2 California—Gold discoveries

Originally published by Yale University Press

Contents: Spanish days; American occupation; Law—military and civil; Gold; Across the plains; The Mormons; Way by Panama; The diggings; Urban Forty-niner; Ordeal by fire; Vigilantes of '51; San Francisco in transition; Storm gathers; Storm breaks; Vigilantes of '56; Triumphs of the Vigilantes; Bibliographical note

979.5   Oregon

Skinner, Constance L.

Adventurers of Oregon; a chronicle of the fur trade. U.S. Pubs. Assn. 1920 290p (The Chronicles of America ser. v22) $4.45 **979.5**

1 Oregon—History 2 Fur trade

Originally published by Yale University Press

Contents: River on the West; Lewis and Clark; Reign of the trapper; The Tonquin; Astor's Overlanders; Astoria under the Northwesters; King of Old Oregon; Fall of the fur kingdom; Bibliographical note

979.8   Alaska

Mathews, Richard

The Yukon; illus. by Bryan Forsyth. Holt 1968 313p illus map (Rivers of America) $7.50   **979.8**

1 Yukon River 2 Alaska—History 3 Canada—History

The author describes the "history and lore of the Yukon River from its source in the Yukon Territory of Canada to its end after 1900 miles in Alaska in the Bering Sea." McClurg. Book News

"An excellent survey of the Yukon's ethnology, history, and economics. The book deals in detail with both early and present-day peoples who settled along the river and the impact of Russian and American explorations and occupations. Stories of the wild Klondike gold stampede, the King salmon run, the dramatic annual spring ice break, and the colorful characters of the territory make this enjoyable reading as well as a useful curriculum adjunct." Library J

Bibliography: p303-08

980   South America

Crow, John A.

The epic of Latin America. Rev. ed. Doubleday 1971 xxvi, 879p illus $12.50   **980**

1 Latin America—History 2 Latin America—Civilization

First published 1946

The author "traces the origin and progress of Latin American civilization from the great pre-Columbian cultures through conquest, colonization and revolution to the militants, militarists and democrats of today." Publisher's note

The book "is well balanced between the 300-year Spanish colonial period and the 150-year post-independence period—between history and culture, religion and economics, politics and international relations. In certain areas it is not wholly satisfying—superficial in treating key figures, too general in analyzing contemporary Latin America. But especially when writing of the past the author's vivid style greatly enhances his subject matter." Pub W

References: p841-48. Map on lining-papers

Gunther, John, 1901-

Inside South America. Harper 1967 610p maps $7.95   **980**

1 South America—Politics 2 South America—Biography 3 South America—Civilization

Supersedes: Inside Latin America, published 1941

"Using the struggle between democracy and Communism to focus the problems and perspectives facing each nation, [the author] gives general impressions, describes leading personalities whom he met, and sketches historical and descriptive background material. Numerous facts crowd the pages." Library J

The author "knows how to do the job. The book is informative, well written, and nicely seasoned with anecdotes and vignettes of personalities. . . . The book, however, lacks depth, and the catchy chapter titles—'Uruguay on the Rocks'—give the impression that the author is less serious than he actually is." Atlantic

Acknowledgements and bibliography: p535-43

Herring, Hubert

A history of Latin America, from the beginnings to present, by Hubert Herring with the assistance of Helen Baldwin Herring. 3d ed. Knopf 1968 xxii, 1002, xxv p maps $14.95   **980**

1 Latin America—History

First published 1955

The story of the Latin American experience from the Indian, Iberian and African backgrounds. Political, cultural, and economic personalities who have appeared in this area are portrayed

This is a "synthesis of a complicated human experience. It is, in fact, an 'Inside Latin America' report which truly penetrates not only the surface area of politics but also the depths of the past that have so clearly conditioned the present reality of our indispensable 'Good Neighbors.'" N Y Her Trib Books

Bibliography: p981-1002

Peck, Anne Merriman

The pageant of South American history; with photogravures and maps. 3d ed. McKay 1962 432p illus maps $6.50   **980**

1 South America—History

Peck, Anne M.—_Continued_
First published 1941 by Longmans
The book is divided into five sections: Native peoples; The conquest of South America; Colonial empires; South American colonies become nations; South America in the twentieth century
"The bibliography is divided to correspond with the five sections, and a lengthy relative index is appended. The author has brought together in impressive fashion social, political, cultural, and economic aspects of history. . . . Section five, South America Today, is less concentrated than preceding sections and can serve well as a guide to the contemporary [i.e. 1962] scene." Chicago. Children's Book Center

Rippy, J. Fred
Latin America; a modern history. New ed. rev. and enl. Univ. of Mich. Press 1968 594, xxii p illus maps (Univ. of Mich. History of the modern world) $10   **980**
1 Latin America—History
First published 1958
"A condensed and yet very full history of the many Latin American nations, including Central and South America, Mexico and several of the West Indies islands; from pre-Columbian times to the [1960's]. Economic social, literary and political aspects of Latin American history are succinctly narrated and appraised. There are useful comparisons to early developments in Europe and North America and some excellent chapters on foreign relations and economic ties to the rest of the world." Pub W
"Mr. Rippy has wisely allotted considerable space to the cultural contributions of the several countries, with some excellent material on the poetry, novels and historical writing of each." N Y Her Trib Books
Suggested readings: p585-94

Shepherd, William R.
The Hispanic nations of the New World; a chronicle of our southern neighbors. U.S. Pubs. Assn. 1919 251p (The Chronicles of America ser. v50) $4.45   **980**
1 Latin America—History
Originally published by Yale University Press
Contents: Heritage from Spain and Portugal; "Our old King or none"; "Independence or death"; Ploughing the sea; Age of the dictators; Peril from abroad; Greater states and lesser; "On the margin of international life"; Republics of South America; Mexico in revolution; Republics of the Caribbean; Pan-Americanism and the Great War; Bibliographical note

980.3 Incas

Métraux, Alfred
The history of the Incas. Tr. from the French by George Ordish. Pantheon Bks. 1969 205p illus map $5.95   **980.3**
1 Incas
Originally published 1961 in French
"A concise but remarkably comprehensive and readable account of a unique civilization, its origins, achievements and decline, describing its social and political structure, the daily life of the people, their religion and their architecture, and the impact of Spanish conquest on the empire and its people to the present day." Am News of Bks
The "ethnologist author is not led astray, like so many romantic utopians, by the supposed ideal socialism of this fascinating Peruvian society. On the contrary, he discards many of the traditional myths that obscure the true nature of Inca civilization; and while deeply sympathetic towards both people and culture, he depicts this primitive collectivist state in the light of our increasing knowledge of other comparable societies. From this standpoint the book deals competently with the Empire's history." Va Q R
Bibliography: p203-05

982 Argentina

Ferns, H. S.
Argentina. Praeger 1969 284p illus maps (Nations of the modern world) $8.50   **982**
1 Argentine Republic—History
The first part of this book "gives the historical background of Argentina until the Great Depression of the 1930's. . . . [The author covers the] rule of Rosas and the . . . achievements of the civilian statesmen Mitre, Pellegrini, Roque Sáenz Peña, and Yrigoyen and explains how the military came to power after the coup of 1943. Under Perón, social and political upheaval upset traditions of authority based on the landed classes. . . . Ferns examines the efforts in present-day Argentina to find a new elite and the place in society of the various classes—the armed forces, landowners, business interest, trade unions." Publisher's note
"Written in a lucid, graceful, highly readable style, beautifully illustrated, and including a marvelous foldout map, this book is essential for university and college libraries, and a valuable addition to public library collections as well." Library J
Bibliography: p267-69

985 Peru

Prescott, William Hickling
History of the conquest of Peru. Introduction by Thomas Seccombe. Dutton 1963 xl, 648p $2.95   **985**
1 Peru—History 2 Incas
"Everyman's library"
"Written in 1847, it remains the standard work on the Spanish conquistadores in the New World." A Guide to Reading in Am History

990 Pacific Ocean islands

Grattan, C. Hartley
The Southwest Pacific since 1900; a modern history; Australia, New Zealand, the Islands, Antarctica. Univ. of Mich. Press 1963 759, xxviii p maps (The Univ. of Mich. History of the modern world) $10   **990**
1 Islands of the Pacific 2 Australia 3 New Zealand 4 Antarctic regions
"Comprehensive political, economic, and cultural history. . . . The book shows Australia and New Zealand growing into vigorous nations increasingly concerned with their place in the world. the islands developing in their economic and strategic importance, and Antarctica becoming a scientific preserve involved in climactic episodes in the nationalistic struggles of several nations for possession of its territory. . . . A colorful narrative." Library J
Includes bibliography

994 Australia

Turnbull, Clive
A concise history of Australia; with 210 illustrations. Viking [1966 c1965] 192p illus $8.50   **994**
1 Australia—History 2 Australia—Civilization
"A Studio book"
This book "describes the transformation of Australia from a penal settlement and pioneering camp to . . . a modern nation with its own national consciousness, its distinctive art and literature, and its individual role in the world today." Publisher's note
"One feels that the text is something of an intrusion on the illustrations. Perhaps it could hold its own, without becoming less readable, if it contained more quotations from original sources, say Captain Cook's journal, or the letters of early settlers, to match the magnificence of lithograph and engraving." New Statesman
Bibliography: p185-86

996.9 Hawaii

Day, A. Grove

Hawaii and its people. Rev. ed. With illus. by John V. Morris. Meredith 1968 356p illus $6.95   **996.9**

1 Hawaii—History

First published 1955

The author shows the life of Hawaii through all its changing eras, covering the period from its discovery by Captain James Cook to the present time. (Publisher)

"A comprehensive one-volume history of the Hawaiian Islands, tightly and interestingly written, tracing the sometimes bloody, sometimes merry track of Hawaii from its discovery." Springf'd Republican

A handy glossary of Hawaiian terms: p327-30. Map on lining-papers

FICTION

It is not possible in a classified catalog to give a comprehensive list of fiction. While it is hoped that the following list is a fair representation of those authors with whom a present-day high school student should be acquainted, it should not be considered as including all the works by these authors that might be suitable. For those users of the Catalog who would like to supplement this list, it is suggested that they consult the eighth edition of FICTION CATALOG, published in 1971

A number of subjects have been added to the books in this section to help in curriculum work. It is not necessarily recommended that these subjects be used in the card catalog

Abé, Kobo

The woman in the dunes; tr. from the Japanese by E. Dale Saunders. With drawings by Marchi Abé. Knopf 1961 239p illus $4.95 **Fic**

1 Japan—Fiction 2 Sand dunes—Fiction

"A symbolic novel about a Japanese entomologist trapped in a strange sanddune village while looking for desert beetles along the coast. In the village the houses are at the bottom of pits, and the villagers spend their lives fighting the encroaching sand. The entomologist, left in such a pit with a widow, tries desperately to escape but in vain." Bk Buyer's Guide

The author "follows with meticulous precision his hero's constantly shifting physical, emotional and psychological states. He also presents the most minute descriptions of the trivia of everyday existence in a sandpit with such compelling realism that these passages serve both to heighten the credibility of the bizarre plot and subtly increase the interior tensions of the novel." N Y Times Bk R

Achebe, Chinua

Arrow of God. Day [1967 c1964] 287p $5.95
Fic

1 Nigeria—Fiction 2 British in Nigeria—Fiction 3 Ibo tribe—Fiction

First published 1964 in England

"Authenticity and simplicity in the telling characterize this story [set in the Ibo villages] of Nigeria where the age-old tribal customs are in continuous conflict with the thoughts and ways of westernization. Ironically it is Ezeulu, Chief Priest of Ulu, who is the one man of all the tribe to send his son to missionary school. Ezeulu and his son are the chief characters, with the English administrator, Captain Winterbottom playing a significant, if secondary role. It is the son's overzealous conversion to Christianity that brings the final clash between Ezeulu and Winterbottom, and ends in tragedy for the Chief Priest." Pub W

Things fall apart. McDowell, Obolensky 1959 215p $5.95   **Fic**

1 Nigeria—Fiction 2 Ibo tribe—Fiction

"The setting is a remote Nigerian village in the late 19th century. The white man and his civilization have not yet made their impact. The life of the village still follows the formal, stately rhythm that has come down through the centuries. For a self-made man like Okonkwo there was pleasant security in this old order of things. A stern but upright man, he lived only to further himself and to insure an untroubled world for his three wives and his numerous children. The conversion of one of his favorite sons to Christianity was the utmost indignity that could befall him. It killed him and it killed his world." N Y Her Trib Books

The story is written in English by a Nigerian. "No European ethnologist could so intimately present this medley of mores of the Ibo tribe, nor detail the intricate formalities of life in the clan. . . . The flashbacks of the book are confusing, the narration undisciplined, but as an objective view of the Ibo customs it is of both interest and value." Sat R

Adams, Andy

The log of a cowboy; pictures by R. Farrington Elwell. Houghton 1927 324p illus $4.75   **Fic**

1 Cowboys—Fiction 2 The West—Fiction

"Riverside bookshelf"

First published 1903

"The journal of a cattle drive, with a herd of several thousand, from Texas through Arkansas and Wyoming to the Blackfoot Agency in Montana. The account is admitted to be an extremely accurate picture of a bygone phase of existence in the Far West." Baker's Historical

Aldrich, Bess Streeter

A lantern in her hand   **Fic**

1 Family—Fiction 2 Frontier and pioneer life —Fiction 3 Nebraska—Fiction

Some editions are:
Appleton $3.50
Grosset $2.95
First published 1928

"The story of a pioneer woman who, as a bride, followed the covered-wagon trail to the Nebraska prairies and lived there the rest of her eighty years. A devoted wife and mother, Abbie Deal brought a large and united family through poverty and hardship." Cleveland

The author "does make bearing children, and loving them, and teaching them, and cheerfully giving up all the world that they might have it instead, seem worth doing." Sat R

Allen, Hervey

Anthony Adverse; decorations by Allan McNab. Rinehart 1933 1224p illus $8.50 **Fic**

1 Adventure and adventurers—Fiction

"This vast romantic novel recounts the story of Anthony—born in 1775, illegitimate, orphaned, left to die in a Catholic convent, educated by the Church, and apprenticed to a wealthy Italian merchant whose heir he became. His business interests were world wide: in early manhood, a slave trader, he was later connected with the financial interests of Napoleon in France, England, Spain, and the new world. Anthony carried with him through life his one link to the past, a beautiful small figure of the Madonna that identified him to others though he himself never learned his identity." Booklist

"Only a scholar could have assembled the enormous knowledge that has gone into the book and only a poet and a critic could have caught so acutely the implications of that knowledge as idea and emotion in human beings. The triumph of the book, however, is that this wealth of fact and feeling is fused by the gusto of the true story-teller." N Y Her Trib Books

Allen, T. D.

Doctor in buckskin. Harper 1951 277p lib. bdg. $4.43   **Fic**

1 Missionaries—Fiction 2 Frontier and pioneer life—Fiction 3 Whitman, Marcus—Fiction 4 Whitman, Narcissa (Prentiss)—Fiction

"This is a novel, based on fact, of the West in the days when the first wagon trains were pushing their way beyond the Rockies, Hudson's Bay men ruled in Oregon, and the Indian fought to keep his land. It is the true story of an American doctor and his wife in the frontier wilderness. Dr. Marcus Whitman and his bride were almost the only white people in the Oregon wilderness when they arrived. The Whitmans learned the language of the Indians, shared their short supplies with their neighbors, nursed them through epidemics. But Indian resentment flared at the unjust actions of some other white people, and they began to lose faith in white man's medicine. Marcus needed help, but help wasn't forthcoming. The tragedy that followed is one of the most moving and dramatic stories of pioneer days." Publisher's note

Amado, Jorge

The violent land; tr. from the Portuguese (Terras do sem fim) by Samuel Putnam; with a new foreword by the author. Knopf 1965 336p $6.95   **Fic**

1 Brazil—Fiction 2 Plantation life—Fiction 3 Cacao—Fiction

First American edition 1945

"The story of a bloody feud between two landowning Brazilian families for the possession of a tract of virgin forest to which neither has any right. The background is the wild, lush countryside of eastern Brazil during a ['cacao rush']." New Yorker

"To the raw violence and action of one of our gold-rush, claim-jumping, frontier tales, this novel adds an exuberant, tropical lyricism. Only study of one or more characters in depth is lacking to complete the full humanity of the work—largely because its true concern is not the individual human being but a society, a region and an industry." N Y Her Trib Books

Ambler, Eric

The Intercom conspiracy. Atheneum Pubs. 1969 241p $5.95   **Fic**

1 Spies—Fiction 2 Switzerland—Fiction

In Geneva, two top intelligence officers plot to get paid off—for their silence. "The pawn in their game is a hard-drinking, irascible, but shrewd ex-reporter who is running a newsletter that up to now has been pushing ultra-right wing propaganda. In the hands of the two plotters it is put to a sinister new use that draws down the wrath of Americans, Russians, West Germans alike." Pub W

"The tale is ingenious and expertly told. Not quite the cliff-hanging thriller but suspenseful enough to carry one to the last page." Best Sellers

Anatoli, A.

Babi Yar   **Fic**

1 World War, 1939-1945—Fiction 2 Russia—Fiction

Some editions are:

Dial Press $5.95 Translated by Jacob Guralsky; illustrated by S. Brodsky

Farrar, Straus $10 [Uncensored and expanded version] Translated by David Floyd

Original Russian edition published 1966 in censored form in Yunost. First American edition published 1967 by Dial Press under author's former name Anatoly Kuznetsov

A documentary novel about the period from 1941 to 1943 in which the Germans systematically murdered some 200,000 people, including 50,000 Jews, at the ravine on the outskirts of Kiev known as Babi Yar. The author, who was twelve years old at the time, based his work on interviews, newspaper clippings, diaries and other documents of the time. (Publisher)

"Compassionate and deeply moving but not for timid souls." Top of the News

Anderson, Paul L.

With the eagles. Biblo & Tannen 1965 [c1929] 279p illus $4.50   **Fic**

1 Gaul—History—Fiction

"Roman life and times series"

First published 1929 by Appleton

In this volume, a brave Gallic boy joins Caesar's army and goes out to battle, eventually winning a place in Caesar's famous Tenth Legion. The narrative pictures a magnificent and thrilling time. (Publisher)

Andrews, Mary Raymond Shipman

The perfect tribute; drawing by Rudolph Ruzicka. Scribner 1956 48p $4.50   **Fic**

1 Lincoln, Abraham, President U.S.—Fiction

First published 1906

" 'The perfect tribute' on the Gettysburg speech is rendered directly to Lincoln, in a Washington hospital, by a wounded soldier who had read the address in a morning newspaper. . . . Leaving veracity out of consideration, it must be confessed that the little story is written with a tenderness of touch and a delicacy of diction." Dial

Armah, Ayi Kwei

The beautiful ones are not yet born; a novel. Houghton 1968 215p $4.95   **Fic**

1 Ghana—Fiction

This novel "presents the case of a poor but honest ('beautyful') man in a rotten world. A middle-class government worker, eager to do right but just managing to feed his wife and three children, is constantly tempted to partake of the petty, common, accepted corruptions of Nkrumaist Ghana. Looming large and wealthy before him is a former schoolmate who has gone the usual route and has thereby become a government Minister. Mr. Armah's hero is greatly bothered, but something within him compels him to refuse to compromise, though he suffers daily for his stand. Then comes the 1966 coup that ousts Nkrumah from office and reorders the seats of power. But what difference does it make to the man? Or indeed to the nation?" Book of the Month Club News

Arnold, Elliott

Blood brother; illus. by Dale Nichols. Duell 1950 558p illus $7.95   **Fic**

1 Apache Indians—Fiction 2 Cochise, Apache chief—Fiction

First published 1947

"This long, readable book tells the tragic story of the Chiricahua Apaches and their great chief, Cochise. . . . Of all the Apaches, the Chiricahuas were fiercest, raiding for centuries into Mexico. But when the Americans took over their country, Cochise with great intelligence saw his people could not fight the invaders. After some sporadic raids, Cochise controlled the majority of his people, a few headed by the notorious Geronimo breaking away. But the American contractors for Army stores wanted conflict, and only the tight-lipped intervention of Tom Jefford, blood brother of Cochise, kept the peace. Filled with authentic lore and the sweep of Arizona's deserts and mountains, this is a book to be read slowly and savored well." Literary Guild

Arnow, Harriette Simpson

The dollmaker. Macmillan (N Y) 1954 549p $7.95   **Fic**

Also available in large type edition $8.95

"Gertie Nevels, a courageous and unselfish Kentucky countrywoman who has a talent amounting to a passion for whittling small objects out of wood, is forced by the war to leave the happy, although poverty-stricken, community where she has spent her life and go to Detroit, where her husband has found work in a factory. The meanness, squalor, and lack of privacy of her new surroundings, and the debasing effect of the city on her husband and on some of their children, oppress her, but she maintains her integrity and her faith in her fellow human beings." New Yorker

Arnow, Harriette S.—*Continued*

"It is hard to believe that anyone who opens its pages will soon forget the big woman and her sufferings as traced in Harriette Arnow's long, heavily packed masterwork." N Y Times Bk R

The weedkiller's daughter. Knopf 1970 [c1969] 371p $6.95   Fic

"Susan Marie Schnitzer, the weedkiller's daughter, is fifteen years old, a straight-A student with science and mathematics her particular forte, a delightful and precocious project of upper suburbia and the Eden Hills High School in a suburb of Detroit. Outwardly a model student and docile daughter, Susie has worked out a private and personal life totally fascinating and totally necessary to the preservation of her own self. Susie functions on two levels simultaneously, switching on her personal 'IBM computer' or 'radar' while she does her homework, rides her bicycle, or carries on any habitual activity. Thus, she is able to carry on one activity under automatic control while her mind is busy rebuilding the past or plotting solutions for the future. This is not a straight-forward novel whose plot can be summed up in a few words or briefly outlined. It is definitely Susie's story—how she grew up in her fifteenth year and managed to preserve both her identity and her ideals. At the same time it portrays an entire family; and aspects of life in suburban Eden Hills and its High School—a small segment of life, with Susie as its focal point. The book is beautifully and skillfully written with insight and understanding on many levels. Susie and her friends are a nice crowd to know." Best Sellers

Ashton-Warner, Sylvia

Greenstone. Simon & Schuster 1966 217p $4.50   Fic

1 Maoris—Fiction 2 New Zealand—Fiction

The author "chronicles ten years in the lives of the Considines of New Zealand: Richard, crippled with arthritis; his wife, energetic, plain, but full of love for her husband; and their twelve children, not to mention a half-Maori granddaughter." Bk Buyer's Guide

"A bit thin and perhaps too mistily poetic sometimes, Greenstone is a happy, lovely, comic novel that touches on the sadness of the streaming away of time." Book of the Month Club News

Includes a glossary of Maori words

Three; a novel. Knopf 1970 241p $5.95 Fic

"When Julian, a young university lecturer, becomes seriously ill in London his estranged French wife and his Australian mother are summoned from their temporary home in India. In the tense, witty, Ashton-Warner style, the mother, recently widowed and grieving, tells the story, a version of the classic triangle. She first hopes for a reknitting of her son's marriage. Then, as he begins to recuperate and turn towards his wife, she finds her need to be needed is most important." Library J

Asimov, Isaac

Fantastic voyage; a novel. Based on the screenplay by Harry Kleiner from the original story by Otto Klement and Jay Lewis Bixby. Houghton 1966 239p $4.95   Fic

1 Science fiction 2 Spies—Fiction

Jan Benes, a brilliant refugee scientist, has a secret vital to the Free World's survival. Victim of an attempted assassination, he lies in a coma with a potentially fatal blood clot in his brain. Other scientists "decide to miniaturize a team of doctors and technicians with all their equipment . . . and inject them into Benes's circulatory system to attack and destroy the blood clot from the inside." Publisher's note

A "highly entertaining fantasy. . . . The moral, as always, is that science conquers all. A jolly tale which, fortunately, nobody will take seriously." Best Sellers

Auchincloss, Louis

The embezzler. Houghton 1966 277p $4.95   Fic

1 Stock exchange—Fiction 2 New York (City) —Fiction

"Guy Prime, scion of a New York Establishment family, misappropriates some bonds to keep afloat a little while longer during the Depression. He is caught and brought to trial. The New Deal pillories him as a flagrant example of the kind of men who run Wall Street as though it were their own private club. He serves his term in the penitentiary and then exiles himself to Panama City. . . . [The author] delivers his embezzler to us in the form of three-first person memoirs, Prime's, that of his friend, Rex Geer, and that of Angelica, Prime's wife." N Y Times Bk R

"The overlapping and mutually contradictory versions create patterns of ambiguity. . . . The result is a tantalizing psychological and moral mystery of human motivation. . . . Auchincloss rejects all simple-minded and portentous analyses. He creates the world in which the events happen and he brings to life the people who inhabit it—which is the novelist's true function. And then having completed this work of imaginative composition, he leaves us to ponder the genesis of the climactic act. The mystery echoes in the mind." Newsweek

Austen, Jane

Emma   Fic

1 Great Britain—Fiction

Some editions are:
Dodd (Great illustrated classics) $4.50 With illustrations of the author and her environment and pictures from early editions of the book, together with an introduction by Frederic E. Faverty
Dutton $3.95
Dutton (Everyman's lib) $3.25
Oxford (The Oxford Illustrated Jane Austen v4) $8
Oxford (World's classics) $2.25

First published 1815

"The heroine is a pretty [English] girl with a feminine rage for match-making." Lenrow. Reader's Guide to Prose Fiction

"Less brilliant than 'Pride and Prejudice,' 'Emma' is equally rich in humor, in the vivid portraiture of character, and a never-ending delight in human absurdities, which the fascinated reader shares from chapter to chapter." Keller's Reader's Digest of Books

Mansfield Park   Fic

1 Great Britain—Fiction

Some editions are:
Dutton $3.95
Dutton (Everyman's lib) $3.25
Oxford (Oxford Illustrated Jane Austen v3) $8
Oxford (World's classics) $2.50 Introduction by Mary Lascelles

First published 1814

"Presents a houseful of young people in love with the right or the wrong person. Thru the device of marrying off three sisters into different ranks, upper middle-class distinctions come in for amusing comparisons." Lenrow. Reader's Guide to Prose Fiction

Northanger Abbey   Fic

1 Great Britain—Fiction

Some editions are:
Dutton $3.95
Oxford (World's classics) $2

First published 1818

"The heroine is a girl in the first innocent bloom of youth, whose entry into life is attended by the collapse of many illusions." Lenrow. Reader's Guide to Prose Fiction

"The origin of the story is the desire to ridicule tales of romance and terror such as Mrs. Radcliffe's 'Mysteries of Udolpho' and to contrast with these life as it really is." Oxford Companion to English Literature

Persuasion   Fic

1 Great Britain—Fiction

Some editions are:
Dutton $3.95
Oxford (The World's classics) $2.50 With an introduction by Forest Reid
Watts, F. lib. bdg. $4.50. Ultra type edition

Austen, Jane—*Continued*

First published 1818
"In this, Miss Austen's last work, satire and ridicule take a milder form, the tone is graver and tenderer, and the interest lies in a more subtle interplay of the characters; indeed, it is a matter of tradition that a love-story of Jane's own life is reflected in Anne Elliot's." Oxford Companion to English Literature

Pride and prejudice   Fic

1 Great Britain—Fiction

Some editions are:
Dodd (Great illustrated classics) $4.50 With an introductory sketch of the author and with illustrations of the Jane Austen country
Dutton $3.95 Illustrated by C. E. Brock
Dutton (New American edition. Everyman's lib) $3.45 Introduction by R. B. Johnson
Harcourt (The Harcourt Lib. of English and American classics) $3.95
Macmillan (N Y) (The Macmillan classics) $3.95, lib. bdg. $4.24 Illustrated by Bernarda Bryson; afterword by Clifton Fadiman
Oxford (The Oxford Illustrated Jane Austen v2) $8
Oxford (World's classics) $2.50
Watts, F. $8.95 Large type edition complete and unabridged. A Keith Jennison book
Watts, F. $4.50. Ultra type edition. With a critical and biographical profile of Jane Austen by John W. Loofbourow
First published 1813
"Concerned mainly with the conflict between the prejudice of a young lady and the well-founded though misinterpreted pride of the aristocratic hero. The heroine's father and mother cope in very different ways with the problem of marrying off five daughters. A masterpiece of gentle humor." Good Reading
"The characters are drawn with humor, delicacy, and the intimate knowledge of men and women that Miss Austen always shows." Keller's Reader's Digest of Books

Sense and sensibility   Fic

1 Great Britain—Fiction

Some editions are:
Dodd (Great illustrated classics) $4.50 With illustrations reproducing drawings for early editions and photographs of historical scenes together with an introductory biographical sketch of the author and anecdotal captions by Basil Davenport
Dutton (Everyman's lib) $3.25
Harcourt (The Harcourt Lib. of English and American classics) $3.95
Oxford (The Oxford Illustrated Jane Austen v 1 $8
Oxford (World's classics) $2.25
First published 1811
"The story tells of two sisters: Elinor, who has sense, and Marianne, who has sensibility. Their unfortunate love affairs form the basis of the narrative. Edward Ferrars, with whom Elinor is in love, is entangled with a sly, avaricious girl, Lucy Steele. His mother, upon learning this, disinherits him. Lucy, being without scruple, then jilts him for his younger brother, now the heir. So Edward returns to Elinor, who takes him back. Marianne's lover, the handsome and dashing John Willoughby, is a heartless rascal. He leaves her and goes to London. Romantic by nature, she follows him to the city, but his insolent conduct soon disillusions her. She then sacrifices her childish and absurd romanticism for the joys of a sensible marriage with staid, middle-aged Colonel Brandon." Haydn. Thesaurus of Book Digests

Baldwin, James

Go tell it on the mountain. Dial Press 1963 [c1953] 253p $4.95   Fic

1 Negroes—Fiction 2 Harlem, New York (City)—Fiction

A reissue of the title first published 1953 by Knopf
"A story of religious experience among Harlem Negroes. The account of young John's conversion on his fourteenth birthday, is set against the story of his forefathers, told in flashbacks covering the lives and sins of three generations." Book Rev Digest

"His people have an enormous capacity for sin, but their capacity for suffering and repentance is even greater. I think that is the outstanding quality of this work, a sometimes majestic sense of the failings of men and their ability to work through their misery to some kind of peaceful salvation." Commonweal

Ball, John

In the heat of the night. Harper 1965 184p boards $5.95   Fic

1 Mystery and detective stories 2 Negroes—Fiction

A novel "introducing a Negro detective, Virgil Tibbs, a homicide expert, a clever, sophisticated man from Pasadena, California. Tibbs uses unusual methods to find information, but he does succeed in pinning down a murderer who has killed a distinguished musician. . . . The scene is a small town in the Carolinas where Tibbs, innocently waiting for a train, is brought in as a murder suspect and then, on request, assists the unhappy, baffled local police, who don't really want him, but do need him." Pub W
"This book combines humor with an understanding both of social problems and of detection." Library J

Johnny get your gun; a novel. Little 1969 227p boards $6.50   Fic

1 California—Fiction 2 Negroes—Fiction

In Pasadena, "nine-year-old Johnny McGuire's greatest treasure was a transistor radio. When bullying Billy Hotchkiss snatched it away and accidently broke it, Johnny got his father's gun and set out to kill Billy. Black policeman Virgil Tibbs was called in and eventually saved Johnny from a Negro mob." Bk Buyer's Guide
Sympathetic to the problems of the police, for a change, it is possible the author goes too far. . . . The story is engrossing and touching!" Best Sellers

Balmer, Edwin

When worlds collide, by Edwin Balmer and Philip Wylie. Lippincott 1950 2v in 1 illus $6.95   Fic

1 Science fiction

An "omnibus edition of 'When Worlds Collide' [1933] and 'After Worlds Collide' [1934]. The former describes the earthy crisis which followed the discovery that this planet was about to be destroyed by collision with another body approaching through space, and the design and launching of an atomic space ship in which a few humans were able to make their escape. [The latter] continues the story of the intrepid pioneers on a new planet." Huntting

Balzac, Honoré de

Eugénie Grandet; introduction by Marcel Girard. Dutton 1956 235p $2.95   Fic

1 Wealth—Fiction 2 France—Fiction

"Everyman's library"
First appeared 1833 as one of the "Scenes of provincial life series." Published in this edition 1907, translated by Ellen Marriage
"Grandet, a rich miser, has an only child, Eugénie. She falls in love with her charming but spoiled young cousin Charles. When she learns he is financially ruined, she lends him her savings. But her father will never consent to her marrying a bankrupt's son. Charles goes to the West Indies, secretly engaged to marry Eugénie on his return. Years go by, Grandet dies and Eugénie becomes an heiress. But Charles, ignorant of her wealth, writes her to ask for his freedom: he wants to marry a rich girl. Eugénie releases him, pays his father's debts, and marries without love an old friend of the family." Haydn. Thesaurus of Book Digests

Père Goriot   Fic

1 France—Fiction

Some editions are:
Dodd (Great illustrated classics) $4.50 Translated by Jane Minot Sedgwick. With illustrations of the author and his environment

Balzac, Honoré de—*Continued*

and reproductions of drawings for early editions of the book together with an introduction and descriptive captions by Allen Klots, Jr.

Dutton (Everyman's lib) $3.25 Translated by Ellen Marriage. Introduction by Marcel Girard. Has title: Old Goriot

First published 1835 in France

"Goriot, a retired manufacturer of vermicelli, is a good man and weak father. He has given away his money in order to ensure the marriage of his two daughters, Anastasie and Delphine. Because of his love for them, he has to accept all kinds of humiliations from his sons-in-law, one a 'gentilhomme,' M. de Restaud, and the other a financier, M. de Nucingen. Both young women are ungrateful. They gradually abandon him. He dies without seeing them at his bedside, cared for only by young Rastignac, a law student who lives at the same boarding house, the pension Vauquer." Haydn. Thesaurus of Book Digests

This "can be regarded as the most typical, and the most popular, of all Balzac's novels. It was written, said George Saintsbury, 'when his genius was at its very height . . .,' when the scheme of the "Comedie Humaine" was not quite finally settle, but elaborated to a considerable extent.' . . . Few readers of the book ever forget Madame Vauquer's 'pension' in the Rue Neuve-Sainte-Geneviève, or the characters." The Reader's Guide to Everyman's Library

Barnes, Margaret Campbell

The Tudor rose. Macrae Smith Co. 1953 313p $5.95   **Fic**

1 Elizabeth, consort of Henry VII, King of England—Fiction 2 Great Britain—History—Wars of the Roses, 1455-1485—Fiction 3 Henry VII, King of England—Fiction

"This is a complex and moving historical novel with its main character [Elizabeth] the daughter of Edward IV, whose marriage to Henry of Lancaster ended the Wars of the Roses and began the Tudor dynasty. There are plots and counterplots. . . . There are frank descriptions of Edward's many mistresses and of Elizabeth's dissatisfaction with her marriage, but there is nothing sensational in the manner. What emerges is understanding of the hardships and tragedies which women of the times met with courage." Horn Bk

Barrett, William E.

The lilies of the field; drawings by Burt Silverman. Doubleday 1962 92p illus $3.50
                                                        Fic

1 Negroes—Fiction 2 Monasticism and religious orders for women—Fiction

"An amiable southern Negro, driving through the Southwest after getting out of the Army, stops to help four German refugee nuns build a church, stays to finish the job, with one spell of restless wandering away, and then disappears, leaving behind him the legend of his faithful help." Pub W

"This refreshing and haunting novelette projects a situation which the reader would like to believe. There are moments of humor and pathos." Wis Lib Bul

Barrie, J. M.

The little minister   **Fic**

1 Scotland—Fiction

Some editions are:
Grosset $2.95
Scribner $5.95

First published 1891

"A romantic fantasia on the Thrums motive: the love affairs of the Auld Licht minister and a beautiful and 'sprightly Egyptian,' who is a lady in disguise. . . . The sketches of character and of Scottish manners and religious sentiments are very humorous, and there are passages of concentrated pathos." Baker's Best

"Aside from its intrinsic interest, there is much skillful portrayal of the complexities of Scotch character, and much sympathy with the homely lives of the poverty-stricken weavers, whose narrow creed may make them cruel, but never dishonorable." Keller's Reader's Digest of Books

Beach, Edward L.

Run silent, run deep; illus. with line drawings. Holt 1955 364p illus $4.95   **Fic**

1 Submarines—Fiction 2 World War, 1939-1945—Fiction

This novel is a "tribute to the brave men of the silent service which operates deep below the ocean's surface. Ingeniously framed as a first-person account tape recorded by one Commander Richardson, the narrative combines simple, accurate, and detailed description of submarine training, patrolling, and fighting with clear portraits of the commander and his crew and a tensely dramatic story of revenge on a deadly Japanese sub hunter. A grippingly realistic novel of submarine activity in the Pacific during World War II, with peripheral love interest and somewhat incidental plot." Booklist

Beagle, Peter S.

The last unicorn. Viking 1968 218p boards $4.95   **Fic**

1 Unicorns

In this novel, a unicorn searches for others of her kind. "Enroute she is captured by members of Mommy Fortuna's Midnight Carnival, and then freed by a melancholy magician named Schmendrick. She and the magician who joins her in her search for King Haggard and the Red Bull, encounter a fifth-rate Robin Hood, Captain Cully, and add to their party one of his followers, Molly Grue, who has recognized the unicorn. . . . When the unicorn is attacked by the Red Bull, Schmendrick . . . saves her by giving her a human form. Prince Lir falls in love with her in this form, and there are numerous complications before the unicorn frees all the other unicorns from the Red Bull." Sat R

"Like many good fantasies this is oblique commentary on matters of good and evil, tyranny and freedom, but can be enjoyed also simply for the poetically sensitive writing and imagery." Booklist

Bellamy, Edward

Looking backward: 2000-1887   **Fic**

1 Utopias—Fiction

Some editions are:
Hendricks House $3 Edited by Frederic R. White
Modern Lib $2.95 With an introduction by Robert L. Shurter
Harvard Univ. Press (The John Harvard lib) $5.95 A Belknap Press book. Edited by John L. Thomas

First published 1888

"Julian West, a wealthy Bostonian, after spending the evening with his fiancee Edith Bartlett, finds that he cannot fall asleep. Hypnotized by Dr. Pillsbury, he awakens to find that it is 113 years later. Still retaining the vigor and appearance of his youth in 2000 A.D., he falls in love with another Edith, the great-granddaughter of his first fiancee. She guides him on a tour of the cooperative commonwealth which has come into existence. Labor is the cornerstone of society: all work and share alike. The State is the Great Trust. Economic security and a healthy moral environment have reduced crime. The cultural level has risen. Julian dreams that he is again in the old society, which now appalls him as ruthless, greedy, and unjust. To his relief, however, he awakens and finds himself still in the new Utopia." Haydn. Thesaurus of Book Digests

Bellow, Saul

Herzog. Viking 1964 341p $5.75   **Fic**

1 Jews in the U.S.—Fiction

National Book Award for 1965

"A novel which is a vehicle for the outpourings of the hero, a Jewish scholar, about himself, about his friends, about the state of the country and of life in general. Moses Herzog is in a great state of emotional confusion after his humiliating second divorce. He vents frustration and irritation in visualizing frank, sarcastic letters—letters to the N.Y. Times, to his psychiatrist, to his son, to his second

Bellow, Saul—*Continued*

mother-in-law. He is on the verge of a nervous breakdown. His predicament has pathos, humor, silliness, and, oddly enough, a Rabelaisian humor, too, but readers should not expect a dramatic entity, a novel with developing plot. What they will find instead is a sequence of pointed satirical comment—on modern women, marriage, politics, philosophy—and a characterization of a present-day American Jewish intellectual." Pub W

"There is nothing in any novel I have read quite like these letters Herzog writes. In no sense formal in tone, they represent at once a fictional device and a prodigiously productive aggression of the mind. . . . Among the elements back of [Bellow's style] is, no doubt, a deep sense of humor specifically derived from his Jewish background and thoroughly assimilated to his sensibility. This style is sensibility in action." Book Week

Mr Sammler's planet. Viking 1970 313p
boards $6.95   **Fic**

1 Jews—Fiction
SBN 670-33319-0

National Book award for 1970
"Although he is in his seventies, in the concluding years of a life that has known more than its share of adventure and tragedy, Arthur Sammler's planet extends far beyond the Upper West Side of New York, where he lives with his widowed niece. It encompasses both his memories—the prewar years as a Polish journalist in London, where he knew many of the best minds and talents of the period, the terrible time in a Nazi prison camp—and the events of the present. It is a present that includes such things as a bizarre encounter with a debonair black pickpocket, and the theft of an esoteric manuscript by Mr. Sammler's daughter. In between, Mr. Sammler finds time for a metaphysical musing on the state of mankind, the world, America, his own self." Pub W

"There are readers who have always felt . . . portions of Bellow's novels to be digressive or pretentious . . . [but] Bellow is a man of high intelligence so that his generalized commentary is intrinsically absorbing, and . . . he has the rare gift of transforming dialectic into drama, casuistry into comedy, so that one is steadily aware of the close relationship between his discursive passages and the central narrative." Harper

Benét, Stephen Vincent

The Devil and Daniel Webster; illus. by Harold Denison. Rinehart 1937 61p illus $3
Fic

1 Webster, Daniel—Fiction

"The story is of a poor New Hampshire farmer, the devil in new guise and New Hampshire's famous native son, Daniel Webster. . . . A twentieth century version of the familiar Faust legend." Boston Transcript

"It is slight only in length, for it is rare to find so much natural humor and true characterization in so short a space. The author has long excelled in his ability to recapture in brief, graphic word pictures scenes and heroes of the past and make these a part of our present. It is to be doubted if, even in his acknowledged masterpiece, 'John Brown's body,' he has surpassed this short prose portrait of Daniel Webster." Christian Science Monitor

Bennett, Arnold

The old wives' tale. Modern Lib. 640p $2.95   **Fic**

1 Great Britain—Fiction

First published 1908; in this edition, 1931
"It is the story of the lives of two middle-class sisters who came from the Five Towns—the pottery district of England." Dickinson. The World's Best Books

"A faithful piece of realism describing the commonplace, sordid life of a small English industrial town with keen observation, convincing psychology, and a somewhat grim humor." Pratt Alcove

Bennett, Jack

Mister fisherman. Little 1964 180p $5.50
Fic

1 Africa, South—Fiction 2 Race problems—Fiction 3 Sea stories

The Negro fisherman, Pillay, and his white tourist-passenger, young "Faraday, have fished throughout the day as strangers separated by the force of racial difference. Now, miles off a remote stretch of South African coast, the engine of the small fishing boat has broken down. They face gale storms and killer whales. Old hatreds dissolve in new fears: Faraday must depend upon Pillay for his survival." Publisher's note

"A spare, moving [tale]. . . . Aside from its being a good story of man against the sea, this is also a commentary on man's inhumanity to man." Horn Bk

Bjorn, Thyra Ferré

Papa's wife. Rinehart 1955 305p $4.50 **Fic**

1 Family—Fiction 2 Swedes in the U.S.—Fiction

"A sober Swedish pastor marries his young housekeeper after she makes a trip to America to prove he needs her. Their life in Swedish Lapland, their move to New England, the births, childhood, school days and marriages of their many children provide a leisurely family story." Horn Bk

Borland, Hal

The amulet. Lippincott 1957 224p $4.95
Fic

1 U.S.—History—Civil War—Fiction

"As a young man, Quincy Scott felt the need to join a contingent of Confederate sympathizers and take a man's part in the world. He left his Denver home and his girl, Rhoda, who gave him an amulet as a token for his safe return. The little band lived on the land and in the open as it crept ahead, avoiding a brush with the enemy. Quincy had time for reflection on the meaning of war, and, as he buried his comrades after the battle of Wilson Creek, he decided to turn back. This story portrays a little known segment of life in that period, and it presents a young man's problems in growing up." Wis Lib Bul

When the legends die. Lippincott 1963 288p $4.95   **Fic**

1 Ute Indians—Fiction 2 Rodeos—Fiction 3 Colorado—Fiction

A story "about a Ute Indian boy, child of outlaws, brought up in the Colorado wilderness in the old ways and in friendship with a bear cub. His boyhood—when he is torn away from his mountains and 'civilized' against his will—and his young manhood are harsh and brutal: he becomes a bronc-buster with a reputation for a murderous riding style. The time is from 1910 up into 1920's." Pub W

In this story, the author illustrates "the love of animal and nature which has always been so admirable in the American Indian. . . . [In the end] broken physically by rodeo life 'Tom returns to his native land for rest. There he acts out the final struggle of his life: to find himself. . . . In that debate comes a final maturity [and acceptance of his heritage] which makes the last chapters thrilling and uplifting." Best Sellers

Boulle, Pierre

The bridge over the River Kwai; tr. by Xan Fielding   **Fic**

1 World War, 1939-1945—Fiction 2 Great Britain. Army—Officers—Fiction 3 Thailand—Fiction

Some editions are:
Vanguard $5.95
Watts, F. $7.95 Large type edition complete and unabridged. A Keith Jennison book

First published 1952 in France
A satire "on a certain type of British officer, a colonel who, even in a Japanese prison camp, [during World War II] keeps a stiff upper lip and clings to discipline. Put in charge of building a bridge with prison labor he carries out the job so satisfactorily that when a team of commandos arrives to blow up his handiwork he indignantly exposes them to the Japanese." Pub W

"This is a stirring and imaginative book. Whatever Monsieur Boulle may think of Kipling standards he has, to his advantage, soaked in the Master's atmosphere Ably seconded by an excellent translation he has

Boulle, Pierre—*Continued*

achieved . . . [a] brisk yet laconic style, the unforgettable character sketches, the technical details, the story-telling magic." New Statesman & Nation

Planet of the Apes; tr. by Xan Fielding. Vanguard 1963 246p boards $5.95   **Fic**

1 Science fiction 2 Apes—Stories

The time in this science fiction novel "is the year 2052. Ulysse Méron, a journalist, is one of a small party from earth which lands on a planet in the 300-light-year-distant constellation of Betelgeuse. They find to their horror that man is in a wild state and that apes—gorillas, chimpanzees, and orangutans—run the planet, in some ways better than civilized man runs his own planet. Their cities, vehicles, clothes, even, are much like what people have on earth, and they have eliminated war. They keep men in zoos and use them for biological experiments, because of all creatures men are physically closest to the simian. In this Swiftian fable Boulle gives full play to his not inconsiderable gift for irony and satire." Library J

Bradford, Richard

Red sky at morning; a novel. Lippincott 1968 256p $4.95   **Fic**

1 New Mexico—Fiction

"When World War II begins Josh Arnold's father Frank joins the Navy and sends his wife and son from Mobile, Alabama to tiny Sagrado, New Mexico where the family had spent previous summers. Josh's observations of life among the motley Mexican and Anglo inhabitants of Sagrado and his disarming schoolmates and his concern for his Southern mother and for the nearly permanent house guest Jim-bob Buel result in a humorous, honest, and affirmative portrayal of a teen-ager's seventeenth summer." Booklist

This novel "is warm and funny and yet has a sharp bite to it, like the snap of fangs crunching through corn pone. The genteel Old South hasn't taken such a beating since Sherman's day. . . . But what makes the book a true delight is the dead-pan, irreverent humor with which Josh tells the story." Book World

Bristow, Gwen

Calico Palace. Crowell 1970 589p $7.95   **Fic**

1 San Francisco—Fiction 2 California—Gold discoveries—Fiction

"San Francisco in the days of the Gold Rush (1849) is the setting for this . . . novel, which follows Kendra Logan through two relatively unhappy marriages, the birth and death of a baby, and friendship with Marny, glamourous proprietress of Calico Palace, a gambling hall. In the eventual, traditional happy ending, both girls find true love." Library J

"If Miss Bristow's story line is pretty conventional, there's plenty of good historical detail and San Francisco lore to make up for it." Pub W

Celia Garth. Crowell 1959 406p $6.95 **Fic**

1 U.S.—History—Revolution—Fiction 2 Spies —Fiction 3 Charleston, S.C.—Fiction

This story "takes its background from South Carolina during the Revolutionary War. Its heroine is Celia Garth, a spirited orphan girl working as an apprentice dressmaker in Charleston, who witnesses the British siege of the city and returns during the occupation to become a spy for the rebels." Booklist

"Celia Garth's story is adventurous and romantic, patriotic and sentimental. Miss Bristow's historical novel presents abundant terror, but it is the terror endured by civilians more than the terror of bloody battle. The general public will find no trace of the realistic, detailed description of love and war that so often characterizes this variety of fiction. Nevertheless, the book successfully brings to life the patriotic Revolutionary fighters." Best Sellers

Jubilee Trail. Crowell 1950 564p $7.50 **Fic**

1 Frontier and pioneer life—Fiction 2 Santa Fé Trail—Fiction 3 California—Fiction

"The story of Garnet Cameron, who, in 1844, exchanges wealth and position for an adventurous pioneer life with Oliver Hale. After a glamorous honeymoon in New Orleans, where they meet the beautiful and mysterious Florinda, they travel via St. Louis to Santa Fe, and then start in the difficult trek over the Jubilee Trail to Los Angeles. There she learned, tragically, of her young husband's weakness, and faced treachery and despair. And there, too, she learned how to meet life without compromise and, finally, with the help of John Ives, found the real meaning of love." Huntting

"A long but colorful novel which recreates vividly the arduous journey over the Santa Fe trail and the crudeness of the early California settlements." Booklist

Brontë, Charlotte

Jane Eyre   **Fic**

1 Great Britain—Fiction

Some editions are:
Dodd (Great illustrated classics) $4.50 With illustrations made up of drawings by contemporary artists and photographs from the Jane Eyre country, together with an introductory biographical sketch of the author and anecdotal captions by Basil Davenport
Dutton (Everyman's lib) $3.25
Harcourt (The Harcourt Lib. of English and American classics) $3.95
Macmillan (N Y) (The Macmillan classics) $4.95 Illustrated by Ati Forberg; afterword by Clifton Fadiman
Modern Lib. $2.95
Oxford (World's classics) $2.75
Watts, F. $8.95 Large type edition complete and unabridged. A Keith Jennison book
Watts, F. $5.50 Ultratype edition. With a critical and biographical profile of Charlotte Brontë by Inga-Stina Ewbank

First published 1847
Told in the first person, this is a novel of a strong woman who rebelled against the narrow social and religious conventions of her day. As a heroine, Jane is described as a plain faced creature, who loved the ugly but forceful Rochester whose wife was a madwoman. Many dramatic episodes occur before a tragedy finally reunites them

"A tale with an extraordinary atmosphere of passion and a 'Byronic hero with a sinful past,' Mr Rochester, it has remained the most popular of Charlotte's novels." The Reader's Guide to Everyman's Library

The professor   **Fic**

1 Brussels—Fiction 2 Teachers—Fiction

Some editions are:
Dutton (Everyman's lib) $2.95
Oxford (World's classics) $2.50

First published 1857
William Crimsworth is a young English orphan who upon leaving Eton is faced with a decision regarding his future. He shuns his mother's family's offer of a wife and position as an Anglican clergyman and works in his brother's mill. Unhappy over his mistreatment there, he travels to Brussels and becomes a teacher of English and Latin in a private school. Successful both in his academic pursuits and his personal life, he is able to retire and return to England while still in middle age

Brontë, Emily

Wuthering Heights   **Fic**

1 Great Britain—Fiction

Some editions are:
Dodd (Great illustrated classics) $4.50 With illustrations from paintings by contemporary artists and photographs from the Wuthering Heights country together with an introductory biographical sketch of the author and anecdotal captions by Basil Davenport
Harcourt (The Harcourt Lib. of English and American classics) $3.95
Macmillan (N Y) (The Macmillan classics) $4.95 Illustrated by Bernarda Bryson. Afterword by Clifton Fadiman
Oxford (World's classics) $2 With a preface and memoir of Emily and Anna Brontë by Charlotte Brontë and introduction by H. W. Garrod

Brontë, Emily—*Continued*

Watts, F. $8.95 Large type edition complete and unabridged. A Keith Jennison book

Watts, F. $4.50 Ultratype edition

First published 1847

Set against a somber background of the moorlands, this novel about Catherine Earnshaw and Heathcliff starts at Wuthering Heights, Catherine's childhood home in Yorkshire

"A wild tale of terror and hatred among the rough people of the Yorkshire moors. The solitary novel of the sister of Charlotte Brontë. It is a work of true genius, most brilliant contribution of the gifted Brontë sisters." Pratt Alcove

Bryher

Beowulf; a novel. Pantheon Bks. 1956 201p $5.95

Fic

1 World War, 1939-1945—Fiction 2 London—Fiction

"Originally published in French to acquaint the British author's friends on the continent with wartime conditions in London. . . . It is a series of impressions of two elderly British ladies who run a tea shop, their staff, customers, and the assorted roomers who occupy the upper floors of the building. Their reactions, before and after the Warming Pan [tea shop] is blitzed, are homely lifelike exemplifications of the English spirit in adversity, as symbolized by the life-sized plaster bulldog which one of the ladies brings home for a mascot." Booklist

"The traces of sentimentality in the book are more the result of embarrassment in the face of great feeling than they are evidence of softness in the writer or in any of her many appealing people. It is a touching work, with a splendidly characteristic last line." New Yorker

Buck, Pearl S.

Nobel Prize in literature, 1938

Dragon seed. Day 1942 378p $8.95

Fic

1 China—History—Fiction

The story of the farmer Ling Tan, and his wife and sons and daughters. The scene is outside and inside the walls of Nanking just before the Japanese assault and the fall of the city

"As war propaganda, the message which this book brings is terrific. And, to Mrs. Buck's honor, be it recorded that it is not so much anti-Japanese propaganda as a wider and deeper propaganda which becomes antibestiality and antidictatorship wherever that monster lifts its head." Christian Science Monitor

The good earth

Fic

1 China—Fiction

Some editions are:

Day $7.50, lib. bdg. $5.97

Watts, F. $9.95 Larke type edition complete and unabridged. A Keith Jennison book

First published 1931

Pulitzer Prize, 1932

A "story of a Chinese peasant and his passionate, dogged accumulation of land and more land, while weathering famine and drought and revolution. Authentic." N Y Libraries

"There is simple dignity of style, easy flow of narrative, firmness of character drawing, above all wealth of detail in The Good Earth, detail which builds up solidly and securely a scene in which men and women move and grow and meet and act upon one another as in life." Outlook

Imperial woman; a novel. Day 1956 376p $8.95

Fic

1 China—History—Fiction 2 Tz'u-hsi, Empress dowager of China—Fiction

"A biographical novel about Tzu-hsi, last Empress of China, known as Old Buddha. Her life is pictured from the day she received the Imperial summmons to appear before the Emperior, to her death in 1908." Book Rev Digest

"The accuracy or lack of accuracy will probably be of no particular concern to the readers of 'Imperial Woman.' . . . The details of the secluded life in the Forbidden City, the political jugglings of the court, and the increasing pressure from the Western powers as the Manchu Dynasty breaks up—these contribute to the novel's movement." N Y Times Bk R

Letter from Peking; a novel. Day 1957 252p $6.95

Fic

1 China—Fiction

This novel "deals largely with the devotion of an American wife of a part-Chinese university president, living in Vermont with her teenaged son while her husband remains at his post in Peking. Even when her husband asks her permission to take another wife, the heroine's love for him does not falter. There is also the story of the son's problems in growing up." Pub W

A "story of two worlds and divided loyalties unfolds, involving three generations in [a] rich study of the relations of people, families, bloods, and nations." Sec Ed Brd

Mandala. Day 1970 361p $8.95

Fic

1 India—Fiction

In this novel of present day India "Prince Jagat has lost most of his wealth and all of his royal titles, but he can never give up his responsibility to his people. His son Jai, who feels it is his duty to fight, has a premonition of death and actually dies in one of the battles between India and China. Prince Jagat and an American girl set out to find out if Jai really is dead. There ensues a delicate romance as well as a quest into the Himalayas to seek the wisdom of the Lama." Library J

"Pearl Buck writes gently and mystically of love's flowering, the meeting of East and West, the changing of an ancient society. 'Mandala's' evocation of India and Indians is constantly perceptive and meaningful." Pub W

Bulwer-Lytton, Sir Edward

The last days of Pompeii

Fic

1 Pompeii—Fiction 2 Rome—History—Empire, 30 B.C.-476 A.D.—Fiction

Some editions are:

Dodd (Great illustrated classics) $4.50 Illustrated with a portrait of the author and photographs and drawings of Pompeii. With an introduction by Curtis Dahl

Dutton (Everyman's lib) $3.25 Introduction by the Earl of Lytton

First published 1834

"The simple story relates principally to two young people of Grecian origin, Glaucus and Ione, who are deeply attached to each other. The former is a handsome young Athenian, impetuous, high-minded, and brilliant, while Ione is a pure and lofty-minded woman. Arbaces, her guardian, the villian of the story, under a cloak of sanctity and religion, indulges in low and criminal designs. His character is strongly drawn; and his passion for Ione, and the struggle between him and Glaucus, form the chief part of the plot. . . . The book, full of learning and spirit, is not only a charming novel, but contains many minute and interesting descriptions of ancient customs; among which, those relating to the gladiatorial combat, the banquet, the bath, are most noteworthy." Keller's Reader's Digest of Books

Bunyan, John

The Pilgrim's progress

Fic

1 Christian life—Fiction

Some editions are:

Dodd (Great illustrated classics) $4.50 Including an introduction to the book and a note on the William Blake designs by A. K. Adams, together with an essay on John Bunyan by Thomas Babington Macaulay. Sixteen pages of illustrations including reproductions of the frontispiece and eight designs for the first part by William Blake

Dutton $3.95 Illustrated by Frank C. Papé

Dutton (Everyman's lib) $3.25 Introduction and notes by G. B. Harrison

Grosset $2.95 Illustrated by Leonard Vosburgh. Has title: The Pilgrim's progress from this world to that which is to come

Oxford (World's classics) $2.25 Has title: The Pilgrim's progress from this world to that which is to come

First published 1678

Bunyan, John—*Continued*

"The 'immortal allegory,' next to the Bible the most widely known book in religious literature. It was written in Bedford jail, where Bunyan was for twelve years a prisoner for his convictions. It describes the troubled journey of Christian and his companions through this life to a triumphal entrance into the Celestial city. Bunyan 'wrote with virgin purity utterly free from mannerisms and affectations; and without knowing himself for a writer of fine English, produced it.'" Pratt Alcove

Burdick, Eugene

Fail-safe, by Eugene Burdick & Harvey Wheeler. McGraw 1962 286p boards $6.95

Fic

1 Atomic warfare—Fiction

"What might happen, sometime in the future, if in a missile raid warning which proved a false alarm, one group of bombers was by fateful accident, not given its recall and flew on towards Moscow with nuclear bombs. The scene is, mostly, Washington, the President's air raid shelter, where he has a private telephone wire to Khrushchev." Pub W

"The President's agonizing solution—which the reader lives through fully with him—brings a finale that shows convincingly how no one can win in nuclear war. . . . A science-fiction atmosphere surrounds much of the plot, but never incredibly; and occasional departures from the command centers into the private lives of the agents offer further reassurance about the reality of the whole performance. . . . It proves that excitement can be both intellectual and emotional." Best Sellers

Burgess, Anthony

A clockwork orange. Norton [1963 c1962] 184p boards $3.95   Fic

1 London—Fiction

First published 1962 in England

"In Mr. Burgess's Slav-oriented state of the future, the Lower Orders are in ascendence and happy hooligans roam the London streets, bashing senior citizens in the eyes with bicycle chains. The protagonist is a 15-year-old psychopath named Alex who undergoes a corrective brainwashing that makes him allergic to violence." N Y Times Bk R

"'A Clockwork Orange' is a gruesome fable. Its poisonous culture has obvious roots in our own. It is a nightmare world, made terrifyingly real through Burgess' extraordinary use of language." N Y Her Trib Books

Butler, Samuel

The way of all flesh   Fic

1 Great Britain—Fiction

Some editions are:

Dodd (Great illustrated classics) $4.50 With illustrations of the author, his environment and the setting of the book, together with an introduction and captions by Louis B. Salomon

Dufour $4.50 With drawings by Donna Nachsen

Dutton (Everyman's lib) $3.25 Introduction by A. J. Hoppé

Watts, F. $5.50 Ultratype edition

Published posthumously 1903

A semi-autobiographical account of a son struggling to find himself and break free of the restrictions of Victorian convention and [British] parental authority. Ernest Pontifex has the doubts and struggles that we now recognize as modern. One of the best books ever written about education—in both the narrow and the broad sense." Good Reading

It "is generally regarded as a very original work; it exercised considerable influence on later English writers." Haydn. Thesaurus of Book Digests

Caidin, Martin

Four came back; a novel. McKay 1968 275p boards $5.95   Fic

1 Science fiction

"The story of eight astronauts orbiting in the internationally sponsored space station 'Epsilon.' They are stricken by a mysterious and apparently fatal disease. The plot revolves around their attempts to discover the causes

and the cure for the affliction, and their decision whether to sacrifice themselves rather than bring a 'plague from space' to a panic-stricken world. . . . The authenticity of the space technology and the breathless pace of action make the novel a thoroughly enjoyable adventure story, one which makes the reader forget any short-comings of style. Only those offended by fairly explicit sexual scenes are likely to find this story anything but exciting and highly entertaining." Library J

Caldwell, Taylor

Dear and glorious physician. Doubleday 1959 574p $7.50   Fic

1 Luke, Saint—Fiction 2 Church history—Primitive and early church—Fiction

This novel about Lucanus, or Luke, "physician and author of one of the Gospels, depicts him as an individual apart, plainly marked out for the service of God in spite of his almost lifelong protest against a deity who inflicted pain on men. Antioch, scene of his boyhood; Rome, where he visited his family in the intervals between his restless travels; Alexandria, where he was educated; and Judaea, where he learned the story of Jesus from his mother Mary and acknowledged him as the Christ, provide a background." Booklist

Great lion of God. Doubleday 1970 629p $7.95   Fic

1 Paul, Saint, apostle—Fiction 2 Palestine—Fiction

Based on the life of St Paul "this very long novel covers Paul's life from the time of his birth and ends with his departure from Palestine for Rome, covering too the Biblical story of Jesus as it related to Paul, his first disbelief in the new Messiah and his conversion after the Crucifixion and Resurrection. The meticulous background of life in Palestine is marvelously created so that the reader feels he is there." Pub W

Camus, Albert

Nobel Prize in literature, 1957

The fall; tr. from the French by Justin O'Brien. Knopf 1957 [c1956] 147p boards $4.50   Fic

Original French edition published 1956

"The hero of this novel tells his story to a stranger whom he has picked up in a sailors' bar in Amsterdam. He was once a successful Parisian lawyer noted for his modesty and kindly thoughtfulness for the poor and the defeated. At heart, however, he despised all but himself. Two insignificant experiences cause him to be revealed to himself in all his insincerity, sham, and shameless immorality. He sets about to reveal his true self to all which soon brings about his calamitous descent to disgrace. In him, Camus mirrors the vices and the despair of his generation." Library J

"Though 'The Fall' seems at times a meditation rather than a novel, it is an irresistibly brilliant examination of the modern conscience. Only a very obdurate reader could finish it without finding himself much more honest about the character of his motives and the contradictions in his values. Despite its external ambiguity and apparent negations, the book has a positive effect of a uniquely personal kind. This is existentialism in practice." N Y Times Bk R

The plague; tr. from the French by Stuart Gilbert   Fic

1 Plague—Fiction 2 Algeria—Fiction

Some editions are:

Knopf $5.95

Modern Lib. $2.95

Original French edition, 1947

"A coastal city in Algeria is struck by bubonic plague and shut off from the world while the pestilence rages for months. The impact on a small group of people and their ways of meeting the catastrophe make the story." Booklist

"Sober, tautly written . . . it creates a situation of soul-revealing crisis, and peoples that situation with very real and well differentiated characters. . . . In telling their story of brave resistance, Albert Camus has accomplished a

Camus, Albert—*Continued*

perfect achievement which, despite the unrelieved grimness of the theme, contains great variety, gay humor and stimulating philosophy." New Repub

The stranger; tr. from the French by Stuart Gilbert. Knopf 1946 154p $4.95 **Fic**

1 Murder—Fiction 2 Algeria—Fiction 3 French in Algeria—Fiction

First French edition published 1942. Published in England with title: The outsider

"An ordinary little clerk living in Algiers is the subject of this novel. . . . The little man lives quietly and for the most part unemotionally until he becomes involved in another man's folly. He shoots an Arab, is tried for murder, and condemned to die. As he contemplates his fate he does seem on the verge of a bit of human emotion." Book Rev Digest

"This is an excellent piece of short fiction, in the classic French tradition. Like many French novelists before him, Camus excels in delineating the narrowness of French provincial life. The handling of the shooting on the beach would almost serve as a model to many American writers of the tough school. The trial itself is reported with a detached irony which makes the underlying horror only the more noticeable. Stuart Gilbert's translation merits unreserved praise. Camus emerges as a master craftsman who never wastes a word." Sat R

Cannon, LeGrand

Look to the mountain, by LeGrand Cannon, Jr. **Fic**

1 Frontier and pioneer life—Fiction 2 New Hampshire—Fiction

Some editions are:
Holt $5.95
Watts, F. $9.95 Large type edition. A Keith Jennison book

First published 1942 by Holt

"This historical novel about the American dream of personal freedom—tells the story of Whit and Melissa who became pioneers so that they might be together and fashion a home and a future for their children. The struggle was relentless from the moment they set forth up the Connecticut to their goal under the peak of Chocorua; but they never questioned their decision or their hardships. An engaging, unpretentious and memorable tale of life in New Hampshire before the Revolution." Huntting

Capote, Truman

A Christmas memory. Random House [1966 c1956] 45p $5 **Fic**

1 Christmas stories

Appeared originally in Mademoiselle, and later in the author's "Breakfast at Tiffany's"

"This beautiful, bittersweet story evokes Alabama 'coming-of-winter' mornings, 'fruitcake weather' and the special joys of Christmas preparations shared by a small boy and his best friend [an elderly cousin]." McClurg. Book News

Other voices, other rooms **Fic**

1 Louisiana—Fiction

Some edtions are:
Modern Lib. $2.95
Random House $6.95

First published 1948

A "novel describing the abnormal maturing of a loveless thirteen-year-old boy who goes to live with his father in a run-down Louisiana mansion peopled with eccentric characters." Book Rev Digest

"Much may still be desired in this tale of a pilgrimage through adolescence whose sources appear to be first-hand and autobiographical despite the apparent influences of McCullers, Barnes, Faulkner and Proust. 'Other Voices, Other Rooms' must be reckoned with as a fascinating experiment in symbols and images . . . notwithstanding the immediate reservations made by those who prefer obscure substance to definite shadow." Commonweal

The Thanksgiving visitor. Random House [1968 c1967] 63p boards $4.95 **Fic**

1 Thanksgiving Day—Stories

This autobiographical story is about "Odd Henderson, a twelve-year-old bully; Buddy, his

victim; and Miss Sook, Buddy's spinster [cousin] and best friend, who insisted on inviting Odd to Thanksgiving dinner." Bk Buyer's Guide

"Truman Capote's brief story is as wispy as Buddy himself must have been at the age of 8, but it has that peculiar Capote blend of energy and whimsy. . . . Minor Capote, but warm and pleasant." Book of the Month Club News

Capps, Benjamin

A woman of the people; a novel. Duell 1966 242p boards $5.95 **Fic**

1 Comanche Indians—Fiction

Captured in 1854 by Comanche Indians, nine-year-old Helen Morrison "yearned to escape, but over the years the tribe absorbed her into their ways, and the love of her adopted family and, later of her husband, tied emotional bonds. Her slow change from white to Indian, the nomadic way of life, the tribe's pursuit of the buffaloes, and the tragic last years of the tribe as the white men raided, killed, and destroyed are . . . portrayed." Pub W

" 'A Woman of the People' tells a dramatic story of the Morrison girl's captivity, but it tells also in copious and apparently authentic detail about 19th-century Comanche life; how 'the people' dressed, what they ate, how they hunted, traded, sang, tended their sick and wounded, buried their dead." Book of the Month Club News

Cather, Willa

Death comes for the archbishop. Knopf 1927 303p $5.95 **Fic**

1 Catholic Church—Missions—Fiction 2 New Mexico—Fiction

"Miss Cather tells the story of a French priest who in the middle years of the last century went to New Mexico, as vicar apostolic and became archbishop of Santa Fé. With him went also Father Joseph Vaillant, friend of his seminary days in France. The two labored together devotedly and by their love and wisdom won the Southwest for the Catholic Church. It was after nearly forty years of good works in his diocese that death came for the archbishop and he lay before the high altar in the church he had built. He died 'of having lived.' " Book Rev Digest

"A mature and beautiful novel by one of our great . . . prose writers. Serene and contemplative in manner, it is typical of Miss Cather's best work, symbolizing the fruition of her literary artistry." Independent

My Antonia **Fic**

1 Czechs in the U.S.—Fiction 2 Frontier and pioneer life—Fiction 3 Nebraska—Fiction

Some editions are:
Houghton $6.95 With illustrations by W. T. Benda
Watts, F. $9.95 Large type edition. A Keith Jennison book

First published 1918

"Story is told by a New York lawyer who reviews his Nebraska boyhood days and his friendship with a young Bohemian girl, the strong and simple Antonia Shimerda, who is the central figure in the novel. A convincing picture of pioneering conditions and of America's assimilation of the immigrant." N Y State Lib

"The story is simply and faithfully told with appreciation of character and a strong feeling for the stubborn country and the rich rewards of its final yielding." Cleveland

O pioneers! **Fic**

1 Frontier and pioneer life—Fiction 2 Nebraska—Fiction

Some editions are:
Houghton $4
Watts, F. $9.95 Large type edition. A Keith Jennison book

First published 1913

"The heroic battle for survival of simple pioneer folk in the Nebraska country of the 1880's. John Bergson, a Swedish farmer, struggles desperately with the soil but dies unsatisfied. His daughter Alexandra resolves to vindicate his faith, and her strong character carries her

Cather, Willa—*Continued*

weak older brothers and her mother along to a new zest for life. Years of privation are rewarded on the farm. But when Alexandra falls in love with Carl Linstrum, and her family objects because he is poor, he leaves to seek a different career. After Alexandra's younger brother Emil is killed by the jealous husband of the French girl Marie Shabata, however, Carl gives up his plans to go to the Klondike, returns to marry Alexandra and take up the life of the farm." Haydn. Thesaurus of Book Digests

"The land itself, 'the Divide,' is made almost a character in the narrative and supplies that sense of conflict with the elemental forces of life which is essential to real tragedy. It is written with sympathy and power, compactly and with perfect restraint." Pittsburgh

One of ours. Knopf 1922 459p $6.95   **Fic**

1 Nebraska—Fiction 2 European War, 1914-1918—Fiction

Pulitzer Prize 1923

"A spiritual biography of a young American brought up on a Nebraska farm, with a mediocre education, married to a prim and passionless wife, living a life which he could not make seem real until [the First World War] saved him and gave him something big to do that seemed worth doing." Pittsburgh

"A fine achievement. The first portion dealing with a farm life in Nebraska could not be matched by any one else now writing. The second part, in France and at the war, is more removed, but has its poignant beauty." Int Bk R

Sapphira and the slave girl. Knopf 1940 295p $5.95   **Fic**

1 Slavery in the U.S.—Fiction 2 Virginia—Fiction

"Having married below her social rank, Sapphira Colbert, before the Civil War, exiled herself to a backwoods Virginia farm, with her husband, a miller, and her family slaves, and now aging and dropsical she puts an erroneous construction on her husband's interest in Nancy, a golden-skinned slave, once her own favorite. How Sapphira not only spoils a sweet companionship but sets about to persecute the once happy and devoted girl and even to bring about her downfall by keeping a rakish young nephew about the house is related." Bookmark

"It shows in its central character the tangible passion and struggle, in its secondary characters the honest virtue and credible humility, and in its general atmosphere of fear and obsession a dramatic force that lift the tale out of its exaggerated moralism and dramatic simplicity into its own kind of truth and power. Its people rise above the flat dimensions of moral humors." Nation

Shadows on the rock. Knopf 1931 280p $5.95   **Fic**

1 Quebec (City)—Fiction 2 Frontenac, Louis de Buade, comte de—Fiction

"In this charming idyll of the French colony at Quebec in the time of Frontenac and Bishop Laval, Willa Cather has again chosen a background of Roman Catholic civilization. It is hardly a novel—rather a series of pictures and anecdotes of the homes, the marketplace, the Ursuline convent, the hunters, and the missionary priests of old Canada." Booklist

"In this quiet book, one steps back three and a half centuries and shares, through the glowing magic of a deeply understanding prose, the life of the French colony, dwelling on the gray mountain rock, 'Kebec.' Characters, historic or imagined are finely created, and the aspect of the rock itself . . . is lovingly portrayed through the changing seasons." N Y Libraries

The song of the lark. Houghton 1915 580p $5   **Fic**

1 Singers—Fiction

"The story of the development of a great American singer. The old broken down music master in Moonstone, Colorado, told Mrs. Kronborg, wife of the Swedish minister, that the little girl, Thea, had talent. From that moment Thea's career was determined on. She must practice four hours a day and become a piano teacher. It is not until she goes to Chicago to continue her studies that she learns

that her future lies in her voice. Three men believe in Thea, Ray Kennedy, the freight train conductor, Howard Archie, the Moonstone doctor, and Fred Ottenburg, the millionaire brewer. Each in his way helps her, and she justifies their faith. She leaves Moonstone far behind her, but she never gets away from its influence." Book Rev Digest

"It is not so much the feeling of life that I get here, as the sense of something less common than life: namely, art as it exists in life, —A very curious and elusive thing, but so beautiful, when one gets it, that one forgets all else." Dial

Cervantes, Miguel de

Don Quixote de la Mancha   **Fic**

1 Spain—Fiction

Some editions are:

Dodd (Great illustrated classics. Titan editions) $5.50 Introduction by John Kenneth Leslie. Has title: The adventures of Don Quixote de la Mancha

Dutton (The Children's illustrated classics) $3.95 Illustrated with 8 pages of colour plates and drawings in the text by W. Heath Robinson. Has title: The adventures of Don Quixote de la Mancha

Dutton (Everyman's lib) 2v ea $3.25 Introduction by J. G. Lockhart. Translated by Motteux

Grosset $4.95 Has title: The adventures of Don Quixote, man of la Mancha

Modern Lib. $2.95 Complete in two parts. A new translation from the Spanish, with a critical text based upon the first editions of 1605 and 1615, and with variant readings, variorum notes, and with an introduction by Samuel Putnam. Has title: The ingenious gentleman Don Quixote de la Mancha

Modern Lib. (Modern Lib. giants) $4.95 Ozell's revision of the translation of Peter Motteux; introduction by Herschel Brickell

Viking $8.95 Complete in two parts. A new translation from the Spanish, with a critical text based upon the first editions of 1605 and 1615, and with variant readings, variorum notes, and an introduction by Samuel Putnam. Has title: The ingenious gentleman Don Quixote de la Mancha

"Treats of the pleasant manner of the knighting of that famous gentleman, Don Quixote, of the dreadful and never-to-be imagined adventure of the windmills, of the extraordinary battle he waged with what he took to be a giant, and of divers other rare and notable adventures and strange enchantments which befell this valorous and witty knight-errant." Pittsburgh

"By the time of the death of the Knight, Sancho Panza [his squire] has become an altogether lovable, quixotic character, so that the reader parts from them and their exciting world of marvels with deeply felt regret. The novel which obviously had for its genesis the satire of romances of chivalry, gradually grew into a vast panorama of Spanish life and into a most entertaining work of fiction, the first modern novel, read and admired to this day as one of the world's great literary achievements." Haydn. Thesaurus of Book Digests

Chase, Mary Ellen

The edge of darkness. Norton 1957 235p $5.95   **Fic**

1 Maine—Fiction

"The day of Sarah Holt's funeral discloses her impact on her son, her neighbors, the fishermen, and the children of the Maine village where she lived for thirty years. No intrigue, no real plot, not much action—just fine writing and a glimpse of life and beauty that lingers on." Sec Ed Brd

Christie, Agatha

Hallowe'en party. Dodd 1969 248p $5.95   **Fic**

1 Mystery and detective stories 2 Great Britain—Fiction

This Hercule Poirot mystery brings "the mustachioed old master out of his retirement in England to find the murderer of a 13-year-old girl at a children's Hallowe'en party. The

Christie, Agatha—*Continued*

unknown had taken the means at hand, holding Joyce's head under water in an apple-bobbing pail. There was no apparent motive. Most people in Woodleigh Common decided that [it] was a pathological killer until Poirot began probing into the past lives of both children and adults in the town." Pub W

"If you are familiar with Miss Christie's works and her methods you may suspect the correct criminal half-way through; but even then you will not be sure until the end." Best Sellers

The murder of Roger Ackroyd. Dodd [1967 c1926] 288p $3.95 **Fic**

1 Mystery and detective stories 2 Great Britain—Fiction

"The Greenway edition"
First published 1926
"The story is told in the first person by Dr. Sheppard the physician in a small English village called King's Abbott. Roger Ackroyd is murdered one night under particularly perplexing circumstances. Strong suspicions centre on his stepson, Ralph Payton, who had not only the best of motives, but also disappeared immediately following the murder. The case is taken over by Hercule Poirot. Matters become more and more complicated, till one surprising fact after another begins to reveal itself." Book Rev Digest

"Miss Christie's dedication of the book is to one 'who likes an orthodox detective story, murder, inquest, and suspicion falling on every one in turn!' So she set herself to write such an orthodox story, with the strange result that she has succeeded in producing one of the few notable for originality." Sat R

Churchill, Winston, 1871-1947

The crisis. Macmillan (N Y) 1951 [c1901] 516p $6.50 **Fic**

1 U.S.—History—Civil War—Fiction

First published 1901
The hero of this historical novel "is Stephen Brice, an anti-slavery New Englander who accepts a job in [a] judge's law office and meets Virginia Carvel, descendant of Richard Carvel. The young people fall in love, but Virginia, because of her Southern convictions, renounces Stephen's affection and becomes engaged to her cousin, Clarence Colfax, a Confederate cavalier. Stephen is wounded with the Union Army, and becomes an aide to Lincoln. Virginia finally breaks with Clarence, who is taken as a spy, and while visiting Lincoln to seek his pardon, is reunited with Stephen." Haydn. Thesaurus of Book Digests

"The novel shows the inevitability of the Civil War, yet stresses the fact that neither side wanted it. The book includes a notable portrait of Lincoln." Benét. The Reader's Encyclopedia

Chute, B. J.

Greenwillow; drawings by Erik Blegvad. Dutton 1956 237p illus boards $5.95 **Fic**

"An enigmatic novel describing life in a small English village where for a time two pastors seek to save the souls of the inhabitants. The Reverend Lapp preached hell fire, but the mysterious Reverend Birdsong was more gentle, and it was doubtless the latter who was responsible for breaking the curse of the Briggs family." Book Rev Digest

"Creating its own reality as it goes along, conjuring up a pastoral microcosm that exists outside space and time, eloquently celebrating the natural world, 'Greenwillow' is a work of sheer, happy imagination—one of those small brave books that defy literary fashions." N Y Her Trib Books

Chute, Marchette

The innocent wayfaring; with decorations by the author. Dutton [1955 c1943] 199p illus $3.95 **Fic**

1 Great Britain—Fiction

First published 1943 by Scribner
"A tale of young love in Chaucer's England. Anne, daughter of Sir Hugh Richmond, runs away from the convent, presided over by an aunt, and joins a young poet, also in revolt over parental wishes. In three days wayfaring along the roads of southern England, the young couple fall in love, and decide to go home and be married and live happily ever after." Book Rev Digest

Clarke, Arthur C.

2001: a space odyssey. . . . New Am. Lib. Distributed by Norton. 1968 221p boards $6.95 **Fic**

1 Science fiction

"Based on a screenplay by Stanley Kubrick and Arthur C. Clarke." Title page
This novel depicts the interplanetary voyage "of the spacecraft 'Discovery,' hurtling its human voyagers . . . toward a confrontation with an unknown Intelligence." Publisher's note

The book "cannot convey the film's amazing visual effects, but it does make the story of earth's first indisputable contact with alien intelligence a little easier to follow." Library J

Cleary, Jon

The sundowners. [Young people's ed] Scribner [1965 c1952] 383p $5.95, lib. bdg. $5.09 **Fic**

1 Sheep—Stories 2 Australia—Fiction

A special edition for young people of the title originally published 1952
Ida and Paddy Carmody are sundowners, people who roam Australia during the 1920's earning a living as sheep drovers and shearers. Ida and her 14-year-old son, Sean, longing for a permanent home, are frustrated by Paddy's wanderlust. (Publisher)

"The author's restraint never allows the book to become overly sentimental. . . . [It] is notable not so much for the action it develops as for the human qualities it depicts." N Y Her Trib Books

Notes: p379-80. Glossary: p381-83

Collins, Wilkie

The moonstone **Fic**

1 Mystery and detective stories

Some editions are:
Dodd (Great illustrated classics) $4.50 With illustrations of the author and the setting of the book together with an introduction and descriptive captions by Basil Davenport
Dutton (Everyman's lib) $3.25
Oxford (World's classics) $2.50
Watts, F. $9.95 Large type edition, complete and unabridged. A Keith Jennison book

First edition 1868
This novel "concerns the disappearance of the Moonstone, an enormous diamond that once adorned a Hindu idol and came into the possession of an English officer. The heroine, Miss Verinder, believes her lover, Franklin Blake, to be the thief; other suspects are Blake's rival and three mysterious Brahmins. The mystery is solved by Sergeant Cuff, possibly the first detective in English fiction." Benét. The Reader's Encyclopedia

The woman in white; introduction by Maurice Richardson. Dutton 569p $2.95 **Fic**

1 Mystery and detective stories

"Everyman's library"
First published 1873
"Practically the first English novel to deal with the detection of crime. The plot is based on the resemblance between the heroine and a mysterious woman in white, and involves an infamous attempt to obtain the heroine's money." Lenrow. Reader's Guide to Prose Fiction

Conrad, Joseph

Lord Jim **Fic**

1 Islands of the Pacific—Fiction

Some editions are:
Dodd (Great illustrated classics) $4.50 With pictures of the author and his environment and illustrations of the setting of the book together with an introduction by Edward Ellsberg

Conrad, Joseph—*Continued*

Doubleday $5.95
Modern Lib. $2.95 Introduction by J. Donald Adams
Watts, F. $8.95 Large type edition. A Keith Jennison book
First published 1899
A psychological study, combined with descriptions of the East, this is the story of a young Englishman's loss of honor in a panic, his settlement in a Malay village, and the final triumph of his sense of courage

The Nigger of the Narcissus; a tale of the forecastle. Doubleday 1959 190p $3.95 **Fic**

1 Sea stories

First published 1897 with title: Children of the sea
"Less narrative than a study of men's characters under stress, the story is centered on a Negro sailor, James Wait, who is dying of tuberculosis. The brooding presence of death brings out the best and the worst in the crew of the 'Narcissus.' In this tense atmosphere Donkin, a mean-spirited agitator, almost manages to stir the crew to mutiny." Benét. The Reader's Encyclopedia
"A wonderfully realistic description of rough seafaring life, by one who has been a seaman, and has moreover a poetic imagination." Baker's Best

Typhoon, and other tales of the sea; with photographs of the author and his environment as well as illustrations from early editions, together with an introduction by Edouard A. Stackpole. Dodd 1963 371p illus $4.50 **Fic**

1 Sea stories

"Great illustrated classics"
First published 1962 in England
Contains: Typhoon (1903); The nigger of the "Narcissus" and two short stories: Youth and Heart of Darkness
The first three sea stories and the last tale set in Africa all reflect this well known author's own experiences

Victory. Modern Lib. 385p $2.95 **Fic**

1 Islands of the Pacific—Fiction

First published 1915 by Doubleday
"'Enchanted Heyst,' a detached, introspective Swedish nobleman, lives alone on an island in the South Seas. Pity obliges him to rescue a girl from a travelling 'Ladies orchestra' and to take her to his retreat upon which exciting and tragic happenings follow. There is more of action than in most of his books."
N Y State Lib

Cooper, James Fenimore
The Deerslayer   **Fic**

1 Frontier and pioneer life—Fiction 2 Indians of North America—Fiction 3 New York (State) —Fiction

Some editions are:
Dodd (Great illustrated classics) $4.50 Biographical sketch by Basil Davenport. Illustrations reproducing drawings for early editions and photographs of historical scenes
Scribner (The Scribner Illustrated classics) $6 With pictures by N. C. Wyeth
First published 1841
This is the first of five books which comprise the author's Leatherstocking tales in which the chief character is Natty Bumppo, also known as Leatherstocking
Set in New York State this "is a record of Natty Bumppo's early days as a young hunter brought up among the Delaware Indians, engaged in warfare against the Hurons. He helps defend the family of Tom Hutter, a settler, from attack. Judith, who is really not Tom's daughter, but a girl of noble birth, loves Natty Bumppo and begs him not to return to the Iroquois, who have released him on parole from capture. Bumppo does return, but is rescued by the intervention of Judith, who thereafter disappears, and the Delaware Chief Chingachgook, who remains a lifelong friend." Haydn. Thesaurus of Book Digests
Followed by: The last of the Mohicans.

The last of the Mohicans   **Fic**

1 Frontier and pioneer life—Fiction 2 Indians of North America—Fiction 3 New York (State)—Fiction 4 U.S.—History—French and Indian War, 1755-1763—Fiction

Some editions are:
Dodd (Great illustrated classics) $4.50 Introduction and captions by Basil Davenport with illustrations from contemporary artists
Scribner (The Scribner Illustrated classics $6 Illustrated by N. C. Wyeth
Watts, F. $7.95 Large type edition, complete and unabridged. A Keith Jennison book
Sequel to: The Deerslayer
First published 1826
The second in the Leatherstocking tales "presents Chingachgook and his son Uncas as the last of the Iroquois aristocracy. Natty Bumppo, the scout Hawkeye, is in the prime of his career in the campaign of Fort William Henry on Lake George under attack by the French and Indians. The commander's daughters, Cora and Alice Munro, with the latter's fiancé Major Duncan Heyward, are captured by a traitorous Indian but rescued and conveyed to the fort by Hawkeye. Later Munro surrenders to Montcalm, and the girls are seized again by Indians. Uncas and Cora are killed, and the others return to civilization." Haydn. Thesaurus of Book Digests
Followed by: The Pathfinder

The Pathfinder   **Fic**

1 Frontier and pioneer life—Fiction 2 Indians of North America—Fiction 3 New York (State)—Fiction 4 U.S.—History—French and Indian War, 1755-1763—Fiction

Some editions are:
Dodd (Great illustrated classics) $4.50 With illustrations of the author and his environment and reproductions of drawings for early editions of the book together with an introduction and descriptive captions by Allen Klots, Jr.
Dutton (Everyman's lib) $3.25
Sequel to: The last of the Mohicans, this is the third of the Leatherstocking tales, published 1840
This book "finds Natty Bumppo at the age of forty. A small outpost on Lake Ontario is under attack. Mabel Dunham helps in the defense, and with the aid of Pathfinder, Chingachgook, and Jasper Western, a young sailor, the Iroquois are routed. Lieutenant Muir arrests Jasper as a traitor, but when Muir is revealed as the guilty one, he is killed by Arrowhead, a Tuscarora Indian. Jasper wins the love of Mabel." Haydn. Thesaurus of Book Digests
Followed by: The pioneers

The pioneers; with illus. of the author and his environment and reproductions of pictures for early editions of the book, together with a foreword and descriptive captions by Allen Klots, Jr. Dodd 1958 477p illus $4.50 **Fic**

1 Frontier and pioneer life—Fiction 2 New York (State)—Fiction

"Great illustrated classics"
Sequel to: The Pathfinder
First published 1822
"The character of Natty Bumppo here makes his first appearance in print as an older man, who has witnessed the coming of civilization to the wilderness. The story takes place in upper New York State. . . . The central conflict in the book concerns the opposition between the laws of nature, upheld by Natty, and the laws of civilization. Symbolic of this opposition are two incidents; in the first, Natty kills a deer for food, in Indian fashion. The white settlement seeks to punish him for failing to respect the seasonal hunting laws it has established. On the other hand, there is the wholesale slaughter of pigeons by the civilized inhabitants of . . . [the town] with no purpose but sport. . . . [In the end, Natty] heads for the far West to escape confining civilization." Benét. The Reader's Encyclopedia
Followed by: The prairie

The prairie; introduction by Basil Davenport. Dodd 1954 453p $4.50 **Fic**

1 Frontier and pioneer life—Fiction 2 Indians of North America—Fiction

Cooper, James F.—*Continued*

"Great illustrated classics"
First published 1827
Sequel to: The pioneers

This last Leatherstocking tale relates the story of the last days of Bumppo, "now an exile whom civilization has driven westward to the great prairies beyond the Mississippi. Here the old scout becomes a trapper, and here as everywhere, there are captives for him to rescue and numerous adventures for him to undertake. Finally, the old trapper dies in the arms of friends." Benét. The Reader's Encyclopedia

The spy; with illus. of contemporary scenes and a foreword by Curtis Dahl. Dodd 1949 333p illus $4.50   Fic

1 U.S.—History—Revolution—Fiction 2 New York (State)—Fiction

"Great illustrated classics"
Written in 1821-1822

A story of the American Revolution. The hero, the spy, is a cool, shrewd, fearless man, who is employed by General Washington in service which involves great personal danger and little glory

Covers "the locality 'between the royal barracks in New York City and the American outposts on the Hudson,' where a mixed population of loyalists and British sympathisers mistrusted one another. Not many historic figures or events are introduced . . . but the tale well illustrates the later Revolution period, and is full of allusions to such men as Burgoyne, Gates, Tarleton, Sumter, etc." Nield

Costain, Thomas B.

The black rose. Doubleday 1945 403p $5.95   Fic

1 Great Britain—History—Plantagenets, 1154-1399—Fiction

This novel laid in the 13th century is the story of a young English nobleman who fights his way to the heart of the Mongol empire and returns to find that he must choose between an English heiress and a girl of the East

"Its background of history is richly furnished with information and local color. . . . [It is] a story that, in spite of the attention given to the romance, derives its major interest from the remarkable tapestry of history against which it is enacted." Christian Science Monitor

Map on lining-papers

The darkness and the dawn; a novel. Doubleday 1959 478p $6.95   Fic

1 Attila—Fiction 2 Rome—History—Empire, 30 B.C.-476 A.D.—Fiction

An historical novel of the 5th century Europe when Attila the Hun, determind to conquer the world, set forth to capture Rome. Chief protagonists in the story are: Attila, the Scourge of God; Aetius, the dictator of Rome; Honoria, the love-minded imperial princess; Leo, the courageous pope; and, Nicolan the hero of the story. (Publisher)

"The color and liveliness that characterize the works of this author are [here] present in abundance." Christian Science Monitor

Map on lining-papers

The last love. Doubleday 1963 434p $6.95   Fic

1 Napoléon I, Emperor of the French—Fiction 2 Balcombe, Betsy—Fiction

"In three parts; 'A guest in the house,' 'Betsy grows up,' and 'The twilight falls' telling of Napoleon's stay with the Balcombes on the island of St. Helena while his living quarters were being prepared and of fifteen-year-old Betsy's romantic admiration." Bk Buyer's Guide

"The intimate portrait of Napoleon during his decline is tragically revealing. His amours are delicately treated; the story unrolls vividly and dramatically." Library J

The silver chalice; a novel; illus. by Burt Silverman. Doubleday [1964 c1952] 533p illus $6.95   Fic

1 Grail—Fiction 2 Church history—Primitive and early church—Fiction

A reissue with new illustrations of the title first published 1952

A story about the cup used by Christ at the Last Supper with his disciples. Basil of Antioch, a young skilled artisan, purchased from slavery to create a decorative casing for the precious chalice, pursues his project, braving the perils of Christian persecution. Set in Antioch, Jerusalem, and ancient Rome

In this long novel "Costain paints a tremendous canvas filled with warm color and life. . . . As those known who have read his many vigorous re-creations of the past, Costain has a magnificent talent for breaking life into history. . . . But over and above this the novel does something else. It will make real for thousands, perhaps for the first time, the whole world of the New Testament." Chicago Sunday Tribune

Courlander, Harold

The African; a novel. Crown 1967 311p $5.95   Fic

1 Slavery in the U.S.—Fiction

"An African boy taken into slavery and brought to the U.S. in the early 1800's is the subject of a clear review of American Negro history in an excellent well-written novel." Bruno. Books for School Libraries, 1968

"Courlander, an expert on African history and folklore, emphasizes the influence of their cultural heritage on American Negroes and in a suspenseful, moving story without excessive emotion or sentimentality, depicts the effect on both Negroes and whites." Booklist

Includes: Some words, African and other, appearing in this tale

Crane, Stephen

The red badge of courage   Fic

1 Chancellorsville, Battle of, 1863—Fiction

Some editions are:
Dutton (Children's illustrated classics) $4.50 With colour plates by Charles Mozley. Has subtitle: an episode of the American Civil War
Hawthorn Bks. $3.95
Macmillan (N Y) (The Macmillan classics) $3.95 Afterword by Clifton Fadiman; illustrations by Herschel Levit
Modern Lib. $2.95
Watts, F. $7.95 Large type edition. A Keith Jennison book

First published 1895

"A young Union soldier, Henry Fleming, tells of his feelings when he is under fire for the first time during the battle of Chancellorsville. He is overcome by fear and runs from the field. Later he returns to lead a charge that re-establishes his own reputation as well as that of his company. One of the great novels of the Civil War." Cincinnati

Crichton, Michael

The Andromeda strain. Knopf 1969 295p illus boards $5.95   Fic

1 Science fiction

"An American unmanned space satellite lands on the edge of a small Arizona town. Almost at once it becomes clear that something has gone terribly wrong. All of the town's inhabitants die suddenly and grotesquely, and the first investigators, die suddenly and grotesquely, and the first investigators, when a rescue team arrives they find alive only a squalling two-month old baby and an old man who has been quieting his ulcer with massive doses of aspirin and drinking Sterno. 'The Andromeda Strain' is the story of a frantic race against time and death carried out by four handpicked scientists in a vast underground government lab. Their job: to find out what the contaminating agent from outer space is, and how to fight it." Pub W

The author "reveals his ability to conceive an imaginative idea and construct a plot that is commendable for its scientific and medical verisimilitude. Although, like most science-fiction writers, he fails to create characters of human dimension, he is concerned with moral values, and makes graphic the dangers of exploiting science for such goals as the perfection of chemical- and biological-warfare techniques." Newsweek

References: p292-95

Cronin, A. J.

The citadel. Little 1937 401p $6.95   Fic

1 Physicians—Fiction 2 Wales—Fiction

"Story of the career of a conscientious, brilliant young doctor, from his start in a mining town in Wales, to the realization of his ambition for a London practice. After many years of struggle against mediocrity and indifference, he decided to capitalize on personal charm and make money. But success meant forgetting honor and ideals, and brought estrangement from a gallant life, until a tragic error brought him to his senses. A restrained, but scathing expose of certain aspects of the British medical profession, which makes a moving and absorbing novel." Wis Lib Bul

The green years. Little 1944 347p $6.95   Fic

1 Adolescence—Fiction 2 Irish in Scotland—Fiction

"A story of adolescence, it covers ten years in the life of Robert Shannon, who after the death of his parents in Ireland comes to Scotland to live with his mother's people. There is no room for Robie in the crowded household where every penny is counted with miserly thrift. There isn't even a place for him to sleep. But to compensate for his miseries there is Grandpa. Grandpa (great grandfather really) is a memorable character, vain and boastful and intemperate, but one who understands small boys, and who, in the end, with one magnificent gesture, settles the problem of Robert's future." Wis Lib Bul

The keys of the kingdom. Little 1941 344p $6.95   Fic

1 Missionaries—Fiction 2 China—Fiction

"This story of Father Francis Chisholm, dedicated Catholic priest, begins when he was about nine years of age. He lost his parents as the indirect result of religous persecution and was taken in by his warmhearted Aunt Polly and her husband. They sent him to Holywell to be educated, and when he has a young man, he decided to devote his life to his religion. . . . [At the turn of this century, he becomes a vicar] in China where he found, not the flourishing mission he had been promised, but instead the remnants of a crumbling church with no congregation. Realizing that the people needed medical aid, he opened a small dispensary and gradually made friends and won real converts to the Church. The story of Father Chisholm's [30] years in China is a dramatic one. . . . Famine and civil war tested the courage of Father Chisholm and his co-workers, and at one time he and his Protestant missionary friends were captured and tortured by bandits before making a daring escape. Finally replaced by two younger priests, he came home, weary but indomitable, to spend his remaining years in his native Scotland." Doors to More Mature Reading

Davis, William Stearns

A victor of Salamis; a tale of the days of Xerxes, Leonidas, and Themistocles. Macmillan (N Y) 1935 [c1907] 450p $5.95 Fic

1 Greece—History—Fiction

First published 1907

This novel "describes the Isthmian games, the Pan-Athenaic festival, and the battles of Thermopylae, Salamis, and Plataea (481-479 B.C.)." Baker's Best

Dayan, Yael

Death has two sons; a novel. McGraw 1967 191p $4.95   Fic

1 Israel—Fiction

"The terrible memory that haunts . . . [Daniel Kalinsky] is that of his father choosing between him and his brother, under Nazi directive, as to which should live. Ironically, Daniel, the son he did not choose, is the only one to survive and now the old man, dying of cancer, and with a second family, has come to Israel where Daniel is trying to come to terms with his feelings about his father." Pub W

Miss Dayan "is writing about the horrors of war, the conflict of generations, the riddle of love. She is also writing about human beings—the father a good if ordinary man forced into an inhuman decision and unable to atone for it; the son a 'child of death' who cannot escape war (his best friend is killed in the Sinai) or the bitterness of his existence." Book of the Month Club News

Defoe, Daniel

The fortunes and misfortunes of the famous Moll Flanders   Fic

Some editions are:
Dutton (Everyman's lib) $3.25
Harcourt (The Harcourt Lib. of English and American classics) $3.95

First published 1722

"Moll went to the bad in early life, was five times married (bigamously or legitimately she little cared), a thief and a harlot, and eventually a penitent. She tells her story with a plain sincerity that both captivates and appalls." Baker's Best

"Defoe allows Moll always to speak for herself, voicing her righteousness, explaining the necessity for being 'temporarily' wicked. Sterile as her morality is, she nevertheless permits herself an occasional flash of intense self-awareness—which she must promptly forget in order to survive in the jungle of her times." The College and Adult Reading List

A journal of the plague year   Fic

1 London—Plague, 1665—Fiction

Some editions are:
Dutton (Everyman's lib) $2.95 Has subtitle: Written by a citizen who continued all the while in London
Oxford $6.75 Edited with an introduction by Louis Landa. Has subtitle: Being observations or memorials of the most remarkable occurrences, as well publick as private, which happened in London during the last Great Visitation in 1665

First published 1722

This is an "account of the epidemic of bubonic plague in England during the summer and fall of 1665. . . . It purports to be an eye-witness report by a resident of London." Benét. The Readers Encyclopedia

"Contemporaries of Defoe thought the Journal was authentic; it gave such persuasive details of the London plague. However, it was instead a clever hoax. The Journal contains precise descriptions of how the frightened citizens fled to the country for safety, how they hid in caves and lived in makeshift huts. To add to the verisimilitude of the tale, Defoe mentions names, dates and places. . . . Defoe wrote of events which had occured during his early childhood; and left us an account of the plague which, if fictionalized, is nevertheless of great historical interest." Haydn. Thesaurus of Book Digests

Robinson Crusoe   Fic

1 Survival (after airplane accidents, shipwrecks, etc.)—Fiction

Some editions are:
Dodd (Great illustrated classics) $4.50 With an introductory sketch of the author and with illustrations by Thomas Stothard
Dutton (Everyman's lib) $3.25
Macmillan (N Y) (The Macmillan classics) $3.95, lib. bdg. $4.24 Illustrated by Federico Castellon. Afterword by Clifton Fadiman
Oxford (The World's classics) $2.25 Has title: The life and adventures of Robinson Crusoe
Scribner (Scribner Illustrated classics) $10 With illustrations by N. C. Wyeth
Watts, F. $7.95 Large type edition. Illustrated by Roger Duvoisin; introduction by May Lamberton Becker. A Keith Jennison book. Has title: The life and adventures of Robinson Crusoe

First published 1719

Robinson Crusoe is shipwrecked "and leads a solitary existence on an uninhabited island near the Orinoco river for 24 years. He meets the difficulties of a primitive existence with wonderful ingenuity. . . . At length he meets a human being, a young native . . . . and makes him his companion and servant." Benét. The Reader's Encyclopedia

De La Roche, Mazo

Jalna. Little 1927 347p $6.95   Fic

1 Family—Fiction 2 Canada—Fiction

De La Roche, Mazo—*Continued*

"Jalna is the family home of the Whiteoaks. Gathered under its roof are representatives of each generation from the time the grandparents drifted to Canada via England from India and there built their homestead on a lavish scale. Rennie, 37, is the present head of the household which includes Gran—a formidable old lady of 99—two uncles, an aunt, an elder sister, and four half-brothers. An affectionate, warring group of strong personalities from the old lady down to Wakefield, the youngest, aged nine." Book Rev Digest

Del Castillo, Michel

Child of our time; tr. from the French by Peter Green. Knopf 1958 281p boards $5.95

Fic

1 Spain—Fiction 2 World War, 1939-1945—Fiction

Originally published 1957 in France

Like the author, Tanguy, the boy in this story, is half-Spanish, half-French. His mother's republicanism during the Spanish Civil War forces them into exile in France. There his father betrays his mother to the police and later Tanguy is interned in a Nazi concentration camp during World War II. After the war Tanguy eventually finds kindness and help in a Jesuit institution in Spain. (Publisher)

"Eloquently portrays a boy's great courage and strength in the face of man's inhumanity." Library J

De Vries, Peter

The blood of the lamb. Little 1961 246p boards $6.50

Fic

This novel "traces the life of a rebellious young man who searches for a belief in religion but finds that he can only rely upon human strength and human courage when his life is shattered by grief. In making his point, Mr. De Vries has drawn his hero's life as unusually hard. When he is a child, his beloved brother dies. He is unlucky in love. His father goes mad. His wife commits suicide. Finally, in scenes that are really very painful to read, his daughter dies a miserable death." Pub W

"A story told with such mastery over the resources of English it would be an event in any season. Moreover De Vries writes of people with such love and insight no reader could withhold for long the impulse to involve himself fully with them. This book will trouble many readers but it is a book that should be read and pondered by everyone who approaches in a forthright challenge to the easy assumptions and affirmations men live by, the substance of great literature." Best Sellers

Dickens, Charles

Barnaby Rudge

Fic

1 Gordon Riots, 1780—Fiction 2 Great Britain—Fiction

Some editions are:
Dodd (Great illustrated classics. Titan eds) $5.50 Foreword by May Lamberton Becker
Dutton (Everyman's lib) $2.95
Oxford (The New Oxford Illustrated Dickens) $7 With 76 illustrations by George Cattermole and Hablot K. Browne 'Phiz' and an introduction by Kathleen Tillotson

First published 1841

"An historical novel giving a lurid tableau of the orgies and incendiarism of the 'No Popery' riots in 1780. Lord George Gordon is an actor, and the principal events are founded on fact. Intertwined is a private story with some characteristic traits, e.g. in the Vardens, the Willets, Miggs and Simon Tappertit." Baker's Best

Bleak House

Fic

1 Trials—Fiction 2 Great Britain—Fiction 3 Lawyers—Fiction

Some editions are:
Dodd (Great illustrated classics. Titan eds) $5.50 Introduction by John Cournos
Dutton (Everyman's lib) $2.95
Oxford (The New Oxford Illustrated Dickens) $7 With 40 illustrations by 'Phiz' and an introduction by Sir Osbert Sitwell

First published 1853

"The heroine is Esther Summerson or rather Esther Hawdon, the illegitimate child of Lady Dedlock and Captain Hawdon. Esther, whom Lady Dedlock believes dead, is the ward of Mr. Jarndyce of the interminable case of Jarndyce and Jarndyce in Chancery Court, and lives with him at Bleak House. Lord Dedlock's lawyer, Mr. Tulkinghorn, gets wind of Lady Dedlock's secret past: and when Tulkinghorn is murdered, Lady Dedlock is suspected, disappears and is later found dead." University Handbook for Readers and Writers

Great expectations

Fic

1 Great Britain—Fiction

Some editions are:
Dodd (Great illustrated classics) $4.50 With illustrations from drawings by Frederic W. Pailthorpe together with an introduction by May Lamberton Becker
Dutton (Everyman's lib) $3.25
Oxford (The New Oxford Illustrated Dickens) $7 With 21 illustrations by F. W. Pailthorpe and an introduction by Frederick Page
Watts, F. $9.95 Large type edition complete and unabridged. A Keith Jennison book
Watts, F. $4.50 Ultratype edition

First published 1861

"The hero is Pip, who is reared by his sister and her husband, Joe Gargery, the blacksmith. Later he is informed that he is to be reared as gentleman of 'great expectations,' as an unknown person has provided money for his education and expects to make him his heir. This patron is Magwitch, a runaway convict to whom the boy Pip had once been of great assistance, Magwitch has made a fortune in New South Wales, but when he secretly returns to England, he is arrested as a returned convict and all his money is confiscated. Pip's love affair is a similar 'great expectation.'" Benét. The Reader's Encyclopedia

Hard times

Fic

1 Great Britain—Fiction

Some editions are:
Dutton (Everyman's lib) $2.95 Introduction by G. K. Chesterton
Oxford (The New Oxford Illustrated Dickens) $7 With 4 illustrations by F. Walker and Maurice Greiffenhagen and an introduction by Dingle Foot. Has title: Hard times for these times

First published 1854

"A tract-novel inspired by Carlyle's Philosophical Radicalism—a protest against tyrannous utilitarianism and political economy divorced from human feeling. The stage is a hideous manufacturing town created by the two apostles of fact, Gradgrind and Bounderby, and the drama is chiefly enacted by Gradgrind's children brought up on facts, and ruined spiritually by the complete neglect of sympathy and sentiment." Baker's Best

Martin Chuzzlewit

Fic

1 Great Britain—Fiction

Some editions are:
Dutton (Everyman's lib) $2.95 Introduction by G. K. Chesterton
Oxford (The New Oxford Illustrated Dickens) $7 With 40 illustrations by 'Phiz' and an introduction by Geoffrey Russell. Has title: The life and adventures of Martin Chuzzlewit

First published 1844

"Because of his love for Mary Graham, the titular hero is forced by his old grandfather to leave home and emigrates to America. He has some sadly disillusioning experiences with real estate in an over-advertised swamp named Eden, and returns to England with little love for anything American. The hypocrite, Pecksniff, is a prominent character, as are the various members of the Chuzzlewit family." Benét. The Reader's Encyclopedia

Nicholas Nickleby

Fic

1 Great Britain—Fiction

Some editions are:
Dodd (Great illustrated classics) $5.50 With illustrations by Cruikshank, "Phiz", and others
Dutton (Everyman's lib) $2.95
Oxford (The New Oxford Illustrated Dickens) $7 With 39 illustrations by 'Phiz' and an introduction by Dame Sybil Thorndike. Has title: The life & adventures of Nicholas Nickleby

Dickens, Charles—*Continued*

First published 1839

"Nicholas Nickleby is the son of a poor country gentleman, and has to make his own way in the world. He first goes as usher to Mr. Squeers, schoolmaster at Dotheboys Hall, in Yorkshire, but leaves in disgust with the tyranny of Squeers and his wife, especially to a poor boy named Smike. Smike runs away from the school to follow Nicholas, and remains his humble follower till death. At Portsmouth, Nicholas joins the theatrical company of Mr. Crummles, but leaves the profession for other adventures. . . . He rises to success as a merchant, and ultimately marries Madeline Bray." Benét. The Reader's Encyclopedia

The old curiosity shop   Fic

1 Great Britain—Fiction

Some editions are:

Dodd (Great illustrated classics) $5.50 With reproductions of the original illustrations by Cruikshank, Phiz, Gilbert and Darley and with an introductory sketch by May Lamberton Becker

Dutton (Everyman's lib) $3.25

Oxford (The New Oxford Illustrated Dickens) $7 With 75 illustrations by Cattermole and Phiz

First published 1841

"The heroine, Nell Trent, better known as Little Nell, lives with her grandfather, an old man who keeps a 'Curiosity shop.' He adores her, but loses what little he has by gambling, and they roam about the country as beggers until finally Little Nell dies. The book relates also the adventures of a boy named Kit Nubbles, employed for a time in the curiosity shop. Later, the hunchback, Daniel Quilp contrives to have him convicted of theft and sentenced to transportation, but he is saved from this fate by the good offices of a girl-of-all-work, nicknamed 'the Marchioness.'" Benét. The Reader's Encyclopedia

Oliver Twist   Fic

1 Great Britain—Fiction

Some editions are:

Dodd (Great illustrated classics) $4.50 With illustrations from drawings by George Cruikshank together with an introduction by May Lamberton Becker

Dutton (Everyman's lib) $3.25 Introduction by G. K. Chesterton

Oxford (The New Oxford Illustrated Dickens) $5 With twenty-four illustrations by George Cruikshank and an introduction by Humphrey House. Has title: The adventures of Oliver Twist

St Martins $4

First published 1837-1838

"A boy from an English workhouse falls into the hands of rogues who train him to be a pickpocket. The story of his struggles to escape from an environment of crime is one of hardship, danger, and the severe obstacles overcome." National Council of Teachers of English

The posthumous papers of the Pickwick Club   Fic

1 Great Britain—Fiction

Some editions are:

Dodd (Great illustrated classics) $5.50 With a foreword by May Lamberton Becker and illustrations by Phiz and others

Dutton (Everyman's lib) $3.25 Has title: Pickwick papers

Modern Lib. $2.95 Has title: Pickwick papers

Oxford (The New Oxford Illustrated Dickens) $7 With forty-three illustrations by Seymour and 'Phiz' and an introduction by Bernard Darwin

St Martins $4.25

First published 1837

"Episodes of the doings and foibles of the Pickwick Club. . . . The book is made up of letters and manuscripts about the club's actions. Among the incidents are: the army parade; trip to Manor Farm; the saving of Rachel Wardle from the villain, Alfred Jingle. Pickwick's landlady, Mrs. Bardell, faints in his arms and compromises the unsophisticated gentleman. She sues him for breach of promise and an amusing court trial follows. Pickwick refuses to pay damages and is put in Fleet prison. Sam Weller, his faithful servant, accompanies him. Mrs Bardell is also incarcerated

for not paying the costs of the trial. When Pickwick is released, he retires to a house outside London with Weller, and the latter's new bride, Mary, as housekeeper. He dissolves the club and spends his time arranging its memoranda." Haydn. Thesaurus of Book Digests

A tale of two cities   Fic

1 France—History—Revolution, 1789-1799—Fiction

Some editions are:

Dodd (Great illustrated classics) $4.50 With illustrations from drawings by "Phiz" (Hablot K. Brown) and Fred Barnard together with an introductory sketch by May Lamberton Becker

Dutton (Everyman's lib) $3.25

Macmillan (N Y) (The Macmillan classics) $4.95. lib. bdg. $4.94

Oxford (The New Oxford Illustrated Dickens) $7 With an introduction by Sir John Schuckburgh and 16 illustrations by Phiz

Watts, F. $8.95 Large type edition complete and unabridged. A Keith Jennison book

Watts, F. $4.50 A Watts Ultratype edition

First published 1859

A novel of the French Revolution. "The two cities are London and Paris. The plot hinges on the physical likeness of Charles Darnay and Sydney Carton, both of whom are in love, with Lucie Manette. Lucie loves Darnay, and Sydney Carton, who is a dissipated, ne'er-do-well never pleads his devotion, but it leads him to go to the guillotine in place of Darnay for the sake of Lucie's happiness." Benét. The Reader's Encyclopedia

Dos Passos, John

Midcentury. Houghton 1961 496p $5.95 Fic

1 Labor and laboring classes—U.S.—Fiction

This novel consitutes a panoramic view of the 20th century American scene with emphasis upon the labor movement. The author quotes "newspaper and magazine headings and stories, and . . . provides interspersed thumbnail biographies of Bridges, Lewis, MacArthur, Eleanor Roosevelt, Sam Goldwyn, Walter Reuther, Young Bob La Follette, and James Dean, among others. There are [also] . . . narrative segments concerning individuals under pressure from labor racketeers." Library J

"The villian of Dos Passos' . . . novel. Midcentury is big unions. This is certainly the most fascinating fact about the book and possibly the most significant. . . . The basic premise of Midcentury is that labor won privileges and power but the individual laborer lost his freedom." Time

Three soldiers. Houghton 1947 [c1921] 433p $6.95   Fic

1 European War, 1914-1918—Fiction 2 Soldiers—Fiction

First published 1921 by Doran

"A novel in which the author presents a bitter invective against what he conceived as the tyranny, misery, and degradation of life in the American army during the great [first World] war." Pittsburgh

U.S.A.; illus. by Reginald Marsh. Houghton 1963 [c1960] 3v in 1 illus $14   Fic

1 U.S.—History—20th century—Fiction

Contents: The 42nd parallel, first published 1930; Nineteen nineteen, first published 1932; The big money, first published 1936

Each novel of this American panorama contains several distinct narratives separated by "News reels" and "The camera eye" made up of quotations from newspapers of the period. Interspersed are short biographical sketches of prominent men of the time

"Technically, 'U.S.A.' is one of the great achievements of the modern novel." Alfred Kazin

Dostoevsky, Fyodor

The adolescent; a new tr. by Andrew R. MacAndrew. Doubleday 1971 xxiii, 585p $10   Fic

1 Russia—Fiction 2 Adolescence—Fiction

Original Russian edition, 1875. First American edition published 1916 by Macmillan (N Y) with title: A raw youth

Dostoevsky, Fyodor—*Continued*

"The story of a nineteen-year-old searching for identity amidst the disorder of Russian society in the 1870s. . . . The young hero/narrator, Arkady Dolgoruky, is himself a living symbol of the spiritual crisis of his time. The illegitimate child of a landowner strongly inspired by the social utopianism of the 1840s and a young serf, the wife of the gardener on the estate, the boy has ties to both the old Russia of his mother and foster father and the shifting new ideas represented by his father." Publisher's note

The brothers Karamazov; tr. from the Russian by Constance Garnett   Fic

1 Russia—Fiction

Some editions are:
Dutton (Everyman's lib) 2v ea $3.25 Introduction by Edward Garnett
Grosset $4.95
Modern Lib. $2.95
Modern Lib. (Modern Lib. giants) $4.95

First appeared as a serial, 1879-1880
"A story which was to have been Dostoevskii's masterpiece but only the first part of which was completed at his death. The brothers Karamazov are the three sons of an old drunkard and sensualist: Ivan, the materialist, Alyosha, the very human and lovable young mystic, and dissolute, impecunious Mitya, tried and convicted for murdering his father. A remarkable work, showing at the worst the author's faults of style and construction, and at their best his profound understanding of human nature and power to depict Russian character." Cleveland
"Beyond the intricate plot and compelling characterizations, the novel gains force from its profound investigations of good, evil, and faith. The climactic novel of Dostoevski's career." Good Reading

Crime and punishment; tr. from the Russian by Constance Garnett   Fic

1 Murder—Fiction 2 Russia—Fiction

Some editions are:
Dodd (Great illustrated classics: Titan ed) $5.50 Introduction by Avrahm Yarmolinsky
Dutton (Everyman's lib) $2.95 Introduction by Nikolay Andreyev
Modern Lib. $2.95 With an introduction by Ernest J. Simmons
Watts, F. lib. bdg. $5.50 Ultratype edition complete and unabridged. With a critical and biographical profile of Fyodor Dostoevsky by Janko Lavrin

Written 1866, translated 1886
A "psychological study, revolving about one incident—the murder of an old woman, a money-lender, and her sister, by a student in St. Petersburg, Raskolnikoff. The circumstances leading to the murder are extreme poverty and the resultant physical and mental depletion." Keller's Reader's Digest of Books
"Dostoevski is concerned with human behavior only as it is symptomatic of the ultimate nature of the self. . . . It is typical of the comprehensive art of Dostoevsky that throughout the book, notably in scenes of terrible human agony like the street show put on by Sonia's mother and the children to raise money, there is hilarious realization of a comic dimension, the ridiculous aspect of the pathetic (usually missed on first reading), which completes the art without mitigating the tragedy." The College and Adult Reading List

The house of the dead   Fic

1 Crime and criminals—Fiction 2 Penal colonies—Fiction 3 Siberia—Fiction

Some editions are:
Dutton (Everyman's lib) $2.95 Translated by H. Sutherland Edwards. Introduction by Nikolay Andreyev
Oxford (World's classics) $3 Translated with a preface by Jessie Coulson Has title: Memoirs from the house of the dead

First published in Russian in 1861-62; in English in 1881 under title: "Buried alive." Variant titles: "Prison life in Siberia," "Memorials of a dead house"; "Memoirs from the house of the dead"
"In this autobiography of a Russian landowner condemned to penal servitude in Siberia. Dostoevsky hardly troubles to disguise his own experiences. He traces the different effects of imprisonment on the moral nature, in the life-stories of a group of criminals. It is a terrible record of the anguish of the prisoner's lot." Baker's Best

The idiot   Fic

1 Mentally handicapped—Fiction 2 Russia—Fiction

Some editions are:
Dutton (Everyman's lib) $2.95 Translated by Eva M. Martin. Introduction by Richard Curle
Modern Lib. (Modern Lib. giants) $4.95 Translated from the Russian by Constance Garnett. Illustrated by Boardman Rabrusin

Written 1868; translated 1887
"Dostoevsky puts into a world of foolishness, vice, pretence, and sordid ambitions, a being who in childhood had suffered from mental disease, and who with an intellect of more than ordinary power retains the simplicity and clear insight of a child. In the 'Idiot,' he tried to realize his idea of 'a truly perfect and noble man': this Prince Myshkin of his, an epileptic like himself, is the champion of humanity. The deeply absorbing drama in which he is a protagonist turns on the salvation of a woman, Nasyasya Filipovna who had been corrupted in young girlhood." Baker's Best

The possessed; tr. from the Russian by Constance Garnett   Fic

1 Russia—Fiction

Some editions are:
Dutton (Everyman's lib) 2v ea $3.25 Introduction by Nikolay Andreyev
Modern Lib. $2.95 With a foreword by Avrahm Yarmolinsky and a translation of the hitherto suppressed chapter "At Tihon's"

Written 1871; English translation 1914
"Traces with infinite and almost wearisome detail yet with undefinable power the development of a Nihilist conspiracy in a Russian provincial town." Pittsburgh
"The criticism of socialism and godlessness, interrelated by Dostoevsky, are implicit in this novel, which is a sort of exposition of the Parable of the Gadarene Swine. It is also in this novel that the author propounds his famous exposition of the man-god, i.e., man as god unto himself, the antithesis of the God-man of Christianity." Haydn. Thesaurus of Book Digests

Douglas, Lloyd C.

The Big Fisherman. Houghton 1948 581p $5.95   Fic

1 Peter, Saint, apostle—Fiction 2 Jesus Christ—Fiction

"The two-fold story of Simon Peter, the fisherman, chosen by Christ to be the leader of his disciples, and the girl Fara, daughter of the Jewish Herod Antipas and an Arabian princess, whose hatred for her father vanishes when she meets Christ." Retail Bookseller
"With the exception of the Arabian scenes, the story follows the biblical account of Peter, necessarily much condensed. The personalities of Peter and others of the disciples receive interesting and plausible interpretations; the modern idiom is used with somewhat startling effect, and frequent references are made to many persons actual and fictitious who appeared in 'The Robe [entered below].'" Booklist

The robe. Houghton 1942 472p $6.95 Fic

1 Jesus Christ—Fiction 2 Rome—History—Empire, 30 B.C.-476 A.D.—Fiction

"A story [in modern language] of the family of the Roman Senator whose son was in charge of the Crucifixion, who got The Robe of the Galilean and who later went to his own death for refusing to recant his Christian belief before Caligula." Am News of Bks
"Perhaps the narrative is a bit too diffuse and attempts to cover too much ground, but on the whole it is an interesting effort at explaining a time of crisis that had many points of similarity to our own. It is skillful storytelling with high intent." Christian Century
Map on lining-papers

Doyle, Sir Arthur Conan

The White Company   **Fic**

1 Hundred Years' War, 1339-1453—Fiction
2 Great Britain—History—Plantagenets, 1154-
1399—Fiction

Some editions are:
Dodd (Great illustrated classics) $4.50 With
biographical illustrations and pictures of the
setting of the story, together with an introduction by Donald J. Harvey
McKay $5.50 Pictures by N. C. Wyeth

First published 1891 in the United States by
Lovell

"The Hampshire hero joins an English Free
Company, and in the course of much wandering through France and the Pyrenees, meets
with stirring adventures and performs many a
deed of valour. The historical situation is
that arising out of the Black Prince's decision
to espouse the cause of Pedro the Cruel of
Castile. Edward III, the Black Prince, Chan-
dos, Sir William Felton, Bertrand du Guesclin,
Don Pedro and others appear." Nield

Dreiser, Theodore

An American tragedy. Illus. by Grant
Reynard; introduction by H. L. Mencken.
World Pub. 1948 874p $10   **Fic**

First published 1925
"The tragedy of a young man brought up in
simple Salvation Army piety who comes East
to find success: money and social acceptance.
Clyde Griffiths loves and is loved by his co-
worker in the collar factory, Roberta, but he
is dazzled by Sondra of the country clubs.
Pregnant, Roberta becomes a threat to the
rise Clyde dreams of. Unlike the hero of Room
at The Top, he lacks the cruel strength to drop
the socially inferior girl for the one who will
help him succeed. Instead, madly, ineptly, un-
certainly, he plans to resolve his dilemma by
drowning Roberta. He is caught easily and easily convicted." College and Adult Reading List

"By making his protagonist a typical American youth, and his opponent the complex and
unconquerable forces of heredity and environment (the modern equivalent of the Fates of
Greek tragedy), he has translated this story
. . . into an American epic comparable to 'Jude
the obscure' or 'The brothers Karamazov.'"
Atlantic

Sister Carrie   **Fic**

1 Chicago—Fiction 2 New York (City)—Fiction

Some editions are:
Modern Lib. $2.95 With a new foreword by the
author
World Pub. $7.95

First published 1900
"A very plain, unassuming, and unconventional history of a young woman [an actress]
led into vice by her love of pleasure, and the
parallel history of the moral deterioration of a
man. The life of the lower middle classes in
New York and Chicago is depicted with the
industrious realism of a Zola." Baker's Best

"When the book appeared it was condemned
because of 'the fact that sin does not meet
what was considered its due punishment.'"
Lenrow. Reader's Guide to Prose Fiction

Drury, Allen

Advise and consent; drawings by Arthur
Shilstone. Doubleday 1959 616p illus $7.95
Fic

1 U.S. Congress. Senate—Fiction 2 U.S.—
Politics and government—Fiction 3 Washington, D.C.—Fiction

Pulitzer Prize, 1960
A novel of the actions "which are set in motion when the Senate is called upon to confirm
the President's nomination to a Cabinet post.
The story is centered on five men who are vitally concerned with the appointment of a new
Secretary of State." McClurg. Book News

"Although the narration dwells on the conflict of personal ambitions and the human frailties of the leaders of the defense and the opposition, it gives a graphic picture of the workings of the Senate and innumerable thumbnail
sketches of individuals in Washington who
figure in the complex political scene. Attempts

to identify the fictional characters with real
persons will no doubt give added interest to
the exciting and suspenseful story." Booklist

It is also a picture of Washington, "its cocktail parties, its hostesses, its crafty legislators
and their parliamentary tricks. . . . There is a
mysterious and incriminating picture about a
Senator's past [and] there is a dash of sex in
the book." Library J

Preserve and protect; a novel. Doubleday 1968 394p $6.95   **Fic**

1 Presidents—U.S.—Fiction 2 U.S.—Politics
and government—Fiction

This novel "describes the chaos that over-
takes America, and the world when the sus-
picious death of the President—just after his
renomination—leaves the incumbent party
without a candidate or a clear-cut way of selecting one." Publisher's note

The author "knows the political climate of
the Savage Seventies, he has infinitely more
than the requisite imagination, and he knows
how to hold on to a reader. He knows people
and he knows political people—the two are not
the same: that's what makes politics and apparently it's also what makes fiction." Best
Sellers

Dumas, Alexandre, 1802-1870

The black tulip; introduction by Marcel
Gerard. Dutton 248p $2.95   **Fic**

1 Netherlands—History—Fiction

"Everyman's library"
Written in 1850. First published in the United
States 1891 by Little

"Love-romance associated with the Haarlem
tulip craze and intertwined with scenes from
Dutch history (1672-5), when William of Orange
lent himself to the agitation against the brothers DeWitt, the patriotic defenders of Dutch
liberty." Baker's Best

The man in the iron mask. With illus. by
J. A. Beaucé Philippoteaux and others, and
a foreword by Emile Van Vliet. Dodd 1944
280p illus $4.50   **Fic**

1 France—History—Bourbons, 1589-1789—Fiction

"Great illustrated classics"
"Identity of the man in the iron mask is an
unsolved mystery. Dumas' iron mask episode
is found toward the end . . . of the third volume of 'The Vicomte De Bragelonne'. . . . The
present volume remains essentially the story
of the . . . closing years of those four men who
had performed such prodigies—attacking
armies, assaulting castles, terrifying death itself—Athos, Porthos, Aramis, and their captain, D'Artagnan." Preface for the reader

Du Maurier, Daphne

The flight of the Falcon. Doubleday 1965
311p $6.95   **Fic**

1 Italy—Fiction

"The story grows out of the accidental involvement of young Armino Fabbio in a murder. Reluctantly he returns to his birthplace in
Italy where he comes to feel that he is haunted
both by the spirit of his beloved elder brother
and the demoniacal Duke Claudio who five
hundred years before, as the Falcon, had victimized the people of the village." Huntting

The glass-blowers. Doubleday 1963 348p
$5.50   **Fic**

1 France—History—Revolution, 1789-1799—
Fiction

The story of a family of master craftsmen,
glass-blowers, in France from 1747 to 1845. The
author touches on a little known aspect of the
French Revolution, the Civil War originating
in the Vendée. She reveals how the lives of
the Busson family were permanently altered by
the Revolution and the Civil War which followed; how it affected in different ways, Ma-
thurin, the father, and the lives of his five
sons and daughters. The story is told through
flashbacks by Sophie, the oldest daughter.
(Publisher)

"Miss du Maurier's book is as readable and
crisp in style as any of her earlier works, but
its main value lies in cutting through the
glamorous surface of a period, thought of too
frequently only in 'Scarlet Pimpernel' terms,
and opening to light its drab and dingy real-

Du Maurier, Daphne—*Continued*

ism. To do this so engagingly is Miss du Maurier's achievement." Christian Science Monitor

Map on lining-papers

The house on the strand. Doubleday 1969 298p $5.95   **Fic**

1 Science fiction 2 Drugs—Fiction

"Richard Young, a British publisher with marital problems . . . borrows a picturesque house in Cornwall from his friend Professor Magnus Lane [a biochemist] with the promise that he will experiment with a drug on which Magnus is working. Magnus warns him only that although the world of the past will seem very real after he takes the drug, he himself will be invisible and must touch only inanimate objects, not people, or he will awaken instantly to the present with nausea and shock. Richard experiments and discovers, after consultation with Magnus, that he has met the very group of 14th-century gentlefolk and servants whom Magnus had seen in previous experiments. But with Richard there is a difference: in the course of repeated 'trips' he falls in love with Isolda, one of the medieval ladies—a development which, among other things, further complicates his already unhappy marriage." Book of the Month Club News

"A suspenseful, colorful story that leaves the reader with an unsolved mystery but with clear evidence of the disastrous effect of the drug." Booklist

The King's general. Doubleday 1946 731p $5.95   **Fic**

1 Great Britain—History—Civil War and Commonwealth, 1642-1660—Fiction 2 Grenville, Sir Richard—Fiction 3 Cornwall—Fiction 4 Physically handicapped—Fiction

"Historical novel of Cornwall in the days of the parliamentary wars. The hero is Sir Richard Grenville: the heroine Honor Harris, who tells the story many years after the events took place. As a girl Honor was in love with the blustering Sir Richard, when an accident crippled her for life, only a few days before their marriage. The rest of the story is told as it seemed to the still beautiful cripple." Book Rev Digest

"A clever blend of fact and fiction, with fewer than usual of the swashbuckling appurtenances of the historical novel, and somewhat more emphasis on the emotional experiences of these hard-living Cornish aristocrats. And the continuity in English life, the persistence of family names and the old castles still standing, adds to the sense of the tale's authenticity." Book of the Month Club News

Rebecca   **Fic**

1 Great Britain—Fiction

Some editions are:
Doubleday $5.95
Modern Lib. $2.95
First published 1938

"Against the setting of a great English estate unfolds the story of Rebecca, its glamorous mistress, who had been dead for eight months. Maxim de Winter's young and frightened second wife gradually realizes that there is some mystery surrounding her death, but it is not until the night of the big costume ball that her suspicions are confirmed and, with an ever-increasing atmosphere of impending disaster, the real story becomes known." Hunting

"Although this is first and last and always a thrilling story, the novel keeps a genuine human value in the person and problem of its heroine, and rises, thus above the level of the theatrical. . . . Miss du Maurier's style in telling her story is exactly suited to her plot and her background, and creates the exact spirit and atomosphere of the novel. The rhythm quickens with the story, is always in measure with the story's beat. And the writing has an intensity, a heady beauty, which is itself the utterance of the story's mood." N Y Her Trib Books

Durrell, Lawrence

The Alexandria quartet: Justine; Balthazar; Mountolive [and] Clea. Dutton 1962 884p $12.50   **Fic**

"A reprint as one work as the author states they were intended to be read, of the four

parts previously published as Justine [1957], Balthazar [1958], Mountolive [1958], and Clea [1960]. This group of novels [is] about a sophisticated somewhat decadent circle of friends in modern Alexandria." Booklist

" 'The Alexandria Quartet' is one of the major achievements of fiction in our time, distinguished not only by its power of language, by its evocation of a place, by its creation of character, by the drama of many of its incidents, but also by its boldly original design." Sat R

Eckert, Allan W.

The great auk; a novel. Little 1963 202p boards $5.95   **Fic**

1 Great auk—Stories

A "book about the life and death of the last great auk of the thousands of these large, flightless, swimming penguin-like birds that annually migrated from their breeding places in the North Atlantic to Cape Hatteras. Natural calamities—storms, killer whales—and massacres by feather-and-meat hunters and by scientists collecting specimens decimated the species till the last of its kind was slaughtered in 1844." Pub W

"Eckert is masterful when describing incidents and places, some purely imaginative: the life of the bird inside the egg and the fledgling immediately after birth; the undersea scenes when the auks, like diminutive submarines, dive for food or for safety; the storms at sea and on land; the predatory actions of the whales; the massacre of the birds by human hunters. These descriptions are vivid, palpable, intensely real. Amazingly he seems most effective when seeing and assessing these things through the eyes and minds of his 'characters,' a tribute to his imaginative genius." Best Sellers

Edmonds, Walter D.

Drums along the Mohawk. Little 1936 592p $6.95   **Fic**

1 U.S.—History—Revolution—Fiction 2 New York (State)—Fiction

"The Mohawk Valley from 1776-1784 is the scene. It is a story of the American revolution as it affected the farmers in that frontier section, when unaided they withstood the raids of British regulars from Canada, and the Iroquois from the surrounding country." Book Rev Digest

"Mr. Edmonds has clearly studied his subject with exemplary thoroughness. He has also studied it with imagination. He possesses the best kind of historical sense. . . . He can do very well in painting a society, a countryside full of people." Sat R

Map on lining-papers

Edwards, Anne

The survivors. Holt 1968 253p $5.95 **Fic**

1 Mystery and detective stories 2 Switzerland—Fiction

"Luanne, in her early thirties, has just been released from a rest home where she had been confined after the unsolved mass murder of her family. On a holiday in the Swiss Alps she meets a man who helps her solve the mystery and find happiness." Cincinnati

"A strangely fascinating story that involves the reader in the dark after-effects of a terrible crime. . . . The suspense holds up all the way, as does an atmosphere of impending horror." Pub W

Eliot, George

Adam Bede   **Fic**

1 Great Britain—Fiction

Some editions are:
Dodd (Great illustrated classics) $4.50 with illustrations of contemporary scenes and a foreword by Curtis Dahl
Dutton (Everyman's lib) $3.25 Introduction by Robert Speaight
First published 1859

Two of George Eliot's best known characters Mrs Poyser and Diana Morris, appear in this novel

" 'Adam Bede' goes into the dark places of human nature, and sets forth a coherent philosophy of conduct and retribution. An innocent country lass is seduced by the young

Eliot, George—*Continued*

squire; and crime, remorse, suffering . . . are the tragic consequences. . . . All the ordinary aspects of country life a hundred years ago are presented with minute strokes of a Dutch painter." Baker's Best

The mill on the Floss   Fic

1 Great Britain—Fiction

Some editions are:
Dodd (Great illustrated classics) $4.50 With photographs of the author and her environment as well as drawings from early editions of the book, and an introduction by Louis B. Salomon
Dutton (Everyman's lib) $3.25 Introduction by Robertson Nicoll
Oxford (The World's classics) $2.75
First published 1860
A tragic story in a setting of English country life. "The conflict of affection and antipathy between a brother and sister is a dominant motive. . . . Among the characters whose humors provide many comic pages the three aunts are famous." Baker's Best

Silas Marner   Fic

1 Great Britain—Fiction

Some editions are:
Dodd (Great illustrated classics) $4.50 With illustrations of contemporary scenes and a foreword by Basil Davenport
Dutton (Everyman's lib) $3.25 Introduction by John Holloway
Watts, F. $7.95 Large type edition complete and unabridged. A Keith Jennison book
First published 1861
"Silas Marner is a handloom weaver, a good man, whose life has been wrecked by a false accusation of theft, which cannot be disproved. For years he lives a lonely life, with the sole companionship of his loom; and he is saved from his own despair by the chance finding of a little child. On this baby girl he lavishes the whole passion of his thwarted nature, and her filial affection makes him a kindly man again. After sixteen years the real thief is discovered, and Silas's good name is restored. On this slight framework are hung the richest pictures of middle and low class life that George Eliot has painted." Keller's Reader's Digest of Books

Ellison, Ralph

Invisible man   Fic

1 Negroes—Fiction

Some edtions are:
Modern Lib. $2.95
Random House $7.50
First published 1952
"The odyssey of a complex, highly sensitive Negro, beginning with his graduation from high school in the South and ending in a fantastic hideaway in Harlem. Surrealistic, nightmarish descriptions of situations and characters." The Negro in the United States

Fairbairn, Ann

Five smooth stones; a novel. Crown 1966 756p $6.95   Fic

1 Negroes—Fiction

This novel "details the life of David Champlin, a Negro born in poverty in New Orleans in the depression, through his escape to college in the North and finally, to Oxford University, his continuing love affair with a white girl whom he eventually marries, his brief but brilliant legal and diplomatic career, his sacrifice of position and comfort to return to the South as a civil rights leader, and his tragic but triumphant end." Pub W
"This is a courageous novel, for its basic element is love shared by a young Negro and a white girl. This story will offend many and be unpopular with those who fear life, but the book is written with such taste and discretion that the intelligent reader, though he may disagree with some of the basic premises of the book, cannot but understand and appreciate what Miss Fairbairn is saying about the way we live today." Library J

Falkner, J. Meade

Moonfleet; illus. by Fritz Kredel. Little 1951 247p illus $5.95   Fic

1 Adventure and adventurers—Fiction 2 Great Britain—Fiction

First published 1898 in England
This "is an adventure tale reminiscent of Stevenson's Treasure Island or Kidnapped, laid in England in the eighteenth century and dealing with hidden treasure, smugglers' caves, and dangers at sea." Book Rev Digest

Fast, Howard

Freedom road. Crown 263p $3.95   Fic

1 Reconstruction—Fiction 2 Negroes—Fiction 3 Race problems—Fiction

A reprint of the title first published 1944 by Duell
"Historical novel based on the reconstruction period in the South following the Civil War, when for a few years Negroes and whites worked together in harmony. Gideon Jackson, the Negro leader, who rose from illiteracy to be a member of Congress, is the central character. The rise of Gideon, his efforts to help his people, the little settlement over which he presided is pictured. Then the Northern troops are withdrawn from the South, and disaster for the Negroes follows." Book Rev Digest

Faulkner, William

Nobel Prize in literature, 1949

Absalom, Absalom!   Fic

1 Mississippi—Fiction

Some editions are:
Modern Lib. $2.95 Introduction by Harvey Breit
Random House $6.95
First published 1936
A "strange story of an old Southern tragedy, which is revived and pieced together by a Harvard freshman who came from the same locality and was only indirectly concerned in the matter. The main story deals with Thomas Sutpen, an ambitious planter who settled near Jefferson, Mississippi in 1833." Book Rev Digest
Faulkner's "violence here and elsewhere is not a means of arousing pointless horror: it is an expression of a whole society which the author sincerely loves and hates and which he perceives to be in a state of catastrophic decay." New Repub

As I lay dying   Fic

1 Southern States—Fiction

Some editions are:
Modern Lib. $2.95
Random House $5.95
First published 1930
"Enclosing their dead mother, Addie Bundren, in a home-made coffin, Cash, Darl, Jewel, Dewey Dell and Vardaman—accompanied by the dazed father Anse—load her on a wagon and travel for several days across a rain-swept country to Jefferson, where Addie wanted to be buried with her folks. Flooding rivers, a decaying corpse, buzzards, and a demented small boy are forced upon the reader's senses thru the subjective medium of the minds of this family of poor whites, and thru the more lucid, objective medium of the reflections of their acquaintances concerning their actions." Book Rev Digest

Intruder in the dust   Fic

1 Mississippi—Race relations—Fiction

Some editions are:
Modern Lib. $2.95
Random House $6.95
First published 1948
"Lucas Beauchamp, a dignified elderly Negro, is charged with murder and held in a Mississippi jail. Evidence to prove his innocence is gathered by two sixteen-year-old boys, one white, one Negro, and an elderly spinster of an aristocratic family." Library J
"Intruder in the Dust makes the reader work, it is not easy reading. But the reward is worth the trouble. It can be read as a detective story, a humorous idyl (a kind of second cousin to Huckleberry Finn), an outraged, descriptive exhortation to Southern society, a parable of modern life. It is also a triumphant work of art." Time

Faulkner, William—*Continued*

Light in August   Fic

Some editions are:
Modern Lib. $2.95
Random House $6.95

First published 1932
"A country girl, well advanced in pregnancy, is seeking the lover who has promised to marry her. She walks shoeless in the warm dust, or rides in friendly wagons, or stays in half willing houses, confidently, because the life force within her makes her confident. And in all this story of murder, rape, lynching, insanity, and remorse, no one hurts her, no one is anything but kind to her, no misadventure comes near her, and even when she learns that her lover is worthless, a husband and father for her child, who is not worthless, is provided." Sat R
"The book is no light novel by any stretch of the imagination, but it has more than a little of Faulkner's humor, which is a rare and precious humor, and it shows that he can be tender when he likes." No Am

The reivers; a reminiscence. Random House 1962 305p $6.95   Fic

Awarded the Pulitzer Prize 1963
"On a summer day in 1905 Lucius Priest, eleven, is persuaded by Boon Hogganbeck to 'borrow' his grandfather's car and make a trip to Memphis. Ned McCaslin, Negro, stows away and the three are off on a heroic odyssey which ends at Miss Reba's bordello. When Ned turns up in the night with a horse for which he has traded the car, the action accelerates wildly . . . into a mad melee of smuggling a horse across country, planning a bizarre race, and ending in jail. The use of the archaic term 'reivers' for stealing and destruction carries a double meaning, for Lucius' innocence is destroyed and Ned consummately destroys the old pattern of subservience to his white relatives." Booklist
The author "treats all classes, white and black, with the same understanding." Best Sellers

The sound and the fury   Fic

1 Southern States—Fiction

Some editions are:
Modern Lib. $2.95
Random House $6.95

First published 1929
"A southern family of gentle blood is shown in decay, its members petty failures, drunkards, suicides, pathological perverts and idiots. Part One presents the tragedy as seen through the eyes of Benjy, the idiot son, a grown man thrown back into childhood by any chance sight or smell. Through his broken thoughts we learn of Caddy, a beloved sister, who has run away from the hideous home and sent back an illegitimate daughter. In Part Two, we move back eighteen years and witness, through the workings of his mind, the last day in the life of Quentin, brother of Benjy and Caddy. Part Three brings us again into the present, where we look through the mean eyes of Jason, the third brother. And in the final part of the novel, in the author's direct narrative, the spectacle of white disintegration is shown and sharpened by the emphasis thrown upon Negro solidity." Outlook

Ferber, Edna

Cimarron. Doubleday 1930 388p $6.95 Fic

1 Frontier and pioneer life—Fiction 2 Petroleum industry and trade—Fiction 3 Oklahoma—Fiction

This novel "deals with the spectacular land rush of 1889 in Oklahoma, beginning when the country was still Indian Territory, continuing through the oil boom and thereafter. The book depicts the degeneration of Yancey Cravat, brilliant editor, lawyer, and wanderer, and the accompanying evolution of his wife Sabra into a practical and tenacious businesswoman, ultimately a congresswoman." Herzberg. The Reader's Encyclopedia of American Literature

Giant. Doubleday 1952 447p $5.95   Fic

1 Texas—Fiction

"Texas and the Texans are subjected to some unfavorable criticism in the story of a Virginia reared woman who marries a Texan.

Bick Benedict, who manages the Benedict family's two and a half million acre ranch, and his friends, who have made their money in cattle, cotton, or oil, have a chance to speak for themselves and defend their brash grand-scale way of living but the final word rests with Bick's wife Leslie. Coming fresh from Virginia as a bookish but spirited young woman, Leslie is shocked by the life she finds and is never reconciled to it although her love for her husband holds her to the ranch." Booklist

So Big. Doubleday 1924 360p $5.95   Fic

1 Farm life—Fiction

Pulitzer Prize, 1925
"Selina DeJong would look up from her work and say, 'How big is my man.' Then little Dirk DeJong would answer in the time-worn way, 'So-o-o big!' And he was so nicknamed. Tho So Big gives the book its title his mother is the outstanding figure. Until Selina was nineteen she traveled with her gambler father. At his sudden death she secured a teacher's post in the Dutch settlement of High Prairie, a community of hardworking farmers and their thrifty, slaving wives—narrow-minded people indifferent to natural beauty. Soon Selina married Pervus DeJong, a plodding, good-natured boy. With her marriage the never-ending drudgery of a farmer's wife began. Thru all the years of hardship she never lost her gay, indomitable spirit. Unfortunately, she was unable to transmit these qualities to her son." Book Rev Digest
"It is a thoughtful book, clean and strong, dramatic at times, interesting always, clearsighted, sympathetic, a novel to read and to remember." N Y Times Bk R

Field, Rachel

All this and heaven too. Macmillan (N Y) 1938 596p $6.95   Fic

1 Field, Henriette (Deluzy-Desportes)—Fiction

"In fiction form the author tells the life story of her great-aunt by marriage [Henriette Deluzy-Desportes Field] the French governess who in 1847 became involved in a famous murder trial, in which she was known as Mademoiselle D. Altho she was acquitted, life became so difficult for her in France that Mademoiselle came to America, where she married an American and presided over a Gramercy Park salon, frequented by William Cullen Bryant, Harriet Beecher Stowe, Samuel Morse, and Fanny Kemble among others." Book Rev Digest
"The author has projected herself into the mind and being of the woman whose life has long fascinated her, and, in giving us the story she has 'always wanted to tell,' she has given us her best and richest fiction." Sat R

And now tomorrow. Macmillan (N Y) 1942 350p $5.95   Fic

1 Deaf—Fiction 2 New England—Fiction

"Emily Blair spent her early years as a member of a prominent family who owned factories in a New England mill town. The river was a barrier protecting her social life from contact with the members of the Polish community who were mill hands. When deafness made Emily reach out for the satisfaction of new values and new friends, young Dr. Vance helps her understand the people who work for their daily bread. Personal contacts and adequate interpretation break down the invisible barriers which cut off one section of a community from another." Reading Ladders
The plot is "obvious . . . but one listens to it because Miss Field has told it so well." Commonweal

Fielding, Henry

The history of Tom Jones, a foundling Fic

1 Great Britain—Fiction

Some editions are:
Dodd (Great illustrated classics. Titan eds) $5.50 With eight pages of illustrations and an introduction by Arthur Sherbo
Dutton (Everyman's lib) 2v ea $3.25 Introduction by A. R. Humphreys
Modern Lib. $2.95
Random House boxed $10 Illustrated by Lawrence Beall Smith

497

Fielding, Henry—*Continued*

First published 1749

"The complete and unexpurgated history of a young man of strong natural impulses, a good disposition, and no overpowering sense of morality. Fielding planned it as a 'Comic Epic,' and built the plot with care, a plot turning on the recognition of Jones's birth and on the fortunes of his love for an adorable girl. Life in country and town in the year 1745; with a great crowd of characters of all sorts and conditions. . . . Of the highest importance in the history of literature, as indicating the lines on which the modern novel of manners was to be written." Baker's Best

Fitzgerald, F. Scott

The Great Gatsby. Scribner 1958 [c1953] 182p $4.95   **Fic**

Also available in large type edition $7.95

First published 1925

"A novel of sordid living and violent death, dealing with the froth of society living on Long Island and having as its central figure, Gatsby, a self-made man whose money is made by various mysterious non-ethical means and spent on disreputable parties. . . . It is memorable for truthfully painting individuals of . . . [the] jazzing post-war time." Cleveland

"Beneath the sparkling surface of 'Gatsby' lie depths of meanings: the American dream fulfilled and desecrated in the selfish dishonesty of the respectable Buchanans and the useless display of the vulgar Alger hero; the once-green island of the New World from which the trees had been cut to make room for ash heaps, garages and echoing hollow mansions." College and Adult Reading List

Tender is the night; a romance. With the author's final revisions. Preface by Malcolm Cowley. Scribner 1951 356p $4.95   **Fic**

First published 1934

"In the hedonistic setting of post-World War I Europe, a wealthy mental patient, Nicole, falls passionately in love with her young psychiatrist, Dick Diver. She finds her cure in marrying him, but as she achieves mental stability and emotional independence, he deteriorates. Finally Nicole leaves him for a man who will be her lover and not her caretaker, and Dick begins an irreversible decline into alcoholism and dissolution." Benét. The Reader's Encyclopedia

"Little appreciated when it appeared, the novel is now widely regarded as one of the finest American novels of our time." Good Reading

This side of Paradise. Scribner 1920 305p $5.95   **Fic**

"Amory Blaine, a handsome, wealthy, spoiled and snobbish young man from the Middle West, attends Princeton University and acquires a refined sense of the proper 'social' values. Lacking all sense of purpose, he interests himself primarily in literary cults, vaguely 'liberal' student activities, and a series of flirtations with some rather predatory young ladies that culminate in a genuine but ill-fated love for Isabelle Borgé, who rejects Amory to marry a wealthier young man. During the war Amory serves as an officer in France, and upon his return home he embarks upon a career in advertising, world-weary, cynical, regretful, and not yet thirty years old. Virtually a record of the 'lost generation' in its college days, the novel treats Fitzgerald's characteristic theme of true love blighted by money-lust and is remarkable for its honest and detailed descriptions of the early 'Jazz Age.'" Benét. The Reader's Encyclopedia

Flaubert, Gustave

Madame Bovary   **Fic**

1 France—Fiction

Some editions are:

Dodd (Great illustrated classics) $4.50
Dutton (Everyman's lib) $2.95 Translated by Eleanor Marx-Aveling. Introduction by George Saintsbury
Modern Lib. $2.95 A new translation by Francis Steegmuller
Watts, F. $4.50 A Watts Ultratype edition

First appeared in French 1857

"Perhaps the most perfect work . . . of realistic art in any language: a faithful and infinitely painstaking interpretation of actual life. . . . It is a plain history of the slow but inevitable moral degeneration of a weak woman. . . . The passionless candour of the narrative, the patient rendering of the squalor and narrowness of provincial life and of its effect on the woman's mind, make this a landmark in the history of naturalism." Baker's Best

Forester, C. S.

The African Queen; with a new foreword by the author. Modern Lib. 1940 307p $2.95   **Fic**

1 Africa, Central—Fiction 2 British in Africa, Central—Fiction 3 Missionaries—Fiction

First published 1935 by Little

"After the death of her brother in an African mission, Rose Sayer, English spinster, resolves to carry on against the German commander who has rounded up her brother's black converts. A gallant little Cockney, Allnutt, comes to her aid with a dilapidated steam launch. They scheme together to blow up the German boat down the lake—but first the long and perilous trip on the river must be made. It is this journey, with many hardships and a constant fight against malaria, which brings out all that is brave and admirable in these two persons so strangely unlike in character and walk of life." Book Rev Digest

Captain Horatio Hornblower; with drawings by N. C. Wyeth. Little 1939 662p illus $6.95   **Fic**

1 Sea stories 2 Great Britain—History—1714-1837—Fiction 3 Adventure and adventurers—Fiction

A trilogy containing the following: Beat to quarters, first published 1937; Ship of the line, first published 1938; Flying colours, first published 1939

"Everyone is bound to enjoy the saga of Horatio Hornblower. . . . When we meet him he's captain of the British frigate Lydia, in the time of the Napoleonic wars, at sea in the Pacific and making for a landfall on the Nicaraguan coast. . . . He is to foment and assist an uprising by Don Julian Alvarado—El Supremo—against the Spanish. . . . He outwits the Spanish man-of-war Natividad, captures her without losing a man, and turns her over to El Supremo. But then when belated news comes in from Europe, he finds that he has to reattack the Natividad. . . . In volume two we find Hornblower helping to blockade the coast of Spain. . . . In the third part we have all the satisfactions of suspense rewarded." Book of the Month Club News

Hornblower during the crisis, and two stories: Hornblower's temptation and The last encounter. Little 1967 174p $5.75   **Fic**

1 Sea stories

"Posthumous novel fragment and two slender stories. The former concerns Hornblower's eventful voyage to London on another man's ship for reassignment on a spy mission to Spain. . . . In one story Mr. Hornblower is almost taken in by a seemingly harmless mission entrusted to him by a young Irishman before his shipboard execution. In the other tale a stranded traveler in distress, helped by Admiral Hornblower and wife, proves to be Napoleon Bonaparte." Booklist

The last nine days of the Bismarck; illus. with maps. Little 1959 138p maps $5.95 **Fic**

1 Bismarck (Battleship)—Fiction 2 World War, 1939-1945—Fiction

"A master of sea writing gives us his reconstruction of the deadly hunt-and-chase which developed in May, 1941, when the 42,000-ton German battleship broke out of the Baltic to attack British shipping in the Atlantic. The few English ships available, inferior in speed and guns, had first to find the 'Bismarck' in foggy, stormy weather and then try to destroy her. This is naval strategy at its best, with reconnaissance, calculation, shrewd guessing, and incredible luck. . . . Forester says he has composed the speeches and conversation himself but the course of events is history." Horn Bk

Forster, E. M.
A passage to India. Harcourt 1949 322p $2.95   Fic

1 British in India—Fiction 2 India—Fiction

"Harbrace Modern classics"
First published 1924
"The story concerns the reactions of two newcomers—Adela Quested and Mrs. Moore, a young and old woman—to Chandrapore. . . . In the background play the vague colors—romantic and unromantic of India and Anglo-India, and the gross misunderstandings that must arise when two races live together—rather apart than together—conscious of an urge to transplant a 'civilization' and of as vigorous an urge to keep one's own. The conflict of these several points of view, in the novel, wells up into a noisy tempest when Miss Quested believes she has been wantonly attacked by a heretofore respectful Indian, Dr. Aziz, in one of the Marabar Caves." Literary Rev
"It is a book abundantly worth reading as a story, but it is even more potent in significance as we realize the subtlety and power with which Mr Foster has revealed to us the Moslem and the Hindu mind and that strange anomaly, the mind of the Anglo-Indian." Boston Transcript

Fowles, John
The collector. Little 1963 305p $6.95 Fic

Frederick Clegg an obscure little clerk and collector of butterflies "becomes obsessed by a pretty art student he has never met. When he wins a fortune in the football pools, he buys a remote cottage in the country; kidnaps the girl and installs her in a prison in the cellar, determined to make her love him. . . . [The author tells] his story first from the demented viewpoint of the man and then from that of the increasingly desperate girl." Pub W
"Mr. Fowles is a powerful writer; this story has a nightmarish reality and immediacy. Both Miranda and Clegg are completely developed characters; the book is at once horrifying and fascinating." Best Sellers

The French lieutenant's woman. Little 1969 467p $7.95   Fic

1 Great Britain—Fiction

"An engrossing love story set in [19th century] Lyme Regis, England, is told in the Victorian manner but is influenced by modern psychology and recent experiments in the composition of the novel. Charles Smithson, a young gentleman of traditional values redeemed by intelligence and a measure of irony is betrothed to Ernestina Freeman, the wealthy, shallow daughter of the proprietor of a London dry goods emporium. Haunting Charles' destiny, however, is the enigmatic, independent Sarah Woodruff whom the citizens of Lyme have castigated for her brief affair with a French sailor." Booklist
"The narrative conventions of the Victorian novel—excursive exposition, incidental comment (some of it in Mr. Fowles's mid-20th-century voice), dramatic confrontations, impossible coincidences—are strikingly employed in a mordant examination of Victorian society and psychopathology. The entire novel resounds with the rich and strangled music of an age of paradox and staggering social and intellectual revolution." Book of the Month Club News

France, Anatole
Nobel Prize in literature, 1921

The crime of Sylvestre Bonnard. Dodd 1890 310p $3.95   Fic

1 France—Fiction

Original French edition, 1881
"Sylvestre Bonnard is a kind-hearted, absent-minded old archeologist. The aged scholar's crime is the kidnapping of Jeanne Alexandre, the orphaned daughter of his former love, from a school in which she is abused and unhappy. Threatening complications results, but when it is discovered that Jeanne's guardian is an embezzler she is made the legal ward of M. Bonnard." Benét. The Reader's Encyclopedia

Frank, Pat
Alas, Babylon; a novel. Lippincott 1959 253p $5.95   Fic

1 Atomic bomb—Fiction 2 Survival (after airplane accidents, shipwrecks, etc.)—Fiction 3 Florida—Fiction

"When a defective missile triggers off World War III and the major cities of the U.S. are demolished by nuclear bombing, the inhabitants of Fort Repose, a small town in central Florida, find themselves cut off from the rest of the world and thrown from machine-age society back into a primitive way of living. Young Randy Bragg accepts the challenge imposed by responsibility for his brother's family and becomes a community leader in the fight for survival against panic and lawlessness, disease, and starvation." Booklist
"The tense excitement and the impact of a nuclear attack on American civilization are made so realistic that the reader feels this could happen here. Older boys and girls are attracted to this book because it provides such a vivid picture of the horror of modern warfare and the obvious need for continuing efforts for peace." Doors to More Mature Reading

Fuller, Iola
The loon feather. Harcourt 1940 419p $5.95   Fic

1 Chippewa Indians—Fiction 2 Mackinac Island—Fiction

The story of Oneta, daughter of Tecumseh, and granddaughter of the chief of the Loon Tribe of the Ojibways. It takes place during the fur trading days on Mackinac Island
An "honest picture of the slow retreat of an old civilization before the advance of a new one." Spring'd Republican
Map on lining-papers

Gaines, Ernest J.
The autobiography of Miss Jane Pittman. Dial Press 1971 245p boards $6.95   Fic

1 Negroes—Fiction 2 Louisiana—Fiction

"These are supposed to be the tape recorded memories of a 110-year-old ex-slave, from the time she is a child of eight or nine watching the plantation receive both Union and Confederate troops on the same day, until the moment a century later when she decides to make her first freedom walk. In between is a very human story of a plucky, stubborn child who never gets beyond the boundaries of Louisiana, geographically speaking, but matures into girlhood and womanhood with a fierce determination to do what she sees as right." Pub W
"Gaines understands his people and knows their history. His command of the Louisiana black and Cajun dialects is masterful. But Gaines's strongest advantage is a controlling sense of art." Sat R

Galbraith, John Kenneth
The triumph; a novel of modern diplomacy. Houghton 1968 239p $4.95   Fic

1 Diplomacy—Fiction 2 U.S.—Foreign relations—Fiction

This novel is centered around a revolution in a small Latin American republic, Puerto Santos. "In the eyes of the U.S. State Department [the dictator] Martínez is a bulwark against Communism. When he is overthrown by a moderate liberal named Miró who threatens to [introduce] . . . democracy and modest land reforms. . . . [Worth Campbell], Assistant Secretary of State for Inter-American affairs, sees the danger at once. . . . Pressure is kept on Miró. He succumbs and Juan Martínez, favorite son of the dictator, is brought back from the University of Michigan to carry on in his father's footsteps. . . . What happened then not even Worth Campbell could have foreseen." Publisher's note
"What Galbraith is concerned to demonstrate is the system of interlocking stupidity in which, he believes, the makers of foreign policy are hopelessly imprisoned." New Repub

Gallico, Paul
The Poseidon adventure. Coward-McCann 1969 347p $6.95 **Fic**

"It was the beginning of the end—seven o'clock in the morning of December 26. The Poseidon was homeward-bound for Lisbon after a Christmas cruise to African and South American ports. It was to be a final appalling voyage; a physical and spiritual nightmare endured by fifteen ordinary, yet eventually extraordinary people. Trapped in a sinking ship for ten dark hours of love, hate, and desperation, they face obstacles known only to adventurers who have conquered the far corners of the earth. At the end of their harrowing experience they emerge wholly different persons from what they were before." Am News of Bks

Galsworthy, John
Nobel Prize in literature, 1932

The Forsyte saga; with a preface by Ada Galsworthy. Scribner 1933 xx, 921p front $12.50 **Fic**

1 Family—Fiction 2 Great Britain—Fiction

A reissue of the title first published in this edition 1922 brings together in one volume the chronicles of the Forsyte family: Man of property (1906) In chancery (1920) and To let (1921) and two interludes: The Indian summer of a Forsyte and Awakening

"Within these pages John Galsworthy has collected his best work as a novelist. It is a compendium of the Victorian epoch and of the first twenty years of the twentieth century. Its characters are verifiably true, and the history of this typical English family is told not only by a first-rate literary artist, but by a thinker who is fundamentally honest and sincere." Lit R

Gann, Ernest K.
The high and the mighty. Morrow 1953 342p $3.95 **Fic**

First published by Sloane

"A group of people, casual travelling companions, approach the critical period in their lives as their plane flies from Hawaii to San Francisco. Love, hate, jealousy, tenderness and faith are revealed as the suspense builds to a climax." Huntting

"Mr. Gann's examination of character under stress, coupled with the superbly sustained suspense of the plane's fight for survival, makes a dramatic novel which is likely to catch and hold the attention of almost any reader. . . . First-rate entertainment." N Y Her Trib Books

In the company of eagles. Simon & Schuster 1966 342p $5.95 **Fic**

1 European War, 1914-1918—Fiction

This novel set in 1917 "recreates the frantic pace of bi-plane battles during World War I. A young French aviator swears vengeance on the German ace who flies without fault and kills without mercy." Cincinnati

This "account of [the combatants'] exhilaration, fatigue, pity, fear, and of the corruptive effect of power, represents faithfully what men have experienced in combat since long before the days of Gideon, Samson or David. Ernest Gann handles his material skillfully. . . . Tension builds honestly, imperceptibly, but steadily to a startling climax. . . . The airman's daily battle for objective control of himself, to sustain life in the midst of death, gives Gann's 'In the Company of Eagles' an enduring quality." America

Gardonyi, Geza
Slave of the Huns; tr. by Andrew Feldmar; illus. and with a foreword by Victor C. Ambrus. Bobbs [1970 c1969] 357p illus $5 **Fic**

1 Huns—Fiction 2 Attila—Fiction 3 Europe—History—To 476—Fiction

Original Hungarian edition, 1901

"Young former slave Zeta accompanies an imperial mission to the camp of Attila the Hun. There he falls in love with Emmo, daughter of a Hunnish nobleman, forges a letter giving himself to Emmo's father, and returns to live among the Huns, first as a domestic slave in Emmo's household, then as a warrior, and finally as Attila's scribe." Booklist

"Historical details are unobtrusively inserted as part of Zeta's personal and emotional experiences, and the everyday life of the Huns is convincingly and realistically portrayed, with touches of sympathy and humor." Horn Bk

Gide, André
Nobel Prize in literature, 1947

The counterfeiters; with Journal of "The counterfeiters." The novel tr. from the French by Dorothy Bussy. The Journal tr. from the French and annotated by Justin O'Brien **Fic**

Some editions are:
Knopf $5.95
Modern Lib. $2.95

First published 1927

"By the term novel Gide understands a narrative work in which there exists a conflict of characters and a conflict of ideas. This is his initial material; what happens thereafter is determined not so much by the shaping hand and brain of the creator as by the volitional force which seems to be generated by those characters themselves and by those ideas themselves. . . . It is not only a desire to portray in unsentimental terms an increasingly obvious revolutionary tendency in sex morals that has led him to examine the young Olivier and his delicate lover Edouard, the vigorous heterosexual Bernard, the depraved 'raffine' Count Passavant; he is drawn to youth and to boyhood because that is the age which presents the hardest and most fruitful problems to an adult novelist." N Y Evening Post

"In an age of experimentation Gide has produced a novel which is original without being experimental, which is large without being unwieldy, and which is intellectual without being dialectic. . . . 'The Counterfeiters' restores the novel to us in all its creative freshness. It is an advance, but a logical advance, in the great tradition." N Y Times Bk R

The immoralist; a new translation by Richard Howard. Knopf 1970 171p $5 **Fic**

Original French edition, 1902

"A somber psychological study of the disintegration of a man's character under the influences of illness and a tropical climate. Michel, formerly an ascetic young scholar, tells his story to his friends, explaining the change in his attitude toward life, and relating the steps of his moral degeneration." Booklist

"Gide, interested between the conflict of puritan and Pagan, examines every oblique angle of human behavior, turns his clear eyes into the obscure corners of the soul. In The Immoralist, he illustrates the conflicting pulls of self-development and self-sacrifice. The moral of the story seems to be that he who loseth his life shall find it, for Michel, having found his life, does not know what to do with it. The Immoralist, like all of Gide's books, is rewarding and provocative reading." Outlook

Giles, Janice Holt
Johnny Osage. Houghton 1960 313p $5.95 **Fic**

1 Osage Indians—Fiction 2 Cherokee Indians—Fiction 3 Frontier and pioneer life—Fiction

"After the War of 1812, Johnny moves westward, opens a trading post in the Arkansas River country, and champions the Osage Indians in the bitter feud with the Cherokees." Patterns in Reading

"The details of the massacres are gruesome, but they are part of truth and are never put in for sensation. What emerges is the reality of men and women who faced dangers courageously and some of whom approached the Indians with friendship and compassion." Horn Bk

Glasgow, Ellen
Vein of iron. Harcourt 1950 462p $2.95 **Fic**

1 Virginia—Fiction

Glasgow, Ellen—*Continued*

"Harbrace Modern classics"
First published 1935
"Concerns the fortunes of the Fincastle family [of Virginia] both material and spiritual and embraces three generations, with brief excursions into the deeper past. Centers quickly in the love story of two young people which grows steadily more dramatic until at the end it has become a remarkable picture of human nature in conflict with fate." Ontario Lib Rev
"A thoughtful, searching study of character under the stress of both immemorial and modern problems." N Y Libraries

Godden, Rumer

The battle of the Villa Fiorita. Viking 1963 312p boards $5   **Fic**

1 British in Italy—Fiction 2 Italy—Fiction

"Hugh, 14, and Caddie, 11, trek by train, ship, and bus from England to Italy to try to prevent their divorced mother's marriage to a movie director. Their invasion of the villa where the couple is enjoying a pre-marital honeymoon starts a complex conflict, intensified by the arrival of the movie director's 10-year-old daughter, Pia. Characterization is good; the setting seems very real; and the plot becomes more gripping as the narrative proceeds and the reader becomes accustomed to the author's technique of shifting tenses to mid-scene." Library J
"An enjoyable novel, even if one cannot quite accept the central situation. Its plot is full of surprises, and its evocation of the Italian setting is vivid." N Y Times Bk R

A candle for St Jude. Viking 1948 252p $5   **Fic**

1 Ballet—Fiction 2 London—Fiction

A day in the ballet school of Madame Holbein in London when the graduate students return for the 50th anniversary performance of an exhibition ballet. Backstage are found the jealousies, the tragedies, the love and the success of the dancers
"Good characterization, and excellent style." Los Angeles. School Libraries

An episode of sparrows; a novel. Viking 1955 247p boards $5.50   **Fic**

1 London—Fiction

Also available in a large type edition, $7.95
This is the story of how two London slum children made a garden from a packet of cornflower seeds dropped on the pavement and how it changed several people's lives; not only the children's, but those of Vincent the restaurant keeper and the rich Misses Chesney who lived in the Square. (Publisher)
"It is a deft, amusing, and touching story of a London neighborhood where wealth adjoins poverty. . . . It is novel which rests lightly on the yearnings of childhood and the dreams of the unworldly. A false touch would tip it over but Miss Godden stays this side of sentiment and of undue irony." Sat R

In this house of Brede. Viking 1969 376p $6.95   **Fic**

1 Monasticism and religious orders for women—Fiction

The author writes "about a cloistered order of English Benedictine nuns (Roman Catholic), the way of life they follow in the 20th century, the very real problems, human and spiritual, with which they must grapple, and above all, the intense inner faith that infuses everything they do. . . . Her story centers on a successful career woman in her forties who renounces the world to enter Brede monastery, and what happens to her thereafter." Pub W
"The reader gets an excellent insight into the daily life, rules, and rituals of a religious order. Miss Godden has maintained her high level of writing; as usual her characters are very much alive. Her six-page description of nature around the abbey as a year passes is a little gem that can be reread time and again. For all fiction collections for Catholic and non-Catholic readers alike." Library J

Gogol, Nikolai

Dead souls   **Fic**

1 Russia—Fiction

Some editions are:
Modern Lib. $2.95 Translated by B. G. Guerney
Oxford (World classics) $3 Translated from the Russian by George Reavey; with an introduction by Maurice Bowra
Published in Russia in 1842. Also published with title: Tchitchikoff's journeys
"A tale of the old days of serfdom, when the peasants were registered and counted as 'souls' and those who died between the registrations were denominated 'dead souls.' An adventurer buys up a large number of these at nominal prices, and then raises money on the certificates. This farcical proceeding gives opportunity for numerous and often bitterly satirical pictures of the Russian landowning class." Baker's Best

Golding, William

Lord of the Flies; introduction by E. M. Forster. Coward-McCann 1962 243p illus $5.95   **Fic**

1 Atomic bomb—Fiction 2 Survival (after airplane accidents, shipwrecks, etc.)—Fiction

First published 1954 in England, 1955 in the United States
It is the "story of a group of boys, evacuated from an atomic holocaust and marooned on a desert island where they try to establish something they can call civilization." Library J
"The hideous accidents that promote the reversion to savagery fill most of the book, and the reader must be left to endure them—and also to embrace them, for somehow or other they are entangled with beauty." Introduction

Goudge, Elizabeth

The child from the sea. Coward-McCann 1970 736p $8.95   **Fic**

1 Walter, Lucy—Fiction 2 Charles II, King of Great Britain—Fiction 3 Great Britain—Fiction

"Lucy Walter is the heroine of a richly detailed historical romance set amid the political upheavals of seventeenth-century England. Resourceful, independent, Lucy was born in a remote Welsh castle and became the beloved although secret wife of Charles II before the shifting course of history brought him to the throne; later events led her to Paris where she died at age twenty-eight. Supporting characters are believably re-created and the drama of the era skillfully depicted." Booklist

A city of bells. Coward-McCann 1936 380p $6.95   **Fic**

1 Great Britain—Fiction

"Jocelyn Irvin, dispirited because of a wound received in the Boer War, traveled down to the peaceful little English cathedral city of Torminster, there to visit his saintly old grandfather, Canon Fordyce. Practically forced to open a bookshop in a tiny house in the city, Jocelyn became interested in the writings of a former occupant, Ferranti, who had disappeared. In the finishing and producing of a play of Ferranti's, Jocelyn helped himself and others, especially the charming child Henrietta, Canon Fordyce's adopted grandchild." Book Rev Digest
"A charming story, very English, told in gay style, with lovely word pictures of Torminster, with its Cathedral, cobbled streets and tiny shops." Wis Lib Bul

The Dean's watch; illus. by A. R. Whitear. Coward-McCann 1960 383p illus $6.95   **Fic**

1 Great Britain—Fiction

A story of "how an engaging pair of waifs help the venerable Dean of a historic English cathedral town of the mid-19th century discover love as the panacea for paralyzing fear and loneliness, and to make a bequest of renewed hope to a circle of spiritual cripples is narrated in a charming tale with Dickensian atmosphere." Bookmark

The scent of water. Coward-McCann 1963 348p boards $6.95   **Fic**

1 Great Britain—Fiction

"A quiet novel of a woman's spiritual regeneration and rebuilding of her life in middle age. The heroine retires at age 50 to an inherited house and garden in the English countryside.

Goudge, Elizabeth—*Continued*

With the inheritance comes a set of the private journals of the elderly cousin who once owned the property. Reading these journals and helping her neighbors in their problems, the heroine finds serene happiness and wisdom." Pub W

Grass, Günter

Cat and mouse; tr. by Ralph Manheim. Harcourt 1963 189p $3.95   **Fic**

1 Poland—Fiction 2 Adolescence—Fiction

"A Helen and Kurt Wolff book"

Original German edition 1961

A novel about Mahlke, a teenager growing up in a Baltic port city during World War II who is set apart from his fellows by his huge Adam's apple. When a classmate attracts a cat to this "mouse" he launches Mahlke on his career, Mahlke becomes an excellent swimmer and athlete, and later a hero to his nation. But the symbolic cat watching him is a society of petty men and Mahlke is eventually doomed. (Publisher)

The tin drum; tr. from the German by Ralph Manheim. Pantheon Bks. [1963 c1962] 591p $8.95   **Fic**

Original German edition 1959, this translation first published 1962 in England

A novel of twentieth century Germany. The author "tells the story of that epoch as seen through the eyes of Oskar Matzerath, a dwarf who deliberately stopped growing when he was three years old and three feet tall. Yet his intellect developed normally—even faster and sharper than normal. . . . From his third year on, Oskar keeps playing on a tin drum. He becomes a virtuoso on the instrument, using it to stimulate his total recall of the past, the histories of his Kashubian ancestors and the city of Danzig, his birthplace; of the outbreak and course of World War II: the defeat; and, finally, the early years of the economic comeback known as the 'Wirtschaftswunder.'" Christian Science Monitor

"Resembling a confessional, this is the autobiography of a strange, deformed figure, embodying the essence of both innocence and evil, hovering at the edge of a world that is absurd and cruel. The myriad of recollections, the jumble of scenes from daily life, and the patches of heightened emotion are molded by varied techniques into a frightening study of modern society made meaningless by the loneliness of its members. In language, description, symbol, and poetic beauty, this is a modern Pilgrim's Progress; a grim, fascinating, depressing, beautiful book." Library J

Grau, Shirley Ann

The keepers of the house. Knopf 1964 309p $6.95   **Fic**

1 Southern States—Fiction 2 Race problems —Fiction

Pulitzer Prize, 1965

In this novel, set in the deep South, "Will Howland, a widower, meets a young Negro who becomes his housekeeper and mistress and bears him children. Years later, Abigail, his only white granddaughter, who has grown up in this mixed-blooded family, marries a segregationist politician, and the Howland past is exposed. The brutal response of the bigoted white community and Abigail's devasting reprisal provide a . . . climax." Publisher's note

"A novel of considerable dramatic force. Miss Grau makes her point—the absurdities as well as the cruelties to which prejudice leads —sharply enough, but this is a story, not a tract." Sat R

Green, Hannah

I never promised you a rose garden; a novel. Holt 1964 300p $5.95   **Fic**

1 Mental illness—Fiction

"The story of a young girl who fought her way back from a severe schizophrenic condition is told in this novel. The heroine is sixteen-year-old Deborah Blau who has suffered a series of traumatic shocks. Starting with her entry into a mental hospital, the book traces her struggle back to sanity with the aid of an extremely able and understanding woman psychiatrist." Huntting

The author "has done a marvelous job of dramatizing the internal warfare in a young psychotic. She has anatomized, in full detail, the relationship between a whole, sick human being and the clinical situation—including doctors, other patients and the abstract forces of institutional life." N Y Times Bk R

Greene, Graham

The heart of the matter. Viking 1948 306p $3.95   **Fic**

1 Africa, West—Fiction

"The corruption of one man in a group of civil servants and natives in a West African colony is the subject of this novel. Scobie, an assistant police commissioner, had maintained his position with integrity for fifteen years. His intense pity for his wife led him to borrow money to send her on a trip. During her absence he fell in love with a young widow. The discovery of his indiscretions by a blackmailer and the sudden return of his wife led Scobie to take the only way out compatible with his conscience. A good portrayal of West African civil service life and a subtle poignant novel that will disappoint some readers and interest others." Ontario Lib Rev

The power and the glory. Viking 1946 301p $4.50   **Fic**

1 Clergy—Fiction 2 Mexico—Fiction

Also available in a large type edition for $8.50

First published 1940 with title: The labyrinthine ways

"A man fleeing for his life, a Mexican Catholic priest, is the central character. Profoundly religious, yet too weak to resist whiskey, the priest alternately runs from the military authorities, and risks his life to bring the comfort of the church to the fearful, browbeaten Mexican peasants." Book Rev Digest

"The atmosphere and detail of this book are convincing. So are the variegated people. So are the squalor and the heat and the venality of man, the sloth and the violence . . . he [Greene] has now proved himself one of the finest craftsmen of story-telling in our time." Sat R

The quiet American   **Fic**

1 Vietnam—Fiction

Some editions are:
Modern Lib. $2.95
Viking $4.40

First published 1955 in England

The scene is Saigon. The principal characters are a skeptical British journalist, his attractive Vietnamese mistress and an eager young American sent out by Washington on a mysterious mission. Local intrigue, a night in a beleaguered outpost, a perilous venture behind the Communist lines are the main ingredients of the story. (Publisher)

"Mr. Greene has always been a master of suspense, and the particular excellence of 'The Quiet American' lies in the way in which he builds up the situation finally to explode the moral problem which for him lies at the heart of the matter." Times (London) Lit Sup

Travels with my aunt; a novel. Viking 1969 244p boards $5.95   **Fic**

SBN 670-72524-2

"Aunt Augusta, in her late 70's embroils her bachelor nephew, an utterly respectable, dahlia-growing, retired bank manager, in a series of wild escapades. The action moves from London, across the European continent to Istanbul, and ends in Paraguay. Most of the characters are from Aunt Augusta's somewhat murky past, although there are contemporary figures such as a C.I.A. agent and his hippie daughter, and Wordsworth from Sierra Leone, who lives with Aunt Augusta as her 'valet.'" Library J

Triple pursuit; a Graham Greene omnibus. Viking [1971 c1958] 435p $6.95   **Fic**

Consists of the following three separately published suspense novels: This gun for hire (1936); The third man (1950); Our man in Havana (1958)

Grosman, Ladislav

The shop on Main Street; tr. from the Czech by Iris Urwin; illus. by Victor Ambrus. Doubleday 1970 123p illus $3.95 **Fic**

1 Jews in the Czechoslovak Republic—Fiction 2 World War, 1939-1945—Fiction

A small Slovak town in 1942 is the setting of this story. Brtko, a good-hearted young carpenter, "is awarded a Jewish shop for Aryanization. Brtko finds himself beguiled by the old woman who keeps the shop; he knows that Mrs. Lautman doesn't understand what is going on and he goes along with her mistaken idea that he has been put in as her assistant. The ending is gently tragic, the writing style adequate, the concept a vital one." Chicago. Children's Book Center

Guareschi, Giovanni

Comrade Don Camillo; tr. by Frances Frenaye. Farrar, Straus 1964 212p illus boards $3.95 **Fic**

1 Clergy—Fiction 2 Communism—Fiction 3 Italians in Russia—Fiction

First published 1963 in Italy

Peppone, the Communist mayor of the Italian town, persuades his constant adversary, Don Camillo, the parish priest, to deposit sweepstake winnings for him secretly. However, the mayor continues his anti-clerical statements. The priest retaliates once more by threatening to disclose Peppone's secret unless the mayor permits Don Camillo to join a group of Party members on a trip to Russia. The wily priest sets off with his prayer book bound in a cover stamped: Maxims of Lenin. (Publisher)

"A neatly turned, very funny satire on Russia and Communism. . . . [It is a] human and warm story; Don Camillo's wit is good-natured." Pub W

Don Camillo meets the flower children; tr. by L. K. Conrad. Farrar, Straus 1969 247p illus $5.95 **Fic**

1 Clergy—Fiction 2 Catholic Church in Italy —Fiction

Translated from the Italian edition

In this Don Camillo story, the country priest has "his problems with the younger generation. First 'Venom,' the communist mayor's son, rides his motorcycle right into Don Camillo's life; then his niece, a cute little hippie from the city, turns up bound to make her uncle's life something less than a bed of roses. . . . [But] Don Camillo gets the best of everyone and the best for everybody at the end." Pub W

The little world of Don Camillo; tr. from the Italian by Una Vincenzo Troubridge. Farrar, Straus 1951 205p illus $4.95 **Fic**

1 Clergy—Fiction 2 Italy—Fiction 3 Communism—Fiction 4 Catholic Church in Italy—Fiction

First published in the United States 1950 by Pellegrini & Cudahy

In post-war Italy, in the Po Valley, there is a small country village that is a stronghold of Communism. The head of the local unit is Peppone, the Mayor. His favorite adversary is Don Camillo, the parish priest, and vice versa. Peppone cannot be a thorough-going Communist because he is a man of conscience. Don Camillo cannot be a thorough-going Christian because he is all too human. Out of this situation the author has woven a series of anecdotes." Rel Bk Club Bul

"Giovanni Guareschi has performed a rather remarkable feat. He has managed to write a delightfully humorous book with a warm, human and tolerant pen, about some of the main issues in the struggle that confronts the world today—Christian principles as opposed to Communist-totalitarian dogmas." N Y Times Bk R

Gulbranssen, Trygve

Beyond sing the woods; tr. by Naomi Walford. Putnam 1936 313p $6.95 **Fic**

1 Norway—Fiction

"Chronicle of fifty years in a Norwegian family living on their huge estate in the hills. The Björndal bred strong men, but they came to tragic ends until one of them, Dag, married a wife from the fertile valley lands, and spent his energies in piling up wealth for himself and his descendants. The tale ends with the engagement of the remaining son of Old Dag, and a beautiful girl from the town." Book Rev Digest

Guthrie, A. B.

Arfive [by] A. B. Guthrie, Jr. Houghton 1971 [c1970] 278p boards $5.95 **Fic**

1 Frontier and pioneer life—Fiction 2 Montana—Fiction

In this novel, set in a small Montana town in the early twenties, the author "has chosen as underlying theme the conflict of midwestern and, by extension, eastern Victorianism with the looser attitudes of a yet uncurried West. To the schoolteacher, Benton Collingsworth, the saloon and the whorehouse are abominations. To Mort Ewing, rancher, they are facts, bad or good or in between. . . . Yet the two men, presented as almost equal protagonists, respect, like, and support each other, even to the point at which their mutual esteem involves violence." Publisher's note

The big sky **Fic**

1 The West—Fiction 2 Frontier and pioneer life—Fiction

Some editions are:
Houghton $6.95
Watts, F. $9.95 Large type edition. A Keith Jennison book
First published 1947 by Sloane

"A novel of the west, period 1830-43, with a strong historical background. It is the story of the development of the mountain country by the white man, fur trapping, Indian fights, but particularly the story of mountain men—how they lived and worked, fought and loved, their rise and fall." Library J

"It is a strong and savory tale of adventure with the first white hunters in the West. Honestly imagined and true to history. It is also a parable of the way the pioneers, as immoderate as children, took their measureless paradise and spoiled it." Time

The way West **Fic**

1 Oregon Trail—Fiction 2 Frontier and pioneer life—Fiction

Some editions are:
Houghton $4.95
Watts, F. $9.95 Large type edition. A Keith Jennison book
Pulitzer Prize, 1950
First published 1949 by Sloane

"A story of an emigrant trek from Independence, Missouri, to Oregon in the 1840's. Dick Summers, one of the principal characters of the author's earlier novel, 'The Big Sky' [entered above] reappears in this." Book Rev Digest

"Where most writers of Western fiction concentrate on what their characters do, Mr. Guthrie concentrates on how they think and feel. It is this emphasis which gives his books depth and sense of reality." Christian Science Monitor

Haggard, H. Rider

King Solomon's mines. With a colour front. and line drawings in the text by A. R. Whitear. Dutton 1963 214p illus $3.95 **Fic**

1 Africa, Central—Fiction 2 Adventures and adventurers—Fiction

First published 1885

"Highly coloured romance of adventure in the wilds of Central Africa in quest of King Solomon's Ophir; full of sensational fights, blood-curdling perils and extraordinary escapes." Baker's Best

Hailey, Arthur

Airport. Doubleday 1968 440p $6.95 **Fic**

1 Airports—Fiction

"From the first paragraph to the last, readers are offered total involvement with the problems of Lincoln Metropolitan Airport during seven hours of a snowbound evening.

Hailey, Arthur—*Continued*

Using many subplots, Hailey has developed a fast-paced story with a bit of everything: a psychotic determined to blow up the plane he is on for the insurance, a disabled aircraft blocking a much-needed runway, a habitual aerial stowaway, and a harassed general manager trying to straighten out his own marital affairs as well as the problems of the airport. A vast amount of research has resulted in an authentic behind-the-scenes look at operations from air traffic control to the cockpit." Library J

Hammett, Dashiell

The novels of Dashiell Hammett. Knopf 1965 726p $8.95   **Fic**

1 Mystery and detective stories

Includes five detective novels. In Red Harvest (1929) a hard-boiled detective arrives in a corrupt town to find his client murdered and remains to clean up the town. The Dain curse (1929) starts with a small diamond theft which serves to introduce the detective-narrator Sam Spade and the events that follow. In Maltese Falcon (1930) a detective seeks the murderer of his partner and runs afoul of the police and people who are after a statuette. The glass key (1931) is a brutal story about detective Ned Beaumont. The thin man (1934) is the story of disappearance, murder and robbery

Hamsun, Knut

Nobel Prize in literature, 1920

Hunger; newly tr. from the Norwegian by Robert Bly; with introductions by Robert Bly and Isaac Bashevis Singer. Farrar, Straus 1967 xxii, 231p $5.95   **Fic**

1 Norway—Fiction

Original Norwegian edition appeared 1890. First published in the United States 1920 by Knopf

"A stream-of-consciousness narrative about a young man, a writer, who is literally starving, giddy with light-headed fancies, and occasionally able to sell an essay for a few kroner—and thus to prolong his suffering. The novel seems entirely modern until one realizes that it was first published in 1890 and is hence the grandfather of a whole range of modern novels, both because of its technique and also because of its fancifulness and humor, which are considerable. Only then does Hamsun's radical originality come clear. 'Hunger' was considered in its day, and must still be considered . . . a great book." Book of the Month Club News

Hardy, Thomas

Far from the madding crowd   **Fic**

1 Farm life—Fiction 2 Great Britain—Fiction

Some editions are:
Dodd (Great illustrated classics) $4.50 With photographs of the author, his environment and the setting of the book, together with an introduction by E. P. Lawrence
Harper $6.95
St Martins $7.50

First published 1874

"Bathsheba Everdene is courted by Gabriel Oak, a young farmer who becomes bailiff of the farm she inherits, by William Boldwood, who owns the neighboring farm, and by Sergeant Troy, a handsome young adventurer. She [first] marries Troy, who spends his money freely . . . [and after many adventures] marries Gabriel Oak." Benét. The Reader's Encyclopedia

"It is concerned with the comedies and tragedies of life among people in humble circumstances. The farm activities, including the lambings, are described with faithful attention to details. . . . Hardy's philosophy of pessimism is apparent but less intense than in 'The Return of the Native [entered below]." Haydn. Thesaurus of Book Digests

Jude the obscure   **Fic**

1 Great Britain—Fiction

Some editions are:
Modern Lib. $2.95
St Martins $7.50

First published 1895

A novel which deals "with the mutual love of Jude Fawley and his cousin, Sue Bridehead. They both marry outsiders, but finally secure divorces to live with each other. After some years, young Jude, the son of Jude's former wife Arabella, murders Jude's two younger children and hangs himself to escape from misery. Broken by this tragedy, Sue returns to her husband and Jude to Arabella. Soon afterward Jude dies." Benét. The Reader's Encyclopedia

"Mr. Hardy's rebellious views of life and religion, and leanings towards naturalistic methods, are given full play in this story of a peasant scholar's foiled ambition, which from beginning to end is sombre and in many of the incidents extremely painful." Baker's Best

The mayor of Casterbridge; the life and death of a man of character. With an introduction by Samuel C. Chew. Modern Lib. [1950] xxiv, 432p $2.95   **Fic**

1 Great Britain—Fiction

First published 1886

"Michael Henchard, a young hay trusser, while intoxicated at a fair sells his wife and child at auction for five pounds to a man named Newson. Eighteen years afterward when Henchard has become the Mayor of Casterbridge, they reappear, and most of the novel deals with the problems and embitterments of his later life. The girl, Elizabeth Jane, who he finally learns, is not his own daughter but Newson's, marries his business rival, Farfrae." Benét. The Reader's Encyclopedia

This Victorian novel is "typical of Hardy's pessimistic philosophy, in which 'happiness was but the occasional episode in a general drama of pain.'" Haydn. Thesaurus of Book Digests

Bibliography: p xxii

The return of the native   **Fic**

1 Great Britain—Fiction

Some editions are:
Dodd (Great illustrated classics) $4.50 With illustrations reproducing drawings for early editions and photographs of contemporary scenes together with an introductory biographical sketch of the author and anecdotal captions by Basil Davenport
Harper $6.95
Watts, F. $8.95 Large type edition. A Keith Jennison book
Watts, F. lib. bdg. $4.50 Ultratype edition

First published 1878

"Clym Yeobright, tired of city life, returns from Paris to open a school on Egdon Heath, and in spite of the opposition of his mother, marries Eustacia Vye. . . . Mrs Yeobright walks over the heath to [her son's] cottage, but Eustacia, entertaining [her lover] Wildeve, does not answer the door. . . . [The mother] is found by Clym, unconscious and dying of adder bite. Clym learns enough to blame Eustacia, who subsequently drowns herself." Benét. The Reader's Encyclopedia

"A drama of passion and nemesis, enacted amidst the wild and solemn scenery of an imaginary heath, and animated profoundly by the author's philosophy and revolt. . . . Fatal misunderstandings between dear relatives, and the subtle and imperceptible yielding to temptation which leads to crime and death, are the determining motives. Clym Yeobright and his mother and the exotic Eustacia Vye are among his finest impersonations of human longing and disillusionment, anguish, and endurance." Baker's Best

Tess of the D'Urbervilles   **Fic**

1 Great Britain—Fiction

Some editions are:
Dodd (Great illustrated classics) $4.50 With photographs of the author, his environment and the setting of the book, together with an introduction by Carl J. Weber
Modern Lib. $2.95
St Martins $7.50

First published in complete form 1891

"The tragic history of a woman betrayed. . . . Tess, the author contends, is sinned

Hardy, Thomas—*Continued*

against, but not a sinner; her tragedy is the work of tyrannical circumstances and of the evil deeds of others in the past and the present, and more particularly of two men's baseness, the seducer, and the well-meaning intellectual who married her. . . . The pastoral surroundings, the varying aspects of field, river, sky, serve to deepen the pathos of stage in the heroine's calamities, or to add beauty and dignity to her tragic personality." Baker's Best

Hartog, Jan de

The captain. Atheneum Pubs. 1966 434p $5.95   **Fic**

1 World War, 1939-1945—Fiction 2 Sea stories

"Martinus Harinxma, apprentice-mate on a Dutch seagoing tugboat, is made captain of the largest rescue ship on the Murmansk run during World War II. Within the framework of a superb sea story, the author relates the battles, the cruel bueaucracy, the futility and final madness of war." Cincinnati

This sea story "is one of those rarities in contemporary fiction a real spellbinder, a he-man story, full of action, in which the hero is brave and likable. . . . The exposure and terror of that long and punishing convoy have never been so powerfully depicted. The art of this book lies in its unforced masculinity, for these men are real." Atlantic

Hawthorne, Nathaniel

The House of the Seven Gables   **Fic**

1 Puritans —Fiction 2 New England—Fiction

Some editions are:

Dodd (Great illustrated classics) $4.50 Biographical introduction by Basil Davenport with contemporary illustrations
Dutton (Everyman's lib) $3.25
Houghton (Riverside bookshelf) $4.25 With illustrations by Helen Mason Grose
Watts, F. $8.95 Large type edition complete and unabridged. A Keith Jennison book
Watts, F. lib. bdg. $4.50 Ultratype edition

First published 1851

"Follows the fortunes of a decayed New England family, consisting of four members —Hephzibah Pyncheon, her brother Clifford, their cousin Judge Pyncheon, and another cousin Phoebe, a country girl. At the time the story opens Hephzibah is living in great poverty at the old homestead, the House of the Seven Gables. With her is [her brother] Clifford, just released from prison. . . . Judge Pyncheon, who was influential in obtaining the innocent Clifford's arrest, that he might hide his own wrong-doing, now seeks to confine him in an asylum on the charge of insanity. Hephzibah's pitiful efforts to shield this brother, to support him and herself by keeping a centshop, to circumvent the machinations of the judge, are described through the greater portion of the novel. The sudden death of the malevolent cousin frees them and makes them possessors of his wealth." Keller's Reader's Digest of Books

"The analysis of character is stern and uncompromising, and the writer marks, as is his wont, upon the endless and incalculable consequences of past mistakes and misdeeds. . . . A picture unsurpassed as a symphony in which background and atmosphere play a dominant part." Baker's Best

The scarlet letter   **Fic**

1 Puritans—Fiction 2 New England—Fiction

Some editions are:

Dodd (Great illustrated classics) $3.95 With contemporary illustrations and a foreword by Basil Davenport
Dutton (Everyman's lib) $3.25 Introduction by Roy Harvey Pierce
Houghton (Riverside lib) $4.95
Modern Lib. $2.95
Watts, F. $8.95 Large type edition. A Keith Jennison book
Watts, F. $4.50 Ultratype edition. With a critical and biographical profile of Nathaniel Hawthorne by Norman Holmes Pearson

First published 1850

"The scene is Boston, two hundred years ago; the chief characters are Hester Prynne; her lover, Arthur Dimmesdale, the young but revered minister of the town; their child, Pearl;

and her husband Roger Chillingworth, an aged scholar." Keller's Reader's Digest of Books

"Hester, who wears the [A, the] visible sign of the sin, finally learns to live with it. . . . [Dimmesdale] is unable to expiate his sin by mortification of the flesh, and finally confesses publicly, but dies immediately thereafter. Chillingworth is revealed as the worst sinner of the three, because he sins out of hate, while the others sin out of love. . . . The novel is not about adultery, for the act occurred before the opening of the story, nor about sin 'per se': but rather it is about the effect of sin on the mind and spirit of the characters." Herzberg. Reader's Encyclopedia of Am Lit

Head, Ann

Mr and Mrs Bo Jo Jones. Putnam 1967 253p $5.95   **Fic**

1 Marriage—Fiction

"A marriage of necessity between two pleasant high school youngsters led astray by their emotions barely holds up against unreadiness for love or marriage and differences in family background and families. After their premature baby's death, Bo Jo and young wife July find their separation, schooling, and return to opposite sides of town assumed and arranged for by their parents. They momentarily yield to seeming reasonableness but, gradually realizing the bonds that have grown between them during a year of marriage, pregnancy, and bereavement, decide to work out their destiny and education together." Booklist

"The appeal of this story is so universal and the problems it deals with so pertinent to modern family life, that it could easily find a wide audience, from teenagers on up to grandparents. The relations between the youngsters and their parents are well handled and made painfully real." Pub W

Heinlein, Robert A.

Stranger in a strange land. Putnam 1961 408p $6.95   **Fic**

1 Science fiction

"Valentine Michael Smith was born on Mars and educated to its strange customs, superhuman abilities and ignorance of sex. A young nurse kidnaps 'The Man from Mars' from a hospital where he was held incommunicado after his arrival on earth and takes him to the Pocono Mountain estate of Jubal Harshaw, who protects him from exploitation by scientists, politicians and newsmen. After several ventures into terrian society and observations of a strange religious sect, Mike becomes pastor and founder of the Church of All Worlds, Inc. The new discipline teaches the Martian language and customs. Because this sect is alien to the mores of the Western culture, conflict brews." Library J

"This is severe social criticism conveyed through a blend of fantasy, satire, and science fiction." Booklist

Three by Heinlein. Doubleday 1965 426p $6.50   **Fic**

1 Science fiction

Contents: The puppet masters (1951); Waldo (1950); Magic, inc. (1950)

The first of these science fiction novels concerns parasitic creatures from outer space who take over men's minds; the second is about a weird inventor and a Pennsylvania Dutch farmer who challenge a power monopoly; and the third involves a protection racket with magical techniques using methods that date back to the early 20th century

Heller, Joseph

Catch-22; a novel   **Fic**

1 World War, 1939-1945—Fiction

Some editions are:

Modern Lib. $2.95
Simon & Schuster $7.95
Simon & Schuster $10.95 A large type edition

First published 1961 by Simon & Schuster

"A broad comedy about a bombardier based in Italy during World War II and his efforts to avoid flying bombing missions while his colonel tries to get him killed by demanding that he fly more and more missions. There is some wonderfully funny dialog and some entertaining zany action. Mr. Heller takes up

Heller, Joseph—*Continued*

just about every aspect of World War II as seen by the comic as well as the cynical novelists who have come before him: pompous officers, malingering soldiers, faking, trading with the enemy and, of course, the pursuit of the local trollops. Eventually the hero deserts." Pub W

"Through the agency of grotesque comedy, Heller has found a way to confront the humbug, hypocrisy, cruelty, and sheer stupidity of our mass society . . . and through some miracle of prestidigitation, Pianosa has become a satirical microcosm for many of the microcosmic idiocies of our time. . . . Catch-22, despite some of the most outrageous sequences since A Night at the Opera, is an intensely serious work." New Repub

Hemingway, Ernest

Nobel Prize in literature, 1954

A farewell to arms. Scribner [1953 c1929] 342p $6.95   **Fic**

1 European War, 1914-1918—Fiction

Also available in a large type edition for $6.95

First published 1929

"An American ambulance officer serving on the Austro-Italian front becomes entangled with an English nurse and deserts to join her after the retreat of Caparetto. Their affair, casual and tawdry at first, becomes a moving and beautiful love story at the tragic end. Using only the minimum of description, Mr Hemingway achieves his effects, many of them highly dramatic, by means of conversations in the staccato repetitive style of average human intercourse." Cleveland

"In spite of the brutality and coarseness of certain passages and the cool description of death agonies, the book achieves the sensitiveness and beauty of fine poetry." Booklist

For whom the bell tolls. Scribner 1940 471p $5.95   **Fic**

1 Spain—History—Civil War, 1936-1939—Fiction

"The frame of the story is a minor incident in the horror that was the war in Spain. Robert Jordan is a young American in the Loyalist ranks who has been detailed to the blowing up of a bridge. . . . Jordan destroys the bridge, but while he is escaping with his companions his horse is knocked from under him by an exploding shell, and we leave him lying on the hillside, his leg crushed by the animal's fall. He sends his companions on and waits with a submachine gun beside him, for the enemy's approach. Those who leave him are, with Jordan, the main figures in the story. Among them is the girl Maria, whom Jordan, in the four-day span of the story's action, has met and loved." N Y Times Bk R

This long novel "sets a new standard for Hemingway in characterization, dialogue, suspense, and compassion for the human being faced with death. . . . He has given us as moving and vivid a story of a group of human beings involved in that war as we are likely to have." Nation

The old man and the sea. Scribner 1952 140p $4.95   **Fic**

1 Fishing—Fiction

Also available in a large type edition for $7.95

Awarded the Pulitzer Prize, 1953

"A brief novel about supreme courage. An old Gulf fisherman, overtaken by hard luck, proves his tenacity and courage when he hooks a monster marlin. He kills his catch but is towed out to sea and then brings what the sharks leave of it back to Havana." Book Rev Digest

"The admirable Santiago, Hemingway's ancient mariner and protagonist of this triumphant short novel, enters the gallery of permanent heroes effortlessly, as if he had belonged there from the beginning. . . . 'The Old Man and The Sea' is a great short novel, told with consummate artistry and destined to become a classic in its kind." Sat R

The sun also rises. Scribner 1926 259p $6.95   **Fic**

In this book "we are introduced to a group of English and American drifters on the continent who have the money and the time to blow where they list from the boulevards of Paris to the bull-fights of Spain, bathing, eating and drinking the while. . . . Yet the book is by no means a bit of sophisticated fluff. It is the hard, acid truth about this group of ineffectuals and conveys the tragedy of their lives. . . . Conversation is the method chiefly used, and it is real talk, not writing." Book Rev Digest

Hémon, Louis

Maria Chapdelaine; a tale of the Lake St John country; tr. by W. H. Blake. Macmillan (N Y) 1921 288p $4.95   **Fic**

1 Quebec (Province)—Fiction 2 Frontier and pioneer life—Fiction

"The daughter of a French-Canadian pioneer in the back country of Quebec, who had lost her first love in a severe snowstorm, eventually had to choose between two others—one a neighbor, the other from the United States." Books for you

Hentoff, Nat

I'm really dragged but nothing gets me down. Simon & Schuster 1968 127p $3.95, lib. bdg. $3.79   **Fic**

"Jeremy Wolf, a high school senior, is beset by deeply conflicting responsibilities—to himself, to his family, to his country. Can his country make him kill? Can his father make him 'respectable'? At school, with friends, with girls, facing the draft, Jeremy is in the process of finding out who he is." Publisher's note

"There is shallowness here, an incompleteness in depth-development of people, and a succession of scenes rather than a plot; but with its authentic dialogue and its sympathetic picture of youth confused and questioning, the book has provocative timeliness." Horn Bk

Hersey, John

A bell for Adano   **Fic**

1 World War 1939-1945—Fiction 2 Italy—Fiction 3 Americans in Italy—Fiction

First published 1944 by Knopf
Awarded Pulitzer Prize, 1945

A novel about Americans in Italy which tells of the Italian American major who tried to rebuild an occupied town along the lines of his own good instincts and democratic upbringing

"Makes very good reading, for in its capable and wholly unpretentious fashion . . . [it] is an entertaining story, a candid report from behind the lines and an effective tract." New Repub

The child buyer. . . . Knopf 1960 257p $4.95   **Fic**

"A novel in the form of hearings before the Standing Committee on Education, Welfare, & Public Morality of a certain State Senate, investigating the conspiracy of Mr. Wissey Jones, with others, to purchase a male child." Title page

The story "of a poor boy of exceptional intelligence and of a representative of a large corporation who seeks to 'buy' him that he may be trained to use his brains for the benefit of the company." Pub W

"In this harsh, satiric, sometimes shocking and profane book, Mr. Hersey is obviously indicating aspects of American education—and other things—with which he disagrees. . . . He lays down a basic irony by having hardly anyone display outrage, or even overwhelming surprise, at the child buyer's proposal. This is all a kind of a tour de force, sometimes entertaining, sometimes sickening. . . . To a reader concerned about educational shortcomings: materialism, mental manipulation, misguided patriotism, the absurdity is uncomfortable, the questions are pressing, the loud clothing of the parable is less important than the thoughts behind it." Christian Science Monitor

Hersey, John—*Continued*

A single pebble. Knopf 1956 181p $4.95 **Fic**

1 Americans in China—Fiction 2 China—Fiction

"An American engineer's trip by junk up the Yangtze to locate a dam site, as he relates it years later in retrospect, symbolizes the contrast between the Western idea of progress and tempo of living and the passive resignation of China's ancient culture and traditions. With mounting tension, the story brings into focus the subtle relationship between the young engineer and the owner of the junk, his wife, and the head tracker, Old Pebble, in a drama heightened by the physical grandeur of the Great River." Booklist

"Written with simplicity and narrative power, this can be read both as high adventure and as a parable of East and West." Horn Bk

The wall **Fic**

1 World War, 1939-1945—Fiction 2 Jews in Warsaw—Fiction 3 Warsaw—Fiction

Some editions are:
Knopf $8.95
Modern Lib. $4.95

First published 1950

On the surface this is the story of the systematic extermination of the Jews of the Warsaw ghetto, and of the heroic resistance of defenseless men and women against the full force of the Germans. But the plot of the story concerns the growth in spirit of a group of friends, so that they emerge undismayed and triumphant in the face of physical annihilation

"Only a true novelist could breathe warmth, compassion, humor, into what a historian would necessarily have pictured as a stark, hopeless, tragic series of events. Only a sensitive novelist could compel us to embark upon such a fearful adventure as this and remain until the end; you do not 'read' 'The Wall'— you live it—and if the experience is shattering it is infinitely rewarding." N Y Times Bk R

Hesse, Hermann

Nobel Prize in literature, 1946

Demian, the story of Emil Sinclair's youth; introduction by Thomas Mann; tr. from the German by Michael Roloff and Michael Lebeck. Harper 1965 171p $4.95 **Fic**

1 Adolescence—Fiction

Original German edition, 1919. First published 1923 in the United States by Boni and Liveright

This novel "is the story of the boy Arthur Sinclair and his growth into young manhood. At school, Arthur is terrified by a bully until a new boy, Max Demian, who has some unusual and hidden power, appears. . . . Demian . . . fascinates but mystifies Arthur. They are separated when Arthur goes off to boarding school, but years later come together as young men. . . . Demian's secret, which marks him off from the run of mankind, is simply that he is one of those rare ones who have found themselves." Atlantic

"Psychological insight into the problems of growth to adulthood combines with the symbolic picture of an age, which through inwardness, tries to replace the lost moral and social order." Library J

Knulp: three tales from the life of Knulp; tr. by Ralph Manheim. Farrar, Straus 1971 114p $4.95 **Fic**

1 Germany—Fiction
SBN 374-1-8216-7

"These three sketches, written in 1915, of Knulp, minor poet, singer of songs, and wanderer through southern Germany show Hesse's developing skills in creating a living, breathing personality through brief but telling actions, and dialog." Pub W

Siddhartha; tr. by Hilda Rosner. New Directions 1951 153p $5 **Fic**

1 Buddha and Buddhism—Fiction

Original German edition first copyrighted 1922

"It is a moral allegory, based on Indian mysticism, which tries to solve the enigma of human loneliness and discontent. The hero, Siddhartha, endowed with all the virtues, goes through the fires of various experiences to emerge to a state of peace and holiness. Before he has achieved this beatitude he has tasted the pleasures of being a mendicant wanderer, then consort to a courtesan, then wealthy man of business, and finally companion to a humble ferryman, whose wisdom comes from the endlessly murmuring river." Sat R

"The cool and strangely simple story makes a beautiful little book, classic in proportion and style." Nation

Steppenwolf; tr. from the German by Basil Creighton **Fic**

Some editions are:
Holt $5.95
Modern Lib. $2.95 Revised by Walter Sorell

Originally published 1927 in German

It is the story of Harry Haller, a man of 50 who considers himself half man, half wolf of the steppes. In Harry Haller, as in intellectual Germany, and as in civilized man of all ages, there is the conflict between nature and spirit

Hilton, James

Lost horizon. Morrow 1933 277p $6.95 **Fic**

1 Tibet—Fiction

"During a revolution in Baskul four people are kidnapped in an airplane and find themselves finally in the mysterious lamasery of Shangri-La, high up in the Kuen-Lun mountains of southern Tibet. The story of their adventures is told by one of their number, Conway, a young Englishman, but the end of the story is left in doubt." Book Rev Digest

"This is a story of drama, of quiet beauty, of satire, and of humor. Readers who enjoy the fantasy of Paul Gallico and Robert Nathan read 'Lost Horizon' with interest and pleasure." Doors to More Mature Reading

Random harvest. Little 1941 326p $5.95 **Fic**

1 Amnesia—Fiction 2 Great Britain—Fiction

"An Atlantic Monthly Press book"

"Charles Rainier, an upper-class English business man and a member of Parliament, with a clever wife and large city and country homes, has, nevertheless, a shadow over his past. There are three years of his life which are perfectly blank—from the time when he was hit by a shell in the World War, until he woke up on a Liverpool park bench in 1919. The story of Rainier's ceaseless efforts to recapture those blank years is told partly by Rainer himself, partly by his secretary. The book closes in 1939, on the eve of the second war, with Rainier in possession of the complete story of his own life." Book Rev Digest

"Those who are interested in any one of a half dozen war problems, 'shell-shock,' the changing social order, and a good love story will like this book immensely. Above all, it is a good story just for the joy of it." Churchman

Holt, Victoria

The legend of the Seventh Virgin. Doubleday 1965 326p $5.95 **Fic**

1 Great Britain—Fiction

"Kerensa Carlee's dream of owning St. Larnston Abbas, the famous convent now the home of Cornwall's leading family, had seemed to be coming true when she married Johnny St. Larnston, but soon her world crumbled as Johnny disappeared and the sinister legendary past of the house enveloped her." McClurg. Book News

This title "has all the ingredients of superior gothic fiction. . . . The Cornish dialect with which Victoria Holt spices her story is a constant delight and a tribute to her skill as a novelist." Best Sellers

The Queen's confession. Doubleday 1968 430p $5.95 **Fic**

1 Marie Antoinette, consort of Louis XVI, King of France—Fiction

This biographical novel, in the form of a memoir written by herself, describes the life of Marie Antoinette as a young Austrian Archduchess; a spoiled Dauphine in the Versailles court; a misunderstood Queen; and as a woman who achieved tragic nobility. (Publisher)

Holt, Victoria—*Continued*

The author "does her work well. Her story is based on hardcore fact and she provides an excellent bibliography, rich in primary sources. Her imagination embroiders the story delicately and makes the entire work believable." Best Sellers

Bibliography: p429-30

Horgan, Paul

A distant trumpet. Farrar, Straus 1960 629p $8.95 **Fic**

1 Apache Indians—Wars, 1883-1886—Fiction

A novel of the Southwest in the 1870's and 1880's. The chief scene of action is at a U.S. Army outpost in Arizona during the Apache Indian Wars. Chief protagonists in the story are Lieutenant Matthew Hazard and his wife, Laura; Major General Alexander Upton Quait, Laura's resourceful eccentric uncle; Colonel and Mrs Prescott and the other officers and their wives; and, White Horn, an Apache scout. (Publisher)

"The author evokes the arid landscape of the Southwest with his usual great skill and feeling; in the characterization of a general officer Mr. Horgan appears to have accomplished a tour de force!" Library J

Whitewater. Farrar, Straus 1970 337p $6.95 **Fic**

1 Texas—Fiction

"The isolated West Texas town of Whitewater becomes, in Horgan's hands, a microcosm in which the chief characters, Phillipson Durham, Billy Breedlove, and Marilee Underwood, represent unsettled, impatient youth. The patterned life of the community is intolerable to these young people, and their association with the characters of the town—the sadistic policemen, prostitutes, a homosexual, an eccentric old maid librarian—serves to emphasize the meaningless, lonesomeness, and barrenness of their existence." Choice

"There is suspense and drive and the breath of life itself. The characters are real; the emotions are gripping; the whole thing rings true. Horgan has the real storyteller's gift." Best Sellers

Household, Geoffrey

Watcher in the shadows; a novel. Little 1960 248p boards $6.95 **Fic**

"An Atlantic Monthly Press book"

"The hero, a Viennese who had served in British intelligence during the war, finds himself hunted down by an old enemy who had, naturally, believed him to be a Nazi at the time when he was posing as one in the line of duty. The two finally settle their differences in hand-to-hand combat in . . . England." Pub W

This "enthralling story reveals past secret service activities, harrowing encounters in the lovely and lonely countryside and a charming romance." Bookmark

Howells, William Dean

The rise of Silas Lapham. With biographical illus. and pictures of the setting of the book, together with an introduction by C. David Mead. Dodd 1964 367p illus $4.50 **Fic**

1 Boston—Fiction

"Great illustrated classics"

First published 1885

"Silas is a crude, uneducated man, who makes his fortune by methods not above criticism, but manly and capable of better things when his conscience is awakened—a compendium of human virtues and vices, drawn with insight, tenderness and humour. The efforts of the prosperous Laphams to get into Boston society, with their mistakes and disillusionments, the sentimental tragi-comedy of the two daughters, in love with the same young man; and Lapham's business troubles, are more or less neatly woven in to make the plot." Baker's Best

Hudson, William H.

Green mansions **Fic**

1 Venezuela—Fiction

Some editions are:

Dodd (Great illustrated classics) $4.50 With illustrations reproducing drawings for early editions and photographs of contemporary scenes together with an introductory biographical sketch of the author and anecdotal captions by Edwin Way Teale

Knopf $12.50 Paintings and drawings by Horacio Butler

Watts, F. $7.95 Large type edition complete and unabridged. A Keith Jennison book

First published 1904

"Based on the naturalist-author's extensive travels in South America. A young man making his way over the Andes falls in with a tribe of savage Indians, discovers in the forest and becomes enamored of a mysterious being, part woman and part bird, and in seeking to unravel her mystery, passes through extreme peril of body and soul." Wis Lib Bul

"'Green Mansions,' the romance of the bird girl Rima, a story actual yet fantastic, immortalizes, I think, as passionate a love of all beautiful things as ever was in the heart of man. In form and spirit the book is unique." John Galsworthy

Hughes, Richard

A high wind in Jamaica **Fic**

1 Pirates—Fiction

Some editions are:

Harper $6.95

Watts, F. lib. bdg. $7.95 Large type edition complete and unabridged. A Keith Jennison book

First published 1929 with title: The innocent voyage

"After the hurricane that razes the Thornton home in the West Indies, the children are sent to England. Word reaches the parents that the children have been captured by pirates and drowned. Actually they continue the voyage on the 'pirate' ship, a voyage that has the quality of a nightmare wherein the most fantastic events are mixed with the natural and real. These events involve both children and crew, yet the minds of the two groups never meet in understanding, either of each other, or of the terrible things that happen." Book Rev Digest

Hugo, Victor

The hunchback of Notre Dame **Fic**

1 France—History—House of Valois, 1323-1589—Fiction 2 Middle Ages—Fiction 3 Paris. Notre Dame Cathedral—Fiction

Some editions are:

Dodd (Great illustrated classics) $4.50 With illustrations of contemporary scenes and a foreword by Curtis Dahl

Dutton (Everyman's lib) $3.25 Introduction by Denis Saurat. Has title: Notre-Dame de Paris Modern Lib. $2.95

Original French edition published 1830

"The first part of the book is a panorama of medieval life—religious, civic, popular, and criminal. . . . These elements are then set in motion in fantastic and grandiose drama, of which the personages are romantic sublimations of human virtues and passions—Quasimodo, the hunchback, faithful unto death; Esmeralda, incarnation of innocence and steadfastness." Baker's Best

Les misérables **Fic**

1 Paris—Fiction

Some editions are:

Dodd $5.50 Illustrated by Mead Schaeffer

Dutton (Everyman's lib) 2v ea $4.95 Translated from the French by Charles E. Wilbour

Modern Lib. (Modern Lib. Giants) Translated from the French by Charles E. Wilbour

First published 1862

"A panorama of French life in the first half of the [nineteenth] century, aiming to exhibit the fabric of civilization in all its details, and to reveal the cruelty of its pressure on the poor, the outcast, and the criminal. Jean Valjean, a man intrinsically noble, thru the tyranny of society becomes a criminal. . . . Valjean, reformed and prosperous, follows in the good bishop's footsteps as an apostle of benevolence, only to be doomed again by the law to

Hugo, Victor—*Continued*

slavery and shame. . . . [A] huge morality, which is thronged with representatives of the good in man and the cruelty of society. Magnificent description. . . . Scenes invested with terror, awe, repulsion, alternate with tedious rhapsodies. Realism mingles with the incredible." Baker's Best

Hulme, Kathryn

The nun's story   **Fic**

1 Nurses and nursing—Fiction

Some editions are:
Little $6.95
Watts, F. $7.95 Large type edition. A Keith Jennison book

First published 1956

"The story, truly based, it is claimed, on the life of a Belgian girl who became a nun, learned tropical nursing and practiced in a hospital much like Dr Schweitzer's deep in the Belgian Congo. In Europe after the Nazi invasion her hospital became a sanctuary for the Underground and it was then that she realized the lack of humility which made it impossible for her to continue in the Order." Am News of Bks

"Some enlightening vignettes of the disciplines of nursing and missionary orders. Occasional clinical reporting of violent scenes which take place in a mental hospital and a mission station in the jungle may limit the appeal of this semi-documentary." Booklist

Huxley, Aldous

Brave new world; a novel; with a foreword for this edition. Harper 1946 xx, 311p $5.95, lib. bdg. $4.43   **Fic**

1 Utopias—Fiction

First published 1932 by Doubleday

A Utopian novel describing an industrialized society in which Ford and his standardized Model T are worshipped

"Dignity, beyond all else, has attended the creation of the classic Utopias, from that of Plato on down to Edward Bellamy's perfectly geared industrial machine. . . . It has remained for Aldous Huxley to build the Utopia to end Utopias. He has satirized the imminent spiritual trustification of mankind, and has made rowdy and impertinent sport of the World State whose motto shall be Community, Identity, Stability." N Y Times Bk R

Point counter point. Harper 432p $5.95 **Fic**

1 London—Fiction

A reprint of the title first published 1928 by Doubleday

The book "presents a satiric picture of London intellectuals and members of English upper-class society during the 1920's. Frequent allusions to literature, painting, music, and contemporary British politics occur throughout the book, and much scientific information is embodied in its background. The story is long and involved, with many characters; it concerns a series of broken marriages and love affairs, and a political assassination. The construction is elaborate, supposedly based on Bach's 'Suite No. 2 in B Minor.' It is also a novel within a novel. Philip Quarles a leading character . . . is himself planning a novel, which echoes or 'counterpoints' the events going on around him." Benét. The Reader's Encyclopedia

Innes, Hammond

The wreck of the Mary Deare. Knopf 1956 296p map $5.95   **Fic**

1 Sea stories

"John Sands saw the 'Mary Deare' briefly that night from the deck of his sailing vessel the 'Sea Witch.' He saw her again the following morning, abandoned and drifting close to the great reef areas of the Channel Islands. And in boarding her and attempting to satisfy his curiosity, he became involved in the mystery of the 'Mary Deare.'" Publisher's note

"A first-rate tale of suspense, betrayal, and heroism involving the discovery of a drifting and deserted ship in the English Channel." A.L.A. Young People's List

Irwin, Margaret

Elizabeth, captive princess. Harcourt 1948 246p illus $4.50   **Fic**

1 Elizabeth I, Queen of England—Fiction
2 Great Britain—History—Tudors, 1485-1603—Fiction

Sequel to: Young Bess, entered below

"Beginning in 1553 with the death of young Edward VI, this novel presents two tempestuous years in the life of Princess Elizabeth and ends with Mary Tudor's long-sought marriage to Philip of Spain." Cleveland

Young Bess. Harcourt 1945 274p $4.95 **Fic**

1 Elizabeth I, Queen of England—Fiction
2 Great Britain—History—Tudors, 1485-1603—Fiction

The story dramatizes the course of the childhood and adolescence of Queen Elizabeth in the tumultuous days of her father's reign and of the sparring for succession following his death

"In the story are the boisterous gayety and strident color that were sixteenth century Court life in England, and the swirl of intrigue. Much of it is based on documents preserved by the Seymour family, on Elizabeth's letters, and young King Edward's journal." Christian Science Monitor

Followed by: Elizabeth, captive princess, entered above

Jackson, Helen Hunt

Ramona; a story; with illus. by N. C. Wyeth; introduction by May Lamberton Becker. Little 1939 424p illus $4.95   **Fic**

1 California—Fiction 2 Indians of North America—Fiction

"First published in 1884, this was primarily an appeal for justice to the American Indian, but it remains a tragic love story and a sympathetic picture of the life and culture of the Indians of Lower California." Toronto

"Ramona Ortegna, a maiden having (unknown to herself) Indian ancestry, is reared as a member of the patriarchal Moreno family, who are trying to hold their estate in spite of American conquests. Their heir, Felipe, falls in love with her, but conceals it from Ramona and from his mother, the aged Señora, who alone knows the secret of Ramona's origin. Ramona marries, out of her caste, the simple Indian peasant Alessandro, and elopes with him to San Diego. Shortly after, he is killed following persecution by the advancing Americans. At the lowest ebb of her fortunes, her foster-brother Felipe comes to the rescue of Ramona and her child. Scorning the 'stigma' of her Indian blood, he marries her. When their estate is lost they go to Mexico." Haydn. Thesaurus of Book Digests

Jackson, Shirley

We have always lived in the castle. Viking 1962 214p $3.95   **Fic**

Also available in a large type edition for $7.95

"Though acquitted by a jury of the arsenic poisoning of four members of her family six years earlier, Constance Blackwood has never been judged anything but guilty by her townspeople, and because of their taunts and cruelty she no longer leaves home at all. But this story, told in the first person, is primarily that of her younger sister, Mary Katherine, now 18: an imaginative, poetic, whimsical and ruthless girl—so ruthless, so strong that she is able to turn aside all inroads." Library J

"The effect of the book does not only depend on mystery or suspense; nor on the casual intimations of evil that Miss Jackson can put in a phrase. . . . The effect depends rather on her ability to specify a real world which is at once more sane and more mad than the world we see. . . . The havoc [Cousin Charles] wreaks, and the unsuspected dénouement of the action, bring into soft focus the human ambivalences of guilt and atonement, love and hate, health and psychosis. . . . Shirley Jackson has once again effected a marvelous elucidation of life in the ageless form of a story full of craft and full of mystery." N Y Times Bk R

James, Henry, 1843-1916

The ambassadors   Fic

1 Americans in France—Fiction

Some editions are:
Dutton (Everyman's lib) $2.95 Introduction by
Frank Swinnerton
Harper $4.95

First published 1903

Chadwick Newsome, expected to return
home and take over his family's New England
mills, remains in Paris. His mother, a widow,
requests her fiancé, Lambert Strether (the
chief ambassador) to go to Europe to rescue
her son. Strether finds Paris, its people and
culture, as delightful as does Chad. He persuades Chad to remain, even though, by remaining, Chad loses the opportunity to become
a rich man. Strether, having failed in his mission, knows he will never marry Mrs. Newsome, but decides to return since the journey
was financed by her. The struggle between the
old-fashioned New England conscience and the
cultured maturity of Paris, is told with subtle
irony in the novel James considered his best

The portrait of a lady; introduction by
Fred B. Millett. Modern Lib. 1951 2v in 1
$2.95   Fic

1 Americans in Europe—Fction 2 Great Britain—Fiction

First published 1881

A story "of a young American woman in
contact with the sophisticated characters and
conditions of European society. Isabel Asher
sets out consciously to explore life, to 'make
her life fine.' Amid scenes in America, London. Paris, and Italy, one follows the development of her personality from girlhood to complex maturity. A long but dramatic work, made
interesting by tragic elements of conflict
and suspense." Lenrow. Reader's Guide to
Prose Fiction

"This is a psychological character novel of
great penetration and a valuable commentary
on the foibles of the human race." Doors to
More Mature Reading

Short novels of Henry James. . . . With
eight full-page illustrations; introduction by
E. Hudson Long. Dodd 1961 530p illus $5.50
                                             Fic

"Great illustrated classics: Titan editions"
Contents: Daisy Miller (1878); Washington
Square (1881); The Aspern papers (1888); The
pupil (1872): The turn of the screw (1898)

"Daisy Miller" is the story of a young American girl abroad who is led into compromising
situations through her innocence of European
conventions. "Washington Square," set in 19th
century New York, tells of the relationship of
Catherine, her romantic aunt, worldly father
and a suitor who is after her money. "The
Aspern papers" concerns a writer who is collecting material, in Italy, on the writer Aspern.
"The pupil" is the story, told by his tutor, of
an American boy abroad, who sees through
his parents' pretensions and false values. "The
turn of the screw" is a ghost story in which
a governess tries to break the spell she believes two evil spirits, former servants, have
cast over the two innocent children in her
charge

The turn of the screw [and] The Aspern
papers; introduction by Kenneth B. Mur-
dock. Dutton [1960 c1935] 299p (Everyman's lib) $2.95   Fic

The turn of the screw, first published 1898, is
"a terrifying ghost story about two children,
haunted by the evil spirits of a man and a woman, former servants, who are determined to
gain possession of the souls of the little boy
and girl. Their young governess encounters
the spectres, and gradually discovers the mysterious power which they exert over the children. . . . Conveys an eerie atmosphere which
constitutes the power of the book." Keller's
Reader's Digest of Books

The latter title: The Aspern papers, first
published 1888, is the story of a writer anxious
to secure certain material on the poet Aspern

Jewett, Sarah Orne

The country of the pointed firs. Large type
ed. complete and unabridged. Watts, F.
[1968] 247p lib bdg. $7.95   Fic

1 Maine—Fiction 2 Large type books

"A Keith Jennison book"
First published 1896 by Houghton

"Thinly bound together by a faint thread of
plot, these sketches describe a Maine community, an isolated seaport town. Local color is
deftly applied, and humor mingles with sentiment in descriptions of characters who are res-
olutely themselves." Herzberg. The Reader's
Encyclopedia of Am Lit

Jhabvala, R. Prawer

The householder. Norton 1960 191p
boards $4.50   Fic

1 India—Fiction

"A story set in modern India, about a young
householder, a teacher, confronting responsibilities and problems he did not know existed
in the days of his carefree youth. How Prem
and his young, pregnant wife deal with their
material affairs, with the worldly wise Mr.
Khanna and his wife, and with their own families provides humorous and poignant reading." Pub W

"A delightfully lively and mobile story. . . .
Mrs Jhabvala has much talent. The detail of
Prem's daily round, school and domestic, is
beautifull done. There are some delicious
little comic scenes between Prem and his
headmaster, Mr Khanna, and his absurd wife,
characters who almost suggest an Indian Dickens. This is a short slight novel but everybody
in it is a character in his own right." New
Statesman

Johnston, Mary

To have and to hold; with illus. by Frank
E. Schoonover. Houghton 1931 331p illus
$4.95   Fic

1 Virginia—History—Fiction 2 U.S.—History
—Colonial period—Fiction

First published 1900

"A beautiful maid-of-honour, ward of the
king, escapes a libertine nobleman, the king's
favourite, by fleeing to Virginia with the cargo
of brides sent out by the Company (1621). She
marries a rough, stanch settler, a famous
swordsman, who defends his wife against the
favourite, and they meet with strange adventures. Daringly and dazzlingly unreal, full of
vigorous movement, characters boldly outlined." Baker's Best

Joyce, James

A portrait of the artist as a young man Fic

1 Adolescence—Fiction 2 Ireland—Fiction

Some editions are:
Viking $3.95
Watts, F. $8.95 Large type edition. A Keith
Jennison book

An autobiographical novel "published in 1915.
It portrays the childhood, schooldays, adolescence, and early manhood of Stephen Dedalus,
later one of the leading characters of Ulysses,
touching upon his unhappy experiences at the
Jesuit school at Clongowes, the bitter conflicts
among the Irish regarding Charles Stewart
Parnell, Stephen's weakening interest in art,
metaphysics, and aesthetics, his first love affairs, and his growing rebellion against his
bigoted and poverty-stricken family background, the Roman Catholic religion, and his
native Ireland itself. This book contains
Joyce's first experiments in the technique of
stream of consciousness." Benét. The Reader's
Encyclopedia

Dedalus' youth is seen through "fitful but
intense flashes, often subjective and difficult
to follow. . . . The account of his spiritual
conflicts is concerned in part with his difficulties over adolescent sex temptations." Lenrow. Reader's Guide to Prose Fiction

Kafka, Franz
Metamorphosis. Vanguard 1946 98p illus
$4.95 **Fic**

Original German edition, 1916. This translation by A. L. Lloyd first published 1937 in England
This is "often regarded as Kafka's most perfect finished work. 'The Metamorphosis' begins as its hero, Gregor Samsa, awakens one morning to find himself changed into a huge insect; the story proceeds to develop the effects of this change upon Gregor's business and family life, and ends with his death. It has been read as everything from a religious allegory to a psychoanalytic case history; but its really attractive qualities are its clarity of depiction and attention to significant detail, which give its completely fantastic occurrences an aura of indisputable truth, so that no allegorical interpretation is necessary to demonstrate its greatness." Benét. The Reader's Encyclopedia

The trial. Definitive edition. Translated from the German by Willa and Edwin Muir; revised and with additional materials by E. M. Butler **Fic**

1 Trials—Fiction

Some editions are:
Knopf $6.95 Illustrations by George Salter
Modern Lib. $2.95
Original German edition published 1924; this translation first published 1937
"A fantastic allegory. . . . In this story, the protagonist K. is a bank clerk leading an innocuous middle-class life. He is suddenly and without apparent cause arrested. Thruout a series of absurd examinations, he tries to defend himself but eventually gives up the struggle against unseen and irresponsible Authority and submits passively to the execution." Book Rev Digest

Kane, Harnett T.
Bride of fortune; a novel based on the life of Mrs Jefferson Davis. Doubleday 1948 301p $4.95 **Fic**

1 Davis, Varina (Howell)—Fiction 2 U.S.—History—Civil War—Fiction 3 Southern States—Fiction

"The human story of the Natchez belle who became First Lady of the Confederacy and rescued her husband from death and oblivion. Exciting, dramatic, poignant—these words best describe the extraordinary life of Varina Howell Davis, a woman who had an unshakable faith in her husband, Jefferson Davis, and the lost cause he represented. In telling her extraordinary story, the author . . . has pictured . . . . the rise and fall of the Confederacy." Huntting
"The great fault of the book is its excessively romantic quality. . . . Yet the book has merits which leave a distinct impression upon the reader: a vivid apprehension of time and place, a real grasp of the complex politics of the era, and above all an understanding of the unusual woman who always holds the center of the piece." Sat R

The lady of Arlington; a novel based on the life of Mrs Robert E. Lee. Doubleday 1953 288p $5.95 **Fic**

1 Lee, Mary Randolph (Custis)—Fiction 2 Lee, Robert Edward—Fiction

"Beginning with her girlhood it tells the story of this great-granddaughter of Martha Washington who defied her adoring parents to marry into the impoverished Lee family, and takes her thru all the vicissitudes of her married life, ending with Robert E. Lee's death." Book Rev Digest
This book "will undoubtedly stimulate in the reader admiration for the courageous woman who was Robert E. Lee's wife, and arouse a desire to learn more about the great general who loved the United States yet fought against it, and who freed his own few slaves and yet fought on the side of the South." Best Sellers

Kantor, MacKinlay
Andersonville. World Pub. 1955 767p map
$8.95 **Fic**

1 Andersonville, Ga. Military Prison—Fiction 2 U.S.—History—Civil War—Fiction 3 Confederate States of America—Fiction

Awarded the Pulitzer Prize 1956
"A lovely woodland in southwestern Georgia was transformed into the Confederacy's largest prison camp administered by a senile general who derived savage satisfaction from watching Yankees die of exposure, starvation, and disease. Individual stories merge to create an indelible impression of sublimity amidst degradation within the prison, and of the shamed helplessness of cultured Southerners unable to counter the inhumanity of the dregs of their armies." Booklist
"This book may repel the squeamish for sometimes it is hideous, as war itself is hideous, and the language is frequently soldiers' language. But there are glory and grandeur in it, too. It is a great war novel." N Y Her Trib Books

Kaufman, Bel
Up the down staircase. Prentice-Hall [1965 c1964] 340p illus $5.95 **Fic**

1 Teaching as a profession—Fiction 2 School stories 3 New York (City)—Public schools—Fiction

A loosely constructed "novel about a New York City high school. The school is overcrowded, chaotic; the students, disorderly, underprivileged, but some of them very promising; the teachers, inspired, good, bad, or neurotic; their paperwork, mountainous. Frantic . . . notes between two excellent teachers, friends and fellow sufferers (one is deciding whether to quit), excerpts from students' compositions, and bureaucratic school announcements tell the story." Pub W
"'Up the Down Staircase' may not be 'classicle' but it should be read by anyone interested in children and education. The teacher who is trying to get through to the pupil succeeds in communicating to us all. Bel Kaufman has an especially good recollection of dialect and dialogue. She is a woman with a forceful message. She may slip and write the same letter twice but what she says can bear repeating." N Y Times Bk R

Kawabata, Yasunari
Nobel Prize in literature, 1968

Snow country and Thousand cranes; the Nobel Prize edition of two novels; tr. from the Japanese by Edward G. Seidensticker. Knopf 1969 2v in 1 $5.95 **Fic**

1 Japan—Fiction
First American editions published 1957 and 1959, respectively
"Snow Country is the story of a geisha, Komako, who gives herself, without illusion and with undismayed directness, to a love affair foredoomed to transience. . . . [In Thousand Cranes] a young man is involved briefly with the two mistresses of his dead father and with the daughter of one of them." Publisher's note

Kazantzakis, Nikos
Zorba the Greek; tr. by Carl Wildman. Simon & Schuster 1952 311p $6 **Fic**

1 Crete—Fiction
"An old Greek workman who is philosopher and hedonist, raconteur and roué, Zorba goes, to Crete with the narrator, a rich and cultivated dilettante, who has been stung into activity by being called a 'bookworm' as a parting shot from his closest friend, en route to fight in Caucasus. He buys a mine and puts Zorba in charge of the workmen. . . . Zorba accomplishes fantastic feats of physical prowess, he tells wild stories of his erotic adventures, he misbehaves badly with his patron's money, he dances, and sings, and talks." Times (London) Lit Sup
"Zorba the Greek is a novel sweet and elate with sunlight, friendship and happiness, with a life full of both sensations and thoughts: it is, in every sense, a minor classic, and Zorba, one feels, is among the significant and permanent characters in modern fiction." New Statesman & Nation

Kellogg, Marjorie

Tell me that you love me, Junie Moon.
Farrar, Straus 1968 216p boards $5.95   Fic

This novel concerns "three patients who meet in a hospital [and] decide to live together because they have no other place to go. The first is Warren, a paraplegic. The second is Arthur, victim of a progressive, undiagnosed neurological disease. The third is Junie Moon, who had been beaten half to death and then had acid poured over her face." Pub W

"It is difficult to convey the humor and humanness of . . . [this] novel. . . . Miss Kellogg is not concerned with picturing the possible psychological crippling which might accompany such physical distortions, but rather in stating the universal importance of love and mutual tolerance in human relationships." Library J

Kemal, Yashar

Memed, my hawk; tr. by Edouard Roditi. Pantheon Bks. 1961 371p $6.95   Fic

1 Turkey—Fiction 2 Robbers and outlaws—Fiction

Originally published 1955 in Istanbul

This novel "is a romantic account of the life of a young Turkish peasant, who is driven from his native village because he defies the local Agha, a kind of twentieth century feudal lord. The hero then takes to the hills where he becomes a celebrated brigand, and eventually a kind of local hero." Pub W

"Yashar Kemal is a powerful storyteller: the constant danger, the elemental struggle against fate mercilessly pull the reader along. His mountains, towns, tents, battles, people are superbly described. He re-creates for us not only Memed's thoughts and feelings, but an age-old way of life still to be found in odd corners of the world. Anyone thinking of living or working in the Near East, indeed in a primitive society anywhere, should read this novel. As should anyone interested in a good, strong story." Book of the Month Club News

Kemelman, Harry

Sunday the rabbi stayed home   Fic

1 Mystery and detective stories

Some editions are:

Lanewood Press $7.50 Large type edition complete and unabridged
Putnam $5.95

First published 1969

In this "encounter with a murder case, the New England rabbi detective is faced with pot being pushed locally to tempt the young people of the temple; a feud among the middle-aged lay leaders that threatens to tear the temple apart; and—in one brisk encounter with an antagonistic Negro—a touch of black anti-Semitism." Pub W

"Mr. Kemelman is quite aware of the issues of the day, and is an avid student of the contemporary scene among youth and in religious circles." Christian Science Monitor

Kesey, Ken

One flew over the cuckoo's nest; a novel. Viking 1962 311p $6   Fic

1 Mentally ill—Care and treatment—Fiction

"Novel about events in a mental institution, centering around a struggle for power between the head nurse and one of the men patients that leads up to a . . . climax of hate, violence and death. The story is told as if by a long-term inmate, a half-Indian." Springf'd Republican

"This is at times a boisterous, ribald book . . . at times touching and pathetic. The characters are real. Their world, seen as sometimes foggy, sometimes painfully clear through the eyes of the narrator, is unforgettable." Library J

Keyes, Daniel

Flowers for Algernon. Harcourt 1966 274p $5.95   Fic

1 Mentally handicapped—Fiction 2 Science fiction

This is "a novel which consists of the poignant journal of a mentally retarded adult, who in the course of the story changes from an amiable, likable dull man with a yearning to be smart, into a genius. . . . Scientists operate on the brain of Charlie Gordon, I.Q. 68, and raise his I.Q. to 185. He is brilliant but miserable—he can't completely reject his old retarded personality and he is tormented by memories of his earlier life, when people were cruel to him and his family rejected him. . . . 'The Algernon' of the title is the name of a mouse who had been subjected to the first such operation." Pub W

This "is a good example of that kind of science fiction which uses a persuasive hypothesis to explore emotional and moral issues. By doing more justice than is common to the complexity of the central character's responses it gives body to its speculations." Times (London) Lit Sup

Kingsley, Charles

Westward ho!   Fic

1 Armada, 1588—Fiction 2 Great Britain—History—Tudors, 1485-1603—Fiction

Some editions are:

Dodd (Great illustrated classics) $5.50 With illustrations from sixteenth century originals and from photographs of the "Westward ho!" country together with an introductory biographical sketch of the author and anecdotal captions
Dutton (Everyman's lib) $3.25 Introduction by J. A. Williamson
Scribner (The Scribner Illustrated classics) $6 Pictures by N. C. Wyeth

First published 1855

"Story of adventure and sea fights with the Spaniards in the time of Queen Elizabeth. Gives an account of the Great Armada, and introduces Hawkins, Drake and other British naval heroes." N Y Pub Lib

"The English novelist re-creates here the glorious days of Queen Elizabeth, when her subjects sailed the seas of the New World searching for gold and the Spaniard, or wrote sonnets in her honor at court. . . . The colorful style and ready wit of the writer capture the spirit of Elizabethan England excellently." Haydn. Thesaurus of Book Digests

Kipling, Rudyard

Nobel Prize in literature, 1907

The light that failed. Doubleday 1936 289p $3.95   Fic

1 Painters—Fiction 2 Blind—Fiction

First published 1890

"Through his experience as an illustrator in the Sudan, the hero, Dick Heldar, wins both professional success and a firm friend in the war correspondent Torpenhow. He is in love with his foster sister Maisie, now also an artist, but Maisie is shallow and selfish and does not appreciate his devotion. Dick gradually goes blind from a sword cut received in the Sudan, working courageously against time on his painting, 'Melancholia.' Although Maisie is summoned by Torpenhow, she heartlessly leaves Dick to his fate, and he carries out his plan of dying at the front." Benét. The Reader's Encyclopedia

Knebel, Fletcher

Convention, by Fletcher Knebel and Charles W. Bailey, II. Harper 1964 343p boards $6.95   Fic

1 Political conventions—Fiction

Charles B. Manchester appeared to be the obvious choice for presidential candidate at the thirtieth convention of the Republican Party. Then, at a press conference Manchester uttered a politically naïve phrase which boomeranged. "In an incredibly short time the odds changed, confusingly and appallingly; the line-up shifted, the pledges evaporated. The convention that had started as a quiet formality swiftly became a political Donnybrook." Publisher's note

Night of Camp David. Harper 1965 336p $7.95   Fic

1 U.S.—Politics and government—Fiction

"A junior Senator, one of those tapped by the dynamic President of the United States as a possible running-mate for the President's

Knebel, Fletcher—*Continued*

second-term campaign, spends hours talking politics, personalities and international relations with the President. Slowly and with horror, he realizes that the President is a dangerous paranoiac, and that very little can be done about it." Pub W

Seven days in May, by Fletcher Knebel and Charles W. Bailey, II. Harper 1962 341p $6.95 **Fic**

1 U.S.—Politics and government—Fiction

Also available in a large type edition for $8.95

"The story, set against a . . . political Washington background, is about a military plot to take over the government. Its hero is a President of the U.S. in the 1970's, who with six men he trusts, sets out to prove the plot exists and to foil it." Pub W

"The reporter-authors, inquisitively familiar with the Washington scene, have made character and incident so satisfyingly genuine, the drama of action at the high ramparts of power is so vivid, and the odds against quietly smashing the plot are so severe, that the reader is as anxious to know the outcome as if this were a well-plotted whodunit. . . . The concern which grips the reader, beyond the adventure, is the question whether the United States Government as we know it, could survive a well-laid plot." Christian Science Monitor

Vanished. Doubleday 1968 407p $5.95 **Fic**

1 Washington, D.C.—Fiction 2 U.S.—Politics and government—Fiction

"Centering on the furor caused by the mysterious disappearance of a prominent Washington lawyer, adviser and close friend of the President, this is a long but suspenseful novel of high-level governmental intrigue." Booklist

"There is no violence, no sex to speak of, no pornography, no gods from the machine, no hare-brained adventures—in short no 007's to jerk us into disbelief. [Knebel operates] strictly within the ground rules of the possible: his expertise in government military intelligence and political know-how is lively and wide-ranging; and his story . . . is just implausible enough to be convincing." N Y Times Bk R

Knowles, John

The paragon; a novel. Random House 1971 210p boards $5.95 **Fic**

1 Colleges and universities—Fiction

The author's "model or pattern of perfection for youth and manhood is a seeking, nonconforming, erratically brilliant and socially maladjusted college student. . . . Bounced from the Marines as unfit for service after eight months, Lou [Colfax] dresses in black, wears an alarm wristwatch, drives a beat-up Morgan. . . . He comes back to classy Yale in 1953 carrying his possessions in a duffel bag and sporting a Soviet flag." N Y Times Bk R

"In this novel Knowles has successfully hit upon the quintessence of the maturing process, the endeavor to achieve and to understand humanity." Sat R

A separate peace; a novel. Macmillan (N Y) 1960 [1959] 186p $4.95 **Fic**

1 School stories

Also available in a large type edition for $6.95
First published 1959 in England

"After fifteen years, Gene Forrester returns to Devon School, one of those private schools in New England that seem never to change, and almost succeeds in recapturing those crucial years when the War was on in 1942, and he and his classmates, especially his closest friend and roommate, Finny, were marking time and, as he comes to realize, fighting their own private war. Finny was a natural athlete. . . . Gene was a good scholar . . . and there was, underneath their comradeship, a rivalry. . . . The deceptively quiet summer comes to a climax when Finny is hurt and Gene is at least partly responsible; but matters come to a tragic end that fall when Finney returns, wearing a cast. Others among their fellow students,

too, meet their fate in quiet but dreadfully personal and important crises. Beautifully written, this is a memorable novel that contains meaning deeper than its surface events." Best Sellers

Koestler, Arthur

Darkness at noon **Fic**

1 Communism—Fiction 2 Russia—Fiction

Some editions are:
Macmillan (N Y) $6.95
Modern Lib. $2.95

First published 1940 in England

An almost plotless "recreation and interpretation of the famous Moscow trials which in its portrayal of the psychology of a loyal Communist throws light on the Russian conflict [the Communist Party, and a prisoner's philosophy]. Rubashov, People's Commissar, is arrested on the charge of plotting against the State, and the plot focuses on his fight with two examining magistrates: the cynic, who wishes to capitulate; and the fanatic, who represents the dictatorship and condemns mistakes." Huntting

La Farge, Oliver

Laughing Boy. Houghton 1929 302p $5.95 **Fic**

1 Navaho Indians—Fiction

Awarded the Pulitzer Prize, 1930

"A lovely idyll of the Navajo country. Laughing Boy, cunning artificer of silver and maker of songs, loves Slim Girl who, tainted and embittered as the result of her American schooling, is trying to find her way back into the heart of her people. The story tells how together they fared along the Trail of Beauty, the final tragedy leaving Laughing Boy bereft but not despairing." Cleveland

"Noted for its sensitive and accurate depiction of Navajo culture and psychology." Benét. The Reader's Encyclopedia

Lampedusa, Giuseppe di

The Leopard; tr. from the Italian by Archibald Colquhoun. Pantheon Bks. 1960 319p $7.95 **Fic**

1 Italy—History—Fiction 2 Sicily—Fiction

Originally published posthumously in Italy 1958

Set in Italy in the last half of the 19th century, this novel is based on the life of the author's great grandfather, Don Fabrizio, Prince of Salina. The "Leopard" of the title, he was a tolerant despot who ruled over a large domain in Sicily. The story traces the effect upon Don Fabrizio of the crumbling of this feudal domain and of the aristocracy after Garibaldi's overthrow of the Bourbon monarchy in Naples. (Publisher)

"Captivating as story; winning in its patrician truthfulness; vital in characterization." Good Reading

Lawrence, D. H.

Sons and lovers. Modern Lib. 1963 517p $2.95 **Fic**

1 Great Britain—Fiction

First published 1913

A story "in which the relationship of mother and son is the predominating theme. There are two other women in Paul Morel's life; Miriam, highly sensitive and spiritual, who appeals only to his higher nature; and Clara, a woman of fire and passion, who draws him with the lure of the senses. Neither satisfies him; and neither can wean him from devotion to his mother." Book Rev Digest

"A semi-autobiographical novel, powerfully dramatizing the sexually inhibiting force of excessive mother-love." Good Reading

Le Carré, John

The spy who came in from the cold **Fic**

1 Spies—Fiction

Some editions are:
Coward-McCann boards $5.95
Watts, F. $8.95 Large type edition. A Keith Jennison book

First published 1963 in England

In this spy novel, "Mundt, of the East German Abteilung, had just killed off the last effective agent British Alec Leamas had behind

Le Carré, John—*Continued*

the Iron Curtain. So the British had Leamas apparently become a defector 'to trap Mundt and destroy him.'" Bk Buyer's Guide

"The plot that finally unfolds itself so that the novel ends where it began . . . at The Wall, is very ingenious and, despite its occasional sluggishness, absorbing. . . . What Mr. le Carré makes undeniably real—through his skill in drawing character, especially the character of the innocent girl who loves Leamas, and through his awareness of humanity's weakness and prejudices—is the horrible, pragmatic destructiveness of espionage systems that are inevitable in our divided, jealous world." Best Sellers

Lee, Harper

To kill a mockingbird **Fic**

1 Alabama—Fiction

Some editions are:

Lippincott $5.50

Watts, F. $9.95 Large type edition complete and unabridged. A Keith Jennison book

Pulitzer Prize 1961

In this Southern novel "eight-year-old Jean Louise, nicknamed Scout, tells about growing up as the daughter of a widowed lawyer, Atticus Finch, in the small town of Maycomb, Alabama during the 1930's. She and her older brother Jem happily occupy themselves with resisting 'progressive education,' bedeviling the neighbors, and stalking the local bogeyman—until their father's courageous defense of a Negro falsely accused of rape introduces them to the problems of race prejudice and brings adult injustice and violence into their childhood world." Booklist

"A first novel of such rare excellence that it will no doubt make a great many readers slow down to relish the more fully its simple distinction. . . . The style is bright and straightforward; the unaffected young narrator uses adult language to render the matter she deals with, but the point of view is cunningly restricted to that of a perceptive, independent child, who doesn't always understand fully what's happening, but who conveys completely, by implication, the weight and burden of the story." Chicago Sunday Tribune

L'Engle, Madeleine

The love letters. Farrar, Straus 1966 365p boards $6.95 **Fic**

1 Portugal—Fiction

A "counterpoint tale of two young women, three centuries apart in time, tormented by their experience of love, each needing to understand love in its deepest sense for her salvation. One is Mariana, long-ago Portuguese nun, won from her vow and soon deserted by a French soldier. The other is Charlotte Napier whose disintegrating marriage, built on an emotionally insecure childhood, has sent her in flight to Beja, Portugal. Learning about Mariana, lingering over her published letters, and pondering her fate, Charlotte comes to understand what love demands of her." Booklist

Lewis, C. S. (no)

Out of the silent planet. Macmillan (N Y) 1943 174p $4.95 **Fic**

1 Science fiction

Also available in a large type edition for $6.95

First published 1938 in England

"A philologist, kidnaped by a physicist and a promoter, is taken via space-ship from England to Malacandra (Mars). There he escapes and goes on the run. Philological, philosophical, social and religious overtones, plus human-interest detail on the Malacandrians make this a credible and stimulating 'tour de force.'" Library J

Lewis, Hilda

Harold was my king. McKay [1970 c1968] 246p $4.95 **Fic**

1 Great Britain—History—Norman period, 1066-1154—Fiction 2 Harold, II, King of England—Fiction 3 William I, the Conqueror, King of England—Fiction

First published 1968 in England

"Pillaging and burning countless English villages, killing anyone who stood in his way, William the Conqueror was relentless in his drive to be crowned King of England. Edmund Edmundson, loyal squire to Harold, served his King devotedly until Harold was killed by William's forces at the Battle of Hastings. Refusing to swear an oath of allegiance to William, Edmund became a servant on his own estate, which had been given to the lovely Norman, Adelais de Conches. Eventually, Edmund was forced to admit that William had brought justice, order and peace to England. And William returned his land to him and gave him Adelais to wed." Library J

Lewis, Sinclair

Nobel Prize in literature, 1930

Lewis at zenith; a three novel omnibus. Harcourt 1961 914p $5.95 **Fic**

Contents: Main Street (1920); Babbitt (1922); Arrowsmith (1925)

Main Street tells the story of "Carol, college-bred girl with a liking for 'high-brow' drama and a hobby for town planning [who] marries a small-town doctor and tries to uplift the natives of Gopher Prairie, Minnesota." Cleveland

In Babbitt, the author satirizes "American middle-class life in a good-sized city. George F. Babbitt is a successful real estate man, a regular fellow, booster, rotarian, Elk, Republican, who . . . molds his opinions of those of the Zenith Advocate-Times and believes in 'a sound business administration in Washington.'" Book Rev Digest

In Arrowsmith, winner of the Pulitzer Prize, 1926, the author depicts a physician who is torn between his innate humanitarianism and his scientific training. He traces the career of Martin Arrowsmith from medical school through experiences as a small-town doctor, as a health department officer, as fighter of the plague on a West Indian island, and director of a medical institute

Lindbergh, Anne Morrow

Dearly beloved; a theme and variations. Harcourt 1962 202p $5 **Fic**

1 Marriage—Fiction

"A Helen and Kurt Wolff book"

A novel which "acts out a philosophy of the meaning of marriage. It portrays a New England family's reactions to the wedding ceremony of a first grandchild. For each of the friends and kinsmen, the ceremony crystallizes some fear, love, hate, or unhappiness and sharpens awareness of the enduring quality of perfect love." Pub W

"Mrs. Lindbergh writes with style and distinction; her chiseled, cadenced, almost classic prose delights the eye, the ear and the tongue. . . . 'Dearly Beloved' is for everyone: the young will respond to its affirmation; men will be stimulated, possibly disturbed, by its courageous honesty; women will welcome its revealing wisdom; all will enjoy its refreshing approach to simple verities." Best Sellers

Llewellyn, Richard

How green was my valley. Macmillan (N Y) 1941 [c1940] 495p $6.95 **Fic**

1 Coal mines and mining—Fiction 2 Wales—Fiction

"The youngest son of a Welsh miner, looking back upon the days of his youth, tells how the slag heaps from the mines encroach upon the valley and destroy its green loveliness. Into this valley come unemployment and mine disturbances which affect the happiness of his family and of the entire community. Shows how experiences of growing up are influenced by economic insecurity in workingmen's homes." Reading Ladders

"A remarkably beautiful novel of Wales. And although it follows stirringly in the romantic traditions, there is the resonance of a profound and noble realism in its evocation, its intensity and reach of truth." N Y Times Bk R

Lofts, Norah

How far to Bethlehem? A novel. Doubleday 1965 353p $5.95   Fic

1 Jesus Christ—Nativity—Fiction

A "retelling, as a novel, of the Bible story of Mary and the birth of Jesus. The story begins with Mary's vision of the angel [follows the journey to Bethlehem] and ends with the three wise men . . . in the stable paying homage to Jesus." Pub W

The author presents "some of the characters involved in a different light. The imagination is teased, and the reader wonders if perhaps this might be a better picture than that given us by tradition." Library J

The lost queen. Doubleday 1969 302p $5.95   Fic

1 Caroline Mathilde, consort of Christian VII, King of Denmark—Fiction 2 Denmark—History—Fiction

"Caroline Matilda, sister of George III of England, is married off to Christian, Crown Prince of Denmark, while both are in their teens. It is not a happy marriage. Christian, who becomes king, is egocentric, sadistic, plagued by syphilis, and dominated by power-hungry courtiers. Caroline is accused of adultery, her children taken from her and imprisoned at Elsinore until George III sends a warship for her." Pub W

"The book is rich in the atmosphere of the 18th century. Both extremes of the economic scale are revealed and the great social cruelties and injustices of the time come to light in the author's skillful weaving of the plot." Best Sellers

London, Jack

Martin Eden. Library ed. Macmillan (N Y) 1957 381p $5.95   Fic

First published 1909, recopyrighted 1936

Partly autobiographical, this "is the story of an unsuccessful writer who is rejected by his wealthy fiancée; only Russ Brissenden, a socialist poet, appreciates his work. When Eden becomes rich and famous, the very people who once rejected him try to court his favor. In disgust, he leaves for the South Seas, but commits suicide on the way." Benét. The Reader's Encyclopedia

The sea-wolf. Macmillan (N Y) 1958 366p $4.95   Fic

1 Sea stories

Also available in large type edition for $7.95

First published 1904

"Wolf Larsen, ruthless captain of the tramp steamer 'Ghost,' receives as unexpected passenger on the high seas Humphrey Van Weyden, a wealthy ne'er-do-well. In spite of his selfish brutality, Larsen becomes an instrument for good. The treatment he gives to the dilettante Van Weyden teaches the latter to stand on his own legs. He and the poet Maude Brewster, whom the 'Sea-Wolf' loves also, escape to an island as the 'Ghost' sinks and Larsen, mortally sick, is deserted. The lovers later return to civilization." Haydn. Thesaurus of Book Digests

"Years after its publication London stated that he wrote 'The Sea Wolf' to show that a superman could not survive in modern society." Herzberg. The Reader's Encyclopedia of Am Lit

McCullers, Carson

The heart is a lonely hunter. Houghton 1940 356p $4.95   Fic

1 Southern States—Fiction 2 Deaf—Fiction

"The story has for its scene a southern town and covers in time about a year. . . . Its chief character is one John Singer, a deaf mute, who, when the story opens loses his only friend, another mute, committed to an insane hospital. Forced to listen and not to 'talk,' Singer becomes the recipient of the confidences of several other residents of the town—the proprietor of a quick-lunch counter, a little girl, an intellectual Negro doctor, a half-crazy, drunken radical." Book Rev Digest

"There is real beauty, poetry, and power, as well as heartbreak in this strange, authentic story about people who work grimly for their living, uncomplaining, each one shut up with his own secret trouble and pain, each one longing for more serenity, more peace, more harmony." Book of the Month Club News

The member of the wedding. Houghton 1946 195p $4.95   Fic

1 Adolescence—Fiction 2 Georgia—Fiction

"A fictional study of child psychology. Twelve-year-old Frankie is utterly bored until she hears about her older brother's wedding. He returns from Alaska to his Georgia home, and Frankie decides she will go, uninvited, on the honeymoon. The few days of excitement of the wedding are pictured in terms of Frankie's reactions, with her six-year-old cousin, and the Negro cook as chorus." Book Rev Digest

"The tremendous feeling of the world lost, and meaning lost; of life recovered and meaning recovered; the merciful power of the young to forget, and thus be healed of fractures, is one of the realest things about this fine book." Commonweal

MacInnes, Helen

Above suspicion. Harcourt 1954 333p $5.95   Fic

1 Germany—Fiction 2 Spies—Fiction

A reissue of the title first published 1941 by Little

"An Oxford don and his very attractive young wife are chosen for a dangerous mission in Germany, in the summer of 1939. They are selected just because they are taking their usual summer vacation on the continent, and can act like ordinary tourists, while following out their work. Their mission is to discover the whereabouts of an anti-Nazi agent. The summer is exciting, nearly ending in tragedy several times, but they come thru successfully." Book Rev Digest

The Salzburg connection. Harcourt 1968 406p $5.95   Fic

1 Austria—Fiction

"In a deep, forbidding lake surrounded by the silent Austrian Alps, the Nazis hid a sealed chest. Now, more than twenty years later, only a handful of people know that the chest exists. Certainly Bill Mathison, a young attorney representing a New York book publisher and arriving in Switzerland on that firm's business, has no such knowledge. He considers his trip little more than routine. Yet, unwittingly, he makes a connection." Am News of Bks

"A fascinating exercise in wide-screen spymanship. . . . The appeal [of the author's books] lies in [her] unfailing eye for vivid backgrounds; in her deft control of complex story-lines; in her clean-cut presentation of each important member of casts. These combined qualities have given her fiction a kind of grandeur." N Y Times Bk R

MacLean, Alistair

The guns of Navarone. Doubleday 1957 320p $6.95   Fic

1 World War, 1939-1945—Fiction

"A taut well-plotted adventure tale of World War II takes five hand-picked British soldiers and saboteurs into the rock-rimmed Greek island of Navarone where they are to silence the devastating guns and free 1200 British men pinned down on a neighboring island. . . . This ranks high for authentic atmosphere, sharp character delineation, and excitement." Horn Bk

H.M.S. Ulysses. Doubleday 1956 [c1955] 316p illus map $5.95   Fic

1 World War, 1939-1945—Fiction 2 Sea stories

First published 1955 in England

"The murderous and tragic World War II sea route to Murmansk, in Arctic Russia, is the subject. . . . A blend of naval tactics and high powered dramatics 'HMS Ulysses' tells of the week-long disintegration of a British light cruiser and its overworked 'zombie' crew while shepherding a convoy in gale-lashed Arctic waters between Iceland and Sweden's North Cape." San Francisco Chronicle

MacLean, Alistair—*Continued*

The book "is more a legend than a novel of real flesh and blood people. Like most legends, it is larger than life. This does not gainsay the truth of its elements. . . . And despite one's foreboding of the denouement, despite even theatrical, sometimes melodramatic touches, the Ulysses and her officers and men come to have personal meaning. The result is a moving and thrilling book." N Y Her Trib Books

Ice Station Zebra. Doubleday 1963 276p $5.95   Fic

1 Atomic submarines—Fiction 2 Arctic regions —Fiction

A novel of suspense and intrigue that begins on "a bitter-cold morning in Holy Loch, Scotland, when a British doctor with top-level endorsements from the American and British military forces seeks admission to an American nuclear submarine. The submarine is slated for a perilous trip to rescue the starving, freezing British crew of a meteorological station situated on an ice flow in the Arctic." Pub W

"Intrigue is electric throughout, but more exciting is the unceasing battle against the elements and the machine." Book Week

Night without end. Doubleday 1960 287p $5.95   Fic

1 Greenland—Fiction

"An airliner crash lands on the Greenland icecap near a small I.G.Y. observation station. It soon becomes clear that the landing was planned and certain of the passengers and crew murdered for reasons unknown, while at least eight of the 10 survivors were drugged into insensibility—the other two of course, being the killers. But which two? . . . A sometimes barely credible, but always absorbing, thriller that combines elements of the espionage story and murder mystery with those of the 'castaways' adventure tale." Library J

Mailer, Norman

The naked and the dead   Fic

1 Soldiers—U.S.—Fiction 2 World War, 1939-1945—Fiction

Some editions are:
Holt $7.95
Modern Lib. $2.95

First published 1948

"A long novel based on the reactions of the members of an American platoon to their part of the invasion and occupation of a Japanese-held island—presumably in 1944. The action is divided into three dramatc stories: the landing on the island; a Japanese counter-attack by night; and a daring patrol of the platoon behind the enemy lines." Book Rev Digest

"It is distinguished primarily for simple realism, a forthright, almost childlike honesty, a command of ordinary speech, a cool and effortless narrative style, quickened here & there with a mild, understated humor. The battle scenes are so vivid as to suggest Tolstoy's War and Peace, the common soldiers as clearly visualized as Tolstoy's peasants." Time

Malamud, Bernard

The assistant. Farrar, Straus 1957 246p $6.95   Fic

1 Jews in New York (City)—Fiction

"Novel about a poverty-stricken Jewish family living in New York City. Bad luck seems to follow the footsteps of the Bobers in every thing and in every way. The only son dies, their grocery store is a failure, the daughter cannot achieve her desire to go to college, the assistant at the store steals from the Bobers. After the death of the grocer, the assistant takes over." Book Rev Digest

"'The Assistant' will reaffirm his talent as a writer about simple people struggling to make their lives better in a world of bad luck. The clarity and concreteness of his style, the warm humanity over his people, the tender wit that keeps them firm and compassionate, will delight many." N Y Times Bk R

The fixer. Farrar, Straus 1966 335p $6.95   Fic

1 Jewish question—Fiction 2 Russia—History —Fiction

Awarded the Pulitzer Prize, 1967

In Kiev "a handy man becomes a hero in spite of himself when he is unjustly accused of a murder as part of an anti-Semitic movement. Set in Czarist Russia." Pub W

"What Mr. Malamud has done in this novel his fourth, is to present a study of human suffering in which the sufferer, a common ordinary man, manages to rise above his suffering and to remain alive when death seems easier, simply as a symbol of truth. . . . The Christian reads these pages with a sense of shocked outrage as the worst accusations of the Middle Ages are hurled against the Jews in the present century, including, most horribly, that of ritualistic blood-murder." Best Sellers

"The prose is transparently simple, like that of an old legend. The atmosphere of the long-ago period is remarkably conveyed." Book of the Month Club News

Malraux, André

Man's fate (La condition humaine)   Fic

1 China—Fiction

Some editions are:
Modern Lib. $2.95 Translated by Haakon M. Chevalier
Random house $6.95

First published in the United States by Smith & Haas in 1934. Published in England under title: Storm in Shanghai

"Out of the conspiracy, the bombing, and the bloodshed of the Shanghai insurrection of 1927, and against a background of Oriental vice, emerges a small group of revolutionaries. They are French, Russian, Japanese, and Chinese, but are all engaged in the same social struggle to free the Chinese workers. . . . The problem of the novel is the dilemma with which these men find themselves abruptly confronted—namely, the determination of the value of human life. Written with skillful and unusual technique, but filled with bloodshed and sadism." Booklist

Mann, Thomas

Nobel Prize in literature, 1929

Buddenbrooks; tr. from the German by H. T. Lowe-Porter. Together with Lübeck as a way of life and thought; a lecture delivered by the author on June 5, 1926, on the 700th anniversary of its founding. Tr. from the German by Richard and Clara Winston. Knopf 1964 xxiv, 604p $8.95   Fic

1 Germany—Fiction

First published in America, 1924, in two volumes. Reset and published in one volume in 1938

"The chronicle of the Buddenbrook family through four generations. In the first generation of 1830, we see Johann Buddenbrook the respected head of a prosperous family of Lübeck's merchant nobility; in the next, with Consul Buddenbrook, all the appearances of prosperity and success are still there, but in the third generation of Thomas and Christian a decline is noticeable. . . . In the last generation, Hanno, the weak, dreamy ineffectual artist, symbolizes the extinction of a great family through over-refinement." Publisher's note

"Interesting for its delineation of social changes; of temperaments, motives, marriages, and measures among the Buddenbrooks and their connections." Good Reading

Doctor Faustus; the life of the German composer Adrian Leverkühn, as told by a friend; tr. from the German by H. T. Lowe-Porter   Fic

1 Germany—Fiction

Some editions are:
Knopf $7.95
Modern Lib. $2.95

Original German edition, 1947

In this novel "the intense and tragic career of the hero Adrian Leverkühn, a composer is made to parallel the collapse of Germany in World War II. To achieve this end, Mann employs the device of having another character, Serenus Zeitblom, narrate Leverkühn's story from memory, while the war is going on, and intersperse his narrative with remarks about

Mann, Thomas—*Continued*

the present situation. In this way, it is implied that it is the same demonic and always potentially destructive energy inherent in Leverkühn's music that is also, on a larger scale, behind the outburst of Nazism. Mann thus suggests that the violent 'Faustian' drive, when it is not diverted into art, or when there is no single artistic genius to harness it into creative process, will be perverted and result in grossly sub-human degradation." Benét. The Reader's Encyclopedia

Joseph and his brothers; tr. from the German by H. T. Lowe-Porter; with an introduction by the author. Knopf 1948 xxi, 1207p $13.95 **Fic**

1 Joseph the Patriarch—Fiction 2 Bible— History of Biblical events—Fiction

An omnibus edition of four titles published separately, now all out of print

Contents: The tales of Jacob (1934); Young Joseph (1935); Joseph in Egypt (1938); Joseph the provider (1944)

"Mann has expanded the original [Biblical] story tremendously, but most of the added episodes and digressions contribute not so much to the tale itself as to the characters' depth and symbolic significance. In its all-over attitude, the Joseph tetralogy is neither ambiguous like the Magic Mountain, nor tragic like Doktor Faustus, but unqualifiedly redemptive." Benét. The Reader's Encyclopedia

The magic mountain (Der Zauberberg); tr. from the German by H. T. Lowe-Porter. Knopf 1927 900p $8.95 **Fic**

1 Tuberculosis—Fiction

"Hans Castorp, a young German, goes to the International Sanitorium of Berghof to visit a tubercular cousin for three weeks, but, discovering that he too is diseased, stays on for seven years, only released by his call to the Great [First World] War." Open Shelf

"The novel is much more than a discussion of the effects of disease in an isolated group; it is a tremendous philosophical and prophetic treatise on contemporary society, and all the issues and ideas of the 20th century western world enter into it. The sanatorium itself, as a community organized with exclusive reference to ill health, stands as a symbol of the diseased capitalistic society of prewar Europe —the world which made war inevitable. This outer world is seen thru the diseased minds of the patients, and the book ends in fact with society plunged into the maelstrom of the World War. Similarly the ostensible hero, a young engineer of no great importance in himself, assumes profund importance as a representative of humanity subjected to the stress of primal experiences." Lenrow. Reader's Guide to Prose Fiction

Markandaya, Kamala

A handful of rice; a novel. Day 1966 297p $7.95 **Fic**

1 India —Fiction

This "is the story of Ravi, [an Indian] who comes to the city young and hopeful only to find that its shining promise is nothing but a light burning in his own imagination. His ambition is relentlessly ground away between two millstones: the sheer struggle for existence among too many people, and his own character." Publisher's note

"Recommended as a depressing but honest portrayal of a culture with too many people and scarcely the material means to satisfy their barest needs." Library J

Nectar in a sieve; a novel. Day 1955 [c1954] 248p $6.50 **Fic**

1 India—Fiction

First published 1954 in England

"Ruckamani was the wife of a peasant farmer in southern India. Her marriage, arranged by her parents, was as happy as possible in a land where droughts and floods caused severe hardships to those whose living came from the land. In telling Ruckamani's story the author gives a vivid picture of life in an Indian village." Huntting

"A simple, unaffected story of human suffering [which] does more than a shelf of books on history and economics to explain the people of India." Time

Some Indian words: p[249]

Marquand, John P.

The late George Apley; a novel in the form of a memoir. Little 1937 354p $6.95 **Fic**

1 Boston—Fiction

Pulitzer Prize, 1938

"The supposed author of this 'novel in the form of a memoir' is one Horatio Willing, who has been requested by the son of George Apley to write his father's biography. George Apley was a member of an old Boston family, resident upon Beacon Hill for many years. The span of his life ended in 1933 at the age of sixty-six. From family notes and letters, supplemented by his own memoirs, Horatio Willing builds up the picture of an age, a class, a locality in his story of the life of George Apley." Book Rev Digest

"This is a delightful satire on Boston and its rigid mores. It also portrays the lack of understanding between generations and the futility of attempting to mold youth in older behavior patterns." Doors to More Mature Reading

Point of no return. Little 1949 559p $6.95 **Fic**

The first and third parts of this new novel "deal with a few days in April, 1947, in the life of Charles Gray, an assistant vice-president in the conservative Stuyvesant Bank in New York. But the main and perhaps the more significant scenes, as related in the much longer second part of the novel, lie in the town where Charles was born and brought up—Clyde, Massachusetts, some thirty miles north of Boston. A combination of present and of retrospect gives a vivid picture of the vicissitudes of small-town and middle-class life in the twentieth century." Huntting

Masefield, John

Jim Davis; illus. by Bob Dean. Macmillan (N Y) 1951 242p illus $4.95 **Fic**

1 Smuggling—Fiction 2 Adventure and adventurers—Fiction 3 Great Britain—Fiction

Also published under title: The captive of the smugglers

First published 1911 by Stokes

"Jim was a small boy in South Devon some hundred years ago, and partly by accident and partly by cleverness he found out more about the local smugglers than his mysterious friend Mr. Gorsuch (who was really their captain) could approve of; so to stop his tongue, he was carried off and made two most exciting trips with them. His narrative . . . has all the atmosphere of the time towards the end of the French wars; it's moral moreover is unimpeachable for Mr. Gorsuch after being severely wounded settled down ashore in a respectable occupation." Sat R

Mather, Melissa

One summer in between. Harper 1967 213p boards $6.95 **Fic**

1 Vermont—Fiction

"Harriet Brown, Negro college student from Abbot's Level, South Carolina, comes north to Vermont for the summer. She needs money for her college tuition, and the Daleys need help with their six children. It is Harriet's first trip north, and the novel is her impression of the Vermont summer 'via' her diary. This is a . . . book, brim full of children, preserves, vegetable gardening, the building of a new house, beautiful rural Vermont. It would be a mistake to read this book for a message, the last word about Negro-white relations; better to enjoy it for Harriet Brown's cross-grained humor and for a record of the growth of a friendship between Harriet and the Daleys." Pub W

Maugham, W. Somerset

The moon and sixpence. Modern Lib. 1935 314p $2.95 **Fic**

1 Gauguin, Paul—Fiction

Maugham, W. S.—*Continued*

First published 1919 by Doran
"Based closely on the life of the French painter Paul Gauguin. It tells of Charles Strickland, a conventional London stock broker, who in middle life becomes interested in painting, changes completely in character, and deserts his wife, family, and business in order to live and paint in Tahiti, where he takes a native mistress and eventually dies of leprosy." Benét. The Reader's Encyclopedia
"The painter, in this novel, is an incarnate example of the 'divine tyranny of art' in his quest of the moon, in which the six-pence in every conventional form—home, family, food, the opinion of mankind, fame, decency itself—is contemptuously thrown aside." Booklist

Of human bondage   **Fic**

Some editions are:
Doubleday $6.95   Illustrated   by   Randolph Schwabe
Modern Lib. $2.95

First published 1915
"Realistic portrayal of the life of a youth handicapped by deformity whose early life was a process of self-torture. When he escapes from the cruelty of his school-fellows and the uncongenial atmosphere of his hypocritical and selfish uncle it is only to plunge deeper into gloom as a lonely lad in London, as a student at Heidelberg, and as a would-be artist in the Latin quarter in Paris." Pittsburgh
"The book traces Philip's development from uncertainty and bewilderment to maturity and spiritual freedom, when he is finally able to achieve a satisfying philosophy of life and face the future with confidence, courage, and humor." Doors to More Mature Reading

The razor's edge; a novel. Doubleday 1944 343p $5.95   **Fic**

"Character study of a young American, a flyer in World War I, who returns to his home in Chicago in 1919, vaguely conscious that he is missing something. To the horror of the girl who wants to marry him, he will not take a job; he wants to 'loaf.' He goes to Paris and then to India in search of his ideal, and finds a certain measure of personal peace, but succeeds in making life even more difficult for those who have tried to make him lead a conventional life." Book Rev Digest

Means, Florence Crannell

Our cup is broken. Houghton 1969 229p $3.95   **Fic**

1 Hopi Indians—Fiction
"Sarah's parents died when she was young and she was forced to leave her Hopi village. Her foster parents were kind but an automobile accident put her into the care of others who wanted to do 'the right things' for her. Well intentioned but insensitive they made life unbearable for Sarah. She ran from them and back to her native village. Once there she was raped by a young man who belonged to her clan and therefore could not marry her. She found a husband, if not a soul mate, in Benny, and gradually was able to work her way to self-realization. A beautifully told story, that traces Sarah's struggle with an alien culture and the difficulties of trying to bridge the gap between old and new. There is compassion here but no artificial sentimentality." Pub W

Melville, Herman

Billy Budd, foretopman; illus. by Robert Quackenbush. Watts, F. 1968 126p illus $3.75   **Fic**

1 Sea stories
Also available in a large type edition for $7.95, with title: Herman Melville's Billy Budd, foretopman
Written in 1891 but in a still "unfinished" manuscript stage when Melville died. First publication 1924 in England as part of the standard edition of Melville's complete works
This is the "tragic story of Billy Budd, the 'handsome sailor,' whose innocence in the face of evil is his undoing. When a jealous officer aboard the 'Indomitable' accuses him falsely of a mutinous conspiracy, Billy—speechless in disbelief—strikes him a fatal blow. The Captain is required by regulations to order the death penalty for Billy." Publisher's note

Moby Dick   **Fic**

1 Whaling—Fiction 2 Sea stories
Some editions are:
Dodd $5.50 Illustrated by Mead Shaeffer
Dutton $3.25 (Everyman's lib)
Hendricks House $6.50 Edited by Luther S. Mansfield and Howard P. Vincent
Macmillan (N Y) $4.95 Illustrated by Robert Shore; afterword by Clifton Fadiman
Modern Lib. $2.95
Oxford $2.50 (The World's classics)
Watts, F. $9.95 Large type edition complete and unabridged. A Keith Jennison book
Watts, F. $5.50 Ultratype edition complete and unabridged. With a critical and biographical profile of Herman Melville by Tyrus Hillway
First published 1851
"Moby Dick, the great white whale, is pursued by the monomaniacal Captain Ahab, whose ivory leg is testimony to their last encounter. The crew of Ahab's ship, the 'Pequod,' is composed of a mixture of races and religions, including the God-fearing mate Starbuck; three primitive harpooners, Queequeg, Daggoo, and Tashtego; the Negro cabin boy, Pip; and the fire-worshipping Parsee. The whale, perhaps representing knowledge of reality, is hunted by Ahab at the cost of his own dehumanization and the sacrifice of his crew." Benét. The Reader's Encyclopedia
"The novel is larded with chapters on the natural history of the whale, marveling rhapsodically upon its fearful and wonderful attributes. Melville in 'Moby-Dick' strove to synthesize all the turbulent and painful torments of his inner spirit. The book, which stands as one of the epic adventure stories of the sea, is equally a ponderous, impressive allegory of man's struggle against the malignant and imponderable forces of the universe, typified in the white whale." Haydn. Thesaurus of Book Digests

Typee; illus. by Mead Schaeffer. Dodd [1951?] 289p illus $5   **Fic**

1 Marquesas Islands—Fiction 2 Whaling—Fiction

First published 1846
A romance of the South Seas "recording the adventures of a whaling voyage in the Pacific. 'Typee' (Taipi) is a valley in one of the Marquesas where Melville was kept captive by the natives. The book goves a vivid picture of a civilized man in contact with the exotic dreamlike life of the tropics. Its popularity was revived by the South Sea furor of the 1920's." Benét. The Reader's Encyclopedia

Meriwether, Louise

Daddy was a number runner. Prentice-Hall 1970 208p $5.95   **Fic**

1 Harlem, New York (City)—Fiction 2 Negroes—Fiction
SBN 13-197103-4
"Twelve-year-old Francie faces the usual crises of a girl her age, but her growing up as the daughter of a numbers runner in Harlem in the late 1930's adds [another dimension]. . . . Francie's family disintegrates as a result of the economic and social pressures of ghetto living." Library J
"In her perceptive and moving first novel . . . [the author] reaches deeply into the lives of her characters to say something about the way black people relate to each other. . . . It is her expression of this tribal or communal quality of black life, its group solidarity and sharing, that lends such strength and humanity to the novel." N Y Times Bk R

Michener, James A.

The bridges at Toko-ri. Random House 1953 146p $5.95   **Fic**

1 Korean War, 1950-1953—Fiction
A story of the men of a naval task force operating in the icy waters off the Korean shore with a vital mission to perform: to destroy with jet bombers the heavily guarded bridges at Toko-ri and thus to stop essential supplies from moving to the Communist front lines
"A tense and exciting book, enthralling in its picture of life aboard an aircraft carrier and of the valor, the judgment and the skill which such service entails. Though focused about the figure of a pilot named Brubaker, its interest

Michener, James A.—*Continued*

lies not only in his individual fortunes but also in the life aboard ship." Book of the Month Club News

Caravans; a novel. Random House 1963 341p $6.95 **Fic**

1 Americans in Afghanistan—Fiction 2 Diplomats—Fiction 3 Afghanistan—Fiction

The story, set in Afghanistan in the year 1946, "of Ellen Jasper, an American bored with her native land, who flees to Afghanistan to become the second wife of a man named Nazrullah. Her parents haven't heard from her in 13 months and Mark Miller, of the U.S. Embassy in that country, is sent to investigate. The search takes Miller into unknown territory. He joins a nomad tribe and experiences a love affair of rare beauty with Mira, daughter of the Great Zulfiqar, chieftain of all of the nomadic peoples scattered around Afghanistan. [The novel describes] Ellen's degeneration into a sensualist, [and] the encounter of Miller (a Jew) with an ex-Nazi who tortured Jews." America

Map on lining-papers

The drifters; a novel. Random House 1971 751p $10 **Fic**

ISBN 0-394-46200-9

This "novel narrated by a 60-year-old American financier who roams Europe and Africa in search of good investments, follows six young adults as they travel in search of something else. . . . Each young person has a special set of circumstances, with which to contend. . . . There is Joe, the idealistic draft-evader; Cato, the black militant. . . . Gretchen, bluestocking Boston folksinger; Yigal, the serious Israeli; . . . Monica, pathetic drug-addict daughter of a British ex-colonial; and Britta, the sexually dead Scandinavian beauty in search of the sun." N Y Times Bk R

"The Drifters is something of a guidebook loosely dressed up as fiction: a guide to quaint and colorful places, especially on the Iberian peninsula, and to the life-styles of the rebellious young." Sat R

Map on lining-papers

Hawaii. Random House 1959 937p $10 **Fic**

1 Hawaii—History—Fiction

A fictional history of the Hawaiian Island from the faraway time when the volcanic islands rose from the sea to their present status as our fiftieth state. The author has told this story in terms of the personal triumphs and tragedies of some highly individual characters, men and women of the many peoples of Hawaii, the Polynesians, American missionaries, Chinese, Japanese, and Filipinos. (Publisher)

"High-domed, long-haired 'littérateurs' may argue that Michener's characters are often as paper-thin as the colorad image in which 'Hawaii' is held by mainland tourists, but 'Hawaii' is still a masterful job of research, an absorbing performance of story telling, and a monumental account of the islands from geologic birth to sociological emergence as the newest, and perhaps the most interesting of the United States." Sat R

Maps on lining-papers

The source; a novel. Random House 1965 909p illus maps $10 **Fic**

1 Archeology—Fiction 2 Palestine—Fiction 3 Israel—Fiction

This book consists of a chain of "stories from mankind's past, strung on the thread of an account of an archaeological expedition in Western Galilee (Israel). The stories are told about significant objects discovered. . . . The main story, about the small contemporary group of archaeologists, their romances, and their participation, in, and in some cases frustration by, modern Israeli customs, is necessarily distributed through the book." Pub W

"Told with remarkable erudition and moving human detail, The Source is a monumental and imaginative study in depth of the old-new nation Israel." Sat R

Mishima, Yukio

Nobel Prize in literature, 1969

After the banquet; tr. from the Japanese by Donald Keene. Knopf 1963 [c1960] 270p $5.95 **Fic**

1 Japan—Fiction

Original Japanese edition 1960

"Kazu, a middle-aged woman who believes that love has long since been put out of her life, is proprietress of a highly successful restaurant in Tokyo that is much frequented by retired diplomats and politicians. One of the latter is Noguchi, a slightly threadbare but haughty aristocrat. Kazu . . . is a woman of the people who harbors a very romantic heart beneath the veneer of a successful professional woman. The opposites attract each other, fall in love, and get married. . . . When [Noguchi] attempts a comeback in politics, Kazu throws herself into the campaign; but her methods in going directly to the people scandalize her husband, and the marriage breaks up." Atlantic

An "illuminating picture of Japanese culture for the Westerner." Booklist

The sound of waves; tr. by Meredith Weatherby; drawings by Yoshinori Kinoshita. Knopf 1956 182p illus $4.95 **Fic**

1 Japan—Fiction

"The scene of this novel is a Japanese fishing village. The hero, Shinji, a young fisherman, falls in love with the daughter of the wealthiest man of the village. The story is of the hazards which had to be overcome before the young people could be married." Book Rev Digest

"'The Sound of Waves' is a simple and satisfying story, concerned with human relationships as timeless as the sea, and far removed from the complexities and strife of urban industrial society." N Y Her Trib Books

Mitchell, Margaret

Gone with the wind; illus. by Ben Stahl. Macmillan (N Y) 1961 954p illus $6.95 **Fic**

1 U.S.—History—Civil War—Fiction 2 Southern States—Fiction 3 Reconstruction—Fiction

Also available in a large type edition for $13.95

An illustrated edition of a book first published 1936

Pulitzer Prize, 1937

"A story of the years before, during and after the Civil war, in [Georgia]. Its heroine, Scarlett O'Hara, is anything but the usual Southern belle, and once freed from the shackles of ladyhood in which she has been bred, she emerges as a forceful and ruthless woman. Matching her is Rhett Butler, the blockade runner, as engaging a scoundrel as has appeared in fiction for many a day. There are dozens of other characters representing the old and the new forces in the South. A long novel but one in which interest never falters." Wis Lib Bul

"For sheer story value this is one of the finest Civil War epics of all time. . . . Miss Mitchell has shown amazing restraint in dealing with two characters as dramatic and colorful as Scarlett and Rhett. That restraint has strengthened every fiber of her story. She is never for a moment guilty of sentimentalizing or of explaining and inviting sympathy." America

Monsarrat, Nicholas

The cruel sea. Knopf 1951 509p $6.95 **Fic**

1 World War, 1939-1945—Fiction 2 Sea stories

A "novel of contemporary history—of convoy duty aboard the corvette, 'Compass Rose,' during the Battle of the North Atlantic from 1939-1945. Old sea dogs, young officers, the captain—all are pitted against a relentless and merciless sea." Huntting

This "is an impressive work of fiction, portraying the war at sea with great emotion and restraint, with drama, tenderness, and terror, and with deep humanity. It is a somber and compassionate novel." Chicago Sunday Tribune

Morley, Christopher

The haunted bookshop; illus. by Douglas Gorsline. Lippincott 1955 253p illus $4.95 **Fic**

1 Booksellers and bookselling—Fiction 2 Mystery and detective stories

Sequel to: Parnassus on wheels, entered below
First published in 1919 by Doubleday. Reset in 1955 with added illustrations
"Roger Mifflin, whom we met in the author's 'Parnassus on wheels,' here keeps a secondhand bookshop in Brooklyn, N.Y. He takes in the young daughter of a friend to learn the book trade, and immediately a mystery develops. There is much good discussion of books and reading sandwiched in with the plot." Wis Lib Bul

Parnassus on wheels; illus. by Douglas Gorsline. Lippincott 1955 160p illus $5.50 **Fic**

1 Booksellers and bookselling—Fiction

First published 1917 by Doubleday. Reset 1955 with an introduction by John T. Winterich and added illustrations
"The title is derived from a wagon bookshop drawn by Pegasus, a sleek, well-fed horse. The owner of this wandering bookstore is Roger Mifflin, who takes his affectionate dog, Boccaccio, along with him on his journeys. He sells the outfit to Helen McGill, who describes herself disparagingly as a fat spinster of thirty-eight; Mifflin goes along to show her the business, successfully fights off her big brother who wants her back as his maid-of-all-work, gets thrown into jail wrongfully, and is duly rescued to marry Helen." Herzberg. Reader's Encyclopedia of Am Lit
Followed by: The haunted bookshop

Morris, Edita

The flowers of Hiroshima. Viking 1959 187p $4.95 **Fic**

1 Atomic bomb—Physiological effect—Fiction 2 Americans in Japan—Fiction 3 Hiroshima—Fiction

"Told in the first person by Yuka Nakamura, this is the poignant story of the effects of radiation on one Japanese family, fourteen years after the atom bomb was dropped on Hiroshima. A young American business man, taken as a boarder to help finances, becomes close to the family, and is made aware of the dreadful plight of many of the Japanese people today." Ontario Lib Rev

The seeds of Hiroshima. Braziller [1966 c1965] 118p $4 **Fic**

1 Atomic bomb—Physiological effect—Fiction 2 Hiroshima—Fiction

A sequel to: The Flowers of Hiroshima, entered above
First published 1965 in England
The author continues the story of Yuka and her sister, survivors of the Hiroshima holocaust. Small sister Ohatsu marries, but the seeds of Hiroshima are tainted, and she commits suicide upon giving birth to a monstrous baby. (Publisher)

Mphahlele, Ezekiel

The wanderers; a novel. Macmillan (N Y) 1971 351p $6.95 **Fic**

1 Africa—Fiction

"The Wanderers are outcasts on their own continent, condemned to drift across Africa in search of the home they cannot find. Timi Tabane, journalist-teacher, has fled with his family from South Africa. Steve Cartwright, a white reporter, fights a retreating battle for human rights. Beautiful, black Naledi discovers that love has no color and no country. Felang, the rebel, lives and dies rootless and violent. Intellectuals and political refugees, they are the undoing of a continent—and the source of . . . [a] powerful, unique and wide-ranging novel." Publisher's note

Muntz, Hope

The golden warrior; the story of Harold and William; with a foreword by G. M. Trevelyan. Scribner 1949 354p $5.95 **Fic**

1 Harold II, King of England—Fiction 2 William I, the Conqueror, King of England—Fiction 3 Great Britain—History—Norman period—1066-1154—Fiction

This "historical novel recreates the life of King Harold of England and illumines what was perhaps the most climactic chapter of English history—the Norman invasion. At Hastings, in the year 1066, Harold's great English army was defeated by the Normans under William the Conqueror, and Harold himself lost his life—but in that battle he won everlasting fame and a permanent place in English hearts." Huntting

Murdoch, Iris

A fairly honourable defeat. Viking 1970 436p boards $6.95 **Fic**

1 London—Fiction
SBN 670-30533-2

This novel is concerned with a "happily married couple, a dropout son, a sister who has 'a compulsive genius for muddles,' her estranged husband, and a homosexual younger brother living . . . with an older man. The sister's former lover . . . sets out to show how . . . [both] loving couples can be detached from their loyalties. In his role as puppet master, he manipulates their vanities to ends which he had not quite intended." Publisher's note

"As is usual with a Murdoch novel, the action in summary seems preposterous. But given her inventiveness, her Gothic imagination, her gift for melodrama and suspense, she creates a world that becomes an effective vehicle for her moral vision. The action, much of which is erotic, takes place during a spell of excessively hot London weather. Some of the scenes are wildly contrived and comic. There are long stretches of dialogue . . . some of which are run through with the philosophic subtlety readers have come to expect of Murdoch." Choice

Murphy, Robert

The golden eagle; illus. by John Schoenherr. Dutton 1965 157p illus $4.95 **Fic**

1 Eagles—Stories

A nature story of the development of Kira, the golden eagle. "Many things happen to her on her hazardous journey to maturity; there are many narrow escapes from death and many lessons well learned: near starvation during her first snow [and] a bitter battle with one of the toughest fighters in the natural world, the weasel." Publisher's note

The peregrine falcon; illus. by Teco Slagboom. Houghton 1964 [c1963] 157p illus $5.95 **Fic**

1 Falcons—Stories

The story of the first year in the life of a falcon and of a perilous journey, "the first migration of Varda, the peregrine, from her birthplace in northern Canada to the Florida Keys. . . . [There are] background facts about hawks and the training of the falcon." Library J

"There is true suspense in the story, a great deal to fascinate bird-lovers about the falcon, her prey, and her equals among birds, and some sharp comments on the ways in which man may mistreat or sometimes aid the birds in their passage. . . . The illustrations, by Teco Slagboom, are very special. They are majestic, soaring pictures of the hawks and other birds and of the wild lands they love." Pub W

The Pond; illus. by Teco Slagboom. Dutton 1964 254p illus $5.50 **Fic**

1 Outdoor life—Fiction

Winner of the Dutton Animal book award, 1964

"Fourteen-year-old Joey and his friend Bud drove to the [Virginia] Pond in a Model-T in 1917 to fish and hunt. But the great cypresses, the Pond, old Mr. Ben the caretaker, and even Charley, Sam White's dog, woke in Joey a protective understanding for all wild life." Bk Buyer's Guide

Murphy, Robert—*Continued*

"There is little or no plot to 'The Pond': just the day-by-day adventures of a boy in the woods who is learning to understand dogs, coon hunting, camping techniques—and human beings. Simple—deceptively simple—and appealing." Book of the Month Club News

Nabokov, Vladimir

Pale fire; a novel. Putnam 1962 315p $6.95

Fic

"The story is told in the form of a poem and a commentary on the poem and deals with the escapades of a desposed Balkan King in a New England college town. . . . The poem itself . . . a thousand lines long, divided into four cantos, . . . purports to be the composition of John Shade, a white-thatched and venerable poet in residence at a New England university. . . . The commentator—hence, the first person singular of the novel—is revealed in the beginning as Charles Kinbote, a queer 'émigreé' teaching at Shade's university. . . . He is, in fact, the deposed King of Zembla, identified only as 'a distant northern land.' . . . A secret agent, Gradus, is dispatched from Zembla to kill the King, and his progress across continents is followed step by step in Kinbote's commentary until he arrives. . . . By mistake, Gradus kills John Shade. Modern dictatorships spare the buffoon (Kinbote) but kill the poet (Shade)." Atlantic

"That the novel is intended as a kind of spoof of scholarly textual criticism and its apparatus, something of a satire on cloak and dagger tales, and a mild swipe at academic life seems apparent. That the poem is frequently lyric and touching, even reminiscent of Conrad Aiken in spots, is not surprising. The whole thing is perhaps caviar for the general, but it is delectable, too." Best Sellers

Narayan, R. K.

The vendor of sweets. Viking [1969 c1967] 184p $6.95

Fic

1 India—Fiction 2 Large type books

"A Viking Largetype book"
First published 1967
In this novel about the imaginary town in India of Malgudi, the "major personage is a candy-maker named Jagan, who caters to the sweet tooth of his townsmen, especially the young, in his shop on the main street, and lives in widowed comfort in a house at what used to be the edge of town. . . . [The book presents] another version of the eternal theme of the old against the young." Publisher's note

"At first gance, Jagan appears to be a simple village shopkeeper, but essentially he is a far more complex personage. He is a merchant but he is also a patriot. . . . However, at the same time he earnestly counts the daily take, plus a little portion he puts aside and does not report for tax purposes. . . . Narayan also gives valuable insight into the Indian culture and its timeless rituals that, for a Westerner, cloak the East in fascinating mystery." Best Sellers
Glossary: p183-84

Nathan, Robert

The Devil with love. Knopf 1963 200p boards $4.95

Fic

"Alfred Sneeden, a repairer of electrical devices in the town of Parish, develops a wild longing for shiny-haired, 17-year-old Gladys Milhouser, daughter of a local tycoon. . . . He invokes the devil to aid him. Lucifer hears Alfred Sneeden. . . . He decides to leave Alfred's soul alone and dispatches an emissary to take his heart instead. Two days later, when a new doctor comes to town and sets up as a specialist in rejuvenating processes, Sneeden has already forgotten what he told the devil. It is the other people in the town—the old general practitioner, the druggist, the post mistress, and above all the parish priest, Father Deener—who look with suspicion upon Dr. Samuel Hod [Samael of Hod]." N Y Times Bk R

The elixir. Knopf 1971 176p $5.95

Fic

1 Great Britain—Fiction
ISBN 0-394-47175-X
"An American historian has a brief but deeply felt affair with a mysterious girl met at Stonehenge. In their time-hopping progress across centuries and continents in many transformations there is more than a hint that the lovers are reincarnations of legendary Arthurian figures and that the elusive Niniane (or Nimue?) will once more outwit Merlin and rejoin the historian in America." Bookist

"This American innocent abroad is enriched and spellbound with love's magic, entwined in the romance of legend and history. That old Merlin, Robert Nathan, charms again as he fashions a bittersweet tale of past and present." Pub W

Portrait of Jennie

Fic

1 Painters—Fiction
Some editions are:
Knopf $4.95
Watts. F. lib. bdg. $7.95 Large type edition. A Keith Jennison book
First published 1939
"A young artist, his courage gone and desperate at the world's indifference, meets a little girl in an old-fashioned dress one night, playing alone on a New York street, who ask him to wait for her to grow up. How in the following months, Jennie, transcending time and space, and on each visit several years older comes to him, waiting and longing, and how he paints her portrait which is to make him famous, and through Jennie finds meaning in life and love and beauty is delicately revealed in a fantasy whose gossamer threads are as real as the realities with which they are interwoven." Bookmark

Nordhoff, Charles

The Bounty trilogy . . . by Charles Nordhoff and James Norman Hall; illus. by N. C. Wyeth. Little 1946 691p illus $8.50 **Fic**

1 Bounty (Ship)—Fiction 2 Islands of the Pacific—Fiction 3 Sea stories
"An Atlantic Monthly Press book"
"Comprising the three volumes: Mutiny on the Bounty, Men against the sea & Pitcairn's Island." Title page
A reissue of the combined volume first published in 1936

Norris, Frank

The octopus; a story of California. Doubleday 1947 361p $6.50 **Fic**

1 Railroads—Fiction 2 Wheat—Fiction 3 California—Fiction
This story of social protest describes the war between California wheat growers and the railroads
"One cannot read it without a thrill at the breadth of purpose, the earnestness, the astonishing verbal power of its author. The characters are rather dwarfed by the main conception." F. T. Cooper

O'Connor, Edwin

All in the family. Little 1966 434p $6.95

Fic

1 U.S.—Politics and government—Fiction
"An Atlantic Monthly Press book"
"The Kinsellas are a wealthy, Irish Massachusetts family, dominated—at first—by the father, who insists that his sons enter politics to clean up a thoroughly corrupt political situation. One son is elected Governor, but political power subtly affects him, ethical problems evoke sharp differences and cause the eventual break-up of the family." Library J

The best and the last of Edwin O'Connor; ed. with an introduction by Arthur Schlesinger, Jr. and with contributions by Edmund Wilson and John V. Kelleher. Little 1970 465p $10 **Fic**

"An Atlantic Monthly Press book"
Selections from the author's "published work ('The Oracle,' 'The Last Hurrah,' 'Benjy,' a children's book, 'The Edge of Sadness,' 'All

O'Connor, Edwin—*Continued*

in the family' [and 'I was Dancing']) plus an article and a talk he wrote, fragments of two novels unfinished at his death in 1968, the 'Cardinal' and 'Boy,' and 'Baldini,' a memoir and collaboration on which he was working, put down by his collaborator, Edmund Wilson." Pub W

The last hurrah. Little 1956 427p $6.95 **Fic**

1 Irish in the U.S.—Fiction 2 U.S.—Politics and government—Fiction

"Frank Skeffington had kept his power as mayor of a large eastern U.S. city for almost 40 years. During the course of his last campaign . . . he is seen not only as the corrupt grafter ruthless with his enemies but also as a man of infinite charm who truly loved his city. . . . Some [high-lights of the story are] the descriptions of the Irish groups who were Skeffington's chief supporters." Booklist

The author "uses some words and expressions which we cannot approve, but fortunately these lapses from good taste are few and far between. . . . [It is] an interesting analysis of how the old-time political boss rose to and remained in power for so long." Best Sellers

Oldenbourg, Zoé

The heirs of the kingdom; tr. from the French by Anne Carter. Pantheon Bks. 1971 563p $8.95 **Fic**

1 Crusades—Fiction 2 Middle Ages—Fiction
ISBN 0-394-46835-X

Original French edition, 1970

This novel centers on a group of weavers from Arras who join the first crusade. "There is Jacques, an out-of-work weaver and his sensitive young wife Marie, who has visions. There is Alix of the Thirty Pieces, a repentant prostitute, Brother Barnabé . . . Elie de Gréle . . . and Saint-John, a simple-minded armorer's son who believes he is the Evangelist in a new body. We follow them from their initial response to Peter the Hermit until, three years later, they storm Jerusalem, helped by trained knights." Book World

"A historical novel is the art of persuading one's contemporaries to believe in a time and a place and a girl at several centuries removed. Zoé Oldenbourg is a French master of this genre who has assimilated the Middle Ages so thoroughly that one follows the large tapestry of her narratives with credulity. [This novel is] . . . faultlessly translated." Atlantic

Orwell, George

Animal farm; illus. by Joy Batchelor and John Halas. Harcourt 1954 155p illus $4.50 **Fic**

1 Animals—Stories

First published 1945 in England

"A political satire, written in the guise of an allegory. The animals on a certain farm rise, overthrow their drunken master, and take over the running of the farm themselves. The pigs, being more intelligent, are the leaders. Gradually the utopian stage passes and dictatorship seeps in; the situation is no better than it was before." Book Rev Digest

"It is absolutely first-rate. . . . Mr. Orwell has worked out his theme with a simplicity, a wit, and a dryness that are closer to La Fontaine and Gay, and has written in a prose so plain and spare, so admirably proportioned to his purpose, that 'Animal Farm' even seems very creditable if we compare it with Voltaire and Swift." New Yorker

Nineteen eighty-four; a novel. Harcourt 1949 314p $7.50 **Fic**

1 Totalitarianism—Fiction

"A satirical novel. . . . Set in the society of the future, toward which Orwell believed both extreme right- and left-wing totalitarianism were heading, it is the story of a man and a girl who rebel. In this terrifying society there is no place for truth, for historical records are destroyed and propaganda replaces information. Thought and love are punished, while privacy is impossible. Placards everywhere say: 'Big Brother is watching you.' Big Brother represents Stalin, and the satire is chiefly directed against Russia." Benét. The Reader's Encyclopedia

Page, Elizabeth

The tree of liberty. Farrar 1939 985p $7.50 **Fic**

1 U.S.—History—Revolution—Fiction 2 U.S.—History—1783-1809—Fiction

In time the narrative runs from 1754 to 1806. "Here is a vast panorama of the beginnings of American national life and national philosophy, as three generations of an American family have their part in great national events." N Y Her Trib Books

"It is all very old-fashioned, and a little unreal. . . . Yet this is not to disparage either the historical authenticity or the sincerity of Miss Page's performance. An immense amount of research is skillfully concealed in the narrative and it cannot be said that the book does injustice to any of the important characters or episodes of our history. And the story itself—clear, straight-forward, skillfully contrived and gracefully told has a vitality that sustains it to the end." N Y Times Bk R

Parks, Gordon

The learning tree. Harper 1963 303p $6.95 **Fic**

1 Negroes—Fiction 2 Kansas—Race relations—Fiction

"A small town in Kansas in the 1920's is setting for the story of a year in the life of a teen age boy. The usual personal and family crises, degrees of understanding and misunderstanding between children and adults, first experience of sex, and a touching first experience of love are parts of Newt's growing up. But also part of his experience is consciousness of being a Negro in a community where the behavior of the individual Negro affects the community's reaction to all Negroes." Booklist

"This first novel by versatile (sometime musician, renowned photographer) Gordon Parks is not written with resentment, but rather with rueful reminiscence, even humor. It is an unassuming and thoroughly conventional book, but it has freshness, sincerity, and charm." Library J

Pasternak, Boris

Nobel Prize in literature, 1958

Doctor Zhivago [Tr. from the Russian by Max Hayward and Manya Harari] **Fic**

1 Communism—Russia—Fiction 2 Russia—History—Fiction

Some editions are:
Modern Lib. $4.95
Pantheon Bks. $7.95

First published 1957 in Italy

A "long novel, which traces the life of a Russian from 1900 to 1929. . . . It is a powerful and enormously interesting work, which . . . gives a vivid picture of what it was like to be a Russian in those years and to feel the impact of the tremendous events of the times. There are dozens of characters. The hero [Zhivago, physician and poet] his wife, from whom he is separated by the Bolsheviks, and another woman whom he loves are especially fine creations." Pub W

"By its sweep, its understanding of man's fate, its deep humanity and religious feeling, its sense of tragedy and joyous love of life, [this novel] is in the tradition of the great Russian novels of the nineteenth century." N Y Her Trib Books

Paton, Alan

Cry, the beloved country **Fic**

1 Africa, South—Fiction 2 Race problems—Fiction

Some editions are:
Scribner $3.95 Subtitle: A story of comfort in desolation
Watts, F. $9.95 Large type edition. A Keith Jennison book

First published 1948

"Novel of South Africa, where the murder of a progressive white industrialist by the son of a patient Zulu parson catalyzes a new understanding of the tropic race problem in the heart of the old parson and the victim's father, owner of the land and lord of the natives in the valley." Retail Bookseller

Paton, Alan—*Continued*

"As it stands, 'Cry, the Beloved Country' commends itself to readers as an outstanding example of a creative effort embodying social comment. The story, the characters, and the problems are all memorable. The book suggests that there are men of good intentions everywhere, but not enough of them to rebuild society in terms of justice, equality, and generosity." Survey G

Too late the phalarope. Scribner 1953 276p $4.95   **Fic**

1 Africa, South—Fiction

"The story is basically that of a well loved white police lieutenant who in his need turns to a native girl. He is betrayed, reported and thus brings shame on himself and his family The narrator of the story is an aunt who fills in the entire picture of family pride, righteous disdain, unbending adherence to an imposed restriction ,and the falsity of many basic customs in parts of South Africa." Library J

"The book is written with superb simplicity. It is cadenced but unaffected; it will inevitably be called Biblical and yet there is no conscious parodying of scriptural prose. It flows relentlessly to its crisis, and sometimes we cry out at its power. The people are all clear and real, the South African backgrounds are colorfully and deeply etched. The conflicts are diverse but they all contribute to the basic struggle; father and son, races, languages, prejudices." Christian Science Monitor

Plaidy, Jean

The captive Queen of Scots. Putnam 1970 410p $6.95   **Fic**

1 Mary Stuart, Queen of the Scots—Fiction 2 Great Britain—History—Tudors, 1485-1603 —Fiction

"The story of the last 18 years of Queen Mary's life, during which she was first a prisoner of her Scottish enemies and later, after a dramatic escape and flight to England, the captive of her archenemy, Queen Elizabeth. Treated with at least some of the respect due a queen, Mary is pictured with her retinue of loyal friends and servants, living in varying degrees of discomfort and confinement as she moved from one castle to another at the whim of Elizabeth. She emerges as a generous, overly trustful, emotional victim, attractive even as she grew older though not wiser, who met her tragic fate because she could not cope with the treachery and intrigue of both friends and enemies." Booklist

Portis, Charles

True grit; a novel. Simon & Schuster 1968 215p $4.95   **Fic**

1 The West—Fiction 2 Frontier and pioneer life—Fiction

Also available in a large type edition for $6.95 Fourteen-year-old Mattie Ross, the main character, describes how she left "a Yell County farm one winter in the 1800's to go to Ft. Smith, Arkansas where her father had just been murdered by a farm tenant. . . . [She convinced] Rooster Cogburn, a U.S. marshal . . . [with] 'true grit,' to join her in tracking down the murderer." Library J

"As delightful to a twelve-year-old as to a cultivated adult. [it] is lively, uproarious high adventure. It is also a commentary on the American character, then and now. Although the tale is straightforward, told in an ingenious nineteenth-century style, its nuances are endless. . . . Portis destroys absurdity by overwhelming it with truth. Mattie Ross is nineteenth-century America; it is impossible to doubt her, impossible to doubt the tale that she tells. Hers is a yarn with swagger, color and song." Sat R

Potok, Chaim

The chosen; a novel. Simon & Schuster 1967 284p $4.95   **Fic**

1 Jews in New York (City)—Fiction

Also available in large type edition for $7.95 "Danny and Reuven grew up in the Williamsburg section of Brooklyn, but lived in entirely different worlds. They met at a baseball game between their two Jewish parochial schools which turned into a holy war. This is a story of friendship; of fathers and sons; and a fine portrayal of Orthodox and Hasidic beliefs." English Speaking Union

"A deeply considered exegesis of modern Judaism. . . . The plot is simple and slight, though strong and graceful." Book Week

The promise. Knopf 1969 358p $6.95 **Fic**

1 Jews in New York (City)—Fiction

"Reuven Malter and Danny Saunders, the two close friends encountered in the author's earlier novel 'The chosen' [entered above] are, in this sequel, young men whose lives are beginning to take shape around their chosen vocations: for Reuven the rabbinate, for David, clinical psychology. Their two worlds, increasingly separated by occupational and personal involvements, are brought in touch again through a complex situation centering on Michael Gordon, a brilliant adolescent heading toward a complete breakdown." Booklist

"The somewhat mechanical writing exhibited in 'The Chosen' shows up again. Yet, the characters continue to be recognizable and moving, not literary abstractions." Best Sellers

Priestley, J. B.

The good companions. Harper 1929 640p $7.75   **Fic**

1 Adventure and adventurers—Fiction

"Three people, set forth to solitary high adventure: Oakroyd, a Yorkshire factory hand with a nagging wife; the gentle lady of a Cotswold manor, with a small legacy in hand and thirty-seven monotonous years behind her, and Inigo Jollifant, a Cambridge man with a distaste for teaching small boys and a talent for airy improvisation on the piano. These amateur vagabonds unite in taking over a traveling dramatic company which has gone on the rocks." Cleveland

It suffices to call The Good Companions a robust and diverting tale, told in meandering fashion, lit by rich humor and warm sentiment and centered about a group of perennially engaging characters." Outlook

Proust, Marcel

The past recaptured; tr. from the French by Andreas Mayor. Random House 1970 272p $7.95   **Fic**

Published in England with title: Time regained. It is a new translation of the final part of Remembrance of things past, entered below

This book carries the narrator and the various characters down to the time of World War I, showing the effect of the war on their lives and thoughts, and presents generalizations by the author on the subject of time and memory." Benét. The Reader's Encyclopedia

Remembrance of things past. Random House v 1, 1934; v2, 1932 2v ea $15 **Fic**

Translated by C. K. Scott Moncrieff and Frederick A. Blossom

Contents: v 1: Swann's way; Within a budding grove; The Guermantes way. v2: Cities of the plain; The captive; The sweet cheat gone; The past recaptured

"Into this long and complex psychological study and panorama of an epoch in social history there has been introduced some of the finest writing of our time on the subject of art in general, painting, music, acting, literature, architecture, and the like, as well as on our reaction to these arts. . . . And the long series as a whole is really an experiment—remarkably successful—in making the author's past live again in the eternity of art." Lenrow. Reader's Guide to Prose Fiction

Rama Rau, Santha

The adventuress; a novel. Harper 1970 327p $6.95   **Fic**

1 East (Far East)—Fiction

"The story opens during the American occupation of Japan. Kay is a young Filipino girl who becomes the mistress of Charles Beaver,

Rama Rau, Santha—*Continued*

an American member of the Occupation administration, loves him but lies to him and loses him; moves on to Manila and, for reasons of passport convenience, marries Jeremy Wilson, a British pilot. In pre-Communist Shanghai, she becomes the mistress of David Marius, a collector of jade." Book Rev Digest

"A skilled liar, determined to live at any cost, Kay assumes identities and invents self-histories with unusual grace and effectiveness, conning both men and women, keeping the 'truth' about herself a secret even from the reader." Book World

Remember the house. Harper 1956 241p $5.95   **Fic**

1 India—Fiction

This novel of modern India "is a story of a young Indian girl, daughter of a wealthy aristocratic family, who samples the influence of the western world (it is the last year of the British occupation) and then finds peace and fulfillment in her own people's traditions and moral values." Pub W

"The understanding that comes to Baba will come to many . . . as they read this book filled with the authentic flavor of India and offering as it does, a key to the philosophy of Indian life." Library J

Rand, Ayn

Atlas shrugged. Random House 1957 1168p $8.95   **Fic**

"A long, complicated novel about what the author believes to be the outcome of today's world. She pictures America as ruined by false leaders who persecute the doers and builders for earning large amounts of money. . . . Her heroes are a copper tycoon, a great steel maker and an inventor. Her heroine is vice-president of a trans-continental railroad system." Pub W

"Miss Rand is as convinced as is Nietzsche that to help the weak or to live for others is a betrayal of the soul of man. aMny readers will reject her views with fury. Few will deny the narrative power and cunning construction of 'Atlas Shrugged.'" Book of the Month Club News

The fountainhead. Bobbs 1943 754p $8.95   **Fic**

1 Architecture—Fiction

"Unusual story of struggle for success among New York architects. Careers of Keating and Roark are followed up, from day one graduates with honors from his alma mater and other is expelled because of unruliness, although he is real genius. Interesting insights into methods by which, for a while, people may gain glory and money, but creative artist wins out. No lack of romance, but amorous ways of Dominique Francon may not appeal to all." Library J

"A dramatic, action-filled book, set against a fascinating background, and based on an uncompromising belief in the importance of the individual—and on the provocative idea that man's ego is the fountainhead of progress." Huntting

Raucher, Herman

The summer of '42. Putnam 1971 251p $5.95   **Fic**

1 Adolescence—Fiction

"A middle-aged man returns to Packett Island off the New England coast and summons up memories of the summer of 1942 when he and his two buddies were 15. Hermie, the 'intellectual,' develops a crush on Dorothy, young wife of a serviceman off to war. The three boys are occupied and preoccupied with sex. They brood about it, talk about it, and read about it in a manual. They also try to turn theory into practice in a movie house and on the beach. When Hermie stumbles into Dorothy's house the night she learns of her husband's death, they have sex and never see each other again. Thirty years later the man still recalls with feeling the summer of '42." Library J

Reade, Charles

The cloister and the hearth   **Fic**

1 Middle Ages—Fiction 2 Reformation—Fiction

Some editions are:

Dodd (Great illustrated classics) $5.50 With illustrations by Charles Keene from old prints, and a foreword

Dutton (Everyman's lib) $3.25

First published 1861

"The action takes place on the Continent in the latter years of the 15th century. Among the historical characters of note whom Reade introduces into the narrative are Froissart, Gringoire, Deschamps, Luther, Villon, and—as a child—Erasmus. The story centers around the tragically thwarted love of Erasmus' parents: Gerard, a talented young writer, and the red-haired Margaret, daughter of Peter Brandt. A forged letter convinces Gerard of Margaret's death; and, after a period of despair and wild living, he becomes a monk of the Dominican order, unaware that Margaret has given birth to Erasmus, his son. When after many adventures and misadventures the pair meet again, Gerard is unable, because of his vows, to live with his family. He manages, however, to settle nearby. Margaret soon dies of the plague, and the heartbroken Gerard dies shortly thereafter." Benét. The Reader's Encyclopedia

Remarque, Erich Maria

All quiet on the western front; tr. from the German by A. W. Wheen. Little 1929 291p $5.95   **Fic**

1 European War, 1914-1918—Fiction

"The narrator of this apparently autobiographical story is a young German private who with three of his classmates is snatched away from school at the age of nineteen to serve in the trenches. Though the author is a German, the book transcends nationality. A simple written life of the common soldier, told without anger or passion, and with an almost unendurable realism and pathos, the book is a powerful indictment of war. When the Armistice comes Paul is the sole survivor of his group of comrades, but it is his flesh only that has escaped. His spirit is destroyed." Book Rev Digest

"The book is powerful, no so much because of the unspeakable horrors which fill its pages but because of the matter-of-factness, the terrible stoicism with which they are related." Wis Lib Bul

Renault, Mary

The bull from the sea   **Fic**

1 Theseus—Fiction 2 Greece—Fiction 3 Mythology, Classical—Fiction

Some editions are:

Modern Lib. $2.95

Pantheon Bks. $7.95

Sequel to: The king must die entered below

First published 1962

A "tale that continues the adventures of Theseus. . . . It is about Theseus as King of Athens, as lover of the Amazon Hippolyta (there is great dramatic intensity in this long episode), and as husband of the Cretan princess, Phaedra." Pub W

"A superb historical novel. It is brilliantly and convincingly imagined, artistically presented, at once mind-stretching and deeply moving. . . . Miss Renault has not only integrated what can be known of Theseus' life and time and contemporaries into her story, but has made the elements intelligible and coherent." N Y Her Trib Books

Fire from heaven. Pantheon Bks. 1969 375p $7.95   **Fic**

1 Alexander the Great—Fiction 2 Greece—History—Fiction

The author tells the story of Alexander's life from childhood to the age of twenty when he succeeded his murdered father, King Philip of Macedon. The book also describes the court and peasant life, the military and political events of the time, as well as the impact of such figures as Aristotle and Demosthenes. (Publisher)

The author expertly "recreates and reinterprets myth and legend and recorded history so that one feels that this must have been the way it was. . . . [She] suggests but does not depict Alexander's homosexual relation with Hephaistion [and] suggests but does not detail Philip's lusting. . . . The whole novel is rich and expertly controlled." Best Sellers

Map on lining-papers

Renault, Mary—*Continued*

The king must die. Pantheon Bks. 1958 338p $6.95   **Fic**

1 Theseus—Fiction 2 Crete—Fiction 3 Mythology, Classical—Fiction

This novel, based on history and legend, tells of Theseus, slayer of monsters, abductor of princesses, King of Athens, sent to destroy the matriarchal pattern of Eleusis and Crete. The core and climax of the novel is the Cretan adventure. (Publisher)

"Author Renault ably dramatizes the cultural clash between Mycenean Greece (masculine, simple-souled and semiprimitive), and Minoan Crete (effeminate, sophisticated and decadent). She has obviously lived her period, which is the closest a historical novelist can ever come to making a period live." Time

The last of the wine   **Fic**

1 Greece—History—Fiction

Some editions are:
Modern Lib. $2.95
Pantheon Bks. $6.95

First published 1956

"In this re-creation of ancient Greece, the author tells the story of Alexias, a young Athenian of good family, who reaches manhood in the last phase of the Peloponnesian War. Against this background develops the friendship of Alexias and Lysis, both of whom have fallen under the spell of Socrates. In their relationship the author shows the impact of Socrates' teaching on the ethics of his time." McClurg. Book News

"A well-rounded personalized picture of ancient Greek culture, including the prevalence of homosexuality, presented according to the contemporary point of view as the ideal type of human love. For the discriminating reader who appreciates meticulous research and fine writing." Booklist

The mask of Apollo. Pantheon Bks. 1966 371p $6.95   **Fic**

1 Actors and actresses—Fiction 2 Greece—Fiction

"A novel set in Syracuse and Athens in the fourth century B.C. which concerns Nikeratos, the actor, who carries an antique mask of Apollo with him on his travels. The mask becomes by degrees his artistic conscience. Niko narrates the struggle for power between Dion, philosopher and soldier, the friend of Plato, and the tyrant Dionysios the Younger." Book Rev Digest

"The story is masterfully told, one gets the feel of the era, hears great heroes talk, learns how backstage life in the Greek theater went on, what ingenious devices were used for the production of the dramatic effects. One also is aware throughout of the acceptance of a kind of homosexuality which, however, insofar as Miss Renault handles it in her story, might have been quite Platonic, for there is none of the need for anatomical 'realism' in this novel." Best Sellers

Richter, Conrad

The awakening land: I The trees; II The fields; III The town. Knopf 1966 3v in 1 (630p) $10   **Fic**

1 Frontier and pioneer life—Fiction 2 Ohio—Fiction

An anthology of the author's three novels published 1940, 1946 and 1950, respectively, and entered separately

A country of strangers. Knopf 1966 169p map $4.95   **Fic**

1 Indians of North America—Fiction 2 Frontier and pioneer life—Fiction

"The tragic conflict of a young white girl, captured and adopted by Indians in her childhood and happy with her Indian husband and son, who is forced against her will to return to the white world. . . . With husband dead and son killed, she stoically accepts—for a time—her miserable lot as little more than a slave to her white family, which rejects her. In a hopeful ending, she joins her life with that of True Son, hero of 'The Light in the Forest,' [entered below] whose experiences have been somewhat similar, and together they flee from 'civilization.' In particular, it is a haunting tale of an innocent victim caught between two

cultures, but in general, it is a denunciation of hypocrisy, prejudice, and inhumanity." Horn Bk

The fields. Knopf 1946 288p $5.95   **Fic**

1 Frontier and pioneer life—Fiction 2 Ohio—Fiction

Sequel to: The trees, entered below
Follows the story of Sayward as a wife and mother, working with her own brood on that hard frontier to create a durable home and the aspects of civilization in a region where life was still difficult and where towns were just beginning to appear
Followed by: The town

The lady. Knopf 1957 191p $4.50   **Fic**

1 Frontier and pioneer life—Fiction 2 New Mexico—Fiction

"Young Jud tells the story of his ruthless, yet charming and beautiful aunt, Dona Ellen, whose streak of violence leaves its mark on those around her in the sheepmen-cattlemen struggle in New Mexico during the 1890's." Cleveland

"This short novel is bathed in the light and the legends of territorial New Mexico, Dona Ellen is the only fully developed character, but she is enough." Sat R

The light in the forest. Knopf 1953 179p $4.50   **Fic**

1 Delaware Indians—Fiction 2 Frontier and pioneer life—Fiction

Companion volue to: A country of strangers, entered above

"A boy stolen in early childhood and brought up by the Delawares at fifteen suddenly returned to the family he has forgotten. He resents his loss of independence, hates the brutality of the white man's civilization and longs only for a return to the Indians whom he remembers as peace-loving and kind. His return to the Delaware does not, however, bring him peace; rather, he must make a bitter choice between helping his Indian brothers kill a group of unsuspecting white men or helping the white men escape. This is both a vivid recreation of outdoor life and a provocative study in conflicting loyalties." Horn Bk

The sea of grass   **Fic**

1 Southwest, Old—Fiction

Some editions are:
Knopf $4.95
Watts, F. $7.95 Large type edition. A Keith Jennison book

First published 1937

"The heroine, a delicate refined, lovely lady, leaves her husband and children and the life on a huge cattle ranch to return to the city. Twenty years later, her youngest son, who is not, according to the whispers of the country, her husband's child, is killed as a desperado, and Lutie Brewton comes back to the man who has loved her in spite of everything." Book Rev Digest

The town. Knopf 1950 433p $5.95   **Fic**

1 Frontier and pioneer life—Fiction 2 Ohio—Fiction

Pulitzer Prize, 1951

Last of the trilogy of which The trees, and The fields, are the first parts

"In this novel the town grows and even changes its name. Sayward Wheeler and her husband move from the old cabin into a mansion, and one by one the children set up their own homes. Chancey, the youngest, delicate and spoiled by his mother, is one of the central characters. The book closes with Sayward's death." Book Rev Digest

"Even in its drier passages The Town is always readable, full of a sweet nostalgia that only occasionally spills over into sentimentality. . . . A good bit of fictional Americana." Time

The trees   **Fic**

1 Frontier and pioneer life—Fiction

Some editions are:
Knopf $5.95
Watts, F. $8.95 Large type edition complete and unabridged. A Keith Jennison book

First published 1940

First in a trilogy of American pioneer life

"The Lucketts were the first family to cross the Ohio into the new territory so soon to be

Richter, Conrad—*Continued*

opened up to settlement. It was a land of un-touched virgin forest in which Worth Luckett, his rifle in the crook of his elbow, felt at home, but Jary, his wife, looked up thru the all but impenetrable branches and longed for the sun. Sayward, the eldest daughter, could take it, and make the best of it, while to the young ones it was a paradise. The trees shape the des-tinies of all of them, and shape them different-ly. Only Sayward remains at the end, strong and serene, and ready to take up the new ways of clearing and cultivation." Wis Lib Bul

"It's a period piece, with no great preten-sions to exciting storytelling, but craftily done, with all the detail convincing and quite with-out the usual pioneer-hero sentimentality." New Yorker

Followed by: The fields

Roberts, Kenneth

Arundel; a chronicle of the province of Maine and of the secret expedition led by Benedict Arnold against Quebec. Double-day 1933 632p $5.95   Fic

1 U.S.—History—Revolution—Fiction 2 Ar-nold, Benedict—Fiction 3 Canadian Invasion, 1775-1776—Fiction

A revised shortened version of a novel pub-lished 1931

"An historical novel of the Revolutionary period, the setting of which is the garrison house at Arundel in southern Maine. Steven Nason, the hero of the story, goes with his friend Benedict Arnold on a hazardous expedi-tion against Quebec. Young Nason has a very personal interest in the success of the enter-prise, since Mary Mallinson, the girl he loves, has been taken by the Indians and is a captive in Quebec. Steven's recollections of the hard-ships, and dangers of the expedition, and its blunders and failure in spite of individual acts of heroism, make up the bulk of the narra-tive." Book Rev Digest

Northwest Passage. Doubleday 1959 [c1937] 709p $5.95   Fic

1 U.S.—History—French and Indian War, 1775-1763—Fiction 2 Rogers, Robert—Fiction

"The central figure of this historical novel is Major Robert Rogers, American ranger com-mander who led the expedition against the In-dian town of St Francis in 1759, and whose dream was to find an overland passage to the Pacific. The narrator is one Longdon Towne, from Kittery, Maine whose two ambitions were to paint the Indians as they really looked, and to follow Rogers. The book falls into three sections, the first dealing with the St Francis expedition; the second with the interlude in London, when Rogers was attempting to gain influential friends and money and Towne was learning to paint; and the third dealing with Rogers' career as governor of Michilimackinac, his court martial, and Towne's success as a painter." Book Rev Digest

"There are love and humor in this mag-nificent book and flavor in the full sensory meaning of the word. Best of all, after the first impetuous pleasure of the story itself, there remains the satisfying knowledge of a shrewd and fresh approach to pre-Revolution-ary American history." Forum

Maps on lining-papers

Oliver Wiswell. Doubleday 1940 836 $6.95   Fic

1 U.S.—History—Revolution—Fiction

The background for this novel of the Ameri-can Revolution is Boston, New York, Paris, Kentucky, and South Carolina. The story is told by Oliver Wiswell, New Englander, who is loyal to the mother country

"The present novel, which is history for all its fictional form, will startle every man, wo-man and child who has been taught to believe that the American Revolution was fought and won by bands of angels. It is, in short, the Revolution as seen by men whom the Revolu-tionary fathers called Tories and who called themselves Loyalists. In it all the bitterness of a horrible civil war is powerfully and dramat-ically brought back to life." N Y Times Bk R

Maps on lining-papers

Rolvaag, O. E.

Giants in the earth; a saga of the prairie; tr from the Norwegian. Harper 1927 465p $5.95, lib. bdg. $4.99   Fic

1 Norwegians in the U.S.—Fiction 2 Frontier and pioneer life—Fiction 3 Farm life—Fic-tion 4 South Dakota—Fiction

"The Norwegian immigrant as a pioneer in America is finely viewed through the character-ization of Per Hansa to whom the Dakota prairie meant life, exhilarating struggle, and freedom, and through the characterization of Beret, his well-loved wife, to whom it brought loneliness, terror, and despair. Professor Rol-vaag, a Norwegian who has lived in the United States . . . first wrote his story in his native language and then translated it into English." Pittsburgh

"It is half an adventure story, a realistic de-scription of the physical facts of the home-steader's life 50 miles from anywhere on the Dakota plains, and half a penetrating study of pioneer psychology: and it is hard to say which is better done." Sat R

Sabatini, Rafael

Captain Blood, his odyssey. Houghton 1927 437p illus $4.95   Fic

1 Pirates—Fiction

"Riverside bookshelf"

First published 1922

"Peter Blood was many things in his time—soldier, country doctor, slave, pirate, and fi-nally Governor of Jamaica. Incidentally, he was an Irishman. Round his humorous-heroic fig-ure Mr Sabatini has written an exciting ro-mance of the Spanish Main, the facts of which he alleges to have been found in the diary and logbooks of one Jeremiah Pitt, a follower of Monmouth in 1685 and Blood's faithful com-panion in adventure." Times (London) Lit Sup

Scaramouche, the king-maker. Houghton 1931 420p $5.95   Fic

1 France—History—Revolution, 1789-1799—Fiction

First published 1921

A story of the French Revolution, colorful and romantic, with a plot of cunning construc-tion. The hero, André-Louis Moreau, to avenge the death of his friend at the hands of a rich noble, adopted that friend's revolutionary creed and used his own powers of eloquence to further the republican cause

Salinger, J. D.

The catcher in the rye   Fic

1 Adolescence—Fiction 2 New York (City)—Fiction

Some editions are:

Little $5.95

Watts, F. $9.95 Large type edition. A Keith Jennison book

First published 1951

"Just before Christmas young Holden Caul-field, knowing that he is to be dropped by his school, decides to leave early and not report home until he has to. He spends three days and nights in New York City and this is the story in his own words, of what he did and saw and suffered." Book Rev Digest

"The author presents an understanding and sincere account of the mental gropings and disillusionment of a sensitive and precocious adolescent boy. . . . The dangers he encounters are terrifying to the adult mind; the language he uses to describe his adventures is downright bad; but the soul of the boy is pure and in-nocent and wholly honest. He rejects the un-wholesome and the evil, not heroically but in a very matter of fact manner and because he is fundamentally decent. He gains knowledge but without sacrifice of his integrity." Ontar-io Lib Rev

Franny and Zooey. Little 1961 201p $5.95   Fic

1 New York (City)—Fiction

Contains two stories: Franny, and Zooey. Both belong to a series of tales about the Glass family of twentieth century New York City. In the first story "college girl Franny has a date

Salinger, J. D.—*Continued*

spoiled by her conversion through a religious book, and [in the second longer story] Zooey, her older brother, tries to make her see that it is her job to become an actress." Bk Buyer's Guide

"The language is incandescent, violent, and convincing." Sec Ed Brd

Raise high the roof beam, carpenters, and Seymour: an introduction. Little [1963 c1959] 248p $5.95   Fic

Two long stories originally written for the New Yorker containing episodes from the life of the Glass family with Seymour Glass, a poet and the oldest child, as the central character. Since Seymour never appears the episodes are recounted by his brother Buddy, an English teacher at a girls' college

"Mr. Salinger's obsessions continue to be Zen Buddhism, Oriental philosophy, and generally the pursuit of some ecstatic and beatific perception that will redeem a stale and ugly world. The protagonist in this search for beatitude is Seymour . . . who has already committed suicide." Atlantic

Sandburg, Carl

Remembrance Rock. Harcourt 1948 1067p $12   Fic

1 U.S.—History—Fiction

"Long historical novel which attempts to tell the story of the American dream in terms of some of the people who have been responsible for furthering it. The book is divided into three sections. The first describes the life and times of the Pilgrim fathers; the second is about the north Atlantic seaboard during the Revolutionary period; and the third section is about the Middle West during the 1850's and the Civil War period. The prolog and epilog are set in . . . [twentieth century] America." Book Rev Digest

Saroyan, William

The human comedy; illus. by Don Freeman; ed. by Marion C. Sheridan. Harcourt 1944 299p illus $5.75   Fic

1 Family—Fiction

First published 1943

"A beautiful and strangely moving book. Made up of little things, trifling episodes in the life of one family living in Ithaca, California. Homer, fourteen years old and a student in Ithaca high school, is night messenger in the telegraph office where he watches the human comedy, and tragedy, as it clicks off the wires. Marcus, the oldest, is in the Army. At home there are Mrs. Macauley and Bess, and Ulysses, viewing the world with solemn four-year old eyes. A simple book, but profound in what it has to say of war—this war, all war—and of the forces of hate, and love." Wis Lib Bul

"The story is typically Saroyan and depends upon devices which are always effective when well handled. The principal device is the creation of a number of thoroughly good characters, good in a sense far exceeding the usual senses, good in a way that human nature never is good. Their every thought, action, word is kindly and wise and unselfish." Commonweal

Schaefer, Jack

Shane; illus. by John McCormack. Houghton 1954 214p illus $3.50   Fic

1 Ranch life—Fiction 2 The West—Fiction

Illustrated edition of the title first published 1949

A story of the impact of a softspoken drifter, Shane, on the fourteen year old son of the homesteader, Starrett, when Shane joins the Starrett's Wyoming household and takes up their fight against the man who is trying to force them from the valley

"The author's skill in depicting character, situation and mood gives the story a quality that makes it superior to most 'westerns.' " Wis Lib Bul

Schmitt, Gladys

Rembrandt; a novel. Random House 1961 657p $10   Fic

1 Rembrandt Hermanszoon van Rijn—Fiction

A fictional biography of the famous 17th century Dutch painter. It follows Rembrandt's life "from his birth as the son of a mill owner, through his marriage to Saskia and his great success as an artist, his spendthrift ways and his rudeness, to the death of Saskia, his affair with his housekeeper, and his declining success." Bk Buyer's Guide

Obviously, an enormous amount of research has gone into the writing of this book, and the period atmosphere is excellent. The characters, especially Rembrandt himself, come alive through the masses of detail that Miss Schmitt has so carefully assembled and imparted about them." Pub W

Scott, Sir Walter

Kenilworth   Fic

1 Great Britain—History—Tudors, 1485-1603 —Fiction 2 Elizabeth I, Queen of England— Fiction

Some editions are:

Dodd (Great illustrated classics) $4.50 With a portrait of the author, pictures of contemporary scenes and drawings with an introduction and captions by Basil Davenport

Dutton (Everyman's lib) $2.95

First published 1821

A novel "famous for its portrayal of Queen Elizabeth. Aside from Her Majesty, the chief characters are the Earl of Leicester, who entertains ambitions of becoming king-consort, and his beautiful, unhappy wife, Amy Robsart. She suffers neglect, insult and finally death at his hands." Benét. The Reader's Encyclopedia

Quentin Durward   Fic

1 France—History—House of Valois, 1328-1589—Fiction 2 Middle Ages—Fiction

Some editions are:

Dodd (Great illustrated classics) $4.50 With illustrations in color by Percy Tarrant

Dutton (Everyman's lib) $3.25 Preface and glossary by W. M. Parker

Scribner (The Scribner Illustrated classics) $5

First published 1823

"A story of French history. In this novel are introduced Louis XI and his Scottish Guards, Oliver le Dane and Tristan l'Hermite, Cardinal Balue, De la Marck (The 'Wild Boar of Ardennes') Charles the Bold, Philip des Comines, Le Glorieux (the court jester), and other well-known historic characters. The main plot has to do with the love of the gallant young Quentin Durward, a member of the Scottish Guards, and Isabelle, Countess of Croye. The hero saves the King's life in a boar hunt and later wins the hand of the Countess from his rival, the Duke of Orleans." Benét. The Reader's Encyclopedia

The talisman   Fic

1 Crusades—Fiction 2 Richard I, King of England—Fiction

Some editions are:

Dodd (Great illustrated classics) $4.50 With illustrations from drawings by Rowland Wheelwright, together with an introductory sketch of the author by Basil Davenport

Dutton (Everyman's lib) $3.25 Preface and glossary by W. M. Parker

First published 1829

"Relating the adventures of Sir Kenneth, Prince Royal of Scotland, as a knight in disguise in the Holy Land [during the third Crusade] under Richard Coeur De Lion. Richard and his noble enemy, Saladin, are leading characters. Hearing of Richard's illness. Saladin assumes the disguise of the physician Adonbec al Hakim and gives his patient a healing drink of spring water into which he has dipped his 'talisman.' At the end of the novel, Sir Kenneth marries the kinswoman, Lady Edith Plantagenet." Benét. The Reader's Encyclopedia

Segal, Erich

Love story. Harper 1970 131p boards $4.95   Fic

1 Marriage—Fiction

Segal, Erich—*Continued*

"Oliver is Harvard, rich, a big campus athlete. Jenny is a Radcliffe scholarship student in music from a poor Italian Catholic background. They meet, fall in love, and marry, even though the boy's father wants him to go to law school first. Jenny gives up the chance to study in Paris and works to put her young husband through law school—and they win out to the beginnings of a great life and a promising career for him. Then tragedy steps in." Pub W

"A very professionally crafted short first novel. . . . The story is all on the surface. But it is funny and sad." Library J

Selinko, Annemarie

Désirée. Morrow 1953 594p $8.95   **Fic**

1 Desideria, consort of Charles XIV John, King of Sweden and Norway—Fiction 2 France—History—Consulate and Empire, 1799-1815—Fiction

A story about the wife of General Jean Baptiste Bernadotte, the general of Napoleon who was elected to the throne of Sweden in 1810. The novel follows Désirée's whole life from her birth in Marseilles, her broken engagement with Napoleon to make way for Josephine, her ups and downs at Napoleon's court, and her reluctant acceptance of her role as Queen of Sweden. It also details a large part of Napoleon's rise and fall, including his maneuverings to get his family and aids into positions of power

Seton, Anya

Avalon. Houghton 1965 440p $5.95   **Fic**

1 Great Britain—History—To 1066—Fiction 2 Northmen—Fiction

The romance in this story "is a deep lifelong attachment between a wandering French prince, an idealistic, poetic man, and a Cornish girl of peasant and Viking blood. The story opens in a courtly, gentle mood which changes to fury, lust and murderous greed when the scene shifts to the English court, and to adventure and exploration when the girl is captured by her father's people and the Vikings take the center of the stage." Pub W

"Late tenth- and early eleventh-century life in England and in the lands colonized by the Norsemen is re-created from early Anglo-Saxon chronicles, French manuscripts, and secondary sources. . . . An epilog sketches events between the end of the story and the Norman Conquest of 1066 and lists sources." Booklist

Devil Water. Houghton 1962 526p maps $6.95   **Fic**

1 Radcliffe, Charles—Fiction 2 Great Britain—History—Fiction 3 Virginia—History—Fiction

"In this biographical novel about England and Virginia in the early eighteenth century, about the two Jacobite rebellions, the Radcliffe family and that of William Byrd of Westover, I have adhered scrupulously to facts, when they can be found." Author's note

The action centers around "Charles Radcliffe, who escaped from Newgate prison after his brother's execution, of Jenny, his daughter by a secret marriage, and of the strong affection between them, which endured through years of separation and despite conflicting beliefs and loyalties." Publisher's note

"Devil Water contains many moving pictures of eighteenth-century high life in Northumberland, London, and Virginia, with copious descriptions of manners and customs." Times (London) Lit Sup

Katherine. Houghton 1954 588p $6.95 **Fic**

1 Katherine, Duchess of Lancaster—Fiction 2 John of Gaunt, Duke of Lancaster—Fiction 3 Great Britain—History—Plantagenets, 1154-1399—Fiction

"The story of John of Gaunt and Katherine Swynford . . . [set in] the England of Geoffrey Chaucer and John Wyclif, of the Black Death and of the Peasants' Revolt. Here John of Gaunt fought for power and lost his heart to Katherine." Huntting

"The novelist's scrupulous use of findings based on careful research, combined with her own interpretations, produces a warm alive

picture of the fourteenth century, convincing characterizations, and a touching romance." Booklist

The Winthrop woman. Houghton 1958 586p $6.95   **Fic**

1 Hallet, Elizabeth (Fones) Winthrop Feake—Fiction 2 Puritans—Fiction 3 Massachusetts—History—Fiction

"The heroine is an attractive, high-spirited woman who dared to flout the conventions of her day. Elizabeth Fones was the niece of John Winthrop, governor of Massachusetts Bay, and wife of his son. Widowed at twenty, she came to Boston and managed to survive tragedy, disease, famine, childbirth, and Indian hostilities. This is the story of her three marriages and her hopeless love for her cousin John. It is also an authoritative account of the Massachusetts Bay and Connecticut Colonies." Huntting

"This is all an amazing story, too little known before. Anya Seton has not distorted or trifled with it, or sought to embellish it. She has clothed the name of Elizabeth, and those about her, with flesh and blood to make them real to us. The novel is noteworthy for its insights into the Puritan 'Bible Commonwealth.' " Sat R

Shellabarger, Samuel

Captain from Castile. Little 1945 632p $6.95   **Fic**

1 Mexico—Fiction

A long historical romance of Mexico and Spain centering on Pedro de Vargas, who "found himself a fugitive in Cuba because of an old family enemy whose weapon was the Inquisition. With an eye to the main chance. De Vargas joined the forces of Cortes and became a Captain with the Conquistadors. The author has successfully interwoven the passions of love and hate, of war and intrigue, of action and suspense, against the vivid background of the early 16th century, rich in the spirit of the modern man, irrevocably changed by the Renaissance, but closely tied to a feudal past." Huntting

The King's cavalier. Little 1950 377p illus $6.95   **Fic**

1 France—History—House of Valois, 1328-1589—Fiction 2 Francis I, King of France—Fiction

The story of a young Frenchman and a young Englishwoman who were caught in the wild plots and counterplots surrounding the Bourbon conspiracy against Francis I

"Mr. Shellabarger is a scholar. Not only does he contrive vivid scenes and live characters—often all good or all bad—but his detailed knowledge of those times cloaks this tale of olden days with authenticity. . . . Tops of its kind." Spring'd Republican

Maps on lining-papers

Prince of foxes. Little 1947 433p $6.95 **Fic**

1 Italy—History—Fiction

"A romantic novel of the Renaissance period in Italy, particularly of the years during which Cesare Borgia rose to power—and fell. At the beginning of the tale, the chief character, a mysterious soldier of fortune, is a protege of the Borgias. Andrea Orsini falls in love with one of the Cesare's intended victims, changes sides, and eventually defeats his master's purposes in one small city state in Italy." Book Rev Digest

"In addition to spinning a lively tale of love and intrigue, [the author] has a fine touch with historical background." Atlantic

Shelley, Mary W.

Frankenstein; or, The modern Prometheus. Dutton 242p $2.95   **Fic**

1 Science fiction

"Everyman's library"

First published 1818: in this edition 1912

"The best of the tales of mystery and horror written in friendly competition by Shelley, Byron, Polidori, and Mrs Shelley at Geneva. . . . It is ghastly extravaganza, built up on the idea of a monster created on pseudo-scientific principles, and endowed with life, by a young

Shelley, Mary W.—*Continued*

German, whom the monster forthwith turns upon and keeps in anxiety and torment." Baker's Best

"The story is one of unrelieved gloom, but in its invention and conduct exhibits unquestioned genius." Keller's Reader's Digest of Books

Sholokhov, Mikhail

Nobel Prize in literature, 1965

The silent Don; tr. from the Russian by Stephen Garry. Knopf 2v $14.95   Fic

1 Cossacks—Fiction 2 European War, 1914-1918—Fiction 3 Russia—History—Revolution, 1917-1921—Fiction

Also available separately at $7.95

Contents: v 1 And quiet flows the Don (1934); v2 The Don flows home to the sea (1941)

Set during the Revolution this novel follows the fortunes of a group of Cossacks living along the Don River

"The book unquestionably has qualities that raise it to the level of a great work of art. Its virility and stark realism in tracing the story of a Don Cossack village through peace, war, revolution and civil strife grip the reader's attention, even though he be appalled at times by the grim horror, the savage brutality or the bestial lust of the pictures presented to him." Sat R

Shute, Nevil

The legacy; a novel. Morrow 1950 308p $4.95   Fic

1 World War, 1939-1945—Fiction 2 Australia—Fiction

Published in England with title: A town like Alice

"This story of Jean Paget, a London typist unknown to fame in her native country, falls into two parts, held together by the fact that an uncle had left her a fortune and the man who became her trustee became interested in her life before and after she received the legacy. First there is the story of Jean's experiences in Malaya during the war when she was an unwanted prisoner of the Japanese, and then comes the story of her return to Malaya and eventually to Australia, to pay her debt of gratitude to the Malayans and to the Australian soldier who had once befriended her." Book Rev Digest

On the beach. Morrow 1957 320p $6.95 Fic

1 Atomic bomb—Fiction 2 Australia—Fiction

"In 1963 in Melbourne, Australia, people are gradually coming to accept the fact that they will die very soon. The results of an atomic war have wiped out all life in the Northern Hemisphere and the infection is moving southward. The story deals with the way these people face the inevitable end." Book Rev Digest

"Despite its grim premise that the world may destroy itself in the near future by atomic warfare, this is a book to be read by mature readers of all ages. Mr. Shute shows marvelous understanding of and sympathy for the people who can be gallant as they await the inevitable results of a war they did not start. Poignant, but not bitter and not without humor." Library J

Sienkiewicz, Henryk

Nobel Prize in literature, 1905

Quo vadis   Fic

1 Church history—Primitive and early church —Fiction 2 Rome—History—Empire, 30 B.C.-476 A.D.—Fiction

Some editions are:

Dodd (Great illustrated classics) $4.50 Translated by Jeremiah Curtin; with illustrations of the author and the setting of the book together with an introduction and descriptive captions by Allen Klots, Jr.

Dutton (Everyman's lib) $3.25 Translated by C. J. Hogarth

Little $6.95 translated from the Polish by Jeremiah Curtin; with illustrations from paintings by Howard Pyle and Evert Van Muyden. Has subtitle: A narrative of the time of Nero

First published 1896

This historical novel deals "with the Rome of Nero and the early Christian martyrs. The Roman noble, Petronius, a worthy representative of the dying paganism, is perhaps the most interesting figure, and the struggle between Christianity and paganism supplies the central plot, but the canvas is large. . . . The beautiful Christian Lygia [who] is the object of unwelcome attentions from Vinicius, one of the Emperor's guards [also figures in the story]." Benét. The Reader's Encyclopedia

"A theatrical picture of Roman life bringing into salient contrast the licentiousness of paganism and the spiritual beauty of Christianity. Scenes of court life and of Christian worship, the burning of Rome, and the massacres in the amphitheatre, are woven into a rapid narrative." Baker's Best

Silone, Ignazio

Bread and wine. A new version tr. from the Italian by Harvey Fergusson II; with a new preface by the author. Atheneum Pubs. 1962 331p $5   Fic

1 Fascism—Italy—Fiction 2 Italy—Fiction

First published in the United States 1937 by Harper

"Translated from the edition revised by the author to modify the political concepts of the original." Pub W

"The hero, Peitro Spina, returns to his native Abruzzi after 15 years of exile to continue his antifascist agitation. As he travels through the country, disguised as a priest, he sees the inroads made upon the Italian character by Mussolini's rule. Finding that the underground movement is in chaos and doubting the validity of his old revolutionary slogans, he eventually flees to avoid certain arrest." Benét. The Reader's Encyclopedia

Simenon, Georges

The confessional; tr. from the French by Jean Stewart. Harcourt [1968 c1967] 155p $4.95   Fic

1 Adolescence—Fiction 2 France—Fiction

"A Helen and Kurt Wolff book"

Original French edition 1966. This translation published 1967 in England

"André, a high school boy [in France], comes to realize that his mother has a lover. He himself is the battlefield for his parents, each trying to win him over to his or her side. . . . [The father] is more discreet, more rational, more put upon than the strident, egocentric mother. The mother packs her bags and attempts to leave, but in the end a weary armistice is achieved, and the boy decides to try to hold on to his sanity, to keep his faith in love, to pass his exams, and to eventually begin his own life as a man." Am News of Bks

"The whole theme is delicately and effectively handled to make this another achievement in psychological understanding of the human condition." Best Sellers

Five times Maigret. Harcourt 1964 525p $5.95   Fic

1 Mystery and detective stories

Originally published 1962 in England with title: A Maigret omnibus

Contents: Maigret right and wrong (Maigret in Montmartre & Maigret's mistake); Maigret has scruples; Maigret and the reluctant witnesses; Maigret goes to school. English translations first published separately in England 1954, 1958, 1959 and 1957 respectively

"Because Simenon writes with such compression, it is good to have the five together, and this collection makes a proper introduction to Maigret." Library J

Smith, Betty

Joy in the morning. Harper 1963 308p $7.95   Fic

1 Marriage—Fiction

"A story of young married love in a Midwest college town during the 1930's in which an eighteen-year-old girl and a twenty-year-old boy struggle with problems of finance, education, and pregnancy, all of which are solved by the child bride through her optimism, charm, and the directness of her vision of life." Booklist

Smith, Betty—*Continued*

"This human hearted song of joy is more than a pen sketch of human nature. The characterization is essentially dramatic and the dialogue is a marvel of accuracy. . . . As always in [Betty Smith's] writing this adroit naturalness and conciseness keeps the reader interested. The flashes of warm reality, of wit, and of truth, give universal interest to the simple tale." Best Sellers

A tree grows in Brooklyn; a novel; with drawings by Richard Bergere. Harper 1947 420p $7.95, lib. bdg. $6.11   Fic

1 Brooklyn—Fiction

First published 1943
"Warm-hearted book tells of the life of a sensitive child Francie Nolan, growing up in a city slum, and of Francie's parents, her lovable drunkard father and tender, determined mother." Benét. The Reader's Encyclopedia
"There is little story, or plot, as the reader encounters it in the average novel. This is rather a stringing together of memory's beads and the workmanship is extraordinarily good. . . . Above all, it is a faithful picture of a part of Brooklyn that was mostly slums and misery." N Y Times Bk R

Smith, Dodie

I capture the castle. Little [1962 c1948] 343p illus $5.95   Fic

1 Great Britain—Fiction

"An Atlantic Monthly Press book"
A reissue of a title first published 1948. Illustrations by Ruth Steed from sketches by the author
The heroine, Cassandra Mortmain, in her girlish diary, unfolds the tale of her eccentric family living precariously in a ruined English castle. With the arrival of two young American bachelors, who have inherited the castle, humorous situations embroil the entire family
"Still fresh and delightful. . . . [This is] basically a love story." Horn Bk

Sneider, Vern

The Teahouse of the August Moon. Putnam 1951 282p $5.95   Fic

1 U.S. Army—Fiction 2 Japan—History—Allied Occupation, 1945-1952—Fiction 3 Okinawa—Fiction

This "novel centers around Captain Fisby, member of a Government Team in Okinawa, his colonel, and Plan B for the welfare of the natives. The plan would have gone according to schedule if Fisby hadn't received a gift of two geishas, and if Miss Higa Jiga and other maiden ladies hadn't felt that they must compete on an equitable basis with the geishas. The chicanery of the ladies, and Fisby's coping with the situation make this a wonderfully humorous and satirical story." Library J

Snow, C. P.

The masters. Scribner [1960 c1951] 374p (Strangers and brothers) $6.95   Fic

1 Colleges and universities—Fiction 2 Great Britain—Fiction

First published 1951 by Macmillan
Narrated by Lewis Eliot, a young lawyer, this story is set at an English college in 1937 "at the time when the master is dying and a new one must be chosen. The forces set in motion—vanity, ambition, scandal, jealousy, and bitterness—are . . . portrayed." Huntting
"For a quiet novel of subtle characterization this one contains a surprising element of suspense." Ontario Lib Rev

Solzhenitsyn, Alexander

Nobel Prize in literature, 1970

One day in the life of Ivan Denisovich Fic

1 Russia—Fiction

Some editions are:
Dutton $4.50 With an introduction by Marvin L. Kalb; foreword by Alexander Tvardovsky. Translated from the Russian by Ralph Parker
Farrar, Straus $7.95 Translated by Gillon Aitken
Praeger $5.50 Translated by Max Hayward and Ronald Hingley; introduction by Max Hayward and Leopold Labedz

First Russian edition, 1962
A novel describing one day in the life of a Russian citizen imprisoned for a ten year sentence in a slave labor camp during the Stalin era. The chief character, an innocent man falsely accused, meets numerous people in prison, experiences brutality and constant struggles to survive. (Publisher)

Spark, Muriel

The prime of Miss Jean Brodie. Lippincott 1962 [c1961] 187p $3.95   Fic

1 Teachers—Fiction

"Set in Edinburgh in the thirties, it is largely a character sketch of a middle-aged school teacher who has a tremendous influence over a small group of girls attending the school in which she teaches. Eventually, one of them turns on her and brings about her dismissal." Pub W
"It is a story that is funny, true, unpleasant, and in the end, gloriously human—or ingloriously human—both, actually. Along the way there are uncanny glimpses of the young, in all their mercurial mystery, equally inclined to hero-worship and treachery." N Y Her Trib Books

Steinbeck, John

Nobel Prize in literature, 1962

Cannery Row   Fic

1 Monterey, Calif.—Fiction

Some editions are:
Viking $4
Watts, F. $8.95. Large type edition complete and unabridged. A Keith Jennison book
First published 1945
The "bravura sketch of the sardine-fishing foreshore of Monterey is not unlike Bret Harte's famous tale. . . . It is the wastrels, bums, loafers, and hard cases, the whorehouse madams or the vacant-lot squatters, who are truly generous and relaxed and salt the earth with genuine romance. . . . [Its highlight is] the first party [the boys] planned for Doc. . . . The best of it is very acute comedy and strong feeling." Book of the Month Club News
"When you have finished reading 'Cannery Row' you know that John Steinbeck has passed another of his small miracles. . . . This goes back in style and substance . . . to Monterey County in California again, where once we met Lennie and George, and Danny and the paisanos [of Tortilla Flats, entered below]. Add to these the people of Cannery Row: Doc, and Mac, and the boys, and the bright-haired Dora, for they are likely to seem as memorable. They are caught up alive for us, stirring and functioning, in the whole, integral atmosphere of their row of shacks along the shore line." Sat R

The grapes of wrath   Fic

1 Migrant labor—Fiction 2 California—Fiction

Some editions are:
Viking $7.50
Watts, F. $9.95 Large type edition. A Keith Jennison book
First published 1939 by Viking
Pulitzer Prize, 1940
"Driven through no fault of their own from the dusty farm in Oklahoma, which their family had owned for years, the Joads, numbering 13, started for California to find work, lured there by the glowing handbills of fruit growers who would benefit by cheap labor. . . . They found only disillusion, exploitation, and hunger. The close family ties, the tenderness, understanding, and courage of the simple people, life on the highway and in the miserable workers' camps in California, are told in a rich narrative that moves the reader profoundly." Booklist
"The book is profane and sometimes shocking in its detail. So is that segment of America which Steinbeck describes with such truth." Atlantic

Of mice and men   Fic

1 Migrant labor—Fiction 2 Ranch life—Fiction 3 Mentally handicapped—Fiction 4 California—Fiction

Some editions are:
Modern Lib. $2.95 With an introduction by Joseph Harry Jackson
Viking $4
Viking $6.50 A Viking Large type book

Steinbeck, John—*Continued*

First published 1937 by Covici
George and Lennie are two drifting ranch hands who "have never been able to work up a stake because big, blundering, simple-witted [amazingly strong] Lennie keeps getting them into trouble. . . . George feels that Lennie has been given into his keeping. He controls him by talking about the rabbit farm they will have one day, where Lennie may look after the rabbits if he is good—for George too is webbed in the dream. They come to work in the Salinas Valley and it is there, among the people they meet at the ranch, that their story is worked out." New Repub
"The story is simple but superb in its understatements, its realisms which are used, not to illustrate behavior, but for character and situation. . . . Its style is right for its subject matter, and that subject matter is deeply felt, richly conceived, and perfectly ordered." Sat R

The pearl; with drawings by José Clemente Orozco   **Fic**

1 Mexico—Fiction

Some editions are:
Viking $4.95
Watts, F. $7.95 Large type edition. A Keith Jennison book
First published 1947 by Viking
Based on an old Mexican folk tale, this is the story of the great pearl, how it was found, and how it was lost again. It is the story, too, of a family, the special solidarity of a man and a woman and their child: Kino, the fisherman, his wife, Juana, and the baby Coyotito
"One can take this as a parable or as an active and limpid narrative whose depth, like that of the tropical waters which Steinbeck so beautifully describes, is far more than one would suspect." Atlantic

The red pony   **Fic**

1 Horses—Stories

Some editions are:
Viking lib. bdg. $3.37 With illustrations by Wesley Dennis
Watts, F. $7.95 Large type edition. A Keith Jennison book
First published 1937 by Covici
Four episodes in the life of Jody, a boy on a California ranch
"No one, I think, has ever caught the ecstasy of a small boy with his first horse more movingly. . . . John Steinbeck can pack into a few paragraphs what many stretch out over a whole book." N Y Her Trib Books

The short novels of John Steinbeck. With an introduction by Joseph Henry Jackson. [New ed. completely reset in 1963] Viking [1963 c1953] 527p $6   **Fic**

An omnibus volume first published 1953. All the titles are entered separately, except The moon is down, o.p. 1971
Contents: Tortilla Flat (1935); The red pony (1937); Of mice and men (1937); The moon is down (1942); Cannery Row (1945); The pearl (1947)
In his novels, "Steinbeck is always aware of mankind's weaknesses, frustrations, failures, grotesqueries. But he is also always the artist. . . . He earnestly wishes to make people understand one another." Introduction

Tortilla Flat   **Fic**

1 Monterey, Calif.—Fiction

Some editions are:
Modern Lib. $2.95 With a foreword by the author; illustrated by Ruth Gannett
Viking $4.50
First published 1935 by Covici
"Tortilla Flat was a tumble-down section of Monterey, California. The paisanos who lived there were a mixed race of Spanish, Indian, Mexican and Caucasion bloods. The central character is one of the paisanos, Danny, who came back from the [first] World War to discover that he had inherited two houses in Tortilla Flat. There he gathered his friends around him and they lived their carefree, unmoral lives with gay abandon until their beloved Danny died." Book Rev Digest
"Mr. Steinbeck exploits with ingenuity and talent the sentimental appeal of vagabondage, companionship in poverty, drink, simple-mindedness, crime altruistically committed, dogs and funerals." Spectator

The winter of our discontent. Viking 1961 311p $6   **Fic**

1 Ethics—Fiction 2 New England—Fiction

Ethan Allen Hawley, the impoverished heir to an upright New England tradition is the focus of this story. Ethan, under pressure from his restless wife and discontented children who want more of this world's goods than his grocery store job provides, decides to take a holiday from his scrupulous standards to achieve wealth and success. What happens as he compromises with his integrity makes up this story. (Publisher)
This is "an internal conflict novel in which the central issue between nobility and expediency, while it is joined, is never satisfactorily resolved. . . . A highly readable novel which bristles with disturbing ideas." N Y Times Bk R

Stendhal

The red and the black   **Fic**

1 France—History—1799-1914—Fiction

Some editions are:
Liveright (The Black and gold lib) $6.95 Translated from the French by C. K. Scott-Moncrieff
Modern Lib. $2.95 Translated by C. K. Scott-Moncrieff
Original French edition published 1830
"The most celebrated novel of Stendhal, published in 1830. It deals with the rise to power of Julien Sorel, a handsome, cold, and intensely egotistical young man who uses his love affairs to serve his ambition and tries to murder his first mistress when she betrays him to her successor in his interest. The title refers to the colors of the military class, represented by Napoleon, the author's hero, and of the clergy, which Stendhal detested. The novel is noted for its psychological analysis and exposition of the character of Sorel." Benét. The Reader's Encyclopedia

Stevenson, Robert Louis

The strange case of Dr Jekyll and Mr Hyde. Illus. by Rick Schreiter. Watts, F. 1967 90p illus lib. bdg. $3.75   **Fic**

Also available in a large type edition for $7.95
First published 1886
This is "the disturbing tale of the dual personality of Dr. Jekyll, a physician. A generous and philanthropic man, he is preoccupied with the problems of good and evil and with the possibility of separating them into distinct personalities. He develops a drug that transforms him into the demonic Mr. Hyde, in whose person he exhausts all the latent evil in his nature. He also creates an antidote that will restore him to his respectable existence as Dr. Jekyll. Gradually, however, the unmitigated evil of his darker self predominates, and finally he performs an atrocious murder. . . . Unable to procure one of the ingredients for the mixture of redemption, and on the verge of being discovered, he commits suicide." Benét. The Reader's Encyclopedia

Stewart, George R.

Fire. Houghton 1971 [c1948] 336p $6.95   **Fic**

1 Forest fires—Fiction
ISBN 0-395-12548-0
First published 1948 by Random House
This novel "relates the life history of a forest fire, from its birth as the result of a lightning stroke, thru its obscure, puny infancy to the days of its might and terror, and its final defeat. Against this story of the fire itself are set glimpses of the lives, hopes, fears and sorrows of the men and women who are called upon to fight it." Book Rev Digest
Map on lining-papers

Storm; a novel; with a new introduction by the author. Modern Lib. 1947 349p $2.95   **Fic**

1 Storms—Fiction 2 California—Fiction

First published 1941 by Random House
"A veritable deluge envelops the entire Pacific coast, disrupting traffic, communications, and power lines. A young man in the Weather Bureau at San Francisco has seen the storm

Stewart, George R.—*Continued*

coming all the way from the coast of China—and he has named it Maria. Mr. Stewart's story concerns itself mainly with things that happen while the storm is raging in California." Hunting

"An unusual and dramatic story. . . . Worth the effort of weathering a somewhat slow and technical beginning." Los Angeles. School Libraries

Stewart, Mary

Airs above the ground. Mill 1965 286p boards $6.95   **Fic**

1 Circus—Fiction 2 Lippizaner horses—Stories 3 British in Austria—Fiction

In this suspense novel, the author describes "the remote mountain villages of Austria, a small traveling circus, and a secret involving one of the famous Lippizaner white stallions. The heroine this time is . . . a young married Englishwoman on the track of an errant husband. Among the other characters are a charming German equestrienne, a 17-year-old English boy escaping an over-possessive mother [and] a sinister Hungarian high-wire performer, and a railroad train named 'Fiery Elijah.' " Pub W

"Its background is authentic, the action fast, the characterizations quite credible, the situations wonderfully adaptable to a film-thriller. And there is wonderful dash in the long chase to the finish." Best Sellers

The crystal cave. Morrow 1970 521p maps $7.95   **Fic**

1 Great Britain—Fiction 2 Middle Ages—Fiction

"Merlin, the baseborn son of royalty in fifth-century Britain, uses magic to outwit his enemies until finally, he sets the stage for the birth of Arthur, the future king of Britain." Top of the News

"Describing Merlin's adventures and education in the magic arts from childhood to the year of Arthur's birth, when Merlin was in his early twenties, she creates a dramatic and colorful picture of fifth-century England, Wales, and Brittany, showing Welsh, Saxons, and Britons in a bitter power struggle while Christians sought to destroy the old druidic and Roman religions." Booklist

My brother Michael   **Fic**

1 British in Greece, Modern—Fiction 2 Greece, Modern—Fiction

Some editions are:
Mill boards $7.95
Watts, F. $8.95 Large type edition. A Keith Jennison book
First Published 1960

In this story of suspense and adventure "the young vacationing heroine is drawn with a most capable English schoolmaster into a search, viciously opposed, into the circumstances of his brother's murder by Greek guerrillas in the confused hill fighting at the end of War II." Am News of Bks

"Slightly sentimental overtones, but the Greek landscape and—much more subtle—the Greek character are splendidly done." Spectator

This rough magic   **Fic**

1 British in Greece, Modern—Fiction 2 Corfu—Fiction

Some editions are:
Mill $5.95
Watts, F. $8.95 Large type edition complete and unabridged. A Keith Jennison book
First published 1964

A story "in which the heroine, an out-of-work young English actress, encounters high adventure on the Greek island of Corfu. She is visiting her sister, who is married to a wealthy Italian with an estate on the island. A distinguished, retired Shakespearian actor takes a hand in events. So does an amiable dolphin who plays with the heroine when she is in swimming. Also prominently present are a perfidious villian and a . . . romantic hero." Pub W

Stinetorf, Louise A.

White witch doctor; decorated by Don McDonough. Westminster Press 1950 276p illus $3.95   **Fic**

1 Missions, Medical—Fiction 2 Congo (Democratic Republic)—Fiction

"Interesting autobiographical novel describing the adventures of a medical missionary in the Belgian Congo. After she is forty. 'Dr. Ellen' takes her nurse's training and goes out to Africa where for twenty years she does heroic work against terrific odds. Cannibals, pygmies and witch doctors all play their parts as do unusually faithful and intelligent servants. Local color is vivid and picturesque characters are clearly delineated." Library J

Stoker, Bram

Dracula   **Fic**

Some editions are:
Dodd (Great illustrated classics) $4.50 With illustrations of the author and the setting of the story, together with an introduction by James Nelson
Doubleday $4.95
Modern Lib. $2.95
Watts, F. $8.95 Large type edition. A Keith Jennison book
First published 1897

"A very successful handling of horrible sensations in a realistic way. . . . A terrible baron in a Transylvanian castle is the chief of an army of human vampires that prey on mankind and pursue their ravages as far as London, demanding all the determination and resource of the hero and his friends to exterminate them." Baker's Best

Stone, Irving

Adversary in the house. Doubleday 1947 432p $6.95   **Fic**

1 Debs, Eugene Victor—Fiction 2 Debs, Katherine (Metzel))—Fiction

Based on the life of "Eugene V. Debs, famous for his fanatic devotion to the cause of the working man. It's the tragic story of a man who married a woman who became his staunch adversary. She opposed him in his work until the end of his days, while the woman he lost remained unswervingly loyal to him." Literary Guild

"Accepting Stone's thesis [of Deb's marriage] as supportable, the novel is an interesting one, told with a sensitive humanism." N Y Times Bk R

The agony and the ecstasy; a novel of Michelangelo. Doubleday 1961 664p $8.95 **Fic**

1 Michelangelo Buonarroti—Fiction 2 Italy—History—Fiction

"Carefully researched biographical novel re-creating the life and times of the great Florentine sculptor, painter, engineer, architect and poet from the time of his apprenticeship at 13 to Ghirlandaio, through his work for his patron Lorenzo de' Medici, his love affairs and brilliant achievements." Bookmark

"Almost every character in the book is well-drawn, although those who are Medici are perhaps drawn with the most understanding and vividness. . . . As fiction, [this book] is an outstanding and readable performance." N Y Times Bk R
Glossary: p659-61

Immortal wife; the biographical novel of Jessie Benton Fremont. Doubleday 1944 456p $6.95   **Fic**

1 Frémont, Jessie (Benton)—Fiction 2 Frémont, John Charles—Fiction

"Full length biographical novel about Jessie Benton Frémont, the indomitable wife of the American explorer and geographer, John Frémont." Book Rev Digest

"Recommended as a novel of exciting historical events (accurately told), as a fine love story and as an excellent character study." Library J
Note on sources: p452-56

Lust for life; the novel of Vincent van Gogh. Doubleday 1937 399p illus $7.95 **Fic**

1 Gogh, Vincent van—Fiction

A reissue of the title first published 1934 by Longmans

"A novelized version of the career of Van Gogh, the mad genius. With apparent fidelity to the sources, but with imagined dialog, the author follows his whole tortured life that ended at thirty-seven in suicide—his early apprenticeship as an art dealer, his agonizing years as

Stone, Irving—*Continued*

a religious worker among the coal miners, his love for half a dozen women, some of them prostitutes, and his long, frenzied striving for a technique of painting. Almost too painful in parts but probably true in essentials." Booklist

The passions of the mind; a novel of Sigmund Freud. Doubleday 1971 808p xxxiip $10   **Fic**

1 Freud, Sigmund—Fiction

The subject is Sigmund Freud and this novel 'is crammed with details about Freud's life, his marriage, his associates, his teachers, his critics, his patients. The Vienna in which he lived, the background of the psychoanalytical movement as a whole, the particular techniques he devised—Mr. Stone seems to take care to leave nothing out. . . . The reader has a sense of participation in historic events; the people, places and dates are real, even if the dialogue isn't. . . . [This is] an example of the novelist's art—in terms of stylistic quality and subtlety of characterization." Book of the Month Club News

The President's lady; a novel about Rachel and Andrew Jackson. Doubleday 1951 338p $6.95   **Fic**

1 Jackson, Rachel (Donelson) Robards—Fiction 2 Jackson, Andrew, President U.S.—Fiction 3 U.S.—History—1815-1861—Fiction

The "story of Rachel and Andrew Jackson and of the vital part they played in [this country's] development. The story is one of continual failure and ultimate success; and of a woman's devotion to one of America's greatest men." Huntting

"No writer of fiction could desire more fascinating and romantic characters than Mr. Stone draws from history for this biographical novel." N Y Her Trib Books

Bibliography: p333-35

Those who love; a biographical novel of Abigail and John Adams. Doubleday 1965 662p $7.95   **Fic**

1 Adams, John, President U.S.—Fiction 2 Adams, Abigail (Smith)—Fiction 3 U.S.—History—Revolution—Fiction

A novel portraying the love story of the second President of the United States and his wife against the background of the American Revolution

Much of the book has been "taken straight from the writings and letters of Adams and his wife. The story is leisurely, lengthy, and solid, filled with important issues. . . . One of the high points [of the book] is Adams' period abroad as ambassador to England and France; stimulating comparisons of national viewpoints are given here. Lesser known events at home, the XYZ papers, the Alien and Sedition Acts, are brought into clear focus." Best Sellers

Bibliography: p651-62

Struther, Jan

Mrs Miniver. Harcourt 1942 298p $4.95 **Fic**

1 Great Britain—Fiction

First published 1939 in England; 1940 in the United States. This 1942 edition adds a new episode

A succession of episodes relating the daily occurrences over a period of two years in the life of the humorous, perceptive, contented Mrs Miniver

This "is a small book of sketches about very small things. But it is not trivial. She is sentimental, playful, domestic. . . . Yet [underneath her] domestic sentiment . . . lie perceptions, not at all original but deeply humane and humorous." New Yorker

Stuart, Jesse

Mr Gallion's school. McGraw 1967 337p boards $6.95   **Fic**

1 School stories 2 Kentucky—Fiction

A story set in the Kentucky hill country. When George Gallion, retired principal, learned that Kensington High might not be able to open that fall, he ignored his doctor's warnings

and his wife's pleas. Into terrible social conditions, made worse by the economic conditions threatening the Valley, strode Mr Gallion with his old-fashioned ideas about courage and discipline. He turned delinquents into students, ruffians into football heroes, and scraped together a first-class band. (Publisher)

Styron, William

The confessions of Nat Turner   **Fic**

1 Turner, Nat—Fiction 2 Southampton Insurrection, 1831—Fiction

Some editions are:
Modern Lib. $2.95
Random house $7.95

Pulitzer Prize, 1968
First published 1967

A biographical novel of Nat Turner, an educated slave, who was condemned to death in 1831 for leading a Negro revolt in [Southampton] Virginia in which more than fifty whites were slaughtered. Narrated by Nat himself, this "story ranges over the whole of Nat's life, reaching its inevitable . . . climax that bloody day in August." Publisher's note

The author "maintains throughout his narrative a consistent and highly imaginative realism not only on the objective plane . . . but also by recreating the intimate psychology of his characters. . . . Styron thoroughly explores the Negro militant's hatred of whites [as well as] . . . the position of the whites . . . without rancor or even a hint of political 'parti pris' on the author's part. It is Nat who sees them, knows and judges them." N Y Rev of Books

Sutcliff, Rosemary

The flowers of Adonis. Coward-McCann 1970 [c1969] 383p $6.95   **Fic**

1 Alcibiades—Fiction 2 Greece—History—Peloponnesian War, 431-404 B.C.—Fiction

First published 1969 in England

The story of "Alkibiades, the godlike Athenian general of Peloponnesian War fame, is told . . . through the first-person reminiscences of a cast of characters consisting of citizens, soldiers, sailors, courtesans, and Spartans and Persians as well as Athenians." Horn Bk

"The technique used is interesting. The story is told entirely in the first person, but with several different 'I's' doing the teling, each one remembering a brief or prolonged relationship with this mysterious and fascinating man, a hero and a traitor, who died by assassination." Pub W

Map on lining-papers

Swarthout, Glendon

Bless the beasts and children. Doubleday 1970 205p $5.95   **Fic**

1 Camps—Fiction 2 Bison—Fiction 3 Adolescence—Fiction

"A group of poor little rich boys shipped to an expensive [Arizona] western camp by their parents are brutally shocked by the slaughter of buffalo. They break out of camp, commandeer a truck, and set off to drive the remaining buffalo to safety in a game preserve. Their ingenuity and determination in the ensuing adventures and misadventures are used by Swarthout to prove the indestructability of human goodness in the most adverse circumstances." Booklist

Tarkington, Booth

Alice Adams; illus. by Arthur William Brown. Grosset 434p illus $2.95   **Fic**

Awarded the Pulitzer Prize, 1922

First published 1921 by Doubleday

'Alice feels inadequate both because she is snubbed by a clique that has false standards and because she discredits her own good qualities. Finally taking stock of the practical possibilities before her, she decides a business course will enable her to help her father through financial difficulties. This story shows the growing pains of a high school girl who failed to crash small-town society." Reading Ladders

"Alice is a pathetic figure, at once amusing, appealing and irritating, as are her self-sacrificing but one-ideaed mother and her simpleminded goaded father. A lightly-handled albeit penetrating study." Cleveland

Tarkington, Booth—*Continued*

Monsieur Beaucaire; illus. by C. D. Williams. Doubleday 1915 127p illus $2.50 **Fic**

1 Great Britain—Fiction

First published 1900

"A French duke in the days of Louis XV, seeking adventure, goes to England as a barber in order to find just the right bride. He falls in love with the beautiful Lady Mary Carlisle, but eventually returns to France to marry his cousin." Benét. The Reader's Encyclopedia

"No one but a born romanticist could have written that dainty and consistent bit of artistry. Its best excuse was the blitheness of its mood, the symmetry of its form, the tingling vitality of it." F. T. Cooper

Tey, Josephine

Three by Tey. With an introduction by James Sandoe. Macmillan (N Y) 1954 3v in 1 (Murder revisited ser) $6.95 **Fic**

1 Mystery and detective stories 2 Great Britain—Fiction

"A Cock Robin mystery"

Contents: Miss Pym disposes (1947); The Franchise affair (1948); Brat Farrar (1949)

In these English novels, a psychologist finds herself involved in a college "accident" that's really a murder, a lawyer defends two women accused of cruelty and witchcraft, and an orphan finds both a family and a murder

Thackeray, William Makepeace

The history of Henry Esmond, esquire; with an introductory sketch of the author and with illustrations of characters and scenes belonging to the novel. Dodd 1945 434p $4.50 **Fic**

1 Great Britain—Fiction

"Great illustrated classics"

Written in 1852

"Written in the first person, supposedly by Henry Esmond. He is brought up by Francis Esmond, heir to the Castlewood estate with Francis' own children, Beatrix and Frank, and grows up in the belief that he is the illegitimate son of Thomas Esmond, the deceased viscount of Castlewood. On his deathbed Francis confesses to [Henry] that he is the lawful heir, but [Henry] keeps the information secret. He and Frank Esmond are ardent supporters of James the Pretender, who, however, falls in love with Beatrix and ruins his chances for the throne. Beatrix joins the Prince abroad and Harry, who has been in love with her, renounces the Pretender, marries her mother Rachel, Lady Castlewood, instead, and takes her to America." Benét. The Reader's Encyclopedia

Vanity fair   **Fic**

1 Great Britain—Fiction

Some editions are:
Dodd (Great illustrated classics) $5.50 With reproductions of the original illustrations by Thackeray and with an introductory biographical sketch of the author by Basil Davenport
Dutton (Everyman's lib) $3.25 Introduction by M. R. Ridley

First published 1848

"A picture of society on a broad canvas, embracing a great variety of characters and interests, the object being to depict mankind with all its faults and meannesses, without idealization or romance. . . . The careers of Becky Sharp, the adventuress, and her husband, Rawdon Crawley, make an apt contrast to the humdrum lives of the good hero and heroine, Dobbin and Amelia. The nobility, fashionable people about town, the mercantile aristocracy and the needy classes below them, are all portrayed in the most lifelike way. . . . Thackeray combines comment with narrative. . . . To many readers, indeed, his sarcastic dissertations are the chief intellectual delight." Baker's Best

Thane, Elswyth

Dawn's early light. Duell 1943 317p $5.95 **Fic**

1 U.S.—History—Revolution—Fiction 2 Williamsburg, Va.—Fiction

"When, in May 1774, young fatherless Julian Day arrives in Virginia from London, he is uncertain of his next step, but the friendliness of St John Sprague impels him to stay on in Williamsburg as a teacher, and soon Julian, the Loyalist, is strangely interested in the activities of the Colonial government and in the personalities of men like Washington and Jefferson. . . . Authentic atmosphere and the vital spirit of the new republic are pleasantly conveyed in this historical romance, which leaves the once shy schoolmaster, Julian, a major in the Continental Army and confident of the future." Bookmark

Thurber, James

The 13 clock; illus. by Mark Simont. Simon & Schuster 1950 124p illus $4.95 **Fic**

1 Fairy tales

This tale "concerns the cruel Duke, the lovely Princess Saralinda (kept a prisoner by the Duke), a monster called Todal, and other fanciful characters presented with the author's special type of affectionate humor." Retail Bookseller

"I don't know just what it is [Thurber] has done this time—a fairy tale, a comment on human cruelty and human sweetness or a spell, an incantation compounded of poetry and logic and wit." N Y Her Trib Books

The white deer; illus. by the author and Don Freeman. Harcourt 1945 115p illus $4.95 **Fic**

1 Fairy tales

"A fantasy written in the guise of a fairy tale, with three princes, an enchanted princess, and a happy outcome." Book Rev Digest

The wonderful O; illus. by Marc Simont. Simon & Schuster 1957 72p illus boards $4.95 **Fic**

1 Fairy tales

An "adult fairy tale. . . . It involves a hidden treasure, a tyrannical villain named Black whose mother got stuck in a porthole, and Black's consequent attempts to ban everything spelled with the letter o from the peaceful island of Ooroo. Though the moral—Black's discovery that he cannot destroy hope, love, valor, and freedom—is obvious, details are ingeniously and subtly worked out." Booklist

"It is extremely clever, sometimes to the point of seeming synthetically so. . . . On the whole Mr. Thurber manages to imbue his ingenious cipher-game [with] that kind of amazed freshness which is so characteristic of the Thurberian world." Christian Science Monitor

Tolkien, J. R. R.

The hobbit; or, There and back again; illus. by the author. Houghton 1938 310p illus $4.95 **Fic**

1 Fairy tales

"Hobbits are very small people, smaller than dwarfs but much larger than Lilliputians. The hero of this tale was a well-to-do hobbit who somehow found himself, accompanied by [a] wizard and dwarfs, off on a mad journey over the edge of the wilds to wrest from Smaug the dragon his hoard of long-forgotten gold." Hunting

"The background of the story is full of authentic bits of mythology and magic and the book has the rare quality of style. It is written with a quiet humor and the logical detail in which children take delight. . . . But this is a book with no age limits. All those, young or old, who love a finely imagined story, beautifully told, will take the Hobbit to their hearts." Horn Bk

The lord of the rings. 2d ed. Houghton 1967 [c1966] 3v map ea $7.50 **Fic**

1 Fairy tales

A revised edition of a trilogy first published 1954-1956

Tolkien, J. R. R.—*Continued*

Contents: v 1 The fellowship of the ring; v2 The two towers; v3 The return of the king

In volume one "Frodo, a home-loving young hobbit, inherits the magic ring which his uncle Bilbo brought back from the adventures described in the . . . fantasy 'The hobbit' [entered above]. This sequel, . . . is the first of a three-part saga that tells of Frodo's valiant journey undertaken to prevent the ring from falling into the hands of the powers of darkness." Booklist

In volume two "the Companions of the Ring, separated, meet Saruman the wizard, cross the Dead Marshes, and prepare for the Great War in which the power of the Ring will be undone." Library J

Volume three "brings the War of the Rings to a close with the success of the forces for good in their fight against the Dark Lord of evil. It also carries Frodo and Sam, bearers of the Ring, to Mount Doom where the Ring is destroyed. Several lengthy appendixes add scholarly information on the past history of Middle Earth and its inhabitants—elves, dwarfs, men, and hobbits." Book Rev Digest

It should be noted that this is not light reading and that there are some people who will be put off by the repetitious ritual and especially the laying of the groundwork in a good part of the first volume. However, once into the adventure, the reader finds it not an easy one to put down." Pub W

Tolstoy, Leo

Anna Karenina   **Fic**

1 Russia—Fiction

Some editions are:

Dodd (Great illustrated classics: Titan eds) $5.50 Foreword by E. Hudson Long

Dutton (Everyman's lib) 2v ea $3.25 Translated by Rochelle S. Townsend. Introduction by Nikolay Andreyev

Modern Lib. $2.95 Edited and introduced by Leonard J. Kent and Nina Berberova. The Constance Garnett translation has been revised throughout by the editors

Modern Lib. (Modern Lib. giants) $4.95

Oxford (The World's classics) $3.75 Translated by Louise and Aylmer Maude. With a preface and notes by Aylmer Maude

Watts, F. Ultratype edition $5.50

First published in English, 1901

Set in Russia this work "gives a direct, truthful, unsentimentalized and unheightened transcript of life in all its multitudinous and complex phases. . . . The main action is profoundly tragic—a woman of fine nature forsakes husband for lover, and after a bitter experience finds rest in suicide." Baker's Best

"For its artistic qualities, Anna Karenina stands foremost among the many beautiful things Tolstoi has written. It is also a work of high moral import, for without sacrificing its value as a masterpiece of art Tolstoi demonstrates through its characters and events that a generous soul cannot live outside the moral law." Pratt Alcove

War and peace   **Fic**

1 Napoleon I, Emperor of the French—Fiction 2 Russia—History—Fiction

Some editions are:

Dutton (Everyman's lib) 3v ea $3.25 Introduction by Vicomte de Vogué

Grosset $4.95

Modern Lib. (Modern Lib. giants) $4.95 Translated from the Russian by Constance Garnett

Oxford (The World's classics) $7.25 Translated by Louise and Aylmer Maude

"The most famous novel of Leo Tolstoi (1865-1872), dealing with Russia and France at the time of Napoleon Bonaparte, giving an epic picture of the invasion of Russia by Napoleon and his army, and presenting the author's theories of history." Benét. The Reader's Encyclopedia

"A multitude of characters are presented, officers and men, both French and Russian, the hostile emperors and their suites, gentry living quietly in Moscow or on their estates, great people of fashion, serfs, and all intermediate classes. The more important are portrayed from the inside, and the reader sees through their eyes . . . the entire life of the nation throughout this tremendous epoch. . . . Real personages occupy almost as much space as the fictitious, and are drawn with the same unerring insight." Baker's Best

Trollope, Anthony

Barchester Towers   **Fic**

1 Clergy—Fiction 2 Great Britain—Fiction

Some editions are:

Dutton (Everyman's lib) $3.25 Introduction by Michael Sadleir

Harcourt (The Harcourt Lib. of English and American classics) $3.95

Oxford (The World's classics) $3

First published 1857

Contains a "picture of [British] clerical society with its peculiar humors and foibles. The chief incidents are connected with the appointments of a new bishop, the troubles and disappointments this involves, and the intrigues and jealousies of the clergy: the henpecked bishop, the ambitious archdeacon, and the dean, canons, and others, with their wives. The picture of the eccentric Stanhope family is particularly delicious." Lenrow. Reader's Guide to Prose Fiction

Turgenev, Ivan

Fathers and sons   **Fic**

1 Russia—Fiction

Some editions are:

Dutton (Everyman's lib) $3.25 Translated by Avril Pyman; introduction by Nikolay Andreyev. Has title: Fathers and children

Modern Lib. $2.95 Newly translated from the Russian by Bernard Guilbert Guerney. With the author's comments on his book and a foreword by the translator

First published 1861

The book "is a description of the tendencies of Young Russia in the [eighteen] sixties, expressed through the hero Bazarov. These tendencies have since become widely known by the name of nihilism." Introduction

"The theme of this novel is the frequent conflict between the older and the younger generation, which the author has rendered particularly touching by his representation of 'the confused efforts of the father to understand his son's new ideas, and the young man's vain efforts to convert his father." Pratt Alcove

Turnbull, Agnes Sligh

The Bishop's mantle. Macmillan (N Y) 1947 359p $6   **Fic**

1 Clergy—Fiction

"There is drama, humor, pathos, adventure in the daily round of Hilary Evans, young Episcopal rector and grandson of a bishop as he tries to live his faith, his idealism, and his enthusiasm for his chosen profession." Cleveland

"Arguments on topics ranging from the tenement situation of the city to the subject-matter of the Sunday sermon take up a goodly portion of the novel and give it a flavor of concrete reality that is so often missing from stories of professions. A flock of wonderful minor characters round out the pattern nicely." N Y Times Bk R

The gown of glory. Houghton 1952 403p $5.95   **Fic**

1 Clergy—Fiction 2 Pennsylvania—Fiction

"A wholesome and sentimental story of a minister and his family in a small Pennsylvania town in the early part of this century. Though constantly hoping for larger opportunities, David Lyall and his wife, Mary, have created an enviable home and community life and their final happiness and fulfillment in these surroundings leaves the reader with a feeling of warm pleasure and a deep sense of peace." Ontario Lib Rev

Whistle and I'll come to you; an idyll. Houghton 1970 243p $5.95   **Fic**

"When British-born Robin Adair arrives to visit his elderly and wealthy American cousins, everyone as is the way of small towns, suspects him of fortune hunting, especially the banker, when Robin falls in love with his daughter." Pub W

Twain, Mark

A Connecticut Yankee in King Arthur's court   **Fic**

1 Arthur, King—Fiction 2 Chivalry—Fiction 3 Great Britain—Fiction

Twain, Mark—*Continued*

Some editions are:

Dodd (Great illustrated classics) $4.50 With photographs of Mark Twain and his environment as well as drawings from early editions of the book, together with an introduction by E. Hudson Long

Harcourt (The Harcourt Lib. of English and American classics) $3.95

Harper $5

Harper (Holiday eds) $3.95, lib. bdg. $4.43

First published 1889. Published in England with title: Yankee at the court of King Arthur

"Burlesque of the historical romance. A Yankee of the most arrant modern type is plumped down in the middle of King Arthur's England." Baker's Best

"A rather extraordinary flight into fantasy—for Mark Twain—combined with his characteristic idiomatic realism. . . . [The Yankee] goes through a series of hair-raising adventures to expose the 'fol-de-rol' of knight-errantry and the bitter injustice of sixth century English laws. This is the real purpose of the book, as its brief but stinging preface shows." Haydn. Thesaurus of Book Digests

Personal recollections of Joan of Arc, by the Sieur Louis de Conte (her page and secretary) illus. by G. B. Cutts. Harper 1926 596p illus $6.95   **Fic**

1 Joan of Arc, Saint—Fiction 2 France—History—House of Valois, 1328-1589—Fiction

First published 1896

"De Conte, who tells the story in the first person, has been reared in the same village with its subject, has been her daily playmate there, and has followed her fortunes in later life, serving her to the end, his being the friendly hand that she touches last. After her death, he comes to understand her greatness; he calls her 'the most noble life that was ever born into this world save only One.' Beginning with a scene in her childhood that shows her innate sense of justice, goodness of heart, and unselfishness, the story follows her throughout her stormy career. We have her audiences with the king; her marches with her army her entry into Orleans; her fighting; her trial; her execution; all simply and naturally and yet vividly told. The historical facts are closely followed." Keller's Reader's Digest of Books

Pudd'nhead Wilson; a tale; with an introduction by F. R. Leavis. Harcourt 1962 214p $3.95   **Fic**

1 Missouri—Fiction

"The Harcourt Library of English and American classics"

First published 1894

Pudd'nhead Wilson is "a story of a sober kind, picturing life in a little town of Missouri. . . . The principal incidents relate to a slave of mixed blood and her almost pure white son, whom she substitutes for her master's baby. The slave by birth grows up in wealth and luxury, but turns out a peculiarly mean scoundrel, and perpetrating a crime, meets with due justice. The science of fingerprints is practically illustrated in detecting the fraud." Baker's Best

"The title character is the village atheist, whose maxims doubtless express much of the author's own disillusion." Lenrow. Reader's Guide to Prose Fiction

Ullman, James Ramsey

The White Tower. Lippincott 1945 479p $6.95   **Fic**

1 Mountaineering—Fiction 2 Alps—Fiction

"When Martin Ordway's plane crashed over Switzerland, he came down into a little valley in the Alps which he had known years before the war. Overshadowing the valley is the Weissturm, [White Tower] a high peak never climbed from that side. While he is waiting for an opportunity to get back home Martin succumbs to a long felt desire to try the climb and with five others he makes the attempt. The story combines the account of the adventure of climbing with the meditations and reminiscences of the various members of the group." Book Rev Digest

The novel "has a love-story in it and contains a lot of philosophizing about modern civilization and it presents a simplified picture of the opposition between the fascist and democratic views of life." Book of the Month Club News

Undset, Sigrid

Nobel Prize in literature, 1928

Kristin Lavransdatter; tr. from the Norwegian. Knopf 3v in 1 $8.95   **Fic**

1 Norway—Fiction

Contains the novels originally published separately as follows: The Bridal wreath (1923); The mistress of Husaby (1925); The cross (1927)

Set in Catholic Norway of the 13th and 14th centuries, this trilogy describes Kristin's life as daughter, mistress, wife and mother

The master of Hestviken; tr. from the Norwegian by Arthur G. Chater. Knopf 4v in 1 $8.95   **Fic**

1 Norway—Fiction

Contains four volumes originally published separately as follows: The axe (1928); The snake pit (1929); In the wilderness (1929); The son avenger (1930)

"This presents a rich picture of Norwegian life in the Middle ages and resembles the 'Kristin Lavransdatter' trilogy [entered above] in that it is concerned with the secret sin of a pair of young lovers, their suffering and final atonement." Cleveland

"No one . . . in the historical novel has given such realness to bygone days and such genius to the evocation of the past." N Y Her Trib Books

Updike, John

The poorhouse fair. Knopf 1959 [c1958] 185p $4.50   **Fic**

1 Old age—Fiction 2 Aged—Dwellings—Fiction 3 New Jersey—Fiction

This novel concerns the lives of a handful of marvelously eccentric and understandable people in a poorhouse on the undulating plains of central New Jersey. It begins on the morning of the annual Fair, an innovation of Conner, the new and very ambitious Prefect. Connor's struggle to institutionalize old age inevitably meets the stiff opposition of those who want to individualize it. (Publisher)

"This is a wise book with much to say on individualism and conformity, mechanization and craftsmanship, the 'welfare state' and the 'old days'—and, foremost, on 'death' as it is looked upon by the aged and the young. Updike's old people are memorable." Library J

Rabbit, run. Knopf 1960 307p $5.95   **Fic**

1 Pennsylvania—Fiction

"Harry (Rabbit) Angstrom is twenty-six, an ex-basketball star who demonstrates kitchen gadgets in dime stores, and man tired of his marriage and his pregnant wife. Leaving home suddenly, he begins a trip south but turns back to Pennsylvania and lives with a prostitute until the birth of his child brings him home again. The baby's accidental death ends the marriage, and Rabbit again runs away from his wife, the prostitute, and his responsibilities." Booklist

"This is a book that is likely to cause something of a stir in the literary world, because life, or lack of it, of the leading character." Pub W

Uris, Leon

Exodus. Doubleday 1958 626p maps boards $7.50   **Fic**

1 Zionism—Fiction 2 Israel—History—Fiction

"A long novel about the fight of the dedicated Zionists against their enemies to establish the young nation of Israel. Scenes shift from the DP camps and ghettos which are the miserable sources of emigration and hope to the battles against active British restrictions of entry and against the Arabs' guerrilla warfare. Half a dozen leading characters include a young American gentile widow drawn actively into the fight as a nurse." Am News of Bks

Uris, Leon—*Continued*

Mila 18. Doubleday 1961 539p $6.95 **Fic**

1 Jews in Poland—Fiction 2 Warsaw—Fiction 3 World War, 1939-1945—Fiction

The author has recreated the World War II story of Warsaw Ghetto freedom fighters. For 42 days and nights in 1943 they fought off the German Army as it carried out the Nazis' plan for the systematic extermination of the Warsaw Jews. Headquarters were set up at Mila 18, where a brave band of men and women led a suicidal fight that lighted a flame of hope and ultimate victory for a handful of survivors. (Publisher)

"The novel is at its best in its non-fictional aspects: its historical passage, its descriptions of Ghetto life, its battle scenes. It is less successful, sometimes embarrassingly clumsy, in its love scenes and attempts at character delineation. Mr. Uris is a poor hand at realistic dialogue, and his grammar is appalling; yet a reader is likely to overlook these flaws as he is swept along by the force of the narrative and the momentousness of the events described." Book of the Month Club News

Van Dyke, Henry

The story of the other wise man; with many drawings in color and line, by J. R. Flanagan. Harper 1923 72p illus $4.95 **Fic**

1 Christmas stories

First published 1896

"Persia, Palestine, Egypt, at the beginning of the Christian era. A finely-conceived extension of the ancient story of the Magi. The general atmosphere of the little tale, as well as certain allusions to world events, may fairly be taken as bringing it under the historical category." Nield

Vining, Elizabeth Gray

Take heed of loving me. Lippincott [1964 c1963] 352p $6.95 **Fic**

1 Donne, John, 1573-1631—Fiction 2 Great Britain—History—Stuarts, 1603-1714—Fiction 3 More, Anne—Fiction

Set in Elizabethan and Jacobean England, this novel concerns "the great poet John Donne and Anne More, who defied her father and risked her inheritance to marry the man she loved." Publisher's note

"To the reader's eyes, Donne becomes a very real, lustful, lyrical young man, then a loving fiancé and faithful husband though oppressed by poverty and lack of preferment, finally an eloquent churchman, in spite of his early worldly life. Donne's poetry winds through the story." Pub W

The Virginia exiles. Lippincott 1955 317p $6.95 **Fic**

1 U.S.—History—R e v o l u t i o n—Fiction 2 Friends, Society of—Fiction

"During the American Revolution, twenty Quakers were held prisoners without trial for their refusal to take a loyalty oath. This novel based on their experiences and what these meant to democratic beliefs implies much about the freedoms of Americans today." Books for You

"Around this incident Mrs. Vining has woven a fascinating novel, yet one that sticks closely to the known facts and presents an accurate picture of all that happened. It is true that she introduces the inevitable love plot into the story, but it neither adds nor detracts markedly from the narration. Authentic to her story is, it is obviously a moral lesson for our times, for, as Mrs Vining comments, 'the problems faced by the exiles' are before us again in only slightly different form." Chicago Sunday Tribune

Vonnegut, Kurt

Cat's cradle. Delacorte Press [1971 c1963] 231p $6 **Fic**

1 Caribbean area—Fiction 2 Science fiction 3 Atomic bomb—Fiction

First published 1963 by Holt

"A facetious, wildly satirical fantasy built up from Felix Hoenikker, father of the atomic bomb; his production of ice-nine, a seed-ice that could set off a chain reaction more deadly than that of nuclear fission; a dictator-ruled Carribean island, where the three Hoenikker children had taken their fatal ice-nine; and other unusual ingredients." Bk Buyer's Guide

The sirens of Titan. Delacorte Press [1971 c1959] 240p $6 **Fic**

1 Science fiction 2 Interplanetary voyages —Fiction

First copyrighted 1959 by Houghton

"At the same time a deep and comic reflection on the human dilemma, this [science fiction] novel follows the richest man in America, Malachi Constant, as he gives up a life of unequaled indulgence [and sets off in a private space ship] to pursue the irresistible Sirens of Titan." Publisher's note

Slaughterhouse-five; or, The children's crusade; a duty-dance with death, by Kurt Vonnegut, Jr. . . . Delacorte Press 1969 186p $6 **Fic**

1 Science fiction

"A Seymour Lawrence book"

"A fourth-generation German-American now living in easy circumstances on Cape Cod [and smoking too much], who, as an American infantry scout 'Hors De Combat,' as a prisoner of war, witnessed the fire-bombing of Dresden, Germany, 'The Florence of the Elbe,' a long time ago, and survived to tell the tale. This is a novel somewhat in the telegraphic schizophrenic manner of tales of the planet Traifamadore, where the flying saucers come from. Peace." Title page

The hero of this novel "is one Billy Pilgrim, a successful optician from Ilium, New York, who goes to war, is captured by Germans and held in an old slaughterhouse in Dresden at the time of the Allied air raids and who later helps—as did Vonnegut—dig out the ash-filled city. But Billy Pilgrim also believes that he has been taken to the distant planet of Tralfamadore (where the flying saucers come from), where he is exhibited naked in the zoo with the beautiful film actress Montana Wildhack, his mate. Billy is able to fall in and out of time, and. . . is often able to know what is going to happen without being able to remember what already has happened. The novel is Billy's story full of all the lackluster details of life in Ilium juxtaposed with the horror of Dresden and the exotica of Tralfamadore." Book of the Month Club News

Walker, Margaret

Jubilee. Houghton 1966 497p $6.95 **Fic**

1 U.S.—History—Civil War—Fiction 2 Reconstruction—Fiction

"A Houghton Mifflin Literary fellowship book"

"To Vyry, the heroine of Jubilee, a slave since her birth and the daughter of a slave, the first murmurings of freedom meant little. . . . But as the murmurings became more insistent her mind began to fill with wishes, and dreams, and possibilities. Her wish was a home of her own—her dream, an education for her children. When the war ended and the Negroes were freed the possibility of her dream coming true seemed almost more remote than it had in the kitchen of the Big House. But Vyry fought, and was defeated and fought again, and in the end she won." Publisher's note

"Each of the fifty-eight chapters [of this novel] opens with lines from a spiritual or popular song of the day . . . suggesting folk ways of thinking or folk wisdom. . . . With a fidelity to fact and detail, [Margaret Walker] presents the little-known everyday life of the slaves, their modes of behavior, patterns and rhythms of speech, emotions, frustrations, and aspirations. Never done on such a scale before, this is the strength of her novel." Sat R

Walker, Mildred

The quarry. Harcourt 1947 407p $5.95 **Fic**

1 Vermont—Fiction

"Life in a Vermont village from 1857 to 1914 is the background of this novel. The central

Walker, Mildred—*Continued*

character is Lyman Converse. All his life Lyman seemed destined to lose the things he loved most, but his friendship with Easy, the escaped slave who became his firm friend never failed. The title of the book refers to the soapstone quarry from which the Converse family made their living." Book Rev Digest

Winter wheat. Harcourt 1944 306p $3.50
                                          Fic

1 Montana—Fiction

"To Ellen Webb wheat-growing was a thing of pride and joy and deep satisfaction. But Gilbert Borden saw only bleak loneliness, her Russian mother's peasant stolidity, her New England father's frustration. He went away—afraid to marry her—and Ellen, seeing her parents through his eyes, lost her faith in the value of their life together. Only her own love of the land did not desert her—it helped her grow in understanding—and from this recognition of reality, hope came to her again." Huntting
"A simple uncomplicated story, which though it lacks powerful action is full of moving incidents. In what is essentially a novel of character and place rather than plot, the creation of Ellen's mother, Anna Petrovna Webb, and the vivid sense of place and region are themselves major achievements." Sat R

Wallace, Lew

Ben Hur   **Fic**

1 Jews—Fiction 2 Church history—Primitive and early church—Fiction 3 Rome—History—Empire, 30 B.C.—476 A.D.—Fiction

Some editions are:
Dodd (Great illustrated classics) $4.50 With 16 full-page illustrative and biographical pictures together with introductory remarks and captions by Basil Davenport
Harper lib. bdg. $6.48

First published 1880
"The hero, Judah Ben-Hur, head of a rich Jewish family, is sentenced to life at the galleys, after being accused by his former friend Messala of attempting to assassinate the new Governor of Jerusalem. His fortune is confiscated; his mother and young sister Tirzah are walled up in a forgotten prison cell, where they contract leprosy. The novel concerns Ben-Hur's escape during an exciting chariot race, his search for his mother and sister and their miraculous cure by Christ, who (with His followers) is an important character. The family is converted to Christianity, and the crucifixion on Calvary is graphically described." Haydn. Thesaurus of Book Digests

Walpole, Hugh

Fortitude; introduction by Hugh Walpole. Modern Lib. 1930 497p $2.95   **Fic**

1 Great Britain—Fiction

First published 1913 by Doran
"The author tells us the story of one Peter Westcott from childhood to maturity, taking us from the grim home in Cornwall to a disreputable Devonshire school, and on to a boardinghouse in Bloomsbury, to poverty in the East End, to success in literature, to love and marriage, and at last to a catastrophe by which most would mark the end. Here, however, there is more to come. Peter is going back to the struggle, for the circle of life is not completed, and for all the author's apparent pessimism we do not yet know whether he would call that circle vicious." Sat R

Waltari, Mika

The Egyptian; a novel; tr. by Naomi Walford. Putnam 1949 503p $6.95   **Fic**

1 Egypt—Fiction

First published 1945 in Finland
Set in Egypt, more than a thousand years before Christ, this novel encompasses all of the then-known world. It is told by Sinuhe, physician to the Pharaoh, and is the story of his life and adventures. Through his eyes are seen innumerable characters of the ancient world
"We see, feel, smell, and taste Waltari's Egypt. He writes in a pungent, easy style." Sat R
Map on lining-papers

The Roman. . . . English version by Joan Tate. Putnam 1966 637p $6.95   **Fic**

1 Rome—History—Empire, 30 B.C.-476 A.D.—Fiction

"The memoirs of Minutus Lausus Manilianus, who has won the Insignia of a Triumph, who has the rank of Consul, who is Chairman of the Priests' Collegium of the god Vespasian and a member of the Roman Senate." Title page
Original Finnish edition published 1964. This is the final volume of the trilogy, begun with: The Egyptian, entered separately, followed by The Etruscan, o.p. 1971
The novel "offers through the life of Minutus, a Roman knight, a panorama of the Empire in the reigns of Claudius and Nero. Social custom, the spread of Christianity, and the persecution of Christians also come into the story as Minutus dies a Christian during the reign of Domitian." Booklist
"Though Minutus is somewhat wooden, his adventures are astonishing." Pub W
Map on lining-papers

Warren, Robert Penn

All the king's men   **Fic**

1 U.S.—Politics and government—Fiction
2 Southern States—Fiction

Some editions are:
Harcourt $7.50
Modern Lib. $2.95 With a new introduction by the author
Random House $4.50
First published 1946. Awarded Pulitzer Prize, 1947
A novel about a political boss, Willie Stark, as told by his publicity man. Stark, a young back-country Southern lawyer becomes a power in his state and then abuses his position
"The story of a corn-pone dictator, undoubtedly based on Huey Long. Remarkable not only for dramatic . . . scenes but also for its flashbacks written in ripe Victorian-type prose and telling about a mid-American journey before the Civil War." Good Reading

Waugh, Evelyn

The end of the battle. Little 1961 319p $4.95   **Fic**

1 World War, 1939-1945—Fiction

Sequel to: Officers and gentlemen
First published in England with title: Unconditional surrender
This story describes "the experiences of Guy Crouchback, scion of an old, English Catholic family, in World War II. In it, a war-weary Crouchback sees action in Yugoslavia, remarries his former wife and, after her death, nobly devotes himself to bringing up her illegitimate child." Pub W

Men at arms; a novel. Little 1952 342p $5.95   **Fic**

"An English Catholic gentleman brought up in Italy and no longer very young returns to his homeland in the hope of getting into the armed forces just before World War II. How he succeeds, his desires and ambitions, his adventures and mis-adventures with his comrades in the renowned Halberdier Regiment are told with inimitable skill and quiet restraint. It is a far more mellow Evelyn Waugh than has thus far appeared—less caustic and biting but none the less deadly in showing up the sins and foibles of army life." Library J
Followed by: Officers and gentlemen

Officers and gentlemen. Little 1955 339p $4.95   **Fic**

1 World War, 1939-1945—Fiction

Sequel to: Men at arms
"As in 'Men at Arms' the central figure is Guy Crouchback whose military career in the early days of World War II is followed through to the catastrophic British defeat at Crete." McClurg. Book News
Followed by: The end of the battle

Wersba, Barbara

Run softly, go fast. Atheneum Pubs. 1970 205p $4.95   **Fic**

On the day of his father's funeral nineteen-year-old David begins a diary to examine their estrangement. This is the record of his thoughts which "lead him back to a conventional childhood in New York, to his disillusionment with this successful father, and to his sudden flight towards the East Village, drugs and freedom." Publisher's note

"The strength of the book is that it rings true. In spite of its preoccupation with the Establishment, hippies, drugs, and sex, the book succeeds in clearly and forcefully conveying basic human weakness and blindness as well as the universal need for love and understanding, which must begin in the individual himself." Horn Bk

West, Jessamyn

Except for me and thee; a companion to The friendly persuasion. Harcourt 1969 309p $5.95   **Fic**

1 Friends, Society of—Fiction 2 U.S.—History—Civil War—Fiction

This episodic narrative of the lives of Jess and Eliza Birdwell, the hero and heroine of The friendly persuasion, entered below, begins "at the time when Jess, 21 and experiencing his own brand of youthful rebellion against his parents and their Quaker teachings, finds himself engaged to three girls at the same time. Wisely, he marries Eliza. . . . The author describes how the Birdwells meet the challenges of their new home: facing the death of a young daughter . . . becoming involved with helping runaway slaves along the Underground Railway, finally seeing their lives affected by the onset of the Civil War. [Anyone who enjoyed the earlier volume] is likely to find this . . . equally appealing. . . . A pleasant look back at the American past." Pub W

The friendly persuasion. Harcourt 1945 214p $4.95   **Fic**

1 Friends, Society of—Fiction 2 Indiana—Fiction

Episodic chapters about the Birdwell family, nineteenth century Quakers living in Indiana during the period following the Civil War

"Miss West, whose first book this is, has produced neither a standard piece of period nostalgia nor the equally standard album of lovable eccentrics, and it is even more to her credit that she has had the sense and taste not to patronize or exploit the gentle piety that directs the loves of her characters." New Yorker

West, Morris L.

The ambassador. Morrow 1965 275p boards $5.95   **Fic**

1 Vietnamese Conflict, 1961- —Fiction

"A fictionalized facsimile of the U.S. dilemma in Vietnam uses the episode of the assassination of Ngo Dinh Diem as a pattern. The result is a timely dramatization of the failure of the Western mind to grasp the Eastern view of reality. The narrator, the American ambassador Amberley, in telling his own tragic involvement in the happenings shows the religious, political, and national complexities of the situation and brings out American internecine disagreements. A polemic rather than a literary work." Booklist

The Devil's advocate. Morrow 1959 319p $5.95   **Fic**

1 Clergy—Fiction 2 Italy—Fiction

"Monsignor Blaise Meredith of the Vatican is assigned to examine the case of the late Giacomo Nerone, a candidate for sainthood. Meredith's involvement with a variety of villagers, each of whom loved or hated Nerone, not only reveals the truth about the English soldier who altered their lives but gives Meredith a hitherto unexperienced concern and affection for his fellow men. A . . . moving novel." Booklist

"Rarely has the vocation of a priest or the problems of leading a Christian life been explored with such dramatic passion and compassion." Time

The shoes of the fisherman; a novel. Morrow 1963 374p boards $5.95   **Fic**

1 Catholic Church—Fiction 2 Popes—Fiction

"Eloquent and moving novel of the dilemma of a modern man, victim of, and victor over, Communist persecution, elected Pope. The machinery of election, the pomp and circumstance, the loneliness, the fear, and the exaltation of this man, Kiril I, become the heart of a novel. . . . The minor characters, the seamy side of life in Rome are realistically portrayed, but always the main interest of the story centers on Kiril and on his relationship to Kamenev, the Russian premier who had been his persecutor." Library J

"The work is a complex of stories involving a variety of individuals . . . [including] a Jewess who had become a Catholic and then left the church and is now recovering from a breakdown; and a homosexual Roman politician who wants to head his country." Newsweek

Westheimer, David

Von Ryan's Express. Doubleday 1964 327p $4.95   **Fic**

1 World War, 1939-1945—Prisoners and prisons—Fiction 2 Escapes—Fiction

"A thousand British and American soldiers in a prisoner-of-war camp in Italy are augmented by one American colonel who outranks them all and whose strict discipline in bringing order into the camp earns him the Prussian title 'von.' When Italy surrenders and the Germans load the men in boxcars to be sent to Germany, Ryan with the assistance of his next in command with much derring-do plus commando tactics takes over the train and carries the men to Switzerland." Booklist

"There is a great deal of killing of the German guards on the train, necessary for the takeover, and readers with queasy stomachs will find some of it much too much for their sensitivities. But the suspense builds, with unforeseen obstacles cropping up and nick-o'-time rescues and diversions about equal, so that it is safe to bet that most will not want to put the novel down until the end." Best Sellers

Wharton, Edith

The age of innocence   **Fic**

1 New York (City)—Fiction

Some editions are:
Modern Lib. $2.95
Scribner $5.95 Introduction by R. W. B. Lewis
Pulitzer Prize, 1921
First published 1920

"The novel gives an excellent picture of New York 'Society' in the 1870's, the age of propriety and inexorable convention, of clan spirit and tribal solidarity in support of prescribed amenities. The author lays bare the destructive powers of social codes when confronted by an exceptional person. A woman who has incurred scandal is loved by a man who has sufficient vision to penetrate the crust of conventionality but has not quite the courage to break with the conventions. . . . Later, when [this man's] children are full grown, he has the satisfaction of seeing them step out freely on the road that had been denied him." Lenrow. Reader's Guide to Prose Fiction

Ethan Frome   **Fic**

Some editions are:
Scribner $6.95 With an introduction by Bernard De Voto
Watts, F. lib. bdg. $7.95 Large type edition. A Keith Jennison book. With an introduction written for this edition
First published 1911 by Scribner

"A grim tale of retribution told in so masterly a manner that the story seems a transcription from real life. The three characters are a discouraged New England farmer, his hypochondriac wife, and a girl who still finds some joy in living." Booklist

"Although not considered representative of Edith Wharton's works, Ethan Frome is probably the best and most popular of her novels. . . . Through the flash-back technique, Edith

Wharton, Edith—*Continued*

Wharton permits us to glimpse the fate of Ethan Frome at the beginning, but we must wait until the end of the book to see how that fate is brought about. Although we know that the story is to have an unhappy ending, the author's crushing use of irony makes the conclusion come as a surprise." Masterpieces of World Literature

The house of mirth; with a foreword by Marcia Davenport. Scribner 1951 329p $5.95
                                Fic

1 New York (City)—Fiction

First published 1905

"The title is ironical, in keeping with this book's implicit criticism of the garish life and shallow ethics of exclusive New York society [of the times]. . . . Lily Bart, the orphaned child of a New York merchant, endowed with beauty, exquisite in physical charm, keen to seize advantages, alert in social crises, calmly prepares campaigns to marry for the power and luxury that money gives, despite the fact that she is impelled toward Lawrence Selden, a lawyer of moderate means, by everything fine in her nature. Relentlessly she is enmeshed in the toils of debt incurred at bridge; in scandal, the price of a trip upon a friend's yacht; and almost in a loveless marriage. . . . Unable to intrigue successfully and the victim of circumstances at every turn, Lily has no other way out save death." Lenrow. Reader's Guide to Prose Fiction

The reef. Scribner 1965 367p $5.95 Fic

1 Americans in France—Fiction 2 France—Fiction

First published 1912 by Appleton. The 1965 edition includes an introduction by Louis Auchincloss

Set in early twentieth-century France, this novel "concerns [the American] Anna's discovery that the man she is about to marry has had an affair with her daughter's governess, whom her stepson wants to marry." Bk Buyer's Guide

According to Louis Auchincloss, this is Miss Wharton's most Jamesian novel

White, Edward Lucas

The unwilling vestal; a tale of Rome under the Caesars. Dutton 1918 317p $5.95 Fic

1 Rome—History—Emperor, 30 B.C.-476 A.D.—Fiction 2 Aurelius Antoninus Marcus, Emperor of Rome—Fiction

"Rome, A.D. 161-191. A story dealing with the time of Marcus Aurelius and his son, Commodus: both figures appear prominently. Illustrates especially the status of the Vestals. The characters converse in modern familiar language—the author insisting on this method of presenting ancient life as fundamentally truer and more illuminating than a more strained or pedantic method." Nield

White, T. H.

The once and future king. Putnam 1958 677p $7.95

1 Arthur, King—Fiction

An omnibus volume of the author's complete story of the Arthurian epic which includes: The sword in the stone (1939); The witch in the wood (1939), under the new title: The Queen of Air and Darkness; The ill-made knight (1940); and The candle in the wind (published for the first time)

"Realistic portrayal of the legendary figures, matter-of-fact treatment of fantasy imaginative interpretation of setting, and an obvious enjoyment in the telling of the tale again characterize the writing." Booklist

Wibberley, Leonard

The mouse on the moon. Morrow 1962 191p boards $5.95 Fic

In this sequel to: The Mouse that roared, entered below "the Duchy of Grand Fenwick, the world's smallest nation, succeeds in a space exploit and, incidentally, picks up enough income to modernize the ducal castle's plumbing and buy a sable coat for the beautiful duchess." Pub W

It is a "wonderful spoof and delicate political satire." Library J

The mouse on Wall Street. Morrow 1969 159p boards $4.95 Fic

This is another story about the Duchy of Grand Fenwick, introduced first in: The mouse that roared, entered below

Gloriana XII, duchess of this fictitious postage stamp sized European country, faces the problem of a surplus of six million dollars. "Since all this cash could ruin the delicate balance of the Fenwickian economy and destroy incentive, Grand Fenwick decides to invest in stocks sold on Wall Street, a near guarantee of how to lose money." Pub W

The mouse that roared. Little 1955 279p boards $5.95 Fic

The tiny Duchy of Grand Fenwick "undertakes to rehabilitate its national economy by declaring war on the U.S., since that nation takes tender care of its defeated enemies. This clever, amusing fantasy . . . tells how the Fenwickian invasion force of 23 longbowmen not only won the war, but seized the newly invented quadium bomb and by virtue of its possession compelled the cessation of the armament race." Booklist

"Along with his beautifully cockeyed humor, his lovely faculty for needle-sharp, ironic jabs delivered where they'll do the most good, and his nice talent for story-telling, Mr. Wibberley has serious things to suggest and he suggests them admirably." San Francisco Chronicle

Wiesel, Elie

Dawn; tr. from the French by Frances Frenaye. Hill & Wang 1961 89p $3.50 Fic

1 Concentration camps—Fiction 2 Palestine—Fiction 3 British in Palestine—Fiction

Original French edition, 1960

"Elisha, an eighteen-year-old Jewish guerrilla in British-controlled Palestine, is ordered to shoot a captured British officer in reprisal for the execution of a Jewish prisoner. During the interminable night before the killing Elisha is haunted by persons from his past, many of whom died in German concentration camps. His horror at killing the Englishman deepens when, just before dawn, he spends some time with the condemned man and sees him not as an enemy but as a man who could be his friend. A very brief but telling indictment of war's tragedy." Booklist

Wilde, Oscar

The picture of Dorian Gray. Modern Lib. 248p $2.95 Fic

First published 1891 in England. Variant title: Dorian Gray

This "novel is a moral preachment against the crimes of soulless hedonism. The story concerns a beautiful youth, Dorian Gray, who has his portrait painted by Basil Hallward, an artist with a flair for the morbid. The portrait proves to have supernatural qualities, and becomes the mirror of its subject's inner life, so that whatever Dorian feels or thinks is reflected in the portrait, Dorian himself retaining his youth and beauty. Through Hallward, Dorian meets Lord Henry Wotton, a cynic and 'bon vivant,' who has mastered all the secret vices. . . . He degenerates still further [and this is recorded in the painting]." Haydn. Thesaurus of Book Digests

Wilder, Thornton

The bridge of San Luis Rey. Harper [1967 c1927] 148p $4.95 Fic

1 Peru—Fiction

Also available in a large type edition for $6.95

First published 1927 by Boni. Awarded Pulitzer Prize, 1928

"One midsummer day nearly two centuries ago an osier bridge built by the Incas collapsed and precipitated five Peruvian travellers into the abyss below. The story is supposed to be a retelling and interweaving of the minute inquiries into the secret lives of the five victims, made by the Franciscan Brother Juniper to prove that here was not a mere accident but rather the culmination of the finite pattern of each life, according to God's plan." Cleveland

Wilder, Thornton—*Continued*

"The essence of Mr. Wilder's book is really the feeling in it; it is a 'notation of the heart' with sympathy. Gaily or sadly, but always with understanding, a belief in the miracle of love runs through it all." Times (London) Lit Sup

The ides of March. Harper 1948 246p $6.95
Fic

1 Caesar, Caius Julius—Fiction 2 Rome—History—Republic, 510-30 B.C.—Fiction

An "historical novel or fantasy which portrays the life of Julius Caesar and some other Romans during the months preceding Caesar's assassination. The narrative device consists of a series of imaginary documents: private letters; entries in journals; and reports of Caesar's secret police. Altho part of the events are historical the author has tampered with history to the extent of transposing some happenings of 62 B.C. to the year 45 B.C." Book Rev Digest

It is "a fascinating book, and while it owes some of its fascination to the period with which it deals, perhaps the most exciting of our history, a great deal of its charm is entirely the author's, who manages to depict with high effectiveness a number of vivid, glowing and powerful personalities." N Y Her Trib Books

Williams, Ben Ames

House divided. Houghton 1947 1514p $14.95
Fic

1 U.S.—History—Civil War—Fiction 2 Virginia—Fiction

"A long narrative about the American Civil War and its effect on the Currain family. As an old Virginia family with plantations in Virginia, and North and South Carolina, and houses in Richmond, the Currains were loyal to the Confederate cause and felt the full impact of the war. General James Longstreet is introduced as a friend of the Currains and his activities and the battles in which he took part are followed in considerable detail. An alleged relationship between the Currains and Abraham Lincoln adds . . . to a story that, in spite of its length, does not flag in interest." Booklist

Wolfe, Thomas

Look homeward, angel; a story of the buried life; with an introduction by Maxwell E. Perkins. Scribner 1957 522p $5.95 **Fic**

1 Family—Fiction

First published 1929

This novel, autobiographical in character, "describes the childhood and youth of Eugene Gant in the town of Altamont, state of Catawba (said to be Asheville, North Carolina) as he grows up, becomes aware of the relations among his family, meets the eccentric people of the town, goes to college, discovers literature and ideas, has his first love affairs, and at last sets out alone on a mystic and romantic 'pilgrimage.'" Benét. The Reader's Encyclopedia

"There is such mammoth appreciation of experience and of living that the intention of the novel cannot be articulated. It comes through to you like fumes or like one supreme mood of courage that you can never forget, and with it all the awe, the defilement and grandeur of actual life." N Y Her Trib Books

Followed by: Of time and the river

Of time and the river. Scribner 1935 912p $10
Fic

Sequel to: Look homeward, angel

"Eugene Gant, youngest son of the family made famous in 'Look homeward, Angel,' takes leave of his mother and sister and starts off for his three years at Harvard. The experiences here, the agonized waiting to hear whether or not his first play is accepted, the years of teaching, his sojourn in England and France, all these form the background against which are thrown all the varied personalities and experiences he encountered, written in equally varied style running the entire range from utter lack of taste to heights of sheer beauty. A work of genius." Wis Lib Bul

"If you look for a plot, a story in the usual sense in 'Of Time and the River' you will not find it; but you will find a hundred stories and five years of life, richly experienced, deeply felt, minutely and lyrically recorded." N Y Her Trib Books

The web and the rock. Harper 1939 695p $8.95
Fic

"This novel marks not only a turning away from the books I have written in the past, but a genuine spiritual and artistic change. It is the most objective novel that I have written. I have invented characters who are compacted from the whole amalgam and consonance of seeing, feeling, thinking, loving, and knowing many people. I have sought, through free creation, a release of my inventive power." The Author

"In fictional form, but probably based on Wolfe's own life, it is the story of one George Webber—his youth in a Southern town, his college days, his teaching, trip abroad, and his unhappy love affair. Thru the whole book runs the account of George's unsuccessful quest for an understanding of the meaning of life." Book Rev Digest

Followed by: You can't go home again

You can't go home again. Harper 1940 743p $7.50, lib. bdg. $6.11
Fic

Sequel to: The web and the rock

A novel of life in America and Europe, which continues "the story of George Webber from the late nineteen twenties to the middle thirties. The book is divided into several sections, dealing respectively with Webber's experiences as a home-town visiting author, a traveler in England, and a sojourner in Germany during the early Nazi years there." Book Rev Digest

"Excellent characterizations; the book shows the same evidences of genius as are found in his other works." Booklist

Wolff, Ruth

A crack in the sidewalk; a novel. Day 1965 281p boards $6.50 **Fic**

1 Family—Fiction 2 Singers—Fiction

"As young Linsey Templeton narrates her story, the Templeton family comes to life—her tubercular, Bible-strict father, her mother who lives vicariously through the lives of others, her beautiful older sister, and the younger children including mentally retarded Pleas. Living on the second floor of a drab building surrounded by cement Linsey dreams of a better life and finds the means through her lovely voice by becoming a folk singer." Booklist

Wouk, Herman

The Caine mutiny; a novel of World War II. Doubleday 1951 494p $6.95 **Fic**

1 U.S. Navy—Fiction 2 World War, 1939-1945—Fiction

Awarded Pulitzer Prize, 1952

"One of the best naval yarns of World War II is this story of the old American destroyer 'Caine' and the men who sailed in her. The action shifts from the bridge to the wardroom and from scenes of petty tyranny to fierce action and heroism. From the time Ensign Willie Keith comes aboard, on through the mutiny and the trial of the paranoiac Captain Queeg it is a novel of action, character development and intrigue." Ontario Lib Rev

"There is a romance in his new novel that might fit in with some of his previous writing, but the Navy material is something else again. Mr. Wouk has a profound understanding of what Navy men should be, and against some who fell short of the mark he has fired a deadly broadside." N Y Times Bk R

City boy; the adventures of Herbie Bookbinder. 20th anniversary ed. Doubleday 1969 317p $5.95
Fic

1 New York (City)—Fiction

First published 1948 by Simon & Schuster

"Story of an eleven-year-old boy plagued by the troubles of his age: bullies, first loves and frustrations, camp life, etc. The humor of the story is relieved by some sharp gibes at the adults who further complicate Herbie's life." Retail Bookseller

Wren, Percival Christopher
Beau Geste; with illus. by Helen McKie.
Lippincott 1927 579p illus $5.95   **Fic**
1 Africa—Fiction 2 France. Army. Foreign Legion—Fiction

First published by Stokes
A suspense story, turning on the disappearance of a valuable gem, which eventually causes three English brothers to enlist in the Foreign Legion in Northern Africa. It includes adventures, mysteries, and thrills in full measure, with descriptions of life in the Foreign Legion

"The behavior of the three Gestes from first to last was nobly idiotic. But the author's knowledge of the North African terrain, its inhabitants and customs, is extensive and colorful and bears the stamp of accuracy." N Y Her Trib Books

Wright, Richard
Native son; with an introduction: "How 'Bigger' was born," by the author. Harper [1969 c1940] xxxiv, 392p $7.50   **Fic**
1 Negroes—Fiction 2 Crime and criminals—Fiction 3 Chicago—Race relations—Fiction

Reissue of title first published 1940
"In this story of a frustrated, inarticulate Chicago Negro whose bewildered resentment of life can only be expressed by violence and murder, there is a melodrama as well as stark realism, but above all there is unusual power, an understanding of Negro psychology, and compassion that never becomes special pleading. It is a disturbing book, and it will horrify many readers, not only by its frank brutalities, but by the menace that is implied in its revelation of Negro misery and degradation." Booklist

"As a Southerner I may be suspect, but I think this book is better as a headlong, hard-boiled narrative than as any preaching about race relations in America, North or South. Certainly no sensible Southerner will deny the authenticity of Mr. Wright's picture of the plight of his race. But not only Negro boys in pool rooms and slums in Chicago feel caught and find a distorted manhood in violence. The rules of an insensitive world may be more binding, more hope-denying among them. But every order creates its rats and rebels and every civilization—so far in existence—deserves them." Sat R

Zindel, Paul
I never loved your mind; a novel. Harper 1970 181p $3.95, lib. bdg. $3.79   **Fic**
The author "explores the relationship between two teen-agers working in a hospital—two bright, zany, and lost high-school dropouts, who can't find what they want together, and who can't stop trying to find something important in a world they think is unbearable." Publisher's note

"Dewey's sincerity and openness to people are contrasted with Yvette's pseudo-idealism and cynicism, but the irritating self-consciousness of his narrative strains reader empathy for both characters. . . . Still, flawed as this book is, it makes better reading than most simply because Zindel is a more technically proficient writer than most producing novels for post-child, pre-adult readers." Library J

S C   STORY COLLECTIONS

Books in this class contain both collections of short stories by one author and collections by more than one author. Those revolving around one character are classed with Fiction. Folklore is in class 398 and its subdivisions. General literature collections are in class 808.8

Abrahams, William
(ed.) Fifty years of the American short story; from the O. Henry Awards, 1919-1970; ed. and with an introduction by William Abrahams. Doubleday 1970 2v $14.95   **S C**
1 Short stories

"For half a century . . . editors have made annual picks of the 'best' short stories to appear in this country and published them as the O. Henry Awards. . . . The 50 collections contained 889 stories by 569 authors: The present collection contains 60 stories by 53 authors. [The editor's] criterion was not relevance or timeliness, he says, but excellence—that is, literary and affective qualities. All the 889 stories he re-examined are listed alphabetically by author—the same order he follows in his present selections." N Y Times Bk R

Akutagawa, Ryūnosuke
Japanese short stories; tr. by Takashi Kojima; introduction by John McVittie; with very unusual illus. by Masakazu Kuwata. Liveright 1961 224p illus $5.95   **S C**
1 Japan—Fiction 2 Short stories

Contents: The hell screen; A clod of soil; "Nezumi-Kozo"—the Japanese Robin Hood; Heichu, the amorous genius; Genkaku-Sanbo; Otomi's virginity; The spider's thread; The nose; The tangerines; The story of Yonosuke

Anderson, Sherwood
Winesburg, Ohio   **S C**
1 Short stories

Some editions are:
Modern Lib. $2.95 Introduction to Ernest Boyd. Has subtitle: A group of tales of Ohio small-town life
Viking $5.95 Introduction by Malcolm Cowley
First published 1919 by Huebsch
"A portrait gallery of the frustrated men and women of a small town at the end of the last century." Good Reading

Asimov, Isaac
Asimov's mysteries. Doubleday 1968 228p (Doubleday Science fiction) $5.95   **S C**
1 Science fiction 2 Short stories

"Culled from Asimov's prodigious output in the science-fiction genre are these [14] stories which include elements of crime and detection. The backdrops are scientific and often planetary, with the added elements of Who did it? or How? . . . The mysteries include a murder in a library, a goose which lays a golden egg, and a strange device missing on the lunar surface. Particularly engaging is the author's candor, most evident in Forewords and Afterwords." Horn Bk

I, robot. Doubleday 1963 [c1950] 218p $4.95   **S C**
1 Robots 2 Science fiction 3 Short stories
First published 1950 by Gnome Press
The book contains nine related stories about robots

Nightfall, and other stories. Doubleday 1969 343p (Doubleday Science fiction) $6.95   **S C**
1 Science fiction 2 Short stories
Here are 20 of the author's science fiction "stories, selected by him as some he thinks are his best and a few he thinks deserve a second chance, arranged in the order of their original publication. There is a uniformity of excellence in the author's work." Pub W

Nine tomorrows; tales of the near future. Doubleday 1959 236p $4.95   **S C**
1 Science fiction 2 Short stories
A collection of "nine short stories that combine pointed social satire with intriguing scientific theory." Booklist

(ed.) Where do we go from here? Doubleday 1971 441p $6.95   **S C**
1 Science fiction 2 Short stories
"There are 17 first-rate science fiction stories in this collection, by writers like Arthur Clarke, Hal Clement, James Gunn, and Lester del Rey, but Isaac Asimov has designed the anthology for readers who want some facts with their fiction. In a commentary following each story he explains how good the author's science is or how consistently a purely hypothetical tale is

Asimov, Isaac—*Continued*
developed, and he asks questions about the story to prod the reader's curiosity and imagination. Among the themes: man's knowledge of Mars (dated 1934), the possibility or unlikelihood of neutron stars, the mysteries of moon dust, the biology of microorganisms, isotopes, and the Moebius strip." Pub W

Baldwin, James
Going to meet the man. Dial Press 1965 294p $4.95
S C
1 Negroes—Fiction 2 Short stories
"Eight stories that, with the exception of an expatriate's experiences, focus on American Negroes in their home environment." Booklist

The **Best** American short stories, 1964-1971; & the Yearbook of the American short story; ed. by Martha Foley and David Burnett. Houghton 1964-1971 7v 1964-1965 ea $5.95; 1966 $6.95; 1967 $6; 1969-1970 ea $6.95; 1971 $7.50
S C
1 Short stories
An annual collection of the best short stories written by American writers (from the United States and Canada) that have appeared in magazines are included in these anthologies.
"All collections of The Best American Short Stories have been pretty eclectic, so varied are the kinds of short stories Americans write. As far as I can determine, there seems to be no one predominant aspect to those in this volume except that they are all exceedingly well written." Foreword to 1970 edition

Best detective stories of the year; 22d, 24th-25th annual collection. . . . Dutton 1967, 1970-1971 3v 1967 $4.50, 1970-1971 ea $5.95
S C
1 Mystery and detective stories 2 Short stories
Editors: 1967: Anthony Boucher; 1970-1971 Allen J. Hunin. The 23d annual collection is o.p. 1971
"Like its precursors in this series [it] contains not only detective stories but examples of many of the types of the fiction of crime and suspense . . . pure formal detection, private-eye capers, espionage, police procedure, and an unusually fine serious study of the murderer-victim relationship. But a number of these stories . . . take a most unserious view of the serious matters of crime and death." Introduction [to 22d edition]

The **Best** from Fantasy and Science Fiction; 19th ser. ed. by Edward L. Ferman. Doubleday 1971 286p illus $5.95
S C
1 Science fiction 2 Short stories
This anthology includes six cartoons by Gahan Wilson and fifteen stories from The Magazine of Fantasy and Science Fiction, by such authors as Avram Davidson, Robert Silverberg, Charles W. Runyon and Bruce McAllister

Borges, Jorge Luis
The Aleph, and other stories, 1933-1969; together with commentaries and an autobiographical essay; ed. and tr. by Norman Thomas di Giovanni in collaboration with the author. Dutton 1970 286p $7.95
S C
1 Short stories
SBN 0-525-05154-6
This selection of twenty stories covers the author's forty-year career as a short story writer. Eleven of the stories have never before appeared in book form in English. (Publisher)
The author's "theme in this collection is almost always the same: two men confront one another as enemies, only to find at the last moment that they are the same man." Christian Science Monitor

Bradbury, Ray
I sing the Body Electric! Stories. Knopf 1969 305p $6.95
S C
1 Science fiction 2 Short stories
In these seventeen stories and one poem, the author "conducts the reader on a tour through time and space—into the unbounded dimensions of the future, and through remapped patterns of the past—as he intermingles the bizarre with the familiar and brings tomorrow and yesterday closer to today." Publisher's note
"All of the stories are 100-proof Bradbury which means that all will be wanted by Bradbury buffs. For those unfortunates as yet unfamiliar with his work this collection is a perfect introduction to a continually interesting and unusual storyteller." Library J

The illustrated man. Doubleday 1951 251p $5.95
S C
1 Science fiction 2 Short stories
"A tattooed man, whose pictures come to life at night and act out their stories, is made the vehicle for [eighteen] science-fiction tales —of a nursery room whose walls change at the whim of precocious children; of an unknown planet just visited by Christ; of the last white men's petition to be accepted on a Negro planet [etc]." Retail Bookseller

The Martian chronicles; prefatory note by Clifton Fadiman. Doubleday 1958 222p $4.95
S C
1 Science fiction 2 Short stories
A reprint with a prefatory note by Clifton Fadiman of the title first published 1950
"Connected episodes on the settlement and abandonment of Mars during the 21st century." Retail Bookseller

R is for rocket. Doubleday 1962 233p $3.95
S C
1 Science fiction 2 Short stories
"Space cadets, sea serpents, solar energy, life on Venus and Mars, rockets, time travel, and people are some of the subjects of these 17 short stories, reprinted from magazines and other anthologies." Library J

Buck, Pearl S.
The good deed, and other stories of Asia, past and present. Day 1969 254p $6.95 S C
1 Asia—Fiction 2 Short stories
"Ten different short stories displaying different insights into life among the Asian peoples, ranging in time and in theme from World War II to the present, from the grimness of war to blithe young romance. . . . Many of the tales are frankly sentimental, but in the last one, dealing with a Hindu student at Harvard who is summoned home to conduct the rituals of his father's burial ghat burning, Pearl Buck's writing is at its most realistic, sharply contrasting the ways of old and new." Pub W

Camus, Albert
Nobel Prize in literature, 1957
Exile and the kingdom; tr. from the French by Justin O'Brien. Knopf 1958 213p boards $4.50
S C
1 Africa, North—Fiction 2 Short stories
Original French edition published 1957
"Discipline of thought and style characterize six short stories by a noted French author-philosopher. The distinguishing marks of locales ranging from North Africa to Brazil are etched with telling detail, but it is the landscape of man's inner life which is most important here. The diverse protagonists—and it is intimated all men—are exiled from themselves, others, and the life of the spirit, but now and again a word or an action renews their courage to continue the pilgrimage." Booklist

Capote, Truman
Breakfast at Tiffany's; a short novel and three stories. Random House 1958 179p $4.95
S C
1 Short stories

Capote, Truman—*Continued.*

"The novella which gives the book its title is the tale of a Manhattan playgirl, Holly Golightly. Completing the volume are three short stories: House of Flowers, A Diamond Guitar, and A Christmas Memory." Book Rev Digest

Cather, Willa

Willa Cather's Collected short fiction, 1892-1912; introduction by Mildred R. Bennett. Univ. of Neb. Press 1965 3v in 1 (xli, 594p) $8.50   S C

1 Short stories

"An anthology of forty-four stories, seventeen of them previously uncollected traces the road Willa Cather traveled from her earliest fiction experiments up to O Pioneers." McClurg. Book News

Includes bibliographies

Chekhov, Anton

The image of Chekhov; forty stories in the order in which they were written. Newly tr. and with an introduction, by Robert Payne. Knopf 1963 xxxvii, 344p front $6.95   S C

1 Russia—Fiction 2 Short stories

These translations have been made from the twelve-volume edition of Chekhov's Collected works, edited by W. W. Yermilov and published in Moscow, 1950

"Payne has written an introductory essay on Chekhov's life and writings, including critical comments on many of the stories included in this volume. As a translator Payne has had his difficulties with Chekhov's idiomatic nineteenth-century Russian, but the effect is generally fresh and has a comparatively modern tone." Booklist

The stories of Anton Tchekov; ed. with an introduction by Robert N. Linscott. Modern Lib. [1959 c1932] 448p $2.95   S C

1 Russia—Fiction 2 Short stories

A reissue of a title first published 1932

"The number and excellence of Chekhov's maturer stories precludes a completely satisfying collection within the bounds of a single volume, particularly as some of the best . . . are almost of novel length." p x

Chesterton, G. K.

The Father Brown omnibus. . . . [New and rev. ed] Dodd 1951 993p $6   S C

1 Mystery and detctive stories 2 Short stories

First published in omnibus form 1933

"Including The innocence of Father Brown, The incredulity of Father Brown, The scandal of Father Brown, The wisdom of Father Brown, The secret of Father Brown, The vampire of the village [short story]" Subtitle

"Here is every Father Brown story Chesterton wrote—a cycle of fifty or more—stories previously published in five separate volumes. It [also] . . . contains an interesting introduction about the origin of Father Brown and his significant role in detective story literature." Huntting

Chute, B. J.

One touch of nature, and other stories. Dutton 1965 250p front boards $4.95   S C

1 Short stories

"Though varied in mood the [thirteen] stories are all positive in approach and concerned mainly with the significance of everyday events, relationships between human beings, and moments of crisis or self-discovery in the lives of ordinary people. Despite their conventional form . . . they reveal a high degree of perceptivity." Booklist

"Miss Chute is an accomplished craftsman and storyteller in all her work. She writes sensitively, aware that illumination of the significance of quietly dramatic moments is one of the purposes fiction serves best. She is adroit in the choice of words, has a fine appreciation of sentence rhythms and the color of speech." Sat R

Clarke, John Henrik

(ed.) American Negro short stories. Hill & Wang 1966 355p $5.95   S C

1 Negroes—Fiction 2 Short stories

"These 31 stories written by and about Negro Americans present their problems, hopes, sorrows, tragedies and humour. Outstanding writers such as James Baldwin, Richard Wright, Langston Hughes and Arna Bontemps are represented. . . . A true picture of Negro American life [is] presented honestly and with little bitterness." Bruno. Books for School Libraries, 1968

Conklin, Groff

(ed.) Invaders of earth. Vanguard 1952 333p $5.95   S C

1 Science fiction 2 Short stories

"Twenty-one science-fiction stories, all of invasions of this planet from outer space . . . [including] the full script of the sensational Orson Welles' broadcast of 'Invasion from Mars.' " Retail Bookseller

Costain, Thomas B.

(ed.) Read with me. Doubleday 1965 623p $6.50   S C

1 Short stories

An "anthology of the editor's favorite short stories, selected from the work of 31 distinguished authors. . . . A brief commentary by the editor introduces each writer." Booklist

Crane, Stephen

The complete short stories & sketches of Stephen Crane; ed. with an introduction by Thomas A. Gullason. Doubleday 1963 790p $7.95   S C

1 Short stories

A "collection and arrangement of all of Crane's short stories, his literary essays, and journalistic sketches and features. A 14-page preface makes significant comment on the works, cites other sources of criticism, and gives Mr. Gullason's reasons for the near-chronological arrangement of the selections. [In] a 27-page introduction . . . he shows how the author's family background and subsequent rebellion and riotous life influenced his works." Library J

Day, A. Grove

(ed.) The greatest American short stories; twenty classics of our heritage. McGraw 1953 359p $5.95   S C

1 Short stories

"Editor Day chose these twenty short stories by such authors as Hawthorne, Poe, Bierce, Steinbeck Cather, O. Henry, Faulkner, and other great narrators to illustrate the development of the short story in America. An introductory essay and brief critiques add value." Cincinnati

Dinesen, Isak

Seven Gothic tales; with an introduction by Dorothy Canfield. Modern Lib. 1961 420p $2.95   S C

1 Short stories

First published 1934 by H. Smith and R. Haas

"These tales are a modern refinement of German romanticism. . . . They are peopled, or haunted, by ghosts of a past age, voluptuaries dreaming of the singers and ballerinas of the operas of Mozart and Gluck, young men who are melancholy to enjoy love or too perverse to profit by it, maidens dedicated to chastity and others hopeful of a gentlemanly seduction; their generally fantastic adventures are exquisitely played, with punctilious attention to the rules of the game." N Y Times Bk R

Doyle, Adrian C.

The exploits of Sherlock Holmes, by Adrian C. Doyle and John Dickson Carr. Random House 1954 338p $4.95   S C

1 Mystery and detective stories 2 Short stories

"Twelve reconstructions of Sherlock Holmes tales each of which takes its beginning from a reference to the case in an old Sherlock Holmes." Book Rev Digest

"Not all the king's horses could persuade me to say that these uncanonical tales compete successfully with the authentic adventures of Sherlock Holmes; but no Sherlockian should dismiss them without a reading." Chicago Sunday Tribune

Doyle, Sir Arthur Conan

The complete Sherlock Holmes; with a preface by Christopher Morley. Doubleday 1953 [c1930] 2v (1323p) illus $12.50   S C

1 Mystery and detective stories 2 Short stories

Also available in a one-volume edition for $7.95

First published 1930

Fifty-eight Sherlock Holmes stories which were originally published in nine separate volumes: A study in scarlet (1887); The sign of the four (1890); Adventures of Sherlock Holmes (1892); Memoirs of Sherlock Holmes (1894); The Return of Sherlock Holmes (1905); The hound of the Baskervilles (1902); The valley of fear (1915); His last bow (1917); The case book of Sherlock Holmes (1927)

Sherlock Holmes' greatest cases; introduction by Howard Haycraft. Large type ed. complete and unabridged. Watts, F. [1967] 463p $9.95   S C

1 Mystery and detective stories 2 Large type books 3 Short stories

"A Keith Jennison book"

"A few years ago the Baker Street Irregulars conducted a combined contest and poll to determine . . . the 'best' Sherlock Holmes tales, by pro and con vote. There were two ballots, one consisting of the four Sherlock Holmes novels, the other of the fifty-six short stories. When the returns were in, 'The Hound of the Baskervilles'—which opens the present volume —placed first among the novels. . . . [The top stories were:] 'The Adventure of the Speckled Band, The Red-Headed League, The Adventure of the Blue Carbuncle, Silver Blaze, A Scandal in Bohemia and The Musgrave Ritual.' These also have been included in the present volume."
Introduction

Bibliographical material included in Introduction

Dulles, Allen

(ed.) Great spy stories from fiction. Harper 1969 433p $6.95   S C

1 Spies—Fiction 2 Short stories

"A Giniger book"

A collection of thirty-two examples of spy stories by such writers as Leon Uris, Joseph Conrad, A. Conan Doyle, Vladimir Nabokov, John Le Carré and Ian Fleming. Some of the stories are based on historical fact or persons; others demonstrate current practices in spying

Faulkner, William

Nobel Prize in literature, 1949

Collected stories of William Faulkner. Random House 1950 900p $7.95   S C

1 Short stories

"Forty-two short stories, including all from These Thirteen (1931), all but two from Doctor Martino and Other Stories (1934) and seventeen published in magazines, 1932-1948, for the first time printed in book form. They have been arranged here under headings (The Country, The Village, The Wilderness, etc.) which present Faulkner as a chronicler of the South; many of the stories deal with characters and incidents related to those in his novels set in the mythical Yoknapatawpha County, Mississippi." Library J

"The final impression left by Faulkner's work is that he is a writer of incomparable talents who has used and misused those talents superbly and recklessly. But his book has the excitement that comes from never knowing when, amidst pages of failure, there will come a masterpiece." Time

The Faulkner reader; selections from the works of William Faulkner. Modern Lib. 1959 682p $4.95   S C

1 Short stories

"Modern Library giant"

A reprint of the title first published 1954 by Random House

This omnibus volume contains short stories; excerpts from the author's longer works and The sound and the fury, entered in Fiction class

The portable Faulkner; rev. and expanded edition. Ed. by Malcolm Cowley. Viking 1967 xxxvii, 724p map $6.50   S C

1 Short stories

"The Viking Portable library"

First published 1946

This collection contains "four of Faulkner's stories dealing with early days in Yoknapatawpha Country; with the Indians, the first white settlers, and the McCaslin plantation. Brief critical and historical notes precede each section; useful appendix of characters." Bruno. Books for School Libraries, 1968

Selected short stories of William Faulkner. Modern Lib. 1961 306p $2.95   S C

1 Short stories

A variety of the author's output, diverse in method and subject matter, ranging in original publication dates from 1930 to 1955

Contents: Barn burning; Two soldiers; A rose for Emily; Dry September; That evening sun; Red leaves; Lo; Turnabout; Honor; There was a queen; Mountain victory; Beyond; Race at morning

Fitzgerald, F. Scott

The Fitzgerald reader; ed. by Arthur Mizener. Scribner 1963 xxvii, 509p boards $8.95   S C

1 Short stories

This representative selection of Scott Fitzgerald's work "includes the whole of his best novel, 'The Great Gatsby,' and considerable parts of his other two important novels, 'Tender Is the Night' and 'The Last Tycoon.' It also includes two novelettes ('May Day' and 'The Rich Boy'), the four or five best short stories from each period of his career, and his four most famous essays." Foreword

"Mizener's penetrating introduction reveals four distinct periods in Fitzgerald's writing, periods around which the selections are organized. Of particular value as an overview or introduction to Fitzgerald." Booklist

The stories of F. Scott Fitzgerald; a selection of 28 stories with an introduction by Malcolm Cowley. Scribner 1951 xxv, 473p $6.95   S C

1 Short stories

"The first selected edition of Fitzgerald's stories. There are twenty-eight stories, of which eighteen were first published in four different books; the remaining ten have not been collected before." Book Rev Digest

"At his best, Fitzgerald was an immensely suggestive writer, a wizard with the language, and—a point that is usually overlooked—a fine humorist." Commonweal

Foley, Martha

(ed.) Fifty best American short stories, 1915-1965. Houghton 1965 814p $12.50   S C

1 Short stories

Supersedes the collection: The Best of the Best American short stories, 1915-1950

A chronological collection "selected from the outstanding hundreds which have appeared in the annual volumes of 'The Best American Short Stories' [anthologies] from 1915 to 1965." McClurg. Book News

Forester, C. S.

Gold from Crete; 10 stories. Little 1970 263p boards $5.95   **S C**

1 World War, 1939-1945—Fiction 2 Short stories

Collected in book form for the first time. "These 10 stories depict the courage, self-sacrifice, and cool resourcefulness of Allied fighting men engaged in the all-out struggle against Nazi Germany." Booklist

Garrity, Devin A.

(ed.) 44 Irish short stories; an anthology of Irish short fiction from Yeats to Frank O'Connor. Devin-Adair 1955 500p boards $6.95   **S C**

1 Short stories

"From Wilde to newcomer James Plunkett, the shanachies are here—Joyce, Stephens, O'Faolain, and the rest, all except MacManus and Colum. Compositely they have portrayed Ireland's everyman, impossible and irresistible heir of an ancient race that lived by dreams when there was no bread. More sensitively and richly than the social historians they have shown forth the way of the Gael." Sat R

Godden, Rumer

Gone; a thread of stories. Viking 1968 213p boards $4.95   **S C**

1 Short stories

These twelve "rare strands of fiction are unravelings from the two-world life of the author, some set in India, some in England. Loss, partings, and days past create the title 'Gone' because each story is 'founded on a moment of experience, felt or seen or touched, that has long since gone, but that has left a small sediment or shape behind.' Included are a young girl who unwittingly gives her uncle a book of erotica as a Christmas gift, another girl who doggedly resists family pressure and becomes a nun, and an American boy who dies because he believes in Indians." Horn Bk

Harte, Bret

The best of Bret Harte; selected by Wilhelmina Harper and Aimée M. Peters; illus. by Paul Brown. Houghton 1947 434p illus $5.95   **S C**

1 Short stories

Eighteen "selections, mostly short stories, which were judged the most characteristic of Bret Harte's writings." Booklist

"It's a good collection, in which you will find almost anything you want to run down in Harte's shorter tales." San Francisco Chronicle

The best short stories of Bret Harte; ed. and with an introduction by Robert N. Linscott. Modern Lib. 1947 517p $2.95   **S C**

1 Short stories

In selecting a group of stories representative of the author's work, the editor has included both the most famous and less well-known tales. They are set in the golden days of early California and portray the life of the mining camp, the barrooms and gambling halls

Havighurst, Walter

(ed.) Masters of the modern short story. 2d ed. Harcourt 1955 453p $7.95   **S C**

1 Short stories

First published 1945

"This anthology of 24 short stories by the foremost writers of fiction of our time has the purpose of showing what writers have accomplished in this era with a form of writing which appears to be as old as literature itself." Springf'd Republican

Hawthorne, Nathaniel

Hawthorne's Short stories   **S C**

1 Short stories

Some editions are:

Dodd (Great illustrated classics) $4.50 With sixteen full-page illustrations of Nathaniel Hawthorne, his environment and the setting of the stories, together with an introduction by Louis B. Salomon

Knopf $5.95 Edited and with an introduction by Newton Arvin

Twenty-nine selections from Twice-told tales, Mosses from an old manse, and The snow image

Hawthorne's "stories, to be sure, have an old-fashioned ring to the ear that listens to the loud and obvious notes only, but at their core they deal with the timeless issues of human experience. . . . Handle these stories carefully. Their edges, though concealed, are sharp and they cut more ways than one." Introduction to Dodd edition

Haycraft, Howard

(ed.) A treasury of great mysteries [by] Agatha Christie [and others]; ed. by Howard Haycraft and John Beecroft. Doubleday [1969 c1957] 2v $7.95   **S C**

1 Mystery and detective stories 2 Short stories

This anthology first published 1957 by Simon & Schuster

Contains 10 short stories, 5 novelettes and the following novels in full: Murder in the Calais coach (1933) by A. Christie; Journey into fear (1940) by E. Ambler; The big sleep (1939) by R. Chandler; Rebecca (1938) by D. Du Maurier, entered separately in Fiction class

Heinlein, Robert A.

Robert A. Heinlein's The past through tomorrow; "future history" stories. Putnam 1967 667p $6.95   **S C**

1 Science fiction 2 Short stories

"Arranged chronologically by time of happening these [twenty-one] adventurous science fiction stories, including the novel' Methuselah's children,' show Heinlein's ideas of possible technological and social developments." Booklist

Hemingway, Ernest

Nobel Prize in literature, 1954

In our time; stories. Scribner 1930 212p $4.50   **S C**

1 Short stories

"With a striking economy of words Mr Hemingway secures his most telling effects. Several of these 'stories' picture episodes in the life of a growing boy in the timber country of the Middle West." Book Rev Digest

"Of 'stories' in the commonly accepted sense of the word there are few; the best of the lot a beautifully executed tale of the racetracks which Mr. Anderson himself could not have bettered. Most of the others are psychological episodes, incidents, sketches . . . call them what you will. They are soundly and movingly done; Mr. Hemingway uses the vernacular with skill. In the curious brief pieces scattered through his pages he does remarkable things with a mere handful of words." Literary Rev

The short stories of Ernest Hemingway. Scribner 1953 499p $8.95   **S C**

1 Short stories

This collection originally published 1938 with title: The fifth column [play] and the first forty-nine stories

"I don't see how you can go through this book without being convinced that Hemingway is the best short-story writer . . . using English." New Yorker

The snows of Kilimanjaro, and other stories. Scribner 1961 154p $4.95   **S C**

1 Short stories

Hemingway, Ernest—*Continued*

First copyright 1927

A sampling of the work of an author whose prose style influenced and continues to influence generations of American writers. Included are such famous stories as: A clean, well-lighted place; The killers and Fifty grand

Henry, O.

The best short stories of O. Henry; selected and with an introduction by Bennett A. Cerf and Van H. Cartmell. Modern Lib. 1945 338p $2.95   S C

1 Short stories

"This varied collection was written by the master of the surprise ending [and contains 38 stories]." Books for You

The complete works of O. Henry; foreword by Harry Hansen. Doubleday 1953 1692p front $8.95   S C

1 Short stories

Also available in two volumes for $15

"All of O. Henry's short stories together with selected and random pieces, are contained [in these volumes]. Included are unabridged versions of [previously published volumes] 'The Four Million,' 'The Heart of the West,' 'The Gentle Grafter,' 'Roads of Destiny,' 'Cabbages and Kings,' 'Options,' 'Sixes and sevens,' 'Rolling Stones,' 'Whirligigs' 'The Voice of the City,' 'Trimmed lamp,' 'Strictly Business' and 'Waifs and Strays.'" Huntting

The four million. Doubleday 261p $3.95   S C

1 New York (City)—Fiction 2 Short stories

First published 1906 by McClure, Phillips

"Original sketches of New York city life, showing an acquaintance with its seamy as well as its Bohemian side." A. L. A. 1904-11

Hesse, Hermann

Nobel Prize in literature, 1946

Klingsor's last summer; tr. by Richard and Clara Winston. Farrar, Staus 1970 217p $6.50   S C

1 Short stories
SBN 374-1-8166-7

"Originally published in 1920, this is the first publication in English of these three novellas. . . . Each story explores the meaning of life, death and guilt by concentrating on a brief period of intense emotional turmoil in each of three sensitive individuals. In 'A Child's Heart,' the character is a boy of 11. It is a prudent middle-class civil servant turned thief and fugitive in 'Klein and Wagner,' and an exuberant avant garde expressionist painter in 'Klingsor's Last Summer.'" Pub W

Hitchcock, Alfred

(ed.) Alfred Hitchcock presents: A month of mystery. Random House 1969 428p $6.95   S C

1 Mystery and detective stories 2 Short stories

This anthology of horror and mystery tales "consists of 31 stories, some by well-known authors, others by those whose names are less familiar. The material is rationed out as 'A Week of Crime.' 'A Week of Suspense,' 'A Week of Detection,' 'A Week of the Macaber,' and 'A Short Week of Long Ones.' . . . [The contributors] know how to keep you guessing and in a state of considerable nervous excitement." Pub W

Hughes, Langston

(ed.) The best short stories by Negro writers; an anthology from 1899 to the present; ed. and with an introduction by Langston Hughes. Little 1967 508p $8.95   S C

1 Short stories

Forty-seven stories ranging "in locale from the Caribbean to Chicago, New York, California, the deep South. Whether the subject is a Southern sheriff or a Harlem dancer, a sharecropper or a politician, Mr. Hughes has chosen stories that move, amuse, surprise. Some are complex, some not, but all are good reading. Langston Hughes raises some interesting questions about the scope of the Negro writer in his introduction. Brief biographies of the authors are included." Pub W

Fourteen of these stories are published for the first time in this volume. Among the authors represented are Charles W. Chesnutt; Paul Laurence Dunbar; Zora Neale Hurston; Richard Wright; Willard Motley; Ralph Ellison; Frank Yerby; James Baldwin; Ronald Milner; Robert Boles; Alice Walker

Joyce, James

Dubliners   S C

1 Ireland—Fiction 2 Short stories

Some editions are:
Modern Lib. $2.95 Introduction by Padraic Colum
Viking $4.50

First published 1914

"By dealing successively with incidents in the childhood, adolescence, maturity, and public life of Dubliners, Joyce provides a picture of the paralyzing world from which he fled. Most of the characters and scenes are mean and petty, sometimes tragic; they are drawn from ordinary Catholic middle-class life." Bén-ét. The Reader's Encyclopedia

Kafka, Franz

Selected short stories of Franz Kafka; tr. by Willa and Edwin Muir; introduction by Philip Rahv. Modern Lib. 1952 328p $2.95   S C

1 Short stories

"Searching, strikingly [15] original commentaries on modern life presented in terms of grotesque imagery and fantastic symbols." Good Reading

Kipling, Rudyard

Nobel Prize in literature, 1907

The best short stories of Rudyard Kipling; ed. by Randall Jarrell. Hanover House 1961 693p $7.95   S C

1 India—Fiction 2 Short stories

Contains 50 stories including many of the author's stories about India under British rule as well as several animal and adventure tales

Maugham's Choice of Kipling's best; sixteen stories selected and with an introductory essay by W. Somerset Maugham. Doubleday 1953 [c1952] xxviii, 324p $5.50   S C

1 Short stories

First published 1952 in England with title: A choice of Kipling's prose

"In these stories, set mainly in the northwest of India, aswarm with Muslims, soldiers, and colonial administrators, Kipling's genius for description and incident came to fulfillment." Booklist

Lagerkvist, Pär

Nobel Prize in literature, 1951

The eternal smile; three stories. Hill & Wang 1971 206p $5.95   S C

ISBN 0-8090-4309-2

"The stories that make up this book are three of [the author's] most important: 'The Eternal Smile' and 'The Guest of Reality,' both translated by Erik Mesterton and Denys W. Harding, and 'The Executioner,' translated by David O'Gorman." Publisher's note

Lardner, Rex

(ed.) Rex Lardner selects the best of sports fiction, ed. with an introduction by Rex Lardner. Grosset 1966 249p $2.95   S C

1 Sports—Fiction 2 Short stories

"In this collection of sports fiction, sport is approached from many points of view. There are humorous stories of overriding ambition and preoccupation with success, tales of fakery and fixes, a sporting mystery, a glimpse of an intriguing sport of the future, and a saga of sport used as a tool of pride and breadwinning. The sports covered run the gamut from baseball, prizefighting and golf, to hunting, polo and marble-shooting. And more. Many of the authors have illustrious names. Some are more noted for their writing in other areas. . . . It is hoped that these [12] stories will provide solid mental nourishment and some chuckles for anyone who has enjoyed the zest of competitive sport and is also a student of human frailty." Introduction

Lardner, Ring

The best short stories of Ring Lardner. Scribner 1957 346p $4.50   S C

1 Short stories

"A selection of twenty-five stories by one of the most original figures in American literature, the colorful personality who was noted as a sports writer, humorist and columnist, as well as short-story writer." N Y Her Trib Books

The Ring Lardner reader; ed. by Maxwell Geismar. Scribner 1963 xxxiv, 661p $7.50 S C

This book is divided into six parts to show the dominant themes in Lardner's work (stories, plays, etc.) and to describe the social development of the period in which he lived. These parts are: Provincial life; On the make; Success story, U.S.A.; Little tales of Suburbia; The popular arts; Native dada

"The bulk of his work stands up remarkably well. Geismar has written an informative introductory essay. This work will probably remain the standard collection for a number of years to come." Library J

Ring Lardner: bibliography: p[663]

Lederer, William J.

The ugly American [by] William J. Lederer and Eugene Burdick. Norton 1958 285p $4.95   S C

1 U.S.—Diplomatic and consular service—Fiction 2 East (Far East)—Fiction 3 Short stories

"A 'fictional' account of actual happenings in the East concerning American diplomatic policy. Readable stories with obvious morals. A factual chapter of hints for students who wish to be diplomats is added." Ontario Lib Rev

This "is a fiery indictment of the kind of American abroad who misrepresents America. . . . Fortunately, these characters are balanced by the kind of American who does good service for our ideas." Horn Bk

Lessing, Doris

African stories. Simon & Schuster 1965 636p boards $7.95   S C

1 Africa—Fiction 2 Short stories

An assemblage of the author's "African-inspired short and longer stories . . . from several earlier collections including some never printed in the U.S. The author's firsthand knowledge of Africa from her 25-year sojourn there and her discontent with white society and its scorn or abuse of black Africa lend sharpness and intensity to tales which taken together reflect myriad aspects of African existence." Booklist

London, Jack

Best short stories of Jack London. Garden City Bks. 1953 [c1945] 311p $4.95   S C

1 Short stories

First published 1945 by Sun Dial

"Stories of action, violence, and atmosphere, set from the Far North to the South Seas." Good Reading

Jack London's Tales of adventure; ed. by Irving Shepard. Doubleday 1956 531p illus $6.95   S C

1 Short stories

"A collection of over fifty pieces written by Jack London between 1893 and 1916, including articles and war dispatches, short stories and selections from his novels. Some of the material has not been published before in book form." Book Rev Digest

Stories of Hawaii; ed. by A. Grove Day. Appleton 1965 282p boards $5.95   S C

1 Hawaii—Fiction 2 Short stories

Thirteen short stories and two other brief pieces written when London was living in Hawaii. "With a wide range of themes he covers many superstitions, beliefs, problems, and pleasures of those glamorous and fascinating islands and captures the flavor of life there at the turn of the century." Library J

Mansfield, Katherine

The short stories of Katherine Mansfield. Knopf 1954 [c1937] 688p $7.95   S C

1 Short stories

"In this comprehensive edition Katherine Mansfield's [88] stories are arranged approximately in chronological order, with one conspicuous exception, namely, that 'At the Bay' is printed immediately after 'Prelude' although it was written four years later." Introduction

"Katherine Mansfield is not the major writer some people once thought. But she was a first-rate minor writer. Her imitators have, by contrast, proved her originality, and this collection establishes her vitality." Sat R

Maugham, W. Somerset

The best short stories of W. Somerset Maugham; selected, and with an introduction, by John Beecroft. Modern Lib. 1957 489p $2.95   S C

1 Short stories

Rain, The vessel of wrath, Lord Mountdrago and The letter are included in this collection of seventeen stories

Maugham's "themes both in novels and short stories are the unpredictability of human behavior and the enslavement of man by his passions." The New Century Handbook of English Literature

Maupassant, Guy de

Guy de Maupassant's Short stories; tr. by Marjorie Laurie; introduction by Gerald Gould. Dutton 1934 335p $2.95   S C

1 Short stories

"Everyman's library"

Thirty-two tales or contés about a wide range of subjects, priests and prostitutes, lovers and the Devil, illustrating the irony of life

The odd number; thirteen tales; tr. by Jonathan Sturges; an introduction by Henry James. Harper 1917 226p front $4.95   S C

1 Short stories

A selection from the author's famous short stories, largely written between 1880 and 1890

"Admirable examples of the literary art that made Maupassant the acknowledged master of the short story. All show an acute realization of the irony of life." Keller's Reader's Digest of Books

Selected short stories; with a critical and biographical profile of Guy de Maupassant by Jean-Albert Bédé. Watts, F. 1969 312p lib. bdg. $4.95   S C

1 France—Fiction 2 Short stories

"A Watts Ultratype edition"

This selection of the author's works includes 22 of his most famous stories

Michener, James A.

Tales of the South Pacific. Macmillan (N Y) 1947 325p $5.95   S C

1 Short stories 2 Islands of the Pacific—Fiction

Also available in large type edition for $7.95

Pulitzer Prize, 1948

"The [18] tales are told by a young naval officer whose duties on an Admiral's staff take him up and down the islands. He meets many people, both service men and the original inhabitants, and hears their stories." Publisher's note

Mishima, Yukio

Nobel Prize in literature, 1969

Death in midsummer, and other stories New Directions 1966 181p $5.50   S C

1 Japan—Fiction 2 Short stories

In these "nine stories and a play the author . . . displays the qualities that have made him one of the most celebrated of Japan's current generation of writers. Characters, settings, and motivations reveal aspects of undiluted Japanese culture and psychology which are comprehensible though alien to Western minds. Fatalism is a prominent motif in stories that generally have a seemingly inconclusive ending but a delayed impact." Booklist

Moore, Robin

The green berets. Crown 1965 341p $5.95
                                              S C

1 U.S. Army. Special Forces—Fiction 2 Vietnamese Conflict, 1961- —Fiction 3 Short stories

Nine "short stories based on the operations of United States Special Forces in South Vietnam. The author served as correspondent, and in preparation [for his book], underwent the [training given to all Green Berets]." Book Rev Digest

"Some of the tangle of misery, cruelty, corruption and hatred afflicting Vietnam . . . comes alive in the vividly unpleasant fictionalized tales of Mr. Moore." N Y Times Bk R

Mystery Writers of America

Crime without murder; an anthology of stories by the Mystery Writers of America; ed. by Dorothy Salisbury Davis. Scribner 1970 301p boards $5.95   S C

1 Mystery and detective stories 2 Short stories

This volume includes twenty-five stories about virtually every sort of crime except murder, by such authors as Georges Simenon, Ellery Queen, Eric Ambler, and Stanley Ellin. (Publisher)

The New Yorker

Stories from The New Yorker, 1950-1960. Simon & Schuster 1960 780p $7.50   S C

1 Short stories

"The [47] stories in this collection are, of course, the best The New Yorker has published in the . . . [1950's] but apart from that they are representative of its editors' judgment. By limiting most of the fiction they publish to a verisimilar representative of contemporary life and to an unobtrusive voice, they have bridged the gap between the high culture of the intellectuals and the urban culture of a large section of the popular audience." N Y Times Bk R

Nourse, Alan E.

R for tomorrow; tales of science fiction, fantasy and medicine. McKay 1971 216p $4.95
                                              S C

1 Science fiction 2 Short stories

"Space medicine is one of the challenges of science today, and in these [11] tales . . . Nourse turns his imagination to situations and problems that may arise. While fantasy plays a part in some of these stories, most of them are quite within the realm of possibility: computerized diagnosis is, for example, already on the horizon. The style is tight, the stories have a variety of plot and mood, the theme of medicine in an advanced technological world of the future is intriguing, and . . . the technical and medical details are accurate." Sat R

Paton, Alan

Tales from a troubled land. Scribner 1961 128p $3.95   S C

1 Africa, South—Fiction 2 Short stories

"Before he became a writer, Alan Paton was the director of a reformatory for African boys. . . . [Here] he has turned his pen to a collection of [ten] short stories about life for non-whites in South Africa, dealing primarily with characters and incidents from his reformatory days." Christian Science Monitor

Pei, Mario

Tales of the natural and supernatural; designs by Laura Torbet. Devin-Adair 1971 310p $5.95   S C

1 Short stories

This collection of thirteen assorted stories plus the longer piece The sparrows of Paris, first published 1958, run "the gamut from political intrigue and ghost visitations to quiz programs and the hint after Christmas, reflecting the author's eclectic and occult interests and his scholarly background." Library J

Poe, Edgar Allan

The complete tales and poems of Edgar Allan Poe; with an introduction by Hervey Allen. Modern Lib. 1938 1026p $4.95 S C

1 Mystery and detective stories 2 Short stories

"Modern Library giant"

"The tales of mystery and suspense from the pen of one of the great mystery writers of all times." Nat Educ Association

Edgar Allan Poe; selected and ed. with an introduction and notes, by Philip Van Doren Stern. Viking 1945 xxxviii, 664p $5.50 S C

1 Mystery and detective stories 2 Short stories

"The Viking Portable library"

Cover title: The portable Poe

"A collection which includes twenty-four tales—of fantasy, horror and mystery,—some letters, critical articles, and poems." Book Rev Digest

"This volume succeeds in both format and content. It is one of the most compact and judiciously inclusive compendiums of Poe that I know of." N Y Times Bk R

Porter, Katherine Anne

The collected stories of Katherine Anne Porter. Harcourt 1965 495p $7.50   S C

1 Short stories

Pulitzer Prize, 1966

Contains three collections of stories: Flowering Judas, and other stories (1935); The leaning tower, and other stories (1944); Pale horse, pale rider (1939). The short stories; Virgin Violeta, and The martyr have been added to the first collection; Holiday, and The fig tree [a sketch] to the second

Pale horse, pale rider; three short novels. Harcourt 1939 264p $5.75   S C

1 Short stories

"These three short novels include the title story, which concerns a young newspaperwoman in love with a soldier who dies in the 1918 influenza epidemic; 'Noon Wine,' the narrative of a shooting in the glare of a Texas midday; and 'Old Mortality,' a three-stage account of a Southern family that tries to believe its own myths about itself." Good Reading

Prize stories, 1970-1971: The O. Henry Awards; ed. and with an introduction by William Abrahams. Doubleday 1970-1971 2v 1970 $4.95; 1971 $5.95   S C

1 Short stories

The 1970 collection contains seventeen stories including such writers as Bernard Malamud, John Updike, James Alan McPherson, Joyce Carol Oates and others of less celebrity. The first prize story is Robert Hemenway's The girl who sang with the Beatles; the second prize story is William Eastlake's The biggest thing since Custer; the third prize story is Norval Rindfleisch's A cliff of fall

The 1971 collection includes seventeen stories by established writers. The first prize story is Florence M. Hecht's Twin bed bridge; second prize story is Guy A. Cardwell's Did you once see Shelley; third prize story is Alice Adams' Gift of grass

Saki

The short stories of Saki (H. H. Munro); with an introduction by Christopher Morley. Modern Lib. 1958 718p $2.95   S C

1 Short stories

An anthology first published 1930 by Viking, and reprinted with renewed copyright 1958. Includes the following stories, which were published separately as follows: Reginald, and Reginald in Russia (1921); The chronicles of Clovis (1927); Beasts and super-beasts (1928); The toys of peace (1928); The square egg (1924)

Concludes with a biography of Saki, by his sister: Ethel M. Munro

Index of titles: p717-18

Salinger, J. D.

Nine stories. Little 1953 302p $5.95   S C

1 Short stories

"J. D. Salinger's writing is original, first rate, serious and beautiful. Here are nine of his stories, and one further reason that they are so interesting, and so powerful seen all together, is that they are paradoxes. From the outside, they are often very funny; inside, they are about heartbreak, and convey it; they can do this because they are pure." N Y Times Bk R

"Most of J. D. Salinger's stories are distinguished by the same qualities which made his first novel, 'The Catcher in the Rye' [entered in Fiction] a refreshing departure from the routine naturalistic story of adolescence." Sat R

The Saturday Evening Post

Best modern short stories; selected from The Saturday Evening Post. Curtis Bks. [distributed by Doubleday] 1965 494p $5.95   S C

1 Short stories

"Thirty stories by Carson McCullers, Graham Greene, James Gould Cozzens, John Updike, Stanley Elkin, and others including a number of newcomers." Bk Buyer's Guide

Although varied in subject and style "the stories are basically about contemporary society or, with three exceptions, at least about the twentieth century. . . . They are also essentially urban and generally big-city." Introduction

Scammell, Michael

(ed.) Russia's other writers; selections from Samisdat literature; selected and introduced by Michael Scammell; foreword by Max Hayward. Praeger [1971 c1970] 216p $6.95   S C

1 Short stories

First published 1970 in England

"Knowledgeable about Russian literature, Scammell has collected nine line prose pieces, most written by Russians living in Russia. . . . [This is both] an anthology of subversive literature and an anthology of material not otherwise available in English. . . . The first half of the book is Maximov's novella [House in the Clouds]. In the other half is prose by Osip Mandelstam, the poet who died in a labor camp 32 years ago, and Victor Velsky, a religious philosopher who died seven years ago. The remaining pages are stories by Ulyansky, Rostopchin, Goryushkin, Shalamov, Bukovsky, and Ktorova." Choice

Schaefer, Jack

The collected stories of Jack Schaefer; with an introduction by Winfield Townley Scott. Houghton 1966 520p $10   S C

1 The West—Fiction 2 Short stories

Thirty-two short stories evoking the mood and manner of the West, in both a bygone era and its aftermath. Many of these stories have appeared in other publications

"The author's mastery of narrative technique, his excellent character development, and his consistently concise description combine in avoiding the unfortunate aspects of typical 'Western' fiction and melodrama." Library J

The **Scribner** treasury; 22 classic tales, by Mary Raymond Shipman Andrews [and others]. Introduction and notes by J. G. E. Hopkins. Scribner 1953 689p $6   S C

1 Short stories

"An anthology of stories published by Scribner from as early as 1881 to as late as 1932, including such authors as George W. Cable, Edith Wharton, Richard Harding Davis, John Galsworthy, and James Barrie. Each story is prefaced by a short note on the author." Pub W

Seltzer, Thomas

(comp.) Best Russian short stories; comp. and ed. by Thomas Seltzer. Modern Lib. [1970 c1925] 556p $2.95   S C

1 Russia—Fiction 2 Short stories

A reissue of a title first published 1917 by Liveright

"This volume contains twenty-two short stories by seventeen famous Russian writers." Publisher's note

Among the authors included are Pushkin, Gogol, Turgenev, Chekhov, Dostoyevsky, Tolstoy, Gorky, Andreyev and Bunin

Seventeen

Seventeen from Seventeen; an anthology of stories; selected by Babette Rosmond. Macmillan (N Y) 1967 268p $4.95   S C

1 Short stories

"An anthology of the best stories which have . . . appeared in 'Seventeen' magazine. The stories, which involve teen-agers in situations from the romantic to the bizarre, are by writers such as Susan Lardner, Paul Darcy Boles, and M. J. Amft." McClurg. Book News

Stories from Seventeen; selected by Bryna Ivens. Lippincott 1955 214p $5.50   S C

1 Short stories

"Although the [fourteen] stories vary in quality, they are generally well-written and deal with fairly mature themes, ranging from the hazards of pickups to the facing of death, with a leavening of love and dates." Chicago. Children's Book Center

Sholokhov, Mikhail

Nobel Prize in literature, 1965

Tales of the Don; tr. from the Russian by H. C. Stevens. Knopf 1962 [c1961] 310p $5.95   S C

1 Russia—Fiction 2 Communism—Russia—Fiction 3 Short stories

"A collection of sixteen short stories written by the Soviet novelist between 1924 and 1926. The tales are concerned with peasant life along the river Don." Book Rev Digest

This book "contains all the elements that later made Sholokhov a master of representational narrative: tense dramatic plots, fresh landscape, catching humor and a racy, uninhibited popular idiom." N Y Times Bk R

Singer, Isaac Bashevis
An Isaac Bashevis Singer reader. Farrar, Straus 1971 560p $10.95   S C
1 Short stories
ISBN 0-374-17747-3
"A fiction anthology by Yiddish author Singer contains among works previously published in journals and other collections, 15 short stories, a novel 'The magician of Lublin,' and four episodes not included in the English translation of 'In my father's court.' Trenchant prose, often humorous and occasionally grim, illumines vagaries and grotesqueries in the lives of Singer's earthy characters in a variety of settings." Booklist

Solzhenitsyn, Alexander
Nobel Prize in literature, 1970
Stories and prose poems; tr. by Michael Glenny. Farrar, Straus 1971 267p $7.95 S C
1 Short stories
SBN 374-2-7033-3
Included in this collection are sixteen prose poems, the novella: For the good of the cause, and five short stories
"The prose poems present in clear detail the true depth of Solzhenitsyn's genius. . . . By their brevity (running to an average of 35 to 40 lines), Solzhenitsyn is able to bring to bear in a concentrated from the full power of his evocative prose on a variety of subjects." Best Sellers

Spark, Muriel
Collected stories: I. Knopf [1968 c1967] 359p $6.95   S C
1 Short stories
First published 1967 in England
This collection includes stories that appeared in the earlier volumes, "The go-away bird, and other stories," and "Voices at play," a collection of stories and plays, together with four new stories she has written in the last few years. (Publisher)
"The settings of these stories are English and African and Mrs. Spark evokes both backgrounds with ease and assurance. Her characters, as always gain one's confidence immediately. . . . But perhaps the author's greatest skill is her ability to capture one's complete attention quickly and to hold it unwaveringly until the very last word has been said." Pub W

Stevenson, Robert Louis
The complete short stories of Robert Louis Stevenson; with a selection of the best short novels; ed. and with an introduction by Charles Neider. Doubleday 1969 xxx, 678p $10   S C
1 Short stories
Contains four short novels: The story of a lie; The merry men; Strange case of Dr Jekyll and Mr Hyde (1886); and The beach of Falesá; as well as New Arabian Nights (which includes The suicide club) and nine additional short stories

The strange case of Dr Jekyll and Mr Hyde, and other famous tales; with photographs of the author and his environment as well as illus. from early editions of the stories, together with an introduction by W. M. Hill. Dodd 1961 339p illus $4.50   S C
1 Short stories
"Great illustrated classics"
An edition of the fantastic title story, published 1886, depicting the dual nature of good and evil, and seven other "thrillers" including the three part story "The suicide club"

Stuart, Jesse
Come back to the farm. McGraw 1971 246p $6.95   S C
1 Appalachian region—Fiction 2 Short stories
SBN 07-062239-6

This "collection of 16 stories, 7 of which have been previously published in periodicals, is an evocation of the Appalachian people and their country. Touching love stories, a tale about a pregnant woman at the mercy of her mother-in-law's ignorance and superstition, and stories of old men like giant trees are told with eloquent simplicity." Booklist

Plowshare in heaven; stories. McGraw [1958 c1956] 273p $5.50   S C
1 Kentucky—Fiction 2 Short stories
"Throughout the twenty-one stories in this collection, the Kentucky hill country is a persuasive, evocative background. It is in this land of sharp contrasts and powerful traditions . . . that a proud and violent people act out the daily drama of their lives, here recorded by Stuart's sensitive pen." Publisher's note
"Mr Stuart has command of the language, and uses fine expressive prose. He handles the flavored dialect judiciously, so it comes across without any sense of constraint upon the reader." N Y Her Trib Books

Tolstoy, Leo
Short novels. . . . Selected and introduced by Ernest J. Simmons. Modern Lib. 1965-1966 2v ea $2.95   S C
1 Russia—Fiction 2 Short stories
v 1 "Stories of love, seduction and peasant life." v2 "Stories of God, sex and death." Title pages
All but two of the novels in this collection were translated by Louise and Aylmer Maude
Contents; v 1 Two hussars (1856); A landlord's morning (1856); Family happiness (1859); Polikúshka (1863); The Cossacks: a tale of 1852 (1863). v2 The death of Iván Ilych (1886); The Devil (1911); The Kreutzer sonata (1901); A talk among leisured people (1893); Walk in the light while there is light (1893); Master and man (1895); Father Sergius (1911); Hadji Murád (1911); The forged coupon (1911)

Short stories; selected and introduced by Ernest J. Simmons. Modern Lib. 1964-1965 2v ea $2.95   S C
1 Russia—Fiction 2 Short stories
Volume 1 "contains all Tolstoy's early efforts in the genre before he embarked on . . . War and Peace. [Volume 2 contains] the short stories he wrote . . . from 1870 to his death in 1910." (Introduction to Volume 2)

Twenty-three tales; tr. by Louise and Aylmer Maude. Oxford 298p $2.75   S C
1 Russia—Fiction 2 Short stories
"The World's classics"
First published in this edition 1906
"These twenty-three stories are arranged under seven heads: Tales for children, published about 1872 when Tolstoy was interested in the education of peasant children; Popular stories, including What men live by; A fairy tale, which contains Tolstoy's indictment of militarism and commercialism; Stories written to pictures, intended to help the sale of cheap reproductions of good drawings; Folktales retold; Adaptations from the French; and Stories given to aid the persecuted Jews." Book Rev Digest

Twain, Mark
The complete short stories of Mark Twain; now collected for the first time; ed. with an introduction by Charles Neider. Hanover House 1957 xxiv, 676p $6.50   S C
1 Short stories
"Contains a total of sixty stories, thirteen of them gathered from works of non-fiction. They cover the entire span of Twain's writing life, from 1865 to 1916, six years after his death. The stories are arranged chronologically according to the years of first publication, and alphabetically within a given year." Editor's note
"Mr. Neider's anthology offers a convenient basis for reappraisal; the sixty pieces which are here hospitably called short stories illustrate both the weaknesses and the strengths of Mark Twain as a writer of fiction." N Y Times Bk R

Undset, Sigrid

Nobel Prize in literature, 1928

Four stories; tr. from the Norwegian by Naomi Walford. Knopf 1959 245p $4.95 **S C**

1 Norway—Fiction 2 Short stories

Norway, at the turn of the century, is the setting for these "long, somber stories about the tragic lives of four who are unloved and no longer young." Chicago

"Under the magic of Sigrid Undset's somewhat massive approach, her sympathetic fidelity to the noble and the ignoble things people do, these stories take on the rare glow of life revealed as only authentic art can reveal it." Cath World

Updike, John

Bech: a book. Knopf 1970 206p $5.95 **S C**

"The seven witty and intelligent interrelated Updike stories about Henry Bech, 'moderately well-known' Jewish writer, brought together here with an amusing 'foreword' by Bech and a couple of tongue-in-cheek appendices, chronicling Bech's work. . . . Bech is seen as a visiting American on cultural exchange behind the Iron Curtain . . . in swinging London, on Martha's Vineyard where he tries with hysterically funny results to turn on via pot, and in several other serio-comic turns that depict his all-too-human weaknesses." Pub W

"Bech is a fine, rich character and a difficult one for waspy John Updike to undertake. That he brings him off, without strain, with a truly entertaining grace, seems to me just wonderful." Harper

Pigeon feathers, and other stories. Knopf 1962 278p boards $4.95 **S C**

1 Short stories

"These carefully polished stories of America today are filled with gentle humor and irony. Youth, marriage, and family life provide most of the themes." Cincinnati

Wells, H. G.

The complete short stories of H. G. Wells. St Martins [1971 c1927] 1038p boards $6.95 **S C**

1 Short stories

First published 1927 in England with title: The short stories of H. G. Wells

A collection of 62 short stories and the complete work: The time machine, first published 1895

"A fat, heavy volume packed with humour, strangeness, horror and imaginative stimulus. Many stories were written 50 years ago and it is astonishing how well they have worn." Daily Telegraph

28 science fiction stories. Dover 1952 915p $5 **S C**

1 Science fiction 2 Short stories

Twenty-six short stories and two unabridged novels, Men like Gods, and Star begotten, make up this collection. Subjects include time, space, exploration, war, pestilence and invention

Wharton, Edith

The collected short stories of Edith Wharton; ed. and with an introduction by R. W. B. Lewis. Scribner 1968 2v ea $8.95 **S C**

1 Short stories

Contains ten collections of stories: The greater inclination (1899); Crucial instances (1901); The descent of man (1904); The hermit and the wild woman (1908); Tales of men and ghosts (1910); Xingu (1916); Here and beyond (1926); Certain people (1930); Human nature (1933); The world over (1936). Also included are thirteen miscellaneous stories, two dramatic sketches and some articles about the short story and ghost stories

The Edith Wharton reader; ed. by Louis Auchincloss. Scribner 1965 700p boards $7.50 **S C**

1 Short stories

The selection opens and closes with excerpts from the author's autobiography, A backward glance. Also included are: the first halves of two novels, The house of mirth and The age of innocence; two novelettes, Ethan Frome and Bunner sisters; two of the four novelettes from Old New York: False dawn and The old maid; five short stories; and a poem. (Publisher)

"One can readily agree with Mr. Auchincloss . . . that Mrs. Wharton's work, a reflection of the first quarter of this century in America, deserves a measure of rediscovery." Best Sellers

Wolfe, Thomas

The hills beyond; with a note on Thomas Wolfe; by Edward C. Aswell. Harper 1941 386p $6.95 **S C**

1 Short stories

"The first half of the book is about the Joyner clan, which settled in North Carolina in the early nineteenth century. The rest of the book is made up of short character studies, many of them satirical." Book Rev Digest

The short novels of Thomas Wolfe; ed. with an introduction and notes by C. Hugh Holman. Scribner 1961 xx, 323p $7.95 **S C**

1 Short stories

"Five short novels—'A Portrait of Bascom Hawke,' 'The Web of Earth,' 'No Door,' 'I Have a Thing to Tell You' and 'The Party at Jack's'—originally published in magazines [between 1932 and 1939], with an introduction and notes by the editor. Several of these were modified later and woven in Wolfe's long novels." N Y Her Trib Books

"As a representative sample of Wolfe's best writing they should encourage new readers to embark upon the mammoth but immensely rewarding project of 'reading Wolfe.'" San Francisco Chronicle

PART 2

AUTHOR, TITLE, SUBJECT, AND ANALYTICAL INDEX

AUTHOR, TITLE, SUBJECT, AND ANALYTICAL INDEX

This index to the books in the Classified Catalog includes author, title, subject and analytical entries, arranged in one alphabet. Added entries for joint authors are also included.

References in the Index are to Dewey Decimal Classification number in Part I, not to pages in this catalog. These numbers are given in boldfaced type.

Analytical entries are introduced by the word *In* or the phrase *See also pages in the following book.* These give (1) the page numbers in the book where the material is to be found, (2) the classification number of the book.

Title entries are provided for most books. However, no title entry is given for non-distinctive titles, e.g., "Complete works." When a title of the book and its subject heading are so similar that both are not needed, no title entry is made. The same is true when the title of a biography is the name of the subject of the biography. In this case the book will appear under the name of the person about whom it is written, but with the name inverted.

For further directions for the use of this Index, see pages viii-x.

A & P. See Great Atlantic and Pacific Tea Company

A & P. Updike, J.
In Updike, J. Pigeon feathers, and other stories   **S C**

The **AAAS** Science book list. Deason, H. J. comp.   **016.5**

The **ABC** of lettering. Biegeleisen, J. I. **745.6**

A.L.A. Cataloging rules for author and title entries. See Anglo-American cataloging rules   **025.3**

ALA Rules for filing catalog cards   **025.37**

ALA Rules for filing catalog cards. Abridged   **025.37**

ASPCA guide to pet care. Henley, D. **636**

Aandahl, Vance
An adventure in the Yolla Bolly Middle Eel Wilderness
In The Best from Fantasy and Science Fiction, 19th ser. p245-66   **S C**

Abad Queipo, Manuel, Bp.
See pages in the following book:
Worcester, D. E. Makers of Latin America p45-53   **920**

Abailard, Pierre. See Abélard, Pierre

Abbeys. See Cathedrals

Abbott, Edwin A.
Flatland   **513**

Abbott, George
Three men on a horse
In Gassner, J. ed. Twenty best plays of the modern American theatre p511-59   **812.08**

About
See pages in the following book:
Ewen, D. The story of America's musical theater p221-32   **782.8**

Abbreviations
Dictionary of foreign phrases and abbreviations   **808.88**
See also pages in the following book:
Becker, E. R. The successful secretary's handbook p165-80   **651.02**
See also Acronyms

Dictionaries
Gale Research Company. Acronyms and initialisms dictionary   **421.03**
Schwartz, R. J. comp. The complete dictionary of abbreviations. Large type ed.   **421.03**

Abd al-Rahaman Azzam. See 'Azzām, 'Abd-al-Rahmān

Abduction. See Kidnapping

Abdul, Raoul
(jt. ed.) Lomax, A. ed. 3000 years of Black poetry   **808.81**

Abé, Kobo
The woman in the dunes   **Fic**

Abe Lincoln grows up. Sandburg, C.   **92**

Abe Lincoln in Illinois. Sherwood, R. E. **812**
also in Gassner, J. ed. Best plays of the modern American theatre; 2d ser. p725-73   **812.08**

Abel, Niels Henrik
See pages in the following book:
Bell, E. T. Men of mathematics p307-26   **920**

Abelard, Peter. See Abélard, Pierre

Abélard, Pierre
See pages in the following books:
Adams, H. Mont-Saint-Michel and Chartres p282-315   **726**
Durant, W. The age of faith p931-48 **940.1**

Abels, Jules
The degeneration of our Presidential election   **329**

Ability
Testing
See pages in the following book:
Sargent, S. S. Basic teachings of the great psychologists p27-37   **150**

Abolition of slavery. See Abolitionists; Slavery

Abolitionists
Bontemps, A. Free at last; the life of Frederick Douglass   **92**
Douglass, F. Life and times of Frederick Douglass   **92**
Hoexter, C. K. Black crusader: Frederick Douglass   **92**

Abolitionists—*Continued*
Macy, J. The anti-slavery crusade   **973.6**
Oates, S. B. To purge this land with blood;
  a biography of John Brown   **92**
Quarles, B. Black abolitionists   **326**
Quarles, B. ed. Frederick Douglass   **92**
    See also pages in the following books:
Holbrook, S. H. Lost men of American
  history p154-77   **920**
Lynd, S. ed. Nonviolence in America: a
  documentary history p25-108   **323**
Sloan, I. J. Our violent past p68-83 **301.18**
Aborigines. See Indians of North America
Abortion
Friends, Society of. American Friends
  Service Committee. Who shall live? **301.3**
    See also pages in the following books:
Ehrlich, P. R. Population, resources, en-
  vironment p221-26   **301.3**
Pierce, R. I. Single and pregnant p47-56
    362.8
About three kings, Uncle Herman's uniform,
  and Christmas night in the Tyrol.
  Bemelmans, L.
  In Becker, M. L. ed. The home book of
    Christmas p519-22   **394.26**
Above suspicion. MacInnes, H.   **Fic**
Abraham Lincoln and the Union. Stephen-
  son, N. W.   **973.7**
Abrahams, William
  (ed.) Fifty years of the American short
  story   **S C**
  (ed.) Prize stories, 1970-1971: The O. Henry
  Awards. See Prize stories, 1970-1971:
  The O. Henry Awards   **S C**
Abridged Dewey Decimal classification and
  relative index. Dewey, M.   **025.4**
Abridged Readers' guide to periodical litera-
  ture. See Readers' guide to periodical
  literature   **051**
Absalom, Absalom! Faulkner, W.   **Fic**
Absence of Mr Glass. Chesterton, G. K.
  In Chesterton, G. K. The Father Brown
    omnibus p229-44   **S C**
Absolute monarchy. See Monarchy
Absolution. Fitzgerald, F. S.
  In Fitzgerald, F. S. The Fitzgerald read-
    er p76-90   **S C**
  In Fitzgerald, F. S. The stories of F.
    Scott Fitzgerald p159-72   **S C**
Abstinence. See Temperance
Abstract art. See Art, Abstract
Abubakar, Sir Alhaji. See Balewa, Sir Abu-
  bakar Tafewa
Academic freedom
    See pages in the following book:
MacLeish, A. A continuing journey p130-
  40   **818**
The **academy.** Ely, D.
  In The Best American short stories, 1966
    p59-68   **S C**
The **academy.** Fratti, M.
  In Richards, S. ed. Best short plays of
    the world theatre, 1958-1967 p85-95
    808.82
Acadians
    Poetry
Longfellow, H. W. Evangeline   **811**

Accadians (Sumerians) See Sumerians
Accident. Christie, A.
  In Costain, T. B. ed. Read with me
    p165-74   **S C**
The **accident.** Stuart, J.
  In The Best American short stories, 1967
    p279-89   **S C**
Accidents
    See also First aid in illness and injury;
    Traffic accidents; and subjects with
    the subdivision Accidents, e.g. Aeronau-
    tics—Accidents
    Prevention
    See also Safety education
Accioly, Breno
  João Urso
  In Cohen, J. M. ed. Latin American writ-
    ing today p235-46   **860.8**
Acclimatization. See Adaptation (Biology);
  Man—Influence of environment
According to their lights. Henry, O.
  In Henry, O. The complete works of O.
    Henry p1446-51   **S C**
Accredited institutions of higher education.
  American Council on Education   **378.73**
Acculturation
Handlin, O. ed. Children of the uprooted
    325.73
Handlin, O. The uprooted   **325.73**
The **Acharnians.** Aristophanes
  In Oates, W. J. ed. The complete Greek
    drama v2 p429-73   **882.08**
Achebe, Chinua
  Arrow of God   **Fic**
  Things fall apart   **Fic**
Acheson, Dean
  Morning and noon   **92**
  Present at the creation   **973.918**
Acheson, Patricia C.
  America's colonial heritage   **973.2**
  Our federal government: how it works **353**
  The Supreme Court   **347.9**
The **achievement** of the cat. Saki
  In Saki. The short stories of Saki p624-
    26   **S C**
Acids
    See pages in the following book:
Snively, W. D. The sea of life p113-25 **612**
Acme rooms and sweet Marjorie Russell.
  Hunt, H. A.
  In The Best American short stories, 1967
    p135-50   **S C**
Acoma Indians
    Wars
    See pages in the following book:
Hall-Quest, O. Conquistadors and Pueblos
    p75-91   **979.1**
Acoustics. See Hearing; Sound
Acquisitions (Libraries) See Book selection
Acrobats. Horovitz, I.
  In The Best short plays, 1970 p217-31
    808.82
Acronyms
Pugh, E. A dictionary of acronyms & ab-
  breviations   **603**
Acronyms and initialisms dictionary. Gale
  Research Company   **421.03**

Adult education

See pages in the following book:

Barzun, J. Teacher in America p253-68
371.1

Anecdotes, facetiae, satire, etc.

Ross, L. Q. The education of H*Y*M*A*N
K*A*P*L*A*N   817

The **adulterous** woman. Camus, A.
In Camus, A. Exile and the kingdom
S C

The **Advanced** Lady. Mansfield, K.
In Mansfield, K. The short stories of
Katherine Mansfield p99-108   S C

Adventure. Anderson, S.
In Anderson, S. Winesburg, Ohio (Modern Lib) p123-34   S C
In Anderson, S. Winesburg, Ohio (Viking) p112-20   S C

Adventure and adventurers

American Heritage. The American Heritage Book of great adventures of the Old
West   978

National Geographic Society. Great adventures with National Geographic
910.9

See also Escapes; Explorers; Sea stories; Seafaring life; Voyages and travels

Fiction

Allen, H. Anthony Adverse   Fic

Falkner, J. M. Moonfleet   Fic

Forester, C. S. Captain Horatio Hornblower   Fic

Haggard, H. R. King Solomon's mines
Fic

Masefield, J. Jim Davis   Fic

Priestley, J. B. The good companions Fic

An **adventure** in the Yolla Bolly Middle Eel
Wilderness. Aandahl, V.
In The Best from Fantasy and Science
Fiction; 19th ser. p245-66   S C

The **adventure** of Black Peter. Doyle, Sir
A. C.
In Doyle, Sir A. C. The complete Sherlock Holmes v2 p651-67   S C

The **adventure** of Charles Augustus Milverton. Doyle, Sir A. C.
In Doyle, Sir A. C. The complete Sherlock Holmes v2 p667-80   S C

Adventure of Foulkes Rath. Doyle, A. C.
In Doyle, A. C. The exploits of Sherlock Holmes p178-204   S C

The **adventure** of Prince Florizel and a detective. Stevenson, R. L.
In Stevenson, R. L. The complete short
stories of Robert Louis Stevenson
p188-95   S C

The **adventure** of six Napoleons. Doyle, Sir
A. C.
In Doyle, Sir A. C. The complete Sherlock Holmes v2 p680-96   S C

Adventure of the Abbas Ruby. Doyle, A. C.
In Doyle, A. C. The exploits of Sherlock Holmes p205-30   S C

The **adventure** of the Abbey Grange. Doyle,
Sir A. C.
In Doyle, Sir A. C. The complete Sherlock Holmes v2 p743-60   S C

The **adventure** of the Beryl Coronet. Doyle,
Sir A. C.
In Doyle, Sir A. C. The complete Sherlock Holmes v 1 p343-61   S C

Adventure of the black baronet. Doyle, A. C.
In Doyle, A. C. The exploits of Sherlock Holmes p121-46   S C

The **adventure** of the blanched soldier. Doyle,
Sir A. C.
In Doyle, Sir A. C. The complete Sherlock Holmes v2 p1179-93   S C

The **adventure** of the Blue Carbuncle. Doyle,
Sir A. C.
In Doyle, Sir A. C. The complete Sherlock Holmes v 1 p276-91   S C
In Doyle, Sir A. C. Sherlock Holmes'
greatest cases p433-63   S C

The **adventure** of the Bruce-Partington plans.
Doyle, Sir A. C.
In Doyle, Sir A. C. The complete Sherlock Holmes v2 p1074-96   S C

The **adventure** of the cardboard box. Doyle,
Sir A. C.
In Doyle, Sir A. C. The complete Sherlock Holmes v2 p1043-59   S C

The **adventure** of the copper beeches. Doyle,
Sir A. C.
In Doyle, Sir A. C. The complete Sherlock Holmes v 1 p361-80   S C

The **adventure** of the creeping man. Doyle,
Sir A. C.
In Doyle, Sir A. C. The complete Sherlock Holmes v2 p1261-76   S C

The **adventure** of the dancing men. Doyle,
Sir A. C.
In Doyle, Sir A. C. The complete Sherlock Holmes v2 p593-612   S C

Adventure of the Dark Angels. Doyle, A. C.
In Doyle, A. C. The exploits of Sherlock Holmes p231-57   S C

Adventure of the Deptford horror. Doyle,
A. C.
In Doyle, A. C. The exploits of Sherlock Holmes p283-310   S C

The **adventure** of the devil's foot. Doyle,
Sir A. C.
In Doyle, Sir A. C. The complete Sherlock Holmes v2 p1123-42   S C

The **adventure** of the dying detective. Doyle,
Sir A. C.
In Doyle, Sir A. C. The complete Sherlock Holmes v2 p1096-1108   S C

The **adventure** of the empty house. Doyle,
Sir A. C.
In Doyle, Sir A. C. The complete Sherlock Holmes v2 p559-75   S C

The **adventure** of the engineer's thumb.
Doyle, Sir A. C.
In Doyle, Sir A. C. The complete Sherlock Holmes v 1 p311-26   S C

Adventure of the gold hunter. Doyle, A. C.
In Doyle, A. C. The exploits of Sherlock Holmes p34-59   S C

The **adventure** of the golden pince-nez.
Doyle, Sir A. C.
In Doyle, Sir A. C. The complete Sherlock Holmes v2 p709-27   S C

The **adventure** of the hansom cab. Stevenson, R. L.
In Stevenson, R. L. The complete short stories of Robert Louis Stevenson p87-109 **S C**
In Stevenson, R. L. The strange case of Dr Jekyll and Mr Hyde, and other famous tales p319-39 **S C**

Adventure of the Highgate miracle. Doyle, A. C.
In Doyle, A. C. The exploits of Sherlock Holmes p88-120 **S C**

The **adventure** of the illustrious client. Doyle, Sir A. C.
In Doyle, Sir A. C. The complete Sherlock Holmes v2 p1160-79 **S C**

The **adventure** of the lion's mane. Doyle, Sir A. C.
In Doyle, Sir A. C. The complete Sherlock Holmes v2 p1276-90 **S C**

The **adventure** of the Mazarin stone. Doyle, Sir A. C.
In Doyle, Sir A. C. The complete Sherlock Holmes v2 p1193-1206 **S C**

The **adventure** of the missing three-quarter. Doyle, Sir A. C.
In Doyle, Sir A. C. The complete Sherlock Holmes v2 p727-43 **S C**

The **adventure** of the noble bachelor. Doyle, Sir A. C.
In Doyle, Sir A. C. The complete Sherlock Holmes v 1 p327-43 **S C**

The **adventure** of the Norwood builder. Doyle, Sir A. C.
In Doyle, Sir A. C. The complete Sherlock Holmes v2 p575-93 **S C**

The **adventure** of the priory school. Doyle, Sir A. C.
In Doyle, Sir A. C. The complete Sherlock Holmes v2 p627-51 **S C**

The **adventure** of the red circle. Doyle, Sir A. C.
In Doyle, Sir A. C. The complete Sherlock Holmes v2 p1059-74 **S C**

The **adventure** of the red leech. Derleth, A.
In Best detective stories of the year [1967] p39-59 **S C**

Adventure of the red widow. Doyle, A. C.
In Doyle, A. C. The exploits of Sherlock Holmes p311-38 **S C**

The **adventure** of the retired colour-man. Doyle, Sir A. C.
In Doyle, Sir A. C. The complete Sherlock Holmes v2 p1312-23 **S C**

Adventure of the sealed room. Doyle, A. C.
In Doyle, A. C. The exploits of Sherlock Holmes p147-77 **S C**

The **adventure** of the second stain. Doyle, Sir A. C.
In Doyle, Sir A. C. The complete Sherlock Holmes v2 p761-80 **S C**

Adventure of the seven clocks. Doyle, A. C.
In Doyle, A. C. The exploits of Sherlock Holmes p3-33 **S C**

The **adventure** of the Shoscombe Old Place. Doyle, Sir A. C.
In Doyle, Sir A. C. The complete Sherlock Holmes v2 p1299-1311 **S C**

The **adventure** of the solitary cyclist. Doyle, Sir A. C.
In Doyle, Sir A. C. The complete Sherlock Holmes v2 p612-27 **S C**

The **adventure** of the speckled band. Doyle, Sir A. C.
In Doyle, Sir A. C. The complete Sherlock Holmes v 1 p292-311 **S C**
In Doyle, Sir A. C. Sherlock Holmes' greatest cases p292-330 **S C**

The **adventure** of the Sussex vampire. Doyle, Sir A. C.
In Doyle, Sir A. C. The complete Sherlock Holmes v2 p1218-30 **S C**

The **adventure** of the three gables. Doyle, Sir A. C.
In Doyle, Sir A. C. The complete Sherlock Holmes v2 p1206-18 **S C**

The **adventure** of the three Garridebs. Doyle, Sir A. C.
In Doyle, Sir A. C. The complete Sherlock Holmes v2 p1230-42 **S C**

The **adventure** of the three students. Doyle, Sir A. C.
In Doyle, Sir A. C. The complete Sherlock Holmes v2 p696-709 **S C**

Adventure of the two women. Doyle, A. C.
In Doyle, A. C. The exploits of Sherlock Holmes p258-82 **S C**

The **adventure** of the veiled lodger. Doyle, Sir A. C.
In Doyle, Sir A. C. The complete Sherlock Holmes v2 p1290-99 **S C**

Adventure of the wax gamblers. Doyle, A. C.
In Doyle, A. C. The exploits of Sherlock Holmes p60-87 **S C**

The **adventure** of Wisteria Lodge. Doyle, Sir A. C.
In Doyle, Sir A. C. The complete Sherlock Holmes v2 p1021-43 **S C**

Adventure on Cocos Island. Charroux, R.
In Armstrong, R. ed. Treasure and treasure hunters **910.4**

Adventurers in the wilderness. Wissler, C.
In Pageant of America v 1 **973**

Adventurers of Oregon. Skinner, C. L. **979.5**

Adventures in the Arctic, Peter Freuchen's. Freuchen, P. **919.8**

The **adventures** of Don Quixote de la Mancha. See Cervantes, M. de. Don Quixote de la Mancha **Fic**

The **adventures** of Oliver Twist. See Dickens, C. Oliver Twist **Fic**

The **adventures** of Shamrock Jolnes. Henry, O.
In Henry, O. The complete works of O. Henry p904-08 **S C**

Adventures of Sherlock Holmes. Doyle, Sir A. C.
In Doyle, Sir A. C. The complete Sherlock Holmes v 1 p177-380 **S C**

The **adventuress**. Rama Rau, S. **Fic**

Adversary in the house. Stone, I. **Fic**

Advertising
Packard, V. The hidden persuaders **659.1**
See also pages in the following books:
Cross, J. The supermarket trap p27-42 **658.87**
Wagner, S. The Federal Trade Commission p170-89 **381.061**
See also Posters

Advertising, Pictorial. See Posters

Advise and consent. Drury, A. **Fic**

Afghanistan—*Continued*

Fiction

Michener, J. A. Caravans   **Fic**

Africa

Coughlin, R. Tropical Africa   916.7
Moore, C. D. ed. Africa yesterday and today   916
See also pages in the following books:
Ashabranner, B. A moment in history: the first ten years of the Peace Corps p50-92, 102-14   309.2
Bowles, C. ed. The conscience of a liberal p164-84   327.73
Du Bois, W. E. B. W. E. B. Du Bois: a reader p357-403   301.451
Rama Rau, S. Gifts of passage p125-52 **92**
See also Pan-Africanism

Antiquities

Clark, J. D. The prehistory of Africa   913.6
Davidson, B. The lost cities of Africa   913.6
See also pages in the following book:
Horizon Magazine. The light of the past p190-210   901.9

Biography

Polatnick, F. T. Shapers of Africa   920

Civilization

Clark, L. E. ed. Through African eyes: cultures in change   916
Davidson, B. The African genius   916
Davidson, B. African kingdoms   960
Davidson, B. The lost cities of Africa   913.6
See also pages in the following book:
Horizon Magazine. The light of the past p190-210   901.9

Description and travel

Carr, A. The land and wildlife of Africa   574.9
Johnson, O. I married adventure   92
Moorehead, A. No room in the ark   916
See also pages in the following book:
Halliburton, R. Richard Halliburton's Complete book of marvels v2   910.4

Discovery and exploration

Moorehead, A. The Blue Nile   962.6
Moorehead, A. The White Nile   962

Economic conditions

See pages in the following book:
The New Cambridge Modern history v7 p566-79   909

Fiction

Lessing, D. African stories   **S C**
Mphahlele, E. The wanderers   **Fic**
Wren, P. C. Beau Geste   **Fic**

Foreign relations—United States

See pages in the following book:
Schlesinger, A. M. A thousand days p551-84   973.922

History

Davidson, B. Africa in history   960
Davidson, B. African kingdoms   960
Hallett, R. Africa to 1875   960
McEwan, P. J. M. comp. Twentieth century Africa   960

Moorehead, A. The Blue Nile   962.6
Moorehead, A. The White Nile   962
Polatnick, F. T. Shapers of Africa   920
Thompson, E. B. Africa: past and present   960
See also pages in the following book:
The New Cambridge Modern history v11 p593-640   909

Politics

See pages in the following book:
The New Cambridge Modern history v9 p572-90   909

Religion

Parrinder, G. Religion in Africa   209

Social life and customs

See pages in the following books:
Franklin, J. H. From slavery to freedom p23-41   301.451
Wernecke, H. H. ed. Celebrating Christmas around the world p5-23   394.26

Africa, Central

See pages in the following book:
Hallett, R. Africa to 1875 p209-24   960

Description and travel

Martelli, G. Livingstone's river   916.7

Fiction

Forester, C. S. The African Queen   **Fic**
Haggard, H. R. King Solomon's mines   **Fic**

Politics

See pages in the following book:
Hallett, R. Africa to 1875 p325-35   960

Africa, East

See pages in the following book:
Hallett, R. Africa to 1875 p225-34   960
See also Kenya

History

Davidson, B. Black mother   967

Politics

See pages in the following book:
Hallett, R. Africa to 1875 p336-46   960

Africa, North

See pages in the following book:
Hallett, R. Africa to 1875 p73-110   960

Fiction

Camus, A. Exile and the kingdom   **S C**

History

See pages in the following book:
Von Hagen, V. W. Roman roads p45-76   625.7

Politics

See pages in the following book:
Hallett, R. Africa to 1875 p274-87   960

Africa, Northwest

See pages in the following book:
Hallett, R. Africa to 1875 p111-35   960

Politics

See pages in the following book:
Hallett, R. Africa to 1875 p288-99   960

Africa, South

Hopkinson, T. South Africa   916.8

Fiction

Bennett, J. Mister fisherman   **Fic**
Paton, A. Cry, the beloved country   **Fic**
Paton, A. Tales from a troubled land   **S C**
Paton, A. Too late the phalarope   **Fic**

The age of big business. Hendrick, B. J. 338
The Age of chivalry 914
The age of chivalry. Bulfinch, T.
  In Bulfinch, T. Bulfinch's Mythology
    v2 291
Age of Enlightenment. Gay, P. 901.93
Age of exploration. Hale, J. R. 910.9
The age of fable. Bulfinch, T.
  In Bulfinch, T. Bulfinch's Mythology
    v 1 291
Age of fable [selections]. See Bulfinch, T.
  A book of myths 292
The age of faith. Durant, W. 940.1
Age of faith. Fremantle, A. 940.1
An age of fiction: the nineteenth century
  British novel. Karl, F. R. 823.09
The age of fighting sail. Forester, C. S.
    973.5
The age of innocence. Wharton, E. Fic
The age of innocence (book 1) Wharton, E.
  In Wharton, E. The Edith Wharton
    reader p385-511 S C
The age of invention. Thompson, H. 608
The age of Jackson. Schlesinger, A. M.
    973.5
Age of kings. Blitzer, C. 940.2
The age of Louis XIV. Durant, W. 940.2
The age of mountaineering. Ullman, J. R.
    796.5
The age of Napoleon, The Horizon Book of.
  Horizon Magazine 944.04
The age of reason begins. Durant, W. 940.2
The age of reform. Hofstadter, R. 973.91
Age of responsibility. Adams, J. T.
  In Adams, J. T. The march of democracy
    v6 973
The age of revolution. Churchill, W. S.
  In Churchill, W. S. A history of the
    English-speaking peoples v3 942
The Age of Roosevelt
  Schlesinger, A. M. The coming of the New
    Deal 973.917
  Schlesinger, A. M. The crisis of the old
    order, 1919-1933 973.91
  Schlesinger, A. M. The politics of up-
    heaval 973.917
Age of Shakespeare and the Stuart period.
  Trevelyan, G. M.
  In Trevelyan, G. M. Illustrated English
    social history v2 942
The age of steel and steam: 1877-1890. Weis-
  berger, B. A.
  In Life (Periodical) The Life History
    of the United States v7 973
The age of the great depression, 1929-1941.
  Wecter, D. 973.917
Age of the guerrilla. Sully, F. 355.4
The age of the moguls. Holbrook, S. H.
    920
The age of the Rococo. Schwarz, M. 759.04
The age of Voltaire. Durant, W. 940.2
Aged
  See pages in the following books:
  Gardner, J. W. No easy victories p153-62
    309.173
  United States. Department of Agriculture.
    A place to live p45-56 301.3
  See also Old age

Dwellings—Fiction
  Updike, J. The poorhouse fair Fic
Agee, James
  The collected poems of James Agee 811
  Letters of James Agee to Father Flye 92
  A mother's tale
    In Foley, M. ed. Fifty best American
    short stories, 1915-1965 p488-507
      S C
  Permit me voyage
    In Agee, J. The collected poems of James
    Agee 811
Agee, Warren K.
  (ed.) Mass media in a free society 301.16
The ageless Chinese. Li, Dun J. 951
Aggressiveness (Psychology)
  Montague, M. F. A. ed. Man and aggres-
    sion 152.4
Agnew, Spiro T.
  Lucas, J. G. Agnew: profile in conflict 92
  Marsh, R. Agnew, the unexamined man
    92
Agnosticism
  See pages in the following book:
  Look. Religions in America p195-203 280
The agony and the ecstasy. Stone, I. Fic
Agrarian question. See Agriculture and state
Agribusiness and industry, Careers in. Stone,
  A. A. 338.1
Agricultural administration
  United States. Department of Agriculture.
    Farmer's world 338.1
  See also pages in the following book:
  Cochrane, W. W. The world food prob-
    lem p177-221 338.1
Agricultural botany. See Botany, Economic
Agricultural chemistry. See Fertilizers and
  manures; Soils
Agricultural credit
  See pages in the following books:
  Stone, A. A. Careers in agribusiness and
    industry p243-54 338.1
  United States. Department of Agriculture.
    Contours of change p117-23 630
Agricultural engineering
  United States. Department of Agriculture.
    Power to produce 631.3
Agricultural laborers. See Migrant labor
Agricultural machinery
  United States. Department of Agriculture.
    Power to produce 631.3
  See also pages in the following books:
  Langdon, W. C. Everyday things in
    American life, 1776-1876 p303-25 917.3
  See pages in the following books:
  National Geographic Society. Those inven-
    tive Americans p46-75 608
  Stone, A. A. Careers in agribusiness and
    industry p175-94 338.1
  Thompson, H. The age of invention p110-
    27 608
  United States. Department of Agriculture.
    After a hundred years p384-476 353.81
  See also Harvesting machinery
Agricultural pests. See Aeronautics in agri-
  culture; Fungi; Plant diseases

Ainu

See pages in the following book:

National Geographic Society. Vanishing peoples of the earth p92-113   **572**

Air

See pages in the following book:

United Nations Educational, Scientific and Cultural Organization. 700 science experiments for everyone p76-91   **507.2**

See also Atmosphere

Pollution

Aylesworth, T. G. This vital air, this vital water   **614**

Goldman, M. I. ed. Controlling pollution   **333.9**

Herber, L. Crisis in our cities   **614**

Linton, R. M. Terracide   **614**

McClellan, G. S. ed. Protecting our environment   **614**

See also pages in the following books:

Cronkite, W. Eye on the world p3-51   **909.82**

Ehrlich, P. R. Population, resources, environment p117-26   **301.3**

Halacy, D. S. Habitat p135-56   **574.5**

Isenberg, I. ed. The city in crisis p127-36   **301.3**

Nader, R. Unsafe at any speed p147-69   **629.2**

Our poisoned planet: can we save it? p93-116   **614**

United States. Department of Agriculture. A place to live p121-32   **301.3**

The **air** around us. Chandler, T. J.   **551.5**

Air crashes. See Aeronautics—Accidents

Air cushion vehicles. See Ground effect machines

Air pilots

Balchen, B. Come north with me   **92**

Brickhill, P. Reach for the sky; the story of Douglas Bader   **92**

Burke, J. Winged legend; the story of Amelia Earhart   **92**

Everest, F. K. The fastest man alive   **92**

Goerner, F. The search for Amelia Earhart   **92**

Reynolds, Q. They fought for the sky   **940.4**

Richtofen, M. F. Freiherr von. The Red Baron   **92**

See also pages in the following book:

National Geographic Society. Great adventures with National Geographic p459-67   **910.9**

Air planes. See Airplanes

Air pollution. See Air—Pollution

Air warfare. See Airplanes, Military; also names of wars with the subdivision Aerial operations, e.g. European War, 1914-1918—Aerial operations

Aircraft. See Airplanes

Airman's odyssey. Saint Exupéry, A. de   **629.13**

Airplanes

Stever, H. G. Flight   **629.132**

See also pages in the following book:

Ridley, A. An illustrated history of transportation p95-103, 133-64   **380.5**

History

Bonney, W. T. The heritage of Kitty Hawk   **629.13**

Pilots

See Air pilots

Airplanes, Military

Green, W. The warplanes of the Third Reich   **623.7**

Airplanes in agriculture. See Aeronautics in agriculture

Airport. Hailey, A.   **Fic**

Airports

Fiction

Hailey, A. Airport   **Fic**

Airs above the ground. Stewart, M.   **Fic**

The **airstrip** at Konora. Michener, J.

In Michener, J. Tales of the South Pacific p237-56   **S C**

Aix-les-Bains

See pages in the following book:

Twain, M. The complete essays of Mark Twain p48-59   **814**

Ajax. Sophocles

In Oates, W. J. ed. The complete Greek drama v 1 p315-60   **882.08**

Akbar, Emperor of Hindustan

See pages in the following book:

Schulberg, L. Historic India p161-77   **954**

Aken, Hieronymus van. See Bosch, Hieronymus

Akers, Susan Grey

Simple library cataloging   **025.3**

Akihito, Crown Prince of Japan

Simon, C. M. The sun and the birch   **92**

Vining, E. G. Windows for the Crown Prince   **92**

Akkadians

See pages in the following book:

Asimov, I. The Near East p28-41   **939**

Aku-aku. Heyerdahl, T.   **572.996**

Akutagawa, Ryūnosuke

Japanese short stories   **S C**

Contents: The hell screen; A clod of soil; "Nezumi-Kozo"—the Japanese Robin Hood; Heichu, the amorous genius; Genkaku-Sanbo; Otomi's virginity; The spider's thread; The nose; The tangerines; The story of Yonosuke

Alabama

Fiction

Lee, H. To kill a mockingbird   **Fic**

Alamo

Siege, 1836

Lord, W. A time to stand   **976.4**

See also pages in the following books:

American Heritage. The American Heritage Book of great adventures of the Old West p106-25   **978**

Chidsey, D. B. The War with Mexico p22-30   **973.6**

Alarms and diversions. Thurber, J.   **818**

Alas, Babylon. Frank, P.   **Fic**

Alaska

Smith, R. A. The frontier states: Alaska [and] Hawaii   **917.3**

See also pages in the following book:

Fish, C. R. The path of empire p39-53   **327.73**

Alexander the Great—*Continued*

Plutarch. Lives from Plutarch. Abridged p97-141   920

Sarton, G. A history of science v 1 p467-500   509

Fiction

Renault, M. Fire from heaven   Fic

Alexander, David

Love will find a way

In Hitchcock, A. ed. Alfred Hitchcock presents: A month of mystery p51-60   S C

Alexander, Gerard L.

(jt. auth.) Kane, J. N. Nicknames and sobriquets of U.S. cities and states 910.3

Alexander, Rae Pace

(comp.) Young and Black in America 920

Alexander, Robert J.

Prophets of the revolution   920

Alexander Hamilton and the Constitution. Rossiter, C.   342.73

Alexandra, consort of Nicholas II, Emperor of Russia

Massie, R. K. Nicholas [II] and Alexandra   92

Alexandria

Civilization

See pages in the following book:

Sarton, G. A history of science v2 p3-28   509

The **Alexandria** quartet: Justine; Balthazar; Mountolive [and] Clea. Durrell, L. Fic

Alfred the Great, King of England

See pages in the following book:

Sutcliff, R. Heroes and history p35-49 920

Alfred, William

Hogan's goat

In Gassner, J. ed. Best American plays; 6th ser. p137-84   812.08

Algae

See pages in the following books:

Idyll, C. P. The sea against hunger p47-63   639

Time-Life Books. A guide to the natural world, and Index to the Life Nature library p24-33   574

Zim, H. S. Plants p105-45   581

Algebra

Asimov, I. Realm of algebra   512

See also pages in the following book:

Hogben, L. Mathematics for the million p521-615   510

Alger, Horatio

See pages in the following book:

Holbrook, S. H. Lost men of American history p229-40   920

Algeria

Fiction

Camus, A. The plague   Fic

Camus, A. The stranger   Fic

Algiers

See pages in the following book:

Camus, A. Lyrical and critical essays p80-92   844

Description

See pages in the following book:

Camus, A. The myth of Sisyphus, and other essays p139-54   844

Algonkian Indians. See Algonquian Indians

Algonquian Indians

Winslow, O. E. John Eliot: "apostle to the Indians"   92

Algren, Nelson

The moon of the arfy darfy

In The Saturday Evening Post. Best modern short stories p390-401 S C

Alibi Ike. Lardner, R.

In Lardner, R. The best short stories of Ring Lardner p35-52   S C

In Lardner, R. The Ring Lardner reader p477-95   S C

In White, E. B. ed. A subtreasury of American humor; abridged p85-102   817.08

Alice Adams. Tarkington, B.   Fic

Alice Doane's appeal. Hawthorne, N.

In Hawthorne, N. Hawthorne's Short stories p411-22   S C

Alice Long's dachshunds. Spark, M.

In Spark, M. Collected stories: I p289-301   S C

Alice Sit-by-the-Fire. Barrie, J. M.

In Barrie, J. M. The plays of J. M. Barrie p247-316   822

Alice's restaurant. Guthrie, A.   781.9

Alien blood. Sholokhov, M.

In Sholokhov, M. Tales of the Don p202-24   S C

The **alien corn.** Maugham, W. S.

In Maugham, W. S. The best short stories of W. Somerset Maugham p200-41   S C

Alisky, Marvin

Uruguay, a contemporary survey   918.95

Alkalies

See pages in the following book:

Snively, W. D. The sea of life p113-25 612

Alkibiades. See Alcibiades

Alkoran. See Koran

All about language. Pei, M.   400

All about the months. Krythe, M. R. 394.2

All around the town. Benét, S. V.

In Benét, S. V. Selected works of Stephen Vincent Benét v2   818

All God's chillun got wings. O'Neill, E.

In O'Neill, E. Ah, wilderness! And two other plays: All God's chillun got wings, and Beyond the horizon p143-96   812

In O'Neill, E. Nine plays p91-133   812

In O'Neill, E. Plays v2 p301-42   812

All Gold Canyon. London, J.

In London, J. Best short stories of Jack London p248-64   S C

In London, J. Jack London's Tales of adventure   S C

All in the family. O'Connor, E.   Fic

All men are brothers. Gandhi, M. K.   92

All my sons. Miller, A.

In Gassner, J. ed. Best American plays; 3d ser. p281-316   812.08

All on her own. Rattigan, T.

In The Best short plays, 1970 p251-61   808.82

Alphabeting. See Files and filing

Alphabets. See Lettering

An **Alpine** idyll. Hemingway, E.
In Hemingway, E. The short stories of Ernest Hemingway p343-49 **S C**

Alpine plants
See pages in the following book:
Carlquist, S. Hawaii: a natural history p358-74 **574.9**

Alps
See pages in the following book:
Ullman, J. R. The age of mountaineering p24-76 **796.5**
Fiction
Ullman, J. R. The White Tower **Fic**

Alter, Dinsmore
Pictorial astronomy **523**

Alternating currents. See Electric currents, Alternating

Alternatives to violence. Bernstein, A. **301.43**

Altitude, Influence of. See Man—Influence of environment

Aluminum
See pages in the following book:
Asimov, I. Building blocks of the universe p122-34 **546**

Alvarado, Pedro de
See pages in the following books:
Innes, H. The Conquistadors p41-50, 180-86 **973.1**
Lloyd, A. The Spanish centuries p132-42 **946**

Álvarez Quintero, Serafín
Malvaloca
In Dickinson, T. H. ed. Chief contemporary dramatists, 3d ser. p413-56 **808.82**
Sunny morning
In Cerf, B. ed. Thirty famous one-act plays p243-50 **808.82**

Always the young strangers. Sandburg, C. **92**

Alyósha. Tolstoy, L.
In Tolstoy, L. Short stories v2 p294-300 **S C**

Am I insane? Maupassant, G. de
In Maupassant, G. de. Selected short stories p256-59 **S C**

Am Strande von Tanger. Salter, J.
In Prize stories, 1970: The O. Henry Awards p113-25 **S C**

Amacher, Richard E.
Edward Albee **812.09**

Amado, Jorge
The violent land **Fic**

Amaranth. Robinson, E. A.
In Robinson, E. A. The collected poems of Edwin Arlington Robinson p1311-93 **811**

The **amateur**. Gilbert, M.
In Hitchcock, A. ed. Alfred Hitchcock presents: A month of mystery p134-44 **S C**

The **amateur** astronomer. See Moore, P. Amateur astronomy **523**

Amateur astronomy. Moore, P. **523**

The **Amateur** photographer's handbook **770.2**

Amateur theatricals. See Make-up, Theatrical

Amazing: the miracle of the Mets. Durso, J. **796.357**

The **Amazon.** Murneaux, R. **918.1**

Amazon River
Furneaux, R. The Amazon **918.1**
Schreider, H. Exploring the Amazon **918**

Amazon Valley
Schreider, H. Exploring the Amazon **918**

The **Ambassador.** Spingarn, L. P.
In The Best American short stories, 1968 p315-22 **S C**

The **ambassador**. West, M. L. **Fic**

The **ambassador** and the working press. Lederer, W. J.
In Lederer, W. J. The ugly American p87-92 **S C**

Ambassador world atlas, Hammond's. Hammond, Incorporated **912**

The **ambassadors**. James, H. **Fic**

Ambassador's journal. Galbraith, J. K. **327.73**

Ambassador's report. Bowles, C. **915.4**

Amberson, Rosanne
Raising your cat **636.8**

The **ambitious** guest. Hawthorne, N.
In Day, A. G. ed. The greatest American short stories p39-49 **S C**
In Hawthorne, N. Hawthorne's Short stories p130-37 **S C**

Ambler, Eric
Belgrade, 1926
In Dulles, A. ed. Great spy stories from fiction p235-52 **S C**
The Intercom conspiracy **Fic**
Journey into fear
In Haycraft, H. ed. A treasury of great mysteries v 1 p437-576 **S C**
Spy-haunts of the world
In Mystery Writers of America. Crime without murder p 1-17 **S C**

America
See also Latin America
Antiquities
Ceram, C. W. The first American **913.7**
Leonard, J. N. Ancient America **913.7**
Stuart, G. E. Discovering man's past in the Americas **913.7**
See also pages in the following book:
Ceram, C. W. ed. Hands on the past p319-84 **913.03**
Discovery and exploration
Cheyney, E. P. European background of American history, 1300-1600 **940.2**
De Voto, B. The course of empire **973.1**
Horgan, P. Conquistadors in North American history **973.1**
Innes, H. The Conquistadors **973.1**
Lamb, H. New found world **973.1**
Morison, S. E. Admiral of the ocean sea: a life of Christopher Columbus **92**
Morison, S. E. Christopher Columbus, mariner **92**

American literature—*Continued*

History and criticism

Brooks, V. The confident years: 1885-1915
810.9

Brooks, V. The flowering of New England
810.9

Brooks, V. New England: Indian summer
810.9

Brooks, V. Our literary heritage 810.9

Brooks, V. The times of Melville and Whitman
810.9

Brooks, V. The world of Washington Irving
810.8

The Cambridge History of American literature
810.9

Curley, D. N. ed. A library of literary criticism: Modern American literature
810.9

Downs, R. B. Books that changed America
810.9

Kazin, A. On native grounds 810.9

Literary history of the United States 810.9

Miller, P. The New England mind: The seventeenth century
917.4

Parrington, V. L. Main currents in American thought
810.9

Rourke, C. American humor 817.09

Spiller, R. E. ed. The American literary revolution, 1783-1837
810.9

See also pages in the following books:

American Heritage. The nineties p80-89
917.3

Commager, H. S. The American mind p55-74, 108-61, 247-92
917.3

Macy, J. The story of the world's literature p519-59
809

Mencken, H. L. The American scene p55-110
818

Nye, R. B. The cultural life of the new nation, 1776-1830 p235-67
917.3

The United States p91-101 917.3

Wright, L. B. The cultural life of the American colonies, 1607-1763 p154-75
917.3

New England

Brooks, V. The flowering of New England
810.9

Brooks, V. New England: Indian summer
810.9

Miller, P. The New England mind: From colony to province
917.4

Miller, P. The New England mind: The seventeenth century
917.4

Southern States

See pages in the following book:

Osborne, J. The old South p149-73 917.5

The American magazine: a compact history. Tebbel, J.
051

American manners & morals. Cable, M.
917.3

An American melodrama. Chester, L. 329

American men and women of science 920.03

American men of science: The physical and biological sciences. See American men and women of science
920.03

American men of science: The social and behavorial sciences
920.03

American militarism, 1970. Knoll, E. ed.
355.03

The American mind. Commager, H. S. 917.3

American modern dancers: the pioneers. Maynard, O.
920

American moderns: from rebellion to conformity. Geismar, M.
813.09

American Museum of Natural History, New York

Anderson, M. D. Through the microscope
576

Audubon, J. J. Audubon, by himself 92

Carlquist, S. Hawaii: a natural history
574.9

Chandler, T. J. The air around us 551.5

Davies, D. Fresh water 333.9

Fiennes, R. The natural history of dogs
636.7

Gordon, B. L. ed. Man and the sea 551.4

McHarg, I. L. Design with nature 711

Matthews, W. H. A guide to the national parks
917.3

Mead, M. Culture and commitment
301.43

Sterland, E. G. Energy into power 621

Vroman, L. Blood 612

Zappler, L. The world after the dinosaurs
599

American music. See Music, American

American musicians. See Musicians, American

American names. See Names, Personal—United States

American national characteristics. See National characteristics, American

American Nazi Party

See pages in the following book:

O'Connor, R. The German-Americans p436-52
301.453

American Negro art. Dover, C. 709.73

American Negro folklore. Brewer, J. M. 398

American Negro poetry. Bontemps, A.
811.08

The American Negro reference book. Davis, J. P. ed.
301.451

American Negro short stories. Clarke, J. H. ed.
S C

American newspapers

Hohenberg, J. The news media: a journalist looks at his profession
071

Mott, F. L. American journalism 071

See also pages in the following book:

Libarle, M. ed. The high school revolutionaries p238-58
371.8

History

Solomon, L. America goes to press 071

Tebbel, J. The compact history of the American newspaper
071

See also pages in the following books:

Walker, R. H. Everyday life in the age of enterprise, 1865-1900 p175-206 917.3

Wright, L. B. The cultural life of the American colonies, 1607-1763 p238-46
917.3

American nicknames. Shankle, G. E. 929.4

The American novel. Stegner, W. ed. 813.09

The American novel, 1789-1939. Van Doren, C.
813.09

American novelists. See Novelists, American

American orations
Hurd, C. comp. A treasury of great American speeches   815.08
Lott, D. N. ed. The Presidents speak   815.08
Representative American speeches   815.08

History and criticism
See pages in the following book:
Boorstin, D. J. The Americans: The national experience p307-24   917.3
American painters. See Painters, American
American painting. See Painting, American
American painting in the twentieth century. Geldzahler, H.   759.13
American painting, 1900-1970. Time-Life Books   759.13
American paintings. See Paintings, American
The **American party systems.** Chambers, W. N. ed.   329
The **American people in the twentieth century.** Handlin, O.   301.45
American periodicals
See pages in the following book:
Hohenberg, J. The news media: a journalist looks at his profession p58-70   071

History
Tebbel, J. The American magazine: a compact history   051

Indexes
Readers' guide to periodical literature   051
American philosophy. See Philosophy, American
American philosophy in the twentieth century. Kurtz, P. ed.   191.08
American place-names. Stewart, G. R.   910.3
The **American Plutarch.** Dictionary of American biography   920
American poetry   811
See also Negro poetry

Collections
Adoff, A. ed. Black out loud   811.08
Adoff, A. ed. I am the darker brother   811.08
Aiken, C. ed. A comprehensive anthology of American poetry   811.08
Aiken, C. ed. Twentieth-century American poetry   811.08
Auslander, J. comp. The winged horse anthology   821.08
Benét, W. R. ed. An anthology of famous English and American poetry   821.08
Bontemps, A. ed. American Negro poetry   811.08
Brooks, C. ed. Understanding poetry   821.08
Ciardi, J. ed. How does a poem mean?   821.08
Ciardi, J. ed. Mid-century American poets   811.08
Coffin, C. M. ed. The major poets: English and American   821.08
Cole, W. ed. A book of love poems   821.08
Cole, W. ed. The fireside book of humorous poetry   821.08
Dunning, S. comp. Some haystacks don't even have any needle, and other complete modern poems   811.08

Eastman, M. Enjoyment of poetry, with Anthology for Enjoyment of poetry   808.1
Engle, P. ed. Poet's choice   821.08
Felleman, H. ed. Poems that live forever   821.08
Hughes, L. ed. New Negro poets U.S.A.   811.08
Hughes, L. ed. The poetry of the Negro, 1746-1970   811.08
Johnson, J. W. ed. The book of American Negro poetry   811.08
Lee, A. ed. The major young poets   811.08
Lowenfels, W. ed. The writing on the wall   811.08
Nash, O. ed. Everybody ought to know   821.08
The Oxford Book of American verse   811.08
The Oxford Book of light verse   821.08
The Oxford Book of modern verse, 1892-1935   821.08
Reeves, J. ed. The Cassell Book of English poetry   821.08
Schreiber, R. ed. 31 new American poets   811.08
Shapiro, K. ed. American poetry   811.08
Sitwell, E. ed. The Atlantic book of British and American poetry   821.08
Stevenson, B. E. comp. The home book of modern verse   821.08
Stevenson, B. E. comp. The home book of verse, American and English   821.08
Untermeyer, L. ed. An anthology of the New England poets   811.08
Untermeyer, L. ed. Modern American poetry   811.08
Untermeyer, L. ed. Modern American poetry [and] Modern British poetry   821.08
Untermeyer, L. ed. A treasury of great poems: English and American   821.08
Van Doren, M. Introduction to poetry   821.08
Williams, O. ed. A little treasury of American poetry   811.08
Williams, O. ed. A little treasury of great poetry, English and American from Chaucer to the present day   821.08
Williams, O. ed. A little treasury of modern poetry, English & American   821.08

Dictionaries
Spender, S. ed. The concise encyclopedia of English and American poets and poetry   821.03
History and criticism
Drew, E. Poetry: a modern guide to its understanding and enjoyment   808.1
Larrick, N. ed. Somebody turned on a tap in these kids   811.09
Rosenthal, M. L. The new poets   821.09
Unger, L. ed. Seven modern American poets   811.09
Untermeyer, L. The forms of poetry   808.1
Untermeyer, L. Lives of the poets   920
Untermeyer, L. The paths of poetry   920
Van Doren, M. Introduction to poetry   821.08

See also pages in the following book:
Nye, R. The unembarrassed muse: the popular arts in America p88-137   917.3

Americanization. See United States—Foreign population; United States—Immigration and emigration

The **Americans.** Frost, D.   917.3

The **Americans.** Furnas, J. C.   917.3

The **Americans.** Handlin, O.   973

The **Americans:** a conflict of creed and reality. Segal, R.   917.3

Americans before Columbus. Baity, E. C.   970.1

Americans in Afghanistan
Fiction
Michener, J. A. Caravans   Fic

Americans in China
Fiction
Hersey, J. A single pebble   Fic

Americans in Europe
Fiction
James, H. The portrait of a lady   Fic

Americans in France
Fiction
James, H. The ambassadors   Fic
Wharton, E. The reef   Fic

Americans in Italy
Fiction
Hersey, J. A bell for Adano   Fic

Americans in Japan
Fiction
Morris, E. The flowers of Hiroshima Fic

Americans in Mexico
Treviño, E. B. de. My heart lies south 92
Treviño, E. B. de. Where the heart is 92

Americans on Everest. Ullman, J. R.   915.4

The **Americans:** The colonial experience. Boorstin, D. J.   917.3

The **Americans:** The national experience. Boorstin, D. J.   917.3

America's ancient treasures. Folsom, F.   913.7074

America's colonial heritage. Acheson, P. C.   973.2

America's concentration camps. Bosworth, A. R.   301.45

America's first civilizations. Coe, M. D.   970.3

America's frontier heritage. Billington, R. A.   978

America's historic houses. Country Beautiful   917.3

America's historylands. National Geographic Society   917.3

America's horses and ponies. Brady, I.   636.1

America's place in the world economy. Forman, B.   338.973

America's receding future. See Segal, R. The Americans: a conflict of creed and reality   917.3

America's rise to world power, 1898-1954. Dulles, F. R.   327.73

America's Robert E. Lee. Commager, H. S.   92

America's ski book. Ski Magazine   796.9

America's wonderlands. National Geographic Society   917.3

Ames, Louise Bates
(jt. auth.) Gesell, A. Youth: the years from ten to sixteen   155.5

Amft, M. J.
Memento, memento
In Seventeen. Seventeen from Seventeen p18-30   S C
No boy. I'm a girl!
In Seventeen. Seventeen from Seventeen p107-21   S C

Amish Mennonites. See Mennonites

Ammianus Marcellinus
See pages in the following book:
Grant, M. The ancient historians p358-84   920

Amnesia
Fiction
Hilton, J. Random harvest   Fic

Amorites
See pages in the following book:
Asimov, I. The Near East p42-57   939

Amos, William H.
The life of the pond   574.92

Amphibia
Cochran, D. M. Living amphibians of the world   597
Cochran, D. M. The new field book of reptiles and amphibians   598.1
Conant, R. A field guide to reptiles and amphibians of the United States and Canada east of the 100th meridian   598.1
Stebbins, R. C. A field guide to Western reptiles and amphibians   598.1
See also Frogs

Amphitryon. Plautus
In Davenport, B. ed. The portable Roman reader p22-74   870.8

Amphitryon 38. Giraudoux, J.
In Cerf, B. A. comp. Sixteen famous European plays p515-68   808.82

Amster, L. J.
Center of gravity
In The Best American short stories, 1965 p 1-44   S C
In The Saturday Evening Post. Best modern short stories p327-67   S C

The **amulet.** Borland, H.   Fic

Amusements
See pages in the following books:
Brogan, D. W. France p144-60   914.4
Horizon Magazine. The Horizon Book of the Middle Ages p188-206   940.1
Wright, L. B. Everyday life in colonial America p186-216   917.3
See also Games; Mathematical recreations; Moving pictures; Puzzles; Recreation; Riddles

Amy Foster. Conrad, J.
In Conrad, J. The portable Conrad p155-91   828

Ana Maria. Donoso, J.
In Cohen, J. M. ed. Latin American writing today p152-66   860.8

Anderson, Maxwell—*Continued*

About

See pages in the following books:

Gould, J. Modern American playwrights p118-34   **812.09**

Krutch, J. W. The American drama since 1918 p27-60, 286-318   **812.09**

Anderson, Paul L.
With the eagles   **Fic**

Anderson, Robert
Silent night, lonely night
  In Gassner, J. ed. Best American plays; 5th ser. p313-39   **812.08**

Tea and sympathy
  In Gassner, J. ed. Best American plays; 4th ser. p279-313   **812.08**

You know I can't hear you when the water's running
  In Gassner, J. ed. Best American plays; 6th ser. p335-65   **812.08**

Anderson, Sherwood
Brother Death
  In Havighurst, W. ed. Masters of the modern short story p49-65   **S C**

Death in the woods
  In Abrahams, W. ed. Fifty years of the American short story v 1 p 1-11   **S C**

I'm a fool
  In Day, A. G. ed. The greatest American short stories p237-49   **S C**
  In Foley, M. ed. Fifty best American short stories, 1915-1965 p38-48 **S C**

Winesburg, Ohio   **S C**
Contents: The book of grotesque; Hands; Paper pills; Mother; The philosopher; Nobody knows; Godliness; A man of ideas; Adventure; Respectability; The thinker; Tandy; The strength of God; The teacher; Loneliness; An awakening; "Queer"; The untold lie; Drink; Death; Sophistication; Departure

Winesburg, Ohio; criticism
  In Stegner, W. ed. The American novel p154-65   **813.09**

About

See pages in the following book:

Kazin, A. On native grounds p205-26   **810.9**

Anderson, William R.
Nautilus 90 north   **623.82**

Andersonville, Ga.

Military, Prison—**Fiction**
Kantor, M. Andersonville   **Fic**

Andersonville. Kantor, M.   **Fic**

Andes, Eugene
Practical macramé   **746.4**

Andes

See pages in the following book:

Ullman, J. R. The age of mountaineering p134-54   **796.5**

Andrada e Silva, José Bonifacio de

See pages in the following book:

Worcester, D. E. Makers of Latin America p62-70   **920**

André. Dunlap, W.
  In Quinn, A. H. ed. Representative American plays p80-108   **812.08**

Andrea da Pontedera. See Pisano, Andrea

Andrea del Sarto. See Sarto, Andrea del

The **Andrech** samples. Gores, J.
  In Best detective stories of the year, 1971 p174-81   **S C**

Andreev, Leonid Nikolaevich. See Andreyev, Leonid

Andretti, Mario
What's it like out there?   **92**

About

Engel, L. K. Mario Andretti   **92**

Andrew. Morgan, B.
  In The Best American short stories, 1967 p187-92   **S C**

Andrews, Charles M.
The colonial background of the American Revolution   **973.2**
Colonial folkways   **917.3**
The fathers of New England   **974**

Andrews, Mary Raymond Shipman
The counsel assigned
  In The Scribner treasury p495-508 **S C**
The perfect tribute   **Fic**
—Same
  In The Scribner treasury p317-31 **S C**

Andreyev, Leonid
He who gets slapped
  In Dickinson, T. H. ed. Chief contemporary dramatists, 3d ser. p473-515   **808.82**
  In Tucker, S. M. ed. Twenty-five modern plays p485-525   **808.82**

Lazarus
  In Seltzer, T. comp. Best Russian short stories p320-46   **S C**

The red laugh
  In Seltzer, T. comp. Best Russian short stories p437-521   **S C**

The seven that were hanged
  In Seltzer, T. comp. Best Russian short stories p347-436   **S C**

Androcles and the lion. Shaw, B.
  In Shaw, B. Androcles and the lion, Overruled, Pygmalion p 1-57 **822**
  In Shaw, B. Complete plays, with prefaces v5 p429-71   **822**
  In Shaw, B. Saint Joan, Major Barbara, Androcles and the lion p323-479   **822**

Androcles and the lion, Overruled, Pygmalion. Shaw, B.   **822**

Andromache. Euripides
  In Oates, W. J. ed. The complete Greek drama v 1 p847-78   **882.08**

The **Andromeda** strain. Crichton, M.   **Fic**

Andros, Sir Edmund

See pages in the following book:

Craven, W. F. The colonies in transition, 1660-1713 p215-22   **973.2**

Anecdotes
Cerf, B. comp. Bennett Cerf's The sound of laughter   **817.08**
Cerf, B. ed. Good for a laugh   **817.08**
Cerf, B. ed. Laugh day   **817.08**
  See also subjects with the subdivision Anecdotes, facetiae, satire, etc. e.g. Students—Anecdotes, facetiae, satire, etc.

Angel, Juvenal L.
How and where to get scholarships & loans   **378.3**

Antarctic regions

Byrd, R. E.   Alone   92

Dufek, G. J.   Operation Deepfreeze   919.9

Grattan, C. H.   The Southwest Pacific
since 1900   990

See also pages in the following books:

Balchen, B.   Come north with me p148-92
92

Stefánsson, V. ed.   Great adventures and
explorations p713-78   910.9

See also South Pole

The **antheap.** Lessing, D.

In Lessing, D.   African stories p353-403
S C

Anthologies. See American poetry—Collections; English poetry—Collections; Poetry—Collections

Anthology for Enjoyment of poetry. Eastman, M.

In Eastman, M.   Enjoyment of poetry,
with Anthology for Enjoyment of
poetry v2   808.1

An **anthology** of famous English and American poetry. Benét, W. R. ed.   821.08

An **anthology** of the New England poets.
Untermeyer, L. ed.   811.08

An **anthology** of world poetry. Van Doren,
M. ed.   808.81

Anthony, Susan Brownell

See pages in the following books:

Stoddard, H.   Famous American women
p36-47   920

Untermeyer, L.   Makers of the modern
world p60-65   920

Vance, M.   The lamp lighters p155-196   920

Anthony Adverse. Allen, H.   Fic

Anthropogeography

Huntington, E.   The red man's continent
970.1

See also Man—Influence of environment

Anthropologists

Mulvey, M. W.   Digging up Adam; the
story of L. S. B. Leakey   92

Anthropology

Benedict, R.   Patterns of culture   572

Benedict, R.   Race: science and politics 572

Chase, S.   The proper study of mankind
300

Coon, C. S.   The story of man   572

Mead, M. ed.   The golden age of American anthropology   572.97

Montagu, A.   Man: his first two million
years   572

See also pages in the following book:

Newman, J. R. ed.   What is science? p319-
57   508

See also Anthropogeography; Archeoloy; Ethnology; also names of races
and tribes

Antibiotics

See pages in the following book:

Kavaler, L.   Mushrooms, molds, and miracles p130-48   589

The **antichrist.** Nietzsche, F. W.

In Nietzsche, F. W.   The portable Nietzsche p565-656   193

Antigone. Anouilh, J.

In Block, H. M. ed.   Masters of modern
drama p781-99   808.82

Antigone. Sophocles

In Bentley, E. comp.   The great playwrights v 1 p155-88   808.82

In Fitts, D. ed.   Greek plays in modern
translation p455-99   882.08

In Oates, W. J. ed.   The complete Greek
drama v 1 p423-59   882.08

Anti-intellectualism in American life. Hofstadter, R.   917.3

Antin, Mary

The promised land   92

Antipathies. See Prejudices and antipathies

Antique automobiles. Bird, A.   629.209

The **antique** ring. Hawthorne, N.

In Hawthorne, N.   Hawthorne's Short
stories p399-410   S C

Antiques

American Heritage.   The American Heritage History of American antiques from
the Revolution to the Civil War   745.1

American Heritage.   The American Heritage History of colonial antiques   745.1

Antiquities. See Archeology; Bible—Antiquities; Classical antiquities; Indians—
Antiquities; Man—Origin and antiquities; and names of countries, etc. with
the subdivision Antiquities, e.g. Egypt—
Antiquities

Antiquities, Biblical. See Bible—Antiquities

Antiquities, Classical. See Classical antiquities

Antisemitism. See Jewish question

The **anti-slavery** crusade. Macy, J.   973.6

Antony, Marc

See pages in the following books:

Durant, W.   Caesar and Christ p198-208
937

Plutarch.   Lives from Plutarch. Abridged
p259-84   920

Antony, Mark. See Antony, Marc

Antonyms. See English language—Synonyms
and antonyms

Ants

Chauvin, R.   The world of ants   595.7

Antwerp

Economic conditions

See pages in the following book:

The New Cambridge Modern history v2
p50-69   909

Any friend of Nicholas Nickleby's is a friend
of mine. Bradbury, R.

In Bradbury, R.   I sing the Body Electric! p200-29   S C

Anyplace but here. Bontemps, A.   301.451

Anything but the truth. McGaffin, W.   071

Anything can happen. Papashvily, G.   92

Anyuta. Chekhov, A.

In Chekhov, A.   The image of Chekhov
p106-11   S C

Apache Indians
Geronimo. Geronimo: his own story   92
See also pages in the following book:
Brown, D. Bury my heart at Wounded Knee p191-217, 392-413   970.4

Fiction
Arnold, E. Blood brother   Fic

Wars, 1883-1886—Fiction
Horgan, P. A distant trumpet   Fic

Apartment houses. See Housing

The **apartment** hunter. Moore, B.
In The Best American short stories, 1967 p175-85   S C

Apel, Willi
The Harvard Brief dictionary of music   780.3

Apes
See also Gorillas

Stories
Boulle, P. Planet of the Apes   Fic

Aphorisms and apothegms
The Viking Book of aphorisms   808.88
See also pages in the following book:
Tomkins, C. Eric Hoffer an American odyssey p[70-115]   818

Apiculture. See Bees

Apollo: lunar landing. Haggerty, J. J.   629.45

The **Apollo** of Bellac. Giraudoux, J.
In Cerf, B. ed. 24 favorite one-act plays p308-32   808.82

Apollo project
Associated Press. Footprints on the moon   629.45
First on the moon   629.45
Haggerty, J. J. Apollo: lunar landing   629.45
Lindbergh, A. M. Earth shine   818
Mailer, N. Of a fire on the moon   629.45
Moore, P. Moon flight atlas   629.45
See also pages in the following book:
Von Braun, W. Space frontier p149-251   629.4

Apollonios of Pergé
See pages in the following book:
Sarton, G. A history of science v2 p87-98   509

An apology. Henry, O.
In Henry, O. The complete works of O. Henry p1048-49   S C

The **apology** of Socrates. Plato
In Turlington, B. Socrates: the father of Western philosophy   92

The **apostate.** London, J.
In London, J. Jack London's Tales of adventure   S C

Apostles
See pages in the following book:
Durant, W. Caesar and Christ p575-95   937

Appalachian Mountains
Social conditions
Caudill, R. My Appalachia   309.175

Appalachian patriarch. Stuart, J.
In Stuart, J. Come back to the farm p 1-18   S C

Appalachian region
Fiction
Stuart, J. Come back to the farm   S C

Appalachian Trail
See pages in the following book:
National Geographic Society. Vacationland U.S.A. p170-85   917.3

Apparatus, Electronic. See Electronic apparatus and appliances

Apparatus, Scientific. See Scientific apparatus and instruments

Apparitions. See Demonology; Ghosts

The **apple.** Wells, H. G.
In Wells, H. G. The complete short stories of H. G. Wells p394-402   S C

The **apple cart.** Shaw, B.
In Shaw, B. Complete plays, with prefaces v4 p233-313   822

The **apple tree.** Galsworthy, J.
In The Scribner treasury p551-605   S C

Appleman, Roy E.
(jt. auth.) Quaife, M. M. The history of the United States flag   929.9

Appleton's New Cuyás English-Spanish and Spanish-English dictionary. Cuyás, A.   463

Appliances, Electric. See Household appliances, Electric

Appliances, Electronic. See Electronic apparatus and appliances

The **application.** Neugeboren, J.
In The Best American short stories, 1965 p251-58   S C

Applied art. See Art industries and trade

Applied psychology. See Psychology, Applied

Applied science. See Technology

Appointment on the moon. Lewis, R. S.   629.4

Appomattox Campaign, 1865
Davis, B. To Appomattox   973.7

Appraisal of books. See Book reviews; Books and reading—Best books; Criticism

The **appraiser.** Wood, M.
In The Saturday Evening Post. Best modern short stories p376-89   S C

Appreciation of art. See Esthetics

Appreciation of art. Benson, S.
In White, E. B. ed. A subtreasury of American humor; abridged p168-74   817.08

Appreciation of music. See Music—Analysis, appreciation

Apprentices
See pages in the following books:
Arnold, A. Career choices for the '70s p101-08   331.7
Wright, L. B. Everyday life in colonial America p101-30   917.3

The **approach** to al-Mu'tasim. Borges, J. L.
In Borges, J. L. The Aleph, and other stories, 1933-1969 p45-52   S C

April showers. Wharton, E.
  In Wharton, E. The collected short sto-
    ries of Edith Wharton v 1 p189-96
    S C

April 2000: the third expedition. Brad-
    bury, R.
  In Bradbury, R. The Martian chronicles
    p49-66   **S C**

April 2003: the musicians. Bradbury, R.
  In Bradbury, R. The Martian chronicles
    p114-15   **S C**

April 2005: Usher II. Bradbury, R.
  In Bradbury, R. The Martian chronicles
    p132-48   **S C**

April 2026: the long years. Bradbury, R.
  In Bradbury, R. The Martian chronicles
    p193-204   **S C**

Aptheker, Herbert
  (ed.) A documentary history of the Negro
    people in the United States   **301.451**

Aptitude testing. See Ability—Testing

Aquariums
  Wainwright, N. Tropical aquariums   **639**
    See also pages in the following book:
  National Geographic Society. Wondrous
    world of fishes p238-46   **597**

Aquatic animals. See Marine animals

Aquatic birds. See Water birds

Aquatic plants. See Fresh-water plants

Aquatic sports. See Water sports

Aquinas, Thomas, Saint. See Thomas
    Aquinas, Saint

Arab art. See Art, Islamic

Arab civilization. See Civilization, Arab

Arab countries
              Politics
    See pages in the following book:
  Comay, J. The UN in action p35-45, 56-59
                                  341.13

Arab-Jewish relations. See Jewish-Arab re-
    lations

The Arab world. Stewart, D.   **915.3**

Arabia
          Social life and customs
  Lawrence, T. E. Seven pillars of wisdom
                                  940.4

Arabian nights
  The Arabian nights' entertainment **398.2**

The Arabian nights' entertainment. Arabian
    nights   **398.2**

Arabic art. See Art, Islamic

Arabic language
    See pages in the following book:
  Pei, M. Talking your way around the
    world p203-25   **418**

Arabs
  Lawrence, T. E. Seven pillars of wisdom
                                  940.4
  Stewart, D. The Arab world   **915.3**
    See also pages in the following book:
  Asimov, I. The Near East p214-29 **939**
              History
  Glubb, Sir J. A short history of the Arab
    peoples   **953**
  Hitti, P. K. The Arabs   **953**
The Arabs. Hitti, P. K.   **953**

Arabs in Africa
    See pages in the following book:
  Davidson, B. The lost cities of Africa
    p202-10   **913.6**

Arabs in Spain
    See pages in the following book:
  Hitti, P. K. The Arabs p61-72, 124-32 **953**

Araby. Joyce, J.
  In Garrity, D. A. ed. 44 Irish short sto-
    ries p126-32   **S C**
  In Joyce, J. Dubliners p33-41   **S C**

Aransas National Wildlife Refuge
  McNulty, F. The whooping crane   **598**

Arbela, Battle of, 331 B.C. See Gaugamela,
    Battle of, 331 B.C.

Arbitration, International. See United Na-
    tions

The arbitration. Menander of Athens
  In Oates, W. J. ed. The complete Greek
    drama v2 p1147-71   **882.08**

Arbman, Holger
  The Vikings   **914.8**

Archaeology. See Archeology

Archangel. Updike, J.
  In Updike, J. Pigeon feathers, and other
    stories   **S C**

Archeologists
  Ceram, C. W. ed. Hands on the past
                                  913.03

Archeology
  Ceram, C. W. ed. Hands on the past
                                  913.03
  Cottrell, L. Lost cities   **913.03**
  Cottrell, L. The quest for Sumer **913.35**
  Cousteau, J. Y. The living sea   **627.7**
  Deetz, J. Invitation to archaeology **913**
  Horizon Magazine. The search for early
    man   **913.03**
  Muley, M. W. Digging up Adam: the
    story of L. S. B. Leakey   **92**
  Poole, L. Carbon-14, and other science
    methods that date the past   **913**
  Silverberg, R. Frontiers in archeology
                                  913.03
  Throckmorton, P. Shipwrecks and archae-
    ology   **913.03**
  White, A. T. Lost worlds   **913.03**
    See also pages in the following books:
  Feigenbaum, L. H. Israel: crossroads of
    conflict p123-38   **915.694**
  National Geographic Society. Great ad-
    ventures with National Geographic p210-
    25   **910.9**
    See also Bible—Antiquities; Bronze
    age; Classical antiquities; Indians of
    North America—Antiquities; Iron age;
    Man, Prehistoric; Stone implements;
    and names of countries, cities, etc. with
    the subdivision Antiquities, e.g. United
    States—Antiquities
            Dictionaries
  Bray, W. The American Heritage Guide
    to archaeology   **913.03**
  The Concise encyclopedia of archaeology
                                  913.03
              Fiction
  Michener, J. A. The source   **Fic**

AUTHOR, TITLE, SUBJECT, AND ANALYTICAL INDEX
TENTH EDITION, 1972

Archeology—*Continued*

History

Ceram, C. W. Gods, graves, and scholars
913.03

Ceram, C. W. The march of archaeology
913.03

Archeology, Biblical. See Bible—Antiquities

Archeology, Classical. See Classical antiquities

Archer, Elsie

Let's face it 646.7

Archer, Jules

The extremists: gadflies of American society 973

Thorn in our flesh: Castro's Cuba 972.91

Archer, William

The green goddess

In Cerf, B. A. comp. Sixteen famous British plays p251-306 822.08

Archery

See pages in the following books:

American Association for Health, Physical Education, and Recreation. Physical education for high school students p29-43
613.7

Shakespeare's England v2 p376-88 822.3

Archimedes

See pages in the following books:

Bell, E. T. Men of mathematics p19-34
920

Newman, J. R. ed. The world of mathematics v 1 p179-87 510.8

Sarton, G. A history of science v2 p68-86
509

Architects

Forsee, A. Men of modern architecture
920

See also pages in the following book:

Fermi, L. Illustrious immigrants p233-41
325.73

Architecture

Sullivan, L. The testament of stone 720.1

See also pages in the following books:

Cooper, M. The inventions of Leonardo da Vinci p38-43 608

The New Cambridge Modern history v11 p154-76 909

Toffler, A. Future shock p50-57 301.24

See also Building

Addresses and essays

Wright, F. L. Frank Lloyd Wright: writings and buildings 720.973

Designs and plans

See Architecture, Domestic—Designs and plans

Fiction

Rand, A. The fountainhead Fic

History

Fletcher, Sir B. A history of architecture on the comparative method 720.9

Hamlin, T. F. Architecture through the ages 720.9

Jordan, R. F. A concise history of Western architecture 720.9

Mansbridge, J. Graphic history of architecture 720.9

See also pages in the following book:

The New Cambridge Modern history v5 p149-75 909

Architecture, American

Forsee, A. Men of modern architecture
920

Mumford, L. Sticks and stones 720.973

The Rise of an American architecture
720.973

Scully, V. Frank Lloyd Wright 720.973

Smith, N. K. Frank Lloyd Wright
720.973

Whiffen, M. American architecture since 1780 720.973

Wright, F. L. Frank Lloyd Wright: writings and buildings 720.973

See also pages in the following books:

The Arts in America: The colonial period p41-145 709.73

Commager, H. S. The American mind p391-405 917.3

Mendelowitz, D. M. A history of American art p48-59, 69-89, 129-64, 245-70, 339-71 709.73

Montagu, A. The American way of life p154-63 917.3

Myron, R. Art in America p168-81 709.73

Nye, R. B. The cultural life of the new nation, 1776-1830 p268-74 917.3

Rose, B. American art since 1900 p270-94
709.73

Wright, L. B. The cultural life of the American colonies, 1607-1763 p196-203
917.3

Architecture, Ancient. See Architecture, Greek

Architecture, British

See pages in the following books:

Burton, E. The pageant of Elizabethan England p44-71 914.2

Burton, E. The pageant of Georgian England p67-108 914.2

Shakespeare's England v2 p50-73 822.3

Williams, P. Life in Tudor England p77-99 914.2

Architecture, Colonial

See pages in the following book:

Langdon, W. C. Everyday things in American life, 1607-1776 p 1-17, 125-46
917.3

Architecture, Domestic

Country Beautiful. America's historic houses 917.3

Le Corbusier. Towards a new architecture
724.9

Wright, F. L. The natural house 728

See also pages in the following book:

Driver, H. E. Indians of North America p116-35 970.1

See also Houses

Designs and plans

House & Garden. House & Garden Book of modern houses and conversions 728.6

Wright, F. L. The natural house 728

585

Architecture, Ecclesiastical. See Church architecture

Architecture, English. See Architecture, British

Architecture, Gothic
See pages in the following books:
Larousse Encyclopedia of Byzantine and medieval art p323-400   **709.02**
Rees, G. The Rhine p138-44   **914.3**
Thorndike, L. The history of medieval Europe p492-506   **940.1**

Architecture, Greek
See pages in the following book:
Horizon Magazine. The Horizon Book of ancient Greece p219-39, 207-16   **913.38**

Architecture, Japanese
See pages in the following book:
Leonard, J. N. Early Japan p147-58 **915.2**

Architecture, Latin American
History
Castedo, L. A history of Latin American art and architecture   **709.8**

Architecture, Medieval. See Castles; Cathedrals

Architecture, Modern
20th century
Forsee, A. Men of modern architecture   **920**
House & Garden. House & Garden Book of modern houses and conversions **728.6**
Le Corbusier. Towards a new architecture   **724.9**
The Rise of an American architecture   **720.973**
Scully, V. Frank Lloyd Wright **720.973**
Smith, N. K. Frank Lloyd Wright   **720.973**
Wright, F. L. The natural house   **728**
See also pages in the following book:
Janson, H. W. History of art p553-68 **709**

20th century—Dictionaries
Encyclopedia of modern architecture   **724.903**

Architecture, Roman
Le Corbusier. Towards a new architecture   **724.9**
See also pages in the following book:
Bailey, C. ed. Legacy of Rome p385-427   **913.37**

The **architecture** of molecules. Pauling, L.   **541**

Architecture through the ages. Hamlin, T. F.   **720.9**

Archy and Mehitabel. Kleinsinger, G.
In The Best short plays, 1957-1958 p23-39   **808.82**

Archy and Mehitabel. Marquis, D.   **817**
also in Marquis, D. The lives and times of Archy & Mehitabel p19-166 **817**

Archy does his part. Marquis, D.
In Marquis, D. The lives and times of Archy & Mehitabel p279-477 **817**

Archy's life of Mehitabel. Marquis, D.
In Marquis, D. The lives and times of Archy & Mehitabel p169-276 **817**

Arctic adventure. See Freuchen, P. Peter Freuchen's Adventures in the Arctic   **919.8**

Arctic regions
Anderson, W. R. Nautilus 90 north   **623.82**
Balchen, B. Come north with me   **92**
Freuchen, P. Peter Freuchen's Adventures in the Arctic   **919.8**
Lindbergh, A. M. North to the Orient   **629.13**
See also North Pole

Fiction
MacLean, A. Ice Station Zebra   **Fic**

Ardennes, Battle of the, 1944-1945
Eisenhower, J. S. D. The bitter woods   **940.54**
Toland, J. Battle: the story of the Bulge   **940.54**

Ardrey, Robert
The territorial imperative   **591**
The territorial imperative; criticism
In Montagu, M. F. A. ed. Man and aggression   **152.4**

Are you running with me, Jesus? Boyd, M.   **242**

Areopagitica. Milton, J.
In Milton, J. The portable Milton p151-205   **828**

Arezzo, Guido d'. See Guido Aretinus

Arfive. Guthrie, A. B.   **Fic**

Argentina. Ferns, H. S.   **982**

Argentine Republic
Ferguson, J. H. The River Plate republics   **918**
See also pages in the following book:
Gunther, J. Inside South America p164-291   **980**
History
Ferns, H. S. Argentina   **982**
See also pages in the following book:
Crow, J. A. The epic of Latin America p345-80, 565-603, 782-92   **980**

Argonauts
See pages in the following books:
Grant, M. Myths of the Greeks and Romans p284-303   **292**
Hamilton, E. Mythology p159-79   **292**
Quennell, M. Everyday things in ancient Greece p3-13   **913.38**

The **Argonauts** of the air. Wells, H. G.
In Wells, H. G. The complete short stories of H. G. Wells p346-58 **S C**
In Wells, H. G. 28 science fiction stories p462-74   **S C**

Argonne, Battle of the, 1918
See pages in the following book:
Armstrong, O. K. The fifteen decisive battles of the United States p270-98 **973**

Arguedas, Antonio
See pages in the following book:
Harris, R. Death of a revolutionary; [Ernesto] Che Guevara's last mission p181-96   **92**

Argumentation. See Debates and debating; Logic

Aria da capo. Millay, E. St V.
In Cerf, B. ed. Thirty famous one-act
plays p465-78   **808.82**
In Gassner, J. ed. Twenty-five best plays
of the modern American theatre;
early ser. p712-20   **812.08**

Aristides the Just
See pages in the following book:
Plutarch. Lives from Plutarch. Abridged
p23-32   **920**

Aristocracy
See pages in the following books:
Avery, G. Victorian people p37-52   **914.2**
Hofstadter, R. Anti-intellectualism in
American life p145-71   **917.3**
See also Nobility; Upper classes

Aristocracy versus hash. Henry, O.
In Henry, O. The complete works of O.
Henry p1042-43   **S C**

Aristophanes
The Acharnians
In Oates, W. J. ed. The complete Greek
drama v2 p429-73   **882.08**
The birds
In Oates, W. J. ed. The complete Greek
drama v2 p733-98   **882.08**
The clouds
In Oates, W. J. ed. The complete Greek
drama v2 p541-99   **882.08**
The Ecclesiazusae
In Oates, W. J. ed. The complete Greek
drama v2 p1007-53   **882.08**
The frogs
In Oates, W. J. ed. The complete Greek
drama v2 p919-95   **882.08**
The knights
In Oates, W. J. ed. The complete Greek
drama v2 p481-532   **882.08**
Lysistrata
In Oates, W. J. ed. The complete Greek
drama v2 p809-59   **882.08**
Peace
In Oates, W. J. ed. The complete Greek
drama v2 p671-721   **882.08**
Plutus
In Oates, W. J. ed. The complete Greek
drama v2 p1063-1115   **882.08**
The Thesmophoriazusae
In Oates, W. J. ed. The complete Greek
drama v2 p867-912   **882.08**
The wasps
In Oates, W. J. ed. The complete Greek
drama v2 p609-61   **882.08**

About
See pages in the following books:
Gassner, J. Masters of the drama p79-91
    809.2
Hamilton, E. The Greek way p126-58
    880.9
Nicoll, A. World drama p90-106   **809.2**
Payne, R. Ancient Greece p307-20   **913.38**

Aristotile da San Gallo. See San Gallo,
Bastiano da, known as Aristotile

Aristotle
The basic works of Aristotle   **888**
Metaphysics
In Aristotle. The basic works of Aris-
totle p689-926   **888**

Nicomachean ethics
In Aristotle. The basic works of Aris-
totle   **888**
On generation and corruption
In Aristotle. The basic works of Aris-
totle p470-531   **888**
On the soul
In Aristotle. The basic works of Aris-
totle p535-603   **888**
Organon
In Aristotle. The basic works of Aris-
totle p 1-212   **888**
Parva naturalia
In Aristotle. The basic works of Aris-
totle p607-30   **888**
Physica
In Aristotle. The basic works of Aris-
totle p213-394   **888**
Poetics   **808.1**
also in Aristotle. The basic works of
Aristotle p1455-87   **888**
Politics
In Aristotle. The basic works of Aris-
totle p1127-316   **888**

About
Farrington, B. Aristotle   **92**
See also pages in the following books:
Durant, W. The story of philosophy p41-
74   **109**
Hamilton, E. The echo of Greece p94-103
    880.9
Moore, R. The earth we live on p12-24
    551.09
Payne, R. Ancient Greece p396-405   **913.38**
Russell, B. A history of Western philoso-
phy p159-207   **109**
Sarton, G. A history of science v 1 p467-
564   **509**
Thomas, H. Understanding the great
philosophers p104-18   **109**

Arithmetic
Adler, I. A new look at arithmetic   **512**
Friend, J. N. More Numbers: fun & facts
    793.7
Friend, J. N. Numbers: fun & facts   **793.7**
Friend, J. N. Still More Numbers: fun &
facts   **793.7**
See also pages in the following books:
Ball, W. W. R. Mathematical recreations
& essays p2-75   **793.7**
Newman, J. R. ed. The world of mathe-
matics v 1 p418-543   **510.8**

Arizin, Paul
See pages in the following book:
Pepe, P. Greatest stars of the NBA p195-
206   **920**

Arizona
Santee, R. Cowboy   **917.8**

Arkansas
Goodwyn, L. The South Central States
    917.6

Arkin, Frieda
The broomstick on the porch
In The Best American short stories,
1964 p 1-14   **S C**

Arlen, Harold
See pages in the following book:
Ewen, D. Great men of American popular
song p245-58   **920**

Arm, Walter
The policeman 352
Armada, 1588
Horizon Magazine. The Spanish Armada 942.05
Lewis, M. The Spanish Armada 942.05
Mattingly, G. The Armada 942.05
See also pages in the following books:
Creasy, Sir E. S. Fifteen decisive battles of the world p233-311 904
Horizon Magazine. The Horizon Book of The Elizabethan world p275-91 940.2
Mitchell, J. B. Twenty decisive battles of the world p151-67 904
Fiction
Kingsley, C. Westward ho! Fic
Armah, Ayi Kwei
The beautiful ones are not yet born Fic
Armaments. See Disarmament; Gunnery; Munitions
Armbrister, Trevor
A matter of accountability 327
Armbruster, Maxim Ethan
The Presidents of the United States, and their administrations from Washington to Nixon 920
Armed forces. See Armies
Armenia
Civilization
Der Nersessian, S. The Armenians 915.66
History
Der Nersessian, S. The Armenians 915.66
The **Armenians.** Der Nersessian, S. 915.66
Armer, L. A.
A Navaho Christmas
In Wernecke, H. H. ed. Celebrating Christmas around the world p199-204 394.26
Armies
See pages in the following book:
The New Cambridge Modern history v10 p302-30, v 11 p204-42 909
See also Military service, Compulsory; War; also names of countries with the subhead Army, e.g. Rome. Army
The **armies** of labor. Orth, S. P. 331.88
Armor. See Arms and armor
Armour, Richard
The classics reclassified 817
Going around in academic circles 817
It all started with stones and clubs 355.02
Arms and armor
See pages in the following books:
Cooper, M. The inventions of Leonardo da Vinci p140-57 608
Foreign Policy Association. Toward the year 2018 p 1-22 901.9
Kelly, F. M. Shakespearian costume p61-76 792
O'Brien, R. Machines p28-51 621.9
See also Firearms
History
Norman, A. V. B. A history of war and weapons, 449 to 1660 355.09
Tunis, E. Weapons 399

See also pages in the following books:
Shakespeare's England v 1 p127-40 822.3
Simpson, J. Everyday life in the Viking age p120-37 914.8
Arms and the man. Shaw, B.
In Shaw, B. Complete plays, with prefaces v3 p125-96 822
In Shaw, B. Seven plays p123-96 822
Arms, industry and America. Davis, K. S. ed. 355.03
Armstrong, Louis
See pages in the following books:
Hadlock, R. Jazz masters of the twenties p13-49 920
Williams, M. The jazz tradition p47-59 781.5
Armstrong, Neil
First on the moon. See First on the moon 629.45
Armstrong, O. K.
The fifteen decisive battles of the United States 973
Armstrong, Richard
A history of seafaring 910.9
The magic calabash
In Armstrong, R. ed. Treasure and treasure hunters p83-95 910.4
(ed.) Treasure and treasure hunters 910.4
The **army** of the Potomac. See Catton, B. Mr Lincoln's army 973.7
The **Army Times**
D-Day 940.54
Arnold, Arnold
Career choices for the '70s 331.7
Arnold, Benedict
Fiction
Roberts, K. Arundel Fic
Arnold, Elliott
Blood brother Fic
Arnold, Matthew
The portable Matthew Arnold 828
About
See pages in the following book:
Daiches, D. A critical history of English literature v2 p972-80, 1008-15 820.9
Arnold, Pauline
Food facts for young people 641.1
Arnolfo di Cambio
See pages in the following book:
Vasari, G. The lives of the painters, sculptors and architects v 1 p28-39 920
Arnolfo di Lapo. See Arnolfo di Cambio
Arnott, Peter D.
The Romans and their world 913.37
Arnow, Harriette Simpson
The dollmaker Fic
The weedkiller's daughter Fic
Arrhenius, Svante August
See pages in the following book:
Jones, B. Z. ed. The golden age of science p638-59 920
Arribas, Antonio
The Iberians 913.36
The **arrogance** of power. Fulbright, J. W. 327.73
Arrow of God. Achebe, C. Fic

The **arrow** of God. Charteris, L.
 In Haycraft, H. A treasury of great mysteries v2 p171-88 **S C**

Arrow of heaven. Chesterton, G. K.
 In Chesterton, G. K. The Father Brown omnibus p454-80 **S C**

Arrowsmith. Lewis, S.
 In Lewis, S. Lewis at zenith p585-914
            Fic

Arsenic and old lace. Kesselring, J.
 In Gassner, J. ed. Best plays of the modern American theatre; 2d ser. p459-510 **812.08**

Art
 Faulkner, R. Art today **700**
 Gombrich, E. H. Art and illusion **701**
 Kuh, K. Art has many faces **701**
 War and peace **704.94**
 See also pages in the following books:
 Durant, W. The Reformation p820-48
            940.2
 Mueller, C. G. Light and vision p178-91
            535
 The New Cambridge Modern history v10 p143-55, v11 p154-76 **909**
 See also Archeology; Art objects; Collage; Drawing; Futurism (Art); Graphic arts; Photography, Artistic; Surrealism

    Bibliography
 National Council of Teachers of English. Committee on College and Adult Reading List. The college and adult reading list of books in literature and the fine arts **016**

    Dictionaries
 Encyclopedia of world art **703**
 Mayer, R. A dictionary of art terms and techniques **703**
 Murray, P. Dictionary of art and artists
            703
 The Oxford Companion to art **703**
 The Praeger Picture encyclopedia of art
            703
 Quick, J. Artists' and illustrators' encyclopedia **703**
 The Reader's encyclopedia **803**

    France
 See Art, French

   Galleries and museums
 See names of countries, cities, etc. with the subdivision Galleries and museums; and names of particular galleries and museums, e.g. New York (City) Museum of Modern Art

    History
 Cheney, S. A new world history of art
            709
 Clark, K. Civilisation **709**
 Gardner, H. Gardner's Art through the ages **709**
 Gombrich, E. H. The story of art **709**
 Hamilton, G. H. 19th and 20th century art: painting, sculpture, architecture
            709.04
 Janson, H. W. History of art **709**
 Janson, H. W. A history of art & music
            700

Larousse Encyclopedia of Byzantine and medieval art **709.02**
Larousse Encyclopedia of prehistoric and ancient art **709.01**
The Praeger Picture encyclopedia of art
            703
Ruskin, A. Nineteenth century art **709.03**
Ruskin, A. 17th & 18th century art **709.03**
Time-Life Books. Seven centuries of art; survey and index **709**
 See also pages in the following books:
Gombrich, E. H. Art and illusion p116-78, 330-89 **701**
Langer, W. L. Political and social upheaval, 1832-1852 p575-613 **940.2**
The New Cambridge Modern history v5 p149-75 **909**
Van Loon, H. W. The story of mankind p433-45 **909**

   History—20th century
Batterberry, M. Twentieth century art
            709.04
Canaday, J. Mainstreams of modern art: David to Picasso **709.03**
Cheney, S. A primer of modern art
            709.03
Cheney, S. The story of modern art
            709.03
Hamilton, G. H. 19th and 20th century art: painting, sculpture, architecture
            709.04
Kuh, K. Art has many faces **701**
Larousse Encyclopedia of modern art
            709.03
Lippard, L. R. ed. Pop art **709.04**
Morris, J. On the enjoyment of modern art **709.73**
 See also pages in the following books:
Gardner, H. Gardner's Art through the ages p688-747 **709**
Janson, H. W. History of art p520-52 **709**
The New Cambridge Modern history v12 p665-83 **909**

    Indexes
Time-Life Books. Seven centuries of art; survey and index **709**

    India
 See Art, Indic

   Islands of the Pacific
Trowell, M. African and Oceanic art
            709.6

    Philosophy
 See pages in the following book:
Hamilton, E. The Greek way p53-69 **880.9**

    Psychology
Froman, R. Science, art, and visual illusions **535**
Gombrich, E. H. Art and illusion **701**

Art, Abstract
 See pages in the following book:
Cheney, S. The story of modern art p613-702 **709.03**
  See also Mobiles (Sculpture)

Art, African
 Trowell, M. African and Oceanic art **709.6**

Art, American

The Arts in America: The colonial period
709.73

Dover, C. American Negro art 709.73

Larkin, O. W. Art and life in America
709.73

Mendelowitz, D. M. A history of American art 709.73

Morris, J. On the enjoyment of modern art 709.73

Myron, R. Art in America 709.73

Rose, B. American art since 1900 709.73

See also pages in the following books:

American Heritage. The nineties p64-79
917.3

Colby, V. ed. American culture in the sixties p85-113, 118-26 917.3

Good things about the U.S. today p114-25
917.3

Nye, R. B. The cultural life of the new nation, 1776-1830 p268-94 917.3

Schlesinger, A. M. The birth of the Nation p202-14 917.3

The United States p102-11 917.3

Art, Ancient

Larousse Encyclopedia of prehistoric and ancient art 709.01

Müller, A. The Seven Wonders of the World 913

See also pages in the following book:

Gardner, H. Gardner's Art through the ages p28-59 709

See also Classical antiquities

Art, Arabic. See Art, Islamic

Art, Baroque

Larousse Encyclopedia of Renaissance and Baroque art 709.03

See also pages in the following books:

Gardner, H. Gardner's Art through the ages p552-619 709

Janson, H. W. History of art p405-52 709

Art, British

Halliday, F. E. An illustrated cultural history of England 709.42

See also pages in the following books:

Durant, W. Rousseau and revolution p746-58 940.2

Lippard, L. R. ed. Pop art p27-67 709.04

Ruskin, A. 17th & 18th century art p122-43
709.03

Shakespeare's England v2 p 1-14 822.3

Souchal, F. Art of the early Middle Ages p86-91 709.02

Art, Byzantine

Larousse Encyclopedia of Byzantine and medieval art 709.02

See also pages in the following books:

Gardner, H. Gardner's Art through the ages p250-73 709

Janson, H. W. History of art p169-83 709

Sherrard, P. Byzantium p141-59 949.5

Art, Chinese

Batterberry, M. Chinese & Oriental art
709.5

Fitzgerald, C. P. China: a short cultural history 915.1

See also pages in the following books:

Durant, W. Our Oriental heritage p735-59
950

Larousse Encyclopedia of Byzantine and medieval art p195-213, 709.02

Art, Christian. See Christian art and symbolism

Art, Classical. See Art, Greek

Art, Cretan

See pages in the following book:

Ruskin, A. Greek & Roman art p11-33
709.38

Art, Decorative. See Needlework; Pottery

Art, Dutch

Koningsberger, H. The world of Vermeer, 1632-1675 92

See also pages in the following books:

Durant, W. The age of reason begins p462-76 940.2

Ruskin, A. 17th & 18th century art p78-115
709.03

Art, Ecclesiastical. See Christian art and symbolism

Art, Egyptian

See pages in the following books:

Casson, L. Ancient Egypt p117-28 913.32

Gardner, H. Gardner's Art through the ages p60-89 709

Gombrich, E. H. Art and illusion p116-45
701

Janson, H. W. History of art p33-49 709

Art, English. See Art, British

Art, Etruscan

See pages in the following book:

Ruskin, A. Greek & Roman art p122-44
709.38

Art, European

See pages in the following book:

The New Cambridge Modern history v 1 p127-93, v7 p66-84, v8 p96-114, v9 p209-28 909

Art, Flemish

See pages in the following book:

Ruskin, A. 17th & 18th century art p78-115 709.03

Art, French

Art treasures in France 709.44

Canaday, J. Mainstreams of modern art: David to Picasso 709.03

Huyghe, R. Art treasures of the Louvre
708

See also pages in the following books:

Ruskin, A. 17th & 18th century art p144-79 709.03

Souchal, F. Art of the early Middle Ages p14-85 709.02

Art, German

Russell, F. The world of Dürer, 1471-1528 92

See also pages in the following books:

Rees, G. The Rhine p132-53 914.3

Souchal, F. Art of the early Middle Ages p100-57 709.02

Art, Gothic

See pages in the following book:

Janson, H. W. History of art p229-82 709

Art, Primitive
See pages in the following books:
Cheney, S. Sculpture of the world p15-32
730.9
Davidson, B. African kingdoms p142-66
960
Gardner, H. Gardner's Art through the ages p12-27
709
Horizon Magazine. The light of the past p32-35, 44-47
901.9
Janson, H. W. History of art p18-32
709
Larousse Encyclopedia of prehistoric and ancient are p72-111
709.01
Montagu, A. Man: his first two million years p219-30
572
See also Cave drawings; Indians of North America—Art; also names of countries, cities, etc. with subdivision Antiquities, e.g. Egypt—Antiquities

Exhibitions
New York (City) Museum of Primitive Art. Art of Oceania, Africa, and the Americas, from the Museum of Primitive Art
709

Art, Renaissance
Batterberry, M. Art of the early Renaissance
709.02
Cellini, B. The autobiography of Benvenuto Cellini; abridged
92
Larousse Encyclopedia of Renaissance and Baroque art
709.03
See also pages in the following books:
Cheney, S. Sculpture of the world p364-401
730.9
Gardner, H. Gardner's Art through the ages p368-55
709
Janson, H. W. History of art p283-373, 388-404
709
Hale, J. R. Renaissance p97-138
940.2
Simon, E. The Reformation p143-50
940.2

Art, Rococo
Schwarz, M. The age of the Rococo
759.04

Art, Roman
Ruskin, A. Greek & Roman art
709.38
See also pages in the following books:
Bailey, C. ed. Legacy of Rome p385-427
913.37
Durant, W. Caesar and Christ p338-62
937
Gardner, H. Gardner's Art through the ages p172-231
709
Janson, H. W. History of art p130-56
709

Art, Romanesque
Souchal, F. Art of the early Middle Ages
709.02
See also pages in the following books:
Gardner, H. Gardner's Art through the ages p300-25
709
Janson, H. W. History of art p208-28
709
Larousse Encyclopedia of Byzantine and medieval art p261-322
709.02

Art, Russian
Horizon Magazine. The Horizon Book of the arts of Russia
709.47
See also pages in the following book:
Salisbury, H. E. ed. The Soviet Union: the fifty years p158-74
914.7

Art, Scandinavian
See pages in the following book:
Souchal, F. Art of the early Middle Ages p158-63
709.02

Art, Spanish
See pages in the following books:
Durant, W. The age of reason begins p314-32
940.2
Ruskin, A. 17th & 18th century art p62-77
709.03
Souchal, F. Art of the early Middle Ages p202-50
709.02
Wertenbaker, L. The world of Picasso, 1881-
92

Art and illusion. Gombrich, E. H.
701

Art and life in America. Larkin, O. W. 709.73

Art and mankind
Larousse Encyclopedia of Byzantine and medieval art
709.02
Larousse Encyclopedia of modern art
709.03
Larousse Encyclopedia of prehistoric and ancient art
709.01
Larousse Encyclopedia of Renaissance and Baroque art
709.03

Art and mental illness
See pages in the following book:
Wilson, J. R. The mind p136-51
150

Art and religion. See Christian art and symbolism

The art and science of color. Hellman, H.
535.6

Art and society
Sullivan, L. The testament of stone 720.1
See also pages in the following book:
Camus, A. The myth of Sisyphus, and other essays p205-12
844

Art and the bronco. Henry, O.
In Henry, O. The complete works of O. Henry p400-08
S C

Art appreciation. See Esthetics

Art for money's sake. Sandaval, J.
In Mystery Writers of America. Crime without murder p245-51
S C

Art forgeries. See Forgery of works of art

Art has many faces. Kuh, K.
701

Art in America. Myron, R.
709.73

Art industries and trade
Faulkner, R. Art today
700

Assyria
See pages in the following book:
Saggs, H. W. F. Everyday life in Babylonia & Assyria p124-36
913.35

Babylonia
See pages in the following book:
Saggs, H. W. F. Everyday life in Babylonia & Assyria p124-36
913.35

China
See pages in the following book:
Loewe, M. Everyday life in early Imperial China p180-88
913.31

Europe
See pages in the following book:
Gay, P. Age of Enlightenment p164-81
901.93

Astrodynamics. See Astronautics; Space flight

Astrology

See pages in the following books:

Christopher, M. ESP, seers & psychics p101-14   **133**

Moore, P. Suns, myths and men p53-63 **523**

Shakespeare's England v 1 p444-61   **822.3**

Astronautics

Shelton, W. R. Man's conquest of space   **629.4**

See also pages in the following book:

Moore, P. Suns, myths and men p116-30   **523**

See also Artificial satellites; Interplanetary voyages; Manned space flight; Outer space; Rocketry; Space flight; Space flight to the moon; Space sciences; Space ships; Space stations; Space vehicles

Dictionaries

The McGraw-Hill Encyclopedia of space   **629.403**

The New Space encyclopaedia   **629.403**

Turnill, R. The language of space **629.403**

Russia

See pages in the following book:

Salisbury, H. E. ed. The Soviet Union: the fifty years p342-57   **914.7**

United States

Lewis, R. S. Appointment on the moon   **629.4**

See also pages in the following book:

Good things about the U.S. today p191-205   **917.3**

Astronauts

Gagarin, Y. Survival in space   **629.45**

Mailer, N. Of a fire on the moon   **629.45**

We seven   **629.45**

See also Manned space flight

Nutrition

See pages in the following book:

Gagarin, Y. Survival in space p11-17   **629.45**

The astronomer. Updike, J.

In Updike, J. Pigeon feathers, and other stories   **S C**

Astronomers

Fermi, L. Galileo and the scientific revolution   **92**

Geymonat, L. Galileo Galilei   **92**

Ley, W. Watchers of the sky   **523.09**

Astronomical instruments

See pages in the following book:

Rudaux, L. Larousse Encyclopedia of astronomy p451-77   **520.3**

Astronomical observatories

See pages in the following book:

Hodge, P. W. The revolution in astronomy p146-54   **523**

Astronomical spectroscopy. See Spectrum

Astronomy

Alter, D. Pictorial astronomy   **523**

Bergamini, D. The universe   **523.1**

Calder, N. Violet universe   **523**

Hawkins, G. S. Stonehenge decoded **913.36**

Hodge, P. W. The revolution in astronomy   **523**

Howard, N. E. The telescope handbook and star atlas   **522**

Menzel, D. H. A field guide to the stars and planets   **523**

Moore, P. Amateur astronomy   **523**

Moore, P. The atlas of the universe   **523**

Moore, P. Suns, myths and men   **523**

Rudaux, L. Larousse Encyclopedia of astronomy   **520.3**

Scientific American. Frontiers in astronomy   **520**

See also pages in the following books:

Asimov, I. The new intelligent man's guide to science p17-86   **500**

Asimov, I. The stars in their courses p3-46   **508**

Boy Scouts of America. Fieldbook for Boy Scouts, explorers, scouters, educators, outdoorsmen p512-29   **369.43**

Halacy, D. S. Habitat p20-35   **574.5**

Hammond, Incorporated. Earth and space p7-64   **551**

Newman, J. R. ed. What is science? p66-96   **508**

Sarton, G. A history of science v2 p53-67, 295-342   **509**

Shakespeare's England v 1 p444-61   **822.3**

Time-Life Books. A guide to science, and Index to the Life Science library p94-105   **500**

United Nations Educational, Scientific and Cultural Organization. 700 science experiments for everyone p67-75   **507.2**

Warshofsky, F. The new age of exploration p151-71   **500**

See also Astrology; Life on other planets; Moon; Planets; Quasars; Solar system; Space sciences; Stars; Sun; Tides

Atlases

See Stars—Atlases

Dictionaries

The New Space encyclopaedia   **629.403**

History

Ley, W. Watchers of the sky   **523.09**

See also pages in the following book:

Sarton, G. A history of science v 1 p275-97, 431-54, 501-21   **509**

Asylums. See Mentally ill—Care and treatment

At arms with Morpheus. Henry, O.

In Henry, O. The complete works of O. Henry p850-53   **S C**

At home in India. Bowles, C.   **915.4**

At Lehmann's. Mansfield, K.

In Mansfield, K. The short stories of Katherine Mansfield p72-78   **S C**

At the Bay. Mansfield, K.

In Mansfield, K. The short stories of Katherine Mansfield p263-99 **S C**

At the end of the passage. Kipling, R.

In Kipling, R. The best short stories of Rudyard Kipling p25-40   **S C**

In Kipling, R. Maugham's Choice of Kipling's best p65-82   **S C**

At the great 'Ecbo.' Cabrera Infante, G.
In Cohen, J. M. ed. Latin American writing today p203-15   860.8

At the hawk's well. Yeats, W. B.
In Block, H. M. ed. Masters of modern drama p429-32   808.82
In Yeats, W. B. Collected plays of W. B. Yeats p135-45   822

At the Hemingways. Sanford, M. H.   92

At the pit door. Crane, S.
In Crane, S. The complete short stories & sketches of Stephen Crane p769-72   S C

At the pit's mouth. Kipling, R.
In Kipling, R. The best short stories of Rudyard Kipling p5-9   S C

At the post office. Chekhov, A.
In Chekhov, A. The image of Chekhov p57-58   S C

Atatürk, Kamâl, President Turkey
See pages in the following book:
Stewart, D. Turkey p71-81   915.61

The atavism of John Tom Little Bear. Henry, O.
In Henry, O. The complete works of O. Henry p957-67   S C

Atheism
See pages in the following book:
Durant, W. The age of Voltaire p605-22   940.2

Athens
See pages in the following books:
Bowra, C. M. Classical Greece p93-104 938
Durant, W. The life of Greece p245-312   938
Horizon Magazine. The Horizon Book of ancient Greece p162-81   913.38
Mills, D. The book of the ancient Greeks p91-107, 171-231, 276-321   938

Parthenon
See pages in the following book:
Payne, R. Ancient Greece p260-66 913.38

Social life and customs
Davis, W. S. A day in old Athens 913.38
Webster, T. B. L. Everyday life in classical Athens   913.38

Athletes
See pages in the following book:
MacInnes, C. Australia and New Zealand p119-31   919.4

Athletes, Negro. See Negro athletes

Athletics
Cretzmeyer, F. X. Bresnahan and Tuttle's Track and field athletics   796.4
See also Physical education and training; Olympic games; Sports; Track athletics; and names of specific athletic activities, e.g. Boxing

Atkinson, J. Edward
(ed.) Black dimensions in contemporary American art   759.13

Atlanta Braves
See pages in the following book:
Durso, J. Amazing: the miracle of the Mets p169-78   796.357

The Atlantic book of British and American poetry. Sitwell, E. ed.   821.08

Atlantic Community. See North Atlantic region

Atlantic declaration, August 14, 1941
See pages in the following book:
Van Loon, H. W. The story of mankind p505-13   909

Atlantic Ocean
Masselman, G. The Atlantic: sea of darkness   910.9

The Atlantic: sea of darkness. Masselman, G.   910.9

Atlantis
Bowman, J. S. The quest for Atlantis 913
See also pages in the following books:
Ley, W. Another look at Atlantis, and fifteen other essays p 1-15   508
Schreiber, H. Vanished cities p28-38 913.03

Atlas. Darby, H. C. ed.
In The New Cambridge Modern history v14   909

Atlas of American history. Adams, J. T. ed.   911

Atlas of American history. See Hammond, Incorporated. History atlas of America   911

An atlas of Latin American affairs. Schneider, R. M.   918

Atlas of the classical world. Heyden, A. A. M. van der, ed.   911

The atlas of the universe. Moore, P.   523

Atlas of the world. Time-Life Books   912

An atlas of world history. Vries, S. de 911

Atlas of world history, Rand McNally. Rand McNally and Company   911

Atlas shrugged. Rand, A.   Fic

Atlases
Britannica atlas   912
Goode, J. P. Goode's World atlas   912
Hammond, Incorporated. Hammond Contempory world atlas   912
Hammond, Incorporated. Hammond World atlas   912
Hammond, Incorporated. Hammond's Ambassador world atlas   912
National Geographic Society. National Geographic Atlas of the world   912
The New Cambridge Modern history v14   909
Rand McNally and Company. The international atlas   912
Rand McNally and Company. Rand McNally Cosmopolitan world atlas   912
Rand McNally and Company. Rand McNally Pictorial world atlas   912
Time-Life Books. Atlas of the world 912
The Times, London. The Times Atlas of the world   912
See also pages in the following book:
Brown, L. A. Map making p104-18   526.8
See also Bible—Geography; and names of countries, cities, etc. with the subdivision Maps, e.g. U.S.—Maps

Atlases, Astronomical. See Stars—Atlases

Atlases, Historical
Gilbert, M. Recent history atlas: 1870 to the present day   911
Historical atlas of the world   911
Rand McNally and Company. Rand McNally Atlas of world history   911
Shepherd, W. R. Historical atlas   911
Vries, S. de. An atlas of world history   911

Atmosphere
Chandler, T. J. The air around us   551.5
See also pages in the following books:
Asimov, I. The new intelligent man's guide to science p143-201   500
Chapman, S. IGY: year of discovery p43-54   551

Atmosphere, Upper
See pages in the following books:
Beiser, A. The earth p57-79   551
Chapman, S. IGY: year of discovery p55-67   551

Atomic bomb
Chinnock, F. W. Nagasaki: the forgotten bomb   940.54
Osada, A. comp. Children of the A-bomb   940.54
See also pages in the following books:
Divine, R. A. ed. American foreign policy since 1945 p30-37   327.73
Stokley, J. The new world of the atom p68-82, 233-51   621.48

Fiction
Frank, P. Alas, Babylon   Fic
Golding, W. Lord of the Flies   Fic
Shute, N. On the beach   Fic
Vonnegut, K. Cat's cradle   Fic

Physiological effect
Hachiya, M. Hiroshima diary   940.54
Hersey, J. Hiroshima   940.54

Physiological effect—Fiction
Morris, E. The flowers of Hiroshima   Fic
Morris, E. The seeds of Hiroshima   Fic

Atomic energy
Fermi, L. Atoms for the world   621.48
Glasstone, S. Sourcebook on atomic energy   539.7
Stokley, J. The new world of the atom   621.48
See also pages in the following books:
Our poisoned planet: can we save it, p117-26   614
Sterland, E. G. Energy into power p76-101, 140-49   621
Warshofsky, F. The new age of exploration p37-56   500

Economic aspects
See pages in the following book:
Stokley, J. The new world of the atom p284-301   621.48

Atomic medicine
See pages in the following book:
Stokley, J. The new world of the atom p302-21   621.48

Atomic nuclei. See Nuclear physics
Atomic piles. See Nuclear reactors

Atomic power. See Atomic energy
Atomic power plants
Curtis, R. Perils of the peaceful atom   621.48
See also pages in the following book:
Stokley, J. The new world of the atom p107-30   621.48

Atomic submarines
Baar, J. Polaris!   623.4

Fiction
MacLean, A. Ice Station Zebra   Fic
Atomic theory. See Quantum theory
Atomic warfare
See pages in the following book:
Schweitzer, A. The teaching of reverence for life p53-55, 59-63   179
See also Atomic bomb; Atomic weapons

Fiction
Burdick, E. Fail-safe   Fic
Atomic weapons
See pages in the following books:
Cleveland, H. NATO: the transatlantic bargain p34-76   341.18
Divine, R. A. ed. American foreign policy since 1945 p233-40   327.73
See also Atomic bomb; Ballistic missiles

Atomic weapons and disarmament. See Disarmament

Atoms
Adler, I. The elementary mathematics of the atom   539
Romer, A. The restless atom   539.7
See also pages in the following books:
Gamow, G. The creation of the universe p44-73   523.1
Nourse, A. E. Universe, earth, and atom p509-23, 578-87   530.9
Warshofsky, F. The new age of exploration p37-56   500
See also Electrons; Nuclear physics

Atoms for the world. Fermi, L.   621.48
Atoms in the family; my life with Enrico Fermi. Fermi, L.   92

Atrophy. Wharton, E.
In Wharton, E. The collected short stories of Edith Wharton v2 p501-10   S C

Attack on the Gustavus III. Bartlett, J.
In Day, A. G. ed. The spell of Hawaii p59-62   919.69

Attaway, William
Blood on the forge; criticism
In Margolies, E. Native sons p47-64   810.9
The green men
In Margolies, E. A native son's reader p93-100   810.8

Attila
Fiction
Costain, T. B. The darkness and the dawn   Fic
Gardonyi, G. Slave of the Huns   Fic

Attitude (Psychology) See Public opinion

Aucassin et Nicolette
See pages in the following book:
Adams, H. Mont-Saint-Michel and Chartres p229-41   **726**

Auchincloss, Louis
The embezzler   **Fic**
Pioneers & caretakers   **813.09**
Power in trust
In The Saturday Evening Post. Best modern short stories p 1-15   **S C**

The auction. Crane, S.
In Crane, S. The complete short stories & sketches of Stephen Crane p323-25   **S C**

Auction bridge. See Bridge (Game)

Audels Foreign auto repair manual. Anderson, E. P.   **629.28**

Audels Handy book of practical electricity with wiring diagrams. Graham, F. D.   **621.302**

Audels Machinists library. Black, P. O. **621.9**

Auden, W. H.
The collected poetry of W. H. Auden **821**
Collected shorter poems: 1927-1957 **821**
(ed.) The portable Greek reader   **880.8**
(ed.) The Oxford Book of light verse. See The Oxford Book of light verse   **821.08**
(ed.) The Viking Book of aphorisms. See The Viking Book of aphorisms   **808.88**

About
Wright, G. T. W. H. Auden   **821.09**
See also pages in the following books:
Beard, A. E. S. Our foreign-born citizens p242-55   **920**
Untermeyer, L. Makers of the modern world p747-52   **920**

Auden, Wystan Hugh. See Auden, W. H.

Audio-visual education
American Association of School Librarians. Standards for school media programs   **371.33**

See also Moving pictures in education

Bibliography
Rufsvold, M. I. Guides to educational media   **016.3713**

Catalogs
National Information Center for Educational Media. Index to overhead transparencies   **371.33**

Directories
Audio visual market place   **371.33**
Audio visual market place   **371.33**

Audiovisual equipment. Oates, S. C. **371.33**

Audubon, John James
Audubon, by himself   **92**
The birds of America   **598**

About
See pages in the following books:
Beard, A. E. S. Our foreign-born citizens p 1-8   **920**
Brooks, V. The world of Washington Irving p182-200   **810.9**

Auerbach, Arnold M.
See pages in the following book:
Padwe, S. Basketball's Hall of Fame p133-42   **920**

Auerbach, Red. See Auerbach, Arnold M.

Augsburg, League of, War. See Grand Alliance, War of the, 1689-1697

August 1999: the earth men. Bradbury, R.
In Bradbury, R. The Martian chronicles p31-46   **S C**

August 1999: The summer night. Bradbury, R.
In Bradbury, R. The Martian chronicles p28-30   **S C**

August 2001: the settlers. Bradbury, R.
In Bradbury, R. The Martian chronicles p94-95   **S C**

August 2002: night meeting. Bradbury, R.
In Bradbury, R. The Martian chronicles p102-10   **S C**

August 2005: the old ones. Bradbury, R.
In Bradbury, R. The Martian chronicles p149   **S C**

August 2026: there will come soft rains. Bradbury, R.
In Bradbury, R. The Martian chronicles p205-11   **S C**

Augustine, Saint, Bp. of Hippo
See pages in the following books:
Russell, B. A history of Western philosophy p352-66   **109**
Thomas, H. Understanding the great philosophers p168-75   **109**

Augustus, Emperor of Rome
See pages in the following books:
Coolidge, O. Lives of famous Romans p66-89   **920**
Horizon Magazine. The light of the past p89-100   **901.9**
Mills, D. The book of the ancient Romans p282-92   **937**
Payne, R. Ancient Rome p153-77, 179-98   **913.37**

Augustus. Anouilh, J.
In The Best short plays, 1969 p133-45   **808.82**

Augustus does his bit. Shaw, B.
In Shaw, B. Complete plays, with prefaces v5 p71-91   **822**

Auks. See Great auks

Aura. Fuentes, C.
In Cohen, J. M. ed. Latin American writing today p107-37   **860.8**

Auran, John Henry
Ski Magazine. America's ski book **796.9**

Aurelius, Marcus. See Aurelius Antoninus, Marcus, Emperor of Rome

Aurelius Antoninus, Marcus, Emperor of Rome
See pages in the following books:
Coolidge, O. Lives of famous Romans p168-88   **920**
Hamilton, E. The echo of Greece p168-77   **880.9**
Thomas, H. Understanding the great philosophers p141-51   **109**

Fiction
White, E. L. The unwilling vestal   **Fic**

Aurora borealis. See Auroras

Auroras
See pages in the following book:
Chapman, S. IGY: year of discovery p68-73   **551**

Auslander, Joseph
The winged horse 809.1
(comp.) The winged horse anthology 821.08

Austen, Jane
Emma Fic
Emma; criticism
In Drew, E. The novel: a modern guide to fifteen English masterpieces p95-110 823.09
Mansfield Park Fic
Northanger Abbey Fic
Persuasion Fic
Pride and prejudice Fic
Sense and sensibility Fic

About
Becker, M. L. Presenting Miss Jane Austen 92
Craik, W. A. Jane Austen in her time 823.09
Laski, M. Jane Austen and her world 92

See also pages in the following books:
Daiches, D. A critical history of English literature v2 p743-65 820.9
Karl, F. R. An age of fiction: the nineteenth century British novel p27-62 823.09
Trilling, L. The opposing self p206-30 809
Wagenknecht, E. Cavalcade of the English novel p142-51 823.09

Contemporary England
Craik, W. A. Jane Austen in her time 823.09
Laski, M. Jane Austen and her world 92

Austin, Paul Britten
The Swedes 914.85

Australia
Brander, B. Australia 919.4
Grattan, C. H. The Southwest Pacific since 1900 990
MacInnes, C. Australia and New Zealand 919.4
Spate, O. H. K. Australia 919.4

Civilization
Turnbull, C. A concise history of Australia 994

Discovery and exploration
See pages in the following books:
Hale, J. R. Age of exploration p137-46 910.9
Stefánsson, V. ed. Great adventurers and explorations p623-90 910.9

Fiction
Cleary, J. The sundowners. Young People's ed. Fic
Shute, N. The legacy Fic
Shute, N. On the beach Fic

History
Turnbull, C. A concise history of Australia 994

Native races
See pages in the following book:
National Geographic Society. Vanishing peoples of the earth p114-31 572

Australia and New Zealand. MacInnes, C. 919.4

Australian (Aboriginal) mythology. See Mythology, Australian (Aboriginal)

Austria
See pages in the following books:
Life (Periodical) Handbook of the nations and international organizations p81-91 910
The New Cambridge Modern history v10 p522-51 909

Abgeordnetenhaus
See pages in the following book:
Twain, M. The complete essays of Mark Twain p208-35 814

Fiction
MacInnes, H. The Salzburg connection Fic

History
Stadler, K. R. Austria 943.6
See also pages in the following books:
Durant, W. Rousseau and revolution p341-66 940.2
The New Cambridge Modern history v3 p319-46, v6 p572-607, v11 p323-51 909

History—German occupation, 1940-1945
See pages in the following book:
Stadler, K. R. Austria p151-80 943.6

House of Deputies
See Austria. Abgeordnetenhaus

Politics and government
See pages in the following books:
The New Cambridge Modern history v9 p395-411 909
Twain, M. The complete essays of Mark Twain p208-35 814

Austrian Succession, War of, 1740-1748
See pages in the following book:
The New Cambridge Modern history v7 p416-64 909

Authoritarianism. See Totalitarianism

Authors
Cassell's Encyclopaedia of world literature 803
The New Century Handbook of English literature 820.3
See also pages in the following book:
Fermi, L. Illustrious immigrants p255-72 325.73

See also Children as authors; Poets; Women as authors; and classes of writers, e.g. Dramatists

Dictionaries
Fuller, M. ed. More junior authors 920.03
Kunitz, S. J. ed. The junior book of authors 920.03
Kunitz, S. J. ed. Twentieth century authors 920.03
Kunitz, S. J. ed. Twentieth century authors: first supplement 920.03
Magill, F. N. ed. Cyclopedia of world authors 920.03

Automobiles—*Continued*

Driving
See Automobile drivers

Engines
Hot Rod. The complete book of engines
629.2

Handbooks, manuals, etc.
Allen, W. A. Know your car   629.28
Anderson, E. P. Audels Foreign auto repair manual   629.28
Chilton's Auto repair manual   629.28
Glenn, H. T. Glenn's Foreign car repair manual   629.28
Glenn's Auto repair manual   629.28
Stapley, R. The car owner's handbook
629.28

History
Bird, A. Antique automobiles   629.209
Burness, T. Cars of the early twenties
629.209
Georgano, G. N. ed. Encyclopedia of American automobiles   629.22
Oliver, S. H. The Smithsonian collection of automobiles and motorcycles   629.22

Models
Hertz, L. H. The complete book of building and collecting model automobiles
629.22
Musciano, W. A. Building and operating model cars   629.22

Motors
See Automobiles—Engines

Racing
See Automobile racing

Repairing
Allen, W. A. Know your car   629.28
Anderson, E. P. Audels Foreign auto repair manual   629.28
Chilton's Auto repair manual   629.28
Glenn, H. T. Glenn's Foreign car repair manual   629.28
Glenn's Auto repair manual   629.28
Mechanix Illustrated. Car care   629.28
Smith, L. How to fix up old cars   629.28
Stapley, R. The car owner's handbook
629.28

Autres temps. Wharton, E.
In Wharton, E. The collected short stories of Edith Wharton v2 p257-81   S C

Autumn
Teale, E. W. Autumn across America
574.9

Autumn across America. Teale, E. W.
574.9

Autumn full of apples. Wakefield, D.
In The Best American short stories, 1966 p283-87   S C

The **autumn** garden. Hellman, L.
In Gassner, J. ed. Best American plays 3d ser. p205-49   812.08

Autun, France. Saint-Lizare (Cathedral)
See pages in the following book:
Horizon Magazine. The light of the past p110-21   901.9

Avalon. Seton, A.   Fic

Avery, Catherine B.
(ed.) The New Century Classical handbook. See The New Century Classical handbook   913.3803

Avery, Curtis E.
Love and marriage   301.42

Avery, Gillian
Victorian people   914.2

Avesta. See Zoroastrianism

Aviation. See Aeronautics

Aviation medicine. See Space medicine

Aviators. See Air pilots

Avon's harvest. Robinson, E. A.
In Robinson, E. A. The collected poems of Edwin Arlington Robinson p543-91   811

Awake and sing! Odets, C.
In Block, H. M. ed. Masters of modern drama p647-68   808.82
In Gassner, J. ed. Best American plays; supplementary volume, 1918-1958 p501-32   812.08
In Odets, C. Six plays p33-101   812

An **awakening.** Anderson, S.
In Anderson, S. Winesburg, Ohio (Modern Lib) p213-27   S C
In Anderson, S. Winesburg, Ohio (Viking) p179-89   S C

The **awakening.** Corkery, D.
In Garrity, D. A. ed. 44 Irish short stories p32-46   S C

Awakening. Galsworthy, J.
In Galsworthy, J. The Forsyte saga p643-62   Fic

The **awakening** land. Richter, C.   Fic

Awakening minorities: American Indians, Mexican Americans, Puerto Ricans. Howard, J. R. ed.   301.45

The **awakening** of American nationalism, 1815-1828. Dangerfield, G.   973.5

The **axe.** Undset, S.
In Undset, S. The master of Hestviken v 1   Fic

Axelrod, George
The seven year itch
In Gassner, J. ed. Best American plays; 4th ser. p503-33   812.08

Axelrod, Herbert R.
Axelrod's Tropical fish book   639

Axel's castle. Wilson, E.   809

The **Axis** strikes (1939-1942) Reeder, R.
In Reeder, R. The story of the Second World War v 1   940.53

Ayer, Ethan
The promise of heat
In The Best American short stories, 1967 p 1-12   S C

Aylesworth, Thomas G.
This vital air, this vital water   614

Aylward, Gladys
Burgess, A. The small woman   92

Aymar, Brandt
A pictorial history of the world's great trials   343

Azef, Evno Fishelevich
See pages in the following book:
Dulles, A. ed. Great true spy stories p192-205   327

Aztecs
Wauchope, R. ed. The Indian background of Latin American history   **970.3**
See also pages in the following books:
Baity, E. C. Americans before Columbus p188-207   **970.1**
Ceram, C. W. Gods, graves, and scholars p323-47   **913.03**
Crow, J. A. The epic of Latin America p48-60, 75-86   **980**
Innes, H. The conquistadors p88-115 **973.1**
Josephy, A. M. The Indian heritage of America p212-17   **970.1**
Leonard, J. N. Ancient America p62-68, 139-46, 153-61   **913.7**
Lloyd, A. The Spanish centuries p127-40   **946**
Mead, M. ed. The golden age of American anthropology p48-57   **572.97**
Vlahos, O. New world beginnings p264-81   **913.7**

Religion and mythology
See pages in the following book:
Larousse World mythology p460-72   **291**
The **azure** steppe. Sholokhov, M.
In Sholokhov, M. Tales of the Don p190-201   **S C**
'Azzām, 'Abd-al-Rahmān
The eternal message of Muhammad   **297**

B

Baa baa black sheep. Kipling, R.
In Kipling, R. The best short stories of Rudyard Kipling p155-75   **S C**
Baalsrud, Jan
Howarth, D. We die alone   **940.54**
Baar, James
Polaris!   **623.4**
Babbitt, Milton
See pages in the following book:
Ewen, D. Composers of tomorrow's music p129-36   **920**
Babbitt. Lewis, S.
In Lewis, S. Lewis at zenith p337-583   **Fic**
Babes in the jungle. Henry, O.
In Henry, O. The complete works of O. Henry p1499-1503   **S C**
Babi Yar. Anatoli, A.   **Fic**
Baby and child care. Spock, B.   **649**
Baby book, Better Homes & Gardens. Better Homes and Gardens   **649**
The **baby** party. Fitzgerald, F. S.
In Fitzgerald, F. S. The stories of F. Scott Fitzgerald p209-19   **S C**
Baby sitters
Kraft, I. When teenagers take care of children   **649**
Lowndes, M. A manual for baby sitters   **649**

Babylon revisited. Fitzgerald, F. S.
In Fitzgerald, F. S. The Fitzgerald reader p302-22   **S C**
In Fitzgerald, F. S. The stories of F. Scott Fitzgerald p385-402   **S C**
In Foley, M. ed. Fifty best American short stories, 1915-1965 p98-117   **S C**
Babylonia
See pages in the following books:
Ceram, C. W. ed. Hands on the past p223-35   **913.03**
Schreiber, H. Vanished cities p119-34   **913.03**
White, A. T. Lost worlds p219-28   **913.03**
Antiquities
See pages in the following book:
Durant, W. Our Oriental heritage p219-64   **950**
Religion
See Assyro-Babylonian religion
Babylonian literature. See Assyro-Babylonian literature
Babylonian mythology. See Mythology, Assyro-Babylonian
The **Bacchae**. Euripides
In Bentley, E. comp. The great playwrights v 1 p227-68   **808.82**
In Oates, W. J. ed. The complete Greek drama v2 p227-82   **882.08**
Bach, Johann Christian
See pages in the following book:
Chapin, V. Giants of the keyboard p22-36   **920**
Bach, Johann Sebastian
See pages in the following book:
Bauer, M. Music through the ages p281-303   **780.9**
Bernstein, L. The joy of music p225-65   **780.1**
Cross, M. The Milton Cross New encyclopedia of the great composers and their music p15-42   **920.03**
Durant, W. The age of Voltaire p412-30   **940.2**
Ewen, D. ed. The complete book of classical music p90-126   **780.1**
Ewen, D. ed. The world of the great composers p34-53   **920**
Shippen, K. B. The heritage of music p77-90   **780.9**
Bach, Marcus
Had you been born in another faith   **291**
Bacharach, Burt
The Bacharach and David Song book   **784**
The **Bacharach** and David Song book. Bacharach, B.   **784**
Bache, Alexander Dallas
See pages in the following book:
Jones, B. Z. ed. The golden age of science p264-95   **920**
Back to Methuselah. Shaw, B.
In Shaw, B. Complete plays, with prefaces v2 p3-262   **822**
Backgammon
See pages in the following book:
Gibson, W. Family games America plays p101-16   **793**

The **background**. Saki
  In Saki. The short stories of Saki p134-
  37   **S C**
Backward areas. See Underdeveloped areas
Backward children. See Slow learning children
Bacon, Francis, Viscount St Albans
  Bowen, C. D. Francis Bacon   92
    See also pages in the following books:
  Durant, W. The story of philosophy p75-
  112   109
  Horizon Magazine. The light of the past
  p168-83   901.9
  Thomas, H. Understanding the great
  philosophers p187-99   109
Bacon, Nathaniel
    See pages in the following book:
  Johnston, M. Pioneers of the Old South
  p161-87   975
Bacon, Roger
    See pages in the following book:
  Costain, T. B. The magnificent century
  p349-57   942.03
Bacon's Rebellion, 1679
    See pages in the following book:
  Craven, W. F. The colonies in transition,
  1660-1713 p138-46   973.2
Bacteria. See Bacteriology
Bacteriology
  De Kruif, P. Microbe hunters   920
  Encyclopedia of the life sciences v4   574.03
    See also pages in the following book:
  Scientific American. Facets of genetics p30-
  41   575.1
    See also Microorganisms
Bad Bad Jo-Jo. Herlihy, J. L.
  In The Best short plays, 1971 p135-54
                                            808.82
A **bad idea.** Mansfield, K.
  In Mansfield, K. The short stories of
  Katherine Mansfield p658-61 **S C**
Bader, Douglas
  Brickhill, P. Reach for the sky   92
The **badge** of policeman O'Roon. Henry, O.
  In Henry, O. The complete works of O.
  Henry p1401-04   **S C**
Badminton
  Sports Illustrated. Sports Illustrated Book
  of badminton   796.34
    See also pages in the following book:
  American Association for Health, Physical
  Education, and Recreation. Physical edu-
  cation for high school students p45-57
                                            613.7
Baedeker, Karl
  Autoguides   910.2
  Handbooks   910.2
Baez, Joan
  Daybreak   92
The **bag.** Saki
  In Saki. The short stories of Saki p82-87
                                            S C
Bagley, J. J.
  Life in medieval England   914.2
Baiæ
    See pages in the following book:
  Schreiber, H. Vanished cities p170-79
                                            913.03

Baigell, Matthew
  A history of American painting   759.13
Bailey, Adrian
  The cooking of the British Isles   641.5
Bailey, Charles W.
  (jt. auth.) Knebel, F. Convention   Fic
  (jt. auth.) Knebel, F. Seven days in May
                                         Fic
Bailey, Cyril
  (ed.) The legacy of Rome   913.37
Bailey, Stephen K.
  (ed.) American politics and government 353
Bailout. Dwiggins, D.   797.5
Bains Turcs. Mansfield, K.
  In Mansfield, K. The short stories of
  Katherine Mansfield p159-64 **S C**
Bainton, Roland H.
  Here I stand; a life of Martin Luther 92
  Horizon Magazine. The Horizon History
  of Christianity   270
Baird, A. Craig
  (ed.) Representative American speeches.
  See Representative American speeches
                                          815.08
Baity, Elizabeth Chesley
  Americans before Columbus   970.1
Bakeless, John
  Signers of the Declaration   920
  Spies of the Confederacy   973.7
Bakeless, Katherine
  (jt. auth.) Bakeless, J. Signers of the
  Declaration   920
Baker, Carlos
  Ernest Hemingway   92
  Hemingway: the writer as artist 813.09
Baker, Laura Nelson
  Maybe next week
  In Seventeen. Stories from Seventeen
  p99-115   **S C**
  (jt. auth.) Stoutenburg, A. Explorer of the
  unconscious: Sigmund Freud   92
Baker, Leonard
  Roosevelt and Pearl Harbor   973.917
Baker, Liva
  Felix Frankfurter   92
Baker, Louise
  Out on a limb   92
Baker, Sheridan
  Ernest Hemingway   813.09
Baker v. Carr
    See pages in the following book:
  Fribourg, M. G. The Supreme Court in
  American history p162-79   347.9
Bakers and bakeries
    See pages in the following book:
  Kefauver, E. In a few hands: monopoly
  power in America p137-59   338.8
The **baker's dozen.** Saki
  In Saki. The short stories of Saki p99-
  104   **S C**
Baking
    See pages in the following books:
  Brown, D. American cooking p166-83
                                          641.5
  Brown, D. The cooking of Scandinavia
  p160-81   641.5
    See also Cake; Pastry

Bakst, Aaron
Mathematical puzzles and pastimes 793.7
Balance of power
See pages in the following book:
Halle, L. J. The cold war as history
p 1-9 909.82
Balanchine, George
Balanchine's New complete stories of the
great ballets 792.8
Balboa, Vasco Núñez de
See pages in the following books:
Richman, I. B. The Spanish conquerors
p69-90 973.1
Stefánsson, V. ed. Great adventures and
explorations p225-33 910.9
Balchen, Bernt
Come north with me 92
Balcombe, Betsy
Fiction
Costain, T. B. The last love Fic
Bald eagle
Mannix, D. The last eagle 598
The bald soprano. Ionesco, E.
In Block, H. M. ed. Masters of modern
drama p1120-31 808.82
In Ionesco, E. Four plays p7-42 842
Balderston, John Lloyd
Berkeley Square
In Gassner, J. ed. Twenty-five best
plays of the modern American
theatre; early ser. p647-85 812.08
Baldwin, Faith
Still is the night
In Becker, M. L. ed. The home book of
Christmas p674-78 394.26
Baldwin, James
Blues for Mister Charlie 812
—Same
In Gassner, J. ed. Best American plays;
6th ser. p47-96 812.08
Come out the wilderness
In Abrahams, W. ed. Fifty years of
the American short story v 1 p12-
33 S C
Equal in Paris
In Engle, P. ed. On creative writing
p109-25 808.02
Exodus
In Clarke, J. H. ed. American Negro
short stories p197-204 S C
The fire next time 301.451
Go tell it on the mountain Fic
Going to meet the man S C
Contents: The rockpile; The outing; The man
child; Previous condition; Sonny's blues; This
morning, this evening, so soon; Come out the
wilderness; Going to meet the man
Nobody knows my name 301.451
Notes of a native son 301.451
The outing
In Margolies, E. A native son's reader
p255-80 810.8
Tell me how long the train's been gone
In The Best American short stories,
1968 p 1-28 S C
This morning, this evening, so soon
In Foley, M. ed. Fifty best American
short stories, 1915-1965 p618-55
S C
In Hughes, L. ed. The best short sto-
ries by Negro writers p213-52
S C

About
See pages in the following book:
Margolies, E. Native sons p102-26 810.9
Baldwin, Marshall Whithed
(jt. auth.) Hayes, C. J. H. History of
Western civilization since 1500 940.2
Balewa, Sir Abubakar Tafewa
See pages in the following book:
Kenworthy, L. S. Leaders of new nations
p48-64 920
Balkan Peninsula
Stillman, E. The Balkans 914.96
The Balkans. Stillman, E. 914.96
Ball, John
In the heat of the night Fic
Johnny get your gun Fic
Ball, W. W. Rouse
Mathematical recreations & essays 793.7
Ball four. Bouton, J. 92
Ball games. See names of games, e.g. Soccer
Ball-of-Fat. Maupassant, G. de
In Maupassant, G. de. Selected short
stories p 1-53 S C
Ballads
The Viking Book of folk ballads of the
English-speaking world 808.81
See also pages in the following books:
Auslander, J. The winged horse p139-46
809.1
Stevenson, B. E. comp. The home book of
modern verse p643-85 821.08
Ballads, American
Fife, A. ed. Ballads of the great West
811.08
Lomax, J. A. comp. American ballads and
folk songs 784.4
Lomax, J. A. comp. Cowboy songs and
other frontier ballads 784.4
Lomax, J. A. ed. Folk song: U.S.A. 784.4
Sandburg, C. ed. The American songbag
784.4
See also pages in the following book:
Ewen, D. Great men of American popular
song p45-52 920
Ballads, English
The Oxford Book of ballads 821.08
See also pages in the following book:
Shakespeare's England v2 p511-38 822.3
Ballads, Scottish
The Oxford Book of ballads 821.08
See also pages in the following book:
The Oxford Book of Scottish verse p264-
304 821.08
Ballads for sale. Lowell, A.
In Lowell, A. The complete poetical
works of Amy Lowell p534-89 811
Ballads of a Cheechako. Service, R.
In Service, R. Collected poems of Robert
Service p77-164 811
Ballads of the great West. Fife, A. ed. 811.08
Ballet
Balanchine, G. Balanchine's New complete
stories of the great ballets 792.8

Bar-room ballads. Service, R.
    In Service, R. Collected poems of Robert
        Service p601-728   811
Bar sinister. Davis, R. H.
    In The Scribner treasury p243-71   **S C**
Barbados
        See pages in the following book:
    Williams, E. From Columbus to Castro:
        the history of the Caribbean, 1492-1969
        p95-119   972.9
Barbados. Marshall, P.
    In Hughes, L. ed. The best short-sto-
        ries by Negro writers p309-24
                                           S C
Barbara's wedding. Barrie, J. M.
    In Barrie, J. M. The plays of J. M.
        Barrie p803-19   822
Barbarian Europe. Simons, G.   940.1
Barbecue cooking. See Outdoor cookery
Barbed wire. Canzoneri, R.
    In The Best American short stories,
        1971 p74-85   **S C**
Barber, Samuel
        See pages in the following book:
    Cross, M. The Milton Cross New en-
        cyclopedia of the great composers and
        their music p43-51   920.03
    Ewen, D. ed. The new book of modern
        composers p53-61   920
Barbizon school
        See pages in the following book:
    Cheney, S. The story of modern art p87-
        98   709.03
Barbour, John A.
    In the wake of the whale   599
    Associated Press. Footprints on the moon
                                          629.45
Barbour, Philip L.
    Pocahontas and her world   975.5
Barchester Towers. Trollope, A.   Fic
Bardach, John
    Harvest of the sea   333.9
Bardeen, John
        See pages in the following book:
    National Geographic Society. Those inven-
        tive Americans p208-16   608
Barefoot in the park. Simon, N.   812
Barendsz, Willem
        See pages in the following book:
    Stefánsson, V. ed. Great adventures and
        explorations p428-40   910.9
Barents, William. See Barendsz, Willem
Barker, Granville
    The Madras House
    In Dickinson, T. H. ed. Chief contem-
        porary dramatists [first series]
        p149-206   808.82
    For a work edited by this author see
    Granville-Barker, Harley
Barker, James N.
    Superstition
    In Gassner, J. ed. Best plays of the early
        American theatre p38-72   812.08
    In Quinn, A. H. ed. Representative
        American plays p109-40   812.08

Barker, Lucius J.
    (ed.) Civil liberties and the Constitution
                                          342.73
Barker, Twiley W.
    (jt. ed.) Barker, L. J. ed. Civil liberties
        and the Constitution   342.73
Barker, Will
    Familiar insects of America   595.7
Barlow, Peter
    Barlow's Tables of squares, cubes, square
        roots, cube roots and reciprocals of all
        integers, up to 12,500   510.21
Barlow's Tables of squares, cubes, square
    roots, cube roots and reciprocals of all
    integers, up to 12,500. Barlow, P. 510.21
Barn burning. Faulkner, W.
    In Abrahams, W. ed. Fifty years of the
        American short story v 1 p254-70
                                          S C
    In Faulkner, W. Collected stories of Wil-
        liam Faulkner p3-25   **S C**
    In Faulkner, W. The Faulkner reader
                                          S C
    In Faulkner, W. Selected short stories
        of William Faulkner p3-27   **S C**
    In Havighurst, W. ed. Masters of the
        modern short story p66-85   **S C**
Barn burning. Vidal, G.
    In Vidal, G. Visit to a small planet, and
        other television plays p235-52 812
Barnaby Rudge. Dickens, C.   Fic
Barnes, Clive
    (jt. ed.) Gassner, J. ed. Best American
        plays; 6th ser.   812.08
Barnes, Margaret Campbell
    The Tudor rose   Fic
Barnett, Lincoln
    The university and Dr Einstein   530.1
    Life (Periodical) The wonders of life on
        earth   574
Barney, Joshua
        See pages in the following book:
    Roscoe, T. True tales of bold escapes p135-
        76   904
Barnhart, Clarence L.
    (ed.) The American college dictionary. See
        The American college dictionary   423
    (ed.) The New Century Cyclopedia of
        names. See The New Century Cyclopedia
        of names   031
    (ed.) The New Century Handbook of
        English literature. See The New Cen-
        tury Handbook of English literature
                                          820.3
    (ed.) Thorndike-Barnhart Comprehensive
        desk dictionary. See Thorndike-Barnhart
        Comprehensive desk dictionary   423
    (ed.) The World book dictionary. See The
        World book dictionary   423
Barnum, Phineas Taylor
    Wallace, I. The fabulous showman   92
The Baron. Mansfield, K.
    In Mansfield, K. The short stories of
        Katherine Mansfield p41-44 **S C**
Baronage. See Nobility
Baroque art. See Art, Baroque

Barraclough, E. M. C.
(ed.) Flags of the world. See Flags of the world   929.9

Barraclough, Geoffrey
(ed.) Eastern and Western Europe in the Middle Ages. See Eastern and Western Europe in the Middle Ages   940.1

Barrett, E. C.
Viewing weather from space   551.59

Barrett, Elizabeth. See Browning, Elizabeth Barrett

Barrett, S. M.
(ed.) Geronimo. Geronimo: his own story
92

Barrett, William E.
The lilies of the field   Fic
—Same
In Costain, T. B. ed. Read with me p37-80   S C

The **Barretts** of Wimpole Street. Besier, R.
822

—Same
In Cerf, B. A. comp. Sixteen famous British plays p673-745   822.08

Barrie, J. M.
The little minister   Fic
The plays of J. M. Barrie   822
Contents: Peter Pan; Quality Street; The admirable Crichton; Alice Sit-by-the-Fire; What every woman knows; A kiss for Cinderella; Dear Brutus; Mary Rose; Pantaloon; Half an hour; Seven women; Old friends; Rosalind; The will; The twelve-pound look; The new word; A well-remembered voice; Barbara's wedding; The old lady shows her medals; Shall we join the ladies
Farewell Miss Julie Logan
In The Scribner treasury p643-89   S C

Twelve-pound look
In Cerf, B. ed. Thirty famous one-act plays p115-29   808.82

What every woman knows
In Cerf, B. A. comp. Sixteen famous British plays p123-84   822.08

Barron's Guide to the two-year colleges
378.73

Barron's Handbook of American college financial aid. Proia, N. C.   378.3

Barron's Handbook of junior and community college financial aid. Proia, N. C.
378.3

Barron's How to prepare for college entrance examinations. Brownstein, S. C.
371.26

Barron's How to prepare for the high school equivalency examination reading interpretation tests. Farley, E. J.   371.27

Barron's Profiles of American colleges. Fine, B.   378.73

Barrows. See Mounds and mound builders

Barry, Philip
The animal kingdom
In Gassner, J. ed. Twenty best plays of the modern American theatre p325-70   812.08

Here come the clowns
In Gassner, J. ed. Best American plays; supplementary volume, 1918-1958 p533-69   812.08

Paris bound
In Gassner, J. ed. Twenty-five best plays of the modern American theatre; early ser. p257-93   812.08
In Quinn, A. H. ed. Representative American plays p1059-99   812.08

The Philadelphia story
In Gassner, J. ed. Best plays of the modern American theatre; 2d ser. p411-58   812.08
About
See pages in the following books:
Gould, J. Modern American playwrights p78-98   812.09
Shannon, W. V. The American Irish p281-90   301.453

Barrymore, Ethel
See pages in the following book:
Stoddard, H. Famous American women p48-58   920

Barth, John
Lost in the funhouse
In Abrahams, W. ed. Fifty years of the American short story v 1 p34-54
S C

Barthelme, Donald
See the moon
In Abrahams, W. ed. Fifty years of the American short story v 1 p55-64
S C

Bartholomew, Carol
My heart has seventeen rooms   915.4

Bartholomew, John & Son ltd.
The Times, London. The Times Atlas of the world   912

Bartlett, John
Attack on the Gustavus III
In Day, A. G. ed. The spell of Hawaii p59-62   919.69
(comp.) Familiar quotations   808.88

Bartók, Béla
See pages in the following books:
Cross, M. The Milton Cross New encyclopedia of the great composers and their music p52-64   920.03
Ewen, D. ed. The new book of modern composers p62-74   920
Shippen, K. B. The heritage of music p240-42   780.9

Barton, Clara Harlowe
Ross, I. Angel of the battlefield   92
See also pages in the following books:
Dodge, B. S. The story of nursing p59-74   610.73
Stoddard, H. Famous American women p59-70   920

Barton, Mary Neill
Enoch Pratt Free Library, Baltimore, Md. Reference books   016

Barton, Otis
See pages in the following book:
Soule, G. The greatest depths p69-81 551.4

Baruch, Bernard Mannes
Baruch: my own story   92

Baruch, Dorothy W.
Glass house of prejudice   301.45

Barzun, Jacques
The American university   378.73
The modern researcher   808.02
Teacher in America   371.1
(ed.) Follett, W. Modern American usage   428

Baseball
Mantle, M. The education of a baseball player   92
Mays, W. My secrets of playing baseball   796.357
Sports Illustrated. Sports Illustrated Baseball   796.357
See also pages in the following books:
American Association for Health, Physical Education, and Recreation. Physical education for high school students p59-78   613.7
Catton, B. Prefaces to history p191-201   973.7
Friendlich, D. Panorama of sports in America p3-15   796

Biography
Bouton, J. Ball four   92
Gibson, B. From ghetto to glory: the story of Bob Gibson   92
Mantle, M. The education of a baseball player   92
Mantle, M. The quality of courage   920
Mays, W. Willie Mays: my life in and out of baseball   92
Musial, S. Stan Musial: "The Man's" own story   92
Piersall, J. Fear strikes out   92
Robinson, F. My life is baseball   92
Silverman, A. Joe Di Maggio: the golden year 1941   92
Williams, T. My turn at bat   92
See also pages in the following book:
Orr, J. The Black athlete: his story in American history p55-79   920

History
Allen, L. The American League story   796.357
Allen, L. The National League story   796.357

Statistics
The Baseball encyclopedia   796.357
The Baseball encyclopedia   796.357
Basic bibliography of science and technology, McGraw-Hill   016.5
Basic documents in American history. Morris, R. B. ed.   973
A basic history of the United States. See Beard, C. A. The Beards' New basic history of the United States   973
Basic machine shop practice. Black, P. O.
In Black, P. O. Audels Machinists library v 1   621.9
Basic teachings of the great psychologists. Stansfeld, S. S.   150
The basic works of Aristotle. Aristotle   888
Basie, Count. See Basie, William

Basie, William
See pages in the following book:
Williams, M. The jazz tradition p107-19   781.5
Basil and Cleopatra. Fitzgerald, F. S.
In Fitzgerald, F. S. The Fitzgerald reader p276-94   S C
Basketball
Sports Illustrated. Sports Illustrated Basketball   796.32
See also pages in the following books:
American Association for Health, Physical Education, and Recreation. Physical education for high school students p81-95   613.7
Friendlich, D. Panorama of sports in America p62-73   796

Biography
Padwe, S. Basketball's Hall of Fame   920
Pepe, P. Greatest stars of the NBA   920
See also pages in the following book:
Orr, J. The Black athlete: his story in American history p125-33   920

History
Hollander, Z. ed. Basketball's greatest games   796.32
Basketball's greatest games. Hollander, Z. ed.   796.32
Basketball's Hall of Fame. Padwe, S.   920
Bassan, Maurice
(ed.) Stephen Crane   818
Bassett, Mrs Clarence
Juanito and Maria's Christmas
In Wernecke, H. H. ed. Celebrating Christmas around the world p186-90   394.26
Bassett, John Spencer
Makers of a new nation
In Pageant of America v9   973
Bassett, Margaret
Profiles & portraits of American Presidents & their wives   920
Bastille
See pages in the following book:
Horizon Magazine. The light of the past p224-31   901.9
Bâtard. London, J.
In London, J. Jack London's Tales of adventure   S C
Bateman, James
Animal traps and trapping   799
Bates, Marston
The forest and the sea   574.5
Man in nature   573
(ed.) Darwin, C. The Darwin reader   574
Bathhurst, Gambia
Lindbergh, A. M. Listen! The wind   629.13
Bathyscaphe
Cousteau, J. Y. ed. Captain Cousteau's Underwater treasury   627.7
Batlle y Ordóñez, José
See pages in the following books:
Alexander, R. J. Prophets of the revolution p9-30   920
Worcester, D. E. Makers of Latin America p190-95   920

Beale, Howard K.
Theodore Roosevelt and the rise of America to world power   327.73
Beals, Carleton
The nature of revolution   323
Bean (L. L.) inc. Freeport, Me.
See pages in the following book:
Mahoney, T. The great merchants p299-309   658.87
The bear. Faulkner, W.
In Day, A. G. ed. The greatest American short stories p309-26   S C
In Faulkner, W. The Faulkner reader   S C
In Faulkner, W. The portable Faulkner p197-320   S C
A bear hunt. Faulkner, W.
In Faulkner, W. Collected stories of William Faulkner p63-79   S C
The bear-hunt. Tolstoy, L.
In Tolstoy, L. Short stories v2 p39-47   S C
In Tolstoy, L. Twenty-three tales p40-49   S C
Beard, Annie E. S.
Our foreign-born citizens   920
Beard, Charles
(jt. auth.) Cunnington, C. W. A dictionary of English costume   391.03
Beard, Charles A.
American foreign policy in the making, 1932-1940   327.73
The Beards' New basic history of the United States   973
An economic interpretation of the Constitution of the United States   342.73
An economic interpretation of the Constitution of the United States; criticism
In Downs, R. B. Books that changed America p185-96   810.8
The rise of American civilization   973
The Supreme Court and the Constitution   342.73
Beard, Mary R.
(jt. auth.) Beard, C. A. The Beards' New basic history of the United States   973
(jt. auth.) Beard, C. A. The rise of American civilization   973
Beard, William
(ed.) Beard, C. A. The Beard's New basic history of the United States   973
Bears
Haynes, B. D. ed. The grizzly bear   599
Leslie, R. F. The bears and I   599
Olsen, J. Night of the grizzlies   599
The bears and I. Leslie, R. F.   599
Beasts and super-beasts. Saki
In Saki. The short stories of Saki p259-438   S C
Beasts in my bed. Durrell, J.   591
Beat to quarters. Forester, C. S.
In Forester, C. S. Captain Horatio Hornblower p 1-220   Fic

The Beatles
Davies, H. The Beatles   920
See also pages in the following book:
Shaw, A. The rock revolution p80-94   781.5
Beau Geste. Wren, P. C.   Fic
Beaumont, William
Experiments and observations on the gastric juice and the physiology of digestion; criticism
In Downs, R. B. Books that changed America p36-46   810.9
Beautiful light and black our dreams. King, W.
In Hughes, L. ed. The best short stories by Negro writers p438-47   S C
The beautiful ones are not yet born. Armah, A. K.   Fic
The beautiful suit. Wells, H. G.
In Wells, H. G. The complete short stories of H. G. Wells p139-43   S C
Beauty, Personal. See Grooming, Personal
Beauty is truth. Guest, A.
In Seventeen. Stories from Seventeen p66-76   S C
Beauvoir, Simone de
See pages in the following book:
Durant, W. Interpretations of life p163-206   809
Beccafumi, Domenico
See pages in the following book:
Visari, G. The lives of the painters, sculptors and architects v3 p140-50   920
Bech: a book. Updike, J.   S C
Bech takes pot luck. Updike, J.
In Prize stories, 1970: The O. Henry Awards p185-203   S C
Becht, Sidney
See pages in the following book:
Williams, M. T. ed. The art of jazz p3-10   781.5
Becker, Carl
The Declaration of Independence   973.3
The eve of the Revolution   973.2
Becker, Esther R.
The successful secretary's handbook   651.02
Becker, Marion Rombauer
(jt. auth.) Rombauer, I. S. Joy of cooking   641.5
Becker, May Lamberton
(ed.) The home book of Christmas 394.26
Introducing Charles Dickens   92
Presenting Miss Jane Austen   92
Becket, Thomas à. See Thomas à Becket, Saint, Abp. of Canterbury
Becket. Anouilh, J.
In Richards, S. ed. Best plays of the sixties p 1-117   808.82
Beckett, Samuel
Endgame
In Block, H. M. ed. Masters of modern drama p1104-17   808.82
About
Esslin, M. ed. Samuel Beckett   848

Behrman, S. N.
Biography
In Cerf, B. A. ed. Sixteen famous American plays p207-73   812.08
In Gassner, J. ed. Best American plays; supplementary volume, 1918-1958 p253-95   812.08
End of summer
In Gassner, J. ed. Twenty best plays of the modern American theatre p275-323   812.08
The second man
In Gassner, J. ed. Twenty-five best plays of the modern American theatre; early ser. p333-70   812.08
Jacobowsky and the Colonel; adaptation. See Werfel, F. Jacobowsky and the Colonel

About
See pages in the following book:
Krutch, J. W. The American drama since 1918 p180-205   812.09
Behrman, Samuel Nathaniel. See Behrman, S. N.
Beiderbecke, Bix. See Beiderbecke, Leon Bismarck
Beiderbecke, Leon Bismarck
See pages in the following books:
Hadlock, R. Jazz masters of the twenties p76-105   920
Williams, M. The jazz tradition p60-69   781.5
Williams, M. T. ed. The art of jazz p59-73   781.5

Beiser, Arthur
The earth   551
Belasco, David
Madame Butterfly
In Quinn, A. H. ed. Representative American plays p621-36   812.08
A **belated** promotion. Cooper, D.
In Dulles, A. ed. Great spy stories from fiction p294-307   S C
The **belated** Russian passport. Twain, M.
In Twain, M. The complete short stories of Mark Twain p409-23   S C
Belaúnde, Fernando, President Peru
See pages in the following book:
Gunther, J. Inside South America p321-38   980

Belfrage, Sally
Freedom summer   323.4
Belgian Congo. See Congo (Democratic Republic)
Belgium
Rachlis, E. The Low Countries   914.92
Belgrade, 1926. Ambler, E.
In Dulles, A. ed. Great spy stories from fiction p235-52   S C
Belisarius
See pages in the following book:
Asimov, I. Constantinople p71-80   949.6
Bell, Alexander Graham
Costain, T. B. The chord of steel   92
National Geographic Society. Those inventive Americans   608
See also pages in the following book:
Beard, A. E. S. Our foreign-born citizens p30-37   920

Bell, Eric Temple
Mathematics   510.9
Men of mathematics   920
Bell, book and candle. Van Druten, J.
In Gassner, J. ed. Best American plays 3d ser. p593-626   812.08
Bell family
Costain, T. B. The chord of steel [biography of Alexander Graham Bell]   92
A **bell** for Adano. Hersey, J.   Fic
The **bell** of charity. Kentfield, C.
In The New Yorker. Stories from The New Yorker, 1950-1960 p119-36 S C
The **bell-ringer** of Angel's. Harte, B.
In Harte, B. The best of Bret Harte p229-67   S C
Bell Wethers. Phelan, J.
In Garrity, D. A. ed. 44 Irish short stories p365-77   S C
Bellamy, Edward
Looking backward: 2000-1887   Fic
Looking backward, 2000-1887; criticism
In Downs, R. B. Books that changed America p100-09   810.9
Bellavita. Pirandello, L.
In Richards, S. ed. Best short plays of the world theatre, 1958-1967 p275-85   808.82
Belles on their toes [biography of Lillian Gilbreth]. Gilbreth, F. B.   92
Bellflower. Maupassant, G. de
In Maupassant, G. de. Selected short stories p198-204   S C
Bellini family
See pages in the following book:
Vasari, G. The lives of the painters, sculptors and architects v2 p44-53   920
Bello, Andrés
See pages in the following book:
Worcester, D. E. Makers of Latin America p98-106   920
Belloc, Hilaire
The mowing of a field
In Parker, E. ed. I was just thinking p65-77   824.08
Bellow, Saul
A father-to-be
In The New Yorker. Stories from The New Yorker, 1950-1960 p309-18 S C
The Gonzaga manuscripts
In Abrahams, W. ed. Fifty years of the American short story v 1 p65-88 S C
Herzog   Fic
The last analysis
In Gassner, J. ed. Best American plays; 6th ser. p97-136   812.08
Mr Sammler's planet   Fic
Belmont, August
See pages in the following book:
O'Connor, R. The German-Americans p243-50   301.453
Bemelmans, Ludwig
About three kings, Uncle Herman's uniform, and Christmas night in the Tyrol
In Becker, M. L. ed. The home book of Christmas p519-22   394.26

Benito Cereno. Melville, H.
In Kearns, F. E. ed. The Black experience p86-167   810.8
Benjamen burning. Winslow, J. M.
In The Best American short stories, 1969 p290-307   S C
Bennett, Arnold
Milestones
In Cerf, B. A. comp. Sixteen famous British plays p189-246   822.08
The old wives' tale   Fic

About
See pages in the following book:
Wagenknecht, E. Cavalcade of the English novel p441-57   823.09
Bennett, Gordon A.
Red Guard; the political biography of Dai Hsiao-ai   92
Bennett, Hal
Dotson Gerber resurrected
In The Best American short stories, 1971 p10-23   S C
Bennett, Jack
Mister fisherman   Fic
Bennett, James V.
I chose prison   365
Bennett, Lerone
Before the Mayflower: a history of the Negro in America, 1619-   301.451
The convert
In Clarke, J. H. ed. American Negro short stories p282-96   S C
What manner of man; a biography of Martin Luther King, Jr.   92
Bennett, Louise B.
Baum, R. ed. China in ferment   951.05
Benny and the bird-dogs. Rawlings, M. K.
In White, E. B. ed. A subtreasury of American humor; abridged p2-17
817.08
Benson, Sally
Appreciation of art
In White, E. B. ed. A subtreasury of American humor; abridged p168-74
817.08
Ben Suc, Vietnam
Schell, J. The village of Ben Suc   915.97
The bent backs of Chang 'Dong. Lederer, W. J.
In Lederer, W. J. The ugly American p232-38   S C
Bentley, E. C.
Greedy night
In Hitchcock, A. ed. Alfred Hitchcock presents: A month of mystery p235-46   S C
Bentley, Elizabeth
See pages in the following book:
Goodman, W. The Committee p244-55
328.73
Bentley, Eric
(comp.) The great playwrights   808.82
A time to live
In The Best short plays, 1969 p283-320
808.82
Bentley, Gerald E.
Shakespeare and his theatre   822.3

Bentley, Phyllis
The Brontës and their world   920
Miss Phipps and the invisible murderer
In Best detective stories of the year [1967] p60-80   S C
Benton, Thomas Hart
See pages in the following books:
Kennedy, J. F. Profiles in courage (Harper) p101-20   920
Kennedy, J. F. Profiles in courage. Large type ed. (Watts, F.) p113-35   920
Beowulf
Beowulf   829
About
Sutcliff, R. Beowulf   398.2
Beowulf. Bryher   Fic
Berciu, D.
Romania   913.39
Berenice. Poe, E. A.
In Poe, E. A. The complete tales and poems of Edgar Allan Poe p642-48
S C
In Poe, E. A. Edgar Allan Poe p208-18
S C
In Poe, E. A. Selected poetry and prose p83-90   818
Berg, Alban
See pages in the following books:
Cross, M. The Milton Cross New encyclopedia of the great composers and their music p106-15   920.03
Ewen, D. ed. The new book of modern composers p75-85   920
Berg, Gertrude
See pages in the following book:
David, J. ed. Growing up Jewish p275-80
920
Bergamini, David
Mathematics   510
The universe   523.1
Bergeijk, Willem A. van. See Van Bergeijk, Willem A.
Bergen, Candice
The freezer
In The Best short plays, 1968 p47-58
808.82
Berger, Melvin
Tools of modern biology   574.028
Bergin, Thomas G.
Petrarch   851.09
Bergman, Mort N.
Bergman, P. M. The chronological history of the Negro in America   301.451
Bergman, Peter M.
The chronological history of the Negro in America   301.451
Bergson, Henri Louis
See pages in the following books:
Durant, W. The story of philosophy p338-50   109
Russell, B. A history of Western philosophy p791-810   109
Thomas, H. Understanding the great philosophers p292-99   109
Untermeyer, L. Makers of the modern world p281-86   920

Berkebile, Donald H.
(jt. auth.) Oliver, S. H. The Smithsonian collection of automobiles and motor-cycles   **629.22**

Berkeley, George, Bp. of Cloyne
See pages in the following book:
Russell, B. A history of Western philosophy p647-59   **109**

Berkeley Square. Balderston, J. L.
In Gassner, J. ed. Twenty-five best plays of the modern American theatre; early ser. p647-85   **812.08**

Berland, Theodore
The fight for quiet   **614**

Berlin, Irving
See pages in the following books:
Ewen, D. Composers for the American musical theatre p84-102   **920**
Ewen, D. Great men of American popular song p100-15   **920**

Berlin
See pages in the following book:
Prittie, T. Germany p105-16   **914.3**

Description
See pages in the following book:
Twain, M. The complete essays of Mark Twain p87-98   **814**

History—Allied occupation, 1945-
See Berlin wall (1961-)

Berlin, Battle of, 1945
Ryan, C. The last battle   **940.54**

Berlin crisis. See Berlin question (1945-)

Berlin question (1945-)
See pages in the following books:
Kohler, F. D. Understanding the Russians p304-39   **947.084**
Schlesinger, A. M. A thousand days p379-405   **973.922**
Sorensen, T. C. Kennedy [biography of John Fitzgerald Kennedy] p583-601   **92**
See also Berlin wall (1961-)

Berlin wall (1961-)
Heaps, W. A. The wall of shame   **943.087**

Berlioz, Hector
See pages in the following books:
Bauer, M. Music through the ages p444-67   **780.9**
Cross, M. The Milton Cross New encyclopedia of the great composers and their music p116-31   **920.03**
Ewen, D. ed. The complete book of classical music p429-44   **780.1**
Ewen, D. ed. The world of great composers p179-94   **920**
Shippen, K. B. The heritage of music p169-75   **780.9**

Bermel, Albert
The mountain chorus
In The Best short plays, 1968 p159-82   **808.82**

Bernadette. Gallant, M.
In The New Yorker. Stories from The New Yorker, 1950-1960 p96-118 **S C**

Bernardini, Gilberto
(jt. auth.) Fermi, L. Galileo and the scientific revolution   **92**

Bernhardt, Sarah
Skinner, C. O. Madame Sarah   **92**

Bernhardt, William F.
(ed.) Granger's Index to poetry. See Granger's Index to poetry   **808.81**
(ed.) Granger's Index to poetry: supplement. See Granger's Index to poetry: supplement   **808.81**

Bernice bobs her hair. Fitzgerald, F. S.
In Fitzgerald, F. S. The stories of F. Scott Fitzgerald p39-60   **S C**

Bernini, Giovani Lorenzo
See pages in the following books:
Blitzer, C. Age of kings p85-95   **940.2**
Wallace, R. The world of Bernini, 1598-1680   **92**

Bernoulli family
See pages in the following book:
Bell, E. T. Men of mathematics p131-38   **920**

Bernstein, Leonard
The infinite variety of music   **780.1**
The joy of music   **780.1**
Laurents, A. West Side story   **812**

About
Ewen, D. Leonard Bernstein   **92**
See also pages in the following books:
Ewen, D. Composers for the American musical theatre p244-52   **920**
Ewen, D. Famous modern conductors p89-104   **920**

Bernstein, Saul
Alternatives to violence   **301.43**

Bernstein, Theodore M.
Watch your language   **428**

Berra, Lawrence Peter
See pages in the following book:
Mantle, M. The quality of courage p39-45   **920**

Berra, Yogi. See Berra, Lawrence Peter

Berriault, Gina
The birthday party
In The Saturday Evening Post. Best modern short stories p421-28 **S C**

Berrigan, Daniel
No bars to manhood   **261.8**
The trial of the Catonsville nine   **343**

Berry, Martha McChesney
Kane, H. T. Miracle in the mountains   **92**

Berry Schools, Mount Berry, Ga.
Kane, H. T. Miracle in the mountains [biography of Martha McChesney Berry]   **92**

Berryman, John
See pages in the following book:
Rosenthal, M. L. The new poets p118-30   **821.09**

Bertalan, Frank J.
(ed.) The junior college library collection   **011**

Bertaux, Pierre
See pages in the following book:
White, T. H. Fire in the ashes p102-29   **940.55**

Berthelot, Marcellin Pierre Eugene
See pages in the following book:
Jones, B. Z. ed. The golden age of science p514-30   **920**

Between rounds. Henry, O.
  In Henry, O. The complete works of
    O. Henry p15-19   **S C**
  In Henry, O. The four million p36-46
                         S C

Between the wars: America, 1919-1941.
  Shannon, D. A.   **973.91**

Bewitched. Wharton, E.
  In Wharton, E. The collected short sto-
    ries of Edith Wharton v2 p403-20
                         S C

Bexar scrip no. 2692. Henry, O.
  In Henry, O. The complete works of
    O. Henry p1051-58   **S C**

Beyond. Faulkner, W.
  In Faulkner, W. Collected stories of
    William Faulkner p781-98   **S C**
  In Faulkner, W. Selected short stories
    of William Faulkner p266-84 **S C**

Beyond human power. Björnson, B.
  In Dickinson, T. H. ed. Chief contempo-
    rary dramatists [1st ser] p573-97
                        808.82

Beyond sing the woods. Gulbranssen, T. **Fic**
Beyond the glass mountain. Stegner, W.
  In Abrahams, W. ed. Fifty years of the
    American short story v2 p337-46
                         S C

Beyond the horizon. O'Neill, E.
  In O'Neill, E. Ah, wilderness! And two
    other plays: All God's chillun got
    wings, and Beyond the horizon
    p197-306   **812**
  In O'Neill, E. Plays v3 p81-169   **812**
  In Quinn, A. H. ed. Representative
    American plays p929-79   **812.08**

Beyond the melting pot. Glazer, N. **301.45**
Beyond Vietnam: the United States and
  Asia. Reischauer, E. O.   **327.73**

Biafra. See Nigeria
Biafran Conflict, 1967-1970. See Nigeria—
  History—Civil War, 1967-1970

Bibby, Geoffrey
  Four thousand years ago   **913.03**
  Looking for Dilmun   **913.03**

Bible
  The Anchor Bible; criticism
  In Daiches, D. More literary essays
    p248-67   **820.9**
  The Holy Bible   **220.5**
  The Jerusalem Bible   **220.5**
  The new American Bible   **220.5**
  The new English Bible   **220.5**

Bible. Selections
  See pages in the following book:
  Smith, R. ed. The tree of life p335-444 **291**

Bible (as subject)
            Antiquities
  Keller, W. The Bible as history   **220.9**
  National Geographic Society. Everyday
    life in Bible times   **220.9**
  Wright, G. E. Biblical archaeology **220.9**

            Concordances
  Harper's Topical concordance   **220.2**
  Nelson's Complete concordance of the Re-
    vised standard version Bible   **220.2**
  Stevenson, B. comp. Home book of Bible
    quotations   **220.2**

            Dictionaries
  Harper's Bible dictionary   **220.3**
  Hastings, J. ed. Dictionary of the Bible
                        220.3
  The New Westminster Dictionary of the
    Bible   **220.3**
  See also Bible—Concordances

            Geography
  Kraeling, E. G. Rand McNally Bible atlas
                        220.9
  The Westminster Historical atlas to the
    Bible   **220.9**

     History of Biblical events
  Keller, W. The Bible as history   **220.9**
  Kraeling, E. G. Rand McNally Bible atlas
                        220.9
  National Geographic Society. Everyday
    life in Bible times   **220.9**

 History of Biblical events—Fiction
  Mann, T. Joseph and his brothers   **Fic**

            Indexes
  See Bible—Concordances; Bible—Dictionaries

            Introductions
  See Bible—Study

        Literary character
  See Bible as literature

            Maps
  See Bible—Geography

        Natural history
  Farb, P. The land, wildlife, and peoples
    of the Bible   **220.8**
            Study
  Chase, M. E. The Bible and the common
    reader   **220.88**

Bible. Old Testament
            Antiquities
  Heaton, E. W. Everyday life in Old
    Testament times   **221.9**

     History of Biblical events
  Oursler, F. The greatest book ever writ-
    ten   **221.9**

            Stories
  Oursler, F. The greatest book ever writ-
    ten   **221.9**

Bible. Old Testament. Job
   Criticism, interpretation, etc.
  See pages in the following book:
  Daiches, D. More literary essays p268-74
                        820.9

Bible. New Testament
            Antiquities
  Bouquet, A. C. Everyday life in New
    Testament times   **225.9**

     History of Biblical events
  Oursler, F. The greatest story ever told
                        232.9

The Bible and the common reader. Chase,
  M. E.   **220.88**

The Bible as history. Keller, W.   **220.9**

Bible as literature
Chase, M. E. The Bible and the common reader 220.88
Henn, T. R. The Bible as literature 220.88
See also pages in the following book:
Macy, J. The story of the world's literature p39-69 809
Bible atlas, Rand McNally. Kraeling, E. G. 220.9
Bible study. See Bible—Study
Biblical archaeology. Wright, G. E. 220.9
Biblical archeology. See Bible—Antiquities
Bibliography
Cumulative book index 015
Subject guide to Books in print 015
See also names of persons, places and subjects with the subdivision Bibliography, e.g. Shakespeare, William—Bibliography; Asia—Bibliography; Mathematics —Bibliography

Best books
See Books and reading—Best books

Editions
See also Paperback books

Paperback editions
See Paperback books

Reference books
See Reference books

Bichat, Marie François Xavier
See pages in the following book:
Moore, R. The coil of life p46-53 574.09
Bickerdyke, Mary Ann (Ball)
See pages in the following book:
Dodge, B. S. The story of nursing p75-81 610.73
Biedermann and the firebugs. Frisch, M.
In Block, H. M. ed. Masters of modern drama p1162-84 808.82
Biegeleisen, J. I.
The ABC of lettering 745.6
Careers and opportunities in teaching 371.1
Bierce, Ambrose
An occurrence at Owl Creek Bridge
In Day, A. G. ed. The greatest American short stories p123-34 S C

About
See pages in the following book:
Brooks, V. The confident years: 1885-1915 p196-210 810.9
Big blonde. Parker, D.
In Abrahams, W. ed. Fifty years of the American short story v2 p67-86 S C
The big bounce. Trevis, W. S.
In Asimov, I. ed. Where do we go from here? p400-13 S C
Big Boy leaves home. Wright, R.
In Margolies, E. A native son's reader p101-39 810.8
The big brown trout. Travers, R.
In The Best American short stories, 1967 p303-13 S C
The big change. Allen, F. L. 973.91
The Big Fisherman. Douglas, L. C. Fic

Big game hunt. Clarke, A. C.
In Lardner, R. ed. Rex Lardner selects the best of sports fiction p185-94 S C
Big meeting. Hughes, L.
In Hughes, L. The Langston Hughes reader p66-76 818
The big money. Dos Passos, J.
In Dos Passos, J. U.S.A. v3 Fic
Big round world. Hughes, L.
In Hughes, L. The Langston Hughes reader p216-19 818
The big sky. Guthrie, A. B. Fic
The big sleep. Chandler, R.
In Haycraft, H. ed. A treasury of great mysteries v2 p3-130 S C
The big stretch. Matthews, C.
In Best detective stories of the year, 1971 p32-46 S C
Big two-hearted river. Hemingway, E.
In Hemingway, E. In our time p175-212 S C
In Hemingway, E. The short stories of Ernest Hemingway p207-32 S C
Big Volodya and Little Volodya. Chekhov, A.
In Chekhov, A. The image of Chekhov p204-18 S C
The biggest thing since Custer. Eastlake, W.
In Abrahams, W. ed. Fifty years of the American short story v 1 p243-53 S C
In Prize stories, 1970: The O. Henry Awards p17-28 S C
Bill of rights. See United States. Constitution—Amendments
The Bill of Rights. Hand, L. 342.73
Bill of Rights reader. Konvitz, M. R. 342.73
The billiard ball. Asimov, I.
In Asimov, I. Asimov's mysteries p209-27 S C
A billiard-marker's notes. Tolstoy, L.
In Tolstoy, L. Short stories v 1 p56-75 S C
Billie Atkins went to Omaha. Crane, S.
In Crane, S. The complete short stories & sketches of Stephen Crane p163-69 S C
Billings, William
See pages in the following book:
Ewen, D. Great men of American popular song p 1-7 920
Billington, Ray Allen
America's frontier heritage 978
The far Western frontier, 1830-1860 978
Westward expansion 973
Bills of credit. See Paper money
Bills of fare. See Menus
Billy Budd. Coxe, L. O.
In Gassner, J. ed. Best American plays 3d ser. p365-93 812.08
Billy Budd, foretopman. Melville, H. Fic
Billy Budd, Twentieth century interpretations of. Vincent, H. P. ed. 813.09
Billy's last stand. Hines, B.
In The Best short plays, 1971 p3-50 808.82

Binary system (Mathematics)
See pages in the following book:
Kadesch, R. R. Math menagerie p20-34
   793.7

Bingham, Hiram
Lost city of the Incas   913.85

Bingham, June
U Thant   92

Bio-bibliography. See Authors; names of
persons with the subdivision Bibliography; and general subjects and names
of countries, cities, etc. with the subdivision Bio-bibliography, e.g. American
literature—Bio-bibliography; U.S.—Bio-bibliography

Biochemistry
Asimov, I. The chemicals of life 612
Asimov, I. The genetic code 575.1
Asimov, I. Life and energy 612
Moore, R. The coil of life 574.09
See also pages in the following book:
Newman, J. R. ed. What is science? p198-225 508
 See also Metabolism

Biogeography. See Anthropogeography
Biographical dictionary, Chambers's 920.03
Biographical dictionary, Webster's 920.03
Biographical encyclopedia of philosophy.
Thomas, H. 920.03
Biographical encyclopedia of science and
technology, Asimov's 920.03

Biography
Canning, J. ed. 100 great events that
changed the world 902
Commager, H. S. Crusaders for freedom
   920
Thomas, N. Great dissenters 920
Untermeyer, L. Makers of the modern
world 920
 See also names of classes of persons,
e.g. Authors; names of countries, cities,
etc. and special subjects with the subdivision Biography, e.g. U.S.—Biography; Negroes—Biography; also names
of persons for biographies of individuals

   Bibliography
Biography index 920.02
Nicholsen, M. E. People in books 920.02

   Dictionaries
Current biography yearbook 920.03
The New Century Cyclopedia of names 031
Webster's Biographical dictionary 920.03
Who's who in the world 920.03

   Indexes
Biography index 920.02
Nicholsen, M. E. People in books 920.02

Biography (as a literary form)
Bowen, C. D. Biography: the craft and
the calling 808.06
 See also pages in the following book:
MacLeish, A. A continuing journey p277-358 818

Biography. Behrman, S. N.
In Cerf, B. A. ed. Sixteen famous
American plays p207-73 812.08
In Gassner, J. ed. Best American plays;
supplementary volume, 1918-1958
p253-95 812.08
Biography index 920.02
Biography of physics. Gamow, G. 530.9
Biography: the craft and the calling. Bowen,
C. D. 808.06
Biological chemistry. See Biochemistry
Biological physics. See Biophysics
The **biological** time bomb. Taylor, G. R.
   577
Biologists. See Naturalists

Biology
Darwin, C. Darwin for today 574
Darwin, C. The Darwin reader 574
Handler, P. ed. Biology and the future
of man 574
Ward, R. R. The living clocks 574.1
 See also pages in the following book:
Newman, J. R. ed. What is science? p231-52 508
  See also Adaptation (Biology); Botany; Cells; Evolution; Genetics; Life
(Biology); Marine biology; Microbiology; Natural history; Sex; Zoology

   Dictionaries
The Encyclopedia of the biological sciences 570.3
Encyclopedia of the life sciences 574.03
Henderson, I. F. A dictionary of biological terms 574.03

   Ecology
 See Ecology

   History
Moore, R. The coil of life 574.09

   Research
Berger, M. Tools of modern biology
   574.028
Taylor, G. R. The biological time bomb
   577

Biology, Marine. See Marine biology
Biology and the future of man. Handler, P.
ed. 574
Biology of mammals. Van Gelder, R. G.
   599
The **biology** of marine mammals. Andersen,
H. T. ed. 599

Bioluminescence
Klein, H. A. Bioluminescence 574.1
 See also pages in the following book:
Scientific American. The living cell p122-34 574.8

Bionics
Halacy, D. S. Bionics 001.5
Wells, R. Bionics 001.5

Biophysics
Asimov, I. Life and energy 612
 See also Bionics; Cells

The **biosphere.** Scientific American 551
Biotechnology. See Bionics
Biplanes. See Airplanes
Bird, Anthony
Antique automobiles 629.209

Birth rate
See pages in the following book:
Ehrlich, P. R. Population, resources, environment p239-45   **301.3**
See also Birth control; Population

A **birthday.** Mansfield, K.
In Mansfield, K. The short stories of Katherine Mansfield p82-91   **S C**

The **birthday party.** Berriault, G.
In The Saturday Evening Post. Best modern short stories p421-28   **S C**

Birthday party. Jackson, S.
In The Best American short stories, 1964 p161-71   **S C**

Birthdays
        Bibliography
Hazeltine, M. E. Anniversaries and holidays   **394.2**

The **birthmark.** Hawthorne, N.
In Hawthorne, N. Hawthorne's Short stories p177-93   **S C**

The **birthmark.** Sholokhov, M.
In Sholokhov, M. Tales of the Don p3-15   **S C**

Bishop, Claire Huchet
Here is France   **914.4**

Bishop, Elizabeth
Brazil   **918.1**
In the village
In The New Yorker. Stories from The New Yorker, 1950-1960 p290-308   **S C**

Bishop, James Alonzo. See Bishop, Jim

Bishop, Jim
The day Christ died   **232.9**
A day in the life of President Kennedy   **92**
The day Kennedy was shot [biography of John Fitzgerald Kennedy]   **92**
The day Lincoln was shot   **92**

Bishop, Morris
The Middle Ages   **940.1**
Horizon Magazine. The Horizon Book of the Middle Ages   **940.1**

Bishop, Washington Irving
See pages in the following book:
Christopher, M. ESP, seers & psychics p58-75   **133**

The **Bishop.** Chekhov, A.
In Chekhov, A. The image of Chekhov p304-22   **S C**

Bishops' Committee of the Confraternity of Christian Doctrine. See Confraternity of Christian Doctrine. Bishops' Committee

The **Bishop's** mantle. Turnbull, A. S.   **Fic**

Bismarck, Otto, Fürst von
Hollyday, F. B. M. ed. Bismarck   **92**
See also pages in the following books:
Carr, A. Men of power p149-75   **920**
Dill, M. Germany p146-87   **943**

Bismarck-Schönhausen, Karl Otto Edward Leopold von, Prince. See Bismarck, Otto, Fürst von

Bismarck (Battleship)
        Fiction
Forester, C. S. The last nine days of the Bismarck   **Fic**

Bison
Haines, F. The buffalo   **978**
See also pages in the following book:
Brown, D. Bury my heart at Wounded Knee p241-71   **970.4**
        Fiction
Swarthout, G. Bless the beasts and children   **Fic**

A **bit o' love.** Galsworthy, J.
In Galsworthy, J. Plays p285-314   **822**

Bitter, Francis
Magnets: the education of a physicist **538**

The **bitter heritage.** Schlesinger, A. M.   **327.73**

The **bitter woods.** Eisenhower, J. S. D.   **940.54**

The **bitter years:** 1935-1941. United States. Farm Security Administration   **301.3**

Bixby, Jerome
The holes around Mars
In Asimov, I. ed. Where do we go from here? p244-65   **S C**

Bizet, Georges
See pages in the following book:
Cross, M. The Milton Cross New encyclopedia of the great composers and their music p132-40   **920.03**

Bjorn, Thyra Ferré
Papa's wife   **Fic**

Björnson, Björnstjerne
Beyond human power
In Dickinson, T. H. ed. Chief contemporary dramatists [1st ser] p573-97   **808.82**

Black, Davidson
Moore, R. Man, time, and fossils p256-81   **573.2**

Black, Hillel
Buy now, pay later   **332.7**

Black, Max
Language and reality
In Kurtz, P. ed. American philosophy in the twentieth century p462-74   **191.08**

Black, Perry O.
Audels Machinists library   **621.9**

Black abolitionists. Quarles, B.   **326**

The **Black American.** Fishel, L. H. ed.   **301.451**

Black and white. Brink, W.   **301.451**

Black armour. Wylie, E.
In Wylie, E. Collected poems p43-103   **811**

Black art. See Witchcraft

The **Black** athlete. Olsen, J.   **301.451**

The **Black** athlete: his story in American history. Orr, J.   **920**

Black boy. Wright, R.   **92**

The **black** cap. Mansfield, K.
In Mansfield, K. The short stories of Katherine Mansfield p305-10   **S C**

The **black** cat. Poe, E. A.
In Poe, E. A. The complete tales and poems of Edgar Allan Poe p223-30   **S C**
In Poe, E. A. Edgar Allan Poe p296-308   **S C**
In Poe, E. A. Selected poetry and prose p280-88   **818**

Black crusader: Frederick Douglass. Hoexter, C. K.   92
Black **death.** See Plague
Black dimensions in contemporary American art. Atkinson, J. E. ed.   759.13
The black dog. Crane, S.
   In Crane, S. The complete short stories & sketches of Stephen Crane p80-84   S C
The Black experience. Kearns, F. E. ed.   810.8
Black fire. Jones, L. ed.   810.8
Black ice; play. Patterson, C.
   In Jones, L. ed. Black fire p559-65   810.8
Black like me. Griffin, J. H.   301.451
The Black Madonna. Lessing, D.
   In Lessing, D. African stories p11-24   S C
The Black Madonna. Spark, M.
   In Spark, M. Collected stories: I p53-76   S C
The black mare. Sheehy, E.
   In Garrity, D. A. ed. 44 Irish short stories p416-30   S C
The black monk. Chekhov, A.
   In Chekhov, A. The stories of Anton Chekhov p115-50   S C
Black mother. Davidson, B.   967
Black music. Faulkner, W.
   In Faulkner, W. Collected stories of William Faulkner p799-821   S C
Black music. Jones, L.   781.7
Black Muslims
   Baldwin, J. The fire next time   301.451
   Clarke, J. H. ed. Malcolm X   301.451
   Malcolm X. The autobiography of Malcolm X   301.451
   See also pages in the following books:
   Bontemps, A. Anyplace but here p216-46   301.451
   Draper, T. The rediscovery of Black nationalism p69-85   301.451
   Lomax, L. E. The Negro revolt p164-77   301.451
   Silberman, C. E. Crisis in black and white p145-61   301.451
Black nationalism in America. Bracey, J. H. ed.   301.451
Black nationalism, The rediscovery of. Draper, T.   301.451
Black out loud. Adoff, A. ed.   811.08
Black Panther Party
   See pages in the following books:
   Draper, T. The rediscovery of Black nationalism p91-117   301.451
   Goldman, P. Report from Black America p133-39   301.451
The black pits of Luna. Heinlein, R. A.
   In Heinlein, R. A. Robert A. Heinlein's The past through tomorrow p232-42   S C
Black poetry, 300 years of. Lomax, A. ed.   808.81
Black power. See Negroes—Politics and suffrage
Black profiles. Metcalf, G. R.   920
The black rose. Costain, T. B.   Fic

Black snowflakes. Horgan, P.
   In The Best American short stories, 1964 p137-51   S C
Black troubadour: Langston Hughes. Rollins, C. H.   92
The black tulip. Dumas, A.   Fic
The black wedding. Singer, I. B.
   In Singer, I. B. An Isaac Bashevis Singer reader p93-103   S C
Blackfoot Indians. See Siksika Indians
The blackjack bargainer. Henry, O.
   In Henry, O. The best short stories of O. Henry p215-31   S C
   In Henry, O. The complete works of O. Henry p1177-88   S C
Blackmer, Donald L. M.
   (jt. ed.) Millikan, M. F. ed. The emerging nations: their growth and United States policy   309.2
Blaine, James Gillespie
   See pages in the following book:
   Stone, I. They also ran p231-50   920
Blair, Clay
   (jt. auth.) Anderson, W. R. Nautilus 90 north   623.82
Blair, Eric Arthur. See Orwell, George
Blake, George
   A modern development
   In Prize stories, 1970: The O. Henry Awards p71-82   S C
   A place not on the map
   In The Best American short stories, 1967 p13-23   S C
Blake, James
   The widow, bereft
   In The Best American short stories, 1971 p24-66   S C
Blake, William
   Poems of William Blake   821
   The portable Blake   828
   Songs of innocence and experience
   In Blake, W. The portable Blake   828
   William Blake   821
   About
   Daugherty, J. William Blake   92
   See also pages in the following books:
   Auslander, J. The winged horse p227-32   809.1
   Cheney, S. The story of modern art p66-74   709.03
   Daiches, D. A critical history of English literature v2 p862-75   820.9
   Ruskin, A. Nineteenth century art p60-66   709.03
   Untermeyer, L. Lives of the poets p286-311   920
   Untermeyer, L. The paths of poetry p90-100   920
Blake to Bernard Shaw. Ward, A. C.
   In Ward, A. C. Illustrated history of English literature v3   820.9
Blake's design. Brown, K. H.
   In The Best short plays, 1969 p237-82   808.82
Blakey, Art
   See pages in the following book:
   Goldberg, J. Jazz masters of the fifties p45-61   920

Blancké, W. Wendell
The Foreign Service of the United States
353.1

Bland, James A.
See pages in the following book:
Ewen, D. Great men of American popular
song p32-35   920

Blanshard, Brand
Reason and analysis; excerpts
In Kurtz, P. ed. American philosophy
in the twentieth century p477-98
191.08

Blanzaco, André
VD: facts you should know   616.9

Blast furnaces
See pages in the following book:
Fisher, D. A. Steel: from the iron age to
the space age p20-30   669.1

Blast of the book. Chesterton, G. K.
In Chesterton, G. K. The Father Brown
omnibus p857-72   S C

Blattner, W. W.
Sound of a drunken drummer
In Foley, M. ed. Fifty best American
short stories, 1915-1965 p720-59
S C

A blaze. Mansfield, K.
In Mansfield, K. The short stories of
Katherine Mansfield p119-24 S C

Bleak House. Dickens, C.   Fic

Bleat Blodgette. Phillips, J.
In The Best American short stories,
1968 p283-314   S C

Blegdamsvej "Faust"
In Gamow, G. Thirty years that shook
physics p165-214   530.1

Blenheim, Battle of, 1704
See pages in the following books:
Creasy, Sir E. S. Fifteen decisive battles
of the world p31-36   904
Mitchell, J. B. Twenty decisive battles of
the world p168-83   904

Bless the beasts and children. Swarthout, G.
Fic

The blessed man of Boston. Updike, J.
In Updike, J. Pigeon feathers, and other stories   S C

Blind
Dahl, B. I wanted to see   92
Frank, M. First lady of the Seeing Eye
636.7
Hartwell, D. Dogs against darkness 636.7
Keller, H. The story of my life   92
Education
Waite, H. E. Valiant companions: Helen
Keller and Anne Sullivan Macy   92

Fiction
Kipling, R. The light that failed   Fic
Blind, Dogs for the. See Seeing eye dogs
Blind man's holiday. Henry, O.
In Henry, O. The complete works of
O. Henry p1223-38   S C
The blind spot. Saki
In Saki. The short stories of Saki p326-
31   S C

Blish, James
Surface tension
In Asimov, I. ed. Where do we go from
here? p171-216   S C

Bliss, A. J.
Dictionary of foreign words and phrases
in current English   422.03

Bliss. Mansfield, K.
In Mansfield, K. The short stories of
Katherine Mansfield p337-50 S C

Blitzer, Charles
Age of kings   940.2

Blitzstein, Marc
See pages in the following book:
Copland, A. The new music, 1900-1960
p135-44   780.9

Blobo's boy. Zuckerman, A. J.
In The Best short plays of 1958-1959
p113-34   808.82

Bloch, Ernest
See pages in the following books:
Cross, M. The Milton Cross New encyclopedia of the great composers and
their music p141-52   920.03
Ewen, D. ed. The new book of modern
composers p86-97   920

Bloch, Raymond
The Etruscans   913.37
The origins of Rome   913.37

Block, Haskell M.
(ed.) Masters of modern drama   808.82

Block, Lawrence
Death wish
In Hitchcock, A. ed. Alfred Hitchcock
presents: A month of mystery
p145-54   S C

Blom, Eric
(ed.) Grove's Dictionary of music and musicians. See Grove's Dictionary of music
and musicians   780.3
(ed.) Grove's Dictionary of music and musicians; supplementary volume. See
Grove's Dictionary of music and musicians; supplementary volume   780.3

The blond beast. Wharton, E.
In Wharton, E. The collected short
stories of Edith Wharton v2 p131-
51   S C

Blood
Vroman, L. Blood   612
See also pages in the following book:
Snively, W. D. The sea of life p189-98
612

Blood. Singer, I. B.
In Singer, I. B. An Isaac Bashevis
Singer reader p167-90   S C

Blood. Vroman, L.   612

Blood brother. Arnold, E.   Fic

The Blood-feud of Toad-Water. Saki
In Saki. The short stories of Saki p60-
63   S C

Blood letting. Gerald, J. B.
In The Best American short stories,
1970 p108-14   S C

The blood of the lamb. De Vries, P.   Fic

Blood of the martyrs. Benét, S. V.
In Benét, S. V. Selected works of Stephen Vincent Benét v2   818

Blood-photo. Friedman, E.
In The Best short plays, 1969 p443-75
808.82

Blood wedding. Garcia Lorca, F.
In Block, H. M. ed. Masters of modern
drama p551-72   808.82

Bloodflowers. Valgardson, W. D.
In The Best American short stories, 1971
p329-46   S C

Bloody Marsh, Battle of, 1742
See pages in the following book:
Armstrong, O. K. The fifteen decisive
battles of the United States p 1-18   973

Bloomgarden, Henry S.
American history through commemorative
stamps   383.2

Blossoming rod. Cutting, M. S.
In Becker, M. L. ed. The home book of
Christmas p277-91   394.26

Blount, Mildred E.
See pages in the following book:
Bontemps, A. We have tomorrow p15-25
920

Blowups happen. Heinlein, R. A.
In Heinlein, R. A. Robert A. Heinlein's
The past through tomorrow p60-97
S C

The Blue and the Gray. Commager, H. S.
973.7

A blue blonde in the sky over Pennsylvania.
Lynds, D.
In The Best American short stories, 1965
p223-39   S C

The blue book of occupational education.
Russell, M. M. ed.   371.42

Blue cross. Chesterton, G. K.
In Chesterton, G. K. The Father Brown
omnibus p3-23   S C

The Blue guides   910.2

The blue hotel. Crane, S.
In Crane, S. The complete short stories
& sketches of Stephen Crane p484-
507   S C

Blue lawns. Brodeur, P.
In Seventeen. Seventeen from Seventeen p147-62   S C

The Blue Nile. Moorehead, A.   962.6

Blue Nile River
Moorehead, A. The Blue Nile   962.6

Blues (Songs, etc.)
Jones, L. Blues people   781.7
Shaw, A. The world of soul   781.7

The blues begins. Leaks, S.
In Hughes, L. ed. The best short stories by Negro writers p275-87 S C

Blues for Mister Charlie. Baldwin, J.   812
also in Gassner, J. ed. Best American
plays; 6th ser. p47-96   812.08

Blues people. Jones, L.   781.7

Blum, Daniel
A pictorial history of the American theatre, 1860-1970   792.09
(ed.) Theatre world. See Theatre world
792.025

A blunder. Chekhov, A.
In Chekhov, A. The image of Chekhov
p96-98   S C

Boadicea, Queen
See pages in the following book:
Trease, G. Seven sovereign queens p30-45
920

The boar-pig. Saki
In Saki. The short stories of Saki p272-
77   S C

The boarding house. Joyce, J.
In Joyce, J. Dubliners p74-84   S C

Boarding schools. See Private schools

Boardman, Fon W.
Economics: ideas and men   330.1

A boar's tooth. Michener, J.
In Michener, J. Tales of the South
Pacific p205-22   S C

Boas, George
The history of ideas   109

The boat. MacLeod, A.
In The Best American short stories, 1969
p98-116   S C

The boat who wouldn't float. Mowat, F.
910.4

Boatner, Mark Mayo
The Civil War dictionary   973.703

Boats, Submarine. See Submarine

Boats and boating
See pages in the following books:
Boy Scouts of America. Fieldbook for
Boy Scouts, explorers, scouters, educa-
tors, outdoorsmen p218-39   369.43
National Geographic Society. Men, ships
and the sea p405-29   387.2
See also Houseboats; Sailing; Ships

Boccaccio, Giovanni
See pages in the following book:
Highet, G. The classical tradition p81-103
809

Bock, Jerry
Stein, J. Fiddler on the roof   812
About
See pages in the following book:
Ewen, D. Composers for the American
musical theatre p230-43   920

Body, Human. See Anatomy; Physiology

The body. Nourse, A. E.   612

Body and mind. See Mind and body

Body fluids
Brooks, S. M. The sea inside us: water in
the life processes   612
Snively, W. D. The sea of life   612

Body language. Fast, J.   153

The body-snatcher. Stevenson, R. L.
In Stevenson, R. L. The complete short
stories of Robert Louis Stevenson
p419-41   S C

Body weight control. See Weight control

Boegehold, Alan L.
Robinson, C. A. Ancient history from prehistoric times to the death of Justinian
930

Boer War, 1899-1902. See South African
War, 1899-1902

Bogart, Gary L.
(ed.) Junior high school library catalog.
See Junior high school library catalog
011

The bogey man. Plimpton, G.   796.352

Boggains in the Bronx. Kober, A.
In White, E. B. ed. A subtreasury of
American humor; abridged p77-81
817.08

Bogs. See Marshes

Bohannan, Paul
Love, sex and being human   612.6

The Bohemian girl. Cather, W.
In Cather, W. Willa Cather's Collected
short fiction, 1892-1912 v 1 p 1-146
S C

The Bohemian girl [short story]. Cather,
W.
In Cather, W. Willa Cather's Collected
short fiction, 1892-1912 v 1 p3-41
S C

Bohemianism. See Hippies

Bohemians in the United States. See Czechs
in the United States

Bohle, Bruce
(comp.) The home book of American quotations   808.88

Bohlen, Marie Nonnast
(illus.) Milne, L. North American birds
598

Bohner, Charles H.
Robert Penn Warren   818

Bohr, Niels Henrik David
See pages in the following book:
Gamow, G. Thirty years that shook
physics p29-61   530.1

Boilers
See pages in the following book:
Sterland, E. G. Energy into power p132-
39   621

Boitelle. Maupassant, G. de
In Maupassant, G. de. Guy de Maupassant's Short stories p220-27 S C

Boker, George Henry
Francesca da Rimini
In Quinn, A. H. ed. Representative
American plays p313-68   812.08

Boles, Paul Darcy
A talent for delight
In Seventeen. Seventeen from Seventeen
p186-97 S C

Boles, Robert
The engagement party
In Hughes, L. ed. The best short sto-
ries by Negro writers p479-89
S C

Bolian, Polly
Growing up slim   613.2

Bolívar, Simón
Bushnell, D. ed. The liberator, Simón
Bolívar   92
See also pages in the following books:
Carr, A. Men of power p123-45   920
Crow, J. A. The epic of Latin America
p429-58, 477-92   980
Peck, A. M. The pageant of South Ameri-
can history p231-50, 272-76   980

Bolivia
Johnson, W. W. The Andean republics
918
See also pages in the following book:
Gunther, J. Inside South America p389-
416   980

Foreign relations—United States
See pages in the following book:
Harris, R. Death of a revolutionary;
[Ernesto] Che Guevara's last mission
p169-78   92
History
Harris, R. Death of a revolutionary;
[Ernesto] Che Guevara's last mission
92

Bolshevism. See Communism

Bolt, Robert
A man for all seasons   822
also in Cerf, B. ed. Plays of our time
p631-719   812.08

The bolted door. Wharton, E.
In Wharton, E. The collected short sto-
ries of Edith Wharton v2 p3-35
S C

Bolton, William
What to do until the doctor comes 614.8

The bomb. Keen, M. L.
In Best detective stories of the year
[1969] p153-59 S C

Bombs. See Atomic bomb

Bonaparte, Napoléon. See Napoléon I, Emperor of the French

Bon-Bon. Poe, E. A.
In Poe, E. A. The complete tales and
poems of Edgar Allan Poe p522-34
S C

Bond, Julian
Neary, J. Julian Bond: Black rebel 92

Bondi, Hermann
Relativity and common sense   530.1
The universe at large   523.1

Bonds. See Stocks

The bone of contention. Sayers, D. L.
In Haycraft, H. ed. A treasury of great
mysteries v2 p131-70 S C

The bones of Charlemagne. Pei, M.
In Pei, M. Tales of the natural and supernatural p73-110 S C

The bones of Kahekili. London, J.
In London, J. Stories of Hawaii p134-58
S C

Bonhoeffer, Dietrich
See pages in the following book:
Berrigan, D. No bars to manood p117-30
261.8

Boni, Margaret Bradford
(ed.) Fireside book of folk songs 784.4

Bonney, Walter T.
The heritage of Kitty Hawk   629.13

Bontemps, Arna
(ed.) American Negro poetry   811.08
Anyplace but here   301.451
Free at last; the life of Frederick Douglass   92
(ed.) Great slave narratives   920
100 years of Negro freedom   301.451
A summer tragedy
In Clarke, J. H. ed. American Negro
short stories p54-63 S C
In Hughes, L. ed. The best short stories by Negro writers p60-69 S C
We have tomorrow   920
(jt. ed.) Hughes, L. ed. The book of Negro folklore   398
(jt. ed.) Hughes, L. ed. The poetry of the
Negro, 1746-1970   811.08

The Booklist and Subscription Books Bulletin
Subscription Books Bulletin reviews 011
See also The Booklist

The Bookman's manual. See The Reader's adviser 011

Books
Downs, R. B. ed. The first freedom 323.44
See also pages in the following books:
Davis, W. S. A day in old Rome p207-19 913.37
Gies, J. Life in a medieval city p166-82 914.4
Macy, J. The story of the world's literature p3-15 809
See also Libraries

Appraisal
See Book reviews; Book selection; Books and reading; Criticism; Literature—History and criticism

Catalogs
See Catalogs, Classified; Catalogs, Publishers'; Catalogs, Subject

Censorship—Bibliography
Haight, A. L. Banned books 098

Reviews
See Book reviews

Selection
See Book selection

Books, Paperback. See Paperback books

Books and reading
Downs, R. B. Books that changed America 810.9
Downs, R. B. Books that changed the world 809
Edwards, M. A. The fair garden and the swarm of beasts 027.62
Fader, D. N. Hooked on books: program & proof 028.5
Highet, G. People, places and books 809
Pilgrim, G. H. Books, young people, and reading guidance 028.5
See also pages in the following books:
Barzun, J. Teacher in America p148-64 371.1
Parker, E. ed. I was just thinking p10-31, 42-45 824.08
See also Libraries; Reference books

Best books
Bertalan, F. J. ed. The junior college library collection 011
The Booklist 011
Books for secondary school libraries 028.52
Carlsen, G. R. Books and the teen-age reader 028.52
Choice: books for college libraries 028.1
The Committee on College Reading. Good reading 028
Emery, R. C. High interest—easy reading for junior and senior high school reluctant readers 028.52
National Council of Teachers of English. Books for you 028.52

National Council of Teachers of English. Committee on College and Adult Reading List. The college and adult reading list of books in literature and the fine arts 016
New York. Public Library. Books for the teen age 028.52
Public Library Association. Starter List for New Branch & New Libraries Collection Committee. Books for public libraries 011
The Reader's adviser 011
Strang, R. Gateways to readable books 028.52
University Press Books for secondary school libraries 028.52
Walker, E. comp. Book bait 028.5
See also Book selection

Books and the teen-age reader. Carlsen, G. R. 028.52

Books for college libraries. See Choice: books for college libraries 028.1

Books for public libraries. Public Library Association. Starter List for New Branch & New Libraries Collection Committee 011

Books for secondary school libraries 028.52

Books for the teen age. New York. Public Library 028.52

Books for you. National Council of Teachers of English 028.52

Books in American history. Wiltz, J. E. 016.973

Books in print 015

Books in print, Large type. Landau, R. A. ed. 015

The books of American Negro spirituals. Johnson, J. W. ed. 784.7

Books that changed America. Downs, R. B. 810.9

Books that changed the world. Downs, R. B. 809

Books, young people, and reading guidance. Pilgrim, G. H. 028.5

Booksellers and bookselling
See pages in the following book:
Shakespeare's England v2 p212-39 822.3

Fiction
Morley, C. The haunted bookshop Fic
Morley, C. Parnassus on wheels Fic

Boole, George
See pages in the following book:
Bell, E. T. Men of mathematics p433-47 920

The boom in the "Calavera Clarion." Harte, B.
In Harte, B. The best short stories of Bret Harte p332-52 S C

Boone, Daniel
Skinner, C. L. Pioneers of the Old Southwest 976
See also pages in the following book:
Udall, S. L. The quiet crisis p25-31 333.7

The boor. Chekhov, A. P.
In Cerf, B. ed. Thirty famous one-act plays p103-12 808.82

Botanical specimens
Collection and preservation
See Plants—Collection and preservation

Botanists. See Naturalists

Botany
Gray, A. Gray's Manual of botany 582
Hylander, C. J. The world of plant life 581
Scientific American. Plant agriculture 581
Went, F. W. The plants 581
Zim, H. S. Plants 581
See also pages in the following book:
Encyclopedia of the life sciences v3 574.03
See also Plant physiology
Ecology
Farb, P. The forest 581
Sears, P. B. Lands beyond the forest 581
Pathology
See Plant diseases
Pictures, illustrations, etc.
Harlow, W. M. Patterns of life 581

Botany, Economic
Bates, M. Man in nature 573
Scientific American. Plant agriculture 581
See also pages in the following books:
Christensen, C. M. The molds and man p183-207 589
Encyclopedia of the life sciences v3 574.03
Kavaler, L. Mushrooms, molds, and miracles p33-99, 237-74 589
See also Grasses

Botany, Fossil. See Plants, Fossil

Bothwell, Francis Stewart Hepburn, 5th Earl of. See Hepburn, Francis Stewart, 5th Earl of Bothwell

Botkin, B. A.
(ed.) A Civil War treasury of tales, legends and folklore 973.7
(ed.) A treasury of American folklore 398
(ed.) A treasury of New England folklore 398
(ed.) A treasury of Southern folklore 398
(ed.) A treasury of Western folklore 398

Botticelli, Sandro
See pages in the following book:
Horizon Magazine. Lorenzo de' Medici and the Renaissance p120-30 92

The bottle imp. Stevenson, R. L.
In Day, A. G. ed. The spell of Hawaii p217-45 919.69
In Stevenson, R. L. The complete short stories of Robert Louis Stevenson p539-74 S C

A bottle of Perrier. Wharton, E.
In Wharton, E. The collected short stories of Edith Wharton v2 p511-31 S C
In Wharton, E. The Edith Wharton reader p626-50 S C

The bottomless well. Terry, W.
In The Best American short stories, 1966 p269-82 S C

Boucher, Anthony
Greatest Tertian
In Conklin, G. ed. Invaders of earth p330-33 S C

(ed.) Best detective stories of the year [1967]. See Best detective stories of the year [1967] S C

Boucicault, Dion
The octoroon
In Gassner, J. ed. Best plays of the early American theatre p185-215 812.08
In Quinn, A. H. ed. Representative American plays p369-98 812.08

Boudicca, Queen. See Boadicea, Queen

Boule de Suif. Maupassant, G. de
In Maupassant, G. de. Guy de Maupassant's Short stories p 1-37 S C

Boulez, Pierre
See pages in the following book:
Ewen, D. Composers of tomorrow's music p78-93 920

Boulle, Pierre
The bridge over the River Kwai Fic
Planet of the Apes Fic

Bound east for Cardiff. O'Neill, E.
In O'Neill, E. The long voyage home p34-54 812
In O'Neill, E. Plays v 1 p477-90 812

Boundaries
See pages in the following book:
Brown, L. A. Map making p166-90 526.8
See also United States—Boundaries

Bounty (Ship)
Fiction
Nordhoff, C. The Bounty trilogy Fic
The Bounty trilogy. Nordhoff, C. Fic

Bouquet, A. C.
Everyday life in New Testament times 225.9

Bourgeoisie. See Middle classes

Bourget, Charles Joseph Paul. See Bourget, Paul Charles Joseph

Bourget, Paul Charles Joseph
See pages in the following book:
Twain, M. The complete essays of Mark Twain p166-89 814

Bourguiba, Habib, President Tunisia
See pages in the following book:
Kenworthy, L. S. Leaders of new nations p130-55 920

Bourke-White, Margaret
Portrait of myself 92

Bourlière, François
The natural history of mammals 599

Bouton, Jim
Ball four 92

Bova, Ben
In quest of quasars 523.8

Bow and arrow. See Archery

Bowen, Catherine Drinker
Biography: the craft and the calling 808.06
Family portrait 920
Francis Bacon 92
John Adams and the American Revolution 92
Miracle at Philadelphia 342.73
Yankee from Olympus; Justice Holmes and his family 92

Bowen, Ezra
The Middle Atlantic States 917.4

Bowen, John
Trevor
In The Best short plays, 1970 p67-124
808.82

Bowers, Claude G.
Jefferson and Hamilton   973.4
Jefferson in power   973.4
The tragic era   973.8
The young Jefferson, 1743-1789   973.4

Bowie, Walter
See pages in the following book:
Kane, H. T. Spies for the Blue and Gray
p157-75   973.7

Bowie, John
England   942
Henry VIII   92

Bowles, Chester
Ambassador's report   915.4
The conscience of a liberal   327.73
Promises to keep   92

Bowles, Cynthia
At home in India   915.4

Bowles, Paul
The echo
In Abrahams, W. ed. Fifty years of the
American short story v 1 p102-15
S C

Bowling
See pages in the following book:
American Association for Health, Physical Education, and Recreation. Physical education for high school students p97-104
613.7

Bowman, John S.
The quest for Atlantis   913

Bowra, C. M.
Classical Greece   938

Boxers
See pages in the following book:
Lord, W. The good years p9-40   973.91

Boxing
See pages in the following book:
Friendlich, D. Panorama of sports in America p75-83   796

Biography
Patterson, F. Victory over myself   92
Robinson, S. R. Sugar Ray   92
See also pages in the following book:
Orr, J. The Black athlete: his story in American history p25-53   920

Drama
Sackler, H. The great white hope   812

The boy in the green hat. Klein, N.
In The Best American short stories, 1969 p69-80
S C

Boy meets girl. Spewack, B.
In Cerf, B. A. ed. Sixteen famous American plays p537-97   812.08
In Gassner, J. ed. Twenty best plays of the modern American theatre p371-413
812.08

Boy Scouts
Boy Scouts of America. Fieldbook for Boy Scouts, explorers, scouters, educators, outdoorsmen   369.43

Boy Scouts of America
Fieldbook for Boy Scouts, explorers, scouters, educators, outdoorsmen   369.43

The boy who painted Christ black. Clarke, J. H.
In Clarke, J. H. ed. American Negro short stories p108-14   S C

Boyar, Burt
Davis, S. Yes I can   92

Boyar, Jane
Davis, S. Yes I can   92

Boyd, Belle
See pages in the following book:
Kane, H. T. Spies for the Blue and Gray
p129-55   973.7

Boyd, Malcolm
Are you running with me, Jesus?   242
As I live and breathe   92
Malcolm Boyd's Book of days   818

Boyd, Mildred
Man, myth and magic   133.4

Boyd, Waldo T.
The world of cryogenics   621.5

Boyden, David D.
An introduction to music   780.1

Boyle, Kay
The ballet of Central Park
In The Saturday Evening Post. Best modern short stories p236-49 S C
Nothing ever breaks except the heart
In Foley, M. ed. Fifty best American short stories, 1915-1965 p270-77
S C
The white horses of Vienna
In Abrahams, W. ed. Fifty years of the American short story v 1 p116-29
S C
The wild horses
In The Best American short stories, 1967 p25-36   S C

Boyle, Robert H.
The Hudson River   917.47

Boyle, Ted E.
Brendan Behan   822.09

Boys and girls together. Saroyan, W.
In The Saturday Evening Post. Best modern short stories p138-56 S C

Boys and sex. Pomeroy, W. B.   612.6

The boys in the band. Crowley, M.
In Richards, S. ed. Best plays of the sixties p801-900   808.82

A boy's will. Frost, R.
In Frost, R. Complete poems of Robert Frost, 1949 p5-43   811
In Frost, R. The poetry of Robert Frost p3-30   811

Bracey, John H.
(ed.) Black nationalism in America
301.451

Brad Halloran. Kilcrin, I.
In Seventeen. Stories from Seventeen p199-214   S C

Bradbury, Ray
I sing the Body Electric!   S C
Contents: The Kilimanjaro device; The terrible conflagration up at the place; Tomorrow's child; The women; The inspired chicken motel; Downwind from Gettysburg; Yes, we'll gather at the river; The cold wind and the warm; Night call, collect; The haunting of the new; I sing the Body Electric; The Tombling day; Any friend of Nicholas Nickleby's is a friend of mine; Heavy-set; The Man in the Rorschach Shirt; Henry the Ninth; The lost city of Mars

Bradbury, Ray—*Continued*

The illustrated man   **S C**

Contents: The veldt; Kaleidoscope; The other foot; The highway; The man; The long rain; The Rocket Man; The fire balloons; The last night of the world; The exiles; No particular night or morning; The fox and the forest; The visitor; The concrete mixer; Marionettes, inc; The city; Zero hour; The rocket

The Martian chronicles   **S C**

Contents: January 1999: rocket summer; February 1999: Ylla; August 1999: the summer night; August 1999: the earth men; March 2000: the taxpayer; April 2000: the third expedition; June 2001:—and the moon be still as bright; August 2001: the settlers; December 2001: the green morning; February 2002: the locusts; August 2002: night meeting; October 2002: the shore; February 2003: interim; April 2003: the musicians; June 2003: way in the middle of the air; 2004-2005: the naming of names; April 2005: Usher II; August 2005: the old ones; September 2005: the Martian; November 2005: the luggage store; November 2005: the off season; November 2005: the watchers; December 2005: the silent towns; April 2026: the long years; August 2026: there will come soft rains; October 2026: the million-year picnic

The other foot

In Foley, M. ed. Fifty best American short stories, 1915-1965 p453-65   **S C**

R is for rocket   **S C**

Contents: R is for rocket; The end of the beginning; The Fog Horn; The rocket; The Rocket Man; The golden apples of the sun; A sound of thunder; The long rain; The exiles; Here there be tygers; The strawberry window; The dragon; The gift; Frost and fire; Uncle Einar; The Time Machine; The sound of summer running

Braden, Waldo W.

(ed.) Representative American speeches. See Representative American speeches   **815.08**

Bradford, Barbara Taylor

The complete encyclopedia of homemaking ideas   **640**

Bradford, Benjamin

Where are you going, Hollis Jay?

In The Best short plays, 1970 p265-81   **808.82**

Bradford, Richard

Red sky at morning   **Fic**

Bradford, Roark

How come Christmas?

In Becker, M. L. ed. The home book of Christmas p194-201   **394.26**

Bradshaw, George

A portrait reversed

In Costain, T. B. ed. Read with me p133-46   **S C**

Brady, Irene

America's horses and ponies   **636.1**

Brahmanism

Moore, C. D. ed. India yesterday and today p103-12   **915.4**

See also Hinduism

Brahms, Johannes

See pages in the following books:

Bernstein, L. The infinite variety of music p229-62   **780.1**

Cross, M. The Milton Cross New encyclopedia of the great composers and their music p163-92   **920.03**

Ewen, D. ed. The complete book of classical music p673-710   **780.1**

Ewen, D. ed. The world of great composers p341-55   **920**

Seroff, V. Men who made musical history p147-71   **920**

Shippen, K. B. The heritage of music p152-58   **780.9**

Brain

Asimov, I. The human brain   **612**

Calder, N. The mind of man   **612**

Elliott, H. C. The shape of intelligence   **153**

Halacy, D. S. Man and memory   **612**

Wilson, J. R. The mind   **150**

See also pages in the following books:

Halacy, D. S. Bionics p96-116   **001.5**

Halacy, D. S. Man alive p145-64   **574**

Lessing, L. DNA: at the core of life itself p55-77   **574.8**

Van Bergeijk, W. A. Waves and the ear p144-70   **534**

Brainwashing

Huxley, A. Brave new world revisited   **301.15**

Braithwaite, E. R.

Paid servant   **362.7**

To Sir, with love   **92**

Bramble bush. Nourse, A. E.

In Nourse, A. E. R for tomorrow p165-84   **S C**

Brander, Bruce

Australia   **919.4**

The River Nile   **916.2**

Brandon, S. G. F.

(ed.) A dictionary of comparative religion   **291.03**

Brandon, William

American Heritage. The American Heritage Book of Indians   **970.1**

Bransten, Thomas R.

(comp.) Ben-Gurion, D. Memoirs   **92**

Brantford, Ontario

Costain, T. B. The chord of steel [biography of Alexander Graham Bell]   **92**

Brasch, R.

How did sports begin?   **796.09**

Brat Farrar. Tey, J.

In Tey, J. Three by Tey v3   **Fic**

Brattain, Walter Houser

See pages in the following book:

National Geographic Society. Those inventive Americans p208-16   **608**

Braun, Wernher von. See Von Braun, Wernher

Brave new world. Huxley, A.   **Fic**

Brave new world revisited. Huxley, A.   **301.15**

Bravery. See Courage

Bray, Warwick

The American Heritage Guide to archaeology   **913.03**

Brazil

Bishop, E. Brazil   **918.1**

See also pages in the following books:

Gunther, J. Inside South America p 1-103   **980**

Schneider, R. M. An atlas of Latin American affairs p106-23   **918**

Brazil—*Continued*

Fiction

Amado, J. The violent land   **Fic**

History
See pages in the following books:

Crow, J. A. The epic of Latin America p136-45, 225-54, 381-97, 531-57, 796-806   **980**

Rippy, J. F. Latin America p75-81, 115-28, 289-301, 460-68   **980**

A Bread and Butter miss. Saki
  In Saki. The short stories of Saki p484-89   **S C**

Bread and wine. Silone, I.   **Fic**

Breakfast at Tiffany's. Capote, T.   **S C**

Brebner, J. Bartlet
  Canada   **971**

Brecher, Ed
  (ed.) Consumer Reports. The Consumers Union report on smoking and the public interest   **613.8**

Brecher, Ruth
  (ed.) Consumer Reports. The Consumers Union report on smoking and the public interest   **613.8**

Brecht, Bertolt
  The Caucasian chalk circle
    In Bentley, E. comp. The great playwrights v2 p2173-2247   **808.82**
  The good woman of Setzuan
    In Block, H. M. ed. Masters of modern drama p872-908   **808.82**
  Mother Courage
    In Bentley, E. comp. The great playwrights v2 p2091-2160   **808.82**
    In Block, H. M. ed. Masters of modern drama p843-70   **808.82**

Breckinridge, Mary
  See pages in the following book:
  Dodge, B. S. The story of nursing p201-08   **610.73**

Breeding. See Plant breeding

Breeds there a man . . . ? Asimov, I.
  In Asimov, I. Nightfall, and other stories p94-128   **S C**

Breen, Jon L.
  The Lithuanian eraser mystery
    In Best detective stories of the year [1969] p186-95   **S C**

Brennan, Bernard P.
  William James   **191**

Brennan, Maeve
  The eldest child
    In The Best American short stories, 1969 p 1-8   **S C**
  The rose garden
    In The New Yorker. Stories from The New Yorker, 1950-1960 p616-31   **S C**

Brenner, Joseph H.
  Drugs & youth   **613.8**

Brentano's, inc.
  See pages in the following book:
  Mahoney, T. The great merchants p133-48   **658.87**

Bresnahan and Tuttle's Track and field athletics. Cretzmeyer, F. X.   **796.4**

Bresson, Henri Cartier- See Cartier-Bresson, Henri

Brewer, E. Cobham
  The reader's handbook of famous names in fiction, allusions, references, proverbs, plots, stories, and poems   **803**
  Brewer's Dictionary of phrase and fable. See Brewer's Dictionary of phrase and fable   **803**

Brewer, J. Mason
  American Negro folklore   **398**

Brewer's Dictionary of phrase and fable **803**

Brewton, John E.
  (jt. comp.) Brewton, S. comp. Christmas bells are ringing   **808.81**

Brewton, Sara
  (comp.) Christmas bells are ringing **808.81**

Brickdust row. Henry, O.
  In Henry, O. The complete works of O. Henry p1404-10   **S C**

Brickhill, Paul
  The great escape   **940.54**
  Reach for the sky; the story of Douglas Bader   **92**

Bridal customs. See Marriage customs and rites

The bridal night. Mayer, P. A.
  In The Best short plays, 1968 p79-107   **808.82**

The bridal party. Fitzgerald, F. S.
  In Fitzgerald, F. S. The stories of F. Scott Fitzgerald p271-86   **S C**

The bridal wreath. Undset, S.
  In Undset, S. Kristin Lavransdatter v 1   **Fic**

The bride. Chekhov, A.
  In Chekhov, A. The image of Chekhov p323-[45]   **S C**

The bride comes to Yellow Sky. Crane, S.
  In Crane, S. The complete short stories & sketches of Stephen Crane p383-92   **S C**

Bride of fortune. Kane, H. T.   **Fic**

The Brides' School Complete book of engagement and wedding etiquette. See Wilson, B. The complete book of engagement and wedding etiquette   **395**

Bridge, Paul
  Designs in wood   **684**

Bridge (Game)
  Goren, C. H. Goren's Bridge complete   **795.4**
  See also pages in the following book:
  Gibson, W. B. Hoyle's Simplified guide to the popular card games p259-300   **795.4**

The bridge at Andau. Michener, J. A. **943.9**

Bridge complete, Goren's. Goren, C. H.   **795.4**

Bridge of San Luis Rey
  See pages in the following book:
  Ceram, C. W. ed. Hands on the past p373-79   **913.03**

The bridge of San Luis Rey. Wilder, T.   **Fic**

The bridge over the River Kwai. Boulle, P.
Fic

Bridge to the sun. Terasaki, G.   952.03

Bridges, William
The New York Aquarium Book of the water world   591.92

Bridges
Jacobs, D. Bridges, canals & tunnels   624
Overman, M. Roads, bridges, and tunnels
    624
Smith, H. S. The world's great bridges
    624
See also pages in the following books:
Langdon, W. C. Everyday things in American life, 1776-1876 p50-64   **917.3**
Owen, W. Wheels p122-45   **380.5**
Von Hagen, V. W. Roman roads p137-50
    625.7

The **bridges** at Toko-ri. Michener, J. A. **Fic**

Bridges, canals & tunnels. Jacobs, D.   624

Bridgwater, William
(ed.) The Columbia encyclopedia. See The Columbia encyclopedia   031
(ed.) The Columbia-Viking Desk encyclopedia. See The Columbia-Viking Desk encyclopedia   031

The **brief début** of Tildy. Henry, O.
In Henry, O. The complete works of O. Henry p103-08   **S C**
In Henry, O. The four million p251-61
    S C

The **brief swinging career** of Dan and Judy Smythe. Wilson, C.
In The Best from Fantasy and Science Fiction; 19th ser. p95-100   **S C**

Brieux, Eugène
The red robe
In Dickinson, T. H. ed. Chief contemporary dramatists [1st ser] p471-516   **808.82**

Bright and morning star. Wright, R.
In Clarke, J. H. ed. American Negro short stories p75-108   **S C**
In Foley, M. ed. Fifty best American short stories, 1915-1965 p214-46
    S C

Bright children. See Gifted children

Brightman, Frank H.
The Oxford Book of flowerless plants. See The Oxford Book of flowerless plants
    586

Bringing it all back home. McNally, T.
In The Best short plays, 1969 p79-105
    808.82

Brinton, Crane
Ideas and men   901.9
The shaping of modern thought   901.93

Brink, William
Black and white   301.451

Brinnin, John Malcolm
(ed.) Twentieth century poetry: American and British (1900-1970)   821.08
William Carlos Williams
In Unger, L. ed. Seven modern American poets p83-118   811.09

Briscoe, Robert
See pages in the following book:
David, J. ed. Growing up Jewish p87-101
    920

Brissie, Leland
See pages in the following book:
Mantle, M. The quality of courage p95-101   920

Brissie, Lou. See Brissie, Leland

Bristow, Gwen
Calico Palace   Fic
Celia Garth   Fic
Jubilee Trail   Fic

Britain. Osborne, J.   914.2

Britannica atlas   912

Britannica Yearbook of science and the future   505

British architecture. See Architecture, British

British art. See Art, British

British authors. See Authors, English

British authors before 1800. Kunitz, S. J. ed.
    920.03

British authors of the nineteenth century. Kunitz, S. J. ed.   920.03

British Columbia
Description and travel
Leslie, R. F. The bears and I   599
See also pages in the following book:
Angier, B. How to live in the woods on pennies a day p83-102   917.1

British Commonwealth of Nations. See Commonwealth of Nations

British cookery. See Cookery, British

British drama. Nicoll, A.   822.09

British Everest Expedition. See Mount Everest Expedition, 1953

British in Africa, Central
Fiction
Forester, C. S. The African Queen   Fic

British in Austria
Fiction
Stewart, M. Airs above the ground   Fic

British in China (People's Republic of China)
Grey, A. Hostage in Peking   92

British in Greece, Modern
Fiction
Stewart, M. My brother Michael   Fic
Stewart, M. This rough magic   Fic

British in India
See pages in the following book:
Moore, C. D. ed. India yesterday and today p113-50   915.4
Drama
Rama Rau, S. A passage to India   822
Fiction
Forster, E. M. A passage to India   Fic

British in Italy
Fiction
Godden, R. The battle of the Villa Fiorita
    Fic

British in Nigeria
Fiction
Achebe, C. Arrow of God   Fic

British in Palestine

Fiction

Wiesel, E. Dawn   **Fic**

British literature. See English literature

British painting. See Painting, British

British poetry. See English poetry

British Statesmen. See Statesmen, British

Britten, Benjamin. See Britten, Edward Benjamin

Britten, Edward Benjamin

See pages in the following books:

Cross, M. The Milton Cross New encyclopedia of the great composers and their music p193-209   920.03

Ewen, D. ed. The new book of modern composers p98-107   920

Brittin, Norman A.

Edna St Vincent Millay   811.09

Broadcasting. See Radio broadcasting; Television broadcasting

Broadway. Dunning, P.

In Gassner, J. ed. Twenty-five best plays of the modern American theatre; early ser. p215-56   812.08

Brodeur, Paul

Blue lawns

In Seventeen. Seventeen from Seventeen p147-62   **S C**

Brodkey, Harold

Sentimental education

In The New Yorker. Stories from The New Yorker, 1950-1960 p206-28   **S C**

Broeg, Bob

Musial, S. Stan Musial: "The Man's" own story   92

Brogan, Denis William

The era of Franklin D. Roosevelt   973.917

France   914.4

Broglie, Louis, Prince de

See pages in the following book:

Gamow, G. Thirty years that shook physics p80-97   530.1

The **Brogue.** Saki

In Saki. The short stories of Saki p277-82   **S C**

The **broken** globe. Kreisel, H.

In The Best American short stories, 1966 p155-65   **S C**

The **broker** of Bogota. Bird, R. M.

In Quinn, A. H. ed. Representative American plays p193-235   812.08

Bromley, J. S.

(ed.) The rise of Great Britain and Russia, 1688-1715/25

In The New Cambridge Modern history v6   909

Brontë, Charlotte

Jane Eyre   **Fic**

The professor   **Fic**

About

Gaskell, E. C. The life of Charlotte Brontë   92

Gregor, I. ed. The Brontës   823.09

See also pages in the following book:

Karl, F. R. An age of fiction: the nineteenth century British novel p90-103   823.09

Brontë, Emily

Wuthering Heights   **Fic**

Wuthering Heights; criticism

In Drew, E. The novel: a modern guide to fifteen English masterpieces p173-90   823.09

Wuthering Heights; criticism [another essay]

In Vogler, T. A. ed. Twentieth century interpretations of Wuthering Heights   823.09

About

Gregor, I. ed. The Brontës   823.09

Hewish, J. Emily Brontë: a critical and biographical study   823.09

See also pages in the following book:

Karl, F. R. An age of fiction: the nineteenth century British novel p77-103   823.09

Brontë, Patrick

See pages in the following book:

Bentley, P. The Brontës and their world p5-15   920

Brontë family

Bentley, P. The Brontës and their world   920

See also pages in the following book:

Wagenknecht, E. Cavalcade of the English novel p304-18   823.09

The **Brontës.** Gregor, I. ed.   823.09

The **Brontës** and their world. Bentley, P.   920

Bronze age

See pages in the following book:

Quennell, M. Everyday life in prehistoric times p149-80   913.03

See also Iron age

The **brooch.** Faulkner, W.

In Faulkner, W. Collected stories of William Faulkner p647-65   **S C**

Brooke, Edward William

See pages in the following book:

Metcalf, G. R. Black profiles p279-305   920

Brooke, Rupert

The collected poems of Rupert Brooke   821

Lithuania

In Cerf, B. ed. Thirty famous one-act plays p361-74   808.82

Brooklyn

Fiction

Smith, B. A tree grows in Brooklyn   **Fic**

Brooklyn Bridge

See pages in the following book:

Jacobs, D. Bridges, canals & tunnels p83-94   624

Brooks, Cleanth

(ed.) Understanding poetry   821.08

William Faulkner: the Yoknapatawpha country   813.09

Brooks, Gwendolyn

In the Mecca   811

Selected poems   811

We're the only colored people here

In Hughes, L. ed. The best short stories by Negro writers p202-04   **S C**

Bulletin boards
Coplan, K. Guide to better bulletin boards
371.33
Bullfights
Collins, L. Or I'll dress you in mourning ₍biography of Manuel Benítez Pérez₎
92

See also pages in the following books:
Michener, J. A. Iberia p622-75   914.6
Porter, K. A. The collected essays and occasional writings of Katherine Anne Porter p91-101   818
Bullins, Ed
Clara's ole man
In The Best short plays, 1969 p107-31
808.82

The gentleman caller
In The Best short plays, 1970 p235-48
808.82

How do you do; play
In Jones, L. ed. Black fire p595-604
810.8
Bullock, Alan
Hitler   92
Bullock's inc.
See pages in the following book:
Mahoney, T. The great merchants p273-85   658.87
Bulls. See Cattle
Bulwer-Lytton, Sir Edward
The last days of Pompeii   Fic
Bunce, Oliver Bell
Mr Bluff's experiences of holidays
In Schauffler, R. H. ed. Christmas p270-81   394.26
Bunin, Ivan
The gentleman from San Francisco
In Seltzer, T. comp. Best Russian short stories p522-56   S C
Bunner, H. C.
Story of a New York house
In The Scribner treasury p71-138   S C
Bunner sisters. Wharton, E.
In Wharton, E. The Edith Wharton reader p303-80   S C
Bünning, Erwin
See pages in the following book:
Ward, R. R. The living clocks p145-63
574.1
Bunsen, Robert Wilhelm Eberhard
See pages in the following book:
Jones, B. Z. ed. The golden age of science p364-400   920
Bunting, James E.
(ed.) Private independent schools. See Private independent schools   370.25
Bunyan, John
The Pilgrim's progress   Fic
Bunzel, Ruth L.
(jt. ed.) Mead, M. ed. The golden age of American anthropology   572.97
Buonamico di Christofano
See pages in the following book:
Vasari, G. The lives of the painters, sculptors and architects v 1 p109-22 920
Buonarroti, Michel Angelo. See Michelangelo Buonarroti
Buoyant billion. Shaw, B.
In Shaw, B. Complete plays, with prefaces v 1 p753-804   822

Burack, A. S.
(ed.) The Writer's handbook. See The Writer's handbook   808.02
Burbank, Rex
Thornton Wilder   813.09
Burchell, S. C.
Horizon Magazine. Building the Suez ₍Canal   962
Burckel, Christian E.
(ed.) The College blue book. See The College blue book   378.73
The **burden** and the glory. Kennedy, J. F.
973.922
Burdick, Eugene
Fail-safe   Fic
Rest camp on Maui
In Day, A. G. ed. The spell of Hawaii p309-22   919.69
(jt. auth.) Lederer, W. J. The ugly American   S C
Bureau of Labor Statistics. See United States. Bureau of Labor Statistics
The **Bureau of Land Management.** Clawson, M.   353.3
Bureau of the Budget. See United States. Bureau of the Budget
The **Bureau of the Budget.** Brundage, P. F.
353.061
Bureau of the Census. See United States. Bureau of the Census
Bureaucracy
See pages in the following book:
Morison, E. E. Men, machines, and modern times p45-66   609
Burgess, Alan
The small woman [biography of Gladys Alyward]   92
Burgess, Anthony
A clockwork orange   Fic
Burgess, Robert F.
The sharks   597
Sinkings, salvages, and shipwrecks 910.4
The **burglar.** Bethune, L.
In Hughes, L. ed. The best short stories by Negro writers p458-64   S C
The **burglar's** Christmas. Cather, W.
In Cather, W. Willa Cather's Collected short fiction, 1892-1912 v3 p557-66
S C
Burgoyne's Invasion, 1777
Furneaux, R. The Battle of Saratoga
973.3
Burial. See Funeral rites and ceremonies; Mounds and mound builders; Mummies
The **burial.** Ervine, St J.
In Garrity, D. A. ed. 44 Irish short stories p86-90   S C
The **burial** of Esposito. Ribman, R.
In The Best short plays, 1971 p157-70
808.82
Burial of the guns. Page, T. N.
In The Scribner treasury p157-79 S C
Buried alive. See Dostoevsky, F. The house of the dead   Fic
Buried cities. See Cities and towns, Ruined, extinct, etc.

Bushmen
Van der Post, L. The heart of the hunter
916.8
See also pages in the following book:
National Geographic Society. Vanishing
peoples of the earth p58-75 **572**
Bushnell, David
(ed.) The liberator, Simón Bolívar **92**
About
See pages in the following book:
Holbrook, S. H. Lost men of American
history p62-69 **920**
Business
See pages in the following book:
Vogue's Book of etiquette and good man-
ners p505-24 **395**
See also Corporations
History
Chamberlain, J. The enterprising Ameri-
cans: a business history of the United
States **330.973**
See also pages in the following book:
Gies, J. Life in a medieval city p98-108
914.4
Philosophy
See pages in the following book:
Hofstadter, R. Anti-intellectualism in
American life p233-96 **917.3**
Business and government. See Industry and
state
Business combinations. See Trusts, Industrial
Business correspondence. See Business let-
ters
Business cycles
Galbraith, J. K. The great Crash, 1929
338.54
See also pages in the following book:
Leighton, I. ed. The aspirin age, 1919-
1941 p214-31 **917.3**
See also Depressions
Business depressions. See Depressions
Business education. See Secretaries
Business letters
Cloke, M. The modern business letter
writer's manual **651.7**
Taintor, S. A. The secretary's handbook
651.7
The business man. Poe, E. A.
In Poe, E. A. The complete tales and
poems of Edgar Allan Poe p413-20
S C
Businesses. See Occupations
The businessmen. Zuroy, M.
In Best detective stories of the year,
1971 p47-62 **S C**
Busoni, Ferruccio Benvenuto
See pages in the following book:
Chapin, V. Giants of the keyboard p156-
64 **920**
Busoni, Rafaello
The man who was Don Quixote; the
story of Miguel Cervantes [Saavedra]
92
But not in shame. Toland, J. **940.54**
Butcher, Devereux
Our national parks in color **917.3**

Butler, Audrey
(ed.) Everyman's Dictionary of dates.
See Everyman's Dictionary of dates
903
Butler, Frank
To the wilderness I wander
In Foley, M. ed. Fifty best American
short stories, 1915-1965 p573-601
S C
Butler, Samuel, 1835-1902
The way of all flesh **Fic**
About
See pages in the following book:
Karl, F. R. An age of fiction: the nine-
teenth century British novel p327-33
823.09
Butterflies
Klots, A. B. A field guide to the butter-
flies of North America, east of the
Great Plains **595.7**
The butterfly and the tank. Hemingway, E.
In Hemingway, E. The Fifth Column,
and four stories of the Spanish
Civil War p101-09 **818**
Butters, Dorothy Gilman
Sorrow rides a fast horse
In Engle, P. ed. On creative writing
p67-77 **808.02**
Buy now, pay later. Black, H. **332.7**
Buyer beware! Trump, F. **339.4**
The buyer from Cactus City. Henry, O.
In Henry, O. The complete works of
O. Henry p1396-1401 **S C**
Buyers' guides. See Consumer education
Buying. See Consumer education
By courier. Henry, O.
In Henry, O. The complete works of
O. Henry p96-98 **S C**
In Henry, O. The four million p232-
38 **S C**
By the river. Oates, J. C.
In The Best American short stories,
1969 p196-214 **S C**
By the waters of Babylon. Benét, S. V.
In Benét, S. V. Selected works of
Stephen Vincent Benét v2 **818**
Byer, Curtis O.
(jt. auth.) Jones, K. L. Drugs and al-
cohol **613.8**
Byrd, Manford
See pages in the following book:
Drotning, P. T. Up from the ghetto p157-
69 **920**
Byrd, Richard E.
Alone **92**
Byrd Antarctic Expedition, 2d, 1933-1935
Byrd, R. E. Alone **92**
Byron, George Gordon Noël Byron, 6th
Baron
Poems of George Gordon, Lord Byron
821
About
Marchand, L. A. Byron: a portrait **92**
Parker, D. Byron and his world **92**
Trueblood, P. G. Lord Byron **821.09**
See also pages in the following books:
Arnold, M. The portable Matthew Arnold
p354-78 **828**

Caesar, Caius Julius
Coolidge, O. Caesar's Gallic War   937
See also pages in the following books:
Coolidge, O. Lives of famous Romans
p36-65   920
Durant, W. Caesar and Christ p167-97
   937
Grant, M. The ancient historians p181-94
   920
Hamilton, E. The Roman way p99-126
   870.9
Mills, D. The book of the ancient Romans p257-75   937
Payne, R. Ancient Rome p134-51, 153-63   913.37
Plutarch. Lives from Plutarch. Abridged
p223-56   920
Drama
White, T. H. Caesar at the Rubicon
   812

Fiction
Wilder, T. The ides of March   Fic
Caesar, Julius. See Caesar, Caius Julius
Caesar and Christ. Durant, W.   937
Caesar and Cleopatra. Shaw, B.
In Shaw, B. Complete plays, with prefaces v3 p363-470   822
In Shaw, B. Four plays p79-209   822
In Shaw, B. Pygmalion, and other plays
p221-359   822
In Shaw, B. Seven plays p355-481   822
Caesar at the Rubicon. White, T. H.   812
Caesar's Gallic War. Coolidge, O.   937
Cage, John
See pages in the following book:
Ewen, D. Composers of tomorrow's music p137-56   920
Cagliostro, Alessandro, conte di
See pages in the following book:
Boyd, M. Man, myth and magic p155-64
   133.4
Cahn, Sammy
See pages in the following book:
Ewen, D. Great men of American popular song p329-39   920
Caidin, Martin
Four came back   Fic
Cain, Arthur H.
Young people and drinking   178
Young people and drugs   613.8
Young people and parents   301.42
Young people and religion   291
Young people and sex   176
Young people and smoking   613.8
The Caine mutiny. Wouk, H.   Fic
The Caine mutiny court-martial. Wouk, H.
   812
also in Gassner, J. ed. Best American plays; 4th ser. p439-77   812.08
Cain's mark. Pronzini, B.
In Best detective stories of the year, 1971 p256-77   S C
Cake
Better Homes and Gardens. Better Homes and Gardens Pies and cakes   641.8

Calcium
See pages in the following books:
Asimov, I. Building blocks of the universe
p162-72   546
Snively, W. D. The sea of life p89-100
   612
Calculus
See pages in the following book:
Hogben, L. Mathematics for the million
p454-520   510
Calcutta metropolitan area
See pages in the following book:
Scientific American. Cities p58-74   309.2
Calder, Nigel
The mind of man   612
Violent universe   523
Calderón de la Barca, Pedro
Life is a dream
In Bentley, E. comp. The great playwrights v 1 p801-65   808.82

About
See pages in the following book:
Nicol, A. World drama p208-39   809.2
Caldwell, Ben
Prayer meeting; play
In Jones, L. ed. Black fire p589-94
   810.8
Caldwell, Erskine
Country full of Swedes
In Abrahams, W. ed. Fifty years of the American short story v 1 p157-70   S C
Caldwell, Janet Taylor. See Caldwell, Taylor
Caldwell, Taylor
Dear and glorious physician   Fic
Great lion of God   Fic
Calendars
Asimov, I. The clock we live on   529
Hazeltine, M. E. Anniversaries and holidays   394.2
Calhoun, John Caldwell
See pages in the following books:
Dictionary of American biography. The American Plutarch p209-25   920
Hofstadter, R. The American political tradition and the men who made it p67-91   973
Calico Palace. Bristow, G.   Fic
California
See pages in the following book:
Montagu, A. The American way of life
p190-97   917.3
Description and travel
See pages in the following book:
National Geographic Society. Vacationland U.S.A. p284-99   917.3

Fiction
Ball, J. Johnny get your gun   Fic
Bristow, G. Jubilee Trail   Fic
Jackson, H. H. Ramona   Fic
Norris, F. The octopus   Fic
Steinbeck, J. The grapes of wrath   Fic
Steinbeck, J. Of mice and men   Fic
Stewart, G. R. Storm   Fic

California—*Continued*

Gold discoveries

Chidsey, D. B. The California gold rush
979.4

White, S. E. The Forty-niners   979.4
See also pages in the following books:

American Heritage. The American Heritage Book of great adventures of the Old West p192-209   978

Billington, R. A. The far Western frontier, 1830-1860 p218-42   978

Gold discoveries—Fiction

Bristow, G. Calico Palace   Fic

History

White, S. E. The Forty-niners   979.4

The California gold rush. Chidsey, D. B.
979.4

California State Prison, San Quentin

Sands, B. My shadow ran fast   364.8

The Californian's tale. Twain, M.
In Twain, M. The complete short stories of Mark Twain p266-72   S C

Caligula. Camus, A.
In Block, H. M. ed. Masters of modern drama p819-40   808.82

Caligula & 3 other plays. Camus, A.   842

The caliph and the cad. Henry, O.
In Henry, O. The complete works of O. Henry p928-31   S C

The caliph, cupid and the clock. Henry, O.
In Henry, O. The complete works of O. Henry p76-81   S C
In Henry, O. The four million p186-96
S C

Calisher, Hortense

In Greenwich there are many gravelled walks
In Foley, M. ed. Fifty best American short stories, 1915-1965 p438-52 S C

Little did I know
In The Saturday Evening Post. Best modern short stories p314-26 S C

Calisthenics. See Gymnastics

The call. Inge, W.
In The Best short plays, 1968 p27-46
808.82

A call loan. Henry, O.
In Henry, O. The complete works of O. Henry p229-33   S C

The call of the tame. Henry, O.
In Henry, O. The complete works of O. Henry p1529-33   S C

Callaghan, Morley

The faithful wife
In Foley, M. ed. Fifty best American short stories, 1915-1965 p82-86 S C

Callahan, Parnell J. T.

Sloan, I. J. Youth and the law   340

Callahan, Philip S.

Insect behavior   595.7
Insects and how they function   595.7

Calligraphy. See Writing

Calliope and Gherkin and the Yankee Doodle thing. Smith, E. E.
In The Best from Fantasy and Science Fiction; 19th ser. p119-59   S C

Calloway's code. Henry, O.
In Henry, O. The complete works of O. Henry p1121-26   S C

Calories and carbohydrates. Kraus, B.   641.1

Calvary. Yeats, W. B.
In Yeats, W. B. Collected plays of W. B. Yeats p287-94   822

Calvin, John
See pages in the following books:

Durant, W. The Reformation p459-90
940.2

Horizon Magazine. The Horizon Book of The Elizabethan world p109-19   940.2

The New Cambridge Modern history v2 p112-19   909

Calypso (Ship)

Cousteau, J. Y. The living sea   627.7

Cambodia
See pages in the following book:

Salisbury, H. E. Orbit of China p26-41
915.1

The Cambridge Ancient history   930

Cambridge Bibliography of English literature, 600-1950, The concise. Watson, G. ed.   016.82

The Cambridge History of American literature   810.9

Cambridge History of English literature, The concise. Sampson, G.   820.9

The Cambridge Medieval history   940.1

Cambridge Medieval history, The Shorter
940.1

The camel. Crane, S.
In Crane, S. The complete short stories & sketches of Stephen Crane p60-61   S C

Camelot. Lerner, A. J.   812

Camels
See pages in the following book:

Milne, L. Water and life p165-78   551.4

The camera. Time-Life Books   771.3

Cameras

Time-Life Books. The camera   771.3
See also pages in the following book:

Time-Life Books. The studio p141-70
778.28

Cameron, Gail

Rose; a biography of Rose Fitzgerald Kennedy   92

Camino Real. Williams, T.
In Cerf, B. ed. Six American plays for today p 1-114   812.08

Camp, L. Sprague de. See De Camp, L. Sprague

Camp cooking. See Outdoor cookery

Campaigns, Political. See Politics, Practical

Campaigns, Presidential. See Presidents—United States—Election

Campanella, Roy
See pages in the following book:

Mantle, M. The quality of courage p128-33   920

Campania
See pages in the following book:

Schreiber, H. Vanished cities p270-80
913.03

Caribbean area—*Continued*
History
Williams, E. From Columbus to Castro: the history of the Caribbean, 1492-1969
    972.9

Immigration and emigration
See pages in the following book:
Williams, E. From Columbus to Castro: the history of the Caribbean, 1492-1969 p347-60
    972.9
Caricatures. See Cartoons and caricatures
Carlquist, Sherwin
  Hawaii: a natural history   574.9
Carlsbad Caverns National Park
  See pages in the following book:
National Geographic Society. America's wonderlands p245-59   917.3
Carlsen, G. Robert
  Books and the teen-age reader   028.52
Carlyle, Thomas
  The French Revolution   944.04
  On heroes, hero-worship and the heroic in history   824
  About
  See pages in the following book:
Daiches, D. More literary essays p115-32
    820.9
Carmer, Carl
  The Hudson   974.7
Carnap, Rudolf
  Empiricism, semantics, and ontology
  In Kurtz, P. ed. American philosophy in the twentieth century p416-32
    191.08
Carnation. Mansfield, K.
  In Mansfield, K. The short stories of Katherine Mansfield p321-24 **S C**
Carnegie, Andrew
  Simon, C. M. The Andrew Carnegie story
    92
  See also pages in the following books:
Beard, A. E. S. Our foreign-born citizens p9-21   920
Fisher, D. A. Steel: from the iron age to the space age p66-75   669.1
Holbrook, S. H. The age of the moguls p74-83   920
Carnets. See Camus, A. Notebooks   848
Caroline Mathilde, consort of Christian VII, King of Denmark

  Fiction
Lofts, N. The lost queen   **Fic**
Carols
  See pages in the following book:
Boni, M. B. ed. Fireside book of folk songs p231-71   784.4
Carols of an old codger. Service, R.
  In Service, R. Later collected verse p 1-185   811
Carousel. Hammerstein, O.
  In Hammerstein, O. 6 plays p91-170 812
Carpenter, Frederic I.
  Eugene O'Neill   812.09
Carpenter, Malcolm Scott
  See pages in the following book:
We seven p43-51, 119-27, 142-47, 246-59, 329-46   629.45

Carpentier, Alejo
  Journey to the seed
  In Cohen, J. M. ed. Latin American writing today p53-66   860.8
Carpentry. See Woodwork
Carpetbag rule. See Reconstruction
Carpio, Lope Félix de Vega. See Vega Carpio, Lope Félix de
Carr, Albert
  Men of power   920
Carr, Archie
  The land and wildlife of Africa   574.9
Carr, John Dickson
  The footprint in the sky
  In Mystery Writers of America. Crime without murder p19-34 **S C**
  The incautious burglar
  In Haycraft, H. ed. A treasury of great mysteries v 1 p333-44 **S C**
  (jt. auth.) Doyle, A. C. The exploits of Sherlock Holmes **S C**
  For another work by this author see Dickson, Carter
Carr, William H. A.
  The du Ponts of Delaware   920
Carreño, Teresa
  See pages in the following book:
Chapin, V. Giants of the keyboard p138-46   920
The carriage-lamps. Crane, S.
  In Crane, S. The complete short stories & sketches of Stephen Crane p663-71 **S C**
Carrington, Richard
  The mammals   599
Carroll, Charles
  See pages in the following book:
Bakeless, J. Signers of the Declaration p233-40   920
Carroll, John M.
  The story of the laser   621.32
Carroll, Joseph T.
  The French   914.4
Carroll, Paul Vincent
  Shadow and substance
  In Cerf, B. A. comp. Sixteen famous European plays p991-1052 808.82
  She went by gently
  In Garrity, D. A. ed. 44 Irish short stories p 1-8 **S C**
Carrucci, Jacopo. See Pontormo, Jacope
Carruth, Gorton
  (ed.) The encyclopedia of American facts and dates   973.03
Cars (Automobiles) See Automobiles
Cars of the early twenties. Burness, T.
    629.209
Carson, Byrta
  How you look and dress   646
Carson, Rachel
  The edge of the sea   574.92
  The sea around us   551.4
  The sense of wonder   574
  Silent spring   632
  Silent spring; criticism
  In Downs, R. B. Books that changed America p260-68   810.9
  Silent spring; criticism [another essay]
  In Graham, F. Since Silent spring 632
  Under the sea-wind   591.92

Carsten, F. L.
(ed.) The ascendancy of France, 1648-88
In The New Cambridge Modern history
v5   909
Carstensz, Jan
See pages in the following book:
Stefánsson, V. ed. Great adventures and
explorations p633-41   910.9
Carstenszoon, Jan. See Carstensz, Jan
Cartels. See Trusts, Industrial
Carter, Hodding
Man and the river: the Mississippi   917.7
Carter, John Stewart
The keyhole eye
In Foley, M. ed. Fifty best American
short stories, 1915-1965 p760-84 **S C**
To a tenor dying old
In The Best American short stories, 1964
p27-84   **S C**
Carter, M. Arkley
The long ride to the city
In Seventeen. Seventeen from Seventeen
p225-41   **S C**
Carthage
See pages in the following books:
Arnott, P. D. The Romans and their
world p53-63   913.37
Schreiber, H. Vanished cities p253-60
                                              913.03
Civilization
Charles-Picard, G. Daily life in Carthage
at the time of Hannibal   913.39
History
See Punic Wars
Social life and customs
Charles-Picard, G. Daily life in Carthage
at the time of Hannibal   913.39
Cartier-Bresson, Henri
The world of Henri Cartier Bresson   779
Cartledge, T. M.
(jt. ed.) Shaw, M. ed. National anthems of
the world   784.7
Cartmell, Van H.
(jt. ed.) Cerf, B. A. ed. Sixteen famous
American plays   812.08
(jt. comp.) Cerf, B. A. comp. Sixteen
famous British plays   822.08
(jt. comp.) Cerf, B. A. comp. Sixteen
famous European plays   808.82
(jt. ed.) Cerf, B. ed. Thirty famous one-
act plays   808.82
(jt. ed.) Cerf, B. ed. 24 favorite one-act
plays   808.82
Carthography. See Map drawing; Maps
A cartoon history of United States foreign
policy since World War I. Foreign Pol-
icy Association   327.73
Cartoons and caricatures
Foreign Policy Association. A cartoon history of United States foreign policy
since World War 1   327.73
See also pages in the following book:
Gombrich, E. H. Art and illusion p330-58
                                              701

See also American wit and humor, Pic-
torial; Comic books, strips, etc.
History
Rogers, W. G. Mightier than the sword
                                              741.5

Carvajal, Gaspar de
See pages in the following book:
Stefánsson, V. ed. Great adventures and
explorations p275-320   910.9
Carver, George Washington
Elliott, L. George Washington Carver   92
Holt, R. George Washington Carver   92
Carver, Raymond
Will you please be quiet, please?
In The Best American short stories, 1967
p37-65   **S C**
Carving, Wood. See Wood carving
Casals, Pablo
Forsee, A. Pablo Casals: cellist for free-
dom   92
Cascade, Idaho
Description
See pages in the following book:
Moyers, B. Listening to America p157-62
                                              917.3
Cascade Range
Douglas, W. O. Of men and mountains
                                              92
The case book of Sherlock Holmes, Doyle,
Sir A. C.
In Doyle, Sir A. C. The complete Sher-
lock Holmes v2 p1160-1323   **S C**
The case for compulsory birth control.
Chasteen, E. R.   301.3
A case of identity. Doyle, Sir A. C.
In Doyle, Sir A. C. The complete Sher-
lock Holmes v 1 p212-26   **S C**
The case of the crimson kiss. Gardner, E. S.
In Haycraft, H. ed. A treasury of great
mysteries v 1 p147-87   **S C**
The case of the white elephant. Alling-
ham, M.
In Haycraft, H. ed. A treasury of great
mysteries v 1 p399-412   **S C**
The case that will not die. Ehrmann, H. B.
                                              364.1
Cash, W. J.
The mind of the South; criticism
In Downs, R. B. Books that changed
America p229-38   810.9
The cask of Amontillado. Poe, E. A.
In Day, A. G. ed. The greatest Ameri-
can short stories p51-60   **S C**
In Poe, E. A. The complete tales and
poems of Edgar Allan Poe p274-79
                                              S C
In Poe, E. A. Edgar Allan Poe p309-17
                                              S C
In Poe, E. A. Selected poetry and prose
p323-29   818
Cass, James
Comparative guide to American colleges
                                              378.73
Comparative guide to two-year colleges &
four-year specialized schools and pro-
grams   378.73
Cass, Lewis
See pages in the following book:
Stone, I. They also ran p251-66   920
Cassatt, Mary
See pages in the following book:
Stoddard, H. Famous American women
p90-100   920
The Cassell Book of English poetry. Reeves,
J. ed.   821.08

Cassell's Encyclopaedia of world literature 803

Cassell's French dictionary, The New 443

Cassell's German dictionary, The New 433

Cassell's Italian dictionary: Italian-English, English-Italian 453

Cassell's New compact German-English, English-German dictionary 433

Cassell's New compact Latin-English, English-Latin dictionary 473

Cassell's New compact Spanish-English, English-Spanish dictionary 463

Cassell's New Latin dictionary: Latin-English, English-Latin 473

Cassell's Spanish dictionary: Spanish-English, English-Spanish 463

Casson, Lionel
Ancient Egypt 913.32

Castaway. Williams, R. M.
In Conklin, G. ed. Invaders of earth p22-36 **S C**

Castaways. See Survival (after airplane accidents, shipwrecks, etc.)

Caste
Hazari. Untouchable 915.4
See also pages in the following book:
Moore, C. D. ed. India yesterday and today p90-101, 103-12 915.4

Castedo, Leopoldo
A history of Latin American art and architecture 709.8

Castelnuovo-Tedesco, Mario
See pages in the following book:
Ewen, D. ed. The new book of modern composers p108-16 920

Castle in the village. Woskoff, V.
In The Best short plays of 1958-1959 p45-68 808.82

Castles
See pages in the following book:
Tomkeieff, O. G. Life in Norman England p30-37 914.2

Castro, Fidel
Lockwood, L. Castro's Cuba, Cuba's Fidel 917.291
Matthews, H. L. Fidel Castro 92
About
See pages in the following books:
Alexander, R. J. Prophets of the revolution p267-86 920
Williams, E. From Columbus to Castro: the history of the Caribbean, 1492-1969 p481-98 972.9

Castro's Cuba. See Archer, J. Thorn in our flesh: Castro's Cuba 972.91

Castro's Cuba, Cuba's Fidel. Lockwood, L. 917.291

Cat and mouse. Grass, G. **Fic**

The cat and the cornfield. MacMahon, B.
In Garrity, D. A. ed. 44 Irish short stories p218-26 **S C**

The cat and the moon. Yeats, W. B.
In Yeats, W. B. Collected plays of W. B. Yeats p295-302 822

Cat book. See Bryant, D. Doris Bryant's New cat book 636.8

Cat in the rain. Hemingway, E.
In Hemingway, E. In our time p115-22 **S C**
In Hemingway, E. The short stories of Ernest Hemingway p165-70 **S C**

Cat nipped. Schaefer, J.
In Schaefer, J. The collected stories of Jack Schaefer p352-71 **S C**

Cat on a hot tin roof. Williams, T.
In Gassner, J. ed. Best American plays; 4th ser. p37-90 812.08

Catalog cards, ALA Rules for filing 025.37

Catalog cards, ALA Rules for filing. Abridged 025.37

Cataloging
Akers, S. G. Simple library cataloging 025.3
Anglo-American cataloging rules 025.3
Non-book materials 025.3
Piercy, E. J. Commonsense cataloging 025.3

Catalogs, Classified
Bertalan, F. J. ed. The junior college library collection 011
Junior high school library catalog 011
Public Library Association. Starter List for New Branch & New Libraries Collection Committee. Books for public libraries 011
Public library catalog 011
The School Library Journal Book review 011

Catalogs, Publishers'
Books in print 015
Subject guide to Books in print 015

Catalogs, Subject
Subject guide to Books in print 015

Catalogue of colour reproductions of paintings prior to 1860 759

Catalogue of colour reproductions of paintings—1860 to [date] 759

A catalogue of the world's most popular coins. Reinfeld, F. 737.4

A catastrophe. Wells, H. G.
In Wells, H. G. The complete short stories of H. G. Wells p502-11 **S C**

The catbird seat. Thurber, J.
In Foley, M. ed. Fifty best American short stories, 1915-1965 p330-38 **S C**

Catch that rabbit. Asimov, I.
In Asimov, I. I, robot p78-98 **S C**

Catch-22. Heller, J. **Fic**

The catcher in the rye. Salinger, J. D. **Fic**

Caterpillars. See Butterflies

Catharine of Aragon, consort of Henry VIII, King of England
Roll, W. The pomegranate and the rose 92

Cathedrals
See pages in the following books:
Gies, J. Life in a medieval city p135-53 914.4
Thorndike, L. The history of medieval Europe p484-506 940.1
See also Architecture, Gothic
Europe
Horizon Magazine. The Horizon Book of great cathedrals 726

Cather, Willa
The Bohemian girl
In Cather, W. Willa Cather's Collected short fiction, 1892-1912 v 1 p 1-146 **S C**
Death comes for the archbishop **Fic**

Catholic converts. See Converts, Catholic

Catholics in the United States
See pages in the following books:
Glock, C. Y. ed. Prejudice U.S.A. p17-64
   301.45
Sloan, I. J. Our violent past p113-29 301.18

Cato, Marcus Porcius, Censorius. See Cato, the elder

Cato, the elder
See pages in the following book:
Plutarch. Lives from Plutarch. Abridged
p165-79   920

Cats
Amberson, R. Raising your cat   636.8
Bryant, D. Doris Bryant's New cat book
   636.8
Whitney, L. F. The complete book of cat
care   636.8
See also pages in the following book:
Henley, D. ASPCA guide to pet care p35-
49   636

Cat's cradle. Vonnegut, K.   Fic

Cattell (Jaques) Press, Temple, Ariz.
American men and women of science. See
American men and women of science
   920.03
American men of science: The social and
behavioral sciences. See American men
of science: The social and behavioral sciences   920.03

Cattle
See pages in the following book:
Goodwyn, L. The South Central States
p85-95   917.6

Cattle trade
The West
See pages in the following book:
Hollon, W. E. The Great American Des-
ert p120-40   917.8

Catton, Bruce
America goes to war   973.7
(ed.). American Heritage. See American
Heritage   973.05
The coming fury   973.7
Glory Road   973.7
Grant moves south   92
Grant takes command   92
Mr Lincoln's army   973.7
Never call retreat   973.7
Prefaces to history   973.7
A stillness at Appomattox   973.7
Terrible swift sword   973.7
This hallowed ground   973.7
U. S. Grant and the American military tra-
dition   92
American Heritage. The American Heri-
tage Picture history of the Civil War
   973.7
(jt. auth.) Catton, W. Two roads to Sum-
ter   973.6

Catton, William
Two roads to Sumter   973.6

The Caucasian chalk circle. Brecht, B.
In Bentley, E. comp. The great playwrights v2 p2173-2247   808.82

Cauchy, Augustin Louis
See pages in the following book:
Bell, E. T. Men of mathematics p270-93
   920

Caudill, Rebecca
My Appalachia   309.175

Caught. Henry, O.
In Henry, O. The complete works of
O. Henry p576-84   S C

Cavalcade. Coward, N.
In Cerf, B. A. comp. Sixteen famous
British plays p545-90   822.08

Cavalcade of the American novel. Wagenknecht, E.   813.09

Cavalcade of the English novel. Wagenknecht, E.   823.09

The cave. Michener, J.
In Michener, J. Tales of the South Pacific p52-78   S C

Cave drawings
Ogg, O. The 26 letters   411
See also pages in the following books:
Horizon Magazine. The search for early
man p89-112   913.03
Simak, C. D. Prehistoric man p125-46
   573.2

The cave dwellers. Saroyan, W.
In Gassner, J. ed. Best American plays;
5th ser. p459-82   812.08

The cave of night. Gunn, J. E.
In Asimov, I. ed. Where do we go from
here? p279-99   S C

Cavender's house. Robinson, E. A.
In Robinson, E. A. The collected poems
of Edwin Arlington Robinson p961-
1007   811

Caves
See pages in the following books:
Horizon Magazine. The search for early
man p11-29   913.03
National Geographic Society. Vacation-
land U.S.A. p22-31   917.3

Cayley, Arthur
See pages in the following books:
Bell, E. T. Men of mathematics p378-405
   920
Newman, J. R. ed. The world of mathe-
matics v 1 p340-65   510.8

Cazamian, Louis
A history of French literature   840.9

Cecil, Robert
Life in Edwardian England   914.2

Cecil Rhodes and the shark. Twain, M.
In Twain, M. The complete short stories
of Mark Twain p332-37   S C

The celebrated jumping frog of Calaveras
County. Twain, M.
In Day, A. G. ed. The greatest Ameri-
can short stories p81-89   S C

Celebrating Christmas around the world.
Wernecke, H. H. ed.   394.26

The celestial railroad. Hawthorne, N.
In Hawthorne, N. Hawthorne's Short
stories p234-50   S C

Celia Garth. Bristow, G.   Fic

The cell. Pfeiffer, J.   574.8

Cellini, Benvenuto
The autobiography of Benvenuto Cellini;
abridged   92

Cervantes, Miguel de—*Continued*
About
Busoni, R. The man who was Don Quixote   **92**
Diaz-Plaja, F. Cervantes   **92**
See also pages in the following books:
Lloyd, A. The Spanish centuries p162-72
   946
National Geographic Society. The Renaissance p309-49   **940.2**
Cervantes Saavedra, Miguel de. See Cervantes, Miguel de
Ceylon
See pages in the following book:
Rama Rau, S. Gifts of passage p170-87 **92**
History
Pakeman, S. A. Ceylon   **954.93**
Politics and government
Pakeman, S. A. Ceylon   **954.93**
Social conditions
Pakeman, S. A. Ceylon   **954.93**
Cézanne, Paul
Murphy, R. W. The world of Cézanne, 1839-1906   **92**
See also pages in the following books:
Cheney, S. The story of modern art p205-36   **709.03**
Untermeyer, L. Makers of the modern world p149-55   **920**
Chaco Canyon
See pages in the following book:
National Geographic Society. America's wonderlands p288-95   **917.3**
Chains of fire. Wilcoxson, K. H. **551.2**
The **chair** of philanthromathematics. Henry, O.
In Henry, O. The complete works of O. Henry p282-87   **S C**
Chairman of the Revolutionary Military Committee of the Republic. Sholokhov, M.
In Sholokhov, M. Tales of the Don p44-49   **S C**
The **chairs.** Ionesco, E.
In Ionesco, E. Four plays p111-60 **842**
Chakravarty, Amiya
(ed.) Tagore, R. A Tagore reader **891.4**
Châli. Maupassant, G. de
In Maupassant, G. de. Selected short stories p226-39   **S C**
The **challenge.** Borges, J. L.
In Borges, J. L. The Aleph, and other stories, 1933-1969 p139-43 **S C**
The **challenge** of crime in a free society. United States. President's Commission on Law Enforcement and Administration of Justice   **364**
The **challenge** of war, 1914-1916. See Gilbert, M. Winston S. Churchill, v3: The challenge of war, 1914-1916   **92**
The **challenge** of world poverty. Myrdal, G.
   338.91
Châlons, Battle of, 451
See pages in the following books:
Creasy, Sir E. S. Fifteen decisive battles of the world p143-58   **904**
Mitchell, J. B. Twenty decisive battles of the world p94-104   **904**

Chamber music
See pages in the following book:
The New York Times. Guide to listening pleasure p69-101   **780.1**
Chamberlain, John
The enterprising Americans: a business history of the United States **330.973**
Chamberlain, Wilt. See Chamberlain, Wilton Norman
Chamberlain, Wilton Norman
See pages in the following books:
Pepe, P. Greatest stars of the NBA p79-92   **920**
Sports Illustrated. The wonderful world of sport p285-87   **796**
Chamberlin E. R.
Everyday life in Renaissance times **940.2**
Chamberlin, Thomas Chrowder
See pages in the following book:
Moore, R. The earth we live on p258-77
   551.09
Chambers, Bradford
(ed.) Chronicles of Negro protest **301.451**
Chambers, William Nisbet
(ed.) The American party systems **329**
Political parties in a new nation: the American experience, 1776-1809 **329**
Chambers's Biographical dictionary **920.03**
Chambers's encyclopaedia   **032**
Champion. Lardner, R.
In Lardner, R. The best short stories of Ring Lardner p109-26   **S C**
In Lardner, R. The Ring Lardner reader p239-58   **S C**
The **champion** of the weather. Henry, O.
In Henry, O. The complete works of O. Henry p844-47   **S C**
The **champion** of the world. Dahl, R.
In The New Yorker. Stories from The New Yorker, 1950-1960 p467-89
   S C
The **champions.** Stuart, J.
In Stuart, J. Plowshare in heaven p206-15   **S C**
A **chance** to go to college. College Entrance Examination Board   **378.73**
Chancellorsville, Battle of, 1863
Fiction
Crane, S. The red badge of courage **Fic**
Chandalika; play. Tagore, R.
In Tagore, R. A Tagore reader p169-79
   891.4
Chandler, Maurice
Ceramics in the modern world   **666**
Chandler, Raymond
The big sleep
In Haycraft, H. ed. A treasury of great mysteries v2 p3-130   **S C**
Chandler, T. J.
The air around us   **551.5**
Chandra Gupta Maurya
See pages in the following book:
Schulberg, L. Historic India p73-78 **954**
Change, Social. See Social change
Changing America and the Supreme Court. Habenstreit, B.   **347.9**

Chanson de Roland
See pages in the following book:
Adams, H. Mont-Saint-Michel and Chartres p13-31 726
Chaos, disorder and the late show. Miller, W.
In The Saturday Evening Post. Best modern short stories p297-302 **S C**
A chaparral Christmas gift. Henry, O.
In Henry, O. The complete works of O. Henry p1205-09 **S C**
A chaparral prince. Henry, O.
In Henry, O. The complete works of O. Henry p252-59 **S C**
Chapin, Kim
King, B. J. Tennis to win 796.34
Chapin, Victor
Giants of the keyboard 920
The violin and its masters 920
Chaplains. See Clergy
The Chaplet. Saki
In Saki. The short stories of Saki p160-63 **S C**
Chaplin, Charles Spencer
See pages in the following book:
Untermeyer, L. Makers of the modern world p669-77 920
Chapman, Gerald W.
(ed.) Essays on Shakespeare 822.3
Chapman, John
(ed.) The Best plays of 1919/1920-1969/1970. See The Best plays of 1919/1920-1969/1970 808.82
Chapman, Sydney
IGY: year of discovery 551
Character. See Behavior
Characters and characteristics in literature
Magill, F. N. ed. Cyclopedia of literary characters 803
See also pages in the following book:
Daiches, D. The novel and the modern world p12-24 823.09
See also Negroes in literature and art
Charlemagne
Horizon Magazine. Charlemagne 92
See also pages in the following books:
Asimov, I. The Dark Ages p141-71 940.1
Mills, D. The Middle Ages p57-78 940.1
Simons, G. Barbarian Europe p101-12 940.1
Thorndike, L. The history of medieval Europe p201-16 940.1
Charlemagne (Romances, etc.)
Bulfinch, T. Bulfinch's Mythology 291
Charles I, King of Great Britain
See pages in the following book:
Aymar, B. A pictorial history of the world's great trials p51-61 343
Charles I, King of Spain. See Charles V, Emperor of the Holy Roman Empire
Charles II, King of Great Britain
Fiction
Goudge, E. The child from the sea **Fic**
Charles III, King of Spain
See pages in the following book:
Lloyd, A. The Spanish centuries p252-65 946

Charles IV, King of Spain
See pages in the following book:
Lloyd, A. The Spanish centuries p265-74 946
Charles V, Emperor of the Holy Roman Empire
See pages in the following books:
Durant, W. The Reformation p357-63, 631-43 940.2
The New Cambridge Modern history v2 p301-33 909
Charles XII, King of Sweden
See pages in the following book:
The New Cambridge Modern history v6 p648-80 909
Charles, Ray
See pages in the following book:
Goldberg, J. Jazz masters of the fifties p168-88 920
Charles-Picard, Colette
(jt. auth.) Charles-Picard, G. Daily life in Carthage at the time of Hannibal 913.39
Charles-Picard, Gilbert
Daily life in Carthage at the time of Hannibal 913.39
Charles the Second. Payne, J. H.
In Gassner, J. ed. Best plays of the early American theatre p73-96 812.08
In Quinn, A. H. ed. Representative American plays p141-64 812.08
Charleston, S.C.
Fiction
Bristow, G. Celia Garth **Fic**
Charlie Brown & Charlie Schulz. Mendelson, L. 741.5
Charlotte, consort of Maximilian, Emperor of Mexico
O'Connor, R. The cactus throne; the tragedy of Maximilian and Carlotta 92
Charm incorporated. Wharton, E.
In Wharton, E. The collected short stories of Edith Wharton v2 p743-62 **S C**
Charroux, R.
Adventure on Cocos Island
In Armstrong, R. ed. Treasure and treasure hunters 910.4
Charteris, Leslie
The arrow of God
In Haycraft, H. ed. A treasury of great mysteries v2 p171-88 **S C**
Chartography. See Map drawing; Maps
Chartres, France. Notre Dame (Cathedral)
Adams, H. Mont-Saint-Michel and Chartres 726
Charts. See Maps
Chase, Marian Tyler
Chase, S. Power of words 412
Chase, Mary
Harvey
In Gassner, J. ed. Best American plays; supplementary volume, 1918-1958 p571-607 812.08
Chase, Mary Ellen
The Bible and the common reader 220.88
The edge of darkness **Fic**
Chase, Richard
Melville 813.09

Chennault and the Flying Tigers. Chennault, A. 940.54

Cherchez la femme. Henry, O.
In Henry, O. The complete works of O. Henry p444-50 **S C**

Cherokee Indians
See pages in the following book:
Wax, M. L. Indian Americans: unity and diversity p88-132 970.1

Cherokee Indians
Fiction
Giles, J. H. Johnny Osage **Fic**

Government relations
Van Every, D. Disinherited: the lost birthright of the American Indian 970.5

The cherry orchard. Chekhov, A.
In Block, H. M. ed. Masters of modern drama p196-215 808.82
In Chekhov, A. Best plays p226-96 891.7
In Dickinson, T. H. ed. Chief contemporary dramatists [1st ser] p627-57 808.82
In Tucker, S. M. ed. Twenty-five modern plays p263-92 808.82

Chesnutt, Charles Waddell
The goophered grapevine
In Clarke, J. H. ed. American Negro short stories p11-20 **S C**
Po' Sandy
In Margolies, E. A native son's reader p43-53 810.8
The sheriff's children
In Hughes, L. ed. The best short stories by Negro writers p 1-16 **S C**

Chess
Horowitz, I. A. First book of chess, with pocket chessboard 794.1
Reinfeld, F. Chess for young people 794.1
Reinfeld, F. The complete chessplayer 794.1
See also pages in the following book:
Gibson, W. Family games America plays p63-90 793

Chess for young people. Reinfeld, F. 794.1

Chessman, G. Wallace
Theodore Roosevelt and the politics of power 92

Chester, Lewis
An American melodrama 329

Chesterfield, Philip Dormer Stanhope, 4th Earl of
Letters of Lord Chesterfield to his son 826

Chesterton, G. K.
The Father Brown omnibus **S C**
The short stories included are: Absence of Mr. Glass; Actor and the alibi; Arrow of heaven; Blast of the book; Blue cross; Chief mourner of Marne; Crime of the Communist; Curse of the golden cross; Dagger with wings; Doom of the Darnaways; Duel of Dr Hirsch; Eye of Apollo; Fairy tale of Father Brown; Flying stars; Ghost of Gideon; Wise; God of the Gongs; Green Man; Hammer of God; Head of Caesar; Honour of Israel Gow; Insoluble problem; Invisible Man; Man in the passage; Man with two beards; Miracle of Moon Crescent; Mirror of the magistrate; Mistake of the machine; Oracle of the dog; Paradise of thieves; Perishing of the Pendragons; Point of a pin; Purple wig; Pursuit of Mr Blue; Queer feet; Quick One; Red Moon of Meru; Resurrection of Father Brown; Salad of Colonel Cray; Scandal of Father Brown; Secret garden; Secret of Father Brown; Secret of Flambeau; Sign of the broken sword; Sins of Prince Saradine; Song of the flying fish; Strange crime of John Boulnoise; Three tools of death; Vampire of the village; Vanishing of Vaudrey; Worst crime in the world; Wrong shape
Incredulity of Father Brown
In Chesterton, G. K. The Father Brown omnibus p433-630 **S C**
Innocence of Father Brown
In Chesterton, G. K. The Father Brown omnibus p 1-226 **S C**
A piece of chalk
In Parker, E. ed. I was just thinking p78-83 824.08
The queer feet
In Costain, T. B. ed. Read with me p147-64 **S C**
Scandal of Father Brown
In Chesterton, G. K. The Father Brown omnibus p813-993 **S C**
Secret of Father Brown
In Chesterton, G. K. The Father Brown omnibus p631-811 **S C**
Wisdom of Father Brown
In Chesterton, G. K. The Father Brown omnibus p227-431 **S C**

Cheyenne Indians
See pages in the following book:
Brown, D. Bury my heart at Wounded Knee p331-49 970.4

Wars, 1864
See Sand Creek, Battle of, 1864

Cheyney, Edward Potts
European background of American history, 1300-1600 940.2

Cheyney, Peter
A defector who didn't make it
In Dulles, A. ed. Great spy stories from fiction p163-77 **S C**

Chiang, Kai-shek
Curtis, R. Chiang Kai-shek 92
See also pages in the following books:
Li, Dun J. The ageless Chinese p466-71 951
Snow, E. Red star over China p373-90 951.04
Tuchman, B. W. Stilwell and the American experience in China, 1911-45 p90-122 327.73

Chibcha Indians
See pages in the following book:
Vlahos, O. New world beginnings p215-21 913.7

Chicago
See pages in the following books:
American Heritage. The nineties p12-29 917.3
Steffens, L. The shame of the cities p162-94 352
Fiction
Dreiser, T. Sister Carrie **Fic**

Haymarket Square Riot, 1886
See pages in the following book:
Gurko, M. Clarence Darrow p53-60 92

Race relations—Fiction
Wright, R. Native son **Fic**

Chinese drama
> *See pages in the following book:*
Gassner, J. Masters of the drama p123-26
809.2

Chinese in Africa
> *See pages in the following book:*
Davidson, B. The lost cities of Africa p181-91 **913.6**

Chinese in the United States
Wong, J. S. Fifth Chinese daughter 92
> *See also pages in the following books:*
Heaps, W. A. Riots, U.S.A. 1765-1970 p61-71 **301.18**
Sloan, I. J. Our violent past p143-56 **301.18**

Chinese-Indian Border Dispute, 1957- See Sino-Indian Border Dispute, 1957-

Chinese-Japanese Conflict, 1937-1945. See Sino-Japanese Conflict, 1937-1945

Chinese journey. Myrdal, J. **309.151**

Chinese language
> *See pages in the following books:*
Pei, M. Talking your way around the world p172-86 **418**
Schafer, E. H. Ancient China p141-50 **913.31**

Chinese mythology. See Mythology, Chinese

Chinese philosophy. See Philosophy, Chinese

Chinese poetry
Collections
Rexroth, K. ed. One hundred poems from the Chinese **895.1**

Chinese sculpture. See Sculpture, Chinese

Chinese thought from Confucius to Mao Tsê-tung. Creel, H. G. **181**

Chinnock, Frank W.
Kim: a gift from Vietnam **362.7**
Nagaski: the forgotten bomb **940.54**

Chinoiserie. McCloy, H.
In Hitchcock, A. ed. Alfred Hitchcock presents: A month of mystery p377-400 **S C**

Chinoy, Helen Krich
(jt. ed.) Cole, T. ed. Actors on acting 792

Chippewa Indians
Burnford, S. Without reserve **970.4**
> *See also pages in the following book:*
Vlahos, O. New world beginnings p64-79 **913.7**

Fiction
Fuller, I. The loon feather **Fic**

Chips off the old Benchley. Benchley, R. **817**

Chips on the shoulder. Hughes, L.
In Hughes, L. The Langston Hughes reader p234-36 **818**

Chisholm, Shirley
Unbought and unbossed **92**

About
> *See pages in the following book:*
Drotning, P. T. Up from the ghetto p132-42 **920**

Chitra. Tagore, R.
In Tagore, R. Collected poems and plays of Rabindranath Tagore p149-73 **891.4**

Chivalry
Bulfinch, T. Bulfinch's Mythology **291**
> *See also pages in the following books:*
Mills, D. The Middle Ages p153-70 **940.1**
Norman, A. V. B. A history of war and weapons, 449 to 1660 p35-43 **355.09**
> *See also* Civilization, Medieval; Knights and knighthood

Fiction
Twain, M. A Connecticut Yankee in King Arthur's court **Fic**

Chlorine
> *See pages in the following book:*
Asimov, I. Building blocks of the universe p87-102 **546**

Choctaw Indians. See Five Civilized Tribes

The Choephori. Aeschylus
In Oates, W. J. ed. The complete Greek drama v 1 p229-67 **882.08**

The choice. Wharton, E.
In Wharton, E. The collected short stories of Edith Wharton v2 p345-56 **S C**

Choice: books for college libraries **028.1**

Choice of books. See Books and reading

A choice of Kipling's prose. See Kipling, R. Maugham's Choice of Kipling's best **S C**

Chommie, John C.
The Internal Revenue Service **353.2**

Chomsky, Noam
American power and the new mandarins **327.73**

Chopin, Frédéric François
> *See pages in the following books:*
Bauer, M. Music through the ages p421-43 **780.9**
Cross, M. The Milton Cross New encyclopedia of the great composers and their music p223-41 **920.03**
Ewen, D. ed. The world of great composers p255-69 **920**
Seroff, V. Men who made musical history p127-46 **920**
Shippen, K. B. The heritage of music p159-68 **780.9**

Chopin. Stewart, N.
In The New Yorker. Stories from The New Yorker, 1950-1960 p137-40 **S C**

Choral music
> *See pages in the following book:*
The New York Times. Guide to listening pleasure p117-33 **780.1**

The chord of steel [biography of Alexander Graham Bell]. Costain, T. B. 92

Choreography. See Ballet; Dancing

The chosen. Potok, C. **Fic**

The chosen one. Davies, R.
In Best detective stories of the year [1967] p233-72 **S C**

Chotzinoff, Samuel
> *See pages in the following book:*
David, J. ed. Growing up Jewish p66-86 **920**

Chou, En-lai
   See pages in the following books:
Snow, E. Red China today p102-29   **915.1**
Snow, E. Red star over China p69-76
                       951.04

Choukas, Michael
   Propaganda comes of age   **301.15**

Christ and the fine arts. Maus, C. P. comp.
                       232.9

Christ in concrete. Di Donato, P.
   In Foley, M. ed. Fifty best American
     short stories, 1915-1965 p190-202
                         S C

Christensen, Clyde M.
   The molds and man   **589**

Christensen, Erwin O.
   A guide to art museums in the United
    States   **708**

Christian art and symbolism
   See pages in the following books:
Gardner, H. Gardner's Art through the
   ages p234-50   **709**
Horizon Magazine. The light of the past
   p110-21   **901.9**
Janson, H. W. History of art p157-69 **709**

Christian art and symbolism
Larousse Encyclopedia of Byzantine and
   medieval art p23-46   **709.02**
Schwarz, M. The age of the Rococo p144-
   59   **759.04**
    See also Church architecture; Jesus
   Christ—Art

Christian biography. See Missionaries

Christian Church (Disciples) See Disciples
   of Christ

Christian ethics
Tolstoy, L. The law of love and the law
   of violence   **172**
   See also pages in the following book:
Veblen, T. The portable Veblen p480-506
                       330.1

Christian life
Lewis, C. S. The Screwtape letters [and]
   Screwtape proposes a toast   **248**

Fiction
Bunyan, J. The Pilgrim's progress   **Fic**

Christian Science
   See pages in the following book:
Look. Religions in America p38-48   **280**

The Christian Science Monitor
James, H. Crisis in the courts   **347.9**

Christian sociology. See Sociology, Christian

Christianity
   See pages in the following books:
Gaer, J. How the great religions began
   p285-332   **291**
Gaer, J. The wisdom of the living religions
   p45-90   **291**
Payne, R. Ancient Rome p291-309   **913.37**
Savage, K. The story of world religions
   p141-57, 195-223, 243-72   **291**
Smith, H. The religions of man p266-308
                       291

Vail, A. Transforming light p107-99   **291**
Voss, C. H. In search of meaning: living
   religions of the world p122-41   **291**
   See also Protestantism; Reformation;
   and names of Christian churches and
   sects, e.g. Catholic Church; Huguenots

Dictionaries
The Oxford Dictionary of the Christian
   Church   **203**

History
   See Church history

Christianity and other religions
   See pages in the following book:
Hayes, C. J. H. Contemporary Europe
   since 1870 p239-63, 537-43   **940.2**
   See also Paganism

Christianity and politics. See Church and
   state

Christianity and science. See Religion and
   science

Christie, Agatha
   Accident
   In Costain, T. B. ed. Read with me p165-
     74   **S C**
   Hallowe'en party   **Fic**
   Murder in the Calais coach
   In Haycraft, H. ed. A treasury of great
     mysteries v 1 p9-146   **S C**
   The murder of Roger Ackroyd   **Fic**

Christina, Queen of Sweden. See Kristina,
   Queen of Sweden

Christmas
Becker, M. L. ed. The home book of
   Christmas   **394.26**
Schauffler, R. H. ed. Christmas   **394.26**
Wernecke, H. H. ed. Celebrating Christ-
   mas around the world   **394.26**
Wernecke, H. H. Christmas customs
   around the world   **394.26**

Poetry
   See Christmas poetry

Stories
   See Christmas stories

Christmas at Bracebridge Hall. Irving, W.
   In Becker, M. L. ed. The home book of
     Christmas p532-40   **394.26**
   In Wernecke, H. H. ed. Celebrating
     Christmas around the world p95-103
                       394.26

Christmas at Concord. Alcott, L. M.
   In Becker, M. L. ed. The home book of
     Christmas p386-406   **394.26**

Christmas at Dingley Dell. Dickens, C.
   In Becker, M. L. ed. The home book of
     Christmas p527-32   **394.26**

The Christmas banquet. Hawthorne, N.
   In Hawthorne, N. Hawthorne's Short
     stories p283-300   **S C**

Christmas bells are ringing. Brewton, S.
   comp.   **808.81**

Christmas by injunction. Henry, O.
   In Henry, O. The complete works of O.
     Henry p243-52   **S C**

Christmas calories. Denison, M.
   In Becker, M. L. ed. The home book of
     Christmas p229-41   **394.26**

Church history—Middle Ages—*Continued*
Fremantle, A. Age of faith p31-40 **940.1**
Gies, J. Life in a medieval city p120-34 **914.4**
Hussey, M. comp. Chaucer's world p116-35 **821.09**

See also Crusades

Primitive and early church
Horizon Magazine. The Holy Land in the time of Jesus **913.33**
See also pages in the following books:
Durant, W. The age of faith p44-79 **940.1**
Durant, W. Caesar and Christ p596-619, 646-64 **937**

Primitive and early church—Fiction
Caldwell, T. Dear and glorious physician **Fic**
Costain, T. B. The silver chalice **Fic**
Sienkiewicz, H. Quo vadis **Fic**
Wallace, L. Ben Hur **Fic**

Reformation
See Reformation

Church music
See pages in the following book:
Bauer, M. Music through the ages p103-25 **780.9**

Church of Christ (Disciples) See Disciples of Christ

Church of Christ, Scientist. See Christian Science

Church of Christ of Latter-Day Saints. See Mormons and Mormonism

Church schools
See pages in the following book:
Lineberry, W. P. ed. New trends in the schools p30-40 **370.8**

The church with an overshot-wheel. Henry, O.
In Henry, O. The complete works of O. Henry p892-900 **S C**

Churches. See Cathedrals; Church architecture

Churchill, Allen
The Roosevelts: American aristocrats **920**

Churchill, Clementine Ogilvy (Hozier) Spencer, Lady
Fishman, J. My darling Clementine **92**

Churchill, Jennie (Jerome) Lady Randolph Churchill
Martin, R. G. Jennie: the life of Lady Randolph Churchill **92**

Churchill, R. C.
(ed.) Sampson, G. The concise Cambridge History of English literature **820.9**

Churchill, Randolph S.
The six day war **956**
Winston S. Churchill v 1-2 **92**
The young statesman, 1901-1914
In Churchill, R. S. Winston S. Churchill v2 **92**
Youth, 1874-1900
In Churchill, R. S. Winston S. Churchill v 1 **92**

Churchill, Sir Winston, 1620?-1688
Rowse, A. L. The Churchills: the story of a family **920**

Churchill, Winston, 1871-1947
The crisis **Fic**

Churchill, Sir Winston Leonard Spencer
The age of revolution
In Churchill, W. S. A history of the English-speaking peoples v3 **942**
The birth of Britain
In Churchill, W. S. A history of the English-speaking peoples v 1 **942**
The Churchill wit **827**
Churchill's History of the English-speaking peoples; abridged **942**
Closing the ring **940.53**
The gathering storm **940.53**
The grand alliance **940.53**
The great democracies
In Churchill, W. S. A history of the English-speaking peoples v4 **942**
Great destiny **942.082**
The hinge of fate **940.53**
A history of the English-speaking peoples **942**
Memoirs of the Second World War **940.53**
The new world
In Churchill, W. S. A history of the English-speaking peoples v2 **942**
Their finest hour **940.53**
Triumph and tragedy **940.53**

About
Churchill, R. S. Winston S. Churchill v 1-2 **92**
Fishman, J. My darling Clementine; the story of Lady Churchill **92**
Gilbert, M. Winston S. Churchill v3: The challenge of war, 1914-1916 **92**
Life (Periodical) The unforgettable Winston Churchill **92**
Rowse, A. L. The Churchills: the story of a family **920**
The Times, London. The Churchill years, 1874-1965 **92**
See also pages in the following book:
Untermeyer, L. Makers of the modern world p484-99 **920**

Churchill, Winston S. 1940-
(jt. auth.) Churchill, R. S. The six day war **956**

Churchill anthology. See Churchill, Sir W. Great destiny **942.082**

Churchill family
Rowse, A. L. The Churchills: the story of a family **920**

The Churchill wit. Churchill, W. S. **827**

The Churchill years, 1874-1965. The Times, London **92**

The Churchills (1958); abridged. Rowse, A. L.
In Rowse, A. L. The Churchills: the story of a family p252-577 **920**

Churchill's History of the English-speaking peoples; abridged. Churchill, W. S. **942**

The Churchills: the story of a family. Rowse, A. L. **920**

Chute, B. J.
Greenwillow   Fic
One touch of nature, and other stories S C

Contents: Mr Bodley's oak; The peaceable
kingdom; January thaw; One touch of nature;
The web; Fly away home; A really important
person; The sheltered bachelor; Thief in the
night; The face on the laundry room floor;
Thank you, Dr Russell; Come of age; Merry
Christmas to all

Chute, Marchette
Ben Jonson of Westminster   92
The first liberty   324.73
Geoffrey Chaucer of England   92
The innocent wayfaring   Fic
An introduction to Shakespeare   822.3
Shakespeare of London   822.3
Stories from Shakespeare   822.3
The worlds of Shakespeare   822.3

Ciardi, John
(ed.) How does a poem mean?   821.08
(ed.) Mid-century American poets   811.08
Person to person   811
This strangest everything   811

Cibola
See pages in the following book:
Ceram, C. W. The first American p29-56
    913.7

Cicero, Marcus Tullius
See pages in the following books:
Arnott, P. D. The Romans and their world
p133-66   913.37
Coolidge, O. Lives of famous Romans p4-
35   920
Hamilton, E. The Roman way p78-126
    870.9
Payne, R. Ancient Rome p124-42, 155-59
    913.37
Plutarch. Lives from Plutarch. Abridged
p203-20   920

La cigale. Chekhov, A.
In Chekhov, A. The stories of Anton
Chekhov p77-102   S C

Cigarettes
Cain, A. H. Young people and smoking
    613.8
Consumer Reports. The Consumers Union
report on smoking and the public interest
    613.8
Diehl, H. S. Tobacco & your health: the
smoking controversy   613.8
United States. Surgeon General's Advisory
Committee on Smoking and Health.
Smoking and health   613.8

Cimabue, Giovanni
See pages in the following book:
Vasari, G. The lives of the painters, sculp-
tors and architects v 1 p21-28   920

Cimarron. Ferber, E.   Fic

Cimon
See pages in the following books:
Plutarch, Lives from Plutarch. Abridged
p35-46   920

Cinema. See Moving pictures

Ciphers
See pages in the following book:
Ball, W. W. R. Mathematical recreations
& essays p379-409   793.7

The **circle.** Maugham, W. S.
In Cerf, B. A. comp. Sixteen famous
British plays p361-415   822.08

A **circle** in the fire. O'Connor, F.
In Foley, M. ed. Fifty best American
short stories, 1915-1965 p524-41
    S C

The **circular** ruins. Borges, J. L.
In Borges, J. L. The Aleph, and other
stories, 1933-1969 p55-62   S C

Circumnavigation. See Voyages around the
world

Circus
Fenner, M. S. ed. The circus, lure and
legend   791.3
Fiction
Stewart, M. Airs above the ground   Fic

The **circus,** lure and legend. Fenner, M. S.
ed.   791.3

The **citadel.** Cronin, A. J.   Fic

Cities. Scientific American   309.2

Cities and towns
Hellman, H. The city in the world of the
future   711
Mumford, L. The urban prospect   711
Rudofsky, B. Streets for people   711
Scientific American. Cities   309.2
See also pages in the following books:
Gardner, J. W. The recovery of confi-
dence p147-84   309.2
Hoffer, E. First things, last things p13-40
    309.173
See also Sociology, Urban; Tenement
houses
Argentine Republic
See pages in the following book:
Gunther, J. Inside South America p194-
207   980
Brazil
See pages in the following book:
Gunther, J. Inside South America p64-86
    980
Chile
See pages in the following book:
Gunther, J. Inside South America p285-
91   980
China
See pages in the following book:
Liu, J. T. C. ed. Traditional China p42-
49   915.1
Civic improvement
See also City planning
Colombia
See pages in the following book:
Gunther, J. Inside South America p466-
79   980
England
See pages in the following book:
Tomkeieff, O. G. Life in Norman En-
gland p70-85   914.2
Europe
See pages in the following books:
Chamberlin, E. R. Everyday life in Ren-
aissance times p107-28   940.2
Mills, D. The Middle Ages p202-14
    940.1
France
Gies, J. Life in a medieval city   914.4

Civilization, Greek—*Continued*
Larousse Encyclopedia of prehistoric and
ancient art p234-91   **709.01**
McNeill, W. H. A world history p88-100,
131-62   **901.9**
Russell, B. A history of Western philos-
ophy p3-24, 218-28   **109**
Spiller, R. E. ed. The American literary
revolution, 1783-1837 p73-87, 284-318
                                      810.9
See also Hellenism

Dictionaries
The Praeger Encyclopedia of ancient Greek
civilization   **913.3803**

Civilization, Islamic
Stewart, D. Early Islam   **915.6**
See also pages in the following books:
Durant, W. The age of faith p153-344 **940.1**
Durant, W. The Reformation p663-94
                                      940.2

Civilization, Jewish. See Jews—Civilization
Civilization, Medieval
The Age of chivalry   **914**
Bishop, M. The Middle Ages   **940.1**
Durant, W. The age of faith   **940.1**
Eastern and Western Europe in the Middle
Ages   **940.1**
Fremantle, A. Age of faith   **940.1**
Gies, J. Life in a medieval city   **914.4**
Hindley, G. The medieval establishment,
1200-1500   **901.92**
Horizon Magazine. Charlemagne   **92**
Horizon Magazine. The Horizon Book of
the Middle Ages   **940.1**
Rowling, M. Everyday life in medieval
times   **914**
Thorndike, L. The history of medieval
Europe   **940.1**
See also Chivalry; Feudalism; Middle
Ages

Pictures, illustrations, etc.
Hussey, M. comp. Chaucer's world **821.09**
Loomis, R. S. A mirror of Chaucer's
world   **914.2**
Serraillier, I. Chaucer and his world **821.09**

Civilization, Minoan
Cottrell, L. The mystery of Minoan civilization   **913.39**

Civilization, Modern
Brinton, C. The shaping of modern thought
                                     901.93
Colton, J. G. Twentieth century   **901.94**
Ferkiss, V. C. Technological man: the
myth and the reality   **301.24**
Gay, P. Age of Enlightenment   **901.93**
Toffler, A. Future shock   **301.24**
See also History, Modern; Renaissance

Civilization, Mohammedan. See Civilization,
Islamic
Civilization, Mycaenean
Baumann, H. Lion gate and labyrinth
                                     913.38
Taylour, Lord W. The Mycenaeans **913.39**
See also pages in the following books:
Horizon Magazine. The light of the past
p8-25   **901.9**
Payne, R. Ancient Greece p39-50 **913.38**

Civilization, Occidental
Brinton, C. Ideas and men   **901.9**
Fromm, E. The sane society   **323.4**
Hayes, C. J. H. History of Western civili-
zation   **940.2**
See also pages in the following books:
McNeill, W. H. A world history p409-31,
481-506   **901.9**
Mead, M. ed. The golden age of American
anthropology p621-28   **572.97**
Civilization, Oriental
Durant, W. Our Oriental heritage   **950**
Reischauer, E. O. A history of East Asian
civilization   **915**
See also pages in the following books:
McNeill, W. H. A world history p101-11,
165-72   **901.9**
Sarton, G. A history of science v2 p196-
215, 520-25   **509**
Civilization, Slavic
Eastern and Western Europe in the Mid-
dle Ages   **940.1**
Civilization, Sumerian. See Sumerians
Civilization and science. See Science and
civilization
Civilization and technology. See Technology
and civilization
Claiborne, Robert
Climate, man, and history   **551.59**
Clairvoyance. See Extrasensory perception;
Thought transference
The **clan** of no-name. Crane, S.
In Crane, S. The complete short sto-
ries & sketches of Stephen Crane
p526-39   **S C**
Clancy, Edward P.
The tides   **525**
Clapesattle, Helen
The Doctors Mayo   **920**
Clara's ole man. Bullins, E.
In The Best short plays, 1969 p107-31
                                    808.82
Clarence. Tarkington, B.
In Gassner, J. ed. Best American plays;
supplementary volume, 1918-1958
p 1-45   **812.08**
Clarence Day's Life with father and Life
with mother. Lindsay, H.   **812**
Clarence Day's Life with mother. Lindsay,
H.
In Lindsay, H. Clarence Day's Life
with father and Life with mother
v2   **812**
The **clarion** call. Henry, O.
In Henry, O. The complete works of
O. Henry p1337-43   **S C**
Clark, Blake
Hawaii the 49th State; excerpt
In Day, A. G. ed. The spell of Hawaii
p63-72   **919.69**
(jt. auth.) Frank, M. First lady of the
Seeing Eye   **636.7**
Clark, Eugenie
See pages in the following book:
Burgess, R. F. The sharks p111-18 **597**
Clark, Gerald
Canada: the uneasy neighbor   **917.1**
Clark, J. Desmond
The prehistory of Africa   **913.6**

Clark, Kenneth
Civilisation   **709**

Clark, Kenneth B.
Dark ghetto   **301.451**

Clark, Leon E.
(ed.) The African past and the coming of the European
In Clark, L. E. ed. Through African eyes: cultures in change p225-350   **916**

(ed.) The colonial experience: an inside view
In Clark, L. E. ed. Through African eyes: cultures in change p353-470   **916**

(ed.) Coming of age in Africa: continuity and change
In Clark, L. E. ed. Through African eyes: cultures in change p3-104   **916**

(ed.) From tribe to town: problems of adjustment
In Clark, L. E. ed. Through African eyes: cultures in change p107-221   **916**

(ed.) Nation-building: Tanzania and the world
In Clark, L. E. ed. Through African eyes: cultures in change p603-744   **916**

(ed.) The rise of nationalism: freedom regained
In Clark, L. E. ed. Through African eyes: cultures in change p473-600   **916**

(ed.) Through African eyes: cultures in change   **916**

Clark, Ramsey
Crime in America   **364.1**

About
Harris, R. Justice   **353.5**

Clark, Ronald W.
The Huxleys   **920**

Clark, Sydney
All the best in . . .   **910.2**

Clark, Thomas D.
The emerging South   **917.5**

Clark, Walter Van Tilburg
The wind and the snow of winter
In Abrahams, W. ed. Fifty years of the American short story v 1 p208-19   **S C**
In Foley, M. ed. Fifty best American short stories, 1915-1965 p375-86   **S C**

Clark, William, 1770-1838
Chidsey, D. B. Lewis and Clark   **973.4**
Dillon, R. Meriwether Lewis   **92**

Clarke, Arthur C.
Big game hunt
In Lardner, R. ed. Rex Lardner selects the best of sports fiction p185-94   **S C**
The deep range
In Asimov, I. ed. Where do we go from here? p266-78   **S C**
Man and space   **629.4**

Mogul silver
In Armstrong, R. ed. Treasure and treasure hunters   **910.4**
2001: a space odyssey   **Fic**

Clarke, Austin
See pages in the following book:
Rosenthal, M. L. The new poets p263-72   **821.09**

Clarke, Desmond
The Islandman
In Garrity, D. A. ed. 44 Irish short stories p9-21   **S C**

Clarke, John Henrik
(ed.) American Negro short stories   **S C**
The boy who painted Christ black
In Clarke, J. H. ed. American Negro short stories p108-14   **S C**
(ed.) Malcolm X   **301.451**
Santa Claus is a white man
In Hughes, L. ed. The best short stories by Negro writers p181-87   **S C**

Clarke, Kenny
See pages in the following book:
Gitler, I. Jazz masters of the forties p175-82   **920**

Class conflict. See Social classes

Class distinction. See Social classes

The **classic** myths in English literature and in art. Gayley, C. M. ed.   **292**

Classical antiquities
Higgins, R. Minoan and Mycenaean art   **709.39**
Ruskin, A. Greek & Roman art   **709.38**
See also Archeology; Art, Greek; Mythology, Classical; also names of countries, etc. with the subdivision Antiquities, e.g. Greece—Antiquities

Classical archeology. See Classical antiquities

Classical art. See Art, Greek

Classical dictionaries
The New Century Classical handbook   **913.3803**
The Oxford Classical dictionary   **913.3803**
The Praeger Encyclopedia of ancient Greek civilization   **913.3803**

Classical geography. See Geography, Ancient

Classical Greece. Bowra, C. M.   **938**

Classical handbook, The New Century   **913.3803**

Classical languages. See Latin language

Classical literature
Grant, M. Myths of the Greeks and Romans   **292**
See also pages in the following book:
Highet, G. The classical tradition p 1-21, 70-80   **809**
See also Greek literature; Latin literature

Dictionaries
Feder, L. Crowell's Handbook of classical literature   **880.3**
The Oxford Companion to classical literature   **880.3**

Classical music, The complete book of. Ewen, D.   **780.1**

Classical mythology. See Mythology, Classical

The **classical** tradition. Highet, G.   809

The **classics** reclassified. Armour, R.   817

Classification
Books
See Classification, Decimal

Classification, Decimal
Dewey, M. Abridged Dewey Decimal classification and relative index   025.4
Dewey, M. Dewey Decimal classification and relative index   025.4

Classified catalogs. See Catalogs, Classified

The **classless** society. Hardwick, E.
In The New Yorker. Stories from The New York, 1950-1960 p728-47 **S C**

Claus Spreckels and the Hawaiian Revolution of 1893. Adler, J.
In Day, A. G. ed. The spell of Hawaii p260-71   919.69

Clawson, Marion
The Bureau of Land Management   353.3

The **Claxtons.** Huxley, A.
In Havighurst, W. ed. Masters of the modern short story p277-305 **S C**

Clay, Henry
See pages in the following books:
Dictionary of American biography. The American Plutarch p195-208   920
Stone, I. They also ran p35-58   920

Clay. Joyce, J.
In Joyce, J. Dubliners p123-32   **S C**

Clay industries
Chandler, M. Ceramics in the modern world   666

Clayton, Horace R.
See pages in the following book:
Bontemps, A. We have tomorrow p26-33   920

Clea. Durrell, L.
In Durrell, L. The Alexandria quartet: Justine; Balthazar; Mountolive [and] Clea p653-884   **Fic**

A **clean** well-lighted place. Hemingway, E.
In Hemingway, E. The short stories of Ernest Hemingway p379-83   **S C**
In Hemingway, E. The snows of Kilimanjaro, and other stories p29-33   **S C**

Cleary, Jon
The sundowners. Young people's ed.   **Fic**

Cleaver, Eldridge
The flashlight
In The Best American short stories, 1970 p20-52   **S C**
In Prize stories, 1971: The O. Henry Awards p226-60   **S C**
Soul on ice   301.451
About
See pages in the following books:
Berrigan, D. No bars to manhood p147-56   261.8
Metcalf, G. R. Black profiles p369-400 920

The **clemency** of the court. Cather, W.
In Cather, W. Willa Cather's Collected short fiction, 1892-1912 v3 p515-22   **S C**

Clemens, Samuel Langhorne
A curious experience
In Dulles, A. ed. Great spy stories from fiction p308-25   **S C**
Roughing it; excerpt
In Day, A. G. ed. The spell of Hawaii p144-54   916.69
About
Brooks, V. The ordeal of Mark Twain 818
Kaplan, J. Mr Clemens and Mark Twain 92
Smith, H. N. ed. Mark Twain   813.09
Twain, M. The autobiography of Mark Twain   92
Wecter, D. Sam Clemens of Hannibal 92
See also pages in the following books:
Brooks, V. The times of Melville and Whitman p291-309, 459-75   810.9
Daiches, D. More literary essays p238-47   820.9
Foster, R. ed. Six American novelists of the nineteenth century p118-54   813.09
Literary history of the United States p917-39   810.9
Quinn, A. H. American fiction p243-56   813.09
Rourke, C. American humor p165-75   817.09
Untermeyer, L. Makers of the modern world p139-48   920
Van Doren, C. The American novel, 1789-1939 p137-62   813.09
Wagenknecht, E. Cavalcade of the American novel p109-26   813.09
For other works by this author see Twain, Mark

Clement, Hal
Dust rag
In Asimov, I. ed. Where do we go from here? p300-24   **S C**
Proof
In Asimov, I. ed. Where do go from here? p127-48   **S C**

Clementi, Muzio
See pages in the following book:
Chapin, V. Giants of the keyboard p37-44   920

Cleminshaw, Clarence H.
(jt. auth.) Alter, D. Pictorial astronomy 523

Cleopatra, Queen of Egypt
See pages in the following book:
Trease, G. Seven sovereign queens p 1-29   920

Cleopatra. Mudrick, M.
In Abrahams, W. ed. Fifty years of the American short story v 1 p490-99   **S C**

Clergy
Boyd, M. As I live and breathe   92
Marshall, C. A man called Peter [Marshall]   92
See also Monasticism and religious orders
Fiction
Greene, G. The power and the glory **Fic**
Guareschi, G. Comrade Don Camillo **Fic**
Guareschi, G. Don Camillo meets the flower children   **Fic**
Guareschi, G. The little world of Don Camillo   **Fic**

Clergy—Fiction—*Continued*
Trollope, A. Barchester Towers **Fic**
Turnbull, A. S. The Bishop's mantle **Fic**
Turnbull, A. S. The gown of glory **Fic**
West, M. L. The Devil's advocate **Fic**
Cleveland, Grover, President U.S.
Tugwell, R. G. Grover Cleveland 92
See also pages in the following book:
Abels, J. The degeneration of our Presidential election p198-206 329
Cleveland, Harlan
NATO: the transatlantic bargain 341.18
The Cleveland era. Ford, H. J. 973.8
The clicking of Cuthbert. Wodehouse, P. G.
In Costain, T. B. ed. Read with me p599-613 **S C**
In Lardner, R. ed. Rex Lardner selects the best of sports fiction p195-214 **S C**
A cliff of fall. Rindfleisch, N.
In Prize stories, 1970: The O. Henry Awards p29-49 **S C**
Clifford, James L.
(ed.) Twentieth century interpretations of Boswell's Life of Johnson 828
Climate
Chandler, T. J. The air around us 551.5
Claiborne, R. Climate, man, and history 551.59
See also pages in the following book:
Carlquist, S. Hawaii: a natural history p63-80 574.9
See also Meteorology; Weather
Climate, man, and history. Claiborne, R. 551.59
Climatology. See Climate
Climbing plants
Petrides, G. A. A field guide to trees and shrubs 582
Clingerman, Mildred
Minister without portfolio
In Conklin, G. ed. Invaders of earth p215-22 **S C**
The cloak. Gogol, N. V.
In Seltzer, T. comp. Best Russian short stories p40-81 **S C**
The clock we live on. Asimov, I. 529
Clocks and watches
Asimov, I. The clock we live on 529
Bruton, E. Clocks and watches, 1400-1900 681
Clocks and watches, 1400-1900. Bruton, E. 681
A clockwork orange. Burgess, A. **Fic**
The clod. Beach, L.
In Cerf, B. ed. Thirty famous one-act plays p451-60 808.82
In Gassner, J. ed. Twenty-five best plays of the modern American theatre; early ser. p688-94 812.08
A clod of soil. Akutagawa, R.
In Akutagawa, R. Japanese short stories p78-96 **S C**
Cloete, Stuart
Christmas in Matabeleland
In Wernecke, H. H. ed. Celebrating Christmas around the world p18-23 394.26

The cloister and the hearth. Reade, C. **Fic**
Cloke, Marjane
The modern business letter writer's manual 651.7
A close-up of Domba Splew. Lardner, R.
In Lardner, R. The Ring Lardner reader p647-50 **S C**
Close-up photography. Eastman Kodak Company 778.3
Closing the ring. Churchill, W. S. 940.53
Clothe the naked. Parker, D.
In Costain, T. B. ed. Read with me p405-14 **S C**
Clothing and dress
Carson, B. How you look and dress 646
Esquire. Esquire Good grooming for men 646.7
Harris, C. Figleafing through history: the dynamics of dress 391.09
Seventeen. The Seventeen Book of fashion and beauty 646.7
See also pages in the following books:
Archer, E. Let's face it p131-54 646.7
United States. Department of Agriculture. Consumers all p339-90 640.73
See also Costume; Dressmaking
Cloud physics and cloud seeding. Battan, L. J. 551.59
Cloud seeding. See Weather control
Clouds
Battan, L. J. Cloud physics and cloud seeding 551.59
See also pages in the following book:
Milne, L. Water and life p90-105 551.4
The clouds. Aristophanes
In Oates, W. J. ed. The complete Greek drama v2 p541-99 882.08
Clovis on parental responsibilities. Saki
In Saki. The short stories of Saki p377-80 **S C**
Clovis on the alleged romance of business. Saki
In Saki. The short stories of Saki p629-30 **S C**
Clutter family
Capote, T. In cold blood 364.1
Cnossus, Crete
See pages in the following book:
White, A. T. Lost worlds p54-90 913.03
The coach. Holland, G.
In Sports Illustrated. The wonderful world of sport p275-79 796
Coad, Oral Sumner
The American stage
In Pageant of America v14 973
Coal mines and mining
Fiction
Llewellyn, R. How green was my valley **Fic**
Coates, Robert M.
The net
In Foley, M. ed. Fifty best American short stories, 1915-1965 p261-69 **S C**
Return
In The New Yorker. Stories from The New Yorker, 1950-1960 p666-77 **S C**

Coats, Alice M.
Flowers and their histories   635.9

Cobb, Boughton
A field guide to the ferns and their related families of northeastern and central North America   587

Cobb, Charlie
Ain't that a groove
In Jones, L. ed. Black fire p519-24 810.8

Cobb, Irvin S.
The plural of moose is mise
In Lardner, R. ed. Rex Lardner selects the best of sports fiction p131-50 S C

Coburn, Alvin Frederick
See pages in the following book:
De Kruif, P. Men against death p342-54   920

The cobweb. Saki
In Saki. The short stories of Saki p295-301   S C

Cochise, Apache chief
See pages in the following book:
Brown, D. Bury my heart at Wounded Knee p192-217   970.4

Fiction
Arnold, E. Blood brother   Fic

Cochran, Doris M.
Living amphibians of the world   597
The new field book of reptiles and amphibians   598.1

Cochrane, Willard W.
The world food problem   338.1

Cock-a-doodle dandy. O'Casey, S.
In Block, H. M. ed. Masters of modern drama p459-86   808.82
In O'Casey, S. The Sean O'Casey reader p435-528   828

The cockfight. Buck, P. S.
In Buck, P. S. The good deed, and other stories of Asia, past and present p167-86   S C

Cockroaches
See pages in the following book:
Ward, R. R. The living clocks p229-41   574.1

The cocktail party. Eliot, T. S.
In Eliot, T. S. The complete plays of T. S. Eliot p123-212   812
In Eliot, T. S. Complete poems and plays, 1909-1950 p295-388   818

Cocoons. See Butterflies

Cocteau, Jean
The infernal machine
In Tucker, S. M. ed. Twenty-five modern plays p839-78   808.82
Orphée
In Block, H. M. ed. Masters of modern drama p534-48   808.82

About
Steegmuller, F. Cocteau   92

The code. Gill, R. T.
In The New Yorker. Stories from The New Yorker, 1950-1960 p180-90 S C

Cody, William Frederick
Buffalo Bill's life story (Colonel W. F. Cody)   92

Coe, Michael D.
America's first civilizations   970.3
Mexico   917.2

Coeducation. See Education of women

The coffee-house of Sura. Tolstoy, L.
In Tolstoy, L. Twenty-three tales p241-49   S C

Coffin, Charles M.
(ed.) The major poets: English and American   821.08

Coffin, Tristram P.
(ed.) Folklore in America   398

Cognition. See Knowledge, Theory of

Cohan, George Michael
See pages in the following books:
Ewen, D. Composers for the American musical theatre p49-60   920
Ewen, D. Great men of American popular song p87-99   920

Cohen, Allan Y.
(jt. auth.) Marin, P. Understanding drug use   613.8

Cohen, Arthur A.
The communism of Mao Tse-tung   335.4

Cohen, Hennig
(jt. ed.) Coffin, T. P. ed. Folklore in America   398

Cohen, J. M
(ed.) Latin American writing today   860.8

Cohen, Morris R.
Reason and nature; excerpts
In Kurtz, P. ed. American philosophy in the twentieth century p373-83   191.08

Cohen, Sidney
The drug dilemma   615

Cohn, Nik
Rock from the beginning   781.5

The coil of life. Moore, R.   574.09

Coin collecting. See Coins

Coin collectors' handbook. Reinfeld, F.   737.4

Coins
Davis, N. M. The complete book of United States coin collecting   737.4
Reed, M. Cowles Complete encyclopedia of U.S. coins   737.4
Reinfeld, F. A catalogue of the world's most popular coins   737.4
Reinfeld, F. Coin collectors' handbook   737.4
Reinfeld, F. How to build a coin collection   737.4
Reinfeld, F. A treasury of American coins   737.4
Reinfeld, F. Treasury of the world's coins   737.4
See also Numismatics

Dictionaries
Hobson, B. Illustrated encyclopedia of world coins   737.4

Coins in the Fracati Fountain. Powell, J.
In Best detective stories of the year, 1971 p200-48   S C

Coit, Margaret L.
The growing years: 1789-1829
In Life (Periodical) The Life History of the United States v3   973

Coit, Margaret L.—*Continued*
The sweep westward: 1829-1849
   In Life (Periodical) The Life History
     of the United States v4   973
Colbert, Edwin H.
   Men and dinosaurs   568
Colbert, Jean-Baptiste
    See pages in the following book:
   Williams, E. From Columbus to Castro:
    the history of the Caribbean, 1492-1969
    p159-68   972.9
Colby, Vineta
   (ed.) American culture in the sixties
    917.3
   (jt. ed.) Kunitz, S. J. ed. European au-
    thors, 1000-1900   920.03
   (jt. ed.) Kuntz, S. J. ed. Twentieth cen-
    tury authors: first supplement   920.03
Cold. See Low temperatures
Cold war. See World politics—1945-
The cold war as history. Halle, L. J.   909.82
The cold wind and the warm. Bradbury, R.
   In Bradbury, R. I sing the Body Elec-
    tric! p100-18   S C
Colditz, Germany. Castle
   Reid, P. R. The Colditz story   940.54
The Colditz story. Reid, P. R.   940.54
Cole, Charles Woolsey
   (jt. auth.) Hayes, C. J. H. History of
    Western civilization since 1500   940.2
Cole, Ernest
   House of bondage   301.451
Cole, Thomas, 1801-1848
    See pages in the following book:
   Baigell, M. A history of American paint-
    ing p107-16   759.13
Cole, Toby
   (ed.) Actors on acting   792
Cole, Tom
   Saint John of the Hershey Kisses: 1964
    In Prize stories, 1970: The O. Henry
    awards p149-83   S C
Cole, William
   (ed.) A book of love poems   821.08
   (ed.) The fireside book of humorous
    poetry   821.08
Coleman, Henry
   (jt. ed.) Shaw, M. ed. National anthems of
    the world   784.7
Coleman, Ornette
    See pages in the following books:
   Goldberg, J. Jazz masters of the fifties
    p228-46   920
   Williams, M. The jazz tradition p207-20
    781.5
Coleridge, Samuel Taylor
   Poems of Samuel Taylor Coleridge   821
   The portable Coleridge   828
   The rime of the ancient mariner
    In Coleridge, S. T. Poems of Samuel
    Taylor Coleridge p21-43   821
    In Coleridge, S. T. The portable Cole-
    ridge p80-105   828
      About
    See pages in the following books:
   Coleridge, S. T. The portable Coleridge
    p 1-54   828

Daiches, D. A critical history of English
   literature v2 p888-902   820.9
Untermeyer, L. Lives of the poets p338-70
    920
Untermeyer, L. The paths of poetry p118-
   25   920
Coles, Manning
   Guarding the Zeppelins
    In Dulles, A. ed. Great spy stories from
    fiction p153-62   S C
Coles, Robert
   Children of crisis   301.451
   The middle Americans   301.44
   Still hungry in America   330.973
   (jt. auth.) Brenner, J. H. Drugs & youth
    613.8
Colfax, Wash.
      Description
    See pages in the following book:
   Moyers, B. Listening to America p163-77
    917.3
Collaborationists. See Treason
Collage
   Lynch, J. How to make collages   745.59
The collapse of the Third Republic. Shirer,
   W. L.   944.081
Collected and new poems, 1924-1963. Van
   Doren, M.   811
The collected essays and occasional writings
   of Katherine Anne Porter. Porter, K. A.
    818
Collected poems (1909-1935). Eliot, T. S.
    In Eliot, T. S. Complete poems and
    plays, 1909-1950   818
Collected poems, 1909-1962. Eliot, T. S. 811
Collected poems, 1917-1952. MacLeish, A. 811
Collected short fiction, 1892-1912, Willa
   Cather's. Cather, W.   S C
The collected shorter poems. Rexroth, K.
    811
Collected shorter poems: 1927-1957. Auden,
   W. H.   821
A collection of essays. Orwell, G.   824
Collections of literature. See Poetry—Collec-
   tions; Short stories
Collective bargaining
   Marx, H. L. ed. Collective bargaining for
    public employees   350
    See also Labor unions
Collective bargaining for public employees.
   Marx, H. L. ed.   350
Collective farms. See Agriculture, Coopera-
   tive
Collective settlements
    See pages in the following book:
   Snow, E. Red China today p89-95, 404-40,
    460-76   915.1
Collectivism. See Communism
The collector. Fowles, J.   Fic
Collectors and collecting. See names of ob-
   jects collected, e.g. Postage stamps
The college and adult reading list of books
   in literature and the fine arts. National
   Council of Teachers of English. Com-
   mittee on College and Adult Reading
   List   016

College and school journalism
Birmingham, J. ed. Our time is now **373.1**
Magmer, J. Photograph & printed word
371.89
Medlin, C. J. Yearbook editing, layout, and management **371.89**
Shaff, A. L. The student journalist and the critical review **371.89**
The College blue book **378.73**
College costs. See Education—Finance
College Entrance Examination Board
A chance to go to college **378.73**
College entrance requirements. See Colleges and universities—Entrance requirements
The college game is best. Underwood, J.
In Sports Illustrated. The wonderful world of sport p237-39 **796**
College guide, Lovejoy's. Lovejoy, C. E.
378.73
College journalism. See College and school journalism
College libraries. See Libraries, College and university
College sports. See Baseball
The college student's handbook. Lass, A. H.
378.102
College teachers. See Teachers
College thesaurus in dictionary form, The New American Roget's **424**
Colleges and universities
See also Education, Higher; Junior colleges; Scholarships, fellowships, etc.

Entrance requirements
Brownstein, S. C. Barron's How to prepare for college entrance examinations
371.26
Fine, B. How to be accepted by the college of your choice **378.1**
Turner, D. R. Scoring high on college entrance tests **371.26**

Europe
Garraty, J. The new guide to study abroad **378.3**
See also pages in the following book:
The New Cambridge Modern history v2 p414-37 **909**

Fiction
Knowles, J. The paragon **Fic**
Snow, C. P. The masters **Fic**

Great Britain
See pages in the following books:
Hussey, M. comp. Chaucer's world p76-86 **821.09**
Shakespeare's England v 1 p238-50 **822.3**

Handbooks, manuals, etc.
Lass, A. H. The college student's handbook **378.102**

United States
Bander, E. J. ed. Turmoil on the campus
378.1
Barzun, J. The American university
378.73
Lovejoy, C. E. Lovejoy's Scholarship guide **378.3**
Pope, L. The right college **378.73**

United States. President's Commission on Campus Unrest. The report of the President's Commission on Campus Unrest
378.1
See also pages in the following books:
Barzun, J. Teacher in America p177-94
371.1
Boorstin, D. P. The Americans: The colonial experience p171-84 **917.3**
Boorstin, D. J. The Americans: The national experience p152-61 **917.3**
Du Bois, W. E. B. W. E. B. Du Bois: a reader p157-200 **301.451**
Fortune (Periodical) Youth in turmoil p120-32 **301.43**
Gardner, J. W. No easy victories p85-104
309.173
Nye, R. B. The cultural life of the new Nation, 1776-1830 p171-94 **917.3**
United States. National Commission on the Causes and Prevention of Violence. To establish justice, to insure domestic tranquility p177-87 **301.18**

United States—Directories
American Council on Education. Accredited institutions of higher education
378.73
American universities and colleges **378.73**
Cass, J. Comparative guide to American colleges **378.73**
Cass, J. Comparative guide to two-year colleges & four-year specialized schools and programs **378.73**
The College blue book **378.73**
College Entrance Examination Board. A chance to go to college **378.73**
Fine, B. Barron's Profiles of American colleges **378.73**
Hawes, G. R. The New American Guide to colleges **378.73**
Lovejoy, C. E. Lovejoy's College guide
378.73
Collier, Basil
The Second World War: a military history **940.54**
Collier, John
The lady on the grey
In Garrity, D. A. ed. 44 Irish short stories p22-31 **S C**
Collier's encyclopedia **031**
Collier's encyclopedia year book. See Collier's encyclopedia **031**
Collins, A. Frederick
The Amateur photographer's handbook. See The Amateur photographer's handbook **770.2**
The radio amateur's handbook **621.3841**
Collins, Bob
Andretti, M. What's it like out there? **92**
Collins, Larry
Is Paris burning? **944.081**
Or I'll dress you in mourning [biography of Manuel Benítez Pérez] **92**
Collins, Michael
Freedom fighter
In Mystery Writers of America. Crime without murder p35-45 **S C**
First on the moon. See First on the moon
629.45

Communism—*Continued*

Douglas, W. O. America challenged p31-74   917.3

MacLeish, A. A continuing journey p59-76   818

Ward, B. Five ideas that change the world p117-49   320

Ward, B. The rich nations and the poor nations p62-85   338.91

Austria
See pages in the following book:

Stadler, K. R. Austria p168-77, 238-42, 259-62   943.6

Bolivia
See pages in the following book:

Harris, R. Death of a revolutionary [Ernesto] Che Guevara's last mission p145-67   92

China

Latourette, K. S. China   951

Snow, E. Red star over China   951.04

See also pages in the following book:

Li, Dun J. The ageless Chinese p476-509   951

China (People's Republic of China)

Bennett, G. A. Red Guard; the political biography of Dai Hsiao-ai   92

Cohen, A. A. The communism of Mao Tse-tung   335.4

Mao, Tsê-tung. The political thought of Mao Tse-tung   320.5

Mao, Tsê-tung. Quotations from Chairman Mao Tse-tung   320.5

Schram, S. Mao Tse-tung   951.05

Europe
See pages in the following book:

White, T. H. Fire in the ashes p318-55   940.55

Fiction

Guareschi, G. Comrade Don Camillo **Fic**

Guareschi, G. The little world of Don Camillo   **Fic**

Koestler, A. Darkness at noon   **Fic**

India
See pages in the following book:

Bowles, C. Ambassador's report p119-42   915.4

Russia

Payne, R. The life and death of Lenin   92

Rieber, A. J. A study of the USSR and communism: an historical approach   914.7

Vladimirov, L. The Russians   914.7

See also pages in the following books:

Camus, A. The rebel p159-214   170

Koutaissoff, E. The Soviet Union p23-68   914.7

Salisbury, H. E. ed. The Soviet Union: the fifty years p402-20   914.7

Russia—Fiction

Pasternak, B. Doctor Zhivago   **Fic**

Sholokhov, M. Tales of the Don   **S C**

United States

Draper, T. The roots of American communism   335.4

Hoover, J. E. Masters of deceit   335.4

See also pages in the following book:

Taft, P. Organized labor in American history p618-30   331.88

The communism of Mao Tse-tung. Cohen, A. A.   335.4

Communist Party of the United States of America

Draper, T. The roots of American communism   335.4

Hoover, J. E. Masters of deceit   335.4

Community and school
See pages in the following book:

Gross, B. ed. Radical school reform p125-38   370.8

Community antenna television
See pages in the following book:

Johnson, N. How to talk back to your television set p149-68   384.55

Community colleges. See Junior colleges

The compact history of the American newspaper. Tebbel, J.   071

Companies. See Corporations

Companion to American history, The Oxford. Johnson, T. H.   973.03

Companion to American literature, The Oxford. Hart, J. D.   810.3

Companion to classical literature, The Oxford   880.3

Companion to English literature, The Oxford   820.3

Companion to French literature, The Oxford   840.3

A companion to Shakespeare studies. See Muir, K. ed. A new companion to Shakespeare studies   822.3

Companion to the theatre, The Oxford   792.03

Comparative guide to American colleges. Cass, J.   378.73

Comparative guide to two-year colleges & four-year specialized schools and programs. Cass, J.   378.73

Comparative literature. See Literature, Comparative

Comparative psychology. See Psychology, Comparative

Comparative religion. See Christianity and other religions; Religions

Compass
See pages in the following book:

Boy Scouts of America. Fieldbook for Boy Scouts, explorers, scouters, educators, outdoorsmen p14-31   369.43

Competition. See Monopolies; Trusts, Industrial

Competitive debate. Musgrave, G. M.   808.53

The complete book of building and collecting model automobiles. Hertz, L. H.   629.22

The complete book of cat care. Whitney, L. F.   636.8

The complete book of classical music. Ewen, D. ed.   780.1

The complete book of engagement and wedding etiquette. Wilson, B.   395

The complete book of engines. Hot Rod
629.2
The complete book of fashion modeling.
Lenz, B.   659.15
The complete book of horses & ponies. Self,
M. C.   798
Complete book of marvels, Richard Halli-
burton's. Halliburton, R.   910.4
Complete book of the American musical
theater, New. Ewen, D.   782.8
The complete book of the Siamese cat. Den-
ham, S.   636.8
The complete book of twentieth century
music. See Ewen, D. The world of
twentieth century music   780.1
The complete book of United States coin
collecting. Davis, N. M.   737.4
The complete chessplayer. Reinfeld, F.
794.1
The complete dictionary of abbreviations.
Large type ed. Schwartz, R. J. comp.
421.03
The complete dog book. American Kennel
Club   636.7
The complete encyclopedia of homemaking
ideas. Bradford, B. T.   640
The complete English poetry of John Mil-
ton. See Milton, J. The complete poeti-
cal works of John Milton   821
A complete field guide to nests in the United
States. Headstrom, R.   598
The complete Greek drama. Oates, W. J.
ed.   882.08
The complete guide to embroidery stitches
and crewel. Bucher, J.   746.4
Complete Hoyle, Foster's. Foster, R. F.
795
The complete humorous sketches and tales
of Mark Twain. Twain, M.   817
The complete life of John Hopkins. Henry,
O.
In Henry, O. The complete works of
O. Henry p1257-61   S C
Complete manual of home repair, The New
York Times. Gladstone, B.   643
Complete opera book, Kobbé's. Kobbé, G.
782.1
The complete photographer. Feininger, A.
770.2
Complete plays, with prefaces. Shaw, B.
822
The complete poems and plays, 1909-1950.
Eliot, T. S.   818
Complete poems of Robert Frost, 1949.
Frost, R.   811
The complete poetic and dramatic works of
Robert Browning. Browning, R.   821
Complete secretary's handbook. Doris, L.
651.02
The complete Sherlock Holmes. Doyle, Sir
A. C.   S C
The complete short stories & sketches of
Stephen Crane. Crane, S.   S C
Complete stories of the great operas, The
new Milton Cross'. Cross, M.   782.1
The complete tales and poems of Edgar
Allan Poe. Poe, E. A.   S C
Complete woodworking handbook. Adams,
J. T.   684
Complexion.   See Cosmetics; Grooming,
Personal

Compliments of the season. Henry, O.
In Henry, O. The complete works of
O. Henry p1575-82   S C
Composers
Chapin, V. The violin and its masters
920
Ewen, D. ed. The complete book of clas-
sical music   780.1
Ewen, D. Composers of tomorrow's mu-
sic   920
Ewen, D. David Ewen introduces mod-
ern music   780.9
Ewen, D. ed. The new book of modern
composers   920
Ewen, D. ed. The world of great com-
posers   920
Ewen, D. The world of twentieth cen-
tury music   780.1
Seroff, V. Men who made musical his-
tory   920
Shippen, K. B. The heritage of music
780.9
Dictionaries
Cross, M. The Milton Cross New en-
cyclopedia of the great composers and
their music   920.03
Ewen, D. ed. Composers since 1900 920.03
Ewen, D. ed. Great composers, 1300-1900
920.03
Composers, American
Dobrin, A. Aaron Copland: his life and
times   92
Ewen, D. Composers for the American
musical theatre   920
Ewen, D. George Gershwin: his journey
to greatness   92
Ewen, D. Great men of American popular
song   920
Ewen, D. Leonard Bernstein   92
Ewen, D. The life and death of Tin Pan
Alley   784
Ewen, D. New Complete book of the
American musical theater   782.8
Ewen, D. The story of America's musical
theater   782.8
Ewen, D. With a song in his heart; the
story of Richard Rodgers   92
Dictionaries
Ewen, D. ed. Popular American composers,
from Revolutionary times to the present
920.03
Composers, Austrian
Valentin, E. Mozart and his world   92
Composers, German
Marek, G. R. Beethoven, biography of a
genius   92
Composers for the American musical theatre.
Ewen, D.   920
Composers of today. See Ewen, D. ed. Com-
posers since 1900   920.03
Composers of tomorrow's music. Ewen, D.
920
Composers of yesterday. See Ewen, D. ed.
Great composers, 1300-1900   920.03
Composers since 1900. Ewen, D. ed. 920.03
Composition (Rhetoric) See Rhetoric; and
names of languages with the subdivision
Composition and exercises, e.g. English
language—Composition and exercises

A **comprehensive** anthology of American poetry. Aiken, C. ed.   811.08

Comprehensive desk dictionary, Thorndike-Barnhart   423

The **comprehensive** high school. Conant, J. B.   373.73

Compton's Dictionary of the natural sciences   570.3

Compton's Encyclopedia and fact-index 031

Compton's Pictured encyclopedia. See Compton's Encyclopedia and fact-index 031

Compton's Yearbook. See Compton's Encyclopedia and fact index   031

Compulsory military service. See Military service, Compulsory

Computer control. See Automation

Computer data processing and programming. Gildersleeve, T. R.   651.8

Computer science   651.8

Computers, Electronic. See Electronic computers

Computers and society. Nikolaieff, G. A. ed.   510.78

Computers—the machines we think with. Halacy, D. S.   510.78

Comrade Don Camillo. Guareschi, G.   **Fic**

Comrades. Strindberg, A.
In Tucker, S. M. ed. Twenty-five modern plays p43-69   808.82

Comstock Lode
See pages in the following books:
American Heritage. The American Heritage Book of great adventures of the Old West p222-39   978
Stone, I. Men to match my mountains p237-65, 302-13   979.1

Conant, James B.
The comprehensive high school   373.73
The education of American teachers 370.7

Conant, Roger
A field guide to reptiles and amphibians of the United States and Canada east of the 100th meridian   598.1

Concentration camps
Bosworth, A. R. America's concentration camps   301.45
Schnabel, E. Anne Frank: a portrait in courage   92
Fiction
Wiesel, E. Dawn   **Fic**

Conception
Prevention
See Birth control

Conchology. See Shells

The **concise** Cambridge bibliography of English literature, 600-1950. Watson, G. ed.   016.82

The **concise** Cambridge History of English literature. Sampson, G.   820.9

Concise Dictionary of American biography   920.03

The **concise** dictionary of national biography. See The Dictionary of national biography. The concise dictionary   920.03

The **Concise** encyclopedia of archaeology   913.03

The **concise** encyclopedia of English and American poets and poetry. Spender, S. ed.   821.03

Concise encyclopedia of Greek and Roman mythology. Oswalt, S. G.   292.03

The **Concise** encyclopedia of modern world literature   803

A **concise** history of Australia. Turnbull, C.   994

The **concise** history of costume and fashion. Laver, J.   391.09

A **concise** history of East Asia. Fitzgerald, C. P.   950

A **concise** history of England. Halliday, F. E.   942

A **concise** history of France. Johnson, D. 944

A **concise** history of modern painting. Read, H.   759.06

A **concise** history of modern sculpture. Read, H.   735

The **concise** history of theatre. Hartnoll, P.   792.09

A **concise** history of Western architecture. Jordan, R. F.   720.9

The **Concise** Oxford Dictionary of current English   423

The **Concise** Oxford Dictionary of English literature   820.3

The **concise** Oxford Dictionary of music. Scholes, P. A.   780.3

Concord rebel; a life of Henry D. Thoreau. Derleth, A.   92

Concordances. See Bible—Concordances

The **concrete** mixer. Bradbury, R.
In Bradbury, R. The illustrated man p189-210   **S C**

Il **conde.** Conrad, J.
In Conrad, J. The portable Conrad p609-29   828

The **Condensed** chemical dictionary   540.3

Condon, Edward U.
Colorado. University. Final report of the scientific study of unidentified flying objects   629.133

Condon, Richard
The trigger
In Dulles, A. ed. Great spy stories from fiction p339-43   **S C**

Conduct of life. See Behavior

The **conduct** of life. Mumford, L.   128

Conducting
See pages in the following book:
Bernstein, L. The joy of music p120-51   780.1

Conductors (Music)
Ewen, D. Famous modern conductors 920
Ewen, D. Leonard Bernstein   92
See also Conducting

The **cone.** Wells, H. G.
In Wells, H. G. The complete short stories of H. G. Wells p457-69 **S C**

Coney Island's failing days. Crane, S.
In Crane, S. The complete short stories & sketches of Stephen Crane p181-86   **S C**

Congressional committees. Morrow, W. L. 328.73

Conkle, E. P.
Heaven is a long time to wait
In The Best short plays of 1958-1959 p135-46   808.82
Minnie Field
In Gassner, J. ed. Twenty-five best plays of the modern American theatre; early ser. p749-52   812.08

Conklin, Groff
(ed.) Invaders of earth   S C

Connecticut

Politics and government
See pages in the following book:
Bowles, C. ed. The conscience of a liberal p293-316   327.73
A **Connecticut** Yankee in King Arthur's court. Twain, M.   Fic

Connell, Evan S.
I came from yonder mountain
In Abrahams, W. ed. Fifty years of the American short story v 1 p220-26   S C
The suicide
In The Saturday Evening Post. Best modern short stories p279-96   S C

Connelly, Marc
The green pastures   812
—Same
In Cerf, B. A. ed. Sixteen famous American plays p147-202   812.08
In Gassner, J. ed. Twenty best plays of the modern American theatre p191-231   812.08
The traveler
In Cerf, B. ed. 24 favorite one-act plays p219-28   808.82
About
Nolan, P. T. Marc Connelly   812.09

Connery, Donald S.
The Irish   914.15

Connolly, James Brendan
The trawler
In The Scribner treasury p511-32   S C

Connor, John M.
(comp.) Ottemiller's Index to plays in collections. See Ottemiller's Index to plays in collections   808.82

The **conquering** family. Costain, T. B. 942.03

The **conquerors.** See Costain, T. B. The conquering family   942.03

Conquest, Robert
The great terror   947.084

Conquest by man. Herrmann, P.   910.9

The **conquest** of Everest. Hunt, J.   915.4

The **conquest** of New France. Wrong, G. M. 971.01

Conquistador. MacLeish, A.
In MacLeish, A. Collected poems, 1917-1952 p233-326   811

Conquistadors. See America—Discovery and exploration

The **Conquistadors.** Innes, H.   973.1

Conquistadors and Pueblos. Hall-Quest, O. 979.1

Conquistadors in North American history. Horgan, P.   973.1

Conrad, Joseph
Lord Jim   Fic
Lord Jim: criticism
In Drew, E. The novel: a modern guide to fifteen English masterpieces p156-72   823.09
Mr Vladimir and Mr Verloc
In Dulles, A. ed. Great spy stories from fiction p74-85   S C
The Nigger of the Narcissus   Fic
also in Conrad, J. The portable Conrad p292-453   828
also in Conrad, J. Typhoon, and other tales of the sea p91-236   Fic
The portable Conrad   828
Contains the following stories: Prince Roman; Warrior's soul; Youth; Amy Foster; Outpost of progress; Heart of darkness; Il conde; The lagoon; The secret sharer
Typhoon
In Conrad, J. The portable Conrad p192-287   828
Typhoon, and other tales of the sea   Fic
Short stories included are: Youth; Heart of darkness
Victory   Fic
Youth
In Havighurst, W. ed. Masters of the modern short story p 1-32   S C
About
Gurko, L. The two lives of Joseph Conrad   92
See also pages in the following books:
Daiches, D. The novel and the modern world p25-62   823.09
Wagenknecht, E. Cavalcade of the English novel p423-40   823.09

Conroy, Jack
(jt. auth.) See Bontemps, A. Anyplace but here   301.451

Conscience in art. Henry, O.
In Henry, O. The complete works of O. Henry p310-14   S C

The **conscience** of a liberal. Bowles, C. 327.73

Conscientious objectors
See pages in the following books:
Lynd, S. ed. Nonviolence in America: a documentary history p173-215, 271-305   323
Polenberg, R. ed. America at war p115-23   309.173

Consciousness. See Self

Conscription, Military. See Military service, Compulsory

Conservation Foundation
Osborn, F. ed. Our crowded planet   301.3

Conservation: now or never. Roosevelt, N. 333.7

Conservation of energy. See Force and energy

Conservation of forests. See Forests and forestry

Conservation of natural resources. See Natural resources

Conservation of the soil. See Soil conservation

Conservation of wild life. See Wild life—Conservation

Conservatism
Rossiter, C. Conservatism in America
320.5
Sigler, J. A. ed. The conservative tradition in American thought   320.5
Conservatism in America. Rossiter, C. 320.5
The conservative tradition in American thought. Sigler, J. A. ed.   320.5
Consolidated Edison Company of New York, inc.
See pages in the following book:
Boyle, R. H. The Hudson River p153-74
917.47
Conspiracy up to the ears. Goul, R.
In Dulles, A. ed. Great spy stories from fiction p49-62   **S C**
Constable, John
See pages in the following book:
Cheney, S. The story of modern art p49-56
709.03
Constantine I, the Great, Emperor of Rome
See pages in the following books:
Asimov, L. Constantinople p21-31   949.6
Coolidge, O. Lives of famous Romans p209-43   920
Payne, R. Ancient Rome p286-89, 291-98
913.37
Constantine II, King of the Hellenes
See pages in the following book:
Papandreou, A. Democracy at gunpoint: the Greek front p142-242, 246-65 949.5
Constantinople. See Istanbul
Constantinople. Asimov, I.   949.6
Constellations. See Astronomy; Stars
Constitution. See United States. Constitution
Constitutional amendents

United States
See United States. Constitution—Amendments
Constitutional history. See United States—Constitutional history
Constitutional law. See United States—Constitutional law
Construction. See Architecture; Building
The consul. Davis, R. H.
In The Scribner treasury p473-92   **S C**
Consumer beware! Hunter, B. T.   664
Consumer credit. See Credit
Consumer education
Klamkin, C. If it doesn't work, read the instructions   640.73
Nader, R. What to do with your bad car
629.22
Trump, F. Buyer beware!   339.4
United States. Department of Agriculture. Consumers all   640.73
See also Shopping
Consumer protection
Cox, E. F. 'The Nader report' on the Federal Trade Commission   381.061
McClellan, G. S. ed. The consuming public
339.4

Trump, F. Buyer beware!   339.4
See also pages in the following book:
Wagner, S. The Federal Trade Commission p190-201   381.061
See also Food adulteration and inspection
Consumer Reports
The Consumers Union report on smoking and the public interest   613.8
Consumers all. United States. Department of Agriculture   640.73
Consumers' guides. See Consumer education
The Consumers Union report on smoking and the public interest. Consumer Reports   613.8
The consuming public. McClellan, G. S. ed.
339.4
Consumption (Economics)
McClellan, G. S. ed. The consuming public
339.4
Packard, V. The waste makers   339.4
Contact lenses. See Eyeglasses
Contagion and contagious diseases
Zinsser, H. Rats, lice and history 616.9
Contamination crew. Nourse, A. E.
In Nourse, A. E. R for tomorrow p34-54
S C
Contemplation in a world of action. Merton, T.   248
Contemporary authors   920.03
Contemporary authors; semi-annual 920.03
Contemporary Europe since 1870. Hayes, C. J. H.   940.2
Contemporary poets of the English language. Murphy, R. ed.   920.03
Contemporary world atlas, Hammond. Hammond, Incorporated   912
The contest for Aaron Gold. Roth, P.
In Foley, M. ed. Fifty best American short stories, 1915-1965 p549-62 **S C**
The continent we live on. Sanderson, I. T.
574.9
Continental drift
See pages in the following book:
Scientific American. Frontiers in astronomy p4-15   520
A continuing journey. MacLeish, A.   818
Contours of change. United States. Department of Agriculture   630
Contraception. See Birth control
Contract. Lardner, R.
In Lardner, R. The Ring Lardner reader p379-91   **S C**
Contract bridge. See Bridge (Game)
Contract bridge complete. See Goren, C. H. Goren's Bridge complete   795.4
Contracting Parties to the General Agreement on Tariffs and Trade
See pages in the following book:
United States. Department of Agriculture. Farmer's world p482-94   338.1
Contractions. See Ciphers
Contracts
Laws and regulations
See pages in the following book:
Sloan, I. J. Youth and the law p31-44 **340**

The **contrast**. Tyler, R.
  In Gassner, J. ed. Best plays of the early
    American theatre p 1-37   **812.08**
  In Quinn, A. H. ed. Representative
    American plays p43-77   **812.08**
Controlling pollution. Goldman, M. I. ed.
                          333.9
The **convalescence** of Jack Hamlin. Harte, B.
  In Harte, B. The best short stories of
    Bret Harte p475-502   **S C**
Convention. Knebel, F.   **Fic**
Conventions, Political. See Political con-
  ventions
Convents. See Monasticism and religious
  orders for women
Conversation in foreign languages. See
  Languages, Modern—Conversation and
  phrase books
Conversation of Eiros and Charmion. Poe,
  E. A.
  In Poe, E. A. The complete tales and
    poems of Edgar Allan Poe p452-56
                          S C
  In Poe, E. A. Selected poetry and prose
    p149-54   **818**
A **conversation** on the train. West, R.
  In Dulles, A. ed. Great spy stories from
    fiction p63-73   **S C**
Conversion. See Converts, Catholic
The **conversion** of Sum Loo. Cather, W.
  In Cather, W. Willa Cather's Collected
    short fiction. 1892-1912 v3 p323-31
                          S C
The **convert**. Bennett, L.
  In Clarke, J. H. ed. American Negro
    short stories p282-96   **S C**
Converts, Catholic
  Merton, T. The seven storey mountain **92**
Convicts. See Crime and criminals
Cook, Dorothy E.
  (comp.) Short story index. See Short story
    index   **808.83**
  (comp.) Short story index: supplement,
    1950-1954. See Short story index: sup-
    plement, 1950-1954   **808.83**
Cook, George Cram
  See pages in the following book:
  Gould, J. Modern American playwrights
    p26-49   **812.09**
Cook, James, 1728-1779
  Villiers, A. Captain James Cook   **92**
  See also pages in the following books:
  Day, A. G. Hawaii and its people p4-15
                          996.9
  Hale, J. R. Age of exploration p143-59
                          910.9
  Stefánsson, V. ed. Great adventures and
    explorations p659-713   **910.9**
Cook, Margaret G.
  The new library key   **028.7**
Cook books. See Cookery
Cook Islands
  See pages in the following book:
  Shadbolt, M. Isles of the South Pacific
    p34-48   **919**
Cooke, Jacob E.
  Adams, J. T. The march of democracy **973**

Cooke, Jay
  See pages in the following book:
  Holbrook, S. H. The age of the moguls
    p51-56   **920**
Cookery
  Adams, C. The teen-ager's menu cookbook
                          641.5
  American Heritage. The American Heri-
    tage cookbook   **641.5**
  American Heritage. The American Heri-
    tage Cookbook, and illustrated history
    of American eating & drinking   **641.5**
  Better Homes and Gardens. Better Homes
    & Gardens New cook book   **641.5**
  Crocker, B. Betty Crocker's Good and
    easy cookbook   **641.5**
  De Knight, F. The Ebony cookbook: a
    date with a dish   **641.5**
  Farmer, F. The Fannie Farmer cook-
    book   **641.5**
  Field, M. A quintet of cuisines   **641.5**
  Good Housekeeping Institute. New York.
    The new Good Housekeeping cookbook
                          641.5
  Hale, W. H. The Horizon Cookbook and
    illustrated history of eating and drinking
    throughout the ages   **641.5**
  McCall's. McCall's Cook book   **641.5**
  Rombauer, I. S. Joy of cooking   **641.5**
  Rosengarten, F. The book of spices
                          641.6
  United States. Department of Agricul-
    ture. Food for us all   **641**
  Wilson, J. American cooking: the East-
    ern heartland   **641.5**
  See also pages in the following book:
  Wernecke, H. H. Christmas customs
    around the world p153-68   **394.26**
    See also Cake; Food; Outdoor cook-
    ery; Pastry
            Cranberries
  See pages in the following book:
  Leonard, J. N. American cooking: New
    England p113-24   **641.5**
            Dictionaries
  De Sola, R. comp. A dictionary of cook-
    ing   **641.503**
            Fish
  See pages in the following book:
  National Geographic Society. Wondrous
    world of fishes p348-65   **597**
            Fruits
  See pages in the following book:
  Wolfe, L. The cooking of the Carib-
    bean Islands p107-27   **641.5**
            Hawaii
  See pages in the following book:
  Steinberg, R. Pacific and Southeast Asian
    cooking p8-31   **641.5**
            History
  Hale, W. H. The Horizon Cookbook and
    illustrated history of eating and drinking
    throughout the ages   **641.5**
          Maple sugar
  See pages in the following book:
  Leonard, J. N. American cooking: New
    England p147-67   **641.5**

Cottages. See Houses

Cotton
Dodd, W. E. The cotton kingdom   975
  See also pages in the following book:
United States. Department of Agriculture.
  Contours of change p39-46   630
The cotton kingdom. Dodd, W. E.   975

Cotton manufacture and trade
  See pages in the following book:
Stone, A. A. Careers in agribusiness and
  industry p155-72   338.1

Cottrell, Leonard
Egypt   916.2
Five queens of ancient Egypt   913.32
Hannibal, enemy of Rome   92
Life under the Pharaohs   913.32
Lost cities   913.03
The lost Pharaohs   913.32
The mystery of Minoan civilization 913.39
The quest for Sumer   913.35
The secrets of Tutankhamen's tomb
    913.32
The warrior Pharaohs   932
(ed.) The Concise encyclopedia of archae-
  ology. See The Concise encyclopedia of
  archaeology   913.03

Couch, Arthur Quiller- See Quiller-Couch,
  Arthur

Coughlan, Robert
Tropical Africa   916.7
The world of Michelangelo, 1475-1564 92

Coughlin, Charles Edward
  See pages in the following books:
Leighton, I. ed. The aspirin age, 1919-
  1941 p232-57   917.3
Shannon, W. V. The American Irish p295-
  319   301.453

Coulson, E. H.
Test tubes and beakers   540.72

Coulson, J.
(ed.) Oxford Illustrated dictionary. See
  Oxford Illustrated dictionary   423

Council on Foreign Relations
Political handbook and atlas of the world.
  See Political handbook and atlas of the
  world   329
The World this year. See The World this
  year   329
Reston, J. The artillery of the press
    323.44

The counsel assigned. Andrews, M. R. S.
  In The Scribner treasury p495-508 **S C**

Counseling. See Vocational guidance

The count and the wedding guest. Henry,
  O.
  In Henry, O. The best short stories of
    O. Henry p315-22 **S C**
  In Henry, O. The complete works of O.
    Henry p1461-64 **S C**

The Count of Crow's Nest. Cather, W.
  In Cather, W. Willa Cather's Collected
    short fiction, 1892-1912 v3 p449-71
    S C

The Count of Monte Cristo. Fechter, C.
  In Gassner, J. ed. Best plays of the early
    American theatre p216-61   812.08

The count who wished he were a peasant;
  a life of Leo Tolstoy. Philipson, M. 92

Counter Reformation
  See pages in the following book:
The New Cambridge Modern history v2
  p275-300   909
The Counter-Reformation and price revolu-
  tion, 1559-1610. Wernham, R. B. ed.
  In The New Cambridge Modern history
    v3   909

Counterblast. McLuhan, M.   001.5

The counterfeiters. Gide, A.   **Fic**

Counterparts. Joyce, J.
  In Garrity, D. A. ed. 44 Irish short
    stories p133-45 **S C**
  In Joyce, J. Dubliners p106-22 **S C**

The Countess Cathleen. Yeats, W. B.
  In Yeats, W. B. Collected plays of W. B.
    Yeats p 1-32   822

Country Beautiful
America's historic houses   917.3
Freeman, O. L. The national forests of
  America   917.3
Thoreau, H. D. America the beautiful
    574.9
Udall, S. L. The national parks of Amer-
  ica   917.3

Country doctor. Kafka, F.
  In Kafka, F. Selected short stories of
    Franz Kafka p148-56 **S C**

Country doctor. Morrison, W.
  In Asimov, I. ed. Where do we go from
    here? p217-43 **S C**

Country editor's boy. Borland, H.   92

A country excursion. Maupassant, G. de
  In Maupassant, G. de. Selected short
    stories p299-312 **S C**

Country full of Swedes. Caldwell, E.
  In Abrahams, W. ed. Fifty years of the
    American short story v 1 p157-70
    S C

The country husband. Cheever, J.
  In The New Yorker. Stories from The
    New Yorker, 1950-1960 p755-78
    S C

Country life
  See also Outdoor life

      Connecticut
Borland, H. The dog who came to stay
    636.7

      North Carolina
Ruark, R. The Old Man and the boy   92

The country love story. Stafford, J.
  In Abrahams, W. ed. Fifty years of the
    American short story v2 p289-300
    S C

The country of elusion. Henry, O.
  In Henry, O. The complete works of O.
    O. Henry p1464-71 **S C**

A country of strangers. Richter, C.   **Fic**

The country of the blind. Wells, H. G.
  In Wells, H. G. The complete short sto-
    ries of H. G. Wells p167-92 **S C**
  In Wells, H. G. 28 science fiction stories
    p310-35 **S C**

The country of the pointed firs. Jewett,
  S. O.   **Fic**

Country schools. See Rural schools

Coup de grâce. Moore, R.
In Moore, R. The green berets p139-63
    S C

The **coup** of Long Lance. Schaefer, J.
In Schaefer, J. The collected stories of Jack Schaefer p451-67   **S C**

Coups d'états. *See* Revolutions

Courage
Kennedy, J. F. Profiles in courage. Memorial ed.   920
Mantle, M. The quality of courage   920

Courbet, Gustave
See pages in the following books:
Cheney, S. The story of modern art p126-32   709.03
Schneider, P. The world of Manet, 1832-1883 p37-43   92

Courlander, Harold
The African   Fic

The **course** of empire. De Voto, B.   973.1

Courses of study. *See* Education—Curricula

Court life. *See* Courts and courtiers

Courtesy. *See* Behavior; Etiquette

The **courthouse.** Faulkner, W.
In Faulkner, W. The Faulkner reader
    S C
In Faulkner, W. The portable Faulkner p21-56   **S C**

Courtiers. *See* Courts and courtiers

Courtney, Winifred F.
(ed.) The Reader's adviser. *See* The Reader's adviser   011

Courts
See also Jury; Justice, Administration of

United States
James, H. Crisis in the courts   347.9

Courts and courtiers
See pages in the following books:
Ashley, M. Life in Stuart England p91-102
    914.2
Bagley, J. J. Life in medieval England p7-13   914.2
Chamberlin, E. R. Everyday life in Renaissance times p34-62   940.2
Saggs, H. W. F. Everyday life in Babylonia & Assyria p56-71   913.35
Shakespeare's England v 1 p79-111 822.3

A **courtship.** Faulkner, W.
In Faulkner, W. Collected stories of William Faulkner p361-80   **S C**

The **courtyards** of peace. Buck, P. S.
In Buck, P. S. The good deed, and other stories of Asia, past and present p7-67   **S C**

Cousin Teresa. Saki
In Saki. The short stories of Saki p342-46   **S C**

Cousteau, Jacques-Yves
(ed.) Captain Cousteau's Underwater treasury   627.7
Jacques-Yves Cousteau's World without sun   551.4
Life and death in a coral sea   551.4
The living sea   627.7
The shark: splendid savage of the sea 597
The silent world   627.7
The silent world; excerpt
In Ceram, C. W. ed. Hands on the past p394-403   913.03

Cousteau, Philippe
(jt. auth.) Cousteau, J. Y. The shark: splendid savage of the sea   597

Cousy, Bob. *See* Cousy, Robert

Cousy, Robert
See pages in the following book:
Pepe, P. Greatest stars of the NBA p15-31
    920

Coventry. Heinlein, R. A.
In Heinlein, R. A. Robert A. Heinlein's The past through tomorrow p471-508   **S C**

The **cow-catcher** on the caboose. Devany, E. H.
In The Best short plays of 1958-1959 p 1-31   808.82

Coward, Noël
Cavalcade
In Cerf, B. A. comp. Sixteen famous British plays p545-90   822.08
Come into the garden Maud
In Richards, S. ed. Best short plays of the world theatre, 1958-1967 p53-72
    808.82
Fumed oak
In Cerf, B. ed. Thirty famous one-act plays p499-515   808.82
Hands across the sea
In Cerf, B. ed. 24 favorite one-act plays p151-69   808.82

About
Levin, M. Noel Coward   822.09

A **coward.** Maupassant, G. de
In Maupassant, G. de. The odd number p19-36   **S C**

A **coward.** Wharton, E.
In Wharton, E. The collected short stories of Edith Wharton v 1 p127-39   **S C**

Cowboy. Santee, R.   917.8

Cowboy songs and other frontier ballads. Lomax, J. A. comp.   784.4

Cowboys
Durham, P. The Negro cowboys   978
James, W. Lone cowboy   92
Santee, R. Cowboy   917.8
See also pages in the following book:
Goodwyn, L. The South Central states p75-84   917.6

Fiction
Adams, A. The log of a cowboy   Fic

Songs and music
Lomax, J. A. comp. Cowboy songs and other frontier ballads   784.4

Cowell, F. R.
Everyday life in ancient Rome   913.37

Cowie, Leonard W.
Martin Luther: leader of the reformation 92

Cowles Complete encyclopedia of U.S. coins. Reed, M.   737.4

Cowley, Malcolm
(ed.) Faulkner, W. The portable Faulkner
    S C

Cox, C. B.
(ed.) Dylan Thomas   821.09

Cox, Edward F.
'The Nader report' on the Federal Trade Commission   381.061

Crawford, Francis Marion
See pages in the following book:
Quinn, A. H. American fiction p385-407
813.09

Crawley, C. W.
(ed.) War and peace in an age of upheaval, 1793-1830
In The New Cambridge Modern history v9
909

Crawling Arnold. Feiffer, J.
In Richards, S. ed. Best short plays of the world theatre, 1958-1967 p73-83
808.82

Crayton, Pearl
The day the world almost came to an end
In Hughes, L. ed. The best short stories by Negro writers p325-31 **S C**

Crazy Sunday. Fitzgerald, F. S.
In Fitzgerald, F. S. The Fitzgerald reader p332-49 **S C**
In Fitzgerald, F. S. The stories of F. Scott Fitzgerald p403-18 **S C**

Creamer, J. Shane
A citizen's guide to legal rights 342.73

Creasy, Sir Edward S.
Fifteen decisive battles of the world 904
(jt. auth.) Mitchell, J. B. Twenty decisive battles of the world 904

Creation. See Evolution; Universe

Creation (Literary, artistic, etc.)
See pages in the following books:
Camus, A. Lyrical and critical essays p154-61
844
Gombrich, E. H. Art and illusion p93-115
701

The **creation** of the universe. Gamow, G.
523.1

Creative film-making. Smallman, K. 778.5

The **creative** writer. Mathieu, A. M. ed.
808.06

Credit
Black, H. Buy now, pay later 332.7
See also pages in the following book:
Smith, C. The Time-Life Book of family finance p26-45
339.4

Credit, Agricultural. See Agricultural credit

Credos and curios. Thurber, J. 818

Cree Indians
Burnford, S. Without reserve 970.4

Creeger, George R.
(ed.) George Eliot 823.09

Creek Indians. See Five Civilized Tribes

Creekmore, Hubert
(ed.) A little treasury of world poetry
808.81

Creel, Herrlee Glessner
Chinese thought from Confucius to Mao Tsê-tung
181

Creely, Robert
See pages in the following book:
Rosenthal, M. L. The new poets p148-59
821.09

Cretan art. See Art, Cretan

Crete
Antiquities
Baumann, H. Lion gate and labyrinth
913.38
Cottrell, L. The mystery of Minoan civilization
913.39

Willetts, R. F. Everyday life in ancient Crete 913.39
See also pages in the following books:
Ceram, C. W. Gods, graves, and scholars p56-72
913.03
Mills, D. The book of the ancient Greeks p6-21
938
Civilization
Cottrell, L. The mystery of Minoan civilization
913.39
Willetts, R. F. Everyday life in ancient Crete
913.39
Fiction
Kazantzakis, N. Zorba the Greek **Fic**
Renault, M. The king must die **Fic**
Religion
See pages in the following book:
Willetts, R. F. Everyday life in ancient Crete p164-79
913.39
Social life and customs
Willetts, R. F. Everyday life in ancient Crete
913.39

Cretzmeyer, Francis X.
Bresnahan and Tuttle's Track and field athletics
796.4

Crevasse. Faulkner, W.
In Faulkner, W. Collected stories of William Faulkner p465-74 **S C**

Crewel, The complete guide to embroidery stitches and. Bucher, J. 746.4

Cribbage
See pages in the following book:
Gibson, W. B. Hoyle's Simplified guide to the popular card games p71-85 795.4

Crichton, Michael
The Andromeda strain **Fic**
Five patients 362.1

Crick, Francis Harry Compton
See pages in the following book:
Moore, R. The coil of life p272-86 574.09

Cricket
See pages in the following book:
Sports Illustrated. The wonderful world of sport p252-54
796

Crime and criminals
See also Criminal law; Justice, Administration of; Juvenile delinquency; Murder; Prisons; Punishment; Riots; Trials
Fiction
Dostoevsky, F. The house of the dead **Fic**
Wright, R. Native son **Fic**
Great Britain
Wood, J. P. Scotland Yard 352
See also pages in the following book:
Avery, G. Victorian people p227-48 914.2
Rehabilitation
Sands, B. My shadow ran fast 364.8
Russia
See pages in the following book:
Vladimirov, L. The Russians p125-33 914.7
United States
Clark, R. Crime in America 364.1
Horan, J. D. The Pinkertons 364.12
Lewin, S. ed. Crime and its prevention 364.1

Crime and criminals—United States—*Cont.*
  Maas, P. The Valachi papers   **364.1**
  Toland, J. The Dillinger days   **364.1**
  Tully, A. The FBI's most famous cases
    353.5
  Tyler, G. ed. Organized crime in America
    364.1
  United States. National Commission the
    Causes and Prevention of Violence. Vio-
    lent crime   **364.1**
  United States. President's Commission on
    Law Enforcement and Administration of
    Justice. The challenge of crime in a free
    society   **364**
    See also pages in the following books:
  Ebony. The Negro handbook p99-111
    301.451
  Lindsay, J. V. The city p164-88   **974.71**
  United States. National Commission on
    the Causes and Prevention of Violence.
    To establish justice, to insure domestic
    tranquility p15-49   **301.18**
Crime and its prevention. Lewin, S. ed. **364.1**
Crime and punishment. Dostoevsky, F. **Fic**
Crime in America. Clark, R.   **364.1**
The crime of Sylvestre Bonnard. France, A.
    Fic
Crime of the Communist. Chesterton, G. K.
  In Chesterton, G. K. The Father Brown
    omnibus p914-33   **S C**
Crime prevention. *See* Crime and criminals
Crime without murder. Mystery Writers of
  America   **S C**
Crimean War, 1853-1856
    See pages in the following book:
  The New Cambridge Modern history v10
    p468-92   **909**
Crimes, Political. *See* Political crimes and
  offenses
Criminal investigation
  Creamer, J. S. A citizen's guide to legal
    rights   **342.73**
  Orbaan, A. Dogs against crime   **636.7**
    See also Police
Criminal law
    See pages in the following book:
  Sloan, I. J. Youth and the law p55-62 **340**
    See also Capital punishment; Punish-
    ment; Trials; and names of crimes, e.g.
    Murder
Criminals. *See* Crime and criminals
Cripples. *See* Physically handicapped
The crisis. Churchill, W.   **Fic**
Crisis. Grendon, E.
  In Conklin, G. ed. Invaders of earth
    p245-54   **S C**
A crisis. Maupassant, G. de
  In Maupassant, G. de. Selected short
    stories p248-55   **S C**
Crisis in black and white. Silberman, C. E.
    301.451
Crisis in our cities. Herber, L.   **614**
Crisis in the classroom. Silberman, C. E. **370**
Crisis in the courts. James, H.   **347.9**
The crisis of the old order, 1919-1933.
  Schlesinger, A. M.   **973.91**

Crisp new bills for Mr Teagle. Sullivan, F.
  In Becker, M. L. ed. The home book of
    Christmas p215-20   **394.26**
Crispen, Frederic Swing
  Dictionary of technical terms   **603**
Critical fable. Lowell, A.
  In Lowell, A. The complete poetical
    works of Amy Lowell p389-434 **811**
A critical history of English literature.
  Daiches, D.   **820.9**
Criticism
  Curley, D. N. ed. A library of literary
    criticism: Modern American literature
    810.9
  Daiches, D. English literature   **801**
  Shaff, A. L. The student journalist and
    the critical review   **371.89**
    See also pages in the following books:
  Arnold, M. The portable Matthew Arnold
    p234-67   **828**
  Eliot, T. S. On poetry and poets p113-31
    808.1
  Mencken, H. L. The American scene
    p177-89   **818**
    See also Shakespeare, William—Criti-
    cism, interpretation, etc.; also literature
    and music subjects with the subdivision
    History and criticism, e.g. English
    drama—History and criticism; Music—
    History and criticism
Critique of pure reason. Kant, I.   **193**
Croce, Benedetto
    See pages in the following books:
  Durant, W. The story of philosophy p350-
    57   **109**
  Thomas, H. Understanding the great phi-
    losophers p300-12   **109**
Crocker, Betty
  Betty Crocker's Good and easy cookbook
    641.5
Crocodiles
    See pages in the following books:
  Ditmars, R. L. Reptiles of North Amer-
    ica p3-9   **598.1**
  Ditmars, R. L. Reptiles of the world p3-23
    598.1
Cromwell, John
  Opening night
  In The Best short plays, 1968 p237-58
    808.82
Cromwell, Oliver
  Ashley, M. ed. Cromwell   **92**
    See also pages in the following book:
  Carr, A. Men of power p47-70   **920**
Crone, Ruth
  (jt. auth.) Brown, M. M. Willa Cather **92**
Cronin, A. J.
  The citadel   **Fic**
  The green years   **Fic**
  The keys of the kingdom   **Fic**
Cronin, Vincent
  Louis XIV   **92**
Cronkite, Walter
  Eye on the world   **909.82**
Crooked bone. Kersh, G.
  In Hitchcock, A. ed. Alfred Hitchcock
    presents: A month of mystery
    p330-53   **S C**

The **crooked** man. Doyle, Sir A. C.
In Doyle, Sir A. C. The complete Sherlock Holmes v 1 p473-87   **S C**

The **crooked** road. Gaby, A.
In Hitchcock, A. ed. Alfred Hitchcock presents: A month of mystery p103-17   **S C**

Crop dusting. *See* Aeronautics in agriculture

Crops. *See* Farm produce

Cross, Colin
The fall of the British Empire, 1918-1968
942.082

Cross, Eric
Saint Bakeoven
In Garrity, D. A. ed. 44 Irish short stories p58-69   **S C**

Cross, F. L.
(ed.) The Oxford Dictionary of the Christian Church. *See* The Oxford Dictionary of the Christian Church   203

Cross, Jennifer
The supermarket trap   658.87

Cross, Milton
Milton Cross' More stories of the great operas   782.1
The Milton Cross New encyclopedia of the great composers and their music   920.03
The new Milton Cross Complete stories of the great operas   782.1

Cross, Wilbur
A job with a future in computers   651.8

The **cross.** Undset, S.
In Undset, S. Kristin Lavransdatter v3   **Fic**

Cross-country running. *See* Track athletics

Cross country snow. Hemingway, E.
In Hemingway, E. In our time p137-47   **S C**
In Hemingway, E. The short stories of Ernest Hemingway p181-88   **S C**

Cross currents. Saki
In Saki. The short stories of Saki p92-98   **S C**

Crossbow
See pages in the following book:
Ley, W. Another look at Atlantis, and fifteen other essays p42-56   508

Crossland, Austin
(jt. auth.) Bridge, P. Designs in wood   684

Crothers, Rachel
He and she
In Quinn, A. H. ed. Representative American plays p891-928   812.08
(jt. auth.) Lindsay, H. Clarence Day's Life with father and Life with mother   812
(jt. auth.) Lindsay, H. The sound of music   812

About
See pages in the following book:
Gould, J. Modern American playwrights p140-50   812.09

Crow, John A.
The epic of Latin America   980

The **crow** in the woods. Updike, J.
In Updike, J. Pigeon feathers, and other stories   **S C**

Crowder, Richard
Carl Sandburg   818

Crowds. *See* Mobs; Riots

Crowell's Handbook for readers and writers. *See* The Reader's encyclopedia   803

Crowell's Handbook of classical literature. Feder, L.   880.3

Crowell's Handbook of classical mythology. Tripp, E.   292.03

Crowell's Spanish-English & English-Spanish dictionary   463

Crowley, Ellen T.
(ed.) Gale Research Company. Acronyms and initialisms dictionary   421.03

Crowley, Mart
The boys in the band
In Richards, S. ed. Best plays of the sixties p801-900   808.82

Crowley, Thomas H.
Understanding computers   510.78

Crowther, Samuel Adjai
See pages in the following book:
Polatnick, F. T. Shapers of Africa p76-107   920

Crowther, Samuel Ajayi. *See* Crowther, Samuel Adjai

Crucial instances. Wharton, E.
In Wharton, E. The collected short stories of Edith Wharton v 1 p227-343   **S C**

The **crucible.** Miller, A.   812
—Same
In Gassner, J. ed. Best American plays; 4th ser. p347-402   812.08

The **cruel** sea. Monsarrat, N.   **Fic**

The **cruel** years. Werstein, I.   946.081

Cruelty to children, Prevention of. *See* Child welfare

Cruising. *See* Sailing

Crusade in Europe. Eisenhower, D. D.   940.54

Crusaders for freedom. Commager, H. S.   920

Crusades
Duggan, A. The story of the crusades, 1097-1291   940.1
Lamb, H. The crusades   940.1
Treece, H. The crusades   940.1
See also pages in the following books:
Durant, W. The age of faith p585-613   940.1
Fremantle, A. Age of faith p53-60   940.1
Glubb, Sir J. A short history of the Arab peoples p154-68   953
Hitti, P. K. The Arabs p168-83   953
Horizon Magazine. The light of the past p122-28   901.9
Mills, D. The Middle Ages p179-201   940.1
Rowling, M. Everyday life in medieval times p106-12   914
Stewart, D. Early Islam p140-48   915.6
Thorndike, L. The history of medieval Europe p322-41   940.1
See also Chivalry

Fiction
Oldenbourg, Z. The heirs of the kingdom   **Fic**
Scott, Sir W. The talisman   **Fic**

Cunningham, Merce
See pages in the following book:
McDonagh, D. The rise and fall and rise of modern dance p52-76   793.3

Cunningham, Noble E.
(ed.) The making of the American party system, 1789-1809   329

Cunnington, C. Willett
A dictionary of English costume   391.03
Handbook of English mediaeval costume   391.09

Cunnington, Phillis
Costumes of the seventeenth and eighteenth century   391.09
Costumes of the nineteenth century   391.09
Medieval and Tudor costume   391.09
(jt. auth.) Cunnington, C. W. A dictionary of English costume   391.03
(jt. auth.) Cunnington, C. W. Handbook of English mediaeval costume   391.09

A **cup** of cold water. Wharton, E.
In Wharton, E. The collected short stories of Edith Wharton v 1 p151-72   S C

A **cup** of tea. Mansfield, K.
In Mansfield, K. The short stories of Katherine Mansfield p584-91   S C

The **cupboard** of the yesterdays. Saki
In Saki. The short stories of Saki p594-98   S C

Cupid à la carte. Henry, O.
In Henry, O. The complete works of O. Henry p189-202   S C

Cupid's exile number two. Henry, O.
In Henry, O. The complete works of O. Henry p584-88   S C

Cuppy, Will
If Christmas comes
In Becker, M. L. ed. The home book of Christmas p139-42   394.26

Cuppy, William Jacob. See Cuppy, Will

The **curfew** tolls. Benét, S. V.
In Benét, S. V. Selected works of Stephen Vincent Benét v2   818

Curie, Eve
Madame Curie   92

Curie, Marie (Sklodowska)
Curie. E. Madame Curie   92
See also pages in the following book:
Untermeyer, L. Makers of the modern world p368-78   920

Curiosities
Guinness Book of world records   032
Kane, J. N. Famous first facts   031

A **curious** dream. Twain, M.
In Twain, M. The complete short stories of Mark Twain p32-39   S C

A **curious** experience. Clemens, S. L.
In Dulles, A. ed. Great spy stories from fiction p308-25   S C
In Twain, M. The complete short stories of Mark Twain p163-86   S C

Curley, Daniel
A story of love, etc.
In The Best American short stories, 1964 p85-93   S C

Curley, Dorothy Nyren
(ed.) A library of literary criticism: Modern American literature   810.9

Curley, James Michael
See pages in the following book:
Shannon, W. V. The American Irish p201-32   301.453

Curley, Jim. See Curley, James Michael

Currency question
Great Britain
See pages in the following book:
Shakespeare's England v 1 p311-40   822.3

United States
See pages in the following books:
American Heritage. The American Heritage History of the confident years p279-86   973.8
Koenig, L. W. Bryan p118-29   92

Current American usage. Bryant, M. M.   428

Current biography yearbook   920.03

Current-Garcia, Eugene
O. Henry   813.09

Currents, Alternating. See Electric currents, Alternating

Curricula (Courses of study) See Education —Curricula

Curry, Joe
See pages in the following book:
White, T. H. Fire in the ashes p216-33   940.55

Curse of the golden cross. Chesterton, G. K.
In Chesterton, G. K. The Father Brown omnibus p531-58   S C

The **curtain** blown by the breeze. Spark, M.
In Spark, M. Collected stories: I p35-52   S C

Curtains. See Drapery

Curti, Merle
The growth of American thought   917.3

Curtis, Maxine
Mission: romance!
In Seventeen. Stories from Seventeen p166-80   S C

Curtis, Richard
Chiang Kai-shek   92
Perils of the peaceful atom   621.48

Curtiss, Glenn Hammond
See pages in the following book:
Bonney, W. T. The heritage of Kitty Hawk p116-29   629.13

Cush
See pages in the following book:
Davidson, B. The lost cities of Africa p36-50   913.6

Cushing, Luther Stearns
Manual of parliamentary practice   328.1

Cushman, Charlotte Saunders
See pages in the following book:
Vance, M. The lamp lighters p92-127   920

Cushman, Pauline
See pages in the following book:
Kane, H. T. Spies for the Blue and Gray p177-91   973.7

Custer, Elizabeth Bacon
Boots and saddles   92
About
Randall, R. P. I Elizabeth   92

Custer, George Armstrong
Custer, E. B. Boots and saddles   92
Randall, R. P. I Elizabeth [Custer]   92
Sandoz, M. The Battle of the Little Big-
horn   973.8
Custer died for your sins. Deloria, V.   970.1
Custis, George Washington Parke
Pocahontas
In Quinn, A. H. ed. Representative
American plays p165-92   812.08
Customs, Social. See names of countries with
subdivision Social life and customs, e.g.
United States—Social life and customs
Cuthrell, Faith (Baldwin) See Baldwin,
Faith
Cutting, Mary Stewart
Blossoming rod
In Becker, M. L. ed. The home book of
Christmas p277-91   394.26
Cuvier, Georges, Baron
See pages in the following books:
Jones, B. Z. ed. The golden age of science
p118-44   920
Moore, R. The earth we live on p113-31
551.09
Cuyás, Arturo
Appleton's New Cuyás English-Spanish
and Spanish-English dictionary   463
Cybernetics
See pages in the following books:
Newman, J. R. ed. What is science? p385-
436   508
Newman, J. R. ed. The world of mathe-
matics v4 p2066-2133   510.8
See also Bionics; Electronic computers
The **cycle** of spring. Tagore, R.
In Tagore, R. Collected poems and plays
of Rabindranath Tagore p331-401
891.4
Cycles, Motor. See Motorcycles
Cyclopedia of literary characters. Magill,
F. N. ed.   803
Cyclopedia of world authors. Magill, F. N.
ed.   920.03
The **cyclops.** Euripides
In Oates, W. J. ed. The complete Greek
drama v2 p395-419   882.08
Cyprus
Politics and government
See pages in the following book:
Comay, J. The UN in action p60-65
341.13
Cyrano de Bergerac, Savinien
Drama
Rostand, E. Cyrano de Bergerac   842
Cyrano de Bergerac. Rostand, E.   842
—Same
In Cerf, B. A. comp. Sixteen famous
European plays p305-439   808.82
In Tucker, S. M. ed. Twenty-five
modern plays p159-223   808.82
Cytology. See Cells
Czechoslovak Republic
Description and travel
See pages in the following book:
McDowell, B. Gypsies: wanderers of the
world p76-95   397

History
Szulc, T. Czechoslovakia since World
War II   943.7

History—Intervention, 1968-
See pages in the following book:
Szulc, T. Czechoslovakia since World
War II p377-433   943.7

Politics and government
Sterling, C. The Masaryk case   364.12
Czechoslovakia. See Czechoslovak Republic
Czechoslovakia since World War II. Szulc, T.
943.7
Czechs in the United States
Fiction
Cather, W. My Antonia   Fic
Czerny, Carl
See pages in the following book:
Chapin, V. Giants of the keyboard p72-76
920

D

D Day. See Normandy, Attack on, 1944
D-Day. The Army Times   940.54
D-Day, The secret of. Perrault, G.   940.54
D Day, the sixth of June, 1944. Howarth, D.
940.54
DDT (Insecticide)
See pages in the following book:
Ehrlich, P. R. Population, resources, en-
vironment p168-74   301.3
DNA
Lessing, L. DNA: at the core of life it-
self   574.8
See also pages in the following books:
Asimov, I. The genetic code p105-60 575.1
Beadle, G. The language of life p154-85
575.1
Fried, J. J. The mystery of heredity p45-
47   575.1
Moore, R. Evolution p88-96   575
Scientific American. Facets of genetics
p248-55   575.1
DNA: at the core of life itself. Lessing, L.
574.8
Daddy was a number runner. Meriwether, L.
Fic
The **daemon** lover. Jackson, S.
In Jackson, S. The magic of Shirley
Jackson p3-17   818
Daft dream adyin'. Grainger, T.
In The Best short plays, 1969 p147-207
808.82
Dagger in the dark. Buck, P. S.
In Buck, P. S. The good deed, and
other stories of Asia, past and
present p89-103   S C
Dagger with wings. Chesterton, G. K.
In Chesterton, G. K. The Father Brown
omnibus p559-82   S C
Dahl, Borghild
I wanted to see   92

Dahl, Roald
The champion of the world
In The New Yorker. Stories from The
New Yorker, 1950-1960 p467-89
S C

Dai, Hsiao-ai
Bennett, G. A. Red Guard   92

Daiches, David
A critical history of English literature
820.9
English literature   801
More literary essays   820.9
The novel and the modern world   823.09
Robert Burns   821.09
About
See pages in the following book:
David, J. ed. Growing up Jewish p102-20
920

Daily life at Versailles in the seventeenth
and eighteenth centuries. Levron, J.
914.43
Daily life in Carthage at the time of Han-
nibal. Charles-Picard, G.   913.39
Daily life in the French Revolution. Robi-
quet, J.   914.4
The **Dain** curse. Hammett, D.
In Hammett, D. The novels of Dashiell
Hammett p143-292   Fic

Dairying
See pages in the following book:
Stone, A. A. Careers in agribusiness and
industry p81-94   338.1
Daisy Miller. James, H.
In James, H. Short novels of Henry
James p 1-58   Fic
Daisy Overend. Spark, M.
In Spark, M. Collected stories: I p185-
95   S C

Dakota Indians
See pages in the following book:
Brown, D. Bury my heart at Wounded
Knee p38-65, 123-49, 416-38   970.4
Wars, 1862-1865
See pages in the following book:
Brown, D. Bury my heart at Wounded
Knee p103-20   970.4
Wars, 1876
See pages in the following book:
Brown, D. Bury my heart at Wounded
Knee p273-313   970.4

Dalai Lama XIV
My land and my people   92

Dale, Sir Thomas
See pages in the following book:
Johnston, M. Pioneers of the Old South
p73-92   975

Daley, Arthur
(jt. auth.) Kieran, J. The story of the
Olympic games: 776 B.C. to [date] 796.4

Dalli Regoli, Gigetta
National Gallery, London. See National
Gallery, London   708

Dalton, Katharina
The menstrual cycle   612.6

Daly, Saralyn R.
Katherine Mansfield   823.09

D'Ambrosio, Richard
No language but a cry   155.45

Dameron, Tadd. See Dameron, Tadley
Ewing
Dameron, Tadley Ewing
See pages in the following book:
Gitler, I. Jazz masters of the forties p262-
82   920

Dampier, Sir William Cecil
A history of science and its relations with
philosophy & religion   509

Dams
See pages in the following books:
Davies, D. Fresh water p82-97   333.9
Overman, M. Water p69-107   333.9

Dan Emmonds. Crane, S.
In Crane, S. The complete short stories & sketches of Stephen Crane
p61-65   S C

Dana, Richard Henry, 1815-1882
Two years before the mast   910.4
About
Gale, R. L. Richard Henry Dana, Jr. 818
Dana's Manual of mineralogy   549
The **dance** at Chevalier's. Cather, W.
In Cather, W. Willa Cather's Collected
short fiction, 1892-1912 v3 p547-55
S C

Dance music
See pages in the following book:
The New York Times. Guide to listening
pleasure p169-83   780.1
See also Jazz music
Dance of the divorced. Gold, H.
In The Saturday Evening Post. Best
modern short stories p270-78 S C
Dance to the piper. De Mille, A.   92
Dance world   793.3025

Dancers
Dance world   793.3025
De Mille, A. And promenade home   92
De Mille, A. Dance to the piper   92
Maynard, O. American modern dancers:
the pioneers   920

Dancing
De Mille, A. To be a young dancer 792.8
See also pages in the following book:
American Association for Health, Phys-
ical Education, and Recreation. Phys-
ical education for high school students
p107-19   613.7
See also Ballet
History
Haskell, A. L. The wonderful world of
dance   793.3
Maynard, O. American modern dancers:
the pioneers   920
United States
Dance world   793.3025
The **dancing** boy. Eastlake, W.
In The Best American short stories,
1971 p107-17   S C
Danger—men talking! Chase, S.   412
Dangerfield, George
The awakening of American nationalism,
1815-1828   973.5

Da Silva Rondon, Cândido Mariano. See Rondon, Cândido Mariano da Silva

Data processing. See Electronic data processing

Data processing terms, Funk & Wagnall's Dictionary of. Rodgers, H. A.   651.803

Data storage and retrieval systems. See Information storage and retrieval systems

Date etiquette. See Dating (Social customs)

Date to remember. Temple, W. F.
  In Conklin, G. ed. Invaders of earth p61-74   **S C**

A date with a dish. See De Knight, F. The Ebony cookbook: a date with a dish
  641.5

Dates. See Chronology, Historical

Dates, Everyman's Dictionary of   903

Dating, Radiocarbon. See Radiocarbon dating

Dating (Social customs)
  See pages in the following books:
  Post, E. L. The Emily Post Book of etiquette for young people p139-64   **395**
  Sugarman, D. A. The Seventeen Guide to knowing yourself p38-49   **155.5**
  See also Love; Marriage

Daugherty, James
  William Blake   92
  (ed.) Thoreau, H. D. Henry David Thoreau   818
  (ed.) Whitman, W. Walt Whitman's America   818

A daughter of the Aurora. London, J.
  In London, J. Best short stories of Jack London p142-50   **S C**

A daughter of the Samurai. Sugimoto, E. I.
  92

The daughters of the late colonel. Mansfield, K.
  In Mansfield, K. The short stories of Katherine Mansfield p463-83 **S C**

Daumas, Maurice
  (ed.) A history of technology & invention
  609

Daumier, Honoré Victorin
  See pages in the following book:
  Cheney, S. The story of modern art p98-120   **709.03**

The daunt Diana. Wharton, E.
  In Wharton, E. The collected short stories of Edith Wharton v2 p50-60
  S C

Davenport, Basil
  (ed.) The portable Roman reader   870.8

David, Edward E.
  (jt. auth.) Van Bergeijk, W. A. Waves and the ear   534

David, Hal
  (jt. auth.) Bacharach, B. The Bacharach and David Song book   784

David, Heather M.
  Wernher von Braun   92

David, Jacques Louis
  See pages in the following books:
  Cheney, S. The story of modern art p 1-16
  709.03
  Ruskin, A. Nineteenth century art p12-18
  709.03

David, Jay
  (ed.) Growing up Jewish   920

Davidson, Avram
  The lord of Central Park
  In Best detective stories of the year, 1971 p85-126   **S C**
  The man who killed sailors
  In Best detective stories of the year [1969] p32-77   **S C**
  Selectra Six-Ten
  In The Best from Fantasy and Science Fiction; 19th ser. p29-35   **S C**

Davidson, Basil
  Africa in history   960
  The African genius   916
  African kingdoms   960
  Black mother   967
  The lost cities of Africa   913.6

Davidson, H. R. Ellis
  Pagan Scandinavia   913.48

Davidson, Marshall B.
  American Heritage. The American Heritage History of American antiques from the Revolution to the Civil War   745.1
  American Heritage. The American Heritage History of colonial antiques   745.1

Davies, Delwyn
  Fresh water   333.9

Davies, Hunter
  The Beatles   920

Davies, Sir John
  See pages in the following book:
  Eliot, T. S. On poetry and poets p149-55
  808.1

Davies, Rhys
  The chosen one
  In Best detective stories of the year [1967] p233-72   **S C**

Davies, Ruth Ann
  The school library   027.8

Da Vinci, Leonardo. See Leonardo da Vinci

Davis, Arthur P.
  How John Boscoe outsung the Devil
  In Clarke, J. H. ed. American Negro short stories p156-64   **S C**

Davis, Benjamin Oliver, 1912-
  See pages in the following book:
  Bontemps, A. We have tomorrow p118-31   920

Davis, Burke
  To Appomattox   973.7

Davis, Dorothy Salisbury
  (ed.) Mystery Writers of America. Crime without murder   **S C**

Davis, J. D.
  The New Westminster Dictionary of the Bible   220.3

Davis, Jefferson
  Catton, W. Two roads to Sumter   973.6
  See also pages in the following books:
  Catton, B. Prefaces to history p141-48
  973.7
  Dictionary of American biography. The American Plutarch p227-43   920

Davis, John P.
  (ed.) The American Negro reference book
  301.451
  The overcoat
  In Clarke, J. H. ed. American Negro short stories p36-41   **S C**

Davis, John William
  See pages in the following book:
  Stone, I. They also ran p321-39   **920**
Davis, Kenneth S.
  (ed.) Arms, industry and America **355.03**
  (ed.) The paradox of poverty in America **330.973**
  American Heritage. Eisenhower, American hero **92**
  (jt. auth.) Leopold, L. B. Water **551.4**
Davis, Miles Dewey
  See pages in the following books:
  Goldberg, J. Jazz masters of the fifties p62-86 **920**
  Williams, M. The jazz tradition p186-96 **781.5**
Davis, Morton D.
  Game theory **519**
Davis, Norman M.
  The complete book of United States coin collecting **737.4**
Davis, Olivia
  The other child
  In The Best American short stories, 1970 p74-83 **S C**
Davis, Owen
  Ethan Frome
  In Gassner, J. ed. Best American plays; supplementary volume, 1918-1958 p373-410 **812.08**
  The world we live in; adaptation. See Čapek, J. The world we live in
Davis, Richard Harding
  Bar sinister
  In The Scribner treasury p243-71 **S C**
  The consul
  In The Scribner treasury p473-92 **S C**
  The deserter
  In The Scribner treasury p535-47 **S C**
  An epic of treasure recovery
  In Armstrong, R. ed. Treasure and treasure hunters **910.4**
Davis, Sammy
  Yes I can **92**
Davis, Varina (Howell)
        Fiction
  Kane, H. T. Bride of fortune **Fic**
Davis, William Stearns
  A day in old Athens **913.38**
  A day in old Rome **913.37**
  Life in Elizabethan days **914.2**
  A victor of Salamis **Fic**
Davison, Frederic Ellis
  See pages in the following book:
  Drotning, P. T. Up from the ghetto p102-18 **920**
Dawn. Wiesel, E. **Fic**
  —Same
  In Costain, T. B. ed. Read with me p545-98 **S C**
Dawn attack. Forester, C. S.
  In Forester, C. S. Gold from Crete p29-44 **S C**
Dawn of remembered spring. Stuart, J.
  In Foley, M. ed. Fifty best American short stories, 1915-1965 p323-29 **S C**
Dawn of zoology. Ley, W. **590**
Dawn's early light. Thane, E. **Fic**

Day, A. Grove
  (ed.) The greatest American short stories **S C**
  Hawaii and its people **996.9**
  James A. Michener **813.09**
  (ed.) The sky clears: poetry of the American Indians **897**
  (ed.) The spell of Hawaii **919.69**
Day, Clarence
  The best of Clarence Day **818**
  God and my father
  In Day, C. The best of Clarence Day p3-48 **818**
  Life with father **818**
  also in Day, C. The best of Clarence Day p49-210 **818**
  Life with father; dramatization. See Lindsay, H. Clarence Day's Life with father and Life with mother
  Life with mother
  In Day, C. The best of Clarence Day p211-374 **818**
  Life with mother; dramatization. See Lindsay, H. Clarence Day's Life with father and Life with mother
  The noblest instrument
  In White, E. B. ed. A subtreasury of American humor; abridged p296-303 **817.08**
  This simian world
  In Day, C. The best of Clarence Day p375-428 **818**
Day, Donald
  (ed.) Rogers, W. The autobiography of Will Rogers **92**
The day after Saturday. García Márquez, G.
  In Cohen, J. M. ed. Latin American writing today p182-202 **860.8**
A day at Niagara. Twain, M.
  In Twain, M. The complete short stories of Mark Twain p16-22 **S C**
The day Christ died. Bishop, J. **232.9**
A day for surprises. Guare, J.
  In The Best short plays, 1970 p285-94 **808.82**
A day in old Athens. Davis, W. S. **913.38**
A day in old Rome. Davis, W. S. **913.37**
A day in operations. Grinstead, D.
  In Prize stories, 1970: The O. Henry Awards p205-17 **S C**
A day in the country. Chekhov, A.
  In Chekhov, A. The stories of Anton Chekhov p 1-7 **S C**
A day in the life of President Kennedy. Bishop, J. **92**
The day is done. Del Rey, L.
  In Asimov, I. ed. Where do we go from here? p64-83 **S C**
The day Kennedy was shot [biography of John Fitzgerald Kennedy]. Bishop, J. **92**
The day Lincoln was shot. Bishop, J. **92**
Day of infamy. Lord, W. **940.54**
The day of the Confederacy. Stephenson, N. W. **973.7**
The day of the funeral. Wharton, E.
  In Wharton, E. The collected short stories of Edith Wharton v2 p669-86 **S C**

The **day** resurgent. Henry, O.
In Henry, O. The complete works of O. Henry p1503-08   **S C**

The **day** the flowers came. Madden, D.
In The Best American short stories, 1969 p117-28   **S C**

The **day** the world almost came to an end. Crayton, P.
In Hughes, L. ed. The best short stories by Negro writers p325-31 **S C**

The **day** we celebrate. Henry, O.
In Henry, O. The complete works of O. Henry p936-40   **S C**

A **day** with Conrad Green. Lardner, R.
In Lardner, R. The best short stories of Ring Lardner p127-38   **S C**
In Lardner, R. The Ring Lardner reader p292-305   **S C**

Dayan, Moshe
Moshe Dayan   **92**

Dayan, Yael
Death has two sons   **Fic**

About
See pages in the following book:
David, J. ed. Growing up Jewish p333-41   **920**

Daybreak. Baez, J.   **92**

Days. See Birthdays

Days of life and death and escape to the moon. Saroyan, W.   **818**

A **day's** wait. Hemingway, E.
In Hemingway, E. The short stories of Ernest Hemingway p436-39   **S C**
In Hemingway, E. The snows of Kilimanjaro, and other stories p34-36   **S C**

Days without end. O'Neill, E.
In O'Neill, E. Plays v3 p493-567   **812**

A **day's** work. Porter, K. A.
In Porter, K. A. The collected stories of Katherine Anne Porter p388-406   **S C**

Dayspring mishandled. Kipling, R.
In Kipling, R. The best short stories of Rudyard Kipling p609-24   **S C**

The **dead.** Joyce, J.
In Joyce, J. Dubliners p224-88   **S C**

A **dead** body. Chekhov, A.
In Chekhov, A. The image of Chekhov p84-89   **S C**

Dead end. Kingsley, S.
In Cerf, B. A. ed. Sixteen famous American plays p453-531   **812.08**
In Gassner, J. ed. Twenty best plays of the modern American theatre p681-738   **812.08**

The **dead** man. Borges, J. L.
In Borges, J. L. The Aleph, and other stories, 1933-1969 p93-99   **S C**

Dead man's story. Rigsby, H.
In Hitchcock, A. ed. Alfred Hitchcock presents: A month of mystery p306-16   **S C**

Dead Sea scrolls
Burrows, M. Dead Sea scrolls   **221.4**
Burrows, M. More light on the Dead Sea scrolls   **221.4**

Noble, I. Treasure of the caves   **221.4**
Wilson, E. The Dead Sea scrolls, 1946-1969   **221.4**
See also pages in the following book:
Ceram, C. W. ed. Hands on the past p312-18   **913.03**

The **Dead** Sea scrolls, 1946-1969. Wilson, E.   **221.4**

Dead souls. Gogol, N.   **Fic**

Deaf
Keller, H. The story of my life   **92**
West, P. Words for a deaf daughter   **155.45**

Education
Waite, H. E. Valiant companions: Helen Keller and Anne Sullivan Macy   **92**

Fiction
Field, R. And now tomorrow   **Fic**
McCullers, C. The heart is a lonely hunter   **Fic**

Deafness
See pages in the following book:
Stevens, S. S. Sound and hearing p144-69   **534**

A **deal.** Maupassant, G. de
In Maupassant, G. de. Guy de Maupassant's Short stories p73-77 **S C**

A **deal** in ostriches. Wells, H. G.
In Wells, H. G. The complete short stories of H. G. Wells p225-29   **S C**

De Alvarado, Pedro. See Alvarado, Pedro de

De Andrada e Silva, José Bonifacio. See Andrada e Silva, José Bonifacio de

De Angeli, Marguerite
Aniela's birthday and Christmas
In Wernecke, H. H. ed. Celebrating Christmas around the world p156-61   **394.26**

The **Dean's** watch. Goudge, E.   **Fic**

Dear Alexandros. Updike, J.
In Updike, J. Pigeon feathers, and other stories   **S C**

Dear and glorious physician. Caldwell, T.   **Fic**

Dear Brutus. Barrie, J. M.
In Barrie, J. M. The plays of J. M. Barrie p473-542   **822**

Dear departed. Houghton, S.
In Cerf, B. ed. Thirty famous one-act plays p269-81   **808.82**

Dear Dr Butts. Hughes, L.
In Hughes, L. The Langston Hughes reader p210-13   **818**

Dearly beloved. Lindbergh, A. M.   **Fic**

Deason, Hilary J.
(comp.) The AAAS Science book list   **016.5**

Death
Lewis, O. A death in the Sánchez family   **309.172**
See also pages in the following book:
Lasagna, L. Life, death, and the doctor p225-43   **610**

The **deluge** at Norderney. Dinesen, I.
In Dinesen, I. Seven Gothic tales p 1-79
S C

Del Vaga, Perino. See Vaga, Perino del

De Maupassant, Guy. See Maupassant, Guy de

Demby, William
Battlecreek; criticism
In Margolies, E. Native sons p173-89
810.9

Catacombs; criticism
In Margolies, E. Native sons p173-89
810.9

De Mendoza, Antonio. See Mendoza, Antonio de

Demian, the story of Emil Sinclair's youth. Hesse, H.
Fic

De Mille, Agnes
And promenade home **92**
Dance to the piper **92**
To a young dancer **792.8**

About
See pages in the following book:
Stoddard, H. Famous American women p111-23 **920**

DeMille, Cecil Blount
See pages in the following book:
Griffith, R. The movies p122-37 **791.43**

Democracy
Dangerfield, G. The awakening of American nationalism, 1815-1828 **973.5**
Ketchum, R. M. What is democracy? **321.8**
Padover, S. K. The meaning of democracy **321.8**
Scholastic Magazines. What you should know about democracy—and why **321.8**
Sullivan, L. The testament of stone **720.1**
Tocqueville, A. de. Democracy in America **309.173**

See also pages in the following books:
Arnold, M. The portable Matthew Arnold p436-69 **828**
Commager, H. S. ed. Living ideas in America p204-51 **973**
Douglas, W. O. America challenged p31-74 **917.3**
Downs, R. B. ed. The first freedom p437-50 **323.44**
Fromm, E. Escape from freedom p240-76 **323.4**
Hofstadter, R. Anti-intellectualism in American life p145-229 **917.3**
Schneider, H. W. A history of American philosophy p99-191 **191**
Stevenson, A. E. Looking outward p249-59 **341.13**
Toffler, A. Future shock p416-30 **301.24**
See also Federal government; Liberty; Socialism

Democracy at gunpoint: the Greek front. Papandreou, A. **949.5**

Democracy in America. Tocqueville, A. de **309.173**

Democratic Party
See pages in the following book:
American Heritage. The American Heritage History of the confident years p199-224 **973.8**

The **Democratic** Republic, 1801-1815. Smelser, M. **973.4**

Demonology
Boyd, M. Man, myth and magic **133.4**
See also Witchcraft
Dictionaries
Robbins, R. H. The encyclopedia of witchcraft and demonology **133.4**

Demonstration for civil rights. See Negroes —Civil rights

The **demonstrators.** Welty, E.
In Abrahams, W. ed. Fifty years of the American short story v2 p423-37
S C

Demosthenes
See pages in the following book:
Hamilton, E. The echo of Greece p105-14 **880.9**

Dempsey, Jack
See pages in the following book:
Leighton, I. ed. The aspirin age, 1919-1941 p152-68 **917.3**

Dempsey, William Harrison. See Dempsey, Jack

Denby, William
Doris and the Count
In Margolies, E. A native son's reader p330-38 **810.8**

Denham, Helen
(jt. auth.) Denham, S. The complete book of the Siamese cat **636.8**

Denham, Sidney
The complete book of the Siamese cat **636.8**

Denison, Merrill
Christmas calories
In Becker, M. L. ed. The home book of Christmas p229-41 **394.26**

Denmark
Jones, W. G. Denmark **948.9**
Antiquities
Klindt-Jensen, O. Denmark before the Vikings **913.489**
History—Fiction
Lofts, N. The lost queen **Fic**

Denmark before the Vikings. Klindt-Jensen, O. **913.489**

Dennis, Patrick
Auntie Mame; dramatization. See Lawrence, J. Mame

Denny, Norman
The Bayeux Tapestry **746.3**

Denominations, Religious. See Sects

Dentist and patient. Saroyan, W.
In The Best short plays, 1968 p67-72 **808.82**

The **denunciation.** Hemingway, E.
In Hemingway, E. The Fifth Column, and four stories of the Spanish Civil War p89-100 **818**

Deoxyribonucleic acid. See DNA

De Paola, Daniel
The returning
In The Best American short stories, 1965 p45-56 **S C**

The **departing.** Snyder, W. H.
In The Best short plays of 1957-1958 p81-119 **808.82**

Department of Agriculture. See United States. Department of Agriculture

Department of Defense. See United States. Department of Defense

The Department of Defense. Borklund, C. W. **353.6**

Department of Health. See United States. Department of Health, Education, and Welfare

The Department of Housing and Urban development. Willmann, J. B. **353.85**

Department of Justice. See United States. Department of Justice

The Department of Justice. Huston, L. A. **353.5**

Department of State. See United States. Department of State

Department of State. Foreign Service. See United States. Department of State. Foreign Service

Department stores
Mahoney, T. The great merchants **658.87**

A departmental case. Henry, O.
In Henry, O. The complete works of O. Henry p487-96 **S C**

Departure. Anderson, S.
In Anderson, S. Winesburg, Ohio (Modern Lib p299-303 **S C**
In Anderson, S. Winesburg, Ohio (Viking) p244-47 **S C**

Depression in the cards. Hughes, L.
In Hughes, L. The Langston Hughes reader p221-23 **818**

Depression, The Great. Goldston, R. **309.173**

Depressions
Galbraith, J. K. The great Crash, 1929 **338.54**
Hoover, H. C. Memoirs **92**
Rublowsky, J. After the Crash **330.973**
Shannon, D. A. ed. The Great Depression **330.973**
Wecter, D. The age of the great depression, 1929-1941 **973.917**
See also pages in the following books:
Allen, F. L. Only yesterday p290-338 **973.91**
American Heritage. The American Heritage History of the 20's & 30's p152-60, 190-201 **917.3**
Colton, J. G. Twentieth century p62-74 **901.94**
Shannon, D. A. Between the wars: America, 1919-1941 p107-25 **973.91**

Depth charge! Forester, C. S.
In Forester, C. S. Gold from Crete p45-55 **S C**

Der Heyden, A. A. M. van. See Heyden, A. A. M. van der

Derleth, August
The adventure of the red leech
In Best detective stories of the year [1967] p39-59 **S C**
Concord rebel; a life of Henry D. Thoreau **92**
Emerson, our contemporary **92**

Der Nersessian, Sirarpie
The Armenians **915.66**

De Sable, Jean Baptiste Pointe. See Pointe de Sable, Jean Baptiste

De Saint Exupéry, Antoine. See Saint Exupéry, Antoine de

Desalting of sea water. See Sea water—Desalting

De Sarasate, Pablo. See Sarasate, Pablo de

Descartes, René
A discourse on method, and selected writings **194**
About
See pages in the following books:
Bell, E. T. Men of mathematics p35-55 **920**
Durant, W. The age of reason begins p636-47 **940.2**
Russell, B. A history of Western philosophy p557-68 **109**
Thomas, H. Understanding the great philosophers p200-06 **109**

A descent into the Maelström. Poe, E. A.
In Poe, E. A. The complete tales and poems of Edgar Allan Poe p127-40 **S C**
In Poe, E. A. Edgar Allan Poe p133-54 **S C**
In Poe, E. A. Selected poetry and prose p197-211 **818**

The descent of man. Wharton, E.
In Wharton, E. The collected short stories of Edith Wharton v 1 p345-490 **S C**

The descent of man [short story]. Wharton, E.
In Wharton, E. The collected short stories of Edith Wharton v 1 p347-63 **S C**

Deschin, Celia S.
The teenager and VD **614.4**

Description. See names of cities with the subdivision Description, e.g. Hartford, Conn.—Description; and names of countries, states and regions with the subdivision Description and travel, e.g. United States—Description and travel

Desegregation. See Negroes—Integration

The desert. Leopold, A. S. **551.4**

Desert animals
Leopold, A. S. The desert **551.4**

Desert plants
Leopold, A. S. The desert **551.4**

The deserter. David, R. H.
In The Scribner treasury p535-47 **S C**

A desertion. Crane, S.
In Crane, S. The complete short stories & sketches of Stephen Crane p136-39 **S C**

Deserts
Hollon, W. E. The Great American Desert **917.8**
Larson, P. Deserts of America **551.4**
Leopold, A. S. The desert **551.4**
See also pages in the following book:
Farb, P. The land and wildlife of North America p50-60 **574.9**

Deserts of America. Larson, P. **551.4**

Desideria, consort of Charles XIV John, King of Sweden and Norway
Fiction
Selinko, A. Désirée **Fic**

Design, Decorative. See Lettering

Design, Industrial. See Systems engineering

Design with nature. McHarg, I. L.   711

Designs, Floral. See Flower arrangement

Designs in wood. Bridge, P.   684

De Siguenza y Gongora, Carlos. See Siguenza y Gongora, Carlos de

Desire under the elms. O'Neill, E.
  In Gassner, J. ed. Twenty-five best plays of the modern American theatre; early ser. p25-56   812.08
  In O'Neill, E. Nine plays p137-206   812
  In O'Neill, E. Plays v 1 p203-69   812
  In O'Neill, E. Selected plays of Eugene O'Neill   812

Désirée. Selinko, A.   Fic

Desmarest, Nicolas
  See pages in the following book:
  Moore, R. The earth we live on p72-80, 91-93   551.09

Desmond, Paul
  See pages in the following book:
  Goldberg, J. Jazz masters of the fifties p154-67   920

Desmond. Mortimer, J.
  In The Best short plays, 1971 p283-95   808.82

De Sola, Dorothy
  (jt. comp.) De Sola, R. comp. A dictionary of cooking   641.503

De Sola, Ralph
  (comp.) A dictionary of cooking   641.503

Desoxyribonucleic acid. See DNA

D'Este, Beatrice, Duchess of Milan. See Este, Beatrice d', Duchess of Milan

D'Este, Isabella, Marchioness of Mantua. See Este, Isabella d', Marchioness of Mantua

Destitution. See Poverty

De Sylva, Buddy
  See pages in the following book:
  Ewen, D. Great men of American popular song p161-68   920

Detached thoughts on books and reading. Lamb, C.
  In Parker, E. ed. I was just thinking p23-31   824.08

A detail. Crane, S.
  In Crane, S. The complete short stories & sketches of Stephen Crane p311-12   S C

The detective detector. Henry, O.
  In Henry, O. The complete works of O. Henry p1670-74   S C

Detective stories. See Mystery and detective stories

Detective story. Kingsley, S.
  In Gassner, J. ed. Best American plays; 3d ser. p317-64   812.08

Detectives. See Crime and criminals; Criminal investigation; Police; United States. Federal Bureau of Investigation

Dethroned. Potapenko, I. N.
  In Seltzer, T. comp. Best Russian short stories p228-53   S C

De Tocqueville, Alexis. See Tocqueville, Alexis de

De Treviño, Elizabeth Borton. See Treviño, Elizabeth Borton de

Detroit
Riot
  See pages in the following books:
  Heaps, W. A. Riots, U.S.A. 1765-1970 p147-71   301.18
  Isenberg, I. ed. The city in crisis p12-23   301.3

Deutsch, A. J.
  A subway named Mobius
  In Asimov, I. ed. Where do we go from here? p149-70   S C

Deutsch, Babette
  The collected poems of Babette Deutsch   811
  Poetry handbook   808.1
  The reader's Shakespeare   822.3

Deutscher, Isaac
  Stalin   92

Deval, Jacques
  Tovarich
  In Cerf, B. A. comp. Sixteen famous European plays p445-509   808.82

De Valera, Eamonn, President Ireland
  Steffan, J. The Long Fellow   92

Devambez, Pierre
  The Praeger Encyclopedia of ancient Greek civilization. See The Praeger Encyclopedia of ancient Greek civilization   913.3803

Devany, Edward H.
  The cow-catcher on the caboose
  In The Best short plays of 1958-1959 p 1-31   808.82
  The red and yellow ark
  In The Best short plays of 1957-1958 p225-53   808.82

De Vaucouleurs, G. See Vaucouleurs, G. de

De Vaux, Roland. See Vaux, Roland de

De Vega, Lope. See Lope de Vega

De Vega Carpio, Lope. See Vega Carpio, Lope Félix de

Developing and administering a comprehensive high school music program. Moses, H. E.   780.7

The developing nations: poverty and progress. Isenberg, I. ed.   338.91

Development. See Evolution; Growth

The development of the American Constitution, 1877-1917. Beth, L. P.   973.8

Devereux, Robert
  See pages in the following book:
  Behrman, D. The new world of the oceans p172-78   551.4

Devil. See Demonology

The Devil. Maupassant, G. de
  In Maupassant, G. de. Guy de Maupassant's Short stories p228-35   S C

The Devil. Tolstoy, L.
  In Tolstoy, L. Short novels v2 p63-113   S C

The **Devil** and Daniel Webster. Benét, S. V.
Fic
—Same
In Abrahams, W. ed. Fifty years of the American short story v 1 p89-101
S C
In Benét, S. V. Selected works of Stephen Vincent Benét v2 **818**
In Day, A. G. ed. The greatest American short stories p265-81 **S C**
The **Devil** and Daniel Webster; play. Benét, S. V.
In Cerf, B. ed. 24 favorite one-act plays p170-93 **808.82**
The **Devil** and O'Flaherty. O'Conaire, P.
In Garrity, D. A. ed. 44 Irish short stories p244-48 **S C**
The **Devil** and television. Stuart, J.
In Stuart, J. Plowshare in heaven p254-66 **S C**
Devil in the belfry. Poe, E. A.
In Poe, E. A. The complete tales and poems of Edgar Allan Poe p736-41 **S C**
Devil Water. Seton, A. **Fic**
The **Devil** with love. Nathan, R. **Fic**
The **Devil's** advocate. West, M. L. **Fic**
The **Devil's** Christmas. Pei, M.
In Pei, M. Tales of the natural and supernatural p21-30 **S C**
The **Devil's** disciple. Shaw, B.
In Shaw, B. Complete plays, with prefaces v3 p271-346 **822**
In Shaw, B. Pygmalion, and other plays p123-219 **822**
In Shaw, B. Seven plays p269-354 **822**
The **Devil's** general. Zuckmayer, C.
In Block, H. M. ed. Masters of modern drama p911-58 **808.82**
De Visser, John
Mowat, F. This rock with the sea: a heritage lost **917.18**
Devlin, Bernadette
The price of my soul **92**
DeVore, Irven
(jt. auth.) Eimerl, S. The primates **599**
The **devotion** of Enriquez. Harte, B.
In Harte, B. The best short stories of Bret Harte p192-222 **S C**
Devotional literature
Seventeen. The Seventeen Book of prayer **242**
De Voto, Bernard
Across the wide Missouri **978**
The course of empire **973.1**
The year of decision: 1846 **978**
De Vries, Hugo. See Vries, Hugo de
De Vries, Peter
The blood of the lamb **Fic**
De Vries, S. See Vries, S. de
The **De Wets** come to Kloof Grange. Lessing, D.
In Lessing, D. African stories p103-28 **S C**
Dewey, John
John Dewey on education **370.1**
[Selections]
In Kurtz, P. ed. American philosophy in the twentieth century p163-218 **191.08**

About
See pages in the following books:
Addams, J. The social thought of Jane Addams p175-83 **309.173**
Durant, W. The story of philosophy p389-95 **109**
Untermeyer, L. Makers of the modern world p287-93 **920**
Dewey, Melvil
Dewey Decimal classification and relative index **025.4**
Dewey Decimal classification and relative index. Abridged **025.4**
Dewey, Thomas Edmund
See pages in the following book:
Stone, I. They also ran p367-402 **920**
Dewey Decimal classification and relative index. Dewey, M. **025.4**
Dewey Decimal classification and relative index. Abridged. Dewey, M. **025.4**
Diagnosis. Wharton, E.
In Wharton, E. The collected short stories of Edith Wharton v2 p723-40 **S C**
The **diamond** as big as the Ritz. Fitzgerald, F. S.
In Fitzgerald, F. S. The stories of F. Scott Fitzgerald p5-38 **S C**
A **diamond** guitar. Capote, T.
In Capote, T. Breakfast at Tiffany's **S C**
The **diamond** maker. Wells, H. G.
In Wells, H. G. The complete short stories of H. G. Wells p252-59 **S C**
The **diamond** necklace. Maupassant, G. de
In Maupassant, G. de. Selected short stories p54-65 **S C**
The **diamond** of Kali. Henry, O.
In Henry, O. The complete works of O. Henry p931-36 **S C**
Diamonds and diamonds. Crane, S.
In Crane, S. The complete short stories & sketches of Stephen Crane p317-20 **S C**
The **diary** of a young girl. Frank, A. **940.54**
also in Frank, A. The works of Anne Frank p25-240 **839.3**
The **diary** of Adam and Eve. Twain, M.
In Twain, M. The complete short stories of Mark Twain p272-94 **S C**
The **diary** of Anne Frank. Goodrich, F. **812**
—Same
In Gassner, J. ed. Best American plays; supplementary volume, 1918-1958 p647-87 **812.08**
Dias, Bartolomeu
See pages in the following book:
Masselman, G. The Atlantic: sea of darkness p76-87 **910.9**
Díaz, Porfirio, President Mexico
See pages in the following books:
Crow, J. A. The epic of Latin America p667-74 **980**
Worcester, D. E. Makers of Latin America p130-42 **920**
Diaz del Castillo, Bernal
See pages in the following book:
Lloyd, A. The Spanish centuries p131-42 **946**

A dictionary of archaeology. See Bray, W. The American Heritage Guide to archaeology 913.03

Dictionary of art and artists. Murray, P. 703

A dictionary of art terms and techniques. Mayer, R. 703

A dictionary of battles. Eggenberger, D. 904

A dictionary of biological terms. Henderson, I. F. 574.03

Dictionary of classical literature and antiquities, Harper's. Peck, H. T. ed. 913.3803

Dictionary of classical mythology. Zimmerman, J. E. 292.03

A dictionary of comparative religion. Brandon, S. G. F. 291.03

A dictionary of contemporary American usage. Evans, B. 428

A dictionary of cooking. De Sola, R. comp. 641.503

The dictionary of costume. Wilcox, R. T. 391.03

Dictionary of data processing terms, Funk & Wagnalls. Rodgers, H. A. 651.803

Dictionary of dates, Everyman's 903

Dictionary of electronics, Funk & Wagnalls 621.3803

A dictionary of English costume. Cunnington, C. W. 391.03

Dictionary of English proverbs, The Oxford 398.9

Dictionary of folklore, mythology and legend, Funk & Wagnalls Standard 398.03

Dictionary of foreign phrases and abbreviations 808.88

Dictionary of foreign words and phrases in current English. Bliss, A. J. 422.03

A dictionary of geography. Monkhouse, F. J. 910.3

Dictionary of modern economics, The McGraw-Hill 330.3

A dictionary of modern English usage. Fowler, H. W. 428

Dictionary of modern Greek (Greek-English) The Oxford 483

Dictionary of music and musicians, Grove's 780.3

Dictionary of music and musicians; Supplementary volume, Grove's 780.3

Dictionary of music, The concise Oxford. Scholes, P. A. 780.3

A dictionary of names, nicknames, and surnames of persons, places and things. Latham, E. 929.4

The Dictionary of national biography: The concise dictionary; pt. 1 920.03

The Dictionary of national biography: The concise dictionary; pt. 2, 1901-1950 920.03

Dictionary of occupational titles. United States. Employment Service 331.703

Dictionary of phrase and fable, Brewer's 803

Dictionary of proper names, Webster's 031

Dictionary of quotable definitions. Brussell, E. E. ed. 808.88

Dictionary of quotations. Evans, B. ed. 808.88

Dictionary of quotations, The Oxford 808.88

Dictionary of scientific biography 920.03

A dictionary of scientific terms. See Henderson, I. F. A dictionary of biological terms 574.03

Dictionary of Shakespeare quotations, Everyman's. Shakespeare, W. 822.3

A dictionary of slang and unconventional English. Partridge, E. 427

Dictionary of synonyms, Webster's New 424

Dictionary of technical terms. Crispin, F. S. 603

Dictionary of textiles, Fairchild's 677.03

Dictionary of the Bible. Hastings, J. ed. 220.3

A dictionary of the Bible. See The New Westminster Dictionary of the Bible 220.3

Dictionary of the English language, The American Heritage 423

Dictionary of the English language, The Random House 423

Dictionary of the English language, The Random House. College ed. 423

Dictionary of the natural sciences, Compton's 570.3

Dictionary of word and phrase origins. Morris, W. 422.03

Dictionary of world literary terms. Shipley, J. T. ed. 803

Dictionary of world literature. See Shipley, J. T. ed. Dictionary of world literary terms 803

Did you once see Shelley? Cardwell, G. A. *In* Prize stories, 1971: The O. Henry Awards p28-57 S C

Diddling. Poe, E. A. *In* Poe, E. A. The complete tales and poems of Edgar Allan Poe p366-75 S C

Diderot, Denis
See pages in the following book:
Durant, W. The age of Voltaire p650-79 940.2

Di Donato, Pietro
Christ in concrete
In Foley, M. ed. Fifty best American short stories, 1915-1965 p190-202 S C

Didrikson, Babe. See Zaharias, Mildred (Didrikson)

Die-hard. Benét, S. V. *In* Benét, S. V. Selected works of Stephen Vincent Benét v2 818

Diebold, John
Man and the computer 301.24

The diehard. Sholokhov, M. *In* Sholokhov, M. Tales of the Don p109-28 S C

Diehl, Harold S.
Tobacco & your health: the smoking controversy 613.8

Dien Bien Phu, Vietnam
Fall, B. B. Hell in a very small place 959.7

Dies, Martin
See pages in the following book:
Goodman, W. The Committee p82-145 328.73

Diesel. Mitchell, D.
In The Best American short stories, 1971
p156-75   **S C**

Diet
See pages in the following books:
Esquire. Esquire Good grooming for men
p82-101   **646.7**
Seventeen. The Seventeen Book of fashion
and beauty p147-86   **646.7**
United States. Department of Agriculture.
Contours of change p124-30   **630**
Wilkinson, B. Bud Wilkinson's Guide to
modern physical fitness p110-24   **613.7**
See also Cookery; Food; Menus; Nu-
trition; Weight control

Dietetics. See Diet

Dietz, Betty Warner
Musical instruments of Africa   **781.9**

Dietz, Howard
See pages in the following book:
Ewen, D. Great men of American popu-
lar song p228-36   **920**

Dieu d'Amour. Wharton, E.
In Wharton, E. The collected short sto-
ries of Edith Wharton v2 p551-69
S C

Diff'rent. O'Neill, E.
In O'Neill, E. Plays v2 p493-549   **812**

Di Gaspari, Vincent M.
(jt. auth.) Proia, N. C. Barron's Handbook of American college financial aid
378.3
(jt. auth.) Proia, N. C. Barron's Handbook of junior and community college
financial aid   **378.3**

Digestion
See pages in the following book:
Sebrell, W. H. Food and nutrition p90-97
641.1

Digging up Adam; the story of L. S. B.
Leakey. Mulvey, M. W.   **92**

Dikeman, May
The woman across the street
In The Best American short stories, 1964
p95-107   **S C**

Di Lampedusa, Giuseppe. See Lampedusa,
Giuseppe di

Dilas, Milovan. See Djilas, Milovan

The dilettante. Wharton, E.
In Wharton, E. The collected short sto-
ries of Edith Wharton v 1 p411-19
S C

Dill, Marshall
Germany   **943**

A dill pickle. Mansfield, K.
In Mansfield, K. The short stories of
Katherine Mansfield p330-37 **S C**

Dillinger, John
Toland, J. The Dillinger days   **364.1**

The Dillinger days. Toland, J.   **364.1**

Dillon, Richard
Meriwether Lewis   **92**

Dilmun
Bibby, G. Looking for Dilmun   **913.03**

Dilsey. Faulkner, W.
In Faulkner, W. The portable Faulkner
p445-80   **S C**

Di Maggio, Joe. See Di Maggio, Joseph
Paul

Di Maggio, Joseph Paul
Silverman, A. Joe Di Maggio: the golden
year, 1941   **92**
See also pages in the following book:
Mantle, M. The quality of courage p134-
42   **920**

Dinesen, Isak
Seven Gothic tales   **S C**
Contents: The deluge at Norderney; The old
chevalier; The monkey; The roads round Pisax;
The supper at Elsinore; The dreamers; The
poet

Dinner. Lardner, R.
In Lardner, R. The Ring Lardner reader p435-43   **S C**

A dinner at—. Henry, O.
In Henry, O. The complete works of
O. Henry p1005-12   **S C**

Dinners and dining. See Cookery; Menus;
Table

Dinosaur National Monument
See pages in the following book:
National Geographic Society. America's
wonderlands p233-39   **917.3**

Dinosaurs
Colbert, E. H. Men and dinosaurs   **568**
See also pages in the following books:
Asimov, I. The solar system and back
p191-217   **508**
Fenton, C. L. The fossil book p330-62
560

Diocletian, Emperor of Rome
See pages in the following book:
Coolidge, O. Lives of famous Romans
p189-208   **920**

Diogenes
See pages in the following book:
Thomas, H. Understanding the great
philosophers p119-28   **109**

Diolé, Philippe
Cousteau, J. Y. Life and death in a coral
sea   **551.4**

Dionne family
See pages in the following book:
Leighton, I. ed. The aspirin age, 1919-
1941 p297-312   **917.3**

Dionysus in doubt. Robinson, E. A.
In Robinson, E. A. The collected poems
of Edwin Arlington Robinson
p859-918   **811**

Diplomacy
See also names of countries with the
subdivision Foreign relations, e.g. United
States—Foreign relations
Fiction
Galbraith, J. K. The triumph   **Fic**

Diplomats
Fiction
Michener, J. A. Caravans   **Fic**

Dirac, Paul Adrien Maurice
See pages in the following book:
Gamow, G. Thirty years that shook phys-
ics p118-38   **530.1**

Direct action. Thelwell, M.
In Hughes, L. ed. The best short stories
by Negro writers p470-78   **S C**

Directory, French, 1795-1799. See France—History—Revolution, 1789-1799

Disabled. See Physically handicapped

Disadvantaged. See Socially handicapped

The disappearance of Crispina Umberleigh. Saki
In Saki. The short stories of Saki p455-60 **S C**

The disappearance of Lady Frances Carfax. Doyle, Sir A. C.
In Doyle, Sir A. C. The complete Sherlock Holmes v2 p1108-23 **S C**

Disarmament
See pages in the following books:
Schlesinger, A. M. A thousand days p450-505 **973.922**
Stevenson, A. E. Looking outward p40-52 **341.13**
White, E. B. The points of my compass p175-92 **818**
See also Peace

Disasters
See pages in the following book:
Gies, J. Life in a medieval city p190-98 **914.4**
See also Shipwrecks; and names of particular disasters, e.g. San Francisco—Earthquake and fire, 1906

Disch, Robert
(ed.) The ecological conscience **301.3**

Disciples of Christ
See pages in the following book:
Look. Religions in America p57-67 **280**

Discography. See Music—Discography

Discord makers. Reynolds, M.
In Conklin, G. ed. Invaders of earth p134-45 **S C**

The discounters of money. Henry, O.
In Henry, O. The complete works of O. Henry p379-84 **S C**

A discourse on method, and selected writings. Descartes, R. **194**

Discover American trees. Platt, R. **582**

Discoverers. See Explorers **962**

The discoverers. Armstrong, R.
In Armstrong, R. A history of seafaring v2 **910.9**

Discoveries (in geography)
Freuchen, P. Peter Freuchen's Book of the Seven Seas **910.4**
Hale, J. R. Age of exploration **910.9**
Herrmann, P. Conquest by man **910.9**
Masselman, G. The Atlantic: sea of darkness **910.9**
National Geographic Society. Great adventures with National Geographic **910.9**
Stefánsson, V. ed. Great adventures and explorations **910.9**
Thomas, L. Lowell Thomas' Book of the high mountains **910.9**
See also pages in the following books:
Shakespeare's England v 1 p170-97 **822.3**

Van Loon, H. W. The story of mankind p224-40 **909**
See also America—Discovery and exploration; Antarctic regions; Arctic regions; Explorers; Scientific expeditions; Voyages and travels; and names of countries with the subdivision Description and travel, e.g. United States—Description and travel

Discoveries (in science) See Inventions; Patents; Science

Discoveries, Maritime. See Discoveries (in geography)

Discovering man's past in the Americas. Stuart, G. E. **913.7**

Discovering poetry. Drew, E. **808.1**

Discovering scientific method. Ruchlis, H. **501**

Discrimination
Stalvey, L. M. The education of a WASP **301.45**
See also Civil rights; Minorities; Negroes—Civil rights; Negroes—Segregation

Discrimination in education
Kozol, J. Death at an early age **371.9**
See also pages in the following book:
Silberman, C. E. Crisis in the classroom p53-112 **370**
See also Segregation in education

Discrimination in employment
See pages in the following book:
Glock, C. Y. ed. Prejudice U.S.A. p151-68 **301.45**
See also names of social or racial groups with the subdivision Employment, e.g. Woman—Employment; Negroes—Employment

Discussion. See Debates and debating

Diseases
Brooks, S. M. The sea inside us: water in the life processes **612**
See also pages in the following book:
Bates, M. Man in nature p82-94 **573**
See also names of specific diseases, e.g. Porphyria; and names of subjects with the subdivision Diseases, e.g. Skin—Diseases

Diseases, Mental. See Mental illness

Diseases and pests. See Fungi; Insects, Injurious and beneficial; Plant diseases

Disinherited: the lost birthright of the American Indian. Van Every, D. **970.5**

Disney, Walt
Schickel, R. The Disney version **92**
The Disney version. Schickel, R. **92**

The disposal. Inge, W.
In Richards, S. ed. Best short plays of the world theatre, 1958-1967 p123-46 **808.82**

Disposal of refuse. See Refuse and refuse disposal

Disraeli, Benjamin. See Beaconsfield, Benjamin Disraeli, 1st Earl of

Dissent in America. Liston, R. A.　301.15

Dissent in three American wars. Morison, S. E.　973

Dissenters, Great. Thomas, N.　920

Dissertations, Academic
Turabian, K. L. A manual for writers of term papers, theses and dissertations　808.02

A distant trumpet. Horgan, P.　Fic

Distribution of wealth. See Wealth

The district doctor. Turgenev, I. S.
In Seltzer, T. comp. Best Russian short stories p82-95　S C

The District of Columbia. Weisberger, B. A.　917.53

District schools. See Rural schools

The disturber of traffic. Kipling, R.
In Kipling, R. The best short stories of Rudyard Kipling p206-17　S C

The ditch. Bannister, E.
In Seventeen. Seventeen from Seventeen p198-214　S C

Ditmars, Raymond L.
The reptiles of North America　598.1
Reptiles of the world　598.1
Snakes of the world　598.1

The divided house. Paton, A.
In Paton, A. Tales from a troubled land p107-16　S C

Dividends. See Stocks

Divination
Douglas, A. How to consult the I Ching　895.1

Divine, Robert A.
(ed.) American foreign policy since 1945　327.73

The Divine comedy. Dante Alighieri
In Dante Alighieri. The portable Dante p3-544　851

Divine healing. See Christian Science

Diving. See Skin and scuba diving

Diving, Submarine. See Bathyscaphe; Skin and scuba diving

Diving vehicles
Cousteau, J. Y. Jacques-Yves Cousteau's World without sun　551.4
Cousteau, J. Y. The living sea　627.7
Soule, G. The greatest depths　551.4
Sweeney, J. B. A pictorial history of oceanographic submersibles　623.82
See also pages in the following books:
Bardach, J. Harvest of the sea p84-105　333.9
Dugan, J. World beneath the sea p29-48, 143-62, 181-200　551.4

Divorce in Naples. Faulkner, W.
In Faulkner, W. Collected stories of William Faulkner p877-93　S C

Dix, Dorothea Lynde
See pages in the following books:
Dodge, B. S. The story of nursing p45-58　610.73
Holbrook, S. H. Lost men of American history p136-42　920
Stoddard, H. Famous American women p136-48　920

Dixon, Dean
See pages in the following book:
Bontemps, A. We have tomorrow p46-58　920

Dixon, Peter L.
Where the surfers are　797.1

Djemila, Algeria
See pages in the following book:
Camus, A. Lyrical and critical essays p73-79　844

Djilas, Milovan
The new class　335.4

Dobie, J. Frank
Some part of myself　92
(ed.) Tales of old-time Texas　398.2

Dobler, Lavinia
(ed.) The Dobler World directory of youth periodicals　016.05

The Dobler International list of periodicals for boys and girls. See Dobler, L. ed. The Dobler World directory of youth periodicals　016.05

The Dobler World directory of youth periodicals. Dobler, L. ed.　016.05

Dobrin, Arnold
Aaron Copland: his life and times　92

Dobu Island
Benedict, R. Patterns of culture　572

Doc Mellhorn and the pearly gates. Benét, S. V.
In Benét, S. V. Selected works of Stephen Vincent Benét v2　818

Doceno. See Gherardi, Christofano, known as Doceno

Dockstader, Frederick J.
Indian art in America　970.6

The doctor. Chekhov, A.
In Chekhov, A. The stories of Anton Chekhov p243-49　S C

A doctor among the addicts. Hentoff, N.　616.86

The doctor and the doctor's wife. Hemingway, E.
In Hemingway, E. In our time p23-31　S C
In Hemingway, E. The short stories of Ernest Hemingway p97-103　S C

Doctor Faustus. Mann, T.　Fic

Dr Heidegger's experiment. Hawthorne, N.
In Hawthorne, N. Hawthorne's Short stories p99-108　S C

Doctor in buckskin. Allen, T. D.　Fic

Dr Jekyll and Mr Hyde, The strange case of. Stevenson, R. L.　Fic

Dr Johnson and his world. Brown, I.　914.2

Doctor Johnson and his world. Halliday, F. E.　92

Dr Martino. Faulkner, W.
In Faulkner, W. Collected stories of William Faulkner p565-85　S C

Doctor Martino, and other stories. Faulkner, W.
In Faulkner, W. Collected stories of William Faulkner　S C

Dr Ox will die at midnight. Kersh, G.
In Best detective stories of the year, 1971 p141-48　S C

Dr Tom Dooley's three great books. Dooley, T. A.　92

The **Don** flows home to the sea. Sholokhov, M.
In Sholokhov, M. The silent Don v2
Fic

Don Juan. See Juan, Don

Don Juan. Molière, J. B. P.
In Bentley, E. comp. The great playwrights v 1 p893-943   808.82

Don Juan in hell. Shaw, B.
In Shaw, B. Complete plays, with prefaces v3 p600-54   822

Don Quixote de la Mancha. Cervantes, M. de
Fic

Donatello
See pages in the following book:
Vasari, G. The lives of the painters, sculptors and architects v 1 p301-14   920

Donato. See Donatello

Donehogawa. See Parker, Eli Samuel, Seneca chief

Donizetti, Gaetano
See pages in the following books:
Cross, M. The Milton Cross New encyclopedia of the great composers and their music p290-98   920.03
Ewen, D. ed. The complete book of classical music p387-94   780.1

Donkey of God. Untermeyer, L.
In Becker, M. L. ed. The home book of Christmas p13-25   394.26

Donne, John, 1573-1631
See pages in the following books:
Untermeyer, L. Lives of the poets p122-36
920
Untermeyer, L. The paths of poetry p57-63   920
Fiction
Vining, E. G. Take heed of loving me
Fic

Donnelly, Ignatius
See pages in the following book:
Holbrook, S. H. Lost men of American history p268-77   920

Donner Party
See pages in the following book:
Stone, I. Men to match my mountains p85-98   979.1

Donnison, F. S. V.
Burma   959.1

Donohue, H. E. F.
Joe College
In Prize stories, 1970: The O. Henry Awards p93-112   S C

Donoso, José
Ana María
In Cohen, J. M. ed. Latin American writing today p152-66   860.8

Donovan, Frank
(ed.) Adams, J. The John Adams papers
92
(ed.) Jefferson, T. The Thomas Jefferson papers   92

Donovan, James A.
The United States Marine Corps   359.9

Donovan, Robert J.
PT 109   940.54

Don't be a drudge. Lardner, R.
In Lardner, R. The Ring Lardner reader p650-53   S C

Don't shoot—we are your children! Lukas, J. A.   301.43

Don't smile until Christmas. Ryan, K. ed.
371.1

Dooley, D. J.
The art of Sinclair Lewis   813.09

Dooley, Thomas A.
Deliver us from evil
In Dooley, T. A. Dr Tom Dooley's three great books p12-122   92
Dr Tom Dooley's three great books   92
The edge of tomorrow
In Dooley, T. A. Dr Tom Dooley's three great books p123-250   92
The night they burned the mountain
In Dooley, T. A. Dr Tom Dooley's three great books p251-383   92

Doolittle, James Harold
Glines, C. V. Doolittle's Tokyo Raiders
940.54

Doolittle's Tokyo Raiders. Glines, C. V.
940.54

Doom of the Darnaways. Chesterton, G. K.
In Chesterton, G. K. The Father Brown omnibus p583-609   S C

The **door** in the wall. Wells, H. G.
In Wells, H. G. The complete short stories of H. G. Wells p144-61 S C

Door of opportunity. Maugham, W. S.
In Havighurst, W. ed. Masters of the modern short story p380-414   S C

The **door** of unrest. Henry, O.
In Henry, O. The complete works of O. Henry p863-71   S C

Doreen. Owen, A.
In The Best short plays, 1971 p99-132
808.82

Doren, Carl van. See Van Doren, Carl

Doren, Charles van. See Van Doren, Charles

Doren, Mark van. See Van Doren, Mark

Dorian Gray. See Wilde, O. The picture of Dorian Gray   Fic

Doris, Lillian
Complete secretary's handbook   651.02

Doris and the Count. Denby, W.
In Margolies, E. A native son's reader p330-38   810.8

Dorland, William Alexander Newman
Dorland's Illustrated medical dictionary. See Dorland's Illustrated medical dictionary   610.3

Dorland's Illustrated medical dictionary
610.3

Dos Passos, John
The big money
In Dos Passos, J. U.S.A. v3   Fic
Easter Island   919.6
The 42nd parallel
In Dos Passos, J. U.S.A. v 1   Fic
The men who made the nation   973.4
Midcentury   Fic
Mr Wilson's war   973.91
Nineteen nineteen
In Dos Passos, J. U.S.A. v2   Fic
The shackles of power   973
Three soldiers   Fic
U.S.A.   Fic

Dos Passos, John—*Continued*
About
See pages in the following book:
Geismar, M. Writers in crisis p87-139
813.09
Doss, Helen
The family nobody wanted 92
Dostoevskiĭ, Fedor Mikhailovich. See Dostoevsky, Fyodor
Dostoevsky, Fyodor
The adolescent Fic
The brothers Karamazov Fic
The Christmas tree and the wedding
In Seltzer, T. comp. Best Russian short stories p96-106 S C
Crime and punishment Fic
The house of the dead Fic
The idiot Fic
The possessed Fic
The possessed; dramatization. See Camus, A. The possessed
About
See pages in the following books:
Posell, E. Z. Russian authors p87-108 920
Untermeyer, L. Makers of the modern world p82-90 920
Dotson Gerber resurrected. Bennett, H.
In The Best American short stories, 1971 p10-23 S C
A double-barreled detective story. Twain, M.
In Twain, M. The complete short stories of Mark Twain p423-69 S C
Double birthday. Cather, W.
In Foley, M. ed. Fifty best American short stories, 1915-1965 p67-81 S C
A double-dyed deceiver. Henry, O.
In Henry, O. The complete works of O. Henry p421-29 S C
Double stars. See Stars
Dougherty's eye-opener. Henry, O.
In Henry, O. The complete works of O. Henry p1266-70 S C
Douglas, Alfred
How to consult the I Ching 895.1
Douglas, George W.
The American book of days 394.2
Douglas, Lloyd C.
The Big Fisherman Fic
The robe Fic
Douglas, Stephen Arnold
Lincoln, A. The Lincoln-Douglas debates of 1858 973.6
About
See pages in the following book:
Stone, I. They also ran p213-30 920
Douglas, William O.
An almanac of liberty 323.4
America challenged 917.3
International dissent: six steps toward world peace 341.6
A living Bill of Rights 342.73
Of men and mountains 92
Points of rebellion 323
A wilderness bill of rights 333.7
Douglass, Frederick
Life and times of Frederick Douglass; abridged 92
The mind and heart of Frederick Douglass 326

About
Bontemps, A. Free at last 92
Hoexter, C. K. Black crusader: Frederick Douglass 92
Quarles, B. ed. Frederick Douglass 92
See also pages in the following book:
Bontemps, A. 100 years of Negro freedom p 1-20, 106-24 301.451
Dover, Cedric
American Negro art 709.73
The Dover Road. Milne, A. A.
In Dickinson, T. H. ed. Chief contemporary dramatists, 3d ser. p117-58 808.82
The doves' nest. Mansfield, K.
In Mansfield, K. The short stories of Katherine Mansfield p622-37 S C
Dovisch in the wilderness. Wilner, H.
In The Best American short stories, 1966 p327-57 S C
Dowd, David L.
Horizon Magazine. The French Revolution 944.04
Down, Oliphant
The maker of dreams
In Cerf, B. ed. 24 favorite one-act plays p256-71 808.82
Down at the dinghy. Salinger, J. D.
In Salinger, J. D. Nine stories p111-30 S C
"Down pens." Saki
In Saki. The short stories of Saki p406-10 S C
Down under the Thames. Godden, R.
In Godden, R. Gone p35-47 S C
Downer, Alan S.
(ed.) Tucker, S. M. ed. Twenty-five modern plays 808.82
Downey, Harris
The vicar-general and the wide night
In The Best American short stories, 1966 p35-57 S C
The downfall of fascism in the Black Ankle County. Mitchell, J.
In White, E. B. ed. A subtreasury of American humor; abridged p304-12 817.08
Downing, Ronald
Rawicz, S. The long walk 910.4
Downs, Elizabeth C.
(jt. auth.) Downs, R. B. How to do library research 028.7
Downs, Robert B.
Books that changed America 810.9
Books that changed the world 809
(ed.) The first freedom 323.44
How to do library research 028.7
The downward path to wisdom. Porter, K. A.
In Abrahams, W. ed. Fifty years of the American short story v2 p87-103 S C
In Porter, K. A. The collected stories of Katherine Anne Porter p369-87 S C
Downwind from Gettysburg. Bradbury, R.
In Bradbury, R. I sing the Body Electric! p72-89 S C

Doyle, Adrian C.

The exploits of Sherlock Holmes   **S C**

Contents: Adventure of the seven clocks; Adventure of the gold hunter; Adventure of the wax gamblers; Adventure of the Highgate miracle; Adventure of the black baronet; Adventure of the sealed room; Adventure of Foulkes Rath; Adventure of the Abbas Ruby; Adventure of the Dark Angels; Adventure of the two women; Adventure of the Deptford horror; Adventure of the red widow

Doyle, Sir Arthur Conan

Adventures of Sherlock Holmes

In Doyle, Sir A. C. The complete Sherlock Holmes v 1 p177-380   **S C**

The Bruce-Partington plans

In Dulles, A. ed. Great spy stories from fiction p119-44   **S C**

The case book of Sherlock Holmes

In Doyle, Sir A. C. The complete Sherlock Holmes v2 p1160-1323   **S C**

The complete Sherlock Holmes   **S C**

Contents for the short stories included in the volumes are as follows:

Adventures of Sherlock Holmes: A scandal in Bohemia; The Red-headed League; A case of identity; The Boscombe Valley mystery; The five orange pips; The man with the twisted lip; The adventure of the Blue Carbuncle; The adventure of the speckled band; The adventure of the engineer's thumb; The adventure of the noble bachelor; The adventure of the Beryl Coronet; The adventure of the copper beeches

Memoirs of Sherlock Holmes: Silver Blaze; The yellow face; The stock-broker's clerk; The "Gloria Scott"; The Musgrave ritual; The Reigate puzzle; The crooked man; The resident patient; The Greek interpreter; The naval treaty; The final problem

The return of Sherlock Holmes: The adventure of the empty house; The adventure of the Norwood builder; The adventure of the dancing men; The adventure of the solitary cyclist; The adventure of the priory school; The adventure of Black Peter; The adventure of Charles Augustus Milverton; The adventure of six Napoleons; The adventure of the three students; The adventure of the golden pince-nez; The adventure of the missing three-quarter; The adventure of the Abbey Grange; The adventure of the second stain

The valley of fear: The tragedy of Birlstone; The Scowrers

His last bow: The adventure of Wisteria Lodge; The adventure of the cardboard box; The adventure of the red circle; The adventure of the Bruce-Partington plans; The adventure of the dying detective; The disappearance of Lady Frances Carfax; The adventure of the Devil's foot; His last bow

The case book of Sherlock Holmes: The adventure of the illustrious client; The adventure of the blanched soldier; The adventure of the Mazarin stone; The adventure of the three gables; The adventure of the Sussex vampire; The adventure of the three Garridebs; The problem of Thor Bridge; The adventure of the creeping man; The adventure of the lion's mane; The adventure of the veiled lodger; The adventure of Shoscombe Old Place; The adventure of the retired colourman

His last bow

In Doyle, Sir A. C. The complete Sherlock Holmes v2 p1021-1155   **S C**

The hound of the Baskervilles

In Doyle, Sir A. C. The complete Sherlock Holmes v2 p783-899   **S C**

In Doyle, Sir A. C. Sherlock Holmes' greatest cases p17-253   **S C**

Memoirs of Sherlock Holmes

In Doyle, Sir A. C. The complete Sherlock Holmes v 1 p383-555   **S C**

The return of Sherlock Holmes

In Doyle, Sir A. C. The complete Sherlock Holmes v2 p559-780   **S C**

Sherlock Holmes' greatest cases   **S C**

Short stories are: The Red-headed League; The adventure of the speckled band; A scandal in Bohemia; The Musgrave ritual; Silver Blaze; The adventure of the Blue Carbuncle

The sign of the four

In Doyle, Sir A. C. The complete Sherlock Holmes v 1 p91-173   **S C**

A study in scarlet

In Doyle, Sir A. C. The complete Sherlock Holmes v 1 p3-88   **S C**

The valley of fear

In Doyle, Sir A. C. The complete Sherlock Holmes v2 p903-1018   **S C**

The White Company   **Fic**

About

Hardwick, M. The man who was Sherlock Holmes   **92**

See also pages in the following book:

Wood, J. P. Scotland Yard p153-61   **352**

Doyle, Paul A.

Pearl S. Buck   **813.09**

Dozer, Donald Marquand

(ed.) The Monroe Doctrine   **327.73**

Dracula. Stoker, B.   **Fic**

Draft, Military. See Military service, Compulsory

Draft Riot, 1863

See pages in the following books:

Heaps, W. A. Riots, U.S.A. 1765-1970 p50-60   **301.18**

Hofstadter, R. ed. American violence p211-17   **301.18**

Drag racing. See Automobile racing

The dragon. Bradbury, R.

In Bradbury, R. R is for rocket p153-56   **S C**

Dragon seed. Buck, P. S.   **Fic**

Drainage

See pages in the following book:

United States. Department of Agriculture. Water p478-575   **631.7**

Drake, Albert

The chicken which became a rat

In The Best American short stories, 1971 p86-106   **S C**

Drake, Sir Francis

Wood, W. Elizabethan sea-dogs   **973.1**

See also pages in the following book:

Lloyd, A. The Spanish centuries p174-89   **946**

Drama

The Best plays of 1919/1920-1969/1970   **808.82**

Highet, G. The classical tradition p127-43   **809**

See also Acting; American drama; Dramatists; English drama; Folk drama; One-act plays; Theater; Tragedy; and subjects with the subdivision Drama

Bibliography

Drury's Guide to best plays   **808.82**

See also pages in the following book:

Ireland, N. O. Index to full length plays, 1944 to 1964 p265-96   **808.82**

Dreamers of the American dream. Holbrook, S. H. 973

The **dreaming** of the bones. Yeats, W. B.
In Yeats, W. B. Collected plays of W. B. Yeats p275-85 822

Dreams
See pages in the following books:
Halacy, D. S. Man and memory p112-32 612
Sugarman, D. A. The Seventeen Guide to knowing yourself p101-15 155.5
See also Sleep

Dreams. Chekhov, A.
In Chekhov, A. The stories of Anton Chekhov p186-95 S C

The **dreamy** kid. O'Neill, E.
In O'Neill, E. Plays v 1 p605-22 812

Dreiser, Theodore
An American tragedy Fic
The lost Phoebe
In Day, A. G. ed. The greatest American short stories p197-214 S C
In Foley, M. ed. Fifty best American short stories, 1915-1965 p8-22 S C
Sister Carrie Fic
Sister Carrie; criticism
In Stegner, W. ed. The American novel p106-16 813.09

About
See pages in the following books:
Brooks, V. The confident years: 1885-1915 p294-313 810.9
Kazin, A. On native grounds p73-90 810.9
Literary history of the United States p1197-1207 810.9
Mencken, H. L. The American scene p111-56 818
Untermeyer, L. Makers of the modern world p434-43 920
Van Doren, C. The American novel, 1789-1939 p245-59 813.09
Wagenknecht, E. Cavalcade of the American novel p281-93 813.09

Dress. See Clothing and dress

Dresser, Paul
See pages in the following book:
Ewen, D. Great men of American popular song p45-52 920

Dressmaking
Better Homes and Gardens. Better Homes and Gardens Sewing book 646.4
Carson, B. How you look and dress 646
Johnson, M. Sewing the easy day 646.4
McCall's Sewing book 646.4
Margolis, A. P. How to make clothes that fit and flatter 646.4
Rosenberg, S. The illustrated hassle-free make your own clothes book 646.4
Simplicity Sewing book 646.4
See also Sewing

Drew, Daniel
See pages in the following book:
Holbrook, S. H. The age of the moguls p21-26, 29-35 920

Drew, Elizabeth
Discovering poetry 808.1
The novel: a modern guide to fifteen English masterpieces 823.09
Poetry: a modern guide to its understanding and enjoyment 808.1

Dreyfus, Alfred
Schechter, B. The Dreyfus affair 944.081
Werstein, I. I accuse 92
See also pages in the following books:
Aymar, B. A pictorial history of the world's great trials p201-19 343
Shirer, W. L. The collapse of the Third Republic p48-69 944.081
Tuchman, B. W. The proud tower p171-226 909.82

The **Dreyfus** affair. Schechter, B. 944.081

Dried rose petals in a silver bowl. Winn, J. B.
In The Best American short stories, 1968 p331-41 S C

Driesch, Hans Adolf Eduard
See pages in the following book:
Moore, R. The coil of life p162-77 574.09

The **drifters.** Michener, J. A. Fic

Drink. Anderson, S.
In Anderson, S. Winesburg, Ohio (Modern Lib) p254-67 S C
In Anderson, S. Winesburg, Ohio (Viking) p210-19 S C

A **drink** in the passage. Paton, A.
In Paton, A. Tales from a troubled land p117-28 S C

Drink question. See Liquor problem

Drinker family
Bowen, C. D. Family portrait 920

The **drive** against illiteracy. Isenberg, I. ed. 379

Driver, Harold E.
Indians of North America 970.1

Drivers, Automobile. See Automobile drivers

Dropout. Ritchie, J.
In Best detective stories of the year [1969] p125-34 S C

The **dropout:** causes and cures. Cervantes, L. F. 371.2

Dropouts
Cervantes, L. F. The dropout: causes and cures 371.2

Drotning, Phillip T.
Up from the ghetto 920

Drowne's wooden image. Hawthorne, N.
In Hawthorne, N. Hawthorne's Short stories p300-12 S C

The **drug** dilemma. Cohen, S. 615

Drug habit. See Narcotic habit

The **drug** scene. Louria, D. B. 613.8

Drugs
Brenner, J. H. Drugs & youth 613.8
Cain, A. H. Young people and drugs 613.8
Cohen, S. The drug dilemma 615
Fort, J. The pleasure seekers: the drug crisis, youth and society 613.8
Houser, N. W. Drugs 613.8
Hyde, M. O. ed. Mind drugs 613.8
Louria, D. B. Overcoming drugs 613.8

Drugs—*Continued*
Marin, P. Understanding drug use **613.8**
Modell, W. Drugs **615**
What everyone needs to know about drugs **613.8**
See also pages in the following books:
Halacy, D. S. Man and memory p202-19 **612**
Kefauver, E. In a few hands: monopoly power in America p8-79 **338.8**
Lasagna, L. Life, death, and the doctor p290-319 **610**
Wilson, J. R. The mind p152-67 **150**
See also names of drugs, e.g. Marihuana

Dictionaries
Lingeman, R. R. Drugs from A to Z: a dictionary **613.8**

Fiction
Du Maurier, D. The house on the strand **Fic**

Drugs and alcohol. Jones, K. L. **613.8**
Drugs & youth. Brenner, J. H. **613.8**
Drugs from A to Z: a dictionary. Lingeman, R. R. **613.8**
Drum beat. Marlowe, S.
In Hitchcock, A. ed. Alfred Hitchcock presents: A month of mystery p19-22 **S C**
Drums along the Mohawk. Edmonds, W. D. **Fic**
The **drums** of Father Ned. O'Casey, S.
In O'Casey, S. The Sean O'Casey reader p529-600 **828**
Drums of Oude. Strong, A.
In Cerf, B. ed. Thirty famous one-act act plays p287-301 **808.82**
The **drums** of the Fore and Aft. Kipling, R.
In Kipling, R. The best short stories of Rudyard Kipling p91-115 **S C**
The **drunkard**. O'Connor, F.
In Garrity, D. A. ed. 44 Irish short stories p249-60 **S C**
Drunkenness. See Temperance
Drury, Allen
Advise and consent **Fic**
Preserve and protect **Fic**
Drury, F. K. W.
(ed.) Drury's Guide to best plays. See Drury's Guide to best plays **808.82**
Drury's Guide to best plays **808.82**
Dry rot. Michener, J.
In Michener, J. Tales of the South Pacific p116-34 **S C**
Dry rot. Sholokhov, M.
In Sholokhov, M. Tales of the Don p294-310 **S C**
Dry September. Faulkner, W.
In Faulkner, W. Collected stories of William Faulkner p169-83 **S C**
In Faulkner, W. The Faulkner reader **S C**
In Faulkner, W. Selected short stories of William Faulkner p62-77 **S C**
Dryden, John
See pages in the following books:
Daiches, D. A critical history of English literature v2 p544-46, 558-83 **820.9**

Durant, W. The age of Louis XIV p321-28 **940.2**
Untermeyer, L. Lives of the poets p193-209 **920**
Dubček, Alexander
See pages in the following book:
Szulc, T. Czechoslovakia since World War II p259-329 **943.7**
Duberman, Martin B.
In white America
In Gassner, J. ed. Best American plays; 6th ser. p471-94 **812.08**
The recorder: a history
In The Best short plays, 1970 p327-48 **808.82**
Dubinsky, David
See pages in the following book:
Beard, A. E. S. Our foreign-born citizens p164-89 **920**
Dublin
Social life and customs
Anderson, C. G. James Joyce and his world **92**
Dubliners. Joyce, J. **S C**
Dubois, Eugène
See pages in the following book:
Moore, R. Man, time, and fossils p233-55 **573.2**
Du Bois, W. E. B.
On being crazy
In Clarke, J H. ed. American Negro short stories p8-10 **S C**
The souls of Black folk **301.451**
W. E. B. Du Bois: a reader **301.451**
About
Lacy, L A. Cheer the lonesome traveler **92**
See also pages in the following books:
Bontemps, A. 100 years of Negro freedom p125-57 **301.451**
Ducas, G. ed. Great documents in Black American history p167-200 **301.451**
Metcalf, G. R. Black profiles p55-84 **920**
Du Bois, William Edward Burghardt. See Du Bois, W. E. B.
Dubos, René
So human an animal **301.3**
Dubus, Andre
If they knew Yvonne
In The Best American short stories, 1970 p84-107 **S C**
Duc De l'Omelette. Poe, E. A.
In Poe, E. A. The complete tales and poems of Edgar Allan Poe p708-10 **S C**
In Poe, E A. Selected poetry and prose p60-63 **818**
Ducas, George
(ed.) Great documents in Black American history **301.451**
The **Duchess** at prayer. Wharton, E.
In Wharton, E. The collected short stories of Edith Wharton v 1 p229-44 **S C**
Due to circumstances beyond our control. Friendly, F. W. **384.55**
Due to lack of interest tomorrow has been canceled. Kampen, I. **378.1**

The duel. Henry, O.
In Henry, O. The complete works of O. Henry p1623-27   **S C**

A duel. Maupassant, G. de
In Maupassant, G. de. Guy de Maupassant's Short stories p192-96   **S C**

Duel of Dr Hirsch. Chesterton, G. K.
In Chesterton, G. K. The Father Brown omnibus p264-79   **S C**

Duel of the four minute men. O'Neill, P.
In Sports Illustrated. The wonderful world of sport p229-30   **796**

The duel that was not fought. Crane, S.
In Crane, S. The complete short stories & sketches of Stephen Crane p205-10   **S C**

Duel with the clock. Edwards, J.
In Hughes, L. ed. The best short stories by Negro writers p301-08   **S C**

Dueling
    See pages in the following book:
Shakespeare's England v2 p401-07   **822.3**
    See also Fencing

Duerrenmatt, Friedrich
The visit
In Block, H. M. ed. Masters of modern drama p1134-59   **808.82**

Duet for organ and strings. Macdonagh, D.
In Garrity, D. A. ed. 44 Irish short stories p176-83   **S C**

Duet in Asia. Buck, P. S.
In Buck, P. S. The good deed, and other stories of Asia, past and present p187-212   **S C**

Dufek, George J.
Operation Deepfreeze   **919.9**

Dugan, James
Cousteau, J. Y. The living sea   **627.7**
World beneath the sea   **551.4**
(jt. ed.) Cousteau, J. Y. ed. Captain Cousteau's Underwater treasury   **627.7**

Duggan, Alfred
The falcon and the dove; a life of Thomas Becket of Canterbury   **92**
The Romans   **937**
The story of the crusades, 1097-1291   **940.1**

Dulles, Allen
The craft of intelligence   **327**
(ed.) Great spy stories from fiction   **S C**
(ed.) Great true spy stories   **327**

Dulles, Foster R.
America's rise to world power, 1898-1954   **327.73**
The United States since 1865   **973**

Dumas, Alexandre, 1802-1870
The black tulip   **Fic**
The general of the order
In Dulles, A. ed. Great spy stories from fiction p89-104   **S C**
The man in the iron mask   **Fic**

About
Maurois, A. Alexandre Dumas   **92**

Dumas, Frederic
Cousteau, J. Y. The silent world   **627.7**

Dumas, Henry
Fon
In Jones, L ed. Black fire p455-66   **810.8**

Du Maurier, Daphne
The flight of the Falcon   **Fic**
The glass-blowers   **Fic**
The house on the strand   **Fic**
The King's general   **Fic**
Rebecca   **Fic**
—Same
In Haycraft, H. ed. A treasury of great mysteries v2 p301-576   **S C**

Dumb (Deaf mutes) See Deaf

The dumb Dutchman. Forester, C. S.
In Forester, C. S. Gold from Crete p165-82   **S C**

The Dummy. Matthews, C.
In Best detective stories of the year [1969] p212-24   **S C**

Dumont, René
The hungry future   **338.1**

Dunan, Marcel
(ed.) Larousse Encyclopedia of ancient and medieval history. See Larousse Encyclopedia of ancient and medieval history   **909**
(ed.) Larousse Encyclopedia of modern history, from 1500 to the present day. See Larousse Encyclopedia of modern history, from 1500 to the present day   **909**

Dunaway, James O.
Sports Illustrated Track and field: running events   **796.4**

Dunbar, Ann
(jt. ed.) Moore, C. D. ed. Africa yesterday and today   **916**

Dunbar, Paul Laurence
The complete poems of Paul Laurence Dunbar   **811**
The lynching of Jube Benson
In Clarke, J. H. ed. American Negro short stories p 1-8   **S C**
Lyrics of love and laughter
In Dunbar, P. L. The complete poems of Paul Laurence Dunbar p259-371   **811**
Lyrics of lowly life
In Dunbar, P. L. The complete poems of Paul Laurence Dunbar p 1-138   **811**
Lyrics of sunshine and shadow
In Dunbar, P. L. The complete poems of Paul Laurence Dunbar p379-479   **811**
Lyrics of the hearthside
In Dunbar, P. L. The complete poems of Paul Laurence Dunbar p139-258   **811**
The scapegoat
In Hughes, L. ed. The best short stories by Negro writers p17-29   **S C**

About
    See pages in the following book:
Bontemps, A. Anyplace but here p92-97   **301.451**

Duncan, Isadora
    See pages in the following books:
Maynard, O. American modern dancers: the pioneers p30-69   **920**

Duncan, Isadora—*Continued*
Stoddard, H. Famous American women p149-61   **920**

Untermeyer, L. Makers of the modern world p522-32   **920**

Duncan, Norman
Christmas Eve at Topmast Tickle
In Becker, M. L. ed. The home book of Christmas p678-88   **394.26**
Christmas with Dr Grenfell
In Wernecke, H. H. ed. Celebrating Christmas around the world p171-81   **394.26**

Duncan, Robert
See pages in the following book:
Rosenthal, M. L. The new poets p174-84   **821.09**

Dunham, Katherine
Afternoon into night
In Hughes, L. ed. The best short stories by Negro writers p145-50   **S C**

Dunlap, Joseph R.
(comp.) Debate index   **016.301**

Dunlap, William
André
In Quinn, A. H. ed. Representative American plays p80-108   **812.08**
See also pages in the following book:
Brooks, V. The world of Washington Irving p156-81   **810.9**

Dunn, C. J.
Everyday life in traditional Japan   **915.2**

Dunn, Robert
See pages in the following book:
McDonagh, D. The rise and fall and rise of modern dance p77-94   **793.3**

Dunne, Finley Peter
Mr Dooley on the education of the young
In White, E. B. ed. A subtreasury of American humor; abridged p222-25   **817.08**

Dunning, Philip
Broadway
In Gassner, J. ed. Twenty-five best plays of the modern American theatre; early ser. p215-56   **812.08**

Dunning, Stephen
(comp.) Reflections on a gift of watermelon pickle . . . and other modern verse   **811.08**

(comp.) Some haystacks don't even have any needle, and other complete modern poems   **811.08**

Dunsany, Edward John Moreton Drax Plunkett, 18th Baron. See Dunsany, Lord

Dunsany, Lord
The jest of Hahalaba
In Cerf, B. ed. 24 favorite one-act plays p367-76   **808.82**
The kith of the Elf-folk
In Garrity D. A. ed. 44 Irish short stories p70-85   **S C**
Night at an inn
In Cerf, B. ed. Thirty famous one-act plays p255-63   **808.82**

Dunway, James O.
Sports Illustrated. Sports Illustrated Book of track and field: running events **796.4**

The **duplicity** of Hargraves. Henry, O.
In Henry, O. The best short stories of O. Henry p173-88   **S C**
In Henry, O. The complete works of O. Henry p871-81   **S C**

Du Pont de Nemours (E. I.) and Company
Carr, W. H. A. The du Ponts of Delaware   **920**
See also pages in the following books:
Bowen, E. The Middle Atlantic States p127-36   **917.4**
Holbrook, S. H. The age of the moguls p247-77   **920**
Mark, H. F. Giant molecules p105-21 **668.4**

Du Pont de Nemours family
Carr, W. H. A. The du Ponts of Delaware   **920**
See also pages in the following book:
Holbrook, S. H. The age of the moguls p247-77   **920**

The **du Ponts** of Delaware. Carr, W. H. A.   **920**

Dupuy, R. Ernest
The encyclopedia of military history **355.09**

Dupuy, Trevor N.
(jt. auth.) Dupuy, R. E. The encyclopedia of military history   **355.09**

Durant, Alice
(jt. auth.) Durant, J. Pictorial history of American Presidents   **920**

Durant, Ariel
(jt. auth.) Durant, W. The age of Louis XIV   **940.2**
(jt. auth.) Durant, W. The age of reason begins   **940.2**
(jt. auth.) Durant, W. The age of Voltaire   **940.2**
(jt. auth.) Durant, W. Interpretations of life   **809**
(jt. auth.) Durant, W. The lessons of history   **901**
(jt. auth.) Durant, W. Rousseau and revolution   **940.2**

Durant, John
Pictorial history of American Presidents   **920**
Pictorial history of American sports **796.09**

Durant, Will
The age of faith   **940.1**
The age of Louis XIV   **940.2**
The age of reason begins   **940.2**
The age of Voltaire   **940.2**
Caesar and Christ   **937**
Interpretations of life   **809**
The lessons of history   **901**
The life of Greece   **938**
Our Oriental heritage   **950**
The Reformation   **940.2**
The Renaissance   **940.2**
Rousseau and revolution   **940.2**
The story of philosophy   **109**

Duration. Wharton, E.
In Wharton, E. The collected short stories of Edith Wharton v2 p859-71   **S C**

Dürer, Albrecht
Russell, F. The world of Dürer, 1471-1528
92
See also pages in the following books:
Durant, W. The Reformation p311-20 **940.2**
Newman, J. R. ed. The world of mathematics v 1 p600-21 **510.8**

Durham, Philip
The Negro cowboys 978

Durrell, Gerald
Birds, beasts, and relatives 574.9
Two in the bush 591

About
Durrell, J. Beasts in my bed 591

Durrell, Jacquie
Beasts in my bed 591

Durrell, Lawrence
The Alexandria quartet: Justine; Balthazar; Mountolive |and| Clea **Fic**
Balthazar
In Durrell, L. The Alexandria quartet: Justine; Balthazar; Mountolive [and] Clea p205-390 **Fic**
Clea
In Durrell, L. The Alexandria quartet: Justine; Balthazar; Mountolive [and] Clea p653-884 **Fic**
I.A.
In Dulles, A. ed. Great spy stories from fiction p191-98 **S C**
Justine
In Durrell, L. The Alexandria quartet: Justine; Balthazar; Mountolive [and] Clea p653-884 **Fic**
Mountolive
In Durrell, L. The Alexandria quartet: Justine; Balthazar; Mountolive [and] Clea p291-652 **Fic**

Durso, Joseph
Amazing: the miracle of the Mets **796.357**

Dusk. Saki
In Saki. The short stories of Saki p331-35 **S C**

Dussek, Jan Ladislav
See pages in the following book:
Chapin, V. Giants of the keyboard p45-49
920

The **dust** of death. Asimov, I.
In Asimov, I. Asimov's mysteries p96-107 **S C**

Dust rag. Clement, H.
In Asimov, I. ed. Where do we go from here? p300-24 **S C**

The **dusty** drawer. Muheim, H.
In Hitchcock, A. ed. Alfred Hitchcock presents: A month of mystery p3-18 **S C**

Dutch, Robert A.
The Original Roget's Thesaurus of English words and phrases. See The Original Roget's Thesaurus of English words and phrases 424

The **Dutch** and English on the Hudson. Goodwin, M. W. **974.7**

Dutch art. See Art, Dutch

Dutch in the United States
Goodwin, M. W. The Dutch and English on the Hudson **974.7**

Dutch painters. See Painters, Dutch
Dutch painting. See Painting, Dutch

Dutton, Brian
(comp.) Cassell's New compact Spanish-English, English-Spanish dictionary. See Cassell's New compact Spanish-English, English-Spanish dictionary 463

Dutton, Clarence Edward
See pages in the following book:
Moore, R. The earth we live on p242-57
551.09

Duval, Evelyn Millis
Faith in families **301.42**

Duvall, Sylvanus M.
Before you marry **301.42**

Dvořák, Anton
See pages in the following books:
Bernstein, L. The infinite variety of music p149-69 **780.1**
Cross, M. The Milton Cross New encyclopedia of the great composers and their music p299-317 **920.03**
Ewen, D. ed. The complete book of classical music p782-98 **780.1**
Ewen, D. ed. The world of great composers p363-72 **920**

Dwellings. See Architecture, Domestic; Houses

Dwiggins, Don
Bailout **797.5**

The **Dybbuk.** Ansky, S.
In Cerf, B. A. comp. Sixteen famous European plays p259-300 **808.82**
In Dickinson, T. H. ed. Chief contemporary dramatists; 3d ser. p605-38 **808.82**
In Gassner, J. ed. Twenty best European plays on the American stage p626-54 **808.82**

A **dying** man's confession. Twain, M.
In Twain, M. The complete short stories of Mark Twain p225-39 **S C**

The **dying** night. Asimov, I.
In Asimov, I. Asimov's mysteries p54-79 **S C**
In Asimov, I. Nine tomorrows p86-112 **S C**

Dykeman, Wilma
The border states **917.5**

Dylan, Bob
See pages in the following books:
Ewen, D. Great men of American popular song p347-61 **920**
Shaw, A. The rock revolution p51-79 **781.5**

Dynamics. See Force and energy

Dynamo. O'Neill, E.
In O'Neill, E. Plays v3 p421-89 **812**

E

ESP. See Extrasensory perception
ESP: a scientific evaluation. Hansel, C. E. M. **133.8**

Easter Island
Dos Passos, J. Easter Island   919.6
See also pages in the following book:
Stefánsson, V. ed. Great adventures and explorations p89-106   910.9

Antiquities
Heyerdahl, T. Aku-aku   572.996

The **Easter** of the soul. Henry, O.
In Henry, O. The complete works of O. Henry p1319-23   **S C**

The **Easter** procession. Solzhenitsyn, A.
In Solzhenitsyn, A. Stories and prose poems p125-31   **S C**

Eastern and Western Europe in the Middle Ages   940.1

Eastern churches. See Orthodox Eastern Church

Eastern Empire. See Byzantine Empire

Eastern question (Far East)
See pages in the following book:
Fish, C. R. The path of empire p218-39   327.73

Eastlake, William
The biggest thing since Custer
In Abrahams, W. ed. Fifty years of the American short story v 1 p243-53   **S C**
In Prize stories, 1970: The O. Henry Awards p17-28   **S C**
The dancing boy
In The Best American short stories, 1971 p107-17   **S C**
A long day's dying
In The Best American short stories, 1964 p109-23   **S C**
In Foley, M. ed. Fifty best American short stories p785-98   **S C**

Eastman, Max
Anthology for Enjoyment of poetry
In Eastman, M. Enjoyment of poetry, with Anthology for Enjoyment of poetry v2   808.1
Enjoyment of poetry, with Anthology for Enjoyment of poetry   808.1

Eastman Kodak Company, Rochester, N.Y.
Close-up photography   778.3
Home movies made easy   778.5
How to make good pictures   770.2

An **easy** introduction to the slide rule. Asimov, I.   510.78

Easy money. Poverman, H.
In The Best short plays of 1958-1959 p147-65   808.82

Easy motorcycle riding. Wallach, T.   629.28

Eaton, William J.
(jt. auth.) Cormier, F. Reuther   92

Eban, Abba
Voice of Israel   956.94

Ebenstein, William
Today's isms   335

Eberhard, Mary Jane West
(jt. auth.) Evans, H. E. The wasps   595.7

Eble, Kenneth
F. Scott Fitzgerald   813.09

Ebony
The Negro handbook   301.451
The white problem in America   323.4

The **Ebony** cookbook: a date with a dish. De Knight, F.   641.5

The **Ecclesiazusae.** Aristophanes
In Oates, W. J. ed. The complete Greek drama v2 p1007-53   882.08

The **echo.** Bowles, P.
In Abrahams, W. ed. Fifty years of the American short story v 1 p102-15   **S C**

The **echo** of Greece. Hamilton, E.   880.9

Eckert, Allan W.
The great auk   **Fic**

The **ecological** conscience. Disch, R. ed.   301.3

Ecology
Amos, W. H. The life of the pond   574.92
Bates, M. The forest and the sea   574.5
Bates, M. Man in nature   573
Carr, A. The land and wildlife of Africa   574.9
Carson, R. Silent spring   632
Disch, R. ed. The ecological conscience   301.3
Dubos, R. So human an animal   301.3
Ecotactics: the Sierra Club handbook for environment activists   333.7
Farb, P. Ecology   574.5
Graham, F. Since Silent spring   632
Halacy, D. S. Habitat   574.5
Ketchum, R. M. The secret life of the forest   574.5
Larson, P. Deserts of America   551.4
Scientific American. The biosphere   551
See also pages in the following book:
Ehrlich, P. R. Population, resources, environment p157-67   301.3
See also Adaptation (Biology); Botany —Ecology

Economic assistance
Myrdal, G. The challenge of world poverty   338.91
See also pages in the following books:
Bowles, C. ed. The conscience of a liberal p79-118   327.73
Douglas, W. O. International dissent: six steps toward world peace p72-96   341.6
Ehrlich, P. R. Population, resources, environment p295-310   301.3
Fulbright, J. W. The arrogance of power p223-41   327.73
Paddock, W. Famine—1975! p205-29   338.1
United States. Department of Agriculture. Farmer's world p495-508   338.1
See also Underdeveloped areas

Economic assistance, Domestic
Davis, K. S. ed. The paradox of poverty in America   330.973
Gladwin, T. Poverty U.S.A.   330.973
See also pages in the following book:
Bernstein, S. Alternatives to violence p67-88   301.43
See also Poverty

Economic botany. See Botany, Economic

Economic conditions
See pages in the following books:
Foreign Policy Association. Toward the year 2018 p148-64   901.9

Education—*Continued*

The New Cambridge Modern history v10 p104-20, v11 p177-203 **909**

Tagore, R. A Tagore reader p205-23 **891.4**

Toffler, A. Future shock p352-78 **301.24**

See also Audio-visual education; Correspondence schools and courses; Culture; Illiteracy; International education; Scholarhip, fellowships, etc.; Students; Teachers; Vocational education; and names of special classes of people and social and ethnic groups with the subdivision Education, e.g. Deaf—Education; Negroes—Education

Africa, South
See pages in the following book:

Cole, E. House of bondage p96-109 **301.451**

Aims and objectives

Parker, D. H. Schooling for what? **370.1**

Silberman, C. E. Crisis in the classroom **370**

See also pages in the following book:

Gross, B. ed. Radical school reform p98-106 **370.8**

Assyria
See pages in the following book:

Saggs, H. W. F. Everyday life in Babylonia & Assyria p72-87 **913.35**

Atlantic States
See pages in the following book:

Bowen, E. The Middle Atlantic States p151-56 **917.4**

Babylonia
See pages in the following book:

Saggs, H. W. F. Everyday life in Babylonia & Assyria p72-87 **913.35**

China (People's Republic of China)
See pages in the following book:

Snow, E. Red China today p226-42 **915.1**

Curricula
See pages in the following book:

Gross, B. ed. Radical school reform p161-78 **370.8**

Europe
See pages in the following books:

Mills, D. The Middle Ages p252-66 **940.1**

The New Cambridge Modern history v2 p414-37, v8 p143-73, v9 p179-208 **909**

Experimental methods

Ashton-Warner, S. Teacher **371.9**

See also pages in the following book:

Gross, B. ed. Radical school reform p178-89, 227-73 **370.8**

Finance

Angel, J. L. How and where to get scholarships & loans **378.3**

France
See pages in the following book:

Carroll, J. T. The French p121-37 **914.4**

Germany (Federal Republic)
See pages in the following book:

Walton, H. Germany p122-30 **914.3**

Great Britain
See pages in the following books:

Ashley, M. Life in Stuart England p121-31 **914.2**

Bagley, J. J. Life in medieval England p89-106 **914.2**

Davis, W. S. Life in Elizabethan days p106-30 **914.2**

Shakespeare's England v 1 p224-50 **822.3**

Silberman, C. E. Crisis in the classroom p207-64 **370**

Williams, P. Life in Tudor England p120-38 **914.2**

Greece
See pages in the following books:

Mills, D. The book of the ancient Greeks p221-31 **938**

Robinson, C. E. Everyday life in ancient Greece p139-50 **915.38**

History
See pages in the following books:

The New Cambridge Modern history v3 p427-52 **909**

Rowling, M. Everyday life in medieval times p135-54 **914**

Tomkeieff, O. G. Life in Norman England p105-16 **914.2**

Ireland
See pages in the following book:

Lyons, F. S. L. Ireland since the famine p76-86, 633-46 **941.5**

Israel
See pages in the following book:

Feigenbaum, L. H. Israel: crossroads of conflict p72-79 **915.694**

Italy
See pages in the following book:

Bryant, A. The Italians p130-36 **914.5**

Kenya
See pages in the following book:

Roberts, J. S. A land full of people p177-97 **916.76**

New England
See pages in the following book:

McCarthy, J. New England p138-48 **917.4**

Philosophy

Dewey, J. John Dewey on education **370.1**

Holt, J. What do I do Monday? **370.1**

Rome
See pages in the following books:

Davis, W. S. A day in old Rome p189-204 **913.37**

Mills, D. The book of the ancient Romans p317-30 **937**

Russia
See pages in the following books:

Koutaissoff, E. The Soviet Union p141-77 **914.7**

Salisbury, H. E. ed. The Soviet Union: the fifty years p79-124 **914.7**

Study and teaching
See Teachers—Training

United States

Gross, B. ed. Radical school reform **370.8**

Herndon, J. How to survive in your native land **373.2**

Holt, J. What do I do Monday? **370.1**

Lineberry, W. P. ed. New trends in the schools **370.8**

Parker, D. H. Schooling for what? **370.1**

Postman, N. Teaching as a subversive activity **370**

Educational psychology
See pages in the following book:
Dewey, J. John Dewey on education p195-285   370.1

Educational sociology
See pages in the following book:
Dewey, J. John Dewey on education p289-310   370.1

Educational tests and measurements. See Ability—Testing

Educators
Holt, R. Mary McLeod Bethune   92
Kane, H. T. Miracle in the mountains [biography of Martha McChesney Berry]   92
Washington, B. T. Up from slavery   92
See also Teachers

Edward I, King of England
Costain, T. B. The three Edwards   942.03

Edward II, King of England
Costain, T. B. The three Edwards   942.03

Edward III, King of England
Costain, T. B. The three Edwards   942.03

Edward VII, King of Great Britain
Priestley, J. B. The Edwardians   914.2
See also pages in the following book:
Cecil, R. Life in Edwardian England p 1-20   914.2

Edward VIII, King of Great Britain
See pages in the following book:
Leighton, I. ed. The aspirin age, 1919-1941 p364-82   917.3

Edward Mills and George Benton: a tale. Twain, M.
In Twain, M. The complete short stories of Mark Twain p144-49   **S C**

Edward the Second. Marlowe, C.
In Marlowe, C. The plays of Christopher Marlowe p281-369   822

Edwardes, Michael
Everyday life in early India   913.34

Edwardian England, Life in. Cecil, R.   914.2

The Edwardians. Priestley, J. B.   914.2

Edwards, Anne
The survivors   **Fic**

Edwards, Gus
See pages in the following book:
Ewen, D. Great men of American popular song p64-69   920

Edwards, Jonathan
See pages in the following book:
Literary history of the United States p71-81   810.9

Edwards, Junius
Duel with the clock
In Hughes, L. ed. The best short stories by Negro writers p301-08   **S C**
Mother dear and Daddy
In Margolies, E. A native son's reader p205-16   810.8

Edwards, Margaret A.
The fair garden and the swarm of beasts   027.62

Edwards, Paul
(ed.) The Encyclopedia of philosophy. See The Encyclopedia of philosophy   103

Edwards, Sherman
Stone, P. 1776   812

Eel by the tail. Lang, A. K.
In Conklin, G. ed. Invaders of earth p50-66   **S C**

Efficiency, Household. See Home economics

Efficiency, Industrial
See pages in the following book:
United States. Department of Agriculture. Power to produce p317-31   631.3

An egg for the major. Forester, C. S.
In Forester, C. S. Gold from Crete p137-54   **S C**

Eggenberger, David
A dictionary of battles   904

Egotism. Hawthorne, N.
In Hawthorne, N. Hawthorne's Short stories p270-82   **S C**

Egypt
Brander, B. The River Nile   916.2

Antiquities
Casson, L. Ancient Egypt   913.32
Chubb, M. Nefertiti lived here   913.32
Cottrell, L. Five queens of ancient Egypt   913.32
Cottrell, L. Life under the Pharaohs   913.32
Cottrell, L. The lost Pharaohs   913.32
Cottrell, L. The secrets of Tutankhamen's tomb   913.32
Murray, M. A. The splendor that was Egypt   913.32
Wells, E. Nefertiti   92
See also pages in the following books:
Ceram, C. W. Gods, graves, and scholars p75-207   913.03
Ceram, C. W. ed. Hands on the past p111-210   913.03
Durant, W. Our Oriental heritage p137-217   950
Falls, C. B. The first 3000 years: ancient civilizations of the Tigris, Euphrates, and Nile River valleys, and the Mediterranean Sea p55-65, 94-99   913.03
White, A. T. Lost worlds p93-165   913.03

Civilization
Casson, L. Ancient Egypt   913.32
Cottrell, L. Five queens of ancient Egypt   913.32
Cottrell, L. Life under the Pharaohs   913.32
Murray, M. A. The splendor that was Egypt   913.32
See also pages in the following books:
Larousse Encyclopedia of prehistoric and ancient art p123-60   709.01
Sarton, G. A history of science v 1 p19-56   509

Description and travel
Cottrell, L. Egypt   916.2

Fiction
Waltari, M. The Egyptian   **Fic**

History
Horizon Magazine. Pharaohs of Egypt   932
See also pages in the following book:
Hallett, R. Africa to 1875 p73-110   960

History, Military
Cottrell, L. The warrior Pharaohs   932
See also pages in the following book:
Casson, L. Ancient Egypt p61-69   913.32

Eleanor of Acquitaine, consort of Henry II
Kelly, A. Eleanor of Aquitaine and the four kings   **92**
Pernoud, R. Eleanor of Aquitaine   **92**

Eleanor's house. Cather, W.
In Cather, W. Willa Cather's Collected short fiction, 1892-1912 v 1 p95-111   **S C**

Election districts
See pages in the following book:
Fribourg, M. G. The Supreme Court in American history p162-79   **347.9**

Electioneering. See Politics, Practical

Elections
See also Presidents—United States—Election
United States
Scammon, R. M. The real majority   **329**
U.S. politics—inside and out   **329**

Electoral college. See Presidents—United States—Election

Electra. Euripides
In Oates, W. J. ed. The complete Greek drama v2 p67-105   **882.08**

Electra. Giraudoux, J.
In Block, H. M. ed. Masters of modern drama p701-29   **808.82**

Electra. Hofmannsthal, H. van
In Dickson, T. H. ed. Chief contemporary dramatists, 3d ser. p261-86   **808.82**

Electra. Sophocles
In Fitts, D. ed. Greek plays in modern translation p59-105   **882.08**
In Oates, W. J. ed. The complete Greek drama v 1 p505-49   **882.08**

Electric apparatus and appliances
See also Household appliances, Electric
Repairing
See pages in the following book:
Gladstone, B. The New York Times Complete manual of home repair p367-402   **643**

Electric appliances. See Household appliances, Electric

Electric circuits. See Electronic circuits

Electric communication. See Telecommunication

Electric currents, Alternating
See pages in the following book:
Pearce, W. E. Transistors and circuits p78-100   **621.381**

Electric engineering
Buban, P. Understanding electricity and electronics   **621.3**
See also Telegraph
Handbooks, manuals, etc.
Graham, F. D. Audels Handy book of practical electricity with wiring diagrams   **621.302**

Electric household appliances. See Household appliances, Electric

Electric wiring. See Telegraph

Electricity
See pages in the following books:
Coulson, E. H. Test tubes and beakers p62-83   **540.72**
Gamow, G. Biography of physics p124-57   **530.9**
O'Brien, R. Machines p122-42   **621.9**
Thomason, H. The age of invention p194-219   **608**
United Nations Educational, Scientific and Cultural Organization. 700 science experiments for everyone p164-90   **507.2**
See also Magnetism

Electricity in agriculture
See pages in the following books:
Stone, A. A. Careers in agribusiness and industry p299-319   **338.1**
United States. Department of Agriculture. A place to live p222-27   **301.3**
United States. Department of Agriculture. Power to produce p69-86   **631.3**

Electricity on the farm. See Electricity in agriculture

Electromagnetism
See pages in the following books:
Pearce, W. E. Transistors and circuits p34-63   **621.381**
United Nations Educational, Scientific and Cultural Organization. 700 science experiments for everyone p175-83   **507.2**

Electronic apparatus and appliances
Pearce, W. E. Transistors and circuits   **621.381**
Steckler, L. Simple transistor projects for hobbyists & students   **621.381**
See also Electronic computers

Electronic brains. See Electronic computers

Electronic calculating machines. See Electronic computers

Electronic circuits
Steckler, L. Simple transistor projects for hobbyists & students   **621.381**

Electronic computers
Adler, I. Thinking machines   **510.78**
Benice, D. D. Introduction to computers and data processing   **651.8**
Cross, W. A job with a future in computers   **651.8**
Crowley, T. H. Understanding computers   **510.78**
Diebold, J. Man and the computer   **301.24**
Halacy, D. S. Computers—the machines we think with   **510.78**
Nikolaieff, G. A. ed. Computers and society   **510.78**

See also pages in the following books:
Foreign Policy Association. Toward the year 2018 p97-113   **901.9**
Longmore, D. Machines in medicine p121-51   **610**
Morison, E. E. Men, machines, and modern times p76-97   **609**
National Geographic Society. Those inventive Americans p144-53   **608**
Warshofsky, F. The new age of exploration p3-36   **500**
Programming
See Programming (Electronic computers)

Electronic data processing
Benice, D. D. Introduction to computers and data processing   **651.8**
Cross, W. A job with a future in computers   **651.8**
Gildersleeve, T. R. Computer data processing and programming   **651.8**
Halacy, D. S. Computers—the machines we think with   **510.78**
See also pages in the following book:
National Geographic Society. Those inventive Americans p144-53   **608**
See also Mathematics—Electronic data processing
Dictionaries
Rodgers, H. A. Funk & Wagnalls Dictionary of data processing terms **651.803**

Electronics
Buban, P. Understanding electricity and electronics   **621.3**
Pearce, W. E. Transistors and circuits   **621.381**
See also pages in the following book:
National Geographic Society. Those inventive Americans p179-95, 208-17 **608**
See also Electronic apparatus and appliances; Electronic circuits; Electronic computers; High-fidelity sound systems; Transistors
Dictionaries
Funk & Wagnalls Dictionary of electronics   **621.3803**

Electronics for young experimenters. See Pearce. W. E. Transistors and circuits   **621.381**

Electrons
See pages in the following book:
Nourse, A. E. Universe, earth, and atom p532-39   **530.9**
See also Electronics

Elegant, Robert S.
Mao's great revolution   **951.05**

Elegant economy. Templeton, E.
In The New Yorker. Stories from The New Yorker, 1950-1960 p396-412   **S C**

Elementary education. See Education, Elementary

The **elementary** mathematics of the atom. Adler, I.   **539**

Elementary particles (Physics) See Particles (Nuclear physics)

Elements, Chemical. See Chemical elements

The **elements** of style. Strunk, W.   **808**

Eleanora. Poe, E. A.
In Poe, E. A. The complete tales and poems of Edgar Allan Poe p649-53   **S C**
In Poe, E. A. Edgar Allan Poe p95-102   **S C**
In Poe, E. A. Selected poetry and prose p217-22   **818**

The **elephant** shooter. Paton, A.
In Paton, A. Tales from a troubled land p69-76   **S C**

Eleven plays of Henrik Ibsen. Ibsen, H.   **839.8**

Eleven verse plays, 1929-1939. Anderson, M.   **812**

Elgar, Sir Edward William
See pages in the following books:
Cross, M. The Milton Cross New encyclopedia of the great composers and their music p318-29   **920.03**
Ewen, D. ed. The new book of modern composers p160-72   **920**

El-hi Textbooks in print   **016.371**

Elias. Tolstoy, L.
In Tolstoy, L. Short stories v2 p133-37   **S C**

Elijah Muhammed. See Poole, Elijah

Eliot, Alexander
Greece   **914.95**

Eliot, George
Adam Bede   **Fic**
The mill on the Floss   **Fic**
The mill on the Floss; criticism
In Drew, E. The novel: a modern guide to fifteen English masterpieces p127-40   **823.09**
Silas Marner   **Fic**
About
Creeger, G. R. ed. George Eliot   **823.09**
See also pages in the following books:
Karl, F. R. An age of fiction: the nineteenth century British novel p253-93   **823.09**
Wagenknecht, E. Cavalcade of the English novel p319-35   **823.09**

Eliot, John, 1604-1690
Winslow, O. E. John Eliot: "apostle to the Indians"   **92**

Eliot, T. S.
The cocktail party
In Eliot, T. S. The complete plays of T. S. Eliot p123-212   **812**
In Eliot, T. S. Complete poems and plays, 1909-1950 p295-388   **818**
Collected poems (1909-1935)
In Eliot, T. S. Complete poems and plays, 1909-1950   **818**
Collected poems, 1909-1962   **811**
The complete plays of T. S. Eliot   **812**
Contents: Murder in the cathedral; The family reunion; The cocktail party; The confidential clerk; The elder statesman
The complete poems and plays, 1909-1950   **818**
The confidential clerk
In Eliot, T. S. The complete plays of T. S. Eliot p215-91   **812**
The elder statesman
In Eliot, T. S. The complete plays of T. S. Eliot p293-355   **812**
In Eliot, T. S. Complete poems and plays, 1909-1950 p223-94   **818**
The family reunion
In Eliot, T. S. The complete plays of T. S. Eliot p55-122   **812**
Four quartets
In Eliot, T. S. Collected poems, 1909-1962 p173-209   **811**
In Eliot, T. S. The complete poems and plays, 1909-1950 p117-45   **818**

Eliot, T. S.—*Continued*
Murder in the cathedral   812
—Same
   In Eliot, T. S. The complete plays of T. S. Eliot p9-54   812
   In Eliot, T. S. Complete poems and plays, 1909-1950 p173-221   818
   In Tucker, S. M. ed. Twenty-five modern plays p879-903   808.82
Old Possum's book of practical cats
   In Eliot, T. S. Complete poems and plays, 1909-1950 p149-71   818
On poetry and poets   808.1
Poems written in early youth   811
The waste land, and other poems   811

About
Kenner, H. ed. T. S. Eliot   811.09
Tate, A. ed. T. S. Eliot: the man and his work   811.09
   See also pages in the following books:
Durant, W. Interpretations of life p90-101   809
Highet, G. People, places and books p77-85   809
Unger, L. ed. Seven modern American poets p191-228   811.09
Untermeyer, L. Makers of the modern world p650-61   920
Wilson, E. Axel's castle p93-131   809
Eliot, Thomas Stearns. See Eliot, T. S.
The elixir. Nathan, R.   Fic
Elizabeth I, Queen of England
Jenkins, E. Elizabeth the Great   92
Strachey, L. Elizabeth and Essex: a tragic history   92
   See also pages in the following books:
Durant, W. The age of reason begins p3-45   940.2
Horizon Magazine. The Horizon Book of The Elizabethan world p75-107, 379-91   940.2
Lloyd, A. The Spanish centuries p176-85   946
National Geographic Society. The Renaissance p350-91   940.2

Fiction
Irwin, M. Elizabeth, captive princess   Fic
Irwin, M. Young Bess   Fic
Scott, Sir W. Kenilworth   Fic
Elizabeth II, Queen of Great Britain
White, R. M. The royal family   920
Elizabeth, consort of Henry VII, King of England

Fiction
Barnes, M. C. The Tudor rose   Fic
Elizabeth. Jackson, S.
   In Jackson, S. The magic of Shirley Jackson p76-108   818
Elizabeth and Essex: a tragic history. Strachey, L.   92
Elizabeth, captive princess. Irwin, M.   Fic
Elizabeth the queen. Anderson, M.
   In Anderson, M. Eleven verse plays, 1929-1939 v 1   812
Elizabethan days, Life in. Davis, W. S.   914.2

Elizabethan England, The pageant of. Burton, E.   914.2
Elizabethan sea-dogs. Wood, W.   973.1
The Elizabethan world. See Horizon Magazine. The Horizon Book of The Elizabethan world   940.2
The Elizabethans at home. See Burton, E. The pageant of Elizabethan England   914.2
The elk. Poe, E. A.
   In Poe, E. A. Selected poetry and prose p289-93   818
The elk. Saki
   In Saki. The short stories of Saki p401-06   S C
Elkin, Stanley
Perlmutter at the East Pole
   In The Saturday Evening Post. Best modern short stories p172-99   S C
The transient
   In The Best American short stories, 1965 p57-91   S C
Ellacott, S. E.
A history of everyday things in England: 1914-1968
   In A History of everyday things in England v5   914.2
Ellin, Stanley
The nine-to-five man
   In Mystery Writers of America. Crime without murder p47-62   S C
Ellington, Duke
   See pages in the following book:
Williams, M. The jazz tradition p87-106   781.5
Elliott, George P.
The NRACP
   In Foley, M. ed. Fifty best American short stories, 1915-1965 p407-37   S C
Elliott, H. Chandler
The shape of intelligence   153
Elliott, Lawrence
George Washington Carver   92
The legacy of Tom Dooley   362.1
Ellis, William
A narrative of a tour through Hawaii; excerpt
   In Day, A. G. ed. The spell of Hawaii p129-43   919.69
Ellison, John W.
(comp.) Nelson's Complete concordance of the Revised standard version Bible. See Nelson's Complete concordance of the Revised standard version Bible   220.2
Ellison, Ralph
Flying home
   In Hughes, L. ed. The best short stories by Negro writers p151-70   S C
Invisible man   Fic
The invisible man; criticism
   In Margolies, E. Native sons p127-48   810.9
Riot
   In Margolies, E. A native son's reader p184-202   810.8
Elly. Faulkner, W.
   In Faulkner, W. Collected stories of William Faulkner p207-14   S C

Elocution. See Public speaking

An eloquence of grief. Crane, S.
  In Crane, S. The complete short stories
    & sketches of Stephen Crane p321-
    22   **S C**

Elpenor. MacLeish, A.
  In MacLeish, A. Collected poems, 1917-
    1952 p327-41   **811**

Elsie in New York. Henry, O.
  In Henry, O. The complete works of O.
    Henry p1478-83   **S C**

Elsner, Robert Wellington
  See pages in the following book:
  Behrman, D. The new world of the oceans
    p36-45   **551.4**

Elton, G. R.
  (ed.) The Reformation, 1520-1559
  In The New Cambridge Modern history
    v2   **909**

Elvie Burdette. Schaefer, J.
  In Schaefer, J. The collected stories of
    Jack Schaefer p148-65   **S C**

Ely, David
  The academy
  In The Best American short stories,
    1966 p59-68   **S C**

The **emancipation** of Billy. Henry, O.
  In Henry, O. The complete works of
    O. Henry p469-77   **S C**

Emancipation of slaves. See Slavery in the
  United States

Emancipation of women. See Woman—
  Rights of women

The **embarkment** for Cythera. Cheever, J.
  In Abrahams, W. ed. Fifty years of the
    American short story v 1 p182-207
                                              S C

The **embezzler.** Auchincloss, L.   **Fic**

Embree, Ainslie T.
  (ed.) Asia Society. Asia: a guide to paper-
    backs   **016.95**

Embroidery
  Bucher, J. The complete guide to embroid-
    ery stitches and crewel   **746.4**

Embryology. See Reproduction

Emergencies. See First aid in illness and injury

Emergency medical guide. Henderson, J.
                                              614.8

The **emerging** Japanese superstate: challenge
  and response. Kahn, H.   **309.152**

The **emerging** nations: their growth and
  United States policy. Millikan, M. F. ed.
                                              309.2

The **emerging** South. Clark, T. D.   **917.5**

Emerson, Ralph Waldo
  Essays, first and second series   **814**
  Journals. Abridged   **92**
  Poems of Ralph Waldo Emerson   **811**

About

  Derleth, A. Emerson, our contemporary
                                              92
  Konvitz, M. R. ed. Emerson   **818**
  See also pages in the following books:
  Brooks, V. The flowering of New England
    p203-16, 261-76   **810.9**
  Literary history of the United States p358-
    87   **810.9**
  Thomas, H. Understanding the great
    philosophers p315-23   **109**

Emery, Raymond C.
  High interest—easy reading for junior and
    senior high school reluctant readers
                                              028.52

Emigration. See Immigration and emigration

Emma. Austen, J.   **Fic**

Emmet Dutrow. Schaefer, J.
  In Schaefer, J. The collected stories of
    Jack Schaefer p33-47   **S C**

Emmett, Daniel Decatur
  See pages in the following book:
  Ewen, D. Great men of American popular
    song p14-22   **920**

Emotionally disturbed children. See Problem children

Emotions
  See pages in the following books:
  Gagarin, Y. Survival in space p91-121
                                              629.45
  Sargent, S. S. Basic teachings of the great
    psychologists p193-210   **150**
  Sugarman, D. A. The Seventeen Guide to
    knowing yourself p85-100, 116-78 **155.5**
  See also Love

The **Emperor** Jones. O'Neill, E.
  In Block, H. M. ed. Masters of modern
    drama p575-86   **808.82**
  In Dickinson, T. H. ed. Chief contempo-
    rary dramatists, 3d ser. p 1-20
                                           808.82
  In O'Neill, E. The Emperor Jones, Anna
    Christie [and] The hairy ape p 1-
    58   **812**
  In O'Neill, E. Nine plays p3-35   **812**
  In O'Neill, E. Plays v3 p173-204   **812**
  In O'Neill, E. Selected plays of Eugene
    O'Neill   **812**
  In Six modern American plays p 1-31
                                           812.08

The **Emperor** Jones, Anna Christie [and]
  The hairy ape. O'Neill, E.   **812**

Emperors. See Kings and rulers; Roman
  emperors; also names of individual emperors, e.g. Peter I, the Great, Emperor of Russia

The **empire** of the ants. Wells, H. G.
  In Wells, H. G. The complete short sto-
    ries of H. G. Wells p92-108   **S C**
  In Wells, H. G. 28 science fiction stories
    p269-85   **S C**

Empiricism
  See pages in the following book:
  Schneider, H. W. A history of American
    philosophy p431-91   **191**

Employees
                Training
  See Apprentices

Employment. See Negroes—Employment

Employment discrimination. See Discrimination in employment

Employment of women. See Woman—Employment

Employment opportunities abroad. Lederer,
  W. J.
  In Lederer, W. J. The ugly American
    p77-82   **S C**

Empresses. See Queens

The **empty** drum. Tolstoy, L.
In Tolstoy, L. Short stories v2 p222-30
S C
In Tolstoy, L. Twenty-three tales p231-40
S C
An **empty** spoon. Decker, S. 371.9
Emrich, Duncan
(comp.) The folklore of weddings and marriage 392
Enamel paints. See Varnish and varnishing
Encarnacion, Rosario de Jesus
See pages in the following book:
Roland, A. Profiles from the new Asia p112-32 920
Encarnacion, Silvino
See pages in the following book:
Roland, A. Profiles from the new Asia p112-32 920
In Cather, W. Willa Cather's Collected short fiction, 1892-1912 v 1 p69-77
S C
The **enchanted** kiss. Henry, O.
In Henry, O. The complete works of O. Henry p477-87 S C
The **enchanted** profile. Henry, O.
In Henry, O. The best short stories of O. Henry p96-104 S C
In Henry, O. The complete works of O. Henry p384-89 S C
Enchanting Jenny Lind. Benét, L. 92
An **encounter**. Joyce, J.
In Joyce, J. Dubliners p20-32 S C
An **encounter**. Maupassant, G. de
In Maupassant, G. de. Guy de Maupassant's Short stories p315-22 S C
Encounter groups, Carl Rogers on. Rogers, C. R. 616.89
Encyclopaedia Britannica
Britannica Yearbook of science and the future. See Britannica Yearbook of science and the future 505
Encyclopaedia Britannica 031
Encyclopaedia Britannica World atlas. See Britannica atlas 912
Encyclopaedia Britannica World atlas international. See Britannica atlas 912
Encyclopaedia of the social sciences 303
Encyclopaedia of world literature, Cassell's 803
The **Encyclopedia** Americana 031
Encyclopedia international 031
Encyclopedia of American automobiles. Georgano, G. N. ed. 629.22
The **encyclopedia** of American facts and dates. Carruth, G. ed. 973.03
Encyclopedia of American history. Morris, R. B. ed. 973.03
Encyclopedia of ancient and medieval history, Larousse 909
Encyclopedia of ancient Greek civilization, Praeger 913.3803
Encyclopedia of animal life, The Larousse 591
Encyclopedia of astronomy, Larousse. Rudaux, L. 520.3
Encyclopedia of Byzantine and medieval art 709.02
Encyclopedia of child care and guidance, The New 649

Encyclopedia of English and American poets and poetry, The concise. Spender, S. ed. 821.03
Encyclopedia of golf, Golf Magazine's 796.352
Encyclopedia of homemaking ideas, The complete. Bradford, B. T. 640
The **encyclopedia** of jazz in the sixties. Feather, L. 781.503
The **encyclopedia** of jazz, The new edition of. Feather, L. 781.503
Encyclopedia of mathematics, The Universal 510.3
The **encyclopedia** of military history. Dupuy, R. E. 355.09
Encyclopedia of modern architecture 724.903
Encyclopedia of modern art, Larousse 709.03
Encyclopedia of modern history, from 1500 to the present day, Larousse 909
Encyclopedia of modern literature, The Concise 803
Encyclopedia of mythology, New Larousse 291.03
The **encyclopedia** of oceanography. Fairbridge, R. W. ed. 551.4
The **Encyclopedia** of philosophy 103
Encyclopedia of prehistoric and ancient art, Larousse 709.01
Encyclopedia of Renaissance and Baroque art, Larousse 709.03
Encyclopedia of science and technology, McGraw-Hill 503
Encyclopedia of science, The Harper 503
Encyclopedia of skiing, Ski Magazine's. Ski Magazine 796.9
Encyclopedia of space, The McGraw-Hill 629.403
The **encyclopedia** of sports. Menke, F. G. 796.03
The **Encyclopedia** of the biological sciences 570.3
Encyclopedia of the earth, Larousse. Bertin, L. 550
Encyclopedia of the great composers and their music, The Milton Cross New. Cross, M. 920.03
Encyclopedia of the life sciences 574.03
Encyclopedia of the modern world, Harper 909.08
Encyclopedia of the nations, Worldmark 910.3
Encyclopedia of the opera. See Ewen, D. The new Encyclopedia of the opera 782.103
Encyclopedia of the social sciences, International 303
The **encyclopedia** of witchcraft and demonology. Robbins, R. H. 133.4
Encyclopedia of world art 703
An **encyclopedia** of world history. Langer, W. L. ed 902
Encyclopedias and dictionaries
Chambers's encyclopaedia 032
Collier's encyclopedia 031
The Columbia encyclopedia 031
The Columbia-Viking Desk encyclopedia 031
Compton's Encyclopedia and fact index 031

English poetry—Collections—*Continued*

Benét, W. R. ed. An anthology of famous English and American poetry   821.08

Brinnin, J. M. ed. Twentieth century poetry: American and British (1900-1970)   821.08

Brooks, C. ed. Understanding poetry   821.08

Ciardi, J. ed. How does a poem mean?   821.08

Coffin, C. M. ed. The major poets: English and American   821.08

Cole, W. ed. A book of love poems   821.08

Cole, W. ed. The fireside book of humorous poetry   821.08

Eastman, M. Enjoyment of poetry, with Anthology for Enjoyment of poetry   808.1

Engle, P. ed. Poet's choice   821.08

Felleman, H. ed. Poems that live forever   821.08

Nash, O. ed. Everybody ought to know   821.08

The Oxford Book of English verse, 1250-1918   821.08

The Oxford Book of light verse   821.08

The Oxford Book of medieval English verse   821.08

The Oxford Book of modern verse, 1892-1935   821.08

The Oxford Book of nineteenth-century English verse   821.03

The Oxford Book of seventeenth century verse   821.08

Palgrave, F. T. comp. The golden treasury of the best songs & lyrical poems in the English language   821.08

Reeves, J. ed. The Cassell Book of English poetry   821.08

Sitwell, E. ed. The Atlantic book of British and American poetry   821.08

Stevenson, B. E. comp. The home book of modern verse   821.08

Stevenson, B. E. comp The home book of verse, American and English   821.08

Untermeyer, L. ed. Modern American poetry [and] Modern British poetry   821.03

Untermeyer, L. ed. Modern British poetry   821.08

Untermeyer, L. ed. A treasury of great poems: English and American   821.08

Van Doren, M. Introduction to poetry   821.08

Williams, O. ed. A little treasury of British poetry   821.08

Williams, O. ed. A little treasury of great poetry, English and American, from Chaucer to the present day   821.08

Williams, O. ed. A little treasury of modern poetry, English & American   821.08

Dictionaries

Spender, S. ed. The concise encyclopedia of English and American poets and poetry   821.03

History and criticism

Drew, E. Discovering poetry   808.1

Drew, E. Poetry: a modern guide to its understanding and enjoyment   808.1

Rosenthal, M. L. The new poets   821.09

Untermeyer, L. The forms of poetry   808.1

Untermeyer, L. Lives of the poets   920

Untermeyer, L. The paths of poetry   920

Van Doren, M. Introduction to poetry   821.08

See also pages in the following books:

Auslander, J. The winged horse p127-332, 365-413   809.1

Daiches, D. More literary essays p 1-18   820.9

Horizon Magazine. The Horizon Book of The Elizabethan world p248-55   940.2

Macy, J. The story of the world's literature p295-310, 334-52, 382-98   809

English poets. See Poets, English

English pottery. See Pottery, English

English prose literature

History and criticism

See pages in the following book:

Macy, J. The story of the world's literature p311-14, 320-33, 370-81   809

English-Russian dictionary. Müller, V. K. comp.   491.7

English social history. Trevelyan, G. M.   942

English social history, Illustrated. Trevelyan, G. M.   942

English wit and humor

See pages in the following book:

Daiches, D. More literary essays p19-41   820.9

Engraving

See pages in the following book:

Brown, L. A. Map making p100-18   526.8

Engravings

Museum of Graphic Art. American printmaking, the first 150 years   769

Enjoyment of poetry, with Anthology for Enjoyment of poetry. Eastman, M.   808.1

Enlightenment, Age of. Gay, P.   901.93

Enoch Pratt Free Library, Baltimore, Md. Reference books   016

The enormous radio. Cheever, J. *In* Foley, M. ed. Fifty best American short stories, 1915-1965 p387-96   S C

Enos Carr. Schaefer, J. *In* Schaefer, J. The collected stories of Jack Schaefer p468-84   S C

Enough rope. Parker, D. *In* Parker, D. The collected poetry of Dorothy Parker p3-89   811

Enrichment mathematics for high school. National Council of Teachers of Mathematics   510

Ensana, Joel Please, no flowers *In* The Best short plays, 1969 p321-42   808.82

Ensigns. See Flags

The enterprising Americans: a business history of the United States. Chamberlain, J.   330.973

Entertainers

Davis, S. Yes I can   92

See also Dancers

Entertaining
See pages in the following books:
Good Housekeeping Institute, New York. The new Good Housekeeping cookbook p54-75   **641.5**
Haupt, E. A. The Seventeen Book of etiquette & entertaining p257-90   **395**
Post, E. L. The Emily Post Book of etiquette for young people p198-233 **395**
Vogue's Book of etiquette and good manners p321-424   **395**
   See also Etiquette; Games; Showers (Parties)

Entomology. See Insects

Entomology, Economic. See Insects, Injurious and beneficial

Entrance requirements for colleges and universities. See Colleges and universities—Entrance requirements

Entrapping a lady. Orczy, Baroness
In Dulles, A. ed. Great spy stories from fiction p105-15   **S C**

Environment. See Adaptation (Biology); Anthropogeography; Man—Influence of environment

Environment and state. See Environmental policy

Environmental careers, Opportunities in. Fanning, O.   **614.069**

Environmental policy

United States
Fanning, O. Opportunities in environmental careers   **614.069**
McClellan, G. S. ed. Protecting our environment   **614**
McHarg, I. L. Design with nature   **711**
Our poisoned planet: can we save it? **614**
Ridgeway, J. The politics of ecology **301.3**
  See also pages in the following books:
Disch, R. ed. The ecological conscience p130-40, 154-68   **301.3**
United States. Department of Agriculture. Contours of change p213-29   **630**

Enzymes
See pages in the following books:
Asimov, I. The chemicals of life p17-92   **612**
Asimov, I. Life and energy p240-60   **612**

Eolithic period. See Stone age

Ephrata Community
See pages in the following book:
Langdon, W. C. Everyday things in American life, 1607-1776 p74-86   **917.3**

The epic of America. Adams, J. T.   **973**

Epic of industry. Keir, M.
In Pageant of America v5   **973**

The epic of Latin America. Crow, J. A. **980**

An epic of treasure recovery. Davis, R. H.
In Armstrong, R. ed. Treasure and treasure hunters   **910.4**

Epic poetry
History and criticism
See pages in the following books:
Auslander, J. The winged horse p79-88   **809.1**
Highet, G. The classical tradition p144-61   **809**

Epictetus
See pages in the following books:
Hamilton, E. The echo of Greece p157-68   **880.9**
Thomas, H. Understanding the great philosophers p141-51   **109**

Epicurus
See pages in the following book:
Thomas, H. Understanding the great philosophers p129-40   **109**

Epigrams. See Quotations

Episcopal Church. See Protestant Episcopal Church in the U.S.A.

An episode of sparrows. Godden, R.   **Fic**

An episode of war. Crane, S.
In Crane, S. The complete short stories & sketches of Stephen Crane p653-56   **S C**

Epithets. See Names

Epstein, Benjamin R.
The radical Right   **323.2**

Equal in Paris. Baldwin, J.
In Engle, P. ed. On creative writing p109-25   **808.02**

Equality
See pages in the following books:
Arnold, M. The portable Matthew Arnold p573-608   **828**
Myrdal, G. The challenge of world poverty p49-77   **338.91**
  See also Social classes

Equiano, Olaudah
The life of Olaudah Equiano or Gustavus Vassa, the African
In Bontemps, A. ed. Great slave narratives p 1-192   **920**

Era of colonization 1492-1689. Hart, A. B. ed.
In Hart, A. B. ed. American history told by contemporaries v 1   **973**

The era of Franklin D. Roosevelt. Brogan, D. W.   **973.917**

The era of Theodore Roosevelt, 1900-1912. Mowry, G. E.   **973.91**

The era of violence. See Mowat, C. L. ed. The shifting balance of world forces, 1898-1945   **909**

Erasmus, Desiderius
See pages in the following books:
Durant, W. The Reformation p271-92, 427-37   **940.2**
Russell, B. A history of Western philosophy p512-22   **109**

Eric Hermannson's soul. Cather, W.
In Cather, W. Willa Cather's Collected short fiction, 1892-1912 v3 p359-79   **S C**

Erie, Lake, Battle of, 1813
See pages in the following books:
Armstrong, O. K. The fifteen decisive battles of the United States p99-119   **973**

Ernst, Earle
The Kabuki theatre   **792.09**

Ernst, Morris L.
Censorship: the search for the obscene   **343**

Erosion
See pages in the following book:
Leopold, L. B. Water p74-101   551.4
United States. Department of Agriculture. Water p121-59   631.7
See also Soil conservation

Errors of Santa Claus. Leacock, S.
In Becker, M. L. ed. The home book of Christmas p479-82   394.26

Ervine, St John
The burial
In Garrity, D. A. ed. 44 Irish short stories p86-90   S C
John Ferguson
In Tucker, S. M. ed. Twenty-five modern plays p527-71   808.82

Esarhaddon, king of Assyria. Tolstoy, L.
In Tolstoy, L. Short stories v2 p231-37   S C
In Tolstoy, L. Twenty-three tales p256-63   S C

Escape! Asimov, I.
In Asimov, I. I, robot p146-69   S C

Escape. Galsworthy, J.
In Galsworthy, J. Plays p607-38   822

The **escape.** Mansfield, K.
In Mansfield, K. The short stories of Katherine Mansfield p431-36   S C

Escape from freedom. Fromm, E.   323.4

Escapes
Brickhill, P. The great escape   940.54
Rawicz, S. The long walk   910.4
Roscoe, T. True tales of bold escapes   904

Fiction
Westheimer, D.   Von Ryan's Express   Fic

Eskimo pies. Somerlott, R.
In The Best American short stories, 1965 p291-98   S C

Eskimos
See pages in the following books:
Josephy, A. M. The Indian heritage of America p57-64   970.1
Ley, W. The Poles p129-42   919.8
National Geographic Society. Vanishing peoples of the earth p132-51   572
Smith, R. A. The frontier states: Alaska [and] Hawaii p33-53   917.3

Social life and customs
Freuchen, P. Peter Freuchen's Adventures in the Arctic   919.8

Eskow, Seymour
Barron's Guide to the two-year colleges. See Barron's Guide to the two-year colleges   378.73

Esmé. Saki
In Saki. The short stories of Saki p111-16   S C

An **Esmeralda** of Rocky Canon. Harte, B.
In Harte, B. The best short stories of Bret Harte p316-31   S C

Espenshade, Edward B.
(ed.) Goode, J. P. Goode's World atlas   912

Esperanto
See pages in the following book:
Pei, M. Talking your way around the world p114-27   418

Espionage. See Spies

The **Esquimau** maiden's romance. Twain, M.
In Twain, M. The complete short stories of Mark Twain p294-307   S C

Esquire
Esquire Good grooming for men   646.7

Essay and general literature index   080

Essays
Indexes
Essay and general literature index   080

Essays, first and second series. Emerson, R. W.   814

The **essays** of Elia and The last essays of Elia. Lamb, C.   824

Essays on Shakespeare. Chapman, G. W. ed.   822.3

Essex, Robert Devereux, Earl of
Strachey, L. Elizabeth and Essex: a tragic history   92

Esslin, Martin
(ed.) Samuel Beckett   848

Estate planning
See pages in the following book:
Smith, C. The Time-Life Book of family finance p362-85   339.4

Este, Beatrice d', Duchess of Milan
See pages in the following book:
Horizon Magazine. The Horizon Book of the Renaissance p361-68   940.2

Este, Isabella d', Marchioness of Mantua
See pages in the following book:
Horizon Magazine. The Horizon Book of the Renaissance p361-68   940.2

Estenssoro, Victor Paz. See Paz Estenssoro, Victor, President Bolivia

Esther Kreindel the second. Singer, I. B.
In The Saturday Evening Post. Best modern short stories p157-71   S C

Esthetics
Eastman, M. Enjoyment of poetry, with Anthology for Enjoyment of poetry   808.1
Faulkner, R. Art today   700
See also pages in the following book:
Dewey, J. John Dewey on education p141-65   370.1
See also Art

Esty, Katharine
The Gypsies, wanderers in time   397

The **eternal** message of Muhammad. Azzām, 'Abd-al-Rahmān   297

The **eternal** smile. Lagerkvist, P.   S C

The **eternal** smile [short story]. Lagerkvist, P.
In Lagerkvist, P. The eternal smile p7-72   S C

Ethan Brand. Hawthorne, N.
In Hawthorne, N. Hawthorne's Short stories p375-90   S C

Ethan Frome. Davis, O.
In Gassner, J. ed. Best American plays; supplementary volume, 1918-1958 p373-410   812.08

Ethan Frome. Wharton, E.   Fic
also in Wharton, E. The Edith Wharton reader p217-302   S C

An **ethic** for survival. Stevenson, A.   327

Ethics
Schweitzer, A. The teaching of reverence for life 179
See also pages in the following books:
Dewey, J. John Dewey on education p23-38 370.1
Mencken, H. L. The American scene p383-93 818
See also Behavior; Christian ethics; Good and evil; Medical ethics; Sexual ethics; Social ethics

Fiction
Steinbeck, J. The winter of our discontent Fic

Ethics, Legal. See Legal ethics
Ethics, Medical. See Medical ethics
Ethics, Political. See Political ethics
Ethics, Sexual. See Sexual ethics
Ethics, Social. See Social ethics
The **ethics** of pig. Henry, O.
In Henry, O. The complete works of O. Henry p347-54 S C

Ethiopia
See pages in the following books:
Davidson, B. The lost cities of Africa p215-24 913.6
Thompson, E. B. Africa: past and present p96-108 960

Ethnology
Coon, C. S. The living races of man 572
Coon, C. S. The origin of races 572
National Geographic Society. Vanishing peoples of the earth 572
See also pages in the following books:
Benedict, R. Race: science and politics p169-93 572
Wells, H. G. The outline of history p55-123 909
See also Anthropogeography; Costume; Language and languages; Race; Race problems; Society, Primitive; also names of races, tribes, and peoples, e.g. Negroes; and names of countries with the subdivision Social life and customs, e.g. United States—Social life and customs

Polynesia
Heyerdahl, T. Kon-Tiki 910.4
Ethridge, James M.
(ed.) Contemporary authors. See Contemporary authors 920.03
(ed.) Contemporary authors; semi-annual. See Contemporary authors; semi-annual 920.03

Etiquette
Haupt, E. A. The new Seventeen Book of etiquette and young living 395
Haupt, E. A. The Seventeen Book of etiquette & entertaining 395
Post, E. Emily Post's Etiquette 395
Post, E. L. The Emily Post Book of etiquette for young people 395
Post, E. L. The wonderful world of weddings 395
Vanderbilt, A. Amy Vanderbilt's New complete book of etiquette 395

Vogue's Book of etiquette and good manners 395
Wilson, B. The complete book of engagement and wedding etiquette 395
See also pages in the following book:
Archer, E. Let's face it p155-80 646.7

Etrurians
Bloch, R. The Etruscans 913.37
See also pages in the following book:
Payne, R. Ancient Rome p3-23 913.37
Etruscan art. See Art, Etruscan
Etruscans. See Etrurians
The **Etruscans.** Bloch, R. 913.37
Etymology. See English language—Etymology

Euchre
See pages in the following book:
Gibson, W. B. Hoyle's Simplified guide to the popular card games p194-200 795.4

Euclid
See pages in the following book:
Sarton, G. A history of science v2 p35-52 509

Eudoxus
See pages in the following book:
Bell, E. T. Men of mathematics p19-34 920

Eugenics. See Birth control
Eugénie Grandet. Balzac, H. de Fic
Euler, Leonhard
See pages in the following book:
Bell, E. T. Men of mathematics p139-52 920

The **Eumenides.** Aeschylus
In Fitts, D. ed. Greek plays in modern translation p107-43 882.08
In Oates, W. J. ed. The complete Greek drama v 1 p271-307 882.08

Euripides
Alcestis
In Fitts, D. ed. Greek plays in modern translation p297-344 882.08
In Oates, W. J. ed. The complete Greek drama v 1 p677-716 882.08
Andromache
In Oates, W. J. ed. The complete Greek drama v 1 p847-78 882.08
The Bacchae
In Bentley, E. comp. The great playwrights v 1 p227-68 808.82
In Oates, W. J. ed. The complete Greek drama v2 p227-82 882.08
The Cyclops
In Oates, W. J. ed. The complete Greek drama v2 p395-419 882.08
Electra
In Oates, W. J. ed. The complete Greek drama v2 p67-105 882.08
Hecuba
In Oates, W. J. ed. The complete Greek drama v 1 p807-40 882.08
Helen
In Oates, W. J. ed. The complete Greek drama v2 p7-58 882.08
The Heracleidae
In Oates, W. J. ed. The complete Greek drama v 1 p885-912 882.08

European War, 1914-1918—Aerial operations
—*Continued*
Rickenbacker, E. V. Fighting the Flying Circus   940.4
See also pages in the following book:
American Heritage. The American Heritage History of flight p158-95   629.13

Campaigns and battles
See names of battles, campaigns and sieges

Campaigns and battles—Turkey and the Near East
Lawrence, T. E. Seven pillars of wisdom   940.4

Canada
See pages in the following book:
Brebner, J. B. Canada p391-410   971

Causes
Fay, S. B. The origins of the World War   940.3
Parkinson, R. The origins of World War One   940.3
Tuchman, B. W. The Zimmermann telegram   940.3

Fiction
Cather, W. One of ours   Fic
Dos Passos, J. Three soldiers   Fic
Gann, E. K. In the company of eagles   Fic
Hemingway, E. A farewell to arms   Fic
Remarque, E. M. All quiet on the western front   Fic
Sholokhov, M. The silent Don   Fic

Germany
See pages in the following book:
Dill, M. Germany p218-42, 270-78   943

Naval operations
Hough, R. The long pursuit   940.4

Peace
See pages in the following book:
Addams, J. The social thought of Jane Addams p246-61   309.173

Personal narratives
See pages in the following books:
Darrow, D. The story of my life p210-25   92
MacArthur, D. Reminiscences p51-73   92

Sources
Snyder, L. L. ed. Historic documents of World War I   940.3

Switzerland
See pages in the following book:
Martin, W. Switzerland, from Roman times to the present p254-71   949.4

United States
Leuchtenburg, W. E. The perils of prosperity, 1914-32   330.973
Seymour, C. Woodrow Wilson and the World War   973.91
See also pages in the following book:
Hart, A. B. ed. American history told by contemporaries v5 p695-807   973

European War, 1939-1945. See World War, 1939-1945

Eusebius Pamphili, Bp. of Caesarea
See pages in the following book:
Grant, M. The ancient historians p343-57   920

Evacuation of civilizations. See World War, 1939-1945—Evacuation of civilians
Evaluation of literature. See Book reviews; Criticism
Evangeline. Longfellow, H. W.   811

Evans, Alice Catherine
See pages in the following book:
De Kruif, P. Men against death p146-75   920

Evans, Sir Arthur John
Baumann, H. Lion gate and labyrinth   913.38
See also pages in the following book:
White, A. T. Lost worlds p56-83   913.03

Evans, Bergen
A dictionary of contemporary American usage   428
(ed.) Dictionary of quotations   808.88

Evans, Cornelia
(jt. auth.) Evans, B. A dictionary of contemporary American usage   428

Evans, Howard E.
The wasps   595.7

Evans, Ivor H.
Brewer's Dictionary of phrase and fable. See Brewer's Dictionary of phrase and fable   803

Evans, Mary
Costume throughout the ages   391.09
The eve of the Revolution. Becker, C. 973.2

Eveline. Joyce, J.
In Joyce, J. Dubliners p42-48   S C

Everest, Frank K.
The fastest man alive   92

Everest, Mount
Hunt, J. The conquest of Everest   915.4
Tenzing, N. Tiger of the snows   92
Ullman, J. R. Americans on Everest 915.4
See also pages in the following book:
Ullman, J. R. The age of mountaineering p234-85   796.5

Everglades National Park
See pages in the following book:
National Geographic Society. America's wonderlands p420-49   917.3
The everlasting witness. Shedd, M.
In Abrahams, W. ed. Fifty years of the American short story v2 p279-88   S C

Evers, Medgar Wiley
Evers, Mrs M. For us, the living   92
See also pages in the following book:
Metcalf, G. R. Black profiles p195-218 920

Evers, Mrs Medger
For us, the living [biography of Medgar Wiley Evers]   92

Every number wins. Almaz, M.
In The Best short plays, 1968 p183-236   808.82

Everybody loves Joe Bing. Lederer, W. J.
In Lederer, W. J. The ugly American p66-73   S C

Everybody ought to know. Nash, O. ed.   821.08

Everybody was very nice. Benét, S. V.
In Benét, S. V. Selected works of Stephen Vincent Benét v2   818
Everybody's Pepys; abridged. Pepys, S. 92

Everyday life in ancient Crete. Willetts, R. F. **913.39**

Everyday life in ancient Egypt. White, J. M. **913.32**

Everyday life in ancient Greece. Robinson, C. E. **913.38**

Everyday life in ancient Rome. Cowell, F. R. **913.37**

Everyday life in Anglo-Saxon, Viking and Norman times. See Quennell, M. Everyday life in Roman and Anglo-Saxon times **913.42**

Everyday life in Babylonia & Assyria. Saggs, H. W. F. **913.35**

Everyday life in Bible times. National Geographic Society **220.9**

Everyday life in classical Athens. Webster, T. B. L. **913.38**

Everyday life in colonial America. Wright, L. B. **917.3**

Everyday life in early Imperial China. Loewe, M. **913.31**

Everyday life in early India. Edwardes, M. **913.34**

Everyday life in medieval times. Rowling, M. **914**

Everyday life in New Testament times. Bouquet, A. C. **225.9**

Everyday life in Old Testament times. Heaton, E. W. **221.9**

Everyday life in prehistoric times. Quennell, M. **913.03**

Everyday life in Renaissance times. Chamberlin, E. R. **940.2**

Everyday life in Roman and Anglo-Saxon times. Quennell, M. **913.42**

Everyday life in Roman Britain. See Quennell, M. Everyday life in Roman and Anglo-Saxon times **913.42**

Everyday life in Rome in the time of Caesar and Cicero. Treble, H. A. **913.37**

Everyday life in the age of enterprise, 1865-1900. Walker, R. H. **917.3**

Everyday life in the new stone, bronze and early iron age. See Quennell, M. Everyday life in prehistoric times **913.03**

Everyday life in the old stone age. See Quennell, M. Everyday life in prehistoric times **913.03**

Everyday life in the Viking age. Simpson, J. **914.8**

Everyday life in traditional Japan. Dunn, C. J. **915.2**

Everyday things in American life, 1607-1776. Langdon, W. C. **917.3**

Everyday things in American life, 1776-1876. Langdon, W. C. **917.3**

Everyday things in ancient Greece. Quennell, M. **913.38**

Everyman's Dictionary of dates **903**

Everyman's Dictionary of Shakespeare quotations. Shakespeare, W. **822.3**

Everyman's Thesaurus of English words and phrases. Roget, P. **424**

Everyman's United Nations. United Nations. Office of Public Information **341.13**

Everyone but thee and me. Nash, O. **811**

Everyone has ears. Lederer, W. J.
In Lederer, W. J. The ugly American p93-109 **S C**

Everything that rises must converge. O'Connor, F.
In Abrahams, W. ed. Fifty years of the American short story v2 p 1-14 **S C**

Evidence. Asimov, I.
In Asimov, I. I, robot p170-94 **S C**

Evil. See Good and evil

Evil allures, but good endures. Tolstoy, L.
In Tolstoy, L. Short stories v2 p127-29 **S C**

In Tolstoy, L. Twenty-three tales p162-64 **S C**

The evitable conflict. Asimov, I.
In Asimov, I. I, robot p195-218 **S C**

Evolution
Darwin, C. The Darwin reader **574**
De Camp, L. S. The great monkey trial **343**
Horizon Magazine. Charles Darwin and The origin of species **92**
Howell, F. C. Early man **573.2**
Huxley, T. H. On a piece of chalk **575**
Jastrow, R. Red giants and white dwarfs **523.1**
Life (Periodical) The wonders of life on earth **574**
Montagu, A. On being human **301**
Moore, R. Evolution **575**
Moore, R. Man, time, and fossils **573.2**
Scopes, J. T. Center of the storm **343**
Vlahos, O. Human beginnings **573.2**
Zappler, L. The world after the dinosaurs **599**

See also pages in the following books:
Ardrey, R. The territorial imperative p8-17 **591**

Asimov, I. The new intelligent man's guide to science p684-747 **500**

Beadle, G. The language of life p20-46 **575.1**

Carrington, R. The mammals p35-53 **599**

Fried, J. J. The mystery of heredity p129-43 **575.1**

Newman, J. R. ed. What is science? p256-89 **508**

Schneider, H. W. A history of American philosophy p275-371 **191**

Scientific American. Facets of genetics p210-74 **575.1**

See also Adaptation (Biology); Man—Influence of environment; Man—Origin and antiquity; Social change

Evreinov, Nikolai Nikolaevich. See Yevreinov, Nikolai Nikolayevich

Evtushenko, Evgenii Aleksandrovich
See pages in the following books:
Durant, W. Interpretations of life p332-40 **809**

Posell, E. Z. Russian authors p236-53 **920**
For a work by this author see Yevtushensko, Yevgeny

Ewald, Carl
My little boy
In The Scribner treasury p275-314 **S C**

Ewen, David
(ed.) American popular songs   784.03
The Cole Porter story   92
(ed.) The complete book of classical music
  780.1
Composers for the American musical theatre   920
Composers of tomorrow's music   920
(ed.) Composers since 1900   920.03
David Ewen introduces modern music
  780.9
Famous modern conductors   920
George Gershwin: his journey to greatness
  92
(ed.) Great composers, 1300-1900   920.03
Great men of American popular song   920
Leonard Bernstein   92
The life and death of Tin Pan Alley   784
(ed.) The new book of modern composers
  920
New Complete book of the American musical theater   782.8
The new Encyclopedia of the opera
  782.103
(ed.) Popular American composers, from Revolutionary times to the present
  920.03
The story of America's musical theater
  782.8
With a song in his heart; the story of Richard Rodgers   92
(ed.) The world of great composers   920
The world of twentieth century music
  780.1
(jt. auth.) Cross, M. The Milton Cross New encyclopedia of the great composers and their music   920.03
Ewing, Maurice
See pages in the following book:
Behrman, D. The new world of the oceans p234-41   551.4
Ex Parte. Lardner, R.
In Lardner, R. The best short stories of Ring Lardner p179-88   **S C**
In Lardner, R. The Ring Lardner reader p401-11   **S C**
Ex parte Milligan
See pages in the following book:
Fribourg, M. G. The Supreme Court in American history p79-90   347.9
The **exact** science of matrimony. Henry, O.
In Henry, O. The complete works of O. Henry p292-96   **S C**
Exactly eight thousand dollars exactly. O'Hara, J.
In Costain, T. B. ed. Read with me p383-91   **S C**
Examinations
Brownstein, S. Barron's How to prepare for college entrance examinations 371.26
Turner, D. R. Scoring high on college entrance tests   371.26
Excavations (Archeology)
Bibby, G. Looking for Dilmun   913.03
Ceram, C. W. ed. Hands on the past
  913.03
See also pages in the following book:
Deetz, J. Invitation to archaeology p11-19
  913

Israel
Pearlman, M. The Zealots of Masada
  913.33
North America
Ceram, C. W. The first American 913.7
Folsom, F. America's ancient treasures
  913.7074
Except for me and thee. West, J.   **Fic**
Excepting Mrs Pentherby. Saki
In Saki. The short stories of Saki p523-28   **S C**
Exceptional children
West, P. Words for a deaf daughter
  155.45
    See also Gifted children; Problem children; Slow learning children
Exchange. See Commerce
The **executioner.** Lagerkvist, P.
In Lagerkvist, P. The eternal smile p153-206   **S C**
Executive ability
Townsend, R. Up the organization 658.4
Executive power
United States
Cunliffe, M. The American Heritage History of the Presidency   353.03
Pusey, M. J. The way we go to war
  353.03
Rossiter, C. The American Presidency
  353.03
Schlesinger, A. M. Congress and the Presidency: their role in modern times
  353.03
The **executive** secretary: handbook to success. Ingoldsby, P.   651.02
Exercise
Cooper, K. H. Aerobics   613.7
Cooper, K. H. The new Aerobics 613.7
  See also pages in the following books:
Bolian, P. Growing up slim p100-20 613.2
Esquire. Esquire Good grooming for men p101-10   646.7
Seventeen. The Seventeen Book of fashion and beauty p125-44   646.7
  See also Physical education and training; Physical fitness
Exhibitions. See Art, Primitive—Exhibitions
Exile and the kingdom. Camus, A.   **S C**
The **exiles.** Bradbury, R.
In Bradbury, R. The illustrated man p131-45   **S C**
In Bradbury, R. R is for rocket p111-26
  S C
Existentialism
Scott, N. A. The unquiet vision   142
Exodus. Baldwin, J.
In Clarke, J. H. ed. American Negro short stories p197-204   **S C**
Exodus. Uris, L.   **Fic**
Expédition française á l'Himalaya, 1950
Herzog, M. Annapurna   915.4
Experience of the McWilliamses with membranous croup. Twain, M.
In Twain, M. The complete short stories of Mark Twain p99-104   **S C**

An **experiment** in luxury. Crane, S.
In Crane, S. The complete short stories & sketches of Stephen Crane p147-54   **S C**

An **experiment** in misery. Crane, S.
In Crane, S. The complete short stories & sketches of Stephen Crane p139-47   **S C**

Experimental methods in education. See Education—Experimental methods

Experiments for young chemists. See Coulson, E. H. Test tubes and beakers 540.72

Expert driving, The book of. Fales, E. D.   629.28

Expiation. Wharton, E.
In Wharton, E. The collected short stories of Edith Wharton v 1 p438-56   **S C**

The **exploits** of Sherlock Holmes. Doyle, A. C.   **S C**

Explorations. See America—Discovery and exploration; Discoveries (in geography); Explorers

Explorer of the unconscious: Sigmund Freud. Stoutenburg, A.   92

Explorers
Byrd, R. E. Alone   92
Hale, J. R. Age of exploration   910.9
Moorehead, A. The white Nile   962
Morison, S. E. Admiral of the ocean sea; a life of Christopher Columbus   92
Morison, S. E. Christopher Columbus, mariner   92
Stefánsson, V. ed. Great adventures and explorations   910.9
Villiers, A. Captain James Cook   92
See also pages in the following books:
American Heritage. The American Heritage History of the thirteen colonies p50-63   973.2
Horizon Magazine. The Horizon Book of The Elizabethan world p338-53   940.2
Sanderson, I. T. Ivan Sanderson's Book of great jungles p369-472   910.9
Thompson, E. B. Africa: past and present p137-51   960
See also America—Discovery and exploration; Discoveries (in geography); Voyages and travels

Exploring Canada from sea to sea. National Geographic Society   917.1

Exploring the Amazon. Schreider, H.   918

An **explosion** of seven babies. Crane, S.
In Crane, S. The complete short stories & sketches of Stephen Crane p98-99   **S C**

Exports. See Commerce

Express highways. See Roads

Extinct animals
Philip, Duke of Edinburgh. Wildlife crisis   333.7
See also pages in the following book:
Ley, W. Another look at Atlantis, and fifteen other essays p80-89   508

Extinct cities. See Cities and towns, Ruined, extinct, etc.

Extinct plants. See Plants, Fossil

Extract from Captain Stormfield's visit to Heaven. Twain, M.
In Twain, M. The complete short stories of Mark Twain p564-97   **S C**

Extradited from Bohemia. Henry, O.
In Henry, O. The complete works of O. Henry p1343-48   **S C**

Extrasensory perception
Hansel, C. E. M. ESP: a scientific evaluation   133.8
Rhine, L. E. ESP in life and lab   133.8
See also pages in the following book:
Christopher, M. ESP, seers & psychics p8-54   133

Extremism (Political science) See Right and left (Political science)

The **extremists**: gadflies of American society. Archer, J.   973

Eye
Seeman, B. Your sight   612
See also Vision

The **eye** of Allah. Kipling, R.
In Kipling, R. The best short stories of Rudyard Kipling p678-93   **S C**

Eye of Apollo. Chesterton, G. K.
In Chesterton, G. K. The Father Brown omnibus p176-92   **S C**

Eye on the world. Cronkite, W.   909.82

Eyeglasses
See pages in the following books:
Seeman, B. Your sight p183-200   612
Seventeen. The Seventeen Book of fashion and beauty p51-56   646.7

The **eyes.** Wharton, E.
In Wharton, E. The collected short stories of Edith Wharton v2 p115-30   **S C**
In Wharton, E. The Edith Wharton reader   **S C**

Eyes do more than see. Asimov, I.
In Asimov, I. Nightfall, and other stories p334-36   **S C**

Eyvind of the hills. Sigurjónsson, J.
In Dickinson, T. H. ed. Chief contemporary dramatists; 3d ser. p639-73   808.82

Ezra Alcorn and April. Stuart, J.
In Stuart, J. A Jesse Stuart reader p83-95   818

F

FAO. See Food and Agriculture Organization of the United Nations

F.B.I. See United States. Federal Bureau of Investigation

The **FBI** in our open society. Overstreet, H.   353.5

The **FBI's** most famous cases. Tully, A. 353.5

FCC. See United States. Federal Communications Commission

FDA. See Food and Drug Administration

FDR: architect of an era. Tugwell, R. G.   973.917

Faber, Harold
The Kennedy years [biography of John Fitzgerald Kennedy]. See The Kennedy years [biography of John Fitzgerald Kennedy]   92
A fable. Twain, M.
    In Twain, M. The complete short stories of Mark Twain p597-99   S C
Fables
        See pages in the following book:
Highet, G. The anatomy of satire p177-90
                                                      809.7
Fables from Aesop. Rees, E.   398.2
Fabre, J. Henri
    The insect world of J. Henri Fabre 595.7
Fabric pictures. See Collage
Fabrics. See Textile industry and fabrics
The fabulous showman; the life and times of P. T. Barnum. Wallace, I.   92
A fabulous tale. Stockton, R. F.
    In The Best short plays of 1957-1958 p59-80   808.82
The face on the laundry room floor. Chute, B. J.
    In Chute, B. J. One touch of nature, and other stories p189-97   S C
Facetiae. See Anecdotes
Facets of genetics. Scientific American 575.1
Fact book of the countries of the World, The U.S. Department of State. United States. Department of State   910
Factory and trade waste. See Water—Pollution
The facts. Lardner, R.
    In Becker, M. L. ed. The home book of Christmas p143-67   394.26
    In Lardner, R. The Ring Lardner reader p99-122   S C
Facts about the Presidents. Kane, J. N. 920
The facts in the case of M. Valdemar. Poe, E. A.
    In Poe, E. A. The complete tales and poems of Edgar Allan Poe p96-103   S C
    In Poe, E. A. Edgar Allan Poe p268-80   S C
    In Poe, E. A. Selected poetry and prose p315-23   818
The facts in the great beef contract. Twain, M.
    In Twain, M. The complete short stories of Mark Twain p40-45   S C
The facts of life. Maugham, W. S.
    In Maugham, W. S. The best short stories of W. Somerset Maugham p328-48   S C
Facts on File, inc. N.Y. See News dictionary   909.82
Faculty (Education) See Teachers
Fader, Daniel N.
    Hooked on books: program & proof 028.5
Fadiman, Clifton
    (ed.) The American treasury, 1455-1955   810.8
    (ed.) Fantasia mathematica   808.8
    (ed.) The mathematical magpie   808.8
Faeroe Islands. See Faroe Islands
Fail-safe. Burdick, E.   Fic

Fair, Ronald L.
    Life with Red Top
    In Jones, L. ed. Black fire p500-09 810.8
    Miss Luhester gives a party
    In Hughes, L. ed. The best short stories by Negro writers p403-07   S C
Fair employment practice. See Discrimination in employment
The fair garden and the swarm of beasts. Edwards, M. A.   027.62
Fairbairn, Ann
    Five smooth stones   Fic
Fairbank, Alfred
    The story of handwriting   411
Fairbank, John K.
    (jt. auth.) Reischauer, E. O. A history of East Asian civilization   915
Fairbridge, Rhodes W.
    (ed.) The encyclopedia of oceanography   551.4
Fairchild's Dictionary of textiles   677.03
The fairest hour. Johnson, N.
    In Seventeen. Seventeen from Seventeen p65-83   S C
A fairly honourable defeat. Murdoch, I. Fic
Fairs
        See pages in the following books:
Langdon, W. C. Everyday things in American life, 1776-1876 p368-82   917.3
National Geographic Society. Vacationland U.S.A. p258-69   917.3
Fairy tale of Father Brown. Chesterton, G. K.
    In Chesterton, G. K. The Father Brown omnibus p417-31   S C
Fairy tales
    Thurber, J. The 13 clocks   Fic
    Thurber, J. The white deer   Fic
    Thurber, J. The wonderful O   Fic
    Tolkien, J. R. R. The hobbit   Fic
    Tolkien, J. R. R. The lord of the rings Fic
        See also Folklore
The faith healer. Moody, W. V.
    In Quinn, A. H. ed. Representative American plays p771-805   812.08
Faith in families. Duvall, E. M.   301.42
The faithful wife. Callaghan, M.
    In Foley, M. ed. Fifty best American short stories, 1915-1965 p82-86 S C
Faithfull, Starr
        See pages in the following book:
Leighton, I. ed. The aspirin age, 1919-1941 p258-74   917.3
The falcon and the dove; a life of Thomas Becket of Canterbury. Duggan, A.   92
Falconry
        See pages in the following book:
Shakespeare's England v2 p351-66   822.3
Falcons
                Stories
    Murphy, R. The peregrine falcon   Fic
Fales, E. D.
    The book of expert driving   629.28
Falk, Signi Lenea
    Tennessee Williams   812.09
Falkland Islands, Battle of the, 1914
        See pages in the following book:
Hough, R. The long pursuit p135-59 940.4

Falkner, J. Meade
Moonfleet — Fic

Fall, Bernard B.
Anatomy of a crisis — 959.4
Hell in a very small place — 959.7
The two Viet-Nams — 959.7

Fall. See Autumn

The fall. Camus, A. — Fic

The fall of the British Empire. Cross, C. — 942.082

The fall of the city. MacLeish, A.
In Gassner, J. ed. Twenty best plays of the modern American theatre p764-74 — 812.08

The fall of the high-flying Dutchman. Simenon, G.
In Mystery Writers of America. Crime without murder p253-63 — S C

The fall of the House of Usher. Poe, E. A.
In Poe, E. A. The complete tales and poems of Edgar Allan Poe p231-45 — S C
In Poe, E. A. Edgar Allan Poe p244-68 — S C
In Poe, E. A. Selected poetry and prose p115-31 — 818

Falla, Manuel de
See pages in the following books:
Cross, M. The Milton Cross New encyclopedia of the great composers and their music p330-42 — 920.03
Ewen, D. ed. The new book of modern composers p173-84 — 920

Fallacies. See Logic

Fallon, Gabriel
Sean O'Casey: the man I knew — 92

Fallon, Padraic
Something in a boat
In Garrity, D. A. ed. 44 Irish short stories p91-109 — S C

Falls, C. B.
The first 3000 years: ancient civilizations of the Tigris, Euphrates, and Nile River valleys, and the Mediterranean Sea — 913.03

False dawn. Wharton, E.
In Wharton, E. The Edith Wharton reader p513-59 — S C

The false gems. Maupassant, G. de
In Maupassant, G. de. Selected short stories p290-98 — S C

Familiar insects of America. Barker, W. — 595.7

Familiar quotations. Bartlett, J. comp. — 808.88

Family
Duvall, E. M. Faith in families — 301.42
Frazier, E. F. The Negro family in the United States; abridged — 301.451
Lewis, O. The children of Sánchez — 309.172
Mead, M. Family — 301.42
Smith, S. L. Nobody said it's easy — 155.5
See also pages in the following books:
Driver, H. E. Indians of North America p222-41 — 970.1
Handlin, O. The uprooted p227-58 — 325.73
Mead, M. ed. The golden age of American anthropology p495-506 — 572.97
Polenberg, R. ed. America at war p124-39 — 309.173

Schlesinger, A. M. The birth of the Nation p17-32 — 917.3
Toffler, A. Future shock p211-30 — 301.24
See also Marriage; Parent and child

Fiction
Aldrich, B. S. A lantern in her hand — Fic
Bjorn, T. F. Papa's wife — Fic
De La Roche, M. Jalna — Fic
Galsworthy, J. The Forsyte saga — Fic
Saroyan, W. The human comedy — Fic
Wolfe, T. Look homeward, angel — Fic
Wolff, R. A crack in the sidewalk — Fic

Pictures, illustrations, etc.
Mead, M. Family — 301.42

Family budget. See Budgets, Household

Family games America plays. Gibson, W. — 793

Family happiness. Tolstoy, L.
In Tolstoy, L. Short novels v 1 p127-213 — S C

Family in the wind. Fitzgerald, F. S.
In Fitzgerald, F. S. The Fitzgerald reader p350-68 — S C
In Fitzgerald, F. S. The stories of F. Scott Fitzgerald p419-35 — S C

Family life education. See Finance, Personal

A family man. Galsworthy, J.
In Galsworthy, J. Plays p391-427 — 822

A family man. Hutter, D.
In The Best American short stories, 1965 p167-85 — S C

A family man. Sholokhov, M.
In Sholokhov, M. Tales of the Don p67-75 — S C

The family nobody wanted. Doss, H. — 92

The family of man. New York (City) Museum of Modern Art — 799

Family portrait. Bowen, C. D. — 920

Family relations. See Family

The family reunion. Eliot, T. S.
In Eliot, T. S. The complete plays of T. S. Eliot p55-122 — 812
In Eliot, T. S. Complete poems and plays, 1909-1950 p223-94 — 818

Family reunion. Nash, O. — 811

Family tree. Hughes, L.
In Hughes, L. The Langston Hughes reader p178-80 — 818

Famine—1975! Paddock, W. — 338.1

Famous American women. Stoddard, H. — 920

Famous first facts. Kane, J. N. — 031

Famous literary prizes and their winners. See Literary and library prizes — 807.9

Famous modern conductors. Ewen, D. — 920

Fancy free. Hughes, L.
In Hughes, L. The Langston Hughes reader p197-201 — 818

The Fannie Farmer cookbook. Farmer, F. — 641.5

Fanning, Odom
Opportunities in environmental careers — 614.069

Fanny's first play. Shaw, B.
In Shaw, B. Complete plays, with prefaces v6 p93-171 — 822

Fantasia mathematica. Fadiman, C. ed. — 808.8

Fantastic voyage (Moving picture)
See pages in the following book:
Asimov, I. The solar system and back
p137-48   508
Fantastic voyage. Asimov, I.   Fic
The fantasticks. Jones, T.
In Gassner, J. ed. Best American plays;
6th ser. p185-225   812.08
Far East. See East (Far East)
Far Eastern question. See Eastern question
(Far East)
Far from home. Leasor, J.
In Dulles, A. ed. Great spy stories from
fiction p199-211   S C
Far from the madding crowd. Hardy, T. **Fic**
The far side of paradise; a biography of F.
Scott Fitzgerald. Mizener, A.   92
The far Western frontier, 1830-1860. Billing-
ton, R. A.   978
Faraday, Michael
Chemical history of a candle   540.8
About
See pages in the following book:
Jones, B. Z. ed. The golden age of science
p217-45   920
Farb, Peter
Ecology   574.5
The forest   581
The land and wildlife of North America
    574.9
The land, wildlife, and peoples of the Bible
    220.8
Farewell Miss Julie Logan. Barrie, Sir J.
In The Scribner treasury p643-89   **S C**
A farewell to arms. Hemingway, E.   **Fic**
A farewell to arms, Twentieth century in-
terpretations of. Gellens, J. ed. 813.09
Farewell to Cuba. Cozzens, J. G.
In Abrahams, W. ed. Fifty years of the
American short story v 1 p227-42
    S C
Farfetched fables. Shaw, B.
In Shaw, B. Complete plays, with pre-
faces v6 p491-521   822
Farge, Oliver la. See La Farge, Oliver
Farley, Eugene J.
Barron's How to prepare for the high
school equivalency examination reading
interpretation tests   371.27
Farm animals. See Domestic animals
Farm credit. See Agricultural credit
Farm engines. See Agricultural engineering
Farm implements. See Agricultural ma-
chinery
The farm labourer. Sholokhov, M.
In Sholokhov, M. Tales of the Don p245-
93   S C
Farm life
Fiction
Ferber, E. So Big   Fic
Hardy, T. Far from the madding crowd
    Fic
Rolvaag, O. E. Giants in the earth   Fic
Great Britain
See pages in the following book:
Reader, W. J. Life in Victorian England
p38-49   914.2

United States
See pages in the following books:
American Heritage. The American Heri-
tage History of the confident years p145-
59, 241-66   973.8
United States. Department of Agriculture.
After a hundred years p658-76   353.81
United States. Department of Agriculture.
Contours of change p143-61   630
Farm machinery. See Agricultural machinery
Farm mechanics. See Agricultural engineer-
ing; Agricultural machinery
Farm produce
See pages in the following books:
United States. Department of Agriculture.
Contours of change p3-10   630
United States. Department of Agriculture.
Farmer's world p291-308   338.1
United States. Department of Agriculture.
Water p341-405   631.7
Marketing
United States. Department of Agriculture.
Food for us all   641
See also pages in the following books:
United States. Department of Agriculture.
After a hundred years p478-504 353.81
United States. Department of Agriculture.
Contours of change p70-78, 95-113, 255-81
    630
United States. Department of Agriculture.
Power to produce p276-307   631.3
Farm Security Administration. See United
States. Farm Security Administration
Farm tenancy
See pages in the following book:
Avery, G. Victorian people p79-105 914.2
Farmer, Fannie
The Fannie Farmer cookbook   641.5
Farmer, Gene
First on the moon. See First on the moon
    629.45
Farmer, James
See pages in the following book:
Drotning, P. T. Up from the ghetto p189-
201   920
Farmers' Alliance
Hicks, J. D. The Populist revolt   329
Farmers' cooperatives. See Agriculture, Co-
operative
Farmer's world. United States. Department
of Agriculture   338.1
Farming. See Agriculture
Farms
See pages in the following book:
United States. Department of Agriculture.
Contours of change p229-36   630
Faroe Islands
See pages in the following book:
Jones, W. G. Denmark p228-35   948.9
Farrand, Max
The fathers of the Constitution   973.3
The framing of the Constitution of the
United States   342.73
Farrell, James T.
An American student in Paris
In The Best American short stories, 1968
p43-73   S C

Faulkner, William—*Continued*
The Faulkner reader   S C
Short stories included are: The bear; Old man; Spotted horses; A rose for Emily; Barn burning; Dry September; That evening sun; Turnabout; Shingles for the Lord; A justice; Wash; An odor of verbena; Percy Grimm; The courthouse
Hand upon the waters
In Foley, M. ed. Fifty best American short stories, 1915-1965 p247-60 S C
Intruder in the dust   Fic
Kentucky: May: Saturday
In Sports Illustrated. The wonderful world of sport p291-92   796
Light in August   Fic
Light in August; criticism
In Minter, D. L. ed. Twentieth century interpretations of Light in August   813.09
Mr Acarius
In The Best American short stories, 1966 p69-82   S C
The portable Faulkner   S C
Contents: A justice; The Courthouse (A name for the city); Red leaves; Was; Raid; Wash; An odor of verbena; The bear; Spotted horses; That evening sun; Ad astra; A rose for Emily; Dilsey; Old man; Death drag; Uncle Bud and the three madams; Percy Grimm; Delta autumn; The jail
The reivers   Fic
Selected short stories of William Faulkner   S C
Contents: Barn burning; Two soldiers; A rose for Emily; Dry September; That evening sun; Red leaves; Lo; Turnabout; Honor; There was a queen; Mountain victory; Beyond; Race at morning
The sound and the fury   Fic
also in Faulkner, W. The Faulkner reader   S C
The sound and the fury; criticism
In Stegner, W. ed. The American novel p219-28   813.09
These thirteen
In Faulkner, W. Collected stories of William Faulkner   S C

About
Brooks, C. William Faulkner: the Yoknapatawpha country   813.09
See also pages in the following books:
Durant, W. Interpretations of life p11-27   809
Geismar, M. Writers in crisis p141-83 813.09
O'Connor, W. V. ed. Seven modern American novelists p118-52   813.09
Untermeyer, L. Makers of the modern world p702-11   920

Fauna. See Zoology
Faure, Gabriel Urbain
See pages in the following book:
Cross, M. The Milton Cross New encyclopedia of the great composers and their music p343-51   920.03
Fauves (School of art) See Fauvism
Fauvism
See pages in the following books:
Batterberry, M. Twentieth century art p15-27   709.04
Cheney, S. The story of modern art p347-84   709.03
Russell, J. The world of Matisse, 1869-1954 p57-63   92

Fay, Sidney Bradshaw
The origins of the World War   940.3
Fear. Maupassant, G. de
In Maupassant, G. de. Guy de Maupassant's Short stories p52-57   S C
Fear strikes out. Piersall, J.   92
"The **fear** that walks by noonday." Cather, W.
In Cather, W. Willa Cather's Collected short fiction, 1892-1912 v3 p505-14   S C
The **feast** of Nemesis. Saki
In Saki. The short stories of Saki p356-60   S C
Feast of Ortolans. Anderson, M.
In Anderson, M. Eleven verse plays, 1929-1939 v9   812
Feasts. See Fasts and feasts
Feather, Leonard
The book of jazz: from then till now **781.5**
The encyclopedia of jazz in the sixties   781.503
The new edition of The encyclopedia of jazz   781.503
The **feather** cloak of Hawaii. Andersen, J. C.
In Day, A. G. ed. The spell of Hawaii p21-25   919.69
Feathertop: a moralized legend. Hawthorne, N.
In Hawthorne, N. Hawthorne's Short stories p251-69   S C
February 1999: Ylla. Bradbury, R.
In Bradbury, R. The Martian chronicles p14-27   S C
February 2002: the locusts. Bradbury, R.
In Bradbury, R. The Martian chronicles p101   S C
February 2003: interim. Bradbury, R.
In Bradbury, R. The Martian chronicles p113   S C
Fechner, Gustav Theodor
See pages in the following book:
Newman, J. R. ed. The world of mathematics v2 p1148-66   510.8
Fechter, Charles
The Count of Monte Cristo
In Gassner, J. ed. Best plays of the early American theatre p216-61   812.08
Feder, Lillian
Crowell's Handbook of classical literature   880.3
Federal budget. See Budget—United States
Federal Bureau of Investigation. See United States. Federal Bureau of Investigation
Federal Communications Commission. See United States. Federal Communications Commission
Federal courts. See Courts—United States
Federal government
See pages in the following book:
Boorstin, D. J. The Americans: The national experience p393-406   917.3
Federal Housing Administration
See pages in the following book:
Willmann, J. B. The Department of Housing and Urban Development p60-72   353.85

Fermi, Laura
Atoms for the world   621.48
Atoms in the family; my life with Enrico Fermi   92
Galileo and the scientific revolution   92
Illustrious immigrants   325.73
Mussolini   92

Fern. Toomer, J.
In Hughes, L. ed. The best short stories by Negro writers p30-34   S C

Fernald, James C.
Funk & Wagnalls Standard handbook of synonyms, antonyms, and prepositions   424

Fernald, Merritt Lyndon
Gray, A. Gray's Manual of botany   582

Fernandez, Justino
A guide to Mexican art: from its beginnings to the present   709.72

Fernandez de Córdoba, Gonzalo
See pages in the following book:
Lloyd, A. The Spanish centuries p99-115   946

Fernández de Lizardi, José Joaquin
See pages in the following book:
Porter, K. A. The collected essays and occasional writings of Katherine Anne Porter p357-84   818

Ferns, H. S.
Argentina   982

Ferns
Cobb, B. A field guide to the ferns and their related families of northeastern and central North America   587
See also pages in the following books:
The Oxford Book of flowerless plants p184-91   586
Zim, H. S. Plants p194-207   581

Ferrari, Erma
(jt. auth.) Kenworthy, L. S. Leaders of new nations   920

The **ferry** of unfulfilment. Henry, O.
In Henry, O. The complete works of O. Henry p1471-74   S C

Fertilizers and manures
Slack, A. V. Defense against famine   631.8
See also pages in the following book:
Scientific American. Plant agriculture p152-62   581
See also Nitrates; Phosphates

Fessler, Loren
China   915.1

Festival! Hopkins, J.   781.5

The **festival** of Saint Nicholas. Dodge, M. M.
In Wernecke, H. (H. ed. Celebrating Christmas around the world p127-34   394.26

Festivals
See also Holidays; Music festivals

Canada
Meyer, R. Festivals U.S.A. & Canada   394.2

United States
Douglas, G. W. The American book of days   394.2
Meyer, R. Festivals U.S.A. & Canada   394.2

Festivals U.S.A. & Canada. Meyer, R.   394.2

Feudalism
See pages in the following books:
Durant, W. The age of faith p552-79   940.1
Fremantle, A. Age of faith p11-20   940.1
Leonard, J. N. Early Japan p137-58   915.2
Mills, D. The Middle Ages p144-52   940.1
Rowling, M. Everyday life in medieval times p19-48   914
Simons, G. Barbarian Europe p147-63   940.1
Thorndike, L. The history of medieval Europe p249-83   940.1
See also Chivalry; Middle Ages; Peasantry

Feuille d'album. Mansfield, K.
In Mansfield, K. The short stories of Katherine Mansfield p324-30   S C

Fiat money. See Paper money

Fibers
See pages in the following book:
United States. Department of Agriculture. Farmer's world p218-60   338.1

Fickle fortune or how Gladys hustled. Henry, O.
In Henry, O. The complete works of O. Henry p1046-48   S C

Fiction
Forster, E. M. Aspects of the novel   808.3
See also American fiction; Animals—Stories; English fiction; Fables; Fairy tales; Folklore; Ghost stories; Historical fiction; Mystery and detective stories; Novelists; School stories; Science fiction; Short stories; also names of historical characters with the subdivision Fiction, e.g. Mary Stuart, Queen of the Scots—Fiction

Bibliography
Fiction catalog   016.8

Dictionaries
Brewer, E. C. The reader's handbook of famous names in fiction, allusions, references, proverbs, plots, stories, and poems   803

Indexes
Fiction catalog   016.8

Technique
Mathieu, A. M. ed. The creative writer   808.06
See also pages in the following book:
Engle, P. ed. On creative writing p163-80   808.02

Fiction, American. See American fiction

Fiction, English. See English fiction

Fiction, Historical. See Historical fiction

Fiction catalog   016.8

Fiddler on the roof. Stein, J.   812
—Same
In Gassner, J. ed. Best American plays; 6th ser. p399-433   812.08
In Richards, S. ed. Best plays of the sixties p241-328   808.82

Fiddler, play fast—play faster
In Wernecke, H. H. ed. Celebrating Christmas around the world p104-10   394.26

Fidell, Estelle A.
(ed.) Fiction catalog. See Fiction catalog
     016.8
(ed.) Junior high school library catalog.
  See Junior high school library catalog
     011
(ed.) Play index, 1953-1960. See Play index,
  1953-1960
     808.82
(ed.) Play index, 1961-1967. See Play index,
  1961-1967
     808.82
(ed.) Public library catalog. See Public
  library catalog
     011
(comp.) Short story index: supplement,
  1950-1954. See Short story index: supplement, 1950-1954
     808.83
(comp.) Short story index: supplement,
  1955-1958. See Short story index: supplement, 1955-1958
     808.83
(comp.) Short story index: supplement,
  1959-1963. See Short story index: supplement, 1959-1963
     808.83
(comp.) Short story index: supplement,
  1964-1968. See Short story index: supplement, 1964-1968
     808.83
Fiefs. See Feudalism
Field, Eugene
First Christmas tree
  In Becker, M. L. ed. The home book of
    Christmas p435-39
     394.26
Mouse that didn't believe in Santa Claus
  In Becker, M. L. ed. The home book of
    Christmas p452-57
     394.26
Field, Frances
(jt. auth.) Field, M. A quintet of cuisines
     641.5
Field, George Wallis
Hermann Hesse
     833.09
Field, Henriette (Deluzy-Desportes)
Fiction
Field, R. All this and heaven too
     Fic
Field, John
  See pages in the following book:
Chapin, V. Giants of the keyboard p60-71
     920
Field, Michael
A quintet of cuisines
     641.5
Field, Noel Haviland
  See pages in the following book:
Dulles, A. ed. Great true spy stories p240-
  50
     327
Field, Rachel
All this and heaven too
     Fic
And now tomorrow
     Fic
Field book of common rocks and minerals.
  Loomis, F. B.
     549
Field book of insects of the United States
  and Canada, aiming to answer common
  questions. Lutz, F. E.
     595.7
A **field** guide to animal tracks. Murie, O. J.
     591
A **field** guide to reptiles and amphibians of
  the United States and Canada east of
  the 100th meridian. Conant, R.
     598.1
A **field** guide to rocks and minerals. Pough,
  F. H.
     549
A **field** guide to shells of the Pacific Coast
  and Hawaii. Morris, P. A.
     594
A **field** guide to the birds. Peterson, R. T.
     598

A **field** guide to the butterflies of North
  America, east of the Great Plains. Klots,
  A. B.
     595.7
A **field** guide to the ferns and their related
  families of northeastern and central
  North America. Cobb, B.
     587
A **field** guide to the insects of America north
  of Mexico. Borror, D. J.
     595.7
A **field** guide to the mammals. Burt, W. H.
     599
A **field** guide to the shells of our Atlantic
  and Gulf Coasts. Morris, P. A.
     594
A **field** guide to the stars and planets. Men-
  zel, D. H.
     523
A **field** guide to trees and shrubs. Petrides,
  G. A.
     582
A **field** guide to Western birds. Peterson,
  R. T.
     598
A **field** guide to Western reptiles and am-
  phibians. Stebbins, R. C.
     598.1
A **field** guide to wildflowers of northeastern
  and north-central North America. Peter-
  son, R. T.
     582
Field hockey
  See pages in the following book:
American Association for Health, Physical
  Education, and Recreation. Physical edu-
  cation for high school students p135-48
     613.7
Field sports. See Hunting; Sports
Fieldbook for Boy Scouts, explorers, scouters,
  educators, outdoorsmen. Boy Scouts of
  America
     369.43
Fieldbook for boys and men. See Boy Scouts
  of America. Fieldbook for Boy Scouts,
  explorers, scouters, educators, outdoors-
  men
     369.43
Fielding, Henry
The history of Tom Jones, a foundling **Fic**
Tom Jones; criticism
  In Drew, E. The novel: a modern guide
    to fifteen English masterpieces p59-
    74
     823.09
      About
  See pages in the following books:
Daiches, D. A critical history of English
  literature v2 p713-27
     820.9
Durant, W. The age of Voltaire p193-99
     940.2
Wagenknecht, E. Cavalcade of the English
  novel p58-68
     823.09
Fielding's Travel guide to Europe
     914
Fields, Julia
Not your singing, dancing spade
  In Jones, L. ed. Black fire p479-85 **810.8**
The **fields.** Richter, C.
     Fic
  also in Richter, C. The awakening land
    p171-329
     Fic
Fiennes, Alice
(jt. auth.) Fiennes, R. The natural history
  of dogs
     636.7
Fiennes, Richard
The natural history of dogs
     636.7
Fiestas. See Festivals
Fife, Alta
(jt. ed.) Fife, A. ed. Ballads of the great
  West
     811.08
Fife, Austin
(ed.) Ballads of the great West
     811.08

First on the moon   **629.45**

First things, last things. Hoffer, E. **309.173**

The **first** 3000 years: ancient civilizations of the Tigris, Euphrates, and Nile River valleys, and the Mediterranean Sea. Falls, C. B.   **913.03**

The **first** to fly. Harris, S.   **629.13**

First views of the enemy. Oates, J. C.
   In The Best American short stories, 1965 p259-70   **S C**

Fischer, Emil
   See pages in the following book:
Moore, R. The coil of life p144-61 **574.09**

Fish, Carl Russell
The path of empire   **327.73**

Fish, Robert L.
A matter of honor
   In Mystery Writers of America. Crime without murder p63-78   **S C**

Fish. See Cookery—Fish; Fishes

Fish as food. See Sea food

Fish culture
Idyll, C. P. The sea against hunger **639**

Fish hatcheries. See Fish culture

Fishel, Leslie H.
(ed.) The Black American   **301.451**

Fisher, Douglas Alan
Steel: from the iron age to the space age
    669.1

Fisher, Graham
(jt. auth.) White, R. M. The royal family
    920

Fisher, James
Wildlife in danger   **333.7**
(jt. auth.) Peterson, R. T. Wild America
    574.9
(jt. auth.) Philip, Duke of Edinburgh. Wildlife crisis   **333.7**

Fisher, M. F. K.
The cooking of provincial France   **641.5**

Fisher, Ronald Aylmer
   See pages in the following book:
Moore, R. Man, time, and fossils p192-210
    573.2

Fisher, Rudolph
The city of refuge
   In Clarke, J. H. ed. American Negro short stories p21-36   **S C**
Miss Cynthie
   In Hughes, L. ed. The best short stories by Negro writers p35-47   **S C**

Fisher, Sydney G.
The Quaker colonies   **973.2**

Fisheries
Idyll, C. P. The sea against hunger **639**
   See also pages in the following books:
Bardach, J. Harvest of the sea p115-63
    333.9
Ehrlich, P. R. Population, resources, environment p101-09   **301.3**
Gaskell, T. F. World beneath the oceans p123-33, 147-49   **551.4**
   See also Whaling

United States
Wright, L. B. Everyday life in colonial America   **917.3**
   See also pages in the following book:
Winter, R. Poisons in your food p98-118
    614

Fishes
Herald, E. S. Living fishes of the world
    597
National Geographic Society. Wondrous world of fishes   **597**
Ommanney, F. D. The fishes   **597**
   See also pages in the following books:
Boy Scouts of America, Fieldbook for Boy Scouts, explorers, scouters, educators, outdoorsmen p420-35   **369.43**
Fenton, C. L. The fossil book p263-79 **560**
Fisher, J. Wildlife in danger p339-51 **333.7**
Gaskell, T. F. World beneath the oceans p116-33   **551.4**
Headstrom, R. A complete field guide to nests in the United States p419-32 **598**
Lorenz, K. Z. King Solomon's ring p22-38
    591
Ricard, M. The mystery of animal migration p143-68   **591**
   See also Aquariums; Fisheries; Sea food; Tropical fishes; and names of fish, e.g. Sharks

United States
   See pages in the following books:
Dodd, E. Careers for the '70: conservation p147-53   **333.7069**
McClung, R. M. Lost wild America p206-16   **333.7**

Fishin' Jimmy. Slosson, A. T.
   In The Scribner treasury p205-20 **S C**

Fishing
Bryant, N. Fresh air, bright water   **799**
National Geographic Society. Wondrous world of fishes   **597**
   See also pages in the following books:
American Association for Health, Physical Education, and Recreation. Physical education for high school students p13-26
    613.7
Idyll, C. P. The sea against hunger p162-85   **639**
Ormond, C. Outdoorsman's handbook p83-114   **796.5**

Fiction
Hemingway, E. The old man and the sea
    Fic

New York
   See pages in the following book:
Boyle, R. H. The Hudson River p213-30
    917.47

Fishing industry. See Fisheries

A **fishing** village. Crane, S.
   In Crane, S. The complete short stories & sketches of Stephen Crane p380-83   **S C**

Fishman, Jack
My darling Clementine: the story of Lady Churchill   **92**

Fishwick, Marshall W.
American Heritage. Jamestown   **975.5**

The flag paramount. Henry, O.
In Henry, O The complete works of O.
Henry p609-16 **S C**

Flags
Flags of the world 929.9
Pedersen, C. F. The international flag
book in color 929.9
Quaife, M. M. The history of the United
States flag 929.9
Smith, W. The flag book of the United
States 929.9

Flags of the world 929.9

Flaherty, Thomas
Cole, E. House of bondage 301.451

The **flame** of Islam. See Lamb, H. The
crusades 940.1

Flanagan and his short filibustering adventure. Crane, S.
In Crane, S. The complete short stories
& sketches of Stephen Crane p365-
77 **S C**

The **flashlight**. Cleaver, E.
In The Best American short stories, 1970
p20-52 **S C**
In Prize stories, 1971: The O. Henry
Awards p226-60 **S C**

Flatland. Abbott, E. A. 513

The **flattering** word. Kelly, G.
In Cerf, B. ed. 24 favorite one-act plays
p272-300 808.82

Flaubert, Gustave
Madame Bovary **Fic**

About
See pages in the following books:
Trilling, L. The opposing self p173-205 809
Untermeyer, L. Makers of the modern
world p91-101 920

Flavia and her artists. Cather, W.
In Cather, W. Willa Cather's Collected
short fiction, 1892-1912 v2 p149-72
S C

Flavours of exile. Lessing, D.
In Lessing, D. African stories p547-54
S C

The **fleecy** jacket. Ulyansky, A.
In Scammell, M. ed. Russia's other
writers p115-21 **S C**

Fleming, Sir Alexander
See pages in the following book:
Untermeyer, L. Makers of the modern
world p559-64 920

Fleming, Ian
The end of James
In Dulles, A. ed Great spy stories from
fiction p360-69 **S C**

Fleming, Thomas
The man from Monticello; an intimate life
of Thomas Jefferson 92

Fleming, Walter Lynwood
The sequel of Appomattox 973.8

Flemish art. See Art, Flemish

Flemish painters. See Painters, Flemish

Flemish painting. See Painting, Flemish

Flesch, Rudolf
The art of clear thinking 153.4
How to be brief 808

How to write, speak, and think more effectively 808
(ed.) The new book of unusual quotations
808.88

Fletcher, Sir Banister
A history of architecture on the comparative method 720.9

Fletcher, Lucille
Sorry, wrong number
In Cerf, B. ed. 24 favorite one-act plays
p117-32 808.82

Flexner, Abraham
Medical education in the United States and
Canada; criticism
In Downs, R. B. Books that changed
America p152-64 810.9

Flexner, James Thomas
George Washington and the new nation
(1783-1793) 92
George Washington in the American Revolution (1775-1783) 92
George Washington: the forge of experience (1732-1775) 92
The world of Winslow Homer, 1836-1910
92

Flexner, Stuart Berg
(jt. ed.) Wentworth, H. ed. Dictionary of
American slang 427

Flies, Artificial. See Fly-casting

Flies. Asimov, I.
In Asimov, I. Nightfall, and other stories
p225-31 **S C**

Flight
Stever, H. G. Flight 629.132
See also pages in the following books:
Cooper, M. The inventions of Leonardo da
Vinci p52-61 608
Halacy, D. S. Bionics p61-67 001.5

Flight. Lessing, D.
In Lessing, D. African stories p578-82
S C

Flight. Steinbeck, J.
In Havighurst, W. ed. Masters of the
modern short story p332-51 **S C**
In Steinbeck, J. The portable Steinbeck
p3-25 818

Flight. Updike, J.
In Updike, J. Pigeon feathers, and other
stories **S C**

The **flight** of the Falcon. Du Maurier, D. **Fic**

The **flight** that failed. Pei, M.
In Pei, M. Tales of the natural and supernatural p55-67 **S C**

Flight to Arras. Saint Exupéry, A. de.
In Saint Exupéry, A. de. Airman's odyssey p281-437 629.13

Flight to the moon. See Space flight to the
moon

Flint implements. See Stone implements

Floan, Howard R.
William Saroyan 818

Flood control
See pages in the following book:
Moss, F. E. The water crisis p95-108 333.9

Flora. See Botany

Flora: a biography [of Flora Macdonald].
Vining, E. G. 92

Floral decoration. See Flower arrangement

A fog in Santone. Henry, O.
In Henry, O. The complete works of
O. Henry p992-97   **S C**

Fogel, Samuel J.
Gymnastics handbook   796.4

Foley, Martha
(ed.) The Best American short stories,
1964-1971. See The Best American
short stories, 1964-1971   **S C**
(ed.) Fifty best American short stories,
1915-1965   **S C**

Folk and festival costume of the world.
Wilcox, R. T.   391

Folk dancing
See pages in the following book:
American Association for Health, Physical Education, and Recreation. Physical education for high school students
p107-19   613.7

Folk dancing, English
See pages in the following book:
Shakespeare's England v2 p437-50   822.3

Folk drama
See pages in the following book:
Coffin, T. P. ed. Folklore in America
p195-225   398

Folk lore. See Folklore

Folk music. See Folk songs

Folk plays. See Folk drama

Folk singers. See Singers

Folk song: U.S.A. Lomax, J. A. ed.   784.4

Folk songs
Boni, M. B. ed. Fireside book of folk
songs   784.4
See also pages in the following books:
Bauer, M. Music through the ages p151-
74   780.9
The New York Times. Guide to listening
pleasure p200-09   780.1
See also Ballads

New England
See pages in the following book:
Botkin, B. A. ed. A treasury of New En-
gland folklore p525-91   398

Southern States
See pages in the following book:
Botkin, B. A. ed. A treasury of Southern
folklore p654-74, 699-762   398

United States
American Heritage. The American Heri-
tage songbook   784.4
Lomax, A. ed. The folk songs of North
America in the English language   784.4
Lomax, J. A. comp. American ballads
and folk songs   784.4
Lomax, J. A. comp. Cowboy songs and
other frontier ballads   784.4
Lomax, J. A. ed. Folk song: U.S.A.   784.4
Sandburg, C. ed. The American songbag
    784.4
See also pages in the following books:
Botkin, B. A. ed. A treasury of American
folklore p818-918   398
Coffin, T. P. ed. Folklore in America
p47-99   398

The West
See pages in the following book:
Botkin, B. A. ed. A treasury of Western
folklore p279-98   398

Folk songs, African
Makeba, M. ed. The world of African
song   784.4

Folk songs, American. See Folk songs—
United States

Folk songs, Irish
See pages in the following book:
Colum, P. ed. A treasury of Irish folk-
lore p588-613   398

Folk songs, Negro (America) See Negro
songs

The **folk** songs of North America in the
English language. Lomax, A. ed.   784.4

Folk tales. See Folklore

Folklore
Rugoff, M. ed. Harvest of world folk
tales   398.2

Arabia
Arabian nights. The Arabian nights' entertainment   398.2

Dictionaries
Funk & Wagnalls Standard dictionary of
folklore, mythology and legend   398.03

Europe
Bulfinch, T. Bulfinch's Mythology   291

Great Britain
See pages in the following book:
Shakespeare's England. v 1 p516-46   822.3

Greece, Modern
Megas, G. A. ed. Folktales of Greece   398.2

Ireland
Colum, P. ed. A treasury of Irish folklore
    398

Mexico
Paredes, A. ed. Folktales of Mexico   398.2
Toor, F. A treasury of Mexican folkways
    398

New England
Botkin, B. A. ed. A treasury of New England folklore   398

Southern States
Botkin, B. A. ed. A treasury of Southern
folklore   398

Texas
Dobie, J. F. ed. Tales of old-time Texas
    398.2

United States
Botkin, B. A. ed. A Civil War treasury of
tales, legends and folklore   973.7
Botkin, B. A. ed. A treasury of American
folklore   398
Brewer, J. M. American Negro folklore
    398
Coffin, T. P. ed. Folklore in America   398
Hughes, L. ed. The book of Negro folk-
lore   398
Williams, B. Lost legends of the West
    917.8
See also pages in the following book:
Literary history of the United States p703-
27   810.9

The West
Botkin, B. A. ed. A treasury of Western
folklore   398

Folklore, Indian. See Indians of North America—Legends

Folklore, Jewish
Nahmad, H. M. ed. A portion in paradise, and other Jewish folktales   **398.2**
Noy, D. ed. Folktales of Israel   **398.2**

Folklore, Negro
Brewer, J. M. American Negro folklore   **398**
Hughes, L. ed. The book of Negro folklore   **398**

Folklore in America. Coffin, T. P. ed.   **398**

Folklore of plants. See Plant lore

The folklore of weddings and marriage. Emrich, D. comp.   **392**

Folktales of Greece. Megas, G. A. ed.   **398.2**

Folktales of Israel. Noy, D. ed.   **398.2**

Folktales of Mexico. Paredes, A. ed.   **398.2**

Folkways. See Manners and customs

Follett, Wilson
Modern American usage   **428**

Folsom, Franklin
America's ancient treasures   **913.7074**

Fon. Dumas, H.
In Jones, L. ed. Black fire p455-66 **810.8**

Food
Arnold, P. Food facts for young people   **641.1**
Sebrell, W. H. Food and nutrition **641.1**
United States. Department of Agriculture. Protecting our food   **641.3**
See also pages in the following books:
Brogan, D. W. France p88-97   **914.4**
Burton, E. The pageant of Elizabethan England p134-63   **914.2**
United States. Department of Agriculture. Consumers all p391-480   **640.73**
United States. Department of Agriculture. Farmer's world p118-205   **338.1**
See also Cookery; Diet; Nutrition; Sea food; Vitamins

Analysis
Kraus, B. Calories and carbohydrates   **641.1**

Laws and regulations
See Food adulteration and inspection

Preservation
See pages in the following book:
Angier, B. How to live in the woods on pennies a day p137-49   **917.1**
See also Food, Frozen

Food, Frozen
See pages in the following books:
Better Homes and Gardens. Better Homes & Gardens New cook book p134-62 **641.5**
Good Housekeeping Institute, New York. The new Good Housekeeping cookbook p700-14   **641.5**
McCall's. McCall's Cook book p345-54   **641.5**

Food adulteration and inspection
Hunter, B. T. Consumer beware!   **664**
Winter, R. Poisons in your food   **614**

Food and Agriculture Organization of the United Nations
See pages in the following books:
Comay, J. The UN in action p80-87 **341.13**
United States. Department of Agriculture. Farmer's world p434-42   **338.1**

Food and Drug Administration
See pages in the following book:
Terrell, J. U. The United States Department of Health, Education, and Welfare p116-35   **353.84**

Food and nutrition. Sebrell, W. H.   **641.1**

Food chains (Ecology)
See pages in the following book:
Ehrlich, P. R. Population, resources, environment p157-62   **301.3**

Food chemistry. See Food—Analysis

The food commissar. Sholokhov, M.
In Sholokhov, M. Tales of the Don p37-43   **S C**

Food control. See Dams; Food supply

Food facts for young people. Arnold, P. **641.1**

Food for us all. United States. Department of Agriculture   **641**

Food industry and trade
Cross, J. The supermarket trap   **658.87**
Hunter, B. T. Consumer beware!   **664**
United States. Department of Agriculture. Protecting our food   **641.3**
See also pages in the following books:
Stone, A. A. Careers in agribusiness and industry p51-79   **338.1**
United States. Department of Agriculture. Contours of change p80-89   **630**

Food inspection. See Food adulteration and inspection

Food plants. See Plants, Edible

Food poisoning
Winter, R. Poisons in your food   **614**

Food preservation. See Food—Preservation

Food supply
Cochrane, W. W. The world food problem   **338.1**
Dumont, R. The hungry future   **338.1**
Freeman, O. L. World without hunger   **338.1**
Harmer, R. M. Unfit for human consumption   **632**
Idyll, C. P. The sea against hunger   **639**
Paddock, W. Famine—1975!   **338.1**
United States. Department of Agriculture. Food for us all   **641** ✓
United States. Department of Agriculture. Protecting our food   **641.3**
See also pages in the following books:
Ehrlich, P. R. Population, resources, environment p81-115   **301.3**
Foreign Policy Association. Toward the year 2018 p126-35   **901.9**
Hyde, M. O. This crowded planet p18-45, 95-102   **301.3**
Scientific American. The biosphere p95-103   **551**
Scientific American. Plant agriculture p206-14   **581**
United States. Department of Agriculture. Contours of change p326-33   **630**
See also Food—Preservation

Food trade. See Farm produce—Marketing

The fool-killer. Henry, O.

In Henry, O. The complete works of O. Henry p1323-29   **S C**

Foot

See pages in the following book:

Archer, E. Let's face it p76-90   **646.7**

Football

Plimpton, G. Paper Lion   **796.33**

Sports Illustrated. Sports Illustrated Book of football   **796.33**

See also pages in the following books:

American Association for Health, Physical Education, and Recreation. Physical education for high school students p307-19   **613.7**

Friendlich, D. Panorama of sports in America p16-30   **796**

Biography

Kramer, J. ed. Lombardi: winning is the only thing   **92**

Sullivan, G. Pro football's all-time greats   **920**

See also pages in the following book:

Orr, J. The Black athlete: his story in American history p81-101   **920**

Football. Kavanagh, P.

In Garrity, D. A. ed. 44 Irish short stories p146-51   **S C**

Foote, Timothy

The world of Bruegel, c.1525-1569   **92**

Footlick, Jerrold K.

(ed.) The National Observer. Careers for the seventies   **331.7**

The footprint in the sky. Carr, J. D.

In Mystery Writers of America. Crime without murder p19-34   **S C**

Footprints on the moon. Associated Press   **629.45**

For Esmé—with love and squalor. Salinger, J. D.

In Salinger, J. D. Nine stories p131-73   **S C**

For I have wept. Stein, G.

In The Best American short stories, 1965 p325-43   **S C**

For the duration of the war. Saki

In Saki. The short stories of Saki p598-603   **S C**

For the good of the cause. Solzhenitsyn, A.

In Solzhenitsyn, A. Stories and prose poems p53-123   **S C**

For the sake of argument. Hughes, L.

In Hughes, L. The Langston Hughes reader p188-93   **818**

For us, the living [biography of Medgar Wiley Evers] Evers, Mrs M.   **92**

For whom the bell tolls. Hemingway, E. **Fic**

For you departed [biography of Doris Francis Paton]. Paton, A.   **92**

Forage plants

United States. Department of Agriculture. Grass   **633**

See also Corn

Forbes, Esther

Paul Revere & the world he lived in   **92**

Forbes, Kathryn

Mama's bank account; dramatization. See Van Druten, J. I remember mama

The forbidden buzzards. Saki

In Saki. The short stories of Saki p368-72   **S C**

Force and energy

Sterland, E. G. Energy into power   **621**

Wilson, M. Energy   **531**

See also pages in the following books:

Asimov, I. The neutrino p23-44   **539.7**

Ehrlich, P. R. Population, resources, environment p53-58   **301.3**

Foreign Policy Association. Toward the year 2018 p114-25   **901.9**

Nourse, A. E. Universe, earth, and atom p97-120, 169-91   **530.9**

Scientific American. The biosphere p14-36, 107-14   **551**

United Nations Educational, Scientific and Cultural Organization. 700 science experiments for everyone p122-30   **507.2**

See also Motion

Forced labor. See Slavery

Ford, Alice

(ed.) Audubon, J. J. Audubon, by himself   **92**

Ford, Charles A.

(ed.) Compton's Dictionary of the natural sciences. See Compton's Dictionary of the natural sciences   **570.3**

Ford, Edward Charles

See pages in the following book:

Mantle, M. The quality of courage p22-27   **920**

Ford, Henry, 1863-1947

Nevins, A. Ford   **92**

See also pages in the following books:

Holbrook, S. H. The age of the moguls p201-12   **920**

Untermeyer, L. Makers of the modern world p321-28   **920**

Ford, Henry Jones

The Cleveland era   **973.8**

Washington and his colleagues   **973.4**

Ford, Jesse Hill

How the mountains are

In Abrahams, W. ed. Fifty years of the American short story v 1 p271-79   **S C**

Ford, Whitey. See Ford, Edward Charles

Ford Foundation

See pages in the following book:

Nevins, A. Ford v3 p409-26   **92**

Ford Motor Company

Nevins, A. Ford   **92**

See also pages in the following book:

Holbrook, S. H. The age of the moguls p203-12   **920**

Forecasting, Weather. See Weather forecasting

Foreign aid program. See Economic assistance; Technical assistance

Foreign auto repair manual, Audels. Anderson, E. P.   **629.28**

Foreign car repair manual, Glenn's. Glenn, H. T.   **629.28**

Foreign economic relations. See International economic relations

Forster, E. M.—*Continued*
Road from Colonus
In Havighurst, W. ed. Masters of the modern short story p86-98 **S C**
The **Forsyte** saga. Galsworthy, J. **Fic**
Forsythe, Alexandra I.
Computer science. See Computer science 651.8
Fort, Harriet
Uncle Hobey
In Seventeen. Seventeen from Seventeen p 1-17 **S C**
Fort, Joel
The pleasure seekers: the drug crisis, youth and society 613.8
Fortitude. Walpole, H. **Fic**
Fortune (Periodical)
Youth in turmoil 301.43
Lessing, L. DNA: at the core of life itself 574.8
Silberman, C. E. The myths of automation 301.24
Fortune. See Probabilities
Fortune telling
See pages in the following book:
Christopher, M. ESP, seers & psychics p91-100 133
Fortunes. See Income
The **fortunes** and misfortunes of the famous Moll Flanders. Defoe, D. **Fic**
44 Irish short stories. Garrity, D. A. ed. **S C**
The **Forty**-niners. White, S. E. 979.4
The **42nd** parallel. Dos Passos, J.
In Dos Passos, J. U.S.A. v 1 **Fic**
Foscari, Francesco
See pages in the following book:
Horizon Magazine. The Horizon Book of the Renaissance p273-80 940.2
The **fossil** book. Fenton, C. L. 560
Fossil mammals. See Mammals, Fossil
Fossil plants. See Plants, Fossil
Fossil reptiles. See Reptiles, Fossil
Fossils
Fenton, C. L. The fossil book 560
See also pages in the following books:
Bertin, L. Larousse Encyclopedia of the earth p350-412 550
Engle, L. The sea p44-53 551.4
See also Reptiles, Fossil
Foster, Julian
(ed.) Protest! Student activism in America 378.1
Foster, R. F.
Foster's Complete Hoyle 795
Foster, Richard
(ed.) Six American novelists of the nineteenth century 813.09
Foster, Ruel E.
Jesse Stuart 818
Foster, Stephen Collins
See pages in the following book:
Ewen, D. Great men of American popular song p23-31 920
Foster home care. See Adoption
Foucquet, Nicolas. See Fouquet, Nicolas, vicomte de Melun et le Vaux

Foundation Franklin (Tugboat)
Mowat, F. The grey seas under 387.5
The **foundations.** Galsworthy, J.
In Galsworthy, J. Plays p315-48 822
The **fountain.** O'Neill, E.
In O'Neill, E. Plays v 1 p377-449 812
The **fountainhead.** Rand, A. **Fic**
Fouquet, Nicolas, vicomte de Melun et de Vaux
See pages in the following book:
Horizon Magazine. The light of the past p184-89 901.9
Four beasts in one. Poe, E. A.
In Poe, E. A. The complete tales and poems of Edgar Allan Poe p510-16 **S C**
Four came back. Caidin, M. **Fic**
Four days; the historical record of the death of President Kennedy. United Press International 92
The **four** guardians of La Grange. Harte, B.
In Harte, B. The best short stories of Bret Harte p426-41 **S C**
Four men in a cave. Crane, S.
In Crane, S. The complete short stories & sketches of Stephen Crane p66-69 **S C**
The **four** million. Henry, O. **S C**
also in Henry, O. The complete works of O. Henry p 1-108 **S C**
The **four** minute mile. Bannister, R. 92
Four plays. Inge, W. 812
Four plays. Ionesco, E. 842
Four plays. Shaw, B. 822
Four plays of Ibsen. Ibsen, H. 839.8
Four quartets. Eliot, T. S.
In Eliot, T. S. Collected poems, 1909-1962 p173-209 811
In Eliot, T. S. Complete poems and plays, 1909-1950 p117-45 818
Four stories. Undset, S. **S C**
Four thousand years ago. Bibby, G. 913.03
Fourier, Jean Baptiste Joseph, Baron
See pages in the following book:
Bell, E. T. Men of mathematics p183-205 920
The **fourposter.** Hartog, J. de
In Gassner, J. ed. Best American plays; 4th ser. p479-501 812.08
Fourteen VC POW's. Moore, R.
In Moore, R. The green berets p223-41 **S C**
Fourth dimension
Abbott, E. A. Flatland 513
The **fourth** in Salvador. Henry, O.
In Henry, O. The complete works of O. Henry p461-69 **S C**
Fourth man. Russell, J.
In Day, A. G. ed. The greatest American short stories p215-36 **S C**
Fourth prose. Mandelstam, O.
In Scammell, M. ed. Russia's other writers p130-45 **S C**
Fowler, H. W.
(ed.) The Concise Oxford Dictionary of current English. See The Concise Oxford Dictionary of current English 423
A dictionary of modern English usage 428

France—*Continued*

History—Revolution, 1789-1799—Fiction
Dickens, C. A tale of two cities   **Fic**
Du Maurier, D. The glass-blowers **Fic**
Sabatini, R. Scaramouche, the king-maker   **Fic**

History—Consulate and Empire,1799-1815
Horizon Magazine. The Horizon Book of The age of Napoleon   **944.04**
Maurois, A. Napoleon [I]   **92**

History—Consulate and Empire, 1799-1815—Fiction
Selinko, A. Désirée   **Fic**

History—1799-1914
See pages in the following books:
Dill, M. Germany p69-85   **943**
The New Cambridge Modern history v10 p442-67, v11 p300-22   **909**

History—1799-1914—Fiction
Stendhal. The red and the black   **Fic**

History—Second Empire, 1852-1870
Guérard, A. Napoleon III   **92**

History—Third Republic, 1870-1940
Schechter, B. The Dreyfus affair   **944.081**
Shirer, W. L. The collapse of the Third Republic   **944.081**
Werstein, I. I accuse; the story of the Dreyfus case   **92**

History—Commune, 1871
See Paris—History—Commune, 1871

History—German occupation, 1940-1945
Collins, L. Is Paris burning?   **944.081**

Kings and rulers
Cronin, V. Louis XIV   **92**

Politics and government
Schoenbrun, D. The three lives of Charles de Gaulle   **92**
See also pages in the following books:
The New Cambridge Modern history v4 p411-34, v7 p214-40, v9 p337-66   **909**
White, T. H. Fire in the ashes p79-129   **940.55**

Politics and government—1589-1789
See pages in the following book:
The New Cambridge Modern history v8 p565-617   **909**

Politics and government—1958-
See pages in the following book:
Carroll, J. T. The French p41-68   **914.4**

Presidents
Schoenbrun, D. The three lives of Charles de Gaulle   **92**

Social life and customs
Levron, J. Daily life at Versailles in the seventeenth and eighteenth centuries   **914.43**
Robiquet, J. Daily life in the French Revolution   **914.4**

Francesca da Rimini. Boker, G. H.
In Quinn, A. H. ed. Representative American plays p313-68   **812.08**
Francesco de' Rossi. See Salviati, Francesco
Franchere, Ruth
Stephen Crane   **92**

The **Franchise** affair. Tey, J.
In Tey, J. Three by Tey v2   **Fic**
Francia, José Gaspar Rodriguez, Dictator of Paraguay
See pages in the following books:
Crow, J. A. The epic of Latin America p559-64   **980**
Worcester, D. E. Makers of Latin America p88-96   **920**
Francis of Assisi, Saint
Almedingen, E. M. St Francis of Assisi   **92**
Francis I, King of France
See pages in the following book:
National Geographic Society. The Renaissance p255-85   **940.2**

Fiction
Shellabarger, S. The King's cavalier **Fic**
Francis, H. E.
One of the boys
In The Best American short stories, 1967 p67-83   **S C**
Franciscans
See pages in the following book:
Russell, B. A history of Western philosophy p463-75   **109**
Franck, César Auguste
See pages in the following books:
Cross, M. The Milton Cross New encyclopedia of the great composers and their music p352-64   **920.03**
Ewen, D. ed. The complete book of classical music p630-41   **780.1**
Ewen, D. ed. The world of great composers p270-80   **920**
Franco, Battista
See pages in the following book:
Vasari, G. The lives of the painters, sculptors and architects v4 p15-27   **920**
Franco, Francisco
See pages in the following book:
Carr, A. Men of power p237-51   **920**
Franco, Jean
An introduction to Spanish American literature   **860.9**
Franco-German War, 1870-1871
See pages in the following book:
Roscoe, T. True tales of bold escapes p177-227   **904**
Frank, Anne
The diary of a young girl   **940.54**
also in Frank, A. The works of Anne Frank p25-240   **839.3**
The diary of a young girl; dramatization. See Goodrich, F. The diary of Anne Frank
The works of Anne Frank   **839.3**

About
Schnabel, E. Anne Frank: a portrait in courage   **92**
Steenmeijer, A. G. ed. A tribute to Anne Frank   **92**
See also pages in the following book:
David, J. ed. Growing up Jewish p121-38   **920**
Frank, Charles P.
Edmund Wilson   **818**

Freeman, Mary E. Wilkins
Jimmy Scarecrow's Christmas
In Becker, M. L. ed. The home book of
Christmas p513-18   394.26

About
See pages in the following book:

Brooks, V. New England: Indian summer p475-84   810.9

Freeman, Orville L.
The National Forests of America   917.3
World without hunger   338.1

Freeman, R. A.
Indoro Bush College
In Angoff, C. ed. African writing today
p175-81   896
For another work by this author see
Ashdown, Clifford

Freeways. See Roads

The freezer. Bergen, C.
In The Best short plays, 1968 p47-58   808.82

Frei Montalva, Eduardo, President Chile
See pages in the following book:
Gunther, J. Inside South America p257-79   980

Freidel, Frank
(ed.) The New Deal and the American
people   973.917
(jt. auth.) Morison, S. E. Dissent in three
American wars   973
National Geographic Society. Our country's Presidents   920

A freight car incident. Crane, S.
In Crane, S. The complete short stories
& sketches of Stephen Crane p272-76   S C

Freitag, George H.
An old man and his hat
In The Best American short stories, 1968
p75-78   S C

Fremantle, Anne
Age of faith   940.1

Frémont, Jessie (Benton)
Randall, R. P. I Jessie   92

Fiction
Stone, I. Immortal wife   Fic

Frémont, John Charles
Randall, R. P. I Jessie [Frémont]   92
See also pages in the following books:
Stone, I. Men to match my mountains
p61-75, 80-88, 124-30   979.1
Stone, I. They also ran p139-58   920

Fiction
Stone, I. Immortal wife   Fic

French, Herbert E.
Of rivers and the sea   551.4

French, Warren
J. D. Salinger   813.09

The French. Carroll, J. T.   914.4

French and Indian War, 1755-1763. See
United States—History—French and Indian War, 1755-1763

The French and Indian War. Chidsey, D. B.   973.2

The French and Indian Wars. Hamilton,
E. P.   973.2

French art. See Art, French

French authors. See Authors, French

The French Chef cookbook. Child, J.   641.5

French cookery. See Cookery, French

French drama   842

History and criticism
See pages in the following books:
Gassner, J. Masters of the drama p263-314, 346-53, 397-423, 707-25   809.2
Nicoll, A. World drama p200-07, 299-334,
586-97   809.2

French essays   844

French fiction

History and criticism
See pages in the following book:
Camus, A. Lyrical and critical essays
p210-18   844

The French impressionists and their century.
Kelder, D.   759.4

French in Algeria
Fiction
Camus, A. The stranger   Fic

French language
See pages in the following book:
Pei, M. Talking your way around the
world p43-57   418

Dictionaries
Mansion's Shorter French and English
dictionary   443

The French lieutenant's woman. Fowles, J.   Fic

French literature
Bio-bibliography
The Oxford Companion to French literature   840.3
Dictionaries
The Oxford Companion to French literature   840.3
History and criticism
Cazamian, L. A history of French literature   840.9
See also pages in the following books:
Durant, W. The age of Louis XIV p104-63   940.2
Highet, G. The classical tradition p48-69,
390-407   809
Macy, J. The story of the world's literature p177-85, 210-42, 399-438   809
Maurois, A. From Proust to Camus   840.9

French national characteristics. See National characteristics, French

French painters. See Painters, French

French painting. See Painting, French

French philosophy. See Philosophy, French

French poetry
History and criticism
See pages in the following book:
Macy, J. The story of the world's literature p422-38   809

French prose literature
History and criticism
See pages in the following book:
Macy, J. The story of the world's literature p210-28, 399-421   809

French Revolution. See France—History—
Revolution, 1789-1799

The **French** Revolution. Carlyle, T. **944.04**

The **French** Revolution. Horizon Magazine
944.04

The **French** scarecrow. Maxwell, W.
In The New Yorker. Stories from The
New Yorker, 1950-1960 p167-79 **S C**

French sculptors. See Sculptors, French

French sculpture. See Sculpture, French

Fresco painting. See Mural painting and
decoration

Fresh air, bright water. Bryant, N. **799**

Fresh water. Davies, D. **333.9**

Fresh-water animals
Bridges, W. The New York Aquarium
Book of the water world **591.92**
See also Marine animals

Fresh-water biology
Amos, W. H. The life of the pond **574.92**
See also Fresh-water animals; Marine
biology

Fresh-water plants
See pages in the following book:
Axelrod, H. R. Axelrod's Tropical fish
book p16-25 **639**

The **freshest** boy. Fitzgerald, F. S.
In Fitzgerald, F. S. The stories of
F. Scott Fitzgerald p326-45 **S C**

Freuchen, Dagmar
(ed.) Freuchen, P. Peter Freuchen's Adventures in the Arctic **919.8**

Freuchen, Peter
Peter Freuchen's Adventures in the Arctic
919.8
Peter Freuchen's Book of the Seven Seas
910.4

Freud, Sigmund
Interpretation of dreams; criticism
In Downs, R. B. Books that changed the
world p174-85 **809**
About
Stoutenburg, A. Explorer of the uncon-
scious: Sigmund Freud **92**
See also pages in the following books:
Untermeyer, L. Makers of the modern
world p238-61 **920**
Wilson, J. R. The mind p90-103 **150**
Fiction
Stone, I. The passions of the mind **Fic**

Fribourg, Marjorie G.
The Supreme Court in American history
347.9

Fried, John J.
The mystery of heredity **575.1**

Friedlander, Joanne K.
Stock market ABC **332.6**

Friedman, Albert B.
(ed.) The Viking Book of folk ballads of
the English-speaking world. See The
Viking Book of folk ballads of the English-speaking world **808.81**

Friedman, Edward
Blood-photo
In The Best short plays, 1969 p443-75
808.82

Friel, Brian
Philadelphia, here I come!
In Richards, S. ed. Best plays of the
sixties p329-417 **808.82**

Friend, J. Newton
More Numbers: fun & facts **793.7**
Numbers: fun & facts **793.7**
Still More Numbers: fun & facts **793.7**

A **friend** of Kafka. Singer, I. B.
In Singer, I. B. An Isaac Bashevis
Singer reader p269-83 **S C**

Friendlich, Dick
Panorama of sports in America **796**

Friendly, Fred W.
Due to circumstances beyond our control
384.55

Friendly brook. Kipling, R.
In Kipling, R. The best short stories of
Rudyard Kipling p566-74 **S C**

The **friendly** call. Henry, O.
In Henry, O. The complete works of
O. Henry p998-1005 **S C**

The **Friendly** persuasion. West, J. **Fic**

Friends, Society of
Fisher, S. G. The Quaker colonies **973.2**
Gray, E. J. Penn **92**
See also pages in the following books:
Boorstin, D. J. The Americans: The colo-
nial experience p33-69 **917.3**
Langdon, W. C. Everyday things in
American life, 1607-1776 p48-62 **917.3**
Look. Religions in America p163-75 **280**
Lynd, S. ed. Nonviolence in America: a
documentary history p3-23 **323**
American Friends Service Committee
Who shall live? **301.3**
Fiction
Vining, E. G. The Virginia exiles **Fic**
West, J. Except for me and thee **Fic**
West, J. The friendly persuasion **Fic**

Friends. Wharton, E.
In Wharton, E. The collected short sto-
ries of Edith Wharton v 1 p197-214
S C

Friends in San Rosario. Henry, O.
In Henry, O. The complete works of
O. Henry p451-61 **S C**

Friendship. See Love

Friml, Rudolf
See pages in the following book:
Ewen, D. Composers for the American
musical theatre p20-28 **920**

Frings, Ketti
Look homeward, angel
In Gassner, J. ed. Best American plays;
5th ser. p237-76 **812.08**

Frisch, Karl von
See pages in the following book:
Ward, R. R. The living clocks p186-99
574.1

Frisch, Max
Biedermann and the firebugs
In Block, H. M. ed. Masters of modern
drama p1162-84 **808.82**
The firebugs
In Richards, S. ed. Best short plays of
the world theatre, 1958-1967 p97-
121 **808.82**

Fulbright, J. William
The arrogance of power   327.73
Fulks, Joe
See pages in the following book:
Pepe, P. Greatest stars of the NBA p139-48   920
Full circle. Wharton, E.
In Wharton, E. The collected short stories of Edith Wharton v2 p73-91   S C
A full moon in March. Yeats, W. B.
In Yeats, W. B. Collected plays of W. B. Yeats p389-96   822
Fuller, C. H.
A love song for seven little boys called Sam
In Jones, L. ed. Black fire p467-78   810.8
Fuller, Hoyt W.
The Senegalese
In Clarke, J. H. ed. American Negro short stories p226-45   S C
Fuller, Iola
The loon feather   Fic
Fuller, Margaret. See Ossoli, Sarah Margaret (Fuller) Marchesa d'
Fuller, Muriel
(ed.) More junior authors   920.03
(jt. ed.) Dobler, L. ed. The Dobler World directory of youth periodicals   016.05
Fuller, Richard Buckminster
Rosen, S. Wizard of the dome: R. Buckminster Fuller, designer for the future   92
The fullness of life. Wharton, E.
In Wharton, E. The collected short stories of Edith Wharton v 1 p12-20   S C
Fumed oak. Coward, N. P.
In Cerf, B. ed. Thirty famous one-act plays p499-515   808.82
Fun with a pencil. Loomis, A.   741.2
Fundamental reference sources. Cheney, F. N.   016
Fundamentals of watercolor painting. Richmond, L.   751.4
Funeral rites and ceremonies
Lewis, O. A death in the Sánchez family   309.172
Mitford, J. The American way of death   393
See also pages in the following book:
Gies, J. Life in a medieval city p68-75   914.4
Fungi
Christensen, C. M. The molds and man   589
Kavaler, L. Mushrooms, molds, and miracles   589
See also pages in the following books:
The Oxford Book of flowerless plants p30-37, 102-57   586
Zim, H. S. Plants p150-69   581
Funk, Charles Earle, 1881-1957
Thereby hangs a tale   422
Funk, Peter V. K.
It pays to increase your word power   428.2

Funk, Wilfred
Word origins and their romantic stories   422
Funk & Wagnalls Dictionary of data processing terms. Rodgers, H. A.   651.803
Funk & Wagnalls Dictionary of electronics   621.3803
Funk & Wagnalls Modern guide to synonyms and related words   424
Funk & Wagnalls New Standard dictionary of the English language   423
Funk & Wagnalls Standard college dictionary   423
Funk & Wagnalls Standard dictionary of folklore, mythology and legend   398.03
Funk & Wagnalls Standard dictionary of the English language. International ed.   423
Funk & Wagnalls Standard handbook of synonyms, antonyms, and prepositions. Fernald, J. C.   424
Funnies. See Comic books, strips, etc.
Funnyhouse of a Negro. Kennedy, A.
In The Best short plays, 1970 p127-47   808.82
Fur. Saki
In Saki. The short stories of Saki p422-27   S C
Fur trade
De Voto, B. Across the wide Missouri   978
Skinner, C. L. Adventurers of Oregon   979.5
Furman, Lucy
Christmas on Bee Tree
In Becker, M. L. ed. The home book of Christmas p649-60   394.26
Furnaces. See Blast furnaces
Furnas, C. C.
The engineer   620
Furnas, J. C.
The Americans   917.3
Goodbye to Uncle Tom   326
Furneaux, Robin
The Amazon   918.1
Furneaux, Rupert
The Battle of Saratoga   973.3
The furnished room. Henry, O.
In Henry, O. The best short stories of O. Henry p63-70   S C
In Henry, O. The complete works of O. Henry p98-103   S C
In Henry, O. The four million p239-50   S C
Furniture
Repairing
See pages in the following book:
Gladstone, B. The New York Times Complete manual of home repairs p403-29   643
Furniture, American
See pages in the following books:
The Arts in America: The colonial period p253-318   709.73
Langdon, W. C. Everyday things in American life, 1607-1776 p18-37, 147-57   917.3
Mendelowitz, D. M. A history of American art p166-78   709.73

Galois, Evariste
See pages in the following book:
Bell, E. T. Men of mathematics p362-77
920

Galsworthy, John
The apple tree
In The Scribner treasury p551-605 **S C**
The Forsyte saga **Fic**
Short stories included are: The Indian summer of a Forsyte; Awakening
In chancery
In Galsworthy, J. The Forsyte saga p363-639 **Fic**
Little man
In Cerf, B. ed. Thirty famous one-act plays p213-26 **808.82**
Loyalties
In Cerf, B. A. comp. Sixteen famous British plays p421-72 **822.08**
The man of property
In Galsworthy, J. The Forsyte saga p3-309 **Fic**
Plays **822**
Contents: The silver box; Joy; Strife; The eldest son; Justice; The little dream; The pigeon; The fugitive; The mob; A bit o' love; The foundations; The skin game; A family man; Loyalties; Windows; The forest; Old English; The show; Escape; The first and the last; The little man; Hall-marked; Defeat; The sun; Punch and go
Strife
In Dickinson, T. H. ed. Chief contemporary dramatists [1st ser] p111-47 **808.82**
To let
In Galsworthy, J. The Forsyte saga p665-921 **Fic**
About
See pages in the following book:
Wagenknecht, E. Cavalcade of the English novel p477-93 **823.09**

Gama, Vasco da
See pages in the following book:
Stefánsson, V. ed. Great adventures and explorations p163-88 **910.9**

Gambetta, Léon Michel
See pages in the following book:
Roscoe, T. True tales of bold escapes p177-227 **904**

The **gambler**, the nun, and the radio. Hemingway, E.
In Hemingway, E. The short stories of Ernest Hemingway p468-87 **S C**
In Hemingway, E. The snows of Kilimanjaro, and other stories p37-54 **S C**

Gambling. See Cards; Probabilities

Game and game birds
National Geographic Society. Water, prey, and game birds of North America **598**
See also Trapping

Game of chess. Goodman, D. S.
In Cerf, B. ed. Thirty famous one-act plays p347-56 **808.82**

Game preserves
Murphy, W. Wild sanctuaries **333.7**

Game theory
Davis, M. D. Game theory **519**

A **game** to catch. Wilbur, R.
In The New Yorker. Stories from The New Yorker, 1950-1960 p392-95 **S C**

Games
Foster, R. F. Foster's Complete Hoyle **795**
Gibson, W. Family games America plays **793**
Mulac, M. E. Games and stunts for schools, camps, and playgrounds **790**
See also pages in the following books:
Coffin, T. P. ed. Folklore in America p171-93 **398**
Lowndes, M. A manual for baby sitters p165-79 **649**
Shakespeare's England v2 p451-83 **822.3**
See also Amusements; Cards; Olympic games; Sports; also names of games, e.g. Chess

Games, Olympic. See Olympic games

Games and stunts for schools, camps, and playgrounds. Mulac, M. E. **790**

The **games** that we played. Weathers, W.
In The Best American short stories, 1968 p323-29 **S C**

Gamow, George
Biography of physics **530.9**
The creation of the universe **523.1**
Gravity **531**
One two three . . . infinity **500**
A planet called earth **551**
Thirty years that shook physics **530.1**

Gandhi, Indira (Nehru)
Lamb, B. P. The Nehrus of India **920**
Mohan, A. Indira Gandhi **92**

Gandhi, Mohandas K.
All men are brothers **92**
Gandhi's autobiography **92**
Gandhi on non-violence **323**
About
Payne, R. The life and death of Mahatma Gandhi **92**
See also pages in the following books:
Brown, J. D. India p75-85 **915.4**
Moore, C. D. ed. India yesterday and today p161-94 **915.4**
Thomas, H. Understanding the great philosophers p347-58 **109**
Thomas, N. Great dissenters p169-220 **920**
Untermeyer, L. Makers of the modern world p389-98 **920**

Ganges River
See pages in the following book:
Leopold, L. B. Water p128-43 **551.4**

Gangs. See Juvenile delinquency

Gann, Ernest K.
The high and the mighty **Fic**
In the company of eagles **Fic**

Gannett, Deborah (Sampson)
See pages in the following book:
Holbrook, S. H. Lost men of American history p55-62 **920**

Gannon, Robert
Walsh, J. Time is short and the water rises **333.7**

Gant, Matthew
The uses of intelligence
In Hitchcock, A. ed. Alfred Hitchcock
presents: A month of mystery p39-
50 **S C**
Garbage. See Refuse and refuse disposal
Garcia, Eugene Current- See Current-Garcia, Eugene
García Lorca, Federico
Blood wedding
In Block, H. M. ed. Masters of modern
drama p551-72 **808.82**
About
Lewis, R. ed. Still waters of the air
861.08
See also pages in the following book:
Stamm, J. R. A short history of Spanish
literature p209-15 **860.9**
García Márquez, Gabriel
The day after Saturday
In Cohen, J. M. ed. Latin American
writing today p182-202 **860.8**
García Moreno, Gabriel
See pages in the following book:
Crow, J. A. The epic of Latin America
p627-33 **980**
Garden design. See Landscape gardening
The **garden** lodge. Cather, W.
In Cather, W. Willa Cather's Collected
short fiction, 1892-1912 v2 p187-97
S C
The **garden**-party. Mansfield, K.
In Mansfield, K. The short stories of
Katherine Mansfield p534-49 **S C**
Gardening
See pages in the following books:
Driver, H. E. Indians of North America
p66-83 **970.1**
United States. Department of Agriculture. Consumers all p214-78 **640.73**
United States. Department of Agriculture. Water p451-77 **631.7**
Dictionaries
Wyman, D. Wyman's Gardening encyclopedia **635.03**
Gardening as a profession
See pages in the following book:
Stone, A. A. Careers in agribusiness and
industry p215-24 **338.1**
Gardening encyclopedia, Wyman's. Wyman,
D. **635.03**
Gardens
See pages in the following book:
Burton, E. The pageant of Elizabethan
England p211-34 **914.2**
The **gardens** of Mont-Saint-Michel. Maxwell, W.
In The Best American short stories,
1970 p174-93 **S C**
Gardner, Albert Ten Eyck
New York (City) Metropolitan
Museum of Art. American sculpture
730.973
Gardner, Erle Stanley
The case of the crimson kiss
In Haycraft, H. ed. A treasury of great
mysteries v 1 p147-87 **S C**

Gardner, Gary
A train going somewhere
In The Best short plays, 1968 p311-26
808.82
Gardner, Helen
Gardner's Art through the ages **709**
Gardner, Herb
A thousand-clowns
In Gassner, J. ed. Best American plays;
5th ser. p419-58 **812.08**
Who is Harry Kellerman and why is he
saying those terrible things about me?
In The Best American short stories,
1968 p79-100 **S C**
Gardner, John W.
No easy victories **309.173**
The recovery of confidence **309.2**
Gardner, Martin
Martin Gardner's New mathematical diversions from Scientific American **793.7**
Relativity for the million **530.1**
The unexpected hanging, and other mathematical diversions **793.7**
Gardonyi, Geza
Slave of the Huns **Fic**
Gargal, Berry
Katz, B. comp. Magazines for libraries
016.05
Garland, Hamlin
A son of the middle border **92**
Garment making. See Dressmaking
Garner, Wightman Wells
See pages in the following book:
Ward, R. R. The living clocks p113-33
574.1
Garraty, John A.
The new guide to study abroad **378.3**
(ed.) Quarrels that have shaped the Constitution **342.73**
Garrett, George
The old army game
In Foley, M. ed. Fifty best American
short stories, 1915-1965 p691-701
S C
Garrett, Jimmy
We own the night; play
In Jones, L. ed. Black fire p527-40 **810.8**
Garrity, Devin A.
(ed.) 44 Irish short stories **S C**
Garshin, V. M.
The signal
In Seltzer, T. comp. Best Russian short
stories p165-77 **S C**
Garvey, Marcus
See pages in the following book:
Bontemps, A. Anyplace but here p191-94,
198-204, 211-15 **301.451**
Garvey, Mona
Library displays **021.7**
Gary, Romain
A humanist
In Hitchcock, A. ed. Alfred Hitchcock
presents: A month of mystery
p277-82 **S C**
In The Saturday Evening Post. Best
modern short stories p47-51 **S C**

Gary, Ind.
Description
See pages in the following book:
Moyers, B. Listening to America p58-78
917.3

Gas. Kaiser, G.
In Tucker, S. M. ed. Twenty-five modern plays p603-39   808.82

Gas and oil engines. See Automobiles—Engines

Gases
See pages in the following book:
Ley, W. Another look at Atlantis, and fifteen other essays p155-69   508

Gaskell, Elizabeth Cleghorn
The life of Charlotte Brontë   92

Gaskell, T. F.
World beneath the oceans   551.4

Gass, William H.
In the heart of the heart of the country
In The Best American short stories, 1968 p101-23   S C

Gassner, John
(ed.) Best American plays; supplementary volume, 1918-1958   812.08
(ed.) Best American plays; 3d ser.-6th ser.   812.08
(ed.) Best plays of the early American theatre   812.08
(ed.) Best plays of the modern American theatre; 2d. ser.   812.08
Masters of the drama   809.2
(ed.) Twenty best European plays on the American stage   808.82
(ed.) Twenty best plays of the modern American theatre   812.08
(ed.) Twenty-five best plays of the modern American theatre; early ser.   812.08
(ed.) The Reader's encyclopedia of world drama. See The Reader's encyclopedia of world drama   809.203

Gassner, Mollie
(jt. auth.) Gassner, J. ed. Best plays of the early American theatre   812.08

Gaster, Theodor H.
(ed.) Frazer, Sir J. G. The new Golden bough   291

Gaston, Edwin W.
Conrad Richter   813.09

Gastronomy. See Cookery; Food; Menus

Gates, Jean Key
Guide to the use of books and libraries   028.7

The **gateway** to history. Nevins, A.   907

Gateways to readable books. Strang, R.   028.52

The **gathering** storm. Churchill, W. S.   940.53

Gauchos. See Cowboys

Gaugamela, Battle of, 331 B.C.
See pages in the following books:
Creasy, Sir E. S. Fifteen decisive battles of the world p57-84   904
Mitchell, J. B. Twenty decisive battles of the world p39-55   904

Gauguin, Paul
See pages in the following books:
Cheney, S. The story of modern art p237-68   709.03
Wallace, R. The world of Van Gogh, 1853-1890 p80-87, 117-27   92
Fiction
Maugham, W. S. The moon and sixpence   Fic

Gaul
History—Fiction
Anderson, P. L. With the eagles   Fic

Gaulle, Charles de, President France
Schoenbrun, D. The three lives of Charles de Gaulle   92
See also pages in the following book:
Schlesinger, A. M. A thousand days p349-58   973.922

Gauss, Karl Friedrich
See pages in the following books:
Bell, E. T. Men of mathematics p218-69   920
Newman, J. R. ed. The world of mathematics v 1 p294-339   510.8

Gautier, Théophile
Mademoiselle de Maupin; criticism
In Ernst, M. L. Censorship: the search for the obscene p56-65   343

Gavell, Mary Ladd
The rotifer
In The Best American short stories, 1968 p125-36   S C

Gaver, Mary Virginia
(jt. auth.) Hook, L. The research paper   808.02

Gay, Peter
Age of Enlightment   901.93

Gay-Lussac, Joseph Louis
See pages in the following book:
Jones, B. Z. ed. The golden age of science p187-216   920

Gayley, Charles Mills
(ed.) The classic myths in English literature and in art   292

Gazetteers. See Names, Geographical

Gazzo, Michael V.
A hatful of rain
In Gassner, J. ed. Best American plays; 4th ser. p179-209   812.08

Gbadamossi, Rasheed A.
Bats and babies
In Angoff, C. ed. African writing today p114-18   896
In the beginning
In Angoff, C. ed. African writing today p119-20   896
The sexton's deaf son
In Angoff, C. ed. African writing today p121-24   896

Gear, Brian
A pretty row of pretty ribbons
In The Best short plays, 1970 p351-69   808.82

Gebauer, Emanuel L.
(jt. auth.) Cornberg, S. A stage crew handbook   792

Gehman, Henry Snyder
The New Westminster Dictionary of the Bible. See The new Westminster Dictionary of the Bible   220.3

Geismar, Maxwell
American moderns: from rebellion to conformity   **813.09**
Writers in crisis   **813.09**
(ed.) Lardner, R. The Ring Lardner reader   **S C**

Gelder, Richard G. van. See Van Gelder, Richard G.

Geldzahler, Henry
American painting in the twentieth century   **759.13**

Gellens, Jay
(ed.) Twentieth century interpretations of A farewell to arms   **813.09**

Gems
Baxter, W. T. Jewelry, gem cutting, and metalcraft   **739.27**
See also Precious stones

Gems for the taking. Brown, M. L. T.   **553**

Gemstones and minerals: how and where to find them. See Sinkankas, J. Prospecting for gemstones and minerals   **553**

General Agreement on Tariffs and Trade. See Contracting Parties to the General Agreement on Tariffs and Trade

The **general** of the order. Dumas, A.
In Dulles, A. ed. Great spy stories from fiction p89-104   **S C**

General Pingley. Schaefer, J.
In Schaefer, J. The collected stories of Jack Schaefer p135-47   **S C**

General woodworking. Groneman, C. H. **684**

Generals
American Heritage. Eisenhower, American hero   **92**
Catton, B. Grant moves south   **92**
Catton, B. Grant takes command   **92**
Catton, B. U. S. Grant and the American military tradition   **92**
Commager, H. S. America's Robert E. Lee   **92**
Freeman, D. S. Lee of Virginia   **92**
Gunther, J. The riddle of MacArthur   **92**
Lewis, L. Captain Sam Grant   **92**
MacArthur, D. Reminiscences   **92**
Miers, E. S. Robert E. Lee   **92**
Young, D. Rommel, the desert fox   **92**

Generation gap. See Conflict of generations

Genes. See Heredity

The **genetic** code. Asimov, I.   **575.1**

Genetics
Asimov, I. The genetic code   **575.1**
Beadle, G. The language of life   **575.1**
Fried, J. J. The mystery of heredity **575.1**
Scientific American. Facets of genetics   **575.1**
See also pages in the following books:
Halacy, D. S. Man alive p71-88   **574**
Newman, J. R. ed. What is science? p256-89   **508**
Osborn, F. ed. Our crowded planet p51-68   **301.3**
Scientific American. The living cell p148-58   **574.8**
Taylor, G. R. The biological time bomb p158-85   **577**
See also Evolution; Life (Biology); Reproduction

Geneva. Shaw, B.
In Shaw, B. Complete plays, with prefaces v5 p651-759   **822**

Genius. See Gifted children

The **genius** of American politics. Boorstin, D. J.   **973**

Genkaku-Sanbo. Akutagawa, R.
In Akutagawa, R. Japanese short stories p145-70   **S C**

The **gentle** boy. Hawthorne, N.
In Hawthorne, N. Hawthorne's Short stories p33-63   **S C**

The **gentle** grafter. Henry, O.
In Henry, O. The complete works of O. Henry p267-354   **S C**

The **gentle** vultures. Asimov, I.
In Asimov, I. Nine tomorrows p127-43   **S C**

The **gentleman** caller. Bullins, E.
In The Best short plays, 1970 p235-48   **808.82**

The **gentleman** from San Francisco. Bunin, I.
In Seltzer, T. comp. Best Russian short stories p522-56   **S C**

A **gentleman** of La Porte. Harte, B.
In Harte, B. The best short stories of Bret Harte p503-17   **S C**

Gentlemen. See Behavior

Gentlemen, be seated. Heinlein, R. A.
In Heinlein, R. A. Robert A. Heinlein's The past through tomorrow p223-31   **S C**

Gentlemen of the press. Wolfe, T.
In Wolfe, T. The hills beyond p49-65   **S C**

Gentlemen, start your engines. Shaw, W. **92**

Gentry, Curt
Powers, F. G. Operation Overflight **327**

Geochemistry
Scientific American. The biosphere **551**

Geographical atlases. See Atlases

Geographical dictionary, Webster's   **910.3**

Geographical distribution of animals and plants
See pages in the following book:
Halacy, D. S. Habitat p87-109   **574.5**
See also Alpine plants; Animals—Migration; Desert animals; Fresh-water plants

Geographical distribution of man. See Anthropogeography; Ethnology

Geographical names. See Names, Geographical

Geography
Life (Periodical) Handbook of the nations and international organizations   **910**
See also Anthropogeography; Atlases; Boundaries; Discoveries (in geography); Ethnology; Maps; Physical geography; Voyages and travels; also names of countries, states, etc. with the subdivision Description and travel, e.g. United States—Description and travel

Dictionaries

The Columbia Lippincott Gazetteer of the world   **910.3**
Monkhouse, F. J. A dictionary of geography   **910.3**

Geography—Dictionaries—*Continued*
The New Century Cyclopedia of names
031
Webster's Geographical dictionary   910.3
Worldmark Encyclopedia of the nations
910.3

Geography, Ancient
See pages in the following books:
Sarton, G. A history of science v 1 p299-330   509
Sarton, G. A history of science v2 p99-116, 413-33   509
Maps
Heyden, A. A. M. van der, ed. Atlas of the classical world   911

Geography, Biblical. See Bible—Geography

Geography, Commercial
Maps
Goode, J. P. Goode's World atlas   912

Geography, Economic. See Geography, Commercial

Geography, Historical
Maps
See Atlases, Historical

Geography, Physical. See Physical geography

Geography, Social. See Anthropogeography

Geological physics. See Geophysics

Geologists
Moore, R. The earth we live on   551.09

Geology
Beiser, A. The earth   551
Bertin, L. Larousse Encyclopedia of the earth   550
Gamow, G. A planet called earth   551
See also pages in the following books:
Hammond, Incorporated. Earth and space p65-122   551
Time-Life Books. A guide to science, and Index to the Life Science library p80-93   500

See also Earth; Glaciers; Mineralogy; Rocks

Hawaii
See pages in the following book:
Carlquist, S. Hawaii: a natural history p 1-63   574.9
History
Moore, R. The earth we live on   551.09

United States
Matthews, W. H. A guide to the national parks   917.3

Geology, Economic. See Mines and mineral resources

Geology, Historical. See Geology, Stratigraphic

Geology, Stratigraphic
See pages in the following book:
Quennell, M. Everyday life in prehistoric times p23-33   913.03

Geometry
See pages in the following books:
Ball, W. W. R. Mathematical recreations & essays p76-128, 326-49   793.7
Hogben, L. Mathematics for the million p343-401   510

Newman, J. R. ed. The world of mathematics v 1 p235-53, 647-68   510.8
Nourse, A. E. Universe, earth, and atom p355-63   530.9

Geometry, Projective
Newman, J. R. ed. The world of mathematics v 1 p622-41   510.8

Geophysics
Chapman, S. IGY: year of discovery   551
Hammond, Incorporated. Earth and space   551
See pages in the following book:
Scientific American. The biosphere   551
Scientific American. The planet earth   551
See also pages in the following book:
Claiborne, R. Climate, man, and history p101-15   551.59

Geopolitics. See World politics

Georgano, G. N.
(ed.) Encyclopedia of American automobiles   629.22

George, David Lloyd. See Lloyd George, David Lloyd George, 1st Earl

George, Henry
Heilbroner, R. L. The worldly philosophers   330.1

George Peabody College for Teachers, Nashville, Tenn.
Free and inexpensive learning materials
016.3713

Georgia
Fiction
McCullers, C. The member of the wedding   Fic
History
See pages in the following book:
Boorstin, D. J. The Americans: The colonial experience p71-96   917.3

Georgian England, The pageant of. Burton, E.   914.2

The Georgians at home. See Burton, E. The pageant of Georgian England   914.2

Georgia's ruling. Henry, O.
In Henry, O. The complete works of O. Henry p1213-23   S C

Gerald, John Bart
Blood letting
In The Best American short stories, 1970 p108-14   S C
Walking wounded
In The Best American short stories, 1969 p37-48   S C

Gerber, Philip L.
Robert Frost   811.09

The German-Americans. O'Connor, R.
301.453

German art. See Art, German

German artists. See Artists, German

German composers. See Composers, German

German cookery. See Cookery, German

German drama
History and criticism
See pages in the following book:
Gassner, J. Masters of the drama p317-41, 446-94, 705-07   809.2

German language
See pages in the following book:
Pei, M. Talking your way around the world p29-42   418

Germination

See pages in the following book:

Scientific American. Plant agriculture p57-63 **581**

Germs. See Bacteriology; Microorganisms

Geronimo, Apache chief

Geronimo: his own story **92**

About

See pages in the following books:

American Heritage. The American Heritage Book of great adventures of the Old West p330-61 **978**

Brown, D. Bury my heart at Wounded Knee p392-413 **970.4**

Gerontology. See Aged

Gershwin, George

Ewen, D. George Gershwin: his journey to greatness **92**

See also pages in the following books:

Cross, M. The Milton Cross New encyclopedia of the great composers and their music p365-83 **920.03**

Ewen, D. Composers for the American musical theatre p103-21 **920**

Ewen, D. Great men of American popular song p169-87 **920**

Ewen, D. ed. The new book of modern composers p185-200 **920**

Ewen, D. The story of America's musical theater p89-93, 112-20, 141-47 **782.8**

Shippen, K. B. The heritage of music p271-73 **780.9**

Untermeyer, L. Makers of the modern world p721-16 **920**

Gershwin, Ira

See pages in the following books:

Ewen, D. George Gershwin: his journey to greatness p158-68, 316-21 **92**

Ewen, D. Great men of American popular song p169-87 **920**

Gerstenberg, Alice

Overtones

In Cerf, B. ed. Thirty famous one-act plays p483-93 **808.82**

Gesell, Arnold

Youth: the years from ten to sixteen **155.5**

Gesner, Clark

You're a good man, Charlie Brown **812**

Gessler, Clifford

Hawaii: Isles of enchantment; excerpt

In Day, A. G. ed. The spell of Hawaii p286-97 **919.69**

Gessner, Robert

The moving image **791.43**

The gesture. Groshong, J.

In The Best American short stories, 1965 p99-112 **S C**

Get a horse! Niven, L.

In The Best from Fantasy and Science Fiction; 19th ser. p195-210 **S C**

Getting high in government circles. Buchwald, A. **817**

Getting married. Shaw, B.

In Shaw, B. Complete plays, with prefaces v4 p393-492 **822**

Getting off the altitude. Lessing, D.

In Lessing, D. African stories p555-70 **S C**

Getting to Williamstown. Hood, H.

In The Best American short stories, 1966 p113-24 **S C**

Gettysburg, Battle of, 1863

See pages in the following books:

Armstrong, O. K. The fifteen decisive battles of the United States p219-50 **973**

Catton, B. Prefaces to history p25-33 **973.7**

Getzel the monkey. Singer, I. B.

In Singer, I. B. An Isaac Bashevis Singer reader p257-68 **S C**

Geymonat, Ludovico

Galileo Galilei **92**

Ghana

See pages in the following book:

Davidson, B. The lost cities of Africa p81-90 **913.6**

Fiction

Armah, A. K. The beautiful ones are not yet born **Fic**

Politics and government

See pages in the following book:

Kenworthy, L. S. Leaders of new nations p65-91 **920**

Gherardi, Christofano, known as Doceno

See pages in the following book:

Vasari, G. The lives of the painters, sculptors and architects v3 p219-34 **920**

Ghiberti, Lorenzo

See pages in the following book:

Vasari, G. The lives of the painters, sculptors and architects v 1 p239-54 **920**

Ghirlandaio, Domenico

See pages in the following book:

Vasari, G. The lives of the painters, sculptors and architects v2 p68-79 **920**

A ghost. Maupassant, G. de

In Maupassant, G. de. The odd number p167-82 **S C**

Ghost dance

See pages in the following book:

Brown, D. Bury my heart at Wounded Knee p416-38 **970.4**

A ghost of a chance. Henry, O.

In Henry, O. The complete works of O. Henry p854-59 **S C**

Ghost of Gideon Wise. Chesterton, G. K.

In Chesterton, G. K. The Father Brown omnibus p610-30 **S C**

The ghost sonata. Strindberg, A.

In Block, H. M. ed. Masters of modern drama p113-25 **808.82**

Ghost stories

See pages in the following book:

Hughes, L. ed. The book of Negro folklore p163-82 **398**

A ghost story. Twain, M.

In Twain, M. The complete short stories of Mark Twain p244-49 **S C**

Ghost town. Schaefer, J.

In Schaefer, J. The collected stories of Jack Schaefer p270-74 **S C**

Ghosts

Holzer, H. Gothic ghosts **133.1**

See also Demonology

Ghosts. Ibsen, H.
In Block, H. M. ed. Masters of modern drama p68-91   808.82
In Ibsen, H. Eleven plays of Henrik Ibsen p95-173   839.8
In Ibsen, H. Six plays p83-153   839.8

A ghoul's accountant. Crane, S.
In Crane, S. The complete short stories & sketches of Stephen Crane p77-79   S C

Giant. Ferber, E.   Fic

Giant molecules. Kaufman, M.   668.4

Giant molecules. Mark, H. F.   668.4

Giants in the earth. Rolvaag, O. E.   Fic

Giants of the keyboard. Chapin, V.   920

Giard, Alfred Mathiew
See pages in the following book:
Moore, R. Man, time, and fossils p95-108   573.2

Gibbon, Edward
The decline and fall of the Roman Empire   937
The decline and fall of the Roman Empire. Abridged   937

About
See pages in the following book:
Durant, W. Rousseau and revolution p795-808   940.2

Gibbons, James Cardinal
See pages in the following books:
O'Connor, R. The German-Americans p350-60   301.453
Shannon, W. V. The American Irish p114-30   301.453

Gibbons v. Ogden
See pages in the following book:
Fribourg, M. G. The Supreme Court in American history p58-73   347.9

Gibbs, Wolcott
Ring out, wild bells
In White, E. B. ed. A subtreasury of American humor; abridged p343-46   817.08

Gibran, Khalil
The Prophet   892.7

Gibson, Althea
I always wanted to be somebody   92

Gibson, Bob
From ghetto to glory: the story of Bob Gibson   92

Gibson, Walter
Family games America plays   793
Hoyle's Simplified guide to the popular card games   795.4

Gibson, William
The miracle worker   812
Two for the seesaw
In Gassner, J. ed. Best American plays; 5th ser. p341-78   812.08

Gide, André
The counterfeiters   Fic
The immoralist   Fic

About
See pages in the following book:
Durant, W. Interpretations of life p138-49   809

Gideon, Clarence Earl
Lewis, A. Gideon's trumpet   347.9

Gideon, Earl. See Gideon, Clarence Earl

Gideon. Chayefsky, P.
In Gassner, J. ed. Best American plays; 5th ser. p553-88   812.08

Gideon's trumpet. Lewis, A.   347.9

Gies, Frances
(jt. auth.) Gies, J. Life in a medieval city   914.4

Gies, Joseph
Harry S. Truman   92
Life in a medieval city   914.4

The gift. Bradbury, R.
In Bradbury, R. R is for rocket p157-59   S C

The gift bearer. O'Connor, P. F.
In The Best American short stories, 1971 p217-36   S C

A gift for numbers. Nourse, A. E.
In Nourse, A. E. R for tomorrow p74-87   S C

Gift from the sea. Lindbergh, A. M.   818

Gift of grass. Adams, A.
In Prize stories, 1971: The O. Henry Awards p58-66   S C

The gift of the Magi. Henry, O.
In Becker, M. L. ed. The home book of Christmas p201-07   394.26
In Day, A. G. ed. The greatest American short stories p165-72   S C
In Henry, O. The best short stories of O. Henry p 1-7   S C
In Henry, O. The complete works of O. Henry p7-11   S C
In Henry, O. The four million p16-25   S C

Gifted children
See pages in the following book:
Sargent, S. S. Basic teachings of the great psychologists p249-56   150

Gifts of passage. Rama Rau, S.   92

Gilbert, Bil
The bird, the vow and the child
In Sports Illustrated. The wonderful world of sport p242-45   796

Gilbert, Cynthia S.
Catherine
In Seventeen. Seventeen from Seventeen p136-46   S C

Gilbert, Elliot L.
Link in the chain
In Best detective stories of the year [1969] p160-65   S C

Gilbert, Martin
American history atlas   911
Jewish history atlas   911
(ed.) Lloyd George   92
Recent history atlas: 1870 to the present day   911
Winston S. Churchill, v3: The challenge of war, 1914-1916   92

Gilbert, Michael
The amateur
In Hitchcock, A. ed. Alfred Hitchcock presents: A month of mystery p134-44   S C

Gilbert, Michael—*Continued*
The system
In Best detective stories of the year, 1971 p69-84 **S C**
In Mystery Writers of America. Crime without murder p79-91 **S C**
Gilbert, Sir William Schwenck
The complete plays of Gilbert and Sullivan 782.8
Contents: Thespis; Trial by jury; The sorcerer; H.M.S. Pinafore; The pirates of Penzance; Patience; Iolanthe; Princess Ida; The Mikado; The Yeoman of the Guard; Ruddigore; The gondoliers; Utopia Limited; The Grand Duke
Martyn Green's Treasury of Gilbert & Sullivan 782.8
Operettas included are: Trial by jury; The sorcerer; H.M.S. Pinafore; The pirates of Penzance; Patience; Iolanthe; Princess Ida; The Mikado; Ruddigore; The Yeomen of the Guard; The gondoliers
Poems of W. S. Gilbert 821
Gilbert of Mons. See Gislebertus
Gilbreth, Frank B. 1911-
Belles on their toes [biography of Lillian Gilbreth] 92
Cheaper by the dozen [biography of Frank B. Gilbreth, Sr]. 1963 edition 92
Cheaper by the dozen [biography of Frank B. Gilbreth, Sr] c1948 Large type ed. 92
Time out for happiness [biography of Lillian Gilbreth] 92
Gilbreth, Frank Bunker, 1868-1924
Gilbreth, F. B. Cheaper by the dozen. 1963 edition 92
Gilbreth, F. B. Cheaper by the dozen. c1948 Large type ed. 92
Gilbreth, F. B. Time out for happiness [biography of Lillian Gilbreth] 92
Gilbreth, Lillian Evelyn (Moller)
Gilbreth, F. B. Belles on their toes 92
Gilbreth, F. B. Time out for happiness 92
See also pages in the following book:
Stoddard, H. Famous American women p193-200 920
Gilbreth family
Gilbreth, F. B. Belles on their toes [biography of Lillian Gilbreth] 92
Gilbreth, F. B. Cheaper by the dozen [biography of Frank B. Gilbreth, Sr]. 1963 edition 92
Gilbreth, F. B. Cheaper by the dozen [biography of Frank B. Gilbreth, Sr]. c1948 Large type ed. 92
Gilchrist, Jack
Opening day
In The Best American short stories, 1965 p93-98 **S C**
The gilded six-bits. Hurston, Z. N.
In Clarke, J. H. ed. American Negro short stories p63-74 **S C**
In Hughes, L. ed. The best short stories by Negro writers p74-85 **S C**
Gildersleeve, Thomas R.
Computer data processing and programming 651.8
Giles, Janice Holt
Johnny Osage **Fic**
Gill, Sir David
See pages in the following book:
Jones, B. Z. ed. The golden age of science p551-63 920

Gill, Richard T.
The code
In The New Yorker. Stories from The New Yorker, 1950-1960 p180-90 **S C**
Gillespie, Alfred
Tonight at nine thirty-six
In The Best American short stories, 1970 p115-37 **S C**
Gillespie, Charles Coulston
(ed.) Dictionary of scientific biography. See Dictionary of scientific biography 920.03
Gillespie, Dizzy. See Gillespie, John Birks
Gillespie, John Birks
See pages in the following book:
Gitler, I. Jazz masters of the forties p58-109 920
Gillette, William
Secret service
In Gassner, J. ed. Best plays of the early American theatre p277-360 812.08
In Quinn, A. H. ed. Representative American plays p545-620 812.08
Gillhoff, Gerd A.
Crowell's Spanish-English & English-Spanish dictionary. See Crowell's Spanish-English & English-Spanish dictionary 463
Gillies, Mary Davis
The new How to keep house 640
Gilroy, Frank D.
The subject was roses
In Gassner, J. ed. Best American plays; 6th ser. p567-94 812.08
Gimbutas, Marija Alseikaite
The Balts 913.47
Gimpel the fool. Singer, I. B.
In Singer, I. B. An Isaac Bashevis, Singer reader p3-21 **S C**
Gin and bitterness. Richards, S.
In The Best short plays of 1958-1959 p69-93 808.82
Ginsberg, Allen
See pages in the following books:
Rosenthal, M. L. The new poets p89-112 821.09
Roszak, T. The making of a counter culture p124-54 301.24
Ginsbury, Norman
The shoemaker and the Devil
In The Best short plays, 1968 p109-30 808.82
Giotto di Bondone
See pages in the following book:
Vasari, G. The lives of the painters, sculptors and architects v 1 p65-86 920
Gipsies. See Gypsies
Gipson, Lawrence Henry
The coming of the Revolution, 1763-1775 973.2
Gipsy Moth IV (Ketch)
Chichester, Sir F. Gipsy Moth circles the world 910.4
Gipsy Moth circles the world. Chichester, Sir F. 910.4

Girard, Denis
(ed.) The New Cassell's French dictionary: French-English, English-French. See The New Cassell's French dictionary: French-English, English-French
443

Giraudoux, Jean
Amphitryon 38
In Cerf, B. A. comp. Sixteen famous European plays p515-68 **808.82**
The Apollo of Bellac
In Cerf, B. ed. 24 favorite one-act plays p308-32 **808.82**
Electra
In Block, H. M. ed. Masters of modern drama p701-29 **808.82**
The madwoman of Chaillot
In Block, H. M. ed. Masters of modern drama p731-56 **808.82**
In Gassner, J. ed. Twenty best European plays on the American stage p241-77 **808.82**
Ondine
In Gassner, J. ed. Twenty best European plays on the American stage p200-40 **808.82**
Tiger at the gates
In Gassner, J. ed. Twenty best European plays on the American stage p55-89 **808.82**

"Girl." Henry, O.
In Henry, O. The complete works of O. Henry p1134-38 **S C**
The **girl** and the graft. Henry, O.
In Henry, O. The complete works of O. Henry p1525-29 **S C**
The **girl** and the habit. Henry, O.
In Henry, O. The complete works of O. Henry p1593-97 **S C**
Girl from Samos. Menander of Athens
In Oates, W. J. ed. The complete Greek drama v2 p1125-41 **882.08**
Girl on the bus. Sansom, W.
In Havighurst, W. ed. Masters of the modern short story p367-79 **S C**
The **girl** who recruited. Lederer, W. J.
In Lederer, W. J. The ugly American p83-85 **S C**
The **girl** who sang with the Beatles. Hemenway, R.
In Abrahams, W. ed. Fifty years of the American short story v 1 p367-80 **S C**
In Prize stories, 1970: The O. Henry awards p 1-16 **S C**
The **girl** with the green eyes. Fitch, C.
In Quinn, A. H. ed. Representative American plays p637-74 **812.08**

Girls
Sugarman, D. A. The Seventeen Guide to knowing yourself **155.5**

Girls and sex. Pomeroy, W. B. **612.6**

Gislebertus
See pages in the following book:
Horizon Magazine. The light of the past p110-21 **901.9**

Gissing, George Robert
See pages in the following book:
Karl, F. R. An age of fiction: the nineteenth century British novel p343-48 **823.09**

Gitler, Ira
Jazz masters of the forties **920**
Gittelsohn, Roland B.
The meaning of Judaism **296**
Giulia Lazzari. Maugham, W. S.
In Dulles, A. ed. Great spy stories from fiction p370-96 **S C**
Giulio Romano
See pages in the following book:
Vasari, G. The lives of the painters, sculptors and architects v3 p97-112 **920**
Give Charlie a little time. Stuart, J.
In Stuart, J. Come back to the farm p21-38 **S C**
Glacial epoch
See pages in the following books:
Claiborne, R. Climate, man, and history p80-86, 116-41 **551.59**
Fenton, C. L. The fossil book p436-47 **560**
Glacier National Park
Olsen, J. Night of the grizzlies **599**
See also pages in the following book:
National Geographic Society. America's wonderlands p111-37 **917.3**
Glaciers
See pages in the following books:
Chapman, S. IGY: year of discovery p28-34 **551**
Thomas, L. Lowell Thomas' Book of the high mountains p62-69 **910.9**
Gladstone, Bernard
The New York Times Complete manual of home repair **643**
Gladstone, William Ewart
See pages in the following book:
Strachey, L. Queen Victoria p327-66 **92**
Gladwin, Thomas
Poverty U.S.A. **330.973**
Glamour. Benét, S. V.
In Benét, S. V. Selected works of Stephen Vincent Benét v2 **818**
Glands, Ductless. See Hormones
Glasgow, Ellen
Vein of iron **Fic**
About
See pages in the following books:
Auchincloss, L. Pioneers & caretakers p56-91 **813.09**
Kazin, A. On native grounds p247-64 **810.9**
Quinn, A. H. American fiction p670-82 **813.09**
Wagenknecht, E. Cavalcade of the American novel p267-80 **813.09**
Glaspell, Susan
Suppressed desires
In Cerf, B. ed. Thirty famous one-act plays 327-41 **808.82**
Trifles
In Cerf, B. ed. 24 favorite one-act plays p333-46 **808.82**
In Gassner, J. ed. Twenty-five best plays of the modern American theatre; early ser. p695-702 **812.08**
About
See pages in the following book:
Gould, J. Modern American playwrights p26-49 **812.09**

Glass
Maloney, F. J. T. Glass in the modern
world   666
See also pages in the following books:
Langdon, W. C. Everyday things in
American life, 1607-1776 p199-210 917.3
National Geographic Society. Vacation-
land U.S.A. p364-71   917.3
The glass-blowers. Du Maurier, D.   Fic
The glass giant of Palomar. Woodbury,
D. O.   522
Glass house of prejudice. Baruch, D. W.
   301.45
Glass in the modern world. Maloney, F. J. T.
   666
The glass key. Hammett, D.
In Hammett, D. The novels of Dashiell
Hammett p441-588   Fic
Glass manufacture
Maloney, F. J. T. Glass in the modern
world   666
The glass menagerie. Williams, T.   812
—Same
In Block, H. M. ed. Masters of modern
drama p991-1017   808.82
In Gassner, J. ed. Best plays of the mod-
ern American theatre; 2d ser. p 1-
38   812.08
In Six modern American plays p271-340
   812.08
Glass painting and staining
See pages in the following book:
Adams, H. Mont-Saint-Michel and Char-
tres p128-41   726
Glasstone, Samuel
Sourcebook on atomic energy   539.7
Glazer, Nathan
American Judaism   296
Beyond the melting pot   301.45
Glazes
See pages in the following book:
Chandler, M. Ceramics in the modern
world p89-111   666
Glendower, Owen
See pages in the following book:
Sutcliff, R. Heroes and history p115-29
   920
Glenn, Harold T.
Glenn's Auto repair manual. See Glenn's
Auto repair manual   629.28
Glenn's Foreign car repair manual 629.28
Honda: repair & tune-up guide   629.28
Glenn, John Herschel
See pages in the following book:
We seven p25-38, 99-107, 137-42, 157-70,
233-46, 281-327   629.45
Glenn's Auto repair manual   629.28
Glenn's Foreign car repair manual. Glenn,
H. T.   629.28
Glenn's New auto repair manual. See Glenn's
Auto repair manual   629.28
A glimpse. Wharton, E.
In Wharton, E. The collected short sto-
ries of Edith Wharton v2 p687-705
   S C
The glimpse of reality. Shaw, B.
In Shaw, B. Complete plays, with pref-
aces v4 p727-45   822

A glimpse of the domesticity of Franklyn
Barnabas. Shaw, B.
In Shaw, B. Complete plays, with pref-
aces v2 p cxi-clii   822
Glines, Carroll V.
Doolittle's Tokyo Raiders   940.54
Global satellite communications systems. See
Artificial satellites in telecommunication
The Globe Playhouse. Adams, J. C. 792.09
Globe Theatre. See Southwark, England.
Globe Theatre
Glock, Charles Y.
(ed.) Prejudice U.S.A.   301.45
The "Gloria Scott." Doyle, Sir A. C.
In Doyle, Sir A. C. The complete Sher-
lock Holmes v 1 p429-43   S C
Glory, God and gold. Wellman, P. I. 979.1
Glory in the daytime. Parker, D.
In White, E. B. ed. A subtreasury of
American humor; abridged p64-77
   817.08
Glory in the flower. Inge, W.
In Cerf, B. ed. 24 favorite one-act plays
p133-50   808.82
The glory of Negro history; a pageant.
Hughes, L.
In Hughes, L. The Langston Hughes
reader p465-80   818
The glory of the nightingales. Robinson,
E. A.
In Robinson, E. A. The collected poems
of Edwin Arlington Robinson
p1011-73   811
Glory Road. Catton, B.   973.7
The glory that was Greece. Stobart, J. C.
   913.38
Glossaries. See name of language or subject
with the subdivision Dictionaries, e.g.
English language—Dictionaries; Chem-
istry—Dictionaries, etc.
Glubb, Sir John
A short history of the Arab peoples 953
Gluck, Christoph Willibald, Ritter von
See pages in the following books:
Cross, M. The Milton Cross New encyclo-
pedia of the great composers and their
music p384-95   920.03
Durant, W. Rousseau and revolution p367-
73   940.2
Ewen, D. ed. The complete book of classi-
cal music p164-75   780.1
Ewen, D. ed. The world of the great com-
posers p74-86   920
Shippen, K. B. The heritage of music p91-
97   780.9
Glückel of Hameln. See Hameln, Glückel of
Glyn, Anthony
The Seine   914.43
Glyndwr, Owen. See Glendower, Owen
The go-away bird. Spark, M.
In Spark, M. Collected stories: I p302-
59   S C
Go tell it on the mountain. Baldwin, J. Fic
God
See pages in the following book:
Boas, G. The history of ideas p187-211
   109
God and my father. Day, C.
In Day, C. The best of Clarence Day
p3-48   818

God bless America. Killens, J. O.
  In Clarke, J. H. ed. American Negro short stories p204-09 **S C**
God of the Gongs. Chesterton, G. K.
  In Chesterton, G. K. The Father Brown omnibus p368-84 **S C**
God rest ye, merry gentlemen. Crane, S.
  In Crane, S. The complete short stories & sketches of Stephen Crane p539-54 **S C**
God rest you merry, gentlemen. Hemingway, E.
  In Hemingway, E. The short stories of Ernest Hemingway p392-96 **S C**
God sees the truth, but waits. Tolstoy, L.
  In Seltzer, T. comp. Best Russian short stories p107-17 **S C**
  In Tolstoy, L. Short stories v2 p 1-9 **S C**
  In Tolstoy, L. Twenty-three tales p2-9 **S C**
Goddard, Robert Hutchings
  See pages in the following book:
  Von Braun, W. History of rocketry & space travel p43-56 **629.403**
Godden, Jon
  Two under the Indian sun **92**
Godden, Rumer
  The battle of the Villa Fiorita **Fic**
  A candle for St Jude **Fic**
  An episode of sparrows **Fic**
  Gone **S C**
  Stories included are: No more Indians; Down under the Thames; The little fishes; Why not live sweetly; Telling the time by the starlings; Lily and the sparrows; To Uncle, with love; Fireworks for Elspeth; You need to go upstairs; L'Élégance; Whither the swans and turtles go; Time is a stream
  Hans Christian Andersen **92**
  In this house of Brede **Fic**
  Mooltiki
    In Costain, T. B. ed. Read with me p227-45 **S C**
  (jt. auth.) Godden, J. Two under the Indian sun **92**
Godfrey, Thomas
  Prince of Parthia
    In Quinn, A. H. ed. Representative American plays p 1-42 **812.08**
Godliness. Anderson, S.
  In Anderson, S. Winesburg, Ohio (Modern Lib) p55-109 **S C**
  In Anderson, S. Winesburg, Ohio (Viking) p63-102 **S C**
Gods
  See pages in the following books:
  Hamilton, E. Mythology p21-76 **292**
  Payne, R. Ancient Greece p51-73 **913.38**
    See also Religions
Gods, graves, and scholars. Ceram, C. W. **913.03**
God's lonely man. Wolfe, T.
  In Wolfe, T. The hills beyond p186-97 **S C**
Gods of the lightning. Anderson, M.
  In Gassner, J. ed. Twenty-five best plays of the modern American theatre; early ser. p531-65 **812.08**
God's trombones. Johnson, J. W. **811**

The godson. Tolstoy, L.
  In Tolstoy, L. Short stories v2 p203-21 **S C**
  In Tolstoy, L. Twenty-three tales p208-27 **S C**
Goerner, Fred
  The search for Amelia Earhart **92**
Goethe, Johann Wolfgang von
  See pages in the following books:
  Durant, W. Rousseau and revolution p555-67, 580-628 **940.2**
  Eliot, T. S. On poetry and poets p240-64 **808.1**
  Schweitzer, A. Reverence for life; ed. by T. Kiernan p12-20 **193**
    Parodies, travesties, etc.
    See pages in the following book:
  Gamow, G. Thirty years that shook physics p165-214 **530.1**
Goggan, John Patrick. See Patrick, John
Gogh, Vincent van
  Van Gogh's "diary" **92**
    About
  Wallace, R. The world of Van Gogh, 1853-1890 **92**
    See also pages in the following books:
  Cheney, S. The story of modern art p268-98 **709.03**
  Untermeyer, L. Makers of the modern world p228-37 **920**
    Fiction
  Stone, I. Lust for life **Fic**
Gogol, Nikolai
  The cloak
    In Seltzer, T. comp. Best Russian short stories p40-81 **S C**
  Dead souls **Fic**
    About
    See pages in the following book:
  Posell, E. Z. Russian authors p44-64 **920**
Goin, Coleman J.
  (jt. auth.) Cochran, D. M. The new field book of reptiles and amphibians **598.1**
Going around in academic circles. Armour, R. **817**
Going home. Buck, P. S.
  In Buck, P. S. The good deed, and other stories of Asia, past and present p213-26 **S C**
Going the rounds on Christmas Eve with the Mellstock choir. Hardy, T.
  In Becker, M. L. ed. The home book of Christmas p207-12 **394.26**
Going to meet the man. Baldwin, J. **S C**
Going to meet the man [short story]. Baldwin, J.
  In Baldwin, J. Going to meet the man p227-49 **S C**
Gold, Herbert
  Dance of the divorced
    In The Saturday Evening Post. Best modern short stories p270-78 **S C**
Gold, Ivan
  The nickel misery of George Washington Carver Brown
    In Abrahams, W. ed. Fifty years of the American short story v 1 p296-333 **S C**

Gold
See pages in the following book:
Asimov, I. Building blocks of the universe p184-96   **546**
Gold. O'Neill, E.
In O'Neill, E. Plays v2 p623-92 **812**
The gold-bug. Poe, E. A.
In Poe, E. A. The complete tales and poems of Edgar Allan Poe p42-70 **S C**
In Poe, E. A. Edgar Allan Poe p462-506 **S C**
In Poe, E. A. Selected poetry and prose p248-80 **818**
Gold Coast. McPherson, J. A.
In The Best American short stories, 1969 p166-84 **S C**
Gold from Crete. Forester, C. S. **S C**
Gold from Crete [short story]. Forester, C. S.
In Forester, C. S. Gold from Crete p3-27 **S C**
Gold rush. See California—Gold discoveries; Klondike gold fields
The gold that glittered. Henry, O.
In Henry, O. The complete works of O. Henry p1493-99 **S C**
Goldberg, Joe
Jazz masters of the fifties **920**
Goldberger, Joseph
See pages in the following book:
Sebrell, W. H. Food and nutrition p107-13 **641.1**
Golden, Harry
Carl Sandburg **92**
Only in America **917.3**
About
See pages in the following book:
David, J. ed. Growing up Jewish p219-35 **920**
The golden age of American anthropology. Mead, M. ed. **572.97**
The golden age of science. Jones, B. Z. ed. **920**
The golden apples of the sun. Bradbury, R.
In Bradbury, R. R is for rocket p71-78 **S C**
The golden axe. Scholl, R.
In The Best short plays of 1957-1958 p199-223 **808.82**
Golden bough, The new. Frazer, Sir J. G. **291**
Golden boy. Odets, C.
In Gassner, J. ed. Twenty best plays of the modern American theatre p775-818 **812.08**
In Odets, C. Six plays p231-321 **812**
Golden Cobwebs
In Schauffler, R. H. ed. Christmas p296-99 **394.26**
The golden eagle. Murphy, R. **Fic**
Golden Fleece. See Argonauts
The Golden Fleece. Gurney, A. R.
In The Best short plays, 1969 p209-36 **808.82**

The golden honeymoon. Lardner, R. W.
In Foley, M. ed. Fifty best American short stories, 1915-1965 p23-37 **S C**
In Lardner, R. The best short stories of Ring Lardner p189-203 **S C**
In Lardner, R. The Ring Lardner reader p340-55 **S C**
In The Scribner treasury p609-25 **S C**
Golden land. Faulkner, W.
In Faulkner, W. Collected stories of William Faulkner p701-26 **S C**
The golden treasury of the best songs & lyrical poems in the English language. Palgrave, F. T. comp. **821.08**
The golden warrior. Muntz, H. **Fic**
The golden west. Fuchs, D.
In The New Yorker. Stories from The New Yorker, 1950-1960 p19-39 **S C**
Golding, William
Lord of the Flies **Fic**
Goldman, Erich F.
The tragedy of Lyndon Johnson **973.923**
Goldman, James
The lion in winter
In Gassner, J. ed. Best American plays; 6th ser. p277-309 **812.08**
Goldman, Marshall I.
(ed.) Controlling pollution **333.9**
Goldman, Peter
Report from Black America **301.451**
Goldring, David
See pages in the following book:
Lukas, J. A. Don't shoot—we are your children! p9-61 **301.43**
Goldsby, Richard A.
Race and races **572**
Goldschmidt, Victor Moritz
See pages in the following book:
Moore, R. The earth we live on p345-47, 352-55 **551.09**
Goldsmith, Oliver
She stoops to conquer **822**
also in Goldsmith, O. The Vicar of Wakefield, and other writings **828**
The Vicar of Wakefield, and other writings **828**
About
See pages in the following book:
Durant, W. Rousseau and revolution p813-17 **940.2**
Goldston, Robert
The Great Depression **309.173**
The life and death of Nazi Germany **943.086**
The Russian Revolution **947.084**
Suburbia: civic denial **301.3**
Goldwater, Robert
What is modern sculpture? **735**
Golenpaul, Dan
Information please almanac. See Information please almanac **317.3**
Golf
Golf Magazine. Golf Magazine's Tips from the teaching pros **796.352**
Golf Magazine's Encyclopedia of golf **796.352**

Goodyear, Charles
See pages in the following book:
National Geographic Society. Those inventive Americans p80-87   608

The **goophered** grapevine. Chestnutt, C. W.
In Clarke, J. H. ed. American Negro short stories p11-20   **S C**

Gordimer, Nadine
Six feet of the country
In The New Yorker. Stories from The New Yorker, 1950-1960 p687-97   **S C**

Gordon, Arthur
American Heritage. The American Heritage History of flight   629.13

Gordon, Bernard L.
(ed.) Man and the sea   551.4

Gordon, Caroline
Old Red
In Abrahams, W. ed. Fifty years of the American short story v 1 p334-50   **S C**

Gordon, Dexter
See pages in the following book:
Gitler, I. Jazz masters of the forties p201-25   920

Gordon Riots, 1780
Fiction
Dickens, C. Barnaby Rudge   **Fic**

Goren, Charles H.
Goren's Bridge complete   795.4

Gores, Joe
The Andrech samples
In Best detective stories of the year, 1971 p174-81   **S C**
South of Market
In Hitchcock, A. ed. Alfred Hitchcock presents: A month of mystery p23-38   **S C**

Gorillas
Schaller, G. B. The year of the gorilla   599

Gorki, Maxim. See Gorky, Maxim

Gorky, Maxim
Her lover
In Seltzer, T. comp. Best Russian short stories p276-83   **S C**
The lower depths
In Block, H. M. ed. Masters of modern drama p218-44   808.82
In Cerf, B. A. comp. Sixteen famous European plays p197-253   808.82
In Tucker, S. M. ed. Twenty-five modern plays p225-62   808.82
One autumn night
In Seltzer, T. comp. Best Russian short stories p263-75   **S C**
About
See pages in the following book:
Posell, E. Z. Russian authors p159-83 920

Gorsline, Douglas
What people wore   391.09

Goryushkin, V.
Before sunrise
In Scammell, M. ed. Russia's other writers p146-51   **S C**

Gothic architecture. See Architecture, Gothic
Gothic art. See Art, Gothic
Gothic ghosts. Holzer, H.   133.1

Gottlieb, Alex
Stud
In The Best short plays, 1969 p365-403   808.82

Gottschalk, Louis Moreau
See pages in the following book:
Chapin, V. Giants of the keyboard p112-23   920

Goudge, Elizabeth
The child from the sea   **Fic**
A city of bells   **Fic**
The Dean's watch   **Fic**
The scent of water   **Fic**

Goul, Roman
Conspiracy up to the ears
In Dulles, A. ed. Great spy stories from fiction p49-62   **S C**

Goulart, João Belchior Marques, President Brazil
See pages in the following book:
Gunther, J. Inside South America p36-46   980

Goulart, Ron
Confessions
In The Best from Fantasy and Science Fiction; 19th ser. p175-94   **S C**
The tin ear
In Best detective stories of the year [1967] p195-206   **S C**

Gould, Jay
See pages in the following book:
Holbrook, S. H. The age of the moguls p29-48   920

Gould, Jean
Modern American playwrights   812.09

Gounod, Charles François
See pages in the following books:
Cross, M. The Milton Cross New encyclopedia of the great composers and their music p396-404   920.03
Ewen, D. ed. The complete book of classical music p641-50   780.1
Ewen, D. ed. The world of great composers p281-89   920

Gouzenko, Igor
See pages in the following book:
Dulles, A. ed. Great true spy stories p219-32   327

Gove, Philip Babcock
(ed.) Webster's Third new international dictionary of the English language. See Webster's Third new international dictionary of the English language   423

Government. See Political science; and names of countries with the subdivision Politics and government, e.g. United States—Politics and government

Government, Local. See Local government

Government employees. See Civil service

Government Printing Office. See United States. Government Printing Office

The **Government** Printing Office. Kling, R. E.   **655.061**

Government publications. See United States —Government publications

Governmental investigations
  Goodman, W. The Committee   **328.73**

The Governor's lady. Mercer, D.
  In Richards, S. ed. Best short stories of the world theatre, 1958-1967 p227-40   **808.82**

Gow, James Ellis
  Tomorrow the world
  In Gassner, J. ed. Best plays of the modern American theatre; 2d ser. p597-640   **812.08**

Gowers, Sir Ernest
  Fowler, H. W. A dictionary of modern English usage   **428**

The gown of glory. Turnbull, A. S.   **Fic**

Goya y Lucientes, Francisco José de
  Schickel, R. The world of Goya, 1746-1828   **92**
  See also pages in the following books:
  Cheney, S. The story of modern art p39-46   **709.03**
  Durant, W. Rousseau and revolution p300-09   **940.2**
  Ruskin, A. Nineteenth century art p34-40   **709.03**

Goyen, William
  Figure over the town
  In The Best American short stories, 1964 p125-35   **S C**
  In The Saturday Evening Post. Best modern short stories p303-13 **S C**

Gracchus, Caius Sempronius
  See pages in the following book:
  Plutarch. Lives from Plutarch. Abridged p183-200   **920**

Gracchus, Gaius Sempronius. See Gracchus, Caius Sempronius

Gracchus, Tiberius Sempronius
  See pages in the following book:
  Plutarch. Lives from Plutarch. Abridged p183-200   **920**

Grace, Joyce, J.
  In Joyce, J. Dubliners p190-223   **S C**

Graff, Henry F.
  (jt. auth.) Barzun, J. The modern researcher   **808.02**

Graham, Frank
  Since Silent spring   **632**
  Woodward, S. Sportswriter   **070.4**

Graham, Frank D.
  Audels Handy book of practical electricity with wiring diagrams   **621.302**

Graham, Hugh Davis
  (ed.) The history of violence in America: historical and comparative perspectives   **301.18**
  (ed.) Huey Long   **92**

Graham, James, 1st Marquis of Montrose. See Montrose, James Graham, 1st Marquis of

Graham, Martha
  See pages in the following books:
  Maynard, O. American modern dancers: the pioneers p105-25   **920**
  Stoddard, H. Famous American women p201-10   **920**

Grail
Fiction
  Costain, T. B. The silver chalice   **Fic**

Grain. See Corn; Wheat

A **grain** as big as a hen's egg. Tolstoy, L.
  In Tolstoy, L. Short stories v2 p200-02   **S C**
  In Tolstoy, L. Twenty-three tales p204-07   **S C**

Grain industry and trade
  See pages in the following book:
  Stone, A. A. Careers in agribusiness and industry p97-113   **338.1**

Grainger, Tom
  Daft dream adyin'
  In The Best short plays, 1969 p147-207   **808.82**

Grammar
  Pei, M. Invitation to linguistics   **410**
  See pages in the following book:
  Pei, M. ed. Language today p128-47   **410**

Gramophone. See Phonograph

Granatelli, Andy. See Granatelli, Anthony

Granatelli, Anthony
  They call me Mister 500   **92**

Grand Alliance, War of the, 1689-1697
  See pages in the following book:
  The New Cambridge Modern history v6 p223-53   **909**

The grand alliance. Churchill, W. S.   **940.53**

Grand Canyon National Park
  See pages in the following book:
  National Geographic Society. America's wonderlands p161-81   **917.3**

The grand Convention. See Rossiter, C. 1787: the grand Convention   **342.73**

The **Grand Duke.** Gilbert, Sir W. S.
  In Gilbert, Sir W. S. The complete plays of Gilbert and Sullivan p649-711   **782.8**

Grand Hotel. Baum, V.
  In Cerf, B. A. comp. Sixteen famous European plays p857-937   **808.82**

Grand Rounds. Nourse, A. E.
  In Nourse, A. E. R for tomorrow p146-64   **S C**

Grand Teton National Park
  See pages in the following book:
  National Geographic Society. America's wonderlands p93-109   **917.3**

Grandma Moses. Moses, A. M. R.   **92**

Grandpa. Stuart, J.
  In Stuart, J. Plowshare in heaven p248-53   **S C**

Granger, Edith
  Granger's Index to poetry. See Granger's Index to poetry   **808.81**
  Granger's Index to poetry: supplement. See Granger's Index to poetry: supplement   **808.81**

Granger's Index to poetry   **808.81**

Granger's Index to poetry: supplement
808.81

The **Granny** Woman. Hughes, D. B.
In Mystery Writers of America. Crime without murder p135-54   **S C**

Grant, Frederick C.
(ed.) Hastings, J. Dictionary of the Bible
220.3

Grant, Julius
(ed.) Hackh's Chemical dictionary, American and British usage. See Hackh's Chemical dictionary, American and British usage
540.3

Grant, M. Earl
See pages in the following book:
Drotning, P. T. Up from the ghetto p119-31
920

Grant, Maxwell. See Gibson, Walter

Grant, Michael
The ancient historians   920
Myths of the Greeks and Romans   292

Grant, Neil
Benjamin Disraeli [biography of Benjamin Disraeli Beaconsfield]   92

Grant, Ulysses Simpson, President U.S.
Catton, B. Grant moves south   92
Catton, B. Grant takes command   92
Catton, B. U.S. Grant and the American military tradition   92
Lewis, L. Captain Sam Grant   92
See also pages in the following books:
American Heritage. The American Heritage History of the confident years p54-64
973.8
Catton, B. Prefaces to history p35-62
973.7
Dictionary of American biography. The American Plutarch p301-20   920

Grant moves south. Catton, B.   92
Grant takes command. Catton, B   92

Grantham, Dewey W.
(ed.) Theodore Roosevelt   92

Grantz, Gerald J.
Home book of taxidermy and tanning   579

Granville-Barker, Harley
(ed.) Muir, K. ed. A new companion to Shakespeare studies   822.3
For a work by this editor see Barker, Granville

Grapes. See Wine and wine making

The **grapes** of wrath. Steinbeck, J.   **Fic**

Graphic arts
Dictionaries
Stevenson, G. A. Graphic arts encyclopedia   655

Graphic arts, American
See pages in the following book:
Mendelowitz, D. M. A history of American art p465-81   709.73

Graphic arts encyclopedia. Stevenson, G. A.   655

Graphic history of architecture. Mansbridge, J.   720.9

The **graphic** story of The American Presidents. Whitney, D. C.   920

Grass, Günter
Cat and mouse   **Fic**
The tin drum   **Fic**

Grass. United States. Department of Agriculture   633

Grasses
Sears, P. B. Lands beyond the forest   581
United States. Department of Agriculture. Grass   633
See also pages in the following book:
Farb, P. The land and wildlife of North America p116-26   574.9

Grasshoppers. See Locusts

Grassi, Battista
See pages in the following book:
De Kruif, P. Microbe hunters p278-310
920

Grattan, C. Hartley
The Southwest Pacific since 1900   990

Grau, Shirley Ann
The beach party
In The Best American short stories, 1966 p83-94   **S C**
The keepers of the house   **Fic**

Grauer, Ben
(ed.) National Broadcasting Company, inc. NBC News. NBC News Picture book of the year   909.82

Graus, F.
Eastern and Western Europe in the Middle Ages. See Eastern and Western Europe in the Middle Ages   940.1

Graveney, Charles
Woodcarving for beginners   736

Graves, Robert
Greek myths   292
Poems, 1938-1945   821
Poems, 1965-1968   821
The siege and fall of Troy   883

Graves, William
Hawaii   919.69

Graves. See Funeral rites and ceremonies; Mounds and mound builders

Gravitation
Gamow, G. Gravity   531
See also pages in the following books:
Newman, J. R. ed. The world of mathematics v2 p1094-1106   510.8
Nourse, A. E. Universe, earth, and atom p66-81   530.9

Gravity. See Gravitation
Gravity. Gamow, G.   531
Gravity free state. See Weightlessness

Gray, Asa
Gray's Manual of botany   582
About
See pages in the following book:
Jones, B. Z. ed. The golden age of science p340-63   920

Gray, Edward
(jt. comp.) Velázquez de la Cadena, M. comp. New revised Velázquez Spanish and English dictionary   463

Gray, Elizabeth Janet
Penn   92
For other works by this author see Vining, Elizabeth Gray

Gray, Genevieve S.
(ed.) Douglass, F. Life and times of Frederick Douglass; abridged   92

Gray, Henry
Gray's Anatomy of the human body **611**
Gray, Len
The little old lady from Cricket Creek
In Best detective stories of the year
[1969] p225-29 **S C**
Gray, Peter
Handbook of basic microtechnique **578**
(ed.) The Encyclopedia of the biological
sciences. See The Encyclopedia of the
biological sciences **570.3**
The Gray Champion, Hawthorne, N.
In Hawthorne, N. Hawthorne's Short
stories p3-10 **S C**
A gray sleeve. Crane, S.
In Crane, S. The complete short stories
& sketches of Stephen Crane p226-
38 **S C**
Grayson, Esther C.
(jt. auth.) Rockwell, F. F. The Rock-
wells' New complete book of flower ar-
rangement **745.92**
Grazia, Alfred de. See De Grazia, Alfred
Greased samba. Deck, J.
In The Best American short stories,
1968 p29-42 **S C**
Great adventure and explorations. Stefáns-
son, V. ed. **910.9**
Great adventures of the Old West, The
American Heritage Book of. American
Heritage **978**
Great adventures with National Geographic.
National Geographic Society **910.9**
The **great** age of change: from 1945. Leuch-
tenburg, W. E.
In Life (Periodical) The Life History of
the United States v12 **973**
The **great** age of Greek literature. See Ham-
ilton, E. The Greek way **880.9**
The **Great** American Desert. Hollon, W. E.
917.8
Great Atlantic and Pacific Tea Company
See pages in the following book:
Mahoney, T. The great merchants p172-
83 **658.87**
Great auk
Stories
Eckert, A. W. The great auk **Fic**
Great Britain
Osborne, J. Britain **914.2**
See also England
Agriculture
See Agriculture—Great Britain
Animals
See Aimals—Great Britain
Antiquities
Ashe, G. The quest for Arthur's Britain
913.42
Hawkins, G. S. Stonehenge **913.36**
Hodges, H. Ancient Britons **913.36**
Horizon Magazine. The search for King
Arthur **913.42**
Quennell, M. Everyday life in Roman and
Anglo-Saxon times **913.42**
Wilson, D. The Anglo-Saxons **913.42**
Architecture
See Architecture, English

Army
See pages in the following book:
Shakespeare's England v 1 p112-26 **822.3**
Army—Officers—Fiction
Boulee, P. The bridge over the River Kwai
Fic
Art
See Art, British
Bio-bibliography
The Dictionary of national biography. The
concise dictionary; pt. 1 **920.03**
The Dictionary of national biography: The
concise dictionary; pt. 2, 1901-1950
920.03
Biography
Sutcliff, R. Heroes and history **920**
Biography—Dictionaries
The Dictionary of national biography. The
concise dictionary; pt. 1 **920.03**
The Dictionary of national biography: The
concise dictionary; pt. 2, 1901-1950 **920.03**
Who's who **920.03**
Church history
See pages in the following book:
The New Cambridge Modern history v2
p226-50 **909**
Civilization
Avery, G. Victorian people **914.2**
Bowle, J. England **942**
Quennell, M. Everyday life in Roman and
Anglo-Saxon times **913.42**
See also pages in the following books:
Arnold, M. The portable Matthew Arnold
p469-573 **828**
Durant, W. The age of reason begins p3-
221 **940.2**
Colleges and universities
See Colleges and universities—Great
Britain
Colonies
Andrews, C. M. The colonial background
of the American Revolution **973.2**
Cross, C. The fall of the British Empire,
1918-1968 **942.082**
See also pages in the following book:
The New Cambridge Modern history v6
p480-508 **909**
Currency question
See Currency question—Great Britain
Description and travel
See pages in the following book:
Shakespeare's England v 1 p198-223 **822.3**
Economic conditions
See pages in the following book:
Williams, P. Life in Tudor England p23-45
914.2
Education
See Education—Great Britain
Fiction
Austen, J. Emma **Fic**
Austen, J. Mansfield Park **Fic**
Austen, J. Northanger Abbey **Fic**
Austen, J. Persuasion **Fic**
Austen, J. Pride and prejudice **Fic**
Austen, J. Sense and sensibility **Fic**

Great Britain—*Continued*

Bennett, A. The old wives' tale	Fic
Brontë, C. Jane Eyre	Fic
Brontë, E. Wuthering Heights	Fic
Butler, S. The way of all flesh	Fic
Christie, A. Hallow'en party	Fic
Christie, A. The murder of Roger Ackroyd	Fic
Chute, M. The innocent wayfaring	Fic
Dickens, C. Barnaby Rudge	Fic
Dickens, C. Bleak House	Fic
Dickens, C. Great expectations	Fic
Dickens, C. Hard times	Fic
Dickens, C. Martin Chuzzlewit	Fic
Dickens, C. Nicholas Nickleby	Fic
Dickens, C. The old curiosity shop	Fic
Dickens, C. Oliver Twist	Fic
Dickens, C. The posthumous papers of the Pickwick Club	Fic
Du Maurier, D. Rebecca	Fic
Eliot, G. Adam Bede	Fic
Eliot, G. The mill on the Floss	Fic
Eliot, G. Silas Marner	Fic
Falkner, J. M. Moonfleet	Fic
Fielding, H. The history of Tom Jones, a foundling	Fic
Fowles, J. The French lieutenant's woman	Fic
Galsworthy, J. The Forsyte saga	Fic
Goudge, E. The child from the sea	Fic
Goudge, E. A city of bells	Fic
Goudge, E. The Dean's watch	Fic
Goudge, E. The scent of water	Fic
Hardy, T. Far from the madding crowd	Fic
Hardy, T. Jude the obscure	Fic
Hardy, T. The mayor of Casterbridge	Fic
Hardy, T. The return of the native	Fic
Hardy, T. Tess of the D'Urbervilles	Fic
Hilton, J. Random harvest	Fic
Holt, V. The legend of the Seventh Virgin	Fic
James, H. The portrait of a lady	Fic
Lawrence, D. H. Sons and lovers	Fic
Masefield, J. Jim Davis	Fic
Nathan, R. The elixir	Fic
Smith, D. I capture the castle	Fic
Snow, C. P. The masters	Fic
Stewart, M. The crystal cave	Fic
Struther, J. Mrs Miniver	Fic
Tarkington, B. Monsieur Beaucaire	Fic
Tey, J. Three by Tey	Fic
Thackeray, W. M. The history of Henry Esmond, esquire	Fic
Thackeray, W. M. Vanity fair	Fic
Trollope, A. Barchester Towers	Fic
Twain, M. A Connecticut Yankee in King Arthur's court	Fic
Walpole, H. Fortitude	Fic

Folklore

See Folklore—Great Britain

Gentry

See pages in the following books:

Ashley, M. Life in Stuart England p68-80
914.2

Reader, W. J. Life in Victorian England p17-37
914.2

History

Ashley, M. Great Britain to 1688   942

Bowle, J. England   942

Churchill, W. S. Churchill's History of the English-speaking peoples; abridged
942

Churchill, W. S. A history of the English-speaking peoples
942

Halliday, F. E. A concise history of England
942

Smellie, K. B. Great Britain since 1688
942

Trevelyan, G. M. English social history
942

Trevelyan, G. M. History of England 942

Trevelyan, G. M. Illustrated English social history
942

Trevelyan, G. M. Illustrated History of England
942

See also pages in the following books:

Durant, W. The age of Louis XIV p183-206, 244-311   940.2

Horizon Magazine. The Horizon Book of The age of Napoleon p208-24   944.04

The New Cambridge Modern history v6 p193-222, 254-83   909

Van Loon, H. W. The story of mankind p279-95   909

History—To 1066

Ashe, G. The quest for Arthur's Britain
913.42

See also Anglo-Saxons

History—To 1066—Fiction

Seton, A. Avalon	**Fic**

History—Norman period, 1066-1154

Costain, T. B. The conquering family
942.03

Tomkeieff, O. G. Life in Norman England
914.2

See also Hastings, Battle of, 1066; Normans

History—Norman period, 1066-1154—Fiction

Lewis, H. Harold was my king	**Fic**
Muntz, H. The golden warrior	**Fic**

History—Plantagenets, 1154-1399

Costain, T. B. The conquering family 942.03

Costain, T. B. The last Plantagenets 942.03

Costain, T. B. The magnificent century
942.03

Costain, T. B. The three Edwards 942.03

Kelly, A. Eleanor of Aquitaine and the four kings   92

Tomkeieff, O. G. Life in Norman England
914.2

See also pages in the following book:

Boyd, M. Man, myth and magic p123-33
133.4

History—Plantagenets, 1154-1399—Drama

Eliot, T. S. Murder in the cathedral 812

History—Plantagenets, 1154-1399—Fiction

Costain, T. B. The black rose	**Fic**
Doyle, Sir A. C. The White Company	**Fic**
Seton, A. Katherine	**Fic**

History—Lancaster and York, 1399-1485

Costain, T. B. The last Plantagenets 942.03

History—Wars of the Roses, 1455-1485—Fiction

Barnes, M. C. The Tudor rose	**Fic**

Great Britain—*Continued*

Politics and government

Cheyney, E. P. European background of American history, 1300-1600   **940.2**

Politics and government—Stuarts, 1603-1714

See pages in the following book:

Blitzer, C. Age of kings p138-48   **940.2**

Politics and government—Civil War and Commonwealth, 1642-1660

Ashley, M. ed. Cromwell   **92**

Politics and government—1714-1837

Paine, T. The rights of man   **323.4**

The New Cambridge Modern history v7 p241-68, v8 p537-64   **909**

Politics and government—19th century

Grant, N. Benjamin Disraeli [biography of Benjamin Disraeli Beaconsfield]   **92**

Politics and government—20th century

The Times London. The Churchill years, 1874-1965   **92**

See also pages in the following books:

Cecil, R. Life in Edwardian England p21-42   **914.2**

Priestley, J. B. The Edwardians p109-22   **914.2**

Race relations

Braithwaite, E. R. Paid servant   **362.7**

Religion

See pages in the following books:

Avery, G. Victorian people p137-64   **914.2**

Page, R. I. Life in Anglo-Saxon England p27-44   **914.2**

Shakespeare's England v 1 p48-78   **822.3**

Williams, P. Life in Tudor England p139-59   **914.2**

Social conditions

Avery, G. Victorian people   **914.2**

Notestein, W. The English people on the eve of colonization, 1603-1630   **942.06**

Trevelyan, G. M. English social history   **942**

Trevelyan, G. M. Illustrated English social history   **942**

See also pages in the following books:

Horizon Magazine. The Horizon Book of The age of Napoleon p225-39   **944.04**

Muir, K. ed. A new companion to Shakespeare studies p168-79   **822.3**

White, T. H. Fire in the ashes p189-233   **940.55**

Social life and customs

Ashley, M. Life in Stuart England   **914.2**

Brown, I. Dickens and his world   **914.2**

Brown, I. Shakespeare and his world   **822.3**

Brown, I. Shakespeare in his time   **822.3**

Cecil, R. Life in Edwardian England   **914.2**

A History of everyday things in England   **914.2**

Martin, R. G. Jennie: the life of Lady Randolph Churchill   **92**

Pepys, S. Everybody's Pepys; abridged   **92**

Priestley, J. B. The Edwardians   **914.2**

Quennell, M. Everyday life in Roman and Anglo-Saxon times   **913.42**

Reader, W. J. Life in Victorian England   **914.2**

Shakespeare's England   **822.3**

White, R. J. Life in Regency England   **914.2**

Theater

See Theater—Great Britain

Great Britain since 1688. Smellie, K. B.   **942**

Great Britain to 1688. Ashley, M.   **942**

The Great Carbuncle. Hawthorne, N.
In Hawthorne, N. Hawthorne's Short stories p72-85   **S C**

Great cathedrals, The Horizon Book of. Horizon Magazine   **726**

Great Catherine. Shaw, B.
In Shaw, B. Complete plays, with prefaces v4 p569-606   **822**

The Great Cherokee Bill. Stuart, J.
In Stuart, J. A Jesse Stuart reader p108-20   **818**

Great composers, 1300-1900. Ewen, D. ed.   **920.03**

The great conspiracy. Chidsey, D. B.   **973.4**

The great Crash, 1929. Galbraith, J. K.   **338.54**

The great democracies. Churchill, W. S.
In Churchill, W. S. A history of the English-speaking peoples v4   **942**

The Great Depression. Goldston, R.   **309.173**

The Great Depression. Shannon, D. A. ed.   **330.973**

Great Depression, 1929-1941. Hoover, H. C.
In Hoover, H. C. Memoirs v3   **92**

Great destiny. Churchill, Sir W.   **942.082**

Great dissenters. Thomas, N.   **920**

The Great Divide. Moody, W. V.
In Dickinson, T. H. ed. Chief contemporary dramatists [1st ser] p283-315   **808.82**
In Gassner, J. ed. Best plays of the early American theatre p361-97   **812.08**

Great documents in Black American history. Ducas, G. ed.   **301.451**

The great escape. Brickhill, P.   **940.54**

Great expectations. Dickens, C.   **Fic**

The Great Gatsby. Fitzgerald, F. S.   **Fic**
also in Fitzgerald, F. S. The Fitzgerald reader p105-238   **S C**

The great god Brown. O'Neill, E.
In O'Neill, E. Nine plays p307-77   **812**
In O'Neill, E. Plays v3 p257-325   **812**
In O'Neill, E. Selected plays of Eugene O'Neill   **812**
In Tucker, S. M. ed. Twenty-five modern plays p765-99   **808.82**

Great goodness of life. Jones, L.
In Richards, S. ed. Best short plays of the world theatre, 1958-1967 p147-53   **808.82**

Great historic places, The American Heritage Book of. American Heritage   **917.3**

Great issues in American history. Hofstadter, R. ed.   **973**

Great Lakes

Havighurst, W. ed. The Great Lakes reader   **977**

The Great Lakes reader. Havighurst, W.   **977**

Great lion of God. Caldwell, T.　Fic

Great men of American popular song. Ewen, D.　920

The great merchants. Mahoney, T.　658.87

A great mistake. Crane, S.
In Crane, S. The complete short stories & sketches of Stephen Crane p157-58　S C

The great monkey trial. De Camp, L. S.　343

Great Negroes past and present. Adams, R. L.　920

Great paintings from the Metropolitan Museum of Art. New York (City). Metropolitan Museum of Art　708

The great patent medicine era. Hechtlinger, A. comp.　615

Great Plains
Jones, E. The Plains States　917.8

The great playwrights. Bentley, E. comp.　808.82

Great Presidential decisions. Morris, R. B. ed.　973

The great psychologists from Aristotle to Freud. Watson, R. I.　150.9

The great rehearsal. Van Doren, C.　342.73

The great religions of the modern world. Jurji, E. J. ed.　291

The great separation. Chidsey, D. B.　973.2

Great slave narratives. Bontemps, A. ed.　920

Great Smoky Mountains National Park
See pages in the following book:
National Geographic Society. America's wonderlands p450-61　917.3

Great spy stories from fiction. Dulles, A. ed.　S C

The Great Stone Face. Hawthorne, N.
In Hawthorne, N. Hawthorne's Short stories p357-75　S C

The great struggle. Werstein, I.　331.88

The great terror. Conquest, R.　947.084

Great true spy stories. Dulles, A. ed.　327

Great Wall of China. Kafka, F.
In Kafka, F. Selected short stories of Franz Kafka p129-47　S C

The great white hope. Sackler, H.　812
—Same
In Richards, S. ed. Best plays of the sixties p901-1036　808.82

The Greater Coney. Henry, O.
In Henry, O. The complete works of O. Henry p911-14　S C

The greater inclination. Wharton, E.
In Wharton, E. The collected short stories of Edith Wharton v 1 p65-185　S C

The greatest American short stories. Day, A. G. ed.　S C

The greatest book ever written. Oursler, F.　221.9

The greatest depths. Soule, G.　551.4

The greatest game of all my life in golf. Nicklaus, J.　92

The greatest man in the world. Thurber, J.
In White, E. B. ed. A subtreasury of American humor; abridged p201-07　817.08

Greatest stars of the NBA. Pepe, P.　920

The greatest story ever told. Oursler, F.　232.9

Greatest Tertian. Boucher, A.
In Conklin, G. ed. Invaders of earth p330-33　S C

Grebstein, Sheldon Norman
Sinclair Lewis　813.09

A Grecian legend. Pei, M.
In Pei, M. Tales of the natural and supernatural p171-76　S C

Greece
See pages in the following book:
Falls, C. B. The first 3000 years: ancient civilizations of the Tigris, Euphrates, and Nile River valleys, and the Mediterranean Sea p153-67　913.03

Antiquities
Horizon Magazine. The Horizon Book of ancient Greece　913.38
Quennell, M. Everyday things in ancient Greece　913.38
See also pages in the following book:
Ceram, C. W. ed. Hands on the past p69-110　913.03

Biography
Plutarch. Lives from Plutarch. Abridged　920

Civilization
See Civilization, Greece

Fiction
Renault, M. The bull from the sea　Fic
Renault, M. The mask of Apollo　Fic

History
Asimov, I. The Greeks: a great adventure　938
Bowra, C. M. Classical Greece　938
Bury, J. B. A history of Greece to the death of Alexander the Great　938
Durant, W. The life of Greece　938
Mills, D. The book of the ancient Greeks　938
Payne, R. Ancient Greece　913.38
See also pages in the following book:
Quennell, M. Everyday things in ancient Greece p87-107, 231-47　913.38

History—Fiction
Davis, W. S. A victor of Salamis　Fic
Renault, M. Fire from heaven　Fic
Renault, M. The last of the wine　Fic

History—Peloponnesian War, 431-404 B.C.
Thucydides. The history of the Peloponnesian War　938

History—Peloponnesian War, 431-404 B.C.—Fiction
Sutcliff, R. The flowers of Adonis　Fic

History—Persian Wars, 500-449 B.C.
Herodotus. The histories of Herodotus　938
See also pages in the following book:
Bowra, C. M. Classical Greece p69-78　938

Religion
See pages in the following books:
Durant, W. The life of Greece p175-202　938
Hamilton, E. The Greek way p284-302　880.9

Green Bay Packers (Football team)
Kramer, J. Instant replay   796.33
Green Bay, Wis. Football Club (National League) See Green Bay Packers (Football team)
The **green** bay tree. Shairp, M.
    In Cerf, B. A. comp. Sixteen famous British plays p03-64   822.08
A **green** beret—all the way. Moore, R.
    In Moore, R. The green berets p17-66   **S C**
The **green** berets. Moore, R.   **S C**
Green cockatoo. Schnitzler, A.
    In Cerf, B. ed. Thirty famous one-act plays p135-63   808.82
The **green** door. Henry, O.
    In Henry, O. The complete works of O. Heny p62-68   **S C**
    In Henry, O. The four million p151-64   **S C**
The **green** goddess. Archer, W.
    In Cerf, B. A. comp. Sixteen famous British plays p251-306   822.08
Green grass, blue sky, white house. Morris, W.
    In The Best American short stories, 1970 p194-206   **S C**
Green grow the lilacs. Riggs, L.
    In Gassner, J. ed. Best American plays; supplementary volume, 1918-1958 p129-68   812.08
The **green** helmet. Yeats, W. B.
    In Yeats, W. B. Collected plays of W. B. Yeats p147-59   822
The **green** hills of Earth. Heinlein, R. A.
    In Heinlein, R. A. Robert A. Heinlein's The past through tomorrow p294-303   **S C**
Green Man. Chesterton, G. K.
    In Chesterton, G. K. The Father Brown omnibus p873-93   **S C**
Green mansions. Hudson, W. H.   **Fic**
The **green** men. Attaway, W.
    In Margolies, E. A native son's reader p93-100   810.8
The **green** pastures. Connelly, M.   812
—Same
    In Cerf, B. A. ed. Sixteen famous American plays p147-202   812.08
    In Gassner, J. ed. Twenty best plays of the modern American theatre p191-231   812.08
Green patches. Asimov, I.
    In Asimov, I. Nightfall, and other stories p38-52   **S C**
The **green** sari. Buck, P. S.
    In Buck, P. S. The good deed, and other stories of Asia, past and present p105-25   **S C**
Green Scythe. Chekhov, A.
    In Chekhov, A. The image of Chekhov p27-44   **S C**
The **green** years. Cronin, A. J.   **Fic**
Greenbacks. See Paper money
Greenberg, Eliezer
    (jt. ed.) Howe, I. ed. A treasury of Yiddish poetry   892.49
Greenberg, Milton
    (jt. auth.) Plano, J. C. The American political dictionary   320.03

Greene, Ann Bosworth
A Vermont Christmas
    In Wernecke, H. H. ed. Celebrating Christmas around the world p221-24   394.26
Greene, Donald
Samuel Johnson   828
Greene, Graham
Across the bridge
    In Havighurst, W. ed. Masters of the modern short story p266-76   **S C**
The heart of the matter   **Fic**
The inventive Mr Wormold
    In Dulles, A. ed. Great spy stories from fiction p422-33   **S C**
Our man in Havana
    In Greene, G. Triple pursuit   **Fic**
The power and the glory   **Fic**
The quiet American   **Fic**
The root of all evil
    In The Saturday Evening Post. Best modern short stories p107-18   **S C**
The third man
    In Greene, G. Triple pursuit   **Fic**
This gun for hire
    In Greene, G. Triple pursuit   **Fic**
Travels with my aunt   **Fic**
Triple pursuit   **Fic**
Greene, Philip L.
The dichotomy
    In Prize stories, 1971: The O. Henry Awards p267-83   **S C**
Greenhow, Rose (O'Neal)
    See pages in the following book:
Kane, H. T. Spies for the Blue and Gray p17-67   973.7
The **greening** of America. Reich, C. A.   917.3
Greenland
Freuchen, P. Peter Freuchen's Adventures in the Arctic   919.8
    See also pages in the following books:
Jones, W. G. Denmark p236-42   948.9
Stefánsson, V. ed. Great adventures and explorations p52-85   910.9
    Fiction
MacLean, A. Night without end   **Fic**
Greenstone. Ashton-Warner, S.   **Fic**
Greenwald, Douglas
The McGraw-Hill Dictionary of modern economics. See The McGraw-Hill Dictionary of modern economics   330.3
Greenwillow. Chute, B. J.   **Fic**
Greeting: you are hereby ordered for induction. Liston, R.   355.2
Gregor, Ian
    (ed.) The Brontës   823.09
Gregory, Dick
Nigger   92
Gregory, Isabella Augusta (Persse) Lady. See Gregory, Lady
Gregory, Lady
Rising of the moon
    In Cerf, B. ed. Thirty famous one-act plays p91-98   808.82
    In Dickinson, T. H. ed. Chief contemporary dramatists [1st ser.] p227-35   808.82
Spreading the news
    In Cerf, B. ed. 24 favorite one-act plays p417-33   808.82

Growth
Tanner, J. M. Growth   612.6
  See also Growth (Plants)
Growth (Plants)
  See pages in the following book:
Scientific American. Plant agriculture p38-69   581
The **growth** of American thought. Curti, M.   917.3
The **growth** of the American Republic. Morison, S. E.   973
Gruenberg, Sidonie Matsner
  (ed.) The New Encyclopedia of child care and guidance. See The New Encyclopedia of child care and guidance   649
Grunert, K.
  Enemies in space
  In Conklin, G. ed. Invaders of earth p182-92   S C
The **guardian** of the Accolade. Henry, O.
  In Henry, O. The complete works of O. Henry p372-79   S C
Guarding the Zeppelins. Coles, M.
  In Dulles, A. ed. Great spy stories from fiction p153-62   S C
Guare, John
  A day for surprises
  In The Best short plays, 1970 p285-94   808.82
Guareschi, Giovanni
  Comrade Don Camillo   Fic
  Don Camillo meets the flower children   Fic
  The little world of Don Camillo   Fic
Guayana. See Cuidad Guayana
Guenther, John
  Everest, F. K. The fastest man alive   92
Guérard, Albert
  France   944
  Napoleon III   92
Guerber, Helene Adeline
  Myths of Greece & Rome   292
The **Guermantes** way. Proust, M.
  In Proust, M. Remembrance of things past v 1   Fic
Guernsey, Otis L.
  (ed.) The Best plays of 1919/1920-1969/1970. See The Best plays of 1919/1920-1969/1970   808.82
Guerrilla warfare
  Harris, R. Death of a revolutionary; [Ernesto] Che Guevara's last mission   92
  Sully, F. Age of the guerrilla   355.4
Guest, Anna
  Beauty is truth
  In Seventeen. Stories from Seventeen p66-76   S C
The **guest.** Camus, A.
  In Camus, A. Exile and the kingdom   S C
The **guest.** Morton, F.
  In The Best American short stories, 1965 p241-49   S C
Guest of reality. Lagerkvist, P.
  In Lagerkvist, P. The eternal smile p73-152   S C
The **guests.** Saki
  In Saki. The short stories of Saki p470-74   S C

Guettard, Jean Étienne
  See pages in the following book:
  Moore, R. The earth we live on p55-70   551.09
Guevara, Che. See Guevara, Ernesto
Guevara, Ernesto
  Harris, R. Death of a revolutionary   92
  Sinclair, A. Che Guevara   92
Guggenheim family
  See pages in the following book:
  Holbrook, S. H. The age of the moguls p277-302   920
Guiana
  McEoin, G. Colombia and Venezuela and the Guianas   918
Guichard-Meili, Jean
  Matisse   759.4
A **guide** book of modern United States currency. Shafer, N.   332.5
Guide for young homemakers, Good Housekeeping's. Good Housekeeping   640.3
Guide to American history, Webster's 973.03
Guide to archaeology, The American Heritage. Bray, W.   913.03
A **guide** to art museums in the United States. Christensen, E. O.   708
Guide to best plays, Drury's   808.82
Guide to better bulletin boards. Coplan, K.   371.33
Guide to colleges, The New American. Hawes, G. R.   378.73
A **guide** to historical fiction. Irwin, L. B. comp.   016.8
A **guide** to historical reading: non-fiction. Irwin, L. B. comp.   016.9
Guide to knowing yourself, The Seventeen. Sugarman, D. A.   155.5
Guide to listening pleasure. The New York Times   780.1
A **guide** to Mexican art: from its beginnings to the present. Fernandez, J.   709.72
Guide to modern physical fitness, Bud Wilkinson's. Wilkinson, B.   613.7
A **guide** to paperbacks on Asia. See Asia Society. Asia: a guide to paperbacks   016.95
Guide to pet care, ASPCA. Henley, D. 636
Guide to reference books. Winchell, C. M.   016
Guide to reference books. First supplement, 1965-1966. Winchell, C. M.   016
Guide to reference books. Second supplement, 1967-1968. Winchell, C. M.   016
A **guide** to reference books. See Enoch Pratt Free Library, Baltimore, Md. Reference books   016
A **guide** to science, and Index to the Life Science library. Time-Life Books   500
A **guide** to study abroad. See Garraty, J. A. The new guide to study abroad   378.3
A **guide** to the national parks. Matthews, W. H.   917.3
A **guide** to the natural world, and Index to the Life Nature library. Time-Life Books   574
A **guide** to the planets. See Moore, P. The planets   523.4

A **guide** to the religions of America. See Look. Religions in America   280

Guide to the two-year colleges, Barron's   378.73

Guide to the use of books and libraries. Gates, J. K.   028.7

Guided missiles

See pages in the following book:

Stevenson, A. E. Looking outward p79-99, 100-12   341.13

See also Ballistic missiles; Polaris (Missile)

Guides to educational media. Rufsvold, M. I.   016.3713

Guides to newer educational media. See Rufsvold, M. I. Guides to educational media   016.3713

Guides to straight thinking. Chase, S.   160

Guido Aretinus

See pages in the following book:

Shippen, K. B. The heritage of music p27-29   780.9

Guilds. See Labor and laboring classes

"The **guilty** party." Henry, O.

In Henry, O. The complete works of O. Henry p1441-46   S C

Guinagh, Kevin

(comp.) Dictionary of foreign phrases and abbreviations. See Dictionary of foreign phrases and abbreviations   808.88

Guinness Book of world records   032

Guitar. Hughes, L.

In Hughes, L. The Langston Hughes reader p167-73   818

Gulbranssen, Trygve

Beyond sing the woods   Fic

Gulf Stream

Piccard, J. The sun beneath the sea 551.4

See also pages in the following book:

Soule, G. The greatest depths p147-58   551.4

Gullible's travels. Lardner, R.

In Lardner, R. The Ring Lardner reader p34-67   S C

Gullick, J. M.

Malaysia   959.5

Gumm, Harry. See Von Tilzer, Harry

Gunn, James E.

The cave of night

In Asimov, I. ed. Where do we go from here? p279-99   S C

Gunn, Thom

See pages in the following book:

Rosenthal, M. L. The new poets p251-57   821.09

Gunner's passage. Shaw, I.

In Abrahams, W. ed. Fifty years of the American short story v2 p264-78   S C

Gunnery

See pages in the following book:

Morison, E. E. Men, machines, and modern times p17-44   609

Gunning. See Hunting; Shooting

Guns. See Firearms; Gunnery; Rifles; Shotguns

The **guns** of August. Tuchman, B. W. 940.3

The **guns** of Navarone. McLean, A.   Fic

Gunston, Bill

Hydrofoils and hovercraft   629.3

Gunther, John, 1901-1970

Death be not proud [a biography of his son]   92

Inside South America   980

The riddle of MacArthur   92

Gunther, John, 1929-1947

Gunther, J. Death be not proud   92

Guptill, Arthur L.

Pencil drawing step-by-step   741.2

Guralnik, David B.

(ed.) Webster's New World dictionary of the American language. 2d college ed. See Webster's New World dictionary of the American language. 2d college ed.   423

Gurion, David Ben- See Ben-Gurion, David

Gurko, Leo

Ernest Hemingway and the pursuit of heroism   813.09

The two lives of Joseph Conrad   92

Gurko, Miriam

Clarence Darrow   92

Restless spirit; the life of Edna St Vincent Millay   92

Gurney, A. R.

The Golden Fleece

In The Best short plays, 1969 p209-36   808.82

The love course

In The Best short plays, 1970 p297-324   808.82

Turn of the century

In The Best short plays of 1957-1958 p 1-21   808.82

Gurr, Ted Robert

(jt. ed.) Graham, H. D. ed. The history of violence in America: historical and comparative perspectives   301.18

Gusev. Chekhov, A.

In Chekhov, A. The image of Chekhov p154-70   S C

Guss, Carolyn

(jt. auth.) Rufsvold, M. I. Guides to educational media   016.3713

Guthrie, A. B.

Arfive   Fic

The big sky   Fic

The way West   Fic

Guthrie, Arlo

Alice's restaurant   781.9

Guthrie, Tyrone

Tyrone Guthrie on acting   792

Guttmacher, Alan F.

Understanding sex: a young person's guide   612.6

Guzman Blanco, Antonio, President Venezuela

See pages in the following book:

Worcester, D. E. Makers of Latin America p176-84   920

Gymnastics

Fogel, S. J. Gymnastics handbook   796.4

See also pages in the following book:

American Association for Health, Physical Education, and Recreation. Physical education for high school students p165-203   613.7

See also Physical education and training

Gymnastics handbook. Fogel, S. J.   796.4

Gypsies
Esty, K. The Gypsies, wanderers in time   397
McDowell, B. Gypsies: wanderers of the world   397
Yoors, J. The Gypsies   397
The **Gypsies,** wanderers in time. Esty, K.   397

Gypsies: wanderers of the world. McDowell, B.   397

The **gypsy** student. Schwartz, J.
In Seventeen. Seventeen from Seventeen p46-63   S C

H

H.E.W. See United States. Department of Health, Education, and Welfare
H.M.S. Pinafore. Gilbert, Sir W. S.
In Gilbert, Sir W. S. The complete plays of Gilbert and Sullivan p101-37   782.8
In Gilbert, Sir W. S. Martyn Green's Treasury of Gilbert & Sullivan   782.8
H.M.S. Ulysses. MacLean, A.   Fic
Haas, Ernst
See pages in the following book:
Time-Life Books. Color p129-66   779.6
Habeas corpus
See pages in the following book:
Fribourg, M. G. The Supreme Court in American history p74-90   347.9
Habenstreit, Barbara
Changing America and the Supreme Court   347.9
Haber, Tom Burns
A. E. Housman   821.09
Habitat. Halacy, D. S.   574.5
An habitation enforced. Kipling, R.
In Kipling, R. The best short stories of Rudyard Kipling p461-85   S C
Habitations, Human. See Architecture, Domestic; Houses; Housing
Habitations of animals. See Animals—Habitations
Habits of animals. See Animals—Habits and behavior
Habsburg, House of
See pages in the following books:
Dill, M. Germany p45-68   943
The New Cambridge Modern history v2 p334-58, v3 p319-46, v4 p503-30, v5 p474-99, v6 p572-607, v8 p279-305   909
Stadler, K. R. Austria p28-37   943.6
Hachiya, Michihiko
Hiroshima diary   940.54
Hacienda. Porter, K. A.
In Porter, K. A. The collected stories of Katherine Ann Porter p135-70 S C
Hackett, Albert
(jt. auth.) Goodrich, F. The diary of Anne Frank   812

Hackh, Ingo Waldemar Dagobert
Hackh's Chemical dictionary, American and British usage. See Hackh's Chemical dictionary, American and British usage   540.3
Hackh's Chemical dictionary, American and British usage   540.3
Had he been a Kohen. Singer, I. B.
In Singer, I. B. An Isaac Bashevis Singer reader p307-13   S C
Had you been born in another faith. Bach, M.   291
Hadas, Moses
Imperial Rome   937
Hadji Murád. Tolstoy, L.
In Tolstoy, L. Short novels v2 p372-502   S C
Hadlock, Richard
Jazz masters of the twenties   920
Hadrian, Emperor of Rome
See pages in the following book:
Coolidge, O. Lives of famous Romans p150-67   920
Hadrian VII. Luke, P.
In Richards, S. ed. Best plays of the sixties p713-800   808.82
Hagan, William T.
American Indians   970.1
Hagedorn, Hermann
The Roosevelt family of Sagamore Hill   92
Hagen, Anders
Norway   913.36
Hagen, Victor W. von. See Von Hagen, Victor W.
Haggard, H. Rider
King Solomon's mines   Fic
Haggerty, James J.
Apollo: lunar landing   629.45
(jt. auth.) Sebrell, W. H. Food and nutrition   641.1
(jt. auth.) Stever, H. G. Flight   629.132
Hahn, Emily
The cooking of China   641.5
Haight, Anne Lyon
Banned books   098
Haiku
Henderson, H. G. ed. An introduction to haiku   895.6
Hailey, Arthur
Airport   Fic
Haines, Francis
The buffalo   978
Horses in America   636.109
Haines, William Wister
Command decision
In Quinn, A. H. ed. Representative American plays p1149-91   812.08
Hair
See pages in the following books:
Archer, E. Let's face it p57-75   646.7
Seventeen. The Seventeen Book of fashion and beauty p57-102   646.7
Sternberg, T. H. More than skin deep p47-88   616.5
Hair. Faulkner, W.
In Faulkner, W. Collected stories of William Faulkner p131-48   S C

Haircut. Lardner, R.
In Day, A. G. ed. The greatest American short stories p251-63   **S C**
In Lardner, R. The best short stories of Ring Lardner p23-33   **S C**
In Lardner, R. The Ring Lardner reader p68-78   **S C**
In The Scribner treasury p629-39   **S C**
The hairless Mexican. Maugham, W. S.
In Maugham, W. S. The best short stories of W. Somerset Maugham p89-129   **S C**
Hairston, Loyle
The winds of change
In Clarke, J. H. ed. American Negro short stories p297-304   **S C**
"The hairy ape." O'Neill, E.
In Gassner, J. ed. Twenty-five best plays of the modern American theatre; early ser. p 1-24   **812.08**
In O'Neill, E. The Emperor Jones, Anna Christie [and] The hairy ape p181-260   **812**
In O'Neill, E. Nine plays p39-88   **812**
In O'Neill, E. Plays v3 p207-54   **812**
In O'Neill, E. Selected plays of Eugene O'Neill   **812**
Haiti
See pages in the following book:
Williams, E. From Columbus to Castro: the history of the Caribbean, 1492-1969 p237-54   **972.9**
Halacy, Daniel S.
Bionics   **001.5**
Computers—the machines we think with   **510.78**
Habitat   **574.5**
Man alive   **574**
Man and memory   **612**
The water crisis   **333.9**
The halberdier of the little Rheinschloss. Henry, O.
In Henry, O. The complete works of O. Henry p529-35   **S C**
Halberstam, David
Ho [biography of Ho-chi Minh]   **92**
The unfinished odyssey of Robert Kennedy   **92**
Haldane, John Burdon Sanderson
See pages in the following book:
Moore, R. Man, time, and fossils p171-91   **573.2**
Hale, Edward Everett
Christmas waits in Boston
In Becker, M. L. ed. The home book of Christmas p171-81   **394.26**
Hale, George Ellery
Woodbury, D. O. The glass giant of Palomar   **522**
Hale, John R.
Age of exploration   **910.9**
Renaissance   **940.2**
Hale, Lucretia P.
The Peterkins celebrate the Fourth of July
In White, E. B. ed. A subtreasury of American humor; abridged p162-68   **817.08**
Peterkins' Christmas tree
In Becker, M. L. ed. The home book of Christmas p430-35   **394.26**

Hale, Nancy
The bubble
In The New Yorker. Stories from The New Yorker, 1950-1960 p632-40   **S C**
The most elegant drawing room in Europe
In Abrahams, W. ed. Fifty years of the American short story v 1 p351-66   **S C**
Who lived and died believing
In Foley, M. ed. Fifty best American short stories, 1915-1965 p286-304   **S C**
Hale, William Harlan
The Horizon Cookbook and illustrated history of eating and drinking throughout the ages   **641.5**
Horizon Magazine. The Horizon Book of ancient Greece   **913.38**
The world of Rodin, 1840-1917   **92**
Haley, Alex
Malcolm X. The autobiography of Malcolm X   **301.451**
Half an hour. Barrie, J. M.
In Barrie, J. M. The plays of J. M. Barrie p631-48   **822**
A half-century of expansion. Adams, J. T.
In Adams, J. T. The march of democracy v2   **973**
Hall, Donald
(jt. ed.) Spender, S. ed. The concise encyclopedia of English and American poets and poetry   **821.03**
Hall, Holworthy. See Porter, Harold Everett
Hall, James
See pages in the following book:
Moore, R. The earth we live on p200-15   **551.09**
Hall, James B.
A view of the beach
In Engle, P. ed. On creative writing p43-50   **808.02**
Hall, James Norman
(jt. auth.) Nordhoff, C. The Bounty trilogy   **Fic**
Hall, Lawrence Sargent
The ledge
In Foley, M. ed. Fifty best American short stories, 1915-1965 p602-17   **S C**
Hall, Richard P.
Protozoa   **593**
Hall-marked. Galsworthy, J.
In Galsworthy, J. Plays p667-74   **822**
Hall of Fame. See New York University. Hall of Fame
Hall-Quest, Olga
Conquistadors and Pueblos   **979.1**
Halle, Louis J.
The cold war as history   **909.82**
Hallet, Elizabeth (Fones) Winthrop Feake
Fiction
Seton, A. The Winthrop woman   **Fic**
Hallett, Robin
Africa to 1875   **960**
Halliburton, Richard
Richard Halliburton's Complete book of marvels   **910.4**

Harlem, New York (City)—*Continued*
Fiction
Baldwin, J. Go tell it on the mountain
    Fic
Meriwether, L. Daddy was a number runner   Fic
Social conditions
Brown, C. Manchild in the promised land   92
Clark, K. B. Dark ghetto   301.451
A Harlem tragedy. Henry, O.
  In Henry, O. The best short stories of O. Henry p295-301   S C
  In Henry, O. The complete works of O. Henry p1437-41   S C
Harley-Davidson repair and tune-up guide, Chilton's. Ritch, O.   629.28
Harling, Robert
  (ed.) House & Garden. House & Garden Book of modern houses and conversions   728.6
Harlow, William M.
  Patterns of life   581
Harmer, Ruth Mulvey
  Unfit for human consumption   632
Harmony. Lardner, R.
  In Lardner, R. The best short stories of Ring Lardner p149-66   S C
The harness. Steinbeck, J.
  In Steinbeck, J. The portable Steinbeck p39-55   818
Harnick, Sheldon
  Stein, J. Fiddler on the roof   812
Harold II, King of England
Fiction
Lewis, H. Harold was my king   Fic
Muntz, H. The golden warrior   Fic
Harold was my king. Lewis, H.   Fic
The Harper Encyclopedia of science   503
Harper Encyclopedia of the modern world   909.08
Harper's Bible dictionary   220.3
Harper's Topical concordance   220.2
Harrap's Shorter French and English dictionary. See Mansion's Shorter French and English dictionary   443
Harrell, Mary Ann
  (jt. auth.) Brander, B. Australia   919.4
Harrer, Heinrich
  Seven years in Tibet   915.15
Harriman, Edward Henry
  See pages in the following book:
Holbrook, S. H. The age of the moguls p195-201   920
Harriman, W. Averell
  America and Russia in a changing world   327.73
Harrington, Michael
  The other America   301.44
Harris, Christie
  Figleafing through history: the dynamics of dress   391.09
Harris, Joel Chandler
  Free Joe and the rest of the world
  In The Scribner treasury p141-53 S C
  The wonderful Tar-Baby story
  In Day, A. G. ed. The greatest American short stories p105-12   S C

About
  See pages in the following book:
Quinn, A. H. American fiction p374-84   813.09
Harris, Louis
  (jt. auth.) Brink, W. Black and white   301.451
Harris, MacDonald
  Trepleff
  In The Best American short stories, 1967 p85-99   S C
Harris, Richard
  Death of a revolutionary; [Ernesto] Che Guevara's last mission   92
  Justice   353.5
Harris, Roy
  See pages in the following books:
Copland, A. The new music, 1900-1960 p118-26   780.9
Cross, M. The Milton Cross New encyclopedia of the great composers and their music p455-67   920.03
Ewen, D. ed. The new book of modern composers p201-10   920
Harris, Sherwood
  The first to fly   629.13
Harris, Theodore F.
  Pearl S. Buck   92
Harris, Townsend
  See pages in the following book:
Tamarin, A. Japan and the United States p174-232   327.52
Harrison, E. L. T.
  See pages in the following book:
Stone, I. Men to match my mountains p268-336   979.1
Harrison, Hal H.
  The world of the snake   598.1
Harrison, John
  See pages in the following book:
Brown, L. A. Map making p152-65 526.8
Harrison, Michael
  Wit's end
  In Best detective stories of the year, 1971 p11-31   S C
Harrison, S. G.
  The Oxford Book of food plants. See The Oxford Book of food plants   581
Harrison, William
  The snooker shark
  In The Best American short stories, 1968 p149-60   S C
Harrison, William Henry, President U.S.
  See pages in the following book:
Lawson, D. The War of 1812 p15-48, 89-98   973.5
Hart, Albert Bushnell
  (ed.) American history told by contemporaries   973
Hart, B. H. Liddell. See Liddell Hart, B. H.
Hart, James D.
  The Oxford Companion to American literature   810.3
Hart, Larry. See Hart, Lorenz Milton
Hart, Lorenz Milton
  See pages in the following books:
Ewen, D. Great men of American popular song p188-207   920
Ewen, D. The story of America's musical theater p102-06, 126-33, 169-75   782.8

Hazel, Robert
White Anglo-Saxon Protestant
In The Best American short stories,
1967 p101-34   **S C**

Hazel Kirke. MacKaye, S.
In Quinn, A. H. ed. Representative
American plays p432-71   **812.08**

Hazeltine, Mary E.
Anniversaries and holidays   **394.2**

Hazelton, Nika Standen
The cooking of Germany   **641.5**

Hazlitt, William
On going a journey
In Parker, E. ed. I was just thinking—
p125-34   **824.08**

He. Porter, K. A.
In Porter, K. A. The collected stories of
Katherine Anne Porter p49-58 **S C**

He also serves. Henry, O.
In Henry, O. The complete works of O.
Henry p747-54   **S C**

He and she. Crothers, R.
In Quinn, A. H. ed. Representative
American plays p891-928   **812.08**

He don't plant cotton. Powers, J. F.
In Havighurst, W. ed. Masters of the
modern short story p201-11   **S C**

He who gets slapped. Andreyev, L.
In Dickinson, T. H. ed. Chief contemporary dramatists; 3d ser. p473-515
808.82

In Tucker, S. M. ed. Twenty-five modern
plays p485-525   **808.82**

Head, Ann
Mr and Mrs Bo Jo Jones   **Fic**

Head
Hogarth, B. Drawing the human head **743**
Loomis, A. Drawing the head and hands
743

See also Brain

The head-hunter. Henry, O.
In Henry, O. The complete works of
O. Henry p764-73   **S C**

Head of Caesar. Chesterton, G. K.
In Chesterton, G. K. The Father Brown
omnibus p315-31   **S C**

Headstrom, Richard
A complete field guide to nests in the
United States   **598**

Health. See Hygiene

Health, Mental. See Mental health

Health, Public. See Public health

Health card. Yerby, F.
In Hughes, L. ed. The best short stories
by Negro writers p192-201   **S C**

Health, Education, and Welfare Department.
See United States. Department of Health,
Education, and Welfare

Health of children. See Children—Care and
hygiene

Health of infants. See Infants—Care and
hygiene

Heaps, Willard A.
Riots, U.S.A. 1765-1970   **301.18**
The wall of shame   **943.087**
Wandering workers   **331.6**

Hearing
Stevens, S. S. Sound and hearing **534**
Van Bergeijk, W. A. Waves and the ear
534
See also pages in the following book:
Asimov, I. The human brain p243-68 **612**

Hearn, Lafcadio
See pages in the following books:
Brooks, V. The confident years: 1885-1915
p232-46   **810.9**
Quinn, A. H. American fiction p509-20
813.09

Hearst, William Randolph
Swanberg, W. A. Citizen Hearst   **92**
See also pages in the following books:
Holbrook, S. H. The age of the moguls
p302-19   **920**
Untermeyer, L. Makers of the modern
world p311-20   **920**

The heart is a lonely hunter. McCullers, C.
Fic

Heart of darkness. Conrad, J.
In Conrad, J. The portable Conrad p490-
603   **828**
In Conrad, J. Typhoon, and other tales
of the sea p273-371   **Fic**

Heart of gold. Lavin, M.
In The Best American short stories, 1965
p199-222   **S C**

The heart of the hunter. Van der Post, L.
916.8

The heart of the matter. Greene, G.   **Fic**

Heart of the West. Henry, O.
In Henry, O. The complete works of O.
Henry p109-266   **S C**

The heart of this or that man. Gropman, D.
In The Best American short stories, 1968
p137-48   **S C**

Heartache. Chekhov, A.
In Chekhov, A. The image of Chekhov
p99-105   **S C**

Heartbreak House. Shaw, B.
In Shaw, B. Bernard Shaw's plays p75-
149   **822**
In Shaw, B. Complete plays, with pref-
aces v 1 p489-598   **822**
In Shaw, B. Four plays p323-473   **822**

The heartland: Ohio, Indiana, Illinois.
Havighurst, W.   **977**

Hearts (Game)
See pages in the following book:
Gibson, W. B. Hoyle's Simplified guide
to the popular card games p86-92 **795.4**

Hearts and crosses. Henry, O.
In Henry, O. The complete works of
O. Henry p109-18   **S C**

Hearts and hands. Henry, O.
In Henry, O. The complete works of
O. Henry p1666-67   **S C**

Heat
See pages in the following books:
Asimov, I. Life and energy p41-51 **612**
United Nations Educational, Scientific
and Cultural Organization. 700 science
experiments for everyone p141-55 **507.2**
See also Thermodynamics

Heat engines. See Steam engines

Heath, F. W.
(ed.) Churchill, Sir W. Great destiny
942.082

An **heiress** of Red Dog. Harte, B.
  In Harte, B. The best short stories of
    Bret Harte p127-44   **S C**
The **heirs** of the kingdom. Oldenbourg, Z.
                            Fic
Heisenberg, Werner
    See pages in the following book:
  Gamow, G. Thirty years that shook phy-
    sics p98-117   **530.1**
Heiser, Victor
  An American doctor's odyssey   **92**
Helen. Euripides
  In Oates, W. J. ed. The complete
    Greek drama v2 p7-58   **882.08**
Helena's husband. Moeller, P.
  In Cerf, B. ed. Thirty famous one-act
    plays p307-22   **808.82**
Helium
    See pages in the following book:
  Asimov, I. Building blocks of the universe
    p52-60   **546**
Hell in a very small place. Fall, B. B. **959.7**
The **hell** screen. Akutagawa, R.
  In Akutagawa, R. Japanese short stories
    p29-77   **S C**
Hellenism
  Sarton, G. A history of science   **509**
Heller, John H.
  Of mice, men and molecules   **619**
Heller, Joseph
  Catch-22   **Fic**
Hellman, Hal
  The art and science of color   **535.6**
  The city in the world of the future   **711**
Hellman, Lillian
  The autumn garden
    In Gassner, J. ed. Best American plays
      3d ser. p205-49   **812.08**
  The children's hour
    In Gassner, J. ed. Twenty best plays of
      the modern American theatre p561-
      98   **812.08**
  The lark; adaptation. See Anouilh, J. The
    lark
  The little foxes
    In Cerf, B. A. ed. Sixteen famous Ameri-
      can plays p799-852   **812.08**
    In Six modern American plays p199-269
                          812.08
  Toys in the attic
    In Cerf, B. ed. Six American plays for
      today p505-91   **812.08**
  Watch on the Rhine
    In Gassner, J. ed. Best plays of the
      modern American theatre; 2d ser.
      p641-82   **812.08**
          About
    See pages in the following book:
  Gould, J. Modern American playwrights
    p168-85   **812.09**
Hello out there. Saroyan, W.
  In Cerf, B. ed. Thirty famous one-act
    plays p549-61   **808.82**
Helmholtz, Hermann Ludwig Ferdinand von
    See pages in the following book:
  Jones, B. Z. ed. The golden age of science
    p436-47   **920**

Helping the other fellow. Henry, O.
  In Henry, O. The complete works of
    O. Henry p967-73   **S C**
Helping youth avoid four great dangers:
  smoking, drinking, VD, narcotics ad-
  diction. Vermes, H.   **613.8**
Hemenway, Robert
  The girl who sang with the Beatles
    In Abrahams, W. ed. Fifty years of the
      American short story v 1 p367-80
                          S C
    In Prize stories, 1970: The O. Henry
      Awards p 1-16   **S C**
Hemingway, Ernest
  A farewell to arms   **Fic**
  A farewell to arms; criticism
    In Gellens, J. ed. Twentieth century in-
      terpretations of A farewell to arms
                          813.09
    In Stegner, W. ed. The American novel
      p192-205   **813.09**
  The Fifth Column; play
    In Hemingway, E. The Fifth Column,
      and four stories of the Spanish Civil
      War p3-85   **818**
  The Fifth Column, and four stories of the
    Spanish Civil War   **818**
  Short stories are: The denunciation; The
  butterfly and the tank; Night before battle;
  Under the ridge
  For whom the bell tolls   **Fic**
  In another country
    In Costain, T. B. ed. Read with me
      p265-71   **S C**
  In our time   **S C**
  Contents: On the quai at Smyrna; Indian
  camp; The doctor and the doctor's wife; The
  end of something; The three day blow; The
  battler; A very short story; Soldier's home;
  The revolutionist; Mr and Mrs Elliot; Cat in
  the rain; Out of season; Cross country snow;
  My old man; Big two-hearted river
  The killers
    In Abrahams, W. ed. Fifty years of the
      American short story v 1 p381-89
                          S C
  A moveable feast   **92**
  My old man
    In Foley, M. ed. Fifty best American
      short stories, 1915-1965 p49-60 **S C**
  The old man and the sea   **Fic**
  The short stories of Ernest Hemingway
                          S C
  Contents: The short happy life of Francis
  Macomber; The capital of the world; The
  snows of Kilimanjaro; Old man at the bridge;
  Up in Michigan; On the quai at Smyrna;
  Indian camp; The doctor and the doctor's
  wife; The end of something; The three-day
  blow; The battler; A very short story; Sol-
  dier's home; The revolutionist; Mr and Mrs
  Elliot; Cat in the rain; Out of season; Cross-
  country snow; My old man; Big two-hearted
  river; The undefeated; In another country;
  Hills like white elephants; The killers; Che
  ti dice la patria; Fifty grand; A simple enquiry; Ten Indians; A canary for one; An
  Alpine idyll; A pursuit race; Today is Friday;
  Banal story; Now I lay me; After the storm;
  A clean, well-lighted place; The light of the
  world; God rest you merry, gentlemen; The
  sea change; A way you'll never be; The
  mother of a queen; One reader writes; Homage to Switzerland; A day's wait; A natural
  history of the dead; Wine of Wyoming; The
  gambler, the nun, and the radio; Fathers and
  sons

Hemingway, Ernest—*Continued*
The snows of Kilimanjaro, and other stories
S C

Contents: The snows of Kilimanjaro; A clean, well-lighted place; A day's wait; The gambler, the nun, and the radio; Fathers and sons; In another country; The killers; A way you'll never be; Fifty grand; The short happy life of Francis Macomber
The sun also rises   Fic
The undefeated
   In Havighurst, W. ed. Masters of the modern short story p171-200 S C

About
Baker, C. Ernest Hemingway   92
Baker, C. Hemingway: the writer as artist   813.09
Baker, S. Ernest Hemingway   813.09
Gurko, L. Ernest Hemingway and the pursuit of heroism   813.09
Hotchner, A. E. Papa Hemingway   92
Rovit, E. H. Ernest Hemingway   813.09
Sanford, M. H. At the Hemingways   92
   See also pages in the following books:
Durant, W. Interpretations of life p28-42
       809
Geismar, M. Writers in crisis p37-85
       813.09
O'Connor, W. V. ed. Seven modern American novelists p153-88   813.09
Sports Illustrated. The wonderful world of sport p273-74   796
Stirling, N. Who wrote the modern classics? p235-83   920
Untermeyer, L. Makers of the modern world p717-25   9920
Wagenknecht, E. Cavalcade of the American novel p368-81   813.09

Hemingway family
Sanford, M. H. At the Hemingways   92

Hémon, Louis
Maria Chapdelaine   ·   Fic
One thousand Aves
   In Becker, M. L. ed. The home book of Christmas p242-58   394.26

Hemphill, George
Allen Tate
   In Unger, L. ed. Seven modern American poets p228-63   811.09

The hen. Saki
   In Saki. The short stories of Saki p283-88   S C

Henderson, Fletcher Hamilton
   See pages in the following book:
Hadlock, R. Jazz masters of the twenties p194-218   920

Henderson, Harold G.
(ed.) An introduction to haiku   895.6

Henderson, I. F.
A dictionary of biological terms   574.03

Henderson, John
Emergency medical guide   614.8

Henderson, John W.
The United States Information Agency   353.061

Henderson, Ray
   See pages in the following book:
Ewen, D. Great men of American popular song p161-68   920

Henderson, Robert
Immortality
   In The New Yorker. Stories from The New Yorker, 1950-1960 p141-51   S C

Henderson, W. D.
(jt. auth.) Henderson, I. F. A dictionary of biological terms   574.03

Henderson, W. O.
(jt. auth.) Vries, S. de. An atlas of world history   911

Hendrick, Burton J.
The age of big business   338

Hendrick, George
Katherine Anne Porter   813.09

Henley, Diana
ASPCA guide to pet care   636

Henn, T. R.
The Bible as literature   220.88

Henry II, King of England
Duggan, A. The falcon and the dove; a life of Thomas Becket of Canterbury
       92
Pernoud, E. Eleanor of Aquitaine   92

Henry III, King of England
Costain, T. B. The magnificent century
       942.03

Henry VII, King of England
Fiction
Barnes, M. C. The Tudor rose   Fic

Henry VIII, King of England
Bowle, J. Henry VIII   92
Roll, W. The pomegranate and the rose; the story of Katharine of Aragon   92
   See also pages in the following books:
Durant, W. The Reformation p523-78
       940.2
Horizon Magazine. The Horizon Book of The Elizabethan world p47-52, 58-69   940.2
The New Cambridge Modern history v2 p226-50   909
Norman, A. V. B. A history of war and weapons, 449 to 1660 p145-76   355.09

Henry IV, King of France
   See pages in the following book:
Durant, W. The age of reason begins p356-73   940.2

Henry the Navigator, Prince of Portugal
   See pages in the following book:
Masselman, G. The Atlantic: sea of darkness p52-66   910.9

Henry, Algernon P.
   See pages in the following book:
Bontemps, A. We have tomorrow p99-107
       920

Henry, Inez
(jt. auth.) Kane, H. T. Miracle in the mountains [biography of Martha McChesney Berry]   92

Henry, Joseph
   See pages in the following books:
Jones, B. Z. ed. The golden age of science p264-95   920
Oehser, P. H. The Smithsonian Institution p27-40   507.4

Henry, O.

The best short stories of O. Henry **S C**

Contents: A gift of the Magi; A cosmopolite in a café; Man about town; The cop and the anthem; The love-philtre of Ikey Shoenstein; Mammon and the archer; Springtime à la carte; From the cabby's seat; An unfinished story; The romance of a busy broker; The furnished room; Roads of destiny; The enchanted profile; The passing of Black Eagle; A retrieved reformation; The renaissance at Charleroi; Shoes; Ships; The hiding of Black Bill; The duplicity of Hargreaves; The ransom of Red Chief; The marry month of May; The whirligig of life; The blackjack bargainer; A lickpenny lover; The defeat of the city; Squaring the circle; Transients in Arcadia; The trimmed lamp; The pendulum; Two Thanksgiving Day gentlemen; The making of a New Yorker; The lost blend; A Harlem tragedy; A midsummer knight's dream; The last leaf; The count and the wedding guest; A municipal report

Cabbages and kings

In Henry, O. The complete works of O. Henry p551-679 **S C**

The complete works of O. Henry **S C**

Contents: The four million: Tobin's palm; The gift of the Magi; A cosmopolite in a café; Between rounds; The skylight room; A service of love; The coming-out of Maggie; Man about town; The cop and the anthem; An adjustment of nature; Memoirs of a yellow dog; The love-philtre of Ikey Shoenstein; Mammon and the archer; Springtime à la carte; The green door; From the cabby's seat; An unfinished story; The caliph, Cupid and the clock; Sisters of the golden circle; The romance of a busy broker; After twenty years; Lost on dress parade; By courier; The furnished room; The brief début of Tildy

Heart of the West: Hearts and crosses; The ransom of Mack; Telemachus friend; The handbook of Hymen; The pimienta pancakes; Seats of the haughty; Hygeia at the Solito; An afternoon miracle; The higher abdication; Cupid à la carte; The caballero's way; The sphinx apple; The missing chord; A call loan; The princess and the puma; The Indian Summer of Dry Valley Johnson; Christmas by injunction; A chaparral prince; The reformation of Calliope

The gentle grafter: The octopus marooned; Jeff Peters as a personal magnet; Modern rural sports; The chair of philanthromathematics; The hand that riles the world; The exact science of matrimony; A midsummer masquerade; Shearing the wolf; Innocents of Broadway; Conscience in art; The man higher up; A tempered wind; Hostages to Momus; The ethics of pig

Roads of destiny: Roads of destiny; The guardian of the Accolade; The discounters of money; The enchanted profile; "Next reading matter"; Art and the bronco; Phoebe; A doubledyed deceiver; The passing of Black Eagle; A retrieved reformation; Cherchez la femme; Friends in San Rosario; The fourth in Salvador; The emancipation of Billy; The enchanted kiss; A departmental case; The renaissance at Charleroi; On behalf of the management; Whistling Dick's Christmas stocking; The halberdier of the little Rheinschloss; Two renegades; The lonesome road

Cabbages and Kings: The proem: By the carpenter; "Fox-in-the-morning"; The lotus and the bottle; Smith; Caught; Cupid's exile number two; The phonograph and the graft; Money maze; The admiral; The flag paramount; The shamrock and the palm; The remnants of the code; Shoes; Ships; Masters of arts; Dicky; Rouge et noir; Two recalls; The vitagraphoscope

Options: "Rose of Dixie"; The third ingredient; The hiding of Black Bill; Schools and school; Thimble, thimble; Supply and demand; Buried treasure; To him who waits; He also serves; The moment of victory; The headhunter; No story; The higher pragmatism; Best-seller; Rus in Urbe; A poor rule

Sixes and sevens: The last of the troubadors; The sleuths; Witches' loaves; The pride of the cities; Holding up a train; Ulysses and the dogman; The champion of the weather; Makes the whole world kin; At arms with Morpheus; A ghost of a chance; Jimmy Hayes and Muriel; The door of unrest; The duplicity of Hargraves; Let me feel your pulse; October and June; The church with an overshot-wheel; New York by camp fire light; The adventures of Shamrock Jolnes; The Greater Coney; Law and order; Transformation of Martin Burney; The caliph and the cad; The diamond of Kali; The day we celebrate

Rolling stones: The dream; A ruler of men; The atavism of John Tom Little Bear; Helping the other fellow; The marionettes; The Marquis and Miss Sally; A fog in Santone; The friendly call; A dinner at—; Sound and fury; Fictocq; Tracked to doom; A snap-shot at the President; An unfinished Christmas story; The unprofitable servant; Aristocracy versus hash; The prisoner of Zembla; A strange story; Fickle fortune or how Gladys hustled; An apology; Lord Oakhurst's curse; Bexar scrip no. 2692; Queries and answers

Whirligigs: The world and the door; The theory and the hound; The hypotheses of failure; Calloway's code; A matter of mean elevation; "Girl"; Sociology in serge and straw; The ransom of Red Chief; The marry month of May; A technical error; Suite homes and their romance; The whirligig of life; A sacrifice hit; The roads we take; A blackjack bargainer; The song and the sergeant; One dollar's worth; A newspaper story; Tommy's burglar; A chaparral Christmas gift; A little local color; Georgia's ruling; Blind man's holiday; Madame Bo-Peep of the ranches

The voice of the city: The voice of the city; The complete life of John Hopkins; A lickpenny lover; Dougherty's eye-opener; "Little speck in garnered fruit"; The harbinger; While the auto waits; A comedy in rubber; One thousand dollars; The defeat of the city; The shocks of doom; The Plutonian fire; Nemesis and the candy man; Squaring the circle; Roses, ruses and romance; The city of dreadful night; The Easter of the soul; The fool-killer; Transients in Arcadia; The rathskeller and the rose; The clarion call; Extradited from Bohemia; A philistine in Bohemia; From each according to his ability; The memento

The trimmed lamp: The trimmed lamp; A Madison Square Arabian night; The rubaiyat of a Scotch highball; The pendulum; Two Thanksgiving Day gentlemen; The assessor of success; The buyer from Cactus City; The badge of policeman O'Roon; Brickdust row; The making of a New Yorker; Vanity and some sables; The social triangle; The purple dress; The foreign policy of Company 99; The lost blend; A Harlem tragedy; "The guilty party"; According to their lights; A midsummer knight's dream; The last leaf; The count and the wedding guest; The country of elusion; The ferry of unfulfilment; The tale of a tainted tenner; Elsie in New York

Strictly business: Strictly business; The gold that glittered; Babes in the jungle; The day resurgent; The fifth wheel; The poet and the peasant; The robe of peace; The girl and the graft; The call of the tame; The unknown quantity; The thing's the play; A ramble in Aphasia; A municipal report; Psyche and the skyscraper; A bird of Bagdad; Compliments of the season; A night in new Arabia; The girl and the habit; Proof of the pudding; Past one at Rooney's; The ventures; The duel; "What you want"

Waifs and strays: The red roses of Tonia; Round the circle; The rubber plant's story; Out of Nazareth; Confessions of a humorist; The sparrows in Madison Square; Hearts and hands; The cactus; The detective detector; The dog and the playlet; A little talk about mobs; The snow man

The four million **S C**

Contents: The four million: Tobin's palm; The gift of the Magi; A cosmopolite in a café; Between rounds; The skylight room; A service of love; The coming-out of Maggie; Man about town; The cop and the anthem; An adjustment of nature; Memoirs of a yellow dog; The love philtre of Ikey Schoenstein; Mammon and the archer; Springtime à la carte; The green door; From the cabby's seat; An unfinished story; The caliph, Cupid and the clock; Sisters of

Henry, O.—*Continued*
the golden circle; The romance of a busy broker; After twenty years; Lost on dress parade; By courtier; The furnished room; The brief début of Tildy
   also in Henry, O. The complete works of O. Henry p 1-108   **S C**
The gentle grafter
   In Henry, O. The complete works of O. Henry p267-354   **S C**
The gift of the Magi
   In Becker, M. L. ed. The home book of Christmas p201-07   394.26
   In Day, A. G. ed. The greatest American short stories p165-72   **S C**
Heart of the West
   In Henry, O. The complete works of O. Henry p100-266   **S C**
Options
   In Henry, O. The complete works of O. Henry p680-810   **S C**
Roads of destiny
   In Henry, O. The complete works of O. Henry p355-550   **S C**
Rolling stones
   In Henry, O. The complete works of O. Henry p941-1060   **S C**
Sixes and sevens
   In Henry, O. The complete works of O. Henry p811-940   **S C**
Strictly business
   In Henry, O. The complete works of O. Henry p1484-1631   **S C**
The trimmed lamp
   In Henry, O. The complete works of O. Henry p1365-1483   **S C**
The voice of the city
   In Henry, O. The complete works of O. Henry p1253-1364   **S C**
Waifs and strays
   In Henry, O. The complete works of O. Henry p1632-92   **S C**
Whirligigs
   In Henry, O. The complete works of O. Henry p1094-1252   **S C**
   For material about this author see Porter, William Sydney
Henry IV. Pirandello, L.
   In Block, H. M. ed. Masters of modern drama p510-31   808.82
Henry the Ninth. Bradbury, R.
   In Bradbury, R. I sing the Body Electric! p254-61   **S C**
Henson, Philip
   See pages in the following book:
Kane, H. T. Spies for the Blue and Gray p193-212   973.7
Hentoff, Nat
A doctor among the addicts   616.86
I'm really dragged but nothing gets me down   **Fic**
A political life; the education of John V. Lindsay   92
Hepburn, Francis Stewart, 5th Earl of Bothwell
   See pages in the following book:
Boyd, M. Man, myth and magic p134-44   133.4
Her first ball. Mansfield, K.
   In Mansfield, K. The short stories of Katherine Mansfield p512-18   **S C**

Her lover. Gorky, M.
   In Seltzer, T. comp. Best Russian short stories p276-83   **S C**
Her son. Wharton, E.
   In Wharton, E. The collected short stories of Edith Wharton v2 p619-68   **S C**
The **heracleidae.** Euripides
   In Oates, W. J. ed. The complete Greek drama v 1 p885-912   882.08
Heracles. Euripides
   In Oates, W. J. ed. The complete Greek drama v 1 p1017-53   882.08
Heraclius, Byzantine Emperor
   See pages in the following book:
Asimov, I. Constantinople p93-106   949.6
Herakles (adaptation) Euripides
   In Browning, R. The complete poetic and dramatic works of Robert Browning p660-75   821
Herald, Earl S.
Living fishes of the world   597
Heraldry
   See pages in the following book:
Shakespeare's England v2 p74-90   822.3
   See also Flags
Herber, Lewis
Crisis in our cities   614
Herbert, Frederick Hugh
The moon is blue
   In Gassner, J. ed. Best American plays; 3d ser. p627-63   812.08
Herbert, Victor
   See pages in the following books:
Ewen, D. Composers for the American musical theatre p 1-19   920
Ewen, D. Great men of American popular song p70-86   920
Ewen, D. The story of America's musical theater p13-27   782.8
Herbs
   See pages in the following book:
McCall's Cook book p556-63   641.5
     History
Coats, A. M. Flowers and their histories   635.9
Hercules
   See pages in the following books:
Grant, M. Myths of the Greeks and Romans p253-74   292
Hamilton, E. Mythology p224-43   292
The **herdsman.** Sholokhov, M.
   In Sholokhov, M. Tales of the Don p16-29   **S C**
Here and beyond. Wharton, E.
   In Wharton, E. The collected short stories of Edith Wharton v2 p371-500   **S C**
Here come the clowns. Barry, P.
   In Gassner, J. ed. Best American plays; supplementary volume, 1918-1958 p533-69   812.08
Here I stand; a life of Martin Luther. Bainton, R. H.   92
Here is France. Bishop, C. H.   914.4

High schools—*Continued*
  Libarle, M. ed. The high school revolutionaries   371.8
    See also Education, Secondary; also names of cities with the subdivision Public schools, e.g. Boston—Public schools
High schools, Junior. See Junior high schools
High society. See Upper classes
High speed aeronautics. See Rockets (Aeronautics)
High Tor. Anderson, M.
  In Anderson, M. Eleven verse plays, 1929-1939 v7   812
  In Gassner, J. ed. Twenty best plays of the modern American theatre p45-91   812.08
High treason. See Treason
High-water mark. Harte, B.
  In Harte, B. The best of Bret Harte p114-24   S C
High, wide and lonesome. Borland, H. G. 92
A high wind in Jamaica. Hughes, R. Fic
The higher abdication. Henry, O
  In Henry, O. The complete works of O. Henry p174-89   S C
Higher education. See Education, Higher
The higher pragmatism. Henry, O.
  In Henry, O. The complete works of O. Henry p780-85   S C
The highest bidder. Stuart, J.
  In Stuart, J. Come back to the farm p133-52   S C
The highest heights. Chekhov, A.
  In Chekhov, A. The image of Chekhov p51-52   S C
Highet, Gilbert
  The anatomy of satire   809.7
  The art of teaching   371.1
  The classical tradition   809
  People, places and books   809
  The powers of poetry   809.1
The highway. Bradbury, R.
  In Bradbury, R. The illustrated man p58-62   S C
The highway and the city. Mumford, L.   301.3
Highway engineering. See Roads
Highways. See Roads
Hiking. See Walking
Hiku and Kawelu. Andersen, J. C.
  In Day, A. G. ed. The spell of Hawaii p25-28   919.69
Hill, Arnold
  Miss Gillespie and the Micks
  In Garrity, D. A. ed. 44 Irish short stories p110-17   S C
Hill, Frank Ernest
  (jt. auth.) Auslander, J. The winged horse   809.1
  (jt. comp.) Auslander, J. comp. The winged horse anthology   821.08
  (jt. auth.) Nevins, A. Ford   92
Hill, Helen
  Christmas in Provence
  In Wernecke, H. H. ed. Celebrating Christmas around the world p114-21   394.26

Hill, James Jerome
  See pages in the following book:
  Holbrook, S. H. The age of the moguls p191-201   920
Hillary, Sir Edmund
  Hunt, J. The conquest of Everest   915.4
The hills beyond. Wolfe, T.   S C
The hills beyond [short story]. Wolfe, T.
  In Wolfe, T. The hills beyond p201-348   S C
Hills like white elephants. Hemingway, E.
  In Hemingway, E. The short stories of Ernest Hemingway p273-78   S C
Hillway, Tyrus
  Herman Melville   813.09
Hillyer, Robert
  In pursuit of poetry   808.1
Hilton, James
  Lost horizon   Fic
  Random harvest   Fic
  Twilight of the wise
  In Becker, M. L. ed. The home book of Christmas p662-70   394.26
Hilton, Timothy
  Keats and his world   92
Himalaya Mountains
  See pages in the following books:
  Mehta, V. Portrait of India p167-278 915.4
  Ullman, J. R. The age of mountaineering p167-295   796.5
Himes, Chester
  Mama's missionary money
  In Clarke, J. H. ed. American Negro short stories p170-75   S C
  Marihuana and a pistol
  In Hughes, L. ed. The best short stories by Negro writers p104-06   S C
  Morning after
  In Margolies, E. A native son's reader p323-29   810.8
    About
  See pages in the following book:
  Margolies, E. Native sons p87-101   810.9
Himmler, Heinrich
  Smith, B. F. Heinrich Himmler: a Nazi in the making, 1900-1926   92
Hinchliffe, Arnold P.
  Harold Pinter   822.09
Hindemith, Paul
  See pages in the following books:
  Cross, M. The Milton Cross New encyclopedia of the great composers and their music p497-515   920.03
  Ewen, D. ed. The new book of modern composers p211-32   920
Hindley, Geoffrey
  The medieval establishment, 1200-1500   901.92
Hindu mythology. See Mythology, Hindu
Hinduism
  See pages in the following books:
  Bach, M. Had you been born in another faith p 1-19   291
  Brown, J. D. India p32-38   915.4
  Cain, A. H. Young people and religion p47-56   291
  Gaer, J. The wisdom of the living religions p115-45   291

Hinduism—*Continued*
Jurji, E. J. ed. The great religions of the modern world p44-89   **291**
Moore, C. D. ed. India yesterday and today p39-53   **915.4**
Savage, K. The story of world religions p52-72   **291**
Schulberg, L. Historic India p113-33   **954**
Smith, H. The religions of man p13-79   **291**
Smith, R. ed. The tree of life p71-114   **291**
Voss, C. H. In search of meaning: living religions of the world p27-45   **291**
See also Caste

Hines, Barry
Billy's last stand
In The Best short plays, 1971 p3-50   **808.82**

Hines, Earl
See pages in the following book:
Hadlock, R. Jazz masters of the twenties p50-75   **920**

Hines, Theodore C.
(ed.) McGraw-Hill Basic bibliography of science and technology. See McGraw-Hill Basic bibliography of science and technology   **016.5**

The hinge of fate. Churchill, W. S.   940.53

Hinsley, F. H.
(ed.) Material progress and world-wide problems, 1870-1898
In The New Cambridge Modern history v11   **909**

Hippies
Time, inc. The hippies   **301.43**
See also pages in the following book:
Louria, D. B. The drug scene p165-76   **613.8**

Hippocrates
See pages in the following book:
Sarton, G. A history of science v 1 p331-83   **509**

Hippolytus. Euripides
In Fitts, D. ed. Greek plays in modern translation p241-96   **882.08**
In Oates, W. J. ed. The complete Greek drama v 1 p763-800   **882.08**

Hiraoka, Kimitake. See Mishima, Yukio

Hirohito, Emperor of Japan
Mosley, L. Hirohito, Emperor of Japan   **92**

Hiroshima
Lifton, B. J. Return to Hiroshima   **915.2**
Bombardment, 1945
Hachiya, M. Hiroshima diary   **940.54**
Hersey, J. Hiroshima   **940.54**
Osada, A. comp. Children of the A-bomb   **940.54**
Fiction
Morris, E. The flowers of Hiroshima   **Fic**
Morris, E. The seeds of Hiroshima   **Fic**

Hiroshima diary. Hachiya, M.   940.54

Hirsch, Sylvia
The art of table setting and flower arrangement   **642**

Hirschfelder, Arlene B.
(comp.) American Indian authors   **016.9701**

Hirshberg, Al
Piersall, J. Fear strikes out   **92**

His father's son. Wharton, E.
In Wharton, E. The collected short stories of Edith Wharton v2 p36-49   **S C**

His last bow. Doyle, Sir A. C.
In Doyle, Sir A. C. The complete Sherlock Holmes v2 p1021-1155   **S C**

His last bow [short story]. Doyle, Sir A. C.
In Doyle, Sir A. C. The complete Sherlock Holmes v2 p1143-55   **S C**

His new mittens. Crane, S.
In Crane, S. The complete short stories & sketches of Stephen Crane p475-84   **S C**

His son. Maupassant, G. de
In Maupassant, G. de. Guy de Maupassant's Short stories p64-72   **S C**

The Hispanic nations of the New World. Shepherd, W. R.   **980**

Hispano-American War, 1898. See United States—History—War of 1898

Hiss, Alger
See pages in the following book:
Goodman, W. The Committee p252-69   **328.73**

Histology. See Cells

Historians
See pages in the following books:
Fermi, L. Illustrious immigrants p353-64   **325.73**
Sarton, G. A history of science v2 p434-58   **509**
See also Archeologists

Historians, American
See pages in the following books:
Commager, H. S. The American mind p293-309   **917.3**
Literary history of the United States p526-40   **810.9**

Historians, Greek
Grant, M. The ancient historians   **920**

Historians, Roman
Grant, M. The ancient historians   **920**

Historic costume. Lester, K. M.   **391.09**

Historic decisions of the Supreme Court. United States. Supreme Court   **347.9**

Historic documents of World War I. Snyder, L. L. ed.   **940.3**

Historic houses, etc. See United States—Historic houses, etc.

Historic India. Schulberg, L.   **954**

Historical atlas. Shepherd, W. R.   **911**

Historical atlas of the world   **911**

Historical atlas to the Bible, The Westminster   **220.9**

Historical atlases. See Atlases, Historical

Historical chronology. See Chronology, Historical

Historical fiction
  Bibliography
Dickinson, A. T. American historical fiction   016.813
Irwin, L. B. comp. A guide to historical fiction   016.8
Historical fiction. See Irwin, L. B. comp. A guide to historical fiction   016.8
Historical geography. See Atlases, Historical; also names of modern countries or regions with the subdivision Historical geography, e.g. United States—Historical geography
Historical non-fiction. See Irwin, L. B. comp. A guide to historical reading: non-fiction   016.9
The histories of Herodotus. Herodotus 938
Historiography
Nevins, A. The gateway to history   907
  See also pages in the following books:
Horizon Magazine. The light of the past p278-88   901.9
Sarton, G. A history of science v 1 p565-83   509
The United States p29-36   917.3
History
Prescott, O. ed. History as literature 908
  See also Biography; Ethnology; Historians; Historical fiction; Military history; Political sciences; World history; and subjects with the subdivision History, or, for literature and music headings, History and criticism, e.g. Civilization—History; American poetry—History and criticism
  Atlases
See Atlases, Historical
  Bibliography
Irwin, L. B. comp. A guide to historical reading: non-fiction   016.9
  Chronology
See Chronology, Historical
  Criticism
See Historiography
  Dictionaries
Canning, J. ed. 100 great events that changed the world   902
Everyman's Dictionary of dates   903
  Historiography
See Historiography
  Outlines, syllabi, etc.
Langer, W. L. ed. An encyclopedia of world history   902
  Philosophy
Durant, W. The lessons of history   901
  See also pages in the following book:
Horizon Magazine. The light of the past p278-88   901.9
  See also Civilization
  Sources
See United States—History—Sources
  Study and teaching
  See pages in the following book:
Barzun, J. Teacher in America p103-14   371.1

Yearbooks
National Broadcasting Company, inc. NBC News. NBC News Picture book of the year   909.82
Year: the encyclopedia news annual 909.82
History, Ancient
The Cambridge Ancient history   930
Grant, M. The ancient historians   920
Herodotus. The histories of Herodotus 938
Larousse Encyclopedia of ancient and medieval history   909
Robinson, C. A. Ancient history from prehistoric times to the death of Justinian   930
  See also pages in the following books:
Van Loon, H. W. The story of mankind p22-130   909
  See also Archeology; Civilization, Ancient; Classical dictionaries; Geography, Ancient; also names of ancient races and peoples, e.g. Hittites; and names of countries of antiquity
History, Biblical. See Bible—History of Biblical events
History, Military. See Military history; and names of countries with the subdivision History, Military, e.g. United States—History, Military
History, Modern
Gilbert, M. Recent history atlas: 1870 to the present day   911
Harper Encyclopedia of the modern world   909.08
Larousse Encyclopedia of modern history, from 1500 to the present day   909
The New Cambridge Modern history 909
  See also Civilization, Modern; Reformation; Renaissance

  20th century
Cronkite, W. Eye on the world   909.82
Halle, L. J. The cold war as history 909.82
Overseas Press Club of America. How I got that story   070
  See also European War, 1914-1918; Twentieth century; World War, 1939-1945
  20th century—Sources
Snyder, L. L. ed. Fifty major documents of the twentieth century   327
  20th century—Yearbooks
News dictionary   909.82
Year: the encyclopedia news annual 909.82
  Philosophy
  See History—Philosophy
History, Natural. See Natural history
History, Naval. See Naval history
History, Universal. See World history
History as literature. Prescott, O. ed. 908
History atlas of America. Hammond, Incorporated   911
History of American antiques from the Revolution to the Civil War, The American Heritage. American Heritage   745.1
A history of American art. Mendelowitz, D. M.   709.73

A history of war and weapons, 449 to 1660. Norman, A. V. B. 355.09

History of Western civilization since 1500. Hayes, C. J. H. 940.2

A history of Western philosophy. Russell, B. 109

The history of world religion's. See Savage, K. The story of world religions 291

History of World War I, The American Heritage. American Heritage 940.3

A history of yesterday, Tolstoy, L.
In Tolstoy, L. Short stories v 1 p 1-22 S C

Histrionics. See Acting; Theater

Hit 'em where they live. Moore, R.
In Moore, R. The green berets p261-338 S C

Hitchcock, Alfred
(ed.) Alfred Hitchcock presents: A month of mystery S C

About
See pages in the following book:
Beard, A. E. S. Our foreign-born citizens p211-23 920

Hitchens, Dolores
If you see this woman
In Mystery Writers of America. Crime without murder p97-111 S C

Hitler, Adolf
Mein Kampf 92
Mein Kampf; criticism
In Downs, R. B. Books that changed the world p118-29 809

About
Bullock, A. Hitler 92
Goldston, R. The life and death of Nazi Germany 943.086
Herzstein, R. E. ed. Adolf Hitler and the Third Reich, 1933-1945 943.086
Shirer, W. L. The rise and fall of the Third Reich 943.086
Speer, A. Inside the Third Reich 943.086
See also pages in the following books:
Carr, A. Men of power p201-16 920
Perrault, G. The secret of D-Day p166-74 940.54
Reeder, R. The story of the Second World War v 1 p16-26 940.53
Untermeyer, L. Makers of the modern world p678-90 920

Hitti, Philip K.
The Arabs 953
The Near East in history 956
A short history of the Near East 956

Hittite mythology. See Mythology, Hittite

Hittites
Ceram, C. W. The secret of the Hittites 939

Ho [biography of Ho-chi Minh]. Halberstam, D. 92

Hoagland, Edward
The final fate of the alligators
In Prize stories, 1971: The O. Henry Awards p330-40 S C

Hobbes, Thomas
See pages in the following books:
Durant, W. The age of Louis XIV p548-64 940.2
Russell, B. A history of Western philosophy p546-57 109

The hobbit. Tolkien, J. R. R. Fic

Hobby, Oveta (Culp)
See pages in the following book:
Stoddard, H. Famous American women p218-24 920

Hobson, Burton
Illustrated encyclopedia of world coins 737.4
Reinfeld, F. A catalogue of the world's most popular coins 737.4
Reinfeld, F. Coin collectors' handbook 737.4
Reinfeld, F. How to build a coin collection 737.4
Reinfeld, F. Stamp collectors' handbook 383.2

Hobson, John Atkinson
Heilbroner, R. L. The worldly philosophers 330.1

Hoch, Edward D.
The magic bullet
In Best detective stories of the year [1969] p230-45 S C
The oblong room
In Hitchcock, A. ed. Alfred Hitchcock presents: A month of mystery p283-92 S C
The theft of the brazen letters
In Mystery Writers of America. Crime without murder p113-24 S C
The theft of the clouded tiger
In Best detective stories of the year [1967] p23-38 S C
The theft of the Coco loot
In Best detective stories of the year, 1971 p182-99 S C

Ho-chi Minh, President Democratic Republic of Vietnam
Halberstam, D. Ho 72
Lacouture, J. Ho Chi Minh 92

Hochstein, Rolaine
(jt. auth.) Sugarman, D. A. Seventeen Guide to knowing yourself 155.5

Hockey
See pages in the following book:
Friendlich, D. Panorama of sports in America p98-105 796
See also Field hockey

Hodge, Paul W.
The revolution in astronomy 523

Hodges, C. Walter
Shakespeare & the players 822.3
Shakespeare's theatre 792.09

Hodges, Henry
Ancient Britons 913.36
Technology in the ancient world 609

Hodgman, Charles
CRC Handbook of chemistry and physics. See CRC Handbook of chemistry and physics 540.21

Hodgson, Godfrey
(jt. auth.) Chester, L. An American melodrama 329

Home to India. Rama Rau, S.   915.4

Home to Nanette. Moore, R.
    In Moore, R. The green berets p164-222   S C

The homecoming. Yerby, F.
    In Clarke, J. H. ed. American Negro short stories p147-56   S C

Homer
    The complete works of Homer   883
    The Iliad   883
    also in Homer. The complete works of Homer v 1   883
    The Iliad; criticism
    In Grant, M. Myths of the Greeks and Romans p27-69   292
    In Horizon Magazine. The light of the past p8-25   901.9
    The Odyssey   883
    also in Homer. The complete works of Homer v2   883
    The Odyssey; criticism
    In Grant, M. Myths of the Greeks and Romans p70-96   292
    In Horizon Magazine. The light of the past p8-25   901.9

About
    Graves, R. The siege and fall of Troy 883
    See also pages in the following books:
    Arnold, M. The portable Matthew Arnold p204-28   828
    Auslander, J. The winged horse p19-29   809.1
    Horizon Magazine. The Horizon Book of ancient Greece p87-93   913.38
    Payne, R. Ancient Greece p74-89   913.38
    Quennell, M. Everyday things in ancient Greece p14-58   913.38
    Sarton, G. A history of science v 1 p130-53   509

Adaptations
    MacInnes, H. Home is the hunter   812

Parodies, travesties, etc.
    MacInnes, H. Home is the hunter   812

Homer, Winslow
    Flexner, J. T. The world of Winslow Homer, 1836-1910   92
    Goodrich, L. Winslow Homer's America   760.9
    See also pages in the following book:
    Baigell, M. A history of American painting p158-67   759.13

Homes for the aged. See Aged—Dwellings

Homestead Strike, 1892
    See pages in the following book:
    Heaps, W. A. Riots, U.S.A. 1765-1970 p72-84   301.18

Honda: repair & tune-up guide. Glenn, H. T.   629.28

Honegger, Arthur
    See pages in the following books:
    Cross, M. The Milton Cross New encyclopedia of the great composers and their music p516-25   920.03
    Ewen, D. ed. The new book of modern composers p233-42   920

Honesty. Mansfield, K.
    In Mansfield, K. The short stories of Katherine Mansfield p666-70   S C

Honey and salt. Sandburg, C.   811
    also in Sandburg, C. The complete poems of Carl Sandburg p706-71   811

Honeymoon. Mansfield, K.
    In Mansfield, K. The short stories of Katherine Mansfield p578-83   S C

Honor. Faulkner, W.
    In Faulkner, W. Collected stories of William Faulkner p551-64   S C
    In Faulkner, W. Selected short stories of William Faulkner p195-209   S C

Honour of Israel Gow. Chesterton, G. K.
    In Chesterton, G. K. The Father Brown omnibus p101-16   S C

Hood, Hugh
    Getting to Williamstown
    In The Best American short stories, 1966 p113-24   S C

Hook, Lucyle
    The research paper   808.82

Hook, Sidney
    [Selections]
    In Kurtz, P. ed. American philosophy in the twentieth century p523-42 191.08

Hooked on books: program & proof. Fader, D. N.   028.5

Hooker, Joseph
    See pages in the following book:
    O'Connor, R. The German-Americans p144-50   301.453

Hooker, Sir Joseph Dalton
    See pages in the following book:
    Jones, B. Z. ed. The golden age of science p418-35   920

Hoover, Herbert Clark, President U.S.
    Memoirs   92
    The ordeal of Woodrow Wilson   92
    #### About
    Faulkner, H. U. From Versailles to the New Deal   973.91
    See also pages in the following books:
    American Heritage. The American Heritage History of the 20's & 30's p177-84   917.3
    Hofstadter, R. The American political tradition and the men who made it p279-310   973
    Shannon, D. A. Between the wars: America, 1919-1941 p126-46   973.91
    Warren, S. The President as world leader p153-64   327.73

Hoover, J. Edgar
    Masters of deceit   335.4

Hop-frog. Poe, E. A.
    In Poe, E. A. The complete tales and poems of Edgar Allan Poe p502-09   S C
    In Poe, E. A. Edgar Allan Poe p317-29   S C
    In Poe, E. A. Selected poetry and prose p329-37   818

Hope (Hospital ship)
    Walsh, W. B. A ship called Hope   362.1

Hopi Indians
    See pages in the following books:
    National Geographic Society. Vanishing peoples of the earth p170-85   572
    Vlahos, O. New world beginnings p199-212   913.7

House in the clouds. Vladimir, M.
In Scammell, M. ed. Russia's other writers p32-114 **S C**

House of bondage. Cole, E. **301.451**

The **House** of Connelly. Green, P.
In Gassner, J. ed. Best American plays; supplementary volume, 1918-1958 p169-215 **812.08**

House of flowers. Capote, T.
In Capote, T. Breakfast at Tiffany's **S C**

House of Habsburg. See Habsburg, House of

The **house** of Madame Tellier. Maupassant, G. de
In Maupassant, G. de. Guy de Maupassant's Short stories p93-119 **S C**

The **House** of Mapuhi. London, J.
In London, J. Best short stories of Jack London p271-90 **S C**

The **house** of mirth. Wharton, E. **Fic**

The **house** of mirth (book 1) Wharton, E.
In Wharton, E. The Edith Wharton reader p45-191 **S C**

The **house** of pride. London, J.
In London, J. Stories of Hawaii p23-37 **S C**

House of Stuart. See Stuart, House of

House of the blues. Wiser, W.
In The Best American short stories, 1967 p315-31 **S C**

The **house** of the dead. Dostoevsky, F. **Fic**

The **House** of the Dead Hand. Wharton, E.
In Wharton, E. The collected short stories of Edith Wharton v 1 p507-29 **S C**

The **house** of the famous poet. Spark, M.
In Spark, M. Collected stories: I p263-73 **S C**

The **House** of the Seven Gables. Hawthorne, N. **Fic**

The **house** of the sun. London, J.
In Day, A. G. ed. The spell of Hawaii p286-97 **919.69**

The **house** on the strand. Du Maurier, D. **Fic**

House painting
Goodheart-Willcox's Painting and decorating encyclopedia **698**
See also pages in the following book:
Gladstone, B. The New York Times Complete manual of home repair p245-317 **643**

House plans. See Architecture—Domestic—Designs and plans

House repairing. See Houses—Repairing

The **house** with the mezzanine. Chekhov, A.
In Chekhov, A. The image of Chekhov p240-61 **S C**

Houseboats
See pages in the following book:
National Geographic Society. Vacationland U.S.A. p248-57 **917.3**

Household, Geoffrey
Children's crusade
In Costain, T. B. ed. Read with me p273-88 **S C**
Watcher in the shadows **Fic**

Household appliances. See Household equipment and supplies

Household appliances, Electric
Klamkin, C. If it doesn't work, read the instructions **640.73**
See also pages in the following book:
O'Brien, R. Machines p132-43 **621.9**

Household equipment and supplies
See pages in the following books:
Cooper, M. The inventions of Leonardo da Vinci p62-69 **608**
United States. Department of Agriculture. Consumers all p121-49 **640.73**
Vogue's Book of etiquette and good manners p233-70 **395**
See also Household appliances, Electric

Household management. See Home economics

The **householder.** Jhabvala, R. P. **Fic**

Housekeeping. See Home economics

Houser, Norman W.
Drugs **613.8**

Houses
See pages in the following books:
Page, R. I. Life in Anglo-Saxon England p136-54 **914.2**
Smith, C. The Time-Life Book of family finance p166-233 **339.4**
United States. Department of Agriculture. Consumers all p 1-80 **640.73**
See also Building—Repair and reconstruction; Housing

Repairing
Gladstone, B. The New York Times Complete manual of home repair **643**

Houshower, Margaret B.
(jt. auth.) Emery, R. C. High interest—easy reading for junior and senior high school reluctant readers **028.52**

Housing
See pages in the following books:
Heaps, W. A. Wandering workers p123-36 **331.6**
Hellman, H. The city in the world of the future p34-48 **711**

Housing and Urban Development Department. See United States. Department of Housing and Urban Development

Housman, A. E.
The collected poems of A. E. Housman **821**
Last poems
In Housman, A. E. The collected poems of A. E. Housman p93-151 **821**
More poems
In Housman, A. E. The collected poems of A. E. Housman p153-211 **821**
A Shropshire lad
In Housman, A. E. The collected poems of A. E. Housman p9-91 **821**

About
Haber, T. B. A. E. Housman **821.09**
See also pages in the following book:
Untermeyer, L. Makers of the modern world p275-80 **920**

How to live in the woods on pennies a day. Angier, B. 917.1

How to make animated movies. Kinsey, A. 778.5

How to make clothes that fit and flatter. Margolis, A. P. 646.4

How to make collages. Lynch, J. 745.59

How to make good pictures. Eastman Kodak Company, Rochester, N.Y. 770.2

How to make movies. Ferguson, R. 778.5

How to prepare for college entrance examinations, Barron's. Brownstein, S. C. 371.26

How to prepare for the high school equivalency examination reading interpretation tests, Barron's. Farley, E. J. 371.27

How to read better and faster. Lewis, N. 428.4

How to select, train, and breed your dog. Whitney, L. F. 636.7

How to solve it. Polya, G. 510

How to survive in your native land. Herndon, J. 373.2

How to take a chance. Huff, D. 519

How to talk back to your television set. Johnson, N. 384.55

How to write a Blackwood article. Poe, E. A.
In Poe, E. A. The complete tales and poems of Edgar Allan Poe p338-45 **S C**

How to write, speak, and think more effectively. Flesch, R. 808

How you look and dress. Carson, B. 646

Howard, Bronson
Shenandoah
In Quinn, A. H. ed. Representative American plays p473-512 812.08

Howard, Clark
We spy
In Best detective stories of the year, 1971 p166-73 **S C**

Howard, Jane
Please touch 301.4

Howard, John R.
(ed.) Awakening minorities: American Indians, Mexican Americans, Puerto Ricans 301.45

Howard, Marjorie Maitland
Hodges, H. Ancient Britons 913.36

Howard, Maureen
Sherry
In The Best American short stories, 1965 p125-65 **S C**

Howard, Neale E.
The telescope handbook and star atlas 522

Howard, Sidney
The late Christopher Bean
In Gassner, J. ed. Twenty best European plays on the American stage p443-89 808.82
The silver cord
In Dickinson, T. H. ed. Chief contemporary dramatists; 3d ser. p65-116 808.82
In Quinn, A. H. ed. Representative American plays p1011-58 812.08
In Tucker, S. M. ed. Twenty-five modern plays p675-720 808.82

They knew what they wanted
In Cerf, B. A. ed. Sixteen famous American plays p5-54 812.08
In Gassner, J. ed. Twenty-five best plays of the modern American theatre; early ser. p91-122 812.08
Yellow Jack
In Gassner, J. ed. Best American plays; supplementary volume, 1918-1958 p451-500 812.08

About
See pages in the following books:
Gould, J. Modern American playwrights p21-25 812.09
Krutch, J. W. The American drama since 1918 p27-60 812.09

Howard, William E.
(jt. auth.) Baar, J. Polaris! 623.4

Howarth, David
D Day, the sixth of June, 1944 940.54
The sledge patrol 940.54
We die alone 940.54

Howarth, William L.
(ed.) Twentieth century interpretations of Poe's tales 813.09

Howe, George Locke
Happy, the Joe
In Dulles, A. ed. Great spy stories from fiction p23-30 **S C**

Howe, Irving
(ed.) Edith Wharton 813.09
(ed.) A treasury of Yiddish poetry 892.49

Howe, Julia (Ward)
Tharp, L. H. Three saints and a sinner: Julia Ward Howe, Louisa, Annie, and Sam Ward 920

Howell, F. Clark
Early man 573.2

Howells, William Dean
The mouse-trap
In Gassner, J. ed. Best plays of the early American theatre p262-76 812.08
The rise of Silas Lapham **Fic**
The rise of Silas Lapham; criticism
In Stegner, W. ed. The American novel p73-85 813.09

About
See pages in the following books:
Brooks, V. New England: Indian summer p24-45, 209-55, 382-404 810.9
Foster, R. ed. Six American novelists of the nineteenth century p155-90 813.09
Literary history of the United States p878-98 810.9
Quinn, A. H. American fiction p257-78 813.09
Trilling, L. The opposing self p76-103 809
Van Doren, C. The American novel, 1789-1939 p120-36 813.09
Wagenknecht, E. Cavalcade of the American novel p127-44 813.09

Howland, Harold
Theodore Roosevelt and his times 973.91

Hoyle, Edmond
Gibson, W. B. Hoyle's Simplified guide to the popular card games 795.4

Hoyle's Simplified guide to the popular card games. Gibson, W. B. 795.4

Hugo Kertchak, builder. Schaefer, J.
In Schaefer, J. The collected stories of
Jack Schaefer p299-317 **S C**

Huguenots
See pages in the following books:
Commager, H. S. Crusaders for freedom
p176-81, 204-10 **920**
Horizon Magazine. The Horizon Book of
The Elizabethan world p166-73 **940.2**

Hull, Isaac
See pages in the following book:
Lawson, D. The War of 1812 p99-106
973.5

Hull, Raymond
(jt. auth.) Peter, L. J. The Peter Principle **817**

Hull, William
See pages in the following book:
Lawson, D. The War of 1812 p58-76
973.5

Hull House, Chicago
Addams, J. Twenty years at Hull-House
361
Meigs, C. Jane Addams: pioneer for so-
cial justice **92**
Wise, W. E. Jane Addams of Hull-House
92
See also pages in the following book:
Addams, J. The social thought of Jane
Addams p44-61 **309.173**

Hulme, Kathryn
The nun's story **Fic**

Hulsker, Jan
(ed.) Gogh, V. van. Van Gogh's "diary"
92

Human beginnings. Vlahos, O. **573.2**
Human body. See Anatomy; Physiology
The **human** body. Asimov, I. **612**
The **human** brain. Asimov, I. **612**
The **human** comedy. Saroyan, W. **Fic**
Human ecology. See Environmental policy
Human engineering. See Life support sys-
tems (Space environment)
The **Human** machine: Adjustments
In Encyclopedia of the life sciences v7
574.03
The **Human** machine: Disorders
In Encyclopedia of the life sciences v6
574.03
The **Human** machine: Mechanisms
In Encyclopedia of the life sciences v5
574.03
Human nature. Wharton, E.
In Wharton, E. The collected short sto-
ries of Edith Wharton v2 p617-740
S C
Human potential movement. See Howard, J.
Please touch **301.4**
Human race. See Anthropology; Man
Human relations
Howard, J. Please touch **301.4**
Montagu, A. On being human **301**
See also pages in the following book:
Toffler, A. Future shock p86-111 **301.24**
See also Conflict of generations;
Family; Prejudices and antipathies;
Psychology, Applied

Human rights. See Civil rights; Religious
liberty
The **human** touch. Easman, R. S.
In Angoff, C. ed. African writing today
p31-37 **896**

Humanism
See pages in the following books:
Brinton, C. The shaping of modern
thought p22-53 **901.93**
Horizon Magazine. Lorenzo de' Medici
and the Renaissance p97-115 **92**
See also Learning and scholarship;
Renaissance

A **humanist.** Gary, R.
In Hitchcock, A. ed. Alfred Hitchcock
presents: A month of mystery
p277-82 **S C**
In The Saturday Evening Post. Best
modern short stories p47-51 **S C**

Humanities. See Art; Literature; Music;
Philosophy

Hume, David
Price, J. V. David Hume **192**
See also pages in the following books:
Durant, W. The age of Voltaire p140-61
940.2
Russell, B. A history of Western philos-
ophy p659-74 **109**

Hummel, Johann Nepomuk
See pages in the following book:
Chapin, V. Giants of the keyboard p55-59
920

Humor. See Wit and humor
Humorists
Rogers, W. The autobiography of Will
Rogers **92**

Humorous pictures. See Cartoons and caricatures; Comic books, strips, etc.

Humorous poetry. See Nonsense verses

Humorous poetry, The fireside book of.
Cole, W. ed. **821.08**

Humorous quotations, A treasury of. Prochnow, H. V. comp. **808.88**

Humorous stories. See Wit and humor

Humphrey, Doris
See pages in the following book:
Maynard, O. American modern dancers:
the pioneers p125-51 **920**

Humphrey, Hubert Horatio
See pages in the following book:
White, T. H. The making of the President,
1968 p353-66 **329**

Humphrey, William
The pump
In The Best American short stories, 1964
p153-60 **S C**

The **hunchback** of Notre Dame. Hugo, V.
Fic

Hundred Years' War, 1339-1453
See pages in the following books:
Mills, D. The Middle Ages p301-24 **940.1**
Thorndike, L. The history of medieval
Europe p541-62 **940.1**

Fiction
Doyle, Sir A. C. The White Company
Fic

I am a camera. Van Druten, J.
  In Gassner, J. ed. Best American plays;
    4th ser. p 1-36   812.08

I am the darker brother. Adoff, A. ed.
              811.08

I came from yonder mountain. Connell,
  E. S.
  In Abrahams, W. ed. Fifty years of the
    American short story v 1 p220-26
              S C

I can find my way out. Marsh, N.
  In Haycraft, H. ed. A treasury of great
    mysteries v2 p189-207   S C

I can't breathe. Lardner, R.
  In Lardner, R. The best short stories
    of Ring Lardner p11-21   S C
  In Lardner, R. The Ring Lardner read-
    er p214-24   S C

I can't imagine tomorrow. Williams, T.
  In The Best short plays, 1971 p77-95
              808.82

I capture the castle. Smith, D.   Fic

I chose prison. Bennett, J. V.   365

"I didn't get over." Fitzgerald, F. S.
  In Fitzgerald, F. S. The Fitzgerald
    reader p429-36   S C

I Elizabeth [Custer]. Randall, R. P. 92

I have a dream   323.4

"I have a thing to tell you." Wolfe, T.
  In Wolfe, T. The short novels of
    Thomas Wolfe p236-78   S C

I Jessie [Frémont]. Randall, R. P. 92

I know why the caged bird sings. Angelou, M.   92

I live on your visits. Parker, D.
  In The New Yorker. Stories from The
    New Yorker, 1950-1960 p529-38
              S C

I married adventure. Johnson, O. 92

I Mary [Lincoln]. Randall, R. P. 92

I never loved your mind. Zindel, P. Fic

I never promised you a rose garden.
  Green, H.   Fic

I remember, I remember. See Maurois, A.
  Memoirs, 1885-1967   92

I remember mama. Van Druten, J. 822
  —Same
  In Gassner, J. ed. Best plays of the
    modern American theatre; 2d ser.
    p85-129   812.08

I, robot. Asimov, I.   S C

I sing the Body Electric! Bradbury, R. S C

I sing the Body Electric [short story].
  Bradbury, R.
  In Bradbury, R. I sing the Body Elec-
    tric! p150-90   S C

I take care of things. Cady, J.
  In The Best American short stories,
    1971 p67-73   S C

I walked with heroes. Romulo, C. P. 92

I wanna woman. O'Casey, S.
  In O'Casey, S. The Sean O'Casey read-
    er p967-81   828

I wanted to see. Dahl, B.   92

I was an outcast. See Hazari. Untouchable
           915.4

I was just thinking. Parker, E. ed. 824.08

Iba, Henry Payne
  See pages in the following book:
  Padwe, S. Basketball's Hall of Fame p103-
    11   920

Iberia. Michener, J. A.   914.6

Iberian Peninsula. See Portugal

The Iberians. Arribas, A.   913.36

Ibn Hakkan al-Bokhari, dead in his labyrinth. Borges, J. L.
  In Borges, J. L. The Aleph, and other
    stories, 1933-1969 p115-25 S C

Ibo tribe
  See pages in the following book:
  Hatch, J. Nigeria p75-91   966.9
           Fiction
  Achebe, C. Arrow of God   Fic
  Achebe, C. Things fall apart Fic

Ibsen, Henrik
  Eleven plays of Henrik Ibsen 839.8
  Contents: A doll's house; Ghosts; An enemy
  of the people; The master builder; Pillars of
  society; Hedda Gabler; John Gabriel Borkman;
  The wild duck; League of youth; Rosmersholm;
  Peer Gynt
  Four plays of Ibsen   839.8
  Contents: When we dead awaken; The mas-
  ter builder; Little Eyolf; The wild duck
  Ghosts
  In Block, H. M. ed. Masters of modern
    drama p68-91   808.82
  Peer Gynt
  In Block, H. M. ed. Masters of modern
    drama p13-66   808.82
  Rosmersholm
  In Bentley, E. comp. The great play-
    wrights v2 p1307-73   808.82
  In Tucker, S. M. ed. Twenty-five mod-
    ern plays p 1-41   808.82
  Six plays   839.8
  Contents: A doll's house; Ghosts; An enemy
  of the people; Rosmersholm; Hedda Gabler;
  The master builder
  The wild duck
  In Bentley, E. comp. The great play-
    wrights v2 p1207-93   808.82
  In Cerf, B. A. comp. Sixteen famous
    European plays p5-84   808.82
          About
  See pages in the following books:
  Gassner, J. Master of the drama p354-83
           809.2
  Nicoll, A. World drama p524-46 809.2
  Untermeyer, L. Makers of the modern
    world p113-20   920

Icarus (Planets, Minor)
  See pages in the following book:
  Scientific American. Frontiers in astron-
    omy p59-68   520

Ice age. See Glacier epoch

The ice palace. Fitzgerald, F. S.
  In Fitzgerald, F. S. The stories of F.
    Scott Fitzgerald p61-82   S C

Ice sports. See Winter sports

Ice Station Zebra. MacLean, A. Fic

Iceland
  See pages in the following book:
  Stefánsson, V. ed. Great adventures and
    explorations p29-52   910.9

The **iceman** cometh. O'Neill, E.   812
—Same
  In Block, H. M. ed. Masters of modern
    drama p588-644   **808.82**
  In Cerf, B. ed. Plays of our time p 1-144
    812.08
  In Gassner, J. ed. Best American plays;
    3d ser. p95-171   **812.08**
  In O'Neill, E. Plays v3   812
  In O'Neill, E. Selected plays of Eugene
    O'Neill   812

I Ching
  Douglas, A. How to consult the I Ching
  p53-236   **895.1**
Ichthyology. See Fishes
An **ideal** family. Mansfield, K.
  In Mansfield, K. The short stories of
    Katherine Mansfield p505-11   **S C**
An **ideal** husband. Wilde, O.
  In Wilde, O. The plays of Oscar Wilde
    v2 p 1-125   **822**
Ideal states. See Utopias
Ideas and men. Brinton, C.   **901.9**
Identity, Personal. See Personality
The **ides** of March. Wilder, T.   **Fic**
Idiocy. See Mentally handicapped
Idioms. See English language—Idioms
The **idiot.** Dostoevsky, F.   **Fic**
Idiot's delight. Sherwood, R. E.
  In Gassner, J. ed. Twenty best plays of
    the modern American theatre p93-
    136   **812.08**
Idle beauty. Maupassant, G. de
  In Maupassant, G. de. Guy de Mau-
    passant's Short stories p297-314
    S C
Idyll, C. P.
  The sea against hunger   **639**
The **idyll** of Red Gulch. Harte, B.
  In Harte, B. The best of Bret Harte
    p65-76   **S C**
Idylls of the King. Tennyson, A. T. 1st
  Baron   **821**
If Christmas comes. Cuppy, W.
  In Becker, M. L. ed. The home book
    of Christmas p139-42   **394.26**
If Hitler had invaded England. Forester,
  C. S.
  In Forester, C. S. Gold from Crete
    p183-263   **S C**
If it don't work, read the instructions.
  Klamkin, C.   **640.73**
If men played cards as women do. Kauf-
  man, G. S.
  In Cerf, B. ed. Thirty famous one-act
    plays p423-27   **808.82**
If they knew Yvonne. Dubus, A.
  In The Best American short stories,
    1970 p84-107   **S C**
"If this goes on—" Heinlein, R. A.
  In Heinlein, R. A. Robert A. Heinlein's
    The past through tomorrow p361-
    470   **S C**
If you marry outside your faith. Pike, J. A.
    301.42
If you see this woman. Hitchens, D.
  In Mystery Writers of America. Crime
    without murder p97-111   **S C**

Ignacio de Loyola, **Saint.** See Loyola, Igna-
  cio de, Saint
Ile. O'Neill, E.
  In Gassner, J. ed. Twenty-five best
    plays of the modern American
    theatre; early ser. p703-11   **812.08**
  In O'Neill, E. The long voyage home
    p117-43   812
  In O'Neill, E. Plays v 1 p535-52   812
Ilg, Frances L.
  (jt. auth.) Gesell, A. Youth: the years
    from ten to sixteen   **155.5**
The **Iliad.** Homer   **883**
  also in Homer. The complete works of
    Homer v 1   883
The **Iliad** of Sandy Bar. Harte, B.
  In Harte, B. The best short stories of
    Bret Harte p55-68   **S C**
I'll call you. Inman, R.
  In Prize stories, 1971: The O. Henry
    Awards p168-96   **S C**
I'll crack your head "Kotsun." Murayama,
  M.
  In Day, A. G. ed. The spell of Hawaii
    p323-35   **919.69**
The **ill**-made Knight. White, T. H.
  In White, T. H. The once and future
    king p325-544   **Fic**
**Illía, Arturo Umberto, President Argentine
Republic**
  See pages in the following book:
  Gunther, J. Inside South America p189-
  97   **980**
Illinois
History
  Havighurst, W. The heartland: Ohio, In-
    diana, Illinois   **977**
Illiteracy
  Isenberg, I. ed. The drive against illiteracy
    379
  Medary, M. Each one teach one; Frank
    Laubach, friend to millions   **92**
Illumination of books and manuscripts
  See pages in the following book:
  Bagley, J. J. Life in medieval England
    p143-50   **914.2**
An **illusion** in red and white. Crane, S.
  In Crane, S. The complete short stories
    & sketches of Stephen Crane p726-
    30   **S C**
Illusions. See Optical illusions
An **illustrated** cultural history of England.
  Halliday, F. E.   **709.42**
Illustrated encyclopedia of world coins.
  Hobson, B.   **737.4**
Illustrated English social history. Trevel-
  yan, G. M.   **942**
The **illustrated** hassle-free make your own
  clothes book. Rosenberg, S.   **646.4**
An **illustrated** history of Black Americans.
  Franklin, J. H.   **301.451**
Illustrated History of England. Trevelyan,
  G. M.   **942**
Illustrated history of English literature.
  Ward, A. C.   **820.9**
An **illustrated** history of Germany. Mau-
  rois, A.   **943**
An **illustrated** history of transportation.
  Ridley, A.   **380.5**

The **illustrated** man. Bradbury, R. **S C**

Illustrated medical dictionary, Dorland's
610.3

Illustrations, Humorous. See American wit and humor, Pictorial; Cartoons and caricatures

Illustrators

Dictionaries

Fuller, M. ed. More junior authors 920.03

Kunitz, S. J. ed. The junior book of authors 920.03

Illustrious immigrants. Fermi, L. 325.73

Ilyás. Tolstoy, L.
In Tolstoy, L. Twenty-three tales p168-73 **S C**

I'm a fool. Anderson, S.
In Day, A. G. ed. The greatest American short stories p237-49 **S C**
In Foley, M. ed. Fifty best American short stories, 1915-1965 p38-48 **S C**

I'm in Marsport without Hilda. Asimov, I.
In Asimov, I. Asimov's mysteries p110-24 **S C**
In Asimov, I. Nine tomorrows p113-26 **S C**

I'm really dragged but nothing gets me down. Hentoff, N. **Fic**

The **image** of Chekhov. Chekhov, A. **S C**

The **Image** of the Lost Soul. Saki
In Saki. The short stories of Saki p589-91 **S C**

Imagination's other place. Plotz, H. comp.
808.81

Imbecility. See Mentally handicapped

Immigration and emigration

See pages in the following books:

American Heritage. The American Heritage History of the confident years p305-19 **973.8**

McCarthy, J. New England p100-15 **917.4**

See also names of countries with the subdivision Immigration and emigration, e.g. United States—Immigration and emigration

The **immodest** Mr Pomfret. Moore, R.
In Moore, R. The green berets p242-60 **S C**

Immoral literature. See Literature, Immoral

The **immoralist.** Gide, A. **Fic**

The **immortal** lovers: Elizabeth Barrett and Robert Browning. Winwar, F. **92**

The **immortal** Sergeant Hanks. Moore, R.
In Moore, R. The green berets p67-87 **S C**

Immortal wife. Stone, I. **Fic**

Immortality. Henderson, R.
In The New Yorker. Stories from The New Yorker, 1950-1960 p141-51 **S C**

The **immortals.** Borges, J. L.
In Borges, J. L. The Aleph, and other stories, 1933-1969 p169-74 **S C**

The **imp** and the crust. Tolstoy, L.
In Tolstoy, L. Short stories v2 p179-82 **S C**
In Tolstoy, L. Twenty-three tales p182-85 **S C**

The **imp** of the perverse. Poe, E. A.
In Poe, E. A. The complete tales and poems of Edgar Allan Poe p280-84 **S C**
In Poe, E. A. Selected poetry and prose p309-14 **818**

The **imperfect** union. Hutchinson, J. **331.88**

Imperial Rome. Hadas, M. **937**

Imperial woman. Buck, P. S. **Fic**

Imperialism. See names of countries with the subdivision Foreign relations, e.g. United States—Foreign relations

Implements, utensils, etc. See Agricultural machinery; Household equipment and supplies; Stone implements

The **importance** of being Earnest. Wilde, O. **822**

—Same
In Bentley, E. comp. The great playwrights v2 p1437-1536 **808.82**
In Cerf, B. A. comp. Sixteen famous British plays p69-117 **822.08**
In Tucker, S. M. ed. Twenty-five modern plays p125-58 **808.82**
In Wilde, O. The plays of Oscar Wilde v 1 p45-132 **822**

Imports. See Commerce

Impressionism (Art)

Kelder, D. The French impressionists and their century **759.4**

Rewald, J. The history of impressionism **759.05**

Schneider, P. The world of Manet, 1832-1883 **92**

See also pages in the following books:

Cheney, S. The story of modern art p174-93 **709.03**

Gardner, H. Gardner's Art through the ages p664-73 **709**

Gombrich, E. H. Art and illusion p203-41 **701**

Janson, H. W. History of art p489-504 **709**

Ruskin, A. Nineteenth century art p100-40 **709.03**

See also Postimpressionism (Art)

Imprisonment. See Prisons

Impulse. Russell, E. F.
In Conklin, G. ed. Invaders of earth p37-47 **S C**

In a cafe. Lavin, M.
In The New Yorker. Stories from The New Yorker, 1950-1960 p247-61 **S C**

In a few hands: monopoly power in America. Kefauver, E. **338.8**

In a good cause—. Asimov, I.
In Asimov, I. Nightfall, and other stories p166-90 **S C**

In a Park Row restaurant. Crane, S.
In Crane, S. The complete short stories & sketches of Stephen Crane p186-88 **S C**

In a Persian kitchen. Mazda, M. **641.5**

In Abraham's bosom. Green, P.
In Dickinson, T. H. ed. Chief contemporary dramatists; 3d ser. p21-63 **808.82**

In another country. Hemingway, E.
In Costain, T. B. ed. Read with me p265-71   **S C**
In Hemingway, E. The short stories of Ernest Hemingway p267-72   **S C**
In Hemingway, E. The snows of Kilimanjaro, and other stories p65-70   **S C**

In chancery. Galsworthy, J.
In Galsworthy, J. The Forsyte saga p363-639   **Fic**

In clean hay. Kelly, E. P.
In Becker, M. L. ed. The home book of Christmas p26-34   **394.26**

In cold blood. Capote, T.   **364.1**

"In conference." Lardner, R.
In Lardner, R. The Ring Lardner reader p275-80   **S C**

In defense of liberty. Wood, W.
In Pageant of America v7   **973**

In exile. Chekhov, A.
In Chekhov, A. The image of Chekhov p193-203   **S C**
In Chekhov, A. The stories of Anton Chekhov p171-80   **S C**

"In good King Charles's golden days." Shaw, B.
In Shaw, B. Complete plays, with prefaces v6 p11-84   **822**

In Greenwich there are many gravelled walks. Calisher, H.
In Foley, M. ed. Fifty best American short stories, 1915-1965 p438-52   **S C**

In late youth. Rush, N.
In The Best American short stories, 1971 p275-90   **S C**

In our time. Hemingway, E.   **S C**

In pursuit of poetry. Hillyer, R.   **808.1**

In quest of quasars. Bova, B.   **523.8**

In quest of quiet. Still, H.   **614**

In search of meaning: living religions of the world. Voss, C. H.   **291**

In sheep's clothing. Nourse, A. E.
In Nourse, A. E. R for tomorrow p55-73   **S C**

In shock. Litwak, L. E.
In The Best American short stories, 1968 p201-14   **S C**

In the abyss. Wells, H. G.
In Wells, H. G. The complete short stories of H. G. Wells p377-93   **S C**
In Wells, H. G. 28 science fiction stories p493-509   **S C**

In the Avu observatory. Wells, H. G.
In Wells, H. G. The complete short stories of H. G. Wells p212-19   **S C**
In Wells, H. G. 28 science fiction stories p352-59   **S C**

In the beginning. Gbadamossi, R. A.
In Angoff, C. ed. African writing today p119-20   **896**

In the cemetery. Chekhov, A.
In Chekhov, A. The image of Chekhov p64-66   **S C**

In the clearing. Frost, R.   **811**
also in Frost, R. The poetry of Robert Frost p409-73   **811**

In the company of eagles. Gann, E. K.   **Fic**

In the country. Maupassant, G. de
In Maupassant, G. de. Guy de Maupassant's Short stories p58-63   **S C**

In the footsteps of Lewis and Clark. Snyder, G. S.   **973.4**

In the heart of the heart of the country. Gass, W. H.
In The Best American short stories, 1968 p101-23   **S C**

In the heat of the night. Ball, J.   **Fic**

In the horsecart. Chekhov, A.
In Chekhov, A. The image of Chekhov p262-72   **S C**

"In the interests of the brethren." Kipling, R.
In Kipling, R. The best short stories of Rudyard Kipling p586-97   **S C**

In the interlude, poems, 1945-1960. Pasternak, B.   **891.7**

In the land of the morning calm, déjà vu. Siegel, J.
In The Best American short stories, 1970 p288-307   **S C**

In the land of the tiger. Kraft, V.
In Sports Illustrated. The wonderful world of sport p267-72   **796**

In the Mecca. Brooks, G.   **811**

In the modern vein. Wells, H. G.
In Wells, H. G. The complete short stories of H. G. Wells p491-501   **S C**

In the penal colony. Kafka, F.
In Kafka, F. Selected short stories of Franz Kafka p90-128   **S C**

In the region of ice. Oates, J. C.
In Abrahams, W. ed. Fifty years of the American short story v 1 p500-15   **S C**

In the rukh. Kipling, R.
In Kipling, R. The best short stories of Rudyard Kipling p176-96   **S C**

In the shadow of the glen. Synge, J. M.
In Cerf, B. ed. 24 favorite one-act plays p377-90   **808.82**

In the spring. Maupassant, G. de
In Maupassant, G. de. Guy de Maupassant's Short stories p156-61   **S C**

In the storm country. McNeely, M. H.
In Becker, M. L. ed. The home book of Christmas p259-77   **394.26**

In the Tenderloin: a duel between an alarm clock and a suicidal purpose. Crane, S.
In Crane, S. The complete short stories & sketches of Stephen Crane p308-11   **S C**

In the village. Bishop, E.
In The New Yorker. Stories from The New Yorker, 1950-1960 p290-308   **S C**

In the wake of the whale. Barbour, J. A.   **599**

In the wilderness. Undset, S.
In Undset, S. The master of Hestviken v3   **Fic**

In the zone. O'Neill, E.
In Cerf, B. ed. Thirty famous one-act plays p405-18   **808.82**
In O'Neill, E. The long voyage home p85-114   **812**
In O'Neill, E. Plays v 1 p513-32   **812**

In the zoo. Stafford, J.
  In Abrahams, W. ed. Fifty years of the American short story v2 p301-19
      S C
  In The New Yorker. Stories from The New Yorker, 1950-1960 p596-615
      S C

In their own words. Meltzer, M. ed. **301.451**
In this house of Brede. Godden, R.   **Fic**
In touch. Steinbeck, J.   **92**
In trust. Wharton, E.
  In Wharton, E. The collected short stories of Edith Wharton v 1 p616-31   **S C**

In white America. Duberman, M. B.
  In Gassner, J. ed. Best American plays; 6th ser. p471-94   **812.08**

An inadvertence. Chekhov, A.
  In Chekhov, A. The stories of Anton Chekhov p110-14   **S C**

The Inca of Perusalem. Shaw, B.
  In Shaw, B. Complete plays, with prefaces v5 p97-121   **822**

Incas
  Bingham, H. Lost city of the Incas **913.85**
  Métraux, A. The history of the Incas
      980.3
  Prescott, W. H. History of the conquest of Peru   **985**
  Wauchope, R. ed. The Indian background of Latin American history   **970.3**
  See also pages in the following books:
  Baity, E. C. Americans before Columbus p209-27   **970.1**
  Crow, J. A. The epic of Latin America p22-44, 95-101   **980**
  Innes, H. The Conquistadors p244-82
      973.1
  Leonard, J. N. Ancient America p79-93, 146-52   **913.7**
  Thomas, L. Lowell Thomas' Book of the high mountains p223-37   **910.9**
  Vlahos, O. New world beginnings p282-301   **913.7**

The incautious burglar. Carr, J. D.
  In Haycraft, H. ed. A treasury of great mysteries v 1 p333-44   **S C**

An incident at Krechetovska Station. Solzhenitsyn, A.
  In Solzhenitsyn, A. Stories and prose poems p167-240   **S C**

Income
  Miller. H. P. Rich man, poor man   **339**

Income tax
  See pages in the following book:
  Smith, C. The Time-Life Book of family finance p278-99   **339.4**

Income tax. Hughes, L.
  In Hughes, L. The Langston Hughes reader p183-85   **818**

The incredible A. J. Foyt. Engel, L. K. **92**
Incredible victory. Lord, W.   **940.54**
Incredulity of Father Brown. Chesterton, G. K.
  In Chesterton, G. K. The Father Brown omnibus p433-630   **S C**

Index to 8mm motion cartridges. National Information Center for Educational Media   **371.33**
Index to full length plays, 1944 to 1964
      808.82
Index to overhead transparencies. National Information Center for Educational Media   **371.33**
Index to plays in collections, Ottemiller's
      808.82
Index to poetry, Granger's   **808.81**
Index to poetry and recitations. See Granger's Index to poetry   **808.81**
Index to 16mm educational films. National Information Center for Educational Media   **371.33**
Index to the Life Nature library. See Time-Life Books. A guide to the natural world, and Index to the Life Nature library   **574**
Index to the Life Science Library. See Time-Life Books. A guide to science, and Index to the Life Science Library
      500
Index to 35mm filmstrips. National Information Center for Educational Media
      371.33
Indexing. See Cataloging; Files and filing

India
  Brown, J. D. India   **915.4**
  Mehta, V. Portrait of India   **915.4**
  See also pages in the following books:
  Ashabranner, B. A moment in history: the first ten years of the Peace Corps p120-33, 189-208   **309.2**
  Ehrlich, P. R. Population, resources, environment p85-90, 96-99, 236-42   **301.3**
  Salisbury, H. E. Orbit of China p83-94
      915.1
  Tagore, R. A Tagore reader p181-204
      891.4

  Antiquities
  Edwardes, M. Everyday life in early India
      913.34
  See also pages in the following book:
  Durant, W. Our Oriental heritage p391-415, 440-502   **950**

  Civilization
  Edwardes, M. Everyday life in early India
      913.34
  Moore, C. D. ed. India yesterday and today   **915.4**
  Schulberg, L. Historic India   **954**
  Taylor, E. Richer by Asia   **915.4**
  See also pages in the following books:
  Durant, W. Our Oriental heritage p526-54, 613-33   **950**
  Larousse Encyclopedia of prehistoric and ancient art p368-80   **709.01**

  Description and travel
  Bowles, C. Ambassador's report   **915.4**
  Bowles, C. At home in India   **915.4**
  Rama Rau, S. Home to India   **915.4**
  Rama Rau, S. This is India   **915.4**

  Drama
  Rama Rau, S. A passage to India   **822**

Indians of North America—History—*Cont.*

La Farge, O. A pictorial history of the American Indian   **970.1**

Wissler, C. Indians of the United States   **970.1**

See also pages in the following book:

Udall, S. L. The quiet crisis p3-12   **333.7**

Industries

Dockstader, F. J. Indian art in America   **970.6**

Legal status, laws, etc.

See Indians of North America—Government relations

Legends

Marriott, A. American Indian mythology   **398.2**

Mythology

See Indians of North America—Religion and mythology

Pictures, illustrations, etc.

La Farge, O. A pictorial history of the American Indian   **970.1**

Poetry

Day, A. G. ed. The sky clears: poetry of the American Indians   **897**

Religion and mythology

See pages in the following books:

Larousse World mythology p449-57   **291**

Smith, R. ed. The tree of life p17-43   **291**

Social conditions

Wax, M. L. Indian Americans: unity and diversity   **970.1**

Wars

Brown, D. Bury my heart at Wounded Knee   **970.4**

See also pages in the following book:

American Heritage. The American Heritage Book of great adventures of the Old West p264-81, 310-29   **978**

See also Little Big Horn, Battle of the, 1876; United States—History—French and Indian War, 1755-1763

The West

Brown, D. Bury my heart at Wounded Knee   **970.4**

Indians of North America. Driver, H. E.   **970.1**

Indians of South America

See pages in the following book:

National Geographic Society. Vanishing peoples of the earth p152-69   **572**

See also names of families or tribes, e.g. Incas

Antiquities

Leonard, J. N. Ancient America   **913.7**

Brazil

See pages in the following book:

National Geographic Society. Great adventures with National Geographic p430-37   **910.9**

Religion and mythology

See pages in the following book:

Larousse World mythology p481-91   **291**

Indians of the United States. Wissler, C.   **970.1**

Indic art. See Art, Indic

Indic cookery. See Cookery, Indic

Indic drama

History and criticism

See pages in the following book:

Gassner, J. Masters of the drama p113-22   **809.2**

Indic literature

History and criticism

See pages in the following book:

Durant, W. Our Oriental heritage p555-83   **950**

Indic philosophy. See Philosophy, Indic

Indic poetry

Collections

Aldan, D. comp. Poems from India   **891**

Indic sculpture. See Sculpture, Indic

An **indiscreet** journey. Mansfield, K.

In Mansfield, K. The short stories of Katherine Mansfield p183-97   **S C**

Individuality

Whyte, W. H. The organization man   **301.15**

See also pages in the following book:

Parker, D. H. Schooling for what? p132-50   **370.1**

See also Conformity; Personality; Self

Indo-Europeans. See Aryans

Indonesia

See pages in the following book:

Rama Rau, S. Gifts of passage p161-69   **92**

Politics and government

See pages in the following book:

Kenworthy, L. S. Leaders of new nations p310-35   **920**

Social conditions

Walsh, W. B. A ship called Hope   **362.1**

Indoor games. See Games

Indoro Bush College. Freeman, R. A.

In Angoff, C. ed. African writing today p175-81   **896**

Induction (Logic) See Logic

Indus Valley

Civilization

See pages in the following book:

Schreiber, H. Vanished cities p313-25   **913.03**

Industrial arts. See Technology; names of specific industries, arts, trades, e.g. Printing; and names of countries, cities, etc. with the subdivision Industries, e.g. United States—Industries

Industrial arts education. See Woodwork

Industrial combinations. See Trusts, Industrial

Industrial efficiency. See Efficiency, Industrial

Industrial mergers. See Trusts, Industrial

Industrial mobilization

Janeway, E. The struggle for survival   **355.2**

Industrial painting. See Painting, Industrial

Industrial revolution. See Industry—History

Industrial trusts. See Trusts, Industrial

Inman, Douglas Lamar
See pages in the following book:
Behrman, D. The new world of the oceans
p143-50   551.4
Inman, Robert
I'll call you
In Prize stories, 1971: The O. Henry
Awards p168-96   **S C**
Innes, Hammond
The Conquistadors   **973.1**
Scandinavia   **914.8**
The wreck of the Mary Deare   **Fic**
Innocence of Father Brown. Chesterton,
G. K.
In Chesterton, G. K. The Father Brown
omnibus p 1-226   **S C**
The **innocence** of Reginald. Saki
In Saki. The short stories of Saki p40-
42   **S C**
The **innocent** voyage. See Hughes, R. A
high wind in Jamaica   **Fic**
The **innocent** wayfaring. Chute, M.   **Fic**
The **innocents** abroad. Twain, M.   **817**
Innocents of Broadway. Henry, O.
In Henry, O. The complete works of O.
Henry p305-10   **S C**
An **inquiry** into the nature and causes of the
wealth of nations. Smith, A.   **330.1**
Insane. See Mental illness
Insane—Care and treatment. See Mentally
ill—Care and treatment
Insanity. See Mental illness
Inscriptions. See Hieroglyphics
Inscriptions, Cuneiform. See Cuneiform in-
scriptions
Inscriptions, Linear B
See pages in the following book:
Ceram, C. W. ed. Hands on the past p102-
10   **913.03**
Insect behavior. Callahan, P. S.   **595.7**
The **insect** world of J. Henri Fabre. Fabre,
J. H.   **595.7**
Insecticides
Carson, R. Silent spring   **632**
United States. Department of Agriculture.
Insects   **632**
See also pages in the following books:
Asimov, I. Twentieth century discovery
p 1-31   **500**
Winter, R. Poisons in your food p9-37 **614**
See also DDT (Insecticide); Insects,
Injurious and beneficial
Insects
Barker, W. Familiar insects of America
595.7
Borror, D. J. A field guide to the insects
of America north of Mexico   **595.7**
Callahan, P. S. Insect behavior   **595.7**
Callahan, P. S. Insects and how they func-
tion   **595.7**
Fabre, J. H. The insect world of J. Henri
Fabre   **595.7**
Lutz, F. E. Field book of insects of the
United States and Canada, aiming to
answer common questions   **595.7**
See also pages in the following books:
Boy Scouts of America. Fieldbook for Boy
Scouts, explorers, scouters, educators,
outdoorsmen p408-19   **369.43**

Fenton, C. L. The fossil book p246-51 **560**
Headstrom, R. A complete field guide to
nests in the United States p389-415 **598**
Ricard, M. The mystery of animal migra-
tion p169-88   **591**
See also names of specific insects, e.g.
Wasps
Insects, Destructive and useful. See Insects,
Injurious and beneficial
Insects, Injurious and beneficial
Swan, L. A. Beneficial insects   **632**
United States. Department of Agriculture.
Insects   **632**
See also pages in the following books:
United States. Department of Agriculture.
After a hundred years p334-82   **353.81**
United States. Department of Agriculture.
Protecting our food p26-38   **641.3**
See also Aeronautics in agriculture
Insects and how they function. Callahan,
P. S.   **595.7**
Insert knob A in hole B. Asimov, I.
In Asimov, I. Nightfall, and other stories
p282-83   **S C**
Inside Latin America. See Gunther, J. Inside
South America   **980**
Inside South America. Gunther, J.   **980**
Inside Summerhill. Popenoe, J.   **371**
Inside the Third Reich. Speer, A.   **943.086**
Insignia. See United States—Armed Forces
—Insignia
Insoluble problem. Chesterton, G. K.
In Chesterton, G. K. The Father Brown
omnibus p956-74   **S C**
Insomnia. See Sleep
Inspection of food. See Food adulteration
and inspection
The **inspired** chicken motel. Bradbury, R.
In Bradbury, R. I sing the Body Elec-
tric! p61-71   **S C**
Instalment plan
Black, H. Buy now, pay later   **332.7**
Instant replay. Kramer, J.   **796.33**
Instead of evidence. Stout, R.
In Haycraft, H. ed. A treasury of great
mysteries v2 p209-44   **S C**
Instinct
Ardrey, R. The territorial imperative **591**
See also pages in the following book:
Tinbergen, N. Animal behavior p127-36
591
Instruction. See Education; Teaching
Instruments, Musical. See Musical instru-
ments
Instruments, Scientific. See Scientific ap-
paratus and instruments
Insull, Samuel, 1859-1938
See pages in the following book:
Holbrook, S. H. The age of the moguls
p230-46   **920**
Insurance
See pages in the following book:
Weinberg, A. ed. The muckrakers p283-96
309.173
Insurance, Life
See pages in the following book:
Smith, C. The Time-Life Book of family
finance p106-33   **339.4**

Irish in the United States
Shannon, W. V. The American Irish
301.453

See also pages in the following books:
Greeley, A. M. Why can't they be like us? p135-47 301.45
O'Connor, R. The German-Americans p349-60 301.453
Fiction
O'Connor, E. The last hurrah **Fic**
Irish national characteristics. See National characteristics, Irish
Iron
See pages in the following book:
Asimov, I. Building blocks of the universe p135-48 546
Iron age
Hagen, A. Norway 913.36
See also pages in the following books:
Fisher, D. A. Steel: from the iron age to the space age p10-16 669.1
Quennell, M. Everyday life in prehistoric times p181-220 913.03
The iron city. Thompson, L.
In Foley, M. ed. Fifty best American short stories, 1915-1965 p165-89 **S C**

Iron industry and trade
See pages in the following book:
Langdon, W. C. Everyday things in American life, 1607-1776 p158-68 917.3
Iron men and saints. See Lamb, H. The crusades 940.1
The iron of war. Lederer, W. J.
In Lederer, W. J. The ugly American p115-31 **S C**
Iroquois Indians
See pages in the following book:
Vlahos, O. New world beginnings p182-95 913.7
Irrigation
United States. Department of Agriculture. Water 631.7
See also pages in the following books:
Davies, D. Fresh water p106-27 333.9
Hollon, W. E. The Great American Desert p160-80 917.8
Overman, M. Water p86-92 333.9
See also Dams
Irving, Sir Henry
See pages in the following book:
Trease, G. Seven stages p140-67 920
Irving, Washington
The art of book-making
In Parker, E. ed. I was just thinking p13-22 824.08
Christmas at Bracebridge Hall
In Becker, M. L. ed. The home book of Christmas p532-40 394.26
In Wernecke, H. H. ed. Celebrating Christmas around the world p95-103 394.26
Knickerbocker's History of New York 974.7

Rip Van Winkle
In Day, A. G. ed. The greatest American short stories p19-37 **S C**
Rip Van Winkle; dramatization. See Jefferson, J. Rip Van Winkle

About
Wagenknecht, E. Washington Irving: moderation displayed 818
See also pages in the following books:
Brooks, V. The world of Washington Irving p201-20, 328-36 810.9
Literary history of the United States p242-52 810.9
Quinn, A. H. American fiction p40-52 813.09
Irwin, Leonard B.
(comp.) A guide to historical fiction 016.8
(comp.) A guide to historical reading: non-fiction 016.9
Irwin, Margaret
Elizabeth, captive princess **Fic**
Young Bess **Fic**
Is he living or is he dead? Twain, M.
In Twain, M. The complete short stories of Mark Twain p307-14 **S C**
Is Paris burning? Collins, L. 944.081
Is there a doctor in the barn? Yates, E. 636.089

Isabel I, Queen of Spain
Horizon Magazine. Ferdinand and Isabella 946
See also pages in the following book:
Trease, G. Seven sovereign queens p71-96 920
Iselin, Fred
Invitation to modern skiing 796.9
Isenberg, Irwin
(ed.) The city in crisis 301.3
(ed.) The developing nations: poverty and progress 338.91
(ed.) The drive against illiteracy 379
(ed.) The outlook for western Europe 330.94
(ed.) The Russian-Chinese rift 327.47
Isherwood, Benjamin Franklin
See pages in the following book:
Morison, E. E. Men, machines, and modern times p100-22 609
Islam
'Azzām, 'Abd-al-Rahmān. The eternal message of Muhammad 297
Stewart, D. Early Islam 915.6
See also pages in the following books:
Bach, M. Had you been born in another faith p121-45 291
Cain, A. H. Young people and religion p85-104 291
Gaer, J. How the great religions began p335-74 291
Gaer, J. The wisdom of the living religions p221-46 291
Jurji, E. J. ed. The great religions of the modern world p178-223 291
McNeill, W. H. A world history p207-16, 236-45 901.9
Mills, D. The Middle Ages p48-57 940.1
Savage, K. The story of world religions p158-77 291
Smith, H. The religions of man p193-224 291
Smith, R. ed. The tree of life p445-65 291
Thompson, E. B. Africa: past and present p70-83 960
Thorndike, L. The history of medieval Europe p155-84 940.1

Italian painters. See Painters, Italian

Italian painting. See Painting, Italian

The Italians. Bryant, A.   914.5

Italians in New York (City)
See pages in the following book:
Glazer, N. Beyond the melting pot p181-216   301.45

Italians in Russia
Fiction
Guareschi, G. Comrade Don Camillo   Fic

Italy
Bryant, A. The Italians   914.5
Grindrod, M. Italy   945
Kubly, H. Italy   914.5

Antiquities
Trump, D. Central and southern Italy before Rome   913.37

Art
See Art, Italian

Church history
See pages in the following book:
The New Cambridge Modern history v2 p251-74   909

Civilization
Durant, W. The Renaissance   940.2
See also pages in the following books:
Durant, W. The age of faith p703-31 940.1
Durant, W. The age of reason begins p225-73   940.2

Education
See Education—Italy

Fiction
Du Maurier, D. The flight of the Falcon
                                       Fic
Godden, R. The battle of the Villa Fiorita   Fic
Guareschi, G. The little world of Don Camillo   Fic
Hersey, J. A bell for Adano   Fic
Silone, I. Bread and wine   Fic
West, M. L. The Devil's advocate   Fic

History
Jucker, N. Italy   945
See also pages in the following books:
Durant, W. The age of Louis XIV p428-45
                                     940.2
The New Cambridge Modern history v8 p378-96   909

History—Fiction
Lampedusa, G. di. The Leopard   Fic
Shellabarger, S. Prince of foxes   Fic
Stone, I. The agony and the ecstasy Fic

History—To 1559
Coughlan, R. The world of Michelangelo, 1475-1564   92
Horizon Magazine. Lorenzo de' Medici and the Renaissance   92
See also pages in the following book:
Hale, J. R. Renaissance p139-48   940.2

History—1559-1789
See pages in the following book:
Durant, W. Rousseau and revolution p217-58, 310-40   940.2
The New Cambridge Modern history v5 p458-73   909

History—1815-1915
See pages in the following book:
The New Cambridge Modern history v10 p552-76   909

History—1914-1946
See pages in the following book:
Beals, C. The nature of revolution p155-73   323

Politics and government
See pages in the following book:
The New Cambridge Modern history v9 p412-38   909

Politics and government—1914-1946
Fermi, L. Mussolini   92

Politics and government—1946-
See pages in the following book:
Bryant, A. The Italians p37-66   914.5

It's a long time ago. Cardoso, O. J.
In Cohen, J. M. ed. Latin American writing today p251-59   860.8

It's cold out there. Buchan, P.
In Prize stories, 1970: The O. Henry Awards p51-70   S C

"It's great to be back!" Heinlein, R. A.
In Heinlein, R. A. Robert A. Heinlein's The past through tomorrow p243-57   S C

It's such a beautiful day. Asimov, I.
In Asimov, I. Nightfall, and other stories p245-66   S C

Ivan III, Czar of Russia
See pages in the following book:
Horizon Magazine. The Horizon History of Russia p74-90   947

Ivan IV, the Terrible, Czar of Russia
See pages in the following books:
Horizon Magazine. The Horizon History of Russia p91-100   947
Wallace, R. Rise of Russia p77-84   947

Ivens, Bryna
(ed.) Seventeen. Stories from Seventeen
                                      S C

Ives, Charles Edward
See pages in the following books:
Copland, A. The new music, 1900-1960 p109-17   780.9
Ewen, D. Composers of tomorrow's music p 1-23   920

Ivy day in the committee room. Joyce, J.
In Joyce, J. Dubliners p148-70   S C

Iwo Jima, Battle of, 1945
Newcomb, R. F. Iwo Jima   940.54

J

J. B. MacLeish, A.
In Gassner, J. ed. Best American plays; 5th ser. p589-633   812.08

Jack, Ian
(ed.) Browning, R. Poetical works, 1833-1864   821

Jack. Ionesco, E.
In Ionesco, E. Four plays p79-110 842

Jack-a-Boy. Cather, W.
In Cather, W. Willa Cather's Collected short fiction, 1892-1912 v3 p311-22   S C

Jainism—*Continued*
Gaer, J. The wisdom of the living religions p149-60 **291**
Voss, C. H. In search of meaning: living religions of the world p46-53 **291**
Jalna. De La Roche, M. **Fic**
James I, King of Great Britain
See pages in the following book:
Durant, W. The age of reason begins p131-61 **940.2**
James VI, King of Scotland. See James I, King of Great Britain
James, Edward T.
(ed.) Dictionary of American biography. The American Plutarch **920**
James, Glenn
(ed.) James & James Mathematics dictionary **510.3**
James, Henry, 1843-1916
The ambassadors **Fic**
The Aspern papers
In James, H. Short novels of Henry James p257-354 **Fic**
In James, H. The turn of the screw [and] The Aspern papers p161-299 **Fic**
Daisy Miller
In James, H. Short novels of Henry James p 1-58 **Fic**
The madonna of the future
In Havighurst, W. ed. Masters of the modern short story p133-70 **S C**
The portrait of a lady **Fic**
The portrait of a lady; criticism
In Drew, E. The novel: a modern guide to fifteen English masterpieces p224-44 **823.09**
The portrait of a lady; criticism [another essay]
In Stegner, W. ed. The American novel p47-60 **813.09**
The pupil
In James, H. Short novels of Henry James p355-405 **Fic**
Short novels of Henry James **Fic**
The turn of the screw
In James, H. Short novels of Henry James p407-530 **Fic**
The turn of the screw [and] The Aspern papers **Fic**
Washington Square
In James, H. Short novels of Henry James p59-256 **Fic**
About
See pages in the following books:
Brooks, V. New England: Indian summer p229-55, 283-303, 405-18 **810.9**
Foster, R. ed. Six American novelists of the nineteenth century p191-255 **813.09**
Literary history of the United States p1039-64 **810.9**
Porter, K. A. The collected essays and occasional writings of Katherine Anne Porter p233-48 **818**
Quinn, A. H. American fiction p279-304 **813.09**
Rourke, C. American humor p186-208 **817.09**
Trilling, L. The opposing self p104-17 **809**
Untermeyer, L. Makers of the modern world p190-97 **920**

Van Doren, C. The American novel, 1789-1939 p163-89 **813.09**
Wagenknecht, E. Cavalcade of the American novel p145-65 **813.09**
James, Howard
Children in trouble **364.36**
Crisis in the courts **347.9**
James, Robert Clarke
(jt. ed.) James, G. ed. James & James Mathematics dictionary **510.3**
James, Will
Lone cowboy **92**
James, William
[Selections]
In Kurtz, P. ed. American philosophy in the twentieth century p105-59 **191.08**
About
Brennan, B. P. William James **191**
See also pages in the following books:
Commager, H. S. The American mind p91-107 **917.3**
Durant, W. The story of philosophy p381-89 **109**
Thomas, H. Understanding the great philosophers p324-34 **109**
Untermeyer, L. Makers of the modern world p182-89 **920**
James & James Mathematics dictionary. James, G. ed. **510.3**
Jamestown, Va.
History
American Heritage. Jamestown **975.5**
Barbour, P. L. Pocahontas and her world **975.5**
See also pages in the following book:
Woodward, G. S. Pocahontas p51-62 **92**
Jan, the unrepentant. London, J.
In London, J. Jack London's Tales of adventure **S C**
Jane. Sitati, P.
In Angoff, C. ed. African writing today p103-13 **896**
Jane Eyre. Brontë, C. **Fic**
The Janeites. Kipling, R.
In Kipling, R. The best short stories of Rudyard Kipling p625-38 **S C**
Janeway, Eliot
The struggle for survival **355.2**
The janissaries of Emilion. Copper, B.
In Hitchcock, A. ed. Alfred Hitchcock presents: A month of mystery p357-76 **S C**
Janson, Dora Jane
Janson, H. W. History of art **709**
Janson, H. W. A history of art & music **700**
Janson, H. W.
History of art **709**
A history of art & music **700**
January 1999: rocket summer. Bradbury, R.
In Bradbury, R. The Martian chronicles p3-13 **S C**
January thaw. Chute, B. J.
In Chute, B. J. One touch of nature, and other stories p47-68 **S C**

Japan

Halloran, R. Japan: images and realities
915.2

Seidensticker, E. Japan   915.2

Antiquities

Kidder, J. E. Japan before Buddhism
913.52

Art

See Art, Japanese

Civilization

Benedict, R. The chrysanthemum and the
sword   915.2
Buck, P. S. The people of Japan   915.2
Dunn, C. J. Everyday life in traditional
Japan   915.2
Kidder, J. E. Japan before Buddhism
913.52
Leonard, J. N. Early Japan   915.2
See also pages in the following book:
Durant, W. Our Oriental heritage p825-
938   950

Description and travel—Views

Van der Post, L. A portrait of Japan
915.2

Economic conditions

Kahn, H. The emerging Japanese superstate: challenge and response   309.152

Fiction

Abé, K. The woman in the dunes   Fic
Akutagawa, R. Japanese short stories S C
Kawabata, Y. Snow country and Thou-
sand cranes   Fic
Mishima, Y. After the banquet   Fic
Mishima, Y. Death in midsummer, and
other stories   S C
Mishima, Y. The sound of waves   Fic

Foreign relations

Kahn, H. The emerging Japanese superstate: challenge and response   309.152

Foreign relations—United States

Neumann, W. L. America encounters Ja-
pan: from Perry to MacArthur   327.73
Reischauer, E. O. The United States and
Japan   327.73
Tamarin, A. Japan and the United States
327.52

See also pages in the following book:
Reischauer, E. O. Beyond Vietnam: the
United States and Asia p105-39   327.73

History

Reischauer, E. O. Japan: the story of a
nation   952
See also pages in the following books:
Fitzgerald, C. P. A concise history of
East Asia p119-98   950
The New Cambridge Modern history v11
p464-86, v12 p329-72   909

History—To 1867

Leonard, J. N. Early Japan   915.2

History—Allied occupation, 1945-1952

Gunther, J. The riddle of MacArthur 92
Terasaki, G. Bridge to the sun   952.03
See also pages in the following book:
MacArthur, D. Reminiscences p269-324
92

History—Allied occupation, 1945-1952—Fiction

Sneider, V. The Teahouse of the August
Moon   Fic

Kings and rulers

Mosley, L. Hirohito, Emperor of Japan
92

Population

See pages in the following book:
Osborn, F. ed. Our crowded planet p165-
72   301.3

Religion

See pages in the following book:
Savage, K. The story of world religions
p104-20   291

Social conditions

Kahn, H. The emerging Japanese superstate: challenge and response   309.152

Social life and customs

Benedict, R. The chrysanthemum and the
sword   915.2
Buck, P. S. The people of Japan   915.2
Dunn, C. J. Everyday life in traditional
Japan   915.2
Hatano, I. Mother and son   92
Simon, C. M. The sun and the birch; the
story of Crown Prince Akihito and
Crown Princess Michiko   92
Sugimoto, E. I. A daughter of the Sa-
murai   92
Vining, E. G. Windows for the Crown
Prince [Akihito]   92

Japan and the United States. Tamarin, A.
327.52

Japan before Buddhism. Kidder, J. E.
913.52

Japan: images and realities. Halloran, R.
915.2

Japan: the story of a nation. Reischauer,
E. O.   952

Japanese cookery. See Cookery, Japanese

Japanese drama

History and criticism

Ernst, E. The Kabuki theatre   792.09
See also pages in the following books:
Gassner, J. Masters of the drama p128-35
809.2
Nicoll, A. World drama p647-57   809.2

Japanese in the United States

Bosworth, A. R. America's concentration
camps   301.45
Sone, M. Nisei daughter   92
Sugimoto, E. I. A daughter of the Sa-
murai   92
See also pages in the following book:
Polenberg, R. ed. America at war p97-107
309.173

Japanese language

See pages in the following book:
Pei, M. Talking your way around the
world p187-202   418

Japanese mythology. See Mythology, Japanese

Japanese national characteristics. See National characteristics, Japanese

Japanese poetry. See Haiku

Japanese sculpture. See Sculpture, Japanese

Japanese short stories. Akutagawa, R. S C

Jews—*Continued*

Language

See Hebrew language

Persecutions

See pages in the following book:

Herzstein, R. E. ed. Adolf Hitler and the Third Reich, 1933-1945 p85-93   943.086

Religion

See Judaism

Jews in Germany

See pages in the following book:

Herzstein, R. E. ed. Adolf Hitler and the Third Reich, 1933-1945 p85-93   943.086

Jew in New York (City)

See pages in the following book:

Glazer, N. Beyond the melting pot p137-80   301.45

Fiction

Malamud, B. The assistant   Fic
Potok, C. The chosen   Fic
Potok, C. The promise   Fic

Jews in Poland

Fiction

Uris, L. Mila 18   Fic

Jews in Russia

See pages in the following book:

Salisbury, H. E. ed. The Soviet Union: the fifty years p421-37   914.7

Drama

Stein, J. Fiddler on the roof   812

Jews in Shushan. Kipling, R.

In Kipling, R. The best short stories of Rudyard Kipling p58-60   S C

Jews in the Czechoslovak Republic

Fiction

Grosman, L. The shop on Main Street   Fic

Jews in the Netherlands

Frank, A. The diary of a young girl 940.54

Drama

Goodrich, F. The diary of Anne Frank   812

Jews in the United States

Antin, M. The promised land   92
Glazer, N. American Judaism   296

See also pages in the following books:

Fortune (Periodical) Youth in turmoil p94-107   301.43
Glock, C. Y. ed. Prejudice U.S.A. p17-64   301.45
O'Connor, R. The German-Americans p241-66   301.453

Fiction

Bellow, S. Herzog   Fic

Jews in Warsaw

Werstein, I. The uprising of the Warsaw Ghetto, November 1940-May 1943 940.54

Fiction

Hersey, J. The wall   Fic

Jhabvala, R. Prawer

The householder   Fic

The interview

In The New Yorker. Stories from The New Yorker, 1950-1960 p585-95   S C

The **jilting** of Granny Weatherall. Porter, K. A.

In Havighurst, W. ed. Masters of the modern short story p234-44 **S C**

In Porter, K. A. The collected stories of Katherine Anne Porter p80-89   **S C**

The **jilting** of Jane. Wells, H. G.

In Wells, H. G. The complete short stories of H. G. Wells p483-90 **S C**

Jim Crow's funeral. Hughes, L.

In Hughes, L. The Langston Hughes reader p225-27   818

Jim Davis. Masefield, J.   **Fic**

Jiménez, Juan Ramón

Lewis, R. ed. Still waters of the air 861.08

Jiménez de Quesada, Gonzalo

See pages in the following book:

Crow, J. A. The epic of Latin America p116-26   980

Jimmy Goggles the god. Wells, H. G.

In Wells, H. G. The complete short stories of H. G. Wells p913-26 **S C**

Jimmy Hayes and Muriel. Henry, O.

In Henry, O. The complete works of O. Henry p859-63   **S C**

Jimmy Scarecrow's Christmas. Freeman, M. E. W.

In Becker, M. L. ed. The home book of Christmas p513-18   394.26

Jinnah, Mohammed Ali

See pages in the following book:

Kenworthy, L. S. Leaders of new nations p244-44   920

Jitta's atonement. Shaw, B.

In Shaw, B. Complete plays, with prefaces v6 p381-452   822

Joachim, Joseph

See pages in the following book:

Chapin, V. The violin and its masters p151-62   920

Joan of Arc, Saint

See pages in the following books:

Aymar, B. A pictorial history of the world's great trials p15-29   343
Boyd, M. Man, myth and magic p111-22   133.4
Durant, W. The Reformation p81-88 940.2

Drama

Anouilh, J. The lark   842

Fiction

Twain, M. Personal recollections of Joan of Arc   **Fic**

João Urso. Accioly, B.

In Cohen, J. M. ed. Latin American writing today p235-46   860.8

Job analysis. See Motion study

Job discrimination. See Discrimination in employment

A **job** with a future in computers. Cross, W.   651.8

Jobs. See Occupations

The **jockey.** McCullers, C.

In Abrahams, W. ed. Fifty years of the American short story v 1 p485-89   **S C**

K

Kafka, Sherry
The man who loved God
In The Best short plays, 1968 p361-88
808.82

Kahn, Herman
The emerging Japanese superstate: challenge and response 309.152

Kaiser, Georg
The coral
In Tucker, S. M. ed. Twenty-five modern plays p573-601 808.82
From morn to midnight
In Block, H. M. ed. Masters of modern drama p489-507 808.82
In Dickinson, T. H. ed. Chief contemporary dramatists; 3d ser. p229-59
808.82
In Gassner, J. ed. Twenty best European plays on the American stage p655-79 808.82
Gas—Part I
In Tucker, S. M. ed. Twenty-five modern plays p603-39 808.82

Kaiulani, Princess of Hawaii
Webb, N. Kaiulani: Crown Princess of Hawaii 92

Kalahari Desert
Description and travel
Van der Post, L. The heart of the hunter
916.8

Kaleidoscope. Bradbury, R.
In Bradbury, R. The illustrated man p32-41 **S C**

Kālidāsa
See pages in the following book:
Gassner, J. Masters of the drama p113-22
809.2

Kamakau, S. M.
The ruling chiefs of Hawaii; excerpt
In Day, A. G. ed. The spell of Hawaii p43-53 919.69

Kamehameha I, the Great, King of the Hawaiian Islands
See pages in the following book:
Day, A. G. Hawaii and its people p28-49
996.9

Kampen, Irene
Due to lack of interest tomorrow has been canceled 378.1
The **Kanaka** surf. London, J.
In London, J. Stories of Hawaii p232-61
S C

Kandyce is the winner. Pei, M.
In Pei, M. Tales of the natural and supernatural p177-87 **S C**

Kane, Harnett T.
Bride of fortune **Fic**
The lady of Arlington **Fic**
Miracle in the mountains [biography of Martha McChesney Berry] 92
Spies for the Blue and Gray 973.7

Kane, Joseph Nathan
Facts about the Presidents 920
Famous first facts 031
Nicknames and sobriquets of U.S. cities and states 910.3

Kanin, Garson
Born yesterday
In Gassner, J. ed. Best plays of modern American theatre; 2d ser. p181-227
812.08

Kansas
Fiction
Parks, G. The learning tree **Fic**

Kansas. University. William Allen White School of Journalism and Public Information
Agee, W. K. ed. Mass media in a free society 301.16

Kant, Immanuel
Critique of pure reason 193
About
See pages in the following books:
Durant, W. Rousseau and revolution p531-51 940.2
Durant, W. The story of philosophy p192-220 109
Russell, B. A history of Western philosophy p701-18 109
Thomas, H. Understanding the great philosophers p250-59 109

Kantor, MacKinlay
Andersonville **Fic**
Lobo
In Costain, T. B. ed. Read with me p289-320 **S C**

Kaplan, Justin
Mr Clemens and Mark Twain 92

Karajan, Herbert von
See pages in the following book:
Ewen, D. Famous modern conductors p118-29 920

Karate
Pfluger, A. Karate: basic principles 796.8

Karen. Killilea, M. 616.8

Karl XII, King of Sweden. See Charles XII, King of Sweden

Karl, Frederick R.
An age of fiction: the nineteenth century British novel 823.09

The **Karl Marx** play. Owens, R.
In The Best short plays, 1971 p223-45
808.82

Karmel-Wolfe, Henia
The month of his birthday
In The Best American short stories, 1965 p187-97 **S C**

Karna and Kunti. Tagore, R.
In Tagore, R. Collected poems and plays of Rabindranath Tagore p559-65
891.4

Karnow, Stanley
Southeast Asia 915.9

Kashmir
Politics and government
See pages in the following book:
Comay, J. The UN in action p16-19 341.13

Kashtanka. Chekhov, A.
In Chekhov, A. The stories of Anton Chekhov p14-37 **S C**

Kassam, Sadru
The water tap
In Angoff, C. ed. African writing today p207-08 896

Katharine of Aragon. See Catharine of Aragon, consort of Henry VIII, King of England

Katherine, Duchess of Lancaster
Fiction
Seton, A. Katherine   Fic
Katherine. Seton, A.   Fic
Katmai National Monument
See pages in the following book:
National Geographic Society. America's
wonderlands p524-33   917.3
Katz, Bill
(comp.) Magazines for libraries   016.05
Katz, William Loren
Teachers' guide to American Negro history
     016.3014
Kaufman, Bel
Up the down staircase   Fic
Kaufman, Edgar
(ed.) The Rise of an American architec-
ture. See The Rise of an American
architecture   720.973
Kaufman, George S.
Beggar on horseback
In Gassner, J. ed. Twenty-five best plays
of the modern American theatre;
early ser. p123-61   812.08
If men played cards as women do
In Cerf, B. ed. Thirty famous one-act
plays p423-27   808.82
The man who came to dinner
In Gassner, J. ed. Best plays of the
modern American theatre; 2d ser.
p317-64   812.08
In Six modern American plays p117-97
     812.08
The solid gold Cadillac
In Gassner, J. ed. Best American plays;
4th ser. p611-41   812.08
The still alarm
In Cerf, B. ed. 24 favorite one-act plays
p229-37   808.82
You can't take it with you
In Gassner, J. ed. Twenty best plays of
the modern American theatre p233-
73   812.08
About
See pages in the following books:
Gould, J. Modern American playwrights
p154-67   812.09
Krutch, J. W. The American drama since
1918 p136-52   812.09
Kaufman, Morris
Giant molecules   668.4
Kaufmann, R. J.
(ed.) G. B. Shaw   822.09
Kavaler, Lucy
Mushrooms, molds, and miracles   589
Kavanagh, Patrick
Football
In Garrity, D. A. ed. 44 Irish short
stories p146-51   S C
Kavanagh, Patrick Joseph Gregory
See pages in the following book:
Rosenthal, M. L. The new poets p275-83
     821.09
Kawabata, Yasunari
Snow country
In Kawabata, Y. Snow country and
Thousand cranes v 1   Fic

Snow country and Thousand cranes **Fic**
Thousand cranes
In Kawabata, Y. Snow country and
Thousand cranes v2   **Fic**
Kazan, Nicolás. See Kazantzakis, Nikos
Kazantzakis, Nikos
Zorba the Greek   Fic
About
See pages in the following book:
Durant, W. Interpretations of life p269-
98   809
Kazin, Alfred
On native grounds   810.9
About
See pages in the following book:
David, J. ed. Growing up Jewish p243-58
     920
Kearney, Paul W.
How to drive better and avoid accidents
     629.28
Kearns, Francis E.
(ed.) The Black experience   810.8
Keating, Bern
Alaska   917.98
The mighty Mississippi   917.7
Keating, L. Clark
Andre Maurois   848
Keats, John, 1795-1821
Poems of John Keats   821
The poetical works   821
About
Hilton, T. Keats and his world   92
Ward, A. John Keats   92
See also pages in the following books:
Auslander, J. The winged horse p283-302
     809.1
Daiches, D. A critical history of English
literature v2 p912-22   820.9
MacLeish, A. Poetry and experience p173-
99   809.1
Trilling, L. The opposing self p3-49 809
Untermeyer, L. Lives of the poets p444-77
     920
Untermeyer, L. The paths of poetry p146-
55   920
Keefauver, John
Special handling
In Hitchcock, A. ed. Alfred Hitchcock
presents: A month of mystery p301-
05   S C
Keen, Elizabeth
See pages in the following book:
McDonagh, D. The rise and fall and rise
of modern dance p270-82   793.3
Keen, Martin L.
The bomb
In Best detective stories of the year
[1969] p153-59   S C
The keepers of the house. Grau, S. A. **Fic**
Keewatin
Mowat, F. Never cry wolf   599
Kefauver, Estes
In a few hands: monopoly power in Amer-
ica   338.8
Keintpoos. See Kintpuash, Modoc chief

Kennedy, John F. President U.S.—About
—*Continued*
United Press International. Four days 92
See also pages in the following books:
Shannon, W. V. The American Irish p392-438   301.453
Warren, S. The President as world leader p417-38   327.73

Assassination
Bishop, J. The day [President] Kennedy was shot   92
Manchester, W. The death of a President; November 20-November 25, 1963   92
United Press International. Four days; the historical record of the death of President Kennedy   92
United States. Warren Commission on the Assassination of President Kennedy. The official Warren Commission report on the assassination of President John F. Kennedy   364.12

Kennedy, Robert F.
The enemy within   331.88
Thirteen days   973.922

About
Associated Press. Triumph and tragedy 920
Halberstam, D. The unfinished odyssey of Robert Kennedy   92
Newfield, J. Robert Kennedy   92
Sorensen, T. C. The Kennedy legacy
                                                            973.922
Stein, J. American journey   92
See also pages in the following book:
White, T. H. The making of the President, 1968 p150-87   329

Kennedy, Rose (Fitzgerald)
Cameron, G. Rose   92

Kennedy family
Associated Press. Triumph and tragedy 920
Bishop, J. A day in the life of President Kennedy   92
Cameron, G. Rose; a biography of Rose Fitzgerald Kennedy   92
The **Kennedy** lagacy. Sorensen, T. C.
                                                            973.922
The **Kennedy** years [biography of John Fitzgerald Kennedy]   92
The **Kennedy** years. Adams, J. T.
In Adams, J. T. The march of democracy v7   973

Kenner, Hugh
(ed.) T. S. Eliot   811.09

Kenneth, J. H.
(ed.) Henderson, I. F. A dictionary of biological terms   574.03

Kent State. See Ohio. State University, Kent

Kentfield, Calvin
The bell of charity
In The New Yorker. Stories from The New Yorker, 1950-1960 p119-36
                                                               S C

Kentucky
Dykeman, W. The border state   917.5
Stuart, J. A Jesse Stuart reader   818

Description and travel
See pages in the following book:
National Geographic Society. Vacationland U.S.A. p186-95   917.3

Fiction
Stuart, J. Mr Gallion's school   Fic
Stuart, J. Plowshare in heaven   S C

History
Skinner, C. L. Pioneers of the Old Southwest   976

Kentucky: May: Saturday. Faulkner, W.
In Sports Illustrated. The wonderful world of sports p291-92   796

Kenworthy, Leonard S.
Leaders of new nations   92

Kenya
Mulvey, M. W. Digging up Adam; the story of L. S. B. Leakey   92
Roberts, J. S. A land full of people 916.76

Description and travel
Adamson, J. The spotted sphinx   599

History
MacPhee, A. M. Kenya   967.6

Politics and government
See pages in the following book:
Kenworthy, L. S. Leaders of new nations p29-47   920

Kenya Colony and Protectorate

Description and travel
Adamson, J. Born free   599

Kenyan art. See Art, Kenyan

Kenyatta, Jomo
See pages in the following books:
Kenworthy, L. S. Leaders of new nations p29-47   920
Rama Rau, S. Gifts of passage p131-52 92

Kepler, Johann
See pages in the following book:
Newman, J. R. ed. The world of mathematics v 1 p220-34   510.8

Kerfol. Wharton, E.
In Wharton, E. The collected short stories of Edith Wharton v2 p282-300   S C

Kerman, Joseph
Janson, H. W. A history of art & music
                                                                700

Kern, Jerome David
See pages in the following book:
Ewen, D. Composers for the American musical theatre p61-83   920
Ewen, D. Great men of American popular song p123-43   920
Ewen, D. The story of America's musical theater p77-86, 110-13, 159-65   782.8

Kerner, Fred
(ed.) Lincoln, A. A treasury of Lincoln quotations   818

Kerner Report. See United States. National Advisory Commission on Civil Disorders. Report of the National Advisory Commission on Civil Disorders   301.18

Kerr, Annie B.
"Here is Joseph and here is Mary"
In Wernecke, H. H. ed. Celebrating Christmas around the world p190-96   394.26

Kerr, Jean
Mary, Mary
In Gassner, J. ed. Best American plays;
5th ser. p379-417 **812.08**
Please don't eat the daisies **817**
The snake has all the lines **817**

Kerr, Rose Netzerg
(jt. auth.) Lester, K. M. Historic costume
391.09

Kerrigan, Evans E.
American badges and insignia **355.1**

Kersh, Gerald
Crooked bone
In Hitchcock, A. ed. Alfred Hitchcock
presents: A month of mystery p330-
53 **S C**
Dr Ox will die at midnight
In Best detective stories of the year, 1971
p141-48 **S C**

Kesey, Ken
One flew over the cuckoo's nest **Fic**

Kesselring, Joseph
Arsenic and old lace
In Gassner, J. ed. Best plays of the
modern American theatre; 2d ser.
p459-510 **812.08**

Kessle, Gun
Myrdal, J. Chinese journey **309.151**

Ketchum, Richard M.
The secret life of the forest **574.5**
(ed.) What is communism? **335.4**
(ed.) What is democracy? **321.8**
American Heritage. The American Heritage Book of great historic places **917.3**
(ed.) American Heritage. The American
Heritage Book of the Revolution **973.3**
(ed.) American Heritage. The American
Heritage Picture history of the Civil
War **973.7**

Key, Francis Scott
See pages in the following book:
Lawson, D. The War of 1812 p114-32 **973.5**

The **key**. Asimov, I.
In Asimov, I. Asimov's mysteries p178-
208 **S C**

The **key**. Singer, I. B.
In The Best American short stories, 1970
p308-17 **S C**

Key Largo. Anderson, M.
In Anderson, M. Eleven verse plays,
1929-1939 v11 **812**

Keyes, Daniel
Flowers for Algernon **Fic**

The **keyhole** eye. Carter, J. S.
In Foley, M. ed. Fifty best American
short stories, 1915-1965 p760-84
S C

Keynes, John Maynard
See pages in the following books:
Boardman, F. W. Economics: ideas and
men p88-103 **330.1**
Heilbroner, R. L. The worldly philosophers
330.1
Newman, J. R. ed. The world of mathe-
matics v2 p1355-59 **510.8**

The **keys** of the kingdom. Cronin, A. J. **Fic**

Khatchaturian, Aram
See pages in the following book:
Cross, M. The Milton Cross New encyclopedia of the great composers and their
music p526-32 **920.03**

Khayyam, Omar. See Omar Khayyam

Khrushchev, Nikita Sergeevich
Khrushchev remembers **947.084**
About
Crankshaw, E. Khrushchev **92**
See also pages in the following book:
Kohler, F. D. Understanding the Russians
p106-31 **947.084**

The **Kicking-Twelfth**. Crane, S.
In Crane, S. The complete short stories
& sketches of Stephen Crane p671-
79 **S C**

The **kid** who fractioned. Sturm, C.
In The Best American short stories, 1967
p291-301 **S C**

Kidder, J. E.
Japan before Buddhism **913.52**

Kidnapping
See pages in the following book:
Tully, A. The FBI's most famous cases
p3-55 **353.5**

Kidneys
See pages in the following books:
Milne, L. Water and life p152-61 **551.4**
Snively, W. D. The sea of life p42-53 **612**

Kiely, Benedict
The white wild bronco
In The New Yorker. Stories from The
New Yorker, 1950-1960 p459-66 **S C**

Kieran, John
An introduction to wild flowers **582**
The story of the Olympic games: 776 B.C.
to [date] **796.4**

Kierkegaard, Søren Aabye
See pages in the following books:
Scott, M. A. The unquiet vision **142**
Untermeyer, L. Makers of the modern
world p7-11 **920**

Kilcrin, Isabel
Brad Halloran
In Seventeen. Stories from Seventeen
p199-214 **S C**

The **Kilimanjaro** device. Bradbury, R.
In Bradbury, R. I sing the Body Electric! p3-14 **S C**

Killens, John O.
God bless America
In Clarke, J. H. ed. American Negro
short stories p204-09 **S C**
The stick up
In Hughes, L. ed. The best short stories
by Negro writers p188-91 **S C**

The **killers**. Hemingway, E.
In Abrahams, W. ed. Fifty years of the
American short story v 1 p381-89
S C
In Hemingway, E. The short stories of
Ernest Hemingway p279-89 **S C**
In Hemingway, E. The snows of Kili-
manjaro, and other stories p71-81
S C

The **king's** threshold. Yeats, W. B.
  In Yeats, W. B. Collected plays of W. B.
    Yeats p69-94   822
Kingsbury, Robert C.
  Schneider, R. M. An atlas of Latin Amer-
    ican affairs   918
Kingsley, Charles
  Westward ho!   Fic
Kingsley, Sidney
  Darkness at noon
    In Gassner, J. ed. Best American plays;
      3d ser. p505-43   812.08
  Dead end
    In Cerf, B. A. ed. Sixteen famous Amer-
      ican plays p453-531   812.08
    In Gassner, J. ed. Twenty best plays of
      the modern American theatre p681-
      738   812.08
  Detective story
    In Gassner, J. ed. Best American plays
      3d ser. p317-64   812.08
  Men in white
    In Gassner, J. ed. Best American plays;
      supplementary volume, p411-50
                      812.08
  The patriots
    In Gassner, J. ed. Best plays of the
      modern American theatre; 2d ser.
      p683-724   812.08
Kinsella, Thomas
  See pages in the following book:
  Rosenthal, M. L. The new poets p283-97
                    821.09
Kinsey, Anthony
  How to make animated movies   778.5
Kinsley, James
  (ed.) The Oxford Book of ballads. See
    The Oxford Book of ballads   821.08
Kinsman of his blood. Wolfe, T.
  In Wolfe, T. The hills beyond p66-76 **S C**
Kintpuash, Modoc chief
  See pages in the following book:
  Brown, D. Bury my heart at Wounded
    Knee p219-40   970.4
Kipling, Rudyard
  The best short stories of Rudyard Kipling
                    S C
  Contents: Lispeth; At the pit's mouth; A
  wayside comedy; The story of Muhammad Din;
  A bank fraud; At the end of the passage;
  Without benefit of clergy; Jews in Shushan;
  The return of Imray; The phantom 'rickshaw;
  Moti Guj——mutineer; The drums of the Fore
  and Aft; On Greenhow Hill; The man who
  would be king; Baa, baa, black sheep; In the
  rukh; A matter of fact; The disturber of traffic; "The finest story in the world"; "Brug-
  glesmith"; The Children of the Zodiac; The
  Maltese Cat; The miracle of Purun Bhagat;
  The undertakers; Kaa's hunting; The King's
  ankus; Red Dog; A Centurion of the Thirtieth;
  On the Great Wall; The Winged Hats; Mark-
  lake witches; "Wireless"; A Sahib's war; As
  easy as A.B.C.; "They"; An habitation enforced; The village that voted the earth was
  flat; Regulus; The propagation of knowledge;
  "My son's wife"; Friendly brook; Mary Postgate; "In the interests of the brethren"; A
  madonna of the trenches; Dayspring mishandled; The Janeites; The wish house; The manner of men; Unprofessional; The eye of Allah
  The light that failed   Fic
  The Maltese cat
    In Lardner, R. ed. Rex Lardner selects
      the best of sports fiction p107-30
                    S C

The **man** who was
  In Costain, T. B. ed. Read with me p321-
    34   **S C**
Maugham's Choice of Kipling's best **S C**
  Contents: The finest story in the world;
  The man who was; Tomb of his ancestors; At
  the end of the passage; 'Wireless'; On Green-
  how Hill; 'Love-o'-women'; The brushwood
  boy; The man who would be king; William the
  Conqueror; 'They'; Tods' amendment; Mowgli's
  brothers; The miracle of Purun Bhagat; With-
  out benefit of clergy; The village that voted the
  earth was flat
A message to Umballa
  In Dulles, A. ed. Great spy stories from
    fiction p181-90   **S C**
Rudyard Kipling's verse   821
             About
  See pages in the following books:
Eliot, T. S. On poetry and poets p265-94
                   808.1
Untermeyer, L. The paths of poetry p213-17
                   920
Kirchshofer, Rosl
  (ed.) The world of zoos   590.74
Kirkland, Jack
  Tobacco road
    In Gassner, J. ed. Twenty best plays of
      the modern American theatre p599-
      642   812.08
The **kiss.** Chekhov, A.
  In Chekhov, A. The stories of Anton
    Chekhov p151-70   **S C**
A **kiss** for Cinderella. Barrie, J. M.
  In Barrie, J. M. The plays of J. M. Bar-
    rie p401-72   822
Kissane, James D.
  Alfred Tennyson   821.09
Kissinger, Henry A.
  American foreign policy   327.73
Kitching, Jessie
  (jt. ed.) Bertalan, F. J. ed. The junior
    college library collection   011
The **kith** of the Elf-folk. Dunsany, Lord
  In Garrity, D. A. ed. 44 Irish short
    stories p70-85   **S C**
Kittura Remsberg. Schaefer, J.
  In Schaefer, J. The collected stories of
    Jack Schaefer p118-34   **S C**
Kivikoski, Ella
  Finland   913.471
Klamkin, Charles
  If it doesn't work, read the instructions
                   640.73
Klass, Philip J.
  UFOs—identified   629.133
The **Klausners.** Tushnet, L.
  In The Best American short stories,
    1971 p316-28   **S C**
Kleber on murder in 30 volumes. Powell, J.
  In Best detective stories of the year
    [1969] p111-24   **S C**
Klein, Aaron E.
  (jt. auth.) Coulson, E. H. Test tubes and
    beakers   540.72
  (jt. auth.) Pearce, W. E Transistors and
    circuits   621.381
Klein, H. Arthur
  Bioluminescence   574.1
  Holography   535.5

Kurtz, Paul
(ed.) American philosophy in the twentieth century   **191.08**

Kush. See Cush

Kutnetsov, Anatoly. See Anatoli, A.

Kuznetsov, Pavel
See pages in the following book:
Dulles, A. ed. Great true spy stories p145-57   **327**

Kwakiutl Indians
Benedict, R. Patterns of culture   **572**
See also pages in the following books:
Riesman, D. The lonely crowd p271-82   **155.8**
Vlahos, O. New world beginnings p113-27   **913.7**

Kyoto
Description
See pages in the following book:
Van der Post, L. A portrait of Japan p113-39   **915.2**

L

LSD. See Lysergic acid diethylamide

Laas, William
(ed.) Good Housekeeping. Good Housekeeping's Guide for young homemakers   **640.3**

Labedz, Leopold
(ed.) Solzhenitsyn: a documentary record   **92**

Labor and laboring classes
See also Labor unions; Middle classes; Migrant labor; Occupations; Peasantry; Proletariat; also names of countries, cities, etc. with the subdivision Social conditions, e.g. United States—Social conditions

Europe
See pages in the following book:
Chamberlin, E. R. Everyday life in Renaissance times p86-106   **940.2**

Great Britain
See pages in the following books:
Avery, G. Victorian people p189-207 **914.2**
Page, R. I. Life in Anglo-Saxon England p78-96   **914.2**
Reader, W. J. Life in Victorian England p71-113   **914.2**

Housing
See Housing

Laws and regulations
See pages in the following books:
Marx, H. L. ed. American labor today p112-39   **331.88**
United States. President's Commission on the Status of Women. American women p54-59, 128-35   **301.41**

Sweden
See pages in the following book:
Jenkins, D. Sweden and the price of progress p132-53   **309.1485**

United States
Werstein, I. The great struggle   **331.88**
See also pages in the following books:
Addams, J. The social thought of Jane Addams p62-84   **309.173**
Chase, S. American credos p90-105 **301.15**
Degler, C. N. Out of our past p237-72 **973**
Leighton, I. ed. The aspirin age, 1919-1941 p383-402   **917.3**
Riesman, D. The lonely crowd p307-25   **155.8**
Schlesinger, A. M. The birth of the Nation p55-72   **917.3**
Sloan, I. J. Our violent past p174-220   **301.18**
Weinberg, A. ed. The muckrakers p340-84, 408-29   **309.173**

United States—Fiction
Dos Passos, J. Midcentury   **Fic**

Labor disputes. See Collective bargaining

Labor management relations act. See United States. Laws, statutes, etc. Labor management relations act, 1947

Labor organizations. See Labor unions

Labor unions
Kennedy, R. F. The enemy within **331.88**
Marx, H. L. ed. American labor today   **331.88**
See also pages in the following books:
Bowen, E. The Middle Atlantic States p82-90   **917.4**
See also Collective bargaining

History
Hutchinson, J. The imperfect union   **331.88**
Orth, S. P. The armies of labor   **331.88**
Taft, P. Organized labor in American history   **331.88**
Werstein, I. The great struggle **331.88**
See also pages in the following books:
Lord, W. The good years p150-79 **973.91**
Lynd, S. ed. Nonviolence in America: a documentary history p217-70 **323**
Lyons, F. S. L. Ireland since the famine p660-70   **941.5**
Shannon, D. A. Between the wars: America, 1919-1941 p186-93 **973.91**
Weinberg, A. ed. The muckrakers p40-53   **309.173**

Laborers. See Labor and laboring classes

The labyrinthine ways. See Greene, G. The power and the glory   **Fic**

Lacouture, Jean
Ho Chi Minh   **92**

Lacquer and lacquering
See pages in the following book:
Newell, A. C. Coloring, finishing and painting wood p375-443   **698.3**

Lacy, Leslie Alexander
Cheer the lonesome traveler; the life of W. E. B. Du Bois   **92**

Lader, Lawrence
Margaret Sanger: pioneer of birth control   **92**

The lady. Richter, C.   **Fic**

Lady Eleanore's mantle. Hawthorne, N.
In Hawthorne, N. Hawthorne's Short stories p108-21   **S C**

Lancelot. Robinson, E. A.
 In Robinson, E. A. The collected poems of Edwin Arlington Robinson p365-449 **811**

Land
 McClellan, G. S. ed. Land use in the United States **333**
 See also pages in the following books:
Scientific American. Cities p122-32 **309.2**
United States. Department of Agriculture. Contours of change p189-96, 204-12 **630**
 See also Agriculture

Land, Reclamation of. See Reclamation of land

The land and wildlife of Africa. Carr, A. **574.9**

The land and wildlife of North America. Farb, P. **574.9**

The land below the wind. Keith, A. N. **919.11**

A land beyond the river. Stuart, J.
 In Stuart, J. Plowshare in heaven p36-60 **S C**

A land full of people. Roberts, J. S. **916.76**

The land God made in anger. White, J. M. **916.8**

The land ironclads. Wells, H. G.
 In Wells, H. G. The complete short stories of H. G. Wells p115-38 **S C**
 In Wells, H. G. 28 science fiction stories p286-309 **S C**

The Land of Heart's Desire. Yeats, W. B.
 In Yeats, W. B. Collected plays of W. B. Yeats p33-47 **822**

Land tenure. See Farm tenancy

Land use in the United States. McClellan, G. S. ed. **333**

The land, wildlife, and peoples of the Bible. Farb, P. **220.8**

Landau, Robert A.
 (ed.) Large type books in print **015**

The landing on Kuralei. Michener, J.
 In Michener, J. Tales of the South Pacific p304-19 **S C**

Landlord and tenant. See Farm tenancy

A landlord's morning. Tolstoy, L.
 In Tolstoy, L. Short novels v 1 p71-126 **S C**

Landon, Alfred Mossman
 See pages in the following book:
Stone, I. They also ran p305-19 **920**

Landon, Margaret
 Anna and the King of Siam **915.93**

Landor's cottage. Poe, E. A.
 In Poe, E. A. The complete tales and poems of Edgar Allan Poe p616-25 **S C**

Lands beyond the forest. Sears, P. B. **581**

Landscape architecture. See Landscape protection

Landscape gardening
 See pages in the following book:
United States. Department of Agriculture. Consumers all p279-98 **640.73**

Landscape painting
 See pages in the following book:
Schwarz, M. The age of the Rococo p111-26 **759.04**

Landscape protection
 McHarg, I. L. Design with nature **711**
 Roosevelt, N. Conservation: now or never **333.7**

Landström, Björn
 The ship **623.82**

Lane, Estella Hitchcock
 Why Santa Claus chose the reindeer
 In Becker, M. L. ed. The home book of Christmas p509-13 **394.26**

Lane Bryant, inc.
 See pages in the following book:
Mahoney, T. The great merchants p244-58 **658.87**

Lang, Allan Kim
 Eel by the tail
 In Conklin, G. ed. Invaders of earth p50-66 **S C**
 Murder is a gas
 In Best detective stories of the year [1967] p130-72 **S C**

Lang, Eddie
 See pages in the following book:
Hadlock, R. Jazz masters of the twenties p239-55 **920**

Lang, Gladys Engel
 (ed.) Mental health **616.8**

Langdon, William C.
 Everyday things in American life, 1607-1776 **917.3**
 Everyday things in American life, 1776-1876 **917.3**

Lange, Dorothea
 See pages in the following book:
Stoddard, H. Famous American women p245-54 **920**

Lange, Norbert Adolph
 (ed.) Handbook of chemistry **660.21**

Langer, Lawrence
 Another way out
 In Cerf, B. ed. Thirty famous one-act plays p433-46 **808.82**

Langer, Susanne Katherina (Knauth)
 See pages in the following book:
Stoddard, H. Famous American women p255-62 **920**

Langer, William L.
 (ed.) An encyclopedia of world history **902**
 Political and social upheaval, 1832-1852 **940.2**

Langford, Anna Riggs
 See pages in the following book:
Drotning, P. T. Up from the ghetto p44-57 **920**

Langland, Joseph
 (jt. ed.) Engle, P. ed. Poet's choice **821.08**

Langland, William
 Vision of Piers Plowman **821**

Langley, Samuel Pierpont
 See pages in the following books:
Bonney, W. T. The heritage of Kitty Hawk p37-51 **629.13**
Jones, B. Z. ed. The golden age of science p531-50 **920**

Language, Universal. See Esperanto

Lardner, Ring—*Continued*

Old folks' Christmas

In Becker, M. L. ed. The home book of Christmas p291-301   394.26

On conversation

In White, E. B. ed. A subtreasury of American humor; abridged p235-37   817.08

The Ring Lardner reader   **S C**

Stories included are: You know me Al; Gullible's travels; Haircut; The Maysville minstrel; Travelogue; The facts; Anniversary; Quick returns; Lady Perkins; Three without, doubled; A visit to the Garrisons; Some like them cold; I can't breathe; Zone of quiet; Champion; A caddy's diary; "In conference"; The love nest; A day with Conrad Green; Mr Frisbie; Sun cured; Now and then; The golden honeymoon; Who dealt?; Liberty Hall; Contract; Old folks' Christmas; Ex parte; The young immigrunts; Symptoms of being 35; Dinner; There are smiles; Say it with oil; Marriage made easy; Table manners; Dogs; Alibi Ike; My roomy; Hurry Kane; Nora; Rhythm; A bedtime story; A close-up of Domba Splew; Don't be a drudge; Segregate the fats; What of it?

The tridget of Greva

In Cerf, B. ed. 24 favorite one-act plays p301-07   808.82

About

See pages in the following books:

Geismar, M. Writers in crisis p 1-36   813.09

Untermeyer, L. Makers of the modern world p626-31   920

Lardner, Susan

Where have you been all my life?

In Seventeen. Seventeen from Seventeen p163-68   **S C**

Large print books. See Large type books

Large type books

Anderson, M. My Lord, what a morning   92

Arnow, H. The dollmaker   Fic

Austen, J. Pride and prejudice   Fic

Baldwin, J. The fire next time   301.451

Boulle, P. The bridge over the River Kwai   Fic

Brontë, C. Jane Eyre   Fic

Brontë, E. Wuthering Heights   Fic

Buck, P. S. The good earth   Fic

Butler, S. The way of all flesh   Fic

Cannon, L. Look to the mountain   Fic

Carson, R. L. The sea around us   551.4

Cather, W. My Antonia   Fic

Cather, W. O pioneers!   Fic

Cerf, B. ed. Laugh day   817.08

Collins, W. The moonstone   Fic

The Columbia-Viking Desk encyclopedia   031

Conrad, J. Lord Jim   Fic

Crane, S. The red badge of courage   Fic

Day, C. Life with father   818

Defoe, D. Robinson Crusoe   Fic

Dickens, C. Great expectations   Fic

Dickens, C. A tale of two cities   Fic

Dostoevsky, F. Crime and punishment   Fic

Doyle, Sir A. C. Sherlock Holmes' greatest cases   **S C**

Eliot, G. Silas Marner   Fic

Fitzgerald, F. S. The Great Gatsby   **Fic**

Flaubert, G. Madame Bovary   **Fic**

Frank, A. The diary of a young girl   940.54

Franklin, B. The autobiography of Benjamin Franklin   92

Fromm, E. The art of loving   152.4

Frost, R. Come in & other poems   811

Gilbreth, F. B. Cheaper by the dozen [biography of Frank B. Gilbreth, Sr]. c1948   92

Godden, R. An episode of sparrows   Fic

Goodspeed, E. J. A life of Jesus   232.9

Greene, G. The power and the glory   Fic

Gunther, J. Death be not proud [a biography of his son]   92

Guthrie, A. B. The big sky   Fic

Guthrie, A. B. The way West   Fic

Hamilton, E. The Greek way   880.9

Hamilton, E. Mythology   292

Hardy, T. The return of the native   Fic

Hawthorne, N. The House of the Seven Gables   Fic

Hawthorne, N. The scarlet letter   Fic

Hayes, H. On reflection   92

Heilbroner, R. L. The worldly philosophers   330.1

Heller, J. Catch-22   Fic

Hemingway, E. A farewell to arms   Fic

Hemingway, E. The old man and the sea   Fic

Hersey, J. A bell for Adano   Fic

Heyerdahl, T. Kon-Tiki   910.4

Homer. The Odyssey   883

Hudson, W. H. Green mansions   Fic

Hughes, R. A high wind in Jamaica   Fic

Jackson, S. We have always lived in the castle   Fic

Jewett, S. O. The country of the pointed firs   **S C**

Joyce, J. A portrait of the artist as a young man   Fic

Kemelman, H. Sunday the rabbi stayed home   Fic

Kennedy, J. F. Profiles in courage. Memorial ed.   920

Kennedy, R. F. Thirteen days   973.922

Knebel, F. Seven days in May   Fic

Knowles, J. A separate peace   Fic

La Carré, J. The spy who came in from the cold   Fic

Lee, H. To kill a mockingbird   Fic

Lewis, C. S. Out of the silent planet   Fic

Lewis, C. S. The Screwtape letters [and] Screwtape proposes a toast   248

Liebman, J. Peace of mind   158

Lindbergh, A. M. Gift from the sea   818

London, J. The sea-wolf   Fic

Lord, W. Incredible victory   940.54

Lord, W. A night to remember   910.4

McKenney, R. My sister Eileen   817

McNeill, W. H. A world history [1967 edition]   901.9

Manchester, W. Portrait of a President; John F. Kennedy in profile   92

Maupassant, G. de. Selected short stories   **S C**

Melville, H. Billy Budd, foretopman   Fic

The last encounter. Forester, C. S.
  In Forester, C. S. Hornblower during the crisis, and two stories: Hornblower's temptation and the last encounter p157-74   **Fic**

The last essays of Elia. Lamb, C.
  In Lamb, C. The essays and The last essays of Elia   **824**

The last flower. Thurber, J.
  In Thurber, J. Alarms and diversions p335-67   **818**

The last hero: Charles A. Lindbergh. Ross, W. S.   **92**

The last house call. Nourse, A. E.
  In Nourse, A. E. Rx for tomorrow p124-45   **S C**

The last hurrah. O'Connor, E.   **Fic**

The last leaf. Henry, O.
  In Henry, O. The best short stories of O. Henry p308-15   **S C**
  In Henry, O. The complete works of O. Henry p1455-59   **S C**

The last love. Costain, T. B.   **Fic**

The last night of the world. Bradbury, R.
  In Bradbury, R. The illustrated man p126-30   **S C**

The last nine days of the Bismarck. Forester, C. S.   **Fic**

The last of the belles. Fitzgerald, F. S.
  In Fitzgerald, F. S. The stories of F. Scott Fitzgerald p240-53   **S C**

Last of the legions. Benét, S. V.
  In Benét, S. V. Selected works of Stephen Vincent Benét v2   **818**

The last of the Mohicans. Cooper, J. F. **Fic**

The last of the troubadours. Henry, O.
  In Henry, O. The complete works of O. Henry p811-19   **S C**

The last of the wine. Renault, M.   **Fic**

The last 100 days. Toland, J.   **940.53**

The last Plantagenets. Costain, T. B. **942.03**

Last poems. Housman, A. E.
  In Housman, A. E. The collected poems of A. E. Housman p93-151   **821**

The last question. Asimov, I.
  In Asimov, I. Nine tomorrows p177-90   **S C**

The last rite. Yu-Hwa, L.
  In The Best American short stories, 1965 p371-84   **S C**

The last rodeo. Haycox, E.
  In Lardner, R. ed. Rex Lardner selects the best of sports fiction p57-74   **S C**

The last unicorn. Beagle, P. S.   **Fic**

Latcha, A. G.
  How do you figure it?   **793.7**

Late at night. Mansfield, K.
  In Mansfield, K. The short stories of Katherine Mansfield p299-301 **S C**

The late Christopher Bean. Howard, S.
  In Gassner, J. ed. Twenty best European plays on the American stage p443-89   **808.82**

Late eighteenth century drama, 1750-1800. Nicoll, A.
  In Nicoll, A. A history of English drama, 1660-1900 v3   **822.09**

The late George Apley. Marquand, J. P.   **Fic**

Late Mr Elvesham. Wells, H. G.
  In Wells, H. G. 28 science fiction stories p475-92   **S C**

Late nineteenth century drama, 1850-1900. Nicoll, A.
  In Nicoll, A. A history of English drama, 1660-1900 v5   **822.09**

Later collected verse. Service, R.   **811**

Latham, Edward
  A dictionary of names, nicknames, and surnames of persons, places and things   **929.4**

Latin America
  Schneider, R. M. An atlas of Latin American affairs   **918**
  See also pages in the following books:
  Ashabranner, B. A moment in history: the first ten years of the Peace Corps p153-66   **309.2**
  Bowles, C. ed. The conscience of a liberal p185-94   **327.73**
  Halliburton, R. Richard Halliburton's Complete book of marvels v 1   **910.4**
  Stefánsson, V. ed. Great adventures and explorations p189-221   **910.9**
  See also Pan-Americanism

    Bibliography
  Farrell, R. V. comp. Latin America   **016.98**

    Biography
  Alexander, R. J. Prophets of the revolution   **920**
  Worcester, D. E. Makers of Latin America   **920**

    Cities and towns
  See Cities and towns—Latin America

    Civilization
  Crow, J. A. The epic of Latin America   **980**
  See also pages in the following book:
  The New Cambridge Modern history v7 p487-99   **909**

    History
  Crow, J. A. The epic of Latin America   **980**
  Herring, H. A history of Latin America, from the beginnings to present   **980**
  Richman, I. B. The Spanish conquerors   **973.1**
  Rippy, J. F. Latin America   **980**
  Shepherd, W. R. The Hispanic nations of the New World   **980**
  Worcester, D. E. Makers of Latin America   **920**
  See also pages in the following books:
  The New Cambridge Modern history v4 p707-26, v8 p398-420, v11 p516-41, v12 p584-61   **909**

    Intellectual life
  See pages in the following book:
  Rippy, J. F. Latin America p302-26, 469-509   **980**

    Maps
  Schneider, R. M. An atlas of Latin American affairs   **918**

Latin America—*Continued*

Politics

Alexander, R. J. Prophets of the revolution   **920**

See also pages in the following books:

Myrdal, G. The challenge of world poverty p452-90   **338.91**

The New Cambridge Modern history v9 p612-38   **909**

Population

See pages in the following book:

Osborn, F. ed. Our crowded planet p175-84   **301.3**

Statistics

The South American handbook   **918**

Yearbooks

The South American handbook   **918**

Latin America. Farrell, R. V. comp.   **016.98**

Latin American architecture. See Architecture, Latin American

Latin American art. See Art, Latin American

Latin American cookery. See Cookery, Latin American

Latin American cooking. Leonard, J. N.   **641.5**

Latin American literature

Collections

Cohen, J. M. ed. Latin American writing today   **860.8**

History and criticism

France, J. An introduction to Spanish American literature   **860.9**

Latin American poetry

Collections

Resnick, S. ed. Spanish-American poetry   **861.08**

Latin American writing today. Cohen, J. M. ed.   **860.8**

Latin drama

History and criticism

See pages in the following book:

Nicoll, A. World drama p107-37   **809.2**

Latin historians. See Historians, Roman

Latin language

See pages in the following book:

Pei, M. Talking your way around the world p128-45   **418**

Dictionaries

Cassell's New compact Latin-English, English-Latin dictionary   **473**

Cassell's New Latin dictionary: Latin-English, English-Latin   **473**

History

See pages in the following book:

Bailey, C. ed. Legacy of Rome p351-84   **913.37**

Latin literature

See also Classical literature

Collections

Davenport, B. ed. The portable Roman reader   **870.8**

History and criticism

Hamilton, E. The Roman way   **870.9**

See also pages in the following books:

Bailey, C. ed. Legacy of Rome p325-50   **913.37**

Durant, W. Caesar and Christ p146-66, 233-58   **937**

Macy, J. The story of the world's literature p131-61   **809**

Sarton, G. A history of science v2 p459-89   **509**

Latin poetry

History and criticism

See pages in the following book:

Macy, J. The story of the world's literature p138-54   **809**

Latitude

See pages in the following book:

Brown, L. A. Map making p119-32   **526.8**

Latourette, Kenneth Scott

China   **951**

A history of Christianity   **270**

A short history of the Far East   **950**

Latter-Day Saints. See Mormons and Mormonism

Laubach, Frank Charles

Medary, M. Each one teach one   **92**

Lauer, Pierre

Hussein, King of Jordan. Hussein of Jordan: My "war" with Israel   **956**

Laugh day. Cerf, B.   **817.08**

Laughing Boy. La Farge, O.   **Fic**

The **laughing** man. Salinger, J. D.

In Salinger, J. D. Nine stories p83-110   **S C**

Laughter. See Wit and humor

Laura. Saki

In Saki. The short stories of Saki p267-72   **S C**

Laurents, Arthur

Home of the brave

In Gassner, J. ed. Best plays of the modern American theatre; 2d ser. p557-96   **812.08**

West Side story   **812**

Lautrec Monfa, Henri Marie Raymond de Toulouse- See Toulouse-Lautrec Monfa, Henri Marie Raymond de

Laver, James

The concise history of costume and fashion   **391.09**

Costume in the theatre   **792.09**

Costume through the ages   **391.09**

Lavin, Mary

Happiness

In The Best American short stories, 1969 p81-97   **S C**

Heart of gold

In The Best American short stories, 1965 p199-222   **S C**

In a cafe

In The New Yorker. Stories from The New Yorker, 1950-1960 p247-61   **S C**

Lavin, Mary—*Continued*
One summer
  In The Best American short stories,
    1966 p167-202   **S C**
The story of the widow's son
  In Garrity, D. A. ed. 44 Irish short
    stories p152-65   **S C**

Lavine, Harold
Central America   917.28

Lavoisier, Antoine Laurent
  See pages in the following book:
Moore, R. The coil of life p7-45 574.09

Law
  See also Justice

Assyria
  See pages in the following book:
Saggs, H. W. F. Everyday life in Baby-
  lonia & Assyria p137-55   913.35

Babylonia
  See pages in the following book:
Saggs, H. W. F. Everyday life in Baby-
  lonia & Assyria p137-55   913.35

China
  See pages in the following book:
Liu, J. T. C. ed. Traditional China p92-
  108   915.1

Great Britain
  See pages in the following book:
Shakespeare's England v 1 p381-412 822.3

History
  See pages in the following book:
Bailey, C. ed. Legacy of Rome p173-208
                             913.37
  See pages in the following book:
Tomkeieff, O. G. Life in Norman England
  p124-33   914.2

Rome
  See pages in the following book:
Durant, W. Caesar and Christ p391-406
                             937

Southern States
  See pages in the following book:
Boorstin, D. J. The Americans: The na-
  tional experience p199-206 917.3

United States
Holmes, O. W. The mind and faith of
  Justice Holmes   340
Lewis, A. Gideon's trumpet   347.9
Sloan, I. J. Youth and the law 340
  See also pages in the following books:
Boorstin, D. J. The Americans: The
  colonial experience p195-205 917.3
Commager, H. S. The American mind
  p359-90   917.3

Law and order. Henry, O.
  In Henry, O. The complete works of
    O. Henry p914-24   **S C**

Law as a profession
Asbell, B. What lawyers really do: six
  lawyers talk about their life and work
                             340.69
Law enforcement
Lewin, S. ed. Crime and its prevention
                             364.1

United States. President's Commission on
  Law Enforcement and Administration
  of Justice. The challenge of crime in
  a free society   364
  See also pages in the following book:
United States. National Commission on
  the Causes and Prevention of Violence.
  To establish justice, to insure domestic
  tranquility p119-45   301.18
  See also Police
The law of life. London, J.
  In London, J. Best short stories of Jack
    London p150-56   **S C**
  In London, J. Jack London's Tales of
    adventure   **S C**
The law of love and the law of violence.
  Tolstoy, L.   172
Lawn tennis. See Tennis
Lawns. See Grasses
Lawrence, D. H.
  D. H. Lawrence: poems selected for young
    people   821
  Lady Chatterley's lover; criticism
  In Porter, K. A. The collected essays
    and occasional writings of Kath-
    erine Anne Porter p14-28 818
  Odor of chrysanthemums
  In Havighurst, W. ed. Masters of the
    modern short story p245-65 **S C**
  Sons and lovers   **Fic**
  Women in love; criticism
  In Drew, E. The novel: a modern guide
    to fifteen English masterpieces
    p208-23   823.09

About
  See pages in the following books:
Daiches, D. The novel and the modern
  world p138-86   823.09
Highet, G. People, places and books p37-
  44   809
Untermeyer, L. Makers of the modern
  world p632-42   920
Wagenknecht, E. Cavalcade of the En-
  glish novel p494-504   823.09
Lawrence, David Herbert. See Lawrence,
  D. H.
Lawrence, Jerome
  Inherit the wind
  In Gassner, J. ed. Best American plays;
    4th ser. p403-38   812.08
  Mame   812
Lawrence, T. E.
  Seven pillars of wisdom   940.4
Lawrence, Kan.
Description
  See pages in the following book:
Moyers, B. Listening to America p83-122
                             917.3
Lawson, Don
  The War of 1812   973.5
Lawson, Thomas William
  See pages in the following book:
Holbrook, S. H. The age of the moguls
  p169-75   920
Lawyers
Darrow, C. The story of my life 92
Gurko, M. Clarence Darrow   92
  See also Law as a profession; Legal
  ethics

Leclair, Jean Marie, 1697-1764
See pages in the following book:
Chapin, V. The violin and its masters p56-63 **920**

Le Corbusier
Towards a new architecture **724.9**
The **lecture.** Singer, I. B.
In Singer, I. B. An Isaac Bashevis Singer reader p235-55 **S C**

Lederer, William J.
A nation of sheep **327.73**
The ugly American **S C**
Contents: Lucky, Lucky Lou #1; Lucky, Lucky Lou #2; Nine friends; Everybody loves Joe Bing; Confidential and personal; Employment opportunities abroad; The girl who got recruited; The ambassador and the working press; Everyone has ears; The Ragtime Kid; The iron of war; The lessons of war; What would you do if you were president; How to buy an American junior grade; The six-foot Swami from Savannah; Captain Boning, USN; The ugly American; The ugly American and the ugly Sarkhanese; The bent backs of Chang 'Doing'; Senator, Sir . . . ; The sum of tiny things

The **ledge.** Hall, L. S.
In Foley, M. ed. Fifty best American short stories, 1915-1965 p602-17 **S C**

Lee, Al
(ed.) The major young poets **811.08**

Lee, Ezra
Holbrook, S. H. Lost men of American history p62-69 **920**

Lee, Harper
To kill a mockingbird **Fic**

Lee, Lawrence
The heroic journey
In The Best American short stories, 1967 p151-60 **S C**

Lee, Mary Randolph (Custis)
Fiction
Kane, H. T. The lady of Arlington **Fic**

Lee, Richard Henry, 1732-1794
See pages in the following book:
Bakeless, J. Signers of the Declaration p79-87 **920**

Lee, Robert E.
(jt. auth.) Lawrence, J. Mame **812**

Lee, Robert Edward
Commager, H. S. America's Robert E. Lee **92**
Freeman, D. S. Lee of Virginia **92**
Miers, E. S. Robert E. Lee **92**
See also pages in the following books:
Commager, H. S. ed. The Blue and the Gray p1060-79 **973.7**
Dictionary of American biography. The American Plutarch p283-300 **920**
Fiction
Kane, H. T. The lady of Arlington **Fic**

Lee, Russel V.
The physician **610.69**

Lee's lieutenants. Freeman, D. S. **973.7**

Leeuwenhoek, Anthony van
See pages in the following book:
De Kruif, P. Microbe hunters p3-24 **920**

Leffland, Ella
The forest
In The Best American short stories, 1970 p138-60 **S C**

Left and right (Political science) See Right and left (Political science)

Left out on Lone Star Mountain. Harte, B.
In Harte, B. The best of Bret Harte p398-430 **S C**

The **leg.** Faulkner, W.
In Faulkner, W. Collected stories of William Faulkner p823-42 **S C**

The **legacy.** Shute, N. **Fic**

The **legacy.** Woolf, V.
In Costain, T. B. ed. Read with me p615-23 **S C**

The **legacy** of Rome. Bailey, C. ed. **913.37**

The **legacy** of Tom Dooley. Elliott, L. **362.1**

Legal aid
See pages in the following book:
James, H. Crisis in the courts p126-42 **347.9**

Legal ethics
See pages in the following book:
James, H. Crisis in the courts p168-79 **347.9**

Legal holidays. See Holidays

Legal status of young adults. See Sloan, I. J. Youth and the law **340**

Legal tender. See Paper money

The **legend.** Wharton, E.
In Wharton, E. The collected short stories of Edith Wharton v2 p92-114 **S C**

The **legend** of Joe Lee. MacDonald, J. D.
In Hitchcock, A. ed. Alfred Hitchcock presents: A month of mystery p317-29 **S C**

Legend of the Capitoline Venus. Twain, M.
In Twain, M. The complete short stories of Mark Twain p22-27 **S C**

The **legend** of the Seventh Virgin. Holt, V. **Fic**

Legendre, Adrien Marie
See pages in the following book:
Jones, B. Z. ed. The golden age of science p93-117 **920**

Legends
See also Folklore; Mythology
Dictionaries
Funk & Wagnalls Standard dictionary of folklore, mythology and legend **398.03**
Germany
See pages in the following book:
Rees, G. The Rhine p112-31 **914.3**

Legends, Indian. See Indians of North America—Legends

Legends. Lowell, A.
In Lowell, A. The complete poetical works of Amy Lowell p245-99 **811**

Legends of Charlemagne. Bulfinch, T.
In Bulfinch, T. Bulfinch's Mythology v3 **291**

Lehrburger, Egon. See Larsen, Egon

Leibniz, Gottfried Wilhelm, Freiherr von
See pages in the following books:
Bell, E. T. Men of mathematics p117-30 **920**
Durant, W. The age of Louis XIV p658-81 **940.2**
Russell, B. A history of Western philosophy p581-96 **109**

Leicester, Simon of Montfort, Earl of. See Montfort, Simon of, Earl of Leicester, 1208?-1265

Leidy, W. Philip
A popular guide to government publications **015.73**

Leigh, Mitch
Wasserman, D. Man of La Mancha **812**

Leighton, Isabel
(ed.) The aspirin age, 1919-1941 **917.3**

Leinsdorf, Erich
See pages in the following books:
Beard, A. E. S. Our foreign-born citizens p256-69 **920**
Ewen, D. Famous modern conductors p60-74 **920**

Leinster, Murray
This star shall be free
In Conklin, G. ed. Invaders of earth p2-19 **S C**

Leish, Kenneth W.
(ed.) American Heritage. The American Heritage Pictorial history of the Presidents of the United States **920**
(ed.) Cunliffe, M. The American Heritage of the Presidency **353.03**

Leisure
See pages in the following book:
Riesman, D. The lonely crowd p342-67 **155.8**
See also Recreation; Retirement

Leisure class
Veblen, T. The theory of the leisure class **339**

L'Élégance. Godden, R.
In Godden, R. Gone p153-77 **S C**

L'Engle, Madeleine
The love letters **Fic**

Lenin, Nikolai. See Lenin, Vladimir Il'ich

Lenin, Vladimir Il'ich
Payne, R. The life and death of Lenin **92**
Trotsky, L. Lenin **92**
See also pages in the following book:
Untermeyer, L. Makers of the modern world p410-19 **920**

Leningrad
See pages in the following book:
Horizon Magazine. The Horizon History of Russia p171-85 **947**

Siege, 1941-1944
Salisbury, H. E. The 900 days **940.54**
See also pages in the following book:
Reeder, R. The story of the Second World War v 1 p220-27 **940.53**

Lenormand, Henri René
This is a dream
In Dickinson, T. H. ed. Chief contemporary dramatists; 3d ser. p311-35 **808.82**

Lenz, Bernie
The complete book of fashion modeling **659.15**

Leo X, Pope
See pages in the following book:
Durant, W. The Renaissance p477-522 **940.2**

Leon of Modena. See Leone da Modena

Leonard, Jonathan Norton
American cooking: New England **641.5**
Ancient America **913.7**
Early Japan **915.2**
Latin American cooking **641.5**

Leonardo da Vinci
Cooper, M. The inventions of Leonardo da Vinci **608**
Hale, J. R. Renaissance **940.2**
Horizon Magazine. Leonardo da Vinci **92**
Wallace, R. The world of Leonardo, 1452-1519 **92**
See also pages in the following books:
Durant, W. The Renaissance p199-228 **940.2**
Horizon Magazine. The Horizon Book of the Renaissance p185-200 **940.2**
National Geographic Society. The Renaissance p98-142 **940.2**
Vasari, G. The lives of the painters, sculptors and architects v2 p156-68 **920**

Leone de Modena
See pages in the following book:
David, J. ed. Growing up Jewish p4-14 **920**

Leonowens, Ann Harriette (Crawford)
Landon, M. Anna and the King of Siam **915.93**

The Leopard. Lampedusa, G. di **Fic**

"Leopard" George. Lessing, D.
In Lessing, D. African stories p189-214 **S C**

Leopold, A. Starker
The desert **551.4**

Leopold, Luna B.
Water **551.4**

Leopold, Nathan Freudenthal
See pages in the following books:
Darrow, C. The story of my life p226-43 **92**
Gurko, M. Clarence Darrow p195-206 **92**

Lepidoptera. See Butterflies

Lerner, Alan Jay
Camelot **812**
My fair lady **812**
About
See pages in the following book:
Ewen, D. Great men of American popular song p299-309 **920**

Leslie, Robert Franklin
The bears and I **599**

Lesseps, Ferdinand Marie, vicomte de
Horizon Magazine. Building the Suez Canal **962**

Lesser, Milton
Pen pal
In Conklin, G. ed. Invaders of earth p146-59 **S C**

Lessing, Doris
African stories **S C**
Contents: The Black Madonna; The trinket box; The pig; Traitors; The old chief Mshlanga; A sunrise on the veld; No witchcraft for sale; The second hut; The nuisance; The De Wets come to Kloof Grange; Little Tembi; Old John's place; "Leopard" George; Winter in July; A home for the highland cattle; Eldorado; The antheap; Hunger; The words he said; Lucy Grange; A mild attack of locusts; Flavours of exile; Getting off the altitude; A road to the big city; Flight; Plants and girls; The sun between their feet; A letter from home; The new man; The story of two dogs

Lessing, Gotthold Ephraim
See pages in the following book:
Durant, W. Rousseau and revolution p508-17   **940.2**
Lessing, Lawrence
DNA: at the core of life itself   **574.8**
The **lesson.** Ionesco, E.
In Ionesco, E. Four plays p43-78   **842**
The **lessons of history.** Durant, W.   **901**
The **lessons of war.** Lederer, W. J.
In Lederer, W. J. The ugly American p132-43   **S C**
Lester, Julius
Search for a new land   **973.92**
Lester, Katherine Morris
Historic costume   **391.09**
Let me feel your pulse. Henry, O.
In Henry, O. The complete works of O. Henry p881-90   **S C**
Let my people go. Luthuli, A.   **92**
Let's face it. Archer, E.   **646.7**
Let's get out of here. Welch, R.
In The Best short plays of 1957-1958 p41-57   **808.82**
Let's play chess. See Horowitz, I. A. First book of chess   **794.1**
The **letter.** Maugham, W. S.
In Maugham, W. S. The best short stories of W. Somerset Maugham p3-39   **S C**
The **letter.** Wharton, E.
In Wharton, E. The collected short stories of Edith Wharton v 1 p493-506   **S C**
A **letter from home.** Lessing, D.
In Lessing, D. African stories p599-607   **S C**
Letter from Peking. Buck, P. S.   **Fic**
Letter home. Buck, P. S.
In Buck, P. S. The good deed, and other stories of Asia, past and present p69-87   **S C**
Letter writing
See pages in the following books:
Post, E. L. The Emily Post Book of etiquette for young people p79-95   **395**
Vogue's Book of etiquette and good manners p425-94   **395**
See also Business letters
Lettering
Biegeleisen, J. I. The ABC of lettering   **745.6**
Letters
Schuster, M. L. ed. A treasury of the world's great letters, from ancient days to our own time   **808.86**
The **letters.** Wharton, E.
In Wharton, E. The collected short stories of Edith Wharton v2 p177-206   **S C**
Letters of James Agee to Father Flye. Agee, J.   **92**
Letters of Lord Chesterfield to his son. Chesterfield, P. D. S. 4th Earl of   **826**
The **letters of Robert Frost to Louis Untermeyer.** Frost, R.   **92**
Letters of the alphabet. See Alphabet

Letters to Karen: on keeping love in marriage. Sheed, C. W.   **301.42**
Leuchtenburg, William E.
Franklin D. Roosevelt and the New Deal, 1932-1940   **973.917**
The great age of change: from 1945
In Life (Periodical) The Life History of the United States v12   **973**
New Deal and global war: 1933-1945
In Life (Periodical) The Life History of the United States v11   **973**
The perils of prosperity, 1914-32   **330.973**
Leuders, Edward
(ed.) National Council of Teachers of English. Committee on College and Adult Reading List. The college and adult reading list of books in literature and the fine arts   **016**
Levenson, Samuel
See pages in the following book:
David, J. ed. Growing up Jewish p236-42   **920**
Leviant, Curt
Mourning call
In The Best American short stories, 1966 p203-18   **S C**
Levin, Ira
No time for sergeants   **812**
—Same
In Gassner, J. ed. Best American plays; 4th ser. p573-609   **812.08**
Levin, Milton
Noel Coward   **822.09**
Levron, Jacques
Daily life at Versailles in the seventeenth and eighteenth centuries   **914.43**
Levy, Leonard W.
(ed.) Freedom of the press from Zenger to Jefferson   **323.44**
Lewin, Leonard C.
(ed.) A treasury of American political humor   **817.08**
Lewin, Stephen
(ed.) Crime and its prevention   **364.1**
Lewis, Anthony
Gideon's trumpet   **347.9**
Lewis, C. S.
Letters of C. S. Lewis   **826**
Out of the silent planet   **Fic**
The Screwtape letters [and] Screwtape proposes a toast   **248**
Screwtape proposes a toast
In Lewis, C. S. The Screwtape letters [and] Screwtape proposes a toast   **248**
Lewis, Clarence Lewis
[Selections]
In Kurtz, P. ed. American philosophy in the twentieth century p388-414   **191.08**
Lewis, Harry Sinclair. See Lewis, Sinclair
Lewis, Hilda
Harold was my king   **Fic**
Lewis, John
See pages in the following book:
Williams, M. The jazz tradition p156-66   **781.5**

Lewis, Lloyd
Captain Sam Grant   92
Lewis, Lucille
The man who talked with books
In Mystery Writers of America. Crime
    without murder p173-76   **S C**
Lewis, Meriwether
History of the expedition under the command of Captains Lewis and Clark; criticism
In Downs, R. B. Books that changed
    America p14-25   810.9

About
Chidsey, D. B. Lewis and Clark   973.4
Dillon, R. Meriwether Lewis   92
Lewis, Michael
The Spanish Armada   942.05
Lewis, Norman
How to read better and faster   428.4
Thirty days to better English   428
(ed.) The New Roget's Thesaurus of the
    English language in dictionary form.
    See The New Roget's Thesaurus of the
    English language in dictionary form 424
Lewis, Oscar
The children of Sánchez   309.172
A death in the Sánchez family   309.172
La vida   301.453
Lewis, Pryce
    See pages in the following book:
Kane, H. T. Spies for the Blue and Gray
    p74-86   973.7
Lewis, Richard
(ed.) Still waters of the air   861.08
Lewis, Richard S.
Appointment on the moon   629.4
Lewis, Sinclair
Arrowsmith
In Lewis, S. Lewis at zenith p585-914
                     Fic
Babbitt
In Lewis, S. Lewis at zenith p337-583
                     Fic
Lewis at zenith   **Fic**
Main Street
In Lewis, S. Lewis at zenith p 1-335
                     Fic
Main Street; criticism
In Stegner, W. ed. The American novel
    p166-79   813.09

About
Dooley, D. J. The art of Sinclair Lewis
                     813.09
Grebstein, S. N. Sinclair Lewis   813.09
O'Connor, R. Sinclair Lewis   92
Schorer, M. Sinclair Lewis   92
    See also pages in the following books:
Kazin, A. On native grounds p205-26
                     810.9
Literary history of the United States
    p1222-29   810.9
O'Connor, W. V. ed. Seven modern American novelists p46-80   813.09
Stirling, N. Who wrote the modern classics? p45-79   920
Untermeyer, L. Makers of the modern
    world p619-25   920

Van Doren, C. The American novel, 1789-
    1939 p303-14   813.09
Wagenknecht, E. Cavalcade of the American novel p354-67   813.09
Lewis, W. H.
(ed.) Lewis, C. S. Letters of C. S. Lewis
                     826
Lewis and Clark. Chidsey, D. B.   973.4
Lewis and Clark Expedition
Chidsey, D. B. Lewis and Clark   973.4
Dillon, R. Meriwether Lewis   92
Snyder, G. S. In the footsteps of Lewis
    and Clark   973.4
    See also pages in the following book:
American Heritage. The American Heritage Book of great adventures of the Old
    West p8-31   978
Lewis at zenith. Lewis, S.   **Fic**
Lewiton, Mina
(ed.) Longfellow, H. W. Evangeline   811
Ley, Willy
Another look at Atlantis, and fifteen other
    essays   508
Dawn of zoology   590
The Poles   919.8
Rockets, missiles, and men in space 629.4
Watchers of the skies   523.09
Li, Dun J.
The ageless Chinese   951
Liar! Asimov, I.
In Asimov, I. I, robot p99-117   **S C**
Libarle, Marc
(ed.) The high school revolutionaries 371.8
Libby, Willard Frank
    See pages in the following book:
Moore, R. Man, time, and fossils p378-402
                     573.2
The liberal tradition in American thought.
    Volkomer, W. E. ed.   320.5
Liberalism
Volkomer, W. E. ed. The liberal tradition in American thought   320.5
The liberator, Simón Bolívar. Bushnell,
    D. ed.   92
Liberty
Commager, H. S. Crusaders for freedom
                     920
Commager, H. S. Freedom, loyalty, dissent   323.44
Fromm, E. Escape from freedom   323.4
Fromm, E. The sane society   323.4
Ketchum, R. M. ed. What is democracy?
                     321.8
Packard, V. The naked society   323.44
Paine, T. The rights of man   323.4
Rossiter, C. Seedtime of the Republic
                     342.73
    See also pages in the following books:
Chase, S. American credos p152-67 **301.15**
Commager, H. S. ed. Living ideas in
    America p366-435   973
    See also Civil rights; Religious liberty
Liberty Hall. Lardner, R.
In Lardner, R. The best short stories of
    Ring Lardner p53-63   **S C**
In Lardner, R. The Ring Lardner reader p368-79   **S C**
Liberty of the press. See Freedom of the
    press

Libraries
Public library catalog   011
The World book encyclopedia. Library   020
See also pages in the following books:
MacLeish, A. A continuing journey p115-29   818
Wright, L. B. The cultural life of the American colonies, 1607-1763 p126-53   917.3
See also School libraries

Automation
Meetham, R. Information retrieval   029.7

Censorship
Merritt, L. C. Book selection and intellectual freedom   025.2

Handbooks, manuals, etc.
Downs, R. B. How to do library research   028.7

History
See pages in the following book:
Sarton, G. A history of science v2 p141-57   509

Public relations
See Public relations—Libraries

Libraries, Children's. See Libraries, Young adults'

Libraries, College and university
Bertalan, F. J. ed. The junior college library collection   011
Choice: books for college libraries   028.1

Libraries, School. See School libraries

Libraries, Young adults'
Edwards, M. A. The fair garden and the swarm of beasts   027.62

Libraries and Negroes
See pages in the following book:
Ebony. The Negro handbook p173-84   301.451

Libraries and readers
Hook, L. The research paper   808.02

Handbooks, manuals, etc.
Toser, M. A. Library manual   028.7

Libraries and schools. See School libraries

Library. The World book encyclopedia   020

Library bill of rights. See American Library Association. Intellectual Freedom Committee. Freedom of inquiry   323.44

Library displays. Garvey, M.   021.7

Library key, The new. Cook, M. G.   028.7

Library manual. Toser, M. A.   028.7

A **library** of literary criticism: Modern American literature. Curley, D. N. ed.   810.9

Library science. See Cataloging

Library service
Cook, M. G. The new library key   028.7
Gates, J. K. Guide to the use of books and libraries   028.7
Rossoff, M. Using your high school library   028.7
Toser, M. A. Library manual   028.7
The World book encyclopedia. Library   020
See also Libraries and readers

Librettos. See Operas—Stories, plots, etc.; also musical forms with the subdivision Librettos, e.g. Operas—Librettos

Libya
See pages in the following book:
Ashabranner, B. A moment in history: the first ten years of the Peace Corps p335-44   309.2

Description and travel
Keith, A. N. Children of Allah   916.1

History
Wright, J. Libya   961

Social life and customs
Keith, A. N. Children of Allah   916.1

Lichens
See pages in the following book:
The Oxford Book of flowerless plants p62-67, 74-79, 158-73   586

A **lickpenny lover.** Henry, O.
In Henry, O. The best short stories of O. Henry p232-38   S C
In Henry, O. The complete works of O. Henry p1261-66   S C

Liddell Hart, B. H.
History of the Second World War   940.54

Lieber, Lillian R.
The education of T. C. Mits   510
The Einstein theory of relativity   530.1
Mits, wits and logic   164

Liebig, Justus, Freiherr von
See pages in the following book:
Moore, R. The coil of life p54-70   574.09

Liebman, Joshua
Peace of mind. Large type ed.   158

Life (Periodical)
Handbook of the nations and international organizations   910
The Life History of the United States   973
The unforgettable Winston Churchill   92
The wonders of life on earth   574
Bishop, E. Brazil   918.1
Carr, A. The land and wildlife of Africa   574.9
Fessler, L. China   915.1
Innes, H. Scandinavia   914.8
Johnson, W. W. The Andean republics   918
Lavine, H. Central America   917.28
McCarthy, J. Ireland   914.15
MacInnes, C. Australia and New Zealand   919.4
Mueller, C. G. Light and vision   535
Stillman, E. The Balkans   914.96
Thayer, C. W. Russia   914.7
Thomas, H. Spain   914.6
Went, F. W. The plants   581

Life
Lindbergh, A. M. Gift from the sea   818
Mumford, L. The conduct of life   128
Schweitzer, A. The teaching of reverence for life   179
See also pages in the following book:
Camus, A. The myth of Sisyphus, and other essays p3-65   844

Liston, Robert A.
Dissent in America   301.15
Greeting: you are hereby ordered for induction   355.2
Slavery in America   326
Liszt, Franz
See pages in the following books:
Bauer, M. Music through the ages p421-43   780.9
Chapin, V. Giants of the keyboard p87-102   920
Cross, M. The Milton Cross New encyclopedia of the great composers and their music p543-60   920.03
Ewen, D. ed. The complete book of classical music p507-21   780.1
Ewen, D. ed. The world of great composers p303-19   920
Shippen, K. B. The heritage of music p176-83   780.9
Literacy. See Illiteracy
Literary and library prizes   807.9
Literary awards. See Literary prizes
Literary characters. See Characters and characteristics in literature
Literary criticism. See Criticism
Literary history of the United States   810.9
Literary life of Thingum Bob, Esq. Poe, E. A.
In Poe, E. A. The complete tales and poems of Edgar Allan Poe p322-37   S C
Literary prizes
Literary and library prizes   807.9
Stuckey, W. J. The Pulitzer Prize novels   813.09
Literary prizes and their winners. See Literary and library prizes   807.9
Literature
See also Authorship; Biography (as a literary form); Classical literature; Devotional literature; Short story; Symbolism in literature; Wit and humor; and names of literatures, e.g. English literature

Addresses and essays
Highet, G. People, places and books   809
Trilling, L. The opposing self   809

Bibliography
Emery, R. C. High interest—easy reading for junior and senior high school reluctant readers   028.52
Irwin, L. B. comp. A guide to historical reading: non-fiction   016.9
National Council of Teachers of English. Committee on College and Adult Reading List. The college and adult reading list of books in literature and the fine arts   016
New York. Public Library. Books for the teen age   028.52
Strang, R. Gateways to readable books   028.52

Bio-bibliography
Cassell's Encyclopaedia of world literature   803
The Concise encyclopedia of modern world literature   803
The Reader's adviser   011
See also Authors

Biography
See Authors

Collections
Day, A. G. ed. The spell of Hawaii   919.69
Fadiman, C. ed. Fantasia mathematica   808.8
Fadiman, C. ed. The mathematical magpie   808.8
Handlin, O. ed. Children of the uprooted   325.73
Haynes, B. D. ed. The grizzly bear   599
See also Letters; Quotations; Short stories; *also* names of literatures and names of literary forms with the subdivision Collections, e.g. English literature—Collections; Poetry—Collections

Dictionaries
Brewer, E. C. The reader's handbook of famous names in fiction, allusions, references, proverbs, plots, stories, and poems   803
Brewer's Dictionary of phrase and fable   803
Cassell's Encyclopaedia of world literature   803
The Concise encyclopedia of modern world literature   803
Magill, F. N. ed. Cyclopedia of world authors   920.03
Shipley, J. T. ed. Dictionary of world literary terms   803
The Reader's encyclopedia   803
See also Literature—Indexes

Evaluation
See Book reviews; Books and reading—Best books; Criticism; Literature—History and criticism

History and criticism
Downs, R. B. Books that changed the world   809
Durant, W. Interpretations of life   809
Highet, G. The classical tradition   809
Macy, J. The story of the world's literature   809
Trilling, L. The opposing self   809
Wilson, E. Axel's castle   809
See also pages in the following books:
Hayes, C. J. H. Contemporary Europe since 1870 p221-30, 529-31   940.2
Langer, W. L. Political and social upheaval, 1832-1852 p547-74   940.2
The New Cambridge Modern history v2 p359-86, v11 p121-53, v12 p613-43   909
See also Authors; Criticism

Indexes
Essay and general literature index   080
Magill, F. N. ed. Cyclopedia of literary characters   803
See also Literature—Dictionaries

Prizes
See Literary prizes; and names of prizes, e.g. Newbery Medal books

The little old lady from Cricket Creek. Gray, L.
In Best detective stories of the year [1969] p225-29   **S C**

A little piece of Hungary. Deighton, L.
In Dulles, A. ed. Great spy stories from fiction p329-35   **S C**

A little pilgrimage. Crane, S.
In Crane, S. The complete short stories & sketches of Stephen Crane p765-68   **S C**

The little regiment. Crane, S.
In Crane, S. The complete short stories & sketches of Stephen Crane p276-90   **S C**

Little Rock, Ark.
Description
See pages in the following book:
Moyers, B. Listening to America p284-308   **917.3**

Little Roger's night in the church. Coolidge, S.
In Schauffler, R. H. ed. Christmas p256-69   **394.26**

Little soldier. Maupassant, G. de
In Maupassant, G. de. The odd number p185-99   **S C**

"Little speck in garnered fruit." Henry, O.
In Henry, O. The complete works of O. Henry p1270-74   **S C**

A little talk about mobs. Henry, O.
In Henry, O. The complete works of O. Henry p1677-79   **S C**

Little Tembi. Lessing, D.
In Lessing, D. African stories p129-51   **S C**

A little treasury of American poetry. Williams, O. ed.   **811.08**

A little treasury of British poetry. Williams, O. ed.   **821.08**

A little treasury of great poetry, English and American, from Chaucer to the present day. Williams, O. ed.   **821.08**

A little treasury of modern poetry, English & American. Williams, O. ed.   **821.08**

A little treasury of world poetry. Creekmore, H. ed.   **808.81**

A little walk. Maupassant, G. de
In Maupassant, G. de. Selected short stories p260-67   **S C**

The little wife. March, W.
In Foley, M. ed. Fifty best American short stories, 1915-1965 p87-97 **S C**

The little world of Don Camillo. Guareschi, G.   **Fic**

Littlejohns, J.
(jt. auth.) Richmond, L. Fundamentals of watercolor painting   **751.4**

Littlewood, Cyril
The world's vanishing animals: the mammals   **599**

Litwak, Leo E.
In shock
In The Best American short stories, 1968 p201-14   **S C**

Liu, James T. C.
(ed.) Traditional China   **915.1**

The lives and times of Archy & Mehitabel. Marquis, D.   **817**

Lives from Plutarch. Abridged. Plutarch   **920**

Lives of famous Romans. Coolidge, O.   **920**

The lives of the painters. Canaday, J.   **920**

The lives of the painters, sculptors and architects. Vasari, G.   **920**

Lives of the poets. Untermeyer, L.   **920**

Livestock. See Cattle; Domestic animals

Living amphibians of the world. Cochran, D. M.   **597**

Living authors. See Kunitz, S. J. ed. Twentieth century authors   **920.03**

A living Bill of Rights. Douglas, W. O.   **342.73**

The living cell. Scientific American   **574.8**

The living clocks. Ward, R. R.   **574.1**

Living fishes of the world. Herald, E. S. **597**

Living ideas in America. Commager, H. S. ed.   **973**

Living in space. Sharpe, M. R.   **629.45**

Living invertebrates of the world. See Buchsbaum, R. The lower animals   **592**

Living mammals of the world. Sanderson, I. T.   **599**

The Living organism
In Encyclopedia of the life sciences **v 1**   **574.03**

The living races of man. Coon, C. S.   **572**

The living sea. Cousteau, J. Y.   **627.7**

Livingstone, David
Martelli, G. Livingstone's river   **916.7**
See also pages in the following book:
Thompson, E. B. Africa: past and present p152-64   **960**

Livingstone's river. Martelli, G.   **916.7**

Livvie. Welty, E.
In Havighurst, W. ed. Masters of the modern short story p33-48   **S C**

Livvie is back. Welty, E.
In Abrahams, W. ed. Fifty years of the American short story v2 p410-22   **S C**

Livy
See pages in the following book:
Grant, M. The ancient historians p217-42   **920**

Lizardi, José Fernández de. See Fernández de Lizardi, José

Lizards
See pages in the following books:
Conant, R. A field guide to reptiles and amphibians of the United States and Canada east of the 100th meridian p74-108   **598.1**
Ditmars, R. L. Reptiles of North America p13-116   **598.1**
Ditmars, R. L. Reptiles of the world p27-114   **598.1**

Llewellin ap Gryffyd. See Llywelyn ab Gruffydd

Llewellyn, Richard
How green was my valley   **Fic**

Llewelyn II. See Llywelyn ab Gruffydd

Lloyd, Alan
The Spanish centuries   **946**

Lloyd, C.
Pacific plunder
In Armstrong, R. ed. Treasure and treasure hunters   **910.4**

Lloyd, Norman
(comp.) American Heritage. The American Heritage Songbook **784.4**
Lloyd, Ruth
(comp.) American Heritage. The American Heritage Songbook **784.4**
Lloyd George, David Lloyd George, 1st Earl
Gilbert, M. ed. Lloyd George **92**
Llywelyn ab Gruffydd
See pages in the following book:
Sutcliff, R. Heroes and history p62-72 **920**
Lo! Faulkner, W.
In Faulkner, W. Collected stories of William Faulkner p381-403 **S C**
In Faulkner, W. Selected short stories of William Faulkner p132-56 **S C**
Loaded with money. Marsh, A.
In Mystery Writers of America. Crime without murder p187-92 **S C**
Loan funds, Student. See Student loan funds
Lobachevskiĭ, Nikolaĭ Ivanovich
See pages in the following book:
Bell, E. T. Men of mathematics p294-306 **920**
Lobatchewsky, Nikolai Ivanovitch. See Lobachevskiĭ, Nikolaĭ Ivanovich
Loble, Lester H.
Delinquency can be stopped **364.36**
Lobo. Kantor, M.
In Costain, T. B. ed. Read with me p289-320 **S C**
Lobos, Heitor Villa- See Villa-Lobos, Heitor
Local government
The American Assembly. The states and the urban crisis **309.2**
See also pages in the following books:
Gies, J. Life in a medieval city p199-210 **914.4**
United States. Department of Agriculture. A place to live p249-67 **301.3**
Local transit
Reische, D. ed. Problems of mass transportation **380.5**
See also pages in the following book:
Scientific American. Cities p133-55 **309.2**
Locke, John
See pages in the following books:
Durant, W. The age of Louis XIV p575-90 **940.2**
Russell, B. A history of Western philosophy p604-47 **109**
Thomas, H. Understanding the great philosophers p218-27 **109**
Lockwood, Lee
Castro's Cuba, Cuba's Fidel **917.291**
Locomotion. See Flight; Transportation
Locusts
See pages in the following book:
American Heritage. The American Heritage Book of great adventures of the Old West p282-95 **978**
A lodging for the night. Stevenson, R. L.
In Stevenson, R. L. The complete short stories of Robert Louis Stevenson p 1-24 **S C**
In Stevenson, R. L. The strange case of Dr Jekyll and Mr Hyde, and other famous tales p128-49 **S C**

Loeb, Richard A.
See pages in the following books:
Darrow, C. The story of my life p226-43 **92**
Gurko, M. Clarence Darrow p195-206 **92**
Loesser, Frank
See pages in the following books:
Ewen, D. Composers for the American musical theatre p215-29 **920**
Ewen, D. Great men of American popular song p259-71 **920**
Loewe, Frederick
Lerner, A. J. Camelot **812**
Lerner, A. J. My fair lady **812**
About
See pages in the following books:
Ewen, D. Composers for the American musical theatre p199-214 **920**
Ewen, D. Great men of American popular song p299-309 **920**
Loewe, Michael
Everyday life in early Imperial China **913.31**
Loewy, Raymond Fernand
See pages in the following book:
Beard, A. E. S. Our foreign-born citizens p190-200 **920**
Lofts, Norah
How far to Bethlehem? **Fic**
The lost queen **Fic**
Log cabins
See pages in the following book:
Angier, B. How to live in the woods on pennies a day p165-75 **917.1**
The log of a cowboy. Adams, A. **Fic**
Logan, Sir William Edmond
See pages in the following book:
Moore, R. The earth we live on p181-99 **551.09**
Logarithms
See pages in the following book:
Hogben, L. Mathematics for the million p402-52 **510**
Logasa, Hannah
Irwin, L. B. comp. A guide to historical fiction **016.8**
Irwin, L. B. comp. A guide to historical reading: non-fiction **016.9**
Logic
Chase, S. Guides to straight thinking **160**
Flesch, R. The art of clear thinking **153.4**
See also pages in the following books:
Flesch, R. How to write, speak, and think more effectively p210-17 **808**
Newman, J. R. ed. The world of mathematics v3 p1852-1931 **510.8**
See also Thought and thinking
Logic, Symbolic and mathematical
Lieber, L. R. Mits, wits and logic **164**
Logic of empire. Heinlein, R. A.
In Heinlein, R. A. Robert A. Heinlein's The past through tomorrow p304-40 **S C**
Logsdon, Gene
Wyeth people; a portrait of Andrew Wyeth as he is seen by his friends and neighbors **92**

A loint of paw. Asimov, I.
    In Asimov, I. Asimov's mysteries p108-
    24   S C
Loken, Newt
    Cheerleading   371.89
Lolos, Kimon
    Mule No. 095
    In The Best American short stories, 1964
    p191-201   S C
Lomax, Alan
    (ed.) The folk songs of North America
    in the English language   784.4
    (ed.) 3000 years of Black poetry   808.81
    (jt. comp.) Lomax, J. A. comp. American
    ballads and folk songs   784.4
    (jt. comp.) Lomax, J. A. comp. Cowboy
    songs and other frontier ballads   784.4
    (jt. ed.) Lomax, J. A. ed. Folk songs:
    U.S.A.   784.4
Lomax, John A.
    (comp.) American ballads and folk songs
                                       784.4
    (comp.) Cowboy songs and other fron-
    tier ballads   784.4
    (ed.) Folk song: U.S.A.   784.4
Lomax, Louis E.
    The Negro revolt   301.451
Lombardi, Vince
    Kramer, J. ed. Lombardi: winning is the
    only thing   92
London, Jack
    Best short stories of Jack London S C
    Contents: The white silence; To build a fire;
    An odyssey of the North; The league of the
    old men; Lost face; A piece of steak; The
    heathen; Samuel; On the Makaloa mat; A
    daughter of the Aurora; The law of life; The
    story of Jees Uck; To the man on trail; The
    story of Keesh; The wit of Porportuk; Love of
    life; The Mexican; All Gold Canyon; The wis-
    dom of the trail; The House of Mapuhi; The
    pearls of Parlay
    The house of the sun
    In Day, A. G. ed. The spell of Hawaii
    p286-97   919.69
    Jack London's Tales of adventure S C
    Short stories included are: To the man on
    trail; The white silence; An odyssey of the
    North; Jan, the unrepentant; The man with
    the gash; The law of life; The one thousand
    dozen; Bâtard; All Gold Canyon; The apostate;
    Love of life; The passing of Marcus O'Brien;
    To build a fire; Flush of gold; Lost face; A
    piece of steak; The seed of McCoy; The Mexi-
    can; The strength of the strong; War; The
    pearls of Parlay; The race for number three;
    Samuel; Told in the drooling ward; The prin-
    cess
    Martin Eden   Fic
    Martin Eden; criticism
    In Stegner, W. ed. The American novel
    p133-43   813.09
    The sea-wolf   Fic
    The sheriff of Kona
    In Day, A. G. ed. The spell of Hawaii
    p272-85   919.69
    Stories of Hawaii   S C
    Short stories are: The house of pride;
    Koolau the leper; Good-by, Jack; Aloha oe;
    Chun Ah Chun; The sheriff of Kona; On the
    Makaloa mat; The bones of Kahekili; When
    Alice told her soul; Shin bones; The water
    baby: The tears of Ah Kim; The Kanaka surf
    Where the trail forks
    In Armstrong, R. ed. Treasure and trea-
    sure hunters   910.4

About
O'Connor, R. Jack London   92
    See also pages in the following book:
Brooks, V. The confident years: 1885-1915
    p221-31   810.9
London
Hibbert, C. London: the biography of a
    city   914.21
Description
    See pages in the following books:
Shakespeare's England v2 p153-81   822.3
White, R. J. Life in Regency England p62-
    84   914.2
Fiction
Bryher. Beowulf   Fic
Burgess, A. A clockwork orange   Fic
Godden, R. A candle for St Jude   Fic
Godden, R. An episode of sparrows   Fic
Huxley, A. Point counter point   Fic
Murdoch, I. A fairly honourable defeat
                                          Fic
History
    See pages in the following books:
Ashley, M. Life in Stuart England p81-90
                                       914.2
Bagley, J. J. Life in medieval England
    p55-64   914.2
Hart, R. English life in the seventeenth
    century p7-18   914.2
Horizon Magazine. The Horizon Book of
    The Elizabethan world p258-73   940.2
National Gallery
National Gallery, London   708
Plague, 1665—Fiction
Defoe, D. The journal of the plague year
                                          Fic
St Paul's Cathedral
    See pages in the following book:
Horizon Magazine. The Horizon Book of
    great cathedrals p172-85   726
Social conditions
Braithwaite, E. R. To Sir, with love   92
Social life and customs
Robertson, D. W. Chaucer's London
                                       914.21
The lone charge of William B. Perkins.
    Crane, S.
    In Crane, S. The complete short stories
    & sketches of Stephen Crane p554-
    57   S C
Lone cowboy. James, W.   92
Lone Star. Fehrenbach, T. R.   976.4
Loneliness. Anderson, S.
    In Anderson, S. Winesberg, Ohio (Mod-
    ern Lib) p197-212   S C
    In Anderson, S. Winesburg, Ohio (Vi-
    king) p167-78   S C
The lonely crowd. Riesman, D.   155.8
Lonely crusader; the life of Florence Night-
    ingale, 1820-1910. Woodham Smith, C.
                                          92
Lonesome cities. McKuen, R.   811
The lonesome road. Henry, O.
    In Henry, O. The complete works of
    O. Henry p544-50   S C
Long, Durward
    (jt. ed.) Foster, J. ed. Protest! Student
    activism in America   378.1

Long, Huey Pierce
Graham, H. D. ed. Huey Long   **92**
See also pages in the following book:
Leighton, I. ed. The aspirin age, 1919-1941 p339-63   **917.3**

Long, John Luther
Madame Butterfly; dramatization. See Belasco, D. Madame Butterfly

A long day in November. Gaines, E. J.
In Hughes, L. ed. The best short stories by Negro writers p359-402   **S C**

A long day's dying. Eastlake, W.
In The Best American short stories, 1964 p109-23   **S C**
In Foley, M. ed. Fifty best American short stories p785-98   **S C**

Long day's journey into night. O'Neill, E.   **812**

The Long Fellow; the story of the Great Irish patriot, Eamon De Valera. Steffan, J.   **92**

The long pursuit. Hough, R.   **940.4**

The long rain. Bradbury, R.
In Bradbury, R. The illustrated man p77-92   **S C**
In Bradbury, R. R is for rocket p94-110   **S C**

The long ride to the city. Carter, M. A.
In Seventeen. Seventeen from Seventeen p225-41   **S C**

The long run. Wharton, E.
In Wharton, E. The collected short stories of Edith Wharton v2 p301-24   **S C**

The long view. Paton, A.   **968**

The long voyage home. O'Neill, E.   **812**
also in O'Neill, E. The long voyage home p57-81   **812**
also in O'Neill, E. Plays v 1 p493-509   **812**

The long walk. Rawicz, S.   **910.4**

The long watch. Heinlein, R. A.
In Heinlein, R. A. Robert A. Heinlein's The past through tomorrow p211-22   **S C**

The long way out. Fitzgerald, F. S.
In Fitzgerald, F. S. The Fitzgerald reader p437-41   **S C**
In Fitzgerald, F. S. The stories of F. Scott Fitzgerald p443-47   **S C**

The longest day: June 6, 1944. Ryan, C.   **940.54**

Longfellow, Henry Wadsworth
The complete poetical works of Henry Wadsworth Longfellow   **811**
Evangeline   **811**
About
Wagenknecht, E. Henry Wadsworth Longfellow: portrait of an American humanist   **92**
See also pages in the following books:
Brooks, V. The flowering of New England p153-77, 313-18, 453-69   **810.9**
Literary history of the United States p587-96   **810.9**
Untermeyer, L. The paths of poetry p171-79   **920**

Longing for America. Rubin, D.
In The Best American short stories, 1967 p257-77   **S C**

Longitude
See pages in the following books:
Brown, L. A. Map making p133-65   **526.8**
Newman, J. R. ed. The world of mathematics v2 p780-819   **510.8**

Longley-Cook, L. H.
New math puzzle book   **793.7**

Longmore, Donald
Machines in medicine   **610**
Spare-part surgery   **617**

Longsworth, Polly
Emily Dickinson   **92**

Longtooth. Pangborn, E.
In The Best from Fantasy and Science Fiction; 19th ser. p37-74   **S C**

Look
Religions in America   **280**

Look back in anger. Osborne, J.
In Block, H. M. ed. Masters of modern drama p1072-1101   **808.82**
In Cerf, B. ed. Plays of our time p469-543   **812.08**

Look homeward, angel. Frings, K.
In Gassner, J. ed. Best American plays; 5th ser. p237-76   **812.08**

Look homeward, angel. Wolfe, T.   **Fic**

Look to the mountain. Cannon, L.   **Fic**

Looking backward: 2000-1887. Bellamy, E.   **Fic**

Looking for Dilmun. Bibby, G.   **913.03**

The looking glass. Wharton, E.
In Wharton, E. The collected short stories of Edith Wharton v2 p844-58   **S C**

Looking outward. Stevenson, A. E.   **341.13**

Loomis, Andrew
Drawing the head and hands   **743**
Fun with a pencil   **741.2**

Loomis, Frederic Brewster
Field book of common rocks and minerals   **549**

Loomis, Roger Sherman
A mirror of Chaucer's world   **914.2**

Loomis, Stanley
Paris in the terror, June 1793-July 1794   **944.04**

Loon, Hendrik Willem Van. See Van Loon, Hendrik Willem

The loon feather. Fuller, I.   **Fic**

Lope de Vega
Fuente Ovejuna
In Bentley, E. comp. The great playwrights v 1 p711-72   **808.82**
For material about this author see Vega Carpio, Lope Félix de

Lorant, Stefan
Lincoln   **92**

Lord, Walter
Day of infamy   **940.54**
The good years   **973.91**
Incredible victory   **940.54**
A night to remember   **910.4**
A time to stand   **976.4**

Lord Jim. Conrad, J.   **Fic**

Lord Mountdrago. Maugham, W. S.
In Maugham, W. S. The best short stories of W. Somerset Maugham p349-74   **S C**

Lord Oakhurst's curse. Henry, O.
In Henry, O. The complete works of O. Henry p1049-51   **S C**

The lord of Central Park. Davidson, A.
In Best detective stories of the year, 1971 p85-126   **S C**

The Lord of the Dynamos. Wells, H. G.
In Wells, H. G. The complete short stories of H. G. Wells p284-93 **S C**

Lord of the Flies. Golding, W.   **Fic**

Lorenz, Konrad Z.
King Solomon's ring   **591**
On aggression; criticism
In Montagu, M. F. A. ed. Man and aggression   **152.4**

The lord of the rings. Tolkien, J. R. R. **Fic**

Lorenzo de' Medici. *See* Medici, Lorenzo d', il Magnifico

Los Angeles
Riots, 1965
See pages in the following book:
Isenberg, I. ed. The city in crisis p50-63   **301.3**

Loss of breath. Poe, E. A.
In Poe, E. A. The complete tales and poems of Edgar Allan Poe p395-404   **S C**

Lost at sea. Maupassant, G. de
In Maupassant, G. de. Guy de Maupassant's Short stories p262-68   **S C**

The lost blend. Henry, O.
In Henry, O. The best short stories of O. Henry p288-94   **S C**
In Henry, O. The complete works of O. Henry p1433-36   **S C**

Lost boundaries. White, W.   **301.451**

The lost boy. Wolfe, T.
In Wolfe, T. The hills beyond p 1-42   **S C**

Lost cities. Cottrell, L.   **913.03**

The lost cities of Africa. Davidson, B. **913.6**

The lost city of Mars. Bradbury, R.
In Bradbury, R. I sing the Body Electric! p262-95   **S C**

Lost city of the Incas. Bingham, H. **913.85**

The lost decade. Fitzgerald, F. S.
In Fitzgerald, F. S. The Fitzgerald reader p451-54   **S C**
In Fitzgerald, F. S. The stories of F. Scott Fitzgerald p470-73   **S C**

Lost face. London, J.
In London, J. Best short stories of Jack London p62-72   **S C**
In London, J. Jack London's Tales of adventure   **S C**

Lost horizon. Hilton, J.   **Fic**

Lost in the funhouse. Barth, J.
In Abrahams, W. ed. Fifty years of the American short story v 1 p34-54   **S C**

The lost inheritance. Wells, H. G.
In Wells, H. G. The complete short stories of H. G. Wells p512-19   **S C**

Lost land of youth. Stuart, J.
In Stuart, J. Come back to the farm p189-201   **S C**

Lost legends of the West. Williams, B. **917.8**

Lost men of American history. Holbrook, S. H.   **920**

Lost on dress parade. Henry, O.
In Henry, O. The complete works of O. Henry p91-96   **S C**
In Henry, O. The four million p221-31   **S C**

The lost Pharaohs. Cottrell, L.   **913.32**

The lost Phoebe. Dreiser, T.
In Day, A. G. ed. The greatest American short stories p197-214   **S C**
In Foley, M. ed. Fifty best American short stories, 1915-1965 p8-22 **S C**

The lost queen. Lofts, N.   **Fic**

The lost sanjak. Saki
In Saki. The short stories of Saki p51-57   **S C**

Lost wild America. McClung, R. M. **333.7**

The lost world. Jarrell, R.
In Jarrell, R. The complete poems **811**

Lost worlds. White, A. T.   **913.03**

Loth, David
Freuchen, P. Peter Freuchen's Book of the Seven Seas   **910.4**
Sanderson, I. T. Ivan Sanderson's Book of great jungles   **910.9**

Lott, Davis Newton
(ed.) The Presidents speak   **815.08**

The lottery. Jackson, S.
In Abrahams, W. ed. Fifty years of the American short story v 1 p390-97   **S C**
In Jackson, S. The magic of Shirley Jackson p137-45   **818**

The lotus and the bottle. Henry, O.
In Henry, O. The complete works of O. Henry p560-68   **S C**

Lou, the prophet. Cather, W.
In Cather, W. Willa Cather's Collected short fiction, 1892-1912 v3 p535-40   **S C**

Louis XIV, King of France
Cronin, V. Louis XIV   **92**
See also pages in the following books:
Blitzer, C. Age of kings p54-75   **940.2**
Horizon Magazine. The light of the past p184-89   **901.9**
Levron, J. Daily life at Versailles in the seventeenth and eighteenth centuries p36-52   **914.43**
Lloyd, A. The Spanish centuries p215-30   **946**

Louis XV, King of France
See pages in the following book:
Levron, J. Daily life at Versailles in the seventeenth and eighteenth centuries p116-32, 151-91   **914.43**

Louis XVI, King of France
See pages in the following book:
Levron, J. Daily life at Versailles in the seventeenth and eighteenth centuries p192-209   **914.43**

Louis. Saki
In Saki. The short stories of Saki p465-69   **S C**

Louise. Saki
In Saki. The short stories of Saki p446-50   **S C**

Lowe, David
Ku Klux Klan: the invisible empire **323.2**

Lowe, Jacques
The Kennedy years [biography of John F. Kennedy]. See The Kennedy years [biography of John F. Kennedy] **92**

Lowell, Amy
Ballads for sale
In Lowell, A. The complete poetical works of Amy Lowell p534-89 **811**
Can Grande's castle
In Lowell, A. The complete poetical works of Amy Lowell p153-201 **811**
The complete poetical works of Amy Lowell **811**
Critical fable
In Lowell, A. The complete poetical works of Amy Lowell p389-434 **811**
A dome of many-coloured glass
In Lowell, A. The complete poetical works of Amy Lowell p 1-25 **811**
East wind
In Lowell, A. The complete poetical works of Amy Lowell p481-533 **811**
Fir-flower tablets
In Lowell, A. The complete poetical works of Amy Lowell p301-88 **811**
Legends
In Lowell, A. The complete poetical works of Amy Lowell p245-99 **811**
Men, women and ghosts
In Lowell, A. The complete poetical works of Amy Lowell p75-151 **811**
Pictures of the floating world
In Lowell, A. The complete poetical works of Amy Lowell p203-43 **811**
Sword blades and poppy seed
In Lowell, A. The complete poetical works of Amy Lowell p27-74 **811**
What's o'clock
In Lowell, A. The complete poetical works of Amy Lowell p435-80 **811**

Lowell, James Russell
Wagenknecht, E. James Russell Lowell **92**
See also pages in the following books:
Brooks, V. The flowering of New England p513-37 **810.9**
Literary history of the United States p601-16 **810.9**

Lowell, Robert
Benito Cereno
In Gassner, J. ed. Best American plays; 6th ser. p367-97 **812.08**
In Richards, S. ed. Best short plays of the world theatre, 1958-1967 p155-85 **808.82**
Notebook **811**
Prometheus bound **812**

About
Fein, R. J. Robert Lowell **811.09**
See also pages in the following book:
Rosenthal, M. L. The new poets p25-78 **821.09**

Lowenfels, Walter
(ed.) The writing on the wall **811.08**
The lower animals. Buchsbaum, R. **592**

The **lower** depths. Gorky, M.
In Block, H. M. ed. Masters of modern drama p218-44 **808.82**
In Cerf, B. A. comp. Sixteen famous European plays p197-253 **808.82**
In Tucker, S. M. ed. Twenty-five modern plays p225-62 **808.82**

Lowndes, Douglas
Film making in schools **778.5**

Lowndes, Marion
A manual for baby sitters **649**

Loyalties. Galsworthy, J.
In Cerf, B. A. comp. Sixteen famous British plays p421-72 **822.08**
In Galsworthy, J. Plays p429-64 **822**

Loyalty
Commager, H. S. Freedom, loyalty, dissent **323.44**
Whyte, W. H. The organization man **301.15**
See also Patriotism

Loyola, Ignacio de, Saint
See pages in the following book:
Horizon Magazine. The Horizon Book of The Elizabethan world p119-26 **940.2**

Lubell, Samuel
The hidden crisis in American politics **329**

Lubis, Mochtar
See pages in the following book:
Roland, A. Profiles from the new Asia p24-56 **920**

Lucas, E. V.
Monkey's revenge
In Becker, M. L. ed. The home book of Christmas p498-502 **394.26**

Lucas, Jim G.
Agnew: profile in conflict **92**

Luce, Clare Boothe
The heaven below
In Sports Illustrated. The wonderful world of sport p311-14 **796**
For another work by this author see Boothe, Clare

Luce, Gay Gaer
Sleep **154.6**

Lucerne. Tolstoy, L.
In Tolstoy, L. Short stories v 1 p306-31 **S C**

The lucid eye in Silver Town. Updike, J.
In The Saturday Evening Post. Best modern short stories p119-27 **S C**

Luck. Twain, M.
In Twain, M. The complete short stories of Mark Twain p249-53 **S C**

The Luck of Roaring Camp. Harte, B.
In Harte, B. The best of Bret Harte p 1-16 **S C**
In Harte, B. The best short stories of Bret Harte p3-15 **S C**

Lucky, Lucky Lou #1. Lederer, W. J.
In Lederer, W. J. The ugly American p11-32 **S C**

Lucky, Lucky Lou #2. Lederer, W. J.
In Lederer, W. J. The ugly American p33-41 **S C**

Lucy Grange. Lessing, D.
In Lessing, D. African stories p534-38 **S C**

Ludwig, Carl. See Ludwig, Karl Friedrich Wilhelm

Ludwig, Karl Friedrich Wilhelm
See pages in the following book:
Jones, B. Z. ed. The golden age of science p401-17 **920**

Lueders, Edward
(jt. comp.) Dunning, S. comp. Reflections on a gift of watermelon pickle . . . and other modern verse **811.08**
(jt. comp.) Dunning, S. comp. Some haystacks don't even have any needle, and other complete modern poems **811.08**

The **Luft** Bad. Mansfield, K.
In Mansfield, K. The short stories of Katherine Mansfield p79-82 **S C**

Luisetti, Angelo Enrico
See pages in the following book:
Padwe, S. Basketball's Hall of Fame p33-40 **920**

Luisetti, Hank. See Luisetti, Angelo Enrico

Lukas, J. Anthony
Don't shoot—we are your children! **301.43**

Luke, Saint
Fiction
Caldwell, T. Dear and glorious physician **Fic**

Luke, Peter
Hadrian VII
In Richards, S. ed. Best plays of the sixties p713-800 **808.82**

The **lull.** Saki
In Saki. The short stories of Saki p301-06 **S C**

Lully, Jean Baptiste de
See pages in the following book:
Chapin, V. The violin and its masters p16-21 **920**

The **lumber-room.** Saki
In Saki. The short stories of Saki p416-22 **S C**

Luminescence. See Phosphorescence

Luminescence, Animal. See Bioluminescence

Lumumba, Patrice Emergy
McKown, R. Lumumba **92**

Lunar bases
Ruzic, N. P. Where the winds sleep **629.45**

Lunar expeditions. See Space flight to the moon

Lunar theory. See Moon

Lungs
See pages in the following book:
Ehrlich, P. R. Population, resources, environment p118-23 **301.3**

Lure of the frontier. Gabriel, R. H.
In Pageant of America v2 **973**

Lure of the sea. Phinizy, C.
In Sports Illustrated. The wonderful world of sport p301-02 **796**

Lussac, Joseph Louis Gay- See Gay-Lussac, Joseph Louis

Lust for life. Stone, I. **Fic**

Luther, Martin
Bainton, R. H. Here I stand **92**
Cowie, L. W. Martin Luther: leader of the reformation **92**
See also pages in the following books:
Durant, .W. The Reformation p341-79, 447-53 **940.2**

The New Cambridge Modern history v2 p70-95 **909**
Simon, E. The Reformation p14-20, 36-44 **940.2**

Lutheran Church
See pages in the following book:
Look. Religions in America p121-30 **280**

Luthuli, Albert
Let my people go **92**

Lutz, Frank E.
Field book of insects of the United States and Canada, aiming to answer common questions **595.7**

Luv. Schisgal, M.
In Cerf, B. ed. Plays of our time p721-82 **812.08**

LuValle, James E.
See pages in the following book:
Bontemps, A. We have tomorrow p108-17 **920**

Luxemburg
Rachlis, E. The Low Countries **914.92**

Luykx, T.
(jt. auth.) Vries, S. de. An atlas of world history **911**

Lycurgus
See pages in the following book:
Plutarch. Lives from Plutarch. Abridged. p3-19 **920**

Lyell, Sir Charles, 1st bart.
See pages in the following book:
Moore, R. The earth we live on p157-78 **551.09**

Lynch, John
How to make collages **745.59**
Metal sculpture **731.4**

The **lynching** of Jube Benson. Dunbar, P. L.
In Clarke, J. H. ed. American Negro short stories p 1-8 **S C**

Lynd, Robert S.
Middletown; criticism
In Downs, R. B. Books that changed America p216-28 **810.9**

Lynd, Staughton
(ed.) Nonviolence in America: a documentary history **323**

Lynds, Dennis
A blue blonde in the sky over Pennsylvania
In The Best American short stories, 1965 p223-39 **S C**

Lynx-hunting. Crane, S.
In Crane, S. The complete short stories & sketches of Stephen Crane p565-70 **S C**

Lyon, Mary
See pages in the following books:
Stoddard, H. Famous American women p263-74 **920**
Vance, M. The lamp lighters p42-65 **920**

Lyons, Augusta Wallace
The first flower
In Foley, M. ed. Fifty best American short stories, 1915-1965 p542-48 **S C**

Lyons, F. S. L.
Ireland since the famine **941.5**

Lyrical and critical essays. Camus, A. **844**

Lyrics of a low brow. Service, R.
In Service, R. More collected verse v3 **811**

Lyrics of love and laughter. Dunbar, P. L.
  In Dunbar, P. L. The complete poems
    of Paul Laurence Dunbar p259-371
    811
Lyrics of lowly life. Dunbar, P. L.
  In Dunbar, P. L. The complete poems
    of Paul Laurence Dunbar p 1-138
    811
Lyrics of sunshine and shadow. Dunbar,
  P. L.
  In Dunbar, P. L. The complete poems
    of Paul Laurence Dunbar p379-479
    811
Lyrics of the hearthside. Dunbar, P. L.
  In Dunbar, P. L. The complete poems
    of Paul Laurence Dunbar p139-258
    811
Lysenko, Trofim Denisovich
  See pages in the following book:
  Vladimirov, L. The Russians p205-13
    914.7
Lysergic acid diethylamide
  See pages in the following books:
  Kavaler, L. Mushrooms, molds, and mir-
    acles p159-83 **598**
  Louria, D. B. The drug scene p122-64
    613.8
Lysistrata. Aristophanes
  In Oates, W. J. ed. The complete Greek
    drama v2 p809-59 **882.08**

M

Ms. found in a bottle. Poe, E. A.
  In Poe, E. A. The complete tales and
    poems of Edgar Allan Poe p118-26
    S C
  In Poe, E. A. Edgar Allan Poe p120-33
    S C
  In Poe, E. A. Selected poetry and prose
    p64-73 **818**
Maas, Peter
  The Valachi papers **364.1**
Maazel, Lorin
  See pages in the following book:
  Ewen, D. Famous modern conductors
    p140-48 **920**
Mabinogion
  Bulfinch, T. Bulfinch's Mythology v2 **291**
McAdam, E. L.
  (ed.) Johnson, S. Johnson's Dictionary
    423
McAllister, Bruce
  Benji's pencil
  In The Best from Fantasy and Science
    Fiction; 19th ser. p273-83 **S C**
McAllister, Mariana K.
  (jt. auth.) Pilgrim, G. H. Books, young
    people, and reading guidance **028.5**
MacArthur, Douglas
  Reminiscences **92**
  About
  Gunther, J. The riddle of MacArthur **92**
  See also pages in the following book:
  Reeder, R. The story of the Second World
    War v2 p179-90 **940.53**

Macauley, Edward
  See pages in the following book:
  Padwe, S. Basketball's Hall of Fame p71-
    79 **920**
Macauley, Pauline
  Monica
  In Richards, S. ed. Best short plays of
    the world theatre, 1958-1967 p187-
    99 **808.82**
McAuliff, John Francis
  See pages in the following book:
  Lukas, J. A. Don't shoot—we are your
    children! p261-96 **301.43**
McCall's
  McCall's Cook book **641.5**
  McCall's Sewing book **646.4**
McCart, Samuel W.
  Trial by jury **347.9**
McCarthy, Eugene J.
  The year of the people **329**
McCarthy, Joe
  Ireland **914.15**
  New England **917.4**
  (jt. auth.) Furnas, C. C. The engineer **620**
McCarthy, Joseph Raymond
  Matusow, A. J. ed. Joseph R. McCarthy
    92
  See also pages in the following books:
  Friendly, F. W. Due to circumstances
    beyond our control p23-67 **384.55**
  Shannon, W. V. The American Irish p367-
    91 **301.453**
McCarthy, Mary
  Ask me no questions
  In Costain, T. B. ed. Read with me p345-
    81 **S C**
  In The New Yorker. Stories from The
    New Yorker; 1950-1960 p353-91
    S C
  The hounds of summer
  In Abrahams, W. ed. Fifty years of the
    American short story v 1 p450-84
    S C
  About
  See pages in the following book:
  Auchincloss, L. Pioneers & caretakers
    p170-86 **813.09**
McCarthy, Stephen R.
  Ordeal above Tesi Lapcha
  In Sports Illustrated. The wonderful
    world of sport p282-84 **796**
McClellan, George Brinton
  Catton, B. Mr Lincoln's army **973.7**
  See also pages in the following book:
  Stone, I. They also ran p159-74 **920**
McClellan, Grant S.
  (ed.) Censorship in the United States
    323.44
  (ed.) Civil rights **323.4**
  (ed.) The consuming public **339.4**
  (ed.) Land use in the United States **333**
  (ed.) Protecting our environment **614**
MacCloskey, Monro
  North Atlantic Treaty Organization **341.18**
McCloy, Helen
  Chinoiserie
  In Hitchcock, A. ed. Alfred Hitchcock
    presents: A month of mystery
    p377-400 **S C**

McClung, Robert M.
Lost wild America   333.7
McCord, Jean
Little dog lost
In Seventeen. Seventeen from Seventeen p215-24   **S C**
McCoy, George Walter
See pages in the following book:
De Kruif, P. Men against death p176-203
    920
McCullers, Carson
The heart is a lonely hunter   Fic
The jockey
In Abrahams, W. ed. Fifty years of the American short story v 1 p485-89
    S C
The member of the wedding   Fic
The member of the wedding; play
In Gassner, J. ed. Best American plays; 3d ser. p171-203   812.08
Sucker
In The Best American short stories, 1964 p217-26   **S C**
In The Saturday Evening Post. Best modern short stories p128-37 **S C**
About
See pages in the following book:
Auchincloss, L. Pioneers & caretakers p161-69   813.09
McCulloch v. Maryland
See pages in the following book:
Fribourg, M. G. The Supreme Court in American history p30-44   347.9
McCully, Helen
(ed.) American Heritage. The American Heritage cookbook   641.5
MacDiarmid, Hugh
See pages in the following book:
Daiches, D. More literary essays p184-210
    820.9
McDonagh, Don
The rise and fall and rise of modern dance
    793.3
Macdonagh, Donagh
"All the sweet butter-milk . . ."
In Garrity, D. A. ed. 44 Irish short stories p166-75   **S C**
Duet for organ and strings
In Garrity, D. A. ed. 44 Irish short stories p176-83   **S C**
Macdonald, Dwight
(ed.) Poe, E. A. Poems of Edgar Allan Poe   811
Macdonald, Flora (Macdonald)
Vining, E. G. Flora: a biography   92
MacDonald, John D.
The legend of Joe Lee
In Hitchcock, A. ed. Alfred Hitchcock presents: A month of mystery p317-29   **S C**
Macdonald, Ross
The singing pigeon
In Hitchcock, A. ed. Alfred Hitchcock presents: A month of mystery p157-90   **S C**
McDougal. Brown, F. L.
In Margolies, E. A native son's reader p287-89   810.8

McDowell, Bart
Gypsies: wanderers of the world   397
The Revolutionary War   973.3
Macedonia
See pages in the following book:
Falls, C. B. The first 3000 years: ancient civilizations of the Tigris, Euphrates, and Nile River valleys, and the Mediterranean Sea p165-76   913.03
Macedonians
See pages in the following book:
Asimov, I. The Near East p141-59   939
MacEoin, Gary
Colombia and Venezuela and the Guianas
    918
McEwan, P. J. M.
(comp.) Twentieth century Africa   960
McFadden, Judith Nies
(jt. ed.) Knoll, E. ed. American militarism, 1970   355.03
(jt. ed.) Knoll, E. ed. War crimes and the American conscience   959.7
McFarland, John W.
(ed.) Plutarch. Lives from Plutarch. Abridged   920
McGaffin, William
Anything but the truth   071
McGee, John M.
See pages in the following book:
Proxmire, W. Report from wasteland p25-34   353.6
McGill, Ralph
The South and the Southerner   917.5
McGinley, Phyllis
Love letters of Phyllis McGinley   811
Sixpence in her shoe   818
Times three   811
A wreath of Christmas legends   811
McGraw-Hill Basic bibliography of science and technology   016.5
The **McGraw-Hill Dictionary of modern economics**   330.3
McGraw-Hill Encyclopedia of science and technology   503
The **McGraw-Hill Encyclopedia of space**
    629.403
McGraw-Hill Modern men of science 920.03
McGraw-Hill Yearbook of science and technology. See McGraw-Hill Encyclopedia of science and technology   503
McGregor, Matthew W.
Porkchops with whiskey and ice cream
In The Best American short stories, 1969 p148-65   **S C**
MacGrian, Michael
Myself and a rabbit
In Garrity, D. A. ed. 44 Irish short stories p184-88   **S C**
Machado y Ruiz, Antonio
Lewis, R. ed. Still waters of the air 861.08
McHarb, Ian L.
Design with nature   711
Machiavelli, Niccolò
The prince   320
The prince; criticism
In Downs, R. B. Books that changed the world p17-27   809
About
See pages in the following book:
Horizon Magazine. The Horizon Book of the Renaissance p56-67   940.2

Machinal. Treadwell, S.
In Gassner, J. ed. Twenty-five best plays of the modern American theatre; early ser. p495-529   812.08

Machine shop. Black, P. O.
In Black, P. O. Audels Machinists library v2   621.9

Machine shop practice
Black, P. O. Audels Machinists library   621.09

Machine shops
    See pages in the following book:
Thompson, H. The age of invention p175-93   608

The machine that won the war. Asimov, I.
In Asimov, I. Nightfall, and other stories p322-27   S C

Machine tools
Black, P. O. Audels Machinists library   621.09

Machinery
O'Brien, R. Machines   621.9
Sterland, E. G. Energy into power   621
    See also pages in the following books ·
Asimov, I. The new intelligent man's guide to science p344-87   500
Cooper, M. The inventions of Leonardo da Vinci p70-89   608
    See also Agricultural machinery; Inventions

    Handbooks, manuals, etc.
Black, P. O. Audels Machinists library   621.9

Machinery in industry. See Automation

Machines. See Machinery

Machines in medicine. Longmore, D.   610

Machinists library, Audels. Black, P. O.   621.9

Machu Picchu, Peru
Bingham, H. Lost city of the Incas 913.85
    See also pages in the following books:
Ceram, C. W. ed. Hands on the past p366-72   913.03
National Geographic Society. Great adventures with National Geographic p151-63   910.9

MacInnes, Colin
Australia and New Zealand   919.4

MacInnes, Helen
Above suspicion   Fic
A confusion of Celts
In Dulles, A. ed. Great spy stories from fiction p277-85   S C
Home is the hunter   812
The Salzburg connection   Fic

McKay, Claude
Truant
In Clarke, J. H. ed. American Negro short stories p41-54   S C

MacKaye, Percy
The scarecrow
In Dickinson, T. H. ed. Chief contemporary dramatists [1st ser] p357-93   808.82
In Gassner, J. ed. Best plays of the early American theatre p677-716   812.08
In Quinn, A. H. ed. Representative American plays p807-44   812.08

MacKaye, Steele
Hazel Kirke
In Quinn, A. H. Representative American plays p432-71   812.08

McKechnie, Jean L.
(ed.) Webster's New twentieth century dictionary of the English language, unabridged. See Webster's New twentieth century dictionary of the English language, unabridged   423

McKelway, St Clair
First marriage
In The New Yorker. Stories from The New Yorker, 1950-1960 p748-54   S C

McKendrick, Melveena
Horizon Magazine. Ferdinand and Isabella   946

McKenna, Richard
The sons of Martha
In The Best American short stories, 1968 p215-33   S C

McKenney, Ruth
My sister Eileen   817

McKenny, Margaret
(jt. auth.) Peterson, R. T. A field guide to wildflowers of northeastern and north-central North America   582

Mackenzie, Sir Alexander
    See pages in the following book:
Stefánsson, V. ed. Great adventures and explorations p323-84   910.9

Mackenzie, Sir Compton
The recruitment of Major Blenkinsop
In Dulles, A. ed. Great spy stories from fiction p413-21   S C

McKimmey, James
Runners in the park
In Best detective stories of the year [1969] p196-211   S C

Mackinac Island
    Fiction
Fuller, I. The loon feather   Fic

Mackinder, Sir Halford John
The geographical pivot of history; criticism
In Downs, R. B. Books that changed the world p107-17   809

McKinley, William, President U.S.
    See pages in the following books:
Abels, J. The degeneration of our Presidential election p242-48   329
American Heritage. The nineties p30-35, 130-38   917.3
Lord, W. The good years p41-66   973.91

McKinley, Mount
    See pages in the following book:
Ullman, J. R. The age of mountaineering p100-16   796.5
    See also Mount McKinley National Park

McKown, Robin
Lumumba   92

McKuen, Rod
Lonesome cities   811

McLaverty, Michael
Father Christmas
In Garrity, D. A. ed. 44 Irish short stories p194-205   S C

McLaverty, Michael—*Continued*
The wild duck's nest
In Garrity, D. A. ed. 44 Irish short
stories p189-93 **S C**
MacLean, Alistair
The guns of Navarone **Fic**
H.M.S. Ulysses **Fic**
Ice Station Zebra **Fic**
Night without end **Fic**
MacLean, Katherine
Pictures don't lie
In Conklin, G. ed. Invaders of earth
p311-29 **S C**
MacLeish, Archibald
Act five
In MacLeish, A. Collected poems, 1917-
1952 p349-69 **811**
Collected poems, 1917-1952 **811**
Colloquy for the states
In MacLeish, A. Collected poems, 1917-
1952 p343-47 **811**
Conquistador
In MacLeish, A. Collected poems, 1917-
1952 p233-326 **811**
A continuing journey **818**
Einstein
In MacLeish, A. Collected poems, 1917-
1952 p225-32 **811**
The Eleanor Roosevelt story **92**
Elpenor
In MacLeish, A. Collected poems, 1917-
1952 p327-41 **811**
The fall of the city
In Gassner, J. ed. Twenty best plays of
the modern American theatre p764-
74 **812.08**
The Hamlet of A. MacLeish
In MacLeish, A. Collected poems, 1917-
1952 p199-223 **811**
J. B.
In Gassner, J. ed. Best American plays;
5th ser. p589-633 **812.08**
Poetry and experience **809.1**
The pot of earth
In MacLeish, A. Collected poems, 1917-
1952 p179-97 **811**
The Trojan horse; play
In MacLeish, A. Collected poems, 1917-
1952 p371-407 **811**
MacLeod, Alistair
The boat
In The Best American short stories,
1969 p98-116 **S C**
McLuhan, Herbert Marshall. See McLuhan,
Marshall
McLuhan, Marshall
Counterblast **001.5**
Culture is our business **301.2**
About
Miller, J. Marshall McLuhan **001.5**
MacMahon, Bryan
The cat and the cornfield
In Garrity, D. A. ed. 44 Irish short
stories p218-26 **S C**
The plain people of England
In Garrity, D. A. ed. 44 Irish short
stories p206-17 **S C**
The Macmillan Book of proverbs, maxims,
and famous phrases **398.9**

The Macmillan Wild flower book **582**
McMorrin, Ian
(jt. ed.) Noyce, W. ed. World atlas of
mountaineering **796.5**
McNally, Terrence
Bringing it all back home
In The Best short plays, 1969 p79-105
808.82
Next
In The Best short plays, 1970 p3-26
808.82
McNamara, Robert Strange
See pages in the following book:
Proxmire, W. Report from wasteland
p124-33 **353.6**
McNear, Robert
Death's door
In Best detective stories of the year
[1969] p83-106 **S C**
McNeely, Marian Hurd
In the storm country
In Becker, M. L. ed. The home book of
Christmas p259-77 **394.26**
McNeil, Elton B.
(jt. auth.) Fader, D. N. Hooked on books:
program & proof **028.5**
McNeill, William H.
A world history **901.9**
McNulty, Faith
The whooping crane **598**
MacPhee, A. Marshall
Kenya **967.6**
McPherson, Aimee Semple
See pages in the following book:
Leighton, I. ed. The aspirin age, 1919-1941
p50-80 **917.3**
McPherson, James Alan
Gold Coast
In The Best American short stories, 1969
p166-84 **S C**
Of cabbages and kings
In Prize stories, 1970: The O. Henry
Awards p237-51 **S C**
MacQueen, John
(ed.) The Oxford Book of Scottish verse.
See The Oxford Book of Scottish verse
821.08
McQueston, Jack. See McQueston, Leroy
Napoleon
McQueston, Leroy Napoleon
See pages in the following book:
Mathews, R. The Yukon p83-97 **979.8**
Macramé
Andes, E. Practical macramé **746.4**
McWhirter, Norris
(ed.) Guinness Book of world records. See
Guinness Book of world records **032**
The **McWilliamses** and the burglar alarm.
Twain, M.
In Twain, M. The complete short stories
of Mark Twain p193-98 **S C**
Macy, Anne (Sullivan)
Keller, H. Teacher: Anne Sullivan Macy
92
Waite, H. E. Valiant companions: Helen
Keller and Anne Sullivan Macy **92**
See also pages in the following book:
Stoddard, H. Famous American women
p234-44 **920**

The **magic** bullet. Hoch, E. D.
  In Best detective stories of the year
    [1969] p230-45   **S C**

The **magic** calabash. Armstrong, R.
  In Armstrong, R. ed. Treasure and trea-
    sure hunters p83-95   **910.4**

Magic, inc. Heinlein, R. A.
  In Heinlein, R. A. Three by Heinlein
    p327-426   **Fic**

Magic, Man, myth and. Boyd, M.   **133.4**

The **magic** mountain. Mann, T.   **Fic**

The **magic** of Shirley Jackson. Jackson, S.
        818

The **magic** poker. Coover, R.
  In The Best American short stories,
    1970 p53-73   **S C**

The **magic** realists. Terry, M.
  In The Best short plays, 1968 p327-59
        808.82

The **magic** shop. Wells, H. G.
  In Wells, H. G. The complete short
    stories of H. G. Wells p848-59 **S C**
  In Wells, H. G. 28 science fiction stories
    p821-32   **S C**

The **Magician** of Lublin. Singer, I. B.
  In Singer, I. B. An Isaac Bashevis Sing-
    er reader p317-560   **S C**

Magill, Frank N.
  (ed.) Cyclopedia of literary characters 803
  (ed.) Cyclopedia of world authors 920.03
  (ed.) Magill's Quotations in context [1st-
    2d ser]   **808.88**
  (ed.) Masterpieces of world literature in
    digest form [1st-4th ser]   **808.8**
  (ed.) Masterpieces of world philosophy in
    summary form   **108**

Magmer, James
  Photograph & printed word   **371.89**

Magnesium
  See pages in the following books:
  Asimov, I. Building blocks of the universe
    p173-83   **546**
  Snively, W. D. The sea of life p101-12 **612**

Magnetic recording for the hobbyist. See
  Zuckerman, A. Tape recording for the
  hobbyist   **621.389**

Magnetic tape and wire recorders. See Tape
  and wire recorders

Magnetism
  Bitter, F. Magnets: the education of a
    physicist   **538**
  See also pages in the following books:
  Chapman, S. IGY: year of discovery p76-
    82   **551**
  United Nations Educational, Scientific and
    Cultural Organization. 700 science ex-
    periments for everyone p156-63   **507.2**
    See also Electromagnetism

Magnetism. Fitzgerald, F. S.
  In Costain, T. B. ed. Read with me
    p187-208   **S C**
  In Fitzgerald, F. S. The stories of F.
    Scott Fitzgerald p220-39   **S C**

Magnets: the education of a physicist. Bitter, F.   **538**

The **magnificient** century. Costain, T. B.
        942.03

Magsaysay, Ramón, President Philippines
  See pages in the following book:
  Kenworthy, L. S. Leaders of new nations
    p336-60   **920**

Mah jong
  See pages in the following book:
  Gibson, W. Family games America plays
    p266-75   **793**

Mahan, Alfred Thayer
  The influence of sea power upon history;
    criticism
  In Downs, R. B. Books that changed the
    world p97-107   **809**
  The influence of sea power upon history,
    1660-1783; criticism
  In Downs, R. B. Books that changed
    America p110-21   **810.9**

Mahatma Gandhi. See Gandhi, Mohandas
  Karamchand

Mahler, Gustav
  See also pages in the following book:
  Cross, M. The Milton Cross New ency-
    clopedia of the great composers and their
    music p561-76   **920.03**
  Ewen, D. ed. The world of great com-
    posers p459-72   **920**

Mahoney, Tom
  The great merchants   **658.87**

Maia, C. Vasconcelos
  Sun
  In Cohen, J. M. ed. Latin American
    writing today p219-32   **860.8**

The **maiden** voyage. Marcus, G.   **910.4**

Maigret and the reluctant witnesses. Simenon, G.
  In Simenon, G. Five times Maigret p323-
    421   **Fic**

Maigret goes to school. Simenon, G.
  In Simenon, G. Five times Maigret p424-
    525   **Fic**

Maigret has scruples. Simenon, G.
  In Simenon, G. Five times Maigret p223-
    320   **Fic**

Maigret in Montmarte. Simenon, G.
  In Simenon, G. Five times Maigret p9-
    116   **Fic**

A **Maigret** omnibus. See Simenon, G. Five
  times Maigret   **Fic**

Maigret's Christmas. Simenon, G.
  In Haycraft, H. ed. A treasury of great
    mysteries v 1 p201-40   **S C**

Maigret's mistake. Simenon, G
  In Simenon, G. Five times Maigret p117-
    219   **Fic**

Mail service. See Postal service

Mailer, Norman
  The naked and the dead   **Fic**
  Of a fire on the moon   **629.45**

Mailliard, Anne Eliza (Ward)
  Tharp, L. H. Three saints and a sinner:
    Julia Ward Howe, Louisa, Annie, and
    Sam Ward   **920**

Maimon, Solomon
  See pages in the following book:
  David, J. ed. Growing up Jewish p23-38
        920

Main currents in American thought. Parrington, V. L.   **810.9**

Main currents of American thought. Shaw, I.
In Havighurst, W. ed. Masters of the modern short story p428-37 **S C**

Main Street. Lewis, S.
In Lewis, S. Lewis at zenith p 1-335 **Fic**

Maine
Description and travel
See pages in the following book:
National Geographic Society. Vacationland U.S.A. p26-41 **917.3**

Fiction
Chase, M. E. The edge of darkness **Fic**
Jewett, S. O. The country of the pointed firs **Fic**

Mainstreams of modern art: David to Picasso. Canaday, J. **709.03**

Maize. See Corn

The **majesty** of the law. O'Connor, F.
In Garrity, D. A. ed. 44 Irish short stories p261-70 **S C**

Major Barbara. Shaw, B.
In Bentley, E. comp. The great playwrights v2 p1643-1725 **808.82**
In Block, H. M. ed. Masters of modern drama p361-96 **808.82**
In Shaw, B. Bernard Shaw's plays p 1-73 **822**
In Shaw, B. Complete plays, with prefaces v 1 p341-446 **822**
In Shaw, B. Saint Joan, Major Barbara, Androcles and the lion p173-322 **822**

Major Burl. Schaefer, J.
In Schaefer, J. The collected stories of Jack Schaefer p 1-17 **S C**

The **major** poets: English and American. Coffin, C. M. ed. **821.08**

The **major** young poets. Lee, A. ed. **811.08**

Make-up (Cosmetics) See Cosmetics

Make-up, Theatrical
Corson, R. Stage makeup **792**

Makeba, Miriam
(ed.) The world of African song **784.4**

The **maker.** Borges, J. L.
In Borges, J. L. The Aleph, and other stories, 1933-1969 p155-57 **S C**

The **maker** of dreams. Down, O.
In Cerf, B. ed. 24 favorite one-act plays p256-71 **808.82**

Makers of a new nation. Bassett, J. S.
In Pageant of America v9 **973**

Makers of Latin America. Worcester, D. E. **920**

Makers of the modern world. Untermeyer, L. **920**

Makes the whole world kin. Henry, O.
In Henry, O. The complete works of O. Henry p847-50 **S C**

Making an orator. Crane, S.
In Crane, S. The complete short stories & sketches of Stephen Crane p625-29 **S C**

Making mobiles. Moorey, A. **731**

Making movies: student films to features. Colman, H. **791.43**

The **making** of a counter culture. Roszak, T. **301.2**

The **making** of a nation: 1775-1789. Morris, R. B.
In Life (Periodical) The Life History of the United States v2 **973**

The **making** of a New Yorker. Henry, O.
In Henry, O. The best short stories of O. Henry p282-88 **S C**
In Henry, O. The complete works of O. Henry p1411-15 **S C**

The **making** of a surgeon. Nolen, W. A. **617**

The **making** of an American. Riis, J. A. **92**

The **making** of the American party system, 1789-1809. Cunningham, N. E. ed. **329**

The **making** of the American theatre. Taubman, H. **792.09**

Making of the Nation, The American Heritage History of the. American Heritage **973**

The **making** of the President, 1960. White, T. H. **329**

The **making** of the President, 1964. White, T. H. **329**

The **making** of the President, 1968. White, T. H. **329**

Making posters. Mills, V. **741.67**

Makowsky, Lucile
The new world
In The Best short plays of 1957-1958 p255-79 **808.82**

Malamud, Bernard
The assistant **Fic**
The fixer **Fic**
The German refugee
In The Best American short stories, 1964 p203-15 **S C**
The magic barrel
In Foley, M. ed. Fifty best American short stories, 1915-1965 p508-23 **S C**
Man in the drawer
In Abrahams, W. ed. Fifty years of the American short story v 1 p412-49 **S C**
My son the murderer
In Prize stories, 1970: The O. Henry Awards p127-33 **S C**
Pictures of Fidelman
In The Best American short stories, 1969 p129-47 **S C**
The refugee
In The Saturday Evening Post. Best modern short stories p52-63 **S C**
About
Richman, S. Bernard Malamud **813.09**

Malaya
History
Gullic, J. M. Malaysia **959.5**

Malaysia
Politics and government
Gullic, J. M. Malaysia **959.5**
See also pages in the following book:
Kenworthy, L. S. Leaders of new nations p290-309 **920**

Malcolm X
The autobiography of Malcolm X **301.451**
About
Clarke, J. H. ed. Malcolm X **301.451**
See also pages in the following books:
Bontemps, A. Anyplace but here p230-44 **301.451**

Man in the moon. Norton, H.
In Conklin, G. ed. Invaders of earth
p301-10 **S C**

Man in the passage. Chesterton, G. K.
In Chesterton, G. K. The Father Brown
omnibus p280-97 **S C**

The Man in the Rorschach Shirt. Bradbury, R.
In Bradbury, R. I sing the Body Electric! p241-53 **S C**

Man must speak. Gallant, R. A. **410**

Man, myth and magic. Boyd, M. **133.4**

The man of destiny. Shaw, B.
In Shaw, B. Complete plays, with prefaces v 1 p697-745 **822**

A man of ideas. Anderson, S.
In Anderson, S. Winesburg, Ohio (Modern Lib) p110-22 **S C**
In Anderson, S. Winesburg, Ohio (Viking) p103-11 **S C**

Man of La Mancha. Wasserman, D. **812**

The man of property. Galsworthy, J.
In Galsworthy, J. The Forsyte saga p3-309 **Fic**

The man of the crowd. Poe, E. A.
In Poe, E. A. The complete tales and
poems of Edgar Allan Poe p475-81 **S C**
In Poe, E. A. Edgar Allan Poe p107-18 **S C**
In Poe, E. A. Selected poetry and prose
p154-62 **818**

Man of the family. Moody, R. **92**

The man of the world. O'Connor, F.
In The New Yorker. Stories from The
New Yorker, 1950-1960 p 1-7 **S C**

Man of tomorrow
In Encyclopedia of the life sciences v8 **574.03**

The man on the threshold. Borges, J. L.
In Borges, J. L. The Aleph, and other
stories, 1933-1969 p129-35 **S C**

The man that corrupted Hadleyburg. Twain, M.
In Twain, M. The complete short stories
of Mark Twain p349-90 **S C**

Man that was used up. Poe, E. A.
In Poe, E. A. The complete tales and
poems of Edgar Allan Poe p405-12 **S C**

Man, time, and fossils. Moore, R. **573.2**

The man who came back. Singer, I. B.
In Singer, I. B. An Isaac Bashevis Singer reader p105-17 **S C**

The man who came to dinner. Kaufman, G. S.
In Gassner, J. ed. Best plays of the
modern American theatre; 2d ser.
p317-64 **812.08**
In Six modern American plays p117-97 **812.08**

The man who could work miracles. Wells, H. G.
In Wells, H. G. The complete short
stories of H. G. Wells p807-25 **S C**
In Wells, H. G. 28 science fiction stories
p692-710 **S C**

The man who died twice. Robinson, E. A.
In Robinson, E. A. The collected poems
of Edwin Arlington Robinson p921-57 **811**

The man who explained miracles. Dickson, C.
In Haycraft, H. ed. A treasury of great
mysteries v2 p265-300 **S C**

The man who invented sin. O'Faoláin, S.
In Havighurst, W. ed. Masters of the
modern short story p415-27 **S C**

The man who killed sailors. Davidson, A.
In Best detective stories of the year
[1969] p32-77 **S C**

The man who learned loving. Sturgeon, T.
In The Best from Fantasy and Science
Fiction; 19th ser. p213-22 **S C**

The man who loved God. Kafka, S.
In The Best short plays, 1968 p361-88 **808.82**

Man who married a dumb wife. France, A.
In Cerf, B. ed. Thirty famous one-act
plays p5-24 **808.82**

The man who never was. Montagu, E. **940.54**

The man who put up at Gadsby's. Twain, M.
In Twain, M. The complete short stories
of Mark Twain p149-53 **S C**

The man who saw through heaven. Steele, W. D.
In Abrahams, W. ed. Fifty years of the
American short story v2 p320-36 **S C**

The man who sold the Moon. Heinlein, R. A.
In Heinlein, R. A. Robert A. Heinlein's
The past through tomorrow p98-172 **S C**

The man who talked with books. Lewis, L.
In Mystery Writers of America. Crime
without murder p173-76 **S C**

The man who was. Kipling, R.
In Costain, T. B. ed. Read with me p321-34 **S C**
In Kipling, R. Maugham's Choice of
Kipling's best p26-37 **S C**

The man who was Don Quixote; the story
of Miguel Cervantes [Saavedra]. Busoni, R. **92**

The man who was Sherlock Holmes [biography of Sir Arthur Conan Doyle].
Hardwick, M. **92**

The man who would be king. Kipling, R.
In Kipling, R. The best short stories
of Rudyard Kipling p128-54 **S C**
In Kipling, R. Maugham's Choice of
Kipling's best p162-92 **S C**

The man with the gash. London, J.
In London, J. Jack London's Tales of
adventure **S C**

The man with the twisted lip. Doyle, Sir A. C.
In Doyle, Sir A. C. The complete Sherlock Holmes v 1 p258-76 **S C**

Man with two beards. Chesterton, G. K.
In Chesterton, G. K. The Father Brown
omnibus p663-83 **S C**

The man without a temperament. Mansfield, K.
In Mansfield, K. The short stories of
Katherine Mansfield p412-25 **S C**

Manacled. Crane, S.
In Crane, S. The complete short stories & sketches of Stephen Crane p762-64   **S C**

Management
Townsend, R. Up the organization **658.4**
See also pages in the following book:
Diebold, J. Man and the computer p107-27   **301.24**

See also Office management

Anecdotes, facetiae, satire, etc.
Peter, L. J. The Peter Principle   **817**

Dictionaries
Pugh, E. A dictionary of acronyms & abbreviations   **603**

Manchester, William
The death of a President, November 20-November 25, 1963 [biography of John Fitzgerald Kennedy]   **92**
Portrait of a President; John F. Kennedy in profile   **92**

Manchild in the promised land. Brown, C.   **92**

Mancini, Henry
See pages in the following book:
Ewen, D. Great men of American popular song p340-46   **920**

Mandala. Buck, P. S.   **Fic**

Mandate for change, 1953-1956. Eisenhower, D. D.
In Eisenhower, D. D. The White House years v 1   **92**

Mandelstam, Osip
Fourth prose
In Scammell, M. ed. Russia's other writers p130-45   **S C**

Manet, Édouard
Schneider, P. The world of Manet, 1832-1883   **92**
See also pages in the following books:
Cheney, S. The story of modern art p132-43   **709.03**
Ruskin, A. Nineteenth century art p100-06   **709.03**

Manhoff, Bill
The owl and the pussycat
In Gassner, J. ed. Best American plays; 6th ser. p495-525   **812.08**

Manila Bay, Battle of, 1898
See pages in the following book:
Armstrong, O. K. The fifteen decisive battles of the United States p251-69 **973**

Mann, Horace
See pages in the following book:
Downs, R. B. Books that changed America p57-68   **810.9**

Mann, Mary Tyler (Peabody)
Tharp, L. H. The Peabody sisters of Salem   **920**

Mann, Matt
Sports Illustrated. Sports Illustrated Book of swimming   **797.2**

Mann, Peggy
Golda [biography of Golda Meir]   **92**

Mann, Thomas
Buddenbrooks   **Fic**
Doctor Faustus   **Fic**
Joseph and his brothers   **Fic**
Joseph in Egypt
In Mann, T. Joseph and his brothers p447-840   **Fic**
Joseph the provider
In Mann, T. Joseph and his brothers p843-1207   **Fic**
The magic mountain   **Fic**
The tales of Jacob
In Mann, T. Joseph and his brothers p3-258   **Fic**
Young Joseph
In Mann, T. Joseph and his brothers p261-444   **Fic**
About
See pages in the following books:
Durant, W. Interpretations of life p219-56   **809**
Untermeyer, L. Makers of the modern world p506-13   **920**

Manned space flight
Clarke, A. C. Man and space   **629.4**
Gagarin, Y. Survival in space   **629.45**
Sharpe, M. R. Living in space   **629.45**
Shelton, W. R. Man's conquest of space   **629.4**
We seven   **629.45**
See also pages in the following book:
Von Braun, W. History of rocketry & space travel p202-22   **629.409**
See also Outer space—Exploration

The **manner** of men. Kipling, R.
In Kipling, R. The best short stories of Rudyard Kipling p651-63   **S C**

Mannerism (Art)
See pages in the following book:
Janson, H. W. History of art p374-87 **709**

Manners, Margaret
The plot
In Mystery Writers of America. Crime without murder p177-85   **S C**

Manners. See Etiquette

Manners and customs
Krythe, M. R. All about the months **394.2**
See also Caste; Costume; Etiquette; Rites and ceremonies; Social classes; also names of countries with the subdivision Social life and customs, e.g. United States—Social life and customs

Mannix, Dan
The last eagle   **598**

Man's best friend. National Geographic Society   **636.7**

Man's conquest of space. Shelton, W. R.   **629.4**

Man's fate. Malraux, A.   **Fic**

Mansa Musa I, Emperor of Mali
See pages in the following book:
Polatnick, F. T. Shapers of Africa p13-38   **920**

Mansbridge, John
Graphic history of architecture   **720.9**

Mansfield, Katherine
The short stories of Katherine Mansfield   **S C**
Contents: The tiredness of Rosabel; How Pearl Button was kidnapped; The journey to Bruges; A truthful adventure; New dresses; Germans at meat; The Baron; The sister of the Baroness; Frau Fischer; Frau Brechenmacher

March, William
The little wife
 In Foley, M. ed. Fifty best American
 short stories, 1915-1965 p87-97 **S C**
The **march** of archaeology. Ceram, C. W.
 913.03
March of commerce. Keir, M.
 In Pageant of America v4 **973**
The **march** of democracy. Adams, J. T. **973**
March 2000: the taxpayer. Bradbury, R.
 In Bradbury, R. The Martian chronicles
 p47-48 **S C**
Marchand, Leslie A.
Byron **92**
Marches for civil rights. See Negroes—Civil
 rights
"Marco Millions." O'Neill, E.
 In O'Neill, E. Nine plays p211-304 **812**
 In O'Neill, E. Plays v2 p347-439 **812**
Marconi, Guglielmo, marchese
 See pages in the following book:
Untermeyer, L. Makers of the modern
 world p478-83 **920**
Marcus, Frank
The killing of Sister George
 In Richards, S. ed. Best plays of the
 sixties p623-711 **808.82**
The window
 In Richards, S. ed. Best short plays of
 the world theatre, 1958-1967 p201-
 12 **808.82**
Marcus, Geoffrey
The maiden voyage **910.4**
Marcus Antonius. See Antony, Marc
Marcus Aurelius. See Aurelius Antoninus,
 Marcus, Emperor of Rome
Marcuse, Herbert
 See pages in the following book:
Roszak, T. The making of a counter cul-
 ture p84-123 **301.24**
Mare, Walter de la. See De La Mare, Walter
Marek, George R.
Beethoven, biography of a genius **92**
Marek, Kurt Wilhelm. See Ceram, C. W.
Margaret Fleming. Herne, J. A.
 In Quinn, A. H. ed. Representative
 American plays p513-44 **812.08**
Margolies, Edward
Native sons **810.9**
(ed.) A native sons reader **810.8**
Margolis, Adele P.
How to make clothes that fit and flatter
 646.4
Maria Chapdelaine. Hémon, L. **Fic**
Maria Concepción. Porter, K. A.
 In Porter, K. A. The collected stories
 of Katherine Anne Porter p3-21
 S C
Maria Theresa, Empress of Austria
 See pages in the following book:
Trease, G. Seven sovereign queens p125-
 48 **920**
Mariánské Lázne, Czechoslovak Republic
 See pages in the following book:
Twain, M. The complete essays of Mark
 Twain p99-109 **814**

Marie-Antoinette, consort of Louis XVI,
 King of France
 See pages in the following book:
Levron, J. Daily life at Versailles in the
 seventeenth and eighteenth centuries
 p204-11 **914.43**
 Fiction
Holt, V. The Queen's confession **Fic**
Marienbad. See Mariánské Lázne, Czecho-
 slovak Republic
Marihuana
Grinspoon, L. Marihuana reconsidered
 613.8
Oursler, W. Marijuana: the facts, the
 truth **613.8**
Steinbeck, J. In touch **92**
Marihuana and a pistol. Himes, C. B.
 In Hughes, L. ed. The best short sto-
 ries by Negro writers p104-06 **S C**
Marihuana reconsidered. Grinspoon, L. **613.8**
Marijuana: the facts, the truth. Oursler, W.
 613.8
Marin, Luis Muñoz
 See pages in the following book:
Alexander, R. J. Prophets of the revolu-
 tion p174-97 **920**
Marin, Peter
Understanding drug use **613.8**
Marine animals
Andersen, H. T. ed. The biology of marine
 mammals **599**
Bridges, W. The New York Aquarium
 Book of the water world **591.92**
Carson, R. Under the sea-wind **591.92**
Cousteau, J. Y. Jacques-Yves Cousteau's
 World without sun **551.4**
 See also pages in the following books:
Engel, L. The sea p15-35, 103-67 **551.4**
Fenton, C. L. The fossil book p55-244 **560**
McClung, R. M. Lost wild America p159-
 66 **333.7**
Zappler, L. The world after the dinosaurs
 p142-54 **599**
 See also Fishes
Marine biology
Carson, R. The edge of the sea **574.92**
Cousteau, J. Y. Life and death in a coral
 sea **551.4**
Cousteau, J. Y. The living sea **627.7**
Cousteau, J. Y. The silent world **627.7**
Engel, L. The sea **551.4**
 See also pages in the following books:
Freuchen, P. Peter Freuchen's Book of
 the Seven Seas p53-85 **910.4**
Halacy, D. S. Bionics p51-60 **001.5**
Scientific American. The ocean p65-79
 551.4
 See also Fresh-water biology; Marine
 animals; Marine resources; Photog-
 raphy, Submarine
Marine Corps. See United States. Marine
 Corps
Marine plants. See Algae
Marine resources
Bardach, J. Harvest of the sea **333.9**
Idyll, C. P. The sea against hunger **639**

Marriage—*Continued*

Fiction

Head, A. Mr and Mrs Bo Jo Jones   **Fic**
Lindbergh, A. M. Dearly beloved   **Fic**
Segal, E. Love story   **Fic**
Smith, B. Joy in the morning   **Fic**

Marriage, Mixed
Pike, J. A. If you marry outside your
faith   301.42

Marriage à la mode. Mansfield, K.
In Mansfield, K. The short stories of
Katherine Mansfield p554-64   **S C**

Marriage customs and rites
Emrich, D. comp. The folklore of wed-
dings and marriage   392
Post, E. L. The wonderful world of wed-
dings   395
Wilson, B. The complete book of engage-
ment and wedding etiquette   395
See also pages in the following book:
Gies, J. Life in a medieval city p68-75
914.4

Marriage made easy. Lardner, R.
In Lardner, R. The Ring Lardner reader p461-64   **S C**

The marriage of Phaedra. Cather, W.
In Cather, W. Willa Cather's Collected
short fiction, 1892-1912 v2 p219-34
S C

A marriage proposal. Chekhov, A.
In Cerf, B. ed. 24 favorite one-act plays
p403-16   808.82

A married man's story. Mansfield, K.
In Mansfield, K. The short stories of
Katherine Mansfield p609-22   **S C**

Marriott, Alice
American Indian mythology   398.2

The marry month of May. Henry, O.
In Henry, O. The best short stories of
O. Henry p201-07   **S C**
In Henry, O. The complete works of
O. Henry p1152-56   **S C**

Mars (Planet)
See pages in the following book:
Scientific American. Frontiers in astron-
omy p48-58   520

Mars revisited. Minot, S.
In Prize stories, 1971: The O. Henry
Awards p284-99   **S C**

Marsh, Anthony
Loaded with money
In Mystery Writers of America. Crime
without murder p187-92   **S C**

Marsh, Dorothy B.
(ed.) Good Housekeeping Institute, New
York. The new Good Housekeeping
cookbook   641.5

Marsh, George Perkins
See pages in the following book:
Udall, S. L. The quiet crisis p71-82   333.7

Marsh, Irving T.
(ed.) Best sports stories. See Best sports
stories   796

Marsh, Ngaio
I can find my way out
In Haycraft, H. ed. A treasury of great
mysteries v2 p189-207   **S C**

Marsh, Robert
Agnew, the unexamined man   92

Marshall, Catherine
A man called Peter; the story of Peter
Marshall   92

Marshall, John, 1755-1835
Corwin, E. S. John Marshall and the Con-
stitution   973.4
Severn, B. John Marshall   92
See also pages in the following books:
Dictionary of American biography. The
American Plutarch p155-75   920
Habenstreit, B. Changing America and
the Supreme Court p23-35   347.9
Koch, A. ed. Jefferson p157-64   92

Marshall, Paule
Barbados
In Hughes, L. ed. The best short sto-
ries by Negro writers p309-24   **S C**
Reena
In Clarke, J. H. ed. American Negro
short stories p264-82   **S C**

Marshall, Peter
Marshall, C. A man called Peter   92

Marshall, S. L. A.
American Heritage. The American Heritage History of World War I   940.3

Marshall, Thurgood
See pages in the following book:
Metcalf, G. R. Black profiles p113-41   920

Marshall, William Martin
See pages in the following book:
Dulles, A. ed. Great true spy stories p145-
57   327

Marshall Field and Company
See pages in the following book:
Mahoney, T. The great merchants p116-
32   658.87

Marshes
See pages in the following books:
Carlquist, S. Hawaii: a natural history
p345-59   574.9
Farb, P. The land and wildlife of North
America p83-93   574.9

Martelli, George
Livingstone's river   916.7

The Martian chronicles. Bradbury, R.   **S C**

A Martian odyssey. Weinbaum, S. G.
In Asimov, I. ed. Where do we go from
here? p 1-35   **S C**

Martin, Alfred Manuel
See pages in the following book:
Mantle, M. The quality of courage p56-63
920

Martin, Billy. See Martin, Alfred Manuel

Martin, Glenn Luther
See pages in the following book:
Bonney, W. T. The heritage of Kitty
Hawk p130-40   629.13

Martin, Ralph G.
Jennie: the life of Lady Randolph Churchill   92

Martin, Terence
Nathaniel Hawthorne   813.09

Martin, William
Switzerland, from Roman times to the
present   949.4

Martin Chuzzlewit. Dickens, C.   **Fic**

Massachusetts

Description and travel

See pages in the following book:
National Geographic Society. Vacationland
U.S.A. p76-93   917.3

History—Fiction

Seton, A. The Winthrop woman   Fic

Massachusetts General Hospital, Boston
Crichton, M. Five patients   362.1

The massacre at Paris. Marlowe, C.
In Marlowe, C. The plays of Christopher
Marlowe p371-414   822

Massaro, Salvatore. See Lang, Eddie

Masselman, George
The Atlantic: sea of darkness   910.9

Massenet, Jules Émile Frédéric
See pages in the following books:
Cross, M. The Milton Cross New encyclopedia of the great composers and their music p577-84   920.03
Ewen, D. ed. The complete book of classical music p806-16   780.1
Ewen, D. ed. The world of great composers p290-302   920

Massey, Estelle. See Osborne, Estelle (Massey)

Massie, Robert K.
Nicholas [II] and Alexandra   92

Massie, Thomas H.
See pages in the following book:
Darrow, C. The story of my life p457-83   92

Master and man. Tolstoy, L.
In Tolstoy, L. Short novels v2 p272-323   S C

The master builder. Ibsen, H.
In Ibsen, H. Eleven plays of Henrik Ibsen p291-383   839.8
In Ibsen, H. Four plays of Ibsen p63-137   839.8
In Ibsen, H. Six plays p429-510   839.8

The master of Hestviken. Undset, S.   Fic

Master of the inn. Herrick, R.
In The Scribner treasury p445-70   S C

Masterpieces of Greek art. Schoder, R. V.   709.38

Masterpieces of world literature in digest form [1st-4th ser]. Magill, F. N. ed.   808.8

Masterpieces of world philosophy in summary form. Magill, F. N. ed.   108

Masterplots. See Magill, F. N. ed. Masterpieces of world literature in digest form [1st-4th ser]   808.8

Masterplots cyclopedia of literary characters. See Magill, F. N. ed. Cyclopedia of literary characters   803

Masterplots cyclopedia of world authors. See Magill, F. N. ed. Cyclopedia of world authors   920.03

Masters, Donald C.
Brebner, J. B. Canada   971

Masters, Edgar Lee
The new Spoon River   811
Spoon River anthology   811

The masters. Snow, C. P.   Fic

The Masters. Wind, H. W.
In Sports Illustrated. The wonderful world of sport p259-61   796

Masters of arts. Henry, O.
In Henry, O. The complete works of O. Henry p646-57   S C

The masters of capital. Moody, J.   332.6

Masters of deceit. Hoover, J. E.   335.4

Masters of modern drama. Block, H. M. ed.   808.82

Masters of the drama. Gassner, J.   809.2

Masters of the modern short story. Havighurst, W. ed.   S C

Mastodon
Silverberg, R. Mammoths, mastodons, and man   569

Masur, Harold Q.
Murder matinee
In Hitchcock, A. ed. Alfred Hitchcock presents: A month of mystery p258-74   S C

The match-maker. Saki
In Saki. The short stories of Saki p116-18   S C

The matchmaker. Wilder, T.
In Block, H. M. ed. Master's of modern drama p961-88   808.82
In Gassner, J. ed. Best American plays; 4th ser. p535-72   812.08
In Wilder, T. Three plays p251-401   812

Material progress and world-wide problems, 1870-1898. Hinsley, F. H. ed.
In The New Cambridge Modern history v11   909

Math menagerie. Kadesch, R. R.   793.7

Math without tears. Hartkopf, R.   510

The mathematical magpie. Fadiman, C. ed.   808.8

Mathematical models
Cundy, H. M. Mathematical models   510.78

Mathematical puzzles and pastimes. Bakst, A.   793.7

Mathematical recreations
Bakst, A. Mathematical puzzles and pastimes   793.7
Ball, W. W. R. Mathematical recreations & essays   793.7
Friend, J. N. More Numbers: fun & facts   793.7
Friend, J. N. Numbers: fun & facts   793.7
Friend, J. N. Still More Numbers: fun & facts   793.7
Gardner, M. Martin Gardner's New mathematical diversions from Scientific American   793.7
Gardner, M. The unexpected hanging, and other mathematical diversions   793.7
Kadesch, R. R. Math menagerie   793.7
Latcha, A. G. How do you figure it?   793.7
Longley-Cook, L. H. New math puzzle book   793.7
See also pages in the following book:
Newman, J. R. ed. The world of mathematics v4 p2366-2469   510.8

Mathematical recreations & essays. Ball, W. W. R.   793.7

Mathematicians
Bell, E. T. Men of mathematics   920
See also pages in the following books:
Ball, W. W. R. Mathematical recreations & essays p350-78   793.7

Mathematicians—*Continued*
Fermi, L. Illustrious immigrants p285-98
    325.73
Newman, J. R. ed. The world of mathematics v 1 p75-416   510.8

Mathematics
Adler, I. The elementary mathematics of the atom   539
Bell, E. T. Mathematics   510.9
Bergamini, D. Mathematics   510
Fadiman, C. ed. Fantasia mathematica
    808.8
Fadiman, C. ed. The mathematical magpie
    808.8
Hartkopf, R. Math without tears   510
Hogben, L. Mathematics for the million
    510
Lieber, L. R. The education of T. C. Mits
    510
Lieber, L. R. The Einstein theory of relativity   530.1
National Council of Teachers of Mathematics. Enrichment mathematics for high school   510
Newman, J. R. ed. The world of mathematics   510.8
Polya, G. How to solve it   510
    See also pages in the following book:
Newman, J. R. ed. What is science? p24-62
    508

    See also Algebra; Logic, Symbolic and mathematical; Numbers, Theory of; Probabilities

Bibliography
Deason, H. J. comp. The AAAS Science book list   016.5
Schaaf, W. L. comp. The high school mathematics library   016.51

Dictionaries
James, G. ed. James & James Mathematics dictionary   510.3
The Universal encyclopedia of mathematics   510.3

Electronic data processing
Computer science   651.8

History
Bell, E. T. Mathematics   510.9
Hogben, L. Mathematics for the million
    510
    See also pages in the following books:
Newman, J. R. ed. The world of mathematics v 1 p75-416   510.8
Sarton, G. A history of science v 1 p275-97, 431-54, 501-21, v2 p280-94   509

Study and teaching
    See pages in the following book:
Barzun, J. Teacher in America p81-87
    371.1

Tables, etc.
Barlow, P. Barlow's Tables of squares, cubes, square roots, cube roots and reciprocals of all integers, up to 12,500
    510.21
Handbook of mathematical tables   510.21
Lange, N. A. ed. Handbook of chemistry
    660.21
The Universal encyclopedia of mathematics   510.3

Mathematics dictionary, James & James. James, G. ed.   510.3
Mathematics for the million. Hogben, L. 510

Mather, Cotton
    See pages in the following book:
Porter, K. A. The collected essays and occasional writings of Katherine Anne Porter p313-51   818

Mather, Frank Jewett
American spirit in art
    In Pageant of America v12   973

Mather, Melissa
One summer in between   **Fic**

Mathews, Mitford M.
American words   427

Mathews, Richard
The Yukon   979.8

Mathieu, Aron M.
(ed.) The creative writer   808.06

Mathis, Tex.
Description
    See pages in the following book:
Moyers, B. Listening to America p223-49
    917.3

Matisse, Henri
Guichard-Meili, J. Matisse   759.4
Russell, J. The world of Matisse, 1869-1954
    92
    See also pages in the following book:
Untermeyer, L. Makers of the modern world p405-09   920

Matrimony. See Marriage

Matryona's house. Solzhenitsyn, A.
    In Solzhenitsyn, A. Stories and prose poems p3-52   **S C**

Matter
Lapp, R. E. Matter   530.4
    See also pages in the following book:
Asimov, I. Twentieth century discovery p67-100   500

A **matter** of accountability. Armbrister, T.
    327

A **matter** of fact. Kipling, R.
    In Kipling, R. The best short stories of Rudyard Kipling p196-205   **S C**

Matter of facts. Payne, L. V.
    In Seventeen. Stories from Seventeen p47-65   **S C**

A **matter** of honor. Fish, R. L.
    In Mystery Writers of America. Crime without murder p63-78   **S C**

A **matter** of mean elevation. Henry, O.
    In Henry, O. The complete works of O. Henry p1127-34   **S C**

A **matter** of pride. Hershman, M.
    In Mystery Writers of America. Crime without murder p93-95   **S C**

A **matter** of seconds. Queen, E.
    In Lardner, R. ed. Rex Lardner selects the best of sports fiction p13-21
    S C

A **matter** of sentiment. Saki
    In Saki. The short stories of Saki p227-31   **S C**

A **matter** of time. Brown, F. L.
    In Clarke, J. H. ed. American Negro short stories p245-48   **S C**

Matterhorn
   See pages in the following book:
Ullman, J. R. The age of mountaineering
   p44-64   **796.5**
Matthews, Clayton
   The big stretch
   In Best detective stories of the year,
      1971 p32-46   **S C**
   The Dummy
   In Best detective stories of the year
      [1969] p212-24   **S C**
Matthews, Herbert L.
   Fidel Castro   **92**
Matthews, Jack
   Another story
   In The Best American short stories, 1970
      p161-73   **S C**
Matthews, Leonard Harrison
   The Whale. See The Whale   **639**
Matthews, William H.
   A guide to the national parks   **917.3**
Matthias at the door. Robinson, E. A.
   In Robinson, E. A. The collected poems
     of Edwin Arlington Robinson
     p1077-1155   **811**
Matthiessen, F. O.
   (ed.) The Oxford Book of American verse.
   See The Oxford Book of American verse
                       811.08
Mattingly, Garrett
   The Armada   **942.05**
The mature mind. Overstreet, H. A.   **155.2**
Matusow, Allen J.
   (ed.) Joseph R. McCarthy   **92**
Maugham, W. Somerset
   The best short stories of W. Somerset
    Maugham   **S C**
   Contents: The letter; The verger; The vessel
of wrath; The hairless Mexican; Mr Harring-
ton's washing; Red; Mr Know-All; The alien
corn; The book-bag; The round dozen; The
voice of the turtle; The facts of life; Lord
Mountdrago; The colonel's lady; The treasure;
Rain; P. & O.
   The circle
   In Cerf, B. A. comp. Sixteen famous
     British plays p361-415   **822.08**
   Door of opportunity
   In Havighurst, W. ed. Masters of the
     modern short story p380-414 **S C**
   Giulia Lazzari
   In Dulles, A. ed. Great spy stories from
     fiction p370-96   **S C**
   The moon and sixpence   **Fic**
   Of human bondage   **Fic**
   The razor's edge   **Fic**
   (ed.) Kipling, R. Maugham's Choice of
    Kipling's best   **S C**
                About
   See pages in the following books:
   Durant, W. Interpretations of life p102-12
                       809
   Stirling, N. Who wrote the modern clas-
     sics? p9-41   **920**
Maugham's Choice of Kipling's best. Kip-
   ling, R.   **S C**
Mau Mau
   See pages in the following book:
   Beals, C. The nature of revolution p203-32
                       323

Maupassant, Guy de
   Guy de Maupassant's Short stories   **S C**
   Contents: Boule de Suif; The necklace; Ven-
detta; Fear; In the country; His son; A deal;
Madame Husson's Rose-king; The house of
Madame Tellier; The hand; Moonlight; Moham-
med-Fripouille; Miss Harriet; In the spring
Madame Parisse; Playing with fire; Love: pages
from a sportsman's diary; Mademoiselle Fifi; A
duel; St Anthony; Julie Romain; The umbrella;
Boitelle; The Devil; The olive grove; Lost at
sea; The hostelry; A portrait; Shali; Idle
beauty; An encounter; The Horla
   The odd number   **S C**
   Contents: Happiness; A coward; The wolf;
The necklace; The piece of string; La mère
Sauvage; Moonlight; The confession; On the
journey; The beggar; A ghost; Little soldier;
The wreck
   Selected short stories   **S C**
   Contents: Ball-of-Fat; The diamond neck-
lace; A piece of string; The story of a farm-
girl; Mme Tellier's excursion; A vagabond; A
Normandy joke; The father; Miss Harriet;
Bellflower; Simon's papa; Waiter; A bock;
Châli; How he got the Legion of Honor;
A crisis; Am I insane; A little walk; Moon-
light; A practical joke; Room no. eleven; The
false gems; A country excursion
Maurier, Daphne Du. See Du Maurier,
   Daphne
Maurois, André
   Alexandre Dumas   **92**
   From Proust to Camus   **840.9**
   An illustrated history of Germany   **943**
   Memoirs, 1885-1967   **92**
   Napoleon [I]   **92**
   Victor Hugo and his world   **92**
                About
   Keating, L. C. Andre Maurois   **848**
Maus, Cynthia Pearl
   (comp.) Christ and the fine arts **232.9**
Mawson, C. O. Sylvester
   The New Roget's Thesaurus of the En-
    glish language in dictionary form. See
    The New Roget's Thesaurus of the En-
    glish language in dictionary form **424**
Maximilian, Emperor of Mexico
   O'Connor, R. The cactus throne   **92**
Maximov, Vladimir
   House in the clouds
   In Scammell, M. ed. Russia's other writ-
     ers p32-114   **S C**
Maxims. See Proverbs
Maxtone Graham, Joyce Anstruther. See
   Struther, Jan
Maxwell, Gavin
   Ring of bright water   **574.9**
Maxwell, William
   The French scarecrow
   In The New Yorker. Stories from The
     New Yorker, 1950-1960 p167-79
                         S C
   Further tales about men and women
   In The Best American short stories, 1966
     p219-33   **S C**
   The gardens of Mont-Saint-Michel
   In The Best American short stories, 1970
     p174-93   **S C**
May, Emmett M.
   See pages in the following book:
   Bontemps, A. We have tomorrow p79-91
                       920

May, Ernest R.
The progressive era: 1901-1917
In Life (Periodical) The Life History of
the United States v9　　　　973
War, boom and bust: 1917-1932
In Life (Periodical) The Life History of
the United States v10　　　973

May Day. Fitzgerald, F. S.
In Fitzgerald, F. S. The Fitzgerald
reader p3-53　　　　　　　**S C**
In Fitzgerald, F. S. The stories of F.
Scott Fitzgerald p83-126　　**S C**

Mayas
Wauchope, R. ed. The Indian background
of Latin American history　　970.3
See also pages in the following books:
Baity, E. C. Americans before Columbus
p156-83　　　　　　　　970.1
Ceram, C. W. Gods, graves, and scholars
p348-416　　　　　　　913.03
Crow, J. A. The epic of Latin America
p 1-21　　　　　　　　　980
Josephy, A. M. The Indian heritage of
America p206-12　　　　　970.1
Lavine, H. Central America p24-39　917.28
Leonard, J. N. Ancient America p40-55
　　　　　　　　　　　913.7
National Geographic Society. Great ad-
ventures with National Geographic p176-
83　　　　　　　　　　910.9
Stuart, G. E. Discovering man's past in
the Americas p61-107　　　913.7
White, A. T. Lost worlds p231-97　913.03

Religion and mythology
See pages in the following books:
Larousse World mythology p473-79　291

Maybe next week. Baker, L. N.
In Seventeen. Stories from Seventeen
p99-115　　　　　　　　**S C**

Maybelle's first-born. Stuart, J.
In Stuart, J. Come back to the farm p39-
54　　　　　　　　　　**S C**

Mayer, Edwin Justus
Children of darkness
In Gassner, J. ed. Best American plays;
supplementary volume, 1918-1958
p216-51　　　　　　　812.08

Mayer, Paul Avila
The bridal night
In The Best short plays, 1968 p79-107
　　　　　　　　　　808.82

Mayer, Ralph
A dictionary of art terms and techniques
　　　　　　　　　　703

Maynard, Olga
American modern dancers: the pioneers
　　　　　　　　　　920

Mayo, Charles Horace
Clapesattle, H. The Doctors Mayo　920

Mayo, William James
Clapesattle, H. The Doctors Mayo　920

Mayo, William Worrall
Clapesattle, H. The Doctors Mayo　920

Mayo Clinic, Rochester, Minn.
Clapesattle, H. The Doctors Mayo　920

The **mayor** of Casterbridge. Hardy, T.　**Fic**

Mayorga, Margaret
(ed.) The Best short plays, 1968-1971. See
The Best short plays, 1968-1971　808.82

Mayors
Hentoff, N. A political life; the education
of John V. Lindsay　　　　92

The **Maypole** of Merry Mount. Hawthorne, N.
In Hawthorne, N. Hawthorne's Short
stories p23-33　　　　　**S C**

Mays, Willie
My secrets of playing baseball　796.357
Willie Mays: my life in and out of base-
ball　　　　　　　　　92

The **Maysville** minstrel. Lardner, R.
In Lardner, R. The best short stories
of Ring Lardner p 1-9　　**S C**
In Lardner, R. The Ring Lardner reader p78-88　　　　　　**S C**

Mazda, Maideh
In a Persian kitchen　　　　641.5

Mazor, Julian
The skylark
In Prize stories, 1971: The O. Henry
Awards p94-136　　　　**S C**

Mazzola, Francesco
See pages in the following book:
Vasari, G. The lives of the painters, sculp-
tors and architects v3 p5-14　　920

Mazzuoli, Francesco. See Mazzola, Francesco

Mboya, Tom
See pages in the following book:
Polatnick, F. T. Shapers of Africa p147-84
　　　　　　　　　　920

Me and Juliet. Hammerstein, O.
In Hammerstein, O. 6 plays p457-527
　　　　　　　　　　812

The **me** nobody knows. Joseph, S. M. ed.
　　　　　　　　　　810.8

Mead, Frank S.
Handbook of denominations in the United
States　　　　　　　　280

Mead, Margaret
Culture and commitment　　301.43
Family　　　　　　　　301.42
(ed.) The golden age of American anthropology　　　　　　　572.97
Male and female　　　　301.41
(ed.) United States. President's Commission on the Status of Women. American
women　　　　　　　301.41
About
See pages in the following book:
Stoddard, H. Famous American women
p275-86　　　　　　　920

Mead, W. R.
Finland　　　　　　　914.71

Meaddough, R. J.
The death of Tommy Grimes
In Hughes, L. ed. The best short sto-
ries by Negro writers p408-13 **S C**

Meade, Ellen
Larson, R. Young filmmakers　791.43

Meagher, Dermot
(jt. auth.) Brenner, J. H. Drugs & youth
　　　　　　　　　　613.8

Meal planning. See Menus; Nutrition

Meals for astronauts. See Astronauts—Nutrition

The **meaning** of democracy. Padover, S. K.
　　　　　　　　　　321.8

The **meaning** of Judaism. Gittelsohn, R. B.
296

The **meaning** of relativity. Einstein, A.   530.1

The **meaning** of treason. See West, R. The new meaning of treason   364.1

Means, Florence Crannel
Our cup is broken   Fic

Measuring. See Mensuration

Meat industry and trade
See pages in the following book:
Stone, A. A. Careers in agribusiness and industry p133-52   338.1

Meat inspection
See pages in the following book:
Winter, R. Poisons in your food p77-97
614

Mecarino, Domenico. See Beccafumi, Domenico

Mechanical brains. See Cybernetics; Electronic computers

Mechanical engineering. See Engines; Power (Mechanics); Steam engineering

Mechanics. See Force and energy; Motion; Wave mechanics

Mechanix Illustrated
Car care   629.28

Mecherino, Domenico. See Beccafumi, Domenico

Mechnikov, Il'ïa Il'ich
See pages in the following book:
De Kruif, P. Microbe hunters p207-33 920

Medals. See United States—Armed Forces—Medals, badges, decorations, etc.

Medary, Marjorie
Each one teach one; Frank Laubach, friend to millions   92

Medea. Euripides
In Fitts, D. ed. Greek plays in modern translation p195-240   882.08
In Oates, W. J. ed. The complete Greek drama v 1 p723-57   882.08

Medea. Jeffers, R.
In Gassner, J. ed. Best American plays; 3d ser. p395-414   812.08

Medea. Seneca
In Davenport, B. ed. The portable Roman reader p487-527   870.8

The **Medes** and Persians. Culican, W. 913.35

Medical care
Crichton, M. Five patients   362.1

Medical colleges. See Medicine—Study and teaching

Medical education. See Medicine—Study and teaching

Medical ethics
Friends, Society of. American Friends Service Committee. Who shall live?   301.3
Lasagna, L. Life, death, and the doctor
610

Medical profession. See Medicine; Medicine as a profession; Physicians

Medical technology
Longmore, D. Machines in medicine   610

Medici, Lorenzo de', il Magnifico, 1449-1492
Horizon Magazine. Lorenzo de' Medici and the Renaissance   92
See also pages in the following book:
Horizon Magazine. The Horizon Book of the Renaissance p145-52   940.2

Medici family
See pages in the following book:
National Geographic Society. The Renaissance p42-86   940.2

Medicine
Lasagna, L. Life, death, and the doctor
610
See also pages in the following books:
Boorstin, D. J. The Americans: The colonial experience p209-39   917.3
Burton, E. The pageant of Elizabethan England p164-86   914.2
Davis, W. S. A day in old Rome p160-69
913.37
Durant, W. The age of Voltaire p586-602
940.2
Encyclopedia of the life sciences v6-8
574.03
Salisbury, H. E. ed. The Soviet Union: the fifty years p323-41   914.7
Shakespeare's England v 1 p413-43   822.3
Snow, E. Red China today p270-77, 297-311   915.1
See also Medical technology; Quacks and quackery; Surgery

Automation
Longmore, D. Machines in medicine   610

Biography
See Physicians

Dictionaries
Dorland's Illustrated medical dictionary
610.3

History
De Kruif, P. Men against death   920
See also pages in the following books:
Burton, E. The pageant of Georgian England p225-67   914.2
Lee, R. V. The physician p8-37   610.69
Rowling, M. Everyday life in medieval times p175-95   914
Sarton, G. A history of science v 1 p331-91, 522-54, v2 p400-12   509
Tomkeieff, O. G. Life in Norman England p118-23   914.2
Williams, P. Life in Tudor England p100-14   914.2

Practice
See pages in the following book:
Montagu, A. The American way of life p135-43   917.3

Research
Heller, J. H. Of mice, men and molecules
619
Taylor, G. R. The biological time bomb
577

Study and teaching
See pages in the following book:
Lee, R. V. The physician p52-77   610.69

Medicine, Atomic. See Atomic medicine

Medicine, Popular
Hechtlinger, A. comp. The great patent medicine era   615

Medicine, Veterinary. See Veterinary medicine

Medicine as a profession
Lee, R. V. The physician   610.69

Medicines, Patent. See Patent medicines

Medieval and Tudor costume. Cunnington, P.   391.09

Medieval art. See Art, Medieval

Medieval civilization. See Civilization, Medieval

Medieval English verse, The Oxford Book of **821.08**

The **medieval** establishment, 1200-1500. Hindley, G. **901.92**

Medieval history. See Middle Ages—History

Medieval history, The Cambridge **940.1**

Medieval literature. See Literature, Medieval

The **medieval** plague. Marks, G. **616.9**

A **medieval** romance. Twain, M.
In Twain, M. The complete short stories of Mark Twain p50-56 **S C**

Medina, José Toribio
See pages in the following book:
Worcester, D. E. Makers of Latin America p106-13 **920**

Mediterranean region
See pages in the following book:
Camus, A. Lyrical and critical essays p189-98 **844**

History
See pages in the following book:
The New Cambridge Modern history v6 p540-71 **909**

Mediterranean Sea
See pages in the following book:
The New Cambridge Modern history v10 p416-40 **909**

Medlin, C. J.
Yearbook editing, layout, and management **371.89**

Meegeren, Hans van
See pages in the following book:
Koningsberger, H. The world of Vermeer, 1632-1675 p174-85 **92**

Meetham, Roger
Information retrieval **029.7**

The **meeting**. Borges, J. L.
In Borges, J. L. The Aleph, and other stories, 1933-1969 p177-84 **S C**

Meeting a Moscow acquaintance in the detachment. Tolstoy, L.
In Tolstoy, L. Short stories v 1 p245-73 **S C**

Megas, Georgios A.
(ed.) Folktales of Greece **398.2**

Mehdevi, Anne Sinclair
Persia revisited **915.5**
Persian adventure **915.5**

Mehta, Ved
Portrait of India **915.4**

Mehta, Zubin
See pages in the following book:
Ewen, D. Famous modern conductors p149-54 **920**

Meier, August
From plantation to ghetto **301.451**
Negro thought in America, 1880-1915 **301.451**
(jt. ed.) Bracey, J. H. ed. Black nationalism in America **301.451**

Meigs, Cornelia
Jane Addams: pioneer for social justice **92**

Meili, Jean Guichard- See Guichard-Meili, Jean

Mein Kampf. Hitler, A. **92**

Meir, Golda
Mann, P. Golda **92**
Syrkin, M. Golda Meir: Israel's leader **92**

Melbourne, William Lamb, 2d Viscount
See pages in the following book:
Strachey, L. Queen Victoria p71-133 **92**

Melfi, Leonard
Birdbath
In Richards, S. ed. Best short plays of the world theatre, 1958-1967 p213-26 **808.82**

Mellon, Andrew William
See pages in the following book:
Holbrook, S. H. The age of the moguls p212-30 **920**

Mellonta Tauta. Poe, E. A.
In Poe, E. A. The complete tales and poems of Edgar Allan Poe p384-94 **S C**

Melon flowers. Johnson, L.
In Angoff, C. ed. African writing today p139-61 **896**

Meltzer, Milton
(ed.) In their own words **301.451**
Langston Hughes **92**
(jt. auth.) Hughes, L. A pictorial history of the Negro in America **301.451**
(jt. auth.) Lader, L. Margaret Sanger: pioneer of birth control **92**
(ed.) Thoreau, H. D. Thoreau: people, principles, and politics **818**

Melville, Herman
Benito Cereno
In Kearns, F. E. ed. The Black experience p86-167 **810.8**
Billy Budd; criticism
In Vincent, H. P. ed. Twentieth century interpretations of Billy Budd **813.09**
Billy Budd, foretopman **Fic**
Moby Dick **Fic**
Moby Dick; criticism
In Stegner, W. ed. The American novel p25-34 **813.09**
Typee **Fic**
About
Chase, R. Melville **813.09**
Hillway, T. Herman Melville **813.09**
Miller, J. E. A reader's guide to Herman Melville **813.09**
See also pages in the following books:
Camus, A. Lyrical and critical essays p288-95 **844**
Foster, R. ed. Six American novelists of the nineteenth century p82-117 **813.09**
Literary history of the United States p441-71 **810.9**
Quinn, A. H. American fiction p149-58 **813.09**
Rourke, C. American humor p154-62 **817.09**
Untermeyer, L. Makers of the modern world p47-59 **920**
Van Doren, C. The American novel, 1789-1939 p84-102 **813.09**
Wagenknecht, E. Cavalcade of the American novel p58-81 **813.09**

A **member** of the family. Spark, M.
   In Spark, M. Collected stories: I p247-62
                               S C
The **member** of the wedding. McCullers, C.
                                Fic
The **member** of the wedding; play. McCullers, C.
   In Gassner, J. ed. Best American plays;
     3d ser. p171-203   **812.08**
Memed, my hawk. Kemal, Y.   **Fic**
The **memento**. Henry, O.
   In Henry, O. The complete works of
     O. Henry p1357-64   **S C**
Memento, memento. Amft, M. J.
   In Seventeen. Seventeen from Seventeen
     p18-30   **S C**
Memoirs. See Biography
Memoirs from the house of the dead. See
   Dostoevsky, F. The house of the dead
                                  Fic
The **memoirs** of a madman. Tolstoy, L.
   In Tolstoy, L. Short stories v2 p247-60
                                S C
Memoirs of a yellow dog. Henry, O.
   In Henry, O. The complete works of
     O. Henry p46-49   **S C**
   In Henry, O. The four million p110-18
                                S C
Memoirs of Sherlock Holmes. Doyle,
   Sir A. C.
   In Doyle, Sir A. C. The complete Sherlock Holmes v 1 p383-555   **S C**
Memoirs of the Second World War. Churchill, W. S.   **940.53**
Memorandum. White, E. B.
   In Parker, E. ed. I was just thinking
     p159-68   **824.08**
Memorials of a dead house. See Dostoevsky, F. The house of the dead   **Fic**
Memories. Huxley, J.   **92**
Memory
   Halacy, D. S. Man and memory   **612**
   See also pages in the following books:
   Lessing, L. DNA: at the core of life itself
     p67-75   **574.8**
   Sargent, S. S. Basic teachings of the great
     psychologists p112-24   **150**
   Wells, R. Bionics p57-66   **001.5**
A **memory** of two Mondays. Miller, A.
   In Cerf, B. ed. 24 favorite one-act plays
     p13-53   **808.82**
Men. See Man
Men against death. De Kruif, P.   **920**
Men against the sea. Nordhoff, C.
   In Nordhoff, C. The Bounty trilogy
     p297-438   **Fic**
Men and dinosaurs. Colbert, E. H. **568**
Men and women: the poetry of love. Untermeyer, L. ed.   **821.08**
Men at arms. Waugh, E.   **Fic**
The **men** in the storm. Crane, S.
   In Crane, S. The complete short stories
     & sketches of Stephen Crane p176-
     81   **S C**
Men in white. Kingsley, S.
   In Gassner, J. ed. Best American plays;
     supplementary volume, 1918-1958
     p411-50   **812.08**

Men like gods. Wells, H. G.
   In Wells, H. G. 28 science fiction stories
     p 1-268   **S C**
Men, machines, and modern times. Morison, E. E.   **609**
Men of mathematics. Bell, E. T.   **920**
Men of modern architecture. Forsee, A. **920**
Men of power. Carr, A.   **920**
Men, ships and the sea. National Geographic Society   **387.2**
Men to match my mountains. Stone, I. **979.1**
Men who made musical history. Seroff, V.   **920**
The **men** who made the nation. Dos Passos, J.   **973.4**
Men, women and ghosts. Lowell, A.
   In Lowell, A. The complete poetical works of Amy Lowell p75-151 **811**
The **menace** from Earth. Heinlein, R. A.
   In Heinlein, R. A. Robert A. Heinlein's The past through tomorrow p341-60   **S C**
Menander of Athens
   The arbitration
   In Oates, W. J. ed. The complete Greek
     drama v2 p1147-71   **882.08**
   Girl from Samos
   In Oates, W. J. ed. The complete Greek
     drama v2 p1125-41   **882.08**
   Shearing of Glycera
   In Oates, W. J. ed. The complete Greek
     drama v2 p1179-99   **882.08**
                     About
   See pages in the following book:
   Hamilton, E. The echo of Greece p139-54
                              880.9
Mencken, H. L.
   The American language [abridged ed] **427**
   The American scene   **818**
   (ed.) A new dictionary of quotations on historical principles from ancient and modern sources   **808.88**
   Prejudices; criticism
   In Downs, R. B. Books that changed America p197-206   **810.9**
                     About
   See pages in the following book:
   Brooks, V. The confident years: 1885-1915 p449-68   **810.9**
Mendel, Gregor Johann
   See pages in the following books:
   Fried, J. J. The mystery of heredity p13-28   **575.1**
   Moore, R. The coil of life p178-206 **574.09**
   Moore, R. Man, time, and fossils p150-70   **573.2**
Mendeleeff, Dmitri. See Mendeleev, Dmitrii Ivanovich
Mendeleev, Dmitrii Ivanovich
   See pages in the following book:
   Newman, J. R. ed. The world of mathematics v2 p919-31   **510.8**
Mendelowitz, Daniel M.
   A history of American art   **709.73**
Mendel's law
   See pages in the following book:
   Beadle, G. The language of life p54-75
                              575.1

Mendelsohn, Eric
See pages in the following book:
Forsee, A. Men of modern architecture p110-30 **920**

Mendelson, Lee
Charlie Brown & Charlie Schulz **741.5**

Mendelssohn, Felix. See Mendelssohn-Bartholdy, Felix

Mendelssohn-Bartholdy, Felix
See pages in the following books:
Bauer, M. Music through the ages p444-67 **780.9**

Cross, M. The Milton Cross New encyclopedia of the great composers and their music p585-605 **920.03**
Ewen, D. ed. The complete book of classical music p450-66 **780.1**
Ewen, D. ed. The world of great composers p219-31 **920**
Seroff, V. Men who made musical history p95-126 **920**
Shippen, K. B. The heritage of music p146-51 **780.9**

Mendes, Helen
The African heritage cookbook **641.5**

Mendoza, Antonio de
See pages in the following book:
Worcester, D. E. Makers of Latin America p22-30 **920**

Menke, Frank G.
The encyclopedia of sports **796.03**

Menken, Adah Isaacs
See pages in the following book:
Bontemps, A. Anyplace but here p122-31 **301.451**

Mennonites
See pages in the following books:
National Geographic Society. Vacationland U.S.A. p102-17 **917.3**
O'Connor, R. The German-Americans p233-40 **301.453**

Menotti, Gian Carlo
See pages in the following books:
Cross, M. The Milton Cross New encyclopedia of the great composers and their music p606-17 **920.03**
Ewen, D. ed. The new book of modern composers p254-64 **920**

The menstrual cycle. Dalton, K. **612.6**

Menstruation. See Woman—Health and hygiene

Mensuration
See pages in the following book:
Cooper, M. The inventions of Leonardo da Vinci p98-111 **608**

Mental deficiency. See Mentally handicapped

Mental diseases. See Mental illness

Mental health
See pages in the following books:
Duvall, S. M. Before you marry p124-43 **301.42**
Hyde, M. O. Psychology in action p13-25 **150**

See also Mental illness; Mind and body
Mental health. Lang, G. E. ed. **616.8**

Mental hospitals. See Mentally ill—Care and treatment

Mental hygiene. See Mental health

Mental illness
Lang, G. E. ed. Mental health **616.8**
Piersall, J. Fear strikes out **92**
See also pages in the following books:
Harrington, M. The other America p121-38 **301.44**
Sargent, S. S. Basic teachings of the great psychologists p257-74 **150**
Snively, W. D. The sea of life p205-15 **612**
Wilson, J. R. The mind p56-79, 136-51 **150**

Fiction
Green, H. I never promised you a rose garden **Fic**

Mental illness and art. See Art and mental illness

Mental tests
See pages in the following books:
Barzun, J. Teacher in America p209-19 **371.1**
Hyde, M. O. Psychology in action p98-116 **150**
Sargent, S. S. Basic teachings of the great psychologists p12-27 **150**

Mentally handicapped
Buck, P. S. The child who never grew **155.45**
See also pages in the following book:
Sargent, S. S. Basic teachings of the great psychologists p242-47 **150**

Fiction
Dostoevsky, F. The idiot **Fic**
Keyes, D. Flowers for Algernon **Fic**
Steinbeck, J. Of mice and men **Fic**

Mentally ill
Care and treatment
Lang, G. E. ed. Mental health **616.8**
See also pages in the following books:
Hyde, M. O. Psychology in action p38-51 **150**
Sargent, S. S. Basic teachings of the great psychologists p275-87 **150**

Care and treatment—Fiction
Kesey, K. One flew over the cuckoo's nest **Fic**

Menus
Adams, C. The teen-ager's menu cookbook **641.5**
American Heritage. The American Heritage Cookbook, and illustrated history of American eating & drinking **641.5**
Hale, W. W. The Horizon Cookbook and illustrated history of eating and drinking throughout the ages **641.5**
See also pages in the following book:
McCall's. McCall's Cook book p708-16 **641.5**

Menzel, Donald H.
A field guide to the stars and planets **523**

Mercer, Charles
Horizon Magazine. Alexander the Great **92**

Mercer, David
The Governor's lady
In Richards, S. ed. Best short plays of the world theatre, 1958-1967 p227-40 **808.82**

Merchandising. See Retail trade
Merchant marine

United States

Paine, R. D. The old merchant marine
387.5

The merchantmen. Armstrong, R.
In Armstrong, R. A history of searfaring v3
910.9

Merchants

See pages in the following book:

Chamberlain, E. R. Everyday life in Renaissance times p63-85
940.2

Mercury

See pages in the following book:

Asimov, I. The solar system p164-76 508

Mercury (Planet)

See pages in the following books:

Asimov, I. Building blocks of the universe p215-25
546

Asimov, I. The solar system and back p5-18
508

Mercury project
We seven
629.45

La mère Sauvage. Maupassant, G. de
In Maupassant, G. de. The odd number p91-105
S C

Meredith, George

See pages in the following books:

Karl, F. R. An age of fiction: the nineteenth century British novel p205-51
823.09

Wagenknecht, E. Cavalcade of the English novel p336-51
823.09

Meredith, James
Three years in Mississippi
370.19

About

See pages in the following book:

Metcalf, G. R. Black profiles p219-54 920

Mergenthaler, Ottmar

See pages in the following book:

Beard, A. E. S. Our foreign-born citizens p68-73
920

Mergers, Industrial. See Trusts, Industrial

Meriwether, Louise
Daddy was a number runner
Fic

Merk, Frederick
(jt. auth.) Morison, S. E. Dissent in three American wars
973

Merlin. Robinson, E. A.
In Robinson, E. A. The collected poems of Edwin Arlington Robinson p235-314
811

Merriam, Eve
Finding a poem
811

Merritt, LeRoy Charles
Book selection and intellectual freedom
025.2

Merry Christmas to all. Chute, B. J.
In Chute, B. J. One touch of nature, and other stories p241-50
S C

The merry men. Stevenson, R. L.
In Stevenson, R. L. The complete short stories of Robert Louis Stevenson p363-418
S C

Merton, Thomas
Contemplation in a world of action 248
The seven storey mountain
92
(ed.) Gandhi, M. K. Gandhi on non-violence
323

Mesa Verde National Park

See pages in the following book:

National Geographic Society. America's wonderlands p297-311
917.3

The mesmeric mountain. Crane, S.
In Crane, S. The complete short stories & sketches of Stephen Crane p99-102
S C

Mesmeric revelation. Poe, E. A.
In Poe, E. A. The complete tales and poems of Edgar Allan Poe p88-95
S C

Mesopotamia

Civilization

Kramer, S. N. Cradle of civilization 913.35

See also pages in the following books:

Larousse Encyclopedia of prehistoric and ancient art p123-34
709.01

Sarton, G. A history of science v 1 p57-99
509

White, A. T. Lost worlds p169-203 913.03

Mesopotamian sculpture. See Sculpture, Mesopotamian

A message to Umballa. Kipling, R.
In Dulles, A. ed. Great spy stories from fiction p181-90
S C

Metabolism
Snively, W. D. The sea of life
612
See also Nutrition

Metal sculpture. Lynch, J.
731.4

Metal work. See Metalwork

Metals

See also Gallium; Mercury

History

See pages in the following book:

Asimov, I. The solar system and back p151-88
508

Metalwork
Baxter, W. T. Jewelry, gem cutting, and metalcraft
739.27

Lynch, J. Metal sculpture
731.4

See also Steel

Metamorphoses. Ovid
871

Metamorphosis. Kafka, F.
Fic
also in Kafka, F. Selected short stories of Franz Kafka p19-89
S C

Metaphysics. See God; Universe

Metaphysics. Aristotle
In Aristotle. The basic works of Aristotle p689-926
888

The metaphysics of the love of the sexes. Schopenhauer, A.
In Schopenhauer, A. The philosophy of Schopenhauer p337-76
193

Metaurus, Battle of the, 207 B.C.

See pages in the following books:

Creasy, Sir E. S. Fifteen decisive battles of the world p85-119
904

Mitchell, J. B. Twenty decisive battles of the world p56-79
904

Metcalf, George R.
Black profiles
920

Metchnikoff, Elie. See Mechnikov, Il'i͡a Il'ich

Meteorology
Barrett, E. C. Viewing weather from
space   **551.59**
Thompson, P. D. Weather   **551.5**
See also pages in the following books:
Beiser, A. The earth p65-79   **551**
Hammond, Incorporated. Earth and space
p149-83   **551**
See also Atmosphere; Climate; Clouds;
Weather
Meteorology in aeronautics
Barrett, E. C. Viewing weather from space
551.59
Meteors
See pages in the following book:
Ley, W. Another look at Atlantis, and
fifteeen other essays p170-79   **508**
Methodist Church
See pages in the following book:
Look. Religions in America p121-30 280
Methodology. See Research
Methuselah's children. Heinlein, R. A.
In Heinlein, R. A. Robert A. Heinlein's
The past through tomorrow p526-
667   **S C**
Métraux, Alfred
The history of the Incas   **980.3**
Metropolitan areas
Goldston, R. Suburbia: civic denial 301.3
Mumford, L. The highway and the city
301.3
See also pages in the following book:
Willmann, J. B. The Department of Hous-
ing and Urban Development p94-123
353.85
See also Cities and towns
Metropolitan Museum of Art. See New
York. Metropolitan Museum of Art
Les **metteurs** en scène. Wharton, E.
In Wharton, E. The collected short
stories of Edith Wharton v 1 p555-
68   **S C**
Metzengerstein. Poe, E. A.
In Poe, E. A. The complete tales and
poems of Edgar Allan Poe p672-
78   **S C**
In Poe, E. A. Selected poetry and prose
p53-60   **818**
The **Mexican.** London, J.
In London, J. Best short stories of Jack
London p226-48   **S C**
In London, J. Jack London's Tales of
adventure   **S C**
Mexican Americans. Moore, J. W.   **301.453**
Mexican Americans, A documentary history
of the. Moquin, W. ed.   **973.08**
Mexican art. See Art, Mexican
Mexican painting. See Painting, Mexican
Mexican sculpture. See Sculpture, Mexican
Mexican War, 1845-1848. See United States
—History—War with Mexico, 1845-
1848
Mexicans in the New Southwest
Moore, J. W. Mexican Americans 301.453
Mexicans in the United States
Howard, J. R. Awakening minorities
301.45

Steiner, S. La Raza   **301.453**
See also pages in the following books:
Heaps, W. A. Wandering workers p58-89
331.6
Miller, H. P. Rich man, poor man p87-
104   **339**
History
Moquin, W. ed. A documentary history of
the Mexican Americans   **973.08**
Mexico
Johnson, W. W. Mexico   **917.2**
Treviño, E. B. de. Here is Mexico 917.2
See also pages in the following books:
Driver, H. E. Indians of North America
p456-78   **970.1**
Schneider, R. M. An atlas of Latin Amer-
ican affairs p26-39   **918**
See also Central America

Antiquities
Coe, M. D. America's first civilizations
970.3
Coe, M. D. Mexico   **917.2**
Fernandez, J. A guide to Mexican art:
from its beginnings to the present **709.72**
See also pages in the following book:
Stuart, G. E. Discovering man's past in
the Americas p61-107   **913.7**

Civilization
Coe, M. D. Mexico   **917.2**

Description and travel
See pages in the following book:
Halliburton, R. Richard Halliburton's
Complete book of marvels v 1   **910.4**

Fiction
Greene, G. The power and the glory **Fic**
Shellabarger, S. Captain from Castile **Fic**
Steinbeck, J. The pearl   **Fic**

History
Horgan, P. Conquistadors in North Amer-
can history   **973.1**
Innes, H. The Conquistadors   **973.1**
O'Connor, R. The cactus throne; the
tragedy of Maxmilian and Carlotta   **92**
Quirk, R. E. Mexico   **972**
See also pages in the following books:
Beals, C. The nature of revolution p107-
23   **323**
Crow, J. A. The epic of Latin America
p45-63, 71-89, 494-504, 649-74, 709-14,
721-36   **980**
Rippy, J. F. Latin America p203-18, 411-
23   **980**
Social life and customs
Toor, F. A treasury of Mexican folkways
398
Treviño, E. B. de. My heart lies south **92**
Treviño, E. B. de. Where the heart is **92**
Mexico (City)
Poor
Lewis, O. The children of Sánchez 309.172
Lewis, O. A death in the Sánchez family
309.172
Social conditions
Lewis, O. The children of Sánchez 309.172
Lewis, O. A death in the Sánchez family
309.172

Meyer, Lewis
See pages in the following book:
David, J. ed. Growing up Jewish p211-18
      920

Meyer, Robert
Festivals U.S.A. & Canada   394.2

Meyerbeer, Giacomo
See pages in the following books:
Cross, M. The Milton Cross New encyclopedia of the great composers and their music p618-26   920.03
Ewen, D. ed. The complete book of classical music p399-406   780.1

Mezada, Israel. See Masada, Israel

Michael and his lost angel. Jones, H. A.
In Dickinson, T. H. ed. Chief contemporary dramatists [1st ser] p73-109
    808.82

Michael and Mary. O'Kelly, S.
In Garrity, D. A. ed. 44 Irish short stories p314-19   S C

Michaels, Leonard
Robinson Crusoe Liebowitz
In Prize stories, 1971: The O. Henry Awards p321-29   S C

Michelangelo Buonarroti
Coughlan, R. The world of Michelangelo, 1475-1564   92
See also pages in the following books:
Horizon Magazine. The Horizon Book of the Renaissance p105-12   940.2
Horizon Magazine. Lorenzo de' Medici and the Renaissance p130-39   92
National Geographic Society. The Renaissance p144-72   940.2
Vasari, G. The lives of the painters, sculptors and architects v4 p108-92   920
Fiction
Stone, I. The agony and the ecstasy **Fic**

Michelin Guides   910.2

Michelozzi, Michelozzo. See Michelozzo di Bartolommeo

Michelozzo di Bartolommeo
See pages in the following book:
Vasari, G. The lives of the painters, sculptors and architects v 1 p314-24   920

Michelson, Albert Abraham, 1852-1931
See pages in the following book:
Nourse, A. E. Universe, earth, and atom p264-70   530.9

Michener, James A.
The bridge at Andau   943.9
The bridges at Toko-ri   **Fic**
Caravans   **Fic**
The drifters   **Fic**
Hawaii   **Fic**
Hawaii; excerpt
In Day, A. G. ed. The spell of Hawaii p3-20   919.69
Iberia   914.6
The quality of life   309.173
Rascals in paradise; excerpt
In Day, A. G. ed. The spell of Hawaii p180-216   919.69
The source   **Fic**

Tales of the South Pacific   **S C**
Contents: Coral Sea; Mutiny; An officer and a gentleman; The cave; The milk run; Alligator; Our heroine; Dry rot; Fo' dolla'; Passion; A boar's tooth; Wine for the mess at Segi; The airstrip at Konora; Those who fraternize; The strike; Frisco; The landing on Kuralei; A cemetery at Hoga Point

About
Day, A. G. James A. Michener   813.09

Michigan
Description and travel
See pages in the following book:
Catton, B. Prefaces to history p209-30
    973.7

Michigan. State Prison, Jackson
See pages in the following book:
Heaps, W. A. Riots, U.S.A. 1765-1970 p138-46   301.18

Michiko, consort of Akihito, Crown Prince of Japan
Simon, C. M. The sun and the birch; the story of Crown Prince Akihito and Crown Princess Michiko   92

Microbe hunters. De Kruif, P.   920

Microbes. See Bacteriology; Microorganisms; Viruses

Microbiology
Anderson, M. D. Through the microscope
    576
See also pages in the following book:
Time-Life Books. A guide to science, and Index to the Life Science library p36-45
    500
See also Bacteriology

Micronesia
See pages in the following book:
Time-Life Books. The U.S. overseas p124-36   917.3

Microorganisms
See pages in the following book:
Asimov, I. The new intelligent man's guide to science p592-641   500
See also Microbiology; Protozoa; Viruses

Microscope and microscopy
Anderson, M. D. Through the microscope   576
Gray, P. Handbook of basic microtechnique   578

Midcentury. Dos Passos, J.   **Fic**

Mid-century American poets. Ciardi, J. ed.
    811.08

Middle Ages
Adams, H. Mont-Saint-Michel and Chartres   726
Asimov, I. The Dark Ages   940.1
Bagley, J. J. Life in medieval England
    914.2
Bishop, M. The Middle Ages   940.1
Hindley, G. The medieval establishment, 1200-1500   901.92
Horizon Magazine. The Horizon Book of the Middle Ages   940.1
Pernoud, R. Eleanor of Aquitaine   92
See also pages in the following books:
Brown, L. A. Map making p58-77 **526.8**
Horizon Magazine. The Horizon Book of The Elizabethan world p11-29   940.2

Milhaud, Darius
See pages in the following books:
Cross, M. The Milton Cross New ency-
clopedia of the great composers and their
music p627-38   920.03
Ewen, D. ed. The new book of modern
composers p265-77   920
Militarism
Knoll, E. ed. American militarism, 1970
                                    355.03
See also Military service, Compulsory;
War
Military aeronautics. See Aeronautics, Mili-
tary
Military airplanes. See Airplanes, Military
Military art and science
See pages in the following book:
Salisbury, H. E. ed. The Soviet Union:
the fifty years p58-84   914.7
See also Arms and armor; Battles;
Spies; War
History
Norman, A. V. B. A history of war and
weapons, 449 to 1660   355.09
See also pages in the following books:
The New Cambridge Modern history v2
p481-509, v3 p171-208, v8 p190-217, v9
p60-76   909
Saggs, H. W. F. Everyday life in Baby-
lonia & Assyria p114-23   913.35
Military biography. See Generals
Military draft. See Military service, Com-
pulsory
Military history
See pages in the following books:
The New Cambridge Modern history v3
p171-208, v4 p202-25, v6 p741-833, v7
p163-90, v9 p60-76   909
See also Battles; also names of coun-
tries with the subhead Marine Corps
or the subdivision History, Military
(e.g. U.S. Marine Corps; U.S.—History,
Military; etc.); and names of wars,
battles, and sieges
Dictionaries
Dupuy, R. E. The encyclopedia of military
history   355.09
Eggenberger, D. A dictionary of battles
                                      904
Military policy. See United States—Military
policy
Military power. See Disarmament; Military
art and science
Military science. See Military art and sci-
ence
Military service, Compulsory
Liston, R. Greeting: you are hereby
ordered for induction   355.2
Reeves, T. The end of the draft   355.2
See also pages in the following books:
Pope, L. The right college p189-200 378.73
Sloan, I. J. Youth and the law p4-12 340
See also Conscientious objectors
Military uniforms. See Uniforms, Military
The **milk run.** Michener, J.
In Michener, J. Tales of the South
Pacific p78-84   S C

The **mill on the Floss.** Eliot, G.   **Fic**
Millay, Edna St Vincent
Aria da capo
In Cerf, B. ed. Thirty famous one-act
plays p465-78   808.82
In Gassner, J. ed. Twenty-five best plays
of the modern American theatre;
early ser. p712-20   812.08
Collected poems   811
Collected sonnets   811
About
Brittin, N. A. Edna St Vincent Millay
                                    811.09
Gurko, M. Restless spirit   92
See also pages in the following book:
Stoddard, H. Famous American women
p287-94   920
Millay, Norma
(ed.) Millay, E. St V. Collected poems 811
Miller, Arthur
All my sons
In Gassner, J. ed. Best American plays;
3d ser. p281-316   812.08
The crucible   812
—Same
In Gassner, J. ed. Best American plays;
4th ser. p347-402   812.08
Death of a salesman   812
—Same
In Block, H. M. ed. Masters of modern
drama p1020-54   808.82
In Cerf, B. ed. Plays of our time p237-
329   812.08
In Gassner, J. ed. Best American plays;
3d ser. p 1-48   812.08
In Tucker, S. M. ed. Twenty-five modern
plays p953-1002   808.82
A memory of two Mondays
In Cerf, B. ed. 24 favorite one-act plays
p13-53   808.82
The price   812
Search for a future
In The Best American short stories,
1967 p161-74   S C
A view from the bridge
In Gassner, J. ed. Best American plays;
4th ser. p315-46   812.08
About
Corrigan, R. W. ed. Arthur Miller 812.09
Moss, L. Arthur Miller   812.09
See also pages in the following book:
Gould, J. Modern American playwrights
p247-63   812.09
Miller, Besse May
(jt. auth.) Doris, L. Complete secretary's
handbook   651.02
Miller, Herman Phillip
Rich man, poor man   339
Miller, James E.
A reader's guide to Herman Melville
                                    813.09
Walt Whitman   811.09
Miller, Jill Nhu Huong
Vietnamese cookery   641.5
Miller, John C.
The Federalist era, 1789-1801   973.4
Miller, Jonathan
Marshall McLuhan   001.5

Miller, Madeleine S.
Harper's Bible dictionary. See Harper's
Bible dictionary   220.3
Miller, Perry
(ed.) The American Puritans: their prose
and poetry   810.8
The New England mind: From colony to
province   917.4
The New England mind: The seventeenth
century   917.4
Miller, Warren
Chaos, disorder and the late show
In The Saturday Evening Post. Best
modern short stories p297-302 **S C**
Millie. Mansfield, K.
In Mansfield, K. The short stories of
Katherine Mansfield p142-47 **S C**
Milligan, Ex parte. See Ex parte Milligan
Millikan, Max F.
(ed.) The emerging nations: their growth
and United States policy   309.2
The **millionairess.** Shaw, B.
In Shaw, B. Complete plays, with pref-
aces v6 p203-78   822
Mills, Dorothy
The book of the ancient Greeks   938
The book of the ancient Romans   937
The Middle Ages   940.1
Renaissance and Reformation times 940.2
Mills, Vernon
Making posters   741.67
Milne, A. A.
The Dover Road
In Dickinson, T. H. ed. Chief contem-
porary dramatists; 3d ser. p117-58
808.82
Mr Pim passes by
In Cerf, B. A. comp. Sixteen famous
British plays p311-55   822.08
The ugly duckling
In Cerf, B. ed. 24 favorite one-act plays
p347-66   808.82
Milne, Lorus
North American birds   598
Water and life   551.4
(jt. auth.) Buchsbaum, R. The lower ani-
mals   592
Milne, Margery
(jt. auth.) Milne, L. North American birds
598
(jt. auth.) Milne, L. Water and life 551.4
Milner, Ronald
Junkie-Joe had some money
In Hughes, L. ed. The best short stories
by Negro writers p465-69   **S C**
Milton, John
Areopagitica
In Milton, J. The portable Milton p151-
205   828
The complete poetical works of John Mil-
ton   821
Paradise lost
In Milton, J. The portable Milton p231-
548   828
Paradise regained
In Milton, J. The portable Milton p549-
609   828
The portable Milton   828
Samson Agonistes
In Milton, J. The portable Milton p610-
64   828

About
Wedgwood, C. V. Milton and his world
914.2
See also pages in the following books:
Auslander, J. The winged horse p190-204
809.1
Daiches, D. A critical history of English
literature v 1 p390-457   820.9
Daiches, D. More literary essays p96-114
820.9
Durant, W. The age of Louis XIV p207-
43   940.2
Eliot, T. S. On poetry and poets p156-83
808.1
Untermeyer, L. Lives of the poets p170-92
920
Untermeyer, L. The paths of poetry p72-
81   920
Bibliography
See pages in the following book:
Daiches, D. English literature p32-48 **801**
Contemporary England
Wedgwood, C. V. Milton and his world
914.2
Milton, John R.
The inheritance of Emmy One Horse
In The Best American short stories,
1969 p185-95   **S C**
Milton and his world. Wedgwood, C. V.
914.2
Mind. See Psychology
The **mind.** Wilson, J. R.   150
Mind and body
Overstreet, H. A. The mature mind **155.2**
Wilson, J. R. The mind   150
See also pages in the following books:
Asimov, I. The new intelligent man's
guide to science p748-98   500
Snively, W. D. The sea of life p208-15 612
See also Mental health; Psychoanalysis;
Sleep
The **mind** and faith of Justice Holmes.
Holmes, O. W.   340
The **mind** and heart of Frederick Douglass.
Douglass, F.   326
Mind cure. See Christian Science
Mind drugs. Hyde, M. O. ed.   613.8
The **mind** of man. Calder, N.   612
Mind reading
See pages in the following book:
Christopher, M. ESP, seers & psychics
p55-77   133
Mineral industries. See Mines and mineral
resources
Mineral resources. See Mines and mineral
resources
Mineralogy
Dana's Manual of mineralogy   549
Fenton, C. L. The rock book   552
Loomis, F. B. Field book of common
rocks and minerals   549
Pough, F. H. A field guide to rocks and
minerals   549
Sinkankas, J. Prospecting for gemstones
and minerals   553
See also pages in the following books:
Hyde, M. O. This crowded planet p54-71
301.3

Mineralogy—*Continued*

Time-Life Books. A guide to the natural world, and Index to the Life Nature library p82-107　　**574**

Minerals. See Mineralogy; Mines and mineral resources

Mines and mineral resources
See pages in the following books:

Beiser, A. The earth p91-103　　**551**

Bertin, L. Larousse Encyclopedia of the earth p201-78　　**550**

Ehrlich, P. R. Population, resources, environment p58-63　　**301.3**

Gaskell, T. F. World beneath the oceans p104-15　　**551.4**

Lowell, T. Lowell Thomas' Book of the high mountains p355-61, 405-16　　**910.9**

See also Coal mines and mining

Africa, South
See pages in the following book:

Cole, E. House of bondage p22-39　**301.451**

United States
See pages in the following books:

Langdon, W. C. Everyday things American life, 1776-1876 p274-302　　**917.3**

Moss, F. E. The water crisis p109-22　　**333.9**

Sprague, M. The Mountain States p118-26　　**917.8**

United States—History

Sloane, H. N. A pictorial history of American mining　　**622.09**

Mingus, Charles
See pages in the following book:

Goldberg, J. Jazz masters of the fifties p132-53　　**920**

Mining. See Mines and mineral resources

Minister without portfolio. Clingerman, M.
In Conklin, G. ed. Invaders of earth p215-22　　**S C**

The **minister's** Black Veil. Hawthorne, N.
In Hawthorne, N. Hawthorne's Short stories p10-23　　**S C**

"Ministers of Grace." Saki
In Saki. The short stories of Saki p240-50　　**S C**

Minneapolis
See pages in the following book:

Steffens, L. The shame of the cities p42-68　　**352**

Politics and government
See pages in the following book:

Weinberg, A. ed. The muckrakers p6-21　　**309.173**

Minnie Field. Conkle, E. P.
In Gassner, J. ed. Twenty-five best plays of the modern American theatre; early ser. p749-52　　**812.08**

Minoan and Mycenaean art. Higgins, R.　　**709.39**

Minoan art. See Art, Minoan

Minoan civilization. See Civilization, Minoan

Minorities

Baruch, D. W. Glass house of prejudice　　**301.45**

Deloria, V. We talk, you listen　　**309.173**

Glazer, N. Beyond the melting pot　**301.45**

Greeley, A. M. Why can't they be like us?　　**301.45**

Huthmacher, J. J. A nation of newcomers　　**301.45**

See also pages in the following books:

Miller, H. P. Rich man, poor man p87-104　　**339**

See also Race problems; also names of races or peoples living within a country, state, or city dominated by another nationality (e.g. Mexicans in the United States); and names of countries with the subdivisions Foreign population and Race relations, e.g. U.S.—Foreign population; U.S.—Race relations

Minot, George Richards
See pages in the following book:

De Kruif, P. Men against death p88-116　　**920**

Minot, Stephen
Mars revisited
In Prize stories, 1971: The O. Henry Awards p284-99　　**S C**

Minter, David L.
(ed.) Twentieth century interpretations of Light in August　　**813.09**

Miracle at Philadelphia. Bowen, C. D.　**342.73**

Miracle in the mountains [biography of Martha McChesney Berry]. Kane, H. T.　　**92**

Miracle of Moon Crescent. Chesterton, G. K.
In Chesterton, G. K. The Father Brown omnibus p505-30　　**S C**

The **miracle** of Puran Bhagat. Kipling, R.
In Kipling, R. The best short stories of Rudyard Kipling p277-87　　**S C**
In Kipling, R. Maugham's Choice of Kipling's best p262-73　　**S C**

A **miracle** of Saint Antony. Maeterlinck, M.
In Cerf, B. ed. Thirty famous one-act plays p169-85　　**808.82**

Miracle of the fifteen murderers. Hecht, B.
In Costain, T. B. ed. Read with me p247-63　　**S C**

The **miracle** worker. Gibson, W.　　**812**

The **miraculous** revenge. Shaw, G. B.
In Garrity, D. A. ed. 44 Irish short stories p392-415　　**S C**

Miriam. Capote, T.
In Abrahams, W. ed. Fifty years of the American short story v 1 p171-81　　**S C**

The **mirror.** Singer, I. B.
In Singer, I. B. An Isaac Bashevis Singer reader p23-34　　**S C**

A **mirror** of Chaucer's world. Loomis, R. S.　　**914.2**

Mirror of the magistrate. Chesterton, G. K.
In Chesterton, G. K. The Father Brown omnibus p642-62　　**S C**

Misalliance. Shaw, B.
In Shaw, B. Complete plays, with prefaces v4 p109-204　　**822**

The **misanthrope.** Molière, J. B. P.
In Bentley, E. comp. The great playwrights v 1 p968-1023　　**808.82**

Misdemeanors (Law) See Criminal law

Les misérables. Hugo, V.　　**Fic**

Missouri River
See pages in the following book:
Snyder, G. S. In the footsteps of Lewis and Clark p61-72, 113-24   **973.4**

Mistake of the machine. Chesterton, G. K.
In Chesterton, G. K. The Father Brown omnibus p298-314   **S C**

Mr Acarius. Faulkner, W.
In The Best American short stories, 1966 p69-82   **S C**

Mr and Mrs Bo Jo Jones. Head, A.   **Fic**

Mr and Mrs Dove. Mansfield, K.
In Mansfield, K. The short stories of Katherine Mansfield p497-505   **S C**

Mr and Mrs Elliot. Hemingway, E.
In Hemingway, E. In our time p107-14   **S C**
In Hemingway, E. The short stories of Ernest Hemingway p159-64   **S C**

Mr and Mrs Fix-it. Lardner, R.
In Lardner, R. The best short stories of Ring Lardner p337-46   **S C**

Mr and Mrs Williams. Mansfield, K.
In Mansfield, K. The short stories of Katherine Mansfield p676-79   **S C**

Mr Binks' day off. Crane, S.
In Crane, S. The complete short stories & sketches of Stephen Crane p169-75   **S C**

Mr Bluff's experiences of holidays. Bunce, O. B.
In Schauffler, R. H. ed. Christmas p270-81   **394.26**

Mr Bodley's oak. Chute, B. J.
In Chute, B. J. One touch of nature, and other stories p13-36   **S C**

Mr Brisher's treasure. Wells, H. G.
In Wells, H. G. The complete short stories of H. G. Wells p981-90   **S C**

Mr Cornelius, I love you. West, J.
In Havighurst, W. ed. Masters of the modern short story p352-66   **S C**

Mr da V. Reed, K.
In Seventeen. Seventeen from Seventeen p169-85   **S C**

Mr Dooley on the education of the young. Dunne, F. P.
In White, E. B. ed. A subtreasury of American humor; abridged p222-25   **817.08**

Mr Dynamite. See Brown, James

Mister fisherman. Bennett, J.   **Fic**

Mr Frisbie. Lardner, R.
In Lardner, R. The best short stories of Ring Lardner p75-85   **S C**
In Lardner, R. The Ring Lardner reader p305-16   **S C**

Mr Gallion's school. Stuart, J.   **Fic**

Mr Harrington's washing. Maugham, W. S.
In Maugham, W. S. The best short stories of W. Somerset Maugham p129-69   **S C**

Mr Iscariot. Brown, R. G.
In The Best American short stories, 1964 p15-25   **S C**

Mr Jones. Wharton, E.
In Wharton, E. The collected short stories of Edith Wharton v2 p594-616   **S C**

Mr Justice Holmes and the Supreme Court. Frankfurter, F.   **347.9**

Mr Know-All. Maugham, W. S.
In Maugham, W. S. The best short stories of W. Somerset Maugham p193-99   **S C**

Mr Ledbetter's vacation. Wells, H. G.
In Wells, H. G. The complete short stories of H. G. Wells p943-62   **S C**

Mr Lincoln's army. Catton, B.   **973.7**

Mr Pim passes by. Milne, A. A.
In Cerf, B. A. comp. Sixteen famous British plays p311-55   **822.08**

Mr Reginald Peacock's day. Mansfield, K.
In Mansfield, K. The short stories of Katherine Mansfield p384-92   **S C**

Mister Roberts. Heggen, T.
In Cerf, B. ed. Plays of our time p331-407   **812.08**
In Gassner, J. ed. Best American plays; 3d ser. p415-53   **812.08**
In Six modern American plays p341-419   **812.08**

Mr Sammler's planet. Bellow, S.   **Fic**

Mr Skelmersdale in Fairyland. Wells, H. G.
In Wells, H. G. The complete short stories of H. G. Wells p884-98   **S C**

Mr Vladimir and Mr Verloc. Conrad, J.
In Dulles, A. ed. Great spy stories from fiction p74-85   **S C**

Mr Wilson's war. Dos Passos, J.   **973.91**

Mistral. Faulkner, W.
In Faulkner, W. Collected stories of William Faulkner p843-76   **S C**

Mrs Kimble. Nair, S.
In Angoff, C. ed. African writing today p212-14   **896**

Mrs McWilliams and the lightning. Twain, M.
In Twain, M. The complete short stories of Mark Twain p153-59   **S C**

Mrs Manstey's views. Wharton, E.
In Wharton, E. The collected short stories of Edith Wharton v 1 p3-11   **S C**

Mrs Miniver. Struther, J.   **Fic**

The **mistress** of Husaby. Undset, S.
In Undset, S. Kristin Lavransdatter v2   **Fic**

Mrs Packletide's tiger. Saki
In Saki. The short stories of Saki p127-30   **S C**

Mrs Skagg's husbands. Harte, B.
In Harte, B. The best of Bret Harte p77-113   **S C**

Mrs Twiller takes a trip. Littke, L. J.
In Best detective stories of the year, 1971 p249-55   **S C**

Mrs Warren's profession. Shaw, B.
In Shaw, B. Complete plays, with prefaces v3 p33-105   **822**
In Shaw, B. Seven plays p 1-105   **822**

The **misunderstanding.** Camus, A.
In Camus, A. Caligula & 3 other plays p75-134   **842**

Mitchell, Billy. See Mitchell, William

Mitchell, Don
Diesel
In The Best American short stories, 1971 p156-75   **S C**

The **modern** soul. Mansfield, K.
In Mansfield, K. The short stories of Katherine Mansfield p63-71   **S C**

Modern world literature, The Concise enclopedia of   803

Modernism (Art)
Canady, J. Mainstreams of modern art: David to Picasso   709.03
Cheney, S. A primer of modern art   709.03
Cheney, S. The story of modern art   709.03
Larousse Encyclopedia of modern art   709.03
Read, H. A concise history of modern painting   759.06
   See also Architecture, Modern—20th century; Art—History—20th century; Cubism; Futurism (Art); Impressionism (Art); Surrealism

Moeller, Philip
Helena's husband
In Cerf, B. ed. Thirty famous one-act plays p307-22   808.82

Mogul silver. Clarke, A. C.
In Armstrong, R. ed. Treasure and treasure hunters   910.4

Mohammed, the prophet
'Assām, 'Abd-al-Rahmān. The eternal message of Muhammad   297
   See also pages in the following books:
Hitti, P. K. The Arabs p23-31   953
Stewart, D. Early Islam p10-20   915.6

Mohammed V, Sultan of Morocco
   See pages in the following book:
Kenworthy, L. S. Leaders of new nations p108-29   920

Mohammed-Fripouille. Maupassant, G. de
In Maupassant, G. de. Guy de Maupassant's Short stories p131-37   **S C**

Mohammedan art. See Art, Islamic

Mohammedanism. See Islam

Mohan, Anand
Indira Gandhi   92

Mohole project
   See pages in the following book:
Behrman, D. The new world of the oceans p188-201   551.4

Molds (Botany)
Kavaler, L. Mushrooms, molds, and miracles   589
   See also Fungi

The **molds** and man. Christensen, C. M.   589

Molecules
Pauling, L. The architecture of molecules   541
   See also pages in the following book:
Asimov, I. The new intelligent man's guide to science p433-86   500

Molière, Jean Baptiste Poquelin
Don Juan; English version by D. M. Frame
In Bentley, E. comp. The great playwrights v 1 p893-943   808.82
The misanthrope; English version by R. Wilbur
In Bentley, E. comp. The great playwrights v 1 p968-1023   808.82

About
   See pages in the following books:
Durant, W. The age of Louis XIV p104-28   940.2
Gassner, J. Masters of the drama p286-300   809.2
Nicoll, A. World drama p316-34   809.2
Trease, G. Seven stages p24-53   920

Moll Flanders. See Defoe, D. The fortunes and misfortunes of the famous Moll Flanders   **Fic**

Mollusks
Morris, P. A. A field guide to shells of the Pacific Coast and Hawaii   594
Morris, P. A. A field guide to the shells of our Atlantic and Gulf Coasts   594

Molnar, Ferenc
Liliom
In Cerf, B. A. comp. Sixteen famous European plays p795-852   808.82
In Dickinson, T. H. ed. Chief contemporary dramatists; 3d ser. p527-68   808.82
In Tucker, S. M. ed. Twenty-five modern plays p361-99   808.82
The play's the thing
In Gassner, J. ed. Twenty best European plays on the American stage p490-522   808.82

A **moment** in history: the first ten years of the Peace Corps. Ashabranner, B.   309.2

The **moment** of victory. Henry, O.
In Henry, O. The complete works of O. Henry p755-63   **S C**

Monarchs. See Kings and rulers; Queens

Monarchy
   See pages in the following book:
The New Cambridge Modern history v4 p104-31   909

Monasteries. See Monasticism and religious orders

Monastic orders. See Monasticism and religious orders

Monasticism and religious orders
Merton, T. Contemplation in a world of action   248
Merton, T. The seven storey mountain   92
   See also pages in the following books:
Bagley, J. J. Life in medieval England p67-88   914.2
Durant, W. The age of faith p785-818   940.1
Hussey, M. comp. Chaucer's world p55-71   821.09
Mills, D. The Middle Ages p130-43   940.1
Page, R. I. Life in Anglo-Saxon England p113-35   914.2
Rowling, M. Everyday life in medieval times p113-34   914
Thorndike, L. The history of medieval Europe p117-37   940.1
Tomkeieff, O. G. Life in Norman England p87-99   914.2

Monasticism and religious orders for women
   Fiction
Barrett, W. E. The lilies of the field   **Fic**
Godden, R. In this house of Brede   **Fic**

The **Monboddo** ape boy. De la Torre, L.
In Mystery Writers of America. Crime without murder p269-87   **S C**

Monet, Claude
See pages in the following books:
Cheney, S. The story of modern art p178-92
709.03
Ruskin, A. Nineteenth century art p107-11
709.03

Money. See Coins; Paper money

Money, Paper. See Paper money

Money maze. Henry, O.
In Henry, O. The complete works of O. Henry p597-604   **S C**

Monge, Gaspard
See pages in the following book:
Bell, E. T. Men of mathematics p183-205
920

Mongkut, King of Siam
Landon, M. Anna and the King of Siam
915.93

Mongolia
See pages in the following book:
Snow, E. Red China today p77-95   915.1
Description and travel
National Geographic Society. Great adventures with National Geographic p92-103
910.9

Mongols
Phillips, E. D. The Mongols   913.39
See also pages in the following book:
Horizon Magazine. The Horizon History of Russia p59-73   947
History
Lamb, H. Genghis Khan, the emperor of all men   92

Mongols in Russia
See pages in the following book:
Wallace, R. Rise of Russia p55-64   947

Monica. Macauley, P.
In Richards, S. ed. Best short plays of the world theatre, 1958-1967 p187-99   808.82

Monje, Mario
See pages in the following book:
Harris, R. Death of a revolutionary; [Ernesto] Che Guevara's last mission p149-64   92

Monk, Meredith
See pages in the following book:
McDonagh, D. The rise and fall and rise of modern dance p174-89   793.3

Monk, Thelonious Sphere
See pages in the following books:
Goldberg, J. Jazz masters of the fifties p24-44   920
Williams, M. The jazz tradition p138-55
781.5

The monkey. Dinesen, I.
In Dinesen, I. Seven Gothic tales p109-63   **S C**

The monkey's paw. Jacobs, W. W.
In Cerf, B. ed. Thirty famous one-act plays p191-207   808.82

Monkey's revenge. Lucas, E. V.
In Becker, M. L. ed. The home book of Christmas p498-502   394.26

Monkhouse, F. J.
A dictionary of geography   910.3

Monks. See Monasticism and religious orders

Monoplanes. See Airplanes

Monopolies
Kefauver, E. In a few hands: monopoly power in America   338.8
See also pages in the following book:
Fribourg, M. G. The Supreme Court in American history p91-107   347.9
See also Trusts, Industrial

Monopoly (Game)
See pages in the following book:
Gibson, W. Family games America plays p124-31   793

Monro, Isabel S.
(comp.) Short story index. See Short story index   808.83

Monro, Kate M.
(jt. auth.) Taintor, S. A. The secretary's handbook   651.7

Monroe, Earl
See pages in the following book:
Pepe, P. Greatest stars of the NBA p93-105   920

Monroe, Harriet
See pages in the following book:
Stoddard, H. Famous American women p305-13   920

Monroe Doctrine
Dozer, D. M. ed. The Monroe Doctrine
327.73
See also pages in the following book:
Fish, C. R. The path of empire p 1-18
327.73

Monsarrat, Nicholas
The cruel sea   **Fic**

Monsieur Beaucaire. Tarkington, B.   **Fic**

The monster. Crane, S.
In Crane, S. The complete short stories & sketches of Stephen Crane p430-75   **S C**

Mont Pelée. See Pelée, Mont

Mont St Michel, France
Adams, M. Mont-Saint-Michel and Chartres   726

Montage of a dream deferred. Hughes, L.
In Hughes, L. The Langston Hughes reader p89-126   818

Montagu, Ashley
The American way of life   917.3
Man: his first two million years   572
On being human   301
For another title by this author see
Montagu, M. F. Ashley

Montagu, Ewen
The man who never was   940.54

Montagu, M. F. Ashley
(ed.) Man and aggression   152.4
For other works by this author see
Montagu, Ashley

Montague, John
See pages in the following book:
Rosenthal, M. L. The new poets p297-306
821.09

Montaigne, Michel Eyquem de
See pages in the following book:
Highet, G. The classical tradition p178-93
809

Montana

Fiction

Guthrie, A. B. Arfive   Fic

Walker, M. Winter wheat   Fic

Politics and government

See pages in the following book:

Weinberg, A. ed. The muckrakers p104-18   309.173

Montaperto, Ronald N.

(jt. auth.) Bennett, G. A. Red Guard; the political biography of Dai Hsiao-ai 92

Montchenu, Jean de, Bp.

See pages in the following book:

Horizon Magazine. The light of the past p144-49   901.9

Montefeltro, Federigo da, duca di Urbino

See pages in the following book:

Horizon Magazine. The Horizon Book of the Renaissance p321-28   940.2

Monterey, Calif.

Fiction

Steinbeck, J. Cannery Row   Fic

Steinbeck, J. Tortilla Flat   Fic

Montesquieu, Charles Louis de Secondat, Baron de la Brede et de

See pages in the following book:

Durant, W. The age of Voltaire p340-60   940.2

Montessori, Maria

The child in the family   301.43

Monteverdi, Claudio

See pages in the following book:

Shippen, K. B. The heritage of music p61-65   780.9

Montezuma II, Emperor of Mexico

See pages in the following book:

Lloyd, A. The Spanish centuries p127-38   946

Montfort, Simon of, Earl of Leicester, 1208?-1265

See pages in the following book:

Costain, T. B. The magnificent century p180-212, 232-318   942.03

Montgomery, Marion

The decline and fall of Officer Fergerson

In The Best American short stories, 1971 p176-201   S C

Montgomery, Ala.

Race relations

King, M. L. Stride toward freedom 323.4

A month in the country. Turgenev, I.

In Gassner, J. ed. Twenty best European plays on the American stage p119-63   808.82

The **month** of his birthday. Karmel-Wolfe, H.

In The Best American short stories, 1965 p187-97   S C

A **month** of mystery. See Hitchcock, A. ed. Alfred Hitchcock presents: A month of mystery   S C

Months

Krythe, M. R. All about the months 394.2

Montorsoli, Fra Giovanni Angelo

See pages in the following book:

Vasari, G. The lives of the painters, sculptors and architects v4 p39-53   920

Montrose, James Graham, 1st Marquis of

See pages in the following book:

Sutcliff, R. Heroes and history p130-47   920

Montross, David

Rape

In Mystery Writers of America. Crime without murder p193-95   S C

Monuments, Natural. See Natural monuments

Moody, John

The masters of capital   332.6

The railroad builders   385.09

Moody, Ralph

Little Britches   92

Man of the family   92

Moody, Sidney C.

(ed.) Associated Press. Triumph and tragedy   920

Moody, William Vaughn

The faith healer

In Quinn, A. H. ed. Representative American plays p771-805   812.08

The Great Divide

In Dickinson, T. H. ed. Chief contemporary dramatists [1st ser] p283-315   808.82

In Gassner, J. ed. Best plays of the early American theatre p361-97   812.08

Mooltiki. Godden, R.

In Costain, T. B. ed. Read with me p227-45   S C

Moon, Charlotte

See pages in the following book:

Kane, H. T. Spies for the Blue and Gray p263-81   973.7

Moon, Virginia

See pages in the following book:

Kane, H. T. Spies for the Blue and Gray p263-81   973.7

Moon

Moore, P. Moon flight atlas   629.45

See also pages in the following books:

Asimov, I. The clock we live on p58-73, 109-23   529

Gamow, G. A planet called earth p25-46   551

Hodge, P. W. The revolution in astronomy p155-64   523

Jastrow, R. Red giants and white dwarfs p72-97   523.1

Menzel, D. H. A field guide to the stars and planets p250-84   523

See also Tides

Moon, Voyages to. See Space flight to the moon

The **moon** and sixpence. Maugham, W. S.   Fic

Moon bases. See Lunar bases

The **moon** child from Wolfe Creek. Stuart, J.

In Stuart J. A Jesse Stuart reader p121-29   818

Moon flight atlas. Moore, P.   629.45

A **moon** for the misbegotten. O'Neill, E.

In Gassner, J. ed. Best American plays; 4th ser. p133-78   812.08

The **moon** is blue. Herbert, F. H.
  In Gassner, J. ed. Best American plays;
    3d ser. p627-63   **812.08**
The **moon** is down. Steinbeck, J.
  In Steinbeck, J. The short novels of
    John Steinbeck p275-354   **Fic**
The **moon** of the arfy darfy. Algren, N.
  In The Saturday Evening Post. Best
    modern short stories p390-401 **S C**
The **moon** of the Caribbees. O'Neill, E.
  In Cerf, B. ed. 24 favorite one-act plays
    p238-55   **808.82**
  In O'Neill, E. The long voyage home
    p 1-32   **812**
  In O'Neill, E. Plays v 1 p455-74 **812**
Moonfleet. Falkner, J. M.   **Fic**
Moonlight. Maupassant, G. de
  In Maupassant, G. de. Guy de Maupas-
    sant's Short stories p126-30 **S C**
  In Maupassant, G. de. The odd number
    p109-19   **S C**
  In Maupassant, G. de. Selected short
    stories p268-73   **S C**
Moonlight on the snow. Crane, S.
  In Crane, S. The complete short stories
    & sketches of Stephen Crane p710-
    19   **S C**
The **moonstone.** Collins, W.   **Fic**
Moore, Anne Carroll
  (ed.) Irving, W. Knickerbocker's History
    of New York   **974.7**
Moore, Brian
  The apartment hunter
  In The Best American short stories, 1967
    p175-85   **S C**
  Canada   **917.1**
Moore, Charles A.
  (jt. ed.) Radhakrishnan, S. ed. A source
    book in Indian philosophy   **181**
Moore, Clark D.
  (ed.) Africa yesterday and today **916**
  (ed.) India yesterday and today **915.4**
Moore, Ferman
  See pages in the following book:
  Goldman, P. Report from Black America
    p192-99   **301.451**
Moore, George
  Julia Cahill's curse
  In Garrity, D. A. ed. 44 Irish short sto-
    ries p227-33   **S C**
Moore, Henry
  Read, H. Henry Moore   **730.942**
Moore, Joan W.
  Mexican Americans   **301.453**
Moore, Marianne
  Collected poems
  In Moore, M. The complete poems of
    Marianne Moore p5-152   **811**
  The complete poems of Marianne Moore
    811
  Like a bulwark
  In Moore, M. The complete poems of
    Marianne Moore p157-74   **811**
  O to be a dragon
  In Moore, M. The complete poems of
    Marianne Moore p177-202   **811**
  Tell me, tell me
  In Moore, M. The complete poems of
    Marianne Moore p205-34   **811**

About
Tomlinson, C. ed. Marianne Moore
    811.09
Moore, Patrick
  Amateur astronomy   **523**
  The atlas of the universe   **523**
  Moon flight atlas   **629.45**
  The planets   **523.4**
  Suns, myths and men   **523**
Moore, Robin
  The green berets   **S C**
  Contents: A green beret—all the way; The
  immortal Sergeant Hanks; The Cao-Dai pagoda;
  Two birds with one stone; Coup de grâce; Home
  to Nanette; Fourten VC POW's; The immodest
  Mr Pomfret; Hit 'em where they live
Moore, Ruth
  The coil of life   **574.09**
  The earth we live on   **551.09**
  Evolution   **575**
  Man, time, and fossils   **573.2**
Moore, Truman
  The slaves we rent   **331.6**
Moorehead, Alan
  The Blue Nile   **962.6**
  No room in the ark   **916**
  The White Nile   **962**
Moorey, Anne
  Making mobiles   **731**
Moorey, Christopher
  (jt. auth.) Moorey, A. Making mobiles
    731
Moorish art. See Art, Islamic
Moquin, Wayne
  (ed.) A documentary history of the Mexi-
    can Americans   **973.08**
Moral conditions. See Negroes—Moral and
  social conditions; United States—Moral
  conditions
Moral philosophy. See Ethics
Morality. See Ethics
Morals. See Behavior
Moravia, Alberto
  A tough nut
  In The Saturday Evening Post. Best
    modern short stories p41-46 **S C**
Moravians
  See pages in the following book:
  Langdon, W. C. Everyday things in Amer-
    ican life, 1607-1776 p87-109 **917.3**
More, Anne
    Fiction
  Vining, E. G. Take heed of loving me **Fic**
More, Sir Thomas, Saint
  Utopia   **321**
    About
  See pages in the following books:
  Durant, W. The Reformation p550-58
    940.2
  Russell, B. A history of Western philos-
    ophy p512-22   **109**
    Drama
  Bolt, R. A man for all seasons   **822**
More collected verse. Service, R. **811**
More friend than lodger. Wilson, A.
  In The New Yorker. Stories from The
    New Yorker, 1950-1960 p641-65
    S C

More junior authors. Fuller, M. ed.   920.03

More light on the Dead Sea scrolls. Burrows, M.   221.4

More literary essays. Daiches, D.   820.9

More Numbers: fun & facts. Friend, J. N.   793.7

More poems. Housman, A. E.
In Housman, A. E. The collected poems of A. E. Housman p153-211   821

More stories of the great operas, Milton Cross. Cross, M.   782.1

More than skin deep. Sternberg, T. H.   616.5

Morella. Poe, E. A.
In Poe, E. A. The complete tales and poems of Edgar Allan Poe p667-71   **S C**
In Poe, E. A. Edgar Allan Poe p218-25   **S C**
In Poe, E. A. Selected poetry and prose p91-95   818

Morelos y Pavon, José María Teclo
See pages in the following book:
Worcester, D. E. Makers of Latin America p36-45   920

Moreno, Gabriel García. See García Moreno, Gabriel

Morgan, Berry
Andrew
In The Best American short stories, 1967 p187-92   **S C**

Morgan, James
Our Presidents   920

Morgan, John Pierpont, 1837-1913
See pages in the following books:
American Heritage. The nineties p60-63, 138-41   917.3
Chamberlain, J. The enterprising Americans: a business history of the United States p167-85   330.973
Holbrook, S. H. The age of the moguls p148-53, 176-79, 335-40   920

Morgan, Thomas Hunt
See pages in the following book:
Moore, R. The coil of life p207-24   574.09

Morgenthau, Hans J.
Politics among nations   341

Moriconi, Virginia
Simple arithmetic
In The Best American short stories, 1964 p227-40   **S C**

Morison, Elting E.
Men, machines, and modern times   609

Morison, Samuel Eliot
Admiral of the ocean sea; a life of Christopher Columbus   92
Christopher Columbus, mariner   92
Dissent in three American wars   973
The growth of the American Republic   973
John Paul Jones   92
The Oxford History of the American people   973
The two-ocean war   940.54

Morley, Christopher
The haunted bookshop   Fic
Parnassus on wheels   Fic
The tree that didn't get trimmed
In Becker, M. L. ed. The home book of Christmas p423-28   394.26

Morley, Edward Williams
See pages in the following book:
Nourse, A. E. Universe, earth, and atom p264-72   530.9

Morlvera. Saki
In Saki. The short stories of Saki p552-56   **S C**

Mormons and Mormonism
See pages in the following books:
American Heritage. The American Heritage Book of great adventures of the Old West p170-91   978
Billington, R. A. The far Western frontier, 1830-1860 p193-217   978
Hollon, W. E. The Great American Desert p88-107   917.8
Look. Religions in America p131-41   280
Sloan, I. J. Our violent past p130-42   301.18
Sprague, M. The Mountain States p139-46   917.8
Stone, I. Men to match my mountains p134-67, 213-39, 266-74, 329-51, 411-23   979.1

Morning after. Himes, C.
In Margolies, E. A native son's reader p323-29   810.8

Morning and noon. Acheson, D.   92

Morning's at seven. Osborn, P.
In Gassner, J. ed. Best American plays; supplementary volume, 1918-1958 p333-72   812.08

Morocco
Politics and government
See pages in the following book:
Kenworthy, L. S. Leaders of new nations p108-29   920

Morons. See Mentally handicapped

Morphett, Tony
Litterbug
In The Best from Fantasy and Science Fiction; 19th ser. p223-42   **S C**

Morris, Desmond
The mammals   599

Morris, Edita
The flowers of Hiroshima   Fic
The seeds of Hiroshima   Fic

Morris, Jerrold
On the enjoyment of modern art   709.73

Morris, Mary
(jt. auth.) Morris. W. Dictionary of word and phrase origins   422.03

Morris, Percy A.
A field guide to shells of the Pacific Coast and Hawaii   594
A field guide to the shells of our Atlantic and Gulf Coasts   594

Morris, Richard B.
The American Revolution reconsidered   973.3
(ed.) Basic documents in American history   973
(ed.) Encyclopedia of American history   973.03
(ed.) Great Presidential decisions   973
(ed.) Harper Encyclopedia of the modern world. See Harper Encyclopedia of the modern world   909.08

Morris, Richard B.—*Continued*
The making of a nation: 1775-1789
In Life (Periodical) The Life History
of the United States v2   973
The new world: Prehistory to 1774
In Life (Periodical) The Life History
of the United States v 1   973
(jt. ed.) Commager, H. S. ed. The spirit
of 'seventy-six   973.3
(ed.) Trevelyan, G. The American Revolution   973.3
Morris, Robert, 1734-1806
See pages in the following book:
Bakeless, J. Signers of the Declaration
p127-36   920
Morris, William
(ed.) The American Heritage Dictionary
of the English language   423
Dictionary of word and phrase origins
422.03
Morris, Wright
Green grass, blue sky, white house
In The Best American short stories,
1970 p194-206   S C
Magic
In The Best American short stories,
1971 p202-16   S C
Morrison, Lillian
(comp.) Sprints and distances   808.81
Morrison, William
Country doctor
In Asimov, I. ed. Where do we go
from here? p217-43   S C
Morro Castle (Steamship)
See pages in the following book:
Leighton, I. ed. The aspirin age, 1919-
1941 p313-38   917.3
Morrow, William L.
Congressional committees   328.73
Morsberger, Robert E.
James Thurber   817.09
A mortal enemy. Sholokhov, M.
In Sholokhov, M. Tales of the Don
p225-44   S C
Le morte d'Arthur. Malory, Sir T. 398.2
Morticians. See Undertakers and undertaking
Mortimer, John
Desmond
In The Best short plays, 1971 p283-95
808.82
Mortimer, Penelope
The parson
In The New Yorker. Stories from The
New Yorker, 1950-1960 p518-28
S C
Morton, Ferdinand Joseph
See pages in the following books:
Bontemps, A. Anyplace but here p248-56
301.451
Williams, M. The jazz tradition p16-46
781.5
Williams, M. T. ed. The art of jazz p33-
42   781.5
Morton, Frederic
The guest
In The Best American short stories,
1965 p241-49   S C
Morton, Jelly Roll. See Morton, Ferdinand
Joseph

Mortuary customs. See Funeral rites and
ceremonies
Moscati, Sabatino
The world of the Phoenicians   913.39
Moscheles, Ignaz
See pages in the following book:
Chapin, V. Giants of the keyboard p77-86
920
Moscow
See pages in the following book:
Horizon Magazine. The Horizon History
of Russia p74-100   947
Mosel, Tad
All the way home
In Gassner, J. ed. Best American plays;
5th ser. p277-311   812.08
The presence of the enemy
In The Best short plays of 1957-1958
p159-98   808.82
Moseley, William
The preacher and Margery Scott
In The Best American short stories,
1968 p235-45   S C
Moselle River and Valley
See pages in the following book:
Rees, G. The Rhine p70-78   914.3
Moses, Anna Mary Robertson
Grandma Moses   92
Moses, Harry E.
Developing and administering a comprehensive high school music program
780.7
Moses, Raphael Jacob
See pages in the following book:
David, J. ed. Growing up Jewish p142-
53   920
**Moshoeshoe II, paramount chief of Basuto-
land**
See pages in the following book:
Polatnick, F. T. Shapers of Africa p108-
46   920
Moslem art. See Art, Islamic
Moslems. See Muslims
Mosley, Leonard
Hirohito, Emperor of Japan   92
On borrowed time   940.53
Moss, Frank E.
The water crisis   333.9
Moss, Leonard
Arthur Miller   812.09
Mosses
See pages in the following book:
The Oxford Book of flowerless plants
p38-45, 86-93, 96-101, 172-83   586
The most elegant drawing room in Europe.
Hale, N.
In Abrahams, W. ed. Fifty years of the
American short story v 1 p351-66
S C
**The most native of sons; a biography of
Richard Wright.** Williams, J. A.   92
The Moth. Wells, H. G.
In Wells, H. G. The complete short
stories of H. G. Wells p302-12
S C
Mother. Anderson, S.
In Anderson, S. Winesburg, Ohio (Modern Lib) p24-37   S C
In Anderson, S. Winesburg, Ohio (Viking) p39-48   S C

A **mother**. Joyce, J.
  In Joyce, J. Dubliners p171-89 **S C**
The **mother**. Schauffler, R. H.
  In Schauffler, R. H. ed. Christmas p325-
    32   **394.26**
Mother and son. Hatano, I.   **92**
Mother Courage. Brecht, B.
  In Bentley, E. comp. The great play-
    wrights v2 p2091-2160   **808.82**
Mother Courage and her children. Brecht, B.
  In Block, H. M. ed. Masters of modern
    drama p843-70   **808.82**
Mother dear and Daddy. Edwards, J.
  In Margolies, E. A native son's reader
    p205-16   **810.8**
The **mother** of a queen. Hemingway, E.
  In Hemingway, E. The short stories
    of Ernest Hemingway p415-19
        S C
Mother to son. Rivers, C. K.
  In Hughes, L. ed. The best short stories
    by Negro writers p356-58 **S C**
A **mother's** tale. Agee, J.
  In Foley, M. ed. Fifty best American
    short stories, 1915-1965 p488-507
        S C
Moti-guj—mutineer. Kipling, R.
  In Kipling, R. The best short stories of
    Rudyard Kipling p86-91 **S C**
Motion
  See pages in the following books:
  Asimov, I. Life and energy p28-40 **612**
  Newman, J. R. ed. The world of mathe-
    matics v2 p734-819   **510.8**
  Nourse, A. E. Universe, earth, and atom
    p136-45   **530.9**
    See also Force and energy
Motion picture almanac, International. See
  International motion picture almanac
    791.43
Motion pictures. See Moving pictures
Motion study
  See pages in the following book:
  United States. Department of Agriculture.
    Power to produce p395-403   **631.3**
Motivation (Psychology)
  See pages in the following book:
  Sargent, S. S. Basic teachings of the great
    psychologists p179-92   **150**
Motley, Constance Baker
  See pages in the following book:
  Stoddard, H. Famous American women
    p314-24   **920**
Motley, Willard
  The almost white boy
  In Hughes, L. ed. The best short stories
    by Negro writers p134-44 **S C**
Motor cars. See Automobiles
Motor cycles. See Motorcycles
Motorcycle troubleshooting guide, Chil-
  ton's. Ritch, O.   **629.28**
Motorcycles
  Wallach, T. Easy motorcycle riding **629.28**
  Yerkow, C. Motorcycles: how they work
    629.22
    Handbooks, manuals, etc.
  Glenn, H. T. Honda: repair & tune-up
    guide   **629.28**

        History
  Oliver, S. H. The Smithsonian collection
    of automobiles and motorcycles **629.22**
        Repairing
  Glenn, H. T. Honda: repair & tune-up
    guide   **629.28**
  Ritch, O. Chilton's Harley-Davidson re-
    pair and tune-up guide   **629.28**
  Ritch, O. Chilton's Motorcycle trouble-
    shooting guide   **629.28**
Motors. See Engines
Mott, Frank Luther
  American journalism   **071**
Mott, Lucretia (Coffin)
  See pages in the following book:
  Stoddard, H. Famous American women
    p325-35   **920**
Mound builders of ancient America. Silver-
  berg, R.   **970.4**
Mounds and mound builders
  Silverberg, R. Mound builders of ancient
    America   **970.4**
  See also pages in the following books:
  Baity, E. C. Americans before Columbus
    p118-37   **970.1**
  Ceram, C. W. The first American p212-30
    913.7
Mount Everest. See Everest, Mount
Mount Everest Expedition, 1953
  Hunt, J. The conquest of Everest **915.4**
  Tenzing, N. Tiger of the snows **92**
  See also pages in the following book:
  National Geographic Society. Great adven-
    tures with National Geographic p366-79
    910.9
Mount Everest Expedition, 1963
  Ullman, J. R. Americans on Everest **915.4**
Mount McKinley National Park
  See pages in the following book:
  National Geographic Society. America's
    wonderlands p511-15   **917.3**
Mount Rainier National Park
  See pages in the following book:
  National Geographic Society. America's
    wonderlands p396-407   **917.3**
  National Geographic Society. Vacation-
    land U.S.A. p406-19   **917.3**
The **mountain** chorus. Bermel, A.
  In The Best short plays, 1968 p159-82
    808.82
Mountain climbing. See Mountaineering
Mountain interval. Frost, R.
  In Frost, R. Complete poems of Robert
    Frost, 1949 p131-95   **811**
Mountain life
        Southern States
  Caudill, R. My Appalachia   **309.175**
  Stuart, J. A Jesse Stuart reader **818**
Mountain plants. See Alpine plants
The **Mountain** States. Sprague, M. **917.8**
Mountain victory. Faulkner, W.
  In Faulkner, W. Collected stories of
    William Faulkner p745-77 **S C**
  In Faulkner, W. Selected short stories
    of William Faulkner p230-65 **S C**

Mountaineering
Douglas, W. O. Of men and mountains
                                          92
Herzog, M. Annapurna   915.4
Hunt, J. The conquest of Everest   915.4
Noyce, W. ed. World atlas of moun-
  taineering   796.5
Tenzing, N. Tiger of the snows   92
Ullman, J. R. The age of mountaineering
                                 796.5
Ullman, J. R. Americans on Everest 915.4
   See also pages in the following book:
National Geographic Society. Great adven-
  tures with National Geographic p332-53
                                 910.9
                Fiction
Ullman, J. R. The White Tower   Fic
Mountaineers of the South. See Mountain
  life—Southern States
Mountains
Noyce, W. ed. World atlas of moun-
  taineering   796.5
Thomas, L. Lowell Thomas' Book of the
  high mountains   910.9
   See also pages in the following book:
Farb, P. The land and wildlife of North
  America p144-72   574.9
    See also Mountaineering
Mountolive. Durrell, L.
  In Durrell, L. The Alexandria quartet:
    Justine; Balthazar; Mountolive
    [and] Clea p391-642   Fic
Mourning becomes Electra. O'Neill, E.
  In O'Neill, E. Nine plays p687-867 812
  In O'Neill, E. Plays v2 p5-179   812
  In O'Neill, E. Selected plays of Eugene
    O'Neill   812
Mourning call. Leviant, C.
  In The Best American short stories,
    1966 p203-18   S C
The mouse. Saki
  In Saki. The short stories of Saki p104-
    08   S C
The mouse on the moon. Wibberley, L. Fic
The mouse on Wall Street. Wibberley, L. Fic
Mouse that didn't believe in Santa Claus.
  Field, E.
  In Becker, M. L. ed. The home book of
    Christmas p452-57   394.26
The mouse that roared. Wibberley, L. Fic
The mouse-trap. Howells, W. D.
  In Gassner, J. ed. Best plays of the
    early American theatre p262-76
                            812.08
Moussorgsky, Modest Petrovich. See Mu-
  sorgskiĭ, Modest Petrovich
A moveable feast. Hemingway, E.   92
Movies. See Moving pictures
The movies. Griffith, R.   791.43
The movies as medium. Jacobs, L. ed. 791.43
The moving finger. Wharton, E.
  In Wharton, E. The collected short
    stories of Edith Wharton v 1 p301-
    13   S C
The moving image. Gessner, R.   791.43
Moving picture cameras. See Cameras

Moving picture cartoons
Kinsey, A. How to make animated movies
                               778.5
Moving picture industry
Schickel, R. The Disney version   92
   See also pages in the following book:
Colby, V. ed. American culture in the
  sixties p164-73   917.3
Moving picture photography
Eastman Kodak Company. Home movies
  made easy   778.5
Ferguson, R. How to make movies 778.5
Kinsey, A. How to make animated movies
                               778.5
Larson, R. Young filmmakers   791.43
Lowndes, D. Film making in schools
                               778.5
Smallman, K. Creative film-making 778.5
Moving picture plays
        History and criticism
Gessner, R. The moving image   791.43
Moving picture projectors. See Projectors
Moving pictures
Ferguson, R. How to make movies 778.5
Jacobs, L. ed. The movies as medium
                               791.43
Larson, R. Young filmmakers   791.43
   See also pages in the following books:
American Heritage. The American Heri-
  tage History of the 20's & 30's p346-53
                                 917.3
Nye, R. The unembarrassed muse: the
  popular arts in America p362-89 917.3
   See also Sound—Recording and re-
  producing
                Biography
International motion picture almanac
                               791.43
                Catalogs
Educational Film Library Association.
  Film evaluation guide, 1946-1964
                            016.3713
                Censorship
   See pages in the following book:
Ernst, M. L. Censorship: the search for
  the obscene p142-59   343
                Directories
International motion picture almanac
                               791.43
                History
Griffith, R. The movies   791.43
Moving pictures as a profession
Colman, H. Making movies: student films
  to features   791.43
Moving pictures in education
                Catalogs
National Information Center for Educa-
  tional Media. Index to 8mm motion
  cartridges   371.33
National Information Center for Educa-
  tional Media. Index to 16mm educational
  films   371.33
National Information Center for Educa-
  tional Media. Index to 35mm filmstrips
                                 371.33
Mowat, C. L.
  (ed.) The shifting balance of world forces,
    1898-1945
  In The New Cambridge Modern history
    v12   909

Mowat, Farley
The boat who wouldn't float   910.4
Canada north   917.1
The dog who wouldn't be   818
The grey seas under   387.5
Never cry wolf   599
The Siberians   915.7
This rock within the sea: a heritage lost   917.18

Mowatt, Anna Cora
Fashion
In Gassner, J. ed. Best plays of the early American theatre p97-135   812.08

Mowgli's brothers. Kipling, R.
In Kipling, R. Maugham's Choice of Kipling's best p245-61   **S C**

The mowing of a field. Belloc, H.
In Parker, E. ed. I was just thinking p65-77   824.08

Mowry, George E.
The era of Theodore Roosevelt, 1900-1912   973.91

Moyers, Bill
Listening to America   917.3

Moynihan, Daniel P.
Toward a national urban policy
In United States. National Commission on the Causes and Prevention of Violence. Violent crime p 1-30   **364.1**
(jt. auth.) Glazer, N. Beyond the melting pot   301.45

Mozart, Johann Chrysostom Wolfgang Amadeus
Valentin, E. Mozart and his world   92
See also pages in the following books:
Bauer, M. Music through the ages p350-69   780.9
Bernstein, L. The infinite variety of music p65-81   780.1
Cross, M. The Milton Cross New encyclopedia of the great composers and their music p639-81   920.03
Durant, W. Rousseau and revolution p382-408   940.2
Ewen, D. ed. The complete book of classical music p213-81   780.1
Ewen, D. ed. The world of the great composers p104-21   920
Seroff, V. Men who made musical history p 1-16   920
Shippen, K. B. The heritage of music p109-19   780.9

Mozart and his world. Valentin, E.   92

Mphahlele, Ezekiel
The wanderers   Fic

The muckrakers. Weinberg, A. ed.   309.173

Mudrick, Marvin
Cleopatra
In Abrahams, W. ed. Fifty years of the American short story v 1 p490-99   **S C**

Mueller, Conrad G.
Light and vision   535

Muhammed. See Mohammed, the Prophet

Muhammedanism. See Islam

Muheim, Harry
The dusty drawer
In Hitchcock, A. ed. Alfred Hitchcock presents: A month of mystery p3-18   **S C**

Muir, John
See pages in the following books:
Beard, A. E. S. Our foreign-born citizens p22-29   920
Udall, S. L. The quiet crisis p109-25   333.7

Muir, Kenneth
(ed.) A new companion to Shakespeare studies   822.3
(ed.) Shakespeare: the comedies   822.3

Muirhead, L. Russell
The Blue guides. See The Blue guides   910.2

Muirhead's Blue guides. See The Blue guides   910.2

Mulac, Margaret E.
Games and stunts for schools, camps, and playgrounds   790

Mulatto. Hughes, L.
In Hughes, L. Five plays p 1-35   812

Mule in the yard. Faulkner, W.
In Faulkner, W. Collected stories of William Faulkner p249-64   **S C**

Mule No. 095. Lolos, K.
In The Best American short stories, 1964 p191-201   **S C**

Mulkerns, Val
The world outside
In Garrity, D. A. ed. 44 Irish short stories p234-43   **S C**

Müller, Artur
The Seven Wonders of the World   913

Muller, Herman Joseph
See pages in the following book:
Moore, R. The coil of life p227-38   574.09

Müller, V. K.
(comp.) English-Russian dictionary   491.7

Mulligan, Gerald Joseph
See pages in the following book:
Goldberg, J. Jazz masters of the fifties p9-23   920

Mulligan, Gerry. See Mulligan, Gerald Joseph

Multimedia materials for Afro-American studies. Johnson, H. A. ed.   016.3014

Mulvey, Mina White
Digging up Adam; the story of L. S. B. Leakey   92

Mumford, Lewis
The city in history   301.3
The conduct of life   128
The highway and the city   301.3
The myth of the machine   901.9
The pentagon of power
In Mumford, L. The myth of the machine v2   901.9
Sticks and stones   720.973
Technics and human development
In Mumford, L. The myth of the machine v 1   901.9
The urban prospect   711

Mummies
See pages in the following book:
Ceram, C. W. The first American p88-96   913.7

Museums

See also United States—Galleries and museums

Directories

The Official museum directory: United States [and] Canada   069.025

Museums directory of the United States and Canada. See The Official museum directory: United States [and] Canada   069.025

Musgrave, George McCoy

Competitive debate   808.53

The **Musgrave** ritual. Doyle, Sir A. C.

In Doyle, Sir A. C. The complete Sherlock Holmes v 1 p444-58   **S C**

In Doyle, Sir A. C. Sherlock Holmes' greatest cases p366-94   **S C**

Mushrooms

Kavaler, L. Mushrooms, molds, and miracles   589

See also Fungi

Mushrooms, molds, and miracles. Kavaler, L.   589

Musial, Stan

Stan Musial: "The Man's" own story   92

Music

See also Jazz music

Analysis, appreciation

Bernstein, L. The infinite variety of music   780.1

Bernstein, L. The joy of music   780.1

Boyden, D. D. An introduction to music   780.1

Copland, A. What to listen for in music   780.1

Ewen, D. ed. The complete book of classical music   780.1

Ewen, D. The world of twentieth century music   780.1

The New York Times. Guide to listening pleasure   780.1

Appreciation

See Music—Analysis, appreciation

Bibliography

National Council of Teachers of English. Committee on College and Adult Reading List. The college and adult reading list of books in literature and the fine arts   016

Bio-bibliography

Ewen, D. ed. Composers since 1900   920.03

Ewen, D. ed. Great composers, 1300-1900   920.03

Biography

See Musicians

Dictionaries

Apel, W. The Harvard Brief dictionary of music   780.3

Grove's Dictionary of music and musicians   780.3

Grove's Dictionary of music and musicians; Supplementary volume   780.3

The Reader's encyclopedia   803

Scholes, P. A. The concise Oxford Dictionary of music   780.3

Scholes, P. A. The Oxford Companion to music   780.3

Thompson, O. ed. The international cyclopedia of music and musicians   780.3

Discography

The New York Times. Guide to listening pleasure   780.1

History and criticism

Bauer, M. Music through the ages   780.9

Boyden, D. D. An introduction to music   780.1

Copland, A. The new music, 1900-1960   780.9

Ewen, D. ed. The complete book of classical music   780.1

Ewen, D. Composers of tomorrow's music   920

Ewen, D. David Ewen introduces modern music   780.9

Ewen, D. The world of twentieth century music   780.1

Janson, H. W. A history of art & music   700

Shippen, K. B. The heritage of music   780.9

Instruction and study

See Music—Study and teaching

Study and teaching

Moses, H. E. Developing and administering a comprehensive high school music program   780.7

See also pages in the following book:

Barzun, J. Teacher in America p115-31   371.1

Music, African

Dietz, B. W. Musical instruments of Africa   781.9

Music, American

See pages in the following books:

Bauer, M. Music through the ages p585-624   780.9

Colby, V. ed. American culture in the sixties p152-61   917.3

Shippen, K. B. The heritage of music p251-80   780.9

See also Negro songs; Negro spirituals

History and criticism

Copland, A. The new music, 1900-1960   780.9

Southern, E. The music of Black Americans: a history   781.7

Spaeth, S. A history of popular music in America   784.09

Music, English

See pages in the following book:

Shakespeare's England v2 p15-49   822.3

Music, European

See pages in the following books:

Gay, P. Age of Enlightenment p120-39   901.93

The New Cambridge Modern history v8 p81-96, v9 p228-49   909

Music, Indic

History and criticism

Shankar, R. My music, my life   781.7

Music, Latin American

See pages in the following book:

The New York Times. Guide to listening pleasure p210-23   780.1

Music, Popular (Songs, etc.)

Bacharach, B. The Bacharach and David Song book   784

Mutation (Biology) See Evolution

Mutiny. Michener, J.
In Michener, J. Tales of the South
  Pacific p14-36   **S C**

Mutiny on the Bounty. Nordhoff, C.
In Nordhoff, C. The Bounty trilogy
  p 1-295   **Fic**

My Antonia. Cather, W.   **Fic**

My apologia. Velsky, V.
In Scammell, M. ed. Russia's other
  writers p185-216   **S C**

My Appalachia. Caudill, R.   **309.175**

My bondage and my freedom; abridged. See
Douglass, F. Life and times of Frederick
Douglass; abridged   **92**

My brother Michael. Stewart, M.   **Fic**

My brother's keeper. Pei, M.
In Pei, M. Tales of the natural and
  supernatural p155-63   **S C**

My darling Clementine; the story of Lady
Churchill. Fishman, J.   **92**

My fair lady. Lerner, A. J.   **812**

My father's friend. Singer, I. B.
In Singer, I. B. An Isaac Bashevis Singer reader p285-90   **S C**

My first aeroplane. Wells, H. G.
In Wells, H. G. The complete short
  stories of H. G. Wells p561-72 **S C**

My Grandmother Millard. Faulkner, W.
In Faulkner, W. Collected stories of
  William Faulkner p667-99   **S C**

My grandmother's thimble, and Fanning
Island. Updike, J.
In Updike, J. Pigeon feathers, and other
  stories   **S C**

My heart has seventeen rooms. Bartholomew, C.   **915.4**

My heart lies south. Treviño, E. B. de   **92**

My Lai 4. Hersh, S. M.   **959.7**

My land and my people. Dalia Lama XIV
     92

My life and hard times. Thurber, J.   **817**

My life and thought. See Schweitzer, A.
Out of my life and thought   **92**

My life in court. Nizer, L.   **343**

My life is baseball. Robinson, F.   **92**

My life with Martin Luther King, Jr. King,
C. S.   **92**

My life with R. H. Macy. Jackson, S.
In Jackson, S. The magic of Shirley
  Jackson p18-21   **818**

My little boy. Ewald, C.
In The Scribner treasury p275-314 **S C**

My Lord, what a morning. Anderson, M. **92**

My music, my life. Shankar, R.   **781.7**

My old man. Hemingway, E.
In Foley, M. ed. Fifty best American
  short stories, 1915-1965 p49-60 **S C**
In Hemingway, E. In our time p149-73
       S C
In Hemingway, E. The short stories of
  Ernest Hemingway p189-205   **S C**

My revelations as a spy. Leacock, S.
In Costain, T. B. ed. Read with me p335-
  43   **S C**

My roomy. Lardner, R.
In Lardner, R. The best short stories
  of Ring Lardner p283-302   **S C**
In Lardner, R. The Ring Lardner reader
  p495-515   **S C**

My Russian journey. Rama Rau, S.   **914.7**

My secrets of playing baseball. Mays, W.
     796.357

My several worlds. Buck, P. S.   **92**

My shadow ran fast. Sands, B.   **364.8**

My sister Eileen. McKenney, R.   **817**

My sister's applegarth. Ktorova, A.
In Scammell, M. ed. Russia's other
  writers p167-84   **S C**

My son the murderer. Malamud, B.
In Prize stories, 1970: The O. Henry
  Awards p127-33   **S C**

My son, the physicist. Asimov, I.
In Asimov, I. Nightfall, and other stories
  p329-32   **S C**

"My son's wife." Kipling, R.
In Kipling, R. The best short stories of
  Rudyard Kipling p543-65   **S C**

My three angels. Spewack, S.
In Gassner, J. ed. Twenty best European
  plays on the American stage p164-
  99   **808.82**

My town. Schaefer, J.
In Schaefer, J. The collected stories of
  Jack Schaefer p230-42   **S C**

My turn at bat. Williams, T.   **92**

My "war" with Israel. See Hussein, King of
Jordan. Hussein of Jordan: My "war"
with Israel   **956**

My watch. Twain, M.
In Twain, M. The complete short stories
  of Mark Twain p57-59   **S C**

Mycenae
Taylour, Lord W. The Mycenaeans **913.39**

Mycenaean art. See Art, Mycenaean

Mycenaean civilization. See Civilization,
Mycenaean

The **Mycenaeans.** Taylour, Lord W. **913.39**

Mycology. See Fungi

Myers, Bernard S.
(ed.) Art treasures in France. See Art
  treasures in France   **709.44**

Myrdal, Gunnar
An American dilemma   **301.451**
An American dilemma; criticism
In Downs, R. B. Books that changed
  America p239-50   **810.9**
The challenge of world poverty   **338.91**

Myrdal, Jan
Chinese journey   **309.151**

Myron, Robert
Art in America   **709.73**

Myself and a rabbit. MacGrian, M.
In Garrity, D. A. ed. 44 Irish short
  stories p184-88   **S C**

Mysteries and miracle plays
See pages in the following book:
Gassner, J. Masters of the drama p142-54
     809.2

The **mysterious** stranger. Twain, M.
In Twain, M. The complete short stories
  of Mark Twain p599-676   **S C**

Mystery and detective stories

Ball, J. In the heat of the night   Fic

Best detective stories of the year, 1967, 1970-1971   S C

Chesterton, G. K. The Father Brown omnibus   S C

Christie, A. Hallowe'en party   Fic

Christie, A. The murder of Roger Ackroyd   Fic

Collins, W. The moonstone   Fic

Collins, W. The woman in white   Fic

Doyle, Sir A. C. The complete Sherlock Holmes   S C

Doyle, Sir A. C. The exploits of Sherlock Holmes   S C

Doyle, Sir A. C. Sherlock Holmes' greatest cases   S C

Edwards, A. The survivors   Fic

Hammett, D. The novels of Dashiell Hammett   Fic

Haycraft, H. ed. A treasury of great mysteries   S C

Hitchcock, A. Alfred Hitchcock presents: A month of mystery   S C

Kemelman, H. Sunday the rabbi stayed home   Fic

Morley, C. The haunted bookshop   Fic

Mystery Writers of America. Crime without murder   S C

Poe, E. A. The complete tales and poems of Edgar Allan Poe   S C

Poe, E. A. Edgar Allan Poe   S C

Simenon, G. Five times Maigret   Fic

Tey, J. Three by Tey   Fic

History and criticism
See pages in the following book:

Nye, R. The unembarrassed muse: the popular arts in America p244-68   917.3

Mystery at the Library of Congress. Queen, E.
In Mystery Writers of America. Crime without murder p223-31   S C

The mystery of animal migration. Ricard, M.   591

The mystery of heredity. Fried, J. J.   575.1

A mystery of heroism. Crane, S.
In Crane, S. The complete short stories & sketches of Stephen Crane p219-26   S C

The mystery of Marie Roget. Poe, E. A.
In Poe, E. A. The complete tales and poems of Edgar Allan Poe p169-207   S C

In Poe, E. A. Edgar Allan Poe p376-439   S C

The mystery of Minoan civilization. Cottrell, L.   913.39

Mystery Writers of America
Crime without murder   S C

Mystification. Poe, E. A.
In Poe, E. A. The complete tales and poems of Edgar Allan Poe p354-60   S C

The myth of Sisyphus, and other essays. Camus, A.   844

The myth of the machine. Mumford, L.   901.9

Mythology

Bulfinch, T. Bulfinch's Mythology   291

Frazer, Sir J. G. The new Golden bough   291

Larousse World mythology   291

See also pages in the following book:

Highet, G. The classical tradition p520-40   809

See also Gods

Dictionaries

Funk & Wagnalls Standard dictionary of folklore, mythology and legend   398.03

New Larousse Encyclopedia of mythology   291.03

Mythology, African
See pages in the following books:

Larousse World mythology p519-43   291

New Larousse Encyclopedia of mythology p473-85   291.03

Mythology, Assyro-Babylonian
See pages in the following books:

Larousse World mythology p63-70   291

New Larousse Encyclopedia of mythology p49-72   291.03

Mythology, Australian (Aboriginal)
See pages in the following book:

Larousse World mythology p511-17   291

Mythology, Babylonian. See Mythology, Assyro-Babylonian

Mythology, Buddhist
See pages in the following book:

Larousse World mythology p252-63   291

Mythology, Celtic
See pages in the following books:

Larousse World mythology p335-56   291

New Larousse Encyclopedia of mythology p222-44   291.03

Mythology, Chinese
See pages in the following book:

Larousse World mythology p271-92   291

Mythology, Classical

Asimov, I, Words from the myths   292

Bulfinch, T. A book of myths   292

Gayley, C. M. ed. The classic myths in English literature and in art   292

Grant, M. Myths of the Greeks and Romans   292

Graves, R. Greek myths   292

Guerber, H. A. Myths of Greece & Rome   292

Hamilton, E. Mythology   292

See also pages in the following books:

Camus, A. The myth of Sisyphus, and other essays p119-23   844

Horizon Magazine. The Horizon Book of ancient Greece p48-111   913.38

Larousse World mythology p97-187   291

New Larousse Encyclopedia of mythology p85-221   291.03

Smith, R. ed. The tree of life p275-306   291

Dictionaries

Oswalt, S. G. Concise encyclopedia of Greek and Roman mythology   292.03

Tripp, E. Crowell's Handbook of classical mythology   292.03

Zimmerman, J. E. Dictionary of classical mythology   292.03

Mythology, Classical—*Continued*

Fiction

Renault, M. The bull from the sea **Fic**
Renault, M. The king must die   **Fic**

Mythology, Egyptian
See pages in the following books:
Larousse World mythology p25-53   **291**
New Larousse Encyclopedia of mythology
p9-48   **291.03**

Mythology, Finno-Ugrian
See pages in the following books:
Larousse World mythology p423-30 **291**
New Larousse Encyclopedia of mythology
p299-308   **291.03**

Mythology, Germanic
See pages in the following books:
Larousse world mythology p357-99   **291**
New Larousse Encyclopedia of mythology
p245-80   **291.03**

Mythology, Greek. See Mythology, Classical

Mythology, Hindu
Coomaraswamy, A. K. Myths of the
Hindus & Buddhists   **294.5**
See also pages in the following books:
Larousse World mythology p208-48 **291**
New Larousse Encyclopedia of mythology
p325-78   **291.03**

Mythology, Hittite
See pages in the following book:
Larousse World mythology p71-83 **291**

Mythology, Hungarian. See Mythology, Finno-Ugrian

Mythology, Indian. See Indians of North America—Religion and mythology

Mythology, Indian (American Indian) See Indians—Religion and mythology; Indians of North America—Religion and mythology

Mythology, Indian (East Indian) See Mythology, Hindu

Mythology, Japanese
See pages in the following book:
Larousse World mythology p293-333 **291**

Mythology, Maya. See Mayas—Religion and mythology

Mythology, Norse
Hamilton, E. Mythology   **292**
See also pages in the following books:
Gayley, C. M. ed. The classic myths in
English literature and in art p373-97
                                    292
Simpson, J. Everyday life in the Viking
age p176-200   **914.8**
Smith, R. ed. The tree of life p45-70 **291**

Mythology, Oceanic
See pages in the following books:
Larousse World mythology p492-509 **291**
New Larousse Encyclopedia of mythology
p449-72   **291.03**

Mythology, Oriental
See pages in the following book:
New Larousse Encyclopedia of mythology
p379-422   **291.03**

Mythology, Persian
See pages in the following books:
Larousse World mythology p189-205 **291**
New Larousse Encyclopedia of mythology
p309-24   **291.03**

Mythology, Phenician
See pages in the following book:
New Larousse Encyclopedia of mythology
p73-84   **291.03**

Mythology, Roman. See Mythology, Classical

Mythology, Russian. See Mythology, Slavic

Mythology, Semitic
See pages in the following book:
Larousse World mythology p85-95   **291**

Mythology, Siberian
See pages in the following book:
Larousse World mythology p431-38 **291**

Mythology, Slavic
See pages in the following books:
Larousse World mythology p401-22 **291**
New Larousse Encyclopedia of mythology
p281-98   **291.03**

Mythology, Slovak. See Mythology, Slavic

Mythology, Sumerian
See pages in the following book:
Larousse World mythology p56-62   **291**

Mythology. Hamilton, E.   **292**

Myths. See Mythology

The **myths** of automation. Silberman, C. E.
                                    301.24

Myths of Greece & Rome. Guerber, H. A.
                                    292

Myths of the Greeks and Romans. Grant, M.
                                    292

Myths of the Hindus & Buddhists. Coomaraswamy, A. K.   **294.5**

N

NAACP. See National Association for the Advancement of Colored People

NAACP. Kellogg, C. F.   **323.4**

NASA. See United States. National Aeronautics and Space Administration

NATO. See North Atlantic Treaty Organization

NATO: the transatlantic bargain. Cleveland, H.   **341.18**

NBC Handbook of pronunciation   **421**

NBC News Picture book of the year. National Broadcasting Company, inc. NBC News   **909.82**

NIH. See National Institutes of Health

The **NRACP.** Elliott, G. P.
In Foley, M. ed. Fifty best American
short stories, 1915-1965 p407-37
                                    S C

Nabokov, Vladimir
The assistant producer
In Dulles, A. ed. Great spy stories from
fiction p215-22   **S C**
Lance
In The New Yorker. Stories from The
New Yorker, 1950-1960 p8-18 **S C**
Pale fire   **Fic**

Nabuco, Joaquim
See pages in the following book:
Worcester, D. E. Makers of Latin America p198-209   **920**

National parks and reserves
See pages in the following book:
Osborn, F. ed. Our crowded planet p71-79   301.3
See also Wilderness areas; *also* names of national parks

United States
Butcher, D. Our national parks in color   917.3
Freeman, O. L. The national forests of America   917.3
Matthews, W. H. A guide to the national parks   917.3
National Geographic Society. America's wonderlands   917.3
Udall, S. L. The national parks of America   917.3
See also pages in the following book:
American Heritage. The American Heritage Pictorial atlas of United States history p353-67   911
The national parks of America. Udall, S. L.   917.3

National planning. See United States—Economic policy

National Pro Football Hall of Fame. See Canton, Ohio. National Pro Football Hall of Fame

National resources. See Natural resources; and names of countries with the subdivision Natural resources, e.g. United States—Economic conditions

National Science Teachers Association
Science looks at itself. See Science looks at itself   508

National socialism
Bullock, A. Hitler   92
Hitler, A. Mein Kampf   92
Zeman, Z. A. B. Nazi propaganda 301.15
See also pages in the following books:
Dill, M. Germany p295-305, 342-80 943
Herzstein, R. E. ed. Adolf Hitler and the Third Reich, 1933-1945 p4-23   943.086
Stadler, K. R. Austria p151-56, 181-89, 228-36, 248-51   943.6
See also Fascism

National songs
Shaw, M. ed. National anthems of the world   784.7
See also Patriotic poetry

National songs, American
History and criticism
Krythe, M. R. Sampler of American songs   784.09

Nationalism
Dangerfield, G. The awakening of American nationalism, 1815-1828   973.5
Ward, B. Nationalism and ideology 320.1
See also pages in the following books:
Schneider, H. W. A history of American philosophy p71-99   191
Ward, B. Five ideas that change the world p13-44   320
See also Patriotism

Nationalism and ideology. Ward, B.   320.1

Native races. See Indians of North America; Race problems

Native son. Wright, R.   Fic
Native sons. Margolies, E.   810.9
A native sons reader. Margolies, E.   810.8

Natural history
Bates, M. The forest and the sea 574.5
Farb, P. The forest   581
Ley, W. Another look at Atlantis, and fifteen other essays   508
Sears, P. B. Lands beyond the forest 581
See also pages in the following book:
Sarton, G. A history of science v2 p379-99   509
See also Botany; Geology

Africa
Carr, A. The land and wildlife of Africa   574.9

Africa, Central
Schaller, G. B. The year of the gorilla 599

Africa, East
Schaller, G. B. The year of the gorilla 599

Corfu
Durrell, G. Birds, beasts, and relatives   574.9

Dictionaries
Compton's Dictionary of the natural sciences   570.3

Handbooks, manuals, etc.
Time-Life Books. A guide to the natural world, and Index to the Life Nature library   574

Hawaii
Carlquist, S. Hawaii: a natural history   574.9

Hudson River
Boyle, R. H. The Hudson River   917.47

Madagascar
See pages in the following book:
Carr, A. The land and wildlife of Africa p151-67   574.9

North America
Farb, P. The land and wildlife of North America   574.9
Peterson, R. T. Wild America   574.9
Sanderson, I. T. The continent we live on   574.9

Outdoor books
See Nature study

Philosophy
Eiseley, L. The unexpected universe 574.01

Pictures, illustrations, etc.
Life (Periodical) The wonders of life on earth   574

Scotland
Maxwell, G. Ring of bright water 574.9

Tropics
Sanderson, I. T. Ivan Sanderson's Book of great jungles   910.9

United States
Krutch, J. W. The best nature writing of Joseph Wood Krutch   574.9
Teale, E. W. Autumn across America   574.9
Teale, E. W. Journey into summer 574.9
Teale, E. W. North with the spring 574.9
Teale, E. W. Wandering through winter   574.9
Thoreau, H. D. America the beautiful   574.9

961

Nature poetry. See Nature in poetry

Nature study
Carson, R. The sense of wonder   574
   See also Animals—Habits and behavior; Botany; Natural history; Zoology

Nautical astronomy
   See pages in the following book:
Hogben, L. Mathematics for the million p294-342   510

Nautilus (Atomic submarine)
Anderson, W. R. Nautilus 90 north 623.82

Nautilus 90 north. Anderson, W. R.   623.82

A Navaho Christmas. Armer, L. A.
   In Wernecke, H. H. ed. Celebrating Christmas around the world p199-204   394.26

Navaho Indians
   See pages in the following books:
Brown, D. Bury my heart at Wounded Knee p14-36   970.4
Sprague, M. The Mountain States p75-82   917.8
      Fiction
La Farge, O. Laughing Boy   Fic

Navajo Indians. See Navaho Indians

Naval architecture. See Shipbuilding

Naval art and science
   See pages in the following books:
The New Cambridge Modern history v8 p174-90, v9 p76-90   909

Naval battles
   See pages in the following book:
Freuchen, P. Peter Freuchen's Book of the Seven Seas p297-359   910.4

Naval biography. See Admirals

Naval history
   See pages in the following books:
The New Cambridge Modern history v4 p226-38, v6 p741-833, v9 p76-90   909
   See also Military history

The naval treaty. Doyle, Sir A. C.
   In Doyle, Sir A. C. The complete Sherlock Holmes v 1 p516-41   S C

Naval uniforms. See Uniforms, Military

Navigation
   See pages in the following books:
Hale, J. R. Age of exploration p72-93   910.9
Ward, R. R. The living clocks p215-27   574.1
   See also Compass; Knots and splices; Nautical astronomy; Sailing

Navigators. See Discoveries (in geography); Explorers

Nazi movement. See National socialism

Nazi propaganda. Zeman, Z. A. B.   301.15

Ne, Win
   See pages in the following book:
Salisbury, H. E. Orbit of China p69-82   915.1

Neal, Jean
(jt. auth.) Friedlander, J. K. Stock market ABC   332.6

Neal, Larry
Sinner man where you gonna run to?
   In Jones, L. ed. Black fire p510-18 810.8
(jt. ed.) Jones, L. ed. Black fire   810.8

Near East
Twain, M. The innocents abroad   817
   See also pages in the following books:
Cronkite, W. Eye on the world p55-87   909.82
Kohler, F. D. Understanding the Russians p398-412   947.084
      Civilization
Asimov, I. The Near East   939
      History
Asimov, I. The Near East   939
Hitti, P. K. The Near East in history 956
Hitti, P. K. A short history of the Near East   956
   See also pages in the following books:
The New Cambridge Modern history v11 p567-92, v12 p269-96   909
      Politics
   See pages in the following book:
The New Cambridge Modern history v9 p525-51   909

The Near East. Asimov, I.   939

Near East cookery. See Cookery, Near East

The Near East in history. Hitti, P. K.   956

Neary, John
Julian Bond: Black rebel   92

Nebraska
      Fiction
Aldrich, B. S. A lantern in her hand Fic
Cather, W. My Antonia   Fic
Cather, W. O pioneers!   Fic
Cather, W. One of ours   Fic

The necklace. Maupassant, G. de
   In Maupassant, G. de. Guy de Maupassant's Short stories p38-46   S C
   In Maupassant, G. de. The odd number p53-70   S C

Necromancy. See Witchcraft

Nectar in a sieve. Markandaya, K.   Fic

Needlework
Better Homes and Gardens. Better Homes & Gardens Stitchery and crafts   746
   See also Embroidery; Sewing

Nefertari, Queen of Egypt
   See pages in the following book:
Cottrell, L. Five queens of ancient Egypt p151-60   913.32

Nefertete. See Nefertiti, Queen of Egypt

Nefertiti, Queen of Egypt
Chubb, M. Nefertiti lived here   913.32
Wells, E. Nefertiti   92
   See also pages in the following book:
Cottrell, L. Five queens of ancient Egypt p73-103   913.32

Nefertiti lived here. Chubb, M.   913.32

Negro actors
Davis, S. Yes I can   92

The Negro American. See Fishel, L. H. ed. The Black American   301.451

The Negro American in paperback 016.3014

Negro art
Atkinson, J. E. ed. Black dimensions in contemporary American art   759.13
Dover, C. American Negro art   709.73
See also pages in the following book:
Du Bois, W. E. B. W. E. B. Du Bois: a reader p247-60   301.451

Negro artists
Atkinson, J. E. ed. Black dimensions in contemporary American art   759.13
Dover, C. American Negro art   709.73
See also pages in the following book:
Ebony. The Negro handbook p353-73   301.451

Negro athletes
Olsen, J. The Black athlete   301.451
Orr, J. The Black athlete: his story in American history   920
See also pages in the following books:
Davis, J. P. ed. The American Negro reference book p775-825   301.451
Ebony. The Negro handbook p337-51   301.451

Negro authors
Margolies, E. Native sons   810.9
Negro cookery. See Cookery, Negro
The **Negro** cowboys. Durham, P.   978
The **Negro** family in the United States; abridged. Frazier, E. F.   301.451
Negro folklore. See Folklore, Negro
The **Negro** handbook. Ebony   301.451
The **Negro** in the making of America. Quarles, B.   301.451
The **Negro** in the United States. Porter, D. B. comp.   016.3014

Negro literature
Hughes, L. ed. The book of Negro humor   817.08
Jones, L. ed. Black fire   810.8
Kearns, F. E. ed. The Black experience   810.8
Margolies, E. ed. A native sons reader   810.8

See also Negro poetry

Bibliography
Dodds, B. Negro literature for high school students   016.81

History and criticism
Dodds, B. Negro literature for high school students   016.81
Margolies, E. Native sons   810.9
See also pages in the following book:
Davis, J. P. ed. The American Negro reference book p850-78   301.451
Negro literature for high shcool students. Dodds, B.   016.81

Negro musicians
Goldberg, J. Jazz masters of the fifties   920
Jones, L. Black music   781.7
Jones, L. Blues people   781.7
Shaw, A. The world of soul   781.7
Southern, E. The music of Black Americans: a history   781.7
See also pages in the following book:
Williams, M. Jazz masters in transition, 1957-69   781.5

Negro nationalism. See Black Muslims
Negro poetry
Adoff, A. ed. Black out loud   811.08
Adoff, A. ed. I am the darker brother   811.08
Bontemps, A. ed. American Negro poetry   811.08
Hughes, L. ed. New Negro poets U.S.A.   811.08
Hughes, L. ed. The poetry of the Negro, 1746-1970   811.08
Johnson, J. W. ed. The book of American Negro poetry   811
Lomax, A. ed. 3000 years of Black poetry   808.81

Collections
See Negro poetry
Negro race. See Negroes
The **Negro** revolt. Lomax, L. E.   301.451
Negro songs
See pages in the following books:
Davis, J. P. ed. The American Negro reference book p731-58   301.451
Ewen, D. Great men of American popular song p22-40   920
Negro spirituals
Johnson, J. W. ed. The books of American Negro spirituals   784.7
Lomax, J. A. comp. American ballads and folk songs   784.4
See also pages in the following books:
Boni, M. B. ed. Fireside book of folk songs p298-316   784.4
Botkin, B. A. ed. A treasury of American folklore p903-18   398
Hughes, L. ed. The book of Negro folklore p279-311   398
Lomax, A. ed. The folk songs of North America in the English language p448-86   784.4
Seventeen. The Seventeen Book of prayer p159-64   242
Negro suffrage. See Negroes—Politics and suffrage
Negro thought in America, 1880-1915. Meier, A.   301.451
Negroes
Baldwin, J. The fire next time   301.451
Baldwin, J. Nobody knows my name   301.451
Baldwin, J. Notes of a native son   301.451
Belfrage, S. Freedom summer   323.4
Bracey, J. H. ed. Black nationalism in America   301.451
Cleaver, E. Soul on ice   301.451
Davis, J. P. ed. The American Negro reference book   301.451
Draper, T. The rediscovery of Black nationalism   301.451
Du Bois, W. E. B. The souls of Black folk   301.451
Du Bois, W. E. B. W. E. B. Du Bois: a reader   301.451
Furnas, J. C. Goodbye to Uncle Tom 326
Goldman, P. Report from Black America   301.451
Hughes, L. The Langston Hughes reader   818

Negroes—Continued

Myrdal, G. An American dilemma   301.451

White, W. Lost boundaries   301.451

See also pages in the following books:

Harrington, M. The other America p61-81   301.44

Michener, J. A. The quality of life p30-43   309.173

Polenberg, R. ed. America at war p107-15   309.173

See also Slavery in the United States; United States—Race relations

Art

See Negro art

Bibliography

Johnson, H. A. ed. Multimedia materials for Afro-American studies   016.3014

The Negro American in paperback   016.3014

Porter, D. B. comp. The Negro in the United States   016.3014

Biography

Adams, R. L. Great Negroes past and present   920

Alexander, R. P. comp. Young and Black in America   920

Anderson, M. My Lord, what a morning   92

Angelou, M. I know why the caged bird sings   92

Bennett, L. What manner of man; a biography of Martin Luther King, Jr.   92

Bontemps, A. Anyplace but here   301.451

Bontemps, A. Free at last; the life of Frederick Douglass   92

Bontemps, A. ed. Great slave narratives   920

Bontemps, A. 100 years of Negro freedom   301.451

Bontemps, A. We have tomorrow   920

Brown, C. Manchild in the promised land   92

Chisholm, S. Unbought and unbossed 92

Douglass, F. Life and times of Frederick Douglass; abridged   92

Drotning, P. T. Up from the ghetto 920

Elliott, L. George Washington Carver 92

Evers, Mrs M. For us, the living [biography of Medgar Wiley Evers]   92

Gibson, A. I always wanted to be somebody   92

Gibson, B. From ghetto to glory: the story of Bob Gibson   92

Gregory, D. Nigger   92

Hoexter, C. K. Black crusader: Frederick Douglass   92

Holt, R. George Washington Carver 92

Holt, R. Mary McLeod Bethune   92

Horne, L. Lena   92

Jackson, G. Soledad brother   92

King, C. S. My life with Martin Luther King, Jr.

Lacy, L. A. Cheer the lonesome; the life of W. E. B. Du Bois   92

Lincoln, C. E. ed. Martin Luther King, Jr.   92

Mays, W. Willie Mays: my life in and out of baseball   92

Meltzer, M. Langston Hughes   92

Metcalf, G. R. Black profiles   920

Neary, J. Julian Bond: Black rebel 92

Oates, S. B. To purge this land with blood; a biography of John Brown 92

Quarles, B. ed. Frederick Douglass 92

Robinson, S. R. Sugar Ray   92

Rollins, C. H. Black troubadour: Langston Hughes   92

Thornbrough, E. L. ed. Booker T. Washington   92

Washington, B. T. Up from slavery 92

Webb, C. Richard Wright   92

Williams, J. A. The most native of sons; a biography of Richard Wright 92

Wright, R. Black boy   92

See also pages in the following book:

Ebony. The Negro handbook p393-418   301.451

Civil rights

Aptheker, H. ed. A documentary history of the Negro people in the United States   301.451

Bennett, L. What manner of man; a biography of Martin Luther King, Jr. 92

Brink, W. Black and white   301.451

Chambers, B. ed. Chronicles of Negro protest   301.451

Ebony. The white problem in America   323.4

Handlin, O. Fire-bell in the night 323.4

I have a dream   323.4

King, M. L. Where do we go from here: chaos or community?   323.4

King, M. L. Why we can't wait   323.4

Lincoln, C. E. ed. Martin Luther King, Jr.   92

Lomax, L. E. The Negro revolt   301.451

McClellan, G. S. ed. Civil rights 323.4

Meier, A. From plantation to ghetto   301.451

Year. Pictorial history of the Black American   301.451

See also pages in the following books:

Barker, L. J. ed. Civil liberties and the Constitution p382-468   342.73

Beth, L. P. The development of the American Constitution, 1877-1917 p191-215   973.8

Davis, J. P. ed. The American Negro reference book p458-83   301.451

Ducas, G. ed. Great documents in Black American history p201-12, 276-90 301.451

Ebony. The Negro handbook p45-98   301.451

Hoexter, C. K. Black crusader: Frederick Douglass p177-89   92

Lacy, L. A. Cheer the lonesome traveler; the life of W. E. B. Du Bois p52-69 92

Lynd, S. ed. Nonviolence in America: a documentary history p379-497   323

Metcalf, G. R. Black profiles   920

Schlesinger, A. M. A thousand days p924-77   973.922

Silverman, C. E. Crisis in black and white p123-61   301.451

Detroit

See pages in the following book:

Darrow, C. The story of my life p304-11   92

Nelson, Horatio Nelson, Viscount
Horizon Magazine. Nelson and the age of fighting sail   92

Nelson, Lowry
(ed.) Cervantes   863.09

Nelson, Robert C.
(jt. auth.) Rieber, A. J. A study of the USSR and communism: an historical approach   914.7

Nelson and the age of the fighting sail. Horizon Magazine   92

Nelson's Complete concordance of the Revised standard version Bible   220.2

Nemesis and the candy man. Henry, O.
In Henry, O. The complete works of O. Henry p1304-08   S C

Nemiroff, Robert
Hansberry, L. To be young, gifted and Black   812

Neo-impressionism (Art) See Impressionism (Art)

Neola
Mad about motors
In Seventeen. Stories from Seventeen p77-90   S C

Neolithic period. See Stone age

Neptune (Planet)
See pages in the following book:
Scientific American. Frontiers in astronomy p78-84   520

Nero, Emperor of Rome
See pages in the following book:
Coolidge, O. Lives of famous Romans p110-30   920

Nersessian, Sirarpie Der. See Der Nersessian, Sirarpie

Nerves. See Nervous system

Nervous system
See pages in the following books:
Asimov, I. The new intelligent man's guide to science p748-60   500
Halacy, D. S. Man alive p145-64   574
See also Brain

Nest egg. Stuart, J.
In Stuart, J. A Jesse Stuart reader p3-16   818

Nests. See Birds—Eggs and nests

The net. Coates, R. M.
In Foley, M. ed. Fifty best American short stories, 1915-1965 p261-69   S C

Netherlands
Frank, A. The works of Anne Frank   839.3
Rachlis, E. The Low Countries   914.92

Art
See Art, Dutch

Civilization
See pages in the following book:
Durant, W. The age of reason begins p436-94   940.2

History
See pages in the following books:
Durant, W. The age of Louis XIV p164-80   940.2
The New Cambridge Modern history v4 p359-84, v5 p275-300, 417-29   909

History—Fiction
Dumas, A. The black tulip   Fic

History—German occupation. 1940-1945—Drama
Goodrich, F. The diary of Anne Frank   812

Nets to catch the wind. Wylie, E.
In Wylie, E. Collected poems p 1-42   811

Neugeboren, Jay
The application
In The Best American short stories, 1965 p251-58   S C

Neumann, William L.
America encounters Japan: from Perry to MacArthur   327.73

Neutra, Richard Joseph
See pages in the following book:
Forsee, A. Men of modern architecture p131-60   920

Neutrality
See pages in the following book:
Stadler, K. R. Austria p273-79, 305-14   943.6

The neutrino. Asimov, I.   539.7

Neutron star. Niven, L.
In Asimov, I. ed. Where do we go from here? p414-37   S C

Never bet the Devil your head. Poe, E. A.
In Poe, E. A. The complete tales and poems of Edgar Allan Poe p482-89   S C

Never call retreat. Catton, B.   973.7

Never cry wolf. Mowat, F.   599

Nevermann, Hans
(jt. auth.) Trowell, M. African and Oceanic art   709.6

Neville, Anthony E.
(jt. auth.) Jacobs, D. Bridges, canals & tunnels   624

Nevins, Allan
Ford: the times, the man, the company   92
The gateway to history   907
The New Deal and world affairs   327.73
Ordeal of the Union   973.6
A short history of the United States   973
The United States in a chaotic world   327.73
(jt. ed.) Commager, H. S. ed. The heritage of America   973
(ed.) Kennedy, J. F. The burden and the glory   973.922

The new accelerator. Wells, H. G.
In Wells, H. G. The complete short stories of H. G. Wells p927-42   S C
In Wells, H. G. 28 science fiction stories p856-70   S C

New advocate. Kafka, F.
In Kafka, F. Selected short stories of Franz Kafka p159-60   S C

The new Aerobics. Cooper, K. H.   613.7

The new age of exploration. Warshofsky, F.   500

The new American Bible. Bible   220.5

The New American Guide to colleges. Hawes, G. R.   378.73

The New American Roget's College thesaurus in dictionary form   424

New basic history of the United States, The Beards'. Beard, C. A.   973

The **new** book of modern composers. Ewen, D. ed. 920

The **new** book of unusual quotations. Flesch, R. 808.88

New Caledonia

See pages in the following book:

Shadbolt, M. Isles of the South Pacific p138-54 919

The **New** Cambridge Modern history 909

The **New** Cassell's French dictionary: French-English, English-French 443

The **New** Cassell's German dictionary: German-English, English-German 433

New cat book, Doris Bryant's. Bryant, D. 636.8

The **New** Century Classical handbook 913.3803

The **New** Century Cyclopedia of names 031

The **New** Century Handbook of English literature 820.3

The **new** class. Djilas, M. 335.4

A **new** companion to Shakespeare studies. Muir, K. 822.3

New complete book of flower arrangement, The Rockwells'. Rockwell, F. F. 745.92

New Complete book of the American musical theater. Ewen, D. 782.8

New complete stories of the great ballets, Balanchine's. Balanchine, G. 792.8

New cook book, Better Homes & Gardens. Better Homes and Gardens 641.5

New Cosmopolitan world atlas, Rand McNally. Rand McNally and Company 912

New Cuyás English-Spanish and Spanish-English dictionary, Appleton's. Cuyás, A. 463

New cyclopedia of practical quotations, Hoyt's. Hoyt, J. K. 808.88

A **new** day. Wright, C.
In Hughes, L. ed. The best short stories by Negro writers p341-46 **S C**

New Deal and global war. Adams, J. T.
In Adams, J. T. The march of democracy v5 973

New Deal and global war: 1933-1945. Leuchtenburg, W. E.
In Life (Periodical) The Life History of the United States v11 973

The **New** Deal and the American people. Freidel, F. ed. 973.917

The **New** Deal and world affairs. Nevins, A. 327.73

A **new** dictionary of quotations on historical principles from ancient and modern sources. Mencken, H. L. ed. 808.88

New dictionary of synonyms, Webster's 424

The **new** dress. Woolf, V.
In Havighurst, W. ed. Masters of the modern short story p212-20 **S C**

New dresses. Mansfield, K.
In Mansfield, K. The short stories of Katherine Mansfield p25-36 **S C**

The **new** edition of The encyclopedia of jazz. Feather, L. 781.503

The **New** Encyclopedia of child care and guidance 649

New Encyclopedia of the great composers and their music, The Milton Cross. Cross, M. 920.03

The **new** Encyclopedia of the opera. Ewen, D. 782.103

New England

Civilization

Brooks, V. The flowering of New England 810.9

Brooks, V. New England: Indian summer 810.9

Description and travel

McCarthy, J. New England 917.4

Fiction

Field, R. And now tomorrow **Fic**

Hawthorne, N. The House of the Seven Gables **Fic**

Hawthorne, N. The scarlet letter **Fic**

Steinbeck, J. The winter of our discontent **Fic**

History—Colonial period

Andrews, C. M. The fathers of New England 974

Miller, P. The New England mind: From colony to province 917.4

Intellectual life

Miller, P. The New England mind: From colony to province 917.4

New England. McCarthy, J. 917.4

New England: Indian summer. Brooks, V. 810.9

New England: Indian summer; condensation. Brooks, V.
In Brooks, V. Our literary heritage p150-79 810.9

The **New** England mind: From colony to province. Miller, P. 917.4

The **New** England mind: The seventeenth century. Miller, P. 917.4

New England poets, An anthology of the. Untermeyer, L. ed. 811.08

The **new** English Bible. Bible 220.5

The **new** field book of reptiles and amphibians. Cochran, D. M. 598.1

New found world. Lamb, H. 973.1

New France

History

See Canada—History—To 1763 (New France)

The **new** Golden bough. Frazer, Sir J. G. 291

The **new** Good Housekeeping cookbook. Good Housekeeping Institute, New York 641.5

The **new** guide to study abroad. Garraty, J. A. 378.3

New Guinea

See pages in the following book:

Shadbolt, M. Isles of the South Pacific p190-206 919

Native races

See pages in the following book:

National Geographic Society. Great adventures with National Geographic p399-411 910.9

New Hampshire

Fiction

Cannon, L. Look to the mountain **Fic**

New Hampshire. Frost, R.
In Frost, R. Complete poems of Robert Frost, 1949 p199-300 811

New York (City)—*Continued*

Metropolitan area
See pages in the following book:
Scientific American. Cities p105-21   309.2

Metropolitan Museum of Art
American sculpture   730.973
Great paintings from the Metropolitan Museum of Art   708
Geldzahler, H. American painting in the twentieth century   759.13
New York (City) Museum of Primitive Art. Art of Oceania, Africa, and the Americas, from the Museum of Primitive Art   709

Museum of Modern Art
The family of man   779

Museum of Primitive Art
Art of Oceania, Africa, and the Americas, from the Museum of Primitive Art   709

Police
Arm, W. The policeman   352

Politics and government
Hentoff, N. A political life; the education of John V. Lindsay   92
Lindsay, J. V. The city   974.71

Poor
See pages in the following book:
Lindsay, J. V. The city p143-63   974.71

Public library
Books for the teen age   028.52

Public schools
Kohl, H. 36 children   371.9

Public schools—Fiction
Kaufman, B. Up the down staircase   Fic

Schools
See New York (City)—Public schools

Social conditions
Lewis, O. La vida   301.453
Lindsay, J. V. The city   974.71
Riis, J. A. The making of an American   92
See also pages in the following book:
Weinberg, A. ed. The muckrakers p308-19   309.173

New York (State)

Fiction
Cooper, J. F. The Deerslayer   Fic
Cooper, J. F. The last of the Mohicans   Fic
Cooper, J. F. The Pathfinder   Fic
Cooper, J. F. The pioneers   Fic
Cooper, J. F. The spy   Fic
Edmonds, W. D. Drums along the Mohawk   Fic

History
Goodwin, M. W. The Dutch and English on the Hudson   974.7
Irving, W. Knickerbocker's History of New York   974.7

Social life and customs
Carmer, C. The Hudson   974.7
The New York Aquarium Book of the water world. Bridges, W.   591.92

New York by camp fire light. Henry, O.
In Henry, O. The complete works of O. Henry p901-04   S C
The New York idea. Mitchell, L.
In Gassner, J. ed. Best plays of the early American theatre p398-457   812.08
In Quinn, A. H. ed. Representative American plays p675-727   812.08

New York Mets
Durso, J. Amazing: the miracle of the Mets   796.357

The New York Times
Guide to listening pleasure   780.1
The New York Times Encyclopedic almanac   317.3
The New York Times Index   071
Divine, R. A. ed. American foreign policy since 1945   327.73
The Kennedy years [biography of John Fitzgerald Kennedy]. See The Kennedy years [biography of John Fitzgerald Kennedy]   92
United States. National Advisory Commission on Civil Disorders. Report of the National Advisory Commission on Civil Disorders   301.18
The New York Times Complete manual of home repair. Gladstone, B.   643
The New York Times Encyclopedic almanac. The New York Times   317.3
The New York Times Index. The New York Times   071

New York University

Hall of Fame
Vance, M. The lamp lighters   920

The New Yorker
The New Yorker album, 1955-1965, fortieth anniversary   741.5
Stories from The New Yorker, 1950-1960   S C
The New Yorker album, 1955-1965, fortieth anniversary. The New Yorker   741.5

The New You and heredity. See Scheinfeld, A. Your heredity and environment   575.1

New Zealand
Grattan, C. H. The Southwest Pacific since 1900   990
MacInnes, C. Australia and New Zealand   919.4
Rowe, J. W. New Zealand   919.31
See also pages in the following book:
Shadbolt, M. Isles of the South Pacific p88-112   919

Fiction
Ashton-Warner, S. Greenstone   Fic

Newbery Medal books
Van Loon, H. W. The story of mankind (1922)   909

Newcomb, Richard F.
Iwo Jima   940.54

The newcomers: Negroes and Puerto Ricans in a changing metropolis. Handlin, O.   301.45

Newell, Adnah Clifton
Coloring, finishing and painting wood   698.3

Newfield, Jack
Robert Kennedy   92
Newfoundland
    See pages in the following book:
    Brebner, J. B. Canada p154-67   971
        Description and travel
    Mowat, F. The boat who wouldn't float
                                        910.4
        Social life and customs
    Mowat, F. This rock within the sea: a
    heritage lost   917.18
Newman, James R.
    (ed.) What is science?   508
    (ed.) The world of mathematics   510.8
    (ed.) The Harper Encyclopedia of science.
    See The Harper Encyclopedia of science
                                        503
Newman, Joseph
    (ed.) What everyone needs to know about
    drugs. See What everyone needs to
    know about drugs   613.8
News broadcasts. See Radio broadcasting;
    Television broadcasting
News dictionary   909.82
The news media: a journalist looks at his
    profession. Hohenberg, J.   071
News photography. See Photography, Jour-
    nalistic
News year. See News dictionary   909.82
A newspaper story. Henry, O.
    In Henry, O. The complete works of
    O. Henry p1198-1201   **S C**
Newspaper work. See Journalism
Newspapers
    See pages in the following books:
    Cecil, R. Life in Edwardian England p182-
    201   914.2
    Langdon, W. C. Everyday things in
    American life, 1776-1876 p152-82   917.3
    See also American newspapers; Free-
    dom of the press; Journalism
        Directories
    Political handbook and atlas of the world
                                        329
        History
    See pages in the following book:
    The New Cambridge Modern history v10
    p121-33   909
Newton, Sir Isaac
    Mathematical principles of natural philos-
    ophy; criticism
    In Downs, R. B. Books that changed
    the world p152-62   809
        About
    See pages in the following books:
    Bell, E. T. Men of mathematics p90-116
                                        920
    Durant, W. The age of Louis XIV p531-
    47   940.2
    Newman, J. R. ed. The world of mathe-
    matics v 1 p254-85   510.8
Next. McNally, T.
    In The Best short plays, 1970 p3-26
                                      808.82
"Next to reading matter." Henry, O.
    In Henry, O. The complete works of
    O. Henry p389-400   **S C**

The next voice you hear. Albee, G. S.
    In Costain, T. B. ed. Read with me p3-
    14   **S C**
Nez Percé Indians
    See pages in the following book:
    Brown, D. Bury my heart at Wounded
    Knee p315-30   970.4
"Nezumi-Lozo"—the Japanese Robin Hood.
    Akutagawa, R.
    In Akutagawa, R. Japanese short sto-
    ries p97-123   **S C**
Nibelungenlied
    See pages in the following book:
    Gayley, C. M. ed. The classic myths in
    English literature and in art p405-30
                                        292
Nicholas I, Emperor of Russia
    See pages in the following book:
    Horizon Magazine. The Horizon History
    of Russia p244-52   947
    The New Cambridge Modern history v10
    p358-69   909
Nicholas II, Emperor of Russia
    Massie, R. K. Nicholas [II] and Alex-
    andra   92
    See also pages in the following book:
    Horizon Magazine. The Horizon History
    of Russia p313-26   947
Nicholas and Alexandra. Massie, R. I.   92
Nicholas Nickleby. Dickens, C.   **Fic**
Nicholsen, Margaret E.
    People in books   920.02
Nicholson, B. E.
    (illus.) The Oxford Book of flowerless
    plants. See The Oxford Book of flower-
    less plants   586
    (illus.) The Oxford Book of food plants.
    See The Oxford Book of food plants
                                        581
Nicholson, Margaret
    A dictionary of American-English usage
                                        428
The nickel misery of George Washington
    Carver Brown. Gold, I.
    In Abrahams, W. ed. Fifty years of the
    American short story v 1 p296-333
                                      S C
Nicklaus, Jack
    The greatest game of all my life in golf
                                         92
Nickles, Harry G.
    Middle Eastern cooking   641.5
Nicknames
    Kane, J. N. Nicknames and sobriquets
    of U.S. cities and states   910.3
    Shankle, G. E. American nicknames 929.4
        Dictionaries
    Latham, E. A dictionary of names, nick-
    names, and surnames of persons, places
    and things   929.4
Nicknames and sobriquets of U.S. cities and
    states. Kane, J. N.   910.3
Nicknames of cities and states of the U.S.
    See Kane, J. N. Nicknames and sobri-
    quets of U.S. cities and states 910.3
Nicodemus. Robinson, E. A.
    In Robinson, E. A. The collected poems
    of Edwin Arlington Robinson
    p1159-1228   **811**

Nicol, John
The cooper and the kings
In Day, A. G. ed. The spell of Hawaii
p54-58 **919.69**
Nicoll, Allardyce
British drama **822.09**
Early eighteenth century drama
In Nicoll, A. A history of English
drama, 1660-1900 v2 **822.09**
Early nineteenth century drama, 1800-1850
In Nicoll, A. A history of English
drama, 1660-1900 v4 **822.09**
A history of English drama, 1660-1900
822.09
Late eighteenth century drama, 1750-1800
In Nicoll, A. A history of English
drama, 1660-1900 v3 **822.09**
Late nineteenth century drama, 1850-1900
In Nicoll, A. A history of English
drama, 1660-1900 v5 **822.09**
Restoration drama, 1660-1700
In Nicoll, A. A history of English
drama, 1660-1900 v 1 **822.09**
A short-title alphabetical catalogue of
plays produced or printed in England
from 1660 to 1900
In Nicoll, A. A history of English
drama, 1660-1900 v6 **822.09**
World drama **809.2**
Nicolls, Richard
See pages in the following book:
Craven, W. F. The colonies in transition,
1660-1713 p68-85 **973.2**
Nicomachean ethics. Aristotle
In Aristotle. The basic works of Aris-
totle **888**
Nietzsche, Friedrich Wilhelm
The antichrist
In Nietzsche, F. W. The portable
Nietzsche p565-656 **193**
Nietzsche contra Wagner
In Nietzsche, F. W. The portable
Nietzsche p661-83 **193**
The portable Nietzsche **193**
Thus spoke Zarathustra
In Nietzsche, F. W. The portable
Nietzsche p103-439 **193**
Twilight of the idols
In Nietzsche, F. W. The portable
Nietzsche p463-563 **193**
About
See pages in the following books:
Camus, A. The rebel p57-71 **170**
Durant, W. The story of philosophy p301-
35 **109**
Russell, B. A history of Western philos-
ophy p760-73 **109**
Scott, M. A. The unquiet vision **142**
Thomas, H. Understanding the great phi-
losophers p283-91 **109**
Untermeyer, L. Makers of the modern
world p209-17 **920**
Nietzsche contra Wagner. Nietzsche, F. W.
In Nietzsche, F. W. The portable
Nietzsche p661-83 **193**

Nigeria
Niven, Sir R. Nigeria **916.69**
See also pages in the following book:
Ashabranner, B. A moment in history: the
first ten years of the Peace Corps p51-
91, 104-11 **309.2**
Fiction
Achebe, C. Arrow of God **Fic**
Achebe, C. Things fall apart **Fic**
History
Hatch, J. Nigeria **966.9**
History—Civil War, 1967-1970
See pages in the following books:
Hatch, J. Nigeria p287-97 **966.9**
Hoepli, N. L. ed. West Africa today p69-
113 **916.6**
Politics and government
See pages in the following book:
Kenworthy, L. S. Leaders of new nations
p48-64 **920**
Nigger. Gregory, D. **92**
The **Nigger** of the Narcissus. Conrad, J.
Fic
also in Conrad, J. The portable Conrad
p292-453 **828**
also in Conrad, J. Typhoon, and other
tales of the sea p91-236 **Fic**
Nikolais, Alwin
See pages in the following book:
McDonagh, D. The rise and fall and rise
of modern dance p206-23 **793.3**
Nile River
Brander, B. The River Nile **916.2**
Moorehead, A. The White Nile **962**
See also pages in the following book:
Casson, L. Ancient Egypt p29-49 **913.32**
See also Blue Nile River
Nilgiri
See pages in the following book:
National Geographic Society. Vanishing
peoples of the earth p76-91 **572**
Nine friends. Lederer, W. J.
In Lederer, W. J. The ugly American
p43-65 **S C**
The **900** days. Salisbury, H. E. **940.54**
Nine planets. Nourse, A. E. **523.4**
Nine plays. O'Neill, E. **812**
Nine stories. Salinger, J. D. **S C**
The **nine-to-five** man. Ellin, S.
In Mystery Writers of America. Crime
without murder p47-62 **S C**
Night. Stuart, D. A.
In Asimov, I. ed. Where do we go from
here? p36-63 **S C**
Night at an inn. Dunsany, Lord
In Cerf, B. ed. Thirty famous one-act
plays p255-63 **808.82**
A **night** at Greenway Court. Cather, W.
In Cather, W. Willa Cather's Collected
short fiction, 1892-1912 v3 p483-92
S C
Night before battle. Hemingway, E.
In Hemingway, E. The Fifth Column,
and four stories of the Spanish
Civil War p110-39 **818**

No boy. I'm a girl! Amft, M. J.
In Seventeen. Seventeen from Seventeen p107-21   **S C**
No cure for it. Wolfe, T.
In Wolfe, T. The hills beyond p43-48   **S C**
No door. Wolfe, T.
In Wolfe, T. The short novels of Thomas Wolfe p158-231   **S C**
No easy victories. Gardner, J. W.   **309.173**
No exit. Sartre, J. P.
In Block, H. M. ed. Masters of modern drama p802-16   **808.82**
In Gassner, J. ed. Twenty best European plays on the American stage p278-99   **808.82**
No hero. Stuart, J.
In Stuart, J. A Jesse Stuart reader p45-58   **818**
No language but a cry. D'Ambrosio, R.   **155.45**
No more Indians. Godden, R.
In Godden, R. Gone p6-30   **S C**
No more roses. Seager, A.
In The Saturday Evening Post. Best modern short stories p200-13 **S C**
No particular night or morning. Bradbury, R.
In Bradbury, R. The illustrated man p146-56   **S C**
No petty thief. Stuart, J.
In Stuart, J. A Jesse Stuart reader p150-61   **818**
No room in the ark. Moorehead, A. **916**
No story. Henry, O.
In Henry, O. The complete works of O. Henry p773-80   **S C**
No time for sergeants. Levin, I.   **812**
—Same
In Gassner, J. ed. Best American plays; 4th ser. p573-609   **812.08**
No trace. Madden, D.
In The Best American short stories, 1971 p134-55   **S C**
No visitors. Benét, S. V.
In Benét, S. V. Selected works of Stephen Vincent Benét v2   **818**
No witchcraft for sale. Lessing, D.
In Lessing, D. African stories p67-84   **S C**
Noah. Obey, A.
In Gassner, J. ed. Twenty best European plays on the American stage p375-400   **808.82**
Nobility
See pages in the following book:
Ashley, M. Life in Stuart England p61-68   **914.2**
See also Aristocracy
Noble, Iris
Treasure of the caves   **221.4**
Noble, Margaret E.
(jt. auth.) Coomaraswamy, A. K. Myths of Hindus & Buddhists   **294.5**
The **noblest** instrument. Day, C.
In White, E. B. ed. A subtreasury of American humor; abridged p296-303   **817.08**

Nobody here but—. Asimov, I.
In Asimov, I. Nightfall, and other stories p232-43   **S C**
Nobody knows. Anderson, S.
In Anderson, S. Winesburg, Ohio (Modern Lib) p49-54   **S C**
In Anderson, S. Winesburg, Ohio (Viking) p58-62   **S C**
Nobody knows my name. Baldwin, J.   **301.451**
Nobody said it's easy. Smith, S. L.   **155.5**
Nocturne on the Rhine; play. Drayton, R.
In Jones, L. ed. Black fire p570-73 **810.8**
Noguchi, Hideyo
See pages in the following book:
Beard, A. E. S. Our foreign-born citizens p80-95   **920**
Noise
See pages in the following books:
Linton, R. M. Terracide p95-121   **614**
Our poisoned planet: can we save it? p145-58   **614**
See also Noise pollution
Noise pollution
Berland, T. The fight for quiet   **614**
Still, H. In quest of quiet   **614**
Nolan, Paul T.
Marc Connelly   **812.09**
Nolen, William A.
The making of a surgeon   **617**
Non-book materials   **025.3**
Nonsense verses
See pages in the following book:
Stevenson, B. E. comp. The home book of verse, American and English p2048-90   **821.08**
Nonverbal communication
Fast, J. Body language   **153**
Nonviolence in America: a documentary history. Lynd, S. ed.   **323**
Non-violent non-cooperation. See Passive resistance to government
Noon wine. Porter, K. A.
In Porter, K. A. The collected stories of Katherine Anne Porter p222-68   **S C**
In Porter, K. A. Pale horse, pale rider p93-176   **S C**
Nora. Lardner, R.
In Lardner, R. The Ring Lardner reader p537-46   **S C**
Nordenskiöld, Nils Adolf Erik fríherre
See pages in the following book:
Stefánsson, V. ed. Great adventures and explorations p446-68   **910.9**
Nordhoff, Charles
The Bounty trilogy   **Fic**
Men against the sea
In Nordhoff, C. The Bounty trilogy p297-438   **Fic**
Mutiny on the Bounty
In Nordhoff, C. The Bounty trilogy p 1-295   **Fic**
Pitcairn's Island
In Nordhoff, C. The Bounty trilogy p441-691   **Fic**
Norman, A. V. B.
A history of war and weapons, 449 to 1660   **355.09**

Norman, Charles
To a different drum; the story of Henry David Thoreau   92
Norman England, Life in. Tomkeieff, O. G.   914.2

Normandy
Description and travel
See pages in the following book:
Adams, H. Mont-Saint-Michel and Chartres p46-60   726

Normandy, Attack on, 1944
The Army Times. D-Day   940.54
Howarth, D. D Day, the sixth of June, 1944   940.54
Perrault, G. The secret of D-Day   940.54
Ryan, C. The longest day: June 6, 1944   940.54
See also pages in the following books:
Armstrong, O. K. The fifteen decisive battles of the United States p327-54   973
Reeder, R. The story of the Second World War v2 p118-56   940.53

A **Normandy** joke. Maupassant, G. de
In Maupassant, G. de. Selected short stories p151-57   S C

Normans
See pages in the following book:
Quennell, M. Everyday life in Roman and Anglo-Saxon times p203-21   913.42
See also Northmen

Norris, Frank
McTeague: A story of San Francisco; criticism
In Stegner, W. ed. The American novel p97-105   813.09
The octopus   Fic
About
See pages in the following book:
Brooks, V. The confident years: 1885-1915 p211-21   810.9

Norris, George William
See pages in the following books:
Kennedy, J. F. Profiles in courage (Harper) p707-30   920
Kennedy, J. F. Profiles in courage. Large type ed. (Watts, F.) p233-60   920

Norse mythology. See Mythology, Norse
Norsemen. See Northmen
North, Sterling
Raccoons are the brightest people   599
North Africa. See Africa, North
North America
See pages in the following book:
The New Cambridge Modern history v7 p500-40   909
Description and travel
Peterson, R. T. Wild America   574.9
Discovery and exploration
See America—Discovery and exploration
Galleries and museums
Folsom, F. America's ancient treasures   913.7074
History
Lamb, H. New found world   973.1
North American birds. Milne, L.   598
North American Indians. See Indians of North America

North American trees (exclusive of Mexico and tropical United States) Preston, R. J.   582
North Atlantic region
See pages in the following book:
Stevenson, A. E. Looking outward p183-93   341.13
North Atlantic Treaty Organization
Cleveland, H. NATO: the transatlantic bargain   341.18
MacCloskey, M. North Atlantic Treaty Organization   341.18
See also pages in the following books:
Acheson, D. Present at the creation p276-84, 551-61, 588-93   973.918
White, T. H. Fire in the ashes p285-317   940.55
North Carolina
Dykeman, W. The border states   917.5
North of Boston. Frost, R.
In Frost, R. Complete poems of Robert Frost, 1949 p47-128   811
North Pole
See pages in the following books:
Ley, W. The Poles p31-58   919.8
Stefánsson, V. ed. Great adventures and explorations p565-622   910.9
North to the Orient. Lindbergh, A. M.   629.13
North with the spring. Teale, E. W.   574.9
Northanger Abbey. Austen, J.   Fic
Northern Ireland
See pages in the following book:
Lyons, F. S. L. Ireland since the famine p682-755   941.5
Politics and government
Devlin, B. The price of my soul   92
Northern lights. See Auroras
Northern Securities Co. et al. v. United States
See pages in the following book:
Fribourg, M. G. The Supreme Court in American history p91-107   347.9
Northmen
Arbman, H. The Vikings   914.8
Simpson, J. Everyday life in the Viking age   914.8
Wilson, D. M. The Vikings and their origins   914.8
See also pages in the following books:
Baity, E. C. Americans before Columbus p111-17   970.1
Claiborne, R. Climate, man, and history p348-63   551.59
Innes, H. Scandinavia p29-41   914.8
Mills, D. The Middle Ages p79-90   940.1
Quennell, M. Everyday life in Roman and Anglo-Saxon times p172-202   913.42
Simons, G. Barbarian Europe p125-44   940.1
Thorndike, L. The history of medieval Europe p217-31   940.1
See also Normans
Fiction
Seton, A. Avalon   Fic
Northwest, Old
Ogg, F. A. The Old Northwest   977

Northwest Passage
See pages in the following books:
Hale, J. R. Age of exploration p117-26
910.9
Stefánsson, V. ed. Great adventures and explorations p473-563　**910.9**
Northwest Passage. Roberts, K.　**Fic**

Northwest Territories, Canada
Description and travel
See pages in the following book:
Angier, B. How to live in the woods on pennies a day p113-23　**917.1**

Norton, Henry
Man in the moon
In Conklin, G. ed. Invaders of earth p301-10　**S C**

Norway, Nevil Shute. See Shute, Nevil

Norway
Antiquities
Hagen, A. Norway　**913.36**
Fiction
Gulbranssen, T. Beyond sing the woods
Fic
Hamsun, K. Hunger　**Fic**
Undset, S. Four stories　**S C**
Undset, S. Kristin Lavransdatter　**Fic**
Undset, S. The master of Hestviken　**Fic**

Norwegians in the United States
Fiction
Rolvaag, O. E. Giants in the earth　**Fic**

The **nose.** Akutagawa, R.
In Akutagawa, R. Japanese short stories p193-205　**S C**

Not only dead men. Van Vogt, A. E.
In Conklin, G. ed. Invaders of earth p160-81　**S C**

Not your singing, dancing spade. Fields, J.
In Jones, L. ed. Black fire p479-85　**810.8**

Notebook. Lowell, R.　**811**

Notebooks. Camus, A.　**848**

Notes from a savage god; play. Drayton, R.
In Jones, L. ed. Black fire p566-69　**810.8**

Notes just prior to the fall. Malzberg, B. N.
In The Best from Fantasy and Science Fiction; 19th ser. p161-73　**S C**

Notes of a native son. Baldwin, J.　**301.451**

Notes on a cowardly lion; the biography of Bert Lahr. Lahr, J.　**92**

Notestein, Wallace
The English people on the eve of colonization, 1603-1630　**942.06**

The **nothing** box. Brooks, T. E.
In Seventeen. Seventeen from Seventeen p84-106　**S C**

Nothing ever breaks except the heart. Boyle, K.
In Foley, M. ed. Fifty best American short stories, 1915-1965 p270-77　**S C**

Nothing is hidden, nothing lost. Hugo, V.
In Armstrong, R. ed. Treasure and treasure hunters　**910.4**

The **notorious** jumping frog of Calaveras County. Twain, M.
In Twain, M. The complete short stories of Mark Twain p 1-6　**S C**

Notre Dame Cathedral. See Paris. Notre Dame Cathedral

Notre Dame de Paris. See Hugo, V. The hunchback of Notre Dame　**Fic**

Nourse, Alan E.
The body　**612**
Nine planets　**523.4**
℞ for tomorrow　**S C**
　Contents: Symptomaticus medicus; ℞; Contamination crew; In sheep's clothing; A gift for numbers; Free Agent; The last house call; Grand Rounds; Bramble bush; Heir apparent; Plague
Universe, earth, and atom　**530.9**

Nova Scotia
See pages in the following book:
Brebner, J. B. Canada p168-80　**971**
Description and travel
See pages in the following book:
National Geographic Society. Exploring Canada from sea to sea p48-66　**917.1**

The **novel:** a modern guide to fifteen English masterpieces. Drew, E.　**823.09**

The **novel** and the modern world. Daiches, D.　**823.09**

Novelists, American
Geismar, M. American moderns: from rebellion to conformity　**813.09**
Geismar, M. Writers in crisis　**813.09**
O'Connor, W. V. ed. Seven modern American novelists　**813.09**

Novels. See Fiction

The **novels** of Dashiell Hammett. Hammett, D.　**Fic**

November 2005: The luggage store. Bradbury, R.
In Bradbury, R. The Martian chronicles p164-65　**S C**

November 2005: The off season. Bradbury, R.
In Bradbury, R. The Martian chronicles p166-78　**S C**

November 2005: The watchers. Bradbury, R.
In Bradbury, R. The Martian chronicles p179-80　**S C**

Novotný, Antonín
See pages in the following book:
Szulc, T. Czechoslovakia since World War II p185-213, 237-58　**943.7**

Now and then. Lardner, R.
In Lardner, R. The Ring Lardner reader p326-37　**S C**

Now I lay me. Hemingway, E.
In Hemingway, E. The short stories of Ernest Hemingway p363-71　**S C**

Noy, Dov
(ed.) Folktales of Israel　**398.2**

Noyce, Wilfrid
(ed.) World atlas of mountaineering　**796.5**

Nu, U
See pages in the following book:
Kenworthy, L. S. Leaders of new nations p270-89　**920**

Nuclear energy. See Atomic energy

Nuclear engineering
Fermi, L. Atoms for the world　**621.48**
Stokley, J. The new world of the atom　**621.48**

Nuclear particles. See Particles (Nuclear physics)

Nuclear physics
Asimov, I. The neutrino   539.7
Fermi, L. Atoms in the family; my life with Enrico Fermi   92
Glasstone, S. Sourcebook on atomic energy   539.7
Romer, A. The restless atom   539.7
Segrè, E. Enrico Fermi: physicist   92
  See also Nuclear engineering; Nuclear reactors; Particles (Nuclear physics)
Nuclear propulsion. See Nuclear reactors
Nuclear reactors
Curtis, R. Perils of the peaceful atom   621.48
  See also pages in the following books:
Asimov, I. The new intelligent man's guide to science p388-429   500
Stokley, J. The new world of the atom p89-106, 223-32   621.48
Nuclear warfare. See Atomic warfare
Nuclear weapons. See Atomic weapons
Nugent, Elliott
  See pages in the following book:
Gould, J. Modern American playwrights p151-54   812.09
The nuisance. Lessing, D.
  In Lessing, D. African stories p96-102   **S C**
Number games. See Mathematical recreations
Number, the language of science. Dantzig, T.   512
Numbers, Theory of
Adler, I. A new look at arithmetic   512
Dantzig, T. Number, the language of science   512
  See also pages in the following books:
Kadesch, R. R. Math menagerie p35-46   793.7
Newman, J. R. ed. The world of mathematics v 1 p442-64   510.8
Numbers: fun & facts. Friend, J. N.   793.7
Numismatics
  See pages in the following book:
Horizon Magazine. The light of the past p101-09   901.9
  See also Coins
Núñez Cabeza de Vaca, Alvar
  See pages in the following book:
Hall-Quest, O. Conquistadors and Pueblos p21-33   979.1
Nuns. See Monasticism and religious orders for women
The nun's story. Hulme. K.   Fic
Nuremberg Trial of Major German War Criminals, 1945-1946
Columbia Broadcasting System, inc. CBS News. Trial at Nuremberg   341.3
  See also pages in the following book:
Aymar, B. A pictorial history of the world's great trials p301-21   343
Nuremberg war crime trials. See Nuremberg Trial of Major German War Criminals, 1945-1946
Nurses and nursing
  See also Home nursing

Biography
Ross, I. Angel of the battlefield; the life of Clara Barton   92
Woodham Smith, C. Lonely crusader; the life of Florence Nightingale, 1820-1910   92
Fiction
Hulme, K. The nun's story   Fic
History
Dodge, B. S. The story of nursing   610.73
Nursing as a profession
Dodge, B. S. The story of nursing   610.73
Nussbaum, Al
Shutterbug
  In Mystery Writers of America. Crime without murder p197-202   **S C**
Nutrition
Arnold, P. Food facts for young people   641.1
Coles, R. Still hungry in America   330.973
Kraus, B. Calories and carbohydrates   641.1
Sebrell, W. H. Food and nutrition   641.1
  See also pages in the following books:
Better Homes and Gardens. Better Homes & Gardens New cook book p3-30   641.5
Ehrlich, P. R. Population, resources, environment p65-79   301.3
McCall's. McCall's Cook book p717-28   641.5
Snively, W. D. The sea of life p126-61, 175-85   612
United States. Department of Agriculture. Contours of change p124-30   630
  See also Diet; Metabolism; Physiology; Vitamins
Nutrition of astronauts. See Astronauts—Nutrition
Nye, Russel
The cultural life of the new Nation, 1776-1830   917.3
The unembarrassed muse: the popular arts in America   917.3
Nyere, Julius Kambarage, President United Republic of Tanzania
  See pages in the following book:
Kenworthy, L. S. Leaders of new nations p2-28   920
Nyren, Dorothy. See Curley, Dorothy Nyren
Nyren, Judith S.
(jt. ed.) Landau, R. S. ed. Large type books in print   015
Nyswander, Marie E.
Hentoff, N. A doctor among the addicts   616.86
Nzingha, Queen of Matomba
  See pages in the following book:
Polatnick, F. T. Shapers of Africa p39-75   920

O

O. Henry. See Henry, O.; Porter, William Sydney
O. Henry. Current-Garcia, E.   813.09

The **O.** Henry Awards. See Prize stories, 1970-1971: The O. Henry Awards **S C**

O pioneers! Cather, W.   **Fic**

O to be a dragon. Moore, M.
In Moore, M. The complete poems of Marianne Moore p177-202   **811**

O ye jigs & juleps! Hudson, V. C.   **817**

Oak Island. Burke, E.
In Armstrong, R. ed. Treasure and treasure hunters   **910.4**

Oakley, Kenneth Page
See pages in the following book:
Moore, R. Man, time, and fossils p357-77   **573.2**

Oates, Joyce Carol
By the river
In The Best American short stories, 1969 p196-214   **S C**
The children
In Prize stories, 1971: The O. Henry Awards p208-25   **S C**
First views of the enemy
In The Best American short stories, 1965 p259-70   **S C**
How I contemplated the world from the Detroit House of Correction and began my life over again
In The Best American short stories, 1970 p207-22   **S C**
In Prize stories, 1970: The O. Henry Awards p275-91   **S C**
In the region of ice
In Abrahams, W. ed. Fifty years of the American short story v 1 p500-15   **S C**
Unmailed, unwritten letters
In Prize stories, 1970: The O. Henry Awards p253-74   **S C**
Upon the sweeping flood
In The Best American short stories, 1964 p241-56   **S C**
In Foley, M. ed. Fifty best American short stories p799-814   **S C**
Where are you going, where have you been?
In Abrahams, W. ed. Fifty years of the American short story v 1 p516-31   **S C**
In The Best American short stories, 1967 p193-209   **S C**

Oates, Stanton C.
Audiovisual equipment   **371.33**

Oates, Stephen B.
To purge this land with blood; a biography of John Brown   **92**

Oates, Whitney J.
(ed.) The complete Greek drama   **882.08**

Obesity. See Weight control

Obey, André
Noah
In Gassner, J. ed. Twenty best European plays on the American stage p375-400   **808.82**

Obituary. Asimov, I.
In Asimov, I. Asimov's mysteries p157-73   **S C**

Oblong box. Poe, E. A.
In Poe, E. A. The complete tales and poems of Edgar Allan Poe p711-19   **S C**

The oblong room. Hoch, E. D.
In Hitchcock, A. ed. Alfred Hitchcock presents: A month of mystery p283-92   **S C**

Obojski, Robert
(jt. auth.) Hobson, B. Illustrated encyclopedia of world coins   **737.4**

O'Brien, Robert
Machines   **621.9**
(jt. auth.) Thompson, P. D. Weather   **551.5**

Obscene literature. See Literature, Immoral

Obscenity (Law)
Censorship: the search for the obscene   **343**

Observatories, Astronomical. See Astronomical observatories

Obstetrics. See Childbirth

Obudo, Nathaniel
They stole our cattle
In Angoff, C. ed. African writing today p215-18   **896**

O'Casey, Sean
Cock-a-doodle dandy
In Block, H. M. ed. Masters of modern drama p459-86   **808.82**
Juno and the paycock
In Block, H. M. ed. Masters of modern drama p435-57   **808.82**
In Dickinson, T. H. ed. Chief contemporary dramatists; 3d ser. p159-94   **808.82**
Nannie's night out
In Richards, S. ed. Best short plays of the world theatre, 1958-1967 p241-56   **808.82**
The plough and the stars
In Tucker, S. M. ed. Twenty-five modern plays p721-63   **808.82**
The Sean O'Casey reader   **828**
Contains the plays: Juno and the paycock; The plough and the stars; The silver Tassie; Within the gates; Purple dust; Red roses for me; Cock-a-doodle dandy; The bedtime story; The drums of Father Ned; and the short story: I wanna woman
Three plays: Juno and the paycock, The shadow of a gunman, The plough and the stars   **822**

About
Fallon, G. Sean O'Casey: the man I knew   **92**

The occasional garden. Saki
In Saki. The short stories of Saki p568-72   **S C**

Occidental civilization. See Civilization, Occidental

Occult sciences
Christopher, M. ESP, seers & psychics   **133**
See also Demonology; Divination; Witchcraft

Occupation, Choice of. See Vocational guidance

Occupational literature. Forrester, G.   **016.3317**

Occupational outlook handbook. United States. Bureau of Labor Statistics **331.7**

Occupations
Fanning, O. Opportunities in environ-
mental careers   614.069
United States. Bureau of Labor Statis-
tics. Occupational outlook handbook
                                331.7
  See also pages in the following book:
Miller, H. P. Rich man, poor man p195-
221   339
  See also Vocational guidance; United
  States—Occupations

Bibliography
Forrester, G. Occupational literature
                                016.3317
Dictionaries
United States. Employment Service. Dic-
tionary of occupational titles   331.703
Occupations: a selected list of pamphlets.
See Forrester, G. Occupational litera-
ture   016.3317
An occurrence at Owl Creek Bridge.
  Bierce, A.
  In Day, A. G. ed. The greatest Ameri-
  can short stories p123-34   **S C**
Ocean
Carson, R. L. The sea around us   551.4
Engel, L. The sea   551.4
Freuchen, P. Peter Freuchen's Book of
the Seven Seas   910.4
Gaskell, T. F. World beneath the oceans
                                551.4
Gordon, B. L. ed. Man and the sea 551.4
Scientific American. The ocean   551.4
  See also pages in the following books:
Bardach, J. Harvest of the sea p13-29
                                333.9
Chapman, S. IGY: year of discovery p35-
41   551
Hyde, M. O. This crowded planet p94-
127   301.3
Economic aspects
  See Marine resources
Ocean currents
          Pacific Ocean
Heyerdahl, T. Kon-Tiki   910.4
Ocean life. See Marine biology
Ocean routes. See Trade routes
Ocean waves
  See pages in the following book:
Gaskell, T. F. World beneath the oceans
p70-81   551.4
Oceania. See Islands of the Pacific
Oceanic art. See Art—Islands of the Pacific
Oceanic mythology. See Mythology, Oceanic
Oceanographic research. See Oceanography
—Research
Oceanography
Bardach, J. Harvest of the sea   333.9
Behrman, D. The new world of the oceans
                                551.4
Cousteau, J. Y. Life and death in a coral
sea   551.4
Gaskell, T. F. World beneath the oceans
                                551.4
Gordon, B. L. ed. Man and the sea 551.4
  See also pages in the following books:
Foreign Policy Association. Toward the
year 2018 p165-77   901.9

Hammond, Incorporated. Earth and space
p123-48   551
Warshofsky, F. The new age of exploration p115-50   500
  See also Marine resources

Dictionaries
Fairbridge, R. W. ed. The encyclopedia of
oceanography   551.4
Research
Behrman, D. The new world of the oceans
                                551.4
Cousteau, J. Y. Jacques-Yves Cousteau's
World without sun   551.4
Dugan, J. World beneath the sea   551.4
Piccard, J. The sun beneath the sea 551.4
Soule, G. The greatest depths   551.4
Sweeney, J. B. A pictorial history of
oceanographic submersibles   623.82
  See also pages in the following books:
Bardach, J. Harvest of the sea p29-53
                                333.9
Ceram, C. W. ed. Hands on the past p394-
403   913.03
United States. Department of Agriculture.
Science for better living p20-32 630.72
  See also Skin and scuba diving
Oceanology. See Oceanography
Ochoa, Severo
  See pages in the following book:
Moore, R. The coil of life p287-300 574.09
Ochsner, Alton
Smoking: your choice between life and
death   613.8
O'Conaire, Padraic
The Devil and O'Flaherty
  In Garrity, D. A. ed. 44 Irish short
  stories p244-48   **S C**
O'Connor, Edwin
All in the family   **Fic**
The best and the last of Edwin O'Connor
                                Fic
The last hurrah   **Fic**
O'Connor, Flannery
A circle in the fire
  In Foley, M. ed. Fifty best American
  short stories, 1915-1965 p524-41
                                S C
Everything that rises must converge
  In Abrahams, W. ed. Fifty years of the
  American short story v2 p 1-14
                                S C
Parker's back
  In The Best American short stories, 1966
  p235-54   **S C**
Revelation
  In Abrahams, W. ed. Fifty years of the
  American short story v2 p15-33
                                S C
O'Connor, Frank
The drunkard
  In Garrity, D. A. ed. 44 Irish short
  stories p249-60   **S C**
A life of your own
  In The Saturday Evening Post. Best
  modern short stories p368-75 **S C**
The majesty of the law
  In Garrity, D. A. ed. 44 Irish short
  stories p261-70   **S C**

O'Connor, Frank—*Continued*
The man of the world
In The New Yorker. Stories from The
New Yorker, 1950-1960 p 1-7 **S C**
Uprooted
In Havighurst, W. ed. Masters of the
modern short story p99-118 **S C**

O'Connor, Patrick
The wooden box
In The Best short plays, 1968 p285-310
808.82

O'Connor, Philip F.
The gift bearer
In The Best American short stories,
1971 p217-36 **S C**

O'Connor, Richard
Bret Harte **92**
The cactus throne; the tragedy of Maxi-
milian and Carlotta **92**
The German-Americans **301.453**
Jack London **92**
O. Henry; the legendary life of William
S. Porter **92**
Sinclair Lewis **92**

O'Connor, William Van
Ezra Pound
In Unger, L. ed. Seven modern American poets p119-54 **811.09**
(ed.) Seven modern American novelists
813.09

October and June. Henry, O.
In Henry, O. The complete works of
O. Henry p890-92 **S C**

October Revolution. See Russia—History—
Revolution, 1917-1921

October 2002: The shore. Bradbury, R.
In Bradbury, R. The Martian chronicles
p111-12 **S C**

October 2026: The million-year picnic. Bradbury, R.
In Bradbury, R. The Martian chronicles
p212-22 **S C**

The octopus. Crane, S.
In Crane, S. The complete short stories
& sketches of Stephen Crane p74-
77 **S C**

The octopus. Norris, F. **Fic**

The octopus marooned. Henry, O.
In Henry, O. The complete works of
O. Henry p267-72 **S C**

The octoroon. Boucicault, D.
In Gassner, J. ed. Best plays of the
early American theatre p185-215
812.08
In Quinn, A. H. ed. Representative
American plays p369-98 **812.08**

The odd couple. Simon, N.
In Gassner, J. ed. Best American plays;
6th ser. p527-65 **812.08**
In Richards, S. ed. Best plays of the
sixties p419-521 **808.82**

The odd number. Maupassant, G. de. **S C**

Odets, Clifford
Awake and sing!
In Block, H. M. ed. Masters of modern
drama p647-68 **808.82**
In Gassner, J. ed. Best American plays;
supplementary volume, 1918-1958
p501-32 **812.08**

Golden boy
In Gassner, J. ed. Twenty best plays of
the modern American theatre p775-
818 **812.08**
Six plays **812**
Contents: Waiting for Lefty; Awake and
sing; Till the day I die; Paradise lost; Golden
boy; Rocket to the moon
Waiting for Lefty
In Cerf, B. A. ed. Sixteen famous American plays p423-47 **812.08**
In Cerf, B. ed. Thirty famous one-act
plays p521-45 **808.82**

About
See pages in the following book:
Gould, J. Modern American playwrights
p186-201 **812.09**

O'Donovan, Michael. See O'Connor, Frank

O'Donovan, Patrick
The United States. See The United States
917.3

Odor of chrysanthemums. Lawrence, D. H.
In Havighurst, W. ed. Masters of the
modern short story p245-65 **S C**

An odor of verbena. Faulkner, W.
In Faulkner, W. The Faulkner reader
S C
In Faulkner, W. The portable Faulkner
p159-96 **S C**

Odysseus. See Ulysses

The Odyssey. Homer **883**
also in Homer. The complete works of
Homer v2 **883**

An odyssey of the North. London, J.
In London, J. Best short stories of
Jack London p23-49 **S C**
In London, J. Jack London's Tales of
adventure **S C**

Oedipus at Colonus. Sophocles
In Fitts, D. ed. Greek plays in modern
translations p383-454 **882.08**
In Oates, W. J. ed. The complete Greek
drama v 1 p613-69 **882.08**

Oedipus the King. Sophocles
In Oates, W. J. ed. The complete Greek
drama v 1 p369-417 **882.08**

Oehser, Paul H.
The Smithsonian Institution **507.4**

Oersted, Hans Christian
See pages in the following book:
Jones, B. Z. ed. The golden age of sci-
ence p163-86 **920**

Of a fire on the moon. Mailer, N. **629.45**

Of cabbages and kings. McPherson, J. A.
In Prize stories, 1970: The O. Henry
Awards p237-51 **S C**

Of course. Jackson, S.
In Jackson, S. The magic of Shirley
Jackson p115-19 **818**

Of human bondage. Maugham, W. S. **Fic**

Of men and mountains. Douglas, W. O. **92**

Of mice and men. Steinbeck, J. **Fic**
—Same
In Gassner, J. ed. Twenty best plays of
the modern American theatre p643-
80 **812.08**
also in Steinbeck, J. The portable Steinbeck p225-323 **818**
also in Steinbeck, J. The short novels of
John Steinbeck p203-72 **Fic**

Of mice, men and molecules. Heller, J. H.
619
Of rivers and the sea. French, H. E.   551.4
Of this time, of that place. Trilling, L.
In Foley, M. ed. Fifty best American short stories, 1915-1965 p339-74
S C
Of time and the river. Wolfe, T.   Fic
O'Faoláin, Sean
The man who invented sin
In Havighurst, W. ed. Masters of the modern short story p415-27   S C
One man, one boat, one girl
In The Saturday Evening Post. Best modern short stories p402-20 S C
Persecution mania
In Garrity, D. A. ed. 44 Irish short stories p291-98   S C
Teresa
In Garrity, D. A. ed. 44 Irish short stories p271-90   S C
Offenbach, Jacques François
See pages in the following book:
Ewen, D. ed. The complete book of classical music p611-19   780.1
Office management
Handbooks, manuals, etc.
Becker, E. R. The successful secretary's handbook   651.02
Doris, L. Complete secretary's handbook
651.02
Hutchinson, L. Standard handbook for secretaries   651.02
Ingoldsby, P. The executive secretary: handbook to success   651.02
Office of Public Information. See United Nations. Office of Public Information
Office of Vocational Rehabilitation. See Vocational Rehabilitation Administration
Office procedures. See Office management
An officer and a gentleman. Michener, J.
In Michener, J. Tales of the South Pacific p36-52   S C
Officers and gentlemen. Waugh, E.   Fic
Official Congressional directory. United States. Congress   328.73
The official encyclopedia of sports. Pratt, J. L. ed.   796.03
The Official museum directory: United States [and] Canada   069.025
Official publications. See United States— Government publications
The official Warren Commission report on the assassination of President John F. Kennedy. United States. Warren Commission on the assassination of President Kennedy   364.12
Offord, Carl Ruthven
So peaceful in the country
In Clarke, J. H. ed. American Negro short stories p123-30   S C
O'Flaherty, Liam
The hawk
In Garrity, D. A. ed. 44 Irish short stories p298-303   S C
The tent
In Garrity, D. A. ed. 44 Irish short stories p304-13   S C

O'Flaherty V.C. Shaw, B.
In Shaw, B. Complete plays, with prefaces v5 p129-51   822
Ogburn, Charlton
The Marauders   940.54
Ogg, Frederic Austin
Builders of the republic
In Pageant of America v8   973
The Old Northwest   977
The reign of Andrew Jackson   973.5
Ogg, Oscar
The 26 letters   411
Oh Dad, poor Dad, Mamma's hung you in the closet and I'm feelin' so sad. Kopit, A. L.
In Gassner, J. ed. Best American plays; 5th ser. p483-508   812.08
O'Halloran's luck. Benét, S. V.
In Benét, S. V. Selected works of Stephen Vincent Benét v2   818
O'Hara, John
Exactly eight thousand dollars exactly
In Costain, T. B. ed. Read with me p383-91   S C
The sun-dodgers
In Costain, T. B. ed. Read with me p393-403   S C
Ohio
Description and travel
See pages in the following book:
Moyers, B. Listening to America p48-57
917.3
Fiction
Richter, C. The awakening land   Fic
Richter, C. The fields   Fic
Richter, C. The town   Fic
History
Havighurst, W. The heartland: Ohio, Indiana, Illinois   977
Ohio. State University, Kent
See pages in the following book:
United States. President's Commission on Campus Unrest. The report of the President's Commission on Campus Unrest p233-410   378.1
Ohio Valley
History
Ogg, F. A. The Old Northwest   977
Ohrbach's, inc.
See pages in the following book:
Mahoney, T. The great merchants p310-23   658.87
Oil. See Petroleum
Ojibwa Indians. See Chippewa Indians
O'Kelly, Seumas
Michael and Mary
In Garrity, D. A. ed. 44 Irish short stories p314-19   S C
Nan Hogan's house
In Garrity, D. A. ed. 44 Irish short stories p320-58   S C
Okinawa
Fiction
Sneider, V. The Teahouse of the August Moon   Fic
Oklahoma
Goodwyn, L. The South Central States
917.6

Oklahoma—*Continued*

Fiction

Ferber, E. Cimarron   **Fic**

Oklahoma. Hammerstein, O.
In Hammerstein, O. 6 plays p7-84   **812**

Okpaku, Joseph O. O.
Under the Iroko tree
In Angoff, C. ed. African writing today p221-94   **896**

"Ol' Bennet" and the Indians. Crane, S.
In Crane, S. The complete short stories & sketches of Stephen Crane p598-603   **S C**

Olatunji, Michael Babatunde
(jt. auth.) Dietz, B. W. Musical instruments of Africa   **781.9**

Old age
See pages in the following book:
Harrington, M. The other America p101-20   **301.44**

See also Aged

Fiction

Updike, J. The poorhouse fair   **Fic**

Old age. Chekhov, A.
In Chekhov, A. The stories of Anton Chekhov p8-13   **S C**

Old age homes. See Aged—Dwellings

Old Anse. Schaefer, J.
In Schaefer, J. The collected stories of Jack Schaefer p243-58   **S C**

The **old** army game. Garrett, G.
In Foley, M. ed. Fifty best American short stories, 1915-1965 p691-701   **S C**

Old blues singers never die. Johnson, C. V.
In Hughes, L. ed. The best short stories by Negro writers p414-27   **S C**

The **old** chevalier. Dinesen, I.
In Dinesen, I. Seven Gothic tales p81-107   **S C**

The **old** chief Mshlanga. Lessing, D.
In Lessing, D. African stories p47-58   **S C**

The **old** curiosity shop. Dickens, C.   **Fic**

The **old** dancers. Williams, T.
In The Saturday Evening Post. Best modern short stories p429-47   **S C**

Old Dick. Stuart, J.
In Stuart, J. Plowshare in heaven p237-47   **S C**

Old English. Galsworthy, J.
In Galsworthy, J. Plays p535-72   **822**

Old Esther Dudley. Hawthorne, N.
In Hawthorne, N. Hawthorne's Short stories p121-30   **S C**

Old folks' Christmas. Lardner, R.
In Becker, M. L. ed. The home book of Christmas p291-301   **394.26**
In Lardner, R. The best short stories of Ring Lardner p139-48   **S C**
In Lardner, R. The Ring Lardner reader p391-400   **S C**

Old friends. Barrie, J. M.
In Barrie, J. M. The plays of J. M. Barrie p667-80   **822**

Old Goriot. See Balzac, H. de. Père Goriot   **Fic**

Old John's place. Lessing, D.
In Lessing, D. African stories p152-88   **S C**

The **old** lady shows her medals. Barrie, J. M.
In Barrie, J. M. The plays of J. M. Barrie p821-51   **822**

The **old** maid. Wharton, E.
In Wharton, E. The Edith Wharton reader p560-624   **S C**

Old man. Faulkner, W.
In Faulkner, W. The Faulkner reader   **S C**
In Faulkner, W. The portable Faulkner p481-581   **S C**

The **old** man. Schaefer, J.
In Schaefer, J. The collected stories of Jack Schaefer p429-50   **S C**

An **old** man and his hat. Freitag, G. H.
In The Best American short stories, 1968 p75-78   **S C**

The **Old** Man and the boy. Ruark, R.   **92**

The **old** man and the sea. Hemingway, E.   **Fic**

Old man at the bridge. Hemingway, E.
In Hemingway, E. The short stories of Ernest Hemingway p78-80   **S C**

An **old** man goes wooing. Crane, S.
In Crane, S. The complete short stories & sketches of Stephen Crane p377-80   **S C**

Old manuscript. Kafka, F.
In Kafka, F. Selected short stories of Franz Kafka p161-64   **S C**

The **old** merchant marine. Paine, R. D.   **387.5**

Old mortality. Porter, K. A.
In Porter, K. A. The collected stories of Katherine Anne Porter p173-221   **S C**
In Porter, K. A. Pale horse, pale rider p3-89   **S C**

The **Old** Northwest. Ogg, F. A.   **977**

Old Op and the Devil. Stuart, J.
In Stuart, J. A Jesse Stuart reader p170-77   **818**

The **old** order. Porter, K. A.
In Porter, K. A. The collected stories of Katherine Anne Porter p321-68   **S C**

Old Possum's book of practical cats. Eliot, T. S.
In Eliot, T. S. Complete poems and plays, 1909-1950 p149-71   **818**

Old Red. Gordon, C.
In Abrahams, W. ed. Fifty years of the American short story v 1 p334-50   **S C**

The **old** regime, 1713-63. Lindsay, J. O. ed.
In The New Cambridge Modern history v7   **909**

The **old** South. Osborne, J.   **917.5**

The **old** town of Pskoff. Saki
In Saki. The short stories of Saki p626-29   **S C**

The **old** wives' tale. Bennett, A.   **Fic**

Oldenbourg, Zoe
Catherine the Great   **92**
The heirs of the kingdom   **Fic**

On the enjoyment of modern art. Morris, J.
709.73

On the Great Wall. Kipling, R.
In Kipling, R. The best short stories of Rudyard Kipling p360-71 **S C**

On the gulls' road. Cather, W.
In Cather, W. Willa Cather's Collected short fiction, 1892-1912 v 1 p79-94 **S C**

On the island. Jacobsen, J.
In Abrahams, W. ed. Fifty years of the American short story v 1 p398-411 **S C**
In The Best American short stories, 1966 p139-53 **S C**

On the journey. Maupassant, G. de
In Maupassant, G. de. The odd number p137-49 **S C**

On the Makaloa mat. London, J.
In London, J. Best short stories of Jack London p122-42 **S C**
In London, J. Stories of Hawaii p107-33 **S C**

On the quai at Smyrna. Hemingway, E.
In Hemingway, E. In our time p9-12 **S C**
In Hemingway, E. The short stories of Ernest Hemingway p87-88 **S C**

On the reef. Stoddard, C. W.
In Day, A. G. ed. The spell of Hawaii p165-79 919.69

On the rocks. Shaw, B.
In Shaw, B. Complete plays, with prefaces v5 p525-620 822

On the soul. Aristotle
In Aristotle. The basic works of Aristotle p535-603 888

On the way. Chekhov, A.
In Chekhov, A. The stories of Anton Chekhov p53-71 **S C**

On the way home. Hughes, L.
In Hughes, L. The Langston Hughes reader p44-50 818

On these I stand. Cullen, C. 811

Onassis, Jacqueline Lee (Bouvier) Kennedy
Wolff, P. A tour of the White House with Mrs John F. Kennedy 975.3
See also pages in the following books:
Galbraith, J. K. Ambassador's journal p305-32 327.73
Salinger, P. With Kennedy [biography of John Fitzgerald Kennedy] p303-18 92

The once and future king. White, T. H. **Fic**

Ondine. Giraudoux, J.
In Gassner, J. ed. Twenty best European plays on the American stage p200-40 808.82

One-act plays
The Best short plays, 1968-1971 808.82
Cerf, B. ed. Thirty famous one-act plays 808.82
Cerf, B. ed. 24 favorite one-act plays 808.82
Richards, S. ed. Best short plays of the world theatre, 1958-1967 808.82

One autumn night. Gorky, M.
In Seltzer, T. comp. Best Russian short stories p263-75 **S C**

One dash—horses. Crane, S.
In Crane, S. The complete short stories & sketches of Stephen Crane p239-49 **S C**

One day in the life of Ivan Denisovich. Solzhenitsyn, A. **Fic**

One dollar's worth. Henry, O.
In Henry, O. The complete works of O. Henry p1193-98 **S C**

One flew over the cuckoo's nest. Kesey, K. **Fic**

One Friday morning. Hughes, L.
In Clarke, J. H. ed. American Negro short stories p114-23 **S C**
In Hughes, L. The Langston Hughes reader p54-62 818

100 great events that changed the world. Canning, J. ed. 902

One hundred ladies. Cozzens, J. G.
In The Saturady Evening Post. Best modern short stories p64-81 **S C**

One hundred poems from the Chinese. Rexroth, K. ed. 895.1

100 years of Negro freedom. Bontemps, A. 301.451

One man, one boat, one girl. O'Faolain, S.
In The Saturday Evening Post. Best modern short stories p402-20 **S C**

One man's honor. Schaefer, J.
In Schaefer, J. The collected stories of Jack Schaefer p412-28 **S C**

One man's meat. White, E. B. 818

The £1,000,000 bank-note. Twain, M.
In Twain, M. The complete short stories of Mark Twain p315-32 **S C**

One night for several samurai. Whitehill, J.
In The Best American short stories, 1966 p289-325 **S C**

One of ours. Cather, W. **Fic**

One of the boys. Francis, H. E.
In The Best American short stories, 1967 p67-83 **S C**

One ordinary day, with Peanuts. Jackson, S.
In Foley, M. ed. Fifty best American short stories, 1915-1965 p563-72 **S C**

One reader writes. Hemingway, E.
In Hemingway, E. The short stories of Ernest Hemingway p420-21 **S C**

One summer. Lavin, M.
In The Best American short stories, 1966 p167-202 **S C**

One summer in between. Mather, M. **Fic**

One thousand Aves. Hémon, L.
In Becker, M. L. ed. The home book of Christmas p242-58 394.26

One thousand dollars. Henry, O.
In Henry, O. The complete works of O. Henry p1285-90 **S C**

The one thousand dozen. London, J.
In London, J. Jack London's Tales of adventure **S C**

One touch of nature. Chute, B. J.
In Chute, B. J. One touch of nature, and other stories p69-91 **S C**

One touch of nature, and other stories. Chute, B. J. **S C**

One two three . . . infinity. Gamow, G. 500

O'Neil, Paul
Duel of the four minute men
In Sports Illustrated. The wonderful world of sport p229-30 796

O'Nolan, Brian
The Martyr's crown
In Garrity, D. A. ed. 44 Irish short
stories p359-64 **S C**
Ontology. See Philosophy
Opaque projectors. See Projectors
The **open** boat. Crane, S.
In Crane, S. The complete short stories
& sketches of Stephen Crane p339-
59 **S C**
In Day, A. G. ed. The greatest Ameri-
can short stories p135-63 **S C**
In Havighurst, W. ed. Masters of the
modern short story p306-31 **S C**
The **open** classroom. Kohl, H. R. 371.3
Open door policy (Far East) See Eastern
question (Far East)
Open letter to the Reverend Dr Hyde of
Honolulu. Stevenson, R. L.
In Day, A. G. ed. The spell of Hawaii
p247-59 919.69
The **open** window. Saki
In Saki. The short stories of Saki p288-
91 **S C**
Opening day. Gilchrist, J.
In The Best American short stories,
1965 p93-98 **S C**
Opening night. Cromwell, J.
In The Best short plays, 1968 p237-58
808.82
Opera
See pages in the following books:
Bauer, M. Music through the ages p204-27,
468-90 780.9
Bernstein, L. The joy of music p266-303
780.1
The New York Times. Guide to listening
pleasure p 1-38 780.1
Nicoll, A. World drama p367-70 809.2
Dictionaries
Ewen, D. The new Encyclopedia of the
opera 782.103
Operas
Librettos
Gilbert, Sir W. S. The complete plays of
Gilbert and Sullivan 782.8
Gilbert, Sir W. S. Martyn Green's Trea-
sury of Gilbert & Sullivan 782.8
Stories, plots, etc.
Cross, M. Milton Cross More stories of
the great operas 782.1
Cross, M. The new Milton Cross' Com-
plete stories of the great operas 782.1
Kobbé, G. Kobbé's Complete opera book
782.1
Operation Deepfreeze. Dufek, G. J. 919.9
Operation Mincemeat. See World War, 1939-
1945—Secret service
Operation Overflight. Powers, F. G. 327
Operation Overlord. See Normandy, At-
tack on, 1944
Operation Pluto. See Cuba—History—In-
vasion, 1961
Operations, Surgical. See Surgery
Operetta
See pages in the following book:
Ewen, D. Great men of American popular
song p70-86 920
See also Musical revues, comedies, etc.

Opiates. See Narcotics
Opinion, Public. See Public opinion
Oppenheim, E. Phillips
A problem of identity
In Dulles, A. ed. Great spy stories from
fiction p255-76 **S C**
Opportunities in environmental careers.
Fanning, O. 614.069
The **opposing** self. Trilling, L. 809
The **opposite** number. Hay, J.
In Best detective stories of the year
[1967] p98-113 **S C**
Optical illusions
Froman, R. Science, art, and visual illu-
sions 535
Optical masers. See Lasers
Optics
Klein, H. A. Holography 535.5
Kock, W. E. Lasers and holography 535.5
See also pages in the following book:
Cooper, M. The inventions of Leonardo
da Vinci p112-19 608
See also Color; Light; Vision
Options. Henry, O.
In Henry, O. The complete works of
O. Henry p680-810 **S C**
Or I'll dress you in mourning [biography
of Manuel Benítez Pérez]. Collins, L.
92
The **oracle** of Change. See Douglas, A. How
to consult the I Ching 895.1
Oracle of the dog. Chesterton, G. K.
In Chesterton, G. K. The Father Brown
omnibus p481-504 **S C**
Oracles. See Divination
Oran, Algeria
Description
See pages in thefollowing books:
Camus, A. Lyrical and critical essays
p109-33 844
Camus, A. The myth of Sisyphus, and
other essays p155-83 844
Orations
Buehler, E. C. Building the contest ora-
tion 808.51
Peterson, H. ed. A treasury of the world's
great speeches 808.851
See also American orations
Oratory. See Public speaking
Orbaan, Albert
Dogs against crime 636.7
Orbit of China. Salisbury, H. E. 915.1
Orbiting vehicles. See Artificial satellites;
Earth satellites
Orcagna, Andrea di Cione
See pages in the following book:
Vasari, G. The lives of the painters, sculp-
tors and architects v 1 p142-51 920
Orchard, Harry. See Horsley, Albert E.
Orchestra. See Conducting
The **orchestra.** Anouilh, J.
In Richards, S. ed. Best short plays of
the world theatre, 1958-1967 p 1-15
808.82

Orton, Charles Wiliam Previté- See Previté-Orton, Charles William

Orton, Joe
The ruffian on the stair
In The Best short plays, 1970 p183-214
808.82

Orwell, George
Animal farm   Fic
A collection of essays   824
Nineteen eighty-four   Fic

About
Williams, R. George Orwell   92
See also pages in the following book:
Trilling, L. The opposing self p151-72
809

Osada, Arata
(comp.) Children of the A-bomb   940.54

Osage Indians
Fiction
Giles, J. H. Johnny Osage   Fic

Osborn, Fairfield
(ed.) Our crowded planet   301.3

Osborn, Paul
Morning's at seven
In Gassner, J. ed. Best American plays; supplementary volume, 1918-1958 p333-72   812.08
On borrowed time
In Gassner, J. ed. Best American plays; supplementary volume, 1918-1958 p297-331   812.08

Osborne, Estelle (Massey)
See pages in the following book:
Dodge, B. S. The story of nursing p135-44
610.73

Osborne, Harold
(ed.) The Oxford Companion to art. See The Oxford Companion to art   703

Osborne, John, 1907-
Britain   914.2
The old South   917.5

Osborne, John, 1929-
Look back in anger
In Block, H. M. ed. Masters of modern drama p1072-1101   808.82
In Cerf, B. ed. Plays of our time p469-543   812.08
A subject of scandal and concern
In Richards, S. ed. Best short plays of the world theatre, 1958-1967 p257-73   808.82

Osler, Sir William, bart.
See pages in the following book:
Highet, G. People, places and books p13-21   809

Ossoli, Sarah Margaret (Fuller) Marchesa d'
See pages in the following book:
Stoddard, H. Famous American women p181-92   920

Ostia
See pages in the following book:
Schreiber, H. Vanished cities p161-70
913.03

Ostrow, Joanna
Celtic twilight
In The Best American short stories, 1968 p247-67   S C

Oswald, Lee Harvey
United States. Warren Commission on the Assassination of President Kennedy. The official Warren Commission report on the assassination of President John F. Kennedy   364.12

Oswalt, Sabine G.
Concise encyclopedia of Greek and Roman mythology   292.03

The other America. Harrington, M. 301.44

The other child. Davis, O.
In The Best American short stories, 1970 p74-83   S C

The other death. Borges, J. L.
In Borges, J. L. The Aleph, and other stories, 1933-1969 p103-11   S C

The other foot. Bradbury, R.
In Bradbury, R. The illustrated man p43-57   S C
In Foley, M. ed. Fifty best American short stories, 1915-1965 p453-65   S C

The other place. Priestley, J. B.
In Costain, T. B. ed. Read with me p447-69   S C

The other side of the river. See Snow, E. Red China today   915.1

The other two. Wharton, E.
In Wharton, E. The collected short stories of Edith Wharton v 1 p380-96   S C

Other versions. Aidoo, A. A.
In Angoff, C. ed. African writing today p199-206   896

Other voices, other rooms. Capote, T.   Fic

Otomi's virginity. Akutagawa, R.
In Akutagawa, R. Japanese short stories p171-86   S C

Ottemiller, John H.
Ottemiller's Index to plays in collections. See Ottemiller's Index to plays in collections   808.82

Ottemiller's Index to plays in collections
808.82

Otters
Maxwell, G. Ring of bright water   574.9
Park, E. The world of the otter   599

Ottoman Empire. See Turkey

Our American heritage. Wallis, C. L. ed.
808.88

Our country's Presidents. National Geographic Society   920

Our crowded planet. Osborn, F. ed. 301.3

Our cup is broken. Means, F. C.   Fic

Our federal government: how it works. Acheson, P. C.   353

Our foreign-born citizens. Beard, A. E. S.
920

Our foreigners. Orth, S. P.   325.73

Our hearts were young and gay. Skinner, C. O.   914

Our heroine. Michener, J.
In Michener, J. Tales of the South Pacific p93-116   S C

Our literary heritage. Brooks, V.   810.9

Our man in Havana. Greene, G.
In Greene, G. Triple pursuit   Fic

Our names. Lambert, E.   929.4

Overland journeys to the Pacific
See pages in the following book:
Billington, R. A. The far Western frontier, 1830-1860 p91-115   **978**

Overman, Michael
Roads, bridges, and tunnels   **624**
Water   **333.9**

Overruled. Shaw, B.
In Shaw, B. Androcles and the lion, Overruled, Pygmalion p59-105 **822**
In Shaw, B. Complete plays, with prefaces v6 p347-71   **822**

Overseas Press Club of America
How I got that story   **070**

The oversight. Saki
In Saki. The short stories of Saki p577-82   **S C**

Overstreet, Bonaro
(jt. auth.) Overstreet, H. The FBI in our open society   **353.5**

Overstreet, Harry
The FBI in our open society   **353.5**
The mature mind   **155.2**

Overtones. Gerstenberg, A.
In Cerf, B. ed. Thirty famous one-act plays p483-93   **808.82**

Overweight. See Weight control

Ovid
Metamorphoses   **871**

Owain ab Gruffydd. See Glendower, Owen

Owen, Alun
Doreen
In The Best short plays, 1971 p99-132   **808.82**

Owen, Sir Richard
See pages in the following book:
Colbert, E. H. Men and dinosaurs p29-37   **568**

Owen, Wilfred
Wheels   **380.5**

Owens, Rochelle
The Karl Marx play
In The Best short plays, 1971 p223-45   **808.82**

The owl and the pussycat. Manhoff, B.
In Gassner, J. ed. Best American plays; 6th ser. p495-525   **812.08**

Owls
Sparks, J. Owls: their natural and unnatural history   **598**

Ownership. See Property

Oxford, Miss.
Race relations
See pages in the following book:
Hofstadter, R. ed. American violence p372-78   **301.18**

The **Oxford** Book of American verse **811.08**
The **Oxford** Book of ballads   **821.08**
The **Oxford** Book of English verse, 1250-1918   **821.08**
The **Oxford** Book of flowerless plants **586**
The **Oxford** Book of food plants   **581**
The **Oxford** Book of light verse   **821.08**
The **Oxford** Book of medieval English verse   **821.08**
The **Oxford** Book of modern verse, 1892-1935   **821.08**

The **Oxford** Book of nineteenth-century English verse   **821.08**
The **Oxford** Book of Scottish verse **821.08**
The **Oxford** Book of seventeenth century verse   **821.08**
The **Oxford** Classical dictionary   **913.3803**
The **Oxford** Companion to American history. Johnson, T. H.   **973.03**
The **Oxford** Companion to American literature. Hart, J. D.   **810.3**
The **Oxford** Companion to art   **703**
The **Oxford** Companion to classical literature   **880.3**
The **Oxford** Companion to English literature   **820.3**
The **Oxford** Companion to French literature   **840.3**
The **Oxford** Companion to music. Scholes, P. A.   **780.3**
The **Oxford** Companion to the theatre   **792.03**
Oxford Dictionary of current English, The Concise   **423**
The **Oxford** Dictionary of English etymology   **422.03**
Oxford Dictionary of English literature, The Concise   **820.3**
The **Oxford** Dictionary of English proverbs   **398.9**
The **Oxford** Dictionary of modern Greek (Greek-English)   **483**
Oxford Dictionary of music, The concise. Scholes, P. A.   **780.3**
The **Oxford** Dictionary of quotations **808.88**
The **Oxford** Dictionary of the Christian Church   **203**
The **Oxford** History of the American people. Morison, S. E.   **973**
Oxford Illustrated dictionary   **423**

Oxygen
See pages in the following books:
Asimov, I. Building blocks of the universe p18-29   **546**
Scientific American. The biosphere p59-68   **551**

Oyster Bay, N.Y.
Hagedorn, H. The Roosevelt family of Sagamore Hill   **92**

Ozark Mountains
See pages in the following book:
National Geographic Society. Vacationland U.S.A. p196-207   **917.3**

Ozick, Cynthia
Yiddish in America
In The Best American short stories, 1970 p236-87   **S C**

P

P. & O. Maugham, W. S.
In Maugham, W. S. The best short stories of W. Somerset Maugham p456-89   **S C**

PT 109. Donovan, R. J.   **940.54**

Pablo Casals: cellist for freedom. Forsee, A.   **92**

The pace of youth. Crane, S.
In Crane, S. The complete short stories & sketches of Stephen Crane p113-21 **S C**

Pacific and Southeast Asian cooking. Steinberg, R. **641.5**

Pacific Crest Trail
See pages in the following book:
National Geographic Society. Vacationland U.S.A. p342-49 **917.3**

Pacific Islands. See Islands of the Pacific

Pacific Ocean
Heyerdahl, T. Kon-Tiki **910.4**
Rickenbacker, E. V. Seven came through **910.4**

Pacific plunder. Lloyd, C.
In Armstrong, R. ed. Treasure and treasure hunters **910.4**

Pacifism
Tolstoy, L. The law of love and the law of violence **172**
See also pages in the following books:
Addams, J. The social thought of Jane Addams p218-46 **309.173**
Lynd, S. ed. Nonviolence in America: a documentary history p173-215, 271-305 **323**

Packaging
See pages in the following book:
Cross, J. The supermarket trap p81-96 **658.87**

Packard, Vance
The hidden persuaders **659.1**
The naked society **323.44**
The status seekers **301.44**
The waste makers **339.4**

Packard, William
Sandra and the janitor
In The Best short plays, 1971 p299-322 **808.82**

Packed dirt, churchgoing, a dying cat, a traded car. Updike, J.
In Updike, J. Pigeon feathers, and other stories **S C**

Packer, Nancy Huddleston
Early morning, lonely ride
In The Best American short stories, 1968 p269-81 **S C**

Paddock, Paul
(jt. auth.) Paddock, W. Famine—1975! **338.1**

Paddock, William
Famine—1975! **338.1**

Paderewski, Ignace Jan
See pages in the following book:
Chapin, V. Giants of the keyboard p147-55 **920**

Padover, Saul K.
The meaning of democracy **321.8**

Padwe, Sandy
Basketballs' Hall of Fame **920**

Pagan Scandinavia. Davidson, H. R. E. **913.48**

Paganini, Nicolò
See pages in the following book:
Chapin, V. The violin and its masters p91-113 **920**

Paganism
See pages in the following book:
Page, R. I. Life in Anglo-Saxon England p27-44 **914.2**

Page, Bruce
(jt. auth.) Chester, L. An American melodrama **329**

Page, Elizabeth
The tree of liberty **Fic**

Page, R. I.
Life in Anglo-Saxon England **914.2**

Page, Thomas Nelson
Burial of the guns
In The Scribner treasury p157-59 **S C**
Shepherd who watched by night
In Becker, M. L. ed. The home book of Christmas p69-80 **394.26**

Pageant of America **973**

The pageant of Canadian history. Peck, A. M. **971**

The pageant of Elizabethan England. Burton, E. **914.2**

The pageant of Georgian England. Burton, E. **914.2**

The pageant of South American history. Peck, A. M. **980**

Pageants
See pages in the following book:
Twain, M. The complete essays of Mark Twain p189-99 **814**

Paid servant. Braithwaite, E. R. **362.7**

Pain was my portion. Harvor, B.
In The Best American short stories, 1971 p118-33 **S C**

Paine, Ralph D.
The fight for a free sea **973.5**
The old merchant marine **387.5**

Paine, Thomas
The American crisis; excerpts
In Paine, T. Common sense, and other political writings p55-70 **320**
Common sense; criticism
In Downs, R. B. Books that changed America p 1-13 **810.9**
In Downs, R. B. Books that changed the world p28-40 **809**
Common sense, and other political writings **320**
The rights of man **323.4**
Rights of man; excerpts
In Paine, T. Common sense, and other political writings p73-151 **320**
About
Coolidge, O. Tom Paine, revolutionary **92**
See also pages in the following books:
Commager, H. S. Crusaders for freedom p16-27 **920**
Paine, T. Common sense, and other political writings p xi-xlix **320**
Thomas, N. Great dissenters p93-128 **920**

Paine, Tom. See Paine, Thomas

A painful case. Joyce, J.
In Joyce, J. Dubliners p133-47 **S C**

Painters
Canaday, J. The lives of the painters **920**
Craven, T. ed. A treasury of art masterpieces **759**
See also Artists; also names of individual painters

Painting, Religious. See Christian art and symbolism

Painting, Spanish
Brown, D. The world of Velázquez, 1599-1660   **92**
Schickel, R. The world of Goya, 1746-1828   **92**
See also pages in the following book:
National Gallery, London p143-52   **708**

Painting and decorating encyclopedia, Goodheart-Willcox's   **698**

Paintings
Craven, T. ed. A treasury of art masterpieces   **759**
National Gallery, London   **708**
Time-Life Books. Seven centuries of art; survey and index   **709**
Walker, J. National Gallery of Art, Washington, D.C.   **708**

Catalogs
Catalogue of colour reproductions of paintings prior to 1860   **759**
Catalogue of colour reproductions of paintings—1860 to [date]   **759**

Color reproductions
See Color prints

Paintings, American
See pages in the following book:
Mendelowitz, D. M. A history of American art p107-21, 184-224, 286-320, 390-464   **709.73**

Pair system. See Binary system (Mathematics)

Paiute Indians
See pages in the following book:
Vlahos, O. New world beginnings p137-47   **913.7**

Pakeman, Sidney Arnold
Ceylon   **954.93**

Pakistan
See pages in the following book:
Life (Periodical) Handbook of the nations and international organizations p124-33   **910**

History
Stephens, I. Pakistan   **954.9**

Politics and government
Stephens, I. Pakistan   **954.9**
See also pages in the following book:
Kenworthy, L. S. Leaders of new nations p224-44   **920**

Pale fire. Nabokov, V.   **Fic**

Pale horse, pale rider. Porter, K. A.   **S C**
also in Porter, K. A. The collected stories of Katherine Anne Porter p173-317   **S C**

Pale horse, pale rider [story]. Porter, K. A.
In Porter, K. A. The collected stories of Katherine Anne Porter p269-317   **S C**
In Porter, K. A. Pale horse, pale rider p179-264   **S C**

Paleobotany. See Plants, Fossil

Paleolithic period. See Stone age

Paleontology. See Fossils

Palestine
See pages in the following book:
Acheson, D. Present at the creation p169-82   **973.918**

Antiquities
Horizon Magazine. The Holy Land in the time of Jesus   **913.33**

Civilization
See pages in the following book:
Durant, W. Our Oriental heritage p299-349   **950**

Fiction
Caldwell, T. Great lion of God   **Fic**
Michener, J. A. The source   **Fic**
Wiesel, E. Dawn   **Fic**

Social life and customs
Bouquet, A. C. Everyday life in New Testament times   **225.9**
Heaton, E. W. Everyday life in Old Testament times   **221.9**

Palestrina, Giovanni Pierluigi da
See pages in the following book:
Shippen, K. B. The heritage of music p37-40   **780.9**

Palgrave, Francis Turner
(comp.) The golden treasury of the best songs & lyrical poems in the English language   **821.08**

Palladino, Eusapia
See pages in the following book:
Christopher, M. ESP, seers & psychics p188-204   **133**

Palmer, Alice Elvira (Freeman)
See pages in the following book:
Vance, M. The lamp lighters p225-54 **920**

Palmer, Joseph
See pages in the following book:
Holbrook, S. H. Lost men of American history p145-53   **920**

Palmer, R. R.
(ed.) Rand McNally and Company. Rand McNally Atlas of world history   **911**

Palmer, Stuart
Rift in the loot
In Haycraft, H. ed. A treasury of great mysteries v2 p245-64   **S C**

Palmerston, Henry John Temple, 3d Viscount
See pages in the following book:
Strachey, L. Queen Victoria p204-52   **92**

Palmyra, Syria
See pages in the following book:
Schreiber, H. Vanished cities p134-48   **913.03**

Palomar Observatory, Calif.
Woodbury, D. O. The glass giant of Palomar   **522**

Pamphlets
Bibliography
George Peabody College for Teachers, Nashville, Tenn. Free and inexpensive learning materials   **016.3713**
Vertical file index   **015**

Indexes
Vertical file index   **015**

Pan-Africanism
See pages in the following book:
Hatch, J. Nigeria p217-36   **966.9**

Pan-Americanism
Dozer, D. M. ed. The Monroe Doctrine
327.73
See also pages in the following book:
Stevenson, A. E. Looking outward p194-203
341.13

Panama Canal
See pages in the following books:
Fish, C. R. The path of empire p240-58
327.73
Time-Life Books. The U.S. overseas p112-23
917.3

Pangborn, Edgar
Angel's egg
In Conklin, G. ed. Invaders of earth p255-89 **S C**
Longtooth
In The Best from Fantasy and Science Fiction; 19th ser. p37-74 **S C**

Pangolin
See pages in the following book:
Ley, W. Another look at Atlantis, and fifteen other essays p90-99 508

Panorama of sports in America. Friedlich, D. 796

Pansing, Nancy Pelletier
The visitation
In The Best American short stories, 1969 p215-35 **S C**

Pantaloon. Barrie, J. M.
In Barrie, J. M. The plays of J. M. Barrie p613-30 822

The **panther** & the lash. Hughes, L. 811

Papa Hemingway. Hotchner, A. E. 92

Papacy
See pages in the following book:
National Geographic Society. The Renaissance p174-208 940.2

Papadopoulos, George
See pages in the following book:
Papandreou, A. Democracy at gunpoint: the Greek front p221-27, 229-35 949.5

Papandreou, Andreas
Democracy at gunpoint: the Greek front
949.5

Papandreou, George
See pages in the following book:
Papandreou, A. Democracy at gunpoint: the Greek front p99-219 949.5

Papa's wife. Bjorn, T. F. Fic

Papashvily, George
Anything can happen 92
(jt. auth.) Papashvily, H. Russian cooking
641.5

Papashvily, Helen
Russian cooking 641.5
(jt. auth.) Papashvily, G. Anything can happen 92

Paper bound books. See Paperback books

Paper crafts
Randlett, S. The art of origami 745.54

Paper folding. See Paper crafts

Paper Lion. Plimpton, G. 796.33

Paper Lion; excerpt. Plimpton, G.
In Sports Illustrated. The wonderful world of sport p318-22 796

Paper money
Shafer, N. A guide book of modern United States currency 332.5

Paper pills. Anderson, S.
In Anderson, S. Winesburg, Ohio (Modern Lib) p18-23 **S C**
In Anderson, S. Winesburg, Ohio (Viking) p35-38 **S C**

Paper poppy. Rugel, M.
In The Best American short stories, 1969 p253-67 **S C**

Paperback books
Asia Society. Asia: a guide to paperbacks
016.95
Fader, D. N. Hooked on books: program & proof 028.5
The Negro American in paperback
016.3014
Paperbound books in print 015
See also pages in the following book:
Daiches, D. English literature p146-52 801

Paperbound books in print 015

Papuans
See pages in the following book:
National Geographic Society. Vanishing peoples of the earth p186-203 572

Parachuting
History
Dwiggins, D. Bailout 797.5

Paradis, Adrian A.
The economics reference book 330.3

Paradise lost. Milton, J.
In Milton, J. The portable Milton p231-548 828

Paradise lost. Odets, C.
In Odets, C. Six plays p155-230 812

Paradise of thieves. Chesterton, G. K.
In Chesterton, G. K. The Father Brown omnibus p245-63 **S C**

Paradise regained. Milton, J.
In Milton, J. The portable Milton p549-609 828

The **paradox** of poverty in America. Davis, K. S. ed. 330.973

The **paragon.** Knowles, J. Fic

Paraguay
Ferguson, J. H. The River Plate republics 918
History
See pages in the following books:
Crow, J. A. The epic of Latin America p558-64 980
Gunther, J. Inside South America p238-56
980

Paralysis agitans
Bourke-White, M. Portrait of myself 92

Parapsychology. See Psychical research

Parasites
See pages in the following book:
Christensen, C. M. The molds and man p87-130, 152-82 589
See also Insects, Injurious and beneficial

Parcheesi
See pages in the following book:
Gibson, W. Family games America plays p116-24 793

Paredes, Américo
(ed.) Folktales of Mexico 398.2

Pasternak, Boris—*Continued*
About
See pages in the following book:
Posell, E. Z. Russian authors p184-203
920

Pasteur, Louis
Vallery-Radot, P. Louis Pasteur   92
See also pages in the following books:
De Kruif, P. Microbe hunters p57-104,
145-83   920
Jones, B. Z. ed. The golden age of science
p448-65   920
Moore, R. The coil of life p104-43   **574.09**
Untermeyer, L. Makers of the modern
world p102-12   920

Pastimes. See Amusements; Games; Recreation; Sports

Pastry
Better Homes and Gardens. Better
Homes and Gardens Pies and cakes
641.8

Pastures
See pages in the following book:
United States. Department of Agriculture.
Water p407-49   **631.7**
See also Grasses

Pat Hobby himself. Fitzgerald, F. S.
In Fitzgerald, F. S. The stories of
F. Scott Fitzgerald p456-63   **S C**

Pâté de foie gras. Asimov, I.
In Asimov, I. Asimov's mysteries p80-
95   **S C**
In Asimov, I. ed. Where do we go from
here? p325-46   **S C**

Patent medicines
Hechtlinger, A. comp. The great patent
medicine era   **615**
See also pages in the following book:
Weinberg, A. ed. The muckrakers p176-
204   **309.173**

The **Patent** Office. Jones, S. V.   **353.82**

Patents
Jones, S. V. The Patent Office   **353.82**
See also pages in the following book:
O'Brien, R. Machines p154-64   **621.9**

The **path** of empire. Fish, C. R.   **327.73**

The **Pathfinder.** Cooper, J. F.   **Fic**

Pathology. See Medicine

The **paths** of poetry. Untermeyer, L.   920

Patience. Gilbert, Sir W. S.
In Gilbert, Sir W. S. The complete
plays of Gilbert and Sullivan p185-
233   **782.8**
In Gilbert, Sir W. S. Martyn Green's
Treasury of Gilbert & Sullivan
782.8

Patients. Strong, J.
In Prize stories, 1970: The O. Henry
Awards p83-91   **S C**

Paton, Alan
Cry, the beloved country   **Fic**
For you departed [biography of Doris
Francis Paton]   92
The long view   968

Tales from a troubled land   **S C**
Contents: Life for a life; Sponono; Ha'penny;
The waste land; The worst thing of his life;
The elephant shooter; Debbie go home; Death
of a tsotsi; The divided house; A drink in the
passage
Too late the phalarope   **Fic**

Paton, Doris Francis
Paton, A. For you departed   92

Patrick, John
The hasty heart
In Gassner, J. ed. Best plays of the
modern American theatre; 2d ser.
p511-55   **812.08**
The Teahouse of the August Moon   **812**
—Same
In Gassner, J. ed. Best American plays;
supplementary volume, 1918-1958
p609-46   **812.08**

Patriotic poetry
See pages in the following books:
Stevenson, B. E. comp. The home book
of modern verse p568-99   **821.08**
Stevenson, B. E. comp. The home book
of verse, American and English p2194-
2326   **821.08**

Patriotic songs. See National songs

Patriotism
See pages in the following book:
Stevenson, A. E. Looking outward p260-
69   **341.13**
See also Loyalty; Nationalism

Patriotism. Mishima, Y.
In Mishima, Y. Death in midsummer,
and other stories p93-118   **S C**

The **patriots.** Kingsley, S.
In Gassner, J. ed. Best plays of the
modern American theatre; 2d ser.
p683-724   **812.08**

Patron of the arts. Hughes, L.
In Hughes, L. The Langston Hughes
reader p80-83   **818**

Patterns of culture. Benedict, R.   **572**

Patterns of life. Harlow, W. M.   **581**

Patterson, Charles
Black ice; play
In Jones, L. ed. Black fire p559-65
810.8

Patterson, Floyd
Victory over myself   92

Patterson, Lindsay
Red bonnet
In Hughes, L. ed. The best short
stories by Negro writers p448-57
S C

Patton, Frances Gray
Two nice girls
In Seventeen. Seventeen from Seventeen p242-68   **S C**

Paul, Saint, apostle
See pages in the following books:
Horizon Magazine. The Holy Land in the
time of Jesus p85-107   **913.33**
Thomas, H. Understanding the great philosophers p155-67   **109**
Fiction
Caldwell, T. Great lion of God   **Fic**

Paul of Tarsus. See Paul, Saint, apostle

Paul I, King of the Hellenes
  See pages in the following book:
  Papandreou, A. Democracy at gunpoint: the Greek front p82-91   949.5

Paulding, James Kirke
  Revenge of Saint Nicholas
  In Becker, M. L. ed. The home book of Christmas p457-65   394.26

Pauli, Wolfgang
  See pages in the following book:
  Gamow, G. Thirty years that shook physics p62-79   530.1

Pauling, Linus
  The architecture of molecules   541

  About
  See pages in the following book:
  Moore, R. The coil of life p321-40   574.09

Paul's case. Cather, W.
  In Cather, W. Willa Cather's Collected short fiction, 1892-1912 v2 p243-61   S C
  In Day, A. G. ed. The greatest American short stories p173-95   S C

Pauperism. See Poverty

The pavilion on the links. Stevenson, R. L.
  In Stevenson, R. L. The strange case of Dr Jekyll and Mr Hyde, and other famous tales p70-127   S C

Pavlova, Anna
  See pages in the following book:
  Trease, G. Seven stages p168-94   920

Pavon, José María Teclo Morelos y. See Morelos y Pavon, José María Teclo

The pawnbroker's wife. Spark, M.
  In Spark, M. Collected stories: I p148-62   S C

Paxton, Steve
  See pages in the following book:
  McDonagh, D. The rise and fall and rise of modern dance p119-33   793.3

Payne, John Howard
  Charles the Second
  In Gassner, J. ed. Best plays of the early American theatre p73-96   812.08
  In Quinn, A. H. ed. Representative American plays p141-64   812.08

Payne, Lucile Vaughan
  Matter of facts
  In Seventeen. Stories from Seventeeen p47-65   S C

Payne, Robert
  Ancient Greece   913.38
  Ancient Rome   913.37
  The life and death of Lenin   92
  The life and death of Mahatma Gandhi   92
  The rise and fall of Stalin   92
  The splendor of Israel   915.694
  The three worlds of Albert Schweitzer   92

Payton, Geoffrey
  (comp.) Webster's Dictionary of proper names. See Webster's Dictionary of proper names   031

Paz Estenssoro, Victor, President Bolivia
  See pages in the following book:
  Alexander, R. J. Prophets of the revolution p198-213   920

Peabody, Elizabeth Palmer
  Tharp, L. H. The Peabody sisters of Salem   920

Peabody family
  Tharp, L. H. The Peabody sisters of Salem   920
  The Peabody sisters of Salem. Tharp, L. H.   920

Peace
  Douglas, W. O. International dissent: six steps toward world peace   341.6
  War and peace   704.94
  See also pages in the following books:
  Commager, H. S. ed. Living ideas in America p605-47   973
  Osborn, F. ed. Our crowded planet p123-33   301.3

  See also Pacifism

Peace. Aristophanes
  In Oates, W. J. ed. The complete Greek drama v2 p671-721   882.08

Peace Corps. See United States. Peace Corps

The Peace Corps. Carey, R. G.   309.2

Peace of mind. Large type ed. Liebman, J.   158

The peace of Mowsle Barton. Saki
  In Saki. The short stories of Saki p205-12   S C

The peace offering. Saki
  In Saki. The short stories of Saki p200-05   S C

Peace under earth. Warde, B.
  In Becker, M. L. ed. The home book of Christmas p716-36   394.26

The peaceable kingdom. Chute, B. J.
  In Chute, B. J. One touch of nature, and other stories p37-46   S C

The peach stone. Horgan, P.
  In Foley, M. ed. Fifty best American short stories, 1915-1965 p305-22   S C

Peanuts
  See pages in the following book:
  Elliott, L. George Washington Carver: the man who overcame p145-85   92

Peanuts classics. Schulz, C. M.   741.5

Peanuts treasury. Schulz, C. M.   741.5

Pearce, W. E.
  Transistors and circuits   621.381

The pearl. Mishima, Y.
  In Mishima, Y. Death in midsummer, and other stories p162-74   S C

The pearl. Steinbeck, J.   Fic
  also in Steinbeck, J. The short novels of John Steinbeck p473-527   Fic

Pearl Harbor, Attack on, 1941
  Baker, L. Roosevelt and Pearl Harbor   973.917
  Lord, W. Day of infamy   940.54
  See also pages in the following book:
  Leighton, I. ed. The aspirin age, 1919-1941 p476-91   917.3

The **pendulum**. Henry, O.
  In Henry, O. The best short stories of
    O. Henry p271-76   **S C**
  In Henry, O. The complete works of
    O. Henry p1383-87   **S C**
Penguins
  See pages in the following book:
  Ley, W. The Poles p83-91   919.8
Penitentiaries. See Prisons
Penkovskiĭ, Oleg Vladimirovich
  See pages in the following book:
  Dulles, A. ed. Great true spy stories p73-
  94   327
Penmanship
  See pages in the following book:
  Shakespeare's England v 1 p284-310 822.3
  See also Writing
Penn, Joseph E.
  (comp.) The Negro American in paper-
  back. See The Negro American in
  paperback   016.3014
Penn, William
  Gray, E. J. Penn   92
  See also pages in the following book:
  Langdon, W. C. Everyday things in
  American life, 1607-1776 p48-62   917.3
Penney (J. C.) Company
  See pages in the following book:
  Mahoney, T. The great merchants p259-
  72   658.87
Pennington, James W. C.
  The fugitive blacksmith
  In Bontemps, A. ed. Great slave narra-
  tives p193-267   920
Pennsylvania
  Bowen, E. The Middle Atlantic States
    917.4
    Fiction
  Turnbull, A. S. The gown of glory   **Fic**
  Updike, J. Rabbit, run   **Fic**
    History
  Fisher, S. G. The Quaker colonies 973.2
  Gray, E. J. Penn   92
  See also pages in the following book:
  Langdon, W. C. Everyday things in
    American life, 1607-1776 p48-124 917.3
Pennsylvania Dutch
  See pages in the following books:
  American Heritage. The American Heri-
  tage History of colonial antiques p299-
  350   **745.1**
  Bowen, E. The Middle Atlantic States
  p113-25   **917.4**
  Langdon, W. C. Everyday things in
  American life, 1607-1776 p63-73 917.3
  National Geographic Society. Vacationland
  U.S.A. p102-17   917.3
  Wilson, J. American cooking: the Eastern
  heartland p32-67   641.5
Pennsylvania Germans. See Pennsylvania
  Dutch
Pennsylvania Station. Faulkner, W.
  In Faulkner, W. Collected stories of
    William Faulkner p609-25   **S C**
Penology. See Punishment
Pension Séguin. Mansfield, K.
  In Mansfield, K. The short stories of
    Katherine Mansfield p148-53   **S C**

Pensions. See Insurance, Social
The **pentagon** of power. Mumford, L.
  In Mumford, L. The myth of the ma-
    chine v2   901.9
Penuchle (Game)
  See pages in the following book:
  Gibson, W. B. Hoyle's Simplified guide to
    the popular card games p231-58 795.4
People in books. Nicholsen, M. E.   920.02
The **people** of Japan. Buck, P. S.   915.2
People, places and books. Highet, G.   809
The **people,** yes. Sandburg, C.   811
  also in Sandburg, C. The complete
    poems of Carl Sandburg p439-617
    811
People's Republic of China. See China (Peo-
  ple's Republic of China)
Pepe, Phil
  Greatest stars of the NBA   920
  Gibson, B. From ghetto to glory: the
    story of Bob Gibson   92
Pepper, Choral
  (jt. auth.) Williams, B. Lost legends of
    the West   917.8
Pepys, Samuel
  Everybody's Pepys; abridged   92
Perception
  See pages in the following books:
  Gombrich, E. H. Art and illusion p3-30,
    242-87   701
  Sargent, S. S. Basic teachings of the great
    psychologists p125-44   150
  Wilson, J. R. The mind p40-55   150
Perceval, Michael
  The Spaniards   914.6
Percy Grimm. Faulkner, W.
  In Faulkner, W. The Faulkner reader
    S C
  In Faulkner, W. The portable Faulkner
    p621-34   **S C**
Père Goriot. Balzac, H. de   **Fic**
The **peregrine** falcon. Murphy, R.   **Fic**
Pérez, Manuel Benítez. See Benítez Pérez,
  Manuel
Perez, Rudy
  See pages in the following book:
  McDonagh, D. The rise and fall and rise
    of modern dance p259-69   793.3
A **perfect** day for bananafish. Salinger, J. D.
  In Salinger, J. D. Nine stories p3-26
    S C
The **perfect** tribute. Andrews, M. R. S. **Fic**
  —Same
  In The Scribner treasury p317-31 **S C**
Performing arts
  See pages in the following book:
  Good things about the U.S. today p103-14
    917.3
Pericles
  See pages in the following books:
  Payne, R. Ancient Greece p239-52 913.38
  Plutarch. Lives from Plutarch. Abridged
    p49-73   920
Pericoli, Niccolò. See Tribolo, Niccolò
The **perils** of prosperity, 1914-32. Leuchten-
  burg, W. E.   330.973
Perils of the peaceful atom. Curtis, R.
    621.48

Phillips, John G.
(jt. auth.) Alter, D. Pictorial astronomy
523
Phillips, Wendell
See pages in the following books:
Hofstadter, R. The American political tradition and the men who made it p135-61 973
Thomas, N. Great dissenters p129-68 920
Philoctetes. Sophocles
In Oates, W. J. ed. The complete Greek drama v 1 p555-607 882.08
Philology. See Language and languages
The philosopher. Anderson, S.
In Anderson, S. Winesburg, Ohio (Modern Lib) p38-48 S C
In Anderson, S. Winesburg, Ohio (Viking) p49-57 S C
Philosophers
Durant, W. The story of philosophy 109
Russell, B. A history of Western philosophy 109
Thomas, H. Understanding the great philosophers 109
See also pages in the following books:
Durant, W. Interpretations of life p150-62 809
Fermi, L. Illustrious immigrants p364-72 325.73

Dictionaries
Thomas, H. Biographical encyclopedia of philosophy 920.03
Philosophers, Ancient
Farrington, B. Aristotle 92
Turlington, B. Socrates: the father of Western philosophy 92
Philosophers, Chinese
See pages in the following book:
Durant, W. Our Oriental heritage p635-93 950
Philosophers, Jewish
Simon, C. M. Martin Buber 92
Philosophy
Dampier, Sir W. C. A history of science and its relations with philosophy & religion 509
Magill, F. N. ed. Masterpieces of world philosophy in summary form 108
See also pages in the following books:
Durant, W. The age of reason begins p613-47 940.2
See pages in the following book:
Muir, K. ed. A new companion to Shakespeare studies p180-98 822.3
The New Cambridge Modern history v5 p73-95 909
Tagore, R. A Tagore reader p255-89 891.4
See also Ethics; Knowledge, Theory of; Logic; Psychology; *also* general subjects with the subdivision Philosophy, e.g. History—Philosophy

Dictionaries
The Encyclopedia of philosophy 103
History
Boas, G. The history of ideas 109
Durant, W. The story of philosophy 109

Russell, B. A history of Western philosophy 109
Thomas, H. Understanding the great philosophers 109
Philosophy, American
Kurtz, P. ed. American philosophy in the twentieth century 191.08
Parrington, V. L. Main currents in American thought 810.9
Schneider, H. W. A history of American philosophy 191
See also pages in the following book:
Nye, R. B. The cultural life of the new Nation p3-53 917.3
Philosophy, Ancient
Aristotle. The basic works of Aristotle 888
See also pages in the following books:
Bailey, C. ed. Legacy of Rome p237-64 913.37
Durant, W. The life of Greece p349-73, 500-37, 640-58 938
Macy, J. The story of the world's literature p113-30 809
Payne, R. Ancient Greece p156-72 913.38
Sarton, G. A history of science v 1 p584-605, v2 p250-79 509
Philosophy, British
See pages in the following book:
Durant, W. The age of Louis XIV p548-97 940.2
Philosophy, Buddhist. See Philosophy, Indic
Philosophy, Chinese
Creel, H. G. Chinese thought from Confucius to Mao Tsê-tung 181
See also pages in the following book:
Liu, J. T. C. ed. Traditional China p109-60 915.1
Philosophy, East Indian. See Philosophy, Indic
Philosophy, English. See Philosophy, British
Philosophy, French
See pages in the following book:
Durant, W. The age of Louis XIV p598-619 940.2
Philosophy, Greek. See Philosophy, Ancient
Philosophy, Hindu. See Philosophy, Indic
Philosophy, Indic
Radhakrishnan, S. ed. A source book in Indian philosophy 181
Philosophy, Medieval
See pages in the following book:
Durant, W. The age of faith p949-83 940.1
Philosophy, Modern
See pages in the following book:
The New Cambridge Modern history v12 p644-56 909
Philosophy, Moral. See Ethics
Philosophy, Roman. See Philosophy, Ancient
Philosophy and religion
See pages in the following book:
Sarton, G. A history of science v2 p158-71 509
Philosophy of history. See History—Philosophy
The philosophy of Schopenhauer. Schopenhauer, A. 193

Pindar
See pages in the following books:
Hamilton, E. The Greek way p85-103
    880.9
Payne, R. Ancient Greece p140-49 **913.38**
Pinero, Arthur Wing
The second Mrs Tanqueray
In Cerf, B. A. comp. Sixteen famous
    British plays p5-64   **822.08**
In Dickinson, T. H. ed. Chief contempo-
    rary dramatists [1st ser.] p31-69
    808.82
The thunderbolt
In Tucker, S. M. ed. Twenty-five mod-
    ern plays p303-60   **808.82**
Pink. Parr, E.
In Seventeen. Stories from Seventeen
    p91-98   **S C**
Pinkerton, Allan
Horan, J. D. The Pinkertons   **364.12**
The Pinkertons. Horan, J. D.   **364.12**
Pinkerton's National Detective Agency, In-
corporated
Horan, J. D. The Pinkertons   **364.12**
Pinochle (Game) See Penuchle (Game)
Pinter, Harold
The caretaker; criticism
In Hinchliffe, A. P. Harold Pinter p87-
    107   **822.09**
The homecoming; criticism
In Hinchliffe, A. P. Harold Pinter p146-
    62   **822.09**
About
Hinchliffe, A. P. Harold Pinter   **822.09**
Pintong, Nilawan
See pages in the following book:
Roland, A. Profiles from the new Asia
    p87-111   **920**
Pioneer life. See Frontier and pioneer life
The pioneers. Cooper, J. F.   **Fic**
Pioneers & caretakers. Auchincloss, L.
    813.09
Pioneers of the Old South. Johnston, M. 975
Pioneers of the Old Southwest. Skinner,
    C. L.   **976**
Piper, H. Beam
Omnilingual
In Asimov, I. ed. Where do we go from
    here? p347-99   **S C**
Pippi, Giulio. See Giulio Romano
Pirandello, Luigi
As you desire me
In Gassner, J. ed. Twenty best European
    plays on the American stage p523-
    60   **808.82**
Bellavita
In Richards, S. ed. Best short plays of
    the world theatre, 1958-1967 p275-
    85   **808.82**
Henry IV
In Block, H. M. ed. Masters of modern
    drama p510-31   **808.82**
Naked
In Dickinson, T. H. ed. Chief contempo-
    rary dramatists; 3d ser. p337-82
    808.82
Right you are
In Bentley, E. comp. The great play-
    wrights v2 p1935-88   **808.82**

Six characters in search of an author
In Bentley, E. comp. The great play-
    wrights v2 p2001-56   **808.82**
In Cerf, B. A. comp. Sixteen famous
    European plays p623-65   **808.82**
Pirates
See pages in the following book:
Crow, J. A. The epic of Latin America
    p183-90   **980**
Fiction
Hughes, R. A high wind in Jamaica **Fic**
Sabatini, R. Captain Blood, his odyssey
    Fic
The pirates of Penzance. Gilbert, Sir W. S.
In Gilbert, Sir W. S. The complete plays
    of Gilbert and Sullivan p141-81
    782.8
In Gilbert, Sir W. S. Martyn Green's
    Treasury of Gilbert & Sullivan
    782.8
Pisano, Andrea
See pages in the following book:
Vasari, G. The lives of the painters, sculp-
    tors and architects v 1 p101-08 **920**
Pisano, Giovanni
See pages in the following book:
Vasari, G. The lives of the painters, sculp-
    tors and architects v 1 p39-53   **920**
Pisano, Niccolò
See pages in the following book:
Vasari, G. The lives of the painters, sculp-
    tors and architects v 1 p39-53   **920**
Piston, Walter
See pages in the following book:
Copland, A. The new music, 1900-1960
    p127-34   **780.9**
The pit and the pendulum. Poe, E. A.
In Poe, E. A. The complete tales and
    poems of Edgar Allan Poe p246-57
    S C
In Poe, E. A. Edgar Allan Poe p154-73
    S C
In Poe, E. A. Selected poetry and prose
    p231-44   **818**
Pitcairn, John James. See Ashdown, Clifford
Pitcairn's Island. Nordhoff, C.
In Nordhoff, C. The Bounty trilogy
    p441-691   **Fic**
Pitt, William, 1759-1806
See pages in the following book:
Williams, E. From Columbus to Castro:
    the history of the Caribbean, 1492-1969
    p255-65   **972.9**
Pittendrigh, Colin Stephenson
See pages in the following book:
Ward, R. R. The living clocks p300-23
    574.1
Pittsburgh
See pages in the following book:
Steffens, L. The shame of the cities p101-
    33   **352**
Pius II, Pope
See pages in the following book:
Horizon Magazine. The Horizon Book of
    the Renaissance p225-32   **940.2**
Piute Indians. See Paiute Indians

Pizarro, Francisco, marqués
Innes, H. The Conquistadors   973.1
  See also pages in the following books:
Crow, J. A. The epic of Latin America
p92-106   980
Leonard, J. N. Ancient America p146-52
    913.7
Richman, I. B. The Spanish conquerors
p154-215   973.1

Pizetti, Idlebrando
  See pages in the following book:
Ewen, D. ed. The new book of modern
composers p278-85   920

Place names. See Names, Geographical

A place not on the map. Blake, G.
  In The Best American short stories,
1967 p13-23   **S C**

A place to live. United States. Department
of Agriculture   301.3

Places we lost. Hedin, M.
  In The Best American short stories,
1966 p95-112   **S C**

Plague
Marks, G. The medieval plague   616.9
        Fiction
Camus, A. The plague   **Fic**

The plague. Camus, A.   **Fic**

Plague! Nourse, A. E.
  In Nourse, A. E. ℞ for tomorrow p205-
16   **S C**

Plaidy, Jean
The captive Queen of Scots   **Fic**

The plain people of England. MacMahon, B.
  In Garrity, D. A. ed. 44 Irish short
stories p206-17   **S C**

The Plains States. Jones, E.   917.8

Planck, Max Karl Ernst Ludwig
  See pages in the following books:
Gamow, G. Thirty years that shook phys-
ics p6-28   530.1
Untermeyer, L. Makers of the modern
world p270-74   920

A planet called earth. Gamow, G.   551

The planet earth. Scientific American   551

Planet of the Apes. Boulle, P.   **Fic**

Planets
Moore, P. The planets   523.4
Nourse, A. E. Nine planets   523.4
  See also pages in the following books:
Asimov, I. The solar system and back
p19-60   508
Asimov, I. Twentieth century discovery
p101-35   500
Gamow, G. A planet called earth p47-65
    551
Hodge, P. W. The revolution in astron-
omy p165-75   523
Jastrow, R. Red giants and white dwarfs
p98-121   523.1
Ley, W. Another look at Atlantis, and
fifteen other essays p180-93   508
Scientific American. Frontiers in astron-
omy p35-84   520
    See also Life on other planets; Solar
system

Planets, Life on other. See Life on other
planets

Plankton
  See pages in the following book:
Idyll, C. P. The sea against hunger p28-46
    639

Planning, City. See City planning

Planning, Economic. See United States—
Economic policy

Planning, National. See United States—Economic policy

Planning, Regional. See Regional planning

Plano, Jack C.
The American political dictionary   320.03

Plant agriculture. Scientific American   581

Plant breeding
  See pages in the following books:
Scientific American. Facets of genetics
p299-307   575.1
Scientific American. Plant agriculture
p133-51   581

Plant diseases
United States. Department of Agriculture.
Plant diseases   632
  See also pages in the following books:
Kavaler, L. Mushrooms, molds, and mir-
acles p187-234   589
United States. Department of Agriculture.
Protecting our food p39-48   641.3

Plant lore
Coats, A. M. Flowers and their histories
    635.9

Plant pathology. See Plant diseases

Plant physiology
Scientific American. Plant agriculture   581
  See also pages in the following book:
Ward, R. R. The living clocks p71-89, 145-
63   574.1

Plant propagation. See Plant breeding

Plantation Christmas. Peterkin, J.
  In Becker, M. L. ed. The home book of
Christmas p187-94   394.26

Plantation life
        Fiction
Amado, J. The violent land   **Fic**

Planting. See Agriculture; Gardening; Landscape gardening

Plants
The Oxford Book of flowerless plants   586
Silverberg, R. Forgotten by time: a book
of living fossils   591
  See also pages in the following books:
Boy Scouts of America. Fieldbook for Boy
Scouts, explorers, scouters, educators,
outdoorsmen p346-403   369.43
Fisher, J. Wildlife in danger p352-60
    333.7
Shakespeare's England v 1 p500-15 822.3
United Nations Educational, Scientific and
Cultural Organization. 700 science ex-
periments for everyone p41-53   507.2
United States. Department of Agriculture.
After a hundred years p100-50   353.81
    See also Alpine plants; Desert plants;
Ferns
    Collection and preservation
Zim, H. S. Plants   581
      Diseases
See Plant diseases

Plotinus
See pages in the following book:
Russell, B. A history of Western philosophy p284-97   109

Plots (Drama, fiction, etc.)
Drury's Guide to best plays   808.82
See also Ballets—Stories, plots, etc.; Operas—Stories, plots, etc.

Plotz, Helen
(comp.) The earth is the Lord's   808.81
(comp.) Imagination's other place   808.81

The plough and the stars. O'Casey, S.
In O'Casey, S. The Sean O'Casey reader p63-131   828
In O'Casey, S. Three plays: Juno and the paycock, The shadow of a gunman, The plough and the stars   822
In Tucker, S. M. ed. Twenty-five modern plays p721-63   808.82

Plowden, David
(comp.) Lincoln and his America, 1809-1865   92

Plowshare in heaven. Stuart, J.   S C

Plowshare in heaven [short story] Stuart, J.
In Stuart, J. Plowshare in heaven p267-73   S C

Plumb, J. H.
Horizon Magazine. The Horizon Book of the Renaissance   940.2

Plumbing
See pages in the following book:
Gladstone, B. The New York Times Complete manual of home repair p318-66   643

Plunkett, James
Weep for our pride
In Garrity, D. A. ed. 44 Irish short stories p378-91   S C

Plupy goes to Sunday school. Shute, H. A.
In Becker, M. L. ed. The home book of Christmas p132-39   394.26

The plural of moose is mise. Cobb, I. S.
In Lardner, R. ed. Rex Lardner selects the best of sports fiction p131-50   S C

Plurality of worlds. See Life on other planets

Plutarch
Lives from Plutarch   920
About
See pages in the following books:
Grant, M. The ancient historians p309-28   920
Hamilton, E. The echo of Greece p179-209   880.9

Plutarch's lives; abridged. See Plutarch. Lives from Plutarch   920

Pluto (Planet)
See pages in the following book:
Asimov, I. The solar system and back p104-18   508

Pluto is the furthest planet. Rothberg, A.
In The Best American short stories, 1966 p255-68   S C

Pluto operation. See Cuba—History—Invasion, 1961

The Plutonian fire. Henry, O.
In Henry, O. The complete works of O. Henry p1299-1304   S C

Plutus. Aristophanes
In Oates, W. J. ed. The complete Greek drama v2 p1063-1115   882.08

Po' Sandy. Chestnutt, C.
In Margolies, E. A native son's reader p43-53   810.8

Pocahontas
Barbour, P. L. Pocahontas and her world   975.5
Woodward, G. S. Pocahontas   92

Pocahontas. Custis, G. W. P.
In Quinn, A. H. ed. Representative American plays p165-92   812.08

Pocahontas and her world. Barbour, P. L.   975.5

The pocket encyclopedia of cacti and succulents in color. Lamb, E.   635.9

The pocketbook game. Childress, A.
In Hughes, L. ed. The best short stories by Negro writers p205-06   S C

Poe, Edgar Allan
The cask of Amontillado
In Day, A. G. ed. The greatest American short stories p51-60   S C
The complete tales and poems of Edgar Allan Poe   S C
Stories included are: Unparalleled adventure of one Hans Pfaall; The gold-bug; The balloon-hoax; Von Kempelen and his discovery; Mesmeric revelation; Facts in the case of M. Valdemar; Thousand-and-second tale of Scheherazade; Ms found in a bottle; Descent into the Maelström; Murders in the Rue Morgue; Mystery of Marie Roget; Purloined letter; The black cat; Fall of the House of Usher; Pit and the pendulum; Premature burial; Masque of the Red Death; Cask of Amontillado; Imp of the perverse; Island of the Fay; Oval portrait; The assignation; Tell-tale heart; System of Doctor Tarr and Professor Fether; Literary life of Thingum Bob, Esq; How to write a Blackwood article; A predicament; Mystification; X-ing a paragrab; Diddling; Angel of the odd; Mellonta Tauta; Loss of breath; Man that was used up; The business man; Maelzel's chessplayer; Power of words; Colloquy of Monos and Una; Conversation of Eiros and Charmion; Shadow—a parable; Silence—a fable; Tale of Jerusalem; The Sphinx; Man of the crowd; Never bet the Devil your head; "Thou art the man"; Hop-Frog; Four beasts in one; Why the little Frenchman wears his hand in a sling; Bon-Bon; Some words with a mummy; Magazine-writing—Peter Snook; Domain of Arnheim; Landor's cottage; William Wilson; Berenice; Eleonora; Ligeia; Morella; Metzengerstein; Tale of the Ragged Mountains; Spectacles; Duc De l'Omelette; Oblong box; King Pest; Three Sundays in a week; Devil in the belfry; Lionizing; Narrative of A. Gordon Pym

The cryptograph
In Armstrong, R. ed. Treasure and treasure hunters   910.4

Edgar Allan Poe   S C
Contents: William Wilson; A tale of the Ragged Mountains; Eleonora; The oval portrait; The man of the crowd; Ms. found in a bottle; A descent into the Maelström; The pit and the pendulum; The premature burial; The assignation; Berenice; Morella; Ligeia; The fall of the House of Usher; The facts in the case of M. Valdemar; The masque of the Red Death; The tell-tale heart; The black cat; The cask of Amontillado; Hop-Frog; The murders in the Rue Morgue; The mystery of Marie Roget; The purloined letter; The gold-bug

Maelzel's chess-player
In Engle, P. ed. On creative writing p98-108   808.02

The purloined letter
In Day, A. G. ed. The greatest American short stories p61-80   S C

Poe, Edgar A.—*Continued*
Selected poetry and prose   818
Stories included are: Metzengerstein; The Duc De l'Omelette; Ms. found in a bottle; The assignation; Berenice; Morella; Shadow; Silence; Ligeia; The fall of the House of Usher; William Wilson; The conversation of Eiros and Charmion; The man of the crowd; The murders in the Rue Morgue; The island of the Fay; A descent into the Maelström; Three Sundays in a week; Eleonora; The oval portrait; The masque of the Red Death; The pit and the pendulum; The tell-tale heart; The gold-bug; The black cat; The elk; The purloined letter; The imp of the perverse; The facts in the case of M. Valdemar; The cask of Amontillado; Hop-Frog; Von Kempelen and his discovery; The light house

About
Howarth, W. L. ed. Twentieth century interpretations of Poe's tales   813.09
Regan, R. ed. Poe   818
Wagenknecht, E. Edgar Allan Poe   92
See also pages in the following books:
Auslander, J. The winged horse p335-47   809.1
Brooks, V. The world of Washington Irving p350-55, 460-73   810.9
Literary history of the United States p321-42   810.9
Quinn, A. H. American fiction p77-101   813.09
Untermeyer, L. The paths of poetry p180-87   920

Poems from Black Africa. Hughes, L. ed.   896
Poems from India. Aldan, D. comp.   891
Poems, 1938-1945. Graves, R.   821
Poems, 1965-1968. Graves, R.   821
Poems that live forever. Felleman, H. ed.   821.08
Poems written in early youth. Eliot, T. S.   811
The **poet**. Dinesen, I.
In Dinesen, I. Seven Gothic tales p357-420   S C
The **poet** and the peasant. Henry, O.
In Henry, O. The complete works of O. Henry p1517-21   S C
The **poet** of Sierra Flat. Harte, B.
In Harte, B. The best short stories of Bret Harte p69-81   S C
Poetics
Aristotle. Poetics   808.1
Deutsch, B. Poetry handbook   808.1
Hillyer, R. In pursuit of poetry   808.1
Untermeyer, L. The forms of poetry   808.1
Untermeyer, L. The pursuit of poetry   808.1
See also pages in the following books:
Drew, E. Poetry: a modern guide to its understanding and enjoyment p13-97   808.1
Engle, P. ed. On creative writing p127-42   808.02
Poetics. Aristotle
In Aristotle. The basic works of Aristotle p1455-87   888
Poetry
Drew, E. Discovering poetry   808.1
Drew, E. Poetry: a modern guide to its understanding and enjoyment   808.1
Eastman, M. Enjoyment of poetry, with Anthology for Enjoyment of poetry   808.1

Eliot, T. S. On poetry and poets   808.1
MacLeish, A. Poetry and experience   809.1
Untermeyer, L. The forms of poetry   808.1
Untermeyer, L. The pursuit of poetry   808.1
See also pages in the following books:
Arnold, M. The portable Matthew Arnold p299-331   828
Disch, R. ed. The ecological conscience p194-204   301.3
Highet, G. The classical tradition p219-54   809
MacLeish, A. A continuing journey p26-45, 188-209   818
Spiller, R. E. ed. The American literary revolution, 1783-1837 p132-53, 416-33   810.9
Tagore, R. A Tagore reader p241-54   891.4
See also Love poetry; and names of famous historical events, places and famous persons with the subdivision Poetry, e.g. Shakespeare, William—Poetry

Addresses and essays
Eliot, T. S. On poetry and poets   808.1

Collections
Brooks, C. ed. Understanding poetry   821.08
Creekmore, H. ed. A little treasury of world poetry   808.81
Morrison, L. comp. Sprints and distances   808.81
Plotz, H. comp. Imagination's other place   808.81
Van Doren, M. ed. An anthology of world poetry   808.81
Van Doren, M. ed. The world's best poems   808.81
See also pages in the following book:
Engle, P. ed. On creative writing p143-62   808.02
See also American poetry—Collections; English poetry—Collections; Negro poetry

Dictionaries
Deutsch, B. Poetry handbook   808.1

History and criticism
Auslander, J. The winged horse   809.1
Ciardi, J. ed. How does a poem mean?   821.08
Eliot, T. S. On poetry and poets   808.1
Highet, G. The powers of poetry   809.1
Hillyer, R. In pursuit of poetry   808.1
MacLeish, A. Poetry and experience   809.1
Untermeyer, L. The pursuit of poetry   808.1
See American poetry—History and criticism; English poetry—History and criticism

Indexes
Granger's Index to poetry   808.81
Granger's Index to poetry: supplement   808.81

Philosophy
See Poetry

Selections
See Poetry—Collections

Poland—*Continued*

History
See pages in the following books:

Durant, W. Rousseau and revolution p472-92   940.2

The New Cambridge Modern history v3 p377-403, v4 p585-619, v5 p559-70, v6 p681-715, v8 p333-59   909

Polar expeditions. See Arctic regions; North Pole; Polar regions; South Pole

Polar regions

Ley, W. The Poles   919.8

See also pages in the following book:

National Geographic Society. Great adventures with National Geographic p12-57   910.9

See also Arctic regions; North Pole; South Pole

Polaris (Missile)

Baar, J. Polaris!   623.4

Polatnick, Florence T.

Shapers of Africa   920

Polenberg, Richard

(ed.) America at war   309.173

The Poles. Ley, W.   919.8

Police

Arm, W. The policeman   352

See also Criminal investigation

United States

Clark, R. Crime in America   364.1

See also pages in the following books:

James, H. Crisis in the courts p91-104   347.9

United States. National Advisory Commission on Civil Disorders. Report of the National Advisory Commission on Civil Disorders p299-322   301.18

The policeman. Arm, W.   352

Polikúshka. Tolstoy, L.

In Tolstoy, L. Short novels v 1 p214-78   S C

Politeness. See Etiquette

Political and social upheaval, 1832-1852. Langer, W. L.   940.2

Political conventions

See pages in the following book:

Koenig, L. W. Bryan p178-208, 376-91, 483-96   92

Fiction

Knebel, F. Convention   Fic

Political corruption. See Corruption (in politics)

Political crimes and offenses

United States. National Commission on the Causes and Prevention of Violence. To establish justice, to insure domestic tranquility   301.18

See also pages in the following book:

Liston, R. A. Dissent in America p119-32   301.15

See also Concentration camps; Treason

Political economy. See Economics

Political economy. Twain, M.

In Twain, M. The complete short stories of Mark Twain p59-64   S C

Political ethics

Machiavelli, N. The prince   320

Political handbook and atlas of the world   329

Political handbook and atlas of the world; 1971 supplement. See The World this year   329

A political life; the education of John V. Lindsay. Hentoff, N.   92

Political parties

Chambers, W. N. ed. The American party systems   329

Chambers, W. N. Political parties in a new nation: the American experience, 1776-1809   329

Cunningham, N. E. ed. The making of the American party system, 1789-1809   329

Hesseltine, W. B. Third-party movements in the United States   329

Orth, S. P. The boss and the machine   329

Political handbook and atlas of the world   329

See also Politics, Practical; Right and left (Political science)

Political parties in a new nation: the American experience, 1776-1809. Chambers, W. N.   329

Political prisoners

Grey, A. Hostage in Peking   92

Political science

Bailey, S. K. ed. American politics and government   353

Machiavelli, N. The prince   320

Paine, T. Common sense, and other political writings   320

Plato. The Republic   888

Ward, B. Five ideas that change the world   320

Ward, B. Nationalism and ideology   320.1

See also pages in the following books:

Fermi, L. Illustrious immigrants p343-53   325.73

The New Cambridge Modern history v2 p438-80, v5 p96-121, 176-99, v11 p101-20   909

See also Church and state; Communism; Democracy; Politics, Practical; Political parties; Power (Social sciences); Right and left (Political science); Socialism; Utopias; World politics; and names of countries with subdivision Politics and government, e.g. United States—Politics and government

Addresses and essays

Boorstin, D. J. The genius of American politics   973

Handbooks, manuals, etc.

Political handbook and atlas of the world   329

The World this year   329

Terminology
See pages in the following book:

Pei, M. The story of language p244-51   400

Yearbooks

The Statesman's year-book   310.25

The political thought of Mao Tse-Tung. Mao, Tsê-tung   320.5

Poor relief. See Economic assistance, Domestic; Public welfare

Poor Richard's almanac. Franklin, B. **818**

Poor Richard's almanac; selections. Franklin, B.

In Franklin, B. The autobiography, and other writings of Benjamin Franklin **818**

A poor rule. Henry, O.

In Henry, O. The complete works of O. Henry p801-10 **S C**

The **poorhouse** fair. Updike, J. **Fic**

Pop art. Lippard, L. R. ed. **709.04**

Pope, Alexander

See pages in the following books:

Daiches, D. A critical history of English literature v2 p621-43 **820.9**

Durant, W. The age of Voltaire p164-78 **940.2**

Johnson, S. The portable Johnson & Boswell p533-643 **828**

Untermeyer, L. Lives of the poets p227-57 **920**

Untermeyer, L. The paths of poetry p82-89 **920**

Pope, Loren

The right college **378.73**

Popé, Pueblo Indian

See pages in the following book:

Hall-Quest, O. Conquistadors and Pueblos p111-16 **979.1**

Pope John [XXIII]. Trevor, M. **92**

Popenoe, Joshua

Inside Summerhill **371**

Popes

Trevor, M. Pope John [XXIII] **92**

See also Papacy

Fiction

West, M. L. The shoes of the fisherman **Fic**

Popular American composers, from Revolutionary times to the present, Ewen, D. ed. **920.03**

The **Popular** arts in America. See Nye, R. The unembarrassed muse: the popular arts in America **917.3**

Popular government. See Democracy

A popular guide to government publications. Leidy, W. P. **015.73**

Popular music. See Music, Popular (Songs, etc.)

Population

Chasteen, E. R. The case for compulsory birth control **301.3**

Cochrane, W. W. The world food problem **338.1**

Dumont, R. The hungry future **338.1**

Ehrlich, P. R. Population, resources, environment **301.3**

Hyde, M. O. This crowded planet **301.3**

Osborn, F. ed. Our crowded planet **301.3**

See also pages in the following books:

Bates, M. Man in nature p48-57 **573**

Foreign Policy Association. Toward the year 2018 p136-47 **901.9**

Linton, R. M. Terracide p3-36 **614**

Michener, J. A. The quality of life p91-105 **309.173**

Myrdal, G. The challenge of world poverty p139-63 **338.91**

Our poisoned planet: can we save it? p35-46 **614**

Paddock, W. Famine—1975! p14-39 **338.1**

Scientific American. Plant agriculture p198-205 **581**

See also Birth control; Migration, Internal; also names of countries with subdivision Population, e.g. United States—Population

Population, Foreign. See names of countries with subdivision Immigration and emigration, e.g. United States—Immigration and emigration; and names of countries, cities, etc. with subdivision Foreign population, e.g. New York (City)—Foreign population

Population, resources, environment. Ehrlich, P. R. **301.3**

Populist Party

Hicks, J. D. The Populist revolt **329**

See also pages in the following book:

Degler, C. N. Out of our past p330-37 **973**

The **Populist** revolt. Hicks, J. D. **329**

Porcelain. See Pottery

Porcelain cups. Cabell, J. B.

In Abrahams, W. ed. Fifty years of the American short story v 1 p142-56 **S C**

The **porcelain** doll. Tolstoy, L.

In Tolstoy, L. Short stories v 1 p419-23 **S C**

Porgy. Heyward, D.

In Gassner, J. ed. Twenty-five best plays of the modern American theatre; early ser. p401-42 **812.08**

Porkchops with whiskey and ice cream. McGregor, M. W.

In The Best American short stories, 1969 p148-65 **S C**

Pornography. See Literature, Immoral; Obscenity (Law)

Porphyria

See pages in the following book:

Scientific American. Facets of genetics p279-87 **575.1**

Porque no tiene, porque la falta. Stone, R.

In The Best American short stories, 1970 p318-43 **S C**

The **portable** Blake. Blake, W. **828**

The **portable** Charles Lamb. Lamb, C. **828**

The **portable** Chaucer. Chaucer, G. **821**

The **portable** Coleridge. Coleridge, S. T. **828**

The **portable** Conrad. Conrad, J. **828**

The **portable** Dante. Dante Alighieri **851**

The **portable** Faulkner. Faulkner, W. **S C**

The **portable** Greek reader. Auden, W. H. **880.8**

The **portable** Johnson & Boswell. Johnson, S. **828**

The **portable** Matthew Arnold. Arnold, M. **828**

The **portable** Milton. Milton, J. **828**

The **portable** Nietzsche. Nietzsche, F. W. **193**

Portraits. See Cartoons and caricatures

Portugal

See pages in the following book:

Life (Periodical) Handbook of the nations and international organizations p73-79 910

Antiquities

Savory, H. N. Spain and Portugal 913.36

Fiction

L'Engle, M. The love letters Fic

Foreign relations—Asia

See pages in the following book:

The New Cambridge Modern history v2 p591-614 909

History

See pages in the following books:

Durant, W. Rousseau and revolution p259-72 940.2

The New Cambridge Modern history v4 p435-73, v5 p384-97, v6 p509-39 909

Politics and government

See pages in the following book:

The New Cambridge Modern history v9 p439-61 909

Portuguese cookery. See Cookery, Portuguese

Portuguese in Africa

See pages in the following book:

Davidson, B. The lost cities of Africa p195-200, 321-32 913.6

Portuguese language

See pages in the following book:

Pei, M. Talking your way around the world p74-88 418

The Poseidon adventure. Gallico, P. Fic

Posell, Elsa Z.

Russian authors 920

The possessed. Camus, A. 842

The possessed. Dostoevsky, F. Fic

Post, Elizabeth L.

The Emily Post Book of etiquette for young people 395

The wonderful world of weddings 395

Post, Emily

Emily Post's etiquette 395

Post, Laurens van der. See Van der Post, Laurens

Post, Melville Davisson

A twilight adventure

In Hitchcock, A. ed. Alfred Hitchcock presents: A month of mystery p247-57 S C

Post-impressionism. See Postimpressionism (Art)

Post office. See Postal service

The post office. Tagore, R.

In Tagore, R. Collected poems and plays of Rabindranath Tagore p223-52 891.4

In Tagore, R. A Tagore reader p148-69 891.4

The Post Office Department. Cullinan, G. 353.4

Postage stamps

Bloomgarden, H. S. American history through commemorative stamps 383.2

Reinfeld, F. Stamp collectors' handbook 383.2

Scott Publications, inc. Scott's Standard postage stamp catalogue 383.2

Scott's New handbook for philatelists 383.2

Postal service

Cullinan, G. The Post Office Department 353.4

See also pages in the following book:

Langdon, W. C. Everyday things American life, 1607-1776 p255-72 917.3

Laws and regulations

See pages in the following book:

Cullinan, G. The Post Office Department p249-58 353.4

Posters

Mills, V. Making posters 741.67

Postgate, Raymond

Wells, H. G. The outline of history 937

The posthumous papers of the Pickwick Club. Dickens, C. Fic

Postimpressionism (Art)

See pages in the following books:

Gardner, H. Gardner's Art through the ages p673-83 709

Janson, H. W. History of art p505-18 709

Ruskin, A. Nineteenth century art p131-79 709.03

See also Futurism (Art); Impressionism (Art); Surrealism

Postman, Neil

Teaching as a subversive activity 370

The postmistress of Laurel Run. Harte, B.

In Harte, B. The best of Bret Harte p183-206 S C

Poston, Ted

The revolt of the evil fairies

In Hughes, L. ed. The best short stories by Negro writers p86-90 S C

The pot of broth. Yeats, W. B.

In Yeats, W. B. Collected plays of W. B. Yeats p59-67 822

The pot of earth. MacLeish, A.

In MacLeish, A. Collected poems, 1917-1952 p179-97 811

Potapenko, I. N.

Dethroned

In Seltzer, T. comp. Best Russian short stories p228-53 S C

Potassium

See pages in the following books:

Asimov, I. Building blocks of the universe p149-61 546

Snively, W. D. The sea of life p73-88 612

The potboiler. Wharton, E.

In Wharton, E. The collected short stories of Edith Wharton v 1 p663-84 S C

Potok, Chaim

The chosen Fic

The promise Fic

Potter, Dan S.

A touch of marble

In The Best short plays of 1958-1959 p167-83 808.82

Potter, G. R.

(ed.) The Renaissance, 1493-1520

In The New Cambridge Modern history v 1 909

Powers, J. F.
Death of a favorite
    In The New Yorker. Stories from The
        New Yorker, 1950-1960 p229-46
        S C
He don't plant cotton
    In Havighurst, W. ed. Masters of the
        modern short story p201-11   **S C**
Lions, harts, leaping does
    In Abrahams, W. ed. Fifty years of the
        American short story v2 p130-50
        S C
The valiant woman
    In Abrahams, W. ed. Fifty years of the
        American short story v2 p151-59
        S C
The powers of poetry. Highet, G.   809.1
Powhatan, Indian chief
    See pages in the following book:
    Woodward, G. S. Pocahontas p84-91 **92**
Powhatan Indians
    Woodward, G. S. Pocahontas   **92**
A practical joke. Maupassant, G. de
    In Maupassant, G. de. Selected short
        stories p274-79   **S C**
Practical macramé. Andes, E.   746.4
Practical politics. See Politics, Practical
The practice of an art. Robinson, L. W.
    In The Best American short stories,
        1965 p271-82   **S C**
Prada, Manuel González. See González
    Prada, Manuel
The Praeger Encyclopedia of ancient Greek
    civilization   913.3803
The Praeger Picture encyclopedia of art 703
Pragmatism
    See pages in the following book:
    Commager, H. S. The American mind
        p91-107   917.3
    See also Empiricism
Prague
    See pages in the following book:
    Camus, A. Lyrical and critical essays
        p40-51   844
The prairie. Cooper, J. F.   Fic
The prairie years; abridged. See Sand-
    burg, C. Abraham Lincoln: The prairie
    years. Abridged   92
The prairie years [condensation]. See Sand-
    burg, C. Abraham Lincoln: The prairie
    years and The war years   92
Prashker, Ivan
    Shirt talk
    In The Best American short stories,
        1971 p266-74   **S C**
Pratt, Fletcher
    War for the world   940.54
Pratt, John Lowell
    (ed.) The official encyclopedia of sports
        796.03
Pratt, Richard Putnam
    (jt. auth.) Smith, C. The Time-Life Book
        of family finance   339.4
Prayer. See Prayers
Prayer meeting; play. Caldwell, B.
    In Jones, L. ed. Black fire p589-94 **810.8**

Prayers
    Boyd, M. Are you running with me, Jesus?
        242
    Seventeen. The Seventeen Book of prayer
        242
The preacher and Margery Scott. Mose-
    ley, W.
    In The Best American short stories,
        1968 p235-45   **S C**
Precious stones
    Brown, M. L. T. Gems for the taking 553
    Sinkankas, J. Prospecting for gemstones
        and minerals   553
Precocious children. See Gifted children
A predicament. Poe, E. A.
    In Poe, E. A. The complete tales and
        poems of Edgar Allan Poe p346-53
        S C
Prefaces to history. Catton, B.   973.7
Pregnancy
    Pierce, R. I. Single and pregnant 362.8
    See also Childbirth
Prehistoric animals. See Fossils
Prehistoric art. See Art, Primitive
Prehistoric man. See Man, Prehistoric
Prehistoric man. Simak, C. D.   573.2
Prehistory. See Archeology; Bronze age;
    Iron age; Stone age; and names of coun-
    tries, cities, etc. with the subdivision
    Antiquities, e.g. Crete—Antiquities
The prehistory of Africa. Clark, J. D. 913.6
Prejudice U.S.A. Glock, C. Y. ed.   301.45
Prejudices and antipathies
    Baruch, D. W. Glass house of prejudice
        301.45
    Glock, C. Y. ed. Prejudice U.S.A. 301.45
    Stalvey, L. M. The education of a WASP
        301.45
Prelude. Mansfield, K.
    In Mansfield, K. The short stories of
        Katherine Mansfield p219-63 **S C**
The premature burial. Poe, E. A.
    In Poe, E. A. The complete tales and
        poems of Edgar Allan Poe p258-
        68   **S C**
    In Poe, E. A. Edgar Allan Poe p173-90
        S C
Pre-Raphaelitism
    See pages in the following book:
    Ruskin, A. Nineteenth century art p94-99
        709.03
Presbyterian Church
    See pages in the following book:
    Look. Religions in America p142-51 **280**
Prescott, Orville
    (ed.) History as literature   908
Prescott, William Hickling
    History of the conquest of Peru   985
    The treasure of Axayacatl
    In Armstrong, R. ed. Treasure and trea-
        sure hunters   910.4
The presence of the enemy. Mosel, T.
    In The Best short plays of 1957-1958
        p159-98   808.82
Present at the creation. Acheson, D. 973.918
Present for Minna. Stern, R. M.
    In Mystery Writers of America. Crime
        without murder p265-68   **S C**

Presidents—United States—Election—*Cont.*

McCarthy, E. J. The year of the people **329**

Roseboom, E. H. A history of Presidential elections **329**

Sayre, W. S. Voting for President **324.73**

White, T. H. The making of the President, 1960 **329**

White, T. H. The making of the President, 1964 **329**

White, T. H. The making of the President, 1968 **329**

See also pages in the following book:

Schlesinger, A. M. A thousand days p62-76 **973.922**

United States—Fiction

Drury, A. Preserve and protect **Fic**

United States—Messages

Filler, L. ed. The President speaks: from William McKinley to Lyndon B. Johnson **973.9**

United States—Wives

Bassett, M. Profiles & portraits of American Presidents & their wives **920**

Johnson, L. B. A White House diary **92**

MacLeish, A. The Eleanor Roosevelt story **92**

Randall, R. P. I Mary [Lincoln] **92**

Randall, R. P. Mary Lincoln **92**

Roosevelt, E. The autobigraphy of Eleanor Roosevelt **92**

See also pages in the following book:

Wolff, P. A tour of the White House with Mrs John F. Kennedy p161-202 **975.3**

President's Commission on Campus Unrest. See United States. President's Commission on Campus Unrest

President's Commission on Law Enforcement and Administration of Justice. See United States. President's Commission on Law Enforcement and Administration of Justice

President's Commission on the Assassination of President Kennedy. See United States. Warren Commission on the Assassination of President Kennedy

President's Commission on the Status of Women. See United States. President's Commission on the Status of Women

The President's lady. Stone, I. **Fic**

The Presidents of the United States, and their administrations from Washington to Nixon. Armbruster, M. E. **920**

The Presidents speak. Lott, D. N. **815.08**

Presidents' wives. See Presidents—United States—Wives

Presley, James

(jt. auth.) Scopes, J. T. Center of the storm **343**

Press, John

(comp.) Palgrave, F. T. comp. The golden treasury of the best songs & lyrical poems in the English language **821.08**

Press. See Freedom of the press; Journalism; Newspapers; Periodicals

Press censorship. See Freedom of the press

Press cuttings. Shaw, B.

In Shaw, B. Complete plays, with prefaces v6 p291-328 **822**

Pressman, Kenneth

Steal the old man's bundle

In The Best short plays, 1971 p173-96 **808.82**

Pressure suits. See Astronauts—Clothing

Preston, Richard J.

North American trees (exclusive of Mexico and tropical United States) **582**

The pretext. Wharton, E.

In Wharton, E. The collected short stories of Edith Wharton v 1 p632-54 **S C**

Pretty mouth and green my eyes. Salinger, J. D.

In Salinger, J. D. Nine stories p174-97 **S C**

A pretty row of pretty ribbons. Gear, B.

In The Best short plays, 1970 p351-69 **808.82**

Prevention of crime. See Crime and criminals

Prevention of cruelty to children. See Child welfare

Previous condition. Baldwin, J.

In Baldwin, J. Going to meet the man p81-100 **S C**

Previté-Orton, Charles William

(ed.) The Shorter Cambridge Medieval history. See The Shorter Cambridge Medieval history **940.1**

Price, Charles

Sports Illustrated. Sports Illustrated Book of golf **796.352**

Price, John Valdimir

David Hume **192**

Price, Reynolds

The names and faces of heroes

In The Best American short stories, 1964 p257-83 **S C**

Waiting at Dachau

In Prize stories, 1971: The O. Henry Awards p67-93 **S C**

The price. Miller, A. **812**

The price of my soul. Devlin, B. **92**

The price of the harness. Crane, S.

In Crane, S. The complete short stories & sketches of Stephen Crane p507-20 **S C**

Prices

See pages in the following book:

Wagner, S. The Federal Trade Commission p126-41 **381.061**

See also Farm produce—Marketing

Pride and prejudice. Austen, J. **Fic**

The pride of the cities. Henry, O.

In Henry, O. The complete works of Henry p827-31 **S C**

Prideaux, Tom

The world of Whistler, 1834-1903 **92**

The priest of Shiga Temple and his love. Mishima, Y.

In Mishima, Y. Death in midsummer, and other stories p59-75 **S C**

Priestley, J. B.

Charles Dickens **92**

Dangerous corner

In Cerf, B. A. comp. Sixteen famous British plays p751-97 **822.08**

Prize stories, 1970-1971: The O. Henry
Awards **S C**
Pro football's all-time greats. Sullivan, G.
920
Probabilities
Adler, I. Probability and statistics for
everyman **519**
Huff, D. How to take a chance **519**
See also pages in the following books:
Hogben, L. Mathematics for the million
p551-615 **510**
Kadesch, R. R. Math menagerie p3-19
793.7
Newman, J. R. ed. The world of mathe-
matics v2 p1316-1414 **510.8**
Probability and statistics for everyman.
Adler, I. **519**
Problem children
D'Ambrosio, R. No language but a cry
155.45

See also Juvenile delinquency
A **problem** of identity. Oppenheim, E. P.
In Dulles, A. ed. Great spy stories
from fiction p255-76 **S C**
The **problem** of Thor Bridge. Doyle, Sir
A. C.
In Doyle, Sir A. C. The complete
Sherlock Holmes v2 p1242-61 **S C**
Problems of mass transportation. Reische,
D. ed. **380.5**
Prochnow, Herbert V. 1897-
(comp.) A treasury of humorous quota-
tions **808.88**
Prochnow, Herbert V. 1931-
(jt. comp.) Prochnow, H. V. comp. A
treasury of humorous quotations **808.88**
Procunier, Edwin R.
Two sides of darkness
In The Best short plays of 1958-1959
p185-205 **808.82**
The **prodigies.** Cather, W.
In Cather, W. Willa Cather's Collected
short fiction, 1892-1912 v3 p411-23
S C
The **proem:** by the carpenter. Henry, O.
In Henry, O. The complete works of
O. Henry p551-54 **S C**
Profession, Choice of. See Vocational guid-
ance
Profession. Asimov, I.
In Asimov, I. Nine tomorrows p16-74
S C
Professional ethics. See Medical ethics
Professions
See also Occupations; Vocational
guidance; also Law as a profession; and
similar headings
Bibliography
Forrester, G. Occupational literature
016.3317
The **professor.** Brontë, C. **Fic**
Professors. See Teachers
The **professor's commencement.** Cather, W.
In Cather, W. Willa Cather's Collected
short fiction, 1892-1912 v3 p283-91
S C
The **professor's yarn.** Twain, M.
In Twain, M. The complete short sto-
ries of Mark Twain p239-44 **S C**

The **profile.** Cather, W.
In Cather, W. Willa Cather's Collected
short fiction, 1892-1912 v 1 p125-35
S C
Profiles & portraits of American Presi-
dents & their wives. Bassett, M. **920**
Profiles from the new Asia. Roland, A.
920
Profiles in courage. Memorial ed. Kennedy,
J. F. **920**
Profiles of American colleges, Barron's.
Fine, B. **378.73**
Programmed instruction. See Teaching
machines
Programming (Electronic computers)
Computer science **651.8**
See also pages in the following book:
Crowley, T. H. Understanding compu-
ters p87-99 **510.78**
Progress
Foreign Policy Association. Toward the
year 2018 **901.9**
See also pages in the following book:
Parker, D. H. Schooling for what? p171-
86 **370.1**
See also Civilization; Science and
civilization; Social change
Progressive education. See Education, Ele-
mentary—Experimental methods
The **progressive** era: 1901-1917. May, E. R.
In Life (Periodical) The Life History
of the United States v9 **973**
Progressive Party (Founded 1912)
See pages in the following books:
Addams, J. The social thought of Jane
Addams p162-74 **309.173**
Degler, C. N. Out of our past p362-78
973
Prohibited books
See pages in the following book:
Ernst, M. L. Censorship: the search for
the obscene p160-68 **343**
Prohibition
Severn, B. The end of the roaring twenties
178
See also pages in the following books:
Allen, F. L. Only yesterday p245-59
973.91
Darrow, C. The story of my life p279-300
92
Leighton, I. ed. The aspirin age, 1919-1941
p34-49 **917.3**
Shannon, D. A. Between the wars: Amer-
ica, 1919-1941 p65-72 **973.91**
Prohibition. Wescott, G.
In Abrahams, W. ed. Fifty years of the
American short story v2 p438-49
S C
Proia, Nicholas C.
Barron's Handbook of American college
financial aid **378.3**
Barron's Handbook of junior and com-
munity college financial aid **378.3**
Project Apollo. See Apollo project
Project Mercury. See Mercury project
Project Saturn. See Saturn project
Projective geometry. See Geometry, Projec-
tive

Pueblo Indians
See pages in the following books:
Hall-Quest, O. Conquistadors and Pueblos p52-62, 111-31   **979.1**
Josephy, A. M. The Indian heritage of America p158-67   **970.1**
See also Zuñi Indians

Puerto Ricans in New York (City)
Handlin, O. The newcomers: Negroes and Puerto Ricans in a changing metropolis   **301.45**
Lewis, O. La vida   **301.453**
See also pages in the following book:
Glazer, N. Beyond the melting pot p86-136   **301.45**

Puerto Ricans in the United States
Howard, J. R. Awakening minorities   **301.45**
Senior, C. The Puerto Ricans: strangers —then neighbors   **301.453**
See also pages in the following book:
Miller, H. P. Rich man, poor man p87-104   **339**
The **Puerto** Ricans: strangers—then neighbors. Senior, C.   **301.453**

Puerto Rico
History
See pages in the following books:
Time-Life Books. The U.S. overseas p41-96   **917.3**
Williams, E. From Columbus to Castro: the history of the Caribbean, 1492-1969 p430-39, 443-65   **972.9**

Puffer (Submarine)
See pages in the following book:
Roscoe, T. True tales of bold escapes p57-81   **904**

Pugh, Eric
A dictionary of acronyms & abbreviations   **603**

Pugilism. See Boxing

Pulitzer, Joseph, 1847-1911
See pages in the following book:
Beard, A. E. S. Our foreign-born citizens p38-44   **920**
The **Pulitzer** Prize novels. Stuckey, W. J.   **813.09**

Pullman Strike, 1894. See Chicago Strike, 1894

The **pump.** Humphrey, W.
In The Best American short stories, 1964 p153-60   **S C**

Punch and go. Galsworthy, J.
In Galsworthy, J. Plays p689-98   **822**

Punctuation
See pages in the following book:
Becker, E. R. The successful secretary's handbook p143-64   **651.02**

Punic War, 2d, 218-201 B.C.
Cottrell, L. Hannibal, enemy of Rome **92**
Lamb, H. Hannibal: one man against Rome   **92**

Punic Wars
See pages in the following book:
Von Hagen, V. W. Roman roads p43-54   **625.7**

Punishment
Lewin, S. ed. Crime and its prevention   **364.1**
Loble, L. H. Delinquency can be stopped   **364.36**
See also pages in the following books:
Lynd, S. ed. Nonviolence in America: a documentary history p150-60   **323**
Weinberg, A. ed. The muckrakers p322-37   **309.173**
See also Prisons; Reformatories

The **pupil.** James, H.
In James, H. Short novels of Henry James p355-405   **Fic**

The **puppet** masters. Heinlein, R. A.
In Heinlein, R. A. Three by Heinlein p 1-215   **Fic**

Purdy, Ken W.
Young people and driving   **629.28**

Pure food. See Food adulteration and inspection

Purgatory. Yeats, W. B.
In Yeats, W. B. Collected plays of W. B. Yeats p429-36   **822**

Puritans
Miller, P. ed. The American Puritans: their prose and poetry   **810.8**
Miller, P. The New England mind: From colony to province   **917.4**
Miller, P. The New England mind: The seventeenth century   **917.4**
See also pages in the following book:
Boorstin, D. J. The Americans: The colonial experience p3-31   **917.3**
Fiction
Hawthorne, N. The House of the Seven Gables   **Fic**
Hawthorne, N. The scarlet letter   **Fic**
Seton, A. The Winthrop woman   **Fic**

The **purloined** letter. Poe, E. A.
In Day, A. G. ed. The greatest American short stories p61-80   **S C**
In Poe, E. A. The complete tales and poems of Edgar Allan Poe p208-22   **S C**
In Poe, E. A. Edgar Allan Poe p439-62   **S C**
In Poe, E. A. Selected poetry and prose p293-309   **818**

The **purple** dress. Henry, O.
In Henry, O. The complete works of O. Henry p1424-28   **S C**

Purple dust. O'Casey, S.
In O'Casey, S. The Sean O'Casey reader p285-364   **828**

The **purple** of the Balkan Kings. Saki
In Saki. The short stories of Saki p591-94   **S C**

The **purple** pileus. Wells, H. G.
In Wells, H. G. The complete short stories of H. G. Wells p470-82   **S C**

Purple wig. Chesterton, G. K.
In Chesterton, G. K. The Father Brown omnibus p332-46   **S C**

The **pursuit** of Admiral von Spee. See Hough, R. The long pursuit   **940.4**

Pursuit of Mr Blue. Chesterton, G. K.
In Chesterton, G. K. The Father Brown omnibus p894-913   **S C**

The **pursuit** of poetry. Untermeyer, L.
808.1

A pursuit race. Hemingway, E.
In Hemingway, E. The short stories of Ernest Hemingway p350-55 **S C**

Pusey, Merlo J.
The way we go to war 353.03

Pushkin, Aleksandr Sergeevich
The queen of spades
In Seltzer, T. comp. Best Russian short stories p3-39 **S C**

About
See pages in the following book:
Posell, E. Z. Russian authors p14-43 920

Puzzle for Poppy. Quentin, P.
In Haycraft, H. ed. A treasury of great mysteries v 1 p201-40 **S C**

Puzzles
Latcha, A. G. How do you figure it?
793.7

See also pages in the following book:
Flesch, R. How to write, speak, and think more effectively p238-47 808

See also Mathematical recreations

Pyddoke, Edward
(jt. auth.) Hodges, H. Ancient Britons
913.36

Pygmalion. Shaw, B.
In Shaw, B. Androcles and the lion, Overruled, Pygmalion p107-224 822
In Shaw, B. Complete plays, with prefaces v 1 p197-281 822
In Shaw, B. Four plays p213-306 822

Pygmalion, and other plays. Shaw, B. 822

Pyle, Howard
How the good gifts were used by two
In Becker, M. L. ed. The home book of Christmas p502-09 394.26

Pynchon, Thomas
The secret integration
In The Saturday Evening Post. Best modern short stories p448-85 **S C**

Under the rose
In Abrahams, W. ed. Fifty years of the American short story v2 p160-85 **S C**

Pyramids
See pages in the following books:
Casson, L. Ancient Egypt p129-39 913.32
Ley, W. Another look at Atlantis, and fifteen other essays p27-41 508

Pythagoras
See pages in the following book:
Sarton, G. A history of science v 1 p199-217 509

Pytheas
See pages in the following book:
Stefánsson, V. ed. Great adventures and explorations p8-17 910.9

The **Python's** dilemma. Njoku, M. C.
In Angoff, C. ed. African writing today p80-97 896

Q

Quaife, Milo M.
See pages in the following book:
Trump, F. Buyer beware! p90-100 339.4
See also Patent medicines

Quaife, Milo M.
The history of the United States flag 929.9

Quail seed. Saki
In Saki. The short stories of Saki p508-14 **S C**

The **Quaker** colonies. Fisher, S. G. 973.2

Quakers. See Friends, Society of

The **quality** of courage. Mantle, M. 920

The **quality** of life. Michener, J. A. 309.173

Quality Street. Barrie, J. M.
In Barrie, J. M. The plays of J. M. Barrie p95-163 822

Quantum mechanics. See Quantum theory

Quantum theory
Gamow, G. Thirty years that shook physics 530.1
See also pages in the following book:
Newman, J. R. ed. The world of mathematics v2 p975-95 510.8
See also Force and energy; Relativity (Physics)

Quarles, Benjamin
Black abolitionists 326
(ed.) Frederick Douglass 92
The Negro in the making of America 301.451
(jt. ed.) Fishel, L. H. The Black American 301.451

Quarrels that have shaped the Constitution.
Garraty, J. A. ed. 342.73

The **quarry.** Walker, M. Fic

Quasars
Bova, B. In quest of quasars 523.8
See also pages in the following books:
Hodge, P. W. The revolution in astronomy p27-40 523
Nourse, A. E. Universe, earth, and atom p444-58 530.9

Quasi-stellar radio sources. See Quasars

Quebec (City)
Fiction
Cather, W. Shadows on the rock Fic

Quebec (Province)
Hémon, L. Marie Chapdelaine Fic

Quebec Campaign, 1759
See pages in the following book:
Armstrong, O. K. The fifteen decisive battles of the United States p19-55 973

Queen, Ellery
The lamp of God
In Haycraft, H. ed. A treasury of great mysteries v 1 p345-98 **S C**

A matter of seconds
In Lardner, R. ed. Rex Lardner selects the best of sports fiction p13-21 **S C**

Mystery at the Library of Congress
In Mystery Writers of America. Crime without murder p223-31 **S C**

Queen Anne's War, 1702-1713. See United States—History—Queen Anne's War, 1702-1713

The **Queen** of Air and Darkness. White, T. H.
 In White, T. H. The once and future king p215-323 **Fic**

The **queen** of spades. Pushkin, A. S.
 In Seltzer, T. comp. Best Russian short stories p3-39 **S C**

Queen Victoria. Strachey, L. 92

Queens
 Cottrell, L. Five queens of ancient Egypt 913.32
 Fraser, A. Mary [Stuart], Queen of Scots 92
 Green, D. Queen Anne 92
 Jenkins, E. Elizabeth the Great 92
 Kelly, A. Eleanor of Aquitaine and the four kings 92
 Oldenbourg, Z. Catherine the Great 92
 Pernoud, R. Eleanor of Aquitaine 92
 Strachey, L. Elizabeth and Essex: a tragic history 92
 Strachey, L. Queen Victoria 92
 Trease, G. Seven sovereign queens 920
 Wells, E. Nefertiti 92
  See also Courts and courtiers; and names of Queens, e.g. Elizabeth II, Queen of Great Britain

The **Queen's** confession. Holt, V. **Fic**

The **queen's** jewel. Holding, J.
 In Hitchcock, A. ed. Alfred Hitchcock presents: A month of mystery p66-75 **S C**

"Queer." Anderson, S.
 In Anderson, S. Winesburg, Ohio (Modern Lib) p228-43 **S C**
 In Anderson, S. Winesburg, Ohio (Viking) p190-201 **S C**

The **queer** feet. Chesterton, G. K.
 In Chesterton, G. K. The Father Brown omnibus p46-66 **S C**
 In Costain, T. B. ed. Read with me p147-64 **S C**

Quennell, C. H. B.
 A History of everyday things in England v 1-4. See A History of everyday things in England v 1-4 914.2
 (jt. auth.) Quennell, M. Everyday life in prehistoric times 913.03
 (jt. auth.) Quennell, M. Everyday life in Roman and Anglo-Saxon times 913.42
 (jt. auth.) Quennell, M. Everyday things in ancient Greece 913.38

Quennell, Marjorie
 Everyday life in prehistoric times 913.03
 Everyday life in Roman and Anglo-Saxon times 913.42
 Everyday things in ancient Greece 913.38

A history of everyday things in England: 1066-1499
 In A History of everyday things in England v 1 914.2

A history of everyday things in England: 1500-1799
 In A History of everyday things in England v2 914.2

A history of everyday things in England: 1733-1851
 In A History of everyday things in England v3 914.2

A history of everyday things in England: 1851-1914
 In A History of everyday things in England v4 914.2

Quentin, Patrick
 Puzzle for Poppy
 In Haycraft, H. ed. A treasury of great mysteries v 1 p241-51 **S C**

Quentin Durward. Scott, Sir W. **Fic**

Queries and answers. Henry, O.
 In Henry, O. The complete works of O. Henry p1058-60 **S C**

Quesada, Gonzalo Jiménez de. See Jiménez de Quesada, Gonzalo

Quest, Olga Hall- See Hall-Quest, Olga

The **quest.** Saki
 In Saki. The short stories of Saki p164-68 **S C**

The **quest** for Arthur's Britain. Ashe, G. 913.42

The **quest** for Atlantis. Bowman, J. S. 913

The **quest** for Sumer. Cottrell, L. 913.35

A **question** of priorities. Higbee, E. 309.2

Quetelet, Lambert Adolphe Jacques
 See pages in the following book:
 Jones, B. Z. ed. The golden age of science p246-63 920

Quick, John
 Artists' and illustrators' encyclopedia 703

Quick One. Chesterton, G. K.
 In Chesterton, G. K. The Father Brown omnibus p833-56 **S C**

Quick returns. Lardner, R.
 In Lardner, R. The Ring Lardner reader p135-54 **S C**

The **quicksand.** Wharton, E.
 In Wharton, E. The collected short stories of Edith Wharton v 1 p397-410 **S C**

Quicksilver. See Mercury

The **quiet** American. Greene, G. **Fic**

The **quiet** crisis. Udall, S. L. 333.7

Quiet pilgrimage. Vining, E. G. 92

A **quiet** wedding. Upson, W. H.
 In Lardner, R. ed. Rex Lardner selects the best of sports fiction p171-84 **S C**

Quietus. Russell, C.
 In Hughes, L. ed. The best short stories by Negro writers p347-55 **S C**

Quiller-Couch, Arthur
 (ed.) The Oxford Book of English verse, 1250-1918. See The Oxford Book of English verse, 1250-1918 821.08

The **quince** tree. Saki
 In Saki. The short stories of Saki p364-68 **S C**

Quine, Willard Van Orman
 Speaking of objects
 In Kurtz, P. ed. American philosophy in the twentieth century p444-60 191.08

Quinn, Arthur Hobson
American fiction   813.09
(ed.) Representative American plays
       812.08

Quinn, Edward
(ed.) The Reader's encyclopedia of world drama. See The Reader's encyclopedia of world drama   809.203

Quintero, Serafín Álvarez. See Álvarez Quintero, Serafín

A quintet of cuisines. Field, M.   641.5

Quirk, Robert E.
Mexico   972

Qumran Community
See pages in the following book:
Noble, I. Treasure of the caves p 1-4, 122-27   221.4

Qumran texts. See Dead Sea scrolls

Quo vadis. Sienkiewicz, H.   Fic

Quotations
Bartlett, J. comp. Familiar quotations   808.88
Bohle, B. comp. The home book of American quotations   808.88
Brussell, E. E. ed. Dictionary of quotable definitions   808.88
Dictionary of foreign phrases and abbreviations   808.88
Evans, B. ed. Dictionary of quotations   808.88
Flesch, R. The new book of unusual quotations   808.88
Hoyt, J. K. Hoyt's New cyclopedia of practical quotations   808.88
Lincoln, A. A treasury of Lincoln quotations   818
Magill, F. N. ed. Magill's Quotations in context [1st-2d ser]   808.88
Mencken, H. L. ed. A new dictionary of quotations on historical principles from ancient and modern sources   808.88
The Oxford Dictionary of quotations   808.88
Prochnow, H. V. comp. A treasury of humorous quotations   808.88
Stevenson, B. comp. Home book of Bible quotations   220.2
Stevenson, B. ed. The home book of quotations   808.88
Tripp, R. T. comp. The international thesaurus of quotations   808.88
Wallis, C. L. ed. Our American heritage   808.88

See also Proverbs

Quotations from Chairman Mao Tse-tung. Mao, Tsê-tung   320.5

Quotations in context, Magill's. Magill, F. N. ed.   808.88

Qur'an. See Koran

R

R is for rocket. Bradbury, R.   S C
R is for rocket [short story]. Bradbury, R.
In Bradbury, R. R is for rocket p11-29
       S C

RNA
Lessing, L. DNA   574.8
See also pages in the following books:
Beadle, G. The language of life p181-207   575.1
Fried, J. J. The mystery of heredity p85-98   575.1

RPG (Computer program language)
Gildersleeve, T. R. Computer data processing and programming   651.8

R.U.R. Čapek, K.
In Cerf, B. A. comp. Sixteen famous European plays p737-88   808.82
In Dickinson, T. H. ed. Chief contemporary dramatists; 3d ser. p569-603   808.82
In Tucker, S. M. ed. Twenty-five modern plays p641-73   808.82

Rx. Nourse, A. E.
In Nourse, A. E. Rx for tomorrow p17-33   S C

Rx for tomorrow. Nourse, A. E.   S C

Rabbit run. Updike, J.   Fic

Rabelais, François
See pages in the following books:
Durant, W. The Reformation p795-807   940.2
Highet, G. The classical tradition p178-93   809

Rabinowitz, Shalom. See Aleichem, Sholem

Raccoons
North, S. Raccoons are the brightest people   599

Raccoons are the brightest people. North, S.   599

Race
Coon, C. S. The living races of man   572
Coon, C. S. The origin of races   572
Goldsby, R. A. Race and races   572
See also pages in the following books:
Bates, M. Man in nature p41-47   573
Claiborne, R. Climate, man, and history p206-19   551.59

Race and races. Goldsby, R. A.   572

Race at morning. Faulkner, W.
In Faulkner, W. Selected short stories of William Faulkner p285-306 S C

The race for number three. London, J.
In London, J. Jack London's Tales of adventure   S C

Race problems
Benedict, R. Race: science and politics   572
See also pages in the following book:
Du Bois, W. E. B. W. E. B. Du Bois: a reader p407-24   301.451
See also names of countries, cities, etc. with subdivision Race relations, e.g. Montgomery, Ala.—Race relations

Drama
Sackler, H. The great white hope   812

Fiction
Bennett, J. Mister fisherman   Fic
Fast, H. Freedom road   Fic
Grau, S. A. The keepers of the house Fic
Paton, A. Cry, the beloved country   **Fic**

Race problems and the church. See Church and race problems

Race relations. Hughes, L.
In Hughes, L. The Langston Hughes
reader p193-94 **818**
Race: science and politics. Benedict, R. **572**
Races of man. *See* Ethnology
Rachlin, Carol K.
(jt. auth.) Marriott, A. American Indian
mythology **398.2**
Rachlis, Eugene
The low countries **914.92**
Rachmaninoff, Sergei. *See* Rachmaninov,
Sergei
Rachmaninov, Sergei
See pages in the following books:
Cross, M. The Milton Cross New ency-
clopedia of the great composers and their
music p739-53 **920.03**
Ewen, D. ed. The new book of modern
composers p311-21 **920**
Racine, Jean Baptiste
Phaedra
In Bentley, E. comp. The great play-
wrights v 1 p1035-86 **808.82**
About
See pages in the following books:
Durant, W. The age of Louis XIV p132-
44 **940.2**
Nicoll, A. World drama p307-15 **809.2**
Racing. *See* Automobile racing; Horse rac-
ing
A racing car driver's world. Caracciola, R.
92
Racketeering
Hutchinson, J. The imperfect union **331.88**
Radar
See pages in the following book:
Hodge, P. W. The revolution in astron-
omy p90-101 **523**
Radcliffe, Charles
Fiction
Seton, A. Devil Water **Fic**
Radcliffe, Donald
Song of the simidor
In The Best American short stories,
1967 p211-37 **S C**
Radhakrishnan, Sarvepalli
(ed.) A source book in Indian philosophy
181
Radiation
Romer, A. The restless atom **539.7**
See also pages in the following book:
Fermi, L. Atoms for the world p171-88
621.48
See also Light; Ultraviolet rays
Physiological effect
See pages in the following book:
Curtis, R. Perils of the peaceful atom p33-
44 **621.48**
See also Atomic medicine
The radical Right. Epstein, B. R. **323.2**
Radical school reform. Gross, B. ed. **370.8**
Radicals and radicalism. *See* Revolutions
Radicals, Young. Keniston, K. **301.43**
Radio
Broadcasting
See Radio broadcasting

Examinations, questions, etc.
Simon, B. Ham radio incentive licensing
guide **621.3841**
Handbooks, manuals, etc.
Collins, A. F. The radio amateur's hand-
book **621.3841**
The Radio amateur's handbook **621.3841**
The Radio amateur's handbook **621.3841**
The radio amateur's handbook. Collins, A. F.
621.3841
Radio astronomy
See pages in the following book:
Hodge, P. W. The revolution in astron-
omy p13-26 **523**
Radio broadcasting
See pages in the following books:
Leighton, I. ed. The aspirin age, 1919-1941
p431-43 **917.3**
Nye, R. The unembarrassed muse: the
popular arts in America p390-406 **917.3**
Radio journalism. *See* Journalism; Radio
broadcasting
Radioactivity
Curtis, R. Perils of the peaceful atom
621.48
See also Nuclear physics
Radiocarbon dating
See pages in the following book:
Deetz, J. Invitation to archaeology p33-
37 **913**
Radiochemistry
Poole, L. Carbon-14, and other science
methods that date the past **913**
Radosh, Ronald
(ed.) Debs **92**
Raffaele Sanzio. *See* Raphael
Raft story. Crane, S.
In Crane, S. The complete short stories
& sketches of Stephen Crane p297-
300 **S C**
The Ragtime Kid. Lederer, W. J.
In Lederer, W. J. The ugly American
p110-14 **S C**
Rahman, Abdul
See pages in the following book:
Kenworthy, L. S. Leaders of new nations
p290-309 **920**
Raid. Faulkner, W.
In Faulkner, W. The portable Faulkner
p111-43 **S C**
The raid: a volunteer's story. Tolstoy, L.
In Tolstoy, L. Short stories v 1 p23-
55 **S C**
The railroad builders. Moody, J. **385.09**
Railroads
See pages in the following book:
White, E. B. The points of my compass
p155-74 **818**
Fiction
Norris, F. The octopus **Fic**
History
Josephson, M. The robber barons **920**
Moody, J. The railroad builders **385.09**
See also pages in the following books:
American Heritage. The American Heri-
tage Book of great adventures of the
Old West p240-63 **978**

The **ransom** of Red Chief. Henry, O.
In Henry, O. The best short stories of
O. Henry p188-201 **S C**
In Henry, O. The complete works of
O. Henry p1144-52 **S C**
Rape. Montross, D.
In Mystery Writers of America. Crime
without murder p193-95 **S C**
The **rape** of Lucrece. Shakespeare, W.
In Shakespeare, W. The sonnets, songs
& poems of Shakespeare p275-332 **821**

Raphael
See pages in the following book:
Vasari, G. The lives of the painters, sculp-
tors and architects v2 p221-49 **920**
Raphael of Urbino. See Raphael
Rapid transit. See Local transit
Rapp, George
See pages in the following book:
O'Connor, R. The German-Americans
p221-29 **301.453**
Rappaccini's daughter. Hawthorne, N.
In Hawthorne, N. Hawthorne's Short
stories p206-34 **S C**
Rappoport, Solomon. See Ansky, S.
Rare animals
Durrell, G. Two in the bush **591**
McClung, R. M. Lost wild America **333.7**
Philip, Duke of Edinburgh. Wildlife crisis **333.7**
Silverberg, R. Forgotten by time: a book
of loving fossils **591**
See also pages in the following book:
Ley, W. Another look at Atlantis, and
fifteen other essays p68-79 **508**
Rascals in paradise; excerpt. Michener, J. A.
In Day, A. G. ed. The spell of Hawaii
p180-216 **919.69**
Rascovich, Mark
Bucher, L. M. Bucher: my story **327**
Rasputin, Gregorii Efimovich
See pages in the following book:
Massie, R. K. Nicholas [II] and Alex-
andra p180-203 **92**
Rathjen, Carl Henry
Jump job
In Mystery Writers of America. Crime
without murder p233-43 **S C**
The **rathskeller** and the rose. Henry, O.
In Henry, O. The complete works of
O. Henry p1333-37 **S C**
Rationalism
See pages in the following book:
Brinton, C. The shaping of modern
thought p82-107 **901.93**
See also Reason
The **rats.** Hauptmann, G.
In Tucker, S. M. ed. Twenty-five mod-
ern plays p401-54 **808.82**
Rats, lice and history. Zinsser, H. **616.9**
Rattigan, Terence
All on her own
In The Best short plays, 1970 p251-61 **808.82**
The Browning version
In Cerf, B. ed. 24 favorite one-act plays
p54-93 **808.82**

Rau, Santha Rama. See Rama Rau, Santha
Raucher, Herman
The summer of '42 **Fic**
Ravel, Maurice
See pages in the following books:
Cross, M. The Milton Cross New encyclo-
pedia of the great composers and their
music p754-72 **920.03**
Ewen, D. ed. The new book of modern
composers p322-33 **920**
Raw materials. See Mines and mineral re-
sources
A **raw** youth. See Dostoevsky, F. The
adolescent **Fic**
Rawicz, Slavomir
The long walk **910.4**
Rawlings, Marjorie Kinnan
Benny and the bird-dogs
In White, E. B. ed. A subtreasury of
American humor; abridged p2-17 **817.08**
Gal young un
In Abrahams, W. ed. Fifty years of the
American short story v2 p186-217 **S C**
Ray, Satyajit
See pages in the following book:
Mehta, V. Portrait of India p408-21 **915.4**
Rays, Ultraviolet. See Ultraviolet rays
La **Raza.** Steiner, S. **301.453**
The **razor's** edge. Maugham, W. S. **Fic**
Reach for the sky; the story of Douglas
Bader. Brickhill, P. **92**
Reaching for empire: 1890-1901. Weisberger,
B. A.
In Life (Periodical) The Life History
of the United States v8 **973**
Reactors (Nuclear physics) See Nuclear re-
actors
Read, Bill
(jt. ed.) Brinnin, J. M. ed. Twentieth cen-
tury poetry: American and British
(1900-1970) **821.08**
Read, Herbert
A concise history of modern painting **759.06**
A concise history of modern sculpture **735**
Henry Moore **730.942**
Read with me. Costain, T. B. ed. **S C**
Reade, Charles
The cloister and the hearth **Fic**
Reader, W. J.
Life in Victorian England **914.2**
The **Reader's** adviser **011**
The **Reader's** encyclopedia **803**
The **Reader's** encyclopedia of American lit-
erature **810.3**
The **Reader's** encyclopedia of Shakespeare **822.3**
The **Reader's** encyclopedia of world drama **809.203**
A **reader's** guide to Herman Melville. Miller,
J. E. **813.09**
Reader's guide to periodical literature **051**
A **reader's** guide to Walt Whitman. Allen,
G. W. **811.09**

The **reader's** handbook of famous names in fiction, allusions, references, proverbs, plots, stories, and poems. Brewer, E. C. 803

The **reader's** Shakespeare. Deutsch, B. 822.3

Reading
Lewis, N. How to read better and faster 428.4
See also Books and reading

Bibliography
Spache, G. D. Good reading for the disadvantaged reader 016.3719

Examinations, questions, etc.
Farley, E. J. Barron's How to prepare for the high school equivalency examination reading interpretation tests 371.27

Study and teaching
See Reading

The **real** majority. Scammon, R. M. 329

Realism
See pages in the following book:
Kurtz, P. ed. American philosophy in the twentieth century p314-48 191.08

Realism in art
See pages in the following book:
Cheney, S. The story of modern art p121-46 709.03

Realism in literature
See pages in the following book:
Nicoll, A. World drama p485-546, 598-610, 682-718, 811-36 809.2

Realities of American foreign policy. Kennan, G. F. 327.73

A **really** important person. Chute, B. J.
In Chute, B. J. One touch of nature, and other stories p131-50 S C

Realm of algebra. Asimov, I. 512

The **reaper** and the flowers. Stuart, J.
In Stuart, J. Plowshare in heaven p113-26 S C

Reapers. See Harvesting machinery

Rear window. Irish, W.
In Haycraft, H. ed. A treasury of great mysteries v 1 p413-36 S C

Reason
Kant, I. Critique of pure reason 193

Reason. Asimov, I.
In Asimov, I. I, robot p59-77 S C

Reason and right. Hughes, L.
In Hughes, L. The Langston Hughes reader p227-30 818

Reason not the need. Stone, W.
In The New Yorker. Stories from The New Yorker, 1950-1960 p553-77 S C

Reasoning. See Logic

Rebecca. Du Maurier, D. Fic

Rebecca. Stout, R.
In Haycraft, H. ed. A treasury of great mysteries v2 p301-576 S C

The **rebel.** Camus, A. 170

Rebora, Piero
(comp.) Cassell's Italian dictionary: Italian-English, English-Italian. See Cassell's Italian dictionary: Italian-English, English-Italian 453

Recent history atlas: 1870 to the present day. Gilbert, M. 911

The **recessional.** Saki
In Saki. The short stories of Saki p223-27 S C

Recipes. See Cookery

The **reckoning.** Wharton, E.
In Wharton, E. The collected short stories of Edith Wharton v 1 p420-37 S C

Reclamation of land
See pages in the following books:
Scientific American. Plant agriculture p123-32 581
United States. Department of Agriculture. Contours of change p197-204 630

The **reconciliation.** Wells, H. G.
In Wells, H. G. The complete short stories of H. G. Wells p551-58 S C

Reconstruction
Bowers, C. G. The tragic era 973.8
Buck, P. H. The road to reunion, 1865-1900 973.8
Fleming, W. L. The sequel of Appomattox 973.8
Franklin, J. H. Reconstruction: after the Civil War 973.8
See also pages in the following books:
Degler, C. N. Out of our past p208-28 973
Hart, A. B. ed. American history told by contemporaries v4 p445-500 973
See also Negroes

Fiction
Fast, H. Freedom road Fic
Mitchell, M. Gone with the wind Fic
Walker, M. Jubilee Fic

Reconstruction (1939-1951)
Europe
White, T. H. Fire in the ashes 940.55

Reconstruction: after the Civil War. Franklin, J. H. 973.8

Record players. See Phonograph

The **recorder:** a history. Duberman, M.
In The Best short plays, 1970 p327-48 808.82

Recorders, Tape. See Tape and wire recorders

Records, Phonograph. See Phonograph records

The **recovery.** Wharton, E.
In Wharton, E. The collected short stories of Edith Wharton v 1 p259-74 S C

The **recovery** of confidence. Gardner, J. W. 309.2

Recreation
American Association for Health, Physical Education, and Recreation. Physical education for high school students 613.7
See also pages in the following books:
Good things about the U.S. today p207-23 917.3
United States. Department of Agriculture. Consumers all p299-338 640.73
The United States p113-30 917.3
See also Amusements; Games; Outdoor recreation

Recreations, Mathematical. See Mathematical recreations

The recruitment of Major Blenkinsop. MacKenzie, Sir C.
    In Dulles, A. ed. Great spy stories from fiction p413-21   S C
The recruitment of the archtraitor. Asprey, R.
    In Dulles, A. ed. Great spy stories from fiction p3-12   S C
Red. Maugham, W. S.
    In Maugham, W. S. The best short stories of W. Somerset Maugham p170-92   S C
The red and the black. Stendhal   Fic
The red and yellow ark. Devany, E. H.
    In The Best short plays of 1957-1958 p225-53   808.82
The red badge of courage. Crane, S.   Fic
The Red Baron. Richthofen, M. Freiherr von   92
Red bonnet. Patterson, L.
    In Hughes, L. ed. The best short stories by Negro writers p448-57   S C
Red China. See China (People's Republic of China)
Red China today. Snow, E.   915.1
Red Cloud, Sioux chief
    See pages in the following book:
    Brown, D. Bury my heart at Wounded Knee p123-49   970.4
Red Cross. United States. American National Red Cross
    American Red Cross Home nursing textbook   649.8
    Basic first aid   614.8
Red Cross. United States. American National Red Cross (as subject)
    Ross, I. Angel of the battlefield; the life of Clara Barton   92
Red Dog. Kipling, R.
    In Kipling, R. The best short stories of Rudyard Kipling p332-49   S C
Red giants and white dwarfs. Jastrow, R.   523.1
Red Guard; the political biography of Dai Hsiao-ai. Bennett, G. A.   92
Red Hanrahan. Yeats, W. B.
    In Garrity, D. A. ed. 44 Irish short stories p482-91   S C
Red harvest. Hammett, D.
    In Hammett, D. The novels of Dashiell Hammett p 1-142   Fic
Red-headed baby. Hughes, L.
    In Hughes, L. The Langston Hughes reader p18-22   818
The Red-headed League. Doyle, Sir A. C.
    In Doyle, Sir A. C. The complete Sherlock Holmes v 1 p194-212   S C
    In Doyle, Sir A. C. Sherlock Holmes' greatest cases p257-91   S C
The red laugh. Andreyev, L. N.
    In Seltzer, T. comp. Best Russian short stories p437-521   S C
Red leaves. Faulkner, W.
    In Faulkner, W. Collected stories of William Faulkner p313-41   S C
    In Faulkner, W. The portable Faulkner p57-84   S C
    In Faulkner, W. Selected short stories of William Faulkner p101-31 S C

The red man's continent. Huntington, E.   970.1
Red Moon of Meru. Chesterton, G. K.
    In Chesterton, G. K. The Father Brown omnibus p764-81   S C
The red pony. Steinbeck, J.   Fic
    also in Steinbeck, J. The portable Steinbeck p325-415   818
    also in Steinbeck, J. The short novels of John Steinbeck p137-200   Fic
Red power. Josephy, A. M. ed.   970.5
The red robe. Brieux, E.
    In Dickinson, T. H. ed. Chief contemporary dramatists [1st ser] p471-516 808.82
The red room. Wells, H. G.
    In Wells, H. G. The complete short stories of H. G. Wells p447-56 S C
Red roses for me. O'Casey, S.
    In O'Casey, S. The Sean O'Casey reader p365-434   828
The red roses of Tonia. Henry, O.
    In Henry, O. The complete works of O. Henry p1632-39   S C
Red sky at morning. Bradford, R.   Fic
Red star over China. Snow, E.   951.04
Redemption. Tolstoy, L.
    In Gassner, J. ed. Twenty best European plays on the American stage p708-33 808.82
The rediscovery of Black nationalism. Draper, T.   301.451
Redl, Alfred
    See pages in the following book:
    Dulles, A. ed. Great true spy stories p353-63   327
Redman, Donald Matthew
    See pages in the following book:
    Hadlock, R. Jazz masters of the twenties p194-218   920
Reducing (Body weight control) See Weight control
Reed, Kit
    Mr da V
    In Seventeen. Seventeen from Seventeen p169-85   S C
Reed, Mark
    Yes, my darling daughter
    In Gassner, J. ed. Twenty best plays of the modern American theatre p467-510 812.08
Reed, Mort
    Cowles Complete encyclopedia of U.S. coins   737.4
Reed, Walter
    See pages in the following book:
    De Kruif, P. Microbe hunters p311-33 920
Reed, Willis
    See pages in the following book:
    Pepe, P. The greatest stars of the NBA p51-64   920
Reeder, Red
    The Allies conquer (1942-1945)
    In Reeder, R. The story of the Second World War v2   940.53
    The Axis strikes (1939-1942)
    In Reeder, R. The story of the Second World War v 1   940.53

Reformation—*Continued*

Van Loon, H. W. The story of mankind
p251-61   909

See also Sixteenth century

Fiction

Reade, C. The cloister and the hearth **Fic**

The **Reformation**. Durant, W.   940.2

The **Reformation**. Simon, E.   940.2

The **Reformation**, 1520-1559. Elton, G. R. ed.
In The New Cambridge Modern history
v2   909

The **reformation** of Calliope. Henry, O.
In Henry, O. The complete works of
O. Henry p259-66   **S C**

Reformatories

See pages in the following book:

James, H. Children in trouble p105-50
                                          364.36

Reformers

See pages in the following book:

Hofstadter, R. Anti-intellectualism in
American life p172-96   917.3

The **refugee**. Malamud, B.
In The Saturday Evening Post. Best
modern short stories p52-63   **S C**

Refugees, Hungarian

Michener, J. A. The bridge at Andau
                                           943.9

Refugees, Vietnamese

Dooley, T. A. Dr Tom Dooley's three
great books   92

The **refugees**. Wharton, E.
In Wharton, E. The collected short stories of Edith Wharton v2 p570-93
                                         S C

Refuse and refuse disposal

See pages in the following book:

Our poisoned planet: can we save it?
p127-44   614

See also Water—Pollution

Regan, Robert
(ed.) Poe   818

Regency England, Life in. White, R. J. 914.2

Reginald. Saki
In Saki. The short stories of Saki p3-6
                                         S C

Reginald at the Carlton. Saki
In Saki. The short stories of Saki p22-
26   **S C**

Reginald at the theatre. Saki
In Saki. The short stories of Saki p11-
13   **S C**

Reginald in Russia. Saki
In Saki. The short stories of Saki p43-
108   **S C**

Reginald in Russia [short story]. Saki
In Saki. The short stories of Saki p45-
48   **S C**

Reginald on besetting sins. Saki
In Saki. The short stories of Saki p26-
28   **S C**

Reginald on Christmas presents. Saki
In Saki. The short stories of Saki p6-8
                                         S C

Reginald on house-parties. Saki
In Saki. The short stories of Saki p20-
22   **S C**

Reginald on tariff. Saki
In Saki. The short stories of Saki p31-
33   **S C**

Reginald on the Academy. Saki
In Saki. The short stories of Saki p8-10
                                         S C

Reginald on worries. Saki
In Saki. The short stories of Saki p18-
20   **S C**

Reginald's choir treat. Saki
In Saki. The short stories of Saki p15-
17   **S C**

Reginald's Christmas revel. Saki
In Saki. The short stories of Saki p33-
36   **S C**

Reginald's drama. Saki
In Saki. The short stories of Saki p28-
31   **S C**

Reginald's Peace poem. Saki
In Saki. The short stories of Saki p13-
15   **S C**

Reginald's rubaiyat. Saki
In Saki. The short stories of Saki p36-
39   **S C**

Regional planning
McHarg, I. L. Design with nature   711
See also City planning

Regoli, Gigetta Dalli. See Dalli Regoli,
Gigetta

Regulus. Kipling, R.
In Kipling, R. The best short stories of
Rudyard Kipling p512-29   **S C**

Rehabilitation, Rural
See pages in the following book:
United States. Department of Agriculture.
Contours of change p173-81   630

Reich, Charles A.
The greening of America   917.3

Reid, P. R.
The Colditz story   940.54

The **Reigate** puzzle. Doyle, Sir A. C.
In Doyle, Sir A. C. The complete Sherlock Holmes v 1 p458-73   **S C**

The **reign** of Andrew Jackson. Ogg, F. A.
                                          973.5

Reign of Terror. See France—History—
Revolution, 1789-1799

Reiman, Donald H.
Percy Bysshe Shelley   821.09

Reinfeld, Fred
A catalogue of the world's most popular
coins   737.4
Chess for young people   794.1
Coin collectors' handbook   737.4
The complete chessplayer   794.1
How to build a coin collection   737.4
Stamp collectors' handbook   383.2
A treasury of American coins   737.4
Treasury of the world's coins   737.4
(jt. auth.) Horowitz, I. A. First book of
chess, with pocket chessboard   794.1

Reischauer, Edwin O.
Beyond Vietnam: the United States and
Asia   327.73
A history of East Asian civilization   915
Japan: the story of a nation   952
The United States and Japan   327.73

Reische, Diana
(ed.) Problems of mass transportation
                                          380.5

The **repentant** sinner. Tolstoy, L.
In Tolstoy, L. Short stories v2 p168-70 **S C**
In Tolstoy, L. Twenty-three tales p228-30 **S C**

A **report**. Chekhov, A.
In Chekhov, A. The image of Chekhov p70 **S C**

Report from Black America. Goldman, P. **301.451**

Report from wasteland. Proxmire, W. **353.6**

Report of the National Advisory Commission on Civil Disorders. United States. National Advisory Commission on Civil Disorders **301.18**

The **report** of the President's Commission on Campus Unrest. United States. President's Commission on Campus Unrest **378.1**

Report on the John Birch Society. See Epstein, B. R. The radical Right **323.2**

Report program generator (Computer program language). See RPG (Computer program language)

Report to an academy. Kafka, F.
In Kafka, F. Selected short stories of Franz Kafka p168-80 **S C**

Report writing
Barzun, J. The modern researcher **808.82**
Hook, L. The research paper **808.02**
Markman, R. H. 10 steps in writing the research paper **808.02**
Turabian, K. L. A manual for writers of term papers, theses and dissertations **808.02**

Reporters and reporting
Overseas Press Club of America. How I got that story **070**
See also Journalism

Reports
Preparation
See Report writing

Representative American plays. Quinn, A. H. ed. **812.08**

Representative American speeches **815.08**

Representative government and representation. See Democracy

Representatives
United States
See United States. Congress. House

Reproduction
See pages in the following books:
Halacy, D. S. Man alive p50-70 **574**
Taylor, G. R. The biological time bomb p22-55 **577**

Reptiles
Cochran, D. M. The new field book of reptiles and amphibians **598.1**
Conant, R. A field guide to reptiles and amphibians of the United States and Canada east of the 100th meridian **598.1**
Ditmars, R. L. The reptiles of North America **598.1**
Ditmars, R. L. Reptiles of the world **598.1**
Stebbins, R. C. A field guide to Western reptiles and amphibians **598.1**
See also pages in the following books:
Fisher, J. Wildlife in danger p322-35 **333.7**

McClung, R. M. Lost wild America p197-205 **333.7**
See also Snakes

Reptiles, Fossil
See pages in the following books:
Asimov, I. The solar system and back p191-217 **508**
Fenton, C. L. The fossil book p297-307, 312-77 **560**
See also Dinosaurs

The **reptiles** of North America. Ditmars, R. L. **598.1**

Reptiles of the world. Ditmars, R. L. **598.1**

The **Republic**. Plato **888**

Republic Steel Company
See pages in the following book:
Leighton, I. ed. The aspirin age, 1919-1941 p383-402 **917.3**

Republican Party
See pages in the following book:
Shannon, D. A. Between the wars: America, 1919-1941 p31-57 **973.91**

Republics. See Democracy; Federal government

Requa I. Olsen, T.
In The Best American short stories, 1971 p237-65 **S C**

Requiem. Heinlein, R. A.
In Heinlein, R. A. Robert A. Heinlein's The past through tomorrow p197-210 **S C**

Rescue work. See First aid in illness and injury

Research
Barzun, J. The modern researcher **808.02**
Heller, J. H. Of mice, men and molecules **619**
See also pages in the following books:
Galin, S. Reference books: how to select and use them p269-84 **016**
Wright, L. B. The cultural life of the American colonies, 1607-1763 p216-37 **917.3**
See also subjects with the subdivision Research, e.g. Medicine—Research

The **research** paper. Hook, L. **808.02**

The **research** paper, 10 steps in writing. Markman, R. H. **808.02**

Reservoirs. See Water supply

Residences. See Architecture, Domestic; Houses

The **resident** patient. Doyle, Sir A. C.
In Doyle, Sir A. C. The complete Sherlock Holmes v 1 p487-501 **S C**

Resistance, rebellion and death. Camus, A. **844**

Resistance to government. See Passive resistance to government

Resnick, Seymour
(ed.) Spanish-American poetry **861.08**

Resources, Marine. See Marine resources

Resources, Natural. See Natural resources

Respectability. Anderson, S.
In Anderson, S. Winesburg, Ohio (Modern Lib) p135-44 **S C**
In Anderson, S. Winesburg, Ohio (Viking) p121-27 **S C**

Respighi, Ottorino
See pages in the following book:
Cross, M. The Milton Cross New encyclopedia of the great composers and their music p773-79   920.03
Rest. See Sleep
Rest camp on Maui. Burdick, E.
In Day, A. G. ed. The spell of Hawaii p309-22   919.69
The **restless** atom. Romer, A.   539.7
Restless spirit; the life of Edna St Vincent Millay. Gurko, M.   92
Reston, James
The artillery of the press   323.44
Restoration drama, 1660-1700. Nicoll, A.
In Nicoll, A. A history of English drama, 1660-1900 v 1   822.09
A **resurrection.** Cather, W.
In Cather, W. Willa Cather's Collected short fiction, 1892-1912 v3 p425-39   S C
The **Resurrection.** Yeats, W. B.
In Yeats, W. B. Collected plays of W. B. Yeats p363-73   822
Resurrection of a life. Saroyan, W.
In Foley, M. ed. Fifty best American short stories, 1915-1965 p138-47   S C
Resurrection of Father Brown. Chesterton, G. K.
In Chesterton, G. K. The Father Brown omnibus p435-53   S C
Retail trade
Mahoney, T. The great merchants **658.87**
See also Supermarkets
Retarded children. See Slow learning children
The **reticence** of Lady Anne. Saki
In Saki. The short stories of Saki p48-51   S C
Retirement
See pages in the following books:
Silberman, C. E. The myths of automation p62-75   301.24
Smith, C. The Time-Life Book of family finance p386-405   339.4
The **retreat** from Moscow. Delderfield, R. F.   944.05
Retribution. Zuroy, M.
In Hitchcock, A. ed. Alfred Hitchcock presents: A month of mystery p61-65   S C
A **retrieved** reformation. Henry, O.
In Henry, O. The best short stories of O. Henry p117-26   S C
In Henry, O. The complete works of O. Henry p438-44   S C
Return. Coates, R. M.
In The New Yorker. Stories from The New Yorker, 1950-1960 p666-77   S C
The **return.** Corkery, D.
In Garrity, D. A. ed. 44 Irish short stories p47-57   S C
The **return** of Imray. Kipling, R.
In Kipling, R. The best short stories of Rudyard Kipling p61-69   S C

The **return** of Sherlock Holmes. Doyle, Sir A. C.
In Doyle, Sir A. C. The complete Sherlock Holmes v2 p559-780   S C
The **return** of the king. Tolkien, J. R. R.
In Tolkien, J. R. R. The lord of the rings v3   Fic
The **return** of the native. Hardy, T.   Fic
The **return** of the prodigal. Wolfe, T.
In Wolfe, T. The hills beyond p108-41   S C
Return to Hiroshima. Lifton, B. J. 915.2
The **returning.** De Paola, D.
In The Best American short stories, 1965 p45-56   S C
Reunion. Lardner, R.
In Lardner, R. The best short stories of Ring Lardner p249-59   S C
Reuther, Walter Philip
Cormier, F. Reuther   92
Revelation. O'Connor, F.
In Abrahams, W. ed. Fifty years of the American short story v2 p15-33   S C
Revelations. Mansfield, K.
In Mansfield, K. The short stories of Katherine Mansfield p425-31 S C
The **revenge.** Crane, S.
In Crane, S. The complete short stories & sketches of Stephen Crane p570-83   S C
Revenge of Saint Nicholas. Paulding, J. K.
In Becker, M. L. ed. The home book of Christmas p457-65   394.26
Revere, Paul
Forbes, E. Paul Revere & the world he lived in   92
Reverence for life [essays]. Schweitzer, A.   193
Reverence for life [sermons]. Schweitzer, A.   252
Reviews. See Book reviews
Revival of letters. See Renaissance
The **revolt** of the evil fairies. Poston, T.
In Hughes, L. ed. The best short stories by Negro writers p86-90 S C
The **revolt** of the masses. Ortega y Gasset, J.   901.9
Revolution, American. See United States—History—Revolution
Revolution, French. See France—History—Revolution, 1789-1799
The **revolution** in astronomy. Hodge, P. W.   523
The **Revolutionary** War. McDowell, B. 973.3
The **revolutionist.** Artzybashev, M. P.
In Seltzer, T. comp. Best Russian short stories p284-97   S C
The **revolutionist.** Hemingway, E.
In Hemingway, E. In our time p103-06   S C
In Hemingway, E. The short stories of Ernest Hemingway p155-58   S C
Revolutions
Beals, C. The nature of revolution   323
See also pages in the following books:
Camus, A. The rebel p148-221   170
Liston, R. A. Dissent in America p29-52   301.15

Revolutions—*Continued*

The New Cambridge Modern history v8 p421-47 **909**

See also France—History—Revolution, 1789-1799; Hungary—History—Revolution, 1956; Russia—History—Revolution, 1917-1921; United States—History—Revolution

Rewald, John

The history of impressionism **759.05**

Rewards (Prizes, etc.) See Literary prizes

Rex Lardner selects the best of sports fiction. Lardner, R. ed. **S C**

Rexroth, Kenneth

The collected shorter poems **811**

(ed.) One hundred poems from the Chinese **895.1**

Reynolds, Mack

Discord makers

In Conklin, G. ed. Invaders of earth p134-45 **S C**

Reynolds, Quentin

They fought for the sky **940.4**

Rhein, Phillip H.

Albert Camus **848**

Rhesus. Euripides

In Oates, W. J. ed. The complete Greek drama v2 p351-88 **882.08**

Rhetoric

Flesch, R. How to be brief **808**

Flesch, R. How to write, speak, and think more effectively **808**

Strunk, W. The elements of style **808**

Taintor, S. A. The secretary's handbook **651.7**

See also pages in the following books:

Barzun, J. Teacher in America p47-80 **371.1**

Muir, K. ed. A new companion to Shakespeare studies p83-98 **822.3**

See also Debates and debating

Rhine, Joseph Banks

See pages in the following book:

Christopher, M. ESP, seers & psychics p19-29, 33-35 **133**

Rhine, Louisa E.

ESP in life and lab **133.8**

The Rhine. Rees, G. **914.3**

Rhine River and Valley

Description and travel

Rees, G. The Rhine **914.3**

A **rhinoceros**, some ladies and a horse. Stephens, J.

In Garrity, D. A. ed. 44 Irish short stories p439-50 **S C**

Rhyme. See English language—Rhyme

Rhymes for my rags. Service, R.

In Service, R. Later collected verse p187-400 **811**

Rhymes of a rebel. Service, R.

In Service, R. More collected verse v4 **811**

Rhymes of a Red Cross man. Service, R.

In Service, R. Collected poems of Robert Service p291-418 **811**

Rhymes of a rolling stone. Service, R.

In Service, R. Collected poems of Robert Service p167-286 **811**

Rhymes of a roughneck. Service, R.

In Service, R. More collected verse v2 **811**

Rhyming dictionary of the English language. Walker, J. **426**

Rhythm. Lardner, R.

In Lardner, R. The Ring Lardner reader p546-55 **S C**

A **ribbon** for Baldy. Stuart, J.

In Stuart, J. A Jesse Stuart reader p178-82 **818**

Ribman, Ronald

The burial of Esposito

In The Best short plays, 1971 p157-70 **808.82**

Ribonucleic acid. See RNA

Ricard, Matthieu

The mystery of animal migration **591**

Ricardo, David

Heilbroner, R. L. The worldly philosophers **330.1**

Rice, Craig

Hard sell

In Hitchcock, A. ed. Alfred Hitchcock presents: A month of mystery p226-34 **S C**

Rice, Elmer

The adding machine

In Gassner, J. ed. Best American plays; supplementary volume, 1918-1958 p95-128 **812.08**

Dream girl

In Gassner, J. ed. Best plays of the modern American theatre; 2d ser. p365-409 **812.08**

Street scene

In Gassner, J. ed. Twenty-five best plays of the modern American theatre; early ser. p567-611 **812.08**

About

See pages in the following books:

Gould, J. Modern American playwrights p8-21 **812.09**

Krutch, J. W. The American drama since 1918 p229-39 **812.09**

Rich, Jack C.

Sculpture in wood **731.4**

The **rich** boy. Fitzgerald, F. S.

In Fitzgerald, F. S. The Fitzgerald reader p239-75 **S C**

In Fitzgerald, F. S. The stories of F. Scott Fitzgerald p177-208 **S C**

Rich man, poor man. Miller, H. P. **339**

Rich men. Stuart, J.

In Stuart, J. Plowshare in heaven p61-72 **S C**

The **rich** nations and the poor nations. Ward, B. **338.91**

Richard I, King of England

See pages in the following book:

Horizon Magazine. The light of the past p122-28 **901.9**

Fiction

Scott, W. The talisman **Fic**

Rise of Russia. Wallace, R.   947

The rise of Silas Lapham. Howell, W. D.   Fic

The rise of the Union. Adams, J. T.
In Adams, J. T. The march of democracy v 1   973

The rise of urban America. Green, C. M.   301.3

The rising of the moon. Gregory, Lady
In Cerf, B. ed. Thirty famous one-act plays p91-98   808.82
In Dickinson, T. H. ed. Chief contemporary dramatists [1st ser] p227-35   808.82

Ritch, Ocee
Chilton's Harley-Davidson repair and tune-up guide   629.28
Chilton's Motorcycle troubleshooting guide   629.28

Ritchie, Anna Cora Mowatt
Fashion
In Quinn, A. H. ed. Representative American plays p277-312   812.08

Ritchie, Barbara
Douglass, F. The mind and heart of Frederick Douglass   326

Ritchie, Jack
Dropout
In Best detective stories of the year [1969] p125-34   S C
Speaking of murder
In Best detective stories of the year [1967] p81-97   S C
A taste for murder
In Hitchcock, A. ed. Alfred Hitchcock presents: A month of mystery p118-22   S C

Rites and ceremonies
See pages in the following book:
Simpson, J. Everyday life in the Viking age p176-200   914.8
See also Marriage customs and rites

Ritual. See Rites and ceremonies

The ritual of Ptah-Mes. Pei, M.
In Pei, M. Tales of the natural and supernatural p111-19   S C

The rivals. Sheridan, R. B.   822

The River Nile. Brander, B.   916.2

River Plate region. See Rio de la Plata region

The River Plate republics. Ferguson, J. H.   918

Rivers, Conrad Kent
Mother to son
In Hughes, L. ed. The best short stories by Negro writers p356-58   S C

Rivers
Pollution
See Water—Pollution

Roach, Max
See pages in the following book:
Gitler, I. Jazz masters of the forties p183-200   920

Road construction. See Roads

Road from Colonus. Forster, E. M.
In Havighurst, W. ed. Masters of the modern short story p86-98   S C

The road not taken. Frost, R.   811

The road to reunion, 1865-1900. Buck, P. H.   973.8

The road to Rome. Sherwood, R. E.
In Gassner, J. ed. Twenty-five best plays of the modern American theatre; early ser. p295-332   812.08

A road to the big city. Lessing, D.
In Lessing, D. African stories p571-77   S C

Roads
Overman, M. Roads, bridges, and tunnels   624
Von Hagen, V. W. Roman roads   625.7
See also pages in the following books:
Langdon, W. C. Everyday things in American life, 1776-1876 p19-37, 66-89   917.3
Owen, W. Wheels p100-07   380.5
United States. Department of Agriculture. A place to live p474-88   301.3

Roads, bridges, and tunnels. Overman, M.   624

The roads must roll. Heinlein, R. A.
In Heinlein, R. A. Robert A. Heinlein's The past through tomorrow p30-59   S C

Roads of destiny. Henry, O.
In Henry, O. The best short stories of O. Henry p71-96   S C
In Henry, O. The complete works of O. Henry p355-550   S C

Roads of destiny [short story]. Henry, O.
In Henry, O. The complete works of O. Henry p355-72   S C

The roads round Pisax. Dinesen, I.
In Dinesen, I. Seven Gothic tales p165-216   S C

The roads we take. Henry O.
In Henry, O. The complete works of O. Henry p1174-77   S C

Roadside. Riggs, L.
In Tucker, S. M. ed. Twenty-five modern plays p801-38   808.82

The robber barons. Josephson, M.   920

Robbers and outlaws
See pages in the following books:
Jones, E. The Plains States p69-81   917.8
Wood, J. P. Scotland Yard p109-36   352
Fiction
Kemal, Y. Memed, my hawk   Fic

Robbie. Asimov, I.
In Asimov, I. I, robot p19-39   S C

The robe. Douglas, L. C.   Fic

The robe of peace. Henry, O.
In Henry, O. The complete works of O. Henry p1521-24   S C

Robert I, King of Scotland
See pages in the following book:
Sutcliff, R. Heroes and history p97-114   920

Robert the Bruce. See Robert I, King of Scotland

Robert, Henry M.
Robert's Rules of order   328.1

Robert, Sarah Corbin
Robert, H. M. Robert's Rules of order   328.1

Robinson Crusoe Liebowitz. Michaels, L.
In Prize stories, 1971: The O. Henry
Awards p321-29   **S C**

Robots
Asimov, I. I, robot   **S C**
The **rock** book. Fenton, C. L.   552

Rock, church. Hughes, L.
In Margolies, E. A native sons reader
p244-54   810.8

Rock climbing. See Mountaineering

Rock from the beginning. Cohn, N.   781.5

The **rock** revolution. Shaw, A.   781.5

Rockefeller, John Davison, 1839-1937
See pages in the following books:
Chamberlain, J. The enterprising Americans: a business history of the United
States p146-56   330.973
Holbrook, S. H. The age of the moguls
p65-74, 131-44   920

The **rocket.** Bradbury, R.
In Bradbury, R. The illustrated man
p241-51   **S C**
In Bradbury, R. R is for rocket p46-57
     S C

Rocket flight. See Space flight

The **Rocket** Man. Bradbury, R.
In Bradbury, R. The illustrated man
p93-105   **S C**
In Bradbury, R. R is for rocket p58-70
     S C

Rocket to the moon. Odets, C.
In Odets, C. Six plays p323-418   812

Rocketry
Ley, W. Rockets, missiles, and men in
space   629.4
Von Braun, W. Space frontier   629.4
See also Rockets (Aeronautics); Space
vehicles

History
Von Braun, W. History of rocketry &
space travel   629.409
See also pages in the following book:
Shelton, W. R. Man's conquest of space
p40-53   629.4

Rockets (Aeronautics)
See pages in the following book:
Stokley, J. The new world of the atom
p210-22   621.48

Rockets, missiles, and men in space. Ley,
W.   629.4

Rockets, missiles, and space. See Ley, W.
Rockets, missiles, and men in space
     629.4

The **rockpile.** Baldwin, J.
In Baldwin, J. Going to meet the man
p13-25   **S C**

Rocks
Fenton, C. L. The rock book   552
Loomis, F. B. Field book of common
rocks and minerals   549
Pough, F. H. A field guide to rocks and
minerals   549
See also Crystallography; Geology;
Mineralogy

Rockwell, F. F.
The Rockwells' New complete book of
flower arrangement   745.92

Rocky Mountain National Park
See pages in the following book:
National Geographic Society. America's
wonderlands p139-46   917.3

Rocky Mountain region
Hollon, W. E. The Great American Desert   917.8
Sprague, M. The Mountain States   917.8

Rocky Mountains
See pages in the following book:
Snyder, G. S. In the footsteps of Lewis
and Clark p134-57   973.4

Rococo art. See Art, Rococo

Rodents
See pages in the following book:
Henley, D. ASPCA guide to pet care
p50-58   636

Rodeos
Fiction
Borland, H. When the legends die   **Fic**

Rodgers, Harold A.
Funk & Wagnalls Dictionary of data
processing terms   651.803

Rodgers, Richard
The Rodgers and Hammerstein Song book
     782.8
Hammerstein, O. 6 plays   812
Lindsay, H. The sound of music   812
About
Ewen, D. With a song in his heart; the
story of Richard Rodgers   92
See also pages in the following books:
Ewen, D. Composers for the American
theatre p145-84   920
Ewen, D. Great men of American popular song p188-207, 272-98   920
Ewen, D. The story of America's musical theater p176-97   782.8

The **Rodgers** and Hammerstein Song book.
Rodgers, R.   782.8

Rodin, Auguste
Hale, W. H. The world of Rodin, 1840-
1917   92
See also pages in the following book:
Untermeyer, L. Makers of the modern
world p170-76   920

Roentgen rays. See X rays

Roethke, Theodore
The collected poems of Theodore Roethke
     811
About
See pages in the following book:
Rosenthal, M. L. The new poets p112-18
     821.09

Rogers, Carl R.
Carl Rogers on encounter groups   616.89

Rogers, Robert
Fiction
Roberts, K. Northwest Passage   **Fic**

Rogers, W. G.
Carl Sandburg, yes   92
Mightier than the sword   741.5

Rogers, Will
The autobiography of Will Rogers   92

Roget, Peter Mark
Everyman's Thesaurus of English words
and phrases 424
The New American Roget's College the-
saurus in dictionary form. See The New
American Roget's College thesaurus in
dictionary form 424
The New Roget's Thesaurus of the En-
glish language in dictionary form. See
The New Roget's Thesaurus of the En-
glish language in dictionary form 424
The Original Roget's Thesaurus of En-
glish words and phrases. See The
Original Roget's Thesaurus of English
words and phrases 424
Roget's International thesaurus. See Ro-
get's International thesaurus 424
Roget's College thesaurus in dictionary form,
The New American 424
Roget's International thesaurus 424
Roget's Thesaurus of English words and
phrases, The Original 424
Roget's Thesaurus of the English language
in dictionary form, The New 424
Rogin, Gilbert
12 days before the mast
In Sports Illustrated. The wonderful
world of sport p240-41 796
Rogues and vagabonds
See pages in the following book:
Shakespeare's England v2 p484-510 822.3
Rohe, Mies van der, Ludwig. See Mies van
der Rohe, Ludwig
Rohmer, Sax
The white hat
In Hitchcock, A. ed. Alfred Hitchcock
presents: A month of mystery
p205-25 S C
Roland, Albert
Profiles from the new Asia 920
Rolfe, John
See pages in the following book:
Woodward, G. S. Pocahontas p160-67 92
Roll, Winifred
The pomegranate and the rose; the story
of Katharine of Aragon 92
Rollett, A. P.
(jt. auth.) Cundy, H. M. Mathematical
models 510.78
Rollier, Auguste
See pages in the following book:
De Kruif, P. Men against death p300-16
920
Rolling stones. Henry, O.
In Henry, O. The complete works of
O. Henry p941-1060 S C
Rollins, Charlemae H.
Black troubadour: Langston Hughes 92
Rollins, Sonny. See Rollins, Theodore Walter
Rollins, Theodore Walter
See pages in the following books:
Goldberg, J. Jazz masters of the fifties
p87-112 920
Williams, M. The jazz tradition p167-77
781.5
Rolvaag, O. E.
Giants in the earth Fic

The Roman. Waltari, M. Fic
Roman antiquities. See Classical antiquities
Roman architecture. See Architecture, Ro-
man
Roman art. See Art, Roman
Roman Bartholow. Robinson, E. A.
In Robinson, E. A. The collected poems
of Edwin Arlington Robinson
p733-856 811
Roman Catholic Church. See Catholic
Church
Roman emperors
Asimov, I. The Roman Empire 937
See also names of Roman emperors,
e.g. Augustus, Emperor of Rome
The Roman Empire. Asimov, I. 937
Roman fever. Wharton, E.
In Wharton, E. The collected short
stories of Edith Wharton v2 p833-
43 S C
Roman historians. See Historians, Roman
Roman literature. See Latin literature
Roman mythology. See Mythology, Classi-
cal
Roman philosophy. See Philosophy, Ancient
The Roman Republic. Asimov, I. 937
Roman roads. Von Hagen, V. W. 625.7
Roman sculpture. See Sculpture, Roman
The Roman way. Hamilton, E. 870.9
Romance languages. See French language
The romance of a busy broker. Henry, O.
In Henry, O. The best short stories
of O. Henry p59-63 S C
In Henry, O. The complete works of
O. Henry p86-88 S C
In Henry, O. The four million p208-
14 S C
The romancers. Saki
In Saki. The short stories of Saki p311-
14 S C
Romances
See pages in the following book:
Highet, G. The classical tradition p162-
77 809
Romanesque art. See Art, Romanesque
Romania. See Rumania
Romania. Berciu, D. 913.39
Romano, Giulio. See Giulio Romano
The Romans. Duggan, A. 937
The Romans and their world. Arnott, P. D.
913.37
Romanticism
See pages in the following books:
Gardner, H. Gardner's Art through the
ages p626-63 709
Janson, H. W. History of art p453-88
709
Stamm, J. R. A short history of Spanish
literature p129-46 860.9
Rombauer, Irma S.
Joy of cooking 641.5

The **rubaiyat** of a Scotch highball. Henry, O.
In Henry, O. The complete works of
O. Henry p1379-83 **S C**

Rubber
See pages in the following book:
Thompson, H. The age of invention p157-74 **608**

Rubber, Artificial
See pages in the following book:
Mark, H. F. Giant molecules p122-31 **668.4**

The **rubber** plant's story. Henry, O.
In Henry, O. The complete works of
O. Henry p1643-46 **S C**

Rubens, Sir Peter Paul
Wedgewood, C. V. The world of Rubens, 1577-1640 **92**

Rubin, David
Longing for America
In The Best American short stories, 1967 p257-77 **S C**

Rubin, Jerry
See pages in the following book:
Lukas, J. A. Don't shoot—we are your children! p343-92 **301.43**

Rubinstein, Anton Gregorovich
See pages in the following book:
Chapin, V. Giants of the keyboard p124-37 **920**

Rublowsky, John
After the Crash **330.973**

Ruchlis, Hy
Discovering scientific method **501**

Rudaux, Lucien
Larousse Encyclopedia of astronomy **520.3**

Ruddigore. Gilbert, Sir W. S.
In Gilbert, Sir W. S. The complete plays of Gilbert and Sullivan p403-57 **782.8**
In Gilbert, Sir W. S. Martyn Green's Treasury of Gilbert & Sullivan **782.8**

Rudofsky, Bernard
Streets for people **711**

Rudolph, Mae
(jt. auth.) Mueller, C. G. Light and vision **535**

Rudwick, Elliott
(jt. ed.) Bracey, J. H. ed. Black nationalism in America **301.451**
(jt. auth.) Meier, A. From plantation to ghetto **301.451**

Rue, Leonard Lee
Pictorial guide to the birds of North America **598**

The **ruffian** on the stair. Orton, J.
In The Best short plays, 1970 p183-214 **808.82**

Rufsvold, Margaret I.
Guides to newer educational media **016.3713**

Rugel, Miriam
Paper poppy
In The Best American short stories, 1969 p253-67 **S C**

Rugoff, Milton
(ed.) Harvest of world folk tales **398.2**

Ruhen, Olaf
(jt. auth.) Shadbolt, M. Isles of the South Pacific **919**

Ruins. See Archeology; Excavations (Archeology)

Ruiz, Juan, Arcipreste de Hita
See pages in the following book:
Stamm, J. R. A short history of Spanish literature p141-48 **860.9**

Ruland, Richard
(ed.) Twentieth century interpretations of Walden **818**

A **ruler** of men. Henry, O.
In Henry, O. The complete works of
O. Henry p944-57 **S C**

Rulers. See Kings and rulers; Queens

Rules for descriptive cataloging in the Library of Congress. See Anglo-American cataloging rules **025.3**

Rules of order. See Parliamentary practice

Rules of order, Robert's. Robert, H. M. **328.1**

Rulfo, Juan
They gave us the land
In Cohen, J. M. ed. Latin American writing today p174-78 **860.8**

The **ruling** chiefs of Hawaii; excerpt. Kamakau, S. M.
In Day, A. G. ed. The spell of Hawaii p43-53 **919.69**

Rum
See pages in the following book:
Wolfe, L. The cooking of the Caribbean Islands p177-95 **641.5**

Rumania
See also Balkan Peninsula
Antiquities
Berciu, D. Romania **913.39**
Description and travel
See pages in the following book:
McDowell, B. Gypsies: wanderers of the world p102-17 **397**

Rummy (Game)
See pages in the following book:
Gibson, W. B. Hoyle's Simplified guide to the popular card games p26-41 **795.4**

Run silent, run deep. Beach, E. L. **Fic**

Run softly, go fast. Wersba, B. **Fic**

Runaround. Asimov, I.
In Asimov, I. I, robot p40-58 **S C**

The **runaway.** Chekhov, A.
In Chekhov, A. The stories of Anton Chekhov p306-13 **S C**

The **runaway** generation. Wein, B. **301.43**

Runcorn, Stanley Keith
See pages in the following book:
Moore, R. The earth we live on p322-28 **551.09**

Runners in the park. McKimmey, J.
In Best detective stories of the year [1969] p196-211 **S C**

Running. See Track athletics

Running a thousand miles for freedom. Craft, W.
In Bontemps, A. ed. Great slave narratives p269-331 **920**

Runyon, Charles W.
Dream patrol
In The Best from Fantasy and Science Fiction; 19th ser. p103-16 **S C**

Runyon, Damon
  Johnny One-Eye
    In Costain, T. B. ed. Read with me p471-
    84   **S C**
  A treasury of Damon Runyon   **817**
Ruoro, Peter
  End of month
    In Angoff, C. ed. African writing today
    p163-69   **896**
Rupp, Adolph Fred
    See pages in the following book:
  Padwe, S. Basketball's Hall of Fame
  p123-32   **920**
Rural electrification. See Electricity in agri-
  culture
Rural life. See Farm life; Outdoor life;
  Peasantry
Rural rehabilitation. See Rehabilitation, Rural
Rural schools
    See pages in the following book:
  United States. Department of Agriculture.
  A place to live p36-44   **301.3**
Rural sociology. See Sociology, Rural
Rus in Urbe. Henry, O.
    In Henry, O. The complete works of
    O. Henry p794-801   **S C**
Rush, Norman
  In late youth
    In The Best American short stories,
    1971 p275-90   **S C**
Rushmore, Robert
  Fanny Kemble   **92**
Ruskin, Ariane
  Greek & Roman art   **709.38**
  Nineteenth century art   **709.03**
  17th & 18th century art   **709.03**
Russell, Bertrand
  A history of Western philosophy   **109**
    About
    See pages in the following books:
  Durant, W. The story of philosophy p357-
  64   **109**
  Newman, J. R. ed. The world of mathe-
  matics v 1 p381-94   **510.8**
  Untermeyer, L. Makers of the modern
  world p450-57   **920**
Russell, Bill. See Russell, William Felton
Russell, Charlie
  Quietus
    In Hughes, L. ed. The best short stories
    by Negro writers p347-55   **S C**
Russell, Eric Frank
  Impulse
    In Conklin, G. ed. Invaders of earth
    p37-47   **S C**
Russell, Francis
  The shadow of Blooming Grove; Warren
  G. Harding in his times   **92**
  The world of Dürer, 1471-1528   **92**
  American Heritage. The American Heri-
  tage History of the confident years **973.8**
  American Heritage. The American Heri-
  tage History of the making of the
  Nation   **973**
Russell, Henry
    See pages in the following book:
  Ewen, D. Great men of American popular
  song p8-13   **920**

Russell, John
  Fourth man
    In Day, A. G. ed. The greatest American
    short stories p215-36   **S C**
  The world of Matisse, 1869-1954   **92**
Russell, Max M.
  (ed.) The blue book of occupational edu-
  cation   **371.42**
  (ed.) The College blue book. See The Col-
  lege blue book   **378.73**
Russell, William Felton
    See pages in the following book:
  Pepe, P. Greatest stars of the NBA p33-
  50   **920**
Russell Cave
    See pages in the following book:
  National Geographic Society. America's
  wonderlands p495-503   **917.3**
Russia
  Koutaissoff, E. The Soviet Union   **914.7**
  Salisbury, H. E. ed. The Soviet Union: the
  fifty years   **914.7**
  Thayer, C. W. Russia   **914.7**
  Vladimirov, L. The Russians   **914.7**
    See also pages in the following book:
  Rama Rau, S. Gifts of passage p189-99 **92**
    Agriculture
    See Agriculture—Russia
    Astronautics
    See Astronautics—Russia
    Church history
    See pages in the following book:
  Horizon Magazine. The Horizon History
  of Russia p101-15   **947**
    Civilization
  Rieber, A. J. A study of the USSR and
  communism: an historical approach
                                             914.7
  Wallace, R. Rise of Russia   **947**
    See also pages in the following book:
  The New Cambridge Modern history v7
  p318-38   **909**
    Communism
    See Communism—Russia
    Description and travel
  Jacob, A. A Russian journey   **914.7**
  Koningsberger, H. Along the roads of the
  new Russia   **914.7**
  Rama Rau, S. My Russian journey **914.7**
  Van Der Post, L. A portrait of all the
  Russians   **914.7**
    Education
    See Education—Russia
    Fiction
  Anatoli, A. Babi Yar   **Fic**
  Chekhov, A. The image of Chekhov **S C**
  Chekhov, A. The stories of Anton Chek-
  hov   **S C**
  Dostoevsky, F. The adolescent   **Fic**
  Dostoevsky, F. The brothers Karamazov
                                               Fic
  Dostoevsky, F. Crime and punishment **Fic**
  Dostoevsky, F. The idiot   **Fic**
  Dostoevsky, F. The possessed   **Fic**
  Gogol, N. Dead souls   **Fic**
  Koestler, A. Darkness at noon   **Fic**
  Seltzer, T. comp. Best Russian short
  stories   **S C**

S

The **sacred** skull. Buck, P. S.
In Buck, P. S. The good deed, and stories of Asia, past and present p125-50 **S C**

A **sacrifice**. Singer, I. B.
In The Best American short stories, 1965 p283-89 **S C**

Sacrifice. Tagore, R.
In Tagore, R. Collected poems and plays of Rabindranath Tagore p501-32 **891.4**

Sacrifice; play. Tagore, R.
In Tagore, R. Tagore reader p125-48 **891.4**

A **sacrifice** hit. Henry, O.
In Henry, O. The complete works of O. Henry p1170-73 **S C**

The **sad** story of a dramatic critic. Wells, H. G.
In Wells, H. G. The complete short stories of H. G. Wells p520-28 **S C**

A **sad** tale's best for winter. Spark, M.
In Spark, M. Collected stories: I p171-77 **S C**

Sade, Donatien Alphonse François, comte, called marquis de
See pages in the following book:
Camus, A. The rebel p32-49 **170**

Sade, Marquis de. See Sade, Donatien Alphonse François, comte, called marquis de

Sadowa, Battle of, 1866. See Königgrätz, Battle of, 1866

Saens, Camille Saint- See Saint-Saens, Camille

Safety education
See pages in the following book:
United States. Department of Agriculture. Consumers all p182-213 **640.73**

Safire, William
The new language of politics: an anecdotal dictionary of catchwords, slogans, and political usage **320.03**

Sagarin, Edward
(jt. auth.) Aymar, B. A pictorial history of the world's great trials **343**

Saggs, H. W. F.
Everyday life in Babylonia & Assyria **913.35**

Sahara
Krüger, C. ed. Sahara **916.6**

A **Sahib's** war. Kipling, R.
In Kipling, R. The best short stories of Rudyard Kipling p409-22 **S C**

Sailing
Chichester, Sir F. Gipsy Moth circles the world **910.4**
Mowat, F. The boat who wouldn't float **910.4**
See also pages in the following book:
National Geographic Society. Vacationland U.S.A. p26-41 **917.3**
See also Boats and boating

Sailors' life. See Seafaring life

The **Saint** and the Goblin. Saki
In Saki. The short stories of Saki p75-78 **S C**

St Anthony. Maupassant, G. de
In Maupassant, G. de. Guy de Maupassant's Short stories p197-204 **S C**

Saint Bakeover. Cross, E.
In Garrity, D. A. ed. 44 Irish short stories p58-69 **S C**

St Clair, Robert
Child of void
In Conklin, G. ed. Invaders of earth p86-99 **S C**

St Denis, Ruth
See pages in the following book:
Maynard, O. American modern dancers: the pioneers p72-85 **920**

Saint Exupéry, Antoine de
Airman's odyssey **629.13**
Flight to Arras
In Saint Exupéry, A. de. Airman's odyssey p281-437 **629.13**
Night flight
In Saint Exupéry, A. de. Airman's odyssey p207-80 **629.13**
Wind, sand, and stars **629.13**
also in Saint Exupéry, A. de. Airman's odyssey p 1-206 **629.13**

Saint-Gaudens, Augustus
See pages in the following book:
Beard, A. E. S. Our foreign-born citizens p45-51 **920**

St Germain, Treaty of, Sept. 10, 1919 (Austria)
See pages in the following book:
Stadler, K. R. Austria p82-105 **943.6**

Saint Joan. Shaw, B.
In Bentley, E. comp. The great playwrights v2 p1747-1837 **808.82**
In Shaw, B. Bernard Shaw's plays p151-227 **822**
In Shaw, B. Complete plays, with prefaces v2 p319-429 **822**
In Shaw, B. Seven plays p745-911 **822**

Saint Joan, Major Barbara, Androcles and the lion. Shaw, B. **822**

St John, David
All's well
In Dulles, A. ed. Great spy stories from fiction p399-410 **S C**

St John, Robert
Ben-Gurion **92**
Israel **915.694**

Saint John of the Hershey Kisses: 1964. Cole, T.
In Prize stories, 1970: The O. Henry awards p149-83 **S C**

Saint-Just, Louis Antoine Léon de
See pages in the following book:
Camus, A. The rebel p89-101 **170**

Saint-Lazare (Cathedral) See Autun, France. Saint-Lazare (Cathedral)

St Louis

Description
See pages in the following book:
Jones, E. The Plains States p141-51 **917.8**

Politics and government
See pages in the following books:
Steffens, L. The shame of the cities p19-41, 69-100 **352**
Weinberg, A. ed. The muckrakers p122-36 **309.173**

St Louis Cardinals (Baseball Club)
Musial, S. Stan Musial: "The Man's" own story **92**

Salisbury, Harrison E.—*Continued*
Orbit of China 915.1
Russia 947
(ed.) The Soviet Union: the fifty years 914.7
War between Russia and China 327.47
Sallust, Gaius Sallustius
See pages in the following book:
Grant, M. The ancient historians p195-213 920
Sally. Asimov, I.
In Asimov, I. Nightfall, and other stories p206-23 S C
Salomé. Wilde, O.
In Cerf, B. ed. Thirty famous one-act plays p63-85 808.82
In Wilde, O. The plays of Oscar Wilde v 1 p 1-41 822
Salomy Jane's kiss. Harte, B.
In Harte, B. The best short stories of Bret Harte p235-58 S C
Salt of the earth. Schaefer, J.
In Schaefer, J. The collected stories of Jack Schaefer p400-11 S C
Salt-water poems and ballads. Masefield, J. 821
Salter, James
Am Strande von Tanger
In Prize stories, 1970: The O. Henry Awards p113-25 S C
Saltykov, M. Y.
How a muzhik fed two officials
In Seltzer, T. comp. Best Russian short stories p118-29 S C
Salvage
Burgess, R. F. Sinkings, salvages, and shipwrecks 910.4
Mowat, F. The grey seas under 387.5
See also Skin and scuba diving
Salvation Nell. Sheldon, E.
In Gassner, J. ed. Best plays of the early American theatre p557-616 812.08
Salviati, Francesco
See pages in the following book:
Vasari, G. The lives of the painters, sculptors and architects v4 p53-72 920
The Salzburg connection. MacInnes, H. Fic
Sam Clemens of Hannibal. Wecter, D. 92
Samachson, Dorothy
The dramatic story of the theatre 792.09
Samachson, Joseph
(jt. auth.) Samachson, D. The dramatic story of the theatre 792.09
Sambrot, William
That touch of genius
In Hitchcock, A. ed. Alfred Hitchcock presents: A month of mystery p93-102 S C
Sammicheli, Michele. See Sanmicheli, Michele
Samoan Islands
See pages in the following book:
Shadbolt, M. Isles of the South Pacific p50-66 919
Sampler of American songs. Krythe, M. R. 784.09

Sampling (Statistics)
See pages in the following book:
Newman, J. R. ed. The world of mathematics v3 p1459-86 510.8
Sampson, Deborah. See Gannett, Deborah (Sampson)
Sampson, George
The concise Cambridge History of English literature 820.9
Samson Agonistes. Milton, J.
In Milton, J. The portable Milton p610-64 828
Samuel. London, J.
In London, J. Best short stories of Jack London p105-22 S C
In London, J. Jack London's Tales of adventure S C
Samuels, Gertrude
The corrupters
In The Best short plays, 1969 p405-42 808.82
Samurai
See pages in the following book:
Leonard, J. N. Early Japan p55-64 915.2
San Francisco
Description
See pages in the following books:
Moyers, B. Listening to America p195-217 917.3
National Geographic Society. Vacationland U.S.A. p300-09 917.3
Earthquake and fire, 1906
Thomas, G. The San Francisco earthquake 979.4
See also pages in the following book:
Lord, W. The good years p120-49 973.91
Fiction
Bristow, G. Calico Palace Fic
The San Francisco earthquake. Thomas, G. 979.4
San Gallo, Antonio de. See Sangallo, Antonio de
San Gallo, Bastiano da, known as Aristotile
See pages in the following book:
Vasari, G. The lives of the painters, sculptors and architects v3 p293-304 920
San Jacinto, Battle of, 1836
See pages in the following book:
Armstrong, O. K. The fifteen decisive battles of the United States p147-68 973
San Juan, P. R.
Social conditions
Lewis, O. La vida 301.453
San Luis Rey, Bridge of. See Bridge of San Luis Rey
San Martín, José de
See pages in the following books:
Crow, J. A. The epic of Latin America p460-85 980
Peck, A. M. The pageant of South American history p251-73 980
San Michele, Michele. See Sanmicheli, Michele
Sand Creek, Battle of, 1864
See pages in the following book:
Brown, D. Bury my heart at Wounded Knee p68-102 970.4

Santiago (Island)
Lindbergh, A. M. Listen! The wind
629.13

Santiago de Compostela. Catedral
See pages in the following book:
Horizon Magazine. The Horizon Book of great cathedrals p250-63   726

Sanyasi. Tagore, R.
In Tagore, R. Collected poems and plays of Rabindranath Tagore p461-79   891.4

Sapphira and the slave girl. Cather, W.
Fic

Sarah. Hamer, M.
In The Best American short stories, 1965 p113-23   S C
In Clarke, J. H. ed. American Negro short stories p311-21   S C

Sarasate, Pablo de
See pages in the following book:
Chapin, V. The violin and its masters p163-70   920

Saratoga Campaign, 1777
Furneaux, R. The Battle of Saratoga
973.3

See also pages in the following books:
Armstrong, O. K. The fifteen decisive battles of the United States p56-59   973
Creasy, Sir E. S. Fifteen decisive battles of the world p351-74   904
Mitchell, J. B. Twenty decisive battles of the world p197-210   904

Sargent, S. Stansfeld
Basic teachings of the great psychologists
150

Saroyan, William
Boys and girls together
In The Saturday Evening Post. Best modern short stories p138-56   S C
The cave dwellers
In Gassner, J. ed. Best American plays; 5th ser. p459-82   812.08
The daring young man on the flying trapeze
In Abrahams, W. ed. Fifty years of the American short story v2 p245-50   S C
Days of life and death and escape to the moon   818
Dentist and patient
In The Best short plays, 1968 p67-72
808.82
The fifty yard dash
In Lardner, R. ed. Rex Lardner selects the best of sports fiction p97-106   S C
Hello out there
In Cerf, B. ed. Thirty famous one-act plays p549-61   808.82
The human comedy   Fic
Husband and wife
In The Best short plays, 1968 p73-78
808.82
The new play
In The Best short plays, 1970 p151-80
808.82
Resurrection of a life
In Foley, M. ed. Fifty best American short stories, 1915-1965 p138-47
S C

The time of your life
In Block, H. M. ed. Masters of modern drama p671-98   808.82
In Cerf, B. A. ed. Sixteen famous American plays p921-78   812.08
In Gassner, J. ed. Best plays of modern American theatre; 2d ser. p39-83   812.08
About
Floan, H. R. William Saroyan   818

Sarto, Andrea del
See pages in the following book:
Vasari, G. The lives of the painters, sculptors and architects v2 p303-25   920

Sarton, George
A history of science   509

Sartre, Jean Paul
No exit
In Block, H. M. ed. Masters of modern drama p802-16   808.82
In Gassner, J. ed. Twenty best European plays on the American stage p278-99   808.82
The words   92
About
Scott, M. A. The unquiet vision   142
See also pages in the following books:
Durant, W. Interpretations of life p163-206   809
Untermeyer, L. Makers of the modern world p741-46   920

Sassanians. See Sassanids

Sassanids
See pages in the following book:
Asimov, I. The Near East p178-213   939

Sasse, H. C.
(comp.) Cassell's New compact German-English, English-German dictionary. See Cassell's New compact German-English, English-German dictionary   433

Satellites, Artificial. See Artificial satellites

Satire
Lewis, C. S. The Screwtape letters [and] Screwtape proposes a toast   248
See also pages in the following book:
Drew, E. Poetry: a modern guide to its understanding and enjoyment p148-69
808.1
History and criticism
Highet, G. The anatomy of satire   809.7
See also pages in the following book:
Highet, G. The classical tradition p303-21   809

The Saturday Evening Post
Best modern short stories   S C

Saturday night. Adams, J.
In Seventeen. Stories from Seventeen p181-98   S C

Saturday's children. Anderson, M.
In Gassner, J. ed. Twenty-five best plays of the modern American theatre; early ser. p371-400   812.08

Saturn (Planet)
See pages in the following book:
Asimov, I. The solar system and back p63-76   508

Schaefer, Jack
The collected stories of Jack Schaefer
S C
Contents: Major Burl; Miley Bennett; Emmet Dutrow; Sergeant Houck; Jeremy Rodock; Cooter James; Kittura Remsberg; General Pingley; Elvie Burdette; Josiah Willett; Something lost; Leander Frailey; Jacob; My town; Old Anse; That Mark horse; Ghost town; Takes a real man; Out of the past; Hugo Kertchak, builder; Prudence by name; Harvey Kendall; Cat nipped; Stalemate; Nate Bartlett's store; Salt of the earth; One man's honor; The old man; The coup of Long Lance; Enos Carr; The fifth man; Stubby Pringle's Christmas

Shane   **Fic**

Schafer, Edward H.
Ancient China   913.31
Schaller, George B.
The year of the gorilla   599
Scharff, Robert
(ed.) Golf Magazine's Encyclopedia of golf. See Golf Magazine's Encyclopedia of golf   796.352
(ed.) Ski Magazine. Ski Magazine's Encyclopedia of skiing   796.9
The **Schartz-Metterklume** method. Saki
In Saki. The short stories of Saki p315-20   **S C**
Schary, Dore
Sunrise at Campobello   812
—Same
In Cerf, B. ed. Six American plays for today p211-98   812.08
Schaudinn, Fritz
See pages in the following book:
De Kruif, P. Men against death p207-28
                                                   920
Schauffler, Robert Haven
(ed.) Christmas   394.26
The mother
In Schauffler, R. H. ed. Christmas p325-32   394.26
Schayes, Adolph
See pages in the following book:
Pepe, P. Greatest stars of the NBA p107-21   920
Schayes, Dolph. See Schayes, Adolph
Schechter, Betty
The Dreyfus affair   944.081
Schecter, Leonard
(ed.) Bouton, J. Ball four   92
Scheffer, Victor B.
The year of the whale   599
Scheinfeld, Amram
Your heredity and environment   575.1
Schell, Jonathan
The village of Ben Suc   915.97
Schickel, Richard
The Disney version   92
The world of Goya, 1746-1828   92
Horne, L. Lena   92
Schiller, Johann Christoph Friedrich von
See pages in the following book:
Durant, W. Rousseau and revolution p569-75, 591-605   940.2
Schirra, Walter Marty
See pages in the following book:
We seven p58-64, 80-93, 109-17   629.45
Schisgal, Murray
Luv
In Cerf, B. ed. Plays of our time p721-82   812.08

Schleiden, Matthias Jacob
See pages in the following book:
Moore, R. The coil of life p71-103   574.09
Schlesinger, Arthur M. 1888-1965
The birth of the Nation   917.3
Schlesinger, Arthur M. 1917-
The age of Jackson   973.5
The bitter heritage   327.73
The coming of the New Deal   973.917
Congress and the Presidency: their role in modern times   353.03
The crisis of the old order, 1919-1933
                                               973.91
The politics of upheaval   973.917
A thousand days   973.922
Schlieker, Willi Hermann
See pages in the following book:
White, T. H. Fire in the ashes p167-88
                                               940.55
Schliemann, Heinrich
Baumann, H. Lion gate and labyrinth
                                               913.38
See also pages in the following book:
White, A. T. Lost worlds p23-56   913.03
Schmitt, Gladys
Rembrandt   **Fic**
The uninvited
In Seventeen. Stories from Seventeen p130-50   **S C**
Schmitt, Marshall L.
(jt. auth.) Buban, P. Understanding electricity and electronics   621.3
Schnabel, Artur
See pages in the following book:
Chapin, V. Giants of the keyboard p165-80   920
Schnabel, Ernst
Anne Frank: a portrait in courage   92
Schneider, Herbert W.
A history of American philosophy   191
Schneider, Pierre
The world of Manet, 1832-1883   92
The world of Watteau, 1684-1721   92
Schneider, Ronald M.
An atlas of Latin American affairs   918
Schnitzler, Arthur
Anatol
In Cerf, B. A. comp. Sixteen famous European plays p669-730   808.82
Green cockatoo
In Cerf, B. ed. Thirty famous one-act plays p135-63   808.82
Light-o'-love
In Tucker, S. M. ed. Twenty-five modern plays p97-123   808.82
La ronde
In Block, H. M. ed. Masters of modern drama p247-69   808.82
Schoder, Raymond V.
Masterpieces of Greek art   709.38
Schoenbaum, S.
(jt. ed.) Muir, K. ed. A new companion to Shakespeare studies   822.3
Schoenberg, Arnold. See Schönberg, Arnold
Schoenbrun, David
The three lives of Charles de Gaulle   92
Schoendienst, Albert Fred
See pages in the following book:
Mantle, M. The quality of courage p64-70   920

Schoendienst, Red. See Schoendienst, Albert Fred

Scholander, Per Fredrik
See pages in the following book:
Behrman, D. The new world of the oceans p24-34   551.4

Scholarship. See Learning and scholarship

Scholarships, fellowships, etc.
Angel, J. L. How and where to get scholarships & loans   378.3
Garraty, J. The new guide to study abroad   378.3
Lovejoy, C. E. Lovejoy's Scholarship guide   378.3
Proia, N. C. Barron's Handbook of American college financial aid   378.3
Proia, N. C. Barron's Handbook of junior and community college financial aid   378.3
Study abroad   378.3
See also pages in the following book:
Arnold, A. Career choices for the '70s p81-90   331.7

Scholastic Magazines
What you should know about democracy —and why   321.8

Scholes, Percy A.
The concise Oxford Dictionary of music   780.3
The Oxford Companion to music   780.3

Scholl, Ralph
The golden axe
In The Best short plays of 1957-1958 p199-223   808.82

Schönberg, Arnold
See pages in the following books:
Cross, M. The Milton Cross New encyclopedia of the great composers and their music p829-50   920.03
Ewen, D. Composers of tomorrow's music p24-65   920
Ewen, D. ed. The new book of modern composers p334-46   920

School administration and organization
See pages in the following book:
Gross, B. ed. Radical school reform p147-60   370.8
See also Teaching

School and community. See Community and school

School attendance. See Dropouts; Education, Compulsory

School District of Abington Township v. Schempp
See pages in the following book:
Fribourg, M. G. The Supreme Court in American history p144-61   347.9

School finance. See Education—Finance

School journalism. See College and school journalism

School libraries
American Association of School Librarians. Standards for school media programs   371.33
Davies, R. A. The school library   027.8
Junior high school library catalog   011
Periodicals for school libraries   016.05

School libraries (High school)
Junior high school library catalog   011
Rossoff, M. Using your high school library   028.7
The school library. Davies, R. A.   027.8
The School Library Journal Book review   011

School management. See School administration and organization

School music. See Music—Study and teaching

School newspapers. See College and school journalism

School organization. See School administration and organization

School stories
Kaufman, B. Up the down staircase   Fic
Knowles, J. A separate peace   Fic
Stuart, J. Mr Gallion's school   Fic

School teaching. See Teaching

Schoolfellows. Stephens, J.
In Garrity, D. A. ed. 44 Irish short stories p431-38   S C

Schooling for what? Parker, D. H.   370.1

Schools
See also Correspondence schools and courses; Education; High schools; Junior high schools; Private schools; Rural schools; and names of cities with the subdivision Public schools, e.g. Boston—Public schools

Administration
See School administration and organization

Canada
See pages in the following book:
Gross, B. ed. Radical school reform p273-96   370.8

Curricula
See Education—Curricula

Management and organization
See School administration and organization

United States
See pages in the following book:
Du Bois, W. E. B. W. E. B. Du Bois: a reader p109-45, 157-200   301.451
Glock, C. Y. ed. Prejudice U.S.A. p136-49   301.45

Schools and schools. Henry, O.
In Henry, O. The complete works of O. Henry p707-15   S C

Schooner Fairchild's class. Benét, S. V.
In Benét, S. V. Selected works of Stephen Vincent Benét v2   818

Schopenhauer, Arthur
The metaphysics of the love of the sexes
In Schopenhauer, A. The philosophy of Schopenhauer p337-76   193
The philosophy of Schopenhauer   193

About
See pages in the following books:
Durant, W. The story of philosophy p227-64   109
Thomas, H. Understanding the great philosophers p260-69   109

Sculpture, American
Craven, W. Sculpture in America 730.973
New York (City) Metropolitan Museum
of Art. American sculpture   730.973
See also pages in the following books:
Mendelowitz, D. M. A history of Ameri-
can art p225-38, 438-509   709.73
Rose, B. American art since 1900 p238-
69   709.73

Sculpture, Chinese
See pages in the following book:
Cheney, S. Sculpture of the world p184-
225   730.9

Sculpture, Early Christian
See pages in the following book:
Cheney, S. Sculpture of the world p294-
363   730.9

Sculpture, Egyptian
See pages in the following book:
Cheney, S. Sculpture of the world p33-60
730.9

Sculpture, French
Hale, W. H. The world of Rodin, 1840-
1917   92

Sculpture, Greek
See pages in the following books:
Cheney, S. Sculpture of the world p87-
131   730.9
Horizon Magazine. The Horizon Book of
ancient Greece p182-97   913.38

Sculpture, Indic
See pages in the following book:
Cheney, S. Sculpture of the world p245-72
730.9

Sculpture, Japanese
See pages in the following book:
Cheney, S. Sculpture of the world p226-
44   730.9

Sculpture, Korean
See pages in the following book:
Cheney, S. Sculpture of the world p226-
44   730.9

Sculpture, Mesopotamian
See pages in the following book:
Cheney, S. Sculpture of the world p61-77
730.9

Sculpture, Mexican
See pages in the following book:
Cheney, S. Sculpture of the world p424-
52   730.9

Sculpture, Persian
See pages in the following book:
Cheney, S. Sculpture of the world p160-83
730.9

Sculpture, Religious. See Christian art and
symbolism

Sculpture, Roman
See pages in the following book:
Cheney, S. Sculpture of the world p132-59
730.9

Sculpture, Southeastern Asian
See pages in the following book:
Cheney, S. Sculpture of the world p273-
93   730.9

Sculpture in America. Craven, W.   730.973
Sculpture in wood. Rich, J. C.   731.4
Sculpture of the world. Cheney, S. 730.9

Sea. See Ocean
The sea. Engel, L.   551.4
The sea against hunger. Idyll, C. P. 639
Sea animals. See Marine animals
The sea around us. Carson, R. L.   551.4
The sea change. Hemingway, E.
In Hemingway, E. The short stories of
Ernest Hemingway p397-401 **S C**
Sea fisheries. See Fisheries
Sea food
See pages in the following book:
Scientific American. The ocean p93-106
551.4
See also Cookery—Sea food
The sea gull. Chekhov, A.
In Block, H. M. ed. Masters of modern
drama p175-94   808.82
In Cerf, B. A. comp. Sixteen famous
European plays p151-91   808.82
In Chekhov, A. Best plays p 1-70 891.7
In Gassner, J. ed. Twenty best Euro-
pean plays on the American stage
p348-74   808.82
The sea inside us: water in the life processes.
Brooks, S. M.   612
Sea laboratories. See Diving vehicles;
Oceanography—Research
Sea life. See Seafaring life
The sea of grass. Richter, C.   Fic
The sea of life. Snively, W. D.   612
Sea power
See pages in the following book:
The New Cambridge Modern history v4
p226-38   909
The sea raiders. Wells, H. G.
In Wells, H. G. The complete short
stories of H. G. Wells p418-29
S C
In Wells, H. G. 28 science fiction stories
p651-61   **S C**
Sea routes. See Trade routes
Sea shells. See Shells
Sea-shore. See Seashore
Sea stories
Bennett, J. Mister fisherman   Fic
Conrad, J. The Nigger of the Narcissus
Fic
Conrad, J. Typhoon, and other tales of
sea   Fic
Forester, C. S. Captain Horatio Horn-
blower   Fic
Forester, C. S. Hornblower during the
crisis, and two stories: Hornblower's
temptation and The last encounter Fic
Hartog, J. de. The captain   Fic
Innes, H. The wreck of the Mary Deare
Fic
London, J. The sea-wolf   Fic
MacLean, A. H.M.S. Ulysses   Fic
Melville, H. Billy Budd, foretopman Fic
Melville, H. Moby Dick   Fic
Monsarrat, N. The cruel sea   Fic
Nordhoff, C. The Bounty trilogy   Fic
Sea water
Desalting
See pages in the following books:
Bardach, J. Harvest of the sea p247-54
333.9

Sea water—Desalting—_Continued_
Halacy, D. S. The water crisis p139-50
            333.9
Moss, F. E. The water crisis p219-30
            333.9
Sea waves. See Ocean waves
The sea-wolf. London, J.   **Fic**
Seafaring life
Dana, R. H. Two years before the mast
            910.4
National Geographic Society. Men, ships
  and the sea   **387.2**
      Drama
O'Neill, E. The long voyage home **812**
      Poetry
Masefield, J. Salt-water poems and ballads
            821
Seager, Allan
No more roses
 _In_ The Saturday Evening Post. Best
  modern short stories p200-13 **S C**
Seamen
Gurko, L. The two lives of Joseph
 Conrad   **92**
 See also Seafaring life
The séance. Singer, I. B.
 _In_ Singer, I. B. An Isaac Bashevis Sin-
  ger reader p203-17   **S C**
Search for a future. Miller, A.
 _In_ The Best American short stories,
  1967 p161-74   **S C**
Search for a new land. Lester, J. **973.92**
The search for Amelia Earhart. Goerner, F.
            92
The search for early man. Horizon Magazine
           913.03
The search for King Arthur. Horizon Maga-
 zine   **913.42**
Search through the streets of the city.
 Shaw, I.
 _In_ Foley, M. ed. Fifty best American
  short stories, 1915-1965 p278-85
           S C
Searchlight. Heinlein, R. A.
 _In_ Heinlein, R. A. Robert A. Heinlein's
  The past through tomorrow p277-
  80   **S C**
Sears, Paul B.
Lands beyond the forest   **581**
Sears, Roebuck and Company
 See pages in the following book:
Mahoney, T. The great merchants p221-
 43   **658.87**
Sears List of subject headings **025.33**
Seashore
 See pages in the following book:
National Geographic Society. Vacation-
 land U.S.A. p150-59   **917.3**
Seasons
 See pages in the following book:
Farb, P. The forest p17-37   **581**
      Poetry
 See pages in the following book:
Stevenson, B. E. comp. The home book of
 modern verse p293-312   **821.08**
Seats of the haughty. Henry, O.
 _In_ Henry, O. The complete works of
  O. Henry p144-54   **S C**

Seattle, Wash.
    Description
  See pages in the following book:
Moyers, B. Listening to America p181-
 93   **917.3**
Seaweeds. See Algae
Sebrell, William H.
Food and nutrition   **641.1**
Second book of marvels: the Orient. See
 Halliburton, R. Richard Halliburton's
 Complete book of marvels **910.4**
The second generation. Crane, S.
 _In_ Crane, S. The complete short stories
  & sketches of Stephen Crane p636-
  52   **S C**
The second hut. Lessing, D.
 _In_ Lessing, D. African stories p75-95
           S C
The second man. Behrman, S. N.
 _In_ Gassner, J. ed. Twenty-five best plays
  of the modern American theatre;
  early ser. p333-70   **812.08**
The second Mrs Tanqueray. Pinero, A. W.
 _In_ Cerf, B. A. comp. Sixteen famous
  British plays p5-64   **822.08**
 _In_ Dickinson, T. H. ed. Chief contem-
  porary dramatists [1st ser] p31-69
          808.82
Second overture. Anderson, M.
 _In_ Anderson, M. Eleven verse plays,
  1929-1939 v10   **812**
The Second Reich: Kaiser Wilhelm II and
 his Germany. Kurtz, H.   **943.08**
The second tree from the corner. White,
 E. B.   **818**
Second violin. Mansfield, K.
 _In_ Mansfield, K. The short stories of
  Katherine Mansfield p673-75 **S C**
The Second World War
 Churchill, W. S. Closing the ring **940.53**
 Churchill, W. S. The gathering storm
          940.53
 Churchill, W. S. The grand alliance **940.53**
 Churchill, W. S. The hinge of fate **940.53**
 Churchill, W. S. Their finest hour **940.53**
 Churchill, W. S. Triumph and tragedy
          940.53
The Second World War; abridgement. See
 Churchill, W. S. Memoirs of the Second
 World War   **940.53**
The Second World War: a military history.
 Collier, B.   **940.54**
Secondary education. See Education, Secon-
 dary
Secondary schools. See Education, Secon-
 dary; High schools; Junior high
 schools; Private schools
The secret. Rinehart, M. R.
 _In_ Haycraft, H. ed. A treasury of great
  mysteries v 1 p253-332   **S C**
Secret garden. Chesterton, G. K.
 _In_ Chesterton, G. K. The Father Brown
  omnibus p24-45   **S C**
The secret integration. Pynchon, T.
 _In_ The Saturday Evening Post. Best
  modern short stories p448-85 **S C**
The secret life of the forest. Ketchum, R. M.
          574.5
The secret life of Walter Mitty. Thurber, J.
 _In_ Day, A. G. ed. The greatest American
  short stories p301-07   **S C**

The secret of D-Day. Perrault, G.   940.54

Secret of Father Brown. Chesterton, G. K.
  In Chesterton, G. K. The Father Brown
    omnibus p631-811   **S C**

Secret of Father Brown [short story].
  Chesterton, G. K.
  In Chesterton, G. K. The Father Brown
    omnibus p633-41   **S C**

Secret of Flambeau. Chesterton, G. K.
  In Chesterton, G. K. The Father Brown
    omnibus p805-11   **S C**

The secret of the Hittites. Ceram, C. W.
  939

Secret service. See Spies

Secret service. Gillette, W.
  In Gassner, J. ed. Best plays of the
    early American theatre p277-360
    812.08
  In Quinn, A. H. ed. Representative
    American plays p545-620   **812.08**

The secret sharer. Conrad, J.
  In Conrad, J. The portable Conrad p648-
    99   **828**

The secret sin of Septimus Brope. Saki
  In Saki. The short stories of Saki p231-
    39   **S C**

Secretaries
  Becker, E. R. The successful secretary's
    handbook   **651.02**
  Doris, L. Complete secretary's handbook
    651.02
  Hutchinson, L. Standard handbook for
    secretaries   **651.02**
  Ingoldsby, P. The executive secretary:
    handbook to success   **651.02**
  Taintor, S. A. The secretary's handbook
    651.7

The secretary's handbook. Taintor, S. A.
  651.7

Secretary's handbook, The successful.
  Becker, E. R.   **651.02**

The secrets of Tutankhamen's tomb. Cottrell, L.   **913.32**

Sects
  Look. Religions in America   **280**
  Mead, F. S. Handbook of denominations
    in the United States   **280**

Securities
  Tyler, P. ed. Securities, exchanges, and
    the SEC   **332.6**

Securities exchange. See Stock exchange

Securities, exchanges, and the SEC. Tyler, P.
  ed.   **332.6**

Security, International. See Peace

Sedgwick, Anne Douglas
  See pages in the following book:
  Quinn, A. H. American fiction p582-95
    813.09

Sedition. See Revolutions

See how they run. Vroman, M. E.
  In Clarke, J. H. ed. American Negro
    short stories p176-97   **S C**
  In Hughes, L. ed. The best short stories
    by Negro writers p253-74   **S C**

See-saw. Mansfield, K.
  In Mansfield, K. The short stories of
    Katherine Mansfield p402-05 **S C**

See the moon. Barthelme, D.
  In Abrahams, W. ed. Fifty years of the
    American short story v 1 p55-64
    S C

The seed of McCoy. London, J.
  In London, J. Jack London's Tales of
    adventure   **S C**

The seed of the faith. Wharton, E.
  In Wharton, E. The collected short
    stories of Edith Wharton v2 p421-
    48   **S C**

Seeds
  United States. Department of Agriculture.
    Seeds   **631.5**
    Germination
    See Germination

The seeds of Hiroshima. Morris, E.   **Fic**

Seedtime of the Republic. Rossiter, C.
  342.73

Seeing double. Hughes, L.
  In Hughes, L. The Langston Hughes
    reader p187-88   **818**

Seeing Eye, Incorporated, Morristown, N.J.
  Frank, M. First lady of the Seeing Eye
    636.7
  Hartwell, D. Dogs against darkness **636.7**

Seeing eye dogs
  Frank, M. First lady of the Seeing Eye
    636.7
  Hartwell, D. Dogs against darkness **636.7**

Seely, Pauline A.
  (ed.) ALA Rules for filing catalog cards.
    See ALA Rules for filing catalog cards
    025.37
  (ed.) ALA Rules for filing catalog cards.
    Abridged. See ALA Rules for filing
    catalog cards. Abridged   **025.37**

Seeman, Bernard
  Your sight   **612**

Segal, Erich
  Love story   **Fic**

Segal, Julius
  (jt. auth.) Luce, G. G. Sleep   **154.6**

Segal, Ronald
  The Americans: a conflict of creed and
    reality   **917.3**

Segrè, Emilio
  Enrico Fermi: physicist   **92**

Segregate the fats. Lardner, R.
  In Lardner, R. The Ring Lardner reader
    p653-55   **S C**

Segregation. See Minorities; also names of
  groups of people with the subdivision
  segregation, e.g. Negroes—Segregation

Segregation in education
  Meredith, J. Three years in Mississippi
    370.19
  See also pages in the following books:
  Clark, K. B. Dark ghetto p111-53 **301.451**
  Ducas, G. ed. Great documents in Black
    American history p253-61   **301.451**
  Fribourg, M. G. The Supreme Court in
    American history p126-43   **347.9**
  Garraty, J. A. ed. Quarrels that have
    shaped the Constitution p243-68 **342.73**
  Glock, C. Y. ed. Prejudice U.S.A. p112-
    35   **301.45**

Segregationist. Asimov, I.
  In Asimov, I. Nightfall, and other
    stories p337-43   **S C**

Seidensticker, Edward
  Japan   **915.2**

Seidlova, Anca
  (jt. auth.) Shippen, K. B. The heritage of
    music   **780.9**

The **seven** storey mountain. Merton, T.   92

The **seven** that were hanged. Andreyev, L. N.
   In Seltzer, T. comp. Best Russian short stories p347-436   **S C**

Seven women. Barrie, J. M.
   In Barrie, J. M. The plays of J. M. Barrie p649-66   822

The **seven** Wonders of the World. Müller, A.   913

The **seven** year itch. Axelrod, G.
   In Gassner, J. ed. Best American plays; 4th ser. p503-33   812.08

Seven years in Tibet. Harrer, H.   915.15

Seven Years' War, 1756-1963
   See pages in the following books:
   Durant, W. Rousseau and revolution p38-64   940.2
   Mitford, N. Frederick the Great p199-215   92
   The New Cambridge Modern history v7 p465-86   909

Seventeen
   The Seventeen Book of fashion and beauty   646.7
   The Seventeen Book of prayer   242
   Seventeen from Seventeen   **S C**
   Stories from Seventeen   **S C**
   Haupt, E. A. The Seventeen Book of etiquette & entertaining   395
   Sugarman, D. A. The Seventeen Guide to knowing yourself   155.5

1787: the grand Convention. Rossiter, C.   342.73

1776. Stone, P.   812

17th & 18th century art. Ruskin, A.   709.03

Seventeenth century
   Blitzer, C. Age of kings   940.2
   Ruskin, A. 17th & 18th century art   709.03
   See also pages in the following book:
   Larousse Encyclopedia of modern history, from 1500 to the present p79-137   909

Seventh-Day Adventists
   See pages in the following book:
   Look. Religions in America p176-84   280

The **seventh** pullet. Saki
   In Saki. The short stories of Saki p320-26   **S C**

73 poems. Cummings, E. E.   811

Severn, Bill
   Adlai Stevenson: citizen of the world   92
   The end of the roaring twenties   178
   John Marshall   92

Sewage disposal
   See pages in the following book:
   United States. Department of Agriculture. Water p644-48   631.7
   See also Water—Pollution

Sewall, Richard B.
   (ed.) Emily Dickinson, a collection of critical essays   811.09

Sewing
   Better Homes and Gardens. Better Homes and Gardens Sewing book   646.4
   Cunningham, G. Singer Sewing book   646.4
   Johnson, M. Sewing the easy way   646.4

McCall's Sewing book   646.4

Margolis, A. P. How to make clothes that fit and flatter   646.4

Rosenberg, S. The illustrated hassle-free make your own clothes book   646.4

Simplicity Sewing book   646.4
   See also Dressmaking

Sewing book, Better Homes and Gardens. Better Homes and Gardens   646.4

Sewing machines
   See pages in the following book:
   Thompson, H. The age of invention p84-109   608

Sewing the easy way. Johnson, M.   646.4

Sex
   Cain, A. H. Young people and sex   176
   Mead, M. Male and female   301.41
   See also pages in the following books:
   Avery, C. E. Love and marriage p135-47   301.42
   Pierce, R. I. Single and pregnant p 1-10   362.8
   Sugarman, D. A. The Seventeen Guide to knowing yourself p179-94   155.5
   See also Reproduction

Sex before twenty. Southhard, H. F.   176

Sex in literature
   See pages in the following book:
   Stuckey, W. J. The Pulitzer Prize novels p68-93   813.09

Sex instruction
   Bahannan, P. Love, sex and being human   612.6
   Guttmacher, A. F. Understanding sex: a young person's guide   612.6
   Johnson, E. W. Love and sex in plain language   612.6
   Pomeroy, W. B. Boys and sex   612.6
   Pomeroy, W. B. Girls and sex   612.6
   Southhard, H. F. Sex before twenty   176
   See also pages in the following books:
   Ernst, M. L. Censorship: the search for the obscene p80-92   343
   Parker, D. H. Schooling for what? p103-31   370.1

The **sex** that doesn't shop. Saki
   In Saki. The short stories of Saki p57-60   **S C**

The **sexton's** deaf son. Gbadamossi, R. A.
   In Angoff, C. ed. African writing today p121-24   896

Sexual education. See Sex instruction

Sexual ethics
   Bohannan, P. Love, sex and being human   612.6
   Cain, A. H. Young people and sex   176
   Deschin, C. S. The teenager and VD   614.4
   Southhard, H. F. Sex before twenty   176
   See also pages in the following book:
   Duvall, S. M. Before you marry p45-67   301.42
   See also Birth control

Sexual hygiene. See Sex instruction; Sexual ethics; Venereal diseases

Seymour, Charles
Woodrow Wilson and the World War
973.91
Seymour, Horatio
See pages in the following book:
Stone, I. They also ran p266-85   920
Seymour, an introduction. Salinger, J. D.
In Salinger, J. D. Raise high the roof
beam, carpenters, and Seymour:
an introduction p109-248   Fic
The shackles of power. Dos Passos, J.   973
Shackleton, Sir Ernest Henry
See pages in the following book:
Stefánsson, V. ed. Great adventures and
explorations p728-36, 739-56   910.9
Shadbolt, Maurice
Isles of the South Pacific   919
The shades, a phantasy. Korolenko, V. G.
In Seltzer, T. comp. Best Russian short
stories p130-64   S C
Shades of yellow. Jordan, H. D.
In Seventeen. Stories from Seventeen
p151-65   S C
Shadow. Poe, E. A.
In Poe, E. A. Selected poetry and
prose p96-98   818
Shadow—a parable. Poe, E. A.
In Poe, E. A. The complete tales and
poems of Edgar Allan Poe p457-
58   S C
Shadow and substance. Carroll, P. V.
In Cerf, B. A. comp. Sixteen famous
European plays p991-1052   808.82
The shadow of a gunman. O'Casey, S.
In O'Casey, S. Three plays: Juno and
the paycock, The shadow of a
gunman, The plough and the stars
822
The shadow of Blooming Grove; Warren
G. Harding in his times. Russell, F.
92
Shadows on the rock. Cather, W.   Fic
The shadowy waters. Yeats, W. B.
In Yeats, W. B. Collected plays of
W. B. Yeats p95-109   822
Shadwell, Wendy J.
Museum of Graphic Art. American print-
making, the first 150 years   769
Shafer, Neil
A guide book of modern United States
currency   332.5
Shaff, A. L.
The student journalist and the critical
review   371.89
Shaffer, Peter
The royal hunt of the sun
In Richards, S. ed. Best plays of the
sixties p523-622   808.82
White lies
In Richards, S. ed. Best short plays of
the world theatre, 1958-1967 p287-
300   808.82
Shafter, William Rufus
See pages in the following book:
Holbrook, S. H. Lost men of American
history p283-94   920
Shainberg, Louis W.
(jt. auth.) Jones, K. L. Drugs and al-
cohol   613.8

Shairp, Mordaunt
The green bay tree
In Cerf, B. A. comp. Sixteen famous
British plays p803-64   822.08
Shakespeare, Anne (Hathaway)
See pages in the following book:
Brown, I. The women in Shakespeare's
life p47-77   822.3
Shakespeare, Judith
See pages in the following book:
Brown, I. The women in Shakespeare's
life p113-23   822.3
Shakespeare, Mary (Arden)
See pages in the following book:
Brown, I. The women in Shakespeare's
life p13-28   822.3
Shakespeare, Susanna
See pages in the following book:
Brown, I. The women in Shakespeare's
life p98-112   822.3
Shakespeare, William
Anthony and Cleopatra; criticism
In Daiches, D. More literary essays
p70-95   820.9
The complete works of William Shake-
speare   822.3
Everyman's Dictionary of Shakespeare
quotations   822.3
Hamlet; criticism
In Chapman, G. W. Essays on Shake-
speare p116-37   822.3
King Lear
In Bentley, E. comp. The great play-
wrights v 1 p417-520   808.82
King Lear; criticism
In Chapman, G. W. ed. Essays on
Shakespeare p138-76   822.3
Love's labour's lost; criticism
In Chapman, G. W. ed. Essays on
Shakespeare p91-115   822.3
The rape of Lucrece; criticism
In Muir, K. ed. A new companion to
Shakespeare studies p116-26   822.3
The sonnets, songs & poems of Shake-
speare   821
Troilus and Cressida
In Bentley, E. comp. The great play-
wrights v 1 p303-401   808.82
Venus and Adonis; criticism
In Muir, K. ed. A new companion to
Shakespeare studies p116-26   822.3

About

Brown, I. The women in Shakespeare's
life   822.3
Chute, M. Shakespeare of London   822.3
Frye, R. M. Shakespeare's life and times
822.3
Halliday, F. E. Shakespeare   822.3
Rowse, A. L. William Shakespeare   822.3
See also pages in the following books:
Auslander, J. The winged horse p164-89
809.1
Coleridge, S. T. The portable Coleridge
p413-27   828
Daiches, D. A critical history of English
literature v 1 p246-308, v2 p780-87
820.9

Shakespeare's England 822.3

Shakespeare's England. Horizon Magazine 822.3

Shakespeare's Globe Playhouse. Smith, I. 792.09

Shakespeare's life and times. Frye, R. M. 822.3

Shakespeare's theater. Thorndike, A. H. 792.09

Shakespeare's theatre. Hodges, C. W. 792.09

Shakespearian costume. Kelly, F. M. 792

Shakespearian costume for stage and screen. See Kelly, F. M. Shakespearian costume 792

Shalamov, Varlam
A good hand
  In Scammell, M. ed. Russia's other writers p152-56 S C

Shali. Maupassant, G. de
  In Maupassant, G. de. Guy de Maupassant's Short stories p287-96 S C

Shall not perish. Faulkner, W.
  In Faulkner, W. Collected stories of William Faulkner p101-15 S C

Shall we join the ladies? Barrie, J. M.
  In Barrie, J. M. The plays of J. M. Barrie p853-71 822

Shame. Crane, S.
  In Crane, S. The complete short stories & sketches of Stephen Crane p656-63 S C

The shame-child. Sholokhov, M.
  In Sholokhov, M. Tales of the Don p76-108 S C

The shame of the cities. Steffens, L. 352

The shamrock and the palm. Henry, O.
  In Henry, O. The complete works of O. Henry p616-27 S C

Shane. Schaefer, J. Fic

Shankar, Ravi
My music, my life 781.7

Shankle, George Earlie
American nicknames 929.4

Shannon, David A.
Between the wars: American 1919-1941 973.91
(ed.) The Great Depression 330.973

Shannon, William V.
The American Irish 301.453

The shape of intelligence. Elliott, H. C. 153

Shapers of Africa. Polatnick, F. T. 920

The shaping of modern thought. Brinton, C. 901.93

The shaping of the modern mind. See Brinton, C. The shaping of modern thought 901.93

Shapiro, Karl
(ed.) American poetry 811.08
Selected poems 811

Shapiro, William E.
(ed.) Columbia Broadcasting System, inc. CBS News. Trial at Nuremberg 341.3

Shares of stock. See Stocks

The shark: splendid savage of the sea. Cousteau, J. Y. 597

Sharks
Burgess, R. F. The sharks 597
Cousteau, J. Y. The shark: splendid savage of the sea 597
  See also pages in the following books:
Engle, L. The sea p131-41 551.4
Heller, J. H. Of mice, men and molecules p69-85 619

Sharp, Twyla
  See pages in the following book:
McDonagh, D. The rise and fall and rise of modern dance p105-18 793.3

Sharpe, Mitchell R.
Living in space 629.45

Shaw, Arnold
The rock revolution 781.5
The world of soul 781.7

Shaw, Bernard
Androcles and the lion, Overruled, Pygmalion 822
Bernard Shaw's plays 822
Contents: Major Barbara; Heartbreak House; Saint Joan; Too true to be good
Complete plays, with prefaces 822
Plays included are: The doctor's dilemma; Pygmalion; Major Barbara; Heartbreak House; Captain Brassbound's conversion; The man of destiny; Buoyant billions; Back to Methuselah; A glimpse of the domesticity of Franklyn Barnabas; Saint Joan; John Bull's other island; The dark lady of the sonnets; Mrs Warren's profession; Arms and the man; Candida; The Devil's disciple; Caesar and Cleopatra; Man and superman; Don Juan in hell; Misalliance; The apple cart; Getting married; Widowers' houses; Great Catherine; Too true to be good; The glimpse of reality; Passion, poison, and petrification; The fascinating foundling; Why she would not; The six of Calais; Annajanska, the Bolshevik Empress; Augustus does his bit; The Inca of Perusalem; O'Flaherty V.C.; The music-cure; The shewing-up of Blanco Posnet; The Admirable Bashville; Androcles and the lion; On the rocks; Geneva; How he lied to her husband; Village wooing; "In good King Charles's golden days"; Fanny's first play; The millionairess; Press cuttings; Overruled; Jitta's atonement; Farfetched fables; The simpleton of the unexpected isles; You never can tell; The philanderer

Four plays 822
Contents: Candida; Caesar and Cleopatra; Pygmalion; Heartbreak House

Major Barbara
  In Bentley, E. comp. The great playwrights v2 p1643-1725 808.82
  In Block, H. M. ed. Masters of modern drama p361-96 808.82

Man and superman
  In Block, H. M. ed. Masters of modern drama p301-59 808.82

The miraculous revenge
  In Garrity, D. A. ed. 44 Irish short stories p392-415 S C

Pygmalion; adaptation. See Lerner, A. J. My fair lady

Pygmalion, and other plays 822
Contents: Pygmalion; The Devil's disciple; Caesar and Cleopatra

Saint Joan
  In Bentley, E. comp. The great playwrights v2 p1747-1837 808.82

Saint Joan, Major Barbara, Androcles and the lion 822

Shelley, Percy B.—About—*Continued*
Daiches, D. A critical history of English literature v2 p905-15   820.9
Twain, M. The complete essays of Mark Twain p119-55   814
Untermeyer, L. Lives of the poets p418-43   920
Untermeyer, L. The paths of poetry p135-45   920

Shells
Morris, P. A. A field guide to the shells of our Atlantic and Gulf Coasts   594
See also pages in the following book:
Carlquist, S. Hawaii: a natural history p180-89   574.9

The sheltered bachelor. Chute, B. J.
In Chute, B. J. One touch of nature, and other stories p151-70   S C

Shelton, William R.
Man's conquest of space   629.4

Shenandoah. Howard, B.
In Quinn, A. H. ed. Representative American plays p473-512   812.08

Shepard, Alan Bartlett
See pages in the following book:
We seven p64-67, 152-55, 173-99, 260-73   629.45

Shepherd, John
See pages in the following book:
Drotning, P. T. Up from the ghetto p143-56   920

Shepherd, William R.
The Hispanic nations of the New World   980
Historical atlas   911

Shepherd who watched by night. Page, T. N.
In Becker, M. L. ed. The home book of Christmas p69-80   394.26

Sherburne, Zoa
From mother . . . with love
In Seventeen. Stories from Seventeen p32-46   S C

Sheridan, Richard Brinsley
The rivals   822

The sheriff of Kona. London, J.
In Day, A. G. ed. The spell of Hawaii p272-85   919.69
In London, J. Stories of Hawaii p90-104   S C

The sheriff's children. Chesnutt, C. W.
In Hughes, L. ed. The best short stories by Negro writers p 1-16   S C

Sherlock Holmes' greatest cases. Doyle, Sir A. C.   S C

Sherman, Allan
See pages in the following book:
David, J. ed. Growing up Jewish p300-04   920

Sherman, Martin
Things went badly in Westphalia
In The Best short plays, 1970 p373-408   808.82

Sherman, Roger
See pages in the following book:
Bakeless, J. Signers of the Declaration p195-202   920

Sherman, William Tecumseh
See pages in the following book:
Catton, B. Prefaces to history p63-70   973.7

Sherrard, Philip
Byzantium   949.5

Sherriff, Robert Cedric
Journey's end
In Cerf, B. A. comp. Sixteen famous British plays p595-668   822.08

Sherry. Howard, M.
In The Best American short stories, 1965 p125-65   S C

Sherwood, Hugh C.
The journalistic interview   070.4

Sherwood, Robert E.
Abe Lincoln in Illinois   812
—Same
In Gassner, J. ed. Best plays of the modern American theatre; 2d ser. p725-73   812.08
Idiot's delight
In Gassner, J. ed. Twenty best plays of the modern American theatre p93-136   812.08
The petrified forest
In Cerf, B. A. ed. Sixteen famous American plays p361-419   812.08
The road to Rome
In Gassner, J. ed. Twenty-five best plays of the modern American theatre; early ser. p295-332   812.08
Roosevelt and Hopkins   973.917

About
See pages in the following books:
Gould, J. Modern American playwrights p99-117   812.09
Krutch, J. W. The American drama since 1918 p213-25   812.09

The shewing-up of Blanco Posnet. Shaw, B.
In Shaw, B. Complete plays, with prefaces v5 p245-76   822

Shibalok's family. Sholokhov, M.
In Sholokhov, M. Tales of the Don p30-36   S C

The shifting balance of world forces, 1898-1945. Mowat, C. L. ed.
In The New Cambridge Modern history v12   909

Shin bones. London, J.
In London, J. Stories of Hawaii p178-202   S C

Shingles for the Lord. Faulkner, W.
In Faulkner, W. Collected stories of William Faulkner p27-43   S C
In Faulkner, W. The Faulkner reader   S C

Shinto
See pages in the following books:
Bach, M. Had you been born in another faith p85-100   291
Gaer, J. How the great religions began p179-96   291
Gaer, J. The wisdom of the living religions p249-56   291
Jurji, E. J. ed. The great religions of the modern world p141-77   291
Voss, C. H. In search of meaning: living religions of the world p87-98   291

Short novels of Henry James. James, H.
Fic

The **short** novels of John Steinbeck. Steinbeck, J.
Fic

The **short** novels of Thomas Wolfe. Wolfe, T.
S C

Short stories

Abrahams, W. ed. Fifty years of the American short story
S C

Akutagawa, R. Japanese short stories **S C**

Anderson, S. Winesburg, Ohio **S C**

Asimov, I. Asimov's mysteries **S C**

Asimov, I. I, robot **S C**

Asimov, I. Nightfall, and other stories
S C

Asimov, I. Nine tomorrows **S C**

Asimov, I. ed. Where do we go from here?
S C

Baldwin, J. Going to meet the man **S C**

The Best American short stories, 1964-1971
S C

Best detective stories of the year, 1967, 1970-1971
S C

The Best from Fantasy and Science Fiction; 19th ser.
S C

Borges, J. L. The Aleph, and other stories, 1933-1969
S C

Bradbury, R. I sing the Body Electric!
S C

Bradbury, R. The illustrated man **S C**

Bradbury, R. The Martian chronicles **S C**

Bradbury, R. R is for rocket **S C**

Buck, P. S. The good deed, and other stories of Asia, past and present **S C**

Camus, A. Exile and the kingdom **S C**

Capote, T. Breakfast at Tiffany's **S C**

Cather, W. Willa Cather's Collected short fiction, 1892-1912 **S C**

Chekhov, A. The image of Chekhov **S C**

Chekhov, A. The stories of Anton Chekhov
S C

Chesterton, G. K. The Father Brown omnibus **S C**

Chute, B. J. One touch of nature, and other stories **S C**

Clarke, J. H. American Negro short stories
S C

Conklin, G. ed. Invaders of earth **S C**

Costain, T. B. ed. Read with me **S C**

Crane, S. The complete short stories & sketches of Stephen Crane **S C**

Day, A. G. ed. The greatest American short stories **S C**

Dinesen, I. Seven Gothic tales **S C**

Doyle, A. C. The exploits of Sherlock Holmes **S C**

Doyle, Sir A. C. The complete Sherlock Holmes **S C**

Doyle, Sir A. C. Sherlock Holmes' greatest cases **S C**

Dulles, A. ed. Great spy stories from fiction **S C**

Faulkner, W. Collected stories of William Faulkner **S C**

Faulkner, W. The Faulkner reader **S C**

Faulkner, W. The portable Faulkner **S C**

Faulkner, W. Selected short stories of William Faulkner **S C**

Fitzgerald, F. S. The Fitzgerald reader
S C

Fitzgerald, F. S. The stories of F. Scott Fitzgerald **S C**

Foley, M. ed. Fifty best American short stories, 1915-1965 **S C**

Forester, C. S. Gold from Crete **S C**

Garrity, D. A. ed. 44 Irish short stories
S C

Godden, R. Gone **S C**

Harte, B. The best of Bret Harte **S C**

Harte, B. The best short stories of Bret Harte **S C**

Havighurst, W. ed. Masters of the modern short story **S C**

Hawthorne, N. Hawthorne's Short stories
S C

Haycraft, H. ed. A treasury of great mysteries **S C**

Heinlein, R. A. Robert A. Heinlein's The past through tomorrow **S C**

Hemingway, E. The Fifth Column, and four stories of the Spanish Civil War
818

Hemingway, E. In our time **S C**

Hemingway, E. The short stories of Ernest Hemingway **S C**

Hemingway, E. The snows of Kilimanjaro, and other stories **S C**

Henry, O. The best short stories of O. Henry **S C**

Henry, O. The complete works of O. Henry **S C**

Henry, O. The four million **S C**

Hess, H. Klingsor's last summer **S C**

Hitchcock, A. Alfred Hitchcock presents: A month of mystery **S C**

Hughes, L. ed. The best short stories by Negro writers **S C**

Jackson, S. The magic of Shirley Jackson
818

Joyce, J. Dubliners **S C**

Kafka, F. Selected short stories of Franz Kafka **S C**

Kipling, R. The best short stories of Rudyard Kipling **S C**

Kipling, R. Maugham's Choice of Kipling's best **S C**

Lardner, R. The best short stories of Ring Lardner **S C**

Lardner, R. ed. Rex Lardner selects the best of sports fiction **S C**

Lederer, W. J. The ugly American **S C**

Lessing, D. African stories **S C**

London, J. Best short stories of Jack London **S C**

London, J. Jack London's Tales of adventure **S C**

London, J. Stories of Hawaii **S C**

Mansfield, K. The short stories of Katherine Mansfield **S C**

Maugham, W. S. The best short stories of W. Somerset Maugham **S C**

Maupassant, G. de. Guy de Maupassant's Short stories **S C**

Maupassant, G. de. The odd number **S C**

Maupassant, G. de. Selected short stories **S C**

Michener, J. A. Tales of the South Pacific
S C

Mishima, Y. Death in midsummer, and other stories **S C**

Moore, R. The green berets **S C**

Short stories—*Continued*
  Mystery Writers of America. Crime without murder **S C**
  The New Yorker. Stories from The New Yorker, 1950-1960 **S C**
  Nourse, A. E. R for tomorrow **S C**
  Paton, A. Tales from a troubled land **S C**
  Pei, M. Tales of the natural and supernatural **S C**
  Poe, E. A. The complete tales and poems of Edgar Allan Poe **S C**
  Poe, E. A. Edgar Allan Poe **S C**
  Poe, E. A. Selected poetry and prose **818**
  Porter, K. A. The collected stories of Katherine Anne Porter **S C**
  Porter, K. A. Pale horse, pale rider **S C**
  Prize stories, 1970-1971: The O. Henry Awards **S C**
  Saki. The short stories of Saki **S C**
  Salinger, J. D. Nine stories **S C**
  The Saturday Evening Post. Best modern short stories **S C**
  Scammell, M. ed. Russia's other writers **S C**
  Schaefer, J. The collected stories of Jack Schaefer **S C**
  The Scribner treasury **S C**
  Seltzer, T. comp. Best Russian short stories **S C**
  Seventeen. Seventeen from Seventeen **S C**
  Seventeen. Stories from Seventeen **S C**
  Sholokhov, M. Tales of the Don **S C**
  Singer, I. B. An Isaac Bashevis Singer reader **S C**
  Solzhenitsyn, A. Stories and prose poems **S C**
  Spark, M. Collected stories: I **S C**
  Stevenson, R. L. The complete short stories of Robert Louis Stevenson **S C**
  Stevenson, R. L. The strange case of Dr Jekyll and Mr Hyde, and other famous tales **S C**
  Stuart, J. Come back to the farm **S C**
  Stuart, J. Plowshare in heaven **S C**
  Tolstoy, L. Short novels **S C**
  Tolstoy, L. Short stories **S C**
  Tolstoy, L. Twenty-three tales **S C**
  Twain, M. The complete short stories of Mark Twain **S C**
  Undset, S. Four stories **S C**
  Updike, J. Pigeon feathers, and other stories **S C**
  Wells, H. G. The complete short stories of H. G. Wells **S C**
  Wells, H. G. 28 science fiction stories **S C**
  Wharton, E. The collected short stories of Edith Wharton **S C**
  Wharton, E. The Edith Wharton reader **S C**
  White, E. B. ed. A subtreasury of American humor; abridged **817.08**
  Wolfe, T. The hills beyond **S C**
  Wolfe, T. The short novels of Thomas Wolfe **S C**
    Indexes
  Short story index **808.83**
  Short story index: supplement, 1950-1954 **808.83**
  Short story index: supplement, 1955-1958 **808.83**

Short story index: supplement, 1959-1963 **808.83**
Short story index: supplement, 1964-1968 **808.83**
Short story
  Dickson, F. A. ed. Handbook of short story writing **808.3**
    See also pages in the following book:
  Engle, P. ed. On creative writing p19-34, 51-66 **808.02**
Short story index **808.83**
Short story index: supplement, 1950-1954 **808.83**
Short story index: supplement, 1955-1958 **808.83**
Short story index: supplement, 1959-1963 **808.83**
Short story index: supplement, 1964-1968 **808.83**
A short-title alphabetical catalogue of plays produced or printed in England from 1660 to 1900. Nicoll, A.
  In Nicoll, A. A history of English drama, 1660-1900 v6 **822.09**
Shorter, Bani
  Nehru **92**
The Shorter Cambridge Medieval history **940.1**
Shorter French and English dictionary, Mansion's **443**
Shostakovich, Dmitriĭ Dmitrievich
    See pages in the following books:
  Cross, M. The Milton Cross New encyclopedia of the great composers and their music p919-39 **920.03**
  Ewen, D. ed. The new book of modern composers p362-74 **920**
Shotguns
  Sports Illustrated. Sports Illustrated Book of the shotgun **799.3**
Should wizard hit mommy. Updike, J.
  In Updike, J. Pigeon feathers, and other stories **S C**
The show. Galsworthy, J.
  In Galsworthy, J. Plays p573-605 **822**
Show me first your penny. Jones, E.
  In Angoff, C. ed. African writing today p70-77 **896**
Showers (Parties)
    See pages in the following book:
  Wilson, B. The complete book of engagement and wedding etiquette p86-94 **395**
"Showin' off." Crane, S.
  In Crane, S. The complete short stories & sketches of Stephen Crane p608-13 **S C**
The shrapnel of their friends. Crane, S.
  In Crane, S. The complete short stories & sketches of Stephen Crane p679-84 **S C**
Shrews
    See pages in the following book:
  Lorenz, K. Z. King Solomon's ring p92-113 **591**
A Shropshire lad. Housman, A. E.
  In Housman, A. E. The collected poems of A. E. Housman p9-91 **821**
Shrubs
  Petrides, G. A. A field guide to trees and shrubs **582**

Shute, Henry Augustus
Plupy goes to Sunday school
In Becker, M. L. ed. The home book of
Christmas p132-39   394.26
Shute, Nevil
The legacy   Fic
On the beach   Fic
Shutterbug. Nussbaum, A.
In Mystery Writers of America. Crime
without murder p197-202   S C
Siam. See Thailand
Siamese cat
Denham, S. The complete book of the
Siamese cat   636.8
Siamese cookery. Wilson, M. M.   641.5
Siamese cooking. See Cookery, Thai
Sibelius, Jean Julius Christian
See pages in the following books:
Cross, M. The Milton Cross New en-
cyclopedia of the great composers and
their music p940-56   920.03
Ewen, D. ed. The new book of modern
composers p375-92   920
Siberia
Description and travel
Mowat, F. The Siberians   915.7
Fiction
Dostoevsky, F. The house of the dead Fic
History
See pages in the following book:
Horizon Magazine. The Horizon History
of Russia p139-47   947
Siberian mythology. See Mythology, Siberi-
an
The Siberians. Mowat, F.   915.7
Sicily
Fiction
Lampedusa, G. di. The Leopard   Fic
Sick. See Home nursing
Siddhartha. Hesse, H.   Fic
Siddons, Sarah (Kemble)
See pages in the following book:
Trease, G. Seven stages p54-82   920
Sidney, Sir Philip
See pages in the following books:
Daiches, D. A critical history of English
literature v 1 p190-200   820.9
Untermeyer, L. The paths of poetry p32-
36   920
The siege and fall of Troy. Graves, R.   883
Siegel, Jules
In the land of the morning calm, déjà vu
In The Best American short stories,
1970 p288-307   S C
Siegelman, Ellen
(jt. ed.) Glock, C. Y. ed. Prejudice U.S.A.
     301.45
Sienkiewicz, Henryk
Quo vadis   Fic
Sierra, Gregorio Martínez. See Martínez
Sierra, Gregorio
Sierra Club, San Francisco
Ecotactics: the Sierra Club handbook for
environment activists. See Ecotactics:
the Sierra Club handbook for environ-
ment activists   333.7

Sight. See Vision
Sight saving books. See Large type books
Sigler, Jay A.
(ed.) The conservative tradition in Ameri-
can thought   320.5
The sign in Sidney Brustein's window.
Hansberry, L.
In Gassner, J. ed. Best American plays;
6th ser. p227-75   812.08
Sign of the broken sword. Chesterton, G. K.
In Chesterton, G. K. The Father Brown
omnibus p193-211   S C
The sign of the four. Doyle, Sir A. C.
In Doyle, Sir A. C. The complete Sher-
lock Holmes v 1 p91-173   S C
Sign painting. See Lettering
The signal. Garshin, V. M.
In Seltzer, T. comp. Best Russian short
stories p165-77   S C
Signals and signaling. See Flags
Signers of the Declaration. Bakeless, J.   920
Signs and signboards. See Posters
Siguenza y Gongora, Carlos de
See pages in the following book:
Worcester, D. E. Makers of Latin Amer-
ica p30-36   920
Sigurjónsson, Johan
Eyvind of the hills
In Dickinson, T. H. ed. Chief contem-
porary dramatists, 3d ser. p639-73
     808.82
Sikhs
See pages in the following book:
Mehta, V. Portrait of India p463-76   915.4
Sikkim
See pages in the following books:
Mehta, V. Portrait of India p234-49   915.4
Salisbury, H. E. Orbit of China p95-106
     915.1
Sikorsky, Igor Ivan
See pages in the following book:
Beard, A. E. S. Our foreign-born citizens
p148-63   920
Siksika Indians
See pages in the following book:
Vlahos, O. New world beginnings p33-48
     913.7
Silas Marner. Eliot, G.   Fic
Silberman, Charles E.
Crisis in black and white   301.451
Crisis in the classroom   370
The myths of automation   301.24
Silence—a fable. Poe, E. A.
In Poe, E. A. The complete tales and
poems of Edgar Allan Poe p459-61
     S C
In Poe, E. A. Selected poetry and prose
p98-101   818
The silent Don. Sholokhov, M.   Fic
The silent men. Camus, A.
In Camus, A. Exile and the kingdom
     S C
Silent night, lonely night. Anderson, R.
In Gassner, J. ed. Best American plays;
5th ser. p313-39   812.08
Silent spring. Carson, R.   632
The silent world. Cousteau, J. Y.   627.7

The silent world; excerpt. Cousteau, J. Y.
In Ceram, C. W. ed. Hands on the past
p394-403   913.03
Silicon
  See pages in the following book:
Asimov, I. Building blocks of the uni-
  verse p77-86   546
Sills, David L.
  (ed.) International Encyclopedia of the
  social sciences. See International En-
  cyclopedia of the social sciences   303
Silone, Ignazio
  Bread and wine   Fic
Silva, José Bonifacio de Andrada e. See
  Andrada e Silva, José Bonifacio de
Silva Rondon, Cândido Mariano da. See
  Rondon, Cândido Mariano da Silva
Silver, Horace
  See pages in the following book:
Williams, M. The jazz tradition p178-85
                                    781.5
Silver, James W.
  Mississippi: the closed society   301.451
Silver
  See pages in the following book:
Asimov, I. Building blocks of the universe
  p184-96   546
  See also Silversmithing
Silver Blaze. Doyle, Sir A. C.
  In Doyle, Sir A. C. The complete Sher-
    lock Holmes v 1 p383-401   S C
  In Doyle, Sir A. C. Sherlock Holmes'
    greatest cases p395-432   S C
The silver box. Galsworthy, J.
  In Galsworthy, J. Plays p 1-32   822
The silver chalice. Costain, T. B.   Fic
The silver cord. Howard, S.
  In Dickinson, T. H. ed. Chief contem-
    porary dramatists, 3d ser. p65-116
                                    808.82
  In Quinn, A. H. ed. Representative
    American plays p1011-58   812.08
  In Tucker, S. M. ed. Twenty-five mod-
    ern plays p675-720   808.82
The silver pageant. Crane, S.
  In Crane, S. The complete short stories
    & sketches of Stephen Crane p195-
    96   S C
The silver Tassie. O'Casey, S.
  In O'Casey, S. The Sean O'Casey read-
    er p133-203   828
Silverberg, Robert
  Forgotten by time: a book of living fossils
                                      591
  Frontiers in archeology   913.03
  Mammoths, mastodons, and man   569
  Mound builders of ancient America 970.4
  Sundance
  In The Best from Fantasy and Science
    Fiction; 19th ser. p77-93   S C
Silverman, Al
  Joe Di Maggio: the golden year, 1941 92
  Robinson, F. My life is baseball   92
Silversmithing
  Forbes, E. Paul Revere & the world he
    lived in   92
  See also pages in the following books:
The Arts in America: The colonial period
  p319-46   709.73
Langdon, W. C. Everyday things in Amer-
  ican life, 1607-1776 p176-91   917.3

Simak, Clifford D.
  Prehistoric man   573.2
Simenon, Georges
  The confessional   Fic
  The fall of the high-flying Dutchman
  In Mystery Writers of America. Crime
    without murder p253-63   S C
  Five times Maigret   Fic
  Maigret and the reluctant witnesses
  In Simenon, G. Five times Maigret
    p323-421   Fic
  Maigret goes to school
  In Simenon, G. Five times Maigret
    p424-525   Fic
  Maigret has scruples
  In Simenon, G. Five times Maigret
    p223-320   Fic
  Maigret in Montmartre
  In Simenon, G. Five times Maigret p9-
    116   Fic
  Maigret's Christmas
  In Haycraft, H. ed. A treasury of great
    mysteries v 1 p201-40   S C
  Maigret's mistake
  In Simenon, G. Five times Maigret
    p117-219   Fic
Simms, D. Harper
  The Soil Conservation Service   353.81
Simms, William Gilmore
  See pages in the following book:
Brooks, V. The world of Washington
  Irving p308-25   810.9
Simon, Bert
  Ham radio incentive licensing guide
                                    621.3841
Simon, Charlie May
  The Andrew Carnegie story   92
  Martin Buber   92
  The sun and the birch; the story of Crown
    Prince Akihito and Crown Princess Mi-
    chiko   92
Simon, Edith
  The Reformation   940.2
Simon, Gus. See Edwards, Gus
Simon, Neil
  Barefoot in the park   812
  The odd couple
  In Gassner, J. ed. Best American plays;
    6th ser. p527-65   812.08
  In Richards, S. ed. Best plays of the
    sixties p419-521   808.82
Simon, Pierre, marquis de Laplace. See
  Laplace, Pierre Simon, marquis de
Simon Magus
  See pages in the following book:
Boyd, M. Man, myth and magic p84-91
                                    133.4
Simon the Magician. See Simon Magus
Simons, Gerald
  Barbarian Europe   940.1
Simon's papa. Maupassant, G. de
  In Maupassant, G. de. Selected short
    stories p205-16   S C
Simonsen. Undset, S.
  In Undset, S. Four stories p199-246 S C
Simple arithmetic. Moriconi, V.
  In The Best American short stories,
    1964 p227-40   S C

A **simple** enquiry. Hemingway, E.
    In Hemingway, E. The short stories of
        Ernest Hemingway p327-30   **S C**
Simple library cataloging. Akers, S. G. **025.3**
Simple stashes back. Hughes, L.
    In Hughes, L. The Langston Hughes
        reader p231-32   **818**
Simple transistor projects for hobbyists &
    students. Steckler, L.   **621.381**
The **simpleton** of the unexpected isles.
    Shaw, B.
    In Shaw, B. Complete plays, with pref-
        aces v6 p543-611   **822**
Simplicity Sewing book   **646.4**
Simplified guide to the popular card games,
    Hoyle's. Gibson, W. B.   **795.4**
Simply heavenly. Hughes, L.
    In Hughes, L. Five plays p113-81 **812**
    In Hughes, L. The Langston Hughes
        reader p244-313   **818**
Simpson, D. P.
    (comp.) Cassell's New compact Latin-En-
        glish, English-Latin dictionary. See Cas-
        sell's New compact Latin-English, En-
        glish-Latin dictionary   **473**
    (comp.) Cassell's New Latin dictionary:
        Latin-English, English-Latin. See Cas-
        sell's New Latin dictionary: Latin-En-
        glish, English-Latin   **473**
Simpson, Jacqueline
    Everyday life in the Viking age   **914.8**
Simpson, Smith
    Anatomy of the State Department **353.1**
Sims, Edward H.
    American aces in great fighter battles of
        World War II   **940.54**
Sims, William Sowden
    See pages in the following book:
    Morison, E. E. Men, machines, and mod-
        ern times p27-38   **609**
Sinai Campaign, 1956
    See pages in the following book:
    Comay, J. The UN in action p35-38 **341.13**
Since Silent spring. Braham, F.   **632**
Sinclair, Andrew
    Che Guevara   **92**
Sinclair, Upton
    The jungle; criticism
    In Downs, R. B. Books that changed
        America p144-51   **810.9**
    About
    See pages in the following book:
    Durant, W. Interpretations of life p43-48
                                          809

Singer, Isaac Bashevis
    The colony
    In The Best American short stories,
        1969 p278-89   **S C**
    Esther Kreindel the second
    In The Saturday Evening Post. Best
        modern short stories p157-71 **S C**
    An Isaac Bashevis Singer reader   **S C**
    Stories included are: Gimpel the fool; The
    mirror; The unseen; The Spinoza of Market
    Street; The black wedding; The man who came
    back; Short Friday; Yentl the Yeshiva boy;
    Blood; The fast; The séance; The slaughterer;
    The lecture; Getzel the monkey; A friend of
    Kafka; My father's friend; Dreamers; A wed-
    ding; Had he been a Kohen

The key
    In The Best American short stories,
        1970 p308-17   **S C**
The Magician of Lublin
    In Singer, I. B. An Isaac Bashevis
        Singer reader p317-560   **S C**
A sacrifice
    In The Best American short stories,
        1965 p283-89   **S C**
    About
    See pages in the following book:
    David, J. ed. Growing up Jewish p53-65
                                          920
Singer Company
    Cunningham, G. Singer Sewing book **646.4**
    See also pages in the following book:
    Mahoney, T. The great merchants p66-77
                                       658.87
Singer Sewing book. Cunningham, G. **646.4**
Singers
    Anderson, M. My Lord, what a morning
                                           92
    Baez, J. Daybreak   **92**
    Benét, L. Enchanting Jenny Lind   **92**
    Horne, L. Lena   **92**
    Shaw, A. The world of soul   **781.7**
    See also Trapp Family Singers
    Fiction
    Cather, W. The song of the lark   **Fic**
    Wolff, R. A crack in the sidewalk   **Fic**
A **singer's** romance. Cather, W.
    In Cather, W. Willa Cather's Collected
        short fiction, 1892-1912 v3 p333-38
                                          S C
The **singing** bell. Asimov, I.
    In Asimov, I. Asimov's mysteries p 1-
        16   **S C**
Singing Dinah's song. Brown, F. L.
    In Hughes, L. ed. The best short sto-
        ries by Negro writers p295-300 **S C**
Singing games
    See pages in the following book:
    Botkin, B. A. ed. A treasury of American
        folklore p768-818   **398**
The **singing** lesson. Mansfield, K.
    In Mansfield, K. The short stories of
        Katherine Mansfield p491-96   **S C**
The **singing** pigeon. Macdonald, R.
    In Hitchcock, A. ed. Alfred Hitchcock
        presents: A month of mystery
        p157-90   **S C**
Single and pregnant. Pierce, R. I.   **362.8**
A **single** pebble. Hersey, J.   **Fic**
The **single** wing epicure. Sisk, F.
    In Best detective stories of the year
        [1969] p166-85   **S C**
Singleton, Benjamin
    See pages in the following book:
    Bontemps, A. Anyplace but here p53-71
                                       301.451
Singmaster, Elsie
    The survivors
    In Foley, M. ed. Fifty best American
        short stories, 1915-1965 p 1-7 **S C**
Sinkankas, John
    Prospecting for gemstones and minerals
                                          553

Sinkings, salvages, and shipwrecks. Burgess, R. F.   910.4
Sinner man where you gonna run to? Neal, L.
 In Jones, L. ed. Black fire p510-18 **810.8**
Sino-Indian Border Dispute, 1957-
   See pages in the following book:
 Galbraith, J. K. Ambassador's journal p428-93   **327.73**
Sino-Japanese Conflict, 1937-1945
   See pages in the following book:
 Tuchman, B. W. Stilwell and the American experience in China, 1911-45 p164-200   **327.73**
Sins of Prince Saradine. Chesterton, G. K.
 In Chesterton, G. K. The Father Brown omnibus p137-57   **S C**
Sioux Indians. See Dakota Indians
Sir Walter Scott: his life and personality. Pearson, H.   **92**
The Sire de Malétroit's door. Stevenson, R. L.
 In Stevenson, R. L. The complete short stories of Robert Louis Stevenson p231-54   **S C**
 In Stevenson, R. L. The strange case of Dr Jekyll and Mr Hyde, and other famous tales p168-89 **S C**
The sirens of Titan. Vonnegut, K.   **Fic**
Siriono Indians
   See pages in the following book:
 Vlahos, O. New world beginnings p80-90   **913.7**
Sisam, Celia
 (ed.) The Oxford Book of medieval English verse. See Oxford Book of medieval English verse   **821.08**
Sisk, Frank
 The leakage
 In Best detective stories of the year, 1971 p63-68   **S C**
 The single wing epicure
 In Best detective stories of the year [1969] p166-85   **S C**
Sister Carrie. Dreiser, T.   **Fic**
The sister of the Baroness. Mansfield, K.
 In Mansfield, K. The short stories of Katherine Mansfield p45-49   **S C**
The sisters. Joyce, J.
 In Joyce, J. Dubliners p7-19   **S C**
Sisters of the golden circle. Henry, O.
 In Henry, O. The complete works of O. Henry p81-85   **S C**
 In Henry, O. The four million p197-207   **S C**
Sitati, Paul
 Jane
 In Angoff, C. ed. African writing today p103-13   **896**
Sitwell, Edith
 (ed.) The Atlantic book of British and American poetry   **821.08**
Six American novelists of the nineteenth century. Foster, R. ed.   **813.09**
Six American plays for today. Cerf, B. ed.   **812.08**

Six characters in search of an author. Pirandello, L.
 In Bentley, E. comp. The great playwrights v2 p2001-56   **808.82**
 In Cerf, B. A. comp. Sixteen famous European plays p623-65   **808.82**
The six day war. Churchill, R. S.   **956**
Six feet of the country. Gordimer, N.
 In The New Yorker. Stories from The New Yorker, 1950-1960 p687-97 p301-05   **S C**
The six-foot Swami from Savannah. Lederer, W. J.
 In Lederer, W. J. The ugly American p174-90   **S C**
Six modern American plays   **812.08**
The six of Calais. Shaw, B.
 In Shaw, B. Complete plays, with prefaces v5 p32-46   **822**
6 plays. Hammerstein, O.   **812**
Six plays. Ibsen, H.   **839.8**
Six plays. Odets, C.   **812**
Six years after. Mansfield, K.
 In Mansfield, K. The short stories of Katherine Mansfield p638-42 **S C**
Sixes and sevens. Henry, O.
 In Henry, O. The complete works of O. Henry p811-940   **S C**
Sixpence. Mansfield, K.
 In Mansfield, K. The short stories of Katherine Mansfield p519-25   **S C**
Sixpence in her shoe. McGinley, P.   **818**
Sixteen famous American plays. Cerf, B. A. ed.   **812.08**
Sixteen famous British plays. Cerf, B. A. comp.   **822.08**
Sixteen famous European plays. Cerf, B. A. comp.   **808.82**
Sixteenth century
   See pages in the following book:
 Larousse Encyclopedia of modern history, from 1500 to the present p13-77   **909**

   See also Reformation
Size and shape
   See pages in the following book:
 Kadesch, R. R. Math menagerie p47-63   **793.7**
Sketching. See Drawing
Ski Magazine
 America's ski book   **796.9**
 Ski Magazine's Encyclopedia of skiing   **796.9**
 The skier's handbook   **796.9**
The skier's handbook. Ski Magazine **796.9**
Skiing. See Skis and skiing
Skiing, Water. See Water skiing
Skin
 Sternberg, T. H. More than skin deep   **616.5**
 Woodburn, J. H. Know your skin **616.5**
   See also pages in the following book:
 Seventeen. The Seventeen Book of fashion and beauty p17-26   **646.7**
   Diseases
 Sternberg, T. H. More than skin deep   **616.5**

Skin and scuba diving

Cousteau, J. Y. ed. Captain Cousteau's Underwater treasury   **627.7**

Cousteau, J. Y. The silent world   **627.7**

Throckmorton, P. Shipwrecks and archaeology   **913.03**

See also pages in the following books:

Bardach, J. Harvest of the sea p54-84   **333.9**

Dugan, J. World beneath the sea p71-90   **551.4**

National Geographic Society. Great adventures with National Geographic p280-331   **910.9**

National Geographic Society. Vacationland U.S.A. p58-69   **917.3**

National Geographic Society. Wondrous world of fishes p156-69   **597**

The **skin** game. Galsworthy, J.

In Galsworthy, J. Plays p349-89   **822**

The **skin** of our teeth. Wilder, T.

In Wilder, T. Three plays p105-250   **812**

Skinner, Constance Lindsay

Adventurers of Oregon   **979.5**

Pioneers of the Old Southwest   **976**

Skinner, Cornelia Otis

Madame Sarah [Bernhardt]   **92**

Our hearts were young and gay   **914**

Skippy. Sackler, H.

In The Best short plays, 1971 p53-74   **808.82**

Skis and skiing

Iselin, F. Invitation to modern skiing   **796.9**

Jerome, J. Sports Illustrated Skiing   **796.9**

Ski Magazine. America's ski book   **796.9**

Ski Magazine. Ski Magazine's Encyclopedia of skiing   **796.9**

Ski Magazine. The skier's handbook   **796.9**

See also pages in the following book:

National Geographic Society. Vacationland U.S.A. p378-91   **917.3**

Skouras, Spyros Panagiotes

See pages in the following book:

Beard, A. E. S. Our foreign-born citizens p201-10   **920**

Skull. See Brain; Head

The **sky** clears: poetry of the American Indians. Day, A. G. ed.   **897**

The **sky** is gray. Gaines, E. J.

In Clarke, J. H. ed. American Negro short stories p321-48   **S C**

Skydiving. See Parachuting

The **skylark.** Mazor, J.

In Prize stories, 1971: The O. Henry Awards p94-136   **S C**

The **skylight** room. Henry, O.

In Henry, O. The complete works of O. Henry p19-24   **S C**

In Henry, O. The four million p47-57   **S C**

Slabs of the sunburnt West. Sandburg, C.

In Sandburg, C. The complete poems of Carl Sandburg p271-314   **811**

Slack, A .V.

Defense against famine   **631.8**

Slang. See English language—Slang

Slang to-day and yesterday. Partridge, E.   **427**

Slater, Elaine

The Sooey pill

In Best detective stories of the year [1969] p78-82   **S C**

The **slaughterer.** Singer, I. B.

In Singer, I. B. An Isaac Bashevis Singer reader p219-34   **S C**

Slaughterhouse-five. Vonnegut, K.   **Fic**

Slave of the Huns. Gardonyi, G.   **Fic**

Slave on the block. Hughes, L.

In Hughes, L. The Langston Hughes reader p11-17   **818**

Slave trade

Davidson, B. Black mother   **967**

See also pages in the following books:

Ducas, G. ed. Great documents in Black American history p39-51   **301.451**

Franklin, J. H. From slavery to freedom p42-70, 175-84   **301.451**

Hatch, J. Nigeria p93-108   **966.9**

Slavery

See also Slave trade

History

See pages in the following books:

Ducas, G. ed. Great documents in Black American history p3-13   **301.451**

Horizon Magazine. The light of the past p56-63   **901.9**

Slavery in America. Liston, R.   **326**

Slavery in Latin America

See pages in the following book:

Franklin, J. H. From slavery to freedom p112-25   **301.451**

Slavery in Rome

See pages in the following book:

Davis, W. S. A day in old Rome p122-38   **913.37**

Slavery in the United States

Aptheker, H. ed. A documentary history of the Negro people in the United States   **301.451**

Bontemps, A. ed. Great slave narratives   **920**

Douglass, F. Life and times of Frederick Douglass; abridged   **92**

Douglass, F. The mind and heart of Frederick Douglass   **326**

Franklin, J. H. From slavery to freedom   **301.451**

Franklin, J. H. An illustrated history of Black Americans   **301.451**

Furnas, J. C. Goodbye to Uncle Tom   **326**

Hoexter, C. K. Black crusader: Frederick Douglass   **92**

Hughes, L. A pictorial history of the Negro in America   **301.451**

Liston, R. Slavery in America   **326**

Macy, J. The anti-slavery crusade   **973.6**

Nevins, A. Ordeal of the Union   **973.6**

Quarles, B. ed. Frederick Douglass   **92**

See also pages in the following books:

Commager, H. S. Crusaders for freedom p61-84   **920**

Smith, Alfred Emanuel
See pages in the following books:
Mencken, H. L. The American scene p447-66   **818**
Shannon, W. V. The American Irish p151-81   **301.453**
Stone, I. They also ran p285-305   **920**

Smith, Bessie
See pages in the following books:
Hadlock, R. Jazz masters of the twenties p219-38   **920**
Williams, M. T. ed. The art of jazz p75-90   **781.5**

Smith, Betty
Joy in the morning   **Fic**
A tree grows in Brooklyn   **Fic**

Smith, Bradford
Captain John Smith: his life & legend   **92**
Heinrich Himmler: a Nazi in the making, 1900-1926   **92**

Smith, Carlton
The Time-Life Book of family finance   **339.4**

Smith, Dodie
I capture the castle   **Fic**

Smith, Edward C.
(ed.) Dictionary of American politics   **320.03**

Smith, Elsdon C.
American surnames   **929.4**

Smith, Evelyn E.
Calliope and Gherkin and the Yankee Doodle thing
In The Best from Fantasy and Science Fiction; 19th ser. p119-59   **S C**

Smith, George
The Dictionary of national biography. The concise dictionary; pt. 1. See The Dictionary of national biography. The concise dictionary; pt. 1   **920.03**

Smith, H. Shirley
The world's great bridges   **624**

Smith, Henry Nash
(ed.) Mark Twain   **813.09**

Smith, Hugh
(jt. comp.) Dunning, S. comp. Reflections on a gift of watermelon pickle . . . and other modern verse   **811.08**
(jt. comp.) Dunning, S. comp. Some haystacks don't even have any needle, and other complete modern poems   **811.08**

Smith, Huston
The religions of man   **291**

Smith, Irwin
Shakespeare's Globe Playhouse   **792.09**

Smith, Jean Wheeler
That she would dance no more
In Jones, L. ed. Black fire p486-99   **810.8**

Smith, John, 1580-1631
Smith, B. Captain John Smith: his life & legend   **92**
See also pages in the following books:
Johnston, M. Pioneers of the Old South p40-56   **975**
Woodward, G. S. Pocahontas p63-73   **92**

Smith, John Caswell
Fighter
In Clarke, J. H. ed. American Negro short stories p135-47   **S C**

Smith, Joseph
The Book of Mormon; criticism
In Downs, R. B. Books that changed America p26-35   **810.9**

Smith, Lacey Baldwin
Horizon Magazine. The Horizon Book of The Elizabethan world   **940.2**

Smith, LeRoi
How to fix up old cars   **629.28**

Smith, Margaret (Chase)
See pages in the following book:
Stoddard, H. Famous American women p387-98   **920**

Smith, Norris Kelly
Frank Lloyd Wright   **720.973**

Smith, Perry Edward
Capote, T. In cold blood   **364.1**

Smith, Richard Austin
The frontier states: Alaska [and] Hawaii   **917.3**

Smith, Ruth
(ed.) The tree of life   **291**

Smith, Sally Liberman
Nobody said it's easy   **155.5**

Smith, Theobald
See pages in the following book:
De Kruif, P. Microbe hunters p234-51   **920**

Smith, Whitney
The flag book of the United States **929.9**

Smith, William George
The Oxford Dictionary of English proverbs. See The Oxford Dictionary of English proverbs   **398.9**

Smith. Henry, O.
In Henry, O. The complete works of O. Henry p568-75   **S C**

Smithson, James
See pages in the following book:
Oehser, P. H. The Smithsonian Institution p4-15   **507.4**

The **Smithsonian** collection of automobiles and motorcycles. Oliver, S. H.   **629.22**

Smithsonian Institution
Coe, M. D. America's first civilizations   **970.3**
Jacobs, D. Bridges, canals & tunnels **624**
Oehser, P. H. The Smithsonian Institution   **507.4**
Oliver, S. H. The Smithsonian collection of automobiles and motorcycles **629.22**

National Collection of Fine Arts
See pages in the following book:
Oehser, P. H. The Smithsonian Institution p135-43   **507.4**

Smog. See Air—Pollution

Smoke. Vidal, G.
In Vidal, G. Visit to a small planet, and other television plays p217-33   **812**

Smoke and steel. Sandburg, C.
In Sandburg, C. The complete poems of Carl Sandburg p149-268   **811**

So Big. Ferber, E.   Fic

So human an animal. Dubos, R.   301.3

So peaceful in the country. Offord, C .R. *In* Clarke, J. H. ed. American Negro short stories p123-30   **S C**

So you want to be a social worker. Perlman, H. H.   361.069

Sobel, Lester A.
(ed.) News dictionary. *See* News dictionary   909.82

Soccer
See pages in the following book:
American Association for Health, Physical Education, and Recreation. Physical education for high school students p219-32   **613.7**

Social change
Diebold, J. Man and the computer 301.24
Hoffer, E. First things, last things   309.173
Mead, M. Culture and commitment 301.43
Millikan, M. F. ed. The emerging nations: their growth and United States policy   309.2
Roszak, T. The making of a counter culture   301.24
Toffler, A. Future shock   301.24

Social classes
Packard, V. The status seekers   301.44
See also pages in the following books:
Billington, R. A. America's frontier heritage p97-116   978
Boas, G. The history of ideas p167-86   109
Degler, C. N. Out of our past p40-48   973
Driver, H. E. Indians of North America p330-44   970.1
Page, R. I. Life in Anglo-Saxon England p45-65   914.2
Riesman, D. The lonely crowd p326-41   155.8
Schlesinger, A. M. The birth of the Nation p128-48   917.3
See also Aristocracy; Caste; Middle classes; Upper classes

Great Britain
See pages in the following books:
Priestley, J. B. The Edwardians p55-78, 97-109   914.2
Williams, P. Life in Tudor England p46-76   914.2

Social conditions. See Economic conditions; Indians of North America—Social conditions; Labor and laboring classes; Negroes—Moral and social conditions; Social problems; and names of countries, cities, etc. with the subdivision Social conditions, e.g. United States—Social conditions

Social conflict. See Conflict of generations

Social conformity. See Conformity

Social customs. See names of countries, cities, etc. with the subdivision Social life and customs, e.g. United States—Social life and customs

Social distinctions. See Social classes

Social equality. See Equality

Social ethics
Friends, Society of. American Friends Service Committee. Who shall live?   301.3
See also Christian ethics; Sexual ethics

Social evolution. See Social change

Social group work
Howard, J. Please touch   301.4

Social hygiene. See Hygiene; Venereal diseases

Social insurance. See Insurance, Social

Social life and customs. See names of countries, cities, etc. with the subdivision Social life and customs, e.g. United States—Social life and customs

Social policy
Millikan, M. F. ed. The emerging nations: their growth and United States policy   309.2
See also names of countries, cities, etc. with the subdivision Social policy, e.g. United States—Social policy

Social problems
Chase, S. The proper study of mankind   300
Harrington, M. The other America 301.44
Weinberg, A. ed. The muckrakers 309.173
See also Migrant labor; Race problems; Social ethics; Tenement houses

Indexes
Dunlap, J. R. comp. Debate index 016.301

Poetry
Lowenfels, W. ed. The writing on the wall   811.08

Social problems and the church. See Church and social problems

Social psychology
Fromm, E. Escape from freedom   323.4
Fromm, E. The sane society   323.4
McLuhan, M. Culture is our business   301.2
Riesman, D. The lonely crowd   155.8
Whyte, W. H. The organization man   301.15
See also pages in the following book:
Sargent, S. S. Basic teachings of the great psychologists p288-320   **150**
See also Human relations

Social sciences
Chase, S. The proper study of mankind   300
See also Economics; Political science; Social change; Sociology

Dictionaries
Encyclopaedia of the social sciences 303
International Encyclopedia of the social sciences   303
The Lincoln library of social studies 031

Social security. See Insurance, Social

Social service. See Social work

Social settlements
See pages in the following book:
Addams, J. The social thought of Jane Addams p28-43, 183-217   309.173

Socrates—*Continued*

Russell, B. A history of Western philosophy p82-93   109

Thomas, H. Understanding the great philosophers p83-93   109

Thomas, N. Great dissenters p19-48   920

Sodium

See pages in the following books:

Asimov, I. Building blocks of the universe p149-61   546

Snively, W. D. The sea of life p54-72   612

Softball

See pages in the following book:

American Association for Health, Physical Education, and Recreation. Physical education for high school students p59-78   613.7

Soil. United States. Department of Agriculture   631.4

Soil conservation

Simms, D. H. The Soil Conservation Service   353.81

See also pages in the following books:

Dodd, E. Careers for the '70s: conservation p140-46   333.7069

Moss, F. E. The water crisis p181-91   333.9

United States. Department of Agriculture. After a hundred years p187-208   353.81

United States. Department of Agriculture. Power to produce p107-13   631.3

See also Erosion

Soil Conservation Service. See United States. Soil Conservation Service

The **Soil** Conservation Service. Simms, D. H.   353.81

Soil erosion. See Erosion

Soil fertility. See Soils

Soils

United States. Department of Agriculture. Soil   631.4

See also pages in the following books:

Ehrlich, P. R. Population, resources, environment p163-67, 184-90   301.3

Scientific American. Plant agriculture p86-95   581

United States. Department of Agriculture. Grass p49-66   633

United States. Department of Agriculture. Water p121-59   631.7

See also Erosion; Fertilizers and manures; Irrigation; Reclamation of land

Sola, Ralph de. See De Sola, Ralph

Solar energy

See pages in the following book:

Sterland, E. G. Energy into power p18-67   621

Solar heat. See Solar energy

Solar physics. See Sun

Solar power. See Solar energy

Solar radiation

See pages in the following book:

Chandler, T. J. The air around us p32-41   551.5

Solar system

Edson, L. Worlds around the sun   523.2

Nourse, A. E. Nine planets   523.4

See also pages in the following books:

Jastrow, R. Red giants and white dwarfs p64-71   523.1

Ley, W. Another look at Atlantis, and fifteen other essays p215-29   508

See also Earth; Moon; Planets; Sun

The **solar** system and back. Asimov, I.   508

Soldier Key. Lanier, S. E.

In Hitchcock, A. ed. Alfred Hitchcock presents: A month of mystery p401-28   S C

Soldiers

See also Generals

Fiction

Dos Passos, J. Three soldiers   Fic

Mailer, N. The naked and the dead   Fic

Soldier's home. Hemingway, E.

In Hemingway, E. In our time p87-101   S C

In Hemingway, E. The short stories of Ernest Hemingway p143-53   S C

Soldiers' songs. See War songs

Soledad brother. Jackson, G.   92

The **solid** gold Cadillac. Kaufman, G. S.

In Gassner, J. ed. Best American plays: 4th ser. p611-41   812.08

Solo on the drums. Petry, A.

In Clarke, J. H. ed. American Negro short stories p165-69   S C

Sologub, F.

Hide and seek

In Seltzer, T. comp. Best Russian short stories p212-27   S C

Solomon, Louis

America goes to press   071

Solomon Islands

See pages in the following book:

Shadbolt, M. Isles of the South Pacific p172-88   919

Solomons, Gus

See pages in the following book:

McDonagh, D. The rise and fall and rise of modern dance p162-73   793.3

Solzhenitsyn, Aleksandr Isaevich. See Solzhenitsyn, Alexander

Solzhenitsyn, Alexander

For the good of the cause

In Solzhenitsyn, A. Stories and prose poems p53-123   S C

One day in the life of Ivan Denisovich   Fic

Stories and prose poems   S C

Short stories included are: Matryona's house; The Easter procession; Zakhar-the-Pouch; The right hand; An incident at Krechetovka Station

About

Labedz, L. ed. Solzhenitsyn: a documentary record   92

See also pages in the following books:

Durant, W. Interpretations of life p321-32   809

Posell, E. Z. Russian authors p218-35   920

Some haystacks don't even have any needle, and other complete modern poems. Dunning, S. comp.   811.08
Some learned fables for good old boys and girls. Twain, M.
In Twain, M. The complete short stories of Mark Twain p105-21 **S C**
Some like them cold. Lardner, R.
In Lardner, R. The best short stories of Ring Lardner p303-20 **S C**
In Lardner, R. The Ring Lardner reader p196-214 **S C**
Some part of myself. Dobie, J. F.   92
Some words with a mummy. Poe, E. A.
In Poe, E. A. The complete tales and poems of Edgar Allan Poe p535-48 **S C**
The somebody. Santiago, D.
In The Best American short stories, 1971 p291-97 **S C**
Somebody turned on a tap in these kids. Larrick, N. ed.   811.09
Somerlott, Robert
Eskimo pies
In The Best American short stories, 1965 p291-98 **S C**
Something childish but very natural. Mansfield, K.
In Mansfield, K. The short stories of Katherine Mansfield p164-83 **S C**
Something in a boat. Fallon, P.
In Garrity, D. A. ed. 44 Irish short stories p91-109 **S C**
Something in common. Hughes, L.
In Hughes, L. The Langston Hughes reader p34-37   818
Something lost. Schaefer, J.
In Schaefer, J. The collected stories of Jack Schaefer p179-98 **S C**
Somme, Battle of the, 1916
Horne, A. Death of a generation   940.4
The son avenger. Undset, S.
In Undset, S. The master of Hestviken v4 **Fic**
Son in the afternoon. Williams, J. A.
In Hughes, L. ed. The best short stories by Negro writers p288-94 **S C**
In Margolies, E. A native son's reader p230-37   810.8
A son of the celestial. Cather, W.
In Cather, W. Willa Cather's Collected short fiction, 1892-1912 v3 p523-28 **S C**
A son of the middle border. Garland, H.   92
Sone, Monica
Nisei daughter   92
Song and garden birds of North America. National Geographic Society   598
The song and the sergeant. Henry, O.
In Henry, O. The complete works of O. Henry p1188-93 **S C**
Song of the flying fish. Chesterton, G. K.
In Chesterton, G. K. The Father Brown omnibus p684-704 **S C**
The song of the lark. Cather, W. **Fic**
Song of the simidor. Radcliffe, D.
In The Best American short stories, 1967 p211-37 **S C**

Song without end; the love story of Clara and Robert Schumann. White, H.   92
Songhai
See pages in the following book:
Davidson, B. The lost cities of Africa p98-107, 117-20   913.6
Songmy, Vietnam
Hersh, S. M. My Lai 4   959.7
Songs
Bacharach, B. The Bacharach and David Song book   784
Gilbert, Sir W. S. Martyn Green's Treasury of Gilbert & Sullivan   782.8
See also pages in the following book:
The New York Times. Guide to listening pleasure p134-45   780.1
See also Music, Popular (Songs, etc.); National songs; Negro songs
Songs, American
American Heritage. The American Heritage Songbook   784.4
Ewen, D. Great men of American popular song   920
Rodgers, R. The Rodgers and Hammerstein Song book   782.8
See also Folk songs—United States
Dictionaries
Ewen, D. ed. American popular songs   784.03
History and criticism
Krythe, M. R. Sampler of American songs   784.09
Songs, Popular. See Music, Popular (Songs, etc.)
Songs after Lincoln. Horgan, P.   811
Songs for my supper. Service, R.
In Service, R. More collected verse v5   811
Songs of a sun-lover. Service, R.
In Service, R. More collected verse v 1   811
Songs of innocence and experience. Blake, W.
In Blake, W. The portable Blake   828
Sonnets from the Portuguese. Browning, E. B.   821
also in Browning, R. How do I love thee? p204-25   92
The sonnets, songs & poems of Shakespeare. Shakespeare, W.   821
Sonny's blues. Baldwin, J.
In Baldwin, J. Going to meet the man p101-41 **S C**
Sons and lovers. Lawrence, D. H. **Fic**
The sons of Martha. McKenna, R.
In The Best American short stories, 1968 p215-33 **S C**
The Sooey pill. Slater, E.
In Best detective stories of the year [1969] p78-82 **S C**
Soper, Tony
(jt. auth.) Sparks, J. Owls: their natural and unnatural history   598
Sophistication. Anderson, S.
In Anderson, S. Winesburg, Ohio (Modern Lib) p285-98 **S C**
In Anderson, S. Winesburg, Ohio (Viking) p233-43 **S C**

Sophocles
Ajax
In Oates, W. J. ed. The complete Greek
drama v 1 p315-60   882.08
Antigone
In Bentley, E. comp. The great play-
wrights v 1 p155-88   808.82
In Fitts, D. ed. Greek plays in mod-
ern translation p455-99   882.08
In Oates, W. J. ed. The complete Greek
drama v 1 p423-59   882.08
Electra
In Fitts, D. ed. Greek plays in mod-
ern translation p59-105   882.08
In Oates, W. J. ed. The complete Greek
drama v 1 p505-49   882.08
King Oedipus
In Bentley, E. comp. The great play-
wrights v 1 p93-122   808.82
In Fitts, D. ed. Greek plays in mod-
ern translation p345-82   882.08
Oedipus; criticism
In Grant, M. Myths of the Greeks and
Romans p215-37   292
Oedipus at Colonus
In Fitts, D. ed. Greek plays in mod-
ern translations p383-454   882.08
In Oates, W. J. ed. The complete
Greek drama v 1 p613-69   882.08
Oedipus the King
In Oates, W. J. ed. The complete
Greek drama v 1 p369-417 882.08
Philoctetes
In Oates, W. J. ed. The complete
Greek drama v 1 p555-607 882.08
The Trachiniae
In Oates, W. J. ed. The complete
Greek drama v 1 p465-99 882.08

About
See pages in the following books:
Gassner, J. Masters of the drama p40-55
809.2
Hamilton, E. The Greek way p258-70
880.9
Nicoll, A. World drama p51-68   809.2
Payne, R. Ancient Greece p270-89 913.38
Sophocles' King Oedipus. Yeats, W. B.
In Yeats, W. B. Collected plays of
W. B. Yeats p303-28   822
Sophocles' Oedipus at Colonus. Yeats,
W. B.
In Yeats, W. B. Collected plays of
W. B. Yeats p329-61   822
Soporifics. See Narcotics
The **sorcerer.** Gilbert, Sir W. S.
In Gilbert, Sir W. S. The complete
plays of Gilbert and Sullivan p61-
97   782.8
In Gilbert, Sir W. S. Martyn Green's
Treasury of Gilbert & Sullivan
782.8
Sorcery. See Occult sciences; Witchcraft
Sorensen, Theodore C.
Kennedy [biography of John Fitzgerald
Kennedy]   92
The Kennedy legacy   973.922
Sorrow rides a fast horse. Butters, D. G.
In Engle, P. ed. On creative writing
p67-77   808.02

Sorry, wrong number. Fletcher, L.
In Cerf, B. ed. 24 favorite one-act
plays p117-32   808.82
Souchal, François
Art of the early Middle Ages   709.02
Soul gone home. Hughes, L.
In Hughes, L. Five plays p37-42 812
In Hughes, L. The Langston Hughes
reader p239-43   818
The **soul** of Laploshka. Saki
In Saki. The short stories of Saki
p78-82   S C
Soul on ice. Cleaver, E.   301.451
Soule, Gardner
The greatest depths   551.4
UFOs and IFOs   629.133
Souls belated. Wharton, E.
In Wharton, E. The collected short
stories of Edith Wharton v 1 p104-
26   S C
The **souls** of Black folk. Du Bois, W. E. B.
301.451
Sound
Stevens, S. S. Sound and hearing   534
See also pages in the following books:
Still, H. In quest of quiet p166-79 614
United Nations Educational, Scientific and
Cultural Organization. 700 science ex-
periments for everyone p131-40   507.2
See also Hearing

Recording and reproducing
Oates, S. C. Audiovisual equipment **371.33**
See also pages in the following book:
Ferguson, R. How to make movies p54-
61   778.5
See also High-fidelity sound systems;
Tape and wire recorders
Sound and fury. Henry, O.
In Henry, O. The complete works of
O. Henry p1012-15   S C
Sound and hearing. Stevens, S. S.   534
The **sound** and the fury. Faulkner, W. Fic
also in Faulkner, W. The Faulkner
reader   S C
Sound of a drunken drummer. Blattner,
W. W.
In Foley, M. ed. Fifty best American
short stories, 1915-1965 p720-59
S C
The **sound** of apples. Young, S.
In The Best short plays of 1957-1958
p121-58   808.82
The **sound** of laughter, Bennett Cerf's. Cerf,
B. comp.   817.08
The **sound** of music. Lindsay, H.   812
The **sound** of summer running. Bradbury, R.
In Bradbury, R. R is for rocket p227-
33   S C
A **sound** of thunder. Bradbury, R.
In Bradbury, R. R is for rocket p79-93
S C
The **sound** of waves. Mishima, Y.   Fic
Sound waves
Kock, W. E. Sound waves and light waves
534
Van Bergeijk, W. A. Waves and the ear
534

Stallings, Laurence—*Continued*
About
See pages in the following book:
Krutch, J. W. The American drama since 1918 p27-60   812.09
Stalvey, Lois Mark
The education of a WASP   301.45
Stamitz, Johann Wenzel-Anton
See pages in the following book:
Chapin, V. The violin and its masters p64-69   920
Stamm, James R.
A short history of Spanish literature 860.9
Stamp collectors' handbook. Reinfeld, F.   383.2
The **stampeding** of Lady Bastable. Saki
In Saki. The short stories of Saki p131-34   **S C**
Stamps, Postage. See Postage stamps
Standard college dictionary, Funk & Wagnalls   423
Standard dictionary of folklore, mythology, and legend, Funk & Wagnalls 398.03
Standard dictionary of the English language, Funk & Wagnalls. International ed. 423
Standard dictionary of the English language, Funk & Wagnalls New   423
Standard handbook for secretaries. Hutchinson, L.   651.02
Standard handbook of synonyms, antonyms, and prepositions, Funk and Wagnalls. Fernald, J. C.   424
Standard postage stamp catalogue, Scott's. Scott Publications, inc.   383.2
Standards for school library programs. See American Association of School Librarians. Standards for school media programs   371.33
Standards for school media programs. American Association of School Librarians   371.33
Standing Bear, Luther, Dakota chief
See pages in the following book:
Brown, D. Bury my heart at Wounded Knee p352-66   970.4
Stanford, Leland
See pages in the following book:
Stone, I. Men to match my mountains p201-03, 231-34, 288-300   979.1
Stanton, Elizabeth (Cady)
See pages in the following book:
Commager, H. S. Crusaders for freedom p153-60   920
Stapley, Ray
The car owner's handbook   629.28
The **star**. Wells, H. G.
In Wells, H. G. The complete short stories of H. G. Wells p644-55 **S C**
In Wells, H. G. 28 science fiction stories p680-91   **S C**
Star begotten. Wells, H. G.
In Wells, H. G. 28 science fiction stories p510-635   **S C**
Star light. Asimov, I.
In Asimov, I. Asimov's mysteries p174-77   **S C**

Stars
Bova, B. In quest of quasars   523.8
See also pages in the following books:
Gamow, G. The creation of the universe p112-36   523.1
Hodge, P. W. The revolution in astronomy p41-53   523
Jastrow, R. Red giants and white dwarfs p38-53   523.1
Nourse, A. E. Universe, earth, and atom p370-77, 381-88, 403-20   530.9
Scientific American. Frontiers in astronomy p120-64   520
See also Astronomy; Solar system
Atlases
Howard, N. E. The telescope handbook and star atlas   522
The **stars** in their courses. Asimov, I. 508
Starter List for New Branch & New Libraries Collection Committee. See Public Library Association. Starter List for New Branch & New Libraries Collection Committee
Starting from scratch. Sheckley, R.
In The Best from Fantasy and Science Fiction; 19th ser. p267-71   **S C**
Stashinskiĭ, Bogdan Nikolaevich
See pages in the following book:
Dulles, A. ed. Great true spy stories p337-50   327
The **State**
Ward, B. Nationalism and ideology 320.1
See also Political science
History
See pages in the following book:
Bailey, C. ed. Legacy of Rome p91-139   913.37
State and agriculture. See Agriculture and state
State and church. See Church and state
State and education. See Education and state
State and environment. See Environmental policy
State and science. See Science and state
State church. See Church and state
State Department. See United States. Department of State
State governments
The American Assembly. The states and the urban crisis   309.2
See also pages in the following book:
James, H. Crisis in the courts p244-60   347.9
See also names of states with the subdivision Politics and government, e.g. Connecticut—Politics and government
Yearbooks
The Book of the States   353.9
State of siege. Camus, A.
In Camus, A. Caligula & 3 other plays p135-232   842
State of the union. Lindsay, H.
In Gassner, J. ed. Best American plays 3d ser. p455-503   812.08
States, New
Kenworthy, L. S. Leaders of new nations   920

Stewart, Desmond
The Arab world   915.3
Early Islam   915.6
Turkey   915.61
Stewart, George R.
American place-names   910.3
Fire   Fic
Storm   Fic
Stewart, John L.
John Crowe Ransom
In Unger, L. ed. Seven modern American poets p155-90   811.09
Stewart, Mary
Airs above the ground   Fic
The crystal cave   Fic
My brother Michael   Fic
This rough magic   Fic
Stewart, Natacha
Chopin
In The New Yorker. Stories from The New Yorker, 1950-1960 p137-40   S C
The **stick** up. Killens, J. O.
In Hughes, L. ed. The best short stories by Negro writers p188-91   S C
Sticks and stones. Mumford, L.   720.973
Stiegel, Henry William
See pages in the following book:
Langdon, W. C. Everyday things in American life, 1607-1776 p199-210   917.3
Stieri, Emanuele
(jt. auth.) Adams, J. T. Complete woodworking handbook   684
Still, Henry
In quest of quiet   614
Still, William
See pages in the following book:
Bontemps, A. Anyplace but here p34-42   301.451
The **still** alarm. Kaufman, G. S.
In Cerf, B. ed. 24 favorite one-act plays p229-37   808.82
Still hungry in America. Coles, R.   330.973
Still is the night. Baldwin, F.
In Becker, M. L. ed. The home book of Christmas p674-78   394.26
Still life. Updike, J.
In Updike, J. Pigeon feathers, and other stories   S C
Still-life painting
See pages in the following book:
Schwarz, M. The age of the Rococo p127-43   759.04
Still More Numbers: fun & facts. Friend, J. N.   793.7
Still waters of the air. Lewis, R. ed.   861.08
Stillman, Edmund
The Balkans   914.96
American Heritage. The American Heritage History of the 20's & 30's   917.3
A **stillness** at Appomattox. Catton, B.   973.7
Stilwell, Joseph Warren
Tuchman, B. W. Stilwell and the American experience in China, 1911-45   327.73
Stimulants
See pages in the following book:
Driver, H. E. Indians of North America p105-15   970.1
See also Alcohol; Narcotics

Stinetorf, Louise A.
White witch doctor   Fic
Stirling, Nora
Who wrote the modern classics?   920
Stitchery and crafts, Better Homes & Gardens. Better Homes and Gardens   746
Stobart, J. C.
The glory that was Greece   913.38
The **stock**-broker's clerk. Doyle, Sir A. C.
In Doyle, Sir A. C. The complete Sherlock Holmes v 1 p415-29   S C
Stock exchange
Friedlander, J. K. Stock market ABC   332.6
Tyler, P. ed. Securities, exchanges, and the SEC   332.6
See also pages in the following book:
Weinberg, A. ed. The muckrakers p261-82   309.173
See also Wall Street
Fiction
Auchincloss, L. The embezzler   Fic
Stock market. See Stock exchange
Stock market ABC. Friedlander, J. K.   332.6
Stockhausen, Karlheinz
See pages in the following book:
Ewen, D. Composers of tomorrow's music p107-19   920
Stockholm
Public works
See pages in the following book:
Scientific American. Cities p75-87   309.2
The **stockings** of Major André. Lancaster, B.
In Dulles, A. ed. Great spy stories from fiction p31-46   S C
Stocks
Friedlander, J. K. Stock market ABC   332.6
See also Stock exchange
Stockton, Frank R.
The lady or the tiger?
In Day, A. G. ed. The greatest American short stories p113-21   S C
In The Scribner treasury p61-67   S C
Stockton, Richard F.
A fabulous tale
In The Best short plays of 1957-1958 p59-80   808.82
Stoddard, Charles Warren
On the reef
In Day, A. G. ed. The spell of Hawaii p165-79   919.69
Stoddard, Hope
Famous American women   920
Stoics
See pages in the following book:
Russell, B. A history of Western philosophy p252-70   109
Stokely, James
(jt. auth.) Dykeman, W. The border states   917.5
Stoker, Bram
Dracula   Fic
Stokley, James
The new world of the atom   621.48
Stokowski, Leopold
See pages in the following book:
Ewen, D. Famous modern conductors p11-30   920

The story of Jees Uck. London, J.
In London, J. Best short stories of Jack
London p156-75 **S C**

The story of Keesh. London, J.
In London, J. Best short stories of Jack
London p183-90 **S C**

The story of language. Pei, M. 400

A story of love, etc. Curley, D.
In The Best American short stories,
1964 p85-93 **S C**

The story of man. Coon, C. S. 572

The story of man and the stars. See
Moore, P. Suns, myths and men 523

The story of mankind. Van Loon, H. W. 909

The story of modern art. Cheney, S. 709.03

The story of Muhammad Din. Kipling, R.
In Kipling, R. The best short stories of
Rudyard Kipling p18-20 **S C**

The story of my experiments with truth. See
Gandhi, M. K. Gandhi's autobiography
92

The story of my life. Darrow, C. 92

The story of my life. Keller, H. 92

The story of nursing. Dodge, B. S. 610.73

The story of philosophy. Durant, W. 109

The story of St Vespaluus. Saki
In Saki. The short stories of Saki p185-
93 **S C**

The story of South Africa. See Marquard, L.
A short history of South Africa 968

The story of the bad little boy. Twain, M.
In Twain, M. The complete short stories
of Mark Twain p6-9 **S C**

Story of the bandbox. Stevenson, R. L.
In Stevenson, R. L. The complete short
stories of Robert Louis Stevenson
p110-37 **S C**

The story of the Common Market.
Savage, K. 382

The story of the crusades, 1097-1291. Duggan, A. 940.1

A story of the days to come. Wells, H. G.
In Wells, H. G. The complete short
stories of H. G. Wells p715-806
S C

In Wells, H. G. 28 science fiction stories
p730-820 **S C**

The story of the English language. Pei, M.
420.9

The story of the good little boy. Twain, M.
In Twain, M. The complete short stories
of Mark Twain p67-70 **S C**

Story of the house with the green blinds.
Stevenson, R. L.
In Stevenson, R. L. The complete short
stories of Robert Louis Stevenson
p154-88 **S C**

The story of the laser. Carroll, J. M. 621.32

The story of the last trump. Wells, H. G.
In Wells, H. G. The complete short
stories of H. G. Wells p589-604
S C

The story of the late Mr Elvesham. Wells,
H. G.
In Wells, H. G. The complete short
stories of H. G. Wells p359-76 **S C**

The story of the Old Ram. Twain, M.
In Twain, M. The complete short stories
of Mark Twain p78-81 **S C**

The story of the Olympic games: 776 B.C. to
[date] Kieran, J. 796.4

The story of the other wise man. Van
Dyke, H. **Fic**

Story of the physician and the Saratoga
trunk. Stevenson, R. L.
In Stevenson, R. L. The complete short
stories of Robert Louis Stevenson
p59-87 **S C**
In Stevenson, R. L. The strange case
of Dr Jekyll and Mr Hyde, and
other famous tales p293-319 **S C**

The story of the Second World War.
Reeder, R. 940.53

The story of the Spanish-American War.
Reeder, R. 973.8

A story of the Stone age. Wells, H. G.
In Wells, H. G. The complete short
stories of H. G. Wells p656-714 **S C**
In Wells, H. G. 28 science fiction stories
p360-417 **S C**

The story of the Trapp Family Singers.
Trapp, M. A. 92

The story of the widow's son. Lavin, M.
In Garrity, D. A. ed. 44 Irish short
stories p152-65 **S C**

The story of the world's literature. Macy, J.
809

Story of the young man in Holy Orders.
Stevenson, R. L.
In Stevenson, R. L. The complete short
stories of Robert Louis Stevenson
p137-54 **S C**

Story of the young man with the cream
tarts. Stevenson, R. L.
In Stevenson, R. L. The complete short
stories of Robert Louis Stevenson
p25-59 **S C**
In Stevenson, R. L. The strange case
of Dr Jekyll and Mr Hyde, and
other famous tales p262-93 **S C**

The story of two dogs. Lessing, D.
In Lessing, D. African stories p616-36
S C

The story of world religions. Savage, K. 291

The story of Yonosuke. Akutagawa, R.
In Akutagawa, R. Japanese short stories
p212-24 **S C**

The story-teller. Saki
In Saki. The short stories of Saki p391-
96 **S C**

A story without an end. Twain, M.
In Twain, M. The complete short stories
of Mark Twain p343-49 **S C**

Stout, Rex
Instead of evidence
In Haycraft, H. ed. A treasury of great
mysteries v2 p209-44 **S C**

Stoutenburg, Adrien
Explorer of the unconscious: Sigmund
Freud 92

The stove. Crane, S.
In Crane, S. The complete short stories
& sketches of Stephen Crane p701-
10 **S C**

Stowe, Harriet Beecher
Christmas Eve in old New England
In Becker, M. L. ed. The home book of
Christmas p615-21 394.26

Streetcorner man. Borges, J. L.
In Borges, J. L. The Aleph, and other stories, 1933-1969 p33-42   S C

Streets
Rudofsky, B. Streets for people   711

Streets for people. Rudofsky, B.   711

The **strength** of God. Anderson, S.
In Anderson, S. Winesburg, Ohio (Modern Lib) p171-83   S C
In Anderson, S. Winesburg, Ohio (Viking) p147-56   S C

The **strength** of the strong. London, J.
In London, J. Jack London's Tales of adventure   S C

Strength to love. King, M. L.   252

Strickland, John Douglas Hipwell
See pages in the following book:
Behrman, D. The new world of the oceans p88-106   551.4

Strictly business. Henry, O.
In Henry, O. The complete works of O. Henry p1484-1631   S C

Strictly business [short story]. Henry, O.
In Henry, O. The complete works of O. Henry p1484-93   S C

Strictly dishonorable. Sturges, P.
In Gassner, J. ed. Twenty-five best plays of the modern American theatre; early ser. p613-46   812.08

Stride toward freedom. King, M. L. 323.4

Strider: the story of a horse. Tolstoy, L.
In Tolstoy, L. Short stories v 1 p377-418   S C

Strife. Galsworth, J.
In Dickinson, T. H. ed. Chief contemporary dramatists [1st ser] p111-47   808.82
In Galsworthy, J. Plays p67-105   822

The **strike.** Michener, J.
In Michener, J. Tales of the South Pacific p278-97   S C

Strikebreaker. Asimov, I.
In Asimov, I. Nightfall, and other stories p268-81   S C

Strikes and lockouts. See Collective bargaining; Labor unions

Strindberg, August
Comrades
In Tucker, S. M. ed. Twenty-five modern plays p43-69   808.82

The father
In Dickinson, T. H. ed. Chief contemporary dramatists [1st ser] p599-625   808.82

The ghost sonata
In Block, H. M. ed. Masters of modern drama p113-25   808.82

Miss Julie
In Bentley, E. comp. The great playwrights v2 p1391-1423   808.82
In Block, H. M. ed. Masters of modern drama p94-111   808.82
In Cerf, B. ed. Thirty famous one-act plays p29-58   808.82

About
See pages in the following book:
Nicoll, A. World drama p547-63   809.2

Stroessner, Alfredo, President Paraguay
See pages in the following book:
Gunther, J. Inside South America p239-45   980

Strong, Austin
Drums of Oude
In Cerf, B. ed. Thirty famous one-act plays p287-301   808.82

Strong, Jonathan
Patients
In Prize stories, 1970: The O. Henry awards p83-91   S C

Xavier Fereira's unfinished book: chapter one
In The Best American short stories, 1971 p298-315   S C

Stroud, Parry
Stephen, P. Stephen Vincent Benét 818

Stroven, Carl
(jt. ed.) Day, A. G. ed. The spell of Hawaii   919.69

The **struggle** for survival. Janeway, E.   355.2

Strunk, William
The elements of style   808

Elements of style; criticism
In White, E. B. The points of my compass p115-23   818

Struther, Jan
Mrs Miniver   Fic

Three stockings
In Becker, M. L. ed. The home book of Christmas p377-79   394.26

Stuart, Don A.
Night
In Asimov, I. ed. Where do we go from here? p36-63   S C

Stuart, Gene S.
(jt. auth.) Stuart, G. E. Discovering man's past in the Americas   913.7

Stuart, George E.
Discovering man's past in the Americas   913.7

Stuart, Jesse
The accident
In The Best American short stories, 1967 p279-89   S C

Come back to the farm   S C
Contents: Appalachian patriarch; Why Menifee wasn't our country; Give Charlie a little time; Maybelle's first-born; Victory and the dream; Wild plums; The best years of our lives; The builders and the dream; Little giant; The highest bidder; A pilgrim out in space; The twelve-pole road; Lost land of youth; Holiday with the Larks; Uncle Mel comes to the aid of his clan; Eighty-one summers

Dawn of remembered spring
In Foley, M. ed. Fifty best American short stories, 1915-1965 p323-29   S C

A Jesse Stuart reader   818
Stories included are: Nest egg; The thing you love; Uncle Jeff had a way; No hero; Rain on Tanyard Hollow; Battle with the bees; Ezra Alcorn and April; Wild plums; The Great Cherokee Bill; The moon child from Wolfe Creek; This farm for sale; As ye sow, so shall ye reap; No petty thief; Miss Anna's asleep; Old Op and the Devil; A ribbon for Baldy; Tradelast; Fight number twenty-five

Mr Gallion's school   Fic

Stuart, Jesse—*Continued*

Plowshare in heaven   **S C**

Contents: Zeke Hammertight; Walk in the moon shadows; A land beyond the river; Rich men; Sylvania is dead; The wind blew east; Sunday afternoon hanging; The reaper and the flowers; How sportsmanship came to Carver College; Love in the spring; Settin'-up with Grandma; Bird-Neck; The chase of the skittish heifer; Before the grand jury; The champions; Death and decision; Alec's cabin; Old Dick; Grandpa; The Devil and television; Plowshare in heaven

The thread that runs so true   92

To teach, to love   92

About

Foster, R. E. Jesse Stuart   818

Stuart, Ruth McEnery

Christmas guest

In Becker, M. L. ed. The home book of Christmas p642-49   394.26

Stuart, House of

See pages in the following book:

The New Cambridge Modern history v4 p531-84   909

Stuart England, Life in. Ashley, M.   914.2

Stubby Pringle's Christmas. Schaefer, J.

In Schaefer, J. The collected stories of Jack Schaefer p508-20   **S C**

Stuckey, W. J.

The Pulitzer Prize novels   813.09

Stud. Gottlieb, A.

In The Best short plays, 1969 p365-403   808.82

The student. Chekhov, A.

In Chekhov, A. The image of Chekhov p219-23   **S C**

Student aid. See Scholarships, fellowships, etc.; Student loan funds

Student guidance. See Vocational guidance

The student journalist and the critical review. Shaff, A. L.   371.89

Student loan funds

Proia, N. C. Barron's Handbook of American college financial aid   378.3

Proia, N. C. Barron's Handbook of junior and community college financial aid   378.3

See also Scholarships, fellowships, etc.

Student Nonviolent Coordinating Committee

Belfrage, S. Freedom summer   323.4

Students

Lass, A. H. The college student's handbook   378.102

See also Education

Anecdotes, facetiae, satire, etc.

Kampen, I. Due to lack of interest tomorrow has been canceled   378.1

United States

Bander, E. J. ed. Turmoil on the campus   378.1

Birmingham, J. ed. Our time is now   373.1

Foster, J. ed. Protest! Student activism in America   378.1

Keniston, K. Young radicals   301.43

Kunen, J. S. The strawberry statement—notes of a college revolutionary   378.1

Libarle, M. ed. The high school revolutionaries   371.8

Pope, L. The right college   378.73

United States. President's Commission on Campus Unrest. The report of the President's Commission on Campus Unrest   378.1

See also pages in the following books:

Fortune (Periodical) Youth in turmoil p47-57   301.43

Gross, B. ed. Radical school reform p139-47   370.8

The studio. Time-Life Books   778

Study, Courses of. See Education—Curricula

Study abroad   378.3

A study in scarlet. Doyle, Sir A. C.

In Doyle, Sir A. C. The complete Sherlock Holmes v 1 p3-88   **S C**

A study of the USSR and communism: an historical approach. Rieber, A. J.   914.7

Sturgeon, Theodore

The man who learned loving

In The Best from Fantasy and Science Fiction; 19th ser. p213-22   **S C**

Tiny and the monster

In Conklin, G. ed. Invaders of earth p100-33   **S C**

Sturges, Preston

Strictly dishonorable

In Gassner, J. ed. Twenty-five best plays of the modern American theatre; early ser. p613-46   812.08

Sturm, Carol

The kid who fractioned

In The Best American short stories, 1967 p291-301   **S C**

Style, Literary. See Rhetoric

Style in dress. See Costume; Fashion

Style manual. United States. Government printing office   655.2

Style manuals. See Printing—Style manuals

Styron, William

The confessions of Nat Turner   **Fic**

Subconsciousness. See Psychoanalysis; Sleep

Subgravity state. See Weightlessness

Subject catalogs. See Catalogs, Subject

Subject guide to Books in print   015

Subject headings

Sears List of subject headings   025.33

A subject of scandal and concern. Osborne, J.

In Richards, S. ed. Best short plays of the world theatre, 1958-1967 p257-73   808.82

The subject was roses. Gilroy, F. D.

In Gassner, J. ed. Best American plays; 6th ser. p567-94   812.08

Submarine! Beach, E. L.   940.54

Submarine boats. See Submarines

Submarine diving. See Skin and scuba diving

Submarine photography. See Photography, Submarine

Submarine warfare. See Submarines

Submarines

Sweeney, J. B. A pictorial history of oceanographic submersibles   **623.82**

See also pages in the following book:

Holbrook, S. H. Lost men of American history p62-69   **920**

See also Nautilus (Submarine)

Fiction

Beach, E. Run silent, run deep   **Fic**

Submarines, Atomic. See Atomic submarines

Subscription Books Bulletin reviews. The Booklist and Subscription Books Bulletin   **011**

A **subtreasury** of American humor; abridged. White, E. B. ed.   **817.08**

Suburban areas. See Metropolitan areas

A **suburban** fairy tale. Mansfield, K.

In Mansfield, K. The short stories of Katherine Mansfield p310-14   **S C**

Suburban life

Goldston, R. Suburbia: civic denial   **301.3**

See also pages in the following book:

Gross, B. ed. Radical school reform p59-92   **370.8**

Suburban tigress. Treat, L.

In Mystery Writers of America. Crime without murder p289-301   **S C**

Suburbia: civil denial. Goldston, R.   **301.3**

Subversive activities

Goodman, W. The Committee   **328.73**

See also Political crimes and offenses; Spies

A **subway** named Mobius. Deutsch, A. J.

In Asimov, I. ed. Where do we go from here? p149-70   **S C**

The **successful** secretary's handbook. Becker, E. R.   **651.02**

Succulent plants

Lamb, E. The pocket encyclopedia of cacti and succulents in color   **635.9**

Such a sweet old lady. Mansfield, K.

In Mansfield, K. The short stories of Katherine Mansfield p664-66   **S C**

Such is life. Wedekind, F.

In Dickinson, T. H. ed. Chief contemporary dramatists, 3d ser. p195-227   **808.82**

Sucker. McCullers, C.

In The Best American short stories, 1964 p217-26   **S C**

In The Saturday Evening Post. Best modern short stories p128-37   **S C**

Sudan

Brander, B. The River Nile   **916.2**

See also pages in the following book:

Davidson, B. The lost cities of Africa p51-124   **913.6**

Sudermann, Hermann

The vale of content

In Dickinson, T. H. ed. Chief contemporary dramatists [1st ser] p439-69   **808.82**

Suetonius Tranquillus, Caius

See pages in the following book:

Grant, M. The ancient historians p329-40   **920**

Suez Canal

Horizon Magazine. Building the Suez Canal   **962**

Suffrage

See also Negroes—Politics and suffrage; Woman—Suffrage

History

Chute, M. The first liberty   **324.73**

Suffragettes. See Woman—Suffrage

Sugar Ray. Robinson, S. R.   **92**

Sugarman, Daniel A.

The Seventeen Guide to knowing yourself   **155.5**

Sugimoto, Etsu Inagaki

A daughter of the Samurai   **92**

Suicide

See pages in the following books:

Camus, A. The myth of Sisyphus, and other essays p93-118   **844**

Leighton, I. ed. The aspirin age, 1919-1941 p403-30   **917.3**

The **suicide.** Connell, E. S.

In The Saturday Evening Post. Best modern short stories p279-96   **S C**

The **suicide;** play. Freeman, C.

In Jones, L. ed. Black fire p631-36   **810.8**

Suite homes and their romance. Henry, O.

In Henry, O. The complete works of O. Henry p1161-65   **S C**

Suiting up for space. Mallan, L.   **629.45**

The **suitor.** Woiwode, L.

In The Best American short stories, 1971 p347-59   **S C**

Sukarno, President Indonesia

See pages in the following book:

Kenworthy, L. S. Leaders of new nations p310-35   **920**

Sukenik, Elazar L.

See pages in the following book:

Noble, I. Treasure of the caves p27-45   **221.4**

Sulfur. See Sulphur

Sullivan, Anne. See Macy, Anne (Sullivan)

Sullivan, Sir Arthur Seymour

Gilbert, Sir W. S. The complete plays of Gilbert and Sullivan   **782.8**

Gilbert, Sir W. S. Martyn Green's Treasury of Gilbert & Sullivan   **782.8**

Sullivan, Frank

Crisp new bills for Mr Teagle

In Becker, M. L. ed. The home book of Christmas p215-20   **394.26**

The Jukes family

In White, E. B. ed. A subtreasury of American humor; abridged p225-30   **817.08**

Sullivan, George

Pro football's all-time greats   **920**

Sullivan, John Lawrence

See pages in the following book:

Shannon, W. V. The American Irish p95-102   **301.453**

Sullivan, Louis

The testament of stone   **720.1**

About

See pages in the following book:

Forsee, A. Men of modern architecture p13-34   **920**

Symbolism of numbers
See pages in the following book:
Hogben, L. Mathematics for the million p167-204   **510**

Symptomaticus medicus. Nourse, A. E.
In Nourse, A. E. R. for tomorrow p 1-16   **S C**

Symptoms of being 35. Lardner, R.
In Lardner, R. The Ring Lardner reader p427-35   **S C**

Synge, John Millington
In the shadow of the glen
In Cerf, B. ed. 24 favorite one-act plays p377-90   **808.82**
The playboy of the Western World
In Bentley, E. comp. The great playwrights v2 p1867-1919   **808.82**
In Block, H. M. ed. Masters of modern drama p405-26   **808.82**
In Cerf, B. A. comp. Sixteen famous European plays p943-84   **808.82**
Riders to the sea
In Block, H. M. ed. Masters of modern drama p399-403   **808.82**
In Cerf, B. ed. Thirty famous one-act plays p231-38   **808.82**
In Dickinson, T. H. ed. Chief contemporary dramatists [1st ser.] p217-26   **808.82**
In Tucker, S. M. ed. Twenty-five modern plays p293-302   **808.82**

About
See pages in the following book:
Gassner, J. Masters of the drama p553-62   **809.2**

Synonyms. See English language—Synonyms and antonyms

Synthetic products
Mark, H. F. Giant molecules   **668.4**

Syphilis. See Venereal diseases

Syracuse
Siege—415-413 B.C.
See pages in the following books:
Creasy, Sir E. S. Fifteen decisive battles of the world p35-56   **904**
Mitchell, J. B. Twenty decisive battles of the world p23-38   **904**

Syrkin, Marie
Golda Meir: Israel's leader   **92**

The **system. Gilbert, M.**
In Best detective stories of the year, 1971 p69-84   **S C**
In Mystery Writers of America. Crime without murder p79-91   **S C**

System of Doctor Tarr and Professor Fether. Poe, E. A.
In Poe, E. A. The complete tales and poems of Edgar Allan Poe p307-21   **S C**

Systems engineering
See pages in the following book:
Furnas, C. C. The engineering p76-85   **620**
See also Bionics

Szell, George
See pages in the following book:
Ewen, D. Famous modern conductors p75-88   **920**

Szulc, Tad
Czechoslovakia since World War II   **943.7**

T

TVA. See Tennessee Valley Authority

Table
Hirsch, S. The art of table setting and flower arrangement   **642**
See also pages in the following book:
Better Homes and Gardens. Better Homes & Gardens New cook book p359-72   **641.5**

See also Cookery; Menus

Table manners. Lardner, R.
In Lardner, R. The Ring Lardner reader p465-70   **S C**

Table setting and decoration. See Table

Tables of squares, cubes, square roots, cube roots and reciprocals of all integers, up to 12,500, Barlow's. Barlow, P.   **510.21**

Tabor, Horace Austin Warner
See pages in the following book:
Stone, I. Men to match my mountains p363-72   **979.1**

Tacitus, Cornelius
See pages in the following book:
Grant, M. The ancient historians p271-305   **920**

Tact. Beer, T.
In Costain, T. B. ed. Read with me p81-98   **S C**

Taddeo di Gaddo. See Gaddi, Taddeo di

Tadpoles. See Frogs

Taft, Philip
Organized labor in American history   **331.88**

Taft, Robert Alphonso
See pages in the following books:
Kennedy, J. F. Profiles in courage (Harper) p231-44   **920**
Kennedy, J. F. Profiles in courage. Large type ed. (Watts, F.) p261-77   **920**

Taft, William Howard, President U.S.
Ross, I. An American family: the Tafts, 1678 to 1964   **920**
See also pages in the following books:
Abels, J. The degeneration of our Presidential election p252-59   **329**
American Heritage. The American Heritage History of the confident years p367-77   **973.8**
Dictionary of American biography. The American Plutarch p395-408   **920**
Warren, S. The President as world leader p50-59   **327.73**

Taft family
Ross, I. An American family: the Tafts, 1678 to 1964   **920**

Templars
> *See pages in the following book:*
Boyd, M. Man, myth and magic p92-103
133.4

Temple, William F.
Date to remember
In Conklin, G. ed. Invaders of earth p61-74 **S C**

Temples
> *See pages in the following books:*
Mills, D. The book of the ancient Greeks p276-86 **938**
Quennell, M. Everyday things in ancient Greece p108-19, 165-88 **913.38**

Templeton, Edith
Elegant economy
In The New Yorker. Stories from The New Yorker, 1950-1960 p396-412 **S C**

Temptation. Hughes, L.
In Hughes, L. The Langston Hughes reader p176-78 **818**

The temptation of Harringay. Wells, H. G.
In Wells, H. G. The complete short stories of H. G. Wells p239-44 **S C**

Ten Indians. Hemingway, E.
In Hemingway, E. The short stories of Ernest Hemingway p331-36 **S C**

10 steps in writing the research paper. Markman. R. H. **808.02**

Ten Vietnamese. Sheehan, S. **915.97**

The tenant. Hudson, H.
In The Best American short stories, 1968 p187-99 **S C**

Tender is the night. Fitzgerald, F. S. **Fic**

Tenement houses
> *See pages in the following books:*
Handlin, O. The uprooted p144-69 **325.73**
Harrington, M. The other American p139-57 **301.44**
Weinberg, A. ed. The muckrakers p308-19 **309.173**

Tenn, William
"Will you walk a little faster"
In Conklin, G. ed. Invaders of earth p290-300 **S C**

Tennessee
Dykeman, W. The border states **917.5**
History
Skinner, C. L. Pioneers of the Old Southwest **976**

Tennessee Valley Authority
Munzer, M. E. Valley of vision **627**
> *See also pages in the following book:*
Dykeman, W. The border states p103-11 **917.5**

Tennessee's partner. Harte, B.
In Harte, B. The best of Bret Harte p17-30 **S C**
In Harte, B. The best short stories of Bret Harte p30-41 **S C**

Tenney, Forrest F.
Yates, E. Is there a doctor in the barn? **636.089**

Tennis
King, B. J. Tennis to win **796.34**
Talbert, W. F. Sports Illustrated Tennis **796.34**
> *See also pages in the following books:*
American Association for Health, Physical Education and Recreation. Physical education for high school students p289-304 **613.7**
Friendlich, D. Panorama of sports in America p51-61 **796**
Wilkinson, B. Bud Wilkinson's Guide to modern physical fitness p66-73 **613.7**
Biography
Gibson, A. I always wanted to be somebody **92**

Tennis to win. King, B. J. **796.34**

Tennyson, Alfred Tennyson, 1st Baron
The complete poetical works of Alfred, Lord Tennyson **821**
Idylls of the King **821**
About
Kissane, J. D. Alfred Tennyson **821.09**
> *See also pages in the following books:*
Auslander, J. The winged horse p303-15 **809.1**
Untermeyer, L. The paths of poetry p188-95 **920**

Tenpins. See Bowling

The tent. O'Flaherty, L.
In Garrity, D. A. ed. 44 Irish short stories p304-13 **S C**

A tent in agony. Crane, S.
In Crane, S. The complete short stories & sketches of Stephen Crane p90-92 **S C**

The tenth man. Chayefsky, P.
In Cerf, B. ed. Six American plays for today p405-504 **812.08**

Tenzing, Norgay
Tiger of the snows **92**

Terasaki, Gwen
Bridge to the sun **952.03**

Terasaki, Hidenari
Terasaki, G. Bridge to the sun **952.03**

Terence
Phormio
In Davenport, B. ed. The portable Roman reader p75-131 **870.8**

Teresa. O'Faolain, S.
In Garrity, D. A. ed. 44 Irish short stories p271-90 **S C**

Terkel, Studs
Hard times **309.173**

Term papers, theses and dissertations, A manual for writers of. Turabian, K. L. **808.02**

Terracide. Linton, R. M. **614**

Terrell, John Upton
American Indian almanac **970.1**
The United States Department of Agriculture **353.81**
The United States Department of Health, Education, and Welfare **353.84**
The United States Department of Justice **353.5**

Terrestrial physics. See Geophysics

The **terrible** conflagration up at the place.
Bradbury, R.
In Bradbury, R. I sing the Body Electric! p15-31 **S C**

Terrible swift sword. Catton, B. **973.7**

The **territorial** imperative. Ardrey, R. **591**

Terror and grief. Tucci, N.
In The New Yorker. Stories from The New Yorker, 1950-1960 p490-517 **S C**

Terry, Louisa (Ward)
Tharp, L. H. Three saints and a sinner: Julia Ward Howe, Louisa, Annie, and Sam Ward **920**

Terry, Megan
The magic realists
In The Best short plays, 1968 p327-59 **808.82**

Terry, Walter
The bottomless well
In The Best American short stories, 1966 p269-82 **S C**

Tess of the D'Urbervilles. Hardy, T. **Fic**

Test pilots. *See* Air pilots

Test tubes and beakers. Coulson, E. H. **540.72**

The **testament** of stone. Sullivan, L. **720.1**

Tests. *See* Mental tests

Teutoburger Wald, Battle of, 9 A.D.
See pages in the following books:
Creasy, Sir E. S. Fifteen decisive battles of the world p121-42 **904**
Mitchell, J. B. Twenty decisive battles of the world p80-93 **904**

Teutonic mythology. *See* Mythology, Germanic

Tevis, Walter S.
The big bounce
In Asimov, I. ed. Where do we go from here? p400-13 **S C**

Texan Sante Fé Expedition, 1841
See pages in the following book:
Hall-Quest, O. Conquistadors and Pueblos p202-18 **979.1**

Texas
Dobie, J. F. Some part of myself **92**
Goodwyn, L. The South Central States **917.6**
Description and travel
See pages in the following book:
Moyers, B. Listening to America p223-83 **917.3**
Fiction
Ferber, E. Giant **Fic**
Horgan, P. Whitewater **Fic**
History
Fehrenbach, T. R. Lone Star **976.4**
Stephenson, N. W. Texas and the Mexican War **973.6**
See also pages in the following book:
Billington, R. A. The far Western frontier, 1830-1860 p116-42 **978**

Texas and the Mexican War. Stephenson, N. W. **973.6**

Textbooks
Bibliography
El-hi Textbooks in print **016.371**

Textbooks in print. *See* El-hi Textbooks in print **016.371**

Textile industry and fabrics
Wilson, J. Weaving is fun **746.1**
See also pages in the following books:
Johnson, M. Sewing the easy way p28-41 **646.4**
Langdon, W. C. Everyday things in American life, 1776-1876 p240-73 **917.3**
See also Cotton manufacture and trade
Dictionaries
Fairchild's Dictionary of textiles **677.03**

Tey, Josephine
Brat Farrar
In Tey, J. Three by Tey v3 **Fic**
The Franchise affair
In Tey, J. Three by Tey v2 **Fic**
Miss Pym disposes
In Tey, J. Three by Tey v 1 **Fic**
Three by Tey **Fic**

Thackeray, William Makepeace
The history of Henry Esmond, esquire **Fic**
Vanity fair **Fic**
Vanity fair; criticism
In Drew, E. The novel: a modern guide to fifteen English masterpieces p111-26 **823.09**
About
See pages in the following books:
Karl, F. R. An age of fiction: the nineteenth century British novel p177-203 **823.09**
Wagenknecht, E. Cavalcade of the English novel p268-85 **823.09**

Thai cookery. *See* Cookery, Thai

Thailand
Thompson, V. Thailand: the new Siam **915.93**
See also pages in the following book:
Salisbury, H. E. Orbit of China p42-53 **915.1**
Fiction
Boulle, P. The bridge over the River Kwai **Fic**
Social life and customs
Landon, M. Anna and the King of Siam **915.93**

Thane, Elswyth
Dawn's early light **Fic**

Thank you, Dr Russell. Chute, B. J.
In Chute, B. J. One touch of nature, and other stories p199-220 **S C**

Thank you, m'am. Hughes, L.
In Hughes, L. ed. The best short stories by Negro writers p70-73 **S C**
In Hughes, L. The Langston Hughes reader p77-80 **818**

Thanksgiving Day
Stories
Capote, T. The Thanksgiving visitor **Fic**

The **Thanksgiving** visitor. Capote, T. **Fic**

Thant, U
Bingham, J. U Thant **92**

Tharp, Louise Hall
The Peabody sisters of Salem   920
Three saints and a sinner: Julia Ward
  Howe, Louise, Annie, and Sam Ward
                             920

That evening sun. Faulkner, W.
  In Faulkner, W. Collected stories of
    William Faulkner p289-309   **S C**
  In Faulkner, W. The Faulkner reader
                             S C
  In Faulkner, W. The portable Faulk-
    ner p391-410   **S C**
  In Faulkner, W. Selected short stories
    of William Faulkner p78-100 **S C**

That good may come. Wharton, E.
  In Wharton, E. The collected short
    stories of Edith Wharton v 1 p21-
    41   **S C**

That Mark horse. Schaefer, J.
  In Schaefer, J. The collected stories of
    Jack Schaefer p259-69   **S C**

That powerful drop. Hughes, L.
  In Hughes, L. The Langston Hughes
    reader p201-02   818

That she would dance no more. Smith,
  J. W.
  In Jones, L. ed. Black fire p486-99
                      810.8

That touch of genius. Sambrot, W.
  In Hitchcock, A. ed. Alfred Hitchcock
    presents: A month of mystery p93-
    102   **S C**

That tree. Porter, K. A.
  In Porter, K. A. The collected stories
    of Katherine Anne Porter p66-79
                        S C

That will be fine. Faulkner, W.
  In Faulkner, W. Collected stories of
    William Faulkner p265-88 **S C**

That word black. Hughes, L.
  In Hughes, L. The Langston Hughes
    reader p208-09   818

Thayer, Charles W.
Russia   914.7

Theater
Guthrie, T. Tyrone Guthrie on acting
                      792

    See also Acting; Actors and actresses;
    Ballet; Moving pictures; Shakespeare,
    William—Stage history

Biography
Trease, G. Seven stages   920

Dictionaries
The Oxford Companion to the theatre
                    792.03

Germany
See pages in the following book:
Nicoll, A. World drama p564-85 809.2

Great Britain
Nicoll, A. British drama   822.09

Great Britain—History
Adams, J. C. The Globe Playhouse 792.09
Hodges, C. W. Shakespeare & the play-
  ers   822.3
Hodges, C. W. Shakespeare's theatre
                    792.09
Horizon Magazine. Shakespeare's England
                  822.3

Nicoll, A. A history of English drama,
  1660-1900   822.09
Thorndike, A. H. Shakespeare's theater
                  792.09
    See also pages in the following books:
Davis, W. S. Life in Elizabethan days
  p341-54   914.2
Horizon Magazine. The Horizon Book
  of The Elizabethan world p292-301
                  940.2
Priestley, J. B. The Edwardians p155-75
                  914.2
Shakespeare's England v2 p283-310 822.3

Greece
See pages in the following book:
Gassner, J. Masters of the drama p17-39
                  809.2

History
Freedley, G. A history of the theatre
                  792.09
Hartnoll, P. The concise history of
  theatre   792.09
Hewitt, B. History of the theatre from
  1800 to the present   792.09
Samachson, D. The dramatic story of the
  theatre   792.09
    See pages in the following book:
Gies, J. Life in a medieval city p183-89
                  914.4

Japan—History
Ernst, E. The Kabuki theatre   792.09

London—History
Bentley, G. E. Shakespeare and his
  theatre   822.3

Production and direction
Cornberg, S. A stage crew handbook 792

Russia
See pages in the following book:
Salisbury, H. E. ed. The Soviet Union:
  the fifty years p146-57   914.7

United States
Hart, M. Act one   92
Theatre world   792.025
    See also pages in the following books:
Colby, V. ed. American culture in the
  sixties p134-52   917.3

United States—History
Blum, D. A pictorial history of the
  American theatre, 1860-1970   792.09
Taubman, H. The making of the Amer-
  ican theatre   792.09
    See also pages in the following books:
American Heritage. The nineties p97-105,
  122-26   917.3
Nye, R. B. The cultural life of the new
  Nation, 1776-1830 p262-67   917.3
Nye, R. B. The unembarrassed muse: the
  popular arts in America p140-98 917.3
Spiller, R. E. ed. The American literary
  revolution, 1783-1837 p319-34 810.9
Wright, L. B. The cultural life of the
  American colonies, 1607-1763 p176-87
                  917.3

Yearbooks
The Best plays of 1919/1920-1969/1970
                808.82

They gave us the land. Rulfo, J.
    In Cohen, J. M. ed. Latin American writing today p174-78 **860.8**
They knew what they wanted. Howard, S.
    In Cerf, B. A. ed. Sixteen famous American plays p5-54 **812.08**
    In Gassner, J. ed. Twenty-five best plays of the modern American theatre; early ser. p91-122 **812.08**
They seek a city. See Bontemps, A. Anyplace but here **301.451**
They stole our cattle. Obudo, N.
    In Angoff, C. ed. African writing today p215-18 **896**
They trample your heart. Porter, K. A.
    In Costain, T. B. ed. Read with me p423-46 **S C**
They were expendable. White, W. L. **940.54**
Thief in the night. Chute, B. J.
    In Chute, B. J. One touch of nature, and other stories p171-88 **S C**
Thieves' carnival. Anouilh, J.
    In Block, H. M. ed. Masters of modern drama p759-79 **808.82**
Thimble, thimble. Henry, O.
    In Henry, O. The complete works of O. Henry p715-24 **S C**
The thin man. Hammett, D.
    In Hammett, D. The novels of Dashiell Hammett p589-726 **Fic**
The thing you love. Stuart, J.
    In Stuart, J. A Jesse Stuart reader p17-31 **818**
Things fall apart. Achebe, C. **Fic**
The thing's the play. Henry, O.
    In Henry, O. The complete works of O. Henry p1538-43 **S C**
Things went badly in Westphalia. Sherman, M.
    In The Best short plays, 1970 p373-408 **808.82**
The thinker. Anderson, S.
    In Anderson, S. Winesburg, Ohio (Modern Lib) p145-65 **S C**
    In Anderson, S. Winesburg, Ohio (Viking) p128-42 **S C**
Thinking. See Thought and thinking
Thinking machines. Adler, I. **510.78**
The third bank of the river. Rosa, J. G.
    In Cohen, J. M. ed. Latin American writing today p97-102 **860.8**
The third ingredient. Henry, O.
    In Henry, O. The complete works of O. Henry p689-98 **S C**
The third man. Greene, G.
    In Greene, G. Triple pursuit **Fic**
Third-party movements in the United States. Hesseltine, W. B. **329**
The 13 clocks. Thurber, J. **Fic**
Thirteen days. Kennedy, R. F. **973.922**
Thirty days to better English. Lewis, N. **428**
Thirty famous one-act plays. Cerf, B. ed. **808.82**
31 new American poets. Schreiber, R. ed. **811.08**

36 children. Kohl, H. **371.9**
The $30,000 bequest. Twain, M.
    In Twain, M. The complete short stories of Mark Twain p497-522 **S C**
Thirty years that shook physics. Gamow, G. **530.1**
Thirty Years' War, 1618-1648
    See pages in the following books:
    Blitzer, C. Age of kings p30-53 **940.2**
    The New Cambridge Modern history v4 p306-58 **909**
This crowded planet. Hyde, M. O. **301.3**
This fabulous century. Time-Life Books **917.3**
This farm for sale. Stuart, J.
    In Stuart, J. A Jesse Stuart reader p130-40 **818**
This flower. Mansfield, K.
    In Mansfield, K. The short stories of Katherine Mansfield p405-08 **S C**
This gun for hire. Greene, G.
    In Greene, G. Triple pursuit **Fic**
This hallowed ground. Catton, B. **973.7**
This I remember [abridged]. Roosevelt, E.
    In Roosevelt, E. The autobiography of Eleanor Roosevelt p127-280 **92**
This is a dream. Lenormand, H. R.
    In Dickinson, T. H. ed. Chief contemporary dramatists; 3d ser. p311-35 **808.82**
This is India. Rama Rau, S. **915.4**
This is my God. Wouk, H. **296**
This is my story [abridged]. Roosevelt, E.
    In Roosevelt, E. The autobiography of Eleanor Roosevelt p 1-125 **92**
This majestic lie. Crane, S.
    In Crane, S. The complete short stories & sketches of Stephen Crane p739-56 **S C**
This morning, this evening, so soon. Baldwin, J.
    In Baldwin, J. Going to meet the man p143-93 **S C**
    In Foley, M. ed. Fifty best American short stories, 1915-1965 p618-55 **S C**
    In Hughes, L. ed. The best short stories by Negro writers p213-52 **S C**
This rock within the sea: a heritage lost. Mowat, F. **917.18**
This rough magic. Stewart, M. **Fic**
This side of Paradise. Fitzgerald, F. S. **Fic**
This simian world. Day, C.
    In Day, C. The best of Clarence Day p375-428 **818**
This star shall be free. Leinster, M.
    In Conklin, G. ed. Invaders of earth p2-19 **S C**
This strangest everything. Ciardi, J. **811**
This vital air, this vital water. Aylesworth, T. G. **614**
This was America. Handlin, O. ed. **917.3**
Thjodolf. Undset, S.
    In Undset, S. Four stories p63-143 **S C**

Thorne, J. O.
(ed.) Chambers's Biographical dictionary. See Chambers's Biographical dictionary
920.03

Thoroughfares. See Streets

Those inventive Americans. National Geographic Society
608

Those who fraternize. Michener, J.
In Michener, J. Tales of the South Pacific p256-78
S C

Those who love. Stone, I.
Fic

"Thou art the man." Poe, E. A.
In Poe, E. A. The complete tales and poems of Edgar Allan Poe p490-501
S C

Thought and thinking
Boas, G. The history of ideas
109
Chase, S. The tyranny of words
412
Flesch, R. The art of clear thinking
153.4
Flesch, R. How to write, speak, and think more effectively
808
Hayakawa, S. I. Language in thought and action
412
See also pages in the following books:
Asimov, I. The human brain p318-31
612
Sargent, S. S. Basic teachings of the great psychologists p145-78
150
See also Logic; Memory

Thought transference
See pages in the following book:
Twain, M. The complete essays of Mark Twain p71-87
814
See also Extrasensory perception; Mind reading

Thousand-and-second tale of Scheherazade. Poe, E. A.
In Poe, E. A. The complete tales and poems of Edgar Allan Poe p104-17
S C

A thousand-clowns. Gardner, H.
In Gassner, J. ed. Best American plays; 5th ser. p419-58
812.08

Thousand cranes. Kawabata, Y.
In Kawabata, Y. Snow country and Thousand cranes v2
Fic

A thousand days. Schlesinger, A. M.
973.922

A thousand springs. Chennault, A.
92

Thrasher, Sue
See pages in the following book:
Lukas, J. A. Don't shoot—we are your children! p117-65
301.43

Thrawn Janet. Stevenson, R. L.
In Stevenson, R. L. The complete short stories of Robert Louis Stevenson p349-61
S C

The thread that runs so true. Stuart, J.
92

The threat. Chekhov, A.
In Chekhov, A. The image of Chekhov p71
S C

The threat. Saki
In Saki. The short stories of Saki p518-23
S C

Three. Ashton-Warner, S.
Fic

Three by Heinlein. Heinlein, R. A.
Fic

Three by Tey. Tey, J.
Fic

Three came home. Keith, A. N.
940.54

The three-day blow. Hemingway, E.
In Hemingway, E. In our time p43-61
S C
In Hemingway, E. The short stories of Ernest Hemingway p113-25
S C

Three deaths. Tolstoy, L.
In Tolstoy, L. Short stories v 1 p362-76
S C

The three Edwards. Costain, T. B.
942.03

The three hermits. Tolstoy, L.
In Tolstoy, L. Short stories v2 p171-78
S C
In Tolstoy, L. Twenty-three tales p174-81
S C

Three hours between planes. Fitzgerald, F. S.
In Fitzgerald, F. S. The stories of F. Scott Fitzgerald p464-69
S C

The three lives of Charles de Gaulle. Schoenbrun, D.
92

Three men on a horse. Abbott, G.
In Gassner, J. ed. Twenty best plays of the modern American theatre p511-59
812.08

Three million yen. Mishima, Y.
In Mishima, Y. Death in midsummer, and other stories p30-42
S C

Three miraculous soldiers. Crane, S.
In Crane, S. The complete short stories & sketches of Stephen Crane p252-72
S C

Three players of a summer game. Williams, T.
In Foley, M. ed. Fifty best American short stories, 1915-1965 p466-87
S C
In The New Yorker. Stories from the New Yorker, 1950-1960 p319-40
S C

Three plays. Wilder, T.
812

Three plays: Juno and the paycock, The shadow of a gunman, The plough and the stars. O'Casey, S.
822

Three questions. Tolstoy, L.
In Tolstoy, L. Short stories v2 p241-45
S C
In Tolstoy, L. Twenty-three tales p267-71
S C

Three saints and a sinner: Julia Ward Howe, Louisa, Annie, and Sam Ward. Tharp, L. H.
920

The three sisters. Chekhov, A.
In Bentley, E. comp. The great playwrights v 2 p1557-1615
808.82
In Chekhov, A. Best plays p137-223
891.7

Three soldiers. Dos Passos, J.
Fic

Three stockings. Struther, J.
In Becker, M. L. ed. The home book of Christmas p377-79
394.26

Three Sundays in a week. Poe, E. A.
In Poe, E. A. The complete tales and poems of Edgar Allan Poe p730-35
S C
In Poe, E. A. Selected poetry and prose p211-17
818

The three taverns. Robinson, E. A.
In Robinson, E. A. The collected poems of Edwin Arlington Robinson p453-539
811

The **tiny** closet. Inge, W.
   In The Best short plays of 1958-1959
      p33-43   **808.82**
Tipasa, Algeria
      See pages in the following books:
Camus, A. Lyrical and critical essays p65-
   72, 162-71   **844**
Camus, A. The myth of Sisyphus, and
   other essays p195-204   **844**
Tips from the teaching pros, Golf Maga-
   zine's. Golf Magazine   **796.352**
Tipton, Charles M.
   (jt. auth.) Cretzmeyer, F. X. Bresnahan
   and Tuttle's Track and field athletics
                                      796.4
The **tiredness** of Rosabel. Mansfield, K.
   In Mansfield, K. The short stories of
      Katherine Mansfield p3-8   **S C**
Titanic (Steamship)
Lord, W. A night to remember   **910.4**
Marcus, G. The maiden voyage   **910.4**
      See also pages in the following book:
Priestley, J. B. The Edwardians p225-32
                                      914.2
Titanium
      See pages in the following book:
Asimov, I. Building blocks of the universe
   p233-40   **546**
Titian
Williams, J. The world of Titian, c.1488-
   1576   **92**
      See also pages in the following book:
Vasari, G. The lives of the painters, sculp-
   tors and architects v4 p199-215   **920**
Tiye, Queen of Egypt
      See pages in the following book:
Cottrell, L. Five queens of ancient Egypt
   p43-52   **913.32**
To a different drum; the story of Henry
   David Thoreau. Norman, C.   **92**
To a tenor dying old. Carter, J. S.
   In The Best American short stories,
      1964 p27-84   **S C**
To a young dancer. De Mille, A.   **792.8**
To Appomattox. Davis, B.   **973.7**
To be young, gifted and Black. Hans-
   berry, L.   **812**
To build a fire. London, J.
   In London, J. Best short stories of Jack
      London p9-22   **S C**
   In London, J. Jack London's Tales of
      adventure   **S C**
To establish justice, to insure domestic tran-
   quility. United States. National Commis-
   sion on the Causes and Prevention of
   Violence   **301.18**
To have and to hold. Johnston, M.   **Fic**
To hell with dying. Walker, A.
   In Hughes, L. ed. The best short sto-
      ries by Negro writers p490-96 **S C**
To him who waits. Henry, O.
   In Henry, O. The complete works of
      O. Henry p739-47   **S C**
To kill a mockingbird. Lee, H.   **Fic**
To let. Galsworthy, J.
   In Galsworthy, J. The Forsyte saga
      p665-921   **Fic**
To my son, the teen-age driver. Felsen,
   H. G.   **629.28**

To purge this land with blood; a biography
   of John Brown. Oates, S. B.   **92**
To Sir, with love. Braithwaite, E. R.   **92**
To teach, to love. Stuart, J.   **92**
To the man on trail. London, J.
   In London, J. Best short stories of Jack
      London p175-83   **S C**
   In London, J. Jack London's Tales of
      adventure   **S C**
To the wilderness I wander. Butler, F.
   In Foley, M. ed. Fifty best American
      short stories, 1915-1965 p573-601
                                   S C
To Uncle, with love. Godden, R.
   In Godden, R. Gone p97-105   **S C**
Toads. See Frogs
Tobacco. See Smoking
Tobacco & your health: the smoking con-
   troversy. Diehl, H. S.   **613.8**
Tobacco road. Kirkland, J.
   In Gassner, J. ed. Twenty best plays of
      the modern American theatre p599-
      642   **812.08**
Tobermory. Saki
   In Saki. The short stories of Saki p119-
      26   **S C**
Tobias, Richard C.
The art of James Thurber   **818**
Tobin's palm. Henry, O.
   In Henry, O. The complete works of
      O. Henry p 1-7   **S C**
   In Henry, O. The four million p3-15
                                   S C
Tocqueville, Alexis de
Democracy in America   **309.173**
Democracy in America; criticism
   In Downs, R. B. Books that changed
      America p47-56   **810.9**
Today is Friday. Hemingway, E.
   In Hemingway, E. The short stories of
      Ernest Hemingway p356-59   **S C**
Today's isms. Ebenstein, W.   **335**
Tods' Amendment. Kipling, R.
   In Kipling, R. Maugham's Choice of
      Kipling's best p240-44   **S C**
Toes. See Foot
Toffler, Alvin
Future shock   **301.24**
Toilers of land and sea. Gabriel, R. H.
   In Pageant of America v3   **973**
The **toilet.** Jones, L.
   In Gassner, J. ed. Best American plays;
      6th ser. p325-34   **812.08**
Tokyo
      Bombardment, 1942
Glines, C. V. Doolittle's Tokyo Raiders
                                      940.54
      Description
      See pages in the following book:
Van der Post, L. A portrait of Japan p31-
   75   **915.2**
Toland, John
Battle: the story of the Bulge   **940.54**
But not in shame   **940.54**
The Dillinger days   **364.1**
The last 100 days   **940.53**
Told in the drooling ward. London, J.
   In London, J. Jack London's Tales of
      adventure   **S C**

Tomorrow's child. Bradbury, R.
  In Bradbury, R. I sing the Body Electric! p32-49   **S C**
Tompkins, Julia
  Stage costumes and how to make them   **792**
Toney, Richard
  A snow statue
  In Seventeen. Seventeen from Seventeen p31-45   **S C**
Tonga Islands
  See pages in the following book:
  Shadbolt, M. Isles of the South Pacific p70-86   **919**
Tonight at nine thirty-six. Gillespie, A.
  In The Best American short stories, 1970 p115-37   **S C**
Too dear. Tolstoy, L.
  In Tolstoy, L. Twenty-three tales p250-55   **S C**
Too early spring. Benét, S. V.
  In Benét, S. V. Selected works of Stephen Vincent Benét v2   **818**
Too late the phalarope. Paton, A.   **Fic**
Too true to be good. Shaw, B.
  In Shaw, B. Bernard Shaw's plays p229-88   **822**
  In Shaw, B. Complete plays, with prefaces v4 p633-720   **822**
Toolmakers handybook. Black, P. O.
  In Black, P. O. Audels Machinists library v3   **621.9**
Tools
  See pages in the following books:
  Boy Scouts of America. Fieldbook for Boy Scouts, explorers, scouters, educators, outdoorsmen p66-83   **369.43**
  Gladstone, B. The New York Times Complete manual of home repair p 1-96   **643**

  See also Agricultural machinery
      History
  See pages in the following book:
  Simak, C. D. Prehistoric man p51-64 **573.2**
Tools of modern biology. Berger, M. **574.028**
Tools of the old and new stone age. Bordaz, J.   **913.03**
Toomer, Jean
  Fern
  In Hughes, L. ed. The best short stories by Negro writers p30-34 **S C**
Toor, Frances
  A treasury of Mexican folkways   **398**
The tooth. Jackson, S.
  In Jackson, S. The magic of Shirley Jackson p120-36   **818**
Tooth of Paul Revere. Benét, S. V.
  In Benét, S. V. Selected works of Stephen Vincent Benét v2   **818**
Top secret. Grinnell, D.
  In Conklin, G. ed. Invaders of earth p48-49   **S C**
Topographical drawing
  See pages in the following book:
  Boorstin, D. J. The Americans: The national experience p241-48   **917.3**
  See also Map drawing
Torre, Lillian de la. See De la Torre, Lillian

Tortesa the usurer. Willis, N. P.
  In Quinn, A. H. ed. Representative American plays p238-76   **812.08**
Tortilla Flat. Steinbeck, J.   **Fic**
  also in Steinbeck, J. The short novels of John Steinbeck p7-133   **Fic**
Tortoises. See Turtles
Toser, Marie A.
  Library manual   **028.7**
Totalitarianism
  Fromm, E. Escape from freedom   **323.4**
  Huxley, A. Brave new world revisited   **301.15**

  See also Communism; Dictators; Fascism; National socialism
      Fiction
  Orwell, G. Nineteen eighty-four   **Fic**
A touch of marble. Potter, D. S.
  In The Best short plays of 1958-1959 p167-83   **808.82**
A touch of realism. Saki
  In Saki. The short stories of Saki p336-41   **S C**
A touch of the poet. O'Neill, E.
  In Gassner, J. ed. Best American plays; 5th ser. p 1-53   **812.08**
A tough nut. Moravia, A.
  In The Saturday Evening Post. Best modern short stories p41-46 **S C**
Toulouse-Lautrec Monfa, Henri Marie Raymond de
  See pages in the following books:
  Cheney, S. The story of modern art p336-46   **709.03**
  Untermeyer, L. Makers of the modern world p329-35   **920**
  Wallace, R. The world of Van Gogh, 1853-1890 p52-67   **92**
A tour of the White House with Mrs John F. Kennedy. Wolff, P.   **975.3**
Tours, Battle of, 732. See Poitiers, Battle of, 732
Tovarich. Deval, J.
  In Cerf, B. A. comp. Sixteen famous European plays p445-509   **808.82**
Tovey, Sir Donald Francis
  See pages in the following book:
  Highet, G. People, places and books p53-60   **809**
Toward a national urban policy. Moynihan, D. P.
  In United States. National Commission on the Causes and Prevention of Violence. Violent crime p 1-30   **364.1**
Toward the year 2018. Foreign Policy Association   **901.9**
Towards a new architecture. Le Corbusier   **724.9**
The tower. Weiss, P.
  In Richards, S. ed. Best short plays of the world theatre, 1958-1967 p301-15   **808.82**
Tower of Babel
  See pages in the following book:
  Ceram, C. W. Gods, graves, and scholars p279-96   **913.03**

Transformation of Martin Burney. Henry, O.
In Henry, O. The complete works of O. Henry p925-28 **S C**

Transforming light. Vail, A. **291**

The transient. Elkin, S.
In The Best American short stories, 1965 p57-91 **S C**

Transients in Arcadia. Henry, O.
In Henry, O. The best short stories of O. Henry p251-57 **S C**
In Henry, O. The complete works of O. Henry p1329-33 **S C**

Transistors
Steckler, L. Simple transistor projects for hobbyists & students **621.381**
See also pages in the following books:
National Geographic Society. Those inventive Americans p208-16 **608**
Pearce, W. E. Transistors and circuits p120-46 **621.381**
Wohlrabe, R. A. Crystals p115-23 **548**

Transistors and circuits. Pearce, W. E. **621.381**

Transit systems. See Local transit

Translating and interpreting
See pages in the following book:
Flesch, R. How to write, speak, and think more effectively p202-09 **808**

Transparencies. See Slides (Photography)

Transplantation of organs, tissues, etc.
Longmore, D. Spare-part surgery **617**
See also pages in the following book:
Taylor, G. R. The biological time bomb p56-81 **577**

Transportation
Reische, D. ed. Problems of mass transportation **380.5**
See also pages in the following books:
Bryant, A. The Italians p137-47 **914.5**
Carroll, J. T. The French p138-51 **914.4**
Foreign Policy Association. Toward the year 2018 p35-47 **901.9**
Rand McNally and Company. Rand McNally Pictorial world atlas p22-37 **912**
Stokley, J. The new world of the atom p198-209 **621.48**
See also Bridges; Canals; Local transit; Railroads; Waterways

History
Owen, W. Wheels **380.5**
Ridley, A. An illustrated history of transportation **380.5**
See also pages in the following books:
Ashley, M. Life in Stuart England p157-62 **914.2**
Cooper, M. The inventions of Leonardo da Vinci p132-39 **608**
Langdon, W. C. Everyday things in American life, 1607-1776 p241-54 **917.3**

Transvaal War, 1899-1902. See South African War, 1899-1902

Trapp, Maria Augusta
The story of the Trapp Family Singers **92**

Trapp family
Drama
Lindsay, H. The sound of music **812**

Trapp Family Singers
Trapp, M. A. The story of the Trapp Family Singers **92**

Trapping
Bateman, J. Animal traps and trapping **639**
See also Hunting

Travel
See pages in the following books:
Haupt, E. A. The Seventeen Book of etiquette & entertaining p102-17 **395**
Parker, E. ed. I was just thinking p110-12, 125-34 **824.08**
Post, E. L. The Emily Post Book of etiquette for young people p167-86 **395**
Vogue's Book of etiquette and good manners p582-608 **395**
See also Voyages and travels; Voyages around the world; and names of countries, cities, etc. with the subdivision Description and travel, e.g. United States—Description and travel

The traveler. Connelly, M.
In Cerf, B. ed. 24 favorite one-act plays p219-28 **808.82**

Travelogue. Lardner, R.
In Lardner, R. The best short stories of Ring Lardner p261-72 **S C**
In Lardner, R. The Ring Lardner reader p88-99 **S C**

Travels. See Voyages and travels; Voyages around the world; and names of countries, states, etc. with the subdivision Description and travel, e.g. United States—Description and travel

Travels in New York: the broken-down van. Crane, S.
In Crane, S. The complete short stories & sketches of Stephen Crane p70-74 **S C**

The travels of Marco Polo. Polo, M. **915**

Travels with Charley. Steinbeck, J. **917.3**

Travels with my aunt. Greene, G. **Fic**

Travers, Robert
The big brown trout
In The Best American short stories, 1967 p303-13 **S C**

The trawler. Connolly, J. B.
In The Scribner treasury p511-32 **S C**

Treadwell, Sophie
Machinal
In Gassner, J. ed. Twenty-five best plays of the modern American theatre; early ser. p495-529 **812.08**

Trease, Geoffrey
Seven sovereign queens **920**
Seven stages **920**

Treason
Werstein, I. I accuse; the story of the Dreyfus case **92**
West, R. The new meaning of treason **364.1**

The treasure. Maugham, W. S.
In Maugham, W. S. The best short stories of W. Somerset Maugham p395-411 **S C**

Treasure and treasure hunters. Armstrong, R. ed. **910.4**

The **treasure** hunt. Stevenson, R. L.
In Armstrong, R. ed. Treasure and treasure hunters   **910.4**

The **treasure** hunt. Wallace, E.
In Haycraft, H. ed. A treasury of great
mysteries v 1 p189-200   **S C**

The **treasure** in the forest. Wells, H. G.
In Armstrong, R. ed. Treasure and
treasure hunters p32-41   **910.4**
In Wells, H. G. The complete short
stories of H. G. Wells p313-21   **S C**

The **treasure** of Axayacatl. Prescott, W. H.
In Armstrong, R. ed. Treasure and
treasure hunters   **910.4**

The **treasure** of Far Island. Cather, W.
In Cather, W. Willa Cather's Collected
short fiction, 1892-1912 v3 p265-82   **S C**

Treasure of the caves. Noble, I.   **221.4**

The **treasure**-ship. Saki
In Saki. The short stories of Saki p292-
95   **S C**

Treasure-trove. See Buried treasure

A **treasury** of American coins. Reinfeld, F.   **737.4**

A **treasury** of American folklore. Botkin,
B. A. ed.   **398**

A **treasury** of American political humor.
Lewin, L. C. ed.   **817.08**

A **treasury** of art masterpieces. Craven, T.
ed.   **759**

A **treasury** of Damon Runyon. Runyon, D.   **817**

Treasury of Gilbert & Sullivan, Martyn
Green's. Gilbert, Sir W. S.   **782.8**

A **treasury** of great American speeches.
Hurd, C. comp.   **815.08**

A **treasury** of great mysteries. Haycraft, H.
ed.   **S C**

A **treasury** of great poems: English and
American. Untermeyer, L. ed.   **821.08**

A **treasury** of humorous quotations. Prochnow, H. V. comp.   **808.88**

A **treasury** of Irish folklore. Colum, P. ed.   **398**

A **treasury** of Lincoln quotations. Lincoln, A.   **818**

A **treasury** of Mexican folkways. Toor, F.   **398**

A **treasury** of New England folklore. Botkin,
B. A. ed.   **398**

A **treasury** of Southern folklore. Botkin,
B. A. ed.   **398**

Treasury of the world's coins. Reinfeld, F.   **737.4**

A **treasury** of the world's great letters, from
ancient days to our own time. Schuster,
M. L. ed.   **808.86**

A **treasury** of the world's great speeches.
Peterson, H. ed.   **808.851**

A **treasury** of Western folklore. Botkin,
B. A. ed.   **398**

A **treasury** of Yiddish poetry. Howe, I. ed.   **892.49**

Treat, Lawrence
Justice magnifique
In Hitchcock, A. ed. Alfred Hitchcock
presents: A month of mystery
p191-204   **S C**

K as in knife
In Best detective stories of the year
[1967] p177-94   **S C**

Suburban tigress
In Mystery Writers of America. Crime
without murder p289-301   **S C**

The verdict
In Best detective stories of the year,
1971 p149-65   **S C**

Treaties. See names of countries with the
subdivision Foreign relations—Treaties,
e.g. United States—Foreign relations—
Treaties

Treaty of Utrecht. See Utrecht, Treaty of,
1713

Treble, H. A.
Everyday life in Rome in the time of
Caesar and Cicero   **917.37**

Treblinka (Concentration camp)
Steiner, J. F. Treblinka   **940.54**

A **tree** grows in Brooklyn. Smith, B.   **Fic**

The **tree** of language. Laird, H.   **400**

The **tree** of liberty. Page, E.   **Fic**

The **tree** of life. Smith, R. ed.   **291**

The **tree** that didn't get trimmed. Morley, C.
In Becker, M. L. ed. The home book of
Christmas p423-28   **394.26**

Treece, Henry
The crusades   **940.1**

Trees
Ketchum, R. M. The secret life of the
forest   **574.5**
See also Forests and forestry; Wood

Hawaii
See pages in the following book:
Carlquist, S. Hawaii: a natural history
p139-57   **574.9**

North America
Petrides, G. A. A field guide to trees and
shrubs   **582**
Preston, R. J. North American trees (ex-
clusive of Mexico and tropical United
States)   **582**

Poetry
See pages in the following book:
Stevenson, B. E. comp. The home book of
modern verse p313-21   **821.08**

United States
Platt, R. Discover American trees   **582**
United States. Department of Agriculture.
Trees   **634.9**

The **trees**. Richter, C.   **Fic**
also in Richter, C. The awakening land
p3-167   **Fic**

Trees, and other poems. Kilmer, J.   **811**

Trench, Charles Chenevix. See Chenevix
Trench, Charles

Trent, William Peterfield
(ed.) The Cambridge History of American
literature. See The Cambridge History
of American literature   **810.9**

Trepleff. Harris, M.
In The Best American short stories,
1967 p85-99   **S C**

Trevelyan, George
The American Revolution   **973.3**

The **trinket** box. Lessing, D.
 In Lessing, D. African stories p25-31
           S C
Triple pursuit. Greene, G.   **Fic**
Tripp, Edward
 Crowell's Handbook of classical mythol-
  ogy   **292.03**
Tripp, Rhoda Thomas
 (comp.) The international thesaurus of
  quotations   **808.88**
Triptych of the three kings. Timmermans, F.
 In Becker, M. L. ed. The home book of
  Christmas p111-15   **394.26**
Tristano, Lenny. See Tristano, Leonard
 Joseph
Tristano, Leonard Joseph
 See pages in the following book:
 Gitler, I. Jazz masters of the forties p226-
  47   **920**
Tristram. Robinson, E. A.
 In Robinson, E. A. The collected poems
  of Edwin Arlington Robinson p595-
  729   **811**
Triton (Atomic submarine)
 See pages in the following book:
 National Geographic Society. Great adven-
  tures with National Geographic p134-45
            910.9
The **triumph.** Galbraith, J. K. **Fic**
Triumph and tragedy. Associated Press **920**
Triumph and tragedy. Churchill, W. S.
            940.53
The **triumph** of night. Wharton, E.
 In Wharton, E. The collected short
  stories of Edith Wharton v2 p325-
  44   **S C**
The **triumphs** of a taxidermist. Wells, H. G.
 In Wells, H. G. The complete short
  stories of H. G. Wells p220-24
            S C
Trivial breath. Wylie, E.
 In Wylie, E. Collected poems p105-66
            811
Troilus and Cressida. Chaucer, G.
 In Chaucer, G. The modern reader's
  Chaucer   **821**
 In Chaucer, G. The poetical works of
  Chaucer   **821**
 In Chaucer, G. The portable Chaucer
  p372-579   **821**
Troilus and Cressida. Shakespeare, W.
 In Bentley, E. comp. The great play-
  wrights v 1 p303-401 **808.82**
The **Trojan** horse; a play. MacLeish, A.
 In MacLeish, A. Collected poems, 1917-
  1952 p371-407   **811**
Trojan War
 Graves, R. The siege and fall of Troy **883**
 Homer. The complete works of Homer
            883
 Homer. The Iliad   **883**
 See also pages in the following books:
 Asimov, I. Words from the myths p177-
  201   **292**
 Gayley, C. M. ed. The classic myths in
  English literature and in art p277-317
            292
 Hamilton, E. Mythology p197-342 **292**
 Quennell, M. Everyday things in ancient
  Greece p14-33   **913.38**

Trojan women. Euripides
 In Fitts, D. ed. Greek plays in modern
  translation p145-93   **882.08**
 In Oates, W. J. ed. The complete Greek
  drama v 1 p959-1010 **882.08**
The **troll** garden. Cather, W.
 In Cather, W. Willa Cather's Collected
  short fiction, 1892-1912 v2 p147-261
            S C
Trollope, Anthony
 Barchester Towers   **Fic**
       About
  See pages in the following books:
 Karl, F. R. An age of fiction: the nine-
  teenth century British novel p337-43
            823.09
 Wagenknecht, E. Cavalcade of the English
  novel p286-303   **823.09**
Troop withdrawal—the initial step. Park-
 er, T.
 In Prize stories, 1971: The O. Henry
  Awards p148-67   **S C**
The **trophy** hunters. Lascelles, K.
 In The Best short plays, 1970 p29-63
            808.82
Tropical Africa. Coughlan, R. **916.7**
Tropical aquariums. Wainwright, N. **639**
Tropical fish
 Axelrod, H. R. Axelrod's Tropical fish
  book   **639**
 Wainwright, N. Tropical aquariums **639**
Tropical fish book, Axelrod's. Axelrod,
 H. R.   **639**
Tropics
 Sanderson, I. T. Ivan Sanderson's Book
  of great jungles   **910.9**
Trotsky, Leon
 Lenin   **92**
Trout fishing
  See pages in the following book:
 Sports Illustrated. The wonderful world of
  sport p261-63   **796**
Trowell, Margaret
 African and Oceanic art   **709.6**
Troy
 Graves, R. The siege and fall of Troy **883**
  See also pages in the following book:
 Schreiber, H. Vanished cities p230-42
            913.03
     Antiquities
  See pages in the following book:
 White, A. T. Lost worlds p23-54 **913.03**
Troyes, France
      History
  See pages in the following book:
 Gies, J. Life in a medieval city p23-33
            914.4
Truant. McKay, C.
 In Clarke, J. H. ed. American Negro
  short stories p41-54   **S C**
True grit. Portis, C.   **Fic**
A **true** story. Twain, M.
 In Twain, M. The complete short stories
  of Mark Twain p94-98 **S C**
True tales of bold escapes. Roscoe, T. **904**
Trueblood, Paul G.
 Lord Byron   **821.09**

Truman, Harry S. President U.S.
Memoirs   92
Year of decisions
In Truman, H. S. Memoirs v 1   92
Years of trial and hope
In Truman, H. S. Memoirs v2   92

About

Gies, J. Harry S. Truman   92
See also pages in the following book:
Warren, S. The President as world leader p283-352   327.73

Trump, David
Central and southern Italy before Rome   913.37
(jt. auth.) Bray, W. The American Heritage Guide to archaeology   913.03

Trump, Fred
Buyer beware!   339.4
The **trumpet** of conscience. King, M. L.   309.173

Trusts, Industrial
Kefauver, E. In a few hands: monopoly power in America   338.8
See also pages in the following books:
Wagner, S. The Federal Trade Commission p3-18, 109-25   381.061
Weinberg, A. ed. The muckrakers p245-60   309.173

See also Monopolies

The **truth.** Fitch, C.
In Dickinson, T. H. ed. Chief contemporary dramatists [1st ser] p237-82   808.82
In Gassner, J. ed. Best plays of the early American theatre p458-510   812.08
The **truth** about Pyecraft. Wells, H. G.
In Wells, H. G. The complete short stories of H. G. Wells p872-83   S C
In Wells, H. G. 28 science fiction stories p845-55   S C
A **truthful** adventure. Mansfield, K.
In Mansfield, K. The short stories of Katherine Mansfield p18-24   S C

Tu, Wei-ming
(jt. ed.) Liu, J. T. C. ed. Traditional China   915.1

Tuberculosis

Fiction

Mann, T. The magic mountain   Fic

Tubman, Harriet (Ross)
See pages in the following books:
Metcalf, G. R. Black profiles p169-94   920
Stoddard, H. Famous American women p421-30   920

Tucci, Niccolò
Terror and grief
In The New Yorker. Stories from The New Yorker, 1950-1960 p490-517   S C

Tuchman, Barbara W.
The guns of August   940.3
The proud tower   909.82
Stilwell and the American experience in China, 1911-45   327.73
The Zimmermann telegram   940.3

Tucker, S. Marion
(ed.) Twenty-five modern plays   808.82

Tudor costume, Medieval and. Cunnington, P.   391

Tudor England, Life in. Williams, P.   914.2
The **Tudor** rose. Barnes, M. C.   Fic
The **Tudors** and the Stuart era. Trevelyan, G. M.
In Trevelyan, G. M. History of England v2   942

Tugwell, Rexford G.
FDR: architect of an era   973.917
Grover Cleveland   92

Tuition. See Education—Finance

Tully, Andrew
CIA: the inside story   351.7
The FBI's most famous cases   353.5

Tumbling
See pages in the following book:
American Association for Health, Physical Education, and Recreation. Physical education for high school students p165-203   613.7

Tumors
See pages in the following book:
Sternberg, T. H. More than skin deep p246-55   616.5

Tunis, Edwin
Colonial living   917.3
Weapons   399

Tunisia

Politics and government

See pages in the following book:
Kenworthy, L. S. Leaders of new nations p130-55   920

Tunnels
Jacobs, D. Bridges, canals & tunnels   624
Overman, M. Roads, bridges, and tunnels   624

Tunney, Gene
See pages in the following book:
Leighton, I. ed. The aspirin age, 1919-1941 p152-68   917.3

Turbian, Kate L.
A manual for writers of term papers, theses and dissertations   808.02

Turgenev, Ivan
The district doctor
In Seltzer, T. comp. Best Russian short stories p82-95   S C
Fathers and sons   Fic
A month in the country
In Gassner, J. ed. Twenty best European plays on the American stage p119-63   808.82

About

See pages in the following book:
Posell, E. Z. Russian authors p65-86   920

Turkey
Stewart, D. Turkey   915.61

Fiction

Kemal, Y. Memed, my hawk   Fic

History

See pages in the following books:
Durant, W. Rousseau and revolution p411-17   940.2
The New Cambridge Modern history v 1 p395-419, v2 p510-33, v3 p347-76, v4 p620-43, v5 p500-18, v6 p608-47, v11 p323-51   909

Turkish cookery. See Cookery, Turkish

Twain, Mark—*Continued*
Russian passport; A double-barreled detective story; The five boons of life; Was it Heaven? Or Hell; A dog's tale; The $30,000 bequest; A horse's tale; Hunting the deceitful turkey; Extract from Captain Stormfield's visit to Heaven; A fable; The mysterious stranger

A Connecticut Yankee in King Arthur's court   Fic

Huck and Jim talk about kings
  In White, E. B. ed. A subtreasury of American humor; abridged p192-95
       817.08

The innocents abroad   817
Life on the Mississippi   817
Personal recollections of Joan of Arc   Fic
Pudd'nhead Wilson   Fic
Roughing it   817
  For other titles by and material about this author see Clemens, Samuel Langhorne

12 days before the mast. Rogin, G.
  In Sports Illustrated. The wonderful world of sport p240-41   796

The **twelve**-hour caper. Marmer, M.
  In Hitchcock, A. ed. Alfred Hitchcock presents: A month of mystery p123-33   S C

Twelve o'clock. Crane, S.
  In Crane, S. The complete short stories & sketches of Stephen Crane p630-35   S C

The **twelve**-pole road. Stuart, J.
  In Stuart, J. Come back to the farm p174-88   S C

The **twelve**-pound look. Barrie, J. M.
  In Barrie, J. M. The plays of J. M. Barrie p737-57   822
  In Cerf, B. ed. Thirty famous one-act plays p115-29   808.82

Twelve stories, and a dream. Wells, H. G.
  In Wells, H. G. The complete short stories of H. G. Wells p827-1038   S C

Twentieth century
  Colton, J. G. Twentieth century   901.94
  MacLeish, A. A continuing journey   818

The **Twentieth** century (Television program)
  Columbia Broadcasting System, inc. CBS News. Trial at Nuremberg   341.4

Twentieth century Africa. McEwen, P. J. M.   960

Twentieth-century American poetry. Aiken, C. ed.   811.08

Twentieth century art. Batterberry, M.   709.04

Twentieth century authors. Kunitz, S. J. ed.   920.03

Twentieth century authors: first supplement. Kunitz, S. J. ed.   920.03

Twentieth century discovery. Asimov, I.   500

Twentieth century interpretations of A farewell to arms. Gellens, J. ed.   813.09

Twentieth century interpretations of Boswell's Life of Johnson. Clifford, J. L. ed.   828

Twentieth century interpretations of Light in August. Minter, D. L. ed.   813.09

Twentieth century interpretations of Poe's tales. Howarth, W. L. ed.   813.09

Twentieth century interpretations of Walden. Ruland, R. ed.   818

Twentieth century interpretations of Wuthering Heights. Vogler, T. A. ed.   823.09

Twentieth century poetry: American and British (1900-1970) Brinnin, J. M. ed.   821.08

Twentieth century United States, 1900-1929. Hart, A. B. ed.
  In Hart, A. B. ed. American history told by contemporaries v5   973

Twenty best European plays on the American stage. Gassner, J. ed.   808.82

Twenty best plays of the modern American theatre. Gassner, J. ed.   812.08

Twenty decisive battles of the world. Mitchell, J. B.   904

28 science fiction stories. Wells, H. G.   S C

Twenty-first century
  Foreign Policy Association. Toward the year 2018   901.9

The **Twenty-first** century (Television program)
  Warshofsky, F. The new age of exploration   500

Twenty-five best plays of the modern American theatre; early ser. Gassner, J. ed.   812.08

Twenty-five modern plays. Tucker, S. M. ed.   808.82

24 favorite one-act plays. Cerf, B. ed.   808.82

Twenty letters to a friend. Alliluyeva, S.   92

27 wagons full of cotton. Williams, T.
  In Cerf, B. ed. 24 favorite one-act plays p94-116   808.82

The **26** letters. Ogg, O.   411

Twenty-three tales. Tolstoy, L.   S C

Twenty years at Hull-House. Addams, J.   361

A **twilight** adventure. Post, M. D.
  In Hitchcock, A. ed. Alfred Hitchcock presents: A month of mystery p247-57   S C

Twilight in southern California. Fuchs, D.
  In Abrahams, W. ed. Fifty years of the American short story v 1 p280-95   S C

Twilight of the idols. Nietzsche, F. W.
  In Nietzsche, F. W. The portable Nietzsche p463-563   193

Twilight of the wise. Hilton, J.
  In Becker, M. L. ed. The home book of Christmas p662-70   394.26

Twin bed bridge. Hecht, F. M.
  In Prize stories, 1971: The O. Henry Awards p 1-27   S C

The **twins**. Spark, M.
  In Spark, M. Collected stories: I p122-33   S C

Two birds with one stone. Moore, R.
  In Moore, R. The green berets p102-38   S C

Two for the seesaw. Gibson, W.
  In Gassner, J. ed. Best American plays; 5th ser. p341-78   812.08

United States—Foreign relations—*Continued*
Reston, J. The artillery of the press 323.44
Stevenson, A. An ethic for survival 327
Stevenson, A. E. Looking outward 341.13
Warren, S. The President as world leader 327.73
White, T. H. Fire in the ashes 940.55
See also pages in the following books:
Chase, S. American credos p41-72 301.15
Commager, H. S. ed. Living ideas in America p648-732 973
Degler, C. N. Out of our past p413-65 973
The New Cambridge Modern history v11 p668-93 909
Snow, E. Red China today p673-704 915.1
Time-Life Books. The U.S. overseas p9-39 917.3
The United States p169-76 917.3

Foreign relations—Africa
See pages in the following book:
Schlesinger, A. M. A thousand days p551-84 973.922

Foreign relations—Asia
Reischauer, E. O. Beyond Vietnam: the United States and Asia 327.73

Foreign relations—Bolivia
See pages in the following book:
Harris, R. Death of a revolutionary; [Ernesto] Che Guevara's last mission p169-78 92

Foreign relations—Caribbean area
See pages in the following book:
Williams, E. From Columbus to Castro: the history of the Caribbean, 1492-1969 p409-27 972.9

Foreign relations—China
Tuchman, B. W. Stilwell and the American experience in China, 1911-45 327.73
See also pages in the following book:
Buck, P. S. China as I see it p216-31 915.1

Foreign relations—China (People's Republic of China)
See pages in the following book:
Snow, E. Red China today p113-24, 597-601, 674-86, 693-98 915.1

Foreign relations—Cuba
See pages in the following books:
Halle, L. J. The cold war as history p400-11 909.82
Stevenson, A. E. Looking outward p79-99 341.13

Foreign relations—Europe
See pages in the following book:
The New Cambridge Modern history v9 p591-611 909

Foreign relations—Fiction
Galbraith, J. K. The triumph Fic

Foreign relations—Great Britain
See pages in the following book:
Degler, C. N. Out of our past p29-36, 58-66 973

Foreign relations—India
Bowles, C. Ambassador's report 915.4
Galbraith, J. K. Ambassador's journal 327.73

Foreign relations—Japan
Newmann, W. L. America encounters Japan: from Perry to MacArthur 327.73
Reischauer, E. O. The United States and Japan 327.73
Tamarin, A. Japan and the United States 327.52

Foreign relations—Russia
Harriman, W. A. America and Russia in a changing world 327.73
Kennedy, R. F. Thirteen days 973.922
See also pages in the following book:
Stevenson, A. E. Looking outward p79-99 341.13

Foreign relations—South America
See pages in the following book:
Gunther, J. Inside South America p138-63 980

Foreign relations—Treaties
See pages in the following book:
Douglas, W. O. International dissent: six steps toward world peace p31-47 341.6

Foreign relations—Vietnam
Schlesinger, A. M. The bitter heritage 327.73

Forest Service
See pages in the following book:
Dodd, E. Careers for the '70s: conservation p18-32 333.7069

Forests and forestry
See Forests and forestry—United States

Furniture
See Furniture, American

Galleries and museums
Christensen, E. O. A guide to art museums in the United States 708
Spaeth, E. American art museums 708

Geography
See United States—Description and travel

Government
See United States—Politics and government

Government Printing Office
Style manual 655.2

Government Printing Office (as subject)
Kling, R. E. The Government Printing Office 655.061

Government publications—Bibliography
Leidy, W. P. A popular guide to government publications 015.73

Graphic arts
See Graphic arts, American

Historic houses, etc.
American Heritage. The American Heritage Book of great historic places 917.3
Country Beautiful. America's historic houses 917.3
National Geographic Society. America's historylands 917.3

Historical geography—Maps
Adams, J. T. ed. Atlas of American history 911
American Heritage. The American Heritage Pictorial atlas of United States history 911

United States—Politics and government—1933-1945—*Continued*

Freidel, F. ed. The New Deal and the American people   973.917

Sherwood, R. E. Roosevelt and Hopkins   973.917

Tugwell, R. G. FDR: architect of an era   973.917

Wecter, D. The age of the great depression, 1929-1941   973.917

Politics and government—1945-1953

Acheson, D. Present at the creation   973.918

Gies, J. Harry S. Truman   92

Matusow, A. J. ed. Joseph R. McCarthy   92

Truman, H. S. Memoirs   92

Politics and government—1953-1961

Eisenhower, D. D. The White House years   92

White, T. H. The making of the President, 1960   329

Politics and government—1961-

Chisholm, S. Unbought and unbossed   92

Goldman, E. F. The tragedy of Lyndon Johnson   973.923

Halberstam, D. The unfinished odyssey of Robert Kennedy   92

Johnson, L. B. A White House diary   92

Kennedy, J. F. The burden and the glory   973.922

Kennedy, R. F. Thirteen days   973.922

Lubell, S. The hidden crisis in American politics   329

Manchester, W. Portrait of a President; John F. Kennedy in profile   92

Newfield, J. Robert Kennedy   92

Schlesinger, A. M. The bitter heritage   327.73

Schlesinger, A. M. A thousand days   973.922

Sorensen, T. C. The Kennedy legacy   973.922

U.S. politics—inside and out   329

White, T. H. The making of the President, 1964   329

White, T. H. The making of the President, 1968   329

Population

See pages in the following book:

Montagu, A. The American way of life p93-102   917.3

Post Office Department

Cullinan, G. The Post Office Department   353.4

Presidents

See Presidents—United States

President's Commission on Campus Unrest

The report of the President's Commission on Campus Unrest   378.1

President's Commission on Law Enforcement and Administration of Justice

The challenge of crime in a free society   364

President's Commission on the Assassination of President Kennedy

See United States. Warren Commission on the Assassination of President Kennedy

President's Commission on the Status of Women

American women   301.41

Prisons

See Prisons—United States

Public documents

See United States—Government publications

Public health

See Public health—United States

Public Health Service

See pages in the following books:

Lee, R. V. The physician p132-45   610.69

Terrell, J. U. The United States Department of Health, Education, and Welfare p17-45   353.84

Public lands

McClellan, G. S. ed. Land use in the United States   333

Race relations

Baldwin, J. The fire next time   301.451

Baldwin, J. Nobody knows my name   301.451

Baldwin, J. Notes of a native son   301.451

Baruch, D. W. Glass house of prejudice   301.45

Bernstein, S. Alternatives to violence   301.43

Bracey, J. H. ed. Black nationalism in America   301.451

Brink, W. Black and white   301.451

Draper, T. The rediscovery of Black nationalism   301.451

Ebony. The white problem in America   323.4

Furnas, J. C. Goodbye to Uncle Tom   326

Goldman, P. Report from Black America   301.451

Handlin, O. The American people in the twentieth century   301.45

Handlin, O. Fire-bell in the night   323.4

Hughes, L. The Langston Hughes reader   818

King, M. L. The trumpet of conscience   309.173

King, M. L. Where do we go from here: chaos or community?   323.4

Lomax, L. E. The Negro revolt   301.451

Malcolm X. The autobiography of Malcolm X   301.451

Meier, A. From plantation to ghetto   301.451

Myrdal, G. An American dilemma   301.451

Senior, C. The Puerto Ricans: strangers —then neighbors   301.453

Silberman, C. E. Crisis in black and white   301.451

Stalvey, L. M. The education of a WASP   301.45

United States. National Advisory Commission on Civil Disorders. Report of the National Advisory Commission on Civil Disorders   301.18

See also pages in the following books:

Archer, J. The extremists: gadflies of American society p91-100   973

Driver, H. E. Indians of North America p479-504   970.1

United States—Social life and customs—
Colonial period—*Continued*
Tunis, E. Colonial living   917.3
Wright, L. B. Everyday life in colonial
America   917.3

Social life and customs—Pictures, illustrations, etc.
Goodrich, L. Winslow Homer's America
                                         760.9

Social policy
The American Assembly. The states and
the urban crisis   309.2
Gardner, J. W. The recovery of con-
fidence   309.2
Higbee, E. A question of priorities   309.2
Tugwell, R. G. FDR: architect of an era
                                         973.917
See also pages in the following book:
United States. National Commission on the
Causes and Prevention of Violence.
Violent crime p 1-30   364.1

Soil Conservation Service
Simms, D. H. The Soil Conservation
Service   353.81

Songs
See Songs, American

State governments
See State governments

Statesmen
See Statesmen, American

Statistics
Information please almanac   317.3
The New York Times. The New York
Times Encyclopedic almanac   317.3
United States. Bureau of the Census.
Statistical abstract of the United States
                                         317.3
The World almanac and book of facts
                                         317.3

Students
See Students—United States

Supreme Court
Historic decisions of the Supreme Court
                                         347.9

Supreme Court (as subject)
Acheson, P. C. The Supreme Court 347.9
Baker, L. Felix Frankfurter   92
Barker, L. J. ed. Civil liberties and the
Constitution   342.73
Beard, C. A. The Supreme Court and the
Constitution   342.73
Bowen, C. D. Yankee from Olympus;
Justice Holmes and his family   92
Corwin, E. S. John Marshall and the
Constitution   973.4
Frankfurter, F. Mr Justice Holmes and
the Supreme Court   347.9
Fribourg, M. G. The Supreme Court in
American history   347.9
Garraty, J. A. ed. Quarrels that have
shaped the Constitution   342.73
Habenstreit, B. Changing America and
the Supreme Court   347.9
Hand, L. The Bill of Rights   342.73
Lewis, A. Gideon's trumpet   347.9
Severn, B. John Marshall   92
See also pages in the following book:
Beth, L. P. The development of the
American Constitution, 1877-1917 p138-
90   973.8

Surgeon General's Advisory Committee on Smoking and Health
Smoking and health   613.8
Smoking and health: criticism
In Cain, A. H. Young people and smok-
ing p36-47   613.8

Tariff
See Tariff—United States

Taxation
See Taxation—United States

Territorial expansion
Billington, R. A. The far Western fron-
tier, 1830-1860   978
Billington, R. A. Westward expansion 973
De Voto, B. The course of empire 973.1
Fish, C. R. The path of empire   327.73

Territories and possessions
Time-Life Books. The U.S. overseas 917.3

Theater
See Theater—United States

Vice-Presidents
See Vice-Presidents—United States

Warren Commission
See United States. Warren Commis-
sion on the Assassination of President
Kennedy

Warren Commission on the Assassination of President Kennedy
The official Warren Commission report on
the assassination of President John F.
Kennedy   364.12

Women
See Women in the United States

World War, 1939-1945
See World War, 1939-1945—United
States
The United States   917.3
The United States and Japan. Reischauer,
E. O.   327.73

United States Capitol Historical Society
We, the people: the story of the United
States Capitol, its past and its promise.
See We, the people: the story of the
United States Capitol, its past and its
promise   975.3
The United States in a chaotic world.
Nevins, A.   327.73

United States Kerner Report. See United
States. National Advisory Commission
on Civil Disorders. Report of the Na-
tional Advisory Commission on Civil
Disorders   301.18
The United States Marine Corps. Donovan,
J. A.   359.9

United States News & World Report. See
U.S. News & World Report
The United States since 1865. Dulles, F. R.
                                         973
The United States to 1865. Kraus, M.   973
The Universal encyclopedia of mathematics
                                         510.3

Universal history. See World history
Universe
Bergamini, D. The universe   523.1
Bondi, H. The universe at large   523.1
Bova, B. In quest of quasars   523.8

Updike, John—*Continued*
Pigeon feathers
In Foley, M. ed. Fifty best American short stories, 1915-1965 p702-19
      S C

Pigeon feathers, and other stories   **S C**
Contents: Walter Briggs; The persistence of desire; Still life; Flight; Should wizard hit mommy; A sense of shelter; Dear Alexandros; Wife-wooing; Pigeon feathers; Home; Archangel; You'll never know, dear, how much I love you; The astronomer; A & P; The doctor's wife; Lifeguard; The crow in the woods; The blessed man of Boston; My grandmother's thimble, and Fanning Island; Packed dirt, churchgoing, a dying cat, a traded car

The poorhouse fair   **Fic**
Rabbit, run   **Fic**

Upon the sweeping flood. Oates, J. C.
In The Best American short stories, 1964 p241-56   **S C**
In Foley, M. ed. Fifty best American short stories p799-814   **S C**

Upper atmosphere. See Atmosphere, Upper

Upper classes
See pages in the following book:
Avery, G. Victorian people p53-78 **914.2**

The **uprising** of the Warsaw Ghetto, November 1940-May 1943. Werstein, I, **940.54**

The **uprooted**. Handlin, O.   **325.73**

Uprooted. O'Connor, F.
In Havighurst, W. ed. Masters of the modern short story p99-118 **S C**

Upson, William Hazlett
A quiet wedding
In Lardner, R. ed. Rex Lardner selects the best of sports fiction p171-84
      S C

The **upturned** face. Crane, S.
In Crane, S. The complete short stories & sketches of Stephen Crane p689-92   **S C**

Uranium
See pages in the following book:
Asimov, I. Building blocks of the universe p254-67   **546**

Urban affairs. See Asbell, B. Careers in urban affairs: six young people talk about their professions in the inner city
      331.7

Urban America, The rise of. Green, C. M.
      301.3

Urban areas. See Metropolitan areas

Urban crisis, The states and the. The American Assembly   **309.2**

Urban League
See pages in the following book:
Lomax, L. E. The Negro revolt p209-20
      301.451

The **urban** prospect. Mumford, L.   **711**

Urban renewal
Isenberg, I. ed. The city in crisis **301.3**
Willmann, J. B. The Department of Housing and Urban Development **353.85**
See also City planning

Urban sociology. See Sociology, Urban

Urbino, Montefeltro Federigo da, duca di.
See Montefeltro, Federigo da, duca di Urbino

Urdang, Laurence
(ed.) The Random House Dictionary of the English language. College ed. See The Random House Dictionary of the English language. College ed.   **423**

Urey, Harold Clayton
See pages in the following book:
Moore, R. The earth we live on p281-98
      551.09

Uris, Leon
The defection of Kuznetov
In Dulles, A. ed. Great spy stories from fiction p13-22   **S C**
Exodus   **Fic**
Mila 18   **Fic**

Uruguay
Alisky, M. Uruguay, a contemporary survey   **918.95**
Ferguson, J. H. The River Plate republics
      918
See also pages in the following book:
Gunther, J. Inside South America p220-37
      980

Useful arts. See Technology

The **uses** of intelligence. Gant, M.
In Hitchcock, A. ed. Alfred Hitchcock presents: A month of mystery p39-50   **S C**

Using your high school library. Rossoff, M.
      028.7

Uta Indians. See Ute Indians

Ute Indians
See pages in the following books:
Brown, D. Bury my heart at Wounded Knee p367-89   **970.4**
Montagu, M. F. A. ed. Man and aggression p103-15   **152.4**
      Fiction
Borland, H. When the legends die   **Fic**

Utopia. More, T.   **321**

Utopia Limited. Gilbert, Sir W. S.
In Gilbert, Sir W. S. The complete plays of Gilbert and Sullivan p585-646
      782.8

Utopias
More, T. Utopia   **321**
Plato. The Republic   **888**
See also pages in the following book:
Horizon Magazine. The light of the past p250-56   **901.9**
      Fiction
Bellamy, E. Looking backward: 2000-1887
      Fic
Huxley, A. Brave new world   **Fic**

Utrecht, Treaty of, 1713
See pages in the following book:
The New Cambridge Modern history v6 p446-79   **909**

V

VD. See Venereal diseases

VD: facts you should know. Blanzaco, A.
      616.9

VRA. See Vocational Rehabilitation Administration

Van Druten, John—*Continued*
I remember mama   822
—Same
  In Gassner, J. ed. Best plays of the modern American theatre; 2d ser. p85-129   812.08
The voice of the turtle
  In Gassner, J. ed. Best plays of the modern American theatre; 2d ser. p229-66   812.08

Van Dyke, Henry
First Christmas tree
  In The Scribner treasury p183-202   **S C**
The story of the other wise man   **Fic**

Vane, Sutton
Outward bound
  In Cerf, B. A. comp. Sixteen famous British plays p477-539   822.08

Van Every, Dale
Disinherited: the lost birthright of the American Indian   970.5

Van Gelder, Richard G.
Biology of mammals   599

Van Gogh, Vincent. See Gogh, Vincent van

Van Heusen, James
  See pages in the following book:
Ewen, D. Great men of American popular song p321-39   920

Vanished. Knebel, F.   **Fic**

Vanished cities. Schreiber, H.   913.03

Vanishing animals. See Rare animals

Vanishing of Vaudrey. Chesterton, G. K.
  In Chesterton, G. K. The Father Brown omnibus p725-45   **S C**

Vanishing peoples of the earth. National Geographic Society   572

Van Itallie, Jean-Claude
The serpent: a ceremony
  In The Best plays of 1969/1970 p232-64   808.82

Vanity and some sables. Henry, O.
  In Henry, O. The complete works of O. Henry p1415-19   **S C**

Vanity fair. Thackeray, W. M.   **Fic**

Vanka. Chekhov, A.
  In Chekhov, A. The image of Chekhov p113-17   **S C**
  In Chekhov, A. The stories of Anton Chekhov p72-76   **S C**
  In Seltzer, T. comp. Best Russian short stories p206-11   **S C**

Van Lew, Elizabeth
  See pages in the following book:
Kane, H. T. Spies for the Blue and Gray p231-49   973.7

Van Loon, Hendrik Willem
The story of mankind   909

Van Meegeren, Han. See Meegeren, Han van

Van Nostrand's International encyclopedia of chemical science. See International encyclopedia of chemical science   540.3

Van Nostrand's Scientific encyclopedia   503

Vannucci, Pietro. See Perugino, Pietro Vannucci, known as

Van Vogt, Alfred Elton
Not only dead men
  In Conklin, G. ed. Invaders of earth p160-81   **S C**

Varèse, Edgard
  See pages in the following book:
Ewen, D. Composers of tomorrow's music p94-106   920

Vargas, Diego de. See Vargas Zapata y Luxán Ponze de Léon, Diego de

Vargas, Getulio, President Brazil
  See pages in the following books:
Alexander, R. J. Prophets of the revolution p219-45   920
Worcester, D. E. Makers of Latin America p209-17   920

Vargas Zapata y Luxán Ponze de Léon, Diego de
  See pages in the following book:
Hall-Quest, O. Conquistadors and Pueblos p136-49   979.1

Variation (Biology) See Adaptation (Biology); Evolution; Mendel's law

Varnish and varnishing
Newell, A. C. Coloring, finishing and painting wood   698.3

Vasari, Giorgio
The lives of the painters, sculptors and architects   920
  See also pages in the following book:
Vasari, G. The lives of the painters, sculptors and architects v4 p257-91   920

Vásquez de Coronado, Francisco
  See pages in the following book:
Hall-Quest, O. Conquistadors and Pueblos p34-51   979.1

Vassals. See Feudalism

Vaucouleurs, G. de
(jt. auth.) Rudaux, L. Larousse Encyclopedia of astronomy   520.3

Vaughan Williams, Ralph
  See pages in the following books:
Cross, M. The Milton Cross New encyclopedia of the great composers and their music p1054-69   920.03
Ewen, D. ed. The new book of modern composers p416-32   920

Vaux, Roland de
  See pages in the following book:
Noble, I. Treasure of the caves p68-111   221.4

Vaux-le-Vicomte
  See pages in the following book:
Horizon Magazine. The light of the past p184-89   901.9

Veblen, Thorstein
The portable Veblen   330.1
The theory of the leisure class   339
The theory of the leisure class [excerpt]
  In Veblen, T. The portable Veblen p53-214   330.1
          About
Heilbroner, R. L. The wordly philosophers   330.1
  See also pages in the following books:
Commager, H. S. The American mind p227-46   917.3
Mencken, H. L. The American scene p200-10   818
Untermeyer, L. Makers of the modern world p262-69   920

Verlaine, Paul Marie
See pages in the following book:
Untermeyer, L. Makers of the modern world p198-203   920

Vermeer, Johannes
Koningsberger, H. The world of Vermeer, 1632-1675   92

Vermes, Hal
Helping youth avoid four great dangers: smoking, drinking, VD, narcotics addiction   613.8

Vermes, Jean
(jt. auth.) Vermes, H. Helping youth avoid four great dangers: smoking, drinking, VD, narcotics addiction 613.8

Vermont
Fiction
Mather, M. One summer in between   Fic
Walker, M. The quarry   Fic

A **Vermont** Christmas. Greene, A. B.
In Wernecke, H. H. ed. Celebrating Christmas around the world p221-24   394.26

Versailles
Levron, J. Daily life at Versailles in the seventeenth and eighteenth centuries   914.43

Versailles, Treaty of, 1919
See pages in the following book:
The New Cambridge Modern history v12 p209-41   909

Vertebrates. See Amphibia; Mammals; Reptiles

Vertical file index   015

Verwoerd, Hendrik Frensch
See pages in the following book:
Paton, A. The long view p268-75   968

A **very** short story. Hemingway, E.
In Hemingway, E. In our time p81-85   S C
In Hemingway, E. The short stories of Ernest Hemingway p139-42   S C

The **vessel** of wrath. Maugham, W. S.
In Maugham, W. S. The best short stories of W. Somerset Maugham p48-88   S C

Vessels (Ships) See Ships

The **veteran.** Crane, S.
In Crane, S. The complete short stories & sketches of Stephen Crane p291-94   S C

Veterinary medicine
Yates, E. Is there a doctor in the barn?   636.089

Viaducts. See Bridges

Vibration. See Light; Sound waves

The **vicar**-general and the wide night. Downey, H.
In The Best American short stories, 1966 p35-57   S C

The **Vicar** of Wakefield, and other writings. Goldsmith, O.   828

Vice. See Crime and criminals

Vice-Presidents
United States
Lucas, J. G. Agnew: profile in conflict   92

Marsh, R. Agnew, the unexamined man   92
Parmet, H. S. Aaron Burr   92

Vicenza, Italy
See pages in the following book:
Camus, A. Lyrical and critical essays p40-51   844

Vicksburg, Miss.
Siege, 1863
See pages in the following books:
Armstrong, O. K. The fifteen decisive battles of the United States p192-218   973
Mitchell, J. B. Twenty decisive battles of the world p243-62   904

The **Vicomte** de Bragelonne; excerpt. See Dumas, A. The man in the iron mask   Fic

A **victor** of Salamis. Davis, W. S.   Fic

Victoria, Queen of Great Britain
Strachey, L. Queen Victoria   92
See also pages in the following book:
Twain, M. The complete essays of Mark Twain p189-99   814

Victoria Regina. Housman, L.
In Cerf, B. A. comp. Sixteen famous British plays p869-931   822.08

Victorian people. Avery, G.   914.2

Victory. Conrad, J.   Fic

Victory. Faulkner, W.
In Faulkner, W. Collected stories of William Faulkner p431-64   S C

Victory and the dream. Stuart, J.
In Stuart, J. Come back to the farm p55-75   S C

The **victory** of the moon. Crane, S.
In Crane, S. The complete short stories & sketches of Stephen Crane p362-64   S C

Victory over myself. Patterson, F.   92

La **vida.** Lewis, O.   301.453

Vidal, Gore
The best man
In Gassner, J. ed. Best American plays; 5th ser. p635-74   812.08
Visit to a small planet, and other television plays   812
About
White, R. L. Gore Vidal   818

Vieira, Antonio
See pages in the following book:
Worcester, D. E. Makers of Latin America p56-62   920

Vierochka. Chekhov, A.
In Chekhov, A. The stories of Anton Chekhov p314-27   S C

Vietnam
Dooley, T. A. Dr Tom Dooley's three great books   92
Hammer, E. Vietnam: yesterday and today   915.97
See also pages in the following books:
Ashabranner, B. A moment in history: the first ten years of the Peace Corps p273-85   309.2
Kohler, F. D. Understanding the Russians p366-97   947.084

Voltaire, François M. A. de—*About*—*Cont.*
Durant, W. The story of philosophy p152-91   **109**
Thomas, H. Understanding the great philosophers p237-49   **109**

Von Braun, Wernher
History of rocketry & space travel **629.409**
Space frontier   **629.4**
About
David, H. M. Wernher von Braun   **92**
See also pages in the following book:
Mailer, N. Of a fire on the moon p63-78   **629.45**

Von Frisch, Karl. See Frisch, Karl von

Von Goethe, Johann Wolfgang. See Goethe, Johann Wolfgang von

Von Hagen, Victor W.
Roman roads   **625.7**

Von Hofmannsthal, Hugo. See Hoffmannsthal, Hugo von

Von Kempelen and his discovery. Poe, E. A.
In Poe, E. A. The complete tales and poems of Edgar Allan Poe p82-87   **S C**
In Poe, E. A. Selected poetry and prose p344-45   **818**

Von Liebig, Justus, Freiherr. See Liebig, Justus, Freiherr von

Vonnegut, Kurt
Cat's cradle   **Fic**
The sirens of Titan   **Fic**
Slaughterhouse-five   **Fic**

Von Richthofen, Manfred, Freiherr. See Richthofen, Manfred, Freiherr von

Von Ryan's Express. Westheimer, D. **Fic**

Von Steuben, Friedrich Wilhelm Ludolf Gerhard Augustin, Baron. See Steuben, Friedrich Wilhelm Ludolf Gerhard Augustin, Baron von

Von Tilzer, Harry
See pages in the following book:
Ewen, D. Great men of American popular song p53-63   **920**

Voss, Carl Hermann
In search of meaning: living religions of the world   **291**

Voting for President. Sayre, W. S. **324.73**

The **voyage.** Mansfield, K.
In Mansfield, K. The short stories of Katherine Mansfield p525-33   **S C**

A **voyage** of discovery into the South Sea and Behring's Strait; excerpt. Kotzebue, O. von
In Day, A. G. ed. The spell of Hawaii p104-19   **919.69**

Voyage round the world, from 1806 to 1818; excerpt. Campbell, A.
In Day, A. G. ed. The spell of Hawaii p97-103   **919.69**

A **voyage** to the Pacific Ocean; excerpt. King, J.
In Day, A. G. ed. The spell of Hawaii p29-42   **919.69**

Voyages and travels
Armstrong, R. A history of seafaring   **910.9**
Dana, R. H. Two years before the mast   **910.4**

Freuchen, P. Peter Freuchen's Book of the Seven Seas   **910.4**
Hale, J. R. Age of exploration   **910.9**
Halliburton, R. Richard Halliburton's Complete book of marvels   **910.4**
Heyerdahl, T. Kon-Tiki   **910.4**
National Geographic Society. Great adventures with National Geographic   **910.9**
National Geographic Society. Men, ships and the sea   **387.2**
Polo, M. The travels of Marco Polo **915**
Rama Rau, S. Gifts of passage   **92**
Twain, M. The innocents abroad   **817**
See also pages in the following books:
Shakespeare's England v 1 p170-97 **822.3**
White, E. B. The points of my compass p205-38   **818**
See also Aeronautics—Flights; Discoveries (in geography); Scientific expeditions; Travel; Voyages around the world; Whaling; also names of countries, continents, etc. with the subdivision Description and travel, e.g. United States—Description and travel

Voyages around the world
Chichester, Sir F. Gipsy Moth circles the world   **910.4**
Villiers, A. Captain James Cook   **92**

Voyages to the moon. See Space flight to the moon

Vries, Hugo de
See pages in the following books:
Moore, R. The coil of life p178-206 **574.09**
Moore, R. Man, time, and fossils p130-49   **573.2**

Vries, Peter de. See De Vries, Peter

Vries, S. de
An atlas of world history   **911**

Vroman, Leo
Blood   **612**

Vroman, Mary Elizabeth
See how they run
In Clarke, J. H. ed. American Negro short stories p176-97   **S C**
In Hughes, L. ed. The best short stories by Negro writers p253-74 **S C**

W

WASP, The education of a. Stalvey, L. M.   **301.45**

WHO. See World Health Organization

Waddell, M. S.
Love me, love me, love me
In Hitchcock, A. ed. Alfred Hitchcock presents: A month of mystery p293-300   **S C**

Waddell, Marie L.
(jt. auth.) Markman, R. H. 10 steps in writing the research paper   **808.02**

Wagenknecht, Edward
Cavalcade of the American novel   **813.09**
Cavalcade of the English novel   **823.09**
Edgar Allan Poe   **92**

Wagenknecht, Edward—*Continued*
Harriet Beecher Stowe: the known and the unknown 92
Henry Wadsworth Longfellow: portrait of an American humanist 92
James Russell Lowell 92
The man Charles Dickens 92
Nathaniel Hawthorne: man and writer 92
The personality of Chaucer 821.09
Washington Irving: moderation displayed 818

Wages
Minimum wage
See pages in the following book:
Fribourg, M. G. The Supreme Court in American history p108-25 347.9
Waging peace, 1956-1961. Eisenhower, D. D.
In Eisenhower, D. D. The White House years v2 92
Wagner, Richard
See pages in the following books:
Bauer, M. Music through the ages p493-514 780.9
Cross, M. The Milton Cross New encyclopedia of the great composers and their music p1095-1135 920.03
Ewen, D. ed. The complete book of classical music p521-61 780.1
Ewen, D. ed. The world of great composers p320-40 920
Shippen, K. B. The heritage of music p185-91 780.9
Twain, M. The complete essays of Mark Twain p59-70 814
Untermeyer, L. Makers of the modern world p12-25 920
Wagner, Susan
The Federal Trade Commission 381.061
Wagner-Jauregg, Julius. See Wagner von Jauregg, Julius, Ritter
Wagner von Jauregg, Julius, Ritter
See pages in the following book:
De Kruif, P. Men against death p249-79 920
Wagner act. See United States. Laws, statutes, etc. National labor relations act
A **Wagner** matinee. Cather, W.
In Cather, W. Willa Cather's Collected short fiction, 1892-1912 v2 p235-42 S C
Wahhabis
Lawrence, T. E. Seven pillars of wisdom 940.4
Waifs and strays. Henry, O.
In Henry, O. The complete works of O. Henry p1632-92 S C
Wainwright, Neil
Tropical aquariums 639
Waite, Helen E.
Valiant companions: Helen Keller and Anne Sullivan Macy 92
Waiter, a bock! Maupassant, G. de
In Maupassant, G. de. Selected short stories p217-25 S C
Waiting at Dachau. Price, R.
In Prize stories, 1971: The O. Henry Awards p67-93 S C
Waiting for Jim. Randal, V.
In The Best American short stories, 1964 p285-97 S C

Waiting for Lefty. Odets, C.
In Cerf, B. A. ed. Sixteen famous American plays p423-47 812.08
In Cerf, B. ed. Thirty famous one-act plays p521-45 808.82
In Odets, C. Six plays p 1-31 812
Wakashan Indians. See Kwakiutl Indians
Wakefield, Dan
Autumn full of apples
In The Best American short stories, 1966 p283-87 S C
Wakefield. Hawthorne, N.
In Hawthorne, N. Hawthorne's Short stories p63-71 S C
Wald, Lillian D.
See pages in the following book:
Dodge, B. S. The story of nursing p184-200 610.73
Walden. Thoreau, H. D. 818
also in Thoreau, H. D. Walden, and other writings p 1-275 818
Walden, and other writings. Thoreau, H. D. 818
Walden, Twentieth century interpretations of. Ruland, R. ed. 818
Waldo. Heinlein, R. A.
In Heinlein, R. A. Three by Heinlein p217-326 Fic
Wales
Drama
Thomas, D. Under milk wood 822
Fiction
Cronin, A. J. The citadel Fic
Llewellyn, R. How green was my valley Fic
Poetry
Thomas, D. Child's Christmas in Wales 821
Walk in the light while there is light. Tolstoy, L.
In Tolstoy, L. Short novels v2 p218-71 S C
Walk in the moon shadows. Stuart, J.
In Stuart, J. Plowshare in heaven p25-35 S C
Walker, Alice
To hell with dying
In Hughes, L. ed. The best short stories by Negro writers p490-96 S C
Walker, Elinor
(comp.) Book bait 028.5
Walker, J.
Rhyming dictionary of the English language 426
Walker, John
National Gallery of Art, Washington, D.C. 708
Walker, Joseph A.
Tribal harangue two
In The Best short plays, 1971 p199-220 808.82
Walker, Margaret
Jubilee Fic
Walker, Mildred
The quarry Fic
Winter wheat Fic
Walker, Robert H.
Everyday life in the age of enterprise, 1865-1900 917.3

Warsaw

Fiction

Hersey, J. The wall   **Fic**

Uris, L. Mila 18   **Fic**

Warsaw Ghetto, November 1940-May 1943, The uprising of the. Werstein, I.   **940.54**

Warshofsky, Fred

The new age of exploration   **500**

(jt. auth.) Stevens, S. S. Sound and hearing   **534**

Warth, Robert D.

Joseph Stalin   **92**

The wartime journals of Charles A. Lindbergh. Lindbergh, C. A.   **92**

Was. Faulkner, W.

In Faulkner, W. The portable Faulkner p85-110   **S C**

Was it Heaven? or Hell? Twain, M.

In Twain, M. The complete short stories of Mark Twain p472-88   **S C**

Wash. Faulkner, W.

In Faulkner, W. Collected stories of William Faulkner p535-50   **S C**

In Faulkner, W. The Faulkner reader   **S C**

In Faulkner, W. The portable Faulkner p144-58   **S C**

Washburn, Sherwood Larned

See pages in the following book:

Moore, R. Man, time, and fossils p403-14   **573.2**

Washington, Booker T.

Up from slavery   **92**

About

Meier, A. Negro thought in America, 1880-1915   **301.451**

Thornbrough, E. L. ed. Booker T. Washington   **92**

See also pages in the following books:

Bontemps, A. 100 years of Negro freedom p21-34, 167-88, 201-27   **301.451**

Ducas, G. ed. Great documents in Black American history p156-64, 167-76   **301.451**

Washington, George, President U.S.

Flexner, J. T. George Washington and the new nation (1783-1793)   **92**

Flexner, J. T. George Washington in the American Revolution (1775-1783)   **92**

Flexner, J. T. George Washington: the forge of experience (1732-1775)   **92**

Ford, H. J. Washington and his colleagues   **973.4**

Wrong, G. M. Washington and his comrades in arms   **973.3**

See also pages in the following books:

Dictionary of American biography. The American Plutarch p27-63   **920**

Highet, G. People, places and books p94-105   **809**

Washington, D.C.

Weisberger, B. A. The District of Columbia   **917.53**

See also pages in the following book:

Myron, R. Art in America p55-69   **709.73**

Capitol

We, the people: the story of the United States Capitol, its past and its promise   **975.3**

Description

See pages in the following books:

Moyers, B. Listening to America p326-40   **917.3**

National Geographic Society. Vacationland U.S.A. p118-27   **917.3**

Fiction

Drury, A. Advise and consent   **Fic**

Knebel, F. Vanished   **Fic**

Johnson, L. B. A White House diary   **92**

White House

Jensen, A. L. The White House and its thirty-five families   **975.3**

White House Historical Association, Washington, D.C. The White House   **975.3**

Wolff, P. A tour of the White House with Mrs John F. Kennedy   **975.3**

Washington and his colleagues. Ford, H. J.   **973.4**

Washington and his comrades in arms. Wrong, G. M.   **973.3**

Washington Square. James, H.

In James, H. Short novels of Henry James p59-256   **Fic**

Wasps

Evans, H. E. The wasps   **595.7**

The wasps. Aristophanes

In Oates, W. J. ed. The complete Greek drama v2 p609-61   **882.08**

Wasserman, Dale

Man of La Mancha   **812**

Waste (Economics)

Proxmire, W. Report from wasteland   **353.6**

Waste disposal. See Refuse and refuse disposal

The waste disposal unit. Brophy, B.

In Richards, S. ed. Best short plays of the world theatre, 1958-1967 p37-51   **808.82**

The waste land. Paton, A.

In Paton, A. Tales from a troubled land p58-61   **S C**

The waste land, and other poems. Eliot, T. S.   **811**

The waste makers. Packard, V.   **339.4**

Watch on the Rhine. Hellman, L.

In Gassner, J. ed. Best plays of the modern American theatre; 2d ser. p641-82   **812.08**

Watch your language. Bernstein, T. M.   **428**

Watcher in the shadows. Household, G.   **Fic**

Watchers of the skies. Ley, W.   **523.09**

Watches. See Clocks and watches

The watchman in the vegetable plots. Sholokhov, M.

In Sholokhov, M. Tales of the Don p50-66   **S C**

Water

Davies, D. Fresh water   **333.9**

French, H. E. Of rivers and the sea   **551.4**

Leopold, L. B. Water   **551.4**

Water supply—*Continued*
Scientific American. Cities p156-69   **309.2**
Sprague, M. The Mountain States p51-73
  917.8

See also Dams; Irrigation

The **water** tap. Kassam, S.
In Angoff, C. ed. African writing today
  p207-08   **896**
Water: the wonder of life. Platt, R.   **551.4**

Waterloo, Battle of, 1815
Horizon Magazine. The Battle of Water-
  loo   **940.2**
See also pages in the following books:
Creasy, Sir E. S. Fifteen decisive battles
  of the world p391-456   **904**
Mitchell, J. B. Twenty decisive batles of
  the world p224-42   **904**

Waters, Aaron Clement
See pages in the following book:
Moore, R. The earth we live on p329-42
  551.09

Waterways
See pages in the following book:
Langdon, W. C. Everyday things in
  American life, 1776-1876 p90-114   **917.3**
See also Rivers

Waterworks. See Water supply

Watkins, Sylvestre C.
See pages in the following book:
Bontemps, A. We have tomorrow p59-67
  920

Watson, Douglas
See pages in the following book:
Bontemps, A. We have tomorrow p68-78
  920

Watson, George
(ed.) The concise Cambridge bibliography
  of English literature, 600-1950   **016.82**
Watson, James Dewey
See pages in the following book:
Moore, R. The coil of life p272-86   **574.09**
Watson, Robert I.
The great psychologists from Aristotle to
  Freud   **150.9**
Watt, William W.
(ed.) White, E. B. An E. B. White read-
  er   **818**
Watteau, Jean Antoine
Schneider, P. The world of Watteau,
  1684-1721   **92**
Wattenberg, Ben J.
(jt. auth.) Scammon, R. M. The real ma-
  jority   **329**
Watts, Alan Wilson
See pages in the following book:
Roszak, T. The making of a counter cul-
  ture p124-54   **301.24**
Wauchope, Robert
(ed.) The Indian background of Latin
  American history   **970.3**
Waugh, Evelyn
The end of the battle   **Fic**
Men at arms   **Fic**
Officers and gentlemen   **Fic**

Wave mechanics
Kock, W. E. Sound waves and light
  waves   **534**
See also pages in the following book:
Newman, J. R. ed. The world of mathe-
  matics v2 p1056-68   **510.8**
The **waveries.** Brown, F.
In Conklin, G. ed. Invaders of earth
  p223-44   **S C**
Waves
See pages in the following books:
Asimov, I. The new intelligent man's
  guide to science p304-43   **500**
Nourse, A. E. Universe, earth, and atom
  p203-15, 236-45   **530.9**
See also Light; Ocean waves; Radia-
  tion; Sound waves; Wave mechanics
Waves and the ear. Van Bergeijk, W. A.
  534
Wax, Murray L.
Indian Americans: unity and diversity
  970.1
The **way** and the road. Sholokhov, M.
In Sholokhov, M. Tales of the Don
  p129-79   **S C**
The **way** of all flesh. Butler, S.   **Fic**
The **way** of the world. Cather, W.
In Cather, W. Willa Cather's Collected
  short fiction, 1892-1912 v3 p395-404
  S C
The **way** to the dairy. Saki
In Saki. The short stories of Saki p193-
  200   **S C**
The **way** we go to war. Pusey, M. J.   **353.03**
The **way** West. Guthrie, A. B.   **Fic**
A **way** you'll never be. Hemingway, E.
In Hemingway, E. The short stories of
  Ernest Hemingway p402-14   **S C**
In Hemingway, E. The snows of Kili-
  manjaro, and other stories p82-94
  S C
A **wayside** comedy. Kipling, R.
In Kipling, R. The best short stories of
  Rudyard Kipling p9-17   **S C**
"**We.**" Lindbergh, C. A.   **92**
"—**we** also walk dogs." Heinlein, R. A.
In Heinlein, R. A. Robert A. Heinlein's
  The past through tomorrow p258-
  76   **S C**
We are not alone. Sullivan, W.   **523.1**
We die alone. Howarth, D.   **940.54**
We have always lived in the castle. Jackson,
  S.   **Fic**
We have tomorrow. Bontemps, A.   **920**
We own the night; play. Garrett, J.
In Jones, L. ed. Black fire p527-40
  810.8
We seven   **629.45**
We spy. Howard, C.
In Best detective stories of the year,
  1971 p166-73   **S C**
We talk, you listen. Deloria, V.   **309.173**
We, the people: the story of the United
  States Capitol, its past and its promise
  975.3

Werfel, Franz
Jacobowsky and the Colonel
  In Gassner, J. ed. Twenty best European plays on the American stage p300-47 **808.82**

Wernecke, Herbert H.
(ed.) Celebrating Christmas around the world **394.26**
Christmas customs around the world **394.26**

Werner, Abraham Gottlob
  See pages in the following book:
Moore, R. The earth we live on p80-93 **551.09**

Wernham, R. B.
(ed.) The Counter-Reformation and price revolution, 1559-1610
  In The New Cambridge Modern history v3 **909**

Wersba, Barbara
Run softly, go fast **Fic**

Werstein, Irving
The cruel years **946.081**
The great struggle **331.88**
I accuse; the story of the Dreyfus case **92**
The uprising of the Warsaw Ghetto, November 1940-May 1943 **940.54**

Wertenbaker, Lael
The world of Picasso, 1881- **92**

Wescott, Glenway
Prohibition
  In Abrahams, W. ed. Fifty years of the American short story v2 p438-49 **S C**

Wesley, John
  See pages in the following book:
Durant, W. The age of Voltaire p128-37 **940.2**

West, Benjamin
  See pages in the following book:
Baigell, M. A history of American painting p64-71 **759.13**

West, Dorothy
The richer, the poorer
  In Hughes, L. ed. The best short stories by Negro writers p130-33 **S C**

West, Dorothy Herbert
(comp.) Play index, 1949-1952. See Play index, 1949-1952 **808.82**

West, Jerry
  See pages in the following book:
Pepe, P. Greatest stars of the NBA p123-38 **920**

West, Jessamyn
Except for me and thee **Fic**
The friendly persuasion **Fic**
Mr Cornelius, I love you
  In Havighurst, W. ed. Masters of the modern short story p352-66 **S C**

West, Mandy
West, P. Words for a deaf daughter **155.45**

West, Morris L.
The ambassador **Fic**
The Devil's advocate **Fic**
The shoes of the fisherman **Fic**

West, Nathanael
  See pages in the following book:
O'Connor, W. V. ed. Seven modern American novelists p226-63 **813.09**

West, Paul
Words for a deaf daughter **155.45**

West, Rebecca
A conversation on the train
  In Dulles, A. ed. Great spy stories from fiction p63-73 **S C**
The new meaning of treason **364.1**

West, Ruth
The teen-age diet book **613.2**

The West
Remington, F. Frederic Remington's own West **917.8**
Williams, B. Lost legends of the West **917.8**
  See also pages in the following books:
American Heritage. The American Heritage History of the confident years p107-34 **973.8**
Haines, F. Horses in America p93-115, 143-73 **636.109**

Description and travel
Parkman, F. The Oregon Trail **978**
Twain, M. Roughing it **817**

Fiction
Adams, A. The log of a cowboy **Fic**
Guthrie, A. B. The big sky **Fic**
Portis, C. True grit **Fic**
Schaefer, J. The collected stories of Jack Schaefer **S C**
Schaefer, J. Shane **Fic**

Folklore
  See Folklore—The West

History
American Heritage. The American Heritage Book of great adventures of the Old West **978**
Billington, R. A. The far Western frontier, 1830-1860 **978**
Billington, R. A. Westward expansion **973**
Brown, D. Bury my heart at Wounded Knee **970.4**
Cody, W. F. Buffalo Bill's life story (Colonel W. F. Cody) **92**
De Voto, B. Across the wide Missouri **978**
De Voto, B. The year of decision: 1846 **978**
Durham, P. The Negro cowboys **978**
Hollon, W. E. The Great American Desert **917.8**
Hough, E. The passing of the frontier **978**
Turner, F. J. The frontier in American history **978**

Poetry
Fife, A. ed. Ballads of the great West **811.08**

West Africa. See Africa, West

West Africa today. Hoepli, N. L. ed. **916.6**

West Coast Hotel Company v. Parrish
  See pages in the following book:
Fribourg, M. G. The Supreme Court in American history p108-25 **347.9**

West-running brook. Frost, R.
  In Frost, R. Complete poems of Robert Frost, 1949 p303-49 **811**

Wharton, Edith—*Continued*

Human nature

In Wharton, E. The collected short stories of Edith Wharton v2 p617-740 **S C**

Madame de Treymes

In The Scribner treasury p391-442 **S C**

The old maid

In Wharton, E. The Edith Wharton reader p560-624 **S C**

The reef **Fic**

Tales of men and ghosts

In Wharton, E. The collected short stories of Edith Wharton v2 p 1-206 **S C**

The world over

In Wharton, E. The collected short stories of Edith Wharton v2 p741-871 **S C**

Xingu

In Wharton, E. The collected short stories of Edith Wharton v2 p207-356 **S C**

About

Coolidge, O. Edith Wharton, 1862-1937 **92**

Howe, I. ed. Edith Wharton **813.09**

See also pages in the following books:

Auchincloss, L. Pioneers & caretakers p20-55 **813.09**

Brooks, V. The confident years: 1885-1915 p275-93 **810.9**

Kazin, A. On native grounds p73-90 **810.9**

O'Connor, W. V. ed. Seven modern American novelists p11-45 **813.09**

Quinn, A. H. American fiction p550-81 **813.09**

Van Doren, C. The American novel, 1789-1939 p273-80 **813.09**

Wagenknecht, E. Cavalcade of the American novel p252-66 **813.09**

What do I do Monday? Holt, J. **370.1**

What every woman knows. Barrie, J. M.

In Barrie, J. M. The plays of J. M. Barrie p317-99 **822**

In Cerf, B. A. comp. Sixteen famous British plays p123-84 **822.08**

What everyone needs to know about drugs **613.8**

What if—. Asimov, I.

In Asimov, I. Nightfall, and other stories p191-204 **S C**

What is communism? Ketchum, R. M. ed. **335.4**

What is democracy? Ketchum, R. M. ed. **321.8**

What is modern sculpture? Goldwater, R. **735**

What is science? Newman, J. R. ed. **508**

What is this thing called love? Asimov, I.

In Asimov, I. Nightfall, and other stories p308-20 **S C**

What lawyers really do: six lawyers talk about their life and work. Asbell, B. **340.69**

What manner of man; a biography of Martin Luther King, Jr. Bennett, L. **92**

What men live by. Tolstoy, L.

In Tolstoy, L. Short stories v2 p49-72 **S C**

In Tolstoy, L. Twenty-three tales p50-74 **S C**

What of it? Lardner, R.

In Lardner, R. The Ring Lardner reader p655-61 **S C**

What people wore. Gorsline, D. **391.09**

What price glory? Stallings, L.

In Gassner, J. ed. Twenty-five best plays of the modern American theatre; early ser. p57-89 **812.08**

What stumped the Bluejays. Twain, M.

In Twain, M. The complete short stories of Mark Twain p159-63 **S C**

What to do until the doctor comes. Bolton, W. **614.8**

What to do with your bad car. Nader, R. **629.22**

What to listen for in music. Copland, A. **780.1**

What we don't know hurts us. Schorer, M.

In Abrahams, W. ed. Fifty years of the American short story v2 p251-63 **S C**

What wood is that? Edlin, H. L. **674**

What would you do if you were president? Lederer, W. J.

In Lederer, W. J. The ugly American p144-54 **S C**

What you hear from 'em. Taylor, P.

In The New Yorker. Stories from The New Yorker, 1950-1960 p191-205 **S C**

What you should know about democracy—and why. Scholastic Magazines **321.8**

"**What** you want." Henry, O.

In Henry, O. The complete works of O. Henry p1627-31 **S C**

What's in a name? Asimov, I.

In Asimov, I. Asimov's mysteries p38-53 **S C**

What's it like out there? Andretti, M. **92**

What's o'clock. Lowell, A.

In Lowell, A. The complete poetical works of Amy Lowell p435-80 **811**

Wheat

See pages in the following books:

Jones, E. The Plains States p115-29 **917.8**

Scientific American. Plant agriculture p142-51 **581**

Fiction

Norris, F. The octopus **Fic**

Wheeler, Harvey

(jt. auth.) Burdick, E. Fail-safe **Fic**

Wheels

Owen, W. Wheels **380.5**

When a man falls a crowd gathers. Crane, S.

In Crane, S. The complete short stories & sketches of Stephen Crane p201-04 **S C**

When Alice told her soul. London, J.

In London, J. Stories of Hawaii p159-77 **S C**

When every one is panic stricken. Crane, S.

In Crane, S. The complete short stories & sketches of Stephen Crane p196-201 **S C**

When shall these three meet again? Dickens, C.

In Becker, M. L. ed. The home book of Christmas p689-701 **394.26**

When teenagers take care of children. Kraft, I. **649**

When we dead awaken. Ibsen, H.
In Ibsen, H. Four plays of Ibsen p 1-61 **839.8**

When worlds collide. Balmer, E. **Fic**

Where are you going, Hollis Jay? Bradford, B.
In The Best short plays, 1970 p265-81 **808.82**

Where are you going, where have you been? Oates, J. C.
In Abrahams, W. ed. Fifty years of the American short story v 1 p516-31 **S C**
In The Best American short stories, 1967 p193-209 , **S C**

Where do we go from here? Asimov, I. ed. **S C**

Where do we go from here: chaos or community? King, M. L. **323.4**

Where have you been all my life? Lardner, S.
In Seventeen. Seventeen from Seventeen p163-68 **S C**

Where I lived, and what I lived for. Thoreau, H. D.
In Parker, E. ed. I was just thinking p50-64 **824.08**

Where love is, God is. Tolstoy, L.
In Tolstoy, L. Short stories v2 p114-26 **S C**
In Tolstoy, L. Twenty-three tales p118-31 **S C**

Where the cross is made. O'Neill, E.
In O'Neill, E. The long voyage home p147-76 **812**
In O'Neill, E. Plays v 1 p555-73 **812**

Where the heart is. Treviño, E. B. de **92**

Where the legends die. Borland, H. **Fic**

Where the surfers are. Dixon, P. L. **797.1**

Where the trail forks. London, J.
In Armstrong, R. ed. Treasure and treasure hunters **910.4**

Where the winds sleep. Ruzic, N. P. **629.45**

Where there is nothing, there is God. Yeats, W. B.
In Garrity, D. A. ed. 44 Irish short stories p492-96 **S C**

Where there's a will, there's a way. Chekhov, A.
In Chekhov, A. The image of Chekhov p67-69 **S C**

Whicher, Stephen E.
(jt. ed.) Konvitz, M. R. ed. Emerson **818**

Whiffen, Marcus
American architecture since 1780 **720.973**

While the auto waits. Henry, O.
In Henry, O. The complete works of O. Henry p1278-82 **S C**

The whirligig of life. Henry, O.
In Henry, O. The best short stories of O. Henry p208-15 **S C**
In Henry, O. The complete works of O. Henry p1165-70 **S C**

Whirligigs. Henry, O.
In Henry, O. The complete works of O. Henry p1094-1252 **S C**

Whispers of intimate things. See Parks, G.
    ⸺⸺n Parks: whispers of intimate **811**

Whist
See pages in the following book:
Gibson, W. B. Hoyle's Simplified guide to the popular card games p186-93 **795.4**

Whistle and I'll come to you. Turnbull, A. S. **Fic**

Whistler, James Abbott McNeill
Prideaux, T. The world of Whistler, 1834-1903 **92**
See also pages in the following book:
Cheney, S. The story of modern art p147-74 **709.03**

Whistling Dick's Christmas stocking. Henry, O.
In Henry, O. The complete works of O. Henry p516-29 **S C**

Whitaker, Thomas R.
William Carlos Williams **818**

White, Anne T.
Lost worlds **913.03**

White, Christopher
Rembrandt and his world **92**

White, E. B.
An E. B. White reader **818**
Memorandum
In Parker, E. ed. I was just thinking p159-68 **824.08**
One man's meat **818**
The points of my compass **818**
The second tree from the corner **818**
(ed.) A subtreasury of American humor; abridged **817.08**
Strunk, W. The elements of style **808**

White, Edward Lucas
The unwilling vestal **Fic**

White, Elwyn Brooks. See White, E. B.

White, Hilda
Song without end; the love story of Clara and Robert Schumann **92**

White, John B.
(jt. auth.) Hawkins, G. S. Stonehenge decoded **913.36**

White, Jon Manchip
Everyday life in ancient Egypt **913.32**
The land God made in anger **916.8**

White, Joseph
The leader; play
In Jones, L. ed. Black fire p605-30 **810.8**

White, Katharine S.
(jt. ed.) White, E. B. ed. A subtreasury of American humor; abridged **817.08**

White, Margaret Bourke- See Bourke-White, Margaret

White, Percival
(jt. auth.) Arnold, P. Food facts for young people **641.1**

White, R. J.
Life in Regency England **914.2**

White, Ralphe M.
The royal family **920**

White, Ray Lewis
Gore Vidal **818**

White, Richard E.
(jt. auth.) Borror, D. J. A field guide to the insects of America north of Mexico **595.7**

White, Robin
Walker's peak
In The Saturday Evening Post. Best modern short stories p214-35 **S C**

Williams, Tennessee—_Continued_
I can't imagine tomorrow
  _In_ The Best short plays, 1971 p77-95
        808.82
The night of the iguana
  _In_ Gassner, J. ed. Best American plays;
    5th ser. p55-104   **812.08**
  _In_ Richards, S. ed. Best plays of the
    sixties p119-39   **808.82**
Orpheus descending
  _In_ Gassner, J. ed. Best American plays;
    5th ser. p509-51   **812.08**
The rose tattoo
  _In_ Gassner, J. ed. Best American plays;
    4th ser. p91-132   **812.08**
A streetcar named Desire   **812**
—Same
  _In_ Cerf, B. ed. Plays of our time p145-
    235   **812.08**
  _In_ Gassner, J. ed. Best American plays;
    3d ser. p49-93   **812.08**
  _In_ Tucker, S. M. ed. Twenty-five mod-
    ern plays p905-52   **808.82**
Summer and smoke
  _In_ Gassner, J. ed. Best American plays;
    3d ser. p665-701   **812.08**
Three players of a summer game
  _In_ Foley, M. ed. Fifty best American
    short stories, 1915-1965 p466-87
        S C
  _In_ The New Yorker. Stories from The
    New Yorker, 1950-1960 p319-40
        S C
27 wagons full of cotton
  _In_ Cerf, B. ed. 24 favorite one-act plays
    p94-116   **808.82**
About
Falk, S. L. Tennessee Williams   **812.09**
  See also pages in the following book:
Gould, J. Modern American playwrights
  p225-46   **812.09**
Williams, Theodore Samuel. See Williams,
  Ted
Williams, Thomas
The old dancers
  _In_ The Saturday Evening Post. Best
    modern short stories p429-47 **S C**
Williams, William Carlos
Whitaker, T. R. William Carlos Williams
        818
  See also pages in the following book:
Unger, L. ed. Seven modern American
  poets p83-118   **811.09**
Williamsburg, Va.
Description
  See pages in the following book:
National Geographic Society. Vacationland
  U.S.A. p128-35   **917.3**
Fiction
Thane, E. Dawn's early light   **Fic**
The willing muse. Cather, W.
  _In_ Cather, W. Willa Cather's Collected
    short fiction, 1892-1912 v 1 p113-23
        S C
Willis, John
(ed.) Dance world. See Dance world
    793.3025
(ed.) Theatre world. See Theatre world
    792.025
(ed.) Blum, D. A pictorial history of the
  American theatre, 1860-1970   **792.09**

Willis, Nathaniel P.
Tortesa the usurer
  _In_ Quinn, A. H. ed. Representative
    American plays p238-76   **812.08**
About
  See pages in the following book:
Brooks, V. The world of Washington
  Irving p443-59   **810.9**
Willkie, Wendell Lewis
  See pages in the following books:
Leighton, I. ed. The aspirin age, 1919-1941
  p444-75   **917.3**
Stone, I. They also ran p340-65   **920**
Willmann, John B.
The Department of Housing and Urban
  Development   **353.85**
Wilmurt, Arthur
Noah; adaptation. See Obey, A. Noah
Wilner, Herbert
Dovisch in the wilderness
  _In_ The Best American short stories,
    1966 p327-57   **S C**
Wilson, Angus
More friend than lodger
  _In_ The New Yorker. Stories from The
    New Yorker, 1950-1960 p641-65
        S C
The world of Charles Dickens   **823.09**
Wilson, Barbara
The complete book of engagement and
  wedding etiquette   **395**
Wilson, Carter
The brief swinging career of Dan and Judy
  Smythe
  _In_ The Best from Fantasy and Science
    Fiction; 19th ser. p95-100 **S C**
Wilson, David
The Anglo-Saxons   **913.42**
The Vikings and their origins   **914.8**
Wilson, Edmund
Axel's castle   **809**
The Dead Sea scrolls, 1946-1969   **221.4**
About
Frank, C. P. Edmund Wilson   **818**
  See also pages in the following book:
Highet, G. People, places and books p29-
  36   **809**
Wilson, Eugene S.
(jt. auth.) Lass, A. H. The college stu-
  dent's handbook   **378.102**
Wilson, F. P.
The Oxford Dictionary of English prov-
  erbs. See The Oxford Dictionary of En-
  glish proverbs   **398.9**
Wilson, H.W. Company, Publisher
Biography index. See Biography Index
    920.02
Book review digest. See Book review di-
  gest   **015**
Cumulative book index. See Cumulative
  book index   **015**
Current biography yearbook. See Current
  biography yearbook   **920.03**
Essay and general literature index. See
  Essay and general literature index **080**
Fiction catalog. See Fiction catalog **016.8**
Junior high school library catalog. See
  Junior high school library catalog **011**

Wilson, H.W. Company, Publisher—*Cont.*
Play index, 1949-1952. See Play index, 1949-1952 **808.82**
Play index, 1953-1960. See Play index, 1953-1960 **808.82**
Play index, 1961-1967. See Play index, 1961-1967 **808.82**
Public library catalog. See Public library catalog **011**
Readers' guide to periodical literature. See Readers' guide to periodical literature **051**
Short story index. See Short story index **808.83**
Short story index: supplement, 1950-1954. See Short story index: supplement, 1950-1954 **808.83**
Short story index: supplement, 1955-1958. See Short story index: supplement, 1955-1958 **808.83**
Short story index: supplement, 1959-1963. See Short story index: supplement, 1959-1963 **808.83**
Short story index: supplement, 1964-1968. See Short story index: supplement, 1964-1968 **808.83**
Wilson, James, 1835-1920
See pages in the following book:
Terrell, J. U. The United States Department of Agriculture p26-35 **353.81**
Wilson, Jean
Weaving is fun **746.1**
Wilson, Jean A.
(ed.) National Council of Teachers of English. Books for you **028.52**
Wilson, John Rowan
The mind **150**
Wilson, José
American cooking: the Eastern heartland **641.5**
Wilson, Marie M.
Siamese cookery **641.5**
Wilson, Mitchell
Energy **531**
Wilson, Robin Scott
Gone fishin'
In The Best from Fantasy and Science Fiction; 19th ser. p11-27 **S C**
Wilson, Woodrow, President U.S.
Dos Passos, J. Mr Wilson's war **973.91**
Hoover, H. The ordeal of Woodrow Wilson **92**
Link, A. S. Woodrow Wilson **92**
Link, A. S. Woodrow Wilson and the progressive era, 1910-1917 **973.91**
Seymour, C. Woodrow Wilson and the World War **973.91**
See also pages in the following books:
American Heritage. The American Heritage History of the 20's & 30's p11-18 **917.3**
Dictionary of American biography. The American Plutarch p321-53 **920**
Hofstadter, R. The American political tradition and the men who made it p234-78 **973**
Koenig, L. W. Bryan p493-507, 510-50 **92**
Lord, W. The good years p289-319 **973.91**

Shannon, D. A. Between the wars: America, 1919-1941 p3-30 **973.91**
Warren, S. The President as world leader p60-138 **327.73**
Wiltz, John E.
Books in American history **016.973**
Winchell, Constance M.
Guide to reference books **016**
Guide to reference books. First supplement, 1965-1966 **016**
Guide to reference books. Second supplement, 1967-1968 **016**
Wind, Herbert Warren
The Masters
In Sports Illustrated. The wonderful world of sport p259-60 **796**
Wind. See Winds
The wind and the snow of winter. Clark, W. V.
In Abrahams, W. ed. Fifty years of the American short story v 1 p208-19 **S C**
In Foley, M. ed. Fifty best American short stories, 1915-1965 p375-86 **S C**
The wind blew east. Stuart, J.
In Stuart, J. Plowshare in heaven p84-96 **S C**
The wind blows. Mansfield, K.
In Mansfield, K. The short stories of Katherine Mansfield p214-19 **S C**
Wind, sand, and stars. Saint Exupéry, A. de **629.13**
also in Saint Exupéry, A. de. Airman's odyssey p 1-206 **629.13**
The window. Marcus, F.
In Richards, S. ed. Best short plays of the world theatre, 1958-1967 p201-12 **808.82**
Windows. Galsworthy, J.
In Galsworthy, J. Plays p465-97 **822**
Windows for the Crown Prince [Akihito]. Vining, E. G. **92**
Winds
See pages in the following book:
Chandler, T. J. The air around us p42-61 **551.5**
The winds of change. Hairston, L.
In Clarke, J. H. ed. American Negro short stories p297-304 **S C**
Windsor, Edward, Duke of. See Edward VIII, King of Great Britain
Windsor, Wallis (Warfield) Duchess of
See pages in the following book:
Leighton, I. ed. The aspirin age, 1919-1941 p364-82 **917.3**
Windsor, House of
White, R. M. The royal family **920**
Wine and wine making
See pages in the following books:
Scientific American. Plant agriculture p178-88 **581**
Wilson, J. American cooking: the Eastern heartland p146-59 **641.5**
Wine for the mess at Segi. Michener, J.
In Michener, J. Tales of the South Pacific p222-37 **S C**

Wolfe, Thomas—*Continued*
The web of earth
  In Wolfe, T. The short novels of
    Thomas Wolfe p76-154   **S C**
You can't go home again   **Fic**

About

Turnbull, A. Thomas Wolfe   **92**
  See also pages in the following books:
Geismar, M. Writers in crisis p185-235
    813.09
O'Connor, W. V. ed. Seven modern American novelists p189-225   **813.09**
Stirling, N. Who wrote the modern classics? p159-95   **920**
Untermeyer, L. Makers of the modern world p726-35   **920**
Van Doren, C. The American novel, 1789-1939 p343-49   **813.09**

Wolff, Perry
A tour of the White House with Mrs John F. Kennedy   **975.3**

Wolff, Ruth
A crack in the sidewalk   **Fic**

Wollheim, Donald
Storm warning
  In Conklin, G. ed. Invaders of earth
    p75-85   **S C**

Wolsey, Thomas, Cardinal
  See pages in the following book:
Durant, W. The Reformation p525-42
    940.2

Wolves
Mowat, F. Never cry wolf   **599**
The **wolves** of Cernogratz. Saki
  In Saki. The short stories of Saki p460-65   **S C**

Woman
Mead, M. Male and female   **301.41**
  See also pages in the following book:
Horizon Magazine. The Horizon Book of the Renaissance p345-59   **940.2**

Biography
  See Actors and actresses; Queens; Women in the U.S.

Diseases
  See Woman—Health and hygiene

Education
  See Education of women

Employment
  See pages in the following books:
Miller, H. P. Rich man, poor man p222-33
    339
Polenberg, R. ed. America at war p131-39
    309.173
United States. President's Commission on the Status of Women. American women p45-53, 118-27   **301.41**

Enfranchisement
  See Woman—Suffrage

Health and hygiene
Dalton, K. The menstrual cycle   **612.6**

History and condition of women
  See pages in the following books:
Asimov, I. The solar system and back p232-46   **508**
Page, R. I. Life in Anglo-Saxon England p66-77   **914.2**

Occupations
  See Woman—Employment

Rights of women
  See pages in the following books:
Cecil, R. Life in Edwardian England p156-81   **914.2**
Commager, H. S. Crusaders for freedom p149-71   **920**
United States. President's Commission on the Status of Women. American women p65-74, 147-57   **301.41**
  See also Woman—Suffrage

Suffrage
  See pages in the following books:
Addams, J. The social thought of Jane Addams p143-62   **309.173**
Lord, W. The good years p272-88   **973.91**
Lynd, S. ed. Nonviolence in America: a documentary history p160-71   **323**
Priestley, J. B. The Edwardians p211-25
    914.2

The **woman** across the street. Dikeman, M.
  In The Best American short stories, 1964 p95-107   **S C**
The **woman** at the store. Mansfield, K.
  In Mansfield, K. The short stories of Katherine Mansfield p124-34   **S C**
The **woman** at the Washington Zoo. Jarrell, R.
  In Jarrell, R. The complete poems   **811**
The **woman** in the dunes. Abé, K.   **Fic**
The **woman** in white. Collins, W.   **Fic**
A **woman** of no importance. Wilde, O.
  In Wilde, O. The plays of Oscar Wilde v2 p129-220   **822**
A **woman** of the people. Capps, B.   **Fic**
A **woman** with a past. Fitzgerald, F. S.
  In Fitzgerald, F. S. The stories of F. Scott Fitzgerald p364-80   **S C**
A **woman's** kingdom. Chekhov, A.
  In Chekhov, A. The stories of Anton Chekhov p196-242   **S C**
Women. See Woman; and headings beginning with the word Women
The **women.** Boothe, C.
  In Cerf, B. A. ed. Sixteen famous American plays p603-76   **812.08**
  In Gassner, J. ed. Twenty best plays of the modern American theatre p415-66   **812.08**
The **women.** Bradbury, R.
  In Bradbury, R. I sing the Body Electric! p50-60   **S C**

Women as authors
Auchincloss, L. Pioneers & caretakers
    813.09

Women in agriculture
  See pages in the following book:
Stone, A. A. Careers in agribusiness and industry p323-34   **338.1**

Women in Great Britain
  See pages in the following books:
Cecil, R. Life in Edwardian England p156-81   **914.2**
Page, R. I. Life in Anglo-Saxon England p66-77   **914.2**

Women in public life
Chisholm, S. Unbought and unbossed   **92**

World politics—1945-   —*Continued.*
Ward, B. The rich nations and the poor
nations   338.91
Worldmark Encyclopedia of the nations
910.3
World records, Guinness Book of   032
World Series (Baseball)
See pages in the following book:
Durso, J. Amazing: the miracle of the
Mets p181-209   796.357
The **World** this year   329
World War, 1914-1918. See European War,
1914-1918
World War, 1939-1945
Churchill, W. S. Closing the ring   940.53
Churchill, W. S. The gathering storm
940.53
Churchill, W. S. The grand alliance 940.53
Churchill, W. S. The hinge of fate 940.53
Churchill, W. S. Memoirs of the Second
World War   940.53
Churchill, W. S. Their finest hour 940.53
Churchill, W. S. Triumph and tragedy
940.53
Liddell Hart, B. H. History of the Sec-
ond World War   940.54
Reeder, R. The story of the Second
World War   940.53
Wright, G. The ordeal of total war, 1939-
1945   940.53
See also pages in the following books:
American Heritage. The American Her-
itage History of the 20's & 30's p383-407
917.3
Ardrey, R. The territorial imperative
p229-42   591
Colton, J. G. Twentieth century p84-107
901.94
Handlin, O. The Americans p371-86 973
Hayes, C. J. H. Contemporary Europe
since 1870 p635-73   940.2
Kennan, G. F. American diplomacy, 1900-
1950 p74-90   327.73
The New Cambridge Modern history v12
p735-77   909
Rowse, A. L. The Churchills: the story of
a family p524-53   920
Van Loon, H. W. The story of mankind
p498-523   909
Aerial operations
Brickhill, P. Reach for the sky; the story
of Douglas Bader   92
Chennault, A. Chennault and The Flying
Tigers   940.54
Sims, E. H. American aces in great fight-
er battles of World War II   940.54
See also pages in the following books:
American Heritage. The American Her-
itage History of flight p286-367   629.13
Von Braun, W. History of rocketry and
space travel p86-119   629.409
See also Tokyo—Bombardment, 1942
Amphibious operations
Howarth, D. D Day, the sixth of June,
1944   940.54
Asia
Taylor, E. Richer by Asia   915.4
Atrocities
Columbia Broadcasting System, inc. CBS
News. Trial at Nuremberg   341.4

Austria
See pages in the following book:
Stadler, K. R. Austria p200-21   943.6
Borneo
Keith, A. N. Three came home   940.54
Burma
Ogburn, C. The Marauders   940.54
Campaigns and battles
Collier, B. The Second World War: a
military history   940.54
Eisenhower, D. D. Crusade in Europe
940.54
Toland, J. Battle: the story of the Bulge
940.54
Young, D. Rommel, the desert fox   92
See also names of battles, sieges, etc.
e.g. Ardennes, Battle of the, 1944-1945
Campaigns and battles—Pacific Ocean
See pages in the following book:
Reeder, R. The story of the Second
World War v2 p177-224   940.53
Canada
See pages in the following book:
Brebner, J. B. Canada p471-96   971
Causes
Baker, L. Roosevelt and Pearl Harbor
973.917
Mosley, L. On borrowed time   940.53
Parkinson, R. The origins of World War
Two   940.53
Taylor, A. J. P. The origins of the Second
World War   940.53
China
Chennault, A. Chennault and The Flying
Tigers   940.54
Tuchman, B. W. Stilwell and the Amer-
ican experience in China, 1911-45
327.73
Civilian evacuation
See World War, 1939-1945—Evacua-
tion of civilians
Denmark
See pages in the following book:
Jones, W. G. Denmark p166-81   948.9
Diplomatic history
Nevins, A. The New Deal and world
affairs   327.73
Drama
Wouk, H. The Caine mutiny court-martial
812
Economic aspects
Janeway, E. The struggle for survival
355.2
Europe
Toland, J. The last 100 days   940.53
Evacuation of civilians
Bosworth, A. R. America's concentration
camps   301.45
Fiction
Anatoli, A. Babi Yar   Fic
Beach, E. Run silent, run deep   Fic
Boulle, P. The bridge over the River Kwai
Fic
Bryher. Beowulf   Fic
Del Castillo, M. Child of our time   Fic
Forester, C. S. Gold from Crete   S C
Forester, C. S. The last nine days of the
Bismarck   Fic

X

X rays
See pages in the following books:
Hodge, P. W. The revolution in astronomy p115-26   **523**
Newman, J. R. ed. The world of mathematics v2 p854-70   **510.8**
Xavier Fereira's unfinished book: chapter one. Strong, J.
In The Best American short stories, 1971 p298-315   **S C**
Xenakis, Yannis
See pages in the following book:
Ewen, D. Composers of tomorrow's music p120-36   **920**
Xenophon
See pages in the following books:
Grant, M. The ancient historians p125-35   **920**
Hamilton, E. The Greek way p204-26   **880.9**
Payne, R. Ancient Greece p362-70   **913.38**
Sarton, G. A history of science v 1 p454-66   **509**
Xingu. Wharton, E.
In Wharton, E. The collected short stories of Edith Wharton v2 p207-356   **S C**
Xingu [short story]. Wharton, E.
In Wharton, E. The collected short stories of Edith Wharton v2 p209-29   **S C**

Y

Yachts and yachting. See Sailing
Yadin, Yigael
See pages in the following book:
Noble, I. Treasure of the caves p171-83   **221.4**
Yahgan Indians
See pages in the following book:
Vlahos, O. New world beginnings p101-12   **913.7**
Yankee from Olympus; Justice Holmes and his family. Bowen, C. D.   **92**
Yanoama Indians
See pages in the following book:
Vlahos, O. New world beginnings p173-81   **913.7**
The **Yarkand** manner. Saki
In Saki. The short stories of Saki p346-51   **S C**
Yates, Elizabeth
Is there a doctor in the barn?   **636.089**
Yates, Norris W.
Robert Benchley   **817.09**
Ybarra, T. R.
Young man of Caracas   **92**
Year
Pictorial history of the Black American   **301.451**
The **year** of decision: 1846. De Voto, B.   **978**
Year of decisions. Truman, H. S.
In Truman, H. S. Memoirs v 1   **92**
The **year** of the gorilla. Schaller, G. B.   **599**

The **year** of the people. McCarthy, E. J.   **329**
The **year** of the whale. Scheffer, V. B.   **599**
Year: the encyclopedia news annual.   **909.82**
Yearbook. United Nations. Office of Public Information   **341.13**
Yearbook editing, layout, and management. Medlin, C. J.   **371.89**
Yearbook of science and technology, McGraw-Hill. See McGraw-Hill Encyclopedia of science and technology   **503**
Yearbook of science and the future, Britannica   **505**
Yearbook of the American short story, 1964-1971. See The Best American short stories, 1964-1971   **S C**
Yearbooks
Medlin, C. J. Yearbook editing, layout, and management   **371.89**
See also names of subjects and organizations with the subdivision Yearbooks, e.g. Science—Yearbooks; United Nations—Yearbooks
Years of adventure, 1874-1920. Hoover, H. C.
In Hoover, H. C. Memoirs v 1   **92**
Years of trial and hope. Truman, H. S.
In Truman, H. S. Memoirs v2   **92**
Year's Pictorial history of the American Negro. See Year. Pictorial history of the Black American   **301.451**
Yeats, William Butler
At the hawk's well
In Block, H. M. ed. Masters of modern drama p429-32   **808.82**
Cathleen ni Houlihan
In Cerf, B. ed. 24 favorite one-act plays p391-402   **808.82**
Collected plays of W. B. Yeats   **822**
Contents: The Countess Cathleen; The Land of Heart's Desire; Cathleen ni Houlihan; The pot of broth; The king's threshold; The shadowy waters; Deirdre; At the hawk's well; The green helmet; On Baile's strand; The only jealousy of Emer; The hour-glass; The unicorn from the stars; The player queen; The dreaming of the bones; Calvary; The cat and the moon; Sophocles' King Oedipus; Sophocles' Oedipus at Colonus The Resurrection; The words upon the window-pane; A full moon in March; The king of the Great Clock Tower; The herne's egg; Purgatory; The death of Cuchulain
Collected poems   **821**
The hour-glass
In Dickinson, T. H. ed. Chief contemporary dramatists [1st ser] p207-16   **808.82**
Red Hanrahan
In Garrity, D. A. ed. 44 Irish short stories p482-91   **S C**
Where there is nothing, there is God
In Garrity, D. A. ed. 44 Irish short stories p492-96   **S C**
(ed.) The Oxford Book of modern verse, 1892-1935. See The Oxford Book of modern verse, 1892-1935   **821.08**
About
See pages in the following books:
Daiches, D. More literary essays p133-49   **820.9**
Eliot, T. S. On poetry and poets p295-308   **808.1**

Yeats, William B.—About—*Continued*
MacLeish, A. A continuing journey p12-25 **818**
MacLeish, A. Poetry and experience p115-47 **809.1**
Untermeyer, L. Makers of the modern world p336-44 **920**
Untermeyer, L. The paths of poetry p218-22 **920**
Wilson, E. Axel's castle p26-63 **809**
The **yellow** brick road. Williams, G.
In Best detective stories of the year [1967]p15-21 **S C**
A **yellow** dog. Harte, B.
In Harte, B. The best short stories of Bret Harte p223-34 **S C**
The **yellow** face. Doyle, Sir A. C.
In Doyle, Sir A. C. The complete Sherlock Holmes v 1 p402-15 **S C**
Yellow Jack. Howard, S.
In Gassner, J. ed. Best American plays; supplementary volume, 1918-1958 p451-500 **812.08**
Yellow Springs, Ohio
Description
See pages in the following book:
Moyers, B. Listening to America p36-47 **917.3**
Yellowstone National Park
See pages in the following book:
National Geographic Society. America's wonderlands p67-91 **917.3**
Yemen
Politics and government
See pages in the following book:
Comay, J. The UN in action p56-59 **341.13**
Yen, James Y. C.
See pages in the following book:
Commager, H. S. Crusaders for freedom p135-47 **920**
Yen, Yang-ch'u. See Yen, James Y. C.
Yen-Nock Bill and his sweetheart. Crane, S.
In Crane, S. The complete short stories & sketches of Stephen Crane p315-17 **S C**
Yentl the Yeshiva boy. Singer, I. B.
In Singer, I. B. An Isaac Bashevis Singer reader p135-66 **S C**
The **yeoman** of the guard. Gilbert, Sir W. S.
In Gilbert, Sir W. S. The complete plays of Gilbert and Sullivan p461-517 **782.8**
In Gilbert, Sir W. S. Martyn Green's Treasury of Gilbert & Sullivan **782.8**
Yerby, Frank
Health card
In Hughes, L. ed. The best short stories by Negro writers p192-201 **S C**
The homecoming
In Clarke, J. H. ed. American Negro short stories p147-56 **S C**
Yerkow, Charles
Motorcycles: how they work **629.22**
Yes I can. Davis, S. **92**

Yes, my darling daughter. Reed, M.
In Gassner, J. ed. Twenty best plays of the modern American theatre p467-510 **812.08**
Yes, we'll gather at the river. Bradbury, R.
In Bradbury, R. I sing the Body Electric! p90-99 **S C**
Yevreinov, Nikolai Nikolayevich
The theatre of the soul
In Dickinson, T. H. ed. Chief contemporary dramatists, 3d ser. p517-26 **808.82**
Yevtushenko, Yevgeny
Yevtushenko poems **891.7**
For material about this author see Evtushenko, Evgenii Aleksandrovich
Yiddish in America. Ozick, C.
In The Best American short stories, 1970 p236-87 **S C**
Yiddish poetry
Collections
Howe, I. ed. A treasury of Yiddish poetry **892.49**
Yoors, Jan
The Gypsies **397**
Yorktown, Va.
Siege, 1781
See pages in the following book:
Armstrong, O. K. The fifteen decisive battles of the United States p80-98 **973**
Yosemite National Park
See pages in the following book:
National Geographic Society. America's wonderlands p339-51 **917.3**
You and heredity. See Scheinfeld, A. Your heredity and environment **575.1**
You and your Congressman. Wright, J. **328.73**
"You are welcome!" Forester, C. S.
In Forester, C. S. Gold from Crete p155-64 **S C**
You can't do that. Marquand, J. P.
In Day, A. G. ed. The spell of Hawaii p73-96 **919.69**
You can't get there from here. Nash, O. **811**
You can't go home again. Wolfe, T. **Fic**
You can't take it with you. Kaufman, G. S.
In Gassner, J. ed. Twenty best plays of the modern American theatre p233-73 **812.08**
You come too. Frost, R. **811**
You could look it up. Thurber, J.
In Lardner, R. ed. Rex Lardner selects the best of sports fiction p151-70 **S C**
You know I can't hear you when the water's running. Anderson, R.
In Gassner, J. ed. Best American plays; 6th ser. p335-65 **812.08**
You know me Al. Lardner, R.
In Lardner, R. The Ring Lardner reader p3-34 **S C**
You need to go upstairs. Godden, R.
In Godden, R. Gone p143-48 **S C**
You never can tell. Shaw, B.
In Shaw, B. Complete plays, with prefaces v6 p615-721 **822**
You should have seen the mess. Spark, M.
In Spark, M. Collected stories: I p196-204 **S C**

You'll never know, dear, how much I love you. Updike, J.
In Updike, J. Pigeon feathers, and other stories   **S C**

Youmans, Vincent
See pages in the following book:
Ewen, D. Great men of American popular song p144-60   **920**

Young, Brigham
See pages in the following books:
American Heritage. The American Heritage Book of great adventures of the Old West p170-91   **978**
Stone, I. Men to match my mountains p94-103, 149-51, 178-84, 266-73, 329-51   **979.1**

Young, Desmond
Rommel, the desert fox   **92**

Young, Lester Willis
See pages in the following book:
Williams, M. The jazz tradition p107-19   **781.5**

Young, Stanley
The sound of apples
In The Best short plays of 1957-1958 p121-58   **808.82**

Young, Whitney Moore
See pages in the following book:
Metcalf, G. R. Black profiles p307-33   **920**

Young adults. See Youth

Young and Black in America. Alexander, R. P. comp.   **920**

Young Bess. Irwin, M.   **Fic**

Young filmmakers. Larson, R.   **791.43**

The **young** gentlemen. Wharton, E.
In Wharton, E. The collected short stories of Edith Wharton v2 p385-402   **S C**

The **young** girl. Mansfield, K.
In Mansfield, K. The short stories of Katherine Mansfield p440-45   **S C**

Young Goodman Brown. Hawthorne, N.
In Hawthorne, N. Hawthorne's Short stories p193-206   **S C**

The **young** immigrants. Lardner, R.
In Lardner, R. The Ring Lardner reader p411-27   **S C**

The **young** Jefferson, 1743-1789. Bowers, C. G.   **973.4**

Young Joseph. Mann, T.
In Mann, T. Joseph and his brothers p261-444   **Fic**

Young man of Caracas. Ybarra, T. R.   **92**

Young people and drinking. Cain, A. H.   **178**

Young people and driving. Purdy, K. W.   **629.28**

Young people and drugs. Cain, A. H.   **613.8**

Young people and parents. Cain, A. H.   **301.42**

Young people and religion. Cain, A. H.   **291**

Young people and sex. Cain, A. H.   **176**

Young people and smoking. Cain, A. H.   **613.8**

Young people's libraries. See Libraries, Young adults'

Young radicals. Keniston, K.   **301.43**

The **young** statesman, 1901-1914. Churchill, R. S.
In Churchill, R. S. Winston S. Churchill v2   **92**

A **young** Turkish catastrophe. Saki
In Saki. The short stories of Saki p64-65   **S C**

Young women. See Girls

The **youngest** Miss Piper. Harte, B.
In Harte, B. The best short stories of Bret Harte p353-72   **S C**

Your book of medieval and Tudor costume. See Cunnington, P. Medieval and Tudor costume   **391**

Your book of nineteenth century costume. See Cunnington, P. Costumes of the nineteenth century   **391.09**

Your book of seventeenth and eighteenth century costume. See Cunnington, P. Costumes of the seventeenth and eighteenth century   **391.09**

Your heredity and environment. Scheinfeld, A.   **575.1**

Your puppy: how to select, raise and train him. See Whitney, L. F. How to select, train, and breed your dog   **636.7**

Your sight. Seeman, B.   **612**

You're a good man, Charlie Brown. Gesner, C.   **812**

Youth
Bernstein, S. Alternatives to violence   **301.43**
Cervantes, L. F. The dropout: causes and cures   **371.2**
Douglas, W. O. Points of rebellion   **323**
Fortune (Periodical) Youth in turmoil   **301.43**
Keniston, K. Young radicals   **301.43**
Lukas, J. A. Don't shoot—we are your children!   **301.43**
Mead, M. Culture and commitment   **301.43**
Steel, R. ed. New light on juvenile delinquency   **364.36**
Time, inc. The hippies   **301.43**
Vermes, H. Helping youth avoid four great dangers: smoking, drinking, VD, narcotics addiction   **613.8**
Wein, B. The runaway generation   **301.43**
What everyone needs to know about drugs   **613.8**

See also pages in the following books:
Addams, J. The social thought of Jane Addams p84-94   **309.173**
Barzun, J. Teacher in America p220-40   **371.1**
Fort, J. The pleasure seekers: the drug crisis, youth and society p209-21   **613.8**
Michener, J. A. The quality of life p57-70   **309.173**
Reeves, T. The end of the draft p3-20   **355.2**
United States. National Commission on the Causes and Prevention of Violence. To establish justice, to insure domestic tranquility p187-205   **301.18**

See also Adolescence; Libraries, Young adults'

DIRECTORY OF PUBLISHERS AND DISTRIBUTORS

A.L.A. American Library Association, Publishing Services, 50 E Huron St, Chicago, Ill. 60611

AMS Press. AMS Press, 56 E 13th St, New York, N.Y. 10003

Abelard-Schuman. Abelard-Schuman, Ltd, 6 W 57th St, New York, N.Y. 10019

Abingdon. Abingdon Press, Hdqrs, 201 8th Av, S, Nashville, Tenn. 37203

Abrams. Harry N. Abrams, Inc, 110 E 59th St, New York, N.Y. 10022

Academic Press. Academic Press, Inc, 111 5th Av, New York, N.Y. 10003

Afro-Am Pub. Co. Afro-Am Publishing Company, Inc, 1727 S Indiana Av, Chicago, Ill. 60616

Aldine Pub. Aldine Publishing Company, 529 S Wabash Av, Chicago, Ill. 60605

Am. Assn. for the Advancement of Science. American Association for the Advancement of Science, 1515 Massachusetts Av, N.W, Washington, D.C. 20005

Am. Bk. American Book Company, 55 5th Av, New York, N.Y. 10003

Am. Council on Educ. American Council on Education, Publications Division, 1785 Massachusetts Av, N.W, Washington, D.C. 20036

Am. Enterprise Inst. American Enterprise Institute for Public Policy Research, 1200 17th St, N.W, Washington, D.C. 20036

Am. Heritage. American Heritage Publishing Company, Inc, 561 5th Av, New York, N.Y. 10017
  Publications distributed by various publishers

Am. Heritage Press. American Heritage Press, 330 W 42d St, New York, N.Y. 10036

Am. Radio. American Radio Relay League, Inc, 225 Main St, Newington, Conn. 06111

Am. Tech. Soc. American Technical Society, 848 E 58th St, Chicago, Ill. 60637

Am. Univ. Press Serv. American University Press Service, Inc, 1 Park Av, New York, N.Y. 10016

Americana. Americana Corporation, 575 Lexington Av, New York, N.Y. 10022

Anchor Bks. Anchor Books, 277 Park Av, New York, N.Y. 10017

Appleton. Appleton-Century-Crofts, 440 Park Av, S, New York, N.Y. 10016

Archon Bks. Archon Books, 995 Sherman Av, Hamden, Conn. 06514

Arco. Arco Publishing Company, Inc, 219 Park Av, S, New York, N.Y. 10003

Asia Society. The Asia Society, 112 E 64th St, New York, N.Y. 10021

Assn. of College & Research Libs. See A.L.A.

Assn. on Am. Indian Affairs. Association on American Indian Affairs, 432 Park Av, S, New York, N.Y. 10016

Assn. Press. Association Press (Nat. Council of Y.M.C.A.'s) 291 Broadway, New York, N.Y. 10007

Associated Press. The Associated Press, Inc, 50 Rockefeller Plaza, New York, N.Y. 10020

Astor-Honor. Astor-Honor, Inc, 205 E 42d St, New York, N.Y. 10017

Atheneum Pubs. Atheneum Publishers, 122 E 42d St, New York, N.Y. 10017

Audel. Theo. Audel & Company, 4300 W 62d St, Indianapolis, Ind. 46206

Barnes, A.S. A. S. Barnes & Company, Box 421, Cranbury, N.J. 08512

Barnes & Noble. Barnes & Noble, Inc, 105 5th Av, New York, N.Y. 10003

Barrons Educ. Ser. Barron's Educational Series, Inc, 113 Crossways Park Dr, Woodbury, N.Y. 11797

Basic Bks. Basic Books, Inc, Publishers, 404 Park Av, S, New York, N.Y. 10016

Beacon Press. Beacon Press, Inc, 25 Beacon St, Boston, Mass. 02108

Bennett. Chas. A. Bennett Company, Inc, Book Publishers, 809 W Detweiller Dr, Peoria, Ill. 61614

Biblo & Tannen. Biblo & Tannen, Inc, 63 4th Av, New York, N.Y. 10003

Bobbs. Bobbs-Merrill Company, Inc, 4300 W 62d St, Indianapolis, Ind. 46206

Bowker. The R. R. Bowker Company, 1180 Av. of the Americas, New York, N.Y. 10036

British Bk. Centre. The British Book Centre, Inc, 996 Lexington Av, New York, N.Y. 10017

Brown, W.C. Wm. C. Brown Company, 135 S Locust St, Dubuque, Iowa 52001

Bruce Pub. Bruce Publishing Company, 400 N Broadway, Milwaukee, Wis. 53201

Bunting & Lyon. Bunting & Lyon, Inc, 238 N Main St, Wallingford, Conn. 06492

Cambridge. Cambridge University Press, 32 E 57th St, New York, N.Y. 10022

Canadian Lib. Assn. Canadian Library Association, Room 606, 63 Sparks St, Ottawa 4

Capricorn Bks. Capricorn Books, 200 Madison Av, New York, N.Y. 10016

Center for Inter-American Relations. Center for Inter-American Relations, 680 Park Av, New York, N.Y. 10021

Chemical Rubber Co. Chemical Rubber Company, 18901 Cranwood Pkwy, Cleveland, Ohio 44128

Chicorel Lib. Pub. Corp. Chicorel Library Publishing Corporation, 330 W 58th St, New York, N.Y. 10019

Chilton Bk. Co. Chilton Book Company, (Chilton Books) 401 Walnut St, Philadelphia, Pa. 19106

Chilton Bks. See Chilton Bk. Co.

Citadel. Citadel Press, 222 Park Av, S, New York, N.Y. 10003

Citation Press. Citation Press, 50 W 44th St, New York, N.Y. 10036

Clarendon Press. See Oxford

Collier. P. F. Collier, Inc, 866 3d Av, New York, N.Y. 10022

Collier Bks. Collier Books, 866 3d Av, New York, N.Y. 10022

Columbia Univ. Press. Columbia University Press, 440 W 110th St, New York, N.Y. 10025

Compton, F. E. Compton & Company, 1000 N Dearborn St, Chicago, Ill. 60610

Cooper Sq. Cooper Square Publishers, Inc, 59 4th Av, New York, N.Y. 10003

Cornell Univ. Press. Cornell University Press, 124 Roberts Pl, Ithaca, N.Y. 14850

Council of State Govs. Council of State Governments, 1313 E 60th St, Chicago, Ill. 60637

Coward-McCann. See Coward, McCann & Geoghegan

Coward, McCann & Geoghegan. Coward, McCann & Geoghegan, Inc, 200 Madison Av, New York, N.Y. 10016

Cowles. Cowles Book Company, Inc, 488 Madison Av, New York, N.Y. 10022

Criterion Bks. Criterion Books, Inc, 6 W 57th St, New York, N.Y. 10019

Crowell. Thomas Y. Crowell Company, 201 Park Av, S, New York, N.Y. 10002

Crowell-Collier Educ. Corp. Crowell-Collier Educational Corporation, 866 3d Av, New York, N.Y. 10022

Crowell-Collier Press. See Collier

Crown. Crown Publishers, Inc, 419 Park Av, S, New York, N.Y. 10016

Day. The John Day Company, 257 Park Av, S, New York, N.Y. 10010

Delacorte Press. Delacorte Press Books, 750 3d Av, New York, N.Y. 10017

Devin-Adair. The Devin-Adair Company, Publishers, 23 E 26th St, New York, N.Y. 10010

Dial Press. The Dial Press, Inc, 750 3d Av, New York, N.Y. 10017

Dodd. Dodd, Mead & Company, Inc, 79 Madison Av, New York, N.Y. 10016

Doubleday. Doubleday & Company, Inc, 277 Park Av, New York, N.Y. 10017

Dover. Dover Publications, Inc, 180 Varick St, New York, N.Y. 10014

Dow-Jones. Dow Jones-Irwin, Inc, (Publishers) (Dow Jones Bks) Box 330, Princeton, N.J. 08540

Dow Jones Bks. See Dow Jones

Duell. Duell, Sloan & Pearce, Inc, 60 E 42d St, New York, N.Y. 10017

Dufour. Dufour Editions, Chester Springs, Pa. 19425

Dutton. E. P. Dutton & Company, Inc, 201 Park Av, S, New York, N.Y. 10003

Eastman Kodak. Eastman Kodak Company, 343 State St, Rochester, N.Y. 14608

Educ. Film. Educational Film Library Association, Inc, 250 W 57th St, New York, N.Y. 10019

Encyclopaedia Britannica. Encyclopaedia Britannica Educational Corporation (Encyclopaedia Britannica Press) 425 N Michigan Av, Chicago, Ill. 60611

Encyclopaedia Britannica Educ. Corp. See Encyclopaedia Britannica

Enoch Pratt. Enoch Pratt Free Library, Cathedral & Mulberry Sts, Baltimore, Md. 21201

Eriksson. Paul S. Eriksson, Inc, 119 W 57th St, New York, N.Y. 10019

Evans, M.&Co. See Lippincott

Fairchild. Fairchild Publications, Inc, Book Division, 7 E 12th St, New York, N.Y. 10002

Farrar. See Holt

Farrar, Straus. Farrar, Straus & Giroux, Inc, 19 Union Sq, W, New York, N.Y. 10003

Faxon. F. W. Faxon Company, 83-91 Francis St, Back Bay, Boston, Mass. 02115

Field Enterprises. Field Enterprises Educational Corporation, 510 Merchandise Mart Plaza, Chicago, Ill. 60654

Fielding. Fielding Publications, Inc, 105 Madison Av, New York, N.Y. 10016

Follett. Follett Publishing Company, 1010 W Washington Blvd, Chicago, Ill. 60607

Forest Press. Forest Press, Inc, 85 Watervliet Av, Albany, N.Y. 12206

Four Winds. The Four Winds Press, 50 W 44th St, New York, N.Y. 10036

Free Press. The Free Press, 60 5th Av, New York, N.Y. 10011

Freeman. W. H. Freeman & Company, Publishers, 660 Market St, San Francisco, Calif. 94104

French & European Publications. French & European Publications, Inc. (Librarie de France) 610 5th Av, New York, N.Y. 10020

Frontier Press. The Frontier Press, 815 Lafayette Bldg, Buffalo, N.Y. 14203

Funk. Funk & Wagnalls Company, Inc, 380 Madison Av, New York, N.Y. 10017

Funk, W. See Funk

G/L Tab Bks. G/L Tab Books, Monterey & Pinola Avs, Blue Ridge, Summit, Pa. 17214

Gale Res. Gale Research Company, 1400 Book Tower, Detroit, Mich. 48226

Garden City Bks. Garden City Books, 277 Park Av, New York, N.Y. 10017

Geis. Bernard Geis Associates, 130 S 56th St, New York, N.Y. 10022

George Peabody College for Teachers. George Peabody College for Teachers, 21st Av, S, Nashville, Tenn. 37203

Ginn. Ginn & Company, Statler Bldg, Boston, Mass. 02117

Golden Press. Golden Press, Publishers, 850 3d Av, New York, N.Y. 10022

Goodheart-Willcox. Goodheart-Willcox, Inc, 123 W Taft Dr, S, Holland, Ill. 60473

Grolier. Grolier, Inc, 575 Lexington Av, New York, N.Y. 10022

Grolier Soc. See Grolier

Grosset. Grosset & Dunlap, Inc, 51 Madison Av, New York, N.Y. 10010

Grossman Pubs. Grossman Publishers, 44 W 56th St, New York, N.Y. 10019

Grove. Grove Press, Inc, 214 Mercer St, New York, N.Y. 10012

Hammond. Hammond Incorporated, 515 Valley St, Maplewood, N.J. 07040

Hammond, C.S. See Hammond

Hanover House. Hanover House, 277 Park Av, New York, N.Y. 10017

Harcourt. Harcourt, Brace Jovanovich, Inc, 757 3d Av, New York, N.Y. 10017

Harper. Harper & Row, Publishers, 49 E 33d St, New York, N.Y. 10016

Harvard Univ. Press. Harvard University Press, Publishing Department, Kittredge Hall, 79 Garden St, Cambridge, Mass. 02138

Harvey House. Harvey House, 5 S Buckhout St, Irvington-on-Hudson, N.Y. 10533

Hastings House. Hastings House, Publishers, Inc, 10 E 40th St, New York, N.Y. 10016

Hawthorn Bks. Hawthorn Books, Inc, 70 5th Av, New York, N.Y. 10011

Hendricks House. Hendricks House, Inc, 103 Park Av, New York, N.Y. 10017

Heritage. Heritage Press, 595 Madison Av, New York, N.Y. 10022

Hill & Wang. Hill & Wang, Inc, 72 5th Av, New York, N.Y. 10011

Holiday. Holiday House, 18 E 56th St, New York, N.Y. 10022

Holt. Holt, Rinehart & Winston, Inc, 383 Madison Av, New York, N.Y. 10017

Horizon Press. Horizon Press, 156 5th Av, New York, N.Y. 10010

Houghton. Houghton Mifflin Company (Riverside Press, Cambridge) 2 Park St, Boston, Mass. 02107

Ind. Univ. Press. Indiana University Press, 10th & Morton Sts, Bloomington, Ind. 47401

Iowa State Univ. Press. Iowa State University Press, Press Bldg, Ames, Iowa 50010

Johns Hopkins Press. The Johns Hopkins Press, Homewood, Baltimore, Md. 21218

Johnson Pub. (Chicago) Johnson Publishing Company, Inc, Book Division, 1820 S Michigan Av, Chicago, Ill. 60616

Kenedy. P. J. Kenedy & Sons, Publishers, 866 3d Av, New York, N.Y. 10022

Knopf. Alfred A. Knopf, Inc, 201 E 50th St, New York, N.Y. 10022

Lanswood Press. Lanewood Press, Inc, 739 Boylston St, Boston, Mass. 02116

Lea. Lea & Febiger Publishers, 600 Washington Sq, Philadelphia, Pa. 19106

Liberal Arts. Liberal Arts Press, Inc, 3 W 57th St, New York, N.Y. 10019

Lion. Lion Press, Inc, 52 Park Av, New York, N.Y. 10016

Lippincott. J. B. Lippincott Company, E Washington Sq, Philadelphia, Pa. 19105

Little. Little, Brown & Company, 34 Beacon St, Boston, Mass. 02106

Liveright. Liveright Publishing Corporation, 386 Park Av, S, New York, N.Y. 10016

London House & Maxwell. See British Bk. Centre

Lothrop. Lothrop, Lee & Shepard Company, Inc, 105 Madison Av, New York, N.Y. 10016

MIT Press. Massachusetts Institute of Technology Press, Room E19-741, 77 Massachusetts Av, Cambridge, Mass. 02139

McDowell, Obolensky. See Astor-Honor

McGraw. McGraw-Hill Book Company, Inc, 330 W 42d St, New York, N.Y. 10036

McKay. David McKay Company, Inc, Publishers, 750 3d Av, New York, N.Y. 10017

McKinley. McKinley Publishing Company, 112 S New Broadway, Brooklawn, N.J. 08030

Macmillan (N Y) The Macmillan Company, Publishers, 866 3d Av, New York, N.Y. 10022

Macrae Smith Co. Macrae Smith Company, Lewis Tower Bldg, 225 S 15th St, Philadelphia, Pa. 19102

Manyland Bks. Manyland Books, Inc, Box 266, Wall St. Station, New York, N.Y. 10005

Marquis. Marquis-Who's Who, Marquis Publications Bldg, 210 E Ohio St, Chicago, Ill. 60611

Meredith. Meredith Press, 1716 Locust St, Des Moines, Iowa 50303

Meridian Bks. See World Pub.

Merriam. G. & C. Merriam Company, 47 Federal St, Springfield, Mass. 01105

Messner. See Simon & Schuster

Midwest Pub. Midwest Publishing Company, Inc, Box 307, 1025 E Maple Rd, Birmingham, Mich. 48012

Mill. M. S. Mill Company, Inc, 105 Madison Av, New York, N.Y. 10016

Modern Lib. Modern Library, Inc, 201 E 50th St, New York, N.Y. 10022

Morgan & Morgan. Morgan & Morgan, Inc, Publishers, 400 Warburton Av, Hastings-on-Hudson, N.Y. 10706

Morrow. William Morrow & Company, Inc, Publishers, 105 Madison Av, New York, N.Y. 10016

Mosby. The C. V. Mosby Company, Publishers, 3207 Washington Blvd, St Louis, Mo. 63103

Mus. of Modern Art. The Museum of Modern Art, 11 W 53d St, New York, N.Y. 10019

N.Y. Graphic. New York Graphic Society, Publishers, Ltd, 140 Greenwich Av, Greenwich, Conn. 06830

N.Y. Public Lib. New York Public Library, Public Relations Office, 5th Av & 42d St, New York, N.Y. 10018

N.Y. Times Co. New York Times Company, 229 W 43d St, New York, N.Y. 10036

N.Y. Univ. Press. New York University Press, 32 Washington Pl, New York, N.Y. 10003

Nat. Council for the Social Studies. The National Council for the Social Studies, National Education Association, 1201 16th St, N.W, Washington, D.C. 20036

Nat. Council of Teachers of English. National Council of Teachers of English, 508 S 6th St, Champaign, Ill. 61820

Nat. Council of Teachers of Mathematics. The National Council of Teachers of Mathematics, 1201 16th St, N.W, Washington, D.C. 20036

Nat. Directory Service. National Directory Service, Box 32065, Cincinnati, Ohio 45232

Nat. Educ. National Education Association of the United States, 1201 16th St, N.W, Washington, D.C. 20036

Nat. Geographic Soc. National Geographic Society, 17th & M Sts, N.W, Washington, D.C. 20036

Natural Hist. Press. Natural History Press, 501 Franklin Av, Garden City, N.Y. 11530

Nelson. Thomas Nelson & Sons, Copewood & Davis Sts, Camden, N.J. 08103

New Am. Lib. The New American Library of World Literature, Inc, 1301 Av. of the Americas, New York, N.Y. 10019

New Directions. New Directions, 333 Av. of the Americas, New York, N.Y. 10014

Northwestern Univ. Press. Northwestern University Press, 1735 Benson Av, Evanston, Ill. 60201

Norton. W. W. Norton & Company, Inc, Publishers, 55 5th Av, New York, N.Y. 10003

Orion. Orion Press, Inc, 150 E 35th St, New York, N.Y. 10016

Oxford. Oxford University Press, Inc, 200 Madison Av, New York, N.Y. 10016

Pantheon Bks. Pantheon Books, Inc, 437 Madison Av, New York, N.Y. 10022

Paragon Bk. Paragon Book Gallery, Ltd, 14 E 38th St, New York, N.Y. 10016

Parents Mag. Press. Parent's Magazine Press, 58 Vanderbilt Av, New York, N.Y. 10017

Pergamon Press. Pergamon Press, Inc, Maxwell House, Fairfield Park, Elmsford, N.Y. 10523

Petersen Pub. Petersen Publishing Company, 5959 Hollywood Blvd, Los Angeles, Calif. 90028

Phaidon. See Praeger

Phillips. S. G. Phillips, Inc, 305 W 86th St, New York, N.Y. 10024

Philosophical Lib. Philosophical Library, Inc, 15 E 40th St, New York, N.Y. 10016

Pitman. Pitman Publishing Corporation, 6 E 43d St, New York, N.Y. 10017

Plays, Inc. Plays, Inc, 8 Arlington St, Boston, Mass. 02116

Potter, C.N. Clarkson N. Potter, Inc, Publisher, 419 Park Av, S, New York, N.Y. 10016

Praeger. Frederick A. Praeger, Inc, Publishers, 111 4th Av, New York, N.Y. 10003

Prentice-Hall. Prentice-Hall, Inc, Route 9W, Englewood Cliffs, N.J. 07632

Princeton Univ. Press. Princeton University Press, Princeton, N.J. 08541

Public Affairs Press. Public Affairs Press, 419 New Jersey Av, S.E. Washington, D.C. 20003

Putnam, G. P. Putnam's Sons, 200 Madison Av, New York, N.Y. 10016

Quadrangle Bks. Quadrangle Books, Inc, 12 E Delaware Av, Chicago, Ill. 60611

Quigley. Quigley Publishing Company, Inc, 1270 6th Av, New York, N.Y. 10020

Rand McNally. Rand McNally & Company, Box 7600, Chicago, Ill. 60680

Random House. Random House, Inc, 201 E 50th St, New York, N.Y. 10022

Regents Pub. Regents Publishing Company, Inc, 1 W 39th St, New York, N.Y. 10018

Regnery. Henry Regnery Company, 114 W Illinois St, Chicago, Ill. 60610

Reilly & Lee. The Reilly & Lee Company, 114 W Illinois St, Chicago, Ill. 60610

Reinhold. See Van Nostrand-Reinhold

Richard W. Baron. Richard W. Baron Publishing Company, Inc, 201 Park Av, New York, N.Y. 10003

Rinehart. See Holt

Ronald. The Ronald Press Company, 79 Madison Av, New York, N.Y. 10016

Rosen, R. Richards Rosen Associates, Inc, 29 E 21st St, New York, N.Y. 10010

Roy Pubs. Roy Publishers, Inc, 30 E 74th St, New York, N.Y. 10021

Rutgers Univ. Press. Rutgers University Press, 30 College Av, New Brunswick, N.J. 08901

Sams. The Howard W. Sams Company, Inc, Box 558, Indianapolis, Ind. 46206

Sargent. Porter E. Sargent, Inc, Publishers, 11 Beacon St, Boston, Mass. 02108

Saunders. W. B. Saunders Company, 218 W Washington Sq, Philadelphia, Pa. 19105

Scarecrow. Scarecrow Press, Inc, 52 Liberty St, Box 656, Metuchen, N.J. 08840

Schocken. Schocken Books, Inc, 67 Park Av, New York, N.Y. 10016

Scott. Scott Foresman & Company, Educational Publishers, 1900 E Lake Av, Glenview, Ill. 60025

Scott Publications. Scott Publications, Inc, 488 Madison Av, New York, N.Y. 10022

Scribner. Charles Scribner's Sons, 597 5th Av, New York, N.Y. 10017

Seabury. The Seabury Press, 815 2d Av, New York, N.Y. 10017

Silver. Silver Burdett Company, 250 James St, Morristown, N.J. 07960
Distributor of Time-Life Books to schools and libraries

Simon & Schuster. Simon & Schuster, Inc, Publishers, 630 5th Av, New York, N.Y. 10020

Sloane. See Morrow

Smith, P. Peter Smith, 6 Lexington Av, Magnolia, Mass. 01930

St Martins. St Martin's Press, Inc, 175 5th Av, New York, N.Y. 10010

Stackpole Bks. Stackpole Books, Cameron & Kelker Sts, Harrisburg, Pa. 17103

Stein & Day. Stein & Day, Publishers, 7 E 48th St, New York, N.Y. 10017

Sterling. Sterling Publishing Company, Inc, 419 Park Av, S, New York, N.Y. 10016

Studio. The Studio Publications, Inc, 625 Madison Av, New York, N.Y. 10022

Supt. of Docs. Superintendent of Documents, Government Printing Office, Washington, D.C. 20402

Taplinger. Taplinger Publishing Company, Inc, 200 Park Av, S, New York, N.Y. 10003

Time, Inc. Time, Inc, Book Division, Time & Life Bldg, Rockefeller Center, New York, N.Y. 10020
See also Silver

Time-Life Bks. See Time, Inc.

Tudor. Tudor Publishing Company, 572 5th Av, New York, N.Y. 10036

Tuttle. Charles E. Tuttle Company, Inc, 28-30 Main St, Rutland, Vt. 05701

Twayne. Twayne Publishers, Inc, 31 Union Sq, W, New York, N.Y. 10003

U.N. See United Nations

UNESCO. United Nations, Sales Department, New York, N.Y. 10017

U.S. Govt. Ptg. Off. See Supt. of Docs.

U.S. News & World Report. U.S. News & World Report, Inc, 2300 N St, N.W, Washington, D.C. 20037

U.S. Pubs. Assn. United States Publications Association, 386 Park Av, S, New York, N.Y. 10003

Underhill, C.S. C. S. Underhill, P.O. Box 8, Williamsville, N.Y. 14221

Ungar. Frederick Ungar Publishing Company, 250 Park Av, New York, N.Y. 10003

United Nations. Office of Public Information. United Nations, Sales Department, New York, N.Y. 10017

United Nations. Statistical Office. United Nations, Sales Department, New York, N.Y. 10017

Univ. of Chicago Press. The University of Chicago Press, 5801 Ellis Av, Chicago, Ill. 60637

Univ. of Ill. Press. University of Illinois Press, Urbana, Ill. 61801

Univ. of Mich. Press. University of Michigan Press, 615 E University Av, Ann Arbor, Mich. 48160

Univ. of Minn. Press. University of Minnesota Press, 2037 University Av, S.E, Minneapolis, Minn. 55455

Univ. of N.C. Press. University of North Carolina Press, Bynum Hall, Chapel Hill, N.C. 27514

Univ. of Neb. Press. University of Nebraska Press, Lincoln, Neb. 60508

Univ. of Okla. Press. University of Oklahoma Press, Faculty Exchange, Norman, Okla. 73069

Univ. Press of Kan. University Press of Kansas, 358 Watson, Lawrence, Kan. 66044

Vanguard. The Vanguard Press, Inc, 424 Madison Av, New York, N.Y. 10017

Van Nostrand. See Van Nostrand-Reinhold

Van Nostrand-Reinhold. Van Nostrand-Reinhold Company, 450 W 33d St, New York, N.Y. 10001

Viking. The Viking Press, Inc, 625 Madison Av, New York, N.Y. 10022

Vintage. See Random House

Walck, H.Z. Henry Z. Walck, Inc, Publishers, 19 Union Sq, W, New York, N.Y. 10003

Walker & Co. Walker & Company, 720 5th Av, New York, N.Y. 10019

Warne. Frederick Warne & Company, Inc, 101 5th Av, New York, N.Y. 10003

Washburn. Ives Washburn, Inc, 750 3d Av, New York, N.Y. 10017

Washington Sq. Press. Washington Square Press, 630 5th Av, New York, N.Y. 10020

Watson-Guptill. Watson-Guptill Publications, 165 W 46th St, New York, N.Y. 10036

Watts, F. Franklin Watts, Inc, 575 Lexington Av, New York, N.Y. 10022

Wesleyan Univ. Press. Wesleyan University Press, 100 Riverview Center, Middletown, Conn. 06457

Westminster Press. Westminster Press, Room 908, Witherspoon Bldg, Walnut & Juniper Sts, Philadelphia, Pa. 19107

Weybright & Talley. Weybright & Talley, Inc, 3 E 54th St, New York, N.Y. 10022

White. David White Company, Publishers, 60 E 55th St, New York, N.Y. 10022

Wiley. John Wiley & Sons, Inc, 605 3d Av, New York, N.Y. 10016

Wilson, H.W. The H. W. Wilson Company, 950 University Av, Bronx, N.Y. 10452

World Pub. The World Publishing Company, 2231 W 110th St, Cleveland, Ohio 44102

Writer. The Writer, Inc, 8 Arlington St, Boston, Mass. 02116

Writers Digest. Writer's Digest, 22 E 12th St, Cincinnati, Ohio 45210

Wyden, P.H. Peter H. Wyden, Inc, 750 3d Av, New York, N.Y. 10017

Yale Univ. Press. Yale University Press, 92A Yale Station, New Haven, Conn. 06511

Year, Inc. Year, Inc, 21 W 45th St, New York, N.Y. 10036

Yoseloff. Thomas Yoseloff, Inc, Publishers, Box 421, Cranbury, N.J. 08512